PRENTICE HALL
LITERATURE
TEACHER'S EDITION • THE BRITISH TRADITION, VOLUME 2

COMMON CORE EDITION ©

ISBN-13: 978-0-13-319631-3
ISBN-10: 0-13-319631-3
5 6 7 8 9 10 V011 15 14 13 12

PEARSON

Contents in Brief

The selections in this book are presented through the lens of three Essential Questions:

What is the relationship between literature and place?

How does literature shape or reflect society?

What is the relationship of the writer to tradition?

Six units explore literature from consecutive periods in British history. Program pacing allows for 3-, 6-, or 9-week intervals.

Each unit develops literary and reading skills, teaching them to mastery.

From Legend to History

The Old English and Medieval Periods (A.D. 449 to 1485)

* INFORMATIONAL TEXT HIGHLIGHTED

Student Edition Pages

Extended Studies provide in-depth exploration of important authors, genres, or themes in history.

Skills workshops provide practice with key language arts skills.

Celebrating Humanity

The English Renaissance Period (1485 to 1625)

Each unit includes an introduction to the historical context and literature of the period.

Grant Wiggins worked with the Pearson development team to identify the Essential Questions that drive the instruction in this program.

Student Edition Pages

UNIT 2

PART TWO: THE INFLUENCE OF THE MONARCHY

World Literature Connections focus on authors, themes, and genres across world cultures.

PART THREE: DRAMA

Vocabulary, Writing, and Grammar activities link to selection content.

Featured unit authors present professional models of writing strategies.

A robust mix of literary and informational texts provides a wide range of reading.

Student Edition Pages

A Turbulent Time

The Seventeenth and Eighteenth Centuries (1625 to 1798)

Snapshot of the Period features present historical information graphically.

Literary History features present information about prominent authors, genres, and themes within the historical context of each period.

Primary Sources documents enhance students' research skills and understanding of literature.

Student Edition Pages

PART FOUR: THE ESSAY

Rebels and Dreamers

The Romantic Period (1798 to 1832)

Students are provided with multiple perspectives on the era through study of graphical data, historical commentary, and scholarly articles.

Contemporary Connections link historical themes and genres with modern ideas and forms of expression.

PHLit Online!
www.PHLitOnline.com

Interactive resources provide personalized instruction and activities online.

Student Edition Pages

PART TWO: **LYRIC POETRY**

Reading for Information features in each unit present nonfiction forms such as manuals, newspaper articles, Web sites, and other real-life readings.

Assessment Workshops prepare students for questions and formats they will encounter on the SAT and ACT tests.

Student Edition Pages

Progress and Decline

The Victorian Period (1833 to 1901)

Essential Questions drive instruction, shaping selection groupings around critical issues.

Student Edition Pages

PART FOUR: **GLOOM AND GLORY**

Performance Tasks, modeled on those in the Common Core framework, enable students to go beyond multiple-choice assessments.

PHLit Online! www.PHLitOnline.com

Interactive resources provide personalized instruction and activities online.

All program resources are available online for classroom presentation or individual study.

A Time of Rapid Change

The Modern and Postmodern Periods (1901 to Present)

Award-winning authors provide scholarly articles that comment on the historical period and related authors and genres.

Comparing Literary Works features support the study of literary and stylistic elements across selections.

Student Edition Pages

PART FOUR: THE POSTMODERN AND BEYOND

Independent Reading suggestions offer opportunities for students to read complex texts independently.

Range of Reading: Complete Contents by Genre

Literature

▶ Stories

▶ Drama

▶ Poetry

Narrative Poems

Odes

Philosophical, Reflective, and Satirical Poems

Informational Text—Literary Nonfiction

Biography

Diary

Essays About Art, Literature, and Language

Essays About History

Essays About Ideas

Historical Accounts and Texts

Journalism

Letters

Personal Essays

Informational Text—Literary Nonfiction

▶ Literature in Context—Reading in the Content Areas

▶ World Literature Connections

Comparing Across World Literature

World Literature Connection

▶ Literary History

Writing Workshops

Communications Workshops

Vocabulary Workshops

SAT PREP ACT Test-Taking Practice

PRENTICE HALL

LITERATURE

TEACHER'S EDITION • THE BRITISH TRADITION, VOLUME 2

COMMON CORE EDITION

ALWAYS LEARNING

PEARSON

Common Core State Standards

- Reading Literature 1, 2, 4, 5, 9
- Reading Informational Text 3, 4, 5, 6, 7, 8
- Writing 1, 2, 3, 5, 6, 7, 8, 9, 10
- Speaking and Listening 1, 3
- Language 1, 2, 3, 4, 5

Rebels and Dreamers

The Romantic Period

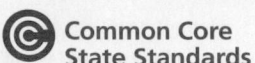

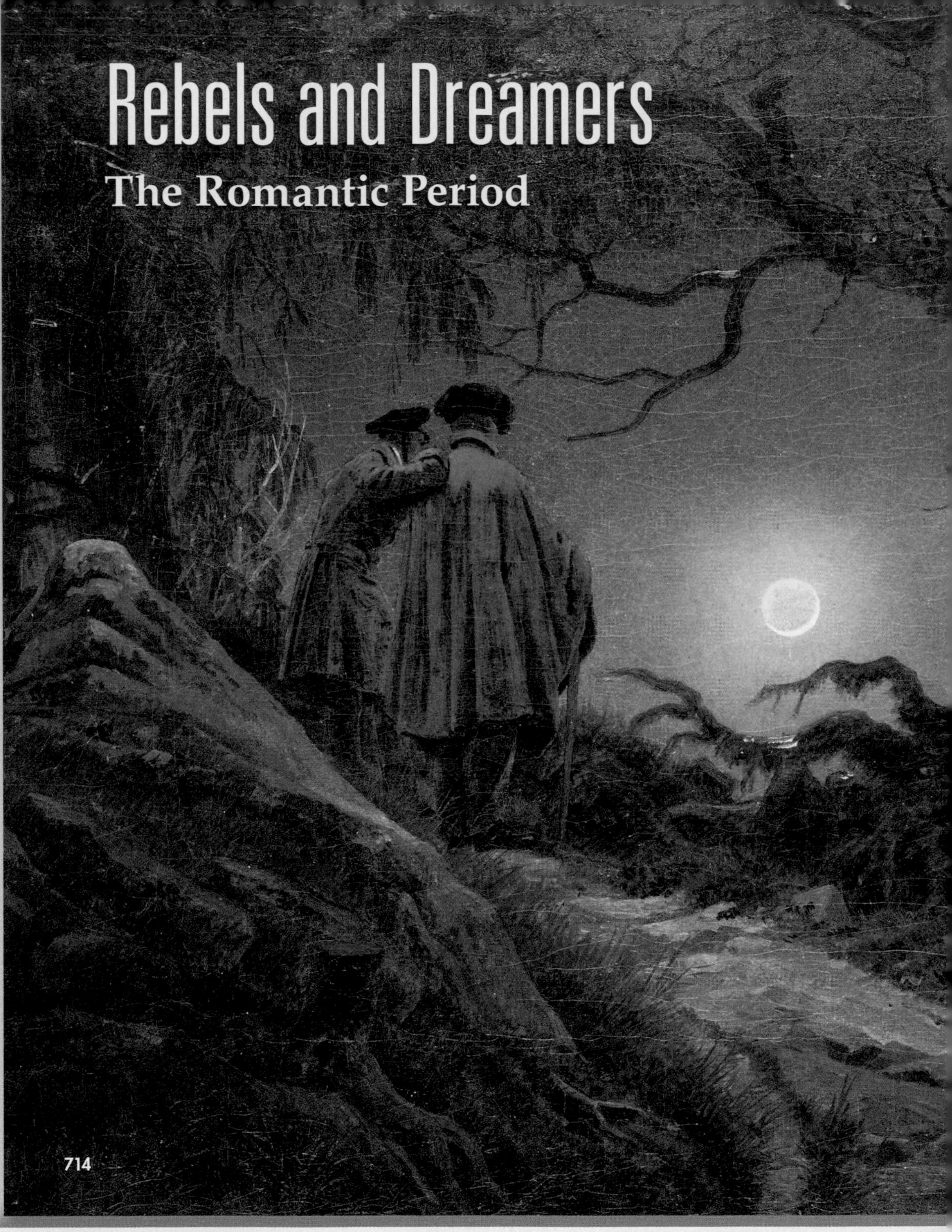

714

PHLit Online!
www.PHLitOnline.com

Teaching From Technology

Enriched Online Student Edition
- full narration of selections
- interactive graphic organizers
- linked **Get Connected** and **Background** videos
- all work sheets and other student resources

Professional Development
- the ***Professional Development Guidebook*** online
- additional professional-development essays by program authors

Planning, Assigning, and Monitoring
- software for online assignment of work to students, individually or to the whole class
- a system for tracking and grading student work

Unit 4
1798–1832

"But oh! that deep Romantic chasm which slanted / Down the green hill, athwart a cedarn cover! / A savage place! as holy and enchanted / As e'er beneath a waning moon was haunted . . ."

—*Samuel Taylor Coleridge*

PHLit Online!
www.PHLitOnline.com

Hear It!
- Selection summary audio
- Selection audio

See It!
- Author videos
- Essential Question video
- Get Connected videos
- Background videos
- More about the authors
- Illustrated vocabulary words
- Vocabulary flashcards

Do It!
- Interactive journals
- Interactive graphic organizers
- Grammar tutorials
- Interactive vocabulary games
- Test practice

Introduce Unit 4

1. Direct students' attention to the title of the Unit, including the time period covered. Have a volunteer read the quotation. **Ask:** What does the quotation suggest about the spirit of the period?
   Possible response: The quotation suggests the many sides of nature: savage, holy, enchanted, haunted.
2. Discuss the artwork, *Two Men Observing the Moon,* by Caspar David Friedrich (1774–1840).
   Ask: Literature of the period often focuses on dreams and the imagination. What elements of this painting strike you as dreamlike?
   Possible response: The coppery mist and burning moon are dreamlike.
3. Have students speculate about the literature of the period, given the quotation and the art.
   Possible response: Romantic writings may focus on dreams and eerie, or haunted, themes.

Unit Resources

Unit 4 Resources includes these pages:

- **Benchmark Tests** assess and monitor student progress.
- **Vocabulary and Reading Warm-ups** provide additional vocabulary support, based on Lexile rankings, for each selection. "A" **Warm-ups** are for students reading two grades below level. "B" **Warm-ups** are for students reading one grade below level.
- **Selection Support**
  - **Reading Skill**
  - **Literary Analysis**
  - **Vocabulary Builder**
  - **Support for Writing**
  - **Enrichment**

Unit Features

Unit Author
Elizabeth McCracken helps introduce the period in the Unit Introduction, provides Recent Scholarship on literature in the Unit, and offers insight in the Writing Workshop.

Extended Study
Students explore in depth the works of William Wordsworth, presented with links to contemporary culture, a Critical Commentary, and a Comparing Literary Works feature.

Comparing Literary Works
Students compare master works in the British tradition with works of world literature.

Primary Sources
Students engage the documents that recorded history as it was made.

Informational Texts
Students learn to use and evaluate various types of informational text.

Themes Across Centuries
Students discover links between canonical literature and the contemporary world.

PHLit Online!
For more about the author, practice with the selection vocabulary, or more background, go online at **www.PHLitOnline.com.**

Reading With Imagination by **Doug Buehl**

"Ultimately, reading triggers a life of the mind..."

What do you see when you read? Ask students this question, and you will likely be met with skeptical looks, as if this was a trick question. "Words, of course," they answer. As proficient readers, we do far more than decipher words on a page. Ultimately, reading triggers a life of the mind, as we re-create for ourselves how things are, or were, or could be, even though we are not actually experiencing them "in the moment." And sometimes, we even transcend the physical act we call reading, the conscious awareness that our eyes are processing lines of print. That bionic DVD player in our heads kicks in, and we feel as if "we were there."

Picturing Reading

Activities that ignite readers' imaginations are fundamental to improving reading comprehension. In their seminal work applying research to comprehension instruction, Keene and Zimmerman (2007) characterize readers' use of sensory and emotional imagery as "bringing text to life." However, many students regard reading as essentially a word identification exercise, and they struggle with picturing in their imaginations what an author is using language to convey.

Students benefit from classroom practices that engage them in eliciting sensory images, especially in response to written texts (Gambrell & Koskinen, 2002). Visualization strategies help students make connections to the background knowledge and experiences they bring to reading, and such strategies "personalize" students' understanding and appreciation of texts. Students read with a deeper engagement with a text, as they use their imaginations to infer how things might be if they were experienced live.

Imagination Tune-Ups

Powers of Observation Provide students with opportunities to practice becoming precise observers. Wilhelm (2004) recommends a progression of visualization activities as "warm-ups" for stimulating imagination. Allow students to carefully examine an interesting object, to notice it in great detail. Then have them close their eyes and imagine the object with as much specificity as they can. As a follow-up, have them verbalize what they are "seeing" with a partner, or quick-sketch the item.

Transition students to visualizing objects not physically present, which requires them to draw extensively on their memories. For example, you might have them visualize familiar objects (such as from their home). Then ask them to "hit the play button" in their minds, and view action sequences, with all their senses alert for a graphic mental trip through the scene.

Guided Imagery As a frontloading activity to help students envision a setting, take them through a guided imagery scenario. Ask students to close their eyes and follow your suggestions as they imagine they are personally experiencing what you are describing. As you talk, use vividly descriptive language that evokes sensory responses: "What would it be like if you were actually there?"

For example, take students into the streets of 1790s Paris as the French people breathe in the euphoria of freedom from an oppressive monarchy. What would they be seeing? Smelling? Hearing? Or place students on an 1800s British sailing ship, as they imagine how it would be to spend arduous months on this small and fragile vessel. Guided imagery sensitizes students to language that cues a sensory response from readers.

You Ought to be in Pictures Photographs and illustrations are often provided in texts to help students visualize what an author is describing. Ask students to insert themselves into the picture (Buehl, 2001). For example, ask them to imagine what they would be seeing, hearing, feeling, as they wander through the ruins of Tintern Abbey. What sensation would they experience if they touched the ancient columns with their hands? How would the light penetrate the ruins? What might the wind sound like? If people are portrayed in the picture, ask students to select one of them, and imagine they are that person. What would this individual be noticing? What emotions might he or she be feeling?

Sparking Sensory Responses

Dramatic Readings Oral interpretations of literary works can also prompt students to "power up" their imaginations.

- **Read Alouds.** Teacher modeling through read-alouds has great potential for helping students perceive the sensory layers of a passage. Intonation, emotional content, and even gestures and body language take students beyond a "monotone" understanding of the words. Pause periodically and encourage students to share with partners what they imagine as you read.
- **Reader's Theater.** Short excerpts of a selection can be quickly refashioned as reader's theater presentations. Students must decide on how to interpret their lines so that sensory aspects cued by author language are communicated. Reader's theater prompts students to consider: "What would this be like if it were live?"

Text Coding Students use sticky notes to text code language that engages their imaginations: "When the author said . . . I could imagine seeing . . . hearing . . . feeling . . ."

Eyewitness Accounts Ask students to read as if they were "eyewitnesses" to the events and scenarios described by an author. Eyewitness accounts can be relayed to a partner after reading, or can be delivered as testimony in writing. What did they see? Hear? Smell? Feel? Or have students provide a first-person retelling of meeting a character, and have them pinpoint the language from the text that is the basis for their impressions.

Modeled Strategy

See pp. 750 and 822 for a point-of-use note modeling these strategies.

Teacher Resources

- ***Professional Development Guidebook***
- ***Classroom Strategies and Teaching Routines cards***

PHLit Online!

Log on as a teacher at **www.PHLitOnline.com** to access a library of all Professional Development articles by the Contributing Authors of Prentice Hall *Literature.*

Doug Buehl

Doug Buehl is a teacher, author, and national literacy consultant. His 33 years with the Madison Metropolitan School District, Madison, WI, included experiences as a reading teacher and district adolescent literacy support teacher.

Supporting Research

Buehl, D. (2001). *Classroom strategies for interactive learning.* Newark, DE: International Reading Association.

Gambrell, L. & Koskinen, P. (2002) Imagery: A strategy for enhancing comprehension. In Block, C. & Pressley, M. Ed. *Comprehension Instruction: Research-based Practices.* New York: Guilford, 305–318.

Keene, E. & Zimmerman, S. (2007). *Mosaic of thought: The power of comprehension strategy instruction, 2nd Ed.* Portsmouth, NH: Heinemann.

Wilhelm, J. (2004) *Reading Is Seeing.* Scholastic, New York.

Reading the Unit Introduction

Rebels and Dreamers

Explain to students that this unit covers literature of the Romantic period, which spanned from 1798–1832. The Unit Introduction includes these components:

—a **Snapshot** offering a quick glimpse at the period

—a **Historical Background** section discussing major events

—a **Timeline** that covers the period from 1798 to 1832 over a span of 10 pages

—a **Unit Essay** examining the literature of the period through the lens of three Essential Questions

—**Following Through** activities

—a **Contemporary Commentary**

Applying the Essential Question

1. Introduce each of the Essential Questions on the student page.
2. Show the **Essential Question** video on the ***See It!*** **DVD.** Help students relate the Essential Questions to the unit and their own experiences by asking the following:

   Literature and Place What do you do when you feel the need to "escape" from everyday life? Is there a physical place where you can go, or do you find refuge in an imaginary world, such as in a book or a game?

   Literature and Society Think of a current example of a writer, musician, or artist who uses his or her work to comment on politics. What position does the artist take? How effective is his or her message?

   Writer and Tradition Choose one tradition that you think people should abandon. Why is the tradition no longer useful or necessary? What do you think should replace it?
3. Explain to students that the ideas they have considered in answering these questions also apply to the history of the Romantic period. Have them begin reading the Unit Introduction, telling them to look as they read for ideas related to their answers.

Snapshot of the Period

During the Romantic period, all the attitudes and assumptions of eighteenth-century classicism and rationalism were dramatically challenged, in part by social and political upheavals. The French Revolution, which began on July 14, 1789, shook the established order in the name of democratic ideals. Fearing the events in France, the English ruling class also felt threatened by unrest at home. British authorities tried to repress workers' efforts to organize, going so far as to kill a number of peaceful demonstrators in Manchester (1819). Another type of revolution, the Industrial Revolution, boosted the growth of manufacturing but also brought poverty and suffering for those who worked or failed to find work in slum-ridden cities. British Romantic writers responded to the climate of their times. For many of them, the faith in science and reason, so characteristic of eighteenth-century thought, no longer applied in a world of tyranny and factories.

▶ In 1819, thousands of workers and their families demonstrated peacefully at St. Peter's Fields in Manchester to protest desperate economic conditions and to gain parliamentary reforms. Soldiers dispersed the crowd, injuring about 500 people and killing 11.

As you read the selections in this unit, you will be asked to think about them in view of three key questions:

What is the **relationship** between literature and *place?*

How does literature **shape or reflect** *society?*

What is the relationship of the writer to *tradition?*

Teaching Resources

The following resources can be used to support, enrich, or extend the instruction for the Unit 4 Introduction.

Unit 4 Resources

- **Names and Terms to Know Worksheet,** p. 2
- **Essential Question Worksheets,** pp. 3–5
- **Follow-Through Activities, p.6**

Common Core Companion, pp. 9–14; 33–38

Professional Development Guidebook

- **Cross-Curricular Enrichment Worksheets, pp. 231, 232, 237**

See It! **DVD**

- **Elizabeth McCracken, segment 2**

PHLit Online! All resources are available online at **www.PHLitOnline.com.**

Integration of Knowledge and Ideas In the image below, the cracked façade and the pictures whirling out of it dramatize the way in which Romantic values challenged earlier Neoclassical beliefs in order and balance. Which of these Romantic values, described in the captions, are still influential today? Which seem historically interesting but no longer directly relevant to us today?

TEACH

Background

History

The French Revolution began on July 14, 1789, when a mob stormed the Bastille, a Paris prison for political prisoners. The successful revolutionaries placed limits on the powers of King Louis XVI, established a new government, and approved a document called the Declaration of the Rights of Man and of the Citizen, which affirmed the principles of "liberty, equality, and fraternity." France became a constitutional monarchy.

In England, most intellectuals, including such important writers of the Romantic Age as William Wordsworth, at first enthusiastically supported the revolution and the democratic ideals on which it was based.

Critical Viewing

Interpreting Illustrations

1. Draw students' attention to the illustrations on the Snapshot pages. **Ask** the questions on the student page.
   Possible response: Wandering as a rebel and outcast, gaining forbidden knowledge, and honoring the common person are still influential. Outcasts are still a common theme in books, movies, and television. There is debate over what knowledge is "forbidden" to the public, including issues such as censorship and freedom of information. Many forms of media, including television, the Internet, and popular music, claim to represent the experiences of the common person. On the other hand, seeking the faraway, creating the fantastic, and feeling awe for nature do not seem as relevant.

Differentiated Instruction for Universal Access

Support for Less Proficient Readers
Explain that during the Romantic period, many writers challenged old beliefs and established new ideas, some of which are still relevant today. Have students preview important themes of the Romantic era by looking at the illustrations on page 717.

EL Background for English Learners
Have students examine the captions of the illustrations on page 717. Ask students to suggest other images that would match the captions. Encourage them to explain what ideas the images communicate to the viewer.

Strategy for Advanced Readers
Have students think of modern-day examples of works that display the themes illustrated on page 717.

PHLit Online!
Show or assign the **Essential Question** video for this Unit online at **www.PHLitOnline.com**.

Teaching the Historical Background

The Historical Background section discusses the most significant events of this period: the English defeat of Napoleon, industrialization and urbanization in the British Empire, and political turbulence centered around the corruption and ineptitude of the English monarchy.

1. Point out that the story of this period is one of people reacting against war, urbanization, and demands for reform.
2. Have students read the Background.
3. Then, **ask** them to identify major social trends during the Romantic period.
   Possible response: England was at war with both France and America during the period. In addition, increasing industrialization and urbanization was taking place, changing many people's lives. Also, the Reform Bill of 1832 allowed more people in England to vote. Still, all working-class and many lower middle-class people were not allowed to vote. In addition, the British monarchy became less and less popular because of corruption and indifference to the British people.

Teaching the Timeline

1. Tell students that the Timeline for the period from 1798 to 1832 appears on pages 718–727 of this Unit Introduction. Each portion of the Timeline identifies and illustrates some of the major events in the British Empire and in the world for that period.
2. Have students survey the entire Timeline before they read the rest of the Unit Introduction.
3. Encourage students to identify a few additional events from the period and share them with the class.

COMMON CORE ▪ MULTIPLE PERSPECTIVES ON THE ERA

Historical Background

The Romantic Period (1798–1832)

For the first half of the Romantic period, England was at war with France. At home, the period was marked by growing urbanization and industrialization and demands for reform. At the end, a wasteful monarchy was redeemed by the succession of a shy, eighteen-year-old girl, Victoria.

English Victories Over Napoleon

Revolutionary France, led by Napoleon Bonaparte, declared war on Britain in 1793. In the ensuing conflict, two national heroes emerged for England. At sea, Lord Horatio Nelson shattered the French fleet at the Battle of Trafalgar (1805), ensuring that Britannia would rule the waves for the next century. Nelson, dying at his moment of triumph, passed immediately into legend. On land, the Duke of Wellington defeated Napoleon at Waterloo (1815).

With Napoleon in exile, the victors met in the conference known as the Congress of Vienna (1814–15) and tried to restore Europe to what it had been before the French Revolution. However, the ideas unleashed by that revolution and the earth-shaking changes of the Industrial Revolution were more powerful than any reactionary politician imagined.

Napoleon Bonaparte

Industrialization and Urbanization

In 1807, Robert Fulton launched his steamboat, and, in 1814, George Stephenson built a steam locomotive. Railroads changed the face of England, and steamships shrank oceans. It was the textile industry, however, that was at the forefront of change. Inventions, from the spinning jenny to the power loom, changed the way cloth was woven and moved the weaver from the spinning wheel in the kitchen to the factory.

Water power and then coal drove the machines that ran the mills that created the cities in which the workers lived. Wealth no longer depended on land, and workers, separated from the land, realized that they would have to unite in political action. The Reform Bill of 1832, the product of democratic impulses and changing economic conditions, was

TIMELINE

1798

1799: Egypt Rosetta Stone, key to deciphering hieroglyphics, discovered. ▶

1801: Act of Union creates United Kingdom of Great Britain and Ireland.

1801: Union Jack becomes official flag of Great Britain and Ireland. ▶

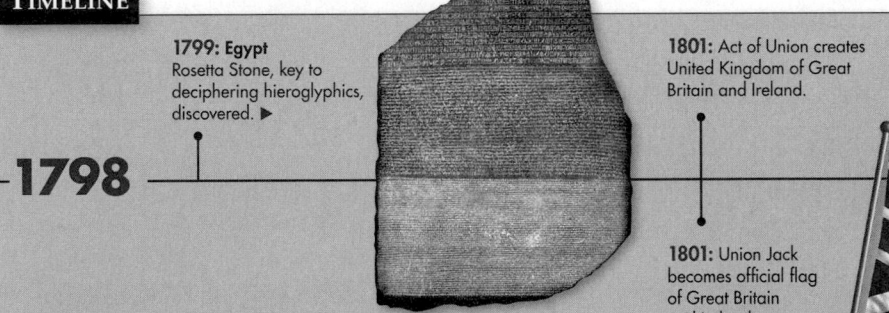

Enrichment: Analyzing Historical Patterns, Trends, and Periods

Exporting the French Revolution

Explain to students that the French Revolution quickly became an international force. As Napoleon's troops swept through Europe, he reformed the governments of the conquered countries, replacing the remains of feudal society with an order based on wealth, merit, and equality.

Activity: Analyze a Historical Trend Have students use the **Analyzing Historical Patterns, Trends, and Periods** worksheet, ***Professional Development Guidebook,*** page 231, to help them analyze the spread of revolutionary ideals throughout Europe during the reign of Napoleon. Students should consider the characteristics of this trend, as well as its causes and effects. Have students research to find important dates to add to the Timeline.

a first step in extending the right to vote. It increased the voting rolls by 57 percent, but the working classes and some members of the lower middle classes were still unable to vote. In 1833, after the period ended, Parliament abolished slavery in the British Empire.

An Out-of-Touch Monarchy

The struggle for increased political rights was a difficult one. Those in power and those who wanted reform collided tragically at St. Peter's Field, Manchester, in 1819. Workers had assembled in a peaceful demonstration for economic and political reform. A cavalry charge killed eleven and wounded many women and children. Called the Peterloo Massacre, the incident inspired Shelley to write "England in 1819" which opens: "An old, mad, blind, despised and dying King."

Cruelly accurate, the line describes George III, who had been declared insane in 1811. His son, named Prince Regent, was designated to rule in his place (a regent substitutes for a ruler). This gave the period its name, The Regency, and the Regent's conduct gave it its scandalous reputation.

Extravagant, obese, separated from his wife in an ugly and very public marital quarrel, he was unaware of the great changes taking place around him. The Regent became George IV in 1820. In 1830, he was succeeded by his brother William, who had ten illegitimate children with his common-law wife, but no legitimate heir. When William died in 1837, the daughter of his younger brother was next in the royal line.

That daughter, Victoria, was determined to restore morality and dignity to the throne. She became the queen and then the symbol of an era in which political reform and industrial might made England the most powerful country in the world.

Key Historical Theme: Political Oppression vs. Political Reform

- Conservative European rulers tried to roll back revolutionary ideas.
- In England, industrialization prompted workers to organize.
- Police killed peacefully protesting workers in Manchester in 1819.
- The Reform Bill of 1832 extended the right to vote but not to the working classes.

1803: United States Louisiana Territory purchased from France.

1804: Germany Beethoven composes *Symphony No. 3.*

◀ **1804: France** Napoleon crowns himself emperor.

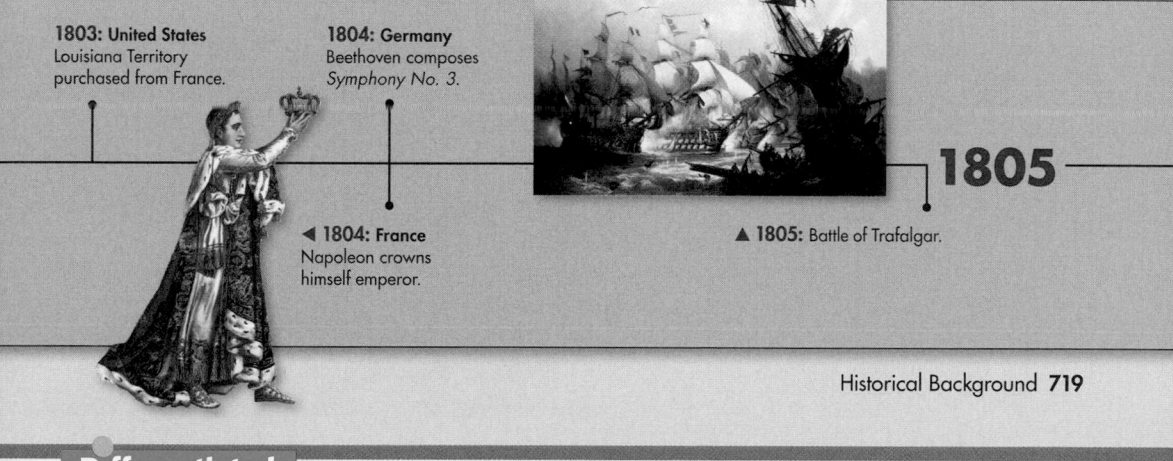

▲ **1805:** Battle of Trafalgar.

1805

Connecting to the Literature

1. Point out to students that many Romantic writers saw a downside to industrialization. Blake's "The Chimney Sweeper," page 751, offers an early, sympathetic view of the human cost of the Industrial Revolution.
2. Explain that nature was a common theme in Romantic works. Some examples of writings dealing with this subject include Shelley's "Ode to the West Wind," page 870, and Keats's "Ode to a Nightingale," page 886.

Key Historical Theme

1. Explain to students that this section of the Historical Background calls out three major historical themes from the whole period.
2. **Ask** students to think of a song that reminds them of each historical theme.
   Possible response: Songs for English Victories Over Napoleon might include "Waterloo" by ABBA; songs for Industrialization and Urbanization might include "Around My Way" by Talib Kweli; songs for An Out-of-Touch Monarchy might include "King and Queen" by Mary J. Blige.

Critical Viewing

1. Call students' attention to the painting on page 719 of the Battle of Trafalgar.
2. **Ask** students to speculate on what it was like to take part in a sea battle.
   Possible response: The turmoil of the scene suggests that participating in a sea battle must have been an overwhelming experience, involving confusing sights and noises.

Differentiated Instruction for Universal Access

Strategy for Less Proficient Readers

Define *romantic* for students. Encourage them to add to this definition based on personal experience. Ask students to keep that definition in mind as they read literature of the Romantic Age.

EL Strategy for English Learners

Inform students that this period is called the Romantic Age. Have them define the word *romantic,* using the dictionary if necessary. Then, have them add to their definition by reading Rebels and Dreamers.

Strategy for Advanced Readers

Using a definition of *romantic,* challenge students to predict the life of a rebel or a dreamer in the Romantic Age. Have them compare and contrast their original perceptions with the knowledge they acquire reading Rebels and Dreamers.

Teaching the Essential Questions

As students read "Rebels and Dreamers," they will examine its information through the lens of three Essential Questions. Each Essential Question is broken down into "stepping-stone," or intermediate questions. Work through each "stepping-stone" question with the class. Then, have students pose answers to the Essential Question as it applies to the period.

What is the relationship between literature and place?

1. Before they read this section of the essay, tell students that English Romanticism embraced the exotic and unfamiliar, as opposed to the everyday and mundane.
2. Have students read this section of the essay. Then, pose the first stepping-stone question. **Ask:** How did Romantics emphasize strange and faraway places?
   Possible response: The Romantics wrote about places that were not well-known, such as Cape Horn. They used settings that represented luxury and mystery, such as Xanadu.
3. Then, **ask** the second stepping-stone question: What worlds became refuges from the smoky cities?
   Possible response: The Lake District was a real place that served as a refuge for Wordsworth, who wrote about the beauty of the natural world. Keats and Shelley wrote about taking refuge in imagination.

Critical Viewing

Interpreting Illustrations

1. Direct students to the illustration of the steamboat on page 720.
2. **Ask** students what they think the steamboat represented to Romantic writers.
   Possible response: The steamboat may have represented progress and also the human costs of progress.

COMMON CORE • MULTIPLE PERSPECTIVES ON THE ERA

Essential Questions Across Time

The Romantic Period (1798–1832)

What is the relationship between literature and *place?*

English Romanticism was born in and inspired by a real place—the Lake District. (See the feature on the next page.) However, since Romanticism defines itself by opposition to the commonplace and familiar, much of the literature of the period is also set in exotic and faraway locations.

How did Romantics emphasize strange and faraway places?

In poetry, the Romantics took readers to distant lands, both real and imaginary. For example, Samuel Taylor Coleridge's Ancient Mariner sails around Cape Horn to the edge of Antarctica, which was just then being explored. He returns to narrate his strange adventures. In Coleridge's "Kubla Khan," the fabulous emperor dwells in a place that has come to symbolize luxury and mystery: Xanadu. Similarly, Percy Bysshe Shelley's poem "Ozymandias" takes us to "an antique land," the Egypt of the pharaohs, which had recently been invaded and plundered by Napoleon.

What worlds became refuges from the smoky cities?

Whether or not they wrote of exotic lands, the Romantic poets all sought something beyond this world, turning to nature and the imagination for transcendence. The worlds they explored were alternatives to the spreading stain of the cities; to what the poet William Blake called the "dark, Satanic mills," factories that seemed to chew up people.

The Lake District William Wordsworth, who settled in the beautiful Lake District—far from the urban blight of London, Manchester, and Birmingham—wrote of the natural world in a religious way. A "worshipper of Nature," he saw the landscape bathed in a heavenly light.

ESSENTIAL QUESTION VOCABULARY

These Essential Question words will help you think and write about literature and place:

exotic (eg zŏt´ ik) *adj.* foreign; strange or different in a way that is striking

secular (sek´ yə lər) *adj.* relating to worldly things as opposed to religion

residential (rez´ ə den´ shəl) *adj.* characterized by private homes

TIMELINE

1805

1806: Germany Prussia declares war on France.

1806: Western Europe Official end of Holy Roman Empire.

1807: United States Fulton's steamboat navigates Hudson River. ▼

Enrichment: Understanding Political Science

Political Thought: Burke and Bentham
In response to the French Revolution, philosopher Jeremy Bentham (1748–1832) argued that actions, including the laws passed by government, should be judged by the standard of "utility" alone—that is, by their usefulness in satisfying people's interest. A rational government was one that created the greatest pleasure for the greatest number. Bentham's principles, known as Utilitarianism, influenced numerous reformist politicians.

Activity: Evaluate Political Ideas Invite students to find out more about Utilitarianism. Have students record their findings in the **Enrichment: Understanding Political Science** worksheet, ***Professional Development Guidebook,*** page 237.

Going Beyond Wordsworth was a native of the Lake District; he had climbed its mountains and rowed across its lakes. He saw ideal beauty in the land that spread out before him. However, when Shelley writes of the skylark and John Keats of the nightingale, they are not concerned with describing these birds in their natural settings. Each celebrates the song and the flight of a bird that lures the poet beyond the bounds of earth.

The urban world the Romantics fled was not, as Wordsworth discovered, completely bleak. Wordsworth, poet of nature and the countryside, had a moment of stunned revelation when, at dawn on a clear September morning, he saw London from Westminster Bridge. "Earth," he wrote, "has not anything to show more fair . . ."

The City Improved—or Blighted London had indeed been improved. The architect John Nash contributed to the secular beautification of London as Christopher Wren had to the ecclesiastical, with the rebuilding of St. Paul's Cathedral after the Great Fire of 1666. Nash built the Brighton Pavilion, modeled in part on India's Taj Mahal, another example of the period's taste for the exotic and fantastic.

Bath, a city forever connected with Regency novelist Jane Austen, created its beautiful crescents, or curved streets, during this time. However, these Regency splendors were the exception. What the novelist Charles Dickens would later call "Coketown," a dirty, soul-destroying city, stands for the world from which the Romantic poets struggled to escape.

The **BRITISH TRADITION**

CLOSE-UP ON GEOGRAPHY

The Lake District, Cradle of Romanticism

The cradle of English Romanticism is the Lake District. Located in the northwest of England, this picturesque region contains some of the country's most impressive mountains and lakes. The Romantic poet William Wordsworth was born in the Lake District, wandered there as a boy, lived there as a man, and wrote poems inspired by its beauty. In the following passage, Wordsworth captures the mystery and thrill of his boyhood climbing expeditions in the region.

. . . Oh! at that time,
While on the perilous ridge I hung alone,
With what strange utterance did the loud dry wind
Blow through my ears! the sky seemed not a sky
Of earth, and with what motion moved the clouds.
—from *The Prelude*

▲ **1810: South America** Simón Bolívar leads rebellion against Spanish rule.

1812: United States War with Britain declared.

1812

1812: Byron publishes *Childe Harold's Pilgrimage.* ▶

Applying the Essential Question

1. Summarize the class discussion of the "stepping-stone" questions on pages 720–721.
2. Then, **ask** students this question: Do you think that the Romantic view of urbanization applies to life in cities today? Why or why not?
   Possible response: No, life in cities has changed considerably since the Romantic period. Cities are cleaner and more pleasant places to live than they used to be. There is less of a need to escape them.

The British Tradition

Close-Up on Geography

1. Remind students that the Lake District was one of the locations idealized by Romantic writers. This region of cool, clear lakes, mountains, and woodlands represented a refuge from the industrial world.
2. **Ask** students how the Lake District contrasted with urban areas, such as London. Students should support their answers using the passage quoted.
   Possible response: The passage describes being alone on a ridge, feeling the wind and watching the clouds move. This contrasts to the city, where it would be more difficult to experience solitude and nature.

Differentiated Instruction for Universal Access

Strategy for Less Proficient Readers
Define words such as *perilous* and *utterance* for students. Have students work together to read the excerpts in the British Tradition sidebar. Have students read the passage aloud. Ask volunteers to explain what aspects of nature are described in the passage.

Strategy for Advanced Readers
Remind students that nature was a common subject of Romantic works. Have students think of a scene from nature that they have witnessed and write a paragraph describing it. Encourage students to use vivid descriptive language and figures of speech in their writing.

Teaching the Essential Questions

How does literature shape or reflect society?

1. Before they read this section of the essay, tell students that Romantic authors were influenced by the events of their time. In turn, their writings helped to shape the era.
2. Have students read this section of the essay. Then, pose the first stepping-stone question. **Ask:** How did political and industrial revolutions affect society?
   Possible response: The ideals that spawned the French Revolution eventually led to the abolition of slavery in England and its empire, as political reform. The Industrial Revolution advanced society with economic progress, yet exacted a human toll.
3. Then, **ask** the second stepping-stone question: How did writers react to revolutionary changes?
   Possible response: Writers reacted directly and indirectly. Some spoke out on issues they believed were important. Others looked inward or to faraway, exotic locations.

Applying the Essential Question

1. Summarize the class discussion of the "stepping-stone" questions on pages 722–723.
2. Then, **ask** students to name a person who speaks out on important issues today. How has this person influenced society?
   Possible response: Answers will vary. Students should name a person and explain how his or her ideas have influenced people.

Critical Viewing

Interpreting Illustrations

1. Direct students to the illustration on page 722 of the men working on the early steam engine (1814).
2. **Ask:** What does the dress of the men suggest about their occupation?
   Possible response: Their top hats and collars suggest that they are the designers of the engine, not men employed to run it.

How does literature shape or reflect *society?*

The French Revolution hit Europe like a tidal wave. The Industrial Revolution, which owes so much to inventor James Watt's improvements to the steam engine, is still shaping the world today. The social history of the period is the story of how people in general, and writers in particular, reacted to the shocks of these revolutions.

How did political and industrial revolutions affect society?

"Bliss was it in that dawn to be alive . . ." In his autobiographical epic, *The Prelude*, William Wordsworth looks back on the heady days when he and the French Revolution were young. Europe, he says, was "thrilled with joy" at the prospect of "human nature seeming born again." (Book 6, lines 340–342) More personally and poignantly: "Bliss was it in that dawn to be alive, / But to be young was very Heaven." (Book 11, lines 108–109)

Disillusionment Sets In The Revolution, however, turned blindly destructive, and England and France went to war. The young poet's bliss faded quickly, as did that of many who had such hope in the beginning. Napoleon's crowning himself emperor ended any belief that human nature had been born again.

Trying to Bring Back the Old Order In the aftermath of Napoleon's defeat, those in power were determined that human nature would not be reborn, and that the old order would be restored—the privileged few would continue to rule. However, the forces of democratic reform had been unleashed and could not be suppressed.

Ideas That Would Not Die The original message of the Revolution, the one that had thrilled Wordsworth, was that people were to be free in their personal lives and free to choose their government—that all people were equally "citizens." Although the later course of the Revolution might have distorted these ideas, the ideas themselves would not die.

ESSENTIAL QUESTION VOCABULARY

These Essential Question words will help you think and write about literature and society:

privileged (priv′ ə lijd) *adj.* having rights or advantages denied to others

institution (in′ stə to͞o′ shən) *n.* established law, custom, or practice

industrial (in dus′ trē əl) *adj.* of or connected with industries or manufacturing

TIMELINE

1812

1813: Jane Austen publishes *Pride and Prejudice.*

1814: George Stephenson constructs first successful steam locomotive. ▶

1813: Mexico independence declared.

◀ **1815: Belgium** Napoleon defeated at Waterloo.

Think Aloud

Vocabulary: Using Context

Direct students' attention to the word *poignantly* in paragraph 2 on this page. Use the following "think aloud" to model the skill of using context to infer the meaning of the word. Say to students:

I may not know the meaning of the word *poignantly*. When I read the sentence, however, I realize that the writer is using *poignantly* to describe poetry written by Wordsworth. We also learn that these lines are more personal than the preceding ones. So I think *poignantly* refers to the personal feelings evoked in the reader by Wordsworth's reflections on his youth.

In England, a group of men and women, mostly Quakers, led by William Wilberforce, were determined that one ancient social institution would be abolished. Thanks to them, slavery was ended in England and in the empire.

The Reform Bill of 1832 was another part of the peaceful revolution that transformed England. It extended the right to vote to many males previously disqualified by lack of wealth. The 1832 bill was a step in a century-long journey that, in the end, gave all citizens voting rights.

The Application of Power to Work Revolutions are about power, and the Industrial Revolution was about the application of power to work: the creation of machines that work while human beings feed and "tend" them.

Unfortunately, the mills—and the cities that grew up around them—crushed and destroyed many who came from the countryside looking for new opportunities. Economic progress exacted an enormous human price.

How did writers react to revolutionary changes?

Direct Responses Some writers directly addressed the problems of their changing world. Mary Wollstonecraft, a witness to the French Revolution, urged a radical transformation of society in her *Vindication of the Rights of Woman.* Among other social institutions, she criticized "a false system of education" geared to make women marriageable rather than knowledgeable.

The BRITISH TRADITION

THE CHANGING ENGLISH LANGUAGE BY RICHARD LEDERER

The Romantic Age

During the Romantic Age, Britannia ruled the waves, and English ruled much of the land. As British ships traveled throughout the world, they left the language of the mother country in their wake but also came home from foreign ports laden with cargoes of words from other languages freighted with new meanings for English speakers.

The biggest and fattest unabridged English dictionaries hold more than 600,000 words, compared to German in second place with 185,000 words. One reason we have accumulated the world's largest and most varied vocabulary is that English continues to be the most hospitable and democratic language that has ever existed, unique in the number and variety of its borrowed words.

The following are words that became part of the English language as a result of England's great economic expansion.

Africa *banana, boorish, chimpanzee, gorilla, gumbo,* and *zebra*

Asia *gingham, indigo, mango,* and *typhoon*

Australia *boomerang* and *kangaroo*

India *bandanna, bungalow, calico, cashmere, china, cot, curry, juggernaut, jungle, loot, nirvana, polo, punch* (beverage), *thug,* and *verandah*

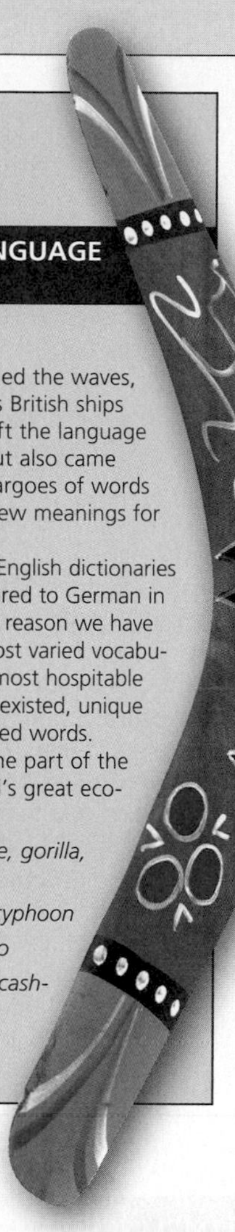

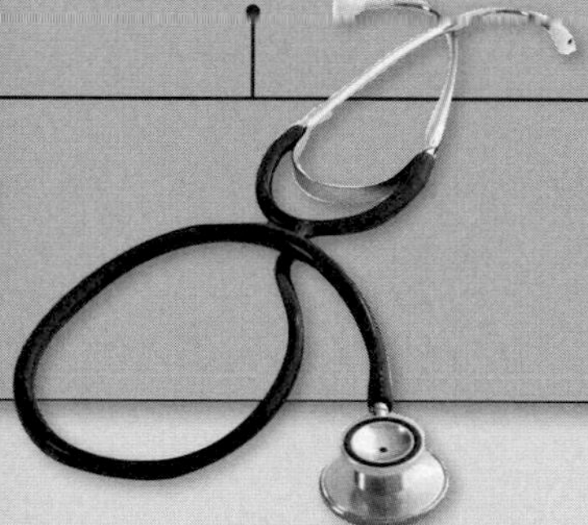

1816: France René Laënnec invents stethoscope. ▼

1818: Mary Wollstonecraft Shelley publishes *Frankenstein, or the Modern Prometheus.* ▲

1819: Peterloo Massacre in Manchester.

1819

The British Tradition

The Changing English Language

1. Have students read the sidebar feature about words that entered English as a result of the expansion of the British Empire.
2. Explain that the English language is unique in the sheer volume of its inclusion of words originating in other languages.
3. **Ask** students to note patterns and categories represented in the words listed in the sidebar. What are two prominent categories of objects represented by the lists of words?
   Possible response: *Banana, gumbo, mango, curry,* and *punch* refer to food and drink. *Chimpanzee, gorilla, zebra,* and *kangaroo* refer to animals.
4. **Ask** students why they think words referring to foods, animals, games, and fabrics are likely to come from other languages.
   Possible response: As people traveled from England throughout the world, they encountered foods, animals, games, and fabrics they had not seen before. They adapted the local names of these things and made the words part of the English language.

Background

Social Studies

Horatio Nelson, Viscount Nelson, and Arthur Wellesley, Duke of Wellington, were among the greatest heroes of their time. Nelson was in the naval service during the American Revolution. When he destroyed a French squadron in 1798, he became a celebrity. Nelson guaranteed his place in British history when, at the Battle of Trafalgar, he crippled the French and Spanish fleet, thereby averting an invasion of Britain. Wounded during that battle, he held onto life until he heard that fifteen enemy ships had been captured. His last words were, "Now I am satisfied. Thank God I have done my duty."

Wellington led a small force to victory in the Peninsular Wars. By 1814, he had pushed the French out of Portugal and Spain. When Napoleon was defeated once and for all at Waterloo, it was Wellington who led the British forces. Wellington's military prowess made him one of the most respected men in Europe.

Critical Viewing

Interpreting Photographs

1. Direct students to the photograph on page 724 of the Grecian urn.
2. **Ask:** Why do you think an object like this one would have appealed to the Romantic writers?
   Possible response: Because of the political turmoil of the Romantic period, writers may have wanted to idealize the ancient past. The image of the urn might appeal to this impulse.

© COMMON CORE ▪ MULTIPLE PERSPECTIVES ON THE ERA

Blake made his readers look at the reality of child labor in "The Chimney Sweeper." Lord Byron spoke "In Defense of the Lower Classes" when Parliament debated using the death penalty against protesting unemployed weavers. This rebellious aristocrat, who would later die in the Greek War of Independence, declared, "I have been in some of the most oppressed provinces of Turkey; but never . . . did I behold such squalid wretchedness as I have seen since my return, in the very heart of a Christian country."

Shelley's poem "Men of England" later became the anthem of the British Labour Party:

Men of England, wherefore plough
For the lords who lay ye low?
Wherefore weave with toil and care
The rich robes your tyrants wear?

Other Ways Some writers reminded people of other ways of being. Nature in the poetry of Wordsworth is not the artificial world of pastoral poetry. His nature is a cleaner, greener world in which human nature can be, if not reborn, at least restored. He writes in "Tintern Abbey": "Nature never did betray / The heart that loved her."

Revolution on a Page Not only that, Wordsworth's focus on common people and their language was a translation of the political goals of the French Revolution—"liberty, equality, fraternity"—into literature. If revolution had turned to terror on the stage of history, it still might be successful on the page.

An Era of Change The people of the time faced unprecedented changes. No political order could ever again be seen as unchangeable. That all people should be free and free to choose their leaders were ideas whose time had come. That economic progress could only be had at the cost of blighting the world was an idea to be challenged.

Some writers spoke out against the ills they saw; others looked inward or far away to see worlds that might be. Human nature was not born again, but human beings were changed profoundly.

Tintern Abbey

TIMELINE

1819

1819: Percy Bysshe Shelley writes "Ode to the West Wind."

1819: First steamship crosses Atlantic. ▶

1820: John Keats publishes "Ode on a Grecian Urn." ▶

Enrichment: Analyzing an Image from Fine Art

Frosty Morning, by J. M. W. Turner

The Romantic movement in literature found echoes in the other arts. The painter J. M. W. Turner (1775–1851) was noted for his depictions of scenes at sea as well as landscapes. His emphasis on the effects of light at the expense of objects suggests, perhaps, a perception of the spirit in nature comparable to Wordsworth's—"A presence that disturbs me with the joy / Of elevated thoughts . . . / Whose dwelling is the light of setting suns . . ."

Activity: Examine Art Have students view Turner's *Frosty Morning* on page 59 of the **Fine Art Transparencies, Volume 1.** Have them fill out the **Analyzing an Image from Fine Art** worksheet, ***Professional Development Guidebook,*** page 232.

What is the relationship of the writer to *tradition?*

No writer of the period called himself or herself "Romantic," but later critics applied the term because they saw consistent themes and attitudes in the literature. *Romantic* in this sense does not mean love stories. It means everything that is the opposite of the drab, the ordinary, the conventional, the routine, the predictable, and the expected.

The Faraway and Exotic Romantic literature can be realistic, as in Scottish poet Robert Burns's "To a Louse," but the emphasis is on the faraway and exotic, as in the Xanadu of Coleridge's "Kubla Khan" and the fantastic and supernatural of his *The Rime of the Ancient Mariner.*

In what ways did Romantics reject previous traditions?

Discarding Eighteenth-Century Forms Romantics were by nature rebellious, unhappy with and unwilling to settle for the status quo. They cast aside the literary forms and subjects that had dominated the previous century—no more conventions and artificialities, satires and heroic couplets. Such forms were to be swept away, as the French Revolution had swept away powdered wigs and knee breeches. Prefigured by Burns and Blake, the new literature was to be authentic and sincere.

Using Ordinary Speech The use of ordinary speech in Romantic literature gave it its authentic feel. The poems of Burns and Joanna Baillie, written in Scottish dialect, proved to be popular with people of the common, or uneducated, class. Romantics achieved sincerity by revealing their personal thoughts and feelings. For example, Wordsworth charts the development of his consciousness with sincerity in *The Prelude.*

Political Rebels Writers were also rebelling against a political order that had, after victory over Napoleon's tyranny, itself become reactionary and repressive. They rebelled against an economic system that turned men, women, and children into factory "hands." They idolized seventeenth-century writer John Milton, in whom they saw a poet who stood up to kings and valued poetry for its prophetic strain.

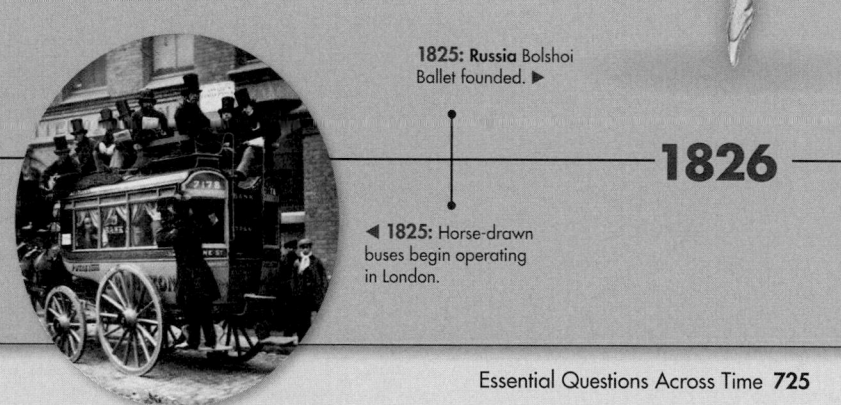

1825: Russia Bolshoi Ballet founded. ▶

1826

◀ **1825:** Horse-drawn buses begin operating in London.

Teaching the Essential Question

What is the relationship of the writer to tradition?

1. Before they read this section of the essay, tell students that Romantic authors rejected some traditions while reviving others. In addition, the period generated its own traditions, which have lasted through the years.
2. Have students read this section of the essay. Then, pose the first stepping-stone question. **Ask:** In what ways did Romantics reject previous traditions?
   Answer: They discarded forms from the eighteenth century, such as satires and heroic couplets, in favor of more authentic forms. They used ordinary speech in their work. They also rebelled against the political and economic order of the time.
3. Then, **ask** the second stepping-stone question: What poetical traditions did the Romantics revive?
   Answer: They revived the sonnet and the ode.
4. Then, **ask** the third stepping-stone question: What mysterious literary figure did the Romantics create?
   Answer: They created the Byronic hero.
5. **Ask** the fourth and final stepping-stone question: What prose genres did the Romantics invent?
   Answer: They invented a comic novel that focused on the lives of middle-class families as well as the Gothic horror novel.

Differentiated Instruction for Universal Access

Culture Focus

Explain to students that English society was extremely stratified during the Romantic period. Great barriers separated different classes from one another. One of these barriers was the way people spoke, or their dialects. For many years, literature had been written in the English of the aristocracy. One way that Romantic writers sought to break down class barriers was by using ordinary speech in their writing. One example of this is the dialect poems of Robert Burns. Have students discuss the importance of dialect in literature and consider why the Romantic's use of ordinary speech was significant.

Applying the Essential Question

1. Summarize the class discussion of the "stepping-stone" questions on pages 725–726.
2. Then, **ask** students these questions: Do people today respect tradition more or less than the Romantics did? Do you think that respect for cultural and social traditions is important? Why or why not?
   Possible response: People today respect tradition less than the Romantics did.

Critical Viewing

Interpreting Illustrations

1. Direct students to the illustration on page 726 of the railway.
2. **Ask:** How did changes in technology parallel the Romantics' rejection of previous traditions?
   Possible response: The Romantic era saw huge changes in technology because of the Industrial Revolution. At the same time that the Romantics were trying new ways of expressing themselves artistically, people were developing new methods of travel and manufacturing.

Background

Science

The railroad, which had its beginnings in the early nineteenth century, was to change the face of the nation. Businesses could ship materials and products more quickly, more reliably, and in greater quantities than ever before. Better transportation encouraged industry to grow even faster. By the middle of the century, extensive, fast travel was available even to the poor—Parliament decreed that certain trains take passengers for only a penny per mile. The first steam-powered locomotive, built in 1814, ran at 5 miles per hour. By the 1850s, trains would average speeds around 20 miles per hour—quadruple their original speed.

Ask students to speculate about how life might have changed for the average Briton when passenger service began on trains.
Possible response: Students may answer that families spread out more, or that it became easier to maintain relations over a distance.

COMMON CORE ▪ MULTIPLE PERSPECTIVES ON THE ERA

What poetical traditions did the Romantics revive?

The Sonnet Romantic poets revived the sonnet, which had virtually disappeared after Milton. Wordsworth used it as a political form in "London, 1802" and Shelley as a visionary form in "Ozymandias" and in "Ode to the West Wind," which is made up of linked sonnets.

The Ode In addition, the Romantics brought to perfection one of the oldest forms of poetry—the ode. Odes were written by Wordsworth, Coleridge, Shelley and, most notably, twenty-four-year-old John Keats.

What mysterious literary figure did the Romantics create?

The Byronic Hero Lord Byron embodies in his life the spirit of the age. A handsome, club-footed aristocrat who scorned the rules of society, he was described as "mad, bad and dangerous to know." Byron created in his person and in his characters the Byronic Hero—mysterious, brooding, threatening. That hero is the distant ancestor of today's mysterious outsiders, whether in film, literature, or the graphic novel.

What prose genres did the Romantics invent?

The leading novelists of the period were Jane Austen and Sir Walter Scott. Austen created a kind of comic novel that focused on the manners of middle-class people, depicting the follies and foibles of families. Her insights into human behavior and her comic touches have inspired today's directors to make film versions of Austen's *Emma* and *Pride and Prejudice*. Scott, regarded as the inventor of the historical novel, took readers back into the history, myths, and legends of England and Scotland. A best seller of his time and the creator of an enduring genre, he fed the Romantic hunger for the distant and the exotic.

The Gothic Mary Shelley wrote *Frankenstein*, influenced by the relatively new tradition of the horror-filled Gothic novel. Doctor Frankenstein, in creating his monster, acts out the great Romantic theme of going beyond the limit. The novel reveals the disquieting shadow cast by science and reason. Frankenstein's monster, in his immense solitude, also seems to warn of a darker side of Romantic ideals—of a humanity that, seeking to redefine itself, is, instead, cut off from its origins.

ESSENTIAL QUESTION VOCABULARY

These Essential Question words will help you think and write about the writer and tradition:

conventional (kən ven′ shə nəl) *n.* usually an adjective, it refers as a noun to whatever follows rules and is not original

routine (ro͞o tēn′) *n.* regular, customary procedure

foibles (foi′ bəlz) *n.* small weaknesses in character

TIMELINE

1826

1827: System for purifying London water installed.

1829: Robert Peel establishes Metropolitan Police in London. ▶

1830: Liverpool–Manchester railway opens. ▼

The **BRITISH TRADITION**

CONTEMPORARY CONNECTION

Jane Austen, Movie Star

At first glance, Jane Austen, a nineteenth-century novelist, seems an improbable box-office draw.

She never married, lived with her mother and sister, and died at age 41. Her novels lack sensation of the kind that modern audiences might be thought to crave. They mostly depict the lives of well-brought-up young ladies as they embark on the marriage-go-round.

Yet, since the 1990s, there have been literally dozens of successful film adaptations of Austen's books.

Some have been faithful to the original setting of her works, such as the 2005 *Pride and Prejudice* starring Keira Knightley. Other movies, such as *Clueless*, have transplanted plot and characters to more contemporary settings.

In 2007, the film *Becoming Jane* was made about Austen's own life, a fact that would certainly have brought a wry smile to her face.

As Hollywood has discovered, Austen's portrayal of human nature hits the mark every time. Her heroes and heroines may wear top hats and layers of petticoats. They may ride sedately in horse-drawn carriages. However, in their king's English, they speak directly to today's audiences, who see in these characters' dilemmas and decisions reflections of their own.

1831: Michael Faraday demonstrates electromagnetic induction. ▶

◀ **1831: United States** Edgar Allan Poe publishes *Poems*.

1832

1832: First Reform Act extends voting rights.

The British Tradition

Contemporary Connection

Discuss with students what makes a story timeless. Encourage students to name some old stories that they think have remained relevant over time. What elements do these tales share? Explain that many people consider the novels of Jane Austen to be relevant today. In fact, numerous film adaptations have been made of her novels. Have interested students view one of the film adaptations of Austen's novels. Ask students to discuss what makes the stories timeless.

Differentiated Instruction for Universal Access

Strategy for Special-Needs Students
Some students may find the account of the Romantics' relationship to tradition difficult to follow. Encourage students to read sections of the text chorally to help their comprehension.

Strategy for Less Proficient Readers
Provide students with examples of sonnets and odes. Point out the features of each type of poetry. Explain that although the Romantics rejected many traditions, they also idealized some aspects of the past, such as these forms of poetry.

Strategy for Advanced Readers
Ask students to choose a hero from a book, film, or television show whom they consider to be an example of the Byronic hero. Have students discuss what people find appealing about this character.

Recent Scholarship

Elizabeth McCracken

1. Elizabeth McCracken introduces the unit and provides insights into early nineteenth-century literature. Her commentary on the "Introduction to Frankenstein" appears later in the unit on pages 756–757.
2. Have students read the Meet the Author feature about Elizabeth McCracken. Tell them that McCracken draws on experiences from her own life as inspiration for her work. Both McCracken and Shelley wrote novels that were inspired by personal experiences.
3. Use the ***See It!* DVD** to introduce Elizabeth McCracken. Show Segment 1 to provide insight into her writing career. After students have watched the segment, **ask** how Romanticism has affected McCracken's work.
   Possible response: She draws on Romantic ideals, such as originality, imagination, and love. Her unique characters are formations of these Romantic virtues.

Creating a Legend

1. Explain to students that the creature from Jewish folklore that McCracken refers to is known as a *golem.* A golem is not intelligent and could accidentally turn on and harm its creator. **Ask** students how this is similar to the legend of Frankenstein.
   Possible response: the hubris of people thinking they have the godlike power to create life, and the creature turning on its maker
2. Tell students that the earliest automata were toys used in ancient Greece for demonstrating scientific principles. Leonardo da Vinci included a sketch in his notebooks for a complex automaton that could move. During the eighteenth century, clockwork mechanisms were perfected that allowed automata to write and draw.

PHLit Online!

All video resources are available online at **www.PHLitOnline.com.**

Ⓒ COMMON CORE ▪ MULTIPLE PERSPECTIVES ON THE ERA

Recent Scholarship

Creating a Legend

Mary Shelley wasn't the first person to imagine creating a living being out of something dead. The subtitle of *Frankenstein—The Modern Prometheus*—refers to the mythological Greek titan who made men out of clay. In a famous Jewish myth, a learned rabbi creates a creature out of clay to protect the Jewish people. Throughout the eighteenth century, inventors created increasingly complicated automata—early robots—who could eat, make musical instruments, and even play chess. People have always been fascinated by trying to create life, or the appearance of it, using nonliving material.

Science Explained

But Mary Shelley was the first writer to explain the notion of someone creating an actual living, breathing being using scientific methods. She was the product of her times. The eighteenth century was a time of enormous scientific discovery, including the work of Isaac Newton, the father of modern physics; the chemist Antoine Lavoisier; and Benjamin Franklin, with his experiments into electricity. Scientists and philosophers of the eighteenth century spoke of "The New Science," meaning that the universe could be understood by human beings who observed the natural world.

About the Author

Born in in 1966 in Boston, Massachuset[ts] to editor/writer parents, Elizabeth McCracken worked full time as a librarian until 1995. She draws on her love of that profession in the novel *The Giant's House: A Romance* (1996), which was a National Book Award finalist for fiction. Other work[s] include the notable collection of short works, *Here's Your Hat, What's Your Hurry* (1993).

PROMETHÉE

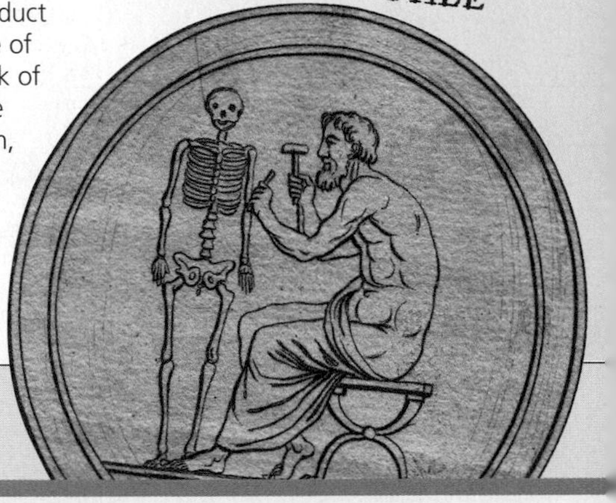

Science Explained

1. Have students read the description of the science of the period.
2. **Ask** students which of these advances they think Mary Shelley might have been likely to draw upon in her fiction.
   Possible responses: The research into electricity or the new discoveries in the field of chemistry might have been used by Mary Shelley's scientist to animate the creature.

Part of the Natural World

In the early nineteenth century, writing and science became more aligned than ever before. Percy Shelley was a passionate student of all the sciences. His college room was filled with his experiments. John Keats studied as a doctor. The "Dr. Darwin" mentioned in Mary Shelley's introduction is Charles's grandfather, Erasmus Darwin, who was not only a doctor, botanist, and inventor, but also a best-selling poet. William Wordsworth, Lord Byron, Percy Shelley, and John Keats all read Darwin and took what they learned about the natural world and applied it to their poetry. To be a human being was to be part of the natural world, and to write about nature, you had to study it very carefully. When the Romantic poets wrote about nature, they were also writing about the human condition. We are nature, and nature is us.

And, Mary Shelley might suggest, we better not mess with it. *Frankenstein* is filled with real and imagined science, but one of the reasons it's been popular for so long is that, at the dawn of modern science, Mary Shelley talked about how it was both exciting and dangerous. Before writing *Frankenstein*, Mary Shelley had had a child who died a few days after birth, and in her journal she writes of a dream in which the baby "came to life again . . . it had only been cold . . . and we rubbed it before the fire, and it lived." She knew the pain of wanting to bring something that was dead back to life, and then she wrote a book about the dangers.

Frankenstein had many children—characters from *Blade Runner, Robocop,* and *The Terminator,* clones and androids in any number of science fiction novels. You give something life, and then it goes amuck. Even now, when people argue about the latest scientific advances—transplants of animal organs, artificial organs, and of course cloning—*Frankenstein* is often the cautionary tale. We are nature, and nature is us, and we can never hope to completely master it.

▶ **Critical Viewing** In what way is a figure like this one a "Son of Frankenstein"?

Research and Technology: Synthesizing Information

As Elizabeth McCracken points out, Mary Shelley's *Frankenstein* influenced many horror movies about scientists going too far in their investigations. Working with a partner, create an **annotated filmography** of such films. Entitled "Frankenstein's Children," your filmography should include this information for each entry: title of movie, year of release, director, main actors, plot summary, and relationship to the Frankenstein theme of meddling with nature. For your research, use books on film and online resources like the Internet Movie Database. Consider using a simple *database* or *Excel chart* for your filmography and *integrating it into a word-processed document.*

Part of the Natural World

1. Have students read McCracken's commentary on the relationship between science and nature.
2. McCracken explains the effects of scientific discovery on the writers of the early nineteenth century. **Ask:** How has scientific advancement continued to affect writers since the nineteenth century? **Possible answer:** Writers throughout the years have used scientific discoveries as sources of inspiration. Science fiction, for example, is filled with knowledge and possibilities gained from science.
3. Tell students that they will also read a commentary by Elizabeth McCracken in Part 1 of this unit, in which she explains her love of the horror genre.

Research and Technology

Synthesizing Information

1. Review the assignment with students.
2. Discuss keyword terms that students might use to find titles to include in their filmographies, such as *robots, automata,* and *monsters.* Remind them to include a plot summary and the connections they see to the Frankenstein story.
3. After students compile the filmographies, have them discuss their findings in class. Have students share their responses.
4. To help conduct the discussion, use the Discussion Guide, in the *Professional Development Guidebook,* page 65.

Critical Viewing

Possible response: He is also an artificial creature and is very dangerous and destructive.

ASSESS

Answers

Common Core State Standards

- **Reading Informational Text 7**
- **Speaking and Listening 1, 1.c**

Integrate and Evaluate Information

1. Review the chart assignment with the class. Then, ask students to use the Activity A chart in the **Following Through** worksheet (p. 6 in ***Unit 4 Resources***) to complete this activity.
   Possible responses: Literature and Place: Author—Coleridge; Key Concept—Use of exotic and faraway locations. Literature and Society: Author—Byron; Key Concept—Reaction to revolutionary changes.
2. **Possible responses:** The pamphlet on p. 716 helps express the belief that common people had basic rights and that industry was becoming tyrannical. The painting on p. 720 shows a steamboat, a symbol of "progress," but its dark shadows and smoke suggest the dark side of technology. The photo on p. 721 depicts the natural beauty that inspired the Romantics' imaginations.
3. **Possible responses:** Students may cite the Industrial Revolution and note the disparate perspectives of the wealthy industrialists, who gained financially, and the workers, who suffered. Students might also cite the French Revolution, urbanization, or new poetic forms, all of which championed the new over the old.
4. Some students may respond that people in today's world no longer identify with nature but instead exploit its resources for profit. Others may point to the "green" movement—a growing collective understanding that if we harm nature, we harm ourselves.

Integrate and Evaluate Information

1. Use a chart like the one shown to determine the key ideas expressed in the Essential Question essays on pages 720–726. Fill in two ideas related to each Essential Question and note the authors most closely associated with each concept. One example has been done for you.

Essential Question	Author	Key Concept
Literature and Place		
Literature and Society		
Writer and Tradition	William Wordsworth	Using ordinary speech

2. How do the visual sources in this section—artifacts, paintings, photographs, and illustrations—add to your understanding of the ideas expressed in words? Cite specific examples.
3. The Romantic period was characterized by innovation and a rejection of tradition. Sometimes these innovations led to positive changes and a greater degree of freedom. Other times, they created new problems. Choose one innovation or change that emerged during this period and describe the various perspectives of those it affected. Who gained something from the change? Who lost something or was harmed by it? Cite evidence from the multiple sources presented on pages 718–726 in your answer.
4. **Address a Question** According to Elizabeth McCracken, the Romantic poets understood that "we are nature, and nature is us." What do you think McCracken means by this? In your view, is this idea mostly honored or ignored in today's world? Integrate information from this textbook and other sources to support your ideas.

Speaking and Listening: Press Conference

Romantic poets challenged earlier literary practices. With a group, stage a **press conference** in which Wordsworth; his sister, Dorothy; and Coleridge answer questions about their Romantic beliefs. The questioners are journalists who pose challenging queries like these:

- Why do Romantics reject refined language?
- Why do Romantics promote dangerous revolutionary ideas?
- Why are Romantics prejudiced against cities?

Solve a Research Problem: This assignment requires you to integrate information and distinguish nuances in Romantic beliefs. To prepare, research Romantic ideas about language, politics, and nature. Identify print and media sources that provide reliable information about Romanticism. Consider using various types of sources, including

- **primary sources,** or the poets' written works; and
- **secondary sources,** or books and articles about this era.

Create a list of sources you used to prepare.

Common Core State Standards

Reading Informational Text
7. Integrate and evaluate multiple sources of information presented in different media or formats as well as in words in order to address a question or solve a problem.

Speaking and Listening
1. Initiate and participate effectively in a range of collaborative discussions with diverse partners on *grades 11–12 topics, texts, and issues,* building on others' ideas and expressing their own clearly and persuasively.
1.c. Propel conversations by posing and responding to questions that probe reasoning and evidence; ensure a hearing for a full range of positions on a topic or issue; clarify, verify, or challenge ideas and conclusions; and promote divergent and creative perspectives.

ESSENTIAL QUESTION VOCABULARY

Use these words in your responses:

Literature and Place
exotic
secular
residential

Literature and Society
privileged
institution
industrial

The Writer and Tradition
conventional
routine
foibles

Speaking and Listening

1. Review the assignment, pointing out that students are to stage a press conference on Romantic beliefs.
2. Analyze the activity and identify its key terms: *press conference; refined language; revolutionary ideas; distinguish nuances; primary sources; secondary sources.*
3. Then, have students complete Activity B in the **Following Through** worksheet (p. 6 of ***Unit 4 Resources***).
4. After students have completed their press conferences, have them discuss which arguments they found most compelling.

Fantasy and Reality

PART 1

Text Complexity: At a Glance

This chart gives a general text complexity rating for the selections in this part of the unit to help guide instruction. For additional text complexity support, see the Test Complexity Rubric at point of use.

To a Mouse	**More Complex**	The Tyger	**More Accessible**
To a Louse	**More Complex**	The Chimney Sweeper	**More Complex**
Woo'd and Married and A'	**More Accessible**	Infant Sorrow	**More Accessible**
The Lamb	**More Accessible**	Introduction to Frankenstein	**More Complex**

Selection Planning Guide

The selections that follow may be described as wild imaginings or as glimpses of real life. Each straddles the line between fantasy and reality.

The poems of Robert Burns take a down-to-earth view of life, presented through fanciful addresses to two creatures he encounters. William Blake's poems, as well as his personal beliefs and philosophies, are strange but compelling combinations of reality and fancy.

Mary Shelley's "Introduction to *Frankenstein*" is the author's true account of how she came to write the novel. Imbedded in the account are the author's remembrances of fantastic dreams and visions that inspired the tale of horror.

Humanities

Jacob's Ladder, 1806, by William Blake

A large part of poet and artist William Blake's (1757–1827) work consists of illustrated poems, also referred to as "illuminated printing." *Jacob's Ladder*, however, is one of his watercolor paintings. This piece depicts the scene described in the biblical book of Genesis in which a ladder reaching from Earth to heaven appears to Jacob as he lies sleeping.

1. Ask students to discuss in which ways this painting is realistic and in which ways it is fantastic.
2. Next, **ask:** How does this art connect to the theme "Fantasy and Reality"?
   Possible response: This piece is an artist's rendering of a dream. It is often during dreams that the line between fantasy and reality is blurred. People sometimes describe even the most outrageous dreams as seeming very real.

Monitoring Progress

Before students read the poetry by Robert Burns and Joanna Baillie, refer to the results for the Vocabulary in Context items on **Benchmark Test 8 (*Unit 4 Resources*, pp. 201-203).** Use this diagnostic portion of the test to guide your choice of selections to teach as well as the depth of prereading preparation you will provide, based on students' readiness for the Reading and Vocabulary skills.

COMMON CORE
Time and Resource Manager

To a Mouse • To a Louse • Woo'd and Married and A'
Lesson Pacing Guide

DAY 1 Preteach

- Administer the Reading and Vocabulary Warm-ups (*Unit 4 Resources,* pp. 7–10) as necessary.
- Introduce the Literary Analysis concept: Dialect.
- Introduce the Reading Strategy: Analyzing Text Features.
- Teach the selection vocabulary.
- Build background with the author and Background features.
- Develop thematic thinking with Connecting to the Essential Question.

DAYS 2–3 Preteach/Teach/Assess

- Distribute copies of the appropriate graphic organizer for Reading Strategy (*Graphic Organizer Transparencies,* pp. 128–129).
- Distribute copies of the appropriate graphic organizer for Literary Analysis (*Graphic Organizer Transparencies,* pp. 130–131)
- Prepare students to read with the Activating Prior Knowledge activities (TE).
- Informally monitor comprehension while students read.
- Use the Reading Check questions to confirm comprehension.
- Develop students' understanding of dialect using the Literary Analysis prompt.
- Develop students' ability to analyze text features using the Reading Strategy prompt.
- Reinforce vocabulary with the Vocabulary notes.
- Assess students' comprehension and mastery of the skills by having them answer the Critical Reading, Literary Analysis, and Reading Strategy questions.
- Have students complete the Vocabulary Lesson.

DAY 4 Extend/Assess

- Have students complete the Writing Lesson and write a persuasive speech. (You may assign as homework.)
- Administer Selection Test A or B (*Unit 4 Resources,* pp. 19–21 or 22–24).

Common Core State Standards

Reading Literature 4. Determine the meaning of words and phrases as they are used in the text, including figurative and connotative meanings; analyze the impact of specific word choices on meaning and tone, including words with multiple meanings or language that is particularly fresh, engaging, or beautiful.

Writing 1.b. Develop claim(s) and counterclaims fairly and thoroughly, supplying the most relevant evidence for each while pointing out the strengths and limitations of both in a manner that anticipates the audience's knowledge level, concerns, values, and possible biases.

Language 5.b. Analyze nuances in the meaning of words with similar denotations.

Additional Standards Practice
Common Core Companion,* *pp. 41–48; 185–195; 332–335

Daily Block Scheduling
Each day in this Lesson Pacing Guide represents a 40–50 minute period. Teachers using block scheduling may combine days to revise pacing. In addition, teachers may differentiate and support core instruction by integrating components for extended and intensive support as students require. See the Guide to Selected Leveled Resources (facing page).

Guide to Selected Leveled Resources

	RTI **Tier 1** (students performing on level)	To a Mouse • To a Louse • Woo'd and Married and A'
Warm Up	**Practice, model,** and **monitor** fluency, working **with the whole class** or **in groups.**	Vocabulary and Reading Warm-ups B, *Unit 4 Resources,* pp. 7–8, 10
Comprehension/Skills	**Support** and **monitor** comprehension and skills development, having students complete the activities, graphic organizers, and interactive prompts **independently** or **as a class.**	• ***Reader's Notebook,*** adapted instruction and full selection EL ***Reader's Notebook: English Learner's Version,*** adapted instruction and adapted selection • **Reading Strategy Graphic Organizer B, *Graphic Organizer Transparencies,*** p. 133 • **Literary Analysis Graphic Organizer B, *Graphic Organizer Transparencies,*** p. 135
Monitor Progress	**Monitor** student progress with the differentiated curriculum-based assessment in the *Unit Resources.*	• **Selection Test B, *Unit 4 Resources,*** pp. 22–24 • **Open-Book Test, *Unit 4 Resources,*** pp. 16–18

	RTI **Tier 2** (students requiring intervention)	To a Mouse • To a Louse • Woo'd and Married and A'
Warm Up	**Practice, model,** and **monitor** fluency **in groups** or **with individuals.**	• **Vocabulary and Reading Warm-ups A, *Unit 4 Resources,*** pp. 7–9 • ***Hear It!* Audio CD (adapted text)**
Comprehension/Skills	• **Support** and **monitor** comprehension and skills development, working **in small groups** or **with individuals.** • As students complete the selection in the appropriate version of the *Reader's Notebook,* **monitor** comprehension frequently with group questions and individual instruction. • **Model** strategies while guiding students in completing the activities and prompts in the *Reader's Notebook,* as well as the graphic organizers. • **Practice** skills and **monitor** mastery with the *Reading Kit* worksheets.	• ***Reader's Notebook: Adapted Version,*** adapted instruction and adapted selection EL ***Reader's Notebook: English Learner's Version,*** adapted instruction and adapted selection • **Reading Strategy Graphic Organizer A, *Graphic Organizer Transparencies,*** p. 132 • **Literary Analysis Graphic Organizer A, *Graphic Organizer Transparencies,*** p. 134 • ***Reading Kit,*** Practice worksheets
Monitor Progress	**Monitor** student progress with the differentiated curriculum-based assessment in the *Unit Resources* and in the *Reading Kit.*	• **Selection Test A, *Unit 4 Resources,*** pp. 19–21 • ***Reading Kit,*** Assess worksheets

TIER 3 Tier 3 intervention may require consultation with the student's special-education or dyslexia specialist. For additional support, see the Tier 2 activities and resources listed above.

One-on-one teaching **Group work** **Whole class instruction** **Independent work** **A Assessment**

For a complete guide to selection support, including support for Advanced students, see the Overview of Resources in the frontmatter.

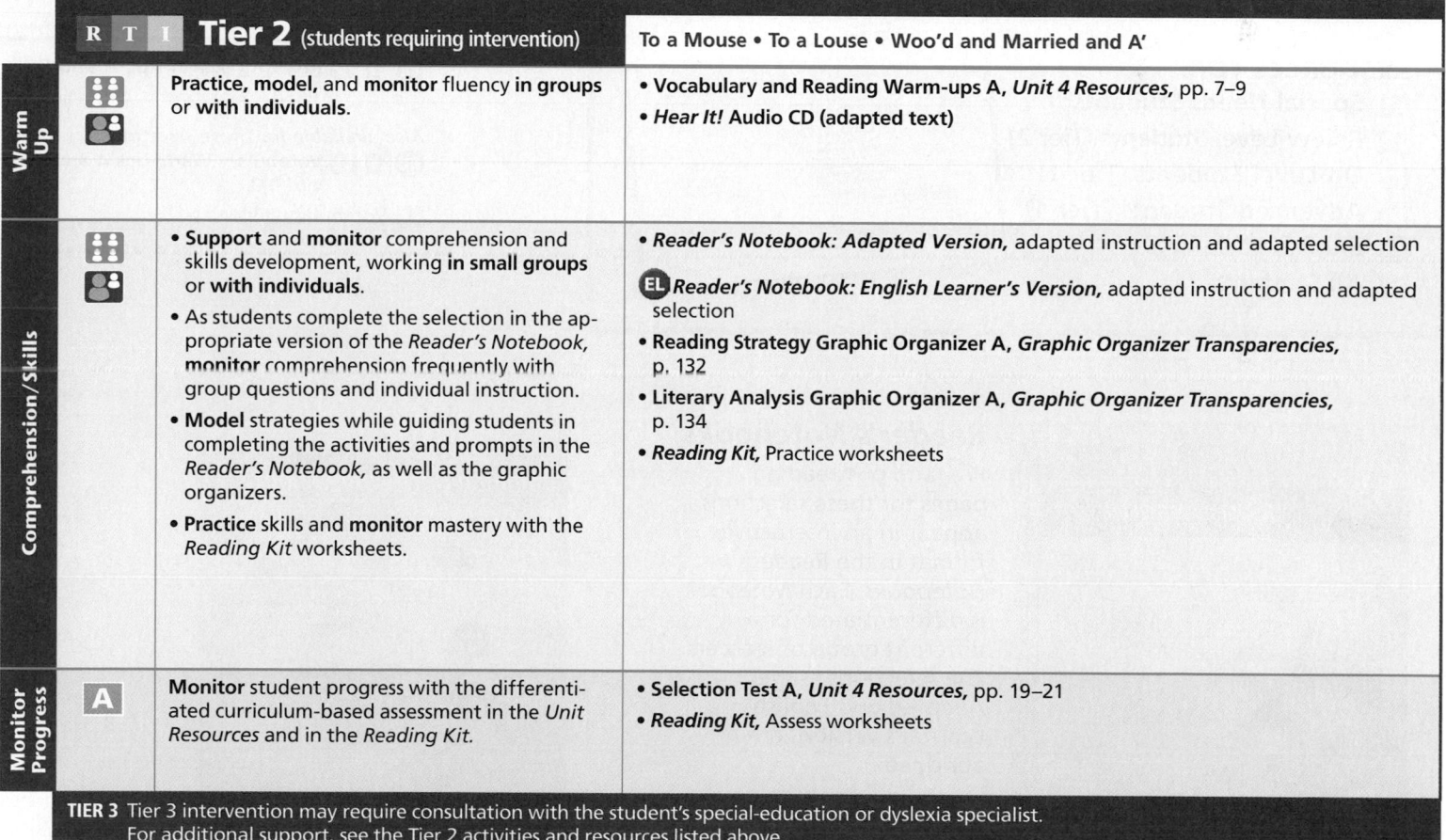

To a Mouse • To a Louse • Woo'd and Married and A'

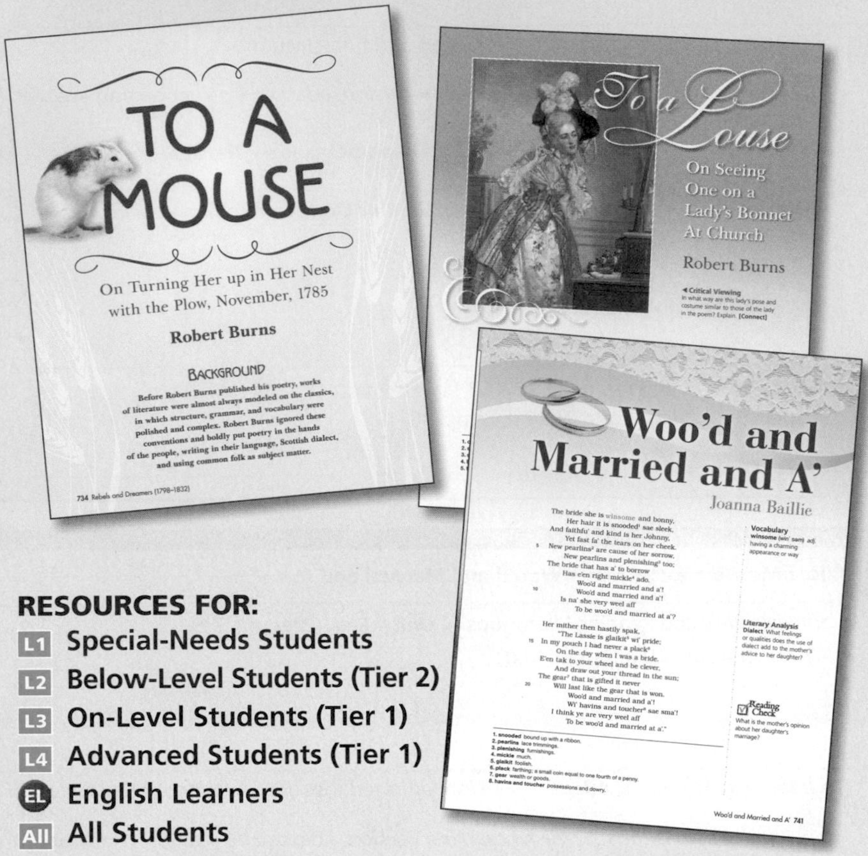

TO A MOUSE

On Turning Her up in Her Nest with the Plow, November, 1785

Robert Burns

BACKGROUND

Before Robert Burns published his poetry, works of literature were almost always modeled on the classics, in which structure, grammar, and vocabulary were polished and complex. Robert Burns ignored these conventions and boldly put poetry in the hands of the people, writing in their language, Scottish dialect, and using common folk as subject matter.

734 Rebels and Dreamers (1798–1832)

To a Louse

On Seeing One on a Lady's Bonnet At Church

Robert Burns

◄ Critical Viewing
In what way are this lady's pose and costume similar to those of the lady in the poem? Explain. [Connect]

Woo'd and Married and A'

Joanna Baillie

The bride she is winsome and bonny,
Her hair it is snooded¹ sae sleek,
And faithfu' and kind is her Johnny,
Yet fast fa' the tears on her cheek.
New pearlins² are cause of her sorrow,
New pearlins and plenishing³ too;
The bride that has a' to borrow
Has e'en right mickle⁴ ado.
Woo'd and married and a'!
Woo'd and married and a'!
Is na' she very weel aff
To be woo'd and married at a'?

Her mither then hastily spak,
"The Lassie is glaikit⁵ wi' pride;
In my pouch I had never a plack⁶
On the day when I was a bride.
E'en tak to your wheel and be clever,
And draw out your thread in the sun;
The gear⁷ that is gifted it never
Will last like the gear that is won.
Woo'd and married and a'!
Wi' havins and toucher⁸ sae sma'!
I think ye are very weel aff
To be woo'd and married at a'."

1. snooded bound up with a ribbon.
2. pearlins lace trimmings.
3. plenishing furnishings.
4. mickle much.
5. glaikit foolish.
6. plack farthing; a small coin equal to one fourth of a penny.
7. gear wealth or goods.
8. havins and toucher possessions and dowry.

Vocabulary
winsome (win' səm) adj. having a charming appearance or way

Literary Analysis
Dialect What feelings or qualities does the use of dialect add to the mother's advice to her daughter?

Reading Check
What is the mother's opinion about her daughter's marriage?

Woo'd and Married and A' 741

RESOURCES FOR:

- L1 Special-Needs Students
- L2 Below-Level Students (Tier 2)
- L3 On-Level Students (Tier 1)
- L4 Advanced Students (Tier 1)
- EL English Learners
- All All Students

Vocabulary/Fluency/Prior Knowledge

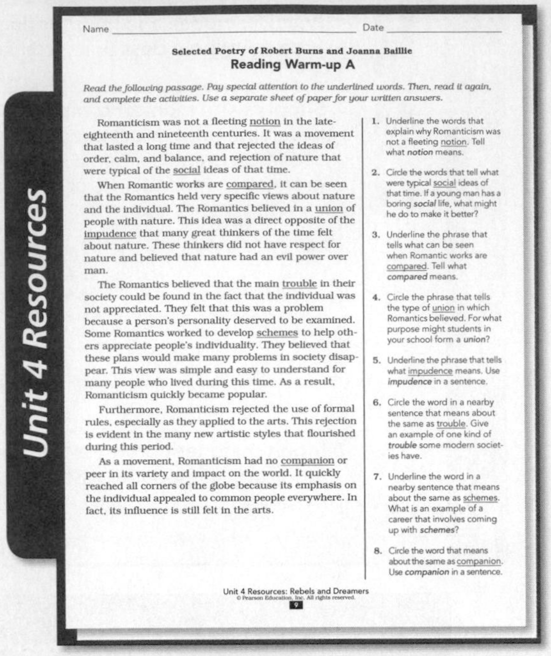

Unit 4 Resources

Name ______________________ Date ______________

Selected Poetry of Robert Burns and Joanna Baillie
Reading Warm-up A

Read the following passage. Pay special attention to the underlined words. Then, read it again, and complete the activities. Use a separate sheet of paper for your written answers.

Romanticism was not a fleeting notion in the late-eighteenth and nineteenth centuries. It was a movement that lasted a long time and that rejected the ideas of order, calm, and balance, and rejection of nature that were typical of the social ideas of that time.

When Romantic works are compared, it can be seen that the Romantics held very specific views about nature and the individual. The Romantics believed in a union of people with nature. This idea was a direct opposite of the impudence that many great thinkers of the time felt about nature. These thinkers did not have respect for nature and believed that nature had an evil power over man.

The Romantics believed that the main trouble in their society could be found in the fact that the individual was not appreciated. They felt that this was a problem because a person's personality deserved to be examined. Some Romantics worked to develop schemes to help others appreciate people's individuality. They believed that these plans would make many problems in society disappear. This view was simple and easy to understand for many people who lived during this time. As a result, Romanticism quickly became popular.

Furthermore, Romanticism rejected the use of formal rules, especially as they applied to the arts. This rejection is evident in the many new artistic styles that flourished during this period.

As a movement, Romanticism had no companion or peer in its variety and impact on the world. It quickly reached all corners of the globe because its emphasis on the individual appealed to common people everywhere. In fact, its influence is still felt in the arts.

1. Underline the words that explain why Romanticism was not a fleeting notion. Tell what *notion* means.
2. Circle the words that tell what were typical social ideas of that time. If a young man has a boring *social* life, what might he do to make it better?
3. Underline the phrase that tells what can be seen when Romantic works are compared. Tell what *compared* means.
4. Circle the phrase that tells the type of union in which Romantics believed. For what purpose might students in your school form a *union*?
5. Underline the phrase that tells what impudence means. Use *impudence* in a sentence.
6. Circle the word in a nearby sentence that means about the same as trouble. Give an example of one kind of *trouble* some modern societies have.
7. Underline the word in a nearby sentence that means about the same as schemes. What is an example of a career that involves coming up with *schemes*?
8. Circle the word that means about the same as companion. Use *companion* in a sentence.

Unit 4 Resources: Rebels and Dreamers
© Pearson Education, Inc. All rights reserved.
9

EL L1 L2 **Reading Warm-ups A and B,** pp. 9–10

Also available for these selections:

EL L1 L2 **Vocabulary Warm-ups A and B,** pp. 7–8

All **Vocabulary Builder,** p. 13

Reader's Notebooks

Pre- and postreading pages for these selections appear in an interactive format in the *Reader's Notebooks.* Each *Notebook* is differentiated for a different group of learners. The selections in the Adapted and English Learner's versions are abridged.

L2 L3 ***Reader's Notebook***

L1 ***Reader's Notebook: Adapted Version***

EL ***Reader's Notebook: English Learner's Version***

EL ***Reader's Notebook: Spanish Version***

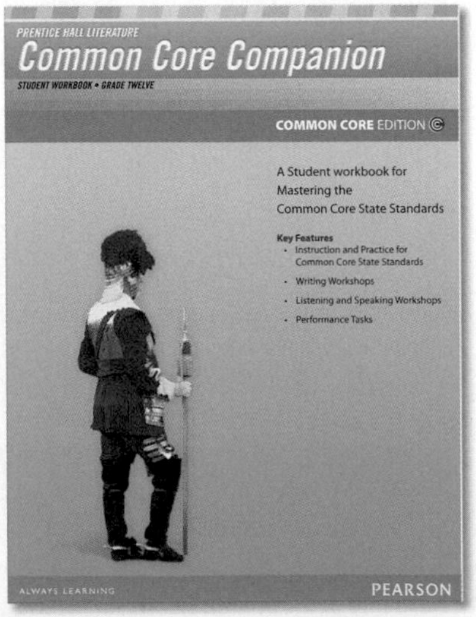

Common Core Companion

Additional instruction and practice for each Common Core State Standard

Selection Support

Graphic Organizer Transparencies

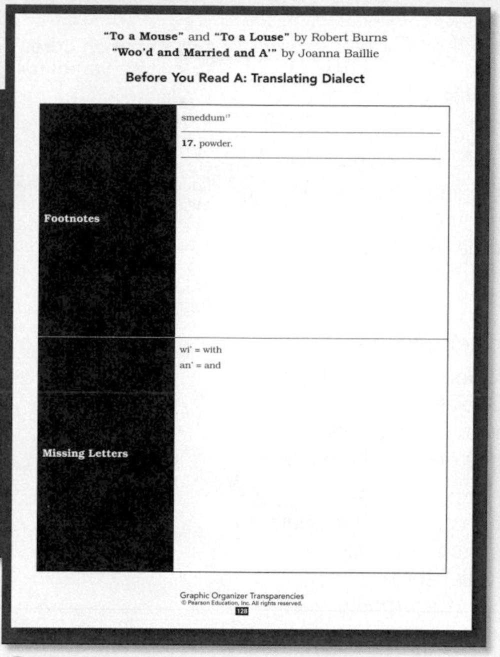
"To a Mouse" and "To a Louse" by Robert Burns
"Woo'd and Married and A'" by Joanna Baillie
Before You Read A: Translating Dialect

Footnotes	smeddum[17] 17. powder.
Missing Letters	wi' = with an' = and

Graphic Organizer Transparencies
© Pearson Education, Inc. All rights reserved.
128

EL L1 L2 **Reading: Graphic Organizer A** (partially filled in), p. 128

Also available for these selections:

EL L3 **Reading: Graphic Organizer B,** p. 129

EL L1 L2 **Literary Analysis: Graphic Organizer A** (partially filled in), p. 130

EL L3 **Literary Analysis: Graphic Organizer B,** p. 131

Skills Development/Extension

Unit 4 Resources

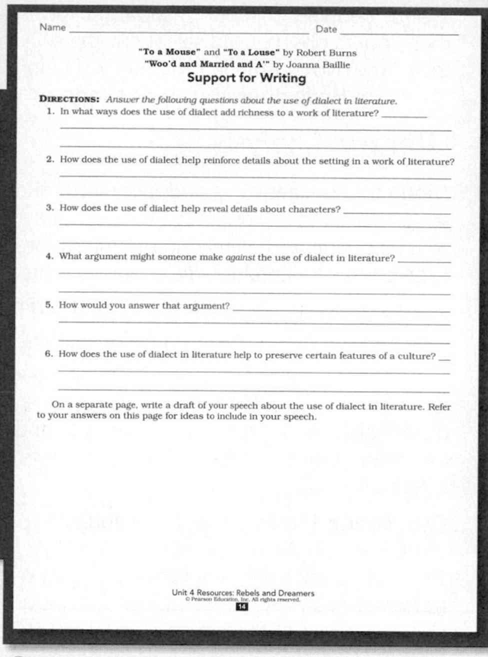
Name ______ Date ______

"To a Mouse" and "To a Louse" by Robert Burns
"Woo'd and Married and A'" by Joanna Baillie
Support for Writing

Directions: *Answer the following questions about the use of dialect in literature.*

1. In what ways does the use of dialect add richness to a work of literature? ______
2. How does the use of dialect help reinforce details about the setting in a work of literature?
3. How does the use of dialect help reveal details about characters? ______
4. What argument might someone make *against* the use of dialect in literature? ______
5. How would you answer that argument? ______
6. How does the use of dialect in literature help to preserve certain features of a culture? ______

On a separate page, write a draft of your speech about the use of dialect in literature. Refer to your answers on this page for ideas to include in your speech.

Unit 4 Resources: Rebels and Dreamers
© Pearson Education, Inc. All rights reserved.
14

EL L3 L4 **Support for Writing,** p. 14

Also available for these selections:

All **Literary Analysis,** p. 11

All **Reading,** p. 12

L4 **Enrichment,** p. 15

Assessment

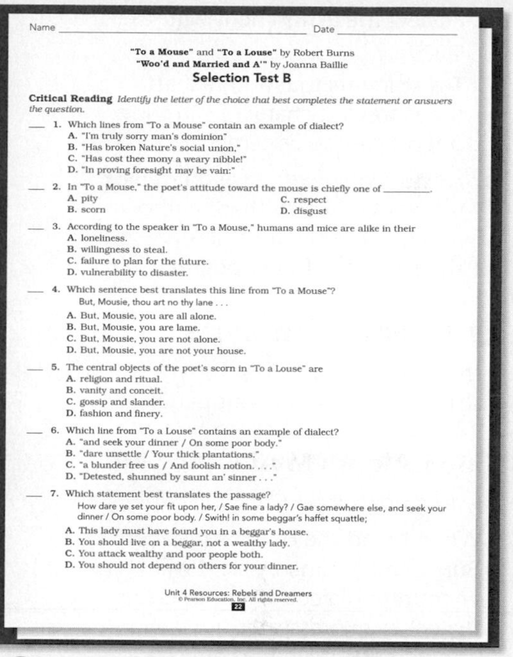
Name ______ Date ______

"To a Mouse" and "To a Louse" by Robert Burns
"Woo'd and Married and A'" by Joanna Baillie
Selection Test B

Critical Reading *Identify the letter of the choice that best completes the statement or answers the question.*

___ 1. Which lines from "To a Mouse" contain an example of dialect?
A. "I'm truly sorry man's dominion"
B. "Has broken Nature's social union,"
C. "Has cost thee mony a weary nibble!"
D. "In proving foresight may be vain:"

___ 2. In "To a Mouse," the poet's attitude toward the mouse is chiefly one of ______.
A. pity
B. scorn
C. respect
D. disgust

___ 3. According to the speaker in "To a Mouse," humans and mice are alike in their
A. loneliness.
B. willingness to steal.
C. failure to plan for the future.
D. vulnerability to disaster.

___ 4. Which sentence best translates this line from "To a Mouse"?
But, Mousie, thou art no thy lane . . .
A. But, Mousie, you are all alone.
B. But, Mousie, you are lame.
C. But, Mousie, you are not alone.
D. But, Mousie, you are not your house.

___ 5. The central objects of the poet's scorn in "To a Louse" are
A. religion and ritual.
B. vanity and conceit.
C. gossip and slander.
D. fashion and finery.

___ 6. Which line from "To a Louse" contains an example of dialect?
A. "and seek your dinner / On some poor body."
B. "dare unsettle / Your thick plantations."
C. "a blunder free us / And foolish notion. . . ."
D. "Detested, shunned by saunt an' sinner . . ."

___ 7. Which statement best translates the passage?
How dare ye set your fit upon her, / Sae fine a lady? / Gae somewhere else, and seek your dinner / On some poor body. / Swith! in some beggar's haffet squattle;
A. This lady must have found you in a beggar's house.
B. You should live on a beggar, not a wealthy lady.
C. You attack wealthy and poor people both.
D. You should not depend on others for your dinner.

Unit 4 Resources: Rebels and Dreamers
© Pearson Education, Inc. All rights reserved.
22

EL L3 L4 **Selection Test B,** pp. 22–24

Also available for these selections:

L3 L4 **Open-Book Test,** pp. 16–18

EL L1 L2 **Selection Test A,** pp. 19–21

PHLit Online!
www.PHLitOnline.com

- complete narrated selection text
- a thematically related video with writing prompt
- an interactive graphic organizer
- highlighting feature
- access to all student print resources, adapted to individual student needs
- Spanish and English summaries
- adapted selection translations in Spanish

Online Resources: All print materials are also available online.

Get Connected!

Also available:

Background Video
All videos are available in Spanish.

Vocabulary Central (tools and activities for studying vocabulary)

Also available:

Writer's Journal (with graphics feature)

PREETEACH

1 ## Connecting to the Essential Question

1. Review the assignment with the class.
2. Tell students that authors' attitudes toward characters in their poems can be discerned.
3. As students read, have them look for ways in which these authors make clear their attitudes toward the subjects of their poems.

2 Literary Analysis

Introduce the skill using the instruction on the student page.

Think Aloud: Model the Skill

Say to students:

When I read the poems of Robert Burns and Joanna Baillie, I will encounter dialect. These poets use dialect to express specific details about Scottish life that only language itself can express.

3 Reading Strategy

1. Introduce the skill using the instruction on the student page.
2. Give students a copy of **Reading Strategy Graphic Organizer B,** page 129 in ***Graphic Organizer Transparencies,*** to fill out as they read.

Think Aloud: Model the Skill

Say to students:

Dialect in poetry and prose can be confusing. I know that by using context clues and footnotes, I can more easily determine the meaning of words and phrases in dialect.

4 Vocabulary

1. Pronounce each word, giving its definition, and have students say it aloud.
2. For more guidance, see the ***Classroom Strategies and Teaching Routines*** card for introducing vocabulary.

Before You Read

To a Mouse • To a Louse • Woo'd and Married and A'

1 **Connecting to the Essential Question** These poets have a sharp eye for people's behavior in social situations. As you read, consider what these poets observe and say about the social customs and attitudes of their time. Noting this information will help you answer the Essential Question: **How does literature shape or reflect society?**

Common Core State Standards

Reading Literature
4. Determine the meaning of words and phrases as they are used in the text, including figurative and connotative meanings; analyze the impact of specific word choices on meaning and tone, including words with multiple meanings or language that is particularly fresh, engaging, or beautiful.

2 Literary Analysis

Dialect is the language, and particularly the speech habits, of a specific social class, region, or group. A dialect may vary from the standard form of a language in grammar, in pronunciation, and in the use of certain expressions. In literature, dialect helps achieve these goals:

- Establishing character, mood, and setting
- Adding "texture" or charm for readers who do not speak the dialect

By using dialect, Burns and Baillie broke with tradition and made their work accessible to the common folk who spoke that dialect. Their use of dialect also adds a sense of authenticity and freshness to the poems. As you read, note the ways in which the poets infuse the dialect with poetic effects.

Comparing Literary Works In addition to using dialect, Romantic poets like Burns and Baillie also introduced subjects drawn from everyday life. This shift away from lofty topics was part of the artistic rebellion known as *Romanticism*. As you read, compare how effectively these poets write about daily life in the language of common folk. Consider factors such as their ability to convey *mood*, or emotional atmosphere, and *meaning*.

3 Reading Strategy

Preparing to Read Complex Texts Even if you do not know Scottish dialect, you can **analyze information from text features** to interpret words. As you read, pay attention to features such as footnotes and apostrophes indicating missing letters in a word. Use a chart like the one shown to help you translate the dialect.

Footnotes	
sleekit[3]	**3.** sleek
Missing Letters	
woo'd, a'	wooed, all

4 Vocabulary

dominion (də min′ yən) *n.* rule; authority (p. 735)

impudence (im′ pyo͞o dəns) *n.* lack of shame; rudeness (p. 737)

winsome (win′ səm) *adj.* having a charming appearance or way (p. 741)

discretion (di skresh′ ən) *n.* good judgment; prudence (p. 742)

inconstantly (in kän′ stənt lē) *adv.* changeably; in a fickle way (p. 742)

PHLit Online! www.PHLitOnline.com

Vocabulary Development

Vocabulary Knowledge Rating

Create a **Vocabulary Knowledge Rating Chart** (***Professional Development Guidebook,*** p. 33) for the vocabulary words on the student page. Give each student a copy of the chart with the words on it. Read the words aloud, and have students mark their ratings in the Before Reading column. Urge students to attend to these words as they read and discuss the selections.

In order to gauge how much instruction you need to provide, tally how many students are confident in their knowledge of each word. As students read, point out the words and their context.

PHLit Online! **Vocabulary Central,** featuring tools and activities for studying vocabulary, is available online at **www.PHLitOnline.com.**

5 Robert Burns

(1759–1796)

Author of "To a Mouse" • "To a Louse"

Known as "The Voice of Scotland," Robert Burns wrote his first verse when he was fifteen. It was a love poem to a girl named Nellie, who was helping the Burns family with the harvest on their farm in Scotland. "Thus with me," Burns later wrote, "began Love and Poesy."

Poor But Learned Beginnings Burns was born at Alloway, in Ayrshire. Although poverty kept him from a full formal education, with his father's encouragement he read widely, studying the Bible, Shakespeare, and Alexander Pope. His mother, though herself illiterate, instilled in him a love of Scottish folk songs, legends, and proverbs.

Literary Triumph In 1786, Burns published his first collection of poems, *Poems, Chiefly in the Scottish Dialect,* through a small local press. The collection, which included "To a Mouse," was a huge success, applauded by critics and country folk alike. The new literary hero was invited to the Scottish capital, where he was swept into the social scene and hailed as the "heaven-taught plowman." When he died, thousands of people from all social levels followed his coffin to the grave.

A Lasting Contribution Although Burns died while just in his thirties, having suffered for years from a weak heart, his brief career resulted in a lasting contribution to literature. Burns's poems, written for the most part in dialect, are marked by their natural, direct, and spontaneous quality. Burns certainly drew on the ballad tradition of Scotland, but while some of the poet's work had its origins in folk tunes, "it is not," as critic James Douglas writes, "easy to tell where the vernacular ends and the personal magic begins."

"My heart's in the Highlands . . ."

Daily Bellringer

For each class during which you will teach these poems, have students complete one of the five activities for the appropriate week in the *Daily Bellringer Activities* booklet.

Multidraft Reading

To assist struggling readers and to enhance reading for all, assign the text in chunks, as warranted by length, and apply multidraft reading protocols. For each reading, have students set the purpose indicated:

- **First reading**—identifying key ideas and details and answering any Reading Checks.
- **Second reading**—analyzing craft and structure and responding to the side-column prompts.
- **Third reading**—integrating knowledge and ideas, connecting to other texts and the world, and answering the end-of-selection questions.

For more guidance, refer to the ***Classroom Strategies and Teaching Routines*** card on Multidraft Reading.

5 Background

More About the Author

Robert Burns was one of seven children born to a farmer and his wife near Alloway in Ayrshire. He was a voracious reader, who read as much literature—particularly Shakespeare—as he could. Burns's spare time in his childhood was devoted to helping his family as a plowman on their farm. In 1785, Burns's financial and domestic problems became so acute that he considered emigrating to Jamaica, but instead he continued to write prolifically, sent his poems to a publisher, and met immediate success upon their publication in 1786.

PHLit Online!

www.PHLitOnline.com

Teaching From Technology

Preparing to Read

Go to **www.PHLitOnline.com** and display the ***Get Connected!*** slideshow for these selections. Have the class brainstorm responses to the writing prompt, entering ideas in the interactive journal. Then, have students complete their written responses as homework.

To build background, display the Background and More About the Author feature.

Using the Interactive Text

Go to **www.PHLitOnline.com** and display the Enriched Online Student Edition. As the class reads the selections or listens to the narration, record answers to side-column prompts using the graphic organizers accessible on the interactive page. Alternatively, have students use the online edition individually, answering the prompts as they read.

TEACH

❶ About the Selection

The unexpected encounter with a field mouse, whose home he has inadvertently destroyed with his plow, prompts the sympathetic speaker to apologize to the mouse. However, in the final two stanzas, the speaker uses the incident to generalize on the similarities between the mouse's situation and that of human beings Just as the mouse's plans for a winter home have come to nothing, so too do humans' plans often come undone.

❷ Activating Prior Knowledge

Point out to students that Robert Burns and Joanna Baillie wrote their poetry in the Scottish dialect—in the language of the people. Much like rap stars of today, who write their songs in the vernacular of urban youth, Burns and Baillie used the vernacular of the Scottish people in their poetry. Ask students to offer examples of vernacular language with which they might already be familiar. Direct students to write a short paragraph describing examples of vernacular language.

Concept Connector →

Tell students they will return to their responses after reading the selection.

❶
❷

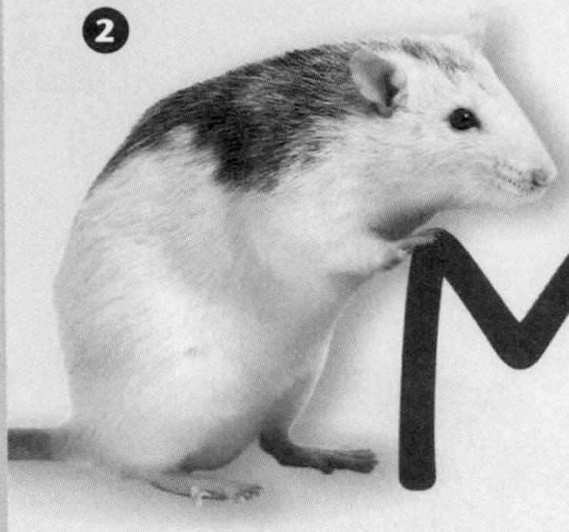

TO A MOUSE

On Turning Her up in Her Nest with the Plow, November, 1785

Robert Burns

BACKGROUND

Before Robert Burns published his poetry, works of literature were almost always modeled on the classics, in which structure, grammar, and vocabulary were polished and complex. Robert Burns ignored these conventions and boldly put poetry in the hands of the people, writing in their language, Scottish dialect, and using common folk as subject matter.

Text Complexity Rubric

	To a Mouse	To a Louse	Woo'd and Married and A'
Qualitative Measures			
Context/ Knowledge Demands	Pre-Romantic; cultural knowledge demands 1 2 ③ 4 5	Pre-Romantic 1 2 ③ 4 5	Pre-Romantic 1 2 ③ 4 5
Structure/Language Conventionality and Clarity	Scottish dialect 1 2 3 ④ 5	Scottish dialect 1 2 3 ④ 5	Scottish dialect 1 2 ③ 4 5
Levels of Meaning/ Purpose/Concept Level	Challenging (human nature) 1 2 3 ④ 5	Moderate (vanity) 1 2 ③ 4 5	Accessible (marriage) 1 ② 3 4 5
Quantitative Measures			
Lexile/Text Length	NP / 266 words	NP / 274 words	NP / 410 words
Overall Complexity	**More complex**	**More complex**	**More accessible**

Wee, sleekit,[1] cow'rin', tim'rous beastie,
O, what a panic's in thy breastie!
Thou need na start awa sae hasty,
Wi' bickering brattle![2]
I wad be laith[3] to rin an' chase thee
Wi' murd'ring pattle![4]

I'm truly sorry man's **dominion**
Has broken Nature's social union,
An' justifies that ill opinion,
Which makes thee startle,
At me, thy poor, earth-born companion,
An' fellow-mortal!

I doubt na, whyles,[5] but thou may thieve;
What then? poor beastie, thou maun[6] live!
A daimen icker in a thrave[7]
'S a sma' request:
I'll get a blessin' wi' the lave,[8]
And never miss't!

Thy wee bit housie, too, in ruin!
Its silly wa's[9] the win's are strewin'!
An' naething, now, to big[10] a new ane,
O' foggage[11] green!
An' bleak December's winds ensuin',
Baith snell[12] an' keen!

Thou saw the fields laid bare and waste,
An' weary winter comin' fast,
An' cozie here, beneath the blast,
Thou thought to dwell,
Till crash! the cruel coulter[13] past
Out through thy cell.

1. **sleekit** sleek.
2. **Wi' . . . brattle** with a quick pattering sound.
3. **wad be laith** would be loath.
4. **pattle** paddle for cleaning a plow.
5. **whyles** at times.
6. **maun** must.
7. **A . . . thrave** an occasional ear of grain in a bundle.
8. **lave** rest.
9. **silly wa's** feeble walls.
10. **big** build.
11. **foggage** rough grass.
12. **snell** sharp.
13. **coulter** plow blade.

Vocabulary
dominion (də min′ yən)
n. rule; authority

Spiral Review
Conceit In what ways does the poem build a conceit about the mouse as the speaker's companion or equal?

❸ **Reading Strategy**
Analyzing Text Features
Use context clues and nearby footnotes to determine the meaning of "win's" in line 20.

❹ **Reading Check**
How does the speaker uncover the mouse?

Spiral Review
Conceit

1. Remind students that they studied conceit in an earlier lesson.
2. **Ask** students the Spiral Review question.
   Possible response: Burns uses references to dispossession, charity, abuse, and theft driven by necessity to draw out the comparison between a mouse and less fortunate classes of his time. He makes the unlikely comparision explicit when he calls the mouse "earth born companion an' fellow mortal."

❸ Reading Strategy
Analyzing Text Features

1. Direct students to the word *win's* in line 20.
2. Remind students that they can determine the meaning of many unfamiliar dialect words from context.
3. Have students **follow** the Reading Strategy prompt.
   Answer: Students should see that *win's* is dialect for *winds.*

❹ Reading Check
Answer: The speaker uncovers the mouse when he turns up her nest with a plow.

Text Complexity: Reader and Task Suggestions

	To a Mouse	To a Louse	Woo'd and Married and A'
Preparing to Read the Texts • Using the Background on p. 733, discuss how Burns's background as a farmer might affect the content and imagery of his poems. • Discuss why a poet might write in dialect instead of standard English. • Guide students to use Multidraft Reading strategies (TE p. 733).	**Leveled Tasks** ***Levels of Meaning*** If students will have difficulty with the poem's ideas, have them sum up the mouse's situation. Then, have them try to state the basic comparison and contrast in the last two stanzas. ***Analyzing*** If students will not have difficulty with the poem's ideas, have them explain the speaker's conclusions and how he reaches them.	**Leveled Tasks** ***Structure/Language*** If students will have difficulty with the dialect, have them first get a general idea of the situation. Then, have them use context clues and footnotes to help them understand the speaker's main points. ***Evaluating*** If students will not have difficulty with the dialect, have them consider how effectively the poem communicates the theme of vanity.	**Leveled Tasks** ***Knowledge Demands*** If students will have difficulty with the cultural context, clarify the reasons the bride is sad about her poverty. Then, as they reread, have them focus on what makes her happy in the end. ***Evaluating*** If students will not have difficulty with the context, have them evaluate the realism of the characters' language and behavior.

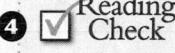

ASSESS

Answers

Before students respond, you may wish to have them write a brief objective summary of the selection. As they answer the questions below, remind them to support their answers with evidence from the text.

1. (a) The speaker has plowed up its home. (b) The speaker is not concerned with the grain the mouse steals. (c) **Possible response:** Students may say that the speaker forgives theft for survival, as he expresses in the lines like: "I doubt na, whyles, but thou may thieve; / What then? poor beastie, thou maun live!"
2. (a) It has been ruined by the plow. (b) *I'm truly sorry man's dominion / Has broken Nature's social union.* (c) **Possible response:** It's sad that human actions sometimes destroy the work of nature.
3. (a) The speaker compares the mouse's absorption in the present with the human ability to regret the past and fear the future. (b) **Possible responses:** Students may point out that taking responsibility for the past and planning for the future are part of human dignity, though they involve suffering beyond what animals experience. Some may agree that the mouse's ignorance of past and future is a blessing because of the worry it saves the mouse.
4. **Possible response:** Students may value foresight as part of intellect, though it leads to more anxiety.
5. **Possible response:** Some students may feel that dialect adds a folksy, country element of wisdom to the poem; others may find the dialect translation impedes their enjoyment of the poem's meaning.

BUT, MOUSIE, thou art no thy lane, In proving foresight may be vain:

That wee bit heap o' leaves an' stibble,
Has cost thee mony a weary nibble!
Now thou's turned out, for a' thy trouble,
    But[14] house or hald,[15]
To thole[16] the winter's sleety dribble,
    An' cranreuch[17] cauld!

But, Mousie, thou art no thy lane,[18]
In proving foresight may be vain:
The best laid schemes o' mice an' men
    Gang aft a-gley,[19]
An' lea'e us nought but grief an' pain,
    For promised joy.

Still thou art blest, compared wi' me!
The present only toucheth thee:
But, och! I backward cast my e'e
    On prospects drear!
An' forward, though I canna see,
    I guess an' fear!

14. **But** without.
15. **hald** property.
16. **thole** withstand.
17. **cranreuch** (kran´ rəkh) frost.
18. **no thy lane** not alone.
19. **Gang aft a-gley** go often awry.

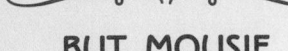

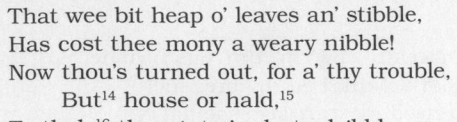

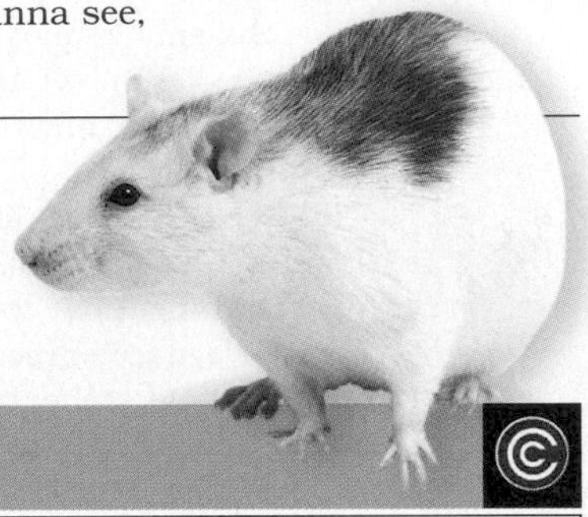

Critical Reading

Cite textual evidence to support your responses.

1. **Key Ideas and Details (a)** For what reason does the speaker apologize to the mouse? **(b) Infer:** How does the speaker feel about the grain the mouse steals? **(c) Interpret:** What does the speaker's reaction show about his ideas of justice?
2. **Key Ideas and Details (a) Infer:** What has happened to the mouse's attempt to prepare for winter? **(b) Interpret:** Which two famous lines in the poem express the poem's theme? **(c) Paraphrase:** Restate the theme in your own words.
3. **Key Ideas and Details (a) Interpret:** What comparison does the speaker draw between himself and the mouse in the last stanza? **(b) Evaluate:** Do you agree with the speaker about the mouse's advantage? Explain.
4. **Integration of Knowledge and Ideas** What value do you place on foresight? Explain.
5. **Craft and Structure** Does dialect add to the quality of folk-wisdom in the poem, or does it distract from the meaning? Explain.

Enrichment: Investigating Artistic Schools and Movements

The Romantic Movement
Robert Burns is a forerunner of the Romantic Movement in art and literature. Unlike the Age of Enlightenment, in which nature was often seen as something to be conquered, Romantics viewed nature as a source of truths with which people should try to harmonize. Hence, Burns apologizes for man's intrusion with the plow into nature's "social union."

Activity: Investigating the Romantic Movement Have students work in small groups, each researching a different aspect of the Romantic Movement. Some groups might focus on literature, others on art or music. Students can record their findings on the **Investigating Artistic Schools and Movements** worksheet, ***Professional Development Guidebook***, page 220.

To a Louse

On Seeing One on a Lady's Bonnet At Church

Robert Burns

6

5

7 ◄ Critical Viewing
In what way are this lady's pose and costume similar to those of the lady in the poem? Explain. **[Connect]**

Ha! whare ye gaun, ye crowlin' ferlie![1]
Your impudence protects you sairly:[2]
I canna say but ye strunt[3] rarely,
 Owre gauze and lace;
5 Though faith! I fear ye dine but sparely
 On sic a place.

Ye ugly, creepin', blastit wonner,[4]
Detested, shunned by saunt an' sinner,
How dare ye set your fit[5] upon her,

1. **crowlin' ferlie** crawling wonder.
2. **sairly** wondrously.
3. **strunt** strut.
4. **blastit wonner** blasted wonder.
5. **fit** foot.

Vocabulary
impudence (im′ pyo͞o dəns)
n. lack of shame; rudeness

8 Reading Check
Where is the louse crawling?

To a Louse **737**

5 **About the Selection**
In "To a Louse," Burns sees a louse (the singular form of *lice,* a parasite like a flea) on the bonnet of a well-dressed lady and uses the incident to satirize conceited behavior.

6 **Humanities**
The Bow, by Talbot Hughes

This painting depicts a fashionable woman who is fastening her bonnet by tying its ribbon in a bow under her chin. Point out to students that the woman is elaborately costumed and made up according to the dictates of fashion of the times.

Use these questions for discussion:

1. How well does the subject of this painting fit the description of the lady in "To a Louse"? **Answer:** Like the lady in the poem, the lady in the painting wears delicate lace, ribbons, a bonnet, and possible gauze. However, the bonnet lacks the balloon shape of a Lunardi.

2. Burns's poem suggests there is a difference between how we see ourselves and how others see us. Judging from the woman's expression, how do you think she sees herself? How might others see her?
Answer: She appears to make an effort to appear well-groomed and seems quite satisfied with the results. Other people might see her as filled with vanity and a false sense of superiority.

7 **Critical Viewing**
Answer: The dainty manner in which the lady ties her bow and her primping pose suggest a self-importance like that of the woman in the poem.

8 **Reading Check**
Answer: The louse is crawling across the clothing of a well–dressed lady.

Differentiated Instruction for Universal Access

Enrichment for Less Proficient Readers
Tell students that an imaginary new TV series called *The Robert Burns Show* is scheduled to air next fall. The producers have hired them to plan an animated short for the premier, which will be based on "To a Mouse" or "To a Louse." Have students select a poem and develop a storyboard for it. Students should break the poem into segments and create an illustration for each segment.

Enrichment for Gifted/Talented Students
Tell students that an imaginary new TV series called *The Robert Burns Show* is scheduled to air next fall. The producers have hired them to choreograph and score an interpretation of "To a Mouse." Students can assign roles, select music and other effects, and then rehearse, and stage their interpretation.

❾ The British Tradition

The Literature of Scotland

The Scottish dialect is an offshoot of the Northumbrian dialect of Anglo–Saxon, the forerunner of modern English spoken from A.D. 500 to 1100. Scottish dialect has a strong Norse element in vocabulary and in vowel and consonant sounds. Over time, Gaelic, French, and Dutch linguistic elements were mixed in.

Political union between Scotland and England began with James I (1566–1625). James, already king of Scotland, became king of England as well in 1603. By the 1700s, the Scottish dialect had been displaced by English as Scotland's major language for written works. Allan Ramsay (1686–1758), Burns, and others revived the dialect, nicknamed "Lallans," in the eighteenth century.

Connect to the Literature Explain to students that American literature has also been affected by movements to preserve or revive local dialects and indigenous languages. Native Americans have struggled to increase the use of their languages in schools and in literature, and African Americans have incorporated their vocabulary and speech patterns into their literature. **Ask** students why a group of people might find it important to preserve their language or way of speaking. **Possible response:** People feel that preserving their language patterns builds a sense of identity and cultural worth.

Have students read aloud lines 7–12. Then, **ask** the Connect to the Literature question.

Possible response: The dialect adds to the sense of outrage at the thought of a low creature touching a fine lady.

❾ *The* BRITISH TRADITION

The Literature of Scotland

Burns's dialect poems were part of a long struggle over Scottish identity. From the late thirteenth century to the middle of the sixteenth century, the Lowlands area of Scotland—Burns's native region—frequently warred with England. A distinctive culture blossomed in the region, yielding famous ballads such as "Barbara Allan."

When Scotland united with England in 1707, important Scottish authors of the time, such as economist Adam Smith, wrote in English as the English spoke it. However, there was a backlash, and Scotland was swept by a literary enthusiasm for things distinctly Scottish. In the poems of Burns, Baillie, and others, as well as in a new passion for collecting the old ballads, the Scottish past reasserted itself even as it faded.

Connect to the Literature

Read aloud lines 7–12. What effect does the Scottish dialect of selected words have on the entire stanza?

Sae fine a lady?
Gae somewhere else, and seek your dinner
On some poor body.

Swith![6] in some beggar's haffet[7] squattle;[8]
There ye may creep, and sprawl, and sprattle[9]
Wi' ither kindred, jumping cattle,
In shoals and nations:
Whare horn nor bane[10] ne'er dare unsettle
Your thick plantations.

Now haud[11] ye there, ye're out o' sight,
Below the fatt'rels,[12] snug an' tight;
Na, faith ye yet![13] ye'll no be right
Till ye've got on it,
The vera tapmost, tow'ring height
O' Miss's bonnet.

My sooth! right bauld ye set your nose out,
As plump and gray as onie grozet;[14]
O for some rank, mercurial rozet,[15]
Or fell,[16] red smeddum,[17]
I'd gie you sic a hearty dose o't,
Wad dress your droddum![18]

I wad na been surprised to spy
You on an auld wife's flannen toy;[19]
Or aiblins some bit duddie boy,[20]
On's wyliecoat;[21]

6. **Swith** swift.
7. **haffet** locks.
8. **squattle** sprawl.
9. **sprattle** struggle.
10. **horn nor bane** comb made of horn or bone.
11. **haud** hold.
12. **fatt'rels** ribbon ends.
13. **Na, faith ye yet!** "Confound you!"
14. **onie grozet** (gräz′ it) any gooseberry.
15. **rozet** (räz′ it) rosin.
16. **fell** sharp.
17. **smeddum** powder.
18. **Wad . . . droddum** "would put an end to you."
19. **flannen toy** flannel cap.
20. **Or . . . boy** or perhaps on some little ragged boy.
21. **wyliecoat** (wī′ lē kōt′) undershirt.

Enrichment: Building Context

Class in Context

Between 1750 and 1850, industrialization had taken hold in Western Europe. Social and economic classes evolved in this period, as society shifted from an agricultural to an industrial economy. In short, changing economic structures created new social divisions and relations.

Activity: Class in Context Have students research social and economic classes in Western Europe during Burns's lifetime, roughly 1750–1800. Students can record their findings on the **Enrichment: Building Context** worksheet, ***Professional Development Guidebook***, page 222. Ask students to consider how their understanding of evolving class relations helps them understand "To a Louse."

But Miss's fine Lunardi![22] fie,
How daur ye do't?

O, Jenny, dinna toss your head,
An' set your beauties a' abread![23]
Ye little ken what cursèd speed
The blastie's[24] makin'!
Thae[25] winks and finger-ends, I dread,
Are notice takin'!

O wad some Pow'r the giftie gie us
To see oursels as ithers see us!
It wad frae monie a blunder free us
And foolish notion:
What airs in dress an' gait wad lea'e us,
And ev'n devotion!

What airs in dress an' gait wad lea'e us, And ev'n devotion!

22. **Lunardi** balloon-shaped bonnet, named for Vincenzo Lunardi, a balloonist of the late 1700s.
23. **abread** abroad.
24. **blastie's** creature's.
25. **Thae** those.

Critical Reading

Cite textual evidence to support your responses.

1. **Key Ideas and Details (a)** What is the louse doing? **(b)** What does the speaker command it to do instead? **(c) Interpret:** What social assumptions about cleanliness does the speaker's command reflect?
2. **Key Ideas and Details (a) Draw Conclusions:** What impression of Jenny does the speaker create? **(b) Analyze:** How do the references to her clothing and the contrast between her and "some poor body" contribute to this impression?
3. **Key Ideas and Details (a) Infer:** In lines 37–42, why does the speaker warn Jenny against tossing her head? **(b) Infer:** What is the reaction of others in the church to Jenny's gesture? **(c) Draw Conclusions:** Why is the contrast between this gesture and the progress of the louse particularly embarrassing?
4. **Integration of Knowledge and Ideas (a) Interpret:** Paraphrase the generalization that the speaker makes in the last stanza. **(b) Evaluate:** Do you agree that we would profit if we could "see oursels as ithers see us"? Explain.
5. **Integration of Knowledge and Ideas** Do you think caring about the impression we make on others is foolish vanity? Explain.

ASSESS

Answers

Before students respond, you may wish to have them write a brief objective summary of the selection. As they answer the questions below, remind them to support their answers with evidence from the text.

1. (a) The louse is crawling on a well-dressed lady's clothing. (b) The speaker commands it to go crawl on some poor beggar. (c) Beggars are expected to have lice; well-dressed ladies are not.
2. (a) Jenny is vain and wants others to admire her. (b) Her "fatt'rels, snug an' tight" and other finery show that she has dressed to show off; along with the condescending references to the "beggar," they reinforce impressions of her snobbery and vanity.
3. (a) The speaker wants her not to toss her head and send the louse elsewhere on her body. (b) Others in the church notice and point ("winks and finger-ends"). (c) Jenny is about to toss her head in order to draw attention to her beautiful hair, but the louse crawling on her bonnet will make the gesture ridiculous.
4. (a) The speaker says that if we could see ourselves as others see us, that ability would free us from making embarrassing mistakes. (b) **Possible response:** Students may agree that we would profit because we would not waste time with foolish vanity.
5. **Possible response:** Self-respect demands that we care to some extent about how others see us; vanity is an excessive concern with appearances.

Differentiated Instruction for Universal Access

Support for Special-Needs Students
Have students read the final stanzas of the poem with your guidance. For students who have difficulty analyzing how dialect can reinforce or enhance subject matter, use **Reading Strategy Graphic Organizer B,** page 129 in ***Graphic Organizer Transparencies,*** to show how effective dialect functions.

Strategy for Less Proficient Readers
Have students read the final stanzas of the poem in small groups. Ask each group to discuss why Burns wrote about an insect crawling on someone's hat in dialect instead of Standard English. Students should then share their ideas in a roundtable discussion.

Enrichment for Advanced Readers
Have students write essays in which they compare Burns's poems "To a Mouse" and "To a Louse." Students should consider the author's use of language in each poem, as well as his themes, rhythm, and rhyme.

⑩ More About the Author

Scottish playwright and poet Joanna Baillie is best known for her *Plays on the Passion,* in which each drama shows the effects of one particular passion. *Basil,* on the subject of love, and *De Montfort,* on the subject of hatred, were the most successful. The dramas garnered Baillie a great deal of attention, most notably in a friendship with Sir Walter Scott, but they also were heavily criticized. Baillie's most revered drama, *The Family Legend,* based on a Scottish feud, established her as a literary success and was produced in 1810.

⑩ Joanna Baillie (1762–1851)

Author of "Woo'd and Married and A'"

When Joanna Baillie's (bā′ lēz) *Plays on the Passions* was published anonymously in 1798, it created a great literary sensation in London. Debates raged over which famous man of letters had written the plays. It was not until 1800 that the true author was revealed—an unassuming thirty-eight-year-old Scottish woman named Joanna Baillie. Even her literary friends were astounded, and she became an instant celebrity.

A Gregarious Tomboy Born in Lanarkshire, Scotland, the daughter of a minister, young Joanna Baillie was a tomboy who loved horseback riding and who resisted the stern moral education given by her father. She blossomed when she and her sister, Agnes, were sent away to boarding school in 1772. Joanna Baillie became an outgoing leader who led the other girls on boisterous outdoor adventures and staged plays that she herself wrote.

A Spinster's Life in London When Baillie's father died in 1778, the family depended on the kindness of a wealthy uncle for support. He provided the two sisters with a lifetime income. When their brother married in 1791, the sisters and their mother started a household of their own. They began a busy social life amid London's bustling literary scene, welcoming many important writers of the day into their home.

Success and Critical Acclaim With Baillie's literary success, the two sisters were able to travel, and they often returned to Scotland to visit Sir Walter Scott, who helped in the production of Baillie's plays. Best known in her day for her dramatic works, Baillie also wrote poetry. Like her fellow Scot, Robert Burns, she wrote poems in the dialect of her homeland, many of them on nature and rustic manners.

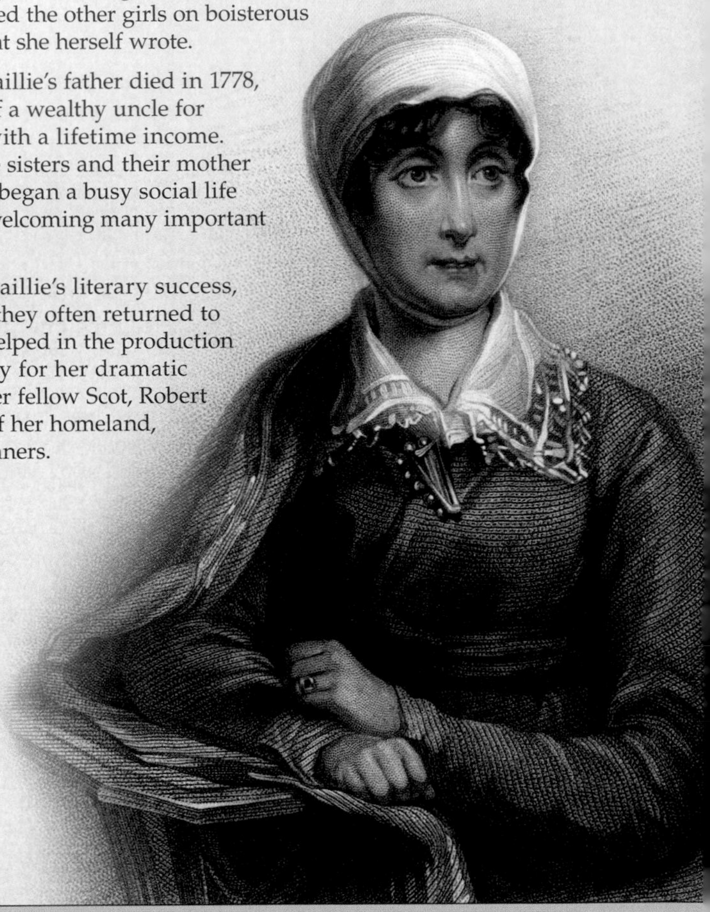

"Pampered vanity is a better thing perhaps than starved pride."

Enrichment: Investigating Culture

Marriage
The institution of marriage is an important tradition in many cultures, fostered by spiritual and secular societies alike. In some cultures, marriage is a fairly informal event. In other societies, marriage is characterized by a highly complex series of ritual behaviors and gestures that begin with courtship—the indication of romantic interest—and conclude with the marriage ceremony itself. As in Baillie's poem, though, most cultures allow a place for a humorous view of marriage.

Activity: Investigating Marriage Have students research marriage customs, rituals and ceremonies of different cultures around the world. Students can record their findings on the **Enrichment: Investigating Culture** worksheet in the ***Professional Development Guidebook,*** page 223.

PHLit Online!

For more about the author, go online at **www.PHLitOnline.com**

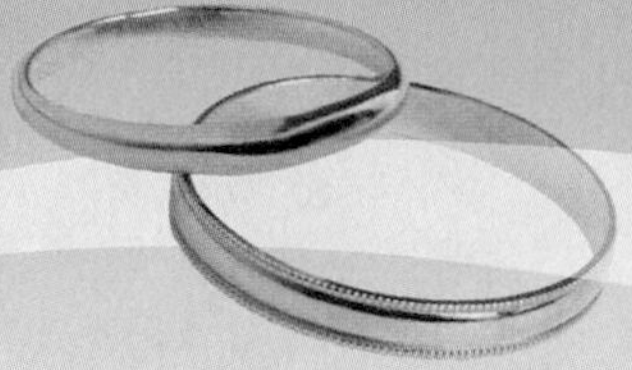

⓫

Woo'd and Married and A'

Joanna Baillie

The bride she is **winsome** and bonny,
    Her hair it is snooded[1] sae sleek,
And faithfu' and kind is her Johnny,
    Yet fast fa' the tears on her cheek.
New pearlins[2] are cause of her sorrow,
    New pearlins and plenishing[3] too;
The bride that has a' to borrow
    Has e'en right mickle[4] ado.
        Woo'd and married and a'!
        Woo'd and married and a'!
    Is na' she very weel aff
        To be woo'd and married at a'?

Her mither then hastily spak,
    "The Lassie is glaikit[5] wi' pride;
In my pouch I had never a plack[6]
    On the day when I was a bride.
E'en tak to your wheel and be clever,
    And draw out your thread in the sun; ⓬
The gear[7] that is gifted it never
    Will last like the gear that is won.
        Woo'd and married and a'!
        Wi' havins and toucher[8] sae sma'!
    I think ye are very weel aff
        To be woo'd and married at a'."

1. **snooded** bound up with a ribbon.
2. **pearlins** lace trimmings.
3. **plenishing** furnishings.
4. **mickle** much.
5. **glaikit** foolish.
6. **plack** farthing; a small coin equal to one fourth of a penny.
7. **gear** wealth or goods.
8. **havins and toucher** possessions and dowry.

Vocabulary
winsome (win′ səm) *adj.* having a charming appearance or way

Literary Analysis
Dialect What feelings or qualities does the use of dialect add to the mother's advice to her daughter?

⓭ **Reading Check**
What is the mother's opinion about her daughter's marriage?

Differentiated Instruction for Universal Access

EL Strategy for English Learners

Explain to students that the words used in the poem "Woo'd and Married and A'" are difficult for most English speakers. Have students work in pairs to make a list of words and phrases in the poem that they find difficult. For each word, have them include an example of its use from the poem and explain what the word means in that context.

Enrichment for Gifted/Talented Students

If possible, have students work in groups of four, reenacting the various figures in the poem "Woo'd and Married and A'." Have students plan a presentation in which each member of the group recites the portion of the poem relevant to the character he or she chooses to portray.

TEACH

⓫ About the Selection

"Woo'd and Married and A'" offers insight into the motives for marriage. The poem begins with the bride sorrowing over her lack of finery and possessions and the prospect of marrying someone who has no more wealth than she. The bride's parents chastise the bride, declaring that she is fortunate to find anyone to marry her at all, given her poverty. The bridegroom, though, knows how to manage her anxiety: He proclaims that the bride herself is wealth enough for him. Pleased by the flattery, she gives up her worrying, and goes off to be married.

⓬ Literary Analysis

Dialect

1. Review with students that dialect is often used to establish character, mood, and setting, and to add charm and "texture."
2. Then, **ask** the Literary Analysis question.
   Answer: Students should recognize that the dialect enriches the mother's remarks by suggesting an entire way of life. Expressions such as "tak to your wheel" (line 17)—a reference to spinning thread—add to the reader's impression of the life of these poor farming folk. The unique words and pronunciations emphasize the fact that the mother is steeped in this way of life and helps the reader identify her as a distinctive personality. In this way, the use of dialect adds sincerity and force to the mother's indignation.

⓭ Reading Check

Answer: The mother believes that although the daughter may need to work for money because her dowry is small, the match is a good one.

⑭ Humanities

The Village Wedding, (detail) by Sir Luke Fildes

Sir Luke Fildes (1844–1927) began his career as a magazine illustrator in London. He illustrated Dickens's last unfinished novel, *The Mystery of Edwin Drood,* before turning to painting in the 1870s. His paintings are part of the social realism movement, which sought to truly depict both the beauty and evils of contemporary life.

Fildes's works were very popular and were often made available as engravings. He was knighted in 1906.

Use these questions for discussion:

1. Which moment in the poem might the painting represent? **Possible response:** Students may say the painting captures the last stanza, in which the bride blushes, smiles, and looks down bashfully.
2. Judging from the expressions of the people in the painting, was this wedding solemn or festive? **Possible response:** Students may point out that the bride and groom seem serious and solemn, whereas the surrounding guests seem happy and animated.

⑮ Critical Viewing

Answer: The village setting depicted in the painting parallels the humble surroundings suggested indirectly in the poem. The dress of the groom and those following him appear to be finer than one might expect in the scene in the poem.

14

The Village Wedding, (detail) Sir Luke Fildes, Christopher Wood Gallery, London

⑮ ▲ Critical Viewing
Compare and contrast the setting and costumes in this painting with the scene described in the poem. **[Compare and Contrast]**

Vocabulary

discretion (di skresh′ ən) *n.* good judgment; prudence

inconstantly (in kän′ stənt lē) *adv.* changeably; in a fickle way

"Toot, toot," quo' her gray-headed faither,
 "She's less o' a bride than a bairn,[9]
She's ta'en like a cout[10] frae the heather,
 Wi' sense and **discretion** to learn.
Half husband, I trow, and half daddy,
 As humor **inconstantly** leans,
The chiel maun be patient and steady[11]
 That yokes wi' a mate in her teens.
  A kerchief sae douce[12] and sae neat
  O'er her locks that the wind used to blaw!
I'm baith like to laugh and to greet[13]
  When I think of her married at a'!"

Then out spak the wily bridegroom,
 Weel waled[14] were his wordies, I ween,
"I'm rich, though my coffer be toom,[15]
 Wi' the blinks o' your bonny blue e'en.[16]
I'm prouder o' thee by my side,

9. **bairn** child.
10. **cout** colt.
11. **The chiel maun . . . steady** The man must be patient and steady.
12. **douce** respectable.
13. **greet** weep.
14. **waled** chosen.
15. **toom** empty.
16. **e'en** eyes.

Vocabulary Development

Vocabulary Knowledge Rating
When students have completed reading and discussing the selection, have them take out their **Vocabulary Knowledge Rating Charts** for the story. Read the words aloud and have students rate their knowledge of words again in the After Reading column. Clarify any words that are still problematic. Have students write their own definitions and example or sentence in the appropriate column. Then, have students complete the Vocabulary Practice at the end of the selection. Encourage students to use the words in further discussion and written work about the selection. Remind them that they will be accountable for these words on the **Selection Test,** ***Unit 4 Resources,*** pages 19–21 or 22–24.

Though thy ruffles or ribbons be few,
Than if Kate o' the Croft were my bride
Wi' purfles[17] and pearlins enow.
Dear and dearest of ony!
Ye're woo'd and buikit[18] and a'!
And do ye think scorn o' your Johnny,
And grieve to be married at a'?"

She turn'd, and she blush'd, and she smiled,
And she looked sae bashfully down;
The pride o' her heart was beguiled,
And she played wi' the sleeves o' her gown.
She twirled the tag o' her lace,
And she nipped her boddice sae blue,
Syne blinkit sae sweet in his face,
And aff like a maukin[19] she flew.
Woo'd and married and a'!
Wi' Johnny to roose[20] her and a'!
She thinks hersel very weel aff
To be woo'd and married at a'!

---

17. purfles embroidered trimmings.
18. buikit "booked"; entered as married in the official registry.
19. maukin hare.
20. roose praise.

Critical Reading

Cite textual evidence to support your responses.

1. **Key Ideas and Details (a)** How does the bridegroom respond to his bride's unhappiness? **(b) Analyze Cause and Effect:** Describe the effect the bridegroom's words have on his young bride. **(c) Draw Conclusions:** How would you describe the personality of the bridegroom?
2. **Key Ideas and Details (a)** Which speaker succeeds in changing the bride's outlook? **(b) Draw Conclusions:** Judging from the final stanza, do you think the marriage will be a happy one? Explain.
3. **Integration of Knowledge and Ideas** Do you think the poet is unkind to the young bride, or does she show insight into people? Explain.
4. **Integration of Knowledge and Ideas** What are the poets' attitudes toward the behaviors they describe in these poems? In your response, use at least two of these Essential Question words: *traditional, role, spirit. [Connecting to the Essential Question: How does literature shape or reflect society?]*

ASSESS

Answers

Before students respond, you may wish to have them write a brief objective summary of the selection. As they answer the questions below, remind them to support their answers with evidence from the text.

1. (a) The bridegroom responds to his bride's unhappiness by saying that her company and beautiful eyes are wealth enough for him. (b) The bridegroom's words cause the bride to blush and content her. (c) **Possible response:** The bridegroom, described as "wily" (line 37) is a clever diplomat and, perhaps, an optimist.
2. (a) The bridegroom succeeds in changing the bride's outlook. (b) The final stanza suggests the marriage will be a happy one, since the bride and bridegroom are happy with each other, despite their lack of wealth. The bridegroom knows how to soothe and flatter his bride.
3. **Possible response:** Students may think that the poet is unkind to the young bride because she shows the bride's worries put to rest with a little flattery, suggesting that the bride is vain and empty-headed. Others may feel that the poet shows real insight into the bride's personality and motives and that the overall cheerfulness of the poem makes the portrayal realistic, not unkind.
4. **Possible response:** Students' responses will vary. Ensure students use at least two of the following words: *traditional, role, spirit.*

Concept Connector

Reading Strategy Graphic Organizer

Ask students to review the graphic organizers in which they have analyzed text features of the poems. Then, have students share their organizers and compare how they have translated Scottish dialect.

Activating Prior Knowledge

Have students return to their responses to the Activating Prior Knowledge activity. Ask them to explain whether their thoughts have changed and if so, how.

Writing About the Essential Question

Have students compare their responses to the prompt before they completed reading the poems with their thoughts afterward. Have them work individually or in groups, writing or discussing their thoughts, to formulate new responses. Then, lead a class discussion, probing for what students have learned that confirms or invalidates their initial thoughts. Encourage students to cite specific textual details to support their responses.

Answers

1. The speaker's language suggests that he is one of the common folk.
2. The dialect of "Woo'd and Married and A'" emphasizes the humble, rural setting.
3. (a) Examples include *cow'rin'* (line 1), *strewin'* (line 20), and *comin'* (line 26). (b) Examples include *sae* for "so" (line 3), *ane* for "one" (line 21), and *aft* for "oft" (line 40).
4. The characters would not seem as true to life.
5. "To a Mouse": Subject: uprooting of a mouse's nest; Message: Plans can go awry. "To a Louse": Subject: a louse crawling on a lady; Message: Mind your behavior. "Woo'd...": Subject: young bride upset about a lack of wealth; Message: Love makes up for material wants.
6. (a) Because all people make plans for the future, "To a Mouse" applies most generally. (b) The message of "Woo'd..." applies specifically to a wedding.
7. **Possible responses:** Yes: everyday subjects of the poems prevent addressing truths from exceptional situations. No: both poets succeed in drawing general truths from their subjects.
8. Students should offer a generalization about contemporary culture.
9. **Possible responses:** *beastie*=animal; *naething*=nothing; *stibble*=stubble; *gaun*=gone; *havins* and *toucher*=possessions and dowry; *bairn*=child; *douce*=respectable; *greet*=weep.
10. (a) **Possible response:** Stanza 1 of "To A Mouse": Poor little, scared thing! You're terrified of me! You don't need to run away from me. I would never chase you. (b) The rhythm and charm of original text is missing.
11. (a) Students' lines of poetry should use Scottish dialect. (b) Students' responses will vary. (c) Students might suggest writing poetry in dialect is difficult.
12. Mass media standardizes communication, and so dialects and regional differences disappear.

After You Read

To a Mouse • To a Louse • Woo'd and Married and A'

Literary Analysis

1. **Craft and Structure** What does the use of **dialect** in the poems by Burns suggest about the speaker's social status?
2. **Craft and Structure** What does dialect contribute to the setting of Joanna Baillie's "Woo'd and Married and A'"?
3. **Craft and Structure** Find at least two examples in "To a Mouse" of the following pronunciation patterns for Scottish English: **(a)** Final consonants are dropped, and **(b)** the letter *o* is replaced by either *ae* or *a*.
4. **Craft and Structure** How would the overall effect of these poems have been different if they had been written in Standard English?
5. **Comparing Literary Works** Using a chart like the one shown, analyze the subject matter of the poems in this grouping.

Poem	Subject	Message

6. **Comparing Literary Works (a)** Which poem conveys a message that applies most generally? Explain. **(b)** Which poem conveys a message that applies only to some people? Explain.
7. **Comparing Literary Works** Do you think the use of everyday subjects in these poems limits the messages they convey? Explain.
8. **Integration of Knowledge and Ideas** The use of everyday subjects in poetry is our inheritance from poets like these. What subject matter, if any, would you be surprised to find in poetry today? Explain.

Reading Strategy

9. List and define ten words in dialect that appear in these poems. For each, explain how you **analyzed information from text features** to interpret it.
10. **(a)** Choose one stanza from a Burns or Baillie poem, and translate it into Standard English. **(b)** Compare and contrast the original with your version, indicating what has been gained or lost in the translation.
11. **(a)** Use text aids to write one or two lines of poetry in Scottish dialect. **(b)** Does dialect work better for poetry meant to be read aloud? Why or why not? **(c)** What are the pros and cons of writing poetry in dialect?
12. How could a mass medium like television, aimed at a nation of common folk, cause the dialects spoken by common folk to vanish?

Common Core State Standards

Language

5.b. Analyze nuances in the meaning of words with similar denotations. *(p. 745)*

Writing

1.b. Develop claim(s) and counterclaims fairly and thoroughly, supplying the most relevant evidence for each while pointing out the strengths and limitations of both in a manner that anticipates the audience's knowledge level, concerns, values, and possible biases. *(p. 745)*

Assessment Practice

Critical Thinking (For more practice, see *All-in-One Workbook*.)

Many tests require students to draw conclusions based upon evidence provided in a passage. Use the following sample test item:

"Toot, toot," quo' her gray–headed faither,
She's less o'bride than a bairn,
She's ta'en like a cout frae the heather,
Wi' sense and discretion to learn.
Half husband, I trow, and half daddy,
As humor inconstantly leans,
The chiel maun be patient and steady

What conclusion can you draw about the groom?

A He will be cared for by his bride.
B He is handsome.
C He is wild and inconstant.
D He will have to guide his impulsive bride.

Point out that lines 29 and 31 state that the bridegroom will be *half husband...*and *half daddy* and must be *patient and steady*. Students should then see that **D** is the correct answer.

PERFORMANCE TASKS

Integrated Language Skills

Vocabulary Acquisition and Use

Word Analysis: Anglo-Saxon Suffix *-some*

Baillie calls the bride in her poem *winsome*, meaning "charming." The Anglo-Saxon suffix *-some* means "tending to" or "tending toward being." Literally, *winsome* means "tending to win over or to delight." Use this meaning of the suffix to infer the meaning of each of these words. If necessary, use a *dictionary* to check your educated guesses.

1. awesome
2. handsome
3. lithesome
4. loathsome
5. tiresome
6. worrisome

Then, invent your own new adjective using the suffix *-some*, and explain how the suffix helps create the word's meaning.

Vocabulary: Synonyms

Synonyms are words that share similar denotations, or dictionary definitions. Write the letter of the word that is the best synonym of each word from the vocabulary list on page 732. Then, use a dictionary to explain any nuances in meaning between the synonyms in each pair.

1. dominion: **(a)** incapability **(b)** rule **(c)** pride
2. impudence: **(a)** rudeness **(b)** shyness **(c)** test
3. winsome: **(a)** competitive **(b)** bold **(c)** attractive
4. discretion: **(a)** quiet **(b)** caution **(c)** gratitude
5. inconstantly: **(a)** changeably **(b)** emptily **(c)** sadly

Writing

Argumentative Text Both Burns and Baillie use dialect, the distinctive language of a group's everyday speech, in their poems. Suppose you have been invited to speak at a literary festival on the use of dialect in literature. Prepare a three- to five-minute **editorial** speech in which you argue that using dialect is or is not a valuable literary technique.

Prewriting Develop a list of claims both for and against using dialect. Based on those claims, decide which position you will take. Use your list of claims to develop an outline for your speech. Be sure to include the opposing arguments, or counterclaims, in your outline; use the ones you favor to refute them.

Drafting Draft your speech following your outline. Present evidence for your position by using examples from the Burns and Baillie poems. Use persuasive techniques such as *appeals to authority, appeals to emotion, rhetorical questions,* and *irony* to make your speech more persuasive.

Model: Revising to Add Supporting Evidence
Burns's poetry may seem difficult, but context can reveal the words hidden beneath strange spellings. In "To a Louse," the context of lines 11 and 12 clearly shows that "Gae" means "go."

Using examples from the poems will support your claims.

Revising Rehearse your delivery, timing yourself and focusing on *performance details.* Make sure the arguments and evidence you present are clear and convincing. Revise the text to fix any trouble spots you find.

ASSESS/EXTEND

Answers

Vocabulary Acquisition and Use

1. Introduce the skill, using the instruction on the student page.
2. Have students complete the Word Analysis activity and the Vocabulary practice.

Word Analysis

1. tending to awe
2. tending toward being attractive
3. tending toward being supple
4. tending toward being unwilling
5. tending to exhaust
6. tending to trouble

Vocabulary

1. b
2. a
3. c
4. b
5. a

Writing

1. To guide students in writing this argumentative text on the use of dialect in literature, give them the Support for Writing page (*Unit 4 Resources,* p. 14).
2. Remind students that their speeches should clearly state their cases for or against using dialect and include persuasive elements.
3. Encourage students to utilize examples of dialect from the Burns and Baillie poems in their persuasive speeches.
4. Use the **Speaking: Delivering a Persuasive Speech** rubric, ***Professional Development Guidebook,*** p. 301, to evaluate students' work.

Assessment Resources

Unit 4 Resources

L1 L2 EL **Selection Test A,** pp. 19–21. Administer Test A to less advanced readers.

L3 L4 EL **Selection Test B,** pp. 22–24. Administer Test B to on-level students and more advanced students.

L3 L4 **Open-Book Test,** pp. 16–18. As an alternative, give the Open-Book Test.

All **Customizable Test Bank**

All **Self-tests**
Students may prepare for the **Selection Test** by taking the **Self-test** online.

PHLit Online! All assessment resources are available at **www.PHLitOnline.com.**

The Lamb • The Tyger • The Chimney Sweeper • Infant Sorrow

Lesson Pacing Guide

DAY 1 Preteach

- Administer the Reading and Vocabulary Warm-ups (*Unit 4 Resources,* pp. 25–28) as necessary.
- Introduce the Literary Analysis concept: Archetypes and Social Commentary.
- Introduce the Reading Strategy: Applying Critical Perspectives.
- Build background with the author and Background features.
- Develop thematic thinking with Connecting to the Essential Question.
- Teach the selection vocabulary.

DAYS 2–3 Preteach/Teach/Assess

- Distribute copies of the appropriate graphic organizer for the Reading Strategy (*Graphic Organizer Transparencies,* pp. 132–133).
- Distribute copies of the appropriate graphic organizer for Literary Analysis (*Graphic Organizer Transparencies,* pp. 134–135).
- Prepare students to read with the Activating Prior Knowledge activities (TE).
- Informally monitor comprehension while students read.
- Develop students' understanding of archetypes and social commentary using the Literary Analysis prompts.
- Develop students' ability to apply critical perspectives using the Reading Strategy prompts.
- Reinforce vocabulary with the Vocabulary notes.
- Assess students' comprehension and mastery of the skills by having them answer the Critical Reading, Literary Analysis, and Reading Strategy questions.
- Have students complete the Vocabulary Lesson.

DAY 4 Extend/Assess

- Have students complete the Conventions and Style Lesson.
- Have students complete the Writing Lesson and write an essay. (You may assign as homework.)
- Administer Selection Test A or B (*Unit 4 Resources,* pp. 38–40 or 41–43).

Common Core State Standards

Reading Literature 2. Determine two or more themes or central ideas of a text and analyze their development over the course of the text, including how they interact and build on one another to produce a complex account.

Writing 2.a. Introduce a topic; organize complex ideas, concepts, and information so that each new element builds on that which precedes it to create a unified whole; include formatting, graphics, and multimedia when useful to aiding comprehension.

Language 3.a. Vary syntax for effect, consulting references for guidance as needed. **4.a.** Use context as a clue to the meaning of a word or phrase.

Additional Standards Practice
Common Core Companion, pp. 15–22; 196–207; 322–331

Daily Block Scheduling
Each day in this Lesson Pacing Guide represents a 40–50 minute period. Teachers using block scheduling may combine days to revise pacing. In addition, teachers may differentiate and support core instruction by integrating components for extended and intensive support as students require. See the Guide to Selected Leveled Resources (facing page).

Guide to Selected Leveled Resources

RTI Tier 1 (students performing on level)			The Lamb • The Tyger • The Chimney Sweeper • Infant Sorrow
Warm Up	Whole class instruction; Group work	**Practice, model,** and **monitor** fluency, working **with the whole class** or **in groups.**	**Vocabulary and Reading Warm-ups B, *Unit 4 Resources,*** pp. 25–26, 28
Comprehension/Skills	Whole class instruction; Group work; Independent work	**Support** and **monitor** comprehension and skills development, having students complete the activities, graphic organizers, and interactive prompts **independently** or **as a class.**	• ***Reader's Notebook,*** adapted instruction and full selection EL ***Reader's Notebook: English Learner's Version,*** adapted instruction and adapted selection • **Reading Strategy Graphic Organizer B, *Graphic Organizer Transparencies,*** p. 137 • **Literary Analysis Graphic Organizer B, *Graphic Organizer Transparencies,*** p. 139
Monitor Progress	A	**Monitor** student progress with the differentiated curriculum-based assessment in the *Unit Resources.*	• **Selection Test B, *Unit 4 Resources,*** pp. 41–43 • **Open-Book Test, *Unit 4 Resources,*** pp. 35–37

RTI Tier 2 (students requiring intervention)			The Lamb • The Tyger • The Chimney Sweeper • Infant Sorrow
Warm Up	Group work; One-on-one teaching	**Practice, model,** and **monitor** fluency **in groups** or **with individuals.**	• **Vocabulary and Reading Warm-ups A, *Unit 4 Resources,*** pp. 25–27 • ***Hear It!* Audio CD (adapted text)**
Comprehension/Skills	Group work; One-on-one teaching	• **Support** and **monitor** comprehension and skills development, working **in small groups** or **with individuals.** • As students complete the selection in the appropriate version of the *Reader's Notebook,* **monitor** comprehension frequently with group questions and individual instruction. • **Model** strategies while guiding students in completing the activities and prompts in the *Reader's Notebook,* as well as the graphic organizers. • **Practice** skills and **monitor** mastery with the *Reading Kit* worksheets.	• ***Reader's Notebook: Adapted Version,*** adapted instruction and adapted selection EL ***Reader's Notebook: English Learner's Version,*** adapted instruction and adapted selection • **Reading Strategy Graphic Organizer A, *Graphic Organizer Transparencies,*** p. 136 • **Literary Analysis Graphic Organizer A, *Graphic Organizer Transparencies,*** p. 138 • ***Reading Kit,*** Practice worksheets
Monitor Progress	A	**Monitor** student progress with the differentiated curriculum-based assessment in the *Unit Resources* and in the *Reading Kit.*	• **Selection Test A, *Unit 4 Resources,*** pp. 38–40 • ***Reading Kit,*** Assess worksheets

TIER 3 Tier 3 intervention may require consultation with the student's special-education or dyslexia specialist. For additional support, see the Tier 2 activities and resources listed above.

One-on-one teaching **Group work** **Whole class instruction** **Independent work** **A Assessment**

For a complete guide to selection support, including support for Advanced students, see the Overview of Resources in the frontmatter.

The Lamb • The Tyger • The Chimney Sweeper • Infant Sorrow

RESOURCES FOR:

- L1 Special-Needs Students
- L2 Below-Level Students (Tier 2)
- L3 On-Level Students (Tier 1)
- L4 Advanced Students (Tier 1)
- EL English Learners
- All All Students

Vocabulary/Fluency/Prior Knowledge

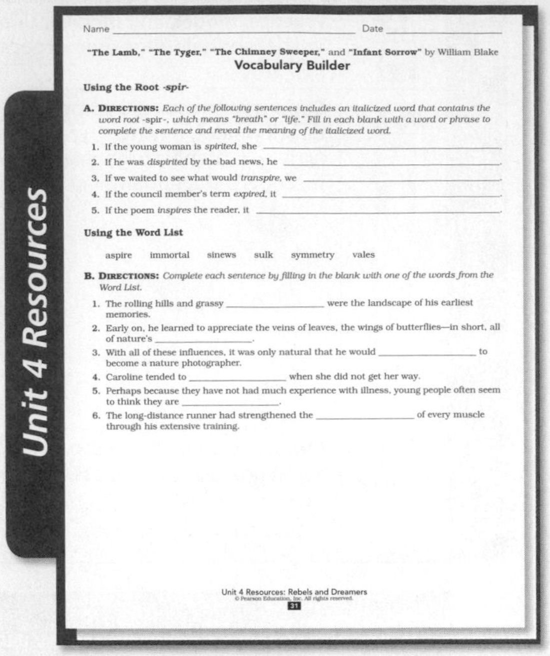

Name ______________________ Date ______________

"The Lamb," "The Tyger," "The Chimney Sweeper," and "Infant Sorrow" by William Blake

Vocabulary Builder

Using the Root -spir-

A. Directions: *Each of the following sentences includes an italicized word that contains the word root -spir-, which means "breath" or "life." Fill in each blank with a word or phrase to complete the sentence and reveal the meaning of the italicized word.*

1. If the young woman is *spirited*, she ______________
2. If he was *dispirited* by the bad news, he ______________.
3. If we waited to see what would *transpire*, we ______________
4. If the council member's term *expired*, it ______________
5. If the poem *inspires* the reader, it ______________

Using the Word List

aspire   immortal   sinews   sulk   symmetry   vales

B. Directions: *Complete each sentence by filling in the blank with one of the words from the Word List.*

1. The rolling hills and grassy ______________ were the landscape of his earliest memories.
2. Early on, he learned to appreciate the veins of leaves, the wings of butterflies—in short, all of nature's ______________.
3. With all of these influences, it was only natural that he would ______________ to become a nature photographer.
4. Caroline tended to ______________ when she did not get her way.
5. Perhaps because they have not had much experience with illness, young people often seem to think they are ______________.
6. The long-distance runner had strengthened the ______________ of every muscle through his extensive training.

Unit 4 Resources: Rebels and Dreamers
© Pearson Education, Inc. All rights reserved.
31

All **Vocabulary Builder,** p. 31

Also available for these selections:

EL L1 L2 **Vocabulary Warm-ups A and B,** pp. 25–26

EL L1 L2 **Reading Warm-ups A and B,** pp. 27–28

Reader's Notebooks

Pre- and postreading pages for these selections appear in an interactive format in the *Reader's Notebooks.* Each *Notebook* is differentiated for a different group of learners. The selections in the Adapted and English Learner's versions are abridged.

L2 L3 ***Reader's Notebook***

L1 ***Reader's Notebook: Adapted Version***

EL ***Reader's Notebook: English Learner's Version***

EL ***Reader's Notebook: Spanish Version***

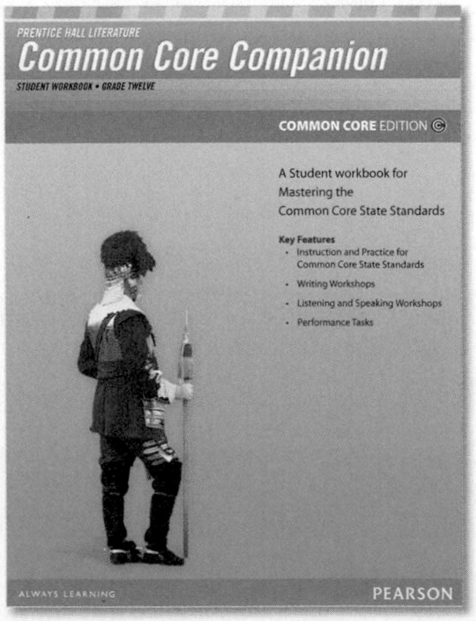

Common Core Companion

Additional instruction and practice for each Common Core State Standard

Selection Support

Graphic Organizer Transparencies

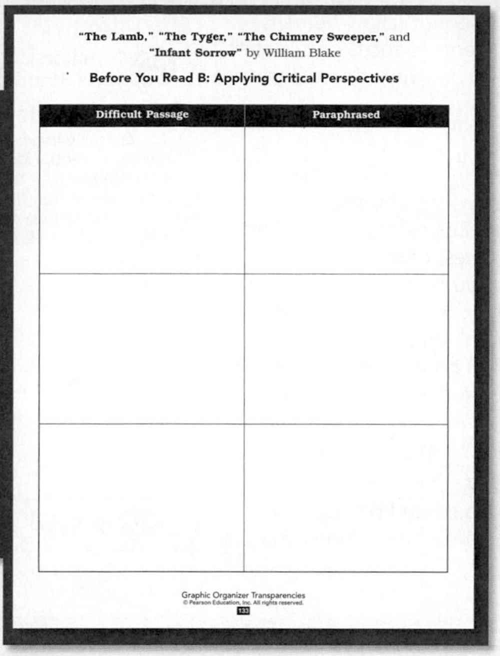
"The Lamb," "The Tyger," "The Chimney Sweeper," and "Infant Sorrow" by William Blake

Before You Read B: Applying Critical Perspectives

Difficult Passage	Paraphrased

Graphic Organizer Transparencies
© Pearson Education, Inc. All rights reserved.
133

EL L3 **Reading: Graphic Organizer B,** p. 133

Also available for these selections:

EL L1 L2 **Reading: Graphic Organizer A,** p. 132

EL L1 L2 **Literary Analysis: Graphic Organizer A** (partially filled in), p. 134

EL L3 **Literary Analysis: Graphic Organizer B,** p. 135

Skills Development/Extension

Unit 4 Resources

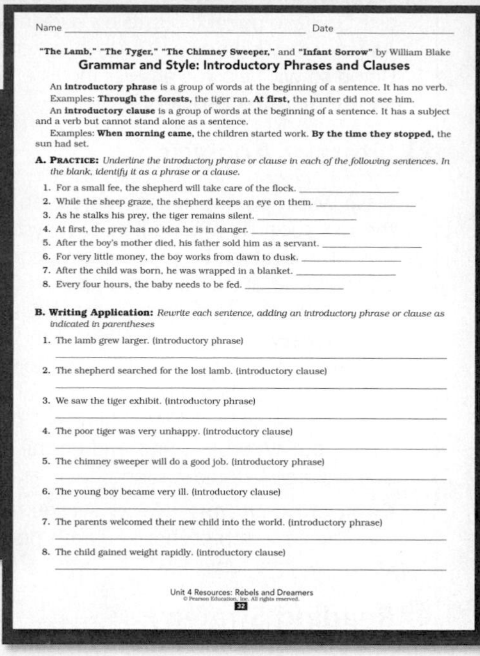
Name ______________ Date ______________

"The Lamb," "The Tyger," "The Chimney Sweeper," and "Infant Sorrow" by William Blake

Grammar and Style: Introductory Phrases and Clauses

An **introductory phrase** is a group of words at the beginning of a sentence. It has no verb.
Examples: **Through the forests,** the tiger ran. **At first,** the hunter did not see him.
An **introductory clause** is a group of words at the beginning of a sentence. It has a subject and a verb but cannot stand alone as a sentence.
Examples: **When morning came,** the children started work. **By the time they stopped,** the sun had set.

A. Practice: *Underline the introductory phrase or clause in each of the following sentences. In the blank, identify it as a phrase or a clause.*

1. For a small fee, the shepherd will take care of the flock. ______
2. While the sheep graze, the shepherd keeps an eye on them. ______
3. As he stalks his prey, the tiger remains silent. ______
4. At first, the prey has no idea he is in danger. ______
5. After the boy's mother died, his father sold him as a servant. ______
6. For very little money, the boy works from dawn to dusk. ______
7. After the child was born, he was wrapped in a blanket. ______
8. Every four hours, the baby needs to be fed. ______

B. Writing Application: *Rewrite each sentence, adding an introductory phrase or clause as indicated in parentheses.*

1. The lamb grew larger. (introductory phrase)
2. The shepherd searched for the lost lamb. (introductory clause)
3. We saw the tiger exhibit. (introductory phrase)
4. The poor tiger was very unhappy. (introductory clause)
5. The chimney sweeper will do a good job. (introductory phrase)
6. The young boy became very ill. (introductory clause)
7. The parents welcomed their new child into the world. (introductory phrase)
8. The child gained weight rapidly. (introductory clause)

Unit 4 Resources: Rebels and Dreamers
© Pearson Education, Inc. All rights reserved.
32

EL L3 L4 **Grammar & Style,** p. 32

Also available for these selections:

All **Literary Analysis,** p. 29

All **Reading,** p. 30

EL L3 L4 **Support for Writing,** p. 33

L4 **Enrichment,** p. 34

Assessment

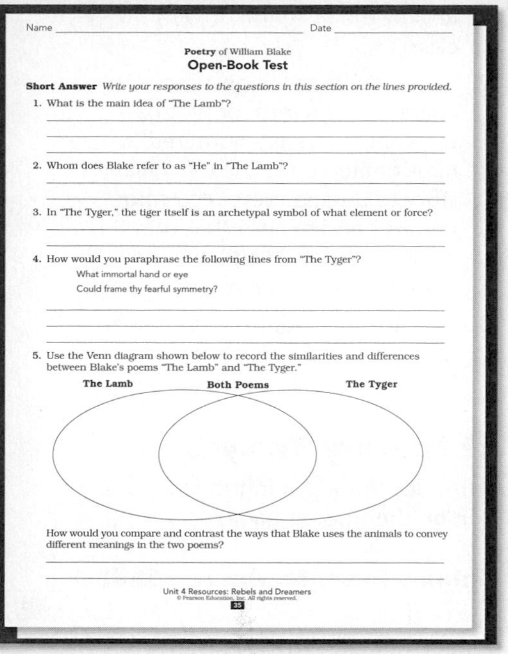
Name ______________ Date ______________

Poetry of William Blake

Open-Book Test

Short Answer *Write your responses to the questions in this section on the lines provided.*

1. What is the main idea of "The Lamb"?
2. Whom does Blake refer to as "He" in "The Lamb"?
3. In "The Tyger," the tiger itself is an archetypal symbol of what element or force?
4. How would you paraphrase the following lines from "The Tyger"?
What immortal hand or eye
Could frame thy fearful symmetry?
5. Use the Venn diagram shown below to record the similarities and differences between Blake's poems "The Lamb" and "The Tyger."

The Lamb — Both Poems — The Tyger

How would you compare and contrast the ways that Blake uses the animals to convey different meanings in the two poems?

Unit 4 Resources: Rebels and Dreamers
© Pearson Education, Inc. All rights reserved.
35

L3 L4 **Open-Book Test,** pp. 35–37

Also available for these selections:

EL L1 L2 **Selection Test A,** pp. 38–40

EL L3 L4 **Selection Test B,** pp. 41–43

PHLit Online!
www.PHLitOnline.com

- complete narrated selection text
- a thematically related video with writing prompt
- an interactive graphic organizer
- highlighting feature
- access to all student print resources, adapted to individual student needs
- Spanish and English summaries
- adapted selection translations in Spanish

Online Resources: All print materials are also available online.

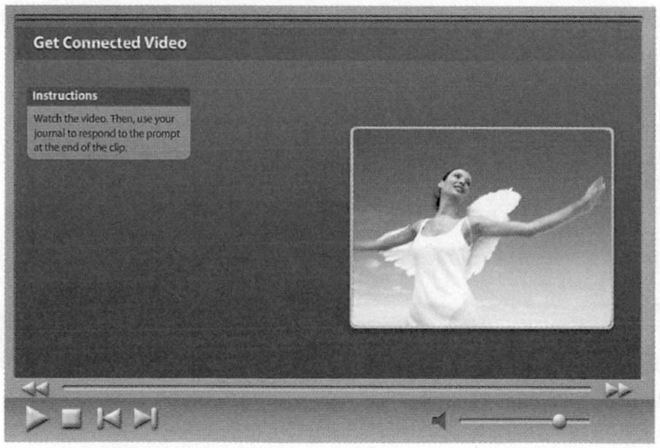

Get Connected! (thematic video with writing prompt)

Also available:

Background Video
All videos are available in Spanish.

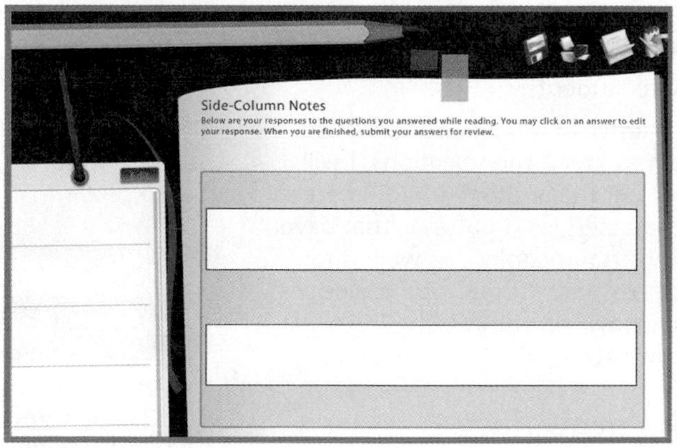

Writer's Journal (with graphics feature)

Also available:

Vocabulary Central (tools and activities for studying vocabulary)

PRETEACH

❶ Connecting to the Essential Question

1. Review the assignment with the class.
2. Ask students to suggest recurring characters, themes, or plot patterns they have encountered in films or literature. Use a familiar story to discuss these recurring patterns and explain that they are archetypes. Then have them complete the assignment.
3. As students read, have them look for passages that focus on problems of industrial society.

❷ Literary Analysis

Introduce the skill using the instruction on the student page.

Think Aloud: Model the Skill

Say to students:

To identify the character or situational archetypes in a literary work, I would start by listing the elements that seem familiar and then try to match them with a pattern I have encountered before.

❸ Reading Strategy

1. Introduce the skill using the instruction on the student page.
2. Give students a copy of **Reading Strategy Graphic Organizer B**, page 133 in ***Graphic Organizer Transparencies***, to fill out as they read.

Think Aloud: Model the Skill

Say to students:

To arrive at a deeper understanding as I read the selections, I will look at the author's use of images, characters, and patterns that have universal meaning, as well as for details that suggest oppression, to see how they fit into the historical context.

❹ Vocabulary

1. Pronounce each word, giving its definition, and have students say it aloud.
2. For more guidance, see the *Classroom Strategies and Teaching Routines* card for introducing vocabulary.

Before You Read

The Lamb • The Tyger • The Chimney Sweeper • Infant Sorrow

❶ Connecting to the Essential Question Like many modern-day artists, Blake pointed out to his audience the misery of fellow humans. As you read, identify passages in which Blake seems to focus on social ills. Doing so will help you answer the Essential Question: **How does literature shape or reflect society?**

Common Core State Standards

Reading Literature

2. Determine two or more themes or central ideas of a text and analyze their development over the course of the text, including how they interact and build on one another to produce a complex account.

❷ Literary Analysis

Blake was a poet who had one eye on mystical visions and the other on the real social ills around him. His mystical visions were based on a perception of **archetypes**—plot patterns, character types, or ideas with emotional power and widespread appeal. Critics argue that archetypes reveal in symbolic form universal truths about humanity. Blake often expressed such archetypes in paired poems, like "The Lamb" and "The Tyger."

Blake is perhaps less well known for his **social commentary**—his criticism of the ills caused by the Industrial Revolution and political tyranny. This Blake, author of "The Chimney Sweeper," had his eye not on the clouds but on urban slums and on the factories in which men, women, and children labored for long hours and little pay.

Comparing Literary Works As you read, compare and contrast these two thematic approaches in Blake's poems: the archetypal visions and the social commentary.

❸ Reading Strategy

Preparing to Read Complex Texts Applying critical perspectives will help you better understand Blake's complex vision of society. As you read, use the following perspectives as ways of understanding Blake's use of archetypes and social commentary:

- *Historical and political perspective*: look for details that suggest economic or political oppression.
- *Archetypal perspective*: look for images, characters, and patterns that have universal meaning and a strong emotional charge.

Use a chart like the one shown to apply both of these perspectives.

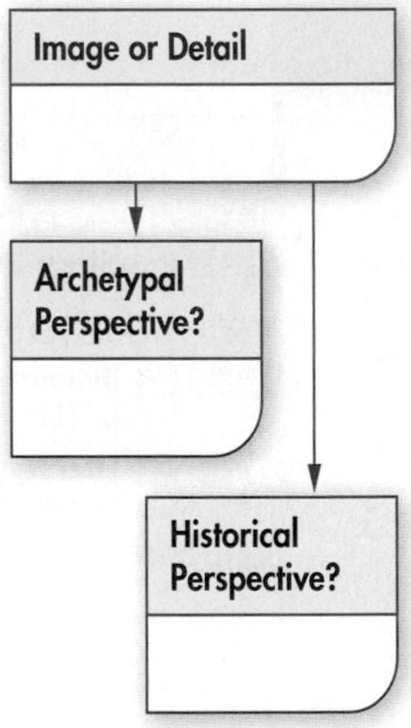

❹ Vocabulary

vales (vālz) *n.* valleys; depressed stretches of ground (p. 748)

immortal (i môrt′ əl) *adj.* living or lasting forever; not dying (p. 749)

symmetry (sim′ ə trē) *n.* balanced, beautiful form; the beauty resulting from such balance (p. 749)

aspire (ə spīr′) *v.* have high ambitions; yearn or seek after (p. 749)

sinews (sin′ yo͞oz) *n.* tendons (p. 749)

sulk (sulk) *v.* show resentment by refusing to interact with others (p. 752)

PHLit Online! www.PHLitOnline.com

Vocabulary Development

Vocabulary Knowledge Rating

Create a **Vocabulary Knowledge Rating Chart** (*Professional Development Guidebook*, p. 33) for the vocabulary words on the student page. Give each student a copy of the chart with the words on it. Read the words aloud, and have students mark their ratings in the Before Reading column. When students have completed reading and discussing the group of selections, have them take out their **Vocabulary Knowledge Rating Charts** for the selections. Read the words aloud and have students rate their knowledge again in the After Reading column. Clarify any words that are still problematic. Then have students complete the Vocabulary practice at the end of the selections.

PHLit Online! **Vocabulary Central,** featuring tools and activities for studying vocabulary, is available online at **www.PHLitOnline.com**.

❺ William Blake

(1757–1827)

Author of **"The Lamb"** • **"The Tyger"** • **"The Chimney Sweeper"** • **"Infant Sorrow"**

"I must create a system or be enslaved by another man's." So spoke William Blake, an artist and poet who strove in his work to break free from the patterns of thought that defined common experience. As if to underscore the difference between his views and the ordinary, he claimed that mystical visions were the source of his inspiration.

Finding His Way Blake's visions began when, at the age of four, he thought he saw God at his window. Four years later, Blake said, he saw a tree filled with angels. While Blake's "spells" might have seemed a cause for concern, Blake's parents were followers of the mystical teachings of Emanuel Swedenborg, a Swedish spiritualist. They believed that their son had a "gift of vision" and did all they could to nurture this gift.

Blake's father was a poor Londoner who owned a small hosiery shop. He sent Blake to drawing school, and Blake pursued his own education at home through wide reading. He became an engraver's apprentice and then went on to study at the Royal Academy.

Striking Out on His Own Formal study did not last long, however. The rebellious Blake left the school and eventually set up his own print shop. He was to live most of his days eking out a living as an engraver, barely making enough to support himself and his wife, Catherine.

Innocence and Experience When Blake was thirty-two, he published *Songs of Innocence*, a series of poems that he had composed when he was younger. In these poems, Blake suggested that by recapturing the wonderment of childhood, we can achieve the goal of true self-knowledge and integration with the world. In 1794, he brought out a companion to *Songs of Innocence*, entitled *Songs of Experience.*

A Mature Vision Exploring the darker side of life, *Songs of Experience* reflected Blake's growing disillusionment and more mature vision. He came to believe that a return to innocence was not, at least by itself, sufficient for people to attain true self-awareness. Blake's credo was that there must be a fusion of innocence and experience.

Blake's talent was barely recognized by his peers or by the public during his lifetime. Despite the lack of recognition, Blake filled his seventy years with constant creative activity. Years after his death, he came to be regarded as one of the most important poets of his time.

Daily Bellringer

For each class during which you will teach these selections, have students complete one of the five activities for the appropriate week in the *Daily Bellringer Activities* booklet.

Multidraft Reading

To assist struggling readers and to enhance reading for all, assign the text in chunks, as warranted by length, and apply multidraft reading protocols. For each reading, have students set the purpose indicated:

- **First reading**—identifying key ideas and details and answering any Reading Checks.
- **Second reading**—analyzing craft and structure and responding to the side-column prompts.
- **Third reading**—integrating knowledge and ideas, connecting to other texts and the world, and answering the end-of-selection questions.

For more guidance, refer to the ***Classroom Strategies and Teaching Routines*** card, Multidraft Reading.

❺ Background

More About the Author

William Blake is remembered today as a visionary who anticipated nineteenth-century developments in poetry and philosophy. His works are a record of his own evolving personal mythology.

Blake's radical views tended to set him apart from others. Modern critics tend to see in Blake's extreme statements and complex images not madness, but irony and a deliberate effort to outrage. Perhaps Blake sought to shock readers and so jolt them free from preconceived ideas.

PHLit Online!

www.PHLitOnline.com

Teaching From Technology

Preparing to Read

Go to **www.PHLitOnline.com** and display the *Get Connected!* slide show for this selection. Have the class brainstorm responses to the writing prompt, entering ideas in the interactive journal. Then, have students complete their written responses as homework.

To build background, display the Background and More About the Author feature.

Using the Interactive Text

Go to **www.PHLitOnline.com** and display the Enriched Online Student Edition. As the class reads the selection or listens to the narration, record answers to side-column prompts using the graphic organizers accessible on the interactive page. Alternatively, have students use the online edition individually, answering the prompts as they read.

TEACH

❶ About the Selection

In this sprightly poem, a child talks to a lamb about their creator, and both the child and the lamb emerge as archetypes of innocence.

❷ Activating Prior Knowledge

Write the word pairs *good/evil; right/wrong;* and *heaven/hell* on the chalkboard. Tell the class that Blake believed that pure opposites such as these are ultimately false. The truth, in Blake's vision, involves overturning these simple terms to find a new vision of life. Have students write a paragraph about the opposites and challenges to conventional dichotomies they discover in Blake's poetry.

Concept Connector →

Tell students they will return to their responses after reading the selection.

❸ Humanities

Illustrated manuscript of **"The Lamb,"** by William Blake

A boy converses with a sheep. He stands outside the simple hut of a shepherd; it has a thatched roof and open window. The vines and leaves that encircle the poem create a pastoral frame for the scene.

Use this question for discussion:

Why do you think the boy is shown with his arms outstretched?

Answer: The gesture expresses the harmonious relationship between child and lamb, and between humanity and nature, as depicted in the poem.

❸

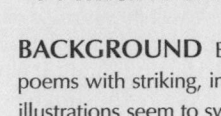

From a manuscript of "The Lamb" by William Blake, Lessing J. Rosenwald Collection, Library of Congress, Washington, D.C.

❹ **▲ Critical Viewing**
What view of nature is expressed by the style of Blake's drawing? **[Infer]**

❶ ❷

The Lamb

William Blake

BACKGROUND Blake illustrated his poems with striking, integrated designs. These illustrations seem to swirl through the words and become part of their meaning. Blake claimed that many of the images he drew as illustrations were likenesses of his inner visions. They have a childlike feeling and are very different from the strict, formal styles of his time.

Little Lamb who made thee
Dost thou know who made thee
Gave thee life & bid thee feed.
By the stream & o'er the mead;
Gave thee clothing of delight,
Softest clothing wooly bright;
Gave thee such a tender voice,
Making all the **vales** rejoice!
Little Lamb who made thee
Dost thou know who made thee

Little Lamb I'll tell thee,
Little Lamb I'll tell thee!
❺ He is called by thy name,
For he calls himself a Lamb:
He is meek & he is mild,
He became a little child:
I a child & thou a lamb,
We are called by his name.
Little Lamb God bless thee.
Little Lamb God bless thee.

Vocabulary
vales (vālz) *n.* valleys; hollows; depressed stretches of ground

Literary Analysis
Archetypes What types of people or human conditions does a lamb usually represent?

Text Complexity Rubric

	The Lamb	The Tyger	The Chimney Sweeper	Infant Sorrow
Qualitative Measures				
Context/Knowledge Demands	Romantic poem 1 ② 3 4 5	Romantic poem 1 ② 3 4 5	Romantic poem; historical knowledge demands 1 2 ③ 4 5	Romantic poem 1 ② 3 4 5
Structure/Language Conventionality and Clarity	Archaic diction; simple vocabulary 1 ② 3 4 5	Archaic diction and spelling 1 ② 3 4 5	Simple vocabulary 1 ② 3 4 5	Simple vocabulary 1 ② 3 4 5
Levels of Meaning/ Purpose/Concepts	Accessible (innocence) 1 ② 3 4 5	Accessible (nature, experience) 1 2 ③ 4 5	Moderate (child labor) 1 2 ③ 4 5	Moderate (birth) 1 2 ③ 4 5
Quantitative Measures				
Lexile/Text Length	NP / 114 words	NP / 141 words	NP / 223 words	NP / 45 words
Overall Complexity	**More accessible**	**More accessible**	**More complex**	**More accessible**

❻ # The TYGER

William Blake

Vocabulary

immortal (i môrt′əl) *adj.* living or lasting forever; not dying

symmetry (sim′ ə trē) *n.* balanced form; the beauty resulting from such balance

aspire (ə spīr′) *v.* have high ambitions; yearn or seek after

sinews (sin′ yo͞oz) *n.* tendons

Tyger Tyger, burning bright,
In the forests of the night;
What immortal hand or eye,
Could frame thy fearful symmetry?

In what distant deeps or skies
Burnt the fire of thine eyes!
On what wings dare he aspire?
What the hand, dare seize the fire?

And what shoulder, & what art,
Could twist the sinews of thy heart?
And when thy heart began to beat,
What dread hand? & what dread feet?

❼ What the hammer? what the chain,
In what furnace was thy brain?
What the anvil? what dread grasp,
Dare its deadly terrors clasp?

When the stars threw down their spears
And water'd heaven with their tears:
Did he smile his work to see?
Did he who made the Lamb make thee?

Tyger, Tyger burning bright,
In the forests of the night:
What immortal hand or eye,
Dare frame thy fearful symmetry?

Literary Analysis
Social Commentary
To what type of worker does Blake compare the tiger's creator?

❹ Critical Viewing

Answer: Nature appears harmonious and unthreatening, as can be inferred from the trust shown between the lamb and the boy.

❺ Literary Analysis

Archetypes

1. Direct students' attention to the bracketed lines on page 748.
2. **Ask** the Literary Analysis question.
   Answer: A lamb usually represents an innocent sacrifice; it is often a biblical reference to Christ.

❻ About the Selection

The voice of this poem shares the chanting, nursery-rhyme quality of the voice in "The Lamb," but the scene is wilder and grimmer. Darkness replaces light, night replaces day; experience replaces innocence. This poem also asks about the creator and the creature. It measures the character of the tiger's creator against the ferocity and power of the tiger, suggesting that the creator of the tiger has burning, passionate energy. However, it leaves its question about the creator unanswered.

❼ Literary Analysis

Social Commentary

1. Direct students' attention to the bracketed lines on page 749.
2. **Ask** the Literary Analysis question.
   Answer: a blacksmith or other metal worker

Text Complexity: Reader and Task Suggestions

	The Lamb; The Tyger	The Chimney Sweeper	Infant Sorrow
Preparing to Read the Texts • Explain that Blake's *Songs of Innocence* and *Songs of Experience* contain parallel poems that convey his sense of the world's duality. • Discuss Blake's idea that truths can be found in the contrast of opposite concepts. • Guide students to use Multidraft Reading strategies (TE p. 747).	**Leveled Tasks** ***Levels of Meanings*** If students will have difficulty with the poems' ideas, have them first focus on the lamb and tiger. Then, have students consider what aspects of the world the two creatures represent. ***Synthesizing*** If students will not have difficulty with the ideas, have them contrast the poems to explain how they together express a dual world view.	**Leveled Tasks** ***Knowledge Demands*** If students will have difficulty with the historical context, have them focus on the chimney sweepers' ages and the kinds of lives they lead. Then, have them decide the main point the poem makes. ***Analyzing*** If students will not have difficulty with the context, have them analyze what the imagery and details suggest about child labor.	**Leveled Tasks** ***Levels of Meaning*** If students will have difficulty with the meaning, have them focus on the connotations of the words. Then, with that in mind, have them decide what the poem is saying about the human condition. ***Evaluating*** If students will not have difficulty with the meaning, have them decide if the poem likely appeared in *Songs of Innocence* or *Songs of Experience*.

❽ Humanities

Illustrated manuscript of **"The Tyger,"** by William Blake

This engraving of a tiger shows a strong-looking animal, with muscular haunches and a stance that prepares it to pounce or run. Its eye appears to "burn bright" with an intense yellow light. Use this question for discussion:

What effect do the tree branches have on the layout of this poem?

Answer: The branches divide the poem into stanzas or pairs of stanzas. The tree is an otherworldly color, outlined in the tiger's orange. It unifies text and illustration and adds to the dark mood of the poem.

❾ Critical Viewing

Answer: The tiger's expression in the illustration—perhaps a mischievous smile—seems far less threatening than its image in the poem.

❽

❾ ▲ **Critical Viewing**
Compare and contrast the tiger's expression with the poem's image of the animal. **[Compare and Contrast]**

Enrichment: Investigating Daily Life

Child Labor

Throughout history, children have been put to work in various forms of labor. For many families, the economic necessities outweighed the burden on the child who was put to work. During the Industrial Revolution in England, children were regularly used in factories. Small children also did the work of cleaning accumulations of flammable soot out of chimneys because they could easily climb into the chimneys and scrape them clean, as described in Blake's poem, "The Chimney Sweeper."

Activity: Investigate Labor Laws In the United States today, strict labor laws prevent the regular employment of children. Ask students to investigate the social, cultural, economic, and historical forces that led to the establishment of laws that regulate the employment of underage workers. Suggest that they record their analysis in the **Enrichment: Investigating Daily Life** worksheet, ***Professional Development Guidebook,*** page 224.

THE Chimney Sweeper

William Blake

When my mother died I was very young,
And my father sold me while yet my tongue,
Could scarcely cry weep weep weep weep.
So your chimneys I sweep & in soot I sleep.

There's little Tom Dacre, who cried when his head
That curl'd like a lambs back, was shav'd, so I said.
Hush Tom never mind it, for when your head's bare,
You know that the soot cannot spoil your white hair.

And so he was quiet, & that very night,
As Tom was a sleeping he had such a sight,
That thousands of sweepers Dick, Joe, Ned & Jack
Were all of them lock'd up in coffins of black

And by came an Angel who had a bright key,
And he open'd the coffins & set them all free.
Then down a green plain leaping laughing they run
And wash in a river and shine in the Sun.

Then naked & white, all their bags left behind,
They rise upon clouds, and sport in the wind.
And the Angel told Tom if he'd be a good boy,
He'd have God for his father & never want joy.

And so Tom awoke and we rose in the dark
And got with our bags & our brushes to work.
Tho' the morning was cold, Tom was happy & warm,
So if all do their duty, they need not fear harm.

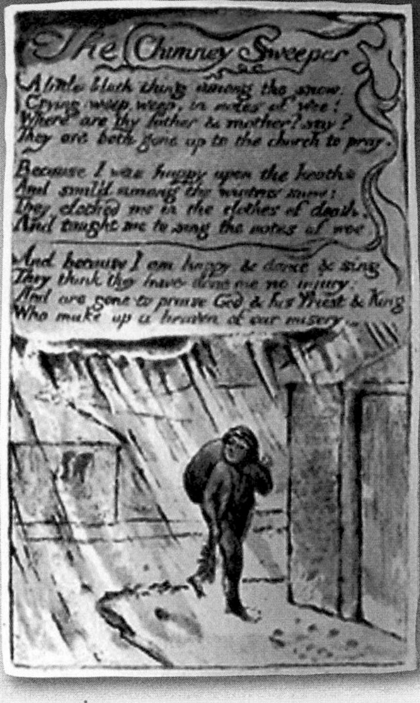

12 ▲ Critical Viewing Compare and contrast Blake's image of a chimney sweeper in his engraving with the image he creates in his poem. **[Compare and Contrast]**

13 Reading Strategy
Applying Critical Perspectives
Which details in this poem suggest economic oppression? Which details have a strong emotional charge?

10 About the Selection

Religious beliefs pervade this short poem about the miseries suffered by child laborers. Tom recounts a dream in which an angel rescues the boys from their coffins, takes them to a sunny meadow, and tells him that if he is good, God will provide.

11 Critical Thinking

Compare and Contrast

1. Explain that Blake wrote two different poems with the same title. The first appeared in his volume *Songs of Innocence* in 1789. The companion poem appeared in his volume *Songs of Experience* in 1794, which is illustrated in the engraving. The point of view of the narrators is very different.
2. **Ask** students to read the poem shown with the engraving and compare its message with Blake's earlier poem.
   Possible response: The second poem focuses on child labor as a social ill. In the first, the children have a positive outlook on life and do not fear death. In the second, the child blames society for allowing these conditions to occur.
3. **Ask** students how they would account for the difference.
   Possible response: Students may suggest that the second poem presents Blake's growing disillusionment with the ills of industrial society.

12 Critical Viewing

Answer: The image in the engraving is much darker and more critical than the mood of Blake's poem.

13 Reading Strategy

Applying Critical Perspectives

1. Direct students' attention to the bracketed passages.
2. **Ask** the first Reading Strategy question.
   Answer: The boy's father sold the boy for economic advantage.
3. **Ask** the second Reading Strategy question.
   Answer: the description of thousands of young boys in coffins

Differentiated Instruction for Universal Access

Strategy for Special-Needs Students
Have students examine and discuss Blake's illustration of a tiger. Then, have students read a section from "The Tyger" with your guidance. Ask students to visualize each line as they reread the entire poem to themselves.

Enrichment for Gifted/Talented Students
Remind students that Blake created art to illustrate his poetry. Encourage them to review Blake's artwork. Then, tell them that their assignment is to reverse the process and choose an illustration or painting they like and write a poem about it. Have them compare their results with Blake's illustrated poetry.

Enrichment for Advanced Readers
Tell students that Blake's poem "The Chimney Sweeper" depicts children working under cruel and inhumane conditions in Britain during the Industrial Revolution. Have students work in small groups to create a script for a short television news segment about child labor.

⑭ About the Selection

Like "The Tyger," this is a song of experience. Turning the stereotype of the joy of new life on its head, this poem presents a newborn that is not received with joy and that struggles, fights, and sulks.

⑮ Critical Viewing

Possible response: The poem says the mother groaned, but she appears to be patiently trying to diaper her struggling infant.

ASSESS

Answers

Before students respond, you may wish to have them write a brief objective summary of the selection. As they answer the questions below, remind them to support their answers with evidence from the text.

1. "The Lamb" urges meek acceptance of the human condition, while "The Tyger" glorifies nature and the jungle.
2. (a) The child in the first stanza of "The Chimney Sweeper" was sold to his employer by his father. (b) These events suggest that the sweeper's life was one of misery and hardship.
3. Yes, the infant's final reaction was one of surrender to weariness, and it is a common reaction when pressures become too much to bear.
4. **Possible response:** Reading about the harsh working conditions that existed for young people during the period in which Blake wrote his poetry makes me *modify* my faith in the essential goodness and *justice* of modern society. Unless people take *responsibility* and demand reforms, there will be some who will exploit others who are weaker than they are.

⑮ ▲ **Critical Viewing** Does the relationship of mother and child in the engraving match that in the poem? Explain. **[Connect]**

Vocabulary
sulk (sulk) *v.* show resentment by refusing to interact with others

⑭ INFANT *Sorrow*

William Blake

My mother groand![1] my father wept.
Into the dangerous world I leapt,
Helpless, naked, piping loud;
Like a fiend hid in a cloud.

Struggling in my father's hands,
Striving against my swaddling bands;
Bound and weary, I thought best
To **sulk** upon my mother's breast.

1. **groand** groaned; an example of Blake's often eccentric spelling.

Critical Reading

Cite textual evidence to support your responses.

1. **Integration of Knowledge and Ideas** In what ways do "The Lamb" and "The Tyger" represent opposite sides of human existence?
2. **Key Ideas and Details (a)** How does the child in the first stanza of "The Chimney Sweeper" get his job? **(b) Interpret:** What do these events suggest about the life of a chimney sweep?
3. **Integration of Knowledge and Ideas** In "Infant Sorrow," is the infant's final reaction characteristic of the way people deal with frustration? Explain.
4. **Integration of Knowledge and Ideas** How do these poems prompt you to rethink assumptions about society? Use two of these Essential Question words in your response: *modify, responsibility, justice.* ***[Connecting to the Essential Question: How does literature shape or reflect society?]***

Concept Connector

Reading Strategy Graphic Organizer

Ask students to review the graphic organizers in which they have listed images or details in the poems that have universal meaning or historical significance. Then, have students share their organizers and compare the images and details that they identified.

Activating Prior Knowledge

Have students return to their responses to the Activating Prior Knowledge activity. Ask them to explain whether their thoughts have changed and, if so, how.

Writing About the Essential Question

Have students compare their responses to the prompt, completed before reading the poems, with their thoughts afterward. Have them work individually or in groups, writing or discussing their thoughts, to formulate new responses. Then, lead a class discussion, probing for what students have learned that confirms or invalidates their initial thoughts. Encourage students to cite specific textual details to support their responses.

After You Read

The Lamb • The Tyger • The Chimney Sweeper • Infant Sorrow

Literary Analysis

1. **Key Ideas and Details** "The Lamb" and "The Tyger" come, respectively, from Blake's paired books *Songs of Innocence* and *Songs of Experience*. **(a)** Why is the lamb, as Blake presents it, an **archetype,** or universal symbol, of innocence? **(b)** Why is the tiger an archetype of experience? **(c)** Does Blake have a good reason for presenting archetypes in pairs? Explain.
2. **Craft and Structure** Blake uses a great deal of repetition in "The Lamb" and "The Tyger." Do you think this repetition increases the archetypal power of the images in these poems? Why or why not?
3. **Integration of Knowledge and Ideas** **(a)** How does the archetypal symbolism of "The Lamb" add to your understanding of the second stanza of "The Chimney Sweeper"? **(b)** How does the symbolism of "The Lamb" help you understand "Infant Sorrow"?
4. **Comparing Literary Works** **(a)** Using a chart like the one shown, compare the **social commentary** presented in "The Chimney Sweeper" with that in "Infant Sorrow." **(b)** Does the ending of each poem confirm or challenge the poem's perspective? Explain.

Who Is Suffering?	Why?	Significance to Time Period

5. **Analyze Visual Information** Explain the humor of the cartoon below.

Common Core State Standards

Writing
2.a. Introduce a topic; organize complex ideas, concepts, and information so that each new element builds on that which precedes it to create a unified whole; include formatting, graphics, and multimedia when useful to aiding comprehension. *(p. 754)*

Language
3.a. Vary syntax for effect, consulting references for guidance as needed. *(p. 755)*
4.a. Use context as a clue to the meaning of a word or phrase. *(p. 754)*

Reading Strategy

6. **Apply an archetypal perspective** in reading these poems. **(a)** Can you find examples of archetypal symbols in each of them? Why or why not? **(b)** Which poems are best explained by an archetypal perspective? Support your choices with references to the poems.
7. **Apply a historical perspective** in reading these poems. **(a)** Can you find references to social ills in each of them? Why or why not? **(b)** Which of the poems are best explained by a historical perspective? Support your choices by making specific references to the poems.
8. Consider how you can blend the archetypal and historical perspectives in reading these poems. For example, could the archetypal "fire" in "The Tyger" be linked with the fires of the oppressive factories of the Industrial Revolution? Explain.

"WHAT IMMORTAL HAND OR EYE COULD FRAME THY FEARFUL SYMMETRY?"

"WHAT IMMORTAL HAND OR EYE COULD FRAME THY FEARFUL SYMMETRY?" ▶

Assessment Practice

Critical Reasoning (For more practice, see *All-in-One Workbook*.)

Many tests require students to judge the relevant facts in a writer's argument. Have students read "The Chimney Sweeper" and then ask them the following question to show students how to identify a fact that does not support the writer's argument.

Which of these does not support Blake's message about the life of a chimney sweep?

A Chimney sweeping was dangerous.
B Some chimney sweepers were quite content.
C Children were forced to work as chimney sweeps.
D Chimney sweepers were not well paid.

Lead students to recognize that Blake's intent was to portray the life of a chimney sweep as a miserable one. Choices ***A***, ***C***, and ***D*** support this message. Students should determine that **B** is the correct answer.

Answers

1. (a) The lamb is an archetype of innocence because it is meek and mild. (b) The tiger is an archetype for experience because it is an experienced hunter. (c) He presents archetypes in pairs to contrast these differences.
2. Since archetypes are recurring patterns, the repetition does help strengthen their emotional power.
3. (a) The lamb is an archetype for childhood innocence. Blake compares the sweeper to a lamb by describing his hair as curled like a lamb's back. (b) The lamb is compared to a little child, meek and mild. In "Infant Sorrow" a child struggles in a dangerous world.
4. (a) "The Chimney Sweeper"—The boy sweepers suffer because their lives are hard; Significance: child labor; "Infant Sorrow"—The child is weary and his parents suffer because it is a dangerous world; Significance: The image contrasts sharply with the period's picture of childhood innocence. (b) The positive ending of "The Chimney Sweeper" challenges the poem's image of hardships. The ending of "Infant Sorrow" confirms the poem's perspective. Students should explain their answers with details from the poems.
5. The cartoon shows a domestic cat comparing itself with the words Blake used to describe the predatory tiger.
6. (a) Each poem has archetypal symbols because they represent common themes for understanding the world. (b) "The Lamb" and "The Tyger" are best explained using an archetypal perspective. The reference to the furnace in "The Tyger" may symbolize evil or hell. The meek mild lamb is a symbol for Christ.
7. (a) The religious theme in "The Lamb" does not comment on social ills, but the other poems do. (b) The dangerous world in "Infant Sorrow" and child labor in "The Chimney Sweeper" are best explained from a historical perspective.
8. "The Tyger" uses words like *hammer, chain, furnace,* and *anvil,* which relate to industry.

ASSESS/EXTEND

Answers

Vocabulary Acquisition and Use

1. Introduce the skill using the instruction on the student page.
2. Have students complete the Word Analysis activity and the Vocabulary practice.

Word Analysis

1. *respiration:* breathing or taking air in and out of the body
2. *respirator:* a device used to help people breathe
3. *transpiration:* way that plants give off gases or breathe through pores in their leaves
4. *aspirate:* to draw breath into the lungs by suction
5. *spiracle:* a breathing hole of a land arthropod, found along each side of its thorax and abdomen
6. *spirometer:* an instrument for measuring the air entering and leaving the lungs during breathing

Vocabulary

1. The opposite of hills are *vales*.
2. By using even numbers: two and four, each description has *symmetry*.
3. *Lofty* suggests having high ambitions.
4. Tendons or *sinews* connect muscles.
5. The example suggests a situation someone might *resent*.
6. *Always* suggests something that lives forever.

Writing

1. To guide students in writing a multi-genre analysis of an author's assumptions, give them the Support for Writing Page (***Unit 4 Resources***, p. 33).
2. In the prewriting stage, tell students to refer back to their graphic organizers and walk students through the process of creating a diagram.
3. Remind students to include accurate and detailed references to the texts to support their work.
4. Use the rubrics for Response to Literature in the ***Professional Development Guidebook***, pages 250–251, to evaluate students' work.

PERFORMANCE TASKS

Integrated Language Skills

Vocabulary Acquisition and Use

Word Analysis: Latin Root *-spir-*

In "The Tyger," Blake uses the word *aspire*, meaning "to yearn or seek after." *Aspire* contains the Latin root *-spir-*, meaning "breath" or "life." When you aspire to something, you "live for it." Many scientific words that have to do with breathing contain the root *-spir-*. Look up the meaning of each word below. Then, write a definition of your own for each word, incorporating the meaning of *-spir-*.

1. respiration
2. respirator
3. transpiration
4. aspirate
5. spiracle
6. spirometer

Vocabulary: Context Clues

For each item below, explain how a context clue, or a hint from surrounding words, helps you identify the meaning of the italicized vocabulary word.

1. We traveled through *vales* and over hills.
2. The *symmetry* of the animal's body—two bright eyes, four strong and balanced legs—made it look graceful and powerful.
3. Even though it is a lofty goal, the students *aspire* to attend a top college.
4. After spraining her ankle, the runner received a massage of her muscles and *sinews*.
5. You are not going to *sulk* because we ordered pizza instead of burgers, are you?
6. His work is *immortal*; it will always be read.

Writing

Explanatory Text Write an **essay** on "The Tyger" and "The Chimney Sweeper," applying an archetypal analysis to the former and a social analysis to the latter. Support your analysis with diagrams of archetypes and of social forces.

Prewriting In your thesis, express Blake's vision in each work, and explain whether it is archetypal or social. Also, sketch a diagram that will help readers picture Blake's visions—for "Tyger," it might be a web showing qualities associated with an archetypal symbol and for "Chimney Sweeper," a diagram showing the effects of industrialization.

Drafting Analyze the perspective presented in each poem and show how it affects literary elements such as *tone, imagery,* and *setting*. Refine your diagrams and include *accurate and detailed references* to the texts to support your work.

Revising Review your essay, circling particularly striking details or ideas. Consider moving these details to the beginning or end of a paragraph to add emphasis. Be sure that your diagrams clearly support your analysis.

Model: Revising Placement for Emphasis

The tiger burns with the fires of passion and ambition and perhaps of cruelty. Can one and the same world contain the innocent lamb and the terrors of the tiger? Therefore, Blake seems to suggest, both the world and its creator contain more power and mystery than we care to admit.

At the beginning of the paragraph, the circled sentence will lend greater emphasis.

Assessment Resources

Unit 4 Resources

L1 L2 EL **Selection Test A**, pp. 38–40. Administer Test A to less advanced readers.

L3 L4 EL **Selection Test B**, pp. 41–43. Administer Test B to on-level students and more advanced students.

L3 L4 **Open-Book Test**, pp. 35–37. As an alternative, give the Open-Book test.

All **Customizable Test Bank**

All **Self-tests** Students may prepare for the **Selection Test** by taking the **Self-test** online.

PHLit Online! All assessment resources are available at **www.PHLitOnline.com**.

Conventions and Style: Using Introductory Phrases and Clauses

One way to improve your writing style is to vary your sentence structure. For example, instead of using a subject, you can use phrases and clauses to introduce a sentence. A **phrase** is a group of words that acts as one part of speech but that lacks a subject and a verb. A **clause** is a group of words that has a subject and a verb.

Varying Sentence Beginnings

Blake was writing simple poems by the age of twelve.
By the age of twelve, Blake was writing simple poems. (prepositional phrase)

He read widely at home and was able to get an education on his own.
Reading widely at home, he was able to get an education on his own. (participial phrase)

Blake entered the Royal Academy to continue his studies.
To continue his studies, Blake entered the Royal Academy. (infinitive phrase)

Blake's parents believed him although his visions were unusual.
Although Blake's visions were unusual, his parents believed him. (subordinate clause)

Punctuation Tip Use a comma after introductory elements, except when they are very brief and omitting a comma would not cause confusion.

Practice Revise each sentence by using the italicized part as an introductory phrase or clause. Hint: In some cases, you will need to make slight changes to the original wording.

1. Blake developed his own unique etching process *to print his works.*
2. He could produce only a few books *since the printing process took so long.*
3. Blake's illustrations were *characterized by a childlike mood* and differed from the more formal styles of the time.
4. Blake describes the magnificence of the tiger *in this powerful poem.*
5. The speaker *answers his own question* and says that Christ made the lamb. (Change *answers* to *answering.*)
6. The reader must understand symbolism *to appreciate these poems.*
7. The father sold the boy as a chimney sweep *after the mother died.*
8. Little Tom is *comforted by his friend's words* and has a dream about an angel.
9. The angel opens all the coffins *with his special, bright key.*
10. The boys *rise up into the clouds* and fly toward heaven. (Change *rise* to *rising.*)

Writing and Speaking Conventions

A. Writing Use each phrase or clause to begin a sentence.

1. during his lifetime
2. working as an engraver
3. to support himself
4. after the boy had a dream

Example: during his lifetime
Sentence: During his lifetime, Blake's talent went virtually unnoticed.

B. Speaking Write and present to the class a paragraph contrasting the lamb and the tiger. Use at least four phrases or clauses to begin sentences.

PH WRITING COACH
Further instruction and practice are available in *Prentice Hall Writing Coach.*

Extend the Lesson

Sentence Modeling
Share these lines with students:
When the stars threw down their spears
And water'd heaven with their tears;
Did he smile his work to see? ("The Tyger")
Into the dangerous world I leapt. ("Infant Sorrow")

Ask students what they notice about the sentences. Elicit from them that Blake introduced the sentence from "The Tyger" with a clause, and he introduced the sentence from "Infant Sorrow" with a prepositional phrase.

Have students imitate the sentences on a topic of their own choosing, matching the stylistic features discussed. Collect the sentences and share them with the class.

Conventions and Style

1. Introduce and discuss the skill using the instruction on the student page.
2. Have students complete the Practice and Grammar in Your Writing activities.

Practice

1. To print his works, Blake developed his own etching process.
2. Since the printing process took so long, he could only produce a few books.
3. Characterized by a childlike mood, Blake's illustrations differed from the more formal styles of the period.
4. In this powerful poem, Blake describes the magnificence of the tiger.
5. Answering his own question, the speaker says that Christ made the lamb.
6. To appreciate these poems, the reader must understand symbolism.
7. After the boy's mother died, his father sold the boy as a chimney sweep.
8. Comforted by his friend's words, Little Tom has a dream about an angel.
9. With his special, bright key, the angel opens all the coffins.
10. Rising up into the clouds, the boys fly toward heaven.

Writing and Speaking Conventions

A. Possible responses:

1. During his lifetime, Blake wrote any poems criticizing social ills using archetypes.
2. Working as an engraver, Blake illustrated many of his own works.
3. To support himself, Blake worked as an engraver.
4. After the boy had a dream, he was more content with his lot in life.

B. Ensure that students' responses use at least four phases or clauses to compare and contrast the lamb and the tiger.

PH WRITING COACH Grade 12

Students will find additional information on using introductory phrases and clauses in Chapter 15.

TEACH

Themes Across Centuries

Elizabeth McCracken

1. Tell students that Elizabeth McCracken's fiction is noted for its inventiveness and imagination. Her books reflect her love of characters. She says, "To me that is one of the pleasures of fiction; getting to know characters in a complex way—in a way that you sometimes don't get to know mere acquaintances."
2. Show Segment 2 on McCracken on the *See It!* **DVD** to provide insight into her imagination and writing process. Then **ask:** How is McCracken's work similar to Mary Shelley's?
   Answer: Both focus on "odd" characters that drive their plots.

Dreaming Up Monsters

1. Have students read the first part of McCracken's comments. **Ask:** What elements of McCracken's recurring nightmare were especially frightening?
   Answer: The monster was half human and half robot. It chased her out of a scary cave.
2. **Ask:** Why might young Elizabeth not want to be comforted?
   Possible response: She realized she was safe in her own bedroom and may have secretly enjoyed the excitement of a world with caves and creatures so very different from her normal life.

The Thrill of the Terrifying

1. Have students read the second part of the McCracken commentary. **Ask:** Why do readers enjoy being terrified?
   Answer: Frightening tales allow readers to explore ideas in their imaginations.
2. **Ask:** If she had not lived in a safe suburban world, might scary literature Elizabeth read have been as appealing to her?
   Possible response: No, McCracken's interest in monsters grew from wanting a change from her safe environment. If she experienced genuine threats, those stories would not be as entertaining.

Elizabeth McCracken Introduces

FRANKENSTEIN

BY MARY WOLLSTONECRAFT SHELLEY

Dreaming Up Monsters I had only one recurring nightmare as a child. It starred a Frankenstein monster—or at least the kind of Frankenstein monster my seven-year-old dreaming self could come up with, half-human and half-robot, inspired by scraps of movies I had seen, with bolts on his neck and a flashing red ambulance light on top of his head. Certainly he was nothing like the articulate and much scarier monster from Mary Shelley's novel. In the first half of the dream, the monster was my friend. In the second, we went into a cave, and then he chased me out. He could not recognize me. I woke up feeling his fingers on my back.

I remember sitting upright in bed, panting, but it was only a dream. Monsters made up of odd parts did not exist. I didn't live in a world of caves and creatures who chased small girls. My world was a single bed with a brown blanket, my older brother sleeping in one nearby room and my parents in another. They would have told me that I was safe. I didn't want to hear that.

The Thrill of the Terrifying Maybe I liked being scared, but mostly I think I liked the privacy of my nightmare. Like most seven-year-olds, I was never really alone except in dreams. Someone was *always* in a nearby room. I liked the terrifying movies I saw on TV, so many different versions of Frankenstein—*Frankenstein, Bride of Frankenstein, Abbott*

About the Author

Elizabeth McCracken's novel *Niagara Falls All Over Again* won the L. L. Winship/PEN New England Award. For her work, she was awarded grants from the Guggenheim Foundation and the Michener Foundation.

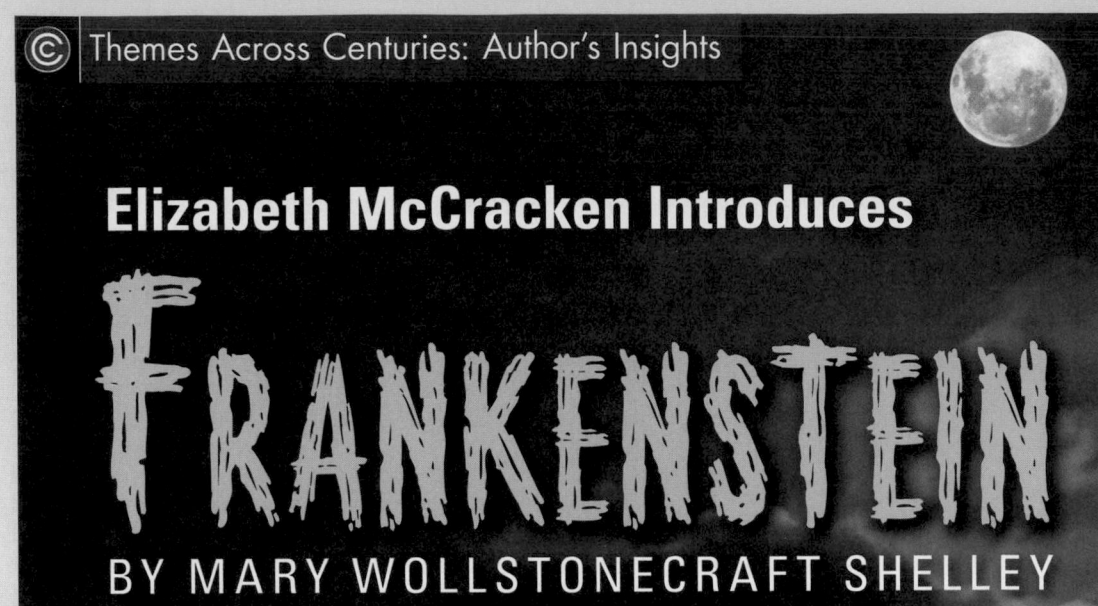

Teaching Resources

Unit 4 Resources
Contemporary Commentary: Elizabeth McCracken, p. 44
Listening and Viewing, Elizabeth McCracken, p. 45
***See It!* DVD**
Elizabeth McCracken, Segment 2

PHLit Online! All resources are available at **www.PHLITOnline.com.**

and Costello Meet Frankenstein. I liked fairy tales with dark woodcuts of dense forests that might hide any number of monsters. Fear was the only room I had to myself. When I read awful books—ghost stories as I got older, then true crime books about murderers, cannibals, disasters at sea—the safe suburban world around me disappeared, and I was alone and strangely happy.

Where Do Great Characters Come From?
I certainly never had to wonder what Mary Shelley says she was so often asked: "How I, then a young girl, came to think of, and to dilate upon, so very hideous an idea." Young girls—young boys, too, of course—love hideous ideas. My dream about a Frankenstein monster impressed me, because my own brain had come up with it—even if I'd ripped off most of the details. He scared me. He belonged to me. My dream-self wanted to go back to it, the way I would reread a particularly terrifying book. When I woke up in my own solid, real, boring bedroom, all the objects surrounding me were briefly as frightening as the dead fingers that had brushed my back.

It's the same reason I became a fiction writer. I wanted to make up people, and then, later, I wanted to wonder where they came from.

▶ **Critical Viewing**
Which details in this image of Frankenstein's monster convey terror? Explain. **[Analyze]**

Critical Reading

1. **Key Ideas and Details (a)** What types of frightening movies and books did McCracken enjoy as a child? **(b) Connect:** What does her enjoyment of these tales suggest about her relationship to "the safe suburban world around" her?
2. **Key Ideas and Details** What do you think McCracken means when she says, "I liked the privacy of my nightmare"?
3. **Integration of Knowledge and Ideas** Do you agree or disagree with McCracken's statement that young people "love hideous ideas"? Why or why not?

As You Read *Introduction to* Frankenstein . . .

4. Look for the inspiration that helped Mary Shelley write *Frankenstein.*
5. Note the connections between Shelley's fiction and the real-life foundations of her novel.

Where Do Great Characters Come From?

1. Point out McCracken's comment that young children "love hideous ideas."
2. **Ask** students whether they think a child's under-the-bed monster can be the beginning of great fiction, and why.
   Answer: McCracken's example suggests that children who enjoy being entertained by frightening stories may continue to make up characters and stories about those characters.

Critical Viewing

Answer: his huge size, the fact that he is made up of odd parts, his scar, and his odd skin tone

ASSESS

1. (a) McCracken liked terrifying movies like *Frankenstein,* fairy tales, ghost stories, books about cannibals and sea disasters, and later, true crime novels. (b) Because her suburban environment was safe, the scary literature provided thrills that were not part of her regular, daily life.
2. McCracken says she was never really alone. The nightmare was something that belonged to her alone, and it was exciting as well as scary.
3. **Possible responses:** Yes, because they appeal to the imagination and curiosity about the unknown. No, because some young people prefer to avoid unpleasant or hideous things.
4. Mary Shelley was inspired to write *Frankenstein* by a "waking vision" prompted by hearing a conversation about experiments with electricity that attempted to give life to the dead.
5. Shelley's fiction featured a scientist who tried to impart life to dead tissue, just as the experiment she heard about was an attempt to animate inanimate matter.

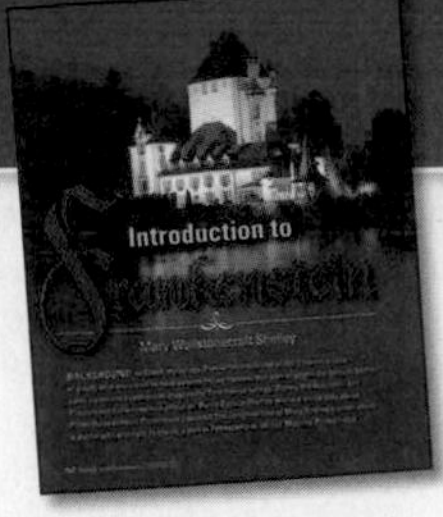

• Introduction to *Frankenstein*

Lesson Pacing Guide

DAY 1 Preteach

- Administer the Reading and Vocabulary Warm-ups (*Unit 4 Resources,* pp. 46–49) as necessary.
- Introduce the Literary Analysis concept: Gothic Literature.
- Introduce the Reading Strategy: Making Predictions.
- Build background with the author and Background features.
- Develop thematic thinking with Connecting to the Essential Question.
- Teach the selection vocabulary.

DAYS 2–3 Preteach/Teach/Assess

- Distribute copies of the appropriate graphic organizer for the Reading Strategy (*Graphic Organizer Transparencies,* pp. 136–137).
- Distribute copies of the appropriate graphic organizer for Literary Analysis (*Graphic Organizer Transparencies,* pp. 138–139).
- Prepare students to read with the Activating Prior Knowledge activities (TE).
- Informally monitor comprehension while students read.
- Use the Reading Check questions to confirm comprehension.
- Develop students' understanding of Gothic literature using the Literary Analysis prompts.
- Develop students' ability to make predictions using the Reading Strategy prompts.
- Reinforce vocabulary with the Vocabulary notes.
- Assess students' comprehension and mastery of the skills by having them answer the Critical Reading, Literary Analysis, and Reading Strategy questions.
- Have students complete the Vocabulary Lesson.

DAY 4 Extend/Assess

- Have students complete the Conventions and Style Lesson.
- Have students complete the Writing Lesson and write an autobiography. (You may assign as homework.)
- Have students read and respond to the Contemporary Commentary.
- Administer Selection Test A or B (*Unit 4 Resources,* pp. 59–61 or 62–64).

Common Core State Standards

Reading Informational Text 3. Analyze a complex set of ideas or sequence of events and explain how specific individuals, ideas, or events interact and develop over the course of the text.

Writing 3. Write narratives to develop real or imagined experiences or events, using effective technique, well-chosen details, and well-structured event sequences.
3.b. Use narrative techniques, such as pacing, to develop experiences, events, and/or characters.

Language 4.d. Verify the preliminary determination of the meaning of a word or phrase.

Additional Standards Practice
***Common Core Companion,* pp. 28–35; 208–218; 324–331**

Daily Block Scheduling
Each day in this Lesson Pacing Guide represents a 40–50 minute period. Teachers using block scheduling may combine days to revise pacing. In addition, teachers may differentiate and support core instruction by integrating components for extended and intensive support as students require. See the Guide to Selected Leveled Resources (facing page).

Guide to Selected Leveled Resources

RTI Tier 1 (students performing on level)			Introduction to *Frankenstein*
Warm Up	Whole class instruction; Group work	**Practice, model,** and **monitor** fluency, working **with the whole class** or **in groups.**	**Vocabulary and Reading Warm-ups B,** ***Unit 4 Resources,*** pp. 46–47, 49
Comprehension/Skills	Whole class instruction; Group work; Independent work	**Support** and **monitor** comprehension and skills development, having students complete the activities, graphic organizers, and interactive prompts **independently** or **as a class.**	• ***Reader's Notebook,*** adapted instruction and full selection EL ***Reader's Notebook: English Learner's Version,*** adapted instruction and adapted selection • **Reading Strategy Graphic Organizer B,** ***Graphic Organizer Transparencies,*** p. 141 • **Literary Analysis Graphic Organizer B,** ***Graphic Organizer Transparencies,*** p. 143
Monitor Progress	A	**Monitor** student progress with the differentiated curriculum-based assessment in the *Unit Resources.*	• **Selection Test B,** ***Unit 4 Resources,*** pp. 62–64 • **Open-Book Test,** ***Unit 4 Resources,*** pp. 56–58

RTI Tier 2 (students requiring intervention)			Introduction to *Frankenstein*
Warm Up	Group work; One-on-one teaching	**Practice, model,** and **monitor** fluency **in groups** or **with individuals.**	• **Vocabulary and Reading Warm-ups A,** ***Unit 4 Resources,*** pp. 46–48 • ***Hear It!*** **Audio CD (adapted text)**
Comprehension/Skills	Group work; One-on-one teaching	• **Support** and **monitor** comprehension and skills development, working **in small groups** or **with individuals.** • As students complete the selection in the appropriate version of the *Reader's Notebook,* **monitor** comprehension frequently with group questions and individual instruction. • **Model** strategies while guiding students in completing the activities and prompts in the *Reader's Notebook,* as well as the graphic organizers. • **Practice** skills and **monitor** mastery with the *Reading Kit* worksheets.	• ***Reader's Notebook: Adapted Version,*** adapted instruction and adapted selection EL ***Reader's Notebook: English Learner's Version,*** adapted instruction and adapted selection • **Reading Strategy Graphic Organizer A,** ***Graphic Organizer Transparencies,*** p. 140 • **Literary Analysis Graphic Organizer A,** ***Graphic Organizer Transparencies,*** p. 142 • ***Reading Kit,*** Practice worksheets
Monitor Progress	A	**Monitor** student progress with the differentiated curriculum-based assessment in the *Unit Resources* and in the *Reading Kit.*	• **Selection Test A,** ***Unit 4 Resources,*** pp. 59–61 • ***Reading Kit,*** Assess worksheets

TIER 3 Tier 3 intervention may require consultation with the student's special-education or dyslexia specialist. For additional support, see the Tier 2 activities and resources listed above.

One-on-one teaching **Group work** **Whole class instruction** **Independent work** **A Assessment**

For a complete guide to selection support, including support for Advanced students, see the Overview of Resources in the frontmatter.

• Introduction to *Frankenstein*

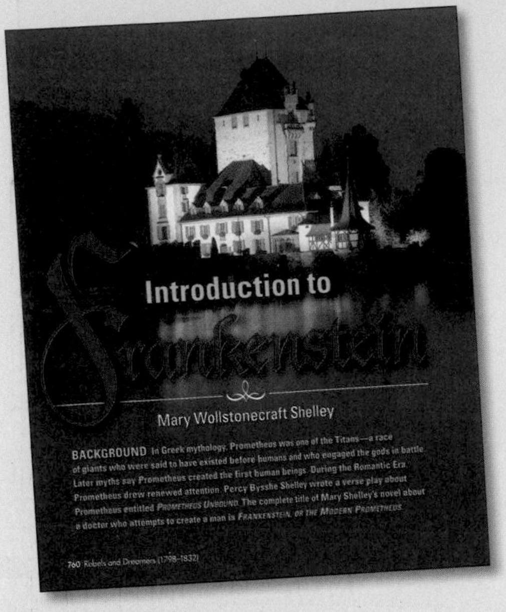

RESOURCES FOR:

- L1 Special-Needs Students
- L2 Below-Level Students (Tier 2)
- L3 On-Level Students (Tier 1)
- L4 Advanced Students (Tier 1)
- EL English Learners
- All All Students

Vocabulary/Fluency/Prior Knowledge

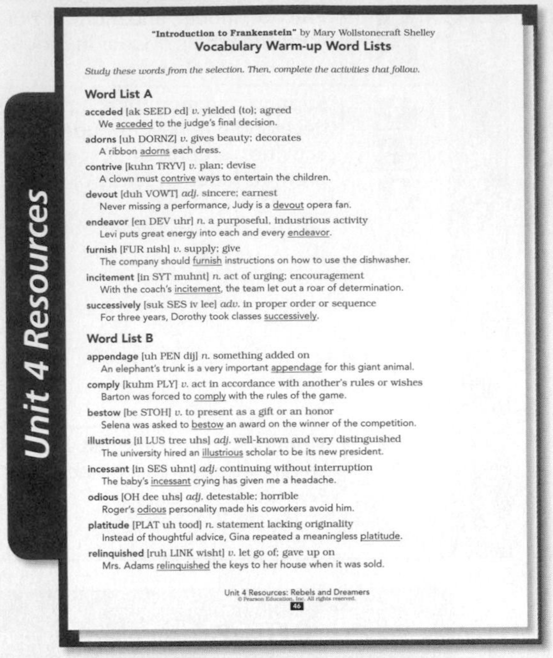
Unit 4 Resources

"Introduction to Frankenstein" by Mary Wollstonecraft Shelley
Vocabulary Warm-up Word Lists

Study these words from the selection. Then, complete the activities that follow.

Word List A

acceded [ak SEED ed] *v.* yielded (to); agreed
We acceded to the judge's final decision.

adorns [uh DORNZ] *v.* gives beauty; decorates
A ribbon adorns each dress.

contrive [kuhn TRYV] *v.* plan; devise
A clown must contrive ways to entertain the children.

devout [duh VOWT] *adj.* sincere; earnest
Never missing a performance, Judy is a devout opera fan.

endeavor [en DEV uhr] *n.* a purposeful, industrious activity
Levi puts great energy into each and every endeavor.

furnish [FUR nish] *v.* supply; give
The company should furnish instructions on how to use the dishwasher.

incitement [in SYT muhnt] *n.* act of urging; encouragement
With the coach's incitement, the team let out a roar of determination.

successively [suk SES iv lee] *adv.* in proper order or sequence
For three years, Dorothy took classes successively.

Word List B

appendage [uh PEN dij] *n.* something added on
An elephant's trunk is a very important appendage for this giant animal.

comply [kuhm PLY] *v.* act in accordance with another's rules or wishes
Barton was forced to comply with the rules of the game.

bestow [be STOH] *v.* to present as a gift or an honor
Selena was asked to bestow an award on the winner of the competition.

illustrious [il LUS tree uhs] *adj.* well-known and very distinguished
The university hired an illustrious scholar to be its new president.

incessant [in SES uhnt] *adj.* continuing without interruption
The baby's incessant crying has given me a headache.

odious [OH dee uhs] *adj.* detestable; horrible
Roger's odious personality made his coworkers avoid him.

platitude [PLAT uh tood] *n.* statement lacking originality
Instead of thoughtful advice, Gina repeated a meaningless platitude.

relinquished [ruh LINK wisht] *v.* let go of; gave up on
Mrs. Adams relinquished the keys to her house when it was sold.

Unit 4 Resources: Rebels and Dreamers
© Pearson Education, Inc. All rights reserved.
46

EL L1 L2 **Vocabulary Warm-ups A and B,** pp. 46–47

Also available for these selections:

EL L1 L2 **Reading Warm-ups A and B,** pp. 48–49

All **Vocabulary Builder,** p. 52

Reader's Notebooks

Pre- and postreading pages for this selection appear in an interactive format in the *Reader's Notebooks.* Each *Notebook* is differentiated for a different group of learners. The selections in the Adapted and English Learner's versions are abridged.

L2 L3 ***Reader's Notebook***

L1 ***Reader's Notebook: Adapted Version***

EL ***Reader's Notebook: English Learner's Version***

EL ***Reader's Notebook: Spanish Version***

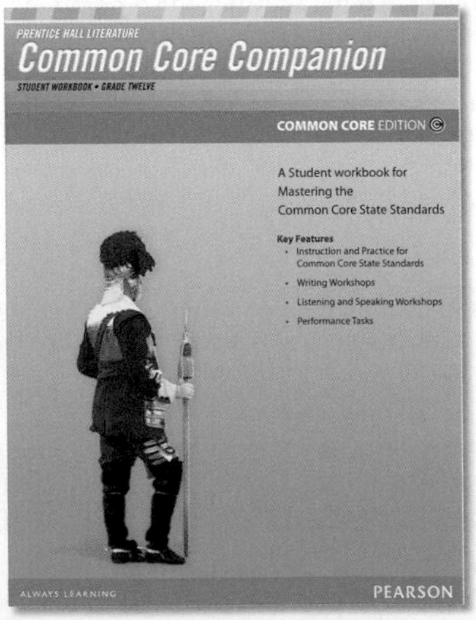

Common Core Companion

Additional instruction and practice for each Common Core State Standard

Selection Support

Graphic Organizer Transparencies

"Introduction to *Frankenstein*" by Mary Wollstonecraft Shelley

After You Read A: The Gothic Tradition

Gothic Characteristic	Example in Shelley
horror and dread	clasping a ghost; withering of innocent children
supernatural events	ghost bride of deserted lover; kiss of death

Graphic Organizer Transparencies

138

EL L1 L2 **Literary Analysis: Graphic Organizer A** (partially filled in), p. 138

Also available for these selections:

EL L1 L2 **Reading: Graphic Organizer A** (partially filled in), p. 136

EL L3 **Reading: Graphic Organizer B,** p. 137

EL L3 **Literary Analysis: Graphic Organizer B,** p. 139

Skills Development/Extension

Unit 4 Resources

Name ______________________ Date ____________

Introduction to Frankenstein by Mary Wollstonecraft Shelley

Enrichment: Science

Mary Shelley published *Frankenstein* in 1818. Scientists in the 1800s, like the fictional Dr. Frankenstein, would have had access to some basic tools, such as microscopes and thermometers. However, nineteenth-century science was very different from modern science in many respects. For example, at the beginning of the nineteenth century, doctors still tried to cure disease by bleeding or applying leeches to the patient. The chart below contrasts nineteenth- and twentieth-century science.

Some scientific developments that occurred by or in the nineteenth century	Some of the scientific developments of the twentieth century
• scientific method	• X-rays
• discovery of atoms	• discovery of structure of the atom
• basic genetics	• discovery of DNA
• electricity	• computers
• magnets	• laser technology
• telescopes	• satellites
• microscopes	• rockets/space shuttle
• partial periodic table of elements	• nuclear physics

Directions: *Refer to the chart as you answer the questions below.*

1. Name three activities of doctors or scientists today that would have been impossible in the nineteenth century.

2. If Shelley were alive today and wrote a new novel about the dangers of technology used for the wrong purposes, what might the plot be?

Unit 4 Resources: Rebels and Dreamers

55

L4 **Enrichment,** p. 55

Also available for these selections:

All **Literary Analysis,** p. 50

All **Reading,** p. 51

EL L3 L4 **Grammar and Style,** p. 53

EL L3 L4 **Support for Writing,** p. 54

Assessment

Name ______________________ Date ____________

Introduction to Frankenstein by Mary Wollstonecraft Shelley

Selection Test A

Critical Reading *Identify the letter of the choice that best answers the question.*

___ 1. According to the Introduction, what were Shelley, her husband, Byron, and Polidori doing during the summer they wrote the ghost stories?
A. They were living in different countries.
B. They were on a summer vacation.
C. They were mourning the loss of a friend.
D. They were working in London.

___ 2. Which of Shelley's statements in the Introduction helps you predict that the friends will write ghost stories?
A. "The Publishers of the Standard Novels, in selecting *Frankenstein* for one of their series, expressed a wish that I should furnish them with some account of the origin of the story."
B. "But it proved a wet, ungenial summer, and incessant rain often confined us for days to the house. Some volumes of ghost stories . . . fell into our hands."
C. "In the summer of 1816, we visited Switzerland, and became the neighbors of Lord Byron."
D. "At first we spent our pleasant hours on the lake or wandering on its shores; and Lord Byron, who was writing the third canto of *Childe Harold*, was the only one among us who put his thoughts upon paper."

___ 3. What were Percy Bysshe Shelley and Lord Byron talking about that gave Mary Shelley the original idea for *Frankenstein*, according to the Introduction?
A. how it can be proved that ghosts really exist
B. if death can really be passed on with a kiss
C. the consequences of peeping through a keyhole
D. whether life could be created by people

___ 4. What was Shelley doing when she came up with the idea for *Frankenstein*, based on what she says in the Introduction?
A. She was walking along a shore.
B. She was listening to Byron.
C. She was having a waking dream.
D. She was thinking at her desk.

Unit 4 Resources: Rebels and Dreamers

59

EL L1 L2 **Selection Test A,** pp. 59–61

Also available for these selections:

L3 L4 **Open-Book Test,** pp. 56–58

EL L3 L4 **Selection Test B,** pp. 62–64

PHLit Online!
www.PHLitOnline.com

- complete narrated selection text
- a thematically related video with writing prompt
- an interactive graphic organizer
- highlighting feature
- access to all student print resources, adapted to individual student needs
- Spanish and English summaries
- adapted selection translations in Spanish

Online Resources: All print materials are also available online.

Background Video

Also available:

Get Connected! (thematic video with writing prompt)
All videos are available in Spanish.

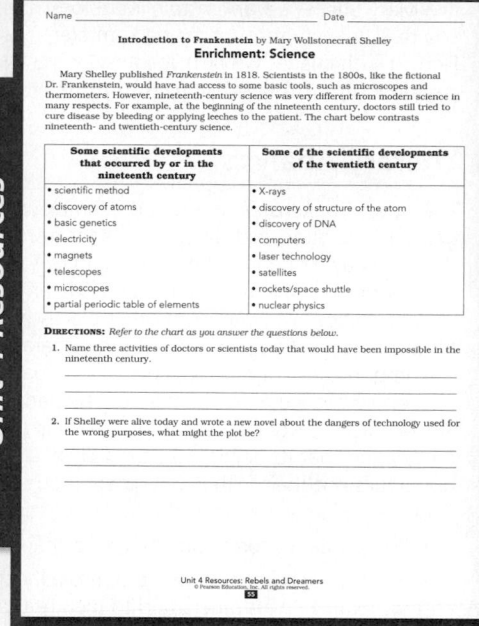

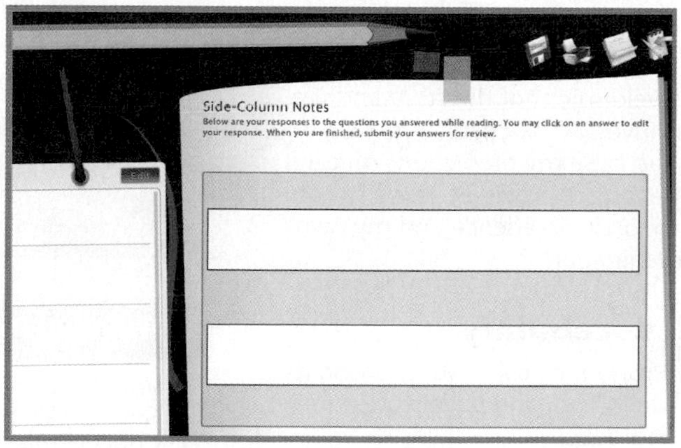

Writer's Journal (with graphics feature)

Also available:

Vocabulary Central (tools and activities for studying vocabulary)

PREACH

❶ Connecting to the Essential Question

1. Review the assignment with the class.
2. Ask students to think about the dark images that they have found especially scary in horror movies they have seen. Then have them complete the assignment.
3. As students read, have them look for the dark, mysterious images that Shelley describes.

❷ Literary Analysis

Introduce the skill using the instruction on the student page.

Think Aloud: Model the Skill

Say to students:

The word *gothic* suggests images of castles, towers, dark passages, and supernatural events. I expect this genre to be highly imaginative and feature elements from folklore and the theme of good versus evil.

❸ Reading Strategy

1. Introduce the skill using the instruction on the student page.
2. Give students a copy of **Reading Strategy Graphic Organizer B,** page 137 in *Graphic Organizer Transparencies,* to fill out as they read.

Think Aloud: Model the Skill

Say to students:

When I make predictions about a story, I must pay attention to the development of the story and the motives of the characters. That way I can base my predictions on clues the author provides, as well as on personal experience and my own imagination.

❹ Vocabulary

1. Pronounce each word, giving its definition, and have students say it aloud.
2. For more guidance, see the *Classroom Strategies and Teaching Routines* card for introducing vocabulary.

Before You Read

Introduction to *Frankenstein*

❶ **Connecting to the Essential Question** Readers of Gothic literature like Mary Shelley's *Frankenstein* were looking for suspense and thrills. As you read, identify some of the dark, mysterious images Shelley describes. Finding such images will help you answer the Essential Question: **What is the relationship of the writer to tradition?**

Common Core State Standards

Reading Informational Text
3. Analyze a complex set of ideas or sequence of events and explain how specific individuals, ideas, or events interact and develop over the course of the text.

❷ Literary Analysis

The novel *Frankenstein* is a classic example of **Gothic literature,** a *subgenre* of literature that takes the reader from the reasoned order of the everyday world into the dark world of the supernatural. Gothic literature, popular in the late eighteenth and early nineteenth centuries, is set in dark castles or towers or in other places with a disquieting, mysterious atmosphere. As you read, note Gothic characteristics in Shelley's work.

The popularity of this form was due in part to the new **Romantic movement** in literature. Romantics rejected two central beliefs of the 18th-century Enlightenment: that reason is the most important human faculty and that its application can fully explain the world. Instead, Romantics put their faith in imagination and the healing powers of nature. They viewed imagination in the following terms:

- It is a creative force comparable to that of nature.
- It is the fundamental source of morality and truth, enabling people to sympathize with others and to picture the world.

As you read, notice how Shelley's account of the creative process reflects the high value the Romantics placed on imagination.

❸ Reading Strategy

Preparing to Read Complex Texts Involved readers naturally try to **make predictions,** or reasoned guesses, about what will happen next in a literary work. As you read, use *text features,* such as titles, background notes, side notes, clues in the text, and your *background knowledge* to make and confirm predictions. Employ a chart like the one shown to record your predictions.

Clue
"Some volumes of ghost stories . . . fell into our hands."

↓

Prediction
Shelley found the idea for *Frankenstein* in another story.

↓

New Information
"'We will each write a ghost story,' said Lord Byron. . ."

↓

Revision
She found her idea while competing in a contest that the stories inspired.

❹ Vocabulary

appendage (ə pen′ dij) *n.* something added on (p. 761)

ungenial (un jē′ nyəl) *adj.* disagreeable; characterized by bad weather (p. 761)

acceded (ak sēd′ id) *v.* yielded (to); agreed (p. 762)

platitude (plat′ ə to͞od′) *n.* statement lacking originality (p. 762)

phantasm (fan′ taz′ əm) *n.* ghost; figment of the imagination (p. 763)

incitement (in sīt′ mənt) *n.* act of urging; encouragement (p. 764)

PHLit Online! www.PHLitOnline.com

Vocabulary Development

Vocabulary Knowledge Rating

Create a **Vocabulary Knowledge Rating Chart** (*Professional Development Guidebook,* p. 33) for the vocabulary words on the student page. Give each student a copy of the chart with the words on it. Read the words aloud, and have students mark their ratings in the Before Reading column. When students have completed reading and discussing the selection, have them take out their **Vocabulary Knowledge Rating Charts** for the story. Read the words aloud and have students rate their knowledge again in the After Reading column. Clarify any words that are still problematic. Then have students complete the Vocabulary practice at the end of the selection.

PHLit Online! **Vocabulary Central,** featuring tools and activities for studying vocabulary, is available online at **www.PHLitOnline.com.**

(5) Mary Wollstonecraft

Shelley

(1797–1851)

Author of *Frankenstein*

Writing was in Mary Shelley's blood. Her mother, Mary Wollstonecraft Godwin (who died at Mary's birth), wrote one of the first feminist books ever published, *A Vindication of the Rights of Woman.* Her father, William Godwin, was a leading reformer, author, and political philosopher.

Four years after his wife's death, Godwin married a widow, Mary Jane Claremont, whom his daughter grew to resent bitterly. It was agreed that to ease the situation in the tense household, the girl, now fourteen, would go to live in Dundee, Scotland, in the home of William Baxter, her father's friend. After two years in Scotland, she returned.

Upon her return, Mary Shelley (then still named Godwin) met her future husband, Percy Bysshe Shelley. He was a radical young poet who had become William Godwin's admirer. Mary, only sixteen, fell in love with Shelley, and the two ran away together to the continent and later married.

Eventually, the couple settled in Italy, where they lived blissfully for an all-too-short time. (Their great friend, Lord Byron, also lived in Italy.) Within a few years, the Shelleys suffered the death of two of their children. Then, in 1822, only eight years after Mary Shelley had first met him, Percy Shelley drowned. His death left the twenty-four-year-old Mary and their two-year-old son penniless.

After Percy's death, Mary returned to England, where she continued writing to support herself and her son. She produced several other novels, including *The Last Man* (1826), a tale of a great plague that destroys the human race.

At the age of forty-eight, Mary Shelley became an invalid. She died six years later of a brain tumor.

Daily Bellringer

For each class during which you will teach this selection, have students complete one of the five activities for the appropriate week in the ***Daily Bellringer Activities*** booklet.

Multidraft Reading

To assist struggling readers and to enhance reading for all, assign the text in chunks, as warranted by length, and apply multidraft reading protocols. For each reading, have students set the purpose indicated:

- **First reading**—identifying key ideas and details and answering any Reading Checks.
- **Second reading**—analyzing craft and structure and responding to the side-column prompts.
- **Third reading**—integrating knowledge and ideas, connecting to other texts and the world, and answering the end-of-selection questions.

For more guidance, refer to the ***Classroom Strategies and Teaching Routines*** card on Multidraft Reading.

(5) Background

More About the Author

Mary Wollstonecraft Shelley wrote several works with Gothic or science fiction premises. Lionel Verney, who begins life as a young shepherd boy and finds himself, after many wanderings, the sole survivor in the ruined grandeur of Rome in the year 2100, narrates *The Last Man,* a novel by Shelley set in the future. Many of her short stories also use Gothic and science fiction elements. They are published in *The Keepsake.*

Shelley's contribution to English literature also includes her efforts to preserve the work of her husband, Percy Bysshe Shelley. After his death, she edited his poems, essays, and letters.

PHLit Online!
www.PHLitOnline.com

Teaching From Technology

Preparing to Read

Go to **www.PHLitOnline.com** and display the ***Get Connected!*** slide show for this selection. Have the class brainstorm responses to the writing prompt, entering ideas in the interactive journal. Then, have students complete their written responses as homework.

To build background, display the Background and More About the Author features.

Using the Interactive Test

Go to **www.PHLitOnline.com** and display the Enriched Online Student Edition. As the class reads the selection or listens to the narration, record answers to side-column prompts using the graphic organizers accessible on the interactive page. Alternatively, have students use the online edition individually, answering the prompts as they read.

TEACH

❶ About the Selection

The nature of a writer's inspiration has been the subject of wonder and speculation since the days of ancient Greece. In this introduction to her novel *Frankenstein,* Mary Shelley offers readers firsthand insight into the process.

❷ Activating Prior Knowledge

Elicit from the class examples of urban myths, tales of alien abductions, or ghost stories. (Examples include stories of alligators in the sewers, a man abducted for his kidneys, and aliens landing in Roswell, New Mexico.) Tell students that two young literary rebels, Percy Bysshe Shelley and Lord Byron, along with nineteen-year-old Mary Shelley and Byron's friend Polidori, indulged in a similar brainstorming activity while vacationing in Italy. The result of the session was Mary Shelley's masterpiece, *Frankenstein,* which helped create both the genre of modern science fiction and the genre of modern horror stories. Have students write a paragraph based on one of these modern urban myths.

Concept Connector →

Tell students they will return to their responses after reading the selection.

❸ Humanities

Castle Oberhofen

This photo features Castle Oberhofen, which stands on the shores of Lake Thun in Oberhofen, Switzerland. The inside of the castle features decor ranging from the 16th to the 19th century.

❸

❶
❷

Introduction to Frankenstein

Mary Wollstonecraft Shelley

BACKGROUND In Greek mythology, Prometheus was one of the Titans—a race of giants who were said to have existed before humans and who engaged the gods in battle. Later myths say Prometheus created the first human beings. During the Romantic Era, Prometheus drew renewed attention. Percy Bysshe Shelley wrote a verse play about Prometheus entitled *Prometheus Unbound.* The complete title of Mary Shelley's novel about a doctor who attempts to create a man is *Frankenstein, or the Modern Prometheus.*

Text Complexity Rubric

Introduction to *Frankenstein*			
Qualitative Measures			
Context/ Knowledge Demands	Gothic novel introduction; literary knowledge demands 1 2 3 (4) 5		
Structure/ Language Clarity	Long sentences; vocabulary 1 2 (3) 4 5		
Levels of Meaning/ Purpose/Concept Level	Challenging (inspiration, horror tale) 1 2 (3) 4 5		
Quantitative Measures			
Lexile	1170L	**Text Length**	1,419 words
Overall Complexity	**More complex**		

Reader and Task Suggestions

Preparing to Read the Text

- Using the information on p. 759 of the student text, explain that Mary Shelley wrote *Frankenstein* as part of a contest to create the best Gothic horror tale.
- Discuss with students the qualities that make a good horror tale.
- Guide students to use Multidraft Reading strategies to deepen their comprehension (TE p. 759).

Leveled Tasks

Levels of Meaning If students will have difficulty with Shelley's ideas about inspiration, have them identify her main goal and her process for achieving it. Then, as they reread, have them focus on the process.

Synthesizing If students will not have difficulty with Shelley's ideas, have them focus on what she reveals about literary inspiration.

The Publishers of the Standard Novels, in selecting *Frankenstein* for one of their series, expressed a wish that I should furnish them with some account of the origin of the story. I am the more willing to comply, because I shall thus give a general answer to the question, so very frequently asked me: "How I, then a young girl, came to think of, and to dilate upon, so very hideous an idea?" It is true that I am very averse to bringing myself forward in print; but as my account will only appear as an **appendage** to a former production, and as it will be confined to such topics as have connection with my authorship alone, I can scarcely accuse myself of a personal intrusion. . . . **5**

In the summer of 1816, we[1] visited Switzerland, and became the neighbors of Lord Byron. At first we spent our pleasant hours on the lake or wandering on its shores; and Lord Byron, who was writing the third canto of *Childe Harold*, was the only one among us who put his thoughts upon paper. These, as he brought them successively to us, clothed in all the light and harmony of poetry, seemed to stamp as divine the glories of heaven and earth, whose influences we partook with him. **6**

But it proved a wet, **ungenial** summer, and incessant rain often confined us for days to the house. Some volumes of ghost stories, translated from the German into French,[2] fell into our hands. There was "The History of the Inconstant Lover,"[3] who, when he thought to clasp the bride to whom he had pledged his vows, found himself in the arms of the pale ghost of her whom he had deserted. There was the tale of the sinful founder of his race,[4] whose miserable doom it was to bestow the kiss of death on all the younger sons of his fated house, just when they reached the age of promise. His gigantic, shadowy form, clothed like the ghost in Hamlet, in complete armor but with the beaver[5] up, was seen at midnight, by the moon's fitful beams, to advance slowly along the gloomy avenue. The shape was lost beneath the shadow of the castle walls; but soon a gate swung back, a step was heard, the door of the chamber opened, and he advanced to the couch of the blooming youths, cradled in healthy sleep. Eternal sorrow sat upon his face as he bent down and kissed the foreheads of the boys, who from that hour withered like flowers snapped upon the stalk. I have not seen these stories since then, but their incidents are as fresh in my mind as if I had read them yesterday.

A View of Chamonix and Mt. Blanc

1. **we** Mary Shelley, her husband Percy Bysshe Shelley, and their two children.
2. **volumes . . . French** *Fantasmagoriana*, or *Collected Stories of Apparitions of Specters, Ghosts, Phantoms, Etc.*, published anonymously in 1812.
3. **"The History . . . Lover"** The true name of the story is "The Dead Fiancée."
4. **the tale . . . race** "Family Portraits."
5. **beaver** hinged piece of armor that covers the face.

4 ◀ **Critical Viewing**
Based on the second paragraph of her essay, do you think Shelley might have liked this image? Why? **[Speculate]**

Vocabulary

appendage (ə pen′ dij) *n.* something added on

ungenial (un jē′ nyəl) *adj.* disagreeable; characterized by bad weather

6 ***Elizabeth McCracken***
Scholar's Insight
Mary Shelley turned nineteen in the summer of 1816, and while I do think—I hope!—that writers get better as they get older, there's also the fact that you can only write your first novel once. That the mix of ambition and fear and, yes, youth, may make it more exciting and fully realized than the books you write when you know what you're doing.

7 **Reading Check**
What has the author set out to explain?

4 Critical Viewing

Possible response: Yes, Shelley reports having fond memories of visiting a similar scene when she visited Switzerland in 1816.

5 Critical Thinking

Speculate

1. Have students read the bracketed passage. Encourage them to use their knowledge of the expectations of women of this time to help them understand this passage in context.
2. Then **ask** students: Why do you suppose Shelley does not like the idea of bringing herself "forward in print"?
   Answer: Many authors prefer to let their work speak for itself. Shelley may fear that it will appear that she is showing too much pride in her work. Also, society at the time discouraged women from asserting themselves.

6 Scholar's Insight

1. Direct students to the Scholar's Insight note. Tell students that Shelley wrote *Frankenstein* when she was about the same age that they are now.
2. **Ask** what might be some advantages of writing a novel at such a young age.
   Possible response: A young person may have new and fresh ideas and may not be restricted by what other people have said or written.

7 Reading Check

Answer: The author set out to explain how she wrote such a terrifying novel at such a young age.

Differentiated Instruction for Universal Access

Strategy for Special-Needs Students
Have students complete the **Before You Read** and the **Making Connections** pages for this selection in the ***Reader's Notebook: Adapted Version.*** These pages provide an abbreviated skills instruction, the Before You Read graphic organizer, and a **Note-taking Guide.**

Support for Less Proficient Readers
Have students complete the **Before You Read** and the **Making Connections** pages for this selection in the ***Reader's Notebook.*** These pages provide abbreviated skills instruction, the **Before You Read** graphic organizer, and a **Note-taking Guide.**

EL Support for English Learners
Have students complete the **Before You Read** and the **Making Connections** pages for this selection in the ***Reader's Notebook: English Learner's Version.*** These pages provide additional vocabulary, vocabulary skills, and vocabulary practice, along with a **Getting Ready to Read** activity.

PHLit Online!
This selection is available in interactive format in the **Enriched Online Student Edition** at **www.PHLitOnline.com,** which includes a thematically related video with writing prompt and an interactive graphic organizer.

8 Scholar's Insight

1. Point out Elizabeth McCracken's comment about her love for ghost stories. **Ask** students to recall what other images from ghost stories they heard as children.
   Possible response: headless horsemen, haunted houses, or rattling chains
2. **Ask** students what other writing may satisfy a desire to feel frightened.
   Possible responses: mystery stories and true crime writing

9 Literary Analysis

Gothic Literature

1. Review with students elements of the Gothic tradition.
2. **Ask** students the Literary Analysis question.
   Answer: The setting includes a castle, typical of the Gothic tradition. The hidden figure in the shadows also adds to the mysterious atmosphere.
3. **Monitor Progress:** Have students identify other Gothic characteristics of the tales described by Shelley.
   Possible responses: Students may note that the supernatural elements in the stories, including ghosts and a family curse, are also Gothic characteristics.
4. **Reteach:** If students have difficulty answering the question, discuss recent examples or spoofs of the Gothic, such as Stephen King novels or TV shows or films like *The Munsters,* or *The Addams Family Values.*

10 Reading Strategy

Making Predictions

1. Remind students that they can make predictions based on prior knowledge and on clues provided in the reading.
2. **Ask** the Reading Strategy question.
   Possible responses: Students may say that Shelley might draw on the dreariness of her environment or that she will expand on ideas discussed with her friends.

Elizabeth McCracken
Scholar's Insight 8
A good ghost story stays in your head forever. I've never gotten over a book of New England ghost stories I had as a child, including one story about a man who buried his murder victim at the base of a tree, only to find that the next year's apples all had a clot of blood in the center of them.

Vocabulary
acceded (ak sēd′ id) *v.* yielded (to); agreed
platitude (plat′ ə to͞od′) *n.* statement lacking originality

9 **Literary Analysis**
Gothic Literature
What elements of the Gothic tradition are incorporated in the image of a shape "lost beneath the shadow of the castle walls"?

10 **Reading Strategy**
Making Predictions
By what means do you think Shelley will find a story idea?

"We will each write a ghost story," said Lord Byron; and his proposition was acceded to. There were four of us.[6] The noble author began a tale, a fragment of which he printed at the end of his poem of Mazeppa. Shelley, more apt to embody ideas and sentiments in the radiance of brilliant imagery, and in the music of the most melodious verse that adorns our language, than to invent the machinery of a story, commenced one founded on the experiences of his early life. Poor Polidori had some terrible idea about a skull-headed lady, who was so punished for peeping through a keyhole—what to see I forget—something very shocking and wrong of course; but when she was reduced to a worse condition than the renowned Tom of Coventry,[7] he did not know what to do with her, and was obliged to despatch her to the tomb of the Capulets,[8] the only place for which she was fitted. The illustrious poets also, annoyed by the platitude of prose, speedily relinquished their uncongenial task.

I busied myself to *think of a story*—a story to rival those which had excited us to this task. One which would speak to the mysterious fears of our nature and awaken thrilling horror—one to make the reader dread to look round, to curdle the blood, and quicken the beatings of the heart. If I did not accomplish these things, my ghost story would be unworthy of its name. I thought and pondered—vainly. I felt that blank incapability of invention which is the greatest misery of authorship, when dull Nothing replies to our anxious invocations. *Have you thought of a story?* I was asked each morning, and each morning I was forced to reply with a mortifying negative. . . .

Many and long were the conversations between Lord Byron and Shelley, to which I was a devout but nearly silent listener. During one of these, various philosophical doctrines were discussed, and among others the nature of the principle of life and whether there was any probability of its ever being discovered and communicated. They talked of the experiments of Dr. Darwin. (I speak not of what the Doctor really did or said that he did, but, as more to my purpose, of what was then spoken of as having been done by him), who preserved a piece of vermicelli in a glass case till by some extraordinary means it began to move with voluntary motion. Not thus, after all, would life be given. Perhaps a corpse would be reanimated: galvanism[9] had given token of such things. Perhaps the component parts of a creature might be manufactured, brought together, and endued with vital warmth.

6. **four of us** Byron, the two Shelleys, and John William Polidori, Byron's physician.
7. **Tom of Coventry** "Peeping Tom" who, according to legend, was struck blind for looking at Lady Godiva as she rode naked through Coventry.
8. **tomb of the Capulets** the place where Romeo and Juliet died.
9. **galvanism** use of electric current to induce twitching in dead muscles.

Enrichment: Investigating Technology

Contemporary Research on Life
Mary Shelley describes Dr. Frankenstein as "the pale student of unhallowed arts" whose experiments "mock" the Creator. The uneasy reactions of critics to modern developments such as cloning and genetic engineering share a good deal with Shelley's reaction. When people reshape the character of life, their actions challenge our sense that life is a gift from the Creator. To some, this research seems dangerously arrogant. Defenders emphasize the value of inquiry and of improving the quality of life.

Activity: Investigate Cloning and Genetic Engineering Research Ask students to learn more about the ethical dilemmas surrounding these techniques for biological research. Suggest that they record their analyses in the **Enrichment: Investigating Technology** worksheet, ***Professional Development Guidebook,*** page 242.

I saw the **hideous** phantasm of a man stretched out, and then, on the working of some powerful engine, show signs of life and stir with an uneasy, half vital motion.

Night waned upon this talk, and even the witching hour had gone by, before we retired to rest. When I placed my head
11 on my pillow, I did not sleep, nor could I be said to think. My imagination, unbidden, possessed and guided me, gifting the successive images that arose in my mind with a vividness far beyond the usual bounds of reverie. I saw—with shut eyes but acute mental vision—I saw the pale student of unhallowed arts kneeling beside the thing he had put together. I saw the hideous **phantasm** of a man stretched out, and then, on the working of some powerful engine, show signs of life and stir with an uneasy, half vital motion. Frightful must it be, for supremely frightful would be the effect of any human endeavor to mock the stupendous mechanism of the Creator of the world. His success would terrify the artist; he would rush away from his odious handiwork, horror-stricken. He would hope that, left to itself, the slight spark of life which he had communicated would fade; that this thing, which had received such imperfect animation, would subside into dead matter; and he might sleep in the belief that the silence of the grave would quench forever the transient existence of the hideous corpse which he had looked upon as the cradle of life. He sleeps; but he is awakened; he opens his eyes; behold the horrid thing stands at his bedside, opening his curtains, and looking on him with yellow, watery, but speculative eyes.

I opened mine in terror. The idea so possessed my mind, that a thrill of fear ran through me, and I wished to exchange the ghastly image of my fancy for the realities around. I see them still: the very room, the dark parquet,[10] the closed shutters, with the moonlight struggling through, and the sense
12 I had that the glassy lake and white high Alps were beyond. I could not so easily get rid of my hideous phantom: still it haunted me. I must try to think of something else. I recurred to my ghost story—my tiresome unlucky ghost story! O! if I could only contrive one which would frighten my reader as I myself had been frightened that night!

10. **parquet** (pär kā′) flooring made of wooden pieces arranged in a pattern.

Elizabeth McCracken
Scholar's Insight
Nothing is worse than wanting to write something but not knowing what. I think it's common for stories to come into your head when you *think* you've given up trying, and are thinking about something else entirely.

Vocabulary
phantasm (fan′ taz′ əm) *n.* ghost; figment of the imagination

Elizabeth McCracken
Scholar's Insight
What surprised me most when I first read *Frankenstein* was that the monster could speak and yearn and accuse. Shelley's Victor Frankenstein did a better job making a creature than the movie version suggested. I've always wondered why they kept him silent in the film.

13 **Reading Check**
That night, what does Mary Shelley imagine?

11 Scholar's Insight

1. Point out McCracken's comment on writer's block and inspiration.
2. **Ask** students if they have ever had a story come to them when they were on the edge of sleep or thinking about something else.
Answer: Students should explain their answers.

12 Scholar's Insight

1. Point out McCracken's comment on the differences between the story and the movie version.
2. **Ask** students why they think a film version would choose to keep the monster silent.
Answer: Students may suggest the decision was made to take away some of the human likeness of the creature. His silence made him scarier because it further alienated him from "normal" people.

13 Reading Check

Answer: Mary Shelley imagines a pale student scientist kneeling beside the body he has perhaps dug up or stitched together from corpses, as well as his terror when it comes to life.

Differentiated Instruction for Universal Access

Support for Special-Needs Students
Review with students their understanding of the various elements of the Gothic tradition. Then, have students read the description of ghost stories in the "Introduction to Frankenstein" with guidance. Ask them to focus on aspects of these stories that seem especially Gothic.

Enrichment for Gifted/Talented Students
Encourage students to illustrate one aspect of Shelley's imaginings that is especially Gothic in its mood. To provide additional guidance, review with students their understandings of the Gothic tradition for additional guidance. Have students display their Gothic art to the rest of the class.

Enrichment for Advanced Readers
Have interested students read a segment of Mary Shelley's *Frankenstein.* Then, ask them to prepare book reviews comparing the *Frankenstein* monster to Shelley's description in her introduction to the work. Ask them to discuss how the book compares with similar novels they have read.

⓮ Scholar's Insight

1. Point out McCracken's comment on death and grief.
2. **Ask** students to identify the tone of the last paragraph in the text. **Answer:** The tone is sad, but hopeful and warm at the same time. Elizabeth McCracken understood this when she said the story was a type of love letter.

ASSESS

Answers

Before students respond, you may wish to have them write a brief objective summary of the selection. As they answer the questions below, remind them to support their answers with evidence from the text.

1. (a) They were kept inside by rain and had books of ghost stories around. (b) Shelley has trouble thinking of a story that she felt spoke to the "mysterious fears" of human nature, while the other writers disliked writing prose.
2. (a) Shelley's idea for a story comes from a discussion she overhears between Byron and her husband about the possibility of creating artificial life. (b) It suggests Mary Shelley finds Dr. Darwin's experiments deeply disturbing for their implications about human power over life.
3. **Possible response:** Students may say that Shelley's dread of science is borne out by inventions such as nuclear weapons and by the possible problems presented by new technologies such as cloning and genetic engineering.
4. **Possible response:** Shelley's use of a dream for her writing idea relates to the high value that Romantics placed on *intuition.* During the Romantic period, *imagination* was considered much more important than logic and *reason.* Ensure that students use at least two of the Essential Question words.

Vocabulary
incitement (in sīt′ mənt) *n.* act of urging; encouragement

Elizabeth McCracken
Scholar's Insight
Death and grief must have been more than mere words to Mary Shelley when she started writing *Frankenstein* at the age of eighteen. Her mother died five days after Mary's birth, and Mary's first child died after being born prematurely. Still, Percy Shelley's death five years after the book's publication redefined those words. The book is, as its author says, a ghost story based on a hideous idea, but it's also a love letter: terrifying, but built during a time of tender memory. ⓮

Swift as light and as cheering was the idea that broke in upon me. "I have found it! What terrified me will terrify others, and I need only describe the specter which had haunted my midnight pillow." On the morrow I announced that I had *thought of a story.* I began that day with the words, *It was on a dreary night of November,* making only a transcript of the grim terrors of my waking dream.

At first I thought but of a few pages—of a short tale—but Shelley urged me to develop the idea at greater length. I certainly did not owe the suggestion of one incident, nor scarcely of one train of feeling, to my husband, and yet but for his incitement, it would never have taken the form in which it was presented to the world. From this declaration I must except the preface. As far as I can recollect, it was entirely written by him.

And now, once again, I bid my hideous progeny go forth and prosper. I have an affection for it, for it was the offspring of happy days, when death and grief were but words, which found no true echo in my heart. Its several pages speak of many a walk, many a drive, and many a conversation, when I was not alone; and my companion was one who, in this world, I shall never see more. But this is for myself: my readers have nothing to do with these associations.

What terrified me will terrify others, and I need only describe the specter which had haunted my midnight pillow.

Critical Reading

1. **Key Ideas and Details (a)** What special set of circumstances inspired the four friends to attempt to write ghost stories? **(b) Compare and Contrast:** Compare the difficulty Shelley has with the reason her companions give up their efforts.
2. **Key Ideas and Details (a)** What gives Shelley her idea for a story? **(b) Connect:** What does the intensity of her vision suggest about her reaction to Dr. Darwin's experiments?
3. **Integration of Knowledge and Ideas Make a Judgment:** In your opinion, has later history borne out Shelley's dread of science? Explain.
4. **Integration of Knowledge and Ideas** Why does Shelley's use of a dream to write her novel confirm Romantic beliefs about the imagination? In your response, use at least two of these Essential Question words: *imagination, reason, intuition.* ***[Connecting to the Essential Question: What is the relationship of the writer to tradition?]***

Cite textual evidence to support your responses.

Concept Connector

Reading Strategy Graphic Organizer

Ask students to review the graphic organizers in which they have listed the text features they used to make and confirm predictions. Then, have students share their organizers and compare the predictions they recorded.

Activating Prior Knowledge

Have students return to their responses to the Activating Prior Knowledge activity. Ask them to explain whether their thoughts have changed and, if so, how.

Writing About the Essential Question

Have students compare their responses to the prompt, completed before reading the selection, with their thoughts afterward. Have them work individually or in groups, writing or discussing their thoughts, to formulate new responses. Then, lead a class discussion, probing for what students have learned that confirms or invalidates their initial thoughts. Encourage students to cite specific textual details to support their responses.

After You Read Introduction to *Frankenstein*

Literary Analysis

1. **Key Ideas and Details** Which characteristics of the **Gothic tradition**—horror, supernatural elements, medieval elements—do the ghost stories described by Shelley in her third paragraph share? List examples in a chart like the one shown.

Gothic Characteristic	Example in Shelley

2. **Key Ideas and Details** In which passage does Shelley describe a connection between the world of reason and a terrifying supernatural world?
3. **Integration of Knowledge and Ideas** Explain why Shelley's idea for *Frankenstein* fits the Gothic tradition.
4. **Integration of Knowledge and Ideas** Compare the ingredients of Gothic tales with those used in current horror movies and books.
5. **Integration of Knowledge and Ideas (a)** How does Shelley respond to the discussion of Darwin's experiments? **(b)** How does her response confirm an assumption of the **Romantic movement**—that the power of imagination is similar to that of nature's creative force?
6. **Integration of Knowledge and Ideas (a)** Contrast Shelley's first efforts to find an idea with her final inspiration. **(b)** How does this contrast reflect the Romantic tendency to value imagination above reason?
7. **Integration of Knowledge and Ideas** What "truth" does Shelley's imagined vision suggest about the dangerous possibilities of science?
8. **Integration of Knowledge and Ideas** Are there areas of scientific investigation in which human beings should not become involved? Explain.
9. **Analyzing Visual Information** Use your knowledge of *Frankenstein* to explain the humor of the cartoon shown on this page.

Common Core State Standards

Writing
3. Write narratives to develop real or imagined experiences or events using effective technique, well-chosen details, and well-structured event sequences. *(p. 766)*
3.b. Use narrative techniques, such as pacing, to develop experiences, events, and/or characters. *(p. 766)*

Language
4.d. Verify the preliminary determination of the meaning of a word or phrase. *(p. 766)*

Reading Strategy

10. Explain whether you were able to **make predictions** as to how Shelley would be affected by the discussion of Darwin's experiments.
11. Based on clues in the Background note, predict what will happen to Victor Frankenstein in the novel. Explain your reasoning.

"Remember how big and clunky the first ones were?" ▶

Assessment Practice

Critical Reasoning (For more practice, see *All-in-One Workbook*.)

Many tests require students to evaluate the assumptions on which an author's argument is based. The first step in mastering this skill is to identify assumptions. Use the following sample item to teach students how to identify an implied assumption. Write this text from the selection on the chalkboard:

> Frightful must it be, for supremely frightful would be the effect of any human endeavor to mock the stupendous mechanism of the Creator of the world.

The assumption behind this statement is—

A re-creation of life is an imitation of God's work.
B God punishes anyone who attempts to create life.
C it is natural for humans to want to play God.
D humans are frightened by science.

Lead students to recognize that the correct answer is **A.** The statement's logic is not supported by the other choices.

Answers

1. Both stories feature supernatural elements—ghosts, one of which delivers a supernatural kiss of death.
2. **Possible response:** Shelley's description of the scientist's animation of the creature he created connects the world of reason and a world of nightmarish horror.
3. Because *Frankenstein* takes readers from the world of reason and science to the world of monsters and terror, it is considered a Gothic tale.
4. **Possible response:** Science-fiction elements, rather than ghosts and ruins, figure prominently in modern tales of horror.
5. (a) Shelley responds to the discussion by fantasizing about the implications of the experiments—and by writing *Frankenstein.* (b) Just as nature produces beings freely by itself, Shelley's imagination produces a story without her conscious participation.
6. (a) Shelley's initial efforts to find an idea were fruitless. Her inspiration did not involve conscious effort, yet gave her a fertile idea. (b) This reflects the Romantic contrast between reason and the imagination. Shelley was only able to arrive at a story idea when she let her imagination dominate over reason.
7. **Possible response:** Science, according to Shelley, may lead to a terrifying unsettling of humanity's place in creation, with humanity attempting to play God.
8. Students may express an opinion that some areas of science are too dangerous for humans to control. Other students may say that scientific discovery is so important that it outweighs the potential dangers. Students should provide reasons and explanations for their opinions.
9. The humor comes from the fact that the tiny Frankenstein monster is no longer frightening and scary.
10. Students should explain why they were or were not able to predict the effect of the discussion on Shelley.
11. Frankenstein is called the "Modern Prometheus" so I predict he may create some kind of new life, like Prometheus did in myths.

ASSESS/EXTEND

Answers

Vocabulary Acquisition and Use

1. Introduce the skill using the instruction on the student page.
2. Have students complete the Word Analysis activity and the Vocabulary practice.

Word Analysis

1. *ambidextrous:* using both hands with equal ease
2. *autodidact:* self taught
3. *fallacy:* false belief
4. *perfervid:* thoroughly exaggerated
5. *retrogression:* to go or be directed backwards
6. *somnambulate:* walk while asleep

Vocabulary

1. incitement
2. platitudes
3. appendage
4. phantasm
5. accede
6. ungenial

Writing

1. To guide students in writing an *Autobiography of a Monster,* give them the Support for Writing Page (*Unit 4 Resources,* p. 54).
2. Encourage students to use a flow chart in the prewriting stage to outline the incidents in the plot before they start to write.
3. Remind students to use sensory and figurative language to make their descriptions of plot events more vivid.
4. Use the rubrics for narrative text, **Professional Development Guidebook,** pages 248–249, to evaluate students' work.

PERFORMANCE TASKS

Integrated Language Skills

Vocabulary Acquisition and Use

Word Analysis: Relate New Words to Familiar Vocabulary

You can often infer the meaning of unfamiliar words by relating them to words you know. For instance, *phantasm*, meaning "figment of the mind," is similar to *fantasy.* Both refer to the imagination. Sometimes, you can use parts from more than one word. The prefix *bi-* ("two") and the root *-ped-* ("foot," as in *pedestrian*, "someone who walks") can help you see that *biped* means "creature with two feet." Infer the meaning of the numbered words by relating them to familiar words. Use a dictionary to confirm your inferences.

1. ambidextrous, *adj.*
2. autodidact, *n.*
3. fallacy, *n.*
4. perfervid, *adj.*
5. retrogression, *n.*
6. somnambulate, *v.*

Vocabulary: Synonyms

A *synonym* is a word that has the same, or similar, meaning as another word. Write a complete sentence to answer each question that follows. In your answer, replace each underlined word with a synonym from the vocabulary list on page 758.

1. Was the king's offer of a royal office a sufficient <u>spur</u> to the noble to change sides?
2. Did the audience accept the tired <u>clichés</u> of the speaker uncritically?
3. Did the <u>attachment</u> in the rear of the car affect its speed?
4. How did the audience react when the <u>ghost</u> of Hamlet's father appeared?
5. Did the dean easily <u>agree</u> to her promotion to college president?
6. Have you ever seen such a sarcastic host or one so <u>disagreeable</u>?

Writing

Narrative Text Typically, monster stories are told from the perspective of the humans confronting the monster. Ask yourself what the monsters think about their treatment, and write a brief **autobiography** of a monster. Choose one you know from literature or film, or invent a new monster. Outline the *sequence of events* in the monster's whole life or focus on events in one episode. Remember to write using the pronoun "I," show the *significance of events*, and gain readers' sympathy, as an autobiography would aim to do.

Prewriting Outline the plot of your narrative. Remember to think about the incidents from the monster's point of view.

Drafting Write your narrative in a serious or humorous way. Use concrete sensory details to add impact. If appropriate, pace the presentation of action to build suspense or sympathy.

Revising Revise your draft to make sure you maintain the monster's point of view and voice. Add figurative language to make your descriptions more vivid.

Model: Revising to Add Figurative Language

like a threatening eye

As the full moon rose, my skin suddenly began to tingle. I saw hair sprouting along my arms.

Using figurative language such as similes makes the description more vivid.

Assessment Resources

Unit 4 Resources

L1 L2 EL **Selection Test A**, pp. 59–61. Administer Test A to less advanced readers.

L3 L4 EL **Selection Test B**, pp. 62–64. Administer Test B to on-level students and more advanced students.

L3 L4 **Open-Book Test**, pp. 56–58. As an alternative, give the Open-Book test.

All **Customizable Test Bank**

All **Self-tests** Students may prepare for the **Selection Test** by taking the **Self-test** online.

PHLit Online! All assessment resources are available at **www.PHLitOnline.com.**

Conventions and Style: Subject-Verb Agreement Problems

Subject-verb agreement means that you use a singular verb with a singular subject and a plural verb with a plural subject, even when a phrase or clause comes between the subject and verb. The antecedent of a relative pronoun determines its agreement with a verb.

Example:
The *publishers* of Mary Shelley's first novel *make* a request.

Example:
The *writer, who is* one of several similar authors, gets the idea while vacationing.

Sentences with inverted order may contain agreement problems. Check the agreement by putting the sentence in normal word order.

Examples:
There *are* constant *rainstorms* in summer.
The *rainstorms* in summer *are* constant.

Sentences with collective nouns or indefinite pronouns may require singular or plural verbs. Titles are always singular.

Examples:
The *group listens* to ghost stories. [group acting as a unit]
The *group* then *writes* their own stories [group acting as individuals]
All of the guests *are* up late.
Romeo and Juliet is a play.

Practice Choose the verb in parentheses that agrees with the subject of each sentence.

1. Lord Byron, who is the Shelleys' neighbor, (proposes, propose) writing ghost stories.
2. Everyone present (agrees, agree) to the idea immediately.
3. Philosophical discussions between Lord Byron and Mary Shelley's husband (includes, include) mentions of Dr. Darwin.
4. There (was, were) experiments by Dr. Darwin, reportedly with a noodle in a glass.
5. The talk that has kept Mary Shelley up late (makes, make) it impossible for her to sleep when she does retire for the night.
6. Before her closed eyes (appears, appear) a series of images.
7. A student, pale and kneeling, (watches, watch) in horror as the creature that he has created (comes, come) to life.
8. When the student wakes, both watery eyes of the creature (is, are) staring at him.
9. Today, the audience for movies based on *Frankenstein* (is, are) huge.
10. *Frankenstein*, one of her many novels, (is, are) Mary Shelley's best-known work.

Writing and Speaking Conventions

A. Writing Complete each sentence by writing a verb that agrees with the subject. Two sentences require more than one answer.

1. Each of the three men _____ quick to give up the task.
2. Mary Shelley, who _____ determined, does not quit.
3. All of Mary Shelley's energy _____ focused on her story.
4. There _____ conversations, but Mary Shelley only _____.
5. The student, who creates the monster, _____ and then _____.

B. Speaking Write and present to the class a paragraph to describe Shelley's imaginings. Use an inverted sentence and two sentences with clauses between the subject and verb.

PH WRITING COACH
Further instruction and practice are available in *Prentice Hall Writing Coach.*

Conventions and Style

1. Introduce and discuss the skill, using the instruction on the student page.
2. Have students complete the Practice and Grammar in Your Writing activities.

Practice

1. proposes
2. agrees
3. include
4. were
5. makes
6. appears
7. watches, comes
8. are
9. is
10. is

Writing and Speaking Conventions

A. **Possible responses:**
1. was
2. is
3. was
4. are; listens
5. sleeps; awakens

B. Ensure that students' responses use an inverted verb and two sentences with clauses between the subject and verb.

PH WRITING COACH Grade 12

Students will find instruction on and practice with subject-verb agreement in Chapter 19, section 1.

Extend the Lesson

Sentence Modeling

Share the sentences given from the selections:

My dream about a Frankenstein monster impressed me, because my own brain had come up with it—even if I'd ripped off most of the details. ("Elizabeth McCracken Introduces *Frankenstein*")

I have an affection for it, for it was the offspring of happy days, when death and grief were but words, which found no true echo in my heart. (Mary Shelley, "Introduction to *Frankenstein*")

Ask students what they notice about the sentence. Elicit from them that the verb must agree with the subject in number. Then ask them what else they notice. (This number agreement is true even when a phrase comes between the subject and the verb.)

Have students imitate the sentence in a sentence of their own choosing, matching each grammatical and stylistic feature discussed. Share them with the class.

Contemporary Connection

"The Curse of Frankenstein" reproduces the transcript of a 2006 skit from the *Saturday Night Live* television show spoofing the mad scientist genre begun by Mary Shelley's now-classic tale, *Frankenstein*. Shelley's monster has come to symbolize uncontrolled science. In fact, Frankenstein is now one of the most famous movie icons in history, rivaled only by the vampire Dracula.

Frankenstein Past and Present

1. Because Frankenstein's monster has become such an icon of popular culture, your students may already be familiar with it. **Ask** volunteers to share what they know and elicit a description of the monster.
   Possible responses: Students may describe the creature's appearance or call him ugly, mute, or beastlike.
2. Explain that the monster in the Shelley novel was anything but silent. Abandoned by his creator, the creature wanders about searching for someone to understand him. He learns to speak, but his attempts to be helpful are misunderstood. Finally he swears revenge on his creator. Then, **ask** students how this tragic creature reflects the beliefs and ideals of the Romantic period.
   Possible response: Writers of the Romantic period emphasized emotion over reason and logic, and Shelley's monster was a very emotional creature. Romantic era writers also rejected the ugliness of the Industrial Age. The novel's twin themes of an arrogant scientist who tries to imitate the Creator and the creature's poignant attempts to be understood fit in well with the Romantic beliefs.

CONTEMPORARY CONNECTION

FRANKENSTEIN Past & Present

In a way, it was the weather that created the monster. The year was 1816, and Mary Wollstonecraft Godwin had traveled to Lake Geneva in Switzerland with her husband-to-be, Percy Bysshe Shelley, to visit their close friend, the poet Lord Byron. The group of friends was forced by the cold and dreary weather to stay indoors, so Lord Byron challenged everyone to a contest to tell the scariest ghost story. Young Miss Wollstonecraft was the hands-down winner. Her story, published anonymously at first, became the novel *Frankenstein*, which has been called a first in the now long-established mad scientist genre.

The influence of Mary Shelley's book went far beyond literature. *Frankenstein* spawned an entire film library, from British director James Whale's 1931 version for Universal that added the "Dr." to Frankenstein's name, to Mel Brooks's hilarious 1974 spoof *Young Frankenstein*, to the 2006 *Saturday Night Live* skit "The Curse of Frankenstein" with British actor Hugh Laurie, star of the popular TV medical drama *House*.

Saturday Night Live

It has been "live from New York" since 1975. Just like Frankenstein, *Saturday Night Live* has created its own place in our culture. When executive producer Lorne Michaels began *SNL* in 1975, he wanted it raw, not polished, more like improv than sitcom. He got his wish, as the show has endured with an amazing array of talented cast members, from John Belushi to Will Ferrell to Tina Fey, who went on from *SNL* to become creator and star of *30 Rock*, a sitcom about a show amazingly like *SNL*.

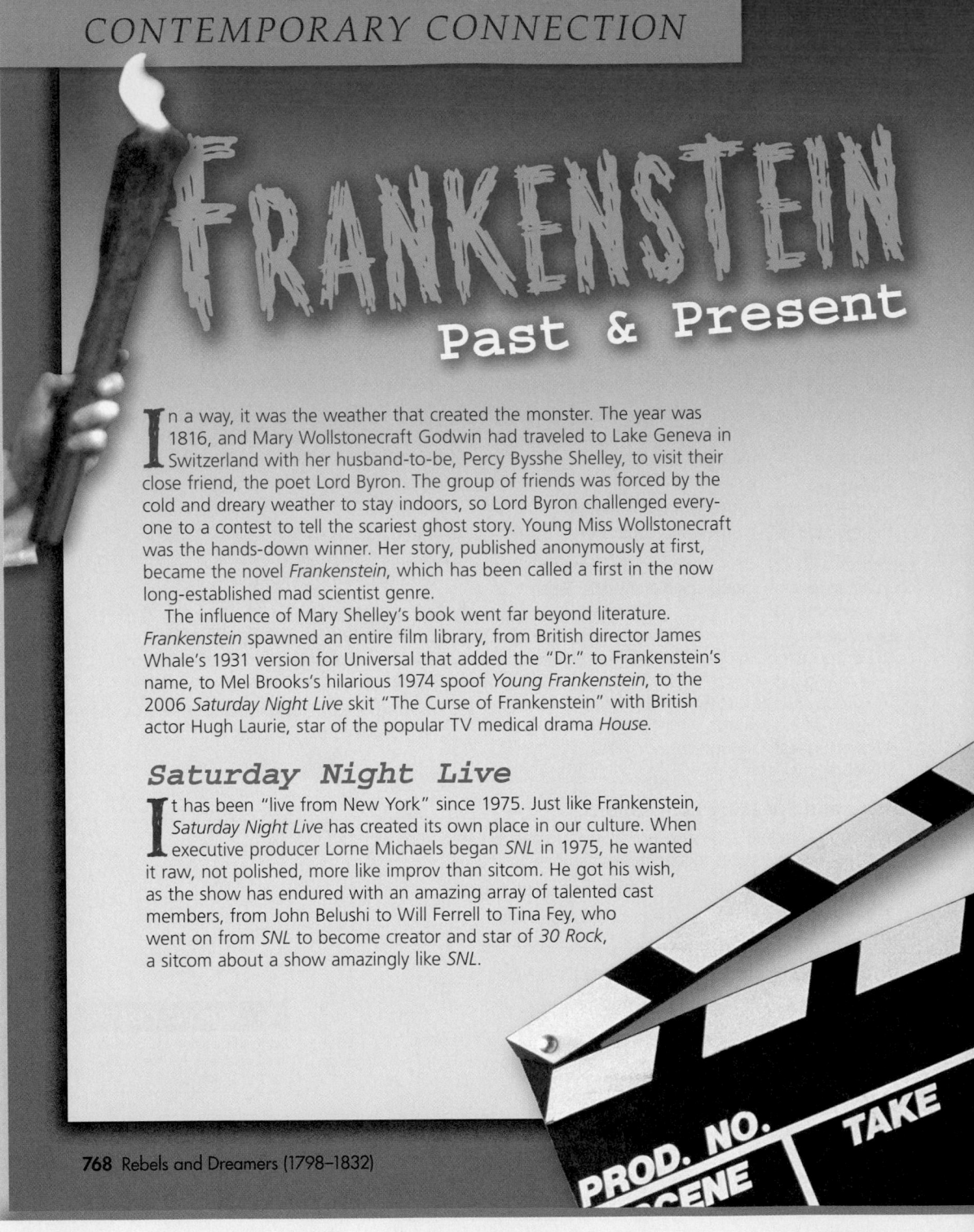

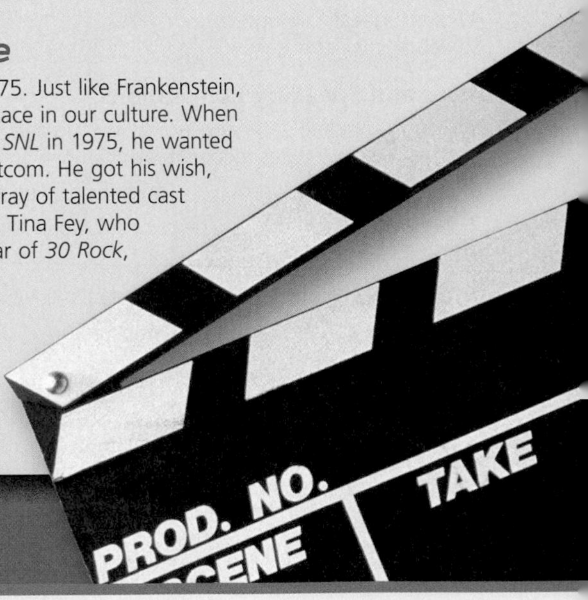

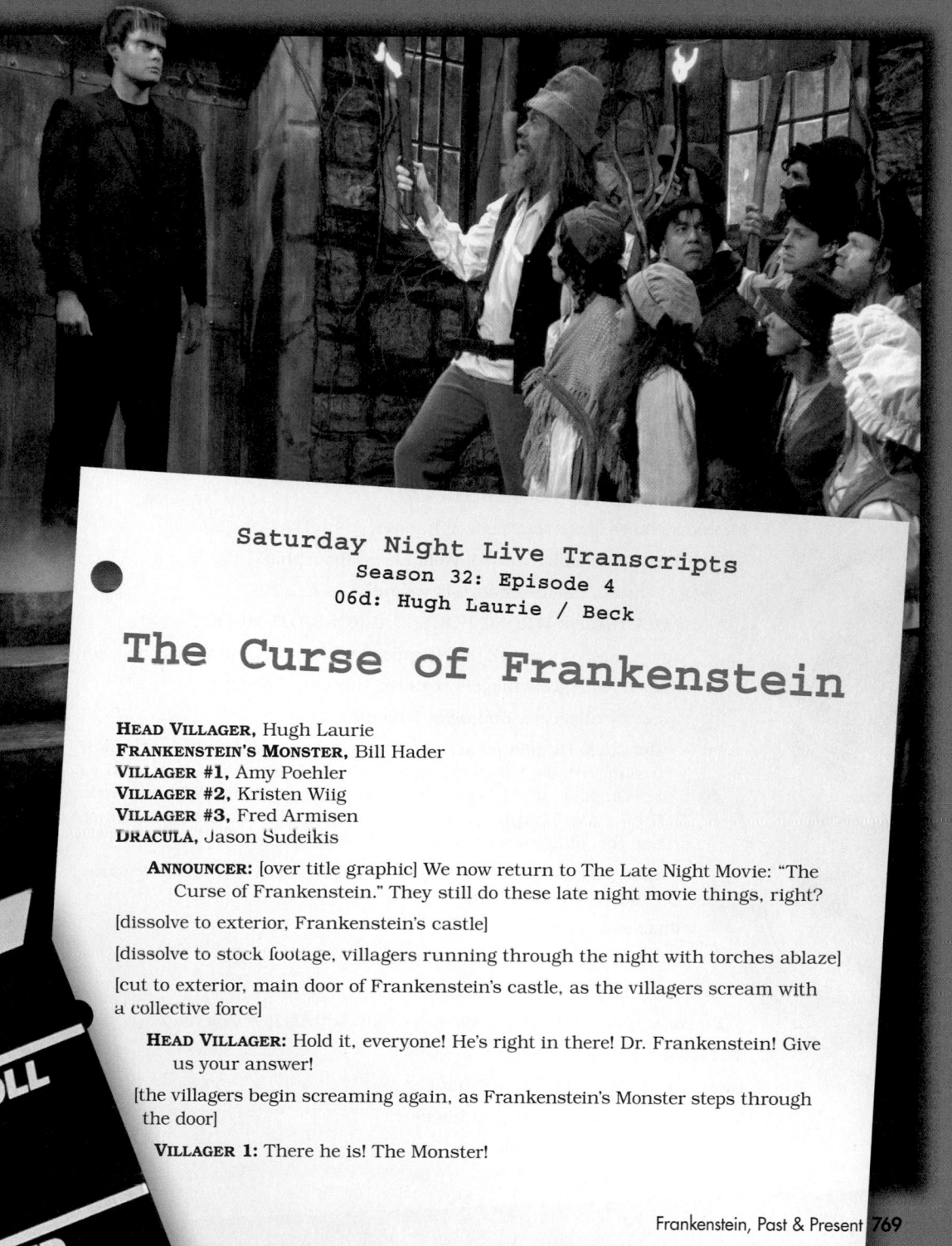

Saturday Night Live Transcripts
Season 32: Episode 4
06d: Hugh Laurie / Beck

The Curse of Frankenstein

HEAD VILLAGER, Hugh Laurie
FRANKENSTEIN'S MONSTER, Bill Hader
VILLAGER #1, Amy Poehler
VILLAGER #2, Kristen Wiig
VILLAGER #3, Fred Armisen
DRACULA, Jason Sudeikis

ANNOUNCER: [over title graphic] We now return to The Late Night Movie: "The Curse of Frankenstein." They still do these late night movie things, right?

[dissolve to exterior, Frankenstein's castle]

[dissolve to stock footage, villagers running through the night with torches ablaze]

[cut to exterior, main door of Frankenstein's castle, as the villagers scream with a collective force]

HEAD VILLAGER: Hold it, everyone! He's right in there! Dr. Frankenstein! Give us your answer!

[the villagers begin screaming again, as Frankenstein's Monster steps through the door]

VILLAGER 1: There he is! The Monster!

Saturday Night Live

1. Review the information about *Saturday Night Live* with students.
2. **Ask** students to share their impressions of the long-running comedy show.
   Possible response: Students may report amazement that the lively comedy show has been on the air for more than 33 years, or they may mention its many talented comedy artists or talk about sketches that they found most memorable.

The Curse of Frankenstein

1. Review with students how to read a broadcast script. Remind them that the words in brackets are stage directions. Tell students that the text on these pages was first broadcast on October 28, 2006, right before Halloween.
2. **Ask:** Why is the announcer's side comment considered humorous?
   Answer: It is a reference to the late-night horror flicks that Elizabeth McCracken referred to in her "Scholar's Insight." In the modern era, of on-demand TV and DVDs very few people need to watch late-night television to view old classic movies like *Frankenstein* or *Dracula.*
3. **Ask** students what Gothic elements they recognize in the opening scenes.
   Possible responses: The castle and the moor are both eerie, supernatural settings common to Gothic romances.

The Curse of Frankenstein

1. Have students continue to read the transcript. **Ask** a volunteer to summarize what happens when the crowd confronts the monster. **Answer:** He shrugs and sends them across the moor to Count Dracula's castle. Dracula in turn tells them that Frankenstein was just messing with their heads and sends them back.
2. **Ask** students to identify familiar images from classic filmed versions of monster stories that can be found in the passage. **Possible responses:** country villagers with torches blazing; the description of the Frankenstein monster as tall, green, with bolts in his neck and stitched hands; and Dracula's fangs, widow's peak, and Inverness cape

FRANKENSTEIN'S MONSTER: Whoa, whoa, whoa, hey, hey, oh!! You guys looking for *Frankenstein?*

CROWD: YES!!!!

FRANKENSTEIN'S MONSTER: [holds up his stitched hands] You guys got the wrong house!

HEAD VILLAGER: What do you mean, we got the wrong house?

VILLAGER #1: YEAH?!! WHAT DO YOU MEAN?!!

FRANKENSTEIN'S MONSTER: SHUT UP!! [they silence] You got the wrong house! Frankenstein lives, uh—[points behind the villagers] Yeah, he lives over *there*. Across the moor.

HEAD VILLAGER: Across the *moor*?

FRANKENSTEIN'S MONSTER: Yeah, yeah, yeah, yeah, yeah! It's, uh—a big castle . . . uh, it's got those, uh—[snaps fingers] oh, what do you call it, those white trees out front, uh—

HEAD VILLAGER: You mean birch trees?

FRANKENSTEIN'S MONSTER: Yeah. Whatever.

HEAD VILLAGER: [embarrassed] Well. Sorry about that.

[Frankenstein's Monster shrugs vacantly]

HEAD VILLAGER: WRONG HOUSE!! ACROSS THE MOOR!!

[the villagers run back in the opposite direction from which they came]

[stock footage of villagers running through the night]

[cut to villagers standing at Dracula's door]

DRACULA: He said *what*?! *I'm* Frankenstein?! [chuckles, as he files his fingernails] I'm sorry, guys—I think someone's messin' with ya'. I'm *Dracula*! See? [shows off his outfit] Cape. Fangs. Widow's peak. Frankenstein's, uh . . . way back *that* way. [points back in the direction the villagers just came from] Across the *moor*.

HEAD VILLAGER: Back *that* way? We just *came* from there. He said Frankenstein lives *here*!

VILLAGER #1: *Yeah!*

VILLAGER #2: Yeah, he said Frankenstein lives HERE!!

[all the villagers join in the chorus]

DRACULA: Hold on, hold on, hold on—what did this guy look like?

VILLAGER #1: He was TALL!

DRACULA: Right, right, okay—what else?

VILLAGER #2: He had BOLTS in his neck!

DRACULA: Uh-huh. What else?

Enrichment: Analyzing Film

Reel-Life Monsters
Mary Shelley's Victor Frankenstein has become the prototype of the celluloid mad scientist who plays God. As early as 1910, Thomas Edison made a 20-minute silent film adaptation. Then, in 1931, Boris Karloff made the version on which the popular culture monster is based. Lon Chaney Jr. took over the part in *The Ghost of Frankenstein* (1942) and Bela Lugosi took the title role in 1943. Other film versions include *The Curse of Frankenstein* (1957) and *Young Frankenstein* (1974).

Activity: Analyze the Film Frankenstein Monster Ask students to view a film version of *Frankenstein.* Have them compare the film with what they know about Mary Shelley's creature and scientist. Suggest that they record their analyses in the **Enrichment: Analyzing Film** worksheet, ***Professional Development Guidebook,*** page 226.

Villager #3: He was *gree-ee-ee-eennnn*!

Dracula: Okay. Tall guy, green, bolts in his neck—yeah, I hate to break it to you, but *that's* Frankenstein!

Head Villager: Okay . . . well, alright. I believe we've made a bit of a mistake. Sorry to trouble you! [to the villagers] Across the moor!!

Crowd: ACROSS THE MOOR!!

[the villagers run back in the opposite direction from which they came]

[stock footage of villagers running through the night]

[cut to villagers standing at Frankenstein's door]

Frankenstein's Monster: Well, uh . . . he's a *li-ar*! That's what!

Head Villager: Well . . . what about the *bolts* in your neck?

Frankenstein's Monster: Oh, great, thanks a lot! I almost forgot about that *spinal injury* I had when I was four-years old! Thanks for bringing back *those* rosy memories! Hey—my dog died last year, why don't you make a few jokes about *that*?!

Villager #1: He's a mon-sterrrr!!

[all the villagers join in the chorus]

Frankenstein's Monster: Hey, now we're *name-calling*! What am I, in the 7th grade, all of a sudden! . . . How do you like that?

Head Villager: Well, how do we know you're *not* Frankenstein's Monster?

Frankenstein's Monster: How do I know *you're* not Frankenstein's Monster, you freakin' genius?! I mean—[glances at villager stepping too close with a lit torch] Hey, dude—get that fire away from me. Alright? I mean,

The Curse of Frankenstein

1. Read aloud from the transcript at the point after the villagers have returned from their confrontation with Count Dracula.
2. **Ask** students how the Frankenstein character explains his unusual appearance to the villagers.
   Answer: He says a spinal cord injury as a small child left him changed.
3. **Ask** students to describe what happens next in the skit.
   Answer: The Frankenstein monster goes on the attack, accusing the villagers of name-calling and making jokes about his bad memories and people with physical deformities.

Differentiated Instruction for Universal Access

EL Support for English Learners

Students may not be familiar with the popular culture images of Frankenstein and Dracula. Build background knowledge by showing pictures and discussing the film versions of these movie monsters. Explain that a *spinal cord injury* may cause paralysis. Also explain that the term *fascist* is commonly used to put down people or groups who do not fit the formal definition of the term, but rather are people who engage in racist behavior or seem intolerant of others.

Enrichment for Gifted/Talented Students

Have interested students take roles and do a dramatic reading of the *SNL* "Curse of Frankenstein" transcript. Tell them to interpret the comedic lines with feeling and broad strokes. Encourage them to rehearse in small groups; obtain simple props, makeup, or costumes; and present their interpretive readings for the class.

The Curse of Frankenstein

1. Point out the use of the term *fascist* in the transcript. Explain its traditional political meaning and how it has been extended to refer to any right-wing extremist group.
2. **Ask** students what is humorous about the monster's use of the term.
   Answer: The monster, generally portrayed as evil in popular culture's representation, acts as if he is the injured party. The rough villagers back off, but attack him when his artificial arm falls off in the final scene.

ASSESS

Answers

Before students respond, you may wish to have them write a brief objective summary of the selection. As they answer the questions below, remind them to support their answers with evidence from the text.

1. (a) The villagers are confused because the monsters accuse them of intolerance and keep refusing to respond in the stereotyped patterns they expect. (b) The success of these films depends in part on our acceptance of stereotyped roles of good and evil. The departure from this pattern makes us laugh and strikes us as humorous.
2. It is the villagers who seem rude and bent on revenge, while the *SNL* Frankenstein monster casts himself in the role of a victim.
3. **Possible response:** You need to know what both monsters look like, the accepted division of the characters into good versus evil, and the fact that Frankenstein is normally presented as brutish and almost silent rather than more educated and actually eloquent in his own defense.

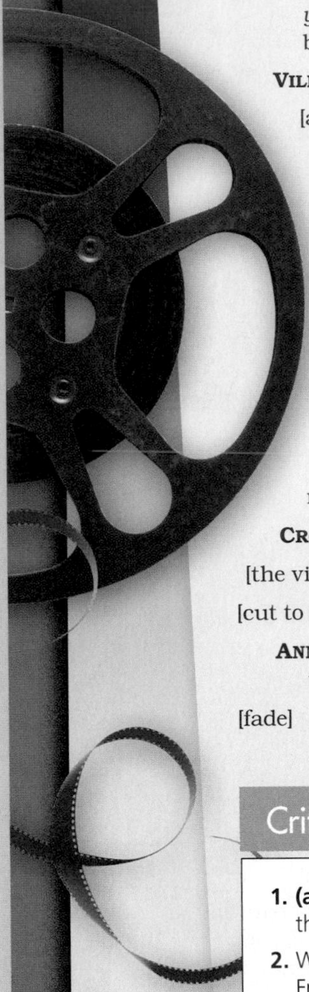

you could be a monster, you know? You got the weird hat, the patchy beard—you know? I mean, you look like a monster to *me*!

VILLAGER #1: [to Head Villager] Well, maybe *you're* the monster!

[all the villagers join in the chorus]

HEAD VILLAGER: [shakes his head] I'm not the monster! [points to Frankenstein's Monster] Look at 'im! He's got a square head and green skin!

FRANKENSTEIN'S MONSTER: Oh, great—now it's a *racial* thing! You know what? You guys are a bunch of fascists! [villager with a lit torch again steps too close] *Seriously*, du-ude! Get that fire away from me! [to the crowd] Here's the deal: I'm a cobbler. I make shoes, and I hang out with my kids. You want to lynch me for *that*—be my guest!

HEAD VILLAGER: Well, I'm sorry. We—we shouldn't have jumped to conclusions. We'll leave you alone.

FRANKENSTEIN'S MONSTER: Uh—how about, apology *not* accepted, Weird Beard! I mean, let a guy live his life, would you? You know what I mean? I mean, it—[his arm suddenly falls off and hits the stone steps] Uhhhhhh—

CROWD: *KILL HIM!!!*

[the villagers storm forward]

[cut to title graphic]

ANNOUNCER: We'll be back with more of The Late Night Movie. I *swear* they haven't done these things in, like, twenty years . . .

[fade]

Critical Reading

1. **(a)** What is confusing the villagers? **(b) Interpret:** In what way is their confusion a humorous comment on monster movies in general?
2. What is surprising and humorous about the way in which Frankenstein's monster talks?

Use this question to focus a group discussion of "The Curse of Frankenstein":

3. What, if anything, should you know about the Frankenstein story to appreciate the humor of this skit?

772

Lyric Poetry

PART 2

Selection Planning Guide

The selections in this section present the lyric poetry of the English Romantic poets Wordsworth, Coleridge, Byron, Shelley, and Keats. In their works, these poets examine humanity's relationship with nature, explore realms of the imagination and of feeling, and contemplate the notions of freedom, beauty, truth, reality, fame, and justice.

Humanities

The Wanderer Over the Sea of Clouds, 1818, by Caspar David Friedrich

This dramatic oil-on-canvas painting of a man standing alone to ponder a fog-covered landscape is emblematic of the Romantic writer contemplating his or her relationship with nature.

Although Caspar David Friedrich was German-born, he studied at the Royal Academy in Copenhagen, Denmark. Many of his paintings, like *The Wanderer,* were landscapes or seascapes capturing human isolation and suggesting people's ultimate impotence against nature's overwhelming force.

Use this question for discussion:

What elements of the painting suggest the Romantics' several views of nature?

Possible response: The light and beauty of the landscape suggest the Romantics' optimistic views about nature, while the dark jagged rocks suggest the Romantics' sense of nature's dangerous powers.

Monitor Progress: **Benchmark** After students have completed the word lyric poetry selections, administer **Benchmark Test 7** (*Unit 4 Resources,* pp. 90–95). If the text reveals that some students need further work, use the appropriate reteaching pages in the **Reading Kit**.

Text Complexity: At a Glance

This chart gives a general text complexity rating for the selections in this part of the unit to help guide instruction. For additional text complexity support, see the Test Complexity Rubric at point of use.

Tintern Abbey	**More Complex**	*from* Don Juan	**More Complex**
The Prelude	**More Complex**	Ozymandias	**More Accessible**
The World Is Too Much With Us	**More Accessible**	Ode to the West Wind	**More Complex**
London, 1802	**More Accessible**	To a Skylark	**More Accessible**
The Rime of the Ancient Mariner	**More Complex**	On First Looking into Chapman's Homer	**More Accessible**
Kubla Khan	**More Accessible**	When I Have Fears	**More Accessible**
She Walks in Beauty	**More Accessible**	Ode to a Nightingale	**More Complex**
from Childe Harold's Pilgrimage	**More Accessible**	Ode on a Grecian Urn	**More Complex**

❶ Defining Lyric Poetry

Explain that lyric poetry gets its name from the lyre, a stringed instrument that poets of ancient Greece used to accompany their songs. Though no longer sung, lyric poems often have a musical feeling and a songlike structure. **Ask:** In what other, similar way is the word *lyric* used?

Answer: The words of a song are called *lyrics.*

❷ Sound Devices and Figurative Language

1. Explain that while the sound devices listed are important poetic elements, poetry has no single recipe. A poem does not require such elements as rhyme, consonance, or metaphor. It can still be a poem while lacking some major elements.
2. Write the following two sentences on the board: *Seeing a rainbow makes me happy* and *My heart leaps up when I behold a rainbow in the sky.* Point out that each statement is saying the same thing. **Ask:** Which sentence is more likely to be a line from a lyric poem? How do you know?

   Possible response: The second sentence might well come from a lyric poem because it employs personification (*My heart leaps up*) and has a distinct rhythm. Out of context, the first sentence has nothing poetic about it.

❸ Close Read: Sound Devices and Figurative Language

1. Read aloud the examples of sound devices and figurative language in the boxes, making sure that students hear and understand the important elements.
2. Point out the highlighted text in the model on page 775. Explain that the color of the highlighting matches the color of the category in the chart. Details that illustrate a given category are highlighted in the color of that category.

"Poetry . . . is . . . a speaking picture."

— Sir Philip Sidney

❶ Defining Lyric Poetry

Lyric poetry expresses the personal thoughts and feelings of a single speaker. Lyric poems often have musical effects and a songlike structure.

Types of Lyric Poems While lyric poems do not have to follow a specific form, many do. The following are traditional lyric forms:

- **Ode:** a serious, often intensely emotional poem that honors a person or thing. In an ode, the speaker directly addresses the subject.
- **Elegy:** a solemn and formal poem about death. The speaker may mourn a person or a more abstract loss, such as the passing of youth.
- **Sonnet:** a 14-line poem with a formal structure, specific meter, and rhyme scheme

❷ **Sound Devices and Figurative Language** In addition to the descriptive, sensory language called **imagery,** one of the most distinctive qualities of poetry is its use of sound devices and figurative language.

Sound devices are patterns of words that use the innate sounds of language to create musical effects. They include the following types:

- **Rhyme:** repetition of sounds at the ends of words, as in *brake* and *lake*
- **Consonance:** repetition of final consonant sounds in stressed syllables that have different vowel sounds, as in *speak* and *break*
- **Repetition:** repeated use of sounds, words, phrases, or sentences

Figurative language is language that is used imaginatively rather than literally. Figurative language includes the following figures of speech:

- **Simile:** comparison of two unlike things using the words *like* or *as*
- **Metaphor:** comparison of two apparently unlike things without using *like* or *as*
- **Oxymoron:** juxtaposing two opposite or contradictory words to reveal a surprising truth

❸ **Close Read: Sound Devices and Figurative Language**
These literary elements appear in the Model text at right.

Sound Device—Alliteration: repetition of initial identical consonant sounds in accented syllables *Example: "All powers of swiftness, subtlety, and strength…" (William Wordsworth)*	**Figurative Language—Personification:** giving human traits to nonhuman things *Example: "These waters, rolling from their mountain springs / With a soft inland murmur…" (William Wordsworth)*
Sound Device—Assonance: repetition of similar vowel sounds in accented syllables *Example: "One shade the more, one ray the less…" (Lord Byron)*	**Figurative Language—Apostrophe:** a figure in which the speaker addresses an absent person *Example: "Milton! thou should'st be living at this hour: / England has need of thee…" (William Wordsworth)*

In This Section

For more practice analyzing lyric poetry, see pages 799, 854, 868, and 882.

EXEMPLAR TEXT

Model

About the Text Pablo Neruda (1904–1973) was one of Chile's most popular poets. In 1971, he was awarded the Nobel Prize in Literature.

"Ode to My Suit" by Pablo Neruda (translated by Margaret Sayers Peden)

Every morning, suit,
(4) you are waiting on a chair
to be filled
by my vanity, my love,
my hope, my body.
Still
only half awake
I leave the shower
to shrug into your sleeves,
my legs seek
the hollow of your legs,
and thus embraced
(5) by your unfailing loyalty
I take my morning walk,
work my way into my poetry;
from my windows I see
the things,
men, women,
events and struggles
constantly shaping me,
constantly confronting me,
setting my hands to the task,
opening my eyes,
creasing my lips,
and in the same way,
suit,
I am shaping you,
poking out your elbows,
wearing you threadbare,
and so your life grows
in the image of my own.
In the wind
you flap and hum
as if you were my soul,
in bad moments
you cling
to my bones,
abandoned, at nighttime
darkness and dream
people with their phantoms
your wings and mine.
I wonder
whether some day
an enemy
(6) bullet
will stain you with my blood,
for then
you would die with me,
but perhaps
it will be
less dramatic,
simple,
and you will grow ill,
suit,
with me,
grow older
with me, with my body,
and together
we will be lowered
into the earth.
That's why
every day
I greet you
with respect and then
you embrace me and I forget you,
because we are one being
and shall be always
in the wind, through the night,
the streets and the struggle,
(7) one body,
maybe, maybe, one day, still.

4 Apostrophe The speaker talks directly to his suit. This use of apostrophe establishes both tone, or emotional attitude, and meaning: the suit is far more than a suit. It is a being for whom the speaker feels admiration and affection.

5 Personification The poem as a whole is based on personification. The speaker attributes human emotion and actions to an inanimate suit. The speaker is actually addressing an aspect of his own being, but doing so through the mechanism of the personified suit.

6 Assonance Repeated vowel sounds are less obvious than rhyme. However, along with other sound devices, they create musical qualities and connections among words.

7 Alliteration In both of the highlighted examples, repetition of the initial consonant sounds helps to link words and stir emotion.

4 Apostrophe

Read aloud the bracketed lines. Point out how the poet separates the word *suit* with commas. Draw students' attention to two other places where the word *suit* appears alone on a line. **Ask:** What effect does this use of the word *suit* have on the poem?

Possible response: It reminds the reader that the speaker is not addressing a person but a suit. It gives the poem a comic formality.

5 Personification

Read aloud the green-highlighted passage. **Ask:** How does the poet give the suit human attributes in these lines?

Answer: He describes himself as "embraced" by the suit and praises its "unfailing loyalty."

6 Assonance

Invite a volunteer to read aloud the bracketed passage. **Ask:** What sounds create assonance in this passage?

Answer: whether, enemy, then

7 Alliteration

Have students read the bracketed passage. Point out the alliteration of the words "streets," "struggle," and "still." **Ask:** What emotions might this alliteration cause the reader to feel?

Possible responses: melancholy, nostalgia

Extend the Lesson

Reading Lyric Poetry

Ask students to notice the quotation from Lord Byron in the chart of sound devices. Explain that the quotation begins the second stanza of "She Walks in Beauty," found on page 855. Read aloud "She Walks in Beauty." Then, ask students the following questions:

- What makes this poem an example of lyric poetry?
- Why is Byron's poem such a personal, even intimate, examination of beauty?

After students discuss the answers to the questions, provide class time for them to preview the poems in this unit and to identify additional examples of lyrical poetry characteristics.

• Poetry of William Wordsworth

Lesson Pacing Guide

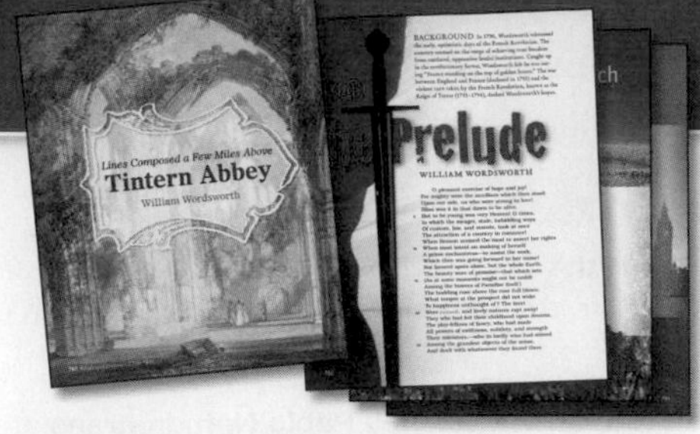

DAY 1 Preteach

- Administer the Reading and Vocabulary Warm-ups (*Unit 4 Resources,* pp. 65–68) as necessary.
- Introduce the Literary Analysis concept: Romanticism.
- Introduce the Reading Strategy: Understanding the Historical Period.
- Build background with the Author in Depth and Background features.
- Develop thematic thinking with Connecting to the Essential Question.
- Teach the selection vocabulary.

DAYS 2–3 Preteach/Teach

- Distribute copies of the appropriate graphic organizer for the Reading Strategy (*Graphic Organizer Transparencies,* pp. 140–141).
- Distribute copies of the appropriate graphic organizer for Literary Analysis (*Graphic Organizer Transparencies,* pp. 142–143).
- Prepare students to read with the Activating Prior Knowledge activities (TE).
- Informally monitor comprehension while students read.
- Use the Reading Check questions to confirm comprehension.
- Develop students' understanding of Romanticism using the Literary Analysis prompts.
- Develop students' ability to understand the historical period using the Reading Strategy prompts.
- Reinforce vocabulary with the Vocabulary notes.

DAY 4 Assess

- Assess students' comprehension and mastery of the skills by having them answer the Critical Reading, Literary Analysis, and Reading Strategy questions.
- Have students complete the Vocabulary Lesson.

DAY 5 Extend/Assess

- Have students complete the Conventions and Style Lesson.
- Have students complete the Writing Lesson and write an essay. (You may assign as homework.)
- Administer Selection Test A or B (*Unit 4 Resources,* pp. 79–81 or 82–84).

Common Core State Standards

Reading Literature 4. Determine the meaning of words and phrases as they are used in the text, including figurative and connotative meanings; analyze the impact of specific word choices on meaning and tone, including words with multiple meanings or language that is particularly fresh, engaging, or beautiful.

Language 1. Demonstrate command of the conventions of standard English grammar and usage when writing or speaking.
4.b. Identify and correctly use patterns of word changes that indicate different meanings or parts of speech.
5.b. Analyze nuances in the meanings of words with similar denotations.

Additional Standards Practice
Common Core Companion, *pp. 41–48; 185–195, 261–266; 324–335*

Daily Block Scheduling
Each day in this Lesson Pacing Guide represents a 40–50 minute period. Teachers using block scheduling may combine days to revise pacing. In addition, teachers may differentiate and support core instruction by integrating components for extended and intensive support as students require. See the Guide to Selected Leveled Resources (facing page).

Guide to Selected Leveled Resources

RTI Tier 1 (students performing on level)

			Poetry of William Wordsworth
Warm Up	Whole class instruction; Group work	**Practice, model,** and **monitor** fluency, working **with the whole class** or **in groups**.	**Vocabulary and Reading Warm-ups B,** ***Unit 4 Resources,*** pp. 65–66, 68
Comprehension/Skills	Whole class instruction; Group work; Independent work	**Support** and **monitor** comprehension and skills development, having students complete the activities, graphic organizers, and interactive prompts **independently** or **as a class**.	• ***Reader's Notebook,*** adapted instruction and full selection EL ***Reader's Notebook: English Learner's Version,*** adapted instruction and adapted selection • **Reading Strategy Graphic Organizer B,** ***Graphic Organizer Transparencies,*** p. 145 • **Literary Analysis Graphic Organizer B,** ***Graphic Organizer Transparencies,*** p. 147
Monitor Progress	A	**Monitor** student progress with the differentiated curriculum-based assessment in the *Unit Resources.*	• **Selection Test B,** ***Unit 4 Resources,*** pp. 82–84 • **Open-Book Test,** ***Unit 4 Resources,*** pp. 76–78
Assess/ Screen	A	**Assess** student progress using Benchmark Test 2.	• **Benchmark Test 7,** ***Unit 4 Resources,*** pp. 90–95

RTI Tier 2 (students requiring intervention)

			Poetry of William Wordsworth
Warm Up	Group work; One-on-one teaching	**Practice, model,** and **monitor** fluency **in groups** or **with individuals**.	• **Vocabulary and Reading Warm-ups A,** ***Unit 4 Resources,*** pp. 65–67 • ***Hear It!*** **Audio CD (adapted text)**
Comprehension/Skills	Group work; One-on-one teaching	• **Support** and **monitor** comprehension and skills development, working **in small groups** or **with individuals**. • As students complete the selection in the appropriate version of the *Reader's Notebook,* **monitor** comprehension frequently with group questions and individual instruction. • **Model** strategies while guiding students in completing the activities and prompts in the *Reader's Notebook,* as well as the graphic organizers. • **Practice** skills and **monitor** mastery with the *Reading Kit* worksheets.	• ***Reader's Notebook: Adapted Version,*** adapted instruction and adapted selection EL ***Reader's Notebook: English Learner's Version,*** adapted instruction and adapted selection • **Reading Strategy Graphic Organizer A,** ***Graphic Organizer Transparencies,*** p. 144 • **Literary Analysis Graphic Organizer A,** ***Graphic Organizer Transparencies,*** p. 146 • ***Reading Kit,*** Practice worksheets
Monitor Progress	A	**Monitor** student progress with the differentiated curriculum-based assessment in the *Unit Resources* and in the *Reading Kit.*	• **Selection Test A,** ***Unit 4 Resources,*** pp. 79–81 • ***Reading Kit,*** Assess worksheets
Assess/ Screen	A	**Assess** student progress using the Benchmark Test.	**Benchmark Test 7,** ***Unit 4 Resources,*** pp. 90–95

TIER 3 Tier 3 intervention may require consultation with the student's special-education or dyslexia specialist. For additional support, see the Tier 2 activities and resources listed above.

One-on-one teaching | Group work | Whole class instruction | Independent work | A Assessment

For a complete guide to selection support, including support for Advanced students, see the Overview of Resources in the frontmatter.

• Poetry of William Wordsworth

RESOURCES FOR:

- L1 Special-Needs Students
- L2 Below-Level Students (Tier 2)
- L3 On-Level Students (Tier 1)
- L4 Advanced Students (Tier 1)
- EL English Learners
- All All Students

Vocabulary/Fluency/Prior Knowledge

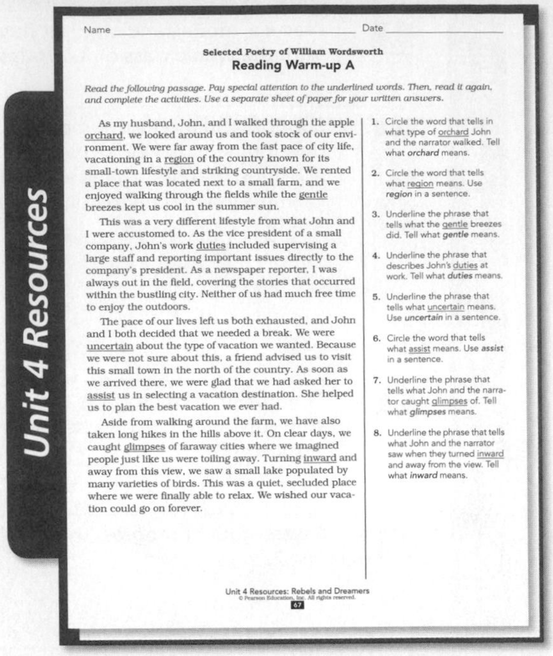

EL L1 L2 **Reading Warm-ups A and B,** pp. 67–68

Also available for these selections:

EL L1 L2 **Vocabulary Warm-ups A and B,** pp. 65–66

All **Vocabulary Builder,** p. 72

Reader's Notebooks

Pre- and postreading pages for these selections, as well as "Lines Composed a Few Miles Above Tintern Abbey," appear in an interactive format in the *Reader's Notebooks.* Each *Notebook* is differentiated for a different group of learners.
The selections in the Adapted and English Learner's versions are abridged.

L2 L3 ***Reader's Notebook***

L1 ***Reader's Notebook: Adapted Version***

EL ***Reader's Notebook: English Learner's Version***

EL ***Reader's Notebook: Spanish Version***

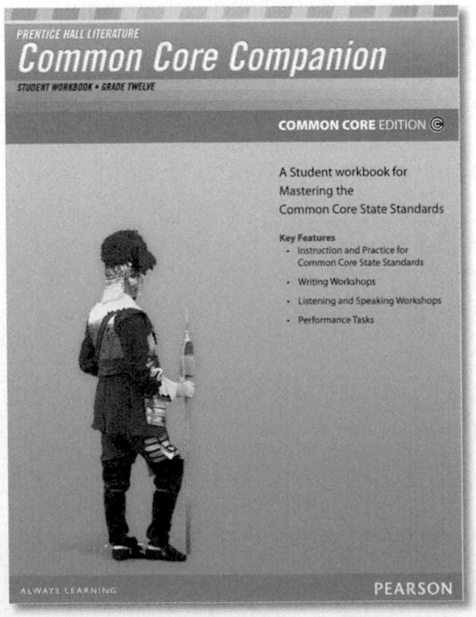

Common Core Companion

Additional instruction and practice for each Common Core State Standard

Selection Support

Graphic Organizer Transparencies

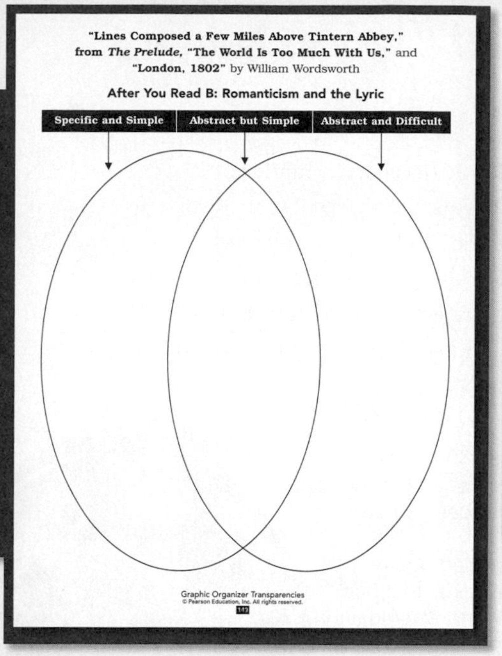

"Lines Composed a Few Miles Above Tintern Abbey," from *The Prelude*, "The World Is Too Much With Us," and "London, 1802" by William Wordsworth

After You Read B: Romanticism and the Lyric

Graphic Organizer Transparencies
© Pearson Education, Inc. All rights reserved.
143

EL L3 Literary Analysis: Graphic Organizer B, p. 143

Also available for these selections:

- **EL L1 L2 Reading: Graphic Organizer A** (partially filled in), p. 140
- **EL L3 Reading Graphic Organizer B,** p. 141
- **EL L1 L2 Literary Analysis: Graphic Organizer A** (partially filled in), p. 142

Skills Development/Extension

Unit 4 Resources

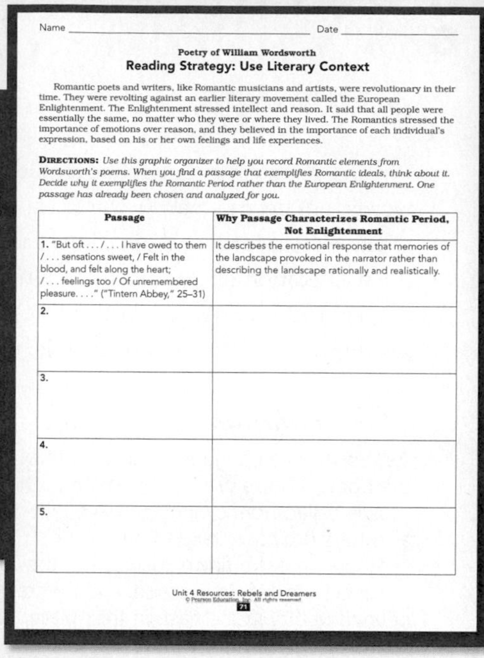

Name ________________ Date ________

Poetry of William Wordsworth

Reading Strategy: Use Literary Context

Romantic poets and writers, like Romantic musicians and artists, were revolutionary in their time. They were revolting against an earlier literary movement called the European Enlightenment. The Enlightenment stressed intellect and reason. It said that all people were essentially the same, no matter who they were or where they lived. The Romantics stressed the importance of emotions over reason, and they believed in the importance of each individual's expression, based on his or her own feelings and life experiences.

Directions: *Use this graphic organizer to help you record Romantic elements from Wordsworth's poems. When you find a passage that exemplifies Romantic ideals, think about it. Decide why it exemplifies the Romantic Period rather than the European Enlightenment. One passage has already been chosen and analyzed for you.*

Passage	Why Passage Characterizes Romantic Period, Not Enlightenment
1. "But oft . . . / . . . I have owed to them / . . . sensations sweet, / Felt in the blood, and felt along the heart; / . . . feelings too / Of unremembered pleasure. . . ." ("Tintern Abbey," 25–31)	It describes the emotional response that memories of the landscape provoked in the narrator rather than describing the landscape rationally and realistically.
2.	
3.	
4.	
5.	

Unit 4 Resources: Rebels and Dreamers
© Pearson Education, Inc. All rights reserved.
71

All Reading, p. 71

Also available for these selections:

- **All Literary Analysis,** p. 69
- **All Literary Analysis,** p. 70
- **EL L3 L4 Grammar and Style,** p. 73
- **EL L3 L4 Support for Writing,** p. 74
- **L4 Enrichment,** p. 75

Assessment

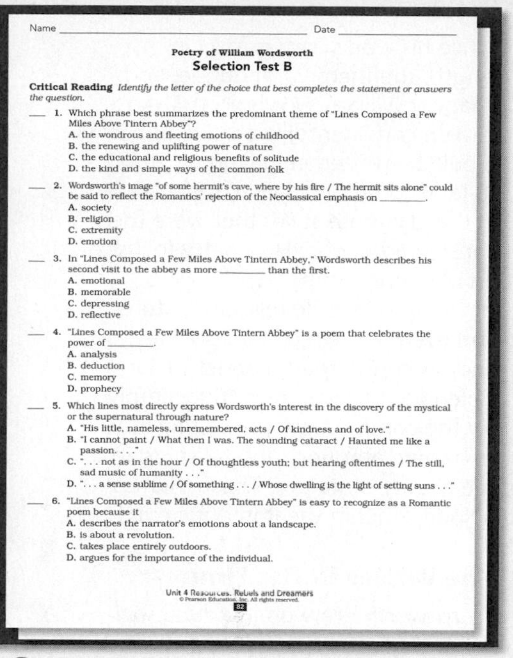

Name ________________ Date ________

Poetry of William Wordsworth

Selection Test B

Critical Reading *Identify the letter of the choice that best completes the statement or answers the question.*

___ 1. Which phrase best summarizes the predominant theme of "Lines Composed a Few Miles Above Tintern Abbey"?
A. the wondrous and fleeting emotions of childhood
B. the renewing and uplifting power of nature
C. the educational and religious benefits of solitude
D. the kind and simple ways of the common folk

___ 2. Wordsworth's image "of some hermit's cave, where by his fire / The hermit sits alone" could be said to reflect the Romantics' rejection of the Neoclassical emphasis on ________.
A. society
B. religion
C. extremity
D. emotion

___ 3. In "Lines Composed a Few Miles Above Tintern Abbey," Wordsworth describes his second visit to the abbey as more ________ than the first.
A. emotional
B. memorable
C. depressing
D. reflective

___ 4. "Lines Composed a Few Miles Above Tintern Abbey" is a poem that celebrates the power of ________.
A. analysis
B. deduction
C. memory
D. prophecy

___ 5. Which lines most directly express Wordsworth's interest in the discovery of the mystical or the supernatural through nature?
A. "His little, nameless, unremembered, acts / Of kindness and of love."
B. "I cannot paint / What then I was. The sounding cataract / Haunted me like a passion. . . ."
C. ". . . not as in the hour / Of thoughtless youth; but hearing oftentimes / The still, sad music of humanity . . ."
D. ". . . a sense sublime / Of something . . . / Whose dwelling is the light of setting suns . . ."

___ 6. "Lines Composed a Few Miles Above Tintern Abbey" is easy to recognize as a Romantic poem because it
A. describes the narrator's emotions about a landscape.
B. is about a revolution.
C. takes place entirely outdoors.
D. argues for the importance of the individual.

Unit 4 Resources: Rebels and Dreamers
© Pearson Education, Inc. All rights reserved.
82

EL L3 L4 Selection Test B, pp. 82–84

Also available for these selections:

- **L3 L4 Open-Book Test,** pp. 76–78
- **EL L1 L2 Selection Test A,** pp. 79–81

PHLit Online!
www.PHLitOnline.com

- complete narrated selection text
- a thematically related video with writing prompt
- an interactive graphic organizer
- highlighting feature
- access to all student print resources, adapted to individual student needs
- Spanish and English summaries
- adapted selection translations in Spanish

Online Resources: All print materials are also available online.

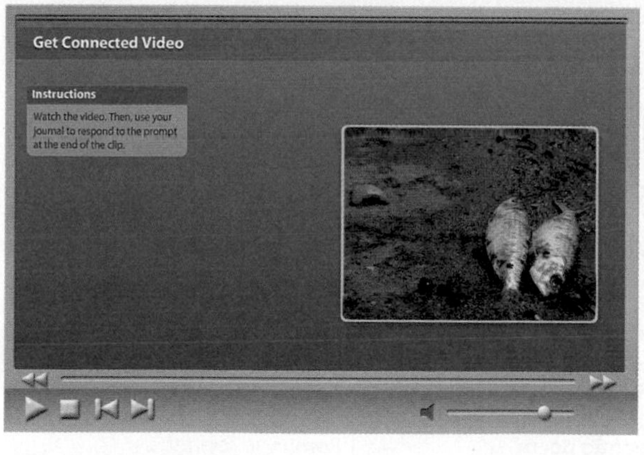

Get Connected! (thematic video with writing prompt)

Also available:

Background Video
All videos are available in Spanish.

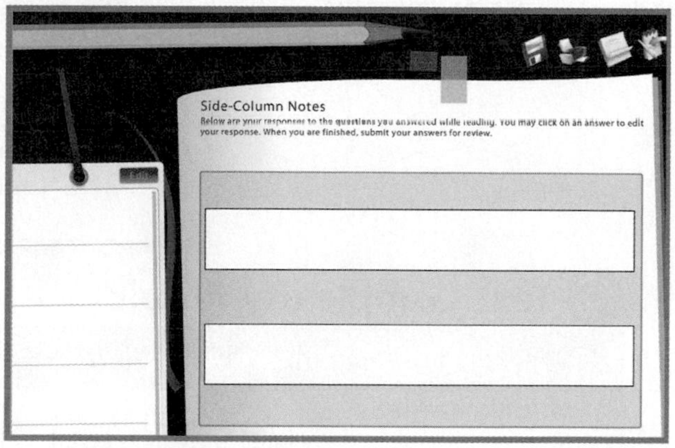

Writer's Journal (with graphics feature)

Also available:

Vocabulary Central (tools and activities for studying vocabulary)

❶ Background

Overview: The Author's Work

While his works vary greatly in length, the themes, language, and imagery William Wordsworth used remain consistent. He believed poetry should be written in the more natural style of common speech, rather than in the elaborate styles that were then considered poetic. His poetry focuses on pleasure, instinct, and feeling. His themes include religion, nature, and even his own childhood. He and his counterpart Samuel Taylor Coleridge believed in writing simply for the common people, connecting to human emotion, and relishing in the beauty of nature. These themes helped usher in the Romantic era.

The Writer in His Time

Wordsworth grew up in a rural society and spent a lot of time playing outdoors. For a time in the early 1790s, he lived in France during the Revolution. His loyalties were with England, while at the same time he felt sympathy toward the revolutionaries. He was driven to philosophy books in an attempt to understand the Reign of Terror in Paris. The harsh realism he found there clashed with his own view of the world, which was much more emotional and soft. He tunneled his emotions into his poetry, resulting in a turning point for English literature. He was poet laureate until his death in 1850—all that time he was considered the most important writer in England.

❶ ❷ William Wordsworth

(1770–1850)

Writing poetry may seem like a quiet, meditative activity, a matter of words, not deeds—hardly the scene of upheavals and crises. Yet in 1798, when Wordsworth and his friend Samuel Taylor Coleridge published the first edition of *Lyrical Ballads,* a revolution shook the world of poetry. Together, Wordsworth and Coleridge rejected all the traditional assumptions about the proper style, words, and subject matter for a poem.

A Revolution in Poetry

As Wordsworth announced in the Preface to the 1802 edition of the book, "There will . . . be found in these volumes little of what is usually called poetic diction; I have taken as much pains to avoid it as others ordinarily take to produce it; . . ."

Gone were the flowery language, the wittily crafted figures of speech, the effusive praise, and the tragic complaints that had defined poetry in the past. In their place, Wordsworth offered an intensified presentation of ordinary life and nature using common language. Wordsworth's revolution took literature in a dramatic new direction, building the movement known as Romanticism.

The Lake District

Wordsworth's revolution was rooted in his early love for nature. Born in the beautiful Lake District of England, Wordsworth spent his youth roaming the countryside. In later years, too, he found peace and reassurance in the gentle hills and serene lakes of this landscape. This region of northwestern England became the cradle of the Romantic Movement, inspiring many personal commentaries and poetic tributes.

Text Complexity Rubric

	Tintern Abbey	*from* The Prelude	The World Is Too Much with Us	London, 1802
Qualitative Measures				
Context/ Knowledge Demands	Romantic meditative poem 1 2 3 ④ 5	Romantic poem 1 2 3 ④ 5	Romantic sonnet 1 2 ③ 4 5	Romantic sonnet 1 2 ③ 4 5
Structure/Language Conventionality and Clarity	Complex syntax 1 2 3 ④ 5	Complex syntax 1 2 3 ④ 5	Long sentences 1 2 ③ 4 5	Archaic diction; long sentences 1 2 ③ 4 5
Levels of Meaning/ Purpose/Concepts	Challenging (nature) 1 2 3 ④ 5	Challenging (disillusionment) 1 2 3 ④ 5	Moderate (social criticism) 1 2 ③ 4 5	Moderate (social criticism) 1 2 ③ 4 5
Quantitative Measures				
Lexile/Text Length	NP / 1,234 words	NP / 642 words	NP / 117 words	NP / 108 words
Overall Complexity	**More complex**	**More complex**	**More accessible**	**More accessible**

Revolution and Love

By the time Wordsworth was thirteen, both his parents had died. Nonetheless, he was able to pursue his education and entered Cambridge University in 1787. After graduating, he traveled through Europe, spending considerable time in France. There, he embraced the ideals of the newly born French Revolution—ideals that stressed social justice and individual rights. Growing emotionally as well as intellectually, Wordsworth fell in love with Annette Vallon.

Disillusionment and Crisis

Wordsworth's involvement with the Revolution and with Vallon ended abruptly when lack of funds and family pressure forced him to return home. Two months later, in 1793, England declared war on France, and the Revolution became increasingly violent. His dreams of liberty betrayed, Wordsworth lapsed into a depression. His beloved sister, Dorothy, and fellow poet Samuel Taylor Coleridge helped him through this crisis.

From Politics to Art

In 1798, Wordsworth published *Lyrical Ballads* with Coleridge. With the publication of this work, Wordsworth translated his revolutionary hopes from politics to literature. His democratic ideals appeared in his use of the language of ordinary people rather than specialized "poetic" words.

Poetry

Critics agree that Wordsworth's greatest work is his autobiography in poetry, *The Prelude.* Wordsworth completed a version of this poem in 1799, which he expanded considerably by 1805. As he wrote to a friend, *The Prelude* told the story of "the growth of my own mind." The poem is not always factually accurate, but, as noted by critic Stephen Gill, in its combination of "satire and narrative, description and meditation, the visionary and the deliberately banal," it was unique.

Eventually, Wordsworth's radical new approach to poetry gained acceptance, while he himself grew more conservative in his politics. A new generation of Romantics, more radical than Wordsworth and Coleridge, arose. Wordsworth's position was secure, however: we remember him as the father of English Romanticism.

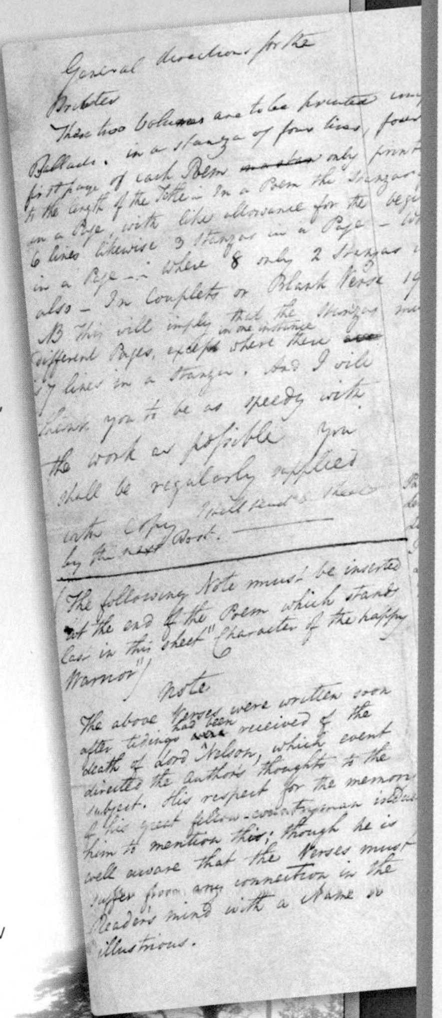

Daily Bellringer

For each class during which you will teach these selections, have students complete one of the five activities for the appropriate week in the ***Daily Bellringer Activities*** booklet.

Multidraft Reading

To assist struggling readers and to enhance reading for all, assign the text in chunks, as warranted by length, and apply multidraft reading protocols. For each reading, have students set the purpose indicated:

- **First reading**—identifying key ideas and details and answering any Reading Checks.
- **Second reading**—analyzing craft and structure and responding to the side-column prompts.
- **Third reading**—integrating knowledge and ideas, connecting to other texts and the world, and answering the end-of-selection questions.

For more guidance, refer to the ***Classroom Strategies and Teaching Routines*** card on Multidraft Reading.

2 Background

More About the Author

Wordsworth's choice of subjects—the rural poor and flowers—and his simple, passionate language offended early reviewers. At best, they saw his artistic decisions as a rejection of good taste. Some may have looked on Wordsworth with distaste for his initially radical political views. Despite such obstacles, and what some critics saw as a decline in creative powers after 1807, Wordsworth's fame and popularity grew. In 1843, his success became official: He was named poet laureate.

C Text Complexity: Reader and Task Suggestions

Tintern Abbey; *from* The Prelude		Wordsworth's Sonnets	
Preparing to Read the Text	**Leveled Tasks**	**Preparing to Read the Text**	**Leveled Tasks**
• Using the Background on TE p. 776, underscore that Wordsworth took lifelong comfort from nature. • Discuss the role of memory in heightening significance and enhancing our understanding of experiences both good and bad. • Guide students to use Multidraft Reading strategies (TE p. 777).	***Levels of Meanings*** If students will have difficulty with the poems' ideas, have them focus on each speaker's feelings and experiences. Then, as they reread, have them consider how those feelings and experiences help convey a particular outlook on life. ***Synthesizing*** If students will not have difficulty with the poems' ideas, have them formulate an understanding of Wordsworth's Romantic outlook based on ideas the poems express.	• Using the About the Selections feature on TE p. 790, explain that the young Wordsworth often felt disillusioned. • Discuss with students how the past is sometimes idealized by those who are unhappy with the present. • Guide students to use Multidraft Reading strategies (TE p. 777).	***Levels of Meaning*** If students will have difficulty with the poems' meanings, help them use sonnet structure to focus on the main point made in the first eight lines and in the last six. Then, have students reread each poem with these points in mind. ***Synthesizing*** If students will not have difficulty with the poems' meanings, have them deepen their understanding of Wordsworth's Romantic outlook based on these sonnets.

PRETEACH

❶ Wordsworth's Mountain Legacy

1. Before reading this page, show students pictures of mountains from the Internet, magazines, posters, or other sources. Have them write down a few words they would use to describe the mountains.
2. Have a volunteer read aloud the two lines of descriptive words at the top of the page. Ask students to identify differences between the words in the top line and the words in the bottom line. Then, read the rest of the page.
3. Have volunteers read the excerpts of Wordsworth's poetry at the bottom of the page. Ask students to describe how his poetry defies the first line of descriptive words at the top of the page. Inform them that Wordsworth's different, more appreciative view of nature, evident in these excerpts, is a defining characteristic of the Romantic era.

❶ WORDSWORTH'S *Mountain Legacy*

Which of these two sets of words would you probably choose to describe Mount Whitney, Mount McKinley, the Rockies, the Alps, or the Himalayas?

massy heaps, disfigurations of the Earth's face, scars, pimples, protuberances, warts

snow-mantled peaks, spectacular beauty, breath-taking scenery, towering spires

The first set of words may seem like a joke to you. Who ever described majestic mountains as if they were ugly? The answer is that many writers did, before William Wordsworth and the Romantic movement changed forever the way we look at and experience lofty peaks. The unflattering terms are not invented. They come from descriptions of mountains written in the centuries leading up to Romanticism. The second group of words comes from web sites describing today's national parks and mountain resorts.

As a boy and later as a man, Wordsworth wandered through England's Lake District, climbing mountains like Scafell Pike and Helvellyn and learning to appreciate their power and beauty. As a young man, he hiked across the Alps, whose awe-inspiring scenery made a deep impression on him.

Most important, Wordsworth expressed in poems his feelings about mountains. Today, these descriptions are part of his mountain legacy to us. Because of what he and others wrote centuries ago, we travel to national parks to view impressive peaks, vacation and camp out in the mountains, and hike on mountain trails.

. . . Oh! when I have hung
Above the raven's nest, by knots of grass
And half-inch fissures in the slippery rock . . .
. . . oh, at that time
While on the perilous ridge I hung alone . . .

—from The Prelude, Book I

. . . in the mountains did he *feel* his faith.
All things responsive to the writing, there
Breathed immortality, revolving life,
And greatness still revolving; infinite:
There littleness was not; the least of things
Seemed infinite . . .

—from The Excursion, Book I

Vocabulary Development

Vocabulary Knowledge Rating

Create a **Vocabulary Knowledge Rating Chart** (***Professional Development Guidebook,*** p. 33) for this selection, using the selection vocabulary from the next page. Give students a copy of the chart. Read the words aloud, and have students mark their ratings in the Before Reading column. Urge them to be alert to these words as they read and discuss the selection.

Tally how many students think they know each word to gauge how much instruction to provide. As students read and discuss the selection, point out the words and their context.

PHLit Online!

Vocabulary Central, featuring student tools for recording and studying vocabulary, is available online at **www.PHLitOnline.com**.

Before You Read

Poetry of William Wordsworth

2 Connecting to the Essential Question Today's rock musicians and environmentalists are descendants of the Romantic movement Wordsworth helped to found. As you read, find passages that show Wordsworth rebelling against eighteenth-century poetic traditions. Identifying these passages will help you answer the Essential Question: **What is the relationship of the writer to tradition?**

3 Literary Analysis

Romanticism was a late-eighteenth-century European literary movement. While the earlier Neoclassical writers, such as Pope and Johnson, favored reason, wit, and outward elegance, the works of many Romantic poets include these elements:

- Simplicity or directness of language
- The expression of spontaneous, intensified feelings
- Responses to nature that lead to a deeper awareness of self

English Romanticism began with William Wordsworth. The **lyric,** a poem in which a single speaker expresses personal emotions and observations, was particularly suited to his vision.

Comparing Literary Works The Romantics adopted a new and freer **diction,** or choice of words. As you read, notice that Wordsworth's poetry favors simple words but that his work also relies heavily on abstract terms. Compare the different types of words Wordsworth chooses—whether specific and concrete like *sycamore* or abstract like *a sense sublime.*

4 Reading Strategy

Preparing to Read Complex Texts You can better understand a work by **evaluating the influence of the historical period** on it. Wordsworth lived in an age of political and social revolutions, and he himself helped bring about a revolution in literature. The relationship between Wordsworth's literary ideas and social and political change are evident in the details in these poems. As you read, use a chart like the one shown to identify the revolutionary *political and philosophical assumptions* that color the view of life in his work.

5 Vocabulary

recompense (rek′ əm pens′) *n.* payment for something (p. 783)

roused (rouzd) *v.* stirred up (p. 786)

presumption (prē zump′ shən) *n.* audacity; nerve (p. 787)

anatomize (ə nat′ ə mīz′) *v.* to dissect in order to examine structure (p. 788)

sordid (sôr′ did) *adj.* dirty (p. 790)

stagnant (stag′ nənt) *adj.* motionless; foul (p. 791)

Common Core State Standards

Reading Literature

4. Determine the meaning of words and phrases as they are used in the text, including figurative and connotative meanings; analyze the impact of specific word choices on meaning and tone, including words with multiple meanings or language that is particularly fresh, engaging, or beautiful.

Historical Ideas

Historical Ideas
Celebration of Common Folk
Love of Nature
Admiration for French Revolution
Loss of Faith in Reason

www.PHLitOnline.com

www.PHLitOnline.com

Teaching From Technology

Preparing to Read

Go to **www.PHLitOnline.com** and display the *Get Connected!* slide show for this selection. Have the class brainstorm responses to the writing prompt, entering ideas in the interactive journal. Then, have students complete their written responses as homework.

To build background, display the **Background** and **More About the Author** features.

Using the Interactive Text

Go to **www.PHLitOnline.com** and display the **Enriched Online Student Edition.** As the class reads the selection or listens to the narration, record answers to side-column prompts using the graphic organizers accessible on the interactive page. Alternatively, have students use the online edition individually, answering the prompts as they read.

2 Connecting to the Essential Question

1. Review the assignment with the class.
2. To prepare students for the assignment, ask them to begin thinking about rock music and environmentalists and how they feel about them.
3. As students read, have them find passages that show Wordsworth rebelling against eighteenth-century poetic traditions.

3 Literary Analysis

Introduce the concept using the instruction on the student page.

Think Aloud: Model the Skill

Say to students:

Romantics wrote poetry characterized by direct language, spontaneous expressions of feelings, and responses to nature. I can recognize a lyric poem by looking for works expressing these elements. I can also keep an eye out for a freer diction.

4 Reading Strategy

1. Introduce the strategy using the instruction on the student page.
2. Give students a copy of **Reading Strategy Graphic Organizer B,** page 141 in *Graphic Organizer Transparencies,* to fill out as they read.

Think Aloud: Model the Skill

Say to students:

Background and assumptions that influence a writer include proper poetic form, language, and subject matter. I will look for ways Wordsworth brought about a change with his work, thereby helping to establish Romanticism.

5 Vocabulary

1. Pronounce each word, giving its definition, and have students say it aloud.
2. For more guidance, see the *Classroom Strategies and Teaching Routines* card for vocabulary instruction.

❶ About the Selection

This poem perfectly illustrates Wordsworth's belief in nature as a healer and teacher. In it, he speaks to his much-loved sister, Dorothy, hoping to share his profound joy in returning to Tintern Abbey after a five-year absence. The poem explores the soothing and uplifting effect the memory of his first visit has had during his absence. Wordsworth then turns to considering his childhood relationship to nature, in which heart and landscape were united in an immediate and spontaneous joy. In contrast, the adult Wordsworth detects in nature a sublime, inexpressible presence—"a motion and a spirit"—that unites all things. He hopes that his sister will share his feelings for the place and that, in the future, she will remember his devotion to nature and their visit to the abbey.

❷ Activating Prior Knowledge

To prepare students for Wordsworth's emotional link to nature, take a nature walk with students, either physically or with pictures or slides, through a beautiful setting. Have students note both the details of the scenes and their own emotional responses. Discuss how the emotions evoked by nature could inspire social or political views. Explain to students that the poetry of William Wordsworth is noted for its focus on nature and that his understanding of his own life, of poetry, and of politics all flow from his relationship with nature.

Concept Connector →

Tell students they will return to their responses after reading the selection.

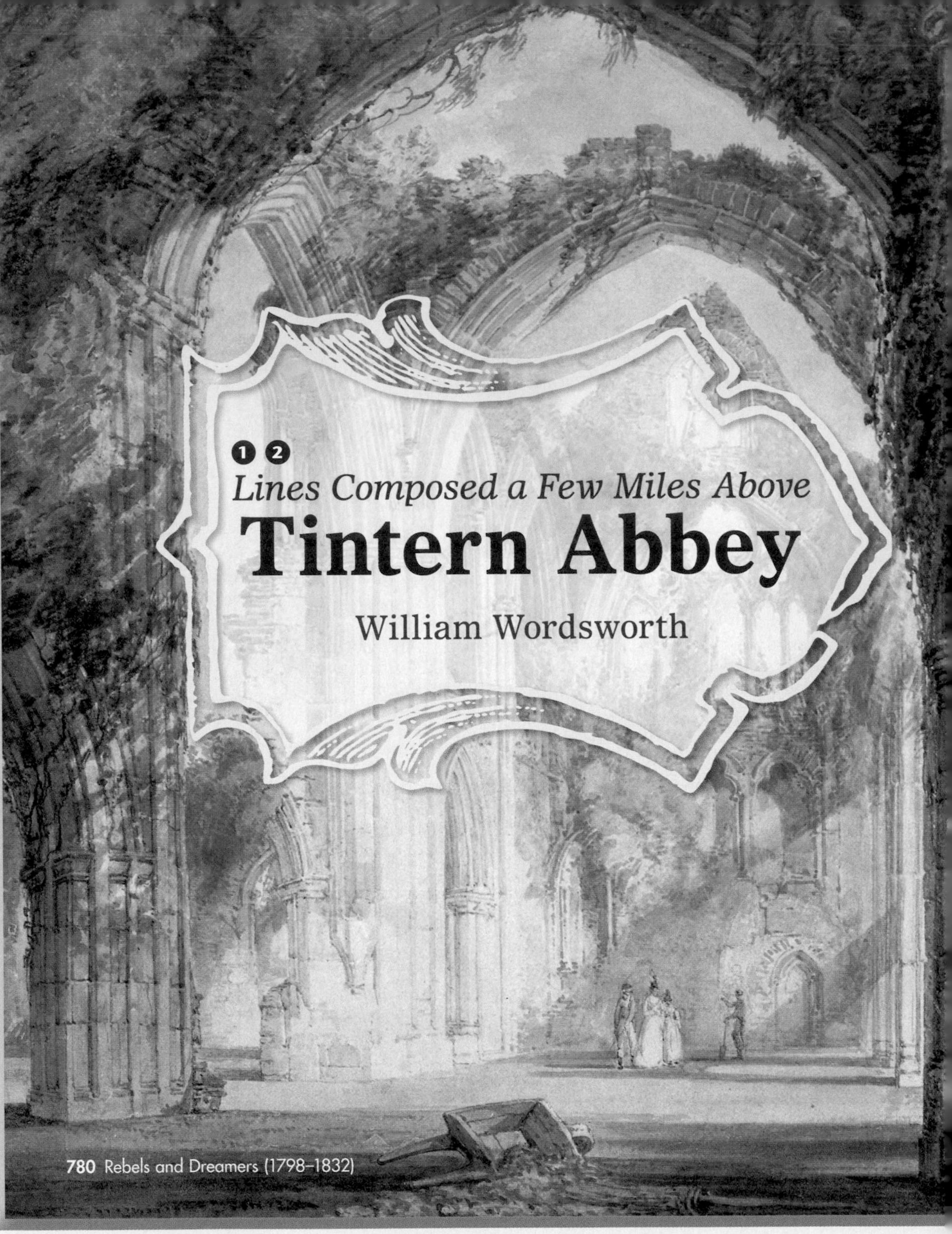

❶ ❷

Lines Composed a Few Miles Above

Tintern Abbey

William Wordsworth

BACKGROUND This poem was written in 1798 during Wordsworth's second visit to the valley of the River Wye and the ruins of Tintern Abbey, once a great medieval church, in Wales. Wordsworth had passed through the region alone five years earlier. This time he brought his sister along to share the experience.

❸
Five years have past; five summers, with the length
Of five long winters! and again I hear
These waters, rolling from their mountain springs
With a soft inland murmur. Once again
Do I behold these steep and lofty cliffs,
That on a wild secluded scene impress
Thoughts of more deep seclusion; and connect
The landscape with the quiet of the sky.
The day is come when I again repose
Here, under this dark sycamore, and view
These plots of cottage ground, these orchard tufts,
Which at this season, with their unripe fruits,
Are clad in one green hue, and lose themselves
'Mid groves and copses. Once again I see
These hedgerows, hardly hedgerows, little lines
Of sportive wood run wild: these pastoral farms,
Green to the very door; and wreaths of smoke
Sent up, in silence, from among the trees!
With some uncertain notice, as might seem
Of vagrant dwellers in the houseless woods,
Or of some hermit's cave, where by his fire
The hermit sits alone.
These beauteous forms,
Through a long absence, have not been to me
As is a landscape to a blind man's eye:
But oft, in lonely rooms, and 'mid the din
Of towns and cities, I have owed to them
In hours of weariness, sensations sweet,
Felt in the blood, and felt along the heart;
And passing even into my purer mind,
With tranquil restoration—feelings too
Of unremembered pleasure: such, perhaps,
As have no slight or trivial influence
On that best portion of a good man's life.
His little, nameless, unremembered, acts
Of kindness and of love. Nor less, I trust,
To them I may have owed another gift,
Of aspect more sublime; that blessed mood,
In which the burthen[1] of the mystery,
In which the heavy and the weary weight

Literary Analysis
Romanticism and the Lyric
How do the sensory observations Wordsworth includes reflect what you know about Romanticism?

❹ ◄ **Critical Viewing**
What elements in this painting help it capture awe and excitement comparable to Wordsworth's on his return to the Wye? **[Connect]**

❺ **Reading Check**
Name two sights that strike Wordsworth on his return to the Wye.

1. **burthen** burden.

❸ Literary Analysis
Romanticism and the Lyric

1. Review with students what they know about Romanticism, including its use of simple language, its spontaneous expression of feelings, and its response to nature.
2. Then, **ask** students the Literary Analysis question.
   Possible response: Students may note Wordsworth's loving attention to the general feeling of the scene—the cliffs that deepen the sense of seclusion—as well as to specific details such as the sycamore tree and unripe fruits. Along with the almost ecstatic tone of his wonder at returning, these details reflect the heartfelt response to nature characteristic of Romantics.

► **Monitor Progress:** Have students identify other Romantic elements in this stanza.
Possible response: Other details include his attention to his own feelings ("sensations sweet")

❹ Critical Viewing

Answer: The glowing walls suggests the excitement of discovery and rediscovery that characterizes Wordsworth's return to the Wye. The light flooding the scene might suggest the sublime, nearly inexpressible sentiments Wordsworth associates with the ruins of Tintern Abbey.

❺ Reading Check

Possible responses: Wordsworth is struck by the "steep and lofty cliffs," the greenery, and the lines of hedgerows.

Differentiated Instruction for Universal Access

Support for Special-Needs Students
Have students complete the **Before You Read** and the **Making Connections** pages for these selections in the ***Reader's Notebook: Adapted Version.*** These pages provide abbreviated skills instruction, a selection summary, the **Before You Read** graphic organizer, and a **Note-taking Guide.**

Support for Less Proficient Readers
Have students complete the **Before You Read** and the **Making Connections** pages for these selections in the ***Reader's Notebook.*** These pages provide abbreviated skills instruction, a selection summary, the **Before You Read** graphic organizer, and a **Note-taking Guide.**

EL Support for English Learners
Have students complete the **Before You Read** and the **Making Connections** pages for these selections in the ***Reader's Notebook: English Learner's Version.*** These pages provide additional vocabulary, vocabulary skills, and vocabulary practice, along with a **Getting Ready to Read** activity.

PHLit Online!
These selections are available in interactive format in the **Enriched Online Student Edition** at **www.PHLitOnline.com**, which includes a thematically related video with writing prompt and an interactive graphic organizer.

❻ Literary Analysis

Romanticism and the Lyric

1. Read aloud the bracketed passage. Review the Romantic concept of a deep sympathy between nature and the people's inner being.
2. Then, **ask** students the Literary Analysis question.
   Answer: The memory of natural scenes lightened the speaker's mood, leaving him so tranquil he became "a living soul." In this mood, he feels able to "see into the life of things"—showing nature can inspire insight. Students should note a bond between nature and soul.

❼ Reading Strategy

Understanding the Historical Period

1. Remind students that literary context is a poet's climate of opinions and traditional beliefs.
2. Then, **ask** students the Reading Strategy question.
   Answer: Childhood, for Wordsworth, is a time "before" reason, and without reflective thought on nature. However, the value he gives this experience relates to the quality of the relationship with nature. The contrast between the adult's possession of reason and the child's lack of it is less important than the changing quality of the speaker's experience of nature. This shift shows that, for Wordsworth, reason is no longer of central importance.

❽ Critical Viewing

Possible response: The landscape in the photograph is similar to Wordsworth's description in that it shows hills, woods, and a prevalence of green.

Literary Analysis
Romanticism and the Lyric
How do the images in lines 40–49 reflect Romantic ideas of the relation between nature and the soul?

❻
Of all this unintelligible world
Is lightened—that serene and blessed mood,
In which the affections gently lead us on—
Until, the breath of this corporeal frame[2]
And even the motion of our human blood
Almost suspended, we are laid asleep
In body, and become a living soul;
While with an eye made quiet by the power
Of harmony, and the deep power of joy,
We see into the life of things.

If this
Be but a vain belief, yet, oh! how oft—
In darkness and amid the many shapes
Of joyless daylight; when the fretful stir
Unprofitable, and the fever of the world,
Have hung upon the beatings of my heart—
How oft, in spirit, have I turned to thee,
O sylvan[3] Wye! thou wanderer through the woods,
How often has my spirit turned to thee!

Reading Strategy
Understanding the Historical Period
What changing attitude about the importance of reason is reflected in Wordsworth's contrast of childhood with adulthood?

And now, with gleams of half-extinguished thought,
With many recognitions dim and faint,
And somewhat of a sad perplexity,
The picture of the mind revives again;
While here I stand, not only with the sense
Of present pleasure, but with pleasing thoughts
That in this moment there is life and food
For future years. And so I dare to hope,
❼ Though changed, no doubt, from what I was when first

❽ **▼ Critical Viewing**
How is the landscape in this photograph similar to the setting Wordsworth describes? **[Connect]**

2. **corporeal** (kôr pôr′ ē əl) **frame** body.
3. **sylvan** (sil′ vən) wooded.

Enrichment: Analyzing Culture

Views of Nature
One's view of nature is strongly influenced by his or her culture. Native Americans, for example, recognize human dependence on nature and strive to maintain harmony with it. Traditional Eastern cultures seek to integrate human existence gracefully with nature. For example, traditional Japanese architecture is always conceived in relation to surrounding landscape and changing seasons. Rock gardens, pools, and streams integrate the human artifice and natural forms.

Activity: Analyzing Other Views Encourage interested students to do further research on cultures' views of nature. Have them record their findings using the **Enrichment: Analyzing Culture** worksheet, ***Professional Development Guidebook,*** page 223.

I came among these hills; when like a roe[4]
I bounded o'er the mountains, by the sides
Of the deep rivers, and the lonely streams,
Wherever nature led: more like a man
❼ Flying from something that he dreads, than one
Who sought the thing he loved. For nature then
(The coarser pleasures of my boyish days,
And their glad animal movements all gone by)
To me was all in all—I cannot paint
What then I was. The sounding cataract
Haunted me like a passion; the tall rock,
The mountain, and the deep and gloomy wood,
Their colors and their forms, were then to me
An appetite; a feeling and a love,
That had no need of a remoter charm,
By thought supplied, nor any interest
Unborrowed from the eye. That time is past,
And all its aching joys are now no more,
And all its dizzy raptures. Not for this
Faint[5] I, nor mourn nor murmur; other gifts
Have followed; for such loss, I would believe,
❿ Abundant **recompense**. For I have learned
To look on nature, not as in the hour
Of thoughtless youth; but hearing oftentimes
The still, sad music of humanity,
Nor harsh nor grating, though of ample power
To chasten and subdue. And I have felt
A presence that disturbs me with the joy
Of elevated thoughts; a sense sublime
Of something far more deeply interfused,
Whose dwelling is the light of setting suns,
And the round ocean and the living air,
And the blue sky, and in the mind of man;
A motion and a spirit, that impels
All thinking things, all objects of all thought,
And rolls through all things. Therefore am I still
A lover of the meadows and the woods
And mountains; and of all that we behold
From this green earth; of all the mighty world
Of eye, and ear—both what they half create,
And what perceive; well pleased to recognize
In nature and the language of the sense,
The anchor of my purest thoughts, the nurse,

4. roe type of deer.
5. Faint lose heart.

❾ *The* **BRITISH TRADITION**

The Evolution of the Self

On returning to the Wye, Wordsworth discovers his own deeper self in experiences of nature bound together by memory. His discovery contributed to a new, Romantic idea of the self. For the Romantics, the self was a journey of self-discovery, not a collection of personal quirks or facts. The Romantic poet set out to recover his or her deeper self through nature, memory, and lyric poetry. For the Romantics, writing a poem became an act of discovery and self-definition.

This Romantic idea of the self—always divided yet always recovering itself—inspired later works such as Tennyson's *In Memoriam, A.H.H.* Centuries later, Wordsworth's vision of the self and its journey still resonates in modern culture.

Connect to the Literature

In lines 88–93, what does the speaker learn about himself and his world?

Vocabulary

recompense (rek′ əm pens′) *n.* payment in return for something

⓫ **Reading Check**

What natural sights inspire in Wordsworth a sense of the unity of things—of "something far more deeply interfused, . . ."?

Differentiated Instruction for Universal Access

Strategy for Special-Needs Students

Have students read "Tintern Abbey" stanza by stanza in small groups with teacher guidance. Discuss each shift in time, place, or the speaker's age as the poem unfolds. Have students identify the major contrasts between each experience in the poem.

Enrichment for Less Proficient Readers

Readers may not recognize that Wordsworth's descriptions in "Tintern Abbey" are rich in appreciation for its natural beauty and what it evokes in him. Have them think of a natural area they have observed that brings out heightened emotions. Then ask them to write a brief poem that describes the place and the emotions they feel when they visit it. Have students compare their poems to Wordsworth's "Tintern Abbey."

❾ The British Tradition

The Evolution of the Self

Wordsworth's poetic use of psychology had an antecedent in prose: In the seventeenth century, Burton's *Anatomy of Melancholy* explored various emotional conditions in a larger inquiry. But Wordsworth's revelations initiated a revelatory writing that allowed confessional poets two centuries later to incorporate personal details into their works. Wordsworth's willingness to focus on himself was a dramatic departure. Most important, though, in the evolution of our culture's idea of the self is the fact that he presents memory and the repetition of past states of the soul as defining himself. Through acts of poetic introspection, Wordsworth discovers or creates himself, apart from social roles and definitions.

Connect to the Literature

Invite students to share any insights they have gained from an experience with nature. Then, **ask** the Connect to the Literature question.

Answer: His reactions to nature have matured, and experiences with nature have helped him reflect on the human condition.

❿ Critical Thinking

Interpret

1. Have students read lines 83–93. Ask them to pay careful attention to Wordsworth's ideas of maturity.
2. **Ask** them: How does Wordsworth feel about the changes maturity has brought to his attitudes about nature?
   Possible response: Wordsworth feels he has lost a vital joy in nature but refuses to mourn for it. The emotion has been replaced by a new sense of the unity of things.

⓫ Reading Check

Answer: The "light of setting suns," the "round ocean," the "living air," "the blue sky," and the "mind of man" inspire him.

Spiral Review

Point of View

Ask students the Spiral Review question.

Possible response: The first-person point of view shows the speaker's appreciation for his sister's vitality, freshness, and openness to nature, as well as his sadness that he has lost those very qualities.

12 Literary Analysis

Romanticism and Diction

1. Review the definition of *diction* as word choice.
2. Read the bracketed passage aloud, asking students to note Wordsworth's diction.
3. Then, **ask** students the Literary Analysis question.
   Answer: Students should recognize that Wordsworth describes old age using simple words that are general, rather than specific.

13 Reading Strategy

Understanding the Historical Period

1. Review the beliefs and assumptions of the Romantics with students, paying special attention to nature.
2. Then, **ask** students the Reading Strategy question.
   Answer: The Romantics had a strong connection with nature. The elaborate and beautiful description of the wind shows evidence of that relationship.

14 Humanities

Tintern Abbey, **watercolor, by Joseph Mallord William Turner** This painting by Wordsworth's contemporary shows Tintern Abbey. J.M.W. Turner (1775–1851) was a premier British landscape painter. Use this question for discussion: Why might ruins have been so attractive to Romantics?

Possible responses: Ruins suggest something no longer present, thereby creating a sense of grandeur, comparable to Wordsworth's "sense sublime." They also reflect the power of nature over human works.

Spiral Review
Point of View
In lines 112–121, how does the use of first-person point of view shape what we know of the speaker's sister?

Literary Analysis
Romanticism and Diction
Does Wordsworth use simple or difficult words to describe old age? Are they specific or general?

Reading Strategy
Understanding the Historical Period How do the lines "let the misty mountain winds be free / To blow against thee" reflect Romantic beliefs and assumptions?

The guide, the guardian of my heart, and soul
Of all my moral being.
Nor perchance,
If I were not thus taught, should I the more
Suffer[6] my genial spirits[7] to decay;
For thou art with me here upon the banks
Of this fair river; thou my dearest Friend,[8]
My dear, dear Friend, and in thy voice I catch
The language of my former heart, and read
My former pleasures in the shooting lights
Of thy wild eyes. Oh! yet a little while
May I behold in thee what I was once,
My dear, dear Sister! and this prayer I make
Knowing that Nature never did betray
The heart that loved her; 'tis her privilege,
Through all the years of this our life, to lead
From joy to joy: for she can so inform
The mind that is within us, so impress
With quietness and beauty, and so feed
With lofty thoughts, that neither evil tongues,
Rash judgments, nor the sneers of selfish men,
Nor greetings where no kindness is, nor all
The dreary intercourse of daily life,
Shall e'er prevail against us, or disturb
Our cheerful faith, that all which we behold
Is full of blessings. Therefore let the moon
Shine on thee in thy solitary walk;
13 And let the misty mountain winds be free
To blow against thee: and, in after years,
When these wild ecstasies shall be matured
Into a sober pleasure; when thy mind
Shall be a mansion for all lovely forms,
Thy memory be as a dwelling place
12 For all sweet sound and harmonies; oh! then,
If solitude, or fear, or pain, or grief,
Should be thy portion, with what healing thoughts
Of tender joy wilt thou remember me,
And these my exhortations! Nor, perchance—
If I should be where I no more can hear
Thy voice, nor catch from thy wild eyes these gleams
Of past existence—wilt thou then forget
That on the banks of this delightful stream
We stood together; and that I, so long
A worshipper of Nature, hither came

6. **Suffer** allow.
7. **genial spirits** creative powers.
8. **Friend** his sister Dorothy.

Enrichment: Investigating Psychology

Psychology and the Child

In "Tintern Abbey," Wordsworth marks a decisive change between childhood and adulthood, a new idea in his time. Today, psychologists study child development. Maturational theorists see nervous system development as key. Behaviorists study the way children learn skills through reinforcement. Cognitive psychologists study motor development. Psychoanalysts, following Sigmund Freud, hold that the structure of the adult personality depends on the repression of childhood fantasies.

Analyze Child Psychology Encourage interested students to do further research on the field of child psychology. Have them record and analyze their findings using the **Enrichment: Investigating Psychology** worksheet, *Professional Development Guidebook,* page 239.

14

Tintern Abbey, J. M. W. Turner, © British Museum

Unwearied in that service: rather say
With warmer love—oh! with far deeper zeal
Of holier love. Nor wilt thou then forget,
That after many wanderings, many years
Of absence, these steep woods and lofty cliffs,
And this green pastoral landscape, were to me
More dear, both for themselves and for thy sake!

15 ▲ Critical Viewing

Compare the appreciation of light and sky shown by Romantic painter J. M. W. Turner with Wordsworth's descriptions in the poem. **[Compare and Contrast]**

Critical Reading

Cite textual evidence to support your responses.

1. **Key Ideas and Details (a)** How long has it been since the poet visited Tintern Abbey? **(b) Infer:** At what time of year does the poet make his second visit to the area? How do you know?
2. **Key Ideas and Details (a)** How have the poet's memories of his first visit helped him? **(b) Interpret:** In line 36 of the poem, the poet mentions "another gift" that his contact with this rural scene bestowed upon him. Briefly describe this gift.
3. **Key Ideas and Details** Explain the difference in the poet's attitude on his first and on his second visit to Tintern Abbey.
4. **Integration of Knowledge and Ideas (a)** What wish for his sister does the poet express toward the end of the poem? **(b) Connect:** What connection can you see between this wish, Wordsworth's thoughts in lines 22–31, and his hopes in lines 62–65?
5. **Integration of Knowledge and Ideas** Does Wordsworth express a deep truth about our relationships with nature, or are his reactions exaggerated? Explain.

15 Critical Viewing

Answer: Students should recognize that Turner's painting shares many qualities with Wordsworth's descriptions in the poem—the delicate treatment of light falling on Tintern Abbey, and the opening of the ruins onto the blue sky, as if revealing the infinite behind the enclosures of human artifice, evoke the elevated spirit of Wordsworth's experience of nature.

ASSESS

Answers

Before students respond, you may wish to have them write a brief objective summary of the selection. As they answer the questions below, remind them to support their answers with evidence from the text.

1. (a) It has been five years. (b) The time of year is summer. We learn this from the "unripe fruits" in line 12.
2. (a) These memories have soothed him and encouraged his kindness. (b) This other gift is a state of harmony with the world in which he sees into "the life of things" (lines 48–49).
3. On his second visit, to his pleasure is added a "sad perplexity" (line 60) and a new pleasure at the thought that his present experience will nourish him when he remembers it.
4. (a) He wishes that his sister will be helped by the memory of their visit. (b) In each case, the memory of nature has, or it is hoped will have, an inspiring effect.
5. **Possible responses:** Some students may say that he mystically exaggerates our ordinary appreciation of nature.

Differentiated Instruction for Universal Access

Strategy for Less Proficient Readers

Some students who have read "Tintern Abbey" with teacher guidance may still have difficulty with comprehension. You may want to consider using the **Reading Strategy Graphic Organizer A**, page 140 in ***Graphic Organizer Transparencies,*** to assess what information they have retained from their reading and to determine what aspects of the poem they still need to study.

Enrichment for Advanced Readers

After students have completed reading "Tintern Abbey," have them reread the section in which Wordsworth discusses his sister. Then, have students write short stories in which they describe a day in the life of Dorothy and William Wordsworth. Encourage students to use as many details from the poem as possible.

16 About the Selection

"The Prelude" is Wordsworth's lament over the failure of the French Revolution to live up to its early possibilities and rebuild society on just and rational principles. The poem describes the excitement stirred up by the original promise of the Revolution, the eventual corruption of its ideals, and the poet's struggle with the implications of the atrocities committed in the name of Revolution.

17 Literary Analysis

Romanticism and the Lyric

1. Remind students that Romanticism reflected the poetic discovery of elevated feelings and truths in the world of common experience.
2. **Ask** students: What connection can you find between the spirit described in these lines and the spirit of Wordsworth's "rebellion" against old styles of poetry?
   Answer: Students should recognize that Wordsworth's enthusiasm for "youth" and for the discovery of romance in the ordinary are motivations both for a new style in poetry and for social change. Just as the Revolution transformed the dry stuff of the law into something out of a fairy tale—by transforming the law, people could transform the world to fit human nature—so Wordsworth's new style transformed the dry, artificial verse of the past into a means of expressing more basic truths about human experience.

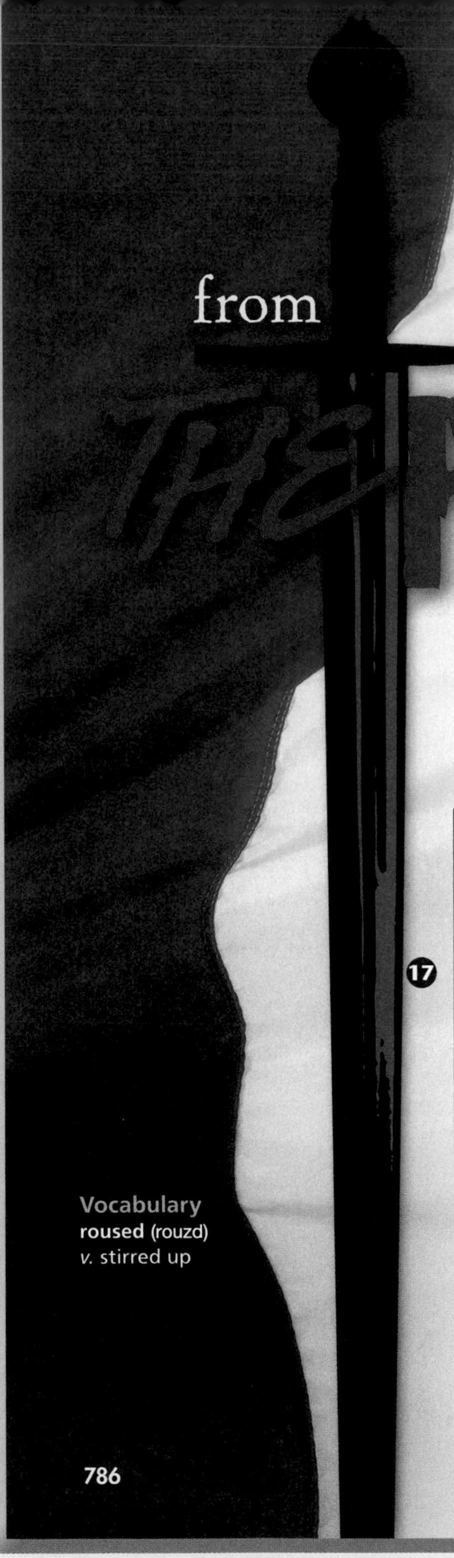

BACKGROUND In 1790, Wordsworth witnessed the early, optimistic days of the French Revolution. The country seemed on the verge of achieving true freedom from outdated, oppressive feudal institutions. Caught up in the revolutionary fervor, Wordsworth felt he was seeing "France standing on the top of golden hours." The war between England and France (declared in 1793) and the violent turn taken by the French Revolution, known as the Reign of Terror (1793–1794), dashed Wordsworth's hopes.

from THE Prelude 16

WILLIAM WORDSWORTH

O pleasant exercise of hope and joy!
For mighty were the auxiliars which then stood
Upon our side, us who were strong in love!
Bliss was it in that dawn to be alive,
But to be young was very Heaven! O times,
In which the meager, stale, forbidding ways
Of custom, law, and statute, took at once
The attraction of a country in romance!
When Reason seemed the most to assert her rights
When most intent on making of herself
A prime enchantress—to assist the work,
Which then was going forward in her name!
Not favored spots alone, but the whole Earth,
The beauty wore of promise—that which sets
(As at some moments might not be unfelt
Among the bowers of Paradise itself)
The budding rose above the rose full blown.
What temper at the prospect did not wake
To happiness unthought of? The inert
Were roused, and lively natures rapt away!
They who had fed their childhood upon dreams,
The play-fellows of fancy, who had made
All powers of swiftness, subtlety, and strength
Their ministers,—who in lordly wise had stirred
Among the grandest objects of the sense,
And dealt with whatsoever they found there

17

Vocabulary
roused (rouzd) *v.* stirred up

Enrichment: Analyzing a Literary Figure

Nature and Literature

Wordsworth's fascination with nature and its beneficial effects on his spirit was echoed in the writings of two American writers, Ralph Waldo Emerson and Henry David Thoreau, known as the American Romantics for the compatibility of their views with those of Wordsworth and Coleridge. Emerson and Thoreau, also known as Transcendentalists, lived in New England in the mid-nineteenth century and were advocates of the same kinds of appreciation of nature that Wordsworth sponsored in his writings. Both of the American writers stressed nature's ability to restore the human soul.

Activity: Researching a Romantic Encourage interested students to do further research on Ralph Waldo Emerson or Henry David Thoreau. Have them record and analyze their findings using the **Enrichment: Analyzing a Literary Figure** worksheet, ***Professional Development Guidebook,*** page 235.

18

19 ▲ Critical Viewing Compare and contrast the impression of the French Revolution conveyed by this poem to the one conveyed by this picture. **[Compare and Contrast]**

As if they had within some lurking right
To wield it;—they, too, who of gentle mood
Had watched all gentle motions, and to these
30 Had fitted their own thoughts, schemers more mild,
And in the region of their peaceful selves;—
Now was it that *both* found, the meek and lofty
Did both find helpers to their hearts' desire,
And stuff at hand, plastic as they could wish,—
35 Were called upon to exercise their skill,
Not in Utopia,—subterranean fields,—
Or some secreted island, Heaven knows where!
But in the very world, which is the world
Of all of us,—the place where, in the end,
40 We find our happiness, or not at all!

But now, become oppressors in their turn,
Frenchmen had changed a war of self-defense
For one of conquest, losing sight of all
Which they had struggled for: now mounted up,
45 Openly in the eye of earth and heaven,
The scale of liberty. I read her doom,
With anger vexed, with disappointment sore,
But not dismayed, nor taking to the shame
Of a false prophet. While resentment rose
50 Striving to hide, what nought could heal, the wounds
Of mortified presumption, I adhered

Vocabulary
presumption (prē zump´
shən) *n.* audacity; nerve

20 ✓ Reading
Check

To which two kinds
of people did the
Revolution appeal?

from The Prelude **787**

18 Humanities

Storming of the Bastille, 14 July 1789, Anonymous

This painting illustrates an important event in the French Revolution. On July 14, 1789, an angry mob protesting actions by King Louis XVI seized control of the long-hated Bastille prison, a symbol of royalty's absolute power. Many of the prisoners in the Bastille had been held without trial or legal cause. July 14 has since been celebrated as a French national holiday. *The Storming of the Bastille, 14 July 1789,* vividly captures the mob's assault on the prison. Use these questions for discussion:

1. How might Wordsworth have responded to the scene depicted in the painting?
Answer: He might have responded with enthusiasm for the spirit of liberation and democracy it represented.

2. How does the painting add to the poem's impact?
Answer: It explains some of the context and creates a visual image of revolutionary fervor.

19 Critical Viewing

Answer: Students should note that the painting depicts the violence and suffering that was involved in the Revolution, whereas this portion of "The Prelude" reveals the philosophical torment that resulted from the failure of the revolutionaries to live up to their ideals.

20 Reading Check

Answer: The Revolution appealed both to people "who had fed their childhood upon dreams" of ordering the world and to contemplative people who had adapted their thoughts to "all gentle motions."

Differentiated Instruction for Universal Access

Strategy for Less Proficient Readers
Have students read "The Prelude" with teacher guidance. Encourage them to focus on Wordsworth's feelings about the French Revolution. Direct students who are having difficulty to **Reading Strategy Graphic Organizer B,** page 141 in *Graphic Organizer Transparencies.*

Strategy for Gifted/Talented Students
Have students read "The Prelude" and create "Before" and "After" posters that express Wordsworth's feelings before and after his disillusionment with the French Revolution. Students may illustrate these changes and include examples.

Enrichment for Advanced Readers
In "The Prelude," Wordsworth describes how his feelings toward the French Revolution have changed. Have students write poems describing something about which they have changed their opinions. Have them compare their poems with an excerpt from "The Prelude."

21 Vocabulary

Forms of *anatomize*

1. Call students' attention to *anatomize*, a word that means "to dissect in order to examine structure." Explain to students that *anatomize* is related to the noun *anatomy* and the adjective *anatomical;* all of them come from the same Greek root.
2. Have students suggest other related words, and list them on the chalkboard.
   Possible responses: *anatomist, atom, atomism*
3. Have students look up any unfamiliar words in a dictionary.

ASSESS

Answers

Before students respond, you may wish to have them write a brief objective summary of the selection. As they answer the questions below, remind them to support their answers with evidence from the text.

1. (a) He characterizes them with the phrase "O pleasant exercise of hope and joy!" (b) This reaction reflects basic values of freedom and social equality. (c) Reason seemed to serve high ideals in the Revolution.
2. (a) The French became "oppressors," conquering other regions. (b) At first, Wordsworth tried to justify continued faith in the Revolution; in the end, he lost all feelings of conviction.
3. (a) When he turned aside from Nature's way, he became so misguided by maxims and creeds that he had to give up all of his convictions. (b) Wordsworth resolves his conflict by giving up his attempts to explain and justify.

More firmly to old tenets, and, to prove
Their temper, strained them more; and thus, in heat
Of contest, did opinions every day
Grow into consequence, till round my mind
They clung, as if they were its life, nay more,
The very being of the immortal soul.

I summoned my best skill, and toiled, intent
21 To anatomize the frame of social life,
Yea, the whole body of society
Searched to its heart. Share with me, Friend! the wish
That some dramatic tale, endued with shapes
Livelier, and flinging out less guarded words
Than suit the work we fashion, might set forth
What then I learned, or think I learned, of truth,
And the errors into which I fell, betrayed
By present objects, and by reasonings false
From their beginnings, inasmuch as drawn
Out of a heart that had been turned aside
From Nature's way by outward accidents,
And which are thus confounded,[1] more and more
Misguided, and misguiding. So I fared,
Dragging all precepts, judgments, maxims, creeds,
Like culprits to the bar; calling the mind,
Suspiciously, to establish in plain day
Her titles and her honors; now believing,
Now disbelieving; endlessly perplexed
With impulse, motive, right and wrong, the ground
Of obligation, what the rule and whence
The sanction; till, demanding formal *proof,*
And seeking it in every thing, I lost
All feeling of conviction, and, in fine,
Sick, wearied out with contrarieties,
Yielded up moral questions in despair.

Vocabulary
anatomize (ə nat′ ə mīz′) *v.* to dissect in order to examine structure

1. **confounded** (kən found′ id) *adj.* confused; mixed together indiscriminately; bewildered

Critical Reading

Cite textual evidence to support your responses.

1. **Key Ideas and Details (a)** With what phrase does the speaker describe the early days of the French Revolution? **(b) Generalize:** What basic values does his reaction reflect? **(c) Interpret:** What role did reason seem to play in the Revolution?
2. **Key Ideas and Details (a)** What change in the course of the French Revolution caused a conflict in Wordsworth? **(b) Interpret:** What two reactions to this turn of events does Wordsworth describe?
3. **Key Ideas and Details (a) Interpret:** What does Wordsworth say happened to him when his heart "had been turned aside / From Nature's way"? **(b) Interpret:** At the end of the excerpt, how has Wordsworth resolved his conflict?

Enrichment: Analyzing Music

Romantic Music

The Romantic movement was not confined to literature. Music was also deeply affected by Romantic ideals, reverberating with new emotional significance. Composers such as Ludwig van Beethoven, Johannes Brahms, Robert Schumann and his wife Clara Schumann, and Felix Mendelssohn created works ranging from symphonies to chamber music to *lieder* (popular songs).

Like Wordsworth's poetry, Romantic music often reflected social events.

Activity: Analyzing Romantic Music
Encourage interested students to do further research on music of the Romantic period. Have them record and analyze their findings using the **Enrichment: Analyzing Music** worksheet, ***Professional Development Guidebook,*** page 236.

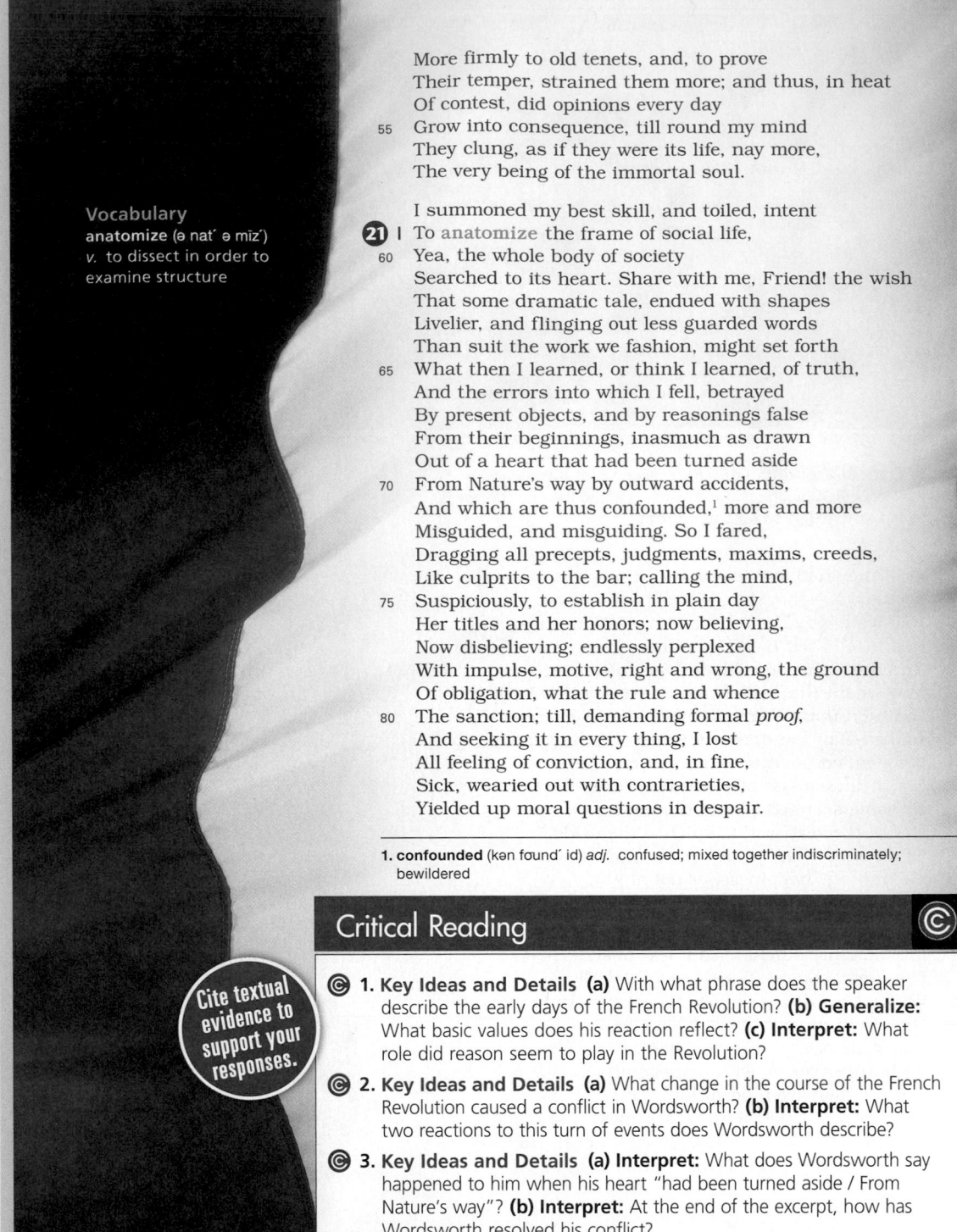

Critical Commentary

"The White Knight's Song"
Lewis Carroll

Lewis Carroll was the pseudonym of Charles Lutwidge Dodgson, the English author who wrote Alice's Adventures in Wonderland*.*

Writers with a well-defined style and beliefs are the most tempting to parody, especially if they do not show much humor themselves. Wordsworth fit these requirements, and therefore was a tempting target for Lewis Carroll, author of *Alice in Wonderland.* Carroll parodied Wordsworth's famous poem "Resolution and Independence," which contains the following account of a meeting with a strange old man:

. . . I saw a Man before me unawares:
The oldest man he seemed that ever wore gray hairs. . . .

Like a sea-beast crawled forth, that on a shelf
Of rock or sand reposeth, there to sun itself;

Such seemed this Man, not all alive or dead,
Nor all asleep—in his extreme old age . . .

The poet then asks this old man, who has been staring at the "muddy water" of a pond, "What occupation do you there pursue?" The man responds as follows:

He told, that to these waters he had come
To gather leeches, being old and poor:
Employment hazardous and wearisome!
And he had many hardships to endure:
From pond to pond he roamed, from moor to moor . . .

Carroll parodied this encounter in "The White Knight's Song":

I'll tell thee everything I can:
There's little to relate.
I saw an aged, aged man,
A-sitting on a gate.

"Who are you, aged man?" I said
"And how is it you live?"
And his answer trickled through my head
Like water through a sieve.
He said, "I look for butterflies
That sleep among the wheat:
I make them into mutton-pies
And sell them in the street. . . .

Key Ideas and Details How does the old man Wordsworth meets in "Resolution and Independence" make his living? In Carroll's parody of Wordsworth's poem, how does the "aged man" make his living?

Parody, a composition that imitates and makes fun of another, is actually a humorous form of literary criticism. In order to ridicule a writer's style, a parodist has to understand and reproduce it accurately enough for the reader to recognize. The parodist then exaggerates some aspect of the style or subject to make the reader laugh. The result is a caricature, rather than a portrait—recognizable, but silly.

David Levine's caricature of William Wordsworth

INTRODUCE/ASSESS

Answers

Critical Commentary

1. Read aloud the excerpt from Wordsworth's poem "Resolution and Independence." Ask students why they think Wordsworth would have written about such a subject.
2. Read aloud the excerpt from Carroll's poem "The White Knight's Song." Ask students if they're able to see Wordsworth's style and/or content reflected in Carroll's work. Have them point out specific examples and how they relate.
3. Review the definition of a parody with students.
4. Discuss with students how Carroll's poem is a parody of Wordsworth's. Steer the discussion to answer the question of whether Carroll's work was meant as an insult or a compliment.

Key Ideas and Details

Answers

1. The old man collects leeches.
2. The aged man collects butterflies, bakes them into pies, and sells the pies on the street.

Enrichment: Analyzing Forms and Genres

Parody

Parody has been a recognized writing form for hundreds of years. One of the earliest examples is a parody of Homer's epic writing style by an anonymous poet of ancient Greece. Shakespeare included parody in the players' scene in *Hamlet* that criticized Christopher Marlowe's dramatic writing style. The first widely successful collection of parodies was *Rejected Addresses,* published in England in 1812 and written by Horace and James Smith. They mimicked poets such as Scott, Byron, Southey, Wordsworth, and Coleridge.

Activity: Analyzing Parody Encourage interested students to do further research on the parody genre. Have them record and analyze their findings using the **Enrichment: Analyzing Forms and Genres** worksheet, ***Professional Development Guide,*** page 227.

㉒ About the Selections

In these sonnets, Wordsworth criticizes social attitudes prevalent in his day. In "The World Is Too Much With Us," he laments the materialism and preoccupation with business that have blinded people to the wonder of being. Wordsworth offers as contrast pagan society, which saw nature not as a mass of "resources" but as the manifestation of the gods.

Wordsworth wrote "London, 1802" after a brief return visit to France. The contrast between what he called the "vanity and parade" of London life and the "desolation" after the Revolution in France moved him to denounce what he saw as the self-absorption and falseness of the English people.

㉓ Critical Viewing

Possible responses: Some students will say that a field of flowers does move us emotionally; others will note that Wordsworth is pointing out that, as a society, we do not appreciate nature as deeply as do cultures that personify its forces.

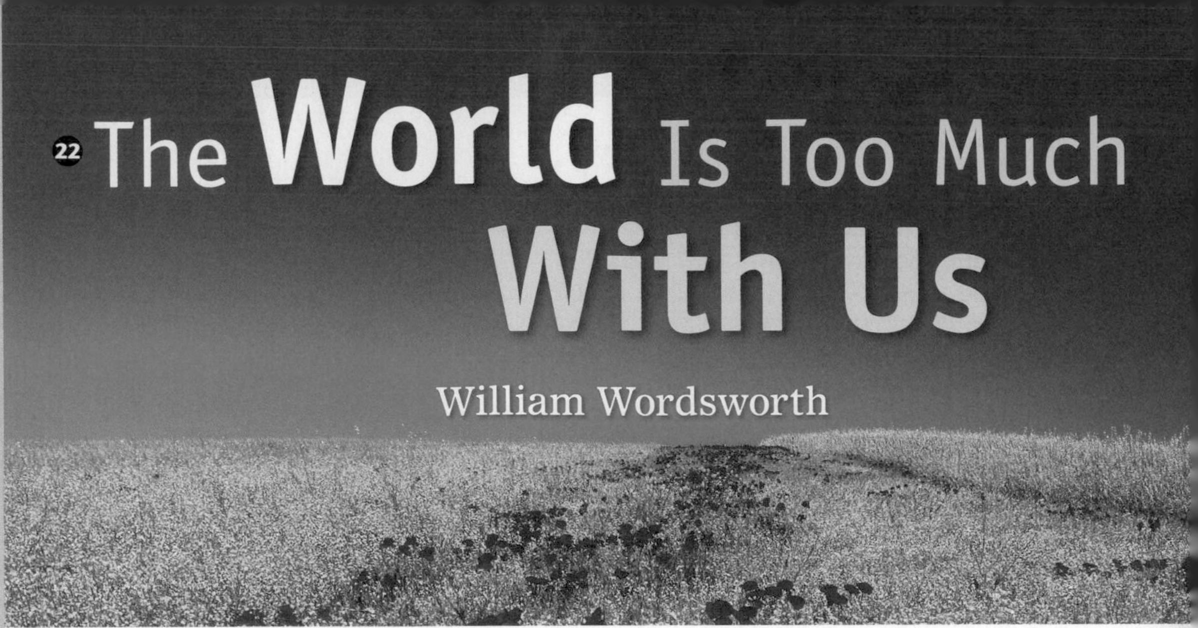

㉒ The World Is Too Much With Us

William Wordsworth

㉓ ▲ **Critical Viewing**
Do you agree with Wordsworth that an image such as this one "moves us not"? Explain. **[Make a Judgment]**

Vocabulary
sordid (sôr′ did) *adj.* dirty

The world is too much with us; late and soon,
Getting and spending, we lay waste our powers:
Little we see in Nature that is ours;
We have given our hearts away, a sordid boon![1]
This Sea that bares her bosom to the moon;
The winds that will be howling at all hours,
And are upgathered now like sleeping flowers;
For this, for everything, we are out of tune;
It moves us not.—Great God! I'd rather be
A Pagan suckled in a creed outworn;
So might I, standing on this pleasant lea,[2]
Have glimpses that would make me less forlorn;
Have sight of Proteus[3] rising from the sea;
Or hear old Triton[4] blow his wreathèd horn.

1. **boon** favor.
2. **lea** meadow.
3. **Proteus** (prō′ tē əs) in Greek mythology, a sea god who could change his appearance at will.
4. **Triton** in Greek mythology, a sea god with the head and upper body of a man and the tail of a fish.

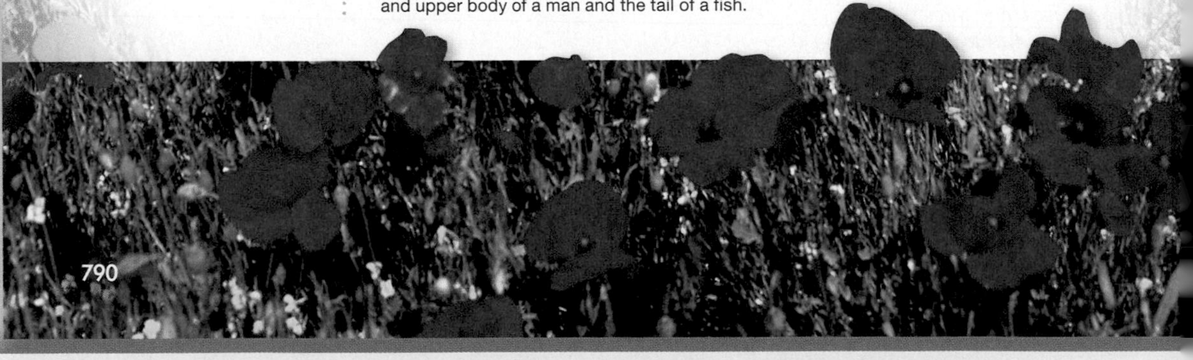

Vocabulary Development

Vocabulary Knowledge Rating

When students have completed reading and discussing the selections, have them take out their **Vocabulary Knowledge Rating Charts** for the story. Read the words aloud and have students rate their knowledge of words again in the After Reading column. Clarify any words that are still problematic. Have students write their own definitions and example or sentence in the appropriate column. Then, have students complete the Vocabulary Practice at the end of the selection. Encourage students to use the words in further discussion and written work about the selection. Remind them that they will be accountable for these words on the **Selection Test,** ***Unit 4 Resources,*** pages 79–81 or 82–84.

22

London, 1802

William Wordsworth

Milton![1] thou should'st be living at this hour:
England hath need of thee: she is a fen[2]
Of **stagnant** waters: altar, sword, and pen,
Fireside, the heroic wealth of hall and bower,
Have forfeited their ancient English dower
Of inward happiness. We are selfish men;
Oh! raise us up, return to us again;
And give us manners, virtue, freedom, power.
Thy soul was like a Star, and dwelt apart:
Thou hadst a voice whose sound was like the sea:
Pure as the naked heavens, majestic, free,
So didst thou travel on life's common way,
In cheerful godliness; and yet thy heart
The lowliest duties on herself did lay.

Vocabulary
stagnant (stag′ nənt) *adj.* motionless; foul

1. **Milton** seventeenth-century English poet John Milton.
2. **fen** (fen) *n.* area of low, flat, marshy land.

Critical Reading

Cite textual evidence to support your responses.

1. **Key Ideas and Details (a)** In "The World Is Too Much With Us," what activities cause people to exhaust their "powers"? **(b) Interpret:** What does the speaker mean by the "world"?
2. **Key Ideas and Details (a)** According to the speaker, with what are we "out of tune"? **(b) Interpret:** Why is being out of tune with these experiences such a loss?
3. **Key Ideas and Details (a)** According to "London, 1802," what is England like? **(b) Analyze:** What lacks or missing qualities have caused this condition? **(c) Interpret:** How would Milton's return help?
4. **Integration of Knowledge and Ideas** What qualities do you find in Wordsworth's poems that make him a poetic rebel? In your response, use at least two of these Essential Question words: *traditional, interpretation, rebellious. [Connecting to the Essential Question: What is the relationship of the writer to tradition?]*

ASSESS

Answers

Before students respond, you may wish to have them write a brief objective summary of the selection. As they answer the questions below, remind them to support their answers with evidence from the text.

1. (a) People waste their powers by "getting and spending." (b) "The world" means material concerns.
2. (a) According to the speaker, we are out of tune with the moonlit, calm sea and with nature generally. (b) Being out of tune with nature means that we live in a world that is cold and sterile; we do not find things of human value and significance in nature ("Little we see in Nature that is ours," line 3).
3. (a) England is stagnant, lacking in "inward happiness," and filled with selfish, mediocre people. (b) This condition results from the fact that the English lack "manners, virtue, freedom, power." (c) Milton's moral vision and example would help restore England to its former ways.
4. Students may refer to Wordsworth's use of nature as inspiration, his romantic word choice, or his use of personification.

Concept Connector

Reading Strategy Graphic Organizer

Ask students to review the graphic organizers in which they have identified revolutionary political and philosophical assumptions in Wordsworth's work. Then, have students share their organizers and compare their findings.

Activating Prior Knowledge

Have students return to their responses to the Activating Prior Knowledge activity. Ask them to explain whether their thoughts have changed and, if so, how.

Writing About the Essential Question

Have students compare their responses to the prompt, completed before reading the poems, with their thoughts afterward. Have them work individually or in groups, writing or discussing their thoughts, to formulate new responses. Then, lead a class discussion, probing for what students have learned that confirms or invalidates their initial thoughts. Encourage students to cite specific textual details to support their responses.

Answers

1. **Possible response:** Wordsworth's idealized feeling for nature is revealed in lines 93–102 of "Tintern Abbey."
2. **Possible response:** Passages such as the one that begins "My dear, dear Friend, . . ." ("Tintern Abbey," line 116) use regular language, but elevate the ideas with adjectives and metaphors.
3. **Possible response:** Students may say that in both "Tintern Abbey" and "The Prelude" Wordsworth shows that losses or changes can lead to growth.
4. Specific and Simple: ". . . I again repose/Here, under this dark sycamore, ..."; Abstract but Simple: "The anchor of my purest thoughts . . ."; Abstract and Difficult: "A motion and a spirit, that impels / All thinking things . . ."
5. **Possible response:** Wordsworth's diction is fairly consistent. Students should quote passages to support their arguments.
6. Student answers will vary, but must be clear representations of Romantic diction.
7. (a) These lines suggest that political idealism, youthful enthusiasm, and a desire for change were important elements of this context. (b) Romantic hopes and dreams could not be satisfied through reliance on reason.
8. **Possible response:** Students may say that the Neoclassical writer would respond with puzzlement at lines that treat nature emotionally. The writer would view Wordsworth's style with disdain, since it does not use the refined vocabulary or polished expressions of ideas.
9. **Possible response:** Wordsworth probably would not have appreciated the way in which computers remove us from nature, but he might have approved of the information they provide, which helps us learn more about nature.

After You Read

Poetry of William Wordsworth

Literary Analysis

1. **Key Ideas and Details** Identify a passage from the poems that illustrates Wordsworth's idealized view of nature.
2. **Key Ideas and Details** Find a passage that reflects the **Romantic** belief in the dignity and importance of ordinary people and common language.
3. **Integration of Knowledge and Ideas** Romantic **lyrics** focus on the speaker's personal development. What lessons from Wordsworth's growth might readers adopt?
4. **Integration of Knowledge and Ideas** Using a chart like the one shown, find examples in the poems of **diction** that is specific and simple, abstract but simple, or abstract and difficult. Then, summarize your results.

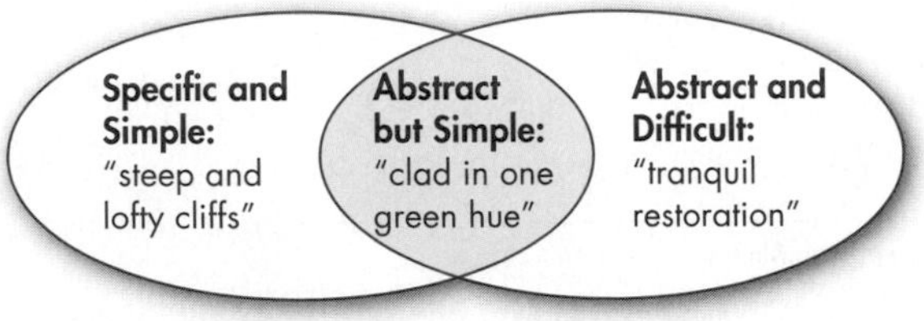

5. **Comparing Literary Works** Wordsworth's subjects in these poems range widely, from natural scenes to politics to modern life. Does his diction vary to match his subject? Support your answer with details from the poems.
6. **Comparing Literary Works** Identify two passages, each from a different poem, whose diction would have seemed revolutionary to Neoclassical poets. Then, explain your choices.

Reading Strategy

7. **(a)** What do the hopes described in *The Prelude* tell you about the *political and philosophical assumptions* of the **historical period** in which Romanticism was born? **(b)** What do lines 66–84 suggest about the Romantics' view of reasoning not guided by the heart? Explain.
8. Imagine that you are a Neoclassical writer—a sociable city-dweller who writes polished, witty, rational verse. Explain how you might react to lines 76–80 of "Tintern Abbey."
9. Would Wordsworth have appreciated modern technology such as computers and the Internet? Support your answer by referring to the political and philosophical assumptions of Romanticism.

Common Core State Standards

Language
4.b. Identify and correctly use patterns of word changes that indicate different meanings or parts of speech. *(p. 793)*
5.b. Analyze nuances in the meanings of words with similar denotations. *(p. 793)*

Assessment Practice

Critical Reasoning (For more practice, see *All-in-One Workbook*.)

Many tests require students to judge the relevance of facts in a writer's argument. Use the following sample item.

These waters, rolling from their mountain springs
With a soft inland murmur. Once again
Do I behold these steep and lofty cliffs,
That on a wild secluded scene impress
Thoughts of more deep seclusion; and connect
The landscape with the quiet of the sky.

Which of these facts would not reinforce the mood Wordsworth is trying to create?

A There is a lark singing in the hedgerows.
B Wordsworth can clearly see the mountains.
C Wordsworth is wearing new boots.
D There is dew beading the grass.

Help students recognize that Wordsworth is emphasizing nature's beauty. Choice **C**, which has nothing to do with this theme, is the correct answer.

PERFORMANCE TASKS

Integrated Language Skills

Vocabulary Acquisition and Use

Word Analysis: Forms of *anatomize*

The verb *anatomize*, meaning "cut into constituent parts," or "dissect," comes from the Greek word *atomos*, meaning "that which cannot be cut further; the smallest part." In *anatomizing* society, Wordsworth attempts to dissect it into the parts that make it up. Several scientific words come from this Greek word. Explain how, as the use of the root changes, each word has a different function or meaning.

1. atom
2. anatomy
3. anatomical
4. atomizer

Root words are modified when affixes are attached. Identify four words with the root *-string-* or *-strict-* ("to draw tight") and explain how each differs in meaning.

Vocabulary: Synonyms

A *synonym* is a word that has the same, or a similar, meaning as another word. Write the letter of the word that is the best synonym of each word from the vocabulary list on page 779. Then, write an original sentence using each vocabulary word.

1. recompense: **(a)** assistance, **(b)** penitence, **(c)** reward
2. roused: **(a)** angered, **(b)** stirred, **(c)** interfered
3. presumption: **(a)** audacity, **(b)** flattery, **(c)** attractive
4. anatomize: **(a)** address, **(b)** dissect, **(c)** respect
5. sordid: **(a)** dirty, **(b)** organized, **(c)** reclassified
6. stagnant: **(a)** direct, **(b)** foul, **(c)** repugnant

Using Resources to Build Vocabulary

Epic Style: Words for Nature

Words have **denotations,** which are their basic meanings, and also **connotations,** which are the feelings or ideas associated with them. For instance, *tired* and *spent* both denote a loss of physical energy from exertion, but *spent* suggests a more extreme state, in which all stamina or tolerance for a difficult situation is gone.

Poets use connotations to add depth and richness to their poems. Wordsworth reveals his feelings for nature through these words from "Tintern Abbey" that he uses to describe it:

sublime (lines 37, 95)

power (line 47)

harmony (line 48)

spirit (line 100)

Use a print or electronic *dictionary* or *thesaurus* to find synonyms of these words. Explain how the connotation of each word differs from that of at least one synonym.

Assessment Resources

Unit 4 Resources

L1 L2 EL **Selection Test A,** pp. 79–81. Administer Test A to less advanced readers.

L3 L4 EL **Selection Test B,** pp. 82–84. Administer Test B to on-level students and more advanced students.

L3 L4 **Open-Book Test,** pp. 76–78. As an alternative, give the Open-Book test.

All **Customizable Test Bank**

All **Self-tests**

Students may prepare for the **Selection Test** by taking the **Self-test** online.

PHLit Online! All assessment resources are available at **www.PHLitOnline.com.**

Vocabulary Acquisition and Use

Word Analysis

Possible responses

1. the smallest part into which something can be divided
2. the study of parts
3. pertaining to the structure of an organism
4. a device used to reduce liquids to a fine spray

constrict "to tighten"

restrict "to limit"

district "a division"

strictness "rigidity"

Vocabulary

Possible responses:

1. C; The recompense for her efforts was a promotion.
2. B; His aggressive posturing roused her defenses.
3. A; The pompous actor had the presumption to assume the role in the play would be his, even without trying out for it.
4. B; She liked to anatomize her father's arguments in order to rebut them.
5. A; Their sordid scheme would be found out in the end.
6. B; The stagnant pool of water emitted a terrible stench.

Using Resources to Build Vocabulary

Possible responses:

1. divine; *sublime* is a stronger description
2. ability; not as strong in connotation as *power*
3. cooperation; *harmony* suggests peace, but *cooperation* suggests teamwork
4. essence; *essence* is related to *essential* while *spirit* is related to *spiritual*

Writing

You may use this Writing Lesson as timed-writing practice, or you may allow students to develop the response as an assignment over several days.

1. To guide students in writing this argumentative text, give them the **Support for Writing Lesson, Unit 4 Resources,** page 74.
2. Explain that in this lesson, students will write responses to a critic's observation about Wordsworth.
3. Remind students that the foundation of a response to criticism is evidence in the text that supports or disproves the critical observation.
4. Remind students to include quotations from Wordsworth's poems to support their thesis statements.
5. Use the Writing Lesson to guide students in developing their responses to criticism.
6. Have students use Rubrics for Response to Literature in the ***Professional Development Guidebook,*** pages 250–251 to evaluate their essays.

PERFORMANCE TASKS

Integrated Language Skills

Writing

Argumentative Text Literary critic Harold Bloom expressed the following insight into Wordsworth's work: "The fear of mortality haunts much of Wordsworth's best poetry, especially in regard to the premature mortality of the Imagination and the loss of its creative joy."

Do you agree or disagree with this evaluation? Prepare an **essay** that refutes or supports Bloom's view.

Prewriting Begin by carefully rereading the poems by Wordsworth in the text.

- After finishing each poem, think about Wordsworth's attitudes toward the loss of imaginative power.
- Note the *imagery, figures of speech, personification,* and *sounds* in the poems that *evoke readers' emotions* and relate to the *theme* of "premature mortality of the Imagination."
- Write a sentence or two to serve as the *thesis* of your essay, and develop an outline that shows how you will support your thesis.

Drafting Write a draft of your essay that follows your outline.

- In the opening paragraph, remember to quote or paraphrase Bloom's insight; to state your thesis clearly, agreeing or disagreeing with Bloom; and to offer a brief explanation of your position.
- Be sure to support your thesis in the body of the essay, making *detailed and accurate references* to the text of Wordsworth's poems.
- Conclude the essay by summarizing what you proved.

Revising Revise your essay to make it clear and effective:

- Review your draft, making sure you have details to support your points. Where they are lacking, find them in the text and add them.
- Determine whether the opening paragraph, in particular, engages the reader's interest as well as setting forth your thesis.
- Check quotations to be sure they are accurate and properly referenced.
- Read the essay carefully to make sure it is grammatically correct and all words are spelled correctly.

Model: Revising to Clearly State Your Position

Much of Wordsworth's work seems to focus on the transience of time. Close reading of his poetry, *however,* suggests that rather than a fear of mortality, his work presents a celebration of life.

Using conjunctions signals agreement or disagreement.

Common Core State Standards

Writing

1.a. Introduce precise, knowledgeable claim(s), establish the significance of the claim(s), distinguish the claim(s) from alternate or opposing claims, and create an organization that logically sequences claim(s), counterclaims, reasons, and evidence.

1.e. Provide a concluding statement or section that follows from and supports the argument presented.

9.a. Apply *grades 11–12 Reading standards* to literature.

Language

1. Demonstrate command of the conventions of standard English grammar and usage when writing or speaking. *(p. 795)*

5.a. Interpret figures of speech in context and analyze their role in the text.

Teaching Resources

Unit 4 Resources

- L3 L4 **Vocabulary Builder,** p. 72
- L3 L4 **Support for Writing Lesson,** p. 74
- L3 L4 **Grammar and Style,** p. 73
- L4 **Enrichment,** p. 75
- All **Interactive Grammar Tutorial:** available under After You Read for this selection
- All **Enriched Online Student Edition Internet Research Activity:** available under After You Read for this selection
- All ***Professional Development Guidebook*** **Rubrics for Self-Assessment: General Writing Rubric,** pp. 298–299

PHLit Online! All resources are available at **www.PHLitOnline.com.**

Conventions and Style: Pronoun-Antecedent Agreement Problems

To write effectively, avoid vague or confusing sentences by using pronouns correctly. Remember that a **pronoun** stands for a noun. The noun is the **antecedent.**

Example: *Wordsworth's* poetry shows *his* love of nature.

Problems in Agreement

Avoid **unintended shifts in person or gender**. It is easy to make accidental errors.

Shift in Person William Wordsworth visited Tintern Abbey, where you saw the ruins.
Revised William Wordsworth visited Tintern Abbey, where he saw the ruins.

Shift in Gender Dorothy Wordsworth, the poet's sister, was himself a very good writer.
Revised Dorothy Wordsworth, the poet's sister, was herself a very good writer.

Watch out for **indefinite pronouns**, such as *all, few, most,* and *none*. Some of them can be either singular or plural.

Most of his *poetry* is read for *its* images.

Most of his *poems* are read for *their* images.

Be sure it is clear to which nouns your pronouns refer.

Unclear Reference Triton and Proteus were sea gods. He was part man and part fish.
Revised Triton was part man and part fish. He and Proteus were sea gods.

Practice Rewrite each sentence, correcting the problem in antecedent and pronoun agreement.

1. Milton and Wordsworth were both English poets. He wrote "London, 1802."
2. There is a poem about the French Revolution in my textbook, but I cannot find it.
3. Poets write of meadows and woods. They are inspiring.
4. Nature is loyal to those who cherish her as it accompanies them through life.
5. The French people lost sight of the reason it fought the French Revolution.
6. Much of the abbey is in ruins, but their former grandeur remains today.
7. Although he has been away five years, the poet remembers the hills for her beauty.
8. One of the landscapes certainly will make their impression.
9. England was going in the wrong direction. They had forgotten manners. They had forgotten freedom.
10. People were interested in worldly things, and you were ignoring nature.

Writing and Speaking Conventions

A. Language Use each pronoun to write a sentence with correct pronoun and antecedent agreement. Choose from these antecedents: *nature, world, beliefs, England, Wordsworth, hope and joy, poets.*

1. he **2.** it **3.** they **4.** her **5.** its

Example: its
Sentence: The *world* offers us *its* beauty to appreciate.

B. Writing As Wordsworth's sister, write a brief letter to Wordsworth after your visit together to Tintern Abbey. Describe the landscape and what you enjoyed about the visit. Use at least two examples of pronoun-antecedent agreement.

PH WRITING COACH
Further instruction and practice are available in *Prentice Hall Writing Coach.*

Extend the Lesson

Sentence Modeling

Present students with this sentence from "Lines Composed a Few Miles Above Tintern Abbey":

My dear, dear Sister! and this prayer
I make / Knowing that Nature never did
betray / The heart that loved her . . .

Ask students what they notice about this sentence. Elicit from them that the poet begins with his sister as the antecedent and later refers to nature as *her*. Ask students if they notice anything else unique about the sentence.

Have students imitate the sentence they analyzed in a sentence on a topic of their own choosing, matching each grammatical and stylistic feature discussed. Collect the sentences and share them with the class.

Conventions and Style

Practice

1. Milton and Wordsworth were both English poets. Wordsworth wrote "London, 1802."
2. There is a poem about the French Revolution in my textbook, but I cannot find the poem.
3. Poets are inspiring. They write of meadows and woods.
4. Nature is loyal to those who cherish her as she accompanies them through life.
5. The French people lost sight of the reason they fought the French Revolution.
6. Much of the abbey is in ruins, but its former grandeur remains today.
7. Although he has been away for five years, the poet remembers the hills for their beauty.
8. One of the landscapes certainly will make its impression.
9. England was going in the wrong direction. It had forgotten manners. It had forgotten freedom.
10. People were interested in worldly things, and they were ignoring nature.

Writing and Speaking Conventions

A. **Sample responses**

1. Wordsworth was a Romantic poet. He was in touch with nature.
2. Wordsworth loved nature and enjoyed writing about it.
3. Sometimes, poets write about experiences they had as children.
4. Nature rewards those who respect her.
5. Our world has its own history.

B. **Sample responses**

Dear William, Thank you so much for taking me to visit Tintern Abbey. It was absolutely beautiful. The view of the sky was gorgeous. It took my breath away. I hope we can go there again sometime! Your sister, Dorothy

PH WRITING COACH Grade 12

Students will find instruction on and practice with pronoun-antecedent agreement in Chapter 13, section 1.

The Muse's Children: Lyric Poets in World Literature

1. Have a volunteer read aloud the paragraph at the top of the page.
2. **Ask** students what the pictures of the writers have in common.
   Answer: They are all playing instruments.
3. **Ask** students what they can deduce about lyric poetry from this similarity.
   Answer: Lyric poetry has a lot to do with music.
4. Tell students this background is why we refer to the words of a song as "lyrics."

Background

Greek Mythology

The ancient Greeks embraced a set of stories about their heroes and gods to explain the ways of the world and the significance of their ways of life. This is what we refer to as Greek mythology. Just as Erato is the Greek goddess of lyric poetry, many other elements of life were associated with a god or goddess. For example, Ares is the god of war, Hades is the god of the dead, Athena is the goddess of courage and wisdom, and Aphrodite is the goddess of beauty and love.

THE *Muse's* CHILDREN: LYRIC POETS IN WORLD LITERATURE

Erato—LYRIC POETRY IS NAMED FOR THE LYRE, A STRINGED INSTRUMENT USED BY THE ANCIENT GREEKS TO ACCOMPANY RECITATIONS OF POETRY. THE GREEKS DEPICTED THE GODDESS ERATO, SHOWN HERE PLAYING THE LYRE, AS THE MUSE OR PATRON OF LYRIC POETRY.

TU FU
(712–770) CHINESE

ONO KOMACHI
(c. 820–c. 900) JAPANESE

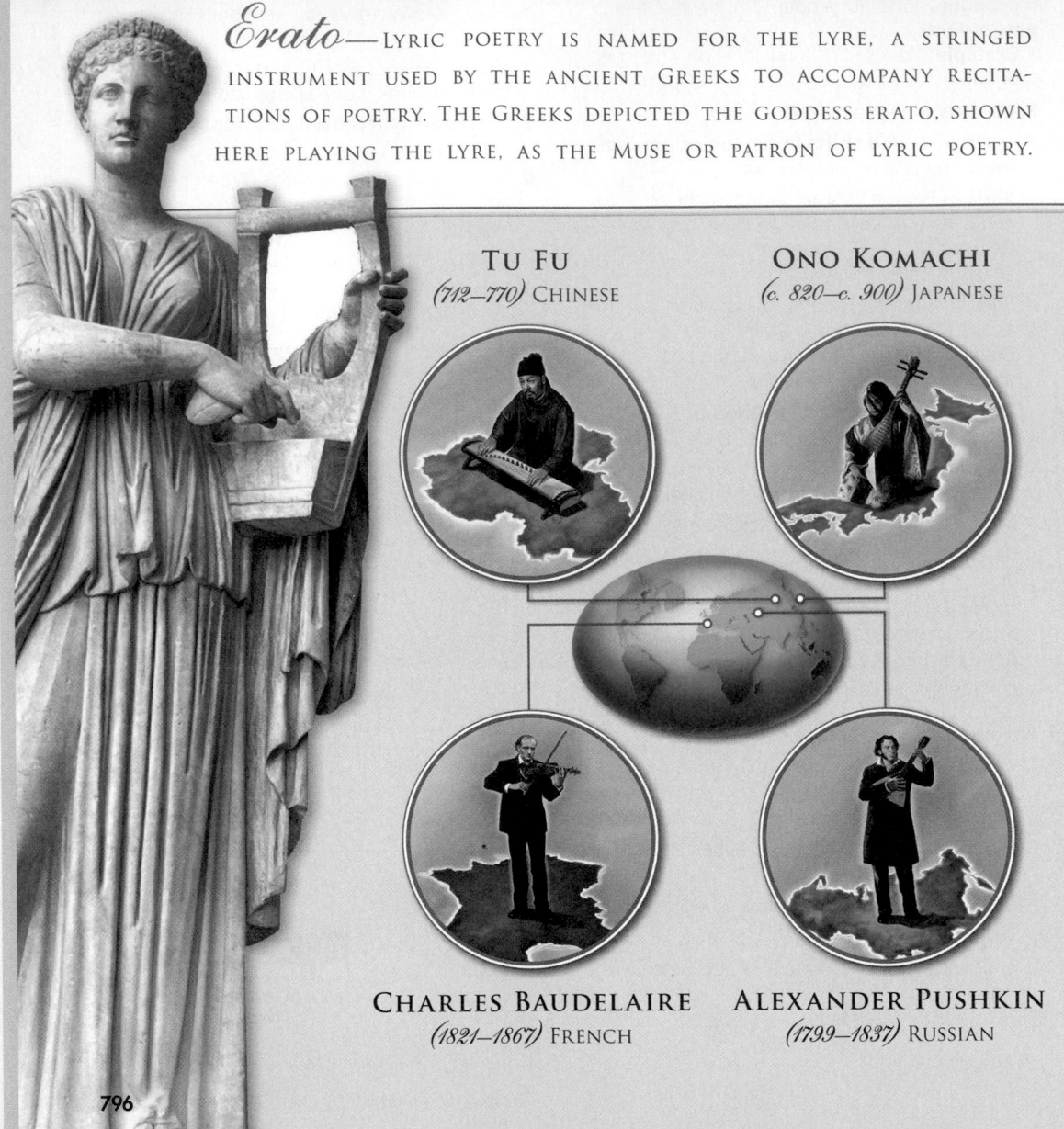

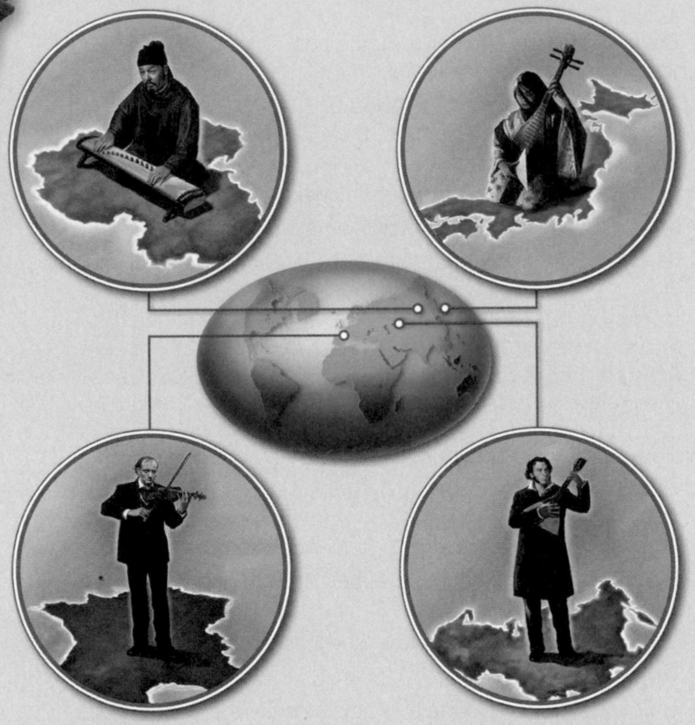

CHARLES BAUDELAIRE
(1821–1867) FRENCH

ALEXANDER PUSHKIN
(1799–1837) RUSSIAN

Comparing Literary Works

Poetry of William Wordsworth • Lyric Poetry from Around the World

Comparing Lyric Poetry from Around the World

Lyric Poetry Lyric poetry began in song. In fact, the word *lyric* comes from *lyre*, the harplike instrument that ancient Greek poets like Sappho played to accompany their lyric poems. Even before the Greeks, however, people were singing poems expressing faith, love, sorrow, joy, and other strong emotions. Love lyrics survive from ancient Egypt's New Kingdom (c. 1570–1070 B.C.). The philosopher Confucius is said to have compiled the *Book of Songs*, collecting Chinese poetry written as early as 1100 B.C.

Lyric poetry typically has these characteristics:

- It is brief and concise.
- It is communicated by a single speaker expressing personal emotions and observations.
- It uses vivid images to convey ideas and evoke emotions.
- It is musical, often employing rhyme, alliteration, and repetition and following a pattern of rhythm (called meter) or a pattern of syllables.

For lyric poems that you read, fill in charts like this one. Then, use your charts to answer comparison-and-contrast questions about the poems.

Common Core State Standards

Reading Literature
5. Analyze how an author's choices concerning how to structure specific parts of a text contribute to its overall structure and meaning as well as its aesthetic impact.

Language
4.c. Consult general and specialized reference materials, both print and digital, to find the pronunciation of a word or determine or clarify its precise meaning, its part of speech, its etymology, or its standard usage.

	"The World Is Too Much With Us"	"I Have Visited Again"
Form and/or lines	Petrarchan sonnet; 14 lines	
Speaker	Lover of nature	
Observations	Society is too materialistic; nature's beauty is unappreciated.	
Emotions	Unhappiness with society; joy and wonder in nature	
Images	Vivid sights and sounds of wild and pagan sea	
Sound devices	Rhyme, meter, some alliteration, assonance	

Gather Vocabulary Knowledge

These lyric poets use words such as *fathomless, treacherous,* and *splendor.* Use a **dictionary** to find each word's part of speech and definition. Then, employ the following references (printed or electronic) to explore these words:

- **History of Language:** Use a history of English to research each word's etymology, or origins.
- **Book of Quotations:** Use a collection of quotations to find a statement containing one of the words. In a paragraph, explain the nuances in meaning that are evident from the context of the quotation.

Comparing References Compare and contrast what you learn about the words from these specialized references.

PHLit Online! www.PHLitOnline.com

Common Core State Standards

- **Reading Literature 5**
- **Language 4.c**

Comparing Lyric Poetry from Around the World

1. Have students write the lyrics to a song they have memorized. If they do not know any, have them find the lyrics to a song on the Internet or provide them with one.
2. Have them compare their lyrics to the characteristics described on the student page. Discuss with students how the lyrics are different and/or similar.
3. Repeat the process with a poem, but have students browse through a few first until they can spot one that uses the characteristics described on the page. Have a few volunteers read their chosen poems aloud to the class. Have the class discuss why they are lyric poems.

Gather Vocabulary Knowledge

Have print and electronic resources available for students to use to explore the origins and meanings of the words. When students search for quotations, encourage them to use related forms of the words. Display the two following quotations and discuss with students how context helps them understand the meanings of *fathomable* and *unfathomable.* Guide students to recognize the nuances of meaning.

"The greatness of truth is unfathomable and it is mightier than anything in this world." Samaveda

"It is of great use to the sailor to know the length of his line, though he cannot with it fathom all the depths of the ocean." John Locke

Guide students to recognize how the different meanings of the words contribute to the layers of meaning in the Locke quotation.

Teaching Resources

The following resources can be used to enrich, extend, or differentiate the instruction.

All *Unit 4 Resources,* pp. 85–87

All **Enriched Online Student Edition**

All *Common Core Companion,* pp. 54–60; 324–331

PHLit Online! All resources are available at www.PHLitOnline.com

Daily Bellringer

As you teach the Comparing Literary Works selection, have students complete the Grammar, Usage, and Mechanics activities that remain for the relevant week in the *Daily Bellringer Activity* booklet.

Multidraft Reading

To assist struggling readers and to enhance reading for all, assign the text in chunks as warranted by length and apply multidraft reading protocols. For each reading, have students set the purpose indicated:

- **First reading**—identifying key ideas and details and answering any Reading Checks.
- **Second reading**—analyzing craft and structure and responding to the side-column prompts.
- **Third reading**—integrating knowledge and ideas, connecting to other texts and the world, and answering the end-of-selection questions.

For more guidance, refer to the ***Classroom Strategies and Teaching Routines*** on **Multidraft Reading.**

Background

More About the Authors

Alexander Pushkin not only wrote poems, but plays as well. His first play, *Boris Godunov,* was notable for several reasons. He based the plot on a legendary incident in Russian history, and his characters were real Russians. Pushkin also experimented with the Romantic tragedy genre, much like Shakespeare. While the play never reached production, it did have some considerable influence on future playwrights and later became the basis of an operatic work.

Charles Baudelaire's work had many influences. He was influenced by the poetry of Edgar Allen Poe, who was seemingly more in touch with the dark side of the imagination. He was also influenced by the paintings of Eugene Delacroix and Edouard Manet, as well as by the music of Richard Wagner. The exotic themes in his writing quickly caught the government's attention. As a result, he was fined for "immorality" and forced to remove some of the poems from his collection. In his anger and frustration, his work turned darker, which provided more influence for future artists.

Alexander Pushkin (1799–1837)

Author of "I Have Visited Again"

Russian author Alexander Pushkin was born in Moscow into an aristocratic family. As a youth, he led a life of relative privilege and wrote with a skill that would hint at his eventual fame. While working in government service in St. Petersburg, he aroused suspicion by associating with political rebels and writing poems advocating government changes. In 1820, the government acted upon its suspicions by reappointing Pushkin to a post in a remote province in southern Russia. During the five years Pushkin spent there, he enhanced his reputation as a writer and began working on his masterpiece, the verse novel *Yevgeny Onegin* (1833). Unfortunately, his unrestrained and sometimes violent behavior resulted in his dismissal from civil service in 1824 and banishment to his family's estate.

Though isolated and unhappy on the estate, Pushkin channeled most of his energy into his writing. He spent much of his time interacting with the peasants who lived on the estate, learning about their lifestyles, and incorporating their legends and folklore into a number of his finest poems.

Acts of Rebellion Pushkin was allowed to return to Moscow in 1826. After marrying Natalya Goncharova in 1831, Pushkin grudgingly returned to government service. In a final act of rebellion, Pushkin entered into a duel that cost him his life.

Charles Baudelaire (1821–1867)

Author of "Invitation to the Voyage"

Charles Baudelaire (shárl bōd ler′) was one of the most colorful, startling, and innovative poets of the nineteenth century. Attempting to break away from the Romantic tradition, Baudelaire created poems that are objective rather than sentimental. Many of his works celebrate the city and the artificial rather than nature.

As a youth, Baudelaire rebelled against his family to pursue a career as a writer. To dissuade him from such a dissolute life, they sent him on an ocean voyage to India. Instead of completing the voyage, he returned to France to claim his share of his late father's fortune. Soon, extravagant living drove him into debt, a problem that would plague him for the rest of his life.

Baudelaire published short stories, translated works by Edgar Allan Poe into French, and both wrote and collected poems for *Flowers of Evil* (1857), which would become his signature work. Although his talents were not widely recognized during his lifetime, Baudelaire's reputation blossomed posthumously, and he came to be considered one of the finest nineteenth-century poets.

798

❶ ❷

I Have Visited Again

Alexander Pushkin, translated by D. M. Thomas

BACKGROUND Initially, Alexander Pushkin found the inspiration to write in the politics of his homeland. His rebellious writings, as well as his unruly behavior, resulted in banishment to his family estate. Such a personality seems distantly related to the speaker of the gentle words and images in "I Have Visited Again." In this poem, the speaker revisits the estate to find that time and nature have hardly stood still in the intervening years.

Differentiated Instruction for Universal Access

Enrichment for Gifted/Talented Students

Encourage students to write their own lyric poems, to prepare them to further understand those in this section. You may suggest a topic or let students choose their own. Remind them of the characteristics of lyric poetry, including the important feature that it is often set to music.

Encourage musically talented students to set their poems to music. Encourage artistic students to illustrate or display their poems creatively. Have students present their poems to the class.

TEACH

❶ About the Selection

"I Have Visited Again" is sad and nostalgic, but a hopeful piece. It describes how a place at which the speaker spent two years of his life appears ten years later. Like his Romantic counterparts, Pushkin shows a strong connection to the natural surroundings.

❷ Activating Prior Knowledge

Survey the class to find if there is anyone who can remember a place from childhood he or she has not seen in a long while. Ask them how they would feel if they returned to that place and saw that it was quite different. If no places come to mind from childhood memories, pose the question about their present location, asking how they would feel coming back ten years later to find that it had changed.

PHLit Online!

These selections are available in the interactive format in the **Enriched Online Student Edition**, at **www.PHLitOnline.com**, which includes a thematically related video with a wrinting prompt and an interactive graphic organizer.

❸ Comparing Lyric Poetry

1. Tell students to pay special attention to Pushkin's treatment and description of nature. Have a volunteer read aloud lines 15–19 to the rest of the class.
2. Then, **ask** students the Comparing Lyric Poetry question.
3. **Possible response:** Students will most likely agree that the speakers share similar views of nature. They could elaborate on how lovingly Pushkin describes nature, which shows a connection. In Wordsworth's poetry, that same deep connection is evident.

Comparing Lyric Poetry
How is the speaker's experience here similar to that of the speaker in Wordsworth's "Lines Composed a Few Miles Above Tintern Abbey"? Do the two speakers share similar views of nature? Explain.

. . . I have visited again
That corner of the earth where I spent two
Unnoticed, exiled years. Ten years have passed
Since then, and many things have changed for me,
And I have changed too, obedient to life's law—
But now that I am here again, the past
Has flown out eagerly to embrace me, claim me,
And it seems that only yesterday I wandered
Within these groves.

Here is the cottage, sadly
Declined now, where I lived with my poor old nurse.
She is no more. No more behind the wall
Do I hear her heavy footsteps as she moved
Slowly, painstakingly about her tasks.

Here are the wooded slopes where often I
Sat motionless, and looked down at the lake,
Recalling other shores and other waves . . .
It gleams between golden cornfields and green meadows,
A wide expanse; across its fathomless waters
A fisherman passes, dragging an ancient net.
Along the shelving banks, hamlets are scattered
—Behind them the mill, so crooked it can scarcely
Make its sails turn in the wind . . .

On the bounds
Of my ancestral acres, at the spot
Where a road, scarred by many rainfalls, climbs
The hill, three pine-trees stand—one by itself,
The others close together. When I rode
On horseback past them in the moonlit night,
The friendly rustling murmur of their crowns
Would welcome me. Now, I have ridden out
Upon that road, and seen those trees again.
They have remained the same, make the same murmur—
But round their ageing roots, where all before
Was barren, naked, a thicket of young pines
Has sprouted; like green children round the shadows
Of the two neighboring pines. But in the distance
Their solitary comrade stands, morose,
Like some old bachelor, and round its roots
All is barren as before.

Vocabulary
ancestral (an ses′ trəl) *adj.* inherited
morose (mə rōs′) *adj.* gloomy; sullen

Enrichment: Analyzing Music

Contemporary Lyric Poets
In today's world, musical artists sometimes combine lyrics and music to convey a message. Play some excerpts from songs that clearly show how lyrics and music work together to convey a message. One example is Simon and Garfunkel's "Bridge Over Troubled Water," which uses hymn-like music to convey a message of comfort and reassurance.

Activity: Analyzing Music Encourage students to look for examples of contemporary lyric poets in their musical repertoires. Each student should locate a song, bring in a recording, introduce and summarize the song, and make a list of attributes that led him or her to believe the song is an example of lyrics and music working together to convey a message. Have them further analyze their song using the **Enrichment: Analyzing Music** worksheet, ***Professional Development Guidebook***, page 236.

I greet you, young
And unknown tribe of pine-trees! I'll not see
Your mighty upward thrust of years to come
When you will overtop these friends of mine
And shield their ancient summits from the gaze
Of passers-by. But may my grandson hear
Your welcome murmur when, returning home
From lively company, and filled with gay
And pleasant thoughts, he passes you in the night,
And thinks perhaps of me . . .

And I have changed too, obedient to life's law—

Critical Reading

1. **Key Ideas and Details** **(a)** Identify four familiar landmarks in the poem that have changed over the years. **(b) Infer:** How has the speaker changed in a similar fashion?
2. **Key Ideas and Details** **(a)** In stanza three, what thoughts occupy the speaker while he looks down at the lake? **(b) Infer:** What does the speaker mean by "other shores"? **(c) Hypothesize:** Why might the speaker have yearned to be in another place?
3. **Craft and Structure** **(a)** Where does the "unknown tribe of pine-trees" grow? **(b) Speculate:** What role will those pines play in the future? **(c) Interpret:** What do those pines symbolize?
4. **Integration of Knowledge and Ideas** Novelist Thomas Wolfe commented on how our lives change by saying that we "can't go home again," a theme shared by "I Have Visited Again." Do you agree or disagree with such a claim? Explain your answer.

Cite textual evidence to support your responses.

ASSESS

Answers

Before students respond, you may wish to have them write a brief objective summary of the selection. As they answer the questions below, remind them to support their answers with evidence from the text.

1. (a) The cottage is "sadly declined," young pine trees now grow, the road is "scarred by many rainfalls," and the mill is "so crooked it can scarcely make its sails turn in the wind." (b) The speaker has grown old, as in the line "obedient to life's law," and now speaks of a grandson.
2. (a) He reflects upon the scenery surrounding the lake and comments on "its fathomless waters." (b) He is talking about other lakes he has seen since he left this one. (c) **Possible response:** He may have yearned to be in another place because he is so upset at how much this place has changed.
3. (a) It grows at the base of the older, taller trees he once rode past. (b) They will be what the speaker's grandson admires, much like the older trees the speaker admired when he was younger. (c) **Possible response:** They symbolize the continuance of life.
4. **Possible response:** Students may agree or disagree with the claim. They must, however, cite specific evidence from the poem to support their answers.

Differentiated Instruction for Universal Access

Culturally Responsive Instruction

Culture Focus Point out to students how in the second stanza, the speaker remembers his nurse and how she "moved / Slowly, painstakingly about her tasks." Explain to students that in Britain, beginning mainly in the seventeenth century, families employed the help of a wet nurse to help raise their children. A wet nurse breastfed and cared for a baby in the mother's place. Nursing was considered unsanitary for the mother and was said to ruin her body. The nurses were often known as *nannies* and remained employed to help raise the children. In the poem, the speaker is referring to the nurse who cared for him and worked for his family when he was young.

❹ About the Selection

The speaker in "Invitation to the Voyage" is eager to get away from his harsh reality and travel to a more ideal world. The speaker writes the poem to describe how beautiful the ideal world would be. Writing in a smooth flow and in rhyme that is pleasing to the ear enhances his descriptions of the ideal world.

❺ Critical Thinking

Infer

1. After students have read the poem, ask them to recall the background information about Charles Baudelaire from the Before You Read section.
2. **Ask** students to use what they know about Baudelaire from the Background information to infer why he would want to write about traveling to such an ideal world with "richness, quietness, and pleasure."
3. **Possible response:** Baudelaire struggled with money and rejection all his life. He probably wrote about such a world because that is what he imagined his own ideal world to be. He wished to be debt free, comfortable, worry free, and surrounded by beauty.

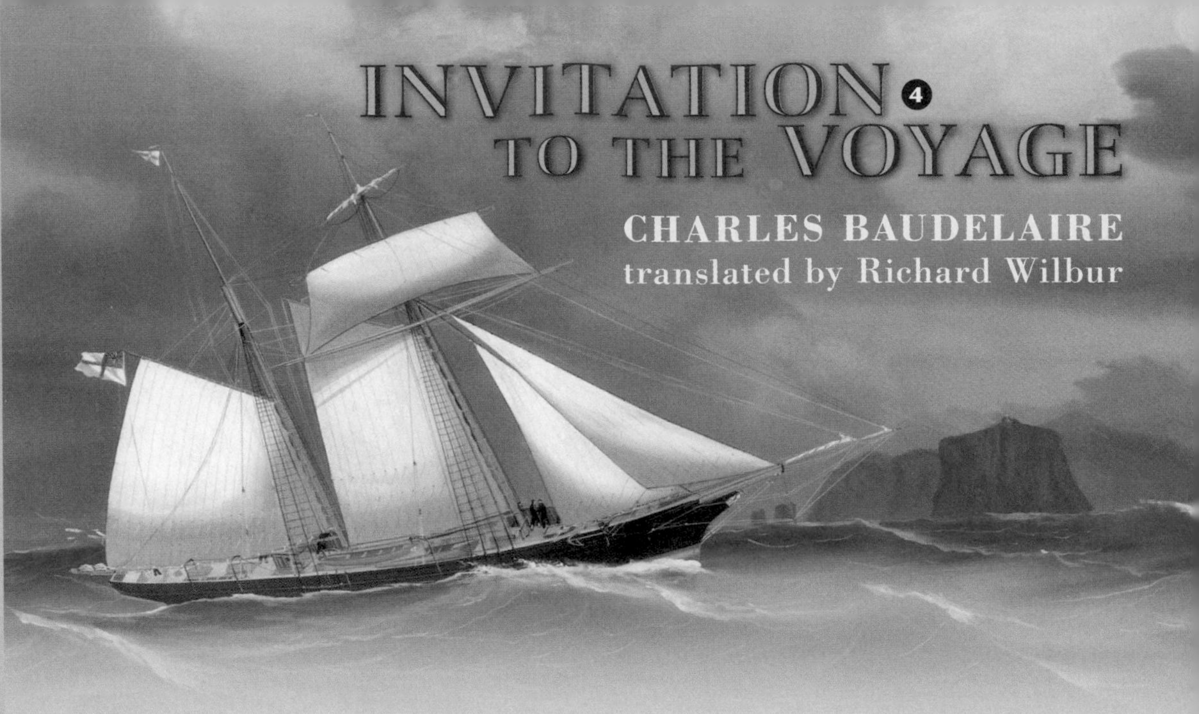

INVITATION TO THE VOYAGE ❹

CHARLES BAUDELAIRE
translated by Richard Wilbur

BACKGROUND There is little doubt that Charles Baudelaire's ocean voyage to India was a significant event in his life. Although the journey was cut short—lasting only eight months instead of eighteen—❺ the experience clearly inspired him as a poet. The voyage, his desire for a life of ease and luxury, and his yearning to escape reality all find expression in his poem "Invitation to the Voyage."

My child, my sister, dream
How sweet all things would seem
Were we in that kind land to live together
And there love slow and long,
There love and die among
Those scenes that image you, that sumptuous[1] weather.
Drowned suns that glimmer there
Through cloud-disheveled[2] air
Move me with such a mystery as appears
Within those other skies
Of your treacherous eyes
When I behold them shining through their tears.

---

1. **sumptuous** (sump´ cho͞o əs) *adj.* magnificent or splendid.
2. **disheveled** (di shev´ əld) *adj.* disarranged and untidy.

Enrichment: Investigating Geography

The Indian Ocean
When Charles Baudelaire went to India by boat, he could not have gotten there without traveling through the Indian Ocean. The Indian Ocean is the smallest of the world's major oceans. It has an area of about 28,360,000 square miles and is more than 6,200 miles wide. Located off the southern coast of Java, the Sunda Deep of the Java Trench is the ocean's deepest point at 24,442 feet.

Activity: A Trip to India Using a map, point out to students that there are many ways to travel from France to India by sea. Have students create a map that depicts a possible route for an ocean voyage from France to India. To begin, have them complete the **Enrichment: Investigating Geography** worksheet, *Professional Development Resources,* page 228.

There, there is nothing else but grace and measure,
Richness, quietness, and pleasure.

Furniture that wears
The luster of the years
Softly would glow within our glowing chamber,
Flowers of rarest bloom
Proffering their perfume
Mixed with the vague fragrances of amber;
Gold ceilings would there be,
Mirrors deep as the sea,
The walls all in an Eastern splendor hung—
Nothing but should address
The soul's loneliness,
Speaking her sweet and secret native tongue.

There, there is nothing else but grace and measure,
Richness, quietness, and pleasure.

See, sheltered from the swells
There in the still canals
Those drowsy ships that dream of sailing forth;
It is to satisfy
Your least desire, they ply
6 Hither through all the waters of the earth.
The sun at close of day
Clothes the fields of hay,
Then the canals, at last the town entire
In hyacinth and gold:
Slowly the land is rolled
Sleepward under a sea of gentle fire.

There, there is nothing else but grace and measure,
Richness, quietness, and pleasure.

Vocabulary
proffering (präf′ ər iŋ) *v.* offering

Comparing Lyric Poetry
How is the landscape described here unlike the landscape described in Pushkin's poem? What feelings does the speaker of each poem seem to have for the landscape he describes?

Critical Reading

1. **Key Ideas and Details (a)** Which details describe the "kind land" in "Invitation to the Voyage"? **(b) Interpret:** What impression of the land do these details convey?
2. **Integration of Knowledge and Ideas** How does the world described in "Invitation to the Voyage" compare to your ideal world?

Cite textual evidence to support your responses.

Differentiated Instruction for Universal Access

Strategy for Special-Needs Students

Have students move a piece of paper down the page to allow them to see only a few lines of the poem at a time. Have them read each chunk of the poem and then summarize it or write what they think it means on a sheet of paper. After reading the entire poem, have them put all their summaries together to figure out the meaning or message behind the poem.

EL Strategy for English Learners

Before reading the poem, review with students the vocabulary words on the page, including any unfamiliar ones. Have them write sentences using the words.

6 Comparing Lyric Poetry

1. Have students recall the attitude Pushkin had for his surroundings in "I Have Visited Again."
2. Then, **ask** students the Comparing Lyric Poetry question: How is the landscape described here unlike the landscape described in Pushkin's poem? What feelings does the speaker of each poem seem to have for the landscape he describes?
3. **Possible response:** Pushkin describes a real landscape that has aged and contains new elements. The landscape in this poem is fictional, ideal, and has not been seen by the speaker. The speaker in Pushkin's poem is nostalgic about the landscape he describes, having fond memories of it flourishing when he was young. The speaker in Baudelaire's poem yearns to be a part of the landscape he describes.

ASSESS

Answers

Before students respond, you may wish to have them write a brief objective summary of the selection. As they answer the questions below, remind them to support their answers with evidence from the text.

1. (a) The main detail that's constantly repeated is that it is a land of "richness, quietness, and pleasure." (b) **Possible response:** It is a place where one is not wanting for material objects, and it is filled with things that make the speaker very happy. It is also a place that is not busy or bustling, and therefore quiet.
2. **Possible response:** Students' answers will vary, but should show an understanding of the world Baudelaire wrote about in his poem.

Background

More About the Authors

Tu Fu failed to pass the imperial civil service examinations and, as a result, spent many years as a wanderer. His poetry reflects the cruelty and corruption of the court and the suffering of the poor. He was at times bitter, yet still managed to be humorous and hopeful.

Ki Tsurayuki helped assemble the poetry anthology *Kokinshu.* He also wrote a prose introduction for the anthology, in which he discusses the styles and nature of the included poetry. His introduction is considered one of the masterpieces of early Japanese prose.

Ono Komachi was a prominent and gifted poet in her day. She was able to weave emotional intensity, multiple entendres, and metaphors together to form elegant poetry.

Priest Jakuren was a renowned court poet. He did not write many poems, but those he did compose were some of the finest of the period. Emperor Gotoba commissioned him to help compile the eighth imperial anthology; however, Priest Jakuren died before the anthology was completed.

Chinese Poets

BOOK OF SONGS

The Book of Songs, also known as *The Book of Odes,* is an anthology of 305 ancient Chinese poems. The poems come from many different regions of China. Most of them were originally folk songs describing people's daily activities. Others, like "Thick Grow the Rush Leaves," focus on love or courtship. All of the songs were originally set to music.

TU FU (712–770)

Author of "Jade Flower Palace"

Tu Fu (do͞o′ fo͞o′) is regarded as the supreme craftsman of Chinese shih (shi) poetry. In all of his poetry—poems dealing with social issues and those that focus on his personal experiences—Tu Fu shows a command of language and a mastery of the shih form. As a result, his poems are admired as much for their form as for their content.

Early in Tu Fu's career, China was relatively peaceful, but later the poet witnessed a major rebellion, the destruction of the capital city, and an invasion by tribes from the northwest. In his poems, Tu Fu gives some of the most vivid accounts of war and destruction in all of Chinese literature.

Japanese Poets

KI TSURAYUKI (died c. 945)

The chief aide of Emperor Daigo (dī′ gō′), Ki Tsurayuki (kē tso͞or′ ī o͞o kē) was one of the leading poets, critics, and diarists of his time. Tsurayuki deserves much of the credit for assembling an anthology of over eleven hundred poems of the Heian (hā′ än′) Age. In addition, his *Tosa Diary* helped to establish the Japanese tradition of the literary diary.

ONO KOMACHI (c. 820–c. 900)

A great beauty with a strong personality, Ono Komachi (ō′ nō′ kō′ mä′ chē′) was an early tanka (täŋ′ kə) poet whose poems are characterized by their passion and energy. Few details of Ono Komachi's life are known.

PRIEST JAKUREN (1139?–1202)

Jakuren (jä′ ko͞o′ ren′) was a Buddhist priest and prominent tanka poet whose poems are filled with beautiful yet melancholic imagery. After entering the priesthood at the age of twenty-three, Jakuren spent much of his time traveling the Japanese countryside, writing poetry and seeking spiritual fulfillment.

Enrichment: Investigating a Key Person in History

Confucius

The Book of Songs was compiled around 600 B.C. According to a first-century B.C. Chinese historian, the 305 poems featured in the book were personally chosen by Confucius from among a collection of more than 3,000. He selected them based on their representation of diplomacy and social harmony. Confucius referred to the chosen poems frequently in his teachings and had his disciples study them carefully. Confucius's advocacy for the book helped it survive.

Activity: Biography Encourage interested students to find out more about Confucius, his life, and his teachings. Have them use the **Enrichment: Investigating a Key Person in History** worksheet, *Professional Development Guidebook,* page 233.

FROM **THE BOOK OF SONGS**

Thick Grow the Rush Leaves

TRANSLATED BY ARTHUR WALEY

Thick grow the rush leaves;
Their white dew turns to frost.
He whom I love
Must be somewhere along this stream.
I went up the river to look for him,
But the way was difficult and long.
I went down the stream to look for him,
And there in mid-water
Sure enough, it's he!

Close grow the rush leaves,
Their white dew not yet dry.
He whom I love
Is at the water's side.
Up stream I sought him;
But the way was difficult and steep.
Down stream I sought him,
And away in mid-water
There on a ledge, that's he!

Very fresh are the rush leaves;
The white dew still falls.
He whom I love
Is at the water's edge.
Up stream I followed him;
But the way was hard and long.
Down stream I followed him,
And away in mid-water
There on the shoals is he!

7

▼ **Critical Viewing**
How is the river in this painting similar to or different from the one in the poem, along which "the way was difficult and long"? **[Compare and Contrast]**

7 Critical Viewing

Possible response: The painting seems to be an illusion. The river does not appear to be very long at first glance. Looking deeper, however, it becomes apparent that the first appearance was deceiving and that the river is quite long. The picture is like the poem in that the speaker always sees her love and attempts to make her way to him, only to find that the road is much longer and more difficult than originally anticipated. In the picture, one may think the end is near at first glance, but then find that it is indeed much farther away than originally anticipated.

Differentiated Instruction for Universal Access

Strategy for Less Proficient Readers
Have students elaborate on the scenes in "Thick Grow the Rush Leaves." List their descriptions on the chalkboard. Then, compare their descriptions with the details in the poem. Discuss how the poet has succeeded in suggesting change through the selection of choice details.

Strategy for Gifted/Talented Students
Have students elaborate on the scenes in "Thick Grow the Rush Leaves." Then, have them illustrate the poem. Compare their illustrations with the details in the poem. Discuss how the poet has succeeded in suggesting change through the selection of choice details.

Strategy for Advanced Readers
Have students elaborate on the scenes in "Thick Grow the Rush Leaves." Then, have them discuss the mood the poem creates and the relationship between the poet and nature that it implies. Discuss how the poet has succeeded in suggesting this mood through the selection of choice details.

8 Critical Viewing

Possible response: The building in the poem is a palace that stands beside cliffs. The building in the picture does not stand beside cliffs and does not look as spectacular as the palace the poem describes, though it is large. The girl in the drawing appears to be dancing and is very colorful.

Jade Flower Palace

TU FU

TRANSLATED BY KENNETH REXROTH

Vocabulary

scurry (skʉr´ ē) *v.* to run hastily; to scamper

pathos (pa´ thəs´) *n.* quality that evokes sorrow or compassion

imperceptibly (im´ pər sep´ tə blē) *adv.* without being noticed

The stream swirls. The wind moans in
The pines. Gray rats **scurry** over
Broken tiles. What prince, long ago,
Built this palace, standing in
Ruins beside the cliffs? There are
Green ghost fires in the black rooms.
The shattered pavements are all
Washed away. Ten thousand organ
Pipes whistle and roar. The storm
Scatters the red autumn leaves.
His dancing girls are yellow dust.
Their painted cheeks have crumbled
Away. His gold chariots
And courtiers are gone. Only
A stone horse is left of his
Glory. I sit on the grass and
Start a poem, but the **pathos** of
It overcomes me. The future
Slips **imperceptibly** away.
Who can say what the years will bring?

8 ▶ **Critical Viewing** How is the building in this photo different from the palace described in "Jade Flower Palace"? How is the girl in the drawing on the facing page like the "dancing girls" found in the poem? **[Connect]**

Enrichment: Analyzing Forms and Genres

Waka

Waka is a term used to describe all forms of Japanese court poetry from the sixth to the fourteenth centuries. The tanka is one such form. Other forms include the sedoka, or "head-repeated poem," which consists of two stanzas of five, seven, and seven syllables each. A poem of indefinite length, made up of alternating lines of five and seven syllables, ending with an extra line of seven syllables is called a *choka*. Renga, "linked verse," and haiku are also forms of waka poetry.

Activity: Waka Poems Have students further research a specific form of waka poetry. Have them record their findings using the **Enrichment: Analyzing Forms and Genres** worksheet, ***Professional Development Guidebook***, page 227. Then have students write a poem of the form they researched.

BACKGROUND All three of the following poems are tanka. The tanka is the most prevalent verse form in traditional Japanese literature. In the original Japanese, each tanka consists of five lines of five, seven, five, seven, and seven syllables. Tanka usually tell a brief story or express a single thought or insight, usually relating to love or nature.

Priest Jakuren

TRANSLATED BY GEOFFREY BOWNAS

9

One cannot ask loneliness
How or where it starts.
On the cypress-mountain,[1]
Autumn evening.

Ki Tsurayuki

TRANSLATED BY GEOFFREY BOWNAS

When I went to visit
The girl I love so much,
That winter night
The river blew so cold
That the plovers[2] were crying.

1. **cypress-mountain** Cypress trees are cone-bearing evergreen trees, native to North America, Europe, and Asia.
2. **plovers** (pluv′ ərz) *n.* wading shorebirds with short tails, long, pointed wings, and short, stout beaks.

9 Critical Thinking

Draw Conclusions

1. Tell students that freezing a single moment in time, these tanka can be likened to Romantic lyric poetry because of their emphasis on nature and emotion. Whether describing the connection between loneliness and an autumn evening, or describing a lover's perilous journey, these tanka demonstrate nature's constant presence in our lives.
2. **Ask** students what mood predominates Priest Jakuren's poem.
   Possible response: The tone is quiet and meditative.
3. **Ask** students what relationship Priest Jakuren sees between loneliness and nature.
   Possible response: Priest Jakuren seems to see humanity through natural objects and scenes, subordinating human concerns to their place in nature.

Differentiated Instruction for Universal Access

Strategy for Less Proficient Readers

Help students understand the poems by identifying key words, such as *loneliness, autumn, love,* and *winter.* Have students determine the importance of each word, first in general, and then in the poem. Have them identify the connections between the words in each poem, thereby extracting a possible meaning.

EL Strategy for English Learners

Help students understand the poems by providing clear definitions for key words, such as *loneliness, autumn, love,* and *winter.* Have students determine the importance of each word, first in general, and then in the poem. Have them identify the connections between the words in each poem, thereby extracting a possible meaning.

⑩ Comparing Lyric Poetry

Answer: The translator best retains the original syllabification in the poem by Ono Komachi.

ASSESS

Answers

Before students respond, you may wish to have them write a brief objective summary of the selection. As they answer the questions below, remind them to support their answers with evidence from the text.

1. (a) The appearance of the rush leaves, the path the speaker took, and where the speaker's love appears change slightly in each stanza. (b) **Possible response:** The images reflect a fish's journey up- and downstream as the seasons change. (c) **Possible response:** Images help convey emotions because they give the reader a different perspective, which helps enforce ideas.
2. (a) All that remains is a stone horse. (b) **Possible response:** Stone represents permanence, while the other elements the poet describes are wistful and subject to change. (c) **Possible response:** Even though most of the prince's legacy is gone, he is not completely gone. He still prevails somewhat in spirit, perhaps.
3. (a) The poem takes place on a winter night. (b) It suggests the speaker's love is strong and impenetrable.
4. (a) The speaker is wondering if the man came to her in her dreams because he was in her thoughts upon falling asleep. (b) She indicated that if the man was in fact the man she wanted, she would not want to have woken up, suggesting she cares for and wants to be with him.

Ono Komachi

TRANSLATED BY GEOFFREY BOWNAS

⑩ **Comparing Lyric Poetry** In which of the three tanka does the translator best retain the original syllabification?

Was it that I went to sleep
Thinking of him,
That he came in my dreams?
Had I known it a dream
I should not have wakened.

Critical Reading

Cite textual evidence to support your responses.

1. **Craft and Structure (a)** In "Thick Grow the Rush Leaves," which images in each stanza are repeated with slight variations? **(b) Infer:** What activity on the river do the images help capture? **(c) Interpret:** How do images help convey the speaker's feelings?
2. **Key Ideas and Details (a)** In "Jade Flower Palace," what remains of the long-gone prince's "glory"? **(b) Compare and Contrast:** In what way does this image contrast with the speaker's description of what used to be in the palace? **(c) Draw Conclusions:** What point might the speaker be making through this contrast?
3. **Craft and Structure (a)** What is the setting of Tsurayuki's poem? **(b) Infer:** What does the speaker's willingness to face that setting suggest about the depth of his love?
4. **Key Ideas and Details (a)** What question does the speaker of Ono Komachi's poem ask? **(b) Infer:** What do her question and her response to that question suggest about her feelings toward the man in her dreams?

Enrichment: Artistic Schools and Movements

Imagism and Haiku

Imagery is a strong feature in tanka poetry and another traditional poetry form: haiku. Though the haiku was developed in seventeenth-century Japan, it influenced many twentieth-century poets. American poet Ezra Pound, inspired in part by the power of images in haiku, founded a movement called Imagism. For Pound, the true content of poetry was the image. As with haiku, Pound's Imagist works do not directly state a message. They create beautiful word-pictures in which sound, sense, and representation form a unified whole.

Activity: Analyzing Imagism Encourage students to research the Imagism movement, recording their findings using the **Enrichment: Investigating Artistic Schools and Movements** worksheet, ***Professional Development Guidebook***, page 220.

After You Read

Poetry of William Wordsworth • Lyric Poetry from Around the World

Comparing Lyric Poetry

1. **Key Ideas and Details** Compare "Thick Grow the Rush Leaves" to the first two tanka poems by Japanese writers. **(a)** What is similar and different about the feelings each poem expresses? **(b)** In which poem does imagery most effectively capture those feelings? Explain.
2. **Key Ideas and Details** **(a)** Compare and contrast the passage of time in "Tintern Abbey," the selection from *The Prelude*, "Jade Flower Palace," and "I Have Visited Again." **(b)** In which two poems are the speakers' experiences of the passage of time most similar? Explain.
3. **Craft and Structure** Of the translations presented here, which lyric poems do you find the most musical? Cite examples from the poems to support your evaluation.

Common Core State Standards

Writing

2. Write informative/explanatory texts to examine and convey complex ideas, concepts, and information clearly and accurately through the effective selection, organization, and analysis of content.

10. Write routinely over extended time frames and shorter time frames for a range of tasks, purposes, and audiences.

Timed Writing

Explanatory Text: Essay

Many of the lyric poems you have read in this section include descriptions of natural settings.

Assignment: Choose two poems by different authors that have vivid descriptions of nature. Write an **essay** in which you *compare and contrast* the two poems by addressing these questions. **[40 minutes]**

- What is the theme or central insight expressed in each poem?
- For each poem, how does the description of nature support the theme?
- What images does each speaker use to describe nature?
- For each poem, what feelings does the description of nature evoke?

As you write, follow the conventions of a strong explanatory essay. Organize your ideas logically. You might focus on the features of one poem and then the features of the other, or you might focus on points of similarity and difference, moving back and forth between the two poems.

USE ACADEMIC VOCABULARY

As you write, use academic language, including the following words or their related forms:

correspond
insight
musicality
perspective

For more on academic language, see the vocabulary charts in the introduction to this book.

5-Minute Planner

Complete these steps before you begin to write:

1. Read the assignment carefully. List key words and phrases.
2. To focus your analysis, scan the poems for evidence that relates to the questions.
3. Create a rough outline for your essay.
4. Reread the prompt, and draft your essay.

Assessment Resources

Unit 4 Resources

L1 L2 L3 L4 EL Selection Test, pp. 88–89.

PHLit Online! All resources are available at www.PHLitOnline.com

Answers

Comparing Lyric Poetry

1. (a) **Possible Response:** The tanka poems express a strong connection with nature. "Thick Grow the Rush Leaves" is hopeful, and tanka poetry is melancholy. (b) **Possible response:** "Thick Grow the Rush Leaves" most effectively expresses a connection with nature because of the detailed descriptions of the river.
2. (a) **Possible response:** All the poems look at the past. The amount of time that has passed differs. (b) **Possible response:** "Tintern Abbey" and "I Have Visited Again" both reflect on the speaker's younger days.
3. **Possible response:** "Jade Flower Palace" seems the most musical because of the flow of the lines.

Timed Writing

1. Teach the Academic Vocabulary. Discuss the words with students, and their related forms, including *insightful* and *musical*. Encourage students to use the academic vocabulary and the words they learned before the selection as they compare and contrast two poems.
2. Use the prompt to help students identify elements and qualities their interpretation of a literary text should have:
   - A thesis statement about the significance of the similarities and differences between two poems
   - An interpretation of the themes
   - Specific text references that illustrate how the themes are developed
   - An interpretation of how the two themes are similar and different in their message, development, and delivery
   - Detailed and specific text references that illustrate and support the interpretation of similarities and differences

   Encourage students to focus on these points when they are planning and revising their essays.

   Tell students they will have 40 minutes to plan and write the essay. Call students' attention to the 5-Minute Planner. Encourage them to budget their time to allow 5 minutes for outlining, 5 minutes for identifying some initial supporting text references in the works, and 10 minutes for revision and proofreading.

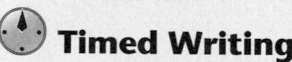

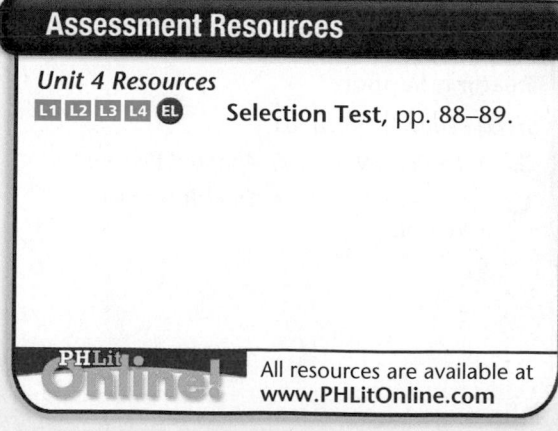

PREACH

Common Core State Standards

- Reading Informational Text 5
- Language 4.d

About the Texts

1. Introduce the government report and travel guide using the instruction on the student page.
2. Tell students they will identify the features of each document as they read the selections.

Reading Strategy

1. Introduce the skill using the instruction and chart on the student page.
2. Tell students they will evaluate information from charts, graphs, and illustrations as they read the two documents.

Think Aloud: Model the Skill

Model the strategy of evaluating information from charts, graphs, and illustrations. Say to students:

Before I begin reading public and consumer documents, I scan them to look for graphic aids. If a document includes charts, graphs, or illustrations, I analyze those closely.

Content-Area Vocabulary

1. Have students say each word aloud.
2. Then, use each word in a sentence that makes its meaning clear. Repeat your sentence with the vocabulary word missing and have students fill in the blank.

For more guidance, consult the ***Classroom Strategies and Teaching Routines*** card on introducing vocabulary.

Reading for Information

Analyzing Functional and Expository Texts

Government Report • Travel Guide

About the Texts

A **government report** is an account of work or a study completed by a government agency. These types of reports often include a description of events or an analysis of an issue; an explanation of how an issue affects different groups; and a description of problems, with proposed solutions, often including actions taken or planned by the government.

A **travel guide** is a document that provides information to people who are planning a trip to a particular destination. Travel guides generally provide an overview of an area and then go into detail about specific attractions, transportation, food, and lodging.

Reading Strategy

Reports and guides provide information in a logical order. Often, the textual information in these types of documents is supplemented by graphics, such as charts and photographs. Graphics may clarify the structure of the text and make it easier to read. They may also make the text more attractive and engaging. As you study these documents, **analyze information from charts, graphs, and illustrations** by evaluating these features:

- a heading or title of a graph that defines its information
- labels that classify different elements of charts and graphs
- captions explaining symbols and images

Use a checklist like the one shown to assess graphics in these texts. Analyze and evaluate how well these structures complement information presented verbally. Consider whether the graphic elements clarify ideas and make the text more interesting or useful to readers.

Features	Yes/No	Content
Graph and chart titles	❑ / ❑	
Graph and chart labels	❑ / ❑	
Photos or images	❑ / ❑	
Captions	❑ / ❑	
Explanations of symbols	❑ / ❑	

Common Core State Standards

Reading Informational Text
5. Analyze and evaluate the effectiveness of the structure an author uses in his or her exposition or argument, including whether the structure makes points clear, convincing, and engaging.

Language
4.d. Verify the preliminary determination of the meaning of a word or phrase. *(p. 817)*

Content-Area Vocabulary

These words may also appear in other subject-area texts:

district (dis′ trikt) *n.* a given area or selected geographical section on a map

trade (trād) *n.* the buying and selling of goods or services

policies (päl′ ə sēz′) *n.* plans of action by a government, business, or political party

geological (jē′ ə läj′ ik əl) *adj.* of or related to the structure of the earth

Teaching Resources

Reading Support

L2 L3 *Reader's Notebook*

L1 *Reader's Notebook: Adapted Version*

EL *Reader's Notebook: English Learner's Version*

Government Report

LAKE DISTRICT
National Park Authority

EDUCATION SERVICE TRAFFIC MANAGEMENT

The Lake **District** National Park is an area of outstandingly beautiful and varied landscape and the scenery is the reason most people give for visiting the Lake District (62%, 1994 All Parks Visitor Survey).

The Lake District remained relatively isolated until the 19th century when new railways allowed the large urban populations of Northwest England to visit the area easily. Both **trade** and early tourism flourished. In the 1940s, it was recognised that areas such as the Lake District would benefit from some kind of special protection. The Lake District was designated a National Park in 1951 to conserve and enhance its special landscape while providing opportunities for the public to enjoy that landscape. At this time, it was expected that "walkers, cyclists, riders and students of nature" would be the main users of the National Park rather than motorists, although National Parks were intended for all to enjoy.

Since then, car ownership has increased and now the vast majority of visitors come by car. Today, over 12 million people visit the National Park annually (staying for 22 million days) while 42,000 people live in the National Park. 89% of visitors come to the National Park by private motor vehicle.

The Lake District National Park Authority (LDNPA) and Cumbria County Council (CCC) have a number of automatic traffic counters around the National Park to help understand traffic movements. Traffic is greatest during the summer months when most visitors come to the National Park and mid-mornings and late afternoons can be exceptionally busy. In recent years, the rate of increase of traffic has slowed down, with recorded increases being largely confined to main roads such as the A591.

The heading "Lake District" and the words "Traffic Management" in the report's heading reveal the focus and purpose of the report.

This paragraph establishes the focus of the report on the issue of car traffic in the park.

TEACH

About Government Reports

1. Tell students this is a report from the National Park Authority, which is a government agency.
2. Have students read the section titled "Education Service Traffic Management."
3. **Ask:** What is the main reason so many people go to the Lake District?
   Answer: It is a beautiful place with a varied landscape.
4. **Ask:** What problem is being described in this report?
   Answer: Traffic has become a problem in the National Park because more than 12 million people visit annually, and 89 percent of those visitors come by car.

Evaluating Information from Charts, Graphs, and Illustrations

1. Explain that as students read this report, they should pay special attention to any charts, graphs, or illustrations that appear.
2. **Ask** students what part of the text on this page could be presented in the form of an illustration.
   Answer: The Lake District is described as a beautiful place. A photo could have enhanced the reader's understanding of the location's beauty.
3. **Ask** students what part of the text on this page could be presented in the form of a chart or graph.
   Answer: The statistics about the number of visitors, residents, and cars could have been presented in a graphic to aid understanding.

Differentiated Instruction for Universal Access

Strategy for Special-Needs Students
A government report often contains high-level vocabulary that will need to be defined for students. Encourage students to read through the report with a partner, looking up words in a dictionary, as needed for comprehension.

Strategy for Less Proficient Readers
To aid understanding, have students organize information from the report in a graphic format. Ask students to gather information from the report to create a timeline with entries for the eighteenth century, nineteenth century, 1940s, 1951, 1994, and today.

Evaluating Information from Charts, Graphs, and Illustrations

1. Have students read the bulleted list of information about the traffic issues.
2. Direct students' attention to the line graph at the bottom of the page. Have them study it for a few minutes.
3. **Ask** students to find the point on the graph that indicates the greatest number of vehicles recorded by the Langdale traffic counter.
   Answer: In 1993, the Langdale traffic counter recorded about 2,300 vehicles passing through the park on an average day.

Government Report

The traffic problems are clearly described in this bulleted list.

Traffic Issues

Large volumes of traffic can lead to a number of issues, especially in an area like the Lake District where roads are often narrow.

- **Pollution:** Motor vehicles emit various pollutants which may reach high levels in certain weather conditions, especially within towns.
- **Noise:** 'Peace and Quiet' is often given as a reason for visiting, so this is an issue, especially when considering development.
- **Visual intrusion:** Lines of parked cars can detract from the natural beauty of the National Park.
- **Congestion:** Congestion can be a problem in certain areas and towns at peak times of day and the year.
- **Reducing visitor traffic:** Traffic Management aims to minimize the impact of traffic and encourage visitors to use public transport rather than private cars.
- **Parking:** A balance needs to be found between provision of parking for visitors and locals and impact on the landscape.
- **Hazards to vulnerable road users:** Walkers, cyclists and horse riders should be at ease on the roads in the Lake District. Actual and perceived hazards to these road users should be minimized.

The graph's clear title, different colors, and sidebar labels make information easy to interpret.

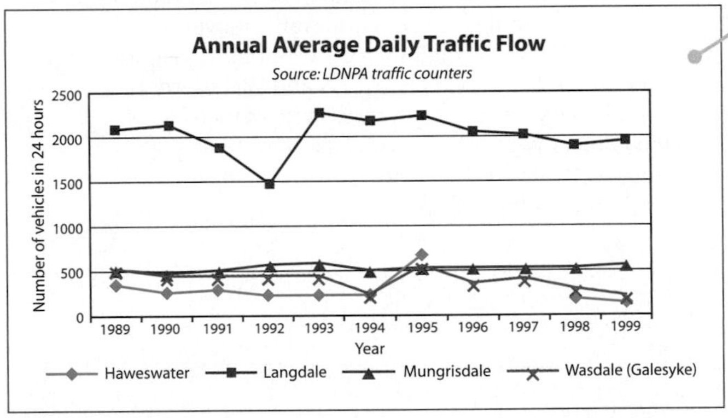

812 Rebels and Dreamers (1798–1832)

Vocabulary Development

Content-Area Vocabulary: Social Studies

Review the definitions of the cross-curricular vocabulary with students: *district, trade,* and *policy*. Then, examine each word in its context in the government report.

When you have finished with the three listed words, ask students to identify other words in the document that fit the context of government regulations, such as *authority, survey, designated,* and *conserve.* Have students look up their definitions in a dictionary and then use the words in sentences about a national park.

Traffic Management in the National Park

The guiding principle underpinning the **policies** of the LDNPA towards transport and traffic is that demand should be managed in order to:

- minimize its impact on the landscape
- improve the quality of life for local residents
- improve the quality of enjoyment for visitors
- encourage use of sustainable means of travel

The policies of the LDNPA are set out in the Lake District National Park Management Plan. These clearly state that increasing road capacity is not an appropriate solution to traffic management in the National Park. Instead, traffic management policy is to tailor traffic to existing roads.

A balance of interests is needed between the purposes of the National Park, local people and visitors to ensure the special qualities of the National Park are not compromised. For example, in 1966 the Lake District Special Planning Board published a "Report on Traffic in the Lake District National Park" suggesting that in the future it might become necessary to restrict all except local traffic along secondary routes. Objections were raised by local residents of Langdale and Borrowdale concerning the impact of these closures on the tourism trade.

This paragraph addresses the different groups the traffic problem and proposed solutions affect.

Monthly Traffic Flow, Waterhead, Ambleside, A591

Source: Lake District Transport Strategy Implementation Plan: Stage One 2000–2005.

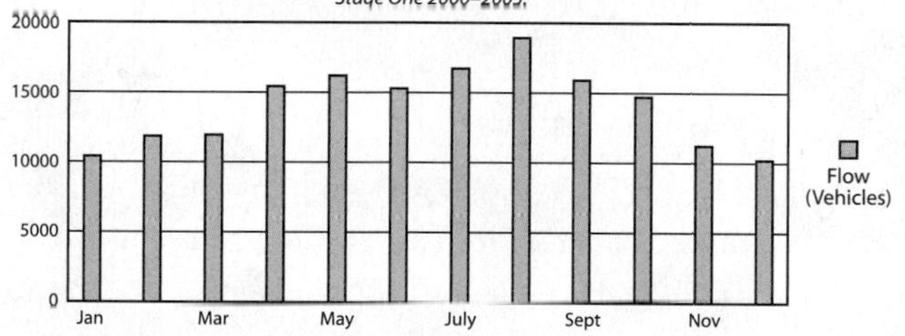

Evaluating Information from Charts, Graphs, and Illustrations

1. Have students read the text under the heading "Traffic Management in the National Park."
2. Direct students' attention to the bar graph at the bottom of the page. Have them study it for a few minutes.
3. **Ask** students to identify the two months with the least traffic.
   Answer: December is the lowest, with January as a close second.

Differentiated Instruction for Universal Access

Culturally Responsive Instruction

Culture Connection This government report is about efforts to manage traffic through a national park. Many public places in the United States and throughout the world have become congested with excessive traffic. Ask students to think of the most crowded place they have ever visited. Have students explain the negative impact of the crowds and traffic on their experiences at the tourist attraction. Ask for volunteers to share any ideas they might have for minimizing traffic in public places.

About Travel Guides

1. Review with students the features of a travel guide, using the instruction on the Preteach page.
2. Have students read the first page of "The North Country."
3. **Ask** students what type of information is provided in this first section of the travel guide.
   Answer: The travel guide starts with general information and a list of attractions. It also mentions lodging.

Evaluating Information from Charts, Graphs, and Illustrations

1. Direct students' attention to the photograph at the bottom of the page. Have them study it for a moment and read its caption.
2. **Ask** students to explain how the captioned photograph aids their understanding of the three paragraphs above it.
   Possible response: The caption explains that this is one of the quieter areas in the district, which implies that other parts are crowded with the tourists mentioned in the text. The beauty of the landscape is described in the text, but seeing it in a photograph makes it more meaningful.

Travel Guide

The North Country

Exploring Lancashire and the Lakes

The lake district's natural scenery outweighs any of its man-made attractions. Its natural features are the result of **geological** upheavals over millennia (see pp 340–41), and four of its peaks are more than 1,000 m (3,300 ft). Human influences have left their mark too: the main activities are quarrying, mining, farming and tourism.

The Lakes are most crowded in summer when activities include lake trips and hill-walking. The best bases are Keswick and Ambleside, while there are also good hotels on the shores of Windermere and Ullswater and in the Cartmel area.

Lancashire's Bowland Forest is an attractive place to explore on foot, with picturesque villages. Further south, Manchester and Liverpool have excellent museums and galleries.

This picture and caption give readers a clearer understanding of the area's "natural scenery" described in the text.

View over Crummock Water, north of Buttermere, one of the quieter Western Lakes

Vocabulary Development

Content-Area Vocabulary: Science

Review the definition of the cross-curricular vocabulary word *geological* with students. Then, examine the word in its context in the travel guide. Also have students locate *district*—a vocabulary word from the government report that reappears in the travel guide.

When you have finished, ask students to identify other words in the document that fit the context of a travel guide, such as *picturesque* and *excursions*. Have students look up their definitions in a dictionary and then use the words in sentences about a tourist attraction.

Preserved docks and Liver Building, Liverpool

This section giving visitors information on traveling to different sites is supplemented by the map on the following page.

Getting Around

For many, the first glimpse of the Lake District is from the M6 near Shap Fell, but the A6 is a more dramatic route. You can reach Windermere by train, but you need to change at Oxenholme, on the mainline route from Euston to Carlisle. Penrith also has rail services and bus links into the Lakes. L'al Ratty, the miniature railway up Eskdale, and the Lakeside & Haverthwaite railway, which connects with the steamers on Windermere, make for enjoyable outings. Regular buses link all the main centres where excursions are organized. One of the most enterprising is the Mountain Goat minibus, in Windermere and Keswick.

Lancaster, Liverpool and Manchester are on the main rail and bus routes and also have airports. For Blackpool, you need to change trains in Preston. Wherever you go in the area, one of the best means of getting around is on foot.

Evaluating Information from Charts, Graphs, and Illustrations

1. Direct students to first examine the photograph at the top of the page.
2. Then, have students read the text that follows.
3. **Ask** students to explain the connection between the photograph and the text.
   Possible responses: The text is about transportation, and the photograph shows boats. The photograph is of Liverpool, which is mentioned in the last paragraph.

Differentiated Instruction for Universal Access

Strategy for Less Proficient Readers
Have each student read through the text with a partner. Then encourage them to look ahead to the map on the next page. This will help them trace the travel routes mentioned in the text for improved understanding.

EL Strategy for English Learners
To aid understanding, have students make a list of the types of transportation mentioned in the text. Suggest that they skim over the capitalized words, which are primarily place names in England. These are less important than the modes of transportation for discerning the overall meaning of the passage.

Evaluating Information from Charts, Graphs, and Illustrations

1. Direct students to study the map for a few minutes on their own.
2. Then, have students work together to locate specific places on the map.
3. **Ask** students to locate two bodies of water that are labeled on the map.
   Answer: Morecambe Bay is number 23, and Northern Fells and Lakes is number 6.

Lancashire and the Lakes

Sights at a Glance

- Ambleside 16
- Blackpool 27
- Borrowdale 10
- Buttermere 9
- Carlisle 1
- Cartmel 21
- Cockermouth 7
- Coniston Water 18
- Dalemain 3
- Duddon Valley 13
- Eskdale 12
- Furness Peninsula 20
- Grasmere and Rydal 15
- Kendal 19
- Keswick 5
- Lancaster 25
- Langdale 14
- Leighton Hall 24
- Levens Hall 22
- Liverpool 29
- Manchester 28
- Morecambe Bay 23
- Newlands Valley 8
- Northern Fells and Lakes 6
- Penrith 2
- Ribble Valley 26
- Ullswater 4
- Wastwater 11
- Windermere 17

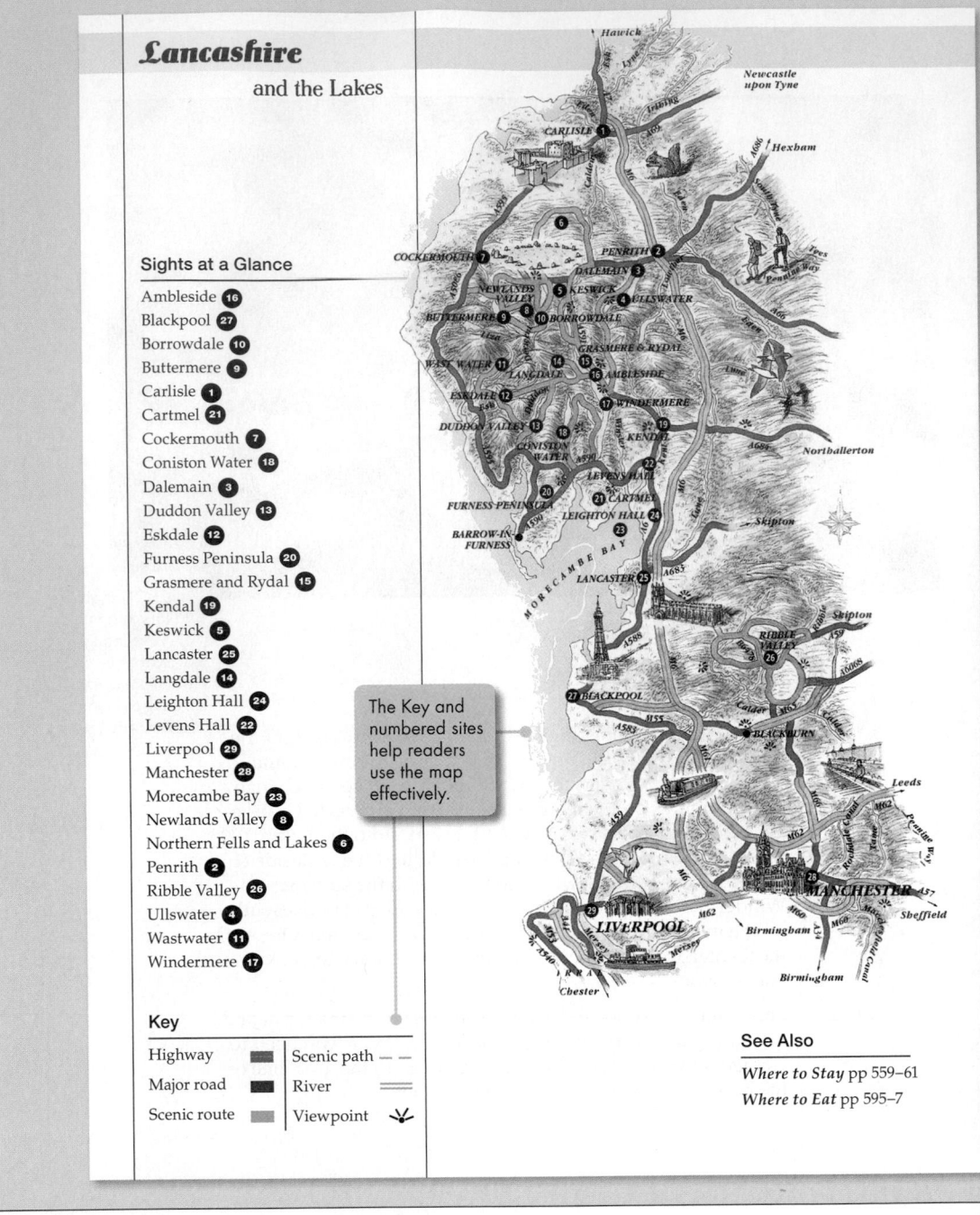

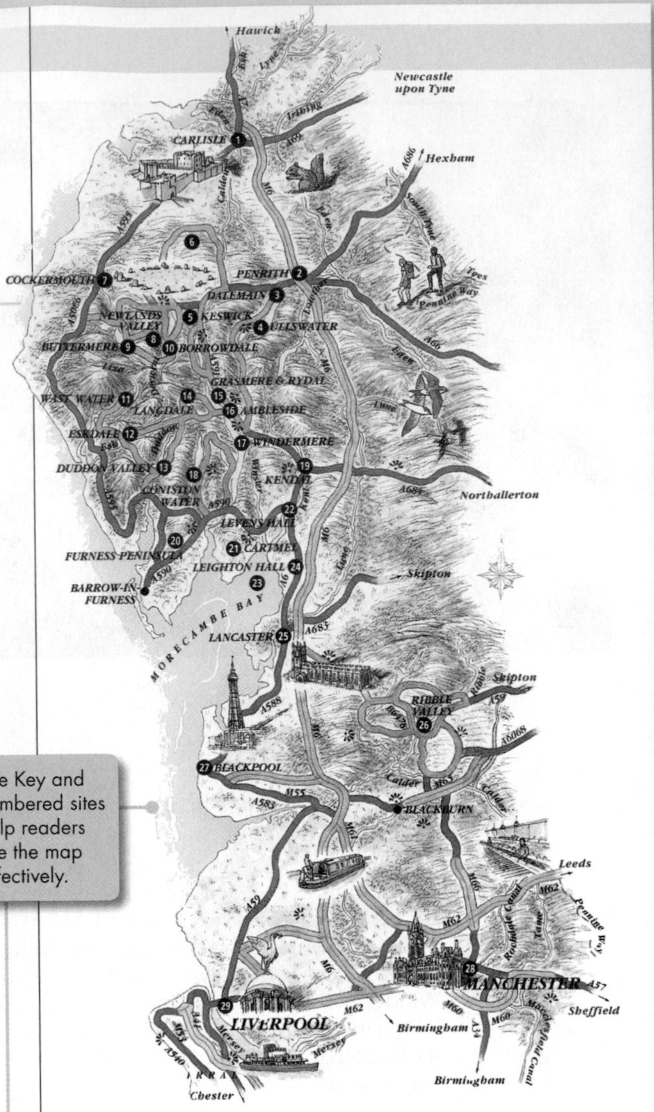

The Key and numbered sites help readers use the map effectively.

Key

Highway		Scenic path	— —
Major road		River	
Scenic route		Viewpoint	

See Also

Where to Stay pp 559–61
Where to Eat pp 595–7

Think Aloud

Reading Strategy: Use Text Features

To model the process of using text features to read a map, use the following "think aloud." Say to students:

When I am given a map to read, I start by studying its key and the types of headings that are used for its labels. For example, if I do not know which symbol represents a river and which represents a highway, I might get confused. Once I understand what the symbols mean, I can begin to analyze the map for more information.

After You Read

Government Report • Travel Guide

Critical Reading

1. **Key Ideas and Details (a)** Based on the government report, what major change has taken place since 1951 in the way visitors tour the Lake District? **(b)** What problems has this change caused? **(c)** What solutions does the report propose?
2. **Key Ideas and Details (a)** Based on the travel guide, what are various transportation options in the Lake District? **(b)** Which option does the guide state is best? **(c)** How does the information in the government report support the opinion expressed in the travel guide?
3. **Craft and Structure** For each document, note at least one way in which its structure and organization reflect and support its content.
4. **Craft and Structure (a)** For each document, note a statement or fact presented verbally that is supported or enhanced by one or more graphics. **(b)** For each document, do the graphic elements make the ideas clearer and more engaging? Why or why not?
5. **Content-Area Vocabulary (a)** The word *policy* derives from the Greek root *-polis-/-polit-*, which means "city." Explain how the meaning of the root informs the meaning of *policy.* **(b)** Define the following words derived from the same root: *political, police,* and *cosmopolitan*. Use a dictionary to verify your definitions.

Timed Writing

Informative Text [40 minutes]

Format
In an **analytical essay,** you break a topic into smaller elements and show how these elements relate to the idea or ideas you are discussing.

Although these documents have different purposes, they are about the same place. Write a brief **analytical essay** in which you use both documents to tell visitors what to expect on a trip to the Lake District. To accomplish your goal, **synthesize ideas and make logical connections** between the texts. Support your ideas with textual evidence, including evidence from the graphs and the map.

Academic Vocabulary
When you **synthesize and make logical connections,** you combine ideas and relate texts logically.

5-Minute Planner

Complete these steps before you begin to write.

1. Read the prompt carefully. Underline key words.
2. Draft a thesis that clearly responds to the prompt.
3. Scan the text for details that relate to the prompt. **TIP** Your scan will help provide the evidence you need to support your points.
4. Reread the prompt, and draft your essay.

Extend the Lesson

Connecting to the Students' World

To give students more practice with public and consumer documents and to help them apply the material to their own world, divide the class into small groups. Have each group look at a government report about a local issue or at a section of a travel guide to your area. Have students gather interesting details from their materials to present to the class.

ASSESS/EXTEND

Answers

Critical Reading

1. (a) Most visitors travel by car. (b) Problems include pollution, noise, and congestion, among others. (c) The report proposes that rather than building new roads, traffic management should focus on existing roads.
2. (a) Transportation options include walking, rail services, buses, airplanes, cars, and steamers. (b) The guide recommends that visitors travel on foot. (c) The report describes problems that could be minimized if more people walked.
3. **Possible response:** The report begins with background, then states the problem, and finally proposes a solution so readers can understand the issue. The travel guide describes the area and then provides helpful information about how to get around.
4. (a) **Possible response:** The report's statement that traffic is greater in summer is supported by the graph. The map in the travel guide supports the text's descriptions of sites and scenic routes. (b) **Possible response:** Yes, the graphic elements add visual interest and emphasis.
5. (a) A *policy* is a guideline that officials use to make decisions. (b) *Political* describes something that relates to politics. The *police* are a group that enforces the law in a city. *Cosmopolitan* describes something or someone that is well suited to life in different cities or areas around the world.

Timed Writing

1. Before students begin the assignment, guide them in analyzing key words in the prompt.
2. Work with students to draw up guidelines for their essays based on the key words.
3. Have students use the 5-Minute Planner to structure their time.
4. Allow students 40 minutes to complete the assignment. Evaluate their work using the guidelines they have developed.

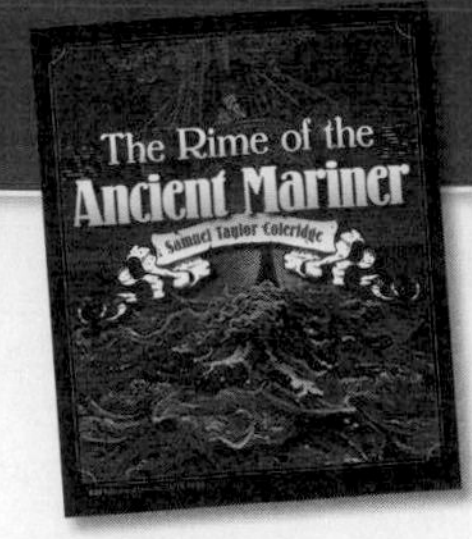

The Rime of the Ancient Mariner • Kubla Khan

Lesson Pacing Guide

DAY 1 Preteach

- Administer the Reading and Vocabulary Warm-ups (*Unit 4 Resources*, pp. 96–99) as necessary.
- Introduce the Literary Analysis concept: Poetic Sound Devices and the Language of Fantasy.
- Introduce the Reading Strategy: Comparing and Contrasting Sound Devices.
- Build background with the author and Background features.
- Develop thematic thinking with Connecting to the Essential Question.
- Teach the selection vocabulary.

DAYS 2–3 Preteach/Teach/Assess

- Distribute copies of the appropriate graphic organizer for the Reading Strategy (*Graphic Organizer Transparencies*, pp. 146–147).
- Distribute copies of the appropriate graphic organizer for Literary Analysis (*Graphic Organizer Transparencies*, pp. 148–149).
- Prepare students to read with the Activating Prior Knowledge activities (TE).
- Informally monitor comprehension while students read.
- Use the Reading Check questions to confirm comprehension.
- Develop students' understanding of poetic sound devices and fantasy language using the Literary Analysis prompts.
- Develop students' ability to compare and contrast sound devices using the Reading Strategy prompts.
- Reinforce vocabulary with the Vocabulary notes.
- Assess students' comprehension and mastery of the skills by having them answer the Critical Reading, Literary Analysis, and Reading Strategy questions.
- Have students complete the Vocabulary Lesson.

DAY 4 Extend/Assess

- Have students complete the Writing Lesson and write a response to literature. (You may assign as homework.)
- Administer Selection Test A or B (*Unit 4 Resources*, pp. 108–110 or 111–113).

Common Core State Standards

Reading Literature 5. Analyze how an author's choices concerning how to structure specific parts of a text contribute to its overall structure and meaning as well as its aesthetic impact.
9. Demonstrate knowledge of eighteenth-, nineteenth-, and early-twentieth-century foundational works of American literature, including how two or more texts from the same period treat similar themes or topics.

Writing 2.b. Develop the topic thoroughly by selecting the most significant and relevant facts, extended definitions, concrete details, quotations, or other information and examples appropriate to the audience's knowledge of the topic.
2.d. Use precise language, domain-specific vocabulary, and techniques such as metaphor, simile, and analogy to manage the complexity of the topic.
9.a. Apply grades 11–12 Reading standards to literature.

Additional Standards Practice
***Common Core Companion**, pp. 54–55, 75–81; 196–207, 261–276*

Daily Block Scheduling
Each day in this Lesson Pacing Guide represents a 40–50 minute period. Teachers using block scheduling may combine days to revise pacing. In addition, teachers may differentiate and support core instruction by integrating components for extended and intensive support as students require. See the Guide to Selected Leveled Resources (facing page).

Guide to Selected Leveled Resources

RTI Tier 1 (students performing on level)			The Rime of the Ancient Mariner • Kubla Khan
Warm Up	Whole class instruction; Group work	**Practice, model,** and **monitor** fluency, working **with the whole class** or **in groups.**	Vocabulary and Reading Warm-ups B, *Unit 4 Resources,* pp. 96–97, 99
Comprehension/Skills	Whole class instruction; Group work; Independent work	**Support** and **monitor** comprehension and skills development, having students complete the activities, graphic organizers, and interactive prompts **independently** or **as a class.**	• *Reader's Notebook,* adapted instruction and full selection EL *Reader's Notebook: English Learner's Version,* adapted instruction and adapted selection • Reading Strategy Graphic Organizer B, *Graphic Organizer Transparencies,* p. 151 • Literary Analysis Graphic Organizer B, *Graphic Organizer Transparencies,* p. 153
Monitor Progress	A	**Monitor** student progress with the differentiated curriculum-based assessment in the *Unit Resources.*	• Selection Test B, *Unit 4 Resources,* pp. 111–113 • Open-Book Test, *Unit 4 Resources,* pp. 105–107

RTI Tier 2 (students requiring intervention)			The Rime of the Ancient Mariner • Kubla Khan
Warm Up	Group work; One-on-one teaching	**Practice, model,** and **monitor** fluency **in groups** or **with individuals.**	• Vocabulary and Reading Warm-ups A, *Unit 4 Resources,* pp. 96–98 • *Hear It!* Audio CD (adapted text)
Comprehension/Skills	Group work; One-on-one teaching	• **Support** and **monitor** comprehension and skills development, working **in small groups** or **with individuals.** • As students complete the selection in the appropriate version of the *Reader's Notebook,* **monitor** comprehension frequently with group questions and individual instruction. • **Model** strategies while guiding students in completing the activities and prompts in the *Reader's Notebook,* as well as the graphic organizers. • **Practice** skills and **monitor** mastery with the *Reading Kit* worksheets.	• *Reader's Notebook: Adapted Version,* adapted instruction and adapted selection EL *Reader's Notebook: English Learner's Version,* adapted instruction and adapted selection • Reading Strategy Graphic Organizer A, *Graphic Organizer Transparencies,* p. 150 • Literary Analysis Graphic Organizer A, *Graphic Organizer Transparencies,* p. 152 • *Reading Kit,* Practice worksheets
Monitor Progress	A	**Monitor** student progress with the differentiated curriculum-based assessment in the *Unit Resources* and in the *Reading Kit.*	• Selection Test A, *Unit 4 Resources,* pp. 108–110 • *Reading Kit,* Assess worksheets

TIER 3 Tier 3 intervention may require consultation with the student's special-education or dyslexia specialist. For additional support, see the Tier 2 activities and resources listed above.

One-on-one teaching **Group work** **Whole class instruction** **Independent work** **A Assessment**

For a complete guide to selection support, including support for Advanced students, see the Overview of Resources in the frontmatter.

The Rime of the Ancient Mariner • Kubla Khan

RESOURCES FOR:

- L1 Special-Needs Students
- L2 Below-Level Students (Tier 2)
- L3 On-Level Students (Tier 1)
- L4 Advanced Students (Tier 1)
- EL English Learners
- All All Students

Vocabulary/Fluency/Prior Knowledge

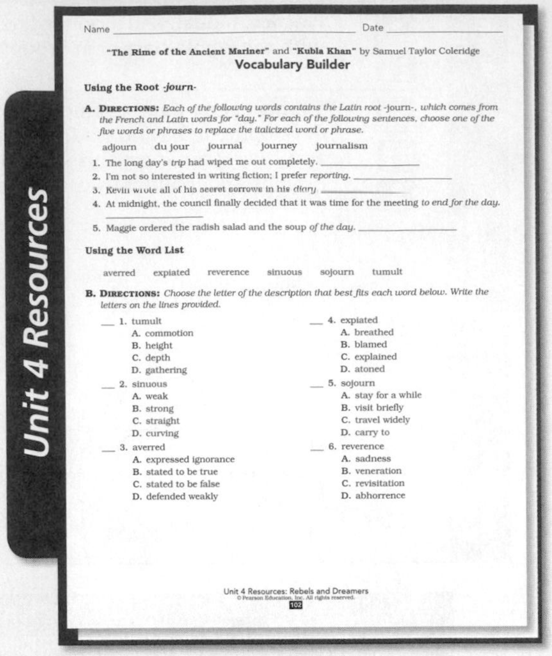

Name ____________ Date ____________

"The Rime of the Ancient Mariner" and **"Kubla Khan"** by Samuel Taylor Coleridge

Vocabulary Builder

Using the Root *-journ-*

A. Directions: *Each of the following words contains the Latin root -journ-, which comes from the French and Latin words for "day." For each of the following sentences, choose one of the five words or phrases to replace the italicized word or phrase.*

adjourn du jour journal journey journalism

1. The long day's *trip* had wiped me out completely. ____________
2. I'm not so interested in writing fiction; I prefer *reporting.* ____________
3. Kevin wrote all of his secret sorrows in his *diary* ____________
4. At midnight, the council finally decided that it was time for the meeting *to end for the day.* ____________
5. Maggie ordered the radish salad and the soup *of the day.* ____________

Using the Word List

averred expiated reverence sinuous sojourn tumult

B. Directions: *Choose the letter of the description that best fits each word below. Write the letters on the lines provided.*

___ 1. tumult
A. commotion
B. height
C. depth
D. gathering

___ 2. sinuous
A. weak
B. strong
C. straight
D. curving

___ 3. averred
A. expressed ignorance
B. stated to be true
C. stated to be false
D. defended weakly

___ 4. expiated
A. breathed
B. blamed
C. explained
D. atoned

___ 5. sojourn
A. stay for a while
B. visit briefly
C. travel widely
D. carry to

___ 6. reverence
A. sadness
B. veneration
C. revisitation
D. abhorrence

Unit 4 Resources: Rebels and Dreamers
© Pearson Education, Inc. All rights reserved.
102

All **Vocabulary Builder,** p. 102

Also available for these selections:

- EL L1 L2 **Vocabulary Warm-ups A and B,** pp. 96–97
- EL L1 L2 **Reading Warm-ups A and B,** pp. 98–99

Reader's Notebooks

Pre- and postreading pages for these selections, as well as *The Rime of the Ancient Mariner,* appear in an interactive format in the *Reader's Notebooks.* Each *Notebook* is differentiated for a different group of learners.
The selections in the Adapted and English Learner's versions are abridged.

- L2 L3 ***Reader's Notebook***
- L1 ***Reader's Notebook: Adapted Version***
- EL ***Reader's Notebook: English Learner's Version***
- EL ***Reader's Notebook: Spanish Version***

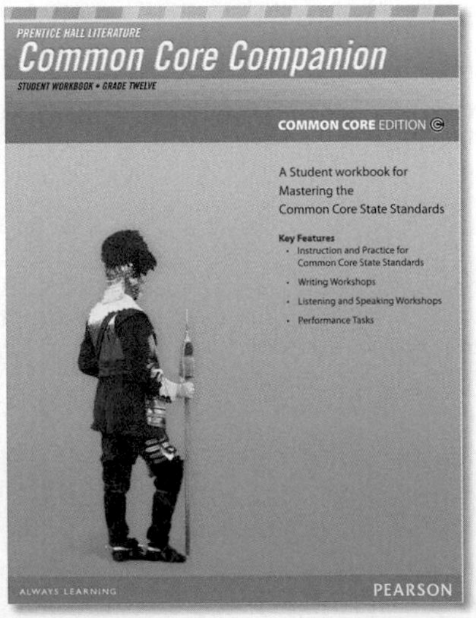

Common Core Companion

Additional instruction and practice for each Common Core State Standard

Selection Support

Graphic Organizer Transparencies

"The Rime of the Ancient Mariner"
and **"Kubla Khan"** by Samuel Taylor Coleridge

Before You Read A: Comparing and Contrasting Sound Devices

"The Rime of the Ancient Mariner"	**"Kubla Khan"**
Passage: "The ice was here, the ice was there,/The ice was all around;/It cracked and growled, and roared and howled,/Like noises in a swound!"	**Passage**
Sound Device: 1. Internal rhyme: "growled/howled" 2. Consonance: "here/there" "cracked/growled/roared/howled"	**Sound Device**
Image: A violent ice storm	**Image**

Graphic Organizer Transparencies
© Pearson Education, Inc. All rights reserved.
146

EL L1 L2 **Reading: Graphic Organizer A** (partially filled in), p. 146

Also available for these selections:

EL L3 **Reading: Graphic Organizer B,** p. 147

EL L1 L2 **Literary Analysis: Graphic Organizer A** (partially filled in), p. 148

EL L3 **Literary Analysis: Graphic Organizer B,** p. 149

Skills Development/Extension

Unit 4 Resources

Name ______________________ Date ______________

"The Rime of the Ancient Mariner" and **"Kubla Khan"** by Samuel Taylor Coleridge

Literary Analysis: Poetic Sound Devices

Alliteration is the repetition of a consonant sound at the beginnings of words. **Consonance** is the repetition of consonant sounds in stressed syllables with dissimilar vowel sounds. **Assonance** is repetition of vowel sounds in stressed syllables with dissimilar consonant sounds. **Internal rhyme** is the use of rhyming words within a line. **Slant rhyme** occurs with the use of sounds that are similar but not identical, such as *shore* and *share*.

DIRECTIONS: *In each of the following passages from "The Rime of the Ancient Mariner" and "Kubla Kahn," certain letters are italicized. For each passage, write on the line the* **sound device** *that is used.*

1. "As who pursued with yell and blow" ______
2. "The ice did split with a thunder-fit" ______
3. "He holds him with his skinny hand" ______
4. "The ship was cheered, the harbor cleared" ______
5. "'From the fiends that plague thee thus!– / Why look'st thou so?' 'With my crossbow / I shot the Albatross.'"
6. "And we did speak only to break" ______
7. "Red as a rose is she" ______
8. "All in a hot and copper sky" ______
9. "The Wedding Guest he beat his breast" ______
10. "The death fires danced at night" ______
11. "The fair breeze blew, the white foam flew" ______
12. " 'Through utter drought all dumb we stood! / I bit my arm, I sucked the blood.' "
13. "His flashing eyes, his floating hair!" ______
14. "A damsel with a dulcimer" ______
15. "For he on honeydew hath fed," ______
16. "And close your eyes with holy dread" ______
17. "And from this chasm, with ceaseless turmoil seething" ______
18. "And 'mid this tumult Kubla heard from far / Ancestral voices prophesying war!" ______

Unit 4 Resources: Rebels and Dreamers
© Pearson Education, Inc. All rights reserved.
100

All **Literary Analysis,** p. 100

Also available for these selections:

All **Reading,** p. 101

EL L3 L4 **Support for Writing,** p. 103

L4 **Enrichment,** p. 104

Assessment

Name ______________________ Date ______________

"The Rime of the Ancient Mariner" and **"Kubla Khan"** by Samuel Taylor Coleridge

Open-Book Test

Short Answer *Write your responses to the questions in this section on the lines provided.*

1. What is the central theme in "The Rime of the Ancient Mariner"? Briefly explain your answer.
2. Locate the passage in "The Rime of the Ancient Mariner" where the spell of the Albatross is broken. What occurrence illustrates the breaking of the spell? Why do you think this event happens?
3. How would you describe the tone displayed by the Mariner throughout his narration? Cite one or two details from the poem to support your answer.
4. What two poetic sound devices does Coleridge employ in the line, "The western wave was all aflame"? Briefly explain your answer.
5. Reread lines 525–532. Pick out the word in this passage that illustrates slant rhyme, and briefly explain your answer.
6. Consider the settings of "The Rime of the Ancient Mariner" and "Kubla Khan." What typical feature of the Romantic Movement do the settings of the two poems have in common?

Unit 4 Resources: Rebels and Dreamers
© Pearson Education, Inc. All rights reserved.
105

L3 L4 **Open-Book Test,** pp. 105–107

Also available for these selections:

EL L1 L2 **Selection Test A,** pp. 108–110

EL L3 L4 **Selection Test B,** pp. 111–113

PHLit Online!
www.PHLitOnline.com

- complete narrated selection text
- a thematically related video with writing prompt
- an interactive graphic organizer
- highlighting feature
- access to all student print resources, adapted to individual student needs
- Spanish and English summaries
- adapted selection translations in Spanish

Online Resources: All print materials are also available online.

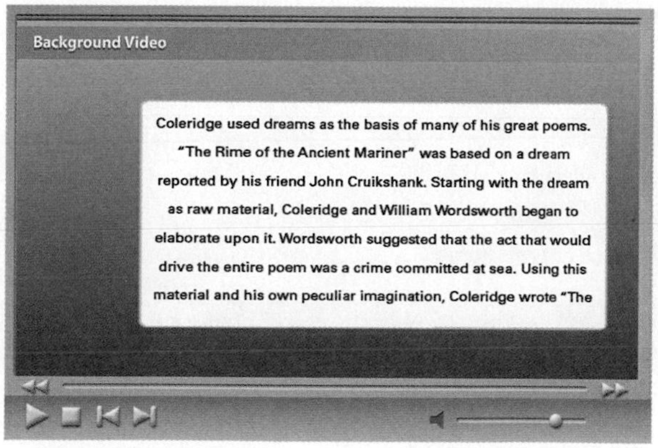

Background Video
Coleridge used dreams as the basis of many of his great poems. "The Rime of the Ancient Mariner" was based on a dream reported by his friend John Cruikshank. Starting with the dream as raw material, Coleridge and William Wordsworth began to elaborate upon it. Wordsworth suggested that the act that would drive the entire poem was a crime committed at sea. Using this material and his own peculiar imagination, Coleridge wrote "The

Background Video

Also available:

Get Connected! (thematic video with writing prompt)
All videos are available in Spanish.

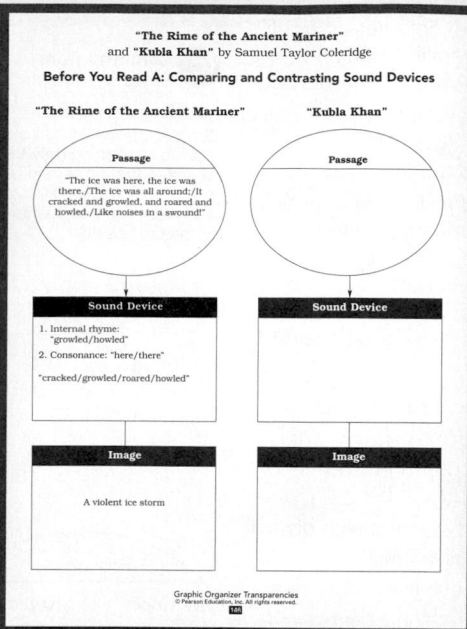

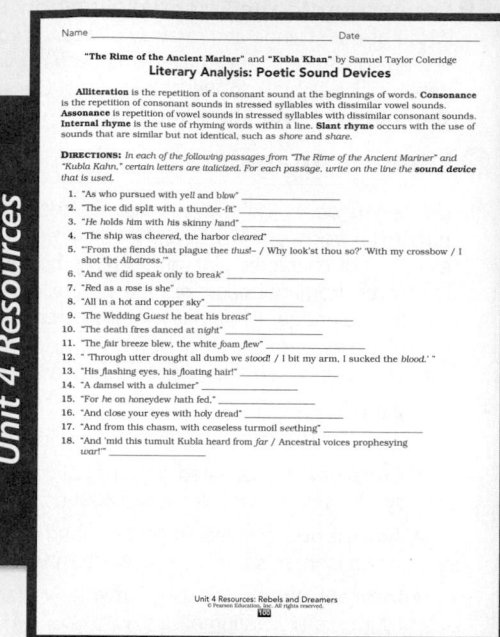

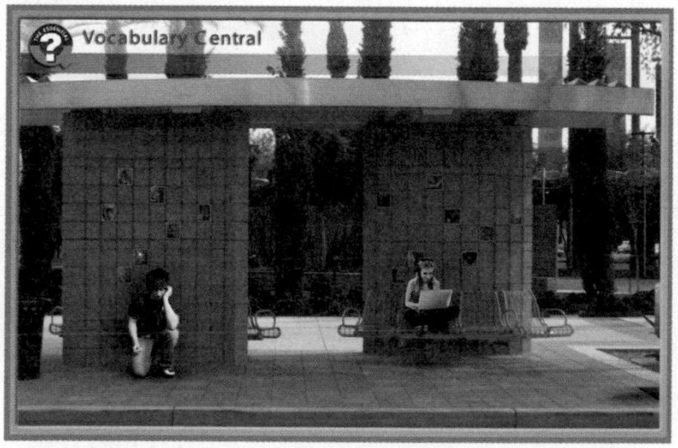

Vocabulary Central (tools and activities for studying vocabulary)

Also available:

Writer's Journal (with graphics feature)

PRETEACH

1 Connecting to the Essential Question

1. Review the assignment with the class.
2. Tell students to note details in the settings of these poems that seem unusual, or dreamlike.

2 Literary Analysis

Introduce the skill using the instruction on the student page.

Think Aloud: Model the Skill

Say to students:

I know that narrative poems are poems that tell a story. In what ways can a poem evoke strong emotions? I know that one way is through the use of poetic sound devices, such as alliteration.

3 Reading Strategy

1. Introduce the skill using the instruction on the student page.
2. Give students a copy of **Reading Strategy Graphic Organizer B,** page 147 in ***Graphic Organizer Transparencies,*** to fill out.

Think Aloud: Model the Skill

Say to students:

I want to analyze the line "seagulls soared across an open ocean." The first thing I notice are the repetitions of sound. The example emphasizes openness with its long *o* sounds and the smoothness of soaring with its *s* sounds.

4 Vocabulary

1. Pronounce each word, giving its definition.
2. For more guidance, see the ***Classroom Strategies and Teaching Routines*** card for introducing vocabulary.

Before You Read

The Rime of the Ancient Mariner • Kubla Khan

1 Connecting to the Essential Question Romantics like Coleridge wrote about strange and faraway places. As you read, note details in the settings of these poems that seem unusual, even dreamlike. Finding such details will help you answer the Essential Question: **What is the relationship between literature and place?**

Common Core State Standards

Reading Literature
5. Analyze how an author's choices concerning how to structure specific parts of a text contribute to its overall structure and meaning as well as its aesthetic impact.

2 Literary Analysis

Unlike *lyric poetry,* which expresses the thoughts and feelings of a speaker, **narrative poetry** tells a story. Narrative poems feature the storytelling elements of character, plot, and setting, but organize them with poetic structures. Romantics admired the storytelling of folk ballads, so it is no wonder Coleridge uses a *ballad stanza* (*abcb*) in much of his narrative poem *The Rime of the Ancient Mariner.* He also uses these **poetic sound devices** to heighten the music and *evoke emotions*:

- **Alliteration,** a repeated consonant sound at the beginnings of words: "The fair breeze blew, the white foam flew, . . ."
- **Consonance**, repeated similar final consonant sounds in stressed syllables with dissimilar vowel sounds: ". . . fiend / . . . behind"
- **Assonance**, a repeated vowel sound in stressed syllables with dissimilar consonant sounds: "The western wave was all aflame."
- **Internal rhyme**, the use of rhymes within a poetic line: "With heavy thump, a lifeless lump, . . ."

Comparing Literary Works Notice how, in both poems, the rhythms propel you forward. At the same time, Coleridge uses sound devices; *archaic,* or old-fashioned, words such as *eftsoons* ("immediately"); and exotic place names ("Xanadu") to create a riveting fantasy.

3 Reading Strategy

Preparing to Read Complex Texts By **comparing and contrasting sound devices** in two of his poems, you can understand how Coleridge evokes a range of moods. As you read, use a chart like the one shown to compare the effects of sound devices in the two poems.

Passages

Mariner	Kubla
The ship drove fast, loud roared the blast,/And southward	

Sound Device	
Internal rhyme, assonance	

4 Vocabulary

averred (ə vurd′) *v.* stated to be true (p. 824)

sojourn (sō′ jurn) *v.* stay for a while (p. 831)

expiated (eks′ pē āt′ id) *v.* atoned for, especially by suffering (p. 838)

reverence (rev′ ər əns) *n.* deep respect (p. 845)

sinuous (sin′ yo͞o əs) *adj.* bending; winding (p. 847)

tumult (to͞o′ mult′) *n.* noisy commotion (p. 848)

PHLit Online! www.PHLitOnline.com

Vocabulary Development

Vocabulary Knowledge Rating

Create a **Vocabulary Knowledge Rating Chart** (***Professional Development Guidebook,*** pp. 32–33) for the vocabulary words on the student page. Give each student a copy of the chart with the words on it. Read the words aloud, and have students mark their ratings in the Before Reading column. Urge students to attend to these words as they read and discuss the selections.

In order to gauge how much instruction you need to provide, tally how many students are confident in their knowledge of each word. As students read, point out the words and their context.

PHLit Online! **Vocabulary Central,** featuring tools and activities for studying vocabulary, is available online at **www.PHLitOnline.com.**

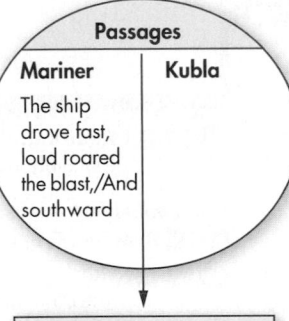

Samuel Taylor Coleridge

(1772–1834)

5 Author of *The Rime of the Ancient Mariner* • "Kubla Khan"

The poetry of Samuel Taylor Coleridge stands at the place where real life slips into dreams and facts are reborn as fantasies. More than any other Romantic poet, he dared to journey inward—deep into the world of the imagination.

Early Fantasies Coleridge was born in Ottery St. Mary on the Devon coast of England, the last of ten children. At an early age, he retreated into a world of books and fantasy. When he was nine, his father died, and Coleridge was sent to school in London. Later, he went to Cambridge University.

Utopian Plans At Cambridge, Coleridge's hunger for new ideas led him into radical politics. He became a friend of the poet Robert Southey. Inspired by the early promise of the French Revolution, the two men planned to form a settlement in Pennsylvania based on their utopian political ideas. The plan collapsed, however, when Southey's aunt refused to fund their project.

"Poetry: the best words in the best order."

A Literary Breakthrough In 1795, Coleridge and his wife, Sara Fricker, moved to Somerset, where he became a friend of poet William Wordsworth. In 1798, the two poets published *Lyrical Ballads*, a joint collection of their works. The four poems that make up Coleridge's contribution to the volume include his masterpiece *The Rime of the Ancient Mariner.* The collection of poems slowly gained critical attention. In the end, it caused a revolution in poetic style and thought, firmly establishing the movement known as Romanticism.

Success and Difficulty As Coleridge's fame grew, he suffered increasingly from asthma and rheumatism. He began to rely heavily on pain-killers, which dulled his creative powers. He sought relief from pain in the warmer climates of Malta and Italy. His travels, however, did not relieve his pain and caused the collapse of his marriage.

Though the end of his life was troubled, Coleridge left a great legacy in poetry and literary criticism. Above all, he helped establish the importance of the imagination in literature and in life.

Daily Bellringer

For each class, have students complete one of the five activities for the appropriate week in the *Daily Bellringer Activities* booklet.

Multidraft Reading

To assist struggling readers and to enhance reading for all, assign the text in chunks. For each reading, have students set the purpose indicated:

- **First reading**—identifying key ideas and details and answering any Reading Checks.
- **Second reading**—analyzing craft and structure and responding to the side-column prompts.
- **Third reading**—integrating knowledge and ideas, connecting to other texts and the world, and answering the end-of-selection questions.

For more guidance, refer to the *Classroom Strategies and Teaching Routines* card on Multidraft Reading.

5 Background

More About the Author

Already well-read when he arrived at Cambridge University, Coleridge found too little to challenge him. Following the collapse of his plans with Robert Southey to set up a colony in Pennsylvania, Coleridge edited a radical Christian journal, *The Watchman.* The end of his marriage, his increasing dissipation from abuse of laudanum (an opium preparation), and the breakup of his friendship with the Wordsworths marked the lowest phase in Coleridge's life. Yet he still managed to produce masterful works.

PHLit Online!
www.PHLitOnline.com

Teaching From Technology

Preparing to Read
Go to **www.PHLitOnline.com** and display the ***Get Connected!*** slide show for these selections. Have the class brainstorm responses to the writing prompt, entering ideas in the interactive journal. Then, have students complete their written responses as homework.

To build background, display the Background and More About the Author features.

Using the Interactive Text
Go to **www.PHLitOnline.com** and display the Enriched Online Student Edition. As the class reads the selections or listens to the narration, record answers to side-column prompts using the graphic organizers accessible on the interactive page. Alternatively, have students use the online edition individually, answering the prompts as they read.

❶ About the Selection

This poem vividly illustrates the torments guilt can create and the horror of complete isolation from society. The central character, the ancient Mariner, recounts the tale of his crime against life—the killing of an albatross—and the physical and emotional punishments his action sets in motion.

❷ Activating Prior Knowledge

Ask students if they can describe how a child who has broken something might behave. Elicit other examples of guilty behavior. Note that guilt introduces a division between the person who feels guilt and other individuals. Have students write a paragraph about a time when they felt guilty, and how they overcame that feeling.

Concept Connector →

Tell students they will return to their responses after reading the selection.

❸ Humanities

Engraving for "The Rime of the Ancient Mariner," 1875, by Gustave Doré

This illustration is a part of a series of illustrations created by Gustave Doré.

Doré, who was born in Strasbourg, France, near the German border, moved to Paris in 1847.

Ask: What elements in the engraving capture the setting of the poem?

Answer: The story within the story is set at sea on the Ancient Mariner's ship, which this engraving captures.

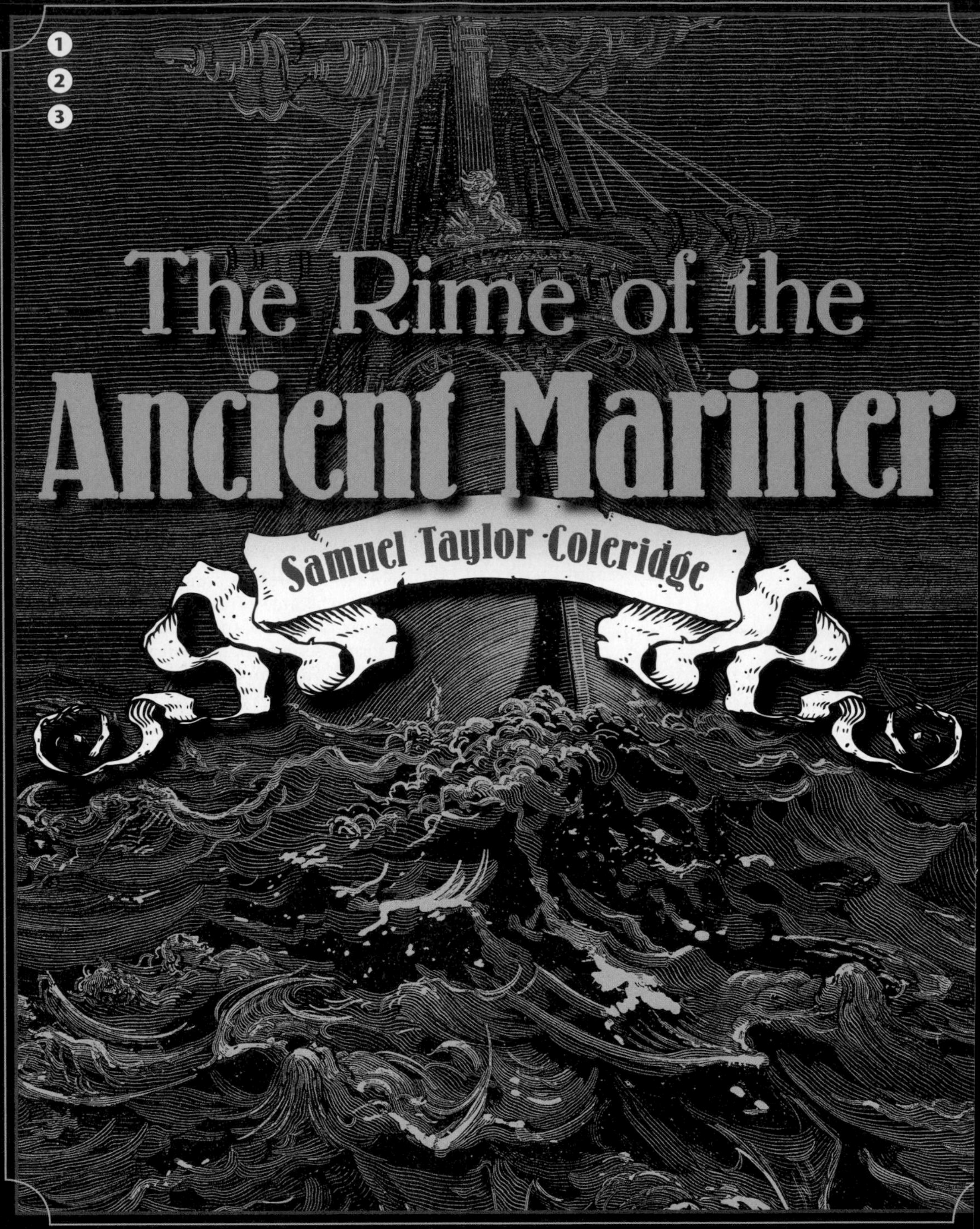

The Rime of the Ancient Mariner

Samuel Taylor Coleridge

Text Complexity Rubric

	The Rime of the Ancient Mariner	Kubla Khan
Qualitative Measures		
Context/ Knowledge Demands	Romantic verse fantasy; cultural knowledge demands 1 2 (3) 4 5	Romantic poem fragment; historical knowledge demands 1 (2) 3 4 5
Structure/Language Conventionality and Clarity	Archaic diction; sailing jargon 1 2 (3) 4 5	Long sentences; sensory language 1 2 (3) 4 5
Levels of Meaning/ Purpose/Concept Level	Challenging (guilt, isolation, supernatural) 1 2 3 (4) 5	Accessible (wild beauty, exotic setting) 1 (2) 3 4 5
Quantitative Measures		
Lexile/Text Length	NP / 3,861 words	NP / 352 words
Overall Complexity	**More complex**	**More accessible**

Background

Coleridge used dreams as the basis of many of his great poems. "The Rime of the Ancient Mariner" was based on a dream reported by his friend John Cruikshank. Starting with the dream as raw material, Coleridge and Wordsworth began to elaborate upon it. Wordsworth suggested that the act that would drive the entire poem was a crime committed at sea. Using this idea and his own lively imagination, Coleridge wrote a poem that has chilled and enthralled audiences to this day. (The margin notes in italics were written by the poet.)

Argument

How a Ship having passed the Line[1] was driven by storms to the cold Country towards the South Pole: and how from thence she made her course to the tropical Latitude of the Great Pacific Ocean; and of the strange things that befell: and in what manner the Ancyent Marinere came back to his own Country.

Part I

An ancient Mariner meeteth three Gallants bidden to a wedding feast and detaineth one.

It is an ancient Mariner,
And he stoppeth one of three.
"By thy long gray beard and glittering eye,
Now wherefore stopp'st thou me?"

"The Bridegroom's doors are opened wide,
And I am next of kin;
The guests are met, the feast is set:
May'st hear the merry din."

The Wedding Guest is spellbound by the eye of the old seafaring man and constrained to hear his tale.

He holds him with his skinny hand,
"There was a ship," quoth he.
"Hold off! unhand me, graybeard loon!"
Eftsoons[2] his hand dropped he.

He holds him with his glittering eye—
The Wedding Guest stood still,

1. **Line** Equator.
2. **Eftsoons** immediately.

4 ◄ **Critical Viewing** Identify two elements in this engraving that create a gloomy, suspense-filled atmosphere. **[Analyze]**

5 **Literary Analysis**
Poetic Sound Devices What examples of internal rhymes and assonance can you find in lines 5–8?

6 **Reading Check** What effect does the ancient Mariner have on the Wedding Guest?

4 Critical Viewing

Possible answer: It is a dark day at sea and the shadows give it a feeling as if something might happen.

5 Literary Analysis

Poetic Sound Devices

1. Review with students the definitions of *internal rhyme* (the use of rhyme within a poetic line) and *assonance* (the repetition of a vowel sound in stressed syllables with different consonant sounds).
2. Have students read lines 5–8 to themselves, and then have a student volunteer read the lines aloud.
3. Then, **ask** students the Literary Analysis question.
   Answer: The internal rhyme is *met/set*. There is assonance in *next/guests/met* (or *set*).

6 Reading Check

Answer: The Mariner has a hypnotic effect on the Wedding Guest. The Wedding Guest is spellbound by his eye and cannot choose but to listen to him.

PHLit Online!

These selections are available in interactive format in the **Enriched Online Student Edition** at **www.PHLitOnline.com**, which includes a thematically related video with writing prompt or an interactive graphic organizer.

Text Complexity: Reader and Task Suggestions

The Rime of the Ancient Mariner		Kubla Khan	
Preparing to Read the Text	**Leveled Tasks**	**Preparing to Read the Text**	**Leveled Tasks**
• Using the Background on SE p. 821, explain that supernatural elements play a strong role in Coleridge's poem. • Explain that the plot of this poem involves a crime against nature committed at sea. • Guide students to use Multidraft Reading strategies (TE p. 819).	***Levels of Meaning*** If students will have difficulty with the levels of meaning, have them focus on the exciting plot in their first reading. Then, as they reread, have them consider the significance of the mariner's crime and punishment. ***Analyzing*** If students will not have difficulty with the levels of meaning, have them focus on how imagery, sound devices, and other style elements help capture the mariner's isolation.	• Using the Background on SE p. 847, discuss why a dream would be likely to inspire writing that expresses Romanticism. • Discuss the devices a poet might use to capture the magnificence of an exotic setting. • Guide students to use Multidraft Reading strategies (TE p. 819).	***Structure/Language*** If students will have difficulty with the sensory imagery, read the poem aloud to them, using the musical sound devices to help them comprehend the setting's mood or atmosphere. Then, as they reread, tell them to use context clues to help them understand the vivid imagery. ***Evaluating*** If students will not have difficulty with the sensory imagery, have them analyze its effectiveness in capturing the mood of the poem.

❼ Humanities

Engraving for "The Rime of the Ancient Mariner," 1875, by Gustave Doré

This engraving illustrates the stanzas of the poem in which the Mariner accosts the Wedding Guest.

French illustrator Gustave Doré was born in 1832 and began his career as a caricaturist for a weekly humor magazine in Paris. A self-taught artist, Doré refined his technique through independent study of engraving at the National Library in Paris. Doré's skillful figure drawing and composition are evident in this drawing.

Use this question for discussion:

What lines in the poem are reflected in the engraving's portrayal of the Mariner's eyes?
Answer: This image suggests lines 3 and 13.

❽ Critical Viewing

Answer: Students may say that the Wedding Guest is annoyed or a bit afraid, but at the same time fascinated by the Mariner.

❽ ▶ **Critical Viewing** From the expression on the Wedding Guest's face (figure on far left), what can you infer about his reaction to the ancient Mariner? **[Infer]**

❼

And listens like a three years' child:
The Mariner hath his will.

The Wedding Guest sat on a stone:
He cannot choose but hear;
And thus spake on that ancient man,
The bright-eyed Mariner.

"The ship was cheered, the harbor cleared,
Merrily did we drop
Below the kirk,[3] below the hill,
Below the lighthouse top.

The Mariner tells how the ship sailed southward with a good wind and fair weather till it reached the Line.

"The Sun came up upon the left,
Out of the sea came he!
And he shone bright, and on the right
Went down into the sea.

"Higher and higher every day,
Till over the mast at noon[4]—"
The Wedding Guest here beat his breast,
For he heard the loud bassoon.

The Wedding Guest heareth the bridal music; but the Mariner continueth his tale.

The bride hath paced into the hall.
Red as a rose is she;

---

3. kirk church.
4. over . . . noon The ship has reached the equator.

Enrichment: Understanding Science

The Albatross

Several different albatross species can be found in the cold regions near Antarctica: the royal albatross, the sooty albatross, and the wandering albatross. All share the ability to glide, sometimes for hours, if there is sufficient wind. In calm weather, its size forces the albatross to rest frequently, on land or water. Albatross often follow ships and feed on scraps of food tossed overboard.

Activity: Understanding the Albatross Have students conduct research on the albatross. Suggest that they record information in the **Enrichment: Investigating Science** worksheet, ***Professional Development Guidebook***, page 241. Have them use the results of their research to write a short paper explaining why they think Coleridge chose the albatross to play a key role in his poem.

Nodding their heads before her goes
The merry minstrelsy.

9
The Wedding Guest he beat his breast,
Yet he cannot choose but hear;
And thus spake on that ancient man
The bright-eyed Mariner.

The ship driven by a storm toward the South Pole.

"And now the Storm blast came, and he
Was tyrannous and strong:
He struck with his o'ertaking wings,
And chased us south along.

"With sloping masts and dipping prow,
As who pursued with yell and blow
Still treads the shadow of his foe,
And forward bends his head,
The ship drove fast, loud roared the blast,
And southward aye[5] we fled.

10
"And now there came both mist and snow.
And it grew wondrous cold;
And ice, mast-high, came floating by,
As green as emerald.

The land of ice, and of fearful sounds, where no living thing was to be seen.

"And through the drifts the snowy clifts[6]
Did send a dismal sheen;
Nor shapes of men nor beasts we ken[7]—
The ice was all between.

"The ice was here, the ice was there,
The ice was all around;
It cracked and growled, and roared and howled,
Like noises in a swound![8]

Till a great sea bird, called the Albatross, came through the snow-fog, and was received with great joy and hospitality.

"At length did cross an Albatross,
Thorough[9] the fog it came;
As if it had been a Christian soul,
We hailed it in God's name.

"It ate the food it ne'er had eat,[10]
And round and round it flew.

---

5. **aye** ever.
6. **clifts** icebergs.
7. **ken** knew.
8. **swound** swoon.
9. **thorough** through.
10. **eat** (et) old form of *eaten.*

Literary Analysis
Poetic Sound Devices What archaic word-form appears in lines 37–40?

Reading Strategy
Comparing and Contrasting Sound Devices Find one line in lines 51–54 that contains the long and the short sound of the same vowel. What emphasis does this alternation create?

11 **Reading Check**
In the Mariner's tale, what happens to the ship shortly after it sets out?

9 Literary Analysis

Poetic Sound Devices and the Language of Fantasy

1. Have students read lines 37–40 to themselves. Ask them to identify any words with which they are not familiar.
2. Then, **ask** students the Literary Analysis question.
   Answer: Students should recognize that the use of *spake* instead of *spoke* is archaic.

10 Reading Strategy

Comparing and Contrasting Sound Devices

Read aloud the bracketed passage to students. Ask students to listen carefully to the vowel sounds as you read.

- **Monitor Progress: Ask** students the Reading Strategy question.
  Possible response: Students may say that the alternation of long and short sounds of the vowel *a* in line 53 ("mast-high, came") and the alternation of long and short sounds of the vowel *e* in line 54 ("As green as emerald") create a wavelike movement; the contrast emphasizes the words with the long sound—*came* and *green.*
- **Reteach:** If students have difficulty with the question, have a volunteer read the stanza out loud. Classmates should volunteer suggestions for which words to emphasize. As the volunteer adapts his or her reading to these suggestions, the class should evaluate which pattern of emphasis best reflects the music of the vowel sounds in the line.

11 Reading Check

Answer: It encounters bad weather.

Differentiated Instruction for Universal Access

Support for Special-Needs Students

Have students consider the engraving on the previous page. Have them explain how the engraving illustrates the opening scene of the poem. For students who are still struggling with comprehension, play **Listening to Literature Audio CDs,** and have students read along to support their comprehension.

Support for Less Proficient Readers

Because "The Rime of the Ancient Mariner" opens with a dialogue between two somewhat mysterious characters, students may have difficulty focusing on the progress of the narrative. Encourage students to read the first few stanzas of the poem, paying special attention to who is speaking and to whom. Then have students reread "The Rime of the Ancient Mariner" silently as they listen to **Listening to Literature Audio CDs.**

⑫ Critical Viewing
Answer: It is innocent and unaware that it is about to be hit.

⑬ Reading Strategy
Comparing and Contrasting Sound Devices

1. Have student volunteers offer definitions for alliteration and internal rhyme. Have a volunteer read aloud lines 91–94.
2. Then, **ask** students the Reading Strategy question.
 Answer: Alliteration and internal rhyme add emphasis to and slow down lines of poetry. They also make the words involved seem to follow one another as if they were fated, since sound as well as sense requires the use of these particular words. In this way, the alliterations *had/hellish, would/work/woe,* and *breeze/blow,* along with the internal rhyme *averred/bird,* make the stanza portentous and contribute to the fatal feeling of the Mariner's action.

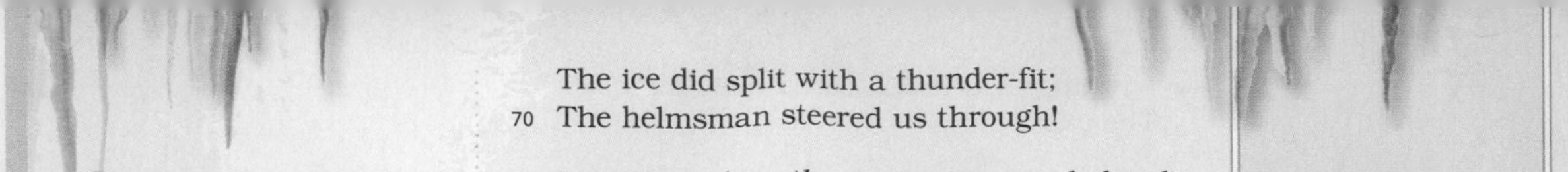

⑫ ▶ Critical Viewing
Based on the details of this illustration, how would you characterize the Albatross?
[Connect]

Reading Strategy
Comparing and Contrasting Sound Devices How does the use of alliteration and internal rhyme in lines 91–94 give a fatal feeling to the Mariner's deed?

Vocabulary
averred (ə vurd′) *v.* stated to be true

The ice did split with a thunder-fit;
70 The helmsman steered us through!

"And a good south wind sprung up behind;
The Albatross did follow,
And every day, for food or play,
Came to the mariner's hollo!

75 "In mist or cloud, on mast or shroud,[11]
It perched for vespers[12] nine;
Whiles all the night, through fog-smoke white,
Glimmered the white Moonshine."

"God save thee, ancient Mariner!
80 From the fiends, that plague thee thus!—
Why look'st thou so?"[13] "With my crossbow
I shot the Albatross."

Part II ●━━━━━

"The Sun now rose upon the right:[14]
Out of the sea came he,
85 Still hid in mist, and on the left
Went down into the sea.

"And the good south wind still blew behind,
But no sweet bird did follow.
Nor any day for food or play
90 Came to the mariners' hollo!

⑬ "And I had done a hellish thing,
And it would work 'em woe:
For all averred, I had killed the bird
That made the breeze to blow.

95 Ah wretch! said they, the bird to slay,
That made the breeze to blow!

"Nor dim nor red, like God's own head,
The glorious Sun uprist;[15]
Then all averred, I had killed the bird
100 That brought the fog and mist.
'Twas right, said they, such birds to slay,
That bring the fog and mist.

11. shroud *n.* ropes stretching from the ship's side to the masthead.
12. vespers evenings.
13. God . . . so spoken by the Wedding Guest.
14. The Sun . . . right The ship is now headed north.
15. uprist arose.

And lo! the Albatross proveth a bird of good omen, and followeth the ship as it returned northward through fog and floating ice.

The ancient Mariner inhospitably killeth the pious bird of good omen.

His shipmates cry out against the ancient Mariner for killing the bird of good luck.

But when the fog cleared off, they justify the same, and thus make themselves accomplices in the crime.

Engraving by Gustave Doré for "The Rime of the Ancient Mariner" by Samuel Taylor Coleridge © 1970 by Dover Publications, Inc.

Enrichment: Understanding Symbols

Birds
Particular birds may mean different things in different cultures. For example, the owl meant death to the ancient Egyptians but wisdom to the ancient Greeks. Traditionally, sailors have attributed a number of meanings to the albatross. Killing an albatross was held to bring bad luck, and some sailors said the birds were inhabited by the souls of dead sea captains.

Activity: Comparing Symbols Have students conduct research on what certain types of birds represent in different cultures. Suggest that they record information in the **Enrichment: Analyzing Themes and Symbols** worksheet, *Professional Development Guidebook,* page 243. Have them use the results to compare the significance certain birds have in different cultures.

14 Humanities

Engraving for "The Rime of the Ancient Mariner," 1875, by Gustave Doré

This illustration depicts the shooting of the albatross, capturing the instant just prior to the arrow's strike.

Use this question for discussion:

What elements in the engraving capture the setting of the poem?
Answer: Elements that capture the setting include icicles on the rigging, the drifting ice, and the grayish sky.

Differentiated Instruction for Universal Access

Culturally Responsive Instruction

Culture Focus Remind students that some sailors are superstitious and think that if they kill an albatross, it will bring bad luck. Point out that many different cultures have their own sets of superstitions. For example, there are certain cultures that believe that spiders in the house are good luck. Ask students to reflect on their home culture or family's country of origin and what superstitions they have. Then have them compare these to the superstitions with which they are familiar that come from the United States.

⓯ Reading Strategy

Comparing and Contrasting Sound Devices

1. Have students read lines 115–119 to themselves. As they read, encourage students to picture the becalmed ship, unable to move.
2. Then, **ask** them the first Reading Strategy question.
   Answer: The repetition of words echoes the ship's condition of rest; like the ship, the line does not move, since the same words keep returning.

⓰ Reading Strategy

Comparing and Contrasting Sound Devices

1. Have students read lines 127–130 to themselves. Encourage them to focus on the sound devices in these lines.
2. Ask students to identify the sound devices in these lines.
3. Then, **ask** students the second Reading Strategy question.
   Answer: Students should recognize that the massing together of sound devices gives these lines the dramatic effect of a chant or incantation.

"The fair breeze blew, the white foam flew,
The furrow[16] followed free;
We were the first that ever burst
Into that silent sea.

The fair breeze continues; the ship enters the Pacific Ocean, and sails northward, even till it reaches the Line. The Ship hath been suddenly becalmed.

"Down dropped the breeze, the sails
dropped down,
'Twas sad as sad could be;
And we did speak only to break
The silence of the sea!

"All in a hot and copper sky,
The bloody Sun, at noon,
Right up above the mast did stand,
No bigger than the Moon.

Reading Strategy **Comparing and Contrasting Sound Devices** How does the repetition of words in lines 115–119 contribute to the image of the stilled ship? ⓯

"Day after day, day after day,
We stuck, nor breath nor motion;
As idle as a painted ship
Upon a painted ocean.

"Water, water, everywhere,
And all the boards did shrink;
Water, water, everywhere,
Nor any drop to drink.

And the Albatross begins to be avenged.

"The very deep did rot: O Christ!
That ever this should be!
Yea, slimy things did crawl with legs
Upon the slimy sea.

Reading Strategy **Comparing and Contrasting Sound Devices** What effect does the increased concentration of sound devices in lines 127–130 have? ⓰

"About, about, in reel and rout[17]
The death fires[18] danced at night;
The water, like a witch's oils,
Burned green, and blue and white.

"And some in dreams assurèd were
Of the Spirit that plagued us so;
Nine fathom deep he had followed us
From the land of mist and snow.

A Spirit had followed them; one of the invisible inhabitants of this planet, neither departed souls nor angels. They are very numerous, and there is no climate or element without one or more.

"And every tongue, through utter drought,
Was withered at the root;
We could not speak, no more than if
We had been choked with soot.

16. **furrow** ship's wake.
17. **rout** disorderly crowd.
18. **death fires** St. Elmo's fire, a visible electrical discharge from a ship's mast, believed by sailors to be an omen of disaster.

Think Aloud

Reading Strategy: Comparing and Contrasting Sound Devices
To model the first Reading Strategy question, use the following "think aloud":

After reading the lines, I notice that "day after day" is repeated, as well as the word *painted.* The repetition of "day after day" seems to emphasize the lack of movement, even in the line, which returns to the same words "day after day." The idea of the scene being similar to a painting suggests the stillness of the ship as well as the stillness of the area in general.

Engraving by Gustave Doré for "The Rime of the Ancient Mariner" by Samuel Taylor Coleridge
© 1970 by Dover Publications, Inc.

17

18 ◄ **Critical Viewing**
What effects does the artist, Gustave Doré, use to capture the eerie mood of the poem? **[Analyze]**

The shipmates, in their sore distress, would fain throw the whole guilt on the ancient Mariner: in sign whereof they hang the dead sea bird round his neck.

"Ah! well a-day! what evil looks
140 Had I from old and young!
Instead of the cross, the Albatross
About my neck was hung.

Part III

The ancient Mariner beholdeth a sign in the element afar off.

"There passed a weary time. Each throat
Was parched, and glazed each eye.
145 A weary time! a weary time!
How glazed each weary eye,
When looking westward, I beheld
A something in the sky.

19

"At first it seemed a little speck,
150 And then it seemed a mist;
It moved and moved, and took at last
A certain shape, I wist.[19]

"A speck, a mist, a shape, I wist!
And still it neared and neared:
155 As if it dodged a water sprite,
It plunged and tacked and veered.

19. wist knew.

**Reading Strategy
Comparing and Contrasting Sound Devices** What poetic effect does Coleridge use in lines 149–153 to build suspense?

20 ☑ Reading Check

What causes the sailors to suffer?

The Rime of the Ancient Mariner **827**

17 **Humanities**
Engraving for "The Rime of the Ancient Mariner," 1875, by Gustave Doré

This illustration depicts the sailors' misery and suffering while stranded at sea: "Water, water, everywhere, / Nor any drop to drink."

Use this question for discussion:

What elements in the engraving reveal the thirst and suffering of the sailors?

Answer: Elements that reveal the sailors' thirst and suffering include a man grasping his head in anguish, a sailor bent over the side of the ship as if imploring the heavens, and the general mass of men lying prostrate or with heads bowed.

18 **Critical Viewing**

Possible Answer: The artist uses the contrast of light and darkness as well as layout to capture the eerie mood of the poem. Most of the suffering sailors lie in the darkest part of the illustration and at the bottom of the illustration. Only a very few sailors are at the top and in the light.

19 **Reading Strategy**
Comparing and Contrasting Sound Devices

1. Have students read lines 149–153 in pairs, paying attention to the poetic effects Coleridge uses.
2. **Ask** the Reading Strategy question.
 Answer: Coleridge uses repetition to build suspense.

20 **Reading Check**

Answer: The relentless heat of the sun and the lack of drinkable water cause the sailors to suffer.

21 Literary Analysis
Poetic Sound Devices and the Language of Fantasy

1. **Read aloud** the bracketed line. Remind students that using fantastic language and archaic vocabulary can contribute to the mood of a poem.

2. **Have students** identify the archaic words in this line.

3. **Ask** them the Literary Analysis question
 Answer: Words like *hither* and *weal* set this line apart from contemporary culture.

22 Critical Viewing

Answer: One would expect the other sailors would experience joy and relief at the sighting of another ship on the horizon. The sailors in the engraving do not look joyful. Some are lost in their despair, while those who seem aware of the other ship's approach still seem grim.

Literary Analysis
Poetic Sound Devices How does the line "Hither to work us weal" give the sense that these events are taking place in a strange, distant era?

22 ▶ Critical Viewing
What reactions to the sighting of the other ship would you expect from the sailors? Can you find such reactions in the engraving? Explain. **[Connect]**

"With throats unslaked, with black lips baked,
We could nor laugh nor wail;
Through utter drought all dumb we stood!
160 I bit my arm, I sucked the blood,
And cried, A sail! a sail!

"With throats unslaked, with black lips baked,
Agape they heard me call:
Gramercy![20] for joy did grin,
165 And all at once their breath drew in,
As they were drinking all.

"See! see! (I cried) she tacks no more!
Hither to work us weal;[21]
Without a breeze, without a tide,
170 She steadies with upright keel!

"The western wave was all aflame.
The day was well nigh done!
Almost upon the western wave
Rested the broad bright Sun;
175 When that strange shape drove suddenly
Betwixt us and the Sun.

"And straight the Sun was flecked with bars,
(Heaven's Mother send us grace!)
As if through a dungeon grate he peered
180 With broad and burning face.

"Alas! (thought I, and my heart beat loud)
How fast she nears and nears!
Are those *her* sails that glance in the Sun,
Like restless gossameres?[22]

185 "Are those *her* ribs through which the Sun
Did peer, as through a grate?
And is that Woman all her crew?
Is that a Death? and are there two?
Is Death that woman's mate?

190 "*Her* lips were red, *her* looks were free,
Her locks were yellow as gold;
Her skin was as white as leprosy,

20. **Gramercy** (grə mʉr´ sē): great thanks.
21. **work us weal** assist us.
22. **gossameres** floating cobwebs.

At its nearer approach, it seemeth him to be a ship; and at a dear ransom he freeth his speech from the bonds of thirst.

A flash of joy:

And horror follows. For can it be a ship that comes onward without wind or tide?

It seemeth him but the skeleton of a ship.

And its ribs are seen as bars on the face of the setting Sun.

The Specter Woman and her Death-mate, and no other on board the skeleton ship.

Like vessel, like crew! Death and Life-in-Death have diced for the ship's crew, and she (the latter) winneth the ancient Mariner.

828 Rebels and Dreamers (1798–1832)

Engraving by Gustave Doré for "The Rime of the Ancient Mariner" by Samuel Taylor Coleridge © 1970 by Dover Publications, Inc.

Enrichment: Understanding Science

Dehydration
Following the killing of the albatross, the sailors suffer dehydration when their water supply runs out. Their suffering is realistic, since water is a necessary requirement for physical performance, as well as for life itself. The normal adult male requires two to three liters of water each day to replace that lost through perspiration and excretion. Without this replacement water, dehydration begins, performance diminishes, and serious health dangers soon develop.

Activity: Investigating Science Have students conduct research on dehydration. Suggest that they record information in the **Enrichment: Investigating Science** worksheet, *Professional Development Guidebook,* page 241. Have them use the results of their research to write short papers on the effects of dehydration on people.

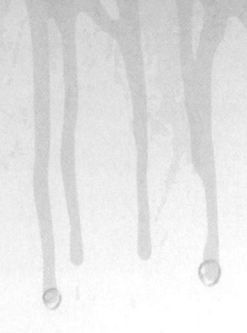

23 Humanities

Engraving for "The Rime of the Ancient Mariner," 1875, by Gustave Doré

This illustration depicts the sailors' hopelessness and suffering while stranded at sea.

Though Doré also worked in painting and sculpture, particularly after 1870, he was never as successful in these arts as he was with book illustrating. Apparently quite obsessed with Coleridge's poem, he created in this series of illustrations some of his most eerie and disturbing images. Although the illustrated volume of Coleridge's poem was not a commercial success, it is considered an artistic triumph for Gustave Doré.

Use these questions for discussion:

1. What details in the engraving convey the peril of the ship?
   Possible responses: Students may cite the sailors' agonized expressions, the calm seas around the ship, and the sailors' desperate efforts to see into the distance and perhaps signal the faraway ship.
2. What mood does this illustration evoke?
   Answer: The mood is despairing and hopeless.

Differentiated Instruction for Universal Access

Culturally Responsive Instruction

Culture Focus The character Death plays a role in this part of the poem. Point out to students that death is not always seen as a frightening aspect of life in all cultures. There are some cultures, such as the Mexican culture, that celebrate the dead. Explain that many Mexicans celebrate Los Días de los Muertos or the Days of the Dead. Ask students to reflect on their home culture or family's country of origin and their attitudes toward death.

24 Literary Analysis

Poetic Sound Devices and the Language of Fantasy

1. After reading aloud the bracketed passage, have students reread the passage with a partner and consider any poetic sound devices or fantastic language.
2. **Ask** students the Literary Analysis question.
   Answer: The name of the woman is like something out of an old legend or nightmare, and it adds to the mysterious feeling of the story.

25 Literary Analysis

Poetic Sound Devices and the Language of Fantasy

1. Point out the phrase "four times fifty men" to students. Ask them how many men this refers to.
2. Then, **ask** them the Literary Analysis question.
   Answer: This archaic way of enumerating makes the story seem more fanciful than real.

Literary Analysis
Poetic Sound Devices In what way does the name of the woman—Life-in-Death—add to the eerie, mysterious atmosphere of the story?

24 The Nightmare Life-in-Death was she,
Who thicks man's blood with cold.

"The naked hulk alongside came,
And the twain were casting dice;
'The game is done! I've won! I've won!'
Quoth she, and whistles thrice.

"The Sun's rim dips; the stars rush out:
At one stride comes the dark;
With far-heard whisper, o'er the sea,
Off shot the specter bark.

No twilight within the courts of the Sun.

"We listened and looked sideways up!
Fear at my heart, as at a cup,
My lifeblood seemed to sip!
The stars were dim, and thick the night,
The steersman's face by his lamp
gleamed white;
From the sails the dew did drip—
Till clomb[23] above the eastern bar
The hornèd[24] Moon, with one bright star
Within the nether tip.

At the rising of the Moon,

"One after one, by the star-dogged Moon,[25]
Too quick for groan or sigh,
Each turned his face with a ghastly pang,
And cursed me with his eye.

One after another,

Literary Analysis
Poetic Sound Devices
How does Coleridge's unusual way of expressing numbers contribute to the fairy-tale atmosphere?

25 "Four times fifty living men,
(And I heard nor sigh nor groan)
With heavy thump, a lifeless lump,
They dropped down one by one.

His shipmates drop down dead.

"The souls did from their bodies fly—
They fled to bliss or woe!
And every soul, it passed me by,
Like the whizz of my crossbow!"

But Life-in-Death begins her work on the ancient Mariner.

Part IV

"I fear thee, ancient Mariner!
I fear thy skinny hand!
And thou art long, and lank, and brown,
As is the ribbed sea sand.

The Wedding Guest feareth that a Spirit is talking to him;

23. clomb climbed.
24. hornèd crescent.
25. star-dogged Moon omen of impending evil to sailors.

Think Aloud

Literary Analysis: Poetic Sound Devices and the Language of Fantasy

To model the first Literary Analysis question, use the following "think aloud":

> I know that for many people, death can be a scary thing, especially if you are stranded at sea. Coleridge names the woman Life-in-Death, which has strong suggestions. The woman is like something out of a nightmare and her name matches this. The name adds to the mysterious and eerie feeling already established in the poem.

But the ancient Mariner assureth him of his bodily life, and proceedeth to relate his horrible penance.

"I fear thee and thy glittering eye,
And thy skinny hand, so brown."
"Fear not, fear not, thou Wedding Guest!
This body dropped not down.

"Alone, alone, all, all alone,
Alone on a wide wide sea!
And never a saint took pity on
My soul in agony.

He despiseth the creatures of the calm,

"The many men, so beautiful!
And they all dead did lie:
And a thousand thousand slimy things
Lived on; and so did I.

And envieth that they should live, and so many lie dead.

26 "I looked upon the rotting sea,
And drew my eyes away;
I looked upon the rotting deck,
And there the dead men lay.

"I looked to heaven, and tried to pray;
But or[26] ever a prayer had gushed,
A wicked whisper came, and made
My heart as dry as dust.

"I closed my lids, and kept them close,
And the balls like pulses beat;
For the sky and the sea and the sea and the sky
Lay like a load on my weary eye,
And the dead were at my feet.

But the curse liveth for him in the eye of the dead men.

"The cold sweat melted from their limbs,
Nor rot nor reek did they;
The look with which they looked on me
Had never passed away.

In his loneliness and fixedness he yearneth towards the journeying Moon, and the stars that still sojourn, yet still move onward; and everywhere the blue sky belongs to them,

"An orphan's curse would drag to hell
A spirit from on high;
But oh! more horrible than that
Is the curse in a dead man's eye!
Seven days, seven nights, I saw that curse,
And yet I could not die.

"The moving Moon went up the sky,
And nowhere did abide:

Reading Strategy
Comparing and Contrasting Sound Devices How does repetition in lines 240–243 emphasize the starkness of the Mariner's situation—the fact that he has "no way out"?

27 **Vocabulary**
sojourn (sō′ jurn) *v.* stay for a while

28 **Reading Check**
What has happened to the other sailors?

---

26. or before.

26 Reading Strategy

Comparing and Contrasting Sound Devices

1. Read the bracketed passage to students. Point out the repetition of "I looked upon the rotting . . ." in these lines. Ask students to describe the effect of this repetition.
2. Then, **ask** them the Reading Strategy question.
   Answer: The repetition in lines 240–243 emphasizes that the Mariner has no place to turn for comfort, finding only dead men on the ship and slimy life in the ocean.

27 Vocabulary Builder

Latin Root: *-journ-*

1. Call students' attention to the margin note for *sojourn,* a word that means "to stay or visit for a short while." Explain to students that *sojourn* contains the root *-journ-*, which is derived from the French and Latin words meaning "day."
2. Have students suggest other words and phrases that contain this Latin root, and list them on the chalkboard.
   Possible responses: adjourn, journey, journal, journalism
3. Have students look up any unfamiliar words in a dictionary.

28 Reading Check

Answer: The other sailors have died with their eyes gaping at the Ancient Mariner.

Spiral Review
Imagery

1. Remind students that they studied imagery in an earlier lesson.

2. **Ask** students the Spiral Review question.

 Possible response: The pattern of imagery contrasting shadows and light reinforces the tone, which contrasts attitudes of isolation and desolation with redemption.

㉙ Literary Analysis
Poetic Sound Devices and the Language of Fantasy

1. Ask students to identify the two events described in these lines.
 Answer: As soon as the Mariner is able to pray, the albatross falls from his neck and sinks into the sea.

 Then, encourage students to focus on the elements of fantasy in these lines.

2. **Ask** students the Literary Analysis question.
 Answer: When he admires and feels love for the water snakes, the Ancient Mariner reconnects himself to nature and the forces of life, so the dead albatross, the symbol of his rejection of nature, falls from around his neck. The coordination of internal events (the Mariner's discovery of love) with external, symbolic events (the dropping off of the albatross) is characteristic of fairy tales.

㉚ Critical Viewing

Answer: There are water snakes, which the artist has skillfully represented moving in "tracks of shining white." I don't see them in tracks that are like a "flash or golden fire," though.

Spiral Review
Imagery How does Coleridge's pattern of imagery in lines 270–276 help set the tone of the poem?

Literary Analysis
Poetic Sound Devices ㉙
What does the connection of the two events in lines 288–291 add to the fairy-tale quality of the story?

㉚ ▶ **Critical Viewing**
How does Coleridge's description of the creatures of the great calm compare and contrast with the artist's representation of them?
[Compare and Contrast]

265 Softly she was going up,
 And a star or two beside—

 "Her beams bemocked the sultry main,[27]
 Like April hoarfrost spread;
 But where the ship's huge shadow lay,
270 The charmèd water burned alway
 A still and awful red.

 "Beyond the shadow of the ship,
 I watched the water snakes:
 They moved in tracks of shining white,
275 And when they reared, the elfish light
 Fell off in hoary flakes.

 "Within the shadow of the ship
 I watched their rich attire:
 Blue, glossy green, and velvet black,
280 They coiled and swam; and every track
 Was a flash of golden fire.

 "O happy living things! no tongue
 Their beauty might declare:
 A spring of love gushed from my heart,
285 And I blessed them unaware;
 Sure my kind saint took pity on me,
 And I blessed them unaware.

 "The selfsame moment I could pray;
 And from my neck so free
290 The Albatross fell off, and sank
 Like lead into the sea.

Part V ◄━━━━━

 "Oh sleep! it is a gentle thing,
 Beloved from pole to pole!
 To Mary queen the praise be given!
295 She sent the gentle sleep from Heaven,
 That slid into my soul.

 "The silly[28] buckets on the deck.
 That had so long remained,
 I dreamed that they were filled with dew;
300 And when I awoke, it rained.

27. **main** open sea.
28. **silly** empty.

and is their appointed rest, and their native country and their own natural homes, which they enter unannounced, as lords that are certainly expected and yet there is a silent joy at their arrival.

By the light of the Moon he beholdeth God's creatures of the great calm.

Their beauty and their happiness.

He blesseth them in his heart.

The spell begins to break.

By grace of the holy Mother, the ancient Mariner is refreshed with rain.

Engraving by Gustave Doré for "The Rime of the Ancient Mariner" by Samuel Taylor Coleridge © 1970 by Dover Publications, Inc.

Enrichment: Understanding Psychology

Dreams

After the Mariner dreams that the buckets are filled with water and then awakens, it rains. In some cultures, this sequence of events could be seen as confirming the prophetic powers of dreams. Psychoanalyst Sigmund Freud's more recent perspective on dreams suggests that they reflect elements of the waking experience that are too painful or difficult to address, except during sleep.

Activity: Understanding Dreams Have students conduct research on the psychology of dreams. Suggest that they record information in the **Enrichment: Investigating Psychology** worksheet, *Professional Development Guidebook,* page 239. Have them use the results of their research to write a one-page description of their findings.

The Rime of the Ancient Mariner 833

31 Humanities

Engraving for "The Rime of the Ancient Mariner," 1875, by Gustave Doré

This engraving illustrates the stanzas of the poem in which the Mariner finds some form of redemption when he blesses the water snakes and the albatross falls from his neck.

Use this question for discussion:

What does the engraving suggest about the attitude of the Mariner at this moment?
Answer: I can see remorse in his eyes as he looks off in the distance.

Differentiated Instruction for Universal Access

Enrichment for Gifted/Talented Students

Have students design a costume for a character in "The Rime of the Ancient Mariner," using details they have gleaned from their reading of the poem. Students should work in pairs, or small groups, to design an appropriate costume for the character they have chosen or been assigned. Encourage students to reread the poem to find clues about that character's appearance if they are having difficulty remembering specifics. Tell students they should use their imaginations in their designs, or they can research the clothing of the time to get ideas.

㉜ Literary Analysis
Poetic Sound Devices

1. Have a volunteer provide an example of alliteration from earlier in the poem.
2. Then, **ask** students the Literary Analysis question
   Answer: Students should note that the repeated *dr* in *drunken*, *dreams*, and *drank* creates alliteration.

㉝ Literary Analysis
Poetic Sound Devices

1. Read aloud the bracketed passage to students.
2. Review with students the definition of *assonance* as the repetition of a vowel sound in stressed syllables with different consonant sounds.
3. Then, **ask** the Literary Analysis question.
   Answer: Students should identify the assonance of the words *groaned* and *uprose* in line 331.

Literary Analysis
Poetic Sound Devices
Which repeated consonant sound in lines 303–304 creates alliteration?

"My lips were wet, my throat was cold,
My garments all were dank;
㉜ Sure I had drunken in my dreams,
And still my body drank.

"I moved, and could not feel my limbs:
I was so light—almost
I thought that I had died in sleep,
And was a blessèd ghost.

"And soon I heard a roaring wind:
It did not come anear;
But with its sound it shook the sails,
That were so thin and sere.[29]

He heareth sounds and seeth strange sights and commotions in the sky and the element.

"The upper air burst into life!
And a hundred fire flags sheen,[30]
To and fro they were hurried about!
And to and fro, and in and out,
The wan stars danced between.

"And the coming wind did roar more loud,
And the sails did sigh like sedge;[31]
And the rain poured down from one
black cloud;
The Moon was at its edge.

"The thick black cloud was cleft, and still
The Moon was at its side:
Like waters shot from some high crag,
The lightning fell with never a jag,
A river steep and wide.

"The loud wind never reached the ship,
Yet now the ship moved on!
Beneath the lightning and the Moon
The dead men gave a groan.

The bodies of the ship's crew are inspired[32] and the ship moves on;

Literary Analysis
Poetic Sound Devices
Find an example of assonance—the repetition of vowel sounds in unrhymed syllables—in lines 331–334.

㉝ "They groaned, they stirred, they all uprose,
Nor spake, nor moved their eyes;
It had been strange, even in a dream,
To have seen those dead men rise.

29. **sere** dried up.
30. **fire flags sheen** the aurora australis, or southern lights, shone.
31. **sedge** *n.* rushlike plant that grows in wet soil.
32. **inspired** inspirited

Enrichment: Understanding Science

The Southern Lights

The Southern Lights, or Aurora Australis, that the Mariner sees can be observed around 70° south latitude. At about 70° north latitude, a similar phenomenon called the Northern Lights, or Aurora Borealis, can be observed. Both displays of light may take many shapes, from arcs or bands to fan-shaped coronas. They originate in the upper atmosphere when auroral electrons and protons collide at high speeds with atoms, causing the atoms to glow.

Activity: Investigating Science Have students conduct research on the Southern Lights. Suggest that they record information in the **Enrichment: Investigating Science** worksheet, ***Professional Development Guidebook***, page 241. Have them use the results of their research to write a short poem about the beauty of the Southern Lights.

"The helmsman steered, the ship moved on:
Yet never a breeze up-blew;
The mariners all 'gan work the ropes,
Where they were wont[33] to do;
They raised their limbs like lifeless tools—
We were a ghastly crew.

"The body of my brother's son
Stood by me, knee to knee:
The body and I pulled at one rope,
But he said nought to me."

But not by the souls of the men, nor by demons of earth or middle air, but by a blessed troop of angelic spirits, sent down by the invocation of the guardian saint.

"I fear thee, ancient Mariner!"
"Be calm, thou Wedding Guest!
'Twas not those souls that fled in pain,
Which to their corses[34] came again,
But a troop of spirits blessed:

34

"For when it dawned—they dropped their arms,
And clustered round the mast;
Sweet sounds rose slowly through
their mouths,
And from their bodies passed.

"Around, around, flew each sweet sound,
Then darted to the Sun;
Slowly the sounds came back again,
Now mixed, now one by one.

"Sometimes a-dropping from the sky
I heard the skylark sing;
Sometimes all little birds that are,
How they seemed to fill the sea and air
With their sweet jargoning![35]

"And now 'twas like all instruments,
Now like a lonely flute;
And now it is an angel's song,
That makes the heavens be mute.

"It ceased; yet still the sails made on
A pleasant noise till noon,
A noise like of a hidden brook
In the leafy month of June,

33. **wont** accustomed.
34. **corses** corpses.
35. **jargoning** singing.

Literary Analysis
Poetic Sound Devices
Find an example of alliteration—the repetition of initial consonant sounds—in lines 350–353.

35 **Reading Check**
What happens to the bodies of the Mariner's shipmates?

34 Literary Analysis

Poetic Sound Devices

1. Have students read lines 350–353 to themselves.
2. Review with students the definition of alliteration.
3. Then, **ask** students the Literary Analysis question.
   Answer: Students should cite the repetition of the *d* sound in "dawned—they dropped" in line 350 and the *s* sound in "Sweet sounds rose slowly . . ." in line 352.

   Monitor Progress: Have students discuss the effects that these sound devices have on the reader of the poem. Make sure they support their responses with details from the poem.
   Possible response: The alliterated *s* sound unifies and emphasizes the image of the slow, sweet sounds, encouraging the reader's wonder at this fantastical event.

35 Reading Check

Answer: The bodies of the Mariner's shipmates become inhabited by angelic spirits.

Differentiated Instruction for Universal Access

Strategy for Less Proficient Readers

Review with students how to analyze poetic sound effects such as assonance, alliteration, consonance, and internal rhyme by using **Reading Strategy Graphic Organizer B**, page 147 in ***Graphic Organizer Transparencies.*** Then, guide students as they read select pages of "The Rime of the Ancient Mariner" as a group. As students identify poetic devices, encourage them to analyze the effects of those devices using the techniques learned from the transparency.

36 Reading Strategy

Comparing and Contrasting Sound Devices

1. Have a student volunteer read aloud lines 373–376. Have students identify the use of alliteration in these lines.
   Answer: Alliteration occurs in the repeated *br* sound in *breeze* and *breathe* and in the repeated *s* sound in *sailed*, *slowly*, and *smoothly*.
2. Then, **ask** the Reading Strategy question.
   Answer: The alliteration enables the language of these lines to flow effortlessly from one word to another, in a fashion that mimics the boat's slow and smooth progress.

37 Humanities

Engraving for "The Rime of the Ancient Mariner," 1875, by Gustave Doré

This illustration depicts the moment when the Mariner's "living life returned" and he collapses "in a swound."

Ask: Which details suggest that it is the spirit "From the land of mist and snow" that is making the ship "go"?

Answer: The white clouds of mist surrounding the ship suggest that something mystical and otherworldly "made the ship to go."

38 Critical Viewing

Answer: The position of the Mariner—flat on his back with hands grasping at the ropes—conveys a mood of hopelessness. The ship's askew position also contributes to the mood.

That to the sleeping woods all night
Singeth a quiet tune.

Reading Strategy
Comparing and Contrasting Sound Devices How does the alliteration in lines 373–376 enhance the description of the boat's smooth progress?

36
"Till noon we quietly sailed on,
Yet never a breeze did breathe;
Slowly and smoothly went the ship,
Moved onward from beneath.

"Under the keel nine fathom deep,
From the land of mist and snow,
The spirit slid; and it was he
That made the ship to go.
The sails at noon left off their tune,
And the ship stood still also.

The lonesome Spirit from the South Pole carries on the ship as far as the Line, in obedience to the angelic troop, but still requireth vengeance.

"The Sun, right up above the mast,
Had fixed her to the ocean:
But in a minute she 'gan stir,
With a short uneasy motion—
Backwards and forwards half her length
With a short uneasy motion.

"Then like a pawing horse let go,
She made a sudden bound:
It flung the blood into my head,
And I fell down in a swound.

The Polar Spirit's fellow demons, the invisible inhabitants of the element, take part in his wrong; and two of them relate, one to the other, that penance long and heavy for the ancient Mariner hath been accorded to the Polar Spirit, who returneth southward.

37

Engraving by Gustave Doré for "The Rime of the Ancient Mariner" by Samuel Taylor Coleridge
© 1970 by Dover Publications, Inc.

38 ▶ **Critical Viewing** Which details convey the mood of hopelessness in this illustration? **[Analyze]**

Enrichment: Understanding Geography

Sea Travel
Given the speed of sea travel in Coleridge's day, one can estimate the duration of the Mariner's journey—from the equator to the Antarctic Circle and back again—at about 78 days. In the 1800s, a sailing ship took approximately four weeks to sail from Liverpool to New York, a distance of approximately 3,320 miles, yielding an average speed of 118 miles a day.

Activity: Mapmaking Have students conduct research on the path the Mariner might have taken. Suggest that they record information in the **Enrichment: Investigating Geography** worksheet, ***Professional Development Guidebook***, page 228. Have them use the results of their research to draw a map with the route the Ancient Mariner might have taken traced on it.

"How long in that same fit I lay,
I have not to declare;
395 But ere my living life returned,
I heard and in my soul discerned
Two voices in the air.

"'Is it he?' quoth one, 'Is this the man?
By him who died on cross,
400 With his cruel bow he laid full low
The harmless Albatross.

"'The spirit who bideth by himself
In the land of mist and snow,
He loved the bird that loved the man
405 Who shot him with his bow.'

"The other was a softer voice,
As soft as honeydew:
Quoth he, 'The man hath penance done,
And penance more will do.'

Part VI

FIRST VOICE

410 "'But tell me, tell me! speak again,
Thy soft response renewing—
What makes that ship drive on so fast?
What is the ocean doing?'

SECOND VOICE

"'Still as a slave before his lord,
415 The ocean hath no blast;
His great bright eye most silently
Up to the Moon is cast—

"'If he may know which way to go;
For she guides him smooth or grim.
420 See, brother, see! how graciously
She looketh down on him.'

FIRST VOICE

"'But why drives on that ship so fast,
Without or wave or wind?'

SECOND VOICE

"'The air is cut away before,
425 And closes from behind.

The Mariner hath been cast into a trance; for the angelic power causeth the vessel to drive northward faster than human life could endure.

Literary Analysis
Poetic Sound Devices How do the two voices contribute to Coleridge's creation of a dream world?

Literary Analysis
Poetic Sound Devices What instance of assonance can you find in lines 414–417?

41 ☑ **Reading Check**
What do the two voices discuss?

The Rime of the Ancient Mariner **837**

39 Literary Analysis
Poetic Sound Devices and the Language of Fantasy

1. Have two student volunteers read aloud lines 402–409. Review with students their understanding of who says what in this passage.

2. Then, **ask** students the first Literary Analysis question.
Answer: The voices that the ancient Mariner overhears are disembodied. They discuss his actions and his fate as if they had complete knowledge of him. These facts suggest that they are supernatural powers, as might be encountered in a dream world.

40 Literary Analysis
Poetic Sound Devices

1. Read the bracketed passage aloud and review with students their understanding of assonance.

2. Then, **ask** students the second Literary Analysis question.
Answer: Students should recognize assonance in words like *ocean* and *no* in line 415 and *eye* and *silently* in line 416.

41 Reading Check
Answer: The two voices discuss whether or not the Ancient Mariner has performed his penance for killing the albatross, and they discuss the progress of the ship.

Differentiated Instruction for Universal Access

Strategy for Special-Needs Students
Have students examine the illustrations throughout the text of "The Rime of the Ancient Mariner." Then, ask them to imagine that they are publishers looking for an artist to illustrate a new edition of Coleridge's poem. Have students make a list of all the scenes they would want illustrated in a new edition. Remind students that they will probably want different scenes from the ones Doré illustrated, or they may want them done in a different manner. Students should write a list of specifications for the artist and any other ideas they have.

42 Humanities

Engraving for "The Rime of the Ancient Mariner," 1875, by Gustave Doré

This illustration, while one of the series created for Coleridge's poem, does not depict any specific event. Rather it evokes the ship's isolation throughout the poem.

The French engraver Gustave Doré shared the exuberance of the Romantic lyric poets and illustrated many other Romantic works.

Use these questions for discussion:

1. How does the light in the illustration relate to the Mariner's description of events?
   Answer: The light is on the boat, just as the wind blows on the Mariner and his ship.
2. What element of the composition reflects the Mariner's spiritual experience?
   Answer: The boat is isolated amidst a sea of dark and turbulent water; the Mariner is spiritually isolated amidst the dark and turbulent experiences of death and despair.

43 Critical Viewing

Possible response: Students may say that this illustration more accurately depicts events very early in the poem, when the ship is storm tossed. In Part V, though the ship sails swiftly, the sailing is "smooth." The image is not portrayed from the Mariner's point of view, but rather from above.

42

43 ▶ **Critical Viewing** How closely can you connect this illustration to the events in the poem? Is the image being portrayed from the Ancient Mariner's point of view? Why or why not? **[Connect]**

"'Fly, brother, fly! more high, more high!
Or we shall be belated:
For slow and slow that ship will go,
When the Mariner's trance is abated.'

"I woke, and we were sailing on
As in a gentle weather:
'Twas night, calm night, the moon was high;
The dead men stood together.

The super-natural motion is retarded; the Mariner awakes, and his penance begins anew.

"All stood together on the deck,
For a charnel dungeon[36] fitter;
All fixed on me their stony eyes,
That in the Moon did glitter.

"The pang, the curse, with which they died,
Had never passed away;
I could not draw my eyes from theirs,
Nor turn them up to pray.

"And now this spell was snapped; once more
I viewed the ocean green,
And looked far forth, yet little saw
Of what had else been seen—

The curse is finally expiated.

Vocabulary
expiated (ĕk′ spē āt′ əd) *v.* atoned; made amends for, especially by suffering

36. charnel dungeon vault where corpses or bones are deposited.

Think Aloud

Critical Viewing
To model the Critical Viewing question, use the following "think aloud":

This does not seem to be from this part of the story, but from a part earlier on, when the ship is tossed in the storm. If it were from the Mariner's point of view, the illustration would be closer up and we would see more detail. The point of view is from above.

"Like one, that on a lonesome road
Doth walk in fear and dread,
And having once turned round
walks on,
And turns no more his head;
Because he knows, a frightful fiend
Doth close behind him tread.

"But soon there breathed a wind
on me,
Nor sound nor motion made:
Its path was not upon the sea,
In ripple or in shade.

"It raised my hair, it fanned my cheek
Like a meadow-gale of spring—
It mingled strangely with my fears,
Yet it felt like a welcoming.

"Swiftly, swiftly flew the ship,
Yet she sailed softly too:
Sweetly, sweetly blew the breeze—
On me alone it blew.

And the ancient Mariner beholdeth his native country.

"Oh! dream of joy! is this indeed
The lighthouse top I see?
Is this the hill? is this the kirk?
Is this mine own countree?

"We drifted o'er the harbor bar,
And I with sobs did pray—
O let me be awake, my God!
Or let me sleep alway.

"The harbor bay was clear as glass,
So smoothly it was strewn![37]
And on the bay the moonlight lay,
And the shadow of the Moon.

"The rock shone bright, the kirk
no less,
That stands above the rock;
The moonlight steeped in silentness
The steady weathercock.

"And the bay was white with
silent light,

37. **strewn** spread.

44 *The* **BRITISH TRADITION**

The Tradition of Fantasy

Coleridge's *Rime of the Ancient Mariner*—written in a dreamlike language, set in an indeterminate past, and filled with supernatural events—is part of the British tradition of fantasy literature. Writers of works of fantasy set out to create a realm distinct from the everyday world of their readers—a never-never land ruled by strange laws.

The fantasy tradition began as long ago as Sir Thomas Malory's *Morte d'Arthur* (p. 185), which is set in a vanished past that had become a myth by Malory's own day. The idea of a vanished past fascinated writers long after Malory, reappearing in the work of Alfred, Lord Tennyson, who resorted to Arthurian and mythological elements in many poems, as in "The Lady of Shalott" (p. 963).

Fantasy writers like Coleridge use strange settings and supernatural tales to break the spell of ordinary life. By plunging us into a wild, unfamiliar world, they remind us that human imagination can always envision worlds beyond the one into which we are born—a power that enables scientific discoveries and social reforms as well as great poetry.

Connect to the Literature

What images in lines 480–499 contribute to the fantastical atmosphere in the poem?

45 **Reading Check**

What familiar things does the Mariner suddenly see from the ship?

44 The British Tradition

The Tradition of Fantasy

The tradition of fantasy in British literature is also echoed by Jonathan Swift in his epic *Gulliver's Travels*, in which unusual worlds like Lilliput and Brobdingnag are inhabited by persons both like and unlike those on Earth. Later works, such as *Alice's Adventures in Wonderland* by Lewis Carroll, Jules Verne's *20,000 Leagues Under the Sea*, and *The Lion, The Witch, and the Wardrobe* by C. S. Lewis, treat imaginary worlds with great liveliness and attention to detail. Many of these works of literature are the antecedents to some popular contemporary fiction that incorporates many of the same elements of fantasy.

Connect to the Literature

Point out to students that fantasy literature is perhaps more popular than ever, especially since the success of J. K. Rowling's Harry Potter novels. Discuss with students the ways in which modern fantasy and science-fiction novels and movies fulfill the same longing for an alternative reality that poems like Coleridge's provided in his day. Then **ask** the Connect to the Literature question.

Answer: Fantastic elements in lines 480–499 include the shapes, shadows, and crimson colors in lines 482–483, the angelic figures that appear by the dead bodies, the "lovely light" given off by the seraphs, and the musical quality of the silence in lines 488–490.

45 Reading Check

Answer: He sees the top of the lighthouse, the hill, the kirk, and his own country.

Differentiated Instruction for Universal Access

Support for Special-Needs Students
Have students read smaller portions of the poem and summarize what they have read so far. To test students' retention and understanding of "The Rime of the Ancient Mariner," consider playing them part of the poem on **Listening to Literature Audio CDs.**

Support for Less Proficient Readers
After students have practiced identifying poetic sound devices using transparencies, have them listen to a portion of "The Rime of the Ancient Mariner" on **Listening to Literature Audio CDs.** Discuss with them the effects of sound devices.

Enrichment for Advanced Readers
Have students analyze the many elements of fantasy in Coleridge's account of the sailors on the ship. Students should write short essays in which they address the ways in which Coleridge makes the crew seem fantastical. Refer them to the British Tradition box for an overview of fantasy literature.

46 Humanities

Engraving for "The Rime of the Ancient Mariner," 1875,

by Gustave Doré

This engraving captures the wonder and dreamlike qualities of "The Rime of the Ancient Mariner". The Mariner, alone on the deck, is left to observe the fantastical spirits and creatures surrounding the ship.

Ask: Which elements of the engraving reveal the influence of the Romantic period in which Doré was born?

Possible Answer: The intricately drawn waves of the sea and the flowing robes of the spirits reveal the influence of the Romantic period.

47 Critical Viewing

Possible Answer: Students might say that this engraving represents the moment in the poem when the spirits leave the bodies of the sailors and move around the ship: "A man all light, a seraph man, / On every corse there stood." (Lines 490–491)

Till rising from the same,
Full many shapes, that shadows were,
In crimson colors came.

The angelic spirits leave the dead bodies,

"A little distance from the prow
Those crimson shadows were:
I turned my eyes upon the deck—
Oh, Christ! what saw I there!

And appear in their own forms of light.

"Each corse lay flat, lifeless and flat,
And, by the holy rood![38]
A man all light, a seraph[39] man,
On every corse there stood.

"This seraph band, each waved
his hand:
It was a heavenly sight!
They stood as signals to the land,
Each one a lovely light;

"This seraph band, each waved
his hand,
No voice did they impart—

---

38. **rood** cross.
39. **seraph** angel.

Engraving by Gustave Doré for "The Rime of the Ancient Mariner" by Samuel Taylor Coleridge

47 ▶ **Critical Viewing** What event from the poem does this engraving represent? **[Connect]**

Think Aloud

Reading Strategy

To model the Reading Strategy question on page 841, use the following "think aloud":

I notice that the language is not as rich in lines 504–513 compared to the other parts of the poem, in which the lines are filled with archaic language and a heavy use of sound devices. I know that Coleridge's use of archaic language and heavy use of sound devices established a mood that was haunting and surreal. I think that the reason why he shifts the language is because he is leaving the nightmarish experience and is about to find his way home.

No voice; but oh! the silence sank
Like music on my heart.

500 "But soon I heard the dash of oars,
I heard the Pilot's cheer;
My head was turned perforce away
And I saw a boat appear.

"The Pilot and the Pilot's boy,
505 I heard them coming fast:
Dear Lord in Heaven! it was a joy
The dead men could not blast.

"I saw a third—I heard his voice:
It is the Hermit good!
510 He singeth loud his godly hymns
That he makes in the wood.
He'll shrieve[40] my soul, he'll
 wash away
The Albatross's blood.

Part VII

"This Hermit good lives in that wood
515 Which slopes down to the sea.
How loudly his sweet voice he rears!
He loves to talk with marineres
That come from a far countree.

"He kneels at morn, and noon,
 and eve—
520 He hath a cushion plump:
It is the moss that wholly hides
The rotted old oak-stump.

"The skiff boat neared; I heard them talk.
'Why, this is strange, I trow![41]
525 Where are those lights so many and fair,
That signal made but now?'

"'Strange, by my faith!' the Hermit said—
'And they answered not our cheer!
The planks looked warped! and see those sails,
530 How thin they are and sere!
I never saw aught like to them,
Unless perchance it were

40. **shrieve** (shrēv) absolve from sin.
41. **trow** believe.

The Hermit of the Wood,

Approacheth the ship with wonder.

The Rime of the Ancient Mariner **841**

48 Reading Strategy
Comparing and Contrasting Sound Devices These lines are less crowded with sound devices than the lines describing the Mariner's nightmarish sea journey. How does this shift in language match the shift in mood?

Literary Analysis
Poetic Sound Devices
Which word in lines 523–526 might Coleridge have borrowed from medieval tales of knights?

50 ☑ **Reading Check**
What does the Mariner think the Hermit will do for him?

48 Reading Strategy
Comparing and Contrasting Sound Devices

1. Have a student volunteer read aloud lines 504–513. Then, review with students their understanding of sound devices, and ask them to reread these lines to detect any sound devices.

2. **Ask** students the Reading Strategy question.
Answer: The language becomes less rich and surreal as the Mariner finds his way home.

49 Literary Analysis
Poetic Sound Devices and the Language of Fantasy

1. Read aloud the bracketed passage to students. Remind students that Coleridge borrowed on medieval traditions in writing his poem.

2. **Ask** students the Literary Analysis question.
Possible response: The word *trow* comes from the lexicon of medieval chivalry.

50 Reading Check
Answer: He thinks the Hermit will absolve him from his sins.

Differentiated Instruction for Universal Access

Strategy for Less Proficient Readers
Guide students as they read Part VII. Encourage students to pay attention to the poetic effects used by Coleridge. If students have difficulty interpreting them, model these skills using **Reading Strategy Graphic Organizer B**, page 147 in *Graphic Organizer Transparencies.*

Enrichment for Gifted/Talented Students
Have students write their own marine legends. When they have completed their works, have each student share his or her tale with a partner.

Strategy for Advanced Readers
Have students analyze Part VII of "The Rime of the Ancient Mariner" in the context of the rest of the poem. Students should analyze the role played by the Hermit, the sinking of the ship, and the nature of the Ancient Mariner's obligation upon his return.

51 Reading Strategy

Comparing and Contrasting Sound Devices

1. Encourage students to identify any poetic effects in the lines.
2. **Ask** students the Reading Strategy question.
   Answer: Students should identify the internal rhyme of *still* and *hill*, the alliteration of the words *whirl/where, sank/ship, still/save,* and the repetition in "round and round" as poetic effects that contribute to the momentum of these lines.

52 Critical Viewing

Answer: The Mariner is rowing, the Hermit is in the hooded garment, and the Pilot is one of the fallen men.

"'Brown skeletons of leaves that lag
My forest brook along;
When the ivy tod[42] is heavy with snow,
And the owlet whoops to the wolf below,
That eats the she-wolf's young.'

"'Dear Lord! it hath a fiendish look'
(The Pilot made reply)
'I am a-feared'— 'Push on, push on!'
Said the Hermit cheerily.

"The boat came closer to the ship,
But I nor spake nor stirred;
The boat came close beneath the ship,
And straight[43] a sound was heard.

"Under the water it rumbled on,
Still louder and more dread:
It reached the ship, it split the bay;
The ship went down like lead.

The ship suddenly sinketh.

"Stunned by that loud and dreadful sound,
Which sky and ocean smote,
Like one that hath been seven days drowned
My body lay afloat;
But swift as dreams, myself I found
Within the Pilot's boat.

The ancient Mariner is saved in the Pilot's boat.

Reading Strategy
Comparing and Contrasting Sound Devices Which poetic effects contribute to the impact of lines 556–559?

51
"Upon the whirl, where sank the ship,
The boat spun round and round;
And all was still, save that the hill
Was telling of the sound.

"I moved my lips—the Pilot shrieked
And fell down in a fit;
The holy Hermit raised his eyes,
And prayed where he did sit.

"I took the oars; the Pilot's boy,
Who now doth crazy go,
Laughed loud and long, and all the while
His eyes went to and fro.
'Ha! ha!' quoth he, 'full plain I see,
The Devil knows how to row.'

52 ▶ **Critical Viewing**
Identify the Pilot, the Mariner, and the Hermit in this engraving. **[Connect]**

42. **tod** bush.
43. **straight** immediately.

Enrichment: Understanding Poetry

The Ballad

Most ballads are narratives; that is, they tell a story. The rhyme scheme is often (but not always) *abcb,* as is seen in "The Rime of the Ancient Mariner." Stanzas typically have four lines. There are four strong beats in the first and third lines and three strong beats in the second and fourth lines. Tell students not to confuse the ballad form with the contemporary term *ballad,* which refers to a slow song.

Activity: Writing Poetry Have students conduct research on ballads. Suggest that they record information in the **Enrichment: Analyzing Forms and Genres** worksheet, ***Professional Development Guidebook,*** page 227. Have them use the results of their research to write a short ballad, narrating an event in their life.

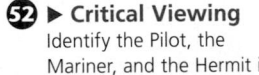

53

53 Humanities

Engraving for "The Rime of the Ancient Mariner," 1875, by Gustave Doré

This engraving illustrates the stanzas of the poem in which the Mariner is saved in the Pilot's boat. Like the other engravings shown with the poem, this engraving was created specifically to accompany Coleridge's poem.

Use this question for discussion:

What lines in the poem are reflected in the depiction of the sinking ship?

Answer: Line 549 reflects the fact that the "ship went down like lead."

Differentiated Instruction for Universal Access

Enrichment for Gifted/Talented Students

Have each student write a ballad, narrating a fantastical journey. Encourage students to reread parts of "The Rime of the Ancient Mariner" to find storytelling strategies that Coleridge used when writing his ballad. After they have written their poems, have them compare and contrast the ballad form with other familiar fixed forms. **Ask:** Which form would be most effective in expressing the contents of your poem? Have students explain their answers.

54 Reading Strategy

Comparing and Contrasting Sound Devices

1. Read aloud the bracketed passage to students. Encourage them to focus on the alliteration in the lines.
2. **Ask** students the Reading Strategy question.
   Answer: Students should say that the alliteration related to the word *tale* emphasizes its centrality to this story—that the Mariner must tell his tale as a continued punishment for killing the albatross.

"And now, all in my own countree,
I stood on the firm land!
The Hermit stepped forth from the boat,
And scarcely he could stand.
"'O shrieve me, shrieve me, holy man!'
The Hermit crossed his brow.[44]
'Say, quick,' quoth he, 'I bid thee say—
What manner of man art thou?'

The ancient Mariner earnestly entreateth the Hermit to shrieve him; and the penance of life falls on him.

"Forthwith this frame of mine was wrenched
With a woeful agony,
Which forced me to begin my tale;
And then it left me free.

"Since then, at an uncertain hour,
That agony returns:
And till my ghastly tale is told,
This heart within me burns.

And ever and anon throughout his future life an agony constraineth him to travel from land to land;

54 "I pass, like night, from land to land;
I have strange power of speech;
That moment that his face I see,
I know the man that must hear me:
To him my tale I teach.

Reading Strategy
Comparing and Contrasting Sound Devices What effect does the alliteration in line 590 featuring *tale*—a word that appears in each of the preceding two stanzas—have?

"What loud uproar bursts from that door!
The wedding guests are there:
But in the garden bower the bride
And bridemaids singing are:
And hark the little vesper bell,
Which biddeth me to prayer!

"O Wedding Guest! this soul hath been
Alone on a wide wide sea:
So lonely 'twas, that God himself
Scarce seemèd there to be.

"O sweeter than the marriage feast,
'Tis sweeter far to me,
To walk together to the kirk
With a goodly company!—

"To walk together to the kirk,
And all together pray,
While each to his great Father bends,

44. **crossed his brow** made the sign of the cross on his forehead.

Think Aloud

Reading Strategy
To model the Reading Strategy skill, use the following "think aloud":

I know that the teaching of the tale to others is central to the story. I know that the *t* sound is repeated in line 590 in the words *tale* and *teach*. I also know that alliteration is often used to emphasize certain sounds or ideas. I think that the repeated *t* sounds emphasize and reinforce the repetitive act of each telling of the tale.

Old men, and babes, and loving friends
And youths and maidens gay!

And to teach, by his own example, love and reverence to all things that God made and loveth.

"Farewell, farewell! but this I tell
To thee, thou Wedding Guest!
He prayeth well, who loveth well
Both man and bird and beast.

"He prayeth best, who loveth best
All things both great and small;
For the dear God who loveth us,
He made and loveth all."

The Mariner, whose eye is bright,
Whose beard with age is hoar,
Is gone; and now the Wedding Guest
Turned from the bridegroom's door.

He went like one that hath been stunned
And is of sense forlorn:
A sadder and a wiser man,
He rose the morrow morn.

Vocabulary
reverence (rev′ ər əns)
n. deep respect

Critical Reading

Cite textual evidence to support your responses.

1. **Key Ideas and Details** **(a)** On what occasion does the Mariner tell his story? **(b) Interpret:** Why do you think Coleridge chose this occasion for the poem?
2. **Key Ideas and Details** **(a)** What contradictory connections does the crew make between the Albatross and the weather? **(b)** What does the Mariner do to the Albatross? **(c) Infer:** Why does the Mariner wear the Albatross around his neck?
3. **Key Ideas and Details** **(a)** What happens to the Mariner's shipmates after the appearance of the Specter Woman and her Death-mate? **(b) Generalize:** What might this symbolize about the effect of guilt on an individual's perceptions of and relations with others?
4. **Craft and Structure** **(a) Infer:** Why does the Albatross finally fall from the Mariner's neck? **(b) Interpret:** What do you think the Albatross symbolizes? Find evidence to support your answer.
5. **Integration of Knowledge and Ideas** **(a)** What is the Mariner's lifelong penance? **(b) Analyze:** How does his story affect his listener? **(c) Draw Conclusions:** What larger lesson about human life might his story suggest?

Differentiated Instruction for Universal Access

Enrichment for Gifted/Talented Students

Show an image of *The Haywain* by John Constable and *Wreck of a Transport Ship* by J.M.W. Turner. Explain that these noted English Romantic painters, like the Romantic poets, celebrated nature. Guide students to see that, while Constable shows nature's tranquility, Turner shows a chaotic nature that threatens to overwhelm the canvas, as well as the ship. Relate the paintings to the poem by exploring ways in which both faces of nature are present in the Mariner's voyage.

ASSESS

Answers

Before students respond, you may wish to have them write a brief objective summary of the selection. As they answer the questions below, remind them to support their answers with evidence from the text.

1. (a) The Mariner tells his story on the occasion of a wedding.
(b) Coleridge may use this occasion because the Mariner's story is a warning about the isolation and guilt brought about by a break with nature and society, while a wedding affirms unity.
2. (a) The crew says that the albatross is responsible for the fog and that the albatross is responsible for the wind that keeps their boat moving. (b) The Mariner kills the albatross.
(c) The Mariner wears the albatross around his neck as a sign of his crime.
3. (a) The Mariner's shipmates drop dead. (b) These deaths might symbolize the ways guilt cuts off an individual from others.
4. (a) **Possible response:** The albatross falls off because his guilt is forgiven. (b) **Possible responses:** The albatross is a symbol of guilt for man's break with nature or the individual's break with a community; it may also symbolize the interconnectedness of all things.
5. (a) The Mariner's lifelong penance is to wander the Earth telling his tale and teaching love for "all things both great and small."
(b) It leaves him "sadder" and "wiser." (c) **Possible response:** Coleridge's poem might suggest that people need to respect nature and community and recognize that every action has consequences.

55 About the Selection

This poem captures the Romantic love of nature and interest in the exotic, the faraway, and the strange. The speaker imagines the pleasure dome of Kubla Khan. By portraying that fantasy so vividly, the speaker demonstrates the extraordinary power of the imagination.

56 Humanities

Box and Cover, first half of the 16th century

This lacquer box cover shows a Chinese palace much like the one Coleridge describes in his poem.

In sixteenth-century China, Ming artisans responded creatively to the demands of an increasingly wealthy—and consumer-oriented—merchant class. A box such as this one was typical of the precise and delicate workmanship prized by wealthy clients. Its picture is pieced together from minute slivers and petals of mother-of-pearl, shaped in myriad ways to represent buildings, natural elements, and figures.

Use this question for discussion.

What elements of the box and cover reflect the sumptuousness of the poem's descriptions?

Answer: The bright and glittering mother-of-pearl and the elaborate detail reflect the luxuriousness of Coleridge's palace.

57 Critical Viewing

Answer: Similarities include settings that feature encircling walks, a garden, an elaborate building with domes, and a river (the stylized arcs at the bottom of the box). Differences may include the scale of the palace, which is smaller on the box with respect to humans than the scale of the palace in the poem, and the lack of ice caves and a chasm in the scene on the box.

55 KUBLA KHAN

Samuel Taylor Coleridge

56

Box and Cover, Ming Dynasty, first half of 16th century, lacquer, black; mother of pearl; wood; fabric. H. 4 in. The Seattle Art Museum

57 ▲ **Critical Viewing**

How do Coleridge's poetic images compare with the details on this sixteenth-century Chinese box cover? **[Compare and Contrast]**

Enrichment: Investigating a Key Person in History

Kubla Khan

Kubla Khan's grandfather, Genghis Khan, began the Mongols' road to conquest by uniting his own people. He then conquered China and parts of Europe in the early thirteenth century. The Mongols raised the status of merchants in China and encouraged trade with the outside world by patrolling the trade route known as the Silk Road. It was the Silk Road that brought Venetian merchant Marco Polo to China later in the thirteenth century.

Activity: About Kubla Khan Have students conduct research on Kubla Khan. Suggest that they record information in the **Enrichment: Investigating a Key Person in History** worksheet, ***Professional Development Guidebook,*** page 233. Have them use the results of their research to write a one-page description of the ruler Kubla Khan.

BACKGROUND

Coleridge claimed to have dreamed his poem "Kubla Khan" line for line after falling asleep while reading a passage from a work about the founder of the great Mongol dynasty. Upon awakening, he transcribed the lines as fast as he could. When he was interrupted by a visitor, however, the lines in his head disappeared, never to be remembered. As a result, Coleridge was unable to complete the poem.

In Xanadu[1] did Kubla Khan
A stately pleasure dome decree:
Where Alph,[2] the sacred river, ran
Through caverns measureless to man
 Down to a sunless sea.
So twice five miles of fertile ground
With walls and towers were girdled round;
And there were gardens bright with **sinuous** rills,[3]
Where blossomed many an incense-bearing tree;
And here were forests ancient as the hills,
Enfolding sunny spots of greenery.

But oh! that deep romantic chasm which slanted
Down the green hill athwart[4] a cedarn cover![5]
A savage place! as holy and enchanted
(58) As e'er beneath a waning moon was haunted
By woman wailing for her demon lover!
And from this chasm, with ceaseless turmoil seething,
As if this earth in fast thick pants were breathing,
A mighty fountain momently was forced;

Vocabulary
sinuous (sin´ yo͞o əs)
adj. bending; winding

Reading Strategy
Comparing and Contrasting Sound Devices What alliteration in lines 15–16 helps you hear the cries of the haunted woman?

1. **Xanadu** (zan´ ə do͞o) indefinite area in China.
2. **Alph** probably derived from the Greek river Alpheus, the waters of which, it was believed in Greek mythology, joined with a stream to form a fountain in Sicily.
3. **rills** brooks.
4. **athwart** across.
5. **cedarn cover** covering of cedar trees.

(58) Reading Strategy

Comparing and Contrasting Sound Devices

1. Read aloud the bracketed passage to students. Review with them the definition of alliteration; then, ask them to identify any examples they find in this passage.
2. **Ask** students the Reading Strategy question.
 Answer: Students should identify the repetition of the *w* sound in *waning, woman,* and *wailing.*

Differentiated Instruction for Universal Access

Background for Less Proficient Readers

Guide students as they read "Kubla Khan" in small groups. Explain to students that Coleridge's account of the "pleasure dome" of Kubla Khan may be based in part on his knowledge of Asia and the riches of the Mongols.

Enrichment for Advanced Readers

Students may find Coleridge's account of Kubla Khan's pleasure dome mesmerizing. Encourage them to find out how much of the wealth and glory of Kubla Khan's regime was exaggerated by Coleridge, and how much was real. Direct students to resources in their school library or on the Internet that will provide more information about Kubla Khan.

59 Humanities

Kubla Khan in council with his courtiers and scribes, c. 1590

This sixteenth-century miniature is an illustration of Kubla Khan in his "stately pleasure dome" at Xanadu, or Shangdu—the name historians often use for Khan's summer residence.

Use the following question for discussion:

Which person in the miniature is most likely Kubla Khan himself? Why?

Possible Answer: The man in the black robe, seated at the center of the semi-circle, is probably Kubla Khan. I think it is Khan because he is the central figure in the piece, and his head and tall headdress rise above the other men's heads—the artist would represent Khan as the most powerful and important.

60 Critical Viewing

Answer: Luxurious details in the work of art include the elegant clothing and the intricate bird decoration on the golden dome of the palace. Such details mimic the luxurious language of Coleridge.

61 Literary Analysis

Poetic Sound Devices

1. Review with students the definitions of *assonance* and *alliteration*; then ask them to reread the passage.
2. Then, **ask** students the Literary Analysis question.
   Answer: Students should identify assonance in *midway/waves* and *heard/measure*; they should identify alliteration in "mingled measure."

59

60 ▶ **Critical Viewing**
Which details in this work of art convey the same sense of luxury as the poem does? **[Connect]**

Vocabulary
tumult (to͞o′ mult′) *n.* noisy commotion

Literary Analysis
Poetic Sound Devices
Find examples of assonance and alliteration in lines 31–34.

Amid whose swift half-intermitted burst
Huge fragments vaulted like rebounding hail,
Or chaffy grain beneath the thresher's flail;
And 'mid these dancing rocks at once and ever
It flung up momently the sacred river.
Five miles meandering with a mazy motion
Through wood and dale the sacred river ran,
Then reached the caverns measureless to man,
And sank in **tumult** to a lifeless ocean:
And 'mid this tumult Kubla heard from far
Ancestral voices prophesying war!
61 The shadow of the dome of pleasure
Floated midway on the waves;
Where was heard the mingled measure
From the fountain and the caves.
It was a miracle of rare device.[6]
A sunny pleasure dome with caves of ice!

6. **device** design.

Vocabulary Development

Vocabulary Knowledge Rating

When students have completed reading and discussing the selections, have them take out their **Vocabulary Knowledge Rating Charts** for the poems. Read the words aloud and have students rate their knowledge of words again in the After Reading column. Clarify any words that are still problematic. Have students write their own definitions and example or sentence in the appropriate column. Then, have students complete the Vocabulary Lesson at the end of the selections. Encourage students to use the words in further discussion and written work about the selections. Remind them that they will be accountable for these words on the **Selection Test, *Unit 4 Resources,*** pages 108–110 or 111–113.

A damsel with a dulcimer[7]
In a vision once I saw:
It was an Abyssinian[8] maid,
And on her dulcimer she played,
Singing of Mount Abora.[9]
Could I revive within me
Her symphony and song,
To such a deep delight 'twould win me,
That with music loud and long,
I would build that dome in air,
That sunny dome! those caves of ice!
And all who heard should see them there,
And all should cry, Beware! Beware!
His flashing eyes, his floating hair!
Weave a circle round him thrice,
And close your eyes with holy dread,
For he on honeydew hath fed,
And drunk the milk of Paradise.

---

7. **dulcimer** (dul′ sə mər) *n.* stringed musical instrument played with small hammers.
8. **Abyssinian** (ab ə sin′ ē ən) Ethiopian.
9. **Mount Abora** probably Mount Amara in Abyssinia.

Critical Reading

1. **Key Ideas and Details (a)** Describe the pleasure dome and its setting. **(b) Analyze:** What makes the pleasure dome and its setting seem beautiful? What makes them sinister?
2. **Integration of Knowledge and Ideas (a)** What comes from the chasm, and what are its effects? **(b) Draw Conclusions:** The pleasure dome might be thought of as a work of art. What does the existence of the chasm on the site of the dome suggest about the relationship between constructive and "chaotic," or "wild," forces in art?
3. **Integration of Knowledge and Ideas (a)** What does the "holy dread" experienced by "all who heard" suggest about the power of art? **(b) Connect:** What connection can you find between this "dread" and the existence of the chasm at the site of the dome?
4. **Integration of Knowledge and Ideas** In what ways do the settings of these poems demonstrate the Romantics' rejection of the dreariness of everyday places and activities? In your response, use at least two of these Essential Question words: *exotic, fantastic, faraway. [Connecting to the Essential Question: What is the relationship between literature and place?]*

Cite textual evidence to support your responses.

ASSESS

Answers

Before students respond, you may wish to have them write a brief objective summary of the selection. As they answer the questions below, remind them to support their answers with evidence from the text.

1. (a) The grounds of the pleasure dome are "twice five miles" in size, and contain gardens, creeks, incense-bearing trees, and sunny spots of greenery. (b) Beautiful elements include "gardens bright with sinuous rills," incense-bearing trees in blossom, and "sunny spots of greenery." Sinister elements include a "sunless sea," a "waning moon," a "woman wailing for her demon lover," the chasm and the emptying fountain, and the "lifeless ocean."
2. (a) A fountain comes from the chasm, and it bursts out of the earth and tosses up fragments of rock as it makes its way to the ocean. (b) **Possible responses:** Wild disorder of the kind present in the chasm might represent the pressures that drive artists to the ordered creation of works of art like the dome. In order to create new patterns, as artists do, it may be necessary to dissolve old patterns in chaos or to start from what is without order.
3. (a) It suggests that art can reveal truths that are dark and disturbing. (b) The dread aroused can be caused by the source or inspiration of the artistic endeavor.
4. **Possible answer:** The settings of these two poems demonstrate the rejection of the everyday by exciting the reader with *faraway* locations and *fantastic* scenarios.

Concept Connector

Reading Strategy Graphic Organizer

Ask students to review the graphic organizers in which they have compared the use of sound devices. Then, have students share their organizers and compare the effects of the sound devices they identified.

Activating Prior Knowledge

Have students return to their responses to the Activating Prior Knowledge activity. Ask them to explain whether their thoughts have changed and, if so, how.

Writing About the Essential Question

Have students compare their responses to the prompt, completed before reading the poems, with their thoughts afterward. Have them work individually or in groups, writing or discussing their thoughts, to formulate new responses. Then, lead a class discussion, probing for what students have learned that confirms or invalidates their initial thoughts. Encourage students to cite specific textual details to support their responses.

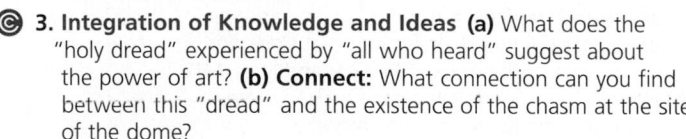

Answers

1. He uses internal rhyme.
2. The initial *h* is repeated in these lines.
3. The internal rhyme words are *night* and *white*.
4. (a) Examples of consonance include *cold/emerald* and *mist/ mast*. (b) Examples of assonance include *both, snow, cold,* and *floating*.
5. Coleridge uses alliteration as the dominant poetic device; *Kubla Khan, dome/decree,* and *sunless/ sea*.
6. (a) Coleridge gives the scene a mood of serenity. (b) The use of the alliterated *s* sound, the assonance of *smoothly/strewn,* and the internal rhyme of *bay/lay* contribute to this mood.
7. **Possible responses:** The archaic words in "Rime" suit its setting in the distant past. They are associated with legends of knights, and so suit the theme of redemption. The exotic words in "Kubla Khan" match its exotic setting, suggesting the allure of the unknown.
8. (a) There's a haunting mood established in "The Rime of the Ancient Mariner" and an exotic feel to the beginning of "Kubla Khan." (b) The use of archaic terms in the first poem establishes that it is from the distant past. The use of alliteration and unknown words in the second establishes a feeling of the exotic.
9. (a) Some words include *incense, Xanadu, chasm,* and *dulcimer*. (b) **Possible responses:** Yes, the poem seems exotic because it is written in a language of a different time.
10. **Possible responses:** "Kubla Khan" creates a greater variety. The mood quickly shifts in the second stanza, when the poem describes the romantic chasm. Rhymes such as *seething/breathing* bring the chasm to life.

After You Read *The Rime of the Ancient Mariner • Kubla Khan*

Literary Analysis

1. **Craft and Structure** What **sound device** does Coleridge use in the line "It cracked and growled, and roared and howled . . ." (*The Rime of the Ancient Mariner,* line 61)?
2. **Craft and Structure** Find an example of **alliteration** in lines 9–12 of *The Rime of the Ancient Mariner.*
3. **Craft and Structure** Which words in the following line create an **internal rhyme**: "Whiles all the night through fog smoke white..."? (*The Rime of the Ancient Mariner,* line 77)
4. **Craft and Structure (a)** Identify an example of **consonance** in lines 51–54 of *The Rime of the Ancient Mariner.* **(b)** Identify an example of **assonance** in the same lines.
5. **Craft and Structure** What device dominates the first stanza of "Kubla Khan"? Give three examples.
6. **Craft and Structure (a)** What mood do lines 472–483 of *The Rime of the Ancient Mariner* create? **(b)** What poetic devices contribute to this mood? Explain.
7. **Comparing Literary Works** Using a chart like the one shown, explain how the characteristics of Coleridge's poetry, including its subjects, settings, events, and uses of language, suit the fantastic subjects he addresses. In discussing his uses of language, specifically consider sound devices.

Poem: ____________

Subject	Setting	Events	Language	Why Suitable?

Common Core State Standards

Reading Literature
9. Demonstrate knowledge of eighteenth-, nineteenth-, and early-twentieth-century foundational works of American literature, including how two or more texts from the same period treat similar themes or topics. *(p. 851)*

Writing
2.b. Develop the topic thoroughly by selecting the most significant and relevant facts, extended definitions, concrete details, quotations, or other information and examples appropriate to the audience's knowledge of the topic. *(p. 851)*
2.d. Use precise language, domain-specific vocabulary, and techniques such as metaphor, simile, and analogy to manage the complexity of the topic. *(p. 851)*
9.a. Apply grades 11–12 Reading standards to literature. *(p. 851)*

Reading Strategy

8. **Compare and contrast sound devices** in these poems by answering these questions. **(a)** Identify the mood, or feeling, that Coleridge evokes in lines 1–12 of *The Rime of the Ancient Mariner* and lines 1–11 of "Kubla Khan." **(b)** How do the sound devices and archaic words used in each poem allow Coleridge to create these moods?
9. **(a)** Identify four words in "Kubla Khan" that contribute to the poem's exotic, or strange and faraway, atmosphere. **(b)** Do archaic words in *The Rime of the Ancient Mariner* also make the setting of this poem seem exotic? Why or why not?
10. Which of these two poems uses sound devices to create a greater variety of moods? Quote specific passages to support your points.

Assessment Practice

Critical Reasoning (For more practice, see *All-in-One Workbook.*)

Many tests require students to evaluate the logic of an argument. Use the following sample item to teach students how to identify faulty logic.

'Twas right, said they, such birds to slay,
That bring the fog and mist.

The reasoning behind this statement can be described as

A faulty, because it is based entirely on coincidence.
B logical, because it is based on the sailors' years of experience.
C faulty, because albatross are good luck.
D logical, because it is based on facts.

Lead students to recognize that the sailors' logic is faulty because it assumes a causal relationship where none exists. The correct answer is **A**.

Integrated Language Skills

Vocabulary Acquisition and Use

Word Analysis: Latin Root *-journ-*

The verb *sojourn*, meaning "to visit for a while," contains the root *-journ-*, derived from French and Latin words meaning "day." In French, the root appears in such words and phrases as *bonjour* ("good day") and *soup du jour* ("soup of the day"). Explain how this root contributes to the meaning of each of these words. If you are unsure of the meaning of any of these words, you may consult a dictionary. Then use each word in an original sentence.

1. adjourn
2. journal
3. journalism
4. journey
5. journeyman

Vocabulary: Antonyms

An antonym is a word that has the opposite meaning of another word. *Freezing* and *boiling* are antonyms, as are *happy* and *sad*. For each word from the vocabulary list on page 818, choose the correct antonym. Then, write an original sentence using both the word and its antonym.

1. averred: **(a)** claimed, **(b)** denied, **(c)** wished
2. sojourn: **(a)** depart, **(b)** rest, **(c)** visit
3. expiated: **(a)** atoned, **(b)** sinned, **(c)** sold
4. reverence: **(a)** contempt, **(b)** hope, **(c)** respect
5. sinuous: **(a)** dark, **(b)** narrow, **(c)** straight
6. tumult: **(a)** peace, **(b)** pleasure, **(c)** wealth

Writing

Explanatory Text Coleridge was not the only nineteenth-century poet to fascinate readers with a mysterious symbolic bird. Find a copy of "The Raven" by the American author Edgar Allan Poe, and read it carefully. Then, write an **essay** comparing the Albatross in *The Rime of the Ancient Mariner* with Poe's Raven as poetic symbols.

Prewriting Gather details about the Albatross and the Raven, grouping them under headings such as "Appearance," "Actions," and "Influence." Remember that symbols are concrete images that stand for a cluster of ideas. For each specific quality or relationship you list in your chart, give the general ideas it suggests.

Drafting As you draft, discuss each category in your chart, linking the details you have listed to your conclusions about the symbolic meaning of each bird. Then, compare the two symbols. Support your ideas with quotations from the works.

Model: Revising for Vivid, Precise Language

The sailors praise the Albatross for bringing good weather, then blame it for bringing ~~bad weather~~ *a deadly calm*. The Polar Spirit also ~~uses weather for its vengeance.~~ *wreaks vengeance through extended drought and fast winds.*

Vivid words and details make the analysis more interesting and precise.

Revising Review your draft to identify flat, unexciting language. Replace such language with vivid, specific descriptions or claims. Make sure that all quotations are accurate and properly cited.

Answers

Vocabulary Acquisition and Use

Word Analysis

1. To adjourn a meeting or a session of a trial is to conclude it for the day. We adjourned the meeting early because of the weather.
2. A journal is something a person writes in every day. I wrote my personal thoughts in my journal.
3. Journalism is the activity or profession of recording the events of the day. Journalism is a good profession for those people who enjoy current events.
4. A journey is a trip that can be measured in days rather than minutes or hours. We took a journey from Wales to Scotland.
5. A journeyman is a type of worker who works by the day. The journeyman worked on the frame of the house.

Vocabulary

1. b, Answers will vary.
2. a, Answers will vary.
3. b, Answers will vary.
4. a, Answers will vary.
5. c, Answers will vary.
6. a, Answers will vary.

Writing

1. To guide students in writing this explanatory text, give them the Support for Writing page (*Unit 4 Resources*, p. 103).
2. Remind students that their explanatory texts should be clearly expressed and supported by lines from the selection.
3. If students have difficulty identifying what the albatross symbolizes, you might wish to have students reflect before writing on what common symbols they know and what they represent.
4. Use the **Rubrics for Response to Literature**, *Professional Development Guidebook*, pages 250–251, to evaluate students' work.

Assessment Resources

Unit 4 Resources

L1 L2 EL **Selection Test A,** pp. 108–110. Administer Test A to less advanced readers.

L3 L4 EL **Selection Test B,** pp. 111–113. Administer Test B to on-level students and more advanced students.

L3 L4 **Open-Book Test,** pp. 105–107. As an alternative, give the Open-Book test.

All **Customizable Test Bank**

All **Self-tests**

Students may prepare for the **Selection Test** by taking the **Self-test** online.

PHLit Online! All assessment resources are available at **www.PHLitOnline.com.**

She Walks in Beauty • Apostrophe to the Ocean • from *Don Juan*

Lesson Pacing Guide

DAY 1 Preteach

- Administer the Reading and Vocabulary Warm-ups (*Unit 4 Resources,* pp. 114–117) as necessary.
- Introduce the Reading Strategy: Questioning.
- Introduce the Literary Analysis concept: Figurative Language.
- Build background with the author and Background features.
- Develop thematic thinking with Connecting to the Essential Question.
- Teach the selection vocabulary.

DAYS 2–3 Preteach/Teach/Assess

- Distribute copies of the appropriate graphic organizer for the Reading Strategy (*Graphic Organizer Transparencies,* pp. 150–151).
- Distribute copies of the appropriate graphic organizer for Literary Analysis (*Graphic Organizer Transparencies,* pp. 152–153).
- Prepare students to read with the Activating Prior Knowledge activities (TE).
- Informally monitor comprehension while students read.
- Use the Reading Check questions to confirm comprehension.
- Develop students' understanding of figurative language using the Literary Analysis prompts.
- Develop students' ability to question using the Reading Strategy prompt.
- Reinforce vocabulary with the Vocabulary notes.
- Assess students' comprehension and mastery of the skills by having them answer the Critical Reading, Literary Analysis, and Reading Strategy questions.
- Have students complete the Vocabulary Lesson.

DAY 4 Extend/Assess

- Have students complete the Writing Lesson and write a monologue. (You may assign as homework.)
- Administer Selection Test A or B (*Unit 4 Resources,* pp. 126–128 or 129–131).

Common Core State Standards

Reading Literature 4. Determine the meaning of words and phrases as they are used in the text, including figurative and connotative meanings.

Writing 3.c. Use a variety of techniques to sequence events so that they build on one another to create a coherent whole and build toward a particular tone and outcome.
3.d. Use precise words and phrases, telling details, and sensory language to convey a vivid picture of the experiences, events, setting, and/or characters.

Language 4.a. Use context as a clue to the meaning of a word or phrase.

Additional Standards Practice
Common Core Companion,* *pp. 41–48; 208–218; 324–331

Daily Block Scheduling
Each day in this Lesson Pacing Guide represents a 40–50 minute period. Teachers using block scheduling may combine days to revise pacing. In addition, teachers may differentiate and support core instruction by integrating components for extended and intensive support as students require. See the Guide to Selected Leveled Resources (facing page).

Guide to Selected Leveled Resources

RTI **Tier 1** (students performing on level)			She Walks in Beauty • Apostrophe to the Ocean • from Don Juan
Warm Up	Whole class instruction; Group work	**Practice, model,** and **monitor** fluency, working **with the whole class** or **in groups.**	**Vocabulary and Reading Warm-ups B, *Unit 4 Resources,*** pp. 114–115, 117
Comprehension/Skills	Whole class instruction; Group work; Independent work	**Support** and **monitor** comprehension and skills development, having students complete the activities, graphic organizers, and interactive prompts **independently** or **as a class.**	• ***Reader's Notebook,*** adapted instruction and full selection EL ***Reader's Notebook: English Learner's Version,*** adapted instruction and adapted selection • **Reading Strategy Graphic Organizer B, *Graphic Organizer Transparencies,*** p. 155 • **Literary Analysis Graphic Organizer B, *Graphic Organizer Transparencies,*** p. 157
Monitor Progress	A	**Monitor** student progress with the differentiated curriculum-based assessment in the *Unit Resources.*	• **Selection Test B, *Unit 4 Resources,*** pp. 129–131 • **Open-Book Test, *Unit 4 Resources,*** pp. 123–125

RTI **Tier 2** (students requiring intervention)			She Walks in Beauty • Apostrophe to the Ocean • from Don Juan
Warm Up	Group work; One-on-one teaching	**Practice, model,** and **monitor** fluency **in groups** or **with individuals.**	• **Vocabulary and Reading Warm-ups A, *Unit 4 Resources,*** pp. 114–116 • ***Hear It!* Audio CD (adapted text)**
Comprehension/Skills	Group work; One-on-one teaching	• **Support** and **monitor** comprehension and skills development, working **in small groups** or **with individuals.** • As students complete the selection in the appropriate version of the *Reader's Notebook,* **monitor** comprehension frequently with group questions and individual instruction. • **Model** strategies while guiding students in completing the activities and prompts in the *Reader's Notebook,* as well as the graphic organizers. • **Practice** skills and **monitor** mastery with the *Reading Kit* worksheets.	• ***Reader's Notebook: Adapted Version,*** adapted instruction and adapted selection EL ***Reader's Notebook: English Learner's Version,*** adapted instruction and adapted selection • **Reading Strategy Graphic Organizer A, *Graphic Organizer Transparencies,*** p. 154 • **Literary Analysis Graphic Organizer A, *Graphic Organizer Transparencies,*** p. 156 • ***Reading Kit,*** Practice worksheets
Monitor Progress	A	**Monitor** student progress with the differentiated curriculum-based assessment in the *Unit Resources* and in the *Reading Kit.*	• **Selection Test A, *Unit 4 Resources,*** pp. 126–128 • ***Reading Kit,*** Assess worksheets

TIER 3 Tier 3 intervention may require consultation with the student's special-education or dyslexia specialist. For additional support, see the Tier 2 activities and resources listed above.

One-on-one teaching **Group work** **Whole class instruction** **Independent work** **A Assessment**

For a complete guide to selection support, including support for Advanced students, see the Overview of Resources in the frontmatter.

She Walks in Beauty • Apostrophe to the Ocean • from *Don Juan*

RESOURCES FOR:

- L1 Special-Needs Students
- L2 Below-Level Students (Tier 2)
- L3 On-Level Students (Tier 1)
- L4 Advanced Students (Tier 1)
- EL English Learners
- All All Students

Vocabulary/Fluency/Prior Knowledge

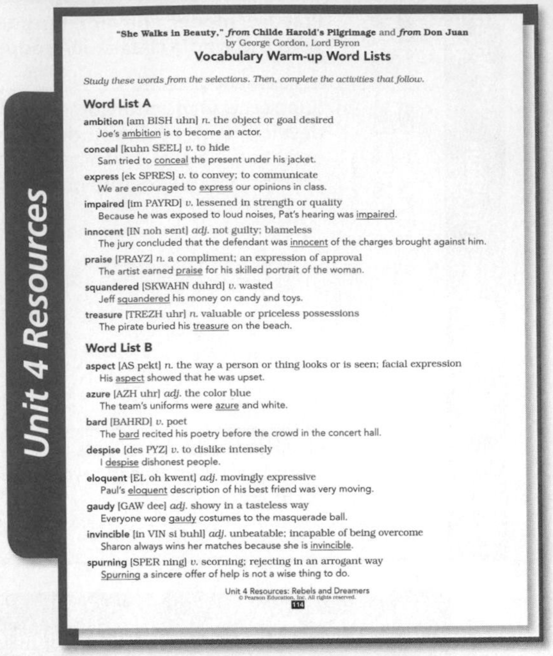

Unit 4 Resources

"She Walks in Beauty," ***from*** **Childe Harold's Pilgrimage** and ***from*** **Don Juan**
by George Gordon, Lord Byron

Vocabulary Warm-up Word Lists

Study these words from the selections. Then, complete the activities that follow.

Word List A

ambition [am BISH uhn] *n.* the object or goal desired
Joe's ambition is to become an actor.

conceal [kuhn SEEL] *v.* to hide
Sam tried to conceal the present under his jacket.

express [ek SPRES] *v.* to convey; to communicate
We are encouraged to express our opinions in class.

impaired [im PAYRD] *v.* lessened in strength or quality
Because he was exposed to loud noises, Pat's hearing was impaired.

innocent [IN noh sent] *adj.* not guilty; blameless
The jury concluded that the defendant was innocent of the charges brought against him.

praise [PRAYZ] *n.* a compliment; an expression of approval
The artist earned praise for his skilled portrait of the woman.

squandered [SKWAHN duhrd] *v.* wasted
Jeff squandered his money on candy and toys.

treasure [TREZH uhr] *n.* valuable or priceless possessions
The pirate buried his treasure on the beach.

Word List B

aspect [AS pekt] *n.* the way a person or thing looks or is seen; facial expression
His aspect showed that he was upset.

azure [AZH uhr] *adj.* the color blue
The team's uniforms were azure and white.

bard [BAHRD] *v.* poet
The bard recited his poetry before the crowd in the concert hall.

despise [des PYZ] *v.* to dislike intensely
I despise dishonest people.

eloquent [EL oh kwent] *adj.* movingly expressive
Paul's eloquent description of his best friend was very moving.

gaudy [GAW dee] *adj.* showy in a tasteless way
Everyone wore gaudy costumes to the masquerade ball.

invincible [in VIN si buhl] *adj.* unbeatable; incapable of being overcome
Sharon always wins her matches because she is invincible.

spurning [SPER ning] *v.* scorning; rejecting in an arrogant way
Spurning a sincere offer of help is not a wise thing to do.

Unit 4 Resources: Rebels and Dreamers
© Pearson Education, Inc. All rights reserved.
114

EL L1 L2 **Vocabulary Warm-ups A and B,** pp. 114–115

Also available for these selections:

EL L1 L2 **Reading Warm-ups A and B,** pp. 116–117

All **Vocabulary Builder,** p. 120

Reader's Notebooks

Pre- and postreading pages for these selections appear in an interactive format in the *Reader's Notebooks.* Each *Notebook* is differentiated for a different group of learners. The selections in the Adapted and English Learner's versions are abridged.

L2 L3 ***Reader's Notebook***

L1 ***Reader's Notebook: Adapted Version***

EL ***Reader's Notebook: English Learner's Version***

EL ***Reader's Notebook: Spanish Version***

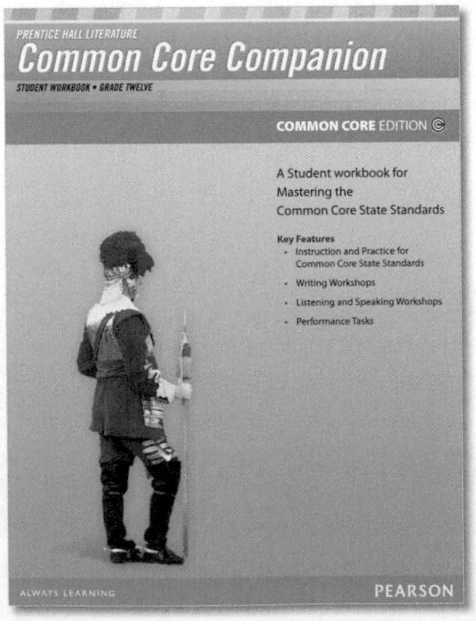

Common Core Companion

Additional instruction and practice for each Common Core State Standard

Selection Support

Graphic Organizer Transparencies

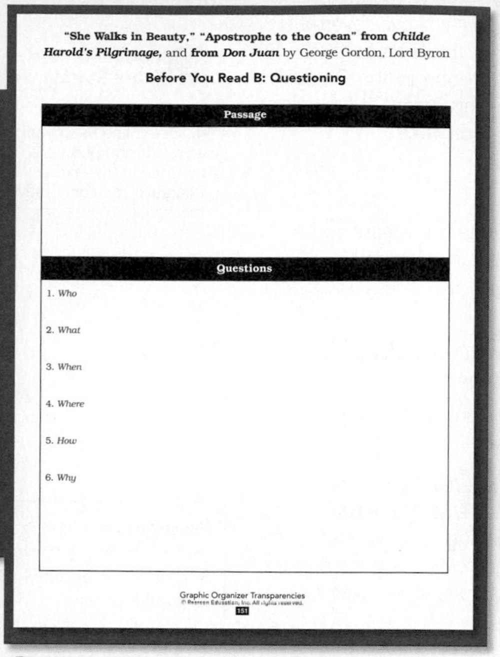
"She Walks in Beauty," "Apostrophe to the Ocean" from *Childe Harold's Pilgrimage*, and from *Don Juan* by George Gordon, Lord Byron

Before You Read B: Questioning

Passage

Questions
1. *Who*
2. *What*
3. *When*
4. *Where*
5. *How*
6. *Why*

Graphic Organizer Transparencies

151

EL L3 **Reading: Graphic Organizer B,** p. 151

Also available for these selections:

EL L1 L2 **Reading: Graphic Organizer A,** (partially filled in), p. 150

EL L1 L2 **Literary Analysis: Graphic Organizer A** (partially filled in), p. 152

EL L3 **Literary Analysis: Graphic Organizer B,** p. 153

Skills Development/Extension

Unit 4 Resources

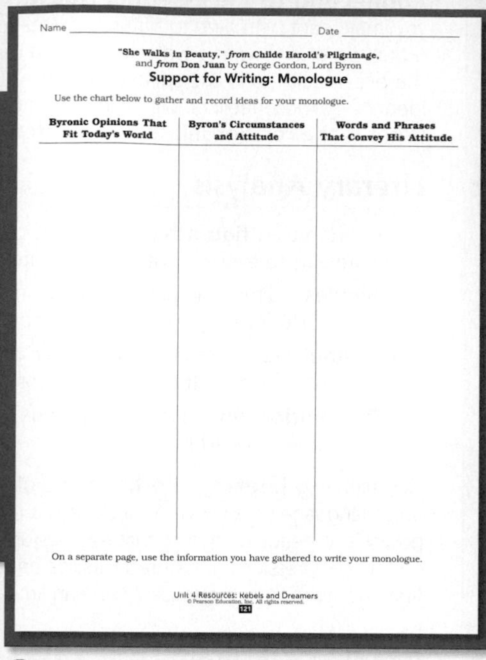
Name ______________________ Date ____________

"She Walks in Beauty," *from* Childe Harold's Pilgrimage, and *from* Don Juan by George Gordon, Lord Byron

Support for Writing: Monologue

Use the chart below to gather and record ideas for your monologue.

Byronic Opinions That Fit Today's World	Byron's Circumstances and Attitude	Words and Phrases That Convey His Attitude

On a separate page, use the information you have gathered to write your monologue.

Unit 4 Resources: Rebels and Dreamers

121

EL L3 L4 **Support for Writing,** p. 121

Also available for these selections:

All **Literary Analysis,** p. 118

All **Reading,** p. 119

L4 **Enrichment,** p. 122

Assessment

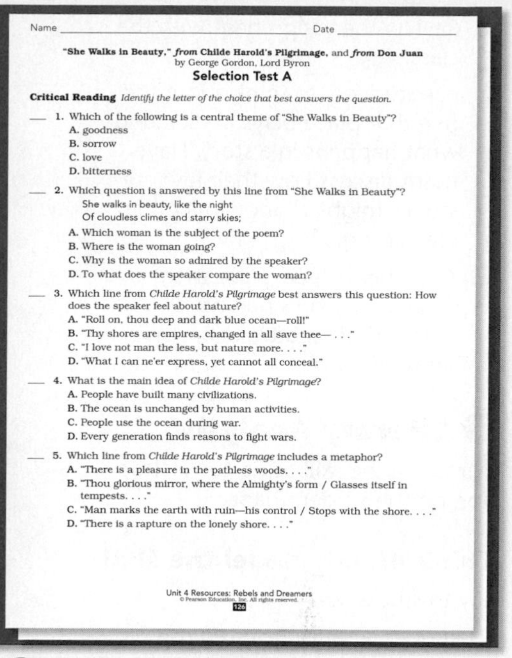
Name ______________________ Date ____________

"She Walks in Beauty," *from* Childe Harold's Pilgrimage, and *from* Don Juan by George Gordon, Lord Byron

Selection Test A

Critical Reading *Identify the letter of the choice that best answers the question.*

___ 1. Which of the following is a central theme of "She Walks in Beauty"?
A. goodness
B. sorrow
C. love
D. bitterness

___ 2. Which question is answered by this line from "She Walks in Beauty"?
She walks in beauty, like the night
Of cloudless climes and starry skies;
A. Which woman is the subject of the poem?
B. Where is the woman going?
C. Why is the woman so admired by the speaker?
D. To what does the speaker compare the woman?

___ 3. Which line from *Childe Harold's Pilgrimage* best answers this question: How does the speaker feel about nature?
A. "Roll on, thou deep and dark blue ocean—roll!"
B. "Thy shores are empires, changed in all save thee— . . ."
C. "I love not man the less, but nature more. . . ."
D. "What I can ne'er express, yet cannot all conceal."

___ 4. What is the main idea of *Childe Harold's Pilgrimage*?
A. People have built many civilizations.
B. The ocean is unchanged by human activities.
C. People use the ocean during war.
D. Every generation finds reasons to fight wars.

___ 5. Which line from *Childe Harold's Pilgrimage* includes a metaphor?
A. "There is a pleasure in the pathless woods. . . ."
B. "Thou glorious mirror, where the Almighty's form / Glasses itself in tempests. . . ."
C. "Man marks the earth with ruin—his control / Stops with the shore. . . ."
D. "There is a rapture on the lonely shore. . . ."

Unit 4 Resources: Rebels and Dreamers

126

EL L1 L2 **Selection Test A,** pp. 126–128

Also available for these selections:

L3 L4 **Open-Book Test,** pp. 123–125

EL L3 L4 **Selection Test B,** pp. 129–131

PHLit Online!
www.PHLitOnline.com

- complete narrated selection text
- a thematically related video with writing prompt
- an interactive graphic organizer
- highlighting feature
- access to all student print resources, adapted to individual student needs
- Spanish and English summaries
- adapted selection translations in Spanish

Online Resources: All print materials are also available online.

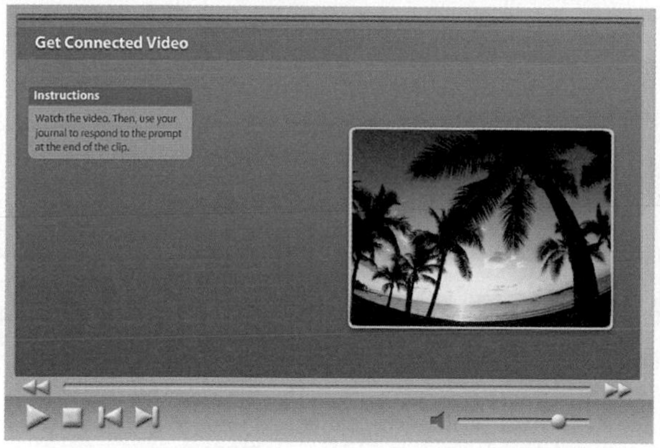

Get Connected! (thematic video with writing prompt)

Also available:

Background Video
All videos are available in Spanish.

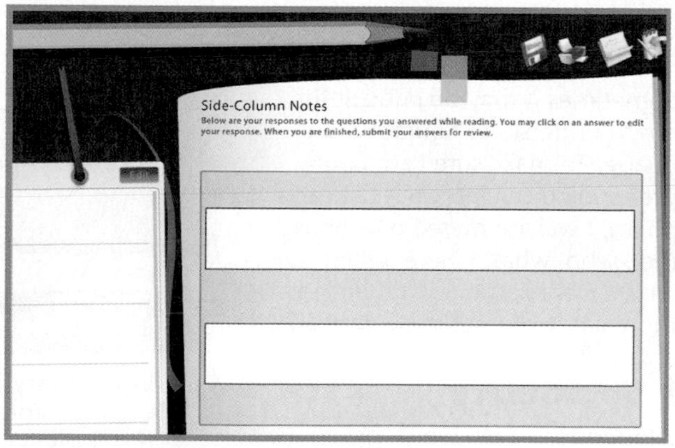

Writer's Journal (with graphics feature)

Also available:

Vocabulary Central (tools and activities for studying vocabulary)

PRETEACH

1 Connecting to the Essential Question

1. Review the assignment with the class.
2. Ask students to think about the role that place plays in dictating what happens in a story. Have them discuss how their favorite stories might change in a different setting.
3. As students read, have them examine Byron's poems for details that create a distinctive sense of place.

2 Literary Analysis

Introduce the skill using the instruction on the student page.

Think Aloud: Model the Skill

Say to students:

I know that authors often use figurative language to convey an image or idea that might be hard to express in literal terms. As I read these poems, I will look for instances where Byron tries to evoke something indefinable.

3 Reading Strategy

1. Introduce the skill using the instruction on the student page.
2. Give students a copy of **Reading Strategy Graphic Organizer A,** page 150 in ***Graphic Organizer Transparencies,*** to fill out as they read.

Think Aloud: Model the Skill

Sometimes it may be difficult for me to understand figurative language. To make sure I am comprehending the intricacies of each poem, I will ask myself questions (i.e., who, what, where, when, why) to break the text down into more easily digestible components.

4 Vocabulary

1. Pronounce each word, giving its definition, and have students say it aloud.
2. For more guidance, see the ***Classroom Strategies and Teaching Routines*** card for introducing vocabulary.

Before You Read

***She Walks in Beauty* • *Apostrophe to the Ocean* •**
from ***Don Juan***

1 **Connecting to the Essential Question** Like some Romantic poets, you may react with awe to nature's dramatic effects—a snow-covered mountain or a towering waterfall. As you read, note the feelings that the ocean calls up in the speaker of Byron's "Apostrophe to the Ocean." Identifying these feelings will help as you consider this Essential Question: **What is the relationship between literature and place?**

Common Core State Standards

Reading Literature
4. Determine the meaning of words and phrases as they are used in the text, including figurative and connotative meanings.

2 Literary Analysis

Poetry often uses **figurative language,** or language not meant to be taken literally, to evoke emotions and state ideas in an imaginative way:

- **Similes**—direct comparisons of dissimilar things using the words *like* or *as:* "Her eyes glowed like the moon."
- **Metaphors**—comparisons in which one thing is identified with another, dissimilar thing: "All the world's a stage."
- **Personification**—giving human qualities to nonhuman subjects: "The trees danced in the wind."

Comparing Literary Works In two of these poems, Byron uses figurative language to express the *sublime*—a Romantic sense of overwhelming power and beauty in nature that escapes understanding. As you read, compare the impressions of nature's sublime beauty and power expressed in the first two lyrics with the sense of human limitations expressed in *Don Juan.*

3 Reading Strategy

Preparing to Read Complex Texts When you do not understand a difficult passage, **question** yourself to *repair your comprehension.* For example, to figure out the subject of a passage, ask yourself "Whom is the speaker talking about?" Begin your questions with *who, what, where, when,* and *why.* Use a chart like the one shown to ask and answer questions as you read.

Passage
She walks in beauty, like the night Of cloudless climes and starry skies;...
Questions
1. *Who* is she? 2. *What* is her relationship with the speaker? 3. To *what* does the speaker compare her?

4 Vocabulary

arbiter (är′ bət ər) *n.* judge; umpire (p. 858)

torrid (tôr′ id) *adj.* very hot; scorching (p. 859)

retort (ri tôrt′) *v.* to respond with a clever answer or wisecrack (p. 861)

credulous (krej′ oo ləs) adj. willing to believe; naive (p. 862)

copious (kō′ pē əs) adj. abundant; plentiful (p. 862)

avarice (av′ ə ris) n. greed; great desire to have wealth (p. 862)

PHLit Online! www.PHLitOnline.com

Vocabulary Development

Vocabulary Knowledge Rating
Create a **Vocabulary Knowledge Rating Chart** (***Professional Development Guidebook,*** p. 33) for the vocabulary words on the student page. Give each student a copy of the chart with the words on it. Read the words aloud, and have students mark their ratings in the Before Reading column. Urge students to attend to these words as they read and discuss the selections.

In order to gauge how much instruction you need to provide, tally how many students are confident in their knowledge of each word. As students read, point out the words and their context.

PHLit Online! **Vocabulary Central,** featuring tools and activities for studying vocabulary, is available online at **www.PHLitOnline.com.**

5 Lord Byron (1788–1824)

Author of "She Walks in Beauty" • "Apostrophe to the Ocean" • *Don Juan*

As famous for the life he led as for the poems he wrote, George Gordon, Lord Byron, came from a long line of handsome but irresponsible aristocrats. Byron lived life in the "fast lane" and was looked on with disapproval by most of his contemporaries.

From Rags to Riches Byron was born in London to a poor but noble family. His father, a handsome ladies' man, died when Byron was just three years old. At the age of ten, Byron inherited his great-uncle's title, baron. He and his mother moved from Scotland to Nottingham, where Byron lived for a time in the ruins of the family hall. When he was seventeen, he left home to attend Trinity College at Cambridge.

A Zest for Life While at Cambridge, Byron made friends, played sports, and spent money. After graduating, he traveled to out-of-the-way corners of Europe and the Middle East. Byron returned home bearing two sections of a book-length poem entitled *Childe Harold's Pilgrimage*, which depicted a young hero not unlike himself—moody, sensitive, and reckless. The work was well received, and Byron became an overnight sensation.

For a time, Byron was the darling of London society. Byron became a celebrity, a public figure of literary genius who in turn thrilled and scandalized his contemporaries. "Mad, bad, and dangerous to know" was Lady Caroline Lamb's famous description of Lord Byron.

The Byronic Hero Although Byron could be quite charming and friendly, his admirers insisted on associating him with the dark, brooding hero, impassioned by a cause, whom he so often described. Because of this persona, or adopted personality, readers throughout the nineteenth century saw Byron as the quintessential Romantic poet.

Italy and Tragedy Byron's fame and infamy grew. When his marriage to Annabella Milbanke broke up, the resulting scandal drove Byron from England in 1816. He would never return to the country of his birth.

A Budding Revolutionary In 1823, Byron, a champion of liberty, joined a group of revolutionaries seeking to free Greece from Turkish rule. Soon after, while training Greek rebel troops, Byron died of a rheumatic fever. To this day he is revered in Greece as a national hero.

Daily Bellringer

For each class during which you will teach these selections, have students complete one of the five activities for the appropriate week in the ***Daily Bellringer Activities*** booklet.

Multidraft Reading

To assist struggling readers and to enhance reading for all, assign the text in chunks, as warranted by length, and apply multidraft reading protocols. For each reading, have students set the purpose indicated:

- **First reading**—identifying key ideas and details and answering any Reading Checks.
- **Second reading**—analyzing craft and structure and responding to the side-column prompts.
- **Third reading**—integrating knowledge and ideas, connecting to other texts and the world, and answering the end-of-selection questions.

For more guidance, refer to the ***Classroom Strategies and Teaching Routines*** card on Multidraft Reading.

5 Background

More About the Author

Byron's poetry was often criticized on moral grounds and frequently condemned by critics, but it remained immensely popular in England and was received even more enthusiastically abroad. In his 1822 journal, Byron noted that his sales were better in Germany, France, and America than in England. Byron was a prolific writer of letters and journals, many of which were written with an eye to publication. They offer a remarkably vivid commentary on his social milieu and his own life.

PHLit Online!
www.PHLitOnline.com

Teaching From Technology

Preparing to Read
Go to **www.PHLitOnline.com** and display the ***Get Connected!*** slide show for this selection. Have the class brainstorm for responses to the writing prompt, entering ideas in the interactive journal. Then, have students complete their written responses as homework
To build background, display the **Background** and **More About the Author** features.

Using the Interactive Text
Go to **www.PHLitOnline.com** and display the **Enriched Online Student Edition**. As the class reads the selection or listens to the narration, record answers to side-column prompts using the graphic organizers accessible on the interactive page. Alternatively, have students use the online edition individually, answering the prompts as they read.

TEACH

❶ About the Selection

This poem vividly describes a woman's beauty, capturing its essential power and linking it to universal images. Byron catalogs the woman's physical charms and spiritual depths, noting her beauty inside and out.

❷ Activating Prior Knowledge

Call students' attention to the information on the Byronic hero on page 855. Have students look for clues to Byron's personality as they read his poems. Then, have them write a paragraph citing an example of a Romantic hero in a favorite film. They should note which aspects of the character match the archetype and which do not.

Concept Connector →

Tell students they will return to their responses after reading the selection.

❸ Humanities

Portrait of Adele Bloch-Bauer I, 1907, by Gustav Klimt

Klimt (1862–1918) was an Austrian Symbolist painter, who became famous for his distinctive portraits of women.

The portrait was the subject of a controversy in 2006. During World War II, it had been stolen from the Jewish Bloch-Bauer family. The painting found its way to the Austrian National Gallery, where it resided until an heir of the Bloch-Bauer family contested ownership. She won her case and sold the painting for $135 million dollars.

❸

❶ ❷

She Walks in Beauty

George Gordon, Lord Byron

854

Text Complexity Rubric

	She Walks in Beauty	*from* Childe Harold's Pilgrimage	*from* Don Juan
Qualitative Measures			
Context/ Knowledge Demands	Romantic lyric poem 1 (2) 3 4 5	Apostrophe from Romantic narrative poem 1 (2) 3 4 5	Monologue from mock-epic 1 2 (3) 4 5
Structure/Language Conventionality and Clarity	Long sentences 1 (2) 3 4 5	Archaic diction; long sentences 1 2 (3) 4 5	Long, interrupted sentences; archaic diction 1 2 3 (4) 5
Levels of Meaning/ Purpose/Concept Level	Accessible (beauty) 1 (2) 3 4 5	Accessible (the sea) 1 (2) 3 4 5	Accessible (aging) 1 2 (3) 4 5
Quantitative Measures			
Lexile/Text Length	NP / 122 words	NP / 498 words	NP / 650 words
Overall Complexity	**More accessible**	**More accessible**	**More complex**

BACKGROUND Lord Byron became so identified with the rebellious heroes he created—brooding figures whose ironic attitude and hidden sorrow only added to their charm—that this kind of figure became known as a Byronic hero. Such heroes are a staple of Romantic literature. They survive in modern times as a Hollywood or rock-and-roll star.

The Byronic attitude may be ironic, but Byron the poet was certainly capable of direct, sincere appreciation of beauty, as this poem demonstrates.

She walks in beauty, like the night
    Of cloudless climes and starry skies;
And all that's best of dark and bright
    Meet in her aspect and her eyes:
Thus mellowed to that tender light
    Which heaven to gaudy day denies.

One shade the more, one ray the less,
    Had half impaired the nameless grace
Which waves in every raven tress,
    Or softly lightens o'er her face;
Where thoughts serenely sweet express
    How pure, how dear their dwelling place.

And on that cheek, and o'er that brow,
    So soft, so calm, yet eloquent,
The smiles that win, the tints that glow,
    But tell of days in goodness spent,
A mind at peace with all below,
    A heart whose love is innocent!

4 Literary Analysis
Figurative Language
With what kind of poetic comparison does Byron capture the reader's imagination in the opening lines?

5 ◄ Critical Viewing
How does the rendering of this woman suggest some of the qualities that Byron attributes to his cousin in the poem? **[Analyze]**

Critical Reading

1. **Key Ideas and Details (a)** To what does the speaker compare the lady's beauty? **(b) Interpret:** What might "that tender light" in line 5 be?
2. **Integration of Knowledge and Ideas (a) Connect:** In lines 11–18, what is the woman's appearance said to reveal about her character? **(b) Compare and Contrast:** How is the focus of the last six lines different from the focus of the opening lines? **(c) Draw Conclusions:** Does Byron's portrayal emphasize the spiritual or the physical aspect of the lady? Explain.

Cite textual evidence to support your responses.

4 Literary Analysis

Figurative Language

1. Have students read the first stanza to themselves.
2. Remind students that figurative language includes similes, metaphors, and personification.
3. **Ask** the Literary Analysis question.
   Answer: Byron uses a simile that compares the woman to a cloudless, starry night sky.

5 Critical Viewing

Possible responses: The subject of the painting appears calm and peaceful, like the woman in the poem.

ASSESS
Answers

Before students respond, you may wish to have them write a brief objective summary of the selection. As they answer the questions below, remind them to support their answers with evidence from the text.

1. (a) The speaker compares her beauty to a cloudless, starry night. (b) The "tender light" is the softer, reflected light given off by the moon.
2. (a) The woman's appearance suggests sweet thoughts, virtuous activity, and innocent love. (b) The focus of the last six lines is on the woman's character, and the focus of the opening lines is on her physical beauty. (c) Byron first emphasizes the physical and then the spiritual; they receive equal space and are presented as if one blends into the other.

Text Complexity: Reader and Task Suggestions

	She Walks in Beauty	*from* Childe Harold's Pilgrimage	*from* Don Juan
Preparing to Read the Texts • Using the Background on p. 855 of the student text, discuss the idea of a Byronic hero as the quintessential Romantic figure. • Discuss with students how a Byronic hero might react to beauty, nature, and aging. • Guide students to use Multidraft Reading strategies (TE p. 853).	**Leveled Tasks** ***Structure/Language*** If students will have difficulty with the poem's long sentences, have them diagram the main points each sentence makes about the woman. Then, have them use arrows to add remaining details that help describe the woman. ***Synthesizing*** If students will not have difficulty with sentences, have them write a one-sentence impression of the woman.	**Leveled Tasks** ***Structure/Language*** If students will have difficulty with the language, have them try to picture the scene. Then, as they reread, have them use context clues to try to understand the images and other details. ***Evaluating*** If students will not have difficulty with the language, have them evaluate the effectiveness of the imagery and figurative language in capturing the ocean.	**Leveled Tasks** ***Levels of Meaning*** If students will have difficulty with the meaning, have them focus their first reading on Don Juan's tone and the traits he displays. Then, as they reread, have them determine the main points Byron is trying to make about him. ***Analyzing*** If students will not have difficulty with the language, have them analyze Don Juan's character based on details from the passage.

❻ About the Selection

This poem expresses Byron's admiration and awe for the ocean. He describes its effects on him: the comfort it offers, the excitement it inspires, the humility its power elicits. Using historical references to great empires and battles, Byron celebrates the ocean's awesome power and its indifference to human political concerns. He discovers in the immeasurable depths, power, and endurance of the ocean an inspiring and reassuring revelation of something larger than humanity.

❼ Reading Strategy

Questioning

1. Read the first stanza aloud to students.
2. Remind them to question aspects of the poem, using *who, what, when, where, how,* and *why* in their interrogatives.
3. Then, **ask** students to complete the Reading Strategy item. **Possible responses:** "What society does the speaker find when he is alone by the ocean?" "Why might someone want to 'steal / From all I may be, . . .'?" "What specific experiences drive the speaker to walk alone by the shore?"

FROM

❻ CHILDE HAROLD'S PILGRIMAGE

APOSTROPHE TO THE Ocean

GEORGE GORDON, LORD BYRON

Reading Strategy
Questioning
List three questions you might ask after reading the first stanza.

❼
There is a pleasure in the pathless woods,
There is a rapture on the lonely shore,
There is society, where none intrudes,
By the deep sea, and music in its roar;
I love not man the less, but nature more,
From these our interviews, in which I steal
From all I may be, or have been before,
To mingle with the universe, and feel
What I can ne'er express, yet cannot all conceal.

Roll on, thou deep and dark blue ocean—roll!
Ten thousand fleets sweep over thee in vain;
Man marks the earth with ruin—his control
Stops with the shore; upon the watery plain
The wrecks are all thy deed, nor doth remain

Enrichment: Investigating Religion and Myth

The Ocean

The human relation to the sea is a conflicted one. The ocean provides food and transportation, but cannot be owned and cultivated as land can. The sea has often been personified because people saw human qualities reflected in its enigmatic depths. Myths about the sea in various cultures date back as far as recorded history. Whether it be as a spiteful god diverting the journey of a hero or a faceless yet sentient force intent on destruction, the sea has always represented aspects of humanity in myth and art.

Activity: The Sea Personified Have students research some sea myths and record their findings on the **Enrichment: Investigating Religion and Myth** worksheet, page 240, ***Professional Development Guidebook.*** Afterwards, have the students discuss what human qualities were attributed to the sea (positive/negative) and why that might have been.

A shadow of man's ravage, save[1] his own,
When, for a moment, like a drop of rain,
He sinks into thy depths with bubbling groan,
Without a grave, unknelled, uncoffined, and unknown.

His steps are not upon thy paths—thy fields
Are not a spoil for him—thou dost arise
And shake him from thee; the vile strength he wields
For earth's destruction thou dost all despise,
Spurning him from thy bosom to the skies,
And send'st him, shivering in thy playful spray
And howling, to his gods, where haply[2] lies
His petty hope in some near port or bay,
And dashest him again to earth—there let him lay.[3]

11

9 ▲ **Critical Viewing**
How does this painting capture the sublime nature of the ocean? **[Analyze]**

10 **Reading Check**
According to the speaker, what impact does humanity's power have on the ocean?

1. **save** except.
2. **haply** perhaps.
3. **lay** A note on Byron's proof suggests that he intentionally made this grammatical error for the sake of the rhyme.

8 Humanities

The Lake of Zug, by Joseph Mallord William Turner, 1843

This painting is one of Joseph Mallord William Turner's "Swiss Series." Turner was a Romantic painter who specialized in topographical watercolors. His focus and interest in nature took him far and wide, traveling and sketching nature scenes which he later transformed into watercolors. This particular work was painted by commission in 1843, and is characteristic of Turner's attention to details with light and atmosphere.

Use this question for discussion:

How does this painting reflect the mood of this poem?
Possible response: Byron's poem speaks to the power of nature, and this watercolor displays nature in all its glory and power.

9 Critical Viewing

Answer: The stillness of the water suggests calm and peacefulness, while the bright tones of the surrounding land suggest warmth and tranquility. People are shown all along the shoreline, suggesting that they are drawn to the water.

10 Reading Check

Answer: Humanity's power has no impact at all on the ocean.

Differentiated Instruction for Universal Access

Support for Special-Needs Students

Some students may have difficulty with the metaphors and similes in "Apostrophe to the Ocean." Have students read the poem with teacher guidance. Model how to understand figurative language using the **Literary Analysis Graphic Organizer B,** page 153 in ***Graphic Organizer Transparencies.***

EL Strategy for English Learners

As students read "Apostrophe to the Ocean," have them say aloud any portions of the text containing unfamiliar words. Have them use context, footnotes, or a dictionary to define these words.

Enrichment for Gifted/Talented Students

Have students design a collage to illustrate scenes from the poem. Students should organize their illustrations and collected objects into a two- or three-dimensional collage. Encourage them to provide sound effects or a spoken accompaniment to their collages.

⓫ Literary Analysis

Figurative Language

1. Have student volunteers read aloud the bracketed passage.
2. Remind them to interpret the language figuratively, not literally.
3. Then, **ask** students the Literary Analysis question.
   Answer: The images suggest that no matter how strong humanity may become, the ocean can still overwhelm it. This idea suggests that the ocean's power is bottomless, and so cannot be measured or comprehended.

▶ **Monitor Progress: Ask** students to analyze the figurative language in lines 19–21. Ask them what figure of speech is being used.
Answer: The ocean's surface is compared to the land through the metaphors "thy paths" and "thy fields" and to a person or animal in the personification or metaphor "thou dost arise / And shake him from thee."

5. **Ask** students in what way these contradictory figures of speech emphasize the ungraspable power of the ocean, even as they present concrete images.
   Answer: Because it is constantly shifting, the ocean has no paths, nor can it be divided into fields. If the ocean shook a person off, the person might very well end up under the ocean. In these ways, Byron's figurative language shows that the ocean exceeds our ability to picture its power.

Vocabulary
arbiter (är′ bət ər) *n.* judge; umpire

⓫ Literary Analysis
Figurative Language
Explain how the images of destructive power in lines 20–36 create a sense of forces of nature beyond human comprehension.

The armaments which thunderstrike the walls
Of rock-built cities, bidding nations quake,
And monarchs tremble in their capitals,
The oak leviathans,[4] whose huge ribs make
⓫ Their clay creator[5] the vain title take
Of lord of thee, and **arbiter** of war—
These are thy toys, and, as the snowy flake,
They melt into thy yeast of waves, which mar
Alike the Armada's[6] pride or spoils of Trafalgar.[7]

Thy shores are empires, changed in all save thee—
Assyria, Greece, Rome, Carthage, what are they?
Thy waters washed them power while they were free,
And many a tyrant since; their shores obey
The stranger, slave, or savage: their decay
Has dried up realms to deserts—not so thou,
Unchangeable, save to thy wild waves' play.
Time writes no wrinkle on thine azure brow;
Such as creation's dawn beheld, thou rollest now.

4. **leviathans** (lə vī′ ə thənz) monstrous sea creatures, described in the Old Testament. Here the word means giant ships.
5. **clay creator** human beings.
6. **Armada's** refers to the Spanish Armada, defeated by the English in 1588.
7. **Trafalgar** battle in 1805 during which the French and Spanish fleets were defeated by the British fleet led by Lord Nelson.

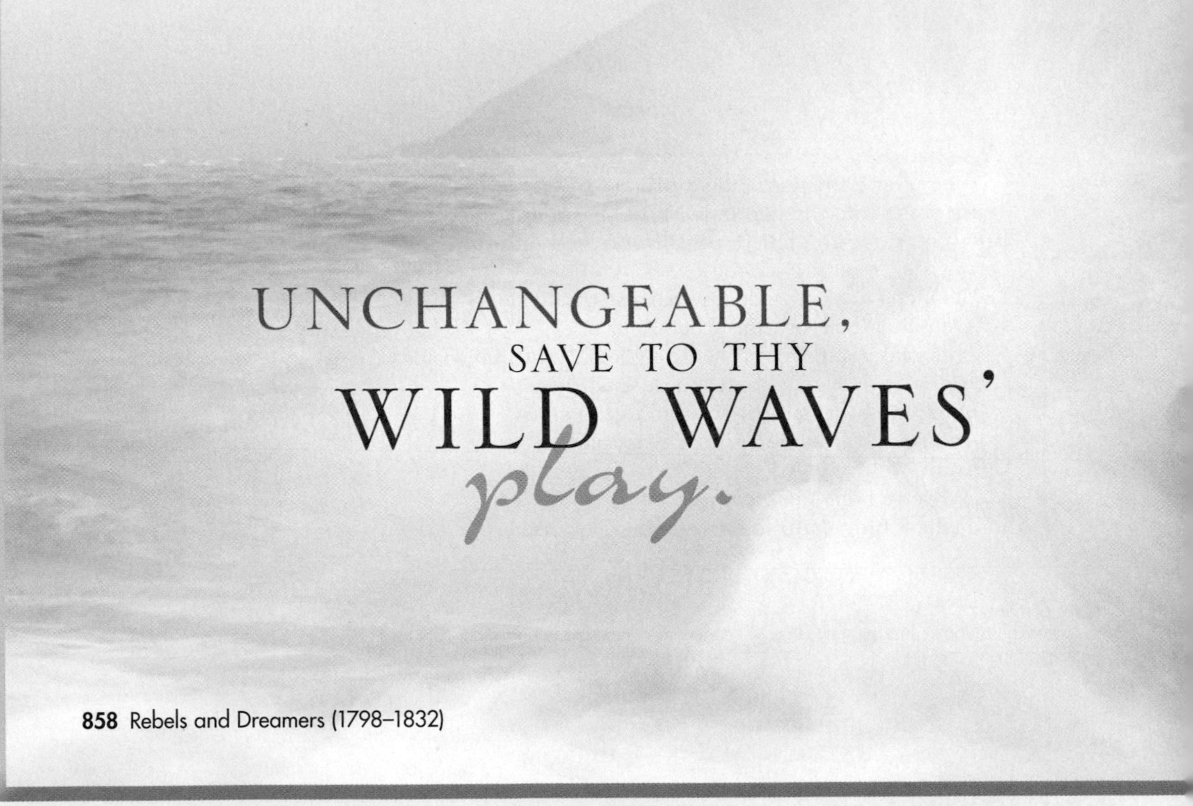

UNCHANGEABLE, SAVE TO THY WILD WAVES' *play.*

Enrichment: Analyzing a Historical Event

The Battle of Trafalgar
The Battle of Trafalgar, mentioned here in line 36, was one of England's most decisive victories in the Napoleonic Wars. In this battle, British fleet routed Napoleon's French and Spanish forces through a combination of strategy engineered by Admiral Nelson and the lucky approach of a storm. However, a number of the captured Spanish ships were later retaken, destroyed by storms, or purposefully sunk by the British to avoid their recapture.

Activity: Battle "Tack-tics" Have students research Admiral Nelson's victorious strategy. They can record their research on the **Enrichment: Analyzing a Historical Event** worksheet, *Professional Development Guidebook,* page 230. Then, using tacks or magnets have them map out the positions of the ships in battle on the board. Many diagrams of various stages of the battle are available.

Thou glorious mirror, where the Almighty's form
Glasses[8] itself in tempests: in all time,
Calm or convulsed—in breeze, or gale, or storm,
Icing the pole, or in the torrid clime
Dark-heaving—boundless, endless, and sublime;
The image of eternity, the throne
Of the Invisible; even from out thy slime
The monsters of the deep are made: each zone
Obeys thee; thou goest forth, dread, fathomless,[9] alone.

And I have loved thee, ocean! and my joy
Of youthful sports was on thy breast to be
Borne, like thy bubbles, onward: from a boy
I wantoned with thy breakers—they to me
Were a delight: and if the freshening sea
Made them a terror—'twas a pleasing fear,
For I was as it were a child of thee,
And trusted to thy billows far and near,
And laid my hand upon thy mane—as I do here.

Vocabulary
torrid (tôr′ id) *adj.* very hot; scorching

8. **Glasses** mirrors.
9. **fathomless** (fa*th*′ əm lis) *adj.* too deep to be measured or understood.

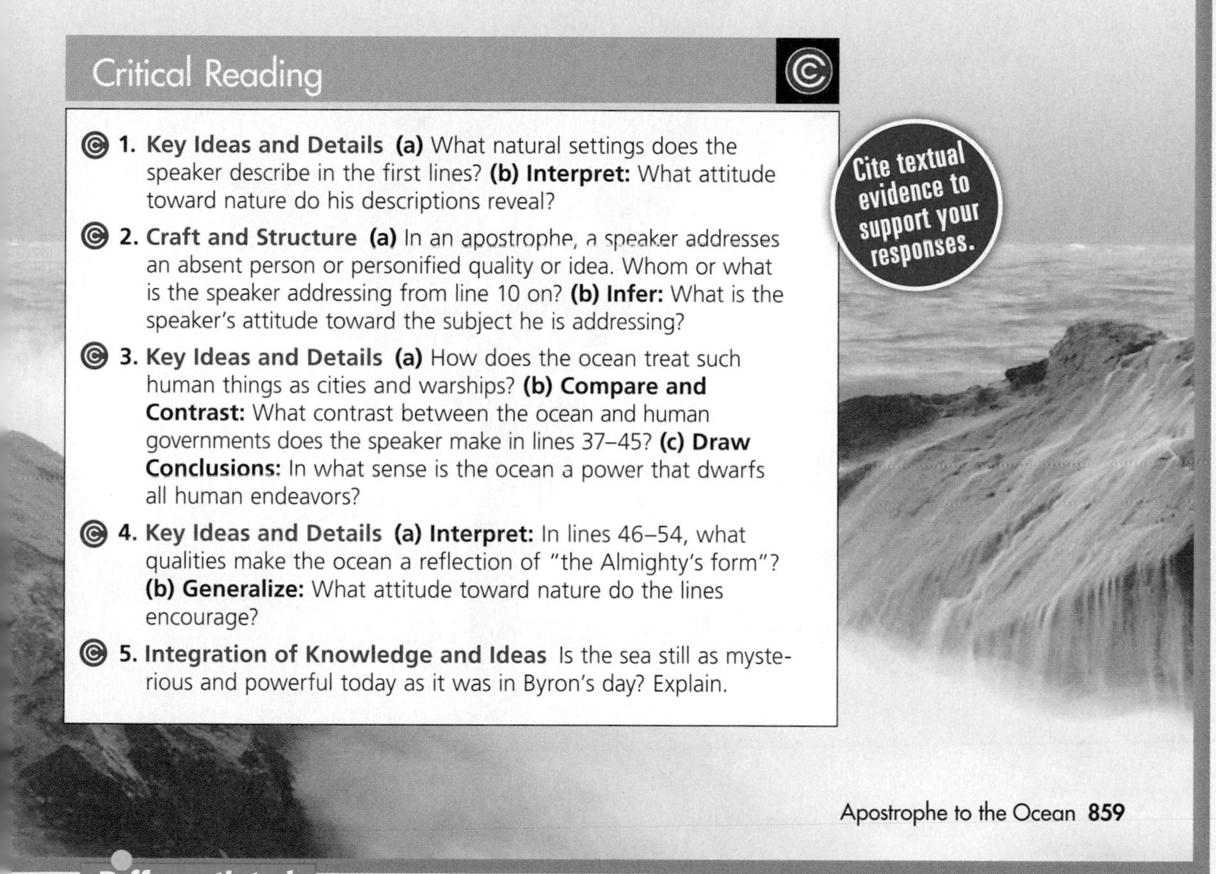

Critical Reading

1. **Key Ideas and Details (a)** What natural settings does the speaker describe in the first lines? **(b) Interpret:** What attitude toward nature do his descriptions reveal?
2. **Craft and Structure (a)** In an apostrophe, a speaker addresses an absent person or personified quality or idea. Whom or what is the speaker addressing from line 10 on? **(b) Infer:** What is the speaker's attitude toward the subject he is addressing?
3. **Key Ideas and Details (a)** How does the ocean treat such human things as cities and warships? **(b) Compare and Contrast:** What contrast between the ocean and human governments does the speaker make in lines 37–45? **(c) Draw Conclusions:** In what sense is the ocean a power that dwarfs all human endeavors?
4. **Key Ideas and Details (a) Interpret:** In lines 46–54, what qualities make the ocean a reflection of "the Almighty's form"? **(b) Generalize:** What attitude toward nature do the lines encourage?
5. **Integration of Knowledge and Ideas** Is the sea still as mysterious and powerful today as it was in Byron's day? Explain.

Cite textual evidence to support your responses.

ASSESS

Answers

Before students respond, you may wish to have them write a brief objective summary of the selection. As they answer the questions below, remind them to support their answers with evidence from the text.

1. (a) The speaker describes the woods, the shore, and the deep sea. (b) He loves nature more than humankind.
2. (a) The speaker is addressing the ocean. (b) The speaker admires the ocean's power.
3. (a) The ocean sinks warships and dashes cities to the ground. (b) Those past empires are subject to the ravages of time, but the ocean is unchangeable. (c) The ocean can destroy everything in its path, including human endeavors.
4. (a) The ocean represents infinite extent, endurance, and power, and as such is a mirror for "the Almighty's form," since God is also infinite. (b) These lines encourage an attitude toward nature that is full of wonder, awe, and supreme admiration.
5. **Possible response:** Despite scientific advances, the ocean remains as wild and powerful as ever.

Differentiated Instruction for Universal Access

Strategy for Less Proficient Readers
Display Art Transparency 11, J. W. M. Turner's *Wreck of a Transport Ship,* in **Art Transparencies, Volume 2.** Have students identify lines in the poem that the painting might illustrate. Then, have students discuss the vision of nature that both works express.

Strategy for Advanced Readers
Display Art Transparency 11 in **Art Transparencies, Volume 2.** Have students discuss the representation of nature in the poem and painting. Encourage them to consider why the idea of untamable nature might have been attractive at the dawn of the scientific and industrial age.

PHLit Online!

This selection is available in interactive format in the **Enriched Online Student Edition** at **www.PHLitOnline.com,** which includes a thematically related video with writing prompt and an interactive graphic organizer.

⓬ About the Selection

This excerpt from the comic epic poem recounts the speaker's thoughts on ambition, aging, and death. The speaker, at 30 years of age, finds himself exhausted, rather disappointed in himself, and somewhat disillusioned by the world around him. He feels that since his chance for romantic passion is past and ambition is a vain idea, he will dispense advice based on his experience. In expressing his poetic philosophy, the speaker takes humorous jabs at contemporary poets Southey and Wordsworth, the first of whom he considers not worth reading and the latter he deems incomprehensible.

⓭ Humanities

Lord Byron, Shaking the Dust of England off His Shoes, 1904, by Max Beerbohm, from "The Poet's Corner"

This caricature depicts Byron's permanent departure from England in 1816 after the breakup of his marriage, which was surrounded by rumors of domestic violence and impropriety on his part. The caricature depicts him as having carelessly dismissed those problems as he embarked upon a series of adventures (and misadventures) around Europe.

Scandal and gossip followed Byron throughout his life, as he constantly flouted the social mores of the day. He even went so far as to keep a bear at school as a way of circumventing the prohibition of dogs on campus.

Use this question for discussion:

Caricatures exaggerate the qualities of their subjects to humorous effect. From what you have read about Byron, what is this cartoon attempting to show about him?

Possible response: Beerbohm's cartoon mocks the perceived arrogance with which Byron dismissed his problems by portraying him with his nose in the air. The flippant movement of his foot cleansing the "dirt" of his scandals from his feet further exaggerates the point.

⓭

⓬ from

Don Juan

George Gordon, Lord Byron

Lord Byron, Shaking the Dust of England off His Shoes, from "The Poet's Corner" pub. William Heinemann, 1904 (engraving by Max Beerbohm) Central Saint Martin's College of Art and Design

860

Enrichment: Analyzing Themes and Symbols

Don Juan

The character of Don Juan has appeared in written and musical works from several cultures over many centuries. One early version, the play *The Deceiver of Seville,* was written by Spanish author Tirso de Molina in 1634. Playwright Molière dramatized Don Juan's life in his 1665 *Don Juan.* The great Austrian composer Wolfgang Amadeus Mozart wrote an opera, *Don Giovanni,* about the legendary rake.

Activity: Character Comparison Don Juan has served as a lens through which authors have explored human characteristics, both positive and negative. Have students contrast several depictions of Don Juan in literature and art. They can record their analyses on the **Enrichment: Analyzing Themes and Symbols** worksheet, ***Professional Development Guidebook,*** page 243.

⓮ **Critical Viewing**

Possible response: Like the speaker of the poem, Byron, as depicted in the drawing, has an air of resigned boredom or world-weariness, suggested by his expression and the way he holds his head.

⓯ **Reading Check**

Answer: The speaker will no longer undergo romantic experiences.

BACKGROUND Though it is unfinished, *Don Juan* (jōō´ ən) is regarded as Byron's finest work. A mock epic described by Shelley as "something wholly new and relative to the age," it satirizes the political and social problems of Byron's time.

Traditionally Don Juan, the poem's hero, is a wicked character driven by his obsession with beautiful women. In Byron's work, Don Juan is an innocent young man whose physical beauty, charm, and spirit prove to be alluring to ladies. As a result, he finds himself in many difficult situations.

During periodic pauses in the story, the narrator drifts away from the subject. In these digressions the narrator comments on the issues of the time and on life in general. In this excerpt the narrator sets aside the adventures of his hero to reflect on old age and death.

But now at thirty years my hair is gray
(I wonder what it will be like at forty?
I thought of a peruke¹ the other day)—
My heart is not much greener; and in short, I
5 Have squandered my whole summer while 'twas May,
And feel no more the spirit to retort; I
Have spent my life, both interest and principal,
And deem not, what I deemed, my soul invincible.

No more—no more—Oh! never more on me
10 The freshness of the heart can fall like dew,
Which out of all the lovely things we see
Extracts emotions beautiful and new,
Hived in our bosoms like the bag o' the bee:
Think'st thou the honey with those objects grew?
15 Alas! 'twas not in them, but in thy power
To double even the sweetness of a flower.

No more—no more—Oh! never more, my heart,
Canst thou be my sole world, my universe!
Once all in all, but now a thing apart,
20 Thou canst not be my blessing or my curse:
The illusion's gone forever, and thou art
Insensible,² I trust, but none the worse,
And in thy stead I've got a deal of judgment,
Though heaven knows how it ever found a lodgment.

Vocabulary
retort (ri tôrt´) *v.* respond with a clever answer or wisecrack

⓮ ◄ **Critical Viewing**
What traits of the poem's narrator does this famous caricature of Byron share? **[Interpret]**

⓯ ☑ **Reading Check**
What type of experience will the speaker no longer undergo?

1. **peruke** (pə rōōk´) wig.
2. **insensible** (in sen´ sə bəl) *adj.* unable to feel or sense anything; numb.

from Don Juan **861**

Differentiated

Instruction for Universal Access

Background for Less Proficient Readers
Remind students that they already know a bit about Byron's life from his biography on page 853. Have them do further research on Byron's life and then write essays comparing him to the speaker of *Don Juan.* Students should address both similarities and differences.

Enrichment for Gifted/Talented Students
Ask students to imagine that the narrator of *Don Juan* had reflected on his life when he was much younger. What might he have said? Have them write a monologue that the speaker might have delivered if he had reflected on life and death at age 20.

Enrichment for Advanced Readers
Byron's *Don Juan* is a satire—it makes fun of Don Juan. "She Walks in Beauty" is just the opposite—it idealizes Byron's cousin. Have students write a satirical version of "She Walks in Beauty" that pokes fun at the lady.

⓰ World Literature in Connection

Byron's Influence on World Literature

Byron's craving for action led him all over Europe and parts of Asia. Soon after turning eighteen he embarked on his first international tour, visiting Portugal, Spain, Turkey, and other destinations along the Mediterranean. His extended stay in Greece in particular colored his poetry; it was there he began writing *Childe Harold's Pilgrimage*. His tie to Greece brought him back when he was thirty-five to aid the Greeks in their revolution against Turkish rule, and it was during his time leading a brigade of Greek soldiers that he contracted an illness and died. His bravery in this pursuit and his poetry lauding Greece helped garner European support for the Greek cause. Today, Lord Byron Street in Athens marks his contribution to the Greek national cause.

Connect to the Literature

Ask students the Connect to the Literature question.

Answer: In "Apostrophe to the Ocean," he mentions the past empires of Greece, Carthage, and Rome. In *Don Juan,* one of the stanzas is about the pharaoh Cheops of Egypt.

Vocabulary

credulous (krej´ oo ləs) *adj.* willing to believe; naive

copious (kō´ pē əs) *adj.* abundant; plentiful

avarice (av´ ə ris) *n.* greed

⓰ World LITERATURE CONNECTION

Byron's Influence on World Literature

Byron's work was translated into many languages, and his fame quickly spread through Europe and beyond. Although the British dismissed Byron because of his wild life, the rest of Europe considered him the most important English poet. They were taken with the dark, brooding heroes described in his poems and were inspired by his life. Byron was a man of action. He made speeches in the House of Lords, defending the rights of workers and religious minorities. He traveled widely and he put his life on the line for liberty, joining the Greek revolutionaries in their fight against Turkish rule.

At a time when much of the world was embroiled in political and economic upheaval, writers found in Byron a model for passionate political and literary engagement. Byron's followers included some of the leading European and Russian poets: Alexander Pushkin and Mikhail Lermontov in Russia, Adam Mickiewicz in Poland, Heinrich Heine in Germany, Alfred de Musset in France, and José de Espronceda in Spain.

Connect to the Literature

What evidence of engagement with the world beyond Britain can you find in Byron's poems?

My days of love are over; me no more
The charms of maid, wife, and still less of widow
Can make the fool of which they made before—
In short, I must not lead the life I did do;
The **credulous** hope of mutual minds is o'er,
The **copious** use of claret is forbid too,
So for a good old-gentlemanly vice,
I think I must take up with **avarice**.

Ambition was my idol, which was broken
Before the shrines of Sorrow and of Pleasure;
And the two last have left me many a token
O'er which reflection may be made at leisure:
Now, like Friar Bacon's brazen head, I've spoken,
"Time is, Time was, Time's past,"[3] a chymic[4] treasure
Is glittering youth, which I have spent betimes—
My heart in passion, and my head on rhymes.

What is the end of fame? 'tis but to fill
A certain portion of uncertain paper:
Some liken it to climbing up a hill,
Whose summit, like all hills, is lost in vapor;
For this men write, speak, preach, and heroes kill,
And bards burn what they call their "midnight taper,"
To have, when the original is dust,
A name, a wretched picture, and worse bust.

What are the hopes of man? Old Egypt's King
Cheops erected the first pyramid
And largest, thinking it was just the thing
To keep his memory whole, and mummy hid:
But somebody or other rummaging
Burglariously broke his coffin's lid:
Let not a monument give you or me hopes,
Since not a pinch of dust remains of Cheops.

But I, being fond of true philosophy,
Say very often to myself, "Alas!
All things that have been born were born to die,
And flesh (which Death mows down to hay) is grass;
You've passed your youth not so unpleasantly,
And if you had it o'er again—'twould pass—
So thank your stars that matters are no worse,
And read your Bible, sir, and mind your purse."

3. **Friar Bacon's . . . Time's past** In Robert Greene's comedy *Friar Bacon and Friar Bungay* (1594), these words are spoken by a bronze bust, made by Friar Bacon.
4. **chymic** (kim´ ik) alchemic: counterfeit.

Vocabulary Development

Vocabulary Knowledge Rating

When students have completed reading and discussing the selection, have them take out their **Vocabulary Knowledge Rating Charts** for the story. Read the words aloud and have students rate their knowledge of words again in the After Reading column. Clarify any words that are still problematic. Have students write their own definitions and example or sentence in the appropriate column. Then, have students complete the Vocabulary Practice at the end of the selection. Encourage students to use the words in further discussion and written work about the selection. Remind them that they will be accountable for these words on the **Selection Test, *Unit 4 Resources,*** pp. 126–128 or 129–131.

But for the present, gentle reader! and
Still gentler purchaser! the bard—that's I—
Must, with permission, shake you by the hand,
And so your humble servant, and good-bye!
We meet again, if we should understand
Each other; and if not, I shall not try
Your patience further than by this short sample—
'Twere well if others followed my example.

"Go, little book, from this my solitude!
I cast thee on the waters—go thy ways!
And if, as I believe, thy vein be good,
The world will find thee after many days."[5]
When Southey's read, and Wordsworth understood,
I can't help putting in my claim to praise—
The four first rhymes are Southey's, every line:
For God's sake, reader! take them not for mine!

5. **Go . . . days** lines from the last stanza of Robert Southey's (1774–1843) Epilogue to *The Lay of the Laureate.*

What are the hopes of man?

Critical Reading

Cite textual evidence to support your responses.

1. **Key Ideas and Details (a)** What subject does the speaker consider in the opening lines? **(b) Analyze:** How would you describe the mood of the speaker's reflections?
2. **Key Ideas and Details (a)** What does the speaker say was the focus of his youth? **(b) Interpret:** In lines 33–40, why does the speaker call "glittering youth" "chymic," or counterfeit, treasure?
3. **Key Ideas and Details (a) Draw Conclusions:** What do lines 65–80 suggest about Byron's attitude toward his own epic poem? **(b) Connect:** Is this attitude consistent with his "true philosophy"? Explain.
4. **Integration of Knowledge and Ideas** Identify a modern character who shares the disillusioned attitude of Byron's speaker.
5. **Integration of Knowledge and Ideas** Which poems express a sense of the sublime, a feeling of fear and wonder inspired by nature? Use at least two of these Essential Question words in your answer: *majestic, capture, preserve. [Connecting to the Essential Question: What is the relationship between literature and place?]*

ASSESS

Answers

Before students respond, you may wish to have them write a brief objective summary of the selection. As they answer the questions below, remind them to support their answers with evidence from the text.

1. (a) The speaker considers his age and how much of his life has passed by. (b) The speaker's mood seems to be wry and somewhat rueful.
2. (a) The speaker says his passion was the focus of his youth. (b) Youth is false treasure because it soon tarnishes and cracks as age sets in.
3. (a) The speaker's attitude toward his own epic poem is one of mocking self-deprecation. He refers to the reader as a "purchaser," as if grateful for the money, invites the reader to leave off reading if he or she is not satisfied with this sample, and notes that he deserves praise, if only because two poets he does not esteem, Southey and Wordsworth, are well regarded. (b) This attitude is consistent with his "true philosophy," which suggests that everything born or created must die—he does not look forward to immortal fame.
4. **Possible responses:** Students may mention characters in advertising campaigns who are presented as having experienced everything the world has to offer (except the advertised product) or sitcom characters who remain unflappable because they have seen it all before.
5. "Apostrophe to the Ocean" *captures* a sense of the *majestic* and indefinable nature of the ocean that has so intrigued and frightened man for centuries. "She Walks in Beauty" attempts to align some of the sublime qualities of nature to the indefinable characteristics in a woman that make her distinctive to the poet.

Concept Connector

Reading Strategy Graphic Organizer

Ask students to review the graphic organizers in which they have listed their questions about the poems. Then, have students share their organizers and compare their questions and the answers that they discovered.

Activating Prior Knowledge

Have students return to their responses to the Activating Prior Knowledge activity. Ask them to explain whether their thoughts have changed, and, if so, how.

Writing About the Essential Question

Have students compare their responses to the prompt, completed before reading the poems, with their thoughts afterwards. Have them work individually or in groups, writing or discussing their thoughts, to formulate new responses. Then, lead a class discussion, probing for what students have learned that confirms or invalidates their initial thoughts. Encourage students to cite specific textual details to support their responses.

Answers

1. simile: "She walks in beauty, like the night…of skies…"; a woman; calm, austere beauty; metaphor: "…thy yeast of waves…"; the appearance of the water; foam and bubbles; personification: "…thou dost arise and shake him from thee…"; the ocean's indifference to man; an irritated person
2. (a) The speaker uses a simile to compare a man in the ocean to "a drop of rain." (b) The comparison suggests that the drowning man is insignificant.
3. (a) metaphor (b) simile
4. **Possible response:** The personification amplifies the sense of the ocean's power in the story.
5. (a) metaphor (b) The comparison conveys his feeling that he has wasted life that he has not even lived yet.
6. (a) By suggesting that she combines light and dark as the night sky combines starlight and darkness, Byron implies that her beauty is as endless as the night sky. (b) These images include the "howling" human being tossed in the "playful spray," and "thy wild waves' play."
7. Both poems are concerned with the ineffable qualities of nature. In "She Walks in Beauty," the focus is on human beauty. In "Apostrophe," the infinite power of the ocean is seen as related to a god.
8. The poem focuses on the narrator's mortality. By mentioning his "gray hair" and the fact that youth is a "chymic treasure," he evokes the fragility of human life. Unlike the mystery and power of the sublime, his life is prosaic and fleeting.
9. (a) Answers will vary. (b) **Possible response:** Most students should say that their questions focused their reading.
10. Who is the speaker referring to? Himself; Why is the speaker concerned? His heart can no longer derive emotion from experience.
11. (a) The title may indicate the subject, so asking questions about it can aid in creating a frame of reference. (b) Who is Don Juan? Who walks in beauty? Why is Byron addressing the ocean?

After You Read

She Walks in Beauty* • *Apostrophe to the Ocean* • from *Don Juan

Literary Analysis

1. **Craft and Structure** Use a chart to list examples from the poems of **figurative language,** finding at least one example each of **simile, metaphor,** and **personification.** Show how each example suggests a number of different associations for what is being described.

Figurative Language	What Is Being Described	Associations Suggested

2. **Craft and Structure (a)** Identify the simile in lines 10–18 of "Apostrophe to the Ocean." **(b)** What does the comparison suggest about the drowning man?
3. **Craft and Structure** Identify and interpret the types of figurative language in the following lines: **(a)** "Thou glorious mirror, where the Almighty's form / Glasses itself. . . ." **(b)** "The freshness of the heart can fall like dew, . . ."
4. **Craft and Structure** In "Apostrophe to the Ocean," what effect does the personification of the ocean have on the poem as a whole?
5. **Craft and Structure** In *Don Juan*, the speaker says he "squandered [his] whole summer while 'twas May." **(a)** What type of figurative language is in this line? **(b)** What meaning does the comparison convey?
6. **Comparing Literary Works (a)** In "She Walks in Beauty," how does Byron use figures of speech and imagery of the night to convey the mysterious, endless power of Lady Horton's beauty? **(b)** Identify three images or figures of speech suggesting the sublime power of nature in "Apostrophe to the Ocean."
7. **Comparing Literary Works** Compare the feelings associated with infinite power or mystery in these two poems.
8. **Comparing Literary Works** In what ways does Byron express the opposite of the sublime in the excerpt from *Don Juan*? Cite specific passages, figures of speech, and images to support your point.

Reading Strategy

9. **(a)** List the questions you asked as you read Byron's poems and the answers you found. **(b)** Did *repairing your comprehension* by **questioning** make your reading more active or focused? Explain.
10. Ask and answer a series of questions to uncover the meaning of lines 9–16 of the excerpt from *Don Juan.*
11. **(a)** In what ways might you apply a questioning strategy to a poem's title before you even begin to read it? **(b)** What questions could you ask and answer about the titles of Byron's poems?

Common Core State Standards

Writing

3.c. Use a variety of techniques to sequence events so that they build on one another to create a coherent whole and build toward a particular tone and outcome. *(p. 865)*

3.d. Use precise words and phrases, telling details, and sensory language to convey a vivid picture of the experiences, events, setting, and/or characters. *(p. 865)*

Language

4.a. Use context as a clue to the meaning of a word or phrase. *(p. 865)*

Assessment Practice

Critical Reasoning (For more practice, see *All-in-One Workbook.*)

Many tests require students to evaluate a writer's implied assumptions. Use this sample test item.

But now at thirty years my hair is gray . . .
My heart is not much greener; and in short, I
Have squandered my whole summer while 'twas May,
And feel no more the spirit to retort; I
Have spent my life . . .

Which potentially invalid assumption does the narrator make in these lines?

A He is on the brink of death.
B He has already experienced the full range of human emotions.
C Absolute power corrupts absolutely.
D He loves the summertime.

The narrator is 30 years old; his assumption that his life is spent is probably invalid. The best choice is ***B.***

PERFORMANCE TASKS

Integrated Language Skills

Vocabulary Acquisition and Use

Word Analysis: Latin Suffix *-ous*

The suffix *-ous* means "full of." The root of the word *credulous*, *cred-*, means "belief." Therefore, *credulous* means "full of belief" or "overly willing to believe." *Strenuous* exercise is "exercise that requires great exertion," or exercise that is "full of strain." Use the meaning of *-ous* to define the listed terms, checking a dictionary if necessary. Then, write an original sentence using each word.

1. furious
2. glorious
3. porous
4. plenteous
5. portentous
6. spacious
7. barbarous
8. querulous

Vocabulary: Context

An unfamiliar word's *context*—words, phrases, or sentences around it—can provide clues to its meaning. Identify the meaning of each italicized vocabulary word below and explain how the context makes that meaning clear.

1. Unable to agree on anything, the two brothers constantly relied on their sister as an *arbiter.*
2. The creek bed became dry after weeks of *torrid* weather.
3. The author's witty *retorts* to the host's questions left the audience laughing.
4. Unable to see her faults, he was always *credulous* with regard to her excuses.
5. The dutiful student filled the pages with *copious*, or plentiful, notes.
6. *Avarice* compelled him to accumulate wealth; selfishness led him to keep it all.

Writing

Narrative Text Write an **interior monologue**—words a character speaks to himself or herself—in which a modern Byronic hero tells his or her story. This type of hero is a brooding loner who may feel impassioned by a cause. If you like, use a real-life celebrity as a model.

Prewriting Jot down some opinions that a Byronic hero might hold today. Think about your hero's circumstances and how he or she might feel about them. Then, list words and phrases that convey this attitude.

Drafting Structure your monologue as the tale of a *sequence of events* that leads to your hero's strongest expression of his or her attitude. As you draft, use precise words to describe the character's feelings.

Revising Read through your draft and think about its *dramatic effect.* Rearrange or change words to intensify the dramatic effect.

Model: Revising to Structure Ideas for Effect

If I am a great actor, it is because my life has been great—not perfect. The films of my long career form an exhibition of my flaws, ~~crimes and mistakes.~~ mistakes, and crimes

Rearranging strengthens the dramatic effect by putting the more powerful word last.

Assessment Resources

Unit 4 Resources

L1 L2 EL **Selection Test A,** pp. 126–128. Administer Test A to less advanced readers.

L3 L4 EL **Selection Test B,** pp. 129–131. Administer Test B to on-level students and more advanced students.

L3 L4 **Open-Book Test,** pp. 123–125. As an alternative, give the Open-Book test.

All **Customizable Test Bank**

All **Self-tests**
Students may prepare for the **Selection Test** by taking the **Self-test** online.

PHLit Online! All assessment resources are available at **www.PHLitOnline.com**.

ASSESS/EXTEND

Answers

Vocabulary Acquisition and Use

Word Analysis

1. full of fury; She was *furious* at her cat for shattering the vase.
2. full of glory; He stopped to photograph the *glorious* sunset.
3. full of pores; The *porous* sponge absorbed the water.
4. full of plenty; The farmer had a *plenteous* harvest because of all the rain.
5. full of portent, ominous; The seer predicted in a *portentous* voice that the king would lose the battle.
6. full of space; He bought the car because of its *spacious* trunk.
7. full of barbarity; The *barbarous* soldiers looted the town.
8. full of complaints; Parker whined in a *querulous* voice.

Vocabulary

1. mediator; The brothers need someone to moderate their disputes.
2. extremely hot; Excessive heat might dry up the creek.
3. responses; The author is being interviewed and must answer the host's questions.
4. gullible; If he is unable to see her flaws, he probably does not think that she would lie.
5. plentiful; A dutiful student would be sure to take thorough notes.
6. greed; People who hoard money are greedy.

Writing

1. To guide students in writing, give them the Support for Writing page (*Unit 4 Resources,* p. 121).
2. If students have difficulty with this character type, refer them to more contemporary versions of the Byronic hero, such as rock-and-roll artists and characters in movies.
3. Use the **Rubrics for a Response to Literature,** ***Professional Development Guidebook,*** pages 250–251, to evaluate students' work.

Ozymandias • Ode to the West Wind • To a Skylark

Lesson Pacing Guide

DAY 1 Preteach

- Administer the Reading and Vocabulary Warm-ups (*Unit 4 Resources,* pp. 132–135) as necessary.
- Introduce the Literary Analysis concept: Imagery and Romantic Philosophy.
- Introduce the Reading Strategy: Comparing Imagery.
- Build background with the author and Background features.
- Develop thematic thinking with Connecting to the Essential Question.
- Teach the selection vocabulary.

DAYS 2–3 Preteach/Teach/Assess

- Distribute copies of the appropriate graphic organizer for the Reading Strategy (*Graphic Organizer Transparencies,* pp. 154–155).
- Distribute copies of the appropriate graphic organizer for Literary Analysis (*Graphic Organizer Transparencies,* pp. 156–157).
- Prepare students to read with the Activating Prior Knowledge activities (TE).
- Informally monitor comprehension while students read.
- Use the Reading Check questions to confirm comprehension.
- Develop students' understanding of imagery and Romantic philosophy using the Literary Analysis prompts.
- Develop students' ability to compare imagery using the Reading Strategy prompts.
- Reinforce vocabulary with the Vocabulary notes.
- Assess students' comprehension and mastery of the skills by having them answer the Critical Reading, Literary Analysis, and Reading Strategy questions.
- Have students complete the Vocabulary Lesson.

DAY 4 Extend/Assess

- Have students complete the Writing Lesson and write a research plan. (You may assign as homework.)
- Administer Selection Test A or B (*Unit 4 Resources,* pp. 144–146 or 147–149).

Common Core State Standards

Reading Literature 1. Cite strong and thorough textual evidence to support analysis of what the text says explicitly as well as inferences drawn from the text, including determining where the text leaves matters uncertain.

Writing 7. Conduct short research projects to answer a question or solve a problem.
8. Gather relevant information from multiple authoritative print and digital sources, using advanced searches effectively; assess the strengths and limitations of each source in terms of the task, purpose, and audience.

Language 4.d. Verify the preliminary determination of the meaning of a word or phrase.
5. Demonstrate understanding of figurative language, word relationships, and nuances in word meanings.

Additional Standards Practice
Common Core Companion, *pp. 2–9; 240–260; 324–335*

Daily Block Scheduling
Each day in this Lesson Pacing Guide represents a 40–50 minute period. Teachers using block scheduling may combine days to revise pacing. In addition, teachers may differentiate and support core instruction by integrating components for extended and intensive support as students require. See the Guide to Selected Leveled Resources (facing page).

Guide to Selected Leveled Resources

RTI Tier 1 (students performing on level)			Ozymandias • Ode to the West Wind • To a Skylark
Warm Up	Whole class instruction; Group work	**Practice, model,** and **monitor** fluency, working **with the whole class** or **in groups.**	Vocabulary and Reading Warm-ups B, *Unit 4 Resources,* pp. 132–133, 135
Comprehension/Skills	Whole class instruction; Group work; Independent work	**Support** and **monitor** comprehension and skills development, having students complete the activities, graphic organizers, and interactive prompts **independently** or **as a class.**	• ***Reader's Notebook,*** adapted instruction and full selection EL ***Reader's Notebook: English Learner's Version,*** adapted instruction and adapted selection • **Reading Strategy Graphic Organizer B, *Graphic Organizer Transparencies,*** p. 159 • **Literary Analysis Graphic Organizer B, *Graphic Organizer Transparencies,*** p. 161
Monitor Progress	A	**Monitor** student progress with the differentiated curriculum-based assessment in the *Unit Resources.*	• **Selection Test B, *Unit 4 Resources,*** pp. 147–149 • **Open-Book Test, *Unit 4 Resources,*** pp. 141–143

RTI Tier 2 (students requiring intervention)			Ozymandias • Ode to the West Wind • To a Skylark
Warm Up	Group work; One-on-one teaching	**Practice, model,** and **monitor** fluency **in groups** or **with individuals.**	• **Vocabulary and Reading Warm-ups A, *Unit 4 Resources,*** pp. 132–134 • ***Hear It!* Audio CD (adapted text)**
Comprehension/Skills	Group work; One-on-one teaching	• **Support** and **monitor** comprehension and skills development, working **in small groups** or **with individuals.** • As students complete the selection in the appropriate version of the *Reader's Notebook,* **monitor** comprehension frequently with group questions and individual instruction. • **Model** strategies while guiding students in completing the activities and prompts in the *Reader's Notebook,* as well as the graphic organizers. • **Practice** skills and **monitor** mastery with the *Reading Kit* worksheets.	• ***Reader's Notebook: Adapted Version,*** adapted instruction and adapted selection EL ***Reader's Notebook: English Learner's Version,*** adapted instruction and adapted selection • **Reading Strategy Graphic Organizer A, *Graphic Organizer Transparencies,*** p. 158 • **Literary Analysis Graphic Organizer A, *Graphic Organizer Transparencies,*** p. 160 • ***Reading Kit,*** Practice worksheets
Monitor Progress	A	**Monitor** student progress with the differentiated curriculum-based assessment in the *Unit Resources* and in the *Reading Kit.*	• **Selection Test A, *Unit 4 Resources,*** pp. 144–146 • ***Reading Kit,*** Assess worksheets

TIER 3 Tier 3 intervention may require consultation with the student's special-education or dyslexia specialist. For additional support, see the Tier 2 activities and resources listed above.

One-on-one teaching **Group work** **Whole class instruction** **Independent work** **A Assessment**

For a complete guide to selection support, including support for Advanced students, see the Overview of Resources in the frontmatter.

Ozymandias • Ode to the West Wind • To a Skylark

RESOURCES FOR:

- L1 Special-Needs Students
- L2 Below-Level Students (Tier 2)
- L3 On-Level Students (Tier 1)
- L4 Advanced Students (Tier 1)
- EL English Learners
- All All Students

Vocabulary/Fluency/Prior Knowledge

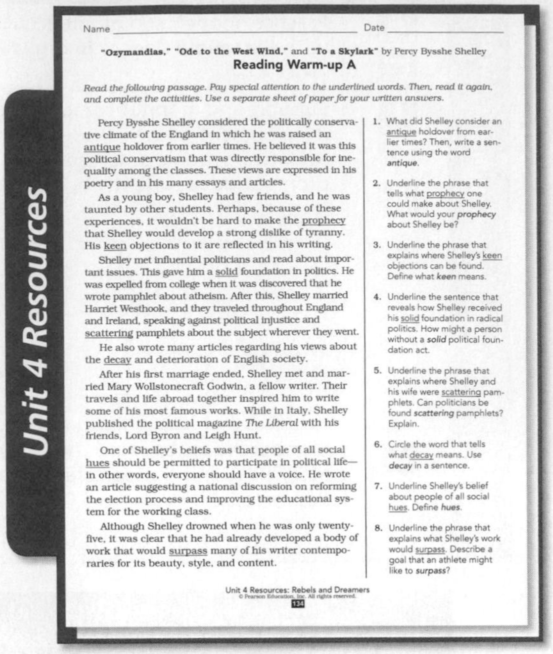

Name ______ Date ______

"Ozymandias," "Ode to the West Wind," and **"To a Skylark"** by Percy Bysshe Shelley
Reading Warm-up A

Read the following passage. Pay special attention to the underlined words. Then, read it again, and complete the activities. Use a separate sheet of paper for your written answers.

Percy Bysshe Shelley considered the politically conservative climate of the England in which he was raised an antique holdover from earlier times. He believed it was this political conservatism that was directly responsible for inequality among the classes. These views are expressed in his poetry and in his many essays and articles.

As a young boy, Shelley had few friends, and he was taunted by other students. Perhaps, because of these experiences, it wouldn't be hard to make the prophecy that Shelley would develop a strong dislike of tyranny. His keen objections to it are reflected in his writing.

Shelley met influential politicians and read about important issues. This gave him a solid foundation in politics. He was expelled from college when it was discovered that he wrote pamphlet about atheism. After this, Shelley married Harriet Westhook, and they traveled throughout England and Ireland, speaking against political injustice and scattering pamphlets about the subject wherever they went.

He also wrote many articles regarding his views about the decay and deterioration of English society.

After his first marriage ended, Shelley met and married Mary Wollstonecraft Godwin, a fellow writer. Their travels and life abroad together inspired him to write some of his most famous works. While in Italy, Shelley published the political magazine *The Liberal* with his friends, Lord Byron and Leigh Hunt.

One of Shelley's beliefs was that people of all social hues should be permitted to participate in political life—in other words, everyone should have a voice. He wrote an article suggesting a national discussion on reforming the election process and improving the educational system for the working class.

Although Shelley drowned when he was only twenty-five, it was clear that he had already developed a body of work that would surpass many of his writer contemporaries for its beauty, style, and content.

1. What did Shelley consider an antique holdover from earlier times? Then, write a sentence using the word ***antique***.
2. Underline the phrase that tells what prophecy one could make about Shelley. What would your ***prophecy*** about Shelley be?
3. Underline the phrase that explains where Shelley's keen objections can be found. Define what ***keen*** means.
4. Underline the sentence that reveals how Shelley received his solid foundation in radical politics. How might a person without a ***solid*** political foundation act.
5. Underline the phrase that explains where Shelley and his wife were scattering pamphlets. Can politicians be found ***scattering*** pamphlets? Explain.
6. Circle the word that tells what decay means. Use ***decay*** in a sentence.
7. Underline Shelley's belief about people of all social hues. Define ***hues***.
8. Underline the phrase that explains what Shelley's work would surpass. Describe a goal that an athlete might like to ***surpass***?

Unit 4 Resources: Rebels and Dreamers
© Pearson Education, Inc. All rights reserved.
134

EL L1 L2 **Reading Warm-ups A and B,** pp. 134–135

Also available for these selections:

EL L1 L2 **Vocabulary Warm-ups A and B,** pp. 132–133

All **Vocabulary Builder,** p. 138

Reader's Notebooks

Pre- and postreading pages for these selections appear in an interactive format in the *Reader's Notebooks.* Each *Notebook* is differentiated for a different group of learners. The selections in the Adapted and English Learner's versions are abridged.

L2 L3 ***Reader's Notebook***

L1 ***Reader's Notebook: Adapted Version***

EL ***Reader's Notebook: English Learner's Version***

EL ***Reader's Notebook: Spanish Version***

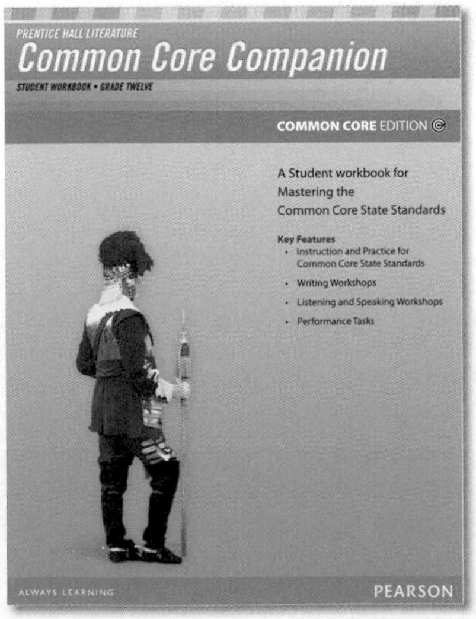

Common Core Companion

Additional instruction and practice for each Common Core State Standard

Selection Support

Graphic Organizer Transparencies

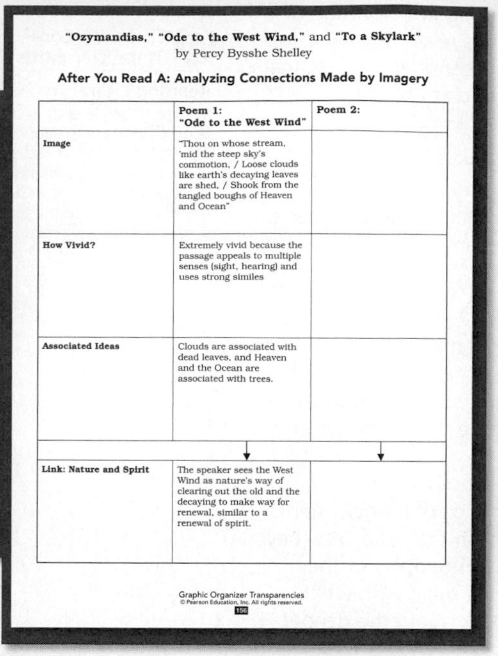

"Ozymandias," "Ode to the West Wind," and **"To a Skylark"**
by Percy Bysshe Shelley

After You Read A: Analyzing Connections Made by Imagery

	Poem 1: "Ode to the West Wind"	**Poem 2:**
Image	"Thou on whose stream, 'mid the steep sky's commotion, / Loose clouds like earth's decaying leaves are shed, / Shook from the tangled boughs of Heaven and Ocean"	
How Vivid?	Extremely vivid because the passage appeals to multiple senses (sight, hearing) and uses strong similes	
Associated Ideas	Clouds are associated with dead leaves, and Heaven and the Ocean are associated with trees.	
Link: Nature and Spirit	The speaker sees the West Wind as nature's way of clearing out the old and the decaying to make way for renewal, similar to a renewal of spirit.	

Graphic Organizer Transparencies

156

EL L1 L2 **Literary Analysis: Graphic Organizer A,** (partially filled in), p. 156

Also available for these selections:

EL L1 L2 **Reading: Graphic Organizer A** (partially filled in), p. 154

EL L3 **Reading: Graphic Organizer B,** p. 155

EL L3 **Literary Analysis: Graphic Organizer B,** p. 157

Skills Development/Extension

Unit 4 Resources

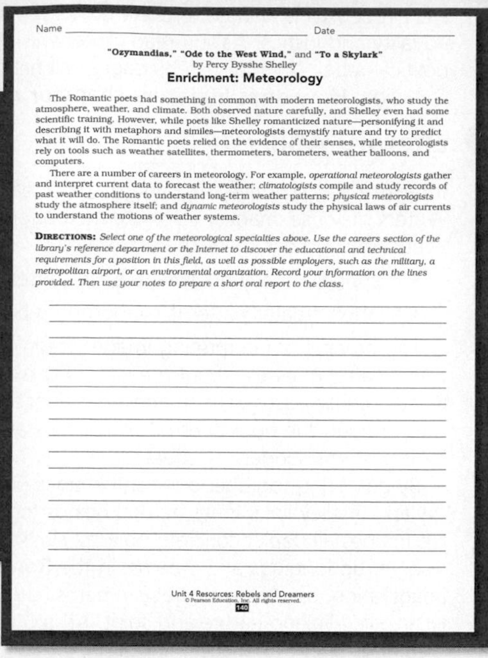

Name ____________________ Date ____________

"Ozymandias," "Ode to the West Wind," and **"To a Skylark"**
by Percy Bysshe Shelley

Enrichment: Meteorology

The Romantic poets had something in common with modern meteorologists, who study the atmosphere, weather, and climate. Both observed nature carefully, and Shelley even had some scientific training. However, while poets like Shelley romanticized nature—personifying it and describing it with metaphors and similes—meteorologists demystify nature and try to predict what it will do. The Romantic poets relied on the evidence of their senses, while meteorologists rely on tools such as weather satellites, thermometers, barometers, weather balloons, and computers.

There are a number of careers in meteorology. For example, *operational meteorologists* gather and interpret current data to forecast the weather; *climatologists* compile and study records of past weather conditions to understand long-term weather patterns; *physical meteorologists* study the atmosphere itself; and *dynamic meteorologists* study the physical laws of air currents to understand the motions of weather systems.

Directions: *Select one of the meteorological specialties above. Use the careers section of the library's reference department or the Internet to discover the educational and technical requirements for a position in this field, as well as possible employers, such as the military, a metropolitan airport, or an environmental organization. Record your information on the lines provided. Then use your notes to prepare a short oral report to the class.*

Unit 4 Resources: Rebels and Dreamers

140

L4 **Enrichment,** p. 140

Also available for these selections:

All **Literary Analysis,** p. 136

All **Reading,** p. 137

EL L3 L4 **Support for Writing,** p. 139

Assessment

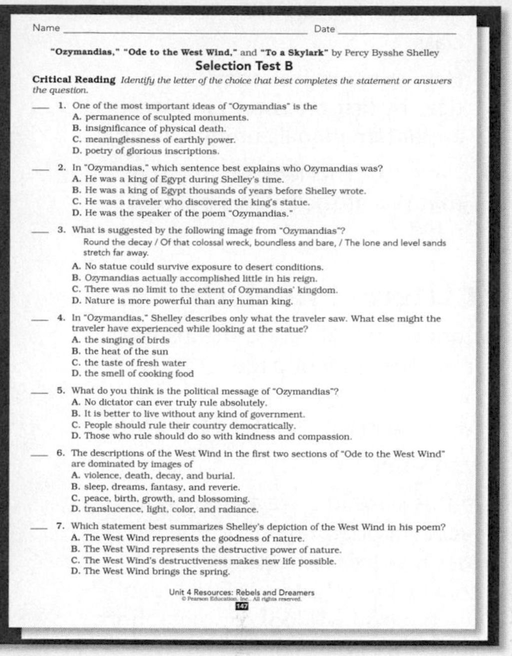

Name ____________________ Date ____________

"Ozymandias," "Ode to the West Wind," and **"To a Skylark"** by Percy Bysshe Shelley

Selection Test B

Critical Reading *Identify the letter of the choice that best completes the statement or answers the question.*

___ 1. One of the most important ideas of "Ozymandias" is the
A. permanence of sculpted monuments.
B. insignificance of physical death.
C. meaninglessness of earthly power.
D. poetry of glorious inscriptions.

___ 2. In "Ozymandias," which sentence best explains who Ozymandias was?
A. He was a king of Egypt during Shelley's time.
B. He was a king of Egypt thousands of years before Shelley wrote.
C. He was a traveler who discovered the king's statue.
D. He was the speaker of the poem "Ozymandias."

___ 3. What is suggested by the following image from "Ozymandias"?
Round the decay / Of that colossal wreck, boundless and bare, / The lone and level sands stretch far away.
A. No statue could survive exposure to desert conditions.
B. Ozymandias actually accomplished little in his reign.
C. There was no limit to the extent of Ozymandias' kingdom.
D. Nature is more powerful than any human king.

___ 4. In "Ozymandias," Shelley describes only what the traveler saw. What else might the traveler have experienced while looking at the statue?
A. the singing of birds
B. the heat of the sun
C. the taste of fresh water
D. the smell of cooking food

___ 5. What do you think is the political message of "Ozymandias"?
A. No dictator can ever truly rule absolutely.
B. It is better to live without any kind of government.
C. People should rule their country democratically.
D. Those who rule should do so with kindness and compassion.

___ 6. The descriptions of the West Wind in the first two sections of "Ode to the West Wind" are dominated by images of
A. violence, death, decay, and burial.
B. sleep, dreams, fantasy, and reverie.
C. peace, birth, growth, and blossoming.
D. translucence, light, color, and radiance.

___ 7. Which statement best summarizes Shelley's depiction of the West Wind in his poem?
A. The West Wind represents the goodness of nature.
B. The West Wind represents the destructive power of nature.
C. The West Wind's destructiveness makes new life possible.
D. The West Wind brings the spring.

Unit 4 Resources: Rebels and Dreamers

147

EL L3 L4 **Selection Test B,** pp. 147–149

Also available for these selections:

L3 L4 **Open-Book Test,** pp. 141–143

EL L1 L2 **Selection Test A,** pp. 144–146

PHLit Online!
www.PHLitOnline.com

- complete narrated selection text
- a thematically related video with writing prompt
- an interactive graphic organizer
- highlighting feature
- access to all student print resources, adapted to individual student needs
- Spanish and English summaries
- adapted selection translations in Spanish

Online Resources: All print materials are also available online.

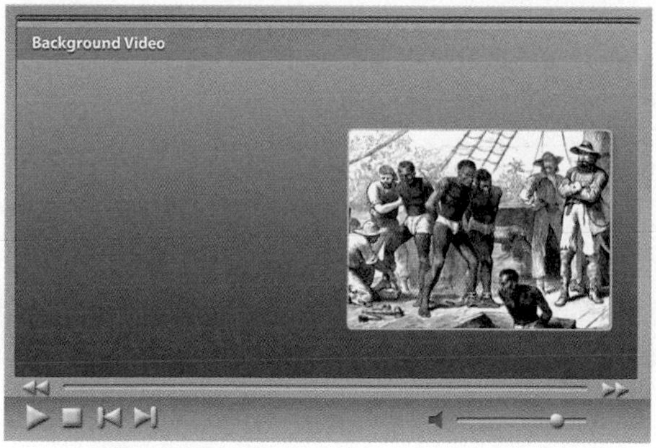

Background Video

Also available:

Get Connected! (thematic video with writing prompt)
All videos are available in Spanish.

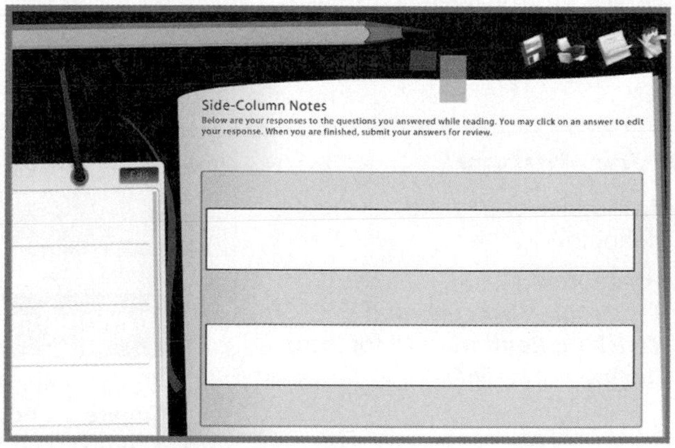

Writer's Journal (with graphics feature)

Also available:

Vocabulary Central (tools and activities for studying vocabulary)

PRETEACH

❶ Connecting to the Essential Question

1. Review the assignment with the class.
2. Help students list today's injustices by first brainstorming local and international current events.
3. Have students look for passages that reveal Shelley as a political rebel.

❷ Literary Analysis

Introduce the skill using the instruction on the student page.

Think Aloud: Model the Skill

Say to students:

In this selection, we are going to focus on poetic imagery. The writer uses imagery to help support or convey his message. When I read the poems I will look for metaphors and other figures of speech that help connect the physical world to the author's thoughts.

❸ Reading Strategy

1. Introduce the skill using the instruction on the student page.
2. Give students a copy of **Reading Strategy Graphic Organizer B,** page 155 in ***Graphic Organizer Transparencies,*** to fill out.

Think Aloud: Model the Skill

Say to students:

As I read Shelley's poetry, I will pay attention to the similarities and differences among the images he uses.

❹ Vocabulary

1. Pronounce each word, giving its definition.
2. For more guidance, see the ***Classroom Strategies and Teaching Routines*** card for introducing vocabulary.

Before You Read

Ozymandias • Ode to the West Wind • To a Skylark

❶ Connecting to the Essential Question Romantic poets like Shelley were rebels who wanted to overthrow tyrants and bring in a new age of equality and justice. As you read, note which passages reveal Shelley as a political rebel. Finding such passages will help as you consider the Essential Question: **How does literature shape or reflect society?**

Common Core State Standards

Reading Literature
1. Cite strong and thorough textual evidence to support analysis of what the text says explicitly as well as inferences drawn from the text, including determining where the text leaves matters uncertain.

❷ Literary Analysis

Imagery is descriptive language that re-creates sensory experience. Writers may use imagery to create metaphors and other figures of speech. Poetic imagery has these characteristics:

- It appeals to any or all of the five senses.
- It often creates patterns supporting a poem's theme.

The process of interpreting imagery requires you to make inferences, or educated guesses, about meaning. For example, in "Ode to the West Wind," Shelley uses wind images that appeal to sight, sound, and touch. Even though the poet does not explicitly state a theme, these images and their patterns suggest his message.

By gathering together powerful images of the west wind or of a skylark, Shelley links these natural beings to the strivings of his own spirit. His images all depict concrete objects, such as leaves in the wind. Yet they also stir up longings and dreams. In the **Romantic philosophy** of the imagination, an image connects what is "outside" the mind with what is "inside," linking nature and spirit. As you read, think about the deeper meanings Shelley's imagery suggests.

❸ Reading Strategy

Preparing to Read Complex Texts You can better understand an author's poetry by **comparing and contrasting elements** from different texts. For example, you might contrast the desert images of "Ozymandias," which suggest the bleakness of tyranny, with the wind images of "Ode to the West Wind," which suggest political rebellion. Use a chart like the one shown to compare the imagery in different poems by Shelley.

Imagery	Poem

❹ Vocabulary

verge (vurj) *n.* edge; rim (p. 870)

sepulcher (sep´ əl kər) *n.* tomb (p. 870)

impulse (im´ puls) *n.* force driving forward (p. 872)

blithe (blīth) *adj.* cheerful (p. 873)

profuse (prō fyo͞os´) *adj.* abundant; pouring out (p. 873)

satiety (sə tī´ ə tē) *n.* state of being filled with enough or more than enough (p. 875)

www.PHLitOnline.com

Vocabulary Development

Vocabulary Knowledge Rating

Create a **Vocabulary Knowledge Rating Chart** (*Professional Development Guidebook,* p. 33) or the vocabulary words on the student page. Give each student a copy of the chart with the words on it. Read the words aloud, and have students mark their ratings in the Before Reading column. Urge students to attend to these words as they read and discuss the selections.

In order to gauge how much instruction you need to provide, tally how many students are confident in their knowledge of each word. As students read, point out the words and their context.

Vocabulary Central, featuring tools and activities for studying vocabulary, is available online at **www.PHLitOnline.com.**

❺ Percy Bysshe Shelley (1792–1822)

Author of **"Ozymandias" • "Ode to the West Wind" • "To a Skylark"**

When he died in a boating accident at 29, Percy Bysshe (bish) Shelley was eulogized by his fellow poet Lord Byron as "without exception the best and least selfish man I ever knew."

A Loner and Rebel Born into the British upper classes, Shelley was raised on a country estate in Sussex. He attended the finest schools, including the prestigious boarding school Eton, but he was never able to settle into the routine of a student. Instead, he spent most of his time wandering the countryside and performing private scientific experiments. At Oxford University, he became a friend of Thomas Jefferson Hogg, a student whose political views were as strong as his own. When, with Hogg's encouragement and support, Shelley published the radical tract *The Necessity of Atheism,* both he and Hogg were expelled from the university.

Love and Art The expulsion estranged Shelley from his father. Instead of going home, Shelley headed for London. There, he met Harriet Westbrook. An unhappy schoolgirl, Westbrook persuaded him to elope, and they married.

Shelley's development as a poet was already under way. In 1813, he had completed "Queen Mab," his first important poem. The work explored ideas of social justice that Shelley had encountered in the philosopher William Godwin's *Political Justice.*

Turmoil, Romance, and Tragedy Shelley's marriage, meanwhile, was in trouble. Harriet felt that she could not keep up with her husband. Then, Shelley fell in love with Mary Wollstonecraft Godwin, daughter of William Godwin and the feminist Mary Wollstonecraft. After Harriet's tragic death in 1816, Shelley married his beloved Mary Godwin.

A Poet and an Outcast His radical politics, his tract about atheism, his separation from his first wife—all helped make Shelley an outcast from England. He and Mary eventually settled in Italy, where Lord Byron, another famous exile, lived.

Shelley wrote many of his finest works in Italy, including "Ode to the West Wind" and "To a Skylark." His early death there, however, meant that he never saw his dreams of social progress come true.

PRETEACH

Daily Bellringer

For each class during which you will teach these selections, have students complete one of the five activities for the appropriate week in the *Daily Bellringer Activities* booklet.

Multidraft Reading

To assist struggling readers and to enhance reading for all, assign the text in chunks, as warranted by length, and apply multidraft reading protocols. For each reading, have students set the purpose indicated:

- **First reading**—identifying key ideas and details and answering any Reading Checks.
- **Second reading**—analyzing craft and structure and responding to the side-column prompts.
- **Third reading**—integrating knowledge and ideas, connecting to other texts and the world, and answering the end-of-selection questions.

For more guidance, refer to the ***Classroom Strategies and Teaching Routines*** card on Multidraft Reading.

❺ Background

More About the Author

Percy Bysshe Shelley, while in his teens, privately published a series of Gothic horror novelettes and verses: *Zastrozzi* (1810), *Original Poetry by Victor and Cazire* (1810), and *St. Irvyne or The Rosicrucian* (1811).

Shelley's early years were characterized by experimental living and radical freethinking. He circulated pamphlets on vegetarianism and on the freedom of the press and tried setting up radical communes of like-minded bohemians.

Later in life, Shelley moved to Pisa, Italy, and was joined by Byron and Leigh Hunt.

PHLit Online! Teaching From Technology

www.PHLitOnline.com

Preparing to Read

Go to **www.PHLitOnline.com** in class or in a lab and display the ***Get Connected!*** slide show for these selections. Have the class brainstorm responses to the slide show writing prompt, entering ideas in the interactive journal. Then, have students complete their written responses individually, in a lab or as homework.

To build background, display the Background and More About the Author features.

Using the Interactive Text

Go to **www.PHLitOnline.com** and display the Enriched Online Student Edition. As the class reads the selection or listens to the narration, record answers to side-column prompts using the graphic organizers accessible on the interactive page. Alternatively, have students use the online edition individually, answering the prompts as they read.

❶ About the Selection

This poem provides an ironic comment on human pride and ambition. In the poem, a traveler describes the ruins of an ancient statue. On its base is an arrogant inscription: "Look on my works, ye Mighty, and despair!" However, what is left of the statue stands in an empty desert; the works of Ozymandias have crumbled under the onslaught of time and nature.

❷ Activating Prior Knowledge

Explain to students that they may already be familiar with the themes and attitudes of the second generation of English Romantics—Byron, Shelley, and Keats. Byron's bad-boy image and Shelley's defiant idealism are not uncommon among modern pop and movie stars. In poems such as "Ozymandias" and "Ode to the West Wind," Shelley taps deep into the mistrust of power and the burning passion for renewal that have characterized youth culture ever since. Think about popular youth culture today and how renewal and the mistrust of power are represented.

Concept Connector →

Tell students they will return to their responses after reading the selection.

❶ ❷ # Ozymandias

Percy Bysshe Shelley

Percy Bysshe Shelley

Text Complexity Rubric

	Ozymandias	Ode to the West Wind	To a Skylark
Qualitative Measures			
Context/ Knowledge Demands	Romantic sonnet 1 (2) 3 4 5	Romantic ode 1 (2) 3 4 5	Romantic ode 1 (2) 3 4 5
Structure/Language Conventionality and Clarity	Inverted syntax; long sentences 1 2 (3) 4 5	Archaic diction; long sentences 1 2 (3) 4 5	Archaic diction; sensory language 1 2 (3) 4 5
Levels of Meaning/ Purpose/Concept Level	Moderate (ambition, mortality) 1 2 (3) 4 5	Challenging (nature, renewal) 1 2 3 (4) 5	Accessible (nature) 1 (2) 3 4 5
Quantitative Measures			
Lexile/Text Length	NP / 112 words	NP / 548 words	NP / 567 words
Overall Complexity	**More accessible**	**More complex**	**More accessible**

Background The Ozymandias of Shelley's poem is based on an actual Egyptian pharaoh, Ramses II ("Ozymandias" was his name in Greek). Ramses II ruled during the thirteenth century B.C. and figures in the biblical story of Moses. He sponsored ambitious building projects and called for huge statues of himself to be built. According to an ancient story, one of these colossal statues was inscribed with this boast about his bold deeds: "I am Ozymandias, king of kings; if anyone wishes to know what I am and where I lie, let him surpass me in some of my exploits."

I met a traveler from an antique land
Who said: Two vast and trunkless legs of stone
Stand in the desert. Near them, on the sand,
Half sunk, a shattered visage[1] lies, whose frown,
And wrinkled lip, and sneer of cold command,
Tell that its sculptor well those passions read
Which yet survive, stamped on these lifeless things,
The hand that mocked them and the heart that fed:
And on the pedestal these words appear:
"My name is Ozymandias, king of kings:
Look on my works, ye Mighty, and despair!"
Nothing beside remains. Round the decay
Of that colossal wreck, boundless and bare,
The lone and level sands stretch far away.

3 ◀ Critical Viewing How is this Egyptian statue like and unlike the one in the poem? **[Compare and Contrast]**

1. **visage** (viz′ ij) *n.* face.

Critical Reading

Cite textual evidence to support your responses.

1. **Key Ideas and Details (a)** How would you describe the expression on the face of Ozymandias? **(b) Infer:** What does his expression suggest about the kind of ruler he was?
2. **Key Ideas and Details (a) Interpret:** What attitude is conveyed by the words on the pedestal? **(b) Compare and Contrast:** Compare this attitude with the opening images of the poem. **(c) Analyze:** In what sense is the inscription ironic?
3. **Integration of Knowledge and Ideas (a) Draw Conclusions:** What is the message of this poem? **(b) Apply:** Do you think that the message is pertinent to today's world? Why or why not?

3 Critical Viewing

Answer: The statue in the photograph is similar because it is large, made of stone, weathered, and on a flat plain. It is different because it has a trunk, its head is still attached, and it is surrounded by grasslands.

ASSESS

Answers

Before students respond, you may wish to have them write a brief objective summary of the selection. As they answer the questions below, remind them to support their answers with evidence from the text.

1. (a) The expression is partially obscured by its deterioration, but it includes a frown, a wrinkled lip, and a sneer. (b) His expression suggests he was a condescending, proud ruler.
2. (a) The inscription conveys an attitude of pride and arrogance. (b) This attitude of arrogance stands in sharp contrast to the opening images of devastation and emptiness. (c) It is ironic because Ozymandias appears to have expected his works to last forever, but the statue on the pedestal, along with his entire civilization, has long since been destroyed.
3. (a) **Possible responses:** Power is fleeting; human beings cannot escape the effects of time. (b) Yes, it puts accomplishments, pride, and power in perspective; no, it is rare to find people creating such self-glorifying monuments in today's world.

Text Complexity: Reader and Task Suggestions

	Ozymandias	Ode to the West Wind	To a Skylark
Preparing to Read the Texts • Using the information on SE p. 867, discuss the role that nature and art might play in the life of someone who feels alienated. • Discuss with students the Romantic ideas of using images from nature to convey human emotions. • Guide students to use Multidraft Reading strategies (TE p. 867).	**Leveled Tasks** ***Structure/Language*** If students will have difficulty with the inverted sentences, have them paraphrase the sentences to clarify meaning. Then, as they reread, have students focus on the irony of the engraved words. ***Synthesizing*** If students will not have difficulty with the inverted sentences, have them explain the relationship between the statue and its surroundings.	**Leveled Tasks** ***Levels of Meaning*** If students will have difficulty with the levels of meaning, have them focus first on the speaker's situation and the comforting lesson of the poem's last line. Then, as they reread, have them examine other feelings. ***Analyzing*** If students will not have difficulty with the levels of meaning, have them analyze wind imagery and key ideas it inspires in the speaker.	**Leveled Tasks** ***Structure/Language*** If students will have difficulty with the poem's language, have them prepare charts showing the comparisons made in the many similes. Then, as they reread, have them use the charts to clarify the speaker's attitude toward the skylark. ***Evaluating*** If students will not have difficulty with the poem's language, have them evaluate the effectiveness of the imagery.

❹ About the Selection

The speaker of this poem describes the elemental force of the West Wind as it drives dead leaves, stirs up the ocean, destroys plants, and heralds winter's arrival. Awed by the wind's natural strength and disillusioned with his own spiritual barrenness, Shelley calls on the wind to lift him up, ravage him, and cleanse him. He concludes by affirming that decay will lead ultimately to the renewal of spring.

❺ Literary Analysis

Imagery

1. Read the bracketed passage aloud to students.
2. Remind them that imagery appeals to the five senses.
3. Then, **ask** the Literary Analysis question.
   Possible response: Students may say that Shelley's description of the wind's "aery surge" elicits appeals to the sense of sight. Point out that the word *surge* also suggests the wind's sound, and its power as it might be detected by touch.

Ode to the ❹ West Wind

Percy Bysshe Shelley

I

O wild West Wind, thou breath of Autumn's being,
Thou, from whose unseen presence the leaves dead
Are driven, like ghosts from an enchanter fleeing,

Yellow, and black, and pale, and hectic red,
Pestilence-stricken multitudes: O thou,
Who chariotest to their dark and wintry bed

The wingèd seeds, where they lie cold and low,
Each like a corpse within its grave, until
Thine azure sister of the Spring[1] shall blow

Her clarion[2] o'er the dreaming earth, and fill
(Driving sweet buds like flocks to feed in air)
With loving hues and odors plain and hill:

Wild Spirit, which art moving everywhere;
Destroyer and preserver; hear, oh, hear!

II

Thou on whose stream, 'mid the steep sky's commotion,
Loose clouds like earth's decaying leaves are shed,
Shook from the tangled boughs of Heaven and Ocean,

Angels[3] of rain and lightning: there are spread
On the blue surface of thine aery surge,
Like the bright hair uplifted from the head

❺

Of some fierce Maenad,[4] even from the dim verge
Of the horizon to the zenith's height,
The locks of the approaching storm. Thou dirge

Of the dying year, to which this closing night
Will be the dome of a vast sepulcher,
Vaulted with all thy congregated might

Literary Analysis
Imagery To which sense does the image in lines 18–23 mostly appeal?

Vocabulary
verge (vʉrj) *n.* edge; rim
sepulcher (sep′ əl kər) *n.* tomb

1. **sister of the Spring** the wind prevailing during spring.
2. **clarion** *n.* trumpet producing clear, sharp tones.
3. **angels** messengers.
4. **Maenad** (mē′ nad) a priestess of Bacchus, the Greek and Roman god of wine and revelry.

Enrichment: Investigating Geography

West Winds

Shelley's poem addresses the West Wind, or wind blowing from the west. Explain to students that this wind usually brings new weather because of Earth's rotation from west to east.

Activity: Investigating West Winds Have students research the West Wind and create a map that demonstrates an understanding of its effect on temperature and climate on Earth. Students should use the **Enrichment: Investigating Geography** worksheet, ***Professional Development Guidebook,*** page 228 to record their notes and plan their projects.

Of vapors, from whose solid atmosphere
Black rain, and fire, and hail will burst: oh, hear!

III

Thou who didst waken from his summer dreams
The blue Mediterranean, where he lay,
Lulled by the coil of his crystalline streams,

Beside a pumice[5] isle in Baiae's bay,[6]
And saw in sleep old palaces and towers
Quivering within the wave's intenser day,

All overgrown with azure moss and flowers
So sweet, the sense faints picturing them!
For whose path the Atlantic's level powers

Cleave themselves into chasms, while far below
The sea-blooms and the oozy woods which wear
The sapless foliage of the ocean, know

Thy voice, and suddenly grow gray with fear,
And tremble and despoil themselves: oh, hear!

IV

If I were a dead leaf thou mightest bear;
If I were a swift cloud to fly with thee;
A wave to pant beneath thy power, and share

5. **pumice** (pum′ is) *n.* volcanic rock.
6. **Baiae's** (bā′ yēz) **bay** site of the ancient Roman resort near Naples, parts of which lie submerged.

6 ▲ Critical Viewing
Which elements in this painting match Shelley's evocation of the west wind in lines 1–8? **[Connect]**

Reading Strategy
Comparing Imagery
Contrast the images in lines 29–36 with those in lines 12–14 of "Ozymandias."

8 Reading Check
In the first three sections, what does the speaker ask the West Wind to do?

6 Critical Viewing

Possible Answer: The red, brownish black, and yellow colors of the field and trees evoke Shelley's words in line 4: "Yellow, and black, and pale, and hectic red." The wind-blown trees and wild sea also suggest the blustery days of Autumn.

7 Reading Strategy

Comparing Imagery

Ask students the Reading Strategy question.
Possible response: Lines 29–36 of "Ode to the West Wind" call to mind calming images of water's soothing effect and of sleep and dreams. Lines 12–14 are resolute and describe the remains of a once glorious statue situated in a barren wasteland.

8 Reading Check

Answer: The speaker asks the West Wind to listen to him.

Differentiated Instruction for Universal Access

Strategy for Special-Needs Students
Have students read a section from "Ode to the West Wind" with teacher guidance. Then, ask students to visualize each line as they read the rest of the poem to themselves.

EL Vocabulary for English Learners
Have students practice reading unfamiliar words in the poem aloud. You may want to play the ***Hear It!*** Audio CDs and have students listen to the sound of the poem, then go back and try to say words with which they are having difficulty.

Enrichment for Advanced Students
Have students write poems in which the West Wind replies to Shelley. Have students divide their poems into five parts, like Shelley's poem, and make sure that each part is a response to the corresponding section of Shelley's work.

9 Literary Analysis

Imagery and Romantic Philosophy

1. Have students read the bracketed passage to themselves.
2. Review with students their understanding of Romantic philosophy and its connection between external and internal sensibilities.
3. Then, **ask** the Literary Analysis question.
   Answer: The speaker sees himself in the bittersweet autumn wind and asks the wind to enable his spirit to be one with that of the wind.

ASSESS

Answers

Before students respond, you may wish to have them write a brief objective summary of the selection. As they answer the questions below, remind them to support their answers with evidence from the text.

1. (a) It is associated with autumn. (b) Shelley associates the West Wind with destruction, frenzy, decay, and fear.
2. (a) The speaker asks the West Wind to lift him up as a wave, leaf, or cloud and carry him. (b) The speaker says he is oppressed by "a heavy weight of hours."
3. (a) Even the bleakest situations are followed by times of renewal and hope. (b) It sums up the poem's theme of hope for a new beginning.

Vocabulary
impulse (im′ puls′) *n.* force driving forward

The impulse of thy strength, only less free
Than thou, O uncontrollable! If even
I were as in my boyhood, and could be

The comrade of thy wanderings over Heaven,
As then, when to outstrip thy skyey speed
Scarce seemed a vision; I would ne'er have striven

As thus with thee in prayer in my sore need.
Oh, lift me as a wave, a leaf, a cloud!
I fall upon the thorns of life! I bleed!

A heavy weight of hours has chained and bowed
One too like thee: tameless, and swift, and proud.

Literary Analysis
Imagery and Romantic Philosophy How do the images in lines 57–63 imply a connection between the speaker and nature?

V

Make me thy lyre,[7] even as the forest is:
What if my leaves are falling like its own!
The tumult of thy mighty harmonies

Will take from both a deep, autumnal tone,
Sweet though in sadness. Be thou, Spirit fierce,
My spirit! Be thou me, impetuous one!

Drive my dead thought over the universe
Like withered leaves to quicken a new birth!
And, by the incantation of this verse,

Scatter, as from an unextinguished hearth
Ashes and sparks, my words among mankind!
Be through my lips to unawakened earth

The trumpet of a prophecy! O Wind,
If Winter comes, can Spring be far behind?

7. **lyre** Aeolian (ē ō′ lē ən) lyre, or wind harp, a stringed instrument that produces musical sounds when the wind passes over it.

Critical Reading

1. **Key Ideas and Details (a)** What season does the poet associate with the west wind? **(b) Interpret:** What feelings does Shelley create around the west wind in sections II and III?
2. **Key Ideas and Details (a)** What does the speaker ask of the wind in section IV? **(b) Infer:** What change in his life prompts this question?
3. **Key Ideas and Details (a)** What does the final line of the poem mean? **(b)** How does it tie together the poem?

Enrichment: Investigating Literary Figures

English Romantics
Activity: Investigating English Romantics Ask students to research more information about Percy Bysshe Shelley or any of the other English Romantics. Students may record their findings in the **Enrichment: Investigating a Literary Figure** worksheet, ***Professional Development Guidebook,*** page 235. Pair students who have researched different figures and allow them to share their findings with each other.

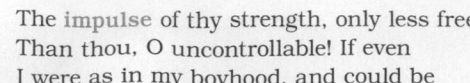

Woman and Bird in Moonlight, 1949, Joan Miro, Tate, London/Art Resource, NY. © Copyright ARS, NY

12 ▲ **Critical Viewing** Which details in this painting capture the freedom and independence of Shelley's skylark? **[Connect]**

10 To a Skylark

Percy Bysshe Shelley

Hail to thee, **blithe** spirit!
  Bird thou never wert,
That from heaven, or near it,
  Pourest thy full heart
In **profuse** strains of unpremeditated art.

Higher still and higher,
  From the earth thou springest
Like a cloud of fire;
  The blue deep thou wingest,
And singing still dost soar, and soaring ever singest.

In the golden lightning
  Of the sunken sun,
O'er which clouds are brightening,
  Thou dost float and run;
Like an unbodied joy whose race is just begun.

Vocabulary
blithe (blīth) *adj.* cheerful
profuse (prō fyo͞os′) *adj.* abundant; pouring out

13 ☑ Reading Check
To what type of cloud does Shelley compare the skylark?

10 About the Selection

This poem honors nature's glorious songs and aspires to its pure joy. Addressed to a bird, the poem captures the skylark's spiraling flight and describes its soaring music, whether in the fading evening or earliest dawn. The unending joy of the skylark's song is contrasted with human experiences of limitation and the contradictions of joy and suffering.

11 Humanities

Woman and Bird in Moonlight, 1949, by Joan Miró

Miró (1893–1983) was a Spanish artist from the region of Catalonia. He is often associated with Surrealism—an artistic and philosophical movement from the early twentieth century. Like Romanticism, Surrealism was a rebellious movement; in particular, Surrealists were attacking and rebelling against the senselessness of war, such as the Spanish Civil War of the 1930s.

Use this question for discussion:

1. Which elements of the painting are rebellious?
   Possible response: The childlike outlines of the figures are a rebellious response to traditional styles and techniques of art from previous centuries.

12 Critical Viewing

Answer: The simplicity of the figures, the open spaces, and the exuberant colors capture the freedom and independence of Shelley's skylark.

13 Reading Check

Answer: Shelley compares the skylark to a cloud of fire.

Differentiated Instruction for Universal Access

Culturally Responsive Instruction

Culture Connection Students may lack the background knowledge or context-building experiences necessary to fully comprehend the selection. Before students read, build background knowledge about some of the places mentioned in the poem: the Mediterranean, Pumice Isle, or Baiae's Bay, for example. Provide images of these places—especially, if possible, as they pertain to their attributes as resort or vacation destinations—and ask students to discuss what they might see and hear if they were there.

⑭ Literary Analysis

Imagery

1. Read the bracketed passage aloud to students.
2. **Ask** the Literary Analysis question.
   Answer: The senses are sight (including the "pale purple" of the evening), sound (the bird's "shrill delight"), and touch (the "melting" of the evening).

Spiral Review

Figurative Lanugage

1. Remind students that they studied figurative language in an earlier lesson.
2. **Ask** students the Spiral Review question.
   Possible response: Similes are used in these stanzas, likening the bird to a star, a poet, a maiden, a glowworm, and a rose. The repeated similes emphasize the skylark's mystery by comparing it to images that people find intriguing and mysterious. Each comparison calls out a quality of something not completely accessible.

Literary Analysis
Imagery To what three senses do lines 16–20 appeal?

Spiral Review
Figurative Language
What type of figure of speech appears throughout these stanzas? How does the repeated use of this figure of speech to describe the skylark emphasize the bird's mystery?

The pale purple even[1]
Melts around thy flight;
⑭ Like a star of heaven,
In the broad daylight
Thou art unseen, but yet I hear thy shrill delight,

Keen as are the arrows
Of that silver sphere,[2]
Whose intense lamp narrows
In the white dawn clear,
Until we hardly see—we feel that it is there.

All the earth and air
With thy voice is loud,
As, when night is bare,
From one lonely cloud
The moon rains out her beams, and Heaven is overflowed.

What thou art we know not;
What is most like thee?
From rainbow clouds there flow not
Drops so bright to see,
As from thy presence showers a rain of melody.

Like a poet hidden
In the light of thought,
Singing hymns unbidden,
Till the world is wrought
To sympathy with hopes and fears it heeded not:

Like a highborn maiden
In a palace tower,
Soothing her love-laden
Soul in secret hour
With music sweet as love, which overflows her bower:

Like a glowworm golden
In a dell of dew,
Scattering unbeholden
Its aerial hue
Among the flowers and grass, which screen it from the view!

⑮ Like a rose embowered
In its own green leaves,

1. **even** evening.
2. **silver sphere** the morning star.

Enrichment: Analyzing Music

Musical Qualities in Shelley's Poetry
"Ode to the West Wind," "To a Skylark," and "Ozymandias" are lyrical poems. Point out to students the specific qualities of Shelley's poetry—figurative language, sound devices, imagery—that help create a musical effect. Remind students that the earliest lyrical poems were sung.

Activity: Analyzing Music Allow students to choose a favorite popular song and to record details about it on the **Enrichment: Analyzing Music** worksheet, ***Professional Development Guidebook,*** page 236. Ask students to look for any of the qualities of lyrical poetry that are in their favorite songs. Divide students into small groups and allow them to compare the characteristics of the songs they chose. Later, with the whole class, discuss how today's popular music is similar to or different than Shelley's work.

15

By warm winds deflowered,[3]
Till the scent it gives
Makes faint with too much sweet those heavy-wingèd thieves.[4]

Sound of vernal[5] showers
On the twinkling grass,
Rain-awakened flowers,
All that ever was
Joyous, and clear, and fresh, thy music doth surpass:

Teach us, sprite or bird,
What sweet thoughts are thine:
I have never heard
Praise of love or wine
That panted forth a flood of rapture so divine.

Chorus Hymeneal,[6]
Or triumphal chant,
Matched with thine would be all
But an empty vaunt,
A thing wherein we feel there is some hidden want.

What objects are the fountains[7]
Of thy happy strain?
What fields, or waves, or mountains?
What shapes of sky or plain?
What love of thine own kind? what ignorance of pain?

With thy clear keen joyance
Languor cannot be;
Shadow of annoyance
Never came near thee;
Thou lovest—but ne'er knew love's sad satiety.

Waking or asleep,
Thou of death must deem[8]
Things more true and deep
Than we mortals dream,
Or how could thy notes flow in such a crystal stream?

We look before and after,
And pine for what is not;
Our sincerest laughter

3. deflowered fully open.
4. thieves the "warm winds."
5. vernal (vʉr´ nəl) *adj.* relating to spring.
6. Chorus Hymeneal (hī´ mə nē´ əl) marriage song, named after Hymen, the Greek god of marriage.
7. fountains sources, inspiration.
8. deem know.

Reading Strategy
Comparing Imagery
Compare the images in lines 51–55 with those in lines 35–36 of "Ode to the West Wind."

Vocabulary
satiety (sə tī´ ə tē) *n.* state of being filled with enough or more than enough

16 **Reading Check**
Through what sense or senses does the speaker perceive the Skylark?

15 Reading Strategy
Comparing Imagery
Ask students the Reading Strategy question.
Possible response: Both sets of lines describe flowers and their scents—scents first full and rich, but then fading.

16 Reading Check
Answer: The speaker perceives the skylark through the sense of hearing (he hears the bird's song).

Differentiated Instruction for Universal Access

Strategy for Special-Needs Students
Have each student present an image from one of the stanzas. Then, discuss what the images have in common—sense appealed to, mood, type of language—and how they differ.

Strategy for Less Proficient Readers
For students who have difficulty interpreting Shelley's imagery, use **Reading Strategy Graphic Organizer B**, page 155 in ***Graphic Organizer Transparencies,*** to model how lines from Shelley's poems appeal to the senses, evoke emotions, and relate to the theme.

Strategy for Advanced Readers
Have students read the final stanzas of the poem in small groups. Review with students their understanding of Romantic philosophy's linking of nature and spirit. Ask them to discuss how Shelley's speaker connects the natural world and the speaker's world.

With some pain is fraught;
Our sweetest songs are those that tell of saddest thought.

Yet if[9] we could scorn
Hate, and pride, and fear;
If we were things born
Not to shed a tear,
I know not how thy joy we ever should come near.

Better than all measures
Of delightful sound,
Better than all treasures
That in books are found,
Thy skill to poet were,[10] thou scorner of the ground!

Teach me half the gladness
That thy brain must know,
Such harmonious madness
From my lips would flow,
The world should listen then, as I am listening now.

---

9. if even if.
10. were would be.

Critical Reading

Cite textual evidence to support your responses.

1. **Key Ideas and Details (a)** In the first stanza, what does the poet claim the skylark is not? **(b) Interpret:** What point is he making? **(c) Analyze:** How do the images of light in lines 6–35 reinforce the point?
2. **Key Ideas and Details (a)** To what four things does the speaker compare the bird in lines 36–55? **(b) Analyze:** What quality or power does each comparison suggest that the bird's song has?
3. **Key Ideas and Details (a)** What comparisons does the poet make between human song and the skylark's? **(b) Analyze:** Based on these comparisons, what does the speaker conclude about similarities and differences between the bird's life and human life?
4. **Craft and Structure** What does the speaker's use of the phrase "harmonious madness" (line 103) suggest about the difference between the skylark's song and human poetry?
5. **Integration of Knowledge and Ideas** In what ways does the sculpture in "Ozymandias" represent tyranny and the wind in "Ode to the West Wind" rebellion? In your response, use at least two of these Essential Question words: *independence, conform, limits.* ***[Connecting to the Essential Question: How does literature shape or reflect society?]***

ASSESS

Answers

Before students respond, you may wish to have them write a brief objective summary of the selection. As they answer the questions below, remind them to support their answers with evidence from the text.

1. (a) The poet claims the skylark is not a bird. (b) He is making the point that the bird's song sounds like something beyond the world of living things. (c) The images of light suggest that the bird is celestial or otherworldly.
2. (a) The poet compares the bird to a poet, a highborn maiden, a glowworm, and a rose. (b) Each comparison suggests that the song can transform the world or a soul. The song is like the poet's hymns, which create new sympathies and fears; the song is like the song of a lovelorn maiden soothing herself; like the glowworm's light, the song permeates the air; like the scent of fallen roses, the song intoxicates.
3. (a) The speaker claims that the skylark's songs are sweeter than any human songs, or any triumphal chants or wedding songs. (b) The speaker concludes that the skylark cannot know annoyance or languor, but that it understands death more deeply. Unlike the bird, humans pine for what is not, and even their laughter is infected with grief.
4. The phrase suggests that the gladness of the skylark is too pure to be understood by people; translated into poetry, it would be startlingly beautiful but would not make sense.
5. The sculpture in "Ozymandias" represents tyranny because it is the image of an arrogant ruler who was not aware of the real *limits* of his power. The wind in "Ode" represents rebellion because it does not *conform* to any rules—it is nature at its most wild and unruly.

Vocabulary Development

Vocabulary Knowledge Rating

When students have completed reading and discussing the selection, have them take out their **Vocabulary Knowledge Rating Charts** for the story. Read the words aloud and have students rate their knowledge of words again in the After Reading column. Clarify any words that are still problematic. Have students write their own definitions and example or sentence in the appropriate column. Then, have students complete the Vocabulary Practice at the end of the selection. Encourage students to use the words in further discussion and written work about the selection. Remind them that they will be accountable for these words on the **Selection Test, *Unit 4 Resources,*** pages 144–146 or 147–149.

LITERATURE IN CONTEXT

SHELLEY AND SCIENCE

Percy Bysshe Shelley was well educated in the science of his day. As a schoolboy, he studied with Adam Walker, a scientist who lectured on natural history, electricity, and meteorology. Later, Shelley, who was an avid reader, followed the latest scientific discoveries with great interest. For example, he read the work of meteorologist Luke Howard and incorporated Howard's theories of cloud formation into his poem "The Cloud":

This cloud sketch is by Luke Howard (1772–1864). Howard kept precise records of the weather in London for forty years and created a classification system for clouds that we still use today. His writings transformed the science of meteorology and inspired Shelley's poem "The Cloud."

. . . I am the daughter of Earth and Water,
And the nursling of the Sky;
I pass through the pores of the ocean and shores;
I change, but I cannot die.

CONNECT TO THE LITERATURE

What evidence of scientific influence can you find in the poems you have read by Shelley?

Concept Connector

Reading Strategy Graphic Organizer

Ask students to review the graphic organizers in which they have compared and contrasted the imagery in Shelley's poetry. Then, have students share their organizers and compare their interpretations of the images and their understanding of each of the texts.

Activating Prior Knowledge

Have students return to their responses to the Activating Prior Knowledge activity. Ask them to explain whether their thoughts have changed and if so, how.

Writing About the Essential Question

Have students compare their responses to the prompt, completed before reading the poems, with their thoughts afterwards. Ask students to formulate new responses supported by specific textual details. Lead a class discussion, probing for what students have learned that confirms or invalidates their initial thoughts.

Background

Meteorology

Today's meteorologists, or atmospheric scientists, specialize not only in forecasting, but in understanding general weather circulation patterns, precipitation processes, global warming, and ozone depletion. Additionally, not all meteorologists need look for work in television and/or radio. The military and the National Weather Service are among the other employers of atmospheric scientists.

Literature in Context

Shelley and Science

Luke Howard, who studied and wrote about science only as a hobby, gave us the first basic cloud classification system, dividing clouds among these types: cumulus (puffy), stratus (layered), cirrus (wispy or curly), and nimbus (rain-producing). He categorized the clouds based on their shapes, recognizing that their appearances reflected their composition. Shelley, who was fascinated by scientific explanations of the world from a young age, read Howard's *Essay on Clouds* and often employed metaphors in his poetry that drew on his knowledge of science and nature.

Howard's system evolved into the system used by meteorologists today, which classifies clouds not only by their shape, but also by their altitude in the atmosphere.

Connect to the Literature

Ask students the Connect to the Literature question.

Answer: In "Ode to the West Wind," Shelley demonstrates an understanding of wind patterns and nature's processes. For example, in lines 16-18 he draws on knowledge of the water cycle and cloud forms, describing rain deriving from both the sky and the ocean. Shelley also mentions clouds and plant life in "To a Skylark.

After You Read

Ozymandias • Ode to the West Wind • To a Skylark

Literary Analysis

1. **Key Ideas and Details** Imagine filming the **imagery** of "Ozymandias." **(a)** Compare the camera placement you would use for lines 4–5, lines 9–11, and the final line. **(b)** Explain how each image helps convey Shelley's message.
2. **Craft and Structure (a)** In "Ode to the West Wind," find three images indicating the power of the wind, and explain to which senses each appeals. **(b)** How do these images support Shelley's message of renewal?
3. **Craft and Structure (a)** How do descriptions of sounds in "To a Skylark" *evoke emotions* by suggesting the bird's "unbodied joy"? **(b)** How does sound show the defect in human joy in lines 86–90?
4. **Comparing Literary Works** Compare Shelley's images of the statue, the west wind, and the skylark. **(a)** Which paints the strongest sensory picture of the object described? Explain. **(b)** Which provides the clearest sense of the ideas and feelings connected with the object? Explain.
5. **Comparing Literary Works** Using a chart like the one shown, compare two poems where an image connects the speaker with nature.

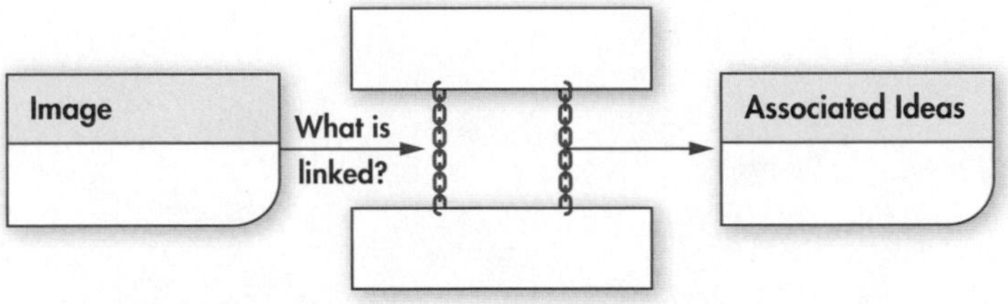

6. **Comparing Literary Works** In **Romantic philosophy,** the imagination connects nature and spirit. **(a)** What images in sections IV and V of "Ode to the West Wind" suggest such a connection? **(b)** Show how Shelley's use of *personification*—treating nonhuman things as if they were human—in two poems also helps link nature and spirit.
7. **Analyzing Visual Information** Using your knowledge of "Ozymandias," explain the humor of the cartoon shown on this page.

Reading Strategy

8. **Compare elements** in Shelley's poems by contrasting the desert imagery of "Ozymandias" with the wind imagery of "Ode to the West Wind." How does each of these patterns of imagery reveal Shelley as a political rebel?
9. **(a)** Using imagery from each poem, contrast the oppressive heaviness of the tyrant in "Ozymandias" with the lightness and ease of the bird in "To a Skylark." **(b)** To what extent do you think Shelley identifies the skylark with imagination itself? Explain.

Common Core State Standards

Writing

7. Conduct short research projects to answer a question or solve a problem. *(p. 879)*

8. Gather relevant information from multiple authoritative print and digital sources, using advanced searches effectively; assess the strengths and limitations of each source in terms of the task, purpose, and audience. *(p. 879)*

Language

4.d. Verify the preliminary determination of the meaning of a word or phrase. *(p. 879)*

5. Demonstrate understanding of figurative language, word relationships, and nuances in word meanings. *(p. 879)*

"My name is Ozymandias, king of kings: Look on my works, ye Mighty, and despair!" ▼

Answers

1. (a) Lines 4–5 and 9–11 are like close-up camera shots; the last line is a panoramic shot of the barren desert. (b) Each image reflects the destruction of Ozymandias's statue and the erasure of all traces of his power.
2. (a) **Possible responses:** The scattering of leaves, the spreading of seeds to the ground, and the flutter of clouds in the sky appeal to sight and sound. (b) The leaves and seeds falling bring about a new season, and the clouds initiate new weather.
3. (a) The descriptions of sounds suggest that the song is everywhere, even in heaven. (b) Humans' "sweetest songs" are ones that "tell of saddest thought" and show that joy and goodness are linked.
4. **Possible responses:** (a) The image of the statue is the strongest because of its simplicity; the image of the wind is the richest because of the wealth of scenes associated with it. (b) The image of the statue presents the clearest sense because of its simplicity.
5. Image: a dead leaf ("West Wind," line 43) Linked: the narrator to a leaf blowing in the wind Associations: weightlessness; the great power and speed of the wind.
6. (a) Images such as "lift me as a wave, a leaf, a cloud," "Make me thy lyre," and "Be thou, Spirit fierce, / My spirit! Be thou me, impetuous one!" suggest the speaker's desire to connect nature and spirit. (b) **Possible answer:** Shelley's personification of the wind—as a being that can listen—links nature and spirit.
7. Answers will vary.
8. **Possible answer:** Shelley uses the desert to show the barren nature of Ozymandias' power and uses the wind imagery to express the defiant and unruly nature of human will.
9. (a) The skylark is "Like a glow-worm golden / In a dell of dew" while the tyrant is described in heavy sounds as "boundless and bare." (b) **Possible answer:** The skylark is like imagination in that it is "harmonious madness."

Assessment Practice

Critical Thinking (For more practice, see *All-in-One Workbook.*)

Many tests require students to judge the relevance of facts in a writer's argument. Use this sample item.

. . . And on the pedestal these words appear:
"My name is Ozymandias, king of kings:
Look on my works, ye Mighty, and despair!"
Nothing beside remains. Round the decay
Of that colossal wreck, boundless and bare,
The lone and level sands stretch far away.

Which of these facts would support the theme of these lines from "Ozymandias"?

A The traveler was from Greece.
B The sculptor is buried in a tomb nearby.
C The writing on the pedestal is so weathered that it is scarcely legible.
D Ruins can survive for centuries in the desert.

The theme of the passage is the transitory nature of human accomplishments. This theme is supported by **C**.

Integrated Language Skills

Vocabulary Acquisition and Use

Word Analysis: Latin Root *-puls-*

The Latin root *-puls-* means "push or drive." It is the base of some common words that are also used for *scientific concepts.* Using your knowledge of the root *-puls-*, write the definition of each numbered word below. Verify your definitions by checking a *dictionary.* Then, write three original sentences, each using a different word on the list.

1. compulsion
2. expulsion
3. impulse
4. propulsion
5. pulse
6. repulse

Vocabulary: Analogies

Analogies show the relationships between pairs of words. Complete each analogy using a word from the vocabulary list on page 866. In each, your choice should create a word pair that matches the relationship between the first two words given. Then, explain your answers.

1. *Penalty* is to *punishment* as ______ is to *brink.*
2. ______ is to *push* as *halt* is to *stop.*
3. *Sad* is to ______ as *ill* is to *healthy.*
4. *Glare* is to *sunlight* as ______ is to *fullness.*
5. ______ is to *building* as *dirge* is to *music.*
6. *Speed* is to *velocity* as ______ is to *excessive.*

Writing

Explanatory Text In lyric poems like "Ode to the West Wind," Shelley drew on the scientific and historical knowledge of his time. Develop a **research plan** for a report on Shelley's use of scientific or historical knowledge—or both—in his poetry. Include a *narrowed topic* to be investigated, *questions* to be answered, a *bibliography* of properly cited sources you will consult, and *annotations* stating the *appropriateness and objectivity* of each source.

Prewriting Use *creative research strategies* to formulate questions and develop a bibliography. Consider interviewing librarians and Shelley scholars. Also consider scanning biographies of Shelley and footnoted editions of his work to uncover scientific and historical influences.

Drafting Based on your reading, identify a narrow topic that could be answered adequately in a short paper. List your sources. Scan introductions, tables of contents, or opening paragraphs of the sources to see how appropriate and reliable each might be. Write specific annotations commenting on the relevance and objectivity of each.

Revising Review your questions to make sure they are clear and focused. Study your bibliography to make sure that you follow the format requested by your teacher.

Model: Making Evaluations Specific
Shelley, Mary. *Notes to the Complete Poetical Works of Percy Bysshe Shelley.* Sydney, Australia: ReadHowYouWant.com, 2006. Comments by his wife might show what reading in history and science Shelley had done.

Use specific information in your evaluations for clarity.

Assessment Resources

Unit 4 Resources

L1 L2 EL **Selection Test A,** pp. 144–146. Administer Test A to less advanced readers.

L3 L4 EL **Selection Test B,** pp. 147–149. Administer Test B to on-level students and more advanced students.

L3 L4 **Open-Book Test,** pp. 141–143. As an alternative, give the Open-Book test.

All **Customizable Test Bank**

All **Self-tests**
Students may prepare for the **Selection Test** by taking the **Self-test** online.

PHLit Online! All assessment resources are available at **www.PHLitOnline.com.**

Answers

Vocabulary Acquisition and Use

1. Introduce the skill, using the instruction on the student page.
2. Have students complete the Word Analysis activity and the Vocabulary practice.

Word Analysis

1. push or drive to behave in a certain way; He felt a compulsion to eat cookies.
2. process of forcing someone to leave a place; Plagiarism was the reason for the student's expulsion.
3. sudden strong drive to act; The child had an irresistible impulse to giggle.
4. the action of pushing forward; The duck uses its webbed feet for propulsion.
5. throbbing of arteries as blood is pushed through; Even after the heart attack, the doctor found a faint pulse.
6. drive back by force; The rebels will repulse the advance of the army.

Vocabulary

1. verge
2. impulse
3. blithe
4. satiety
5. sepulcher
6. profuse

Writing

1. To guide students in writing this explanatory text, give them the **Support for Writing Lesson** page (*Unit 4 Resources,* p. 139).
2. Use the Writing Lesson to guide students in developing their introductory backgrounds.
3. Use the **Rubrics for Research: Research Report** in *Professional Development Guidebook,* pages 268–269, to evaluate students' topic choices.

• Poetry of John Keats

Lesson Pacing Guide

DAY 1 Preteach

- Administer the Reading and Vocabulary Warm-ups (*Unit 4 Resources,* pp. 150–153) as necessary.
- Introduce the Reading Strategy: Paraphrasing.
- Introduce the Literary Analysis concept: The Ode.
- Build background with the author and Background features.
- Develop thematic thinking with Connecting to the Essential Question.
- Teach the selection vocabulary.

DAYS 2–3 Preteach/Teach/Assess

- Distribute copies of the appropriate graphic organizer for the Reading Strategy (*Graphic Organizer Transparencies,* pp. 158–159).
- Distribute copies of the appropriate graphic organizer for Literary Analysis (*Graphic Organizer Transparencies,* pp. 160–161).
- Prepare students to read with the Activating Prior Knowledge activities (TE).
- Informally monitor comprehension while students read.
- Use the Reading Check questions to confirm comprehension.
- Develop students' understanding of odes using the Literary Analysis prompts.
- Develop students' ability to paraphrase using the Reading Strategy prompts.
- Reinforce vocabulary with the Vocabulary notes.
- Assess students' comprehension and mastery of the skills by having them answer the Critical Reading, Literary Analysis, and Reading Strategy questions.
- Have students complete the Vocabulary Lesson.

DAY 4 Extend/Assess

- Have students complete the Writing Lesson and write a response to literature. (You may assign as homework.)
- Administer Selection Test A or B (*Unit 4 Resources,* pp. 162–164 or 165–167).

Common Core State Standards

Reading Literature 5. Analyze how an author's choices concerning how to structure specific parts of a text contribute to its overall structure and meaning as well as its aesthetic impact.

Writing 9.a. Apply *grades 11–12 Reading standards* to literature.

Language 5. Demonstrate understanding of figurative language, word relationships, and nuances in word meanings.

Additional Standards Practice
Common Core Companion,* *pp. 54–55; 261–266; 332–335

Daily Block Scheduling
Each day in this Lesson Pacing Guide represents a 40–50 minute period. Teachers using block scheduling may combine days to revise pacing. In addition, teachers may differentiate and support core instruction by integrating components for extended and intensive support as students require. See the Guide to Selected Leveled Resources (facing page).

Guide to Selected Leveled Resources

RTI Tier 1 (students performing on level)			Poetry of John Keats
Warm Up	Whole class instruction; Group work	**Practice, model,** and **monitor** fluency, working **with the whole class** or **in groups.**	**Vocabulary and Reading Warm-ups B,** ***Unit 4 Resources,*** pp. 150–150, 153
Comprehension/Skills	Whole class instruction; Group work; Independent work	**Support** and **monitor** comprehension and skills development, having students complete the activities, graphic organizers, and interactive prompts **independently** or **as a class.**	• ***Reader's Notebook,*** adapted instruction and full selection EL ***Reader's Notebook: English Learner's Version,*** adapted instruction and adapted selection • **Reading Strategy Graphic Organizer B,** ***Graphic Organizer Transparencies,*** p. 163 • **Literary Analysis Graphic Organizer B,** ***Graphic Organizer Transparencies,*** p. 165
Monitor Progress	A	**Monitor** student progress with the differentiated curriculum-based assessment in the *Unit Resources.*	• **Selection Test B,** ***Unit 4 Resources,*** pp. 165–167 • **Open-Book Test,** ***Unit 4 Resources,*** pp. 159–161

RTI Tier 2 (students requiring intervention)			Poetry of John Keats
Warm Up	Group work; One-on-one teaching	**Practice, model,** and **monitor** fluency **in groups** or **with individuals.**	• **Vocabulary and Reading Warm-ups A,** ***Unit 4 Resources,*** pp. 150–152 • ***Hear It!*** **Audio CD (adapted text)**
Comprehension/Skills	Group work; One-on-one teaching	• **Support** and **monitor** comprehension and skills development, working **in small groups** or **with individuals.** • As students complete the selection in the appropriate version of the *Reader's Notebook,* **monitor** comprehension frequently with group questions and individual instruction. • **Model** strategies while guiding students in completing the activities and prompts in the *Reader's Notebook,* as well as the graphic organizers. • **Practice** skills and **monitor** mastery with the *Reading Kit* worksheets.	• ***Reader's Notebook: Adapted Version,*** adapted instruction and adapted selection EL ***Reader's Notebook: English Learner's Version,*** adapted instruction and adapted selection • **Reading Strategy Graphic Organizer A,** ***Graphic Organizer Transparencies,*** p. 162 • **Literary Analysis Graphic Organizer A,** ***Graphic Organizer Transparencies,*** p. 164 • ***Reading Kit,*** Practice worksheets
Monitor Progress	A	**Monitor** student progress with the differentiated curriculum-based assessment in the *Unit Resources* and in the *Reading Kit.*	• **Selection Test A,** ***Unit 4 Resources,*** pp. 162–164 • ***Reading Kit,*** Assess worksheets

TIER 3 Tier 3 intervention may require consultation with the student's special-education or dyslexia specialist. For additional support, see the Tier 2 activities and resources listed above.

One-on-one teaching **Group work** **Whole class instruction** **Independent work** **A Assessment**

For a complete guide to selection support, including support for Advanced students, see the Overview of Resources in the frontmatter.

• Poetry of John Keats

RESOURCES FOR:

- L1 Special-Needs Students
- L2 Below-Level Students (Tier 2)
- L3 On-Level Students (Tier 1)
- L4 Advanced Students (Tier 1)
- EL English Learners
- All All Students

Vocabulary/Fluency/Prior Knowledge

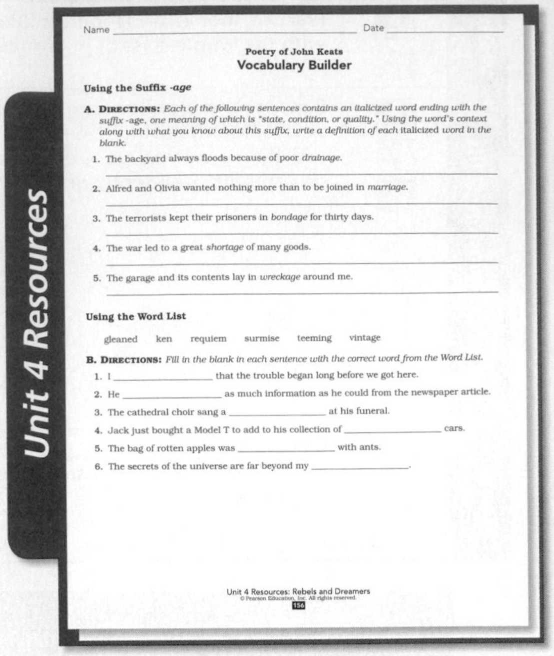

Name ______________________ Date ____________

Poetry of John Keats
Vocabulary Builder

Using the Suffix *-age*

A. Directions: *Each of the following sentences contains an italicized word ending with the suffix -age, one meaning of which is "state, condition, or quality." Using the word's context along with what you know about this suffix, write a definition of each italicized word in the blank.*

1. The backyard always floods because of poor *drainage*.
2. Alfred and Olivia wanted nothing more than to be joined in *marriage*.
3. The terrorists kept their prisoners in *bondage* for thirty days.
4. The war led to a great *shortage* of many goods.
5. The garage and its contents lay in *wreckage* around me.

Using the Word List

gleaned ken requiem surmise teeming vintage

B. Directions: *Fill in the blank in each sentence with the correct word from the Word List.*

1. I ____________ that the trouble began long before we got here.
2. He ____________ as much information as he could from the newspaper article.
3. The cathedral choir sang a ____________ at his funeral.
4. Jack just bought a Model T to add to his collection of ____________ cars.
5. The bag of rotten apples was ____________ with ants.
6. The secrets of the universe are far beyond my ____________.

Unit 4 Resources: Rebels and Dreamers
© Pearson Education, Inc. All rights reserved.
156

All **Vocabulary Builder,** p. 156

Also available for these selections:

EL L1 L2 **Vocabulary Warm-ups A and B,** pp. 150–151

EL L1 L2 **Reading Warm-ups A and B,** pp. 152–153

Reader's Notebooks

Pre- and postreading pages for these selections, as well as "Ode on a Grecian Urn," appear in an interactive format in the *Reader's Notebooks.* Each *Notebook* is differentiated for a different group of learners. The selections in the Adapted and English Learner's versions are abridged.

L2 L3 ***Reader's Notebook***

L1 ***Reader's Notebook: Adapted Version***

EL ***Reader's Notebook: English Learner's Version***

EL ***Reader's Notebook: Spanish Version***

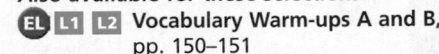

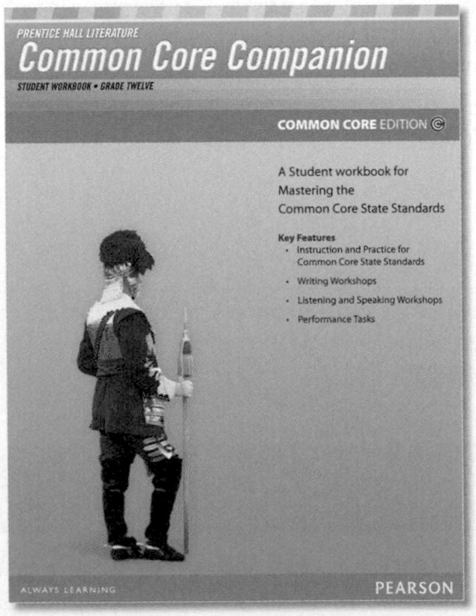

Common Core Companion

Additional instruction and practice for each Common Core State Standard

Selection Support

Graphic Organizer Transparencies

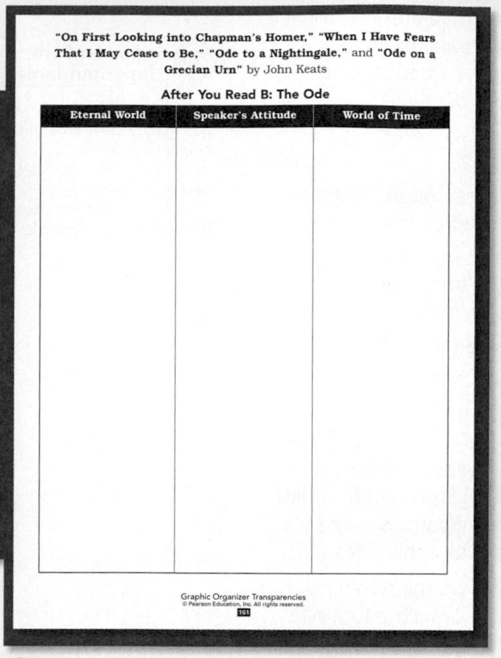
"On First Looking into Chapman's Homer," "When I Have Fears That I May Cease to Be," "Ode to a Nightingale," and "Ode on a Grecian Urn" by John Keats

After You Read B: The Ode

Eternal World	Speaker's Attitude	World of Time

Graphic Organizer Transparencies
© Pearson Education, Inc. All rights reserved.
161

EL L3 **Literary Analysis: Graphic Organizer B,** p. 161

Also available for these selections:

EL L1 L2 **Reading: Graphic Organizer A** (partially filled in), p. 158

EL L3 **Reading: Graphic Organizer B,** p. 159

EL L1 L2 **Literary Analysis: Graphic Organizer A** (partially filled in), p. 160

Skills Development/Extension

Unit 4 Resources

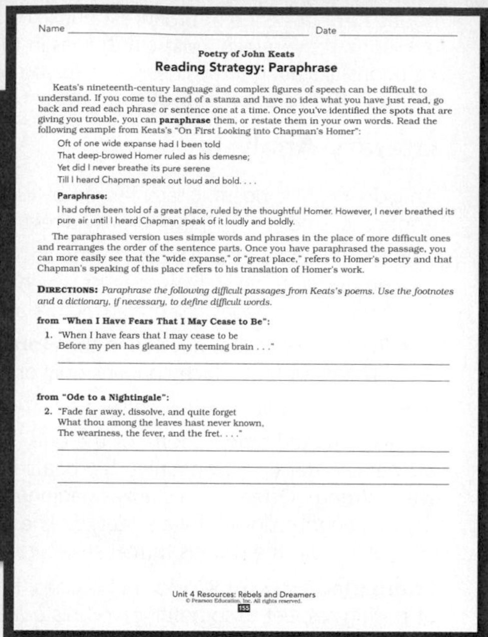
Name ______ Date ______

Poetry of John Keats
Reading Strategy: Paraphrase

Keats's nineteenth-century language and complex figures of speech can be difficult to understand. If you come to the end of a stanza and have no idea what you have just read, go back and read each phrase or sentence one at a time. Once you've identified the spots that are giving you trouble, you can **paraphrase** them, or restate them in your own words. Read the following example from Keats's "On First Looking into Chapman's Homer":

Oft of one wide expanse had I been told
That deep-browed Homer ruled as his demesne;
Yet did I never breathe its pure serene
Till I heard Chapman speak out loud and bold. . . .

Paraphrase:

I had often been told of a great place, ruled by the thoughtful Homer. However, I never breathed its pure air until I heard Chapman speak of it loudly and boldly.

The paraphrased version uses simple words and phrases in the place of more difficult ones and rearranges the order of the sentence parts. Once you have paraphrased the passage, you can more easily see that the "wide expanse," or "great place," refers to Homer's poetry and that Chapman's speaking of this place refers to his translation of Homer's work.

Directions: *Paraphrase the following difficult passages from Keats's poems. Use the footnotes and a dictionary, if necessary, to define difficult words.*

from "When I Have Fears That I May Cease to Be":

1. "When I have fears that I may cease to be
Before my pen has gleaned my teeming brain . . ."

from "Ode to a Nightingale":

2. "Fade far away, dissolve, and quite forget
What thou among the leaves hast never known,
The weariness, the fever, and the fret. . . ."

Unit 4 Resources: Rebels and Dreamers
© Pearson Education, Inc. All rights reserved.
155

All **Reading,** p. 155

Also available for these selections:

All **Literary Analysis,** p. 154

EL L3 L4 **Support for Writing,** p. 157

L4 **Enrichment,** p. 158

Assessment

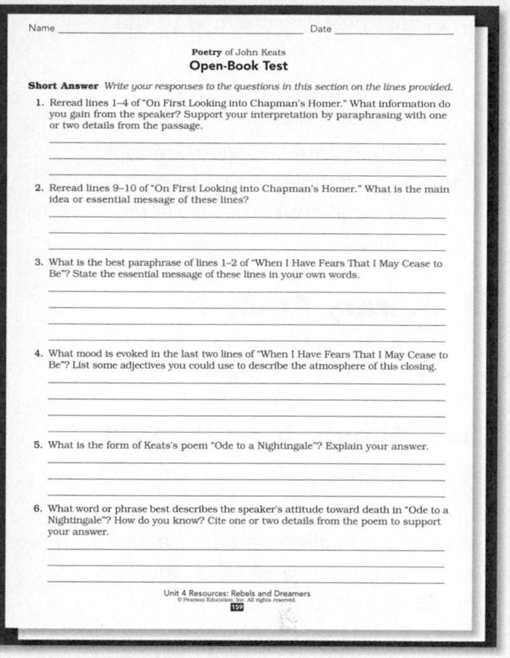
Name ______ Date ______

Poetry of John Keats
Open-Book Test

Short Answer *Write your responses to the questions in this section on the lines provided.*

1. Reread lines 1–4 of "On First Looking into Chapman's Homer." What information do you gain from the speaker? Support your interpretation by paraphrasing with one or two details from the passage.

2. Reread lines 9–10 of "On First Looking into Chapman's Homer." What is the main idea or essential message of these lines?

3. What is the best paraphrase of lines 1–2 of "When I Have Fears That I May Cease to Be"? State the essential message of these lines in your own words.

4. What mood is evoked in the last two lines of "When I Have Fears That I May Cease to Be"? List some adjectives you could use to describe the atmosphere of this closing.

5. What is the form of Keats's poem "Ode to a Nightingale"? Explain your answer.

6. What word or phrase best describes the speaker's attitude toward death in "Ode to a Nightingale"? How do you know? Cite one or two details from the poem to support your answer.

Unit 4 Resources: Rebels and Dreamers
© Pearson Education, Inc. All rights reserved.
159

L3 L4 **Open-Book Test,** pp. 159–161

Also available for these selections:

EL L1 L2 **Selection Test A,** pp. 162–164

EL L3 L4 **Selection Test B,** pp. 165–167

PHLit Online!
www.PHLitOnline.com

- complete narrated selection text
- a thematically related video with writing prompt
- an interactive graphic organizer
- highlighting feature
- access to all student print resources, adapted to individual student needs
- Spanish and English summaries
- adapted selection translations in Spanish

Online Resources: All print materials are also available online.

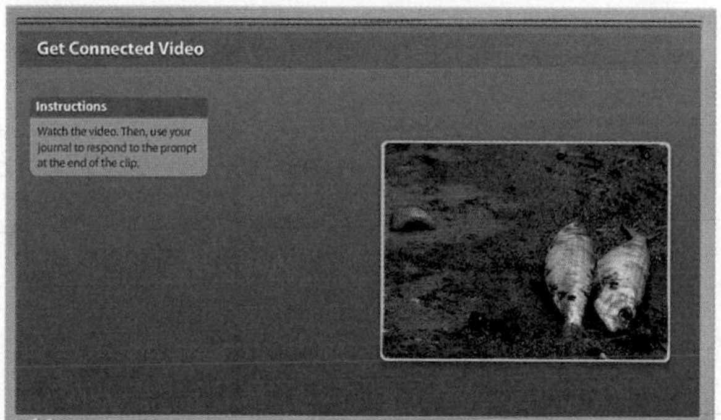

Get Connected! (thematic video with writing prompt)

Also available:

Background Video
All videos are available in Spanish.

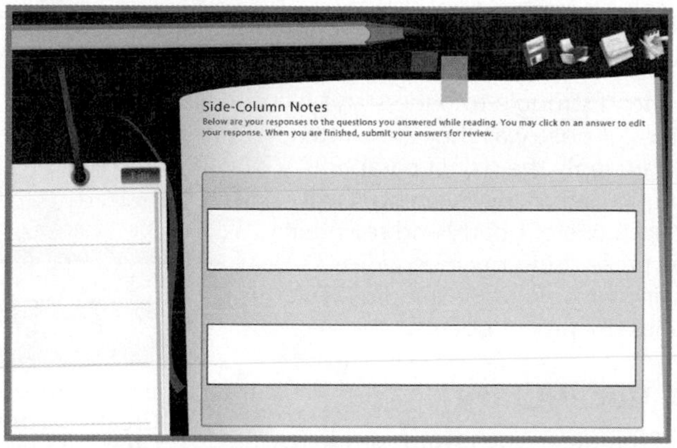

Writer's Journal (with graphics feature)

Also available:

Vocabulary Central (tools and activities for studying vocabulary)

❶ ❓ Connecting to the Essential Question

1. Review the assignment with the class.

2. Tell students that poems are reflections of their authors.

3. As students read, have them look for ways in which Keats reveals his personal concerns, anxieties, and fears.

❷ Literary Analysis

Introduce the skill using the instruction on the student page.

Think Aloud: Model the Skill

Say to students:

I understand that Keats uses a poetic form called an ode. There are different kinds of odes, such as Pindaric, Horatian, and irregular odes. Keats's odes are usually 10-line stanzas of iambic pentameter. I can understand Keats's odes better when I apply an understanding of his poetic structure.

❸ Reading Strategy

1. Introduce the skill using the instruction on the student page.

2. Give students a copy of **Reading Strategy Graphic Organizer B,** page 159 in *Graphic Organizer Transparencies,* to fill out as they read.

Think Aloud: Model the Skill

Say to students:

When I struggle to understand lines of poetry as they are written, I can apply the skill of paraphrasing to determine meaning. I can take a line of poetry and rewrite it as prose using my own words. This skill helps me understand difficult lines or parts of poems.

❹ Vocabulary

1. Pronounce each word, giving its definition, and have students say it aloud.

2. For more guidance, see the *Classroom Strategies and Teaching Routines* card for introducing vocabulary.

880

Before You Read *Poetry of John Keats*

❶ Connecting to the Essential Question Keats adapted the ode—a poetic form designed to broadcast public concerns—to express personal emotions. As you read, note which lines in the odes reveal personal emotions. Locating these lines will help you answer the Essential Question: **What is the relationship of the writer to tradition?**

❷ Literary Analysis

An **ode** is a lyric poem, characterized by heightened emotion, that pays respect to a person or thing, usually directly addressed by the speaker.

- The **Pindaric ode** (named for the ancient Greek poet Pindar) uses groups of three stanzas, one of which differs in form from the other two. Pindar's odes celebrated victors at the Olympic Games.
- Roman poets later developed the **Horatian ode** (also called homostrophic), which contains only one type of stanza.
- The **irregular ode** has no set pattern.

Keats created his own form of the ode, using ten-line stanzas of iambic pentameter (lines containing ten beats with a repeated pattern of weak-strong). Often those stanzas begin with a heroic quatrain (four lines rhymed *abab*) followed by a sestet (six lines rhymed in various ways). As you read, note the various formal structures Keats uses in his odes.

Comparing Literary Works In his odes, Keats follows the tradition of paying respect to something. Yet his odes reveal as much about him as they do about his subjects. As you read, compare the ways in which his odes dramatize a conflict in the speaker. Also, analyze how, in each case, the conflict is brought on by longings for what is unobtainable.

❸ Reading Strategy

Ⓒ **Preparing to Read Complex Texts** You can **determine the main idea** of a passage by *paraphrasing* it—restating it in your own words. Doing so will not only help you clarify the meaning of the specific passage but will also help you see how the ideas in a work connect and develop. Use a chart like the one shown to paraphrase difficult passages in Keats's poems.

❹ Vocabulary

ken (ken) *n.* range of sight or knowledge (p. 883)

surmise (sər mīz´) *n.* guess; assumption (p. 883)

gleaned (glēnd) *v.* collected bit by bit, as when gathering stray grain after a harvest (p. 885)

teeming (tēm´ iŋ) *adj.* filled to overflowing (p. 885)

vintage (vin´ tij) *n.* wine of fine quality (p. 887)

requiem (rek´ wē əm) *n.* musical composition honoring the dead (p. 888)

Ⓒ **Common Core State Standards**

Reading Literature
5. Analyze how an author's choices concerning how to structure specific parts of a text contribute to its overall structure and meaning as well as its aesthetic impact.

Original
"When I have fears that I may cease to be…"

Paraphrase
"When I am afraid that I may die…"

PHLit Online!
www.PHLitOnline.com

880 Rebels and Dreamers (1798–1832)

Vocabulary Development

Vocabulary Knowledge Rating
Create a **Vocabulary Knowledge Rating Chart** (*Professional Development Guidebook,* p. 33) for the vocabulary words on the student page. Give each student a copy of the chart with the words on it. Read the words aloud, and have students mark their ratings in the Before Reading column. Urge students to attend to these words as they read and discuss the selections.

In order to gauge how much instruction you need to provide, tally how many students are confident in their knowledge of each word. As students read, point out the words and their context.

Vocabulary Central, featuring tools and activities for studying vocabulary, is available online at **www.PHLitOnline.com.**

❺ John Keats (1795–1821)

Author of **“On First Looking into Chapman’s Homer” • “When I Have Fears That I May Cease to Be” • “Ode to a Nightingale” • “Ode on a Grecian Urn”**

Although he died at age twenty-five, Keats left his indelible mark on literature, and this makes us wonder what more he might have accomplished had he lived longer.

A Defender of Worthy Causes Unlike his contemporaries Byron and Shelley, John Keats was not an aristocrat. Instead, he was born to working-class Londoners. As a child, he received attention for his striking good looks and his restless spirit. Keats developed a reputation for fighting, but always for a worthy cause. It was not until he and his school-master’s son, Charles Cowden Clarke, became friends that Keats developed an interest in poetry and became an avid reader.

From Medicine to Poetry In 1815, Keats began studying medicine at a London hospital. He had already begun writing poetry, but he earned his pharmacist’s license before abandoning medicine for the literary world. In 1818, he published his first major work, *Endymion*, a long poem that the critics panned. Despite the critical rejection, Keats did not swerve from his new career.

A Year of Sorrow and Joy The year 1818 was significant for Keats in other ways as well. He lost his brother Tom to tuberculosis, but he also met the light of his life, Fanny Brawne, to whom he became engaged. The next year, 1819, was a period of feverish creativity. In just nine months, fired by grief, new-found love, and his own encroaching illness, Keats wrote the poems for which he is most famous, including “The Eve of St. Agnes,” “La Belle Dame sans Merci,” and his odes. Each is recognized as a masterpiece.

An Early Death Keats’s engagement to Fanny and his burst of creativity might have been the prelude to a happy, productive life. Instead, Keats found his health deteriorating. Recognizing that like his brother, he had tuberculosis, Keats moved to Italy, hoping that the warmer climate would reverse the disease. Sadly, that hope proved false, and, in 1821, his battle with tuberculosis ended with his death.

Despite his early death, John Keats remains one of the major influences in English poetry.

Daily Bellringer

For each class during which you will teach these selections, have students complete one of the five activities for the appropriate week in the ***Daily Bellringer Activities*** booklet.

Multidraft Reading

To assist struggling readers and to enhance reading for all, assign the text in chunks, as warranted by length, and apply multidraft reading protocols. For each reading, have students set the purpose indicated:

- **First reading**—identifying key ideas and details and answering any Reading Checks.
- **Second reading**—analyzing craft and structure and responding to the side-column prompts.
- **Third reading**—integrating knowledge and ideas, connecting to other texts and the world, and answering the end-of-selection questions.

For more guidance, refer to the ***Classroom Strategies and Teaching Routines*** card on Multidraft Reading.

❺ Background

More About the Author

The grief Keats experienced at the death of his brother Tom was magnified by the early deaths of his parents. Keats’s father, the manager of a livery stable in Moorfield, a section of London, died when the poet was 8. His mother remarried, but died of tuberculosis when the poet was 14.

PHLit Online!

Teaching From Technology

www.PHLitOnline.com

Preparing to Read

Go to **www.PHLitOnline.com** and display the ***Get Connected!*** slideshow for this selection. Have the class brainstorm responses to the writing prompt, entering ideas in the interactive journal. Then, have students complete their written responses as homework.

To build background, display the Background and More About the Author feature.

Using the Interactive Text

Go to **www.PHLitOnline.com** and display the Enriched Online Student Edition. As the class reads the selection or listens to the narration, record answers to side-column prompts using the graphic organizers accessible on the interactive page. Alternatively, have students use the online edition individually, answering the prompts as they read.

❶ About the Selection

"On First Looking into Chapman's Homer" celebrates Chapman's translations of Homer's *Iliad* and *Odyssey,* which give Keats new insights into the literature. The octave suggests the antiquity of classical poetry. The sestet, in contrast, uses simple language to convey the immediacy and excitement of discovery.

❷ Activating Prior Knowledge

Ask students to bring in recordings of songs that they believe define truth and beauty. Play selected recordings. Discuss how contemporary views of truth and beauty compare with those of a nineteenth-century poet. Have students write a paragraph about how the songs they selected define truth and beauty.

Concept Connector

Tell students they will return to their responses after reading the selection.

❸ Humanities

Ulysses Deriding Polyphemus (oil on canvas), 1829, by Joseph Mallord William Turner, National Gallery, London

J.M.W. Turner (1775–1851) was an English landscape painter known for his treatment of natural light effects in land and marine subjects. Use this sentence for discussion:

Describe Turner's use of light and color in this painting from Homer's *Odyssey.*

Possible response: The ships look like indistinct masses in a glowing haze of color; the color is brilliant and uses diffusion of light.

❶

On First Looking into ❷ Chapman's Homer

John Keats

❸

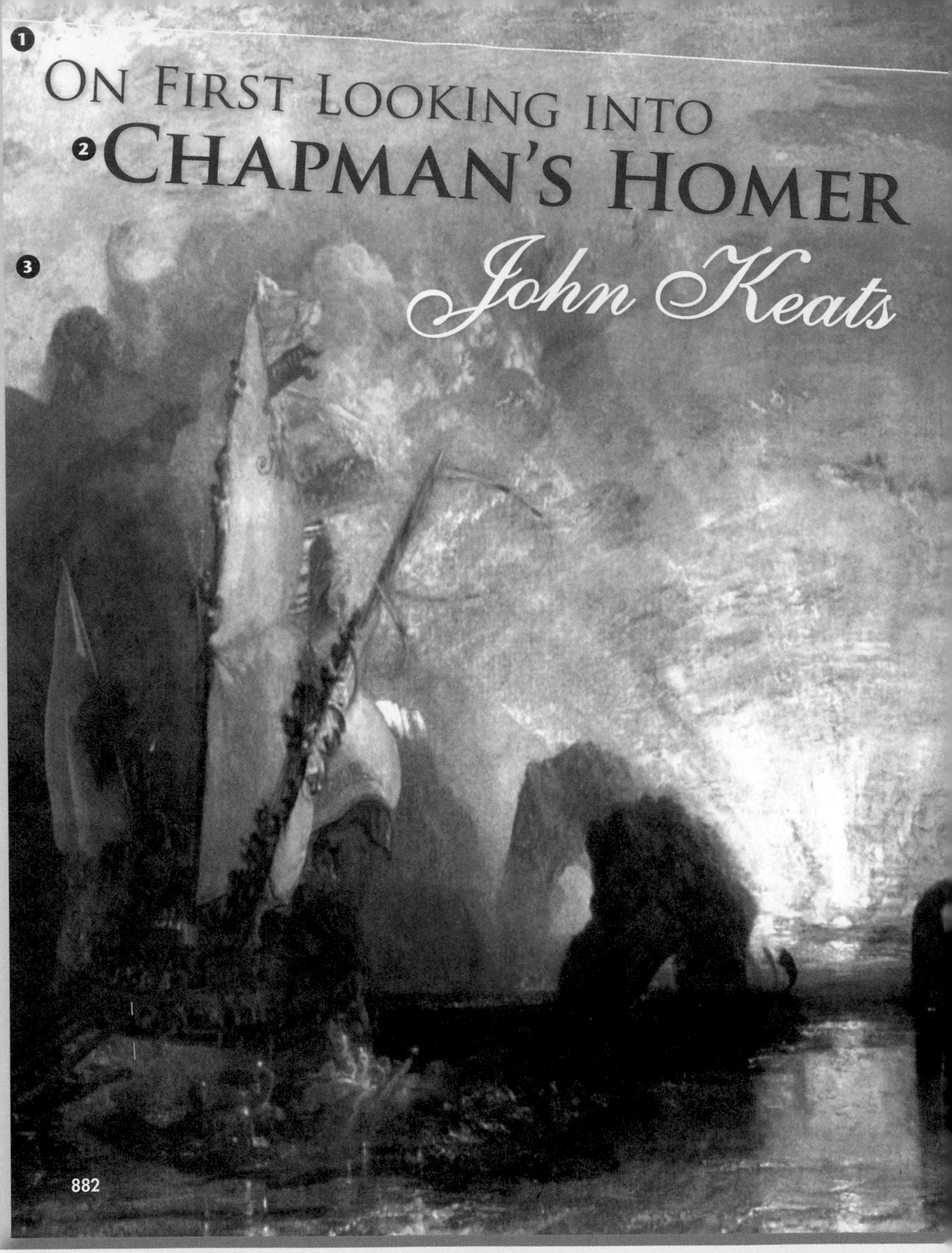

882

Text Complexity Rubric

	Chapman's Homer	When I Have Fears	Ode to a Nightingale	Ode on a Grecian Urn
Qualitative Measures				
Context/ Knowledge Demands	Romantic sonnet 1 2 (3) 4 5	Romantic sonnet 1 (2) 3 4 5	Romantic ode 1 2 3 (4) 5	Romantic ode 1 2 3 (4) 5
Structure/Language Conventionality and Clarity	Archaic diction; long sentences 1 2 (3) 4 5	Long sentences; archaic diction 1 2 (3) 4 5	Archaic diction; long sentences 1 2 3 (4) 5	Archaic diction; long sentences 1 2 (3) 4 5
Levels of Meaning/ Purpose/Concept Level	Accessible (literary appreciation) 1 2 (3) 4 5	Accessible (death and unfulfilled dreams) 1 2 (3) 4 5	Challenging (nature and beauty) 1 2 3 (4) 5	Challenging (art and beauty) 1 2 3 (4) 5
Quantitative Measures				
Lexile/Text Length	NP / 112 words	NP / 113 words	NP / 592 words	NP / 366 words
Overall Complexity	**More accessible**	**More accessible**	**More complex**	**More complex**

BACKGROUND Romantic poets such as Byron, Shelley, and Keats admired the culture of ancient Greece and derived inspiration from its art and literature. Keats's "Ode on a Grecian Urn" (p. 890), for instance, shows his tendency to associate ideas about beauty with antiquities, such as the beautifully adorned vases that ancient Greek society produced.

When Keats was twenty-one, his friend and former schoolmate, Charles Cowden Clarke, introduced him to a translation of Homer by Elizabethan poet George Chapman. The two men spent the evening reading this book, and early the next morning Keats presented this sonnet to Clarke.

Much have I traveled in the realms of gold,
And many goodly states and kingdoms seen;
Round many western islands have I been
Which bards in fealty to Apollo[1] hold.
4 Oft of one wide expanse had I been told
That deep-browed Homer ruled as his demesne;[2]
Yet did I never breathe its pure serene[3]
Till I heard Chapman speak out loud and bold:
Then felt I like some watcher of the skies
When a new planet swims into his **ken**;
Or like stout Cortez[4] when with eagle eyes
He stared at the Pacific—and all his men
Looked at each other with a wild **surmise**—
Silent, upon a peak in Darien.[5]

Reading Strategy
Paraphrasing
Paraphrase lines 5–6, paying special attention to the metaphor of a "demesne."

Vocabulary
ken (ken) *n.* range of sight or knowledge
surmise (sər mīz′) *n.* guess; assumption

1. **Apollo** in Greek and Roman mythology, the god of music, poetry, and medicine.
2. **demesne** (di mān′) realm.
3. **serene** clear air.
4. **Cortez** Here, Keats was mistaken. The Pacific was discovered in 1513 by Balboa, not Cortez.
5. **Darien** (der′ ē ən) the Isthmus of Panama.

5 ◀ **Critical Viewing** How does this image of ships convey the feeling of exploration Keats describes in this sonnet? **[Connect]**

4 Reading Strategy
Paraphrasing
1. Have students read lines 5–6 to themselves.
2. Review with students how to paraphrase, putting phrases or ideas into their own words.
3. Then, have students **respond** to the Reading Strategy item.
Answer: I'd heard a lot about Homer's works as I "traveled" through the "kingdoms" of poets (read their works), and I understood that Homer was superior to all others in his poetry.

5 Critical Viewing
Answer: In this poem, exploration is an exciting adventure, and these ships, which glow because of the treatment of the light, hint at that adventure.

PHLit Online!
These selections are available in interactive format in the **Enriched Online Student Edition** at **www.PHLitOnline.com**, which includes a thematically related video with writing prompt and an interactive graphic organizer.

Text Complexity: Reader and Task Suggestions

Keats's Sonnets: Preparing to Read the Text	Keats's Sonnets: Leveled Tasks	Keats's Odes: Preparing to Read the Text	Keats's Odes: Leveled Tasks
• Using the Background on TE p. 881, stress that Keats's many early losses gave him a deep sense of the transience of life. • Discuss the significance a poet is likely to place on the great works of other poets. • Guide students to use Multidraft Reading strategies (TE p. 881).	***Structure/Language*** If students will have difficulty with the poems' structure, have them summarize the content of the octets, then of the sestets. Once students understand the basic structure, have them focus on the poems' main ideas. ***Synthesizing*** If students will not have difficulty with the poems' structure, have them contrast the moods and world views of the two sonnets.	• Using the About the Selections feature on TE p. 886, discuss the idea of "negative capability." • Discuss with students how nature and art can help human beings escape or transcend the pain or sorrow of the mortal world. • Guide students to use Multidraft Reading strategies (TE p. 881).	***Levels of Meaning*** If students will have difficulty with the meaning, have them focus first on the physical description of each poem's subject. Then, have them focus on the speaker's changing feelings. ***Analyzing*** If students will not have difficulty with the meaning, have them analyze how the imagery describing the nightingale or urn and the speaker's changing feelings in each ode help convey that ode's central theme.

❻ About the Selection

The speaker expresses fears that he will not live to fulfill his potential. This lyric is particularly poignant because Keats died less than three years after he wrote it.

❼ Humanities

John Keats, by Joseph Severn

This painting portrays poet John Keats in a moment of sadness and perhaps doubt.

Joseph Severn, in whose arms Keats died in 1821, was born and raised in England. After apprenticing to a royal engraver and studying at the Royal Academy, Severn risked his connection to the academy to travel to Italy with the ailing Keats. He created this painting after Keats's death, basing it on a moment observed just after the writing of "Ode to a Nightingale" and using memory and masks made of Keats's face both before and after his death.

Use these questions for discussion:

1. What elements of the painting suggest a mood appropriate to "When I Have Fears That I May Cease to Be"?
   Answer: Keats's despondent expression and posture and the dark and somber colors of the carpet and walls create an atmosphere of sadness and doubt.
2. How does the painting's composition reflect the themes of the poem?
   Answer: As in the poem, Keats is shown isolated with his thoughts while the bright world beckons from outside.

❽ Critical Viewing

Answer: Students may say that Keats is serious, contemplative, and moody.

7

John Keats, 1821, Joseph Severn, by courtesy of the National Portrait Gallery, London

Enrichment: Investigating Health and Medicine

Tuberculosis

In the late-eighteenth and early-nineteenth centuries, many famous artists died of tuberculosis. Tuberculosis is a contagious, bacterial disease that affects the lungs. Symptoms include weight loss, fatigue, and a chronic, debilitating cough. Keats's mother and his brother Tom both died of tuberculosis. Because of his medical training, Keats was able to diagnose himself with the disease. Keats died of tuberculosis in 1821.

Activity: Investigating Tuberculosis

Have students research the disease of tuberculosis, its prevalence and emergence as a major health problem during the Industrial Revolution, how it was treated, and what we understand about the disease today. Students can record their findings on the **Enrichment: Investigating Health and Medicine** worksheet, ***Professional Development Guidebook***, page 229.

6 # When I Have Fears That I May Cease to Be

John Keats

9
When I have fears that I may cease to be
    Before my pen has gleaned my teeming brain,
Before high-piled books, in charactery,[1]
    Hold like rich garners[2] the full ripened grain;
When I behold, upon the night's starred face,
    Huge cloudy symbols of a high romance,
9
And think that I may never live to trace
    Their shadows, with the magic hand of chance;
And when I feel, fair creature of an hour,
    That I shall never look upon thee more,
Never have relish in the fairy power
    Of unreflecting love—then on the shore
Of the wide world I stand alone, and think
Till love and fame to nothingness do sink.

Vocabulary
gleaned (glēnd) *v.* collected from bit by bit, as when gathering stray grain after a harvest

teeming (tēm′ iŋ) *adj.* filled to overflowing

8 ◀ **Critical Viewing** From this rendering of Keats, how would you characterize him? **[Infer]**

1. **charactery** written or printed letters of the alphabet.
2. **garners** storehouses for grain.

Critical Reading

Cite textual evidence to support your responses.

1. **Key Ideas and Details (a)** In "On First Looking into Chapman's Homer," what feelings about Chapman's translation do lines 9–14 convey? **(b) Draw Conclusions:** How does the comparison of reading to a journey support these feelings?
2. **Key Ideas and Details (a)** In lines 1–4 of "When I Have Fears," what does the speaker fear he will not accomplish before he dies? **(b) Interpret:** In lines 5–12, what is he concerned about missing? **(c) Evaluate:** Do the last lines offer a convincing resolution to such fears? Explain.
4. **Integration of Knowledge and Ideas** What words describe Keats's character as revealed in these two poems?
5. **Integration of Knowledge and Ideas** Are most young people today as anxious about and thrilled by the future as Keats? Explain.

9 Critical Thinking

Connect

1. Direct student attention to lines 1–4 and lines 7–10 in "When I Have Fears..."
2. **Ask:** What two common fears about dying does Keats express in these lines?

   Possible response: dying before completing his life's work (writing volumes of poetry) and missing his loved ones

ASSESS

Answers

Before students respond, you may wish to have them write a brief objective summary of the selection. As they answer the questions below, remind them to support their answers with evidence from the text.

1. (a) They convey excitement and wonder. (b) The comparison of reading to a journey supports these feelings, because journeys are usually full of delight at the discovery of new, unimagined worlds.
2. (a) The speaker fears dying before he has written a great deal. (b) He is concerned about missing his beloved. (c) The last lines do not resolve the fears, but the speaker annihilates them by thinking until they seem unimportant.
3. Keats's character is pensive and extremely intelligent.
4. Possible response: Youth today face more responsibilities and fewer opportunities than in Keats's day because of the nature of work and the economy. These facts may make them more anxious but less thrilled.

Differentiated Instruction for Universal Access

Enrichment for Less Proficient Readers
Guide students as they read the poem. Remind them that the speaker in the poem is exploring his own fears of dying. Have students write letters—in the voice of Keats—in which they explain the nature of their fears.

EL Strategy for English Learners
Students may find the language and imagistic thoughts in the poem difficult to decode and "translate." Encourage students to paraphrase any difficult ideas and to use the footnotes for additional context.

Enrichment for Gifted/Talented Students
Have students read "When I Have Fears That I May Cease to Be" aloud, listening carefully to the rhythm and meter. Ask students to perform the poem as a song or spoken-word piece, using melody and/or rhythm sensitive to the poem's rhythms and sounds.

⑩ About the Selection

This poem captures what Keats termed "negative capability"—the capacity of a poet to negate himself or herself and enter fully into his or her subject so as to represent it with an especially rich and vibrant objectivity. In this case, the speaker subsumes himself into the joyous nightingale and so transcends the pain of the mortal world.

⑪ Humanities

Birds on a Flowering Plum Branch, attributed to Ma Lin

This painting on silk depicts a bird similar to the poem's nightingale. Like Keats's nightingale, the bird is perched on a plum tree branch.

Ma Lin was a landscape painter of China's Sung Dynasty. The bird and flower were a favored Sung motif. The serenity of the scene suggests the freedom from earthly concerns for which the speaker longs in "Ode to a Nightingale."

Use this question for discussion:

What elements of beauty might Keats admire in this painting?
Answer: He might admire the simple composition of the bird and tree, the delicacy of the blossoms, and the contrast of blank background with subject.

⑫ Critical Viewing

Answer: Students may say that the painting conveys a sense of serenity and timeless beauty that contrasts sharply with the suffering and lack of time described in Stanza III.

⑪

⑩ Ode to a Nightingale

John Keats

BACKGROUND Keats composed the following ode in 1819, while living in Hampstead with his friend Charles Brown. Brown wrote the following description about how the ode was composed: "In the spring of 1819 a nightingale had built her nest near my house. Keats felt a tranquil and continued joy in her song; and one morning he took his chair from the breakfast table to the grass plot under the plum tree, where he sat for two or three hours. When he came into the house, I perceived he had some scraps of paper in his hand, and these he was quietly thrusting behind the books. On inquiry, I found those scraps, four or five in number, contained his poetic feeling on the song of our nightingale."

Enrichment: Analyzing Themes and Symbols

Birds in Song and Story

Like poets, musicians and storytellers have long been inspired by the calls of songbirds. In many cultures, bird flight and birdsong are associated with freedom from material concerns. In Japanese haiku, the nightingale is a symbol invoking spring. Some well-known examples of tunes, poems, and folk tales involving songbirds are Charlie "Bird" Parker's "Ornithology," Hans Christian Andersen's "The Nightingale," Yeats's "Sailing to Byzantium," Oscar Wilde's "The Nightingale and the Rose," and Robert Frost's "Never Again Would Birds' Song Be the Same."

Activity: Analyzing Birds as Symbols Have students research birds as symbols in works of art, literature, or music. Suggest that students record their work in the **Enrichment: Analyzing Themes and Symbols** worksheet, ***Professional Development Guidebook,*** page 243.

I

My heart aches, and drowsy numbness pains
My sense, as though of hemlock[1] I had drunk,
Or emptied some dull opiate to the drains
One minute past, and Lethe-wards[2] had sunk:
'Tis not through envy of thy happy lot,
But being too happy in thine happiness,—
That thou, light-wingèd Dryad[3] of the trees,
In some melodious plot
Of beechen green, and shadows numberless,
Singest of summer in full-throated ease.

II

(13) O, for a draft[4] of **vintage**! that hath been
Cooled a long age in the deep-delved earth,
Tasting of Flora[5] and the country green,
Dance, and Provençal[6] song, and sunburnt mirth!
O for a beaker full of the warm South,
Full of the true, the blushful Hippocrene,[7]
With beaded bubbles winking at the brim,
And purple-stainèd mouth;
That I might drink, and leave the world unseen,
And with thee fade away into the forest dim:

III

(14) Fade far away, dissolve, and quite forget
What thou among the leaves hast never known,
The weariness, the fever, and the fret
Here, where men sit and hear each other groan;
Where palsy shakes a few, sad, last gray hairs,
Where youth grows pale, and specter-thin, and dies;[8]
Where but to think is to be full of sorrow
And leaden-eyed despairs,
Where Beauty cannot keep her lustrous eyes,
Or new Love pine at them beyond tomorrow.

1. **hemlock** poisonous herb.
2. **Lethe-wards** toward Lethe, the river of forgetfulness in Hades, the underworld, in classical mythology.
3. **Dryad** (drī´ əd) in classical mythology, a wood nymph.
4. **draft** drink.
5. **Flora** in classical mythology, the goddess of flowers, or the flowers themselves.
6. **Provencal** (prō´ vən säl´) pertaining to Provence, a region in Southern France, renowned in the late Middle Ages for its troubadours, who composed and sang love songs.
7. **Hippocrene** (hip´ ō krēn´) in classical mythology, the fountain of the Muses on Mt. Helicon. From this fountain flowed the waters of inspiration.
8. **youth . . . dies** Keats is referring to his brother, Tom, who had died from tuberculosis the previous winter.

Birds on a Flowering Plum Branch Attributed to Ma Lin, ink and colors on silk, S Song dynasty (13th c.), The Gotoh Museum

(12) ◀ **Critical Viewing**
Compare the mood of this painting with that of stanza III. **[Compare and Contrast]**

Vocabulary
vintage (vin´ tij) *n.* wine of fine quality

Reading Strategy
Paraphrasing
Restate lines 11–14 in your own words.

Literary Analysis
The Ode Which passages in stanza III seem to express Keats's deep personal feelings? Explain.

(15) ☑ **Reading Check**
What does the speaker wish to do along with the nightingale?

13 Reading Strategy
Paraphrasing

1. Have students read lines 11–14 to themselves.
2. Then, have students **respond** to the Reading Strategy item.
Answer: Oh, for a sip of wine that has been chilled over time in a cellar, tasting of flowers, the country, dance, and song, and happiness of the sun!

14 Literary Analysis
The Ode

1. Have volunteers read Stanza III aloud.
2. Remind students of the definition of an ode: a lyric poem characterized by heightened emotion that pays homage to a person or thing.
3. Then **ask** the Literary Analysis question.
Answer: In lines 22–26, Keats expresses worry, anxiety, and weariness. In lines 29–30, Keats is mourning the loss of youth. These lines reveal his deep personal feelings of anxiety, fear, and suffering.

15 Reading Check

Answer: The speaker wishes to fade away with the nightingale into the forest.

Differentiated Instruction for Universal Access

Strategy for Less Proficient Readers
Have students reread "Ode to a Nightingale" to themselves. Ask them to identify which kind of ode Keats has created and to note the metrical and rhythmic patterns he uses.

EL Strategy for English Learners
Encourage students to break down longer sentences into shorter ones or to paraphrase expressions or phrases that are particularly difficult. You can model how to paraphrase using **Reading Strategy Graphic Organizer B,** page 159 in ***Graphic Organizer Transparencies.***

Strategy for Advanced Readers
Have students write brief essays comparing "Ode to a Nightingale" with "When I Have Fears That I May Cease to Be." Ask them to address what the themes of these poems suggest about Keats's poetic sensibility. Refer students to **www.PHLitOnline.com** for more information about Keats's work.

16 World Literature Connection

Pablo Neruda's Odes

Like Keats, Neruda wrote personal poetry, much of it filled with anguish and hopelessness. His prose is simple; he uses strong metaphors and free verse. His mission as a poet was to enable everyone to read and enjoy poetry. In a very real sense, he was a poet of the people.

Connect to the Literature

Ask students the Connect to the Literature question.

Possible responses: Students might offer that John Keats's audience would have been people of some station, and not necessarily the ordinary, everyday people Pablo Neruda hoped to reach.

17 Reading Strategy

Paraphrasing

1. Have students read Stanza V to themselves.
2. Then have students **respond** to the Reading Strategy item. **Answer:** I cannot see what flowers surround me, what smell is in the air in the darkness; standing in the dark, I guess which blossoms are out in May.

---

16 World LITERATURE CONNECTION

Pablo Neruda's Odes

Keats is considered the master of the 19th-century English ode. However, the master of the 20th-century ode is Pablo Neruda, who wrote in Spanish.

Neruda was born in Chile in 1904. At sixteen, he was already a published poet. As he grew older, Neruda realized that many of the uneducated poor in Latin America would have trouble understanding his ornate, complicated poems. Yet he wanted to reach everyone. "Poetry is like bread," he said. "It should be shared by all."

So Neruda began writing poems with short lines and vivid images. These new poems were tributes to everyday objects: a hat, a pair of socks, an onion, a tomato. Neruda called them odes. He described a watermelon as "a jewel box of water," and he described fire as "jumpy and blind but with studded eyes." Eventually, Neruda achieved his goal: hundreds of thousands of Spanish-speaking people, rich and poor, came to know and love his poetry.

Connect to the Literature

What sort of people do you think John Keats imagined would read "Ode to a Nightingale?"

Vocabulary
requiem (rek´ wē əm) *n.* musical composition honoring the dead

IV

Away! away! for I will fly to thee,
Not charioted by Bacchus[9] and his pards,
But on the viewless[10] wings of Poesy,[11]
Though the dull brain perplexes and retards:
Already with thee! tender is the night,
And haply[12] the Queen-Moon is on her throne,
Clustered around by all her starry Fays;[13]
But here there is no light,
Save what from heaven is with the breezes blown
Through verdurous[14] glooms and winding mossy ways.

V

I cannot see what flowers are at my feet,
Nor what soft incense hangs upon the boughs,
But, in embalmed[15] darkness, guess each sweet
Wherewith the seasonable month endows
17 The grass, the thicket, and the fruit-tree wild;
White hawthorn, and the pastoral eglantine;[16]
Fast fading violets covered up in leaves;
And mid-May's eldest child,
The coming musk-rose, full of dewy wine,
The murmurous haunt of flies on summer eves.

VI

Darkling[17] I listen; and, for many a time
I have been half in love with easeful Death,
Called him soft names in many a mused[18] rhyme,
To take into the air my quiet breath;
Now more than ever seems it rich to die,
To cease upon the midnight with no pain,
While thou art pouring forth thy soul abroad
In such an ecstasy!
Still wouldst thou sing, and I have ears in vain—
To thy high **requiem** become a sod.

---

9. **Bacchus** (bak´ əs) in classical mythology, the god of wine, who was often represented in a chariot drawn by leopards ("pards").
10. **viewless** invisible.
11. **Poesy** poetic fancy.
12. **haply** perhaps.
13. **Fays** fairies.
14. **verdurous** green-foliaged.
15. **embalmed** perfumed.
16. **eglantine** (eg´ lən tīn´) sweetbrier or honeysuckle.
17. **Darkling** in the dark.
18. **mused** meditated.

Think Aloud

Reading Strategy: Paraphrasing

To model the process of working out the answer to the Reading Strategy question on the student page, use the following "think aloud." Say to students:

I may have trouble understanding Keats's poetic verse. I can use the strategy of paraphrasing to decode his meaning. First, I can locate a complete thought or sentence. I can write that sentence down. Then, I can think about that thought or sentence and then write what it means in my own words. This skill of paraphrasing allows me to take verses of poetry that are difficult to access and to make them my own by restating them in my own words.

VII

(18)

Thou wast not born for death, immortal Bird!
No hungry generations tread thee down;
The voice I hear this passing night was heard
In ancient days by emperor and clown:
Perhaps the selfsame song that found a path
Through the sad heart of Ruth,[19] when, sick for home,
She stood in tears amid the alien corn;
The same that ofttimes hath
Charmed magic casements, opening on the foam
Of perilous seas, in fairylands forlorn.

VIII

Forlorn! the very word is like a bell
To toll me back from thee to my sole self!
Adieu! the fancy cannot cheat so well
As she is famed[20] to do, deceiving elf.
Adieu! adieu! thy plaintive anthem fades
Past the near meadows, over the still stream,
Up the hillside; and now 'tis buried deep
In the next valley-glades:
Was it a vision, or a waking dream?
Fled is that music:—Do I wake or sleep?

19. **Ruth** in the Bible (Ruth 2:1–23), a widow who left her home and went to Judah to work in the corn (wheat) fields.
20. **famed** reported.

(18) Literary Analysis
The Ode What element of traditional odes appears in verse VII?

Past the near meadows,
over the still stream,
Up the hillside;
and now 'tis buried deep

Critical Reading

Cite textual evidence to support your responses.

1. **Key Ideas and Details (a)** How does the speaker describe his emotional state in stanza I? **(b) Infer:** What appears to have brought on this state?
2. **Key Ideas and Details (a)** What wish does the speaker express in lines 19–20? **(b) Compare and Contrast:** What differences does he see between the bird's life and his own that cause him to wish this?
3. **Craft and Structure (a) Analyze:** What is the viewpoint from which the speaker describes his surroundings in stanza V? **(b) Connect:** How does this viewpoint reflect the speaker's wish in line 21?
4. **Craft and Structure (a) Analyze:** How does stanza VII "answer" stanza VI? **(b) Synthesize:** What similarity between death and immortality does the speaker imply?
5. **Integration of Knowledge and Ideas** By writing a poem full of extreme feeling, is Keats just being dramatic, or is writing such a poem a way of making peace with strong feelings? Explain.

Differentiated Instruction for Universal Access

Strategy for Special-Needs Students
Students who have read "Ode to a Nightingale" may still have difficulty with comprehension. Reinforce students' learning by using **Reading Strategy Graphic Organizer B**, page 159 in ***Graphic Organizer Transparencies.***

Strategy for Less Proficient Readers
Remind students that direct address of the subject is a feature of most odes. Review how Keats uses personification—or assigning human traits to the nightingale—in this poem. Have students reread the poem and find examples of personification.

Enrichment for Advanced Readers
Have students do research on the figure of the nightingale as it appears in European and Asian art, music, and literature. Students should present their findings in oral reports comparing characterizations of the birds in other works with Keats's depiction.

(18) Literary Analysis
The Ode

1. Have students read verse VII.
2. Review with students the definition of an ode.
3. Then, **ask** the Literary Analysis question.
   Answer: Keats's speaker directly addresses the nightingale, a traditional element of odes.

ASSESS
Answers

Before students respond, you may wish to have them write a brief objective summary of the selection. As they answer the questions below, remind them to support their answers with evidence from the text.

1. (a) He describes his state as a kind of drowsy heartsickness. (b) The ecstasy of the songs of the nightingale has brought on this emotional state.
2. (a) He wishes to leave the world behind and join the nightingale. (b) The real world in which the speaker lives is perplexing and dull; the nightingale's world is one of permanent, dreamlike joy.
3. (a) The speaker cannot see his surroundings. (b) The speaker wishes to disappear into the darkness that engulfs him.
4. (a) Stanza VII suggests that the bird was not born for death, and it "answers" the speaker's musings in Stanza VI that he wishes he could die. (b) The speaker suggests that death is a kind of immortality, since both are states in which nothing changes.
5. **Possible responses:** Some students may say that Keats is overly dramatic in his poetic musings on death; others may feel that he is coming to terms with his own mortality, a subject that deserves the extreme emotion in this poem. By expressing this emotion, he may purge himself of it.

⓳ About the Selection

In this poem, Keats comes to an understanding about the nature of truth and beauty as he gazes at an ancient Greek urn. The scenes depicted on the urn, frozen in time, eternally beautiful and unchanging, symbolize that the urn's beauty embodies the eternity of truth.

⓴ Humanities

Neck-amphora with lid attributed to Exekias (*ca.* 540 BCE)

This terracotta urn shows a woman in a wedding chariot accompanied by a woman and a bearded man. The style is known as black figure painting, in which the painter applies glaze in silhouettes and then incises details of anatomy and drapery. Exekias, one of the greatest black-figure artists, was both the potter and the painter of this well-preserved vase. Athenian vases of this time period show a wealth of detail illustrating aspects of Greek culture, including daily life, athletics, warfare, religion, and mythology.

Use these questions for discussion:

1. How do the decorative elements on this Greek urn help to unify the artwork?

Possible response: The battle scenes below the decorative elements show other scenes from Greek life; while the ornaments, the floral design and the spirals under the handles organize the surface and help to reinforce the shape of the pot.

2. What details about the figures are reflected in Keats's poetry?

Possible response: The bearded man and a fair-skinned woman hold the reins of the wedding chariot. These figures have a great deal of dignity. The figures have been placed perfectly, which reflects the ideal of beauty and harmony that Keats describes in his poem.

⓴ EXEMPLAR TEXT ©

⓳ ODE ON A GRECIAN URN

JOHN KEATS

Vocabulary Development

Vocabulary Knowledge Rating

When students have completed reading and discussing the selection, have them take out their **Vocabulary Knowledge Rating Charts** for the story. Read the words aloud and have students rate their knowledge of words again in the After Reading column. Clarify any words that are still problematic. Have students write their own definitions and example or sentence in the appropriate column. Then, have students complete the Vocabulary Practice at the end of the selection. Encourage students to use the words in further discussion and written work about the selection. Remind them that they will be accountable for these words on the **Selection Test, *Unit 4 Resources,*** pages 162–164 or 165–167.

I

Thou still unravished bride of quietness
  Thou foster child of silence and slow time,
Sylvan[1] historian, who canst thus express
  A flowery tale more sweetly than our rhyme:
What leaf-fringed legend haunts about thy shape
  Of deities or mortals, or of both,
    In Tempe[2] or the dales of Arcady?[3]
  What men or gods are these? What maidens loath?[4]
What mad pursuit? What struggle to escape?
    What pipes and timbrels?[5] What wild ecstasy?

II

Heard melodies are sweet, but those unheard
  Are sweeter; therefore, ye soft pipes, play on;
Not to the sensual[6] ear, but, more endeared,
  Pipe to the spirit ditties of no tone:
(21) Fair youth, beneath the trees, thou canst not leave
  Thy song, nor ever can those trees be bare;
    Bold Lover, never, never canst thou kiss,
Though winning near the goal—yet, do not grieve;
  She cannot fade, though thou hast not thy bliss,
    Forever wilt thou love, and she be fair!

III

Ah, happy, happy boughs! that cannot shed
  Your leaves, nor ever bid the Spring adieu;
And, happy melodist, unwearied,
  Forever piping songs forever new;
More happy love! more happy, happy love!
  Forever warm and still to be enjoyed,
    Forever panting, and forever young;
All breathing human passion far above,
  That leaves a heart high-sorrowful and cloyed,
    A burning forehead, and a parching tongue.

IV

Who are these coming to the sacrifice?
  To what green altar, O mysterious priest,
(24) Lead'st thou that heifer lowing at the skies,
  And all her silken flanks with garlands dressed?

---

1. **Sylvan** rustic, representing the woods or forest.
2. **Tempe** (tem′ pē) beautiful valley in Greece that has become a symbol of supreme rural beauty.
3. **Arcady** (är′ kə dē) region in Greece that has come to represent supreme pastoral contentment.
4. **loath** unwilling.
5. **timbrels** tambourines.
6. **sensual** involving the physical sense of hearing.

Literary Analysis
The Ode
What two figures on Keats's urn are directly addressed in stanza II?

(22) **Reading Check**
Describe two scenes depicted on the urn.

(23) **◀ Critical Viewing**
What stories can you see in the picture above and in the picture decorating the urn to the left? **[Speculate]**

(21) Literary Analysis
The Ode

1. Have students read the bracketed passage to themselves.
2. **Ask** the Literary Analysis question.
   Answer: He directly addresses a youth and a lover.

(22) Reading Check

Possible responses: Students may describe the majestic scene of a wedding chariot drawn by two horses on the belly of the vase and this battle scene from below the floral frieze.

(23) Critical Viewing

Possible responses: The urn has scenes of lovers about to kiss and a priest about to make a sacrifice.

Differentiated Instruction for Universal Access

EL Strategy for English Learners
Have students look at the Grecian urn on the facing page, then read "Ode on a Grecian Urn." Remind them to sound out any difficult words and, wherever possible, to paraphrase any complicated phrases or ideas.

Enrichment for Gifted/Talented Students
Have students draw the vase described by Keats, paying close attention to the imagery and details of the poem. Their drawings should include two components: a picture of a vase in its entire shape and a single panel that shows the images and scenes in continuous form.

Enrichment for Advanced Readers
Explain that the ode was a favorite genre for Keats. Refer students who wish to do more in-depth analysis of Keats and his lyric achievements to additional examples of his work. Have students compare and contrast all of Keats's odes.

24 Literary Analysis

The Ode

1. Have students read Stanza IV to themselves.
2. **Ask** the Literary Analysis question.
   Possible response: The questions suggest that he is imaginative because they attempt to "fill in" what is not shown in the pictures; they also suggest that he is capable of a passionate response to art.

ASSESS

Answers

Before students respond, you may wish to have them write a brief objective summary of the selection. As they answer the questions below, remind them to support their answers with evidence from the text.

1. (a) The scenes depict a youth pursuing his lover against a background of trees and piping musicians. (b) The lover in Stanza II might grieve because he can never attain his beloved. (c) Because even if he can never kiss his beloved, she will always be beautiful and he will always love her.
2. (a) The boughs, the melodist, and love. (b) The boughs cannot shed their leaves, or leave the springtime of the urn. The melodist will never be tired, and his songs will always be new. Love will always be young.
3. That permanent happiness is impossible.
4. (a) The "truth" of imperishable, eternal youth, passion, and beauty. (b) The urn's artistic beauty is unending and true in a way that the real world can never be, because the real world is transitory. (c) Students may say that the "truth" is only partly true—the "truth" of beauty is not the truth of suffering, aging, and death, which are part of life.
5. These odes are traditional in that they employ classic forms of odes and address classic themes. Keats's *authentic* odes are not *conventional* and leave much to his readers' *interpretation.*

---

24 Literary Analysis
The Ode
What do the speaker's questions reveal about his feelings or personality?

24

What little town by river or seashore,
    Or mountain-built with peaceful citadel,
        Is emptied of this folk, this pious morn?
And, little town, thy streets forevermore
    Will silent be; and not a soul to tell
        Why thou art desolate, can e'er return.

V

O Attic[7] shape! Fair attitude! with brede[8]
    Of marble men and maidens overwrought,[9]
With forest branches and the trodden weed;
    Thou, silent form, dost tease us out of thought
As doth eternity: Cold[10] Pastoral!
    When old age shall this generation waste,
        Thou shalt remain, in midst of other woe
Than ours, a friend to man, to whom thou say'st,
    "Beauty is truth, truth beauty,"—that is all
        Ye know on earth, and all ye need to know.

---

7. **Attic** Attica was the region of Greece in which Athens was located; the art of the region was characterized by grace and simplicity.
8. **brede** interwoven pattern.
9. **overwrought** adorned with.
10. **Cold** unchanging.

Critical Reading

Cite textual evidence to support your responses.

1. **Key Ideas and Details (a)** Describe the scenes in stanzas I and II. **(b) Infer:** Why might the lover in stanza II grieve? **(c) Interpret:** Why does the speaker advise him not to grieve?
2. **Key Ideas and Details (a)** Which items are called "happy" in stanza III? **(b) Infer:** What is the reason for their happiness?
3. **Key Ideas and Details Infer:** What do the speaker's comments on these painted scenes indirectly suggest about real life?
4. **Key Ideas and Details (a) Interpret:** In line 49, what is the "truth" represented by the scenes on the urn? **(b) Connect:** How is this truth connected to the fact that the urn will remain after "old age shall this generation waste"? **(c) Make a Judgment:** Is the truth of the urn the "whole truth"? Explain.
5. **Integration of Knowledge and Ideas** In what ways are these poems traditional odes? In what ways has Keats personalized them? In your response, use at least two of these Essential Question words: *authentic, conventional, interpretation. [Connecting to the Essential Question: What is the relationship of the writer to tradition?]*

Concept Connector

Reading Strategy Graphic Organizer

Ask students to review the graphic organizers in which they have paraphrased difficult parts of Keats's work. Then, have students share their organizers and compare their paraphrasing with each other.

Activating Prior Knowledge

Have students return to their responses to the Activating Prior Knowledge activity. Ask them to explain whether their thoughts have changed and, if so, how.

Writing About the Essential Question

Have students compare their responses to the prompt, completed before reading the poems, with their thoughts afterward. Have them work individually or in groups, writing or discussing their thoughts, to formulate new responses. Lead a class discussion, probing for what students have learned that confirms or invalidates their initial thoughts. Encourage students to cite specific textual details to support their responses.

After You Read | Poetry of John Keats

Literary Analysis

1. **Craft and Structure (a)** Identify the rhyme scheme of stanza I of "Ode on a Grecian Urn." **(b)** Is this rhyme scheme used throughout the poem? **(c)** Classify the **ode** as **Pindaric, Horatian,** or **irregular.** Then, explain your choice.
2. **Craft and Structure** What phrase does Keats use to directly address his subject in stanza I of "Ode to a Nightingale"? Identify another such phrase in the poem.
3. **Key Ideas and Details (a)** What do Keats's two odes honor? **(b)** Would you say he treats his subjects with heightened emotion? Why or why not?
4. **Integration of Knowledge and Ideas** What artifacts of today would speak most to the future about our culture, as the urn speaks of ancient Greece? Why?
5. **Comparing Literary Works (a)** Compare the speaker's attitude—wonder? fear? longing?—in each ode. **(b)** In each, an object or event represents something that the speaker desires but does not and perhaps cannot possess. Support this generalization with details from the poems.
6. **Comparing Literary Works** Both "Ode to a Nightingale" and "Ode on a Grecian Urn" show a speaker caught between eternal beauty and the realities of life. Using a chart like the one shown, collect details from each ode that compare the relationship between the eternal and the world of time.

7. **Comparing Literary Works** Explain how each ode contributes to the idea that a person's self is defined by his or her deepest conflicts.
8. **Comparing Literary Works** In what ways are Keats's two sonnets as dramatic as his odes? Cite specific passages to support your points.

Reading Strategy

9. **Paraphrase** lines 9–10 from "Chapman's Homer."
10. Paraphrase at least one passage that you find difficult in stanza VII of "Ode to a Nightingale."
11. Suppose you are telling a friend about Keats's sonnet "When I Have Fears." Paraphrase lines of the poem to explain to your friend exactly what Keats fears.

Common Core State Standards

Writing
9.a. Apply *grades 11–12 Reading standards* to literature. [RL.11-12.5] *(p. 894)*

Language
5. Demonstrate understanding of figurative language, word relationships, and nuances in word meanings. *(p. 894)*

Assessment Practice

Critical Thinking (For more practice, see *All-in-One Workbook.*)

Many tests require students to judge the importance of points in a writer's argument. Use this sample test item.

Which of the following lines from "Ode to a Nightingale" is not an important point in Keats's argument that life is full of suffering?

A I cannot see what flowers are at my feet, / Nor what soft incense hangs upon the boughs
B The weariness, the fever, and the fret / Here, where men sit and hear each other groan
C Where but to think is to be full of sorrow / And leaden-eyed despairs
D Now more than ever seems it rich to die, / To cease upon the midnight with no pain

Choices ***B***, ***C***, and ***D*** support Keats's argument. Therefore, ***A*** is the correct answer.

Answers

1. (a) *abab cdedce* (b) No. (c) The ode is a modified Horatian ode.
2. Keats uses "thou, light-winged Dryad of the trees" and "immortal Bird!"
3. (a) a nightingale and a Grecian urn (b) Yes; he is passionate about classical and natural beauty.
4. **Possible responses:** Students may say our highways or our television programming will speak most about our culture.
5. (a) The speaker's wonder and longing in "Ode to a Nightingale" at the ecstasy of the bird's song is similar to the speaker's enchantment with the perpetual spring of the Grecian urn. (b) In "Ode to a Nightingale," the speaker longs for the complete joy of the bird as exhibited in its songs, but he feels it is not possible in this world. In "Ode on a Grecian Urn," the speaker desires the beauty possible only in art.
6. **Possible responses:** for "Nightingale": Longs for ecstasies experienced by a bird; Eternal World: the nightingale's happy son, can be heard forever. World of Time: fever, fret, groans, grief
7. **Possible responses:** Students may say that in "Ode to a Nightingale," the speaker's desire for contentment can be fulfilled only by death— he could never enjoy the fulfillment of desire. In "Ode on a Grecian Urn," the speaker's desire for beauty and truth can be perfected only in art, which he can only enter through this poem.
8. The subject matter of the two sonnets (a great adventure and human mortality) are just as dramatic as the joy of the nightingale and the beauty of the urn in the two odes.
9. **Possible response:** I felt like an astronomer who sees a new planet in his or her telescope.
10. **Possible response:** (lines 61–70) Nightingale, you are not meant to die. Your voice, heard in ancient times, comforted Ruth and opened the windows of the imagination.
11. In lines 1–4 and 7–10 of "When I Have Fears," Keats fears dying without fulfilling his life's work (of writing poety) and the loss of his beloved.

EXTEND/ASSESS

Answers

Vocabulary Acquisition and Use

Word Analysis

1. Lit.: The lamb raced to its flock. Fig: The teacher spoke softly to her lambs.
2. Lit.: Please varnish the railing. Fig: The child varnished the truth to avoid punishment.
3. Lit.: The airplane was damaged by flak. Fig: I received flak for my ill-timed opinion.
4. Lit.: The small child had trouble speaking into the mouthpiece of the telephone. Fig: Her mouthpiece spoke to the press on her behalf.
5. Lit.: The lights in this room are too dim to see. Fig: He was too dim to understand what was going on.

Vocabulary

1. teeming
2. surmise
3. requiem
4. ken
5. vintage
6. gleaned

Writing

1. To guide students in writing this explanatory text, give them the Support for Writing page (*Unit 4 Resources,* p. 157).
2. Explain that in this lesson, students will write analyses of Keats's use of drama in his poetry.
3. Remind students to cite examples of dramatic images in Keats's poetry and to describe the emotions the images bring to mind.
4. Use the **Response to Literature** rubric, ***Professional Development Guidebook,*** pages 250–251, to evaluate students' work.

PERFORMANCE TASKS

Integrated Language Skills

Vocabulary Acquisition and Use

Word Analysis: Multiple Meanings

Some words have both a literal and a figurative meaning. Literally, *vintage* is "wine of a particular place and season." Figuratively, though, the word *vintage* means "of a particular era" or "best of its class." As you can see, the figurative meaning draws on the literal one. Identify the figurative meaning of each word below and explain how it is related to the literal meaning. Consult a dictionary to verify your answers. Then, write two sentences for each word, one illustrating the literal meaning and one the figurative.

1. lamb, *n.*
2. varnish, *v.*
3. flak, *n.*
4. mouthpiece, *n.*
5. dim, *adj.*

Vocabulary: Sentence Completion

Using words from the vocabulary list on page 880, complete the sentences below. Use each word once. If necessary, change its form. Then, write original sentences with each word.

1. The storage room was ______ with supplies.
2. Despite the evidence, he remained convinced that his initial ______ was correct.
3. At the funeral, the organist played a mournful ______.
4. There are many mysteries beyond our ______.
5. The wine collector carefully organized his bottles according to ______.
6. At harvest time, the birds ______ stray grain from the reaped fields.

Writing

Explanatory Text Critics David Perkins and Walter Jackson Bate have pointed to the dramatic quality of Keats's odes, a quality also found in his lyrics. Write an **essay** analyzing how Keats uses *imagery, personification, figures of speech,* and *sound* to structure his poems, setting up dramatic situations and evoking readers' emotions. Bear in mind that drama springs from internal or external conflicts.

Prewriting Take notes on the poems, recording examples of the kinds of dramatic images and situations Keats presents. Annotate your notes to show how he evokes emotions. Then, use your notes to formulate a thesis statement.

Model: Annotating Notes

Words or Passage	Comment
"Looked at each other with a wild surmise— / Silent, upon a peak in Darien." ("Chapman's Homer," lines 13–14)	Dramatic image: men stunned into silence by what they see.

Taking specific notes will help your writing flow more easily.

Drafting Write your essay, explaining the techniques Keats uses and the effects they have. To make your essay more coherent, organize it to follow the sequence of ideas in your thesis statement.

Revising Revise your draft to make sure you have organized it well, clearly stated your points, and supported your ideas with *accurate and detailed references* to the text.

Assessment Resources

Unit 4 Resources

L1 L2 EL **Selection Test A,** pp. 162–164. Administer Test A to less advanced readers.

L3 L4 EL **Selection Test B,** pp. 165–167. Administer Test B to on-level students and more advanced students.

L3 L4 **Open-Book Test,** pp. 159–161. As an alternative, give the Open-Book test.

All **Customizable Test Bank**

All **Self-tests**

Students may prepare for the **Selection Test** by taking the **Self-test** online.

PHLit Online! All assessment resources are available at **www.PHLitOnline.com.**

The Reaction to Society's Ills

PART 3

Text Complexity: At a Glance

This chart gives a general text complexity rating for the selections in this part of the unit to help guide instruction. For additional text complexity support, see the Test Complexity Rubric at point of use.

On Making an Agreeable Marriage	**More Complex**
from A Vindication of the Rights of Woman	**More Accessible**

Selection Planning Guide

The selections in this section highlight the societal problems that arose during the Industrial Revolution. Russell, Peel, and Macaulay address the need for better treatment of the working class and for political reform. Austen and Wollstonecraft comment on the foibles and unfairness in society, particularly in regard to the status of women.

Humanities

Coalbrookdale by Night, 1801, by Philippe Jacques de Loutherbourg (1740–1812)

Loutherberg was an English artist of French extraction. He was most well-known for revolutionizing set design by incorporating complex lighting and special effects into scenery. He also painted numerous naval battles. *Coalbrookdale by Night* shows how the advent of the Industrial Revolution began to change the landscape. The painting depicts the iron foundries at work, silhouetted against a natural background. Use this question for discussion: How does the composition of the painting reflect the societal reordering engendered by the Industrial Revolution?

Possible response: The exhaust and light from the foundry are the focal points of the piece. The people and buildings in the painting appear as insignificant outlines, indicating the growing primacy of industry over manpower.

Monitoring Progress

After students have completed the excerpt from *A Vindication of the Rights of Woman*, administer **Benchmark Test 8** (***Unit 4 Resources,*** pp. 195–200). If the Benchmark Test reveals that some students need further work, use the Interpretation Guide to determine the appropriate reteaching page in the **Reading Kit** and online **Success Tracker**.

Monitoring Progress

Before students read the poetry by Robert Burns and Joanna Baillie, refer to the results for the Vocabulary in Context items on **Benchmark Test 8** (***Unit 4 Resources,*** **pp. 201-203**). Use this diagnostic portion of the test to guide your choice of selections to teach as well as the depth of prereading preparation you will provide, based on students' readiness for the reading and vocabulary skills.

PRETEACH

Common Core State Standards

- Reading Informational Text 4, 6

1 About the Text Forms

1. Introduce the forms using the instruction on the student page.
2. Tell students they will identify the features of each form as they read the selections.

2 Reading Strategy

Introduce the strategy using the instruction on the student page.

Think Aloud: Model the Skill

Model the skill of analyzing rhetorical devices. Say to students:

When I read a persuasive speech or letter, I look for rhetorical devices being used by the speaker or author. For example, when I read Sir Robert Peele's assertion that the people have been "grossly deceived, grossly deluded," I recognize he is using both repetition and charged language. By emphasizing the strong word "grossly," Peele depicts his opposition as untrustworthy. I can see that defining his opponents negatively is a component of Peele's argument and that he uses this tactic to appeal to his audience's emotions. Analyzing the use of these devices can help me understand the argument being made.

3 How does literature shape or reflect society?

1. Ask for a volunteer to read the Essential Question aloud.
2. Then, discuss how students should approach the selections with the Essential Question in mind, using the instruction on the student page.

COMMON CORE • RESEARCH PROJECT

Primary Sources

Parliamentary Debate
Speech by Lord John Russell
Speech by Sir Robert Peel

Letter
Thomas Babington Macaulay to Thomas Flower Ellis

1 About the Text Forms

A **debate** is a formal argument in which speakers with opposing views try to persuade an audience to support their positions. Debates follow rules, especially if they take place in a legislative body like Parliament.

Those who viewed parliamentary proceedings might provide an eyewitness account of them in a **letter.** Such a communication can provide insights into public opinion as well as the writer's own views.

2 Reading Strategy

A speaker or author arguing for a position may use *rhetorical devices.* **Analyzing rhetorical devices** like these will help you understand how authors try to make their case:

- *charged language and imagery:* words that carry strong emotional associations and stir up the audience's feelings
- *parallelism:* similar ideas expressed in similar grammatical forms
- *dramatic alternatives:* the posing of sharply contrasting alternatives
- *allusions:* references to well-known people, places, and events

As you read, notice how the two debaters and Macaulay use rhetorical devices to clarify their ideas, make them memorable, and engage the audience's emotions.

To fully appreciate rhetoric, first clarify the meaning of the writer's words:

- Be sensitive to word *connotations*—the positive or negative associations of words.
- Interpret words used in a *figurative sense,* such as *similes* (comparisons of unlike things using *like* or *as*).
- Consult references to determine the meaning of *technical terms*—terms specific to a discipline or profession, such as politics.

3 How does literature shape or reflect society?

Lord Russell and Sir Robert Peel were on opposite sides of the debate on the First Reform Bill. As you read, consider how the two served as spokesmen for different social interests. Also consider how the outcome of their argument, as reflected in Macaulay's letter, affected their society.

Common Core State Standards

Reading Informational Text
4. Determine the meaning of words and phrases as they are used in a text, including figurative, connotative, and technical meanings; analyze how an author uses and refines the meaning of a key term or terms over the course of a text.
6. Determine an author's point of view or purpose in a text in which the rhetoric is particularly effective, analyzing how style and content contribute to the power, persuasiveness, or beauty of the text.

PHLit Online! www.PHLitOnline.com

Teaching Resources

All *Unit 4 Resources,* pp. 168–171

All **Enriched Online Student Edition**

PHLit Online! All resources are available at www.PHLITOnline.com

❹ Note-Taking Guide

Primary source documents are a rich source of information for researchers. As you read these documents, use a note-taking guide like this one to organize relevant and accurate information.

1 Type of Document (check one)
☐ Newspaper ☐ Letter ☐ Diary ☐ Map ☐ Speech ☐ Government Form
☐ Advertisement ☐ Memorandum ☐ Other (Specify) ______

2 Date of Document ______

3 Author ______

Author's Position ______

4 Original Audience ______

5 Purpose and Importance

a How does the author try to persuade his audience? ______

Write down two details that support your answer. ______

b List two important ideas, statements, or observations from this document. ______

c What does this document show about life in the time and place in which it was written? ______

Reading Strategy Analyzing Rhetorical Devices As you read, analyze rhetorical devices that authors of public documents, or of private documents relating to public issues, use to support their positions.

This guide was adapted from the **U.S. National Archives** document analysis worksheet.

❺ Vocabulary

measure (mezh´ ər) *n.* a bill, resolution, or something else proposed or enacted to improve a situation (p. 900)

grievances (grēv´ əns əz) *n.* circumstances that cause people to complain (p. 900)

electors (ē lek´ tərz) *n.* those who vote (p. 900)

constituency (kən stich´ o͞o ən sē) *n.* the people making up a body of voters (p. 901)

extravagant (ek strav´ ə gənt) *adj.* going beyond reasonable limits; excessive (p. 902)

reverence (rev´ ər əns) *n.* deep respect (p. 902)

inauspicious (in´ ô spi´ shəs) *adj.* not promising a good outcome; unfavorable (p. 904)

orthodox (ôr´ thə däks´) *adj.* conforming to established beliefs (p. 907)

❹ Note-Taking Guide

1. Point out the sample Note-Taking Guide on the student page.
2. Encourage students to use it to help them analyze the three selections in this lesson.

❺ Vocabulary

1. Have students preview the selection vocabulary, pronouncing the words and reading their definitions. Have students identify any words with which they are already familiar.
2. Use each word in a sentence with sufficient context to define the word. Then, repeat your definitional sentence with the vocabulary word missing, requiring the class to fill in the blank orally. Here is an example:

   An extravagant gift is one that seems excessive, or more than is reasonable. When a person gives someone an excessive amount of money, it is considered an [students say "extravagant"] gift.

PRETEACH

❻ Background

The Story Behind the Documents

Lord John Russell

Russell was not someone who gave up easily. A constant reformer, Russell brought measures before Parliament time and time again, sometimes reintroducing topics years later if they failed to go through during earlier attempts.

Sir Robert Peel

From 1812 to 1817, during Lord Liverpool's time as prime minister, Sir Peel served as chief secretary for Ireland. In this post, he tried to minimize the corruption in Ireland's government, particularly regarding religious discrimination.

Thomas Babington Macaulay

Macaulay wrote several history volumes that earned him lasting fame and recognition. His *History of England* (1849–1861) was one of the bestsellers of the nineteenth century, and it is acknowledged as including one of the most detailed factual accounts of the reign of James II.

❼ Primary Source: Photography

1. Have students look at the Primary Source Photo on the facing page.
2. **Ask** students the Primary Source: Photography question: How does the arrangement of seats in the House of Commons suggest the idea of opposed parties? **Possible response:** The two sides face each other, much as two opposing sports team do on a sports field.

Ⓒ COMMON CORE ▪ RESEARCH PROJECT

❻ THE STORY BEHIND THE DOCUMENTS

Lord John Russell

Lord John Russell (1792–1878) was the British statesman who introduced the Reform Bill of 1832 in Parliament. A champion of reform, Lord Russell was a leading member of the Whig party when it came to power in 1830 with Lord Grey as prime minister. Some years later, after the Whigs had evolved into the Liberal party, Russell himself served twice as Britain's prime minister. Among his later achievements was passage of a law limiting factory labor to ten hours a day.

Sir Robert Peel

Sir Robert Peel (1788–1850) helped lead the Tory party opposition to the Reform Bill of 1832. Peel later served as prime minister twice, first from 1834 to 1835 and later, after reorganizing the Tories as the modern Conservative party, for a much longer period in the 1840s. In 1829, while serving as home secretary in a Tory administration, he established London's police force, whose members are nicknamed "bobbies" in his honor.

Thomas Babington Macaulay

Thomas Babington Macaulay (1800–1859) was a well-known nineteenth-century historian and literary critic. Trained as a lawyer, he was also a Whig member of Parliament who, like Lord Russell, spoke in favor of the Reform Bill of 1832. Macaulay first won literary fame with an essay on John Milton. His influential five-volume *History of England* (1849–1861) offered a Whig interpretation of British history, stressing the value of gradual democratic reform.

The Industrial Revolution brought great change to Britain. Large chunks of the population shifted from rural areas to newly emerging urban centers, where the middle class grew and prospered. Britain's political landscape, however, had not changed with the times. Sparsely populated rural areas had disproportionately large representation, while booming new industrial cities like Manchester had none. Some seats in Parliament were completely controlled by a single nobleman or by small self-interested groups. Additionally, landholding and financial restrictions kept much of the population from voting. The result was a Parliament that strongly favored the interests of landowners at the expense of everyone else. The Reform Bill of 1832—often called the First Reform Bill—was an attempt to correct that situation.

▶ **Primary Source: Photography** How does the arrangement of seats in the House of Commons suggest the idea of opposed parties? **[Analyze]**

❼

Enrichment: Building Context

English Industrial Revolution

Between 1760 and 1830, the production of cotton textiles in England increased twelvefold. This was due in large part to the new inventions that mechanized the spinning and weaving of imported cotton. As this transition began, people who had spent their lives farming or working as artisans left old ways of life to become factory workers. But as one technology quickly replaced the last, their jobs were threatened.

Activity: Research Have students do further research about the English Industrial Revolution. Suggest that they record information in the **Enrichment: Building Context** worksheet, ***Professional Development Guidebook,*** page 222.

SPEECH IN FAVOR OF REFORM

Lord John Russell

❶ **BACKGROUND** When the Whigs came to power in 1830, the number one issue on the party's agenda was reform of Britain's election system. To that end, Lord Russell first proposed the Reform Bill on March 1, 1831. The Tory party opposed the bill, with Sir Robert Peel speaking effectively against it. Extracts from both those speeches are presented here.

On the second reading, the bill passed Parliament's House of Commons by just one vote. Recognizing the need for a greater majority, Lord Grey, the Whig prime minister, dissolved Parliament and called for a new election. The Whigs now won many more seats, and the Reform Bill readily passed in the House of Commons—but it was still rejected in Parliament's other chamber, the House of Lords. Finally, the prime minister forced King William IV to name several new members to the House of Lords—members sympathetic to the reforms—and in July of 1832 the bill passed both Houses of Parliament and became law.

Interior of the Commons Chambers Houses of Parliament, Westminster, United Kingdom

TEACH

❶ Background

History

The two dominant parties in Britain's election system in the 1800s were the Whigs and the Tories. Whigs favored political reform and later became known as the Liberal party.

The Tories were generally monarchists, who favored royal authority. They tended to be against parliamentary reform, preferring instead for the traditional structure to be maintained. This group later became known as the Conservative Party.

PHLit Online!

These selections are available in interactive format in the **Enriched Online Student Edition** at **www.PHLitOnline.com**, which includes a thematically related video with writing prompt and an interactive graphic organizer.

❷ Reading Strategy

Analyzing Rhetorical Devices

1. Ask a volunteer to read the first paragraph aloud for the class. Encourage him or her to read slowly, as the text is written in a formal style that may hinder comprehension.
2. **Ask** the Reading Strategy question in the margin: Identify the emotionally charged language in the first paragraph of Russell's speech.
   Possible response: Emotional language includes such words as *difficult, grievances, complain, confined, evils, farce,* and *deprive.*

❸ Critical Thinking

Connect

1. After students have read the page, have them study the image on the page.
2. **Ask** students to explain the relationship between the text on this page and the artifact that is shown.
   Possible response: The text is talking about election reform, and the document reproduced here is an account of what happened during an election.

© COMMON CORE ▪ RESEARCH PROJECT

Vocabulary
measure (mezh´ ər) *n.* a bill, resolution, or something else proposed or enacted to improve a situation
grievances (grēv´ əns əz) *n.* circumstances that cause people to complain

❷

Reading Strategy
Analyzing Rhetorical Devices Identify the emotionally charged language in the first paragraph of Russell's speech.

I come now to the utmost difficult part of this subject—the explanation of the measure, which, representing the King's Ministers,[1] I am about to propose to the House. . . . The chief grievances of which the people complain are these;—First, the nomination of Members by individuals. Second, the Elections by close Corporations;[2] third, the Expense of Elections. With regard to the first—the nomination by individuals—it may be exercised in one of two ways; either over a place containing scarcely any inhabitants, and with a very extensive right of election, or over a place of wide extent and numerous population, but where the franchise[3] is confined to very few residents. . . . We have addressed ourselves to both these evils, because we have thought it essential to apply a remedy to both; but they must, of course, be dealt with in different ways. With regard to Boroughs[4] where there are scarcely any inhabitants, . . . , it would be evidently a mere farce to take away the right from the person exercising it, and to give it to the borough; and the only Reform that can be justly recommended is, to deprive the borough of its franchise altogether. . . .

An announcement for the first election following the passage of the Reform Bill

❸

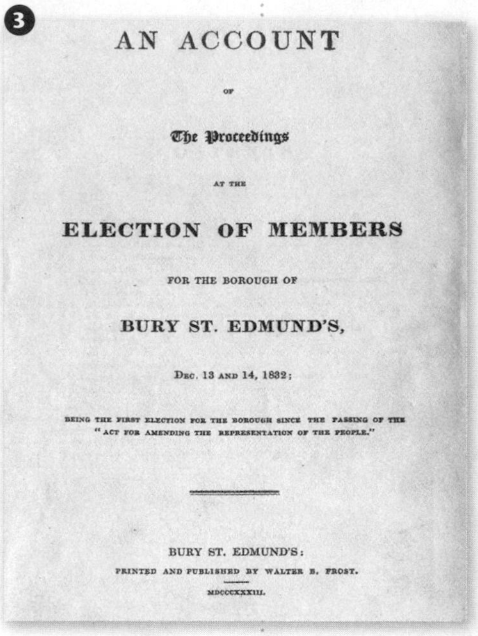
AN ACCOUNT
OF
The Proceedings
AT THE
ELECTION OF MEMBERS
FOR THE BOROUGH OF
BURY ST. EDMUND'S,
DEC. 13 AND 14, 1832;
BEING THE FIRST ELECTION FOR THE BOROUGH SINCE THE PASSING OF THE "ACT FOR AMENDING THE REPRESENTATION OF THE PEOPLE."
BURY ST. EDMUND'S:
PRINTED AND PUBLISHED BY WALTER B. FROST.
MDCCCXXXIII.

But, as I have already said, we do not mean to allow that the remaining boroughs should be in the hands of select Corporations—that is to say, in the possession of a small number of persons, to the exclusion of the great body of the inhabitants, who have property and interest in the place represented. . . . We therefore propose that the right of voting shall be given to householders paying rates[5] for, or occupying a house of, the yearly value of £10. and upwards. Whether he be the proprietor, or whether he only rent the house, the person rated will have the franchise, upon certain conditions hereafter to be named. At the same time, it is not intended to deprive the present electors of their privilege to vote, provided they be resident.

With regard to non-residence, we are of the opinion that it produces much expense, that it is the cause of a great deal of bribery, and that it occasions such manifold and manifest evils, that electors who do not live in a place ought not to be permitted to retain their votes. . . .

Vocabulary
electors (ē lek´ tərz) *n.* those who vote

1. **King's Ministers** Having won the last election, members of Parliament from the Whig party become the King's ministers, taking charge of the different departments of government.
2. **close Corporations** small unelected groups of influential people who controlled all the votes in nearly 200 voting districts.
3. **franchise** (fran´ chīz´) *n.* the right to vote.
4. **Boroughs** (bur´ ōz) *n.* towns or voting districts that send members to Parliament.
5. **rates** *n.* local property taxes.

Enrichment: Analyzing Historical Patterns, Trends, and Periods

The Reform Bill
The Reform Bill was the biggest political issue in England in 1831 and 1832. When it became law in 1832, the Reform Bill resulted in a redistribution of seats in Parliament, which gave more power to the growing industrial cities. It also extended the right to vote to all middle-class men and some artisans. This meant that the electorate was increased by 50 percent in both England and Wales, and by even more in Scotland and Ireland. By extending the vote to more "common" people, the measure weakened the power of both the monarchy and the House of Lords. Thus, it was a giant step toward greater democracy.

Activity: Tracing Election Reform Have each student work with a partner to learn more about the Reform Bill of 1832. Suggest that they take notes in the **Enrichment: Analyzing Historical Patterns, Trends, and Periods** worksheet, *Professional Development Guidebook,* page 231.

I now beg leave to direct the attention of the House to that part of the plan which relates to the expense of long-protracted Polls, and which, while it removes that evil also greatly facilitates the collection of the sense of the elective body. The names of electors are to be enrolled, by which means we hope that the disputes regarding qualification will be in a great measure avoided. We propose that all electors in counties, cities, towns, or boroughs, shall be registered. . . . These regulations are extremely simple, and will prevent all those vexatious and noisy scenes now so often witnessed, regarding disputed votes.

4 The means of ascertaining who are the electors being made thus easy, there will be no reason why the poll should be kept open for eight days, or for a longer period; and it is proposed that, nearly according to the present law, booths shall be erected for the voters of the different parishes, so that the whole poll may be taken in two days. . . . 5 With respect to the manner of proceeding at Elections, we have it in view to introduce a measure which can hardly fail to be an improvement of the present system. Everybody knows, and must have lamented the enormous expense to which candidates are put in bringing voters to the poll. An election in Yorkshire has been known to cost nearly £150,000; and in Devonshire some of the electors are obliged to travel forty miles over rough cross-roads, which occupies one day; the next is consumed in polling, and the third in returning home; the whole scheme being a manifest source of vast expense, and most inconvenient delay. We propose, therefore, that the poll shall be taken in separate districts, into which the counties are to be divided, those districts to be arranged according to circumstances by the Magistrates at Quarter Sessions. . . .[6]

It is my opinion, therefore, that the whole measure will add to the **constituency** of the Commons House of Parliament, about half a million of Persons, and these all connected with the property of the country, having a valuable stake amongst us, and deeply interested in our institutions. They are the persons on whom we can depend in any future struggle in which this nation may be engaged, and who will maintain and support Parliament and the Throne in carrying that struggle to a successful termination. I think that those measures will produce a further benefit to the people, by the great incitement which it will occasion to industry and good conduct. For when a man finds, that by industrious exertion, and by punctuality, he will entitle himself to a place in the list of voters, he will have an additional motive to improve his circumstances, and to preserve his character amongst his neighbors. I think, therefore, that in adding to the constituency, we are providing for the moral as well as for the political improvement of the country. . . .

6. **Magistrates** (maj´ is trāts *or* trits) **at Quarter Sessions** judges in English local courts that sit four times a year.

Primary Sources
What do the details in Russell's next-to-last paragraph show about the actual process of holding elections in Russell's day?

Reading Strategy
Analyzing Rhetorical Devices How does the phrase "Everybody knows" help persuade the audience to accept the statement that follows?

Vocabulary
constituency (kən stich´ o͞o ən sē) *n.* the people making up a body of voters

6 **Reading Check**
To whom does Russell propose to give the right to vote?

4 Primary Sources

Debate

1. Have students read the page silently, rereading paragraphs if necessary for comprehension.
2. **Ask** students the Primary Sources question: What do the details in Russell's next-to-last paragraph show about the actual process of holding elections in Russell's day?
Possible response: The polls stay open for eight days or more, campaign financing is a problem, it is difficult to get people to vote, and they need a better system for polling people.

5 Reading Strategy

Analyzing Rhetorical Devices

1. Have students reread the page, noting the use of the rhetorical device "everybody knows."
2. **Ask** students the Reading Strategy question: How does the phrase "everybody knows" help persuade the audience to accept the statement that follows?
Possible response: The rhetorical device sets up a statement as something that no one could disagree with, when it is actually a matter of opinion that everyone "must have lamented the enormous expense."

6 Reading Check

Answer: He proposes that middle-class householders—owners and renters—be given the right to vote.

Differentiated Instruction for Universal Access

Strategy for Special-Needs Students
Explain that any effort toward reform is a reaction against social conditions of the time. Have students look for descriptions of what needs to be improved, as well as the suggestions being made for how to do so.

EL Vocabulary for English Learners
All students might not be familiar with the word *elector*. Explain that an *elector* is a person who is allowed to vote, and that the full group of people allowed to vote is called the *electorate*. When they do formally cast their votes, that is called an *election*.

❼ Background

Robert Peel continually fought against parliamentary reform. In July 1831 alone, he made almost fifty speeches against reform. In later years, Peel became more moderate, allowing for some reform, while still maintaining traditions.

❽ Reading Strategy

Analyzing Rhetorical Devices

1. Have students reread the page, noting the emotions to which Peel appeals.
2. **Ask** students the Reading Strategy question: In referring to the recent revolution in France, to what emotion does Peel appeal? Explain.
   Possible response: He's appealing to the emotion of fear—England should not press for change so much that a bloody revolution is the result.

❾ Primary Source

Debate

1. Have students review the last paragraph on this page.
2. **Ask** students the Primary Source question: What position on the Reform Bill does Peel state in his last paragraph?
   Answer: Peel states his position as being opposed to the Reform Bill.

COMMON CORE ▪ RESEARCH PROJECT

❼ SPEECH AGAINST REFORM

Sir Robert Peel

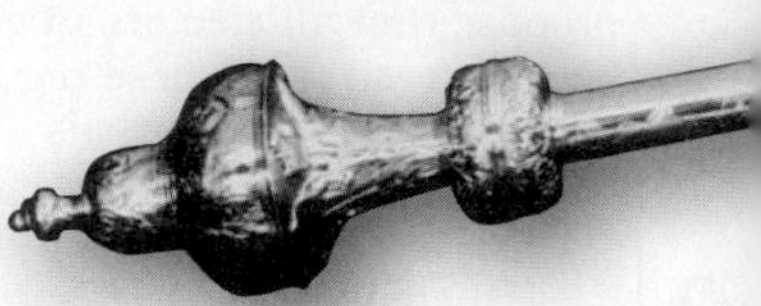

Vocabulary
extravagant (ek strav′ ə gənt) *adj.* going beyond reasonable limits; excessive

Reading Strategy
Analyzing Rhetorical Devices In referring to the recent revolution in France, to what emotion does Peel appeal? Explain.

Primary Source
Debate What position on the Reform Bill does Peel state in his last paragraph?

Vocabulary
reverence (rev′ ər əns) *n.* deep respect

I expected that the present ministers would bring in a reform bill on their acceptance of office; but I believe, in my conscience, that the concessions made by them to the popular demands have been far more extensive than was at all necessary. I was not prepared for so **extravagant** a measure, still less could I have thought that they would venture to bring in so large a measure of reform within ❽ three months after they had taken office, and while the country was yet agitated by the events of the French Revolution.[7]

No issue of this discussion can be satisfactory, for, decide as we may, there must be much irreparable evil. I may be obliged to submit by necessity to a plan of reform which I cannot successfully oppose; but believing, as I do, that the people of this country are grossly deceived, grossly deluded, in their expectations of the practical benefits they will derive from reform, I shall not be precluded from declaring my opinion, and opposing that reform as long as I can. . . .

I am satisfied with the constitution under which I have lived hitherto, which I believe is adapted to the wants and habits of the people. I deplore a disposition, which seems too prevalent, to innovate unnecessarily upon all the institutions of the country. I admit, that to serve the sovereign, and the public in an office of honor and dignity, is an object of honorable ambition; but I am ready to sacrifice that object, rather than incur the responsibility of advocating measures which, I believe on my conscience, will tend to the destruction of the best interests of the country. I will continue my opposition to the last, believing, as I do, that this is the first step, not directly to revolution, but to a series of changes which will affect the property, and totally change the character, of the mixed constitution of this country. . . .

❾ On this ground I take my stand, not opposed to a well-considered reform of any of our institutions which need reform, but opposed to this reform in our constitution, because it tends to root up the feelings of respect, the feelings of habitual **reverence** and attachment, which are the only sure foundations of government. . . .

7. **French Revolution** a second revolution in France, which took place in 1830 and replaced the reactionary monarch Charles X with Louis-Philippe, Duke of Orleans.

Enrichment: Analyzing a Historical Event

French Revolution
The French Revolution, which lasted from 1789 to 1799, is considered one of the most important events in the history of Europe. The goal of the revolution was to overthrow the monarchy and set up a system of democratic government in which members of the middle class could have more of a voice. Many of the changes to France's government were later adopted by other European countries.

Activity: Debate Divide the class in half. Ask one group to defend the reasons for revolution, and ask the other to argue for keeping peace. Then, have students analyze what they have heard, using the **Enrichment: Analyzing a Historical Event** worksheet, ***Professional Development Guidebook,*** page 230.

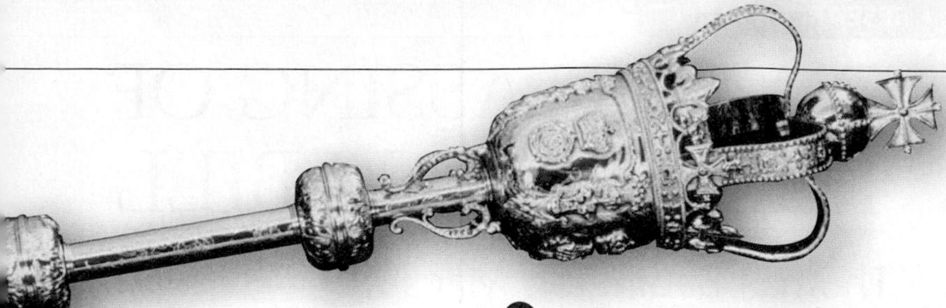

⑩ ▲ **Primary Source: Artifact** Why might this ceremonial mace, which is carried into the House of Commons each day, be an effective symbol of the authority of the Crown and Parliament? **[Analyze]**

11

⑫ ▲ **Primary Source: Art** In the 18th century, British artist William Hogarth created a series of paintings satirizing corrupt politicians. Which details in this depiction of a tavern dinner attended by Whig candidates serve Hogarth's satiric purpose? **[Infer]**

⑩ Primary Source: Artifact

1. Have students look at the Primary Source Artifact on this page.
2. **Ask** students the Primary Source: Artifact question: Why might this ceremonial mace, which is carried into the House of Commons each day, be an effective symbol of the authority of the Crown and Parliament?
   Possible response: The crown is at the top, symbolizing its overall importance. However, the crown is just one part of the whole mace, indicating the balance of power.

⑪ Humanities

An Election Entertainment, William Hogarth, 1755

This painting is one of Hogarth's series *Four Prints of an Election* that depicts the corruption of British politics. This painting shows politicians at a Whig banquet.

⑫ Primary Source: Art

1. Have students look at the Primary Source Art on this page.
2. **Ask** students the Primary Source: Art question: Which details in this depiction of a tavern dinner attended by Whig candidates serve Hogarth's satiric purpose?
   Possible response: The painting shows each corrupt politician eating and drinking, surrounded by people who are attending to him in various ways. Meanwhile, the darkness of Hogarth's painting suggests the corruption.

Differentiated Instruction for Universal Access

Culturally Responsive Instruction

Culture Focus Sir Robert Peel speaks strongly against reform. Discuss with students the costs and benefits of questioning the status quo and seeking change. Consider what types of reforms might be points of discussion in your community. Also ask students to share any examples with which they are familiar, from the past or from other places they have lived.

⓭ Background

With what seems like the whole future of England riding on the vote to pass the Reform Bill, the moments of tallying are tense indeed. Thomas Babington Macaulay recounts them vividly here—and with all the pleasure of the victor (unfortunately, the bill failed to pass the House of Lords after the vote Macaulay reports in the House of Commons). This personal letter to a friend reveals an insider's view of the working of government during an exciting time in England's history.

⓮ Primary Source

Letter

1. Have students skim the letter before reading it more closely.
2. Then, **ask** the Primary Source question: What are two subjects you might learn about by reading this letter?
   Answer: Students may learn about the Reform Bill—what it sought to change, who opposed it, who supported it—and why it was of special importance to Macaulay.

Ⓒ COMMON CORE ▪ RESEARCH PROJECT

ON THE PASSING OF THE REFORM BILL

Thomas Babington Macaulay

⓭ **BACKGROUND Macaulay was elected to Parliament in 1830, when his party, the Whigs, began the fight to pass the First Reform Bill. A talented writer and orator, he was in an excellent position to report on the great debate that was raging over the bill. The following letter, written to his good friend and fellow lawyer Thomas Flower Ellis, describes the excitement of the Reform Bill's passage—by just one vote—in Parliament's House of Commons.**

Dear Ellis,

I have little news for you, except what you will learn from the papers as well as from me. It is clear that the Reform Bill must pass, either in this or in another Parliament. The majority of one does not appear to me, as it does to you, by any means inauspicious. We should perhaps have had a better plea for a dissolution if the majority had been the other way. But surely a dissolution under such circumstances would have been a most alarming thing. If there should be a dissolution now there will not be that ferocity in the public mind which there would have been if the House of Commons had refused to entertain the Bill at all.—I confess that, till we had a majority, I was half inclined to tremble at the storm which we had raised. At present I think that we are absolutely certain of victory, and of victory without commotion.

Such a scene as the division of last Tuesday I never saw, and never expect to see again. If I should live fifty years the impression of it will be as fresh and sharp in my mind as if it had just taken place. It was like seeing Caesar stabbed in the Senate House,[1] or seeing Oliver taking the mace from the table, a sight to be seen only once and never to be forgotten. The crowd overflowed the House in every part. When the strangers were cleared out and the doors locked we had six hundred and eight members present, more by fifty five than

Vocabulary
inauspicious (in´ ô spi´ shəs) *adj.* not promising a good outcome; unfavorable

⓮ **Primary Source**
What are two subjects you might learn something about by reading this letter?

1. **Caesar** (sē´ zər) **stabbed in the Senate House** Emperor Julius Caesar, assassinated in the legislative council of ancient Rome.

Enrichment: Investigating Culture

Letter Writing

Before the days of e-mail, many letters were written by hand. Because of this, the quality of one's handwriting was often a point of pride. By using different types of paper and ink, people could also distinguish their personal letters. Some letter writers developed shorthand versions of common words—similar to what people do today while text messaging.

Activity: Examine Letters Have students locate online or in a local library some handwritten letters from the 1800s. Ask students to examine them closely and record what they learn, using the **Enrichment: Investigating Culture** worksheet, ***Professional Development Guidebook,*** page 223.

ever were at a division before. The Ayes and Noes were like two vollies of cannon from opposite sides of a field of battle. When the opposition went out into the lobby,—an operation by the by which took up twenty minutes or more,—we spread ourselves over the benches on both sides of the House. For there were many of us who had not been able to find a seat during the evening. When the doors were shut we began to speculate on our numbers. Everybody was desponding. "We have lost it. We are only two hundred and eighty at most. I do not think we are two hundred and fifty. They are three hundred. Alderman Thompson has counted them. He says they are two hundred and ninety-nine." This was the talk on our benches. I wonder that men who have been long in parliament do not acquire a better coup d'œil[2] for numbers. The House when only the Ayes were in it looked to me a very fair house,—much fuller than it generally is even

2. **coup d'œil** (ko͞o dëy´) glance.

16 ▲ **Primary Source Art** Does Hogarth's portrayal of voters attending the polling booth for an election suggest that the electoral process is fair? Why or why not? **[Infer]**

17 **Reading Check** What scene does Macaulay describe in his letter?

15 Humanities

The Polling, William Hogarth, 1758

This painting is one of Hogarth's series *Four Prints of an Election* that depicts the corruption of British politics. This painting shows an election for a member of Parliament.

16 Primary Source: Art

1. Have students look at the Primary Source Art on this page.
2. **Ask** students the Primary Source: Art question: Does Hogarth's portrayal of voters attending the polling booth for an election suggest that the electoral process is fair? Why or why not?
   Answer: No; there seems to be a lot of questionable activity in the painting—poor, sickly people being carried in by rich people who are whispering to them—suggesting that the election is corrupt.

17 Reading Check

Answer: Macaulay describes the crowd that gathered to vote for and against the Reform Bill.

Differentiated Instruction for Universal Access

Strategy for Special-Needs Students

Have students read portions of "On the Passing of the Reform Bill" with teacher guidance. Discuss with students what Macaulay's purpose was, who his audience was, and how his letter functioned as a type of political commentary.

Strategy for Less Proficient Readers

Remind students that "On the Passing of the Reform Bill" was a private letter intended to be read by Macaulay's friend and political ally. Encourage students to set a purpose for themselves as they read with teacher guidance, gleaning details and information pertaining to Macaulay's agenda.

⓲ Literature in Context

Vocabulary Connection

The Parliament of England, like the U.S. Congress, is divided into two houses. In Macaulay's day, both had to agree before a bill became a law; since that time, the situation has changed. The House of Lords has virtually no political power in England today. Nor does the king or queen. The elected members of the House of Commons—along with the elected prime minister, who also is a member of the House of Commons—are Britain's lawmakers.

Connect to the Literature

1. Invite volunteers to give a brief description of the U.S. Congress and the ways in which it differs from Parliament.
2. Then, **ask** the Connect to the Literature question: What effect does a knowledge of the terminology have on your ability to understand the message of this work? Explain.
   Possible response: Understanding the terminology makes it easier for readers to follow the action in the piece and to get a feeling for the underlying emotions without being distracted by unfamiliar words.

18 LITERATURE IN CONTEXT

Vocabulary Connection

Government Terms
The following terms in the selection refer to British government:

Parliament the bicameral (two-house) legislative body of Britain

dissolution dismissal of Parliament in order to hold new elections; if major legislation fails, the prime minister resigns and Parliament is dissolved.

House of Commons the house of Parliament made up of elected members and led by the prime minister

House of Lords the house of Parliament whose membership is hereditary or by appointment

mace the symbol of the authority of the Speaker of the House of Commons. By demanding the removal of the mace in 1653, Puritan leader Oliver Cromwell (1599–1658) overrode Parliamentary authority and became virtual dictator of England.

Ayes and Noes respectively, votes in favor of and votes against a bill

tellers those appointed to count votes in Parliament

Connect to the Literature

What effect does a knowledge of the terminology have on your ability to understand the message of this work? Explain.

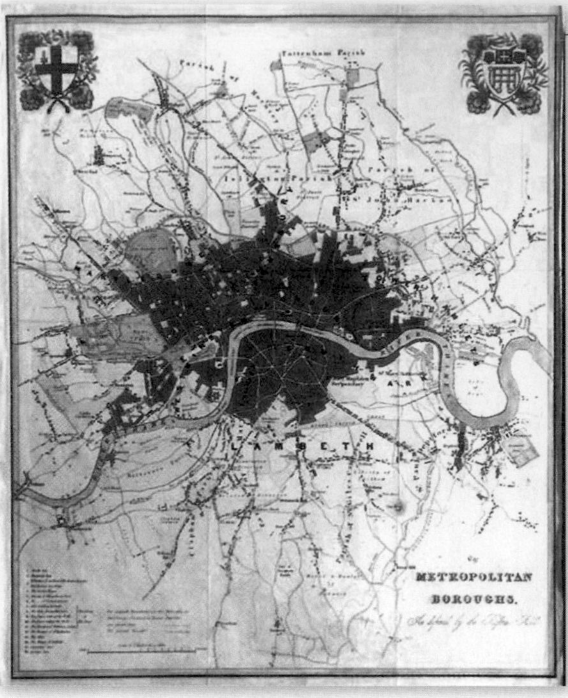

on debates of considerable interest. I had no hope however of three hundred. As the tellers passed along our lowest row on the left hand side the interest was insupportable,—two hundred and ninety-one:—two hundred and ninety-two:—we were all standing up and stretching forward, telling with the tellers. At three hundred there was a short cry of joy, at three hundred and two another—suppressed however in a moment. For we did not yet know what the hostile force might be. We knew however that we could not be severely beaten. The doors were thrown open and in they came. Each of them as he entered brought some different report of their numbers. It must have been impossible, as you may conceive, in the lobby, crowded as they must have been, to form any exact estimate. First we heard that they were three hundred and three—then the number rose to three hundred and ten, then went down to three hundred and seven. Alexander Baring told me that he had counted and that they were three hundred and four. We were all breathless with anxiety, when Charles Wood who stood near the door jumped on a bench and cried out, "They are only three hundred and one." We set up a shout that you might have heard to Charing Cross[3]—waving our hats—stamping against the floor and

3. **Charing Cross** London neighborhood some distance from the Houses of Parliament.

Enrichment: Analyzing Historical Patterns, Trends, and Periods

Voting Reforms

The Reform Bills were a series of laws enacted in England in 1832, 1867, 1884, 1918, and 1928 that expanded the British voting system. Have students research how voting conditions developed in these five steps from 1832 to 1928.

Activity: Timeline Have students work in groups to create timelines that show the progression of voting reform. Suggest that they take notes in the **Enrichment: Analyzing Historical Patterns, Trends, and Periods** worksheet, ***Professional Development Guidebook,*** page 231.

clapping our hands. The tellers scarcely got through the crowd:—for the house was thronged up to the table, and all the floor was fluctuating with heads like the pit of a theater. But you might have heard a pin drop as Duncannon read the numbers. Then again the shouts broke out—and many of us shed tears—I could scarcely refrain. And the jaw of Peel fell; and the face of Twiss[4] was as the face of a damned soul; and Herries[5] looked like Judas taking his neck-cloth off for the last operation. We shook hands and clapped each other on the back, and went out laughing, crying, and huzzaing into the lobby. And no sooner were the outer doors opened than another shout answered that within the house. All the passages and the stairs into the waiting rooms were thronged by people who had waited till four in the morning to know the issue. We passed through a narrow lane between two thick masses of them; and all the way down they were shouting and waving their hats; till we got into the open air. I called a cabriolet—and the first thing the driver asked was, "Is the Bill carried?"—"Yes, by one." "Thank God for it, Sir." And away I rode to Grey's Inn—and so ended a scene which will probably never be equalled till the reformed Parliament wants reforming; and that I hope will not be till the days of our grandchildren—till that truly orthodox and apostolical person Dr. Francis Ellis[6] is an archbishop of eighty.

19 ◂ Critical Viewing
The map shows London electoral boroughs as defined by the Reform Bill. Based on your knowledge of the bill, what can you assume about the voters in these boroughs? **[Apply]**

Vocabulary
orthodox (ôr´ thə däks´) *adj.* conforming to established beliefs

4. **Twiss** Horace Twiss, another Tory who opposed the bill.
5. **Herries** J. C. Herries, another Tory who opposed the bill.
6. **Francis Ellis** six-year-old son of Thomas Ellis.

Critical Reading

1. **Key Ideas and Details (a)** To what two historic events does Macaulay compare the scene of division he witnessed in Parliament? **(b) Interpret:** What do these comparisons stress about the scene?
2. **Craft and Structure (a)** What was the outcome of the vote in the House of Commons for the Reform Bill, as reported by Macaulay? **(b) Analyze:** In what ways does he make the procedure exciting and dramatic?
3. **Integration of Knowledge and Ideas (a)** According to Macaulay, what was happening outside the House of Commons during and after the vote? **(b) Infer:** What do these details suggest about the public's view of the vote on the Reform Bill?

Cite textual evidence to support your responses.

19 Critical Viewing

1. Have students study the map on page 906.
2. Then, **ask** students the Critical Viewing question: Based on your knowledge of the bill, what can you assume about the voters in these boroughs?
Answer: The voters are middle-class men, and most of them have not voted before.

ASSESS

Answers

Before students respond, you may wish to have them write a brief objective summary of the selection. As they answer the questions below, remind them to support their answers with evidence from the text.

1. (a) Macaulay compared the scene to "seeing Caesar stabbed in the Senate House, or seeing Oliver taking the mace from the table." (b) **Possible response:** These comparisons stress that it was a time of great tension, and it was extremely dramatic and memorable.
2. (a) The number of members for passage of the bill was larger, so they won. (b) **Possible response:** By detailing the counting of the members and the votes, Macaulay builds suspense about the outcome.
3. (a) Crowds had gathered outside and stayed until four in the morning to hear the ruling. Upon hearing the bill had passed, the crowd was celebrating. (b) These details show us that the public was very much in favor of the Reform Bill.

Differentiated Instruction for Universal Access

Support for Less Proficient Readers
To aid in understanding, have pairs of students paraphrase the letter, breaking it down into shorter, more manageable sentences. Encourage students to use a dictionary to look up the meanings of any words they do not understand.

EL Support for English Learners
The scene in which the votes are counted can be easier to follow if the counts are written out as numerals. Have students pair up to trace the number count for each side of the debate. Ask them to determine what the exact count was when all votes were in. **Answer:** The vote was 302 to 301.

Answers

Comparing Primary Sources

1. (a) Peel uses an allusion to a world event. (b) Lord Russell uses charged language. (c) **Possible response:** Russell's approach is more effective, because it is more subtle.
2. (a) **Possible response:** evidence—Russell: "election in Yorkshire cost £150,000, Peel: Peel does not provide evidence; inferences—Russell: the current system leads to corruption, Peel: it is not a good time to shake up the country with reforms; assumptions—Russell: "in adding to the constituency, we are providing for the moral....improvement of the country", Peel: "the people of this country are grossly deceived"; claims—Russell: , Peel: "country still agitated by...French Revolution"; relationships among these—Russell: Russell links each of his arguments, Peel: Peel tries to link Reform to social upheaval; evaluation of merits—Russell: adding people to the constituency of Parliament will strengthen the country; Peel: Reform will destroy "the only sure foundations of government..." (b) Students should support their answers.
3. (a) Macaulay uses allusions, inductive reasoning, charged language, and imagery. (b) Macaulay uses these techniques to enhance his description of the events. The other men are having to be formal while trying to persuade people to agree with them and cannot be as creative or free with the language they use.

COMMON CORE ▪ RESEARCH PROJECT

Parliamentary Debate • Letter

Comparing Primary Sources

Refer to your Note-Taking Guide to complete these questions.

1. **(a)** In his opening paragraph, what approach does Sir Robert Peel take to convince others not to support the Reform Bill? **(b)** In contrast, what basic approach does Lord Russell outline in his opening paragraph? **(c)** Which approach seems more effective to you? Why?
2. **(a)** Using a chart like the one below, compare the language that Russell and Peel use in their speeches. Explain the meaning of technical terms and figurative language and the connotations of charged language. **(b)** In your opinion, which man uses language more persuasively? Why?

Type of Language	Lord John Russell	Sir Robert Peel
Precise (including technical) language		
Charged language		
Imagery and figurative language		
Parallelism		

3. **(a)** Which rhetorical devices does Macaulay use? **(b)** Compare and contrast his use of these devices with that of the debaters. Does his purpose differ from theirs? Explain.

Common Core State Standards

Reading Informational Text
8. Delineate and evaluate the reasoning in seminal U.S. texts, including the application of constitutional principles and use of legal reasoning and the premises, purposes, and arguments in works of public advocacy. *(p. 909)*

Writing
7. Conduct short as well as more sustained research projects to answer a question or solve a problem; narrow or broaden the inquiry when appropriate; synthesize multiple sources on the subject, demonstrating understanding of the subject under investigation. *(p. 909)*
9. Draw evidence from literary or informational texts to support analysis, reflection, and research. *(p. 909)*

Language
4.a. Use context as a clue to the meaning of a word or phrase.

Vocabulary Acquisition and Use

Using Context Clues Revise each sentence so that the underlined word is used in a logical way.

1. The miser was typically quite <u>extravagant</u> with his money.
2. Most people show <u>reverence</u> for fools.
3. Her broad grin signaled an <u>inauspicious</u> outcome.

Content-Area Vocabulary For each item, choose the lettered word closest in meaning to the vocabulary word. Explain your answers.

1. electors: **(a)** candidates **(b)** voters **(c)** choices **(d)** elite
2. orthodox: **(a)** disobedient **(b)** spiritual **(c)** open-minded **(d)** conservative
3. grievances: **(a)** complaints **(b)** listings **(c)** armor **(d)** funerals
4. measure: **(a)** conclusion **(b)** question **(c)** remedy **(d)** contract
5. constituency: **(a)** candidates **(b)** voters **(c)** democracy **(d)** election

Etymology Study *Orthodox* combines the Greek word part *ortho-,* which means "straight," with the Greek word *doxa,* meaning "opinion." Someone or something that is *orthodox* conforms to the "straight" or established opinion. Why do you think certain dentists are called *orthodontists?*

Vocabulary Acquisition and Use

Using Context Clues

1. The miser was never <u>extravagant</u> with his money.
2. Few people show <u>reverence</u> for fools.
3. Her deep frown signaled an <u>inauspicious</u> outcome.

Content-Area Vocabulary

1. (b) voters—part of the electorate
2. (d) conservative—orthodox people maintain tradition
3. (a) complaints—things that make you grieve
4. (c) remedy—a measure is something proposed to improve a situation
5. (b) voters—given powers by the constitution

Etymology Study

<u>Orthodontists</u> help make your teeth straight.

Research Task

Topic: The Reform Bill Debate

The debate on the Reform Bill

The debate about reform was a battle between Britain's past and future. Greater representation in Parliament would mean greater economic benefits and more rights for many people, especially city dwellers.

Assignment: Stage a debate on the Reform Bill. Several students should take the roles of debating lords and members of the press, and others should act as the "commoners" who evaluate and judge the proceedings.

Plan your research, gather sources, and synthesize information. As a participant or an evaluator, list questions you need to answer, such as "What were the basic positions on reform?" Then, consult reliable primary and secondary sources, including the speeches and letter on pages 899–907, to gather and synthesize the answers.

Evaluate arguments. Review the arguments for and against reform, noting their strengths and weaknesses. Broaden the debate by consulting important United States works on government, such as the first section of Thomas Paine's *Common Sense.* Compare American arguments with those of the reformers. Debaters may incorporate or answer the strongest of them.

Listen responsively and frame inquiries. Listen carefully and respond effectively, whether as a debater or a member of the press. Take notes to identify the positions taken and the evidence in support of those positions.

Assess persuasiveness and formulate sound arguments. Identify each speaker's strong and weak arguments based on content; diction, or word choice; rhetorical strategies, such as appeals to logic or emotion; and delivery. Use a chart like the one shown.

Model: Questioning a Speaker's Appeal to Logic

Fact	Speaker's Conclusion	My Question
Recent French Revolution	Too soon for major reform in England	Why? Maybe time is just right.

Speak clearly. As a debater, communicate your ideas effectively by using rhetorical devices such as appeals to logic and emotion. Make eye contact and control your speaking rate and volume. Pause for effect. Enunciate words clearly and use purposeful gestures.

RESEARCH TIP

As you do your own research, keep asking yourself, "Is this information my opponent can use against me?" Keep an index of facts and arguments that are "pro and con" (for and against) each issue.

Use a checklist like the one shown to ensure that you have prepared as well as possible.

Research Checklist

- ☐ Have I answered the basic questions about issues and positions?
- ☐ Have I gathered information from reliable sources?
- ☐ Have I organized the information in a useful way?
- ☐ Have I formulated sound arguments?
- ☐ Have I anticipated counter-arguments?

The Reform Bill Debate

Introduce the Assignment

1. Review the research assignment. Point out that all three types of participants—debaters, members of the press, and evaluators—have research tasks and responsibilities. Help students choose the roles they prefer.
2. Ensure that students review in the textbook the relevant historical background, the basic political and social positions, and the debate selections.

Guide Student Research

1. Help students list the questions they need to answer before beginning the debate. These might include the following: What was the status quo and who supported it? Who supported change, and why? Why had reform not taken place before?
2. Students should explore a range of relevant sources. You might suggest that students begin their research with secondary sources, such as history books and encyclopedias, in order to get "the big picture" from scholars who have studied the primary sources. Then, they can move on to research relevant and recommended primary sources for support.

Think Aloud: Model Note-Taking During a Debate

Say to students:

When I am taking notes during a debate, I do not write down everything I hear. I ask myself, "What are the most important points the speaker is making?" I make a kind of shorthand list as I listen, using numbers or letters to identify points worth remembering and facts and expressions worth quoting. For the most part, I do not write down the comments that I want to make because that will take my concentration away from what the speaker is actually saying. If necessary, I can add my own comments later.

Assessment Resources

Unit 4 Resources

All EL **Selection Test A**, pp. 170–171

All **Customizable Test Bank**

All **Self-tests**

Students may prepare for the **Selection Test** by taking the **Self-test** online.

PHLit Online! All resources are available at **www.PHLitOnline.com.**

Guide Student Writing

1. Students should prepare written materials to have at hand during the debate: statements of positions, facts and statistical data for support, questions for the opposition, and responses to anticipated questions.
2. Students may organize their research in a variety of ways so that it is accessible during the debate. Note cards, tabbed pages, colored labels, and computer files can be used to make researched information useful and handy.

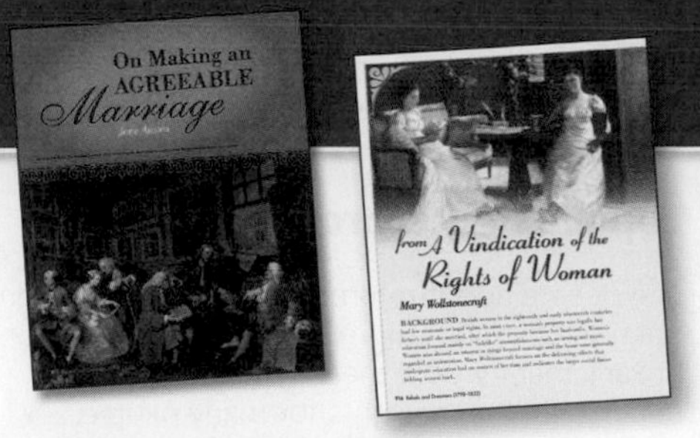

On Making an Agreeable Marriage • from *A Vindication of the Rights of Woman*

Lesson Pacing Guide

DAY 1 Preteach

- Administer the Reading and Vocabulary Warm-ups (*Unit 4 Resources,* pp. 172–175) as necessary.
- Introduce the Literary Analysis concept: Social Commentary.
- Introduce the Reading Strategy: Analyzing the Author's Purpose.
- Build background with the author and Background features.
- Develop thematic thinking with Connecting to the Essential Question.
- Teach the selection vocabulary.

DAY 2 Preteach/Teach/Extend

- Distribute copies of the appropriate graphic organizer for Literary Analysis (*Graphic Organizer Transparencies,* pp. 166–167).
- Distribute copies of the appropriate graphic organizer for the Reading Strategy (*Graphic Organizer Transparencies,* pp. 164–165).
- Prepare students to read with the Activating Prior Knowledge activities (TE).
- Informally monitor comprehension while students read.
- Use the Reading Check questions to confirm comprehension.
- Develop students' understanding of social commentary using the Literary Analysis prompts.
- Develop students' ability to analyze the author's purpose using the Reading Strategy prompt.
- Reinforce vocabulary with the Vocabulary notes.
- Assess students' comprehension and mastery of the skills by having them answer the Critical Reading, Literary Analysis, and Reading Strategy questions.

DAY 3 Assess

- Have students complete the Vocabulary activities.
- Have students complete the Writing Lesson and write an e-mail exchange. (You may assign as homework.)
- Administer Selection Test A or B (*Unit 4 Resources,* pp. 184–186 or 187–189).

Common Core State Standards

Reading Informational Text
6. Determine an author's point of view or purpose in a text in which the rhetoric is particularly effective, analyzing how style and content contribute to the power, persuasiveness, or beauty of the text.

Language 1.a. Apply the understanding that usage is a matter of convention, can change over time, and is sometimes contested.

Additional Standards Practice
***Common Core Companion,* pp. 143–150; 314–317**

Daily Block Scheduling
Each day in this Lesson Pacing Guide represents a 40–50 minute period. Teachers using block scheduling may combine days to revise pacing. In addition, teachers may differentiate and support core instruction by integrating components for extended and intensive support as students require. See the Guide to Selected Leveled Resources (facing page).

Guide to Selected Leveled Resources

RTI Tier 1 (students performing on level)			On Making an Agreeable Marriage • *from* A Vindication of the Rights of Woman
Warm Up	Whole class instruction; Group work	**Practice, model,** and **monitor** fluency, working **with the whole class** or **in groups.**	**Vocabulary and Reading Warm-ups B, *Unit 4 Resources,*** pp. 187–188, 190
Comprehension/Skills	Whole class instruction; Group work; Independent work	**Support** and **monitor** comprehension and skills development, having students complete the activities, graphic organizers, and interactive prompts **independently** or **as a class.**	• ***Reader's Notebook,*** adapted instruction and full selection EL ***Reader's Notebook: English Learner's Version,*** adapted instruction and adapted selection • **Reading Strategy Graphic Organizer B, *Graphic Organizer Transparencies,*** p. 173 • **Literary Analysis Graphic Organizer B, *Graphic Organizer Transparencies,*** p. 175
Monitor Progress	A	**Monitor** student progress with the differentiated curriculum-based assessment in the *Unit Resources.*	• **Selection Test B, *Unit 4 Resources,*** pp. 202–204 • **Open-Book Test, *Unit 4 Resources,*** pp. 196–198
Assess/Screen	A	• **Assess** student progress using Benchmark Test. • **Preassess** instructional needs using the Vocabulary in Context section of the test.	• **Benchmark Test 8, *Unit 4 Resources,*** pp. 210–218, including Vocabulary in Context diagnostic items

RTI Tier 2 (students requiring intervention)			On Making an Agreeable Marriage • *from* A Vindication of the Rights of Woman
Warm Up	Group work; One-on-one teaching	**Practice, model,** and **monitor** fluency **in groups** or **with individuals.**	• **Vocabulary and Reading Warm-ups A, *Unit 4 Resources,*** pp. 187–189 • ***Hear It!* Audio CD (adapted text)**
Comprehension/Skills	Group work; One-on-one teaching	• **Support** and **monitor** comprehension and skills development, working **in small groups** or **with individuals.** • As students complete the selection in the appropriate version of the *Reader's Notebook,* **monitor** comprehension frequently with group questions and individual instruction. • **Model** strategies while guiding students in completing the activities and prompts in the *Reader's Notebook,* as well as the graphic organizers. • **Practice** skills and **monitor** mastery with the *Reading Kit* worksheets.	• ***Reader's Notebook: Adapted Version,*** adapted instruction and adapted selection EL ***Reader's Notebook: English Learner's Version,*** adapted instruction and adapted selection • **Reading Strategy Graphic Organizer A, *Graphic Organizer Transparencies,*** p. 172 • **Literary Analysis Graphic Organizer A, *Graphic Organizer Transparencies,*** p. 174 • ***Reading Kit,*** Practice worksheets
Monitor Progress	A	**Monitor** student progress with the differentiated curriculum-based assessment in the *Unit Resources* and in the *Reading Kit.*	• **Selection Test A, *Unit 4 Resources,*** pp. 199–201 • ***Reading Kit,*** Assess worksheets
Assess/Screen	A	• **Assess** student progress using Benchmark Test. • **Preassess** instructional needs using the Vocabulary in Context section of the test.	**Benchmark Test 8, *Unit 4 Resources,*** pp. 210–218, including Vocabulary in Context diagnostic items

TIER 3 Tier 3 intervention may require consultation with the student's special-education or dyslexia specialist. For additional support, see the Tier 2 activities and resources listed above.

One-on-one teaching **Group work** **Whole class instruction** **Independent work** **A Assessment**

For a complete guide to selection support, including support for Advanced students, see the Overview of Resources in the frontmatter.

On Making an Agreeable Marriage • from *A Vindication of the Rights of Woman*

RESOURCES FOR:

- L1 Special-Needs Students
- L2 Below-Level Students (Tier 2)
- L3 On-Level Students (Tier 1)
- L4 Advanced Students (Tier 1)
- EL English Learners
- All All Students

Vocabulary/Fluency/Prior Knowledge

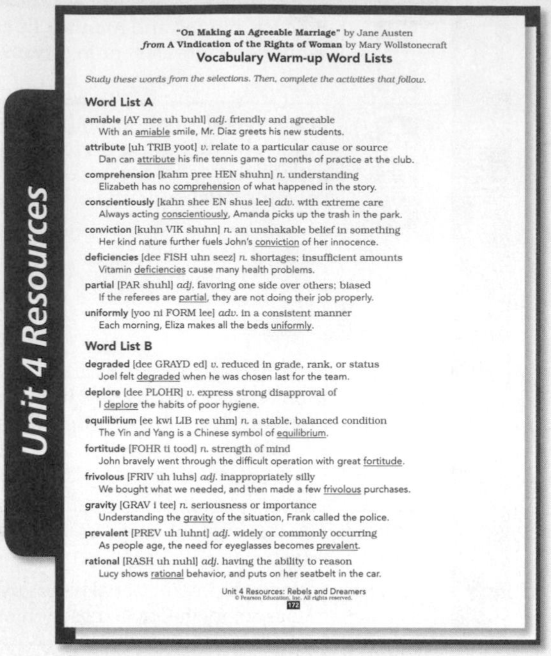
Unit 4 Resources

"On Making an Agreeable Marriage" by Jane Austen
from **A Vindication of the Rights of Woman** by Mary Wollstonecraft
Vocabulary Warm-up Word Lists

Study these words from the selections. Then, complete the activities that follow.

Word List A

amiable [AY mee uh buhl] *adj.* friendly and agreeable
With an amiable smile, Mr. Diaz greets his new students.

attribute [uh TRIB yoot] *v.* relate to a particular cause or source
Dan can attribute his fine tennis game to months of practice at the club.

comprehension [kahm pree HEN shuhn] *n.* understanding
Elizabeth has no comprehension of what happened in the story.

conscientiously [kahn shee EN shus lee] *adv.* with extreme care
Always acting conscientiously, Amanda picks up the trash in the park.

conviction [kuhn VIK shuhn] *n.* an unshakable belief in something
Her kind nature further fuels John's conviction of her innocence.

deficiencies [dee FISH uhn seez] *n.* shortages; insufficient amounts
Vitamin deficiencies cause many health problems.

partial [PAR shuhl] *adj.* favoring one side over others; biased
If the referees are partial, they are not doing their job properly.

uniformly [yoo ni FORM lee] *adv.* in a consistent manner
Each morning, Eliza makes all the beds uniformly.

Word List B

degraded [dee GRAYD ed] *v.* reduced in grade, rank, or status
Joel felt degraded when he was chosen last for the team.

deplore [dee PLOHR] *v.* express strong disapproval of
I deplore the habits of poor hygiene.

equilibrium [ee kwi LIB ree uhm] *n.* a stable, balanced condition
The Yin and Yang is a Chinese symbol of equilibrium.

fortitude [FOHR ti tood] *n.* strength of mind
John bravely went through the difficult operation with great fortitude.

frivolous [FRIV uh luhs] *adj.* inappropriately silly
We bought what we needed, and then made a few frivolous purchases.

gravity [GRAV i tee] *n.* seriousness or importance
Understanding the gravity of the situation, Frank called the police.

prevalent [PREV uh luhnt] *adj.* widely or commonly occurring
As people age, the need for eyeglasses becomes prevalent.

rational [RASH uh nuhl] *adj.* having the ability to reason
Lucy shows rational behavior, and puts on her seatbelt in the car.

Unit 4 Resources: Rebels and Dreamers
© Pearson Education, Inc. All rights reserved.
172

EL L1 L2 Vocabulary Warm-ups A and B, pp. 172–173

Also available for these selections:

EL L1 L2 Reading Warm-ups A and B, pp. 174–175

All **Vocabulary Builder,** p. 178

Reader's Notebooks

Pre- and postreading pages for these selections, as well as the excerpt from *A Vindication of the Rights of Woman,* appear in an interactive format in the *Reader's Notebooks*. Each *Notebook* is differentiated for a different group of learners.
The selections in the Adapted and English Learner's versions are abridged.

L2 L3 ***Reader's Notebook***

L1 ***Reader's Notebook: Adapted Version***

EL ***Reader's Notebook: English Learner's Version***

EL ***Reader's Notebook: Spanish Version***

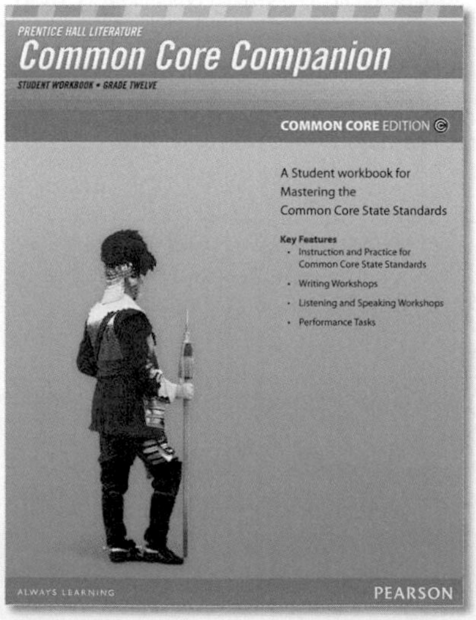

Common Core Companion

Additional instruction and practice for each Common Core State Standard

Selection Support

Graphic Organizer Transparencies

"On Making an Agreeable Marriage" by Jane Austen
from *A Vindication of the Rights of Woman* by Mary Wollstonecraft

Before You Read A: Comparing Appeals

Type of Appeal	Austen	Wollstonecraft
Logic	"he is I dare say such a Scholar as your agreeable, idle Brothers would ill bear a comparison with."	
Ethics	"any objection from his *Goodness*" "up to the precepts of the New Testament"	
Emotion	"And with all my heart I wish I had cautioned you" "unless you really do like him"	

Graphic Organizer Transparencies

164

EL L1 L2 **Reading: Graphic Organizer A,** (partially filled in), p. 164

Also available for these selections:

EL L3 **Reading: Graphic Organizer B,** p. 165

EL L1 L2 **Literary Analysis: Graphic Organizer A** (partially filled in), p. 166

EL L3 **Literary Analysis: Graphic Organizer B,** p. 167

Skills Development/Extension

Unit 4 Resources

Name ______________________ Date ____________

"On Making an Agreeable Marriage" by Jane Austen
***from* A Vindication of the Rights of Woman** by Mary Wollstonecraft
Literary Analysis: Social Commentary

Mary Wollstonecraft and Jane Austen were writers who were enormously gifted in the art of **social commentary.** These women looked closely at the world around them, thought deeply about what they saw, and put their views down on paper for the betterment and enjoyment of others. For example, Austen begins her letter to her niece by gently prodding Fanny to remember all her gentleman friend's wonderful qualities. But Austen's letter slowly transforms into an appeal to consider carefully before accepting a marriage proposal, thereby avoiding a marriage of convenience or a marriage for the sake of money. Her point, in the end, is that there is nothing worse than marriage without mutual affection and respect. Austen, who remained unmarried throughout her brief life, was nonetheless able to view the institution of marriage with great perception and evenhandedness.

Directions: *Read the excerpts from the selections, and answer the questions that follow.*

And from the time of our being in London together, I thought you really very much in love.—But you certainly are not at all—there is no concealing it.—What strange creatures we are!—It seems as if your being secure of him (as you say yourself) had made you Indifferent.

(from "On Making an Agreeable Marriage")

1. What point does Austen make about the fickle nature of some human relationships?

It is acknowledged that they spend many of the first years of their lives in acquiring a smattering of accomplishments; meanwhile strength of body and mind are sacrificed to libertine notions of beauty, to the desire of establishing themselves—the only way women can rise in the world—by marriage. And this desire making mere animals of them, when they marry they act as such children may be expected to act—they dress, they paint, and nickname God's creatures. . . . Can they be expected to govern a family with judgment, or take care of the poor babes whom they bring into the world?

(from *A Vindication of the Rights of Woman*)

2. What point is Wollstonecraft making about women's place in society?

Unit 4 Resources: Rebels and Dreamers

176

All **Literary Analysis,** p. 176

Also available for these selections:

All **Reading,** p. 177

EL L3 L4 **Support for Writing,** p. 179

L4 **Enrichment,** p. 180

Assessment

Name ______________________ Date ____________

"On Making an Agreeable Marriage" by Jane Austen
***from* A Vindication of the Rights of Woman** by Mary Wollstonecraft
Selection Test A

Critical Reading *Identify the letter of the choice that best answers the question.*

___ 1. According to Austen in "On Making an Agreeable Marriage," what is the most important reason for marrying someone?
A. wealth
B. personality
C. affection
D. respect

___ 2. What is Jane Austen's purpose in writing to her niece Fanny in "On Making an Agreeable Marriage"?
A. to tell her about the success of her book
B. to advise her on marriage
C. to share news of the family
D. to discuss their interest in music

___ 3. According to Austen in "On Making an Agreeable Marriage," what are Fanny's two biggest objections to her suitor?
A. He is poor and lives far away.
B. He is generous but lacks confidence.
C. He is selfish and proud.
D. He is too modest and good.

___ 4. Why does Austen tell Fanny in "On Making an Agreeable Marriage" that "I have no hope of writing anything to the purpose"?
A. She knows little about the man who wants to marry Fanny.
B. She knows that events will have changed before Fanny gets her letter.
C. She does not want to appear to tell Fanny what to do about marriage.
D. She realizes that Fanny will ignore anything she says.

___ 5. As social commentary, what does Austen accomplish in "On Making an Agreeable Marriage"?
A. She consciously analyzes marriage customs of the period.
B. She unconsciously depicts society's expectations for marriage.
C. She consciously points out the flaws in how society treats women.
D. She unconsciously criticizes how women allow themselves to be treated.

Unit 4 Resources: Rebels and Dreamers

184

EL L1 L2 **Selection Test A,** pp. 184–186

Also available for these selections:

L3 L4 **Open-Book Test,** pp. 181–183

EL L3 L4 **Selection Test B,** pp. 187–189

PHLit Online!

www.PHLitOnline.com

- complete narrated selection text
- a thematically related video with writing prompt
- an interactive graphic organizer
- highlighting feature
- access to all student print resources, adapted to individual student needs
- Spanish and English summaries
- adapted selection translations in Spanish

Online Resources: **All print materials are also available online.**

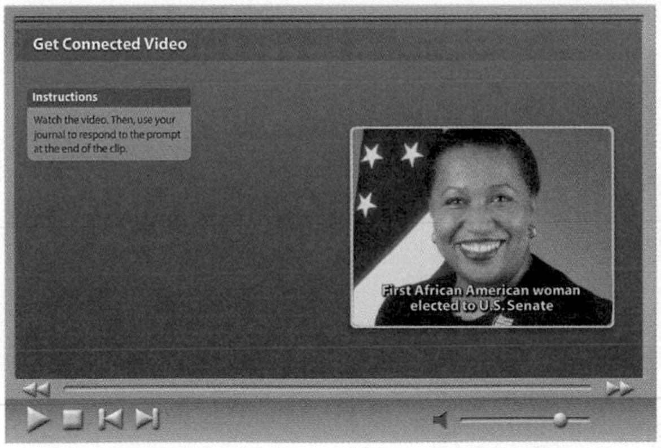

Get Connected! **(thematic video with writing prompt)**

Also available:

Background Video
All videos are available in Spanish.

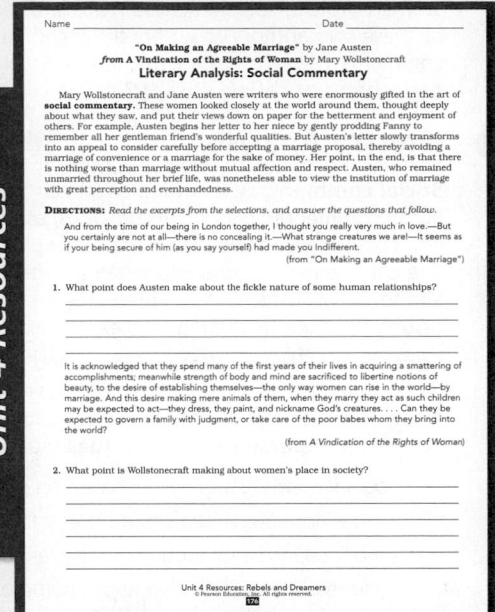

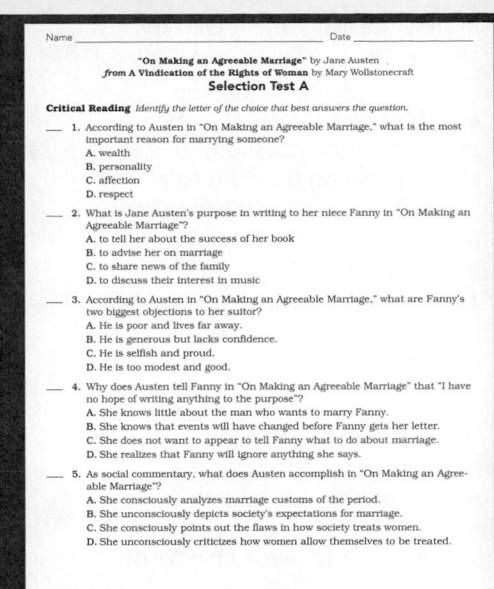

Vocabulary Central **(with graphics feature)**

Also available:

Writer's Journal (tools and activities for studying vocabulary)

PRETEACH

❶ Connecting to the Essential Question

1. Review the assignment with the class.
2. Remind students to consider events of recent history as they think about the question, such as women gaining the right to vote in 1920 and women working in politics. Then, have them complete the assignment.
3. As students read, have them look for ways in which each writer views women.

❷ Literary Analysis

Introduce the concept using the instruction on the student page.

Think Aloud: Model the Skill

Say to students:

In this lesson, we are learning about social commentary. Both Austen and Wollstonecraft speak to different audiences, yet both women offer their insights into society's treatment of women. I am intrigued by the way the two writers use persuasive language to make me think about how women were treated during their time period. As I read these selections, I will look for examples of social customs that may have led to problems for women.

❸ Reading Strategy

1. Introduce the strategy using the instruction on the student page.
2. Give students a copy of **Reading Strategy Graphic Organizer B,** page 165 in ***Graphic Organizer Transparencies,*** to fill out as they read.

❹ Vocabulary

1. Pronounce each word, giving its definition, and have students say it aloud.
2. For more guidance, see the ***Classroom Strategies and Teaching Routines*** card for introducing vocabulary.

Before You Read

On Making an Agreeable Marriage • from ***A Vindication of the Rights of Woman***

❶ **Connecting to the Essential Question** These authors address issues of women's role in society. As you read, find comments that suggest which of these two authors was more advanced for her time. Identifying such comments will help you answer the Essential Question: **How does literature shape or reflect society?**

❷ Literary Analysis

Social commentary is writing or speech that offers insights into society. Social commentary can be *unconscious*, as when a writer points to a problem caused by social customs without explicitly challenging those customs. The commentary is *conscious* when a writer directly attributes a problem to social customs. As you read these selections, *analyze the political assumptions* about women they expose, consciously or unconsciously.

Comparing Literary Works Austen and Wollstonecraft address widely different audiences for different purposes—Austen writes advice to her niece, and Wollstonecraft seeks to persuade the general reader. Both, however, use **persuasive techniques** that take the following forms:

- *Logical appeals:* arguments based on sound reasoning
- *Ethical appeals:* appeals to authority that establish credibility
- *Emotional appeals:* arguments that engage the reader's feelings

As you read, consider each author's purpose for writing. Then, identify how the persuasive appeals each writer uses reflect and support that purpose.

❸ Reading Strategy

Preparing to Read Complex Texts To **analyze the author's purpose,** or goals, use background knowledge and clues, such as the work's title. Then, determine how the purpose *affects the meaning* of passages. (Wollstonecraft's purpose explains her "indignation" in the first sentence.) Use a chart like the one shown.

❹ Vocabulary

amiable (ā′ mē ə bəl) *adj.* friendly; agreeable (p. 914)

vindication (vin′ də kā′ shən) *n.* act of providing justification or support for (p. 917)

fastidious (fas tid′ ē əs) *adj.* particular; difficult to please (p. 917)

specious (spē′ shəs) *adj.* deceptively attractive or valid; false (p. 917)

fortitude (fôrt′ ə to͞od′) *n.* courage; strength to endure (p. 918)

gravity (grav′ i tē) *n.* weight; seriousness (p. 918)

Common Core State Standards

Reading Informational Text
6. Determine an author's point of view or purpose in a text in which the rhetoric is particularly effective, analyzing how style and content contribute to the power, persuasiveness, or beauty of the text.

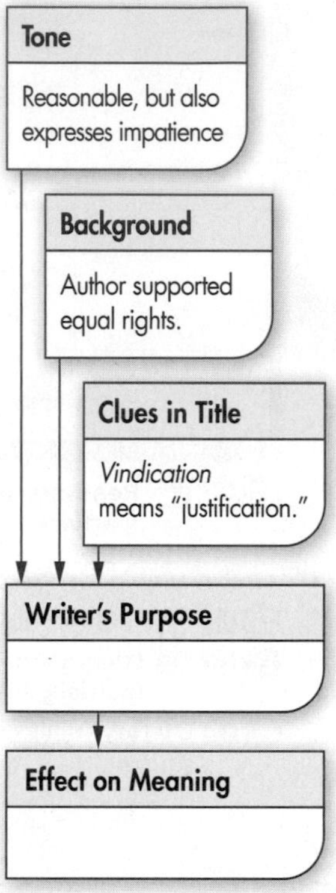

PHLit Online! www.PHLitOnline.com

Vocabulary Development

Vocabulary Knowledge Rating

Create a **Vocabulary Knowledge Rating Chart** (***Professional Development Guidebook,*** p.33) for the vocabulary words on the student page. Give each student a copy of the chart with the words on it. Read the words aloud, and have students mark their ratings in the Before Reading column. Urge students to attend to these words as they read and discuss the selections.

In order to gauge how much instruction you need to provide, tally how many students are confident in their knowledge of each word. As students read, point out the words and their context.

PHLit Online! **Vocabulary Central,** featuring tools, activities, and songs for studying vocabulary, is available online at **www.PHLitOnline.com.**

5

Jane Austen *(1775–1817)*

Author of "On Making an Agreeable Marriage"

Modest about her own genius, Jane Austen lived a quiet life devoted to her family. Although she never married, she nonetheless explored love, beauty, and marriage in her six novels, which include *Pride and Prejudice, Emma,* and *Sense and Sensibility.*

A Reserved Life Austen was born in Steventon, Hampshire, the daughter of a clergyman. The seventh of eight children, she was educated largely at home by her father. In her teens, Austen began writing parodies and skits to amuse her family.

An Anonymous Novelist As an adult, Austen put her gift for keen observation to work in her novels. Capturing the absurdities of social life with satirical wit, she makes brilliant observations on human nature. Like most women writers of the time, Austen published anonymously. As her identity became more widely known, she was honored by the Prince Regent a few years before her death.

(1759–1797) *Mary Wollstonecraft*

Author of *A Vindication of the Rights of Woman*

Mary Wollstonecraft, the mother of writer Mary Wollstonecraft Shelley, is recognized as one of the first major feminists. She wrote revolutionary works attacking the restrictions on women's freedom and education. The movement for women's rights has been influenced by her writings ever since.

A Passionate Educator The daughter of a textile worker and sometime farmer, Mary Wollstonecraft grew up in poverty, yet she pursued an education. She worked at various times as a lady's companion and governess. With her sisters and a friend, she established a girls' school near London. In 1787, she wrote *Thoughts on the Education of Daughters,* criticizing the poor education given to most females of her day.

A Voice for Women In 1790, when the writer Edmund Burke attacked the French Revolution, Wollstonecraft defended it in *A Vindication of the Rights of Man.* Two years later, she produced her most important work, *A Vindication of the Rights of Woman,* a landmark book on women's rights.

Daily Bellringer

For each class during which you will teach these selections, have students complete one of the five activities for the appropriate week in the ***Daily Bellringer Activities*** booklet.

Multidraft Reading

To assist struggling readers and to enhance reading for all, assign the text in chunks, as warranted by length, and apply multidraft reading protocols. For each reading, have students set the purpose indicated:

- **First reading**—identifying key ideas and details and answering any Reading Checks.
- **Second reading**—analyzing craft and structure and responding to the side-column prompts.
- **Third reading**—integrating knowledge and ideas, connecting to other texts and the world, and answering the end-of-selection questions.

For more guidance, refer to the ***Classroom Strategies and Teaching Routines*** card on Multidraft Reading.

5 Background

More About the Authors

Jane Austen

Jane Austen's advice to her niece is interesting in light of her own romantic life. Although she never married, she had several suitors, one of whose proposals she accepted, only to change her mind the next day.

Mary Wollstonecraft

In 1788, Mary Wollstonecraft returned from Ireland, where she had worked as a governess. She spent some years writing reviews and translations for the radical publisher Joseph Johnson, who later published her major works.

PHLit Online!
www.PHLitOnline.com

Teaching From Technology

Preparing to Read

Go to **www.PHLitOnline.com** in class or in a lab and display the ***Get Connected!*** slideshow for these selections. Have the class brainstorm responses to the slideshow writing prompt, entering ideas in the interactive journal. Then, have students complete their written responses individually, in a lab or as homework.

To build background, display the Background and More About the Author feature.

Using the Interactive Text

Go to **www.PHLitOnline.com** and display the Enriched Online Student Edition. As the class reads the selection or listens to the narration, record answers to side-column prompts using the graphic organizers accessible on the interactive page. Alternatively, have students use the online edition individually, answering the prompts as they read.

TEACH

1 About the Selection

Responding in a letter to her niece Fanny Knight, who had recently expressed doubts about her suitor, Austen not only advises her niece but also comments neatly on what makes a desirable marriage in Austen's social class in the early 1800s.

2 Activating Prior Knowledge

Tell students they will be writing an article for a women's magazine at the end of the eighteenth century in England. They should speculate on the rights women did or did not have at that time. Students should use conjecture to discuss women's feelings about careers, education, and marriage.

Concept Connector →

Tell students they will return to their responses after reading the selection.

3 Humanities

Marriage à la Mode: The Marriage Contract, by William Hogarth

This painting, which is the first in a series of six that Hogarth painted, shows the beginning of the marriage: the contract. At the left of the picture sit the bride- and groom-to-be. At the table, the two fathers work out the financial details of the arrangement.

Use this question for discussion:

Is the scene one of social or business activity? Explain.
Answer: The fathers are discussing serious business matters, but they are about a social arrangement.

1 2 On Making an AGREEABLE Marriage

Jane Austen

Marriage à la Mode: The Marriage Contract, 1743, William Hogarth, Reproduced by courtesy of the Trustees, National Gallery of Art, London

3

Text Complexity Rubric

	On Making an Agreeable Marriage	*from* A Vindication of the Rights of Woman
Qualitative Measures		
Context/ Knowledge Demands	Literary letter; cultural knowledge demands 1 2 (3) 4 5	Social commentary; historical knowledge demands 1 2 (3) 4 5
Structure/Language Conventionality and Clarity	Long sentences; informal diction 1 2 3 (4) 5	Long sentences; formal diction 1 2 (3) 4 5
Levels of Meaning/ Purpose/Concept Level	Moderate (social customs) 1 2 (3) 4 5	Moderate (women's rights) 1 2 (3) 4 5
Quantitative Measures		
Lexile/Text Length	1900L / 1,316 words	1730L / 756 words
Overall Complexity	**More complex**	**More accessible**

To Fanny Knight [1]

Friday 18–Sunday 20 November 1814

Chawton Nov: 18.—Friday

4 I feel quite as doubtful as you could be my dearest Fanny as to *when* my Letter may be finished, for I can command very little quiet time at present, but yet I must begin, for I know you will be glad to hear as soon as possible, & I really am impatient myself to be writing something on so very interesting a subject, though I have no hope of writing anything to the purpose.—I shall do very little more I dare say than say over again, what you have said before.—I was certainly a good deal surprised *at first*—as I had no suspicion of any change in your feelings, and I have no scruple in saying that you cannot be in Love. My dear Fanny, I am ready to laugh at the idea—and yet it is no laughing matter to have had you so mistaken as to your own feelings—And with all my heart I wish I had cautioned you on that point when first you spoke to me;—but tho' I did not think you then so *much* in love as you thought yourself, I did consider you as being attached in a degree—quite sufficiently for happiness, as I had no doubt it would increase with opportunity.—And from the time of our being in London together, I thought you really very much in love.—But you certainly are not at all—there is no concealing it.—What strange creatures we are!—It seems as if your being secure of him (as you say yourself) had made you Indifferent.—There was a little disgust I suspect, at the Races—& I do not wonder at it. His expressions then would not do for one who had rather more Acuteness, Penetration & Taste, than Love, which was your case. And yet, after all, I *am* surprised that the change in your feelings should be so great.—He is, just what he ever was, only more evidently & uniformly devoted to *you*. This is all the difference.—How shall we account for it?—My dearest Fanny, I am writing what will not be of the smallest use to you. I am feeling differently every moment, & shall not be able to suggest a single thing that can assist your Mind.—I could lament in one sentence & laugh in the next, but as to Opinion or Counsel I am sure none will [be] extracted worth having from this Letter.—I read yours through the very even[2] I received it—getting away by myself—I could not bear to leave off, when I had once begun.—I was full of curiosity & concern. Luckily Your Aunt C. dined at the other

He is just what he ever was, only more evidently & uniformly devoted to you.

Reading Skill
Analyzing the Author's Purpose What is Austen's purpose in claiming she has "no hope of writing anything to the purpose"?

5 **Reading Check**
What news from Fanny prompts Austen's reaction?

1. **Fanny Knight** Fanny Austen Knight was the daughter of Austen's brother Edward.
2. **even** evening.

6 ◀ **Critical Viewing** In what ways does William Hogarth's (1697–1764) satirical depiction of the signing of a wedding contract echo attitudes in Austen's letter? **[Compare and Contrast]**

4 Reading Strategy

Analyzing the Author's Purpose

1. Have students read the bracketed passage to themselves.
2. Remind students that by using their prior knowledge on the subject and considering the title of a selection, they may be able to determine the writer's purpose.
3. **Ask** the Reading Strategy question.
4. **Possible response:** Austen says this to offset any fear her niece may have that she will attempt to dictate her niece's actions. Indeed, Austen's letter is quite "to the purpose," giving solid advice.

5 Reading Check

Answer: Fanny's revelation that her feelings toward her suitor have changed prompts Austen's letter.

6 Critical Viewing

Answer: Hogarth suggests that the event is a combination of a social affair and a business transaction, echoing Austen's concern with the social conventions and monetary considerations surrounding marriage.

PHLit Online!

This selection is available in interactive format in the **Enriched Online Student Edition**, at **www.PHLitOnline.com**, which includes a thematically related video with writing prompt and an interactive graphic organizer.

Text Complexity: Reader and Task Suggestions

On Making an Agreeable Marriage		*from* A Vindication of the Rights of Woman	
Preparing to Read the Text	**Leveled Tasks**	**Preparing to Read the Text**	**Leveled Tasks**
• Using the Background on TE p. 911, discuss the difficulty of being unmarried when women had few possibilities for careers. • Discuss the tone students would use in trying to influence someone making a life decision. • Guide students to use Multidraft Reading strategies (TE p. 911).	***Knowledge Demands*** If students will have difficulty with the chatty nature of the letter, have them read it, focusing on the details about marriage. Then, have them read it again to identify Austen's basic advice about marriage and potential husbands. ***Evaluating*** If students will not have difficulty with the author's meaning, have them evaluate how effectively Austen achieves her purpose of advising her niece about marriage.	• Explain that most women in Wollstonecraft's time had poor educational opportunities. • Remind students that effective persuasion usually uses a combination of logical, ethical, and emotional appeals. • Guide students to use Multidraft Reading strategies (TE p. 911).	***Levels of Meaning*** If students will have difficulty with the author's meaning, have them read first to determine the main points she wants to convince her audience to accept. Then, as they reread, have them determine the key details she provides. ***Evaluating*** If students will not have difficulty with the author's meaning, have them evaluate how effectively she uses logical, ethical, and/or emotional appeals to achieve her purpose.

❼ Literary Analysis
Social Commentary

1. Have students read the first bracketed passage to themselves.
2. **Ask** the first Literary Analysis question.
Answer: These lines suggest that Austen's society valued social status ("His situation in life"); respectability; good companionship ("His uncommonly amiable mind"); and achievement, including distinction in scholarship.

❽ Literary Analysis
Social Commentary

1. Read the second bracketed passage aloud to students.
2. Review students' understanding of the distinction between conscious and unconscious social commentary.
3. **Ask** students in which category they would put Austen's letter to her niece.
Answer: Students should recognize this letter as unconscious social commentary.
4. **Ask** the second Literary Analysis question.
Answer: Austen suggests that her niece should not commit herself further unless she is prepared to marry her suitor; this advice reveals the assumption that the woman bears as much responsibility as the man in the development of a relationship.

Vocabulary
amiable (ā′ mē ə bəl) *adj.* friendly; agreeable

Literary Analysis
Social Commentary
What do these details reveal about the criteria for judging a suitor in Austen's day?

My dear Fanny, the more I write about him the warmer my feelings become. . .

Literary Analysis
Social Commentary
What assumptions about responsibility in courtship does this passage reveal?

house, therefore I had not to maneuver away from *her;*—& as to anybody else, I do not care.—Poor dear Mr J. P![3]—Oh! dear Fanny, Your mistake has been one that thousands of women fall into. He was the *first* young Man who attached himself to you. That was the charm, & most powerful it is.—Among the multitudes however that make the same mistake with Yourself, there can be few indeed who have so little reason to regret it;—*his* Character & *his* attachment leave you nothing to be ashamed of.—Upon the whole, what is to be done? You certainly *have* encouraged him to such a point as to make him feel almost secure of you—you have no inclination for any other person—His situation in life, family, friends, & above all his Character—his uncommonly **amiable** mind, strict principles, just notions, good habits—*all* that *you* know so well how to value, *All* that really is of the first importance—everything of this nature pleads his cause most strongly.—You have no doubt of his having superior Abilities—he has proved ❼ it at the University—he is I dare say such a Scholar as your agreeable, idle Brothers would ill bear a comparison with.—Oh! my dear Fanny, the more I write about him, the warmer my feelings become, the more strongly I feel the sterling worth of such a young Man & the desirableness of your growing in love with him again. I recommend this most thoroughly.—There *are* such beings in the World perhaps, one in a Thousand, as the Creature You & I should think perfection, where Grace & Spirit are united to Worth, where the Manners are equal to the Heart & Understanding, but such a person may not come in your way, or if he does, he may not be the eldest son of a Man of Fortune, the Brother of your particular friend, & belonging to your own County.—Think of all this Fanny. Mr J. P.– has advantages which do not often meet in one person. His only fault indeed seems Modesty. If he were less modest, he would be more agreeable, speak louder & look Impudenter;—and is not it a fine Character, of which Modesty is the only defect?—I have no doubt that he will get more lively & more like yourselves as he is more with you;—he will catch your ways if he belongs to you. And as to there being any objection from his *Goodness*, from the danger of his becoming even Evangelical,[4] I cannot admit *that.* I am by no means convinced that we ought not all to be Evangelicals, & am at least persuaded that they who are so from Reason & Feeling, must be happiest & safest.—Do not be frightened from the connection by your Brothers having most wit. Wisdom is better than Wit, & in the long run will certainly have the laugh on her side; & don't be frightened by the idea of his acting more strictly up to the precepts of the New Testament than others.—And now, my ❽ dear Fanny, having written so much on one side of the question, I shall turn round & entreat you not to commit yourself farther, & not

3. **Mr J. P.** Fanny's suitor.
4. **Evangelical** of or relating to a group of earnest Church of England members active in social reform movements at the time of the letter.

Enrichment: Investigating Daily Life

The Institution of Marriage

Although marriage is regulated by varying laws all over the world, social and cultural regulations often prove as strong as or stronger than civil law. Endogamy, for example—the tendency of people from a group to stay within that group—often limits marriage partners to members of one's own tribe, religion, or social class.

In Austen's day, endogamy was a key regulatory factor. The families often controlled the marriage, negotiating the dowry, the living arrangements, and other crucial matters related to the union and future lives of the couple involved. The courtship period was characterized by chaperoned visits.

Activity: Investigating Women, Then and Now Encourage students to examine the treatment of women in the late 1700s and early 1800s and today. Suggest that they record their ideas in the **Enrichment: Investigating Daily Life** worksheet, ***Professional Development Guidebook,*** page 224.

8 to think of accepting him unless you really do like him. Anything is to be preferred or endured rather than marrying without Affection; and if his deficiencies of Manner &c &c[5] strike you more than all his good qualities, if you continue to think strongly of them, give him up at once.—Things are now in such a state, that you must resolve upon one or the other, either to allow him to go on as he has done, or whenever you are together behave with a coldness which may convince him that he has been deceiving himself.—I have no doubt of his suffering a good deal for a time, a great deal, when he feels that he must give you up;—but it is no creed of mine, as you must be well aware, that such sort of Disappointments kill anybody.—Your sending the Music was an admirable device,[6] it made everything easy, & I do not know how I could have accounted for the parcel otherwise; for tho' your dear Papa most conscientiously hunted about till he found me alone in the Din[g]-parlor,[7] Your Aunt C. had seen that he had a parcel to deliver.—As it was however, I do not think anything was suspected.—We have heard nothing fresh from Anna. I trust she is very comfortable in her new home. Her Letters have been very sensible & satisfactory, with no *parade* of happiness, which I liked them the better for.—I have often known young married Women write in a way I did not like, in that respect.

You will be glad to hear that the first Edit: of M.P.[8] is all sold.—Your Uncle Henry is rather wanting me to come to Town, to settle about a 2[d] Edit:—but as I could not very conveniently leave home now, I have written him my Will & pleasure, & unless he still urges it, shall not go.—I am very greedy & want to make the most of it;—but as you are much above caring about money, I shall not plague you with any particulars.—The pleasures of Vanity are more within your comprehension, & you will enter into mine, at receiving the *praise* which every now & then comes to me, through some channel or other.—

Anything is to be preferred or endured rather than marrying without Affection . . .

5. **&c &c** et cetera (the & symbol, called an ampersand, stands for et, Latin for "and").
6. **device** trick; ruse; ploy.
7. **Din[g]-parlor** dining room.
8. **M.P.** Austen's novel *Mansfield Park.*

Critical Reading

1. **Key Ideas and Details** What is the problem Austen is trying to help her niece resolve?
2. **Key Ideas and Details (a)** What qualities does Austen find in Mr. J. P.? **(b) Interpret:** What does she mean by "Wisdom is better than Wit"?
3. **Key Ideas and Details Summarize:** In one or two sentences, summarize Austen's advice to her niece about Mr. J. P.

Cite textual evidence to support your responses.

ASSESS

Answers

Before students respond, you may wish to have them write a brief objective summary of the selection. As they answer the questions below, remind them to support their answers with evidence from the text.

1. Austen is trying to help her niece resolve how she should handle her suitor if she doesn't want to commit to marrying him.
2. (a) Mr. J. P.'s "amiable mind," "strict principles," "just notions," and "good habits" recommend him as a suitor. (b) Austen implies that while Mr. J. P. may not be as much fun as others, his steady character is more important than his lack of charm.
3. Austen suggests that Mr. J. P. is a good person and a worthy husband, but if her niece cannot convince herself of this fact, she should break off their relationship immediately in order to prevent giving the wrong impression to Mr. J. P.

Differentiated Instruction for Universal Access

Solutions for All Learners

Enrichment for Special-Needs Students
Students may be intrigued to learn more about the period in which decisions about marriage were discussed with relatives and considered with special care. Suggest that students research marriage customs of the time.

Strategy for Less Proficient Readers
Explain to students that the letters of famous authors often serve as a form of autobiography. Have each student write a letter to a friend, keeping in mind that the letter may turn out to be a historical document. Then, have students compare their letters to Jane Austen's.

Strategy for Advanced Readers
Ask students to discuss how Austen's letter functions as social commentary. Students should address whether the letter is unconscious or conscious social commentary. Direct students to **www.PHLitOnline.com** for more information on Jane Austen and her work.

❾ About the Selection

Wollstonecraft sadly reflects on the fact that women's poor educational opportunities, coupled with society's expectations about feminine beauty, have rendered women silly and vain. In what begins as a sad voice and gradually becomes a more strident one, Wollstonecraft attacks this degradation of women.

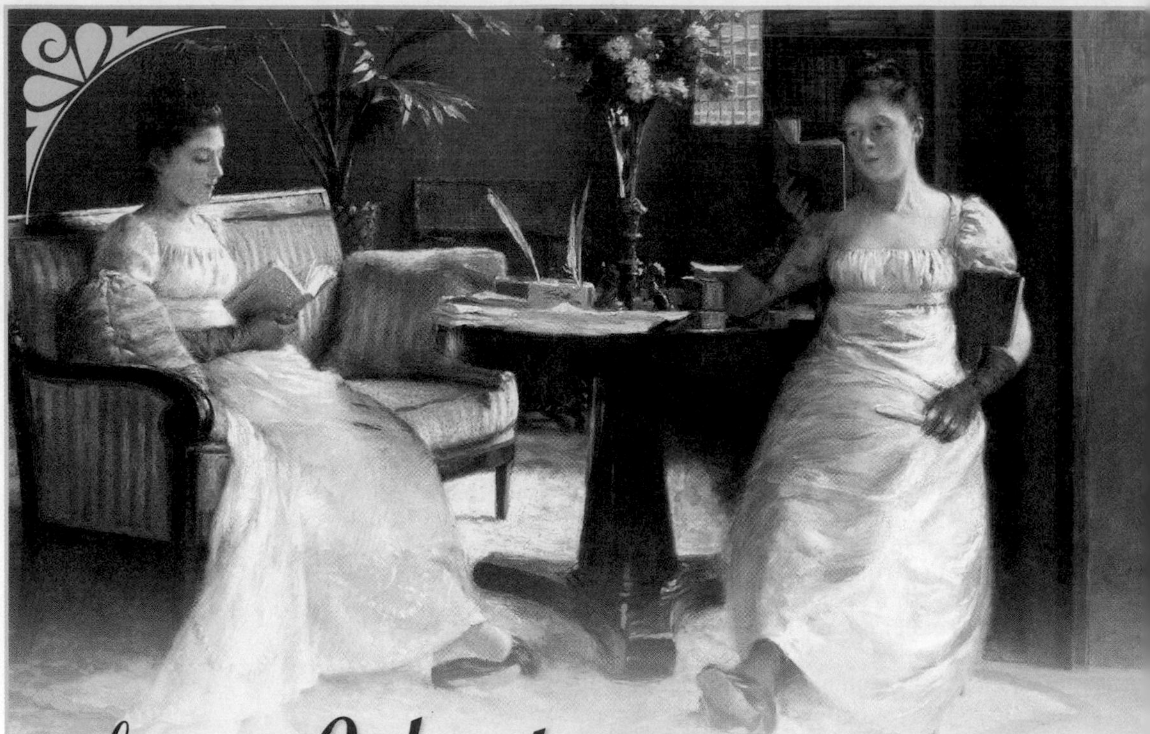

from A Vindication of the ❾ Rights of Woman

Mary Wollstonecraft

BACKGROUND British women in the eighteenth and early nineteenth centuries had few economic or legal rights. In most cases, a woman's property was legally her father's until she married, after which the property became her husband's. Women's education focused mainly on "ladylike" accomplishments such as sewing and music. Women who showed an interest in things beyond marriage and the home were generally regarded as unfeminine. Mary Wollstonecraft focuses on the deforming effects that inadequate education had on women of her time and indicates the larger social forces holding women back.

Vocabulary Development

Vocabulary Knowledge Rating

When students have completed reading and discussing the selection, have them take out their **Vocabulary Knowledge Rating Charts** for the story. Read the words aloud and have students rate their knowledge of words again in the After Reading column. Clarify any words that are still problematic. Have students write their own definitions and example or sentence in the appropriate column. Then, have students complete the Vocabulary Practice at the end of the selection. Encourage students to use the words in further discussion and written work about the selection. Remind them that they will be accountable for these words on the **Selection Test, *Unit 4 Resources***, pages 184–186 or 187–189.

After considering the historic page,[1] and viewing the living world with anxious solicitude the most melancholy emotions of sorrowful indignation have depressed my spirits, and I have sighed when obliged to confess that either Nature has made a great difference between man and man,[2] or that the civilization which has hitherto taken place in the world has been very partial. I have turned over various books written on the subject of education, and patiently observed the conduct of parents and the management of schools; but what has been the result?—a profound conviction that the neglected education of my fellow creatures is the grand source of the misery I deplore, and that women, in particular, are rendered weak and wretched by a variety of concurring causes, originating from one hasty conclusion. The conduct and manners of women, in fact, evidently prove that their minds are not in a healthy state; for, like the flowers which are planted in too rich a soil, strength and usefulness are sacrificed to beauty; and the flaunting leaves, after having pleased a **fastidious** eye, fade, disregarded on the stalk, long before the season when they ought to have arrived at maturity. One cause of this barren blooming I attribute to a false system of education, gathered from the books written on this subject by men who, considering females rather as women than human creatures, have been more anxious to make them alluring . . . than affectionate wives and rational mothers; and the understanding of the sex has been so bubbled by this **specious** homage, that the civilized women of the present century, with a few exceptions, are only anxious to inspire love, when they ought to cherish a nobler ambition, and by their abilities and virtues exact respect . . . .

The education of women has of late been more attended to than formerly; yet they are still reckoned a frivolous sex, and ridiculed or pitied by the writers who endeavor by satire or instruction to improve them. It is acknowledged that they spend many of the first years of their lives in acquiring a smattering of accomplishments; meanwhile strength of body and mind are sacrificed to libertine[3] notions of beauty, to the desire of establishing themselves—the only way women can rise in the world—by marriage. And this desire making mere animals of them, when they marry they act as such children may be expected to act—they dress, they paint, and nick-name God's creatures . . . . Can they be expected to govern a family with judgment, or take care of the poor babes whom they bring into the world?

1. **the historic page** the record of history.
2. **man and man** used here in the generic sense to mean "human being and human being."
3. **libertine** immoral.

⑩ *The* BRITISH TRADITION

The Literature of Protest
Mary Wollstonecraft writes in the tradition of protest in British literature. As early as the seventeenth century, the poet Amelia Lanier was speaking out for women's rights. In the nineteenth century, the Romantics were urging a fair distribution of wealth and power to the working classes. Twentieth-century poets, including Siegfried Sassoon, would chronicle the horrors of war. In the 1950s, the "angry young men," including Alan Sillitoe, would write grim portrayals of working-class lives. Wollstonecraft was an early voice in this tradition of protest.

Connect to the Literature

Identify four words that suggest Wollstonecraft's attitude of protest. Why do they convey this tone?

Vocabulary

vindication (vin′ də kā′ shən) *n.* act of providing justification or support for

fastidious (fas tid′ ē əs) *adj.* particular; difficult to please

specious (spē′ shəs) *adj.* deceptively attractive or valid; false

⑪ ☑ Reading Check

According to Wollstonecraft, for what does the "false system of education" train women?

⑩ The British Tradition

The Literature of Protest

It often takes a long time for protest literature to have a tangible result. Usually it is written on behalf of groups that have little or no power—otherwise they would not need someone else lobbying on their behalf. Also, before people change their behavior, it is necessary that they change their minds, and that is not a speedy process. There is one notable instance where protest literature led to a prompt response to a social ill. In 1906, American writer Upton Sinclair published *The Jungle,* which told the devastating story of the meatpacking industry and the horrifying life of those who worked in it. This led to a huge public outcry—perhaps because most people ate meat—and reform of federal food inspection laws.

Connect to the Literature

Point out that the literature of protest is a form of persuasion: The writer seeks to convince readers of an injustice and of needed corrective action. Invite volunteers to mention persuasive techniques, such as emotionally charged language. Then **ask** the Connect to the Literature question.

Possible response: Wollstonecraft uses the phrases "false system," "prejudices," "mistaken notions," and "artificial weaknesses." These phrases imply that her opponents' arguments are invalid, poorly conceived, and unsupported.

⑪ Reading Check

Answer: The false system of education trains women to be alluring, rather than affectionate wives and rational mothers.

Concept Connector

Reading Strategy Graphic Organizer

Ask students to review the graphic organizers in which they have determined the writer's purpose. Then, have students share their organizers and compare the clues they identified.

Activating Prior Knowledge

Have students return to their responses to the Activating Prior Knowledge activity. Ask them to explain whether their thoughts have changed and if so, how.

Writing About the Essential Question

Have students compare their responses to the prompt, completed before reading the selections, with their thoughts afterward. Have them work individually or in groups, writing or discussing their thoughts, to formulate new responses. Then, lead a class discussion, probing for what students have learned that confirms or invalidates their initial thoughts. Encourage students to cite specific textual details to support their responses.

ASSESS

Answers

Before students respond, you may wish to have them write a brief objective summary of the selection. As they answer the questions below, remind them to support their answers with evidence from the text.

1. Society encourages an idea of the feminine sex as more virtuous and weaker, which in turn produces an artificial weakness in women that "produces a propensity to tyrannize, and gives birth to cunning…which leads them to play off those contemptible infantine airs"—in other words they become manipulative, like children.
2. **Possible answer:** Wollstonecraft expresses a more radical view since she says women "are rendered weak and wretched by a variety of concurring causes." Her conviction is that women lack *independence* since their "strength of body and mind are sacrificed to libertine notions of beauty" and they can only "rise in the world—by marriage." Additionally, she believes "there is little reason to fear that women will acquire too much courage or fortitude"; therefore, it is unlikely that they will be *rebellious*. Her rejection of these societal norms was very radical for her time.

If, then, it can be fairly deduced from the present conduct of the sex, from the prevalent fondness for pleasure which takes place of ambition and those nobler passions that open and enlarge the soul, that the instruction which women have hitherto received has only tended, with the constitution of civil society, to render them insignificant objects of desire—mere propagators of fools!—if it can be proved that in aiming to accomplish them, without cultivating their understandings, they are taken out of their sphere of duties, and made ridiculous and useless when the short-lived bloom of beauty is over, I presume that *rational* men will excuse me for endeavoring to persuade them to become more masculine and respectable.

Vocabulary
fortitude (fôrt′ ə to͞od) *n.* courage; strength to endure

Indeed the word masculine is only a bugbear;[4] there is little reason to fear that women will acquire too much courage or fortitude, for their apparent inferiority with respect to bodily strength must render them in some degree dependent on men in the various relations of life; but why should it be increased by prejudices that give a sex to virtue, and confound simple truths with sensual reveries?

Women are, in fact, so much degraded by mistaken notions of female excellence, that I do not mean to add a paradox when I assert that this artificial weakness produces a propensity to tyrannize, and gives birth to cunning, the natural opponent of strength, which leads them to play off those contemptible infantine[5] airs that undermine esteem even whilst they excite desire. Let me become more chaste and modest, and if women do not grow wiser in the same ratio it will be clear that they have weaker understandings. It seems scarcely necessary to say that I now speak of the sex in general. Many individuals have more sense than their male relatives; and, as nothing preponderates where there is a constant struggle for an equilibrium without it has[6] naturally more gravity, some women govern their husbands without degrading themselves, because intellect will always govern.

Vocabulary
gravity (grav′ i tē) *n.* weight; seriousness

4. **bugbear** frightening imaginary creature, especially one that frightens children.
5. **infantine** infantile; childish.
6. **without it has** without having.

Critical Reading

1. **Key Ideas and Details Summarize:** According to the author, how do her society's notions of femininity encourage women to be childish and manipulative?
2. **Integration of Knowledge and Ideas** Which author expresses a more radical view of women for her day? In your response, use at least two of these Essential Question words: *independence, values, rebellious. [Connecting to the Essential Question: How does literature shape or reflect society?]*

Assessment Practice

Critical Reasoning **(For more practice, see the *All-in-One Workbook.)***

Many tests require students to evaluate the assumptions on which a writer's argument depends. Use this sample test item.

> …[I have] a profound conviction that the neglected education of my fellow creatures is the grand source of the misery I deplore,… for, like the flowers which are planted in too rich a soil, strength and usefulness are sacrificed to beauty….

The author's argument that women would be improved by education is based on the assumption that ________.

A nurture is an important factor in the formation of an individual
B women are less intelligent than men
C women are superior to men
D women are oppressed by their illiteracy

The author's argument is that education can fundamentally alter a person's values, judgment, and personality. The correct answer is **A.**

After You Read

On Making an Agreeable Marriage • from *A Vindication of the Rights of Woman*

Literary Analysis

1. **Key Ideas and Details** What unconscious **social commentary** does Austen's letter offer about the pressures that once limited women's choices?
2. **Key Ideas and Details** Which social and political assumptions about men and women does Wollstonecraft challenge in *A Vindication of the Rights of Woman*?
3. **Key Ideas and Details** Which assumptions about men's motives and desires does Wollstonecraft incorporate into her argument?
4. **Comparing Literary Works** Compare the kinds of appeals used by Wollstonecraft and Austen in a chart like the one shown.

Logic	Ethics	Emotion

5. **Comparing Literary Works** How does each writer's audience affect her choice of **persuasive techniques?**

Common Core State Standards

Language

1.a. Apply the understanding that usage is a matter of convention, can change over time, and is sometimes contested.

Reading Strategy

6. Compare Wollstonecraft's and Austen's purposes in writing, explaining the clues you used to **analyze the author's purpose** in each work.
7. Explain how each author's purpose affected the meaning of a passage.

PERFORMANCE TASKS

Integrated Language Skills

Vocabulary Acquisition and Use

From the vocabulary list on page 910, find a **synonym**—a word with the same or similar meaning—or an **antonym**—a word with the opposite meaning—for each of these words. Then, write an original sentence using each antonym or synonym pair.

1. justification
2. lightness
3. false
4. disagreeable
5. picky
6. cowardice

Writing

Explanatory Text Relatives still give well-meaning advice today, but they are more likely to do so in **e-mails** than in letters.

- Rewrite Austen's letter to her niece as an e-mail, keeping her ideas.
- Update the word choices, syntax, and situation to reflect modern times. For example, consider how you would update this sentence to reflect modern usage: "I read yours through the very even I received it . . . I could not bear to leave off, when I had once begun."

Assessment Resources

Unit 4 Resources

L1 L2 EL **Selection Test A,** pp. 184–186. Administer Test A to less advanced readers.

L3 L4 EL **Selection Test B,** pp. 187–189. Administer Test B to on-level students and more advanced students.

L3 L4 **Open-Book Test,** pp. 181–183. As an alternative, give the Open-Book test.

All **Customizable Test Bank**

All **Self-tests**
Students may prepare for the **Selection Test** by taking the **Self-test** online.

PHLit Online! All assessment resources are available at **www.PHLitOnline.com**.

Answers

1. Austen's letter reflects the pressures on women to choose men they can rely on to support them.
2. She challenges the assumption that women should be alluring.
3. She assumes that men like and encourage the present station of women.
4. **Possible response:** Austen: Logic: He is a good prospect; Ethics: She appeals to the values of Acuteness and taste and the ideas of Grace and Worth; Emotion: Do not marry without affection. Wollstonecraft: Logic: No "rational" man can disagree; Ethics: She calls on the ideals of education and good parenting; Emotion: Her indignation is clear.
5. Austen can make direct appeals to her niece's emotions and ethics. Wollstonecraft's effort to reach the general public requires her to use general arguments in suggesting reform. She employs persuasive language.
6. **Possible response:** Austen's purpose is to advise her niece, as her tactful tone makes clear. Wollstonecraft's purpose is to persuade by argument on a general issue, as is conveyed by her title.
7. Wollstonecraft's work is intended as a social commentary, so it clearly lays out a social problem. Austen's commentary is more subtle; she is writing a personal letter.

Vocabulary Acquisition and Use

1. synonym: vindication. This is a vindication, or justification, for the rights of women.
2. antonym: gravity. He smiled despite the gravity of the situation.
3. synonym: specious. Their specious statements were unconvincing.
4. antonym: amiable. One can't have an amiable relationship with such a disagreeable person.
5. synonym: fastidious. A positive word for picky is fastidious.
6. antonym: fortitude. If you lack fortitude in a difficult situation, you will display cowardice.

Writing

Evaluate students' explanatory texts using **Rubric for Letters,** ***Professional Development Guidebook,*** pages 262–263.

PREETEACH

Common Core State Standards

- Writing 2.a, b, c; 5, 6, 7
- Language 2, 3

Introducing the Writing Assignment

Review the assignment and the criteria, using the instruction on the student page.

Elizabeth McCracken on the Writing Process

Show students Segment 3 on Elizabeth McCracken on the *See It!* **DVD** or via the link in the **Enriched Online Student Edition** at **www.PHLitOnline.com.**

Writing Workshop

Create a Multimedia Presentation

Multimedia Presentation Written text is only one communication tool. Ideas can be communicated through a wide variety of other media, including film, radio, television, digital technology, and the Internet. In a multimedia presentation, a writer organizes words, images, and sounds into a coherent, informative, and lively presentation of a topic. Follow the steps in this workshop to create your own multimedia presentation.

Assignment Research, draft, revise, and present a multimedia presentation on a topic that interests you.

What to Include Your presentation should have these elements:

- an effective combination of words, images, and sounds
- a clear, consistent organization
- a coherent, well-paced flow of sounds, images, and information
- a variety of media appropriate to each aspect of the topic
- a strong, memorable conclusion
- an overall length of ten to fifteen minutes

To preview the criteria on which your multimedia presentation may be assessed, see the rubric on page 927.

Common Core State Standards

Writing

2.a. Introduce a topic; organize complex ideas, concepts, and information so that each new element builds on that which precedes it to create a unified whole; include formatting, graphics, and multimedia when useful to aiding comprehension.

2.b. Develop the topic thoroughly by selecting the most significant and relevant facts, extended definitions, concrete details, quotations, or other information and examples appropriate to the audience's knowledge of the topic.

6. Use technology, including the Internet, to produce, publish, and update individual or shared writing products in response to ongoing feedback, including new arguments or information.

7. Conduct short as well as more sustained research projects to answer a question or solve a problem; narrow or broaden the inquiry when appropriate.

Media Types and Sources

Presentations can include existing media as well as media that you create yourself. When you generate your own media, you begin by using equipment (hardware) to produce the raw material. Then, you use computer programs (software) to edit the media into a final form.

You can use multimedia software to assemble your media elements. Ask your teacher which programs he or she recommends.

PHLit Online! www.PHLitOnline.com

	Sources of Existing Media	Hardware to Generate New Media	Software to Edit Media
text	books, magazines, newspapers, Web sites, CD-ROMs, e-mails	keyboard; scanner; printer	word processor; multimedia software
photographs	books, magazines, newspapers, Web sites, CD-ROMs	digital camera; scanner; printer	photo-editing software
illustrations	books, magazines, newspapers, Web sites, CD-ROMs	keyboard; graphics tablet; scanner; printer	graphics programs
movies	television, DVDs, videos, Web sites, CD-ROMs	digital video camera	digital editor; animation software
sound	radio, CDs, Web sites, CD-ROMs	microphone; digital instruments	sound/music editor

Teaching Resources

- All *Unit 4 Resources*
  Writing Workshop, pp. 190–191
- All *Common Core Companion,*
  pp. 196–207; 226–244; 318–323
- All *Professional Development Guidebook*
  Rubrics for Self-Assessment: Multimedia Report, pp. 266–267
- All *Graphic Organizer Transparencies*
  Rubric for Self-Assessment: Multimedia Presentation, p. 168
- All *See It!* **DVD**
  Elizabeth McCracken, Segments 3 and 4

PHLit Online! All resources, including print and video, are available online at **www.PHLitOnline.com.**

Prewriting and Planning

Choosing Your Topic

Use one of these strategies to choose an appropriate topic:

- **Conduct a media flip-through.** Browse available sources, including magazines, television programs, and the Internet. As you scan for a topic, keep in mind that your presentation should include a variety of media.
- **List and itemize.** Start with a broad category that interests you, such as sports, travel, celebrities, or science. Then, jot down specific ideas that come to mind. Review your list, considering the media you might use to present your ideas. Choose a topic.

Broad Category	Nature
Specific Ideas	National Parks: Yosemite, Zion Canyon, Grand Canyon
Media	slides and video of the park, music, audio of animal sounds park visitors might hear, video interviews
Topic	Zion Canyon National Park: Yesterday and Today

Narrowing Your Topic

Consider time management. Choosing a specific topic can help make your research time more efficient and focused. If your topic is too broad, you might waste time viewing and collecting unnecessary media. For example, "Renaissance art" is too broad because it connects to an overwhelming supply of possible media elements. Instead, choose a specific focus, such as portrait painters or a particular painter, such as Raphael.

Gathering Details

Organize your material. After you have gathered a variety of media, outline your topic. Identify the media elements that best explain, illustrate, or set a mood for each aspect of your subject. Do a rough outline like the one shown, indicating where you expect to use each element.

Renaissance Portraits
I. Raphael
portraits show individuality
Visuals:
– portrait of *Castiglione*
Audio:
– courtly music

II. Later Renaissance Art
Titian (Venice)
Visuals:
– map of Venice
Audio:
– baroque music
(Bach or Vivaldi)

TEACH

Prewriting and Planning

1. Introduce the prewriting strategies using the instruction on the student page.
2. Have students apply the strategies to choose and narrow a topic and gather details.

Teaching the Strategies

1. Have students share topic ideas in small groups.
2. Encourage students to do keyword searches in a search engine to get an idea of the kinds of materials that are available online. Point out that the availability of materials should guide the development of outlines.

Think Aloud: Model List and Itemize

Use the following "think aloud" to model listing and itemizing:

I am interested in baseball. To narrow the topic, I list some things that come to mind: the World Series, the Boston Red Sox, Hank Aaron. Next, I consider what sort of media is available for each topic. I will search for media about the Boston Red Sox and their wins in the World Series.

Six Traits Focus

✔	Ideas		Word Choice
✔	Organization		Sentence Fluency
	Voice		Conventions

PH WRITING COACH Grade 12

Students will find additional information on multimedia presentations in Chapter 11.

Applying Understanding by Design Principles

Clarifying Expected Outcomes: Using Rubrics

- Before students begin work on this assignment, have them preview the **Rubric for Self-Assessment** to learn what qualities their multimedia presentations must have. A copy of this Rubric appears in the ***Professional Development Guidebook,*** pp. 266–267.
- Review the criteria in the Rubric with the class. Before students use the Rubric to assess their own writing, work with them to rate the Student Model (p. 926) using the Rubric.
- If you wish to assess students' multimedia presentations with either a 4-point or 6-point scoring rubric, see the ***Professional Development Guidebook,*** pages 282-283.

Drafting

1. Introduce the drafting strategies using the instruction on the student page.
2. Have students apply the strategies as they draft their multimedia presentation.

Teaching the Strategies

1. Explain to students that their text is not an ancillary to their presentations. It remains the most important part of the multimedia presentation. The images and audio should enhance, not overshadow, the text.
2. Suggest students write the text first and then fill in the "Audio and Video" column of their 2-column planning chart later.
3. Remind students that a multimedia presentation, like an essay, must provide a structure for the audience. It must introduce the topic, give information about it, and then draw a logical conclusion.
4. Point out the "Consider variety and flow" part of the lesson. Using fewer and more varied visuals helps viewers absorb information more thoroughly.

Six Traits Focus

✔	Ideas	✔	Word Choice
✔	Organization		Sentence Fluency
✔	Voice		Conventions

Drafting

Shaping Your Presentation

Select and position media elements. Your report should present information through both text and media elements. Using a two-column planning chart will help you be sure that you achieve an effective balance.

Text	Audio and Video

Follow a logical flow and focus. Before you draft your presentation, try rehearsing it in your mind to make sure that the ideas follow a logical arc, or overall focus. It can be tempting to include too many media elements. Make sure that each of your elements is genuinely appropriate. Remember your target duration of ten to fifteen minutes. Create a timed outline to plan how much time you will devote to each media element.

Providing Elaboration

Consider variety and flow. As you draft, try to create a varied, interesting experience for your audience. Make sure that your presentation flows logically from idea to idea and that each media element supports the focus and mood. These tips will help you avoid some common problems.

Avoid: a series of photographs showing the same scene from different angles

Improvement: a photograph of a scene, followed by a map showing the scene's location

Avoid: one song repeated throughout the entire presentation

Improvement: shorter music clips that set specific moods

Clarify and frame your media. For each transition you make from your script to a multimedia element, include an explanation so listeners can follow the connection. Transitional clauses such as the following can help you introduce media elements:

- This photograph highlights…
- As this chart indicates…
- In this footage, the speaker makes it clear that…
- This audio clip demonstrates…
- Notice how this diagram connects to the photograph…

Imagine that your media elements are like quotations in a literature essay. Just as you would introduce a quotation, you must also introduce a media element and integrate it into your presentation.

Common Core State Standards

Writing

2.c. Use appropriate and varied transitions and syntax to link the major sections of the text, create cohesion, and clarify the relationships among complex ideas and concepts.

Strategies for Using Technology

If students are using word processors to generate their scripts, encourage them to use different fonts or colors for the audio and visual portions of their reports. The different fonts will make it easier for them to make revisions later. Colors and fonts will also provide students with a script in which the speaking parts are easily distinguished from the audiovisual cues.

Writers on Writing

Elizabeth McCracken On the Writing Process

Elizabeth McCracken is the author of "Creating a Legend" (p. 728).

I am a very inefficient writer. I do thousands of drafts and throw out a lot of pages. I keep a journal when I write, a place I can play around with ideas, and I often write a page in the voice of a minor character. I tried it with the librarian as I was writing *The Giant's House*. It turned out she wouldn't shut up. She was cranky and talkative and ended up narrating the entire story. The passage here is one of the oldest passages in the book, which is maybe why I'm fond of it. All around it, I tore out pages and pages and pages—I bet I write at least twice as many pages as ever gets into a book—and somehow it always worked.

"I keep a journal when I write, a place I can play around with ideas."

—Elizabeth McCracken

from *The Giant's House*

People think librarians are unromantic, unimaginative. This is not true. We are people whose dreams run in particular ways. Ask a mountain climber what he feels when he sees a mountain; a lion tamer what goes through his mind when he meets a new lion; a doctor confronted with a beautiful malfunctioning body. The idea of a library full of books, the books full of knowledge, fills me with fear and love and courage and endless wonder. I knew I would be a librarian in college as a student assistant at a reference desk, watching those lovely people at work. "I don't think there's such a book—" a patron would begin, and then the librarian would hand it to them, that very book.

I worried about what my fellow librarians would make of my librarian, who's pretty stereotypically uptight and tweedy. I tried to make up for it by making her very romantic.

I hear my sentences when I write them, and I love semi-colons—they're just another kind of music.

Sometimes phrases stick in my mind for years before they come out in a book.

Elizabeth McCracken on the Writing Process

Review the passage on the student page with the class, using Elizabeth McCracken's comments to deepen students' understanding of the process of writing a multimedia presentation.

Teaching From the Professional Model

1. Show students Segment 4 on Elizabeth McCracken on the *See It!* **DVD** or from this page in the **Enriched Online Student Edition.** Discuss McCracken's approach to the storytelling process and her ability to create interesting characters.
2. Point out McCracken's use of a journal to keep notes and try out ideas for a character's "voice." Tell students that every piece of writing, even a multimedia presentation, has a voice. The voice can reveal the writer's personality, background, and even his or her sense of humor.
3. Review Elizabeth McCracken's comments about her own writing. Ask students to explain how they might "hear" their sentences as they write them, and what they might learn from listening to their writing.

Strategies for Using the Writing Process

Give students these suggestions for using the writing process in their multimedia presentations:

- Try to write many drafts of your multimedia presentation. By writing several drafts, you can play with ideas and how they might connect to your media elements. You can also take the time to step away from the writing—if you put your work aside for a few hours or overnight, awkward writing and transitions will be more apparent.
- Listen to your sentences as you write them. Even better, read your sentences aloud to a classmate and make sure that they flow smoothly and maintain the listener's interest.

PHLit Online!

Enriched Online Student Edition
Show or assign the video online at **www.PHLitOnline.com.**

Revising

1. Introduce the revising strategies using the instruction on the student page.
2. Have students apply the strategies as they revise their multimedia presentations.

Teaching the Strategies

1. Remind students that the audience can become confused if the text of a multimedia presentation and the audiovisual materials are not in sync. Explain that it is important for students to practice giving their presentations in order to find the places where images or audio or video cues may cause problems.
2. Review the concept of pace with students. Suggest that they think of their presentations in terms of a leisurely walk, not a marathon or a dash. If their rehearsals leave them feeling breathless or rushed, they should slow the pace by cutting visuals and using fewer audio cues. If the presentations seem too long, they can pick up the pace by changing or varying cues.
3. Encourage students to follow the example shown in the graphic organizer in which visuals are moved to create better pacing.
4. Emphasize that students should maintain eye contact with their audience and not be distracted by an excess of media elements.

Six Traits Focus

✔	Ideas	✔	Word Choice
✔	Organization	✔	Sentence Fluency
	Voice		Conventions

Revising

Revising Your Overall Structure

Improve your pacing. Practice your presentation, noting places where your pacing feels too rapid, too slow, or incompatible with the technology you are using. You may need to add more text for clarity or cut a media element that makes your presentation feel choppy.

Common Core State Standards

Writing

5. Develop and strengthen writing as needed by revising, focusing on addressing what is most significant for a specific purpose and audience.

Student Model: Revising for Smooth Flow

(Cue AUDIO) The pose exhibits the man's elegant manner, his head and hands ★ ~~(Show SLIDE C)~~ placed in the perfectly calm demeanor that a man of his stature would be expected to display Show SLIDE C; pause, then back to ~~(Show~~ SLIDE B)	AUDIO: selection from Bach's *Well-Tempered Clavier* SLIDE C: Detail of Castiglione's hands SLIDE B: Raphael's *Baldassare Castiglione* Full length

The student postpones showing Slide C to make the delivery smoother and to provide better pacing for the audience.

Revising Your Media

Evaluate your media and delivery. Rehearsal is vital for a successful presentation. Do a run-through, focusing on smooth oral delivery and accurate matching of media elements to ideas. Become comfortable with your script so that you can maintain eye contact with your audience and not read word for word.

Revise media elements. You may decide to improve media elements to make them more effective. Here are some common revisions:

- Shorten video segments that feel too long.
- Add labels or captions to art to emphasize important ideas.
- Crop photos to focus more closely on the subject.
- Adjust sound levels of audio narration or music.

Peer Review: Hold a test run for a small group. Ask them to use the Evaluation Form shown here. Talk with your viewers about elements that were confusing or ineffective and revise accordingly.

Evaluation

Rate from 1 to 5 (5 = very; 1 = not at all)

____ How clear is the overall focus?
____ How logical is the organization of ideas?
____ How appropriate are the media elements?
____ How smooth are transitions between elements?
____ How effectively is the running time used?

Which media element is most effective?
____

Which media element is least effective?
____

What change would most improve the presentation?
____

Strategies for Using a Graphic Organizer

Have students review "Student Model: Revising for Smooth Flow." It demonstrates the use of a two-column chart to synchronize text and audiovisual elements. Point out that the writer uses parentheses to set off cues, and capital letters to indicate words that are not part of the spoken text. The dividing line between the two columns clearly distinguishes the spoken text and cues from the audiovisual content. You may wish to provide students with copies of the Two-column Chart, p. 302 in ***Graphic Organizer Transparencies.***

SIX TRAITS WRITER'S TOOLBOX SIX TRAITS

Organization | Word Choice | Ideas | Conventions | Sentence Fluency | Voice

Developing Your Style

Integrating Media

It is important that all of the media elements work together. Use a chart like the one shown to help you evaluate the integration of these elements.

Media Element	Idea It Expresses or Supports	Is the idea clear? If not, consider how you can improve the way you handle this element or if you should replace it with something else.
Audio interview with art expert	Titian was a perfectionist. It could take him 10 years to finish a painting.	Clear
Video of people in a museum	Renaissance portraits were made for the wealthy, but today anyone can see them in a museum.	Not very clear; add a line of narration to explain the connection.
Brass theme by Mussorgsky	Raphael's portraits have an elegant simplicity.	This point would be better made with another musical selection, perhaps something by Bach.

Find It in Your Reading

Read or review the Student Model on page 926.

1. Locate elements of the presentation that work together.
2. In particular, consider how the audio and video work together.

PH WRITING COACH
Further instruction and practice are available in *Prentice Hall Writing Coach*.

Apply It to Your Writing

Review the script for your multimedia presentation.

1. Evaluate each media element you have included in your presentation. Ask yourself, "Why did I include this element?"
2. Decide whether each element clearly connects to a key idea. Consider adding narration and text labels or changing the order of media elements in order to make the ideas clearer.
3. Experiment with different combinations of images, music, and text. Preview combinations for a group and see if they work.

Developing Your Style

1. Introduce integrating media elements to students using the instruction on the student page.
2. Have students complete the Find It in Your Reading and Apply It to Your Writing activities.

Teaching the Strategies

1. Remind students that skillfully integrating media in a presentation is key to maintaining an attentive audience.
2. Point out that each media element should connect to the text directly. Students might add explicit captions to images or additional narrative text in order to integrate media seamlessly.

Find It in Your Reading

Review the Student Model and emphasize the student's use of tone, transitions, consistent organization, and a memorable conclusion.

Apply It to Your Writing

Repeat to students that rehearsal and practice and experimentation with media elements is the way to develop an outstanding multimedia presentation.

Six Traits Focus

✔	Ideas		Word Choice
✔	Organization		Sentence Fluency
	Voice	✔	Conventions

Differentiated Instruction for Universal Access

Strategy for Less Proficient Readers
Students may have difficulty with adding narration to connect ideas and media elements. Help them by reading essays or magazine articles that contain examples of transitions between ideas. You might also show sample slide presentations from classes you have taught. Challenge students to help each other brainstorm connecting sentences for classmates' presentations.

Enrichment for Gifted/Talented Students
Challenge students to help each other improve their presentations. Have students work in pairs and provide feedback—similar to the notes for the Student Model on p. 926—that highlights the strengths and weaknesses of the integration of media in a classmate's presentation.

Student Model

Review the Student Model with the class, using the annotations to analyze the writer's incorporation of the elements of a multimedia presentation.

Teaching the Strategies

1. Explain that the Student Model is a sample and that student scripts may be longer.
2. Point out how Kate uses slide changes to maintain focus on the topic. **Ask** students how this technique helps her report.
   Possible response: The focus continues to be on the artwork. The visual cues provide an overview of Renaissance art that changes quickly enough to maintain interest.
3. Note that Kate has used the same music at the end of her report as she did at the beginning. Note that reusing music creates a sense of continuity. Listeners will recognize the music, and it will remind them of what they learned at the beginning of the report.

Connecting to Real-Life Writing

1. Point out that multimedia presentations permeate modern life. Today, television is available all day long and in almost every public setting. From news reports to commercials, each segment is carefully scripted to include just the right amount of music, video, and narration in an effort to engage viewers.
2. Discuss with students memorable examples of multimedia, such as televised coverage of a presidential election or the documentary *An Inconvenient Truth*, featuring the slide show presentation created by Vice President Al Gore.

Student Model: Kate Vengraitis, Maplewood, NJ

Raphael's Art of the Portrait

Text	Audio and Video
[Cue AUDIO.] In the fifteenth and sixteenth centuries, art underwent a drastic change. [Cue VIDEO SLIDESHOW.] Each artist developed a unique style, sometimes blatantly trying to break the rules, other times creating innovative techniques. One common focus for Renaissance artists was the portrayal of individual personality. [Fade music.]	AUDIO: brass theme from Mussorgsky's *Pictures at an Exhibition* VIDEO: rapid dissolve from one slide to the next: Raphael's *Baldassare Castiglione* to Bronzio's *Portrait of a Young Man* to Titian's *Man with the Glove*
[Cue SLIDE A.] In the Early Renaissance, portraits remained somewhat formal. By the High Renaissance, though, there is a clear focus on the personality of the subject, as in this portrait by Raphael. [Cue SLIDE B; pause.] In this portrait, *Baldassare Castiglione,* every detail helps communicate the subject's inner self. The background remains a stately neutral shade, free of decoration, appropriate for a man such as Baldassare Castiglione, the author of a handbook on genteel behavior.	SLIDE A: timeline: Early / High Renaissance SLIDE B: Raphael's *Baldassare Castiglione*
[Cue AUDIO.] The pose exhibits the man's elegant manner, his hands folded with the composure that a man of his stature would be expected to display. [Show SLIDE C; pause, then back to SLIDE B.]	AUDIO: selection from Bach's *The Well-Tempered Clavier* SLIDE C: detail of Castiglione's perfectly calm demeanor SLIDE B
[Cue MUSIC.] [Cue VIDEO SLIDESHOW.] As this painting attests, Renaissance painters discovered complex ways to give insight into the individuality of their subjects.	AUDIO: same as at opening VIDEO SLIDESHOW: same as at opening

Dramatic theme music and a sampling of portraits establish the tone and topic of the presentation.

Transitions and pauses keep the flow of the presentation smooth.

Kate chooses music to reflect the melancholy mood of this portrait.

Information is consistently organized, with each new main idea illustrated by a slide.

Both the audiovisual and textual parts of Kate's conclusion are strong and memorable.

Editing and Proofreading

Check your presentation for errors in grammar, usage, punctuation, and spelling.

Focus on proper nouns and titles. Double-check the capitalization of names and places in your text elements, including labels and handouts.

Focus on spelling. Most words ending with the sound *seed* end with the spelling *cede,* as in *concede.* Three English words end in *ceed: exceed, proceed,* and *succeed*. Review your essay, circling words that end with this sound. Make sure your spelling of these words is correct.

Spiral Review: Conventions Earlier in this unit, you learned about correct subject-verb and pronoun-antecedent agreement. Check your presentation to make sure you have used these conventions correctly.

Publishing, Presenting, and Reflecting

Consider one of the following ways to share your writing:

Stage a showing. Deliver your multimedia presentation to your class. Speak slowly and confidently, and allow time for questions and answers.

Post your presentation. Create a final version of your report using multimedia software and post it to a class or school file-sharing site. If possible, invite visitors to post comments, and address readers' concerns or questions by posting updates with new information or additional arguments.

Reflect on your writing. Jot down your thoughts about the experience of creating a multimedia presentation. Answer these questions: What did you learn about presenting your ideas using audio and visual elements as well as words? What surprised you about presenting material to an audience?

Rubric for Self-Assessment

Evaluate your multimedia presentation using the following criteria and rating scale.

Criteria	Rating Scale (not very – very)				
Focus: How clearly do all of your media elements present your topic?	1	2	3	4	5
Organization: How well do you organize the presentation of information?	1	2	3	4	5
Support/Elaboration: How well do you integrate video and audio elements to support each aspect of your topic?	1	2	3	4	5
Style: How coherent and well paced is the flow of sound, images, and information?	1	2	3	4	5
Conventions: How correct are the grammar, spelling, and punctuation in your presentation materials?	1	2	3	4	5

Common Core State Standards

Writing

5. Develop and strengthen writing as needed by editing, focusing on addressing what is most significant for a specific purpose and audience.

6. Use technology, including the Internet, to produce, publish, and update individual or shared writing products in response to ongoing feedback, including new arguments or information.

Language

2. Demonstrate command of the conventions of standard English capitalization, punctuation, and spelling when writing.

3. Apply knowledge of language to make effective choices for meaning or style.

PH WRITING COACH

Further instruction and practice are available in *Prentice Hall Writing Coach.*

Editing and Proofreading

1. Introduce the editing and proofreading focuses, using the instruction on the student page.
2. Have students read their presentations, marking them for line edits.

Teaching the Strategies

1. Remind students that a computer's spelling checker will not accurately check proper nouns.
2. Suggest students use the "two-font rule" when editing visuals and titles. Too many fonts tend to confuse readers.

Six Traits Focus

	Ideas		Word Choice
	Organization		Sentence Fluency
	Voice	✔	Conventions

ASSESS

Publishing, Presenting, and Reflecting

1. Remind students to pay attention to the cues their listeners are sending during their presentations.
2. When preparing a file for sharing on the Internet, remind students to consider the file size of the inserted media elements—very large files will not be accepted by some file-sharing sites.
3. Ask students what changes in their presentations might have made the tone more consistent.

Strategies for Test Taking

A reading passage on the SAT or ACT may be accompanied by visuals and include questions that ask about the relationship between the visual and the test. The visual may be a photograph or illustration, or it may be a graph or chart. Remind students to draw on their own experiences preparing a multimedia presentation when faced with these questions. Students should always take a moment to figure out how a visual supports the text in a test.

Common Core State Standards

- **Speaking and Listening 3**

Identify Purpose of Political Advertising

1. Present the purpose of political advertising, using the instruction on the student page.
2. Have a general discussion about any recent political ads students might have seen.

Negative Techniques Used in Political Ads

1. Present the types of negative techniques used in political ads, using the instruction on the student page.
2. Explain the common logical fallacies as they are presented in the chart on the student page.

MEDIA LITERACY

Communications Workshop

Analyze a Non-Print Political Advertisement

Common Core State Standards

Speaking and Listening
3. Evaluate a speaker's point of view, reasoning, and use of evidence and rhetoric, assessing the stance, premises, links among ideas, word choice, points of emphasis, and tone used.

During an election year, you may see advertisements promoting political candidates in many different forms of media. Non-print political advertisements air on television, the radio, and the Internet. Because they reach a vast audience, these ads can exert great influence on voters' decisions.

Identify Purpose of Political Advertising

Learning how political ads are designed will help you make informed political choices. The goal of a political ad, like that of any ad, is to sell something. However, instead of selling a product, a political ad sells a candidate's ideas and image. Political ads create name recognition and cast a candidate in a favorable light—or, in an attack ad, cast an opponent in a negative light.

Negative Techniques Used in Political Ads

Campaign strategists determine advertising tactics based on their candidate's position in the polls. If a candidate is leading, strategists may simply tout his or her accomplishments. When a race is very close, you may see ads using **propaganda,** biased content that damages an opponent's credibility or image. Some ads use **wrong facts** to intentionally misrepresent an opponent's stance on an issue. Other times, ads use **logical fallacies,** appeals that sound convincing but are based on faulty reasoning.

Common Logical Fallacies

Ad Hominem	Bandwagon	Either-Or
Attacking a candidate's character	Appealing to popularity	Offering only two solutions (when more are possible)
"My opponent spent $400 on a day at the spa. How can she understand the issues facing the poor?"	"The police support our candidate. So should you!"	"You can elect our candidate or watch unemployment skyrocket. What's your choice?"

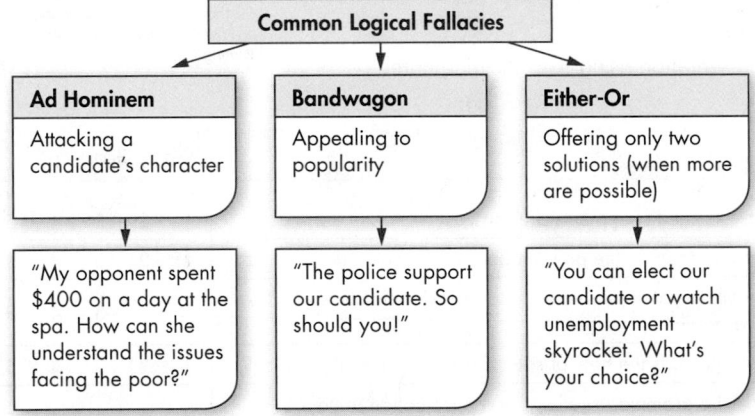

Persuasive Techniques

Other strategies used in a non-print political ad include the following:

- *Editing*: arranging images and sound to create certain effects. A TV clip edited to show a candidate shaking hands with rival politicians creates the impression that he or she can negotiate successfully.
- *Camera Angles:* the direction from which a camera operator shoots images. A low-angle shot makes a person appear tall and confident.
- *Camera Shots:* different ways of framing a subject on camera. A close-up may make an ad feel more personal and intimate.
- *Symbols:* images with positive or negative associations. An ad that depicts a candidate's family suggests he or she understands issues affecting voters with families.
- *Charged Language:* words that carry very positive or negative connotations. A candidate might describe an opponent as a "waffler" to make him or her seem inconsistent.
- *Tone:* the general attitude conveyed by the words used. A phrase like "rising to the challenge" helps create a positive tone.

Activities: Analyze Non-Print Political Ads

Comprehension and Collaboration For both activities, use an evaluation form like the one shown below.

A. Watch a recent political ad on TV or online. Use the evaluation form to analyze the persuasive techniques included in the ad.

B. Using the Internet, find and analyze two opposing non-print political ads from a historical campaign.

Evaluating a Political Ad

Ad Title: ______________________________

Name of Candidate: ______________________________

Year of Production: ______________________________

Primary Audience [pick one]: *Sympathetic* ☐ *Neutral* ☐ *Hostile* ☐

What makes you think so? Tone ☐ Language ☐ Images ☐

Other ______________________________

Visual and Sound Techniques: Angles ☐ Symbols ☐ Charged Language ☐

Other ______________________________

Negative Techniques: Yes ☐ No ☐

If Yes, which ones? ______________________________

How many of the claims made in this ad are true? Consult an unbiased source to find out. ______________________________

Persuasive Techniques

1. Present the five persuasive techniques, using the instruction on the student page.
2. Ask students to provide other examples of symbols and charged language to support the instruction.

Activities: Analyze Non-Print Political Ads

1. Present the purpose of the activity, using the instruction on the student page.
2. Show the class a political ad for a local or national candidate or measure.
3. Allow students to work in pairs or small groups to complete the challenge activity.
4. Remind students to follow the sample evaluation form that is provided on the student page.

Differentiated Instruction for Universal Access

Strategy for Special-Needs Students
Have pairs of students study the chart of logical fallacies. Encourage them to take turns quizzing each other on the fallacies until both of them feel they have mastered the content.

Strategy for Less Proficient Readers
Explain to students that logical fallacies are often used in other types of advertising, as well. Break students into small groups and assign a fallacy to each group. Have each group find examples of their fallacy in actual advertisements and bring them to class to share. Ask students to evaluate whether the ad is persuasive.

EXTEND

Common Core State Standards

- Language 4.a, c

Etymology of Scientific, Medical, and Mathematical Terms

1. Teach the skills, using the instruction and chart on the student page.
2. If possible, supply students with a medical or scientific reference book to use for this lesson. If those references are not available, a dictionary will suffice.

Think Aloud: Model the Skills

Say to students:

When I come across a technical word I do not know, I always begin by breaking it into parts. If I know the meaning of its prefix and suffix, that gives me a good start. If I can identify the root of the word and determine its meaning, too, then I am able to put all the parts together to define the term.

Vocabulary Workshop

Etymology of Scientific, Medical, and Mathematical Terms

Common Core State Standards

Language

4.a. Use context as a clue to the meaning of a word or phrase.

4.c. Consult general and specialized reference materials (e.g., dictionaries, glossaries, thesauruses), both print and digital, to find the pronunciation of a word or determine or clarify its precise meaning, its part of speech, its etymology, or its standard usage.

During the Renaissance, English scholars gained much of their knowledge on medicine, mathematics, and science from ancient Greek and Roman texts. As they absorbed information from these works, the English naturally adopted many of the words they found. From the Renaissance onward, scholars have used these classical languages to describe new scientific and mathematical discoveries.

Study these other affixes and roots commonly found in science and math.

Prefixes	Roots	Suffixes
anthrop- (Greek): human	*angle* (Latin): intersecting lines	*-al* (Latin): characterized by
bio- (Greek): life	*derma* (Greek): skin	*-ar* (Latin): of or relating to, resembling
cosmo- (Greek): universe, world	*morph* (Greek): form	*-ic* (Greek): of or relating to
epi- (Greek): upon, over	*photo* (Greek): light	*-logy* (Greek): science, theory, study
equi- (Latin): equal	*pod* (Greek): foot	*-meter* (Greek): measure
geo- (Greek): Earth	*sphere* (Greek): ball, globe	*-oid* (Greek): resembling, like
pseudo- (Greek): false	*stell* (Latin): star	*-phobia* (Greek): fear
quadr- (Latin): four		*-ty* (Anglo-Saxon): multiplied by ten
thermo- (Greek): heat		

Practice

Directions: Combine the indicated affix or root with others from the chart to create additional terms related to science or math. Define them, using the meanings given in the chart. Check your definitions in a dictionary.

1. thermo
2. bio
3. geo
4. angle
5. sphere
6. anthrop

Directions: Provide an explanation for each question.

7. Why might an amoeba be called a ***pseudopod?***
8. What is an ***equilateral*** triangle?
9. Why might a ***photophobic*** stay in the dark?
10. How can you protect your ***epidermis?***

Practice

Possible answers:

1. *thermal:* "having heat"; *thermosphere:* "global heat"; *thermospheric:* "relating to global heat"
2. *biology:* "the study of life forms"; *biomorphic:* "resembling a life form"; *biosphere:* "life within the globe"; *biospheric:* "relating to life within the globe"
3. *geology:* "the study of Earth"; *geologic:* "relating to geology"; *geomorphic:* "resembling the form of the earth"
4. *angular:* "having intersecting lines"; *quadrangle:* "shape with four intersecting lines"; *quadrangular:* "having four angles"
5. *spheric:* "relating to a globe"; *biosphere:* "life within the globe"; *biospheric:* "relating to life within the globe"; *thermosphere:* "global heat"; *thermospheric:* "relating to global heat"
6. *anthropic:* "relating to humans"; *anthropomorphic:* "relating to the human form"; *anthropology:* "study of humans"
7. A *pseudopod* would be a "false foot." An amoeba extends part of its cell and uses it like a foot to propel itself.
8. An *equilateral* triangle has three equal sides.
9. A *photophobic* person is afraid of light.
10. Your *epidermis* is your outer layer of skin. You can protect it with sunscreen or lotion.

Vocabulary Acquisition and Use: Context Clues

Context clues are words or phrases that help readers clarify the meanings of unfamiliar words in a text. By using context clues, you can determine the word or words that complete a sentence. Sentence Completion questions appear in most standardized tests. In these types of questions, you are given sentences with one or more missing words. Your task is to choose the correct word or words to complete each sentence logically. Try this strategy: (1) Read the entire sentence and look for signal words that indicate whether a missing word is positive or negative. (2) Scan the answer choices and cross out those that do not fit your criteria. (3) Test the rest of the answer choices in the sentence.

Practice

This exercise is modeled after the Sentence Completion exercises that appear in the Critical Reading section of the SAT.

Directions: Each of the following sentences is missing one or two words. Choose the word or set of words that best completes each sentence.

Test-Taking Tip
Eliminate words you know are wrong. Test the rest in the sentence to determine what fits best.

1. William Blake studied painting at the Royal Academy yet was not considered one of the __?__ of art in his time.

A. sepulchers
B. roused
C. arbiters
D. torrid
E. morose

2. Blake was a visionary, but he lived in __?__ conditions, often at the edge of poverty.

A. sordid
B. vintage
C. orthodox
D. copious
E. ancestral

3. He existed on meager sales and the __?__ of his patrons.

A. reverence
B. symmetry
C. mundane
D. fortitude
E. recompense

4. Some of Blake's illustrations are childlike and __?__ while others are marked by __?__ and darkness.

A. incitement . . . sinuous
B. presumption . . . amiable
C. winsome . . . pathos
D. avarice . . . ungenial
E. platitudes . . . teeming

5. Blake used __?__ brushwork in his precise watercolors to create apocalyptic images, including __?__, and otherworldly creatures, giving shape to his poetic vision.

A. stagnant . . . vindications
B. expiated . . . discretions
C. blithe . . . requiems
D. acceded . . . discretions
E. fastidious . . . phantasms

Strategies for Test Taking

Remind students of the importance of reading Sentence Completion test items thoroughly. Tell students that crossing out incorrect answers can help eliminate confusion and ensure that they do not mark incorrect answers.

Practice

1. Introduce the skill, using the instruction on the student page. Be sure students understand how context clues can reveal the meaning of an unknown word.
2. You may wish to go over the first item with students, applying the "look for a relationship with other words" strategy. Read the first item to the class, including all of the answer choices. As you read the list of choices a second time, ask students to raise their hands when they think a choice might work. Point out that the main idea of the sentence is concerned with Blake's studies at the Royal Academy, an achievement associated with gaining knowledge and expertise. Point out that *sepulchers* are tombs; *roused* is associated with waking or becoming active; *torrid* describes something that is hot and dry; and *morose* describes a sullen or gloomy mood. None of these words fits the context of the sentence. *Arbiters* are experts or individuals of authority and influence in their field. After trying the word *arbiters* in the sentence, students may agree that it fits best, selecting C as the correct answer.
3. Assign the remaining items in the Practice Test. Point out that some questions require pairs of words, rather than a single word, for completion. Allow students 6 minutes to complete the questions.

Answers

1. C
2. A
3. E
4. C
5. E

Using the Test-Taking Practice

In this Test-Taking Practice (pp. 932–935), students apply the skills in Unit 4. The Practice is divided into three sections.

1. Before assigning each section, review the relevant Unit skills with students. Discuss the characteristics of each type of test and specific strategies for test questions, using the instruction that precedes each Practice.
2. Set a time limit for the multiple-choice items in each Practice, allowing a little more than 1 minute per question. Use the designated time allowance set for the Timed Writing section.
3. Administer each section. Have students write the starting time at the top of their papers. When half of the time for the multiple-choice items has elapsed, ask students to write the time next to the answer on which they are working. Have them make similar notes when the time is three-quarters through and again when time is up. Follow a similar procedure for the Timed Writing assignment.
4. Review with students the pacing reflected in their notes.

Reteaching

Have students complete each Practice. Then, use the Reteach charts to determine which skills require reteaching, based on the items students answer incorrectly. Reteach these skills prior to assigning the **Benchmark Test** (***Unit 4 Teaching Resources,*** pp. 195–200).

Test-Taking Practice

Reading Test: Long Reading Passages

The **long reading passages** of standardized tests present more substantial texts that require extended concentration. Passages can be as long as 850 words and can present narrative, persuasive, and expository styles. You should spend more time on answering the questions than reading the passages. You must read purposefully to cover the material, to which you can later return for details.

Common Core State Standards

RI.11-12.1, RI.11-12.2, RI.11-12.3, RI.11-12.4, RI.11-12.6; L.11-12.1, L.11-12.2, L.11-12.3, L.11-12.4.a

[For the full wording of the standards, see the standards chart in the front of your textbook.]

Practice

The following exercise is modeled after the SAT Long Passage Critical Reading section. This section usually includes 48 questions.

Directions: Read the following passage, taken from *A Vindication of the Rights of Woman* by Mary Wollstonecraft. Then, choose the best answer to each question.

Indeed the word *masculine* is only a bugbear; there is little reason to fear that women will acquire too much courage or fortitude, for their apparent inferiority with respect to bodily strength must render them in some degree dependent on men in the various relations of life; but why should it be increased by prejudices that give a sex to virtue, and confound simple truths with sensual reveries?

Women are, in fact, so much degraded by mistaken notions of female excellence, that I do not mean to add a paradox when I assert that this artificial weakness produces a propensity to tyrannize and gives birth to cunning, the natural opponent of strength, which leads them to play off those contemptible infantine airs that undermine esteem even whilst they excite desire. Let me become more chaste and modest, and if women do not grow wiser in the same ratio it will be clear that they have weaker understandings. It seems scarcely necessary to say that I now speak of the sex in general. Many individuals have more sense than their male relatives; and, as nothing preponderates where there is a constant struggle for an equilibrium without it has naturally more gravity, some women govern their husbands without degrading themselves, because intellect will always govern.

Strategy

Identify opinions.

- **Scan the passage.** Notice "I" statements and charged language. These may indicate opinions.
- **Determine point of view.** Identify what the author wants readers to feel, understand, or do.
- Use this information to guide your answer choices.

Strategies for Test Taking

Tell students that critical reading is, in part, an exercise in putting themselves in another person's shoes. As they make inferences and look for unstated assumptions, students can ask themselves, "Is the writer afraid of something? Angry at something? What has made the writer feel this way?" Examining the feelings of the writer—or the narrator—can be a first step in making the inferences needed for critical analysis.

SAT® PREP ACT

1. Which of the following is the best statement of the overall purpose of the author's commentary in this passage?
   A. Most men are stronger than women and thus dominate.
   B. Some women dominate because they are smarter.
   C. Women are held back by a fear of their powers.
   D. Women should become more chaste and modest toward men.
   E. Men fear that women will gain too much strength and courage.

2. Which of the following persuasive techniques does the author employ?
   A. anticipating objections of her male readers and countering them
   B. suggesting that all women believe as she does and so should the reader
   C. offering questionable statistics and facts that support only her opinion
   D. challenging established opinions of both men and women of her day
   E. resorting to name-calling and mud-slinging to provoke male readers

3. In line 2, the word *fortitude* means
   A. attractiveness
   B. intelligence
   C. resistance
   D. weakness
   E. strength

4. Which social issue is this author attempting to address?
   A. forces in society that hold women back
   B. the struggle for equality among women
   C. men using physical force against women
   D. peer pressure on young women of the day
   E. career versus motherhood for young women

5. Which of the following quotations from the passage show the author attempting to persuade her audience?
   A. ". . . their apparent inferiority with respect to bodily strength . . ."
   B. ". . . I now speak of the sex in general . . ."
   C. ". . . there is a constant struggle for an equilibrium . . ."
   D. "Let me become more chaste and modest . . ."
   E. ". . . but why should it be increased by prejudices . . ."

6. Which choice best expresses the main idea of the first paragraph?
   A. Women have very little reason to fear men and should take comfort in their own feminine nature.
   B. Women will never be masculine, but their weaknesses should not be multiplied by turning them into virtues.
   C. Men are prejudiced against the virtues of women and have none of their own.
   D. Women will gradually gain power and courage, which poses a threat to men.
   E. Women lack strength and virtue, and always will.

GO ON

Differentiated Instruction for Universal Access

Support for Less Proficient Students

Read the passage with students and help them to summarize it. Then, go over the first test item as a class, guiding students to eliminate incorrect answer choices.

EL Support for English Learners

Read the entire passage with the class and help students to summarize each paragraph. Review the six questions, making sure that students understand *address* in question 4 and *persuade* in question 5. Allow students to ask clarifying questions about any of the question choices, being careful not to reveal correct answers. Once students understand the questions, have them complete the test on their own. Allow 5 minutes for reading the passage and 10 minutes for the questions.

Reading Test

Long Reading Passage

1. Introduce the passage using the instruction on page 932. Be sure students understand the strategy set off in the boxed section.
2. You may wish to go over the first test item with students before they take the test. Have students read the first paragraph silently, then, as a class, analyzing each choice in the first test item.
   A—Wollstonecraft does not say that men dominate entirely due to their bodily strength. Eliminate.
   B—She mentions intellect, but it is not the focus of her argument. Eliminate.
   C—The author never writes that women fear their powers. Eliminate.
   D—Wollstonecraft does not argue for chastity or modesty. Eliminate.
   E—Correct answer. The first line indicates that men "fear that women will acquire too much courage or fortitude."
3. Assign the Practice exercise. Allow 15 minutes for this process, and announce to students when they have 5 minutes and 1 minute remaining.

Answers

1. E
2. D
3. E
4. A
5. E
6. B

Reteach

Question	Pages to Reteach
1	910
2	910
3	919
4	910
5	910
6	880

Grammar and Writing:
Improving Sentences

1. Introduce the skill using the instruction on the student page. Be sure students understand the strategy set off in the boxed section.
2. You may wish to go over the first test item with students, modeling the "rely on your 'ear'" strategy. Read the sentence with each answer choice aloud to the class. As you repeat the sentence and choices more slowly, ask students to raise their hands when the grammar sounds correct throughout the sentence.
3. Point out that the verbs *represent* and *delight* belong to the subject *poem.* The plural forms of the verbs do not agree with the singular subject. Change is required, so Choice *A* is eliminated. Choice *B* only changes *represent* to singular; *B* is eliminated. Choice *C* correctly replaces both the plural verb forms with the singular forms. Choice *D* only changes *delight* to singular; *D* is eliminated. Choice *E* incorrectly changes each verb to plural past perfect; *E* is eliminated. Choice *C* is therefore the best alternative.
4. Have students complete questions 2–7 on their own. Allow students 8 minutes to complete the questions.

Grammar and Writing: Improving Sentences

Improving Sentences exercises often appear in the writing sections of standardized tests. The test items show five different versions of a sentence. Your job is to choose the most effective version. This type of exercise tests your ability to recognize and correct flaws in grammar, usage, and sentence structure.

Practice

This exercise is modeled after the Improving Sentences portion of the SAT Writing Section. The full test has 25 such questions.

Directions: Part or all of each of the following sentences is underlined; beneath each sentence are five ways of phrasing the underlined portion. Choice A will always be the same as the original wording; B–E are different options. If you consider the original sentence to be the most effective sentence, select choice A; otherwise, select one of the other choices.

Strategy

Rely on your "ear." Say possible choices quietly to yourself and let your natural "ear" for proper grammar distinguish what sounds correct.

1. John Keats's great poem "When I Have Fears" represent his finest work and delight millions of readers.
   A. represent his finest work and delight
   B. represents his finest work and delight
   C. represents his finest work and delights
   D. represent his finest work and delights
   E. have represented his finest work and have delighted

2. Readers of Wordsworth are lovers of Romantic ideals.
   A. Readers of Wordsworth are lovers
   B. One of the readers of Wordsworth are lovers
   C. Readers of Wordsworth is lovers
   D. Reader of Wordsworth is a lover
   E. Readers of Wordsworth is a lover

3. There were, it seems in the varied life of Samuel Coleridge, few accomplishments he didn't achieve.
   A. were, it seems in the varied life of Samuel Coleridge, few accomplishments
   B. were, it seem in the varied life of Samuel Coleridge, few accomplishments
   C. were, it seems, in the varied life of Samuel Coleridge, few accomplishments
   D. are, it seem in the varied life of Samuel Coleridge, few accomplishments
   E. are, it seems in the varied lives of Samuel Coleridge, few accomplishments

Strategies for Test Taking

When taking a test that includes a persuasive writing prompt, students should be careful to allow enough time for each step of the process. Though it is likely that a topic will be given, prewriting is still important because this is the stage at which students gather support and determine a position on the topic. Suggest that students take prewriting notes of their opinions. Under each opinion, they should list observations and reasoning they will use to support their arguments.

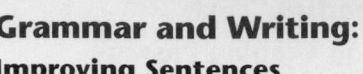

SAT® PREP ACT

4. Lord Byron, while at school, have made friends, has played sports, and spends money like a wastrel.
   A. have made friends, has played sports, and spends
   B. has made friends, has played sports, and has spent
   C. have made friends, have played sports, and spends
   D. made friends, played sports, and spent
   E. make friends, play sports, and spend

5. Percy Bysshe Shelley, born into the British upper classes, were expelled from Oxford University with a friend and were forced to live apart from his family.
   A. born into the British upper classes, were expelled from Oxford University with a friend and were forced
   B. born into the British upper classes, was expelled from Oxford University with a friend and were forced
   C. born into the British upper classes, was expelled from Oxford University with a friend and forced
   D. birthed into the British upper classes, were expelled from Oxford University with a friend and were forced
   E. born into the British upper classes, was expelled from Oxford University with a friend and was forced

6. It were a tragedy that John Keats, like many poets, dies so young and writes his major works in the space of only two years.
   A. It were a tragedy that John Keats, like many poets, dies so young and writes
   B. It was a tragedy that John Keats, like many poets, dies so young and writes
   C. It was a tragedy that John Keats, like many poets, died so young and wrote
   D. It was a tragedy that John Keats, like many poets, dies so young and writes
   E. It is a tragedy that John Keats, like many poets, dies so young and writes

7. *The Prelude*, which many students memorize, and "Ozymandias" are poetry any reader loves for a lifetime.
   A. memorize, and "Ozymandias" are poetry any reader loves
   B. memorizes, and "Ozymandias" are poetry any reader loves
   C. memorize, and "Ozymandias" is poetry any reader loves
   D. memorize, and "Ozymandias" is poetry any reader love
   E. memorize, and "Ozymandias" is poetry any readers loves

Timed Writing: Position Statement [25 minutes]

Mary Wollstonecraft wrote about the condition of women in the late eighteenth century. At that time few women enjoyed a formal education, and all women lacked basic legal rights. Things are entirely different today.

Write an essay in which you discuss whether education is the key to liberation for an oppressed group of people. You are free to take any side of the issue, but be sure to back up your opinions with observations and reasoning. This assignment is similar to the Essay portion of the SAT Writing Section.

Academic Vocabulary
Your **observations** come from things you have noticed or witnessed. You do not have to cite experts or recognized sources of research to include your observations in your essay.

STOP

Answers

1. C
2. A
3. C
4. D
5. E
6. C
7. A

Timed Writing

Position Statement

1. Go over the two paragraphs of the timed writing assignment on the student page.
2. Tell students that they can quickly formulate a thesis statement for their position statements.
3. Encourage students to budget adequate time for prewriting and revising/editing. Students should spend about 8 minutes in the prewriting stage, 12 minutes drafting, and 5 minutes revising and editing. Reinforce this by announcing elapsed time at the 8- and 20-minute marks as students respond to the assignment.
4. Use the **Rubrics for Writing for Assessment,** ***Professional Development Guidebook,*** pages 258–259, to evaluate students' work.

Benchmark

Reteach skills as indicated by students' performance, following the Reteach charts on pages 933 and 935. Then, administer the end-of-unit **Benchmark Test** (*Unit 4 Resources,* pp. 195–200). The Benchmark Test concludes instruction in the Unit skills. Follow the **Interpretation Guide** for the test (*Unit 4 Resources,* p. 204) to assign reteaching pages as necessary in the ***Reading Kit.*** Use **Success Tracker** online to automatically assign these pages.

Reteach

Question	Pages to Reteach
1	767
2	767
3	755
4	767
5	767
6	767
7	767

PHLit Online!

The **Benchmark Tests** and **Success Tracker** are available online at **www.PHLitOnline.com.**

Performance Tasks

Assigning Tasks/Reteaching Skills

Use the chart below to choose appropriate Performance Tasks by identifying which tasks assess lessons in the textbook that you have taught. Use the same lessons for reteaching when students' performance indicates a failure to fully master a standard. For additional instruction and practice, assign the *Common Core Companion* pages indicated for each task.

Task	Where Taught/ Pages to Reteach	*Common Core Companion Pages*
1	95, 296, 794, 866, 928	2–14, 196–207, 261–268
2	723, 732, 766, 793, 797, 818, 852	41–53, 261–268
3	774–775, 797, 806, 818	54–60, 219–225, 322–324
4	719, 746, 774–775, 783, 866	15–27, 297–303
5	747, 760, 899, 902, 904, 910	143–155, 306–312
6	730, 761, 810, 896, 909, 914, 921	136–142, 278–285

Assessment Pacing

In assigning the Writing Tasks on this student page, allow a class period for the completion of a task. As an alternative, assign tasks as homework. In assigning the Speaking and Listening Tasks on the facing page, consider having students do any required preparation as a homework assignment. Then, allow a class period for the presentations themselves.

Evaluating Performance Tasks

Use the rubric at the bottom of this Teacher Edition page to evaluate students' mastery of the standards as demonstrated in their Performance Task responses. Review the rubric with students before they begin work so they know the criteria by which their work will be evaluated.

Performance Tasks

Directions: *Follow the instructions to complete the tasks below as required by your teacher. As you work on each task, incorporate both general academic vocabulary and literary terms you learned in this unit.*

Common Core State Standards

RL.11-12.1, RL.11-12.2, RL.11-12.4, RL.11-12.5; RI.11-12.5, RI.11-12.6; W.11-12.2.a, W.11-12.4, W.11-12.9.a; SL.11-12.1.a, SL.11-12.1.d, SL.11-12.4, SL.11-12.6; L.11-12.3.a

[For the full wording of the standards, see the standards chart in the front of your textbook.]

Writing

Task 1: Literature [RL.11-12.1, W.11-12.2.a, W.11-12.9.a]
Draw Inferences

Write an ***essay*** *in which you cite textual evidence to support inferences drawn from a poem in this unit.*

- Explain which poem you chose. Identify the poem's explicit meaning or key idea. Quote from the text to support your point.
- Identify any ideas or emotions that the speaker suggests but does not explicitly state. Cite details from the poem that help you draw inferences about the speaker's unstated ideas or feelings. Explain how you tied these details together to see connections that suggest implicit meanings.
- Discuss ideas or emotions the poem leaves uncertain or open to interpretation. Consider the reasons for and effects of this ambiguity.
- Organize your ideas so that each new idea builds on the one that precedes it to create a unified whole.

Task 2: Literature [RL.11-12.4, W.11-12.9.a]
Analyze the Impact of Word Choice

Write an ***essay*** *in which you analyze the impact of word choice in a poem from this unit.*

- Choose a poem in which the word choice is particularly interesting to you. Explain which poem you chose and why you chose it.
- Identify at least two words in the poem that carry connotative meanings that are essential to the poet's overall meaning. Explain the shades of meaning each word contributes to the poem as a whole.
- Explain the cumulative, or combined, impact these words have on the tone of the poem.
- Consider how word choices with similar denotations but different connotations would alter the meaning and tone of the poem.

Task 3: Literature [RL.11-12.5, W.11-12.4, L.11-12.3.a]
Analyze Text Structure

Write an ***essay*** *in which you analyze how a poet's choice of structure adds to the overall meaning and aesthetic impact of a poem in this unit.*

- Choose a poem from this unit in which the structure, or form, plays a key role in developing meaning. Explain which poem you chose and why.
- Analyze how the poet's choices of structure in sections of the poem contribute to the structure of the poem as a whole. Consider line length, rhyme scheme, and stanza lengths and divisions.
- Connect the author's choices concerning structure to the meaning as well as to the aesthetic, or artistic and emotional, impact of the poem.
- Clearly develop and organize your ideas while maintaining an appropriate, consistent style and tone in your writing.
- Vary your sentence length and structure to add interest and sophistication to your writing.

Performance Task Rubric: Standards Mastery	Rating Scale (*not very* – *very*)
Critical Thinking: How clearly and consistently does the student pursue the specific mode of reasoning or discourse required by the standard, as specified in the prompt (e.g., comparing and contrasting, analyzing, explaining)?	1 2 3 4 5
Focus: How well does the student understand and apply the focus concepts of the standard, as specified in the prompt (e.g., development of theme or of complex characters, effects of structure, and so on)?	1 2 3 4 5
Support/Elaboration: How well does the student support points with textual or other evidence? How relevant, sufficient, and varied is the evidence provided?	1 2 3 4 5
Insight: How original, sophisticated, or compelling are the insights the student achieves by applying the standard to the text(s)?	1 2 3 4 5
Expression of Ideas: How well does the student organize and support ideas? How well does the student use language, including word choice and conventions, in the expression of ideas?	1 2 3 4 5

Speaking and Listening

Task 4: Literature [RL.11-12.2, SL.11-12.4]
Analyze Development of Theme

*Deliver an **oral presentation** in which you analyze the development of two or more themes in a poem in this unit.*

- State which poem you chose and briefly explain why you chose it.
- Clearly state the themes of your chosen poem. Discuss specific ways in which the author develops each theme throughout the poem. Identify specific details, figurative language, and images that contribute to the expression of each theme.
- Explain how the themes interact and build on one another as the poem progresses.
- Be sure to develop your ideas fully and present them in logical order.
- As you present, demonstrate your command of the conventions of Standard English grammar and usage. Choose language that expresses ideas precisely and concisely, eliminating wordiness.

Task 5: Informational Text [RI.11-12.6, SL.11-12.6]
Determine the Author's Point of View

*Deliver an **oral presentation** in which you examine the author's point of view, rhetoric, and style in a nonfiction work from this unit.*

- Introduce the work you chose. Explain the author's purpose, topic, and central idea.
- Describe the author's point of view. Explain how the author's stance affects his or her discussion of the topic and helps to shape the central idea.
- Discuss specific aspects of the author's rhetoric and style, explaining how they contribute to the power or persuasiveness of the text. Cite details and examples from the text to support your position.
- Be aware of your own uses of rhetoric and style. Use formal English appropriate to an academic discussion.

Task 6: Informational Text [RI.11-12.5, SL.11-12.1.a, SL.11-12.1.d]
Analyze Ideas or Events

*Participate in a **small-group discussion** in which you analyze the structure of an author's exposition or argument in a nonfiction work from this unit.*

- As a group, choose a nonfiction work from this unit. Prepare for the discussion by working independently to conduct your own analysis of the work.
- Identify the structure the author uses to present ideas. Consider whether the structure involves a formal pattern of organization, such as comparison-and-contrast, or combines various patterns.
- Evaluate the clarity and logic of the structure. Consider how the structure helps or hinders readers' understanding and whether it makes ideas more convincing and engaging.
- Discuss your ideas in a small group. Respond thoughtfully to each other's ideas, and work to resolve any contradictions in your interpretations.

What is the relationship of the writer to tradition?

The Voice of a Romantic The voice of the Romantic writer is personal, passionate, and dedicated to expressing a personal imaginative vision. That personal vision colors the writer's reflections.

Assignment Write a **composition** in the voice of a Romantic. You may choose the voice of a particular author or any writer of the time. Use the form of an essay, a book introduction, or a letter to a friend.

Differentiated Instruction for Universal Access

Strategy for Less Proficient Readers
Assign a Performance Task, and then have students meet in groups to review the standard assessed in that task. Remind students of the selections or independent readings to which they have previously applied the standard. Have groups summarize what they learned in applying the standard and then present their summaries. Discuss, clarifying any points of confusion. After students have completed their tasks, have groups meet again to evaluate members' work. Encourage members to revise their work based on the feedback they receive.

EL Strategy for English Learners
For each Performance Task, review the instructions with students. Clarify the meaning of unfamiliar vocabulary, emphasizing classroom words such as *conventions* and *ambiguity* and academic vocabulary such as *purpose*.

Next, have students note ideas for their responses. Pair students, and have them review each other's notes, asking questions to clarify meaning and suggesting improvements. Encourage students to ask for your assistance in supplying English words or expressions they may require.

Supporting Speaking and Listening

1. Consider having students work with partners or in groups to complete Performance Tasks involving listening and speaking. For tasks that you assign for individual work, you may still wish to have students rehearse with partners, who can provide constructive feedback.
2. As students rehearse, have them keep in mind these tips:
   - Present findings and evidence clearly and concisely.
   - Observe conventions of standard English grammar and usage.
   - Be relaxed and friendly but maintain a formal tone.
   - Make eye contact with the audience, pronounce words clearly, and vary your pace.
   - When working with a group, respond thoughtfully to others' positions, modifying your own in response to new evidence.

Linking Performance Tasks to Independent Reading

If you wish to cover the standards with students' independent reading, adapt Performance Tasks of your choice to the works they have selected. (Independent reading suggestions appear on the next page.)

What is the relationship of the writer to tradition?

1. Remind students of the Essential Question, "What is the relationship of the writer to tradition?"
2. Have students complete their responses to the prompt on the student page. Point out that in this unit, they have read a variety of literature from the Romantic period and that they should draw on these selections in their responses. Remind them that they can also draw on their own experiences and what they have learned in other subject areas in formulating their answers.

EXTEND

Independent Reading

Titles featured on the Independent Reading pages at the end of each unit represent a range of reading, including stories, dramas, and poetry, as well as literary nonfiction and other types of informational text. Throughout, labels indicate the works that are CCSS Exemplar Texts. Choosing from among these featured titles will help students read works at increasing levels of text complexity in the grades 11–12 text complexity band.

Using Literature Circles

A literature circle is a temporary group in which students independently discuss a book.

Use the guidance in the *Professional Development Guidebook*, pp. 47–49, as well as the teaching notes on the facing page, for additional suggestions for literature circles.

Meeting Unit 4 CCS Standards

Students can use books listed on this page to apply and reinforce their mastery of the CCS Standards covered in this unit.

Introducing Featured Titles

Have students choose a book or books for independent reading. Assist them by previewing the titles, noting their subject matter and level of difficulty. **Note:** Before recommending a work to students, preview it, taking into account the values of your community as well as the maturity of your students.

COMMON CORE ▪ INDEPENDENT READING

Featured Titles

In this unit, you have read a variety of literature from the Romantic period. Continue to read works related to this era on your own. Select books that you enjoy, but challenge yourself to explore new topics, new authors, and works offering varied perspectives or approaches. The titles suggested below will help you get started.

LITERATURE

Frankenstein
Mary Shelley

Novel This classic story presents an epic battle between man and monster. Frankenstein, a medical student, fashions a creature from the body parts of the dead and brings it to life, setting in motion a chain of events that brings him to the brink of madness.

[Shelley's introduction to Frankenstein *appears on page 760 in this book. Build knowledge by reading the entire work.]*

Pride and Prejudice
Jane Austen — EXEMPLAR TEXT

Novel The setting is the English countryside in the eighteenth century, a world of comfortable homes, tidy fortunes, and respectable families. In this world, Mr. Darcy, handsome and wealthy, would seem to be the ideal match for the charming and pretty Elizabeth Bennet. Their courtship is one of the most treasured love stories of English literature.

The Portable Romantic Poets
Edited by W. H. Auden and Norman Holmes Pearson

Anthology This volume includes works by celebrated British and American poets, such as Robert Burns, William Wordsworth, and Edgar Allan Poe, as well as works by lesser-known writers.

[Poems by Burns and Wordsworth appear earlier in this unit. Build knowledge by reading additional works by these poets.]

The Complete Poetry and Prose of William Blake
Edited by David V. Erdman

Anthology All of Blake's great poetry, including *Songs of Innocence and Experience* and *The Marriage of Heaven and Hell*, appear in this volume. Also included are early poems and many illuminating letters.

[Poems by Blake appear on pages 748–752 of this book. Build knowledge by reading additional poems by Blake.]

INFORMATIONAL TEXT

Historical Texts

A Defence of Poetry and Other Essays
Percy Bysshe Shelley

Essays First published in 1821, "A Defence of Poetry" proclaimed a revolutionary idea—that poets are active political forces, or "the unacknowledged legislators of the world." In these essays, Shelley reflects on the art of poetry.

[Poems by Shelley appear on pages 868–876 of this book. Build knowledge by reading Shelley's essays.]

From Montrose to Culloden: Bonnie Prince Charlie & Scotland's Romantic Age
Sir Walter Scott

History Scott, one of the nineteenth century's most popular novelists, wrote these stories for his grandson. The historical tales bring to life Scotland's colorful and romantic history and feature memorable characters such as Bonnie Prince Charlie and the Duke of Cumberland.

Contemporary Scholarship

The Mirror and the Lamp: Romantic Theory and the Critical Tradition
M. H. Abrams
Oxford University Press, 1971

Scholarship Abrams explains a powerful contrast in the history of literary criticism. Pre-Romantic writers regarded literature as a mirror that reflects the real world. The Romantics, however, saw literature as a lamp that projects the writer's soul.

Romantic Poetry: Recent Revisionary Criticism
Edited by Karl Kroeber and G. Ruoff

Anthology These up-to-date essays reflect key critical views on the English Romantic poets: Blake, Wordsworth, Coleridge, Byron, Shelley, and Keats.

Text Complexity: Aligning Texts With Readers and Tasks

TEXTS	READERS AND TASKS
• *The Complete Poetry and Prose of William Blake* (Lexile: 1130L)	**Below-Level Readers** Allow students to focus on reading for content, and challenge them to interpret multiple perspectives.
• *Frankenstein* (Lexile: 1170L) • *Pride and Prejudice* (Lexile: 1190L) • *The Portable Romantic Poets* • *A Defence of Poetry and Other Essays*	**Below-Level Readers** Challenge students as they read for content. **On-Level Readers** Allow students to focus on reading for content, and challenge them to interpret multiple perspectives. **Advanced Readers** Allow students to focus on interpreting multiple perspectives.
• *From Montrose to Culloden* • *The Mirror and the Lamp* • *Romantic Poetry*	**On-Level Readers** Challenge students as they read for content. **Advanced Readers** Allow students to focus on reading for content, and challenge them to interpret multiple perspectives.

Preparing to Read Complex Texts

Reading for College and Career In both college and the workplace, readers must analyze texts independently, draw connections among works that offer varied perspectives, and develop their own ideas and informed opinions. The questions shown below, and others that you generate on your own, will help you more effectively read and analyze complex college-level texts.

Common Core State Standards

Reading Literature/Informational Text
10. By the end of grade 12, read and comprehend literature, including stories, dramas, and poems, and literary nonfiction at the high end of the grades 11-CCR text complexity band independently and proficiently.

When reading complex texts, ask yourself...

- What idea, experience, or story seems to have compelled the author to write? Has the author presented that idea, experience, or story in a way that I, too, find compelling?
- How might the author's era, social status, belief system, or personal experiences have affected the point of view he or she expresses in the text?
- What key idea does the author state explicitly? What key idea does he or she suggest or imply? Which details in the text help me to perceive implied ideas?
- Do I find multiple layers of meaning in the text? If so, what relationships do I see among these layers of meaning?
- How do details in the text connect or relate to one another? Do I find any details unconvincing, unrelated, or out of place?
- Do I find the text believable and convincing?

Key Ideas and Details

- What patterns of organization or sequences do I find in the text? Do these patterns help me understand the ideas better?
- What do I notice about the author's style, including his or her diction, uses of imagery and figurative language, and syntax?
- Do I like the author's style? Is the author's style memorable?
- What emotional attitude does the author express toward the topic, the story, or the characters? Does this attitude seem appropriate?
- What emotional attitude does the author express toward me, the reader? Does this attitude seem appropriate?
- What do I notice about the author's voice—his or her personality on the page? Do I like this voice? Does it make me want to read on?

Craft and Structure

- Is the work fresh and original?
- Do I agree with the author's ideas entirely or are there elements I find unconvincing?
- Do I disagree with the author's ideas entirely, or are there elements I can accept as true?
- How do the concerns, values, and assumptions of my own era shape my response to the text?
- Based on my knowledge of British literature, history, and culture, does this work reflect the British tradition? Why or why not?

Integration of Ideas

Text Complexity: Reader and Task Support Suggestions

INDEPENDENT READING

Increased Support Suggest that students choose a book that they feel comfortable reading and one that is a bit more challenging.

Pair a more proficient reader with a less proficient reader and have them work together on the more challenging text. Partners can prepare to read the book by reviewing questions on this student page. They can also read difficult passages together, sharing questions and insights. They can use the questions on the student page to guide after-reading discussion.

Increased Challenge Encourage students to integrate knowledge and ideas by combining the Essential Questions and the unit concepts in their approach to two or more featured titles.

For example, students might consider Shelley's essays about the role of poetry in *A Defence of Poetry and Other Essays.* Students can then discuss how the poetry in *The Portable Romantic Poets* lives up to Shelley's ideas about what poetry should accomplish.

Preparing to Read Complex Texts

1. Tell students they can be attentive readers by bringing their experience and imagination to the texts they read and by actively questioning those texts. Explain that the questions they see on the student page are examples of types of questions to ask about works of fiction and nonfiction.
2. Point out that, like writing, reading is a "multidraft" process, involving several readings of complete works or passages, revising and refining one's understanding each time.

Key Ideas and Details

3. Review and amplify the fifth bulleted point in the Key Ideas and Details box. **Ask:** What details in the text reveal the relationships between these layers of meaning?

   Possible response: Students may point to changes in setting, unexpected turns in the plot, or character arcs as details that reveal these relationships.

Craft and Structure

4. **Ask:** How does an author's poetic style differ from his or her prose style?

   Possible responses: Poetic style is more evocative, while prose style strives more for clarity. Poetic style leaves more room for interpretation than prose style.

Integration of Ideas

5. **Ask:** What is it about the work that makes it fresh and original?

   Possible response: Students may point to the author's voice, the rhythm of the writing, or the originality of the characters.
6. Finally, explain to students that they should cite key ideas and details, examples of craft and structure, or instances of the integration of ideas as evidence to support their points during a discussion of poetry, fiction, or nonfiction. After hearing the evidence, the group might reach a consensus or might agree to disagree.

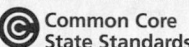

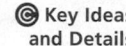

Common Core State Standards

- **Reading Literature 1, 2, 3, 5, 9**
- **Reading Informational Text 3, 5, 6**
- **Writing 1, 2, 4, 5, 6, 7, 8, 9**
- **Speaking and Listening 1, 3**
- **Language 1, 3, 4, 5**

Progress and Decline

The Victorian Period

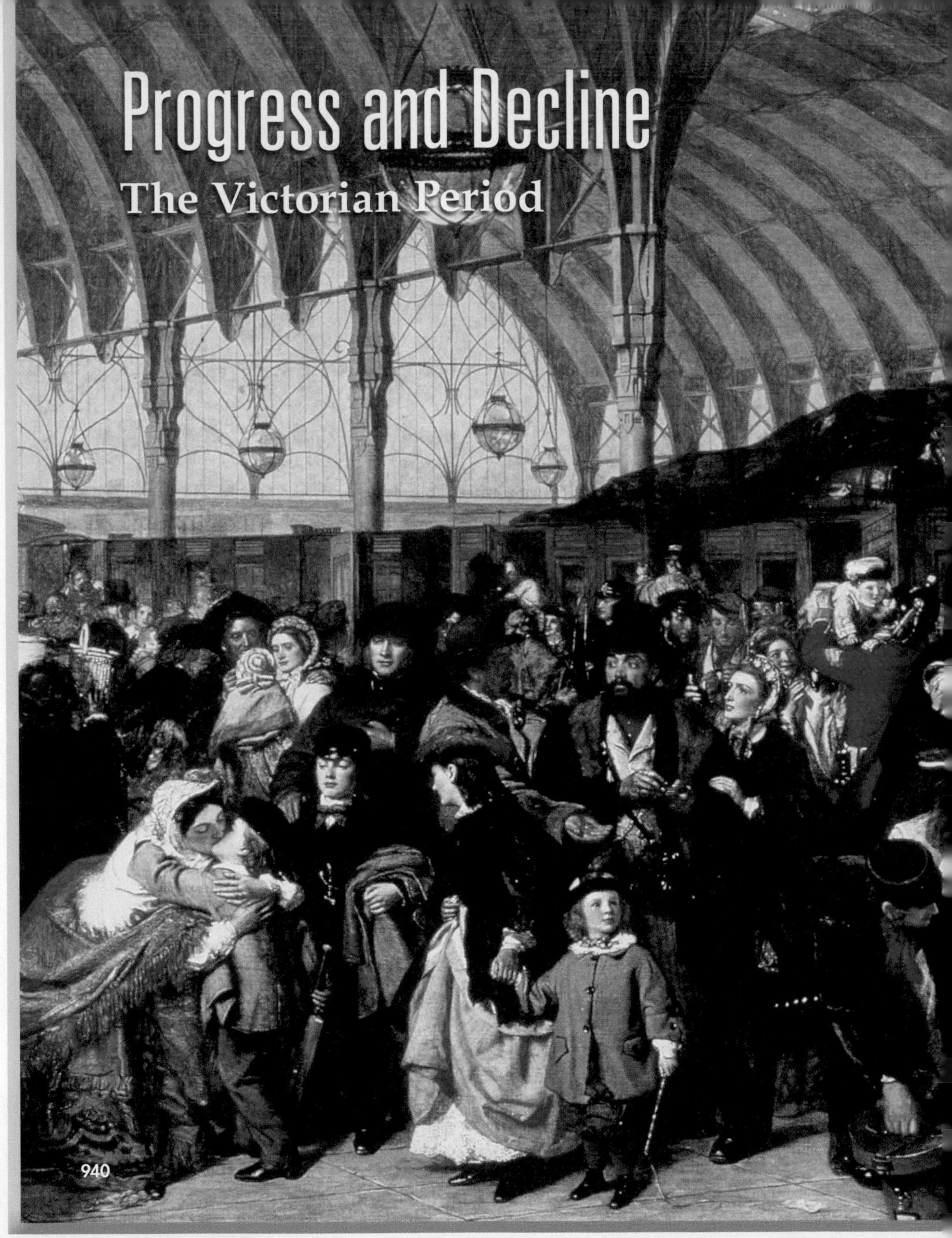

PHLit Online!
www.PHLitOnline.com

Teaching From Technology

Enriched Online Student Edition
- full narration of selections
- interactive graphic organizers
- linked **Get Connected** and **Background** videos
- all work sheets and other student resources

Professional Development
- the ***Professional Development Guidebook*** online
- additional professional-development essays by program authors

Planning, Assigning, and Monitoring
- software for online assignment of work to students, individually or to the whole class
- a system for tracking and grading student work

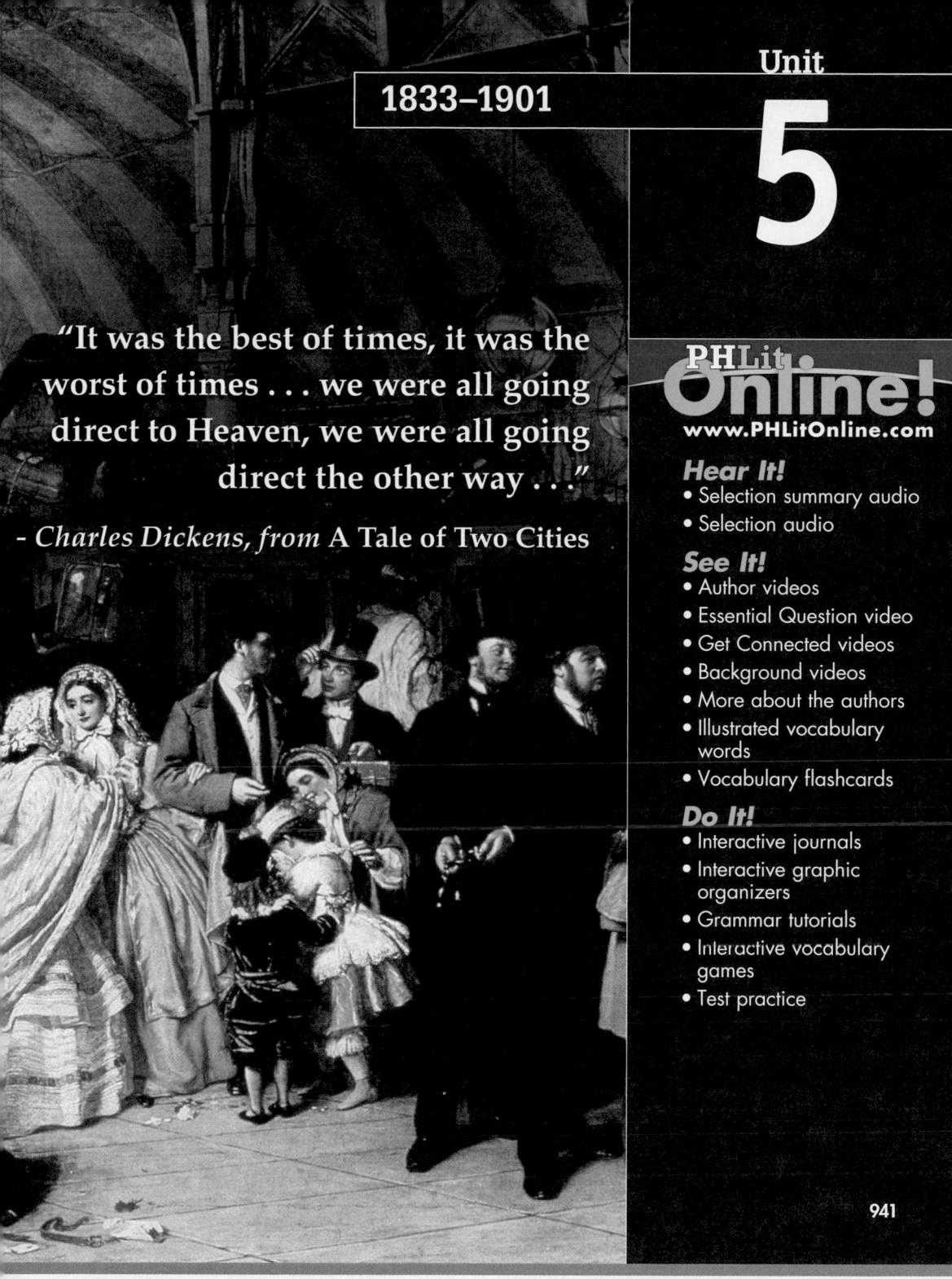

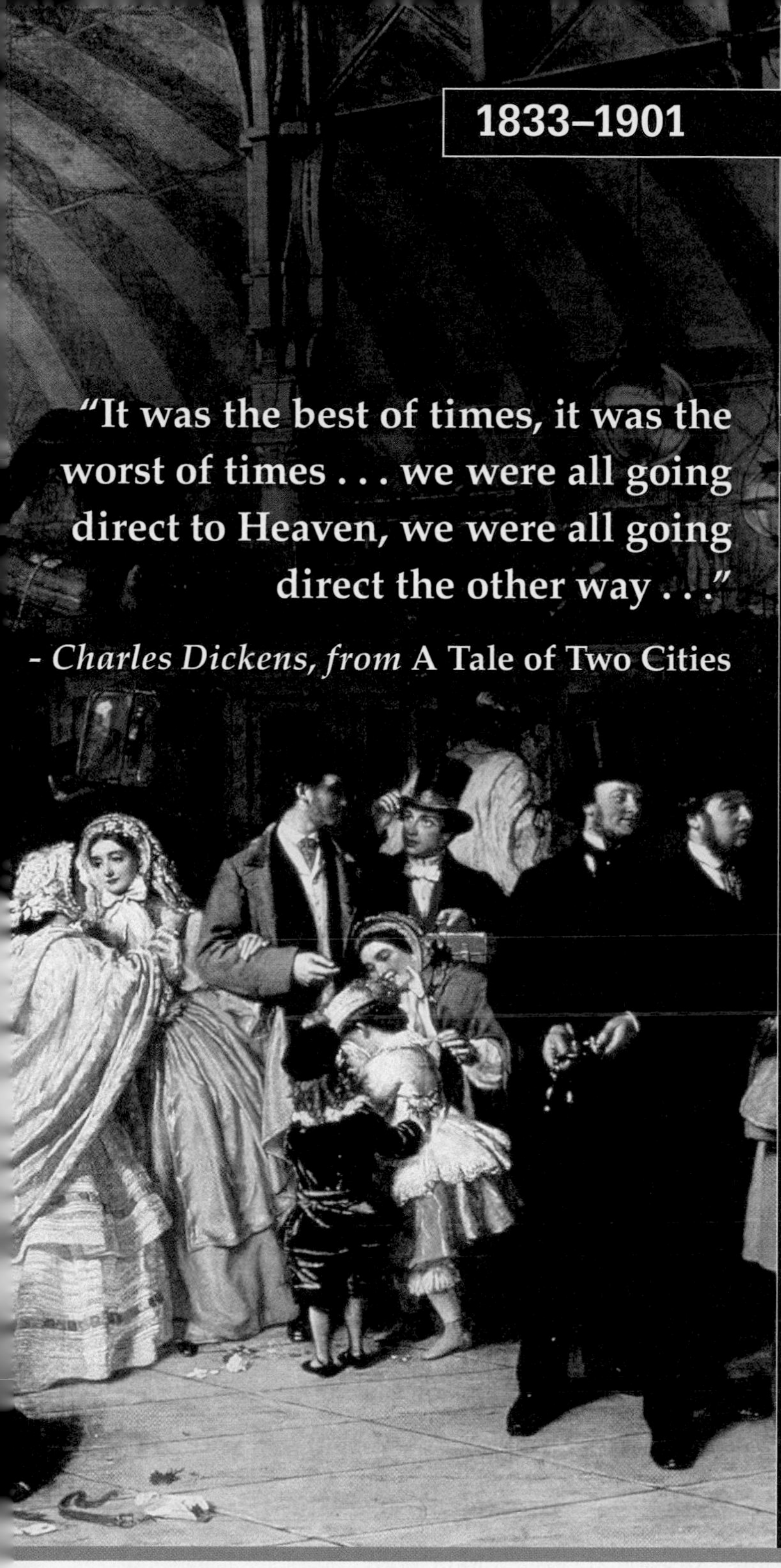

Unit 5

1833–1901

"It was the best of times, it was the worst of times . . . we were all going direct to Heaven, we were all going direct the other way . . ."

- *Charles Dickens, from* A Tale of Two Cities

PHLit Online!

www.PHLitOnline.com

Hear It!
- Selection summary audio
- Selection audio

See It!
- Author videos
- Essential Question video
- Get Connected videos
- Background videos
- More about the authors
- Illustrated vocabulary words
- Vocabulary flashcards

Do It!
- Interactive journals
- Interactive graphic organizers
- Grammar tutorials
- Interactive vocabulary games
- Test practice

Introduce Unit 5

1. Direct students' attention to the title of the Unit. Have a volunteer read the quotation. **Ask:** What does the quotation suggest about the themes of the Victorian period?
   Possible response: The Victorian period is emblematic of two seeming opposites: progress (the best of times) and decline (the worst of times).
2. Discuss the artwork, *The Railway Station,* painted by William Powell Frith in 1862.
   Ask: How might this painting symbolize the best of times and the worst of times in Victorian England?
   Possible response: The Industrial Revolution, of which the railroad is part, led to many innovations. It also led to urbanization which led to crowded urban spaces and poverty.
3. Have students speculate about the literature of the period, given the quotation and the art.
   Possible response: The literature of the Victorian period encompasses themes of beauty and progress, as well as hardship and social criticism.

Unit Resources

Unit 5 Resources includes these pages:

Benchmark Tests assess and monitor student progress.

Vocabulary and Reading Warm-ups provide additional vocabulary support, based on Lexile rankings, for each selection. **"A" Warm-ups** are for students reading two grades below level. **"B" Warm-ups** are for students reading one grade below level.

Selection Support
- **Reading Skill**
- **Literary Analysis**
- **Vocabulary Builder**
- **Support for Writing**
- **Enrichment**

All worksheets and other student resources are also available online at **www.PHLitOnline.com.**

Unit Features

Unit Author
James Berry helps introduce the period in the Unit Introduction, provides Author's Insights on literature in the Unit, and offers insight in the Writing Workshop.

Extended Study
Students explore in depth the works of Charles Dickens, presented with links to contemporary culture, a Critical Commentary, and a Comparing Literary Works feature.

Comparing Literary Works
Students compare master works in the British tradition with works of world literature.

Primary Sources
Students engage the documents that recorded history as it was made.

Informational Texts
Students learn to use and evaluate various types of informational text.

Themes Across Cultures
Students discover links between literature from different cultures.

Reading Difficult Texts: The Habits of Mind of Strong Readers Sheridan Bla

It is often the case that as you understand a text better, you have more questions about it.

Have you ever asked your students to read a difficult passage that you know they can understand, if they would only try hard enough and stick with it? If they are like most students, they looked at the passage for a second or two and then complained that it was above their reading level and too hard for them. The passage was probably hard for you too, when you first read it. But you stuck with the difficult task of reading the passage until you got it. You read the passage again and again. You discovered new problems as you solved old ones. You noticed the difference between what you did and didn't understand, and looked for ways to solve the problems you encountered. Thinking hard and persisting in the task were your primary reading strategies.

Building Strong Readers

The determined will to understand a text often defines the difference between strong readers and weak ones, or between us as teachers and many of our students. We have a higher tolerance for difficulty than our students do. When we encounter a difficult text, we may find ourselves feeling frustrated and momentarily insecure, but we see the problems we encounter as evidence of the difficulty of the text. Students see the same problems as evidence of their insufficiency as readers, and this leads them to give up before they get started. Our job as teachers, then, becomes one of helping our students—especially as they prepare for college and read difficult 12th-grade literature selections—to develop the habits of mind of strong readers, habits that will keep them going when the going gets tough.

The Habits of Strong Readers

- A capacity for sustained focused attention, in spite of difficulty; a willingness to re-read and re-read again.
- Metacognitive awareness: the habit of monitoring one's own understanding
- A willingness to suspend closure: to entertain problems rather than avoid them.

Strategies for Developing Strong Readers

What follows are some strategies designed to help individual students develop these traits of strong readers, which is to say, of productive readers of difficult texts:

Getting What You Pay For

1. Ask students to read a difficult passage or poem **three times** and after each reading do the following:
   - Rate their understanding of the text using a scale of 0–10.

- Take notes about what they don't understand. What lines or phrases confuse or puzzle them? What questions do they have about this reading selection?

2. Have students work with two partners to talk about what happened to each reader over the course of three readings and to give their best collective effort to answering all of their questions.
3. After group members have collaboratively answered as many questions as possible, assign one student from each group to report to the class on the problems or questions that remain unsolved for that group. After each report, ask if other groups solved those questions, and, if so, have them share their answers. Discuss all unsolved questions as a class.
4. Encourage reflection and self-assessment.
   - Ask students whether they raised their rating of their understanding after each reading.
   - Ask how many lowered their rating of their understanding after some reading or after talking with partners.
   - Ask, why? It will inevitably be that the students had more questions than they did before.
   - Ask whether that means that they understood the text better or worse than they did before.
   - Conclude with this observation: It is often the case that as you understand a text better, you have more questions about it.

Learning from Reflection Observe students as they work through this process. Here are some patterns you might notice:

- The questions that students still have about a text after this process will be the questions that strong readers have and that teachers themselves often can't answer.
- Strong readers can understand a text and still have questions about it.
- Readers benefit from talking with other readers about what is hard to understand.
- As student understanding grows, learners frequently have more, not fewer, questions!

Teacher Resources

- ***Professional Development Guidebook***
- ***Classroom Strategies and Teaching Routines cards***

PHLit Online!

Log on as a teacher at **www.PHLitOnline.com** to access a library of all Professional Development articles by the Contributing Authors of Prentice Hall *Literature.*

Sheridan Blau

Sheridan Blau is Professor of English and Education at the University of California, Santa Barbara, where he directs the South Coast Writing Project and the Literature Institute for Teachers. A former President of the National Council of Teachers of English, he has published widely.

REFERENCES:

Blau, Sheridan. 2003 *The Literature Workshop: Teaching Texts and Their Readers.*: Portsmouth NH. Heinemann.

Blau, Sheridan. 1981. "Literacy as a Form of Courage." *Journal of Reading*, 25:2 (November) 101–105.

Dewey, John. 1910. *How We Think.* Buffalo, NY: Prometheus Books, 1991.

Lee, Carol and Peter Smagorinsky (eds.) 2000. *Vygotskian Perspectives on Literary Research: Constructing Meaning Through Collaborative Inquiry,* Cambridge: Cambridge University Press.

Reading the Unit Introduction

Progress and Decline

Explain that this unit covers literature of the Victorian period, which spanned 1833–1901. The Unit Introduction includes these components:

—a **Snapshot** offering a quick glimpse at the period

—a **Historical Background** section discussing major events

—a **Timeline** that covers the period from 1833 to 1901

—a **Unit Essay** examining the literature of the period through the lens of three Essential Questions

—**Following Through** activities

—a **Contemporary Commentary**

Introducing the Essential Questions

1. Introduce each of the Essential Questions on the student page.
2. Show the **Essential Question** video on the ***See It!*** **DVD.** Help students relate the Essential Questions to the unit and their own experiences by asking the following:
   Literature and Place Think of a time when you went beyond a boundary. What did it feel like? Is breaking boundaries generally a positive or negative thing?
   Literature and Society What are some paradoxes and contradictions in American society?
   Writer and Tradition Think of a television series in which a single story is presented in installments. How does the serialized nature of the program affect factors such as suspense, character development, and plot?
3. Explain to students that the ideas they have considered in answering these questions apply to the Victorian period.

COMMON CORE • MULTIPLE PERSPECTIVES ON THE ERA

Snapshot of the Period

The Crystal Palace, on the facing page, is a symbol of Victorian optimism and Victorian faith in progress, technology, and empire. It is true that this period witnessed dramatic technological advances, rapid industrialization, the growth of cities, political reforms, and the development of Britain into a worldwide empire. It is equally true that this era witnessed the spread of poverty, a division of Britain into two nations—one prosperous and the other poverty stricken—and advances in philosophy and science that threatened long-held beliefs. Above all, Victorians were aware that they were living—as a writer of the time put it—"in an age of transition." An old social and political order, dating back to medieval times, was being transformed into a modern democracy. The poet Matthew Arnold expressed the unease of this transition when he described himself as "Wandering between two worlds . . ."

This English cartoon of 1843 reflects the sharp contrast between the rich and the poor. The cartoon was inspired by a government report on the horrific state of workers in coal mines.

As you read the selections in this unit, you will be asked to think about them in view of three key questions:

What is the **relationship** between literature and *place?*

How does literature **shape or reflect** *society?*

What is the relationship of the writer to *tradition?*

Teaching Resources

Unit 5 Resources
- **Names and Terms to Know,** p. 2
- **Essential Question,** pp. 3–5
- **Listening and Viewing,** p. 87
- **Follow-Through Activities,** p. 6

All *Common Core Companion,* pp. 9–14; 33–38

All *Professional Development Guidebook*
- **Content-Area Enrichment,** pp. 224, 225, 231, 242

All *See It! DVD*
- **Essential Question Video: Unit 5**
- **James Berry,** *Segment 1*

PHLit Online! All resources are available at **www.PHLitOnline.com**.

Integration of Knowledge and Ideas The Crystal Palace (shown here), designed by Sir Joseph Paxton for Britain's Great Exhibition of 1851, was a large structure made of iron and glass. Stunningly advanced for its time, this "palace" housed exhibitions dramatizing the themes of empire and progress. If you were designing a Crystal Palace for today, what materials would you use, what would the structure look like, and what kind of exhibitions would it house?

Interior of the Crystal Palace; notice the glass and iron vaulted roof, advanced for its time.

Displays from Tunis, North Africa; Tunisia, whose capital is Tunis, was a French colony, but Britain was poised to expand its colonial holdings in Africa.

The machinery section; new and powerful machines testified to the Victorian belief in progress.

The stained glass gallery; the Victorian fascination with the Middle Ages prompted an interest in the art of the medieval church, including stained-glass windows.

TEACH

Background

History

Tell students that the Great Exhibition of 1851 took place in London. The event's main organizer was Prince Albert himself. Six million people visited the exhibition. The exhibits were varied: Frederick Bakewell demonstrated a device that was later developed into today's fax machine; Mathew Brady garnered admiration for his daguerreotypes, which were early photographs; and visitors marveled at the world's largest diamond. The Great Exhibition was the first in a series of world's fairs that demonstrated technological and cultural advances during the nineteenth century.

Critical Viewing

Interpreting Illustrations

1. Draw students' attention to the illustrations. **Ask** the question on the student page: If you were designing a Crystal Palace for today, what materials would you use, what would the structure look like, and what kind of exhibitions would it house?
   Possible responses: Answers will vary.
2. Then, **ask** students why they think that many Victorians identified this structure with the idea of progress.
   Answer: Glass would appear to be a modern material in contrast to the traditional materials of stone and wood.

Differentiated Instruction for Universal Access

Background for Less Proficient Readers
Have students examine the photographs to look for clues that support the description of the Victorian era as a time of transition. Ask students to list words that describe each photograph.

EL Background for English Learners
Have students write captions for each of the photographs. Ask them to identify details that support the text's description of the Victorian era as a time of change.

Enrichment for Advanced Readers
Ask students to name some buildings that they think represent the modern age. Ask them to explain how architecture can reflect the values of a particular time and place.

PHLit Online!

Show or assign the **Essential Question** video for this Unit online at **www.PHLitOnline.com.**

Teaching the Historical Background

The Historical Background section discusses the most significant events of this period: the rise of the British Empire under Queen Victoria, the struggle for political and economic reform, and the eventual waning of the Empire.

1. Point out that the story of this period is one of colonization and growth, but also of hard times, poverty, and conflict on the horizon.
2. Have students read the Background. Then, **ask** them to identify major social trends during the Victorian period. **Possible response:** The Victorian era was marked by numerous highs and lows. Culture and technology advanced, and the British Empire expanded. However, the seeds of change were planted by the works of Marx and Darwin. Important reforms took place in the British government as well.

Teaching the Timeline

1. Tell students that the Timeline for the period from 1832 to 1901 appears on pages 944–953 of this Unit Introduction. Each portion of the Timeline identifies and illustrates some of the major events in the British Empire and in the world for that period.
2. Have students survey the entire Timeline before they read the rest of the Unit Introduction.
3. Encourage students to identify a few additional events from the period and share with the class why they think the events are significant.

COMMON CORE ▪ MULTIPLE PERSPECTIVES ON THE ERA

Historical Background

The Victorian Period (1833–1901)

Queen Victoria's reign (1837–1901) was marked by triumphs and tragedies. The consequences of some of them, like the mixed legacy of imperialism, were felt well beyond her century.

Shy and diminutive, the young queen set out to restore the reputation of the monarchy. Her marriage in 1840 to her first cousin, Albert of Saxe-Coburg and Gotha, whom she loved dearly, was a model of respectability. That quality, respectability, became a very important concept in her time.

Tragedies and Triumphs of Empire

The first blight on her reign came in 1845, when the potato crop failed in Ireland. The Famine grew worse until by 1849, half the population of Ireland had died or gone into exile. The British government did little or nothing for this quarter of the "United Kingdom." The events and the legends of the Famine fueled the hatred and violence in the relations between the British and the Irish for more than a hundred and fifty years.

The high point of Victoria's reign was the Great Exposition in the Crystal Palace, organized by her husband, the Prince Consort, in 1851. Built in a wholly new style, with iron girders holding over a million feet of glass panels, the building was the cathedral of commerce and empire. A combination of world's fair and industrial show, the Exposition trumpeted to the world the achievements of manufacturing England, colonizing England, and self-satisfied England.

Two works published during Victoria's reign proved as powerful as any of the machinery assembled for the Great Exposition. In 1848, as England watched while revolutions convulsed Europe, Karl Marx published *The Communist Manifesto*. This pamphlet warned that there was "a spectre haunting Europe." That "spectre" was communism, with its prophecy of political revolution. The other book, the work of a gentleman scientist who had seen evidence for biological evolution during his long sea voyage on the *H.M.S. Beagle*, was *On the Origin of Species*. Supporters and attackers alike

Queen Victoria

TIMELINE

1832

1833: Slavery abolished in British empire.

1836 North America The Alamo falls to the Mexican army. ▶

1837: Victoria becomes queen. ▶

1839: Michael Faraday offers general theory of electricity. ▼

944

Enrichment: Understanding Economics

The Engine of Imperialism

In existence for almost 260 years, the British East India Company was the engine powering British imperialism. The East India Company was formed by royal charter in 1600. For much of its existence, the company had a monopoly on British trade with Asia and the area bordering the Persian Gulf.

Activity: Understanding Economics Explain to students that the British East India Company traded largely in cotton, silk, indigo dye, saltpeter, tea, and opium. Have students choose one of these products and research its role in Britain's colonization of Asia. Have students use the **Understanding Economics** worksheet, ***Professional Development Guidebook***, page 225, to help them analyze activities related to the production, distribution, and consumption of the goods they chose.

knew that after Charles Darwin's work, our sense of ourselves and our place in the world would never be the same.

The reform impulse gathered strength throughout the period. Laws regulated the worst abuses of child labor in mills and mines. The Second Reform Bill of 1867 further extended the franchise. The Elementary Education Act of 1870, passed in part to ensure an educated electorate, provided for the education of all children between five and twelve, the first step toward education for all. Nevertheless, poverty continued to be a major problem, especially in rapidly growing cities.

In 1871, Germany, newly unified and serving notice that it was a powerful force in European politics, crushed the French army and occupied Paris. Ominously, Germany began to build a fleet with which to challenge the Royal Navy.

Celebrating Empire

In 1876, Victoria was proclaimed Empress of India. England purchased the Suez Canal from the bankrupt French company that had built it and now had a vital sea link to the vast sub-continent. Few questioned whether it was appropriate for a constitutional monarch to be the Empress of a country half-a-world away. In 1887, Victoria celebrated her Golden Jubilee as queen and the nation rejoiced in fifty years of progress, prosperity and peace. The theme of the Diamond Jubilee in 1897 was The Empire.

When Victoria died in 1901, her eldest son became King Edward VI. His reign proved to be the "Indian summer" of Victorian England. The rise of Germany, France's desire to revenge the defeat of 1871, and squabbles over colonies formed clouds over Europe that would soon thicken and loose the deluge of war that would sweep away all vestiges of Victorian stability.

Key Historical Theme: Imperial Britain

- Under Victoria, Britain's empire expanded, and Britain celebrated progress, prosperity, and peace.
- Darker stories linked to Britain's empire included the Irish Famine, widespread poverty at home, and the rise of Germany as a competing imperial power.

1841 South Pacific
New Zealand becomes a British colony.

1844 United States
Samuel F.B. Morse sends first message over a long-distance telegraph line. ▶

◀ **1843:** William Wordsworth becomes poet laureate.

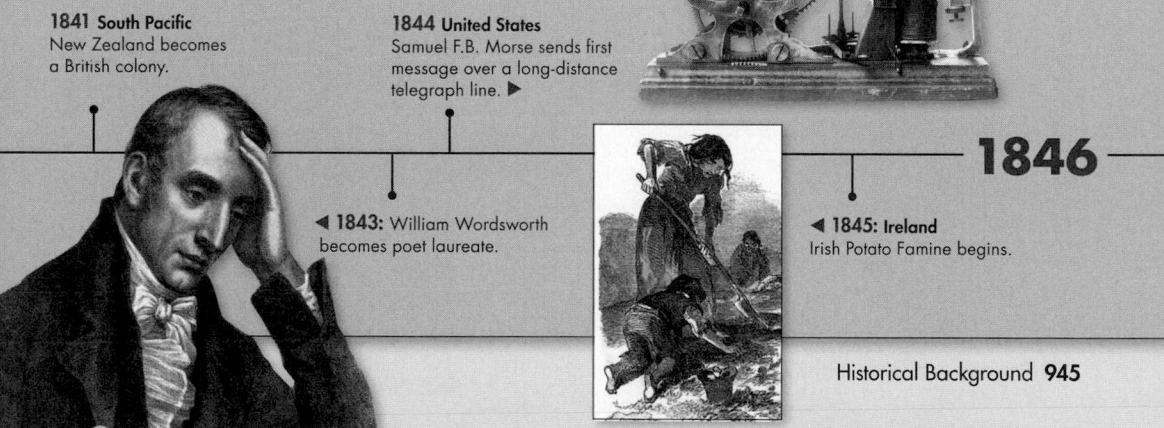

1846

◀ **1845: Ireland**
Irish Potato Famine begins.

Differentiated Instruction for Universal Access

Background for Less Proficient Readers
Explain to students that during this period, some thought society was out of control. Others believed it could solve any problem. Ask students to keep a two-column chart showing these two views as they read "Progress and Decline."

EL Background for English Learners
Explain to students that during this period, some thought society was out of control. Others believed it could solve any problem. Ask students to write a caption for each subhead and picture in the Historical Background.

Enrichment for Advanced Readers
Have students look for new modes of travel, new scientific theories, and new forms of work that affected how people perceived or thought of time. What idea might Victorians have had of the future?

Connecting to the Literature

1. Point out to students that Victorian writers documented both satisfaction with the status quo and a desire to change it. For an example of Victorian optimism, see Sydney Smith's memoir, "Progress in Personal Comfort," page 1065. For an example of the reforming instinct at work, direct students to the excerpt from Dickens's *Hard Times* on page 998.
2. Explain that Victorian authors also dealt with issues arising from colonialism. See Kipling's "Recessional" on page 1045 for a response to the expansion of the British Empire.

Key Historical Theme

1. Explain to students that this section of the Historical Background calls out major historical themes from the whole period.
2. **Ask** each student to make a chart showing the positive and negative sides of the Victorian era.
Possible response: Positive: Queen Victoria restored the reputation of the monarchy, the Great Exposition happened, technology and culture progressed, political reform took place; Negative: the Irish Potato Famine, poverty in cities, the rise of Germany

Critical Viewing

1. Call students' attention to the illustration on page 945 depicting the Potato Famine (1845).
2. **Ask:** From the illustration, what conclusions can you draw about agriculture in Ireland?
Possible response: For some people, farming was small scale and primitive, without draft animals or machinery.

Teaching the Essential Questions

As students read "Progress and Decline," they will examine its information through the lens of three Essential Questions. Each Essential Question is broken down into "stepping-stone," or intermediate, questions. Work through each stepping-stone question with the class. Then, have students pose answers to the Essential Question as it applies to the period.

What is the relationship between literature and place

1. Before they read this section of the essay, tell students that Victorian literature often deals with issues surrounding the growth of the British Empire.
2. Have students read this section of the essay. Then, pose the first stepping-stone question. **Ask:** What was the reach of the United Kingdom's empire?
   Response: The British Empire included Ireland, islands in the Caribbean, the Falkland Islands, New Zealand, Australia, Hong Kong, and India, as well as much of Africa.
3. Then, **ask** the second stepping-stone question: How was the spirit of empire reflected in Victorian literature?
   Possible response: Authors depicted the glory of exploration and conquest.

Applying the Essential Question

1. Summarize the class discussion of the stepping-stone questions.
2. Then, **ask** students this question: What do people think about British imperialism today?
   Possible response: Today, people are generally less positive about the effects of imperialism on the areas under imperial rule; while there are some benefits of imperialism, there are also many negative effects.

Essential Questions Across Time

The Victorian Period (1833–1901)

What is the relationship between literature and *place?*

What was the reach of the United Kingdom's empire?

Imagine a map of the world in 1897, Queen Victoria's Diamond Jubilee year, her sixtieth as queen. The British Empire, centered in the United Kingdom of Great Britain and Ireland, covered the globe. Starting from Great Britain (England, Scotland, and Wales), take an imaginary tour of the Empire. Sail a little to the west to reach Ireland. Then, sail across the Atlantic Ocean, to the vast expanse of Canada. Next, sail southward to the islands of the Caribbean. Continuing southward, pass the Falkland Islands and, rounding Cape Horn at the tip of South America, cross the Pacific Ocean to reach New Zealand and Australia. Traveling northward, dock at the beautiful harbor of Hong Kong. Then, turn southward to reach India, which includes what we now know as India, Pakistan, and Bangladesh. Traveling westward brings you to Africa, where there is almost enough continuous British territory for someone to dream of a railroad connecting Cape Town in South Africa with Cairo in Egypt. Finally, your tour takes you through the British-owned Suez Canal to the Mediterranean, past Gibraltar, and northward back to Britain.

The British flag flew over forty percent of the earth's land, and the Royal Navy patrolled and controlled all the oceans of the world.

How was the spirit of empire reflected in Victorian literature?

Restless Spirit The poem "Ulysses," by Victorian poet Alfred, Lord Tennyson, makes no mention of England or empire, yet it still captures the spirit that produced an empire. Ulysses is the wandering hero of Homer's

ESSENTIAL QUESTION VOCABULARY

These Essential Question words will help you think and write about literature and place:

empire (em´ pīr´) *n.* extensive territory and many peoples under the control of a single country or power

conquest (kän´ kwest´) *n.* act of taking control of a people or territory, especially in war

missionary (mish´ ən er´ ē) *n.* religious person who cares for others, usually in another country, and tries to teach them his or her religion

TIMELINE

1846

1848 Belgium Marx and Engels publish *The Communist Manifesto.* ▶

1848: Women begin attending University of London.

1853 Eastern Europe Crimean War begins. ▶

1854 Japan Trade with West reopened. ▶

Enrichment: Investigating Technology

Victorian Progress

Technological advances abounded throughout the industrializing world during this period. Methods for mass-producing steel were invented in 1865, and steel replaced iron as a major material. By the 1890s, dynamos (electric generators) powered factories.

Progress was not confined to industry. Paved streets, lighting, and improved sewer systems transformed cities. Anesthesia was introduced in surgery. Joseph Lister, an English surgeon, discovered the importance of antiseptics in preventing infections.

Activity: Learn More About Victorian Technology Invite students to choose a Victorian technology to learn more about. They should record their findings in the **Investigating Technology** worksheet, ***Professional Development Guidebook,*** page 242.

Odyssey who finally makes it home and reclaims his kingdom. In later legends, he is depicted as having had so many adventures that he cannot settle down to ordinary life. In these legends, he sails beyond the Pillars of Hercules, the Straits of Gibraltar, into the unknown sea. In Dante's medieval epic, the *Divine Comedy*, Ulysses is in hell, punished for his sin of going beyond an established boundary. To go beyond a limit—in Dante's structured, medieval world—was a grave sin. In Tennyson's fluid Victorian world, to accept a limit was a grave sin. The restless spirit that can never stop exploring, glorified in Tennyson's poem, is the spirit that created an empire.

Even a novel like Charlotte Brontë's *Jane Eyre,* set entirely in England, is connected with empire. When Jane Eyre grows up, she rejects one suitor who wants her to go with him as a missionary to India. She falls in love with the dark, brooding, Byronic Mr. Rochester, who has come back from Jamaica with a fortune and a terrible secret.

Empire's Poet The poet of empire was Rudyard Kipling. Born to British parents in India, he made that country, which he loved, vivid to his countrymen in poems and his panoramic novel *Kim.* Kipling delighted in describing British soldiers, the "Tommies," the thin, red line of heroes who carried the empire on their shoulders. In "The Widow at Windsor," one of those soldiers speaks of his pride and his problems in her service. "Recessional" is Kipling's own solemn warning against the arrogance of power.

The **BRITISH TRADITION**

CLOSE-UP ON ART

The Values of Empire and the Values of Art

While the British empire thrived on progress and expansion, an avant-garde group of Victorian painters sought purity and inward focus by moving backward in time. This group, founded by the painter and poet Dante Gabriel Rossetti (1828–1882), called itself the Pre-Raphaelite Brotherhood. Its members found inspiration in the Gothic style of the Middle Ages, before the time of the Renaissance painter Raphael (hence the group's name). Rossetti is known especially for his portraits of women, such as the one shown here. These portraits emphasize color, texture, and an earthy or sadly spiritual feminine beauty.

Critical Viewing Could this portrait by Rossetti, entitled *Day Dream*, be regarded as a comment on the Victorian belief in empire and progress? Why or why not?

◀ **1857 India** Sepoy Mutiny against British.

1855: London sewers modernized after outbreak of cholera.

1859: Charles Darwin publishes *On the Origin of Species.* ▲

1860

The British Tradition

Close-Up on Art

1. Have students read the sidebar feature about the Pre-Raphaelite Brotherhood.
2. Remind students that not all art and literature of the Victorian period looked favorably on the expansion of the British Empire and the values of mainstream society.
3. **Ask** students to describe how the values of the Pre-Raphaelites differed from those of poets like Tennyson.
   Possible response: While Tennyson glorified empire and progress, the Pre-Raphaelites sought to look inward and move back in time.

Critical Viewing

Answer: This painting could be viewed as a negative commentary on the progress of the Victorian era. The painting is attempting to capture the communication and feeling in medieval art. The simplicity of the figure's face and the simple, relaxed lines of her pose and of the drapery of her robe all suggest a clear, straightforward idea of study, grace, and repose. There are no complicating "psychological" ambiguities or tensions in her expression or manner.

Differentiated Instruction for Universal Access

Culturally Responsive Instruction

Culture Focus Explain to students that the influence of imperialism flowed both ways between the colonizers and the colonized. India was one country where British rule had tremendous economic, political, and cultural influence. Britain's introduction of new technology to the subcontinent changed many people's way of life. The introduction of Western concepts such as utilitarianism and equality before the law were also highly influential.

Teaching the Essential Question

How does literature shape or reflect society?

1. Before they read this section of the essay, tell students that Victorian society was filled with contradictions. Authors such as Charles Dickens attempted to grapple with such contradictions in their work.
2. Have students read this section of the essay. Then, pose the first stepping-stone question. **Ask:** How did literature reflect Victorian contradictions? **Possible response:** Authors such as Sydney Smith described new inventions that helped people live more comfortably. At the same time, other authors chronicled events such as the Boer War. Matthew Arnold encouraged people to enrich their minds, while on the other hand Lewis Carroll encouraged people to enjoy the sillier side of literature. Arnold also wrote about the despair of the time in "Dover Beach," whereas Elizabeth Barrett Browning explored the theme of hope in Sonnet 43. Authors such as Dickens and Brontë explored the paradox of sentimentalized children versus the reality of the life of orphans.

Critical Viewing

Interpret

1. Direct students to the illustration on page 948 of Florence Nightingale (1860).
2. **Ask:** What qualities does the picture of Florence Nightingale convey? Support your answer with details. **Possible response:** Her solitary, perhaps nighttime, vigil (she holds a lantern) over the sick suggests dedication; the viewer is meant to be impressed with her watchful mercy.

How does literature shape or reflect *society?*

"It was the best of times, it was the worst of times…." That is how Charles Dickens begins his novel of the French Revolution, *A Tale of Two Cities*. He goes on to say that this is also true of Victorian England. He knew what he was talking about, and it is helpful to follow Dickens's words as a guide to the contradictions of Victorian society:

". . . it was the age of wisdom, it was the age of foolishness, it was the epoch of belief, it was the epoch of incredulity, it was the season of Light, it was the season of Darkness, it was the spring of hope, it was the winter of despair, we had everything before us, we had nothing before us, we were all going direct to Heaven, we were all going direct the other way . . ."

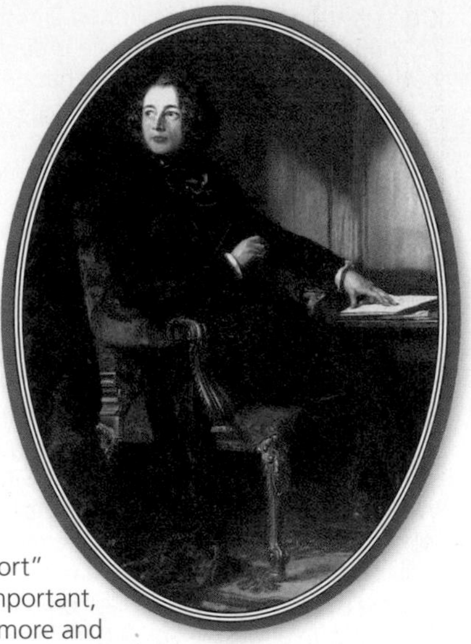

Charles Dickens

How did literature reflect Victorian contradictions?

"best of times" Sydney Smith's essay "Progress in Personal Comfort" lists some of the creature comforts invented in his lifetime. More important, however, is the attitude behind the essay: Life is getting better for more and more people. That optimistic spirit helped England make peaceful progress while Europe was torn by revolutions, assassinations, and war.

"worst of times" In the Irish Famine, two million people starved to death although there was food enough to feed them. From 1899 to 1902, the British fought the Dutch settlers of South Africa in the Boer War. The British army herded the women and children of the Boer guerillas into barbed-wire enclosures, thereby helping to invent the concentration camp.

"wisdom . . . foolishness" Wisdom includes Michael Faraday's experiments in electricity and Joseph Lister's introduction of sterile surgery. Matthew Arnold wrote essays urging his fellow citizens to enrich their minds with the same zeal with which they enriched their bank accounts.

TIMELINE

1860

1860: Florence Nightingale founds school for nurses. ▲

1861 Russia Emancipation of serfs.

1861 United States Civil War begins. ▶

1865 Austria Gregor Mendel proposes laws of heredity. ▶

1865: London Fire Department established.

Think Aloud

Vocabulary: Using Context

Direct students' attention to the word *incredulity* in paragraph 2 on this page. Use the following "think aloud" to model the skill of using context to infer the meaning of the word. Say to students:

I may not know the meaning of the word *incredulity*. When I read the sentence, however, I realize that the writer is using words that are opposites, such as *wisdom* and *foolishness* and *light* and *darkness*. I see that the word *incredulity* is paired with the word *belief*. It must mean "the opposite of belief." So I think *incredulity* refers to the time where some people believed accepted ideas of the time, while others questioned these ideas.

There were two varieties of foolishness. One was creative, a relief from the smug self-satisfaction of the time. Examples of this healthy foolishness are the operettas of W. S. Gilbert and Arthur Sullivan, with their amusing patter, and Lewis Carroll's fantastic tale *Alice in Wonderland* and his nonsense poem "Jabberwocky."

Unhealthy foolishness included using the Thames as an open sewer until one typhoid outbreak in 1861 killed Albert, Victoria's beloved Prince Consort. It also included sending British troops to fight in the Crimea so ill-fed, ill-clothed, and ill-led that the war is best remembered in Tennyson's poem "The Charge of the Light Brigade," which celebrates a suicidal cavalry charge.

"belief . . . incredulity" Problems of belief haunted the Victorians. At the very moment they wanted to think they were God's chosen people, they faced serious challenges to their belief in that God. Historical and scientific investigations undermined literal interpretations of the Bible, but it was Darwin who was the real villain for believers. Newton had distanced God from the universe; more frighteningly, Darwin seemed to distance God from human life.

"hope . . . despair" It is the spring of hope in Elizabeth Barrett Browning's Sonnet 43; it is the winter of despair in Matthew Arnold's "Dover Beach." It is the season of light in Gerard Manley Hopkins's "God's Grandeur"; it is the season of darkness in Emily Brontë's "Remembrance."

The BRITISH TRADITION

THE CHANGING ENGLISH LANGUAGE, BY RICHARD LEDERER

Euphemisms: The Fig Leaves of Language

Prudishness reached its golden age in the straitlaced Victorian era. Take the widely read *Lady Gough's Book of Etiquette.* Among Lady Gough's pronouncements was that under no circumstances should books written by male authors be placed on shelves next to books written by "authoresses." Married writers, however, such as Robert and Elizabeth Barrett Browning could be shelved together without impropriety.

So delicate were Victorian sensibilities that members of polite society would blush at the mention of anything physical. Instead of being *pregnant*, women were in a delicate condition, in a family way, or *expectant*. Their children were not born; rather, they were *brought by the stork* or *came into the world.*

Such words and expressions are called *euphemisms* (from two Greek roots that mean "pleasant speech," "words of good omen"). A euphemism is a mild, indirect word or phrase used in place of one that is more direct or that may have an unpleasant connotation for some people. Using a euphemism is "calling a spade a heart" . . . or "telling it like it isn't."

In the Victorian Age, prudery extended even to animals and things. *Bull* was considered an indecent word, and the proper substitute was *he cow, male cow,* or (gasp!) *gentleman cow.* Victorian standards were so exacting that Victorians could not refer to something as vulgar as legs. They had to call them *limbs*, even when talking about the legs on a chicken or a piano. Instead of asking for a leg of chicken, they would ask for dark meat, and they even went so far as to cover up piano legs with little skirts!

1869: Debtors' prisons abolished.

1872: Ballot Act in Britain introduces voting by secret ballot.

1874

◀ **1869 Egypt** Suez Canal, linking the Mediterranean Sea and the Red Sea, completed.

1872: First international soccer game, England vs. Scotland. ▶

Differentiated Instruction for Universal Access

Support for Special-Needs Students
As students explore the paradoxes of Victorian society, encourage them to make a two-column chart for each pair of contradictions and their examples.

EL Background for English Learners
Encourage students to explore the idea of euphemisms by listing some euphemisms from their own languages. What are more direct ways of communicating the ideas that the euphemisms express?

Enrichment for Gifted and Talented Students
Have students invent their own euphemisms. Encourage them to consider how euphemisms, metaphors, and figures of speech allow people to communicate ideas indirectly.

Applying the Essential Question

1. Summarize the class discussion of the stepping-stone question on page 948.
2. Then, **ask** students whether the contradictions present in Victorian society still exist in modern American culture.
   Possible response: Yes, many of these paradoxes are still with us today. There is still a contrast between wealth and poverty, wisdom and foolishness, and hope and despair.

The British Tradition

The Changing English Language

1. Have students read the sidebar feature about euphemisms in the Victorian era.
2. Explain that euphemisms are used to avoid saying something directly.
3. Explain that many occupations have taken on glorified, euphemistic titles. Nowadays, a garbage collector is called a "sanitation engineer" and a dogcatcher an "animal control warden." **Ask:** What are some other examples of occupations with euphemistic titles?
   Possible response: "Administrative assistant" has replaced "secretary"; "consultant" often replaces "freelance advisor."
4. **Ask:** Are there any situations in which the use of euphemisms would be advisable? Explain your answer.
   Possible response: Students may identify times when euphemisms would protect the feelings of people undergoing stress or grieving for losses.

Critical Viewing

Interpret

1. Direct students to the illustration of *David Copperfield* on page 950.
2. **Ask** the Critical Viewing question: To what extent does the illustrator sentimentalize David? To what extent does the illustrator show David struggling to survive in a hostile world?
   Possible response: The illustrator sentimentalizes David with the work's warm, lush colors as well as the bowed head and crossed arms of the boy. The illustrator shows the boy's struggle for survival with the indifferent gazes of the adults.

COMMON CORE ▪ MULTIPLE PERSPECTIVES ON THE ERA

◀ **Critical Viewing** In this scene from Charles Dickens's autobiographical novel *David Copperfield,* young David (shown at the center) is on a journey from Yarmouth to London. To what extent does the illustrator sentimentalize David? To what extent does the illustrator show David struggling to survive in a hostile world? **[Interpret]**

There was light and hope in The Crystal Palace; despair and darkness in the fetid slums with contaminated water.

"going direct to Heaven . . . going direct the other way" Nowhere is paradox more apparent than in the era's treatment of children. The Victorians frequently sentimentalized their children as little angels. However, in the novels of Dickens and Brontë and many others, we meet orphans and abandoned children struggling to survive in a hostile world. Often we see these children in school where the adults view them as, to use Dickens's phrase, "going direct the other way" unless they are rigorously and painfully kept in line.

All ages have their paradoxes, but the Victorians more than most felt, again in Dickens's words: ". . . we had everything before us, we had nothing before us."

ESSENTIAL QUESTION VOCABULARY

These Essential Question words will help you think and write about literature and society:

zeal (zēl) *n.* intense enthusiam

smug (smug′) *adj.* narrowly self-satisfied; overly contented

undermined (un′ dər mīnd) *v.* injured or weakened, especially in ways that are not immediately obvious

TIMELINE

1874

1875: Public Health Act is passed in Britain.

1876 United States Alexander Graham Bell patents telephone. ▶

Enrichment: Investigating Daily Life

Middle-Class Life

By the middle of the nineteenth century, the modern middle class had evolved its own way of life. The nuclear family lived in a large house or apartment. Even a small middle-class household was expected to have at least a cook and a maid. A strict code of etiquette dictated how to dress for every occasion, when to write letters, and how long to mourn relatives who had died. Parents strictly supervised their children, who were expected to be "seen but not heard."

Activity: Investigate Middle-Class Life Encourage students to research to find more about what everyday life was like for middle-class Victorians. Have them fill out the **Investigating Daily Life** worksheet, ***Professional Development Guidebook,*** page 224.

What is the relationship of the writer to *tradition?*

Literature turned inward in the Victorian period. As the Empire expanded and people talked of progress and prosperity, there was a brooding, melancholic tone to much of Victorian writing. Writers also used old forms in new ways or created new forms. Poets adapted traditional forms like the elegy and the sonnet to address contemporary questions of belief. Robert Browning's dramatic monologue, a new poetic form more vital than many stage plays of the era, reflected an up-to-date understanding of psychology. Novelists developed a genre created in an earlier century and found an eager audience. Published in serial form in magazines, novels generated the same excitement as popular TV sitcoms do today.

How did poets repurpose traditional forms and subjects?

An Elegy with Up-to-Date Themes Tennyson's *In Memoriam, A.H.H.,* his elegy for his friend Arthur Hallam, speaks to the problem of belief and doubt that was central to the age. In this poem, Tennyson struggles to come to terms with Hallam's death at the age of twenty-two, asking whether a benevolent God or an indifferent nature directs the universe. About ten years before Darwin, he writes of "nature red in tooth and claw." One of the most impressive aspects of this elegy is its engagement with the latest scientific discoveries. By the end of the poem, however, Tennyson has regained his belief and declares his faith in a divine plan for the universe.

Old and New Like the Pre-Raphaelite painters and many other artists of the era, Tennyson was fascinated by the Middle Ages. However, he combines this traditional subject with up-to-date concerns. In his epic poem *Idylls of the King*, which retells the story of King Arthur, he warns his contemporaries about what can happen to a powerful kingdom like Victoria's Britain.

A melancholy that is the opposite of faith in empire and progress informs Matthew Arnold's "Dover Beach." The speaker stands at the edge of the island kingdom and contemplates the chaos encroaching on the world. He hopes, almost desperately, that a personal relationship will survive that chaos.

1883: Joseph Swan produces synthetic fiber. ▶

◀ **1883 United States** First skyscraper built in Chicago.

1888: English Lawn Tennis Association founded at Wimbledon. ▶

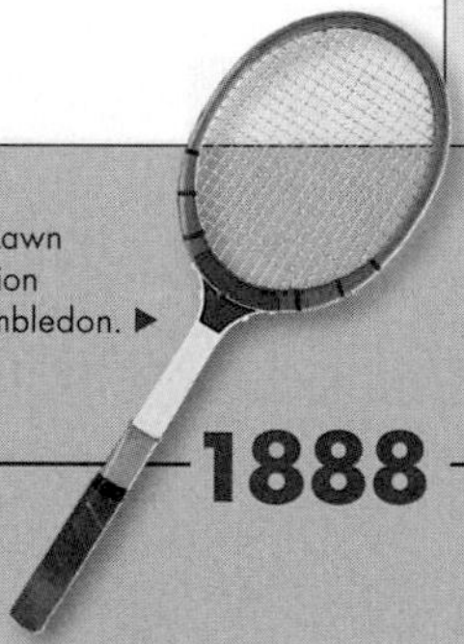

1888

Teaching the Essential Question

What is the relationship of the writer to tradition?

1. Before they read this section of the essay, tell students that Victorian authors adapted old forms to new purposes and invented a new poetic form called the dramatic monologue. In addition, writers further developed the novel.
2. Have students read this section of the essay. Then, pose the first stepping-stone question. **Ask:** How did poets use traditional forms and subjects for contemporary purposes?
   Answer: They used traditional forms such as the elegy to pose questions about the nature of belief; they wrote about traditional subjects such as the Middle Ages in new ways that alluded to current concerns; they wrote sonnets that included references to religion.
3. Then, **ask** the second stepping-stone question: What literary forms did the Victorians invent or perfect?
   Answer: They invented the dramatic monologue and perfected the novel.

Differentiated Instruction for Universal Access

Support for Less Proficient Readers
Explain that religion was a driving force behind much of Victorian art and literature. Yet doubt of faith was also a common theme. Tell students to look for examples of these competing ideas as they read about Victorian writers and tradition.

EL Background for English Learners
Have students look up words such as *brooding* and *melancholic* to help them better understand some of the key characteristics of Victorian writing. Explain phrases such as "nature red in tooth and claw" to students.

Enrichment for Gifted Talented/Students
As students read, encourage them to identify forms and subjects from the Victorian era that remain popular today. Ask students to identify features that give these forms lasting significance.

Applying the Essential Question

1. Summarize the class discussion of the stepping-stone questions on pages 951–952.
2. Then, **ask** students this question: Which kind of writing mentioned in the text is most relevant today? Why?
   Possible response: The novel remains popular today. It is a timeless form that tells a story, which is something that many people enjoy.

Critical Viewing

Interpreting Illustrations

1. Direct students to the illustration on page 952 of a scene from the Sino-Japanese War.
2. **Ask:** How might events such as the Sino-Japanese War have affected the sensibilities of Victorian artists and writers?
   Possible response: Foreign conflicts and the responsibilities that came with empire might have encouraged artists and writers to turn inward more.

© COMMON CORE ▪ MULTIPLE PERSPECTIVES ON THE ERA

The Sonnet In Sonnet 43, Elizabeth Barrett Browning states her belief in the power of love, more positively than Matthew Arnold. She adds a distinctively Victorian note of piety, reverence, and religious belief to her love poem. Victorian poets were as committed to the sonnet as were the Romantics, and none more so than Gerard Manley Hopkins. A Catholic convert and Jesuit priest, he experimented boldly with the form. In "God's Grandeur," a traditional sonnet enhanced by experiments with meter, he proclaims his faith in a divine presence in the world.

What literary forms did the Victorians invent or perfect?

The Dramatic Monologue Robert Browning, Elizabeth Barrett's husband, perfected the dramatic monologue. In this poetic form, a character is speaking to a silent listener and in the process revealing more about himself than he realizes. Browning's strange and chilling speakers are the British cousins of Edgar Allan Poe's mad narrators in stories like "The Cask of Amontillado" and "The Tell-Tale Heart."

The Novel The dramatic monologue takes readers into the mind of a character, as does the popular Victorian genre, the novel. This genre was as central to the Victorian period as the drama was to the Elizabethan. Usually published serially in magazines, each new installment of a novel was eagerly awaited by all levels of society. The novel's social commentary and realistic descriptions presented the Victorians to themselves.

The great theme of these novels is education: the depiction of a hero or heroine learning how to secure a proper place in society.

Note of Melancholy At the end of the era, A. E. Housman does not react as Tennyson did to the premature death of a young man. He does not seek the meaning of such a death in cosmic terms. Rather, in "To an Athlete Dying Young," he offers ironic consolation.

In an age of prosperity and progress, pride and power, England's poets and novelists reminded their countrymen that empires crumble, individuals are fragile and vulnerable, and death awaits us.

ESSENTIAL QUESTION VOCABULARY

These Essential Question words will help you think and write about the writer and tradition:

chaos (kā äs′) *n.* disorder and formlessness

piety (pī′ ə tē) *n.* devotion to religious duties

reverence (rev′ ər ens) *n.* feeling of deep respect, love, and awe

TIMELINE

1888

1890: First English electrical power station opens in Deptford.

1890 United States First entirely steel-framed building erected in Chicago.

1894 Asia Sino-Japanese War begins. ▲

Enrichment: Analyzing Historical Patterns, Trends, and Periods

Domestic Sentiment

The Victorians are remembered for an extreme sentimentalization of the middle-class domestic scene. In paintings, songs, novels, and those famous samplers bearing the words "Home Sweet Home," motherhood, marriage, and domestic duty were glorified.

Home, though, was a "haven in a heartless world." The middle-class husband battled his way through the cruel, indifferent war zone of business, then took shelter in the warm household ordered and filled with love by his dutiful spouse.

Activity: Analyze Domestic Sentiment
Encourage students to learn more about expressions of domesticity in Victorian culture. Have them fill out the **Analyzing Historical Patterns, Trends, and Periods** worksheet, ***Professional Development Guidebook,*** page 231.

The BRITISH TRADITION

CONTEMPORARY CONNECTION

The Brontës: Fantasy Forerunners

For today's readers, the name Brontë evokes two renowned classics, Emily Brontë's *Wuthering Heights* and her sister Charlotte's *Jane Eyre.* Less known is the fact that the Brontës—three sisters, including Anne, as well as their brother, Branwell—were among the pioneer writers of fantasy.

As children, the Brontës lived with their widowed clergyman father in a bleak and isolated region of northern England. Perhaps as a result of their isolation, they immersed themselves in a world of make-believe. Inspired by their play with Branwell's toy soldiers, they invented the lands of Angria and Gondal as settings for their fantasies.

They peopled their make-believe empires with fictional characters and real-life heroes, such as the Duke of Wellington, Napoleon, and various Arctic explorers. Also, they recorded the elaborate adventures of their characters in books, using tiny handwriting that adults needed a magnifying glass to read.

The Brontë children may not have intended their childhood tales to be widely read. These fantasies have been published, however, and have even inspired well-known authors. Not long ago, Joan Aiken published a book entitled *Dangerous Games* that, as she says, uses "bits and pieces" of the Brontes' Angria.

1896 Greece First modern Olympics held. ▶

◀ **1896 Austria** Sigmund Freud first uses the term "psychoanalysis."

1898 France Marie and Pierre Curie discover radium.

1900 China Boxer Rebellion against foreign influence. ▶

1901: Queen Victoria dies.

1901

953

The British Tradition

Contemporary Connection

1. Have students read the sidebar feature about the Brontës.
2. **Ask:** What features did the Brontës' childhood make-believe share with modern fantasy novels?
   Answer: They involved invented lands and make-believe empires.

Differentiated Instruction for Universal Access

Strategy for Special-Needs Students

With students, make a list of characteristics that are found in fantasy works. Read aloud the sidebar text, encouraging students to point out examples of the characteristics they listed.

Strategy for Less Proficient Readers

Have students list books, movies, and television shows that fall into the category of fantasy. Ask students to brainstorm a list of characteristics found in the fantasy genre.

Strategy for Advanced Readers

Have students discuss the appeal of the fantasy genre. To whom does it appeal, and why? Have students research an important work of fantasy and explain why it appeals to people.

Recent Scholarship
James Berry

1. James Berry introduces the unit and provides insights into British colonization during the Victorian era. His own selections, "From Lucy: Englan' Lady," "Time Removed," and "Freedom," and his commentary about them appear later in the unit on pages 1055–1059.
2. Have students read the introductory paragraph about Berry. Tell them that when he moved to London in 1948 he trained to become a telegraphist. He worked for the International Telegraph Department of the Post Office until he became a full-time writer. Berry now divides his time between London and Jamaica. He is an advocate for black writers.
3. Use the ***See It!*** **DVD** to introduce James Berry. Show Segment 1 to provide insight into his writing career. You can also view the video from this page in the Enriched Online Student Edition at **www.PHLitOnline.com.**
4. After students have watched the segment, **ask** why Berry felt it was important to share his culture with British students.
Possible response: Berry felt there was a lack of literature about Caribbean life, and he wanted to fill that gap.

PHLit Online!

All video resources are available online at **www.PHLitOnline.com.**

© COMMON CORE ▪ MULTIPLE PERSPECTIVES ON THE ERA

Recent Scholarship
Growing up in Colonial Jamaica

James Berry

About the Author

Born and raised in rural Jamaica, James Berry (b. 1925) now lives in London. His poetry and prose are enriched by both Creole language and more formal English. In 1993, Berry won the Coretta Scott King Award Honor Book and the Boston Globe–Horn Book Award for *Ajeeman and His Son,* a work of historical fiction set in Jamaica. Berry's books of poetry include *Fractured Circles* and *Lucy's Letters and Loving.*

A British Colonial Child

I grew up as a British colonial child in Jamaica, British West Indies. I was made to feel that there was something special about being British: You were born into honoring the British flag and feeling that the British way of life was best. Yet you also knew in a strange way that there was something alien and inferior about you. I came to realize that this was to do with race. Because we were a black people, we knew that we were different from the rulers of our island, who were white.

We sang songs in praise of Britain, like "Land of Hope and Glory," which glorified Britain's colonial past and power. And once a year, on Empire Day, we sang "Rule Britannia," with its line: "Britons never, never, never shall be slaves." We sang with fervor because Britishness seemed to offer a sense of safety and belonging. But we also knew that our ancestors *had* been slaves and had been enslaved by the British.

As a child growing up, you had these two different histories to contend with. You felt and knew that your colonial existence was strongly influenced by your slave history. It made you feel almost an outsider in the world because there was nowhere you could appeal to.

Schooling

It was the British way of life that constructed our schooling. We received a good, basic education in ordinary subjects like English language, arithmetic, biology, history, and geography. The maps we used showed British territories colored in red, and we were proud of that. We were made to learn a little verse about Queen Victoria setting us free.

Our reading books were not based on Africa or Jamaica. They brought us the culture of the British Isles; the stories and poems in them were all British. Many of the poems were from the eighteenth or nineteenth centuries—they had all the weight of grand English usage.

Most Jamaican children spoke our island dialect every day at home, but if you spoke dialect at school, teachers would shame you. They would say, "This is not a place for bad talk." Speaking English properly was tremendously respected and was connected to further education.

The Mother Country

We grew up with the idea that all the best things came from England. On Sundays, my father liked to ride to church on an English saddle that he had sent to England for. People would save up to order shoes and wedding suits from England.

At church on Sundays, we prayed for the King and the Royal Family. These were our hopeful figureheads, possible sources of influence. On Empire Day, at school, we were issued with tins of sweets with pictures of the King on them. England was our mother country.

Our Jamaican colonial history is different from that of many other colonial peoples because our own mother country sold our ancestors as slaves, and we grew up disconnected from Africa. In this kind of situation, a country takes a long time to recover from its own history. But this history has given Jamaicans a unique status in the world: a connection with Europe as well as a link back to Africa.

©Speaking and Listening: Collaboration

James Berry discusses the positive and negative effects of British colonialism on Jamaica. With a partner, develop a research **plan for a presentation** on the pros and cons of colonialism for Jamaicans like Berry. In formulating your plan, take the following steps:

- Review Berry's essay, listing the pros and cons of colonialism from his perspective.
- Formulate *clear research questions* to explore this topic further.
- Develop *research strategies* that would help you answer these questions; consider such sources as *oral histories*, *interviews*, and *autobiographies*.
- Review sources, *evaluating them for objectivity or bias* and taking preliminary notes on your topic.

After reviewing sources, discuss what you have learned with your partner. Drawing on your reading, decide on a preliminary thesis. Present your plan and thesis to the class and ask for comments and suggestions for improving it.

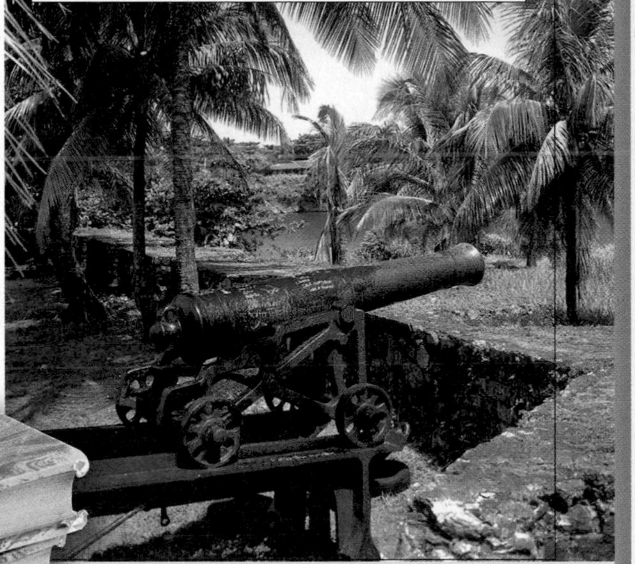

"This is not a place for bad talk."

Speaking and Listening: Collaboration

Plan for a Presentation

1. Review the assignment with students.
2. Have students discuss the pros and cons of colonialism from Berry's perspective. They should then use Berry's opinions to guide the formation of their own research questions.
3. After students have developed their questions, they should discuss possible strategies for answering them. When students have outlined their research plans, they can discuss ways to improve them with the class.
4. To help conduct the discussion, use the **Discussion Guide** in the ***Professional Development Guidebook,*** page 65.

ASSESS

Common Core State Standards

- Reading Informational Text 7
- Speaking and Listening 1.a, 5

Integrate and Evaluate Information

1. Review the chart assignment with the class. Then, ask students to use the Activity A chart in the **Follow-Through** worksheet (p. 6 in ***Unit 5 Resources***). **Possible responses:** Place and Literature: Key Concept—Wandering and exploring; Key Author—Alfred, Lord Tennyson. Writer and Tradition: Key Concept—Melancholy; Key Author—Matthew Arnold.
2. **Possible responses:** The illustrations of the Crystal Palace on p. 943 reflect the "best" of Britain during this period, including its architectural, artistic, and industrial innovations and its colonial wealth and breadth. The illustration of the woman and children on p. 945 represents the "worst" of this period—England's poor relations with Ireland after the famine and its insufficient concern for the workers who made England prosperous.
3. **Possible response:** Citizens who benefited from England's imperial rule—industrialists, military leaders, and politicians—would have agreed that the Empire was cause for celebration. Those living under enforced colonialism abroad and the poor within England's own borders would have had little reason to celebrate.
4. Responses should reflect students' understanding that colonialism can produce a rich mix of cultural elements from both the ruling country and the colonized one— but that some citizens may feel conflicted about accepting one tradition over the other or finding an acceptable balance between the two.

COMMON CORE ▪ MULTIPLE PERSPECTIVES ON THE ERA

Integrate and Evaluate Information

1. Use a chart like the one shown to determine the key ideas expressed in the Essential Question essays on pages 946–952. Fill in two ideas related to each Essential Question and note the authors most closely associated with each concept. An example has been provided for you.

Essential Questions	Key Concepts	Key Author
Place and Literature		
Literature and Society	pride in and cautions about empire	Rudyard Kipling
Writer and Tradition		

2. "It was the best of times, it was the worst of times," wrote Victorian novelist Charles Dickens. Review the images on pages 940–955, and choose one that evokes the "best" of this period and one that evokes the "worst." Describe each image and explain its significance.
3. When Queen Victoria celebrated her Diamond Jubilee in 1897, the theme was "The Empire." Which British citizens would have agreed that the Empire was a cause for celebration? Which citizens might have disagreed? Explain, citing evidence from the multiple sources on pages 942–953, as well as from other sources, such as online encyclopedias.
4. **Address a Question:** In his essay on pages 954–955, James Berry portrays Jamaican culture as a complex intersection of British tradition and local history. Choose an aspect of Jamaican culture, such as the Jamaican dialect of English. Integrating ideas from Berry's essay as well as from other sources, such as online encyclopedias, explain how the element reflects the intersection of—or struggle between—cultures.

Speaking and Listening: Multimedia Presentation

The British Empire was at its height in 1851, when the Crystal Palace was built. Create and deliver a **multimedia presentation** on the Palace, analyzing what its innovative construction and displays implied about Britain's place in the world.

Solve a Research Problem: To create an effective multimedia presentation, combine text, images, and sound from sources like these:

- TV documentaries
- Internet sites
- videos
- Victorian newspapers
- history books
- magazines

Formulate a plan to find and assemble the media you need. Determine how to access each type of source listed above. Then, select and use media strategically. Choose only pieces that clearly illustrate your points, and create pacing by distributing them evenly through the report.

Common Core State Standards

Reading Informational Text

7. Integrate and evaluate multiple sources of information presented in different media or formats as well as in words in order to address a question or solve a problem.

Speaking and Listening

1.a. Come to discussions prepared, having read and researched material under study; explicitly draw on that preparation by referring to evidence from texts and other research on the topic or issue to stimulate a thoughtful, well-reasoned exchange of ideas. *(p. 955)*

5. Make strategic use of digital media in presentations to enhance understanding of findings, reasoning, and evidence and to add interest.

ESSENTIAL QUESTION VOCABULARY

Use these words in your responses:

Literature and Place
empire
conquest
missionary

Literature and Society
zeal
smug
undermine

The Writer and Tradition
chaos
piety
reverence

Speaking and Listening

1. Review the assignment, pointing out that students are to deliver a multimedia presentation on the Crystal Palace.
2. Analyze the activity and identify its key terms: *multimedia presentation; innovative construction; use media strategically.*
3. Then, have students complete Activity B in the **Follow-Through** worksheet (p. 6 of ***Unit 5 Resources***).
4. After students have completed their presentations, have them discuss which elements they found most compelling.

PART 1

Relationships

Text Complexity: At a Glance

This chart gives a general text complexity rating for the selections in this part of the unit to help guide instruction. For additional text complexity support, see the Test Complexity Rubric at point of use.

from In Memoriam, A. H. H.	**More Accessible**	My Last Duchess	**More Complex**
The Lady of Shallot	**More Accessible**	Life in a Love	**More Accessible**
Tears, Idle Tears	**More Accessible**	Porphyria's Lover	**More Accessible**
Ulysses	**More Complex**	Sonnet 43	**More Accessible**

Selection Planning Guide

The selections in this part are poems by Alfred, Lord Tennyson and Robert and Elizabeth Barrett Browning that explore the theme "Relationships." The section opens with excerpts from Tennyson's tribute to his friend Arthur Hallam: "In Memoriam, A.H.H." Other explorations of a relationship between death and love are found in "Tears, Idle Tears" and "The Lady of Shalott." The latter poem is a lyric narrative of a romantic heroine who chooses love and finds death. Tennyson's famous dramatic monologue, "Ulysses," provides contrasts to Browning's "My Last Duchess," "Porphyria's Lover," and "Life in a Love," evoking multiple variations on relationships of love and life. Elizabeth Barrett Browning's famous Sonnet 43 epitomizes a loving relationship between a woman and her husband.

Humanities

Jealousy, by Tihamé von Margitay (1859–1922)

This nineteenth-century scene depicts a courtship between a man and woman. The formal meeting is broken by the man's intimate action of touching the woman's arm. Her small frame and demure behavior embody the ideal woman of the times. The soft colors and naturalistic setting add to the portrayal of courtship. Have students link the art to the focus of Part 1, "Relationships," by answering the following question:

What do you think is going on between the couple in this painting, and what elements of the painting lead you to this idea?

Answer: The man is courting the woman, indicated by his hand gestures, smile, and his relaxed posture. His action of touching her sleeve indicates affection for her, and her posture indicates her shyness. The look on her face shows her reluctance to accept his love as true.

Monitoring Progress

Before students read the poetry by Alfred, Lord Tennyson, refer to the results for the Vocabulary in Context items on **Benchmark Test 9** (*Unit 5 Resources*, pp. 152–157). Use this diagnostic portion of the test to guide your choice of selections to teach, as well as the depth of prereading preparation you will provide, based on students' readiness for the reading and vocabulary skills.

from *In Memoriam, A.H.H.* • The Lady of Shalott • Tears, Idle Tears • Ulysses

Lesson Pacing Guide

DAY 1 Preteach

- Administer the Reading and Vocabulary Warm-ups (*Unit 5 Resources,* pp. 7–10) as necessary.
- Introduce the Literary Analysis concept: Speaker.
- Introduce the Reading Strategy: Analyze an Author's Philosophical Assumptions and Beliefs.
- Build background with the author and Background features.
- Develop thematic thinking with Connecting to the Essential Question.
- Teach the selection vocabulary.

DAYS 2–3 Preteach/Teach/Assess

- Distribute copies of the appropriate graphic organizer for the Reading Strategy (*Graphic Organizer Transparencies,* pp. 169–170).
- Distribute copies of the appropriate graphic organizer for Literary Analysis (*Graphic Organizer Transparencies,* pp. 171–172)
- Prepare students to read with the Activating Prior Knowledge activities (TE).
- Informally monitor comprehension while students read.
- Use the Reading Check questions to confirm comprehension.
- Develop students' understanding of speaker using the Literary Analysis prompts.
- Develop students' ability to analyze an author's philosophical assumptions and beliefs using the Reading Strategy prompts.
- Reinforce vocabulary with the Vocabulary notes.
- Assess students' comprehension and mastery of the skills by having them answer the Critical Reading, Literary Analysis, and Reading Strategy questions.
- Have students complete the Vocabulary Lesson.

DAY 4 Extend/Assess

- Have students complete the Writing Lesson and write a biographical essay. (You may assign as homework.)
- Administer Selection Test A or B (*Unit 5 Resources,* pp. 19–21 or 22–24).

Common Core State Standards

Reading Literature 1. Cite strong and thorough textual evidence to support analysis of inferences drawn from the text.

Writing 2. Write informative/explanatory texts to examine and convey complex ideas, concepts, and information clearly and accurately through the effective selection, organization, and analysis of content.

Language 4.a. Use context as a clue to the meaning of a word or phrase.

Additional Standards Practice
Common Core Companion,* *pp. 2–9; 196–207; 324–325

Daily Block Scheduling
Each day in this Lesson Pacing Guide represents a 40–50 minute period. Teachers using block scheduling may combine days to revise pacing. In addition, teachers may differentiate and support core instruction by integrating components for extended and intensive support as students require. See the Guide to Selected Leveled Resources (facing page).

Guide to Selected Leveled Resources

RTI — Tier 1 (students performing on level)

from **In Memoriam, A.H.H. • The Lady of Shalott • Tears, Idle Tears • Ulysses**

Warm Up — Practice, model, and monitor fluency, working **with the whole class** or **in groups**.	Vocabulary and Reading Warm-ups B, *Unit 5 Resources,* pp. 7–8, 10
Comprehension/Skills — **Support** and **monitor** comprehension and skills development, having students complete the activities, graphic organizers, and interactive prompts **independently** or **as a class**.	• *Reader's Notebook,* adapted instruction and full selection **EL** *Reader's Notebook: English Learner's Version,* adapted instruction and adapted selection • Reading Strategy Graphic Organizer B, *Graphic Organizer Transparencies,* p. 178 • Literary Analysis Graphic Organizer B, *Graphic Organizer Transparencies,* p. 180
Monitor Progress — **Monitor** student progress with the differentiated curriculum-based assessment in the *Unit Resources.*	• **Selection Test B,** *Unit 5 Resources,* pp. 22–24 • **Open-Book Test,** *Unit 5 Resources,* pp. 16–18

RTI — Tier 2 (students requiring intervention)

from **In Memoriam, A.H.H. • The Lady of Shalott • Tears, Idle Tears • Ulysses**

Warm Up — Practice, model, and monitor fluency **in groups** or **with individuals**.	• Vocabulary and Reading Warm-ups A, *Unit 5 Resources,* pp. 7–9 • *Hear It!* Audio CD (adapted text)
Comprehension/Skills — • **Support** and **monitor** comprehension and skills development, working **in small groups** or **with individuals**. • As students complete the selection in the appropriate version of the *Reader's Notebook,* monitor comprehension frequently with group questions and individual instruction. • **Model** strategies while guiding students in completing the activities and prompts in the *Reader's Notebook,* as well as the graphic organizers. • **Practice** skills and **monitor** mastery with the *Reading Kit* worksheets.	• *Reader's Notebook: Adapted Version,* adapted instruction and adapted selection **EL** *Reader's Notebook: English Learner's Version,* adapted instruction and adapted selection • Reading Strategy Graphic Organizer A, *Graphic Organizer Transparencies,* p. 177 • Literary Analysis Graphic Organizer A, *Graphic Organizer Transparencies,* p. 179 • *Reading Kit,* Practice worksheets
Monitor Progress — **Monitor** student progress with the differentiated curriculum-based assessment in the *Unit Resources* and in the *Reading Kit.*	• **Selection Test A,** *Unit 5 Resources,* pp. 19–21 • *Reading Kit,* Assess worksheets

TIER 3 Tier 3 intervention may require consultation with the student's special-education or dyslexia specialist. For additional support, see the Tier 2 activities and resources listed above.

One-on-one teaching **Group work** **Whole class instruction** **Independent work** **A** Assessment

For a complete guide to selection support, including support for Advanced students, see the Overview of Resources in the frontmatter.

from *In Memoriam, A.H.H.* • The Lady of Shalott • Tears, Idle Tears • Ulysses

RESOURCES FOR:

- L1 Special-Needs Students
- L2 Below-Level Students (Tier 2)
- L3 On-Level Students (Tier 1)
- L4 Advanced Students (Tier 1)
- EL English Learners
- All All Students

Vocabulary/Fluency/Prior Knowledge

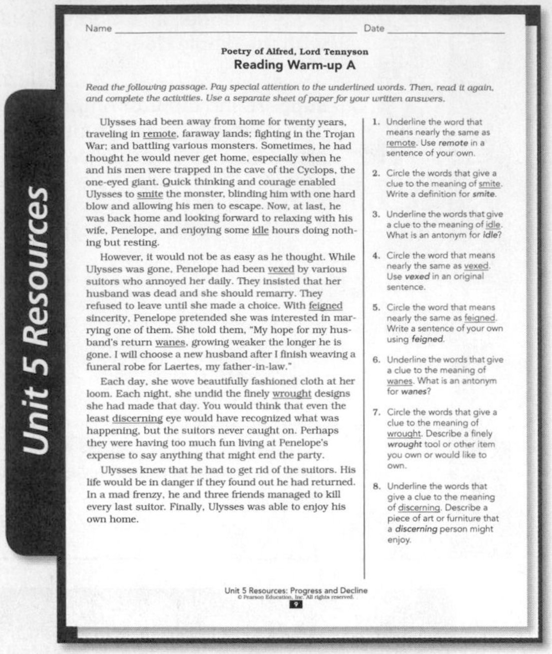

Unit 5 Resources

Name ______________________ Date ____________

Poetry of Alfred, Lord Tennyson
Reading Warm-up A

Read the following passage. Pay special attention to the underlined words. Then, read it again, and complete the activities. Use a separate sheet of paper for your written answers.

Ulysses had been away from home for twenty years, traveling in remote, faraway lands; fighting in the Trojan War; and battling various monsters. Sometimes, he had thought he would never get home, especially when he and his men were trapped in the cave of the Cyclops, the one-eyed giant. Quick thinking and courage enabled Ulysses to smite the monster, blinding him with one hard blow and allowing his men to escape. Now, at last, he was back home and looking forward to relaxing with his wife, Penelope, and enjoying some idle hours doing nothing but resting.

However, it would not be as easy as he thought. While Ulysses was gone, Penelope had been vexed by various suitors who annoyed her daily. They insisted that her husband was dead and she should remarry. They refused to leave until she made a choice. With feigned sincerity, Penelope pretended she was interested in marrying one of them. She told them, "My hope for my husband's return wanes, growing weaker the longer he is gone. I will choose a new husband after I finish weaving a funeral robe for Laertes, my father-in-law."

Each day, she wove beautifully fashioned cloth at her loom. Each night, she undid the finely wrought designs she had made that day. You would think that even the least discerning eye would have recognized what was happening, but the suitors never caught on. Perhaps they were having too much fun living at Penelope's expense to say anything that might end the party.

Ulysses knew that he had to get rid of the suitors. His life would be in danger if they found out he had returned. In a mad frenzy, he and three friends managed to kill every last suitor. Finally, Ulysses was able to enjoy his own home.

1. Underline the word that means nearly the same as remote. Use *remote* in a sentence of your own.
2. Circle the words that give a clue to the meaning of smite. Write a definition for *smite*.
3. Underline the words that give a clue to the meaning of idle. What is an antonym for *idle*?
4. Circle the word that means nearly the same as vexed. Use *vexed* in an original sentence.
5. Circle the word that means nearly the same as feigned. Write a sentence of your own using *feigned*.
6. Underline the words that give a clue to the meaning of wanes. What is an antonym for *wanes*?
7. Circle the words that give a clue to the meaning of wrought. Describe a finely *wrought* tool or other item you own or would like to own.
8. Underline the words that give a clue to the meaning of discerning. Describe a piece of art or furniture that a *discerning* person might enjoy.

Unit 5 Resources: Progress and Decline
© Pearson Education, Inc. All rights reserved.
9

EL L1 L2 **Reading Warm-ups A and B,** pp. 9–10

Also available for these selections:

EL L1 L2 **Vocabulary Warm-ups A and B,** pp. 7–8

All **Vocabulary Builder,** p. 13

Reader's Notebooks

Pre- and postreading pages for these selections appear in an interactive format in the *Reader's Notebooks.* Each *Notebook* is differentiated for a different group of learners. The selections in the Adapted and English Learner's versions are abridged.

L2 L3 ***Reader's Notebook***

L1 ***Reader's Notebook: Adapted Version***

EL ***Reader's Notebook: English Learner's Version***

EL ***Reader's Notebook: Spanish Version***

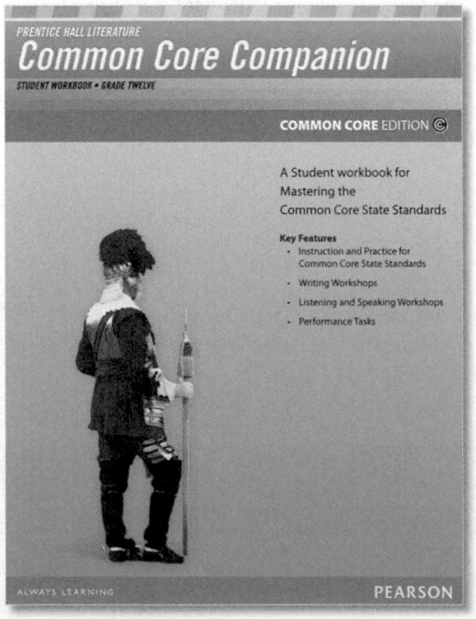

Common Core Companion

Additional instruction and practice for each Common Core State Standard

Graphic Organizer Transparencies

Selection Support

from *In Memoriam, A.H.H.*
"The Lady of Shalott"
from *The Princess:* Tears, Idle Tears
and "Ulysses" by Alfred, Lord Tennyson

Before You Read B: Author's Philosophical Beliefs

Details

↓

Message

↓

My Own Experience

↓

Judgment

Graphic Organizer Transparencies
© Pearson Education, Inc. All rights reserved.
170

EL L3 **Reading: Graphic Organizer B,** p. 170

Also available for these selections:

EL L1 L2 **Reading: Graphic Organizer A,** p. 169

EL L1 L2 **Literary Analysis: Graphic Organizer A,** (partially filled in), p. 171

EL L3 **Literary Analysis: Graphic Organizer B,** p. 172

Unit 5 Resources

Skills Development/Extension

Name ______________________ Date ____________

from **In Memoriam, A.H.H., "The Lady of Shalott," "Ulysses,"** and *from* **The Princess: "Tears, Idle Tears"** by Alfred, Lord Tennyson

Reading Strategy: Analyze Author's Assumptions and Beliefs

If we look beyond the words and images in poetry, we can often find the author's assumptions and beliefs. Depending on when and where the author lived and his or her experiences, those assumptions and beliefs may or may not be familiar to us. As you read a poem, first try to understand the speaker's meaning. The speaker may be the author of the poem or a fictional character. Once you understand what the speaker is saying, figure out the author's assumptions and/or beliefs that underlie the speaker's words.

DIRECTIONS: *In the following chart, record the poet's message and then what you believe to be the underlying assumption or belief in the message.*

Quote From Poem	Speaker's Meaning	Underlying Assumption/ Belief
1. But who shall so forecast the years/And find in loss a gain to match?/Or reach a hand through time to catch/ The far=off interest of tears? ("In Memoriam, A.H.H.")		
2. O Death in Life, the days that are no more. ("Tears, Idle Tears")		
3. I am a part of all that I have met;/ Yet all experience is an arch wherethrough/Gleams that untraveled world, whose margin fades/ Forever and forever when I move. ("Ulysses")		

All **Reading: Analyze an author's philosophical assumptions and beliefs,** p. 12

Also available for these selections:

All **Literary Analysis: Speaker,** p. 11

EL L3 L4 **Support for Writing,** p. 14

L4 **Enrichment,** p. 15

Assessment

Name ______________________ Date ____________

from **In Memoriam, A.H.H., "The Lady of Shalott,"**
from **The Princess: "Tears, Idle Tears,"** and **"Ulysses"**
by Alfred, Lord Tennyson

Selection Test B

Critical Reading *Identify the letter of the choice that best completes the statement or answers the question.*

___ 1. "In Memoriam, A.H.H." was written by Tennyson to commemorate
A. a dead close friend.
B. the end of a love affair.
C. sailors who died in a critical naval battle.
D. the lives of common people.

___ 2. An author of a poem may communicate his own philosophical beliefs or assumptions
A. only if he is speaking in his own voice.
B. either in his own voice or in the voice of a fictional character.
C. only if he has adopted the voice of a fictional character.
D. only if he writes about his poetry in order to explain it.

___ 3. The speaker of "In Memoriam, A.H.H." seems to be
A. a casual acquaintance of A.H.H.
B. someone who never knew A.H.H.
C. one who contemplates death impersonally.
D. Tennyson himself.

___ 4. What is the meaning of the following line in "In Memoriam, A.H.H."?
Far off thou art, but ever nigh
A. The speaker regrets that A.H.H. ever left the country.
B. No matter how much he remembers, death still removes his friend forever.
C. Although A.H.H. is dead, the speaker holds his memory close.
D. Death and life are closer than it may seem.

___ 5. What is the theme of "In Memoriam, A.H.H."?
A. the endurance of love beyond death
B. the tragic termination of friendship
C. the awful injustice of dying young
D. the gradual fading of painful memories

___ 6. In form and content, "The Lady of Shalott" recalls
A. Christian allegories.
B. national epics.
C. medieval romances.
D. classical drama.

EL L3 L4 **Selection Test B,** pp. 22–24

Also available for these selections:

EL L1 L2 **Selection Test A,** pp. 19–21

L3 L4 **Open-Book Test,** pp. 16–18

PHLit Online!
www.PHLitOnline.com

- complete narrated selection text
- a thematically related video with writing prompt
- an interactive graphic organizer
- highlighting feature
- access to all student print resources, adapted to individual student needs
- Spanish and English summaries
- adapted selection translations in Spanish

Online Resources: All print materials are also available online.

Background Video

Also available:

Get Connected! (thematic video with writing prompt)
All videos are available in Spanish.

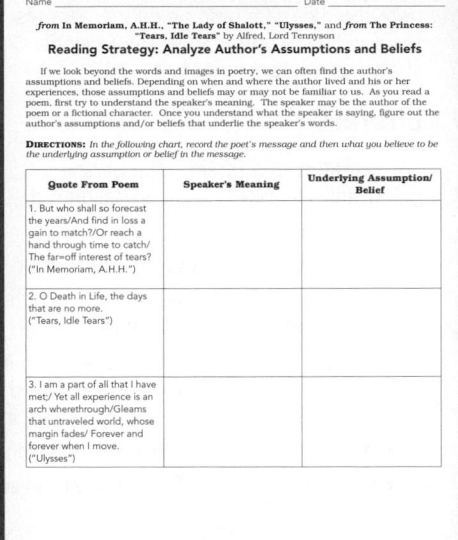

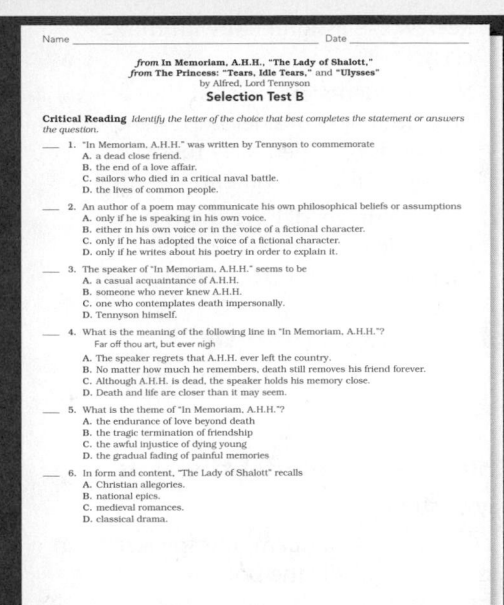

Vocabulary Central (tools and activities for studying vocabulary)

Also available:

Writer's Journal (with graphics feature)

PRETEACH

❶ Connecting to the Essential Question

1. Review the assignment with the class.
2. Have students think about the qualities they consider important to friendship. Then have them complete the assignment.
3. As students read, have them look for the ideas Tennyson explores as a result of his friend's death.

❷ Literary Analysis

Introduce the skill using the instruction on the student page.

Think Aloud: Model the Skill

Say to students:

I know that in a poem, the speaker is not necessarily the poet. It could be written from the perspective of a different person or a fictional character, as is seen in the poem "Ulysses." Clues in the poem will usually help me determine the identity of the speaker.

❸ Reading Strategy

1. Introduce the skill using the instruction on the student page.
2. Give students a copy of **Reading Strategy Graphic Organizer B,** page 170 in ***Graphic Organizer Transparencies,*** to fill out as they read.

Think Aloud: Model the Skill

Say to students:

If I want to understand the author's philosophical assumptions and beliefs, I have to analyze the details provided in the poem. I might look at the poet's diction, or word choice. Or I might look at the tone of the piece.

❹ Vocabulary

1. Pronounce each word, giving its definition, and have students say it aloud.
2. For more guidance, see the ***Classroom Strategies and Teaching Routines*** card for introducing vocabulary.

Before You Read

from ***In Memoriam, A.H.H.* • *The Lady of Shalott* • *Tears, Idle Tears* • *Ulysses***

❶ **Connecting to the Essential Question** *In Memoriam, A.H.H.* is a poem Tennyson wrote in memory of his best friend, Arthur Hallam. As you read, note the ideas Tennyson explores as a result of his friend's death. This focus will help you answer the Essential Question: **How does literature shape or reflect society?**

Common Core State Standards

Reading Literature

1. Cite strong and thorough textual evidence to support analysis of what the text says explicitly as well as inferences drawn from the text, including determining where the text leaves matters uncertain.

❷ Literary Analysis

The **speaker** in a poem—the person who "says" its words—is not necessarily the poet. Speakers fall into the following categories:

- Fictional or real
- Generalized (not described in specific detail) or with a specific identity

As you read, determine the identity of each speaker and analyze the speaker's conflict and motivation.

Comparing Literary Works Some of Tennyson's speakers have histories—they have undergone a change or suffered a loss. Using such speakers, he dramatizes different experiences of time, including the following:

- A perpetual present, in which nothing significant changes
- Restless movement from past achievement into an unknown future
- The loss of the past

Consider whether each poem creates its own "time"—a moment in which the speaker sums up the past, making way for the future.

❸ Reading Strategy

Preparing to Read Complex Texts Analyzing an author's philosophical assumptions and beliefs will help you understand the meaning of a poem. For example, Tennyson's speaker in "Ulysses" expresses a desire "to seek a newer world." The speaker's restless drive to explore suggests that Tennyson, like many Victorians, valued progress. Use what is stated explicitly, or directly, in the text as the basis for making inferences about the author's assumptions and beliefs. As you read, use a chart like the one shown to identify the author's beliefs.

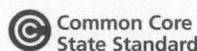

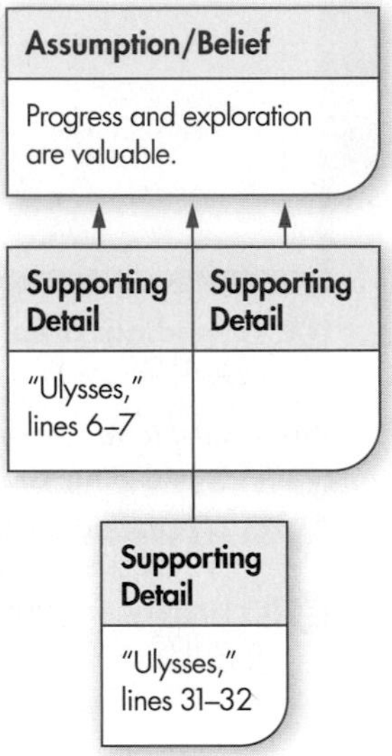

❹ Vocabulary

chrysalis (kris′ l is) *n.* the third stage in the development of a moth or butterfly (p. 961)

diffusive (di fyo͞o′ siv) *adj.* tending to spread out (p. 962)

prosper (präs′ pər) *v.* thrive (p. 962)

waning (wān′ iŋ) *v.* gradually dimming or weakening (p. 967)

prudence (pro͞od′ ns) *n.* careful management of resources; economy (p. 972)

furrows (fur′ ōz) *n.* grooves, such as those made by a plow (p. 972)

PHLit Online! www.PHLitOnline.com

Vocabulary Development

Vocabulary Knowledge Rating

Create a **Vocabulary Knowledge Rating Chart** (***Professional Development Guidebook,*** p. 33) for the vocabulary words on the student page. Give each student a copy of the chart with the words on it. Read the words aloud, and have students mark their ratings in the Before Reading column. Urge students to attend to these words as they read and discuss the selections.

In order to gauge how much instruction you need to provide, tally how many students are confident in their knowledge of each word. As students read, point out the words and their context.

PHLit Online! **Vocabulary Central,** featuring tools and activities for studying vocabulary, is available online at **www.PHLitOnline.com.**

5 Author of *In Memoriam, A.H.H.* • "The Lady of Shalott" • "Tears, Idle Tears" • "Ulysses"

Tennyson was born in the rural town of Somersby in Lincolnshire, the fourth of twelve children. He was a sensitive boy who was charmed by the magical words "far, far away." His father, a clergyman, had a large library and supervised Tennyson's early education, predicting that his son would be "the greatest Poet of the Time." At the same time, Tennyson's father was extremely bitter, having been disinherited by his own father. His anger poisoned the atmosphere of the Tennyson household. As a teenager, Alfred was probably eager to escape to Cambridge University.

The Power of Friendship At first, Tennyson was disappointed by Cambridge. Then, he met the young man who became his closest friend, Arthur Henry Hallam. They were often together, and Hallam intended to marry Tennyson's sister Emily. In 1830, with Hallam's encouragement, Tennyson published *Poems, Chiefly Lyrical.*

A Stunning Tragedy In 1833, however, Hallam died suddenly, leaving a void in Tennyson's life that nearly destroyed him. Soon after Hallam's death, Tennyson began working on a series of short poems that considered questions of death, religious faith, and immortality. This series, which grew over seventeen years into an extended elegy for his friend, was published in 1850 under the title *In Memoriam, A.H.H.*

National Honor The elegy so impressed Prince Albert that in 1850, he encouraged Queen Victoria to appoint Tennyson the poet laureate of England, replacing the recently deceased Wordsworth.

In 1884, Queen Victoria made Tennyson a baron, and so added the title of Lord to his name.

Land, Literature, Long Life When royalties from *In Memoriam, A.H.H.* began to flow in, Tennyson bought a farm on the Isle of Wight. There, he and his wife Emily Sellwood raised two children. Tennyson continued to publish poems into his eighties.

ALFRED, LORD TENNYSON

(1809–1892)

Daily Bellringer

For each class during which you will teach these selections, have students complete one of the five activities for the appropriate week in the ***Daily Bellringer Activities*** booklet.

Multidraft Reading

To assist struggling readers and to enhance reading for all, assign the text in chunks, as warranted by length, and apply multidraft reading protocols. For each reading, have students set the purpose indicated:

- **First reading**—identifying key ideas and details and answering any Reading Checks.
- **Second reading**—analyzing craft and structure and responding to the side-column prompts.
- **Third reading**—integrating knowledge and ideas, connecting to other texts and the world, and answering the end-of-selection questions.

For more guidance, refer to the ***Classroom Strategies and Teaching Routines*** card on Multidraft Reading.

5 Background

More About the Author

Tennyson's reputation as a poet began early in his career at Cambridge University. Tennyson suffered poverty until middle age because his father had been disinherited in favor of his younger brother. Tennyson did not marry until he was forty, and he is believed to have tended toward emotional instability and melancholy for much of his life. The death of his friend Arthur Henry Hallam was a life-altering experience for Tennyson. In addition to the homage he paid him in his monumental *In Memoriam, A.H.H.,* Tennyson named his son Hallam after his dead friend.

PHLit Online!
www.PHLitOnline.com

Teaching From Technology

Preparing to Read
Go to **www.PHLitOnline.com** and display the ***Get Connected!*** slide show for these selections. Have the class brainstorm responses to the writing prompt, entering ideas in the interactive journal. Then, have students complete their written responses individually, in a lab or as homework.

To build background, display the Background and More About the Author features.

Using the Interactive Text
Go to **www.PHLitOnline.com** and display the **Enriched Online Student Edition.** As the class reads the selection or listens to the narration, record answers to side-column prompts using the graphic organizers accessible on the interactive page. Alternatively, have students use the online edition individually, answering the prompts as they read.

❶ About the Selection

In Memoriam, A.H.H., an elegy, or poem that mourns death, was written as a tribute to Tennyson's closest friend, Arthur Henry Hallam, who died at twenty-two.

❷ Activating Prior Knowledge

Ask students to think of tributes they have heard in music or poetry. For example, some may mention Elton John's "Candle in the Wind," as a tribute to Princess Diana. Have students write a paragraph describing how a tribute of their choosing was particularly memorable.

Concept Connector →

Tell students they will return to their responses after reading the selection.

❸ Humanities

The Stages of Life, 1835, by Caspar David Friedrich

Friedrich (1774–1840) is considered the most important of the German Romantic painters. The painting *The Stages of Life* shows Friedrich himself with his family. It was painted shortly after he suffered a stroke, and the central figure, the artist (with the cane), is staring out to sea. The large ship is Friedrich's ship of life, and approaching night (sunset) in the painting symbolizes the artist's death. Use this question for discussion:

How is the use of dark and light in the painting reflected in Tennyson's poem?

Answer: The poet moves through despair into hope, just as the artist looks from the foreground into the sunset.

❸

The Stages of Life, Caspar David Friedrich, Museum der Bildenden Kunst, Leipzig

❶ ❷

FROM In Memoriam, A. H. H.

ALFRED, LORD TENNYSON

❹ **▲ Critical Viewing** This painting, *The Stages of Life,* suggests that life is like a voyage. How would the speaker in the poem react to such a comparison? Explain. **[Speculate]**

1

I held it truth, with him who sings
  To one clear harp in divers[1] tones,
  That men may rise on stepping stones
Of their dead selves to higher things.

But who shall so forecast the years
  And find in loss a gain to match?
  Or reach a hand through time to catch
The far-off interest of tears?

1. divers (dī′ vərz) *adj.* varied; having many parts.

Text Complexity Rubric

	from In Memoriam, A. H. H.	The Lady of Shalott	Tears, Idle Tears	Ulysses
Qualitative Measures				
Context/ Knowledge Demands	Victorian elegy 1 ② 3 4 5	Narrative poem 1 2 ③ 4 5	Victorian lyric 1 ② 3 4 5	Dramatic poem 1 2 3 ④ 5
Structure/Language Conventionality and Clarity	Poetic diction and syntax 1 ② 3 4 5	Poetic diction and syntax 1 2 ③ 4 5	Poetic diction and syntax 1 ② 3 4 5	Poetic diction and syntax 1 2 ③ 4 5
Levels of Meaning/ Purpose/Concepts	Accessible (relationships) 1 2 ③ 4 5	Moderate (Arthurian romance) 1 2 ③ 4 5	Accessible (transience of life) 1 2 ③ 4 5	Moderate (old age, death) 1 2 3 ④ 5
Quantitative Measures				
Lexile/Text Length	NP / 411 words	NP / 992 words	NP / 172 words	NP / 564 words
Overall Complexity	**More accessible**	**More accessible**	**More accessible**	**More complex**

Let Love clasp Grief lest both be drowned,
Let darkness keep her raven gloss.
Ah, sweeter to be drunk with loss,
To dance with death, to beat the ground,

Than that the victor Hours should scorn
The long result of love, and boast,
"Behold the man that loved and lost,
But all he was is overworn."

7

Dark house, by which once more I stand
Here in the long unlovely street,
Doors, where my heart was used to beat
So quickly, waiting for a hand,

5 A hand that can be clasped no more—
Behold me, for I cannot sleep,
And like a guilty thing I creep
At earliest morning to the door.

He is not here; but far away
The noise of life begins again,
And ghastly through the drizzling rain
On the bald street breaks the blank day.

82

I wage not any feud with Death
For changes wrought on form and face;
No lower life that earth's embrace
May breed with him, can fright my faith.

6 Eternal process moving on,
From state to state the spirit walks;
And these are but the shattered stalks,
Or ruined **chrysalis** of one.

Nor blame I Death, because he bare
The use of virtue out of earth;
I know transplanted human worth
Will bloom to profit, otherwhere.

For this alone on Death I wreak
The wrath that garners in my heart;
He put our lives so far apart
We cannot hear each other speak.

He put our lives so far apart
We cannot hear each other speak.

Literary Analysis
The Speaker in Poetry What do you learn about the speaker in lines 21–24?

Reading Strategy
Analyzing Philosophical Beliefs In lines 29–44, what does the poet suggest about the consolations of faith and philosophy?

Vocabulary
chrysalis (kris´ l is)
n. the third stage in the development of a moth or butterfly

7 **Reading Check**

What are two of the main feelings Tennyson conveys in these stanzas?

4 Critical Viewing

Possible response: The speaker would reject the idea that life is like a voyage, since his friend's life was senselessly cut short.

5 Literary Analysis

The Speaker in Poetry

1. Review various kinds of speakers.
2. Have a volunteer read aloud the bracketed passage. **Ask** students to paraphrase the stanza. **Possible response:** I can no longer clasp your hand. I cannot sleep and instead creep about troubled by my guilt and grief.
3. **Ask** the Literary Analysis question: **Answer:** The speaker is grieving for a friend and suffering from insomnia.

6 Reading Strategy

Analyzing Philosophical Beliefs

1. Have students read lines 29–44, paraphrasing each stanza to determine the main idea or image in each.
2. For example, point out the word *chrysalis* in line 36. **Ask** students what the speaker implies about Hallam, based on this image. **Answer:** A chrysalis is a cocoon; this image implies that death is only a transformation.
3. **Ask** the Reading Strategy question: In lines 29–44, what does the poet suggest about the consolations of faith and philosophy? **Answer:** They do not touch him because no explanation or theory will let him speak with his friend.

7 Reading Check

Answer: Tennyson conveys his grief at losing his friend, and his wrath at Death for having separated them.

Text Complexity: Reader and Task Suggestions

	In Memoriam; Tears, Idle Tears	The Lady of Shalott	Ulysses
Preparing to Read the Texts • Using the information on SE p. 959, explain that a friend's early death had a lifelong effect on Tennyson. • Discuss with students the reasons that sorrow might cause a poet to turn to the mythic past. • Guide students to use Multidraft Reading strategies (TE p. 959).	**Leveled Tasks** ***Levels of Meaning*** If students will have difficulty with the poems' ideas, have them first focus on the emotions each speaker expresses. Then, have students consider the effects of those emotions on each speaker's world view. ***Synthesizing*** If students will not have difficulty with the ideas, have them compare the emotions expressed in the two poems and contrast their different causes.	**Leveled Tasks** ***Structure/Language*** If students will have difficulty with the poetic language, have them read portions and concentrate on the poem's music. Then, have them read the whole poem, focusing on the title character. ***Analyzing*** If students will not have difficulty with the language, have them analyze how imagery and sound effects contribute to the poem's mood or atmosphere.	**Leveled Tasks** ***Knowledge Demands*** If students have difficulty with the literary context, help them contrast the clever adventurer-king of the *Odyssey* with the speaker in this poem. Then, have them consider what the speaker's attitudes suggest about old age. ***Analyzing*** If students will not have difficulty with the context, have them analyze the universal themes that Ulysses expresses.

ASSESS

Answers

Before students respond, you may wish to have them write a brief objective summary of the selection. As they answer the questions below, remind them to support their answers with evidence from the text.

1. (a) The speaker had thought men could learn from and elevate themselves through their losses. (b) He argues that grief must be embraced to affirm the value of love.
2. (a) He is standing by the house where his friend had lived. (b) The loss of his friend makes the scene bleak and empty.
3. The speaker is not angered by the thought that his friend's form or body has been destroyed or that the world has been robbed of his friend's virtues. He is angered that Death has separated him from his friend.
4. (a) Although the friend is dead and his voice and physical presence are gone, the speaker feels close to his spirit at all times. (b) Section 130 reconfigures the speaker's complaint that Death has put their "lives so far apart" into the idea that "Far off thou art, but ever nigh."

I prosper, circled with thy voice;
I shall not lose thee though I die.

130

Thy voice is on the rolling air;
    I hear thee where the waters run;
    Thou standest in the rising sun,
And in the setting thou art fair.

What art thou then? I cannot guess;
    But though I seem in star and flower
    To feel thee some **diffusive** power,
I do not therefore love thee less.

My love involves the love before;
    My love is vaster passion now;
    Though mixed with God and Nature thou,
I seem to love thee more and more.

Far off thou art, but ever nigh;
    I have thee still, and I rejoice;
    I **prosper**, circled with thy voice;
I shall not lose thee though I die.

Vocabulary
diffusive (di fyo͞o′ siv) *adj.* tending to spread out
prosper (präs′ pər) *v.* thrive

Critical Reading

Cite textual evidence to support your responses.

1. **Key Ideas and Details (a)** In section 1, what idea does the speaker say he once held as truth but now doubts? **(b) Interpret:** The speaker rejects this truth in favor of a new view of grief. Paraphrase this view.
2. **Key Ideas and Details (a)** By what place is the speaker standing in section 7? **(b) Interpret:** What effect does the loss of his friend have on the scene?
3. **Integration of Knowledge and Ideas** Contrast the facts that, in section 82, the speaker says do not anger him with the one fact that does.
4. **Integration of Knowledge and Ideas (a) Interpret:** Explain the paradox in line 57: "Far off thou art, but ever nigh." **(b) Connect:** How does section 130 answer the speaker's one reason for anger in section 82?

Think Aloud

Critical Reading Question
To model the Critical Reading question 5b, use the following "think aloud":

I know that the speaker's reason for being angry in Section 82 was because Death had separated him from his friend. But how does Section 130 answer this? I know that in Section 130 the speaker states, "Thy voice is on the rolling air." He later states, "Far off thou art, but ever nigh." I think he is saying that although they are apart, the speaker feels him all around. I think he is saying that his thoughts of him bring them closer together, even though Death has separated them.

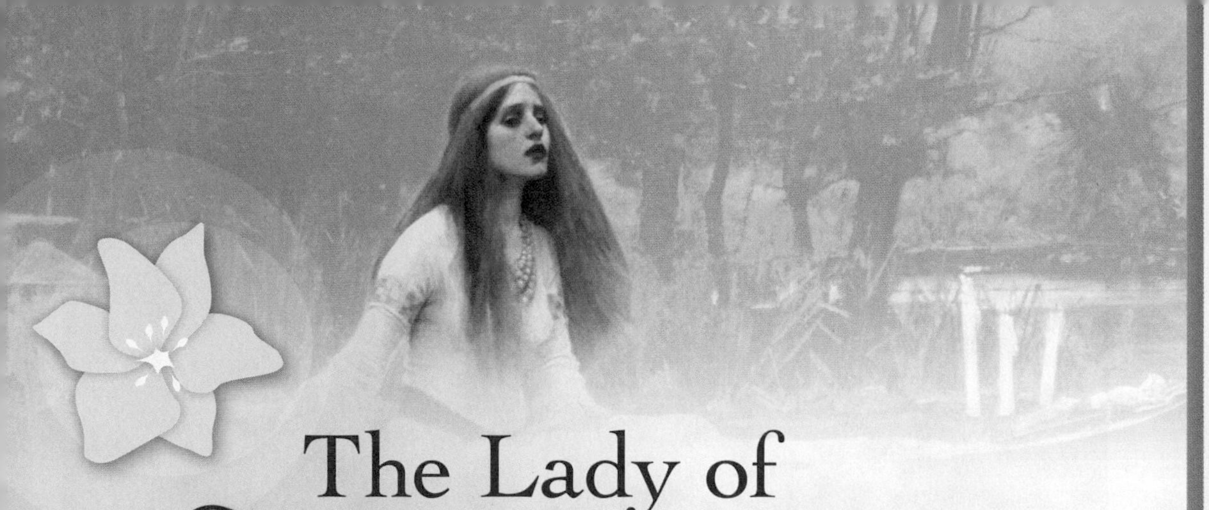

The Lady of SHALOTT

ALFRED, LORD TENNYSON

PART I

On either side the river lie
Long fields of barley and of rye,
That clothe the wold[1] and meet the sky;
And through the field the road runs by
To many-towered Camelot,[2]
And up and down the people go,
Gazing where the lilies blow[3]
Round an island there below,
The island of Shalott.

Willows whiten, aspens quiver,
Little breezes dusk and shiver
Through the wave that runs forever
By the island in the river
Flowing down to Camelot.
Four gray walls, and four gray towers,
Overlook a space of flowers,
And the silent isle imbowers
The Lady of Shalott.

The Lady of Shalott, (detail), John Waterhouse, The Tate Gallery, London

Literary Analysis
The Speaker in Poetry
What does setting this poem in the days of King Arthur suggest about the poet's attitude toward the past?

1. **wold** rolling plains.
2. **Camelot** legendary English town where King Arthur had his court and Round Table.
3. **blow** bloom.

8 About the Selection

"The Lady of Shalott" is a poem based on an Arthurian legend, but it is also about the position of the creative artist in society. The central character, the Lady of Shalott, has lived under a curse barring her from experiencing the real world—under pain of death. The Lady is locked away from the vital life of society, seeing life only through a mirror. In the same way, Tennyson suggests that many artists are locked away from life, looking at it secondhand.

9 Literary Analysis

The Speaker in Poetry

1. Have students read the first stanza to themselves. **Ask** students to explain the significance of the reference to Camelot. Have students consider why the poet would use Camelot as a setting.
   Answer: Camelot was the name of the legendary King Arthur's kingdom.
2. **Then, ask** them the Literary Analysis question: What does setting this poem in the days of King Arthur suggest about the poet's attitude toward the past?
   Answer: The poet is intrigued by the past and feels that it is a rich source of poetic material and inquiry. Perhaps he also feels that the past is a refuge from a confusing or ugly present.

Differentiated Instruction for Universal Access

Strategy for Less Proficient Readers
Have students begin reading "The Lady of Shalott" with teacher guidance. Remind them that the speaker tells the poem from the perspective of a spectator of the Lady. Ask them to consider, in an imaginary diary entry, what Lancelot thought on his way to Camelot, as he stood and "mused a little space."

EL Background for English Learners
Remind students that Tennyson sets his poems in the atmosphere of Arthurian legend, and he cloaks the Lady of Shalott with mystery. Have students begin to read the poem with teacher guidance, sounding out any words that give them difficulty.

⑩ Humanities

The Lady of Shalott, by John Waterhouse

John William Waterhouse (1849–1917) studied and exhibited at the Royal Academy in London. He is considered to be both a Classical and a Pre-Raphaelite painter of mainly romantic and poetic subjects. Much of his work was inspired by the poetry of Tennyson and Keats.

This painting, beautifully detailed and executed, was done in iridescent colors that lend a supernatural feel. Note the Lady's grief-stricken expression, which registers her resignation to her fate. Use these questions for discussion:

1. Does the painting appear to be true to the details of the poem?
   Possible response: In important details, the painting is true to the poem. The Lady in the painting is dressed in white, afloat on a boat that resembles the boat described in the poem. She appears beautiful, mysterious, and very much alone.
2. In what way does the mood of the painting effectively mirror that of the poem?
   Possible response: The painting is dark and sadly romantic, as is the poem's overall mood.

⑪ Critical Viewing

Answer: The chain in the Lady's hand may represent her bondage to fate; the flickering candle suggests the flickering flame of her life.

The Lady of Shalott, John Waterhouse, The Tate Gallery, London

⑪ ▲ Critical Viewing
What symbols of the Lady of Shalott's occupation and eventual fate are in this painting? Explain why they are significant. **[Interpret]**

By the margin, willow-veiled,
Slide the heavy barges trailed
By slow horses; and unhailed
The shallop[4] flitteth silken-sailed
 Skimming down to Camelot:
But who hath seen her wave her hand?
Or at the casement seen her stand?
Or is she known in all the land,
 The Lady of Shalott?

Only reapers, reaping early
In among the bearded barley,
Hear a song that echoes cheerly,
From the river winding clearly,
 Down to towered Camelot:
And by the moon the reaper weary,
Piling sheaves in uplands airy,
Listening, whispers, "'Tis the fairy
 Lady of Shalott."

4. **shallop** light, open boat.

Enrichment: Understanding Legends

Arthurian Legends
Explain to students that many people have written about King Arthur and his knights of the Round Table. Tennyson himself wrote a long poem called *The Idylls of the King,* which is about Arthur's life and death. Other well-known treatments include *Sir Gawain and the Green Knight; A Connecticut Yankee in King Arthur's Court,* written by Mark Twain in 1889; and *The Once and Future King,* published in 1958 by T. H. White.

Activity: Descriptive Writing Have students conduct research on the historical period of the Arthurian legends. Suggest that they record information in the **Enrichment: Building Context** worksheet, ***Professional Development Guidebook,*** page 222. Have them use the results of their research to write a one-page description of what it might be like living during that historical period.

PART II

There she weaves by night and day
A magic web with colors gay.
She has heard a whisper say,
A curse is on her if she stay
    To look down to Camelot.
She knows not what the curse may be,
And so she weaveth steadily,
And little other care hath she,
    The Lady of Shalott.

And moving through a mirror[5] clear
That hangs before her all the year,
Shadows of the world appear.
There she sees the highway near
    Winding down to Camelot:
There the river eddy whirls,
And there the surly village churls,[6]
And the red cloaks of market girls,
    Pass onward from Shalott.

Sometimes a troop of damsels glad,
An abbot on an ambling pad,[7]
Sometimes a curly shepherd lad,
Or long-haired page in crimson clad,
    Goes by to towered Camelot;
And sometimes through the mirror blue
The knights come riding two and two:
She hath no loyal knight and true,
    The Lady of Shalott.

But in her web she still delights
To weave the mirror's magic sights,
For often through the silent nights
A funeral, with plumes and lights
12   And music, went to Camelot:
Or when the moon was overhead,
Came two young lovers lately wed;
"I am half sick of shadows," said
    The Lady of Shalott.

5. **mirror** Weavers placed mirrors in front of their looms, so that they could view the progress of their work.
6. **churls** (chʉrlz) *n.* farm laborers; peasants.
7. **pad** easy-paced horse.

12 Literary Analysis
The Speaker in Poetry
Is the speaker who tells the Lady of Shalott's story also a character in the poem? How can you tell?

13 Reading Check
What does the Lady of Shalott do with her time?

12 Literary Analysis

The Speaker in Poetry

1. Explain to students that sometimes the speaker of a poem is a character involved in the action. In other poems, the speaker is similar to an omniscient narrator who does not participate in the action.
2. Have students read lines 64–72. Ask them to pay careful attention to the speaker's relation to the action being described.
3. Then, **ask** students the Literary Analysis question: Is the speaker who tells the Lady of Shalott's story also a character in the poem? How can you tell?
   Answer: No, the speaker who tells her story is not a character in the poem. This is clear from the fact that the speaker is omniscient and does not participate in events.

13 Reading Check

Answer: Night and day, the Lady of Shalott weaves a tapestry showing the scenes she sees in her magic mirror.

Differentiated Instruction for Universal Access

Support for Special-Needs Students
Students may find the elaborate description of the world of the Lady of Shalott somewhat daunting. Encourage them to read slowly with teacher guidance.

EL Strategy for English Learners
English language learners may find the descriptions of the Lady of Shalott's day-to-day activities and the Arthurian legends behind her story difficult to understand. Encourage them to question the text, to rely on the footnotes and definitions, and to paraphrase passages.

Enrichment for Gifted/Talented Students
As students read from the poem, point out that in "The Lady of Shalott," Camelot is a town populated by common people going about the business of making a living. Have students make drawings of Camelot, with its towers in the background, on a typical day.

(14) The British Tradition

A Crisis of Faith

Charles Darwin's theory of a natural, rather than a divine, origin of species, put forth in *On the Origin of Species* (1859), was a contributing source of anxiety in the Victorian era. He proposed that creatures possessing advantageous mutations survived to reproduce and pass their characteristics on to offspring. In this way, a new species could evolve from an old one. Just as Copernicus shocked the world in his *De Revolutionibus* (1543) with the theory that the planets revolved around the sun and not the Earth, so too did Darwin with his "agnostic" view of the origin of life. Darwin's work gave rise to intense opposition in his lifetime because it seemed to contradict the biblical account of creation.

Connect to the Literature

Encourage students to reflect on the details of the setting in Part III before responding to the Connect to the Literature question.

Possible response: Sir Lancelot's war gear is used for violence, but the tranquil Shalott—filled with barley fields, trees, cloudless blue skies, and rivers—seems to be a place of peace and tranquility.

(15) Critical Thinking

Make Judgments

1. Have students read lines 91–108 to themselves. Encourage them to focus on the description of Lancelot.
2. Then, **ask** students to address how the Lady of Shalott feels about Sir Lancelot: What does he represent to her?
   Possible response: She sees Lancelot as the embodiment of knightly beauty, bravery, and chivalry. He represents the life and love she has missed by staying in her tower.

---

(14) *The* **BRITISH TRADITION**

A Crisis of Faith

When the grief-stricken Tennyson of *In Memoriam* pushes away the comforting philosophies of his day, or when he turns to the mythic past in "The Lady of Shalott," he reflects a broader crisis of faith that rocked Victorian society. The Industrial Revolution and its teeming urban masses had pushed aside the traditional bond between peasant and lord. The comfortable rhythms of a farming society had given way to surging spirals of economic boom and bust. Meanwhile, such intellectual developments as Charles Darwin's theory of evolution challenged religious beliefs.

In the midst of these social and intellectual changes, Victorian artists asked whether their cultural resources—religion, science, art—were still sufficient to guide their lives. From Tennyson to Matthew Arnold to T. S. Eliot to Philip Larkin, the theme of a fractured culture, unable to answer its own questions, persists to this day.

Connect to the Literature

In what way might the isolated Lady of Shalott find the sight of Sir Lancelot a crisis of faith?

PART III

A bow-shot from her bower eaves,
He rode between the barley sheaves,
The sun came dazzling through the leaves,
And flamed upon the brazen greaves[8]
Of bold Sir Lancelot.
A red-cross knight[9] forever kneeled
To a lady in his shield,
That sparkled on the yellow field,
Beside remote Shalott.

The gemmy[10] bridle glittered free,
Like to some branch of stars we see
Hung in the golden Galaxy.[11]
The bridle bells rang merrily
As he rode down to Camelot:
And from his blazoned baldric[12] slung
A mighty silver bugle hung,
And as he rode his armor rung,
Beside remote Shalott.

All in the blue unclouded weather
Thick-jeweled shone the saddle leather,
The helmet and the helmet feather
Burned like one burning flame together,
As he rode down to Camelot.
As often through the purple night,
Below the starry clusters bright,
Some bearded meteor, trailing light,
Moves over still Shalott.

(15)

His broad clear brow in sunlight glowed;
On burnish'd hooves his war horse trode;
From underneath his helmet flowed
His coal-black curls as on he rode,
As he rode down to Camelot.
From the bank and from the river
He flashed into the crystal mirror,
"Tirra lirra," by the river
Sang Sir Lancelot.

8. **greaves** armor that protects the legs below the kneecaps.
9. **red-cross knight** refers to the Redcrosse Knight from *The Faerie Queene* by Edmund Spenser. The knight is a symbol of holiness.
10. **gemmy** jeweled.
11. **Galaxy** the Milky Way.
12. **blazoned baldric** decorated sash worn diagonally across the chest.

Enrichment: Understanding Poetry

Iambic Tetrameter

Tennyson writes this poem in iambic tetrameter. Explain to students that an iamb is a metrical foot of two syllables, with an unstressed syllable followed by a stressed syllable, as in *arise. Tetrameter* means that there are four feet per line. A poem written in iambic tetrameter has eight syllables in a line, with the stress patterns being unstressed, stressed, unstressed, stressed, and so on. Writers often incorporate variations in the meter for expressive moments.

Activity: Writing in Learning Have students research iambic tetrameter. Suggest that they record information in the **Enrichment: Analyzing Forms and Genres** worksheet, ***Professional Development Guidebook,*** page 227. Have them use the results of their research to write one four-line stanza in iambic tetrameter. Encourage students to incorporate rhyme into their writing.

She left the web, she left the loom,
She made three paces through the room,
She saw the waterlily bloom,
She saw the helmet and the plume,
(16) She looked down to Camelot.
Out flew the web and floated wide;
The mirror cracked from side to side;
"The curse is come upon me," cried
The Lady of Shalott.

PART IV

In the stormy east wind straining,
The pale yellow woods were **waning**,
The broad stream in his banks complaining,
Heavily the low sky raining
Over towered Camelot;
Down she came and found a boat
Beneath a willow left afloat,
And round about the prow she wrote
The Lady of Shalott.

And down the river's dim expanse
Like some bold seër in a trance,
Seeing all his own mischance—
With a glassy countenance
Did she look to Camelot.
And at the closing of the day
She loosed the chain, and down she lay;
The broad stream bore her far away,
The Lady of Shalott.

Lying, robed in snowy white
That loosely flew to left and right—
The leaves upon her falling light—
Through the noises of the night
She floated down to Camelot:
And as the boathead wound along
The willowy hills and fields among,
They heard her singing her last song,
The Lady of Shalott.

Heard a carol, mournful, holy,
Chanted loudly, chanted lowly,
Till her blood was frozen slowly,
And her eyes were darkened wholly,
Turned to towered Camelot.

16 Literary Analysis
The Speaker in Poetry
How does the speaker create the sense that a decisive moment has arrived?

Vocabulary
waning (wān′ iŋ) *v.* gradually becoming dimmer or weaker

17 Reading Check
What does the Lady of Shalott do once she sees Sir Lancelot?

16 Literary Analysis
The Speaker in Poetry

1. Have students read lines 109–117 to themselves.
2. Then, **ask** students the Literary Analysis question: How does the speaker create the sense that a decisive moment has arrived?
   Answer: The speaker neutrally describes what the Lady sees. By not interpreting the significance of the waterlily blooming, of Lancelot's plume, or of the sight of Camelot, he lets the reader's imagination fill in the significance and so experience it more profoundly—the Lady is suddenly, decisively overwhelmed by a sense of the richness of life beyond her tower.
   Monitor Progress: Ask students how the scene would have been different if the Lady were the speaker.
   Possible response: The Lady might have explained her thoughts, detracting from the drama.

17 Reading Check

Answer: When she sees Sir Lancelot, the Lady of Shalott looks down to Camelot and then leaves on a boat for the town.

Differentiated Instruction for Universal Access

Enrichment for Gifted/Talented Students
Have students write their own Arthurian legends, borrowing some of the key components used by Tennyson in "The Lady of Shalott." Students may want to use the figure of Sir Lancelot or the Lady in their legends. Encourage students not only to let their imaginations loose in creating their legends, but also to echo Tennyson's use of tetrameter.

Enrichment for Advanced Readers
Have students work in a group to cast, write, rehearse, and present a brief drama of the funeral of the Lady of Shalott. Ask students to consider what kind of service the townspeople would have given her and who would have participated. Tell students to address how Lancelot would have involved himself in the ceremony.

For ere she reached upon the tide
The first house by the waterside,
Singing in her song she died,
    The Lady of Shalott.

Under tower and balcony,
By garden wall and gallery,
A gleaming shape she floated by,
Dead-pale between the houses high,
    Silent into Camelot.
Out upon the wharfs they came,
Knight and burgher, lord and dame,
And round the prow they read her name,
    The Lady of Shalott.

Who is this? and what is here?
And in the lighted palace near
Died the sound of royal cheer;
And they crossed themselves for fear,
    All the knights at Camelot:
But Lancelot mused a little space;
He said, "She has a lovely face;
God in his mercy lend her grace,
    The Lady of Shalott."

Critical Reading

Cite textual evidence to support your responses.

1. **Key Ideas and Details (a)** What does the Lady spend her time doing? Why? **(b) Interpret:** Why does the Lady glimpse only "shadows of the world"? **(c) Interpret:** Why might an artist share the complaint the Lady makes in lines 71–72?
2. **Key Ideas and Details (a)** What does the Lady do after seeing Sir Lancelot in the mirror? **(b) Analyze:** How does the long description of Sir Lancelot make the knight seem like the real-life embodiment of a vision? **(c) Draw Conclusions:** Given this description of Lancelot, explain why the Lady might be said to leave her room in pursuit of her visions.
3. **Key Ideas and Details (a) Draw Conclusions:** What does the fact that the Lady dies before meeting Lancelot suggest about her love for him? **(b) Make a Judgment:** Do you agree with Tennyson's implication that we can never realize our fantasies? Why or why not?
4. **Integration of Knowledge and Ideas** The poem suggests that the life of the imagination isolates one from reality. Do modern media outlets, such as television and the Internet, suggest otherwise? Explain.

ASSESS

Answers

Before students respond, you may wish to have them write a brief objective summary of the selection. As they answer the questions below, remind them to support their answers with evidence from the text.

1. (a) The Lady spends her time weaving, avoiding the real world. (b) The Lady glimpses only "shadows of the world" because she sees the world in the reflected surface of her mirror. (c) Like an artist, the Lady sees life as material for her depictions, and so she is distanced from it.
2. (a) She abandons her weaving and sails for Camelot. (b) The description of Lancelot is poetic, filled with vivid imagery giving Lancelot a legendary stature (the "Galaxy" hangs from his bridle). (c) The Lady leaves her room to pursue Lancelot in real life, yet the description makes him seem more like a figure on her tapestry than a real man. In this sense, what draws the Lady out into the real world is the hope that she will find her visions there.
3. (a) The Lady's love for Lancelot cannot be consummated because it is forbidden by the curse; her love for him, as a love for an unattainable vision, is impossible. (b) **Possible response:** We can never realize our fantasies because the allure of a fantasy is destroyed once it becomes reality.
4. **Possible response:** No, modern media—including "reality" shows—cut one off even more completely from reality than the Lady's curse would, since modern media offer themselves as if they were reality or a direct view of it, while the Lady knows that her visions are not real.

Think Aloud

Critical Reading Question

To model the Critical Reading question 4a, use the following "think aloud":

> What does the Lady of Shallot's death suggest about her love for Lancelot? I know that the Lady of Shalott has a curse on her. I know this from lines 40–41, which state "A curse is on her if she stay / To look down to Camelot." I think it suggests that her love for him is unattainable because of that curse. We see that this is true when she is found "dead-pale" in line 157.

18 TEARS, *Idle* TEARS

ALFRED, LORD TENNYSON

BACKGROUND *The Princess* (1847) is a long narrative poem that contains a number of songs. Some of these songs, including the one that follows, are considered to be among the finest of Tennyson's lyrics.

Tears, idle tears, I know not what they mean,
Tears from the depth of some divine despair
Rise in the heart, and gather to the eyes,
In looking on the happy autumn fields,
And thinking of the days that are no more.

Fresh as the first beam glittering on a sail,
That brings our friends up from the underworld,
Sad as the last which reddens over one
That sinks with all we love below the verge;
So sad, so fresh, the days that are no more.

Ah, sad and strange as in dark summer dawns
The earliest pipe of half-awakened birds
To dying ears, when unto dying eyes
The casement slowly grows a glimmering square;
So sad, so strange, the days that are no more.

Dear as remembered kisses after death,
And sweet as those by hopeless fancy feigned
On lips that are for others; deep as love,
Deep as first love, and wild with all regret;
O Death in Life, the days that are no more.

19 **Reading Check**

What is the speaker's reaction to the thought of "the days that are no more"?

18 About the Selection

"Tears, Idle Tears" from *The Princess* treats a theme common in Tennyson's works: the transience, or fleeting quality, of life and the nearness of death. Tennyson said about this poem: "This song came to me on the yellowing autumn-tide at Tintern Abbey, full for me of its bygone memories. It is the sense of abiding in the transient." The poem focuses on regret for that which passes and cannot be truly possessed—love and the happy times of the past.

19 Reading Check

Answer: The speaker feels "divine despair" and weeps.

Differentiated Instruction for Universal Access

Background for Less Proficient Readers
Guide students as they read the poem. Explain that Tennyson's speaker was moved to tears at a beautiful scene when his thoughts turned to "days that are no more."

EL Vocabulary for English Learners
Have students read "Tears, Idle Tears" from *The Princess* with teacher guidance. Encourage them to visualize the descriptions Tennyson includes in his poem as they read.

Enrichment for Advanced Readers
Remind students that Tennyson wrote "Tears, Idle Tears" after a visit to Tintern Abbey, a site that also inspired William Wordsworth. After students read the poem, have them reread Wordsworth's "Lines Composed a Few Miles Above Tintern Abbey," pages 780–785, and write an essay comparing the poems.

20 About the Selection

"Ulysses" is based on the story of the Greek king who fought at Troy for one decade and then wandered the seas for another. The poem takes place after Ulysses' return home to Ithaca, as he is facing old age. It raises a central question about the speaker, Ulysses himself: Did Tennyson intend him to be a heroic figure, eternally questing and fighting death, or is the poet's portrayal ironic, suggesting that Ulysses is a selfish, self-justifying character who longs to cast off boredom and indulge himself by fleeing a clinging wife and unpleasant kingship?

21 Humanities

Ulysses, by Jean-Auguste-Dominique Ingres

Ingres (1780–1867), a French painter of historical subjects and portraits, was exposed to art by his father, a sculptor. He studied with various artists, the foremost of which was the Neoclassicist Jacques-Louis David.

Ulysses (1827) shows Ingres's mixed commitment to Neoclassicism (the imitation of the aesthetic principles of ancient Greece and Rome). The harmonious lines and restrained colors are perhaps Neoclassical; the shadows and emotion are Romantic. Use this question for discussion:

How does the depiction of Ulysses' gaze reflect the spirit Tennyson captures?

Possible response: Ulysses' upward gaze, makes him seem expectant; the fact that his eyes are in shadow adds to the sense that he is waiting. Like Tennyson's Ulysses, he looks toward the future.

21

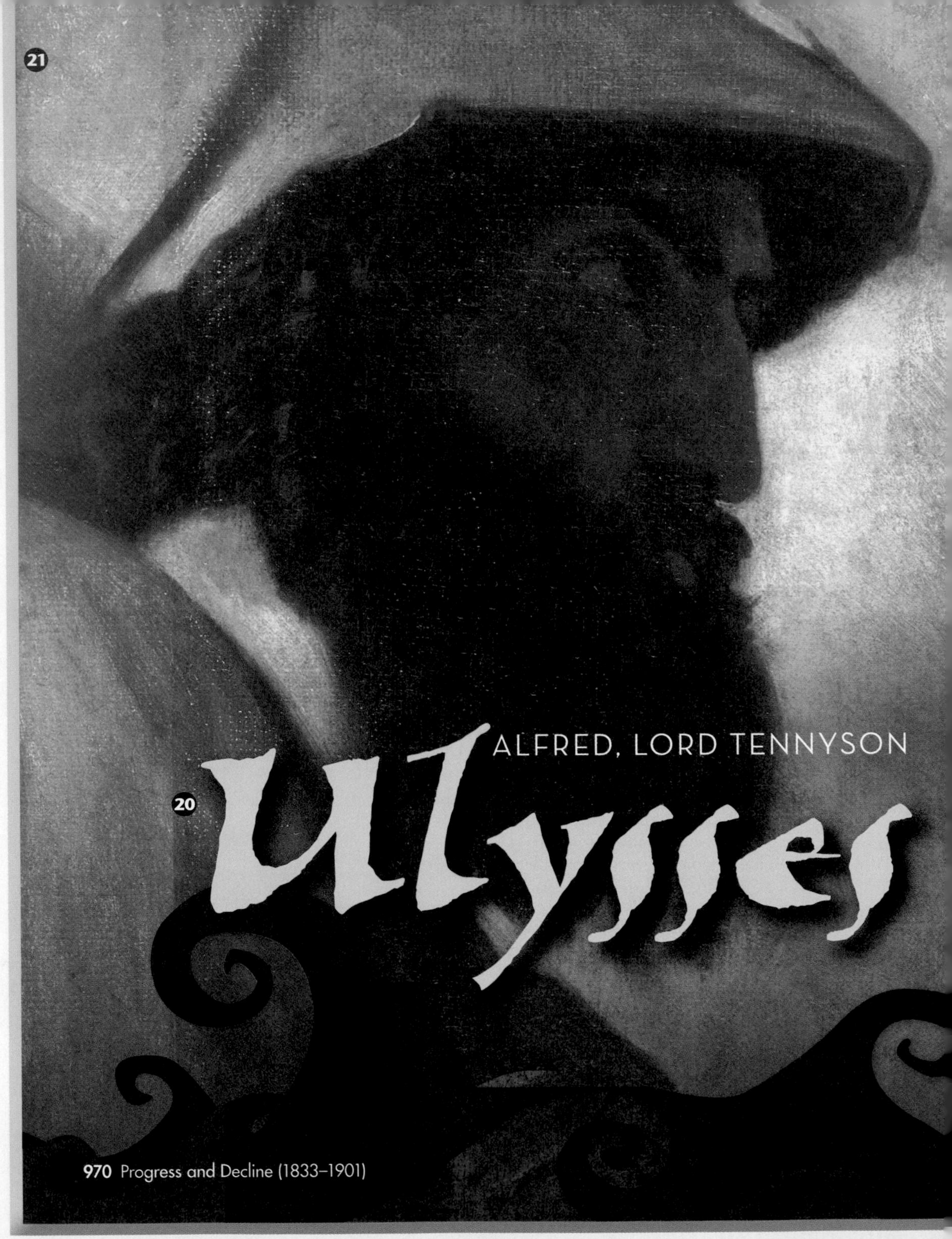

ALFRED, LORD TENNYSON

20 # Ulysses

Enrichment: Understanding Geography

Ulysses' Route

Ulysses, whom Tennyson profiles in his poem, went on many adventures. What follows is just one of many theories about the route he took: From Troy in present-day Turkey, he proceeded briefly northward and then southwestward on the Aegean Sea, passing between the Greek lands of Peloponnesus and Crete. Then, sailing westward on the Mediterranean Sea, he traveled near Sicily. After circling Sicily clockwise, he sailed northeastward and finally reached the Ionian Islands of Greece and his home, Ithaca.

Activity: Mapmaking Have students conduct research on Ulysses' route. Suggest that they record information in the **Enrichment: Investigating Geography** worksheet, ***Professional Development Guidebook,*** page 228. Have them use their results to draw the route that Ulysses might have taken during his adventures.

BACKGROUND In this poem, Tennyson extends the story of Ulysses (yoo lis′ ez′), the hero of Homer's epic the *Odyssey*. Homer's writing ends after Ulysses' triumphant return home to Ithaca. Years later, Tennyson tells us, the hero has grown restless. Although he had been away for twenty long years—ten fighting in the Trojan War and another ten on a long and adventure-filled voyage back—Ulysses finds that he is contemplating yet another journey.

It little profits that an idle king,
By this still hearth, among these barren crags,
Matched with an aged wife, I mete and dole[1]
22 Unequal[2] laws unto a savage race,
That hoard, and sleep, and feed, and know not me.
I cannot rest from travel; I will drink
Life to the lees.[3] All times I have enjoyed
Greatly, have suffered greatly, both with those
That loved me, and alone; on shore, and when
Through scudding drifts the rainy Hyades[4]
Vexed the dim sea. I am become a name;
For always roaming with a hungry heart
Much have I seen and known—cities of men
And manners, climates, councils, governments,
Myself not least, but honored of them all—
And drunk delight of battle with my peers,
Far on the ringing plains of windy Troy.
I am a part of all that I have met;
Yet all experience is an arch wherethrough
Gleams that untraveled world, whose
    margin fades
Forever and forever when I move.
How dull it is to pause, to make an end,
To rust unburnished, not to shine in use!
25 As though to breathe were life. Life piled on life
Were all too little, and of one to me
Little remains; but every hour is saved
From that eternal silence, something more,
A bringer of new things; and vile it were
For some three suns to store and hoard myself,

1. mete and dole measure and give out.
2. unequal unfair.
3. lees sediment.
4. Hyades (hī′ ə dēz′) group of stars whose rising was assumed to be followed by rain.

Jean-Auguste-Dominique Ingres, National Gallery of Art, Washington, D.C.

22 Literary Analysis
The Speaker in Poetry
Who is speaking the words of this poem? How can you tell?

23 ◀ Critical Viewing
Compare the character of Ulysses conveyed by this painting with the speaker in the poem. **[Compare and Contrast]**

24 Reading Check
What has Ulysses encountered on his travels?

22 Literary Analysis
The Speaker in Poetry

1. Remind students that the speaker of the poem may be fictional or real, generalized or specific, and may or may not resemble the poem's author.
2. Have students identify any details in lines 1–7 that help them determine who the speaker of the poem is.
3. Then, **ask** students the Literary Analysis question: Who is speaking the words of this poem? How can you tell?
   Answer: It is Ulysses himself. This fact is apparent because he uses the first-person pronoun *I* to refer to the antecedent, "an idle king."

23 Critical Viewing

Answer: Accept all reasonable responses. Make sure students support their responses with details from the image and the poem.

24 Reading Check

Answer: He has encountered cities, different climates, councils, governments, and battle at Troy.

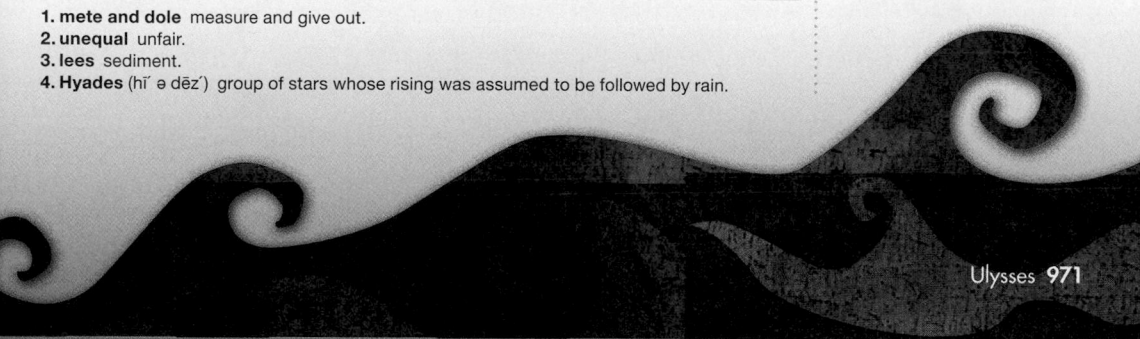

25 Reading Strategy

Analyzing Philosophical Beliefs

1. Have students look at the diction and imagery used in lines 22–32.
2. Then, **ask** the Reading Strategy question: What do lines 22–32 suggest about Tennyson's philosophical beliefs?
   Possible response: These lines suggest that Tennyson believes that people should have purpose-driven lives. He believes that people strive to understand and experience beyond what they have already known. This is particularly telling in the beautiful lines "To follow knowledge like a sinking star, / Beyond the utmost bound of human thought."

25 Reading Strategy
Analyzing Philosophical Beliefs What do lines 22-32 suggest about Tennyson's philosophical beliefs?

Vocabulary
prudence (pro͞od′ ns) *n.* careful management of resources; economy

Vocabulary
furrows (fur′ ōz) *n.* narrow grooves, such as those made by a plow

And this gray spirit yearning in desire
To follow knowledge like a sinking star,
Beyond the utmost bound of human thought.
    This is my son, mine own Telemachus,
To whom I leave the scepter and the isle[5]
Well-loved of me, discerning to fulfill
This labor, by slow **prudence** to make mild
A rugged people, and through soft degrees
Subdue them to the useful and the good.
Most blameless is he, centered in the sphere
Of common duties, decent not to fail
In offices of tenderness, and pay
Meet[6] adoration to my household gods,
When I am gone. He works his work, I mine.
    There lies the port; the vessel puffs her sail;
There gloom the dark broad seas. My mariners,
Souls that have toiled and wrought, and thought with me—
That ever with a frolic welcome took
The thunder and the sunshine, and opposed
Free hearts, free foreheads—you and I are old;
Old age hath yet his honor and his toil;
Death closes all; but something ere the end,
Some work of noble note, may yet be done,
Not unbecoming men that strove with Gods.
The lights begin to twinkle from the rocks;
The long day wanes; the slow moon climbs; the deep
Moans round with many voices. Come, my friends,
'Tis not too late to seek a newer world.
Push off, and sitting well in order smite
The sounding **furrows**; for my purpose holds

---

5. isle Ithaca, an island off the coast of Greece.
6. meet appropriate.

HOW DULL IT IS TO PAUSE, TO MAKE AN END,
TO RUST UNBURNISHED, NOT TO **SHINE IN USE!**

Vocabulary Development

Vocabulary Knowledge Rating

When students have completed reading and discussing the selection, have them take out their **Vocabulary Knowledge Rating Charts** for the poems. Read the words aloud and have students rate their knowledge of words again in the After Reading column. Clarify any words that are still problematic. Have students write their own definitions and example or sentence in the appropriate column. Then, have students complete the Vocabulary Practice at the end of the selection. Encourage students to use the words in further discussion and written work about the selection. Remind them that they will be accountable for these words on the **Selection Test,** ***Unit 5 Resources,*** pages 19–21 or 22–24.

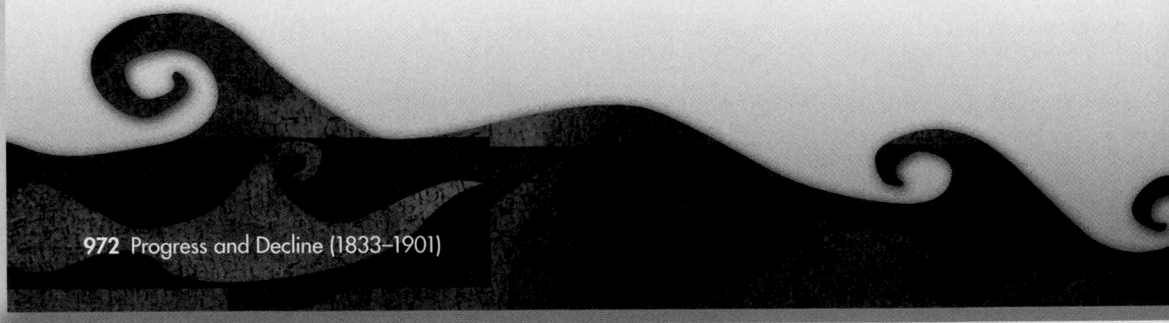

26

To sail beyond the sunset, and the baths
Of all the western stars, until I die.
It may be that the gulfs will wash us down:
It may be we shall touch the Happy Isles,[7]
And see the great Achilles,[8] whom we knew.
Though much is taken, much abides; and though
We are not now that strength which in old days
Moved earth and heaven, that which we are, we are—
One equal temper of heroic hearts,
Made weak by time and fate, but strong in will
To strive, to seek, to find, and not to yield.

7. **Happy Isles** Elysium, or the Islands of the Blessed: in classical mythology, the place heroes went after death.
8. **Achilles** (ə kil′ ēz′) Greek hero of the Trojan War.

Critical Reading

Cite textual evidence to support your responses.

1. **Key Ideas and Details (a)** What three comparisons in "Tears, Idle Tears" describe "the days that are no more"? **(b) Analyze:** What contrast does each comparison involve? **(c) Interpret:** What feelings does the line "Deep as first love, and wild with all regret" capture?
2. **Key Ideas and Details (a)** In "Ulysses," how does Ulysses describe his situation? **(b) Compare and Contrast:** How does this situation contrast with his previous experiences? **(c) Draw Conclusions:** What is Ulysses' attitude toward his experiences?
3. **Key Ideas and Details (a)** According to lines 58–61, what is Ulysses' purpose? **(b) Draw Conclusions:** What are Ulysses' feelings about aging? **(c) Draw Conclusions:** What is his attitude toward life in general?
4. **Integration of Knowledge and Ideas** What values do you think Tennyson celebrates in his poetry? Explain using two of these Essential Question words: *universe, rationalism, curiosity, challenge.* *[Connecting to the Essential Question: How does literature shape or reflect society?]*

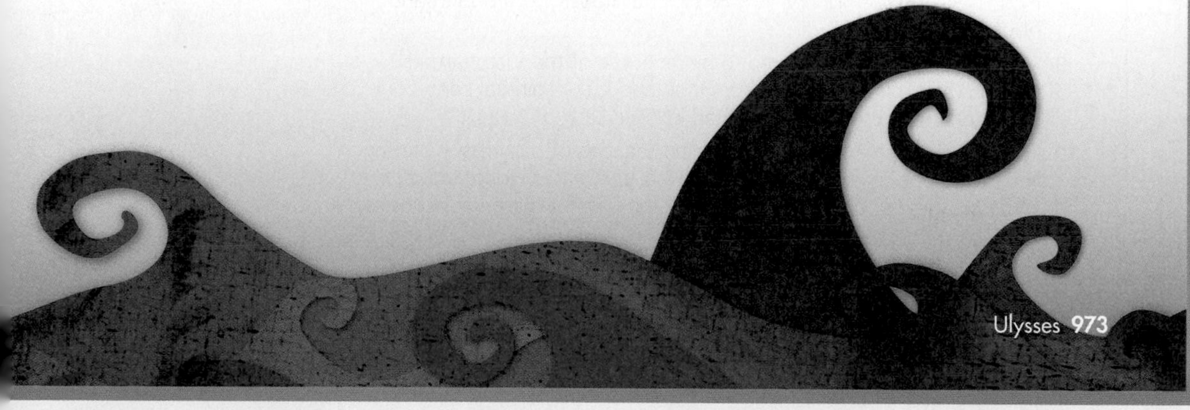

Concept Connector

Reading Strategy Graphic Organizer
Ask students to review the graphic organizers in which they have filled in the assumptions, beliefs and supporting details. Then, have students share their organizers and compare the supporting details they identified.

Activating Prior Knowledge
Have students return to their responses to the Activating Prior Knowledge activity. Ask them to explain whether their thoughts have changed and, if so, how.

Writing About the Essential Question
Have students compare their responses to the prompt, completed before reading the poems with their thoughts afterward. Have them work individually or in groups, writing or discussing their thoughts, to formulate new responses. Then, lead a class discussion, probing for what students have learned that confirms or invalidates their initial thoughts. Encourage students to cite specific textual details to support their responses.

26 Critical Thinking

Connect
1. Have students read lines 60–61. **Ask** them what earlier lines these two lines echo.
   Answer: They echo lines 30–32.
2. **Then, ask** them what the echo of sentiments suggests about his determination to seek new adventures.
   Possible response: The earlier lines suggest that he has a noble cause—"to follow knowledge." The echo reinforces his argument that he leaves with a noble purpose.

ASSESS

Answers

Remind students to support their answers with evidence from the text.

1. (a) The days are: (1) fresh as the first gleam of sunrise and sad as the last ray of sunset; (2) strange as the first peep of birds at sunrise heard by dying ears and sad as fading light seen through a window by dying eyes; and (3) deep as first love and dear as kisses recalled after a loved one's death. (b) Each contrast involves a comparison between beginnings and endings, life and death. (c) The line captures the bittersweet feelings of memories of past love, which call up profound feelings precisely because its time has passed.
2. (a) He says he leads a dull life without adventure or risk. (b) This current situation is in sharp contrast to his many voyages and adventures. (c) Ulysses is proud of his accomplishments and past experiences.
3. (a) Ulysses' aim is to continue seeking challenges until he dies. (b) He sees aging as a process that robs him of his cherished way of life. (c) He sees life as empty unless it is lived in the spirit of striving and openness toward the future.
4. **Possible response:** I think Tennyson wanted to promote the values of resoluteness when facing *challenge* and curiosity in the vast unknown *universe.*

Answers

1 (a) The speaker is a character much like Tennyson. (b) He is grieved by the death of a friend.

2. (a) He is an observer. (b) He is generalized and fictional. He is not identified specifically.

3. The situation of the Lady, who can safely view life through the mirror of art but who is drawn by the pull of real experience, is like that of a poet.

4. (a) He has settled down but longs for adventure. (b) **Possible response:** Tennyson sees Ulysses as heroic (". . . strong in will/To strive, to seek, to find, and not to yield.")

5. "Ulysses": Present: Restless: "How dull it is to pause, to make an end." Future: Open: "I cannot rest from travel; I will drink/Life to the lees." "The Lady of Shalott": Present: Unchanging: "And so she weaveth steadily,/And little other care hath she." Future: Doomed: "She looked down to Camelot . . . 'The curse is come upon me.'"

6. In "Tears," the past is both irrecoverably lost and vividly present in the speaker's longing; in *In Memoriam,* the past is lost, yet is present in the speaker's grief, transformed into faith.

7. **Possible response:** He valued the world of poetry more, given his choice of subjects: mythology, Arthurian legend, and the memory of his friend.

8. **Possible response:** The passages of *In Memoriam* express the belief in an "eternal process"; that is, Tennyson has faith that the spirit's life continues, even after death.

9. **Possible response:** Tennyson assumes that isolation from society can lead to conflicted feelings.

10. **Possible response:** Lines 27–29 suggest that experiencing "new things" is better than sitting around to "hoard." The idea of hoarding appears elsewhere, such as in lines 4–5. He expresses that seeking knowledge is a better goal. Lines 30–32 state this sentiment well, making the pursuit of knowledge seem noble.

After You Read

from *In Memoriam, A.H.H.* • *The Lady of Shalott* • *Tears, Idle Tears* • *Ulysses*

Literary Analysis

1. **Craft and Structure (a)** Who is the **speaker** of *In Memoriam, A.H.H.*? **(b)** Tennyson wrote the poem in direct response to his friend's death. How does the speaker's conflict reflect one that Tennyson might have felt?
2. **Craft and Structure (a)** Who is the speaker of "The Lady of Shalott"? **(b)** Is the speaker fictional or real, generalized or specific? Explain.
3. **Integration of Knowledge and Ideas** Why might Tennyson have identified the situation of a poet with the Lady's situation?
4. **Key Ideas and Details (a)** Describe the conflict faced by the speaker in "Ulysses." **(b)** Does Tennyson see Ulysses as heroic or as selfish and self-justifying? Support your answer by quoting from the poem.
5. **Integration of Knowledge and Ideas** Use a chart like the one shown to compare Ulysses' view of time with the Lady of Shalott's view.

	Past	Present	Future
Ulysses	Remembers it with satisfaction: "I am a part of all that I have met"		
The Lady of Shalott	Considers it identical with the present: "There she weaves by night and day"		

6. **Integration of Knowledge and Ideas** Compare the speaker's relationship with the past in "Tears, Idle Tears" and in *In Memoriam, A.H.H.*
7. **Comparing Literary Works** Which did Tennyson value more—the timeless world of poetry or the perishable real world? Support your view.

Reading Strategy

8. **Analyze the philosophical assumptions and beliefs** Tennyson expresses in *In Memoriam, A.H.H.* What attitudes toward faith and hope can you detect?
9. Tennyson's work is considered to be reflective of the Victorian period. What philosophical assumption about the spiritual condition of Victorian society is demonstrated in "The Lady of Shalott"?
10. Tennyson lived in an age that accepted the idea of progress, believing the acquisition of knowledge would lead to a better world. Identify two passages in "Ulysses" that support this belief. Explain your choices.

Common Core State Standards

Writing
2. Write informative/explanatory texts to examine and convey complex ideas, concepts, and information clearly and accurately through the effective selection, organization, and analysis of content. *(p. 975)*

Language
4.a. Use context as a clue to the meaning of a word or phrase. *(p. 975)*

Assessment Practice

(For more practice, see *All-in-One Workbook*.)

Many tests require students to describe literary elements—sometimes by comparing two passages. Use the following sample item to demonstrate for students how to compare the tones of two passages. Have students read the last five lines of "Ulysses" and "Tears, Idle Tears." Then ask them the following question:

Which of these choices best describes the tone of the passages?

A The lines from "Ulysses" are angry; the lyrics are mournful.
B Both have a nostalgic tone.
C The lines from "Ulysses" are bold; the lyrics are bittersweet.
D Both have a mournful tone.

Because the tone in the two passages is not the same, *B* and *D* are incorrect. The correct answer is **C**.

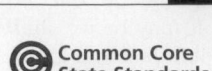

PERFORMANCE TASKS

Integrated Language Skills

Vocabulary Acquisition and Use

Word Analysis: Literal and Figurative Meanings

Many words have both a literal meaning and a figurative one. This is a broader or more symbolic meaning that often draws on the literal meaning. For instance, a *chrysalis* is the stage in the life of a butterfly in which the insect grows in a cocoon before emerging as an adult butterfly. Tennyson, in *In Memoriam, A.H.H.*, uses the word figuratively to refer to stages of human life. His image has a richer meaning, though. In the cocoon, the chrysalis changes from caterpillar to butterfly, just as death may transform a person from physical to spiritual life. Identify the literal and figurative meanings of these other words Tennyson uses:

1. doors (*In Memoriam, A.H.H.*, line 19)
2. bald (*In Memoriam, A.H.H.*, line 28)
3. lees ("Ulysses," line 7)
4. hungry ("Ulysses," line 12)
5. shine ("Ulysses," line 23)

Vocabulary: Context

The context of a word—the lines or phrases around it—can provide clues to the meaning of an unfamiliar word. Identify the contextual meaning of each italicized vocabulary word below and explain how context makes that meaning clear.

1. As the sun rose, its *diffusive* light reached into all the shadows of the night, revealing sharp edges and colors.
2. His popularity *waning*, the actor could no longer command starring roles.
3. When the *chrysalis* turns into the adult butterfly, the empty cocoon remains behind.
4. Her natural *prudence* prevented her from taking any rash action.
5. The *furrows* on his parents' foreheads showed their anxiety.
6. After launching the new business, she worked day and night to ensure it would *prosper*.

Writing

Informative Text Arthur Hallam's death had a decisive influence not only on Tennyson's life but also on his poetry. Writing *In Memoriam, A.H.H.* gave Tennyson the money he needed to buy his own land. Write a **biographical essay** that recounts the details of Tennyson's life and work, examining the *cause-and-effect relationships* between them.

Prewriting Research Tennyson's life and work. Outline the main events of his life and make a chart of his main accomplishments and literary themes. Take notes on ways his life and work affected each other.

Draft Draft your essay, following the *correct sequence of events* and locating incidents in specific places where they occurred. In your draft, explore the significance of major events in Tennyson's life, clarifying the way his life influenced his work and vice versa.

Revising Read through your draft to make sure that you present the correct sequence of events and clearly explain cause-and-effect relationships. Be sure that you have ample evidence or solid reasoning to claim such a relationship. If not, revise your text to support your claim.

Model: Charting Cause-and-Effect Relationships

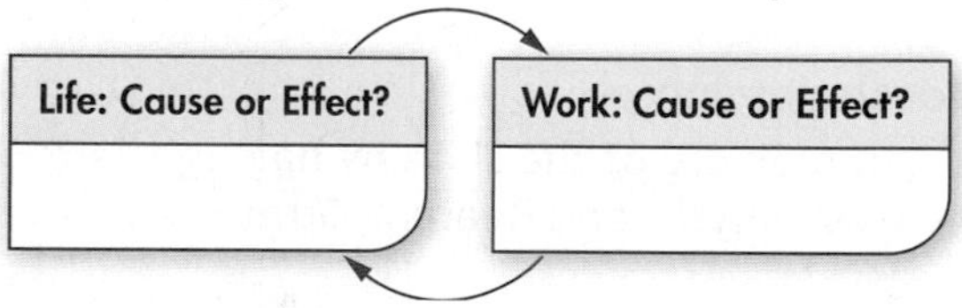

Assessment Resources

Unit 5 Resources

L1 L2 EL **Selection Test A**, pp. 19–21. Administer Test A to less advanced students.

L3 L4 EL **Selection Test B**, pp. 22–24. Administer Test B to on-level students and more advanced students.

L3 L4 **Open-Book Test**, pp. 16–18. As an alternative, give the Open-Book test.

All **Customizable Test Bank**

All **Self-tests**
Students may prepare for the **Selection Test** by taking the **Self-test** online.

PHLit Online! All assessment resources are available at **www.PHLitOnline.com**.

Answers

Vocabulary Acquisition and Use

1. Introduce the skill using the instruction on the student page.
2. Have students complete the Word Analysis activity and the Vocabulary practice.

Word Analysis

1. literal: swinging barriers that open and close an entryway; figurative: blocked off area
2. literal: without hair; figurative: empty
3. literal: the sediment of wine; figurative: experience life to the end
4. literal: desiring food; figurative: eager
5. literal: to emit light; figurative: to perform well in a given situation

Vocabulary

1. scattered
2. declining
3. protective covering
4. caution
5. wrinkles
6. succeed

Writing

1. To guide students in writing this narrative text, give them the Support for Writing Lesson, page 14, in ***Unit 5 Resources.***
2. Tell students to research Tennyson's life and his work and to be careful when making connections between the two, unless these seem justified by facts they find in their research.
3. Encourage students to make a timeline of Tennyson's life, in which they incorporate the dates of composition and publication of his major works.
4. Evaluate their essays using the **Exposition: Cause-and-Effect Essay** rubrics in ***Professional Development Guidebook,*** pages 264–265.

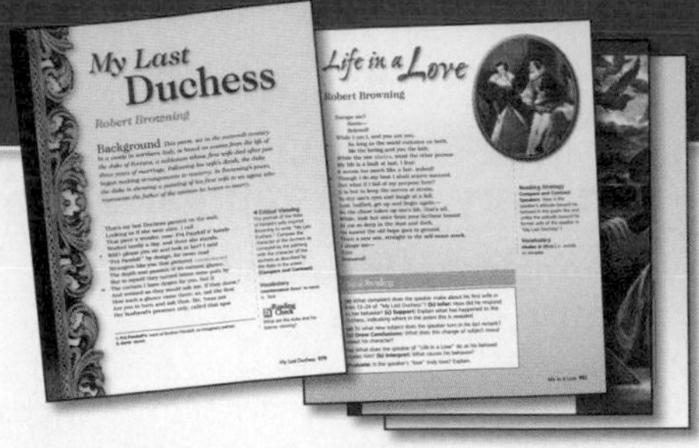

My Last Duchess • Life in a Love • Porphyria's Lover • Sonnet 43

Lesson Pacing Guide

DAY 1 Preteach

- Administer the Reading and Vocabulary Warm-ups (*Unit 5 Resources,* pp. 25–28) as necessary.
- Introduce the Literary Analysis concept: Dramatic Monologue.
- Introduce the Reading Strategy: Compare and Contrast Speakers in Multiple Poems.
- Build background with the author and Background features.
- Develop thematic thinking with Connecting to the Essential Question.
- Teach the selection vocabulary.

DAYS 2–3 Preteach/Teach/Assess

- Distribute copies of the appropriate graphic organizer for the Reading Strategy (*Graphic Organizer Transparencies,* pp. 173–174).
- Distribute copies of the appropriate graphic organizer for Literary Analysis (*Graphic Organizer Transparencies,* pp. 175–176).
- Prepare students to read with the Activating Prior Knowledge activities (TE).
- Informally monitor comprehension while students read.
- Use the Reading Check questions to confirm comprehension.
- Develop students' understanding of dramatic monologue using the Literary Analysis prompts.
- Develop students' ability to compare and contrast speakers in multiple poems using the Reading Strategy prompts.
- Reinforce vocabulary with the Vocabulary notes.
- Assess students' comprehension and mastery of the skills by having them answer the Critical Reading, Literary Analysis, and Reading Strategy questions.
- Have students complete the Vocabulary Lesson.

DAY 4 Extend/Assess

- Have students complete the Writing Lesson and write a detective's report on the duke. (You may assign as homework.)
- Administer Selection Test A or B (*Unit 5 Resources,* pp. 37–39 or 40–42).

Common Core State Standards

Reading Literature 3. Analyze the impact of the author's choices regarding how to develop and relate elements of a story or drama.

Writing 1. Write arguments to support claims in an analysis of substantive topics or texts, using valid reasoning and relevant and sufficient evidence.
1.d. Establish and maintain a formal style and objective tone while attending to the norms and conventions of the discipline in which they are writing.

Language 4.b. Identify and correctly use patterns of word changes that indicate different meanings or parts of speech.

Additional Standards Practice
Common Core Companion, ***pp. 28–35; 185–195; 326–327***

Daily Block Scheduling
Each day in this Lesson Pacing Guide represents a 40–50 minute period. Teachers using block scheduling may combine days to revise pacing. In addition, teachers may differentiate and support core instruction by integrating components for extended and intensive support as students require. See the Guide to Selected Leveled Resources (facing page).

Guide to Selected Leveled Resources

RTI **Tier 1** (students performing on level)		My Last Duchess • Life in a Love • Porphyria's Lover • Sonnet 43
Warm Up	**Practice, model,** and **monitor** fluency, working **with the whole class** or **in groups.**	**Vocabulary and Reading Warm-ups B,** ***Unit 5 Resources,*** pp. 25–26, 28
Comprehension/Skills	**Support** and **monitor** comprehension and skills development, having students complete the activities, graphic organizers, and interactive prompts **independently** or **as a class.**	• ***Reader's Notebook,*** adapted instruction and full selection EL ***Reader's Notebook: English Learner's Version,*** adapted instruction and adapted selection • **Reading Strategy Graphic Organizer B,** ***Graphic Organizer Transparencies,*** p. 182 • **Literary Analysis Graphic Organizer B,** ***Graphic Organizer Transparencies,*** p. 184
Monitor Progress	**Monitor** student progress with the differentiated curriculum-based assessment in the *Unit Resources.*	• **Selection Test B,** ***Unit 5 Resources,*** pp. 40–42 • **Open-Book Test,** ***Unit 5 Resources,*** pp. 34–36

RTI **Tier 2** (students requiring intervention)		My Last Duchess • Life in a Love • Porphyria's Lover • Sonnet 43
Warm Up	**Practice, model,** and **monitor** fluency **in groups** or **with individuals.**	• **Vocabulary and Reading Warm-ups A,** ***Unit 5 Resources,*** pp. 25–28 • ***Hear It!*** **Audio CD (adapted text)**
Comprehension/Skills	• **Support** and **monitor** comprehension and skills development, working **in small groups** or **with individuals.** • As students complete the selection in the appropriate version of the *Reader's Notebook,* **monitor** comprehension frequently with group questions and individual instruction. • **Model** strategies while guiding students in completing the activities and prompts in the *Reader's Notebook,* as well as the graphic organizers. • **Practice** skills and **monitor** mastery with the *Reading Kit* worksheets.	• ***Reader's Notebook: Adapted Version,*** adapted instruction and adapted selection EL ***Reader's Notebook: English Learner's Version,*** adapted instruction and adapted selection • **Reading Strategy Graphic Organizer A,** ***Graphic Organizer Transparencies,*** p. 181 • **Literary Analysis Graphic Organizer A,** ***Graphic Organizer Transparencies,*** p. 183 • ***Reading Kit,*** Practice worksheets
Monitor Progress	**Monitor** student progress with the differentiated curriculum-based assessment in the *Unit Resources* and in the *Reading Kit.*	• **Selection Test A,** ***Unit 5 Resources,*** pp. 37–39 • ***Reading Kit,*** Assess worksheets

TIER 3 Tier 3 intervention may require consultation with the student's special-education or dyslexia specialist. For additional support, see the Tier 2 activities and resources listed above.

One-on-one teaching **Group work** **Whole class instruction** **Independent work** **A Assessment**

For a complete guide to selection support, including support for Advanced students, see the Overview of Resources in the frontmatter.

My Last Duchess • Life in a Love • Porphyria's Lover • Sonnet 43

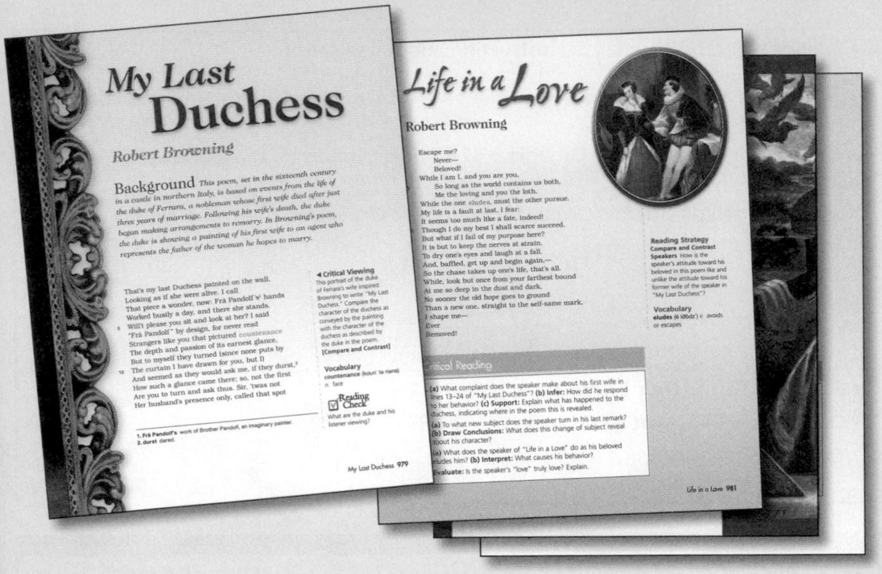

RESOURCES FOR:

- L1 Special-Needs Students
- L2 Below-Level Students (Tier 2)
- L3 On-Level Students (Tier 1)
- L4 Advanced Students (Tier 1)
- EL English Learners
- All All Students

Vocabulary/Fluency/Prior Knowledge

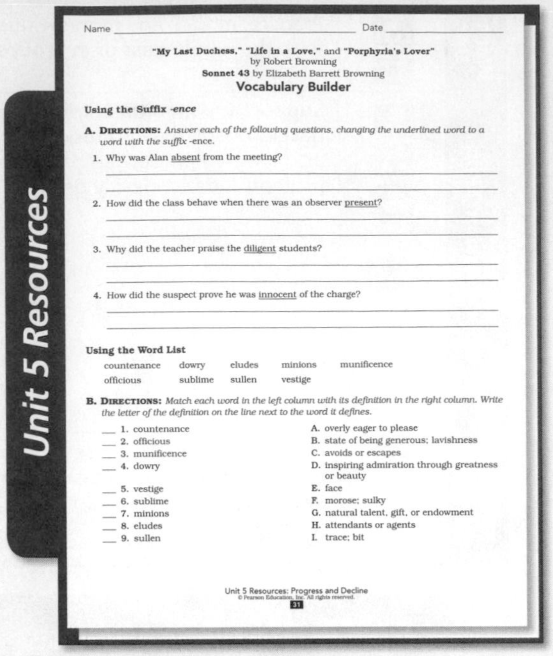

Name ____________ Date ____________

"My Last Duchess," "Life in a Love," and "Porphyria's Lover" by Robert Browning
Sonnet 43 by Elizabeth Barrett Browning
Vocabulary Builder

Using the Suffix *-ence*

A. Directions: *Answer each of the following questions, changing the underlined word to a word with the suffix -ence.*

1. Why was Alan absent from the meeting?
2. How did the class behave when there was an observer present?
3. Why did the teacher praise the diligent students?
4. How did the suspect prove he was innocent of the charge?

Using the Word List

countenance dowry eludes minions munificence
officious sublime sullen vestige

B. Directions: *Match each word in the left column with its definition in the right column. Write the letter of the definition on the line next to the word it defines.*

___ 1. countenance	A. overly eager to please
___ 2. officious	B. state of being generous; lavishness
___ 3. munificence	C. avoids or escapes
___ 4. dowry	D. inspiring admiration through greatness or beauty
___ 5. vestige	E. face
___ 6. sublime	F. morose; sulky
___ 7. minions	G. natural talent, gift, or endowment
___ 8. eludes	H. attendants or agents
___ 9. sullen	I. trace; bit

Unit 5 Resources: Progress and Decline
© Pearson Education, Inc. All rights reserved.
31

All **Vocabulary Builder,** p. 31

Also available for these selections:

EL L1 L2 **Vocabulary Warm-ups A and B,** pp. 25–26

EL L1 L2 **Reading Warm-ups A and B,** pp. 27–28

Reader's Notebooks

Pre- and postreading pages for these selections appear in an interactive format in the *Reader's Notebooks.* Each *Notebook* is differentiated for a different group of learners. The selections in the Adapted and English Learner's versions are abridged.

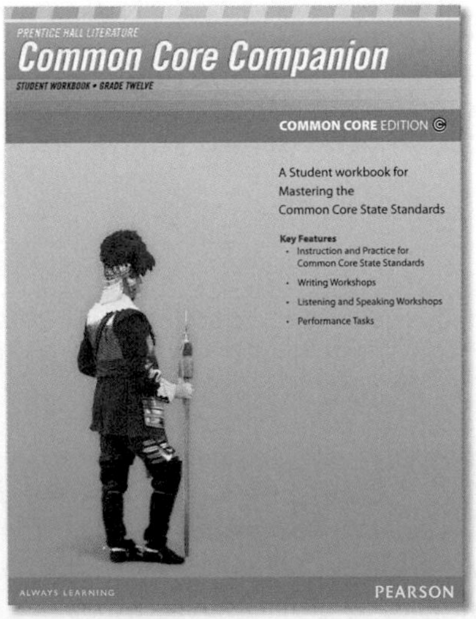

L2 L3 ***Reader's Notebook***

L1 ***Reader's Notebook: Adapted Version***

EL ***Reader's Notebook: English Learner's Version***

EL ***Reader's Notebook: Spanish Version***

Common Core Companion

Additional instruction and practice for each Common Core State Standard

Selection Support

Graphic Organizer Transparencies

"My Last Duchess," "Life in a Love," and **"Porphyria's Lover"**
by Robert Browning; **"Sonnet 43"** by Elizabeth Barrett Browning

After You Read A: Dramatic Monologue

Line 14	Her hus-	-band's pre-	-sence on-	-ly, called	that spot
Natural Pauses	no pause	no pause	no pause	pause	no pause
Line 15	Of joy	into	the Duch-	-ess' cheek:	perhaps
Natural Pauses	no pause	no pause	no pause	pause	no pause
Line 16	Frà Pan-	-dolf chanced	to say	"Her man-	-tle laps
Natural Pauses	no pause	pause	pause	pause	no pause
Line 17	Over	my la-	-dy's wrist	too much,"	or "Paint
Natural Pauses	no pause	no pause	no pause	pause	no pause
Line 18	Must ne-	-ver hope	to re-	produce	the faint
Natural Pauses					
Line 19	Half-flush	that dies	along	her throat";	such stuff
Natural Pauses					
Line 20	Was cour-	-tesy,	she thought,	and cause	enough
Natural Pauses					
Line 21	For call-	-ing up	that spot	of joy.	She had
Natural Pauses					
Line 22	A heart—	how shall	I say?—	too soon	made glad,
Natural Pauses					

Graphic Organizer Transparencies

175

EL L1 L2 **Literary Analysis: Graphic Organizer A,** (partially filled in), p. 175

Also available for these selections:

- EL L3 **Literary Analysis: Graphic Organizer B,** p. 176
- EL L1 L2 **Reading: Graphic Organizer A,** p. 173
- EL L3 **Reading: Graphic Organizer B,** p. 174

Skills Development/Extension

Unit 5 Resources

Name ______________________ Date ____________

"My Last Duchess," "Life in a Love," and **"Porphyria's Lover"**
by Robert Browning
Sonnet 43 by Elizabeth Barrett Browning

Enrichment: Fine Art

Reflections of a Poet's Theme

Like poets who can express a wealth of ideas in a concise form, artists can convey complex meaning in a single image. A piece of fine art accompanies two of the poems you read. These artworks are more than decorations; they reflect the poet's theme.

Directions: *Complete the following chart by listing the main visual details and identifying lines from the poems that support those details. Then, draw conclusions about how each artwork reflects the poet's theme.*

Criteria for Analysis	*Antea* by Parmigianino and "My Last Duchess"	*La Pia de Tolommei* by Dante Gabriel Rossetti and "Porphyria's Lover"
Visual Details		
Related Lines from Poem		
Reflections of Poet's Theme		

L4 **Enrichment,** p. 33

Also available for these selections:

- All **Literary Analysis: Dramatic Monologue,** p. 29
- All **Reading: Compare and Contrast Speakers in Poems,** p. 30
- EL L3 L4 **Support for Writing,** p. 32

Assessment

Name ______________________ Date ____________

Poetry of Robert Browning and Elizabeth Barrett Browning

Open-Book Test

Short Answer *Write your responses to the questions in this section on the lines provided.*

1. In Robert Browning's dramatic monologue "My Last Duchess," to whom is the Duke speaking? Explain your answer.
2. In "My Last Duchess," when the Duke refers to a gift he offered his last duchess (lines 33–34), why does he want his next duchess to appreciate it more fully, and why does he feel his "gift" is valuable?
3. How do you know that "My Last Duchess" is a dramatic monologue?
4. Reread lines 12–15 of "Life in a Love," and decide who or what strains the nerves, causes a fall, and takes up one's life. Explain your answer, using examples.
5. Use an example from "Life in a Love" to show how it works as a dramatic monologue, revealing the most intimate feelings of a single speaker.
6. Where does the turning point occur in the action the speaker describes in "Porphyria's Lover"? Explain your answer.
7. Give *two* examples of run-on lines in "Porphyria's Lover."

L3 L4 **Open-Book Test,** pp. 34–36

Also available for these selections:

- EL L1 L2 **Selection Test A,** pp. 37–39
- EL L3 L4 **Selection Test B,** pp. 40–42

PHLit Online!
www.PHLitOnline.com

- complete narrated selection text
- a thematically related video with writing prompt
- an interactive graphic organizer
- highlighting feature
- access to all student print resources, adapted to individual student needs
- Spanish and English summaries
- adapted selection translations in Spanish

Online Resources: All print materials are also available online.

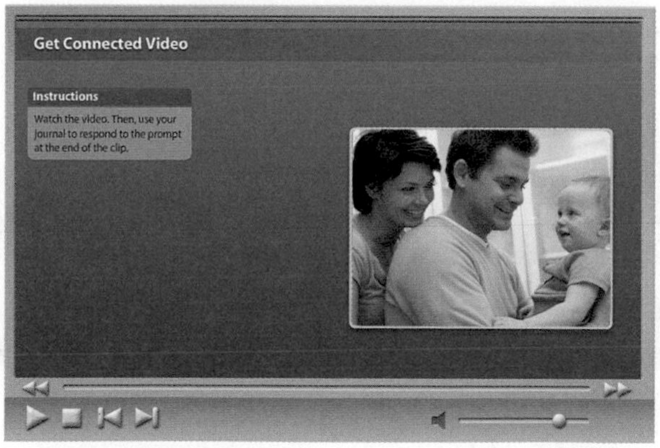

Get Connected! (thematic video with writing prompt)

Also available:

Background Video
All videos are available in Spanish.

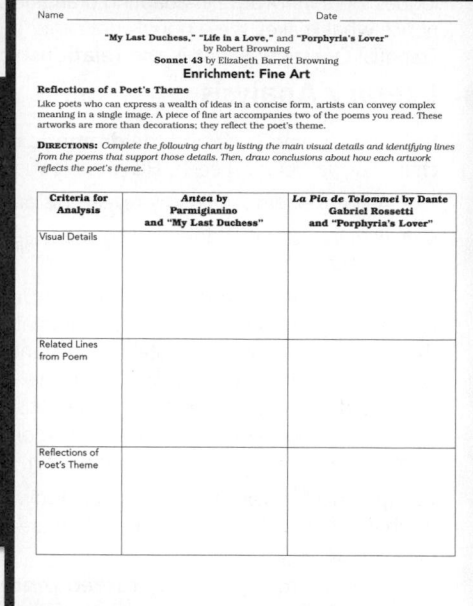

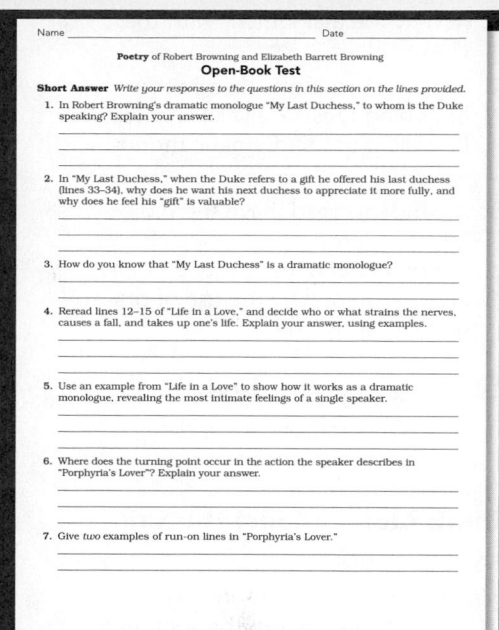

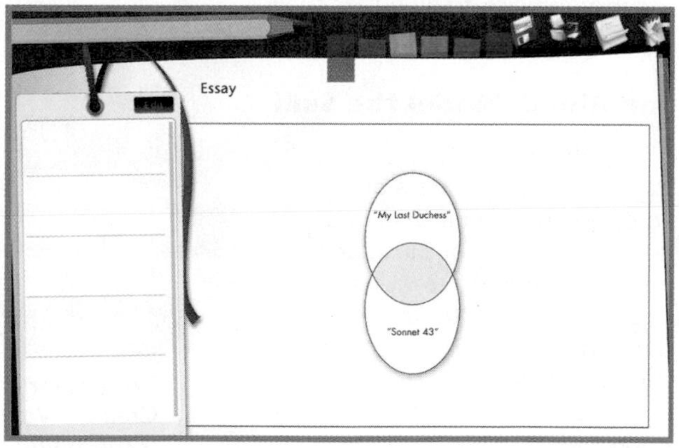

Writer's Journal (with graphics feature)

Also available:

Vocabulary Central (tools and activities for studying vocabulary)

PRETEACH

❶ Connecting to the Essential Question

1. Review the assignment with the class.
2. Explain to students that Robert Browning is especially known for his skillful use of dramatic monologues.
3. As students read, have them look for and identify ways in which the drama and interest of a poem are heightened by the use of dramatic monologue.

❷ Literary Analysis

Introduce the concept using the instruction on the student page.

Think Aloud: Model the Skill

Say to students:

In reading dramatic monologues, I can learn a lot about the speaker, and about the listener. I know that dramatic monologues reveal much about a speaker's frame of mind and his or her character. When I read or hear a dramatic monologue, sometimes I am able to identify the listener, and sometimes I am not.

❸ Reading Strategy

1. Introduce the strategy using the instruction on the student page.
2. Give students a copy of **Reading Strategy Graphic Organizer B,** page 174 in ***Graphic Organizer Transparencies,*** to fill out as they read.

Think Aloud: Model the Skill

Say to students:

I can better appreciate a grouping of poems if I compare and contrast elements of those poems. Comparing two different perspectives on love leads to an understanding of the broad spectrum on which this emotion is expressed.

❹ Vocabulary

1. Pronounce each word, giving its definition, and have students say it aloud.
2. For more guidance, see the ***Classroom Strategies and Teaching Routines*** card for introducing vocabulary.

Before You Read

My Last Duchess • Life in a Love • Porphyria's Lover • Sonnet 43

❶ **Connecting to the Essential Question** Robert Browning's monologues were innovative in adapting dramatic devices to poetry. As you read, notice what makes these poems dramatic. This will help you address the Essential Question: **What is the relationship of the writer to tradition?**

Common Core State Standards

Reading Literature
3. Analyze the impact of the author's choices regarding how to develop and relate elements of a story or drama.

❷ Literary Analysis

Robert Browning perfected the **dramatic monologue,** in which a single character delivers a speech. His monologues contain these elements:

- A speaker who indirectly reveals his or her situation and character
- A silent listener, addressed by the speaker and implied in what the speaker says

Browning's decision to write "My Last Duchess" as a dramatic monologue allows him to develop a dramatic, tension-filled scene in which the reader does not immediately understand who is speaking, who is being addressed, and what has happened to the "last Duchess." Further, having only the duke speaking highlights his egotism. As you read, consider other ways that using the form of a dramatic monologue allows the author to develop the narrative and convey meaning.

Comparing Literary Works Robert Browning's monologues capture the rhythms of speech through **run-on lines**—lines whose natural flow goes past line endings:

But to myself they turned (since none puts by
The curtain I have drawn for you, but I)

He and Elizabeth Barrett also use **end-stopped lines,** which end just where a speaker would pause. Compare the poets' use of these devices.

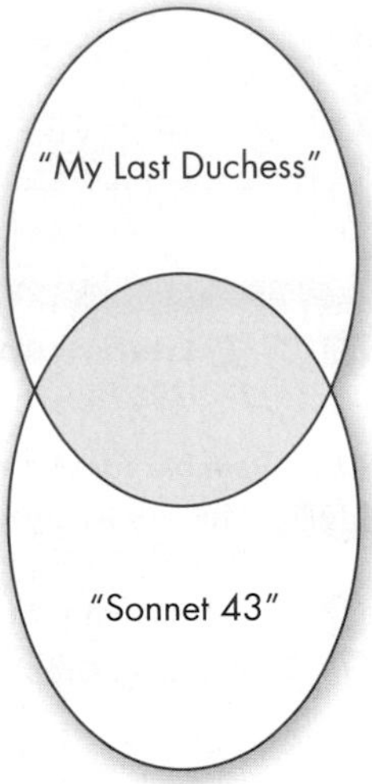

❸ Reading Strategy

Preparing to Read Complex Texts You can better understand the theme of a poem if you **compare and contrast speakers in multiple poems.** For example, you might gain insights into the selfish, possessive love of the speaker in one poem if you compare it to the deep, abiding love of the speaker in another. Use a diagram like the one shown to compare and contrast speakers in these poems.

❹ Vocabulary

countenance (koun′ tə nəns) *n.* face (p. 979)

officious (ə fish′ əs) *adj.* meddlesome (p. 980)

munificence (myo͞o nif′ ə səns) *n.* lavish generosity (p. 980)

dowry (dou′ rē) *n.* property brought by a woman's family to her husband upon their marriage (p. 980)

eludes (ē lo͞odz′) *v.* avoids or escapes (p. 981)

sullen (sul′ ən) *adj.* brooding; morose; sulky (p. 982)

PHLit Online! www.PHLitOnline.com

Vocabulary Development

Vocabulary Knowledge Rating

Create a **Vocabulary Knowledge Rating Chart** (***Professional Development Guidebook,*** p. 33) for the vocabulary words on the student page. Give each student a copy of the chart with the words on it. Read the words aloud, and have students mark their ratings in the Before Reading column. Urge students to attend to these words as they read and discuss the selections.

In order to gauge how much instruction you need to provide, tally how many students are confident in their knowledge of each word. As students read, point out the words and their context.

PHLit Online! **Vocabulary Central,** featuring tools and activities for studying vocabulary, is available online at **www.PHLitOnline.com.**

5 *Robert*
Browning
(1812–1889)

Author of "My Last Duchess" • "Life in a Love" • "Porphyria's Lover"

Young Robert Browning's best teacher may not have been a person, but his father's 6,000-book library. Although he had little schooling, he eagerly devoured those books, hungry for knowledge about history, art, and literature.

Inspiration and Discouragement By the time he was a teenager, Browning had decided to make poetry his life's pursuit. He published his first book, *Pauline,* at the age of twenty-one. Success was a while coming, though. A long and highly personal poem modeled after Shelley's work, *Pauline* did not sell a single copy.

Discouraged, Browning tried his hand at something less personal, a long dramatic poem called *Paracelsus.* He also wrote a play. His work still failed to attract much public notice, and his reputation was eclipsed by that of his wife, the poet Elizabeth Barrett Browning, whom he had married in 1846.

Lasting Fame In 1869, eight years after Elizabeth's death, the publication of *The Ring and the Book* turned Browning's career around. This long poem, based on an actual trial, tells the story of a murder in a series of dramatic monologues, or speeches by characters. *The Ring and the Book* achieved wide recognition for its author. It demonstrated the unique elements that Browning contributed to nineteenth-century poetry: a more down-to-earth, less "poetic" language and a renewal of the dramatic monologue, a literary form ideally suited to reveal character.

Today, Browning ranks with Tennyson as one of the great Victorian poets. His shorter dramatic monologues, such as "My Last Duchess," and "Porphyria's Lover," remain favorites of many.

Daily Bellringer

For each class during which you will teach these selections, have students complete one of the five activities for the appropriate week in the *Daily Bellringer Activities* booklet.

Multidraft Reading

To assist struggling readers and to enhance reading for all, assign the text in chunks, as warranted by length, and apply multidraft reading protocols. For each reading, have students set the purpose indicated:

- **First reading**—identifying key ideas and details and answering any Reading Checks.
- **Second reading**—analyzing craft and structure and responding to the side-column prompts.
- **Third reading**—integrating knowledge and ideas, connecting to other texts and the world, and answering the end-of-selection questions.

For more guidance, refer to the ***Classroom Strategies and Teaching Routines*** card on Multidraft Reading.

5 Background

More About the Author

Robert Browning was influenced most significantly in his youth by his reading of Shelley, Byron, and Keats, and by his mother's Nonconformist piety. At the age of twelve, he wrote a volume of poems, *Incondita,* that no longer survives. After the death of his wife, Elizabeth, Browning lived with his sister and formed a wide circle of acquaintances in London society. He was awarded an honorary degree by Oxford University. Browning died in Venice and is buried in Westminster Abbey.

PHLit Online!
www.PHLitOnline.com

Teaching From Technology

Preparing to Read
Go to **www.PHLitOnline.com** and display the ***Get Connected!*** slide show for these selections. Have the class brainstorm responses to the writing prompt, entering ideas in the interactive journal. Then, have students complete their written responses as homework.

To build background, display the Background and More About the Author feature.

Using the Interactive Text
Go to **www.PHLitOnline.com** and display the Enriched Online Student Edition. As the class reads the selection or listens to the narration, record answers to side-column prompts using the graphic organizers accessible on the interactive page. Alternatively, have students use the online edition individually, answering the prompts as they read.

❶ About the Selection

In "My Last Duchess," Browning skillfully uses the dramatic monologue to provide a brilliant portrait of a jealous, possessive, arrogant man who gave orders to kill his first wife because she displeased him. The duke describes at length his dead wife's supposed faults. As the duke talks, he reveals to the reader his chilling personality.

❷ Activating Prior Knowledge

Have students brainstorm a list of qualities that they would look for in a loved one. Then, make a list of the five most important qualities and keep them to compare and contrast with the qualities they find in these poems.

Concept Connector →

Tell students they will return to their responses after reading the selections.

❸ Humanities

Portrait of Lucrezia de'Medici, by the Workshop of Agnolo Bronzino, 16th century

Use this question for discussion: Do you think the woman in this portrait is happy?

Possible response: No, she looks wealthy but unhappy.

Text Complexity Rubric

	My Last Duchess	Life in a Love	Porphyria's Lover	Sonnet 43
Qualitative Measures				
Context/ Knowledge Demands	Dramatic monologue; cultural knowledge demands 1 2 (3) 4 5	Dramatic monologue 1 (2) 3 4 5	Dramatic monologue 1 2 (3) 4 5	Victorian sonnet 1 (2) 3 4 5
Structure/Language Conventionality and Clarity	Above-level vocabulary; long sentences 1 2 (3) 4 5	Poetic diction 1 (2) 3 4 5	Poetic diction 1 (2) 3 4 5	Archaic diction 1 2 (3) 4 5
Levels of Meaning/ Purpose/Concepts	Moderate (relationships) 1 2 (3) 4 5	Accessible (love) 1 2 (3) 4 5	Moderate (jealousy, madness) 1 2 (3) 4 5	Accessible (love) 1 (2) 3 4 5
Quantitative Measures				
Lexile/Text Length	NP / 452 words	NP / 143 words	NP / 409 words	NP / 125 words
Overall Complexity	**More complex**	**More accessible**	**More accessible**	**More accessible**

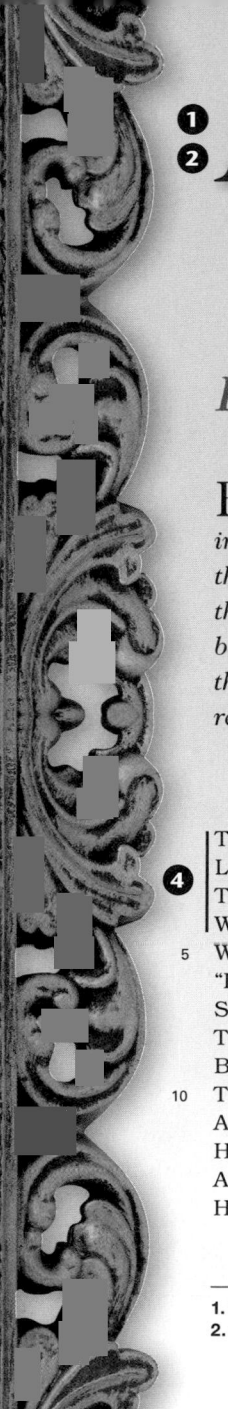

❶ ❷

My Last Duchess

Robert Browning

Background *This poem, set in the sixteenth century in a castle in northern Italy, is based on events from the life of the duke of Ferrara, a nobleman whose first wife died after just three years of marriage. Following his wife's death, the duke began making arrangements to remarry. In Browning's poem, the duke is showing a painting of his first wife to an agent who represents the father of the woman he hopes to marry.*

❹
That's my last Duchess painted on the wall,
Looking as if she were alive. I call
That piece a wonder, now: Frà Pandolf's[1] hands
Worked busily a day, and there she stands.
Will't please you sit and look at her? I said
"Frà Pandolf" by design, for never read
Strangers like you that pictured **countenance**
The depth and passion of its earnest glance,
But to myself they turned (since none puts by
The curtain I have drawn for you, but I)
And seemed as they would ask me, if they durst,[2]
How such a glance came there; so, not the first
Are you to turn and ask thus. Sir, 'twas not
Her husband's presence only, called that spot

---

1. **Frà Pandolf's** work of Brother Pandolf, an imaginary painter.
2. **durst** dared.

❺ **◀ Critical Viewing**
This portrait of the duke of Ferrara's wife inspired Browning to write "My Last Duchess." Compare the character of the duchess as conveyed by the painting with the character of the duchess as described by the duke in the poem. **[Compare and Contrast]**

Vocabulary
countenance (koun′ tə nəns) *n.* face

❻ **Reading Check**
What are the duke and his listener viewing?

❹ Literary Analysis

Dramatic Monologue

1. Remind students that a dramatic monologue is the speech of a single speaker. It contains no stage directions or omniscient narration. Yet poets can deftly set a scene in a monologue through implication.
2. Have a volunteer read lines 1–4 aloud.
3. **Ask** students: In front of what object is the speaker standing in these lines?
   Answer: He is standing in front of the portrait of his former wife.

► **Monitor Progress: Ask** students: What technique does Browning use to convey this information within the form of a dramatic monologue?
Answer: The opening "That's" immediately suggests that the speaker is indicating something. The rest of the line explains what he is saying and implies that he is speaking to a visitor unfamiliar with the painting. The information is conveyed in the speech of the poem's speaker, without outside narration, so it remains within the form of the monologue.

❺ Critical Viewing

Answer: The woman portrayed by the artist seems serious and unsentimental, not warm and lighthearted like the duchess.

❻ Reading Check

Answer: The duke and his listener are looking at a portrait of the duke's deceased wife.

Text Complexity: Reader and Task Suggestions

	My Last Duchess	Life in a Love; Porphyria's Lover	Sonnet 43
Preparing to Read the Texts • Using the information at the bottom of TE p. 982, discuss how a writer can make clear to readers that a speaker is delusional. • Explain to students that some of the Browning poems explore unpleasant relationships. • Guide students to use Multidraft Reading strategies (TE p. 977).	**Leveled Tasks** ***Levels of Meaning*** If students will have difficulty with the meaning, have them read through the poem to see what the duke says about his first marriage. Then, have them reread, asking questions such as *"Is this really true?"* ***Synthesizing*** If students will not have difficulty with the meaning, have them synthesize the telling details to formulate a mental portrait of the duke.	**Leveled Tasks** ***Levels of Meaning*** If students will have difficulty understanding the monologues, have them focus first on the speaker's personality. Then, have students reread each poem, keeping the speaker's personality in mind. ***Evaluating*** If students will not have difficulty with the meaning, have them evaluate how effectively Browning communicates the personalities of his speakers.	**Leveled Tasks** ***Structure/Language*** If students will have difficulty with the language, have them restate it in contemporary English. Then, have them reread it, focusing on the emotions that the speaker expresses. ***Evaluating*** If students will not have difficulty with the language, have them evaluate the effectiveness of the details in communicating the speaker's feelings.

❼ Literary Analysis

Dramatic Monologue

1. Remind students that dramatic monologues often indirectly reveal the situation and character of their speakers.
2. Have students read lines 15–34, paying careful attention to the detail about the duke indirectly revealed by his words.
3. Then, **ask** them the Literary Analysis question: How does the duke indirectly suggest his own deeply jealous nature?
Answer: The duke shows that he could not tolerate the ordinary pleasures his wife took in simple things, since he felt that this pleasure equaled the pleasure she took in his gifts, an equivalence his pride could not accept.

❽ Reading Strategy

Compare and Contrast Speakers

1. Have students reread lines 13–34.
2. Then, **ask** students the Reading Strategy questions: Compare and contrast the speaker and his duchess as characters. Based on the speaker's description lines 13–31, what sort of person was the duchess? In contrast, what do lines 32–34 show about the speaker?
Answer: Students might offer that the duchess seems carefree, and the duke seems overly suspicious and jealous. Other students might suggest that the duchess seems like a trusting person, and that the duke is quite her opposite, being as filled with mistrust in her as he seems. The duke describes the duchess as a flirt, "easily impressed," and "too soon made glad." Lines 32–34 reveal the duke as a jealous man who is insecure and who believes the duchess ranks all gifts she is given as equal to or better than the gifts he gives her.
3. Point out to students that the duke's seeming rationality in thinking is belied by his completely irrational emotional reactions—insane jealousy of his wife's attention to anything besides himself and his rank.

---

❼ Literary Analysis
Dramatic Monologue How does the duke indirectly suggest his own deeply jealous nature?

Vocabulary
officious (ə fish′ əs) *adj.* meddlesome

❽ Reading Strategy
Compare and Contrast Speakers Based on the speaker's description (lines 13–31), what sort of person was the duchess? In contrast, what do lines 32–34 show about the speaker?

Vocabulary
munificence (myo͞o nif′ ə səns) *n.* lavish generosity
dowry (dou′ rē) *n.* property brought by a woman's family to her husband upon their marriage

Of joy into the Duchess' cheek: perhaps
Frà Pandolf chanced to say "Her mantle laps
Over my lady's wrist too much," or "Paint
Must never hope to reproduce the faint
Half-flush that dies along her throat"; such stuff
Was courtesy, she thought, and cause enough
For calling up that spot of joy. She had
A heart—how shall I say?—too soon made glad,
Too easily impressed; she liked whate'er
She looked on, and her looks went everywhere.
Sir, 'twas all one! My favor at her breast,
The dropping of the daylight in the West,
The bough of cherries some **officious** fool
Broke in the orchard for her, the white mule
She rode with round the terrace—all and each
Would draw from her alike the approving speech,
Or blush, at least. She thanked men—good! but
    thanked
Somehow—I know not how—as if she ranked
My gift of a nine-hundred-year-old name
With anybody's gift. Who'd stoop to blame
This sort of trifling? Even had you skill
In speech—(which I have not)—to make your will
Quite clear to such an one, and say, "Just this
Or that in you disgusts me; here you miss,
Or there exceed the mark"—and if she let
Herself be lessoned so, nor plainly set
Her wits to yours, forsooth,[3] and made excuse,
—E'en then would be some stooping; and I choose
Never to stoop. Oh sir, she smiled, no doubt,
Whene'er I passed her; but who passed without
Much the same smile? This grew; I gave commands;
Then all smiles stopped together. There she stands
As if alive. Will 't please you rise? We'll meet
The company below, then. I repeat,
The Count your master's known **munificence**
Is ample warrant that no one just pretense
Of mine for **dowry** will be disallowed;
Though his fair daughter's self, as I avowed
At starting, is my object. Nay, we'll go
Together down, sir! Notice Neptune,[4] though,
Taming a sea horse, thought a rarity,
Which Claus of Innsbruck[5] cast in bronze for me!

3. **forsooth** in truth.
4. **Neptune** in Roman mythology, the god of the sea.
5. **Claus of Innsbruck** imaginary Austrian sculptor.

Enrichment: Investigating Daily Life

Love and Marriage

Share with the class that the relationship we call "love" has been interpreted in widely different ways in various eras and in diverse cultures. In ancient Greece and Rome, as well as in medieval and Renaissance Europe, political marriages among individuals of the upper classes were common. Help students to recognize that the Brownings' romantic courtship was decidedly unconventional by the standards of nineteenth-century England. In many parts of the world today, such a relationship—in defiance of a parent's wishes—would still be regarded with disapproval.

Activity: Investigating Love and Marriage Have students research love and marriage in nineteenth-century England. Students can record their findings on the **Enrichment: Investigating Daily Life** worksheet, ***Professional Development Guidebook***, page 224.

9 Life in a Love

Robert Browning

Escape me?
Never—
Beloved!
While I am I, and you are you,
So long as the world contains us both,
Me the loving and you the loth,
While the one **eludes**, must the other pursue.
My life is a fault at last, I fear:
It seems too much like a fate, indeed!
Though I do my best I shall scarce succeed.
But what if I fail of my purpose here?
It is but to keep the nerves at strain,
To dry one's eyes and laugh at a fall,
And, baffled, get up and begin again,—
So the chase takes up one's life, that's all.
While, look but once from your farthest bound
At me so deep in the dust and dark,
No sooner the old hope goes to ground
Than a new one, straight to the self-same mark,
I shape me—
Ever
Removed!

10 Reading Strategy
Compare and Contrast Speakers How is the speaker's attitude toward his beloved in this poem like and unlike the attitude toward his former wife of the speaker in "My Last Duchess"?

Vocabulary
eludes (ē lo͞odz′) *v.* avoids or escapes

Critical Reading

Cite textual evidence to support your responses.

1. **Key Ideas and Details (a)** What complaint does the speaker make about his first wife in lines 13–24 of "My Last Duchess"? **(b) Infer:** How did he respond to her behavior? **(c) Support:** Explain what has happened to the duchess, indicating where in the poem this is revealed.
2. **Key Ideas and Details (a)** To what new subject does the speaker turn in his last remark? **(b) Draw Conclusions:** What does this change of subject reveal about his character?
3. **Key Ideas and Details (a)** What does the speaker of "Life in a Love" do as his beloved eludes him? **(b) Interpret:** What causes his behavior?
4. **Integration of Knowledge and Ideas** Is the speaker's "love" truly love? Explain.

9 About the Selection

In this dramatic monologue, the male speaker describes his persistence in pursuing a reluctant woman. Attitudes toward this speaker may vary widely. Some may be charmed and amused by his persistence, while others may find it sad or scary.

10 Reading Strategy

Compare and Contrast Speakers

1. Have students reread the poem.
2. **Ask** students the Reading Strategy question.
   Answer: The speakers in both poems seem overly possessive and see their romantic interests as something to be controlled or directed. They differ in that the speaker of "Life in a Love" is commenting on a woman who is still living, and with whom he is still involved. The duke speaks of the duchess in the past tense in "My Last Duchess."

ASSESS

Answers

Remind students to support their answers with evidence from the text.

1. (a) The speaker complains that his first wife was too free with her appreciation for things. (b) He had her killed. (c) This murder is revealed in lines 45–46: "This grew: I gave commands; / Then all smiles stopped together."
2. (a) The speaker turns to the subject of a bronze sculpture as they descend the stairs. (b) The speaker has the same possessive attitude toward the sculpture, the portrait, and the duchess.
3. (a) He keeps pursuing his goal and looking for a sign of encouragement. (b) His behavior is caused by his unrequited love.
4. **Possible response:** The speaker is in love with the "game" of love, rather than with the woman. Or, the speaker really must be in love to subject himself to such constant agony.

Differentiated Instruction for Universal Access

Support for Special-Needs Students
To help students read the poem "Life in a Love," give students a copy of **Literary Analysis Graphic Organizer B**, page 176 in ***Graphic Organizer Transparencies.***

Strategy for Less Proficient Readers
Have students read "Life in a Love" with teacher guidance. Then, have them paraphrase this poem in one or two paragraphs. Remind them that when they paraphrase, they take Browning's words and restate them in their own words.

Enrichment for Advanced Readers
Have students write a parody of Browning's "Life in a Love," in which they take his dramatic monologue of obsessive love to an extreme. Students may want to exploit some of the ideas in Browning's poem for comic effect, or they may choose to manipulate the genre of the obsequious lover in hot pursuit of his beloved.

11 About the Selection

In this, one of Browning's earliest and most shocking dramatic monologues, the speaker describes an incident in which a young woman is murdered by her lover. Narrating using first-person point of view, the nameless man describes the event which has just taken place. Porphyria has come into the man's cottage from a raging storm, bared her shoulder, and explained that she was there in spite of her family's and friends' wishes otherwise. The man believes that at some point in the future, Porphyria will succumb to societal pressures and leave him. Because Porphyria "worshipped" this man, he cannot bear to lose her, so his fairly illogical conclusion is to strangle her.

12 Critical Viewing

Answer: The subject of the painting is in a contemplative state. Some students may say that she is thinking about her romantic interest. Other students may say that she looks sad.

11 PORPHYRIA'S LOVER

Robert Browning

Vocabulary
sullen (səl′ ən) *adj.* brooding; morose; sulky

The rain set early in tonight,
The **sullen** wind was soon awake,
It tore the elm-tops down for spite,
And did its worst to vex the lake:
I listened with heart fit to break.
When glided in Porphyria; straight
She shut the cold out and the storm,
And kneeled and made the cheerless grate
Blaze up, and all the cottage warm;
Which done, she rose, and from her form
Withdrew the dripping cloak and shawl,
And laid her soiled gloves by, untied
Her hat and let the damp hair fall,
And, last, she sat down by my side
And called me. When no voice replied,
She put my arm about her waist,
And made her smooth white shoulder bare,
And all her yellow hair displaced,
And, stooping, made my cheek lie there,
And spread, o'er all, her yellow hair,
Murmuring how she loved me—she
Too weak, for all her heart's endeavor,
To set its struggling passion free
From pride, and vainer ties dissever,

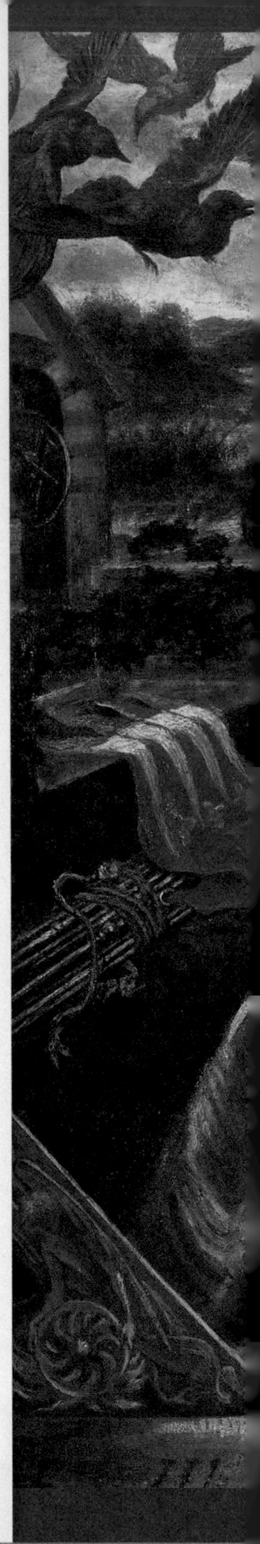

12 ▶ Critical Viewing
Does the subject of this painting seem to be in love, as Porphyria is? Why or why not? **[Infer]**

Enrichment: Investigating Psychology

Delusional Disorder
The male speakers in "My Last Duchess" and "Porphyria's Lover" are clearly mentally unbalanced. Some might conjecture that they suffer from delusional disorder, or the inability to determine real from imagined situations and experiences. Delusional disorder is a serious mental illness that causes many problems for people afflicted with it.

Activity: Investigating Delusional Disorder
Have students research delusional disorder. Students can explore the causes, symptoms, and treatment of this mental illness. Have students record their findings on the **Enrichment: Investigating Psychology** worksheet, ***Professional Development Guidebook,*** page 239.

⓭ Humanities

La Pia de Tolomei, 1881 by Dante Rossetti

In this painting, one of many Rossetti painted to illustrate different Cantos of the *Divine Comedy*, Rossetti features a woman in distress. In *Canto V* of *Purgatorio*, Dante meets La Pia, the wife of a man who has imprisoned her in a fortress. She eventually dies, either through neglect or force.

Use this question for discussion: How does this woman resemble the woman in Browning's poem?

Answer: She is a lover of an irrational man. She eventually meets a bad end.

Differentiated Instruction for Universal Access

Strategy for Less Proficient Readers

Have students read "Porphyria's Lover" with teacher guidance. Assign students to pairs or small groups. Then, ask teams of students to paraphrase the poem in a short paragraph. Students can share paraphrased paragraphs and assist each other in decoding the poem.

Enrichment for Advanced Readers

Have students analyze the poems they have read in this lesson and write essays in which they analyze the different kinds of love expressed in each work. Students should quote directly from each work to support their opinions. For students who are interested in reading more of Elizabeth Barrett Browning's work before they complete their essays, refer them to her Sonnet 14, "If Thou Must Love Me, Let It Be for Nought."

14 Reading Strategy

Compare and Contrast Speakers

1. Point out to students that this dramatic monologue describes the central event from first-person point of view.
2. **Ask** the Reading Strategy question: From the contrast, between the speaker's words and actions, what can you conclude about his mental state?
Answer: The speaker describes Porphyria as happy and affectionate—in short, in love with him. This demeanor dramatically contrasts with the action the speaker takes against her: he murders her. From this action, we can conclude that the mental state of the speaker is unwell, perhaps psychotic.

ASSESS

Answers

Before students respond, you may wish to have them write a brief objective summary of the selection. As they answer the questions below, remind them to support their answers with evidence from the text.

1. Elements of conflict include the woman being at the cottage against her family's and friends' wishes and the man not wanting to lose her. Elements of resolution include the woman's murder. Elements of dialogue include the woman "murmuring" of her love for the man. Elements of stage direction include details of the storm, the woman lighting the fire, approaching the man, and his actions toward her.
2. The last line is dramatic in that the man seems to imply that since God had not yet "said a word," that he was either waiting for punishment or believed that God approved of his actions.

And give herself to me for ever.
But passion sometimes would prevail,
Nor could tonight's gay feast restrain
A sudden thought of one so pale
For love of her, and all in vain:
So, she was come through wind and rain.
Be sure I looked up at her eyes
Happy and proud; at last I knew
Porphyria worshipped me; surprise
Made my heart swell, and still it grew
While I debated what to do.
That moment she was mine, mine, fair,
Perfectly pure and good: I found
A thing to do, and all her hair
In one long yellow string I wound
Three times her little throat around,
And strangled her. No pain felt she;
I am quite sure she felt no pain.
As a shut bud that holds a bee,
I warily oped her lids: again
Laughed the blue eyes without a stain.
And I untightened next the tress
About her neck; her cheek once more
Blushed bright beneath my burning kiss:
I propped her head up as before,
Only, this time my shoulder bore
Her head, which droops upon it still:
The smiling rosy little head,
So glad it has its utmost will,
That all it scorned at once is fled,
And I, its love, am gained instead!
Porphyria's love: she guessed not how
Her darling one wish would be heard.
And thus we sit together now,
And all night long we have not stirred,
And yet God has not said a word!

I AM QUITE SURE SHE FELT NO PAIN

14 Reading Strategy
Compare and Contrast Speakers From the contrast between the speaker's words and actions, what can you conclude about his mental state?

Critical Reading

Cite textual evidence to support your responses.

1. **Craft and Structure** Does this monologue have such dramatic elements as conflict, resolution, dialogue, and stage directions? Explain.
2. **Craft and Structure** What makes the last line especially dramatic? Explain.

Vocabulary Development

Vocabulary Knowledge Rating

When students have completed reading and discussing the selection, have them take out their **Vocabulary Knowledge Rating Charts** for the story. Read the words aloud and have students rate their knowledge of words again in the After Reading column. Clarify any words that are still problematic. Have students write their own definitions and example or sentence in the appropriate column. Then, have students complete the Vocabulary Practice at the end of the selection. Encourage students to use the words in further discussion and written work about the selection. Remind them that they will be accountable for these words on the **Selection Test, *Unit 5 Resources,*** pages 37–39 or 40–42.

(1806–1861)

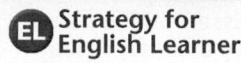

15

ELIZABETH BARRETT *Browning*

Author of Sonnet 43

Like her future husband, young Elizabeth Barrett had no formal education. However, her zest for knowledge spurred her to learn eight languages on her own. By the time she was ten, she had read plays by Shakespeare, passages of *Paradise Lost,* and histories of England, Greece, and Rome. The oldest of eleven children in an upper-middle-class family, she began writing poetry as a child. By the time she reached adulthood, she had published two volumes of verse.

Frailty and Romance Elizabeth Barrett's frail health, caused by a spinal injury, made her something of a recluse. But her poetry attracted much attention, including that of Robert Browning, who wrote her a letter of appreciation. After five months of correspondence, she and Browning met and fell in love. Her father objected to their romance, but Elizabeth and Robert married in 1846 and ran away to Florence, Italy, where they had a son they nicknamed Pen and lived in happy exile. In Italy, Elizabeth Barrett took an interest in politics and wrote denunciations of slavery in the United States. She died in Florence in 1861.

Shifting Reputations It is hard for us to believe today, when Robert Browning's reputation is so great, that Elizabeth was the more famous poet during her lifetime. Her love story in verse, *Aurora Leigh* (1857), was so popular that the income from it helped support the Brownings. Also popular was her *Sonnets from the Portuguese,* a sequence of forty-four love poems written to her husband. Sonnet 43, which comes from this collection, has appeared in countless anthologies and has assured her place in the history of English poetry.

PRETEACH

Background

15 More About the Author

Elizabeth Barrett Browning received a great deal of critical attention in her lifetime. When Wordsworth died in 1850, she was considered to be the most likely successor to the post of poet laureate. Toward the end of her life, she wrote poems that were more politically charged and less popular with her peers. In particular, *Poems Before Congress* (1860) damaged her popularity. She and Robert Browning were friends of Ruskin, Carlyle, Tennyson, Thackeray, Hawthorne, Rossetti, and scores of other literary luminaries of their day.

Differentiated Instruction for Universal Access

EL Strategy for English Learners

Students may struggle with determining the course of events in the poems in this grouping. Read the poems through with students, pausing for comprehension questions and clarification. Students may also need guidance regarding nineteenth-century notions of propriety and gender relations in order to fully understand the poems.

Enrichment for Gifted/Talented Students

Have students research other artistic couples. They can use online search engines or go to the school or local library. Encourage students to look beyond literature and to research creative artistic couples in art and music, as well as literature. Students can present their findings to the class in the form of short biographical sketches.

PHLit Online!

For more about the author, go online at **www.PHLitOnline.com.**

TEACH

⑯ About the Selection

To describe her love for her husband, Elizabeth Barrett Browning proposes the question, "How do I love thee?" and then provides eight answers. Browning's famous sonnet has become a universal tribute to love.

⑰ Reading Strategy

Compare and Contrast Speakers

1. Have a student volunteer read the sonnet aloud.
2. Then, **ask** the questions: Compare and contrast the love expressed here with the speaker's love for Porphyria in "Porphyria's Lover." What, if anything, do the two types of love have in common? How are they different?
   Possible responses: The love expressed in Sonnet 43 is much purer and selfless than the speaker's love in "Porphyria's Lover." The love expressed in both poems is total and complete; however, the love expressed in Sonnet 43 is not based on deluded obsession, but instead on pure, freely given, romantic love.

ASSESS

Answers

Remind students to support their answers with evidence from the text.

1. (a) The speaker asks: In how many ways do I love you? (b) **Possible response:** She loves her beloved to the limits that her soul can reach; her love is always sufficient to the demands of each particular day; she loves with all the passion she has ever been capable of feeling.
2. **Possible responses:** Students should cite songs about various aspects of love and compare their language, attitude, and images to those of Sonnet 43.
3. **Possible response:** The speaker in "Porphyria's Lover" is the most dramatic because he *rationalizes* his *motivation* for killing his lover. One wonders about his *psychological* state.

⑯

Sonnet 43

ELIZABETH BARRETT BROWNING

⑰ Reading Strategy
Compare and Contrast Speakers Compare and contrast the love expressed here with the speaker's love for Porphyria in "Porphyria's Lover." What, if anything, do the two types of love have in common? How are they different?

How do I love thee? Let me count the ways.
I love thee to the depth and breadth and height
My soul can reach, when feeling out of sight
For the ends of Being and ideal Grace.
I love thee to the level of every day's
Most quiet need, by sun and candlelight.
I love thee freely, as men strive for Right;
I love thee purely, as they turn from Praise.
I love thee with the passion put to use
In my old griefs, and with my childhood's faith.
I love thee with a love I seemed to lose
With my lost saints—I love thee with the breath,
Smiles, tears, of all my life!—and, if God choose,
I shall but love thee better after death.

Critical Reading

Cite textual evidence to support your responses.

1. **Key Ideas and Details (a)** In Sonnet 43, what question does the speaker ask? **(b) Paraphrase:** Briefly summarize the speaker's answers to her own question.
2. **Integration of Knowledge and Ideas** Cite a popular song that praises love, and compare its language, attitude, and images with those of Sonnet 43.
3. **Integration of Knowledge and Ideas** Which speakers in these poems are most dramatic? Explain, using three of these Essential Question words: *psychological, emotional, motivation, rationalize, confront.* ***[Connecting to the Essential Question: What is the relationship of the writer to tradition?]***

Concept Connector

Reading Strategy Graphic Organizer

Ask students to review the graphic organizers in which they have compared and contrasted elements of these poems. Then, have students share their organizers and compare their findings with each other.

Activating Prior Knowledge

Have students return to their responses to the Activating Prior Knowledge activity. Ask them to explain whether their thoughts have changed and, if so, how.

Writing About the Essential Question

Have students compare their responses to the prompt, completed before reading the poems, with their thoughts afterward. Have them work individually or in groups, writing or discussing their thoughts, to formulate new responses. Then, lead a class discussion, probing for what students have learned that confirms or invalidates their initial thoughts. Encourage students to cite specific textual details to support their responses.

After You Read

My Last Duchess • Life in a Love • Porphyria's Lover • Sonnet 43

Literary Analysis

1. **Craft and Structure (a)** Who delivers the **dramatic monologue** in "My Last Duchess," and who is the listener? **(b)** How can you tell when the listener interacts with the speaker? Give an example.
2. **Key Ideas and Details (a)** Cite two lines in which the speaker reveals something negative about himself. **(b)** Basing your answer on this monologue, do you think the speaker's next marriage will be successful? Explain.
3. **Key Ideas and Details (a)** Who are the speaker and the listener in "Life in a Love"? **(b)** Do they interact with each other? Explain.
4. **Key Ideas and Details (a)** Characterize the speaker in "Porphyria's Lover." **(b)** Whom do you think he might be addressing?
5. **Craft and Structure (a)** Use a chart like the one shown to analyze the places at which a speaker would naturally pause in lines 14–22 of "My Last Duchess." **(b)** How does the lack of **end-stopped lines** and the use of **run-on lines** and pauses within lines create a conversational rhythm?

Line 14:	Her hus-	-band's pre-	-sence on-	-ly, called	that spot
Natural Pauses	no pause	no pause	no pause	**pause**	no pause

6. **Craft and Structure** Use a similar chart to analyze the rhythms of Elizabeth Barrett Browning's Sonnet 43.
7. **Comparing Literary Works (a)** Compare the rhythms of speech in the two poems. **(b)** Which rhythm is more dramatic? Explain. **(c)** Which better captures general feelings in a memorable manner?
8. **Analyzing Visual Information** What qualities in Robert Browning's work earned it the popularity suggested by this Victorian cartoon?

Common Core State Standards

Writing

1. Write arguments to support claims in an analysis of substantive topics or texts, using valid reasoning and relevant and sufficient evidence. *(p. 988)*

1.d. Establish and maintain a formal style and objective tone while attending to the norms and conventions of the discipline in which they are writing. *(p. 988)*

Language

4.b. Identify and correctly use patterns of word changes that indicate different meanings or parts of speech. *(p. 988)*

Reading Strategy

9. **Compare and contrast the speakers'** behavior in "My Last Duchess" and "Porphyria's Lover." What is similar about their actions? What is different about the reasons for their actions?
10. **(a)** What is similar about the mental state of the speakers in all three poems by Robert Browning? Cite details to support your comparisons. **(b)** How do the tones or attitudes of all three speakers differ?

TRUE LITERARY EXCLUSIVENESS.
"Don't you admire Robert Browning as a poet, Mr. Fitzsnook?" "I used to, once; but everybody admires him now, don'tcherknow—so I've had to give him up!"▶

Assessment Practice

Paired Passages (For more practice, see *All-in-One Workbook.*)

Many tests require students to compare and identify literary elements in two passages. Use the following sample item to teach students how to compare the speakers of two passages. Have students read "Life in a Love" and Sonnet 43 before answering this question:

Which of these characteristics do the speakers in the two poems share?

A devotion
B desperation
C strong religious feelings
D confusion

Suggest that students first list adjectives that describe *each* of the speakers. Then, have them compare their lists. Students should recognize that the only characteristic the speakers share is devotion. Thus, the correct answer is A.

Answers

1. (a) The duke is the speaker; the listener is a messenger from the count whose daughter the duke wants to marry. (b) The listener and the speaker interact when the speaker asks the listener a question (line 5) or addresses him as "you" or "Sir."
2. (a) Students may cite lines 42–43: "I choose / Never to stoop. . ." or lines 45–46 "I gave commands; / Then all smiles stopped together." (b) Given the speaker's treatment of his first wife, he will not have a successful second marriage.
3. (a) The speaker addresses his beloved in his mind. (b) There is no interaction between them as the speaker speaks.
4. (a) The speaker in "Porphyria's Lover" is irrational. (b) The speaker addresses someone to whom he is attempting to justify his actions.
5. (a) Students should note the pause after "cheek" in line 15, before "or" in line 17, before "such" in line 19, after "courtesy" and "thought" in line 20, after "joy" in line 21, and after "heart," "say," and "glad" in line 22. (b) Run-on lines and pauses within lines are closer to the natural rhythms of conversation.
6. Lines 1, 4, 6–8, and 10 are end-stopped. There should also be pauses after the punctuation marks in lines 1, 3, 6–8, 10, 12, and 13.
7. (a) "My Last Duchess" uses more conversational rhythms than Sonnet 43. (b) "My Last Duchess" is more dramatic; the speaker and his personality are vividly present. (c) The end-stopped lines of Sonnet 43 better capture general feelings in a memorable manner.
8. Browning's poetry was popular because he touched on themes many understood.
9. Each speaker is psychologically imbalanced in some way. The speakers differ in the extent of their jealousy, possessiveness, or delusion.
10. (a) The mental state is unbalanced. (b) The duke is cynical and mean. The man in "Life in a Love" is desperate. The speaker in "Porphyria's Lover" is delusional.

Answers

Vocabulary Acquisition and Use

Word Analysis

1. innocence
2. intelligence
3. obedience
4. permanence
5. prominence
6. insistence

Original sentences will vary.

Vocabulary

1. eludes
2. dowry
3. countenance
4. sullen
5. officious
6. munificence

Writing

1. To guide students in writing their argumentative text, give them the **Support for Writing** page (***Unit 4 Resources,*** p. 32).
2. Remind students that their reports should include details from "My Last Duchess."
3. Students should review the poem before prewriting. Students should employ a format that a detective agency might employ. Encourage students to invent dialogue from interview subjects. Finally, in revising their reports, students should be able to relate their observations and conclusions with "facts" from the poem.
4. Use the **Response to Literature** rubric, ***Professional Development Guidebook,*** pages 250–251, to evaluate students' work

PERFORMANCE TASKS

Integrated Language Skills

Vocabulary Acquisition and Use

Word Analysis: Latin Suffix *-ence*

The Latin suffix *-ence* means "quality of," or "state of being." Words with this ending are often nouns that are closely related to adjectives. The adjective *munificent*, for example, means "very generous." Replacing the suffix *-ent* with *-ence* yields the noun *munificence,* "the state of being very generous." Write the noun forms of each of these words and then write an original sentence using each word.

1. innocent
2. intelligent
3. obedient
4. permanent
5. prominent
6. insistent

Vocabulary: Analogies

In an analogy, the relationship between two words is explained by comparing it to the relationship between two other words. Discern the meaning of the words from the vocabulary list on page 976 by using each word once to complete these analogies. Explain each choice.

1. *Building* is to *edifice* as *escapes* is to ______.
2. ______ is to *husband* as *gift* is to *charity.*
3. *Dialogue* is to *play* as ______ is to *portrait.*
4. *Silence* is to *noise* as ______ is to *happy.*
5. ______ is to *annoying* as *attentive* is to *pleasing.*
6. *Starting* is to *stopping* as ______ is to *greed.*

Writing

Argumentative Text The duke in "My Last Duchess" has proposed marriage to another woman. Her father has hired you, a detective, to investigate the duke's history and character. Your task is to write a **report** to the father recommending whether he should allow the marriage to take place.

Prewriting Begin by reviewing the poem, noting what it reveals about the duke's character and first marriage. Draw from it as many facts as you can; infer others that you think are logical outgrowths of the duke's character. Think about the steps you might take to verify these facts so that you can detail those actions in your report. Speculate about what might have caused the duke's behavior.

Drafting Write your report using the *format* a detective might employ. For instance, you might state the date of the assignment and the subject. Include technical words that a detective might use, such as *surveillance, eyewitnesses, suspicions,* or *charges.* Keep in mind that you are a professional working for a client. Choose words, such as *suspect,* that create a formal, businesslike tone, rather than informal words such as *guy.*

Model: Revising to Add Transitional Words

As a result of my observations,
^I have concluded the duke is a cruel and dangerous
Therefore,
man. ^~~and~~ I advise you to reject his proposal to marry your daughter.

Transitional words and phrases highlight causes and effects.

Revising Review your draft, drawing arrows between observations and the conclusions they support. Where needed, add missing transitional words to clarify causes and effects.

Assessment Resources

Unit 5 Resources

L1 L2 EL **Selection Test A,** pp. 37–39. Administer Test A to less advanced students.

L3 L4 EL **Selection Test B,** pp. 40–42. Administer Test B to on-level students and more advanced students.

L3 L4 **Open-Book Test,** pp. 34–36. As an alternative, give the Open-Book test.

All **Customizable Test Bank**

All **Self-tests**
Students may prepare for the **Selection Test** by taking the **Self-test** online.

PHLit Online! All assessment resources are available at **www.PHLitOnline.com.**

Focus on Literary Forms: The Novel

PART 2

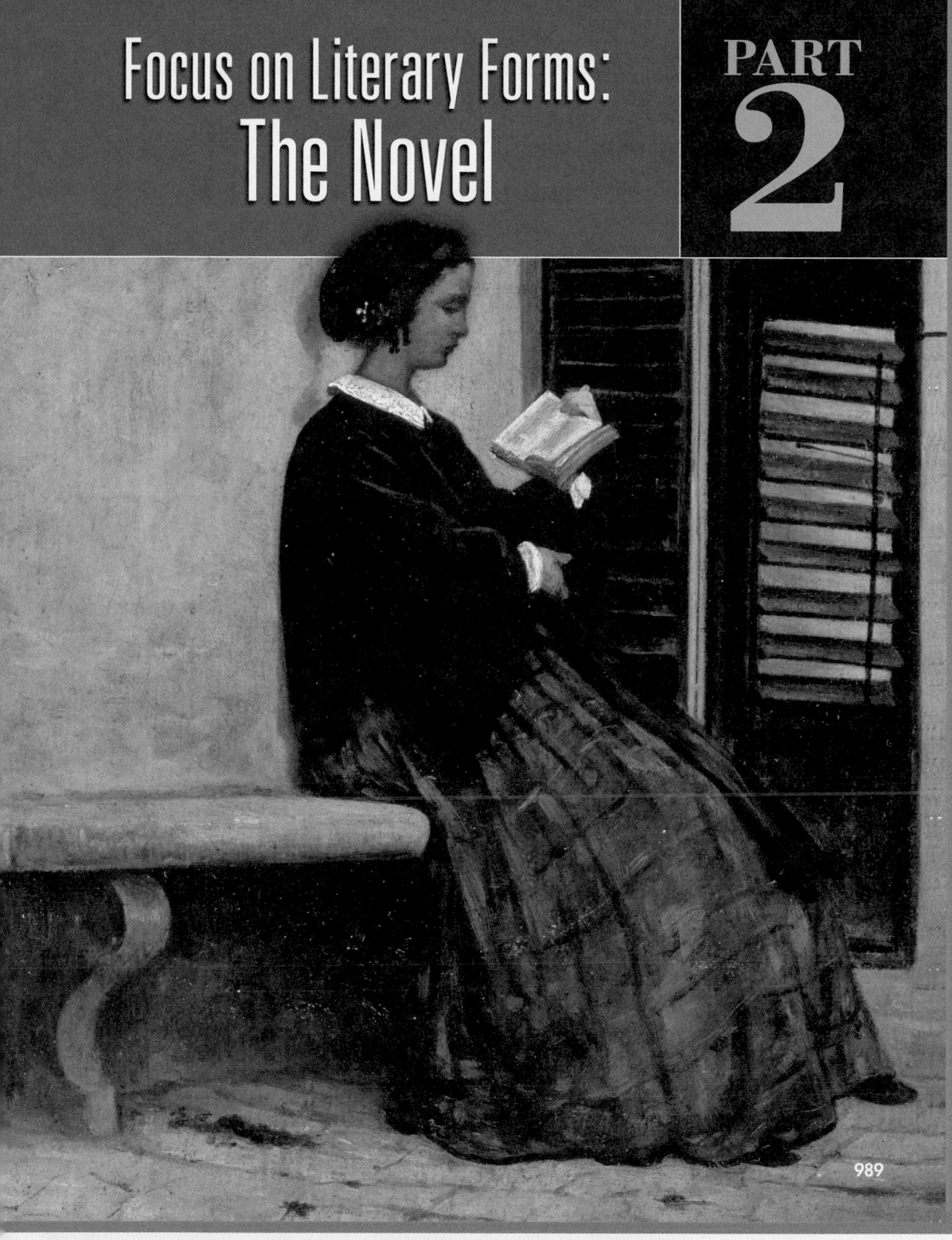

Text Complexity: At a Glance

This chart gives a general text complexity rating for the selections in this part of the unit to help guide instruction. For additional text complexity support, see the Test Complexity Rubric at point of use.

from Hard Times	**More Complex**
from Jane Eyre	**More Accessible**

Selection Planning Guide

The selections in this section reveal how nineteenth-century novelists expressed their views about society and its problems in their works of fiction. In *Hard Times,* Dickens shows how the education system stifled individuality and imagination. The unfairness and meager living conditions in Jane Eyre's school reflect Brontë's opinions about educational institutions for poor girls. "An Upheaval" depicts the confrontation between a headstrong governess and a class system unaccustomed to dissent.

Humanities

The Reader, by Silvestro Lega

Silvestro Lega (1826–1895) was a member of the Macchiaioli. This group of nineteenth-century artists was located principally in Florence, Italy. Their landscapes and portraits were reactions against the academic art of the time. Experimental use of color denotes Macchiaioli artwork.

Encourage students to examine the use of color in this painting. Call attention to the lines of bright color in the woman's skirt.

Have students link the art to Part 2 by answering the following question:

How is the painter's attitude toward literature expressed in the painting?
Answer: The soft colors on the wall and the dark doors suggest a sense of peace and solitude. The vibrant lines of color in the woman's skirt may reflect her joy and passion for reading. Lega appears to appreciate the pleasure that reading can provide.

Monitoring Progress

Before students read the selections in Part 2, refer to the results for the **Vocabulary in Context** items on **Benchmark Test 8 *(Unit 4 Resources, p. 201).*** Use this diagnostic portion of the test to guide your choice of selections to teach, as well as the depth of pre-reading preparation you will provide, based on students' readiness for the reading and vocabulary skills.

❶ Defining the Novel

1. Introduce the concept that novels as a genre are a more recent literary development than poetry, drama, or the epic.
2. Discuss the ways in which individual novels can combine elements of the different types listed on the student page. For example, Charles Dickens's *A Tale of Two Cities,* set during the French Revolution, shows the social and economic conditions of its age. It is both a historical novel and a social novel. **Ask:** How might you classify *The Great Gatsby, To Kill a Mockingbird*, or another novel of your choice?

   Possible responses: *The Great Gatsby:* novel of manners; *To Kill a Mockingbird:* historical novel/ novel of growth

❷ Literary Elements

Review with students the elements of the novel. **Ask:** How might it help a reader to identify with a certain character?

Possible response: Putting oneself in a character's place to understand his or her feelings, needs, problems, and goals can help a reader understand that character, as well as the theme of the novel, more deeply.

❸ Close Read: Novelistic Literary Elements

Review the chart with students. Point out the highlighted text in the model on page 991. Explain that in each case, the color of the highlighting matches the color of the category in the chart. Details that illustrate a given category are highlighted in the color of that category.

"THE NOVEL IS THE HIGHEST FORM OF HUMAN EXPRESSION SO FAR ATTAINED."

—D. H. LAWRENCE

In This Section

For more practice analyzing novels, see page 1030.

❶ Defining the Novel

A novel is a long work of prose fiction. As a genre, the novel is comparatively recent, though it has roots in the narratives of earlier ages. The length of a novel allows a writer great scope, and from its beginnings, the novel tended to survey—and sometimes criticize—a society, a social class, or a way of life as a whole. The English novel began with the work of writers such as Henry Fielding in the eighteenth century and reached full flower during the Victorian era with such classics as *Hard Times* and *David Copperfield* by Charles Dickens.

Types of Novels While novels need not belong to a specific type, many do. The following are traditional types:

- **Picaresque Novel:** relates the adventures of a traveling hero in episodic form
- **Historical Novel:** features characters and events from history
- **Novel of Manners:** shows the effects of social customs on individuals
- **Social Novel:** presents a large-scale portrait of an age, showing the influence of social and economic conditions on characters and events
- ***Bildungsroman* (Novel of Growth):** traces a protagonist's passage to adulthood

❷ **Literary Elements** Nearly all novels contain certain basic literary elements, including **plot,** or an ordered sequence of events; **setting,** or the specific time and place of the action; **characters,** or the people who take part in the action; and a **theme,** or the insight into life conveyed by the work. In addition, as the novel developed historically, it emphasized or led to innovations in the literary elements shown in the chart below.

❸ **Close Read: Novelistic Literary Elements**
These literary elements are called out in the Model text at right.

Narrative Technique: the way in which a writer tells a story. **Example:** *In* Mrs. Dalloway, *Virginia Woolf tells the story through the thoughts of her characters.*	**Philosophical Themes:** general ideas about existence and values. **Example:** *In* Crime and Punishment, *Fyodor Dostoyevsky's main character tries to apply new philosophical ideas, rejecting traditional morality.*
Social Commentary: writing that poses questions about or suggests criticisms of life in a society. **Example:** *In* Oliver Twist, *Charles Dickens's portrayal of the plight of a poor orphan is a call for reforms in England's treatment of its poor.*	**Realistic Description:** writing that attempts to accurately capture life in its details. **Example:** *In* The Jungle, *Upton Sinclair described industrial conditions in his day with grim accuracy.*

EXEMPLAR TEXT

Model

About the Text The Russian novelist Fyodor Dostoyevsky (1821–1881), is noted for keen psychological portraits, including that of Raskolnikov in *Crime and Punishment.*

from **Crime and Punishment**

Fyodor Dostoyevsky (translated by Constance Garnett)

On an exceptionally hot evening early in July a young man came out of the garret in which he lodged in S. Place and walked slowly, as though in hesitation, towards K. bridge.

4 He had successfully avoided meeting his landlady on the staircase. His garret was under the roof of a high, five-storied house and was more like a cupboard than a room. The landlady who provided him with garret, dinners, and attendance, lived on the floor below, and every time he went out he was obliged to pass her kitchen, the door of which invariably stood open. And each time he passed, the young man had a sick, frightened feeling, which made him scowl and feel ashamed. He was hopelessly in debt to his landlady, and was afraid of meeting her. . . .

This evening, however, on coming out into the street, he became acutely aware of his fears.

5 "I want to attempt a thing *like that* and am frightened by these trifles," he thought, with an odd smile. 6 "Hm... yes, all is in a man's hands and he lets it all slip from cowardice, that's an axiom. It would be interesting to know what it is men are most afraid of. Taking a new step, uttering a new word is what they fear most. . . . But I am talking too much. It's because I chatter that I do nothing. Or perhaps it is that I chatter because I do nothing. I've learned to chatter this last month, lying for days together in my den thinking...of Jack the Giant-killer. Why am I going there now? Am I capable of *that*? Is *that* serious? It is not serious at all. It's simply a fantasy to amuse myself; a plaything! Yes, maybe it is a plaything."

7 The heat in the street was terrible: and the airlessness, the bustle and the plaster, scaffolding, bricks, and dust all about him, and that special Petersburg stench, so familiar to all who are unable to get out of town in summer—all worked painfully upon the young man's already overwrought nerves. The insufferable stench from the pot-houses, which are particularly numerous in that part of the town, and the drunken men whom he met continually, although it was a working day, completed the revolting misery of the picture. An expression of the profoundest disgust gleamed for a moment in the young man's refined face. He was, by the way, exceptionally handsome, above the average in height, slim, well-built, with beautiful dark eyes and dark brown hair. Soon he sank into deep thought, or more accurately speaking into a complete blankness of mind; he walked along not observing what was about him and not caring to observe it. From time to time, he would mutter something, from the habit of talking to himself, to which he had just confessed. At these moments he would become conscious that his ideas were sometimes in a tangle and that he was very weak; for two days he had scarcely tasted food.

4 **Realistic Description** The details in this passage realistically depict a poor young man's life, without apology or an attempt to "dress things up."

5 **Narrative Technique** The interior monologue, or direct representation of a character's thoughts, in this passage helps to advance the plot: The young man is plotting something that will require daring. It also helps to develop his character: he is beset by doubts and confusion.

6 **Philosophical Themes** Here, Dostoevsky hints at key philosophical questions in the novel: What are the limits on a person's freedom of choice? Are these limits valid—a matter of morals—or invalid—a matter of fear?

7 **Social Commentary** Details in this passage point to the inhuman, alienating conditions in the city and prompt questions about the society that has created these conditions.

Extend the Lesson

Strategies for Reading a Novel

Ask students to brainstorm a list of their favorite novels. As students name their favorites, ask them to identify which elements of the novel (plot, setting, character, theme) the authors developed. Ask students to classify the novels based on the descriptions on page 990.

Also, ask students to decide which forms their favorite novels fall under. Remind students that novels may combine elements of different forms. When students have finished creating their lists, assess which forms of novels the class prefers overall.

4 Realistic Description

Read the bracketed text. Draw students' attention to the author's artful use of description in setting the scene. **Ask:** What part of this description most powerfully conveys the realism of the scene? Why?

Possible response: "And each time he passed, the young man had a sick, frightened feeling, which made him scowl and feel ashamed." These words present strong emotions that the reader will most likely be able to identify with.

5 Narrative Technique

Point out that one important part of narrative technique is to reveal the thoughts of the main character. **Ask:** In what ways might a novelist reveal a character's thoughts?

Possible response: A novelist may reveal the thoughts directly or have the character speak his or her thoughts aloud.

6 Philosophical Themes

Read aloud the bracketed passage. Point out that although he is confused, the young man is making a serious point. **Ask:** How do you interpret the words " . . . it is all in a man's hands and he lets it slip from cowardice . . ."

Possible response: We all have the freedom to control our own lives, but often we do not have the courage to exercise this freedom.

7 Social Commentary

Have students read the bracketed passage, asking them to pay particular attention to the author's use of detail. **Ask:** If this novel were set in a modern but depressed American city, what details might the author include to create a similar effect?

Possible responses: A modern description might include broken-down cars, vandalized parking meters, broken store windows, piles of litter, cracked sidewalks, and fumes from trucks and buses.

• from *Hard Times*

Lesson Pacing Guide

DAY 1 Preteach

- Administer the Reading and Vocabulary Warm-ups (*Unit 5 Resources,* pp. 43–46) as necessary.
- Introduce the Literary Analysis concept: Ethical and Social Influences.
- Introduce the Reading Strategy: Analyze an Author's Purpose.
- Build background with the Author in Depth and Background features.
- Develop thematic thinking with Connecting to the Essential Question.
- Teach the selection vocabulary.

DAYS 2–3 Preteach/Teach

- Distribute copies of the appropriate graphic organizer for the Reading Strategy (*Graphic Organizer Transparencies,* pp. 177–178).
- Distribute copies of the appropriate graphic organizer for Literary Analysis (*Graphic Organizer Transparencies,* pp. 179–180).
- Prepare students to read with the Activating Prior Knowledge activities (TE).
- Informally monitor comprehension while students read.
- Use the Reading Check questions to confirm comprehension.
- Develop students' understanding of ethical and social influences using the Literary Analysis prompts.
- Develop students' ability to analyze an author's purpose using the Reading Strategy prompts.
- Reinforce vocabulary with the Vocabulary notes.

DAY 4 Assess

- Assess students' comprehension and mastery of the skills by having them answer the Critical Reading, Literary Analysis, and Reading Strategy questions.
- Have students complete the Vocabulary Lesson.

DAY 5 Extend/Assess

- Have students complete the Conventions and Style Lesson.
- Have students complete the Writing Lesson and write a historical investigation: annotated bibliography. (You may assign as homework.)
- Administer Selection Test A or B (*Unit 5 Resources,* pp. 57–59 or 60–62).

Common Core State Standards

Reading Literature 3. Analyze the impact of the author's choices regarding how to develop and relate elements of a story or drama.

Writing 2. Write informative/explanatory texts to examine and convey complex ideas, concepts, and information clearly and accurately through the effective selection, organization, and analysis of content.
8. Gather relevant information from multiple authoritative print and digital sources, using advanced searches effectively; assess the strengths and limitations of each source in terms of the task, purpose, and audience; integrate information into the text selectively to maintain the flow of ideas, avoiding plagiarism and overreliance on any one source, following a standard format for citation.

Language 4.c. Consult general and specialized reference materials, both print and digital, to find the pronunciation of a word or determine or clarify its precise meaning, its part of speech, its etymology, or its standard usage.
4.d. Verify the preliminary determination of the meaning of a word or phrase.

Additional Standards Practice
***Common Core Companion,* pp. 28–35; 196–207; 247–260; 328–331**

Daily Block Scheduling
Each day in this Lesson Pacing Guide represents a 40–50 minute period. Teachers using block scheduling may combine days to revise pacing. In addition, teachers may differentiate and support core instruction by integrating components for extended and intensive support as students require. See the Guide to Selected Leveled Resources (facing page).

Guide to Selected Leveled Resources

RTI Tier 1 (students performing on level)			*from* Hard Times
Warm Up	Whole class instruction; Group work	**Practice, model,** and **monitor** fluency, working **with the whole class** or **in groups.**	Vocabulary and Reading Warm-ups B, *Unit 5 Resources,* pp. 43–44, 46
Comprehension/Skills	Whole class instruction; Group work; Independent work	**Support** and **monitor** comprehension and skills development, having students complete the activities, graphic organizers, and interactive prompts **independently** or **as a class.**	• ***Reader's Notebook,*** adapted instruction and full selection EL ***Reader's Notebook: English Learner's Version,*** adapted instruction and adapted selection • Reading Strategy Graphic Organizer B, ***Graphic Organizer Transparencies,*** p. 186 • Literary Analysis Graphic Organizer B, ***Graphic Organizer Transparencies,*** p. 188
Monitor Progress	A	**Monitor** student progress with the differentiated curriculum-based assessment in the *Unit Resources.*	• Selection Test B, ***Unit 5 Resources,*** pp. 60–62 • Open-Book Test, ***Unit 5 Resources,*** pp. 54–56

RTI Tier 2 (students requiring intervention)			*from* Hard Times
Warm Up	Group work; One-on-one teaching	**Practice, model,** and **monitor** fluency **in groups** or **with individuals.**	• Vocabulary and Reading Warm-ups A, ***Unit 5 Resources,*** pp. 43–45 • ***Hear It!*** Audio CD (adapted text)
Comprehension/Skills	Group work; One-on-one teaching	• **Support** and **monitor** comprehension and skills development, working **in small groups** or **with individuals.** • As students complete the selection in the appropriate version of the *Reader's Notebook,* **monitor** comprehension frequently with group questions and individual instruction. • **Model** strategies while guiding students in completing the activities and prompts in the *Reader's Notebook,* as well as the graphic organizers. • **Practice** skills and **monitor** mastery with the *Reading Kit* worksheets.	• ***Reader's Notebook: Adapted Version,*** adapted instruction and adapted selection EL ***Reader's Notebook: English Learner's Version,*** adapted instruction and adapted selection • Reading Strategy Graphic Organizer A, ***Graphic Organizer Transparencies,*** p. 185 • Literary Analysis Graphic Organizer A, ***Graphic Organizer Transparencies,*** p. 187 • ***Reading Kit,*** Practice worksheets
Monitor Progress	A	**Monitor** student progress with the differentiated curriculum-based assessment in the *Unit Resources* and in the *Reading Kit.*	• Selection Test A, ***Unit 5 Resources,*** pp. 57–59 • ***Reading Kit,*** Assess worksheets

TIER 3 Tier 3 intervention may require consultation with the student's special-education or dyslexia specialist. For additional support, see the Tier 2 activities and resources listed above.

One-on-one teaching | Group work | Whole class instruction | Independent work | A Assessment

For a complete guide to selection support, including support for Advanced students, see the Overview of Resources in the frontmatter.

• from *Hard Times*

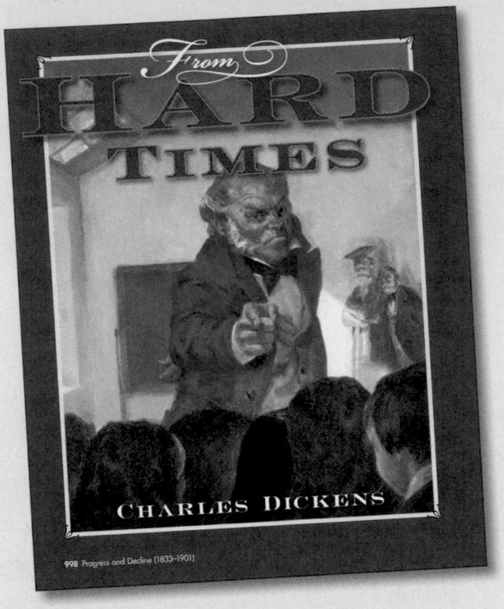

RESOURCES FOR:

- L1 Special-Needs Students
- L2 Below-Level Students (Tier 2)
- L3 On-Level Students (Tier 1)
- L4 Advanced Students (Tier 1)
- EL English Learners
- All All Students

Vocabulary/Fluency/Prior Knowledge

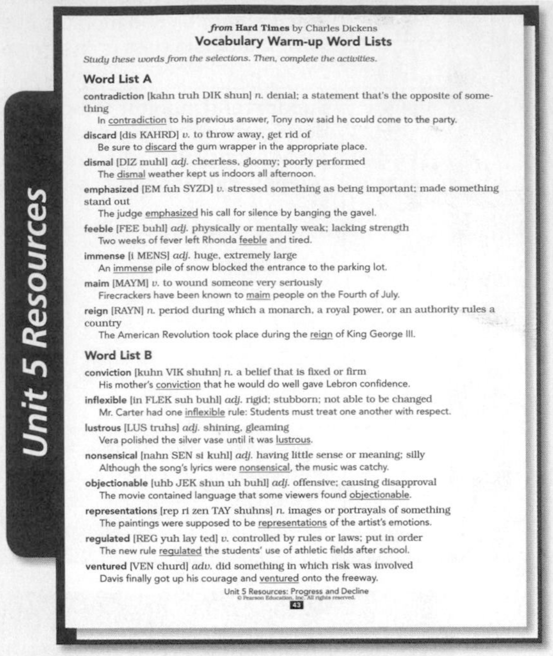

from **Hard Times** by Charles Dickens

Vocabulary Warm-up Word Lists

Study these words from the selections. Then, complete the activities.

Word List A

contradiction [kahn truh DIK shun] *n.* denial; a statement that's the opposite of something
In contradiction to his previous answer, Tony now said he could come to the party.

discard [dis KAHRD] *v.* to throw away, get rid of
Be sure to discard the gum wrapper in the appropriate place.

dismal [DIZ muhl] *adj.* cheerless, gloomy; poorly performed
The dismal weather kept us indoors all afternoon.

emphasized [EM fuh SYZD] *v.* stressed something as being important; made something stand out
The judge emphasized his call for silence by banging the gavel.

feeble [FEE buhl] *adj.* physically or mentally weak; lacking strength
Two weeks of fever left Rhonda feeble and tired.

immense [i MENS] *adj.* huge, extremely large
An immense pile of snow blocked the entrance to the parking lot.

maim [MAYM] *v.* to wound someone very seriously
Firecrackers have been known to maim people on the Fourth of July.

reign [RAYN] *n.* period during which a monarch, a royal power, or an authority rules a country
The American Revolution took place during the reign of King George III.

Word List B

conviction [kuhn VIK shuhn] *n.* a belief that is fixed or firm
His mother's conviction that he would do well gave Lebron confidence.

inflexible [in FLEK suh buhl] *adj.* rigid; stubborn; not able to be changed
Mr. Carter had one inflexible rule: Students must treat one another with respect.

lustrous [LUS truhs] *adj.* shining, gleaming
Vera polished the silver vase until it was lustrous.

nonsensical [nahn SEN si kuhl] *adj.* having little sense or meaning; silly
Although the song's lyrics were nonsensical, the music was catchy.

objectionable [uhb JEK shun uh buhl] *adj.* offensive; causing disapproval
The movie contained language that some viewers found objectionable.

representations [rep ri zen TAY shuhns] *n.* images or portrayals of something
The paintings were supposed to be representations of the artist's emotions.

regulated [REG yuh lay ted] *v.* controlled by rules or laws; put in order
The new rule regulated the students' use of athletic fields after school.

ventured [VEN churd] *adv.* did something in which risk was involved
Davis finally got up his courage and ventured onto the freeway.

Unit 5 Resources: Progress and Decline

43

EL L1 L2 **Vocabulary Warm-ups A and B,** pp. 43–44

Also available for these selections:

EL L1 L2 **Reading Warm-ups A and B,** pp. 45–46

All **Vocabulary Builder,** p. 50

Reader's Notebooks

Pre- and postreading pages for this selection, as well as the excerpt from *Hard Times,* appear in an interactive format in the *Reader's Notebooks.* Each *Notebook* is differentiated for a different group of learners.

The selections in the Adapted and English Learner's versions are abridged.

L2 L3 ***Reader's Notebook***

L1 ***Reader's Notebook: Adapted Version***

EL ***Reader's Notebook: English Learner's Version***

EL ***Reader's Notebook: Spanish Version***

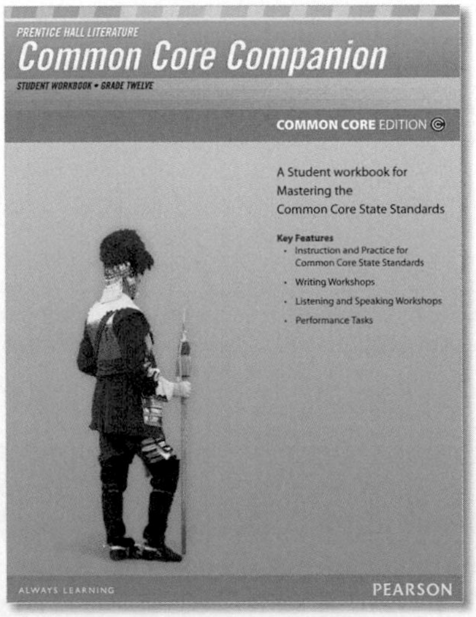

Common Core Companion

Additional instruction and practice for each Common Core State Standard

Selection Support

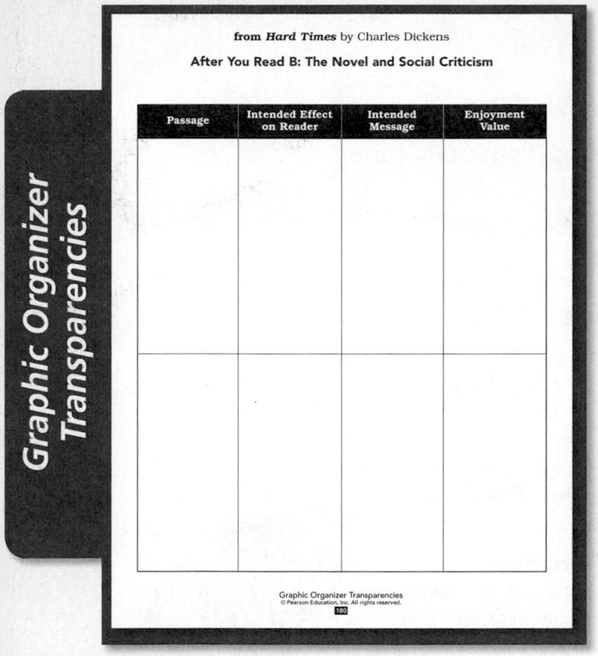
from Hard Times by Charles Dickens

After You Read B: The Novel and Social Criticism

Passage	Intended Effect on Reader	Intended Message	Enjoyment Value

Graphic Organizer Transparencies
© Pearson Education, Inc. All rights reserved.
180

EL L3 **Literary Analysis: Graphic Organizer B,** p. 180

Also available for these selections:

EL L1 L2 **Literary Analysis: Graphic Organizer A** (partially filled in), p. 179

EL L1 L2 **Reading: Graphic Organizer A,** p. 177

EL L3 **Reading: Graphic Organizer B,** p. 178

Skills Development/Extension

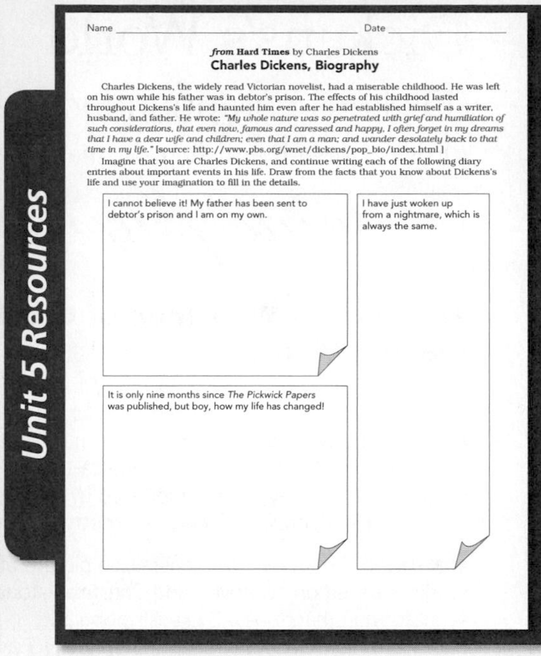
Name ______________________ Date ____________

from Hard Times by Charles Dickens
Charles Dickens, Biography

Charles Dickens, the widely read Victorian novelist, had a miserable childhood. He was left on his own while his father was in debtor's prison. The effects of his childhood lasted throughout Dickens's life and haunted him even after he had established himself as a writer, husband, and father. He wrote: *"My whole nature was so penetrated with grief and humiliation of such considerations, that even now, famous and caressed and happy, I often forget in my dreams that I have a dear wife and children; even that I am a man; and wander desolately back to that time in my life."* [source: http://www.pbs.org/wnet/dickens/pop_bio/index.html]

Imagine that you are Charles Dickens, and continue writing each of the following diary entries about important events in his life. Draw from the facts that you know about Dickens's life and use your imagination to fill in the details.

I cannot believe it! My father has been sent to debtor's prison and I am on my own.

I have just woken up from a nightmare, which is always the same.

It is only nine months since *The Pickwick Papers* was published, but boy, how my life has changed!

All **Biography,** p. 47

Also available for these selections:

All **Literary Analysis: The Novel and Social Influences,** p. 48

All **Reading: Recognize the Writer's Purpose** p. 49

EL L3 L4 **Support for Writing,** p. 52

L4 **Enrichment,** p. 53

Assessment

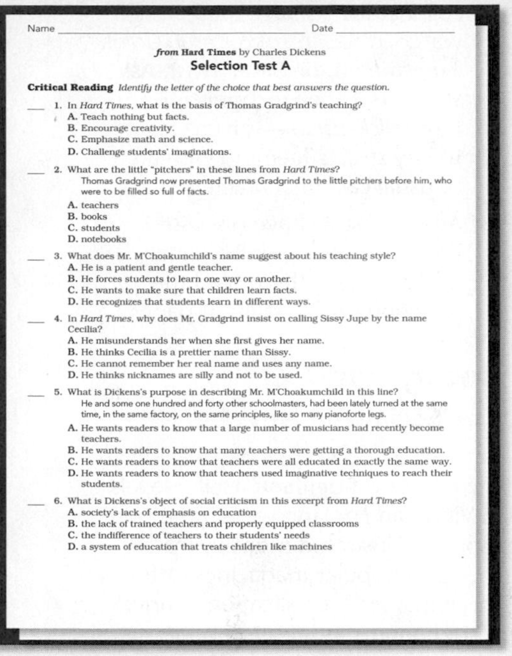
Name ______________________ Date ____________

from Hard Times by Charles Dickens
Selection Test A

Critical Reading *Identify the letter of the choice that best answers the question.*

____ 1. In *Hard Times,* what is the basis of Thomas Gradgrind's teaching?
A. Teach nothing but facts.
B. Encourage creativity.
C. Emphasize math and science.
D. Challenge students' imaginations.

____ 2. What are the little "pitchers" in these lines from *Hard Times?*
Thomas Gradgrind now presented Thomas Gradgrind to the little pitchers before him, who were to be filled so full of facts.
A. teachers
B. books
C. students
D. notebooks

____ 3. What does Mr. M'Choakumchild's name suggest about his teaching style?
A. He is a patient and gentle teacher.
B. He forces students to learn one way or another.
C. He wants to make sure that children learn facts.
D. He recognizes that students learn in different ways.

____ 4. In *Hard Times,* why does Mr. Gradgrind insist on calling Sissy Jupe by the name Cecilia?
A. He misunderstands her when she first gives her name.
B. He thinks Cecilia is a prettier name than Sissy.
C. He cannot remember her real name and uses any name.
D. He thinks nicknames are silly and not to be used.

____ 5. What is Dickens's purpose in describing Mr. M'Choakumchild in this line?
He and some one hundred and forty other schoolmasters, had been lately turned at the same time, in the same factory, on the same principles, like so many pianoforte legs.
A. He wants readers to know that a large number of musicians had recently become teachers.
B. He wants readers to know that many teachers were getting a thorough education.
C. He wants readers to know that teachers were all educated in exactly the same way.
D. He wants readers to know that teachers used imaginative techniques to reach their students.

____ 6. What is Dickens's object of social criticism in this excerpt from *Hard Times?*
A. society's lack of emphasis on education
B. the lack of trained teachers and properly equipped classrooms
C. the indifference of teachers to their students' needs
D. a system of education that treats children like machines

EL L1 L2 **Selection Test A,** pp. 57–59

Also available for these selections:

EL L3 L4 **Selection Test B,** pp. 60–62

EL L3 L4 **Open-Book Test,** pp. 54–56

PHLit Online!
www.PHLitOnline.com

- complete narrated selection text
- a thematically related video with writing prompt
- an interactive graphic organizer
- highlighting feature
- access to all student print resources, adapted to individual student needs
- Spanish and English summaries
- adapted selection translations in Spanish

Online Resources: All print materials are also available online.

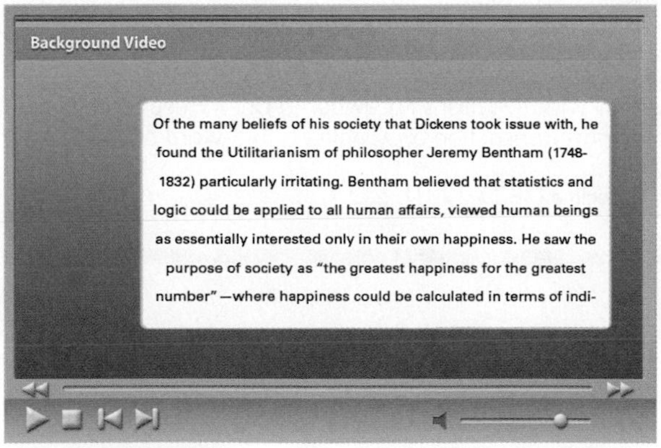

Background Video
Of the many beliefs of his society that Dickens took issue with, he found the Utilitarianism of philosopher Jeremy Bentham (1748-1832) particularly irritating. Bentham believed that statistics and logic could be applied to all human affairs, viewed human beings as essentially interested only in their own happiness. He saw the purpose of society as "the greatest happiness for the greatest number"—where happiness could be calculated in terms of indi-

Background Video

Also available:

Get Connected! (thematic video with writing prompt)
All videos are available in Spanish.

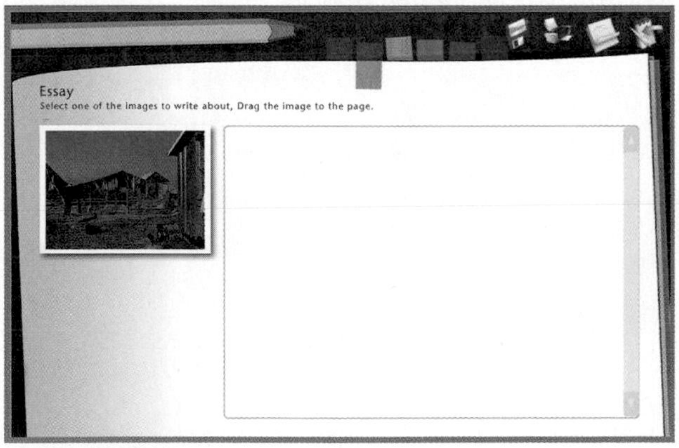

Select one of the images to write about. Drag the image to the page.

Writer's Journal (with graphics feature)

Also available:

Vocabulary Central (tools and activities for studying vocabulary)

Literary History: Dickens's World

1. Discuss with students ways in which they are already familiar with the work of Charles Dickens. Ask if students have read or watched *A Christmas Carol, Great Expectations,* or *Oliver Twist.* Ask students if they recognize the term *Dickensian*—as it refers to city streets teeming with an unusual cast of characters.
2. After students have discussed their experience with Charles Dickens, have them read the selection on the student pages.

Background

The Serialized Novel

The novel in Dickens's day was still in the process of defining itself. Novels in Victorian England were often published in illustrated monthly installments in popular magazines. After this initial serial publication, a novel would appear as a bound book.

The publishing venture that launched Dickens's career, *The Pickwick Papers,* was brought about by serial publishers in 1836. Dickens was commissioned to write text to accompany the sketches of a popular artist. When the artist died, Dickens took over the project. The work was published in monthly installments over nineteen months. Dickens composed chapters to meet monthly deadlines. The work bears the mark of this origin. Episodes often end at a suspenseful moment, to make sure readers return for more, and there is little overall direction to the story in the early parts.

Literary History: Dickens's World

"Dickens compounded characters of peculiar turns of speech and singular mannerisms, some endearing, *some frightening.*"

The Curious Workshop of Charles Dickens: Making Myths

Even if you have never read a novel by Charles Dickens, you have encountered his work. Characters such as the miser Ebenezer Scrooge and the orphan Oliver Twist stepped out from Dickens's books long ago to take up a life as old friends in musicals and cartoons. The very word *Dickensian* conjures obscure city streets populated by leering villains, honest clerks, wide-eyed innocents, and a host of knotty eccentrics.

Defining Dickens This generalized picture of Dickens and his works is based on his novels and Christmas stories, most published in serial form in magazines. Dickens's popularity in his own lifetime was enormous. With his first major effort, *The Pickwick Papers* (1836–1837), and for decades after, he held Victorian England spellbound, raptly awaiting the publication of the next chapter of *Oliver Twist* (1837–1839) or *Great Expectations* (1860–1861). When his character Little Nell of *The Old Curiosity Shop* (1840–1841) died, England was torn by grief.

Reformer and Myth-Maker In Dickens's lifetime, the Industrial Revolution left England overcrowded with the new working class, living in slums and riddled with epidemic fatal diseases. Dickens's stories of hard times and injured innocents challenged the forces that smothered compassion and nursed vice in the new society.

A Curious Workshop Yet Dickens does more than tell stories about social injustice. The most distinctive characteristic of his work might be its mythical or fairy tale–like quality. In the shadow of the factories choking London with smoke and slums, Dickens set up a workshop of the imagination, where he developed new myths of crime and redemption.

"A Perpetual Summer of Being Themselves" There are no John Smiths or Jane Joneses among Dickens's characters. From Samuel Pickwick to Wilkins Micawber to Uriah Heep, each character's name is a distinctive concoction of syllables, a two-word poem. The names reflect the quirkiness of the characters themselves. From the Rumplestiltskin-like Daniel Quilp of *The Old Curiosity Shop* to the hopelessly optimistic Mr. Micawber of *David Copperfield* (1849–1850), Dickens compounded characters of peculiar turns of speech and mannerisms, some endearing, some frightening.

Wicked Woods, Safe Havens Under Dickens's fairy-tale pen, the economic and social challenges of Victorian times reappear as a grotesque landscape, the literary equivalent of the woods in which a wicked witch lives. Here is Dickens's description of landscape surrounding a new railroad:

> Everywhere were bridges that led nowhere; thoroughfares that were wholly impassable; Babel towers of chimneys, wanting half their height; temporary wooden houses and enclosures, in the most unlikely situations; carcasses of ragged tenements, and fragments of unfinished walls and arches, and piles of scaffolding, and wildernesses of bricks, and giant forms of cranes, and tripods straddling above nothing. There were a hundred thousand shapes and substances of incompleteness. . .
> *(*Dombey and Son*, 1846–1848).*

Yet Dickens also creates islands of safety and refuge, such as the permanently beached boat in which David Copperfield finds happiness with the Peggoty family. In settings such as these, both Dickens's social criticism and his childlike attunement to the fairy-tale dimension of life have a place.

Dickens and Victorian England Dickens ruled over the imagination of Victorian England as a kind of father figure, by turns jolly and stern. He amuses his readers even while reprimanding their faults. Though there is much that is simply sentimental in Dickens, there are also depths of realism, an unflagging faith in redemption, and the eternal exuberance in human variety. Modern readers can still warm themselves at the cheerful glow of his work.

Speaking and Listening: Discussion

Comprehension and Collaboration Message Art Dickens was a brilliant novelist and social critic who blended scathing critiques of Victorian society with first-class literary entertainment.

With a group, discuss your thoughts about how modern writers, musicians, and entertainers convey messages of social or political reform. Use these questions to guide your discussion:

- Of the writers, musicians, and entertainers you know, which ones use their art to send a message? What are their messages?
- What effect, if any, do popular entertainers' social or political messages have on others?
- Do you think artists have a responsibility to make public their social or political messages? Explain.

Choose a point person to share your thoughts with the class.

Background

Dickens's Own Character

The compound of energy, caricature, and sentiment in Dickens's work is reflected in his own life. Dickens was a terrific mimic. Early in his career, he hoped to become an actor. His theatrical bent is evident in the characterizations in his novels, which share with the art of mime the art of isolating and exaggerating a mannerism.

When Dickens was a child, his father entered debtors' prison, and young Charles took a job in a factory. He never gave up his bitterness at the abandonment he felt. Later, he was scarred by an ill-fated infatuation and by the death of his young sister-in-law. In each case, Dickens was haunted by the loss. One can perhaps detect Dickens's nostalgia for an unbroken childhood in the cheery fireside scenes and the tragic deaths of innocents in his novels.

Critical Thinking

Speculate

1. Tell students that Dickens's novels were extremely popular.
2. **Ask:** What effect might Dickens's descriptions of the oppression of the poor and the young have had on his society?
   Possible response: Influential citizens may have encouraged legislation to reform schools and workplaces.

Speaking and Listening: Discussion

Message Art

Ask students to select a particular writer, musician, or entertainer who uses his or her art to promote social or political reforms. Then, have each student write out answers to the questions on the student page. Have groups of students discuss their answers and appoint a representative to present their thoughts to the rest of the class.

❶ Background

Overview: The Author's Work

Charles Dickens wrote with a rich imagination and often in a strong comic overtone. Frequently, he gave his characters names that foreshadowed the plot, providing the reader with a slight hint. He also enjoyed making silly, yet meaningful, comparisons, such as party guests to furniture, orphans to shares and stocks, and people to tugboats. His work was often a form of social commentary, as he wrote satirically about the government, politics, and other important issues of the time period.

The Writer in His Time

Charles Dickens lived during England's Industrial Revolution, a time of economic chaos. The gap between the poor and the rich grew even greater. Factory owners forced their employees to work for long hours in cramped, dangerous, and unsanitary conditions. These workers, with little education or job skills, were unable to do much to improve their situations. Dickens, having been a factory worker when he was young, greatly sympathized with the working poor, especially the children. He became involved with a number of organizations that helped to improve the living conditions of the poor. He became a speaker for the Metropolitan Sanitary Organization and worked to clean up the slums to provide the poor with safe, clean, and inexpensive living options. *Hard Times* functioned partly as an attempt to focus the public's attention on the difficult circumstances of the poor he worked so hard to improve.

❶ ❷

CHARLES Dickens

(1812–1870)

No writer since Shakespeare has occupied as important a place in popular culture as Charles Dickens. His novels have held a special appeal for critics and the public alike. They have also been dramatized time and again in plays and films.

A CHILDHOOD OF HARDSHIP

Born in Portsmouth on England's southern coast, Dickens had a generally unhappy childhood. His father was sent to debtors' prison, and the boy was sent to a "prison" of his own—a factory in which he worked long hours pasting labels. Similar experiences, dramatizing the ills of the newly industrialized society, were to figure prominently in Dickens's novels.

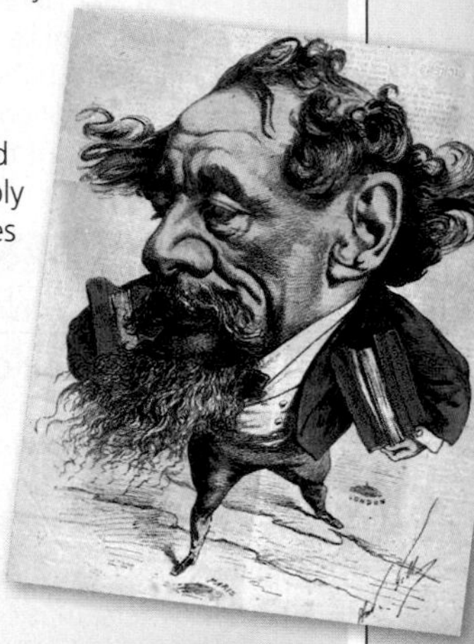

THE BIRTH OF A WRITER

As a young man, Dickens held jobs as a stenographer in the courts and as a reporter for London newspapers. At twenty-one, he began to apply his keen powers of observation to producing humorous literary sketches of everyday life in London. A collection of these, *Sketches by Boz* (1836), earned him a small following, but his first novel, *The Pickwick Papers* (1837), made him the most popular writer of his day. Closely following were *Oliver Twist* (1839) and *Nicholas Nickleby* (1839).

A SERIOUS NOVELIST

The young Dickens reveled in the variety and peculiarity of the human character. Memorable characters like the charming Mr. Pickwick and the evil Fagin abound in his early work, but they are perhaps more like cartoons or natural forces than full-blooded characters. Dickens shows his growing mastery of characterization in *Dombey and Son* (1848) and *David Copperfield* (1850), novels of greater psychological depth. Throughout his work, Dickens offers his distinctive brand of social criticism, which is especially prominent in his masterpiece *Hard Times* (1854).

Text Complexity Rubric

from Hard Times			
Qualitative Measures			
Context/Knowledge Demands	Victorian novel; historical knowledge demands 1 2 ③ 4 5		
Structure/Language Conventionality and Clarity	Long sentences; above-level vocabulary 1 2 ③ 4 5		
Levels of Meaning/ Purpose/Concept Level	Challenging (education, reform) 1 2 3 ④ 5		
Quantitative Measures			
Lexile	1050L	**Text Length**	2,333 words
Overall Complexity	**More complex**		

Reader and Task Suggestions

Preparing to Read the Text

- Explain that *Hard Times* is very critical of the educational methods then being used with poor children.
- Remind students that in satire, they will meet characters who see themselves in one light while the author wants readers to see them in another.
- Guide students to use Multidraft Reading strategies (TE p. 995).

Leveled Tasks

Levels of Meanings If students will have difficulty with Dickens's satire, have them first focus on the characters. Then, have them consider what Dickens wants readers to think about those characters.

Analyzing If students will not have great difficulty with the satire, have them analyze details about the characters to determine what Dickens is ridiculing.

Serialization

Many of Dickens's novels, beginning with *The Pickwick Papers,* were published serially in magazines—a common method of writing and producing fiction at the time. Monthly installments often ended with uncertain or dangerous situations, leaving readers eagerly awaiting the next installment.

Immense Popularity

Dickens developed an avid following, and he thrived on the support of the public. He was widely read in Europe and the United States. Always fond of theater, he gave dramatic public readings from his novels. In 1842, he crossed the Atlantic for a five-month lecture tour in the United States. The American public welcomed him enthusiastically but were less happy with him when he criticized social issues in the United States.

Without doubt, Dickens was the preeminent nineteenth-century novelist. He was both imaginative and prolific. Despite his criticism of his age, he wrote to please his audience. So deeply did he affect his audiences, in fact, that the view of life in his novels has become a part of English tradition.

Daily Bellringer

For each class during which you will teach this selection, have students complete one of the five activities for the appropriate week in the ***Daily Bellringer Activities*** booklet.

Multidraft Reading

To assist struggling readers and to enhance reading for all, assign the text in chunks, as warranted by length, and apply multidraft reading protocols. For each reading, have students set the purpose indicated:

- **First reading**—identifying key ideas and details and answering any Reading Checks.
- **Second reading**—analyzing craft and structure and responding to the side-column prompts.
- **Third reading**—integrating knowledge and ideas, connecting to other texts and the world, and answering the end-of-selection questions.

For more guidance, refer to the ***Classroom Strategies and Teaching Routines*** card on Multidraft Reading.

❷ Background

More About the Author

Charles Dickens experienced tremendous success with the 1843 publication of *A Christmas Carol.* This work, the first in a series of Christmas books, was described by Dickens as "a whimsical sort of masque intended to awaken loving and forebearing thoughts." Dickens wrote many of his novels as serializations in magazines, in which a chapter or portion of the novel would appear each week. Readers would wait breathlessly for the next issue to come off the press to learn what would happen to their favorite characters.

Differentiated Instruction for Universal Access

Enrichment for Gifted/Talented Students

Have students read from *Hard Times* in pairs. Then, have them imagine that they are in charge of teaching Mr. Gradgrind's class for one day. Have students develop a lesson plan that focuses on subjects that are important to them. Tell them to consider using related music, stories, and visual aids. Also, have them take note of the ways they would treat the children differently from how they are treated in the story. Ask them to explain their choices.

PHLit Online!

For more about Charles Dickens, additional background, and a ***Get Connected!*** video, go online at **www.PHLitOnline.com**.

PRETEACH

❶ Dickens and Pop Culture

1. Ask students if they are familiar with any of the elements mentioned on the page. Have them explain the context in which they know the element or have heard of it.
2. Review with students the meanings behind the term *Scrooged.* Have students discuss situations from their own lives or an invented situation in which they could apply the term.
3. Explain to students that there are countless film renditions and adaptations of Charles Dickens's story *A Christmas Carol.* Have students go to a film database Web site, such as www.imdb.com, and do a search for "Christmas Carol." Many results will be displayed. Ask them to identify any they recognize or with which they are familiar. Discuss with students why they believe *A Christmas Carol* is such a timeless story, in that it has been retold so many times and in so many different ways.

The Masterpiece Theatre production of *Bleak House* was originally released on October 27, 2005.

Uriah Heep's album *Very 'Eavy . . . Very 'Umble* was originally released on February 4, 1970.

❶

Dickens's Characters—And Their Words—Live On!

"Bah, humbug!"

"Shake me up, Judy"

"Very 'Eavy... Very 'Umble'"

Scrooged!

What's in a name, Juliet asked in Shakespeare's *Romeo and Juliet.* She was making the point that names do not reveal anything about a person. Well, don't tell that to Charles Dickens. For him, there was a world of meaning in the names he gave his characters—989 in all. In fact, many of the names Dickens coined and the odd phrases he put into characters' mouths are still used today.

- Ever been Scrooged? Even if you are unfamiliar with *A Christmas Carol,* Dickens's tale about a miserly man whose experiences with three spirits on Christmas Eve change him into a kind and generous soul, you probably know how it feels to be the victim of someone else's stinginess. One of the unreformed Scrooge's favorite phrases, "Bah, humbug!," is still used today to express a Scrooge-like view of the world.
- Ever hear the optimistic phrase, "Something will turn up," used in a sarcastic way? If so, the speaker may be ironically quoting the ne'er-do-well Wilkins Micawber, a character from Dickens's autobiographical novel *David Copperfield.* Based on Dickens's father, Micawber was a perennial optimist, despite the evidence of reality.
- Ever listen to the music of the band Uriah Heep? The title of the band's first album, "Very 'Eavy . . . Very 'Umble," quotes a characteristic phrase spoken by the devious, obsequious clerk Uriah Heep, another character from *David Copperfield.* Young David memorably describes Heep as someone "who had hardly any eyebrows, and no eyelashes, and eyes of a red brown, so unsheltered and unshaded, that I remember wondering how he went to sleep." To this day, it is an insult to be called a falsely humble Uriah Heep.

These are just a few of the Dickens characters whose vivid names and twitchy phrases are still part of pop culture today.

Vocabulary Development

Vocabulary Knowledge Rating

Create a **Vocabulary Knowledge Rating Chart** (***Professional Development Guidebook,*** p. 33) for the vocabulary words on the student page. Give each student a copy of the chart with the words on it. Read the words aloud, and have students mark their ratings in the Before Reading column. Urge students to attend to these words as they read and discuss the selections.

In order to gauge how much instruction you need to provide, tally how many students are confident in their knowledge of each word. As students read, point out the words and their context.

PHLit Online! **Vocabulary Central,** featuring tools and activities for studying vocabulary, is available online at **www.PHLitOnline.com.**

Before You Read from *Hard Times*

❷ **Connecting to the Essential Question** In *Hard Times*, Dickens criticizes education that is based on rote learning instead of imagination. As you read, notice how Dickens describes the educational approaches he is criticizing. Focusing on these descriptions will help you answer the Essential Question: **How does literature shape or reflect society?**

Common Core State Standards

Reading Literature
3. Analyze the impact of the author's choices regarding how to develop and relate elements of a story or drama.

❸ Literary Analysis

The novel, a long work of fiction, became popular in the nineteenth century, a period of disturbing social and economic changes. Like other novelists of the time, Dickens included social criticism in his works, calling attention to the **ethical and social influences** that resulted in society's ills. In *Hard Times*, Dickens focuses on misguided educational practices. Through his characters and situations, Dickens reveals his own *philosophical assumptions.* As you read, notice how Dickens turns incidents into dramatizations—and criticisms—of ethical and social issues.

❹ Reading Strategy

Preparing to Read Complex Texts **Analyzing an author's purpose** will help you understand how specific incidents relate to *meaning* in a novel. In *Hard Times*, note how Dickens develops elements such as characterization, setting, and dialogue to reveal the ethical and social influences that he is criticizing. Also note Dickens's use of comic exaggeration to achieve his purpose. Use a chart like the one shown to help you analyze Dickens's purpose and the meaning it reveals.

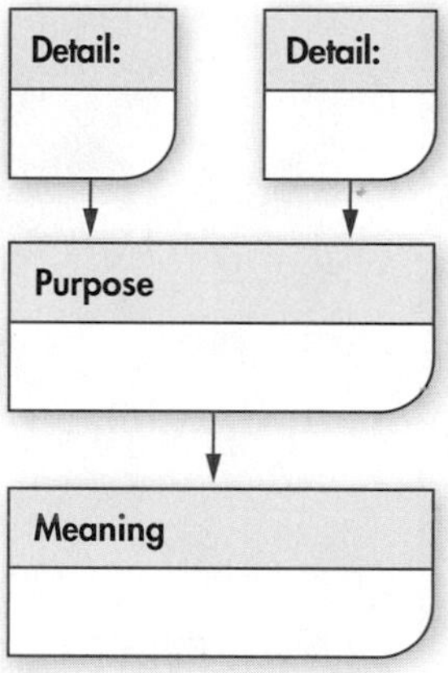

❺ Vocabulary

monotonous (mə nät′ ən əs) *adj.* without variation (p. 999)

obstinate (äb′ stə nət) *adj.* stubborn; dogged (p. 999)

deficient (di fish′ ənt) *adj.* lacking an essential quality (p. 1001)

adversary (ad′ vər ser ē) *n.* opponent; enemy (p. 1002)

indignant (in dig′ nənt) *adj.* outraged; filled with righteous anger (p. 1002)

approbation (ap′ rə bā shən) *n.* official approval (p. 1002)

etymology (et′ ə mol′ ə jē) *n.* the study of word origins (p. 1004)

syntax (sin′ taks) *n.* the study of sentence structure (p. 1004)

PHLit Online! www.PHLitOnline.com

❷ Connecting to the Essential Question

1. Review the assignment with the class.
2. Help students prepare for the writing assignment by discussing school projects or assignments they have completed.
3. As students read, have them look for the words Dickens uses to describe the educational approaches he is criticizing.

❸ Literary Analysis

Introduce the skill using the instruction on the student page.

Think Aloud: Model the Skill

Say to students:

I know that Dickens often weaved social criticism into his writing. Outside influences must have triggered such a writing style. To understand these influences, I must be alert for social criticism and keep in mind what I know about Dickens and the time period.

❹ Reading Strategy

1. Introduce the skill using the instruction on the student page.
2. Give students a copy of **Reading Strategy Graphic Organizer B,** page 178 in *Graphic Organizer Transparencies,* to fill out as they read.

Think Aloud: Model the Skill

Say to students:

I understand that one way to focus on a work of literature is to recognize a writer's purpose. I can do this by making note of details, determining their purposes, and interpreting meaning.

❺ Vocabulary

1. Pronounce each word, giving its definition.
2. For more guidance, see the *Classroom Strategies and Teaching Routines* card for introducing vocabulary.

PHLit Online! www.PHLitOnline.com

Teaching From Technology

Preparing to Read
Go to **www.PHLitOnline.com** in class or in a lab and display the ***Get Connected!*** slide show for this selection. Have the class brainstorm responses to the slide show writing prompt, entering ideas in the interactive journal. Then, have students complete their written responses individually, in a lab or as homework.

To build background, display the Background and More About the Author feature.

Using the Interactive Text
Go to **www.PHLitOnline.com** and display the Enriched Online Student Edition. As the class reads the selection or listens to the narration, record answers to side-column prompts using the graphic organizers accessible on the interactive page. Alternatively, have students use the online edition individually, answering the prompts as they read.

From Hard Times ❶ ❷

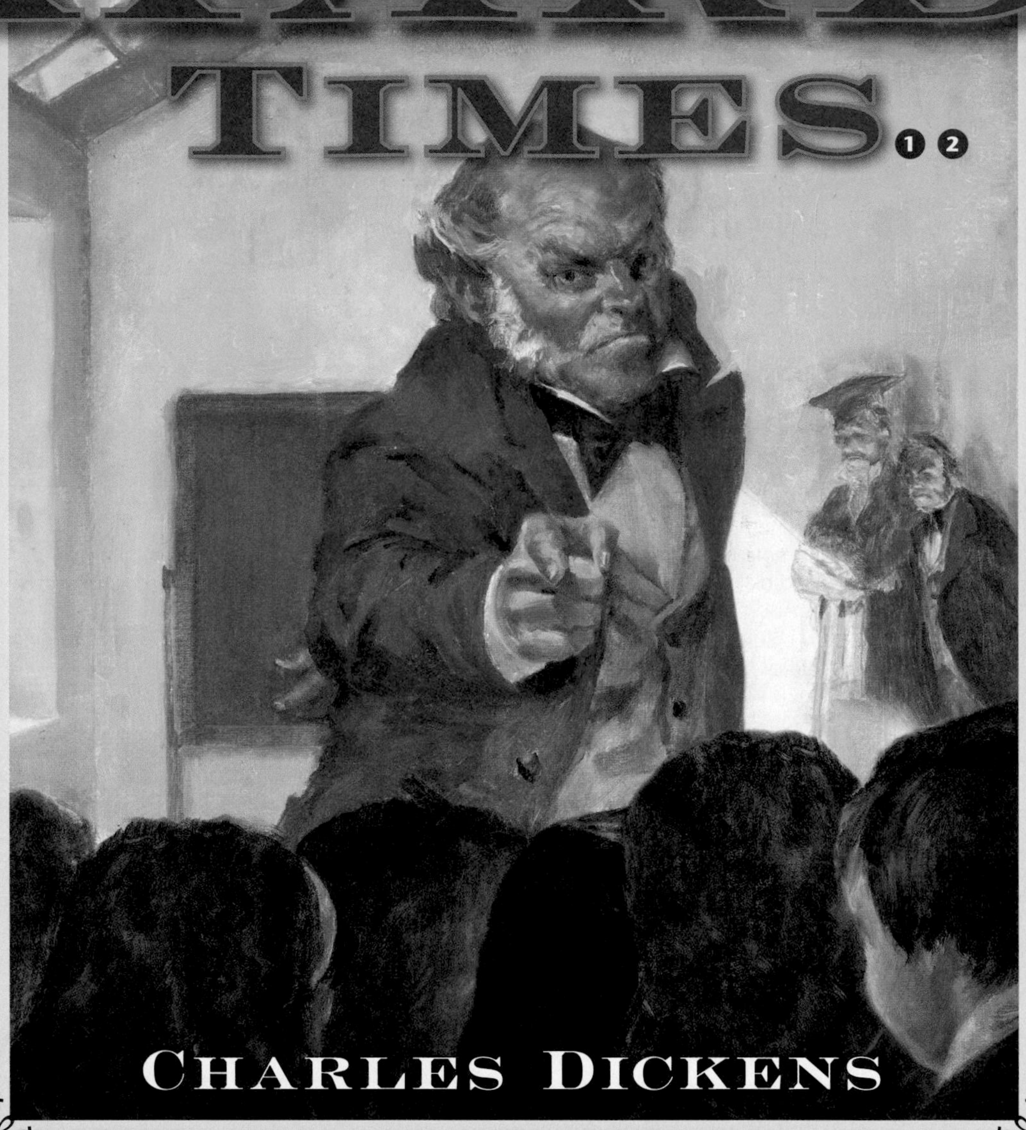

CHARLES DICKENS

❶ About the Selection

In this episode, from the beginning of *Hard Times,* Thomas Gradgrind questions children in his model school. Then, he turns the proceedings over to the schoolmaster, M'Choakumchild. Dickens uses the occasion to satirize the deadening utilitarian philosophy of these "educators," with its devotion to facts at the expense of living knowledge. A student named Sissy Jupe, for example, is the daughter of a man who makes his living from horses. However, her inability to define a horse according to the dictionary is regarded as a deficiency. Dickens uses names—*Gradgrind* speaks volumes—as well as descriptions and dialogue to score more satiric points.

❷ Activating Prior Knowledge

Students may enjoy creating their own illustration of Gradgrind's classroom. They might draw or paint the scene or create a collage. Have each write a paragraph explaining his or her artistic choices.

Concept Connector →

Tell students they will return to their responses after reading the selection.

PHLit Online!

This selection is available in interactive format in the **Enriched Online Student Edition** at **www.PHLitOnline.com**, which includes a thematically related video with writing prompt and an interactive graphic organizer.

Enrichment: Investigating Psychology

Schools and Conformity

Point out that the setting of *Hard Times* is a school and that Dickens explores the theme of conformity and individuality. For young people in many cultures, the pressures to conform produce some of the most powerful conflicts of adolescence. This theme has been developed by many contemporary authors in works such as J. D. Salinger's *The Catcher in the Rye* and John Knowles's *A Separate Peace,* in which school scenes are used to play out these young adult conflicts.

Activity: Conformity and Psychology

Encourage interested students to do further research on the psychological aspects of conformity. Have them record and analyze their findings using the **Enrichment: Investigating Psychology** worksheet, ***Professional Development Guidebook,*** page 239.

BACKGROUND OF THE MANY BELIEFS IN HIS SOCIETY WITH WHICH DICKENS TOOK ISSUE, THE UTILITARIANISM OF PHILOSOPHER JEREMY BENTHAM (1748–1832) PARTICULARLY IRRITATED HIM. BENTHAM BELIEVED THAT STATISTICS AND LOGIC COULD BE APPLIED TO ALL HUMAN AFFAIRS, AND HE VIEWED HUMAN BEINGS AS ESSENTIALLY INTERESTED ONLY IN THEIR OWN HAPPINESS. HE SAW THE PURPOSE OF SOCIETY AS "THE GREATEST HAPPINESS FOR THE GREATEST NUMBER," WITH HAPPINESS CALCULATED IN TERMS OF INDIVIDUAL PLEASURES AND PAINS. DICKENS BELIEVED UTILITARIANISM DISCOUNTED OR EVEN SOUGHT TO NEGATE VIRTUES LIKE IMAGINATION AND SYMPATHY. IN *HARD TIMES,* DICKENS USED HIS CHARACTER MR. GRADGRIND TO POKE FUN AT THIS PHILOSOPHY.

Artist rendering of cover of first edition of *Hard Times*

CHAPTER 1
THE ONE THING NEEDFUL

"Now, what I want is, Facts. Teach these boys and girls nothing but Facts. Facts alone are wanted in life. Plant nothing else, and root out everything else. You can only form the minds of reasoning animals upon Facts: nothing else will ever be of any service to them. This is the principle on which I bring up my own children, and this is the principle on which I bring up these children. Stick to Facts, sir!"

4 The scene was a plain, bare, monotonous vault of a schoolroom, and the speaker's square forefinger emphasized his observations by underscoring every sentence with a line on the schoolmaster's sleeve. The emphasis was helped by the speaker's square wall of a forehead, which had his eyebrows for its base, while his eyes found commodious cellarage in two dark caves, overshadowed by the wall. The emphasis was helped by the speaker's mouth, which was wide, thin, and hard set. The emphasis was helped by the speaker's voice, which was inflexible, dry, and dictatorial. The emphasis was helped by the speaker's hair, which bristled on the skirts of his bald head, a plantation of firs to keep the wind from its shining surface, all covered with knobs, like the crust of a plum pie, as if the head had scarcely warehouse-room for the hard facts stored inside. The speaker's obstinate carriage, square coat, square legs, square shoulders—nay, his very neckcloth, trained to take him by the throat with an unaccommodating grasp, like a stubborn fact, as it was—all helped the emphasis.

"In this life, we want nothing but Facts, sir; nothing but Facts!"

The speaker, and the schoolmaster, and the third grown person present, all backed a little, and swept with their eyes the inclined plane of little vessels, then and there arranged in order, ready to have imperial gallons of facts poured into them until they were full to the brim.

Vocabulary 3
monotonous (mə nät′ ən əs) *adj.* without variation
obstinate (äb′ stə nət) *adj.* stubborn; dogged

◀ Critical Viewing 5
Judging from the details in this illustration, what was school like in England during Victorian times? **[Speculate]**

Reading Check 6
What does Gradgrind aim to do for students?

3 Vocabulary
Greek Prefix: *mono-*

1. Call students' attention to *monotonous,* a word that means "having a single tone, and therefore dull and unvarying."
2. Explain that *monotonous* contains the Greek prefix *mono-,* which means "single" or "alone."
3. Have students suggest other words and phrases that contain this prefix.
   Possible responses: *monogamous, monopoly,* and *monomaniacal*

4 Critical Thinking
Make a Judgment

1. Have a student volunteer read aloud the second paragraph. **Ask** students to consider the distinction between Dickens's speaker's message and Dickens's description of the speaker.
2. Then, **ask** students: What is the relationship between Dickens's description of the speaker and the speaker's message?
   Possible response: Student responses should reflect the utter lack of warmth or softness in the speaker. His geometrical angularity underscores his rigidity of character and viewpoint.

5 Critical Viewing
Answer: Students may observe the harsh look on the instructor's face. Students may conclude from this that instructors were very dominant over their classes and basically scared the children into learning. The classroom was likely an environment where the teacher's word was the bottom line and no one was allowed to argue.

6 Reading Check
Answer: Gradgrind aims to fill the students with facts.

Differentiated Instruction for Universal Access

Support for Special-Needs Students
Have students complete the **Before You Read** and the **Making Connections** pages for this selection in the ***Reader's Notebook: Adapted Version.*** These pages provide abbreviated skills instruction, a selection summary, the **Before You Read** graphic organizer, and a **Note-taking Guide.**

Support for Less Proficient Readers
Have students complete the **Before You Read** and the **Making Connections** pages for this selection in the ***Reader's Notebook.*** These pages provide abbreviated skills instruction, a selection summary, the **Before You Read** graphic organizer, and a **Note-taking Guide.**

EL Support for English Learners
Have students complete the **Before You Read** and the **Making Connections** pages for this selection in the ***Reader's Notebook: English Learner's Version.*** These pages provide additional vocabulary, vocabulary skills, and vocabulary practice, along with a **Getting Ready to Read** activity.

❼ Literary Analysis

Ethical and Social Influences

1. Review with students the various ways in which Gradgrind reveals something about himself in this passage.
2. Then, **ask** the Literary Analysis question: What outlook is Dickens criticizing through Gradgrind's identification of Sissy Jupe by a number?
   Answer: Students may recognize that using numbers rather than names to refer to people is a way to dehumanize them and strip away their individuality.

❽ World Literature Connection

The Ninteenth-Century Novel

The novel is a complex fictional prose narrative of considerable length. Traditionally, the novel features believable characters, a plot structure, and a sense of reality. The novel stems from the desire to write about human character.

The word *novel* is an English transliteration of the Italian word *novella,* which describes a realistic, short tale popular during the medieval period.

Connect to the Literature

Ask the Connect to the Literature question.
Possible answer: Contemporary readers in Dickens's time might have enjoyed the regular "servings" and eagerly waited for each installment—in the same way viewers today look forward to serial television programs.

World
LITERATURE
CONNECTION ❽

The Nineteenth-Century Novel

In the nineteenth century, technological advances allowed newspaper and magazine publishers to print large runs at affordable prices. For the first time, this made reading material widely available to the middle classes. For these publications, writers contributed fiction that was serialized in weekly or monthly issues. British authors Charles Dickens, George Eliot, William Thackeray and Thomas Hardy, French authors Honoré de Balzac and Victor Hugo, and Russian authors Fyodor Dostoyevsky and Leo Tolstoy wrote their novels as serials.

Connect to the Literature

How do you think contemporary readers might have responded to the weekly installments of *Hard Times,* which Dickens joked were "teaspoon" servings?

CHAPTER 2
MURDERING THE INNOCENTS

Thomas Gradgrind, sir. A man of realities. A man of fact and calculations. A man who proceeds upon the principle that two and two are four, and nothing over, and who is not to be talked into allowing for anything over. Thomas Gradgrind, sir—peremptorily Thomas—Thomas Gradgrind. With a rule and a pair of scales, and the multiplication table always in his pocket, sir, ready to weigh and measure any parcel of human nature, and tell you exactly what it comes to. It is a mere question of figures, a case of simple arithmetic. You might hope to get some other nonsensical belief into the head of George Gradgrind, or Augustus Gradgrind, or John Gradgrind, or Joseph Gradgrind (all suppositious, non-existent persons), but into the head of Thomas Gradgrind—no, sir!

In such terms Mr. Gradgrind always mentally introduced himself, whether to his private circle of acquaintance, or to the public in general. In such terms, no doubt, substituting the words "boys and girls," for "sir," Thomas Gradgrind now presented Thomas Gradgrind to the little pitchers before him, who were to be filled so full of facts.

Indeed, as he eagerly sparkled at them from the cellarage before mentioned, he seemed a kind of cannon loaded to the muzzle with facts, and prepared to blow them clean out of the regions of childhood at one discharge. He seemed a galvanizing apparatus, too, charged with a grim mechanical substitute for the tender young imaginations that were to be stormed away.

"Girl number twenty," said Mr. Gradgrind, squarely pointing with his square forefinger, "I don't know that girl. Who is that girl?"

"Sissy Jupe, sir," explained number twenty, blushing, standing up, and curtseying.

"Sissy is not a name," said Mr. Gradgrind. "Don't call yourself Sissy. Call yourself Cecilia."

"It's father as calls me Sissy, sir," returned the young girl in a trembling voice, and with another curtsey.

"Then he has no business to do it," said Mr. Gradgrind. "Tell him he mustn't. Cecilia Jupe. Let me see. What is your father?"

"He belongs to the horse-riding, if you please, sir."

Mr. Gradgrind frowned, and waved off the objectionable calling with his hand.

"We don't want to know anything about that, here. You mustn't tell us about that, here. Your father breaks horses, don't he?"

"If you please, sir, when they can get any to break, they do break horses in the ring, sir."

"You mustn't tell us about the ring, here. Very well, then. Describe

Literary Analysis
Ethical and Social Influences ❼ What outlook is Dickens criticizing through Gradgrind's identification of Sissy Jupe by a number?

Think Aloud

Vocabulary: Using Context
Direct students' attention to the word *galvanizing* on this page. Use the following "think aloud" to model the skill of using context to infer the meaning of the word. Say to students:

> I may not know the meaning of the word *galvanizing.* I see that the writer is using *galvanizing* to describe Mr. Gradgrind. In the previous sentence, the writer compares Mr. Gradgrind to a cannon, ready to suddenly blast the children with information. After the word appears, it says that Mr. Gradgrind was "charged," which tells me that *galvanizing* has something to do with electricity. The comparison to a sudden cannon blast and electricity must mean that *galvanizing* is used to describe something startling and stimulating.

your father as a horsebreaker. He doctors sick horses, I dare say?"

"Oh yes, sir."

"Very well, then. He is a veterinary surgeon, a farrier and horsebreaker. Give me your definition of a horse."

(Sissy Jupe thrown into the greatest alarm by this demand.)

"Girl number twenty unable to define a horse!" said Mr. Gradgrind, for the general behoof of all the little pitchers. "Girl number twenty possessed of no facts, in reference to one of the commonest of animals! Some boy's definition of a horse. Bitzer, yours."

The square finger, moving here and there, lighted suddenly on Bitzer, perhaps because he chanced to sit in the same ray of sunlight which, darting in at one of the bare windows of the intensely whitewashed room, irradiated Sissy. For, the boys and girls sat on the face of the inclined plane in two compact bodies, divided up the center by a narrow interval; and Sissy, being at the corner of a row on the sunny side, came in for the beginning of a sunbeam, of which Bitzer, being at the corner of a row on the other side, a few rows in advance, caught the end. But, whereas the girl was so dark-eyed and dark-haired, that she seemed to receive a deeper and more lustrous color from the sun when it shone upon her, the boy was so light-eyed and light-haired that the self-same rays appeared to draw out of him what little color he ever possessed. His cold eyes would hardly have been eyes, but for the short ends of lashes which, by bringing them into immediate contrast with something paler than themselves, expressed their form. His short-cropped hair might have been a mere continuation of the sandy freckles on his forehead and face. His skin was so unwholesomely **deficient** in the natural tinge, that he looked as though, if he were cut, he would bleed white.

"Bitzer," said Thomas Gradgrind. "Your definition of a horse."

"Quadruped. Graminivorous. Forty teeth, namely twenty-four grinders, four eye-teeth, and twelve incisive. Sheds coat in the spring; in marshy countries, sheds hoofs, too. Hoofs hard, but requiring to be shod with iron. Age known by marks in mouth." Thus (and much more) Bitzer.

"Now girl number twenty," said Mr. Gradgrind. "You know what a horse is."

She curtseyed again, and would have blushed deeper, if she could have blushed deeper than she had blushed all this time. Bitzer, after rapidly blinking at Thomas Gradgrind with both eyes at once, and so catching the light upon his quivering ends of lashes that they looked like the antennae of busy insects, put his knuckles to his freckled forehead, and sat down again.

The third gentleman now stepped forth. A mighty man at cutting and drying, he was; a government officer; in his way (and in most other people's too), a professed pugilist; always in training, always with a system to force down the general throat like a bolus,[1] always to be heard of at the bar of his little Public-office, ready to fight all England. To continue

1. **bolus** small, round mass, often of chewed food.

"GIRL NUMBER TWENTY UNABLE TO DEFINE A HORSE!"

Vocabulary
deficient (di fish′ ənt) *adj.* lacking an essential quality

Spiral Review
Plot How would you summarize the events of *Hard Times* up to this point in the plot?

Reading Check 9

What type of answer to his question does Gradgrind accept?

9 Reading Check

Answer: Gradgrind accepts an extremely clinical and scientific definition of a horse.

Spiral Review

Plot

1. Remind students that they studied plot in an earlier lesson.
2. Have students reread the red-bracketed passage. Then, **ask** students the Spiral Review question.

   Possible response: Gradgrind, a man interested only in facts, has questioned student Sissy Jupe. She is flustered by Gradgrind's harsh attitude, his criticism of her nickname, and her description of her father's profession. When he questions her about the definition of a horse, she is too intimidated to respond, although she is familiar with horses because her father works with them. Gradgrind pronounces her unable to define a horse, and calls on another boy, who supplies many facts. Although Gradgrind praises the boy for the facts provided, the details do not provide a clear picture of what a horse is like.

Differentiated Instruction for Universal Access

Background for Less Proficient Readers

As students read the excerpt from *Hard Times* with teacher guidance, ask them to pay special attention to the way in which the classroom and its instructors are portrayed. Remind them that Dickens may have included materials or details that offer social criticism of his era. To engage students, ask them what Dickens might think about education today.

EL Vocabulary for English Learners

Have students read from *Hard Times* with teacher guidance. If students seem to struggle with vocabulary or the progress of the conversation between Mr. Gradgrind and his students, have them sound out words and paraphrase any concepts that they do not understand. Then, have students reread the selection independently and listen to it on ***Listening to Literature* Audio CDs.**

⑩ Reading Strategy

Analyzing the Author's Purpose

1. Have students read the bracketed passage to themselves. Remind them to keep in mind the writer's purpose for including the information he does in this scene.
2. **Ask** them the Reading Strategy question: What does the reaction of the class hint about Dickens's purpose in this scene?
Answer: Dickens's purpose is to poke fun at theories of education. He shows the ridiculousness of these theories in practice—because the gentleman is more interested in his own ideas than in the true education of students, he is oblivious to the fact that they simply tell him what he wants to hear.

Vocabulary
adversary (ad′ vər ser′ ē) *n.* opponent; enemy

Reading Strategy
Analyzing the Author's Purpose What does the reaction of the class hint about Dickens's purpose in this scene?

"WHAT IS CALLED TASTE, IS ONLY ANOTHER NAME FOR FACT."

Vocabulary
indignant (in dig′ nənt) *adj.* outraged; filled with righteous anger
approbation (ap′ rə bā′ shən) *n.* official approval

in fistic phraseology, he had a genius for coming up to the scratch, wherever and whatever it was, and proving himself an ugly customer. He would go in and damage any subject whatever with his right, follow up with his left, stop, exchange, counter, bore his opponent (he always fought All England[2]) to the ropes, and fall upon him neatly. He was certain to knock the wind out of common sense, and render that unlucky **adversary** deaf to the call of time. And he had it in charge from high authority to bring about the great public-office Millennium, when Commissioners should reign upon earth.

"Very well," said this gentleman, briskly smiling, and folding his arms. "That's a horse. Now, let me ask you girls and boys, Would you paper a room with representations of horses?"

After a pause, one half of the children cried in chorus, "Yes, sir!" Upon which the other half, seeing in the gentleman's face that Yes was wrong, cried out in chorus, "No, sir!"—as the custom is, in these examinations.

"Of course, No. Why wouldn't you?"

A pause. One corpulent slow boy, with a wheezy manner of breathing, ventured the answer, Because he wouldn't paper a room at all, but would paint it. ⑩

"You *must* paper it," said Thomas Gradgrind, "whether you like it or not. Don't tell *us* you wouldn't paper it. What do you mean, boy?"

"I'll explain to you, then," said the gentleman, after another and a dismal pause, "why you wouldn't paper a room with representations of horses. Do you ever see horses walking up and down the sides of rooms in reality—in fact? Do you?"

"Yes, sir!" from one half. "No, sir!" from the other.

"Of course no," said the gentleman, with an **indignant** look at the wrong half. "Why, then, you are not to see anywhere, what you don't see in fact; you are not to have anywhere, what you don't have in fact. What is called Taste, is only another name for Fact."

Thomas Gradgrind nodded his **approbation**.

"This is a new principle, a discovery, a great discovery," said the gentleman. "Now, I'll try you again. Suppose you were going to carpet a room. Would you use a carpet having a representation of flowers upon it?"

There being a general conviction by this time that "No, sir!" was always the right answer to this gentleman, the chorus of No was very strong. Only a few feeble stragglers said Yes; among them Sissy Jupe.

"Girl number twenty," said the gentleman, smiling in the calm strength of knowledge.

Sissy blushed, and stood up.

"So you would carpet your room—or your husband's room, if you were a grown woman, and had a husband—with representations of flowers, would you," said the gentleman. "Why would you?"

---

2. **fought All England** fought according to the official rules of boxing.

Enrichment: Building Context

Victorian Decoration
Dickens could exaggerate to make a point, but sometimes he did not have to go far. In 1852, a Department of Practical Arts was established in Britain to study designs of textiles and other products. Henry Cole, the General Superintendent, decried portrayals of inappropriate subjects. One of his attacks, in fact, was aimed at wallpaper showing representations of horses and at carpets with floral designs.

Activity: Researching Victorian England
Encourage students to do further research on England in the Victorian Era, specifically on decoration. Have them record and analyze their findings using the **Enrichment: Building Context** worksheet, ***Professional Development Guidebook,*** page 222.

"If you please, sir, I am very fond of flowers," returned the girl.

"And is that why you would put tables and chairs upon them, and have people walking over them with heavy boots?"

"It wouldn't hurt them, sir. They wouldn't crush and wither if you please, sir. They would be the pictures of what was very pretty and pleasant, and I would fancy—"

"Ay, ay, ay! but you mustn't fancy," cried the gentleman, quite elated by coming so happily to his point. "That's it! You are never to fancy."

"You are not, Cecilia Jupe," Thomas Gradgrind solemnly repeated, "to do anything of that kind."

"Fact, fact, fact!" said the gentleman. And "Fact, fact, fact!" repeated Thomas Gradgrind. 12

"You are to be in all things regulated and governed," said the gentleman, "by fact. We hope to have, before long, a board of fact, composed of commissioners of fact, who will force the people to be a people of fact, and of nothing but fact. You must discard the word Fancy altogether. You have nothing to do with it. You are not to have, in any object of use or ornament, what would be a contradiction in fact. You don't walk upon
11 flowers in fact; you cannot be allowed to walk upon flowers in carpets. You don't find that foreign birds and butterflies come and perch upon your crockery. You never meet with quadrupeds going up and down walls; you must not have quadrupeds represented upon walls. You must use," said the gentleman, "for all these purposes, combinations and modifications (in primary colors) of mathematical figures which are susceptible of proof and demonstration. This is the new discovery. This is fact. This is taste."

The girl curtseyed, and sat down. She was very young, and she looked as if she were frightened by the matter of fact prospect the world afforded.

"Now, if Mr. M'Choakumchild," said the gentleman, "will proceed to give his first lesson here, Mr. Gradgrind, I shall be happy, at your request, to observe his mode of procedure."

Mr. Gradgrind was much obliged. "Mr. M'Choakumchild, we only wait for you." 13

So, Mr. M'Choakumchild began in his best manner. He and some one hundred and forty other schoolmasters, had been lately turned at the same time, in the same factory, on the same principles, like so many pianoforte legs. He had been put through an immense

Literary Analysis
Ethical and Social Influences What point about imagination does Dickens make through the teacher's literal-minded understanding?

▼ Critical Viewing
What does this picture of Sissy suggest about her relationship with her classmates and Gradgrind? **[Infer]**

Reading Check

Why does the third gentleman object to horses on wallpaper and flowers on rugs?

11 Literary Analysis

Ethical and Social Influences

1. Read the bracketed passage aloud to students, and remind them as they read along in the text to pay attention to the ways in which Dickens's novel reflects the ethical and social influences of the time period.
2. Then, **ask** students the Literary Analysis question: What point about imagination does Dickens make through the teacher's literal-minded understanding?
Answer: By exemplifying Gradgrind's literal-minded understanding to the point of ridiculousness and pairing it up with the imaginative Sissy Jupe, Dickens emphasizes the necessity of one's imagination and shows that facts are not everything.

12 Critical Viewing

Possible response: Students may observe her sad, frustrated, and even tense expression. They may also note the way the instructor is standing so closely and seems so intimidating. Students may conclude that Sissy does not have a very close or comfortable relationship with her classmates or Gradgrind.

13 Reading Check

Answer: He objects to these things because they are not what happens "in fact" in the real world.

Differentiated Instruction for Universal Access

Support for Special-Needs Students
To help students understand the writer's purpose, show them **Reading Strategy Graphic Organizer A** (*Graphic Organizer Transparencies,* p. 177). This sample will model how to interpret details to understand the writer's purpose. Students can use the graphic organizer as a model.

EL Support for English Learners
Students may find the exchange between Sissy Jupe and Mr. Gradgrind incomprehensible because they may not understand the attitudes Dickens is satirizing. Encourage students to ask questions of the text and to paraphrase any words or expressions they find unfamiliar.

Enrichment for Gifted/Talented Students
Have students work in small groups to complete a reading from *Hard Times.* When they have finished, tell them that they must adapt the chapter "Murdering the Innocents" from the novel, turning it into a scene they can perform.

ASSESS

Answers

Before students respond, you may wish to have them write a brief objective summary of the selection. As they answer the questions below, remind them to support their answers with evidence from the text.

1. (a) He sees "facts" as the important element in learning. (b) He discourages the use of imagination or imprecise, but common-sense, reasoning in his class. (c) He sees students as passive, empty vessels to be filled with facts rather than as full people with hearts and imaginations, as well as intellects.
2. (a) Sissy's performance is weak, stumbling, and meandering. Bitzer's performance is a model of the "factual" response: he offers a formal dictionary definition in short, unrelated phrases. (b) Dickens expects the reader to sympathize with Sissy, whose response is more like what most readers would give.
3. **Possible response:** Dickens seems to believe in an educational system that teaches according to an equal balance of *imagination* and *fact*.

Vocabulary

etymology (et′ ə mol′ ə jē) *n.* the study of word origins

syntax (sin′ taks) *n.* the study of sentence structure

variety of paces, and had answered volumes of head-breaking questions. Orthography, etymology, syntax, and prosody, biography, astronomy, geography, and general cosmography, the sciences of compound proportion, algebra, land-surveying and leveling, vocal music, and drawing from models, were all at the ends of his ten chilled fingers. He had worked his stony way into Her Majesty's most Honorable Privy Council's Schedule B, and had taken the bloom off the higher branches of mathematics and physical science, French, German, Latin, and Greek. He knew all about all the Water Sheds of all the world (whatever they are), and all the histories of all the peoples, and all the names of all the rivers and mountains, and all the productions, manners, and customs of all the countries, and all their boundaries and bearings on the two-and-thirty points of the compass. Ah, rather overdone, M'Choakumchild. If he had only learnt a little less, how infinitely better he might have taught much more!

"IF HE HAD ONLY LEARNT A LITTLE LESS... HE MIGHT HAVE TAUGHT MUCH MORE!"

He went to work in this preparatory lesson, not unlike Morgiana in the Forty Thieves:[3] looking into all the vessels ranged before him, one after another, to see what they contained. Say, good M'Choakumchild. When from thy boiling store, thou shalt fill each jar brim full by and by, dost thou think that thou wilt always kill outright the robber Fancy lurking within—or sometimes only maim him and distort him!

3. **Morgiana in the Forty Thieves** In the tale "Ali Baba and the Forty Thieves," Ali Baba's clever servant, Morgiana, saves him from the thieves who are hiding in large jars.

Critical Reading

Cite textual evidence to support your responses.

1. **Key Ideas and Details (a)** What does Mr. Gradgrind believe is the key to all learning? **(b) Connect:** In what ways does he put this belief into practice? **(c) Interpret:** What attitude does the description of the children as "little pitchers" reflect?
2. **Integration of Knowledge and Ideas (a) Compare and Contrast:** Compare and contrast Sissy's and Bitzer's performances in the classroom. **(b) Analyze:** With whom does Dickens's expect the reader to sympathize? Why?
3. **Integration of Knowledge and Ideas** What values does Dickens believe a system of education should teach? Explain, using two of these Essential Question words: *imagination, sympathy, conform, society, fact.* ***[Connecting to the Essential Question: How does literature shape or reflect society?]***

Vocabulary Development

Vocabulary Knowledge Rating

When students have completed reading and discussing the selection, have them take out their **Vocabulary Knowledge Rating Charts** for the story. Read the words aloud and have students rate their knowledge of words again in the After Reading column. Clarify any words that are still problematic. Have students write their own definitions and example or sentence in the appropriate column. Then, have students complete the Vocabulary Practice at the end of the selection. Encourage students to use the words in further discussion and written work about the selection. Remind them that they will be accountable for these words on the **Selection Test, *Unit 5 Resources,*** pages 57–59 or 60–62.

Critical Commentary

"Charles Dickens"
George Orwell

George Orwell (1903–1950), an important author in his own right (see p. 1317), wrote a brilliant and highly readable essay on Charles Dickens. In the essay, Orwell comments specifically on the criticism of Victorian education that Dickens made in Hard Times *and elsewhere.*

. . . Except for the universities and the big public schools, every kind of education then existing in England gets a mauling at Dickens's hands. . . . But as usual, Dickens's criticism is neither creative or destructive. He sees the idiocy of an educational system founded on the Greek lexicon and the wax-ended cane; on the other hand, he has no use for the new kind of school that is coming up in the 'fifties and 'sixties, the "modern" school, with its gritty insistence on "facts." What, then, *does* he want? As always, what he appears to want is a moralized version of the existing thing—the old type of school, but with no caning, no bullying or underfeeding, and not quite so much Greek.

"Charity begins at home, and justice begins next door."

Orwell also explains how he visualizes Dickens and what he values most about him.

When one reads any strongly individual piece of writing, one has the impression of seeing a face somewhere behind the page. It is not necessarily the actual face of the writer. . . . What one sees is the face that the writer *ought* to have. Well, in the case of Dickens I see a face that is not quite the face of Dickens's photographs, though it resembles it. It is the face of a man of about forty, with a small beard and a high color. He is laughing, with a touch of anger in his laughter, but no triumph, no malignity. It is the face of a man who is always fighting against something, but who fights in the open and is not frightened, the face of a man who is *generously angry*—in other words, of a nineteenth-century liberal, a free intelligence, a type hated with equal hatred by all the smelly little orthodoxies which are now contending for our souls.

▼ **Critical Viewing** Does this caricature of Dickens by David Levine capture any of the qualities Orwell discusses? Why or why not? **[Connect]**

Key Ideas and Details According to Orwell, what kind of a school does Dickens favor? What picture of Dickens does Orwell have in mind as he reads the Victorian author?

Answers

Critical Commentary

1. Have students reread the first excerpt of Orwell's essay, and have them pay special attention to his description of the school system Charles Dickens wished for.
2. If students are having a hard time conceptualizing the type of schools Orwell is using as examples, have them do some research.
3. Then, ask students whether or not they agree with Dickens's ideal school. Have them write several sentences explaining their answers.

Critical Viewing

Possible response: The caricature of Dickens by David Levine captures the anger that Dickens had toward the education system in England, which Orwell discusses in his essay. However, Orwell pictures Dickens as "laughing, with a touch of anger," which is not captured in the caricature.

Key Ideas and Details

1. **Answer:** Dickens favors a school that is a balance between the old ways and the new ways. He wants no abuse toward the children and less "insistence on 'facts.'"
2. **Answer:** Orwell pictures Dickens as a pleasantly angry man who does not look quite like the actual photos of him. Orwell recognizes that Dickens is a true and rightful fighter.

Concept Connector

Reading Strategy Graphic Organizer
Ask students to review the graphic organizers in which they have analyzed Dickens's purpose and the meaning it reveals. Then, have students share their organizers and compare their analyses.

Activating Prior Knowledge
Have students return to their responses to the Activating Prior Knowledge activity. Ask them to explain whether their thoughts have changed and, if so, how.

Writing About the Essential Question
Have students compare their responses to the prompt, completed before reading the story, with their thoughts afterward. Have them work individually or in groups, writing or discussing their thoughts, to formulate new responses. Then, lead a class discussion, probing for what students have learned that confirms or invalidates their initial thoughts. Encourage students to cite specific textual details to support their responses.

Answers

1. (a) Details like "plain, bare, monotonous vault" make the setting vivid. (b) The negative connotations of the words Dickens chooses are a direct criticism.
2. (a) He is critical of the belief that children are empty vessels to be filled with facts. (b) **Possible answer:** No, this viewpoint is not respectful of children.
3. (a) calling Sissy "girl number twenty"; the gentleman's ridiculous comment on horse wallpaper; equating taste with facts (b) Dickens's exaggeration reinforces his satire of the classroom and his critique of education.
4. (a) The passage about the definition of a horse is most effective. (b) Details like Bitzer's definition by rote and Sissy's sound reason for using flower carpet (flowers are "pretty and pleasant") reveal Dickens desire to convey a message.
5. (a) Choakumchild sounds like "choke a child"; reveals Dickens's purpose of critiquing education. (b) Gradgrind says, "Sissy is not a name"; Dickens wants to show the lack of respect for children. (c) The "vault of a schoolroom"; reveals Dickens's belief that a schoolroom was often seen as a storage room for children.
6. (a) Sissy would probably write social criticism. (b) Dickens probably includes both to show how adults with closed and open minds come to be.
7. (a) The conclusion is that the adults have far less common sense than the students. (b) The conclusion is that this type of education will produce automatons.
8. **Possible answer:** He might want to reveal inequalities in education or draw attention to standardized testing.

After You Read from *Hard Times*

Literary Analysis

1. **Key Ideas and Details (a)** In the selection from *Hard Times,* which details make the setting vivid? **(b)** How do they contribute to a criticism of the **ethical and social influences** of the time?
2. **Key Ideas and Details (a)** Summarize the viewpoint that Dickens criticizes. **(b)** Do you think there is a positive side to this viewpoint that Dickens may have neglected or deliberately ignored? Why or why not?
3. **Craft and Structure (a)** Identify three examples in which Dickens uses comic exaggeration to criticize Gradgrind and his fellows. **(b)** What does Dickens accomplish through his use of exaggeration, both in characterization and in the character's words? Use a chart like the one shown to examine Dickens's techniques.

Passage	Intended Effect on Reader	Intended Message	Enjoyment Value

4. **Integration of Knowledge and Ideas (a)** Identify the passage that you think is most effective in conveying Dickens's message about education. **(b)** Which details in this passage reveal the writer's desire to convey a message? Explain.

Reading Strategy

5. Choose an example of each of the following elements that help clarify the **author's purpose,** explaining your choice:
   (a) the name of a character
   (b) a character's statement or dialogue
   (c) a description of a place
6. **(a)** If Sissy and Bitzer grew up and became writers, which character would write social criticism and which might not? Explain. **(b)** What does your answer suggest about Dickens's purpose in including both characters?
7. **(a)** What conclusion does Dickens want the reader to draw about the three adults in the classroom? **(b)** What conclusions does Dickens want the reader to draw about the kind of children this type of education will produce?
8. If Dickens were alive today, what purpose or purposes might he have in writing about contemporary educational practices? Explain.

Common Core State Standards

Language
4.c. Consult general and specialized reference materials, both print and digital, to find the pronunciation of a word or determine or clarify its precise meaning, its part of speech, its etymology, or its standard usage. *(p. 1007)*
4.d. Verify the preliminary determination of the meaning of a word or phrase. *(p. 1007)*

Assessment Practice

Tone (For more practice, see *All-in-One Workbook*.)

Many tests require students to identify the tone of a passage. The following sample item can teach students how to identify the tone of a passage. Have students reread Chapter 1 from *Hard Times.*

Which of the following statements best describes the tone of the passage?

A sad, yet hopeful
B humorous
C gloomy
D dramatic

Help students analyze the tone of the selection. *Hard Times* is not hopeful or gloomy, and it is definitely not dramatic, which eliminates answers ***A, C,*** and ***D.*** The correct answer is ***B.***

PERFORMANCE TASKS

Integrated Language Skills

Vocabulary Acquisition and Use

Word Analysis: Greek Prefix *mono-*

The Greek prefix *mono-* means "single" or "alone." Thus, someone who speaks in a *monotonous* way talks in a single, unchanging manner, without varying tone or subject. The prefix is used to form many common words as well as some scientific and technical words. Explain how the prefix *mono-* contributes to the meaning of each of these words. Use a dictionary to confirm the meaning of a word if you are unsure.

1. monochromatic
2. monogamy
3. monologue
4. monopoly
5. monorail
6. monotreme

Write two original sentences using these or any other words with the prefix *mono-*.

Vocabulary: Antonyms

Antonyms are words with opposite or nearly opposite meanings. *Bitter* and *sweet* are antonyms, as are *night* and *day*. For each of the following vocabulary words, identify an antonym. Then, write an original sentence using the word and its antonym.

Example: reality
Antonym: fantasy
Sentence: Gradgrind did not believe in fantasy or the imagination, only in his cold, hard reality.

1. monotonous
2. obstinate
3. deficient
4. adversary
5. indignant
6. approbation

Using Resources to Build Vocabulary

Words for a Utilitarian Perspective

Charles Dickens gives Thomas Gradgrind a particular vocabulary that emphasizes his interest in only the utilitarian aspects of life. Near the beginning of the passage, he declares, "Facts alone are wanted in life." Review this list of utilitarian words that Dickens puts in Gradgrind's mouth—or thoughts.

reason	inflexible
observation	calculation
weigh	mechanical

Use a print or an electronic dictionary to find the **connotations** of these words. Connotations are ideas or emotions associated with a word. Then, use a print or an electronic dictionary or a thesaurus to find antonyms—words with the opposite connotation, such as *illogic* for *reason.* Explain why each word you choose is a suitable antonym.

Assessment Resources

Unit 5 Resources

L1 L2 EL **Selection Test A**, pp. 57–59. Administer Test A to less advanced students.

L3 L4 EL **Selection Test B**, pp. 60–62. Administer Test B to on-level and more advanced students.

L3 L4 **Open-Book Test**, pp. 54–56. As an alternative, give the Open-Book Test.

All **Customizable Test Bank**

All **Self-tests**
Students may prepare for the **Selection Test** by taking the **Self-test** online.

PHLit Online! All assessment resources are available at **www.PHLitOnline.com**.

ASSESS/EXTEND

Answers

Vocabulary Acquisition and Use

Word Analysis

1. using only one color
2. married to one person
3. in a play or movie, a speech by one actor
4. control of supply or trade by one person or company
5. a railroad with a single track
6. mammals with a single opening for urinary, defecatory, and reproductive systems

Possible sentences: The actor stood in the spotlight and performed his monologue.
The design of the set was monochromatic—only tones of blue were used.

Vocabulary

1. interesting; The movie was not monotonous; rather, it was thrilling and interesting.
2. compliant; The child was obstinate and refused to eat, while his brother was compliant and did what he was told.
3. abundant; His diet was deficient in iron but abundant in calcium.
4. ally; You are my adversary on the soccer field but my ally in the classroom.
5. pleased; I was indignant that you suspected me of stealing your pencil, but I was pleased that you found it.
6. criticism; The student hoped for her aunt's approbation, but her ugly behavior elicited the aunt's criticism.

Using Resources to Build Vocabulary

Explanations for answers will vary.

Possible answers:

An antonym for *reason* is *guess.*

An antonym for *observation* is *imagination.*

An antonym for *weigh* is *believe* or *suppose.*

An antonym for *inflexible* is *flexible.*

An antonym for *calculation* is *judgment.*

An antonym for *mechanical* is *conscious* or *thoughtful.*

Writing

You may use this Writing Lesson as in-class practice, or you may allow students to develop the annotated bibliography as a writing assignment over several days.

1. To guide students in writing this informative text, give them the **Support for Writing Lesson** page (*Unit 5 Resources*, p. 52).
2. Encourage students to begin their research in print materials. It may be more efficient to scan a print table of contents—scanning a Web site's contents might be more time-consuming.
3. Review with students how to use relevant and effective keyword searches.
4. To support all students, provide a sample bibliography that includes several types of sources.
5. Define *scope, reliability*, and *validity* in the context of research, and ask for volunteers to give examples of each.

PERFORMANCE TASKS

Integrated Language Skills

Writing

Informative Text The excerpt from *Hard Times* presents a vivid picture of a Victorian school. Were the attitudes and methods used by Gradgrind typical of the period, or was Dickens painting an extreme picture? Answering that question requires a historical investigation.

Compile an **annotated bibliography** of works that could be used in a research paper on the topic. An annotated bibliography includes not only full bibliographic information on sources but also notes that describe the kinds of information each source can offer and an evaluation of its usefulness. In your bibliography, include works with different perspectives, and include both primary sources (books from Victorian times) and secondary sources (those from later periods).

Prewriting Use both print materials and the Internet to locate sources. You might ask a librarian for help in finding appropriate sources.

- Use relevant keywords like *education, Victorian,* and *Britain* to search for sources. Be sure to locate both primary and secondary sources.
- Scan the table of contents, introduction, first chapter, or other key elements of each source to learn what it says about the subject. Consider its scope, what type of education it addresses; its validity, how authoritative the observations seem to be; and its reliability, how free or absent of bias it is.
- Find a copy of the style guide, such as the MLA style guide, that your teacher wants you to use for presenting the bibliographic information for each source.

Drafting Write a draft of your annotated bibliography.

- Prepare an entry for each source you consulted, styling it properly according to the style guide.
- Add an annotation that addresses the scope, reliability, and validity of each source. Use your annotations to show the different perspectives you can gain from this variety of sources.

Model: Drafting Annotations for Primary Sources

Timkins, Charles. *School Days* London: Chapman, 1868.
Timkins's memoir narrates his life in a boarding, or private, school. It reveals the loneliness felt by the boys, the brutality of some teachers, and the tough academic standards students had to meet. Limited in scope to just one school but full of anecdotes.

The annotation shows the unique insight provided by this source.

Revising Review your bibliographical entries for both format and content.

- Be sure the entries conform to the correct style. If not, make any needed changes.
- Review the annotations to make sure they clearly assess each work's usefulness.

Common Core State Standards

Writing

2. Write informative/explanatory texts to examine and convey complex ideas, concepts, and information clearly and accurately through the effective selection, organization, and analysis of content.

8. Gather relevant information from multiple authoritative print and digital sources, using advanced searches effectively; assess the strengths and limitations of each source in terms of the task, purpose, and audience; integrate information into the text selectively to maintain the flow of ideas, avoiding plagiarism and overreliance on any one source and following a standard format for citation.

Teaching Resources

Unit 5 Resources
L3 L4 **Vocabulary Builder**, p. 50.
L3 L4 **Support for Writing Lesson**, p. 52.
L3 L4 **Grammar and Style**, p. 51.
L4 **Enrichment**, p. 53.

All **Enriched Online Student Edition**
Internet Research Activity: available under After You Read for this selection
Interactive Grammar Lesson: available under After You Read for this selection

All ***Professional Development Guidebook***
Rubrics for Self-Assessment: General Writing, pp. 282–283

PHLit Online! All resources are available at **www.PHLitOnline.com**.

Conventions and Style Shifts in Verb Tense

Use **verb tenses** in a logical sequence to show when actions happen in relation to one another. **Avoid shifting tenses** when the actions occur at the same time.

Shifted Tenses: Mr. Gradgrind points to Sissy and asked her name.
Correct: Mr. Gradgrind pointed to Sissy and asked her name.
Correct: Mr. Gradgrind points to Sissy and asks her name.
Note the different forms of verb tenses:

Present:	*wants, is wanting, does want, have wanted, have been wanting*
Past:	*wanted, was wanting, did want, had wanted, had been wanting*
Future:	*will want, will be wanting, will have wanted, will have been wanting*

When actions occur at different times, use the sequence of tenses that indicates the correct times.

Mr. Gradgrind had learned Sissy's name, but he still called her "girl number twenty."

Participle forms (*wanting, wanted, having wanted*) and infinitive forms (*to want, to have wanted*) can also indicate time. Use the form that indicates the timing in relation to the main verb.

Practice Decide whether a sentence uses verb tenses correctly. If it is correct, write *correct*. If it is incorrect, rewrite the sentence correctly

1. Bitzer had learned the definition of a horse, and so he recites it when called on.
2. The gentleman hopes commissioners of fact forced people to use only facts.
3. Once the children learn facts, they will be educated.
4. Having stated his beliefs about facts, Gradgrind begins to call on students.
5. The gentleman had been listening, but then he joins in the examining of students.
6. Half the class had called out "yes" before they see that the gentleman expected "no."
7. Sissy hadn't known the definition of *horse*, but she will be speaking up again.
8. In Mr. Gradgrind's opinion, children are like pitchers to have been filled with facts.
9. Educated with facts, the schoolmaster wanted to see what the children knew.
10. The schoolmaster had learned too many facts, and he is a poorer teacher as a result.

Writing and Speaking Conventions

A. Writing Use the two verbs in a sentence showing actions that happen at the same time. Use the tense given in parentheses.

1. ask, answer (*present*)
2. weigh, measure (*future*)
3. frown, wave (*past*)
4. fill, hold (*present*)

Example: ask, answer
Sentence: The adults ask questions, and the children answer.

B. Speaking Write and present to the class a persuasive argument in which you either agree or disagree with Mr. Gradgrind's point of view about education. Be sure to avoid shifts in verb tense and to include support for your argument.

PH WRITING COACH
Further instruction and practice are available in *Prentice Hall Writing Coach*.

Conventions and Style

Practice

1. incorrect: Bitzer had learned the definition of a horse, and so he recited it when called on.
2. incorrect: The gentleman hopes commissioners of fact force people to use only facts.
3. correct
4. incorrect: Having stated his beliefs about facts, Gradgrind began to call on students.
5. incorrect: The gentleman had been listening, but then he joined in the examining of students.
6. incorrect: Half the class had called out "yes" before they saw that the gentleman expected "no."
7. incorrect: Sissy didn't know the definition of *horse*, but she was speaking up again.
8. incorrect: In Mr. Gradgrind's opinion, children are like pitchers to be filled with facts.
9. correct
10. incorrect: The schoolmaster had learned too many facts, and he was a poorer teacher as a result.

Writing and Speaking Conventions

A. Sample responses:

1. When you ask a question, I always answer.
2. The scientist will weigh the matter, and then she will measure its length.
3. The clown frowned and waved while walking in the parade.
4. The baby holds the glass while her mother fills it with juice.

B. Answers will vary.

Extend the Lesson

Sentence Modeling

Choose the sentence given from the selection students have read:

Indeed, as he eagerly sparkled at them from the cellarage before mentioned, he seemed a kind of cannon loaded to the muzzle with facts, and prepared to blow them clean out of the regions of childhood at one discharge.

Ask students what they notice about this sentence. Elicit from them that all the verbs are in the same tense. Explain to them the importance of avoiding verb shifts. Reread the sentence, changing the tense of a verb or two. Point out how awkward it sounds.

Have students imitate the sentence in a topic of their own choosing, matching each grammatical and stylistic feature discussed. Have volunteers read their sentences aloud.

PH WRITING COACH Grade 12

Students will find practice with and guidance on verb tense in Chapter 17.

The Novelist as Social Critic

1. **Ask** students to think about possible topics of social criticism. **Possible topics:** the educational system, gender roles, racism, social class system, living conditions, environment, war, technological progress
2. **Ask:** Why is social criticism important to society at large? **Possible response:** It is important that individuals reveal social flaws so that people work for social justice.
3. Discuss whether a novelist can or should influence social trends or merely reflect them.
4. Ask students to name authors they have read who provide social criticism and commentary. Have them sum up the theme or central message of each.
5. Ask students to consider social criticism in documentary film and in journalism (e.g. Michael Moore).
6. **Ask:** Are art and literature strong enough influential forces to solve social problems? **Possible response:** Art can influence only a receptive audience. Only the audience members have it within their power to respond and improve society.

Comparing Literary Works

from *Hard Times* by Charles Dickens
• "An Upheaval" by Anton Chekhov

Comparing Social Criticism in Fiction

Social Criticism

In the nineteenth century, **social criticism** began to appear much more frequently in fiction. Writers like Charles Dickens and Anton Chekhov told stories that brought societal ills to public awareness. Slavery, unsafe work or living conditions, colonialism, the class system, injustices in the judicial and education systems—these are some of the issues that authors have criticized over the years. Social criticism often takes these forms:

- **Realism:** Reveals social ills by showing how life is really lived
- **Satire:** Ridicules individuals, institutions, groups, and so on
- **Utopian fiction:** Shows a perfect society, forcing readers to see what needs improvement in their own society
- **Dystopian fiction:** Depicts a dreadful society, forcing readers to see the dangers to which current social ills may lead

Some social criticism is **explicit,** stated directly in the work. More often in fiction, however, it is **implicit,** with readers expected to infer the criticisms based on the work's details. As you read "An Upheaval," compare it to the selection from *Hard Times,* using a chart like this to list your inferences.

"An Upheaval"	
Details	Criticisms

Hard Times	
Details	Criticisms

Common Core State Standards

Reading Literature
1. Cite strong and thorough textual evidence to support analysis of what the text says explicitly as well as inferences drawn from the text, including determining where the text leaves matters uncertain.

Language
6. Demonstrate independence in gathering vocabulary knowledge when considering a word or phrase important to comprehension or expression.

Gather Vocabulary Knowledge

Chekhov uses related forms of the words *shame, resentment,* and *dismay.* Use a **dictionary** to find each word's part of speech and definition. Then, employ the following references to further explore these words:

- **History of English:** Use this work to research each word's origin. Explain the word's emergence in English.
- **Book of Quotations:** Use this resource to find a quotation containing one of the words. Then, explain nuances in meaning that are evident from the context of the quotation.

Comparing References Compare and contrast what you learn about the words from these specialized references.

PRETEACH

Common Core State Standards
- **Reading Literature 1**
- **Writing 1**
- **Language 6**

Comparing Social Criticism in Fiction

1. Introduce the topic using the instruction on the student page.
2. Give students a copy of the **Literary Analysis Graphic Organizer B,** page 182 in ***Graphic Organizer Transparencies,*** to fill out as they read.

Gather Vocabulary Knowledge

Have print and electronic resources available for students to use to explore the origins and meanings of the words. Encourage students to search for quotations using related forms, including *shameful, resent, resentful,* and *dismayed*. Display a key of etymological symbols and ensure that students understand the symbols they will encounter as they research word origins.

Teaching Resources

The following resources can be used to enrich, extend, or differentiate the instruction.

- All *Unit 5 Resources,* pp. 63–67
- All **Enriched Online Student Edition**
- All *Common Core Companion* pp. 2–9; 185–195; 336–337

PHLit Online! All resources are available at **www.PHLitOnline.com**

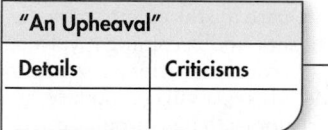

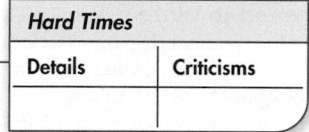

Daily Bellringer

As you teach the Comparing Literary Works selection, have students complete the Grammar, Usage, and Mechanics activities that remain for the relevant week in the *Daily Bellringer Activities* booklet.

Background

More About the Author

To many, Anton Chekhov is known as a dramatist more so than a short story writer. One of his most famous plays is *Uncle Vanya* (1899), which Chekhov based on his four-act comedy *The Wood-Demon* (1889). *Uncle Vanya* was staged at the Moscow Art Theatre in 1899.

Chekhov's wife, Olga Knipper—whom he married in 1901—was an actress. She performed in productions of Chekhov's plays *The Seagull*, *Three Sisters*, and *The Cherry Orchard*.

(1860–1904)

ANTON CHEKHOV

"YOU MUST TRUST AND BELIEVE IN PEOPLE OR LIFE BECOMES IMPOSSIBLE."

Anton Chekhov (än tôn′ chek′ ôf) is one of only a few major writers who also studied and practiced medicine. By applying to his writing the same type of compassion and objectivity that are required of a good doctor, Chekhov was able to establish himself as one of the dominant figures in Russian Realism.

Beginnings The grandson of a serf who had purchased his freedom, Chekhov was born in the small coastal town of Taganrog in southern Russia. After the failure of his father's grocery business, his family moved to Moscow, while he remained in Taganrog to complete his schooling. In 1879, he moved to Moscow to be with his family, and he enrolled in medical school. As a medical student, he began writing comic sketches and light short stories to earn extra money to help support his family.

Devoted to Writing While helping to care for his elderly parents, offering medical treatment to local peasants, and becoming involved in community affairs, Chekhov managed to continue writing prolifically throughout the six years he lived in Melikhovo, a village south of Moscow. Among the most notable short stories that he produced during this period are "Ward Number Six" (1892), the story of a doctor who is ironically committed to the same grim, depressing mental ward that he had previously directed; and "An Anonymous Story" (1893) and "Peasant" (1897), two harshly realistic sketches of Russian peasant life. During this period, Chekhov also wrote one of his finest plays, *The Seagull* (1896), which focuses on the conflict between different generations of people.

Poor Health and High Acclaim Toward the end of the nineteenth century, Chekhov's physical condition began to rapidly deteriorate. No longer able to withstand the cold climate of Melikhovo, he was forced to move to Yalta, a coastal resort on the Black Sea. His ill health did not impair his literary output, however, and in the final years of life he was able to produce two critically acclaimed plays, *The Sisters* (1901) and *The Cherry Orchard* (1904).

AN UPHEAVAL

BY ANTON CHEKHOV

TRANSLATED BY CONSTANCE GARNETT

BACKGROUND THE INDUSTRIAL REVOLUTION WAS SLOW IN COMING TO RUSSIA, BUT BY CHEKHOV'S DAY, TIMES WERE CHANGING. IN 1861, CZAR ALEXANDER II FREED THE SERFS—PEASANTS BOUND TO THE LAND SINCE MEDIEVAL TIMES—THOUGH MOST FREED SERFS REMAINED DESPERATELY POOR PEASANTS. STILL, AS THE NATION MOVED FROM AN AGRARIAN TO AN INDUSTRIAL ECONOMY, NEW OPPORTUNITIES AROSE FOR SOME WHOSE PARENTS OR GRANDPARENTS HAD NOT BEEN WELL BORN. HOWEVER, AMONG THE GENTRY, THOSE WHO COULD NOT ADAPT TO THE CHANGING ECONOMY WERE FINDING IT HARD TO STAY AFLOAT ECONOMICALLY.

TEACH

❶ About the Selection

Mashenka Pavletsky is working as a governess for a wealthy family. She returns home one day to find the mistress of the house going through her belongings. Mashenka is horrified to learn that she—along with all other members of the staff—is suspected of having stolen the lady's brooch. Mashenka is insulted by this utter disrespect and gives up her position in the house.

❷ Activating Prior Knowledge

Tell students that "An Upheaval" is a story in which a young woman is suspected of a crime she did not commit. Based on what they have read in other stories or seen in movies, television shows, and real news stories, ask them to write their predictions of how the young woman might respond to the situation.

PHLit Online!

This selection is available in an interactive format in the **Enriched Online Student Edition**, at **www.PHLitOnline.com**, which includes a thematically related video with a writing prompt and an interactive graphic organizer.

❸ Comparing Social Criticism

1. Have a volunteer read the bracketed text aloud.
2. Then, **ask** students the question on the student page: What explicit commentary does this paragraph contain about the treatment of those in dependent positions?
   Possible response: This paragraph explains that people in dependent positions live with the wealthy but rarely are treated as their equals. They can be mistreated at the whim of their employers.

Vocabulary
turmoil (tur′ moil′) *n.* upheaval; confusion

MASHENKA PAVLETSKY, a young girl who had only just finished her studies at a boarding school, returning from a walk to the house of the Kushkins, with whom she was living as a governess, found the household in a terrible turmoil. Mihailo, the porter who opened the door to her, was excited and red as a crab.

Loud voices were heard from upstairs.

"Madame Kushkin is in a fit, most likely, or else she has quarrelled with her husband," thought Mashenka.

In the hall and in the corridor she met maidservants. One of them was crying. Then Mashenka saw, running out of her room, the master of the house himself, Nikolay Sergeitch, a little man with a flabby face and a bald head, though he was not old. He was red in the face and twitching all over. He passed the governess without noticing her, and throwing up his arms, exclaimed:

"Oh, how horrible it is! How tactless! How stupid! How barbarous! Abominable!"

❸ Comparing Social Criticism What explicit commentary does this paragraph contain about the treatment of those in dependent positions?

❸ Mashenka went into her room, and then, for the first time in her life, it was her lot to experience in all its acuteness the feeling that is so familiar to persons in dependent positions, who eat the bread of the rich and powerful, and cannot speak their minds. There was a search going on in her room. The lady of the house, Fedosya Vassilyevna,[1] a stout, broad-shouldered, uncouth woman with thick black eyebrows, a faintly perceptible moustache, and red hands, who was exactly like a plain, illiterate cook in face and manners, was standing, without her cap on, at the table, putting back into Mashenka's work-bag balls of wool, scraps of materials, and bits of papers. . . . Evidently the governess's arrival took her by surprise, since, on looking round and seeing the girl's pale and astonished face, she was a little taken aback, and muttered:

"*Pardon.* I . . . I upset it accidentally. . . . My sleeve caught in it . . ."

And saying something more, Madame Kushkin rustled her long skirts and went out. Mashenka looked round her room with wondering eyes, and, unable to understand it, not knowing what to think, shrugged her shoulders, and turned cold with dismay. What had Fedosya Vassilyevna been looking for in her workbag? If she really had, as she said, caught her sleeve in it and upset everything, why had Nikolay Sergeitch dashed out of her room so excited and red in the face? Why was one drawer of the table pulled out a little way? The moneybox, in which the governess put away ten kopeck pieces[2] and old stamps, was open. They had opened it, but did not know how to shut it, though they had scratched the lock all over. The whatnot[3]

1. **Fedosya Vassilyevna** Russian names traditionally include a patronymic, or father's name, with the ending *-evich/-ovich* meaning "son of" or *-evna/-ovna* meaning "daughter of"; *Fedosya Vassilyevna*, for example, means "Fedosya, daughter of Vassily."
2. **kopeck pieces** coins each worth a tenth of a **rouble** (ro͞o′ bəl), the chief currency of Russia.
3. **whatnot** *n.* set of open shelves used to display miscellaneous items.

Enrichment: Investigating Daily Life

Nineteenth-Century Russia
The introduction to this story tells us that the setting is nineteenth-century Russia. At that time, Russia's economy was advancing more slowly than other European countries, so there was a great disparity between social classes. Society was split between the wealthy class, or bourgeoisie, and the working class and peasants.

Activity: Research The first page of the story provides details of the characters' daily lives. Have students conduct research on the daily life of Russians in the 1800s. Suggest that students record the information from their research and from Chekhov's story in the **Investigating Daily Life** worksheet, ***Professional Development Guidebook,*** page 224.

"OH, HOW HORRIBLE IT IS! HOW TACTLESS! HOW STUPID!"

with her books on it, the things on the table, the bed—all bore fresh traces of a search. Her linen-basket, too. The linen had been carefully folded, but it was not in the same order as Mashenka had left it when she went out. So the search had been thorough, most thorough. But
4 what was it for? Why? What had happened? Mashenka remembered the excited porter, the general turmoil which was still going on, the weeping servant-girl; had it not all some connection with the search that had just been made in her room? Was she not mixed up in something dreadful? Mashenka turned pale, and feeling cold all over, sank on to her linen-basket.

A maidservant came into the room.

"Liza, you don't know why they have been **rummaging** in my room?" the governess asked her.

"Mistress has lost a brooch worth two thousand," said Liza.

"Yes, but why have they been rummaging in my room?"

"They've been searching every one, miss. They've searched all my things, too. They stripped us . . . and searched us . . . God knows, miss, I never went near her toilet-table, let alone touching the brooch. I shall say the same at the police-station."

"But . . . why have they been rummaging here?" the governess still wondered.

"A brooch has been stolen, I tell you. The mistress has been rummaging in everything with her own hands. She even searched Mihailo, the porter, herself. It's a perfect disgrace! Nikolay Sergeitch simply looks on and cackles like a hen. But you've no need to tremble like that, miss. They found nothing here. You've nothing to be afraid of if you didn't take the brooch."

"But Liza, it's vile . . . it's insulting," said Mashenka, breathless with indignation. "It's so mean, so low! What right had she to suspect me and to rummage in my things?"

"You are living with strangers, miss," sighed Liza. "Though you are a young lady, still you are . . . as it were . . . a servant. . . . It's not like living with your papa and mamma."

Mashenka threw herself on the bed and sobbed bitterly. Never in her life had she been subjected to such an outrage, never had she been so deeply insulted. . . . She, well-educated, refined, the daugh-
8 ter of a teacher, was suspected of theft; she had been searched like a street-walker! She could not imagine a greater insult. And to this feeling of resentment was added an oppressive dread of what would come next. All sorts of absurd ideas came into her mind. If they could suspect her of theft, then they might arrest her . . . and search

Vocabulary
rummaging (rum′ ij iŋ) *v.* thoroughly searching through

5 **Reading Check**
What is happening in the household where Mashenka is governess?

4 Critical Thinking

Infer

1. Ask students to reread the paragraph that spans pages 1014–1015, counting how many questions it includes.
2. Then, **ask** students to infer what Mashenka is feeling, based on the number of questions that cross her mind. **Answer:** She is clearly in a state of anxiety, wondering what is going on and what she has done wrong.

5 Reading Check

Answer: The lady of the house has discovered that an expensive brooch is missing. She immediately suspects that a servant has taken it. She is searching through all their belongings, showing no respect for anyone.

Differentiated Instruction for Universal Access

Culturally Responsive Instruction

Culture Focus Has anyone in your family or community ever been falsely accused of some wrongdoing? This could range from a minor misunderstanding between friends to a false arrest for a crime. What effect, if any, did a difference in cultural background have on the situation? In a small group, share the story and comment on how the experience made the falsely accused person feel.

❻ Humanities

Arrival of the Governess in the House of a Merchant, 1866, by Vasily Perov

Perov (1833–1882) was a Russian artist and one of the founding members of a movement of Russian realist painters.

Use the following question for discussion:

Which elements of the painting reveal Perov's aim to show life as it was really lived?

Possible response: The elegance of the room's decoration reveals the wealth of the family, and the governess's drab dress reveals her social status.

❼ Critical Viewing

Possible response: The painting serves as social criticism of the class system. The governess's head is lowered, showing that she is required to demonstrate humility. The others in the painting are all gawking. It looks like an uncomfortable situation for the young girl.

❽ Comparing Social Criticism

1. Have a volunteer read the paragraph that spans pages 1015–1016 aloud.
2. **Ask** the Comparing Social Criticism question.
Possible response: In nineteenth-century Russia, any woman who needs to work is treated as someone of a lower class. Even though Mashenka is educated, she feels that her employer gives her no more respect than she would give a prostitute. Mashenka feels that she would be powerless to defend herself if her employer formally accused her of a crime.

❼▶ **Critical Viewing** This nineteenth century Russian painting depicts a governess arriving at a merchant's house. What social commentary might the artist be offering? **[Interpret]**

"THEY WILL BELIEVE THAT I COULD NOT BE A THIEF!"

Comparing Social Criticism What social criticism about the plight of young working women does Chekhov imply in this paragraph? ❽

Vocabulary
kindred (kin′ drəd) *n.* family; relatives

her, then lead her through the street with an escort of soldiers, cast her into a cold, dark cell with mice and wood-lice, exactly like the dungeon in which Princess Tarakanov[4] was imprisoned. Who would stand up for her? Her parents lived far away in the Provinces; they had not the money to come to her. In the capital she was as solitary as in a desert, without friends or kindred. They could do what they liked with her.

"I will go to all the courts and all the lawyers," Mashenka thought, trembling. "I will explain to them, I will take an oath. . . . They will believe that I could not be a thief!"

Mashenka remembered that under the sheets in her basket she had some sweetmeats, which, following the habits of her schooldays, she had put in her pocket at dinner and carried off to her room. She

4. **Princess Tarakanov** daughter supposedly born to Russia's Empress Elizabeth (1709–1761) in a secret marriage to a commoner.

felt hot all over, and was ashamed at the thought that her little secret was known to the lady of the house; all this terror, shame, resentment, brought on an attack of palpitation of the heart, which set up a throbbing in her temples, in her heart, and deep down in her stomach.

"Dinner is ready," the servant summoned Mashenka.

"Shall I go, or not?"

9 Mashenka brushed her hair, wiped her face with a wet towel, and went into the dining-room. There they had already begun dinner. At one end of the table sat Fedosya Vassilyevna with a stupid, solemn, serious face; at the other end Nikolay Sergeitch. At the sides there were the visitors and the children. The dishes were handed by two footmen in swallowtails[5] and white gloves. Everyone knew that there was an upset in the house, that Madame Kushkin was in trouble, and everyone was silent. Nothing was heard but the sound of munching and the rattle of spoons on the plates.

The lady of the house, herself, was the first to speak.

"What is the third course?" she asked the footman in a weary, injured voice.

"Esturgeon à la russe,"[6] answered the footman.

"I ordered that, Fenya," Nikolay Sergeitch hastened to observe. "I wanted some fish. If you don't like it, *ma chère,*[7] don't let them serve it. I just ordered it. . . ."

Fedosya Vassilyevna did not like dishes that she had not ordered herself, and now her eyes filled with tears.

"Come, don't let us agitate ourselves," Mamikov, her household doctor, observed in a honeyed voice, just touching her arm, with a smile as honeyed. "We are nervous enough as it is. Let us forget the brooch! Health is worth more than two thousand roubles!"

"It's not the two thousand I regret," answered the lady, and a big tear rolled down her cheek. "It's the fact itself that revolts me! I cannot put up with thieves in my house. I don't regret it—I regret nothing; but to steal from me is such ingratitude! That's how they repay me for my kindness. . . ."

They all looked into their plates, but Mashenka fancied after the lady's words that every one was looking at her. A lump rose in her throat; she began crying and put her handkerchief to her lips.

"Pardon," she muttered. "I can't help it. My head aches. I'll go away."

And she got up from the table, scraping her chair awkwardly, and went out quickly, still more overcome with confusion.

11 "It's beyond everything!" said Nikolay Sergeitch, frowning. "What need was there to search her room? How out of place it was!"

---

5. footmen in swallowtails servants whose uniforms include full dress coats with long tapering tails in the back.

6. *Esturgeon à la russe* Russian sturgeon, the fish whose salted eggs are served as the costly Russian appetizer known as caviar.

7. *ma chère* (mä shâr′) French for "my dear."

Vocabulary
palpitation (pal′ pə tā′ shən) *n.* rapid fluttering of the heart

Comparing Social Criticism What do the presence of "footmen in swallowtails" and so many other servants show about the Kushkin household?

10 **Reading Check**
What did Mashenka hide in her basket?

9 Comparing Social Criticism

1. Ask for a volunteer to read the bracketed paragraph and footnote 5.
2. Then, **ask** the Comparing Social Criticism question: What do the presence of "footmen in swallowtails" and so many other servants show about the Kushkin household?
   Possible response: The Kushkins clearly have a great deal of wealth, or they would not be able to support so many servants. Also, the servants are expected to dress in a formal manner, which suggests that the Kushkins often have important visitors they want to impress.

10 Reading Check

Answer: Mashenka hid some sweets from dinner in her basket.

Differentiated Instruction for Universal Access

Strategy for Less Proficient Readers
Stories from earlier time periods often contain vocabulary or syntax that is difficult for modern readers to understand. Encourage students to read the text aloud with a partner, alternating paragraphs to split up the dialogue and narration.

Strategy for Advanced Readers
Ask advanced readers to compare the behavior of Fedosya Vassilyevna and Mashenka in this scene. Then, have each student write a brief summary of the similarities between the two women.

11 Comparing Social Criticism

1. Have students reread the disagreement between the Kushkins about searching Mashenka's room.
2. Then, **ask** the Comparing Social Criticism question.
   Possible response: The disagreement illustrates that social class determines how a person is treated in nineteenth-century Russia. Nikolay does not question his wife for searching all the servants' rooms, showing them a lack of respect. He only questions her about treating Mashenka, an educated girl, in the same way. He also goes to personally apologize to Mashenka—something he would not consider doing for the lower members of the servant class.

Spiral Review

Conflict

1. Remind students that they studied conflict in an earlier lesson.
2. **Ask** students the Spiral Review question.
   Possible response: The disagreement reveals that social class dictated an individual's rights more than laws did. When Mashenka asks what right the family had to search her room, Liza tells her, "You are a servant." When Mashenka reflects on her position, she realizes that "they can do as they like with her." Finally, during the disagreement, Fedosya points out Fenya has no legal right to search, and she responds, "I know nothing about your laws. All I know is that I've lost my brooch." These details combine to suggest that in practice, those in the upper classes did not think they were disregarding the rights of the lower classes; rather, they believed the lower classes had no rights at all.

Comparing Social Criticism What does the disagreement about whether Mashenka's room should be searched reveal about attitudes toward social class in late-nineteenth-century Russia? 11

Spiral Review
Conflict There is disagreement about whether or not Mashenka's room should be searched. What does this reveal about ideas regarding social class in late-nineteenth-century Russia?

"I don't say she took the brooch," said Fedosya Vassilyevna, "but can you answer for her? To tell the truth, I haven't much confidence in these learned paupers."

"It really was unsuitable, Fenya. . . . Excuse me, Fenya, but you've no kind of legal right to make a search."

"I know nothing about your laws. All I know is that I've lost my brooch. And I will find the brooch!" She brought her fork down on the plate with a clatter, and her eyes flashed angrily. "And you eat your dinner, and don't interfere in what doesn't concern you!"

Nikolay Sergeitch dropped his eyes mildly and sighed. Meanwhile Mashenka, reaching her room, flung herself on her bed. She felt now neither alarm nor shame, but she felt an intense longing to go and slap the cheeks of this hard, arrogant, dull-witted, prosperous woman.

Lying on her bed she breathed into her pillow and dreamed of how nice it would be to go and buy the most expensive brooch and fling it into the face of this bullying woman. If only it were God's will that Fedosya Vassilyevna should come to ruin and wander about begging, and should taste all the horrors of poverty and dependence, and that Mashenka, whom she had insulted, might give her alms![8] Oh, if only she could come in for a big fortune, could buy a carriage, and could drive noisily past the windows so as to be envied by that woman!

But all these were only dreams, in reality there was only one thing left to do—to get away as quickly as possible, not to stay another hour in this place. It was true it was terrible to lose her place, to go back to her parents, who had nothing; but what could she do? Mashenka could not bear the sight of the lady of the house nor of her little room; she felt stifled and wretched here. She was so disgusted with Fedosya Vassilyevna, who was so obsessed by her illnesses and her supposed aristocratic rank, that everything in the world seemed to have become coarse and unattractive because this woman was living in it. Mashenka jumped up from the bed and began packing.

"May I come in?" asked Nikolay Sergeitch at the door; he had come up noiselessly to the door, and spoke in a soft, subdued voice. "May I?"

"Come in."

He came in and stood still near the door. His eyes looked dim and his red little nose was shiny. After dinner he used to drink beer, and the fact was perceptible in his walk, in his feeble, flabby hands.

"What's this?" he asked, pointing to the basket.

"I am packing. Forgive me, Nikolay Sergeitch, but I cannot remain in your house. I feel deeply insulted by this search!"

"I understand. . . . Only you are wrong to go. . . . Why should you? They've searched your things, but you . . . what does it matter to you? You will be none the worse for it."

8. **alms** (ämz) *n.* money, food, clothing, etc., given as charity to the poor.

Think Aloud

Literary Analysis: Comparing Social Criticism

To model the process of working out the answer to the Comparing Social Criticism question on the student page, use the following "think aloud." Say to students:

Remember that social criticism can be explicit, stated directly, or implicit. When it is implicit, the reader has to study the details that are presented in the work and see what message they seem to be sending. If I look at this conversation between husband and wife, I see his efforts to discuss what is legal and proper. He is chastising his wife for mistreating Mashenka. Meanwhile, his wife remains focused on her personal distress over the loss of the brooch and expresses no sympathy for Mashenka. Mashenka's dream of revenge against Fedosya also adds details to the implicit criticism about an unfair society.

Mashenka was silent and went on packing. Nikolay Sergeitch pinched his moustache, as though wondering what he should say next, and went on in an **ingratiating** voice:

"I understand, of course, but you must make allowances. You know my wife is nervous, headstrong; you mustn't judge her too harshly."

Mashenka did not speak.

"If you are so offended," Nikolay Sergeitch went on, "well, if you like, I'm ready to apologize. I ask your pardon."

12 Mashenka made no answer, but only bent lower over her box. This exhausted, irresolute man was of absolutely no significance in the household. He stood in the pitiful position of a dependent and hanger-on, even with the servants, and his apology meant nothing either.

"H'm . . . You say nothing! That's not enough for you. In that case, I will apologize for my wife. In my wife's name. . . . She behaved tactlessly, I admit it as a gentleman. . . ."

Nikolay Sergeitch walked about the room, heaved a sigh, and went on:

"Then you want me to have it rankling here, under my heart. . . . You want my conscience to torment me. . . ."

"I know it's not your fault, Nikolay Sergeitch," said Mashenka, looking him full in the face with her big tearstained eyes. "Why should you worry yourself?"

"Of course, no. . . . But still, don't you . . . go away. I entreat you."

Mashenka shook her head. Nikolay Sergeitch stopped at the window and drummed on a pane with his fingertips.

"Such misunderstandings are simply torture to me," he said. "Why, do you want me to go down on my knees to you, or what? Your pride is wounded, and here you've been crying and packing up to go; but I have pride, too, and you do not spare it! Or do you want me to tell you what I would not tell at Confession? Do you? Listen; you want me to tell you what I won't tell the priest on my deathbed?"

Mashenka made no answer.

"I took my wife's brooch," Nikolay Sergeitch said quickly. "Is that enough now? Are you satisfied? Yes, I . . . took it. . . . But, of course, I count on your discretion. . . . For God's sake, not a word, not half a hint to any one!"

Mashenka, amazed and frightened, went on packing; she snatched her things, crumpled them up, and thrust them anyhow into the box and the basket. Now, after this candid avowal on the part of Nikolay Sergeitch, she could not remain another minute, and could not understand how she could have gone on living in the house before. 13

Vocabulary
ingratiating
(in grā′ shē āt′ iŋ) *adj.* trying to win someone's favor or good opinion

Reading Check
What does Nikolay Sergeitch confess?

"I WILL APOLOGIZE FOR MY WIFE. IN MY WIFE'S NAME..."

12 Critical Thinking

Apply

1. Have students reread the bracketed text silently.
2. Then, **ask** students to think of a time when someone has refused to talk to them, and explain how Nikolay might be feeling as Mashenka continues to pack silently.
   Possible response: Nikolay is completely flustered by Mashenka's silence. He sees that she is very upset, and he struggles to calm her. He gets more uncomfortable and desperate with each attempt, since she remains silent.

13 Reading Check

Answer: He confesses to having taken the brooch.

Differentiated Instruction for Universal Access

Strategy for Less Proficient Readers
Review with students the meaning of *ingratiating* and list possible synonyms on the board. Synonyms might include *insincere, flattering,* and *fawning.* Then encourage students to think of antonyms. Antonyms might include *sincere* or *insulting.*

Strategy for Advanced Readers
The dialogue between Mashenka and her employer may be interpreted differently by different students. Have at least two or three students read the dialogue aloud, beginning on page 1018 with "May I come in?" Encourage each student to read Nikolay's words with varying levels and types of emotion.

⓮ Comparing Social Criticism

1. Read aloud Mr. Kushkin's statement about why he took the brooch.
2. Then, **ask** students the Comparing Social Criticism question.
   Possible response: Mrs. Kushkin did not have any more money than Mashenka when she got married. She has now taken control over all marital property, though, and controls her husband's wealth. Mr. Kushkin suggests that this is a common pattern among people of their economic class.

ASSESS

Answers

Before students respond, you may wish to have them write a brief objective summary of the selection. As they answer the questions below, remind them to support their answers with evidence from the text.

1. (a) Mashenka's room is searched because the lady of the house is missing a brooch and she suspects a servant has taken it. (b) Mashenka has never before been treated with such a lack of respect.
2. (a) Fedosya Vassilyevna says she does not have much confidence in "learned paupers" like Mashenka. (b) Fedosya comes across as a spoiled woman who always puts her own interests above those of others.
3. (a) Nikolay is willing to steal something in order to get some spending cash. For Mashenka, even being suspected of theft is vile. (b) It is ironic because the brooch actually belongs to him. He should not have to steal it.

Comparing Social Criticism What do these details suggest about marriage among people of the Kushkins' economic class? How does Mrs. Kushkin's situation contrast with Mashenka's? ⓮

"And it's nothing to wonder at," Nikolay Sergeitch went on after a pause. "It's an everyday story! I need money, and she . . . won't give it to me. It was my father's money that bought this house and everything, you know! It's all mine, and the brooch belonged to my mother, and . . . it's all mine! And she took it, took possession of everything. . . . I can't go to law with her, you'll admit. . . . I beg you most earnestly, overlook it . . . stay on. *Tout comprendre, tout pardonner.*[9] Will you stay?"

"No!" said Mashenka resolutely, beginning to tremble. "Let me alone, I entreat you!"

"Well, God bless you!" sighed Nikolay Sergeitch, sitting down on the stool near the box. "I must own I like people who still can feel resentment, contempt, and so on. I could sit here forever and look at your indignant face. . . . So you won't stay, then? I understand. . . . It's bound to be so. . . . Yes, of course. . . . It's all right for you, but for me—wo-o-o-o! . . . I can't stir a step out of this cellar. I'd go off to one of our estates, but in every one of them there are some of my wife's rascals . . . stewards, experts, damn them all! They mortgage and remortgage. . . . You mustn't catch fish, must keep off the grass, mustn't break the trees."

"Nikolay Sergeitch!" his wife's voice called from the drawing-room. "Agnia, call your master!"

"Then you won't stay?" asked Nikolay Sergeitch, getting up quickly and going toward the door. "You might as well stay, really. In the evenings I could come and have a talk with you. Eh? Stay! If you go, there won't be a human face left in the house. It's awful!"

Nikolay Sergeitch's pale, exhausted face besought her, but Mashenka shook her head, and with a wave of his hand he went out.

Half an hour later she was on her way.

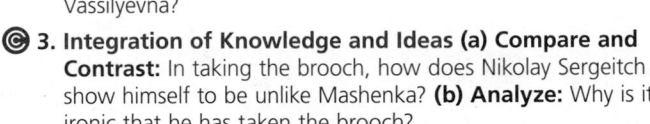

9. ***Tout comprendre, tout pardonner*** (to͞o´ kən prän´ dr to͞o´ pär´ də nā´) a French proverb meaning "To understand all, to forgive all."

Critical Reading

1. **Key Ideas and Details (a)** Why is Mashenka's room searched? **(b) Infer:** Why does the search upset her?
2. **Key Ideas and Details (a)** What does Fedosya Vassilyevna say about her confidence in Mashenka? **(b) Infer:** Based on her remarks and behavior, what sort of person is Fedosya Vassilyevna?
3. **Integration of Knowledge and Ideas (a) Compare and Contrast:** In taking the brooch, how does Nikolay Sergeitch show himself to be unlike Mashenka? **(b) Analyze:** Why is it ironic that he has taken the brooch?

Cite text evidenc support respon

After You Read from *Hard Times* • *An Upheaval*

Comparing Social Criticism

1. **Key Ideas and Details (a)** What is similar about the plight of the schoolchildren in *Hard Times* and Mashenka in "An Upheaval"? **(b)** What is different about their backgrounds?
2. **Key Ideas and Details (a)** How does sticking to a particular social philosophy play a role in the behavior of the teachers in *Hard Times* and the behavior of Mashenka in "An Upheaval"? **(b)** In what way are the two philosophies nearly opposite?
3. **Key Ideas and Details (a)** Where in each selection do characters have trouble communicating? **(b)** What does each selection suggest about the importance of and barriers to communication in society?
4. **Integration of Knowledge and Ideas** What role does the title of the work play in stressing the social criticisms that each selection contains?

Common Core State Standards

Writing

1. Write arguments to support claims in an analysis of substantive topics or texts, using valid reasoning and relevant and sufficient evidence.

Timed Writing

Argumentative Text: Essay

Both Dickens and Chekhov take issue with ethical and social influences prevalent in their times.

Assignment: In an **essay,** compare and contrast the means that each author uses to express criticism of his society.
[40 minutes]

Address these questions, citing details from the selections to support your ideas:

- What main social criticisms does each selection make?
- Which selection uses more realism in its social criticism?
- Which writer uses more satire in his social criticism?
- Which text is more effective in its social criticism?

5-Minute Planner

Complete these steps before you begin to write:

1. Read the assignment carefully. Identify key words and phrases.
2. Weigh the similarities and differences between the two selections. **TIP** As you scan the texts, jot down quotations or details that you might use in your essay.
3. Create a rough outline for your essay.
4. Reread the prompt, and draft your essay.

Answers

Comparing Social Criticism

1. (a) The children's plight is similar to Mashenka's in that they are all powerless in the face of both class divisions and injustices in the social system. (b) Mashenka is educated and from a family with relative status, while the children are probably from middle or lower class families.
2. (a) Sticking to a social philosophy leads to the teachers ignoring common sense and leads to Mashenka leaving the Kushkin home. (b) The philosophies are nearly opposite in that the teachers believe social and class systems must be maintained carefully, while Mashenka believes that respect toward individuals should prevail.
3. (a) Madame Kushkin has trouble communicating when Mashenka finds her in her room; Sissy has trouble speaking when she is asked for the definition of a horse. (b) Both selections suggest there are barriers to communication between social classes and that such barriers amplify injustice.
4. Dickens's title directly addresses the "hard times" the children face; the title "An Upheaval" reveals that Mashenka refuses to accept the social norms.

Timed Writing

1. Review with students key words in the prompt and questions, including *argumentative essay, citing, social criticism, realism,and satire.*
2. Use the prompt to help students identify elements their argumentative essay should have:
   - A thesis statement about the social criticism in the works of Chekhov and Dickens
   - An interpretation of the social criticism in each work
   - Specific text references that support the interpretation
   - A discussion of the similarities and differences between the authors' styles and techniques, including the use of satire and realism
   - Textual evidence that supports points about similarities and differences
   - A conclusion that makes a judgment about the effectiveness of the two authors' social criticism

Assessment Resources

Unit 5 Resources
L1 L2 L3 L4 EL **Selection Test A,** pp. 66–67

PHLit Online! All resources are available at **www.PHLitOnline.com.**

Encourage students to focus on these points when they are planning and revising their essays.

Tell students they will have 40 minutes to plan and write the essay. Call students' attention to the 5-Minute Planner. Encourage students to budget their time to allow 5 minutes for outlining and identifying some initial supporting text references in the works, and 10 minutes for revision and proofreading.

PRETEACH

Common Core State Standards

- Reading Informational Text 5
- Writing 2
- Language 4.d

About the Texts

1. Introduce the forms using the instruction on the student page.
2. Tell students that they will identify the features of public documents as they read.

Reading Strategy

1. Introduce the skill using the instruction and chart on the student page.
2. Tell students that they will predict the content and purpose of each document as they read.

Think Aloud: Model the Skill

Say to students:

When I begin reading a Web site home page or brochure, I first scan text features. I look at the subheadings to identify what types of information the document contains.

Content-Area Vocabulary

1. Have students say each word aloud.
2. Then, use each word in a sentence that makes its meaning clear. Repeat your sentence with the vocabulary word missing and have students fill in the blank.

For more guidance, consult the ***Classroom Strategies and Teaching Routines*** card on introducing vocabulary.

Reading for Information

Analyzing Functional and Expository Texts

Web Site Home Page • Brochure

About the Texts

A **Web site** consists of text and media that is divided into pages and accessed online, via a computer. A **Web site home page** is the opening page of a Web site. Serving as a table of contents, the home page displays links or connections to other pages on the site. In addition, it may provide information on the site's purpose and sponsoring organization.

A park or museum **brochure** is a pamphlet with information about an attraction, including contact and admission information. It also usually includes a map to guide visitors, historical background, and images meant to excite interest.

Reading Strategy

You can **predict the content and purpose** of home pages and brochures by scanning these *text features:*

- Simple section headings
- Introductions providing basic background information
- Sidebars, or sections of information presented in a column down the side of a page
- Captions or explanations of graphics

Once you have used text features to learn how a document is organized, you can more effectively use the text. To *evaluate the effectiveness of a document's organization,* consider how easy it is to follow the sequence of information and to locate specific items. Use a chart like this one to guide your review of the documents.

Checklist	Questions	Responses
☐ Introduction	How helpful is the overview provided?	
☐ Links or Headings	What ordering or subdivision of information do these present? Is this order logical?	
☐ Layout	How is information arranged on the page? Is this layout effective?	
☐ Graphics	How clear is the purpose for and labeling of graphics?	

Common Core State Standards

Reading Informational Text
5. Analyze and evaluate the effectiveness of the structure an author uses in his or her exposition or argument, including whether the structure makes points clear, convincing, and engaging.

Language
4.d. Verify the preliminary determination of the meaning of a word or phrase.

Content-Area Vocabulary

These words appear in the selections that follow. They may also appear in other content-area texts.

manuscripts (man′ yo͞o skripts′) *n.* the unpublished versions of a written work

agricultural (ag′ ri kul′ chərəl) *adj.* pertaining to farming

tenant (ten′ ənt) *adj.* of or for someone who rents property

Teaching Resources

Reading Support

L2 L3 *Reader's Notebook*

L1 *Reader's Notebook: Adapted Version*

EL *Reader's Notebook: English Learner's Version*

Web site

(The site's URL appears here.)

These links to other parts of the Web site help users quickly locate the information they need.

The Dickens Museum Home Page and Virtual Tour Link *London*

The Museum	Private Views	Books & Gifts	Media
Opening Hours	Events	Events	Research
Find Us	Teachers	Hire the Museum	Links
History	Access	Exhibitions	Access
Groups	Learning	Support	

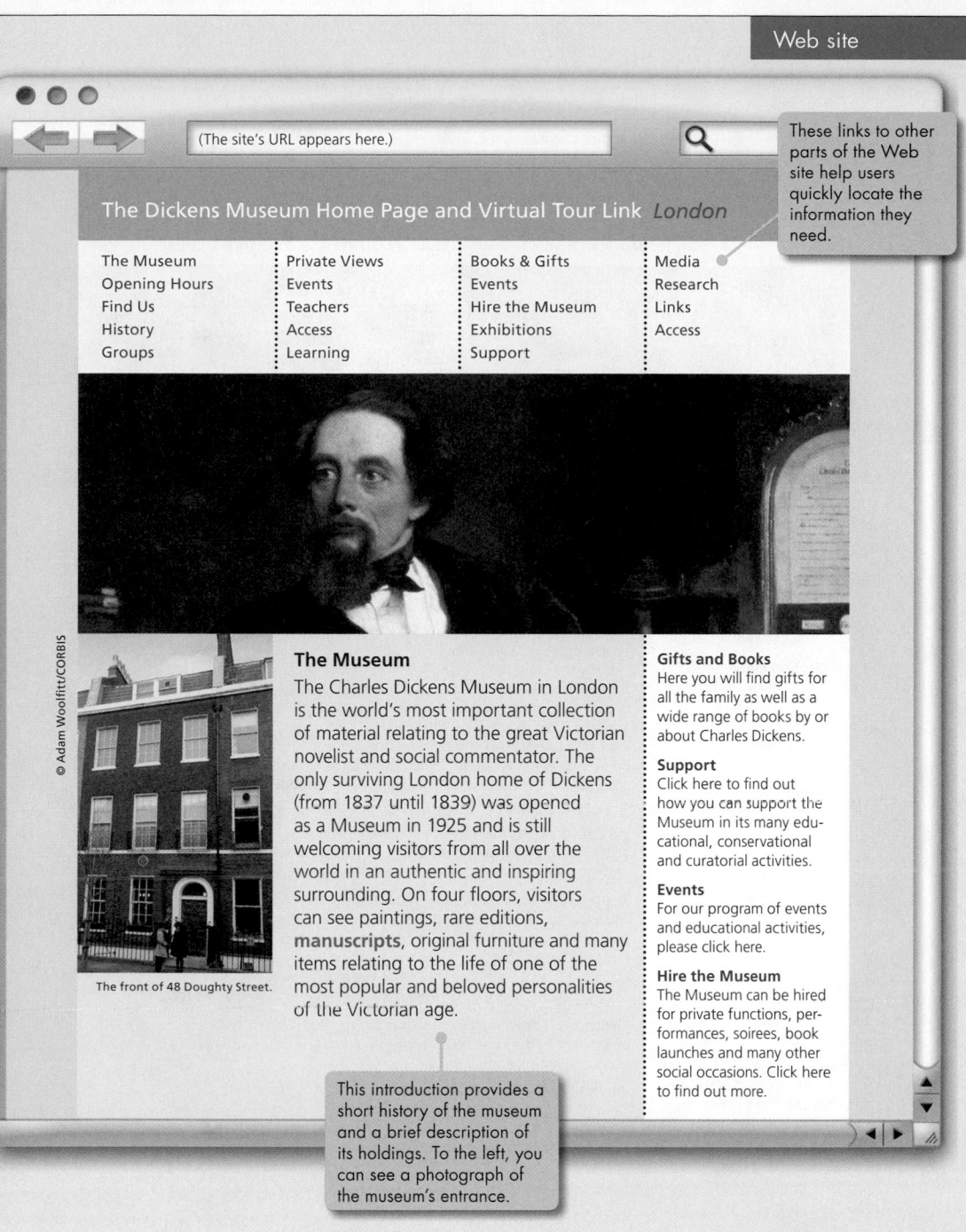

The front of 48 Doughty Street.

The Museum

The Charles Dickens Museum in London is the world's most important collection of material relating to the great Victorian novelist and social commentator. The only surviving London home of Dickens (from 1837 until 1839) was opened as a Museum in 1925 and is still welcoming visitors from all over the world in an authentic and inspiring surrounding. On four floors, visitors can see paintings, rare editions, **manuscripts**, original furniture and many items relating to the life of one of the most popular and beloved personalities of the Victorian age.

Gifts and Books
Here you will find gifts for all the family as well as a wide range of books by or about Charles Dickens.

Support
Click here to find out how you can support the Museum in its many educational, conservational and curatorial activities.

Events
For our program of events and educational activities, please click here.

Hire the Museum
The Museum can be hired for private functions, performances, soirees, book launches and many other social occasions. Click here to find out more.

This introduction provides a short history of the museum and a brief description of its holdings. To the left, you can see a photograph of the museum's entrance.

TEACH

About Web Site Home Pages

1. Point out to students that the first selection is a Web site home page.
2. Refer students to the features of a home page on the Preteach page.
3. **Ask** students to identify the different parts of the Web page.
Answer: The Web page has links at the top and right side, two photos, and a paragraph of text.

Predict the Content and Purpose

1. Refer students to the bulleted information on the Preteach page about how to predict the content and purpose of a document.
2. Point out that they will be scanning the text features as they read the two public documents.

Differentiated Instruction for Universal Access

Support for Less Proficient Readers

To increase students' comprehension of the Web site, begin by giving them a brief introduction to Charles Dickens. Be sure they know that he was a British writer during Victorian times and that his works continue to be popular today. Explain that he lived in London, so this museum is located in his former home.

EL Strategies for English Learners

Ask students to reread the section called "The Museum," which gives an overview of the Charles Dickens Museum. It is important that students understand its main points. Ask them to work in pairs to look up any words they do not understand. Have them summarize the paragraph before reading further.

Predict the Content and Purpose

1. Remind students to scan the text features before making their predictions.
2. **Ask** students to predict the content of this page.
   Possible response: Since the subheading says it is a virtual tour, I predict that this page will tell us about what is inside the museum.
3. **Ask** students to predict the purpose of the page.
   Possible response: The page seems geared toward attracting visitors to the museum. It gives them an idea of what they will see there.

Web site

(The site's URL appears here.)

The Charles Dickens Museum *Virtual Tour*

Main | Museum Map | Museum Guide | Tour Tutorial

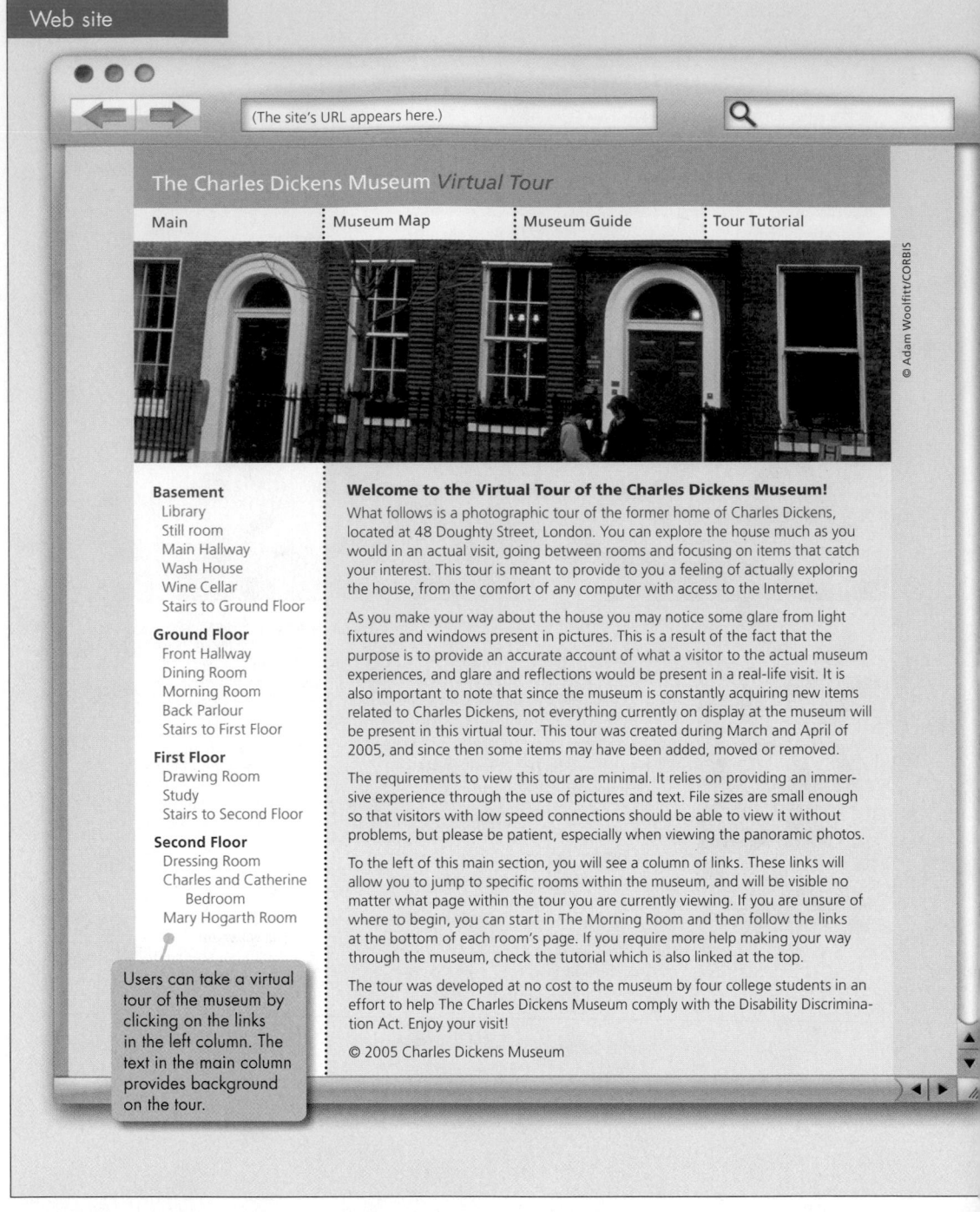

© Adam Woolfitt/CORBIS

Basement
- Library
- Still room
- Main Hallway
- Wash House
- Wine Cellar
- Stairs to Ground Floor

Ground Floor
- Front Hallway
- Dining Room
- Morning Room
- Back Parlour
- Stairs to First Floor

First Floor
- Drawing Room
- Study
- Stairs to Second Floor

Second Floor
- Dressing Room
- Charles and Catherine Bedroom
- Mary Hogarth Room

Users can take a virtual tour of the museum by clicking on the links in the left column. The text in the main column provides background on the tour.

Welcome to the Virtual Tour of the Charles Dickens Museum!

What follows is a photographic tour of the former home of Charles Dickens, located at 48 Doughty Street, London. You can explore the house much as you would in an actual visit, going between rooms and focusing on items that catch your interest. This tour is meant to provide to you a feeling of actually exploring the house, from the comfort of any computer with access to the Internet.

As you make your way about the house you may notice some glare from light fixtures and windows present in pictures. This is a result of the fact that the purpose is to provide an accurate account of what a visitor to the actual museum experiences, and glare and reflections would be present in a real-life visit. It is also important to note that since the museum is constantly acquiring new items related to Charles Dickens, not everything currently on display at the museum will be present in this virtual tour. This tour was created during March and April of 2005, and since then some items may have been added, moved or removed.

The requirements to view this tour are minimal. It relies on providing an immersive experience through the use of pictures and text. File sizes are small enough so that visitors with low speed connections should be able to view it without problems, but please be patient, especially when viewing the panoramic photos.

To the left of this main section, you will see a column of links. These links will allow you to jump to specific rooms within the museum, and will be visible no matter what page within the tour you are currently viewing. If you are unsure of where to begin, you can start in The Morning Room and then follow the links at the bottom of each room's page. If you require more help making your way through the museum, check the tutorial which is also linked at the top.

The tour was developed at no cost to the museum by four college students in an effort to help The Charles Dickens Museum comply with the Disability Discrimination Act. Enjoy your visit!

© 2005 Charles Dickens Museum

Vocabulary Development

Content-Area Vocabulary: Literature

Review the definitions of the cross-curricular vocabulary with students: *manuscript.* Then, examine the word in its context in the Web site.

When you have finished with the listed word, ask students to identify other words on the Web site that relate to the cross-curricular vocabulary. Have students look up their definitions in a dictionary and then use them in sentences about the topic of museums.

Brochure

The brochure provides basic information in the form of frequently asked questions (FAQs) and answers.

ANDALUSIA

home of Flannery O'Connor

Milledgeville, Georgia

Andalusia is open on Monday, Tuesday and Saturday from 10:00 a.m. to 4:00 p.m. or by appointment. Guided trolly tours can be arranged by calling the Milledgeville, Baldwin County Visitors Center at 1-800-653-1804

2628 N. Columbia Street (Hwy 441 N)
Milledgeville, Georgia
www.andalusiafarm.org 478-454-4029

Where was Flannery O'Connor born?

Flannery O'Connor was born in Savannah, Georgia on March 25, 1925, the only child of Edward F. O'Connor, Jr. and Regina Cline O'Connor.

Where did Flannery O'Connor attend school and college?

O'Connor attended St. Vincent's Grammar School and Sacred Heart Parochial School in Savannah, Georgia; St. Joseph's Parochial School and North Fulton High School in Atlanta, Georgia; Peabody High School and Georgia State College for Women in Milledgeville, Georgia; and the State University of Iowa in Iowa City.

How long did Flannery O'Connor live at Andalusia?

Flannery O'Connor lived at Andalusia with her mother, Regina Cline O'Connor, from early 1951 until Flannery's death in 1964. She completed all her published books while living here.

Why is the farm called Andalusia?

In the fall of 1946, before the death of Dr. Bernard Cline, Flannery O'Connor met on a bus to Atlanta a descendant of the original Hawkins family that owned Andalusia. It was the descendant who told her the original name of the place in the 19th century was Andalusia. She wrote her mother, and when her uncle Bernard heard of it, he was pleased and liked the name. From then on the name was Andalusia.

What happened to Flannery's peacocks?

None of the descendants of O'Connor's domestic flock has survived at the farm. Regina Cline O'Connor gave two pair of peafowl to Stone Mountain Mansion, one pair to Our Lady of Perpetual Help Cancer Home in Atlanta, and another pair to the Monastery of the Holy Spirit near Conyers, Georgia.

The cover page of the brochure features a photograph of O'Connor's home and provides contact information for the organization that administers the site.

About Brochures

1. Introduce the form, using the instruction on the Preteach page.
2. Tell students that they will now be examining a brochure.
3. **Ask** students to identify the site or attraction this brochure is advertising.
   Answer: This is a brochure for Andalusia, the home of Flannery O'Connor.

Predict the Content and Purpose

1. Tell students that they are to predict the brochure's content and purpose.
2. Remind students to use the bulleted list under "Reading Strategy" on page 1022.
3. **Ask** students to scan the text features and summarize their predictions about the brochure.
   Answer: The brochure seeks to inform people about the author and the location of her home.

Differentiated Instruction for Universal Access

Culturally Responsive Instruction

Culture Connection Most communities have a famous literary or historical figure connected to them. Often, a museum or memorial site will be established to help people remember the significance of that person or group. Have students research important people from or associated with your community. Create a bulletin board to collect the images and information students find.

Predict the Content and Purpose

1. Remind students to use a chart like the one on the Preteach page to guide their review of the brochure.
2. **Ask** students to predict the content of this page.
   Answer: This provides further information about the author's home and how to get there. It also provides a list of major works by Flannery O'Connor.
3. **Ask** students to predict the purpose of this page.
   Possible response: This information is meant to persuade people to visit Andalusia.

Brochure

Publications by Flannery O'Connor:

Wise Blood — 1952
A Good Man Is Hard To Find — 1955
The Violent Bear It Away — 1960
Everything That Rises Must Converge — 1965
Mystery and Manners — 1969
The Complete Stories, winner of the 1971 National Book Award for Fiction.
The Habit of Being — 1979, winner of the National Book Critics Circle Award.
Flannery O'Connor: Collected Works (Library of America) — 1988

Andalusia is the picturesque farm where American author Flannery O'Connor lived from 1951 until her death from lupus in 1964. Listed on the National Register of Historic Places, Andalusia is brought to life on many occasions in O'Connor's published letters. In the 1950s Andalusia was a dairy farm operated by O'Connor's mother, Regina Cline O'Connor. The **agricultural** setting of Andalusia provided for O'Connor not only a place to live and write, but also a landscape in which to set her fiction.

The farm complex consists of the 19th century Main House, Jack and Louise Hill's house (the home of farm workers), the cow barn, an equipment shed, the milk-processing shed, an additional smaller barn, a parking garage, a water tower, an old well house (storage), a horse stable, a pump house, several small **tenant** houses, a small pond, and nature trails.

Flannery O'Connor did not live a reclusive life at Andalusia. She traveled for various speaking engagements and made frequent visits into town for dining, social events, and to attend Mass regularly at Sacred Heart Catholic Church. She routinely wrote every morning until noon in her downstairs bedroom/study and spent her afternoons and evenings tending to her peafowl and other domestic birds or entertaining visitors.

The brochure provides background information about the house and the author.

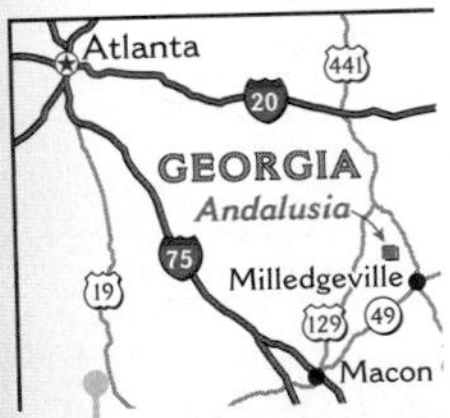

Andalusia is located just north of the shopping center on Hwy 441 North of Milledgeville

The map helps visitors planning a trip to the site.

Vocabulary Development

Content-Area Vocabulary: Social Studies

Review the definitions of the cross-curricular vocabulary with students: *tenant* and *agriculture*. Then, examine each word in its context in the brochure.

When you have finished with the two listed words, ask students to identify other words in the brochure that relate to the cross-curricular vocabulary. Have students look up their definitions in a dictionary and then use them in sentences about the topic of tourist attractions.

Critical Reading

1. **Key Ideas and Details (a)** Based on the Web site home page, where could you access views of Dickens's study? **(b)** How do the links at the top of the home page help visitors navigate the Web site?
2. **Key Ideas and Details (a)** Where in the brochure can you find information about O'Connor's publications and awards? **(b)** Where can you find contact information for the organization that sponsors the site?
3. **Craft and Structure (a)** How does the structure of each text, including the graphic elements, make points clear and engaging? **(b)** Which text has a more effective structure? Explain.
4. **Content-Area Vocabulary (a)** The word *tenant* derives from the Latin verb *tenere,* which means "to hold." Explain how the meaning of the Latin verb informs the meaning of *tenant.* **(b)** Define the following words derived from the same Latin verb: *tenable* and *tenacious.* Use a dictionary to verify your definitions.

Common Core State Standards

Writing

2. Write informative/explanatory texts to examine and convey complex ideas, concepts, and information clearly and accurately through the effective selection, organization, and analysis of content.

Timed Writing

Explanatory Text [40 minutes]

Format

In an **analytical essay,** you present a clear thesis statement in an introductory paragraph and develop it in the body, following a clear organization.

Write an **analytical essay** in which you explain the types of information preserved and published by museums and parks focused on authors' lives. Carefully select and organize information from the Web site home page and the museum brochure to support your explanation. Gather and develop ideas by **synthesizing ideas and making logical connections** between the Web site and the brochure.

Academic Vocabulary

When you **synthesize ideas and make logical connections,** you combine related ideas, focusing on ways in which they reinforce or build on one another, to reach new conclusions.

5-Minute Planner

Complete these steps before you begin to write.

1. Read the prompt carefully, and underline key words.
2. Scan the text for details that relate to the prompt. **TIP** As you consider the various types of information available at museums and parks, consider the types of information that a visitor might gather by inspecting an author's home in person, as well as information that the museum or park might provide in printed materials.
3. Before writing, create an outline to guide you.
4. Reread the prompt, and begin drafting your essay.

ASSESS

Answers

Critical Reading

1. (a) **Answer:** Visitors will find views of the study on the Web site's virtual tour. (b) **Answer:** The links help visitors find information quickly by using keywords.
2. (a) **Answer:** This information is listed under O'Connor's photograph. (b) **Answer:** The contact information is on the front of the brochure, under the photograph of the house.
3. (a) **Possible response:** The Web site uses headings and hyperlinks to organize information. Images help break up the text and add visual interest. The brochure uses a question-and-answer format to engage the reader. (b) **Possible response:** The Web site has a more effective structure because it makes it easy for the reader to find many different kinds of information.
4. (a) **Answer:** A *tenant* is a person who holds property. (b) **Answer:** *Tenable* describes a position or situation that is capable of being held to or maintained. *Tenacious* describes something with a firm hold.

Timed Writing

1. Before students begin the assignment, guide them in analyzing key words and phrases in the prompt, using the highlighted notes.
2. Work with students to draw up guidelines for their analytical essays based on the key words they identified.
3. Have students use the 5-Minute Planner to structure their time.
4. Allow students 40 minutes to complete the assignment. Evaluate their work using the guidelines they have developed.

Extend the Lesson

Connecting to the Students' World

To give students further practice with public documents and to help them apply the material to their own world, divide the class into small groups. Provide each group with a printout of a Web site home page about an author or museum. Students should work together to predict the content and purpose of the site. Ask them to share their predictions with the class.

COMMON CORE
Time and Resource Manager

• from *Jane Eyre*
Lesson Pacing Guide

DAY 1 Preteach

- Administer the Reading and Vocabulary Warm-ups (*Unit 5 Resources,* pp. 68–71) as necessary.
- Introduce the Literary Analysis concept: Philosophical Assumptions.
- Introduce the Reading Strategy: Analyze the Author's Assumptions.
- Build background with the author and Background features.
- Develop thematic thinking with Connecting to the Essential Question.
- Teach the selection vocabulary.

DAY 2 Preteach/Teach/Extend

- Distribute copies of the graphic organizer for the Reading Strategy (*Graphic Organizer Transparencies,* pp. 183–184).
- Distribute copies of the graphic organizer for Literary Analysis (*Graphic Organizer Transparencies,* pp. 185–186).
- Prepare students to read with the Activating Prior Knowledge activities (TE).
- Informally monitor comprehension while students read.
- Use the Reading Check questions to confirm comprehension.
- Develop students' understanding of philosophical assumptions using the Literary Analysis questions.
- Develop students' ability to analyze the author's assumptions using the Reading Strategy prompts.
- Reinforce vocabulary with the Vocabulary notes.
- Assess students' comprehension and mastery of the skills by having them answer the Critical Reading, Literary Analysis, and Reading Strategy questions.

DAY 3 Assess

- Have students complete the Vocabulary Lesson.
- Have students complete the Writing activity and write a school conduct report. (You may assign as homework.)
- Administer Selection Test A or B (*Unit 5 Resources,* pp. 80–82 or 83–85).

Common Core State Standards

Reading Literature 3. Analyze the impact of the author's choices regarding how to develop and relate elements of a story or drama.

Writing 2. Write informative/explanatory texts to examine and convey complex ideas, concepts, and information clearly and accurately through the effective selection, organization, and analysis of content.

Additional Standards Practice
Common Core Companion, pp. 28–35; 196–207

Daily Block Scheduling
Each day in this Lesson Pacing Guide represents a 40–50 minute period. Teachers using block scheduling may combine days to revise pacing. In addition, teachers may differentiate and support core instruction by integrating components for extended and intensive support as students require. See the Guide to Selected Leveled Resources (facing page).

Guide to Selected Leveled Resources

RTI Tier 1 (students performing on level)

			from Jane Eyre
Warm Up	Whole class instruction; Group work	**Practice, model,** and **monitor** fluency, working **with the whole class** or **in groups**.	**Vocabulary and Reading Warm-ups B,** ***Unit 5 Resources,*** pp. 68–69, 71
Comprehension/Skills	Whole class instruction; Group work; Independent work	**Support** and **monitor** comprehension and skills development, having students complete the activities, graphic organizers, and interactive prompts **independently** or **as a class**.	• ***Reader's Notebook,*** adapted instruction and full selection EL ***Reader's Notebook: English Learner's Version,*** adapted instruction and adapted selection • **Reading Strategy Graphic Organizer B,** ***Graphic Organizer Transparencies,*** p. 192 • **Literary Analysis Graphic Organizer B,** ***Graphic Organizer Transparencies,*** p. 194
Monitor Progress	A	**Monitor** student progress with the differentiated curriculum-based assessment in the *Unit Resources.*	• **Selection Test B,** ***Unit 5 Resources,*** pp. 83–85 • **Open-Book Test,** ***Unit 5 Resources,*** pp. 77–79

RTI Tier 2 (students requiring intervention)

			from Jane Eyre
Warm Up	Group work; One-on-one teaching	**Practice, model,** and **monitor** fluency **in groups** or **with individuals**.	• **Vocabulary and Reading Warm-ups A,** ***Unit 5 Resources,*** pp. 68–71 • ***Hear It!*** **Audio CD (adapted text)**
Comprehension/Skills	Group work; One-on-one teaching	• **Support** and **monitor** comprehension and skills development, working **in small groups** or **with individuals**. • As students complete the selection in the appropriate version of the *Reader's Notebook,* **monitor** comprehension frequently with group questions and individual instruction. • **Model** strategies while guiding students in completing the activities and prompts in the *Reader's Notebook,* as well as the graphic organizers. • **Practice** skills and **monitor** mastery with the *Reading Kit* worksheets.	• ***Reader's Notebook: Adapted Version,*** adapted instruction and adapted selection EL ***Reader's Notebook: English Learner's Version,*** adapted instruction and adapted selection • **Reading Strategy Graphic Organizer A,** ***Graphic Organizer Transparencies,*** p. 191 • **Literary Analysis Graphic Organizer A,** ***Graphic Organizer Transparencies,*** p. 193 • ***Reading Kit,*** Practice worksheets
Monitor Progress	A	**Monitor** student progress with the differentiated curriculum-based assessment in the *Unit Resources* and in the *Reading Kit.*	• **Selection Test A,** ***Unit 5 Resources,*** pp. 80–82 • ***Reading Kit,*** Assess worksheets

TIER 3 Tier 3 intervention may require consultation with the student's special-education or dyslexia specialist. For additional support, see the Tier 2 activities and resources listed above.

One-on-one teaching **Group work** **Whole class instruction** **Independent work** **A Assessment**

For a complete guide to selection support, including support for Advanced students, see the Overview of Resources in the frontmatter.

• from *Jane Eyre*

FROM JANE EYRE

Charlotte Brontë

CHAPTER 6

The next day commenced as before, getting up and dressing by rushlight; but this morning we were obliged to dispense with the ceremony of washing; the water in the pitchers was frozen. A change had taken place in the weather the preceding evening, and a keen northeast wind, whistling through the crevices of our bedroom windows all night long, had made us shiver in our beds, and turned the contents of the ewers to ice.

Before the long hour and a half of prayers and Bible reading was over, I felt ready to perish with cold. Breakfast time came at last, and this morning the porridge was not burnt; the quality was eatable, the quantity small; how small my portion seemed! I wished it had been doubled.

Reading Strategy
Analyzing an Author's Assumptions Which details suggest Brontë thinks schools like Lowood are in need of reform?

RESOURCES FOR:

- L1 Special-Needs Students
- L2 Below-Level Students (Tier 2)
- L3 On-Level Students (Tier 1)
- L4 Advanced Students (Tier 1)
- EL English Learners
- All All Students

Vocabulary/Fluency/Prior Knowledge

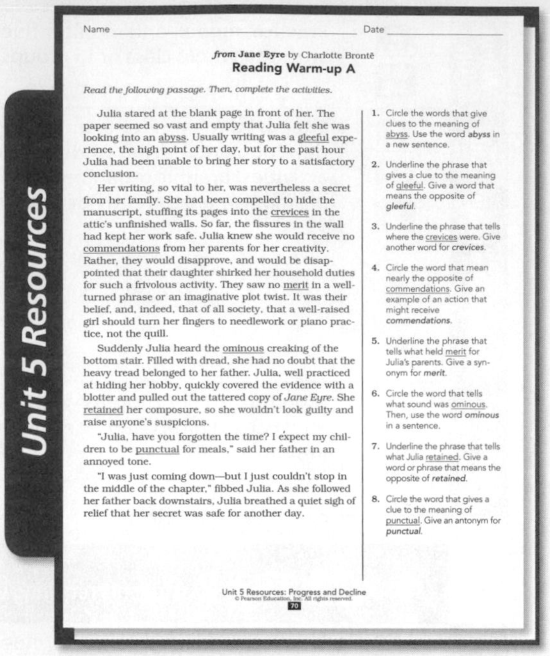
Unit 5 Resources

Name ______________________ Date ______________

from **Jane Eyre** by Charlotte Brontë

Reading Warm-up A

Read the following passage. Then, complete the activities.

Julia stared at the blank page in front of her. The paper seemed so vast and empty that Julia felt she was looking into an abyss. Usually writing was a gleeful experience, the high point of her day, but for the past hour Julia had been unable to bring her story to a satisfactory conclusion.

Her writing, so vital to her, was nevertheless a secret from her family. She had been compelled to hide the manuscript, stuffing its pages into the crevices in the attic's unfinished walls. So far, the fissures in the wall had kept her work safe. Julia knew she would receive no commendations from her parents for her creativity. Rather, they would disapprove, and would be disappointed that their daughter shirked her household duties for such a frivolous activity. They saw no merit in a well-turned phrase or an imaginative plot twist. It was their belief, and, indeed, that of all society, that a well-raised girl should turn her fingers to needlework or piano practice, not the quill.

Suddenly Julia heard the ominous creaking of the bottom stair. Filled with dread, she had no doubt that the heavy tread belonged to her father. Julia, well practiced at hiding her hobby, quickly covered the evidence with a blotter and pulled out the tattered copy of *Jane Eyre*. She retained her composure, so she wouldn't look guilty and raise anyone's suspicions.

"Julia, have you forgotten the time? I expect my children to be punctual for meals," said her father in an annoyed tone.

"I was just coming down—but I just couldn't stop in the middle of the chapter," fibbed Julia. As she followed her father back downstairs, Julia breathed a quiet sigh of relief that her secret was safe for another day.

1. Circle the words that give clues to the meaning of abyss. Use the word *abyss* in a new sentence.
2. Underline the phrase that gives a clue to the meaning of gleeful. Give a word that means the opposite of *gleeful*.
3. Underline the phrase that tells where the crevices were. Give another word for *crevices*.
4. Circle the word that mean nearly the opposite of commendations. Give an example of an action that might receive *commendations*.
5. Underline the phrase that tells what held merit for Julia's parents. Give a synonym for *merit*.
6. Circle the word that tells what sound was ominous. Then, use the word *ominous* in a sentence.
7. Underline the phrase that tells what Julia retained. Give a word or phrase that means the opposite of *retained*.
8. Circle the word that gives a clue to the meaning of punctual. Give an antonym for *punctual*.

Unit 5 Resources: Progress and Decline
© Pearson Education, Inc. All rights reserved.
70

EL L1 L2 **Reading Warm-ups A and B,** pp. 70–71

Also available for these selections:

EL L1 L2 **Vocabulary Warm-ups A and B,** pp. 68–69

All **Vocabulary Builder,** p. 74

Reader's Notebooks

Pre- and postreading pages for these selections, as well as the excerpt from *Jane Eyre,* appear in an interactive format in the *Reader's Notebooks.* Each *Notebook* is differentiated for a different group of learners.
The selections in the Adapted and English Learner's versions are abridged.

L2 L3 ***Reader's Notebook***

L1 ***Reader's Notebook: Adapted Version***

EL ***Reader's Notebook: English Learner's Version***

EL ***Reader's Notebook: Spanish Version***

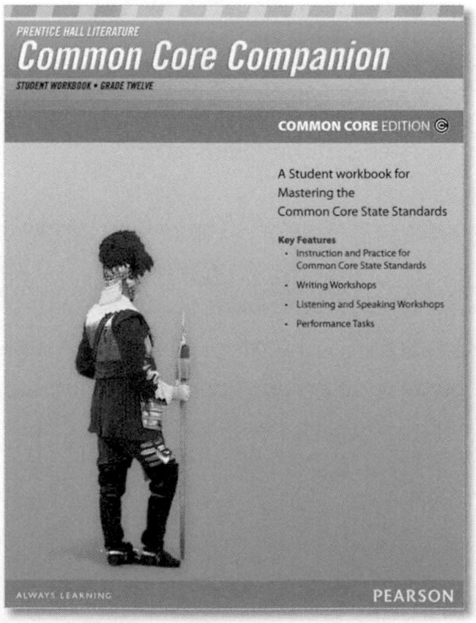

Common Core Companion

Additional instruction and practice for each Common Core State Standard

Selection Support

Graphic Organizer Transparencies

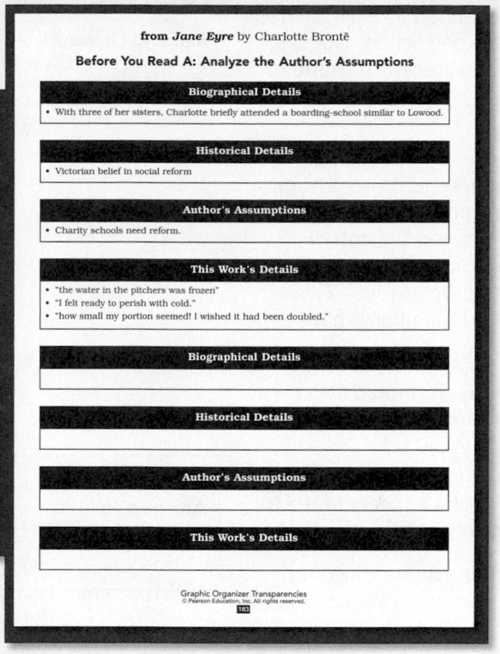

from ***Jane Eyre*** by Charlotte Brontë

Before You Read A: Analyze the Author's Assumptions

Biographical Details
• With three of her sisters, Charlotte briefly attended a boarding-school similar to Lowood.

Historical Details
• Victorian belief in social reform

Author's Assumptions
• Charity schools need reform.

This Work's Details
• "the water in the pitchers was frozen" • "I felt ready to perish with cold." • "how small my portion seemed! I wished it had been doubled."

Biographical Details

Historical Details

Author's Assumptions

This Work's Details

Graphic Organizer Transparencies
© Pearson Education, Inc. All rights reserved.
183

EL L1 L2 **Literary Analysis: Graphic Organizer A** (partially filled in), p. 185

Also available for these selections:

EL L3 **Literary Analysis: Graphic Organizer B**, p. 186

EL L1 L2 **Reading Graphic Organizer A**, p. 183

EL L3 **Reading: Graphic Organizer B**, p. 184

Skills Development/Extension

Unit 5 Resources

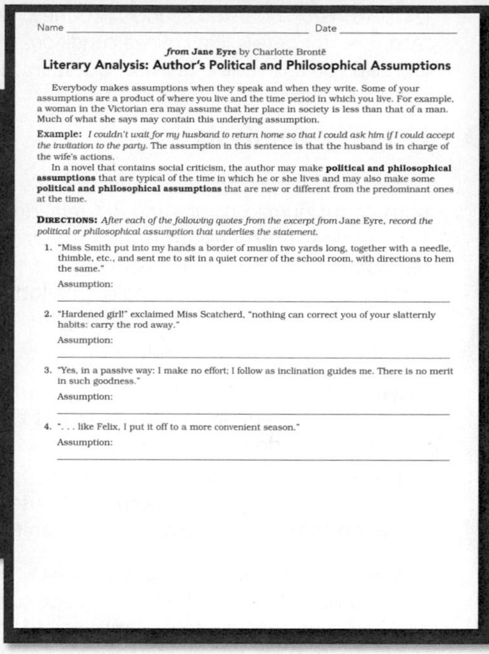

Name ______________ Date ______________

***from* Jane Eyre** by Charlotte Brontë

Literary Analysis: Author's Political and Philosophical Assumptions

Everybody makes assumptions when they speak and when they write. Some of your assumptions are a product of where you live and the time period in which you live. For example, a woman in the Victorian era may assume that her place in society is less than that of a man. Much of what she says may contain this underlying assumption.

Example: *I couldn't wait for my husband to return home so that I could ask him if I could accept the invitation to the party.* The assumption in this sentence is that the husband is in charge of the wife's actions.

In a novel that contains social criticism, the author may make **political and philosophical assumptions** that are typical of the time in which he or she lives and may also make some **political and philosophical assumptions** that are new or different from the predominant ones at the time.

Directions: *After each of the following quotes from the excerpt from* Jane Eyre, *record the political or philosophical assumption that underlies the statement.*

1. "Miss Smith put into my hands a border of muslin two yards long, together with a needle, thimble, etc., and sent me to sit in a quiet corner of the school room, with directions to hem the same."
   Assumption: ______________
2. "Hardened girl!" exclaimed Miss Scatcherd, "nothing can correct you of your slatternly habits: carry the rod away."
   Assumption: ______________
3. "Yes, in a passive way: I make no effort; I follow as inclination guides me. There is no merit in such goodness."
   Assumption: ______________
4. ". . . like Felix, I put it off to a more convenient season."
   Assumption: ______________

All **Literary Analysis: Philosophical Assumptions,** p. 72

Also available for these selections:

All **Reading: Analyze an Author's Assumptions,** p. 73

EL L3 L4 **Support for Writing,** p. 75

L4 **Enrichment,** p. 76

Assessment

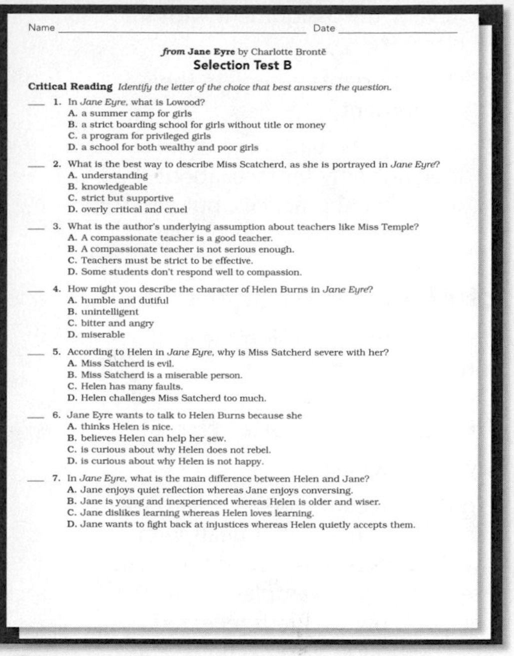

Name ______________ Date ______________

***from* Jane Eyre** by Charlotte Brontë

Selection Test B

Critical Reading *Identify the letter of the choice that best answers the question.*

___ 1. In *Jane Eyre*, what is Lowood?
A. a summer camp for girls
B. a strict boarding school for girls without title or money
C. a program for privileged girls
D. a school for both wealthy and poor girls

___ 2. What is the best way to describe Miss Scatcherd, as she is portrayed in *Jane Eyre*?
A. understanding
B. knowledgeable
C. strict but supportive
D. overly critical and cruel

___ 3. What is the author's underlying assumption about teachers like Miss Temple?
A. A compassionate teacher is a good teacher.
B. A compassionate teacher is not serious enough.
C. Teachers must be strict to be effective.
D. Some students don't respond well to compassion.

___ 4. How might you describe the character of Helen Burns in *Jane Eyre*?
A. humble and dutiful
B. unintelligent
C. bitter and angry
D. miserable

___ 5. According to Helen in *Jane Eyre*, why is Miss Satcherd severe with her?
A. Miss Satcherd is evil.
B. Miss Satcherd is a miserable person.
C. Helen has many faults.
D. Helen challenges Miss Satcherd too much.

___ 6. Jane Eyre wants to talk to Helen Burns because she
A. thinks Helen is nice.
B. believes Helen can help her sew.
C. is curious about why Helen does not rebel.
D. is curious about why Helen is not happy.

___ 7. In *Jane Eyre*, what is the main difference between Helen and Jane?
A. Jane enjoys quiet reflection whereas Jane enjoys conversing.
B. Jane is young and inexperienced whereas Helen is older and wiser.
C. Jane dislikes learning whereas Helen loves learning.
D. Jane wants to fight back at injustices whereas Helen quietly accepts them.

EL L3 L4 **Selection Test B,** pp. 83–85

Also available for these selections:

EL L1 L2 **Selection Test A,** pp. 80–82

L3 L4 **Open-Book Test,** pp. 77–79

PHLit Online!
www.PHLitOnline.com

Online Resources: All print materials are also available online.

- complete narrated selection text
- a thematically related video with writing prompt
- an interactive graphic organizer
- highlighting feature
- access to all student print resources, adapted to individual student needs
- Spanish and English summaries
- adapted selection translations in Spanish

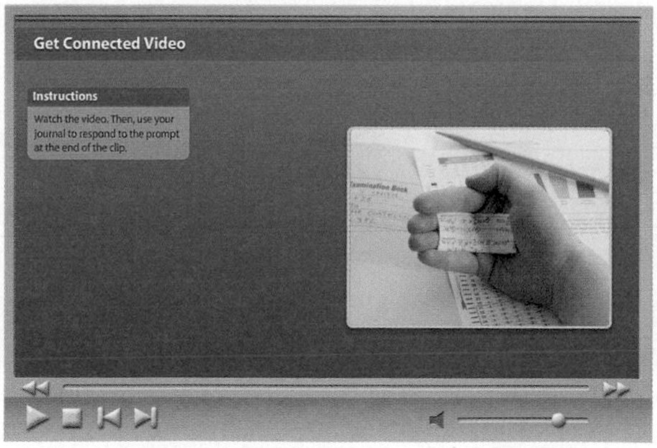

Get Connected! (thematic video with writing prompt)

Also available:

Background Video
All videos are available in Spanish.

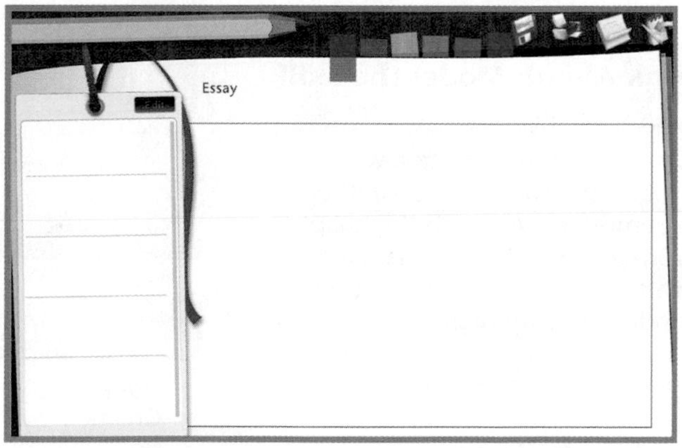

Writer's Journal (with graphics feature)

Also available:

Vocabulary Central (tools and activities and songs for studying vocabulary)

PRETEACH

❶ Connecting to the Essential Question

1. Review the assignment with the class.
2. Have students complete the assignment.
3. As students read, have them look not only for facts about the educational practices, but also for how Brontë feels about them.

❷ Literary Analysis

Introduce the skill using the instruction on the student page.

Think Aloud: Model the Skill

Say to students:

In this selection, we are going to focus on a novel that deals with social criticism. As I read this chapter, I look for examples where the author's own voice is reflected in Jane's thoughts and actions. For example, Jane's comments about how she would react to Miss Scatcherd's cruel treatment seem to reflect how the author feels about the treatment of girls at the boarding school.

❸ Reading Strategy

1. Introduce the skill using the instruction on the student page.
2. Give students a **Reading Strategy Graphic Organizer B,** page 184 in ***Graphic Organizer Transparencies,*** to fill out as they read.

Think Aloud: Model the Skill

Say to students:

One way to respond to a work of literature is to analyze an author's assumptions. As I read this chapter from *Jane Eyre,* I think that Jane feels all people should be treated kindly and with dignity. I think this reflects the author's assumption of equality of poor and rich.

❹ Vocabulary

1. Pronounce each word, giving its definition, and have students say it aloud.
2. For more guidance, see the *Classroom Strategies and Teaching Routines* card for introducing vocabulary.

Before You Read from *Jane Eyre*

❶ **Connecting to the Essential Question** In *Jane Eyre*, Charlotte Brontë criticizes harsh boarding schools like the one she attended as a girl. As you read, look for details that criticize conditions at the Lowood School. Doing so will help you answer the Essential Question: **How does literature shape or reflect society?**

Common Core State Standards

Reading Literature
3. Analyze the impact of the author's choices regarding how to develop and relate elements of a story or drama.

❷ Literary Analysis

Works of fiction often reflect the author's philosophy—his or her assumptions about human nature and our relationships to each other and society. Such **philosophical assumptions** may influence the way the author develops and relates the elements of the story, including characters, settings, and events. For example, Charlotte Brontë develops Jane Eyre's character by contrasting the reactions that Jane and Helen Burns have to their harsh treatment at the Lowood School:

> **Jane:** "When we are struck at without a reason, we should strike back again very hard. . . . so hard as to teach the person who struck us never to do it again."
>
> **Helen:** ". . . Love your enemies; bless them that curse you; do good to them that hate you and despitefully use you. . . . Life appears to me to be too short to be spent in nursing animosity or registering wrongs."

When characters' philosophies conflict, the author may be criticizing one and accepting the other or may see some merit in both. As you read, consider the philosophical assumptions that drive Brontë's narrative.

❸ Reading Strategy

Preparing to Read Complex Texts To **analyze the author's assumptions,** apply information you have about the author and time period to details in the selection itself. For example, if you consider the novel's presentation of the Lowood School along with the strong Victorian belief in social reform and Charlotte Brontë's experience, you can better understand the assumptions the author makes about such schools. As you read, use a chart like the one shown to help you analyze the author's assumptions.

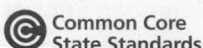

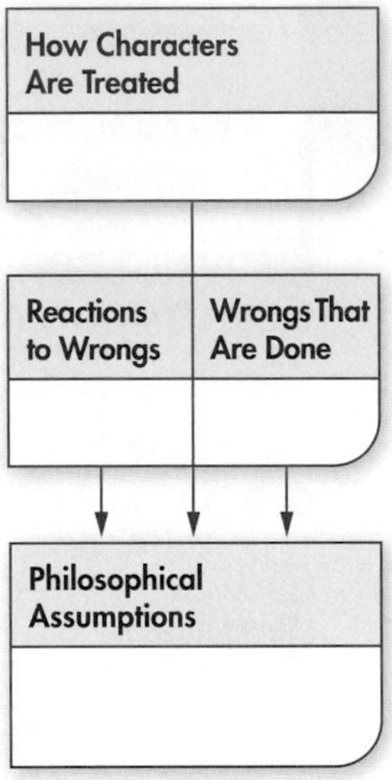

❹ Vocabulary

obscure (əb skyŏŏr´) *adj.* not easily seen; not generally known (p. 1031)

comprised (kəm prīzd´) *v.* consisted of; included (p. 1031)

sundry (sun´ drē) *adj.* various, miscellaneous (p. 1031)

tumult (to͞o´ mult) *n.* noise caused by a crowd (p. 1032)

truculent (truk´ yə lənt) *adj.* cruel; fierce (p. 1036)

PHLit Online! www.PHLitOnline.com

Vocabulary Development

Vocabulary Knowledge Rating

Create a **Vocabulary Knowledge Rating Chart** (***Professional Development Guidebook,*** p. 33) for the vocabulary words on the student page. Give each student a copy of the chart with the words on it. Read the words aloud, and have students mark their ratings in the Before Reading column. Urge students to attend to these words as they read and discuss the selection.

In order to gauge how much instruction you need to provide, tally how many students are confident in their knowledge of each word. As students read, point out the words and their context.

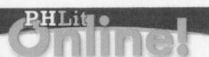

PHLit Online! **Vocabulary Central,** featuring tools and activities for studying vocabulary, is available online at **www.PHLitOnline.com.**

❺ # Charlotte Brontë

(1816–1855)

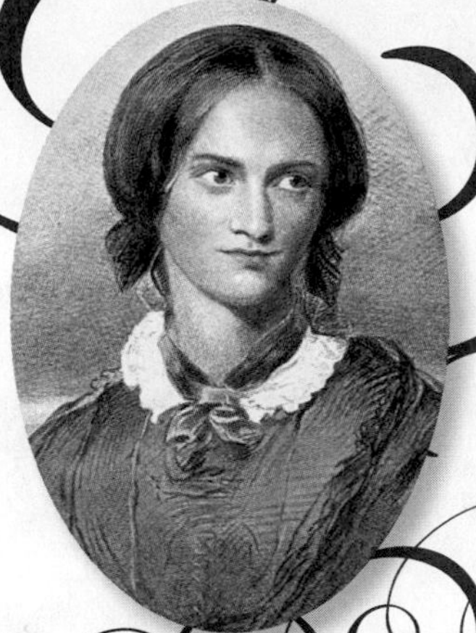

Author of *Jane Eyre*

Charlotte Brontë was part of a renowned literary family: Her sisters Anne and Emily were also writers. Their father, an Anglican clergyman, moved his family to the moors in Yorkshire in 1820, and the children were educated largely at home. Raised without their mother, who had died in 1821, the sisters, together with their brother Branwell, led a rich fantasy life that nurtured their artistic development.

Early Failure With three of her sisters, Charlotte briefly attended a boarding school. Her experiences there provided material for the critical descriptions of boarding-school life at Lowood in *Jane Eyre*. Charlotte spent several years as a teacher, first of her own siblings and then at another school that she herself had briefly attended. She found this job difficult and unappealing, and in 1844 attempted to open her own school near her family home. The school's failure was quick and definite: No pupils enrolled.

Success In 1846, the three sisters published a volume of poems under the pseudonyms Currer, Ellis, and Acton Bell, but the book had little success. Charlotte had also written a novel, *The Professor*, but the book failed to find a publisher. Charlotte persevered, however, and when *Jane Eyre* was published in 1847, it met with immediate popular success.

Personal Struggle The final years of Charlotte Brontë's life were clouded by tragedy. Her brother died in 1848, and Emily and Anne died soon after. Despite her loneliness, Charlotte found the strength to complete the novels *Shirley* (1849) and *Villette* (1853). She married Arthur Bell Nicholls, her father's curate, and died about nine months later.

Daily Bellringer

For each class during which you will teach this selection, have students complete one of the five activities for the appropriate week in the ***Daily Bellringer Activities*** booklet.

Multidraft Reading

To assist struggling readers and to enhance reading for all, assign the text in chunks, as warranted by length, and apply multidraft reading protocols. For each reading, have students set the purpose indicated:

- **First reading**—identifying key ideas and details and answering any Reading Checks.
- **Second reading**—analyzing craft and structure and responding to the side-column prompts.
- **Third reading**—integrating knowledge and ideas, connecting to other texts and the world, and answering the end-of-selection questions.

For more guidance, refer to the ***Classroom Strategies and Teaching Routines*** card on Multidraft Reading.

❺ Background

More About the Author

The loneliness caused by the deaths of Charlotte Brontë's siblings in her later years was abated by her friendship with Mrs. Gaskell, who would later be her celebrated biographer. Even after her identity was known, Brontë continued to use her pseudonym in her publications. Charlotte was the most admired of the three sisters, although she also received the most criticism for what Matthew Arnold called the "hunger, rebellion, and rage" of her mind.

PHLit Online!
www.PHLitOnline.com

Teaching From Technology

Preparing to Read

Go to **www.PHLitOnline.com** in class or in a lab and display the ***Get Connected!*** slide show for this selection. Have the class brainstorm responses to the slide show writing prompt, entering ideas in the interactive journal. Then, have students complete their written responses individually, in a lab or as homework

To build background, display the More About the Author feature.

Using the Interactive Text

Go to **www.PHLitOnline.com** and display the Enriched Online Student Edition. As the class reads the selection or listens to the narration, record answers to side-column prompts using the graphic organizers accessible on the interactive page. Alternatively, have students use the online edition individually, answering the prompts as they read.

❶ About the Selection

In this excerpt from Charlotte Brontë's *Jane Eyre,* Jane is at a boarding school named Lowood. Jane describes the harsh conditions, the lack of sufficient food for the girls, and the cruel way one of the teachers treats a girl named Helen Burns. Later, Jane speaks with Helen in private and is surprised by Helen's meek acceptance of the wrongs done to her. Brontë may not editorialize quite the way Dickens does, but many of her descriptions and dialogues represent criticisms of the conditions suffered by disadvantaged girls like Jane and Helen.

❷ Activating Prior Knowledge

Ask students to imagine that their school will be the site for filming a new television series on teenagers. Have them create the pilot show. Remind them that they can use the show to dramatize problems faced by teenagers. After they have sketched out an episode, explain that in the nineteenth century, novels were as popular as television series are today.

Concept Connector

Tell students that they will return to their responses after reading the selection.

❸ Reading Strategy

Analyzing an Author's Assumptions

1. Remind students that novels are not essays: When a novel offers social criticism, it must create believable and engaging fiction, not just preach. To do so, novelists create situations that clearly and naturally highlight the issues they wish to address.
2. Have a volunteer read aloud the first two paragraphs on page 1030.
3. **Ask** students the Reading Strategy question: Which details suggest Brontë thinks schools like Lowood are in need of reform? **Answer:** The rooms were so cold the water in the washing pitchers was frozen. Breakfast seemed routinely of poor quality and quantity.

EXEMPLAR TEXT

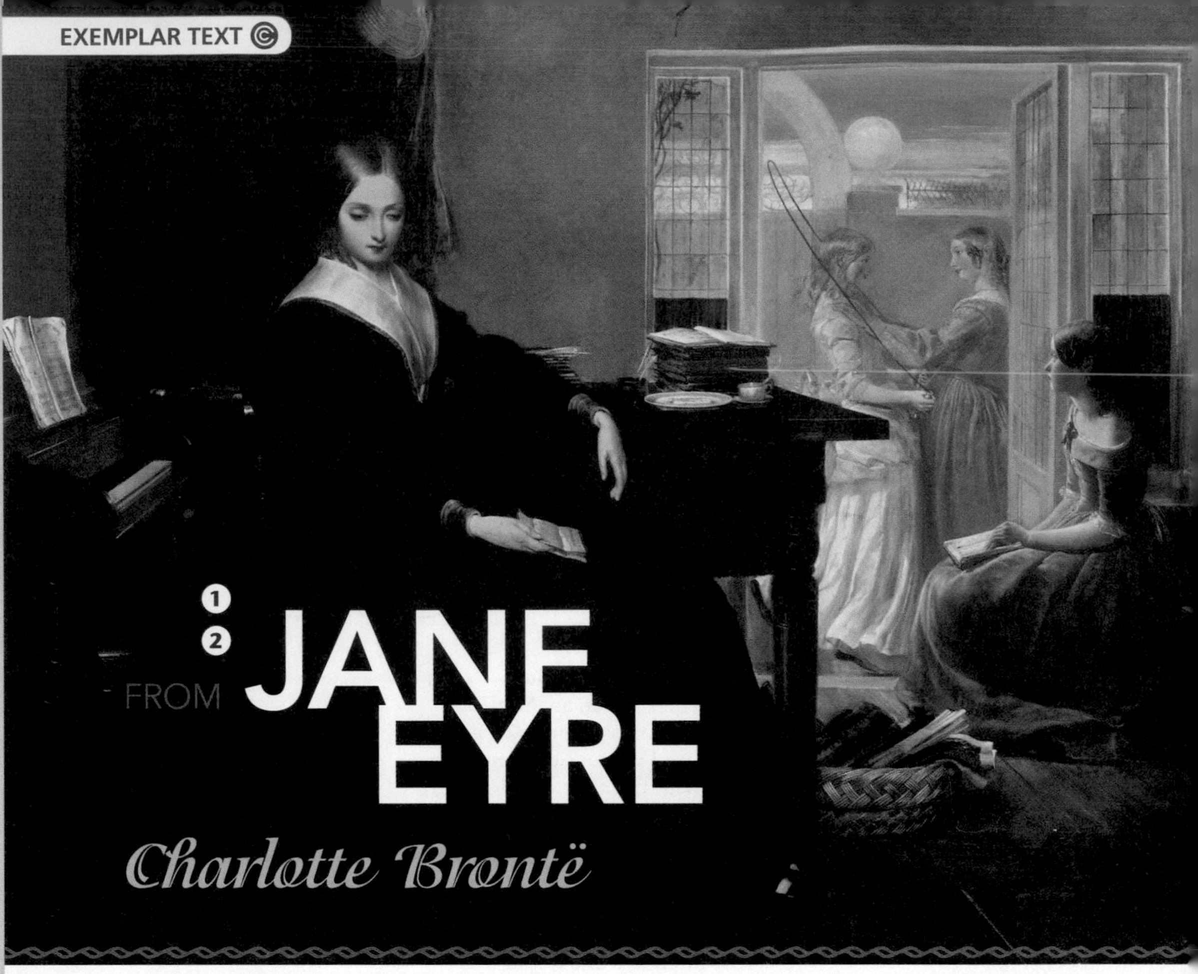

❶ ❷

FROM JANE EYRE

Charlotte Brontë

CHAPTER 6

The next day commenced as before, getting up and dressing by rushlight; but this morning we were obliged to dispense with the ceremony of washing: the water in the pitchers was frozen. A change had taken place in the weather the preceding evening, and a keen northeast wind, whistling through the crevices of our bedroom ❸ windows all night long, had made us shiver in our beds, and turned the contents of the ewers to ice.

Before the long hour and a half of prayers and Bible reading was over, I felt ready to perish with cold. Breakfast time came at last, and this morning the porridge was not burnt; the quality was eatable, the quantity small; how small my portion seemed! I wished it had been doubled.

Reading Strategy
Analyzing an Author's Assumptions Which details suggest Brontë thinks schools like Lowood are in need of reform?

Text Complexity Rubric

from Jane Eyre	
Qualitative Measures	
Context/ Knowledge Demands	Victorian novel; historical and cultural knowledge demands 1 ② 3 4 5
Structure/Language Conventionality and Clarity	Long sentences; above-level vocabulary 1 ② 3 4 5
Levels of Meaning/ Purpose/Concept Level	Accessible (education, reform) 1 2 ③ 4 5
Quantitative Measures	
Lexile/Text Length	930L / 2,852 words
Overall Complexity	**More accessible**

In the course of the day I was enrolled a member of the fourth class, and regular tasks and occupations were assigned to me: hitherto, I had only been a spectator of the proceedings at Lowood, I was now to become an actor therein. At first, being little accustomed to learn by heart, the lessons appeared to me both long and difficult: the frequent change from task to task, too, bewildered me; and I was glad, when, about three o'clock in the afternoon, Miss Smith put into my hands a border of muslin two yards long, together with needle, thimble, etc., and sent me to sit in a quiet corner of the school room, with directions to hem the same. At that hour most of the others were sewing likewise; but one class still stood round Miss Scatcherd's chair reading, and as all was quiet, the subject of their lessons could be heard, together with the manner in which each girl acquitted herself, and the animadversions or commendations of Miss Scatcherd on the performance. It was English history; among the readers, I observed my acquaintance of the verandah; at the commencement of the lesson, her place had been at the top of the class, but for some error of pronunciation or some inattention to stops, she was suddenly sent to the very bottom. Even in that **obscure** position, Miss Scatcherd continued to make her an object of constant notice: she was continually addressing to her such phrases as the following:—

"Burns" (such it seems was her name: the girls here, were all called by their surnames, as boys are elsewhere), "Burns, you are standing on the side of your shoe, turn your toes out immediately." "Burns, you poke your chin most unpleasantly, draw it in." "Burns, I insist on your holding your head up: I will not have you before me in that attitude," etc. etc.

A chapter having been read through twice, the books were closed and the girls examined. The lesson had **comprised** part of the reign of Charles I, and there were **sundry** questions about tonnage and poundage, and ship-money, which most of them appeared unable to answer; still, every little difficulty was solved instantly when it reached Burns: her memory seemed to have retained the substance of the whole lesson, and she was ready with answers on every point. I kept expecting that Miss Scatcherd would praise her attention; but, instead of that, she suddenly cried out:—

"You dirty, disagreeable girl! you have never cleaned your nails this morning!"

Burns made no answer: I wondered at her silence.

"Why," thought I, "does she not explain that she could neither clean her nails nor wash her face, as the water was frozen?"

My attention was now called off by Miss Smith, desiring me to hold a skein of thread: while she was winding it, she talked to me from time to time, asking whether I had ever been at school before, whether I could mark, stitch, knit, etc.; till she dismissed me, I could not pursue my observations on Miss Scatcherd's movements. When I returned to my seat, that lady was just delivering an order, of which I did not catch the import; but Burns immediately left the class, and

4 ◀ Critical Viewing
This picture depicts a governess and her students. In what ways is the situation of these students similar to and different from Jane's? **[Compare and Contrast]**

Vocabulary
obscure (əb skyoor′) *adj.* not easily seen; not generally known

comprised (kəm prīzd′) *v.* consisted of; included

sundry (sun′ drē) adj. various, miscellaneous

5 Reading Check
How has the narrator's role at Lowood changed?

4 Critical Viewing

Possible responses: A similarity between the young women in this painting and the young women in this selection include the fact that older women are teaching younger women. Students might suggest that one difference between the painting and the selection is that the young women in this painting seem to be more well-situated than the girls in the selection.

5 Reading Check

Answer: The narrator now participates in the school day as a student, no longer as a spectator.

Text Complexity: Reader and Task Suggestions

from Jane Eyre	
Preparing to Read the Text • Explain that in this excerpt from *Jane Eyre,* Jane is at a girls' school with harsh conditions similar to those that Charlotte Brontë and her sisters encountered. Remind students that many authors write about social problems—including bad schools—in the hopes of effecting reform. • Discuss the importance of realism in portraying social problems in order to effect change. • Guide students to use Multidraft Reading strategies (TE p. 1029).	**Leveled Tasks** ***Levels of Meanings*** If students will have difficulty with Brontë's meaning, have them focus on the events that unfold as well as characters' situations and relationships. Then, have students consider how Brontë expects readers to react to those events and characters. Finally, have students determine the main points about society that Brontë is making. ***Evaluating*** If students will not have great difficulty with the meaning, have them evaluate the effectiveness with which Brontë portrays the Lowood school and the students and teachers there.

6 Literary Analysis

Author's Philosophical Assumptions

1. Remind students to read the passage for evidence of social commentary or criticism. Have students focus their attention on the details provided about Miss Scatcherd and Burns.
2. Then, **ask** students the Literary Analysis question: What does Miss Scatcherd's reaction suggest about Brontë's assumptions regarding an ideal teacher–student relationship?
   Answer: Brontë's assumptions about the ideal teacher–student relationship are revealed in what the relationship between Miss Scatcherd's and Helen Burns's relationship is *not.*
3. Explain to students that here Brontë is making a comment about the abuse of power. Teachers had total control over their students in Victorian times, as is evident by Miss Scatcherd's ability to punish Helen Burns with impunity.

Spiral Review

Point of View

1. Remind students that they studied point of view in an earlier lesson.
2. **Ask** students the Spiral Review question.
   Possible response: The first-person point of view strengthens readers' connection with Jane because it gives readers insight into her thoughts and feelings. In this passage specifically, the details provide a context for connecting to readers' experiences that evoke feelings similar to the ones Jane describes.

going into the small inner room where the books were kept, returned in half a minute, carrying in her hand a bundle of twigs tied together at one end. This ominous tool she presented to Miss Scatcherd with a respectful courtesy; then she quietly, and without being told, unloosed her pinafore, and the teacher instantly and sharply inflicted on her neck a dozen strokes with the bunch of twigs. Not a tear rose to Burns's eye; and, while I paused from my sewing, because my fingers quivered at this spectacle with a sentiment of unavailing and impotent anger, not a feature of her pensive face altered its ordinary expression.

Literary Analysis **Author's Philosophical Assumptions** What does Miss Scatcherd's reaction suggest about Brontë's assumptions regarding an ideal teacher-student relationship?

6 "Hardened girl!" exclaimed Miss Scatcherd, "nothing can correct you of your slatternly habits: carry the rod away."

Burns obeyed: I looked at her narrowly as she emerged from the book closet; she was just putting back her handkerchief into her pocket, and the trace of a tear glistened on her thin cheek.

Spiral Review **Point of View** How does the novel's first-person narration affect the reader's connection with Jane?

The play-hour in the evening I thought the pleasantest fraction of the day at Lowood: the bit of bread, the draught of coffee swallowed at five o'clock had revived vitality, if it had not satisfied hunger; the long restraint of the day was slackened; the school room felt warmer than in the morning: its fires being allowed to burn a little more brightly to supply, in some measure, the place of candles, not yet introduced; the ruddy gloaming,[1] the licensed uproar, the confusion of many voices gave one a welcome sense of liberty.

On the evening of the day on which I had seen Miss Scatcherd flog her pupil, Burns, I wandered as usual among the forms and tables and laughing groups without a companion, yet not feeling lonely: when I passed the windows, I now and then lifted a blind and looked out; it snowed fast, a drift was already forming against the lower panes; putting my ear close to the window, I could distinguish from the gleeful **tumult** within, the disconsolate moan of the wind outside.

Vocabulary
tumult (to͞o′ mult) *n.* noise caused by a crowd

Probably, if I had lately left a good home and kind parents, this would have been the hour when I should most keenly have regretted the separation: that wind would then have saddened my heart; this obscure chaos would have disturbed my peace: as it was I derived from both a strange excitement, and reckless and feverish, I wished the wind to howl more wildly, the gloom to deepen to darkness, and the confusion to rise to clamor.

Jumping over forms, and creeping under tables, I made my way to one of the fire-places: there, kneeling by the high wire fender, I found Burns, absorbed, silent, abstracted from all round her by the companionship of a book, which she read by the dim glare of the embers.

"Is it still 'Rasselas'?"[2] I asked, coming behind her.

"Yes," she said, "and I have just finished it."

And in five minutes more she shut it up. I was glad of this.

1. **ruddy gloaming** glowing twilight; the sunset.
2. **Rasselas** *The History of Rasselas, Prince of Abyssinia*, a moralizing novel by Samuel Johnson.

Think Aloud

Vocabulary: Using Context

Direct students' attention to the word *slatternly* on this page. Use the following "think aloud" to model the skill of using context to infer the meaning of the word. Say to students:

I may not know the meaning of the word *slatternly.* When I read the sentence, however, I realize that Miss Scatcherd is using *slatternly* as an insult. We know that Miss Scatcherd constantly criticizes and berates Burns for all her perceived faults. The phrases that follow the context tells us that *slatternly* habits are bad so I think *slatternly* must mean "untidy and sloppy."

"HARDENED GIRL!"
exclaimed Miss Scatcherd . . .

"Now," thought I, "I can perhaps get her to talk." I sat down by her on the floor.

"What is your name besides Burns?"

"Helen."

"Do you come a long way from here?"

"I come from a place further north; quite on the borders of Scotland."

"Will you ever go back?"

"I hope so; but nobody can be sure of the future."

"You must wish to leave Lowood?"

"No: why should I? I was sent to Lowood to get an education; and it would be of no use going away until I have attained that object."

"But that teacher, Miss Scatcherd, is so cruel to you?"

"Cruel? Not at all! She is severe: she dislikes my faults."

"And if I were in your place I should dislike her: I should resist her; if she struck me with that rod, I should get it from her hand; I should break it under her nose."

7 ▲ **Critical Viewing**

How well does this still from a movie version of *Jane Eyre* match your vision of Jane and Burns? Explain. **[Evaluate]**

8 **Reading Check**

How does Burns react to her beating by Miss Scatcherd?

7 Critical Viewing

Answer: Students may say that the actresses match their vision of Burns and Jane; the two girls appear to be close friends.

8 Reading Check

Answer: Burns feels that Miss Scatcherd is severe, but not cruel. She accepts the mistreatment as part of her education.

Differentiated Instruction for Universal Access

Support for Less Proficient Readers

Have students read from *Jane Eyre* with teacher guidance. As students read, ask them to picture what the words describe. If students seem to be having difficulty decoding the meaning of the words, consider playing the ***Hear It!* Audio CD** and asking them to read along with the selection.

Enrichment for Advanced Readers

Remind students that *Jane Eyre* examines institutions and attitudes of the early nineteenth century. Have students consider a contemporary social problem or issue. Then have students write short stories that examine their social issues or problems in contemporary society. Encourage students to share their stories with their classmates.

❾ Critical Thinking

Clarify

1. Have two student volunteers read aloud the bracketed dialogue. Then, have students summarize the exchange.
2. Point out Helen's comment at the end of the third paragraph on page 1034: "It is weak and silly to say you *cannot bear* what it is your fate to be required to bear." Have students clarify the meaning of her comment. What do students think Brontë is saying here? **Possible response:** Helen means that, if you are faced with something that you must bear, saying you cannot bear it is simply refusing to face what you cannot avoid.
3. **Ask** students: How does Brontë address both individual ethics and social problems in this dialogue? **Answer:** Brontë's description criticizes the cruelty and hypocrisy of schools in her day, and she shows how Helen's patient, forgiving attitude embodies the ideals of charity and mercy more than does the behavior of the instructors of the school.

❿ Literary Analysis

Author's Philosophical Assumptions

1. Direct students' attention to the fourth paragraph on page 1034, beginning with "I heard her with wonder..."
2. **Ask** students the Literary Analysis question: What do Jane's thoughts suggest about the author's assumptions regarding the relative importance of obedience and independence? **Possible response:** Students might offer that Jane cannot comprehend Helen's acquiescence and forbearance. She thinks, perhaps, Helen is right, and herself wrong, in her doctrine of endurance. Jane's thoughts suggest Brontë's assumption that the more difficult, but more virtuous, road is one of forbearance and endurance.

"Probably you would do nothing of the sort: but if you did, Mr. Brocklehurst would expel you from the school; that would be a great grief to your relations. It is far better to endure patiently a smart which nobody feels but yourself, than to commit a hasty action whose evil consequences will extend to all connected with you—and, besides, the Bible bids us return good for evil."

"But then it seems disgraceful to be flogged, and to be sent to stand in the middle of a room full of people; and you are such a great girl: I am far younger than you, and I could not bear it."

❾ "Yet it would be your duty to bear it, if you could not avoid it: it is weak and silly to say you *cannot bear* what it is your fate to be required to bear."

Literary Analysis
Author's Philosophical Assumptions What do Jane's thoughts suggest about the author's assumptions regarding the relative importance of obedience and independence?

❿ I heard her with wonder: I could not comprehend this doctrine of endurance; and still less could I understand or sympathize with the forbearance she expressed for her chastiser. Still I felt that Helen Burns considered things by a light invisible to my eyes. I suspected she might be right and I wrong; but I would not ponder the matter deeply: like Felix,[3] I put it off to a more convenient season.

"You say you have faults, Helen: what are they? To me you seem very good."

"Then learn from me, not to judge by appearances: I am, as Miss Scatcherd said, slatternly; I seldom put, and never keep, things in order; I am careless; I forget rules; I read when I should learn my lessons; I have no method; and sometimes I say, like you, I cannot *bear* to be subjected to systematic arrangements. This is all very provoking to Miss Scatcherd, who is naturally neat, punctual, and particular."

"And cross and cruel," I added; but Helen Burns would not admit my addition: she kept silence.

"Is Miss Temple as severe to you as Miss Scatcherd?"

At the utterance of Miss Temple's name, a soft smile flitted over her grave face.

"Miss Temple is full of goodness; it pains her to be severe to anyone, even the worst in the school: she sees my errors, and tells me of them gently; and, if I do anything worthy of praise, she gives me my meed liberally. One strong proof of my wretchedly defective nature is

3. **Felix** in the Bible, governor of Judea who released Paul from prison and deferred his trial until a more "convenient season" (Acts 24:25).

". . . it is weak and silly to say you
CANNOT BEAR
what it is your fate to be required to bear."

Vocabulary Development

Vocabulary Knowledge Rating
When students have completed reading and discussing the selection, have them take out their **Vocabulary Knowledge Rating Charts** for the story. Read the words aloud and have students rate their knowledge of words again in the After Reading column. Clarify any words that are still problematic. Have students write their own definitions and example or sentence in the appropriate column. Then, have students complete the Vocabulary Practice at the end of the selection. Encourage students to use the words in further discussion and written work about the selection. Remind them that they will be accountable for these words on the **Selection Test**, ***Unit 5 Resources,*** pages 80–82 or 83–85.

that even her expostulations, so mild, so rational, have not influence to cure me of my faults; and even her praise, though I value it most highly, cannot stimulate me to continued care and foresight."

"That is curious," said I: "it is so easy to be careful."

"For *you* I have no doubt it is. I observed you in your class this morning, and saw you were closely attentive: your thoughts never seemed to wander while Miss Miller explained the lesson and questioned you. Now, mine continually rove away: when I should be listening to Miss Scatcherd, and collecting all she says with assiduity,[4] often I lose the very sound of her voice; I fall into a sort of dream. Sometimes I think I am in Northumberland, and that the noises I hear round me are the bubbling of a little brook which runs through Deepden, near our house;—then, when it comes to my turn to reply, I have to be wakened; and, having heard nothing of what was read for listening to the visionary brook, I have no answer ready."

"Yet how well you replied this afternoon."

11 "It was mere chance: the subject on which we had been reading had interested me. This afternoon, instead of dreaming of Deepden, I was wondering how a man who wished to do right could act so unjustly and unwisely as Charles the First sometimes did; and I thought what a pity it was that, with his integrity and conscientiousness, he could see no farther than the prerogatives of the crown. If he had but been able to look to a distance, and see how what they call the spirit of the age was tending! Still, I like Charles—I respect him—I pity him, poor murdered king! Yes, his enemies were the worst: they shed blood they had no right to shed. How dared they kill him!"

Helen was talking to herself now: she had forgotten I could not very well understand her—that I was ignorant, or nearly so, of the subject she discussed. I recalled her to my level.

"And when Miss Temple teaches you, do your thoughts wander then?"

"No, certainly, not often; because Miss Temple has generally something to say which is newer to me than my own reflections: her language is singularly agreeable to me, and the information she communicates is often just what I wished to gain."

"Well, then, with Miss Temple you are good?"

"Yes, in a passive way: I make no effort; I follow as inclination guides me. There is no merit in such goodness."

"A great deal: you are good to those who are good to you. It is all I ever desire to be. If people were always kind and obedient to those who are cruel and unjust, the wicked people would have it all their own way: they would never feel afraid, and so they would never alter, but would grow worse and worse. When we are struck at without a reason, we should strike back again very hard; I am sure we should—so hard as to teach the person who struck us never to do it again." 12

4. **assiduity** (as´ ə dyōō´ ə tē) *n.* constant care and attention; diligence.

Reading Strategy
Analyzing an Author's Assumptions To what extent is Brontë criticizing or supporting the ideas Helen shares about Charles the First? Explain.

Reading Check

What faults does Helen Burns attribute to herself?

11 Reading Strategy

Analyzing an Author's Assumptions

1. Direct students' attention to the paragraph beginning, "It was mere chance…"
2. **Ask** students the Reading Strategy question: To what extent is Brontë criticizing or supporting the ideas Helen shares about Charles the First?
   Answer: Students might suggest that Brontë herself is critical of Charles the First and his hunger for power. She seemed to view him in light of his humanity: he wanted to do right, but acted unjustly and unwisely.

12 Reading Check

Answer: Helen Burns claims she is slatternly, disordered, careless, forgetful, and not methodical.

Differentiated Instruction for Universal Access

Enrichment for Gifted/Talented Students

After students have read the scene between Jane and Helen in which the two discuss the differences between Miss Scatcherd and Miss Temple, have each write a diary entry from the point of view of Miss Scatcherd. In their entries, students should describe a typical day in the life of Scatcherd and should include information about how the instructor views her life, as well as her view on her students. Particularly creative entries might include dialogue between Miss Scatcherd and some of her pupils.

Enrichment for Advanced Readers

Have students write essays in which they compare the techniques of Miss Scatcherd in *Jane Eyre* with those of Mr. Gradgrind in *Hard Times*. Students should also examine in their essays how Brontë and Dickens might have created their characters as illustrations of some of the social ills of their era. Encourage students to brainstorm how these characters might have been received when these books were published.

⓭ Literary Analysis

Author's Philosophical Assumptions

1. Direct students' attention to the paragraph on page 1036 beginning, "She has been unkind to you, no doubt…"
2. Have a student volunteer read the paragraph aloud.
3. **Ask** students the Literary Analysis question: Does the author favor one girl's argument over the other's?
   Possible responses: Given the length of Helen's response to Jane, and the context in which she casts her response, students might suggest Brontë favors Helen's philosophy toward injustice over Jane's.
4. After students read page 1037, **ask** students: What is the larger context in which Helen sees herself?
   Answer: Helen believes that whatever struggle she endures in this life will fall away when "… only the spark of the spirit will remain…", and where "Eternity" will be "…a rest—a mighty home, not a terror and abyss."

"When we are struck at without a reason, we should

[redacted]TRIKE BACK A[redacted]AIN

very hard"

"You will change your mind, I hope, when you grow older: as yet you are but a little untaught girl."

"But I feel this, Helen: I must dislike those who, whatever I do to please them, persist in disliking me; I must resist those who punish me unjustly. It is as natural as that I should love those who show me affection, or submit to punishment when I feel it is deserved."

". . . Love your enemies; bless them that curse you; do good to them that hate you and despitefully use you."

"Then I should love Mrs. Reed, which I cannot do; I should bless her son John, which is impossible."

In her turn, Helen Burns asked me to explain; and I proceeded forthwith to pour out, in my way, the tale of my sufferings and resentments. Bitter and **truculent** when excited, I spoke as I felt, without reserve or softening.

Vocabulary
truculent (truk´ yə lənt) *adj.* cruel; fierce

Helen heard me patiently to the end: I expected she would then make a remark, but she said nothing.

"Well," I asked impatiently, "is not Mrs. Reed a hard-hearted, bad woman?"

⓭ Literary Analysis
Author's Philosophical Assumptions Does the author favor one girl's argument over the other's? Explain.

"She has been unkind to you, no doubt; because, you see, she dislikes your cast of character, as Miss Scatcherd does mine: but how minutely you remember all she has done and said to you! What a singularly deep impression her injustice seems to have made on your heart! No ill usage so brands its record on my feelings. Would you not be happier if you tried to forget her severity, together with the passionate emotions it excited? Life appears to me too short to be spent in nursing animosity or registering wrongs. We are, and must be, one and all, burdened with faults in this world: but the time will soon come when, I trust, we shall put them off in putting off our corruptible bodies; when debasement and sin will fall from us with this cumbrous frame of flesh, and only the spark of the spirit will remain,—the impalpable principle of life and thought, pure as when it left the Creator to inspire the creature: whence[5] it came it will return; perhaps again to be communicated to some being higher than man—perhaps to pass through gradations of glory, from the pale human soul to brighten to the seraph![6] Surely it will never, on

5. **whence** the place from which.

Concept Connector

Reading Strategy Graphic Organizer

Ask students to review the graphic organizers in which they have analyzed the author's assumptions. Then, have students share their organizers and compare.

Activating Prior Knowledge

Have students return to their responses to the Activating Prior Knowledge activity. Ask them to explain whether their thoughts have changed and, if so, how.

Writing About the Essential Question

Have students compare their responses to the prompt, completed before reading the selection, with their thoughts afterward. Have them work individually or in groups, writing or discussing their thoughts, to formulate new responses. Then, lead a class discussion, probing for what students have learned that confirms or invalidates their initial thoughts. Encourage students to cite specific textual details to support their responses.

the contrary, be suffered to degenerate from man to fiend? No; I cannot believe that: I hold another creed; which no one ever taught me, and which I seldom mention; but in which I delight, and to which I cling: for it extends hope to all: it makes Eternity a rest—a mighty home, not a terror and abyss. Besides, with this creed, I can so clearly distinguish between the criminal and his crime; I can so sincerely forgive the first while I abhor the last: with this creed revenge never worries my heart, degradation never too deeply disgusts me, injustice never crushes me too low: I live in calm, looking to the end."

Helen's head, always drooping, sank a little lower as she finished this sentence. I saw by her look she wished no longer to talk to me, but rather to converse with her own thoughts. She was not allowed much time for meditation: a monitor, a great rough girl, presently came up, exclaiming in a strong Cumberland accent—

"Helen Burns, if you don't go and put your drawer in order, and fold up your work this minute, I'll tell Miss Scatcherd to come and look at it!"

Helen sighed as her reverie fled, and getting up, obeyed the monitor without reply as without delay.

---

6. seraph angel of the highest order.

Critical Reading

Cite textual evidence to support your responses.

1. **Key Ideas and Details (a)** For what offense does Miss Scatcherd punish Helen Burns? **(b) Infer:** When punished, why does Helen make every effort to hold back tears?
2. **Key Ideas and Details (a)** Which teacher does Helen particularly like? **(b) Analyze:** Why does Helen find that there is "no merit" in being good in this teacher's class?
3. **Key Ideas and Details** Describe Jane's personality in a few sentences.
4. **Integration of Knowledge and Ideas (a) Compare and Contrast:** Compare Jane's and Helen's reactions to mistreatment. **(b) Make a Judgment:** Do you think each has something to teach the other? Explain.
5. **Integration of Knowledge and Ideas** Might Helen and Jane be seen as two sides of the author's personality? Why or why not?
6. **Integration of Knowledge and Ideas** How do you think Brontë would like to reform schools like Lowood? In your response, use at least two of these Essential Question words: *education, independence, leadership.* ***[Connecting to the Essential Question: How does literature shape or reflect society?]***

ASSESS

Answers

Before students respond, you may wish to have them write a brief objective summary of the selection. As they answer the questions below, remind them to support their answers with evidence from the text.

1. (a) She punishes Helen for untidiness. (b) Helen would think crying self-indulgent; she feels she must bear ill treatment without complaint.
2. (a) Helen particularly likes Miss Temple. (b) Helen says that it is easy to be good in Miss Temple's class, and for that reason, it is not a test of one's virtues.
3. Jane is independent, intelligent, and observant, and tends to be insubordinate.
4. (a) Jane feels that she "must resist those who punish [her] unjustly." Helen says that people should love their enemies and return good for evil. (b) **Possible response:** Most students will say that each should borrow from the other's point of view to avoid being overly naïve or overly resentful.
5. **Possible response:** Students might offer that Jane might represent the author's passion, and Helen her idealism.
6. In *Jane Eyre,* Brontë is clearly critiquing the *education* system in place for young girls and women. Brontë seems to believe that young women should have the chance to learn *independence* and *leadership,* instead of cowing to untrained instructors bent on imposing their own inconsequential wills.

Assessment Practice

Paired Passages (For more practice, see *All-in-One Workbook.*)

Many tests require students to compare and identify literary elements in two passages. The following sample item can teach students how to identify the tone of two passages. Have students reread Chapter 1 from *Hard Times,* pages 998–1004, and the first eight paragraphs of *Jane Eyre,* pages 1030–1031.

Which of the following statements best describes the tone of each passage?

A Both passages are sad yet hopeful.

B *Hard Times* is humorous; *Jane Eyre* is somber.

C Both passages are gloomy.

D *Hard Times* is satiric; *Jane Eyre* is dramatic.

Help students analyze the tone of each work. Choices ***A*** and ***C*** could describe *Jane Eyre,* but not *Hard Times. Hard Times* is satiric, but *Jane Eyre* is not particularly dramatic, so students should eliminate choice ***D.*** The correct answer is ***B***.

After You Read from *Jane Eyre*

Literary Analysis

1. Integration of Knowledge and Ideas **(a)** Use a chart like the one shown to compare and contrast the two philosophies espoused by Jane and Helen in this excerpt. **(b)** Which do you think best reflects the underlying **philosophical assumptions** that Brontë brings to this story? Explain.

Character's view	*of Miss Scatcherd's actions*	*of education*	→	Assumption

2. Integration of Knowledge and Ideas **(a)** Based on their behavior, what different teaching philosophies do Miss Temple and Miss Scatcherd follow? **(b)** How does the author seem to feel about each teacher's philosophy? Cite details from the selection to support your evaluation.

Common Core State Standards

Writing

2. Write informative/explanatory texts to examine and convey complex ideas, concepts, and information clearly and accurately through the effective selection, organization, and analysis of content.

Reading Strategy

3. **(a)** Begin to **analyze the author's assumptions** in this selection by identifying three details Brontë uses to describe the setting. **(b)** What assumptions about children and education do these details suggest?

4. Early Victorian society taught that women should be docile, domestic creatures with little concern for larger issues. Do Brontë's assumptions seem to agree with that view? Cite details to support your evaluation.

PERFORMANCE TASKS
Integrated Language Skills

Vocabulary Acquisition and Use

For each word, choose the letter of its synonym, and explain your choice.

1. tumult:	**(a)** ache	**(b)** cruelty	**(c)** satisfaction	**(d)** excitement
2. comprised:	**(a)** included	**(b)** suggested	**(c)** pried	**(d)** attached
3. truculent:	**(a)** forgetful	**(b)** ferocious	**(c)** driven	**(d)** peaceful
4. obscure:	**(a)** murky	**(b)** noisy	**(c)** arrogant	**(d)** attentive
5. sundry:	**(a)** shiny	**(b)** outdoor	**(c)** withered	**(d)** diverse

Writing

Informative Text Write the **school conduct report** that Miss Scatcherd might have written about Helen Burns. From the selection, infer Miss Scatcherd's feelings about Helen. Then, set up a formal report with the Lowood School heading, your name (Miss Scatcherd), a date at the top, and an evaluation section that includes grades and comments in categories such as schoolwork, personal hygiene, posture, and effort.

Answers

1. (a) Jane's view: Miss Scatcherd is cruel; education should allow for independent thinking; independent spirits should not be stifled. Helen's view: Miss Scatcherd is strict, but not cruel; education is important to acquire, through whatever means necessary; endure with stoicism. (b) Helen philosophically endures injustice. This seems to best reflect the author's philosophical assumptions—that submission and patience are admirable, and much harder than fighting for what one wants.
2. (a) Miss Scatcherd seems to approach children as though they are beasts to tame. Miss Temple seems to understand that her kindness opens them up to learn more. (b) The author seems to feel Miss Temple's approach is more appropriate, as shown to us through Jane's narration.
3. (a) The first setting is a cold bedroom—details include "a keen northeast wind," "water in the pitchers was frozen," and "shiver in our beds." (b) This immediately puts the reader in a position of sympathy to the poor children who are forced to live in such conditions. It serves as a criticism of the school.
4. There are docile creatures in the novel, but the protagonist is fiercely independent. This suggests that the author is more in line with Jane's approach to life.

Vocabulary Acquisition and Use

1. d; *tumult* is disorder, so *excitement* matches best.
2. a; *comprised* means made of, so *included* matches best.
3. b; *truculent* means aggressively defiant, so *ferocious* matches best.
4. a; something that is *obscured* is difficult to see, so *murky* matches best.
5. d; *sundry* is a variety, so *diverse* matches best.

Writing

Evaluate students' informative texts using the **Rubrics for Response to Literature**, *Professional Development Guidebook*, pages 250–251.

Assessment Resources

Unit 5 Resources

L1 L2 EL **Selection Test A**, pp. 80–82. Administer Test A to less advanced students.

L3 L4 EL **Selection Test B**, pp. 83–85. Administer Test B to on-level students and more advanced students.

L3 L4 **Open-Book Test**, pp. 77–79. As an alternative, give the Open-Book test.

All **Customizable Test Bank**

All **Self-tests**
Students may prepare for the **Selection Test** by taking the **Self-test** online.

PHLit Online! All assessment resources are available at **www.PHLitOnline.com**.

The Empire and Its Discontents

PART 3

Text Complexity: At a Glance

This chart gives a general text complexity rating for the selections in this part of the unit to help guide instruction. For additional text complexity support, see the Test Complexity Rubric at point of use.	
Dover Beach	**More Accessible**
Recessional	**More Accessible**
The Widow at Windsor	**More Complex**

Selection Planning Guide

The selections in this section reveal the opposing forces of the Victorian era. "Progress in Personal Comfort" shows the joyful face of progress. The poems "Dover Beach," "Recessional," and "The Widow at Windsor" reveal the uncertainty and social problems that existed at the height of the British Empire. The poems "from Lucy: Englan' Lady," "Freedom," and "Time Removed" address the effects of the British Empire and its culture on one of its colonies, Jamaica.

Humanities

Derby Day, 1858, by William P. Frith

Derby Day is considered a satirical panorama in that it provides a wide-angle view that, in may ways, pokes fun at a popular Victorian tradition. Explain to students that a derby is a horse race, but that the horses in this piece are barely visible. **Ask:** What are the prominent features of this painting? What does this tell you about the social aspect of Derby Day?

Possible response: People figure prominently in this work. Derby Day was about seeing and being seen. People of different classes came to observe one another.

Also, point out to students that the people in the painting are dressed differently. **Ask:** What can you tell about the subjects from the way they are dressed?

Possible response: The way the subjects are dressed helps identify their social standing.

Monitoring Progress

Before students read the selections in Part 3, refer to the results for the **Vocabulary in Context** items on **Benchmark Test 8** (*Unit 4 Resources,* p. 201). Use this diagnostic portion of the test to guide your choice of selections to teach, as well as the depth of pre-reading preparation you will provide, based on students' readiness for the reading and vocabulary skills.

Dover Beach • Recessional • The Widow at Windsor

Lesson Pacing Guide

DAY 1 Preteach

- Administer the Reading and Vocabulary Warm-ups (*Unit 5 Resources,* pp. 88–91) as necessary.
- Introduce the Literary Analysis concept: Mood and Theme.
- Introduce the Reading Strategy: Connecting Poems to the Historical Period.
- Build background with the author and Background features.
- Develop thematic thinking with Connecting to the Essential Question.
- Teach the selection vocabulary.

DAYS 2–3 Preteach/Teach/Assess

- Distribute copies of the appropriate graphic organizer for the Reading Strategy (*Graphic Organizer Transparencies,* pp. 187–188).
- Distribute copies of the appropriate graphic organizer for Literary Analysis (*Graphic Organizer Transparencies,* pp. 189–190).
- Prepare students to read with the Activating Prior Knowledge activities (TE).
- Informally monitor comprehension while students read.
- Develop students' understanding of mood and theme using the Literary Analysis prompts.
- Develop students' ability to connect poems to the historical period using the Reading Strategy prompts.
- Reinforce vocabulary with the Vocabulary notes.
- Assess students' comprehension and mastery of the skills by having them answer the Critical Reading, Literary Analysis, and Reading Strategy questions.
- Have students complete the Vocabulary Lesson.

DAY 4 Extend/Assess

- Have students complete the Writing Lesson and write a response to literature. (You may assign as homework.)
- Administer Selection Test A or B (*Unit 5 Resources,* pp. 100–102 or 103–105).

Common Core State Standards

Reading Literature 2. Determine two or more themes or central ideas of a text and analyze their development over the course of the text, including how they interact and build on one another to produce a complex account.

Writing 1. Write arguments to support claims in an analysis of substantive topics or texts, using valid reasoning and relevant and sufficient evidence.
1.a. Introduce precise, knowledgeable claim(s), establish the significance of the claim(s), distinguish the claim(s) from alternate or opposing claims, and create an organization that logically sequences claim(s), counterclaims, reasons, and evidence.

Additional Standards Practice
Common Core Companion, pp. 15–22; 186–187

Daily Block Scheduling
Each day in this Lesson Pacing Guide represents a 40–50 minute period. Teachers using block scheduling may combine days to revise pacing. In addition, teachers may differentiate and support core instruction by integrating components for extended and intensive support as students require. See the Guide to Selected Leveled Resources (facing page).

Guide to Selected Leveled Resources

RTI Tier 1 (students performing on level)		Dover Beach • Recessional • The Widow at Windsor
Warm Up	**Practice, model,** and **monitor** fluency, working **with the whole class** or **in groups.**	**Vocabulary and Reading Warm-ups B,** ***Unit 5 Resources,*** pp. 88–89, 91
Comprehension/Skills	**Support** and **monitor** comprehension and skills development, having students complete the activities, graphic organizers, and interactive prompts **independently** or **as a class.**	• ***Reader's Notebook,*** adapted instruction and full selection EL ***Reader's Notebook: English Learner's Version,*** adapted instruction and adapted selection • **Reading Strategy Graphic Organizer B,** ***Graphic Organizer Transparencies,*** p. 196 • **Literary Analysis Graphic Organizer B,** ***Graphic Organizer Transparencies,*** p. 198
Monitor Progress	**Monitor** student progress with the differentiated curriculum-based assessment in the *Unit Resources.*	• **Selection Test B,** ***Unit 5 Resources,*** pp. 103–105 • **Open-Book Test,** ***Unit 5 Resources,*** pp. 97–99

RTI Tier 2 (students requiring intervention)		Dover Beach • Recessional • The Widow at Windsor
Warm Up	**Practice, model,** and **monitor** fluency **in groups** or **with individuals.**	• **Vocabulary and Reading Warm-ups A,** ***Unit 5 Resources,*** pp. 88–90 • ***Hear It!*** **Audio CD (adapted text)**
Comprehension/Skills	• **Support** and **monitor** comprehension and skills development, working **in small groups** or **with individuals.** • As students complete the selection in the appropriate version of the *Reader's Notebook,* **monitor** comprehension frequently with group questions and individual instruction. • **Model** strategies while guiding students in completing the activities and prompts in the *Reader's Notebook,* as well as the graphic organizers. • **Practice** skills and **monitor** mastery with the *Reading Kit* worksheets.	• ***Reader's Notebook: Adapted Version,*** adapted instruction and adapted selection EL ***Reader's Notebook: English Learner's Version,*** adapted instruction and adapted selection • **Reading Strategy Graphic Organizer A,** ***Graphic Organizer Transparencies,*** p. 195 • **Literary Analysis Graphic Organizer A,** ***Graphic Organizer Transparencies,*** p. 197 • ***Reading Kit,*** Practice worksheets
Monitor Progress	**Monitor** student progress with the differentiated curriculum-based assessment in the *Unit Resources* and in the *Reading Kit.*	• **Selection Test A,** ***Unit 5 Resources,*** pp. 100–102 • ***Reading Kit,*** Assess worksheets

TIER 3 Tier 3 intervention may require consultation with the student's special-education or dyslexia specialist. For additional support, see the Tier 2 activities and resources listed above.

One-on-one teaching **Group work** **Whole class instruction** **Independent work** **A Assessment**

For a complete guide to selection support, including support for Advanced students, see the Overview of Resources in the frontmatter.

Dover Beach • Recessional • The Widow at Windsor

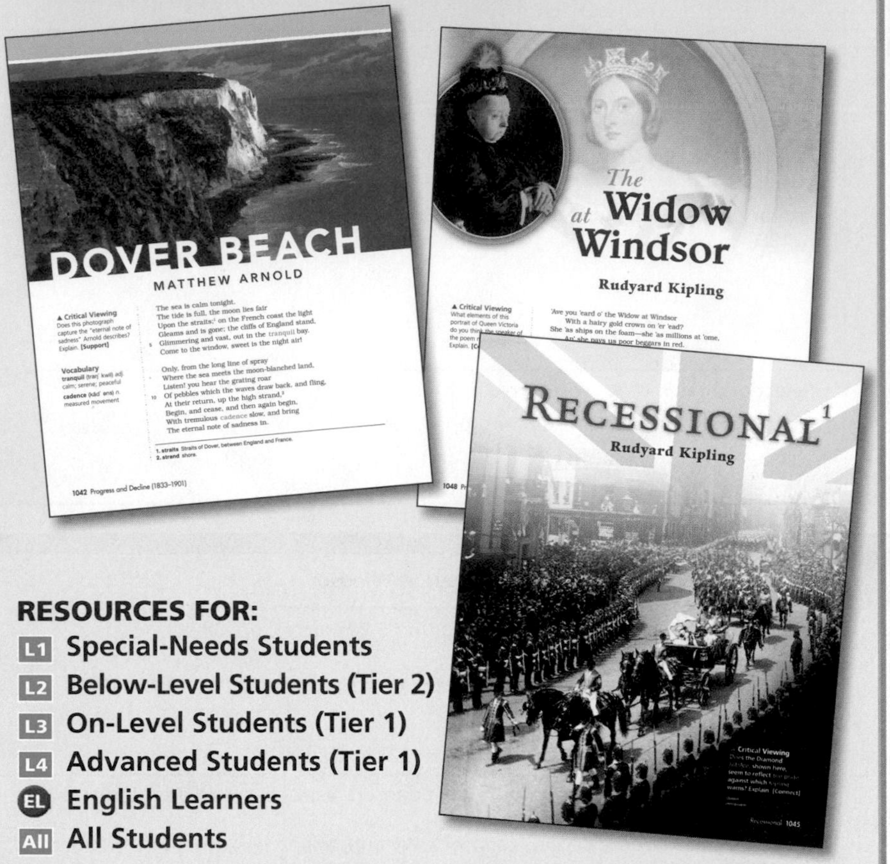

RESOURCES FOR:

- L1 Special-Needs Students
- L2 Below-Level Students (Tier 2)
- L3 On-Level Students (Tier 1)
- L4 Advanced Students (Tier 1)
- EL English Learners
- All All Students

Vocabulary/Fluency/Prior Knowledge

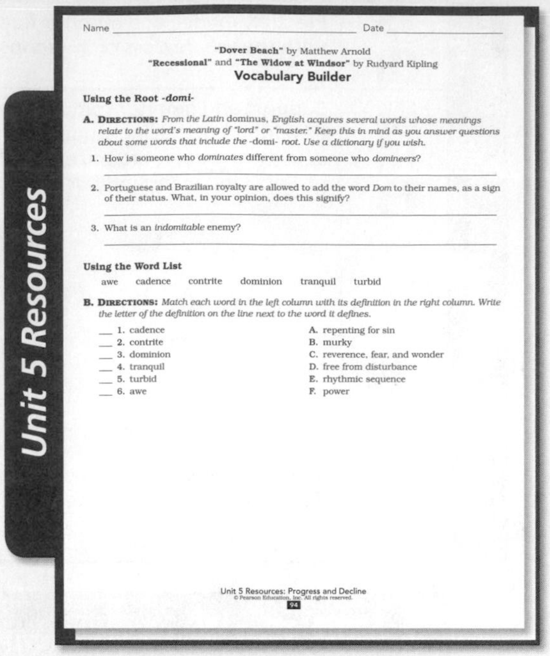

Unit 5 Resources

Name ______ Date ______

"Dover Beach" by Matthew Arnold
"Recessional" and **"The Widow at Windsor"** by Rudyard Kipling
Vocabulary Builder

Using the Root *-domi-*

A. DIRECTIONS: *From the Latin* dominus, *English acquires several words whose meanings relate to the word's meaning of "lord" or "master." Keep this in mind as you answer questions about some words that include the* -domi- *root. Use a dictionary if you wish.*

1. How is someone who *dominates* different from someone who *domineers*?
2. Portuguese and Brazilian royalty are allowed to add the word *Dom* to their names, as a sign of their status. What, in your opinion, does this signify?
3. What is an *indomitable* enemy?

Using the Word List

awe cadence contrite dominion tranquil turbid

B. DIRECTIONS: *Match each word in the left column with its definition in the right column. Write the letter of the definition on the line next to the word it defines.*

___ 1. cadence	A. repenting for sin
___ 2. contrite	B. murky
___ 3. dominion	C. reverence, fear, and wonder
___ 4. tranquil	D. free from disturbance
___ 5. turbid	E. rhythmic sequence
___ 6. awe	F. power

Unit 5 Resources: Progress and Decline

94

All **Vocabulary Builder,** p. 94

Also available for these selections:

EL L1 L2 **Vocabulary Warm-ups A and B,** pp. 88–89

EL L1 L2 **Reading Warm-ups A and B,** pp. 90–91

Reader's Notebooks

Pre- and postreading pages for these selections appear in an interactive format in the *Reader's Notebooks*. Each *Notebook* is differentiated for a different group of learners. The selections in the Adapted and English Learner's versions are abridged.

L2 L3 ***Reader's Notebook***

L1 ***Reader's Notebook: Adapted Version***

EL ***Reader's Notebook: English Learner's Version***

EL ***Reader's Notebook: Spanish Version***

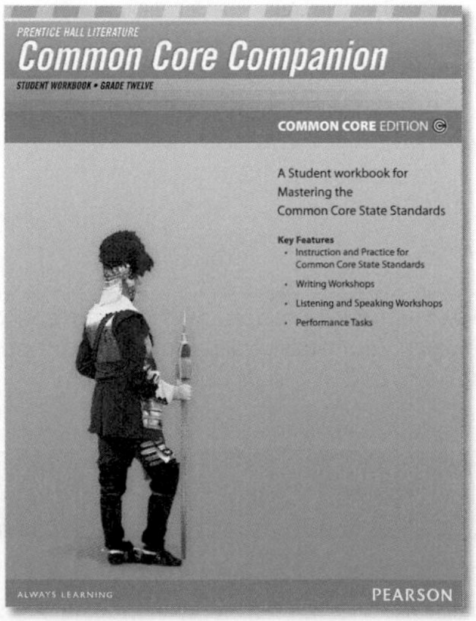

Common Core Companion

Additional instruction and practice for each Common Core State Standard

Selection Support

Graphic Organizer Transparencies

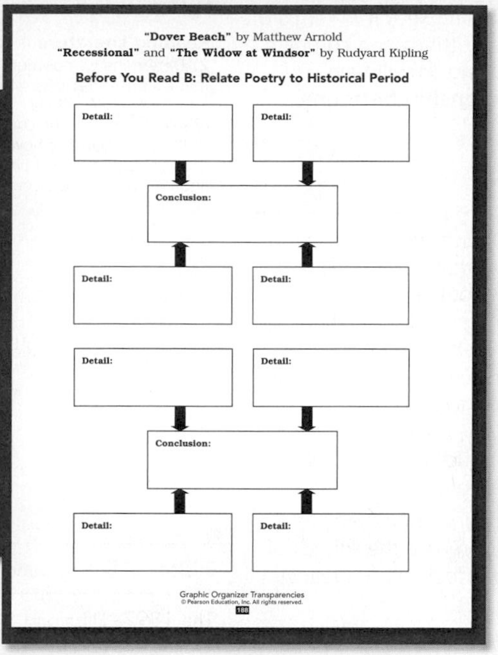

"Dover Beach" by Matthew Arnold
"Recessional" and "The Widow at Windsor" by Rudyard Kipling

Before You Read B: Relate Poetry to Historical Period

Detail: | Detail:
Conclusion:
Detail: | Detail:

Detail: | Detail:
Conclusion:
Detail: | Detail:

Graphic Organizer Transparencies
© Pearson Education, Inc. All rights reserved.
188

EL L3 **Reading: Graphic Organizer B,** p. 188

Also available for these selections:

- EL L1 L2 **Reading: Graphic Organizer A,** p. 187
- EL L1 L2 **Literary Analysis: Graphic Organizer A** (partially filled in), p. 189
- EL L3 **Literary Analysis: Graphic Organizer B,** p. 190

Skills Development/Extension

Unit 5 Resources

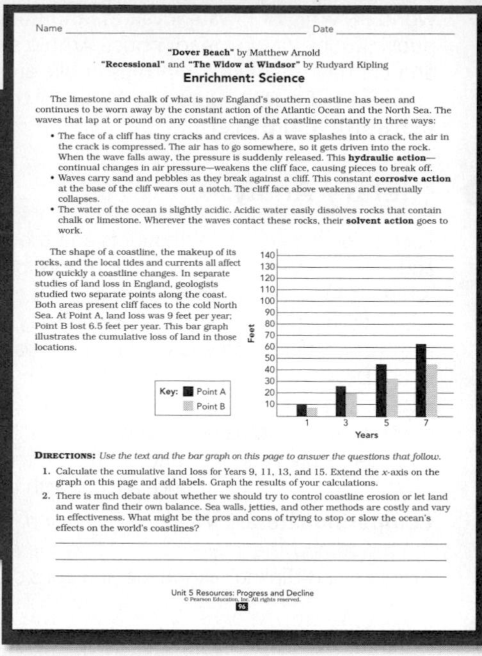

Name ______________ Date ______________

"Dover Beach" by Matthew Arnold
"Recessional" and **"The Widow at Windsor"** by Rudyard Kipling

Enrichment: Science

The limestone and chalk of what is now England's southern coastline has been and continues to be worn away by the constant action of the Atlantic Ocean and the North Sea. The waves that lap at or pound on any coastline change that coastline constantly in three ways:

- The face of a cliff has tiny cracks and crevices. As a wave splashes into a crack, the air in the crack is compressed. The air has to go somewhere, so it gets driven into the rock. When the wave falls away, the pressure is suddenly released. This **hydraulic action**—continual changes in air pressure—weakens the cliff face, causing pieces to break off.
- Waves carry sand and pebbles as they break against a cliff. This constant **corrosive action** at the base of the cliff wears out a notch. The cliff face above weakens and eventually collapses.
- The water of the ocean is slightly acidic. Acidic water easily dissolves rocks that contain chalk or limestone. Wherever the waves contact these rocks, their **solvent action** goes to work.

The shape of a coastline, the makeup of its rocks, and the local tides and currents all affect how quickly a coastline changes. In separate studies of land loss in England, geologists studied two separate points along the coast. Both areas present cliff faces to the cold North Sea. At Point A, land loss was 9 feet per year; Point B lost 6.5 feet per year. This bar graph illustrates the cumulative loss of land in those locations.

Directions: *Use the text and the bar graph on this page to answer the questions that follow.*

1. Calculate the cumulative land loss for Years 9, 11, 13, and 15. Extend the *x*-axis on the graph on this page and add labels. Graph the results of your calculations.
2. There is much debate about whether we should try to control coastline erosion or let land and water find their own balance. Sea walls, jetties, and other methods are costly and vary in effectiveness. What might be the pros and cons of trying to stop or slow the ocean's effects on the world's coastlines?

Unit 5 Resources: Progress and Decline
© Pearson Education, Inc. All rights reserved.
96

L4 **Enrichment,** p. 96

Also available for these selections:

- All **Literary Analysis: Mood and Theme,** p. 92
- All **Reading: Relate Mood and Theme to Historical Period,** p. 93
- EL L3 L4 **Support for Writing,** p. 95

Assessment

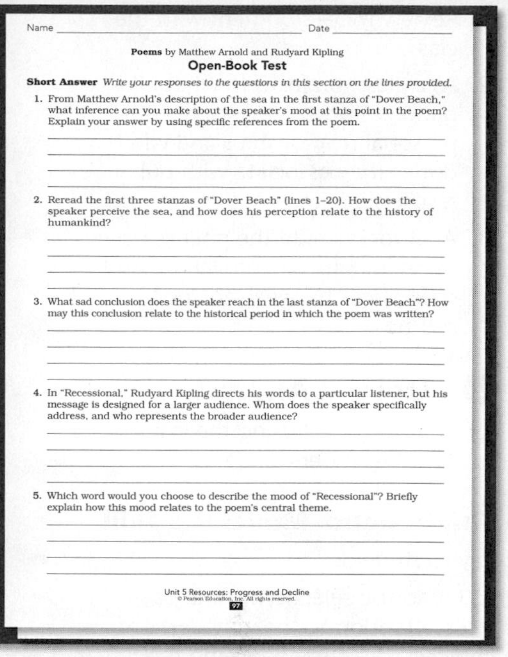

Name ______________ Date ______________

Poems by Matthew Arnold and Rudyard Kipling

Open-Book Test

Short Answer *Write your responses to the questions in this section on the lines provided.*

1. From Matthew Arnold's description of the sea in the first stanza of "Dover Beach," what inference can you make about the speaker's mood at this point in the poem? Explain your answer by using specific references from the poem.
2. Reread the first three stanzas of "Dover Beach" (lines 1–20). How does the speaker perceive the sea, and how does his perception relate to the history of humankind?
3. What sad conclusion does the speaker reach in the last stanza of "Dover Beach"? How may this conclusion relate to the historical period in which the poem was written?
4. In "Recessional," Rudyard Kipling directs his words to a particular listener, but his message is designed for a larger audience. Whom does the speaker specifically address, and who represents the broader audience?
5. Which word would you choose to describe the mood of "Recessional"? Briefly explain how this mood relates to the poem's central theme.

Unit 5 Resources: Progress and Decline
© Pearson Education, Inc. All rights reserved.
97

L3 L4 **Open-Book Test,** pp. 97–99

Also available for these selections:

- EL L1 L2 **Selection Test A,** pp. 100–102
- EL L3 L4 **Selection Test B,** pp. 103–105

PHLit Online!
www.PHLitOnline.com

- complete narrated selection text
- a thematically related video with writing prompt
- an interactive graphic organizer
- highlighting feature
- access to all student print resources, adapted to individual student needs
- Spanish and English summaries
- adapted selection translations in Spanish

Online Resources: All print materials are also available online.

Background Video

Also available:

Get Connected! (thematic video with writing prompt)
All videos are available in Spanish.

Vocabulary Central (tools and activities for studying vocabulary)

Also available:

Writer's Journal (with graphics feature)

PRETEACH

❶ Connecting to the Essential Question

1. Review the assignment with the class.
2. As a class, brainstorm what obligations students associate with personal relationships and what duties they associate with public responsibilities.
3. As students read the poetry, have them look for the similarities and differences between the poems' settings.

❷ Literary Analysis

Introduce the skill using the instruction on the student page.

Think Aloud: Model the Skill

Say to students:

As I read the selections, I will pay close attention to the writer's word choices, use of imagery, and the mood that the poems evoke because emotion and theme are so closely related.

❸ Reading Strategy

1. Introduce the skill using the instruction on the student page.
2. Give students a copy of **Reading Strategy Graphic Organizer B,** page 188 in ***Graphic Organizer Transparencies,*** to fill out as they read.

Think Aloud: Model the Skill

Say to students:

As I read these poems, I will look for references to scientific progress, prosperity, and the British empire that help connect them to the Victorian Age in which these poets were writing.

❹ Vocabulary

1. Pronounce each word, giving its definition, and have students say it aloud.
2. For more guidance, see the ***Classroom Strategies and Teaching Routines*** card for introducing vocabulary.

Before You Read

Dover Beach • Recessional • The Widow at Windsor

❶ **Connecting to the Essential Question** Matthew Arnold sees the world in terms of private loyalties, and Rudyard Kipling sees it in terms of public duties. As you read, notice Arnold's private settings and compare and contrast them with Kipling's public arenas. Doing so will help you answer the Essential Question: **What is the relationship between literature and place?**

Common Core State Standards

Reading Literature
2. Determine two or more themes or central ideas of a text and analyze their development over the course of the text, including how they interact and build on one another to produce a complex account.

❷ Literary Analysis

Poems contain emotional thoughts and thoughtful emotions. With thought and emotion so closely linked, the **mood,** or feeling, that a poem calls up is bound to be related to its **themes**, or messages about life, and to its *aesthetic impact*—its intended *emotional effect* on the reader. Read poetry with your feelings and you will find your way to its ideas.

In "Dover Beach," for example, the crash of waves brings "The eternal note of sadness in." This mood of sadness contributes to an important theme of the poem, which concerns a world with "neither joy, nor love, nor light." This theme interacts with other themes in the poem, such as the loss of certainty and faith, to produce a work with rich layers of meaning.

Comparing Literary Works The *"sound" of language* contributes to the mood and the intended effect on the reader. Compare the sounds of Arnold's and Kipling's language and consider their effects on the reader.

❸ Reading Strategy

Preparing to Read Complex Texts Connecting a poem to the historical period will help you better understand its mood and themes. The Victorian era was marked by scientific progress, material prosperity, and British global domination, yet each success brought fresh anxieties with it:

- Scientific progress brought a greater questioning of religious faith.
- Material prosperity for some brought greater poverty for others.
- Expansion of Britain's empire brought heavy responsibilities as well as political and cultural tensions that often resulted in warfare.

Use a diagram like this to relate the poems to their historical period.

Historical Background

The 1897 "Diamond Jubilee" celebrates the British Empire.

↓

"Recessional" Mood/Themes

The speaker prays for the British Empire while recognizing its greatness is likely temporary.

❹ Vocabulary

tranquil (traŋ´ kwil) *adj.* calm; serene; peaceful (p. 1042)

cadence (kād´ əns) *n.* measured movement (p. 1042)

turbid (tʉr´ bid) *adj.* muddy or cloudy; not clear (p. 1043)

dominion (də min´ yən) *n.* rule; control (p. 1046)

contrite (kən trīt´) *adj.* willing to repent or atone (p. 1046)

awe (ô) *n.* mixed feeling of reverence, fear, and wonder (p. 1046)

PHLit Online! www.PHLitOnline.com

Vocabulary Development

Vocabulary Knowledge Rating

Create a **Vocabulary Knowledge Rating Chart** (***Professional Development Guidebook,*** p. 33) for the vocabulary words on the student page. Give each student a copy of the chart with the words on it. Read the words aloud, and have students mark their ratings in the Before Reading column. Urge students to attend to these words as they read and discuss the selections.

In order to gauge how much instruction you need to provide, tally how many students are confident in their knowledge of each word. As students read, point out the words and their context.

PHLit Online! **Vocabulary Central,** featuring tools and activities for studying vocabulary, is available online at **www.PHLitOnline.com.**

(1822–1888)

MATTHEW ARNOLD

5 Author of "Dover Beach"

Much of Matthew Arnold's poetry concerns a theme as relevant today as it was in the nineteenth century: the isolation of individuals from one another and from society. In fact, in the 1960s, the American novelist Norman Mailer used a modified quotation from Arnold's poem "Dover Beach" for the title of his book about a Vietnam War protest, *Armies of the Night.*

A Social Conscience While attending Oxford University, Arnold developed the social conscience that was to guide his career as a public servant, poet, and literary critic. In 1851, he became Inspector of Schools, and in performing this job he did much to improve education throughout Great Britain. All the while, he remained a poet at heart, although his first two collections, published in 1849 and 1852, met with little success.

Literary Achievement Arnold's literary fortunes changed in 1853 when he published *Poems,* with its long preface that established him as a major critic. *New Poems,* published in 1867, contained Arnold's celebrated "Dover Beach."

A Return to Culture After completing this collection, Arnold believed that he had said everything he could in poetry. From that point on he wrote prose, such as the social criticism of the essays in *Culture and Anarchy* (1869). In this book, he attacks Victorian complacency and materialism, arguing that culture should open our minds to what is true and valuable. Arnold's idea of culture still influences critics today.

"CULTURE IS TO KNOW THE BEST THAT HAS BEEN SAID AND THOUGHT IN THE WORLD."

Daily Bellringer

For each class during which you will teach these selections, have students complete one of the five activities for the appropriate week in the ***Daily Bellringer Activities*** booklet.

Multidraft Reading

To assist struggling readers and to enhance reading for all, assign the text in chunks, as warranted by length, and apply multidraft reading protocols. For each reading, have students set the purpose indicated:

- **First reading**—identifying key ideas and details and answering any Reading Checks.
- **Second reading**—analyzing craft and structure and responding to the side-column prompts.
- **Third reading**—integrating knowledge and ideas, connecting to other texts and the world, and answering the end-of-selection questions.

For more guidance, refer to the ***Classroom Strategies and Teaching Routines*** card on Multidraft Reading.

5 Background

More About the Author

Matthew Arnold

Although "Dover Beach" seems to "throw in the towel" in the fight to find meaning in life, Matthew Arnold is famous for his faith in what he called culture. In *Culture and Anarchy* (1869), he defines culture as "the study of perfection," or the effort to critically assess and expand the spirit of a society.

Arnold abandoned poetry in favor of prose in midlife. Still pursuing questions of faith, he wrote extensively on religion toward the end of his life.

PHLit Online!

www.PHLitOnline.com

Teaching From Technology

Preparing to Read

Go to **www.PHLitOnline.com** and display the ***Get Connected!*** slide show for these selections. Have the class brainstorm responses to the writing prompt, entering ideas in the interactive journal. Then, have students complete their written responses as homework.

To build background, display the Background and More About the Author features.

Using the Interactive Text

Go to **www.PHLitOnline.com** and display the Enriched Online Student Edition. As the class reads the selections or listens to the narration, record answers to side-column prompts using the graphic organizers accessible on the interactive page. Alternatively, have students use the online edition individually, answering the prompts as they read.

TEACH

❶ About the Selection

Looking out a window from the white chalk cliffs of Dover, the speaker describes a moonlit sea, which he takes as an image of the loss of certainty, faith, and peace in the world.

❷ Activating Prior Knowledge

Write on the chalkboard: "Our country, right or wrong." Have students discuss the meaning of the phrase. Ask students if they believe this is an appropriate attitude. Have each student write a paragraph, describing whether he or she agrees or disagrees with the statement, and why. Encourage students to think about the phrase as they read the poems that follow and to consider whether Matthew Arnold and Rudyard Kipling would agree or disagree with the statement.

Concept Connector →

Tell students they will return to their responses after reading the selections.

❸ Critical Viewing

Possible response: Yes, The photograph shows the endless cycle of the waves lapping against the rocky cliffs, which relates to the eternal aspect, while the dark clouds overhead suggest the sadness the poet alludes to.

①② DOVER BEACH

MATTHEW ARNOLD

❸ **▲ Critical Viewing** Does this photograph capture the "eternal note of sadness" Arnold describes? Explain. **[Support]**

Vocabulary

tranquil (traŋ′ kwil) *adj.* calm; serene; peaceful

cadence (kād′ əns) *n.* measured movement

The sea is calm tonight.
The tide is full, the moon lies fair
Upon the straits;[1] on the French coast the light
Gleams and is gone; the cliffs of England stand,
Glimmering and vast, out in the **tranquil** bay.
Come to the window, sweet is the night air!

Only, from the long line of spray
Where the sea meets the moon-blanched land,
Listen! you hear the grating roar
Of pebbles which the waves draw back, and fling,
At their return, up the high strand,[2]
Begin, and cease, and then again begin,
With tremulous **cadence** slow, and bring
The eternal note of sadness in.

1. **straits** Straits of Dover, between England and France.
2. **strand** shore.

Ⓒ Text Complexity Rubric

	Dover Beach	Recessional	The Widow at Windsor
Qualitative Measures			
Context/ Knowledge Demands	Victorian lyric; literary knowledge demands 1 2 ③ 4 5	Victorian lyric; historical knowledge demands 1 2 ③ 4 5	Dramatic poem; historical knowledge demands 1 2 ③ 4 5
Structure/Language Conventionality and Clarity	Long sentences 1 ② 3 4 5	Poetic diction; long sentences 1 2 ③ 4 5	Dialect 1 2 3 ④ 5
Levels of Meaning/ Purpose/Concepts	Moderate (love amid uncertainty) 1 2 ③ 4 5	Moderate (transience of empire) 1 2 ③ 4 5	Challenging (empire, irony) 1 2 ③ 4 5
Quantitative Measures			
Lexile/Text Length	NP / 260 words	NP / 189 words	NP / 327 words
Overall Complexity	**More accessible**	**More accessible**	**More complex**

Sophocles[3] long ago
Heard it on the Aegean,[4] and it brought
Into his mind the **turbid** ebb and flow
Of human misery; we
Find also in the sound a thought,
Hearing it by this distant northern sea.

❹
The Sea of Faith
Was once, too, at the full, and round earth's shore
Lay like the folds of a bright girdle furled.
But now I only hear
Its melancholy, long, withdrawing roar,
Retreating, to the breath
Of the night wind, down the vast edges drear
And naked shingles[5] of the world.

❺
Ah, love, let us be true
To one another! for the world, which seems
To lie before us like a land of dreams,
So various, so beautiful, so new,
Hath really neither joy, nor love, nor light,
Nor certitude, nor peace, nor help for pain;
And we are here as on a darkling[6] plain
Swept with confused alarms of struggle and flight,
Where ignorant armies clash by night.

Vocabulary
turbid (tur´ bid) *adj.* muddy or cloudy; not clear

❹ **Reading Strategy**
Connecting to the Historical Period How does the doubt expressed in lines 21–28 reflect the historical period in which the poem was written?

❺ **Literary Analysis**
Mood as a Key to Theme How do the feelings that the final stanza evokes relate to its message in lines 29–30?

3. **Sophocles** (säf´ ə klēz´) Greek tragic dramatist (496?–406 B.C.).
4. **Aegean** (ē jē´ ən) arm of the Mediterranean Sea between Greece and Turkey.
5. **shingles** *n.* beaches covered with large, coarse, waterworn gravel.
6. **darkling** *adj.* in the dark.

Critical Reading

1. **Key Ideas and Details (a)** Where are the speaker and his "love," and what do they hear and see? **(b) Interpret:** Why do you think the scene suggests to the speaker "the eternal note of sadness"?
2. **Key Ideas and Details (a)** What does the speaker say has happened to "The Sea of Faith"? **(b) Interpret:** What does he mean by this remark?
3. **Key Ideas and Details (a)** In the last stanza, what does the speaker say that he and his "love" should do? **(b) Draw Conclusions:** What problem does the speaker believe that they can alleviate if they follow his urging?
4. **Integration of Knowledge and Ideas** Is Arnold's message in the final stanza a satisfactory response to "human misery" today? Why or why not?

Cite textual evidence to support your responses.

❹ Reading Strategy
Connecting to the Historical Period

1. Have students reread lines 21–28, noting the expression of doubt in these lines.
2. Then, **ask** the Reading Strategy question.
   Possible response: Changing times had brought traditional religious faith into question. Many felt that faith was no longer a clear and certain comfort.

❺ Literary Analysis
Mood as a Key to Theme

1. Remind students that they should be focusing on the relationship between mood and theme as they read the poem.
2. Read aloud the final stanza of the poem. Then, **ask** the Literary Analysis question.
   Answer: The references to the indifference of the world to the fate of human beings creates a sense of isolation. Arnold's response in lines 29–30 is that we must fulfill emotional needs through romantic love.

ASSESS
Answers

Before students respond, you may wish to have them write a brief objective summary of the selection. As they answer the questions below, remind them to support their answers with evidence from the text.

1. (a) They are looking out a window from the white chalk cliffs of Dover, over to France, listening to the sea. (b) **Possible response:** The sea brings in the note of sadness because its ebb and flow call to mind the meaningless repetitions and cycles of human life, which all end in death.
2. (a) It is retreating. (b) He means that faith is on the decline.
3. (a) They should "be true / To one another . . ." (b) He believes they can alleviate, for themselves, the joylessness of the world.
4. Some students may say that love is the only way to navigate a difficult world. Others may argue that we should face conflicts on our own.

Text Complexity: Reader and Task Suggestions

	Dover Beach; Recessional	The Widow at Windsor
Preparing to Read the Texts • Using the information on TE p. 1046, discuss the doubts that late Victorian writers felt about the British Empire. • Discuss how world events can challenge people's faith and fill them with doubt about the future. • Guide students to use Multidraft Reading strategies (TE p. 1041).	**Leveled Tasks** ***Knowledge Demands*** If students will have difficulty with the poems' contexts, clarify each speaker's location. Then, have students read to compare each speaker's feelings about England. ***Evaluating*** If students will not have difficulty with contexts, ask them to judge which poem is more personal and which is more national in scope.	**Leveled Tasks** ***Structure/Language*** If students will have difficulty with the dialect, explain the dropped initial *h* and other consonant sounds. Have students transcribe dialect into standard English. ***Evaluating*** If students will not have difficulty with the dialect, have them consider why the poem's message is more effective when spoken by a solider.

Background

6 More About the Author

Traces of Kipling's life experiences can be found throughout his work. When his parents placed him with relatives back home in England, the young Kipling struggled with lack of affection and dramatically deteriorating eyesight. He documents such an experience in his novel *The Light That Failed.* Even the experiences of Mowgli in *The Jungle Books* reflect Kipling's life. A British citizen born in India, middle-class but a friend of lower-class soldiers, Kipling crossed into many other worlds and learned to speak many tongues, just as Mowgli learns the language of the beasts.

Rudyard Kipling

(1865–1936)

6 Author of "Recessional" • "The Widow at Windsor"

Rudyard Kipling's works are known for their celebration of the British Empire, yet they also warn of the costs of world dominion. While praising the benefits of imperialism, he emphasizes the responsibility of the British to bring their "civilized" ways to other parts of the world.

Early Success Kipling was born to British parents in India, one of Britain's largest colonies. At the age of six, he was placed by his parents in a foster home in England, and later, at a chaotic boarding school. One critic speculates that the theme of self-preservation in Kipling's work was inspired by experiences at the boarding school that tested his courage. Kipling would later immortalize his school days in a collection of stories called *Stalky and Co.* (1899). In 1882, Kipling returned to India to work as a journalist. During the next seven years, he published a number of witty poems and stories, and by the time he returned to England in 1889, he was a celebrity.

Kipling's Achievements Kipling is known as a Victorian author because he produced his best work before the death of Queen Victoria in 1901. In its great variety, that work includes poetry, short stories, and novels. Some of his books, such as *The Jungle Books* (1894, 1895), *Captains Courageous* (1897), and *Kim* (1901), have become children's classics.

For years, Kipling was the most popular English poet, and in 1907 he became the first English writer to receive the Nobel Prize for Literature.

Enrichment: Understanding Planning

Event Coordinator

"Recessional" was written for the national celebration of Queen Victoria's Diamond Jubilee. One can only imagine the amount of planning that went into staging the event. If a similar event were held today, an event coordinator would be hired to oversee the proceedings. Ask students what they know about event coordinators.

Activity: Planning an Event Have students conduct research on what it takes to be an event coordinator. Suggest that they record information in the **Enrichment: Investigating Career Connections** worksheet, ***Professional Development Guidebook,*** page 221. Have them use the results of their research to write a one-page plan for a school fundraiser.

PHLit Online!

For more about the author, go online at **www.PHLitOnline.com.**

7 RECESSIONAL[1]

Rudyard Kipling

8 Critical Viewing Does the Diamond Jubilee, shown here, seem to reflect the pride against which Kipling warns? Explain. [Connect]

Queen Victoria's Diamond Jubilee procession in London in 1897

TEACH

7 About the Selection

As a recessional signals the end of a religious service, this poem heralds the end of the British Empire. Although Rudyard Kipling was a staunch supporter of British imperialism, he recognized the dangers of complacency and overblown pride.

8 Critical Viewing

Answer: The highly formal attire,the military formations, the ornamentation—the pomp and circumstance of the Diamond Jubilee—do indeed reflect the pride of Queen Victoria's British Empire that Kipling warns against when he refers to extinct empires of the past such as Babylonian city of Nineveh and the Phoenician city of Tyre.

Differentiated Instruction for Universal Access

EL Support for English Learners

Before students read the selection, explain that a recessional is a hymn that is played when the clergy and choir exit after a religious service. While students read "Recessional," have them identify why they think Kipling chose this title for his poem.

Enrichment for Advanced Readers

Have students write brief analyses of the poem's form and rhyme scheme. What do they notice about choices Kipling made when writing this poem? How does the poem's form support the content? Have each student share his or her analysis with a partner.

PHLit Online!

These selections are available in an interactive format in the **Enriched Online Student Edition,** at **www.PHLitOnline.com,** which includes a thematically related video with a writing prompt and an interactive graphic organizer.

❾ Vocabulary Builder

The Latin Root *-domi-*

1. Have students read lines 3–4 and ask them if they can determine what *dominion* might mean from the context.
2. Point out that Kipling uses the word *dominion* when referring to the power of the British Empire.
3. Explain to students that this word contains the Latin root *-domi-*, which means "lord" or "master."
4. Have students look for other words in their readings that contain this root and use a dictionary to find the meanings of each word.
   Possible responses: Words with this root include *dominate, domineer, dominant, predominant,* and *domain.*

❿ Critical Thinking

Infer

1. Read aloud lines 3–4 and focus students' attention on the phrase "over palm and pine."
2. Have students draw upon their knowledge of biomes from science class. **Ask:** What does this phrase say about the extent of the boundaries of the empire?
   Answer: It implies that the empire extends from forests characterized by pines to tropical regions, where palms are the dominant trees.

⓫ Background

History

Remind students that an allusion is a reference to a well-known person, place, event, literary work, or work of art. Note that Kipling alludes to the ancient cities of Nineveh and Tyre. No longer glorious, those cities were once the capitals of mighty empires. Kipling's allusion, therefore, reminds Britons that their empire may decline as all previous empires have. Encourage students to find other allusions in the poems of Kipling and Arnold and explain the references.

BACKGROUND In 1897, a national celebration called the "Diamond Jubilee" was held in honor of the sixtieth anniversary of Queen Victoria's reign. The occasion prompted a great deal of boasting about the strength and greatness of the empire. Kipling responded to the celebration by writing this poem, reminding the people of England that the British empire might not last forever.

God of our fathers, known of old—
Lord of our far-flung battle-line—
❿ Beneath whose awful Hand we hold
Dominion over palm and pine—
Lord God of Hosts, be with us yet
Lest we forget—lest we forget!

The tumult and the shouting dies—
The Captains and the Kings depart—
Still stands Thine ancient Sacrifice,
An humble and a **contrite** heart.[2]
Lord God of Hosts, be with us yet,
Lest we forget—lest we forget!

Far-called, our navies melt away—
On dune and headland sinks the fire[3]—
⓫ Lo, all our pomp of yesterday
Is one with Nineveh[4] and Tyre![5]
Judge of the Nations, spare us yet,
Lest we forget—lest we forget!
If, drunk with sight of power, we loose
Wild tongues that have not Thee in **awe**—
Such boasting as the Gentiles use

❾ **Vocabulary**

dominion (də min′ yən) *n.* rule; control

contrite (kən trīt′) *adj.* willing to repent or atone

awe (ô) *n.* mixed feeling of reverence, fear, and wonder

1. **Recessional** hymn sung at the end of a religious service. [footnote in title, previous page]
2. **An . . . heart** allusion to the Bible (Psalms 51:17) "The sacrifices of God are a broken spirit: a broken and contrite heart, O God, thou wilt not despise."
3. **On . . . fire** Bonfires were lit on high ground all over Britain as part of the opening ceremonies of the Jubilee celebration.
4. **Nineveh** (nin′ ə və) ancient capital of the Assyrian Empire, the ruins of which were discovered buried in desert sands in the 1850s.
5. Tyre (tīr) once a great port and the center of ancient Phoenician culture, now a small town in Lebanon.

Enrichment: Building Context

The British Empire

Even as the British Empire expanded, writers expressed doubts about life in the world's most powerful nation. In "Dover Beach," for example, Matthew Arnold laments the decline of religious faith and depicts the world as a place where "ignorant armies clash by night."

Even Kipling, who supported British imperialism, uses "Recessional" to warn against the perils of pride.

Activity: Writing About Empire Have students conduct research on the British Empire during the 1800s. Suggest that they record information in the **Enrichment: Building Context** worksheet, ***Professional Development Guidebook,*** page 222. Have each student use the result of his or her research to write a one-page description of the effects that British imperialism had on the world.

Or lesser breeds without the Law—[6]
(12) Lord God of Hosts, be with us yet,
Lest we forget—lest we forget!

For heathen heart that puts her trust
In reeking tube[7] and iron shard[8]—
All valiant dust that builds on dust,
And guarding calls not Thee to guard—
For frantic boast and foolish word,
Thy mercy on Thy People, Lord!

Literary Analysis
Mood as a Key to Theme
How does the refrain "Lest we forget," create a mood and support the poem's theme?

6. **Such boasting . . . Law** allusion to the Bible (Romans 2:14) "For when the Gentiles, which have not the law, do by nature the things contained in the law, these, having not the law, are a law unto themselves."
7. **tube** barrel of a gun.
8. **shard** fragment of a bombshell.

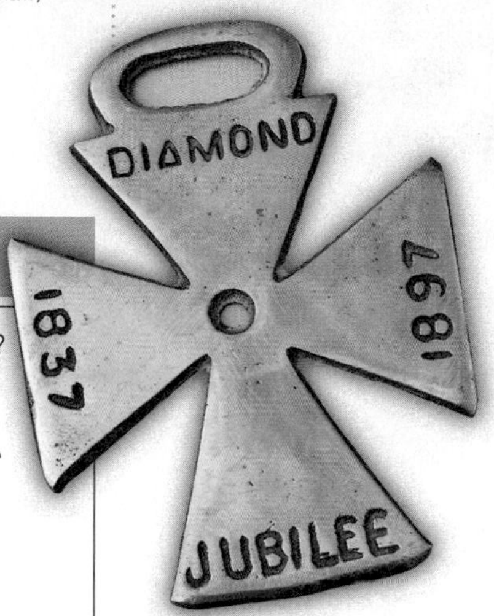

Critical Reading

1. **Key Ideas and Details (a)** To whom is this poem addressed? **(b) Interpret:** For whom is the message of the poem really meant?
2. **Key Ideas and Details (a)** What is the literal meaning of the title of the poem? **(b) Interpret:** What double meaning is contained in the title? **(c) Analyze:** How is this ambiguity appropriate to the mood of the poem?
3. **Key Ideas and Details (a)** Paraphrase the first stanza of the poem. **(b) Analyze:** According to this stanza, what is the relationship between God and empire? Explain.
4. **Key Ideas and Details (a)** In lines 15 and 16, what happens to "our pomp of yesterday"? **(b) Infer:** What qualities and actions does the speaker condemn? **(c) Draw Conclusions:** What is the theme of the poem?
5. **Integration of Knowledge and Ideas** Britain is no longer an empire. Does this fact bear out Kipling's warning? Explain.
6. **Integration of Knowledge and Ideas** Is Kipling condemning the very existence of the British empire, or is he advocating a more humble approach to the responsibilities of empire? Explain.

Cite textual evidence to support your responses.

Differentiated Instruction for Universal Access

Culturally Responsive Instruction

Culture Focus Tell students that it was once said that the sun never set on the British Empire. Explain to students that this meant that the British Empire spanned the globe. One country that Britain controlled during the 1800s was India. India finally gained its independence in 1947, thanks to Mahatma Gandhi's leadership and methods of nonviolent protest. Gandhi's doctrine of nonviolence influenced many people, including Dr. Martin Luther King, Jr. Have students consider how Gandhi and India's struggle for independence from British rule have impacted the lives of people around the world.

(12) Literary Analysis

Mood as a Key to Theme

1. Have students reread the entire poem, noting the repetition of the words "lest we forget."
2. Then, **ask** the Literary Analysis question: How does the refrain "Lest we forget" create a mood and support the poem's theme?
Answer: The refrain creates a vigilant mood. It supports the theme, reminding the reader that the British Empire might not last forever.

ASSESS

Answers

Before students respond, you may wish to have them write a brief objective summary of the selection. As they answer the questions below, remind them to support their answers with evidence from the text.

1. (a) The poem is addressed to God. (b) The poem is meant for the people of England.
2. (a) A recessional is a hymn at the end of a service. (b) The poem concludes the Jubilee and speaks of the receding power of the British Empire. (c) This ambiguity is appropriate because the poem is both a warning and a celebration.
3. (a) God, who preserves our empire, saves us from growing arrogant. (b) God permits the British to hold the empire, ruling over them with his "awful Hand."
4. (a) The pomp has disappeared like empires of old. (b) The speaker condemns pride, lust for power, and lack of humility before God. (c) The theme is the importance of humility over pride.
5. **Possible response:** Yes, the collapse of the British Empire shows that excessive pride in it was inappropriate.
6. **Possible response:** Kipling nowhere in the poem questions Britain's right to rule, only the attitude with which it rules.

13 About the Selection

During the sixty-three-year reign of Queen Victoria, Great Britain reached the height of its power. By the last decade of the nineteenth century, however, cracks in the strength of the British Empire were beginning to show. In "The Widow at Windsor," the speaker is a common soldier who reminds Britons that one country's domination always comes at a price.

14 Background

Victoria's "Nick"

"[H]er nick on the cavalry 'orses" refers to the V.R.I. mark that shows that the horses belong to the queen. The letters stand for "Victoria, Regina Imperatrix," meaning "Victoria, Queen and Empress."

15 Critical Viewing

Possible response: The speaker might say that she has a look of authority.

13 *The* Widow *at* Windsor

Rudyard Kipling

15 ▲ **Critical Viewing**
What elements of this portrait of Queen Victoria do you think the speaker of the poem might point out? Explain. **[Connect]**

'Ave you 'eard o' the Widow at Windsor
With a hairy gold crown on 'er 'ead?
She 'as ships on the foam—she 'as millions at 'ome,
An' she pays us poor beggars in red.
(Ow, poor beggars in red!)
14 | There's 'er nick on the cavalry 'orses,
There's 'er mark on the medical stores—
An' 'er troops you'll find with a fair wind be'ind
That takes us to various wars.
(Poor beggars!—barbarious wars!)
Then 'ere's to the Widow at Windsor,
An' 'ere's to the stores an' the guns,
The men an' the 'orses what makes up the forces
O' Missis Victorier's sons.
(Poor beggars! Victorier's sons!)

Walk wide o' the Widow at Windsor,
For 'alf o' Creation she owns:

Vocabulary Development

Vocabulary Knowledge Rating
When students have completed reading and discussing the selection, have them take out their **Vocabulary Knowledge Rating Charts** for the poems. Read the words aloud and have students rate their knowledge of words again in the After Reading column. Clarify any words that are still problematic. Have students write their own definitions and example or sentence in the appropriate column. Then, have students complete the Vocabulary Practice at the end of the selection. Encourage students to use the words in further discussion and written work about the selection. Remind them that they will be accountable for these words on the **Selection Test,** ***Unit 5 Resources,*** pages 100–102 or 103–105.

We'ave bought 'er the same with the sword an' the flame,
An' we've salted it down with our bones.
(Poor beggars!—it's blue with our bones!)
Hands off o' the sons o' the widow,
Hands off o' the goods in 'er shop.
For the kings must come down an' the emperors frown
When the Widow at Windsor says "Stop!"
(Poor beggars!—we're sent to say "Stop!")
Then 'ere's to the Lodge o' the Widow,
From the Pole to the Tropics it runs—
To the Lodge that we tile with the rank an' the file,
An' open in form with the guns.
(Poor beggars!—it's always they guns!)

We 'ave 'eard o' the Widow at Windsor,
It's safest to leave 'er alone:
For 'er sentries we stand by the sea an' the land
Wherever the bugles are blown.
(Poor beggars!—an' don't we get blown!)
Take 'old o' the Wings o' the Mornin',
An' flop round the earth till you're dead;
But you won't get away from the tune that they play
To the bloomin' old rag over'ead.
(Poor beggars!—it's 'ot over'ead!)
Then 'ere's to the sons o' the Widow,
Wherever, 'owever they roam.
'Ere's all they desire, an' if they require
A speedy return to their 'ome.
(Poor beggars!—they'll never see 'ome!)

16 Literary Analysis
Mood as a Key to Theme
What do the remarks in parentheses suggest about the speaker's attitude toward the empire?

Critical Reading

1. **Key Ideas and Details (a)** Who is the "Widow at Windsor"? **(b) Infer:** What is surprising about the speaker's decision to use this description?
2. **Key Ideas and Details (a)** Who is the speaker of this poem? **(b) Analyze:** Would you describe the speaker's tone as disloyal or disrespectful? Explain.
3. **Key Ideas and Details (a)** What various remarks of the speaker's appear in parentheses? **(b) Make a Judgment:** How would the poem be different if the remarks in parentheses were deleted? Why?
4. **Integration of Knowledge and Ideas** What comment is the speaker making about the extent and power of the British Empire? Use two of these Essential Question words in your answer: *authority, consequence, domination. [Connecting to the Essential Question: What is the relationship between literature and place?]*

Cite textual evidence to support your responses.

16 Literary Analysis

Mood as a Key to Theme

1. Have students finish reading the poem. Draw their attention to the remarks in parentheses.
2. Then, **ask** the Literary Analysis question: What do the remarks in parentheses suggest about the speaker's attitude toward the empire?
   Answer: The parentheses act as asides—that is, they contain short refrains that the speaker is, so to speak, uttering under his breath. They communicate an ironic and bitter attitude toward the empire.

ASSESS

Answers

Before students respond, you may wish to have them write a brief objective summary of the selection. As they answer the questions below, remind them to support their answers with evidence from the text.

1. (a) The "Widow" is Queen Victoria. (b) It is both fondly familiar and disrespectful.
2. (a) The speaker is a common soldier. (b) Students may respond that the tone is disrespectful, but not disloyal. The speaker resents that soldiers are sent off to die for Victoria, but he also takes pride in her power.
3. (a) All the "Poor beggars" lines are in parentheses. (b) Students may respond that the poem would lose much of its mocking, bitter tone if the remarks in parentheses were removed. Other students may point out that without the "interior monologue" of the parenthetical statements, the poem's meaning and intent would lose its clarity.
4. The speaker is commenting that the extent of the British domination and power is great, and that as a consequence the authority of the queen is equally great.

Concept Connector

Reading Strategy Graphic Organizer

Ask students to review the graphic organizers in which they have identified images in each poem that relate to the Victorian Age. Then, have students share their organizers and compare the images they identified.

Activating Prior Knowledge

Have students return to their responses to the Activating Prior Knowledge activity. Ask them to explain whether their thoughts have changed and, if so, how.

Writing About the Essential Question

Have students compare their responses to the prompt, completed before reading the poems, with their thoughts afterward. Have them work individually or in groups, writing or discussing their thoughts, to formulate new responses. Then, lead a class discussion, probing for what students have learned that confirms or invalidates their initial thoughts. Encourage students to cite specific textual details to support their responses.

Answers

1. Possible responses: Image: "ignorant armies clash by night"; Where It Appears: line 37; Mood: dark, foreboding, violent. The theme of the poem is that the human race is driven by conflicts it does not understand.
2. As the poem advances, so does Arnold's pessimism. The opening images of night ("sweet is the night air!") suggest the beauties of night. By line 37, night has come to mean Victorian society's inability to give meaning to human existence.
3. The theme is a warning against pride, taken as an offense against God's majesty, so a solemn, stern mood is appropriate.
4. Kipling is pleading with God to bear with human frailty and with the people of England to relinquish their "frantic boast."
5. The mood, which combines pride in a soldier's profession with a sarcastic acceptance of the indifference of the empire to his fate, supports b.
6. Possible responses: (a) Words like "eternal note of sadness" set a somber mood for "Dover Reach." (b) Clipped lines, such as "Poor beggars! — it's always they guns!" give "The Widow at Windsor" a brisk feeling. (c) Arnold uses sounds of the sea's "ebb and flow" to create a mood of sadness. Kipling uses sound in the repetition of phrases such as "lest we forget" to emphasize his meaning.
7. The last lines of the poem describing the indifference of the world are presented as TV news commentary. People often watch evening news reports with indifference, yet this audience appears to be giving their full attention.
8. These words emphasize the confusion of the era.
9. (a) Kipling's parenthetical remarks make clear the ironic attitude soldiers need in order to cope. (b) Through the words of the soldier, Kipling can point out what is right and what is wrong about the Empire.
10. "Recessional" reflects both the responsibility to God and the danger that arrogance will be the downfall of the empire. "The Widow at Windsor" reflects both the responsibility of empire toward those who maintain it and the danger that it will simply exploit them.

After You Read

Dover Beach • Recessional • The Widow at Windsor

Literary Analysis

Common Core State Standards

Writing

1. Write arguments to support claims in an analysis of substantive topics or texts, using valid reasoning and relevant and sufficient evidence. *(p. 1051)*

1.a. Introduce precise, knowledgeable claim(s), establish the significance of the claim(s), distinguish the claim(s) from alternate or opposing claims, and create an organization that logically sequences claim(s), counterclaims, reasons, and evidence. *(p. 1051)*

1. **Craft and Structure** Fill in a chart like the one shown here by describing the **mood** evoked by images from "Dover Beach." Then, using what you have written as a clue, state the **theme** of the poem.

Image	Where It Appears	Mood It Evokes

2. **Craft and Structure** Review Arnold's descriptions of the night throughout "Dover Beach" and his use of the word "night" in line 37. Do you think his mood is ultimately pessimistic or optimistic? Explain.
3. **Craft and Structure** Explain how the mood of sternness and solemnity in "Recessional" relates to the theme of the poem.
4. **Craft and Structure** Basing your answer on the concluding two lines of each stanza in "Recessional," what conclusion can you draw about Kipling's theme?
5. **Craft and Structure** Use the mood in "The Widow at Windsor" to explain which of these sentences best describes the theme of the poem: **(a)** Maintaining the Empire seems ridiculous to soldiers who must do it. **(b)** Maintaining the Empire is a deadly serious game, played at the expense of soldiers.
6. **Comparing Literary Works** Compare and contrast the effect of the sounds of words and lines of Arnold's and Kipling's poetry. **(a)** Which poet's work is more slow and somber? **(b)** Which poet's work is more clipped and lively? **(c)** Explain how the sound of the language contributes to the mood of each poem and to the poets' aesthetic purposes.
7. **Analyzing Visual Information** Use your knowledge of Arnold's "Dover Beach" to explain the humor of the cartoon on this page.

Reading Strategy

8. **Connect Arnold's work to the historical period** by considering how the phrases "ignorant armies" and "darkling plain" in "Dover Beach" might relate to advances in science and the decline of faith.
9. **(a)** What do Kipling's parenthetical remarks in "The Widow" reveal about the historical period? **(b)** What does Kipling achieve by describing the Empire from the point of view of a common soldier?
10. Relate "Recessional" and "The Widow at Windsor" to the historical period by explaining how the poems reflect different perspectives on the responsibilities and dangers that come with empire.

"Here as on a darkling plain swept with confused alarms of struggle and flight, where ignorant armies clash by night, Matthew Arnold, News." ▶

Assessment Practice

Paired Passages ***(For more practice, see All-in-One Workbook.)***

Many tests require students to compare and identify literary elements in two passages. Use the following sample item to show students how to compare the themes of two passages. Have students read "Dover Beach" and "Recessional" before completing this exercise.

Which of these themes do the two poems share?

A People have become too proud.
B War is a terrible evil.
C History repeats itself.
D In this world, nothing can be certain.

Remind students that a theme is the central idea or ideas in a poem. Choices *A* and *C* are themes in "Recessional," but they do not appear in "Dover Beach." Choice *B* is too peripheral to the poems' central ideas to be called a theme. Students should determine that the correct answer is **D**.

PERFORMANCE TASKS
Integrated Language Skills

Vocabulary Acquisition and Use

Word Analysis: Word-Phrase Relationships

Some words have special meaning when used in phrases. *Dominion,* for instance, means "control." The phrase *dominion over,* which Kipling uses in "Recessional," suggests a responsibility for the beings that the person with dominion controls. Contrast the meanings of each of these words and the phrases in which they also appear. Then, write an original sentence using the phrase.

1. attend; attend on
2. awe; in awe of
3. closed; closed down
4. move; move on
5. see; see through
6. stand; stand by

Vocabulary: Antonyms

Antonyms are words with opposite meanings. *Love* and *hate* are antonyms. For each word from the vocabulary list on page 1040, choose the antonym. Then, write an original sentence using both the word and its antonym.

1. awe: **(a)** attrition **(b)** contempt **(c)** reverence
2. turbid: **(a)** clear **(b)** confused **(c)** separated
3. tranquil: **(a)** calm **(b)** rational **(c)** restless
4. contrite: **(a)** incomplete **(b)** respectful **(c)** unrepentant
5. cadence: **(a)** tempo **(b)** unevenness **(c)** vigor
6. dominion: **(a)** obedience **(b)** rule **(c)** sway

Writing

Argumentative Text Critic Walter E. Houghton writes that the Victorian Age was characterized by "widespread doubt about the nature of man, society, and the universe." Using *evidence* from the poems by Arnold and Kipling, write an **essay** to support or refute this general observation.

Prewriting Review the poems, using a chart like the one shown to gather evidence about the *theme* of Victorian doubt or self-confidence. Note uses of imagery, language, or stylistic devices that illustrate or contradict the doubts that Houghton cites. Based on your examples, decide whether you agree or disagree with Houghton's claim.

Drafting Begin your draft by summarizing Houghton's point and stating your position for or against it. Support your generalizations with evidence from Arnold's and Kipling's poems. Consider organizing your response by devoting a paragraph to each selection.

Model: Gathering Details

Poem:			
	Images	Mood(s)	Theme(s)
Doubt			
Self-confidence			

Revising Review your draft, highlighting generalizations and looking for supporting details for each. Where details are lacking, provide them. Make sure that all quotations are accurate and properly referenced. Also, be sure you have *acknowledged and refuted opposing arguments.*

Assessment Resources

Unit 5 Resources

L1 L2 EL **Selection Test A,** pp. 100–102. Administer Test A to less advanced students.

L3 L4 EL **Selection Test B,** pp. 103–105. Administer Test B to on-level students and more advanced students.

L3 L4 **Open-Book Test,** pp. 97–99. As an alternative, give the Open-Book test.

All **Customizable Test Bank**

All **Self-tests**
Students may prepare for the **Selection Test** by taking the **Self-test** online.

PHLit Online! All assessment resources are available at **www.PHLitOnline.com.**

EXTEND/ASSESS

Answers

Vocabulary Acquisition and Use

1. Introduce the skill using the instruction on the student page.
2. Have students complete the Word Analysis activity and the Vocabulary Practice.

Word Analysis

Ensure student sentences use each phrase correctly.

1. attend: to go to; attend on: to be ready or waiting
2. awe: dread and wonder; in awe of: inspire respect
3. closed: shut; closed down: cease to operate
4. move: transfer position; move on: progress
5. see: to perceive; see through: carry through
6. stand: to stop; stand by: to support

Vocabulary

Sentences should use both the word and its antonym.

1. awe: (b) contempt
2. turbid: (a) clear
3. tranquil: (d) restless
4. contrite: (c) unrepentant
5. cadence: (b) unevenness
6. dominion: (a) obedience

Writing

1. To guide students in writing this argumentative text, give them the Support for Writing page (*Unit 5 Resources,* p. 95)
2. Explain that in their essays students should use evidence from Arnold and Kipling's poetry to either support or refute Houghton's conclusion about the Victorian Age.
3. Remind students to cite specific examples of imagery, language, and stylistic devices in their arguments.
4. Use the ***Response to Literature Rubric Professional Development Guidebook,*** pp. 250–251 to evaluate student's work.

Themes Across Cultures

James Berry

1. You might wish to have students reread James Berry's introduction to the unit on pages 955–956.
2. Show Segment 2 on James Berry on the *See It!* DVD to provide insight into the author's passion for poetry. After students have watched the segment, **ask:** How does the use of dialect add to Berry's poems?
   Answer: Dialect shows his speakers' Caribbean perspective and gives them an authentic voice.

On Growing Up British

1. Review with students the role of the British Empire in Jamaica, and of Berry's Jamaican/British background. Show students a world map and point out the extent of the British Empire in the nineteenth century. Indicate how it had shrunk and was "fading fast" in the 1950s.
2. **Ask** students: How does Berry's background combine both British and Jamaican traditions?
   Answer: Berry's family and heritage are Jamaican, descended from African slaves. However, he is also a British citizen, he speaks English, and he may, like Lucy, feel a loyalty to the Queen.

Themes Across Cultures: Author's Insights

James Berry Introduces "From Lucy: Englan' Lady," "Time Removed," and "Freedom"

On Growing Up British The poems in this selection reflect my different heritages: my Jamaican upbringing, my British identity, and to some extent, my African background. I was one of the peoples "of palm and pine" who grew up under the dominion of the British Empire that is the subject of Kipling's "Recessional" (p. 1045). As pompous as it sounds, Kipling's poem foresees some of the dangers of power and pomp and their likely end—those at the top will have to climb down. Empires are humbled, but sometimes, out of that, new relationships are made and changes happen.

Looking at England from a Caribbean Perspective When I grew up, the British Empire was fading fast, but my Caribbean people had become part of the British way of life. My poem "From Lucy: Englan' Lady" is one of a group of poems that I wrote in Caribbean Creole language and in the voice of Lucy, a Caribbean woman living in England.

Like Lucy, most people who came to Britain in the 1950s were royalists with a natural respect for the Royal Family. To them, the Queen was just like the church. Lucy treats the Queen like an ancient institution, something that will always be there, but at the same time she feels sympathy for her as a woman, for the hard time she has keeping up a show. She feels the Queen belongs to her, so she has a right to comment on her.

About the Author

James Berry has won numerous awards for his work as a poet, novelist, and short-story writer. Among his awards and honors are the Signal Poetry Award in 1989 for *When I Dance* and the Order of the British Empire in 1990.

Teaching Resources

Unit 5 Resources
Contemporary Commentary: James Berry, pp. 86–87

***See It!* DVD**
James Berry, Segment 2

Lucy represents the uncritical, unwavering admiration that so many ordinary people feel for royalty. She comes from the poverty-stricken context of the Caribbean, yet she would give her life for an institution that does nothing positive for her.

Traveling Back to Jamaica The poem "Time Removed" was one I wrote after I'd been in England for some years and following a visit I made back to Jamaica. I was saddened by how little had happened during my absence. My surroundings seemed to be more broken-down and less well maintained than before I went away.

Because I had a wider experience of life now, I could see what was not being done. In England, I had felt a kind of awe for all the work that had gone on over centuries to shape and tame the land. There was a sense of a managed landscape that was kept up and renewed continually through organization and the application of knowledge and skill. In Jamaica, the landscape and the roads were still very undeveloped.

▼ Critical Viewing
Which details in this photograph reflect Berry's recollections in his essay? **[Interpret]**

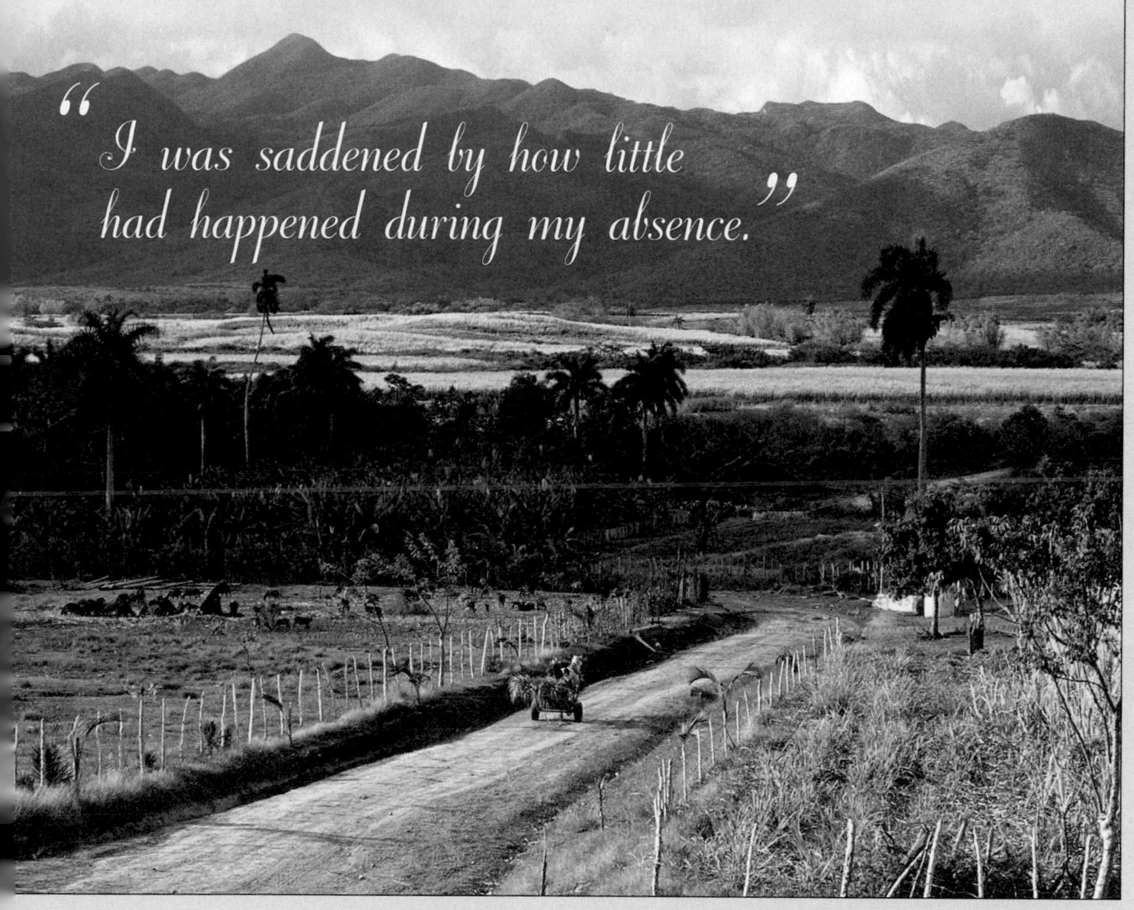
"I was saddened by how little had happened during my absence."

Traveling Back to Jamaica

Before students respond, you may wish to have them write a brief objective summary of the selection. As they answer the questions below, remind them to support their answers with evidence from the text.

1. Berry indicates that he has mixed feelings about Jamaica's ability to govern itself. **Ask:** In what ways does Berry continue to admire the British Empire, even though it once controlled Jamaica?
   Answer: Berry admires British organizational and management skills. Because of knowledge and experience, the British landscape looks well maintained and organized. In contrast, the island of Jamaica looks old-fashioned and undeveloped.
2. Discuss with students the number of colonies that received independence from British dominion after World War II: for example, India and Kenya. **Ask** students: What are some of the "terrible things" that former colonies might remember about their European rulers?
   Answer: Many European countries gave their colonies few freedoms; they imposed strict taxes; they had policies that discriminated against colonized peoples.
3. Refer students to page 1054. Berry says that people in former colonies must "let go of a destructive past." **Ask:** How would he like to see Caribbean people focus their energies?
   Answer: He would like to see Caribbean people focus on positive growth and creating new models for themselves.

Critical Viewing

Answer: The photograph shows an unpaved road and horse-drawn wagon, both of which correspond to Berry's description of Jamaica as "undeveloped."

ASSESS

Answers

1. (a) Berry says that individuals or empires that are at the top eventually will have to climb down. (b) After Britain's power diminished, Berry might have wanted the empire to share more of the benefits of its governing and organizational expertise to help Jamaicans rule themselves.
2. (a) Berry called his poem "Time Removed" because he felt both removed from the time of his childhood in Jamaica, yet still a part of it. (b) Students may say that they are saddened when they see places that were important to them in their childhood falling into disrepair or not being appreciated.
3. In "From Lucy: Englan' Lady," Berry uses warm Caribbean images to describe London: the Queen is like the sun, and her waving hand is like a flying seagull.
4. In "Freedom," Berry speaks of Britain's treatment of Jamaica as "a source of hurt."

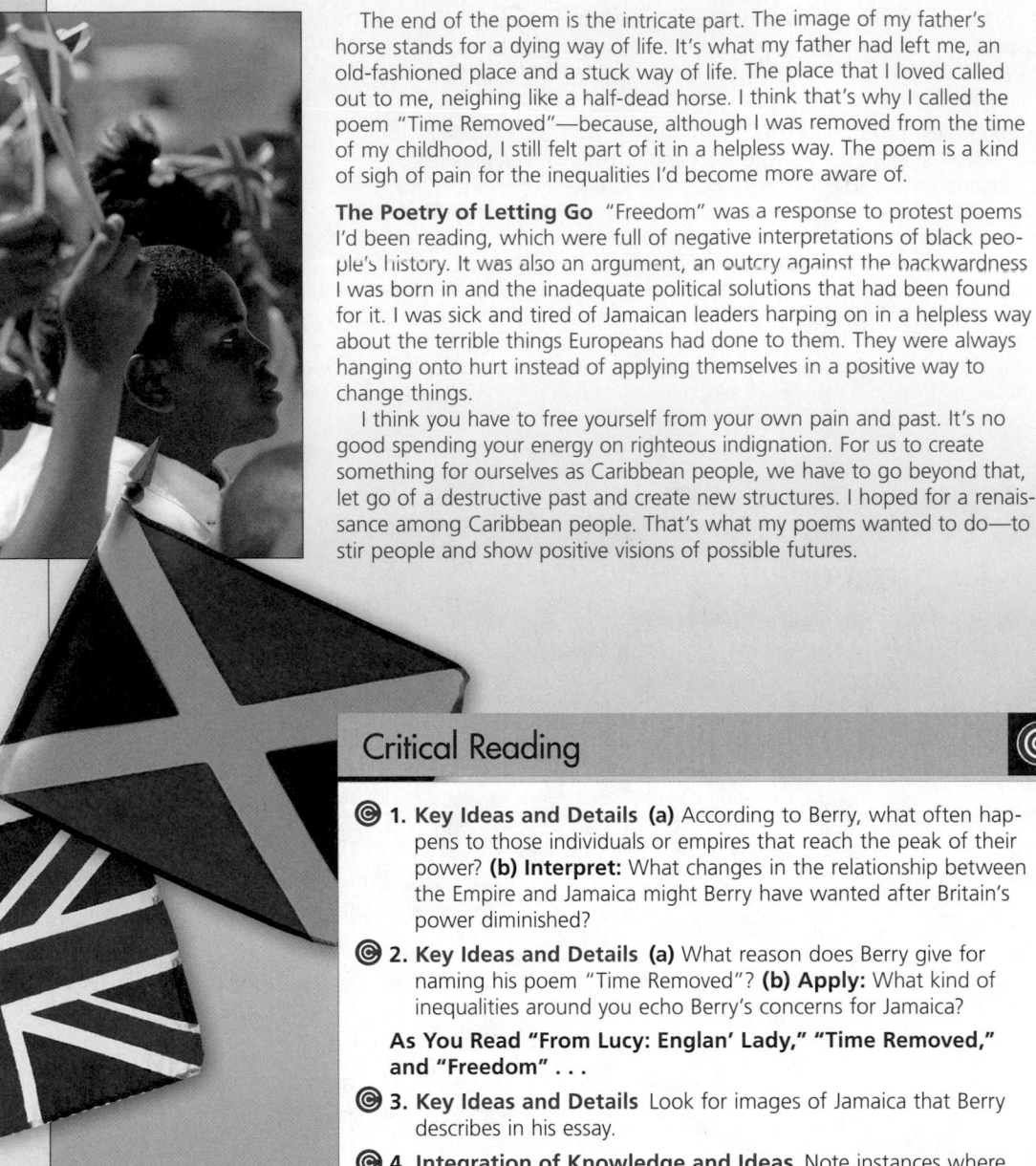

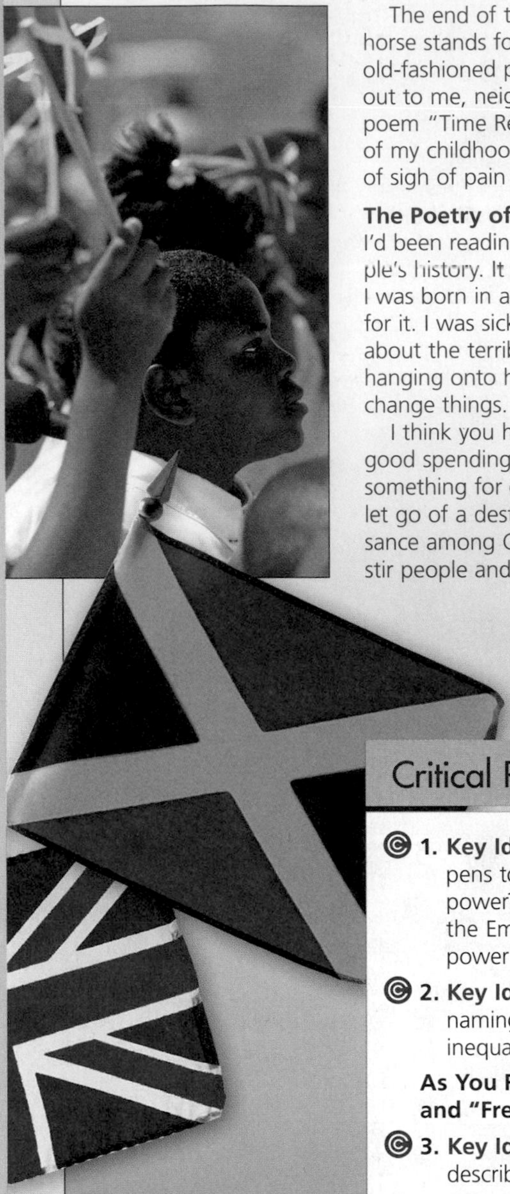

The end of the poem is the intricate part. The image of my father's horse stands for a dying way of life. It's what my father had left me, an old-fashioned place and a stuck way of life. The place that I loved called out to me, neighing like a half-dead horse. I think that's why I called the poem "Time Removed"—because, although I was removed from the time of my childhood, I still felt part of it in a helpless way. The poem is a kind of sigh of pain for the inequalities I'd become more aware of.

The Poetry of Letting Go "Freedom" was a response to protest poems I'd been reading, which were full of negative interpretations of black people's history. It was also an argument, an outcry against the backwardness I was born in and the inadequate political solutions that had been found for it. I was sick and tired of Jamaican leaders harping on in a helpless way about the terrible things Europeans had done to them. They were always hanging onto hurt instead of applying themselves in a positive way to change things.

I think you have to free yourself from your own pain and past. It's no good spending your energy on righteous indignation. For us to create something for ourselves as Caribbean people, we have to go beyond that, let go of a destructive past and create new structures. I hoped for a renaissance among Caribbean people. That's what my poems wanted to do—to stir people and show positive visions of possible futures.

Critical Reading

1. **Key Ideas and Details (a)** According to Berry, what often happens to those individuals or empires that reach the peak of their power? **(b) Interpret:** What changes in the relationship between the Empire and Jamaica might Berry have wanted after Britain's power diminished?
2. **Key Ideas and Details (a)** What reason does Berry give for naming his poem "Time Removed"? **(b) Apply:** What kind of inequalities around you echo Berry's concerns for Jamaica?

As You Read "From Lucy: Englan' Lady," "Time Removed," and "Freedom" . . .

3. **Key Ideas and Details** Look for images of Jamaica that Berry describes in his essay.
4. **Integration of Knowledge and Ideas** Note instances where Berry uses his poems to voice his frustration with Britain's treatment of Jamaica.

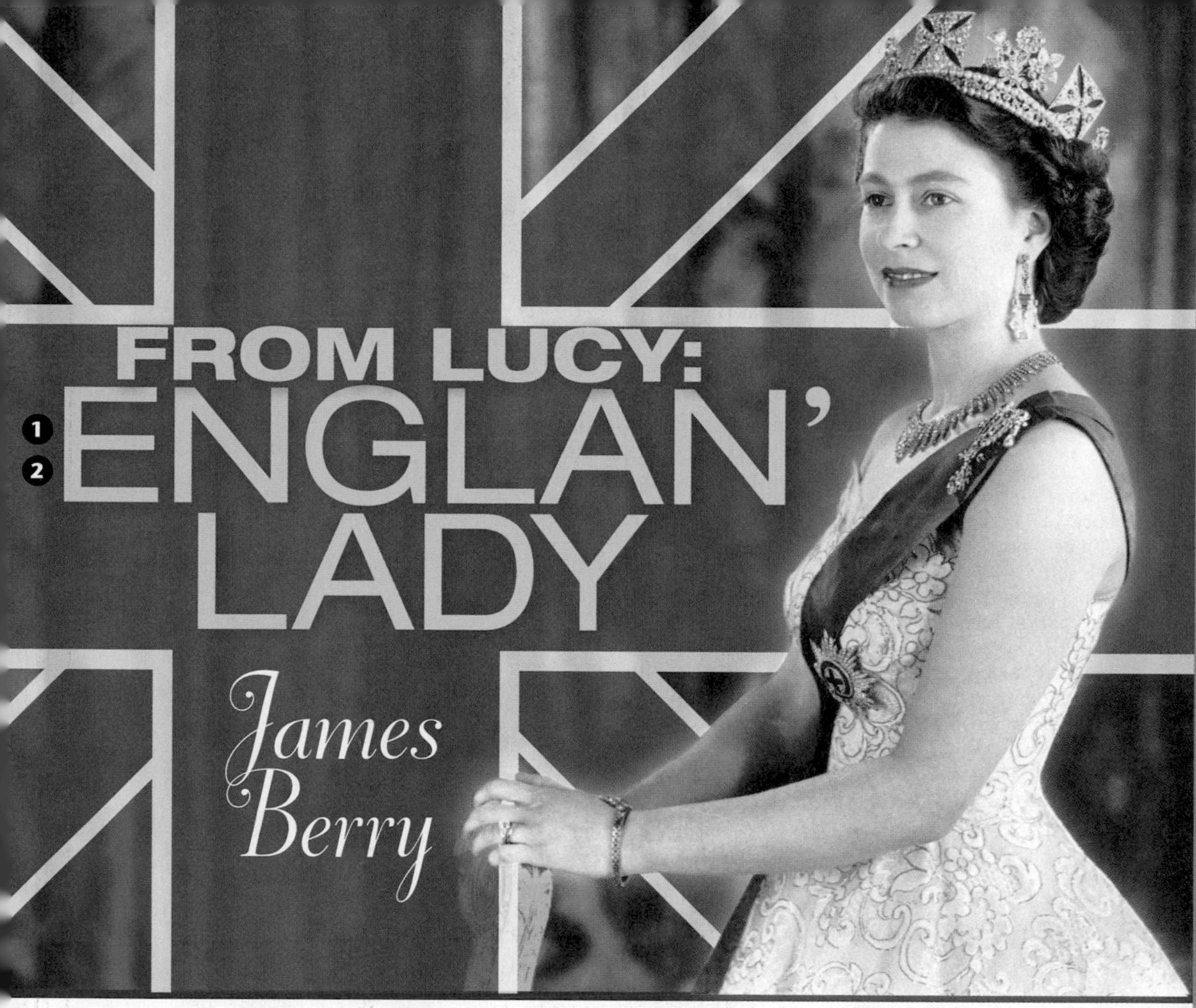

1 2

FROM LUCY: ENGLAN' LADY

James Berry

Queen Elizabeth II

3 You ask me 'bout the lady. Me dear,
old center here still shine
with Queen. She affec' the place
like the sun: not comin' out oft'n
an' when it happ'n everybody's out
smilin' as she wave a han'
like a seagull flyin' slow slow.

James Berry
Author's Insight Lucy has been asked by Leela, her friend back home, whether she has seen the Queen. Every time I go back to the Caribbean people ask me that!

❶ About the Selection

In this poem, a Jamaican immigrant woman living in London expresses her thoughts about Queen Elizabeth in a letter to a friend back home. In Jamaican dialect, she wonders whether the Queen does not find her life as a royal celebrity lonely.

❷ Activate Prior Knowledge

Ask students to imagine that they grew up in one town, but then moved to a new community. After living in the new place for several years, which town would they consider "home"? Have each student write a paragraph about what it means to be from two different places. Encourage students to keep these thoughts in mind when reading Berry's poems.

❸ Author's Insight

1. Read the poem aloud. Direct students to the Author's Insight on this page. Point out that the choice of speaker is effective in describing the Queen and the city of London. Lucy describes much more than celebrities and sights—she describes the gulf between the rich and the poor. Explain that Lucy uses images that will be familiar to Leela—the seagull flying slow and a bird sitting on its nest.
2. Then, **ask** students why they think Jamaicans are so interested in the Queen.
   Possible response: Students might say that they are fascinated by celebrities and royalty. Other students might point out the Jamaican people's loyalty and allegiance to the Queen.

Differentiated Instruction Additional Instruction

EL Strategy for English Learners

Students may find it easier to understand the poem when they hear it spoken. Ask students to reread the entire poem. Explain words or phrases with which they are not familiar. Once they feel comfortable with the poem, have students work in pairs, reading aloud to each other, to practice pronunciation of the Jamaican dialect.

Enrichment for Advanced Readers

Ask students to find a more recent picture of Queen Elizabeth in an online encyclopedia or other reference book. Ask them to compare it with the picture of the Queen on this page. How are her expressions the same or different? Suppose that you are Lucy. Write to tell Leela of the news of the royal family now. Like Lucy, include a description of modern-day London.

PHLit Online!

These selections are available in an interactive format in the Enriched Online Student Edition, at **www.PHLitOnline.com**, which includes a thematically related video with a writing prompt and an interactive graphic organizer.

❹ Author's Insight

1. Refer to the first Author's Insight note on this page. Then, **ask** to what the poet compares the Queen.
   Answer: The Queen is compared to the infrequent appearance of the sun in London—everyone is happy when it is out.
2. Reread lines 8–11. Discuss the effect of the words "dust free," "velvet," and "diamond." Then, **ask** how students think Lucy would describe her former home in Jamaica.
   Possible response: She would probably describe it as dusty and simple, but comfortable and filled with sunshine.

❺ Author's Insight

1. Refer to the second Author's Insight note on this page. Explain that Berry humanizes the Queen by having Lucy describe her loneliness. It makes the Queen seem ordinary, with the same feelings of loneliness and isolation as commoners.
2. **Ask** how Berry's use of the Jamaican dialect affects the tone of the poem.
   Possible response: The choice of dialect creates a distinctive, authentic voice for Lucy. It makes her seem very genuine.
3. Explain that Lucy is an observer and thus able to comment on life in London. This is an effective technique for writers and poets to use, especially when commenting on politics. Then, **ask** the students what comment Berry makes in this poem.
   Possible response: Berry comments on British nobility, which has done nothing for the people of Jamaica but which is respected and admired nonetheless.

James Berry
Author's Insight Lucy connects the Queen with her feeling of the ancient power of British history and with the vast metropolitan character of London.

An' you know she come from
dust free rooms an' velvet
an' diamond. She make you feel
this on-an'-on[1] town, London,
❹ where long long time deeper than mind.[2]
An' han's after han's[3] die away,
makin' streets, putt'n' up bricks,
a piece of brass, a piece of wood
an' plantin' trees: an' it give
a car a halfday job gett'n' through.

An' Leela, darlin', no, I never
meet the Queen in flesh. Yet
sometimes, deep deep, I sorry for her.
Everybody expec' a show
from her, like she a space touris'
on earth. An' darlin', unless
you can go home an' scratch up[4]
you' husban', it mus' be hard
strain keepin' good graces for
❺ all hypocrite faces.

Anyhow, me dear, you know what
ole time people say,
"Bird sing sweet for its nest."[5]

James Berry
Author's Insight
Lucy imagines the Queen at home, where she can be herself and behave naturally—just as a bird at home in its own nest sings most sweetly. I often end my Lucy poems with a Jamaican proverb.

"BIRD SING SWEET FOR ITS NEST"

1. **on-an'-on** extraordinary.
2. **deeper . . . mind** more than can be comprehended.
3. **han's after han's** many generations.
4. **scratch up** lose your temper at.
5. **"Bird . . . nest"** Jamaican proverb, referring to the nightingale's habit of singing loudest near its nest. It means, "Those closest to home are the most contented."

Enrichment: Understanding History

Caribbean Immigration to Great Britain
In a sense, a wave of migration of Caribbean people to Britain was inevitable. Britain had shaped the lives and history of the Caribbean islands for many centuries. The economic conditions on many of the islands pushed people to migrate. It became a matter of leaving to find work, or staying and living in poverty.
Activity: Creating Visuals Have students conduct research on the immigration wave of Caribbeans to Britain from 1955 to 1962. Suggest that they record information in the **Enrichment: Analyzing Historical Patterns, Trends, and Periods worksheet, *Professional Development Guidebook*,** page 231. Have them use the results of their research to create a visual, charting the immigration trend during that period.

PHLit Online!

These selections are available in an interactive format in the Enriched Online Student Edition, at **www.PHLitOnline.com,** which includes a thematically related video with a writing prompt and an interactive graphic organizer.

❻ # Freedom

James Berry

Freedom is not
a helpless grasping
at a source of hurt
or an outpour of oneself
to fixed ends others started

Freedom is not
a hiding in the dust
of righteous indignation
or a merging with shadows

Freedom is not
a becoming the model
of destructive echoes
or a walking in the hands of ghosts

❽ Freedom is not
a reframing of oneself
in the walls of the old prison
or a becoming the tyrant's chain

Freedom is not
excursions of energy
to nowhere
driven and controlled
by someone else's motivation

❾ Freedom is
a letting go like trees grow
a native self unravelling
an adventure of a new
self because of oneself

❼ ***James Berry***
Author's Insight This poem works through a series of images which all in some way suggest a failure to let go of a history of hurt and oppression.

James Berry
Author's Insight My argument in this poem is that people can continue their own imprisonment; if you live with hate and the desire for revenge, you replace one set of chains with another.

James Berry
Author's Insight This last verse sums up the adventure of living and striving to become more.

Differentiated Instruction — Additional Instruction

Strategy for Special-Needs Students

The format of this poem lends itself to choral reading. Ask students to work in small groups. Have them practice saying the poem aloud, with each student taking a verse. Students may be tempted to stop at the end of every line rather than to read to the end of each thought or idea. Help them recognize the correct places at which to pause. Have the groups present the poem to the class.

Enrichment for Gifted/Talented Students

The visual images in this poem are particularly vivid. Have students draw a prison (or prisons) described in "Freedom." Then have them illustrate the negative emotions that can imprison people. Have them discuss their drawings in small groups—and also discuss ways people can free themselves from their emotional prisons.

❻ About the Selection

In "Freedom," James Berry responds to protest poems of oppression and hopelessness by revealing the natural beauty of free will and self-discovery.

❼ Author's Insight

1. Read the poem as a class. Point out the physical appearance of the poem, which emphasizes the line "Freedom is not." Then **ask** what effect the repetition of the lines "Freedom is not" has on the poem.
   Possible response: The repetition makes it clear that the author has deep feelings about freedom.
2. Discuss the impact of the last stanza. By stating what freedom is, Berry underscores the importance of the individual. He also reinforces the beauty of self-discovery.

❽ Author's Insight

1. Direct students to the fourth stanza. **Ask** students to describe ways people imprison themselves.
   Possible response: People who live with hate, prejudice, or other negative emotions live in their own prisons.
2. Then, **ask** students to explain the meaning of "excursions of energy to nowhere."
   Possible response: Students might say that ambition is often futile, leading nowhere. Others might say that the greed that motivates some people to work long hours is a form of imprisonment.

❾ Author's Insight

1. Tell students that Berry wants to emphasize the importance of self-discovery by writing this stanza as he does. **Ask** students the meaning of "a letting go like trees grow."
   Possible response: True freedom is innate and natural.
2. Then, ask students to compare and contrast Berry's comments in the two poems.
   Possible response: Berry makes light of the history of oppression in "Lucy: Englan' Lady." In "Freedom," he rebukes those who will not let go of hurt and oppression.

⑩ About the Selection

In "Time Removed," Berry compares England, with its manicured fields and tarred roads, to his home in Jamaica. Though he still feels a love for his homeland, he realizes how far time has removed it from him.

⑪ Author's Insight

1. **Ask** students whether they have seen a landscape that was ordered like the one Berry describes. Explain that the scene saddens Berry because it was the antithesis of his home on the Caribbean.
2. **Ask** students what words and phrases are clues to Berry's feelings.
   Possible response: Berry uses the words "compulsive hands" to indicate the British obsession with manicured trees and shrubs. The phrase "lands now railed and tarred" indicates that he thinks the British have ruined the landscape with railroads and highways.

⑫ Critical Viewing

Possible response: The top landscape is well-maintained and managed in an organized manner. It is apparent that "compulsive hands have shaped" it. In contrast, the bottom image shows untended fields."

⑬ Author's Insight

1. Explain to students that Berry would not have been familiar with the change of seasons because of the location of the Caribbean islands.
2. Point out that he is impressed with the color of the landscape in late summer, when the tropical heat dries up the landscape in Jamaica.

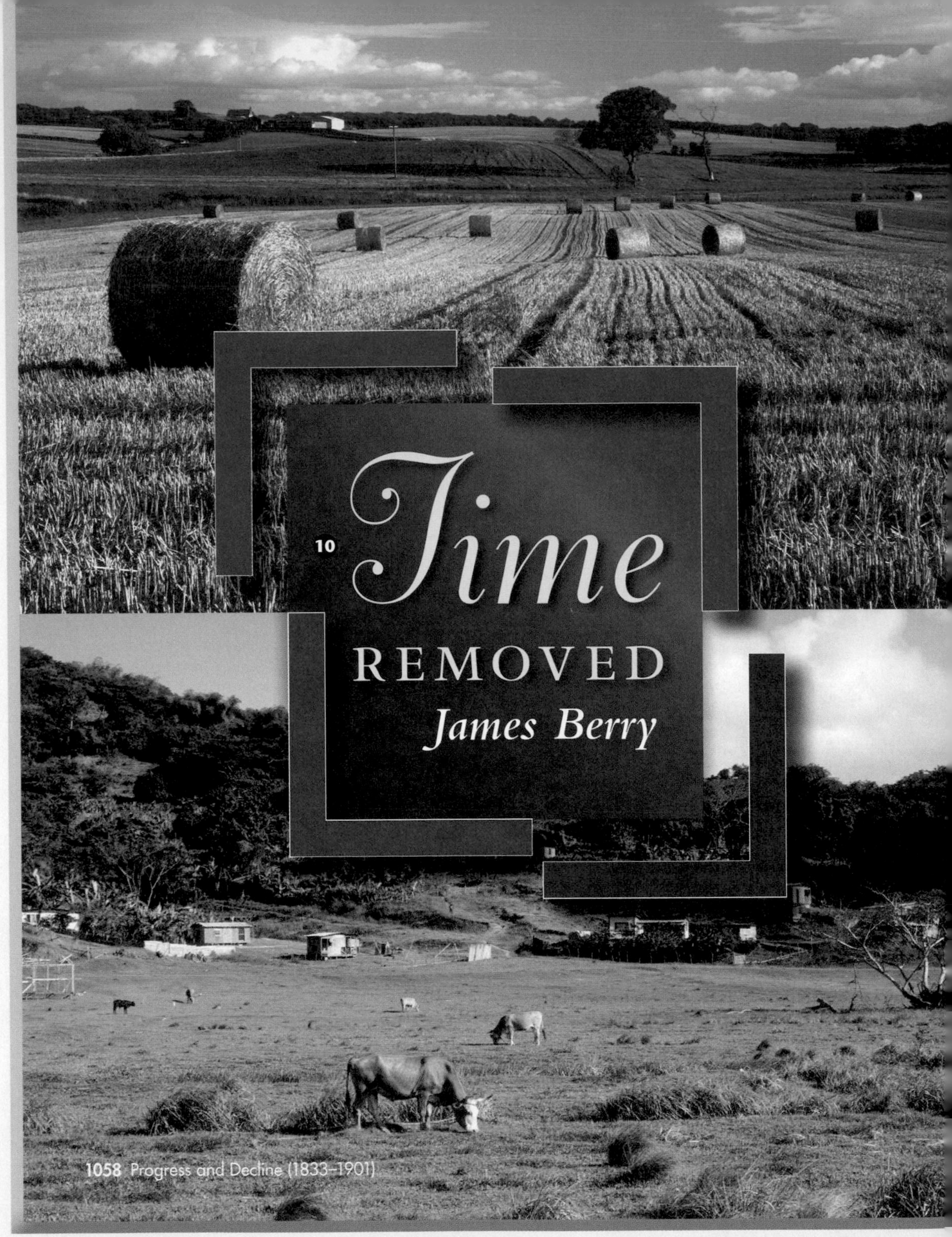

10 *Time* REMOVED

James Berry

I go on and on in England
and walk no ground untrodden.

11 Landscapes are checkered —
tamed out of new years
and recurring generations.

Compulsive hands have shaped
bordered fields
out of scrub,
rivers' faces with bridge,
edifices for trees towering
lands now railed and tarred.

Animals are not bony and bare.
13 Wheels quicken time —
through a late summer
staying fresh as spring.

And here
just as jungles hold my love
every whiff of air evokes a time
14 like the horse my father left
and I after ten years away
found the greyhaired skeleton
neighing to me,
like these days do,
in memories too overlaid to touch.

James Berry
Author's Insight When I first rode through England on a train I was extraordinarily moved by the organization and variety of the landscape, like an ordered checkerboard of fields with different colored crops.

12 ◄ **Critical Viewing**
How do the two landscapes in these photographs dramatize the contrast that Berry makes in the poem? **[Connect]**

James Berry
Author's Insight Coming from the Caribbean, I wasn't used to the change of seasons. I'd thought that grass would go brown and dry up in late summer, but it stayed green all year round.

Critical Reading

Cite textual evidence to support your responses.

1. **Key Ideas and Details (a)** According to Lucy, in what kind of environment does the Queen live? **(b) Summarize:** What challenges does Lucy think the Queen faces as a result of her position? **(c) Analyze:** How do Lucy's perceptions humanize the Queen?
2. **Key Ideas and Details (a) Interpret:** In your own words, explain the meaning of lines 18–22 in "Freedom."
   (b) Support: Provide an example that illustrates your point.
3. **Integration of Knowledge and Ideas** In "Time Removed," Berry writes in lines 3–5 that the landscapes around us are "tamed out" by each new generation. Do you think the landscape around you is improved by each generation or compromised by it? Provide examples to support your response.

14 Critical Thinking

1. Explain to students that in the last stanza, Berry remembers his home in Jamaica. **Ask** students how the last verse explains the title of the poem.
   Possible response: The speaker has been removed from the time of his childhood—from memories of the jungles and his father's horse—to the more modern England.
2. Discuss the image of the "grey-haired skeleton neighing to me." Point out that his memories are bittersweet.
3. **Ask** what message this poem shares with "Lucy: Englan' Lady."
   Possible response: The two poems share a message of inequality between the rich in England and the poor in Jamaica.

ASSESS

Answers

Before students respond, you may wish to have them write a brief objective summary of the selection. As they answer the questions below, remind them to support their answers with evidence from the text.

1. (a) Lucy claims that the Queen lives in "dust free rooms an' velvet an' diamond." (b) Lucy feels that the Queen must suffer loneliness and isolation brought about by always being on display. (c) Lucy humanizes the Queen when she observes "mus' be hard strain keepin' good graces for all hypocrite faces."
2. **Possible response:** (a) The speaker suggests that freedom is not just giving in to someone else's demands, nor is it the energy one spends being angry at oneself for falling victim to someone else's demands. (b) One example might be an individual who complains about his or her situation but does nothing to improve it.
3. **Possible response:** Students might note that "taming out" the landscape often means building huge cities and pouring concrete over the land. Others may note that "civilization" is a direct result of taming the landscape.

Differentiated Instruction — Additional Instruction

Culturally Responsive Instruction

Culture Focus The speaker in the poem returns to his homeland and compares its landscape with the well-maintained fields in England. Like the speaker, many Americans have come from other countries. Many times, if they can, they revisit their homelands.

Have students reflect upon how they would feel if they revisited their homeland. Have them consider what has changed since the last time they were there. If they have not revisited their homeland, have them consider what it would be like to do so.

Contemporary Connection

Explain to students that artists often reference other works or styles, both within and outside of the genres in which they work. Sometimes, these references serve to illustrate a point for which a previous style was particularly well suited, while at other times they create a sense of irony. Either way, this tendency speaks to the understanding of art as a dialogue rather than a series of static statements. **Ask** students if they can think of some examples of contemporary music that make use of past styles.
Possible responses: Rap, house, and R & B music sample from old jazz and soul records. Musical theater may incorporate popular music styles from the era in which the piece is set.

Connecting Victorian Themes

1. Tell students that Victorian art often attempted to articulate concerns about the growing gap between the natural world and the more artificial milieu generated by the rapid industrial development of the time.
2. The lament expressed by "Eli, the Barrow Boy" mirrors the concerns in Matthew Arnold's "Dover Beach." Have students turn back to "Dover Beach" and **ask** them what similarities they note in the two pieces.
   Possible responses: Both the poem and song occur at the border of nature and human habitation; both express the fear of death.

Colin Meloy

1. Tell students that Meloy's literary education informs his lyrics. Have them read the paragraph on Meloy.
2. **Ask** them why Meloy might be concerned about the accessibility of his music.
   Possible response: If Meloy is using Victorian motifs and language to give voice to analogous issues in contemporary society, he might need to eliminate some of the more esoteric elements so that his audience can understand his point.

CONTEMPORARY CONNECTION

CONNECTING VICTORIAN THEMES

Colin Meloy, frontman for lit-rock band The Decemberists, admits he reads a lot of Victorian novels. They have informed his writing style. His lyrics are often couched in the doubts and melancholy of the Victorians, harking back to the era's concerns about the passing of the natural world and the isolation ushered in by the new industrial age. Specifically, Meloy's "Eli, the Barrow Boy" lyrics echo the themes of love and loss in Matthew Arnold's "Dover Beach" as well as the working class voices in Kipling's poems.

COLIN MELOY SONGWRITER

Music is a necessity to Colin Meloy, something "that drives me completely," he says. He is the main songwriter for the indie group The Decemberists, whose music has been described as lit-rock. Meloy's background in literature qualifies him for the "lit" side of that description. He has a Master of Fine Arts (MFA) in creative writing and considers himself a writer of fictional song stories. The songs on the album *Picaresque,* for example, tell stories that seem to come straight out of Victorian Literature 101.

Sometimes, Meloy has to defend himself against charges of using too many big words! "I don't want to be the person who sends everyone to the dictionary when they're listening to music," he said in a 2004 interview, "just because I think that pop music should be a populist thing."

Enrichment: Analyzing Music

Protest Songs
While Victorian social problems were most notably documented in literature, other times of upheaval were marked by musical expressions of revolution. The accessibility of music has proven it to be an effective tool in disseminating the collective concerns of the disenfranchised. Slave spirituals conveyed messages of hope in the face of repression. Rock-and-roll music proposed alternatives to the puritanical mores of 1950s America. Today, musicians sing about topics ranging from homelessness to war overseas.

Activity: Listen for Dissent Have students choose a social problem and research songs that deal with that problem. They should record their observations on the **Enrichment: Analyzing Music** worksheet, ***Professional Development Guidebook,*** page 236. If possible, they should play the chosen songs for the class and discuss the interplay of musical styles and issues explored in the songs.

ELI, THE BARROW BOY

Eli, the barrow boy of the old town
Sells coal and marigolds
And he cries out all down the day

Below the tamaracks he is crying.
"Corncobs and candlewax for the buying!"
All down the day

"Would I could afford to buy my love a fine robe
Made of gold and silk Arabian thread
But she is dead and gone and lying in a pine grove
And I must push my barrow all the day.
And I must push my barrow all the day."

Eli, the barrow boy—when they found him
Dressed all in corduroy, he had drowned in
The river down the way.

They laid his body down in the church yard
But still when the moon is out
With his push cart he calls down the day:

"Would I could afford to buy my love a fine robe
Made of gold and silk Arabian thread
But I am dead and gone and lying in a church ground
But still I push my barrow all the day.
Still I must push my barrow all the day."

"CORNCOBS AND CANDLEWAX FOR THE BUYING!"

Critical Reading

1. **(a)** What does Eli do to make a living? **(b) Summarize:** What is the story behind the poem?
2. **Compare and Contrast:** In what ways do the setting, characters, and details in these lyrics echo those of Victorian literary works? Explain.

Use this question to focus a group discussion of "Eli, The Barrow Boy":

3. What might a contemporary music group gain by connecting with literature from the past?

Differentiated Instruction for Universal Access

Support for Less Proficient Readers
Students may need help in discerning the allegorical nature of the song. As it is a "song story," have students map out the plot in simple terms. They may want to use a graphic organizer to trace the events, setting, and characters. Have them compare the simplified narrative to some of the issues plaguing the Victorian age and note how Eli's suffering parallels that of his working-class compatriots in the new industrial world.

Enrichment for Gifted/Talented Students
The Chartist movement in Victorian England was comprised of working-class people giving voice to their own problems through protests, speeches, and even poetry. Have students research some Chartist poems. They can then contrast these poems, which were often very literal in their descriptions of working-class life, to the euphemistic culture that dominated much of the Victorian age.

"Eli, the Barrow Boy"

1. Have students read the lyrics to "Eli, the Barrow Boy" and, if possible, listen to the song. Discuss with students some of the issues of the Victorian age evoked by this song. The subject of the song belongs to the working class. The exploitation of the working class became increasingly clear as the exponential growth of manufacturing placed growing demands on the labor force. Many in the working class were relegated to filthy slums. Eli appears to be living on the literal and allegorical margin ("below the tamaracks"—a type of tree) between a pastoral existence and the demanding, dirty industrial age.
2. **Ask** students to note parallels between the seemingly Victorian problems in this song and similar problems occurring today.
Possible responses: Students may note that globalization and the digital age mark a cultural and economic shift equivalent to the one motivated by the Industrial Revolution.

ASSESS

Answers

Before students respond, you may wish to have them write a brief objective summary of the selection. As they answer the questions below, remind them to support their answers with evidence from the text.

1. (a) Eli is a barrow boy. (b) He sells items from his barrow as he laments his love's death. He eventually drowns later in the song.
2. The details in these lyrics echo the realism that emerged during this time of rapid social change. The lyrics focus on an ordinary boy facing day-to-day problems.
3. **Possible response:** Drawing from literature and traditions of the past creates certain expectations in the present work. An artist can either use these expectations to point out a common theme or treat the subject in unexpected ways, therefore creating a sense of irony.

PRETEACH

Common Core State Standards

- Reading Informational Text 1, 3

1 About the Text Forms

1. Introduce the forms, using the instruction on the student page.
2. **Ask** students what approaches a writer might use in a newspaper article about technology.
   Possible responses: A writer might use the voice of a witness or judge of technology and its effect on society, use humor to describe technological advances, or offer individual opinions.
3. Explain that an advertisement must have strong visual appeal and be worded such that it persuades its intended audience to buy or use goods or services.
4. **Ask** students what challenges the writer of a print advertisement might face.
   Possible response: The writer must be able to persuade the target audience, using only written language and visual images, to buy or use goods or services.

2 Reading Strategy

Introduce the strategy using the instruction on the student page.

Think Aloud: Model the Skill

Say to students:

I know that writers may choose from a variety of approaches to communicate a message. To determine the mode of persuasion used in a document, I ask myself questions as I read. This helps me evaluate the author's opinions.

3 How does literature shape or reflect society?

Tell students that, as they read, they should watch for modes of persuasion and note whether they think these are intended to influence or reflect social trends.

COMMON CORE ▪ RESEARCH PROJECT

Primary Sources

Newspaper Article
Progress in Personal Comfort

Advertisement
Cook's Railroad Advertisement

1 About the Text Forms

A **newspaper article** is any short piece of prose writing that appears in a newspaper. It may contain straight news, opinions about recent events, or a combination of both.

An **advertisement** is a persuasive piece that attempts to sell people a product or service. Before the invention of radio and television, printed advertisements were the major means of publicizing products. Such advertisements appeared in a variety of formats, including leaflets, newspaper advertisements, billboards, posters, and product labels.

2 Reading Strategy

Analyze the techniques of media messages in advertisements and persuasive newspaper articles by focusing on the following *modes of persuasion:*

- **Logical:** presents factual evidence and arguments that make sense
- **Faulty:** presents arguments that upon close study are not fully sound
- **Deceptive:** presents intentionally misleading information
- **Emotional:** uses status symbols, peer pressure, patriotism, humor, or other appeals to the reader's emotions and desires

Look for these modes of appeal as you read or view the primary sources. To help you identify and analyze appeals in these modes,

- summarize what the text explicitly says
- draw conclusions about what the text implies, or suggests
- analyze the sequence of and interrelationships between ideas. For example, do they follow a logical order? Do they build on one another?

Support your summary and your analysis by citing relevant quotations and other details from the text.

3 How does literature shape or reflect *society?*

Both the newspaper article and the advertisement reflect changes to society in Victorian times. As you read, consider what each document reveals about its times and how each relates to the other.

Common Core State Standards

Reading Informational Text
1. Cite strong and thorough textual evidence to support analysis of what the text says explicitly as well as inferences drawn from the text, including determining where the text leaves matters uncertain.
3. Analyze a complex set of ideas or sequence of events and explain how specific individuals, ideas, or events interact and develop over the course of the text.

PHLit Online! www.PHLitOnline.com

Teaching Resources

All *Unit 5 Resources, pp. 106–109*
All **Enriched Online Student Edition**

PHLit Online! All resources are available at www.PHLitOnline.com.

❹ Note-Taking Guide

Primary source documents are a rich source of information for researchers. As you read these documents, use a note-taking guide like the one shown to organize relevant and accurate information.

1 Type of Document (check one)
☐ Newspaper Article ☐ Letter ☐ Diary ☐ Speech ☐ Map
☐ Government Document ☐ Advertisement ☐ Memorandum ☐ Other

2 Date of Document ______________________

3 Author ______________________

Author's Position ______________________

4 Original Audience ______________________

5 Purpose and Importance

a Does this document or image have a persuasive purpose? ______________________

____

What techniques does it use to accomplish this purpose? Logical argument? Appeals to emotion? Attractive images? ______________________

____

b List two important ideas, statements, or observations from this document.

____

____

c What does this document show about life in the time and place in which it was composed? ______________________

____

Reading Strategy Analyzing Media Messages Identifying a source's persuasive goals, target audience, and techniques is a key to analyzing its message.

This guide was adapted from the **U.S. National Archives** document analysis worksheet.

❺ Vocabulary

depredation (dep′ rə dā′ shən) *n.* act or instance of robbing or laying waste (p. 1065)

Macadam (mə kad′ əm) *n.* road surfacing made of small stones bound with adhesive (p. 1065)

fracture (frak′ chər) *n.* a broken bone (p. 1065)

pulp (pulp) *n.* a soft, formless mass (p. 1065)

gout (gout) *n.* a type of arthritis characterized by painful attacks in the hands and especially the feet (p. 1066)

bilious (bil′ yəs) *adj.* suffering from or caused by too much bile or another liver problem (p. 1066)

privations (prī vā′ shənz) *n.* instances of being deprived; losses or absences of something (p. 1066)

PRETEACH

❹ Note-Taking Guide

1. Walk the class through the Note-Taking Guide, pointing out the different types of information students will be recording.
2. Discuss items 4 and 5 on the Note-Taking Guide with students, asking them to discuss how they might determine this information. For example, discuss questions students might ask themselves to determine the intended audience for a selection, and criteria students can use to identify the purpose and importance of a document.
3. Point out that students can use paraphrasing to help identify the message or main events of a selection for item 5c.

❺ Vocabulary

1. Have students preview the selection vocabulary, pronouncing the words and reading their definitions. Have students identify any words with which they are already familiar.
2. Use each word in a sentence with context to define the word. Then, repeat your definitional sentence with the vocabulary word missing, requiring the class to fill in the blank orally. For example:

The soft, fleshy inner tissue of fruits and vegetables is called pulp.

Peel a banana to get at the inner (students say "pulp").

Differentiated Instruction for Universal Access

Support for Special-Needs Students
Have students complete the **Before You Read** and the **Making Connections** pages for these selections in the ***Reader's Notebook: Adapted Version.*** These pages provide an abbreviated skills instruction, a selection summary, the **Before You Read** graphic organizer, and a **Note-Taking Guide.**

Support for Less Proficient Readers
Have students complete the **Before You Read** and the **Making Connections** pages for these selections in the ***Reader's Notebook.*** These pages provide an abbreviated skills instruction, a selection summary, the **Before You Read** graphic organizer, and a **Note-Taking Guide.**

EL Support for English Learners
Have students complete the **Before You Read** and the **Making Connections** pages for these selections in the ***Reader's Notebook: English Learner's Version.*** These pages provide additional vocabulary, vocabulary skills, and vocabulary practice, along with a **Getting Ready to Read** activity.

PRETEACH

Background

The Story Behind the Documents

The British Empire in the nineteenth century measured itself with a yardstick called *progress.* People wondered whether things were better in the present than they had been in the past, and whether present trends would lead to a more reasonable future.

The idea of progress was perhaps born with the modern newspaper. To even ask whether progress has been made, the mind must first view the world as a collection of measurable facts—the number of people fed, of miles traveled, of diseases cured. By bringing together news from far and near, Victorian newspapers assembled an image of such a world.

In his article from the mid-nineteenth century, Sydney Smith reflects on the scientific and technological advances that have taken place, noting that he can name at least eighteen improvements that have occurred in his lifetime.

Along with bringing news and information to wider audiences, newspapers brought advertisements. Merchants and providers of services soon found that money spent on well-designed, persuasive newspaper ads was quickly recouped through the increased number of consumers these ads attracted. Thomas Cook quickly took advantage of this form of mass communication to reach his desired target customer base: prosperous, literate middle-class Victorians looking for safe forms of adventure and entertainment through travel to the faraway lands they had formerly only been able to know through reading.

COMMON CORE • RESEARCH PROJECT

THE STORY BEHIND THE DOCUMENTS

Sydney Smith

Sydney Smith (1771–1845) was an influential writer and preacher of his time. In 1802, he helped found the *Edinburgh Review,* a popular journal to which he frequently contributed articles. Many of these articles express progressive viewpoints on issues such as parliamentary reform, prisons, slavery, and religious freedom. Ordained in the Church of England, Smith nevertheless was a tireless champion of Catholic Emancipation, arguing that Roman Catholics should enjoy equal rights in Britain, at a time when many Britons still thought they should not.

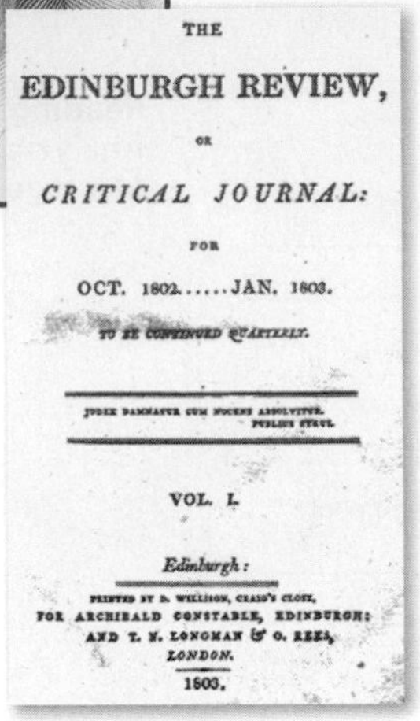

THE
EDINBURGH REVIEW,
OR
CRITICAL JOURNAL:
FOR
OCT. 1802......JAN. 1803.
TO BE CONTINUED QUARTERLY.

VOL. I.

Edinburgh:
1803.

Volume I of *The Edinburgh Review,* co-founded by Sydney Smith

The *Edinburgh Review,* which was published from 1802 to 1929, was a forerunner of today's magazines and journals. It was especially known for its progressive commentaries on politics and its criticism of literary works. Contributors to the journal included famous authors such as the essayist William Hazlitt and the historian Thomas Babington Macaulay (a letter of whose appears in this textbook). The relatively large circulation of this journal—13,500 in 1818—testifies to the growing interest in ideas and literature.

A pioneer of the modern travel industry, **Thomas Cook** (1808–1892) was a devout Baptist who organized his first tour to bring people to a meeting of the temperance movement, a movement to discourage the use of alcoholic beverages. Soon Cook was booking railway excursions all over Britain. He eventually expanded his tours to include Europe, the Middle East, and even North America. In 1872, he led a round-the-world tour that is said to have inspired Jules Verne's novel *Around the World in 80 Days.*

Thomas Cook

Smith's journal and Cook's tours are both evidence of the growth of Victorian Britain's middle class. An increasingly prosperous and literate middle class meant a greater audience for books, magazines, and newspapers. Having more money and leisure time also meant that middle-class Victorians could see a bit more of the world, enjoying the relatively safe and comfortable travel adventures that a Cook's tour provided.

New publications and new means of travel are just two examples of the kind of progress that Victorian Britain valued. Sydney Smith's newspaper article celebrates the innovations, large and small, that contributed to progress in the area of personal comfort—umbrellas, gas streetlights, and adhesive postage stamps, to name just a few. The great strides in transportation that Smith also describes—steamships, better roads, and most of all, railways—were the cornerstone of the new tourist industry promoted in Thomas Cook's advertisement.

Enrichment: Investigating Technology

Mass Communication

Smith's article came just before the rise of mass communication. The invention of transatlantic cable was hailed as a miracle. Formerly, messages traveled by ship, a two-week trip across the Atlantic. Messages sent by cable arrived in minutes. Today, cable and telegraph seem cumbersome—messages had to be sent and received in code by trained operators, then delivered by hand to the recipient. But at the time, the technology revolutionized social communication.

Activity: Research Victorian-era Communication Technology Have student pairs research how the appearance of mass communication—the telegraph and the transatlantic cable—affected Victorian-era society. Have students use the **Enrichment: Investigating Technology** worksheet, ***Professional Development Guidebook,*** page 242.

PROGRESS IN PERSONAL COMFORT

1

Sydney Smith

It is of some importance at what period a man is born. A young man, alive at this period, hardly knows to what improvements of human life he has been introduced; and I would bring before his notice the following eighteen changes which have taken place in England since I first began to breathe in it the breath of life—a period amounting now to nearly seventy-three years.

Gas[1] was unknown: I groped about the streets of London in all but the utter darkness of a twinkling oil lamp, under the protection of watchmen in their grand climacteric,[2] and exposed to every species of **depredation** and insult.

3 I have been nine hours in sailing from Dover to Calais before the invention of steam. It took me nine hours to go from Taunton to Bath, before the invention of railroads, and I now go in six hours from Taunton to London! In going from Taunton to Bath, I suffered between 10,000 and 12,000 severe contusions,[3] before stone-breaking **Macadam** was born.

I paid £15 in a single year for repairs of carriage-springs on the pavement of London; and I now glide without noise or **fracture**, on wooden pavements.

I can walk, by the assistance of the police, from one end of London to the other, without molestation; or, if tired, get into a cheap and active cab, instead of those cottages on wheels, which the hackney coaches[4] were at the beginning of my life.

I had no umbrella! They were little used, and very dear. There were no waterproof hats, and *my* hat has often been reduced by rains into its primitive **pulp**.

---

1. **gas** coal gas, piped under the streets of London and used in streetlights after 1814.
2. **climacteric** (klī mak′ tər ik) *n.* a major turning point in life, referring here to old age.
3. **contusions** (kən tyo͞o′ or to͞o′ zhənz) *n.* bruises.
4. **cheap and active cab . . . hackney coaches** Faster two-wheeled hansom cabs replaced hackney coaches as London's typical vehicles for hire to travel short distances.

2 **Primary Sources: Newspaper Article** What does the article reveal to be the contrasting attitudes of younger and older Victorians toward the progress it describes?

Reading Strategy Analyzing Media Messages Identify the logical reasoning and emotional appeals in the third paragraph.

Vocabulary

depredation (dep′ rə dā′ shən) *n.* act or instance of robbing or laying waste

Macadam (mə kad′ əm) *n.* road surfacing made of small stones bound with adhesive

fracture (frak′ chər) *n.* a broken bone

pulp (pulp) *n.* a soft, formless mass

TEACH

1 Background
History

The rise of newspapers brought opinions and news to a vast public, appealing to it as witness and critic of events, and ushering in the concept of public opinion.

A prolific writer on serious matters, Sydney Smith was famous for his witty essays, and his wit is evident in the article included here. He celebrates the progress made in the area of personal comfort.

2 Primary Sources
Newspaper Article

1. Read the first paragraph aloud to the class. Then briefly describe the pre-computer process of preparing a term paper: by use of manual typewriters, carbon copies, and erasers.
2. Point out that the difference between this method and computer technology is more significant today for older people than for students.
3. Then, **ask** students the Primary Source question: What does the artical reveal to be the contrasting attitudes of younger and older Victorians toward the progress it describes?
4. **Possible response:** Older people may be more aware of technological progress than younger people, who were born at a time when the technology was already in use.

3 Reading Strategy
Analyzing Modes of Persuasion

1. Have students read the third paragraph. Review differences between logical and emotional language.
2. Then, **ask** the Reading Strategy question.
3. **Answer:** The exclamation point following the second sentence and the exaggerated reference "10,000 to 12,000 severe contusions" are emotional appeals. Travel time references present logical reasoning.

❸ Primary Sources
Newspaper Article

1. Have students finish reading the article. Then, have them summarize its content and identify the writer's purpose for writing it.
2. Then, **ask** the Primary Source question: Why do you think Smith does not relate the detailed history of the inventions he cites?

Possible response: Students may respond that by just citing these inventions, almost as if they had appeared out of thin air, Smith manages to express a greater sense of wonder at these technological marvels.

ASSESS/EXTEND
Answers

1. (a) **Possible response:** Smith was approximately 73 years old. (b) **Possible response:** The changes took place before the "young man" was born, or during his childhood and young adulthood, and were interwoven into his daily life.
2. (a) Two changes in public safety were gas street lamps and a more robust police force. Two changes in public transportation were the invention of steamboats and railroads. (b) **Possible response:** Before the changes Smith describes, it was more dangerous to go out at night, transportation was slow and uncomfortable, public health was generally poor, and it took a long time for mail to travel between distant locations.
3. (a) It apparently did not occur to Smith that progress would continue and his "luxurious" lifestyle would later be looked upon as out-of-date and uncomfortable. (b) **Possible response:** Values such as "progress" and "discomfort" are relative to a person's habits and expectations. Smith cannot "see" the discomfort in his own surroundings because he has not had the experience of twentieth- and twenty-first-century conveniences.

❸ Primary Sources
Newspaper Article
Why do you think Smith does not relate the detailed history of the inventions he cites?

Vocabulary

gout (gout) *n.* a type of arthritis that especially affects the feet

bilious (bil′ yəs) *adj.* having a digestive ailment caused by too much bile or another liver problem

privations (prī vā′ shənz) *n.* losses or absences of something

I could not keep my smallclothes in their proper place, for braces were unknown.[5] If I had the gout, there was no colchicum. If I was bilious, there was no calomel. If I was attacked by ague, there was no quinine.[6] There were filthy coffee houses instead of elegant clubs. Game could not be bought. Quarrels about uncommuted tithes[7] were endless. The corruption of Parliament, before Reform, infamous.[8] There were no banks to receive the savings of the poor. The Poor Laws were gradually sapping the vitals of the country; and whatever miseries I suffered, I had no post to whisk my complaints for a single penny[9] to the remotest corners of the empire; and yet, in spite of all these privations, I lived on quietly, and am now ashamed that I was not more discontented, and utterly surprised that all these changes and inventions did not occur two centuries ago.

I forgot to add, that as the basket of stage coaches, in which luggage was then carried, had no springs, your clothes were rubbed all to pieces. . . .

---

5. **smallclothes . . . braces were unknown** There were no suspenders to hold up his trousers.
6. **gout . . . quinine** (kwī′ nīn′) Colchicum, calomel, and quinine were new, more effective medications used to treat the medical conditions mentioned. *Ague* (ā′ gyo͞o′) is an old word for a fever accompanied by chills—the kind of fever that recurs in people suffering from malaria.
7. **uncommuted tithes** (tī*thz*) Beginning with the Tithe Act of 1836, taxes paid to the Church of England in the form of produce were "commuted," or changed to, an equivalent payment in money.
8. **The corruption . . . infamous** Before passage of the Reform Bill of 1832, the House of Commons was dominated by a small number of wealthy, corrupt landowners.
9. **I had no post . . . single penny** Penny postage, in the form of an adhesive stamp, was first introduced to Britain in 1840.

Critical Reading

Cite textual evidence to support your responses.

1. **Key Ideas and Details (a)** How old was Smith when he wrote this newspaper article? **(b) Infer:** Why does he think a young man would "hardly know" the value of the improvements he describes?
2. **Key Ideas and Details (a) Classify:** What are two improvements in public safety and two in public transportation that Smith reports? **(b) Generalize:** What general picture does he draw of life before the various inventions and changes he describes?
3. **Integration of Knowledge and Ideas (a) Assess:** Does Smith consider the possibility that people in the future might find his world uncomfortable? Explain. **(b) Generalize:** What does Smith's attitude toward the past, present, and future show about human attitudes toward progress in general?

Enrichment: Investigating Health and Medicine

Victorian Health Concerns
Smith mentions health concerns that were relieved by medications discovered during his lifetime. Though these advances provided great relief, other health concerns abounded. Rising industrialization brought increased urbanization. Some of the gravest threats to public health— typhus, cholera, and tuberculosis (consumption)—stemmed from lack of knowledge about hygiene and sanitation. These diseases were widespread, even among the wealthy.

Activity: Research Victorian-era Health and Medicine Have students work in small groups to research a common illness or public health threat from the mid-nineteenth century and learn about any advances in medical knowledge and treatment that arose. Suggest that students use the **Enrichment: Investigating Health and Medicine** worksheet, ***Professional Development Guidebook,*** page 229, to guide and record their research.

LITERATURE IN CONTEXT

TECHNOLOGICAL ADVANCES IN THE NINETEENTH CENTURY

As Sydney Smith describes, during the nineteenth century, technology developed at a rapid pace and changed people's lives in important ways. This timeline shows a few of these advances.

▲1824
Englishman **Joseph Aspin** patented Portland Cement, made from hydraulic lime. In 1843, cement was used to build the Thames Tunnel, the world's first underwater tunnel.

▼1835
Fox Talbot, an English chemist, published an article on his discovery of the paper negative, preparing the way for modern photography.

▲1862
French scientist **Louis Pasteur** discovered that, by heating milk, one could kill many harmful organisms in it, thus extending its shelf life. He called the process "pasteurization."

▲1895
The Frenchman **Louis Lumière** invented a portable all-in-one motion-picture camera, film processing unit, and projector called the Cinématographe, which began the era of motion pictures.

►1834
The Analytic Engine—designed by **Charles Babbage,** a British scientist and mathematician—is a forerunner of modern digital computers.

▼1877
The cylinder phonograph, the earliest method of recording sound, was developed by **Thomas Edison.** Soon after, he recorded the voice of Alfred, Lord Tennyson.

CONNECT TO THE LITERATURE

How would you describe Sydney Smith's attitude toward the changes he witnessed during his lifetime?

1067

Literature in Context

Technological Advances in the Nineteenth Century

1. Have students read the first two paragraphs on page 1066.
2. Ask students to imagine their lives without a common modern technology, such as cell phones.

Connect to the Literature

Then, **ask** the Connect to the Literature question: How would you describe Sydney Smith's attitude toward the changes he witnessed during his lifetime?

Possible response: Although he writes with much humor, Smith is in awe of the progress made in technology and excited by the prospect of further advances.

Differentiated Instruction for Universal Access

Culturally Responsive Instruction

Culture Focus Students may lack the background knowledge or context-building experiences necessary to fully comprehend the selection. Before students read, build background knowledge about transportation and communications in Victorian-era Britain. Provide images of several key advances of the Industrial Revolution and discuss these in the context of a typical working-class family. Locate Britain on the globe and point out its location relative to North America. Explain how advances in transportation and communications expanded opportunities for transatlantic communication and the mass emigration that began in the second part of the nineteenth century.

❹ Background

The package tour was born when Thomas Cook arranged to take a group of temperance advocates to a rally. He arranged with the rail company to include tickets and refreshments at a single price per passenger. For arranging the outing, Cook collected a share of the fares.

❺ Reading Strategy

Analyzing Modes of Persuasion

1. Have students describe the advertisement on page 1068.
2. Then, have students indicate the intended audience, the message, and the method of persuasion for each listed element.
3. **Possible responses:** Use of woman as central figure: intended audience is middle-class, married women; message is that seeing the world is exotic and educational; method of persuasion is emotional appeal.

❻ Primary Source

Advertisement

1. Have a student read aloud the text of the advertisement.
2. Then, **ask** students the Primary Source question: What does this advertisement try to persuade people to do?
   Possible response: The advertisement tries to persuade people to travel on a guided tour (a Cook's tour) to distant places.

ASSESS/EXTEND

Answers

1. (a) It will take me anywhere in the world. (b) **Possible response:** It is underlined to emphasize that trips to far-off, exotic locations are possible.
2. (a) **Possible response:** Like modern ads, it is colorful and designed to attract customers; a modern advertisement would use photography and might emphasize travel technology such as WiFi. (b) Yes, modern print ads tend to use color photographs.

COMMON CORE ▪ RESEARCH PROJECT

RAILROAD ADVERTISEMENT

❹ BACKGROUND This Victorian advertisement for a Cook's tour was aimed at Britain's growing middle class.

❺ **Reading Strategy**
Analyzing Media Messages For each of the following elements, indicate the intended audience, the message, and the method of persuasion:
- The use of a woman as the central figure
- The woman's position, body language, and dress
- Other images
- Featured words

❻ **Primary Source**
Advertisement
What does this advertisement try to persuade people to do?

Critical Reading

1. **Key Ideas and Details (a)** Where does the ad say a Cook's tour will take you? **(b) Infer:** Why do you think the word *anywhere* is underlined?
2. **Integration of Knowledge and Ideas (a) Apply:** If this ad were used today, how would a contemporary reader react to it? Explain, citing specific elements of the ad. **(b) Evaluate:** Have the techniques of print advertising changed very much since Victorian times? Explain, giving examples in support.

Cite textual evidence to support your responses.

Enrichment: Investigating Daily Life

Everyday Life in Victorian Britain
Some of the most important technological changes in the nineteenth century were those affecting everyday life. As work became mechanized, people were less tired in the evening and were more inclined to make use of their new leisure time by going out to social events or visiting friends.

Activity: Investigating Daily Life Have students work in pairs or small groups to examine the effects of technological advances on the members of an average family in Victorian Britain. Students can use the **Enrichment: Investigating Daily Life** worksheet, ***Professional Development Guidebook,*** page 224, to guide and record their research.

Newspaper Article • Advertisement

Comparing Primary Sources

Refer to your Note-Taking Guide to answer these questions.

1. **(a)** Summarize the **newspaper article.** Support your answer with quotations from the text. **(b)** What attitudes and ideas does Smith implicitly promote? Explain, citing relevant details. **(c)** Explain how the main ideas in the article reinforce one another.
2. **(a)** What does the appearance of the people in the **advertisement** show about the background, class, and interests of its audience? **(b)** Which details in Smith's article appeal to a similar audience? Organize details in a diagram like the one shown.

Details of People Pictured in Ad	Details in Newspaper Article
↓	↓
Likely Audience	Likely Audience

3. Write a paragraph comparing the modes of persuasion used in the two sources.

Common Core State Standards

Writing

7. Conduct short as well as more sustained research projects to answer a question or solve a problem; narrow or broaden the inquiry when appropriate; synthesize multiple sources on the subject, demonstrating understanding of the subject under investigation. *(p. 1070)*

8. Gather relevant information from multiple authoritative print and digital sources, using advanced searches effectively; assess the strengths and limitations of each source in terms of the task, purpose, and audience; integrate information into the text selectively to maintain the flow of ideas, avoiding plagiarism and overreliance on any one source and following a standard format for citation. *(p. 1070)*

Language

6. Acquire and use accurately general academic and domain-specific words and phrases, sufficient for reading, writing, speaking, and listening at the college and career readiness level; demonstrate independence in gathering vocabulary knowledge when considering a word or phrase important to comprehension or expression.

Vocabulary Acquisition and Use

New Vocabulary Is each statement true or false? Explain.

1. A generous philanthropist will often engage in *depredation*.
2. The *pulp* of the tooth is the hard enamel on the outside.
3. Someone camping in the wild is likely to experience *privations*.

Content-Area Vocabulary Use the italicized vocabulary words to help you answer each question. Then, explain your answer.

1. A person with *gout* would probably **(a)** cough a lot **(b)** sleep a lot **(c)** rest his or her feet on a cushion.
2. A person would most likely feel *bilious* after **(a)** eating **(b)** resting **(c)** trying on shoes.
3. To heal a *fracture*, a person would most likely need **(a)** a cast **(b)** a flu shot **(c)** a warm drink.
4. Supplying new *Macadam* would be the job of **(a)** a chef **(b)** a road builder **(c)** a travel agent.

Etymology Study Macadam is named for John Macadam, the engineer who developed it. Use a dictionary to trace the etymology of these words based on a person's name: *boycott, maverick, silhouette, watt.*

Differentiated Instruction for Universal Access

Support for Special-Needs Students
Lead a quick "selection tour" of Cook's advertisement before students read, focusing their attention on the title, illustrations, and questions in side margins.

Less Proficient Readers
Tell students to find advertisements in two different newspapers or magazines that advertise the same type of product or service. Then, have them use a Venn diagram to compare the two advertisements.

Enrichment for Gifted/Talented Students
Have students create print advertisements for a travel service or particular destination. Encourage students to focus on a new service that arose due to advances in technology, or on an unusual destination the "average" traveler might not have visited. Students may illustrate their advertisements.

ASSESS/EXTEND

Answers

Comparing Primary Sources

1. (a) **Possible response:** He wants readers to embrace changes in technology, because he thinks progressively. (b) **Possible response:** He might have described these as an advance due to improved transportation.
2. (a) **Possible response:** It targets prosperous, educated, middle-class people interested in traveling to locations they have read about. (b) **Possible response:** His descriptions of travel by train across England, concern for proper dress, elegant clubs, and wild game suggest targeting prosperous readers who value travel and elegance.
3. Paragraphs should include accurate details from each document.

Vocabulary Acquisition and Use

True or False

1. False; philanthropists engage in charitable acts, while acts of depredation involve plunder.
2. False; pulp is soft and usually without form, so it could not form a hard outer coating.
3. True; someone camping endures privations such as the lack of running water.

Content-Area Vocabulary

1. C; gout makes the feet sore, so sufferers might rest their feet.
2. A; bilious refers to an unpleasant sensation in the digestive system following a meal.
3. A; fractured bones must be kept immobile to heal properly.
4. B; Macadam is used to build roads, so supplying it is the job of a road builder.

Etymology Study

boycott—C. C. Boycott, an English land agent in Ireland ostracized for dealings with British landlords and tenants

maverick—Samuel A. Maverick, a Texas cattleman who refused to brand his cows

silhouette—Étienne de Silhouette, an unpopular mid-nineteenth century French finance minister

watt—James Watt, a Scottish engineer who invented the steam engine

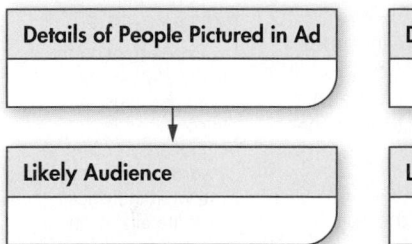

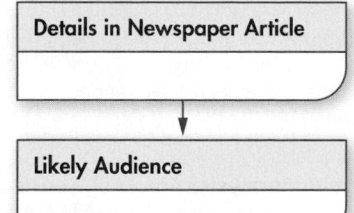

The Theme of "Progress" in the Media

Introduce the Assignment

1. Review the assignment. Point out that the research report calls for students to do two things—*analyze* two ads, and then *evaluate* how these media differ from traditional texts.
2. Mention that few ads will directly discuss the theme of progress. Instead, students are likely to find ads that show the effects of progress—people feeling or doing something because they now have the ability to do so; or people experiencing the negative consequences of "progress," such as dependence on electronics for social interactions.

Guide Student Research

1. Ensure that students formulate two kinds of research questions: *Analysis Questions,* such as "What media techniques are used in the ad?" *Evaluation Questions,* such as "What does this ad do that a traditional text does not or cannot do?"
2. As students gather sources, remind them that the ads do not need to be about the same type of product or idea. They need only make use, in some way, of the theme of progress.

Think Aloud: Model the Skill

Say to students: When I evaluate how media works in ways different from traditional texts, I remind myself that time is a major factor. A television ad may last thirty or sixty seconds, and I can get the idea of a print ad in even less time; however, it might take an hour to read an essay.

Guide Student Writing

1. Point out that students will need to create two charts to help synthesize their insights—one each for the print ad and the television ad.
2. To help students identify the cultural and social views in contemporary print and television media, remind students that ads depend largely on associations and suggestions, not direct statements. Since associations and suggestions are largely subjective, they may have different effects on different people.

© COMMON CORE ▪ RESEARCH PROJECT

Research Task

Topic: The Theme of "Progress" in the Media

In the centuries separating Victorian England from the present, the idea of progress—measured with terms such as "faster," "farther," and "easier"—has acquired a large shadow side. Concerned about everything from pollution to poor diet to cell phones, people today may associate progress with threats to the environment, to health, and even to civility. These days, "progress" may even mean taking a step back.

Assignment: Present a research report in which you analyze the treatment of the theme of "progress" in a television and a print advertisement. Then, evaluate how these media reflect cultural and social views different from those in Sydney Smith's essay and in the Cook's tour advertisement.

Gather sources. Use television recordings, newspapers, magazines, and online and library sources to locate and review possible ads for your report. Narrow or broaden your search as needed to ensure that you find the material you need efficiently. Keep accurate notes of the sources of all material.

Develop questions to guide analysis. Analyzing your chosen advertisements should involve answering questions like these:

- What is the purpose of and audience for the ad?
- What media techniques does the ad use to convey the theme of progress?
- What view of progress—positive, negative, or mixed—does the advertisement present?

Synthesize information. Review each ad, analyzing individual elements such as words, images, graphic elements, and sounds. Create a chart like the one shown to help synthesize your insights.

Model: Synthesizing Information in Media

Words	Images	Graphics	Sounds
Simpler and *purer* suggest progress —away from "progress"!	Images of an elderly farmer suggest tradition.	Logo of a mill suggests return to the past.	Theme played on banjo suggests simpler times.

Conclusion: Ad suggests that the product helps consumers escape the confusion and stress of "progress" to return to simpler times.

Organize and present ideas. Present your analysis of the ads and your comparison of the social and cultural views they reflect with the views found in Smith's essay and the Cook's tour advertisement. To ensure flow, select the strongest examples for each point you make. Avoid plagiarism, citing your sources for images and ideas.

RESEARCH TIP

Pay close attention to the denotations, or literal meanings, and the connotations, or emotional associations, of words used in the ads. Note what individual words literally mean and what connotations they take on in the context of the ads.

Use a checklist like the one shown to evaluate your work.

Research Checklist

- ☐ Have I answered all the questions in my guidelines for analysis?
- ☐ Have I fully analyzed the words and the images?
- ☐ Have I evaluated the impact of the graphics and the sounds?
- ☐ Have I articulated the overall meaning of each ad?
- ☐ Have I successfully compared the social and cultural views reflected in the ads with the views of optimistic Victorians?

Assessment Resources

Unit 3 Reasources

- All **Selection test, pp. 108–109**
- All **Customizable Test Bank**
- All **Self-Test**
  Students may prepare for the **Selection Test** bt taking the **Self-Test** online.

PHLit Online! All resources are available at **www.PHLitOnline.com.**

Gloom and Glory

PART 4

1071

Ⓒ Text Complexity: At a Glance

This chart gives a general text complexity rating for the selections in this part of the unit to help guide instruction. For additional text complexity support, see the Test Complexity Rubric at point of use.	
Remembrance	**More Accessible**
The Darkling Thrush	**More Complex**
"Ah, Are You Digging on My Grave?"	**More Accessible**
God's Grandeur	**More Accessible**
Spring and Fall	**More Accessible**
To an Athlete Dying Young	**More Complex**
When I Was One-and-Twenty	**More Accessible**

Selection Planning Guide

The selections in this section all deal with the theme of gloom and glory. Emily Brontë's "Remembrance" and Thomas Hardy's "'Ah, Are You Digging on My Grave?'" comment on death and love, and Hardy's "The Darkling Thrush" explores how hope can exist even in the midst of loneliness and despair.

In Gerard Manley Hopkins's poem "God's Grandeur," the speaker marvels at the presence of God in nature. In Hopkins's "Spring and Fall," the speaker conjectures that a young girl's sorrow is caused by her sense of mortality. The speaker in A. E. Housman's "To an Athlete Dying Young" tells how a young runner has died in glory but at the peak of his talent. Housman's "When I Was One-and-Twenty" also examines gloom and glory but in a much lighter vein.

Humanities

Past and Present (no. 2), by Augustus Leopold Egg

Augustus Leopold Egg (1816–1863) was a painter and an actor. He performed in Charles Dickens's acting company and painted "genre paintings," which referred to works of novelists such as William Thackeray and Sir Walter Scott. **Ask** students to describe the atmosphere in this painting and to point out elements that contribute to that atmosphere.

Possible response: The painting has a melancholy atmosphere, created by the weeping child, the darkness of the room, and the mother's gaze directed toward the moon.

Monitoring Progress

Before students read the selections in Part 4, refer to the results for the **Vocabulary in Context** items on **Benchmark Test 8** (*Unit 4 Resources,* p. 201). Use this diagnostic portion to guide your choice of selections to teach, as well as the depth of prereading preparation you will provide, based on students' readiness for the reading and vocabulary skills.

Benchmark

After students have completed the poems by Hopkins and Housman, administer **Benchmark Test 9** ***(Unit 5 Resources,*** pp. 152–157). If the test reveals that some students need further work, use the **Interpretation Guide** to determine the appropriate reteaching page in the **Reading Kit.**

Remembrance • The Darkling Thrush • "Ah, Are You Digging on My Grave?"

Lesson Pacing Guide

DAY 1 Preteach

- Administer the Reading and Vocabulary Warm-ups (*Unit 5 Resources,* pp. 110–113) as necessary.
- Introduce the Literary Analysis concept: Stanzas.
- Introduce the Reading Strategy: Pattern of Stanzas.
- Build background with the author and Background features.
- Develop thematic thinking with Connecting to the Essential Question.
- Teach the selection vocabulary.

DAYS 2–3 Preteach/Teach/Assess

- Distribute copies of the graphic organizer for the Reading Skill (*Graphic Organizer Transparencies,* pp. 191–192).
- Distribute copies of the graphic organizer for Literary Analysis (*Graphic Organizer Transparencies,* pp. 193–194).
- Prepare students to read with the Activating Prior Knowledge activities (TE).
- Informally monitor comprehension while students read.
- Use the Reading Check questions to confirm comprehension.
- Develop students' ability to understand the pattern of stanzas using the Reading Strategy prompts.
- Reinforce vocabulary with the Vocabulary notes.
- Assess students' comprehension and mastery of the skills by having them answer the Critical Reading, Literary Analysis, and Reading Strategy questions.
- Have students complete the Vocabulary Lesson.

DAY 4 Extend/Assess

- Have students complete the Conventions and Style Lesson.
- Have students complete the Writing Lesson and write a response to literature. (You may assign as homework.)
- Administer Selection Test A or B (*Unit 5 Resources,* pp. 123–125 or 126–128).

Common Core State Standards

Reading Literature 5. Analyze how an author's choices concerning how to structure specific parts of a text contribute to its overall structure and meaning as well as its aesthetic impact.

Writing 2.b. Develop the topic thoroughly by selecting the most significant and relevant facts, extended definitions, concrete details, quotations, or other information and examples appropriate to the audience's knowledge of the topic.
5. Develop and strengthen writing as needed by planning, revising, editing, rewriting, or trying a new approach, focusing on addressing what is most significant for a specific purpose and audience.

Language 5. Demonstrate understanding of figurative language, word relationships, and nuances in word meaning.

Additional Standards Practice
Common Core Companion,* *pp. 54–55; 198–199; 226–227; 332–335

Daily Block Scheduling
Each day in this Lesson Pacing Guide represents a 40–50 minute period. Teachers using block scheduling may combine days to revise pacing. In addition, teachers may differentiate and support core instruction by integrating components for extended and intensive support as students require. See the Guide to Selected Leveled Resources (facing page).

Guide to Selected Leveled Resources

RTI		Tier 1 (students performing on level)	Remembrance • The Darkling Thrush • "Ah, Are You Digging on My Grave?"
Warm Up	Whole class instruction; Group work	**Practice, model,** and **monitor** fluency, working **with the whole class** or **in groups.**	**Vocabulary and Reading Warm-ups B,** ***Unit 5 Resources,*** pp. 110–111, 113
Comprehension/Skills	Whole class instruction; Group work; Independent work	**Support** and **monitor** comprehension and skills development, having students complete the activities, graphic organizers, and interactive prompts **independently** or **as a class.**	• ***Reader's Notebook,*** adapted instruction and full selection EL ***Reader's Notebook: English Learner's Version,*** adapted instruction and adapted selection • **Reading Strategy Graphic Organizer B,** ***Graphic Organizer Transparencies,*** p. 202 • **Literary Analysis Graphic Organizer B,** ***Graphic Organizer Transparencies,*** p. 204
Monitor Progress	A	**Monitor** student progress with the differentiated curriculum-based assessment in the *Unit Resources.*	• **Selection Test B,** ***Unit 5 Resources,*** pp. 126–128 • **Open-Book Test,** ***Unit 5 Resources,*** pp. 120–122

RTI		Tier 2 (students requiring intervention)	Remembrance • The Darkling Thrush • "Ah, Are You Digging on My Grave?"
Warm Up	Group work; One-on-one teaching	**Practice, model,** and **monitor** fluency **in groups** or **with individuals.**	• **Vocabulary and Reading Warm-ups A,** ***Unit 5 Resources,*** pp. 110–112 • ***Hear It!*** **Audio CD (adapted text)**
Comprehension/Skills	Group work; One-on-one teaching	• **Support** and **monitor** comprehension and skills development, working **in small groups** or **with individuals.** • As students complete the selection in the appropriate version of the *Reader's Notebook,* **monitor** comprehension frequently with group questions and individual instruction. • **Model** strategies while guiding students in completing the activities and prompts in the *Reader's Notebook,* as well as the graphic organizers. • **Practice** skills and **monitor** mastery with the *Reading Kit* worksheets.	• ***Reader's Notebook: Adapted Version,*** adapted instruction and adapted selection EL ***Reader's Notebook: English Learner's Version,*** adapted instruction and adapted selection • **Reading Strategy Graphic Organizer A,** ***Graphic Organizer Transparencies,*** p. 201 • **Literary Analysis Graphic Organizer A,** ***Graphic Organizer Transparencies,*** p. 203 • ***Reading Kit,*** Practice worksheets
Monitor Progress	A	**Monitor** student progress with the differentiated curriculum-based assessment in the *Unit Resources* and in the *Reading Kit.*	• **Selection Test A,** ***Unit 5 Resources,*** pp. 123–125 • ***Reading Kit,*** Assess worksheets

TIER 3 Tier 3 intervention may require consultation with the student's special-education or dyslexia specialist. For additional support, see the Tier 2 activities and resources listed above.

One-on-one teaching | **Group work** | **Whole class instruction** | **Independent work** | **A Assessment**

For a complete guide to selection support, including support for Advanced students, see the Overview of Resources in the frontmatter.

Remembrance • The Darkling Thrush • "Ah, Are You Digging on My Grave?"

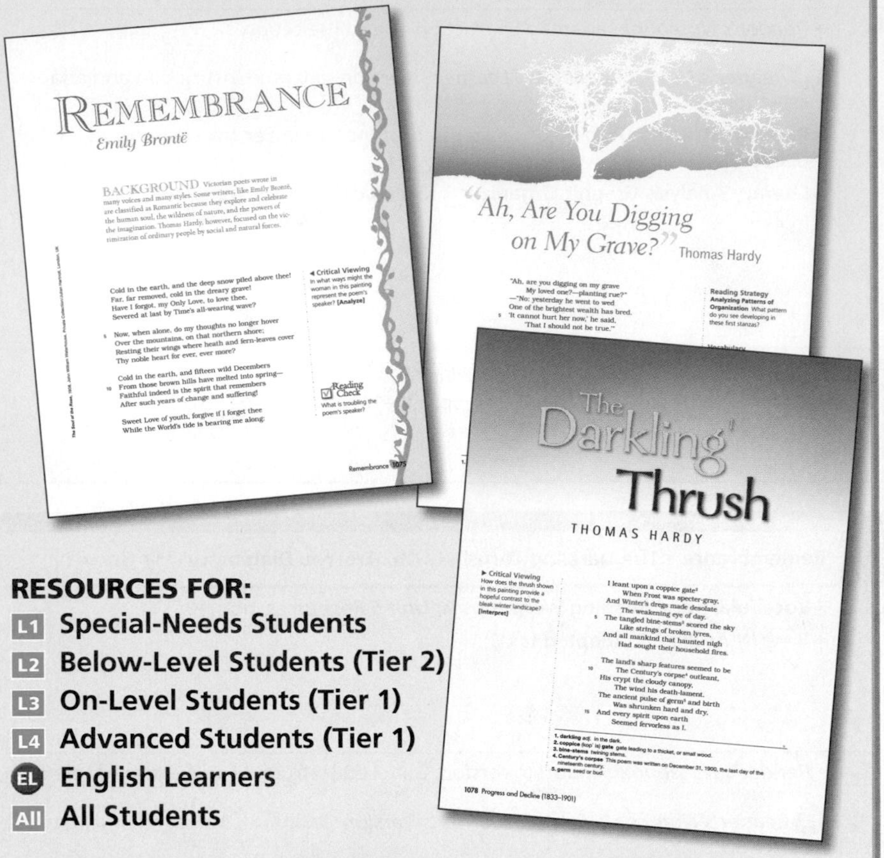

RESOURCES FOR:

- L1 Special-Needs Students
- L2 Below-Level Students (Tier 2)
- L3 On-Level Students (Tier 1)
- L4 Advanced Students (Tier 1)
- EL English Learners
- All All Students

Vocabulary/Fluency/Prior Knowledge

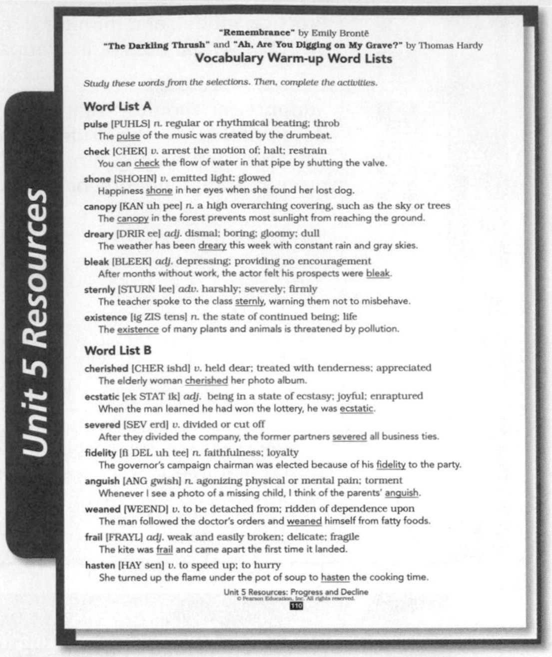
"Remembrance" by Emily Brontë
"The Darkling Thrush" and "Ah, Are You Digging on My Grave?" by Thomas Hardy
Vocabulary Warm-up Word Lists

Study these words from the selections. Then, complete the activities.

Word List A

pulse [PUHLS] *n.* regular or rhythmical beating; throb
The pulse of the music was created by the drumbeat.
check [CHEK] *v.* arrest the motion of; halt; restrain
You can check the flow of water in that pipe by shutting the valve.
shone [SHOHN] *v.* emitted light; glowed
Happiness shone in her eyes when she found her lost dog.
canopy [KAN uh pee] *n.* a high overarching covering, such as the sky or trees
The canopy in the forest prevents most sunlight from reaching the ground.
dreary [DRIR ee] *adj.* dismal; boring; gloomy; dull
The weather has been dreary this week with constant rain and gray skies.
bleak [BLEEK] *adj.* depressing; providing no encouragement
After months without work, the actor felt his prospects were bleak.
sternly [STURN lee] *adv.* harshly; severely; firmly
The teacher spoke to the class sternly, warning them not to misbehave.
existence [ig ZIS tens] *n.* the state of continued being; life
The existence of many plants and animals is threatened by pollution.

Word List B

cherished [CHER ishd] *v.* held dear; treated with tenderness; appreciated
The elderly woman cherished her photo album.
ecstatic [ek STAT ik] *adj.* being in a state of ecstasy; joyful; enraptured
When the man learned he had won the lottery, he was ecstatic.
severed [SEV erd] *v.* divided or cut off
After they divided the company, the former partners severed all business ties.
fidelity [fi DEL uh tee] *n.* faithfulness; loyalty
The governor's campaign chairman was elected because of his fidelity to the party.
anguish [ANG gwish] *n.* agonizing physical or mental pain; torment
Whenever I see a photo of a missing child, I think of the parents' anguish.
weaned [WEEND] *v.* to be detached from; ridden of dependence upon
The man followed the doctor's orders and weaned himself from fatty foods.
frail [FRAYL] *adj.* weak and easily broken; delicate; fragile
The kite was frail and came apart the first time it landed.
hasten [HAY sen] *v.* to speed up; to hurry
She turned up the flame under the pot of soup to hasten the cooking time.

Unit 5 Resources: Progress and Decline
110

EL L1 L2 **Vocabulary Warm-ups A and B,** p. 110–111

Also available for these selections:

EL L1 L2 **Reading Warm-ups A and B,** pp. 112–113

All **Vocabulary Builder,** pp. 116

Reader's Notebooks

Pre- and postreading pages for these selections appear in an interactive format in the *Reader's Notebooks*. Each *Notebook* is differentiated for a different group of learners. The selections in the Adapted and English Learner's versions are abridged.

- L2 L3 ***Reader's Notebook***
- L1 ***Reader's Notebook: Adapted Version***
- EL ***Reader's Notebook: English Learner's Version***
- EL ***Reader's Notebook: Spanish Version***

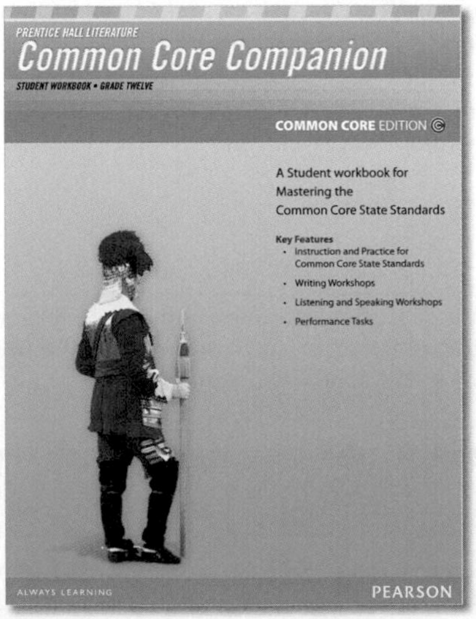

Common Core Companion

Additional instruction and practice for each Common Core State Standard

Selection Support

Graphic Organizer Transparencies

"Remembrance" by Emily Brontë
"The Darkling Thrush" and **"'Ah, Are You Digging on My Grave?'"**
by Thomas Hardy

After You Read A: Stanza Structure

"Remembrance"

Stanza	Number of Lines	Rhyme Scheme	Meter
1 2 3 4 5 6 7 8	4 in each stanza	*abab*	Basically iambic pentameter, with some initial trochees and line-ending unstressed syllables

"The Darkling Thrush"

Stanza	Number of Lines	Rhyme Scheme	Meter
1 2 3 4	8 in each stanza	*abababab*	

"'Ah, Are You Digging on My Grave?'"

Stanza	Number of Lines	Rhyme Scheme	Meter
1 2 3 4 5 6			

Graphic Organizer Transparencies

193

EL L1 L2 **Literary Analysis: Graphic Organizer A** (partially filled in), p. 193

Also available for these selections:

EL L3 **Literary Analysis: Graphic Organizer B,** p. 194

EL L1 L2 **Reading: Graphic Organizer A,** p. 191

EL L3 **Reading: Graphic Organizer B,** p. 192

Skills Development/Extension

Unit 5 Resources

Name ____________________ Date ____________

"Remembrance" by Emily Brontë
"The Darkling Thrush" and **"Ah, Are You Digging on My Grave?"**
by Thomas Hardy

Grammar: Using Active Voice

When it is appropriate to the meaning of your sentence, use the active voice to lend vitality to your writing. The active voice can also help you cut down on unnecessary words. Consider the following example:

There was a deafening noise coming from the refrigerator.

A deafening noise came from the refrigerator.

DIRECTIONS: *Rewrite the following letter, using the active voice where appropriate.*

Dear Ms. Satchel,

Your history class was enjoyed by me this semester. In fact, I think it was enjoyed by all of your students. Liveliness and a great atmosphere in the classroom were created by your sense of humor. Learning history has never been enjoyed by me until now. History was brought alive for me with your teaching. There is sadness in me because the year is ending.

Your future students are envied by me to have you as a teacher. Hopefully, your summer will be great.

Your Student,

Nigel

EL **Grammar and Style,** p. 117

Also available for these selections:

All **Literary Analysis: Stanzas,** p. 114

All **Reading: Pattern of Stanzas,** p. 115

EL L3 L4 **Support for Writing,** p. 118

L4 **Enrichment,** p. 119

Assessment

Name ____________________ Date ____________

"Remembrance" by Emily Brontë
"The Darkling Thrush" and **"Ah, Are You Digging on My Grave?"** by Thomas Hardy

Selection Test A

Critical Reading *Identify the letter of the choice that best answers the question.*

___ 1. What does the speaker remember in "Remembrance"?
A. her home
B. her sister
C. the one she loved
D. her country

___ 2. What is the meaning of this stanza from "Remembrance"?

Cold in the earth, and fifteen wild Decembers
From these brown hills have melted into spring—
Faithful indeed is the spirit that remembers
After such years of change and suffering!

A. It takes a special person to stay faithful to one who has been dead fifteen years.
B. Fifteen cold years have passed and I still think of my beloved as if he were alive.
C. It was cold when my beloved died, and it feels colder now when I remember him.
D. I'll never forget the joys we had, which remind me of spring and the melting snow.

___ 3. What does the speaker in "Remembrance" plan to do?
A. Forget her beloved.
B. Live in mourning forever.
C. Find a new love.
D. Go on with her life.

___ 4. What is ironic about the song of the thrush in "The Darkling Thrush"?
A. It is ironic that the speaker bothers to notice the thrush singing outside.
B. It is ironic that only the thrush is singing when so many other birds are about.
C. It is a winter day and nothing seems alive, but the thrush sings a cheerful song.
D. The thrush is old and frail, and it is ironic that it can sing at all.

___ 5. How does the mood change from the beginning to the end of "The Darkling Thrush"?
A. hopeless to hopeful
B. hopeful to sad
C. joyful to hopeless
D. thoughtful to sad

___ 6. What is the main idea of "The Darkling Thrush"?
A. None but birds would sing during the cold winter.
B. Birds do not understand how sad life can be.
C. Winter is the most difficult of seasons.
D. Hope exists even during the worst of times.

EL L1 L2 **Selection Test A,** pp. 123–125

Also available for these selections:

EL L3 L4 **Selection Test B,** pp. 126–128

L3 L4 **Open-Book Test,** pp. 120–122

PHLit Online!
www.PHLitOnline.com

- complete narrated selection text
- a thematically related video with writing prompt
- an interactive graphic organizer
- highlighting feature
- access to all student print resources, adapted to individual student needs
- Spanish and English summaries
- adapted selection translations in Spanish

Online Resources: All print materials are also available online.

Get Connected! (thematic video with writing prompt)

Also available:

Background Video
All videos are available in Spanish.

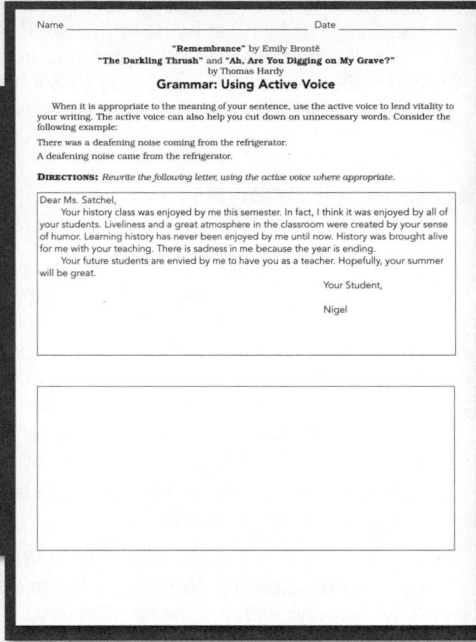

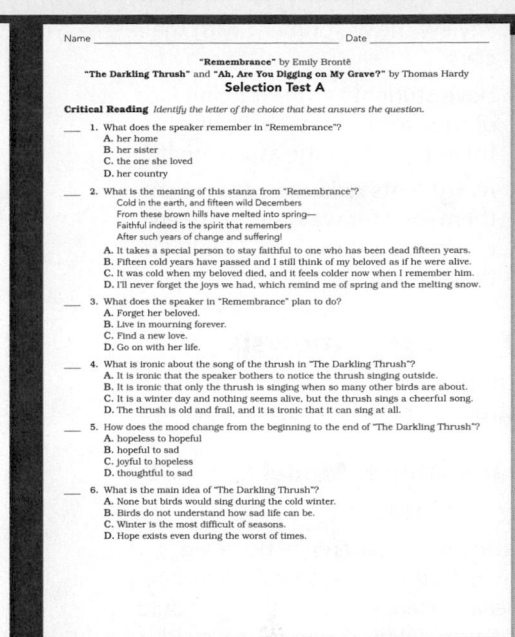

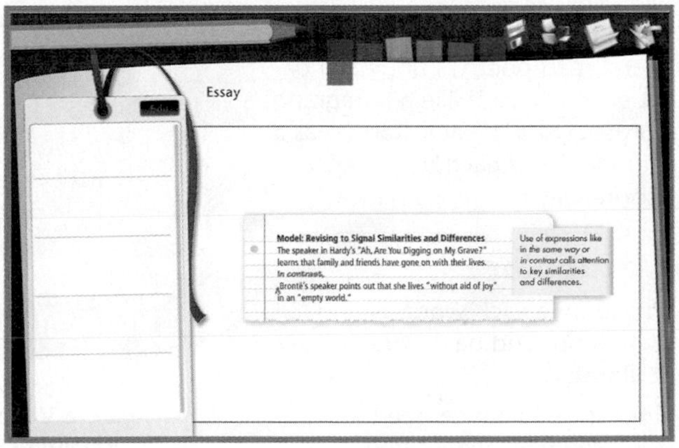

Writer's Journal (with graphics feature)

Also available:

Vocabulary Central (tools and activities for studying vocabulary)

1 Connecting to the Essential Question

1. Review the assignment with the class.
2. Have students suggest definitions of the word *home*. Then, have them complete the assignment.
3. As students read the poems, have them look for ways the speakers express dissatisfaction with where they are.

2 Literary Analysis

Introduce the skill using the instruction on the student page.

Think Aloud: Model the Skill

Say to students:

Irony is the difference between expectation or appearance and reality. Here's an example: It would be ironic if you went into a building to get out of the pouring rain only to have the building's emergency sprinkler system come on and drench you.

3 Reading Strategy

1. Introduce the strategy using the instruction on the student page.
2. Give students a copy of **Reading Strategy Graphic Organizer B,** page 192 in ***Graphic Organizer Transparencies***, to fill out as they read.

Think Aloud: Model the Skill

Say to students:

When I read poetry, I understand that each stanza is like a paragraph of prose. Usually, each stanza has a main idea, and each detail relates in some way to the main idea.

4 Vocabulary

1. Pronounce each word, giving its definition, and have students say it aloud.
2. For more guidance, see the ***Classroom Strategies and Teaching Routines*** card for introducing vocabulary.

Before You Read

Remembrance • The Darkling Thrush • "Ah, Are You Digging on My Grave?"

1 **Connecting to the Essential Question** Brontë and Hardy express the feeling of not being at home in the world. As you read, note the ways in which the speakers in these poems indicate dissatisfaction with the places in which they find themselves. Doing so will help you think about the Essential Question: **What is the relationship between literature and place?**

Common Core State Standards

Reading Literature
5. Analyze how an author's choices concerning how to structure specific parts of a text contribute to its overall structure and meaning as well as its aesthetic impact.

2 Literary Analysis

Poets have a number of ways of addressing a reader's expectations. **Stanzas,** for instance, are repeated groupings of two or more verse lines with a definite pattern of line length, rhythm, and, frequently, rhyme. The **stanza structure** of a poem is the pattern of stanzas from which it is built. While stanza structure creates an expectation of a regular pattern, **irony** challenges expectations by creating a contradiction between reality and appearance or between what is said and what is meant.

Both stanza structure and irony may set up and then fulfill or not fulfill expectations. In reading these poems, for example, notice these patterns:

- The arrangement of the first stanza leads you to expect a similar arrangement in the others.
- Irony surprises you by not fulfilling expectations.

Comparing Literary Works Brontë's and Hardy's poems deal in different ways with the theme of absence—the sense of something missing. Compare the ways in which the speakers in these poems feel about an absence and succeed or fail in handling it.

3 Reading Strategy

Preparing to Read Complex Texts Many poetic stanzas express a single main idea, as paragraphs do in prose. You can **analyze the pattern of stanzas** and how it affects the meaning and aesthetic impact of the poem if you notice how each stanza builds on the preceding one. Use a chart like this one to understand the logical progression of stanzas in each poem.

"Remembrance"

Stanza 1
Speaker had a true love who died and whom she may be forgetting.

↓

Stanza 2

↓

Etc.

4 Vocabulary

obscure (ăb skyo͞or′) *v.* make difficult to see (p. 1076)

languish (laŋ′ gwish) *v.* become weak; suffer from longing (p. 1076)

rapturous (rap′ chər əs) *adj.* filled with joy and love; ecstatic (p. 1076)

gaunt (gônt) *adj.* thin and bony, as from great hunger or age (p. 1080)

terrestrial (tə res′ trē əl) *adj.* relating to the earth or to this world (p. 1080)

prodding (präd′ iŋ) *adj.* poking, jabbing, seeking (p. 1081)

Vocabulary Development

Vocabulary Knowledge Rating

Create a **Vocabulary Knowledge Rating Chart** (***Professional Development Guidebook,*** p. 33) for the vocabulary words on the student page. Give each student a copy of the chart with the words on it. Read the words aloud, and have students mark their ratings in the Before Reading column. Urge students to attend to these words as they read and discuss the selections.

In order to gauge how much instruction you need to provide, tally how many students are confident in their knowledge of each word. As students read, point out the words and their context.

PHLit Online! **Vocabulary Central,** featuring tools and activities for studying vocabulary, is available online at **www.PHLitOnline.com.**

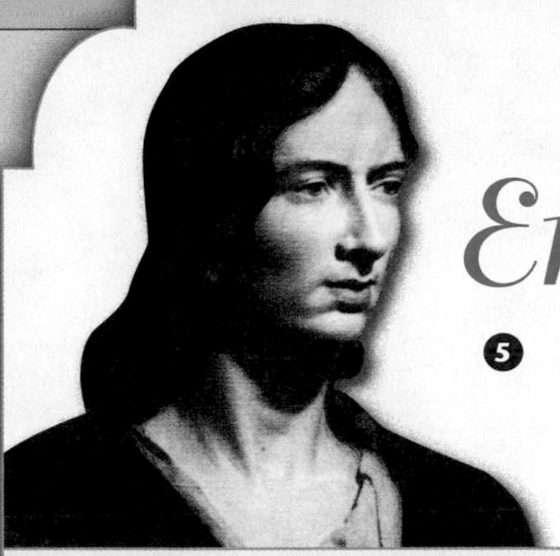

5 Emily Brontë

(1818–1848)

Author of "Remembrance"

Although some literary critics of the time attacked Emily Brontë for the violent passions expressed in her novel *Wuthering Heights* (1847), her dark Romanticism is now regarded as the essence of her genius.

A Writer's Beginnings Brontë grew up in the Yorkshire moorlands, a barren wasteland in the north of England, where her father was a clergyman. When Emily was just three, her mother died. Emily and her sisters, Charlotte and Anne, were educated at home for the most part and were often on their own.

Homesickness In 1835, Charlotte became a teacher at a school some distance from her home. Emily accompanied her as a pupil, but she quickly returned home. Three years later, she took a teaching position herself but resigned after six months.

Several years later, Charlotte and Emily devised another plan to support themselves as teachers. They would establish and run a school for girls in their own town of Haworth. To learn the skills they needed for this enterprise, they traveled to Brussels, Belgium. There, many people they met admired Emily for her Romantic temperament. However, Emily became homesick again and, after learning of her aunt's death, went home for good.

A Career Cut Short As adults, the three sisters published a book of poetry. The twenty-one poems that Emily contributed are considered the best of the collection. Emily's first and only novel, *Wuthering Heights,* was published in 1847. It tells the story of a tragic love affair played out against the mysterious landscape of the Yorkshire moors. The book is now considered a classic.

Wuthering Heights is the culminating expression of Emily's fiery imagination. A year after the book was published, she died of tuberculosis.

Daily Bellringer

For each class during which you will teach these selections, have students complete one of the five activities for the appropriate week in the ***Daily Bellringer Activities*** booklet.

Multidraft Reading

To assist struggling readers and to enhance reading for all, assign the text in chunks, as warranted by length, and apply multidraft reading protocols. For each reading, have students set the purpose indicated:

- **First reading**—identifying key ideas and details and answering any Reading Checks.
- **Second reading**—analyzing craft and structure and responding to the side-column prompts.
- **Third reading**—integrating knowledge and ideas, connecting to other texts and the world, and answering the end-of-selection questions.

For more guidance, refer to the ***Classroom Strategies and Teaching Routines*** card on Multidraft Reading.

5 Background

More About the Author

Emily Brontë

Emily Brontë's reputation rests largely on *Wuthering Heights*, her masterful novel, and the poems that she published with her sisters, Jane and Anne. In her poems, Emily Brontë created the imaginary world of Gondal, which was the setting for many of her finest poems, including "Remembrance." Emily was deeply attached to the landscape of Yorkshire—more so than either of her sisters—and she is remembered as a poet of the moors of England for their repeated appearances in *Wuthering Heights*.

PHLit Online! Teaching From Technology

www.PHLitOnline.com

Preparing to Read

Go to **www.PHLitOnline.com** and display the ***Get Connected!*** slide show for this selection. Have the class brainstorm responses to the writing prompt, entering ideas in the interactive journal. Then, have students complete their written responses as homework.

To build background, display the Background and More About the Author features.

Using the Interactive Text

Go to **www.PHLitOnline.com** and display the **Enriched Online Student Edition**. As the class reads the selection or listens to the narration, record answers to side-column prompts using the graphic organizers accessible on the interactive page. Alternatively, have students use the online edition individually, answering the prompts as they read.

❶ About the Selection

The speaker in Emily Brontë's poem addresses his or her only love, who died fifteen years earlier. The speaker asks forgiveness for not indulging in "memory's rapturous pain."

❷ Activating Prior Knowledge

On the board, make the words *hope* and *despair* the centers of two separate concept maps. Have students suggest related words for each map, and fill these in. Then tell students that the poems in this section are a mixture of both hope and despair. Encourage students to identify each speaker's outlook as they read the poems.

❸ Humanities

My Sweet Rose, by John William Waterhouse

John William Waterhouse (1849–1917) was an English painter who studied at the Royal Academy in London. He is considered to be both a Classical and a Pre-Raphaelite painter of mainly romantic and poetic subjects. Much of his work was inspired by the work of poets.

Use this question for discussion: What is your interpretation of the painting's title, *My Sweet Rose*?

Possible responses: Some students may say that the rose represents the beloved of the woman who is in the painting. Others may say that the title refers to the woman herself—that is, the painting depicts the artist's beloved.

Text Complexity Rubric

	Remembrance	**The Darkling Thrush**	**"Ah, Are You Digging on My Grave?"**
Qualitative Measures			
Context/ Knowledge Demands	Victorian Romantic lyric 1 ② 3 4 5	Victorian Naturalist lyric 1 2 ③ 4 5	Victorian dramatic poem 1 ② 3 4 5
Structure/Language Conventionality and Clarity	Poetic diction and syntax 1 2 ③ 4 5	Poetic diction and syntax 1 2 ③ 4 5	Informal dialogue 1 2 ③ 4 5
Levels of Meaning/ Purpose/Concepts	Accessible (pragmatic vs. romantic views) 1 2 ③ 4 5	Moderate (hope and despair) 1 2 ③ 4 5	Accessible (irony, selfishness) 1 ② 3 4 5
Quantitative Measures			
Lexile/Text Length	NP / 261 words	NP / 163 words	NP / 224 words
Overall Complexity	**More accessible**	**More complex**	**More accessible**

❶ ❷

REMEMBRANCE

Emily Brontë

BACKGROUND Victorian poets wrote in many voices and many styles. Some writers, like Emily Brontë, are classified as Romantic because they explore and celebrate the human soul, the wildness of nature, and the powers of the imagination. Thomas Hardy, however, focused on the victimization of ordinary people by social and natural forces.

The Soul of the Rose, 1908, John William Waterhouse, Private Collection/Julian Hartnoll, London, UK

Cold in the earth, and the deep snow piled above thee!
Far, far removed, cold in the dreary grave!
Have I forgot, my Only Love, to love thee,
Severed at last by Time's all-wearing wave?

❹
Now, when alone, do my thoughts no longer hover
Over the mountains, on that northern shore;
Resting their wings where heath and fern-leaves cover
Thy noble heart for ever, ever more?

Cold in the earth, and fifteen wild Decembers
From those brown hills have melted into spring—
Faithful indeed is the spirit that remembers
After such years of change and suffering!

Sweet Love of youth, forgive if I forget thee
While the World's tide is bearing me along:

❺ ◂ **Critical Viewing**
In what ways might the woman in this painting represent the poem's speaker? **[Analyze]**

❻ ☑ Reading Check
What is troubling the poem's speaker?

❹ Critical Thinking

Essential Question

1. Direct students' attention to the second stanza of the poem.
2. **Ask** students to describe the speaker's feelings in these lines. **Possible response:** The speaker is lonely and is concerned by the growing emotional distance between herself and her dead lover.
3. **Ask** students why the speaker seems dissatisfied with the place she is in. **Possible response:** She finds the world a lonely place without her lover.
4. Remind students to look for similar emotions of loneliness, dissatisfaction, and loss in the other poems.

❺ Critical Viewing

Possible response: Like the speaker in the poem, the woman in the painting is sad and reflective; she looks as if she were thinking of someone or something far away or far in the past.

❻ Reading Check

Answer: The poem's speaker is troubled by the thought of his or her dead lover buried in the ground.

PHLit Online!

These selections are available in interactive format in the **Enriched Online Student Edition** at **www.PHLitOnline.com,** which includes a thematically related video with writing prompt and an interactive graphic organizer.

Text Complexity: Reader and Task Suggestions

	Remembrance	The Darkling Thrush	"Ah, Are You Digging on My Grave?"
Preparing to Read the Texts • Explain that Brontë wrote near the start of the Victorian era, while Hardy wrote at the end. • Contrast the Romantic view of nature as a source of comfort and guidance with the Naturalist view. • Guide students to use Multidraft Reading strategies (TE p. 1073).	**Leveled Tasks** ***Levels of Meaning*** If students will have difficulty with the poem's meaning, have them first focus on the feelings or mood that the images express. Then, as they reread, have them consider the poem's main ideas. ***Evaluating*** If students will not have difficulty with the poem's meaning, have them evaluate the effectiveness of its imagery.	**Leveled Tasks** ***Levels of Meaning*** If students will have difficulty with the poem's meaning, have them first consider the speaker's mood. Then, as they reread, have students focus on the thrush and what it represents. ***Analyzing*** If students will not have difficulty with the poem's meaning, have them analyze how the thrush conveys the poem's Naturalist views.	**Leveled Tasks** ***Structure/Language*** If students will have difficulty with the dialogue, have volunteers perform it aloud. Then, have students sum up the main question and answer in each stanza. ***Analyzing*** If students will not have difficulty with the dialogue, have them consider what the ironic ending suggests about life or human relationships.

7 Reading Strategy

Analyzing Patterns of Organization

1. Remind students that, as they read, they should make connections between stanzas, noticing how each successive stanza builds on the preceding one.
2. Have students use the ***Reading Strategy Graphic Organizer*** to help them understand the progression of ideas in the poem.
3. **Ask** them the Reading Strategy question: How do lines 25–28 elaborate on the idea in lines 21–24?
   Answer: Lines 25–28 suggest that it was only when the speaker is resigned to the death of the beloved that he or she can stop yearning. These lines elaborate on the idea expressed in lines 21–24 that the speaker had to learn to cherish life, even without joy.

ASSESS

Answers

Before students respond, you may wish to have them write a brief objective summary of the selection. As they answer the questions below, remind them to support their answers with evidence from the text.

1. (a) The speaker's love died fifteen years ago. (b) The speaker means that he or she has not fallen in love with anyone else.
2. (a) The speaker plans to "forget" the lost love and move on. (b) The speaker is afraid that old feelings will take over and prevent moving on with life.
3. (a) The basic conflict is between living in a joyless present and giving oneself up to painful memories of a joyous past. (b) The speaker handles this conflict by deciding not to dwell too long on memories.
4. **Possible response:** Students will probably conclude that it is not usually desirable to lead an existence without joy, but that sometimes mourning requires it.
5. Students should choose a music type and give reasons for their views.

Vocabulary
obscure (äb skyo͞or′)
v. make difficult to see

Other desires and other hopes beset me,
Hopes which obscure but cannot do thee wrong.

No later light has lightened up my heaven,
No second morn has ever shone for me:
All my life's bliss from thy dear life was given—
All my life's bliss is in the grave with thee.

Reading Strategy
Analyzing Patterns of Organization
How do lines 25–28 elaborate on the idea in lines 21–24?

But when the days of golden dreams had perished
And even Despair was powerless to destroy,
Then did I learn how existence could be cherished,
Strengthened and fed without the aid of joy;

Then did I check the tears of useless passion,
Weaned my young soul from yearning after thine; (7)
Sternly denied its burning wish to hasten
Down to that tomb already more than mine!

Vocabulary
languish (laŋ′ gwish)
v. become weak; suffer from longing

rapturous (rap′ chər əs)
adj. filled with joy and love; ecstatic

And even yet, I dare not let it languish,
Dare not indulge in Memory's rapturous pain;
Once drinking deep of that divinest anguish,
How could I seek the empty world again?

Critical Reading

Cite textual evidence to support your responses.

1. **Key Ideas and Details (a)** How long ago did the speaker's love die? **(b) Interpret:** What does the speaker mean by, "No later light has lightened up my heaven"?
2. **Key Ideas and Details (a)** What does the speaker plan to do? **(b) Interpret:** Why is the speaker afraid to give in to his or her old feelings?
3. **Key Ideas and Details (a) Draw Conclusions:** In your own words, express the basic conflict of the poem's speaker. **(b) Analyze:** How does the speaker handle this conflict?
4. **Integration of Knowledge and Ideas** Can it be desirable in some circumstances to lead an existence "without . . . joy"? Explain.
5. **Integration of Knowledge and Ideas** In ancient times, lyric poems like this one were accompanied by music. Which of these types of music would make the best accompaniment for this poem: country, jazz, folk, rock, or rap? Explain your choice.

Enrichment: Investigating a Literary Figure

Emily Brontë
Emily Brontë lived in a time when women had strict roles they were expected to play in society. Female writers were rare, and women who did write were expected to focus on such subjects as maintaining a household and raising children. They were not expected to write about such heavy topics as death and grief. Brontë, however, was not afraid to challenge expectations.

Activity: Author Study Have students conduct research on the author to learn more about the breadth of her work and influence. Suggest that they record information in the **Enrichment: Investigating a Literary Figure** worksheet, ***Professional Development Guidebook,*** page 235. Have the class create a bulletin board about the author.

8 Thomas Hardy

(1840–1928)

Author of "The Darkling Thrush" • "Ah, Are You Digging on My Grave?"

Thomas Hardy, who was unusual in being both a great novelist and a great poet, was born in Dorset, a region of southwest England. He used this region as the basis for the imaginary county of Wessex that is the setting of many of his novels.

Early Life The son of a stonemason, Hardy grew up in a rural cottage near a tract of wasteland. He received a fine education at a local school, although he never went on to study at a university. As a teenager, he began working for a local architect, and he eventually became a draftsman for an architect who specialized in churches.

While on a business trip to Cornwall, at the southwestern tip of England, Hardy met the woman who later became his first wife. She encouraged him in his literary activities, and soon he committed himself entirely to writing.

The Novelist When Hardy's early poetry did not gain notice, he turned to writing novels. *Far From the Madding Crowd* was the first to gain success.

Hardy used his fiction writing to elaborate his own pessimistic view of life. In tragic novels like *Tess of the D'Urbervilles* (1891) and *Jude the Obscure* (1895), he showed the difficulty people experience when trying to rise above their circumstances.

The Poet The bleakness of Hardy's fiction disturbed readers, and the response to *Jude the Obscure* was so hostile that Hardy abandoned fiction and returned to writing poetry, a form of writing he had pursued in the 1860s.

A Poetic Legacy Hardy's poetry marks a transition from Victorian verse to the Modernist movement of the twentieth century. In his use of strict meter and stanza structure, Hardy was unmistakably Victorian. However, his nonpoetic language and odd rhymes, his devotion to English characters and the English countryside, and his fatalistic outlook inspired twentieth-century poets like Philip Larkin.

"Time changes everything except something within us which is always surprised by change."

PRETEACH

Background

8 More About the Author

A theme central to much of Thomas Hardy's work—both poetry and prose—is the struggle of man against the indifferent force that governs the world and inflicts on him the sufferings and ironies of life and love. Hardy considered taking Holy Orders, but he lost his religious faith. He lived the life of an architect's apprentice until he found his calling as a writer. In 1885, he moved with his first wife, Emma Gifford, into a house he designed and built himself, Max Gate, near Dorchester. Hardy lived at the house until his death in 1928.

Differentiated Instruction for Universal Access

Vocabulary for Special-Needs Students
Have partners take turns reading paragraphs of the biography aloud. Circulate among the students to monitor the fluency of students' reading. Review difficult words and passages with the class. For example, if students have difficulty with the word *pessimistic* in the fifth paragraph, point out context clues in the surrounding text: *view of life, tragic, difficulty.*

EL Vocabulary for English Learners
If students have difficulty with the word *fatalistic* in the last paragraph, break it into parts for them. They know the word *fatal* means "causing death." Remind them that the suffix *-ist* means "characteristic of," and the suffix *-ic* means "relating to." So, someone with a "fatalistic outlook" would be likely to focus on negative outcomes.

PHLit Online!

For more information about the author, go online at **www.PHLitOnline.com.**

9 About the Selection

Hardy's bleak reflections—and tentative expression of hope—on the eve of the twentieth century are especially poignant as he looks back on both the tragedies and progress of the past.

10 Critical Viewing

Answer: The thrush seems small and vulnerable to the cold. It must deal with a harsh climate, but it keeps singing anyway.

9 The Darkling[1] Thrush

THOMAS HARDY

10 ▶ Critical Viewing
How does the thrush shown in this painting provide a hopeful contrast to the bleak winter landscape?
[Interpret]

I leant upon a coppice gate[2]
When Frost was specter-gray,
And Winter's dregs made desolate
The weakening eye of day.
The tangled bine-stems[3] scored the sky
Like strings of broken lyres,
And all mankind that haunted nigh
Had sought their household fires.

11

The land's sharp features seemed to be
The Century's corpse[4] outleant,
His crypt the cloudy canopy,
The wind his death-lament.
The ancient pulse of germ[5] and birth
Was shrunken hard and dry,
And every spirit upon earth
Seemed fervorless as I.

1. **darkling** *adj.* in the dark.
2. **coppice** (kop′ is) **gate** gate leading to a thicket, or small wood.
3. **bine-stems** twining stems.
4. **Century's corpse** This poem was written on December 31, 1900, the last day of the nineteenth century.
5. germ seed or bud.

Enrichment: Investigating Artistic Schools and Movements

Naturalism
The Naturalist element in Thomas Hardy's writing had important literary counterparts in both France and the United States. In France, the novelist Émile Zola (1840–1902) and the short-story writer Guy de Maupassant (1850–1893) espoused Naturalism. These writers believed that human behavior is rigorously determined by hereditary and environmental factors.

Activity: Investigating Artistic Schools and Movements Encourage interested students to conduct further investigation into Naturalism. Students may also want to research one of the authors mentioned above as an example of this movement. Have them use the **Enrichment: Investigating Artistic Schools and Movements** worksheet, ***Professional Development Guidebook***, page 220. Ask students to share what they discover with their classmates.

⓫ Reading Strategy

Analyzing Patterns of Organization

1. Have students reread the first two stanzas of the poem. **Ask:** What mood does Hardy create with his winter setting in the first stanza?
   Answer: Hardy uses the fading light of a midwinter day to create a bleak, desolate mood.
2. Then **ask:** How does the mood change in his second stanza?
   Possible response: Hardy moves from desolate imagery to death imagery. The closing century is personified as a "corpse," the wind becomes a "death lament."

Differentiated Instruction for Universal Access

Strategy for Less Proficient Readers
Have partners clap to find the poem's rhythm. As one student reads the poem aloud, the other should clap on the stressed syllables. Have students continue the reading and clapping until they successfully identify the rhythm.

Enrichment for Gifted/Talented Students
The speaker of "The Darkling Thrush" refers to the "Century's corpse," an allusion to the poem's date—December 31, 1900. Have students explain how millennia are calculated and why the last day of 1900, rather than the last day of 1899, is the end of the century.

Strategy for Advanced Readers
Tell students that both Brontë and Hardy used nature to symbolize ideas and emotions. Have them write analyses of the symbols in "Remembrance" and "The Darkling Thrush."

ASSESS

Answers

Before students respond, you may wish to have them write a brief objective summary of the selection. As they answer the questions below, remind them to support their answers with evidence from the text.

1. (a) It is wintertime, toward the end of the year. (b) The poet uses the images of "Frost," "Winter's dregs," "desolate," "weakening," and "broken lyres" to suggest a gloomy mood.
2. (a) The speaker hears a thrush singing. (b) The mood in the third stanza differs from that of the first two because it includes the joyful singing of the thrush and lifts the gloom of the preceding stanzas.
3. (a) The speaker thinks that if the thrush sings with such joy at such an otherwise gloomy time, there must be some hope in the air. (b) **Possible responses:** Students may note that the speaker calls the Hope signified by the thrush "blessed"—the speaker desires such hope—but also claims to be "unaware" of any reason for such hope.
4. **Possible response:** In their responses, students should indicate what signs of hope or invitations to pessimism appeared at the end of the twentieth century.

At once a voice arose among
  The bleak twigs overhead
In a full-hearted evensong
  Of joy illimited;
An aged thrush, frail, gaunt, and small,
  In blast-beruffled plume,
Had chosen thus to fling his soul
  Upon the growing gloom.

So little cause for carolings
  Of such ecstatic sound
Was written on terrestrial things
  Afar or nigh around,
That I could think there trembled through
  His happy good-night air
Some blessed Hope, whereof he knew
  And I was unaware.

Vocabulary

gaunt (gônt) *adj.* thin and bony, as from great hunger or age

terrestrial (tə res′ trē əl) *adj.* relating to the earth or to this world

Critical Reading

Cite textual evidence to support your responses.

1. **Key Ideas and Details (a)** In which season and time of year is this poem set? **(b) Classify:** In the first two stanzas, what details and images does Hardy use to convey the mood of the setting?
2. **Key Ideas and Details (a)** What does the speaker suddenly hear and see in the third stanza? **(b) Compare and Contrast:** How does the mood in the third stanza differ from that in the first two?
3. **Integration of Knowledge and Ideas (a)** Summarize what the speaker says in the final stanza. **(b) Draw Conclusions:** Do you agree with critics who assert that Hardy longs to believe there is reason for hope but does not really think so? Why or why not?
4. **Integration of Knowledge and Ideas** If Hardy had seen the end of the twentieth century, do you think he would have felt the same way that he did at the end of the nineteenth? Explain.

Vocabulary Development

Vocabulary Knowledge Rating

When students have completed reading and discussing the poems, have them take out their **Vocabulary Knowledge Rating Charts** for the poems. Read the words aloud and have students rate their knowledge of words again in the After Reading column. Clarify any words that are still problematic. Have students write their own definitions and example or sentence in the appropriate column. Then, have students complete the Vocabulary Lesson at the end of the selections. Encourage students to use the words in further discussion and written work about the selections. Remind them that they will be accountable for these words on the **Selection Test,** ***Unit 5 Resources***, pages 123–125 or 126–128.

12 "Ah, Are You Digging on My Grave?" Thomas Hardy

"Ah, are you digging on my grave
My loved one?—planting rue?"
—"No: yesterday he went to wed
One of the brightest wealth has bred.
'It cannot hurt her now,' he said,
'That I should not be true.'"

13

"Then who is digging on my grave?
My nearest dearest kin?"
—"Ah, no: they sit and think, 'What use!
What good will planting flowers produce?
No tendance of her mound can loose
Her spirit from Death's gin.'"[1]

"But some one digs upon my grave?
My enemy?—prodding sly?"
—"Nay: when she heard you had passed the Gate
That shuts on all flesh soon or late,
She thought you no more worth her hate,
And cares not where you lie."

Reading Strategy
Analyzing Patterns of Organization What pattern do you see developing in these first stanzas?

Vocabulary
prodding (präd´ iŋ)
adj. poking; jabbing; seeking

14 ☑ Reading Check
Who is the speaker of this poem?

1. **gin** *n.* trap.

Differentiated Instruction for Universal Access

Strategy for Special-Needs Students
Have students read "Ah, Are You Digging on My Grave?" with teacher guidance. Encourage them to pay attention to the dialogue in the poem and to note who is speaking and when.

Strategy for Less Proficient Readers
Have students write an epitaph, or inscription for a tombstone. Tell them they might write one for the speaker in "Ah, Are You Digging on My Grave?" Encourage them to use clues from the poem to capture the essence of the person being memorialized.

Strategy for Advanced Readers
Have students write brief essays in which they compare and contrast the two interpretations of "Ah, Are You Digging on My Grave?" Have them explore how the poem might be interpreted as merely humorous or deeply pessimistic.

12 About the Selection

In Hardy's bitterly humorous and ironic poem, a dead woman keeps asking who is digging on her grave—assuming that someone is visiting her. An unidentified voice answers her questions. The voice is finally revealed to be that of her dog. The woman is relieved to find that her dog still remembers her, but—in the poem's final irony—the dog claims he was just burying a bone and had forgotten his mistress was buried there.

13 Reading Strategy

Analyzing Patterns of Organization

1. Have students review the first two stanzas of the poem.
2. **Ask** students the Reading Strategy question: What pattern do you see developing in these first stanzas?
   Answer: Each stanza begins with a question and ends with an answer.

Monitor Progress

3. **Ask** students to explain how stanza structure and irony may function in a poem.
   Answer: Stanza structure sets up expectations; irony occurs when something other than those expectations happens.
4. **Ask** students what they expect to happen in the rest of the poem, based on the first two stanzas.
   Possible response: Students may suggest that the woman's question will be answered and that she will find out that a loved one is digging on her grave out of grief.
5. Point out that ironic poems often set up patterns, then break those patterns to surprise the reader.

Reteach

If students have difficulty recognizing the pattern, have them read the stanzas aloud. Explain that the speaker is asking and answering her own question. Students may find it helpful to speculate what ironic twist the poem might take.

14 Reading Check

Answer: The speaker of this poem is a dead woman.

15 World Literature Connection

The Greek Anthology

Although it was edited and expanded over the years, many of the poems in *The Greek Anthology* were first collected by Meleager of Gadara, a Greek poet who lived during the first century B.C.E.

Meleager introduced the collection with one of his own poems. In it, he compares each writer to a flower. As a result, the collection is called *Stephanos*, which means "garland," or "collection of flowers." It is interesting to note that the word *anthology* comes from the Greek word *anthologia*, which means "flower gathering."

Connect to the Literature

Possible response: Hardy does not seem to echo traditional sentiments about death, which might focus on the significance of the dead person and the grief of those left behind. Instead, Hardy chooses to focus on the insignificance of the dead and the way the living spend little time mourning.

ASSESS

Answers

Remind students to support their answers with evidence from the text.

1. (a) The speaker believes in turn that it is her widower, her relatives, and her enemy digging in the three stanzas. (b) They seldom think about the dead woman.
2. (a) The woman's dog is digging on her grave. (b) Hardy is making the point that we are rarely as important to others as we think we are.
3. **Possible response:** Because the woman is speaking from the grave, Hardy is communicating ideas about death. The ironic twist that the "faithful" dog is only digging on the grave because he buried his bone there communicates the idea that the dead are insignificant to the living, yet this serious idea is expressed in a humorous way.

15 World LITERATURE CONNECTION

The Greek Anthology

Hardy was not the first poet to write in the voice of a deceased person. Many of the poems in *The Greek Anthology,* compiled in the tenth century, are ancient Greek epitaphs written in the voice of the person who died. Like most well-educated people in nineteenth-century Britain, Hardy owned a copy of *The Greek Anthology.* He probably spent hours poring over the little tombstone poems, which commemorate the lives of men, women, children, and even dogs.

Connect to the Literature

Do you think Hardy expresses traditional sentiments about remembering the dead? Why or why not?

"Then, who is digging on my grave?
 Say—since I have not guessed!"
—"O it is I, my mistress dear,
Your little dog, who still lives near,
And much I hope my movements here
 Have not disturbed your rest?"

"Ah, yes! *You* dig upon my grave . . .
 Why flashed it not on me
That one true heart was left behind!
What feeling do we ever find
To equal among human kind
 A dog's fidelity!"

"Mistress, I dug upon your grave
 To bury a bone, in case
I should be hungry near this spot
When passing on my daily trot.
I am sorry, but I quite forgot
 It was your resting-place."

Critical Reading

Cite textual evidence to support your responses.

1. **Key Ideas and Details (a)** In each of the first three stanzas, who does the speaker think is digging? **(b) Infer:** What do the responses tell you about the people thought to be digging?
2. **Key Ideas and Details (a)** Who is actually digging on the grave? **(b) Draw Conclusions:** What point about human vanity and self-esteem is Hardy making in this poem?
3. **Integration of Knowledge and Ideas** How do the places in which the Hardy's speakers find themselves limit their knowledge? Use two of these Essential Question words in your answer: *pessimism, insignificant, humorous, ironic.* ***[Connecting to the Essential Question: What is the relationship between literature and place?]***

Concept Connector

Reading Skill Graphic Organizer

Ask students to review the graphic organizers they completed as they read the poems. Then, have students summarize the logical progression of ideas in each poem. Ask volunteers to share their summaries with the class.

Activating Prior Knowledge

Have students return to their responses to the Activating Prior Knowledge activity. Ask them to explain whether their thoughts have changed and, if so, how.

Writing About the Essential Question

Have students compare their responses to the prompt, completed before reading the poems, with their thoughts afterward. Have them work individually or in groups, writing or discussing their thoughts, to formulate new responses. Then, lead a class discussion, probing for what students have learned that confirms or invalidates their initial thoughts. Encourage students to cite specific textual details to support their responses.

After You Read

Remembrance • The Darkling Thrush • "Ah, Are You Digging on My Grave?"

Literary Analysis

1. **Craft and Structure (a)** Complete a chart like the one shown to determine whether each poem uses a consistent **stanza structure. (b)** Summarize the pattern of stanzas in each of these poems.

Stanza	Number of lines	Rhyme scheme	Meter
1			
2			
3			

2. **Craft and Structure** What is ironic about the phrases "rapturous pain" and "divinest anguish" in the final stanza of "Remembrance"?
3. **Craft and Structure** Explain how repetition in the stanza structure of "Ah, Are You Digging on My Grave?" contributes to Hardy's ironic—and aesthetic—purpose.
4. **Craft and Structure (a)** How do lines 25–30 of "Ah, Are You Digging on My Grave?" disappoint a reader's expectations for an established stanza structure? **(b)** How does the last stanza use **irony** to disappoint a character's expectations in a drastic way?
5. **Integration of Knowledge and Ideas** Compare and contrast the types of absence that these poems address.
6. **Integration of Knowledge and Ideas** Which of the three speakers seems to experience the sorrow of loss most keenly? Why?
7. **Integration of Knowledge and Ideas** Which speaker seems best able to handle the absence of a sign of remembrance or hope? Explain.
8. **Analyzing Visual Information** What qualities of Hardy's poetry—for example, its moods and themes—does the artist capture in the caricature of Hardy on this page? Explain.

Common Core State Standards

Writing

2.b. Develop the topic thoroughly by selecting the most significant and relevant facts, extended definitions, concrete details, quotations, or other information and examples appropriate to the audience's knowledge of the topic. *(p. 1084)*

5. Develop and strengthen writing as needed by planning, revising, editing, rewriting, or trying a new approach, focusing on addressing what is most significant for a specific purpose and audience. *(p. 1084)*

Language

5. Demonstrate understanding of figurative language, word relationships, and nuances in word meaning. *(p. 1084)*

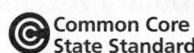

Reading Strategy

9. **Analyze the pattern of stanzas** in "Remembrance" to show how the speaker gradually works out an answer to the question in the first stanza.
10. Explain the function of each stanza in "The Darkling Thrush."
11. **(a)** In "The Darkling Thrush," which stanza introduces a shift in meaning? Explain. **(b)** In "Ah, Are You Digging on My Grave?," what important shift in meaning occurs between the last two stanzas?

Answers

1. (a) Students should chart the information for each poem. (b) "Remembrance": Stanzas contain four lines with a rhyme scheme of *abab*. The meter varies. "The Darkling Thrush": Stanzas contain eight lines with a rhyme scheme of *ababcdcd*. The meter is ballad meter (4–3–4–3 stresses per line). "Ah, Are You Digging on My Grave?": Stanzas contain six lines with a rhyme scheme of *abcccb*. The meter is 4–3–4–4–4–3 stresses per line.
2. These phrases are ironic because they involve contradictions.
3. The first few stanzas set up a pattern of question and answer. In the fourth stanza, the pattern holds true as the woman gets an answer to her question: her dog is the one digging. In the last two stanzas, the pattern is broken, heightening the surprise and irony of the dog's revelation that he had, in fact, forgotten she was buried there.
4. (a) Lines 25–30 disappoint a reader's expectations for an established stanza structure because, in this stanza, the woman expresses her thoughts directly. (b) The last stanza uses irony to upset the dead woman's hopes that she is mourned.
5. "Remembrance" treats the absence of a loved one as a gaping hole in one's life. "The Darkling Thrush" concerns the absence of hope. "Ah, Are You Digging on My Grave?" concerns the absence of the speaker's memory from the hearts of others.
6. **Possible response:** The speaker of "Remembrance" does, because in fifteen years, he or she has not been able to overcome anguish.
7. **Possible response:** The speaker of "Remembrance" does—he or she has reflected on grief for years.
8. The artist captures Hardy's pessimistic views, as is seen in the image of the dark cloud hovering over his head.
9. The speaker asks if he or she has forgotten to love the dead beloved. Each stanza builds toward the realization that the speaker's feelings for the past are a danger.

Answers continued

10. Stanza 1 describes the setting as a bleak winter day. Stanza 2 continues to characterize the landscape as desolate. In stanza 3, the joyful song of a thrush interrupts the speaker's melancholy musings. In stanza 4, the speaker is puzzled by the joyful song and concludes that the thrush has some reason to hope.
11. (a) Stanza 3 introduces a shift in meaning. The voice of the thrush disturbs the speaker's gloomy reverie. (b) The shift in meaning between the last two stanzas suggests that the seeming "remembrance" of the woman's dog is actually forgetfulness—he has forgotten where she is buried.

Answers

Vocabulary Acquisition and Use

1. Introduce the skill.
2. Have students complete the Word Analysis activity and the Vocabulary Practice.

Word Analysis

1. *Extraterrestrial* means "beyond or outside Earth." Sample sentence: The scientists searched for extraterrestrial life.
2. *Subterranean* means "underground." Sample sentence: The subterranean tunnel collapsed.
3. *Terrace* means "a level stretch of ground." Sample sentence: The farmer planted crops on the terrace.
4. *Terrain* means "the surface of the land or ground." Sample sentence: The terrain was too rough to ride bicycles.
5. *Territory* means "an area of land." Sample sentence: My dog barks when squirrels enter her territory.

Vocabulary

1. obscure
2. rapturous
3. gaunt
4. terrestrial
5. prodding
6. languish

Writing

You may use this Writing Lesson as timed-writing practice, or you may allow students to develop the informative text over several days. Tell students to focus on the following:

1. **Focus and Organization** The writer should have a clear thesis and give equal attention to each poem.
2. **Elaboration** The writer should explain the way each speaker speaks about absence, and should provide several points of comparison and contrast to support his or her thesis. Main points should be supported with details and quotes from the poems.
3. **Style** An informative text should have a more formal style, and should use concrete language and examples.

PERFORMANCE TASKS

Integrated Language Skills

Vocabulary Acquisition and Use

Word Analysis: Latin Root *-terr(a)-*

The Latin root *-terr(a)-* comes from the Latin word for "earth." *Terrestrial,* which contains this root, means "of the earth" or "of this world." Write the definition for each *-terr(a)-* word below based on the meaning of the root. Explain how you arrived at your meaning. Then, write an original sentence for each of the words.

1. extraterrestrial
2. subterranean
3. terrace
4. terrain
5. territory

Vocabulary: Analogies

In an analogy, the relationship between two words is compared to the relationship between two other words. To complete these analogies, choose the word from the vocabulary list on page 1072 that creates a word pair that matches the relationship in the other pair. Explain your choices.

1. *Explain* is to *clarify* as ______ is to *conceal.*
2. ______ is to *ecstasy* as *miserable* is to *depression.*
3. ______ is to *emaciated* as *vigorous* is to *fitness.*
4. *Arrival* is to *departure* as ______ is to *heavenly.*
5. *Withdrawn* is to *shy* as *pushy* is to ______.
6. *Longing* is to ______ as *sympathy* is to *assist.*

Writing

Informative Text Brontë's and Hardy's poems deal in different ways with the theme of absence, the sense of something missing, whether that is a loved one, a sign of hope, or the knowledge that people remember the speaker. Write a **comparative analysis** in which you examine the ways in which the speakers in these poems feel about an absence and succeed or fail in handling it.

Prewriting Review the poems, using a chart to take notes on how each speaker perceives and responds to absence. Note uses of *imagery, language, or stylistic devices* that reveal the speaker's feelings. Review your examples to determine whether the speakers' attitudes and feelings are more similar or different. Then develop a thesis statement that expresses your view.

Drafting Begin your draft by stating your thesis. As you write, support your generalizations with quotations from Brontë's and Hardy's poems. Consider analyzing all the similarities first and then the differences if you think the differences are more important—and vice versa.

Model: Revising to Signal Similarities and Differences

The speaker in Hardy's "Ah, Are You Digging on My Grave?" learns that family and friends have gone on with their lives. *In contrast,* Brontë's speaker points out that she lives "without the aid of joy" in an "empty world."

Use of expressions like *in the same way* or *in contrast* calls attention to key similarities and differences.

Revising Review your draft, making sure that you signal similarities and differences. Make sure that all quotations are accurate and properly referenced.

Assessment Resources

Unit 5 Resources

L1 L2 EL **Selection Test A,** pp. 123–125. Administer Test A to less advanced students.

L3 L4 EL **Selection Test B,** pp. 126–128. Administer Test B to on-level and more advanced students.

L3 L4 **Open-Book Test,** pp. 120–122. As an alternative, give the Open-Book Test.

All **Customizable Test Bank**

All **Self-tests** Students may prepare for the **Selection Test** by taking the **Self-test** online.

PHLit Online! All assessment resources are available at **www.PHLitOnline.com**.

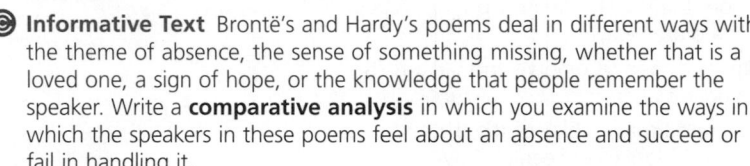

Conventions and Style: Active, Not Passive, Voice

When you write, you can make your sentences more energetic and powerful by using active-voice verbs. A verb is in the **active-voice** when the subject is the doer of the action. A verb is in the **passive voice** when it receives the action of the verb.

The active voice is more direct and concise than the passive voice. However, the passive voice can be appropriate and effective in the following situations:

- You wish to emphasize the receiver of the action rather than the doer.

Hope was symbolized by the tiny thrush.

- The doer of the action is not known or is unimportant to your meaning.

The poem had been written on the last day of the nineteenth century.

The passive voice is constructed from the past participle of the main verb and a form of the verb *be.* Review these examples of active and passive voice.

	Active	Passive
Present	*is digging, digs*	*is dug, is being dug*
Past	*dug, was digging, had dug*	*was dug, was being dug, had been dug*
Future	*will dig, will have dug*	*will be dug, will have been dug*

Practice Identify whether the verb in each sentence is in the active or passive voice. If a sentence in the passive voice should be in the active voice, rewrite it. If the passive voice is appropriate, explain why.

1. Fires were hurried to by people who wanted to sit by them on a winter night.
2. A tiny bird was heard to sing in the middle of the gloomy evening.
3. The branches of a tree are compared to the broken strings of a musical instrument by the speaker.
4. The bird's joy cannot be understood.
5. The speaker, surprised by the joyful singing, believes that something giving hope is known by the bird.
6. The woman buried in the grave was not mourned by her loved one.
7. Flowers won't be planted by relatives.
8. The dead one was disturbed by the digging.
9. The dead are quickly forgotten by the living.
10. Can anyone overlook the faithfulness expressed by a friendly dog?

Writing and Speaking Conventions

A. Writing Use each subject-verb pair in a sentence with the verb in the active voice.

1. **S:** poet, **V:** lean
2. **S:** relatives, **V:** plant
3. **S:** voice, **V:** sing
4. **S:** dog, **V:** disturb
5. **S:** thrush, **V:** know

Example: S: poet, **V:** lean.

Sentence: The poet leans on a gate and sees a winter landscape.

B. Speaking Write and present to the class a brief scene for a play based on the poem "Ah, Are You Digging on My Grave?" Describe the setting, list the character(s) in your scene, and include at least one speech written in the active voice.

PH WRITING COACH
Further instruction and practice are available in *Prentice Hall Writing Coach.*

Extend the Lesson

Sentence Modeling

Display for students the following lines:

But when the days of golden dreams had perished
And even Despair was powerless to destroy,
Then did I learn how existence could be cherished,
Strengthened and fed without the aid of joy;
("Remembrance")

The tangled bine-stems scored the sky
Like strings of broken lyres,
And all mankind that haunted nigh
Had sought their household fires.
("The Darkling Thrush")

Ask students to identify the type of voice used in each—active or passive—and discuss reasons the poet may have had for his or her choice. (*Both are in active voice.*)

Have students imitate both passages on topics of their own choosing, matching the grammatical and stylistic features as much as possible.

Answers

Conventions and Style

1. Introduce and discuss the skill, using the instruction on the student page.
2. Have students complete the Practice.

Practice

1. Passive; People who wanted to sit by fires on a winter night hurried to them.
2. Passive; Correct—the sentence places the attention on the bird, rather than on those who heard it.
3. Passive; The speaker compared the branches of a tree to a string on a broken musical instrument.
4. Passive; Correct—the focus is on the bird.
5. Passive; The speaker, surprised by the joyful singing, believes that the bird knows something that gives it hope.
6. Passive; Correct—the focus is on the woman, not the loved one.
7. Passive; Relatives will not plant flowers.
8. Passive; Digging disturbed the dead one. This would also be correct in passive voice.
9. Passive; The living quickly forget the dead.
10. Active

Writing and Speaking Conventions

A. Possible Responses

1. Sample is given on student page: The poet leans on the gate and sees a winter landscape.
2. The man's relatives planted flowers on his grave.
3. The voice sang a song of hope and joy.
4. A barking dog disturbed the woman's restful sleep.
5. The thrush knows something that I would love to know.

B. Students' scenes should include a speech in which a character speaks in active voice.

PH WRITING COACH Grade 12

Further instruction on narrative writing can be found in Chapter 6.

God's Grandeur • Spring and Fall: To a Young Child • To an Athlete Dying Young • When I Was One-and-Twenty

Lesson Pacing Guide

DAY 1 Preteach

- Administer the Reading and Vocabulary Warm-ups (*Unit 5 Resources,* pp. 129–132) as necessary.
- Introduce the Literary Analysis concept: Rhythm.
- Introduce the Reading Strategy: Analyze the Author's Beliefs
- Build background with the author and Background features.
- Develop thematic thinking with Connecting to the Essential Question.
- Teach the selection vocabulary.

DAYS 2–3 Preteach/Teach/Assess

- Distribute copies of the appropriate graphic organizer for the Reading Strategy (*Graphic Organizer Transparencies,* pp. 195–196).
- Distribute copies of the appropriate graphic organizer for Literary Analysis (*Graphic Organizer Transparencies,* pp. 197–198).
- Prepare students to read with the Activating Prior Knowledge activities (TE).
- Informally monitor comprehension while students read.
- Develop students' understanding of rhythm using the Literary Analysis prompt.
- Develop students' ability to analyze the author's beliefs using the Reading Strategy prompt.
- Reinforce vocabulary with the Vocabulary notes.
- Assess students' comprehension and mastery of the skills by having them answer the Critical Reading, Literary Analysis, and Reading Strategy questions.
- Have students complete the Vocabulary Lesson.

DAY 4 Extend/Assess

- Have students complete the Writing Lesson and write a letter of recommendation. (You may assign as homework.)
- Administer Selection Test A or B (*Unit 5 Resources,* pp. 141–143 or 144–146).

Common Core State Standards

Reading Literature 5. Analyze how an author's choices concerning how to structure specific parts of a text contribute to its overall structure and meaning as well as its aesthetic impact.

Writing 1. Write arguments to support claims in an analysis of substantive topics or texts, using valid reasoning and relevant and sufficient evidence.
1.d. Establish and maintain a formal style and objective tone while attending to the norms and conventions of the discipline in which they are writing.

Language 3. Apply knowledge of language to understand how language functions in different contexts, to make effective choices for meaning or style, and to comprehend more fully when reading or listening.

Additional Standards Practice
Common Core Companion,* *pp. 54–55; 185–195; 322–323

Daily Block Scheduling
Each day in this Lesson Pacing Guide represents a 40–50 minute period. Teachers using block scheduling may combine days to revise pacing. In addition, teachers may differentiate and support core instruction by integrating components for extended and intensive support as students require. See the Guide to Selected Leveled Resources (facing page).

Guide to Selected Leveled Resources

RTI Tier 1 (students performing on level)			God's Grandeur • Spring and Fall: To a Young Child • To an Athlete Dying Young • When I Was One-and-Twenty
Warm Up	Whole class instruction; Group work	**Practice, model,** and **monitor** fluency, working **with the whole class** or **in groups.**	**Vocabulary and Reading Warm-ups B, *Unit 5 Resources,*** pp. 129–130, 132
Comprehension/Skills	Whole class instruction; Group work; Independent work	**Support** and **monitor** comprehension and skills development, having students complete the activities, graphic organizers, and interactive prompts **independently** or **as a class.**	• ***Reader's Notebook,*** adapted instruction and full selection EL ***Reader's Notebook: English Learner's Version,*** adapted instruction and adapted selection • **Reading Strategy Graphic Organizer B, *Graphic Organizer Transparencies,*** p. 206 • **Literary Analysis Graphic Organizer B, *Graphic Organizer Transparencies,*** p. 208
Monitor Progress	A	**Monitor** student progress with the differentiated curriculum-based assessment in the *Unit Resources.*	• **Selection Test B, *Unit 5 Resources,*** pp. 144–146 • **Open-Book Test, *Unit 5 Resources,*** pp. 138–140
Assess/Screen	A	**Assess** student progress using Benchmark Test 2.	• **Benchmark Test 9, *Unit 5 Resources,*** pp. 152–157

RTI Tier 2 (students requiring intervention)			God's Grandeur • Spring and Fall: To a Young Child • To an Athlete Dying Young • When I Was One-and-Twenty
Warm Up	Group work; One-on-one teaching	**Practice, model,** and **monitor** fluency **in groups** or **with individuals.**	• **Vocabulary and Reading Warm-ups A, *Unit 5 Resources,*** pp. 129–131 • ***Hear It!* Audio CD (adapted text)**
Comprehension/Skills	Group work; One-on-one teaching	• **Support** and **monitor** comprehension and skills development, working **in small groups** or **with individuals.** • As students complete the selection in the appropriate version of the *Reader's Notebook,* monitor comprehension frequently with group questions and individual instruction. • **Model** strategies while guiding students in completing the activities and prompts in the *Reader's Notebook,* as well as the graphic organizers. • **Practice** skills and **monitor** mastery with the *Reading Kit* worksheets.	• ***Reader's Notebook: Adapted Version,*** adapted instruction and adapted selection EL ***Reader's Notebook: English Learner's Version,*** adapted instruction and adapted selection • **Reading Strategy Graphic Organizer A, *Graphic Organizer Transparencies,*** p. 205 • **Literary Analysis Graphic Organizer A, *Graphic Organizer Transparencies,*** p. 207 • ***Reading Kit,*** Practice worksheets
Monitor Progress	A	**Monitor** student progress with the differentiated curriculum-based assessment in the *Unit Resources* and in the *Reading Kit.*	• **Selection Test A, *Unit 5 Resources,*** pp. 141–143 • ***Reading Kit,*** Assess worksheets
Assess/Screen	A	**Assess** student progress using the Benchmark Test.	**Benchmark Test 9, *Unit 5 Resources,*** pp. 152–157

TIER 3 Tier 3 intervention may require consultation with the student's special-education or dyslexia specialist. For additional support, see the Tier 2 activities and resources listed above.

One-on-one teaching **Group work** **Whole class instruction** **Independent work** **A Assessment**

For a complete guide to selection support, including support for Advanced students, see the Overview of Resources in the frontmatter.

God's Grandeur • Spring and Fall: To a Young Child • To an Athlete Dying Young • When I was One-and-Twenty

RESOURCES FOR:

- L1 Special-Needs Students
- L2 Below-Level Students (Tier 2)
- L3 On-Level Students (Tier 1)
- L4 Advanced Students (Tier 1)
- EL English Learners
- All All Students

Vocabulary/Fluency/Prior Knowledge

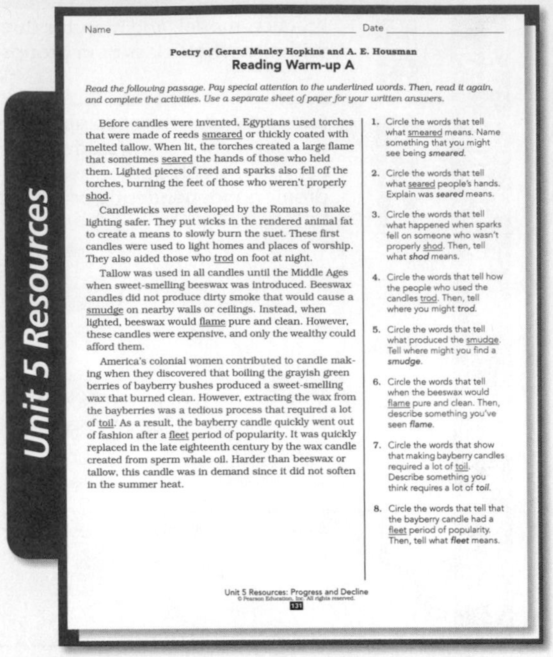

Unit 5 Resources

Name ______________________ Date ____________

Poetry of Gerard Manley Hopkins and A. E. Housman
Reading Warm-up A

Read the following passage. Pay special attention to the underlined words. Then, read it again, and complete the activities. Use a separate sheet of paper for your written answers.

Before candles were invented, Egyptians used torches that were made of reeds smeared or thickly coated with melted tallow. When lit, the torches created a large flame that sometimes seared the hands of those who held them. Lighted pieces of reed and sparks also fell off the torches, burning the feet of those who weren't properly shod.

Candlewicks were developed by the Romans to make lighting safer. They put wicks in the rendered animal fat to create a means to slowly burn the suet. These first candles were used to light homes and places of worship. They also aided those who trod on foot at night.

Tallow was used in all candles until the Middle Ages when sweet-smelling beeswax was introduced. Beeswax candles did not produce dirty smoke that would cause a smudge on nearby walls or ceilings. Instead, when lighted, beeswax would flame pure and clean. However, these candles were expensive, and only the wealthy could afford them.

America's colonial women contributed to candle making when they discovered that boiling the grayish green berries of bayberry bushes produced a sweet-smelling wax that burned clean. However, extracting the wax from the bayberries was a tedious process that required a lot of toil. As a result, the bayberry candle quickly went out of fashion after a fleet period of popularity. It was quickly replaced in the late eighteenth century by the wax candle created from sperm whale oil. Harder than beeswax or tallow, this candle was in demand since it did not soften in the summer heat.

1. Circle the words that tell what smeared means. Name something that you might see being *smeared*.
2. Circle the words that tell what seared people's hands. Explain was *seared* means.
3. Circle the words that tell what happened when sparks fell on someone who wasn't properly shod. Then, tell what *shod* means.
4. Circle the words that tell how the people who used the candles trod. Then, tell where you might *trod*.
5. Circle the words that tell what produced the smudge. Tell where might you find a *smudge*.
6. Circle the words that tell when the beeswax would flame pure and clean. Then, describe something you've seen *flame*.
7. Circle the words that show that making bayberry candles required a lot of toil. Describe something you think requires a lot of *toil*.
8. Circle the words that tell that the bayberry candle had a fleet period of popularity. Then, tell what *fleet* means.

Unit 5 Resources: Progress and Decline
© Pearson Education, Inc. All rights reserved.
131

EL L1 L2 **Reading Warm-ups A and B,** p. 131–132

Also available for these selections:

EL L1 L2 **Vocabulary Warm-ups A and B,** pp. 129–130

All **Vocabulary Builder,** p. 135

L2 L3 ***Reader's Notebook***

L1 ***Reader's Notebook: Adapted Version***

EL ***Reader's Notebook: English Learner's Version***

EL ***Reader's Notebook: Spanish Version***

Reader's Notebooks

Pre- and postreading pages for these selections appear in an interactive format in the *Reader's Notebooks.* Each *Notebook* is differentiated for a different group of learners. The selections in the Adapted and English Learner's versions are abridged.

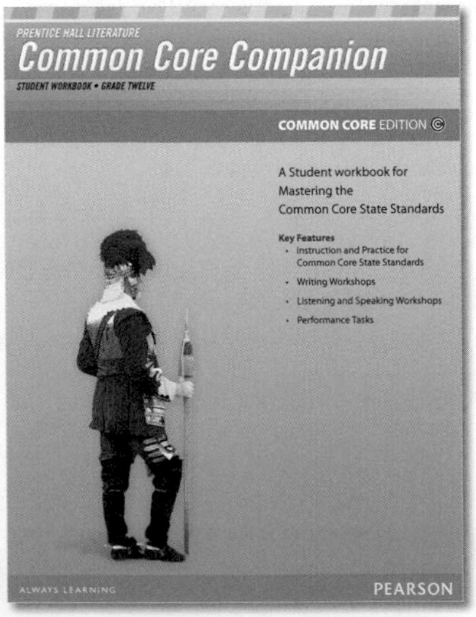

Common Core Companion

Additional instruction and practice for each Common Core State Standard

Selection Support

Graphic Organizer Transparencies

"God's Grandeur" and "Spring and Fall: To a Young Child"
by Gerard Manley Hopkins
"To an Athlete Dying Young" and "When I Was One-and-Twenty"
by A. E. Housman

After You Read B: Rhythm and Meter

Generations have trod, have trod, have trod; . . .

Explain:

Graphic Organizer Transparencies

198

EL L3 **Literary Analysis: Graphic Organizer B,** p. 198

Also available for these selections:

- EL L1 L2 **Literary Analysis: Graphic Organizer A** (partially filled in), p. 197
- EL L1 L2 **Reading: Graphic Organizer A,** p. 195
- EL L3 **Reading: Graphic Organizer B,** p. 196

Skills Development/Extension

Unit 5 Resources

Name ________________ Date ________

"God's Grandeur" and "Spring and Fall: To a Young Child"
by Gerard Manley Hopkins
"To an Athlete Dying Young" and "When I Was One-and-Twenty"
by A. E. Housman

Enrichment: Social Studies

Hopkins and Housman lived and worked in various cities in England, Wales, Scotland, and Ireland during their lifetimes. Modern-day readers often enjoy visiting the places where their favorite authors and poets lived and worked. This map identifies the locations of Hopkins's and Housman's activities.

DIRECTIONS: *Study the map. Then write general directions, using compass points, for modern-day visitors to travel from London to the specified points on the map.*

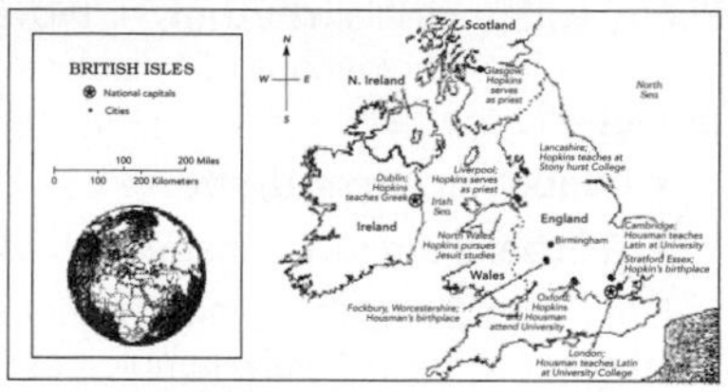

1. Send a traveler to tour places with which only A. E. Housman is connected. ________
2. Send a traveler to learn more about Hopkins's work as a priest. ________
3. Send another traveler to learn specifically about the childhoods of Hopkins and Housman. ________
4. Where should a traveler go who wants to compare the college careers of the two poets? Give directions. ________
5. Finally, send a traveler to learn about Hopkins's work in Ireland. ________

Unit 5 Resources: Progress and Decline

137

L4 **Enrichment,** p. 137

Also available for these selections:

- All **Literary Analysis: Rhythm,** p. 133
- All **Reading: Analyze the Author's Belief's** p. 134
- EL L3 L4 **Support for Writing,** p. 139

Assessment

Name ________________ Date ________

"God's Grandeur" and "Spring and Fall: To a Young Child" by Gerard Manley Hopkins
"To an Athlete Dying Young" and "When I Was One-and-Twenty" by A. E. Housman

Selection Test B

Critical Reading *Identify the letter of the choice that best completes the statement or answers the question.*

___ 1. Gerard Manley Hopkins's "God's Grandeur" contrasts
A. the flame of poetry with the oil of commerce.
B. the splendor of creation with the dullness of mankind.
C. western darkness with eastern light.
D. the sad wisdom of age with the fresh inexperience of youth.

___ 2. What type of rhythm is used in this line from "Spring and Fall: To a Young Child"?
Áh! ás the heart grows older
A. trochaic rhythm
B. sprung rhythm
C. blank rhythm
D. iambic pentameter

___ 3. What characteristic of counterpoint rhythm does this line from "God's Grandeur" illustrate?
World broods with warm breast and with ah! bright wings
A. a regular pattern of stressed syllables
B. the omission of prepositions as connectors
C. two opposing rhythms appearing together
D. the use of iambic tetrameter

___ 4. Which of the lines from "God's Grandeur" is most indicative of Hopkins's religious faith?
A. "Because the Holy Ghost over the bent / World broods with warm breast and with ah! bright wings."
B. "Generations have trod, have trod, have trod; / And all is seared with trade . . ."
C. ". . . the soil / Is bare now, nor can foot feel, being shod."
D. "And for all this, nature is never spent; / There lives the dearest freshness deep down things;"

___ 5. What event occasions Gerard Manley Hopkins's "Spring and Fall: To a Young Child"?
A. the destruction of a forest
B. the death of a child of a family friend
C. a child's sadness at fallen leaves
D. the death of a child's parents

___ 6. In "Spring and Fall: To a Young Child," the image of "wanwood leafmeal" suggests the
A. bounty of harvest.
B. process of decay.
C. mystery of the forest.
D. innocence of childhood.

Unit 5 Resources: Progress and Decline

144

EL L3 L4 **Selection Test B,** pp. 144–146

Also available for these selections:

- EL L1 L2 **Selection Test A,** pp. 141–143
- L3 L4 **Open-Book Test,** pp. 138–140

PHLit Online!
www.PHLitOnline.com

Online Resources: All print materials are also available online.

- complete narrated selection text
- a thematically related video with writing prompt
- an interactive graphic organizer
- highlighting feature
- access to all student print resources, adapted to individual student needs
- Spanish and English summaries
- adapted selection translations in Spanish

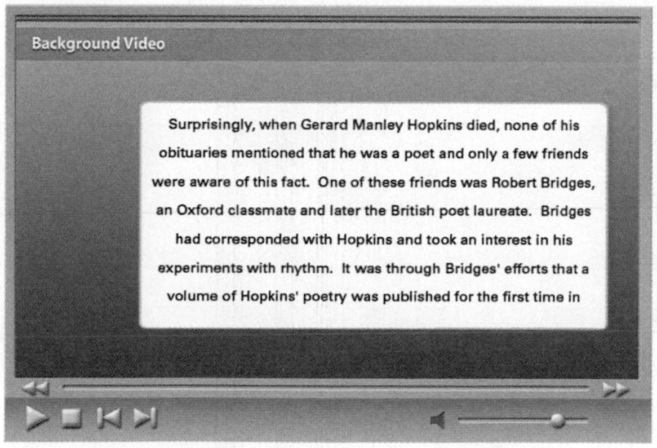

Background Video
Surprisingly, when Gerard Manley Hopkins died, none of his obituaries mentioned that he was a poet and only a few friends were aware of this fact. One of these friends was Robert Bridges, an Oxford classmate and later the British poet laureate. Bridges had corresponded with Hopkins and took an interest in his experiments with rhythm. It was through Bridges' efforts that a volume of Hopkins' poetry was published for the first time in

Background Video

Also available:

Get Connected! (thematic video with writing prompt)
All videos are available in Spanish.

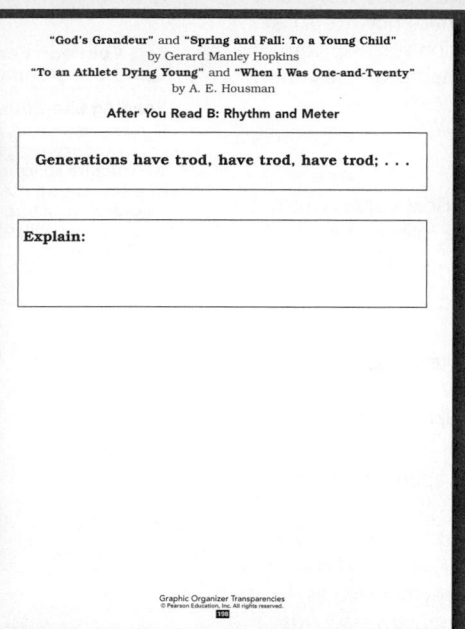

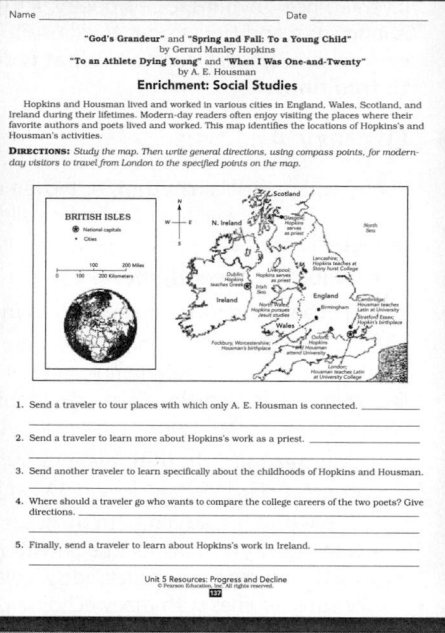

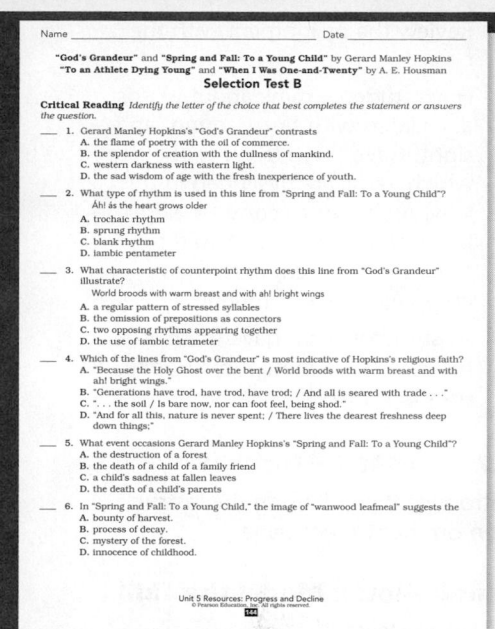

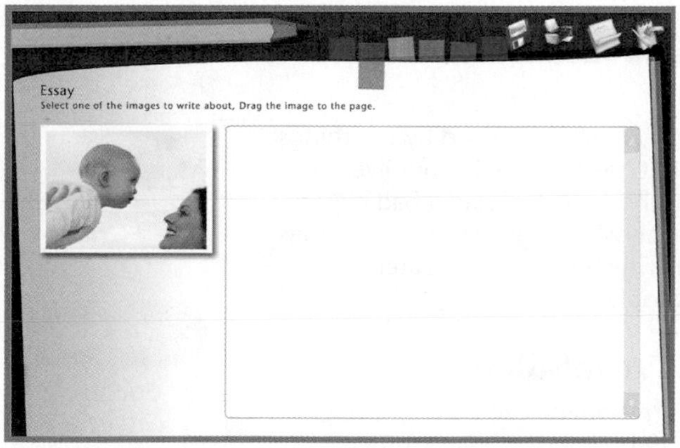

Writer's Journal (with graphics feature)

Also available:

Vocabulary Central (tools and activities for studying vocabulary)

PRETEACH

❶ Connecting to the Essential Question

1. Review the assignment with the class.
2. Have students think about words associated with taste, sound, and sight. Have them think about which items are described in this way. Ask them to consider other kinds of associations related to these items. Then, have them complete the assignment.
3. As students read, have them look for innovative metaphors Hopkins uses in his work.

❷ Literary Analysis

Introduce the skill using the instruction on the student page.

Think Aloud: Model the Skill

Say to students:

We are exposed to rhythm every day, mainly in music. The music's beat is like the stressed syllables in poetry. So, for example, I could tap out the rhythm of poetry just as I might tap out the beat of a song.

❸ Reading Strategy

1. Introduce the skill using the instruction on the student page.
2. Give students a copy of **Reading Strategy Graphic Organizer B,** p.196 in ***Graphic Organizer Transparencies,*** to fill out as they read.

Think Aloud: Model the Skill

Say to students:

We are all influenced by the things that happen to us in our lives. An author who has had a bad experience with dogs might write stories in which dogs are threatening to people.

❹ Vocabulary

1. Pronounce each word, giving its definition, and have students say it aloud.
2. For more guidance, see the ***Classroom Strategies and Teaching Routines*** card for introducing vocabulary.

Before You Read

God's Grandeur • Spring and Fall: To a Young Child • To an Athlete Dying Young • When I Was One-and-Twenty

❶ **Connecting to the Essential Question** Hopkins coined words and invented new rhythms for his poetry. As you read, notice how Hopkins is innovative and Housman is traditional. This distinction will help you explore the Essential Question: **What is the relationship of the writer to tradition?**

Common Core State Standards

Reading Literature
5. Analyze how an author's choices concerning how to structure specific parts of a text contribute to its overall structure and meaning as well as its aesthetic impact.

❷ Literary Analysis

Poetry with a regular **rhythm,** or movement, is **metrical verse,** which is divided into combinations of syllables called **feet.** The following are types of feet and the pattern of stressed and unstressed syllables they contain:

- **Iambic:** unstressed, stressed, as in *the time*
- **Trochaic:** stressed, unstressed, as in *grandeur*

Lines with three, four, and five feet are **trimeter, tetrameter,** and **pentameter,** respectively. Iambic pentameter, for example, is a five-foot line with iambic feet. Housman uses regular meters like iambic and trochaic tetrameter, but Hopkins invents rhythms like these:

- **Counterpoint rhythm:** two opposing rhythms appear together; for example, two trochaic feet in an iambic line:
  The world is charged with the grandeur of God.
- **Sprung rhythm:** all feet begin with a stressed syllable and contain a varying number of unstressed syllables. Sprung rhythm creates densely stressed lines with many echoing consonant and vowel sounds.

As you read, notice which words the poets choose to stress. Consider why the authors may have placed special emphasis on these words and determine if such emphasis adds to the meaning of the poems.

Comparing Literary Works Beauty and mortality are two connected themes these poets explore. Analyze how these themes interact.

❸ Reading Strategy

Preparing to Read Complex Texts Analyzing the author's beliefs will help you understand the ideas and feelings in the poems. Consider details in the author's biography along with details of the poems. Use a diagram like this to analyze the poets' beliefs.

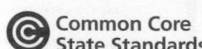

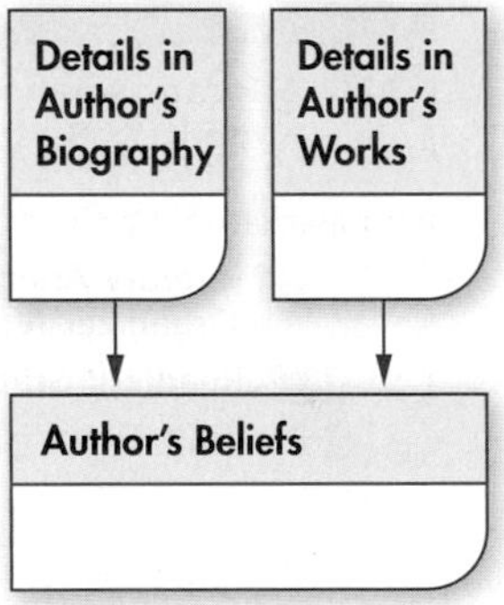

❹ Vocabulary

grandeur (granʹ jər) *n.* splendor; magnificence (p. 1089)

smudge (smŭj) *n.* a smear or stain of dirt (p. 1089)

brink (brĭngk) *n.* edge (p. 1089)

blight (blīt) *n.* condition of withering (p. 1090)

lintel (lĭnʹ tl) *n.* horizontal bar above a door (p. 1092)

rue (ro͞o) *n.* sorrow; regret (p. 1093)

PHLitOnline! www.PHLitOnline.com

Vocabulary Development

Vocabulary Knowledge Rating

Create a **Vocabulary Knowledge Rating Chart** ***(Professional Development Guidebook,*** p. 33) for the vocabulary words on the student page. Give each student a copy of the chart with the words on it. Read the words aloud, and have students mark their ratings in the Before Reading column. Urge students to attend to these words as they read and discuss the selections.

In order to gauge how much instruction you need to provide, tally how many students are confident in their knowledge of each word. As students read, point out the words and their context.

PHLitOnline! **Vocabulary Central,** featuring tools and activities for studying vocabulary, is available online at **www.PHLitOnline.com.**

❺ # GERARD MANLEY HOPKINS

(1844–1889)

Author of "God's Grandeur" • "Spring and Fall: To a Young Child"

Although he was the most innovative poet of the Victorian period, Hopkins never published a collection of his work during his lifetime. It was not until 1918 that his work was published and a generation of poets could read and be influenced by his startling poetry.

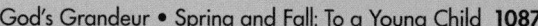

Devotion to God and Nature This quietly rebellious poet was born just outside London, the oldest of nine children in a prosperous middle-class family. Although physically slight, he would perch fearlessly at the top of a tree and sway in the wind while observing the landscape. He began to write poetry in grammar school, a practice he continued at Oxford University, where he studied the classics.

During his third year at Oxford, Hopkins decided to become a Catholic priest in the Jesuit order—a decision that dismayed his parents, who were devout Anglicans. The discipline of Hopkins's religious vocation was sometimes at odds with his writing of verse. He temporarily gave up poetry but continued to keep detailed notebooks that recorded his fascination with words and his love of nature.

Inscape In the mid-1870s, while studying theology in Wales, he began to write poetry again, stimulated by the Welsh language and encouraged by his religious mentor. Somewhat earlier, Hopkins had found in the medieval theologian Duns Scotus a verification of his own ideas about the individuality of all things. Hopkins called this precious individuality *inscape,* and he tried to capture it in highly original poems like "God's Grandeur." He also experimented with new rhythms in his verse.

From early 1884 on, he taught at a Jesuit college in Dublin. There, he died of typhoid fever just before his forty-fifth birthday. Although in many ways he was not typical of the other poets of his age, he is now considered one of the greatest Victorian poets.

Daily Bellringer

For each class during which you will teach these selections, have students complete one of the five activities for the appropriate week in the ***Daily Bellringer Activities*** booklet.

Multidraft Reading

To assist struggling readers and to enhance reading for all, assign the text in chunks, as warranted by length, and apply multidraft reading protocols. For each reading, have students set the purpose indicated:

- **First reading**—identifying key ideas and details and answering any Reading Checks.
- **Second reading**—analyzing craft and structure and responding to the side-column prompts.
- **Third reading**—integrating knowledge and ideas, connecting to other texts and the world, and answering the end-of-selection questions.

For more guidance, refer to the ***Classroom Strategies and Teaching Routines*** card on Multidraft Reading.

❺ Background

More About the Author

One of Gerard Manley Hopkins's most creative periods was ushered in by a disaster. The 1875 sinking of the *Deutschland,* a ship that had been carrying five Franciscan nuns exiled for their faith, led to a period of poetic inspiration for Hopkins, who wrote "The Wreck of the *Deutschland,*" one of his longest poems. Although the poem was rejected as too difficult by the Jesuit journal to which Hopkins submitted it for publication, the renaissance of his creative powers seems to have been the spur for Hopkins to write other works, including "The Windhover" and "Pied Beauty."

PHLit Online!
www.PHLitOnline.com

Teaching From Technology

Preparing to Read
Go to **www.PHLitOnline.com** and display the ***Get Connected!*** slide show for this selection grouping. Have the class brainstorm responses to the writing prompt, entering ideas in the interactive journal. Then, have students complete their written responses as homework.

To build background, display the Background and More About the Author features.

Using the Interactive Text
Go to **www.PHLitOnline.com** and display the Enriched Online Student Edition. As the class reads the selection or listens to the narration, record answers to side-column prompts using the graphic organizers accessible on the interactive page. Alternatively, have students use the online edition individually, answering the prompts as they read.

❶ About the Selection

In "God's Grandeur," Hopkins marvels at how the glory of God shines out through all of nature. In "Spring and Fall," Hopkins reflects on how a young girl is intuitively responding to a sense of her own mortality as she mourns the falling leaves in autumn.

❷ Activating Prior Knowledge

Remind students that poetry is meant to be read aloud, and that the rhythms and sounds of poetry play an important part in the meaning. Have them recall the rhythms and meters of poems they have read. Then, encourage them to meet in small groups and read the following poems aloud.

Concept Connector →

Tell students they will return to their responses after reading the selections.

❶ ❷ GOD'S GRANDEUR

GERARD MANLEY HOPKINS

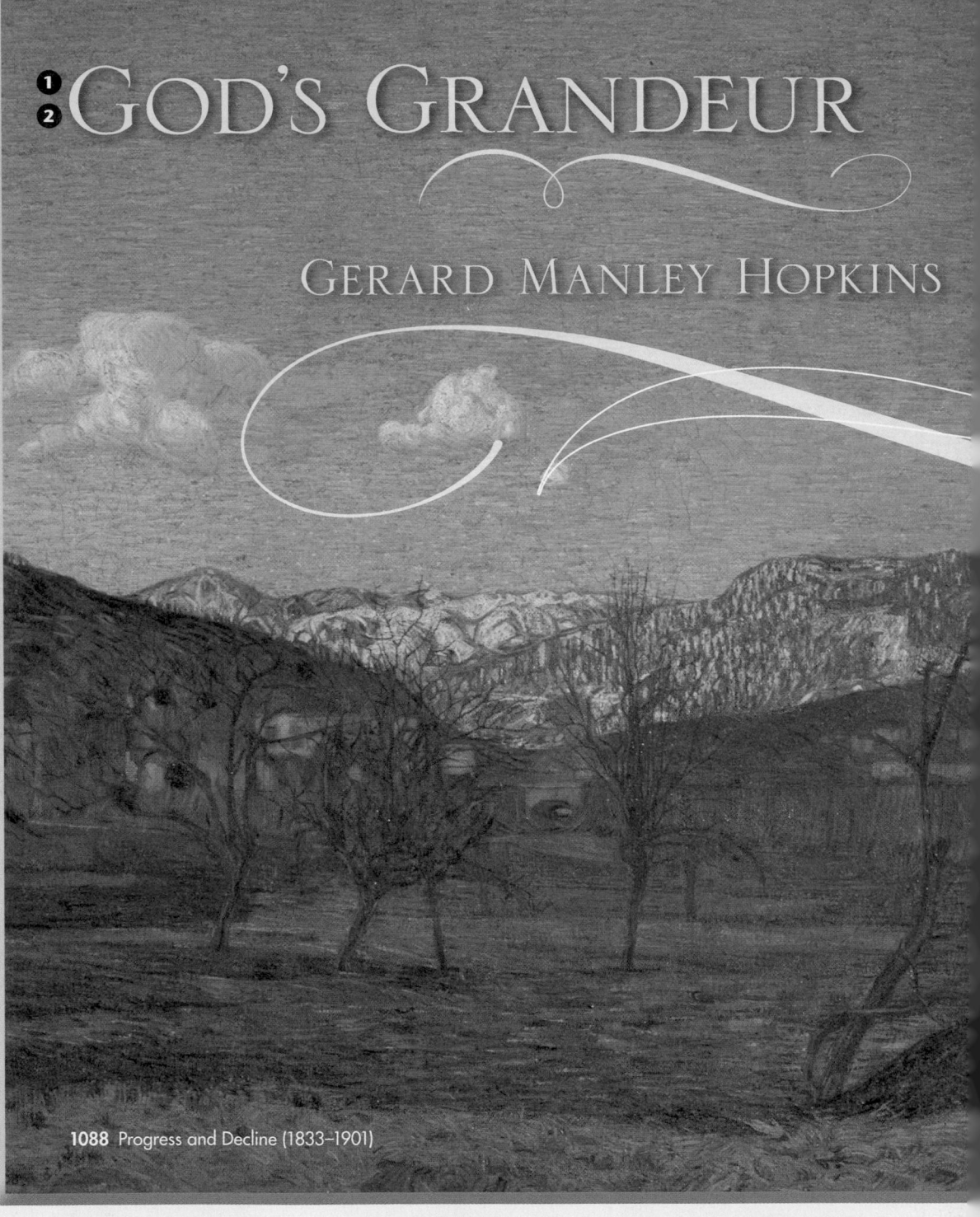

Text Complexity Rubric

	God's Grandeur	Spring and Fall	To an Athlete Dying Young	When I Was One-and-Twenty
Qualitative Measures				
Context/ Knowledge Demands	Victorian lyric 1 ② 3 4 5	Victorian lyric 1 ② 3 4 5	Victorian elegy 1 2 ③ 4 5	Victorian lyric 1 ② 3 4 5
Structure/Language Conventionality and Clarity	Poetic diction 1 2 ③ 4 5	Coined words; simple diction 1 ② 3 4 5	Simple diction; poetic syntax 1 2 ③ 4 5	Poetic diction and syntax 1 2 ③ 4 5
Levels of Meaning/ Purpose/Concepts	Accessible (nature and glory) 1 2 ③ 4 5	Accessible (mortality) 1 2 ③ 4 5	Challenging (transience) 1 2 3 ④ 5	Accessible (rueful humor) 1 ② 3 4 5
Quantitative Measures				
Lexile/Text Length	NP / 411 words	NP / 95 words	NP / 173 words	NP / 84 words
Overall Complexity	**More accessible**	**More accessible**	**More complex**	**More accessible**

BACKGROUND Surprisingly, when Gerard Manley Hopkins died, none of his obituaries mentioned that he was a poet and only a few friends were aware of this fact. One of these friends was Robert Bridges, an Oxford classmate and later the British poet laureate. Bridges had corresponded with Hopkins and took an interest in his experiments with rhythm. It was through Bridges's efforts that a volume of Hopkins's poetry was published for the first time in 1918. Today, Bridges is little known, but his once-obscure friend Gerard Manley Hopkins is a famous Victorian poet.

4
The world is charged with the grandeur of God.
It will flame out, like shining from shook foil;[1]
It gathers to a greatness, like the ooze of oil
Crushed.[2] Why do men then now not reck his rod?[3]
Generations have trod, have trod, have trod;
And all is seared with trade; bleared, smeared with toil;
And wears man's smudge and shares man's smell: the soil
Is bare now, nor can foot feel, being shod.

And for all this, nature is never spent;
There lives the dearest freshness deep down things;
And though the last lights off the black West went
Oh, morning, at the brown brink eastward, springs—
Because the Holy Ghost over the bent
World broods with warm breast and with ah! bright wings.

1. **foil** *n.* tinsel.
2. **crushed** squeezed from olives.
3. **reck his rod** heed God's authority.

Vocabulary
grandeur (gran′ jər) *n.* splendor; magnificence
smudge (smŭj) *n.* a smear or stain of dirt
brink (brĭngk) *n.* edge; margin

3 ◀ **Critical Viewing** How does this painting reflect Hopkins's ideas in "God's Grandeur"? **[Apply]**

3 Critical Viewing

Possible response: The painting reflects Hopkins's ideas because it focuses on small details of nature in an intense way. The vivid colors in the painting reflect the "freshness" of natural glory in the world, a freshness that is never "spent," despite the intrusions of humanity.

4 Critical Thinking

Analyze

1. **Ask** students with what force of nature the verb *charge* is usually associated. Then, ask them what effect the word has as used here.
Answer: The verb *charge* is usually associated with electricity. By using the word here, Hopkins invests God with an electric, dynamic presence.
2. You may find it necessary to explain that in Christian theology, the Holy Ghost, or Holy Spirit, is believed to be one aspect of God. The Holy Ghost is often symbolized by a dove, and that may be why Hopkins uses bird imagery to describe Its presence in the world.

PHLit Online!

These selections are available in an interactive format in the **Enriched Online Student Edition**, at **www.PHLitOnline.com,** which includes a thematically related video with writing prompt and an interactive graphic organizer.

Text Complexity: Reader and Task Suggestions

	God's Grandeur; Spring and Fall	To An Athlete Dying Young	When I Was One-and-Twenty
Preparing to Read the Texts • Discuss with students the idea that the rhythm or meter of a poem can enhance its meaning. • Discuss with students the loss of innocence or hope that some people experience as they grow older. • Guide students to use Multidraft Reading strategies (TE p. 1087).	**Leveled Tasks** ***Structure/Language*** If students will have difficulty with the sprung rhythm, read the poems aloud so that they can hear the rhythm. Then, have students read the poems, concentrating on the emotions conveyed by the poems. ***Synthesizing*** If students will not have difficulty with the meter, have them compare the moods and world views of the poems.	**Leveled Tasks** ***Levels of Meaning*** If students will have difficulty with the levels of meaning, have them focus first on the parallel events recounted in the poem. Then, as they reread, have them consider the logic of the speaker's views on dying. ***Evaluating*** If students will not have difficulty with the meaning, have them support or refute the poem's central idea.	**Leveled Tasks** ***Structure/Language*** If students have difficulty with the poetic diction and syntax, have them restate the poem in contemporary English. Then, have them contrast the speaker's attitude at different ages. ***Evaluating*** If students will not have difficulty with the poem's language, have them evaluate whether its poetic diction and syntax are apt and essential to the poem's effect.

5 Literary Analysis

Rhythm and Meter

1. Remind students that in sprung rhythm, all feet begin with a stressed syllable and contain a varying number of unstressed syllables.
2. Then, **read** the Literary Analysis directive: Identify a visual clue that proves that this poem is written in sprung rhythm.
   Answer: Several of the first syllables are marked with accents.

6 Vocabulary Builder

Coined Words

1. Explain to students that Hopkins sometimes combines old words to make new ones. Point out the words *wanwood* and *leafmeal.*
2. Tell them that *wanwood* means "pale wood," and *leafmeal* means "ground-up, decomposed leaves."
3. Encourage students to coin some words of their own.

ASSESS

Answers

Before students respond, you may wish to have them write a brief objective summary of the selection. As they answer the questions below, remind them to support their answers with evidence from the text.

1. (a) People have tainted nature with trade and toil. (b) Lines 1–8 present an opposition between God's grandeur in nature and the power of humans to obscure it. (c) He asserts that no matter what people do, they can never obliterate God's grandeur in nature.
2. (a) She is unhappy because the leaves are falling off the trees. (b) Margaret will always be sad, but as she grows older, she will be sad for herself.
3. (a) As she grows older, Margaret will mourn for her own mortality. (b) The speaker teaches Margaret that death is a part of the human condition.
4. Yes; because he takes the beauty and integrity of nature as a sign of God's grandeur, it seems likely that Hopkins would support any movement to preserve nature.

SPRING AND FALL: TO A YOUNG CHILD

GERARD MANLEY HOPKINS

Márgarét, áre you gríeving
Over Goldengrove unleaving?
5 Leáves, líke the things of man, you
With your fresh thoughts care for, can you?
Áh! ás the heart grows older
It will come to such sights colder
By and by, nor spare a sigh
6 Though worlds of wanwood[1] leafmeal[2] lie;
And yet you wíll weep and know why.
Now no matter, child, the name:
Sórrow's spríngs áre the same.
Nor mouth had, no nor mind, expressed
What heart heard of, ghost[3] guessed:
It ís the **blight** man was born for,
It is Margaret you mourn for.

Literary Analysis
Rhythm and Meter
Identify a visual clue that proves that this poem is written in sprung rhythm.

Vocabulary
blight (blīt) *n.* condition of withering

1. **wanwood** (wän' wood) pale wood.
2. **leafmeal** ground-up decomposed leaves.
3. **ghost** spirit.

Critical Reading

Cite textual evidence to support your responses.

1. **Key Ideas and Details (a)** According to Hopkins in "God's Grandeur," what has been the impact on nature of humanity's behavior? **(b) Analyze:** What opposition or conflict does he explore in lines 1–8 of "God's Grandeur"? **(c) Draw Conclusions:** How does Hopkins resolve that opposition?
2. **Key Ideas and Details (a)** What makes Margaret unhappy in "Spring and Fall"? **(b) Interpret:** Explain how the poem's speaker suggests that Margaret will both outgrow and not outgrow this sadness.
3. **Key Ideas and Details (a)** According to the speaker, how will Margaret change as she grows older? **(b) Draw Conclusions:** What lesson does the speaker offer to Margaret in this poem?
4. **Integration of Knowledge and Ideas** Judging by "God's Grandeur," would Hopkins support the ecology movement if he were alive today? Explain.

Enrichment: Analyzing a Literary Figure

Discovering Gerard Manley Hopkins

Remind students that Hopkins did not publish a collection of his work during his lifetime. Given the extent to which he influenced twentieth-century poets, students might wonder how and when Hopkins was discovered. Suggest students research more about Hopkins's life, how his work was discovered, and his influence on twentieth-century poetry. Students can record their findings on the **Enrichment: Investigating a Literary Figure** worksheet, ***Professional Development Guidebook,*** page 235.

A. E. Housman (1859–1936)

Author of "To an Athlete Dying Young" • "When I Was One-and-Twenty"

A man of solitary habits and harsh self-discipline, Housman was also capable of creating delicately crafted poems, full of gentle regret.

Challenges of Youth Housman grew up in Worcestershire, a region northwest of London. His childhood came to an end on his twelfth birthday, when his mother died. Later, at Oxford University, his despair over an unrequited love darkened his life still further. Perhaps because of this double grief, his poetry has bitter undertones.

Upon leaving Oxford, where he had studied classical literature and philosophy, Housman went to work in the Patent Office. Determined to prove himself in the classics, he studied Greek and Latin at night and wrote scholarly articles. In 1892, his hard work paid off when he was appointed to a position as professor of Latin at University College in London.

Literary Success Although Housman spent most of his life engaged in teaching and in scholarly pursuits, he is most remembered for three slender volumes of poetry that are as romantic and melancholy as any ever written. His first and most famous collection of verse, *A Shropshire Lad* (1896), has as its central character a young man named Terence. In later years, Housman claimed, ironically, that he had "never spent much time" in Shropshire.

Housman's image is that of an emotionless intellectual, but his poems display deep feelings. In his view, the goal of poetry is to "transfuse emotion," not to transmit thought. A well-written poem, he maintained, should affect the reader like a shiver down the spine or a punch in the stomach.

7 Background

More About the Author

A. E. Housman's *A Shropshire Lad* was published in 1896. Housman was better known as an academic at the time of its publication, which he paid for himself. The collection's sixty-three poems were mostly nostalgic, set in a partly imaginary Shropshire, and they treated issues of childhood and war. Housman's book met with little success initially but became enormously popular during World War I, when Housman was appointed a professor of Latin at Cambridge University.

Background

The Elegy

Housman's poem "To an Athlete Dying Young" belongs to a genre of poetry known as the elegy. An elegy is a lyric poem that mourns the death of a well-known person or hero, a dear friend, or other loved one. An elegy can also be a meditation on the inevitability of death. The elegy often contains a description of a funeral procession, and it usually ends with an acceptance of death as part of life. In the eighteenth century, a type of elegy written by the so-called "graveyard school" of poets developed. These elegies often contained ghoulish or gloomy imagery about the fleeting nature of life. One of the best known of these is Thomas Gray's "An Elegy Written in a Country Church Yard."

American poets also used the elegy. One of the most famous American elegies is Walt Whitman's "When Lilacs Last in the Dooryard Bloom'd," written upon the death of Abraham Lincoln.

Differentiated Instruction for Universal Access

Support for Special-Needs Students
Students may find it difficult to relate to the subject matter of Housman's poem "To an Athlete Dying Young." Ask them to read the poem with teacher guidance, focusing on the ways in which Housman juxtaposes the athlete's former glory with his present state.

Strategy for Less Proficient Readers
Have students gather news articles depicting moments of glory in sports. Have them explain the feelings they associate with each moment. Then, have them write a paragraph, explaining why Housman might consider it enviable for the athlete to die after that moment.

Background for Advanced Readers
A. E. Housman considered himself more of a classical scholar than a poet. It is only natural that he would include classical allusions in his poetry. In "To an Athlete Dying Young," Housman refers to the athlete's "early-laureled head." Ask students why an athlete would have a laurel on his head.

PHLit Online!

For more about the author, go online at **www.PHLitOnline.com.**

8 About the Selections

In two of his most famous poems, "To an Athlete Dying Young" and "When I Was One-and-Twenty," A. E. Housman reflects on the fleeting glories of youth and the inevitable disillusionment that comes with age and experience. However, he gives the theme of disillusionment an ironic, humorous twist by having a young man voice it in a world-weary tone ("When I Was One-and-Twenty").

9 Literary Analysis

Rhythm and Meter

1. Explain that small departures from a metrical scheme can add meaning.
   Monitor Progress: Ask what the metrical scheme of the poem is.
   Answer: The meter is, generally, iambic tetrameter.
2. Then, **ask** which lines in the fifth stanza begin with trochees.
   Answer: Lines 17 and 19 begin with trochees.
3. **Ask** what effects these departures have on meaning.
   Possible responses: The trochee in line 17 stresses "Now," emphasizing the change that has occurred. The trochee in line 19 adds "speed" to the word *runners,* since the stress comes earlier than expected.

8 To an Athlete Dying Young

A. E. Housman

The time you won your town the race
We chaired you through the marketplace;
Man and boy stood cheering by,
And home we brought you shoulder-high.

Today, the road all runners come,
Shoulder-high we bring you home,
And set you at your threshold down,
Townsman of a stiller town.

Smart lad, to slip betimes away
From fields where glory does not stay
And early though the laurel[1] grows
It withers quicker than the rose.

Eyes the shady night has shut
Cannot see the record cut,
And silence sounds no worse than cheers
After earth has stopped the ears:

9 Now you will not swell the rout
Of lads that wore their honors out,
Runners whom renown outran
And the name died before the man.

So set, before its echoes fade,
The fleet foot on the sill of shade,
And hold to the low **lintel** up
The still-defended challenge cup.

And round that early-laureled head
Will flock to gaze the strengthless dead,
And find unwithered on its curls
The garland briefer than a girl's.

Vocabulary
lintel (lĭn′ tl) *n.* horizontal bar above a door

1. **laurel** symbol of victory.

Vocabulary Development

Vocabulary Knowledge Rating

When students have completed reading and discussing the selections, have them take out their **Vocabulary Rating Charts** for the poems. Read the words aloud and have students rate their knowledge of words again in the After Reading column. Clarify any words that are still problematic. Have students write their own definitions and example or sentence in the appropriate column. Then, have students complete the Vocabulary Lesson at the end of the selections. Encourage students to use the words in further discussion and written work about the selections. Remind them that they will be accountable for these words on the **Selection Test, *Unit 5 Resources,*** pages 141–143 or 144–146.

When I Was One-and-Twenty

A. E. Housman

When I was one-and-twenty
I heard a wise man say,
"Give crowns and pounds and guineas[1]
But not your heart away;
Give pearls away and rubies
But keep your fancy free."
But I was one-and-twenty,
No use to talk to me.

When I was one-and-twenty
I heard him say again,
"The heart out of the bosom
Was never given in vain;
'Tis paid with sighs a plenty
And sold for endless rue."
And I am two-and-twenty,
And oh, 'tis true, 'tis true.

10 Reading Strategy
Analyzing an Author's Beliefs In this poem, do the speaker's beliefs about youth correspond with the author's? Why or why not?

Vocabulary
rue (ro͞o) *n.* sorrow; regret

1. crowns . . . guineas

Critical Reading

1. **Key Ideas and Details (a)** In "To an Athlete," what are three advantages of dying young, according to the speaker? **(b) Interpret:** Does the speaker entirely mean what he says about these advantages? Explain.
2. **Key Ideas and Details (a)** In "When I Was One-and-Twenty," what advice does the speaker receive, and how does he react? **(b) Interpret:** What clues are there in the poem that Housman is mocking his speaker?
3. **Integration of Knowledge and Ideas** Which are more effective, Hopkins's inventive rhythms or Housman's more traditional ones? Explain, using two of these Essential Question terms: *meter, sprung rhythm, innovation. [Connecting to the Essential Question: What is the relationship of the writer to tradition?]*

Cite textual evidence to support your responses.

10 Reading Strategy

Analyzing an Author's Beliefs

1. Have students reread the entire poem.
2. Then, **ask** the Reading Strategy question: In this poem, do the speaker's beliefs about youth correspond with the author's? Why or why not?
   Possible response: Students might say that at first their beliefs are different. The speaker, at the age of twenty-one, states that it was "No use to talk to me." As the speaker turns twenty-two, he or she recognizes the advice of the wise man.

ASSESS

Answers

Before students respond, you may wish to have them write a brief objective summary of the selection. As they answer the questions below, remind them to support their answers with evidence from the text.

1. (a) Three advantages of dying young are getting away from a place where glory "does not stay"; not having to be like other athletes, who live on while their former glory disappears; not having to face lack of recognition ("silence") after the "cheers." (b) No, the speaker does not believe that the runner was "smart" to die. He is merely trying to console himself.
2. (a) He was told not to fall in love. He ignored the advice. (b) The line "And I am two-and-twenty" shows that the speaker takes his new wisdom a bit too seriously.
3. **Possible response:** Some students may state they prefer Hopkins's poetry because of its innovation and complexity; others may prefer Housman's poetry because of its direct expression and simplicity of rhythm and meter.

Concept Connector

Reading Strategy Graphic Organizer

Ask students to review the graphic organizers in which they have identified details of the author's life and the author's work, and drawn conclusions about the author's beliefs. Then, have students share their organizers and compare their conclusions.

Activating Prior Knowledge

Have students return to their responses to the Activating Prior Knowledge activity. Ask them to explain whether their thoughts have changed and, if so, how.

Connecting to the Essential Question

Have students compare their responses to the prompt, completed before reading the selections, with their thoughts afterward. Have them work individually or in groups, writing or discussing their thoughts, to formulate their new responses. Then, lead a class discussion, probing for what students have learned that confirms or invalidates their initial thoughts. Encourage students to cite specific textual details to support their responses.

Answers

1. (a) Génĕrátiŏns hăve tród, hăve tród, hăve tród. (b) The line uses two trochees and three iambs; counterpoint rhythm occurs when two opposing rhythms appear together.
2. The line has four feet.
3. (a) The two initial trochees capture the heaviness of generations treading; the three iambs "have trod" capture the mechanical quality of treading. (b) The stressed syllables at the line's beginning emphasize that certain sorrows are inevitable and universal.
4. (a) In "To an Athlete," lines 3, 6, and 8 are trochaic tetrameter; lines 1, 2, 4, 5, and 7 are iambic tetrameter. (b) The trochaic lines interrupt the regular rhythm, introducing a silence where the expected stresses are missing.
5. (a) "Dearest freshness deep down things" reflects Hopkins's belief that nature is beautiful and also enduring. (b) In "Spring and Fall," Hopkins meditates on the passing of seasons; students may say that "God's Grandeur" captures nature's endurance more completely.
6. Students may think these speakers would agree that deep sorrow is the right response to the fleeting qualities of life and beauty—both express this idea.
7. **Possible response:** Students may suggest that "Spring and Fall" conveys the most compassionate view of human mortality, because the speaker recognizes that children begin very early to understand mortality and to grieve for those things that die.
8. "And, for all this, nature is never spent" (line 9) suggests Hopkins's faith in nature's abiding beauty.
9. **Possible response:** The line "Townsman of a stiller town" suggests Housman's sadness. It denotes the athlete's place in the community of the dead.
10. Hopkins's belief in "inscape" is reflected in lines 11–14 of "God's Grandeur," in which he describes the special quality of dawn, which is infused with the spirit of God.
11. **Possible responses:** Students may use examples of "washed-up" athletes or older athletes who find new careers.

After You Read

God's Grandeur • Spring and Fall: To a Young Child • To an Athlete Dying Young • When I Was One-and-Twenty

Literary Analysis

1. **Craft and Structure** **(a)** Use scansion symbols (˘ ´) to identify the **feet** in line 5 of "God's Grandeur," inserting symbols over syllables on a slip of paper like the one shown below. **(b)** Explain how your scan demonstrates that the line uses **counterpoint rhythm.**

   Generations have trod, have trod, have trod;…

2. **Craft and Structure** "Spring and Fall" is written with **sprung rhythm.** Using the stresses in line 11, indicate how many feet that line has.
3. **Craft and Structure** **(a)** How does the counterpoint rhythm in line 5 of "God's Grandeur" support the meaning of the line? **(b)** In "Spring and Fall," how do the three stresses in line 11 reinforce the meaning of the line?
4. **Craft and Structure** **(a)** Show that in lines 1–8 of "To an Athlete," the **meter** includes five **iambic tetrameter** lines and three **trochaic tetrameter** lines. **(b)** How do the trochaic lines reinforce the idea of a "stiller town"?
5. **Integration of Knowledge and Ideas** **(a)** In "God's Grandeur," does Hopkins think the beauty of nature is enduring? Explain. **(b)** In "Spring and Fall," does he express the same perspective on the endurance of nature's beauty as he does in "God's Grandeur"? Explain.
6. **Integration of Knowledge and Ideas** Would the speakers in "Spring and Fall" and "To an Athlete" agree that deep sorrow is the right response to the realization that life and earthly beauty are fleeting? Explain.
7. **Comparing Literary Works** Which poem conveys the most compassionate view of human mortality—"Spring and Fall," "To an Athlete," or "When I Was One-and-Twenty"? Explain.

Reading Strategy

8. **Analyze the author's beliefs** by finding a passage in "God's Grandeur" that reflects Hopkins's love of nature. Then, explain your choice.
9. Find a passage in "To an Athlete" that reflects Housman's underlying sadness. Explain your choice.
10. Hopkins was inspired by his idea of "inscape"—that special individual quality that distinguished one person, object, or emotion from every other. Find a passage that reflects this belief, and explain how this passage conveys the idea of inscape.
11. Do you agree with Housman in "To an Athlete" that aging can bring only sadness to an athlete? Why or why not?

Common Core State Standards

Writing

1. Write arguments to support claims in an analysis of substantive topics or texts, using valid reasoning and relevant and sufficient evidence. *(p. 1095)*

1.d. Establish and maintain a formal style and objective tone while attending to the norms and conventions of the discipline in which they are writing. *(p. 1095)*

Language

3. Apply knowledge of language to understand how language functions in different contexts, to make effective choices for meaning or style, and to comprehend more fully when reading or listening. *(p. 1095)*

Assessment Practice

Paired Passages (For more practice, see *All-in-One Workbook*.)

Many tests require students to identify and compare literary elements in two passages. Use the following sample item to teach students how to compare the speakers of the two poems. Have students read pages 1092–1093 before they answer the item.

Which of these best describes the speakers in the two poems?

A The first speaker is suicidal; the second is brokenhearted.
B Both speakers like to laugh at themselves.
C The first speaker is sad; the second is regretful.
D Both speakers are serious and loyal.

Students should eliminate ***A*** and ***B*** because nothing in "To an Athlete Dying Young" suggests that the speaker is suicidal or self-mocking. Choice ***D*** is not supported by "When I Was One-and-Twenty." The correct answer is **C**.

PERFORMANCE TASKS

Integrated Language Skills

Vocabulary Acquisition and Use

Word Analysis: Coined Words

Hopkins's fascination with language can be seen in the way he coins, or invents, words. For example, he combines *wan*, meaning "pale," and *wood* to make *wanwood*, a new word to describe pale autumn trees. Similarly, he coins *leafmeal* to describe fallen dead leaves ground into a kind of meal. Imitate Hopkins and *create new words from familiar words* to replace each of these phrases. Use concrete or vivid words so that others will understand the meaning you are trying to convey.

1. the very end of summer
2. chilly mornings right after dawn
3. snow-covered lawns
4. tall, bare trees

Vocabulary: Analogies

Analogies compare the relationships between pairs of words. To complete these analogies, choose the word from the vocabulary list on page 1086 that creates a word pair that matches the relationship in the other pair. Explain your choices.

1. *Roof* is to *car* as ______ is to *doorway.*
2. ______ is to *squalor* as *summer* is to *winter.*
3. ______ is to *cliff* as *balcony* is to *building.*
4. *Joy* is to *happiness* as ______ is to *regret.*
5. *Remove* is to *stain* as *wash* is to ______.
6. *Starvation* is to *hunger* as ______ is to *damage.*

Writing

Argumentative Text Hopkins's poetry was virtually unknown during his life. The poet became more widely read only after Robert Bridges, a long-time friend, had his work published in 1918, long after the poet's death. Take the role of Bridges in 1918 and write a **business letter** to a British publishing company recommending that the publisher issue a collected edition of the poetry of Hopkins.

Prewriting Review the background information about Hopkins's theory of sprung rhythm, his idea of inscape, and his use of coined words. Find passages from his poems that illustrate these ideas and Hopkins's unique poetic voice.

Drafting Use the proper format of a business letter, with the date, the name and address of a fictional publisher, salutation, body, and closing. In the body of your letter, give reasons why the publisher should issue the volume you propose. Explain Hopkins's ideas and cite passages from Hopkins's poetry that show his use of *imagery, figures of speech, and sound* to *evoke reader's emotions.*

Revising Review your letter to make sure that it is persuasive, and strengthen parts that need more emphasis. Use the formal language of business and not the less formal tone of everyday speech.

Model: Revising to Use Formal Language

In sum, Hopkins's poetry deserves to reach a wider public.

His ~~awesome style~~ *unique poetic voice* must be heard.

The use of formal language in business letters establishes credibility.

Assessment Resources

Unit 5 Resources

L1 L2 EL **Selection Test A,** pp. 141–143. Administer Test A to less advanced students.

L3 L4 EL **Selection Test B,** pp. 144–146. Administer Test B to on-level and more advanced students.

L3 L4 **Open-Book Test,** pp. 138–140. As an alternative, administer the **Open-Book Test.**

All **Customizable Test Bank**

All **Self-tests**
Students may prepare for the **Selection Test** by taking the **Self-test** online.

PHLit Online! Assessment resources are available at **www.PHLitOnline.com.**

ASSESS/EXTEND

Answers

Vocabulary Acquisition and Use

1. Introduce the skill using the instruction on the student page.
2. Have students complete the Word Analysis activity and the Vocabulary practice.

Word Analysis

Possible responses: Students' coined words will vary considerably. The following are some suggestions:

1. summersend
2. chillmorns
3. snow-lawns
4. tallbare trees

Vocabulary

1. lintel
2. grandeur
3. brink
4. rue
5. smudge
6. blight

Writing

1. To guide students in writing this argumentative text, give them the **Support for Writing** page (*Unit 5 Resources,* p. 136).
2. Remind students that the use of sprung rhythm and coined words was a departure from the standard poetic conventions of the time. They may wish to present Hopkins's poetry as something new and fresh.
3. Point out that this letter is attempting to sell an idea, that of publishing a book of poetry. Encourage students to use techniques of persuasive writing in the body of their letters.
4. Use the **Rubrics for Persuasion, *Professional Development Guidebook,*** pages 256–257, to evaluate students' work.

PRETEACH

Common Core State Standards

- **Writing 2, 2.c, e, f; 4, 5, 7, 8**
- **Language 2**

Introducing the Assignment

Review the assignment and the criteria, using the instruction on the student page.

What Do You Notice?

1. Read the excerpt from "Life in Elizabethan and Jacobean England." Discuss with students how Kermode combines factual information and his own perceptions.
2. Then, have a student read the highlighted sentence aloud. **Ask** what makes it special. **Possible response:** its images; words such as *splendor, keen,* and *magnificence.*
3. Point out that this long sentence contains only one comma, but that its phrases create a natural rhythm that prevents the sentence from rambling. Then read the first clause aloud, emphasizing the stressed syllables (*SPLENdor, RIver, MANsions,* etc.).
4. **Ask** how the rhythms of this clause mimic its subject. (The sentence's smooth, flowing rhythm is like that of a river.)
5. Suggest that students use the arrangement of words and phrases to create rhythm in their own prose.

Writing Workshop

Write a Report

Historical Investigation Conducting a historical investigation can help you analyze and evaluate the historical background of literary works. You can record your findings in a research report. Remember that an effective report does more than simply list facts: it synthesizes information from a variety of primary, secondary, and tertiary sources and connects ideas to present a coherent analysis, explaining any differences in sources. Follow the steps outlined in this workshop to write a historical investigation.

Assignment Write a **historical investigation report** on an event, figure, or topic that relates to the historical context of a work or works of literature.

What to Include Your research report should have these elements:

- A clear thesis statement, supported by a variety of formats and rhetorical strategies
- An analysis that supports and develops personal opinions, as opposed to restating existing information
- Incorporation of the complexities of and discrepancies in information from multiple sources, with anticipation and refutation of counter-arguments
- Proper documentation and listing of sources, using a style manual
- Sufficient length and complexity to address the topic

To preview the criteria on which your research report may be assessed, see the rubric on page 1107.

To get a feel for historical investigation, read this mentor text. Notice how Sir Frank Kermode combines factual information with his version of Shakespeare's perceptions.

***from:* Life in Elizabethan and Jacobean England**

Inflation was unchecked but money flowed freely. Among the expensive luxuries of the day were ostentatious clothes and tobacco, a recent import from the New World. London was a perpetual bustle, noise and display. Imagine how a young man from the provinces, like Shakespeare, might react to it. Shakespeare's Stratford, though a sturdy community with its own guilds and its good grammar school, hardly offered adequate preparation for London, among other things a great port and the gateway to the larger world. The splendor of the river and the mansions lining its bank won the keen admiration of foreign visitors, who compared its magnificence with that of Paris and other great European cities.

Common Core State Standards

Writing

2. Write informative/explanatory texts to examine and convey complex ideas, concepts, and information clearly and accurately through the effective selection, organization, and analysis of content.

7. Conduct short as well as more sustained research projects to answer a question or solve a problem; narrow or broaden the inquiry when appropriate; synthesize multiple sources on the subject, demonstrating understanding of the subject under investigation.

8. Gather relevant information from multiple authoritative print and digital sources, using advanced searches effectively; assess the strengths and limitations of each source in terms of the task, purpose, and audience.

PHLit Online! www.PHLitOnline.com

WRITE GUY
Jeff Anderson, M. Ed.

What Do You Notice?

Read the highlighted sentence several times. Then, with a partner, discuss the qualities that make it special. You might consider the following elements:

- Word choice
- Sentence length
- Rhythm
- Structure

Share your group's observations with the class.

Teaching Resources

All *Unit 5 Resources*
Writing Workshop, pp. 147–148

All *Common Core Companion*,
pp. 196–207, 219–227, 240–260; 318–321

All *Professional Development Guidebook*
Rubric for Self-Assessment: Research Report, pp. 268–269

All *Graphic Organizer Transparencies*
Rubric for Self-Assessment p. 199

All *See It!* DVD
James Berry, Segments 3 and 4

PHLit Online! All resources, including print and video, are available online at www.PHLitOnline.com.

Prewriting and Planning

Choosing Your Topic

To choose a topic suitable for the research sources that are available to you, use one of the following strategies:

- **Notebook and Textbook Review** Reviewing school notebooks, textbooks, and writing journals, list topics that interest you. Also review the selections you have read in this textbook, and consider specific questions you have about the historical context for your favorite works.
- **Research Preview** When you have two good topic choices, spend 10–15 minutes researching each topic on the Internet or at the library. This quick research preview will help you identify how much information is available on each topic. Look for both primary and secondary sources.

  Primary sources: letters, diaries, interviews, eyewitness accounts
  Secondary sources: encyclopedias, nonfiction books, and articles

Narrowing Your Topic

Freewrite to find your focus. If your topic can be divided into significant subheads, each with its own focus, it is probably too broad. Using what you already know or have learned in preliminary research, write freely on your topic for two or three minutes. Review your writing and circle the most important or interesting idea. Continue this process until you arrive at a topic that is narrow enough for your paper.

Gathering Details

Do the research. Use both library and Internet resources to locate information. Evaluate sources for validity and reliability before citing them. Be especially critical of Internet sources, checking that the authors have followed careful academic procedures.

Use source cards and note cards. For every source you consult, create a source card with the author's name, title, publisher, city, and date of publication. Then, create a note card for each relevant fact or opinion. Write the general subject at the top. Then, write the fact or quotation, followed by a keyword, such as the author's name, that links the fact with its source.

Source Card
[Ament]
Ament, Phil. "Charles Babbage." The Great Idea Finder. 15 Jan. 2008 <http://www.ideafinder.com/history/inventors/babbage.htm>

Note card
[Babbage's importance]
he's often called the "Father of Computing"
Source: Ament

Applying Understanding by Design Principles

Clarifying Expected Outcomes: Using Rubrics

1. Before students begin work on this assignment, have them preview the **Rubric for Self-Assessment: Research Report** on p. 1107, to learn what qualities their research reports must have. A copy of this Rubric appears in the ***Professional Development Guidebook,*** page 268.
2. Review the Assessment criteria with the class. Before students use the Rubric to assess their own writing, work with them to rate the Student Model (pp. 1104–1106) using the Rubric.
3. If you wish to assess students' research reports with either a 4-point or 6-point scoring rubric, see the ***Professional Development Guidebook,*** pages 268–269.

TEACH

Prewriting and Planning

1. Introduce the prewriting strategies using the instruction on the student page.
2. Have students apply the strategies to choose and narrow a topic and gather details.

Teaching the Strategies

1. Ask students to identify questions they hope to answer in their research reports and to list these questions in two-column charts.
2. Tell students that if information is scarce, they may need a different topic.
3. Remind students that they will need to identify a topic that is both broad enough to have sufficient research sources and narrow enough to explore fully.
4. Point out to students the sample source information on this page, mentioning each aspect of the information included there.

Think Aloud: Model Choosing Your Topic

Say to students:

To choose a topic for my research report, I will first write a list of possible topics, and then decide on two I find most interesting. Next I will research each topic to see how much information is available. That will help me decide which to choose.

Six Traits Focus

✔	Ideas		Word Choice
✔	Organization		Sentence Fluency
	Voice		Conventions

PH WRITING COACH Grade 12

Students will find additional information on historical investigation in Chapter 11.

Prentice Hall EssayScorer

A writing prompt for this mode of writing can be found on the ***Prentice Hall Essay Scorer*** at **www.PHLitOnline.com.**

Drafting

1. Introduce the drafting strategies using the instruction on the student page.
2. Have students apply the strategies as they draft their research reports.

Teaching the Strategies

1. Remind students that a thesis statement clearly states the main idea or purpose of a research report. Students' opening paragraphs should clearly identify this thesis and provide an introduction so that readers clearly understand the topic.
2. Review the **Effective Methods of Organization** chart with students. Have them determine which type of organization would best suit the topics of their research reports.
3. Tell students that the introduction can make a good or a poor first impression on their reports' readers. As students conduct their research, remind them to look for a well-spoken quotation or a dramatic historical event to use for special effect in the introduction.
4. Review with students how to handle their sources well. Encourage them to use paraphrasing more often than direct quotation, reserving direct quotation for occasions when they cannot adequately express the idea another way. Remind students that direct quotes should always be framed so that the reader understands why they were chosen.

Six Traits Focus

✔	Ideas		Word Choice
✔	Organization		Sentence Fluency
	Voice		Conventions

Drafting

Shaping Your Writing

Develop a thesis statement. Review your notes and draft a statement that reflects a theme in the material you have collected. Your thesis statement should introduce your topic and the point you will develop.

Establish your organizational plan. Decide whether you will present conclusions about your sources as part of your introduction, or build toward your conclusions throughout the paper. Use one of these plans.

Effective Methods of Organization

Introduction	present historical context give thesis statement DRAW CONCLUSION	present historical context establish issue in thesis statement
Body	PROVE CONCLUSION present/analyze/compare sources	present/analyze/compare sources LEAD TO CONCLUSION
Closing	summarize	DRAW CONCLUSION

Write a powerful introduction and conclusion. Use your opening paragraph to introduce the issue, to define unfamiliar terms, and to clarify background details such as the time, place, and relevant social conditions. In your conclusion, emphasize the significance of your findings.

Maintain a formal style and objective tone. As you draft, choose words consistent with a formal style, such as *supplies*, rather than informal words, such as *stuff*. In addition, keep your tone objective. Rather than choosing words that express opinions, such as *outrageous*, choose objective words and phrases such as *widely condemned*.

Providing Elaboration

Handle your sources well. Follow these guidelines when presenting sources:

- Use a mix of paraphrases and direct quotations. Do not string quotations together without interpretation. Instead, frame your quotations so that a reader understands why you chose them.
- Describe and analyze your sources. Explain whether or not primary resources reflect consensus, or general agreement, about a topic. When primary resources offer different perspectives, try to account for these differences. If a writer's perspective is unique, explain it, if possible, by analyzing the writer's circumstances and motives.
- As you draft, underline sentences you will need to document. After you finish drafting, you can format the appropriate citations.
- Be aware of what constitutes *plagiarism*, especially in using media and digital sources. Clearly attribute the words and ideas of others.

Common Core State Standards

Writing

2.c. Use appropriate and varied transitions and syntax to link the major sections of the text, create cohesion, and clarify the relationships among complex ideas and concepts.

2.e. Establish and maintain a formal style and objective tone while attending to the norms and conventions of the discipline in which they are writing.

2.f. Provide a concluding statement or section that follows from and supports the information or explanation presented.

4. Produce clear and coherent writing in which the development, organization, and style are appropriate to task, purpose, and audience.

Strategies for Writing Research Reports

Give students these suggestions for writing research reports.

- Choose a topic about which you would like to learn more. The time you spend reading and researching will be more interesting if you are working on a topic you enjoy.
- Start your research by thinking of your own experiences at home or in your area. For example, the stories a neighbor told you about what your neighborhood was like years ago might lead you to an idea for a research report.
- Not all research will come from books. Think about the different types of sources available to you. People are sources, too, and interviews can be an important source of information. An interview subject also may have photographs, newspaper clippings, or other materials you can use in your research report.

WRITER'S TOOLBOX

Sentence Fluency | Voice | Organization | Word Choice | Ideas | Conventions

Developing Your Style

Check for Coherence

Examine your draft for coherence, the logical, smooth connections of ideas. Vary your syntax and consider adding transitional words and phrases to show the relationships between your thoughts.

Transitional Words and Phrases			
above all	aside from	however	on the whole
accordingly	because	in other words	otherwise
alternatively	consequently	instead	particularly
although	for example	likewise	similarly
as a result	for that reason	on the contrary	therefore
as well as	furthermore	on the other hand	usually

Integrate source material. Another aspect of a coherent report is the careful integration of source material. Be aware of discrepancies among sources and account for them. Also, connect paraphrases or quotations to the subject being discussed and show how they support your point.

Find It in Your Reading

Read the student model research report "Visionaries" on page 1104.

1. Identify and evaluate transitional words and phrases.
2. Analyze how the writer integrates information from other sources.

PH WRITING COACH

Further instruction and practice are available in *Prentice Hall Writing Coach.*

Try It in Your Writing

To check your sentences for coherence, follow these steps:

1. Circle any transitional words and phrases in your writing. Check that each transition is effective and appropriate.
2. Read each paragraph aloud, listening for how the ideas connect. Sudden shifts may indicate that a transition is needed.
3. Review sentences in which you present information from your research. For paraphrases, be sure you have not copied wording. For direct quotations, check that you have introduced and analyzed the quotation effectively.

Developing Your Style

1. Introduce sentence fluency and coherence to students, using the instruction on the student page.
2. Have students complete the Find It in Your Reading and Try It in Your Writing activities

Teaching the Strategies

1. Remind students that transitions show the relationship between ideas. When using source material, it is especially important that it be carefully integrated into the paper. Review with students the strategy for integrating another writer's ideas: introduce the quotation by connecting it to the idea being discussed, present the quoted material, and explain how the quote supports the point being made.
2. Point out that different relationships between ideas are shown with different types of transitions. Write these examples on the board: *because, so that, after, before, next, since, but, neither... nor, compared to.* Challenge students to refer to the transitional words and phrases on the student page to suggest other transitions that could be used in their place.
3. Have students read the first student page and answer the Find It in Your Reading questions.

Find It in Your Reading

Possible responses:

1. *However* is used in paragraph 3. *However* could be replaced by *furthermore. Because* is used in paragraph 4. *Because* could be replaced by *as a result.*
2. Direct quotation: "Father of Computing"; Paraphrasing: The machine was made up of four thousand parts and weighed over three metric tons.

Six Traits Focus

	Ideas		Word Choice
	Organization	✔	Sentence Fluency
	Voice		Conventions

PH WRITING COACH Grade 12

Students will find practice with and guidance on phrases in Chapter 15.

Revising

1. Introduce the revising strategies, using the instruction on the student page.
2. Have students apply the strategies as they revise their research reports.

Teaching the Strategies

1. Review the methods of organizing a research report's structure with students. Discuss with them when it might be appropriate to use each. Point out that different sections of the same paper may be organized differently.
2. Discuss with students how topical paragraphs and topic sentences will make "maps" to guide readers through their papers. Read the excerpt from the Student Model aloud. **Ask** students to identify the topic sentence and explain why the author chose to move it during revision.
   Possible response: The topic sentence is "He is another visionary who has directly affected the world." By moving the topic sentence to the beginning of the paragraph, the focus of the passage is more clearly identified.
3. As students revise, have them highlight their topic sentences to reveal the "maps" they have created for readers. Tell students to draw lines connecting the topic sentences to see whether there is a clear connection between their topic sentences.
4. Have students work in pairs to read each other's topic sentences and make sure that the placement makes sense.
5. Tell students that they should not assume that readers will see the same connections between ideas and events that they do. Transitions make connections clear and are another kind of "map" to guide readers.

Six Traits Focus

✔	Ideas		Word Choice
✔	Organization	✔	Sentence Fluency
	Voice		Conventions

Revising

Common Core State Standards

Writing
5. Develop and strengthen writing as needed by planning, revising, editing, rewriting, or trying a new approach, focusing on addressing what is most significant for a specific purpose and audience.

Revising Your Overall Structure

Organize ideas effectively. Review the flow of ideas in your historical investigation report. This chart shows some common organizational methods you can use throughout your report or in specific sections. For example, you might follow an overall chronological order, but within one section, a problem/solution order may help you clarify an important relationship.

Method	Description
Chronological	Discuss events in time order.
Cause/Effect	Analyze the causes and/or effects of an event.
Problem/Solution	Identify a specific problem or conflict and tell how it was or was not solved.
Parts to Whole	Relate elements of a single event or topic to a whole.
Order of Importance	Present your support from most to least important, or from least to most important.
Comparison and Contrast	When comparing two topics, discuss their similarities and then their differences, or discuss each topic separately.

Peer Review: Ask a partner to review your draft and describe your organizational plan. Did your partner identify the plan you intended to follow? Discuss how you can improve the flow of ideas throughout your report.

Revising Your Paragraphs

Place topic sentences effectively. Each key paragraph should contain a topic sentence and supporting details, but the topic sentence can appear in the first sentence, in the last sentence, or in the body of the paragraph.

Reread each paragraph in your essay. Place brackets around the topic sentence. Then, review the placement of each topic sentence, considering moving it for maximum impact.

Model: Revising Placement of Topic Sentence

Original: In contrast to Babbage and Da Vinci, Bill Gates has been able to directly affect the world in which he lives. He is a visionary of our own time. It seems that this man can literally predict future technology and then develop it.

Revised: A visionary of our own time is Bill Gates. In contrast to Babbage and Da Vinci, Gates has been able to directly affect the world in which he lives. It seems that this man can literally predict future technology and then develop it.

Moving the topic sentence to the beginning of the paragraph presents a clearer focus.

Strategies for Using Technology in Writing

Point out that if students collect their research information electronically, they can use the cut-and-paste feature of their word-processing software to quickly create in-text documentation, as well as their works-cited lists. Students can also use spell check and other revision tools.

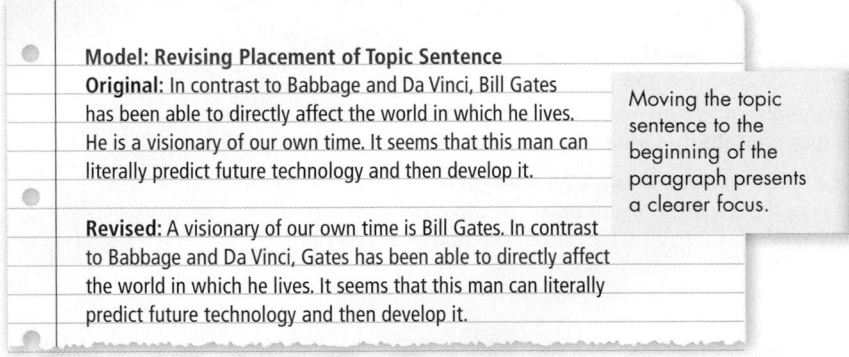

Writers on Writing

James Berry On Research-Based Writing

James Berry is the author of *"From Lucy: Englan' Lady"* (p. 1055).

"To learn more about these times, I read obsessively. . . ."
—James Berry

James Berry on Research-Based Writing

I deliberately set this novel of slavery in the period 1807–1840, so as to take in both the end of the slave trade and life after Emancipation. Writing it, for me, was like traveling through the experiences of my ancestors. My childhood home was only minutes from the ruins of a big slave plantation, so I grew up surrounded by landmarks of slavery. To learn more about these times, I read obsessively, consulting books, maps, and old pictures.

from *Ajeemah and His Son*

Atu saw his father leaving, being taken away by a planter while he was held, already bought by another plantation owner. Led along, Ajeemah looked back, calling desperately, "Atu, my son Atu—freedom! Freedom! Or let us meet in the land of spirits!"

I wanted to show here how family members could be separated forever at the kind of barbaric sales, called "scrambles," where purchasers rushed in and grabbed slaves to gain the right to buy them.

Two hours' ride from Kingston, in the back of the estate horse-drawn carriage with two other male slaves bought with him, and Ajeemah came to his big and busy New World sugar plantation. Nearly four hundred slaves lived and worked here.

I researched in Jamaican libraries for pictures of how four broken-down old estates near my home would have looked when they were flourishing.

Everybody stepped down from the carriage in the center of the estate work yard in a blaze of sunlight. The estate work yard buildings spread out like a little village. The huge windmill that powered the grinding of the sugarcane was near the millhouse where the cane was crushed and where its juice was taken and boiled into the wealth-making sugar, and also rum. Then in a close cluster there were the boiling house, curing house, distilling house and trash house. Ajeemah stared at the windmill; he'd never seen a windmill. He then glanced at the many workshop buildings, the animal houses and the overseer's and headmen's houses. And he could see, separated some good distance away, the huts—the slaves' quarters. . . .

I used Eric Williams's Capitalism and Slavery as a reference in writing this book.

Just at the top of my lane were the ruins of an old slave estate. As a boy, I climbed up inside the windmill tower to look out over the landscape.

James Berry on Research-Based Writing

Review the passage on the student page with the class, using James Berry's comments to deepen students' understanding of the process of writing a research paper.

Teaching From the Professional Model

1. Show students Segment 4 on James Berry on the ***From the Author's Desk* DVD** or from this page in the **Enriched Online Student Edition.** Discuss his advice about the importance of reading and writing often.
2. Point out that James Berry writes fiction based on real events. Tell students that Berry did extensive research to find details that would make his tale accurate and interesting.
3. Review James Berry's comments about his sources. Point out that Berry's story begins with information from his own experience growing up near the ruins of a plantation. Note that Berry also uses pictures from a Jamaican library and a nonfiction book as sources.

PHLit Online!
Enriched Online Student Edition
Show or assign the video online at **www.PHLitOnline.com**.

Providing Appropriate Citations

1. To reinforce the importance of providing appropriate citations, introduce plagiarism to students, using the instruction on the student page.
2. Have students apply the strategies to provide appropriate citations.

Teaching the Strategies

1. Students may have difficulty deciding when and if they need to cite sources. Have students work in pairs to help evaluate when documentation is needed.
2. As a guide to documentation, talk to students about the "voice" they bring to their writing, and the ways in which they form sentences and develop arguments. Tell them that quotations, too, have their own "voice." A sentence that sounds markedly different from other sentences will stand out in a research report. Tell students to review their research reports for sentences that stand out to see whether they should be credited to another author.

Six Traits Focus

	Ideas		Word Choice
	Organization		Sentence Fluency
✓	Voice	✓	Conventions

Providing Appropriate Citations

Common Core State Standards

Writing
8. Integrate information into the text selectively to maintain the flow of ideas, avoiding plagiarism and overreliance on any one source and following a standard format for citation.

You must cite the source for the information and ideas you use in your report. In the body of your paper, include a footnote, an endnote, or a parenthetical citation to identify the source of each fact, opinion, and quotation. At the end of your paper, provide a bibliography or a Works Cited list, a list of all the sources you cite. Follow the format your teacher recommends, such as Modern Language Association (MLA) style or American Psychological Association (APA) style. See page 1103 for more information about how to prepare citations for different kinds of sources.

If you do not give credit for the information you found, you commit the serious offense of plagiarism, presenting someone else's work as your own. Plagiarism is stealing someone else's ideas, so it is both illegal and dishonest. It's easy to prevent this problem by fairly and thoroughly citing every source you use.

Deciding What to Cite

A fact that can be found in three or more reference sources is probably common knowledge and does not need to be cited. However, do cite facts and opinions that are not common knowledge. This chart distinguishes between common knowledge and facts that should be cited.

Reading/Writing Connection
To read the complete student model, see page 1104.

Common Knowledge
• Charles Babbage was born in 1791 and died in 1871. • He was a mathematician and a philosopher. • He invented a machine called The Difference Engine.
Facts to be Cited
• Babbage's early computer greatly impressed some forward-thinking scientists as early as 1833. Source: "Wonderful Machinery." *New York Weekly Messenger.* 13 Feb, 1833. • Babbage was fascinated by machinery and even went backstage at the theater to find out how the staging was created. Source: Lee, J.A.N. "Charles Babbage." 15 Jan. 2008. <http://ei.cs.vt.edu/~history/Babbage.html>.

In your report, you will give credit for the following ideas, opinions, or theories presented by other writers:

- Any facts or statistics that are not common knowledge
- Direct quotations of spoken or written words
- Paraphrases of spoken or written words

Notice that you must still provide a citation even if you paraphrase someone else's ideas. It is appropriate to give credit to someone else's thoughts, whether or not you use his or her exact words. In general, it is a good idea to provide too many citations rather than too few.

WRITER'S TOOLBOX

Conventions | Sentence Fluency | Voice | Organization | Word Choice | Ideas

Developing Your Style

Avoiding Plagiarism

Give proper credit. In a research paper, commonly known facts need not be credited. However, lesser-known facts, as well as quotations and the opinions of other writers, must be acknowledged with proper citations.

Common knowledge: *Charles Babbage was a nineteenth-century British scientist.*

Requires citation: *Charles Babbage planned a calculating machine with [describe the design].*

Never present someone else's ideas or words as though they were your own. To avoid plagiarism—the act of repeating other people's words or ideas without crediting them—follow these steps:

1. Avoid taking notes verbatim, or word for word. Instead, jot down a main idea. When you copy from a source, use quotation marks.
2. Have a partner read your draft and mark any statements that need documentation. Write legibly to avoid miscommunication.
3. Add credits and documentation, as needed.

Find It in Your Reading

Read or review the writing model on page 1104. Notice the way in which this writer gives credit to specific individuals whose ideas she uses.

Sample Works-Cited List

Swade, Doron. *The Difference Engine: Charles Babbage and the Quest to Build the First Computer*. Penguin, 2002.

Ament, Phil. "Charles Babbage." *The Great Idea Finder.* 15 Jan. 2008. <http://www.ideafinder.com/history/inventors/babbage.htm>.

The Life of Leonardo Da Vinci. Dir. Renato Castellani. Questar, 2003.

"Wonderful Machinery." *New York Weekly Messenger*. 13 Feb. 1833.

Indicate the date you accessed information from an Internet site. Content and addresses at Web sites change frequently.

List an anonymous work by title.

Apply It to Your Writing

Review the draft of your research paper. Be sure that your citations are accurate and follow a consistent format. Underline statements in your draft if they are not common knowledge. Then, provide a complete citation for each underlined statement.

PH WRITING COACH
Further instruction and practice are available in *Prentice Hall Writing Coach.*

Developing Your Style

1. To reinforce the importance of providing appropriate citations, discuss how to avoid plagiarism with yourstudents, using the instruction on the student page.
2. Have students apply the strategies to provide appropriate citations.

Teaching the Strategies

1. Point out that the information used in this method of citation should be on the note cards they prepared as they researched their topics.
2. Encourage students to practice citing a variety of sources, including books, journals, personal interviews, and Web sites. Direct them to the Sample Works Cited List on this page for examples.

PH WRITING COACH Grade 12

Students will find additional instruction on avoiding plagiarism in Chapter 11.

Differentiated Instruction for Universal Access

Strategy for Special-Needs Students

After you have reviewed plagiarism and techniques for citing sources with the class, work individually with students to explain the problems that arise from incorrectly cited sources. Give students example quotations and have them practice paraphrasing or using the quotation to illustrate a point made in a larger section of text.

Strategy for Advanced Writers

Discuss with students the difference between quoting and paraphrasing source materials. Remind them that, in a short assignment, they may need to abbreviate quotations to save space. In these situations, citing the source and then restating the source's ideas might be the most efficient strategy. Tell students to use only quotations that are extremely striking or well expressed, saving them for instances in which they cannot state the idea themselves.

Student Model

Review the Student Model with the class, using the annotations to analyze the writer's incorporation of the elements of a research report.

Teaching the Strategies

1. Explain that the Student Model is a sample and that students' research reports may be longer.
2. Point out that the author identifies the thesis in the opening paragraph. **Ask** students to identify the thesis.
   Answer: The ideas and inventions of visionaries have shaped the way we live our lives today.
3. Draw students' attention to the fact that the author provides background information for the reader to provide a historical context for the topic.
4. **Ask** students to identify a direct quotation and a paraphrase within this page of the model.
   Answer: There are two direct quotes about Babbage in the second paragraph, and one about Leonardo da Vinci in the fourth paragraph. All of the other citations in the text represent paraphrasing or attribution of ideas.

Connecting to Real-Life Writing

Explain to students that nearly all college students write research reports as part of the assignments for their classes. Students in the liberal arts write many such works over the course of their college careers. Research reports are also common assignments in the business world and in professions such as law and finance.

Student Model: Nicole Leraas, El Cajon, CA

Visionaries

The world has seen many visionaries whose inventions and concepts would change the world forever and shape the way we live our lives today. Despite the fact that their ideas were not necessarily accepted right away, many people like Charles Babbage, Leonardo Da Vinci, and even Bill Gates, are now regarded as some of the most amazing minds the world has ever seen.

> Nicole states her thesis in the opening paragraph.

One who is not very well known but incredibly influential was Charles Babbage. He was born in 1791 and died in 1871 in the UK. Babbage was a well-known mathematician, philosopher, and engineer who invented the first computer and was so far ahead of the technology of his time that he was unable to complete his machine due to lack of sufficient machinery to build the parts needed. Babbage is now considered the "Father of Computing," but during the early 1800s—the period in which he lived—his plans for the first programmable computer seemed unattainable to most people despite his credibility as a leading mathematician and engineer (Ament). His life was so consumed by his work that even when he went to the theater "[He] went behind the scenes to look at the mechanism" (Lee). In the 1820s and 1830s it was impossible to build his precisely engineered Difference Engine with the technology available to him and the lack of funding that he experienced (Ament). However, more than a century later in the 1990s, several scientists decided to build his machine according to his original plans. The machine was made up of four thousand parts and weighed over three metric tons, but size was not the most impressive part (Ament). His Difference machine worked to perfection and effectively eliminated the high rate of human error in math problems, which was his original motivation for the project.

> Next, Nicole provides readers with general background on her subject.

It's hard to imagine how different the world would be if Babbage had finished his machine and given us the first programmable computer. However, it was not until a century later in the 1940s that Howard Aiken created the Harvard Mark I Calculator, which is the first modern digital computer. Aiken used several ideas from Babbage's original design, including a push card and vacuum tube, both of which were unheard of at the time Babbage envisioned them.

> Nicole provides readers with a sense of Babbage's accomplishments by linking them to modern computer technology.

Another visionary working past simpler innovation was Leonardo Da Vinci. Da Vinci is best known for his paintings that seem to pop off the canvas. He was one of the first painters to use the technique of perspective to achieve this type of picture, which was radically different from the flat paintings of the Middle Ages. He often used mathematics, geometry, and shading to help him plan out the perspective. His paintings show something else that is truly remarkable. They show no brush strokes because of his skill level as well as his use of oil paints while the rest of the painting world was using tempera paints (O'Connor 27).

> Nicole cites sources on her Works Cited list properly, following MLA style.

However, Da Vinci's legacy is more than just his artwork. As he sketched and painted, Da Vinci often drew scientific instruments on the side of his paper. He had a fascination with studying the way things worked and most of all creating his own inventions, ranging from war machines to musical instruments (O'Connor 44). Soon his study and experimentation distracted him from his painting. He began to study the nature of light and how it affects shading and the inner workings of optics. As he studied the human body more closely, he found that human eyes received light rather than giving off particles, which was the common belief at the time. Through this experimentation, Da Vinci began to develop theories that linked sound waves and light. He also studied the way muscles work and greatly contributed to the medical science of his day. These concepts were well ahead of their time.

Nicole provides specific information on Da Vinci's study of optics.

Da Vinci's study of the human body fit in perfectly with his inventions; he noted that joints were like hinges and muscles were like gears and levers. He was fascinated with the thought of motion and how things move. In fact, he once expressed the idea that "motion is the principle of all life" (O'Connor 58). Da Vinci devoted much of his study to how things could move by themselves. He drew several sketches of motors and flying machines that came from his study of the wings of a variety of birds. One of his sketches of his flying machines, called an aerial screw, resembles the modern-day helicopter.

Overall, Leonardo Da Vinci's devotion to the study of the human body, scientific observations, and inventions, and his ground-breaking artistic work became the foundation that many after him would build on.

Another visionary who has directly affected the world is Bill Gates. In contrast to Babbage and Da Vinci, Gates has been able to directly affect the world in which he lives. It seems that this man can literally predict future technology and then develop it.

Notice how Nicole creates a transition between Gates and the previous "visionaries": "In contrast to Babbage and Da Vinci . . ." Such a transition makes the report more coherent.

In the 1980s, Bill Gate's company focused on producing products for individual computer use. Three years later, Microsoft developed a word-processing tool called Word that put words on the screen exactly how they would be printed on paper (Lesinski 41). Later, he made use of a piece of hardware called the mouse, which had been invented by Douglas C. Englebart and Bill English. At that time, the mouse was a breakthrough innovation that made interaction with a computer screen easier for many people.

This, however, was just the beginning. Gates's company went international as he continued to innovate and create new technology. The new technologies he developed have changed the way we communicate, do business, teach, and learn. Due to the contributions of Bill Gates, we can now use computers at home and at school. We can communicate with amazing speed. Recently, Microsoft has expanded into the creation of voice-activated technology to be put in cars. With this technology, driving may become safer and the number of accidents may be reduced. After so many years of creating and innovating, Bill Gates continues to influence the evolution of technology, bringing products to market that people before him could not even imagine.

Notice how Nicole uses language to show causes and effects: "Due to . . ."

It is hard to imagine how the world would be without Bill Gates and his contributions to technology. It is truly amazing that in a matter of seconds

Student Model

Teaching the Strategies

1. Point out citations the author uses in the report. Remind students to refer to their note cards when making citations to their papers.
2. Have students note the materials that the author uses for quotations. Discuss with them why they think particular quotations may have been chosen, and which quotations are particularly effective or interesting.
3. Point out that the author has written sentences of many different lengths. Remind students that variety in sentence length helps keep readers' attention and that not all sentences in a formal research report must be complex.

Differentiated Instruction for Universal Access

Strategy for Special-Needs Students

Encourage students to choose fairly narrow topics for their research reports so they do not become overwhelmed with facts and citations. Tell students that it is perfectly acceptable to narrow their topics midway through the project. The further they progress, the more they will be able to see how large of a topic they have taken on.

EL Strategy for English Learners

Have students work in pairs to read through the Student Model, noting any words or phrases they need to look up for better understanding. Have students make a class list of these words and phrases on the board. As a class, work through the words and phrases, using a dictionary when needed.

Student Model
Teaching the Strategies

1. Draw students' attention to the Works Cited section of the student model. Note that the author has listed both books and Web sites as sources and has credited them properly in this bibliography. Advise students to use an up-to-date guideline for citing sources that will include the proper forms for online sources.
2. Make sure students understand that the bibliography must contain the publication information for every source used in the research report. Students should be able to go through the paper and match up each citation with one of the works in the list.
3. Remind students of the importance of obtaining complete information on their note cards as they conduct their research so they can easily construct bibliographies at the end of their reports. Tell students that spending the time to put source material on note cards can save them the trouble of later recalling or reviewing sources they have cited.

anyone could pull up a Web site about Charles Babbage or Leonardo Da Vinci or communicate incredibly quickly with someone on the other side of the world.

There is no doubt that the world would be a different place if it were not for visionaries like these. These men were not afraid of the limitations of their time. They pursued the what-ifs their minds developed, imagining things that were science fiction in their day. For Babbage and Da Vinci, their ideas would be brought to fruition in future generations. Gates has been able to bring his imaginings from sketch to prototype to best-seller, consistently moving technology past what even he might have thought possible.

Nicole summarizes her report in the final paragraph.

Works Cited

Ament, Phil [pseudonym for employees at Vaunt Design Group, an Internet consulting company in Troy, Michigan]. "Charles Babbage." The Great Idea Finder. 4 May 2006. 15 Jan. 2008 <http://www.ideafinder.com/history/inventors/babbage.htm>.

Lee, J.A.N. "Charles Babbage." History of Computing site. Department of Computer Science at Virginia Tech. Sep. 1994. 15 Jan. 2008. <http://ei.cs.vt.edu/~history/Babbage.html>.

Lesinski, Jeanne M. *Bill Gates.* Minneapolis: Lerner Publications, 2000.

O'Connor, Barbara. *Leonardo Da Vinci: Renaissance Genius.* Minneapolis: Carolrhoda Books, Inc., 2003.

Nicole provides a complete, detailed, and properly formatted list of all the works she has cited in her report.

Strategies for Using Technology

Discuss with students the specialized databases that can be used for particular historical periods. Students may save time by looking at Web sites and other resources that correspond to the specific historical time that they are researching.

Editing and Proofreading

Focus on quotations. Compare each direct quotation in your essay with its source. Make sure that you have recorded exactly what your source said or wrote. To avoid plagiarism, use quotation marks around words, phrases, and sentences that come directly from your sources.

Spiral Review: Conventions Earlier in this unit, you learned about verb tense (p. 1009) and active voice (p. 1085). Check your report to be sure you have used those conventions correctly.

Publishing, Presenting, and Reflecting

Consider one of the following ways to share your writing:

Prepare your Works-Cited list. Your paper is ready for presentation only after you add your Works-Cited list, which provides full bibliographical information on each source you cite. Identify the format your teacher prefers. Then, follow that accepted style to assemble your list. (For more information, see Citing Sources, pp. R21–R23.)

Apply principles of design. Make sure the text of your investigation is appealing to the eye. The lines should be evenly spaced, and the margins of the page should be even, not ragged.

Present your report orally. Use your report as the basis for an oral presentation. Be sure to rehearse well, using clear syntax and accessible diction.

Reflect on your writing. Jot down your thoughts on the experience of writing a research report. Begin by answering these questions:

- What have you learned in this workshop about differing points of view on the same event?
- What aspects of researching one topic in depth surprised you?

Rubric for Self-Assessment

Evaluate your reflective essay using the following criteria and rating scale:

Criteria	Rating Scale (not very → very)
Focus: How clearly does your thesis statement guide your report?	1 2 3 4 5
Organization: How logical and well documented is your presentation?	1 2 3 4 5
Support/Elaboration: How well do you use a variety of primary and secondary sources to support your thesis?	1 2 3 4 5
Style: How clearly and effectively do you state your conclusions?	1 2 3 4 5
Conventions: According to an accepted format, how complete and accurate are your citations?	1 2 3 4 5

Common Core State Standards

Writing
5. Develop and strengthen writing as needed by editing, focusing on addressing what is most significant for a specific purpose and audience.

Language
2. Demonstrate command of the conventions of standard English capitalization, punctuation, and spelling when writing.

PH WRITING COACH

Further instruction and practice are available in *Prentice Hall Writing Coach.*

Editing and Proofreading

1. Introduce the editing and proofreading focus, using the instruction on the student page.
2. Have students read their research reports carefully, marking changes in word choice and corrections in grammar, spelling, and punctuation.

Teaching the Strategies

1. Remind students that a paper that is brilliantly researched but poorly proofread is not likely to convince readers that the author's point is sound.
2. Tell students that double-checking their quotations and works-cited lists should be part of the writing process for every report.

Six Traits Focus

	Ideas		Word Choice
	Organization		Sentence Fluency
	Voice	✓	Conventions

ASSESS

Publishing, Presenting, and Reflecting

1. Tell students that the bibliography is also a courtesy to readers. It not only properly credits sources, but it also shows readers where to find more information on the subject.
2. Before students present their reports orally, have them practice reading their work aloud. Students may want to work in pairs and offer each other suggestions about emphasis and pacing.
3. Ask them what techniques they might use in their next research project.

PH WRITING COACH Grade 12

Students will find additional information on the writing process in Chapter 3.

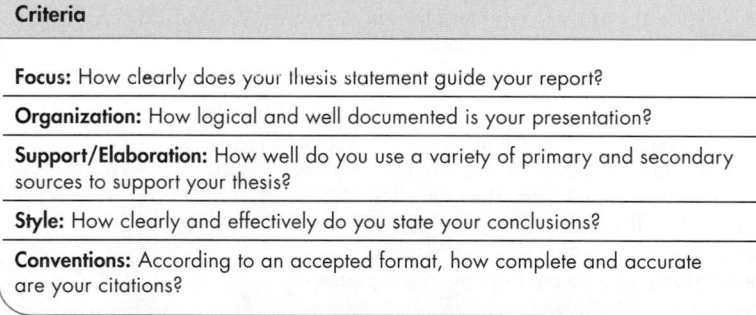

EXTEND

Common Core State Standards

- Speaking and Listening 2

Analyze and Evaluate Entertainment Media

1. Present some of the types of entertainment media using the instruction on the student page.
2. Explain to students that while the primary purpose of this type of media is to entertain, it also serves to represent and shape the audience's perception of reality.
3. Point out that as active recipients of media messages, students should attempt to determine whether the realities constructed by their favorite shows or movies are accurate or misleading.

Media Effects

1. Indicate the reciprocal relationship between media and the culture it seeks to represent or influence, using the diagram on the student page.
2. Emphasize that while diverting the audience may be the most apparent goal of entertainment media, it can serve the dual purpose of educating or persuading viewers. As engaged members of a media audience, encourage students to evaluate the media that they consume for instances of bias and misrepresentation of facts.
3. Discuss with students the role of media as a vehicle for the transmission of cultural values. In seeking to reify the values and perceptions dominating a society, entertainment media often creates overly generalized portraits of certain groups of people that in turn may enter the social lexicon as factual. The unnecessary validation of such stereotypes further demonstrates the necessity of being a critically engaged consumer of media.

SPEAKING AND LISTENING
Communications Workshop

Analyze and Evaluate Entertainment Media

Our culture is saturated with **entertainment media**—movies, TV shows, music videos, and other programming designed primarily for enjoyment rather than for instruction or information. While providing entertainment is the core goal, these media also appeal to our values, offering representations of society that both reinforce those values and shape our perceptions of reality. As a consumer of media, you should determine whether the portrait of reality they present is flawed or misleading.

Common Core State Standards

Speaking and Listening
2. Integrate multiple sources of information presented in diverse formats and media in order to make informed decisions and solve problems, evaluating the credibility and accuracy of each source and noting any discrepancies among the data.

Evaluating Media Credibility

In addition to seeking the primary goal of entertaining audiences, entertainment media makers often influence viewers in these ways:

- *Informing them* and providing a new understanding of historical or current events. Dramatic interpretations of history or current issues, however, may not always be reliable factual accounts.
- *Persuading them* to accept particular viewpoints. By providing only certain perspectives or depicting groups or actions as positive or negative, media can present a *biased* view of an issue.

Entertainment media also cater to audiences' values. For instance, when they tell tales of families reunited, criminals punished, and underdogs who become winners, they are forming a picture of how we think life should be. In this way, they *transmit our own cultural values* back to us. You might envision the relationship between media and culture as a cycle:

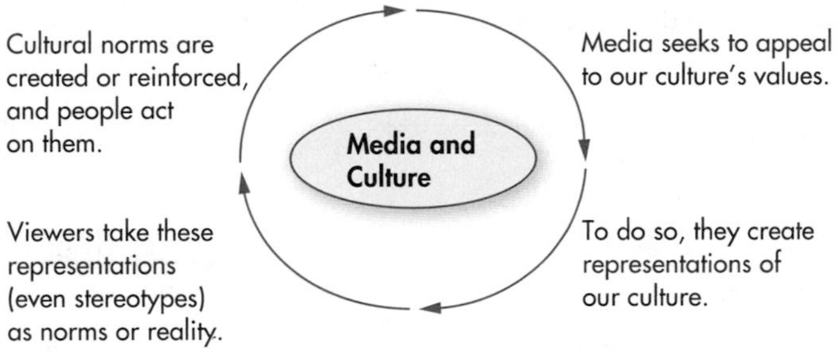
Cultural norms are created or reinforced, and people act on them.
Media seeks to appeal to our culture's values.
Media and Culture
Viewers take these representations (even stereotypes) as norms or reality.
To do so, they create representations of our culture.

Along with the transmission of values, however, come representations of groups of people. Scholars who study the media have examined the effects these representations have upon public perception. They have found that the way groups are portrayed in the media can create **stereotypes,** assumptions about race, gender, or religion that influence a person's attitude and behavior toward individuals who belong to certain groups.

Media Tools and Techniques

The makers of entertainment media use the following *editing techniques*:

- **Special Effects**—technological tricks of sight and sound that produce images, such as flying superheroes and roaming dinosaurs
- **Camera Angles**—the different positions from which a scene is recorded to create different effects
- **Reaction Shots**—close-up shots of an actor's face as he or she responds to another actor or to action in the script
- **Sequencing**—the arrangement of a story's events, such as chronological order or a series of flashbacks
- **Music**—sound added to visual sequences to complement the action or create a particular mood

Activities: Evaluate a Movie, TV Episode, or Skit

Comprehension and Collaboration For both activities, use an evaluation form like the one shown below.

A. Find a movie, show, or skit you like to watch on television or the Internet. Examine the main ideas it presents and analyze how it conveys these ideas. Record your observations on a form like the one below.

B. Search the Internet to find episodes of a television show from the 1960s or 1970s. Consider how a particular group is represented in this show. Then, compare this representation with representations of the same group on television today. Share your observations with your class.

Evaluation Form

Type of Entertainment Media: Movie ☐ TV Episode ☐ Skit ☐

Name of Movie, Show, or Skit: ______________________

What story does this movie, episode, or clip tell? ______________

What cultural values does it appeal to? Idealism ☐ Fear ☐ Family ☐

Justice ☐ Other ______________________

How does it appeal to these values? ______________

Are there stereotypes in this representation? Yes ☐ No ☐

If yes, what are they? ______________________

Identify techniques used in this film: Special effects ☐ Editing ☐

Camera angles ☐ Reaction shots ☐ Sequencing ☐ Music ☐

Explain the effect of two of these techniques. ______________

____

Media Tools and Techniques

1. Using the student page, present the tools and techniques that media professionals use to dramatically represent reality.
2. **Ask** students how exposure to these editing techniques has informed how they perceive their own realities.
   Possible responses: Students may note that a significant event seems to occur in "slow motion" or that a conversation that cues a memory seems like a "flashback."

Activity: Analyze a Movie, TV Episode, or Skit

1. Present the activity using the information on the student page. Ask students to select a contemporary movie or television show to analyze using the form provided.
2. For students seeking more of a challenge, instruct them to find episodes of a show from the 1960s or 1970s. They should analyze the show using the form provided, paying particular attention to the way that various groups are depicted in comparison to how they might be shown today.

Differentiated Instruction for Universal Access

Support for Less Proficient Readers

The media cycle explained on the previous page may not be immediately clear to less proficient readers. Use the diagram from the previous page to chart the cycle. Choose a cultural value (such as "criminals should be punished") and trace the way that this value manifests in the cycle.

EL Support for English Learners

Students not proficient in English may have difficulty ascertaining instances of stereotypes. Walk students through a sitcom that you have selected from the 1960s or 1970s and encourage students to look at the visual and musical representations of certain groups. Ask them what certain costuming or music may be trying to convey about a group of people.

EXTEND

Common Core State Standards

- Language 4.a, 5

Idioms

1. Teach the skill, using the instruction on the student page.
2. **Ask** students to replace the idioms used in the sentences on the page with one of the listed alternatives.
3. Explain to students that idioms can be useful in creating context in a story, as many idioms are representative of a distinct time or place. However, encourage students to be cautious in overusing idioms in favor of more original and vivid language.

Think Aloud: Model the Skill

Say to students:

I know that as I write, idioms can be a useful tool in establishing a social or temporal context. I know that I need to be careful about inserting them, since many have become trite. For example, if I am writing a story about students having an argument, it might be tempting to state that one participant is "tongue-tied." While the meaning of this description is evident, it might be more intriguing to the reader to describe the student as "unable to form the words furiously churning in response."

Vocabulary Workshop

Common Core State Standards

Language

4.a. Use context as a clue to the meaning of a word or phrase.

5. Demonstrate understanding of figurative language, word relationships, and nuances in word meanings.

Idioms

Idioms are figurative expressions that do not mean what the words literally say. For example, describing the weather as *raining cats and dogs* means the rain is torrential. To recognize an idiom, you have to understand *word-phrase relationships*—to realize that in the phrase *raining cats and dogs,* the words have a figurative meaning rather than their usual literal ones.

Idioms can be effective tools in some kinds of writing to convey character or to evoke a particular time period or setting. For example, an American detective of the 1940s might jump in a taxi and growl to the driver, "Step on it." Idioms can also help set a particular mood or tone.

Relying on idioms consistently in your own writing is not always a good idea, however. Because they have been used so often, many of them have lost their originality. Look at the examples below. Note how replacing the idioms can help to communicate meaning in a more precise and lively way.

Idioms	Alternatives
After ten hours of driving in heavy traffic, the trucker ran out of steam.	❑ collapsed over his steering wheel. ❑ sighed and pulled into a rest stop. ❑ radioed his boss and told her he quit.
She was down in the dumps.	❑ too lethargic to get out of bed. ❑ apt to burst into tears if anyone looked at her the wrong way. ❑ in need of a friend to listen to her problems.

Practice

Directions: An analogy shows the relationship between sets of words. Each of the analogies below pairs a word with an idiomatic phrase. Complete each analogy with one of the lettered words provided, creating a pair that matches the other pair in the analogy. Then, write an explanation of the idiomatic expression and the relationships in each pairing.

1. upset : "bent out of shape" :: _______ : "under the weather"
   a. cloudy **b.** sick **c.** wet **d.** forgetful
2. "jump the gun" : _______ :: "shoot the breeze" : deliberate
   a. run quickly **b.** rush **c.** chat **d.** consider
3. "over the moon" : ecstatic :: "fit to be tied" : _______
   a. furious **b.** delighted **c.** sad **d.** fastened

Practice

Answers

1. b; A sick person might say that he or she felt "under the weather," because quick changes in weather can make people ill.
2. b; "Jumping the gun" literally means to start a race before the signal is given, which indicates a rush to start something before the proper time.
3. a; An angry person may act irrationally and therefore need to be "tied up."

Vocabulary Acquisition and Use: Context Clues

Context clues are words or phrases that help readers clarify the meanings of unfamiliar words in a text. By using context clues, you can determine the word or words that complete a sentence. Sentence Completion questions appear in most standardized tests. In these types of questions, you are given sentences with one or more missing words. Your task is to use the context to choose the correct word or words to complete each sentence logically. Try this strategy: (1) Read the sentence. (2) Scan the answer choices. Find synonyms that are simple words or phrases for the choices. (3) Test the synonyms and determine which makes the most sense.

Practice

This exercise is modeled after the Sentence Completion questions that appear in the Reading Comprehension section of the SAT.

Directions: Each of the following sentences is missing one or two words. Choose the word or set of words that best completes each sentence.

Test-Taking Tip
Eliminate any words with similar meanings because a single correct answer choice should be obvious.

1. Charlotte Brontë's work might have remained ___?___ without the popular success of *Jane Eyre*.
   A. truculent
   B. obscure
   C. rapturous
   D. monotonous
   E. obstinate
2. Charlotte and her gifted siblings can be called ___?___ spirits.
   A. agricultural
   B. terrestrial
   C. gaunt
   D. rapturous
   E. kindred
3. Her close-knit family ___?___ six children and a widowed father.
   A. blanched
   B. eluded
   C. comprised
   D. assessed
   E. clasped
4. The ___?___ Charlotte witnessed at boarding school inspired her to write *Jane Eyre*.
   A. depredation
   B. contusion
   C. adversary
   D. approbation
   E. etymology
5. She would never ___?___ her days as a governess, for they led her to write a popular novel from which she would ___?___ .
   A. impel . . . profundity
   B. fracture . . . officious
   C. rue . . . prosper
   D. languish . . . deficient
   E. elude . . . diffusive
6. In the ___?___ years of her life she married, enjoying a brief time of happiness after the ___?___ of her siblings' deaths.
   A. waning . . . turmoil
   B. ingratiating . . . inculcation
   C. ravenous . . . rendezvous
   D. wily . . . malevolence
   E. gaudy . . . predilection

Practice

1. Introduce the skill, using the instruction on the student page. Be sure students understand how context clues can reveal the meaning of an unknown word.
2. You may wish to go over the first item with students, applying the "substitute a simple synonym" strategy. Read the first item to the class, including all of the answer choices. As you read the list of choices a second time, ask students to think of a synonym for each of the choices. As a class, test these synonyms to determine which makes the most sense. Point out the following synonym pairs: *truculent:* defiant; *rapturous:* ecstatic; *monotonous:* repetitious; *obstinate:* stubborn. None of these words fits the context of the sentence. After trying "unrecognized," a synonym of *obscure,* students may agree that *obscure* works better, selecting *B* as their answer.
3. Assign the remaining items in the Practice Test. Point out that some questions require pairs of words, rather than a single word, for completion. Allow students 7 minutes to complete the questions.

Answers

1. B
2. E
3. C
4. A
5. C
6. A

Strategies for Test Taking

On a multiple-choice test, students may be asked to identify the statement that best interprets an idea or a section in a reading passage. Before students read the possible answers, they should return to the passage and form their own interpretation. Then, they should read the answer choices and choose the one that is closest to their own interpretation.

Using the Test-Taking Practice

In this Test-Taking Practice (pp. 1112–1115), students apply the skills in Unit 5. The Practice is divided into three sections.

1. Before assigning each section, review the relevant Unit skills with students. Discuss the characteristics of each type of test and specific strategies for test questions, using the instruction that precedes each Practice.
2. Set a time limit for the multiple-choice items in each Practice, allowing a little more than one minute per question. Use the designated time allowance set for the Timed Writing section.
3. Administer each section. Have students write the starting time at the top of their papers. When half of the time for the multiple-choice items has elapsed, ask students to write the time next to the answer on which they are working. Have them make similar notes when the time is three-quarters through and again when time is up. Follow a similar procedure for the Timed Writing assignment.
4. Review with students the pacing reflected in their notes.

Reteaching

Have students complete each Practice. Then, use the Reteach charts to determine which skills require reteaching, based on the items students answer incorrectly. Reteach these skills prior to assigning the **Benchmark Test** (*Unit 5 Teaching Resources,* pp. 152–157).

Test-Taking Practice

Reading Test: Prose Fiction

Some standardized tests include lengthy prose fiction reading passages drawn from novels and short stories. You will have to demonstrate your basic comprehension as well as your analytical skills. Questions will focus on topics such as main ideas, significant details, causes and effects, and themes. In addition, you may be asked to show understanding of words, statements, and the author's perspective.

Common Core State Standards

RL.11-12.1, RL.11-12.3, RL.11-12.4; L.11-12.1, L.11-12.2, L.11-12.3

[For the full wording of the standards, see the standards chart in the front of your textbook.]

Practice

The following exercise is modeled after the ACT Reading Test, Prose Fiction section.

Directions: Read the following passage, taken from *Jane Eyre,* by Charlotte Brontë. Then, choose the best answer to each question.

It was English history: among the readers I observed my acquaintance of the verandah: at the commencement of the lesson, her place had been at the top of the class, but for some error of pronunciation, or some inattention to stops, she was suddenly sent to the very bottom. Even in that obscure position, Miss Scatcherd continued to make her an object of constant notice: she was continually addressing to her such phrases as the following:—

"Burns" (such it seems was her name: the girls here were all called by their surnames, as boys are elsewhere), "Burns, you are standing on the side of your shoe; turn your toes out immediately." "Burns, you poke your chin most unpleasantly; draw it in." "Burns, I insist on your holding your head up; I will not have you before me in that attitude," etc. etc.

A chapter having been read through twice, the books were closed and the girls examined. The lesson had comprised part of the reign of Charles I, and there were sundry questions about tonnage and poundage and ship-money, which most of them appeared unable to answer; still, every little difficulty was solved instantly when it reached Burns: her memory seemed to have retained the substance of the whole lesson, and she was ready with answers on every point. I kept expecting that Miss Scatcherd would praise her attention; but, instead of that, she suddenly cried out—

"You dirty, disagreeable girl! you have never cleaned your nails this morning!"

Burns made no answer: I wondered at her silence. "Why," thought I, "does she not explain that she could neither clean her nails nor wash her face, as the water was frozen?"

Strategy:

- **Underline time words,** such as dates and time of day, and **transition words,** such as "then," and "afterwards," to clarify sequence.
- As you read, **make a chronological list of the story's events.**
- Refer to your list as you answer the questions.

Strategies for Test Taking

Explain to students that rereading can help them identify the chronological order of details in a passage. For example, when answering the sample test item, students should reenter the passage and underline time clues, such as "next day," "this morning," "preceding evening," and "all night," which indicate the passage of events. Chronologically, the first phrase is "preceding evening." The text that corresponds with this phrase in the passage is "A change had taken place in the weather." Therefore, Choice *C* correctly identifies the first event in a chronological plot summary.

1. Which of the following quotes from the passage demonstrates emotive language and not informative language?
   A. "there were sundry questions about tonnage and poundage"
   B. "she was suddenly sent to the very bottom"
   C. "'You dirty, disagreeable girl!'"
   D. "the girls here were all called by their surnames"

2. The author provides precise dialogue to increase the reader's understanding of her characters' motivations because she wants:
   F. readers to understand what Burns is really like.
   G. to show how the setting affects the characters.
   H. readers to experience the shock the narrator feels.
   J. to show how Burns forces Miss Scatcherd to act.

3. As it is used in line 9, the word *surnames* most nearly means:
   A. nicknames.
   B. last names.
   C. first names.
   D. official titles.

4. Which of the following would be included in a summary of this selection?
   I. Burns was an acquaintance of Jane's.
   II. The lesson they read was about Charles I.
   III. Burns did not mention the frozen wash water.
   F. I and II
   G. I only
   H. III only
   J. I, II, and III

5. Considering the events of the entire passage, it is most reasonable to infer that
   A. Jane would soon become a favorite of the teacher.
   B. Burns knew how to deal with Miss Scatcherd.
   C. Burns would one day be recognized as intelligent.
   D. Jane thought Burns deserved the way she was treated.

6. Which elements of the author's beliefs are demonstrated in her description of Miss Scatcherd's response to Burns's answers?
   F. Good students deserve praise.
   G. Boarding schools are good for character.
   H. Teachers need to be firm with their students.
   J. Cleanliness is an important personal trait.

7. The details and events in the passage suggest that the relationship between Jane and Burns would most accurately be described as:
   A. a misunderstanding.
   B. a rivalry.
   C. sympathetic.
   D. jealousy.

GO ON

Differentiated Instruction for Universal Access

Support for Less Proficient Students
Read the passage with students and help them to summarize it. Then, go over the first test item as a class, guiding students to eliminate incorrect answer choices.

EL Support for English Learners
Read the entire passage with the class and help students to summarize each paragraph. Review the seven questions, making sure that students understand *summary* in question 4 and *infer* in question 5. Allow students to ask clarifying questions about any of the question choices, being careful not to reveal correct answers. Once students understand the questions, have them complete the test on their own. Allow 5 minutes for reading the passage and 12 minutes for the questions.

Reading Test

Prose Fiction

1. Introduce the passage using the instruction on page 1112.
2. You may wish to go over the first test item with students before they take the test. Have students read the passage silently, then, as a class, analyze each choice in the first test item.
   - A—Information regarding the lesson questions. (Eliminate)
   - B—Informs reader of classmate's place in the class. (Eliminate)
   - C—Correct answer. This dialogue carries an angry tone.
   - D—Informative of the names used for the girls. (Eliminate)
3. Assign the Practice exercise. Have students read the passage and answer the questions on their own. Allow 15 minutes for this process, and announce to students when they have 5 minutes and 1 minute remaining.

Answers

1. C
2. H
3. B
4. J
5. B
6. F
7. A

Reteach

Question	Pages to Reteach
1	1040
2	308
3	975
4	1040
5	296
6	958
7	296

Grammar and Writing

Editing in Context

1. Introduce the skill using the instruction on the student page. Be sure students understand the strategy set off in the boxed section.
2. Read the first paragraph of the Practice passage; then, go over the first test item with students, modeling the "what is different?" strategy.
3. Point out that each of the answer choices is a different verb tense. The original sentence begins in past tense, but shifts to present tense. Change is required, so Choice *A* is eliminated. A plural past tense of the verb is necessary. Choice *B* is singular present tense; *B* is eliminated. Choice *C* is past perfect; *C* is eliminated. Choice *D* is plural past tense. Choice *D* is therefore the correct answer.
4. Have students complete questions 2–8 on their own. Allow students 9 minutes to complete the questions.

Grammar and Writing: Editing in Context

Editing-in-context segments appear in some standardized tests. They are made up of a passage with underlined and numbered areas, some of which contain errors in grammar, style, and usage. For each question, you must choose the best way to correct a given sentence.

Practice

This exercise is modeled after the ACT English Test.

Directions: For each underlined sentence or portion of a sentence, choose the best alternative. If an item asks a question about the underlined portion or a numbered sentence, choose the best answer to the question.

[1]

Boarding schools first began in England when boys go[1] to a local monastery for their education. Monks and lay staff would provide a variety of instruction while the boys' housing would be provided by the order that sponsored the monastery.[2] Often a local nobleman would make his estate available to the sons of other nobles. Employing a literate priest from the area.[3] These makeshift academies often became boarding houses for the elite.

[2]

In the twelfth century, all Benedictine monasteries were ordered by the Pope to provide what were known as "charity schools."[4] Followed by what we know today as public schools.[5] Students began to pay their way and attended[6] in greater numbers than ever before.

[3]

Aristocratic families continued to favor private instruction in their homes. [7] The great universities of Cambridge and Oxford provided models. As the British Empire began to expand, the boarding school became well established. [8]

1. **A.** NO CHANGE
   B. goes
   C. have gone
   D. went

Strategy

Try out each answer.

Examine the answer choices with an eye to what makes them different. Various aspects of writing can vary in multiple answers. Make sure each part is effective.

Strategies for Test Taking

Point out to students that in Editing in Context Tests such as the one on this page, some test items simply list choices; students, following the general directions, are expected to choose the best alternative. Items 1, 3, 4, 5, and 6 are of this type.

Other test items are preceded by questions. Often these involve descriptions of the writer's thoughts, sometimes describing a deletion or quoting an insertion the writer is planning to make. Items 2, 7, and 8 are of this type. Tell students to read these questions twice, making sure they understand exactly what change the writer is contemplating before testing out the item's choices.

Since these questions may take more time, students might work through the "short" test items first and then go back to the more detailed test items. Also, if students complete the test with time remaining, they should review their answers to the detailed test items.

2. Which of the following sentences would best make this statement more forceful?
   F. NO CHANGE
   G. the order that sponsored the monastery would provide the boys' housing.
   H. the boys' housing would be sponsored by the order the monastery provided.
   J. the order that sponsored the monastery would be provided by the boys' housing.

3. **A.** NO CHANGE
   B. attach it to previous sentence
   C. attach it to next sentence
   D. OMIT

4. **F.** NO CHANGE
   G. all Benedictine monasteries were ordered to provide what were known as "charity schools" by the Pope.
   H. the Pope ordered all Benedictine monasteries to provide what were known as "charity schools."
   J. the Pope was ordered by all Benedictine monasteries to provide what were known as "charity schools."

5. **A.** NO CHANGE
   B. These were soon followed by what we know today as public schools.
   C. Followed soon is what we know today as public schools.
   D. Public schools what we know today followed soon.

6. **F.** NO CHANGE
   G. began to pay their way and attending
   H. begin to pay their way and attend
   J. begin paying their way and attending

7. The writer wishes to add the following sentence without creating a run-on sentence: *However, elite boarding schools also became fashionable.*
   If added, this would best be placed:
   A. as part of the previous sentence, at its beginning, with new punctuation.
   B. as part of the previous sentence, at its end, joined by a semicolon and a conjunction.
   C. as part of the following sentence at its beginning joined by a comma.
   D. as is, standing alone as a sentence.

8. Which of these alternatives provides the most direct conclusion of Paragraph 3?
   F. To stay attuned to their own culture and attend boarding school, children of British administrators were sent back to England.
   G. Children of British administrators attended boarding school, going back to England and stay attuned to their own culture.
   H. Children of British administrators went back to England attending boarding school and staying attuned to their own culture.
   J. British administrators sent their children back to England to attend boarding school and stay attuned to their own culture.

Timed Writing: Position Statement [30 minutes]

Jane Eyre is sent to Lowood, a private boarding school, and has to deal with strict teachers and harsh conditions. Charlotte Brontë briefly attended a school like Lowood and clearly did not enjoy the experience. But for many students, boarding school life became a wonderful home away from home and a memorable academic experience.

Write an essay in which you discuss the benefits or drawbacks of boarding school. Support your opinions with sound reasoning, and try to anticipate and address counterarguments.

Academic Vocabulary

An essay often argues with itself by first presenting one way of looking at an issue, and then refuting that argument with another viewpoint.

STOP

ASSESS/RETEACH

Answers

1. D
2. G
3. B
4. H
5. B
6. F
7. D
8. J

Timed Writing

Position Statement

1. Go over the two paragraphs of the timed writing assignment on the student page.
2. Tell students that they can quickly formulate a thesis statement for their position statements.
3. Encourage students to budget adequate time for prewriting and revising/editing. Students should spend about 8 minutes in the prewriting stage, 12 minutes drafting, and 5 minutes revising and editing. Reinforce this by announcing elapsed time at the 8- and 20-minute marks as students respond to the assignment.
4. Use the **Rubrics for Writing for Assessment,** *Professional Development Guidebook,* pages 258–259, to evaluate students' work.

Reteach

Question	Pages to Reteach
1	1009
2	1085
3	1099
4	1085
5	1085
6	1009
7	1099
8	1099

Benchmark

Reteach skills as indicated by students' performance, following the Reteach charts on pages 1113 and 1115. Then, administer the end-of-unit **Benchmark Test** (*Unit 5 Resources,* pp. 152–157). The Benchmark Test concludes instruction in the Unit skills. Follow the **Interpretation Guide** for the test (*Unit 5 Resources,* p. 160) to assign reteaching pages as necessary in the *Reading Kit.* Use **Success Tracker** online to automatically assign these pages.

PHLit Online!

The **Benchmark Tests** and **Success Tracker** are available online at **www.PHLitOnline.com.**

Performance Tasks

Assigning Tasks/Reteaching Skills

Use the chart below to choose appropriate Performance Tasks by identifying which tasks assess lessons in the textbook that you have taught. Use the same lessons for reteaching when students' performance indicates a failure to fully master a standard. For additional instruction and practice, assign the *Common Core Companion* pages indicated for each task.

Task	Where Taught/ Pages to Reteach	*Common Core Companion* Pages
1	794, 894, 958, 976, 990, 1011, 1021, 1040	15–27, 196–207, 261–268
2	1072, 1076, 1084, 1086, 1098	54–60, 219–225, 322–323
3	990, 996, 1022, 1028, 1034, 1096	28–40, 196–207, 261–268
4	990, 1011, 1040, 1051, 1060, 1070	15–27, 306–312
5	956, 958, 986, 1022, 1028, 1051, 1084	28–40, 278–285
6	794, 894, 1022, 1062, 1070, 1096, 1100	136–142, 297–303

Assessment Pacing

In assigning the Writing Tasks, allow a class period for the completion of a task. As an alternative, assign tasks as homework. In assigning the Speaking and Listening Tasks, consider having students do preparation as a homework assignment. Then, allow a class period for the presentations.

Evaluating Performance Tasks

Use the rubric at the bottom of this Teacher Edition page to evaluate students' mastery of the standards as demonstrated in their Performance Task responses. Review the rubric with students before they begin work so they know the criteria by which their work will be evaluated.

Performance Tasks

Common Core State Standards

RL.11-12.2, RL.11-12.3, RL.11-12.5; RI.11-12.5; W.11-12.2, W.11-12.9.a, W.11-12.4; SL.11-12.1, SL.11-12.4, SL.11-12.6; L.11-12.3.a

[For the complete wording of the standards, see the standards chart in the front of your textbook.]

Directions: *Follow the instructions to complete the tasks below as required by your teacher. As you work on each task, incorporate both general academic vocabulary and literary terms you learned in this unit.*

Writing

Task 1: Literature [RL.11-12.2; W.11-12.2, W.11-12.9.a]

Analyze Development of Themes

*Write an **essay** in which you analyze the development of two themes in a work of fiction from this unit.*

- Choose a story or a novel excerpt from this unit that expresses multiple themes.
- Briefly summarize the story. Identify two themes that develop in the story.
- Analyze how the author introduces and develops those themes over the course of the story.
- Note ways in which the themes interact and build on one another, and discuss how this interaction creates deeper meaning.
- Use transitions to clearly show the relationships and interactions among story elements.
- Use active, not passive, voice.
- Accurately use academic vocabulary in your writing.

Task 2: Literature [RL.11-12.5; W.11-12.4; L.11-12.3.a]

Analyze Text Structure

*Write an **essay** in which you analyze how a poet's choice of structure adds to the overall meaning and aesthetic impact of a poem in this unit.*

- Choose a poem from this unit in which the structure, or form, plays a key role in developing the poem's meaning. Explain which poem you chose and why.
- Analyze how the poet's choices of structure in sections of the poem contribute to the structure of the poem as a whole. Consider line length, rhyme scheme, and meter, as well as stanza lengths and divisions.
- Connect the author's choices concerning structure to the meaning as well as to the aesthetic, or artistic and emotional, impact of the poem. Cite examples from the text to support your thinking.
- Develop and present your ideas while maintaining an appropriate, consistent style and tone in your writing.
- Vary your sentence length and structure to add interest and sophistication to your writing.

Task 3: Literature [RL.11-12.3; W.11-12.2, W.11.12.9.a]

Analyze Character Development

*Write an **essay** in which you analyze the impact of the author's choices regarding how to introduce and develop characters in a work of fiction from this unit.*

- State which fictional characters you will be discussing in your essay and the reasons for your choice.
- Describe each character, including the points at which important information is revealed. Determine what kinds of details the author provides about each character.
- Analyze the role each character plays in the story and explain each character's goals and motivations.
- Explain the connection between characters and theme.
- Sum up your analysis with a conclusion about how the author's choices regarding character development shaped the work of fiction.
- In your writing, use technical academic vocabulary, standard English grammar, and correct spelling.

Performance Task Rubric: Standards Mastery	Rating Scale (*not very* – *very*)
Critical Thinking: How clearly and consistently does the student pursue the specific mode of reasoning or discourse required by the standard, as specified in the prompt (e.g., comparing and contrasting, analyzing, explaining)?	1 2 3 4 5
Focus: How well does the student understand and apply the focus concepts of the standard, as specified in the prompt (e.g., development of theme or of complex characters, effects of structure, and so on)?	1 2 3 4 5
Support/Elaboration: How well does the student support points with textual or other evidence? How relevant, sufficient, and varied is the evidence provided?	1 2 3 4 5
Insight: How original, sophisticated, or compelling are the insights the student achieves by applying the standard to the text(s)?	1 2 3 4 5
Expression of Ideas: How well does the student organize and support ideas? How well does the student use language, including word choice and conventions, in the expression of ideas?	1 2 3 4 5

Speaking and Listening

Task 4: Literature [RL.11-12.2, SL.11-12.6]
Analyze Related Themes

*Prepare and deliver an **oral presentation** in which you analyze two themes expressed in a literary work in this unit and the way in which those themes interact.*

- Select a work that expresses multiple, related themes. Briefly summarize the work and explain why you chose it.
- Explain how the author develops themes over the course of the work. Consider narrative elements such as plot, setting, and character. Also consider literary elements such as symbolism and imagery.
- Explain how the two themes interact and build on each other during the course of the work.
- Cite specific evidence from the text to support your points.
- As you present, use adequate volume and clear pronunciation. Demonstrate a command of formal English.

Task 5: Literature [RL.11-12.3; SL.11-12.1]
Analyze and Compare Speakers

Prepare and conduct a group discussion comparing speakers in two poems in this unit.

- Choose two poems with distinctive speakers that have a good basis for comparison.
- Analyze the speaker in each poem. Consider the choices the poet made as to the speaker. For example, the speaker may be real or fictional, specific or general. Determine each speaker's motivation and conflict. Draw inferences about the character of each speaker based on evidence from the poems.
- Prepare for the discussion. Create a list of questions designed to promote discussion. Make charts on which to record the main points that are brought up during the discussion.
- During the discussion, clarify or challenge ideas; respond thoughtfully to diverse perspectives; and propel conversation by posing and responding to questions.

Task 6: Informational Text [RI.11-12.5; SL.11-12.4]
Analyze Structure

*Prepare and deliver an **oral presentation** in which you analyze an author's use of text structure as part of exposition in a nonfiction work from this unit.*

- Select a work of nonfiction from this unit in which the structure helps to communicate the author's ideas or argument. Briefly explain why you chose this work.
- Define the text's structure. Explain how it enhances or helps to develop the author's ideas or argument. Consider how the text structure serves the author's purpose as well as how it might affect an audience.
- Be sure to provide examples from the text to support your points. Check the pronunciation of challenging words from the text.
- Present your ideas clearly and completely so that your listeners can follow your reasoning.
- While presenting, use formal English, good pronunciation, and adequate volume.

How does literature shape or reflect society?

Victorian Views in Today's World Which aspects of the Victorian Age have meaning and value for us now?

Assignment Imagine that you are compiling a book of Victorian wit and wisdom to be sold today. It will include nuggets of literature that reflect Victorian values. First, select some quotations you would include. Then, write a **preface to the book,** convincing the reader of the value and relevance of the quotations in today's world.

Supporting Speaking and Listening

1. Consider having students work with partners or in groups to complete Performance Tasks involving listening and speaking. For tasks that you assign for individual work, you may still wish to have students rehearse with partners, who can provide constructive feedback.
2. As students rehearse, have them keep in mind these tips:
   - Present findings and evidence clearly and concisely.
   - Observe conventions of standard English grammar and usage.
   - Be relaxed and friendly but maintain a formal tone.
   - Make eye contact with the audience, pronounce words clearly, and vary your pace.
   - When working with a group, respond thoughtfully to others' positions, modifying your own in response to new evidence.

Linking Performance Tasks to Independent Reading

If you wish to cover the standards with students' independent reading, adapt Performance Tasks of your choice to the works they have selected. (Independent reading suggestions appear on the next page.)

How does literature shape or reflect society?

1. Remind students of the Essential Question, "How does literature shape or reflect society?"
2. Have students complete their responses to the prompt on the student page. Point out that in this unit, they have read a variety of British literature from the Victorian period and that they should draw on these selections in their responses. Remind them that they can also draw on their own experiences and what they have learned in other subject areas in formulating their answers.

Differentiated Instruction for Universal Access

Strategy for Less Proficient Readers
Assign a Performance Task, and then have students meet in groups to review the standard assessed in that task. Remind students of the selections or independent readings to which they have previously applied the standard. Have groups summarize what they learned in applying the standard and then present their summaries. Discuss, clarifying any points of confusion. After students have completed their tasks, have groups meet again to evaluate members' work. Encourage members to revise their work based on the feedback they receive.

EL Strategy for English Learners
For each Performance Task, review the instructions with students. Clarify the meaning of unfamiliar vocabulary, emphasizing classroom words such as *style, motivations,* and *symbolism* and academic vocabulary such as *summarize.*

Next, have students note ideas for their responses. Pair students, and have them review each other's notes, asking questions to clarify meaning and suggesting improvements. Encourage students to ask for your assistance in supplying English words or expressions they may require.

Independent Reading

Titles featured on the Independent Reading pages at the end of each unit represent a range of reading, including stories, dramas, and poetry, as well as literary nonfiction and other types of informational text. Throughout, labels indicate the works that are CCSS Exemplar Texts. Choosing from among these featured titles will help students read works at increasing levels of text complexity in the grades 11–12 text complexity band.

Using Literature Circles

A literature circle is a temporary group in which students independently discuss a book.

Use the guidance in the *Professional Development Guidebook*, pp. 47–49, as well as the teaching notes on the facing page, for additional suggestions for literature circles.

Meeting Unit 5 CCS Standards

Students can use books listed on this page to apply and reinforce their mastery of the CCS Standards covered in this unit.

Introducing Featured Titles

Have students choose a book or books for independent reading. Assist them by previewing the titles, noting their subject matter and level of difficulty. **Note:** Before recommending a work to students, preview it, taking into account the values of your community as well as the maturity of your students.

Featured Titles

In this unit, you have read a variety of British literature from the Victorian period. Continue to read works related to this era on your own. Select books that you enjoy, but challenge yourself to explore new topics, new authors, and works offering varied perspectives or approaches. The titles suggested below will help you get started.

LITERATURE

Wuthering Heights
Emily Brontë

Novel Set on the wild and windy moors of northern Yorkshire, *Wuthering Heights* tells the story of Heathcliff and Catherine, who are desperately in love. The thwarting of their love prompts Heathcliff to seek revenge.

[The poem "Remembrance" by Emily Brontë begins on page 1075. Build knowledge by reading a novel by this author.]

Jane Eyre
Charlotte Brontë — EXEMPLAR TEXT

Novel The title character in this classic novel endures many challenges that give readers insight into the life of a single, middle-class woman in Victorian Britain. After a lonely, difficult childhood, Jane Eyre becomes a governess at the home of Mr. Rochester, a man with a terrible secret.

[An excerpt from Jane Eyre *begins on page 1030 of this book. Build knowledge by reading the complete novel.]*

Hard Times
Charles Dickens

Novel While exposing the harsh realities of poverty in nineteenth-century England, Dickens tells the story of Thomas Gradgrind, a teacher and parent who believes facts alone are all that are needed in life. As life unfolds around him, his views change.

[An excerpt from Hard Times *begins on page 998 of this book. Build knowledge by reading the complete novel.]*

Crime and Punishment
Fyodor Dostoyevsky — EXEMPLAR TEXT

Novel Ex-student Raskolnikov is poor and starving. Though he thinks of himself as a good person, he rationalizes robbing and murdering an old woman by telling himself that she is morally corrupt. His actions soon begin to haunt him, however, and he is forced to face their consequences.

INFORMATIONAL TEXTS

Historical Texts

The Essays of Virginia Woolf
Virginia Woolf
Mariner Books, 1990

Essay This four-volume text includes essays written by Woolf from her early twenties until her death in 1941. Woolf's essays present a personal view of her life, as well as her views on women, writing, literature, and politics.

[Selected works by Virginia Woolf appear on page 1192 of this book. Build knowledge by reading the full text.]

Queen Victoria
Lytton Strachey
Nabu Press, 2010

Biography Get to know Britain's long-reigning and influential queen in this comprehensive and engaging biography—her willful childhood, her joyful marriage to Albert, her sorrow at his death, and her devotion to her servant John Brown.

Contemporary Scholarship

Dickens
Peter Ackroyd

Biography This award-winning biography describes in detail the life of famed British novelist Charles Dickens. Read about his difficult childhood and his rise to popular and critical acclaim as one of the most important writers of his time.

The Ghost Map
Steven Johnson
Riverhead, 2007

Scientific History It is the summer of 1854 and a devastating cholera outbreak has seized London. Dr. John Snow—whose ideas about contagious disease have been dismissed by the scientific community—is spurred into action when his neighbors begin dying.

Text Complexity: Aligning Texts With Readers and Tasks

TEXTS	READERS AND TASKS
• *Wuthering Heights* (Lexile: 880L) • *Jane Eyre* (Lexile: 890L)	**Below-Level Readers** Allow students to focus on reading for content, and challenge them to interpret multiple perspectives.
• *Crime and Punishment* (Lexile: 990L) • *Hard Times* (Lexile: 1060L) • *Dickens* • *The Ghost Map*	**Below-Level Readers** Challenge students as they read for content. **On-Level Readers** Allow students to focus on reading for content, and challenge them to interpret multiple perspectives. **Advanced Readers** Allow students to focus on interpreting multiple perspectives.
• *The Essays of Virginia Woolf* • *Queen Victoria*	**On-Level Readers** Challenge students as they read for content. **Advanced Readers** Allow students to focus on reading for content, and challenge them to interpret multiple perspectives.

Preparing to Read Complex Texts

Reading for College and Career In both college and the workplace, readers must analyze texts independently, draw connections among works that offer varied perspectives, and develop their own ideas and informed opinions. The questions shown below, and others that you generate on your own, will help you more effectively read and analyze complex college-level texts.

Common Core State Standards

Reading Literature/Informational Text
10. By the end of grade 12, read and comprehend literature, including stories, dramas, and poems, and literary nonfiction at the high end of the grade 11-CCR text complexity band independently and proficiently.

When reading analytically, ask yourself...

- What idea, experience, or story seems to have compelled the author to write? Has the author presented that idea, experience, or story in a way that I, too, find compelling?
- How might the author's era, social status, belief system, or personal experiences have affected the point of view he or she expresses in the text?
- How do my circumstances affect what I understand and feel about this text?
- What key idea does the author state explicitly? What key idea does he or she suggest or imply? Which details in the text help me to perceive implied ideas?
- Do I find multiple layers of meaning in the text? If so, what relationships do I see among these layers of meaning?
- How do details in the text connect or relate to one another? Do I find any details unconvincing, unrelated, or out of place?
- Do I find the text believable and convincing?

Key Ideas and Details

- What patterns of organization or sequences do I find in the text? Do these patterns help me understand the ideas better?
- What do I notice about the author's style, including his or her diction, uses of imagery and figurative language, and syntax?
- Do I like the author's style? Is the author's style memorable?
- What emotional attitude does the author express toward the topic, the story, or the characters? Does this attitude seem appropriate?
- What emotional attitude does the author express toward me, the reader? Does this attitude seem appropriate?
- What do I notice about the author's voice—his or her personality on the page? Do I like this voice? Does it make me want to read on?

Craft and Structure

- Is the work fresh and original?
- Do I agree with the author's ideas entirely, or are there elements I find unconvincing?
- Do I disagree with the author's ideas entirely, or are there elements I can accept as true?
- Based on my knowledge of British literature, history, and culture, does this work reflect the British tradition? Why or why not?

Integration of Ideas

Text Complexity: Reader and Task Support Suggestions

INDEPENDENT READING	
Increased Support Suggest that students choose a book that they feel comfortable reading and one that is a bit more challenging. Pair a more proficient reader with a less proficient reader and have them work together on the more challenging text. Partners can prepare to read the book by reviewing questions on this student page. They can also read difficult passages together, sharing questions and insights. They can use the questions on the student page to guide after-reading discussion.	*Increased Challenge* Encourage students to integrate knowledge and ideas by combining the Essential Questions and the unit concepts in their approach to two or more featured titles. For example, students might compare and contrast the motivations of Heathcliff in *Wuthering Heights* to those of Raskolnikov in *Crime and Punishment.* Students should go on to discuss the consequences of each character's actions and how these consequences contribute to the author's theme.

Preparing to Read Complex Texts

1. Tell students they can be attentive readers by bringing their experience and imagination to the texts they read and by actively questioning those texts. Explain that the questions they see on the student page are examples of types of questions to ask about works of fiction and nonfiction.
2. Point out that, like writing, reading is a "multidraft" process, involving several readings of complete works or passages, revising and refining one's understanding each time.

Key Ideas and Details

3. Focus on the second bulleted point in the Key Ideas and Details box. **Ask:** What key ideas and details in the text illustrate this point of view?

   Possible response: Students may cite ideas and details that are directly related to the author's background or details that convey a contrast with the author's background.

Craft and Structure

4. **Ask:** Why might an author vary his or her style from story to story or book to book?

   Possible response: The writing style can contribute to the reader's understanding of the ideas and themes of a piece. Different ideas and themes will be most effectively conveyed using different writing styles.

Integration of Ideas

5. Focus on the third bulleted point in the Integration of Ideas box. **Ask:** Can you remain engaged with a work if you disagree entirely with the author's ideas? Explain.

   Possible response: Students may say they can remain engaged if the author presents compelling, persuasive arguments for his or her ideas and helps the reader view those ideas in a new light.
6. Finally, explain to students that they should cite key ideas and details, examples of craft and structure, or instances of the integration of ideas as evidence to support their points during a discussion of fiction or nonfiction. After hearing the evidence, the group might reach a consensus or might agree to disagree.

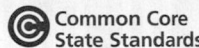

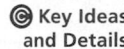

Common Core State Standards

- Reading Literature 1, 2, 3, 4, 5, 9
- Reading Informational Text 2, 3, 4, 5, 6, 13
- Writing 1, 2, 3, 4, 5, 9
- Speaking and Listening 1, 2
- Language 1, 2, 3, 4, 5

A Time of Rapid Change

The Modern and Postmodern Periods

1120

PHLit Online!
www.PHLitOnline.com

Teaching From Technology

Enriched Online Student Edition
- full narration of selections
- interactive graphic organizers
- linked **Get Connected** and **Background** videos
- all work sheets and other student resources

Professional Development
- the *Professional Development Guidebook* online
- additional professional-development essays by program authors

Planning, Assigning, and Monitoring
- software for online assignment of work to students, individually or to the whole class
- a system for tracking and grading student work

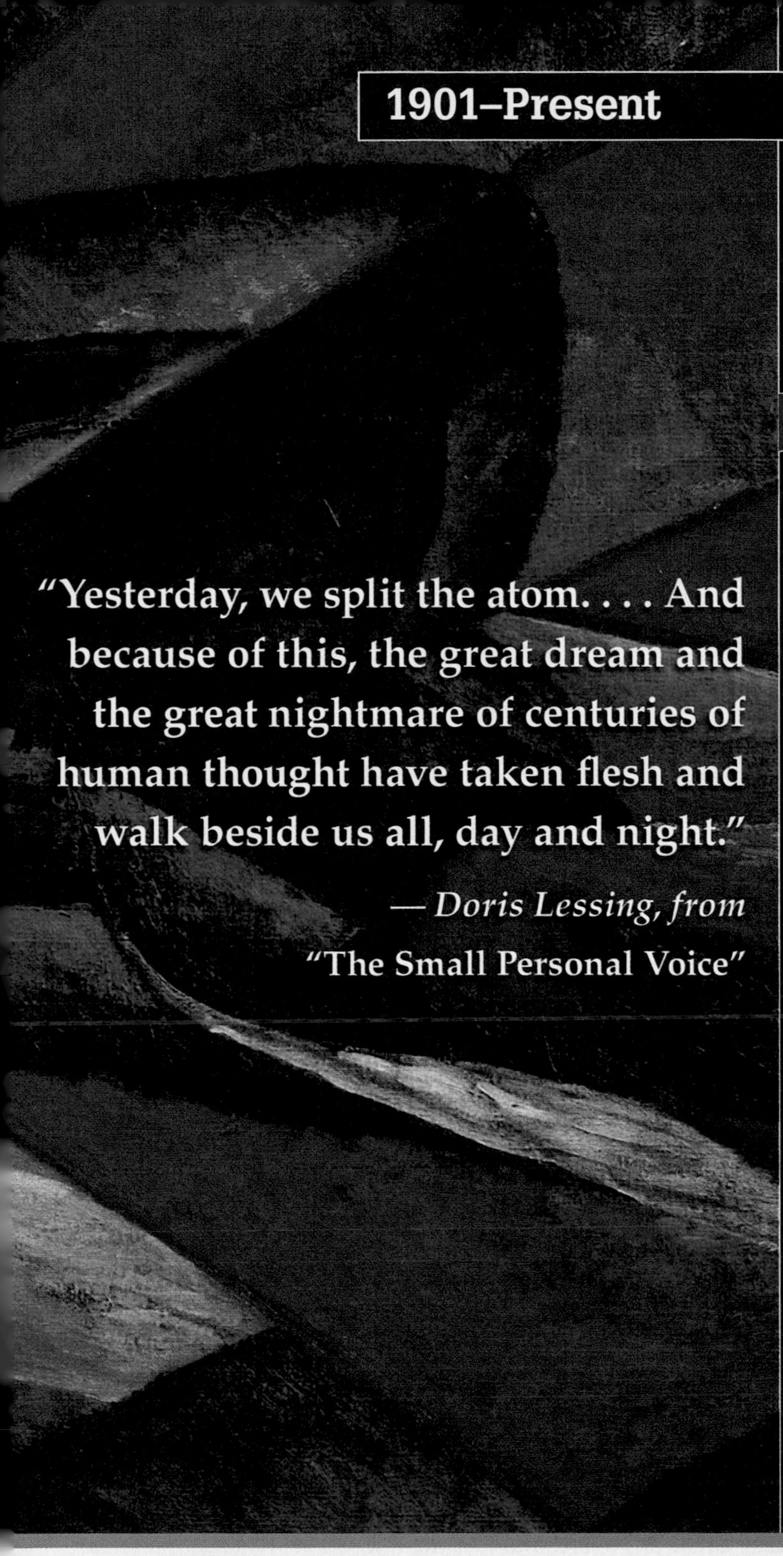

Unit 6

1901–Present

"Yesterday, we split the atom. . . . And because of this, the great dream and the great nightmare of centuries of human thought have taken flesh and walk beside us all, day and night."

— *Doris Lessing, from* "The Small Personal Voice"

PHLit Online!
www.PHLitOnline.com

Hear It!
- Selection summary audio
- Selection audio

See It!
- Author videos
- Essential Question video
- Get Connected videos
- Background videos
- More about the authors
- Illustrated vocabulary words
- Vocabulary flashcards

Do It!
- Interactive journals
- Interactive graphic organizers
- Grammar tutorials
- Interactive vocabulary games
- Test practice

1121

Introduce Unit 6

1. Direct students' attention to the title of the Unit, including the time period covered. Have a volunteer read the quotation. **Ask:** What does the quotation suggest about the attitudes of the Modern and Postmodern periods?
   Possible response: The many changes that occurred in these time periods evoked mixed emotions from people. For example, some saw the benefits of scientific advancements and others saw the dangers of too much power.
2. Discuss the artwork, *The Dynamism of an Automobile*, painted by Luigi Russolo in 1911. **Ask:** What might this abstract representation of automobiles suggest about the literature of the Modern and Postmodern periods?
   Possible response: The abstract painting reinforces the idea that Modern and Postmodern experiences cannot be pictured directly.
3. Have students speculate about the literature of the period, given the quotation and the art.
   Possible response: Themes that might emerge include chaos, disillusionment, courage, and hope.

Unit Resources

Unit 6 Resources includes these pages:

- **Benchmark Tests** assess and monitor student progress.
- **Vocabulary and Reading Warm-ups** provide additional vocabulary support, based on Lexile rankings, for each selection. "A" **Warm-ups** are for students reading two grades below level. "B" **Warm-ups** are for students reading one grade below level.
- **Selection Support**
  - **Reading Skill**
  - **Literary Analysis**
  - **Vocabulary Builder**
  - **Support for Writing**
  - **Enrichment**

PHLit Online!
All worksheets and other student resources are also available online at **www.PHLitOnline.com.**

Unit Features

Unit Author
Anita Desai helps introduce the period in the Unit Introduction, provides Recent Scholarship on literature in the Unit, and offers insight in the Writing Workshop.

Extended Study
Students explore in depth the works of Virginia Woolf, presented with links to contemporary culture, a Critical Commentary, and a Comparing Literary Works feature.

Comparing Literary Works
Students compare master works in the British tradition with works of world literature.

Primary Sources
Students engage the documents that recorded history as it was made.

Informational Texts
Students learn to use and evaluate various types of informational text.

Themes Across Cultures
Students discover links between literature from different cultures.

Pump Up the Writing Volume **Kelly Gallagher**

"I have found that when writing on-demand responses, my students perform better if they take some time *before* they write to plan their essays."

Writing has become a "gate-keeping" skill for our students. Many state tests now have a writing component, writing is now central to the SAT, and increasingly, writing is now being used in the workforce as both a hiring and promotion determinant. Recognizing the importance writing plays in our students' lives, the National Commission on Writing recommends that we *double* the amount of writing our students are doing. Why? Because writing has two immediate benefits: It deepens our students' reading comprehension and enables them to generate new thinking.

Demand More Writing

When considering how to increase the volume of our students' writing, our focus should be on both process writing (multiple-draft) and on-demand writing (the kind of writing students are likely to encounter on tests). The cognitive skills needed to produce an on-demand essay differ somewhat from those necessary to produce a process piece, and as a result, it is critical that my students receive numerous practice opportunities in *both* domains.

The ABC's (and D) of On-Demand Writing In preparation for both the state tests and for the SAT, my students write an on-demand essay every three weeks. I have found that when writing on-demand responses my students perform better if they take some time *before* they write to plan their essays. To help them do this, I teach them the ABC's (and D) of on-demand writing:

1. **A**ttack the prompt. Consider the following question: "Write a composition in which you identify the author's thesis. State whether you agree or disagree with the author's position. Support your answer with details and examples." Before writing, have students re-read the prompt and circle any word that tells them to do something. Students then draw a line from that word to what it is asking them to do. In the prompt above, for example, students would circle "Identify" and draw a line to "author's thesis." They repeat this process for every verb in the prompt. A re-write, in shorthand, of the prompt might look like this:

Identify:	author's thesis
State:	agree or disagree
Support:	with details/examples

Attacking the prompts enables students to simplify the question into understandable fragments. It also helps them to remember that most prompts ask for more than one thing. With practice, students will be able to attack the prompt in two minutes or less.

2. **B**rainstorm for possible answers. Students brainstorm for as many responses as possible for five minutes. I model how to cluster, list, map, and outline, and afterwards I allow my students to select the strategies that work best for them.
3. **C**hoose the order of their response. Once their pre-writing is completed, students take one minute to numerically order their response. Students who begin writing with "roadmaps" in front of them are better equipped to maximize the time allotted to complete the writing task.
4. **D**etect errors by re-reading. It always amazes me how many students turn in essays without having read them for errors. If time permits, I always require my students to re-read before submitting.

Strategies for Encouraging More Process Writing

Donald Graves once said, "If kids don't write at least three times a week, they're dead." Here are two strategies to generate more writing:

Sneezing Rather than write complete essay after complete essay, my students are frequently asked to "sneeze"—that is, to write short blasts of writing (Fletcher, 1993). I want my students to write frequently without fearing how the writing will turn out. Once a student has generated four or five sneezes, she then chooses one of her most promising pieces to take through the entire writing process. Allowing the student some choice establishes more buy-in, which in turn increases the possibility that the revisions necessary in a process paper will be taken more seriously.

Cubing Like most teachers, I get tired of reading the same essay repeatedly. To avoid this, I will often have students "cube" a writing topic (Cowan and Cowan). Here are the "cubing" perspectives students might explore through writing:

1. **Describe It**
   - What characteristics does it have?
   - What does it say? What does it look like?
2. **Compare It**
   - What is it similar to?
   - What is it analogous to?
3. **Associate It**
   - What does it remind you of?
   - How does it connect to other topics/issues/events/people?
4. **Analyze it**
   - How did it happen?
   - Why did it happen?
5. **Apply It**
   - What can you do with it?
   - How can you use it?
   - What lesson(s) did it teach?
   - What understanding did it generate?
6. **Argue for or Against It**
   - I support/oppose this because…
   - This is good/bad

Teacher Resources

- ***Professional Development Guidebook***
- ***Classroom Strategies and Teaching Routines cards***

PHLit Online!

Log on as a teacher at **www.PHLitOnline.com** to access a library of all Professional Development articles by the Contributing Authors of Prentice Hall *Literature*.

Kelly Gallagher

Kelly Gallagher is a full-time English teacher at Magnolia High School in Anaheim, California, where he has taught twenty-two years. He is the author of *Deeper Reading: Comprehending Challenging Texts.*

Supporting Research

Cowan,G. and E. Cowan. 1980. *Writing.* New York: Wiley.

Fletcher, Ralph. 1993. *What a Writer Needs.* Portsmouth, NH: Heinemann.

National Commission on Writing for America's Families, Schools, and Colleges. 2003. *The Neglected 'R': The Need for a Writing Revolution.* New York: The College. www.writingcommission.org/prod_downloads/writingcom/neglectedr.pdf.

INTRODUCE

Reading the Unit Introduction

A Time of Rapid Change

Explain to students that this unit covers literature in Britain during the Modern and Postmodern periods, from 1901 to the present. The Unit Introduction includes these components:

—a **Snapshot** offering a quick glimpse at the period

—a **Historical Background** section discussing major events

—a **Timeline** that covers the period from 1901 to the present, over a span of ten pages

—a **Unit Essay** examining the literature of the period through the lens of three Essential Questions

—**Following-Through** activities

—a **Contemporary Commentary**

Applying the Essential Question

1. Introduce each of the Essential Questions on the student page.
2. Show the Essential Question video on the *See It!* DVD. Help students relate the Essential Questions to the unit and their own experiences by asking the following:

Literature and Place How would you describe the place in which you live? Is the community diverse? Is the economy in the community solid or is it experiencing problems?

Literature and Society How would you describe the status of women in our society today? Do they have the same economic, political, and social opportunities as men do?

Writer and Tradition Do you use the Internet to access literature? What kinds of literature does the Internet provide? How much effect do you think technology will have on literature in the future?

3. Explain to students that the ideas they have considered in answering these questions also apply to Britain's Modern and Postmodern periods. Have them begin reading the Unit Introduction, telling them to look for ideas related to their answers as they read.

COMMON CORE ▪ MULTIPLE PERSPECTIVES ON THE ERA

Snapshot of the Period

A Ride on the London Eye

England celebrated the new millennium with the London Eye, a 443-foot Ferris wheel beside the Thames (see page to the right). Picture this wheel as the symbol of a 2,000-year cycle in time. Looking out from it, we might view England's history—waves of invaders from the Romans to the Normans, performances at Shakespeare's Globe, the changing versions of London known to Dr. Johnson, Charles Dickens, and Virginia Woolf. From the top, we might see how England's empire stretched across the globe in the nineteenth century and how, in the twentieth, two world wars led to the loss of that empire. The ride over, we would step onto the soil of twenty-first-century England, once more a nation rather than an empire. It is a nation, however, whose language is spoken across the globe and whose literature is enriched by writers from St. Lucia to Singapore.

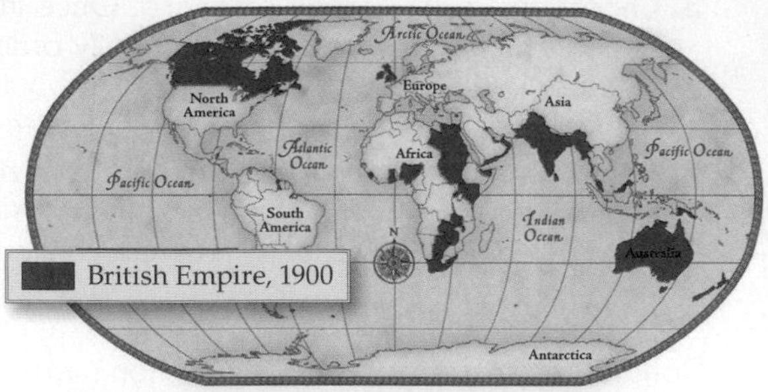

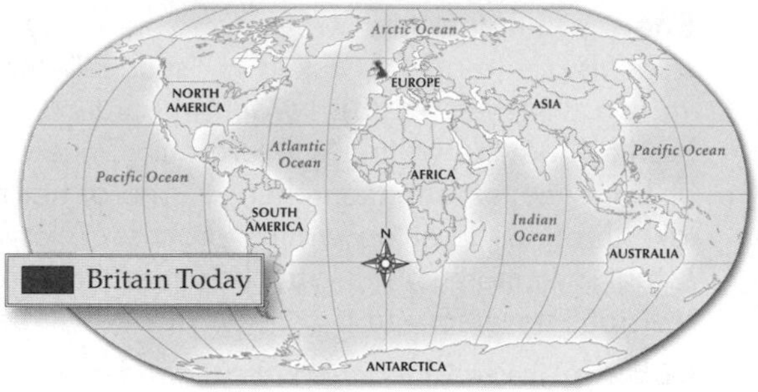

These two maps dramatize Britain's loss of its empire in the twentieth century.

As you read the selections in this unit, you will be asked to think about them in view of three key questions:

What is the **relationship** between literature and *place?*

How does literature **shape or reflect** *society?*

What is the relationship of the writer to *tradition?*

Teaching Resources

Unit 6 Resources
- **Names and Terms to Know Worksheet**, p. 2
- **Essential Question Worksheets**, pp. 3–5
- **Listening and Viewing**, p. 342
- **Following Through**, p. 6

All *Common Core Companion*, pp. 9–14; 33–38

All *Professional Development Guidebook*
- **Cross-Curricular Enrichment Worksheets**, pp. 238, 224, 234, 230
- *See It!* **DVD**
- **Anita Desai**

Integration of Knowledge and Ideas As this London Eye timeline indicates, the end of the British empire was also marked by a renewal of English literature as writers from former colonies made—and are still making—important contributions to the tradition. During what postwar decade did Britain lose most of its colonies? What are three former colonies that have produced Nobel Prize-winning authors who write in English?

Differentiated Instruction for Universal Access

Strategy for Less Proficient Readers

Before students read the Unit Introduction, distribute copies of the **Names and Terms to Know** worksheet (***Unit 6 Resources***, p. 2). Ask students to preview the worksheet. On the board, list the names and terms on the worksheet. Ask students to predict (or guess) the possible significance of these terms. Record several predictions or guesses next to each term on the board. As students read the Unit Introduction, have them check the accuracy of the predictions on the board. Correct each as necessary. Finally, when students have finished reading the Unit Introduction, erase the board, and have the class complete the worksheet, referring back to the Unit Introduction.

Background

Architecture

The London Eye is made up of thirty-two sealed, air-conditioned capsules that seat twenty-five people. The capsules are large enough for passengers to walk around in, if they so choose. Constructing the Ferris wheel was truly a European collaboration. Steel and electrical components were supplied by the United Kingdom, and the steel was manufactured in the Netherlands. The Czech Republic provided the spindle and hub, while Italy provided the glass for the capsules and the cables. The wheel's bearings came from Germany, and France constructed the wheel's capsules.

Critical Viewing

Interpreting Maps and Timelines

1. Draw students' attention to the maps on page 1122. **Ask** students what they notice when they compare the size of the British Empire in 1900 with its extent in the second map. What events led to this drastic change?
   Answer: The British Empire has shrunk to the islands that make up the United Kingdom. The two world wars led to this change.
2. Draw students' attention to the London Eye Timeline on the next page. **Ask** the first question on the student page: During what post-war decade did Britain lose most of its colonies?
   Answer: during the 1960s
3. **Ask** the second question on the student page: What are three former colonies that have produced Nobel Prize-winning authors who write in English?
   Possible response: Ireland, South Africa, and Rhodesia/Zimbabwe

PHLit Online!

Show or assign the **Essential Question** video for this unit online at **www.PHLitOnline.com.**

Teaching the Historical Background

The Historical Background section discusses the most significant events of this period: World War I, the Great Depression, World War II, the end of the British Empire, the end of violence in Northern Ireland, and building of a tunnel under the English Channel.

1. Point out that the story of this period is a story of conflicts and the loss of empire.
2. Have students read the Background. Then, **ask** them to identify the challenges the British faced in each of the following developments: World War I, World War II, and Britain's involvement with Europe at the end of the twentieth century. **Possible responses:** World War I resulted in the death of more than 700,000 soldiers, along with the fight for independence by Irish nationalists, which led to prolonged bloodshed throughout the century. World War II resulted in Britain's victory but it left the nation impoverished, and Britain could no longer sustain its empire. Britain cooperated in drilling a tunnel under the English Channel.

Teaching the Timeline

Tell students that the Timeline for the period from 1901 to the present appears on pages 1124–1133 of this Unit Introduction. Each portion of the Timeline identifies and illustrates some of the major events in Britain and in the world for that period.

Background

Economics

World War II left Britain physically battered and economically drained. In 1945, voters put the Labour party in power. The war helped change old attitudes toward the working class. This government nationalized major industries and expanded social welfare benefits, such as unemployment insurance and old-age pensions. They built housing for the poor and a national health service extended free, low-cost medical care to all citizens. Other programs gave aid to the poor and created an economic cushion to help people through hard times. To pay for all these benefits, taxes rose a great deal.

Historical Background

The Modern and Postmodern Periods (1901–Present)

At dusk on August 3, 1914, Sir Edward Grey, the British Foreign Secretary, clutching the telegram announcing the German invasion of Belgium, walked to the window, looked over a darkening London and said: "The lamps are going out all over Europe; we shall not see them lit again in our lifetime." The next day, Britain declared war on Germany.

World War I and Its Long-Lasting Effects

Many said that the war would be brief, with the troops coming home by Christmas. Instead, the war lasted four long years and 750,000 British soldiers never came home at all. World War I, and the flaws in the treaty with which it was finally settled, influenced much of what followed in the twentieth century.

Germany, for example, wanting to get Russia out of the war and thereby win a victory on the Western Front, transported Lenin to St. Petersburg. There, he led the Bolshevik Revolution that altered the course of Russian and European history.

The war also encouraged Irish nationalists to fight for independence in 1916 while the British army was engaged in France. Their attempted rebellion failed and deepened the hatred between the British and Irish. In 1922, the Irish achieved a measure of independence in the south, but fighting between Catholics and Protestants in the northern, British provinces prolonged the bloodshed for the rest of the century.

The Treaty of Versailles, which settled World War I, led to economic collapse and near-anarchy in Germany, paving the way for Hitler to exact revenge on the Allies.

The horrific slaughter of the war and the crippling effects of the Great Depression forced England into a passive role in the 1930s. Once the mightiest nation in the world, England looked on as a re-armed Germany amassed territory in Europe, and as Japan, perceiving Western powers as weak, occupied much of China.

World War I recruiting poster

TIMELINE

1901

1901: Edward VII becomes king. ▶

1903: Orville and Wilbur Wright build first successful airplane.

1905: Germany Albert Einstein proposes theory of relativity. ▶

1914: Britain enters World War I ▶

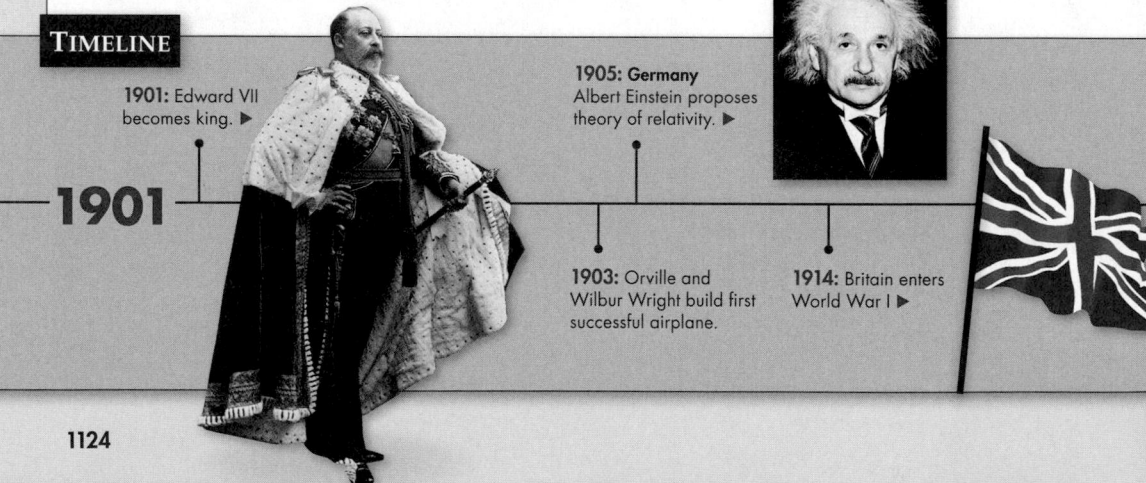

1124

Enrichment: Investigating Popular Culture

The "British Invasion"

In the 1950s, most rock-and-roll music that the British listened to came from the United States. A change developed in the early 1960s when British groups began creating rock-and-roll music of their own. At that time, rock-and-roll music began traveling from Britain to the United States in a movement called the British Invasion. The music of the Beatles, the Rolling Stones, and other British groups became wildly popular.

Activity: Research Report Have students find out more about the British Invasion and its effect on culture in the United States. Students might accompany their reports with examples of the music and the styles from the time period. Suggest that they record their analyses in the **Investigating Popular Culture** worksheet, ***Professional Development Guidebook***, page 238.

World War II and the Loss of the Empire

The aggression of Germany and Japan led inevitably to World War II. When Hitler's armies overran Europe, the English stood defiantly alone, shielded by the English Channel and the Royal Air Force. It was, Winston Churchill said, "their finest hour."

In 1942, Russia blunted the German advance, America was in the war, and the tide turned against the aggressors. After nearly six years of struggle, England emerged from the war victorious, battered, and impoverished.

England's former colonies became independent countries. The Indian subcontinent, where Gandhi had led an independence movement, was divided into the nations of India and Pakistan in 1947.

The imperial British lion gave a dying gasp in 1956 when Britain, France, and Israel invaded Egypt to keep control of the Suez Canal. However, the United States intervened, the Egyptians kept the Canal, and British troops came home to a country ashamed of its government's actions.

Suez was forgotten in the cultural upheaval of the nineteen sixties when British fashion and British rock musicians carried the flag around the world in a kind of cultural conquest. Also, writers from England's former colonies were engaged in their own re-conquest, enriching English literature.

As the century closed, the violence in Northern Ireland seemed to be ending. Also, England pondered its involvement with Europe, not accepting the common currency, the Euro, but cooperating in drilling a tunnel under the English Channel.

Do Sir Edward Grey's words still have a prophetic ring? Many thought the lamps came on again when the Berlin Wall fell. However, countries cobbled together in the aftermath of World War I—Yugoslavia and Iraq—have been the sites of bitter conflict.

Key Historical Theme: Conflicts and the Loss of Empire

- England emerged victorious but weakened from World War I, which influenced events in Europe for years to come.
- England was on the winning side in World War II as well, but it was weakened further and gradually lost all its colonies.

The Spitfire fighter played a major role in defending Britain during World War II.

1917: Austria Sigmund Freud publishes *Introduction to Psychoanalysis.*

◀ **1920: India** Mohandas Gandhi leads nonviolent protests.

1922: Irish Free State formed.

1922

1917: Russia Czar overthrown; Bolsheviks, led by Lenin, seize power. ▶

1918: Women over thirty achieve right to vote in Great Britain.

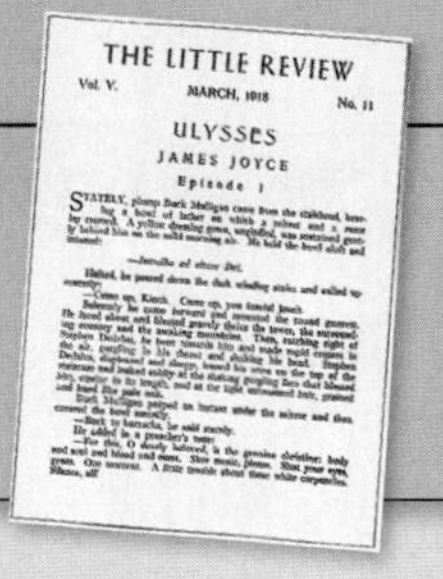
THE LITTLE REVIEW
Vol. V. MARCH, 1918 No. 11
ULYSSES
JAMES JOYCE
Episode I

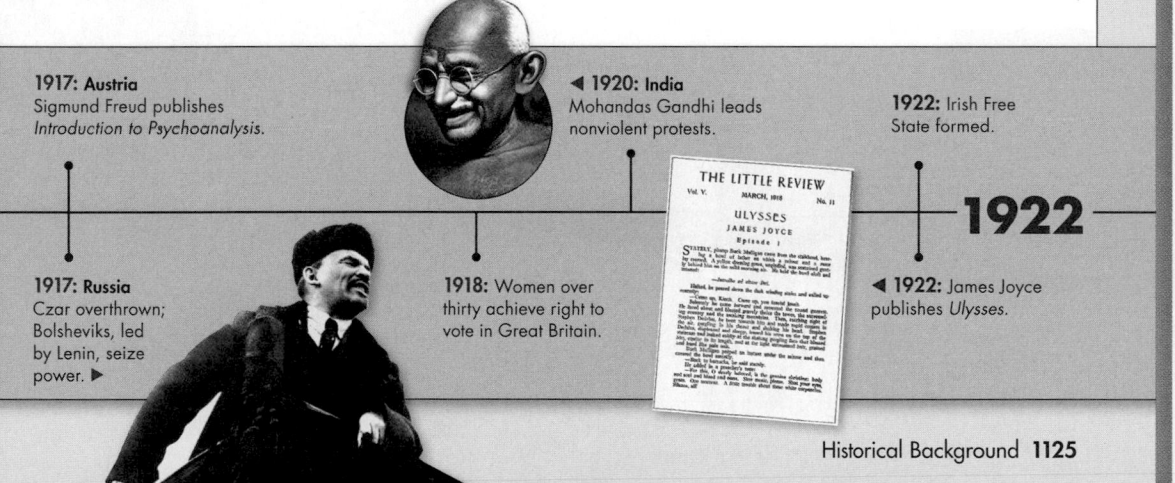

◀ **1922:** James Joyce publishes *Ulysses.*

Differentiated Instruction for Universal Access

Strategy for Less Proficient Readers

Explain to students that during this period, huge wars swept the planet. Instruct them to preview the subheads and the pictures in the Historical Background before reading the selection.

EL Support for English Learners

For each subhead and picture in the Historical Background, have students write a caption as to whether the image concerns war or peacetime, or whether they cannot be sure. Then, have them read the sections, filling in their notes with the name of the war or the important peacetime event that each section concerns.

Strategy for Advanced Readers

Challenge students to trace the events in the Historical Background. What events involve a "forgetting" of the past? What events should be remembered as a warning to the future? What trends attempt to create the utterly new?

Connecting to the Literature

1. To give students a sense of life in the trenches of World War I, and of the effect of war's barbarity on refined sensibilities, have them read the War Poets, Brooke, Sassoon, and Owen, beginning on page 1274.
2. The sufferings of war were widespread during the first half of the twentieth century. W. H. Auden provides a thought-provoking meditation on the place of suffering in art and the world in "Musée des Beaux Arts," page 1176.
3. For a taste of early twentieth-century "quiet despair," students should walk through the brown city smog with T. S. Eliot in the "Preludes," page 1156.
4. Like a ghost returned from the grave, World War II repeated the traumas of World War I—as if nothing had been learned in the meantime. Elizabeth Bowen mirrors the "haunting" of the twentieth century by war in her tale of a woman haunted by her past, "The Demon Lover," page 1298.

Key Historical Theme

1. Explain to students that this section of the Historical Background calls out two major historical themes from the period: international conflict and the loss of empire.
2. **Ask** students to visualize a scene to help them remember these themes.
   Possible response: Possible images for conflict might include an airplane dropping bombs; images of loss of empire might include a map of the Indian subcontinent, with the nations of India and Pakistan labeled.

Critical Viewing

Connect

1. Call students' attention to the illustration of Mohandas Gandhi on the Timeline.
2. **Ask:** What effect do you think Gandhi's nonviolent protests over British rule would have had on the British in India?
   Possible response: It would have worn down the British and eventually led to transition to independence and the end of Britain's overseas empire.

Teaching the Essential Questions

As students read "A Time of Rapid Change," they will examine its information through the lens of three Essential Questions. Each Essential Question is broken down into "stepping-stone" questions. Work through each stepping-stone question with the class. Then have students pose answers to the Essential Question as it applies to the period.

What is the relationship between literature and place?

1. Before they read this section of the essay, tell students that Britain experienced both economic and social changes after World War II.
2. Have students read this section of the essay. Then, pose the stepping-stone question on page 1126. **Ask:** In what ways are the "three Englands" reflected in literature?
   Possible responses: While the English countryside was untouched, the human damage from World War I was reflected in the poetry of the period; large sections of London were destroyed by the bombs of the German blitz, but nothing could break what a contemporary song called "London Pride"; the mythical England, shattered by racial divisions of the postcolonial period, left many in former British colonies feeling betrayed, as in Trinidadian V. S. Naipul's story "B. Wordsworth"; D. H. Lawrence continued the British literary tradition by criticizing the materialism of the period.

Applying the Essential Question

1. Summarize the class discussion of the stepping-stone question.
2. Then **ask** students this question: How have similar conflicts in places such as Vietnam and Iraq affected Americans who lived though those events?
   Possible response: Both of these conflicts have had powerful influences on the American cultural experience. Filmmakers, writers, and historians offer accounts of what happened in Vietnam and in Iraq.

Essential Questions Across Time

A Time of Rapid Change (1901–Present)

What is the relationship between literature and *place?*

England in the twentieth century is, of course, a geographic place—an island nation ravaged and rebuilt to an unprecedented degree. It is also a geopolitical place—a "mother country" that stood as a land of hope and glory to many citizens of her far-flung empire. Lastly, it is a place of imagination, a realm of letters and literature fed by the ever-changing English language.

In what ways are the "three Englands" reflected in literature?

The Land Itself The English landscape was untouched by the terrible destruction of World War I. However, the real devastation was human, as an entire generation of young men was wiped out. The physical and psychological damage of the war is documented in poems by soldier poets.

Postwar Growth and Materialism The most obvious change in the landscape after the war came with the automobile. More people could afford cars, and ribbons of highway covered the landscape. Accompanying this economic growth was a materialistic attitude on the part of many, perhaps inspired by the war's devastation. In his story "The Rocking-Horse Winner" (1926), D. H. Lawrence criticizes such materialism and reveals a stylish home as a place haunted by the need for "more money."

World War II and the Blitz The Blitz, from the German *blitzkrieg,* "lightning warfare," refers to the German bombing of English cities during World War II. Large sections of London were destroyed by bombs and rockets, but nothing could break what a song hailed as "London Pride." Elizabeth Bowen's story "The Demon Lover" reflects not so much the actual damage as

ESSENTIAL QUESTION VOCABULARY

These Essential Question words will help you think and write about literature and place:

generation (jen′ ər ā′ shən) *n.* all the people born and living at the same time

materialism (mə tir′ ē əl iz′ əm) *n.* belief in comfort pleasure, and wealth as the highest values

colonial (kə lō′ nē əl) *adj.* of or relating to the colony or colonies of a mother country

TIMELINE

1922

1927: United States Charles Lindbergh flies solo to Paris. ▼

1939: Europe Hitler invades Poland; World War II begins. ▶

1939: Britain enters World War II. ▼

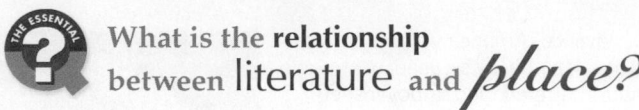

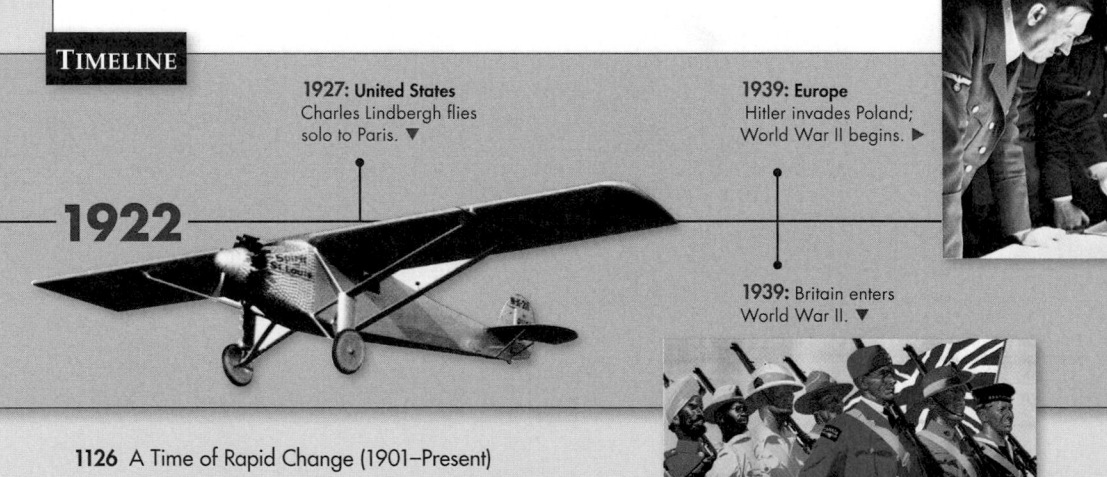

Enrichment: Investigating Daily Life

London During World War II

In preparation for a German invasion of the island, starting in 1940, London experienced frequent bombings by the German air force in a period known as the Blitz. Fires consumed many parts of the city. Residents sought shelter in air-raid shelters and Underground stations. Children were evacuated to the countryside. Londoners dealt with the frequent bombing and tried to maintain normal lives throughout this period.

Activity: Oral Report Have students use the Internet and other sources to research how the bombardment of the Blitz affected daily life in London and the English countryside. Have them present their findings in oral reports. Suggest that they record their analyses in the **Investigating Daily Life** worksheet, ***Professional Development Guidebook,*** page 224.

the psychological aftershocks of this assault. Her wartime London is truly a haunted place.

From the ashes, a new London emerged. Other changes were more problematic. The mill and mining country of the north was no longer the economic heart of the country. Wealth concentrated in the south as banking and technology took command. The economic divide between the rusting north and the booming south grew wider as the century ended. The poet Ted Hughes, a northerner, portrays in his work a vision of nature as both glorious and cruel. That vision may be related to the north-south divide.

The England of Hope and Glory In addition to an economic divide, Britain felt the effects of racial and colonial divisions. In V. S. Naipaul's story "B. Wordsworth," England is the distant land of hope and glory to those living in colonial Trinidad, but the dream may be an empty one.

Until 1950, the typical English man or woman was seen as fair-haired, blue eyed, and Anglican. When people of color, British citizens from the former colonies, began to move to England, the English had to deal with unprecedented diversity. In "Midsummer XXIII," Caribbean poet Derek Walcott writes about riots prompted by racial prejudice.

The Realm of the English Language Walcott also raises questions about the English language itself. To whom does the language and its literary tradition belong? Can writers from former colonies and elsewhere in the world find a home in that language and tradition? The evidence, starting with Walcott's own brilliant work, indicates that the answer is yes.

The **BRITISH TRADITION**

CLOSE-UP ON HISTORY

Planned Town, Unplanned Poet

Sir Ebenezer Howard (1850–1928) was a British social thinker who helped invent the concept of the suburbs. In *Garden Cities of Tomorrow* (1902), Howard described a new kind of planned town surrounded by a ring of farmland. This garden city, as he called it, would combine the advantages of a city with those of the country. Welwyn Garden City, one of the first examples, was built after World War I and inspired the "new towns" that the British government built after World War II. Howard's ideas also inspired Walt Disney's original design for the Experimental Prototype Community of Tomorrow (EPCOT) in Florida.

Unplanned by Howard was the fact that Glyn Maxwell, a talented young poet and playwright, would grow up in a planned town. Humorously calling himself the "Shakespeare of Welwyn Garden City," Maxwell often alludes to Welwyn in his poetry. He has also been known to stage what he calls "large pageant like shows" in his parents' garden. Given Maxwell's skilled use of poetic forms, perhaps it is true that Sir Ebenezer's talent for planning influenced him after all.

1940: Winston Churchill becomes prime minister. ▶

1941: United States Japan bombs Pearl Harbor; United States enters World War II. ▲

1943

The British Tradition

Close-Up on History

1. Have students read the sidebar feature about Sir Ebenezer Howard's planned town and how it affected Glyn Maxwell and his poetry and plays.
2. Tell students that Howard's plan influenced urban planning throughout the world.
3. **Ask** students how Howard's idea for a garden city, which would combine the advantages of a city and the country, is similar to and different from today's suburbs.
   Possible response: Howard's plan for a garden city is similar to a suburb in that it called for combining the advantages of living in the city with the advantages of living in the country. The plan is different from a suburb in that suburbs are generally not surrounded by farmland.

Critical Viewing

Analyze

1. Call students' attention to the photograph of Winston Churchill in the Timeline.
2. **Ask:** What effect did this man's leadership have on England during World War II?
   Possible response: After the fall of France, Britain stood alone defying Hitler. Churchill's leadership enabled the British to defend their island nation and withstand the German Blitz.

Differentiated Instruction for Universal Access

Culturally Responsive Instruction

Culture Focus Students may lack the background knowledge and context-building experiences necessary to comprehend the selection. Before students read, build background knowledge about World War I and the London Blitz. Provide images of the trench warfare during World War I, the deserted No-Man's-Land beyond the barbed wire trenches, the gas masks the men wore, and the devastation of London wrought by the German bombing raids. Discuss how these experiences would have affected the people who lived through them. Explain that Americans had their own planned suburban communities after World War II. Show pictures of Levittown, New York, and point out how it and communities like it changed the American landscape. Then, have students read the essay about the impact of similar events on British literature.

Teaching the Essential Question

How does literature shape or reflect society?

1. Before they read this section, explain to students that the Modern and Postmodern periods saw vast social changes in Britain. One of the strongest socialist movements involved the campaign for women's voting rights.
2. Have students read this section of the essay. Then, pose the first stepping-stone question. **Ask:** In what ways did literature reflect new social freedoms?
   Answer: Virginia Woolf's experimental fiction broke new ground and explored social conditions that helped women succeed in the arts.
3. Then, **ask** the second stepping-stone question: How did writers respond to social crises?
   Possible response: Poets like Auden, MacNeice, and Spender wrote in response to political dishonesty in the Great Depression and Spanish Civil War. Orwell attacked fascism in novels like *Animal Farm* and *1984*.

Critical Viewing

Speculate

1. Call students' attention to the photograph of the mushroom cloud of the atomic bomb shown in the Timeline.
2. **Ask:** How do you think the explosion of the A-bombs that ended World War II affected the literature of the period?
   Possible response: People were probably shocked at the devastation unleashed by atomic weapons. It would have produced speculative fiction about the impact of such weapons on a future international conflict, on the planet, and on the environment.

How does literature shape or reflect *society?*

In what ways did literature reflect new social freedoms?

Women as Bicyclists At the end of the nineteenth and beginning of the twentieth century, the craze for cycling swept England and the Continent. Cycling required a drastic change in the way women dressed. The new freedom in clothing was, however, only a part of the change in pre-World War I England. The strongest social movement of the time was the campaign for women's right to vote. The Suffragettes, women who crusaded for the vote, chained themselves to buildings and went on hunger strikes when arrested. Their victory was slow in coming, but by 1918 women over the age of thirty could vote.

Women as Writers The work of novelist Virginia Woolf revealed a new freedom that women were finding in literature as well. Woolf's experimental fiction broke new ground, and her nonfiction explored the social conditions that would help women succeed in the arts.

The bicycle as product and the right to vote as principle were part of the century-long process of loosening the rigid rules of class, propriety, and morality that had bound the Victorians. This process applied to such areas as access to higher education, health care, marriage laws and customs for ordinary people and the monarchy, home ownership, pensions, and working conditions.

How did writers respond to social crises?

War and Social Change The war of 1914 put most questions of social change on hold, but the men who were "demobbed" (demobilized or discharged) and the women who had coped without them were not going to settle for the old ways. As soldier-poet Siegfried Sassoon wrote of one patrol, "night's misery is ended." However, the years-long "misery" of the war would not be forgotten by those who returned. The

TIMELINE

1943

1945: Japan The United States drops atomic bombs on Hiroshima and Nagasaki. World War II ends as Japan surrenders. ▼

1947: India and Pakistan gain independence.

1948: Middle East Israel established.

1949: China Mao Zedong establishes People's Republic. ▲

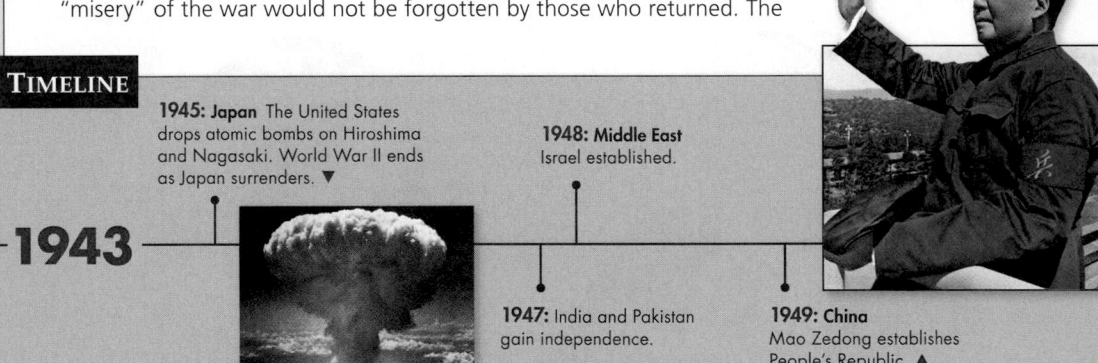

Enrichment: Investigating Language

Other English Dialects

The divisions in English do not stop with the distance between Britain and the United States. Various regions of Britain still have their own distinctive accents, vocabularies, and idioms, as do regions of the United States. Additionally, English, like other languages, has developed a variety of jargon and slang—words and expressions that are used by people practicing a profession or similar lifestyles.

Activity: Research Have students research vocabulary that is particular to a certain region, group, or profession. Direct them to indicate words that have become fashionable with a group wider than the one that introduced them, or have even become part of the larger "official" English language. Suggest that they record their analyses in the **Investigating Language** worksheet from the ***Professional Development Guidebook***, page 234.

aristocracy would have to make do with many fewer servants as men and women found work in new industries (automotive), new jobs (radio), and new forms of entertainment (movies). Higher hemlines and shorter hair signaled that women were freer than ever.

Writers and Politics Then came the 1930s, called by poet W. H. Auden "a low dishonest decade." Auden and fellow poets Louis MacNeice and Stephen Spender responded to such crises as The Great Depression and the Spanish Civil War. In that conflict, the Communist and Fascist tyrannies sparred, foreshadowing the conflict that would come in World War II. Especially shocking was the Nazi-Soviet treaty, a cynical pretense at peace by the totalitarian powers. Men and women on the left and the right were sickened by the callousness of it. Left-wing writer George Orwell, who fought in Spain, would later attack totalitarianism of all kinds in books like *Animal Farm* and *1984*.

Speeches and Poems When war broke out, British Prime Minister Winston Churchill rallied the people for the supreme effort required of them. His radio broadcasts and other speeches—"I have nothing to offer but blood, toil, tears, and sweat"—were classics of their kind. The war indeed brought blood and tears, and the bombs and rockets made all the British combatants and casualties. Literary descendants of the World War I soldier poets, writers like Keith Douglas and Alun Lewis, recorded the cost of conflict.

The BRITISH TRADITION

THE CHANGING ENGLISH LANGUAGE, BY RICHARD LEDERER

Britspeak, A to Zed

At the end of World War II, Winston Churchill tells us, the Allied leaders nearly came to blows over a single word during their negotiations when some diplomats suggested that it was time to "table" an important motion. For the British, table meant that the motion should be put on the table for discussion. For the Americans it meant just the opposite—that it should be put on the shelf and dismissed from discussion.

This confusion serves to illustrate the truth of George Bernard Shaw's pronouncement that "England and America are two countries divided by a common language."

When an American exclaims, "I'm mad about my flat," he is upset about his tire. When a Brit exclaims, "I'm mad about my flat," she's not bemoaning the puncture of her "tyre"; she is delighted with her apartment. When a Brit points out that you have "a ladder in your hose," the situation is not as bizarre as you might at first think. Quite simply, you have a run in your stocking.

With the increasing influence of film, radio, television, and international travel, the two main streams of the English language are rapidly converging like the streets of a circus (British for "traffic circle"). Nonetheless, there are scores of words, phrases, and spellings about which Brits and Yanks still do not agree.

1955: United States Martin Luther King, Jr., leads civil rights bus boycott. ▶

1961: Germany Berlin Wall built.

1964: Vietnam American involvement in the Vietnam War grows.

◀ **1957: Russia** Sputnik I, first satellite, launched.

1963: United States President John F. Kennedy assassinated. ▶

The New York Times.
KENNEDY IS KILLED BY SNIPER AS HE RIDES IN CAR IN DALLAS; JOHNSON SWORN IN ON PLANE

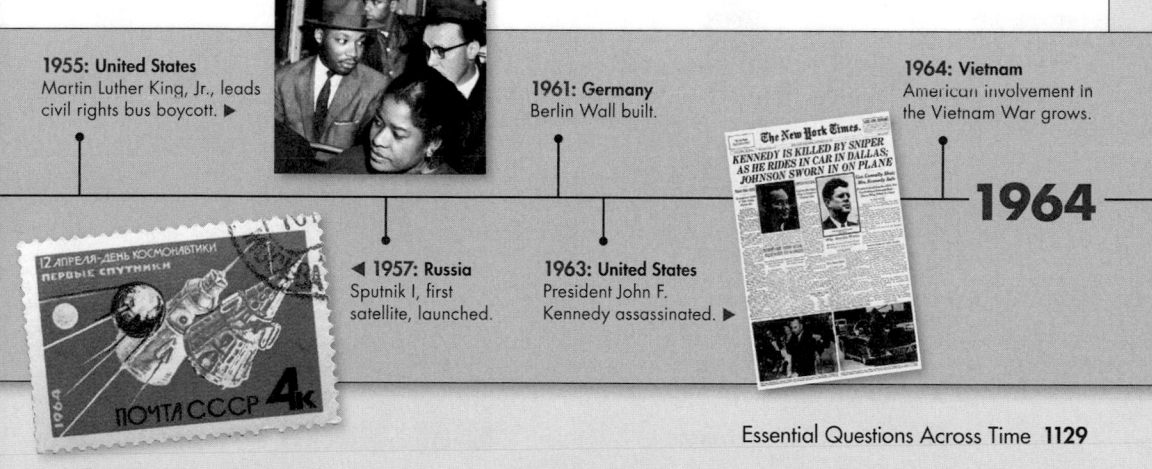

1964

The British Tradition

The Changing English Language

1. Have students read the sidebar feature about the differences in the English language as spoken in the United States and in Britain.
2. Then, **ask** students to name a television program produced in Britain that is shown on American television. Ask them if the dialogue is difficult to follow and to explain where difficulties arise.
   Possible response: Students may name *Masterpiece Theater, Are You Being Served?, The Benny Hill Show,* and *Mr. Bean.* At times the dialogue is difficult to follow if the same words mean something different or speakers use different words to describe the same thing.
3. Then, **ask** students to define the following words in American English first, then British English: *biscuit, braces, chemist, chips, crisp, lift, plaster, pudding, spectacles, tin, torch.*
   Possible response: British definitions: *biscuit* means *cookie; braces, suspenders; chemist, drugstore; chips, French fries; crisp, potato chip; lift, elevator; plaster, bandaid; pudding, sausage; spectacles, eyeglasses; tin, can; torch, flashlight*

Differentiated Instruction for Universal Access

Strategy for Special-Needs Students
Some students may find this account of the relationship between literature and society difficult to follow. Encourage these students to read sections of the text in small groups chorally to improve their comprehension.

Enrichment for Gifted/Talented Students
Have these students research other expressions in which British and American English differ and to make posters illustrating the differences they find. Display the posters around the room. Have students present their posters to the class.

Enrichment for Advanced Readers
Have advanced readers research additional words, phrases, and spellings where American and British English differ sharply. Ask each student to write an imaginary dialogue about an encounter between a Brit and a Yank tourist illustrating these differences.

Teaching the Essential Question

(cont.)

4. **Ask** the third and final stepping-stone question: How did music and literature respond to social changes?
   Possible response: Musicians and poets of the 1960s responded to new freedoms, the civil rights movement, and the Vietnam conflict by criticizing the establishment and introducing new musical styles.

Applying the Essential Question

1. Summarize the class discussion of the stepping-stone questions.
2. Then, **ask** students this question: Do you think contemporary literature is more likely to produce or reflect the changes in modern society? Explain.
   Possible response: Some students may suggest modern literature helps shape society. Others may feel it is more likely to reflect society's values. Students should support their answers with examples.

© COMMON CORE ▪ MULTIPLE PERSPECTIVES ON THE ERA

As soon as the war had ended, however, Churchill was voted out of office and the returning veterans and the survivors of the bombings demanded a new kind of welfare state. Recovery was slow and England was struggling when the twenty-five-year-old Elizabeth became Queen in 1952. She reminded many of Victoria, another shy young woman who had become queen more than a century before, and suddenly things looked brighter.

The Rolling Stones in performance

How did music and literature respond to social changes?

Music and Literature in the Sixties Things were at their brightest in the next decade: the swinging sixties. The Greek philosopher Plato once said: "When the modes of music change, the walls of the city are shaken." The walls were rocked by the Beatles and the Rolling Stones. Not as famous as these songwriters and singers, poets like Ted Hughes and Peter Redgrove nevertheless opened their minds and their styles to a wide range of new influences.

The pendulum slowed in the eighties. Margaret Thatcher, a Conservative Party member and the first female prime minister, reversed many of the socio-economic changes of the previous twenty-five years. Early in her administration, the army and navy crushed Argentina's attempt to seize the Falkland Islands in the South Atlantic. This was the final flick of the imperial lion's tail. She was succeeded by fellow Conservative John Major, but the Labor Party came back into power with Tony Blair's election in 1997.

Literature Celebrates Diversity More capitalistic, more technological, and much more multiracial, the England of Tony Blair entered the twenty-first century in style. That style was maintained in literature as well, as Zadie Smith's acclaimed first novel, *White Teeth* (2000), welcomed the new millennium with a comic celebration of diversity.

ESSENTIAL QUESTION VOCABULARY

These Essential Question words will help you think and write about literature and society:

propriety (prō prī´ ə tē) *n.* display of proper manners or behavior

aristocracy (ar i stä´ krə sē) *n.* ruling class; nobility

fascism (fash´ iz´ əm) *n.* type of government ruled by one party, which puts down all opposition

TIMELINE

1964

1967: The Beatles release *Sgt. Pepper's Lonely Hearts Club Band.* ▲

1969: United States Apollo 11 lands on moon. ▼

1972: Britain imposes direct rule on Northern Ireland.

1975: North Sea oil production begins.

Think Aloud

Vocabulary: Using Context

Direct students' attention to the word *pendulum* in the third paragraph on this page. Use the following "think aloud" to model the skill of using context to infer the meaning of the word. Say to students:

A good way to figure out the meaning of an unknown word is to look carefully at the sentence in which it appears and also to look at sentences before and after it. I may not know the meaning of the word *pendulum* as it is used here. The following sentences discuss changes and reversals that have occurred in Britain in the past 25 years. So I realize that the writer is using *pendulum* here to describe something that changes direction or alternates between opposites.

What is the relationship of the writer to *tradition?*

In the twentieth century, the English literary tradition became more accessible and more inclusive. It was more accessible because inexpensive editions of books and the Internet made all of English literature instantly available for writers and readers. It was more inclusive because writers from the former colonies were now enriching the tradition.

How did writers connect with and renew traditions?

Poet as Prophet It was an "outsider," for example, who, following the examples of Romantic poets Blake and Shelley, continued the tradition of prophetic poetry. Irish poet William Butler Yeats summed up the fears of the century in "The Second Coming": "Things fall apart; the center cannot hold . . ."

New Uses for Traditional Forms Twentieth-century writers found new uses for traditional forms such as the sonnet. In twentieth-century hands, the sonnet dealt with experiences undreamed of by the Elizabethans. The radical change in subject matter and tone can be seen by comparing sonnets written by two different World War I poets. The young and dashing Rupert Brooke wrote, in "The Soldier," of the idealism that spurred many of his generation. However, Wilfred Owen's sonnet "Anthem for Doomed Youth" tells what happened when those idealistic young men encountered the turmoil of the Western Front: "What passing bells for those who die as cattle?"

Echoes of Romanticism Although Ted Hughes's lyric "The Horses" differs in many ways from William Wordsworth's "Tintern Abbey," we can still hear an echo of Wordsworth in Hughes's celebration of nature and his distrust of cities.

The Blossoming of the Modern Short Story The modern short story was invented in the nineteenth century. In the twentieth century, however, it became a global genre. Just a few examples will show how authors were setting their tales everywhere and anywhere in the world: James

◀ **1977: Africa** Djibouti, last remaining European colony, granted independence.

1979: Iran Ayatollah Khomeini overthrows Shah. ▶

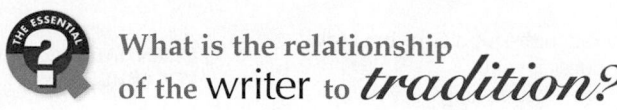

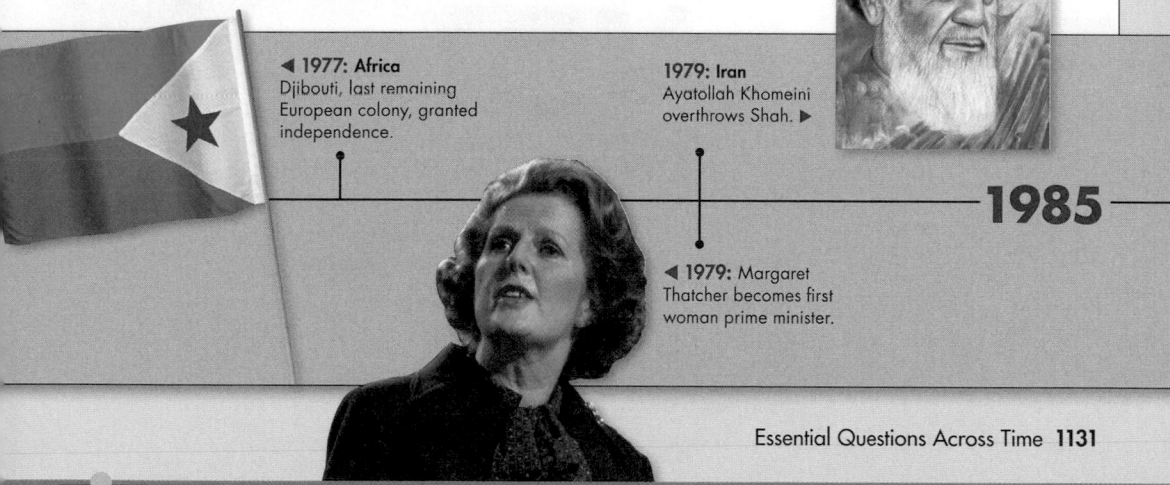

◀ **1979:** Margaret Thatcher becomes first woman prime minister.

1985

Differentiated Instruction for Universal Access

Strategy for Less Proficient Readers
To help students sift through this information-packed text, encourage them to break the text into manageable chunks and to read them one at a time. Have them stop and ask themselves questions such as: What does this tell me about the history or literature of this time?

EL Vocabulary for English Learners
Have students skim this selection together and compile a list of unfamiliar vocabulary words. Give a brief overview of what is being described in each section. Then help students define unfamiliar vocabulary words and ideas as they read.

Enrichment for Gifted/Talented Students
Encourage musically talented students to set some of the poetry from this unit to music. Suggest that they use some of the tunes from the 1960s rock era and record or present dramatic readings for the class.

Teaching the Essential Question

What is the relationship of the writer to tradition?

1. Before they read this section, explain to students that during this time, British literature became more accessible, due to the Internet, and more inclusive, because of the writers from former English colonies adding to the literary tradition.
2. Have students read this section of the essay. Then, **ask** the first stepping-stone question: How did writers connect with and renew traditions?
   Possible responses: Writers like Yeats continued the tradition of prophetic poetry that began with Milton. Writers found new uses for traditional forms of literature. For example, writers such as Rupert Brooke and Wilfred Owen wrote sonnets, but the subject matter differed greatly from the sonnets of the past. Echoes of Romanticism can be heard in modern poets' distrust of cities and celebration of nature. The short story, which was invented in the nineteenth century, became a global genre during this time period, with story settings from all parts of the world. The subjects of the short stories also varied greatly.

Critical Viewing

Speculate

1. Call students' attention to the photograph of the American astronaut on the Timeline.
2. **Ask:** How do you think the moon landing affected literature of this period?
   Possible response: It probably increased public interest in science fiction as a genre. It also produced entertaining nonfiction narrative accounts of the moon landings and the results of exploratory space probes.

Teaching the Essential Question (cont.)

3. Then, **ask** the second stepping-stone question: How did well-crafted poetry capture an unruly world?
   Possible response: Poets such as Seamus Heaney used a well-ordered poem to describe the continuing violence in Ireland. The repetitions in the poem stir up images of the repeated violence.
4. Then, **ask** the third stepping-stone question: What happens to literary traditions in tumultuous times?
   Possible response: They may cause changes in the literary tradition, but they can also result in writers trying to make connections to link the present with the past.

Background

Sestina

The sestina, also known as a sextain, is a sophisticated form of poetry. The structure of this kind of poem consists of thirty-nine lines: six six-line stanzas, ending with a three-line shorter stanza called a tornada. Each line in a stanza recycles the same six words.

Applying the Essential Question

1. Summarize discussion of the three stepping-stone questions on pages 1131–1132.
2. Then, **ask** students what topics short-story writers of today might focus on. Ask them to describe possible settings for the stories.
   Possible response: Students might suggest that short-story writers today might focus on current conflicts in the world, environmental issues, or social concerns. The settings might include the places in which the conflicts or concerns are taking place.

Joyce in the streets of Dublin, Joseph Conrad in the jungles of the Malay Archipelago, and Doris Lessing on the Rhodesian veldt.

The subjects of these stories are as varied as their settings. Joyce writes about the coming of age of an infatuated boy. D. H. Lawrence, in "The Rocking-Horse Winner, tells a chilling story of twisted love and destructive greed. Elizabeth Bowen's "The Demon Lover" links both of the World Wars in a few evocative pages. Doris Lessing and Nadine Gordimer deal with the thorny cultural and racial problems of a fading empire.

How did well-crafted poetry capture an unruly world?

A Sestina on "The Troubles" Poets Seamus Heaney, from Northern Ireland, and Derek Walcott, from St. Lucia, both use well-ordered poetry to express the world's disorder. In the sestina "Two Lorries," Heaney writes of the lingering violence in Ireland resulting from an incomplete separation, violence known as "the Troubles." At first glance, a sestina, with its intricate pattern of repeated end words, seems like the wrong form for capturing such a gritty reality. In this poet's hands, however, the repetitions evoke a repeated nightmare of violence that cannot be shaken.

In "Midsummer XXIII," Walcott writes about the violent racism experienced by people of color in "antic England." Like Heaney's, his poem is deeply rooted in the English poetic tradition—it is filled with allusions to earlier work—but also expresses bitter contemporary realities.

What happens to literary traditions in tumultuous times?

Traditions change, especially in times of conflict, but they also endure and connect a living present with a vital past. T. S. Eliot said that any individual talent is best understood in terms of the tradition within which that talent is working. Eliot, who served as an air-raid warden during the Blitz, wrote his poem "Little Gidding" during that dark time. This work links a perilous present to the literary past by invoking Shelley and Milton and the recently deceased Joyce and Yeats, a communion of writers. It invokes them at "the intersection of" a "timeless moment" that somehow contains both past and present—"the timeless moment" of a work of art.

ESSENTIAL QUESTION VOCABULARY

These Essential Question words will help you think and write about the writer and tradition:

inclusive (in kloo͞′ siv) *adj.* tending to include; taking everything into account

evocative (ē väk′ ə tiv) *adj.* calling up a particular image or reaction

allusions (ə loo͞′ zhənz) *n.* indirect references

TIMELINE

1985

1989: Germany Berlin Wall torn down; reunification of East and West Germany follows. ▶

1994: South Africa Nelson Mandela elected president. ▶

1986: Soviet Union Nuclear accident occurs in Chernobyl. ▶

1991: Eastern Europe Soviet Union dissolved.

Enrichment: Analyzing a Historical Event

End of the Cold War

During World War II, the Soviet Union and Western nations cooperated to defeat Nazi Germany. By 1945, the wartime alliance crumbled. Conflicting ideologies and distrust led to the Cold War. The Soviets installed communist governments in Eastern Europe. The United States and its allies engaged in an arms race with the Soviets. From 1989 to 1991, the Cold War came to an abrupt end. The Berlin Wall, a symbol of the Cold War, was torn down. Soon after, communist dictatorships in Europe collapsed and the Soviet Union fell apart.

Activity: Multimedia Report Ask students to research the events that led to the end of the Cold War. Have them find visuals and sound recordings to enhance the information. Suggest that they record their analyses in the **Analyzing a Historic Event** worksheet from the ***Professional Development Guidebook,*** page 230.

The
BRITISH TRADITION

CONTEMPORARY CONNECTION

George Orwell: More Relevant Than Ever!

Big Brother, Newspeak, and *doublethink* are words that probably sound familiar because you hear them frequently. They were all coined in the 1940s by British author George Orwell for his novel *1984* (published in 1949). After World War II, Orwell was alarmed by a trend toward repressive totalitarian rule. Believing that language is the first weapon dictators use to seize power, he employed his own words as a warning. In the futuristic tyranny portrayed in his novel, words are used to obscure and destroy meaning:

- The official language, *Newspeak,* has been stripped of meaning.
- The tyrannical ruler is deceptively named *Big Brother.*
- Dissenters face torture in the innocently named *Room 101.*
- Citizens are adept at *doublethink,* the ability to accept blatant contradictions, as in the government declaration "War is Peace."

Sixty years later, these terms and others coined by Orwell still ring true. In fact, Orwell's own name is used as an adjective, *Orwellian,* to describe this kind of abuse of language. Pundits, reporters, citizens, and bloggers alike use Orwell's words to criticize Orwellian practices. The year 1984 has come and gone, but Orwell's words live on.

1997: United Kingdom signs Kyoto Protocol against global warming.

2001: United States Hijacked planes crash into the World Trade Center in New York, the Pentagon in Washington, D.C., and a field in rural Pennsylvania. Thousands of lives are lost. ▶

Present

1997: Tony Blair becomes Prime Minister.

◀ **2004:** Tsunami devastates Southeast Asia.

1133

The British Tradition

Contemporary Connection

1. Have students read the sidebar feature about the words that George Orwell introduced to the English language in his novel *1984.*
2. *Then,* **ask** students to find examples of the way the term *Big Brother* is used today. Students might first find the definition of the term in the dictionary, then find examples of the term being used in recent newspaper or magazine articles. Students might point out that *Big Brother* is used today to refer to government surveillance of various groups or individuals. Have students present their articles to the class, and hold a class discussion about the context of the references.

Critical Viewing

Draw Conclusions

1. Call students' attention to the photograph of the World Trade Center bombings in the Timeline.
2. **Ask:** How might these turbulent events affect the literary tradition?
Possible response: They may lead to people trying to reach out and share their emotional responses to world terrorism and the Trade Center bombings with the global community via their writing.

Differentiated Instruction for Universal Access

Strategies for Special-Needs Students

These students may benefit from creating their own outlines to help master this unit's treatment of the three Essential Questions. The main entries of the outline should consist of each of the three Essential Questions. The first subheadings of the outline should consist of the stepping-stone questions for each of the Essential Questions. The second subheadings should consist of details that answer the stepping-stone questions. Students might work with partners to create their outlines.

Enrichment for Gifted/Talented Students

Have artistic students put together collages that illustrate the times and events referred to in this Unit Introduction. The collages should focus on the entire time covered by the Unit. Have students work in small groups and use newspaper headlines, magazine photographs, and self-made drawings to include in their collages. Display completed collages, and hold a class discussion of how the collages depict the time period.

Recent Scholarship

Anita Desai

1. Anita Desai introduces the unit and provides insights into the impact of British language and culture on Indian society. Her own selection, "A Devoted Son," appears later in the unit on pages 1420–1429.
2. Have students read the introductory paragraph about Anita Desai. Tell them that characters in Desai's work struggle with tradition, isolation, and the modern world. She represents a new literary phase in Indian writing because she writes in English.
3. Use the ***See It!*** **DVD** to introduce Anita Desai. Show Segment 1 to provide insight into her writing career. You can also view the video from this page in the **Enriched Online Student Edition** at **www.PHLitOnline.com.**
4. After students have watched the segment, **ask** if they feel Desai made the right decision not to use America as a setting in her work.
   Possible response: Students should provide reasons for their answers.

PHLit Online!

All video resources are available online at **www.PHLITOnline.com.**

© COMMON CORE • MULTIPLE PERSPECTIVES ON THE ERA

Recent Scholarship

ANITA DESAI

The English Language Takes Root in India

The Portuguese, the Dutch, and the French all came to India as traders. So did the British, but they stayed to govern. To trade and to govern, you need a common language with the people. In the French colony of Pondicherry, people were taught French; in the Portuguese colony of Goa, Portuguese. In the rest of India, a few English people did learn some Indian languages—in order to compile dictionaries and to translate the Bible—but it was largely left to Indians to learn English if they wanted jobs or to do business. So schools were set up across the country to teach the English language and also its literature.

Two Languages and Two Worlds to Occupy

I went to such a school myself, Queen Mary's School for Girls in Old Delhi. I was taught to read and write English before my own language, Hindi, and my first books were of English nursery rhymes and fairy stories. This was curious because they had nothing at all to do with our Indian world—its plants and animals, its festivals and seasons—but they did provide me with a rich, imagined world, in addition to the one we lived in and knew. And at home, with our families and neighbors, we spoke our own language. So there were always two languages and two worlds to occupy.

About the Author

Introducing Anita Desai (b. 1937) Born to a German mother and an Ind father, Desai spoke German at home New Delhi, conversed in Hindi with friends, and learned English in school Her works, written in English, often c with the conflict between tradition ar contemporary life.

I went on to read the English classics—Jane Austen and George Eliot, Charles Dickens and Henry James—as well as other literatures translated into English. And all the time, I was writing my own books about my own world—but in this other language, English.

Expressing Indian Thoughts in This Foreign Language, English

There were other Indian writers in those years who were also doing so, while continuing to draw upon the rich Indian-language literatures. Each of us had to experiment to find out how to express Indian thoughts and experiences in this foreign language. Sometimes, we had to combine the languages if, say, we were describing an Indian ceremony or a meal for which there were no English words.

After India won independence in 1947, writing in English was looked on with scorn. The English were gone, so why were we still using their language? We found ourselves having to explain how, after three hundred years, a language could not simply vanish or be thrown aside. It had established roots in India and by now had a tradition—not as old as the literary traditions in the Indian languages but still, a living, growing one that belonged to our own complicated times.

A New Form of the Language: Indian English

Then, in 1980, a book called *Midnight's Children* by Salman Rushdie was published. It was based on our own themes—the fight for freedom and the birth of two nations, India and Pakistan—and used our own epics, the *Mahabharata* and the *Ramayana* as sources. But it was written in the polyglot language of the Indian streets, of newspapers and shop signs, the cinema and school grounds. It was a bold, noisy, loud, and funny language. Rushdie's work won the Booker Prize, which showed that the English, too, were ready to read this new form of their language—Indian English.

It gave many young writers in India the confidence to use Indian English. So things came together at last, and now there is as lively a literature in English as in Bengali and Tamil, Urdu and Hindi, to name just a few of the Indian languages. If you look into it, I think you will find it as crowded and colorful and bustling as an Indian market or fair.

Indian women cheer Lord and Lady Mountbatten, who are followed by Pandit Nehru, the Indian prime minister. This ceremony marks the British departure from India, a newly independent nation (June 25, 1948).

Speaking and Listening: Collaboration

Anita Desai describes the language she uses in her work as a new form of English—Indian English. With a group of classmates, develop a **presentation** on the varieties of English in your school or community. These varieties may include versions of English with different degrees of formality, types of English used by different age groups, and types of English influenced by other languages. Develop a *comprehensive flexible search plan,* using *clear research questions* and *strategies* like these:

- Oral histories—in-depth interviews with individuals
- Field studies—observation and notetaking in public places
- Surveys—use of questionnaires to obtain information from numbers of people

Take steps to ensure that your interviews, observations, and questionnaires are *objective* and *free from bias*—that they don't reflect prejudice against any language uses. Finally, summarize your findings in a presentation to your classmates.

Speaking and Listening: Collaboration

Develop a Presentation

1. Review the assignment with students.
2. Have students discuss the different varieties of English they will include in their presentations. Remind them they are to develop a *comprehensive flexible search plan* using *clear research questions* and *strategies.*
3. After students prepare their presentations, have them present in class. Invite students to share their responses.
4. To help guide the development and discussion of the presentations, use the Discussion Guide in the ***Professional Development Guidebook,*** page 65.

ASSESS

Common Core State Standards

- **Reading Informational Text 7**
- **Speaking and Listening 4, 6**

Integrate and Evaluate Information

1. Review the chart assignment with the class. Then, ask students to use the Activity A chart in the **Follow-Through** worksheet (p. 6 in ***Unit 6 Resources***) to complete this activity.
   Possible responses: Literature and Society: Key Concept—Writers and politics; Author or Group—George Orwell. Writer and Tradition: Key Concept—New uses for traditional forms; Author or Group—Rupert Brooke.
2. **Possible responses:** The photo of Margaret Thatcher on p. 1131 reflects a key social change: the women's rights movement. The images of Hitler and the soldiers on p. 1126 illustrate World War II, which marked the beginning of the end of the Empire. Still, Britain emerged victorious, thanks to technological innovations such as the Spitfire fighter plane shown on p. 1125.
3. **Possible response:** The Empire began to fall apart during World War II, which depleted Britain's resources and stirred up unrest in its colonies. A botched maneuver in the Suez Canal further weakened Britain's world power. In the post-colonial decades, the "center" of the English language has also flown apart as writers in former colonies use local dialects of English to depict their cultures and experiences.
4. Students may contrast the slang-driven English they speak with friends with the more formal English they speak at school; if they speak multiple languages, they may explain when they use each. Students may also note new forms of shorthand used in electronic communications.

COMMON CORE ▪ MULTIPLE PERSPECTIVES ON THE ERA

Integrate and Evaluate Information

1. Use a chart like the one shown to determine the key ideas expressed in the Essential Question essays on pages 1126–1132. Fill in two ideas related to each Essential Question and note the author or group most closely associated with each concept. One example has been done for you.

Essential Question	Key Concept	Author or Group
Literature and Place	Bombing of England in WWII	Winston Churchill
Literature and Society		
Writer and Tradition		

2. For England, as for much of the world, the twentieth century was a time of dramatic social, political, and technological change. Choose three visual sources from this section, one reflecting each kind of change. Describe the image and explain its impact on England during this period.
3. In "The Second Coming," William Butler Yeats wrote that "Things fall apart; the center cannot hold...." How do these words describe the British Empire over the course of the twentieth century? Explain, citing evidence from the multiple sources presented on pages 1122–1133.
4. **Address a Question:** Anita Desai grew up speaking three different languages—German at home, Hindi with friends, and English at school. Even if you speak only one language, you probably use different versions of that language in various social contexts. Explain how you use different "languages" in your life, using information from "Britspeak, A to Zed" on page 1129 as well as other sources to support your ideas.

Speaking and Listening: Book Talk

Authors from former British colonies who write in English often use language that reflects their countries of origin. With a partner, prepare a **book talk** illustrating this idea. Choose four or five contemporary writers from countries such as India, Jamaica, Nigeria, Pakistan, and South Africa. Prepare a talk in which you discuss connections between the authors' cultural experiences and their writing.

Solve a Research Problem: This assignment requires you to research and synthesize a great deal of complex material. Work with your partner to formulate a research plan that includes the authors' writings, biographical materials, and reviews. Consult both print and electronic sources. For each author you cover, provide the following content:

- Name, with correct pronunciation; date of birth; native country
- Titles of one or two books, with brief summaries
- Clear explanation, using formal English, of the author's style, subject matter, and cultural influences
- Brief recitation from the author's work to show the influence of place

Common Core State Standards

Reading Informational Text
7. Integrate and evaluate multiple sources of information presented in different media or formats as well as in words in order to address a question or solve a problem.

Speaking and Listening
4. Present information, findings, and supporting evidence, conveying a clear and distinct perspective.
6. Adapt speech to a variety of contexts and tasks, demonstrating a command of formal English when indicated or appropriate.

ESSENTIAL QUESTION VOCABULARY

Use these words in your responses:

Literature and Place
generation
materialism
colonial

Literature and Society
propriety
aristocracy
fascism

Writer and Tradition
inclusive
evocative
allusions

Speaking and Listening

1. Review the assignment, pointing out that students are to create a book talk illustrating the use of the English language by authors from former British colonies.
2. Analyze the activity and identify its key terms: *countries of origin; book talk; contemporary writers; cultural experiences; influence of place.*
3. Then, have students complete Activity B in the **Follow-Through** worksheet (p. 6 in ***Unit 6 Resources***).
4. After students have written their book talks, have pairs present their talks to the class. Ask students to evaluate each book talk. Evaluations should focus on how thoroughly the book talk addresses the items in the bulleted list in the **Speaking and Listening** box.

Forging Modernism

PART 1

Selection Planning Guide

The selections in this section present the great writers of the twentieth century confronting disillusionment—and the renewal of perception to which disillusionment sometimes leads. Yeats charts the dreams of love, age, and art, as well as the nightmare of history. Disenchantment with modern life finds its own voice in T. S. Eliot's poems. Poets Auden, MacNeice, and Spender question the task of poetry.

Humanities

Woman with Hair Net, 1938, by Pablo Picasso (1881–1973)

Born in Spain, Pablo Picasso studied art in Madrid before arriving in Paris as a young adult. Widely recognized for establishing the Cubist movement, his work includes paintings, collages, etchings, sculptures, stage designs, and ceramics.

Use these questions for discussion:

1. The modern period was marked by hopelessness and disillusionment in response to the ills of society. How might such feelings have provoked artists and writers to question the purpose of the painting or poem?
   Possible response: They may have felt powerless to ease the pain of a broken world. Conveying anguish through self-expression was the only thing left in the artist's control.
2. How does Picasso's innovation with Cubism indicate a weariness of convention and a renewal of perception that is common to Modernists?
   Possible response: Picasso's development of unconventional methods allowed him to portray many angles at once, which the conventional two-dimensional painting had not achieved.

Monitoring Progress

Before students read the poetry selections, refer to students' results on the **Vocabulary in Context** section of **Benchmark Test 8** ***(Unit 4 Resources,*** pp. 201–203). Use this diagnostic portion of the test to guide your choice of selections to teach as well as the depth of prereading preparation you will provide, based on students' readiness for the reading and vocabulary skills.

Text Complexity: At a Glance

This chart gives a general text complexity rating for the selections in this part of the unit to help guide instruction. For additional text complexity support, see the Test Complexity Rubric at point of use.

When You Are Old	**More Accessible**	Journey of the Magi	**More Accessible**
The Lake Isle at Innisfree	**More Accessible**	The Hollow Men	**More Complex**
The Wild Swans at Coole	**More Accessible**	In Memory of W. B. Yeats	**More Accessible**
The Second Coming	**More Complex**	Musée des Beaux Arts	**More Accessible**
Sailing to Byzantium	**More Complex**	Carrick Revisited	**More Complex**
Preludes	**More Accessible**	Not Palaces	**More Complex**

• Poetry of William Butler Yeats

Lesson Pacing Guide

DAY 1 Preteach

- Administer the Reading and Vocabulary Warm-ups (*Unit 6 Resources*, pp. 7–10) as necessary.
- Introduce the Literary Analysis concept: Philosophical System.
- Introduce the Reading Strategy: Analyze Philosophical Assumptions.
- Build background with the author and Background features.
- Develop thematic thinking with Connecting to the Essential Question.
- Teach the selection vocabulary.

DAYS 2–3 Preteach/Teach/Assess

- Distribute copies of the appropriate graphic organizer for the Reading Strategy (*Graphic Organizer Transparencies*, pp. 200–201).
- Distribute copies of the appropriate graphic organizer for Literary Analysis (*Graphic Organizer Transparencies*, pp. 202–203).
- Prepare students to read with the Activating Prior Knowledge activities (TE).
- Informally monitor comprehension while students read.
- Use the Reading Check questions to confirm comprehension.
- Develop students' understanding of philosophical systems using the Literary Analysis prompts.
- Develop students' ability to analyze philosophical assumptions using the Reading Strategy prompts.
- Reinforce vocabulary with the Vocabulary notes.
- Assess students' comprehension and mastery of the skills by having them answer the Critical Reading, Literary Analysis, and Reading Strategy questions.
- Have students complete the Vocabulary Lesson.

DAY 4 Extend/Assess

- Have students complete the Conventions and Style Lesson.
- Have students complete the Writing Lesson and write a response to literature. (You may assign as homework.)
- Administer Selection Test A or B (*Unit 6 Resources,* pp. 20–22 or 23–25).

Common Core State Standards

Reading Literature 4. Determine the meaning of words and phrases as they are used in the text, including figurative and connotative meanings; analyze the impact of specific word choices on meaning and tone, including words with multiple meanings or language that is particularly fresh, engaging, or beautiful.

Writing 1. Write arguments to support claims in an analysis of substantive topics or texts, using valid reasoning and relevant and sufficient evidence.
5. Develop and strengthen writing as needed by planning, revising, editing, rewriting, or trying a new approach, focusing on addressing what is most significant for a specific purpose and audience.

Language 4.d. Verify the preliminary determination of the meaning of a word or phrase.

Additional Standards Practice
Common Core Companion, *pp. 41–48; 185–195; 226–227; 324–331*

Daily Block Scheduling
Each day in this Lesson Pacing Guide represents a 40–50 minute period. Teachers using block scheduling may combine days to revise pacing. In addition, teachers may differentiate and support core instruction by integrating components for extended and intensive support as students require. See the Guide to Selected Leveled Resources (facing page).

Guide to Selected Leveled Resources

RTI Tier 1 (students performing on level)

			Poetry of William Butler Yeats
Warm Up	Whole class instruction; Group work	**Practice, model,** and **monitor** fluency, working **with the whole class** or **in groups**.	**Vocabulary and Reading Warm-ups B, *Unit 6 Resources,*** pp. 7–8, 10
Comprehension/Skills	Whole class instruction; Group work; Independent work	**Support** and **monitor** comprehension and skills development, having students complete the activities, graphic organizers, and interactive prompts **independently** or **as a class**.	• ***Reader's Notebook,*** adapted instruction and full selection EL ***Reader's Notebook: English Learner's Version,*** adapted instruction and adapted selection • **Reading Strategy Graphic Organizer B, *Graphic Organizer Transparencies,*** p. 211 • **Literary Analysis Graphic Organizer B, *Graphic Organizer Transparencies,*** p. 213
Monitor Progress	A	**Monitor** student progress with the differentiated curriculum-based assessment in the *Unit Resources.*	• **Selection Test B, *Unit 6 Resources,*** pp. 23–25 • **Open-Book Test, *Unit 6 Resources,*** pp. 17–19

RTI Tier 2 (students requiring intervention)

			Poetry of William Butler Yeats
Warm Up	Group work; One-on-one teaching	**Practice, model,** and **monitor** fluency **in groups** or **with individuals**.	• **Vocabulary and Reading Warm-ups A, *Unit 6 Resources,*** pp. 7–9 • ***Hear It!* Audio CD (adapted text)**
Comprehension/Skills	Group work; One-on-one teaching	• **Support** and **monitor** comprehension and skills development, working **in small groups** or **with individuals**. • As students complete the selection in the appropriate version of the *Reader's Notebook,* **monitor** comprehension frequently with group questions and individual instruction. • **Model** strategies while guiding students in completing the activities and prompts in the *Reader's Notebook,* as well as the graphic organizers. • **Practice** skills and **monitor** mastery with the *Reading Kit* worksheets.	• ***Reader's Notebook: Adapted Version,*** adapted instruction and adapted selection EL ***Reader's Notebook: English Learner's Version,*** adapted instruction and adapted selection • **Reading Strategy Graphic Organizer A, *Graphic Organizer Transparencies,*** p. 210 • **Literary Analysis Graphic Organizer A, *Graphic Organizer Transparencies,*** p. 212 • ***Reading Kit,*** Practice worksheets
Monitor Progress	A	**Monitor** student progress with the differentiated curriculum-based assessment in the *Unit Resources* and in the *Reading Kit.*	• **Selection Test A, *Unit 6 Resources,*** pp. 20–22 • ***Reading Kit,*** Assess worksheets

TIER 3 Tier 3 intervention may require consultation with the student's special-education or dyslexia specialist. For additional support, see the Tier 2 activities and resources listed above.

One-on-one teaching | **Group work** | **Whole class instruction** | **Independent work** | **A Assessment**

For a complete guide to selection support, including support for Advanced students, see the Overview of Resources in the frontmatter.

• Poetry of William Butler Yeats

RESOURCES FOR:

- L1 Special-Needs Students
- L2 Below-Level Students (Tier 2)
- L3 On-Level Students (Tier 1)
- L4 Advanced Students (Tier 1)
- EL English Learners
- All All Students

Vocabulary/Fluency/Prior Knowledge

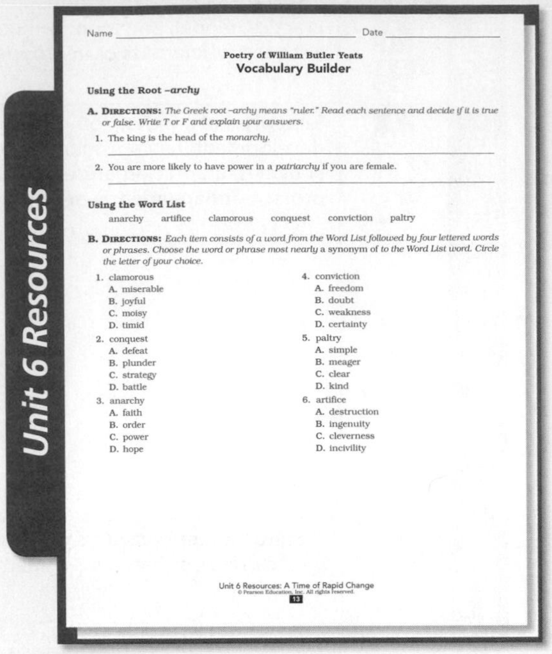
Unit 6 Resources

Name ______ Date ______

Poetry of William Butler Yeats
Vocabulary Builder

Using the Root *-archy*

A. Directions: *The Greek root -archy means "ruler." Read each sentence and decide if it is true or false. Write T or F and explain your answers.*

1. The king is the head of the *monarchy*.
2. You are more likely to have power in a *patriarchy* if you are female.

Using the Word List

anarchy artifice clamorous conquest conviction paltry

B. Directions: *Each item consists of a word from the Word List followed by four lettered words or phrases. Choose the word or phrase most nearly a synonym of to the Word List word. Circle the letter of your choice.*

1. clamorous A. miserable B. joyful C. moisy D. timid
2. conquest A. defeat B. plunder C. strategy D. battle
3. anarchy A. faith B. order C. power D. hope
4. conviction A. freedom B. doubt C. weakness D. certainty
5. paltry A. simple B. meager C. clear D. kind
6. artifice A. destruction B. ingenuity C. cleverness D. incivility

Unit 6 Resources: A Time of Rapid Change
13

All **Vocabulary Builder,** p. 13

Also available for these selections:

EL L1 L2 **Vocabulary Warm-ups A and B,** pp. 7–8

EL L1 L2 **Reading Warm-ups A and B,** pp. 9–10

L2 L3 ***Reader's Notebook***

L1 ***Reader's Notebook: Adapted Version***

EL ***Reader's Notebook: English Learner's Version***

EL ***Reader's Notebook: Spanish Version***

Reader's Notebooks

Pre- and postreading pages for these selections appear in an interactive format in the *Reader's Notebooks*. Each *Notebook* is differentiated for a different group of learners. The selections in the Adapted and English Learner's versions are abridged.

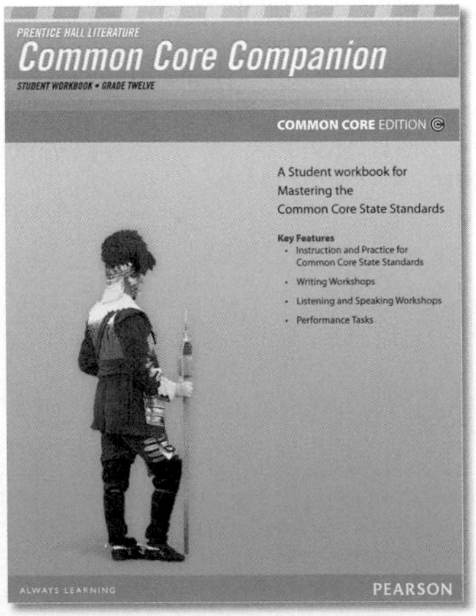

Common Core Companion

Additional instruction and practice for each Common Core State Standard

Selection Support

Graphic Organizer Transparencies

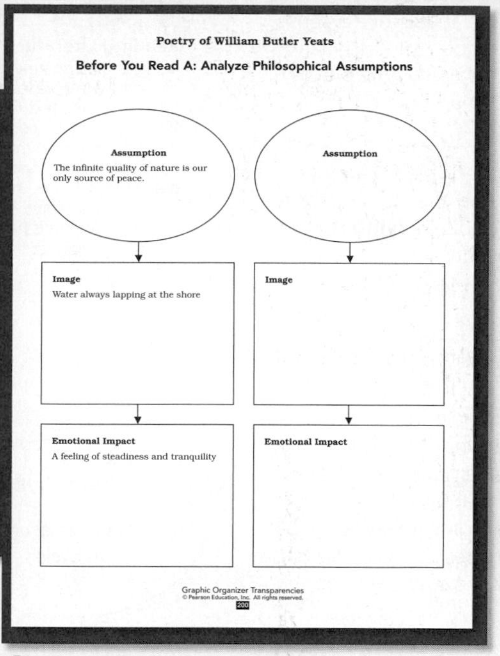
Poetry of William Butler Yeats

Before You Read A: Analyze Philosophical Assumptions

Graphic Organizer Transparencies
© Pearson Education, Inc. All rights reserved.
200

EL L1 L2 **Reading: Graphic Organizer A,** p. 200

Also available for these selections:

EL L3 Reading: Graphic Organizer B, p. 201

EL L1 L2 **Literary Analysis: Graphic Organizer A,** (partially filled in) p. 202

EL L3 **Literary Analysis: Graphic Organizer B,** p. 203

Skills Development/Extension

Unit 6 Resources

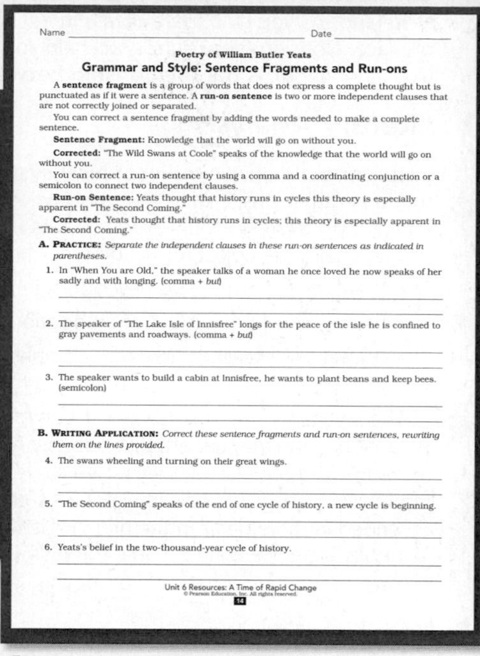
Name ______________________ Date ____________

Poetry of William Butler Yeats

Grammar and Style: Sentence Fragments and Run-ons

A **sentence fragment** is a group of words that does not express a complete thought but is punctuated as if it were a sentence. A **run-on sentence** is two or more independent clauses that are not correctly joined or separated.

You can correct a sentence fragment by adding the words needed to make a complete sentence.

Sentence Fragment: Knowledge that the world will go on without you.

Corrected: "The Wild Swans at Coole" speaks of the knowledge that the world will go on without you.

You can correct a run-on sentence by using a comma and a coordinating conjunction or a semicolon to connect two independent clauses.

Run-on Sentence: Yeats thought that history runs in cycles this theory is especially apparent in "The Second Coming."

Corrected: Yeats thought that history runs in cycles; this theory is especially apparent in "The Second Coming."

A. Practice: *Separate the independent clauses in these run-on sentences as indicated in parentheses.*

1. In "When You Are Old," the speaker talks of a woman he once loved he now speaks of her sadly and with longing. (comma + *but*)
2. The speaker of "The Lake Isle of Innisfree" longs for the peace of the isle he is confined to gray pavements and roadways. (comma + *but*)
3. The speaker wants to build a cabin at Innisfree, he wants to plant beans and keep bees. (semicolon)

B. Writing Application: *Correct these sentence fragments and run-on sentences, rewriting them on the lines provided.*

4. The swans wheeling and turning on their great wings.
5. "The Second Coming" speaks of the end of one cycle of history, a new cycle is beginning.
6. Yeats's belief in the two-thousand-year cycle of history.

Unit 6 Resources: A Time of Rapid Change
© Pearson Education, Inc. All rights reserved.
14

EL L3 L4 **Grammar and Style,** p. 14

Also available for these selections:

All **Literary Analysis: Symbolism,** p. 11

All **Reading: Analyze Philosophical Assumptions,** p. 12

EL L3 L4 **Support for Writing,** p. 15

L4 **Enrichment,** p. 16

Assessment

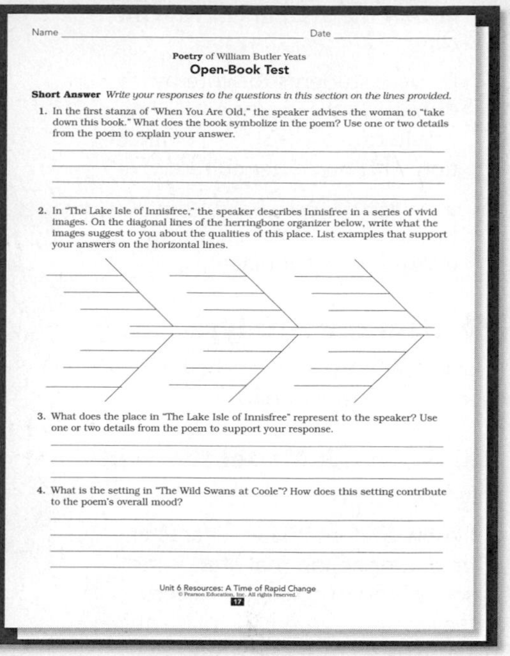
Name ______________________ Date ____________

Poetry of William Butler Yeats

Open-Book Test

Short Answer *Write your responses to the questions in this section on the lines provided.*

1. In the first stanza of "When You Are Old," the speaker advises the woman to "take down this book." What does the book symbolize in the poem? Use one or two details from the poem to explain your answer.
2. In "The Lake Isle of Innisfree," the speaker describes Innisfree in a series of vivid images. On the diagonal lines of the herringbone organizer below, write what the images suggest to you about the qualities of this place. List examples that support your answers on the horizontal lines.
3. What does the place in "The Lake Isle of Innisfree" represent to the speaker? Use one or two details from the poem to support your response.
4. What is the setting in "The Wild Swans at Coole"? How does this setting contribute to the poem's overall mood?

Unit 6 Resources: A Time of Rapid Change
© Pearson Education, Inc. All rights reserved.
17

L3 L4 **Open-Book Test,** pp. 17–19

Also available for these selections:

EL L1 L2 **Selection Test A,** pp. 20–22

EL L3 L4 **Selection Test B,** pp. 23–25

PHLit Online!
www.PHLitOnline.com

- complete narrated selection text
- a thematically related video with writing prompt
- an interactive graphic organizer
- highlighting feature
- access to all student print resources, adapted to individual student needs
- Spanish and English summaries
- adapted selection translations in Spanish

Online Resources: All print materials are also available online.

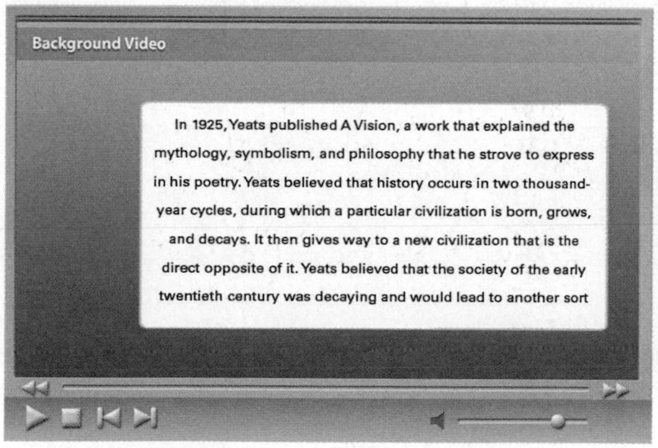

Background Video

Also available:

Get Connected! (thematic video with writing prompt)
All videos are available in Spanish.

Vocabulary Central (tools and activities for studying vocabulary)

Also available:

Writer's Journal (with graphics feature)

PRETEACH

❶ Connecting to the Essential Question

1. Review the assignment with the class.
2. Prepare students to write by discussing the reasons why one would develop a strong connection with his or her culture.
3. As students read, have them look for details in Yeats's poems that evoke a sense of place.

❷ Literary Analysis

Introduce the skill using the instruction on the student page.

Think Aloud: Model the Skill

Say to students:

I know that an image, character, object, or action that stands for something or gives rise to certain feelings is a symbol. I can identify symbols by using background knowledge, common knowledge, and careful reading. As I read, I will make a list of possible symbols in Yeats's poetry to discuss later with the class.

❸ Reading Strategy

1. Introduce the skill using the instruction on the student page.
2. Give students a copy of **Reading Strategy Graphic Organizer B,** page 201 in ***Graphic Organizer Transparencies,*** to fill out as they read.

Think Aloud: Model the Skill

Say to students:

I know symbols can evoke emotional responses. A writer can elicit these responses to convince his readers of certain ideas and assumptions. As I read, I will record and analyze Yeats's philosophical assumptions by paying special attention to the emotional responses his symbols evoke.

❹ Vocabulary

1. Pronounce each word, giving its definition, and have students say it aloud.
2. For more guidance, see the *Classroom Strategies and Teaching Routines* card for introducing vocabulary.

Before You Read

Poetry of William Butler Yeats

❶ **Connecting to the Essential Question** Yeats felt a deep connection to Ireland. As you read, note details in Yeats's poems that evoke a sense of place. Noticing these details will help you think about the Essential Question: **What is the relationship between literature and place?**

Common Core State Standards

Reading Literature
4. Determine the meaning of words and phrases as they are used in the text, including figurative and connotative meanings; analyze the impact of specific word choices on meaning and tone, including words with multiple meanings or language that is particularly fresh, engaging, or beautiful.

❷ Literary Analysis

Yeats created a unique **philosophical system,** or set of ideas about fundamental truths, woven from his own insights and the ideas of many thinkers. To express his philosophy, Yeats used symbols. A **symbol** is an image, character, object, or action with these functions:

- It stands for something beyond itself, such as an abstract idea.
- It gives rise to a number of associations.
- It intensifies feelings and adds complexity to meaning by concentrating these associations together.

The swans in "The Wild Swans at Coole," for example, combine associations of beauty (they are attractive), purity (they are white), freedom (they are wild), and the eternal (they return every year). Over time, Yeats consistently used certain symbols to express his philosophical system, which is described in more detail in the graphic Literature in Context feature on page 1144. As you read, consider how this philosophy shapes the meaning of his poems, particularly "The Second Coming" and "Sailing to Byzantium."

❸ Reading Strategy

Preparing to Read Complex Texts As a poet, Yeats uses vivid language and rich symbols to make his philosophical arguments, relying on the emotional impact of specific word choices and symbolic images to convey meaning and "convince" his readers. As you read, **analyze Yeats's philosophical assumptions** by analyzing the emotional impact of his word choices and symbolic images. Use a chart like the one shown. To ensure you appreciate his word choice, consult a dictionary as needed to determine the connotations as well as the literal meaning of unfamiliar words.

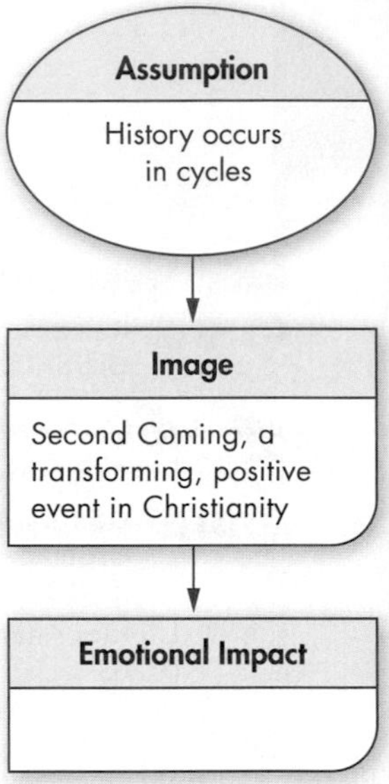

Assumption
History occurs in cycles
Image
Second Coming, a transforming, positive event in Christianity
Emotional Impact

❹ Vocabulary

clamorous (klam′ ər əs) *adj.* loud and confused; noisy (p. 1142)

conquest (kän′ kwest′) *n.* the winning of the submission or affection of (p. 1143)

anarchy (an′ ər kē) *n.* absence of government; disorder (p. 1145)

conviction (kən vik′ shən) *n.* belief; faith (p. 1145)

paltry (pôl′ trē) *adj.* practically worthless; insignificant (p. 1147)

artifice (ärt′ ə fis) *n.* skill; the product of skill, especially a skillful deception (p. 1148)

PHLit Online! www.PHLitOnline.com

Vocabulary Development

Vocabulary Knowledge Rating

Create a **Vocabulary Knowledge Rating Chart** (***Professional Development Guidebook,*** p. 33) for the vocabulary words on the student page. Give each student a copy of the chart with the words on it. Read the words aloud, and have students mark their ratings in the Before Reading column. Urge students to attend to these words as they read and discuss the selections.

In order to gauge how much instruction you need to provide, tally how many students are confident in their knowledge of each word. As students read, point out the words and their context.

PHLit Online! **Vocabulary Central,** featuring tools, activities, and songs for studying vocabulary, is available online at **www.PHLitOnline.com.**

❺ Author of **Poetry of William Butler Yeats**

WILLIAM BUTLER YEATS

(1865–1939)

The twentieth century was a time of change, marked by unprecedented world wars, revolutions, technological innovations, and a mass media explosion. Even as the winds of change threatened to sweep away old traditions, the Irish poet William Butler Yeats delved deep into his nation's mythological past for insight. Winner of the Nobel Prize for Literature in 1923, Yeats is generally regarded as one of the finest poets of the century. His return to the past helped earn him an abiding place in the future.

Born in Dublin, Ireland, Yeats was educated there and in London. His heart lay to the west, though, in County Sligo, where he spent childhood vacations with his grandparents. In the shadow of Sligo's barren mountains, the young Yeats was immersed in the mythology and legends of Ireland. This experience led to a lifelong enthusiasm for the roots of Irish culture.

Philosophical Influences After three years of studying painting in Dublin, Yeats moved to London to pursue a literary career. He became a friend of the poet Arthur Symons, who awakened his interest in the symbolic, visionary poetry of William Blake and the delicate, musical verse of the French Symbolists. Yeats's early poems show Symbolist influences as well as an affinity with the Pre-Raphaelites, a group of nineteenth-century British painters and writers who turned to medieval art as they strove for simplicity and beauty.

From Poetry to Plays to Poetry As the century turned, Yeats became interested in drama. He joined with his friend Lady Augusta Gregory in founding the Irish National Theatre Society. In 1892, Yeats had written *The Countess Cathleen,* a play that was to become one of his most popular dramatic works. With the acquisition and opening of the Abbey Theatre in Dublin, Yeats turned increasingly to writing plays. When Yeats returned to poetry, it was with a new voice, subtler and more powerful than the one he had used before. The poems in *The Tower* (1928) show Yeats at the height of his abilities. "Sailing to Byzantium" dates from this period of his work.

Ireland's Hero On his seventieth birthday, he was hailed by his nation as the greatest living Irishman. Though Yeats's quarrels with the tastes and politics of middle-class Ireland were often fierce, no one could deny his stature. He continued to write up until a day or two before his death in France. One of his last poems contains his famous epitaph: "Cast a cold eye / On life, on death. / Horseman, pass by!"

"THINGS FALL APART; THE CENTER CANNOT HOLD…"

Daily Bellringer

For each class during which you will teach these selections, have students complete one of the five activities for the appropriate week in the *Daily Bellringer Activities* booklet.

Multidraft Reading

To assist struggling readers and to enhance reading for all, assign the text in chunks, as warranted by length, and apply multidraft reading protocols. For each reading, have students set the purpose indicated:

- **First reading**—identifying key ideas and details and answering any Reading Checks.
- **Second reading**—analyzing craft and structure and responding to the side-column prompts.
- **Third reading**—integrating knowledge and ideas, connecting to other texts and the world, and answering the end-of-selection questions.

For more guidance, refer to the ***Classroom Strategies and Teaching Routines*** card on Multidraft Reading.

❺ Background

More About the Author

Yeats had a lifelong involvement with the occult. He joined a branch of the Hermetic Order of the Golden Dawn, which hoped to prove that occult phenomena were possible. The Golden Dawn incorporated traditional magic and astronomy. Yeats adopted as his personal motto within the club "Demon est Deus Inversus" (The Devil Is God Inverted) and rose through the ranks to become a major officer. Maud Gonne was also a member, adopting the motto "Per Ignum, Ad Astra" (Through the Fire, to the Light). Elements of Yeats's fascination with magic and the supernatural are evident in his poems.

PHLit Online! www.PHLitOnline.com

Teaching From Technology

Preparing to Read
Go to **www.PHLitOnline.com** and display the ***Get Connected!*** slide show for these selections. Have the class brainstorm responses to the writing prompt, entering ideas in the interactive journal. Then, have students complete their written responses as homework.

To build background, display the Background and More About the Author features.

Using the Interactive Text
Go to **www.PHLitOnline.com** and display the **Enriched Online Student Edition.** As the class reads the selection or listens to the narration, record answers to side-column prompts using the graphic organizers accessible on the interactive page. Alternatively, have students use the online edition individually, answering the prompts as they read.

❶ About the Selection

All five poems are attempts to overcome the disappointments of mortal life. The first poem, "When You Are Old," offers a softer-edged, more "poetic" strategy to solve this problem.

❷ Activating Prior Knowledge

Write this description on the chalkboard and have students begin to improvise a horror movie based on it: "Somewhere in the sands of the desert is a shape with the body of a lion and the head of a man. The creature, its gaze blank and pitiless, is just beginning to move." After students have launched into their "movies," tell them that the image comes from Yeats's poem "The Second Coming."

Concept Connector →

Tell students they will return to their responses after reading the selection.

❸ Critical Thinking

Make a Judgment

1. Have students reread the poem to themselves.
2. After they have finished reading, **ask:** Do you think this poem is comforting? Why or why not? **Possible response:** The poem might be comforting to the writer, as it allows him revenge without doing any real deed. Imagining her feeling regretful consoles him for the fact that she did not return or ceased to return his love.

❶ ❷

WHEN YOU ARE OLD

WILLIAM BUTLER YEATS

When you are old and gray and full of sleep,
And nodding by the fire, take down this book,
And slowly read, and dream of the soft look
Your eyes had once, and of their shadows deep;

How many loved your moments of glad grace,
And loved your beauty with love false or true,
❸ But one man loved the pilgrim soul in you,
And loved the sorrows of your changing face;

And bending down beside the glowing bars,
Murmur, a little sadly, how Love fled
And paced upon the mountains overhead
And hid his face amid a crowd of stars.

Ⓒ Text Complexity Rubric

	When You Are Old; Lake Isle of Innisfree	The Wild Swans at Coole	The Second Coming	Sailing to Byzantium
Qualitative Measures				
Context/Knowledge Demands	Romantic lyrics 1 ② 3 4 5	Modernist lyric 1 ② 3 4 5	Modernist lyric 1 2 ③ 4 5	Modernist lyric 1 2 ③ 4 5
Structure/Language Conventionality and Clarity	Simple diction 1 ② 3 4 5	Simple diction 1 ② 3 4 5	Poetic diction 1 2 ③ 4 5	Poetic diction 1 2 ③ 4 5
Levels of Meaning/ Purpose/Concepts	Accessible (aging; nature) 1 ② 3 4 5	Moderate (youth, mortality) 1 2 ③ 4 5	Challenging (apocalypse) 1 2 3 ④ 5	Challenging (immortality of art) 1 2 3 ④ 5
Quantitative Measures				
Lexile/Text Length	NP / 101, 122 words	NP / 175 words	NP / 166 words	NP / 231 words
Overall Complexity	**More accessible**	**More accessible**	**More complex**	**More complex**

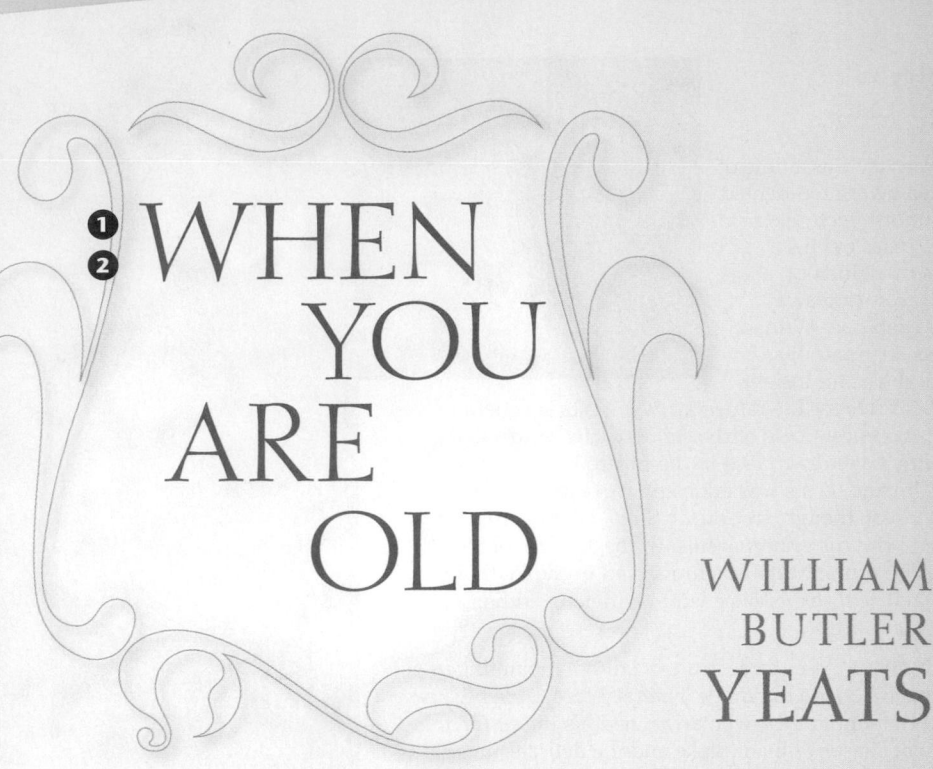

❹ # The Lake Isle of Innisfree

WILLIAM BUTLER YEATS

❺ I will arise and go now, and go to Innisfree,
And a small cabin build there, of clay and wattles[1] made:
Nine bean-rows will I have there, a hive for the honeybee,
And live alone in the bee-loud glade.

And I shall have some peace there, for peace comes dropping slow,
Dropping from the veils of the morning to where the cricket sings;
There midnight's all a glimmer, and noon a purple glow,
And evening full of the linnet's wings.[2]

I will arise and go now, for always night and day
I hear lake water lapping with low sounds by the shore;
While I stand on the roadway, or on the pavements gray,
I hear it in the deep heart's core.

Reading Strategy
Analyzing Philosophical Assumptions What kind of ideal life does Yeats envision in the first stanza?

1. **wattles** stakes interwoven with twigs or branches.
2. **linnet's wings** wings of a European singing bird.

Critical Reading

1. **Key Ideas and Details (a)** What "comes dropping slow" at Innisfree? **(b) Infer:** How does life at Innistree contrast with the speaker's current life?
2. **Integration of Knowledge and Ideas Compare and Contrast:** Do you think that "Innisfree" and "When You Are Old" suggest that writing poetry is a way of compensating for disappointments? Why or why not?

Cite textual evidence to support your responses.

❹ About the Selection

In "The Lake Isle of Innisfree," the softer image is once again presented. The writer imagines a Walden-like retreat to which he can flee from "the pavements gray."

❺ Reading Strategy

Analyzing Philosophical Assumptions

1. Direct students' attention to the first stanza. Have a volunteer read it aloud.
2. Then, **ask** students the Reading Strategy question: What kind of ideal life does Yeats envision in the first stanza?
   Possible response: He saw living alone in a glade. He described a house made of clay, stakes, and wood. He wished to have a bean garden, and to live near a beehive so he could hear the bees buzzing loudly around him. Yeats envisioned a very simple life filled with the pleasures of nature.

ASSESS

Answers

Before students respond, you may wish to have them write a brief objective summary of the selection. As they answer the questions below, remind them to support their answers with evidence from the text.

1. (a) Peace comes dropping slow. (b) Innisfree is probably less hurried and calmer than his current life.
2. **Possible response:** "When You Are Old" acts out a subtle, imaginary revenge; "Lake Isle" creates a desired tranquil mood. In this way, both poems satisfy an unsatisfied or disappointed desire.

Text Complexity: Reader and Task Suggestions

	When You Are Old; Lake Isle; Wild Swans	The Second Coming	Sailing to Byzantium
Preparing to Read the Texts • Use information on SE p. 1144 to explain that Yeats's early works are Romantic nature poems. • Discuss the qualities that make a place ideal and how a person's view of an ideal place might change. • Guide students to use Multidraft Reading strategies (TE p. 1139).	**Leveled Tasks** *Levels of Meaning* If students will have difficulty with the poems' meaning, have them focus first on each poem's imagery and the feelings it conveys. Then, have them reread each poem to decide which key images are used as symbols. *Synthesizing* If students will not have difficulty with the meaning, have them contrast the tone of the three poems.	**Leveled Tasks** *Levels of Meaning* If students will have difficulty with the context of the poem, clarify the Christian idea of the Second Coming. Then, have students contrast that ideal time with Yeats's more sinister impressions. *Analyzing:* If students will not have difficulty with the meaning, have them analyze the poem's imagery and tone.	**Leveled Tasks** *Levels of Meaning* If students have difficulty with the levels of meaning, have them focus first on images that convey the speaker's feelings about his own time. As they reread, have them focus on what Byzantium represents. *Analyzing* If students will not have difficulty with the levels of meaning, have them analyze the poem's key symbols.

6 About the Selection

"The Wild Swans at Coole" exchanges the softness of the previous two poems for a tougher, more impersonal solution to the problems of mortality. This poem is set in Coole Park, the estate of Lady Gregory. She was Yeats's patron as well as his collaborator in establishing the Irish National Theatre Society. Yeats spent a great deal of time at Coole Park, a large estate with ponds, forest paths, and orchards.

7 Critical Viewing

Answer: Students may respond that the curve of the swans' backs and the bend in their necks give them a mysteriously balanced beauty.

8 Critical Thinking

Infer

1. Have students go to page 1143 and read lines 13–24 to themselves. Have them briefly restate the meaning of these lines.
2. **Ask** students to identify what has changed for the speaker over the nineteen years of watching the swans.
   Answer: Students should recognize that the poet has aged and no longer experiences "passion or conquest"; he laments the losses that aging brings.

6 THE WILD SWANS AT COOLE

WILLIAM BUTLER YEATS

7 **▲ Critical Viewing**
Why might Yeats describe swans such as this one as "mysterious" and "beautiful"? **[Infer]**

Vocabulary
clamorous (klam′ ər əs) *adj.* loud and confused; noisy

The trees are in their autumn beauty,
The woodland paths are dry,
Under the October twilight the water
Mirrors a still sky;
Upon the brimming water among the stones
Are nine-and-fifty swans.

The nineteenth autumn has come upon me
Since I first made my count;
I saw, before I had well finished,
All suddenly mount
And scatter wheeling in great broken rings
Upon their clamorous wings.

Enrichment: Investigating Science

A Scientist's View of Swans

There are eight different species of swans, but all share some of the characteristics Yeats describes. Some swans weigh as much as 50 pounds, but they are graceful in flight.

Swans mate for life, producing about six babies (called cygnets) each breeding season. The cygnets are gray or brown; most gradually become white, but a few species have other colorations. Although the male swan, or cob, will defend his family against outsiders, families do merge with others to migrate. Flying at high altitudes, in diagonal or V-formations, swans travel southward in fall and northward in spring.

Activity: Researching Swans Encourage interested students to do further research on swans. Suggest they record their findings in the **Enrichment: Investigating Science** worksheet, ***Professional Development Guidebook,*** page 241.

I have looked upon those brilliant creatures,
And now my heart is sore.
All's changed since I, hearing at twilight,
The first time on this shore,
The bell-beat of their wings above my head,
Trod with a lighter tread.

8

Unwearied still, lover by lover,
They paddle in the cold
Companionable streams or climb the air;
Their hearts have not grown old;
9 Passion or conquest, wander where they will,
Attend upon them still.

But now they drift on the still water,
Mysterious, beautiful;
Among what rushes will they build,
By what lake's edge or pool
Delight men's eyes when I awake some day
To find they have flown away?

Vocabulary
conquest (käŋ′ kwest′) *n.* the winning of the submission or affection of

10 **Literary Analysis**
Symbolism What might the swans symbolize?

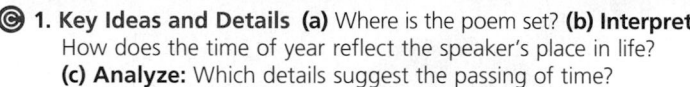

Critical Reading

1. **Key Ideas and Details (a)** Where is the poem set? **(b) Interpret:** How does the time of year reflect the speaker's place in life? **(c) Analyze:** Which details suggest the passing of time?
2. **Key Ideas and Details (a)** When the speaker first counted the swans, what did they suddenly do? **(b) Interpret:** What reflection does the memory of their action prompt in the speaker?
3. **Key Ideas and Details (a) Infer:** What has changed in the speaker since he first heard the swans? **(b) Compare and Contrast:** How does the swans' condition contrast with that of the speaker?
4. **Integration of Knowledge and Ideas (a) Interpret:** The speaker says he will "awake some day / To find they have flown away?" What event might this flight represent for him? **(b) Draw Conclusions:** How does this imagined absence increase the poignancy of the sight of the swans?
5. **Integration of Knowledge and Ideas (a) Interpret:** In what way does the sight of the swans help the speaker measure the passage of time? **(b) Apply:** Compare this experience with another way in which people measure the passage of time.

Cite textual evidence to support your responses.

Differentiated Instruction for Universal Access

Strategy for Less Proficient Readers
Help students understand "The Wild Swans at Coole" by having them make two lists. Title one list "Things That Have Changed" and the other "Things That Have Not Changed." Help them decide what objects in the poem belong in each category, then discuss the results.

EL Strategy for English Learners
Encourage students to use signal words such as *since, before,* and *will* to track past, present, and future in "The Wild Swans at Coole." Then, have them list the poem's events in chronological order.

Enrichment for Advanced Readers
Encourage students to extend the meaning of "The Wild Swans at Coole" by analyzing the depictions of swans in other cultures. Direct them to architectural decorations, book illustrations, fairy tales, fiction, and poetry as possible sources.

9 Vocabulary

Latin Root *-ques-*

1. Point out the word *conquest.* Explain that the root *-ques-* means "to seek or acquire."
2. Explain that a conquest is an acquisition of another's affection or submission. It carries the association of victory.
3. Have students identify other words formed from *-ques-*. **Possible responses:** inquest, request, question, query, and bequest

10 Literary Analysis

Symbolism

1. Explain to students that the thoughts and events linked to an image in a poem contribute to its symbolic value.
2. Pointing out the passage of time since the speaker first counted the swans, **ask** students the Literary Analysis question: What might the swans symbolize?
   Possible response: The swans are connected with youth; they stay the same despite the passage of time.

ASSESS

Answers

Before students respond, you may wish to have them write a brief objective summary of the selection. As they answer the questions below, remind them to support their answers with evidence from the text.

1. (a) The setting is a lake at Coole. (b) Autumn is a common symbol of old age. (c) The swans' flight suggests passing time.
2. (a) The swans suddenly take flight. (b) The speaker realizes how much has changed.
3. (a) The speaker is older, more tired, and less lighthearted. (b) The swans do not change; the speaker does.
4. (a) The flight may represent the end of life. (b) It suggests that life is a passing experience.
5. (a) The speaker measures the passage of time between his first and his present count of them. (b) **Possible response:** Photographs are also reminders of the passage of time.

⓫ Literature in Context

Yeats's Philosophy

Yeats was very interested in the Byzantine Empire. In 306 A.D., Emperor Constantine became ruler of the Roman Empire, which included the lands surrounding the Mediterranean Sea and parts of the Middle East. After 20 years of rule, Constantine built a new imperial capital in Byzantium, an ancient Greek city in the eastern part of the empire. In 330 A.D., the city was renamed Constantinople after its emperor. The city was rich and powerful due to international trade and a strong army. Over time, the Roman Empire split in two—the eastern half stronger by far. Meanwhile, Muslim peoples to the east were growing stronger. In 1453, a force of 70,000 Turks conquered Constantinople, which had been an impenetrable fortress for more than 1,000 years. This marked the end of the Byzantine Empire. Today, we know Byzantium as Istanbul, a city in Turkey.

Connect to the Literature

1. After going over the concept of Yeats's philosophy and its visual symbols, have students reread the captions on the page.
2. **Ask** the Connect to the Literature question: Does knowing some of Yeats's philosophical ideas help you better understand poems like "The Second Coming" and "Sailing to Byzantium"?
   Answer: Yes, knowing Yeats's system of visualizing conflict and completion using different shapes and formations helps in understanding some of his descriptions in his poetry, such as "turning in the widening gyre" in "The Second Coming" (line 1) and "perne in a gyre" in "Sailing to Byzantium" (line 19). Both of these images gain significance when readers know that Yeats pictured all civilizations as spinning cycles that die out and give way to new ones.

⓬ Critical Thinking

Connect

Ask students to identify other aspects of life the gyres could represent, and why they think so.

Answer: Answers will vary, but they should be applicable to the conflict of opposites or two forces struggling against each other.

LITERATURE IN CONTEXT

⓫ YEATS'S PHILOSOPHY

Yeats developed a philosophy that united his interest in history, art, personality, and society. His basic insight was that, in all these fields, conflicting forces are at work. In history, for example, as one kind of civilization grows and eventually dies, an opposite kind of civilization is born to take its place. Similarly, human personalities can be defined as opposites: the creative or subjective person versus the active or objective person.

Gyres
To visualize the conflict of opposites, Yeats uses gyres [jierz]. In two dimensions, these look like triangles.

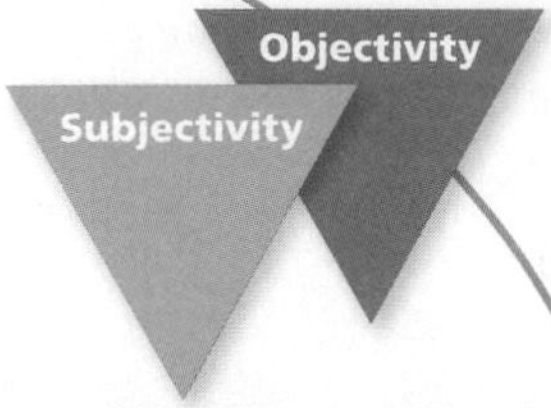

Circles and Wheels
Because Yeats wanted to imagine completion as well as conflict, he placed a circle around the two gyres. This circle he called The Great Wheel. He labeled it with compass points, qualities, and phases of the moon. He said this wheel is "every completed movement of thought or life."

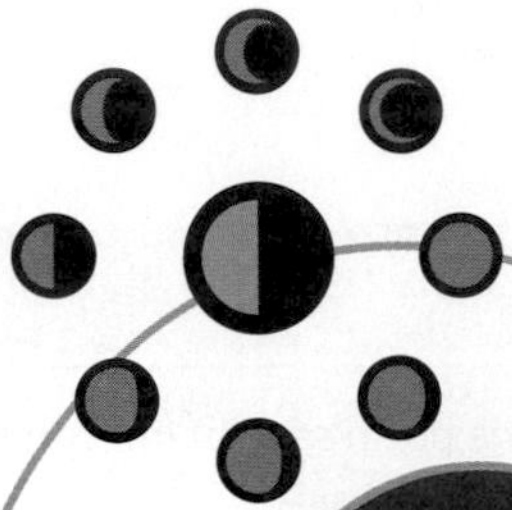

However, Yeats pictured them as helixes, whirling forms of motion.

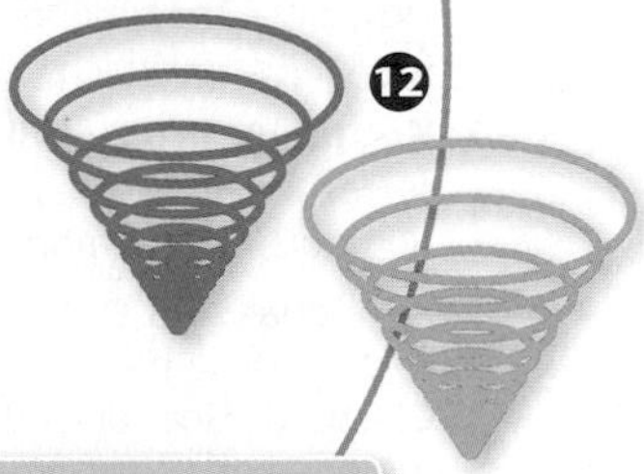

⓬

Interpenetrating gyres showed how two different forces struggled against one another, moving from left to right, and back again. This movement could describe the development of a personality or the rise and fall of civilizations.

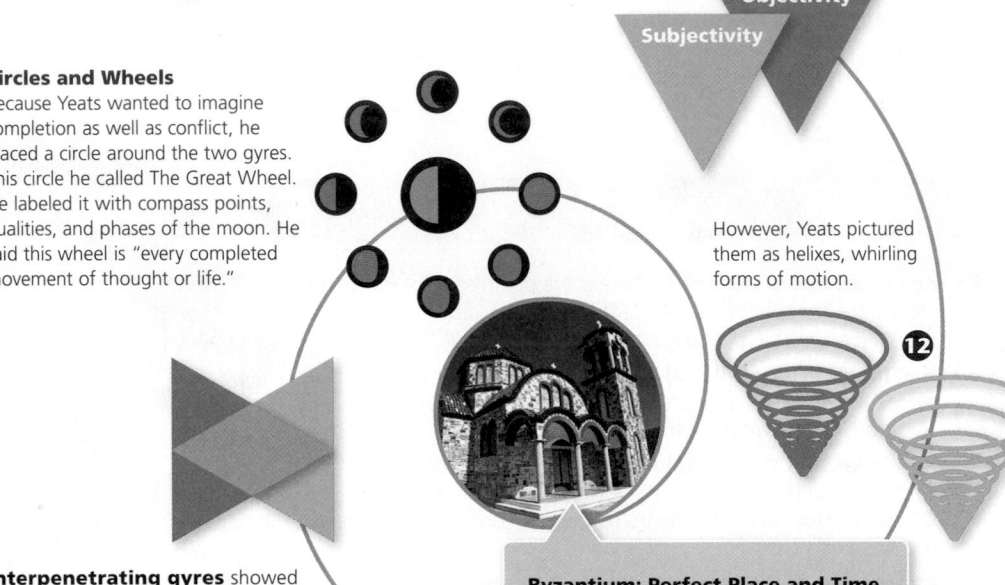

Byzantium: Perfect Place and Time
For Yeats, the perfect era in the cycle was the Byzantine Empire in the early sixth century A.D. It stands for an escape from time's wheel because "in early Byzantium, maybe never before or since . . ., religious, aesthetic and practical life were one." Artists' work spoke directly to the people.

CONNECT TO THE LITERATURE

Does knowing some of Yeats's philosophical ideas help you better understand poems like "The Second Coming" and "Sailing to Byzantium"? Explain.

Enrichment: Analyzing Themes and Symbols

Falconry
Students will not appreciate the opening image in "The Second Coming," and its symbolism, unless they understand something about falconry. This sport involved the use of trained falcons to hunt small birds and animals. After killing its prey, but otherwise leaving it untouched, the falcon returns to the trainer's wrist. Falconry was practiced by the ancient Chinese and was popular among the nobility in Europe during the Middle Ages and the Renaissance. In Yeats's poem, the falcon, flying in wider and wider circles, "cannot hear the falconer" and is therefore out of control.

Activity: The Falcon as a Symbol Encourage interested students to further analyze the falcon as a symbol by using the **Enrichment: Analyzing Themes and Symbols** worksheet, ***Professional Development Guidebook,*** page 243.

The Second Coming

WILLIAM BUTLER YEATS

BACKGROUND **In 1925, Yeats published *A Vision*, a work that explained the mythology, symbolism, and philosophy that he strove to express in his poetry. Yeats believed that history occurs in two-thousand-year cycles, during which a particular civilization is born, grows, and decays. Each civilization then gives way to a new one that is the direct opposite of it. Yeats believed that the society of the early twentieth century was decaying and would lead to another sort of rebirth, very different from the birth of Christ. These ideas are vividly expressed in the poem "The Second Coming."**

14 Turning and turning in the widening gyre
The falcon cannot hear the falconer;
Things fall apart; the center cannot hold;
Mere **anarchy** is loosed upon the world,
The blood-dimmed tide is loosed, and everywhere
The ceremony of innocence is drowned;
The best lack all **conviction**, while the worst
Are full of passionate intensity.[1]

Vocabulary
anarchy (an′ ər kē) *n.* absence of government; disorder
conviction (kən vik′ shən) *n.* belief; faith

1. **Mere . . . intensity** refers to the Russian Revolution of 1917.

13 About the Selection

The fierce and disturbing images in "The Second Coming" represent Yeats's vision of the great cycles of history. Yeats wrote this poem in January 1919, just after World War I came to a close, shortly after the Russian Revolution, and just as war in Ireland was breaking out between the English forces and the Irish patriots. The "blood-dimmed tide" of the poem is therefore an image of the violence that seemed to be filling the world.

14 Literary Analysis

Symbolism

1. Remind students that symbols may be traditional or may reflect the poet's experience.
2. Read lines 1–2, and ask students where they think the symbols of the gyre and falcon derive from.
Possible response: The gyre, or spiral, is probably an obscure traditional symbol that Yeats adapted to his theory of history. Falcons have traditional associations of nobility, obedience, and fierceness.

Differentiated Instruction for Universal Access

Strategy for Less Proficient Readers

To help students understand Yeats's symbolism, explain the historical background and write on the chalkboard "things fall apart." Have students come up with their own images and symbols to convey this idea. Have them compare these symbols to Yeats's.

Enrichment for Gifted/Talented Students

Students with an interest in art may be familiar with paintings that depict chaos. Have them assemble a portfolio of paintings that represent the turmoil and anxiety about civilization expressed in the poem.

Enrichment for Advanced Readers

Have students respond to critic Richard Ellmann's appraisal of this poem: ". . . an awareness of Yeats's mythological system was more useful for writing than it is for reading the poem. . . . It is more necessary that we be familiar with the ancient, traditional myth of a second coming . . . than that we understand Yeats's system."

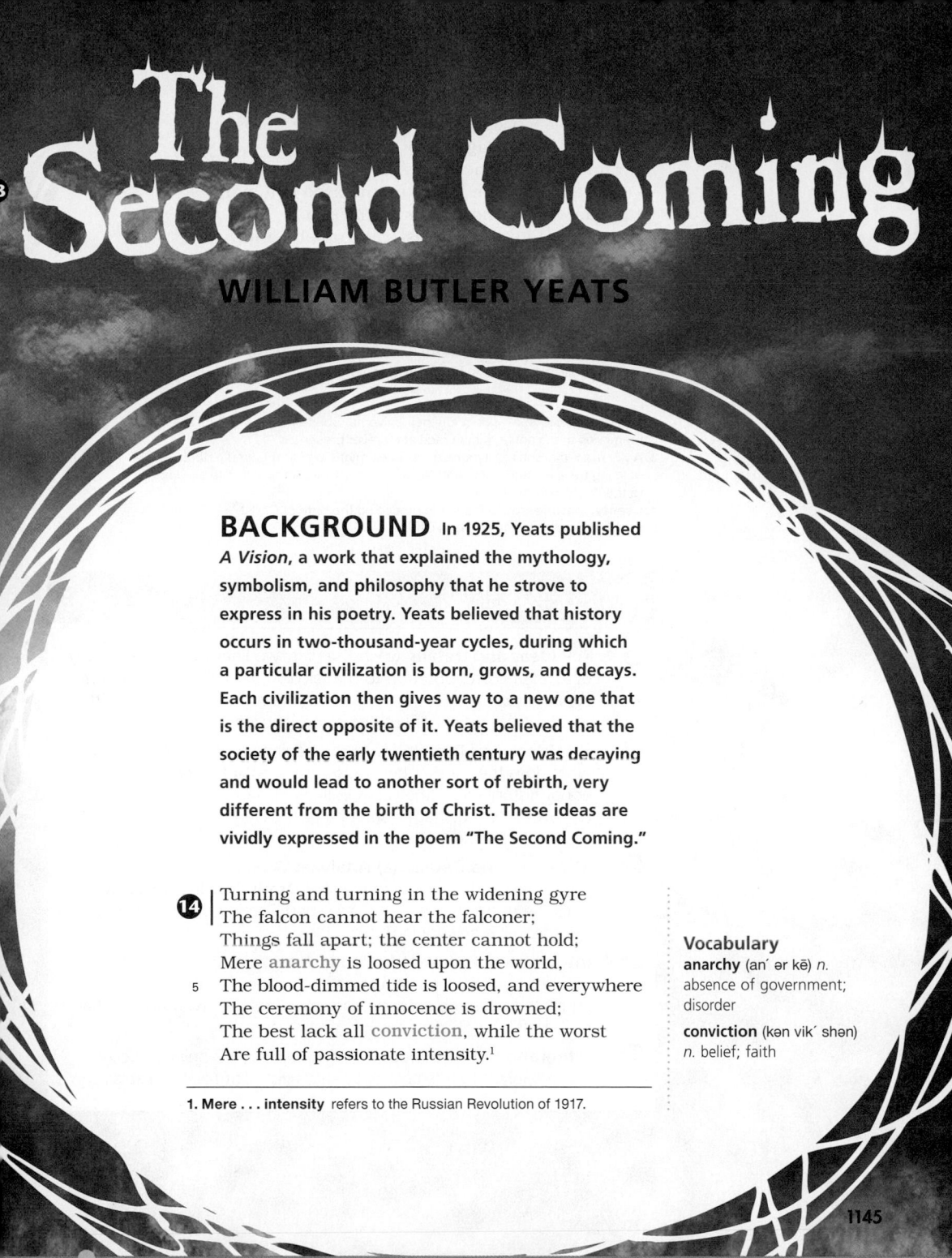

⑮ Literary Analysis

Philosophical System

1. Have students read the poem again, keeping Yeats's philosophy in mind.
2. Then, **ask** students the Literary Analysis question: What elements of Yeats's philosophy does "The Second Coming" contain?
   Possible responses: Yeats compares the falcon's path in the sky to a "widening gyre." The "blood-dimmed tide" is comparable to a gyre. The struggle between light and dark is like the interpenetrating gyres. Also, the cycle of time Yeats describes, starting with the birth of Christ and ending with the birth of a "rough beast," is comparable to the Great Wheel.

ASSESS

Answers

Remind students to support their answers with evidence from the text.

1. (a) The falcon cannot hear its master's voice. (b) The falcon is now out of control and the "order" of authority, falconer over falcon, has broken down; the falcon's disobedience is innocent, though, since it cannot hear the falconer's command.
2. (a) The speaker believes that "some revelation is at hand." (b) The lines may represent the age before Christ's birth, since the Sphinx is a mythological figure of ancient Greece and Egypt. (c) The birth of Christ began a new religion, and the gods of ancient times were abandoned.
3. (a) A "rough beast" is about to be born. (b) In the traditional version, it is Christ who returns at the Second Coming; often symbolized as a lamb, the merciful figure of Christ contrasts with Yeats's ominous "rough beast."
4. **Possible response:** Even though Yeats's strong and vibrant images are unpleasant, one can appreciate the craftsmanship the poem exhibits.
5. **Possible response:** Yes, his vision is manifest today in the violence that is occurring around the world.

Surely some revelation is at hand;
Surely the Second Coming is at hand.
The Second Coming! Hardly are those words out
When a vast image out of *Spiritus Mundi*[2]
Troubles my sight: somewhere in sands of the desert
A shape with lion body and the head of a man,[3]
A gaze blank and pitiless as the sun,
Is moving its slow thighs, while all about it
Reel shadows of the indignant desert birds.
The darkness drops again; but now I know
That twenty centuries[4] of stony sleep
Were vexed to nightmare by a rocking cradle,[5]
And what rough beast, its hour come round at last,
Slouches towards Bethlehem to be born?

⑮ **Literary Analysis**
Philosophical System
What elements of Yeats's philosophy does "The Second Coming" contain?

2. ***Spiritus Mundi*** (spir′ i təs mo͞on′ dē) Universal Spirit or Soul, in which the memories of the entire human race are forever preserved.
3. **A . . . man** the Sphinx, a monster in Greek mythology that posed a riddle to passing travelers and destroyed those who could not answer it. The answer to the riddle was "man."
4. **twenty centuries** historical cycle preceding the birth of Christ.
5. **rocking cradle** cradle of Jesus Christ.

Critical Reading

Cite textual evidence to support your responses.

1. **Key Ideas and Details (a)** In the first two lines of the poem, why does the falcon not return to the falconer, as it ordinarily would? **(b) Analyze:** Why is the image of the falcon an effective introduction to Yeats's ideas about order and innocence?
2. **Key Ideas and Details (a)** At the beginning of the second stanza, what does the speaker believe is at hand? **(b) Interpret:** What era of history might the vision in lines 11–17 represent? Explain. **(c) Interpret:** In what sense did a past birth in Bethlehem bring this era to an end?
3. **Key Ideas and Details (a) Analyze:** What birth does the speaker predict will end the modern era? **(b) Draw Conclusions:** How does the traditional idea of the Second Coming differ from what the speaker is envisioning?
4. **Integration of Knowledge and Ideas** Yeats draws on his own theories of history for the theme and imagery of this poem. Why might the poem be appreciated even by readers who do not share his beliefs?
5. **Integration of Knowledge and Ideas** In your opinion, do any contemporary events bear out Yeats's vision of history? Explain.

Vocabulary Development

Vocabulary Knowledge Rating

When students have completed reading and discussing the group of selections, have them take out their **Vocabulary Knowledge Rating Charts** for the story. Read the words aloud and have students rate their knowledge of words again in the After Reading column. Clarify any words that are still problematic. Have students write their own definitions and example or sentence in the appropriate column. Then, have students complete the Vocabulary Lesson at the end of the selections. Encourage students to use the words in further discussion and written work about the selections. Remind them that they will be accountable for these words on the **Selection Test,** ***Unit 6 Resources,*** pages 20–22 or 23–25.

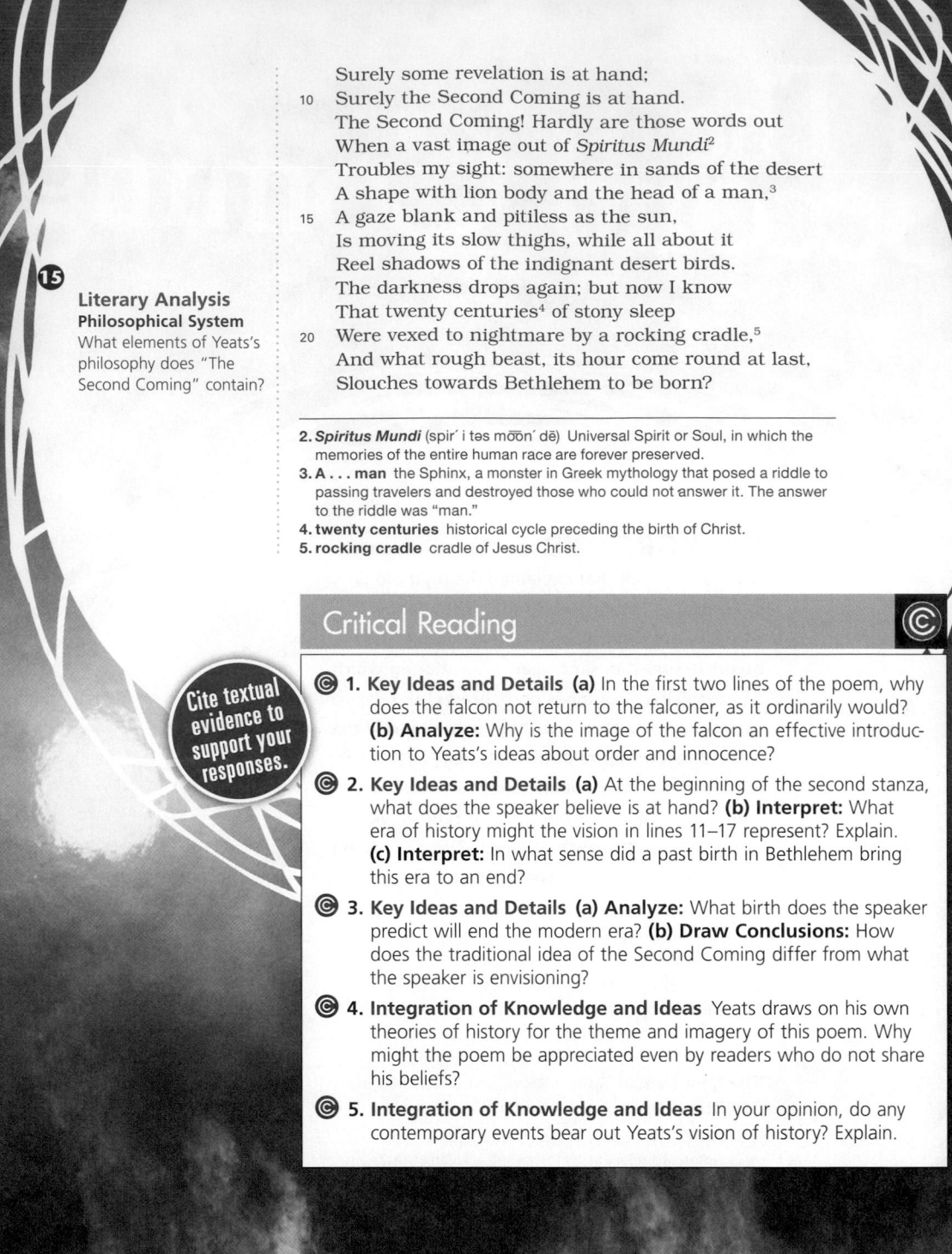

⑯ SAILING TO BYZANTIUM

William Butler Yeats

I

That is no country for old men. The young
In one another's arms, birds in the trees
—Those dying generations—at their song,
The salmon-falls, the mackerel-crowded seas,
Fish, flesh, or fowl, commend all summer long
Whatever is begotten, born, and dies.
Caught in that sensual music all neglect
Monuments of unaging intellect.

II

An aged man is but a paltry thing,
A tattered coat upon a stick, unless
Soul clap its hands and sing, and louder sing
⑰ For every tatter in its mortal dress,
Nor is there singing school but studying
Monuments of its own magnificence;
And therefore I have sailed the seas and come
To the holy city of Byzantium.[1]

III

O sages standing in God's holy fire
As in the gold mosaic of a wall,[2]

Vocabulary
paltry (pôl′ trē) *adj.* practically worthless; insignificant

⑱ **Reading Check**
What does the speaker's age motivate him to do?

1. **Byzantium** (bi zan′ shē əm) ancient capital of the Eastern Roman (or Byzantine) Empire and the seat of the Greek Orthodox Church; today, Istanbul, Turkey. For Yeats, Byzantium symbolized the world of art as opposed to the world of time and nature.
2. **sages . . . wall** wise men portrayed in mosaic on the walls of Byzantine churches.

⑯ About the Selection

"Sailing to Byzantium" is another impersonal poem. It represents attempts to imagine a pattern of existence beyond the individual—the immortality of art.

⑰ Critical Thinking

Draw Conclusions

1. Direct students' attention to the second stanza of the poem.
2. **Ask:** Why must the soul "clap its hands and sing" in line 11?
   Answer: The speaker is urging his soul to clap hands as a symbol for creating beauty and order (song) to compensate for the frailties, wounds, and imperfections of bodily, mortal existence ("for every tatter in its mortal dress").
3. Then, **ask:** What does the second stanza suggest about the reason people create works of art?
   Answer: It suggests that people create works of art to provide themselves with some form of immortality and that they are motivated to do so by the frustrations and disappointments inherent in life.

⑱ Reading Check

Answer: The speaker's age motivates him to sail to Byzantium in an attempt to escape his mortality.

Differentiated Instruction for Universal Access

EL Vocabulary for English Learners

Help students read the poem. On a photocopy of the poem, have them underline words and phrases that apply to the natural world. With another color, they can underline words that apply to the ideal world for which Yeats longed. Help students understand the differences between the two worlds.

Enrichment for Gifted/Talented Students

Have students research Byzantium and its art. Have them pool their findings and list several adjectives that describe the place and the culture. Remind students that Yeats thought of Byzantium as the ideal place, and discuss what attributes may have influenced his thinking.

Enrichment for Advanced Readers

Have students discuss what the golden bird might symbolize for Yeats. Discuss the paradoxical nature of this symbol: The bird symbolizes the artist who has transcended the natural world through his art, but the bird sings about that natural world.

19 Reading Strategy

Analyzing Philosophical Assumptions

1. Direct students' attention to the last stanza of the poem. Have a volunteer read it aloud.
2. Then, **ask** students the Reading Strategy question: What does the last stanza suggest about the artist's relationship to nature and time?
   Answer: The last stanza suggests that when the artist dies, he is no longer a part of the natural world. He becomes his art, which forever speaks of the past, present, and future.

ASSESS

Answers

Before students respond, you may wish to have them write a brief objective summary of the selection. As they answer the questions below, remind them to support their answers with evidence from the text.

1. (a) They commend "Whatever is begotten, born, or dies." They neglect "Monuments of unaging intellect." (b) Yeats means the world of nature and time, not a specific country.
2. (a) An aged man is "a paltry thing, / A tattered coat upon a stick." (b) The passions of the aged have diminished, and they may have already "begotten" young. Therefore, they have no place in nature.
3. (a) He asks the sages to consume his heart and gather him "Into the artifice of eternity"—to change his mortal being into something immortal. (b) The request reveals that the speaker believes works of art provide entry into a world beyond nature and change.
4. **Possible responses:** Byzantium is the dream, because we only really exist in the world of change; the world of nature is a dream, because everything in it passes away like a dream.
5. **Possible response:** Real or imagined places affect Yeats's poetry in that their uses reveal the desire for a more ideal existence, which is a constant theme in his poetry.

Vocabulary
artifice (ärt′ ə fis) *n.* skill; the product of skill, especially a skillful deception

Come from the holy fire, perne in a gyre,[3]
And be the singing-masters of my soul.
Consume my heart away; sick with desire
And fastened to a dying animal
It knows not what it is; and gather me
Into the **artifice** of eternity.

IV

Once out of nature I shall never take
My bodily form from any natural thing,
But such a form as Grecian goldsmiths make
Of hammered gold and gold enameling
To keep a drowsy Emperor awake;
Or set upon a golden bough to sing[4]
To lords and ladies of Byzantium
Of what is past, or passing, or to come.

Reading Strategy
Analyzing Philosophical Assumptions What does the last stanza suggest about the artist's relationship to nature and time?

3. **perne . . . gyre** spin in a spiraling motion.
4. **To . . . sing** Yeats wrote, "I have read somewhere that in the Emperor's palace at Byzantium was a tree made of gold and silver, and artificial birds that sang."

Critical Reading

Cite textual evidence to support your responses.

1. **Key Ideas and Details (a)** What do the people and things of the country referred to in the first stanza "commend"? What do they "neglect"? **(b) Interpret:** What "country" is Yeats describing in the first stanza?
2. **Key Ideas and Details (a)** What is an "aged man," according to the second stanza? **(b) Interpret:** Why might the aged not belong to the "country" of the first stanza?
3. **Key Ideas and Details (a) Interpret:** In the third stanza, what does the speaker ask the sages to change in him? **(b) Draw Conclusions:** What does this request reveal about the speaker's faith in artistic production?
4. **Integration of Knowledge and Ideas Make a Judgment:** In your view, which is a "dream"—Byzantium or the world of what "is begotten, born, and dies"?
5. **Integration of Knowledge and Ideas** How is Yeats's poetry affected by both real and imagined places? Use at least three of these Essential Question words in your response: *ideal, locate, occur, affect, significance, constant. [Connecting to the Essential Question: What is the relationship between literature and place?]*

Concept Connector

Reading Strategy Graphic Organizer

Ask students to review the graphic organizers in which they have found connections between assumptions, imagery, and their emotional impacts. Then, have students share their organizers and compare the connections they made.

Activating Prior Knowledge

Have students return to their responses to the Activating Prior Knowledge activity. Ask them to explain whether their thoughts have changed and, if so, how.

Writing About the Essential Question

Have students compare their responses to the prompt, completed before reading the poems, with their thoughts afterward. Have them work individually or in groups, writing or discussing their thoughts, to formulate their new responses. Then, lead a class discussion, probing for what students have learned that confirms or invalidates their initial thoughts. Encourage students to cite specific textual details to support their responses.

After You Read

Poetry of William Butler Yeats

Literary Analysis

1. **Key Ideas and Details (a)** In "When You Are Old," Yeats refers to "Love" as a person. What ideas are traditionally associated with that character? **(b)** How does the behavior of Love in the poem compare to that traditional image?
2. **Craft and Structure (a)** What associations does the speaker in "The Lake Isle of Innisfree" build around the **symbol** of Innisfree? **(b)** Explain two things Innisfree might symbolize.
3. **Key Ideas and Details** Explain what the dry "woodland paths," "October twilight," and the "still sky" symbolize in "The Wild Swans at Coole."
4. **Key Ideas and Details** "The Second Coming" is a poem strongly influenced by Yeats's **philosophical system. (a)** In the poem, what events does Yeats connect to the end of one civilization and the beginning of another? **(b)** How does humanity respond to these times of crisis?
5. **Craft and Structure** Use a chart like the one below to compare the birds in the first and second stanzas of "The Second Coming." How do these symbols contribute to the meaning of the poem?

Symbol	Associations	Effect on Meaning
Falcon		

6. **Craft and Structure (a)** In "Sailing to Byzantium," what do the monuments in lines 8 and 14 symbolize? **(b)** Find two examples in this poem of Yeats's use of Byzantine art to symbolize perfection.
7. **Integration of Knowledge and Ideas** Based on Yeats's poems, do you think symbols based on personal associations, such as Innisfree, are more compelling than traditional symbols such as the Sphinx?

Common Core State Standards

Writing

1. Write arguments to support claims in an analysis of substantive topics or texts, using valid reasoning and relevant and sufficient evidence. *(p. 1150)*

5. Develop and strengthen writing as needed by planning, revising, editing, rewriting, or trying a new approach, focusing on addressing what is most significant for a specific purpose and audience. *(p. 1150)*

Language

4.d. Verify the preliminary determination of the meaning of a word or phrase. *(p. 1150)*

Reading Strategy

8. **(a)** What emotions does the speaker in "The Lake Isle of Innisfree" feel? **(b)** What does the speaker in "The Wild Swans at Coole" feel? **(c)** Explain how Yeats's word choice helps convey these feelings.
9. **Analyze Yeats's philosophical system** by assessing the emotional impact of his symbols. **(a)** Compare the emotional effect and meaning of the swans in "The Wild Swans at Coole" and the birds in "Sailing to Byzantium." **(b)** Based on those meanings, how do you think Yeats's attitude toward nature changed during his life?
10. How does Yeats use the symbol of the "gyre" in "The Second Coming" and "Sailing to Byzantium"?
11. Compare Yeats's idea of historical cycles with the scientific view of time.

Assessment Practice

Many tests require students to recognize effective stylistic devices and language. Use the following sample test item to teach students how to recognize parallel structure.

How many loved your moments of glad grace,
And loved your beauty with love false or true,
But one man loved the pilgrim soul in you,
And loved the sorrows of your changing face.

Which of the following appears in these lines?

A allusion
B metaphor
C parallel structure
D dangling modifier

Knowing that parallel structure is the repetition of a basic grammatical pattern leads to the correct answer, **C**.

Answers

1. (a) Love is associated with togetherness and affection. (b) "Love" defies this image by representing distance, bitterness, and revenge.
2. (a) He builds associations of youth and peace. (b) Innisfree might symbolize the speaker's youth, or the peace he lacks in his life.
3. The phrases symbolize the speaker's old age. October is near the end of the year, and the speaker is near the end of his life. Twilight is the end of the day; dry paths suggest an end of growth; the "still sky" suggests an end of change.
4. (a) Yeats connects this transition with chaos and darkness. (b) People react with intense violence.
5. The falcon represents obedience. Its flying free emphasizes the idea of civilization spiraling out of control. The desert birds symbolize freedom. Flying angrily, they help emphasize the extent of the chaos at hand.
6. (a) The monuments symbolize cultural achievements of lasting value. (b) **Possible response:** The gold mosaic and artificial bird represent the unchanging perfection of art.
7. Students may say personal symbols are more compelling because they more directly convey passions and experiences. Traditional symbols involve preset associations and responses, so they seem flat or stale.
8. (a) The speaker in "The Lake Isle of Innisfree" feels peace and hope. (b) The speaker in "The Wild Swans at Coole" feels mournful. (c) In "Innisfree," "peace," "glow," and "water lapping" convey tranquility. In "Wild Swans," "October twilight," and "heart is sore" convey sadness.
9. (a) The swans symbolize youth, while the birds symbolize fierceness and chaos. (b) Yeats had a positive view of nature, but it changed for the worse.
10. In "The Second Coming," he used the gyre to represent the end of a civilization. In "Sailing to Byzantium," he used it to represent time.
11. Yeats believed history makes sudden, drastic changes in moral climate every 2,000 years. Scientists mark periods of history as progressive.

EXTEND/ASSESS

Answers

Vocabulary Acquisition and Use

Word Analysis:

1. A *matriarchy* is a society governed by women.
2. A *monarchy* is a society governed by a single person.
3. A group of people ranked one above another is a *hierarchy*.
4. An *oligarchy* is a society governed by a group of people.
5. A *patriarchy* is a society governed by men.

Vocabulary

1. His <u>artifice</u> managed to convince the gullible victim.
2. <u>Anarchy</u> resulted when the government leaders fled.
3. She had the power gained from certainty in her <u>conviction</u>.
4. The <u>paltry</u> sum was hardly sufficient recompense for the damage done.
5. With her final victory in the chess tournament, her <u>conquest</u> was complete.
6. The <u>clamorous</u> crowd shouted the speaker down.

Sample Sentences:
The detective's <u>artifice</u> quickly led him to the perpetrator.
A knight embarked on a <u>conquest</u> to win the love of a lady of the court.

Writing

You may use this Writing Lesson as timed-writing practice, or you may allow students to develop the argumentative text over several days.

1. To give students guidance for writing this argumentative text, give them the **Support for Writing Lesson** page from **Unit 6 Resources,** page 15.
2. Before students begin their writing projects, ask them to read the criticism through once to form a general impression of the critic's intent.
3. During the drafting portion of the activity, remind students to place references in logical order.
4. Use the Critique in the ***Professional Development Guidebook,*** pages 276–277, to evaluate students' work.

PERFORMANCE TASKS

Integrated Language Skills

Vocabulary Acquisition and Use

Word Analysis: Words with the Greek Root *-archy-*

In "The Second Coming," Yeats uses the word *anarchy.* The word combines the prefix *an-*, meaning "not," and the Greek root *-archy*, which means "ruler." *Anarchy,* then, is the condition of having no ruler, or government. Use context to determine the meanings of the italicized words. Explain those meanings in a sentence. You may consult a dictionary to confirm the meanings.

1. In a *matriarchy,* mothers own the land and pass it on to their daughters.
2. The oldest surviving child of the king gains the throne in a *monarchy.*
3. In the army's *hierarchy*, each member obeys the orders of those with higher rank.
4. The Council of Ten was a powerful *oligarchy* that led a country of millions.
5. The family was a *patriarchy*, and the father's word had to be followed.

Vocabulary: Synonyms

A synonym is a word that has a meaning similar to that of another word. Replace each italicized word below with a synonym from the vocabulary list on page 1138. Use each vocabulary word only once. Then write two original sentences, each using one of the vocabulary words.

1. His *trickery* managed to convince the gullible victim.
2. *Chaos* resulted when the government leaders fled.
3. She had the power gained from certainty in her *beliefs.*
4. The *insignificant* sum was hardly sufficient recompense for the damage done.
5. With her final victory in the chess tournament, her *triumph* was complete.
6. The *noisy* crowd shouted the speaker down.

Writing

Argumentative Text Critic Richard Ellmann writes that Yeats's poetry is based on the opposition between "the world of change" and a world of "changelessness." Write a **response** in which you find evidence of this opposition in Yeats's poems.

Prewriting Note uses of imagery, language, or ideas that represent change or changelessness. Review your examples to see if they mainly support or refute Ellmann's claim, and decide whether you agree or disagree with his view.

Drafting Begin your draft by summarizing Ellmann's position and stating your response to it. Support your generalizations with quotations from Yeats's writing. Introduce each quotation and explain how it supports the point you are making.

Revising Review your draft, highlighting generalizations and looking for supporting details. Where details are lacking, look back at Yeats's poems to find supporting details. Be sure that the titles of Yeats's poems and the quotations you use from them are accurate.

Model: Revising References to Be Accurate
In "The Wild Swans at Coole," Yeats laments that, for him at least, "~~All is~~ All's changed."

Review of quotations ensures they are accurate.

Assessment Resources

Unit 6 Resources

L1 L2 EL **Selection Test A,** pp. 20–22. Administer Test A to less advanced readers.

L3 L4 EL **Selection Test B,** pp. 23–25. Administer Test B to on-level students and more advanced students.

L3 L4 **Open-Book Test,** pp. 17–19. As an alternative, give the Open-Book test.

All **Customizable Test Bank**

All **Self-tests**
Students may prepare for the **Selection Test** by taking the **Self-test** online.

PHLit Online! All assessment resources are available at **www.PHLitOnline.com.**

Conventions and Style: Sentence Fragments and Run-ons

In most writing, except for dialogue in fiction, it is important to avoid sentence fragments and run-on sentences. A **sentence fragment** is an incomplete sentence punctuated as a sentence. It may be missing a subject, a verb, or both, and it fails to express a complete thought. Fragments are often phrases or subordinate clauses.

Fragment (lacking a verb): The lover old and gray sitting by the fire.

Add a verb: The lover grew old and gray sitting by the fire.

A **run-on sentence** is two or more sentences punctuated as one. **Fused sentences** and **comma splices** are two types of run-ons:

Fused sentence: The trees are beautiful in the fall the still water reflects the sky.

Corrected by rewriting: The trees are beautiful in the fall when the still water reflects the sky.

Comma splice: Many love a woman's beauty, few will love the inner person.

Corrected by adding a conjunction: Many love a woman's beauty, but few will love the inner person.

Punctuation Tip If the two parts of a run-on sentence are related, you can connect them with a semicolon

Practice: Identify each of the following items as a fragment, a run-on, or a complete sentence. If an item is a fragment or a run-on, rewrite it.

1. The sound of water remains in the memory it gives calm in a cold, gray world.
2. Swans do not seem to weary from the cares of the world as humans do.
3. The swans swim across the water. Or take off and fly through the air.
4. On the still water, swans mysterious and lovely.
5. In fall, swans migrate. In noisy flight.
6. Things that live and breathe must one day die it is the way of the world.
7. When there is no order, things collapse disorder rules the world.
8. People grow old and worthless, monuments are timeless.
9. Art that captures the sound of birds hammered in gold. Lives on through time.
10. Yeats believed in historical cycles of twenty centuries.

Writing and Speaking Conventions

A. Writing Find three fragments and two run-ons in the paragraph below. Rewrite the paragraph so that each sentence is complete.

A small cabin at Innisfree. The cabin is built of clay and sticks, the cabin provides shelter and peace. A place for a garden and hive for the bees. In the morning the cricket sings in the evening songbirds fill the air with music. Outside the water against the shore.

Example: A small cabin at Innisfree.

Rewritten: There's a small cabin at Innisfree.

B. Speaking Write and present to the class a brief explanation of whether you believe Yeats's predictions are proving true or false in the twenty-first century. Be sure to check your writing for fragments and run-ons.

PH WRITING COACH

Further instruction and practice are available in *Prentice Hall Writing Coach.*

Extend the Lesson

Sentence Modeling

Read aloud the line given from the selection students have read:

While I stand on the roadway, or on the pavements gray

Ask students what they notice about this line. Elicit from them that it is a sentence fragment. Have them turn to "The Lake Isle of Innisfree" and ask them what line or lines they need to add to make it a complete sentence. Elicit from them that they must add the line below it to form a complete sentence.

Have students imitate the given sentence in sentences on topics of their own choosing, matching each grammatical and stylistic feature discussed. Collect the sentences, and share them with the class.

Conventions and Style

Practice

1. run-on; The sound of water remains in the memory; it gives calm in a cold, gray world.
2. complete sentence
3. fragment; The swans swim across the water or take off and fly through the air.
4. fragment; On the still water, swans are mysterious and lovely.
5. fragment; In fall, swans migrate in noisy flight.
6. run-on; Things that live and breathe must one day die; it is the way of the world.
7. run-on; When there is no order, things collapse and disorder rules the world.
8. run-on; People grow old and worthless, but monuments are timeless.
9. fragment; Art that captures the sound of birds hammered in gold lives on through time.
10. complete sentence

Writing and Speaking Conventions

A. There is a small cabin at Innisfree. The cabin is built of clay and sticks, and it provides shelter and peace. There is a place for a garden and a hive for the bees. In the morning the cricket sings. In the evening songbirds fill the air with music. Outside the water laps against the shore.

B. **Sample response:** Students may answer positively or negatively. Their answers must contain just support for their opinions and be free of fragments and run-ons.

PH WRITING COACH Grade 12

Further instruction on and practice with writing a response to literature can be found in Chapter 10.

Literary History: T. S. Eliot's World

1. Discuss with students the plethora of styles writers can use to convey their ideas. What sorts of writing styles do they enjoy reading? Do they consider those styles to be conventional?
2. After students have discussed their favorite styles of writing, have them read the article about Modernism and what types of writing styles emerged from the period.

Background

Literature

1. Write the following list on the board:

   Woolf: *stories about a person's train of thought*

   Eliot: *poems composed from "anonymous" images*

   Joyce: *stories in which an individual is disillusioned*
2. Use the following prompt for discussion: Explain how each writer discovered a new subjectivity or a new objectivity in literature.
   Possible response: Woolf: based stories in subjective experience; Eliot: eliminated subjectivity by treating words as objects (allusions and images); Joyce: dramatized the destruction of subjective illusion by an indifferent objective world

Literary History: T. S. Eliot's World

Modernists like T. S. Eliot responded to an increasingly complex and fragmented world with art that was also complex, dark, and multifaceted.

Modernism and Beyond

At the beginning of the twentieth century, the world woke up and discovered that it had changed. Electricity, engines, telephones, radios—the globe crackled with new energy. Airplanes, machine guns, and chemical warfare enabled human beings to destroy each other with horrendous efficiency. The First World War (1914–1918) claimed twenty million lives. Disillusionment with politics and society was common.

In this climate of change and uncertainty, artists broke with the past and began to pursue new ideals and visions. They began to see themselves not just as preservers of culture but as creators of culture; they did not simply follow traditions, they created new ones. These dramatic trends in the arts in the early twentieth century are collectively known as Modernism (1890–1945).

Images of Modernism When you take a photograph, you record and preserve what is happening now. Modernism could be thought of as a complex response to what photographs imply. Some Modernists, such as the American poet Ezra Pound (1885–1972) and the British poet T. S. Eliot (1888–1965), wrote poetry as if they were taking snapshots of the world and then cutting and pasting them into collages. Eliot celebrated what he called objectivity in poetry. He relied on images, well chosen and artfully rendered, to encapsulate a feeling or perspective.

On the other hand, the British Modernist novelist Virginia Woolf (1882–1941) perfected techniques for conveying an individual's moment-by-moment experience. For Woolf, the mind is like a camera filming continuously. Her writing records what the moment looks like to an individual. A photograph shows us exactly what the world looks like; Woolf suggests that what the world looks like depends on who is looking.

Visual Arts Photography makes a good analogy for Modernist literary developments. It had a clear impact on painting. Photography now had the job of recording literal appearances, so artists were freed from the necessity of directly imitating the look of things. The revolutionary French painter Paul Cézanne (1839–1906) began to emphasize the canvas as a two-dimensional arrangement of form and color. His work led to the innovations of Modernists such as Pablo Picasso (1881–1973), whose

Enrichment: Technology

Photography

The first successful technologies for photography were introduced by Louis-Jacques-Mandé Daguerre in 1839. Daguerreotypes, images created using his process, introduced a broad public to the possibilities of recording the moment. Photography quickly took on a public dimension. Pioneers such as Mathew Brady used the camera to record contemporary events. The Photo-Secession group, led by Alfred Stieglitz, brought photography to the status of a fine art. Paul Strand and others explored abstract composition. Henri Cartier-Bresson celebrated the humor or beauty of a moment by squeezing the shutter at the right time in the right place.

Encourage interested students to do further research on photography. Have them record and analyze their findings using the **Enrichment: Analyzing Forms and Genres** worksheet, ***Professional Development Guidebook***, page 227.

Les Desmoiselles d'Avignon is the first Cubist painting—a picture in which multiple perspectives on the subject are depicted simultaneously.

Past, Present, and Future Time is a central theme of Modernism. To a photographer, every moment in time is equal to every other, another present to be captured. Yet Eliot was deeply preoccupied with the thought that the past and present are quite unequal. In a poem like "Journey of the Magi" (p. 1158), Eliot portrays the present as a time of despair, an emptiness left behind when the past has disappeared.

Making the New At the same time that Eliot seemed to mourn the past, Modernism also turned toward the future. Modernist fiction writers broke with traditional narrative methods. Describing how characters saw their lives became more important than constructing a traditional plot, and endings were sometimes unresolved. Modernist poets, too, favored experimentation over traditional forms and rhyme schemes. Their poems draw images from a variety of sources, such as history, everyday life, and other texts and cultures.

Beyond Modernism The Modernist literary movement climaxed in 1922, when both James Joyce's *Ulysses* and T. S. Eliot's *The Waste Land* were published. In ensuing decades, the arts took another turn in the developments known as Postmodernism, a movement that replaced the hopes Modernism placed on innovative artistic breakthroughs with a sometimes cynical questioning of the nature of art and perception. The Modernist legacy lives on, though, in the continuing drive for the new.

In This Section

Speaking and Listening: Discussion

Comprehension and Collaboration Photography was invented in the nineteenth century and evolved aesthetically and technologically through the twentieth century. Today, photography is both an art form and a technology accessible to nearly everyone. With a group, discuss photography's changing role in art and culture. Use the list of questions provided to guide your discussion.

Prepare by researching photography as both popular hobby and art form. Assign group members to specific research tasks, using these questions to focus the work:

- How has digital technology changed photography?
- With the technology to retouch photographs, have we strayed completely from the Modernist idea that an image captures a moment forever?
- If anyone can take a picture, what makes photography an art form?

As a group, assign roles for the discussion, such as moderator and note-taker. Agree upon a set of rules to ensure all members participate fully. Choose a point person to share your conclusions with the class.

Background

Culture

1. Explain to students that while Modernists created new forms, Postmodernists challenge form.
2. Key Postmodernist devices include quotation and context shift. Roy Lichtenstein (1923–1997) quoted from popular culture by painting comic strip panels, raising the question: Is this a painting of a scene or a comic book drawing? Marcel Duchamp (1887–1968) lined a spoon and bowl with fur. By rendering these objects useless, he changed their context from dinner table to museum.
3. Postmodernism might be interpreted as persistent irony in response to meaninglessness or seen as an isolated moment when an object becomes art.

Speaking and Listening: Discussion

Photography Today

1. Review Modernism with the class and encourage students to start thinking beyond what was stated in the text. Here are some additional starter questions: Why is Modernist art more suited to modern life than an epic? Does every era consider itself "modern"?
2. Have students form groups to research Postmodernism and its effects on photography and other art forms.
3. Allow class time for groups to discuss individual findings. Then, have groups present their conclusions to the class.

Preludes • Journey of the Magi • The Hollow Men

Lesson Pacing Guide

DAY 1 Preteach

- Administer the Reading and Vocabulary Warm-ups (*Unit 6 Resources*, pp. 26–29) as necessary.
- Introduce the Literary Analysis concept: Modernism in Poetry.
- Introduce the Reading Strategy: Relate to Historical Period.
- Build background with the author and Background features.
- Develop thematic thinking with Connecting to the Essential Question.
- Teach the selection vocabulary.

DAYS 2–3 Preteach/Teach/Assess

- Distribute copies of the appropriate graphic organizer for the Reading Strategy (*Graphic Organizer Transparencies*, pp. 204–205).
- Distribute copies of the appropriate graphic organizer for Literary Analysis (*Graphic Organizer Transparencies*, pp. 206–207).
- Prepare students to read with the Activating Prior Knowledge activities (TE).
- Informally monitor comprehension while students read.
- Use the Reading Check questions to confirm comprehension.
- Develop students' understanding of Modernism in poetry using the Literary Analysis prompts.
- Develop students' ability to relate to the historical period using the Reading Strategy prompts.
- Reinforce vocabulary with the Vocabulary notes.
- Assess students' comprehension and mastery of the skills by having them answer the Critical Reading, Literary Analysis, and Reading Strategy questions.
- Have students complete the Vocabulary Lesson.

DAY 4 Extend/Assess

- Have students complete the Conventions and Style Lesson.
- Have students complete the Writing Lesson and write a multi-genre response. (You may assign as homework.)
- Administer Selection Test A or B (*Unit 6 Resources,* pp. 39–41 or 42–44).

Common Core State Standards

Reading Literature 1. Cite strong and thorough textual evidence to support analysis of what the text says explicitly as well as inferences drawn from the text, including determining where the text leaves matters uncertain.

Writing 2. Write informative/explanatory texts to examine and convey complex ideas, concepts, and information clearly and accurately through the effective selection, organization, and analysis of content.
4. Produce clear and coherent writing in which the development, organization, and style are appropriate to task, purpose, and audience.

Speaking and Listening 1.a. Come to discussions prepared, having read and researched material under study.
1.b. Work with peers to promote civil, democratic discussions and decision making, set clear goals and deadlines, and establish individual roles as needed.

Language 3.a. Vary syntax for effect.
5. Demonstrate understanding of figurative language, word relationships, and nuances in word meanings.

Additional Standards Practice
***Common Core Companion**, pp. 2–14; 196–207; 219–225; 278–285; 322–323; 332–335*

Daily Block Scheduling
Each day in this Lesson Pacing Guide represents a 40–50 minute period. Teachers using block scheduling may combine days to revise pacing. In addition, teachers may differentiate and support core instruction by integrating components for extended and intensive support as students require. See the Guide to Selected Leveled Resources (facing page).

Guide to Selected Leveled Resources

RTI Tier 1 (students performing on level)			Preludes • Journey of the Magi • The Hollow Men
Warm Up	Whole class instruction; Group work	**Practice, model,** and **monitor** fluency, working **with the whole class** or **in groups**.	Vocabulary and Reading Warm-ups B, *Unit 6 Resources,* pp. 26–27, 29
Comprehension/Skills	Whole class instruction; Group work; Independent work	**Support** and **monitor** comprehension and skills development, having students complete the activities, graphic organizers, and interactive prompts **independently** or **as a class**.	• *Reader's Notebook,* adapted instruction and full selection EL *Reader's Notebook: English Learner's Version,* adapted instruction and adapted selection • Reading Strategy Graphic Organizer B, *Graphic Organizer Transparencies,* p. 215 • Literary Analysis Graphic Organizer B, *Graphic Organizer Transparencies,* p. 217
Monitor Progress	Assessment	**Monitor** student progress with the differentiated curriculum-based assessment in the *Unit Resources.*	• Selection Test B, *Unit 6 Resources,* pp. 42–44 • Open-Book Test, *Unit 6 Resources,* pp. 36–38

RTI Tier 2 (students requiring intervention)			Preludes • Journey of the Magi • The Hollow Men
Warm Up	Group work; One-on-one teaching	**Practice, model,** and **monitor** fluency **in groups** or **with individuals.**	• Vocabulary and Reading Warm-ups A, *Unit 6 Resources,* pp. 26–28 • *Hear It!* Audio CD (adapted text)
Comprehension/Skills	Group work; One-on-one teaching	• **Support** and **monitor** comprehension and skills development, working **in small groups** or **with individuals.** • As students complete the selection in the appropriate version of the *Reader's Notebook,* **monitor** comprehension frequently with group questions and individual instruction. • **Model** strategies while guiding students in completing the activities and prompts in the *Reader's Notebook,* as well as the graphic organizers. • **Practice** skills and **monitor** mastery with the *Reading Kit* worksheets.	• *Reader's Notebook: Adapted Version,* adapted instruction and adapted selection EL *Reader's Notebook: English Learner's Version,* adapted instruction and adapted selection • Reading Strategy Graphic Organizer A, *Graphic Organizer Transparencies,* p. 214 • Literary Analysis Graphic Organizer A, *Graphic Organizer Transparencies,* p. 216 • *Reading Kit,* Practice worksheets
Monitor Progress	Assessment	**Monitor** student progress with the differentiated curriculum-based assessment in the *Unit Resources* and in the *Reading Kit.*	• Selection Test A, *Unit 6 Resources,* pp. 39–41 • *Reading Kit,* Assess worksheets

TIER 3 Tier 3 intervention may require consultation with the student's special-education or dyslexia specialist. For additional support, see the Tier 2 activities and resources listed above.

One-on-one teaching · Group work · Whole class instruction · Independent work · A Assessment

For a complete guide to selection support, including support for Advanced students, see the Overview of Resources in the frontmatter.

Preludes • Journey of the Magi • The Hollow Men

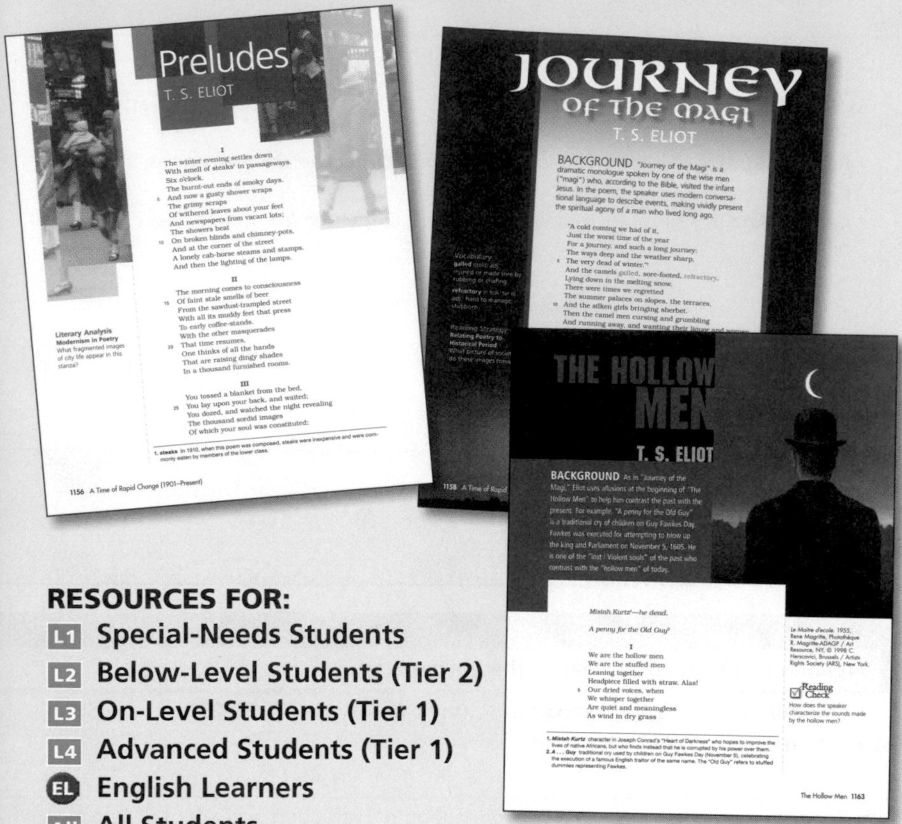

RESOURCES FOR:

- L1 Special-Needs Students
- L2 Below-Level Students (Tier 2)
- L3 On-Level Students (Tier 1)
- L4 Advanced Students (Tier 1)
- EL English Learners
- All All Students

Vocabulary/Fluency/Prior Knowledge

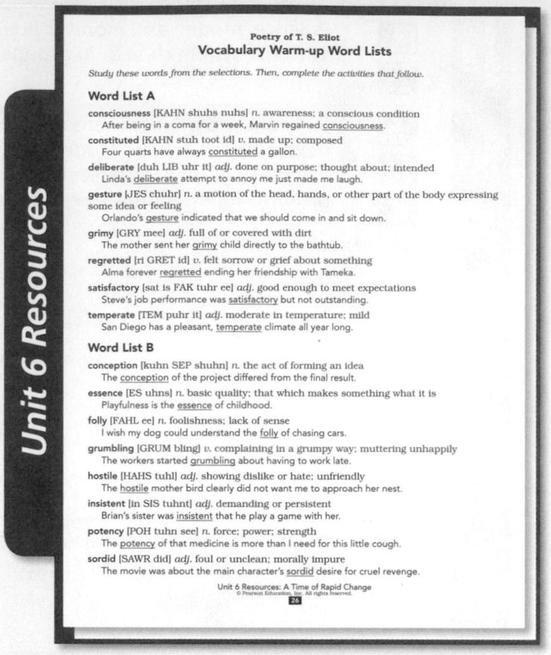
Unit 6 Resources

Poetry of T. S. Eliot

Vocabulary Warm-up Word Lists

Study these words from the selections. Then, complete the activities that follow.

Word List A

consciousness [KAHN shuhs nuhs] *n.* awareness; a conscious condition
After being in a coma for a week, Marvin regained consciousness.

constituted [KAHN stuh toot id] *v.* made up; composed
Four quarts have always constituted a gallon.

deliberate [duh LIB uhr it] *adj.* done on purpose; thought about; intended
Linda's deliberate attempt to annoy me just made me laugh.

gesture [JES chuhr] *n.* a motion of the head, hands, or other part of the body expressing some idea or feeling
Orlando's gesture indicated that we should come in and sit down.

grimy [GRY mee] *adj.* full of or covered with dirt
The mother sent her grimy child directly to the bathtub.

regretted [ri GRET id] *v.* felt sorrow or grief about something
Alma forever regretted ending her friendship with Tameka.

satisfactory [sat is FAK tuhr ee] *adj.* good enough to meet expectations
Steve's job performance was satisfactory but not outstanding.

temperate [TEM puhr it] *adj.* moderate in temperature; mild
San Diego has a pleasant, temperate climate all year long.

Word List B

conception [kuhn SEP shuhn] *n.* the act of forming an idea
The conception of the project differed from the final result.

essence [ES uhns] *n.* basic quality; that which makes something what it is
Playfulness is the essence of childhood.

folly [FAHL ee] *n.* foolishness; lack of sense
I wish my dog could understand the folly of chasing cars.

grumbling [GRUM bling] *v.* complaining in a grumpy way; muttering unhappily
The workers started grumbling about having to work late.

hostile [HAHS tuhl] *adj.* showing dislike or hate; unfriendly
The hostile mother bird clearly did not want me to approach her nest.

insistent [in SIS tuhnt] *adj.* demanding or persistent
Brian's sister was insistent that he play a game with her.

potency [POH tuhn see] *n.* force; power; strength
The potency of that medicine is more than I need for this little cough.

sordid [SAWR did] *adj.* foul or unclean; morally impure
The movie was about the main character's sordid desire for cruel revenge.

Unit 6 Resources: A Time of Rapid Change
© Pearson Education, Inc. All rights reserved.
26

EL L1 L2 **Vocabulary Warm-ups A and B,** pp. 26–27

Also available for these selections:

EL L1 L2 **Reading Warm-ups A and B,** pp. 28–29

All **Vocabulary Builder,** p. 32

Reader's Notebooks

Pre- and postreading pages for these selections, as well as "Journey of the Magi," appear in an interactive format in the *Reader's Notebooks.* Each *Notebook* is differentiated for a different group of learners. The selections in the Adapted and English Learner's versions are abridged.

L2 L3 ***Reader's Notebook***

L1 ***Reader's Notebook: Adapted Version***

EL ***Reader's Notebook: English Learner's Version***

EL ***Reader's Notebook: Spanish Version***

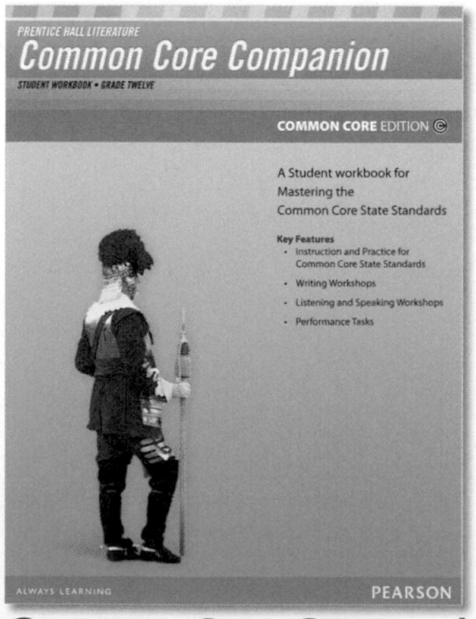

Common Core Companion

Additional instruction and practice for each Common Core State Standard

Selection Support

Graphic Organizer Transparencies

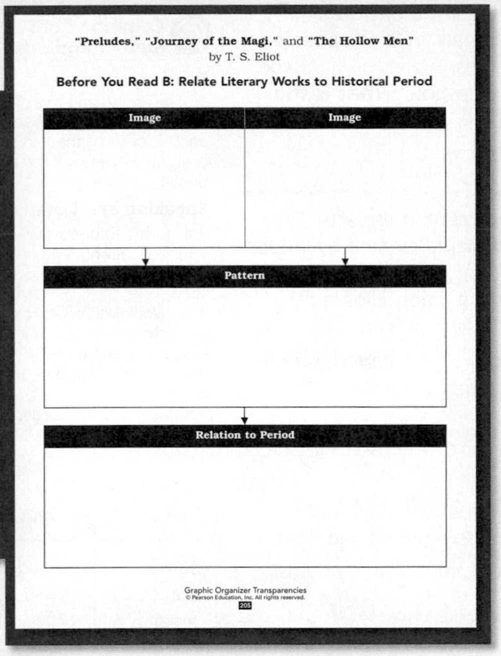
"Preludes," "Journey of the Magi," and "The Hollow Men"
by T. S. Eliot

Before You Read B: Relate Literary Works to Historical Period

Image	Image

Pattern

Relation to Period

Graphic Organizer Transparencies
© Pearson Education, Inc. All rights reserved.
205

EL L3 **Reading: Graphic Organizer B,** p. 205

Also available for these selections:

EL L1 L2 **Reading: Graphic Organizer A,** p. 204

EL L1 L2 **Literary Analysis: Graphic Organizer A,** (partially filled in), p. 206

EL L3 **Literary Analysis: Graphic Organizer B,** p. 207

Skills Development/Extension

Unit 6 Resources

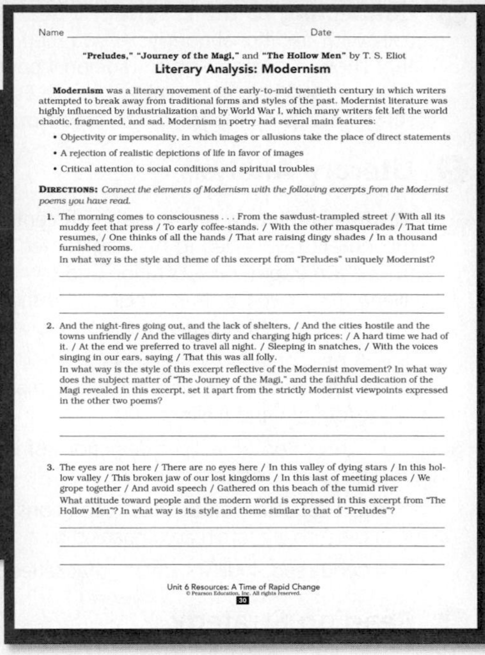
Name ______________________ Date ____________

"Preludes," "Journey of the Magi," and "The Hollow Men" by T. S. Eliot
Literary Analysis: Modernism

Modernism was a literary movement of the early-to-mid twentieth century in which writers attempted to break away from traditional forms and styles of the past. Modernist literature was highly influenced by industrialization and by World War I, which many writers felt left the world chaotic, fragmented, and sad. Modernism in poetry had several main features:

- Objectivity or impersonality, in which images or allusions take the place of direct statements
- A rejection of realistic depictions of life in favor of images
- Critical attention to social conditions and spiritual troubles

Directions: *Connect the elements of Modernism with the following excerpts from the Modernist poems you have read.*

1. The morning comes to consciousness . . . From the sawdust-trampled street / With all its muddy feet that press / To early coffee-stands. / With the other masquerades / That time resumes, / One thinks of all the hands / That are raising dingy shades / In a thousand furnished rooms.
In what way is the style and theme of this excerpt from "Preludes" uniquely Modernist?

2. And the night-fires going out, and the lack of shelters, / And the cities hostile and the towns unfriendly / And the villages dirty and charging high prices: / A hard time we had of it. / At the end we preferred to travel all night, / Sleeping in snatches, / With the voices singing in our ears, saying / That this was all folly.
In what way is the style of this excerpt reflective of the Modernist movement? In what way does the subject matter of "The Journey of the Magi," and the faithful dedication of the Magi revealed in this excerpt, set it apart from the strictly Modernist viewpoints expressed in the other two poems?

3. The eyes are not here / There are no eyes here / In this valley of dying stars / In this hollow valley / This broken jaw of our lost kingdoms / In this last of meeting places / We grope together / And avoid speech / Gathered on this beach of the tumid river
What attitude toward people and the modern world is expressed in this excerpt from "The Hollow Men"? In what way is its style and theme similar to that of "Preludes"?

Unit 6 Resources: A Time of Rapid Change
© Pearson Education, Inc. All rights reserved.
30

All **Literary Analysis: Modernism in Poetry,** p. 30

Also available for these selections:

All **Reading: Relate to Historical Period,** p. 31

EL L3 L4 **Grammar and Style,** p. 33

EL L3 L4 **Support for Writing,** p. 34

L4 **Enrichment,** p. 35

Assessment

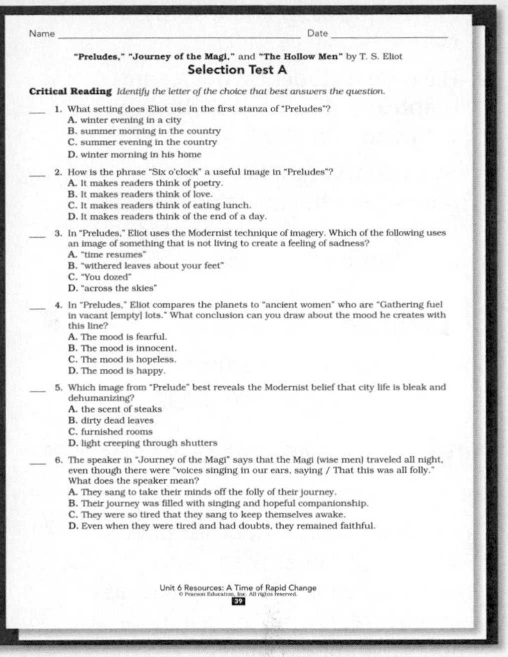
Name ______________________ Date ____________

"Preludes," "Journey of the Magi," and "The Hollow Men" by T. S. Eliot
Selection Test A

Critical Reading *Identify the letter of the choice that best answers the question.*

___ 1. What setting does Eliot use in the first stanza of "Preludes"?
A. winter evening in a city
B. summer morning in the country
C. summer evening in the country
D. winter morning in his home

___ 2. How is the phrase "Six o'clock" a useful image in "Preludes"?
A. It makes readers think of poetry.
B. It makes readers think of love.
C. It makes readers think of eating lunch.
D. It makes readers think of the end of a day.

___ 3. In "Preludes," Eliot uses the Modernist technique of imagery. Which of the following uses an image of something that is not living to create a feeling of sadness?
A. "time resumes"
B. "withered leaves about your feet"
C. "You dozed"
D. "across the skies"

___ 4. In "Preludes," Eliot compares the planets to "ancient women" who are "Gathering fuel in vacant [empty] lots." What conclusion can you draw about the mood he creates with this line?
A. The mood is fearful.
B. The mood is innocent.
C. The mood is hopeless.
D. The mood is happy.

___ 5. Which image from "Prelude" best reveals the Modernist belief that city life is bleak and dehumanizing?
A. the scent of steaks
B. dirty dead leaves
C. furnished rooms
D. light creeping through shutters

___ 6. The speaker in "Journey of the Magi" says that the Magi (wise men) traveled all night, even though there were "voices singing in our ears, saying / That this was all folly." What does the speaker mean?
A. They sang to take their minds off the folly of their journey.
B. Their journey was filled with singing and hopeful companionship.
C. They were so tired that they sang to keep themselves awake.
D. Even when they were tired and had doubts, they remained faithful.

Unit 6 Resources: A Time of Rapid Change
© Pearson Education, Inc. All rights reserved.
39

EL L1 L2 **Selection Test A,** pp. 39–41

Also available for these selections:

L3 L4 **Open-Book Test,** pp. 36–38

EL L3 L4 **Selection Test B,** pp. 42–44

PHLit Online!
www.PHLitOnline.com

- complete narrated selection text
- a thematically related video with writing prompt
- an interactive graphic organizer
- highlighting feature
- access to all student print resources, adapted to individual student needs
- Spanish and English summaries
- adapted selection translations in Spanish

Online Resources: All print materials are also available online.

Get Connected! (thematic video with writing prompt)

Also available:

Background Video
All videos are available in Spanish.

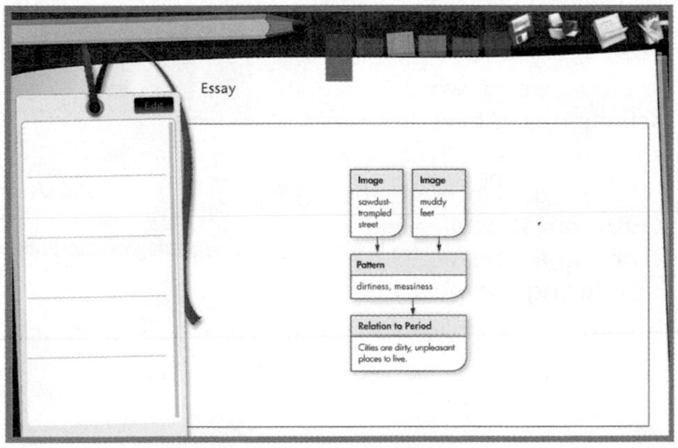

Writer's Journal (with graphics feature)

Also available:

Vocabulary Central (tools and activities for studying vocabulary)

PRETEACH

❶ Connecting to the Essential Question

1. Review the assignment with the class.
2. Have each student write a paragraph about someone who broke with tradition.
3. As students read, have them note where the qualities of Eliot's poetry align with and diverge from those of traditional poetry.

❷ Literary Analysis

Introduce the skill using the instruction on the student page.

Think Aloud: Model the Skill

Say to students:

In reading Eliot's Modernist poetry, I notice that rather than using emotional, subjective language, as some genres do, he takes a more impersonal tone, characterized by bleak snapshots and objective observations. As I read, these juxtaposed images evoke the mundane and depressed atmosphere of modern life.

❸ Reading Strategy

1. Introduce the skill using the instruction on the student page.
2. Give students a copy of **Reading Strategy Graphic Organizer B,** page 205 in ***Graphic Organizer Transparencies,*** to fill out as they read.

❹ Vocabulary

1. Pronounce each word, giving its definition, and have students say it aloud.
2. For more guidance, see the ***Classroom Strategies and Teaching Routines*** card for introducing vocabulary.

Before You Read

Preludes • Journey of the Magi • The Hollow Men

❶ **Connecting to the Essential Question** T. S. Eliot broke dramatically with traditional poetry. As you read, notice details in Eliot's poems that show differences from traditional poetic themes, meter, or language. Doing so will help you think about the Essential Question: **What is the relationship of the writer to tradition?**

❷ Literary Analysis

Modernism was an early-twentieth-century movement in the arts. The movement responded to the fragmented modern world created by industrialization, rapid transportation and communication, and a feeling of alienation caused by mass society and the growth of cities. Eliot led the movement for **Modernism in poetry,** which had several features:

- A new objectivity or impersonality in poetry, in which a work is built from images and allusions rather than from direct statements of thoughts and feelings
- A rejection of realistic depictions of life in favor of the use of images for artistic effect
- Critical attention to social conditions and the spiritual troubles of modern life, often accompanied by a sense of displacement and despair

As you read, look for details that reflect Modernism in Eliot's poems.

❸ Reading Strategy

Preparing to Read Complex Texts Modernist writers found their society bleak and lifeless. They saw crowded cities as places of isolation and loneliness. They believed that the new emphasis on material goods and technology left people adrift spiritually, while factory work dehumanized them. Modernist works do not state these ideas directly. Instead, their emphasis on the oblique suggested meanings requiring readers to draw inferences, or interpret ideas, from images and details. As you read, use a chart like the one shown to **relate Eliot's literary works to the historical period** by identifying images that suggest the Modernist worldview.

❹ Vocabulary

galled (gôld) *adj.* injured or made sore by rubbing or chafing (p. 1158)

refractory (ri frak´ tər ē) *adj.* hard to manage; stubborn (p. 1158)

dispensation (dis´ pən sā´ shən) *n.* religious system or belief (p. 1159)

supplication (sup´ lə kā´ shən) *n.* act of praying or pleading (p. 1164)

tumid (to͞o´ mid) *adj.* swollen (p. 1165)

Common Core State Standards

Reading Literature
1. Cite strong and thorough textual evidence to support analysis of what the text says explicitly as well as inferences drawn from the text.

Speaking and Listening
1.a. Come to discussions prepared, having read and researched material under study.
1.b. Work with peers to promote civil, democratic discussions and decision making, set clear goals and deadlines, and establish individual roles as needed. *(p. 1162)*

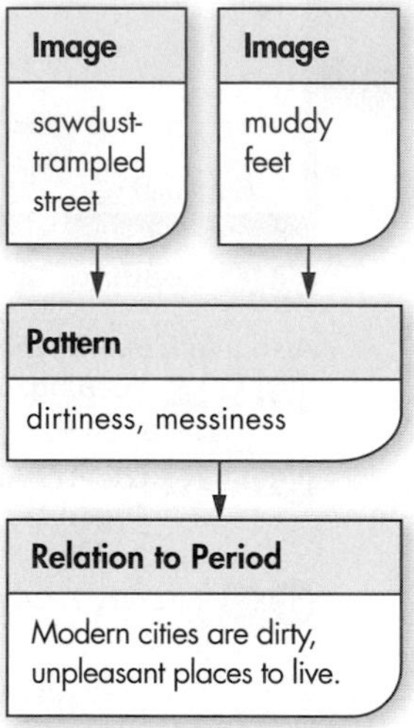

❺ # T. S. ELIOT

(1888–1965)

Author of **"Preludes" • "Journey of the Magi" • "The Hollow Men"**

T. S. Eliot was the most famous English poet of his time. He was also the most influential. His distinctive style and novel ideas affected not only poets, but also critics, fiction writers, playwrights, and even philosophers. From the 1920s on, he was a leader of the artistic movement called Modernism. Eliot and fellow Modernist Ezra Pound transformed English-language poetry, grounding their work in the power of images.

Crossing the Atlantic Born Thomas Stearns Eliot in St. Louis, Missouri, he was educated at Harvard University. He went on to study at Oxford University in England and at the Sorbonne in Paris. The outbreak of World War I in 1914 found Eliot in England, where he settled and eventually became a citizen.

In 1915, Eliot married the sensitive, intelligent, and witty Vivien Haigh-Wood. While writing poetry and critical reviews, Eliot taught school, worked for the banking firm of Lloyd's, and eventually took a position with a publishing company.

Early Work Because of its unconventional style, Eliot's earliest work was greeted with less than universal acclaim, although the American poet Ezra Pound was a vocal supporter from the beginning. Pound saw that Eliot spoke in an authentic new voice and offered an original, if bleak, vision. From *Prufrock and Other Observations* (1917) through *The Waste Land* (1922) and "The Hollow Men" (1925), Eliot portrayed the modern world as one of fragmented experiences and despair. Eliot may have been responding to World War I, an event that damaged the faith of many. At the same time, the war may have prompted readers to catch up with Eliot, who had written works such as "Preludes" and "The Love Song of J. Alfred Prufrock" before the war.

A Spiritual Rebirth Eventually, Eliot found an answer to despair in religion. In 1927, he joined the Church of England and became a devout Anglican. His new faith shaped the writing of "Journey of the Magi" (1927), *Ash Wednesday* (1930), and the *Four Quartets* (1935–1943).

As a literary critic, Eliot had a profound influence on his contemporaries. His re-evaluations of past poetry shaped the tastes of a generation. In 1948, Eliot received the Nobel Prize for Literature.

"WE SHALL NOT CEASE FROM EXPLORATION."

Daily Bellringer

For each class during which you will teach these selections, have students complete one of the five activities for the appropriate week in the ***Daily Bellringer Activities*** booklet.

Multidraft Reading

To assist struggling readers and to enhance reading for all, assign the text in chunks, as warranted by length, and apply multidraft reading protocols. For each reading, have students set the purpose indicated:

- **First reading**—identifying key ideas and details and answering any Reading Checks.
- **Second reading**—analyzing craft and structure and responding to the side-column prompts.
- **Third reading**—integrating knowledge and ideas, connecting to other texts and the world, and answering the end-of-selection questions.

For more guidance, refer to the ***Classroom Strategies and Teaching Routines*** card on Multidraft Reading.

❺ Background

More About the Author

Eliot had a definite affinity for both the metaphysical poets of the seventeenth century (primarily John Donne) and the nineteenth-century French symbolists (including Baudelaire and Laforgue). He combined these influences with the post–World War I generation, whose values and conventions were born of the Victorian era but changed by the harsh realities of war. The later influence of orthodox Christianity turned him more toward social and religious conservatism.

PHLit Online!
www.PHLitOnline.com

Teaching From Technology

Preparing to Read

Go to **www.PHLitOnline.com** and display the ***Get Connected!*** slide show for this selection. Have the class brainstorm responses to the writing prompt, entering ideas in the interactive journal. Then, have students complete their written responses as homework.

To build background, display the Background and More About the Author features.

Using the Interactive Text

Go to **www.PHLitOnline.com** and display the **Enriched Online Student Edition.** As the class reads the selection or listens to the narration, record answers to side-column prompts using the graphic organizers accessible on the interactive page. Alternatively, have students use the online edition individually, answering the prompts as they read.

TEACH

❶ About the Selection

This poem presents a bleak and despairing vision of the world. Yet, Eliot may not just have been reveling in despair; he may have seen it as a necessary "prelude" to spiritual awakening.

❷ Activating Prior Knowledge

People punch the clock every day and wonder why they do it. People cannot encounter something new without asking, "I don't know, what do you think?" For Eliot, this kind of uncertainty and despair characterizes life in modern times. Have students bring in examples (from advertisements, books, films, or their own lives) of modern responses to despair. Discuss what these alternatives—psychiatry, crystals, yoga, exercise, religious reawakening, health food—have in common and how they seek to calm the despair in modern life.

Concept Connector ⟶

Tell students they will return to their responses after reading the selection.

❸ Literary Analysis

Modernism in Poetry

1. Remind students that Modernism is frequently based on despair.
2. **Ask** students the Literary Analysis question: What fragmented images of city life appear in this stanza?
   Answer: The images include stale smells, muddy streets, people buying coffee at a vendor's stand, and poor people raising the blinds to look out at the day.

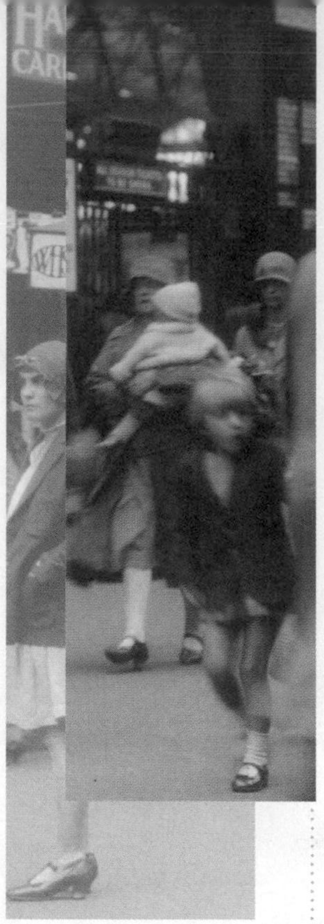

❶ ❷ Preludes

T. S. ELIOT

I

The winter evening settles down
With smell of steaks[1] in passageways.
Six o'clock.
The burnt-out ends of smoky days.
And now a gusty shower wraps
The grimy scraps
Of withered leaves about your feet
And newspapers from vacant lots;
The showers beat
On broken blinds and chimney-pots,
And at the corner of the street
A lonely cab-horse steams and stamps.
And then the lighting of the lamps.

II

The morning comes to consciousness
Of faint stale smells of beer
From the sawdust-trampled street
With all its muddy feet that press
To early coffee-stands. ❸
With the other masquerades
That time resumes,
One thinks of all the hands
That are raising dingy shades
In a thousand furnished rooms.

Literary Analysis
Modernism in Poetry What fragmented images of city life appear in this stanza?

III

You tossed a blanket from the bed,
You lay upon your back, and waited;
You dozed, and watched the night revealing
The thousand sordid images
Of which your soul was constituted;

1. **steaks** In 1910, when this poem was composed, steaks were inexpensive and were commonly eaten by members of the lower class.

Ⓒ Text Complexity Rubric

	Preludes	Journey of the Magi	The Hollow Men
Qualitative Measures			
Context/Knowledge Demands	Modernist lyric 1 ② 3 4 5	Modernist dramatic monologue 1 2 ③ 4 5	Modernist poem 1 2 3 ④ 5
Structure/Language Conventionality and Clarity	Simple diction 1 ② 3 4 5	Fairly simple diction 1 ② 3 4 5	Fairly simple diction 1 ② 3 4 5
Levels of Meaning/ Purpose/Concept Level	Accessible (modern anxiety) 1 2 ③ 4 5	Moderate (realistic biblical retelling) 1 2 ③ 4 5	Challenging (modernist view of human condition) 1 2 3 ④ 5
Quantitative Measures			
Lexile/Text Length	NP / 312 words	NP / 338 words	NP / 426 words
Overall Complexity	**More accessible**	**More accessible**	**More complex**

They flickered against the ceiling.
And when all the world came back
And the light crept up between the shutters
And you heard the sparrows in the gutters,
You had such a vision of the street
As the street hardly understands;
Sitting along the bed's edge, where
You curled the papers from your hair,
Or clasped the yellow soles of feet
In the palms of both soiled hands.

IV

His soul stretched tight across the skies
That fade behind a city block,
Or trampled by insistent feet
At four and five and six o'clock;
And short square fingers stuffing pipes,
And evening newspapers, and eyes
Assured of certain certainties,
The conscience of a blackened street
Impatient to assume the world.

I am moved by fancies that are curled
Around these images, and cling:
The notion of some infinitely gentle
Infinitely suffering thing.

Wipe your hand across your mouth, and laugh;
The worlds revolve like ancient women
Gathering fuel in vacant lots.

Reading Strategy
Relating Poetry to Historical Period
What view of modern life do the last lines in this stanza convey?

Critical Reading

1. **Key Ideas and Details (a)** In Prelude I, what is the time of year and the time of day? **(b) Interpret:** What cycle of time takes place from Prelude I to Prelude IV? **(c) Support:** What effect does the poet achieve by representing this complete cycle?
2. **Key Ideas and Details (a) Draw Conclusions:** What is the character of modern life as Eliot depicts it? **(b) Compare and Contrast:** Contrast this character with "The notion of some infinitely gentle / Infinitely suffering thing" (lines 50–51). **(c) Speculate:** Based on this contrast, what do you think the "thing" might be?
3. **Integration of Knowledge and Ideas** Think of a sight in a modern city that conveys joy. How might Eliot have reacted to that image?

Cite textual evidence to support your responses.

❹ Reading Strategy

Relating Poetry to Historical Period

1. **Ask** students the Reading Strategy question: What view of modern life do the last lines in this stanza convey?
2. **Answer:** The poet appears to encourage amusement in the face of the desolation of modernity.

ASSESS

Answers

Before students respond, you may wish to have them write a brief objective summary of the selection. As they answer the questions below, remind them to support their answers with evidence from the text.

1. (a) It is winter, at 6 P.M. (b) The cycle of time is one day, from evening through the night to morning and back to evening. (c) The poet implies that life is a never-ending cycle, reinforcing the mood of despair.
2. (a) The general character of modern life is monotony, lack of individualism, and lack of spiritual hope. (b) The lines paint a different picture by introducing the idea of compassion and gentleness. (c) **Possible responses:** The "thing" might be Christ; it might be humanity taken in its totality.
3. **Sample response:** A fountain in a park might inspire joy. Eliot might convert it, though, into an image of despair by noting the litter floating in it (for example).

Text Complexity: Reader and Task Suggestions

	Preludes	Journey of the Magi	The Hollow Men
Preparing to Read the Texts • Using the information at the bottom of TE p. 1162, explain that Eliot often includes religious and literary allusions in his poetry. • Discuss with students the disillusionment with modern life that many writers felt after World War I. • Guide students to use Multidraft Reading strategies (TE p. 1155).	**Leveled Tasks** ***Levels of Meaning*** If students will have difficulty with the poem's meaning, have them first focus on the mood that the images express. Then, as they reread, have them consider the main impression the images convey. ***Evaluating*** If students will not have difficulty with the poem's meaning, have them evaluate the effectiveness of the imagery in revealing modern life.	**Leveled Tasks** ***Levels of Meaning*** If students will have difficulty with the poem's meaning, have them focus first on the speaker's experiences, and then on their relevance to modern life. ***Evaluating*** If students will not have difficulty with the poem's meaning, have them evaluate the effectiveness of the dramatic presentation.	**Leveled Tasks** ***Knowledge Demands*** If students will have difficulty with the literary context, have them first read through the poem to get a general idea of its attitudes. Then, have students read the poem for meaning. ***Analyzing*** If students will not have difficulty with the context, have them analyze how the poem's allusions contribute to its meaning.

❺ About the Selection

The speaker, one of the three biblical wise men who honor the baby Jesus, recounts the practical challenges and physical discomforts of the long journey to Bethlehem. By affiliating those discomforts with the religious awakening of Christianity, the speaker acknowledges the difficulties of spiritual growth and change.

❻ Vocabulary

Latin Root -fract-

1. Point out the word *refractory* in line 6. Tell students that the word means "stubborn."
2. Have students suggest other words that contain the root *-fract-*.
   Possible responses: Such words include *fracture* and *fraction.*
3. Then, encourage students to use a dictionary to find out how the meaning of this root contributes to the specific meaning of each word.

❼ Reading Strategy

Relating to Historical Period

1. **Ask** students the Reading Strategy question: What picture of society do these images convey?
2. **Answer:** These images show society as uncaring and dissolute.

❺ JOURNEY OF THE MAGI

T. S. ELIOT

BACKGROUND "Journey of the Magi" is a dramatic monologue spoken by one of the wise men ("magi") who, according to the Bible, visited the infant Jesus. In the poem, the speaker uses modern conversational language to describe events, making vividly present the spiritual agony of a man who lived long ago.

"A cold coming we had of it,
Just the worst time of the year
For a journey, and such a long journey:
The ways deep and the weather sharp,
The very dead of winter."[1]
And the camels galled, sore-footed, refractory,
Lying down in the melting snow.
There were times we regretted
The summer palaces on slopes, the terraces,
And the silken girls bringing sherbet.
Then the camel men cursing and grumbling
And running away, and wanting their liquor and women,
And the night-fires going out, and the lack of shelters,
And the cities hostile and the towns unfriendly
And the villages dirty and charging high prices:
A hard time we had of it.

❻ **Vocabulary**
galled (gôld) *adj.* injured or made sore by rubbing or chafing

refractory (ri frak´ tər ē) *adj.* hard to manage; stubborn

❼ **Reading Strategy**
Relating Poetry to Historical Period
What picture of society do these images convey?

1. **"A . . . winter"** Adapted from a part of a sermon delivered by 17th-century Bishop Lancelot Andrewes: "A cold coming they had of it at this time of year, just the worst time of the year to take a journey, and specially a long journey in. The ways deep, the weather sharp, the days short, the sun farthest off . . . the very dead of winter."

Enrichment: Investigating Religion and Myth

The Magi
In many Christian churches, the commemoration of the Magi's visit is celebrated on January 6 with feasting, bright lights, religious services, and gift giving. Throughout the Spanish-speaking world, *El Día de los Reyes,* "The Day of Kings," is celebrated with a parade in which stand-ins for the three kings ride camels through the streets.

Activity: Research Astrology Some religious groups have translated the word *magi* to mean *astrologers,* as the Christian Bible says that the Magi followed a star to find the birthplace of Jesus. Have students investigate how some people still use astrology to guide their lives, and contrast this with evidence negating the accuracy of such claims. Suggest that they record the information on the **Enrichment: Investigating Religion and Myth** worksheet, ***Professional Development Guidebook,*** page 240.

At the end we preferred to travel all night,
Sleeping in snatches,
With the voices singing in our ears, saying
That this was all folly.

Then at dawn we came down to a temperate valley,
Wet, below the snow line, smelling of vegetation;
With a running stream and a water-mill beating the darkness,
And three trees on the low sky,
And an old white horse galloped away in the meadow.
Then we came to a tavern with vine-leaves over the lintel,
Six hands at an open door dicing for pieces of silver,
And feet kicking the empty wine-skins.
But there was no information, and so we continued
And arrived at evening, not a moment too soon
Finding the place; it was (you may say) satisfactory.

All this was a long time ago, I remember,
And I would do it again, but set down
This set down
This: were we led all that way for
Birth or Death? There was a Birth, certainly,
We had evidence and no doubt. I had seen birth and death,
But had thought they were different; this Birth was
Hard and bitter agony for us, like Death, our death.
We returned to our places, these Kingdoms,
But no longer at ease here, in the old dispensation,
With an alien people clutching their gods.
I should be glad of another death.

Vocabulary
dispensation (dis´ pən sā´ shən) *n.* religious system or belief

Critical Reading

Cite textual evidence to support your responses.

1. **Key Ideas and Details (a)** What event has the speaker in "Journey of the Magi" gone to witness? **(b) Compare and Contrast:** How does the description of the journey compare to the description of the event? **(c) Interpret:** Why might the speaker say so little about one and so much about the other?
2. **Key Ideas and Details** How has the event changed the speaker's relation to his own people?
3. **Integration of Knowledge and Ideas (a) Compare and Contrast:** In what way is Eliot's choice of details similar in the first stanzas of "Preludes" and "Journey of the Magi"? **(b) Draw Conclusions:** What do you think Eliot was trying to achieve in each case?

ASSESS

Answers

Before students respond, you may wish to have them write a brief objective summary of the selection. As they answer the questions below, remind them to support their answers with evidence from the text.

1. (a) The journey is to witness a birth. (b) The journey shows many places, each different, and each in detail. The birth is glossed over. (c) **Possible responses:** The speaker has yet to evaluate the significance of the birth; it is too momentous to be put into words.
2. The speaker is no longer at ease in his old surroundings because he does not share the beliefs of those around him.
3. (a) In both poems, he masses together fragmented details of scenes that he indicates are repeated. (b) **Possible response:** In "Preludes," these details suggest the meaninglessness of modern life; in "Magi," they create a sense of passing time and expectancy: The jumbled events of the journey appear insignificant beside its goal.

Differentiated Instruction for Universal Access

Background for Special-Needs Students
Be sure that students understand that the Magi are the three wise men from Christian stories. Have students relate what they may know about the three wise men. Prepare them for the difference between the conventional picture of the Magi and the picture Eliot presents.

Enrichment for Gifted/Talented Students
Those students with an interest in drama and theater might like to perform this poem. Have students write a monologue from the point of view of one of the Magi who tells of the journey undertaken. Some students may match Eliot's view, while others may present a different view.

Enrichment for Advanced Readers
Eliot makes no mention of the traditional gifts the Magi bore for Jesus: gold, frankincense, and myrrh. Have students research these substances and determine whether they would have supported Eliot's view of the events.

How "The Hollow Men" Was Written

1. Discuss with students their own writing processes. How do they go about constructing stories that they write? Do they ever use ideas that they eliminated from a previous piece for another story?
2. After students have discussed their own writing processes, have them read about Eliot's approach.

Background

More About the Author

1. Explain to students that when Eliot wrote "The Hollow Men," he had already secured international renown with the publication of *The Waste Land* in 1922.
2. In 1927, the year he published the volume containing "The Hollow Men," he also became an English citizen and entered the Anglican Church. The poetry he wrote after this point had a decidedly religious cast.
3. One can already detect his religious interests, though, in "The Hollow Men," which is set in Hell and describes the damnation of those without sufficient spirit to commit evil.
4. Eliot states some of the views implied in the poem in his critical writing. Read the class the following quotation, written by Eliot about Baudelaire:

> It is better, in a paradoxical way, to do evil, than to do nothing: at least we exist. The worst that can be said of most of our malefactors, from statesmen to thieves, is that they are not man enough to be damned.

Literary History: Eliot's "The Hollow Men"

"Eliot's allusions create a distinctive, dreamlike world for a reader to explore."

How "The Hollow Men" Was Written

In 1921, T. S. Eliot began a long poem called *The Waste Land*. He later used sections that had been edited out of *The Waste Land* as the basis for "The Hollow Men." He often worked this way, building a poem from pieces that had been written independently and using discarded fragments of one poem to create the next. He explained this process of working in an interview with Donald Hall (*The Paris Review*, No. 21):

Interviewer: Are any of your minor poems actually sections cut out of longer works? There are two that sound like "The Hollow Men."

Eliot: Oh, those were the preliminary sketches. Those things were earlier. Others I published in periodicals but not in my collected poems . . .

Interviewer: You seem often to have written poems in sections. Did they begin as separate poems? I am thinking of "Ash Wednesday," in particular.

Eliot: Yes, like "The Hollow Men," it originated out of separate poems. As I recall, one or two early drafts of parts of *Ash Wednesday* appeared in *Commerce* [magazine] and elsewhere. Then gradually I came to see it as a sequence. That's one way in which my mind does seem to have worked throughout the years poetically—doing things separately and then seeing the possibility of fusing them together, altering them, and making a kind of whole of them.

Enrichment: Investigating a Key Person in History

Dante's *Divine Comedy*

An important source of references in "The Hollow Men" is the *Divine Comedy,* a poem by Dante Alighieri. In the poem, Dante embarks on a quest that takes him through Hell, Purgatory, and Heaven. Each book in the work, the *Inferno,* the *Purgatorio,* and the *Paradiso,* corresponds to a stage in Dante's journey. In the *Inferno,* Dante meets and speaks with a number of the damned, whose tortures he describes.

Activity: Research the Damned Have students do research on some of the historical figures mentioned in the *Inferno,* such as Brutus, Cassius, Judas Iscariot, and Ulysses. Instruct students to compare Dante's judgment of their flaws to the historical records of their actions. Have students record their findings on the **Enrichment: Investigating a Key Person in History** worksheet, ***Professional Development Guidebook,*** page 233.

The Theme of "The Hollow Men"

It makes sense to assume that "The Hollow Men" and *The Waste Land* are thematically related. *The Waste Land*, as its title suggests, deals with a sense of emotional and spiritual barrenness after the destruction wrought by World War I. "The Hollow Men," published in 1925, also deals with a barren and empty (hollow) existence. It resembles *The Waste Land* in its use of literary allusions to convey this theme of barrenness and to compare the present with other historical eras.

Using Allusions to Interpret the Poem

Critics have identified four key allusions in the poem:

Joseph Conrad's "Heart of Darkness" Kurtz, referred to in a line introducing the poem, is a mysterious character in Conrad's "Heart of Darkness." He travels to the Belgian Congo on a mission to uplift and educate the Congolese people. However, he develops his own little kingdom in which he exercises absolute power over the people he intended to save. It is only when he is dying that he sees the "horror" of what he has done and how he has been, in Conrad's words, a "hollow sham," or fake. His tragic downfall exposes the hollowness of his noble ideals and of the whole colonial enterprise. That enterprise is supported by a host of administrators and clerks who are most like the speakers in Eliot's poem, a chorus of paralyzed nonentities: "We are the hollow men. . . ." Eliot may also be suggesting that this chorus includes his readers.

The Gunpowder Plot The hollow men are also like the effigies of Guy Fawkes, burned to commemorate the uncovering of the Gunpowder Plot of 1605. Fawkes himself was tortured until he revealed the names of his co-conspirators who plotted a powerful explosion that would destroy the king of England and Parliament. As Eliot writes at the end of the poem, "This is the way the world ends / Not with a bang but a whimper." Like Fawkes, so the speakers of Eliot's poem are as helpless and ineffective as straw dummies: "Leaning together / Headpiece filled with straw. Alas!"

Shakespeare's *Julius Caesar* This play deals with another conspiracy to betray a leader. Brutus, a high-minded Roman, is lured by flattery into a plot to assassinate the Roman ruler Julius Caesar. Section V of "The Hollow Men" quotes lines from Shakespeare's play in which Brutus experiences the nightmarelike emptiness of the time before the deed. Like Kurtz in Conrad's story, Brutus is a tragic figure, a self-deluded man who commits murder in the name of high ideals. In this sense, he too is a form of hollow man.

Background

Literature

In 1935, after many had inquired, Eliot revealed the sources for the title "The Hollow Men." He said that the title represents a combination of the titles of two poems by well-known British authors: "The Hollow Land" by William Morris (1834–1896) and "The Broken Man" by Rudyard Kipling (1865–1936).

B. C. Southam, in *A Guide to the Selected Poems of T. S. Eliot,* points out other possible sources for the title in two works that clearly influenced the poem:

1. Shakespeare's *Julius Caesar* (IV.ii):

   But hollow men, like horses
    hot at hand,
   Make gallant show and promise
    of their mettle;
   But when they should endure the
    bloody spur;
   They fail their crests, and, like
    deceitful jades,
   Sink in the trial.

2. Joseph Conrad's *Heart of Darkness:* As is mentioned in the student edition, Kurtz is called a "hollow sham" in Conrad's work.

Background

Eliot and Tradition

1. Explain that Eliot's essay "Tradition and the Individual Talent" has helped shape modern perspectives on and tastes in literature.
2. The essay suggests that it is by "concentrating" together ordinary experiences and emotions not ordinarily associated that art achieves its effects. Eliot concludes that "Poetry is not a turning loose of emotion, but an escape from emotion. . . ."
3. Eliot also argues that poetry is only ever understood by comparing and contrasting it with the body of significant works that precedes it—a tradition.
4. **Ask** students what connection they can see between Eliot's critical theory and his poetic practice in "The Hollow Men."
   Possible answer: By constructing the poem out of allusions, Eliot both celebrates the tradition on which he is drawing and effaces his own personality, since the "speaker" of the poem barely exists.

Critical Thinking

Connect

1. **Ask:** What do Brutus and Guy Fawkes have in common?
   Possible response: Both are traitors who assassinate or attempt to assassinate a ruler.
2. **Ask:** Why are they a suitable contrast with the "hollow men"?
   Possible response: They acted out of principles, however misguided. The "hollow men" drift through life without principle.

Speaking and Listening

Discussion

1. Read the Discussion instructions with the class. Point out that allusions appear in many art forms and that they are not necessarily limited to the art form in which they appear.
2. Have students break into groups to discuss their thoughts and observations about allusions. When they have had sufficient time to discuss, instruct each group to choose a spokesperson who will share the results of the exchange with the class.

Dante's *Divine Comedy* Dante's medieval poems describe the three realms of the afterlife according to Roman Catholic belief: *Inferno, Purgatorio,* and *Paradiso*—hell, purgatory, and heaven. The speakers in Eliot's poem are being punished for their spiritual emptiness in a kind of inferno: a "dead land" (line 39); a "cactus land" (line 40); a "valley of dying stars" (line 54). It does not appear that these speakers will gain salvation, but Eliot uses images drawn from Dante's description of paradise to suggest the existence of higher realms: " . . . the perpetual star / Multifoliate rose . . ." (lines 63–64). In terms of Dante's work, "The Hollow Men" is like an inferno (a realm of punishment) that is almost without the promise of a purgatory or a paradise.

Eliot's Theory of Tradition

Eliot's allusions create a distinctive, dreamlike world for a reader to explore. They also reflect his theory of poetry. In an essay, Eliot compares the poet to a catalyst in a chemical reaction. A catalyst adds nothing of itself, but without it, the reaction will not take place. The poet's mind is the catalyst that causes images and feelings to combine in a poem, but the poem does not necessarily reflect the poet's own life. For Eliot, a tradition of past literature was a key source of ingredients for the reaction. Eliot's allusions reflect both of these values: impersonality and tradition.

Speaking and Listening: Discussion

Comprehension and Collaboration An **allusion** is a device used by many creative artists, not just poets. Filmmakers and composers sometimes incorporate cinematic or musical allusions into their work to enrich the audience's experience. As "The Hollow Men" demonstrates, allusions add depth to a work but can also make it more difficult to understand.

With a group, discuss your thoughts about films and musical works that feature allusions. Set a twenty-minute time limit for the discussion, and use these questions to help you set clear goals:

- Identify a movie or song that alludes to or quotes from another source. What is that source, and what point does the artist make through the allusion?
- In what way does understanding allusions enhance your enjoyment of a work?
- Is it always necessary to fully understand an allusion? Explain.

Encourage each group member to participate. Remind participants to be courteous as they interact. Appoint one person to take notes on the ideas and issues presented. After the discussion, choose a point person to share your thoughts with the class.

Enrichment: Analyzing Themes and Symbols

Religious Imagery

The religious images in this poem are almost exclusively Christian. Christianity is a monotheistic religion, focused around the belief in one god. Judaism and Islam are both monotheistic as well, while Hinduism recognizes one supreme god among many lesser gods. Despite differences among religions, they share many characteristics. Most religions include some form of prayer. Many religions have important symbols as well, just as the star and rose are Christian symbols.

Activity: Religious Symbolism Ask students to investigate the origin of a particular religious symbol. Have them hypothesize why it is that religiously observant people choose symbols to represent their beliefs. Students should record their findings on the **Enrichment: Analyzing Themes and Symbols** worksheet, ***Professional Development Guidebook,*** page 243.

8 9

THE HOLLOW MEN

T. S. ELIOT

BACKGROUND As in "Journey of the Magi," Eliot uses allusions at the beginning of "The Hollow Men" to help him contrast the past with the present. For example, "A penny for the Old Guy" is a traditional cry of children on Guy Fawkes Day. Fawkes was executed for attempting to blow up the king and Parliament on November 5, 1605. He is one of the "lost / Violent souls" of the past who contrast with the "hollow men" of today.

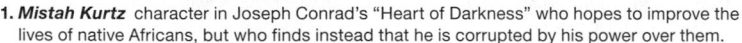

Le Maitre d'ecole. 1955, Rene Magritte, Photothèque R. Magritte-ADAGP / Art Resource, NY, © 1998 C. Herscovici, Brussels / Artists Rights Society (ARS), New York.

Mistah Kurtz[1]*—he dead.*

A penny for the Old Guy[2]

I

We are the hollow men
We are the stuffed men
Leaning together
Headpiece filled with straw. Alas!
Our dried voices, when
We whisper together
Are quiet and meaningless
As wind in dry grass

10 **Reading Check**

How does the speaker characterize the sounds made by the hollow men?

---

1. ***Mistah Kurtz*** character in Joseph Conrad's "Heart of Darkness" who hopes to improve the lives of native Africans, but who finds instead that he is corrupted by his power over them.
2. ***A . . . Guy*** traditional cry used by children on Guy Fawkes Day (November 5), celebrating the execution of a famous English traitor of the same name. The "Old Guy" refers to stuffed dummies representing Fawkes.

8 About the Selection

Perhaps the bleakest of the Eliot poems presented here, "The Hollow Men" describes a world in which people have no faith, no courage, no spirit, and no awareness. Spoken by the hollow men themselves, the poem is a self-portrait of the typical modern person.

9 Background

T. S. Eliot

In addition to the social and political changes of the modern post–World War I experience, Eliot had faced personal despair in caring for his deeply troubled first wife, Vivien Haigh-Wood. She was ultimately unable to function in the world and spent her latter years in a psychiatric hospital.

10 Reading Check

Answer: The voices are characterized as quiet and meaningless.

Differentiated Instruction for Universal Access

Strategy for Less Proficient Readers

To help less proficient readers navigate this difficult poem, suggest contemporary images of "hollow men": slackers and "couch potatoes." Urge students to identify the poem's speakers. As students read on, direct them to continually analyze the speakers' attitudes.

Strategy for Advanced Readers

Point out the apparent contradictions in lines 11–12 of the poem. Have students think about the meaning of the contradictions and how each could be possible, if at all. Is it possible to have "shape without form"? If not, what is the meaning behind these images?

11 Literary Analysis

Modernism in Poetry

Ask students the Literary Analysis question: In what ways does this poem reflect the fragmentation characteristic of Modernism?

Answer: The poem links disparate images that indicate a lack of connection to the dreary modern world.

12 Reading Strategy

Relating Poetry to Historical Period

1. Direct students' attention to the footnote for line 14 at the bottom of the page. Students need not be familiar with *Paradiso* to understand the image Eliot wishes to convey.
2. Discuss the speakers' reaction to those with "direct eyes."
3. Have students determine how the hollow men wish to be remembered by those with "direct eyes." Help students understand that hollow men are not necessarily evil; they have simply not found the religious spirit that will make them complete.
4. Then, **ask** students to analyze the meaning of the pattern of images that Eliot creates in lines 13–21. **Answer:** The pattern of images involves speakers who are afraid of meeting the eyes of the blessed.

---

11 Literary Analysis
Modernism in Poetry
In what ways does this poem reflect the fragmentation characteristic of Modernism?

Vocabulary
supplication (sup′ lə kā′ shən) *n.* act of praying or pleading

Or rats' feet over broken glass
In our dry cellar

Shape without form, shade without color,
Paralyzed force, gesture without motion;
Those who have crossed
With direct eyes, to death's other Kingdom[3]
Remember us—if at all—not as lost
Violent souls, but only
As the hollow men
12 The stuffed men.

II

Eyes I dare not meet in dreams
In death's dream kingdom
These do not appear:
There, the eyes are
Sunlight on a broken column
There, is a tree swinging
And voices are
In the wind's singing
More distant and more solemn
Than a fading star.
Let me be no nearer
In death's dream kingdom
Let me also wear
Such deliberate disguises
Rat's coat, crowskin, crossed staves
In a field[4]
Behaving as the wind behaves
No nearer—

Not that final meeting
In the twilight kingdom

III

This is the dead land
This is cactus land
Here the stone images
Are raised, here they receive
The supplication of a dead man's hand
Under the twinkle of a fading star.

SHAPE
WITHOUT FORM,

SHADE
WITHOUT COLOR

---

3. **Those . . . kingdom** allusion to Dante's *Paradiso*, in which those "with direct eyes" are blessed by God in heaven.
4. **crossed . . . field** scarecrows.

Vocabulary Development

Vocabulary Knowledge Rating

When students have completed reading and discussing the group of selections, have them take out their **Vocabulary Knowledge Rating Charts** for the story. Read the words aloud and have students rate their knowledge of words again in the After Reading column. Clarify any words that are still problematic. Have students write their own definitions and example or sentence in the appropriate column. Then, have students complete the Vocabulary Lesson at the end of the selections. Encourage students to use the words in further discussion and written work about the selections. Remind them that they will be accountable for these words on the **Selection Test, *Unit 6 Resources*,** pages 39–41 or 42–44.

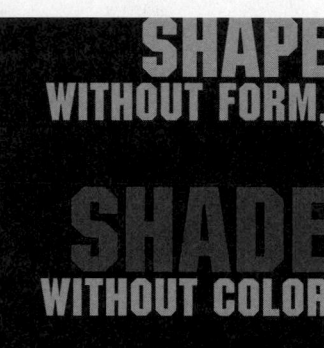

Is it like this
In death's other kingdom
Waking alone
At the hour when we are
Trembling with tenderness
Lips that would kiss
Form prayers to broken stone.

IV

The eyes are not here
There are no eyes here
In this valley of dying stars
In this hollow valley
This broken jaw of our lost kingdoms

In this last of meeting places
We grope together
And avoid speech
Gathered on this beach of the tumid river[5]

Sightless, unless
The eyes reappear
As the perpetual star[6]
Multifoliate rose[7]
Of death's twilight kingdom
The hope only
Of empty men.

V

Here we go round the prickly pear
Prickly pear prickly pear
Here we go round the prickly pear
At five o'clock in the morning.[8]

Between the idea
And the reality
Between the motion
And the act[9]
Falls the Shadow

---

5. **river** from Dante's *Inferno*, the river Acheron, which the dead cross on the way to hell.
6. **star** traditional symbol for Christ.
7. **Multifoliate rose** rose with many leaves. Dante describes paradise as such a rose in his *Paradiso*. The rose is a traditional symbol for the Virgin Mary.
8. **Here . . . morning** adaptation of a common nursery rhyme. A prickly pear is a cactus.
9. **Between . . . act** reference to *Julius Caesar*, Act II, Scene i, 63–65: "Between the acting of a dreadful thing / And the first motion, all the interim is / Like a phantasma or hideous dream."

13 *The* **British Tradition**

The Literary Magazine

No institution played a more important role in the development of Modernism than the literary magazine. These modest periodicals were published on both sides of the Atlantic. In England, Eliot founded *The Criterion* (later called *The New Criterion*) in 1922. In the United States, *The Dial* published the work of Eliot, W. B. Yeats, Ezra Pound, and D. H. Lawrence. Another important journal, *The Egoist*, serialized *A Portrait of the Artist as a Young Man*, James Joyce's first major work, from 1914 to 1915.

These Modernist periodicals dedicated themselves to promoting new trends in art. The profound impact of Eliot's work would perhaps not have been as great if it had not found a home in such journals.

Connect to the Literature

What kinds of readers might enjoy literary magazines featuring poems like "The Hollow Men"?

Vocabulary
tumid (to͞o' mid) *adj.* swollen

14 Reading Check

To what kingdoms does the speaker refer?

13 The British Tradition

The Literary Magazine

Many regions, areas, colleges, and local groups publish literary magazines. Some nationwide literary magazines students may be familiar with are *The New Yorker, Harper's,* and *The Atlantic Monthly.* Eliot's journal, though, like the small literary quarterlies published today, did not try to appeal to a broad public but instead gave a home to new developments in the arts. This aim was particularly important in fostering Modernism, since much Modernist art was difficult and could not hope to achieve immediate, broad public recognition. Eliot's journal helped the movement thrive among a limited but appreciative audience.

Connect to the Literature

Ask students to reflect on the works of Eliot that they have read. Then, **ask** them to imagine who would enjoy literary magazines that feature modern poetry.
Possible responses: Poets, writers, and artistically inclined and literary-minded people might enjoy such a magazine.

14 Reading Check

Answer: The speaker refers to the Kingdom of Heaven.

Differentiated Instruction for Universal Access

Background for Less Proficient Readers
Less proficient readers are unlikely to be familiar with the referenced texts, Dante's *Inferno* or Shakespeare's *Julius Caesar.* Invite students familiar with these works to summarize them briefly, or do so yourself.

EL Support for English Learners
Remind these students that one feature of Modernist poetry is dreamlike jumps from one topic to another. Urge English-language learners to regard Eliot's use of italics as signals of such jumps.

Enrichment for Gifted/Talented Students
Have dramatically inclined students prepare, rehearse, and perform a choral reading of the poem. Allow students time to rehearse, then ask them to perform for the others in the class.

⓯ Literary Analysis
Modernism in Poetry

Ask students the Literary Analysis question: How does Eliot's handling of the line from the Lord's Prayer reflect modernist techniques?
Answer: Eliot uses a fragment of the Lord's Prayer as a motif to represent the faltering of the stability offered by institutions such as religion in the modern world.

ASSESS
Answers

Before students respond, you may wish to have them write a brief objective summary of the selection. As they answer the questions below, remind them to support their answers with evidence from the text.

1. (a) Descriptive words include *hollow, stuffed,* and *leaning together.* (b) Students may infer that what the hollow men say is as meaningless as the noise of the wind; that what they say is produced by outside forces (they say "what everybody is saying"); that their lives have as little substance as and leave as little trace as the wind.
2. (a) The Shadow repeatedly falls. (b) The Shadow can be interpreted as fear. It falls between the idea and the achievement, preventing the hollow men from accomplishing anything.
3. The fragmentation of Eliot's style and his use of free verse constitute a significant break from traditional poetic forms. However, he alludes to more traditional works by Shakespeare and Joseph Conrad.

⓯

For Thine is the Kingdom[10]

Between the conception
And the creation
Between the emotion
And the response
Falls the Shadow

Life is very long[11]

Between the desire
And the spasm
Between the potency
And the existence
Between the essence
And the descent
Falls the Shadow

For Thine is the Kingdom

For Thine is
Life is
For Thine is the

This is the way the world ends
This is the way the world ends
This is the way the world ends
Not with a bang but a whimper.

Literary Analysis
Modernism in Poetry
How does Eliot's handling of the line from the Lord's Prayer reflect modernist techniques?

BETWEEN THE IDEA AND THE REALITY

10. **For . . . Kingdom** from the ending of the Lord's Prayer.
11. **Life . . . long** Quotation from Joseph Conrad's *An Outcast of the Islands.*

Critical Reading

Cite textual evidence to support your responses.

1. **Craft and Structures (a)** Which words are used to describe the hollow men in the first ten lines? **(b) Infer:** What do the images of wind in Parts I and II suggest about the hollow men?
2. **Key Ideas and Details (a)** In Part V, what repeatedly "falls"? **(b) Interpret:** How is this action related to the poem's theme?
3. **Integration of Knowledge and Ideas** In what ways do Eliot's poems both break with tradition and connect to tradition? Use at least two of these Essential Question words in your response: *free verse, fragmentation, allusion, imagery. **[Connecting to the Essential Question: What is the relationship of the writer to tradition?]***

Concept Connector

Reading Skill Graphic Organizer
Ask students to review the graphic organizers in which they have listed observations about modern life made by Eliot. Then, have students share their organizers and compare the observations they have identified and conclusions that they have drawn.

Activating Prior Knowledge
Have students return to their responses to the Activating Prior Knowledge activity. Ask them to explain whether their thoughts have changed and, if so, how.

Connecting to the Essential Question
Have students compare their responses to the prompt, completed before reading the poems, with their thoughts afterward. Have them formulate their new responses. Then, lead a class discussion, probing for what students have learned that confirms or invalidates their initial thoughts. Encourage students to cite specific textual details to support their responses.

After You Read

Preludes • Journey of the Magi • The Hollow Men

Literary Analysis

1. **Craft and Structure** Identify three images in the "Preludes" that suggest the **Modernist** view that modern life is empty. Explain your choices.
2. **Craft and Structure** What Modernist qualities characterize "The Hollow Men"? Use a chart like the one shown to help you in answering.

Passage	Fragmented Images/ Realistic Pictures	Critical of Modern Life?

3. **Key Ideas and Details (a)** What escape from modern despair does "Journey of the Magi" suggest? **(b)** What despair appears in the poem?
4. **Craft and Structure (a)** Quoting passages in support, identify two aspects of Modernism illustrated by the "Preludes." **(b)** Does "Journey of the Magi" also illustrate these aspects? Explain, quoting from the poem.
5. **Craft and Structure** Compare the use of *allusion*—brief references to literature—in "The Hollow Men" with the use of images in the "Preludes." How are they similar?
6. **Integration of Knowledge and Ideas** Which poem is easiest to relate to? Explain.
7. **Integration of Knowledge and Ideas** Why might Eliot have found it necessary to turn to past literature to make a point about what is missing in the present?

Reading Strategy

8. **(a)** What similarities are there in the way Eliot describes people in "Preludes" and "The Hollow Men"? **(b) Relate Eliot's work to the historical period** by determining what vision of modern life these similar images provide.
9. "The Journey of the Magi" is set in ancient times. What aspects of the poem reflect on Eliot's contemporary society? Explain your answer.
10. The Christian religion had been a source of spiritual comfort for the British for many centuries. Both "The Journey of the Magi" and "The Hollow Men" refer to Christian events or ideas. What does Eliot's treatment of these events or ideas suggest about his view of the role of Christianity in his society?
11. To what extent does Eliot's criticism of the hollow men apply to people today? Explain.

Common Core State Standards

Writing

2. Write informative/explanatory texts to examine and convey complex ideas, concepts, and information clearly and accurately through the effective selection, organization, and analysis of content. *(p. 1168)*

4. Produce clear and coherent writing in which the development, organization, and style are appropriate to task, purpose, and audience. *(p. 1168)*

Language

3.a. Vary syntax for effect. *(p. 1169)*

5. Demonstrate understanding of figurative language, word relationships, and nuances in word meanings. *(p. 1168)*

Assessment Practice

Style (For more practice, see *All-in-One Workbook.*)

Many tests require students to recognize effective style. Use the following sample test item to teach students how to recognize the mood of a passage.

The winter evening settles down
With smells of steaks in passageways.
Six o'clock.
The burnt-out ends of smoky days.
And now a gusty shower wraps
The grimy scraps
Of withered leaves about your feet

Which of these words *best* describes the mood of the passage?

A isolation
B suspense
C obscurity
D hopefulness

Knowing that mood describes a piece's prevailing emotional effect, students should eliminate ***C*** because it cannot a describe a mood. ***B*** and ***D*** do not describe the mood of these lines. The correct answer is ***A***.

Answers

1. Images include: "The burnt-out ends of smoky days"; "Of withered leaves about your feet / And newspapers from vacant lots"; and "With the other masquerades / That time resumes." All three images depict waste, decay, or futility.
2. **Possible response:** Passage: "And voices are / In the wind's singing / More distant and more solemn / Than a fading star"; Fragmented Images vs. Realistic Pictures: Fragmented— winds singing, fading star; Critical of Modern Life? Yes: Modern thoughts are weightless; spirituality is fading away.
3. (a) Spirituality offers escape. (b) The speaker despairs at being caught between traditions and new beliefs.
4. (a) **Possible response:** "The showers beat / On broken blinds and chimney-pots" is an image that conveys dreariness and hopelessness. The passage "all the hands / That are raising dingy shades" uses a fragmented image. (b) An image that conveys dreariness and hopelessness is "A cold coming we had of it, / Just the worst time of the year. . . . " The fragmented details from the journey resemble the images in "Preludes."
5. In both cases, an abbreviated part of a thing suggests a world of meaning.
6. The allusions in "The Hollow Men" are not as easy to understand as those in "Preludes."
7. It might contain values that have disappeared from modern life.
8. (a) Both poems describe only parts of people (feet, hair). They also mention the particulate nature of people's souls. (b) These descriptions provide a vision of modernity in which people are disconnected from the world.
9. Though set in ancient times, this poem comments on drunkenness and poverty.
10. It suggests Christianity cannot mitigate the problems of modern life.
11. The advent of the technological age has caused many to become disengaged from their surroundings and to lose their identities.

EXTEND/ASSESS

Answers

Vocabulary Acquisition and Use

Word Analysis

1. A prism *breaks* white light into a spectrum of its component colors.
2. She *broke* the rules.
3. A computer image can be *broken* into the fractals that comprise it.
4. The bone was *broken.*

Vocabulary

1. tumid
2. refractory
3. supplication
4. dispensation
5. galled

Writing

You may use this Writing Lesson as timed-writing practice, or you may allow students to develop the informative text as a writing assignment over several days.

1. To give students guidance for writing this informative text, give them the **Support for Writing Lesson** page from *Unit 6 Resources,* page 34.
2. Before students begin their writing projects, ask them to review some of the techniques that reflect Modernism in Eliot's poetry. Discuss how similar techniques might be implemented in visual art.
3. Explain to students that the Modernist movement had wide-reaching effects in the arts and that the view on life espoused by this school of thought manifested itself in a variety of mediums.
4. During the drafting portion of the activity, remind students to place references in logical order, such as those from one poem together, followed by those from another poem.
5. Use the **Rubrics for Critique** in *Professional Development Guidebook,* pages 276–277, to evaluate student work.

PERFORMANCE TASKS

Integrated Language Skills

Vocabulary Acquisition and Use

Word Analysis: Latin Root *-fract-*

The Latin root *-fract-* means "to break." A *refractory* animal is one that "breaks away," making it difficult to manage. A *fraction* is a part broken away from a larger whole. Explain how the root contributes to the meaning of the italicized words in these sentences.

1. When white light is *refracted* by a prism, it produces a spectrum.
2. Her motives were good, but she was guilty of an *infraction* of the rules.
3. Computer scenery may be formed of *fractals* so tiny you cannot see them.
4. The *fractured* bone needed time to mend.

Vocabulary: Analogies

In an analogy, the relationship between two words is explained by comparing it to the relationship between two other words. Discern the meaning of the words from the vocabulary list on page 1154 by using each word once to complete these analogies. Explain each choice.

1. *Thin* is to *slender* as _______ is to *bloated.*
2. *Emotional* is to *rational* as *obedient* is to _______.
3. *Order* is to *inferior* as _______ is to *superior.*
4. *Belief* is to _______ as *citizenship* is to *nation.*
5. *Medicine* is to *scraped* as *ointment* is to _______.

Writing

Informative Text Eliot's poetry reflects the Modernist movement that swept through other arts as well. He uses words to achieve effects similar to those attained by such artists as Pablo Picasso and Paul Cézanne. Write a **multi-genre response** that responds to Eliot's Modernism in poetry. Analyze his techniques, showing how they contribute to a *comment on life,* and present the art of a Modernist painter, showing how he or she uses comparable devices.

Prewriting Review Eliot's poems to identify imagery, rhythms, and other techniques that reflect Modernism. Take notes on his Modernist themes as well. Using a history of art, find a Modernist work of art that shows comparable techniques or themes in visual form.

Drafting Begin with a thesis statement explaining your main point about Modernism in literature and art. Then, discuss the Modernist techniques in Eliot's poetry and write a caption for the work of art explaining similar Modernist techniques it uses.

Model: Revising to Clarify Generalizations

Eliot's poetry is ^a verbal form of~~like~~ Picasso's cubism. He breaks the soul into a "thousand sordid images"; Picasso breaks the face into dozens of different pieces.

Using vivid language clarifies generalizations.

Revising Review your draft, highlighting generalizations. Where supporting details are lacking, look back at the poems or the artwork to find relevant support. Make sure that all quotations are accurate and properly referenced.

Assessment Resources

Unit 6 Resources

L1 L2 EL **Selection Test A,** pp. 39–41. Administer Test A to less advanced readers.

L3 L4 EL **Selection Test B,** pp. 42–44. Administer Test B to on-level and more advanced students.

L3 L4 **Open-Book Test,** pp. 36–38. As an alternative, give the Open Book Test.

All **Customizable Test Bank**

All **Self-tests**
Students may prepare for the **Selection Test** by taking the **Self-test** online.

PHLit Online! All assessment resources are available at **www.PHLitOnline.com.**

Conventions and Style: Transitional Expressions

To write coherently and smoothly, you must show how your ideas relate to one another. **Transitional expressions** can help you do this by making clear the connection between ideas.

Conjunctive adverbs make a transition between two independent clauses and show the relationship between the ideas in the clauses.

The examples demonstrate how conjunctive adverbs combine choppy sentences and make clear the relationship between ideas.

Choppy: The Magi's journey was long. It was at the worst time of year.

Conjunctive adverb: The Magi's journey was long; *moreover,* it was at the worst time of year.

Below is a chart of some common transitional expressions used as conjunctive adverbs.

Cause-effect	consequently, because of this
Time	in time, afterwards, at present
To illustrate	in other words, for instance
To add to	also, moreover, in addition
Compare	similarly, in like manner
Contrast	however, on the contrary

Punctuation Tip Remember to use a semicolon before the transitional expression.

Practice Rewrite each item using a conjunctive adverb to make a transition and show the relationship between the ideas.

1. Nighttime was dark and dismal. A new day dawned.
2. The modern world appeared lifeless. Former times seemed filled with emotion.
3. Cities, towns, and villages were unwelcoming. The travelers chose to keep on through the night.
4. The journey was long ago. The speaker would make it again.
5. The Magi returned to their homes. They no longer felt comfortable there.
6. Eliot alluded to Mistah Kurtz. He wanted to emphasize that power corrupts.
7. Hollow men had heads filled with straw. They were unthinking and unfeeling.
8. People spoke with dry voices. Their words were meaningless.
9. On Earth, people gathered but avoided speaking. They lived in a world of shadows.
10. Sightless eyes were symbols. They stood for emptiness.

Writing and Speaking Conventions

A. Writing Write an independent clause followed by a semicolon to fill each blank.

1. ______ that is, they had no shape or form.
2. ______ for this reason, he used the cactus image.
3. ______ in other words, it will go out with a quiet groan.

Example: ______ **that is, they had no shape or form.**

Complete Sentence: Eliot wrote of hollow men; that is, they had no shape or form.

B. Speaking Briefly explain to the class why Eliot's poems continue to have meaning. Include at least two conjunctive adverbs as transitional expressions.

PH WRITING COACH
Further instruction and practice are available in *Prentice Hall Writing Coach.*

Extend the Lesson

Sentence Modeling

Choose the lines given from the selection students have read:

". . . And the cities hostile and the towns unfriendly / And the villages dirty and charging high prices: / A hard time we had of it."

"The winter evening settles down / With smell of steaks in passageways. / Six o'clock."

Explain to students that in fragmented, Modernist poetry like Eliot's, transitions are often implied rather than directly stated. The reader mentally supplants the ellipses between the fragmented images with transitions to form a unified impression. Elicit from students that the lack of transitions in Modernist poetry is calculated to mirror the lack of cohesion in the modern milieu.

Have students use a transitional expression to create a complete sentence from one of the above lines from Eliot's poetry. Collect the sentences and share them with the class.

Answers

Conventions and Style

Practice

Introduce and discuss the skill using the instruction on the student page.

1. Nighttime was dark and dismal; however, a new day dawned.
2. The modern world appeared lifeless; on the contrary, former times seemed filled with emotion.
3. Cities, towns, and villages were unwelcoming; consequently, the travelers chose to keep on through the night.
4. The journey was long ago; in time, the speaker would make it again.
5. The Magi returned to their homes; however, they no longer felt comfortable there.
6. Eliot wanted to emphasize that power corrupts; because of this, he alluded to Mistah Kurtz.
7. Hollow men had heads filled with straw; in other words, they were unthinking and unfeeling.
8. People spoke with dry voices; moreover, their words were meaningless.
9. On Earth, people gathered but avoided speaking; at present they lived in a world of shadows.
10. Sightless eyes were symbols; namely, they stood for emptiness.

Writing and Speaking Conventions

A. Writing

Sample answers:

1. The amoebas were amorphous; that is, they had no shape or form.
2. The modern world is desertlike in its desolation; for this reason, he used the cactus image.
3. Eliot writes that the world will go out not with a bang, but a whimper; in other words, it will go out with a quiet groan.

B. Speaking

Students should use at least two conjunctive adverbs as transitional expressions in their explanations.

PH WRITING COACH Grade 12

Further instruction on and practice with expository writing can be found in Chapter 8.

In Memory of W. B. Yeats • Musée des Beaux Arts • Carrick Revisited • Not Palaces

Lesson Pacing Guide

DAY 1 Preteach

- Administer the Reading and Vocabulary Warm-ups (*Unit 6 Resources*, pp. 45–48) as necessary.
- Introduce the Literary Analysis concept: Allegory and Pastoral.
- Introduce the Reading Strategy: Comparing and Contrasting Elements.
- Build background with the author and Background features.
- Develop thematic thinking with Connecting to the Essential Question.
- Teach the selection vocabulary.

DAYS 2–3 Preteach/Teach/Assess

- Distribute copies of the appropriate graphic organizer for the Reading Strategy (*Graphic Organizer Transparencies*, pp. 208–209).
- Distribute copies of the appropriate graphic organizer for Literary Analysis (*Graphic Organizer Transparencies*, pp. 210–211).
- Prepare students to read with the Activating Prior Knowledge activities (TE).
- Informally monitor comprehension while students read.
- Use the Reading Check questions to confirm comprehension.
- Develop students' understanding of allegory and pastoral using the Literary Analysis prompts.
- Develop students' ability to compare and contrast elements using the Reading Strategy prompts.
- Reinforce vocabulary with the Vocabulary notes.
- Assess students' comprehension and mastery of the skills by having them answer the Critical Reading, Literary Analysis, and Reading Strategy questions.
- Have students complete the Vocabulary Lesson.

DAY 4 Extend/Assess

- Have students complete the Writing Lesson and write a poem about an artwork. (You may assign as homework.)
- Administer Selection Test A or B (*Unit 6 Resources,* pp. 57–59 or 60–62).

Common Core State Standards

Reading Literature 1. Cite strong and thorough textual evidence to support analysis of what the text says explicitly as well as inferences drawn from the text, including determining where the text leaves matters uncertain.

Writing 5. Develop and strengthen writing as needed by planning, revising, editing, rewriting, or trying a new approach, focusing on addressing what is most significant for a specific purpose and audience.

Language 3. Apply knowledge of language to understand how language functions in different contexts, to make effective choices for meaning or style, and to comprehend more fully when reading or listening.

Additional Standards Practice
***Common Core Companion**, pp. 2–14; 226–227; 322–323*

Daily Block Scheduling
Each day in this Lesson Pacing Guide represents a 40–50 minute period. Teachers using block scheduling may combine days to revise pacing. In addition, teachers may differentiate and support core instruction by integrating components for extended and intensive support as students require. See the Guide to Selected Leveled Resources (facing page).

Guide to Selected Leveled Resources

RTI Tier 1 (students performing on level)

			In Memory of W.B.Yeats • Musée des Beaux Arts • Carrick Revisited • Not Palaces
Warm Up	Whole class instruction; Group work	**Practice, model,** and **monitor** fluency, working **with the whole class** or **in groups**.	**Vocabulary** and **Reading Warm-ups B,** ***Unit 6 Resources,*** pp. 45–46, 48
Comprehension/Skills	Whole class instruction; Group work; Independent work	**Support** and **monitor** comprehension and skills development, having students complete the activities, graphic organizers, and interactive prompts **independently** or **as a class**.	• ***Reader's Notebook,*** adapted instruction and full selection EL ***Reader's Notebook: English Learner's Version,*** adapted instruction and adapted selection • **Reading Strategy Graphic Organizer B,** ***Graphic Organizer Transparencies,*** p. 219 • **Literary Analysis Graphic Organizer B,** ***Graphic Organizer Transparencies,*** p. 221
Monitor Progress	A	**Monitor** student progress with the differentiated curriculum-based assessment in the *Unit Resources.*	• **Selection Test B,** ***Unit 6 Resources,*** pp. 60–62 • **Open-Book Test,** ***Unit 6 Resources,*** pp. 54–56

RTI Tier 2 (students requiring intervention)

			In Memory of W.B.Yeats • Musée des Beaux Arts • Carrick Revisited • Not Palaces
Warm Up	Group work; One-on-one teaching	**Practice, model,** and **monitor** fluency **in groups** or **with individuals**.	• **Vocabulary and Reading Warm-ups A,** ***Unit 6 Resources,*** pp. 45–47 • ***Hear It!*** **Audio CD (adapted text)**
Comprehension/Skills	Group work; One-on-one teaching	• **Support** and **monitor** comprehension and skills development, working **in small groups** or **with individuals**. • As students complete the selection in the appropriate version of the *Reader's Notebook,* **monitor** comprehension frequently with group questions and individual instruction. • **Model** strategies while guiding students in completing the activities and prompts in the *Reader's Notebook,* as well as the graphic organizers. • **Practice** skills and **monitor** mastery with the *Reading Kit* worksheets.	• ***Reader's Notebook: Adapted Version,*** adapted instruction and adapted selection EL ***Reader's Notebook: English Learner's Version,*** adapted instruction and adapted selection • **Reading Strategy Graphic Organizer A,** ***Graphic Organizer Transparencies,*** p. 218 • **Literary Analysis Graphic Organizer A,** ***Graphic Organizer Transparencies,*** p. 220 • ***Reading Kit,*** Practice worksheets
Monitor Progress	A	**Monitor** student progress with the differentiated curriculum-based assessment in the *Unit Resources* and in the *Reading Kit.*	• **Selection Test A,** ***Unit 6 Resources,*** pp. 57–59 • ***Reading Kit,*** Assess worksheets

TIER 3 Tier 3 intervention may require consultation with the student's special-education or dyslexia specialist. For additional support, see the Tier 2 activities and resources listed above.

One-on-one teaching **Group work** **Whole class instruction** **Independent work** **A Assessment**

For a complete guide to selection support, including support for Advanced students, see the Overview of Resources in the frontmatter.

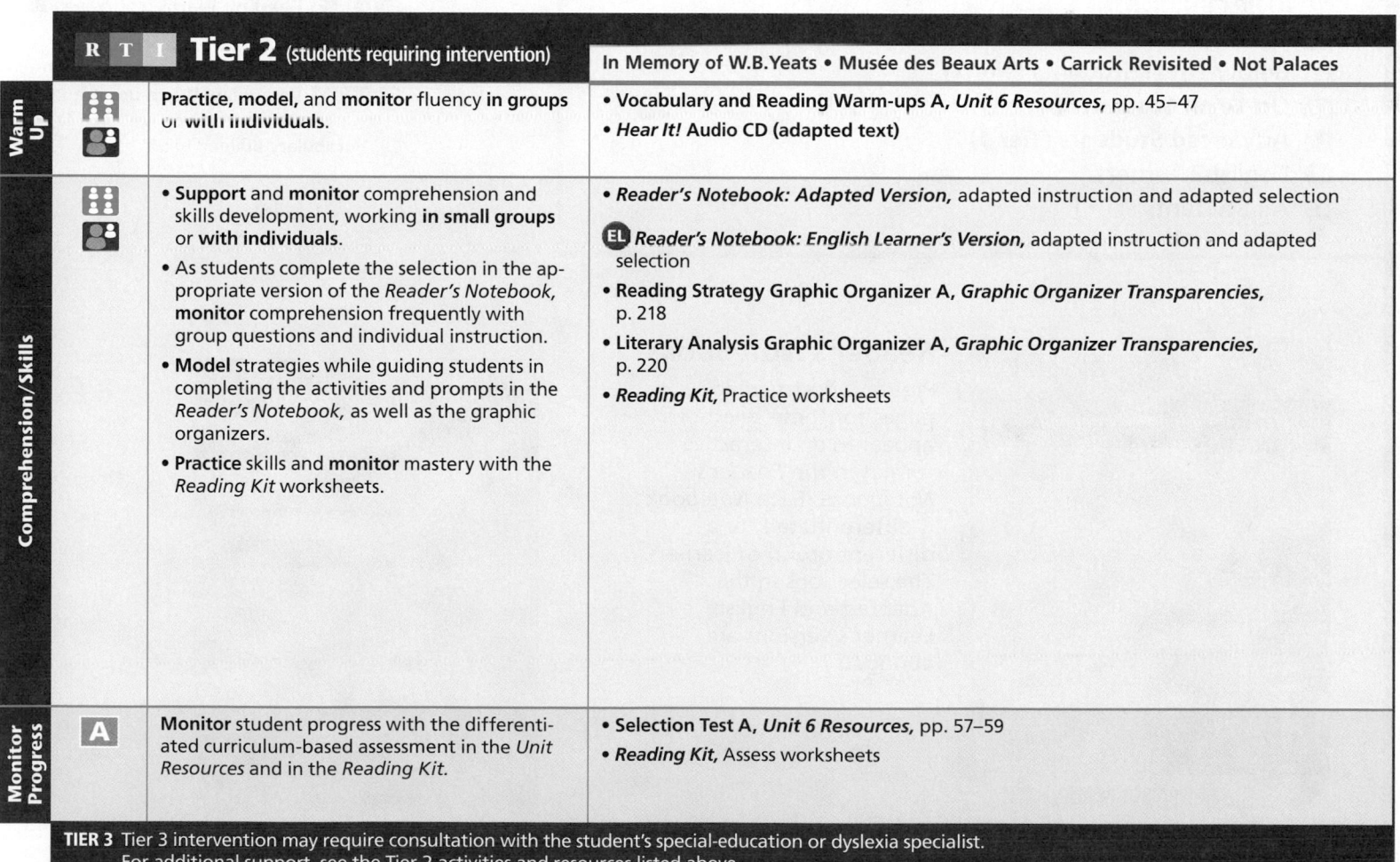

In Memory of W. B. Yeats • Musée des Beaux Arts • Carrick Revisited • Not Palaces

RESOURCES FOR:

- L1 Special-Needs Students
- L2 Below-Level Students (Tier 2)
- L3 On-Level Students (Tier 1)
- L4 Advanced Students (Tier 1)
- EL English Learners
- All All Students

Vocabulary/Fluency/Prior Knowledge

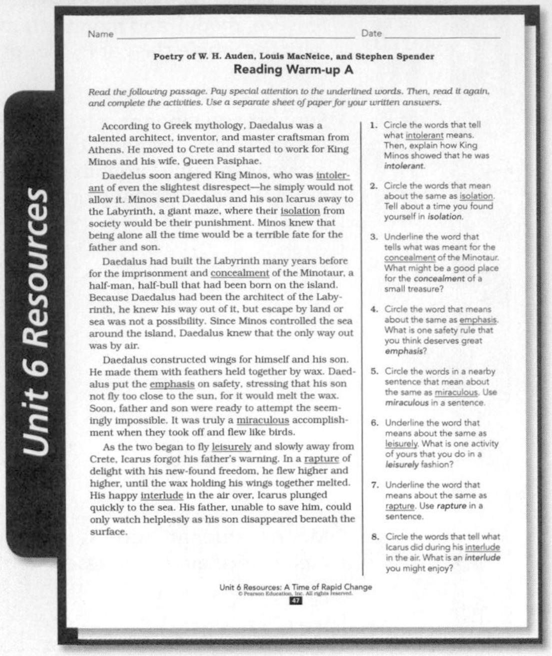
Unit 6 Resources

Name ______ Date ______

Poetry of W. H. Auden, Louis MacNeice, and Stephen Spender
Reading Warm-up A

Read the following passage. Pay special attention to the underlined words. Then, read it again, and complete the activities. Use a separate sheet of paper for your written answers.

According to Greek mythology, Daedalus was a talented architect, inventor, and master craftsman from Athens. He moved to Crete and started to work for King Minos and his wife, Queen Pasiphae.

Daedelus soon angered King Minos, who was intolerant of even the slightest disrespect—he simply would not allow it. Minos sent Daedalus and his son Icarus away to the Labyrinth, a giant maze, where their isolation from society would be their punishment. Minos knew that being alone all the time would be a terrible fate for the father and son.

Daedalus had built the Labyrinth many years before for the imprisonment and concealment of the Minotaur, a half-man, half-bull that had been born on the island. Because Daedalus had been the architect of the Labyrinth, he knew his way out of it, but escape by land or sea was not a possibility. Since Minos controlled the sea around the island, Daedalus knew that the only way out was by air.

Daedalus constructed wings for himself and his son. He made them with feathers held together by wax. Daedalus put the emphasis on safety, stressing that his son not fly too close to the sun, for it would melt the wax. Soon, father and son were ready to attempt the seemingly impossible. It was truly a miraculous accomplishment when they took off and flew like birds.

As the two began to fly leisurely and slowly away from Crete, Icarus forgot his father's warning. In a rapture of delight with his new-found freedom, he flew higher and higher, until the wax holding his wings together melted. His happy interlude in the air over, Icarus plunged quickly to the sea. His father, unable to save him, could only watch helplessly as his son disappeared beneath the surface.

1. Circle the words that tell what intolerant means. Then, explain how King Minos showed that he was *intolerant*.
2. Circle the words that mean about the same as isolation. Tell about a time you found yourself in *isolation*.
3. Underline the word that tells what was meant for the concealment of the Minotaur. What might be a good place for the *concealment* of a small treasure?
4. Circle the word that means about the same as emphasis. What is one safety rule that you think deserves great *emphasis*?
5. Circle the words in a nearby sentence that mean about the same as miraculous. Use *miraculous* in a sentence.
6. Underline the word that means about the same as leisurely. What is one activity of yours that you do in a *leisurely* fashion?
7. Underline the word that means about the same as rapture. Use *rapture* in a sentence.
8. Circle the words that tell what Icarus did during his interlude in the air. What is an *interlude* you might enjoy?

Unit 6 Resources: A Time of Rapid Change
© Pearson Education, Inc. All rights reserved.
47

EL L1 L2 **Reading Warm-ups A and B,** pp. 47–48

Also available for these selections:

EL L1 L2 **Vocabulary Warm-ups A and B,** pp. 45–46

All **Vocabulary Builder,** p. 51

Reader's Notebooks

Pre- and postreading pages for these selections appear in an interactive format in the *Reader's Notebooks*. Each *Notebook* is differentiated for a different group of learners. The selections in the Adapted and English Learner's versions are abridged.

L2 L3 ***Reader's Notebook***

L1 ***Reader's Notebook: Adapted Version***

EL ***Reader's Notebook: English Learner's Version***

EL ***Reader's Notebook: Spanish Version***

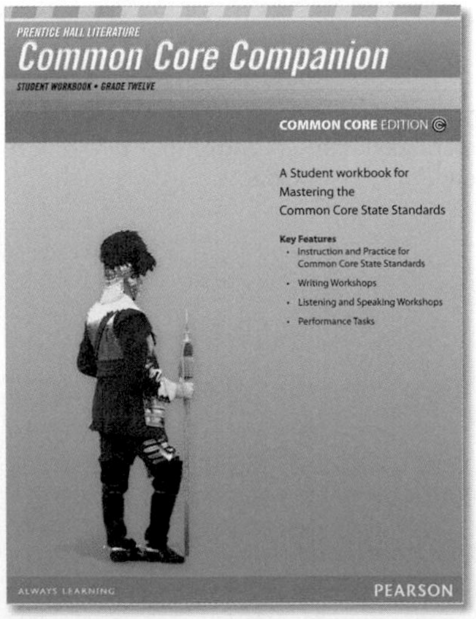

Common Core Companion

Additional instruction and practice for each Common Core State Standard

Selection Support

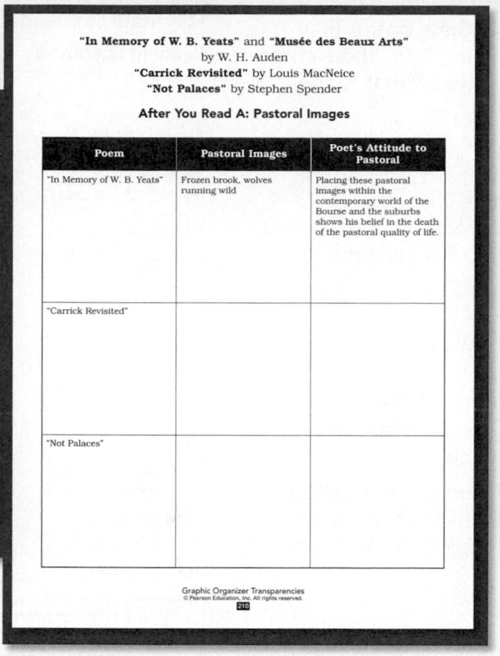
"In Memory of W. B. Yeats" and **"Musée des Beaux Arts"**
by W. H. Auden
"Carrick Revisited" by Louis MacNeice
"Not Palaces" by Stephen Spender

After You Read A: Pastoral Images

Poem	Pastoral Images	Poet's Attitude to Pastoral
"In Memory of W. B. Yeats"	Frozen brook, wolves running wild	Placing these pastoral images within the contemporary world of the Bourse and the suburbs shows his belief in the death of the pastoral quality of life.
"Carrick Revisited"		
"Not Palaces"		

Graphic Organizer Transparencies
© Pearson Education, Inc. All rights reserved.
210

Graphic Organizer Transparencies

EL L1 L2 **Literary Analysis: Graphic Organizer A** (partially filled in), p. 210

Also available for these selections:

EL L1 L2 **Reading: Graphic Organizer A,** p. 208

EL L3 **Reading: Graphic Organizer B,** p. 209

EL L3 **Literary Analysis: Graphic Organizer B,** p. 211

Skills Development/Extension

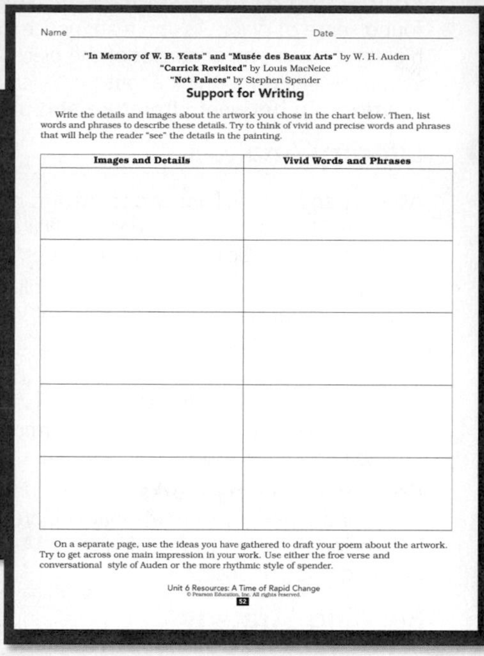
Name ______________________ Date ____________

"In Memory of W. B. Yeats" and **"Musée des Beaux Arts"** by W. H. Auden
"Carrick Revisited" by Louis MacNeice
"Not Palaces" by Stephen Spender
Support for Writing

Write the details and images about the artwork you chose in the chart below. Then, list words and phrases to describe these details. Try to think of vivid and precise words and phrases that will help the reader "see" the details in the painting.

Images and Details	Vivid Words and Phrases

On a separate page, use the ideas you have gathered to draft your poem about the artwork. Try to get across one main impression in your work. Use either the free verse and conversational style of Auden or the more rhythmic style of spender.

Unit 6 Resources: A Time of Rapid Change
© Pearson Education, Inc. All rights reserved.
52

Unit 6 Resources

EL L3 L4 **Support for Writing,** p. 52

Also available for these selections:

All **Literary Analysis: Allegory and Pastoral,** p. 49

All **Reading: Comparing and Contrasting,** p. 50

L4 **Enrichment,** p. 53

Assessment

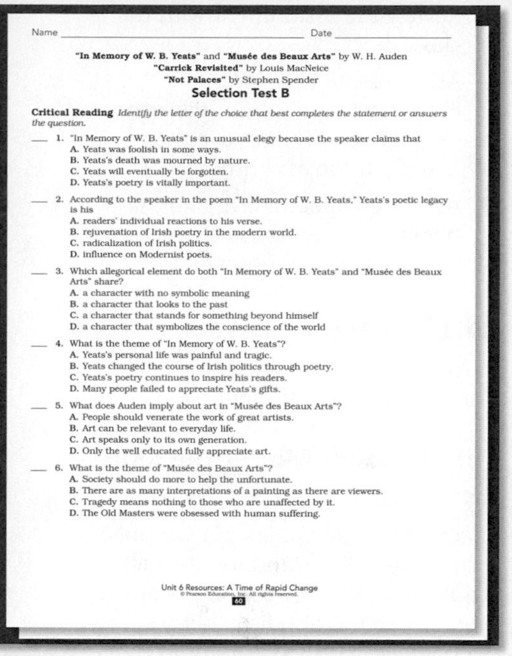
Name ______________________ Date ____________

"In Memory of W. B. Yeats" and **"Musée des Beaux Arts"** by W. H. Auden
"Carrick Revisited" by Louis MacNeice
"Not Palaces" by Stephen Spender
Selection Test B

Critical Reading *Identify the letter of the choice that best completes the statement or answers the question.*

___ 1. "In Memory of W. B. Yeats" is an unusual elegy because the speaker claims that
A. Yeats was foolish in some ways.
B. Yeats's death was mourned by nature.
C. Yeats will eventually be forgotten.
D. Yeats's poetry is vitally important.

___ 2. According to the speaker in the poem "In Memory of W. B. Yeats," Yeats's poetic legacy is his
A. readers' individual reactions to his verse.
B. rejuvenation of Irish poetry in the modern world.
C. radicalization of Irish politics.
D. influence on Modernist poets.

___ 3. Which allegorical element do both "In Memory of W. B. Yeats" and "Musée des Beaux Arts" share?
A. a character with no symbolic meaning
B. a character that looks to the past
C. a character that stands for something beyond himself
D. a character that symbolizes the conscience of the world

___ 4. What is the theme of "In Memory of W. B. Yeats"?
A. Yeats's personal life was painful and tragic.
B. Yeats changed the course of Irish politics through poetry.
C. Yeats's poetry continues to inspire his readers.
D. Many people failed to appreciate Yeats's gifts.

___ 5. What does Auden imply about art in "Musée des Beaux Arts"?
A. People should venerate the work of great artists.
B. Art can be relevant to everyday life.
C. Art speaks only to its own generation.
D. Only the well educated fully appreciate art.

___ 6. What is the theme of "Musée des Beaux Arts"?
A. Society should do more to help the unfortunate.
B. There are as many interpretations of a painting as there are viewers.
C. Tragedy means nothing to those who are unaffected by it.
D. The Old Masters were obsessed with human suffering.

Unit 6 Resources: A Time of Rapid Change
© Pearson Education, Inc. All rights reserved.
60

EL L3 L4 **Selection Test B,** pp. 60–62

Also available for these selections:

L3 L4 **Open-Book Test,** pp. 54–56

EL L1 L2 **Selection Test A,** pp. 57–59

PHLit Online!
www.PHLitOnline.com

- complete narrated selection text
- a thematically related video with writing prompt
- an interactive graphic organizer
- highlighting feature
- access to all student print resources, adapted to individual student needs
- Spanish and English summaries
- adapted selection translations in Spanish

Online Resources: All print materials are also available online.

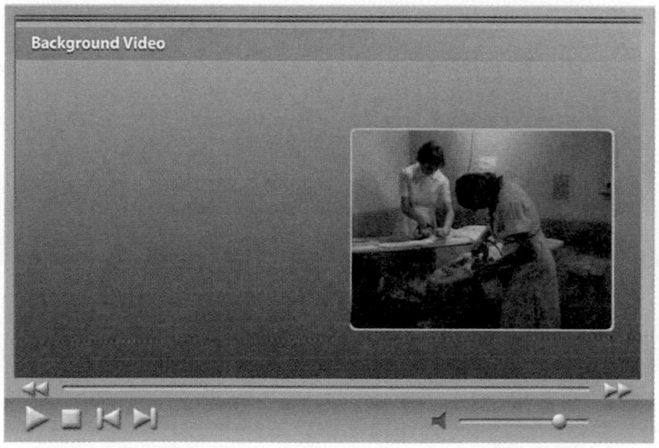
Background Video

Background Video

Also available:

Get Connected! (thematic video with writing prompt)
All videos are available in Spanish.

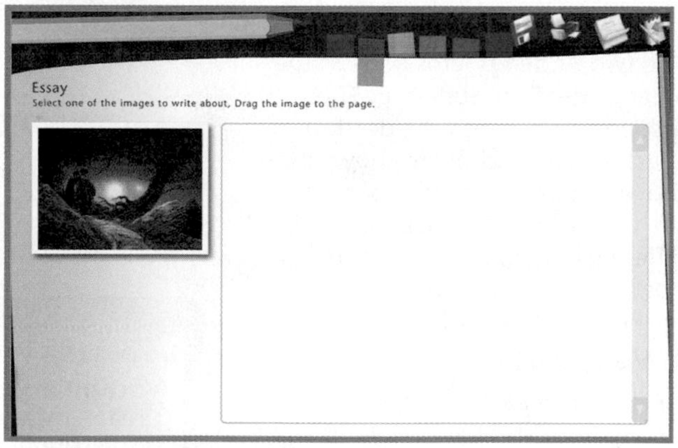
Essay
Select one of the images to write about. Drag the image to the page.

Writer's Journal (with graphics feature)

Also available:

Vocabulary Central (tools and activities for studying vocabulary)

PREACH

PRETEACH

❶ Connecting to the Essential Question

1. Review the assignment with the class.
2. Ask students what most impressed them about their chosen location. Then, have them complete the assignment.
3. As students read, have them find details that reveal the character of the places being described.

❷ Literary Analysis

Introduce the skill using the instruction on the student page.

Think Aloud: Model the Skill

Say to students:

I know that allegories use symbolic characters that stand for abstract qualities. In the upcoming selection, Auden embodies poetry in a brief allegory. I know the word *pastoral* has something to do with nature. I will look for language that deals with nature as I read.

❸ Reading Strategy

1. Introduce the skill using the instruction on the student page.
2. Give students a copy of **Reading Strategy Graphic Organizer B,** page 209 in ***Graphic Organizer Transparencies,*** to fill out as they read.

Think Aloud: Model the Skill

Say to students:

The two Auden poems address the ideas of death or suffering. The first poem describes the death of Yeats; the second poem shows the drowning of Icarus. As I contrast the two poems, I realize that their differences help to highlight the poems' different themes.

❹ Vocabulary

1. Pronounce each word, giving its definition, and have students say it aloud.
2. For more guidance, see the ***Classroom Strategies and Teaching Routines*** card for introducing vocabulary.

Before You Read

In Memory of W. B. Yeats • Musée des Beaux Arts • Carrick Revisited • Not Palaces

❶ **Connecting to the Essential Question** These poems reveal a profound sense of place. As you read, notice details in these poems that highlight the special character of the places being described. These observations will help you think about the Essential Question: **What is the relationship between literature and place?**

Common Core State Standards

Reading Literature

1. Cite strong and thorough textual evidence to support analysis of what the text says explicitly as well as inferences drawn from the text, including determining where the text leaves matters uncertain.

❷ Literary Analysis

Allegory and pastoral are two subgenres of literature with a long tradition. They are called subgenres because these approaches to writing can be found in each major genre—poetry, prose, fiction, and drama.

- In an **allegory,** a writer uses symbolic characters to stand for abstract qualities or traits. In "In Memory of W. B. Yeats," for instance, Auden embodies poetry in a brief allegory. Allegories often teach a moral or lesson.
- In the **pastoral,** writers celebrate nature and those who live in the natural world. In this subgenre, farmers and shepherds are often seen as being wiser or more virtuous than city dwellers.

Comparing Literary Works Many modernist writers rejected traditional forms and styles. These poets may explore allegory or the pastoral not by embracing them but by rejecting them. As you read, look for both positive and negative attitudes.

❸ Reading Strategy

Preparing to Read Complex Texts Both Auden poems address the role of art in the world. The speakers in the MacNeice and Spender poems react in different ways to the traditional pastoral world and the modern human-made one. You can enrich your understanding by **comparing and contrasting elements** that appear in the same poem or different poems. Comparing and contrasting MacNeice's and Spender's presentations of the natural world, for instance, highlights the different themes of their poems and how each poet develops them. As you read, use a chart like the one shown to record similarities and differences in the poems.

MacNeice on Nature
"The child's astonishment not yet cured"

Spender on Nature
"Leave your gardens"

Conclusion
MacNeice is tied to the place and the past; Spender rejects the natural for the new.

❹ Vocabulary

sequestered (si kwes′ tərd) *adj.* kept apart from others (p. 1175)

topographical (täp′ ə graf′ i kəl) *adj.* representing the surface features of a region (p. 1180)

affinities (ə fin′ i tēz) *n.* family connections; sympathies (p. 1181)

prenatal (prē nāt′ əl) *adj.* existing or taking place before birth (p. 1181)

intrigues (in trēgz′) *v.* plots or schemes (p. 1183)

PHLit Online! www.PHLitOnline.com

Vocabulary Development

Vocabulary Knowledge Rating

Create a **Vocabulary Knowledge Rating Chart** (***Professional Development Guidebook***, p. 33) for the vocabulary words on the student page. Give each student a copy of the chart with the words on it. Read the words aloud, and have students mark their ratings in the Before Reading column. Urge students to attend to these words as they read and discuss the selections.

In order to gauge how much instruction you need to provide, tally how many students are confident in their knowledge of each word. As students read, point out the words and their context.

PHLit Online! **Vocabulary Central,** featuring tools and activities for studying vocabulary, is available online at **www.PHLitOnline.com.**

❺ W. H. AUDEN

(1907–1973)

Author of **"In Memory of W. B. Yeats" • "Musée des Beaux Arts"**

Much as T. S. Eliot became established as the poetic voice of the 1920s, so Wystan Hugh Auden emerged as the voice of the 1930s. As a young poet, Auden was greatly influenced by Eliot's work, particularly *The Waste Land*. He soon developed his own poetic style, however, characterized by versatility, wit, and dazzling technique.

Born in York, England, Auden had early dreams of becoming an engineer but gravitated to poetry instead. His commitment to social justice and his opposition to fascism made him a poetic spokesperson for the political left. In 1939, Auden left England for the United States, where he taught at a number of universities. He became an American citizen in 1946. From 1956 to 1960, he taught at Oxford as professor of poetry.

Achievements in Poetry Auden's early poems, along with works by his friends Louis MacNeice and Stephen Spender, appeared in *Oxford Poetry*, a series of annual collections of verse by the university's undergraduates. Auden's first published collection, entitled *Poems*, appeared in 1930. Full of cryptic images and references, Auden's verse struck some readers of the day as impenetrable. His more straightfoward second collection, *On This Island* (1937), generated greater enthusiasm. In 1948, Auden won a Pulitzer Prize for the collection *The Age of Anxiety*.

A Versatile Poet Auden wrote equally well in the idiom of the street or in the archaic measures of *Beowulf*. His voice is original, achieving a kind of personable intimacy even as he makes polished pronouncements on the general human condition. With Yeats and Eliot, he is among the most highly regarded British poets of the twentieth century.

"A REAL BOOK IS NOT ONE THAT WE READ, BUT ONE THAT READS US."

Daily Bellringer

For each class during which you will teach these selections, have students complete one of the five activities for the appropriate week in the *Daily Bellringer Activities* booklet.

Multidraft Reading

To assist struggling readers and to enhance reading for all, assign the text in chunks, as warranted by length, and apply multidraft reading protocols. For each reading, have students set the purpose indicated:

- **First reading**—identifying key ideas and details and answering any Reading Checks.
- **Second reading**—analyzing craft and structure and responding to the side-column prompts.
- **Third reading**—integrating knowledge and ideas, connecting to other texts and the world, and answering the end-of-selection questions.

For more guidance, refer to the *Classroom Strategies and Teaching Routines* card on multidraft reading.

❺ Background

More About the Author

One of Auden's strengths was being able to mimic almost any style of poetry, from the classic poets to the Modernists. His poetry frequently tells, literally or metaphysically, of journeys or quests, backed by his own extensive travels. His early works reflect a Socialist bent and an interest in Freudian psychoanalysis. Later, he became an advocate of modern Protestant theology.

PHLit Online!
www.PHLitOnline.com

Teaching From Technology

Preparing to Read
Go to **www.PHLitOnline.com** and display the ***Get Connected!*** slide show for these selections. Have the class brainstorm responses to the writing prompt, entering ideas in the interactive journal. Then, have students complete their written responses as homework.

To build background, display the Background and More About the Author features.

Using the Interactive Text
Go to **www.PHLitOnline.com** and display the **Enriched Online Student Edition.** As the class reads the selections or listens to the narrations, record answers to side-column prompts using the graphic organizers accessible on the interactive page. Alternatively, have students use the online edition individually, answering the prompts as they read.

❶ About the Selection

This poem celebrates and honors the life of poet W. B. Yeats. Structured as an elegy, the poem sums up Yeats's lifetime accomplishments and crafts a vivid picture of the man. Part 1 describes his all-too-human death and the gap it will leave behind. In Part 2, Auden addresses Yeats directly to reassure him of poetry's enduring qualities. Part 3, addressed both to Earth and to a generic poet, focuses on the nature of poetry. Although it "makes nothing happen," poetry teaches joy in the human condition.

❷ Activating Prior Knowledge

Hold up this textbook, or ask students to examine their own copies. Ask students to consider for a moment the art—poetry, fiction, drama, paintings—the book contains. **Ask:** What is the purpose of art? What does it do? Out of what impulses do people create art? Have students write a paragraph about art they have created. Then have them write about why they created it. State that in three very different ways, each of the poets in this section asks and perhaps answers the questions above.

Concept Connector →

Tell students they will return to their responses at the end of the selection.

❶ ❷ *In Memory of*

W. B. YEATS

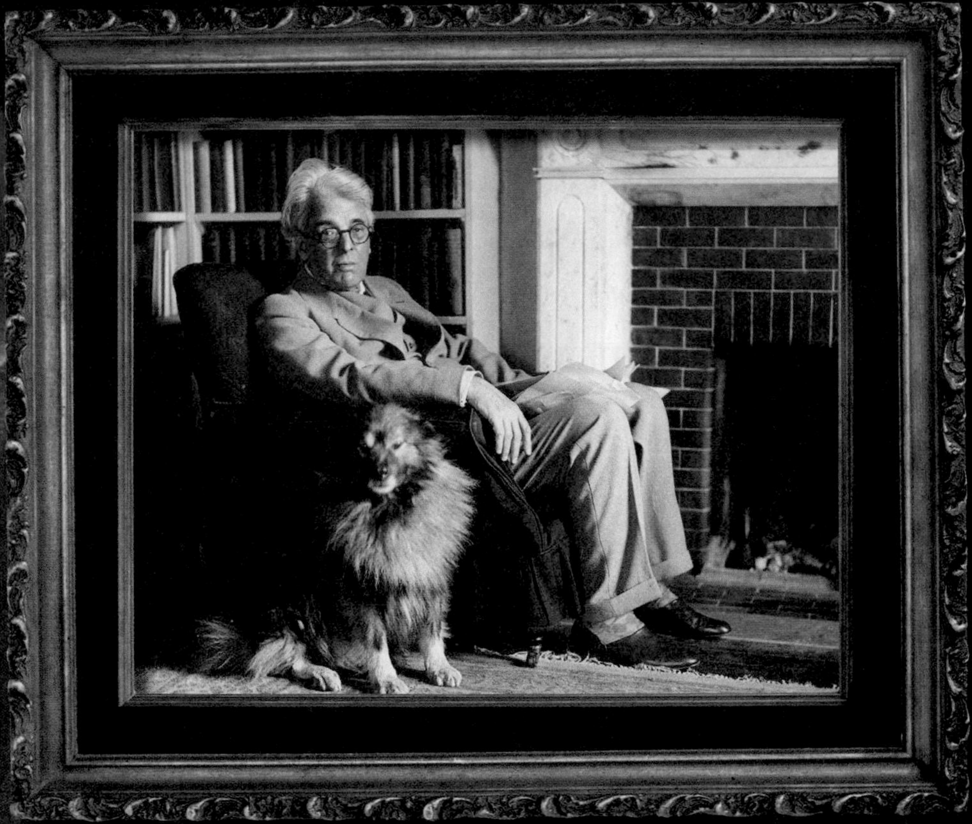

W. H. AUDEN

Text Complexity Rubric

	In Memory of W. B. Yeats	Musée des Beaux Arts	Carrick Revisited	Not Palaces
Qualitative Measures				
Context/Knowledge Demands	Modernist elegy 1 2 ③ 4 5	Modernist lyric 1 2 ③ 4 5	Modernist lyric 1 2 ③ 4 5	Modernist lyric 1 2 ③ 4 5
Structure/Language Conventionality and Clarity	Fairly simple diction 1 ② 3 4 5	Simple diction 1 ② 3 4 5	Challenging diction; long sentences 1 2 ③ 4 5	Challenging diction; long sentences 1 2 ③ 4 5
Levels of Meaning/ Purpose/Concepts	Moderate (poetic achievement) 1 2 ③ 4 5	Moderate (suffering and art) 1 2 ③ 4 5	Challenging (childhood and art) 1 2 3 ④ 5	Challenging (art; social change) 1 2 3 ④ 5
Quantitative Measures				
Lexile/Text Length	NP / 517 words	NP / 186 words	NP / 235 words	NP / 149 words
Overall Complexity	**More accessible**	**More accessible**	**More complex**	**More complex**

BACKGROUND The 1930s was a decade of economic collapse and political turmoil that ended with the world plunged into another great war. The complex concerns of the period are reflected in the poems of the Auden circle, which included Auden himself, Spender, MacNeice, and C. Day Lewis. The political urgencies of the times—the opposition to fascism and the movement for social justice for the working classes—shaped much of the poetry the Auden circle wrote then. Yet along with their social concerns, each of these poets shared a deep sense of a specifically poetic vocation—to make something happen in language.

1

He disappeared in the dead of winter:
The brooks were frozen, the airports almost deserted,
And snow disfigured the public statues;
The mercury sank in the mouth of the dying day.
O all the instruments agree
The day of his death was a dark cold day.

Far from his illness
The wolves ran on through the evergreen forests,
The peasant river was untempted by fashionable quays;[1]
By mourning tongues
The death of the poet was kept from his poems.

But for him it was his last afternoon as himself,
4 An afternoon of nurses and rumors;
The provinces of his body revolted,
The squares of his mind were empty,
Silence invaded the suburbs,
The current of his feeling failed: he became his admirers.

Now he is scattered among a hundred cities
And wholly given over to unfamiliar affections;
To find his happiness in another kind of wood
And be punished by another code of conscience.
The words of a dead man
Are modified in the guts of the living.

But in the importance and noise of tomorrow
When the brokers are roaring like beasts on the floor
of the Bourse,[2]
And the poor have the sufferings to which they are
fairly accustomed,

1. **quays** (kēz) wharfs with facilities for loading or unloading ships.
2. **Bourse** (bo͝ors) Paris Stock Exchange.

3 ◀ Critical Viewing
Does this photograph of Yeats present him as the mortal man described in parts 1 and 2 of Auden's poem or as the great writer eulogized in part 3? Explain. **[Interpret]**

Reading Strategy
Compare and Contrast Elements How does Auden use images of different locations to dramatize Yeats's death?

5 Reading Check
According to the speaker, where is Yeats now?

3 Critical Viewing

Possible response: The photograph presents him as the mortal man seen in the earlier sections of the poem.

4 Reading Strategy

Compare and Contrast Elements

1. Have students read the first five stanzas of the poem.
2. **Ask** students the Reading Strategy question: How does Auden use images of different locations to dramatize Yeats's death?
   Answer: By providing snapshot descriptions of different locations and showing their response or lack of response to Yeats's passing, he dramatizes the scope of Yeats's influence, which is "scattered among a hundred cities." The poem creates a feeling that there was a small community throughout the world that took note of that day.

5 Reading Check

Answer: According to the speaker, Yeats may be found in a hundred different cities—in the libraries of those cities and in the minds of the readers all around the world.

PHLit Online!

These selections are available in interactive format in the **Enriched Online Student Edition,** at **www.PHLitOnline.com,** which includes a thematically related video with writing prompt and an interactive graphic organizer.

Text Complexity: Reader and Task Suggestions

In Memory of W. B. Yeats; Musée des Beaux Arts		Carrick Revisited; Not Palaces	
Preparing to Read the Text • Use the information on SE p. 1173 to discuss the worldwide depression of the 1930s. Note that Yeats died in 1939. • Explain that the role of the artist was a major theme of Modernist literature. • Guide students to use Multidraft Reading strategies (TE p. 1171).	**Leveled Tasks** ***Levels of Meaning*** If students will have difficulty with meanings, have them read to get an impression of what Auden thought of Yeats and Breughel. Then, have students reread each poem, focusing on each artist's insights. ***Evaluating*** If students will not have difficulty with the poems' meanings, have them evaluate the effectiveness with which Auden supports his views about each artist.	**Preparing to Read the Text** • Discuss the role of a writer's background in determining what he or she writes about. • Discuss with students the ways in which setting can be used to create mood or to represent ideas. • Guide students to use Multidraft Reading strategies (TE p. 1171).	**Leveled Tasks** ***Structure/Language*** If students will have difficulty with language, have them first read each poem to find its complete thoughts about the places it describes. Then, have them summarize. ***Synthesizing*** If students will not have difficulty with the poems' language, have them compare and contrast each poem's use of setting images to help convey its meaning.

❻ Literary Analysis

Allegory

1. Have students review section 2 of the poem.
2. **Ask** students the Literary Analysis question: How does Auden create a mini-allegory, or symbolic narrative, in lines 36–41 to describe the creation and progress of poetry?
   Answer: Poetry is a symbol for survival and continuation of life. It is a "way of happening, a mouth" for those who need its comfort.

And each in the cell of himself is almost convinced of
  his freedom;
A few thousand will think of this day
As one thinks of a day when one did something
  slightly unusual.
O all the instruments agree
The day of his death was a dark cold day.

2

You were silly like us: your gift survived it all;
The parish of rich women, physical decay,
Yourself; mad Ireland hurt you into poetry.
Now Ireland has her madness and her weather still,
❻ For poetry makes nothing happen: it survives
In the valley of its saying where executives
Would never want to tamper; it flows south
From ranches of isolation and the busy griefs,
Raw towns that we believe and die in; it survives,
A way of happening, a mouth.

Literary Analysis
Allegory How does Auden create a mini-allegory, or symbolic narrative, in lines 36–41 to describe the creation and progress of poetry?

3

Earth, receive an honored guest;
William Yeats is laid to rest:
Let the Irish vessel lie
Emptied of its poetry.

Time that is intolerant
Of the brave and innocent,
And indifferent in a week
To a beautiful physique,

Worships language and forgives
Everyone by whom it lives;
Pardons cowardice, conceit
Lays its honors at their feet.

Time that with this strange excuse
Pardoned Kipling and his views,[3]
And will pardon Paul Claudel,[4]
Pardons him for writing well.

---

3. **Kipling . . . views** English writer Rudyard Kipling (1865–1936) was a supporter of imperialism.
4. **pardon Paul Claudel** (klō del′) French poet, dramatist, and diplomat. Paul Claudel (1868–1955) had antidemocratic political views, which Yeats at times shared.

Enrichment: Understanding Science

Meteorology

In this poem, both Auden's observations and "the instruments" agree that the weather is very cold. In Auden's time, these instruments would have been much simpler than those used today to evaluate and predict weather. Meteorologists now use computer modeling, satellite photographs, and sophisticated monitoring equipment.

Activity: Writing About Science Have students research different meteorological instruments that aid in evaluating weather. Suggest that they record information in the **Enrichment: Investigating Science** worksheet, ***Professional Development Guidebook,*** page 241. Have them use the results of their research to write two paragraphs, comparing modern methods of evaluating the weather with their own observations.

In the nightmare of the dark
All the dogs of Europe bark,
And the living nations wait,
Each sequestered in its hate;

Intellectual disgrace
Stares from every human face,
And the seas of pity lie
Locked and frozen in each eye.

Follow, poet, follow right
To the bottom of the night,
With your unconstraining voice
Still persuade us to rejoice;

With the farming of a verse
Make a vineyard of the curse,
Sing of human unsuccess
In a rapture of distress;

In the deserts of the heart
Let the healing fountain start,
In the prison of his days
Teach the free man how to praise.

Vocabulary
sequestered (si kwes′ tərd) *adj.* kept apart from others

FOLLOW, POET, FOLLOW RIGHT TO THE BOTTOM OF THE *Night*

Critical Reading

Cite textual evidence to support your responses.

1. **Key Ideas and Details** What does the speaker mean by saying Yeats "became his admirers"?
2. **Key Ideas and Details** What does the second section suggest about the sources and effects of poetry?
3. **Integration of Knowledge and Ideas (a) Interpret:** Considering the kind of fame great past poets enjoy, why does the speaker say that time "Worships language and forgives / Everyone by whom it lives . . ."? **(b) Synthesize:** What kind of poetry might "Sing of human unsuccess / In a rapture of distress . . ."?
4. **Integration of Knowledge and Ideas** Summarize the view of poetry presented in the poem.
5. **Craft and Structure** In phrases such as "ranches of isolation," Auden combines the abstract and the specific. Identify three other images that combine abstract ideas and concrete details.
6. **Craft and Structure** Is Auden's style suited to a poem of mourning? Explain.

ASSESS

Answers

Before students respond, you may wish to have them write a brief objective summary of the selection. As they answer the questions below, remind them to support their answers with evidence from the text.

1. His mourners kept his poems alive, even after his death.
2. Though Yeats the man has died, Yeats the poet, a voice and a source of pleasure, lives on in his readers' enjoyment of his poems.
3. (a) The speaker believes that language will last eternally and that people will forgive any sins committed by the poet. (b) The poetry may very well be in the Modernist style, with topics of human despair but signs of hopefulness.
4. Poetry has little to do with the personal lives or political beliefs of poets; good poetry is immortal; it is the essence of poetry to "Sing of human unsuccess," affirming the human condition in all its limitations.
5. Students may cite "all the instruments agree," "Now Ireland has her madness," and "the farming of a verse."
6. **Possible responses:** Yes, the style suits the elegy, as it praises Yeats and acknowledges his public stature. No, Auden's style is too public and philosophical to express personal grief.

Differentiated Instruction for Universal Access

Support for Special-Needs Students
Have students read along to the recorded version of "In Memory of W. B. Yeats" on the ***Listening to Literature* Audio CDs.** Pause after every stanza to discuss what the speaker is talking about. Have a volunteer recount the ideas in the poem up to that point.

EL Strategy for English Learners
Help English-language learners read the poem by having them pay attention to the punctuation of the lines. Help them construct reasonable sentences, which may or may not conclude at the end of a line or stanza.

Enrichment for Advanced Readers
The poem mentions that Kipling and Claudel will each be forgiven for "his views," and Claudel will be forgiven for "writing well." For what must Yeats be forgiven? Have students research his life to determine what Auden is referring to.

❼ Humanities

The Fall of Icarus, by Pieter Brueghel

This painting illustrates the last scene in the myth of Icarus, in which he falls into the sea. It is a visual depiction of the ideas Auden expresses in the poem. Flemish painter Pieter Brueghel the Elder (he had a son Pieter Brueghel the Younger) served an artistic apprenticeship with Belgian artist Pieter Coecke van Aelst. As he developed his own style, Brueghel often roamed the countryside, making candid drawings of the landscape and its inhabitants for later use in his paintings. *The Fall of Icarus* could be one such painting, in which the everyday people are captured with exquisite detail. Use these questions for discussion:

1. **Ask:** What specific elements from the painting does Auden describe?
   Answer: He describes the ploughman, the sun shining, the white legs disappearing into the water, and the delicate ship sailing on.
2. **Ask:** How do the attitudes of poet and painter toward human indifference compare?
   Possible response: Both draw a lesson about the nature of suffering.

❽ Critical Viewing

Answer: Nobody in the picture is paying any attention to Icarus' fall. In this way, the painting reflects Auden's idea that suffering belongs only to the sufferer and is not part of everyday life.

❼

❽ ▲ **Critical Viewing** In this painting by Brueghel, which inspired Auden's poem, the drowning Icarus appears in the lower right. What is Brueghel implying about the place of suffering in life? **[Interpret]**

Enrichment: Understanding Mythology

Icarus

Daedalus, Icarus' father, designed the labyrinth in which King Minos of Crete imprisoned the Minotaur (a monster half-man, half-bull). Daedalus revealed the labyrinth's secret, enabling the hero Theseus to slay the Minotaur and escape with Minos' daughter Ariadne. When King Minos then imprisoned Daedalus and Icarus, Daedalus fashioned wings of wax and feathers and he and Icarus flew off. Icarus flew too close to the sun; the wax on his wings melted and he plummeted to his death.

Activity: Poetry and Mythology Have students research the myth of Icarus. Suggest that they record information in the **Enrichment: Investigating Religion and Myth** worksheet, ***Professional Development Guidebook,*** page 240. Have each student use the results of this research to write a short poem from the perspective of Icarus.

Musée des Beaux Arts[1]

W. H. Auden

⑨

About suffering they were never wrong,
The Old Masters: how well they understood
Its human position; how it takes place
While someone else is eating or opening a window or just
 walking dully along;
5 How, when the aged are reverently, passionately waiting
For the miraculous birth, there always must be
Children who did not specially want it to happen, skating

1. **Musée des Beaux Arts** Museum of Fine Arts in Brussels, Belgium, which contains Brueghel's *Icarus*.

⑩ ☑ Reading Check

What did the Old Masters understand about suffering?

Musée des Beaux Arts **1177**

⑨ About the Selection

This poem gives depth to the truism that "people suffer, yet the world moves on." Focusing on a painting by Pieter Brueghel, Auden points out how Brueghel's figures ignore Icarus' tragic fall. The world of the painting is innocently indifferent to suffering, and Auden seems sure that this indifference holds a profound truth. This indifference may show that there is something deeply private about an individual's suffering that cannot be shared with others.

⑩ Reading Check

Possible response: The Old Masters understood that the suffering of others is often an afterthought in a person's everyday life or that suffering is just another moment in everyday life.

Differentiated Instruction for Universal Access

Strategy for Less Proficient Readers
Have less proficient readers examine the painting and write what each person is doing. Discuss whether Icarus' death makes a difference. Help students understand the theme of the world's indifference to personal suffering as told in the poem and in the painting.

EL Background for English Learners
English learners may not be familiar with the story of Icarus. Find the story of Icarus and Daedalus in the library. Help students read the story to provide the background necessary to interpret the picture and the poem.

Enrichment for Advanced Readers
Have advanced students research more about the painter Pieter Brueghel the Elder. The story of Icarus is a Greek myth. Was there a relationship between Brueghel and the classical myths? Did he paint more scenes such as this?

⓫ Literary Analysis

Allegory

1. Have students examine the Brueghel painting more closely, looking for allegorical elements in the picture.
2. Then, **ask** the Literary Analysis question.
3. **Possible response:** Icarus represents suffering in the world; those who pass by do not acknowledge the tragic event. The moral is that suffering is a private experience, which cannot be shared with others so readily.

ASSESS

Answers

Before students respond, you may wish to have them write a brief objective summary of the selection. As they answer the questions below, remind them to support their answers with evidence from the text.

1. (a) The Old Masters are Belgian, Italian, and Dutch painters of the thirteenth to sixteenth centuries. (b) They depict momentous events surrounded by indifferent figures pursuing ordinary activities.
2. (a) They witness the fall of Icarus. (b) Although the event is both wondrous and tragic—a winged boy falls to his death—they continue their routine activities.
3. (a) They continue playing in ignorance. (b) Yes, both are disassociated from the important events nearby.
4. (a) The artist implies that the fall is only one event among others. (b) Brueghel realizes that suffering is part of life.
5. Students should provide reasons for their choices. In support of (a), they should note that Auden emphasizes the isolation of the sufferer. In support of (b), they should note that in both painting and poem, the contrast between details of everyday life and extraordinary events emphasizes the significance of both.
6. (a) Students should supply instances of indifference to suffering. Answers will vary. (b) Auden might note that, right or wrong, people cannot share another's suffering or abandon their own concerns entirely.

On a pond at the edge of the wood:
They never forgot
That even the dreadful martyrdom must run its course
Anyhow in a corner, some untidy spot
Where the dogs go on with their doggy life and the
 torturer's horse
Scratches its innocent behind on a tree.

In Brueghel's *Icarus*,[2] for instance: how everything turns away
Quite leisurely from the disaster; the ploughman may
Have heard the splash, the forsaken cry,
But for him it was not an important failure; the sun shone
As it had to on the white legs disappearing into the green
Water; and the expensive delicate ship that must have seen
Something amazing, a boy falling out of the sky,
Had somewhere to get to and sailed calmly on.

⓫ Literary Analysis
Allegory In what way does Brueghel's picture depict an allegorical landscape for Auden? What is the moral of this allegory?

2. **Brueghel's** (brü´ gəlz) ***Icarus*** (ik´ ə rəs) *The Fall of Icarus*, a painting by Flemish painter Pieter Brueghel (1525?–1569). In Greek mythology, Icarus flies too close to the sun. The wax of his artificial wings melts, and he falls into the sea.

Cite textual evidence to support your responses.

Critical Reading

1. **Key Ideas and Details (a)** Who are the "Old Masters"? **(b) Interpret:** What general device used by the Old Masters does the speaker discuss?
2. **Key Ideas and Details (a)** What disaster do the "ploughman" and the "ship" witness? **(b) Compare and Contrast:** How do their responses contrast with the gravity of the event?
3. **Key Ideas and Details (a) Infer:** What is the relation of the children to the important events near them? **(b) Connect:** Is the attitude of the ploughman to Icarus's fall similar? Explain.
4. **Key Ideas and Details (a) Analyze:** Look at Brueghel's *The Fall of Icarus* (p. 1176). What does the artist imply by showing only Icarus's legs in the right corner of the picture? **(b) Infer:** What does Brueghel, an Old Master, realize about the place of suffering in the world?
5. **Integration of Knowledge and Ideas** Consider these two statements: (1) *A person's suffering belongs to him or her in a way that not even pity can change.* (2) *Suffering gives meaning to innocent everyday life, and vice versa.* Which statement better captures the sense of the poem? Support your choice.
6. **Integration of Knowledge and Ideas (a) Apply:** Identify two examples of indifference to suffering today. **(b) Relate:** What might Auden say about them?

Think Aloud

Critical Reading

To model the process of working out the answer to the Critical Reading question 2b on the student page, use the following "think aloud." Say to students:

How do the responses of the ploughman and others contrast with the gravity of the event? I know that the event, a winged boy falling to his death, is both wondrous and tragic. I would have stopped to look or help. But, the ploughman is described as possibly hearing the splash of Icarus in the water and not thinking of it as an important event. He is described as "leisurely" turning away from the disaster. I can see that Auden is describing a response that is different from our expectations—one of indifference.

(1907–1963)

⓬ # Louis MacNeice

Author of "Carrick Revisited"

Louis MacNeice was the son of a Protestant clergyman in Belfast, Northern Ireland. A gifted youth, he began to write poetry at age seven, about the time his mother died. His first collection, *Blind Fireworks*, appeared in 1929, followed six years later by *Poems*, the volume that established his reputation. During the 1930s, MacNeice taught classical literature. In 1941, he joined the British Broadcasting Corporation, writing radio plays in verse.

In a period when Auden and others embraced leftist politics, MacNeice was unwilling to commit to a rigid political program. He once dismissed Marxism by writing that "the evil of the means obscures the good of the end." Proudly Irish, he often returned to the island to enjoy its land and people. At the same time, he lived most of his adult life in England and tried to achieve a balance between the pulls of those two places and Europe as a whole.

T. S. Eliot praised MacNeice as a "poet of genius whose virtuosity can be fully appreciated only by other poets." Critics of his time viewed him less favorably, though. His reputation has since shifted more toward Eliot's judgment. Today, many consider MacNeice second only to Auden among the poets of their generation. His poetry is restrained and precise, with overtones of melancholy. It is the poetry of a man who, as the poet Edwin Muir put it, "is never swept off his feet."

"The evil of the means obscures the good of the end."

⓬ Background

More About the Author

MacNeice taught Greek at Bedford College in London and later became a skilled translator of the Greek classics. He also wrote and produced radio plays for the BBC. His characteristic mood was that of the slightly detached, wryly observant, ironic, and witty commentator.

Differentiated Instruction for Universal Access

Culturally Responsive Instruction

Culture Focus Point out that in the following poem, the poet goes back to his place of birth. He was born in Northern Ireland, but lived for a while in southern England. Have students note that in the United States, there are many people who have emigrated from different countries to live in the United States. Often, they revisit their homelands, if they can, and may have some of the same reactions as MacNeice does in his poem "Carrick Revisited." Invite students to share their knowledge and experiences of leaving or revisiting the countries of their families' origins.

PHLit Online!

For more about the author, go online at **www.PHLITOnline.com.**

⓭ About the Selection

This poem takes readers on a journey back to the poet's birthplace in an effort to understand and define the influences on an artist's identity. The speaker—presumably MacNeice—describes Carrickfergus, with its castle and green hills and its familiar sights and sounds. As he tours the natural and human landscape, recalling the Carrick of his childhood, the poet acknowledges the irrefutable influence of Northern Ireland—a chance "Particular," neither the pure Irish of the west nor the pure English across the water—on his character.

⓮ Literary Analysis

Pastoral

1. Have students read the third stanza, noting the ways in which childhood is presented as a kind of pastoral.
2. Then, **ask** students the Literary Analysis question: In what ways does the third stanza present childhood itself as a kind of pastoral?
   Possible response: Childhood is presented as a kind of pastoral because MacNeice attributes the innocence and curiosity of childhood to feelings and memories of the past.

⓭ Carrick Revisited

Louis MacNeice

Back to Carrick,[1] the castle as plumb assured
As thirty years ago—Which war was which?
Here are new villas, here is a sizzling grid
But the green banks are as rich and the lough[2] as hazily lazy
And the child's astonishment not yet cured.

Who was—and am—dumbfounded to find myself
In a topographical frame—here, not there—
The channels of my dreams determined largely
By random chemistry of soil and air;
Memories I had shelved peer at me from the shelf.

Fog-horn, mill-horn, corncrake and church bell
Half-heard through boarded time as a child in bed
⓮ Glimpses a brangle of talk from the floor below
But cannot catch the words. Our past we know
But not its meaning—whether it meant well.

Vocabulary
topographical (täp′ ə graf′ i kəl) *adj.* representing the surface features of a region

Literary Analysis
Pastoral In what way does the third stanza present childhood itself as a kind of pastoral?

1. **Carrick** shortened form of Carrickfergus, a town in Northern Ireland.
2. **lough** (läkh) lake, specifically Belfast Lough. Carrickfergus is situated on the northern shore of Belfast Lough.

Enrichment: Understanding History

Feudal Ireland

Carrickfergus Castle, mentioned by MacNeice, was built by an Anglo-Norman lord, John de Courci, sometime after he conquered the area in 1175. The Normans, who conquered England in 1066, also conquered parts of Ireland. Soon, though, the kings of England became wary of the independence of the Anglo-Norman lords of Ireland and took steps to limit their power. Thus began the enduring conflict between England and Ireland.

Activity: John de Courci's Perspective
Have students research the life of John de Courci after he conquered the area around 1175. Suggest that they record information in the **Enrichment: Analyzing a Historical Event** worksheet, ***Professional Development Guidebook***, page 230. Have each student use the results of his or her research to write a short one-page description of the land from the perspective of John de Courci.

Time and place—our bridgeheads into reality
But also its concealment! Out of the sea
We land on the Particular and lose
All other possible bird's-eye views, the Truth
That is of Itself for Itself—but not for me.

Torn before birth from where my fathers dwelt,
Schooled from the age of ten to a foreign voice,
Yet neither western Ireland nor southern England
Cancels this interlude; what chance misspelt
May never now be righted by my choice.

Whatever then my inherited or acquired
Affinities, such remains my childhood's frame
Like a belated rock in the red Antrim[3] clay
That cannot at this era change its pitch or name—
And the prenatal mountain is far away.

3. **Antrim** county in Northern Ireland in which Carrickfergus is located.

◀ Carrickfergus Castle, shown on the facing page, was built in 1177.

Vocabulary

affinities (ə fin′ i tēz) *n.* family connections; sympathies

prenatal (prē nāt′ əl) *adj.* existing or taking place before birth

Critical Reading

Cite textual evidence to support your responses.

1. **Key Ideas and Details (a)** Where does the speaker find himself at the beginning of the poem? **(b) Compare and Contrast:** According to the first stanza, what has changed and what has remained the same?
2. **Key Ideas and Details (a)** What discovery dumbfounds the speaker? **(b) Interpret:** What relationship does the speaker discover between the imagination—which enables us to picture ourselves in any circumstances—and the facts of his personal history?
3. **Key Ideas and Details (a) Interpret:** What effect do the specifics of the place have on the speaker's imagination? **(b) Interpret:** What does the speaker mean in saying "Our past we know / But not its meaning . . ."? **(c) Speculate:** What task concerning the past might MacNeice assign to poetry?
4. **Integration of Knowledge and Ideas (a) Interpret:** Why does the speaker call his childhood in Carrick an "interlude"? **(b) Draw Conclusions:** How is MacNeice's identity, as described in this poem, influenced by two cultures but separate from both?
5. **Integration of Knowledge and Ideas** Name two ways in which issues of identity are just as complex for people today.

ASSESS

Answers

Before students respond, you may wish to have them write a brief objective summary of the selection. As they answer the questions below, remind them to support their answers with evidence from the text.

1. (a) He finds himself back at Carrickfergus, where he spent some childhood years. (b) The castle, green hills, and lake are the same, while new houses show change.
2. (a) He is dumbfounded to find himself in territory more familiar than expected. (b) His personal history affects the way he imagines things, yet his imagination lets him discern the arbitrariness of the particulars of his past.
3. (a) The specifics reinforce and add details to his imagination, such as the sounds of "Fog-horn, mill-horn, corncrake and church bell . . . ." (b) We cannot choose our own past, and the past defines who we are. (c) He might expect poetry to record and interpret the past.
4. (a) It is an interlude between his ancestry in the western part of Ireland and his schooling in the south of England. (b) He is influenced by both the Irish and English portions of his life, but he feels as though he does not belong to either totally.
5. Many people today are of mixed ethnic lineage or have relocated to new countries.

Differentiated Instruction for Universal Access

Strategy for Less Proficient Readers

Have less proficient readers recite each stanza of the poem in a choral reading. Remind students to pay attention to the punctuation of the lines, and point out that the end of a line does not always mean the end of a sentence. If you think it would be helpful, provide copies of the poem and ask students to draw a red or blue slash to indicate the end of each sentence.

Enrichment for Gifted/Talented Students

Gifted or talented students might enjoy creating for the class a rendition of their childhood memories. This may be accomplished in art, drama, music, or dance. Encourage students to plan some discussion time after a performance or showing so that other students can determine whether they interpreted the art and its meaning correctly.

⑮ Background

More About the Author

Sir Stephen Harold Spender was influenced by the German poet Rainer Maria Rilke and the Spanish poet Federico Garcia Lorca. His poems were self-critical and compassionate and had a personal, almost autobiographical nature. He was the first non-American to serve as poetry consultant to the Library of Congress. Spender was knighted in 1983.

⑮ Stephen Spender

(1909–1995)

"I think continually of those who were truly great. / Who, from the womb, remembered the soul's history..."

Author of "Not Palaces"

No poet of the 1930s provided a more honest picture of the era between the wars than did Stephen Spender. Much of his early poetry deals with the world of the thirties, the "low dishonest decade"—in W. H. Auden's phrase—that saw many countries struggle with economic depression, experiment with extremist ideologies, and drift inexorably toward war. Yet Spender, never a pessimist, celebrates technology at the same time as he confronts the problems of industrial progress. While many of his poems had political themes, they also reflect his deeply personal responses to the world.

Born in London and educated at Oxford, Spender published his first important book, *Poems* (1933), while he was living in Germany. Early in life, Spender was politically active and—like many other young English college men of the time—embraced communism. He promoted antifascist propaganda in Spain during that country's civil war (1936–1939) but abandoned communism during World War II. In 1949, he joined with others in publishing a work that criticized communism called *The God That Failed*.

Even in his college years, Spender was more than a poet. It was he who published Auden's first collection of poems, privately printing an edition of thirty copies. Starting in the 1940s, Spender became a highly regarded literary critic and commentator. He later coedited the literary magazine *Horizon* and the political, cultural, and literary review *Encounter*. Along with writing poetry, Spender wrote short stories, a novel, verse plays, and volumes of criticism and essays. He continued working at poetry, though, publishing his last collection of poems a year before his death.

Vocabulary Development

Vocabulary Knowledge Rating

When students have completed reading and discussing the group of selections, have them take out their **Vocabulary Knowledge Rating Charts** for the poems. Read the words aloud and have students rate their knowledge of words again in the After Reading column. Clarify any words that are still problematic. Have students write their own definitions and examples or sentence in the appropriate column. Then, have students complete the Vocabulary Lesson at the end of the selections. Encourage students to use the words in further discussion and written work about the selections. Remind them that they will be accountable for these words on the **Selection Test, *Unit 6 Resources,*** pages 57–59 or 60–62.

16 # Not Palaces

Stephen Spender

16 **About the Selection**

This poem contrasts the aesthetic values of art with its potential for social change. The poet discusses and rejects the idea that art should be merely a "palace"—a beautiful home for the imagination, remote from society. He calls emphatically instead for commitment to social action, asking artists to inspire change.

BACKGROUND In this poem's unifying metaphor, Spender says that he will not build old-fashioned poems that are like palaces—beautiful, ornate structures remote from the masses. Instead, he hopes to build active, modern poetry, more like the steel and glass skyscrapers that began with the International and Bauhaus architectural styles of the 1920s and 1930s. These buildings create dynamic spaces by combining strikingly simple forms with superior industrial craftsmanship. Walter Gropius, the founder of the Bauhaus school, sought to integrate architecture and the other arts.

Not palaces, an era's crown
Where the mind dwells, **intrigues**, rests:
Architectural gold-leaved flower
From people ordered like a single mind,
I build: this only what I tell:
It is too late for rare accumulation,
For family pride, for beauty's filtered dusts;

Vocabulary
intrigues (in trēgz′)
v. plots or schemes

Differentiated Instruction for Universal Access

Strategy for Less Proficient Readers
Less proficient readers may need help navigating Spender's poetic structure. Direct them to break down the sentences in the poem and read them, at first, according to punctuation only. Note that often semicolons link what could be several sentences, creating one long sentence instead.

Enrichment for Advanced Readers
Advanced students may enjoy researching to determine to what extent the era of palaces involved a society of "people ordered like a single mind." Have some students investigate society, architecture, painting, and music during the reign of the famous palace builder Louis XIV. Have them put their research together to write essays evaluating Spender's assumption.

17 Reading Strategy

Compare and Contrast Elements

1. Have students reread lines 16–18 of the poem.
2. Then, **ask** the Reading Strategy question: Contrast Spender's definite rejection of pastoral images in lines 16–18 with MacNeice's mixed feelings about the pastoral of childhood.
   Possible response: Spender rejects the pastoral in favor of the new and modern in his poem. On the other hand, MacNeice understands that we are, in part, defined by our places of origin ("our bridgeheads into reality"), though they can limit us in how we understand the world.

ASSESS

Answers

Before students respond, you may wish to have them write a brief objective summary of the selection. As they answer the questions below, remind them to support their answers with evidence from the text.

1. (a) He will not build elaborate monuments or collect rare objects from the past. (b) He is rejecting the vision of art as merely recording reality.
2. (a) Times have changed; it is too late. (b) He wants to use poetry to inspire and motivate others toward social action.
3. (a) The images of flashing glass may refer to modern skyscrapers. (b) These buildings are plainer, more modern, and more functional.
4. (a) Poetry used to be written for the pleasure of those with the leisure to appreciate its elaborate beauty and wit. (b) He thinks it should now be used to communicate views about society.
5. **Possible response:** Yes, some reflect *unique* moments and places, such as the death of Yeats or the revisiting of a childhood location. In setting down in writing these fleeting specific times, though, the poets give them *permanence*.

I say, stamping the words with emphasis,
Drink from here energy and only energy
To will this time's change.
Eye, gazelle, delicate wanderer,
Drinker of horizon's fluid line;
Ear that suspends on a chord
The spirit drinking timelessness;
Touch, love, all senses;
(17) Leave your gardens, your singing feasts,
Your dreams of suns circling before our sun,
Of heaven after our world.
Instead, watch images of flashing glass
That strike the outward sense, the polished will,
Flag of our purpose which the wind engraves.
No spirit seek here rest. But this: No one
Shall hunger: Man shall spend equally;
Our goal which we compel: Man shall be man.

Reading Strategy
Compare and Contrast Elements Contrast Spender's definite rejection of pastoral images in lines 16–18 with MacNeice's mixed feelings about the pastoral of childhood.

1184

Critical Reading

Cite textual evidence to support your responses.

1. **Key Ideas and Details (a)** In lines 1–7, what does the speaker say he will not do? **(b) Interpret:** What vision of art is he rejecting?
2. **Key Ideas and Details (a)** What reason does the speaker give for rejecting the "accumulation" of rarities? **(b) Interpret:** What connection does the speaker make between his poem and social progress in lines 9–10?
3. **Key Ideas and Details (a) Interpret:** What might the speaker mean by "images of flashing glass"? **(b) Compare and Contrast:** How does this image contrast with the palaces described in the poem's opening?
4. **Integration of Knowledge and Ideas (a) Analyze:** What does Spender think the job of poetry once was? **(b) Analyze:** What does he think it should be now?
5. **Integration of Knowledge and Ideas** Do these poems reflect a sense of a particular place or time? Explain. In your response, use at least two of these Essential Question words: *unique, aware, consciousness, permanence.* ***[Connecting to the Essential Question: What is the relationship between literature and place?]***

Concept Connector

Reading Strategy Graphic Organizer

Ask students to review the graphic organizers in which they have recorded similarities and differences in the poems they compared. Then, have students share their organizers and compare the similarities and differences.

Activating Prior Knowledge

Have students return to their responses to the Activating Prior Knowledge activity. Ask them to explain whether their thoughts have changed and, if so, how.

Writing About the Essential Question

Have students compare their responses to the prompt, completed before reading the poems, with their thoughts afterward. Have them work individually or in groups, writing or discussing their thoughts, to formulate their new responses. Then, lead a class discussion, probing for what students have learned that confirms or invalidates their initial thoughts. Encourage students to cite specific textual details to support their responses.

After You Read

In Memory of W. B. Yeats • Musée des Beaux Arts • Carrick Revisited • Not Palaces

Literary Analysis

1. **Craft and Structure** Is it reasonable to say that Auden builds an **allegory** out of Yeats's work and life in the poem "In Memory of W. B. Yeats"? Explain.
2. **Craft and Structure** Auden uses similar images in lines 27 and 76–77 in "In Memory of W. B. Yeats." How do the differences in these two mentions help carry the meaning of the poem?
3. **Craft and Structure** Use a chart like the one shown to trace the use of **pastoral** images in "In Memory of W. B. Yeats," "Carrick Revisited," and "Not Palaces." Then, summarize the way each writer uses pastoral elements in his poems.

Poem	Pastoral Images	Poet's Attitude Toward Pastoral
"In Memory of W. B. Yeats"	Frozen brook; wolves running wild	
"Carrick Revisited"		
"Not Palaces"		

4. **Key Ideas and Details** **(a)** What does MacNeice say we gain from being born in a particular time and place? **(b)** What do we lose?
5. **Comparing Literary Works** Pastoral writers often look to the past, cherishing a time when life was simpler and sometimes portraying that time as a "golden age." **(a)** Does Auden reflect this perspective in "Musée des Beaux Arts"? Explain your answer. **(b)** Does Spender reflect this view in "Not Palaces"? Explain your answer.

Reading Strategy

6. **(a) Compare and contrast** Auden's portrayal of the contemporary world in "In Memory of W. B. Yeats" with Spender's view of the modern world in "Not Palaces." **(b)** With which of these views do you think MacNeice would most agree? Explain your answer.
7. **(a)** How do the language and tone of "Musée des Beaux Arts" and "Not Palaces" differ? **(b)** How do those differences contribute to the feeling and meaning of the poems?
8. Both "In Memory of W. B. Yeats" and "Carrick Revisited" question the connection between the particulars of an artist's life and his or her work. Compare their answers.
9. **(a)** Which of these poets believe that art in some sense rises above life? **(b)** Which do not? Explain, using examples. **(c)** With which poet's view of art do you agree? Why?

Common Core State Standards

Writing
5. Develop and strengthen writing as needed by planning, revising, editing, rewriting, or trying a new approach, focusing on addressing what is most significant for a specific purpose and audience. *(p. 1186)*

Language
3. Apply knowledge of language to understand how language functions in different contexts, to make effective choices for meaning or style, and to comprehend more fully when reading or listening. *(p. 1186)*

Assessment Practice

Many tests require students to recognize effective stylistic devices and language. Use the following sample test item to teach students how to recognize the tone of a passage.

He disappeared in the dead of winter:
The brooks were frozen, the airports almost deserted,
And snow disfigured the public statues;
The mercury sank in the mouth of the dying day.

Which of these best describes the tone of the passage?

A whimsical
B controversial
C melodramatic
D solemn

Guide students to see that words such as *dead, frozen, deserted,* and *dying* lead to a tone best described as **D**, solemn.

Answers

1. **Possible response:** Yes, Yeats is an allegorical figure who symbolizes the enduring quality of poetry.
2. Line 27 provides no resolution to the suffering of the poor. Lines 76–77, though, show that poetry has the capacity to instruct and change people.
3. "In Memory . . ." Attitude: disinterested; "Carrick Revisited" Pastoral Images: green banks; the lough as hazily lazy; Attitude: nostalgic, but with mixed feelings; "Not Palaces" Pastoral Images: gazelle, delicate wanderer; leave your gardens; Attitude: rejection of the pastoral
4. (a) We gain a unique perspective. (b) We lose all other possible perspectives.
5. (a) No, he does not depict their time as a "golden age." (b) No, Spender rejects the pastoral idea that cherishes the past.
6. (a) Auden portrays the world as diverse. Spender prefers the modern world over the past. (b) MacNeice would agree with Auden, who depicts a variety of realities. In MacNeice's own poem, he states that there are many views.
7. (a) "Musée des Beaux Arts" uses language that expresses the tragedy of suffering and the indifference of those who are nearby. Its tone is disinterested. "Not Palaces" is written with very directed language that conveys the urgency of his message. (b) "Not Palaces" expresses a more optimistic feeling about modern life.
8. "In Memory of W. B. Yeats" responds by stating that art rises above life. "Carrick Revisited" responds by stating that artists' perspectives are closely tied to the times and places from which they come.
9. (a) Auden and Spender believe this. Auden describes how Yeats's life continues on through his works. Spender believes that art can be a catalyst for social change. (b) MacNeice believes that art is, in part, created from the perspective of the artist's time and place. (c) **Possible response:** Answers will vary, but the reasoning should be supported by the text.

Vocabulary Acquisition and Use

1. Introduce the skill using the instruction on the student page.
2. Have students complete the Word Analysis activity and the Vocabulary Practice.

Word Analysis

1. Topical ointment is intended for surface application.
2. Topocentric distances are measured from a particular point on Earth's surface.
3. The topography of a place is its surface physical features.
4. Topology is the study of the topographic features of a given place.

Vocabulary

Sentences will vary.

1. intrigues
2. sequestered
3. topographical
4. prenatal
5. affinities

Writing

1. To guide students in writing this poem, give them the **Support for Writing** page (***Unit 6 Resources,*** p. 52).
2. Remind students that their poems should clearly express and maintain a strong, consistent tone.
3. If students have difficulty establishing a clear tone, have them think about what their chosen artwork shows and how they react to the art. Are their reactions positive or negative? Why?
4. Use the **Rubrics for Poem, *Professional Development Guidebook,*** pages 274–275, to evaluate students' work.

PERFORMANCE TASKS

Integrated Language Skills

Vocabulary Acquisition and Use

Word Analysis: Greek Root *-top-*

The Greek root *-top-* means "place" or "surface." The word *topographical,* which MacNeice uses in "Carrick Revisited," means "relating to a map of the surface features of a place." Explain how the root contributes to the meaning of the italicized words in these sentences.

1. The nurse used a *topical* ointment on the bee sting to reduce the swelling.
2. The *topocentric* distances were all measured from the same point of origin.
3. Mapmakers use precise measures to learn the *topography* of a place.
4. *Topology* is only one branch of geography.

Vocabulary: Synonyms

A synonym is a word that has a meaning similar to that of another word. Answer each question below. In your answer, use a word from the vocabulary list on page 1170 that is a synonym for the italicized word in each question.

1. Were the *schemes* of the plotters successful?
2. Were the different conspirators *isolated* from each other or held together?
3. What kind of detail did the *elevation* map show?
4. Do experts agree on the importance of *prebirth* nutrition?
5. Did her *sympathies* affect what charities she gave to?

Writing

Poem Auden's poem "Musée des Beaux Arts" was inspired by a Brueghel painting. Choose another painting or a photograph and respond to it in a **poem** of your own. To convey one main impression, establish and maintain a strong, consistent tone. Demonstrate your understanding of the style of the poets in this collection by using the free verse and conversational tone of Auden or the more energetic, rhythmic style of Spender.

Prewriting Begin by choosing an artwork that you either admire or dislike. Jot notes about what the artwork shows—the use of shapes and colors—and how it makes you feel. Is the work dramatic and stirring? Or is it peaceful and calming? Review your notes, circling important details.

Drafting Choose a logical organization. You might begin with a physical description of the artwork and then reveal your emotional response to it. As you draft, concentrate on choosing natural, fresh, and vivid language that will result in a strong, consistent tone, whether that is wonder, amusement, or disappointment.

Revising Ask a partner to read your poem and share the main impression he or she received. Revise your poem if your partner's impression does not match the one you wanted to convey. Pay special attention to your word choice, revising language as needed to more clearly convey your intended impression.

Model: Revising to Add Descriptive Language

A ^bold^ blue stripe splits the canvas in two, ~~challenging the viewer,~~ ^mocking, laughing—^ "On which side are you?"

Flatly descriptive language is revised to portray stronger images.

Assessment Resources

Unit 6 Resources

L1 L2 EL **Selection Test A,** pp. 57–59. Administer Test A to less advanced readers.

L3 L4 EL **Selection Test B,** pp. 60–62. Administer Test B to on-level students and more advanced students.

L3 L4 **Open-Book Test,** pp. 54–56. As an alternative, give the Open-Book test.

All **Customizable Test Bank**

All **Self-tests**
Students may prepare for the **Selection Test** by taking the **Self-test** online.

PHLit Online! All assessment resources are available at **www.PHLitOnline.com**.

Modernism in Fiction

PART 2

Selection Planning Guide

The selections in this section introduce students to modern experience as expressed through fiction. Narrative techniques explore Modernist ideas concerning the loneliness and isolation of the self and reflect the subjectivity of the self and objectivity of the surrounding world. Through immersion in the minds of characters, narratives are shaped by character development. Woolf, Rulfo, and Castellanos developed stream-of-consciousness narrative. Conrad used the idea of "voyage" to evoke self-discovery, while Joyce employed epiphany to build a psychological climax. The works of Lawrence and Greene imply modern perspectives on the anguish and absurdity of life.

Humanities

Plum Blossoms, Green Background, 1948, by Henri Matisse (1869–1954)
French artist Henri Matisse is known for his use of bold lines and shapes and bright colors. His works range from drawing and painting to collage. This interior scene incorporates a harmony of vibrant color, expressing mood and experience.

Use these questions for discussion:

1. How does Matisse's break from realistic composition relate to the Modernist idea of subjective expression?
   Possible response: Modernism preoccupied itself with individual experience. This painting aims to express the experience of mood rather than to reproduce the appearance of objects.
2. What is emotional realism, given the subjectivity of human experience?
   Possible response: Authentic representation of mood is unique to each individual; its reality cannot be proven.

Monitoring Progress

After students have completed the selections in Part 2, administer **Benchmark Test 10** *(Unit 6 Resources,* pp. 124–132). If the benchmark test reveals that some students need further work, use the **Interpretation Guide** to determine the appropriate reteaching pages in the **Reading Kit.**

Text Complexity: At a Glance

This chart gives a general text complexity rating for the selections in this part of the unit to help guide instruction. For additional text complexity support, see the Test Complexity Rubric at point of use.

The Lady in the Looking Glass	**More Complex**
from Mrs. Dalloway	**More Complex**
Shakespeare's Sister	**More Accessible**
The Lagoon	**More Complex**
Araby	**More Accessible**
The Rocking-Horse Winner	**More Accessible**
A Shocking Accident	**More Complex**

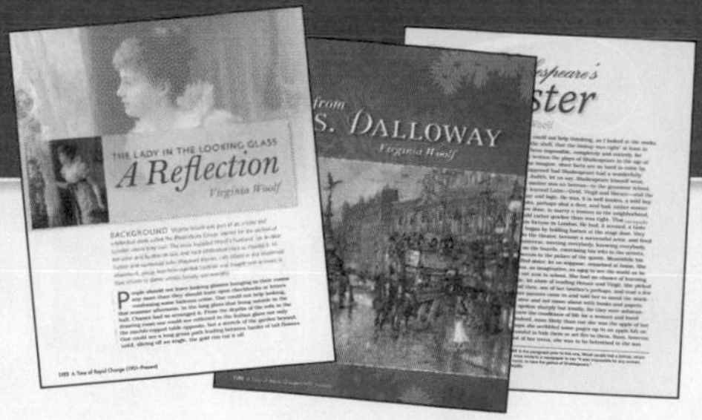

The Lady in the Looking Glass • from *Mrs. Dalloway* • Shakespeare's Sister

Lesson Pacing Guide

DAY 1 Preteach

- Administer the Reading and Vocabulary Warm-ups (*Unit 6 Resources*, pp. 63–66) as necessary.
- Introduce the Literary Analysis concept: Point of View.
- Introduce the Reading Strategy: Repair Comprehension.
- Build background with the Author in Depth and Background features.
- Develop thematic thinking with Connecting to the Essential Question.
- Teach the selection vocabulary.

DAYS 2–3 Preteach/Teach

- Distribute copies of the appropriate graphic organizer for the Reading Strategy (*Graphic Organizer Transparencies*, pp. 212–213).
- Distribute copies of the appropriate graphic organizer for Literary Analysis (*Graphic Organizer Transparencies*, pp. 214–215).
- Prepare students to read with the Activating Prior Knowledge activities (TE).
- Informally monitor comprehension while students read.
- Use the Reading Check questions to confirm comprehension.
- Develop students' understanding of point of view using the Literary Analysis prompts.
- Develop students' ability to repair comprehension using the Reading Strategy prompts.
- Reinforce vocabulary with the Vocabulary notes.

DAY 4 Assess

- Have students read and respond to the Critical Commentray.
- Assess students' comprehension and mastery of the skills by having them answer the Critical Reading, Literary Analysis, and Reading Strategy questions.
- Have students complete the Vocabulary Lesson.

DAY 5 Extend/Assess

- Have students complete the Conventions and Style Lesson.
- Have students complete the Writing Lesson and write a response to literature. (You may assign as homework.)
- Administer Selection Test A or B (*Unit 6 Resources*, pp. 77–79 or 80–82).

Common Core State Standards

Reading Literature 3 Analyze the impact of the author's choices regarding how to develop and relate elements of a story or drama.

Language 4.d. Verify the preliminary determination of the meaning of a word or phrase.

Additional Standards Practice
***Common Core Companion*, pp. 28–35; 324–331**

Daily Block Scheduling
Each day in this Lesson Pacing Guide represents a 40–50 minute period. Teachers using block scheduling may combine days to revise pacing. In addition, teachers may differentiate and support core instruction by integrating components for extended and intensive support as students require. See the Guide to Selected Leveled Resources (facing page).

Guide to Selected Leveled Resources

RTI Tier 1 (students performing on level)			The Lady in the Looking Glass • *from* Mrs. Dalloway • Shakespeare's Sister
Warm Up	Whole class instruction; Group work	**Practice, model,** and **monitor** fluency, working **with the whole class** or **in groups**.	**Vocabulary and Reading Warm-ups B,** ***Unit 6 Resources,*** pp. 63–64, 66
Comprehension/Skills	Whole class instruction; Group work; Independent work	**Support** and **monitor** comprehension and skills development, having students complete the activities, graphic organizers, and interactive prompts **independently** or **as a class**.	• ***Reader's Notebook,*** adapted instruction and full selection EL ***Reader's Notebook: English Learner's Version,*** adapted instruction and adapted selection • **Reading Strategy Graphic Organizer B,** ***Graphic Organizer Transparencies,*** p. 223 • **Literary Analysis Graphic Organizer B,** ***Graphic Organizer Transparencies,*** p. 225
Monitor Progress	A	**Monitor** student progress with the differentiated curriculum-based assessment in the *Unit Resources.*	• **Selection Test B,** ***Unit 6 Resources,*** pp. 80–82 • **Open-Book Test,** ***Unit 6 Resources,*** pp. 74–76

RTI Tier 2 (students requiring intervention)			The Lady in the Looking Glass • *from* Mrs. Dalloway • Shakespeare's Sister
Warm Up	Group work; One-on-one teaching	**Practice, model,** and **monitor** fluency **in groups** or **with individuals**.	• **Vocabulary and Reading Warm-ups A,** ***Unit 6 Resources,*** pp. 63–65 • ***Hear It!*** **Audio CD (adapted text)**
Comprehension/Skills	Group work; One-on-one teaching	• **Support** and **monitor** comprehension and skills development, working **in small groups** or **with individuals**. • As students complete the selection in the appropriate version of the *Reader's Notebook,* **monitor** comprehension frequently with group questions and individual instruction. • **Model** strategies while guiding students in completing the activities and prompts in the *Reader's Notebook,* as well as the graphic organizers. • **Practice** skills and **monitor** mastery with the *Reading Kit* worksheets.	• ***Reader's Notebook: Adapted Version,*** adapted instruction and adapted selection EL ***Reader's Notebook: English Learner's Version,*** adapted instruction and adapted selection • **Reading Strategy Graphic Organizer A,** ***Graphic Organizer Transparencies,*** p. 222 • **Literary Analysis Graphic Organizer A,** ***Graphic Organizer Transparencies,*** p. 224 • ***Reading Kit,*** Practice worksheets
Monitor Progress	A	**Monitor** student progress with the differentiated curriculum-based assessment in the *Unit Resources* and in the *Reading Kit.*	• **Selection Test A,** ***Unit 6 Resources,*** pp. 77–79 • ***Reading Kit,*** Assess worksheets

TIER 3 Tier 3 intervention may require consultation with the student's special-education or dyslexia specialist. For additional support, see the Tier 2 activities and resources listed above.

One-on-one teaching **Group work** **Whole class instruction** **Independent work** **A Assessment**

For a complete guide to selection support, including support for Advanced students, see the Overview of Resources in the frontmatter.

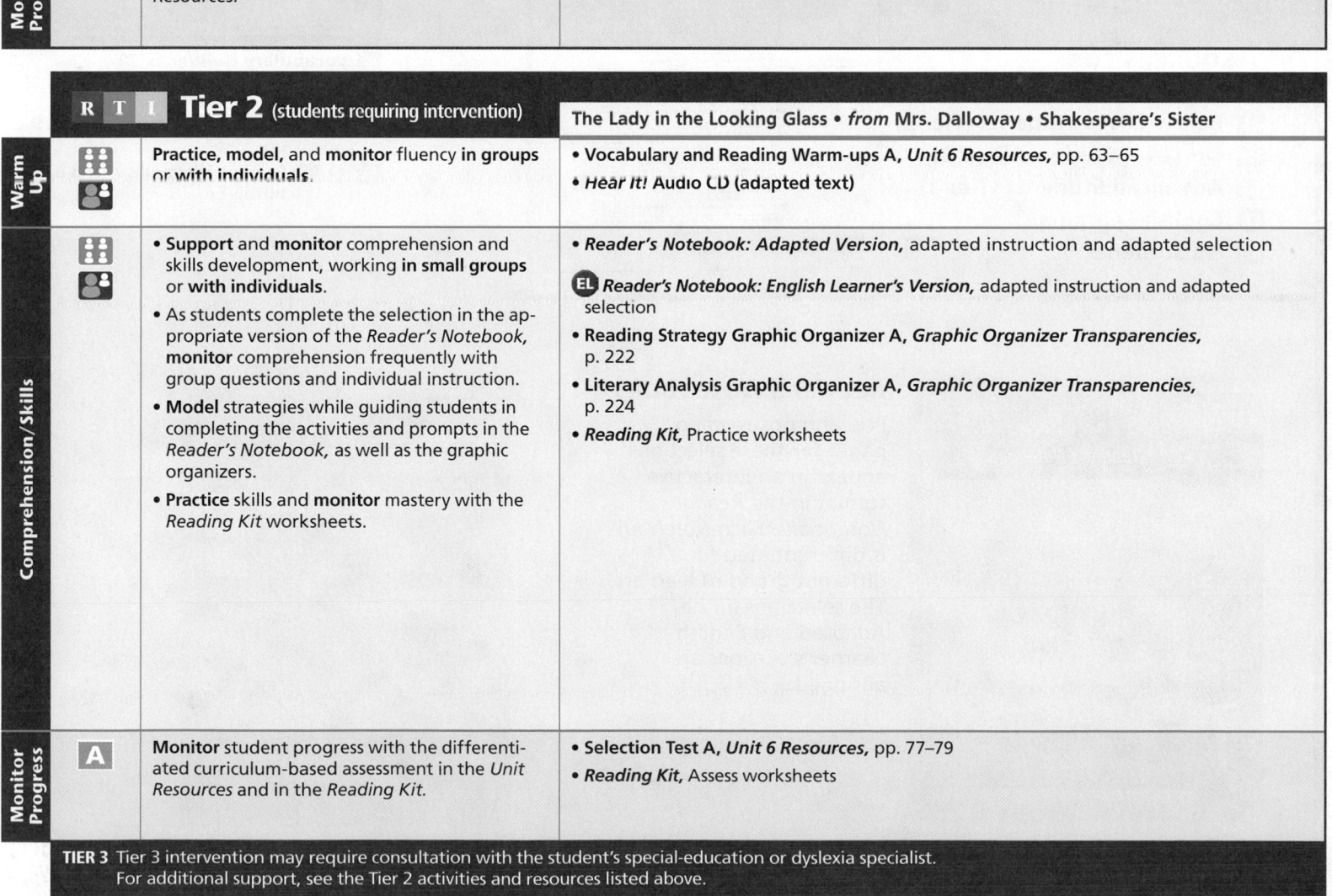

The Lady in the Looking Glass • from *Mrs. Dalloway* • Shakespeare's Sister

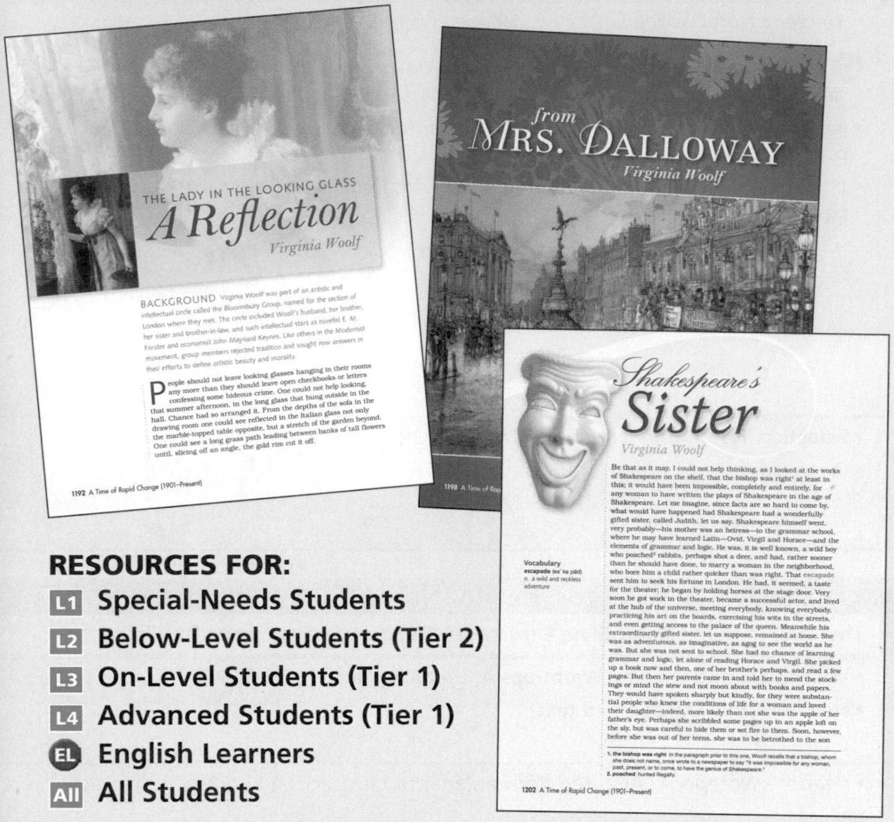

RESOURCES FOR:

- L1 Special-Needs Students
- L2 Below-Level Students (Tier 2)
- L3 On-Level Students (Tier 1)
- L4 Advanced Students (Tier 1)
- EL English Learners
- All All Students

Vocabulary/Fluency/Prior Knowledge

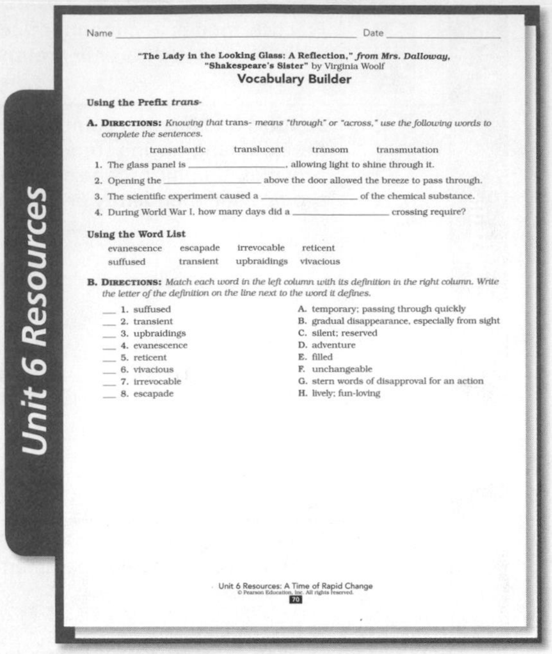
Unit 6 Resources

Name ______________________ Date ____________

"The Lady in the Looking Glass: A Reflection," *from Mrs. Dalloway,* "Shakespeare's Sister" by Virginia Woolf

Vocabulary Builder

Using the Prefix *trans-*

A. Directions: *Knowing that* trans- *means "through" or "across," use the following words to complete the sentences.*

transatlantic   translucent   transom   transmutation

1. The glass panel is ______________, allowing light to shine through it.
2. Opening the ______________ above the door allowed the breeze to pass through.
3. The scientific experiment caused a ______________ of the chemical substance.
4. During World War I, how many days did a ______________ crossing require?

Using the Word List

evanescence   escapade   irrevocable   reticent
suffused   transient   upbraidings   vivacious

B. Directions: *Match each word in the left column with its definition in the right column. Write the letter of the definition on the line next to the word it defines.*

__ 1. suffused	A. temporary; passing through quickly
__ 2. transient	B. gradual disappearance, especially from sight
__ 3. upbraidings	C. silent; reserved
__ 4. evanescence	D. adventure
__ 5. reticent	E. filled
__ 6. vivacious	F. unchangeable
__ 7. irrevocable	G. stern words of disapproval for an action
__ 8. escapade	H. lively; fun-loving

Unit 6 Resources: A Time of Rapid Change
© Pearson Education, Inc. All rights reserved.
70

All **Vocabulary Builder,** p. 70

Also available for these selections:

EL L1 L2 **Vocabulary Warm-ups A and B,** pp. 63–64

EL L1 L2 **Reading Warm-ups A and B,** pp. 65–66

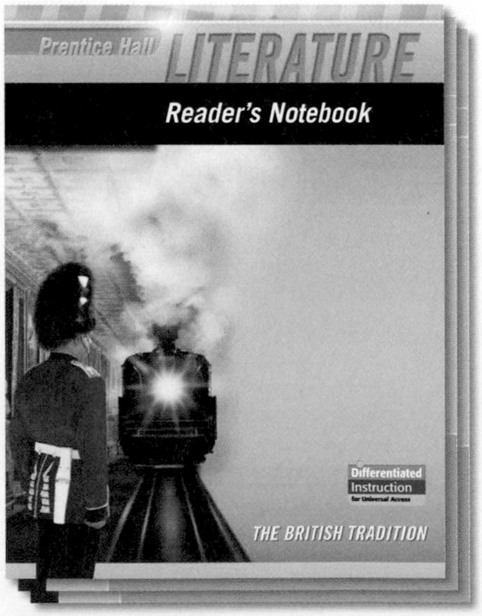

Reader's Notebooks

Pre- and postreading pages for these selections appear in an interactive format in the *Reader's Notebooks*. Each *Notebook* is differentiated for a different group of learners. The selections in the Adapted and English Learner's versions are abridged.

L2 L3 ***Reader's Notebook***

L1 ***Reader's Notebook: Adapted Version***

EL ***Reader's Notebook: English Learner's Version***

EL ***Reader's Notebook: Spanish Version***

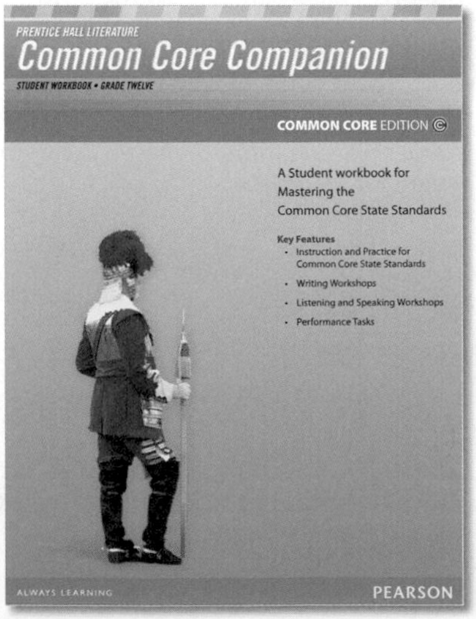

Common Core Companion

Additional instruction and practice for each Common Core State Standard

Selection Support

Graphic Organizer Transparencies

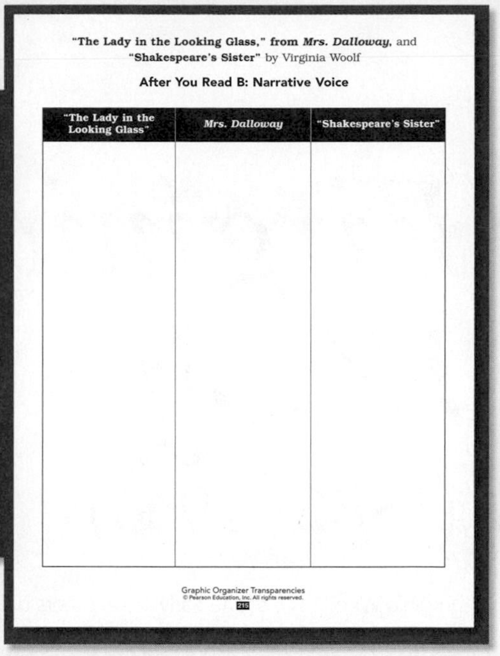
"The Lady in the Looking Glass," from *Mrs. Dalloway,* and "Shakespeare's Sister" by Virginia Woolf

After You Read B: Narrative Voice

"The Lady in the Looking Glass"	*Mrs. Dalloway*	"Shakespeare's Sister"

Graphic Organizer Transparencies

215

EL L3 **Literary Analysis: Graphic Organizer B,** p. 215

Also available for these selections:

EL L1 L2 **Reading: Graphic Organizer A,** p. 212

EL L3 **Reading: Graphic Organizer B,** p. 213

EL L1 L2 **Literary Analysis: Graphic Organizer A,** (partially filled in), p. 214

Skills Development/Extension

Unit 6 Resources

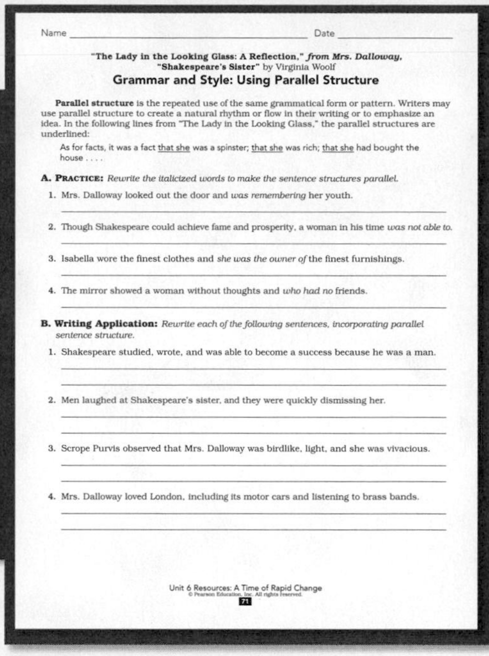
Name ______________ Date ______________

"The Lady in the Looking Glass: A Reflection," *from* ***Mrs. Dalloway,*** **"Shakespeare's Sister"** by Virginia Woolf

Grammar and Style: Using Parallel Structure

Parallel structure is the repeated use of the same grammatical form or pattern. Writers may use parallel structure to create a natural rhythm or flow in their writing or to emphasize an idea. In the following lines from "The Lady in the Looking Glass," the parallel structures are underlined:

As for facts, it was a fact that she was a spinster; that she was rich; that she had bought the house . . . .

A. Practice: *Rewrite the italicized words to make the sentence structures parallel.*

1. Mrs. Dalloway looked out the door and *was remembering* her youth.
2. Though Shakespeare could achieve fame and prosperity, a woman in his time *was not able to.*
3. Isabella wore the finest clothes and *she was the owner of* the finest furnishings.
4. The mirror showed a woman without thoughts and *who had no* friends.

B. Writing Application: *Rewrite each of the following sentences, incorporating parallel sentence structure.*

1. Shakespeare studied, wrote, and was able to become a success because he was a man.
2. Men laughed at Shakespeare's sister, and they were quickly dismissing her.
3. Scrope Purvis observed that Mrs. Dalloway was birdlike, light, and she was vivacious.
4. Mrs. Dalloway loved London, including its motor cars and listening to brass bands.

Unit 6 Resources: A Time of Rapid Change

71

EL L3 L4 **Grammar and Style,** p. 71

Also available for these selections:

All **Literary Analysis: Point of View,** p. 67

All **Literary Analysis: Stream of Consciousness,** p. 68

All **Reading: Repair Comprehension,** p. 69

EL L3 L4 **Support for Writing,** p. 72

L4 **Enrichment,** p. 73

Assessment

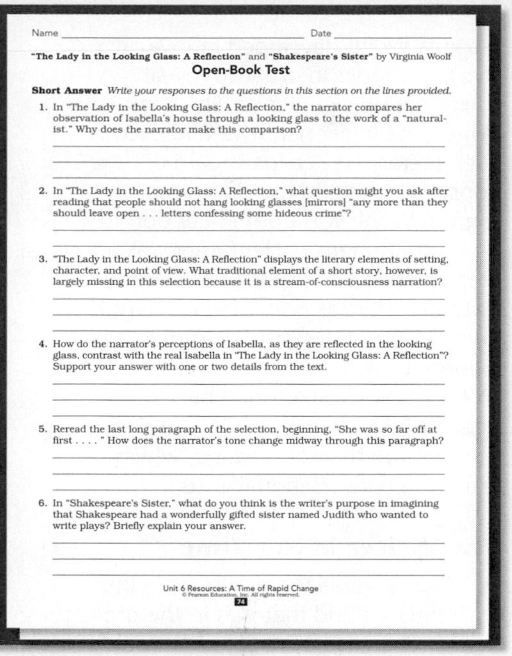
Name ______________ Date ______________

"The Lady in the Looking Glass: A Reflection" and **"Shakespeare's Sister"** by Virginia Woolf

Open-Book Test

Short Answer *Write your responses to the questions in this section on the lines provided.*

1. In "The Lady in the Looking Glass: A Reflection," the narrator compares her observation of Isabella's house through a looking glass to the work of a "naturalist." Why does the narrator make this comparison?
2. In "The Lady in the Looking Glass: A Reflection," what question might you ask after reading that people should not hang looking glasses [mirrors] "any more than they should leave open . . . letters confessing some hideous crime"?
3. "The Lady in the Looking Glass: A Reflection" displays the literary elements of setting, character, and point of view. What traditional element of a short story, however, is largely missing in this selection because it is a stream-of-consciousness narration?
4. How do the narrator's perceptions of Isabella, as they are reflected in the looking glass, contrast with the real Isabella in "The Lady in the Looking Glass: A Reflection"? Support your answer with one or two details from the text.
5. Reread the last long paragraph of the selection, beginning, "She was so far off at first . . . ." How does the narrator's tone change midway through this paragraph?
6. In "Shakespeare's Sister," what do you think is the writer's purpose in imagining that Shakespeare had a wonderfully gifted sister named Judith who wanted to write plays? Briefly explain your answer.

Unit 6 Resources: A Time of Rapid Change

74

L3 L4 **Open-Book Test,** pp. 74–76

Also available for these selections:

EL L1 L2 **Selection Test A,** pp. 77–79

EL L3 L4 **Selection Test B,** pp. 80–82

PHLit Online!
www.PHLitOnline.com

- complete narrated selection text
- a thematically related video with writing prompt
- an interactive graphic organizer
- highlighting feature
- access to all student print resources, adapted to individual student needs
- Spanish and English summaries
- adapted selection translations in Spanish

Online Resources: All print materials are also available online.

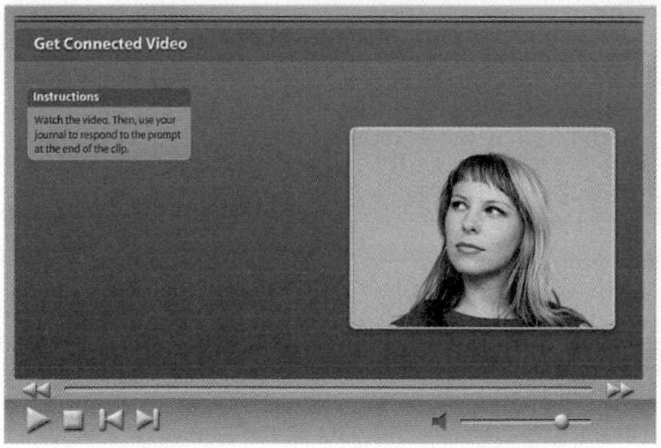

Get Connected! (thematic video with writing prompt)

Also available:

Background Video
All videos are available in Spanish.

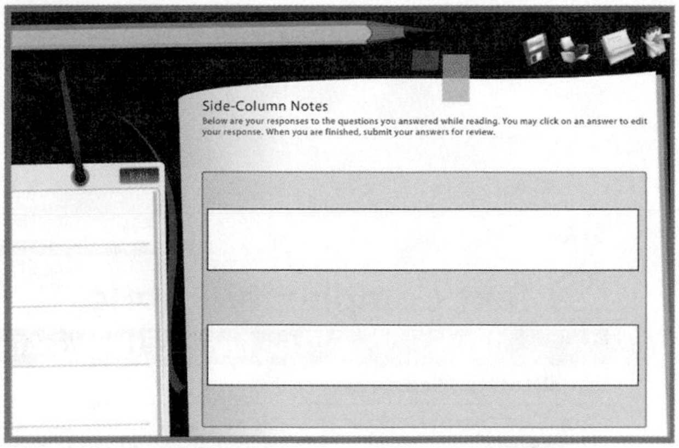

Writer's Journal (with graphics feature)

Also available:

Vocabulary Central (tools and activities for studying vocabulary)

❶ Background

Overview: The Author's Work

Virginia Woolf developed innovative techniques in order to reveal the feminine experience. She abandoned the linear narrative and used such literary devices as stream of consciousness and interior monologues. Woolf was born in London to a publishing family. Her father was a literary critic and the friend of such noted authors as Henry James, Alfred, Lord Tennyson, Matthew Arnold, and George Eliot. With *To the Lighthouse* (1927), Woolf established herself as a leading Modernist writer. She published more than 500 essays, which are often conversational in tone.

The Writer in Her Time

In 1882, Virginia Woolf was born into a Victorian world that was in the process of changing. Though she would later be offered honorary degrees from Cambridge and other universities, at the time she was growing up, women were not even admitted. The Bloomsbury Group that she was part of started out as a weekly meeting of friends and soon became an intense gathering place for ideas and philosophy.

Woolf wrote during a time that was rich with literary experimentation. Her stream-of-consciousness narration was considered extremely modern at the time.

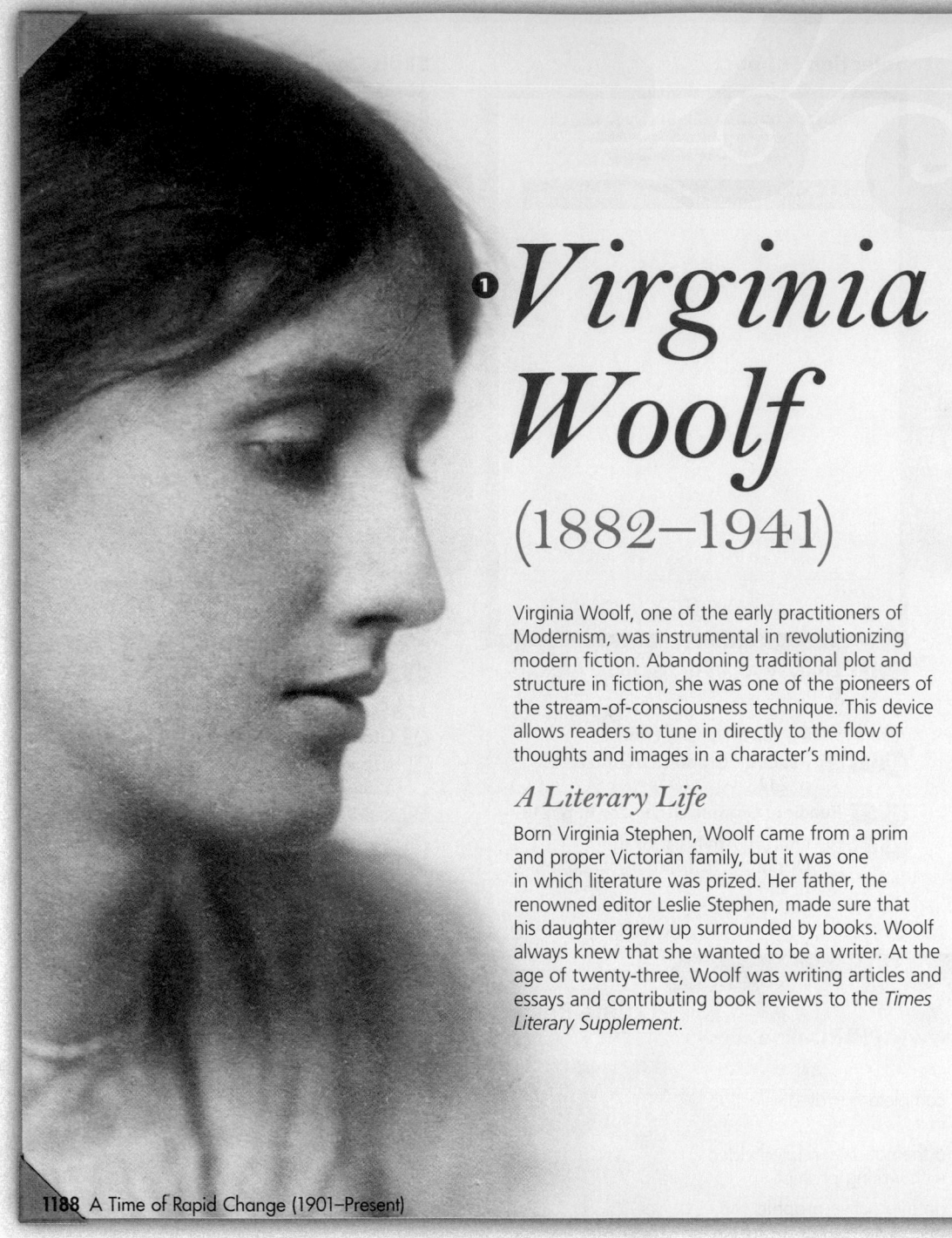

❶ *Virginia Woolf*

(1882–1941)

Virginia Woolf, one of the early practitioners of Modernism, was instrumental in revolutionizing modern fiction. Abandoning traditional plot and structure in fiction, she was one of the pioneers of the stream-of-consciousness technique. This device allows readers to tune in directly to the flow of thoughts and images in a character's mind.

A Literary Life

Born Virginia Stephen, Woolf came from a prim and proper Victorian family, but it was one in which literature was prized. Her father, the renowned editor Leslie Stephen, made sure that his daughter grew up surrounded by books. Woolf always knew that she wanted to be a writer. At the age of twenty-three, Woolf was writing articles and essays and contributing book reviews to the *Times Literary Supplement*.

Text Complexity Rubric

	The Lady in the Looking Glass	*from* Mrs. Dalloway	Shakespeare's Sister
Qualitative Measures			
Context/Knowledge Demands	Modernist story; cultural knowledge and life experience demands 1 2 ③ 4 5	Modernist fiction; cultural knowledge demands 1 2 ③ 4 5	Modernist social criticism; literary knowledge demands 1 ② 3 4 5
Structure/Language Conventionality and Clarity	Stream-of-consciousness structure 1 2 3 ④ 5	Stream-of-consciousness structure 1 2 3 ④ 5	Archaic diction 1 ② 3 4 5
Levels of Meaning/ Purpose/Concepts	Challenging (self-realization) 1 2 3 ④ 5	Moderate (daily activity) 1 2 ③ 4 5	Accessible (women's role) 1 ② 3 4 5
Quantitative Measures			
Lexile/Text Length	1220L / 2,207 words	780L / 540 words	1110L / 764 words
Overall Complexity	**More complex**	**More complex**	**More accessible**

Bloomsbury

After their father died in 1904, Virginia moved with her sister Vanessa and her brothers to a home in the Bloomsbury neighborhood of London. Their house became a meeting place for writers, artists, and thinkers, who gathered to discuss literature, art, and politics. This influential group, known as the Bloomsbury Group, generally rejected the values and morals of Victorianism, instead promoting artistic and personal freedoms.

In 1912, Virginia married Leonard Woolf, a member of this group, who was a journalist, author, and literary editor. Together they founded the Hogarth Press in 1917. Along with Virginia's works, they published the works of other notable writers, including T. S. Eliot, E. M. Forster, and Katherine Mansfield.

In This Section

Revolutionizing Fiction

Woolf's first two novels were not unusual, but she soon established herself as one of the leading writers of Modernism. *Jacob's Room* (1922) shattered the conventions of fiction by telling the story of a young man's life entirely through an examination of his room. (She also uses this device in "The Lady in the Looking Glass: A Reflection.") Woolf continued to refine her fluid, inward-looking style with three more stream-of-consciousness novels—*Mrs. Dalloway* (1925), *To the Lighthouse* (1927), and *The Waves* (1931). In her more revolutionary works, she virtually abolishes a traditional plot, preferring to concentrate on what she called "an ordinary mind on an ordinary day." In *Mrs. Dalloway*, for example, there is little action. The central character, Clarissa Dalloway, spends a day in London preparing for an evening party. Her thoughts move from the present to the past and back to the present.

❷ Depression and Tragedy

Throughout her life, Woolf suffered episodes of severe depression brought on by poor health. She had frequent periods when she was unable to focus enough to read or write. The turmoil of World War II worsened her depression. In 1941, she drowned in the River Ouse near the Woolfs' home in Sussex.

In addition to the considerable number of critical essays she produced in her life, Woolf wrote about fifteen novels. Today she is recognized as one of the greatest contributors to modern fiction.

Daily Bellringer

For each class during which you will teach these selections, have students complete one of the five activities for the appropriate week in the ***Daily Bellringer Activities*** booklet.

Multidraft Reading

To assist struggling readers and to enhance reading for all, assign the text in chunks, as warranted by length, and apply multidraft reading protocols. For each reading, have students set the purpose indicated:

- **First reading**—identifying key ideas and details and answering any Reading Checks.
- **Second reading**—analyzing craft and structure and responding to the side-column prompts.
- **Third reading**—integrating knowledge and ideas, connecting to other texts and the world, and answering the end-of-selection questions.

For more guidance, refer to the ***Classroom Strategies and Teaching Routines*** card on Multidraft Reading.

❷ Background

More About the Author

Virginia Woolf's involvement with the Bloomsbury Group, which began in 1905–1906, was centered in her home at 46 Gordon Square, Bloomsbury, in London. Its members were against the artistic, social, and sexual restrictions of the Victorian period. Many of them radically affected the development of the avant-garde in art and literature in Britain.

Text Complexity: Reader and Task Suggestions

	The Lady in the Looking Glass	*from* Mrs. Dalloway	Shakespeare's Sister
Preparing to Read the Texts • Using the Background on TE p. 1188, discuss the changing role of women in Woolf's day. • Discuss the pioneering work that Woolf did in stream-of-consciousness narration, which reflects a character's flow of ideas. • Guide students to use Multidraft Reading strategies (TE p. 1189).	**Leveled Tasks** ***Levels of Meaning*** If students will have difficulty with the levels of meaning, have them read first to understand the narrator's view of Isabella. Then, as they reread, have students focus on revelations of Isabella's unhappiness. ***Synthesizing*** If students will not have difficulty with meaning, have them note aspects of Isabella's life that might relate to other women's lives.	**Leveled Tasks** ***Structure/Language*** If students will have difficulty with the stream-of-consciousness structure, have them focus on Mrs. Dalloway's point of view. Then, as they reread, have them look for another point of view. ***Evaluating*** If students will not have difficulty with the stream-of-consciousness structure, have them evaluate its effectiveness as reflection of thought.	**Leveled Tasks** ***Levels of Meaning*** If students will have difficulty with the author's meaning, have them read first to determine her main points. Have students reread to decide whether or not they agree with the author. ***Evaluating*** If students will not have difficulty with the author's meaning, have them evaluate how effectively she supports her points to make her argument effective.

❶ Virginia Woolf and Pop Culture

1. Ask students if any of them have ever read anything by Virginia Woolf. If so, ask their reactions to her work.
2. Have students visit the Web site mentioned in the third paragraph.
3. Have students do an Internet search on Virginia Woolf. Ask them to pay special attention to unusual finds, or anything that is not just a biography. Have them share their results and reactions with the class.

❶ Virginia Woolf & Pop Culture

Who's afraid of Virginia Woolf? That punning question—based on the jingle, Who's Afraid of the Big Bad Wolf—was the title of a famous Edward Albee play. Part of the joke behind it is that the author of such sophisticated stream-of-consciousness novels as *Mrs. Dalloway* and *To the Lighthouse* does seem like a forbidding intellectual figure.

Surprisingly, however, this great Modernist author turns up frequently on the Internet. Apparently, no one on the World Wide Web is afraid of her.

Some Woolf sites, such as that of The Virginia Woolf Society, are devoted to a serious-minded discussion of her as an important literary figure. Others, however, blur the line between high and low culture, bringing the upper-class British author into the democracy of the Internet. Another way to view her online popularity would be to say that somehow she has entered into our culture's stream of consciousness.

One of the sites showing no fear of the Woolf is that of the Cosmic Baseball Association, a self-described art project that had the Bloomsbury author playing on one of the league's teams. A dispute between Woolf and her manager, however, led to her being traded.

As these Web shenanigans reveal, Woolf has gone beyond her role as a writer to become a cultural icon—a figure in whom many online constituencies see their own interests and obsessions reflected. In this respect, Woolf is not unlike Marilyn Monroe, another iconic female who has achieved immortality in the culture's stream of consciousness.

Marilyn Monroe, as depicted by Andy Warhol

Director Mike Nichols (left) and part of the cast of the film version of *Who's Afraid of Virginia Woolf* (1966): (from left to right, after Nichols) George Segal, Elizabeth Taylor, and Richard Burton

Nicole Kidman, playing Virginia Woolf in the film *The Hours* (2002)

Vocabulary Development

Vocabulary Knowledge Rating

Create a **Vocabulary Knowledge Rating Chart** (***Professional Development Guidebook,*** p. 33) for this selection, using the selection vocabulary from the next page. Give each student a copy of the chart. Read the words aloud, and have students mark their ratings in the Before Reading column. Urge them to be alert to these words as they read and discuss the selection.

Tally how many students think they know a word to gauge how much instruction to provide. As students read and discuss the selection, point out the words and their context.

PHLit Online! **Vocabulary Central,** featuring student tools for recording and studying vocabulary, is available online at **www.PHLitOnline.com.**

Before You Read

The Lady in the Looking Glass • from *Mrs. Dalloway* • *Shakespeare's Sister*

2 **Connecting to the Essential Question** Think of a song you like. Freewrite about your associations with the song—your thoughts, your feelings, and why you like it. As you read, find details in the fictional selections by Virginia Woolf that differ from the traditional way of telling a story. This will help you think about the Essential Question: **What is the relationship of the writer to tradition?**

Common Core State Standards

Reading Literature
3. Analyze the impact of the author's choices regarding how to develop and relate elements of a story or drama.

3 Literary Analysis

Searching for forms suited to modern experience, writers tested different **points of view,** the perspective from which a story is told.

- A **first-person** narrator tells his or her own story. With this technique, authors can probe the thoughts of the narrator.
- A **third-person** narrator tells what happened to others. An **omniscient third person** has the ability to reveal the thoughts of several characters. A narrator with **limited omniscience** sees only into the mind of one or few characters.
- **Stream-of-consciousness** narration follows the flowing, branching currents of thought in a character's mind.

Writers began using the stream-of-consciousness technique under the influence of the emerging science of psychology. As in psychology, the free association of ideas in stream-of-consciousness narration reveals the dynamic nature of people's minds. As you read, consider how Woolf uses this technique to develop character.

4 Reading Strategy

Preparing to Read Complex Texts Experimental works offer great rewards but also place demands on readers. If you lose your way in a stream-of-consciousness story, you can **repair your comprehension by asking questions** to restore your focus. Use a chart such as the one shown.

Passage
"The room that afternoon was full of such shy creatures..."

↓

Question
Why is the narrator talking about creatures filling the drawing room?

↓

Answer
She is comparing the movements in the room to the movements of shy animals that do not know they are being observed.

5 Vocabulary

suffused (sə fyo͞ozd′) *v.* spread throughout; filled (p. 1193)

transient (tran′ shənt) *n.* that which passes quickly (p. 1193)

upbraidings (up brād′ iŋz) *n.* words of disapproval; scoldings (p. 1194)

evanescence (ev′ ə nes′ əns) *n.* vanishing or tendency to vanish (p. 1196)

reticent (ret′ ə sənt) *adj.* silent; reserved (p. 1196)

vivacious (və vā′ shəs) *adj.* lively, spirited (p. 1199)

irrevocable (i rev′ ə kə bəl) *adj.* not possible to revoke or change (p. 1199)

escapade (es′ kə pād) *n.* a wild and reckless adventure (p. 1202)

PHLit Online! www.PHLitOnline.com

PHLit Online! www.PHLitOnline.com Teaching From Technology

Preparing to Read
Go to **www.PHLitOnline.com** and display the ***Get Connected!*** slide show for this selection. Have the class brainstorm responses to the writing prompt, entering ideas in the interactive journal. Then, have students complete their written responses as homework.

To build background, display the Background and More About the Author features.

Using the Interactive Text
Go to **www.PHLitOnline.com** and display the **Enriched Online Student Edition.** As the class reads the selection or listens to the narration, record answers to side-column prompts using the graphic organizers accessible on the interactive page. Alternatively, have students use the online edition individually, answering the prompts as they read.

2 Connecting to the Essential Question

1. Review the assignment with the class.
2. Briefly discuss with students the many different ways songs are written—such as story songs, poetic lyrics, rap music, and classical music—and how they convey ideas in different ways.
3. As students read, have them find details in the fictional selections by Virginia Woolf that differ from traditional storytelling.

3 Literary Analysis

Introduce the skill using the instruction on the student page.

Think Aloud: Model the Skill

Say to students:

Point of view is the perspective from which a story is told. If a story is told by a character using *I*, the story uses first-person narration. If the narrator is not part of the story, it is third-person narration. If the narration follows the flow of a character's thoughts it is stream-of-consciousness narration.

4 Reading Strategy

1. Introduce the skill using the instruction on the student page.
2. Give students a copy of **Reading Strategy Graphic Organizer B,** page 213 in ***Graphic Organizer Transparencies,*** to fill out as they read.

Think Aloud: Model the Skill

Say to students:

One way I can enhance my understanding of what I am reading is by asking questions and learning new things about what I am reading. I should always ask questions, even if I think I understand completely.

5 Vocabulary

1. Pronounce each word, giving its definition, and have students say it aloud.
2. For more guidance, see the *Classroom Strategies and Teaching Routines* card for introducing vocabulary.

TEACH

❶ About the Selection

Isabella is a wealthy woman who lives alone. The narrator forms a concept of her by examining the objects in her home, partly as they appear in a mirror, and by imagining Isabella in the garden. To the narrator, Isabella's wealth and possessions are signs of happiness and success; her silence implies mystery and passion. When Isabella comes back inside from being in the garden and appears in the mirror, however, the true loneliness and emptiness of her life are revealed. Her letters, which seemed so mysterious, turn out to be only a collection of bills.

❷ Activating Prior Knowledge

Before students read the story by Virginia Woolf, bring in six to ten unrelated objects and place them together on a table in full view of students. Challenge pairs of students to do one of two things: describe the type of character to whom these things belong or contrive some connection between all the items. After students have had time to share their ideas, tell them that in "The Lady in the Looking Glass: A Reflection," the narrator tries to understand a character by viewing her possessions.

Concept Connector ⟶

Tell students they will return to their responses after reading the selection.

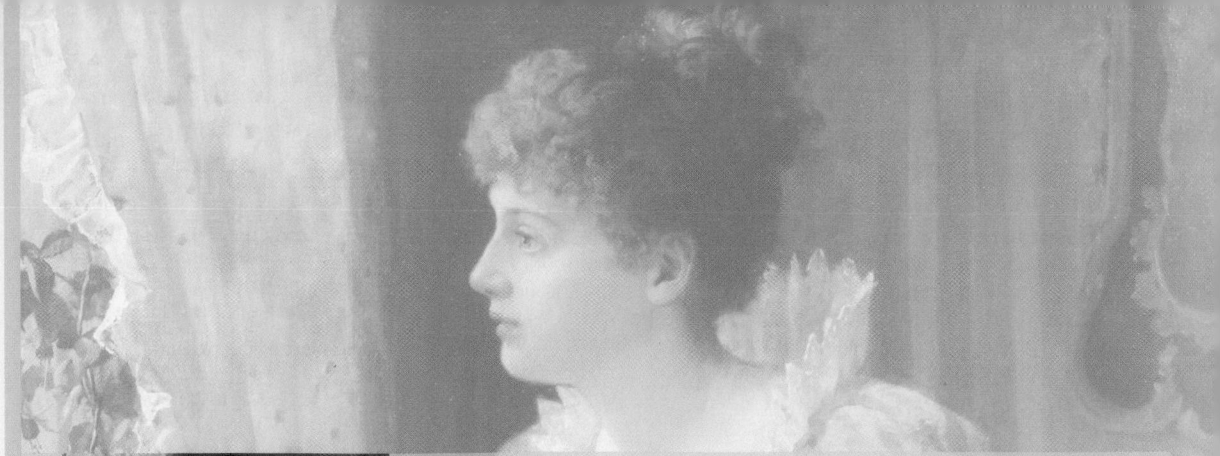

THE LADY IN THE LOOKING GLASS ❶ ❷

A Reflection

Virginia Woolf

BACKGROUND Virginia Woolf was part of an artistic and intellectual circle called the Bloomsbury Group, named for the section of London where they met. The circle included Woolf's husband, her brother, her sister and brother-in-law, and such intellectual stars as novelist E. M. Forster and economist John Maynard Keynes. Like others in the Modernist movement, group members rejected tradition and sought new answers in their efforts to define artistic beauty and morality.

❸ People should not leave looking glasses hanging in their rooms any more than they should leave open checkbooks or letters confessing some hideous crime. One could not help looking, that summer afternoon, in the long glass that hung outside in the hall. Chance had so arranged it. From the depths of the sofa in the drawing room one could see reflected in the Italian glass not only the marble-topped table opposite, but a stretch of the garden beyond. One could see a long grass path leading between banks of tall flowers until, slicing off an angle, the gold rim cut it off.

Think Aloud

Vocabulary: Using Context

Direct students' attention to the word *pirouetting* at the top of page 1193. Use the following "think aloud" to model the skill of using context to infer the meaning of the word. Say to students:

> I may not know the meaning of the word *pirouetting.* When I read the sentence in which it appears, however, I realize that the writer is using *pirouetting* to describe what the "nocturnal creatures" are doing. The writer seems to elaborate on the creatures' movements with the phrase "stepping delicately with high-lifted feet . . . ." *Pirouetting* must be a delicate way of stepping or dancing. I know that ballerinas dance delicately. Perhaps *pirouetting* is something a ballerina would do.

The house was empty, and one felt, since one was the only person in the drawing room, like one of those naturalists who, covered with grass and leaves, lie watching the shyest animals—badgers, otters, king-fishers—moving about freely, themselves unseen. The room that afternoon was full of such shy creatures, lights and shadows, curtains blowing, petals falling—things that never happen, so it seems, if someone is looking. The quiet old country room with its rugs and stone chimney pieces, its sunken bookcases and red and gold lacquer cabinets, was full of such nocturnal creatures. They came pirouetting across the floor, stepping delicately with high-lifted feet and spread tails and pecking allusive beaks as if they had been cranes or flocks of elegant flamingoes whose pink was faded, or peacocks whose trains were veiled with silver. And there were obscure flushes and darkening too, as if a cuttlefish had suddenly **suffused** the air with purple; and the room had its passions and rages and envies and sorrows coming over it and clouding it, like a human being. Nothing stayed the same for two seconds together.

But, outside, the looking glass reflected the hall table, the sunflowers, the garden path so accurately and so fixedly that they seemed held there in their reality unescapably. It was a strange contrast—all changing here, all stillness there. One could not help looking from one to the other. Meanwhile, since all the doors and windows were open in the heat, there was a perpetual sighing and ceasing sound, the voice of the **transient** and the perishing, it seemed, coming and going like human breath, while in the looking glass things had ceased to breathe and lay still in the trance of immortality.

Half an hour ago the mistress of the house, Isabella Tyson, had gone down the grass path in her thin summer dress, carrying a basket, and had vanished, sliced off by the gilt rim of the looking glass. She had gone presumably into the lower garden to pick flowers; or as it seemed more natural to suppose, to pick something light and fantastic and leafy and trailing, traveler's-joy, or one of those elegant sprays of convolvulus that twine round ugly walls and burst here and there into white and violet blossoms. She suggested the fantastic and the tremulous convolvulus rather than the upright aster, the starched zinnia, or her own burning roses alight like lamps on the straight posts of their rose trees. The comparison showed how very little, after all these years, one knew about her; for it is impossible that any woman of flesh and blood of fifty-five or sixty should be really a wreath or a tendril. Such comparisons are worse than idle and superficial—they are cruel even, for they come like the convolvulus itself trembling between one's eyes and the truth. There must be truth; there must be a wall. Yet it was strange that after knowing her all these years one could not say what the truth about Isabella was; one still made up phrases like this about convolvulus and traveler's-joy. As for facts, it was a fact that she was a spinster; that she was rich; that she had bought this house and collected with her own hands—often in the

Reading Strategy
Repairing Comprehension
Is your impression of the narrator clear? Ask a question to clarify your impression.

Vocabulary
suffused (sə fyo͞ozd′)
v. spread throughout; filled

4 **Vocabulary**
transient (tran′ shənt) *n.*
that which passes quickly

5 **Reading Check**
Where is the narrator?

3 Reading Strategy

Repairing Comprehension

1. As they read, encourage students to ask questions of the text to help them understand what is happening. Have students record these questions and any answers they find as they read.
2. **Ask** students the Reading Strategy question: Is your impression of the narrator clear? Ask a question to clarify your impression.
   Possible response: Students may ask why the narrator is so keenly observant.

4 Vocabulary

Latin Prefix: *trans-*

1. Call students' attention to the vocabulary word *transient.* Explain to students that the prefix *trans-* is derived from Latin and means "through" or "across."
2. **Ask** students to suggest other words and phrases that contain this prefix, and list them on the chalkboard.
   Possible responses: translate, transubstantiate, transistor, transatlantic, transitory, transition

5 Reading Check

Answer: The narrator is in "the depths of the sofa in the drawing room."

Differentiated Instruction for Universal Access

Support for Special-Needs Students
Have students complete the **Before You Read** and the **Making Connections** pages for these selections in the ***Reader's Notebook: Adapted Version.*** These pages provide an abbreviated skills instruction, a selection summary, the **Before You Read** graphic organizer, and a **Note-taking Guide.**

Support for Less Proficient Readers
Have students complete the **Before You Read** and the **Making Connections** pages for these selections in the ***Reader's Notebook.*** These pages provide an abbreviated skills instruction, a selection summary, the **Before You Read** graphic organizer, and a **Note-taking Guide.**

EL Support for English Learners
Have students complete the **Before You Read** and the **Making Connections** pages for these selections in the ***Reader's Notebook: English Learner's Version.*** These pages provide additional vocabulary, vocabulary skills, and vocabulary practice, along with a **Getting Ready to Read** activity.

PHLit Online!
There selections are available in interactive format in the **Enriched Online Student Edition** at **www.PHLitOnline.com,** which includes a thematically related video with writing prompt and an interactive graphic organizer.

6 Literary Analysis

Point of View

1. Review with students how the narrator's description of this scene affects the reader's understanding of the story.
2. Then, **ask** the Literary Analysis question: What effect does the narrator's attention to the workings of his or her own mind have on the narration?
   Answer: The narrator's stream-of-consciousness description gives the narration a "you-are-there" immediacy.

7 Critical Viewing

Possible response: Students may say that the painting has the same playful, scattered quality as a stream-of-consciousness narrative, referring to the interplay of light and shadow and the contrast between hard edges and curves. They may say that their eyes are drawn all over the canvas, even off its edge, since only some of the objects shown appear in full view.

most obscure corners of the world and at great risk from poisonous stings and Oriental diseases—the rugs, the chairs, the cabinets which now lived their nocturnal life before one's eyes. Sometimes it seemed as if they knew more about her than we, who sat on them, wrote at them, and trod on them so carefully, were allowed to know. In each of these cabinets were many little drawers, and each almost certainly held letters, tied with bows of ribbon, sprinkled with sticks of lavender or rose leaves. For it was another fact—if facts were what one wanted—that Isabella had known many people, had had many friends; and thus if one had the audacity to open a drawer and read her letters, one would find the traces of many agitations, of appointments to meet, of **upbraidings** for not having met, long letters of intimacy and affection, violent letters of jealousy and reproach, terrible final words of parting—for all those interviews and assignations had led to nothing—that is, she had never married, and yet, judging from the masklike indifference of her face, she had gone through twenty times more of passion and experience than those whose loves are trumpeted forth for all the world to hear. Under the stress of thinking about Isabella, her room became more shadowy and symbolic; the corners seemed darker, the legs of chairs and tables more spindly and hieroglyphic.

Vocabulary
upbraidings (up brād′ iŋz) *n.* stern words of disapproval; scoldings

Suddenly these reflections were ended violently and yet without a sound. A large black form loomed into the looking glass; blotted out everything, strewed the table with a packet of marble tablets veined with pink and gray, and was gone. But the picture was entirely altered. For the moment it was unrecognizable and irrational and entirely out of focus. One could not relate these tablets to any human purpose. And then by degrees some logical process set to work on them and began ordering and arranging them and bringing them into the fold of common experience. One realized at last that they were merely letters. The man had brought the post.

6 **Literary Analysis**
Point of View What effect does the narrator's attention to the workings of his or her own mind have on the narration?

There they lay on the marble-topped table, all dripping with light and color at first and crude and unabsorbed. And then it was strange to see how they were drawn in and arranged and composed and made part of the picture and granted that stillness and immortality which the looking glass conferred. They lay there invested with a new reality and significance and with a greater heaviness, too, as if it would have needed a chisel to dislodge them from the table. And, whether it was fancy or not, they seemed to have become not merely a handful of casual letters but to be tablets graven with eternal truth—if one could read them, one would know everything there was to be known about Isabella, yes, and about life, too. The pages inside those marble-looking envelopes must be cut deep and scored thick with meaning. Isabella would come in, and take them, one by one, very slowly, and open them, and read them carefully word by word, and then with a profound sigh of comprehension, as if she had seen to the bottom of everything, she would tear the envelopes to little bits and tie the letters together and lock the cabinet drawer in her determination to conceal what she did not wish to be known.

7 ▶ **Critical Viewing**
What aspects of this painting mirror the story's setting? **[Connect]**

Enrichment: Analyzing Historical Patterns, Trends, and Periods

Mirrors

For centuries, mirrors were rare and expensive. The first mirrors were made of polished metal; in the Middle Ages, the idea of using glass with a metal backing was introduced. Venice, known for the art of glass blowing during the fifteenth century, was also a center for making mirrors.

The use of mirrors in the main rooms at the Palace of Versailles in France is one reason observers consider it so magnificent. Built for Louis XIV in the seventeenth century, Versailles has a famous Hall of Mirrors named for the huge mirrors that face each window.

Activity: Analyzing the Mirror in History
Encourage interested students to further analyze the mirror and its role in history by using the **Enrichment: Analyzing Historical Patterns, Trends, and Periods** worksheet, ***Professional Development Guidebook,*** page 231.

The thought served as a challenge. Isabella did not wish to be known—but she should no longer escape. It was absurd, it was monstrous. If she concealed so much and knew so much one must prize her open with the first tool that came to hand—the imagination. One must fix one's mind upon her at that very moment. One must fasten her down there. One must refuse to be put off any longer with sayings and doings such as the moment brought forth—with dinners and visits and polite conversations. One must put oneself in her shoes. If one took the phrase literally, it was easy to see the shoes in which she stood, down in the lower garden, at this moment. They were very narrow and long and fashionable—they were made of the softest and most flexible leather. Like everything she wore, they were exquisite. And she would be standing under the high hedge in the lower part of the garden, raising the scissors that were tied to her waist to cut some dead flower, some overgrown branch. The sun would beat down on her face, into her eyes; but no, at the critical moment a veil of cloud covered the sun, making the expression of her eyes doubtful—was it mocking or tender, brilliant or dull? One could only see the indeterminate outline of her rather faded, fine face looking at the sky. She was thinking, perhaps, that she must order a new net for the strawberries; that she must send flowers to Johnson's widow; that it was time she drove over to see the Hippesleys in their new house. Those were the things she talked about at dinner certainly. But one was tired of the things that she talked about at dinner. It

8 Literary Analysis
Point of View In what way does this paragraph illustrate the use of stream-of-consciousness narration?

9 Reading Check
What do the "marble tablets" turn out to be?

THE THOUGHT SERVED AS A CHALLENGE. *Isabella did not wish to be known—but she should no longer escape.*

The Garden of Love, (detail), Walter Richard Sickert, The Fitzwilliam Museum, Cambridge

8 Literary Analysis
Point of View

1. Review with students their understanding of stream-of-consciousness narration.
2. Then, **ask** the Literary Analysis question: In what way does this paragraph illustrate the use of stream-of-consciousness narration?
   Answer: Guide students to notice the stream-of-consciousness style of narration here: from speaking figuratively about putting oneself in Isabella's shoes to imagining seeing those shoes and Isabella in them.

9 Reading Check

Answer: The "marble tablets" are letters that arrived in the mail.

10 Humanities

The Garden of Love, by Walter Richard Sickert

Walter Richard Sickert (1860–1942) was born in Munich, Germany, but moved to Great Britain. Sickert's greatest contribution to British art was his willingness to experiment with, teach, and defend new ideas in art. Use the following question for discussion:

Ask: How does the garden in the painting compare with the garden in the story?
Answer: In the story, the garden—described as "the lower garden"—is more dense with flowers and plants than the garden in the painting; the garden in the story has a path, but no path appears in the painting.

Differentiated Instruction for Universal Access

Support for Special-Needs Students
Have students read from "The Lady in the Looking Glass: A Reflection" with your guidance. Tell students to visualize each word they read or to slow down until they have a clear image of what is being described.

Support for Less Proficient Readers
Students may have difficulty reading "The Lady in the Looking Glass: A Reflection" because of the narrator's complex series of ideas and images and a lack of clear narrative. Review with students what stream of consciousness is, and then have students read the selection.

Strategy for Gifted/Talented Students
Have students examine with a partner the painting *The Garden of Love,* which accompanies "The Lady in the Looking Glass: A Reflection." Ask them to take turns detailing aloud what they see in the painting.

⓫ Critical Viewing

Possible responses: Students may say the woman in the painting seems similar to Isabella because she is alone and does not seem to be engaged in any meaningful activity. Some may respond that she looks like she is sitting and thinking about something, and so she is not like Isabella.

⓬ Critical Thinking

Analyze Cause and Effect

1. Have students read aloud the bracketed paragraph on this page.
2. **Ask** what causes Isabella to consider her own mortality.
   Answer: Cutting an overgrown branch saddens Isabella and causes her to think of her own mortality.

AND THERE WAS NOTHING. *Isabella was perfectly empty. She had no thoughts. She had no friends.*

⓫ ▲ **Critical Viewing** Does the woman in this painting seem, like Isabella, to have "no thoughts"? Why or why not? **[Connect]**

was her profounder state of being that one wanted to catch and turn to words, the state that is to the mind what breathing is to the body, what one calls happiness or unhappiness. At the mention of those words it became obvious, surely, that she must be happy. She was rich; she was distinguished; she had many friends; she traveled—she bought rugs in Turkey and blue pots in Persia. Avenues of pleasure radiated this way and that from where she stood with her scissors raised to cut the trembling branches while the lacy clouds veiled her face.

Here with a quick movement of her scissors she snipped the spray of traveler's-joy and it fell to the ground. As it fell, surely some light came in too, surely one could penetrate a little farther into her being. Her mind then was filled with tenderness and regret. . . . To cut an overgrown branch saddened her because it had once lived, and life was dear to her. Yes, and at the same time the fall of the branch would suggest to her how she must die herself and all the futility and evanescence of things. And then again quickly catching this thought up, with her instant good sense, she thought life had treated her well; even if fall she must, it was to lie on the earth and molder sweetly into the roots of violets. So she stood thinking. Without making any thought precise—for she was one of those reticent people whose minds hold their thoughts enmeshed in clouds of silence—she was filled with thoughts. Her mind was like her room, in which lights advanced and retreated, came pirouetting and stepping delicately, spread their tails, pecked their way; and then her whole being was suffused, like the room again, with a cloud of some profound knowledge, some unspoken regret, and then she was full of locked drawers, stuffed with letters, like her cabinets. To talk of "prizing her open" as if she were an oyster, to use any but the finest and subtlest and most pliable tools upon her was impious and absurd. One must imagine—here was she in the looking glass. It made one start.

Vocabulary

evanescence (ev′ ə nes′ əns) *n.* vanishing or tendency to vanish

reticent (ret′ ə sənt) *adj.* silent; reserved ⓬

Think Aloud

Literary Analysis: Point of View

To model the process of analyzing point of view, use the following "think aloud." Say to students:

> As I read, I keep track of the pronouns. I realize that the narrator uses third-person pronouns such as *she* and *her*, but never *I*. I see that this story is told in third-person point of view. At the same time, I note the way the story is told. The narrator stays quite close, moment by moment, to her character's thoughts and actions. The sentences are long, and they range over a number of topics, just as someone's thoughts might. I realize the writer is using stream-of-consciousness. This technique used by the writer helps to put readers more directly in the mind of Isabella. On this page, we follow along as her thoughts race and she considers how she has spent her life.

She was so far off at first that one could not see her clearly. She came lingering and pausing, here straightening a rose, there lifting a pink to smell it, but she never stopped; and all the time she became larger and larger in the looking glass, more and more completely the person into whose mind one had been trying to penetrate. One verified her by degrees—fitted the qualities one had discovered into this visible body. There were her gray-green dress, and her long shoes, her basket, and something sparkling at her throat. She came so gradually that she did not seem to derange the pattern in the glass, but only to bring in some new element which gently moved and altered the other objects as if asking them, courteously, to make room for her. And the letters and the table and the grass walk and the sunflowers which had been waiting in the looking glass separated and opened out so that she might be received among them. At last there she was, in the hall. She stopped dead. She stood by the table. She stood perfectly still. At once the looking glass began to pour over her a light that seemed to fix her; that seemed like some acid to bite off the unessential and superficial and to leave only the truth. It was an enthralling spectacle. Everything dropped from her—clouds, dress, basket, diamond—all that one had called the creeper and convolvulus. Here was the hard wall beneath. Here was the woman herself. She stood naked in that pitiless light. And there was nothing. Isabella was perfectly empty. She had no thoughts. She had no friends. She cared for nobody. As for her letters, they were all bills. Look, as she stood there, old and angular, veined and lined, with her high nose and her wrinkled neck, she did not even trouble to open them.

People should not leave looking glasses hanging in their rooms.

13 ▼ Critical Viewing Make an analogy comparing an unopened letter like this one with Isabella as seen by the narrator. **[Connect]**

Critical Reading

1. **Key Ideas and Details (a)** Where are the narrator and Isabella, respectively, at the opening of the story? **(b) Infer:** From what perspective does the narrator observe Isabella? **(c) Speculate:** Who might the narrator be? Explain.
2. **Key Ideas and Details (a)** Briefly describe the layout and furnishings of the room in the story. **(b) Summarize:** How does the looking glass "guide" the narrator to an understanding of Isabella? **(c) Interpret:** What does the last sentence of the story, repeated from the beginning, mean?

Cite textual evidence to support your responses.

13 Critical Viewing

Answer: A letter suggests communication with the outside world, but—by virtue of its being unopened—it also suggests a separateness from others. In that way, the letter is like Isabella, who lives alone.

ASSESS

Answers

Before students respond, you may wish to have them write a brief objective summary of the selection. As they answer the questions below, remind them to support their answers with evidence from the text.

1. (a) Isabella is in the garden gathering flowers, and the narrator is in the drawing room. (b) The narrator observes Isabella from the drawing room, gazing at her reflection in the mirror. (c) **Possible response:** Students may say that the narrator is someone well acquainted with the superficial aspects of Isabella's life, perhaps a longtime acquaintance.
2. (a) The room is richly furnished and filled with Isabella's possessions. (b) At first, the looking glass provides a view of Isabella through her possessions. When Isabella herself appears in the looking glass, the narrator sees the true emptiness of her life. (c) It means that the reflections in the mirror and the mental reflections they lead to can be dangerously revealing.

Differentiated Instruction for Universal Access

Support for Special-Needs Students

Students may have difficulty following the story about Isabella Tyson, since it is told almost totally without her direct involvement. Review with students how the narrator describes Isabella's life and personality through what she observes in her home.

EL Vocabulary for English Learners

English learners may find some of the complex vocabulary in Woolf's story an obstacle to their comprehension. Encourage them to sound out any words that are difficult, and to try to grasp their meaning from context if margin definitions and footnotes are not available.

⓮ About the Selection

Mrs. Dalloway takes place in 1923 in London, England. It tells the story of a woman named Clarissa Dalloway, who spends the day preparing for a party. Clarissa's parallel character, Septimus, is a World War I veteran and suffers from the mental illness he developed in the aftermath of the war. As the day progresses, Clarissa has an encounter with an ex-suitor and questions her marriage. During her party, when Clarissa learns Septimus committed suicide, she contemplates whether or not he was right in committing the act. The story frequently bounces from one point of view to another, and it uses free indirect discourse, a technique by which the writer describes the thoughts of characters using third-person singular pronouns. *Mrs. Dalloway* is one of Virginia Woolf's most well-known and celebrated stories. This excerpt is the opening scene of the book.

from ⓮ MRS. DALLOWAY

Virginia Woolf

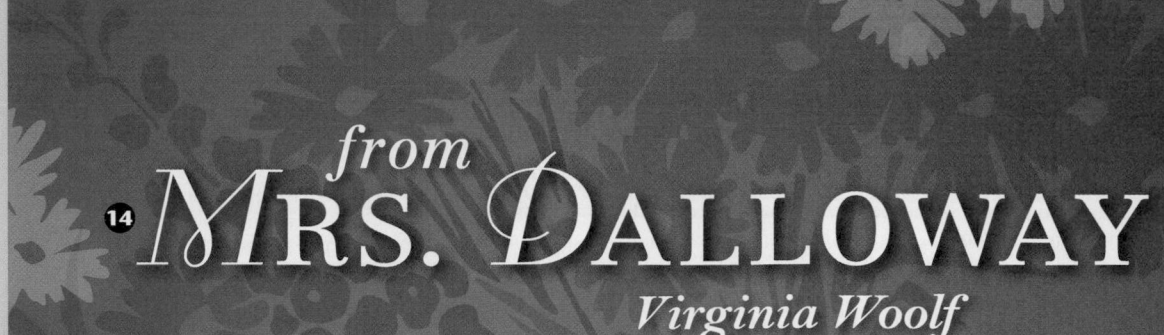

Enrichment: Building Context

Big Ben

Big Ben is one of London's most well-known landmarks. It stands 316 feet tall and is part of the Palace of Westminster, also known as the Houses of Parliament. It looks particularly fantastic at night when the clock faces are illuminated. The clock features a 14-foot-long minute hand, a 9-foot-long hour hand, and 2-foot-high figures. Contrary to popular belief, the name *Big Ben* does not refer to the clock tower, but to the 13-ton bell that hangs within it, named after the first commissioner of works, Sir Benjamin Hall.

Activity: Researching Big Ben

Encourage interested students to conduct further research on Big Ben. Have them record and analyze their findings using the **Enrichment: Building Context** worksheet, ***Professional Development Guidebook,*** page 222.

Mrs. Dalloway said she would buy the flowers herself. For Lucy had her work cut out for her. The doors would be taken off their hinges; Rumpelmayer's men were coming. And then, thought Clarissa Dalloway, what a morning—fresh as if issued to children on a beach.

What a lark! What a plunge! For so it had always seemed to her, when, with a little squeak of the hinges, which she could hear now, she had burst open the French windows and plunged at Bourton into the open air. How fresh, how calm, stiller than this of course, the air was in the early morning; like the flap of a wave; the kiss of a wave; chill and sharp and yet (for a girl of eighteen as she then was) solemn, feeling as she did, standing there at the open window, that something awful was about to happen; looking at the flowers, at the trees with the smoke winding off them and the rooks[1] rising, falling; standing and looking until Peter Walsh said, "Musing among the vegetables?"—was that it?—"I prefer men to cauliflowers"—was that it? He must have said it at breakfast one morning when she had gone out on to the terrace—Peter Walsh. He would be back from India one of these days, June or July, she forgot which, for his letters were awfully dull; it was
15 his sayings one remembered; his eyes, his pocket-knife, his smile, his grumpiness and, when millions of things had utterly vanished—how strange it was!—a few sayings like this about cabbages.

She stiffened a little on the kerb,[2] waiting for Durtnall's van to pass. A charming woman, Scrope Purvis thought her (knowing her as one does know people who live next door to one in Westminster); a touch of the bird about her, of the jay, blue-green, light, **vivacious**, though she was over fifty, and grown very white since her illness. There she perched, never seeing him, waiting to cross, very upright.

For having lived in Westminster—how many years now? over twenty,—one feels even in the midst of the traffic, or waking at night, Clarissa was positive, a particular hush, or solemnity; an indescribable pause; a suspense (but that might be her heart, affected, they said, by influenza) before Big Ben strikes. There! Out it boomed. First a warning, musical; then the hour, **irrevocable**. The leaden circles dissolved in the air. Such fools we are, she thought, crossing Victoria Street. For Heaven only knows why one loves it so, how one sees it so, making it up, building it round one, tumbling it, creating it every moment afresh; but the veriest frumps,[3] the most dejected of miseries sitting on doorsteps (drink their downfall) do the same; can't be dealt with, she felt positive, by Acts of Parliament for that very reason: they love life. In

1. **rooks** crows.
2. **kerb** the curb.
3. **veriest frumps** most plain, unfashionable women.

16 ◄ Critical Viewing
How do the bustle and vividness of this painting mirror the stream-of-consciousness narration of the story? **[Deduce]**

Vocabulary
vivacious (və vā′ shəs) *adj.* lively, spirited
irrevocable (i re′ və kə bəl) *adj.* not possible to revoke or change

17 Reading Check
Where does Mrs. Dalloway live?

15 Critical Thinking

Defend

1. Inform students that critics of this passage may argue that the large amount of seemingly unimportant details is unnecessary and uninteresting.
2. **Ask** students to defend Virginia Woolf's use of details in this selection.
3. **Possible response:** The use of details is important to developing this character. We learn how she perceives the world, and thereby learn how important each detail is to her. This shows that she appreciates life and seems to be a happy person. The way the details are presented also gives the selection an artistic, flowing style that intrigues the reader and encourages further reading.

16 Critical Viewing

Possible response: The stream-of-consciousness narration bounces from one topic to another, just as a viewer's eye moves from one element of the busy scene to another. Every piece of the picture is connected, just as each thought in the story's sequence flows into the next, but each element also has its own interesting details.

17 Reading Check

Answer: She lives in Westminster.

Differentiated Instruction for Universal Access

Strategy for Less Proficient Readers

Encourage students to summarize what they have learned about Mrs. Dalloway. Have them write a sketch of her character, describing her appearance, personality, and motivations.

EL Background for English Learners

Remind students that Virginia Woolf, the author of *Mrs. Dalloway,* wrote during a period in literary history that was full of experimentation. Her use of stream-of-consciousness narration—or narrating whatever thoughts occur in the mind of the speaker—was considered extremely modern at the time. Reading her work aloud can sometimes help with comprehension.

18 Critical Viewing

Possible response: The brightly colored flowers and lack of other people in this scene might prompt Mrs. Dalloway to think about the sights and sounds of the city around her, as she does in the passage.

ASSESS

Answers

Before students respond, you may wish to have them write a brief objective summary of the selection. As they answer the questions below, remind them to support their answers with evidence from the text.

1. (a) She remembers Peter's sayings, eyes, pocketknife, smile, and grumpiness. (b) Scrope Purvis thought her to be lively and spirited, and the narrator quickly says this despite the fact she is over fifty and has grown pale.
   (c) **Possible response:** Some people are not able to see beyond the exterior to the true souls of people, never truly understanding them.
2. (a) The narrator indicates that the suspense she feels may be her heart affected by influenza. (b) Her sickness might have negatively affected her outlook on life for a time, but now she is happy to be alive.
3. (a) Mrs. Dalloway decides to buy the flowers for her party herself. She muses by the window, goes out to the street to begin her trip, and takes in all the sounds and sights of the June day. (b) **Possible response:** In the grand scheme of things, these details do not matter all that much, but at that time, to Mrs. Dalloway, these details mattered a great deal because it was the entirety of her existence at that moment.
4. **Possible response:** I believe Woolf portrays Mrs. Dalloway's thoughts remarkably well. Woolf writes in the way one would think, which is a constant reminder that we are reading her thoughts.

people's eyes, in the swing, tramp, and trudge; in the bellow and the uproar; the carriages, motor cars, omnibuses,[4] vans, sandwich men shuffling and swinging; brass bands; barrel organs; in the triumph and the jingle and the strange high singing of some aeroplane overhead was what she loved; life; London; this moment of June.

4. omnibuses buses

18 ▶ **Critical Viewing** What might Mrs. Dalloway think about on a London street like this? **[Connect]**

Critical Reading

Cite textual evidence to support your responses.

1. **Key Ideas and Details (a)** What does Mrs. Dalloway remember of Peter Walsh? **(b)** How does the narrator call into question Scrope Purvis's understanding of Mrs. Dalloway? **(c) Infer:** What do these comments suggest about the ability of one person to understand another?
2. **Key Ideas and Details (a)** What details suggest that Mrs. Dalloway has not been in the best of health? **(b) Infer:** How might that history affect her outlook on life?
3. **Key Ideas and Details (a) Summarize:** What happens in the passage? **(b) Draw Conclusions:** How important are those events?
4. **Integration of Knowledge and Ideas** How effectively do you think Woolf portrays the inner thoughts of Mrs. Dalloway?

Enrichment: Analyzing a Historical Event

World War I

Mrs. Dalloway takes place in post-World War I England. The war broke out in 1914 between the Allies (Britain, France, Italy, and Russia) and the Central Powers (Germany and Austro-Hungary).

British soldiers from all parts of society were sent to fight in France and Belgium (the Western Front). Many volunteered, but as the war dragged on, many more were forced by the government to join. *Mrs. Dalloway* features a World War I veteran who was so affected by the horrors of war, he becomes mentally unstable.

Activity: Analyzing World War I Encourage interested students to conduct further research on World War I and analyze their findings using the **Enrichment: Analyzing a Historical Event** worksheet, ***Professional Development Guidebook***, page 230.

Critical Commentary

from a Speech on Virginia Woolf

Michael Cunningham

Michael Cunningham is an American writer whose Pulitzer Prize–winning novel The Hours *features Virginia Woolf as a character. In this speech delivered at a PEN America Virginia Woolf tribute, Cunningham describes how, as a high-school student, he first fell in love with her work.*

Michael Cunningham

Mrs. Dalloway is the first great book I ever read. I was fifteen . . . One day I . . . suddenly found myself standing beside the pirate queen of our school. She was beautiful and mean and smart, she had long red fingernails, and long straight hair. Fringe, pretty much everywhere. I found myself standing next to her, and I thought, "Uh oh, uh oh . . . Think fast, be suave, say something that will make her love you forever." So I said something that I thought then—and I think today—was very winning, about the poetry of Bob Dylan and Leonard Cohen. She was kind to me. . . . and said, "Well, yes, they're very good, but how do you feel about T. S. Eliot and Virginia Woolf?"

. . . I never expected I'd have to read either one of them. I went to the library, the Bookmobile, the little trailer where the books were. They didn't have any Eliot, but they did have one book of Woolf's, and it was *Mrs. Dalloway.* I took it out, and I took it home and read it, tried to read it, and I didn't know what was going on. In another way I did get it. I did get the depth and density, and the sentences, and it did turn on some little light inside my stupid skull.

Everybody who reads has a first book—maybe not the first book you read, but the first book that shows you what literature can be. Like a first kiss. And you read other books, you kiss other people, but especially for those who are romantically inclined, that first book stays with you. I felt wedded to *Mrs. Dalloway* in a way I've never felt about any other book. I finally, finally, finally grew up and wrote *The Hours*, in which I tried to take an existing work of great art and make another work of art out of it, the way a jazz musician might play improvisations on a great piece of music.

I learned so much from Woolf as a writer. I think what I learned most importantly was her conviction that the whole of human existence, while it is copiously contained in foreign wars and the death of kings, and the other big subjects for big novels, is also contained in every hour in the life of everybody, very much the way the blueprint for the whole organism is contained in every strand of its DNA. If you look with sufficient penetration, and sufficient art, at any hour in the life of anybody, you can crack it open. And get everything. Virginia Woolf understood that every character, no matter how minor, in a novel she wrote was visiting the novel, from a novel of his or her own, where he or she was the hero of another great tragic and comic tale.

Key Ideas and Details What did Cunningham as a writer learn from reading Virginia Woolf?

Answers

Critical Commentary

1. Ask students what they would consider to be their equivalent of what *Mrs. Dalloway* is to Michael Cunningham.
2. Briefly discuss Cunningham's idea about how your first good book is like your first kiss. Ask students if they agree and why.
3. Ask students how it is possible to make the little goings-on in everyday life seem so meaningful and make them so interesting to read.
4. Ask students to share their reactions to Cunningham's statement about how each character is the star of his or her own novel, visiting those of others from time to time. Ask them how his idea compares to real life.

Enrichment: Analyzing Film

The Hours

Michael Cunningham's book *The Hours* was made into a movie of the same name in 2002. The movie features three women in three different time periods. The women have a common thread: Virginia Woolf's book *Mrs. Dalloway.*

In 1923, Virginia Woolf begins writing *Mrs. Dalloway* and struggles against her mental illness. In 1951, Laura Brown is reading *Mrs. Dalloway* and planning a party for her husband. In 2001, Clarissa Vaughn is planning a party for her friend who is dying of AIDS.

Activity: Analyzing *The Hours* Encourage interested students to watch *The Hours* and further analyze it by using the **Enrichment: Analyzing Film** worksheet, ***Professional Development Guidebook***, page 226.

19 About the Selection

In this selection, Virginia Woolf supports her claim that "it would have been impossible . . . for any woman to have written the plays of Shakespeare in the age of Shakespeare." Woolf introduces the reader to Judith, William Shakespeare's fictional sister, a woman with the same creativity as Shakespeare, but with no support from the public. She would have had no support from her family either, as they would not have allowed her materials or schooling. She would have run away from home, trying to find her creative outlet in the real world; however, she would have eventually committed suicide as a result of her frustration.

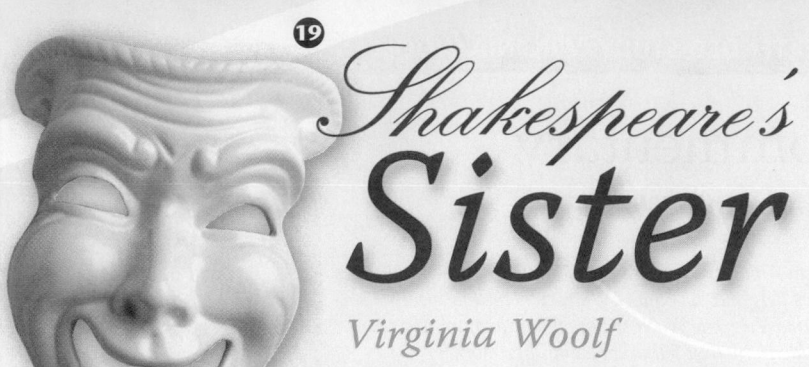

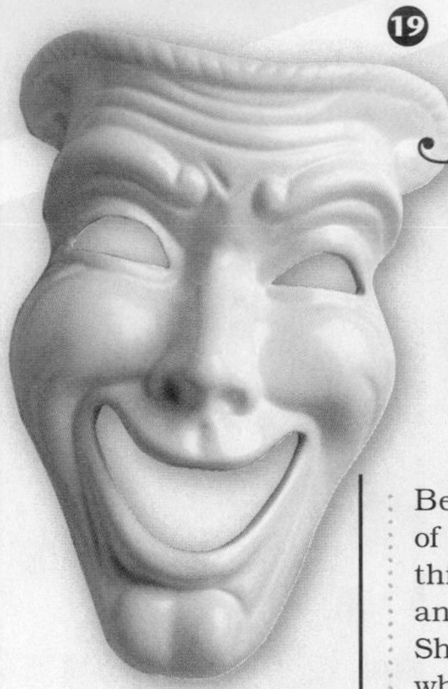

19

Shakespeare's Sister

Virginia Woolf

Be that as it may, I could not help thinking, as I looked at the works of Shakespeare on the shelf, that the bishop was right[1] at least in this; it would have been impossible, completely and entirely, for any woman to have written the plays of Shakespeare in the age of Shakespeare. Let me imagine, since facts are so hard to come by, what would have happened had Shakespeare had a wonderfully gifted sister, called Judith, let us say. Shakespeare himself went, very probably—his mother was an heiress—to the grammar school, where he may have learned Latin—Ovid, Virgil and Horace—and the elements of grammar and logic. He was, it is well known, a wild boy who poached[2] rabbits, perhaps shot a deer, and had, rather sooner than he should have done, to marry a woman in the neighborhood, who bore him a child rather quicker than was right. That **escapade** sent him to seek his fortune in London. He had, it seemed, a taste for the theater; he began by holding horses at the stage door. Very soon he got work in the theater, became a successful actor, and lived at the hub of the universe, meeting everybody, knowing everybody, practicing his art on the boards, exercising his wits in the streets, and even getting access to the palace of the queen. Meanwhile his extraordinarily gifted sister, let us suppose, remained at home. She was as adventurous, as imaginative, as agog to see the world as he was. But she was not sent to school. She had no chance of learning grammar and logic, let alone of reading Horace and Virgil. She picked up a book now and then, one of her brother's perhaps, and read a few pages. But then her parents came in and told her to mend the stockings or mind the stew and not moon about with books and papers. They would have spoken sharply but kindly, for they were substantial people who knew the conditions of life for a woman and loved their daughter—indeed, more likely than not she was the apple of her father's eye. Perhaps she scribbled some pages up in an apple loft on the sly, but was careful to hide them or set fire to them. Soon, however, before she was out of her teens, she was to be betrothed to the son

Vocabulary

escapade (es´ kə pād) *n.* a wild and reckless adventure

20

1. **the bishop was right** In the paragraph prior to this one, Woolf recalls that a bishop, whom she does not name, once wrote to a newspaper to say "it was impossible for any woman, past, present, or to come, to have the genius of Shakespeare."
2. **poached** hunted illegally.

Vocabulary Development

Vocabulary Knowledge Rating

When students have completed reading and discussing the selection, have them take out their **Vocabulary Knowledge Rating Charts** for the selection. Read the words aloud and have students rate their knowledge of words again in the After Reading column. Clarify any words that are still problematic. Have students write their own definitions and example or sentence in the appropriate column. Then, have students complete the Vocabulary Practice at the end of the selection. Encourage students to use the words in further discussion and written work about the selection. Remind them that they will be accountable for these words on the **Selection Test,** ***Unit 6 Resources,*** pages 77–79 or 80–82.

of a neighboring wool-stapler. She cried out that marriage was hateful to her, and for that she was severely beaten by her father. Then he ceased to scold her. He begged her instead not to hurt him, not to shame him in this matter of her marriage. He would give her a chain of beads or a fine petticoat, he said; and there were tears in his eyes. How could she disobey him? How could she break his heart? The force of her own gift alone drove her to it. She made up a small parcel of her belongings, let herself down by a rope one summer's night and took the road to London. She was not seventeen. The birds that sang in the hedge were not more musical than she was. She had the quickest fancy, a gift like her brother's, for the tune of words. Like him, she had a taste for the theater. She stood at the stage door; she wanted to act,[3] she said. Men laughed in her face. The manager—a fat, loose-lipped
20 man—guffawed. He bellowed something about poodles dancing and women acting—no woman, he said, could possibly be an actress. He hinted—you can imagine what. She could get no training in her craft. Could she even seek her dinner in a tavern or roam the streets at midnight? Yet her genius was for fiction and lusted to feed abundantly upon the lives of men and women and the study of their ways. At last—for she was very young, oddly like Shakespeare the poet in her face, with the same grey eyes and rounded brows—at last Nick Greene the actor-manager took pity on her; she found herself with child by that gentleman and so—who shall measure the heat and violence of the poet's heart when caught and tangled in a woman's body?—killed herself one winter's night and lies buried at some cross-roads where the omnibuses now stop outside the Elephant and Castle.

That, more or less, is how the story would run, I think, if a woman in Shakespeare's day had had Shakespeare's genius.

3. **she wanted to act** In Shakespeare's time, women were not allowed to act on stage. Men, dressed as women, played female roles.

Reading Strategy
Repairing Comprehension
If you were wondering whether these events actually occurred, what questions might you ask to clarify that point?

Like him, She had a taste for the theater.

Critical Reading

1. **Key Ideas and Details (a)** What details does Woolf include to give an identity to Shakespeare's sister? **(b) Infer:** What does she hope to accomplish by doing so?
2. **Integration of Knowledge and Ideas** Would Woolf say that the same obstacles blocking Shakespeare's sister existed in Woolf's own time?
3. **Integration of Knowledge and Ideas** How do the selections by Woolf reveal her to be a writer interested in changing tradition? In your response, use at least two of these Essential Question words: *convention, defy, credible, narrative, stream of consciousness.* *[Connecting to the Essential Question: What is the relationship of the writer to tradition?]*

Cite textual evidence to support your responses.

Concept Connector

Reading Strategy Graphic Organizer
Ask students to review the graphic organizers in which they have organized their questions and answers. Then, have students share their organizers and compare their questions and answers.

Activating Prior Knowledge
Have students return to their responses to the Activating Prior Knowledge activity. Ask them to explain whether their thoughts have changed and, if so, how.

Connecting to the Essential Question
Have students compare their responses to the prompt, completed before reading the selections, with their thoughts afterward. Have them work individually or in groups, writing or discussing their thoughts, to formulate new responses. Then, lead a class discussion, probing for what students have learned that confirms or invalidates their initial thoughts. Encourage students to cite specific textual details to support their responses.

20 Reading Strategy
Repair Comprehension

1. Remind students that when they are reading a stream-of-consciousness work, asking questions can help them repair their comprehension.
2. **Ask** the Reading Strategy question: If you are wondering whether these events actually occurred, what questions might you ask to clarify that point? **Possible responses:** How does Woolf introduce Judith? What does Woolf using the words "let us suppose" at the beginning of "Shakespeare's Sister" tell me?

ASSESS
Answers

Before students respond, you may wish to have them write a brief objective summary of the selection. As they answer the questions below, remind them to support their answers with evidence from the text.

1. (a) Judith was "wonderfully gifted," and "as adventurous, as imaginative" as her brother.
   (b) She is saying women are equal to men in potential.
2. **Possible response:** Yes, I believe she would. She may not have been so adamant about her position if she had not had to fight it herself. It may be said that she could identify with Judith.
3. **Possible response:** Woolf wanted to change tradition, especially the idea that women could not produce high-level writing because they were female. Her use of unconventional narrative techniques in "The Lady in the Looking Glass," as well as her arguments against conventional ideas about women in "Shakespeare's Sister," show her interest in changing tradition. If she wrote conventionally, her work would have fallen into a large pool of others like her and not really be recognized. She stands out more because she defied tradition.

Answers

1. **Possible responses:** Students may cite the description of the letters on the marble-topped table, the narrator's account of how she needed to "put oneself in shoes," and the contrast between appearance and reality at the end of the story.
2. (a) The narrator's reflections on Isabella's character end as Isabella appears in the mirror. (b) Isabella is nothing like the person the narrator has imagined her to be; she is empty, lonely, and detached.
3. (a) It starts out as third-person limited and shifts to third-person omniscient. (b) Her technique is very fluid, and the shift happens so smoothly, the reader hardly realizes it.
4. (a) Her style is very fluid and detailed in all three selections. (b) **Possible response:** Woolf gains credibility because she succeeds with that style in three different pieces.
5. (a) The narration is chiefly first-person. (b) This is different because the other selections work with third-person narration.
6. Woolf's use of stream of consciousness shows how the narrator constructs a reality for Isabella out of merely an appearance.
7. The character looks very pensive, reflecting the extended trains of thought in Woolf's work. She is also very prim, like the characters of Isabella and Clarissa.
8. (a) One might ask who the narrator is, why she is in Isabella's house, and what relationship she has to Isabella. (b) The story suggests that she is an acquaintance.
9. (a) **Possible response:** My first impression was of a simple woman who was concerned too much about love. (b) **Possible response:** I would ask what her situation was. (c) Possible response: My opinion changed because she was obviously not simple—she fully appreciated the details of the day.
10. (a) **Possible response:** Based on Woolf's first statement, I did not think Judith would succeed. (b) **Possible response:** I would ask exactly how she tried to achieve her goals and whether or not anyone at all supported her.

After You Read

The Lady in the Looking Glass • from *Mrs. Dalloway* • *Shakespeare's Sister*

Literary Analysis

1. **Craft and Structure** Give three examples of the use of the **stream-of-consciousness** technique in "The Lady in the Looking Glass."
2. **Craft and Structure (a)** How does the literal reflection of Isabella in the mirror serve as a climax for the narrator's mental reflections? **(b)** What does the climax reveal about Isabella?
3. **Craft and Structure (a)** In the excerpt from *Mrs. Dalloway*, how does the focus of the narrator shift? **(b)** How does Woolf's choice of a narrative **point of view** make that shift possible?
4. **Craft and Structure (a)** What is similar in writing style in all three selections? **(b)** What does Woolf gain by using this style?
5. **Craft and Structure (a)** How would you describe Woolf's narrative voice in the essay "Shakespeare's Sister"? **(b)** How does that voice compare to those of the narrators of the other two selections? Use a chart like the one shown to list details about each narrator.

"The Lady in the Looking Glass"	*Mrs. Dalloway*	"Shakespeare's Sister"
Narrator has limited knowledge until end	Omniscient narrator	

6. **Integration of Knowledge and Ideas** What does Woolf's use of the stream-of-consciousness technique show about how we construct a picture of another person?
7. **Analyzing Visual Information** In the caricature of Woolf on this page, what qualities of Woolf or her work does David Levine capture?

Reading Strategy

8. **(a)** In "The Lady in the Looking Glass," what **questions** about the narrator might you ask? **(b)** What answers does the story suggest?
9. **(a)** What impression did you have of Mrs. Dalloway after reading the first long paragraph in the passage? **(b)** What questions would you ask about her to confirm that impression? **(c)** Did you have the same impression after reading the entire passage?
10. **(a)** What did you think would happen to Shakespeare's sister when Woolf introduced her? **(b)** What questions might you have asked to anticipate the ending?

Common Core State Standards

Language
4.d. Verify the preliminary determination of the meaning of a word or phrase. *(p. 1205)*

▲ David Levine caricature of Woolf from November 20, 1980

Assessment Practice

Style (For more practice, see *All-in-One Workbook*.)

Many tests require students to describe recognized stylistic devices and effective language. Use the following sample item to review with students how to recognize the tone of a passage. Have students read pages 1192–1193 before answering the question.

The tone of this selection can *best* be described as—

A whiny.
B dry and academic.
C matter-of-fact.
D hopeful.

Lead students to recognize that the tone is never whiny, so ***A*** is incorrect. It is definitely not "dry and academic," so ***B*** is not correct either. Between the last two choices, "matter-of-fact" does not describe the tone as accurately as "hopeful" does. The correct answer is ***D***.

PERFORMANCE TASKS

Integrated Language Skills

Vocabulary Acquisition and Use

Word Analysis: Latin Root *-trans-*

The Latin root *-trans-*, meaning "through" or "across," appears in the word *transient*, which Woolf uses in "The Lady in the Looking Glass." In that word, the root conveys the idea that an emotion or thought passes quickly, moving *through* a person rapidly. Use the meaning of *-trans-* to define these phrases that include the root.

1. transnational corporation
2. business transaction
3. transatlantic communication
4. transparent proceedings
5. transfer station
6. transformational experience

After defining the phrases, check your meanings by looking up the words in a dictionary.

Vocabulary: Sentence Completions

Use a word from the vocabulary list on page 1191 to complete each sentence, and explain your choice. Use each word only once.

1. The _______ hostess helped everyone at her party have a good time.
2. Constant _______ from his boss convinced the harried worker to resign.
3. The decisions of the Supreme Court are _______ and cannot be appealed.
4. How did the trickster manage to avoid the consequences of that particular _______?
5. The setting sun _______ the room with red-orange light.
6. The shy man was _______ to speak at the crowded meeting.
7. "It is just a passing fad, a _______ movement," declared the critic.
8. The preacher contrasted the _______ of worldly goods with the eternal nature of the spirit.

Using Resources to Build Vocabulary

Precise Words for Movement

Many words have synonyms, or other words with a similar meaning, but each word has a precise meaning. Woolf uses several words to describe the movements of light or objects in "The Lady in the Looking Glass":

pirouetting (p. 1193)	trembling (p. 1193)
pecking (p. 1193)	loomed (p. 1194)

Use a print or electronic dictionary or thesaurus to find synonyms of these words. State whether you think Woolf used the most effective word or whether you would recommend that she use one of the synonyms. Explain your reasoning.

Assessment Resources

Unit 6 Resources

L1 L2 EL **Selection Test A,** pp. 77–79. Administer Test A to less advanced readers.

L3 L4 EL **Selection Test B,** pp. 80–82. Administer Test B to on-level students and more advanced students.

L3 L4 **Open-Book Test,** pp. 74–76. As an alternative, give the Open-Book test.

All **Customizable Test Bank**

All **Self-tests**
Students may prepare for the **Selection Test** by taking the **Self-test** online.

PHLit Online! All assessment resources are available at **www.PHLitOnline.com**.

EXTEND/ASSESS

Answers

Vocabulary Acquisition and Use

Word Analysis

Sample Answers

1. A *transnational corporation* is a business organization that extends across international boundaries.
2. A *business transaction* is an economic event or activity between two or more businesses.
3. *Transatlantic communication* is a means of communicating across the Atlantic Ocean.
4. *Transparent proceedings* are interactions in which everything is out in the open.
5. A *transfer station* is a station where passengers can move from one means of transportation to another.
6. A *transformational experience* is an experience that changes a person.

Vocabulary

Sample Answers

1. vivacious
2. upbraidings
3. irrevocable
4. escapade
5. suffused
6. reticent
7. transient
8. evanescence

Using Resources to Build Vocabulary

Sample Answers

pirouetting: spinning
pecking: biting
trembling: shaking
loomed: appeared
strained: forced

Writing

You may use this Writing Lesson as timed-writing practice, or you may allow students to develop the informative text as an assignment over several days.

Work with students to draw up guidelines, based on the assignment, for their essays:

- **Focus** The writer should clearly present the differences between the original stream-of-consciousness version and his or her "translation" of the passage.
- **Organization** The writer should begin with his or her "translation," then compare the two techniques, ordering points logically.
- **Elaboration** The writer should give details and provide examples from the original version and his or her "translation" to support his or her opinion.
- **Style** The audience is not specified, so a formal style is appropriate.

PERFORMANCE TASKS

Integrated Language Skills

Writing

Informative Text While a traditional omniscient third-person narrator can penetrate the thoughts of characters, the stream-of-consciousness technique gives the author an opportunity to show those thoughts in more complex ways. At the same time, this technique puts demands on readers. Choose a passage from "The Lady in the Looking Glass" or *Mrs. Dalloway* that you think is a good representative of the stream-of-consciousness technique. Then "translate" that passage into the style of a traditional omniscient third-person narrator. Finally, write a brief essay in which you state whether you prefer the original version or your "translation" and explain why.

Prewriting Begin by choosing a passage to "translate."

- Look for a passage that effectively presents the flow of the character's thoughts and feelings.
- Pick a passage that you found difficult to understand.

Drafting Write a "translation" of the passage that converts it to that of a traditional omniscient narrator.

- Remember that an omniscient narrator can reveal the inner thoughts of a character but does not use the fragmented words and phrases or association of ideas that mark stream-of-consciousness narration.
- Draft a brief **essay** that compares the two techniques. You might think about the different opportunities each gives to writers and the demands each places on readers. You might use a graphic organizer like the one below to take notes on the two points of view.

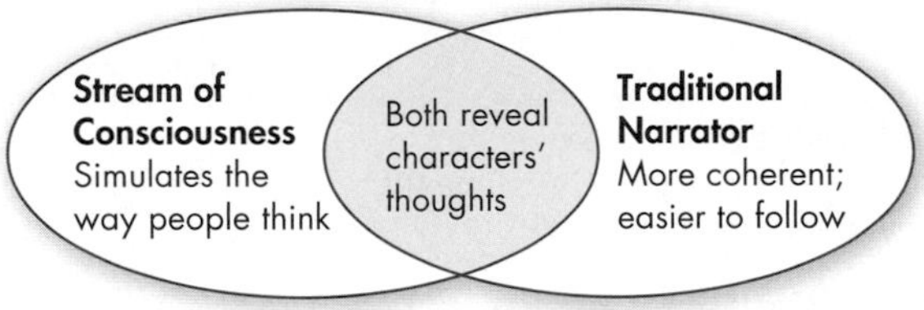

Revising Revise your essay to make it clear and effective:

- Review the draft of your "translation," making sure it is true to the traditional narrative style.
- Review the draft of your essay to ensure that you clearly state your position and cite evidence to support your points.
- Read both drafts carefully to make sure they are grammatically correct and all words are spelled correctly.

Common Core State Standards

Writing
2. Write informative/explanatory texts to examine and convey complex ideas, concepts, and information clearly and accurately through the effective selection, organization, and analysis of content.

Language
1. Demonstrate command of the conventions of standard English grammar and usage when writing or speaking. *(p. 1207)*
2.b. Spell correctly.

Teaching Resources

Unit 6 Resources
L3 L4 **Vocabulary Builder,** p. 70
L3 L4 **Support for Writing Lesson,** p. 72
L3 L4 **Grammar and Style,** p. 71
L4 **Enrichment,** p. 73

All **Interactive Grammar Lesson:** available under After You Read for this selection

All **Enriched Online Student Edition Internet Research Activity:** available under After You Read for this selection

All ***Professional Development Guidebook* Rubrics for Self-Assessment: General Writing Rubric,** pp. 282–283

PHLit Online! All resources are available at **www.PHLitOnline.com**.

Conventions and Style: Parallel Structure

Good writers use **parallel structure,** or similar grammatical forms, to express similar ideas. Parallel structure gives your writing rhythm and emphasizes key ideas. To create parallel structure, use nouns with nouns, phrases with phrases, and clauses with clauses.

Look at the examples below. Notice that coordinating conjunctions *(and, or)* join items of equal importance.

Nonparallel: Look past the room *with its rugs, with its bookcases, and the night creatures that were dancing around.*	**Parallel:** Look past the room *with its rugs, with its bookcases, and with its dancing night creatures.*
Nonparallel: It was a fact *that Isabella was rich, and she took risks to collect objects.*	**Parallel:** It was a fact *that Isabella was rich and that she took risks to collect objects.*
Nonparallel: Isabella went into the garden *because of its flowers rather than because she wanted quiet.*	**Parallel:** Isabella went into the garden *because of its flowers rather than because of its quiet.*

As you edit your writing, check for parallel structure.

Practice Rewrite each item to correct the nonparallel structure.

1. Lights and shadows moved across the room, curtains blew, and there were petals that fell.
2. Rage, envy, and sorrowing seemed to fill the room.
3. Isabella went from the house, down the grass path, and she walked into the garden.
4. Isabella would choose a trailing plant rather than it was an upright, sturdy flower.
5. Because it was hot, the windows and doors were open, letting in sounds of life and to contrast with the scene in the mirror.
6. Isabella bought the house, traveled to far off places, and choosing furnishings.
7. The envelopes lay on the marble table, seeming to be out of order and not focusing.
8. Letters can reveal a person's past—appointments, dates not kept, and breaking promises.
9. She was seen in the looking glass, pausing, straightening a rose, and to lift a bloom to smell it.
10. Was her expression scornful or sensitive, shining or in a dull way?

Writing and Speaking Conventions

A. Writing Use the following items to write sentences with parallel structure:

1. feet, tails, beaks
2. of affection, of jealousy, of parting
3. marble-topped table, long grass path, the sunflowers
4. raising, looking, thinking

Example: feet, tails, beaks
Sentence: The birds lifted their feet, spread their tails, and tapped their beaks.

B. Speaking Consider the letters mentioned in "The Lady in the Looking Glass." Compose and present to the class a letter that might be written by the narrator who is imagining the contents of the drawers. Use at least three examples of parallel structure.

PH WRITING COACH
Further instruction and practice are available in *Prentice Hall Writing Coach.*

Extend the Lesson

Sentence Modeling

Choose the sentence given from the first selection students read:

> They came pirouetting across the floor, stepping delicately with high-lifted feet and spread tails and pecking allusive beaks as if they had been cranes or flocks of elegant flamingoes. . . ."

Ask students what they notice about the sentence. Elicit from them that this is a list of descriptive elements. Then ask what else they notice. Each verb introducing each of the three elements of the list (*pirouetting, stepping, pecking*) is in the same form—present tense with an *-ing* ending. Tell students that because all the verbs are in the same form, this sentence is parallel.

Have students imitate the example sentence in sentences on topics of their own choosing, matching each grammatical and stylistic feature discussed. Collect the sentences, and share them with the class.

Conventions and Style

Practice

1. Lights and shadow moved across the room, curtains blew, and petals fell.
2. Rage, envy, and sorrow seemed to fill the room.
3. Isabella went from the house, down the grass path, and into the garden.
4. Isabella would choose a trailing plant rather than an upright, sturdy flower.
5. Because it was hot, the windows and doors were open, letting in sounds of life and contrasting with the scene in the mirror.
6. Isabella bought the house, traveled to far-off places, and chose furnishings.
7. The envelopes lay on the marble table, out of order and not focused.
8. Letters can reveal a person's past—appointments, dates not kept, and broken promises.
9. She was seen in the looking glass, pausing, straightening a rose, and lifting a bloom to smell it.
10. Was her expression scornful or sensitive, shining or dull?

Writing and Speaking Conventions

A. **Sample answers:**

1. The birds lifted their feet, spread their tails, and tapped their beaks.
2. In his love letter, he spoke of affection, of jealousy, and of parting.
3. Her painting captured the beauty of the marble-topped table, the long grass path, and the sunflowers.
4. Raising her head, looking at the man, and thinking of the past, she decided to speak to him.

B. Students' letters will vary. Make sure each uses three examples of parallel structure.

PH WRITING COACH Grade 12
Further instruction on and practice with fiction narration can be found in Chapter 6.

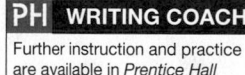

Stream-of-Consciousness Narration

1. Ask students to think about the function of the narrator in books they have read and movies they have seen. Elicit from the students some of the forms that the narrator has taken throughout history, from the omniscient Greek chorus to the meandering twenty-first century blogger relating thoughts and observations about the events of his or her daily life.
2. **Ask** students to think of blogs that they have come across online. Have them consider the ways in which bloggers relate events in contrast to how a news reporter or essayist might describe the same events. **Ask** them what advantages each type of narration provides to the reader.
   Possible answers: A narrator speaking in stream of consciousness, like some bloggers, provides a more subjective point of view. The narrator might provide the reader with more specific insights and realistic thought patterns than a narrator operating from a more removed perspective. On the other hand, by nature of its unstructured and subjective format, stream-of-consciousness narration also allows for the creation of greater ambiguity as to the actual events unfolding.
3. Explain to students that the reliability of stream-of-consciousness narration is often questionable. **Ask** students how, as in the selection from *The Nine Guardians,* the stream-of-consciousness narration of a child might color the story in a way another narrator might not.
   Possible answers: A child's thought process might include misunderstandings of complex events or might offer perspectives unconsidered by an adult mind.

Stream-of-Consciousness

IN WORLD LITERATURE

1208

Enrichment: Investigating Psychology

William James and Stream of Consciousness

In the late nineteenth century, psychologist William James posited that the thought process could be viewed as an unending flow of linked emotions, events, and sensations rather than a discrete, linear progression of ideas. This theory cast thought as subjective, which came into conflict with the widely held belief that scientific analysis was necessarily objective. **Activity: Go with the Flow** Have students research theories on stream-of-consciousness and record their findings in the **Enrichment: Investigating Psychology** worksheet, ***Professional Development Guidebook,*** page 239. Then, have them touch an object, complete a simple action (such as a jumping), and read a paragraph (such as a news article). Have them record their entire thought processes while completing each task and compare their "streams of consciousness."

Comparing Literary Works

"The Lady in the Looking Glass" *by Virginia Woolf* • from *Pedro Páramo by Juan Rulfo* • from *The Nine Guardians by Rosario Castellanos*

Comparing Stream-of-Consciousness Narratives

Stream-of-Consciousness Narration

In the early twentieth century, writers like James Joyce and Virginia Woolf tried to capture all the layers of consciousness observed in the groundbreaking work of Austrian psychoanalyst Sigmund Freud—visual and auditory perceptions, associations, memories, dreams, unconscious impulses—all flowing through the mind in what psychologist William James called the stream of consciousness. **Stream-of-consciousness narration** has these traits:

- Whether it uses first- or third-person point of view, it presents the external world through one or more characters' impressions.
- It leaps abruptly to new mental associations.
- It may shift in time, presenting memories or flashbacks.
- It may include fantasy elements or even dreams.
- It may use symbols that can be interpreted to reveal character.
- It may use long sentences or irregular grammar or punctuation to capture the flow of thoughts.

As you read, use a form like the one shown to help you compare the stream-of-consciousness narration in these selections.

Selection: ______
Character(s) Portrayed: ______
Leaps to New Associations: ______
Time Shifts/Memories or Flashbacks: ______
Fantasies or Dreams: ______
Symbols and Interpretations: ______
Unusual Grammar/Usage/Punctuation: ______

Common Core State Standards

Reading Literature
3. Analyze the impact of the author's choices regarding how to develop and relate elements of a story or drama.

Language
4.c. Consult general and specialized reference materials, both print and digital, to find the pronunciation of a word or determine or clarify its precise meaning, its part of speech, its etymology, or its standard usage.

Gather Vocabulary Knowledge

Rulfo and Castellanos use related forms of the words *sweeping, swirling,* and *lashing.* Use a **dictionary** to find each word's part of speech and definition. Then, employ the following references to further explore these words:

- **History of Language:** Use a history of English to research each word's origins. Write a paragraph about the word's emergence in English.
- **Book of Quotations:** Use an online or print collection of quotations to find a quotation containing one of the words. In a paragraph, explain nuances in meaning that are evident from the context of the quotation.

Comparing References Compare and contrast what you learn about the words from these and other related references (printed or electronic), such as **books of roots and affixes.**

PHLit Online! www.PHLitOnline.com

Common Core State Standards
- Reading Literature 3
- Writing 2, 10
- Language 4.c

Comparing Stream-of-Consciousness Narratives

1. Review the characteristics of stream-of-consciousness narration. Remind students that this style attempts to capture different aspects of consciousness, including visual and auditory perceptions, associations, memories, dreams, and unconscious impulses.
2. Tell students that the selections they are about to read use stream-of-consciousness narration in different ways.
3. Introduce the form on the student page. Explain that students will use it to compare the next two selections to each other and to the story by Virginia Woolf.

Gather Vocabulary Knowledge

Have print and electronic resources available for students to use to explore the definitions and uses of the words. Encourage students to search for quotations using other forms of the words, including *swept, lashed,* and *swirled.* Remind students that the context will sometimes determine what part of speech a word acts as. Display the following quotation and elicit from students that in this context, *lash* is a noun:

"He who has provoked the lash of wit cannot complain that he smarts from it." James Boswell

When students share their quotations, encourage them to indicate the part of speech the target word acts as in the context of the quotation.

Teaching Resources

The following resources can be used to enrich, extend, or differentiate the instruction.

- All *Unit 6 Resources,* pp. 83–87
- All **Enriched Online Student Edition**
- All *Common Core Companion,* pp. 28–40; 196–207; 269–276; 324–331

PHLit Online! All resources are available at **www.PHLitOnline.com.**

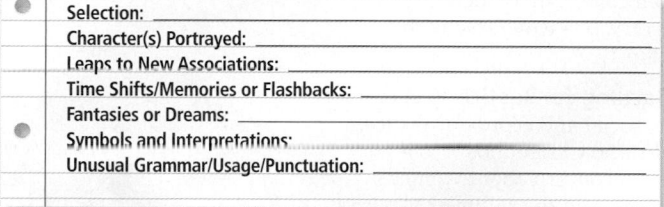

Daily Bellringer

As you teach the Comparing Literary Works selection, have students complete the Grammar, Usage, and Mechanics activities that remain for the relevant week in the *Daily Bellringer Activities* booklet.

Background

More About the Authors

Juan Rulfo

Juan Rulfo spent most of his life working as a bureaucrat in the Mexican government, occasionally writing screenplays for film and television. However, *Pedro Páramo* was the only novel that Rulfo ever wrote. When it was published in Mexico City in 1955, it met with neither critical nor commercial success. However, the novel went on to inspire some of the world's greatest writers. Over the years, *Pedro Páramo* has acquired a reputation as a book that is both highly influential and oddly obscure. Indeed, Gabriel García Márquez once stated that "Juan Rulfo, to the contrary of what happens with the great classic writers, is a writer whom one reads a lot, but of whom one speaks little."

Rosario Castellanos

Rosario Castellanos often wrote about the struggle for social justice from a religious point of view. As a devout Catholic, she expressed both anger at social injustice and wonder at the beauty of creation. She was particularly interested in the work of two religious authors: Saint Teresa of Ávila, a sixteenth-century Spanish author, and Sor Juana Inés de la Cruz, a Mexican nun and poet of the seventeenth century. In addition, Castellanos's poetry was influenced by that of Saint John of the Cross, a famous Christian mystic and Spanish poet.

JUAN RULFO (1918–1986)

The son of wealthy landowners, Juan Rulfo (hwän ro͞ol′ fō) grew up at a time when violent rebellion was tearing the Mexican countryside apart. When his father was killed and his mother died soon after, he lived for a time in an orphanage before moving to Mexico City. There he held a variety of jobs and also wrote fiction and screenplays, drawing on the tormented landscape of his childhood to produce the story collection *The Burning Plain* and the short novel *Pedro Páramo.*

A Literary Pioneer Although he wrote only two major works, Rulfo's influence on Latin American literature has been enormous. One of the first Spanish-language writers to use stream-of-consciousness narration, he also blended reality and fantasy to pioneer the magical realism that became so popular in Latin American fiction. The great magical realist Gabriel García Márquez recognized his debt to Rulfo by including a line from *Pedro Páramo* in his famous novel *One Hundred Years of Solitude.*

ROSARIO CASTELLANOS (1925–1974)

Rosario Castellanos (rō sär′ ē ō käs tel yä′ nōs) grew up in the southern Mexican region of Chiapas, where her family owned sugar and coffee plantations. Here she saw firsthand the poverty of the indigenous Mayan population whose plight she would later portray in her writing. After graduating from college in Mexico City, she began publishing essays and poetry. She won fame with her novel *The Nine Guardians*, published in 1957.

Battling for Justice A champion of social and economic justice, Rosario Castellanos wrote with deep concern about women's rights and the rights of Mexico's indigenous peoples. She also held several government posts and, as a member of the National Indigenous Institute, worked to promote literacy in impoverished parts of the country. She was serving as Mexico's ambassador to Israel when she died in an accident there in 1974.

from
Pedro Páramo
Juan Rulfo

BACKGROUND To fulfill his mother's deathbed request of vengeance against the man who abandoned their family, Juan Preciado goes in search of his father, Pedro Páramo. He travels to Comala, his mother's home town, only to learn that his father has died years before. Comala itself is a ghost town—literally, for the reader gradually comes to realize that all of the people Preciado encounters there are ghosts. The book shifts point of view to some of those people; in the following passage, the voice talking is probably that of Doña Susanita, Pedro Páramo's last wife.

I am lying in the same bed where my mother died so long ago; on the same mattress, beneath the same black wool coverlet she wrapped us in to sleep. I slept beside her, her little girl, in the special place she made for me in her arms.

I think I can still feel the calm rhythm of her breathing; the palpitations and sighs that soothed my sleep. . . . I think I feel the pain of her death. . . . But that isn't true.

Here I lie, flat on my back, hoping to forget my loneliness by remembering those times. Because I am not here just for a while. And I am not in my mother's bed but in a black box like the ones for burying the dead. Because I am dead.

Vocabulary
palpitations
(pal´ pə tā´ shənz) *n.*
rapid beating of the heart

from Pedro Páramo **1211**

TEACH

❶ **About the Selection**
In *Pedro Páramo,* the character of Juan Preciado travels to the town of Comala to find his father, Pedro Páramo. Juan soon discovers that the town is populated by ghosts. This selection is a stream-of-consciousness passage narrated by Pedro Páramo's wife, Doña Susanita.

❷ **Activating Prior Knowledge**
Have students think about some other works they have read in which ghosts appear. Examples might include *Hamlet, A Christmas Carol,* or *The Legend of Sleepy Hollow.* Have each student write a paragraph generalizing about the role of ghosts in works he or she has read.

Differentiated
Instruction for Universal Access

Culturally Responsive Instruction
Culture Focus Explain to students that *Pedro Páramo* was an important influence on the ascendance of magical realism as a style among Latin American authors. Novelists such as Gabriel García Márquez, Isabel Allende, and Jorge Luis Borges all wrote novels in this style, mixing the real with the imaginary to create a portrait of life in places such as Argentina and Colombia. Have students try to find examples of magical realism or stream-of-consciousness storytelling from their own home cultures. Ask students to consider how this work is similar to and different from *Pedro Páramo.* Have students give opinions on whether they think the authors of the works they chose were influenced by Juan Rulfo.

PHLit
Online!

These selections are available in interactive format in the **Enriched Online Student Edition,** at **www.PHLitOnline.com,** which includes a thematically related video with writing prompt and an interactive graphic organizer.

❸ Comparing Stream-of-Consciousness Narratives

1. Review with students their understanding of stream-of-consciousness narration.
2. Then, **ask** which details indicate that this narrative, like that in *Mrs. Dalloway,* uses the stream-of-consciousness technique.
   Answer: The stream-of-consciousness technique is exemplified by the shifts in time between the present, where the narrator is lying in bed, and the past, as she remembers when she was a young girl and when her mother died.

ASSESS

Answers

Before students respond, you may wish to have them write a brief objective summary of the selection. As they answer the questions below, remind them to support their answers with evidence from the text.

1. (a) She has died. (b) It is a coffin. (c) She is lonely and trying to comfort herself.
2. (a) She believes that she should have been miserable and filled with anguish. By contrast, she remembers feeling joyful on the morning of her mother's death. (b) **Possible response:** She was happy because the breeze was blowing.
3. (a) It suggests that people continue to think and feel after they are dead. They may become "trapped" on Earth and feel lonely. (b) The narrator states that although she is dead, she can still think. She says she is lonely, and that she is "not here just for a while."

❸ **Comparing Stream-of-Consciousness Narratives** Which details indicate that this narrative, like that in *Mrs. Dalloway*, uses the stream-of-consciousness technique?

Vocabulary
tendrils (ten´ drəlz) *n.* climbing plants' clinging or coiling stemlike parts

I sense where I am, but I can think. . . .

I think about the limes ripening. About the February wind that used to snap the fern stalks before they dried up from neglect. The ripe limes that filled the overgrown patio with their fragrance.

The wind blew down from the mountains on February mornings. And the clouds gathered there waiting for the warm weather that would force them down into the valley. Meanwhile the sky was blue, and the light played on little whirlwinds sweeping across the earth, swirling the dust and lashing the branches of the orange trees.

The sparrows were twittering; they pecked at the wind-blown leaves, and twittered. They left their feathers among the thorny branches, and chased the butterflies, and twittered. It was that season.

February, when the mornings are filled with wind and sparrows and blue light. I remember. That is when my mother died.

I should have wailed. I should have wrung my hands until they were bleeding. That is how you would have wanted it. But in fact, wasn't that a joyful morning? The breeze was blowing in through the open door, tearing loose the ivy **tendrils**.

Critical Reading

Cite textual evidence to support your responses.

1. **Key Ideas and Details (a)** What has happened to the narrator to cause her to lie in the black box? **(b) Infer:** What is the black box? **(c) Analyze:** Why does she pretend to be a little girl in her mother's bed?
2. **Key Ideas and Details (a) Compare and Contrast:** Contrast the narrator's attitude toward the morning her mother died with the attitude she thinks she is supposed to have. **(b) Analyze:** Why do you think she feels the way she does about the morning?
3. **Integration of Knowledge and Ideas (a) Interpret:** What does the passage suggest about death in general? **(b) Support:** Cite details to support your interpretation.

from

The Nine Guardians

Rosario Castellanos

BACKGROUND Set in the remote towns and countryside of 1930s Chiapas, Mexico, *The Nine Guardians* depicts the harsh poverty of the area's Mayan Indians and the changes to society brought about by government efforts to improve economic conditions. Most of the book is narrated by a nameless seven-year-old girl from a family of ranch owners, through whose eyes and mind we see the social landscape mixed together with the nursery tales and fantasies of childhood. In this passage from early in the book, the narrator walks through the nearby town with Nana, the devoted Indian servant who has cared for her since birth.

Nana leads me through the street by the hand. The pavements are flagstones, polished and slippery. The street is cobbled. Little stones are arranged like petals in a flower. From between the joints grows short grass which the Indians tear up with the points of their machetes.[1] There are carts drawn by sleepy bullocks;[2] and ponies that strike sparks with their hoofs; and old horses tied to posts by their halters. All day they remain there, heads hanging, ears sadly twitching. We've just passed one. I held my breath and pressed close to the wall, afraid that any minute the horse would bare its great yellow teeth—and he has such lots of them—and bite my arm. I'd be ashamed, because my arms are very skinny and the horse might laugh.

The balconies are forever staring into the street, watching it go uphill and down and the way it turns the corners. Watching the gentlemen pass with their mahogany canes; the ranchers dragging their spurs as they walk; the Indians running under their heavy burdens. And at all times the diligent trotting donkeys loaded with water in wooden tubs. It must be nice to be like the balconies, always idle, absent-minded, just looking on. When I'm grown up. . . .

Vocabulary
diligent (dil′ ə jənt) *adj.* persevering and careful

1. **machetes** (mə shet′ *or* chet′ əz) *n.* large, heavy blades used for cutting down sugar cane, dense underbrush, or other plants.
2. **bullocks** (bool′ ə ks) *n.* bulls that have been neutered.

❹ About the Selection

The Nine Guardians takes place in the 1930s in the Chiapas region of Mexico. The story is narrated by a seven-year-old girl from a wealthy land-owning family. She observes the world around her, including the hardships suffered by Mayan Indians who live in the region.

❺ Activating Prior Knowledge

Tell students that the selection is told from the perspective of a seven-year-old girl. Ask students how they think this might affect the point of view of the selection. Have students write paragraphs about events they experienced when they were younger. Students should try to write from the perspective of their younger selves.

Differentiated Instruction for Universal Access

Culturally Responsive Instruction

Culture Focus Tell students that Mayan Indians have lived throughout Mexico and Central America for thousands of years. Explain that people of Indian ancestry in Mexico have often faced obstacles such as poverty and discrimination.

The narrator of *The Nine Guardians* describes the lives of the Indians as difficult. Encourage students to discuss what they can infer about the Indians' position in Mexican society from what they have read.

6 Comparing Stream-of-Consciousness Narration

1. Review with students their understanding of stream-of-consciousness narration. Remind students that this type of writing often presents the external world through the characters' impressions, including abrupt new mental associations.
2. Then, **ask** students: Do any details indicate that this is a child's stream of consciousness, unlike stream-of-consciousness narratives of the mature women in *Pedro Páramo* and *Mrs. Dalloway?*
   Possible response: The narrator says "When I'm grown up…." Also, many of the things described by the narrator are described with an annoyed or impatient perspective indicative of one who is immature.

ASSESS

Answers

Before students respond, you may wish to have them write a brief objective summary of the selection. As they answer the questions below, remind them to support their answers with evidence from the text.

1. (a) The narrator is on her way to school. (b) Nana probably accompanies her because she is young and because the street is crowded with many things the narrator does not understand. (c) Nana's presence suggests that the narrator's family is wealthy and privileged.
2. (a) The narrator describes a woman in a window, a blacksmith, and a group of Indian weavers. She describes ponies, bullocks drawing carts, and old horses tied to posts. The narrator describes the flies buzzing and aspects of some of the products sold in the shops. (b) **Possible response:** The narrator's details imply that the town is forlorn.
3. **Possible responses:** (a) The narrator reacts to the world around her with curiosity and wariness. (b) She has a vivid imagination, as evidenced by her explanation for why the woman in the window is sad and by her fear of being bitten by the horses.

Comparing Stream-of-Consciousness Narration Do any details indicate that this is a child's stream of consciousness, unlike the stream-of-consciousness narratives of the mature women in *Pedro Páramo* and *Mrs. Dalloway*? 6

Now we begin climbing down Market Hill. The butchers' hatchets are ringing inside, and the stupid, sated flies are buzzing. We trip over the Indian women sitting on the ground weaving palm. They are talking together in their odd language, panting like hunted deer. And suddenly they let their sobs fly into the air, high-pitched, without tears. They always frighten me though I've heard them so often.

We skirt past the puddles. Last night came the first shower, the one that brings out the little ants with wings that go *tzisim*. We pass in front of the shops smelling of freshly dyed cloth. Behind the counter the assistant is measuring with a yard-stick. We can hear the grains of rice pattering against the metal scales. Someone is crumbling a handful of cocoa. And through the open street doors goes a girl with a basket on her head, and she screams, afraid that either the dogs or the owners will let fly at her:

"Dumplings—come buy!"

Nana urges me on. Now the only person in the street is a man with squeaking yellow shoes he can't have worn very often. A large door is wide open, and in front of the lighted forge[3] stands the blacksmith, dark from his trade. His chest shows bare and sweating as he hammers. An old maid opens her window just wide enough to watch us furtively. Her mouth is clamped tight as if she'd locked some secret in. She is sad because she knows her hair is turning white.

"Say how-do-you-do, child, she's a friend of your mother."

But we're already some distance off. The last few steps I almost run. I mustn't be late for school.

Vocabulary

sated (sāt′ id) *adj.* with appetite satisfied; full from eating

furtively (fur′ tiv lē) *adv.* in a sneaky or secretive manner

3. **forge** *n.* the place where a blacksmith heats metal and hammers it into shape.

Critical Reading

Cite textual evidence to support your responses.

1. **Key Ideas and Details (a)** Where is the narrator going? **(b) Infer:** Why does Nana accompany her? **(c) Infer:** What does the presence of Nana suggest about the social or economic standing of the narrator's family?
2. **Key Ideas and Details (a)** List some of the people, animals, or things the narrator observes as she walks through the town. **(b) Draw Conclusions:** From the details, what can you conclude the town is like?
3. **Key Ideas and Details (a)** With what emotions does the narrator react to the world around her? **(b) Evaluate:** Would you say she has a vivid imagination? Why or why not?

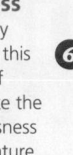

After You Read

The Lady in the Looking Glass • from *Pedro Páramo* • from *The Nine Guardians*

Comparing Stream-of-Consciousness Narration

1. **Craft and Structure** In your estimation, in which of the three selections does the **stream-of-consciousness narration** best capture the way the human mind works? Cite examples to support your opinion.
2. **Integration of Knowledge and Ideas** **(a)** Contrast the point of view in the Woolf story with that of the selections by Rulfo and Castellanos. **(b)** Which narrative has the strongest sense of immediacy, making you feel as if you are there? Why?
3. **Integration of Knowledge and Ideas** **(a)** What do the narrator in Woolf's story and the narrators of the other two selections have in common? **(b)** What are some of their chief differences? **(c)** Which of the three characters seems most in touch with reality? Why?

Common Core State Standards

Writing
2. Write informative/explanatory texts to examine and convey complex ideas, concepts, and information clearly and accurately through the effective selection, organization, and analysis of content.
10. Write routinely over extended time frames and shorter time frames for a range of tasks, purposes, and audiences.

Timed Writing

Informative Text: Analytical Essay

Each of these stream-of-consciousness narratives has to meet a challenge: how to use a character's thought processes, which are often chaotic, to convey a sense of the world around the character.

Assignment: Write an **analytical essay** in which you compare and contrast the ways in which the exterior world is conveyed in the three stream-of-consciousness narratives. **[40 minutes]**

Your essay should address these questions:

- Through whose eyes is the setting conveyed?
- What memories or other associations do the details of setting prompt in this person's mind?
- How do the character's perceptions and memories color your impression of the exterior world?

As you write, follow the conventions of a strong analytical essay:

- Advance a clear thesis statement.
- Support your ideas with relevant and substantial evidence and well-chosen details from the texts.

Remember to write legibly and use appropriate capitalization and punctuation conventions.

5-Minute Planner

Complete these steps before you begin to write:

1. Read the assignment carefully. Identify key words and phrases.
2. Weigh the similarities and differences in the ways in which each selection conveys the setting. **TIP** As you scan the texts, jot down quotations or details that you might use in your essay.
3. Create a rough outline for your essay.
4. Reread the prompt, and draft your essay.

USE ACADEMIC VOCABULARY

As you write, use academic language, including the following words or their related forms:

approximates
clarify
coherent
emerge

For more on academic language, see the vocabulary charts in the introduction to this book.

Assessment Resources

Unit 6 Resources
L1 L2 EL **Selection Test A, pp. 77–79.**
L3 L4 **Selection Test B, pp. 80–82.**
L3 L4 **Open-Book Test, pp. 74–76.**

PHLit Online! All resources are available at **www.PHLitOnline.com.**

Answers

Comparing Stream-of-Consciousness Narration

1. **Possible response:** The excerpt from *The Nine Guardians*, at the end of the second paragraph, for example, the narrator trails off without finishing her thought as she starts to climb the hill.
2. (a) The narrator of Woolf's story seems more removed from the action that is taking place. The stories of Rulfo and Castellanos are narrated in a way that makes them seem like they are the thoughts a person is having. (b) **Possible response:** Castellanos's story; it is made up of a series of impressions described by the narrator as they take place.
3. (a) They all observe the world and relay their impressions of it. (b) They are of different ages and in different circumstances in life. (c) **Possible response:** The narrator of Woolf's story seems the most in touch with reality because she observes everything in close detail.

Timed Writing

1. Teach the Academic Vocabulary and encourage students to use the words as appropriate when writing about characters' thought processes.
2. Use the prompt to help students identify elements and qualities their analytical essay should have.
   - A thesis statement about the ways that the exterior world is conveyed in the stream-of-consciousness narratives.
   - A discussion of the similarities and differences among the narrators and what they relate.
   - An analysis of how setting affects the thoughts and memories of the narrators.
   - Relevant and substantial evidence and well-chosen details from the text.

Encourage students to focus on these points when they are planning and revising their essays.

Tell students they will have 40 minutes to plan and write the essay. Encourage students to budget their time to allow 5 minutes for outlining and identifying some initial supporting text references in the works, and 10 minutes to revise and proofread.

❶ Defining the Contemporary Short Story

Review with students how modern short stories are different from traditional ones. **Ask:** How might the experience of reading a typical nineteenth-century short story differ from the experience of reading a contemporary one?

Possible response: A nineteenth century story would probably be more predictable than a contemporary one. Readers might anticipate a happy or sad ending and perhaps learn a lesson about life. A contemporary story is less likely to provide a satisfying resolution to the characters' conflicts.

❷ Literary Elements

Review the elements of short stories. Point out the similarities between a short story and a novel. **Ask:** Apart from its length, how does a short story differ from a novel?

Possible response: Short stories tend to focus on a brief period of conflict in a character's life. There is no space for the large cast of characters, complex subplots, or detailed descriptions of many novels.

❸ Close Read: Literary Elements

Review the chart with students. Point out the highlighted text in the model on page 1217. Explain that in each case, the color of the highlighting matches the color of the category in the chart. Details that illustrate a given category are highlighted in the color of that category.

THE SHORT STORY IS . . . VISIONARY, AND IS NOT WEIGHED DOWN BY FACTS, EXPLANATION, OR ANALYSIS.

— ELIZABETH BOWEN

In This Section

For more practice analyzing short stories, see pages 1298, 1328, and 1342.

❶ Defining the Contemporary Short Story

A short story is a brief work of fiction that usually features a plot with a distinct beginning, middle, and end. In the late nineteenth century, most writers used a formulaic structure that involved a suspenseful climax and a dramatic ending. In the twentieth century, British writers like Virginia Woolf, Henry Green, and Katherine Mansfield strove to depict life more truthfully and modernized the short story. Later writers such as D. H. Lawrence, Graham Greene, and Doris Lessing continued to develop the form.

❷ **Literary Elements** The short story and the novel share basic narrative elements:

- **Plot:** the ordered sequence of events that explores characters in conflict in many modern stories. The plot builds to a crucial moment in which the conflict is altered, but not necessarily resolved.
- **Conflict:** a struggle between opposing forces
- **Setting:** the time and place of a story's action
- **Character:** a person or creature that participates in the action of a story
- **Theme:** the central idea, message, or insight expressed in a story
- **Point of view:** the vantage point from which a story is told. In *first-person point of view,* the narrator is a character in the story who speaks in the first person. In *third-person point of view,* the narrator is a voice outside the action. A *third-person omniscient* narrator is all-knowing and can reveal all the characters' thoughts and feelings. A *third-person limited* narrator reveals only what a single character experiences, thinks, and feels.

❸ **Close Read: Literary Elements**
These additional narrative elements appear in the Model text at right.

Irony: a discrepancy between appearance and reality, between what is said and what is meant, or between expectation and outcome Example: *"The scientist, who all the time had been leaning back in a big chair, sipping his coffee and smiling with skeptical good humor, chipped in and explained . . . about . . . the progress of science." (Doris Lessing)*	**Flashback:** a type of plot device in which a scene from the past interrupts an ongoing sequence of events Example: *"The young girl talking to the soldier in the garden had not ever completely seen his face. It was dark; they were saying goodbye under a tree." (Elizabeth Bowen)*
Dialogue: the words characters speak; dialogue may advance the story's action and show what characters are like Example: *"Oh!" said the boy. "Then what* is *luck, mother?"* *"It's what causes you to have money. . . ." (D.H. Lawrence)*	**Characterization:** the revelation of characters' personalities through descriptions of their appearances, feelings, thoughts, and actions Example: *"There was a woman who was beautiful, who started with all the advantages, yet she had no luck." (D.H. Lawrence)*

Differentiated Instruction for Universal Access

Strategy for Special-Needs Students

Students may benefit from turning the information on these pages into a chart for future reference. Give each student a copy of the Five-Column Chart, on page 294 of ***Graphic Organizer Transparencies.*** Have them insert the headings *Plot, Conflict, Setting, Character, Theme,* and *Point of View.* Under each heading, students should note information that pertains to that element of the short story.

Strategy for Advanced Readers

Challenge students to identify stories they have read for school or on their own that emphasize each element of a short story discussed above. Talk about how story writers mix and match types of conflict, characterization, narrators, and themes to create an endless number of original stories.

EXEMPLAR TEXT

Model

About the Text One of the dominant figures in Russian Realism, Anton Chekhov (1860–1904) excelled at two literary forms: drama and the short story. His work is noted for both its compassion and objectivity.

from **"Home"**

by Anton Chekhov (translated by Constance Garnett)

"Someone came from the Grigoryevs' to fetch a book, but I said you were not at home. The postman brought the newspaper and two letters. By the way, Yevgeny Petrovitch, I should like to ask you to speak to Seryozha. To-day, and the day before yesterday, I have noticed that he is smoking. When I began to expostulate with him, he put his fingers in his ears as usual, and sang loudly to drown my voice."

4 Yvgeny Petrovitch Bykovsky, the prosecutor of the circuit court, who had just come back from a session and was taking off his gloves in his study, looked at the governess as she made her report, and laughed.

5 "Seryozha smoking . . ." he said, shrugging his shoulders. "I can picture the little cherub with a cigarette in his mouth! Why, how old is he?"

"Seven. You think it is not important, but at his age smoking is a bad and pernicious habit, and bad habits ought to be eradicated in the beginning."

"Perfectly true. And where does he get the tobacco?"

"He takes it from the drawer in your table."

"Yes? In that case, send him to me."

6 When the governess had gone out, Bykovsky. . . called up memories of the long past, half-forgotten time when smoking aroused in his teachers and parents a strange, not quite intelligible horror. . . . Yvegeny Petrovitch remembered the head-master of the high school, a very cultured and good-natured old man, who was so appalled when he found a high-school boy with a cigarette in his mouth that he turned pale, immediately summoned an emergency committee of the teachers, and sentenced the sinner to expulsion. . . .

"What am I to say to him, though?" Yvgeny Petrovitch wondered.

But before he had time to think of anything whatever his son Seryozha, a boy of seven, walked into the study. . . .

"Good evening, papa!" he said, in a soft voice, clambering on to his father's knee and giving him a rapid kiss on his neck. "Did you send for me?" . . .

"Natalya Semyonovna has just been complaining to me that you have been smoking. . . . Is it true? Have you been smoking?"

7 "Yes, I did smoke once. . . . That's true. . . ."

"Now you see you are lying as well," said the prosecutor, frowning to disguise a smile. "Natalya Semyonovna has seen you smoking twice. So you see you have been detected in three misdeeds: smoking, taking someone else's tobacco, and lying. Three faults."

Characterization The passage begins to develop Bilovsky's character—he is a successful lawyer who does not seem to view life, or child rearing, with too much gravity.

Dialogue The conversation between the governess and Bilovsky both reveals differences in the two characters' personalities and sets up the action that is to follow.

Flashback As Bilovsky prepares to scold his son, a flashback in the form of a memory interrupts the narrative. The information it provides helps readers understand Bilovsky's mild reaction to his son's behavior.

Irony The discrepancy between Bilovsky's feelings of amusement and his stern statements is ironic. The irony emphasizes both Bilovsky's understanding of his paternal role and the tenderness he feels toward his son.

4 Characterization

Read aloud the bracketed text. Point out how succinctly Chekhov develops three characters in two brief paragraphs. **Ask:** On the basis of this opening passage, what adjectives might you use to describe the governess, Seriozha, and Bilovsky?

Possible responses: the governess: anxious, conscientious, serious; Seriozha: disobedient, spoiled, curious; Bilovsky: wealthy, irresponsible, confident

5 Dialogue

Invite volunteers to read the bracketed passage of dialogue. **Ask:** What does this exchange tell the reader about Bilovsky's values?

Possible response: Bilovsky considers theft (from his own table) more serious misbehavior than smoking.

6 Flashback

Point out that a flashback in fiction is similar to a vivid memory in real life. **Ask:** How does this flashback help explain Bilovsky's tolerant attitude toward Seriozha's smoking?

Possible response: Bilovsky believes that some people overreact to smoking. He does not wish to behave like this "good-natured" principal.

7 Irony

Read aloud the bracketed passage. Discuss with students the irony in the contradiction between Bilovsky's outward manner and his true feelings. **Ask:** If this story were set in modern society, what other irony regarding attitudes to smoking might a reader detect?

Possible response: A parent who smokes condemns the habit for his or her child.

Extend the Lesson

Evaluating Short Stories

Ask students to read short stories of their own choosing. They might select a short story from a literary magazine or a collection of short stories. Have students determine whether the short story chosen is effective. Tell students to focus on the point of view, the theme, and the conflict of the short story they choose.

After students have read and evaluated their stories, have them work in groups to compare their selections. As a class, determine if particular points of view, themes, or conflicts arise among the students' selections.

COMMON CORE
Time and Resource Manager

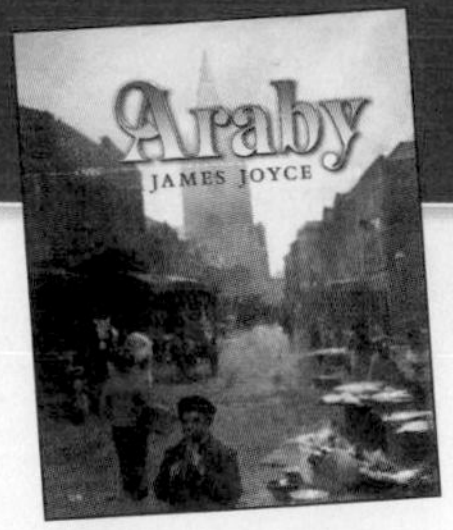

The Lagoon • Araby
Lesson Pacing Guide

DAY 1 Preteach

- Administer the Reading and Vocabulary Warm-ups (*Unit 6 Resources,* pp. 88–91) as necessary.
- Introduce the Literary Analysis concept: Plot Devices.
- Introduce the Reading Strategy: Identify Cause-and-Effect Relationships.
- Build background with the author and Background features.
- Develop thematic thinking with Connecting to the Essential Question.
- Teach the selection vocabulary.

DAYS 2–3 Preteach/Teach/Assess

- Distribute copies of the appropriate graphic organizer for the Reading Strategy (*Graphic Organizer Transparencies,* pp. 218–219).
- Distribute copies of the appropriate graphic organizer for Literary Analysis (*Graphic Organizer Transparencies,* pp. 220–221).
- Prepare students to read with the Activating Prior Knowledge activities (TE).
- Informally monitor comprehension while students read.
- Use the Reading Check questions to confirm comprehension.
- Develop students' understanding of plot devices using the Literary Analysis prompts.
- Develop students' ability to identify cause-and-effect relationships using the Reading Strategy prompts.
- Reinforce vocabulary with the Vocabulary notes.
- Assess students' comprehension and mastery of the skills by having them answer the Critical Reading, Literary Analysis, and Reading Strategy questions.
- Have students complete the Vocabulary Lesson.

DAY 4 Extend/Assess

- Have students complete the Writing Lesson and write a response to literature. (You may assign as homework.)
- Administer Selection Test A or B (*Unit 6 Resources,* pp. 100–102 or 103–105).

Common Core State Standards

Reading Literature 5. Analyze how an author's choices regarding how to structure a text contribute to its overall structure and meaning as well as its aesthetic impact.
9. Demonstrate knowledge of eighteenth-, nineteenth- and early-twentieth-century foundational works of American literature, including how two or more texts from the same period treat similar themes or topics.

Writing 2. Write informative/explanatory texts to examine and convey complex ideas, concepts, and information clearly and accurately through the effective selection, organization, and analysis of content.
2.b. Develop the topic thoroughly by selecting the most significant and relevant facts, extended definitions, concrete details, quotations, or other information and examples appropriate to the audience's knowledge of the topic.
5. Develop and strengthen writing as needed by planning, revising, editing, rewriting, or trying a new approach, focusing on addressing what is most significant for a specific purpose and audience.
9.a. Apply grades 11–12 Reading standards to literature.

Language 5.b. Analyze nuances in the meaning of words with similar denotations.

Additional Standards Practice
***Common Core Companion,* pp. 54–55; 75–76; 185–195; 226–227; 261–266; 332–335**

Daily Block Scheduling
Each day in this Lesson Pacing Guide represents a 40–50 minute period. Teachers using block scheduling may combine days to revise pacing. In addition, teachers may differentiate and support core instruction by integrating components for extended and intensive support as students require. See the Guide to Selected Leveled Resources (facing page).

Guide to Selected Leveled Resources

RTI Tier 1 (students performing on level)

		The Lagoon • Araby
Warm Up	**Practice, model,** and **monitor** fluency, working **with the whole class** or **in groups.**	**Vocabulary and Reading Warm-ups B,** ***Unit 6 Resources,*** pp. 88–89, 91
Comprehension/Skills	**Support** and **monitor** comprehension and skills development, having students complete the activities, graphic organizers, and interactive prompts **independently** or **as a class.**	• ***Reader's Notebook,*** adapted instruction and full selection EL ***Reader's Notebook: English Learner's Version,*** adapted instruction and adapted selection • **Reading Strategy Graphic Organizer B,** ***Graphic Organizer Transparencies,*** p. 229 • **Literary Analysis Graphic Organizer B,** ***Graphic Organizer Transparencies,*** p. 231
Monitor Progress	**Monitor** student progress with the differentiated curriculum-based assessment in the *Unit Resources.*	• **Selection Test B,** ***Unit 6 Resources,*** pp. 103–105 • **Open-Book Test,** ***Unit 6 Resources,*** pp. 97–99

RTI Tier 2 (students requiring intervention)

		The Lagoon • Araby
Warm Up	**Practice, model,** and **monitor** fluency **in groups** or **with individuals.**	• **Vocabulary and Reading Warm-ups A,** ***Unit 6 Resources,*** pp. 88–90 • ***Hear It!*** **Audio CD (adapted text)**
Comprehension/Skills	• **Support** and **monitor** comprehension and skills development, working **in small groups** or **with individuals.** • As students complete the selection in the appropriate version of the *Reader's Notebook,* **monitor** comprehension frequently with group questions and individual instruction. • **Model** strategies while guiding students in completing the activities and prompts in the *Reader's Notebook,* as well as the graphic organizers. • **Practice** skills and **monitor** mastery with the *Reading Kit* worksheets.	• ***Reader's Notebook: Adapted Version,*** adapted instruction and adapted selection EL ***Reader's Notebook: English Learner's Version,*** adapted instruction and adapted selection • **Reading Strategy Graphic Organizer A,** ***Graphic Organizer Transparencies,*** p. 228 • **Literary Analysis Graphic Organizer A,** ***Graphic Organizer Transparencies,*** p. 230 • ***Reading Kit,*** Practice worksheets
Monitor Progress	**Monitor** student progress with the differentiated curriculum-based assessment in the *Unit Resources* and in the *Reading Kit.*	• **Selection Test A,** ***Unit 6 Resources,*** pp. 100–102 • ***Reading Kit,*** Assess worksheets

TIER 3 Tier 3 intervention may require consultation with the student's special-education or dyslexia specialist. For additional support, see the Tier 2 activities and resources listed above.

One-on-one teaching **Group work** **Whole class instruction** **Independent work** **A Assessment**

For a complete guide to selection support, including support for Advanced students, see the Overview of Resources in the frontmatter.

The Lagoon • Araby

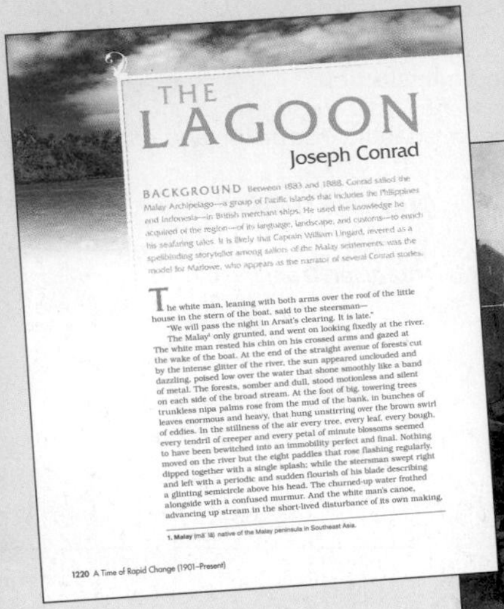

THE LAGOON
Joseph Conrad

BACKGROUND Between 1883 and 1888, Conrad sailed the Malay Archipelago—a group of Pacific islands that includes the Philippines and Indonesia—in British merchant ships. He used the knowledge he acquired of the region—of its language, landscape, and customs—to enrich his seafaring tales. It is likely that Captain William Lingard, revered as a spellbinding storyteller among sailors of the Malay settlements, was the model for Marlowe, who appears as the narrator of several Conrad stories.

The white man, leaning with both arms over the roof of the little house in the stern of the boat, said to the steersman—

"We will pass the night in Arsat's clearing. It is late."

The Malay[1] only grunted, and went on looking fixedly at the river. The white man rested his chin on his crossed arms and gazed at the wake of the boat. At the end of the straight avenue of forests cut by the intense glitter of the river, the sun appeared unclouded and dazzling, poised low over the water that shone smoothly like a band of metal. The forests, somber and dull, stood motionless and silent on each side of the broad stream. At the foot of big, towering trees trunkless nipa palms rose from the mud of the bank, in bunches of leaves enormous and heavy, that hung unstirring over the brown swirl of eddies. In the stillness of the air every tree, every leaf, every bough, every tendril of creeper and every petal of minute blossoms seemed to have been bewitched into an immobility perfect and final. Nothing moved on the river but the eight paddles that rose flashing regularly, dipped together with a single splash; while the steersman swept right and left with a periodic and sudden flourish of his blade describing a glinting semicircle above his head. The churned-up water frothed alongside with a confused murmur. And the white man's canoe, advancing up stream in the short-lived disturbance of its own making,

1. Malay (mā′ lā) native of the Malay peninsula in Southeast Asia.

1220 A Time of Rapid Change (1901–Present)

RESOURCES FOR:

- L1 Special-Needs Students
- L2 Below-Level Students (Tier 2)
- L3 On-Level Students (Tier 1)
- L4 Advanced Students (Tier 1)
- EL English Learners
- All All Students

Vocabulary/Fluency/Prior Knowledge

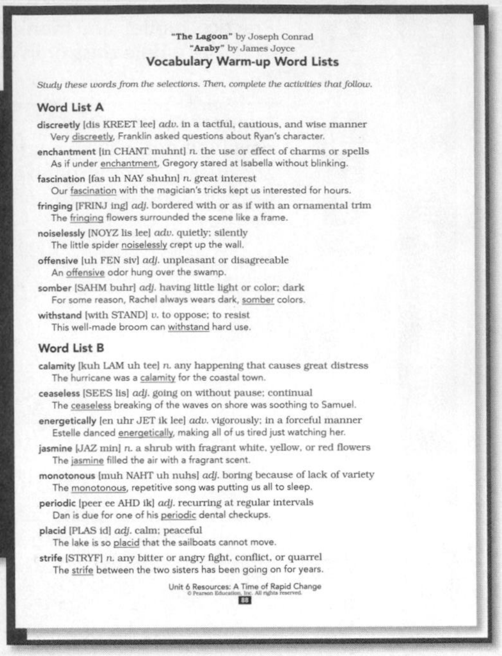

Unit 6 Resources

"The Lagoon" by Joseph Conrad
"Araby" by James Joyce
Vocabulary Warm-up Word Lists

Study these words from the selections. Then, complete the activities that follow.

Word List A

discreetly [dis KREET lee] *adv.* in a tactful, cautious, and wise manner
Very discreetly, Franklin asked questions about Ryan's character.

enchantment [in CHANT muhnt] *n.* the use or effect of charms or spells
As if under enchantment, Gregory stared at Isabella without blinking.

fascination [fas uh NAY shuhn] *n.* great interest
Our fascination with the magician's tricks kept us interested for hours.

fringing [FRINJ ing] *adj.* bordered with or as if with an ornamental trim
The fringing flowers surrounded the scene like a frame.

noiselessly [NOYZ lis lee] *adv.* quietly; silently
The little spider noiselessly crept up the wall.

offensive [uh FEN siv] *adj.* unpleasant or disagreeable
An offensive odor hung over the swamp.

somber [SAHM buhr] *adj.* having little light or color; dark
For some reason, Rachel always wears dark, somber colors.

withstand [with STAND] *v.* to oppose; to resist
This well-made broom can withstand hard use.

Word List B

calamity [kuh LAM uh tee] *n.* any happening that causes great distress
The hurricane was a calamity for the coastal town.

ceaseless [SEES lis] *adj.* going on without pause; continual
The ceaseless breaking of the waves on shore was soothing to Samuel.

energetically [en uhr JET ik lee] *adv.* vigorously; in a forceful manner
Estelle danced energetically, making all of us tired just watching her.

jasmine [JAZ min] *n.* a shrub with fragrant white, yellow, or red flowers
The jasmine filled the air with a fragrant scent.

monotonous [muh NAHT uh nuhs] *adj.* boring because of lack of variety
The monotonous, repetitive song was putting us all to sleep.

periodic [peer ee AHD ik] *adj.* recurring at regular intervals
Dan is due for one of his periodic dental checkups.

placid [PLAS id] *adj.* calm; peaceful
The lake is so placid that the sailboats cannot move.

strife [STRYF] *n.* any bitter or angry fight, conflict, or quarrel
The strife between the two sisters has been going on for years.

Unit 6 Resources: A Time of Rapid Change
© Pearson Education, Inc. All rights reserved.
88

EL L1 L2 **Vocabulary Warm-ups A and B,** pp. 88–89

Also available for these selections:

EL L1 L2 **Reading Warm-ups A and B,** pp. 90–91

All **Vocabulary Builder,** p. 94

Reader's Notebooks

Pre- and postreading pages for these selections, as well as "Araby," appear in an interactive format in the *Reader's Notebooks*. Each *Notebook* is differentiated for a different group of learners.
The selections in the Adapted and English Learner's versions are abridged.

L2 L3 ***Reader's Notebook***

L1 ***Reader's Notebook: Adapted Version***

EL ***Reader's Notebook: English Learner's Version***

EL ***Reader's Notebook: Spanish Version***

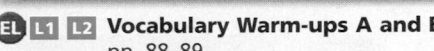

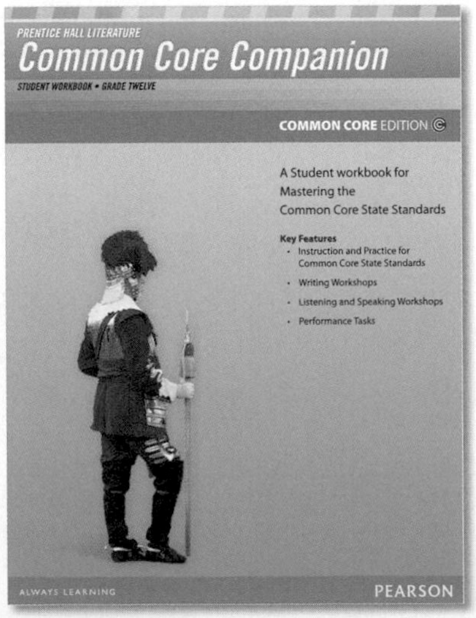

Common Core Companion

Additional instruction and practice for each Common Core State Standard

Selection Support

Graphic Organizer Transparencies

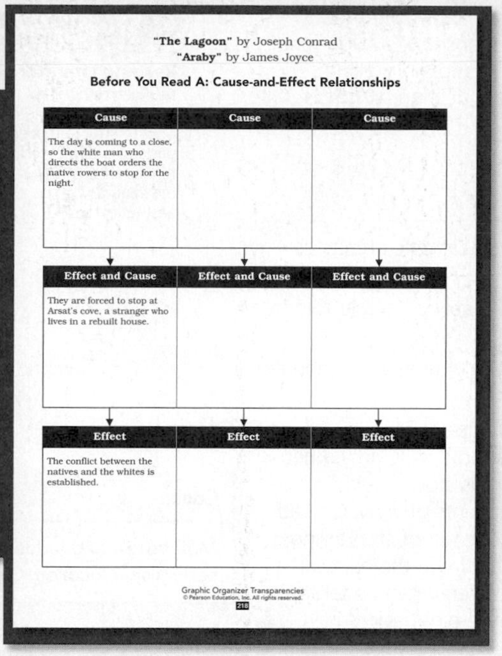

"The Lagoon" by Joseph Conrad
"Araby" by James Joyce

Before You Read A: Cause-and-Effect Relationships

Cause	Cause	Cause
The day is coming to a close, so the white man who directs the boat orders the native rowers to stop for the night.		

Effect and Cause	Effect and Cause	Effect and Cause
They are forced to stop at Arsat's cove, a stranger who lives in a rebuilt house.		

Effect	Effect	Effect
The conflict between the natives and the whites is established.		

Graphic Organizer Transparencies

218

EL L1 L2 **Reading: Graphic Organizer A,** p. 218

Also available for these selections:

EL L3 **Reading: Graphic Organizer B,** p. 219

EL L1 L2 **Literary Analysis: Graphic Organizer A,** (partially filled in), p. 220

EL L3 **Literary Analysis: Graphic Organizer B,** p. 221

Skills Development/Extension

Unit 6 Resources

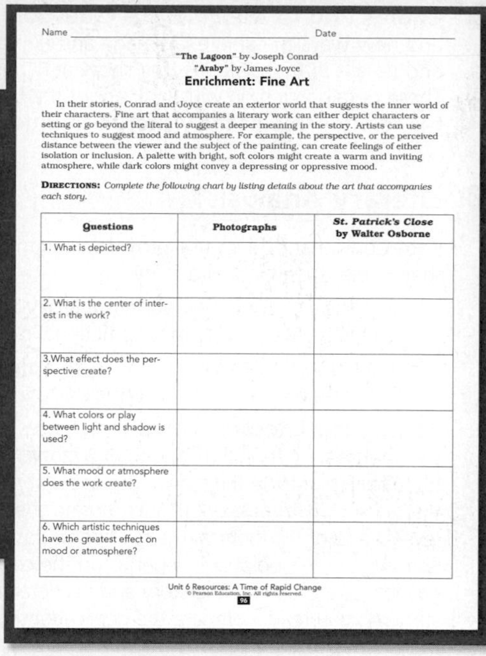

Name ______________________ Date ____________

"The Lagoon" by Joseph Conrad
"Araby" by James Joyce

Enrichment: Fine Art

In their stories, Conrad and Joyce create an exterior world that suggests the inner world of their characters. Fine art that accompanies a literary work can either depict characters or setting or go beyond the literal to suggest a deeper meaning in the story. Artists can use techniques to suggest mood and atmosphere. For example, the perspective, or the perceived distance between the viewer and the subject of the painting, can create feelings of either isolation or inclusion. A palette with bright, soft colors might create a warm and inviting atmosphere, while dark colors might convey a depressing or oppressive mood.

Directions: *Complete the following chart by listing details about the art that accompanies each story.*

Questions	Photographs	*St. Patrick's Close* by Walter Osborne
1. What is depicted?		
2. What is the center of interest in the work?		
3.What effect does the perspective create?		
4. What colors or play between light and shadow is used?		
5. What mood or atmosphere does the work create?		
6. Which artistic techniques have the greatest effect on mood or atmosphere?		

Unit 6 Resources: A Time of Rapid Change

96

L4 **Enrichment,** p. 96

Also available for these selections:

All **Literary Analysis: Plot Devices,** p. 92

All **Reading: Identify Cause-and-Effect Relationships,** p. 93

EL L3 L4 **Support for Writing,** p. 95

Assessment

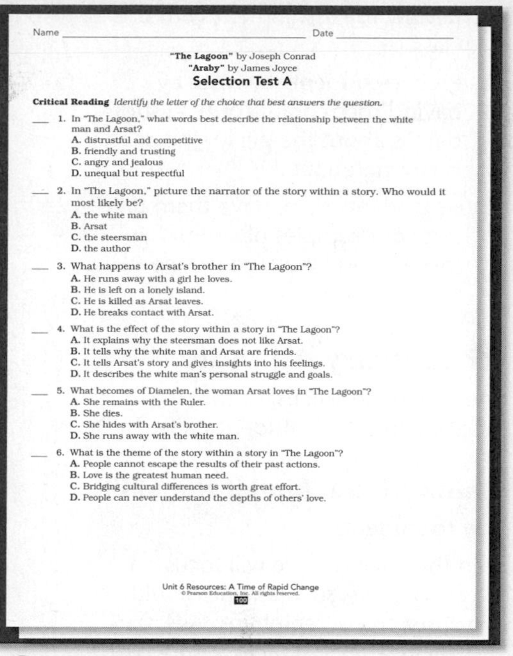

Name ______________________ Date ____________

"The Lagoon" by Joseph Conrad
"Araby" by James Joyce

Selection Test A

Critical Reading *Identify the letter of the choice that best answers the question.*

___ 1. In "The Lagoon," what words best describe the relationship between the white man and Arsat?
A. distrustful and competitive
B. friendly and trusting
C. angry and jealous
D. unequal but respectful

___ 2. In "The Lagoon," picture the narrator of the story within a story. Who would it most likely be?
A. the white man
B. Arsat
C. the steersman
D. the author

___ 3. What happens to Arsat's brother in "The Lagoon"?
A. He runs away with a girl he loves.
B. He is left on a lonely island.
C. He is killed as Arsat leaves.
D. He breaks contact with Arsat.

___ 4. What is the effect of the story within a story in "The Lagoon"?
A. It explains why the steersman does not like Arsat.
B. It tells why the white man and Arsat are friends.
C. It tells Arsat's story and gives insights into his feelings.
D. It describes the white man's personal struggle and goals.

___ 5. What becomes of Diamelen, the woman Arsat loves in "The Lagoon"?
A. She remains with the Ruler.
B. She dies.
C. She hides with Arsat's brother.
D. She runs away with the white man.

___ 6. What is the theme of the story within a story in "The Lagoon"?
A. People cannot escape the results of their past actions.
B. Love is the greatest human need.
C. Bridging cultural differences is worth great effort.
D. People can never understand the depths of others' love.

Unit 6 Resources: A Time of Rapid Change

100

EL L1 L2 **Selection Test A,** pp. 100–102

Also available for these selections:

L3 L4 **Open-Book Test,** pp. 97–99

EL L3 L4 **Selection Test B,** pp. 103–105

PHLit Online!
www.PHLitOnline.com

- complete narrated selection text
- a thematically related video with writing prompt
- an interactive graphic organizer
- highlighting feature
- access to all student print resources, adapted to individual student needs
- Spanish and English summaries
- adapted selection translations in Spanish

Online Resources: All print materials are also available online.

Background Video

Also available:

Get Connected! (thematic video with writing prompt)
All videos are available in Spanish.

Vocabulary Central (tools and activities for studying vocabulary)

Also available:

Writer's Journal (with graphics feature)

❶ Connecting to the Essential Question

1. Review the assignment with the class.
2. Prepare students to write by having them brainstorm a list of details about the person he or she is writing about.
3. As students read, have them take note of examples of Conrad and Joyce using language in a new way.

❷ Literary Analysis

Introduce the skill using the instruction on the student page.

Think Aloud: Model the Skill

Say to students:

In these stories, we will focus on plot devices, such as a story within a story and an epiphany. As I read, I will look for instances where plot devices tie in with the author's theme. For example, in "The Lagoon," a character tells another character a story about betrayal. The story of one brother's betrayal of another relates to the betrayal of one friend who is unable to help another.

❸ Reading Strategy

1. Introduce the skill using the instruction on the student page.
2. Give students a copy of **Reading Strategy Graphic Organizer B,** page 219 in ***Graphic Organizer Transparencies,*** to fill out as they read.

Think Aloud Model the Skill

Say to students:

Looking for causes and effects in a story can help me better understand the plot. For example, in "Araby," the narrator's love for his friend's sister causes him to want to go to the bazaar. This event leads to the climax of the story and the narrator's epiphany.

❹ Vocabulary

1. Pronounce each word, giving its definition, and have students say it aloud.
2. For more guidance, see the ***Classroom Strategies and Teaching Routines*** card for introducing vocabulary.

Before You Read *The Lagoon • Araby*

Common Core State Standards

Reading Literature
5. Analyze how an author's choices regarding how to structure specific parts of a text contribute to its overall structure and meaning as well as its aesthetic impact.

❶ **Connecting to the Essential Question** Conrad and Joyce tried to find new ways to explore language and human relationships. As you read, find details in these stories that show new approaches to storytelling. These details will help you think about the Essential Question: **What is the relationship of the writer to tradition?**

❷ Literary Analysis

Both Conrad and Joyce use **plot devices** to achieve aesthetic effects as they relate the events of a story.

- In "The Lagoon," Conrad tells a **story within a story**—a tale told by a character within a framing fictional narrative.
- In "Araby," Joyce builds toward an **epiphany**—a character's sudden insight—which forms the climax of the story.

Comparing Literary Works Plot devices have a close connection with the **themes,** or central meaning, of a story. "The Lagoon" is told by a neutral narrator outside the story—but the story within this story is told in the first person, with passion. By juxtaposing these two points of view, Conrad reveals one of his themes: the relation of passion to the act of storytelling. Similarly, Joyce's epiphany depends on the contrast between the narrator's passion at the time of the story and his detachment later, when he tells the story. As you read, compare the implications that these plot devices have for the themes of the stories in which they are used.

❸ Reading Strategy

Preparing to Read Complex Texts Plots are a sequence of causally connected events. That is, one event usually causes another, which in turn triggers yet another effect. The sequence continues until the action closes. **Identifying cause-and-effect relationships** in a plot can help you understand the author's themes. As you read, use a graphic organizer like the one shown.

Cause
Man travels to a hidden, eerie jungle location.

↓

Effect and Cause
Arsat narrates a story of loss and sorrow.

↓

Effect

❹ Vocabulary

invincible (in vin′ sə bəl) *adj.* unconquerable (p. 1222)

propitiate (prō pish′ ē āt) *v.* win the goodwill of; appease (p. 1222)

conflagration (kän′ flə grā′ shən) *n.* great fire (p. 1224)

imperturbable (im′ pər tur′ bə bəl) *adj.* calm; not easily ruffled (p. 1237)

garrulous (gar′ ə ləs) *adj.* talkative (p. 1239)

derided (di rīd′ id) *v.* made fun of; ridiculed (p. 1241)

PHLit Online! www.PHLitOnline.com

Vocabulary Development

Vocabulary Knowledge Rating

Create a **Vocabulary Knowledge Rating Chart** (***Professional Development Guidebook,*** p. 33) for the vocabulary words on the student page. Give each student a copy of the chart with the words on it. Read the words aloud, and have students mark their ratings in the Before Reading column. Urge students to attend to these words as they read and discuss the selections.

In order to gauge how much instruction you need to provide, tally how many students are confident in their knowledge of each word. As students read, point out the words and their context.

PHLit Online! **Vocabulary Central,** featuring tools and activities for studying vocabulary, is available online at **www.PHLitOnline.com.**

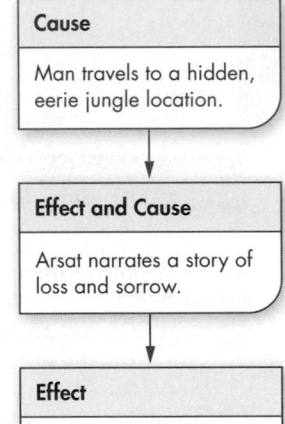

❺ # Joseph Conrad
(1857–1924)

Author of **"The Lagoon"**

It is accomplishment enough to become one of the most distinguished novelists of your age, but to do so in your third language is an achievement almost without parallel. Born in Poland, Joseph Conrad mastered English only after acquiring Polish, his native language, and French.

At Sea in the World Orphaned at the age of eleven, Conrad fled his Russian-occupied homeland when he was sixteen. He landed first in France and later in England. He spent the next six years as an apprentice seaman. The voyages Conrad made to the corners of the globe—Asia, Africa, and South America—became the vivid settings of much of his fiction. In 1886, he became a master mariner and an English citizen.

A Storytelling Life Conrad published his first novel, *Almayer's Folly,* when he was in his late thirties. Three masterpieces followed: *Lord Jim* (1900); *Youth,* a collection of shorter pieces that includes his famous short story "Heart of Darkness" (1902); and *Nostromo* (1904).

Although many of Conrad's works may be read as thrilling tales of the sea, the notion of "voyage" in a work by Conrad translates to a voyage of self-discovery. The question of loyalty, so crucial for the survival of a ship's crew, appears as a question of the general frailty of human relationships and the limits of self-knowledge. The menacing jungles, vast oceans, and exotic people that confront the characters become metaphors for the hidden depths of the self. Telling tales set around the globe, Conrad charts a geography of the human soul.

Daily Bellringer

For each class during which you will teach these selections, have students complete one of the five activities for the appropriate week in the ***Daily Bellringer Activities*** booklet.

Multidraft Reading

To assist struggling readers and to enhance reading for all, assign the text in chunks, as warranted by length, and apply multidraft reading protocols. For each reading, have students set the purpose indicated:

- **First reading**—identifying key ideas and details and answering any Reading Checks.
- **Second reading**—analyzing craft and structure and responding to the side-column prompts.
- **Third reading**—integrating knowledge and ideas, connecting to other texts and the world, and answering the end-of-selection questions.

For more guidance, refer to the ***Classroom Strategies and Teaching Routines*** card on Multidraft Reading.

❺ Background

More About the Author

Joseph Conrad's given name was Jozef Teodor Konrad Korzeniowski. His work was generally panned by critics and the public, and he suffered financial problems for most of his adult life. The 1913 publication of his novel *Chance* brought Conrad his first popular and financial success. By the time of his death, he was considered one of the leading Modernists.

PHLit Online!
www.PHLitOnline.com

Teaching From Technology

Preparing to Read

Go to **www.PHLitOnline.com** and display the ***Get Connected!*** slide show for this selection. Have the class brainstorm responses to the writing prompt, entering ideas in the interactive journal. Then, have students complete their written responses as homework.

To build background, display the Background and More About the Author features.

Using the Interactive Text

Go to **www.PHLitOnline.com** and display the **Enriched Online Student Edition.** As the class reads the selection or listens to the narration, record answers to side-column prompts using the graphic organizers accessible on the interactive page. Alternatively, have students use the online edition individually, answering the prompts as they read.

❶ About the Selection

Two old comrades—a Malay and a European—meet near a Malaysian lagoon. As his beloved lies dying inside the hut, Arsat, the Malay, tells how he betrayed his own brother, impelled by passion for the woman now dying. In leaving Arsat to his misery, the European seems to commit a betrayal as well.

❷ Activating Prior Knowledge

Before assigning "The Lagoon" or "Araby," play the Carly Simon song "Anticipation." Then, have students think back to something they eagerly anticipated, such as a vacation or a special event. Have them share their recollections about which was better: the event itself or the buildup to it. Then, tell students that in "The Lagoon" and "Araby," the main characters' sense of anticipation plays a key role.

Concept Connector →

Tell students they will return to their responses at the end of the selection.

❶ ❷ THE LAGOON

Joseph Conrad

BACKGROUND Between 1883 and 1888, Conrad sailed the Malay Archipelago—a group of Pacific islands that includes the Philippines and Indonesia—in British merchant ships. He used the knowledge he acquired of the region—of its language, landscape, and customs—to enrich his seafaring tales. It is likely that Captain William Lingard, revered as a spellbinding storyteller among sailors of the Malay settlements, was the model for Marlowe, who appears as the narrator of several Conrad stories.

The white man, leaning with both arms over the roof of the little house in the stern of the boat, said to the steersman—

"We will pass the night in Arsat's clearing. It is late."

The Malay[1] only grunted, and went on looking fixedly at the river. The white man rested his chin on his crossed arms and gazed at the wake of the boat. At the end of the straight avenue of forests cut by the intense glitter of the river, the sun appeared unclouded and dazzling, poised low over the water that shone smoothly like a band of metal. The forests, somber and dull, stood motionless and silent on each side of the broad stream. At the foot of big, towering trees trunkless nipa palms rose from the mud of the bank, in bunches of leaves enormous and heavy, that hung unstirring over the brown swirl of eddies. In the stillness of the air every tree, every leaf, every bough, every tendril of creeper and every petal of minute blossoms seemed to have been bewitched into an immobility perfect and final. Nothing moved on the river but the eight paddles that rose flashing regularly, dipped together with a single splash; while the steersman swept right and left with a periodic and sudden flourish of his blade describing a glinting semicircle above his head. The churned-up water frothed alongside with a confused murmur. And the white man's canoe, advancing up stream in the short-lived disturbance of its own making,

1. **Malay** (mā′ lā) native of the Malay peninsula in Southeast Asia.

Text Complexity Rubric

	The Lagoon	Araby
Qualitative Measures		
Context/ Knowledge Demands	Modernist story; cultural knowledge demands 1 2 3 (4) 5	Modernist story; cultural knowledge demands 1 (2) 3 4 5
Structure/Language Conventionality and Clarity	Long sentences; poetic diction 1 2 (3) 4 5	Stream-of-consciousness structure; Irish regionalisms 1 (2) 3 4 5
Levels of Meaning/ Purpose/Concept Level	Challenging (betrayal; life's illusions) 1 2 3 (4) 5	Moderate (come-of-age anguish; life's illusions) 1 2 (3) 4 5
Quantitative Measures		
Lexile/Text Length	1000L / 5,573 words	940L / 2,335 words
Overall Complexity	**More complex**	**More accessible**

seemed to enter the portals[2] of a land from which the very memory of motion had forever departed.

The white man, turning his back upon the setting sun, looked along the empty and broad expanse of the sea-reach. For the last three miles of its course the wandering, hesitating river, as if enticed irresistibly by the freedom of an open horizon, flows straight into the sea, flows straight to the east—to the east that harbors both light and darkness. Astern of the boat the repeated call of some bird, a cry discordant and feeble, skipped along over the smooth water and lost itself, before it could reach the other shore, in the breathless silence of the world.

The steersman dug his paddle into the stream, and held hard with stiffened arms, his body thrown forward. The water gurgled aloud; and suddenly the long straight reach seemed to pivot on its center, the forests swung in a semicircle, and the slanting beams of sunset touched the broadside of the canoe with a fiery glow, throwing the slender and distorted shadows of its crew upon the streaked glitter of the river. The white man turned to look ahead. The course of the boat had been altered at right-angles to the stream, and the carved dragonhead of its prow was pointing now at a gap in the fringing bushes of the bank. It glided through, brushing the overhanging twigs, and disappeared from the river like some slim and amphibious creature leaving the water for its lair in the forests.

2. **portals** (pôr təlz) *n.* doors.

3 ▲ **Critical Viewing**
Judging from this photograph, would it be difficult to escape from an enemy in jungle territory? Why or why not?
[Make a Judgment]

4 **Reading Check**
What is the white man's destination?

3 Critical Viewing

Answer: Students may say that the thick foliage, dark shadows, and wide waterways would probably make escape possible for someone well acquainted with that region.

4 Reading Check

Answer: The man's destination is Arsat's lagoon.

PHLit Online!

This selection is available in interactive format in the **Enriched Online Student Edition** at **www.PHLitOnline.com**, which includes a thematically related video with writing prompt and an interactive graphic organizer.

Text Complexity: Reader and Task Suggestions

The Lagoon		Araby	
Preparing to Read the Text	**Leveled Tasks**	**Preparing to Read the Text**	**Leveled Tasks**
• Using the information on p. 1219 of the student text, discuss the isolation that a sailor experiences at sea. • Discuss with students the topic of loyalty and betrayal. Ask: Has the meaning of these terms changed over time? • Guide students to use Multidraft Reading strategies (TE p. 1219).	***Levels of Meaning*** If students will have difficulty with the levels of meaning, have them first focus on Arsat's present situation and past relationship with his brother. Then, as students reread, have them look for parallels in the European's treatment of Arsat. ***Analyzing*** If students will not have difficulty with the story's meaning, have them analyze the significance of the lagoon setting to the story's plot and themes.	• Using the information at the bottom of TE p. 1236, help clarify the religious ideas and symbols Joyce uses in his writing. • Discuss with students the false illusions that young people may have about romantic relationships. • Guide students to use Multidraft Reading strategies (TE p. 1219).	***Levels of Meaning*** If students will have difficulty with the levels of meaning, have them read first to determine the narrator's feelings about the bazaar. Then, have students reread, tracing ideas and details that lead to the epiphany. ***Evaluating*** If students will not have difficulty with the story's meaning, have them evaluate how realistically he captures the narrator's character and builds to the epiphany.

❺ Reading Strategy

Identifying Cause-and-Effect Relationships

1. Tell students to remain aware of causes and effects as they read.
2. Then, **ask** them the Reading Strategy question: Why is the boat coming to Arsat's? What is the reaction of the Malays to coming here?
   Answer: The boat is coming to Arsat's to pass the night. The Malays are dismayed by this, because they do not like or trust Arsat.

The narrow creek was like a ditch: tortuous, fabulously deep; filled with gloom under the thin strip of pure and shining blue of the heaven. Immense trees soared up, invisible behind the festooned draperies of creepers. Here and there, near the glistening blackness of the water, a twisted root of some tall tree showed amongst the tracery of small ferns, black and dull, writhing and motionless, like an arrested snake. The short words of the paddlers reverberated loudly between the thick and somber walls of vegetation. Darkness oozed out from between the trees, through the tangled maze of the creepers, from behind the great fantastic and unstirring leaves; the darkness, mysterious and **invincible**; the darkness scented and poisonous of impenetrable forests.

Vocabulary
invincible (in vin´ sə bəl) *adj.* unconquerable

The men poled in the shoaling[3] water. The creek broadened, opening out into a wide sweep of a stagnant lagoon. The forests receded from the marshy bank, leaving a level strip of bright green, reedy grass to frame the reflected blueness of the sky. A fleecy pink cloud drifted high above, trailing the delicate coloring of its image under the floating leaves and the silvery blossoms of the lotus. A little house, perched on high piles, appeared black in the distance. Near it, two tall nibong palms, that seemed to have come out of the forests in the background, leaned slightly over the ragged roof, with a suggestion of sad tenderness and care in the droop of their leafy and soaring heads.

The steersman, pointing with his paddle, said, "Arsat is there. I see his canoe fast between the piles."

Reading Strategy
Identifying Cause-and-Effect Relationships
Why is the boat coming to Arsat's? What is the reaction of the Malays to coming here?

❺

The polers ran along the sides of the boat glancing over their shoulders at the end of the day's journey. They would have preferred to spend the night somewhere else than on this lagoon of weird aspect and ghostly reputation. Moreover, they disliked Arsat, first as a stranger, and also because he who repairs a ruined house, and dwells in it, proclaims that he is not afraid to live amongst the spirits that haunt the places abandoned by mankind. Such a man can disturb the course of fate by glances or words; while his familiar ghosts are not easy to **propitiate** by casual wayfarers upon whom they long to wreak the malice of their human master. White men care not for such things, being unbelievers and in league with the Father of Evil, who leads them unharmed through the invisible dangers of this world. To the warnings of the righteous they oppose an offensive pretense of disbelief. What is there to be done?

Vocabulary
propitiate (pro pish´ ē āt´) *v.* win the good will of; appease

So they thought, throwing their weight on the end of their long poles. The big canoe glided on swiftly, noiselessly, and smoothly, toward Arsat's clearing, till, in a great rattling of poles thrown down, and the loud murmurs of "Allah[4] be praised!" it came with a gentle knock against the crooked piles below the house.

3. **shoaling** shallow.
4. **Allah** (al´ ə) Muslim name for God.

Enrichment: Investigating Geography

The British Empire

Write this saying on the chalkboard: "The sun never sets on the British Empire." Explain that at one time, the British Empire was so large that it extended to all parts of the globe, including North, Central, and South America; the Caribbean; the Middle East; Asia; Africa; and the South Pacific.

Point out that Malaysia, where this story is set, was a British colony. Invite students to select Malaysia or another country that was once a British colony. Challenge them to find out about Britain's colonization in those areas and the process by which the regions gained independence.

Activity: Create a Map of a Former Colony Encourage interested students to create maps of the colonies they researched. Suggest that they use the **Enrichment: Investigating Geography** worksheet, ***Professional Development Guidebook***, page 228, to help them complete their maps.

The boatmen with uplifted faces shouted discordantly, "Arsat! O Arsat!" Nobody came. The white man began to climb the rude ladder giving access to the bamboo platform before the house. The juragan[5] of the boat said sulkily, "We will cook in the sampan,[6] and sleep on the water."

"Pass my blankets and the basket," said the white man curtly.

He knelt on the edge of the platform to receive the bundle. Then the boat shoved off, and the white man, standing up, confronted Arsat, who had come out through the low door of his hut. He was a man young, powerful, with a broad chest and muscular arms. He had nothing on but his sarong.[7] His head was bare. His big, soft eyes stared eagerly at the white man, but his voice and demeanor were composed as he asked, without any words of greeting—

"Have you medicine, Tuan?"[8]

"No," said the visitor in a startled tone. "No. Why? Is there sickness in the house?"

"Enter and see," replied Arsat, in the same calm manner, and turning short round, passed again through the small doorway. The white man, dropping his bundles, followed.

In the dim light of the dwelling he made out on a couch of bamboos a woman stretched on her back under a broad sheet of red cotton cloth. She lay still, as if dead; but her big eyes, wide open, glittered in the gloom, staring upward at the slender rafters, motionless and unseeing. She was in a high fever, and evidently unconscious. Her cheeks were sunk slightly, her lips were partly open, and on the young face there was the ominous and fixed expression—the absorbed, contemplating expression of the unconscious who are going to die. The two men stood looking down at her in silence.

"Has she been long ill?" asked the traveler.

"I have not slept for five nights," answered the Malay, in a deliberate tone. "At first she heard voices calling her from the water and struggled against me who held her. But since the sun of today rose she hears nothing—she hears not me. She sees nothing. She sees not me—me!"

6 Reading Check

What is wrong in Arsat's house?

5. juragan (jo͞o rä´ gän) captain or master.
6. sampan small flat-bottomed boat with a cabin formed by mats.
7. sarong long, brightly colored strip of cloth worn like a skirt.
8. Tuan (twan) Malayan for "sir."

SHE LAY STILL
AS IF DEAD...
1223

6 Reading Check

Answer: A woman in Arsat's house is feverish and may die.

Differentiated Instruction for Universal Access

Support for Special-Needs Students

Have students read portions of "The Lagoon" with teacher guidance. Some students may have difficulty understanding the Malay words that Conrad intersperses to heighten the realism of his tale. Remind students that many stories and legends use the language of the milieu to set the scene. Encourage them to look up any words they do not know or to refer to the footnotes.

Support for Less Proficient Readers

Students may find that the exotic setting of Conrad's story "The Lagoon" is sufficiently foreign that they cannot fully enter it. For these students, consider locating a short documentary at a local library that focuses on life in a tropical island setting. Ask students to identify scenes that may remind them of passages in "The Lagoon."

❼ Literary Analysis

Plot Devices

1. Remind students of the various kinds of plot devices Conrad uses to enhance the story.
2. Then, **ask** students the Literary Analysis question: Is the narrator of the story closer in point of view to the white man or Arsat? Explain.
   Possible response: Students may say that the narrator is closer to the white man; his description of the man's affection for Arsat is likened to feelings about a favorite dog.

He remained silent for a minute, then asked softly—

"Tuan, will she die?"

"I fear so," said the white man sorrowfully. He had known Arsat years ago, in a far country in times of trouble and danger, when no friendship is to be despised. And since his Malay friend had come unexpectedly to dwell in the hut on the lagoon with a strange woman, he had slept many times there, in his journeys up and down the river. He liked the man who knew how to keep faith in council and how to fight without fear by the side of his white friend. He liked him—not so much perhaps as a man likes his favorite dog—but still he liked him well enough to help and ask no questions, to think sometimes vaguely and hazily in the midst of his own pursuits, about the lonely man and the long-haired woman with audacious face and triumphant eyes, who lived together by the forests—alone and feared.

Literary Analysis ❼
Plot Devices Is the narrator of the story closer in point of view to the white man or Arsat? Explain.

Vocabulary
conflagration (kän′ flə grā′ shən) *n.* great fire

The white man came out of the hut in time to see the enormous **conflagration** of sunset put out by the swift and stealthy shadows that, rising like a black and impalpable vapor above the treetops, spread over the heaven, extinguishing the crimson glow of floating clouds and the red brilliance of departing daylight. In a few moments all the stars came out above the intense blackness of the earth, and the great lagoon gleaming suddenly with reflected lights resembled an oval patch of night sky flung down into the hopeless and abysmal night of the wilderness. The white man had some supper out of the basket, then collecting a few sticks that lay about the platform, made up a small fire, not for warmth, but for the sake of the smoke, which would keep off the mosquitos. He wrapped himself in his blankets and sat with his back against the reed wall of the house, smoking thoughtfully.

Arsat came through the doorway with noiseless steps and squatted down by the fire. The white man moved his outstretched legs a little.

"She breathes," said Arsat in a low voice, anticipating the expected question. "She breathes and burns as if with a great fire. She speaks not; she hears not—and burns!" He paused for a moment, then asked in a quiet, incurious tone—

"Tuan . . . will she die?"

The white man moved his shoulders uneasily, and muttered in a hesitating manner—

"If such is her fate."

"No, Tuan," said Arsat calmly. "If such is my fate. I hear, I see, I wait. I remember . . . Tuan, do you remember the old days? Do you remember my brother?"

"Yes," said the white man. The Malay rose suddenly and went in.

Enrichment: Investigating Artistic Schools and Movements

Impressionism
Conrad is sometimes termed an Impressionistic writer because he seeks to capture the atmosphere and texture of reality as well as the complexity of subjective experience. Originally, the term *Impressionism* was applied to the work of a group of nineteenth-century painters in Paris. These painters tried to show in their paintings impressions gained from direct observation of nature, rather than precise representations.

Activity: Learn More About Impressionism
Encourage interested students to research to find out more about Impressionism. Suggest that they record their findings on the **Enrichment: Investigating Artistic Schools and Movements** worksheet, ***Professional Development Guidebook,*** page 220.

The other, sitting still outside, could hear the voice in the hut. Arsat said: "Hear me! Speak!" His words were succeeded by a complete silence. "O Diamelen!" he cried suddenly. After that cry there was a deep sigh. Arsat came out and sank down again in his old place.

They sat in silence before the fire. There was no sound within the house, there was no sound near them; but far away on the lagoon they could hear the voices of the boatmen ringing fitful and distinct on the calm water. The fire in the bows of the sampan shone faintly in the distance with a hazy red glow. Then it died out. The voices ceased. The land and the water slept invisible, unstirring and mute. It was as though there had been nothing left in the world but the glitter of stars streaming, ceaseless and vain, through the black stillness of the night.

The white man gazed straight before him into the darkness with wide-open eyes. The fear and fascination, the inspiration and the wonder of death—of death near, unavoidable, and unseen, soothed the unrest of his race and stirred the most indistinct, the most intimate of his thoughts. The ever-ready suspicion of evil, the gnawing suspicion that lurks in our hearts, flowed out into the stillness round him—into the stillness profound and dumb, and made it appear untrustworthy and infamous, like the placid and impenetrable mask of an unjustifiable violence. In that fleeting and powerful disturbance of his being the earth enfolded in the starlight peace became a shadowy country of inhuman strife, a battlefield of phantoms terrible and charming, august[9] or ignoble[10], struggling ardently for the possession of our helpless hearts. An unquiet and mysterious country of inextinguishable desires and fears.

A plaintive murmur rose in the night; a murmur saddening and startling, as if the great solitudes of surrounding woods had tried to whisper into his ear the wisdom of their immense and lofty indifference. Sounds hesitating and vague floated in the air round him, shaped themselves slowly into words; and at last flowed on gently in a murmuring stream of soft and monotonous sentences. He stirred like a man waking up and changed his position slightly. Arsat, motionless and shadowy, sitting with bowed head under the stars, was speaking in a low and dreamy tone—

". . . for where can we lay down the heaviness of our trouble but in a friend's heart? A man must speak of war and of love. You, Tuan, know what war is, and you have seen me in time of danger seek death as other men seek life! A writing may be lost; a lie may be written; but what the eye has seen is truth and remains in the mind!"

8 Reading Strategy
Identifying Cause-and-Effect Relationships
What causes Arsat to speak to the white man?

9 Reading Check
What does Arsat tell Tuan about the woman's health?

9. **august** (ô gust′) *adj.* worthy of great respect; inspiring awe.
10. **ignoble** (ig nō′ bəl) *adj.* of the common people; dishonorable.

8 Reading Strategy
Identifying Cause-and-Effect Relationships

1. Have students review what they know about Arsat. **Ask:** What is Arsat's situation?
   Answer: He is alone, but for the woman in his house, who is very sick. At first she had delusions, but now she is unresponsive and feverish.
2. **Ask** students to speculate how Arsat is feeling.
   Answer: He is filled with worry about the woman's poor health, and he is physically drained from not sleeping in five nights.
3. Then, **ask** students the Reading Strategy Question: What causes Arsat to speak to the white man?
   Answer: His emotional stress over the woman's illness leads him to share his situation with the white man.

9 Reading Check
Answer: She is feverish and does not speak.

Differentiated Instruction for Universal Access

Support for Special-Needs Students
Some students may find the progress of Conrad's account difficult to follow because of its use of poetic effects such as alliteration, assonance, and consonance. Encourage students to read chorally in small groups to help them understand the language of the story.

Support for Less Proficient Readers
As students continue to read "The Lagoon" with teacher guidance, remind them that Conrad uses many plot devices to keep the attention of his reader. Ask students to note these plot devices as they read.

Enrichment for Gifted/Talented Students
In "The Lagoon," Arsat shares his story. Ask students to recall or invent an occasion on which a friend took them into his or her confidence and shared a problem. Have students describe in several paragraphs the emotions they experienced.

⑩ Literary Analysis

Plot Devices

1. Review with students how point of view can alter the interpretation of a passage.
2. Then, **ask** students the Literary Analysis question: What shift in point of view alerts you to the fact that a story within a story begins here?

Answer: Students should recognize Arsat's line "Therefore I shall speak to you of love" as an indication that a story within a story is about to begin. The pause that follows his remark and precedes the story marks a shift in narration.

Spiral Review

Character

1. Remind students that they studied character in an earlier lesson.
2. **Ask** students the Spiral Review question.

Possible response: The strong emotion in Arsat's speech implies even more than his words that the "one who is dying" made everything else in his world seem unimportant.

"I remember," said the white man quietly. Arsat went on with mournful composure—

Literary Analysis
Plot Devices What shift in point of view alerts you to the fact that a story within a story begins here? ⑩

"Therefore I shall speak to you of love. Speak in the night. Speak before both night and love are gone—and the eye of day looks upon my sorrow and my shame; upon my blackened face; upon my burnt-up heart."

A sigh, short and faint, marked an almost imperceptible pause, and then his words flowed on, without a stir, without a gesture.

"After the time of trouble and war was over and you went away from my country in the pursuit of your desires, which we, men of the islands, cannot understand, I and my brother became again, as we had been before, the sword bearers of the Ruler. You know we were men of family, belonging to a ruling race, and more fit than any to carry on our right shoulder the emblem of power. And in the time of prosperity Si Dendring showed us favor, as we, in time of sorrow, had showed to him the faithfulness of our courage. It was a time of peace. A time of deer hunts and cock fights; of idle talks and foolish squabbles between men whose bellies are full and weapons are rusty. But the sower watched the young rice shoots grow up without fear, and the traders came and went, departed lean and returned fat into the river of peace. They brought news too. Brought lies and truth mixed together, so that no man knew when to rejoice and when to be sorry. We heard from them about you also. They had seen you here and had seen you there. And I was glad to hear, for I remembered the stirring times, and I always remembered you, Tuan, till the time came when my eyes could see nothing in the past, because they had looked upon the one who is dying there—in the house."

Spiral Review
Character What inferences can you make about the way "the one who is dying" affected Arsat's relation to his world?

He stopped to exclaim in an intense whisper, "O Mara bahia! O Calamity!" then went on speaking a little louder.

"There's no worse enemy and no better friend than a brother, Tuan, for one brother knows another, and in perfect knowledge is strength for good or evil. I loved my brother. I went to him and told him that I could see nothing but one face, hear nothing but one voice. He told me: 'Open your heart so that she can see what is in it—and wait. Patience is wisdom. Inchi Midah may die or our Ruler may throw off his fear of a woman!'. . . I waited!. . . You remember the lady with the veiled face, Tuan, and the fear of our Ruler before her cunning and temper. And if she wanted her servant, what could I do?

Enrichment: Investigating Culture

Malay

Tuan is a Malay term of respect. The term *tuan* was probably used to describe Captain William Lingard, a local hero at the time Conrad sailed through Malaysia. According to Conrad's biographer, Frederick Karl, Lingard was also known as "Rajah Laut" or "King of the Sea" for his ". . . shrewdness as a trader, daring as a contender with sea pirates for routes and goods, and expertise as a handler of sailing vessels." Men like Arsat probably worked with and fought beside Lingard in a number of his daring adventures.

Activity: Learn More About Malay Culture Encourage interested students to research to find out more about traditional Malay culture. Suggest that they record their findings on the **Enrichment: Investigating Culture** worksheet, ***Professional Development Guidebook,*** page 223.

But I fed the hunger of my heart on short glances and stealthy words. I loitered on the path to the bath houses in the daytime, and when the sun had fallen behind the forest I crept along the jasmine hedges of the women's courtyard. Unseeing, we spoke to one another through the scent of flowers, through the veil of leaves, through the blades of long grass that stood still before our lips; so great was our prudence, so faint was the murmur of our great longing. The time passed swiftly . . . and there were whispers amongst women—and our enemies watched—my brother was gloomy, and I began to think of killing and of a fierce death. . . . We are of a people who take what they want—like you whites. There is a time when a man should forget loyalty and respect. Might and authority are given to rulers, but to all men is given love and strength and courage. My brother said, 'You shall take her from their midst. We are two who are like one.' And I answered, 'Let it be soon, for I find no warmth in sunlight that does not shine upon her.' Our time came when the Ruler and all the great people went to the mouth of the river to fish by torchlight. There were hundreds of boats, and on the white sand, between the water and the forests, dwellings of leaves were built for the households of the Rajahs.[11] The smoke of cooking fires was like a blue mist of the evening, and many voices rang in it joyfully. While they were making the boats ready to beat up the fish, my brother came to me and said, 'Tonight!' I looked to my weapons, and when the time came our canoe took its place in the circle of boats carrying the torches. The lights blazed on the water, but behind the boats there was darkness. When the shouting began and the excitement made them like mad we dropped out. The water swallowed our fire, and we floated back to the shore that was dark with only here and there the glimmer of embers. We could hear the talk of slave girls amongst the sheds. Then we found a place deserted and silent. We waited there. She came. She came running along the shore, rapid and leaving no trace, like a leaf driven by the wind into the sea. My brother said gloomily, 'Go and take her; carry her into our boat.' I lifted her in my arms. She panted. Her heart was beating against my breast. I said, 'I take you from those people. You came to the cry of my heart, but my arms take you into my boat against the will of the great!' 'It is right,' said my brother. 'We are men who take what we want and can hold it against many. We should have taken her in daylight.' I said, 'Let us be off'; for since she was in my boat I began to think of our Ruler's many men.

11. **Rajahs** (rä′ jəz) Malayan chiefs.

11 Reading Strategy
Identifying Cause-and-Effect Relationships What causes Arsat to speak to the woman? What is the result of that action?

12

Reading Check
What do Arsat and his brother decide to do?

"LET IT BE SOON, FOR I FIND NO WARMTH IN SUNLIGHT THAT **DOES NOT SHINE UPON HER.**"

11 Reading Strategy

Identifying Cause-and-Effect Relationships

1. Have students identify and record causes and effects on page 1227.
2. Then, **ask** them the Reading Strategy question: What causes Arsat to speak to the woman? What is the result of that action?
   Answer: He speaks to her because he wants to tell her that he loves her. The result is that she says she loves him too, and they decide to run away.

12 Reading Check

Answer: Arsat and his brother decide to help Arsat's beloved escape during a night ceremony.

Differentiated Instruction for Universal Access

Support for Less Proficient Readers
As students read "The Lagoon" with teacher guidance, they may want to consider the character of Arsat in greater depth. Have them write character descriptions of Arsat and describe his appearance, personality, dreams or goals, and regrets or sorrows, based on what he recounts in the story.

Enrichment for Gifted/Talented Students
Some students who read "The Lagoon" may be fascinated by aspects of the account and their visual representation. You may want to direct these students to research the life and body of work of painter Paul Gauguin. He spent a significant portion of his working life in tropical island settings, pushing the boundaries of the day's artistic conventions.

⑬ Reading Strategy

Identifying Cause-and-Effect Relationships

1. Remind students that a character's actions can shape the outcome of a story.
2. Then, **ask** the Reading Strategy question: What is the effect of the brothers' action? What do you think might happen next?
   Answer: They must leave everything behind. Soon they will be pursued by people who were once their friends.

⑭ Literary Analysis

Plot Devices

1. Have students consider why Arsat pauses during his story.
2. Then, **ask** the Literary Analysis question: What do the pauses in Arsat's story indicate to the white man and the reader about Arsat's emotional state?
   Answer: Arsat's pauses seem to occur at parts of the story that affect his present emotions concerning Diamelen. They heighten the suspense.

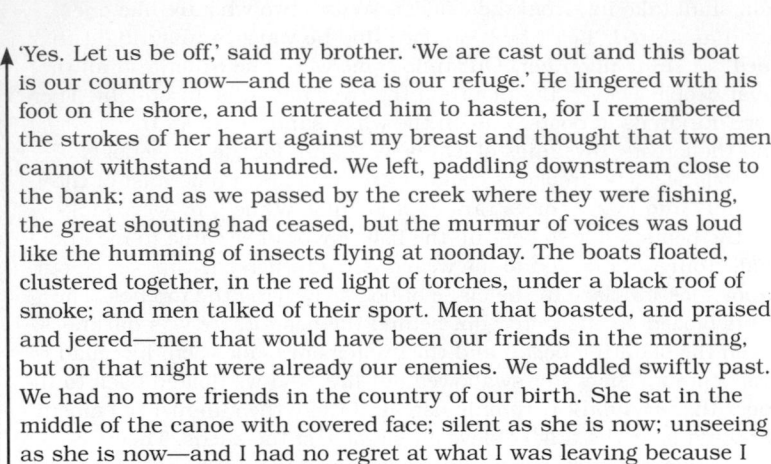

'Yes. Let us be off,' said my brother. 'We are cast out and this boat is our country now—and the sea is our refuge.' He lingered with his foot on the shore, and I entreated him to hasten, for I remembered the strokes of her heart against my breast and thought that two men cannot withstand a hundred. We left, paddling downstream close to the bank; and as we passed by the creek where they were fishing, the great shouting had ceased, but the murmur of voices was loud like the humming of insects flying at noonday. The boats floated, clustered together, in the red light of torches, under a black roof of smoke; and men talked of their sport. Men that boasted, and praised, and jeered—men that would have been our friends in the morning, but on that night were already our enemies. We paddled swiftly past. We had no more friends in the country of our birth. She sat in the middle of the canoe with covered face; silent as she is now; unseeing as she is now—and I had no regret at what I was leaving because I could hear her breathing close to me—as I can hear her now." ⑬

He paused, listened with his ear turned to the doorway, then shook his head and went on.

"My brother wanted to shout the cry of challenge—one cry only—to let the people know we were freeborn robbers who trusted our arms and the great sea. And again I begged him in the name of our love to be silent. Could I not hear her breathing close to me? I knew the pursuit would come quick enough. My brother loved me. He dipped his paddle without a splash. He only said, 'There is half a man in you now—the other half is in that woman. I can wait. When you are a whole man again, you will come back with me here to shout defiance. We are sons of the same mother.' I made no answer. All my strength and all my spirit were in my hands that held the paddle—for I longed to be with her in a safe place beyond the reach of men's anger and of women's spite. My love was so great, that I thought it could guide me to a country where death was unknown, ⑭

Reading Strategy
Identifying Cause-and-Effect Relationships What is the effect of the brothers' action? What do you think might happen next?

Literary Analysis
Plot Devices What do the pauses in Arsat's story indicate to the white man and the reader about Arsat's emotional state?

Enrichment: Analyzing Film

A Joseph Conrad Film Festival

There are many films whose ideas come from the writings of Joseph Conrad. Some of the films are fairly literal versions of the literature.

Invite interested students to get together to view some of the available films based on Conrad's writings: *Victory* (1940), *Outcast of the Islands* (1952), *Lord Jim* (1965), and *Heart of Darkness* (1994). However, you should preview films before recommending them or showing them to students.

Activity: Analyze a Film Encourage interested students to choose one of the films listed above and analyze it. Suggest that they record their analyses on the **Enrichment: Analyzing Film** worksheet, ***Professional Development Guidebook***, page 226.

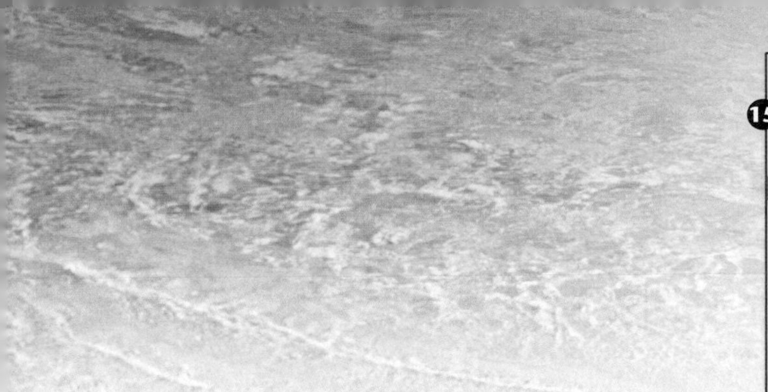

if I could only escape from Inchi Midah's fury and from our Ruler's sword. We paddled with haste, breathing through our teeth. The blades bit deep into the smooth water. We passed out of the river; we flew in clear channels amongst the shallows. We skirted the black coast; we skirted the sand beaches where the sea speaks in whispers to the land; and the gleam of white sand flashed back past our boat, so swiftly she ran upon the water. We spoke not. Only once I said, 'Sleep, Diamelen, for soon you may want all your strength.' I heard the sweetness of her voice, but I never turned my head. The sun rose and still we went on. Water fell from my face like rain from a cloud. We flew in the light and heat. I never looked back, but I knew that my brother's eyes, behind me, were looking steadily ahead, for the boat went as straight as a bushman's dart, when it leaves the end of the sumpitan.[12] There was no better paddler, no better steersman than my brother. Many times, together, we had won races in that canoe. But we never had put out our strength as we did then—then, when for the last time we paddled together! There was no braver or stronger man in our country than my brother. I could not spare the strength to turn my head and look at him, every moment I heard the hiss of his breath getting louder behind me. Still he did not speak. The sun was high. The heat clung to my back like a flame of fire. My ribs were ready to burst, but I could no longer get enough air into my chest. And then I felt I must cry out with my last breath. 'Let us rest!' . . . 'Good!' he answered; and his voice was firm. He was strong. He was brave. He knew not fear and no fatigue . . . My brother!"

12. **sumpitan** (sump´ ə tän) Malayan blowgun that discharges poisonous darts.

15 World LITERATURE Connection

Joseph Conrad, International Author

As a child, Jozeph Konrad Nalecz Korzeniowski (1857-1924) moved between cultures and languages. He was born in Berdichev, a city once part of Poland, that was under Russian rule. Polish was his first language, but he also spoke French and Russian.

When he was eleven, Jozeph was orphaned and went to live with his uncle in Switzerland. There he picked up some Italian and German. At seventeen, he shipped out with the French merchant marine. When he was 29, he earned British citizenship and changed his name to Joseph Conrad. Soon after, he settled in Britain.

Conrad did not begin writing until his early thirties, and when he did, he wrote in English. His first novel, *Almayer's Folly*, was published in 1895. Soon Conrad's fiction was published in French translation too. His work influenced leading French writers including André Gide, Marcel Proust, Louis-Ferdinand Céline, André Malraux, and Jean-Paul Sartre.

Connect to the Literature

What evidence of Conrad's ability to learn languages can you find in "The Lagoon"?

16 Reading Check

Have Arsat, his brother, and Diamelen escaped the Rajah? Explain.

15 World Literature Connection

Joseph Conrad, International Author

Joseph Conrad's facility with languages came from traveling and experiencing different cultures. His time in the French merchant service, which he began at the age of seventeen, brought him to the Venezuelan coast and the Caribbean Islands, when they were still considered the West Indies. When he later served in the British merchant navy, he journeyed to Constantinople (now Istanbul), Bombay (now Mumbai), and areas of the Far East. He recreated many of the destinations he encountered in his writing.

Connect to the Literature

Ask students the Connect to the Literature question: What evidence of Conrad's ability to learn languages can you find in "The Lagoon"?

Answer: Conrad uses many Malay terms in the story, such as *prau*, *sampan*, and *Tuan*.

16 Reading Check

Answer: No; the Rajah has sent a *prau* after them.

Differentiated Instruction for Universal Access

EL Support for English Learners

Have students read portions of "The Lagoon" with teacher guidance. Whenever possible, have them summarize the content of what they have read. Students should be able to articulate the key plot elements, name the main characters, and predict what might happen next.

Enrichment for Gifted/Talented Students

Ask students to assess the ways in which the story Arsat tells in "The Lagoon" seems like a tragedy. Tell students to write brief essays in which they analyze the elements of Arsat's experience, his relationship with his brother, his feelings for Diamelen, and the restrictions on his life.

17 Literary Analysis
Plot Devices

1. Review with students how Conrad's use of a story within a story is an effective plot device.
2. Then, **ask** students the Literary Analysis question: How do the descriptions of the setting in which Arsat tells his tale provide a kind of commentary on his tale? **Answer:** Arsat's story takes place in the blazing heat of the day; the shift to nighttime is identifiable because Conrad describes the starry reflection in the lagoon. The return to the lagoon in the middle of Arsat's story reinforces the concept of isolation—a concept that will become increasingly important in Arsat's tale.

Literary Analysis
Plot Devices How do the descriptions of the setting in which Arsat tells his tale provide a kind of commentary on his tale?

17 A murmur powerful and gentle, a murmur vast and faint; the murmur of trembling leaves, of stirring boughs, ran through the tangled depths of the forests, ran over the starry smoothness of the lagoon, and the water between the piles lapped the slimy timber once with a sudden splash. A breath of warm air touched the two men's faces and passed on with a mournful sound—a breath loud and short like an uneasy sigh of the dreaming earth.

Arsat went on in an even, low voice:

"We ran our canoe on the white beach of a little bay close to a long tongue of land that seemed to bar our road; a long wooded cape going far into the sea. My brother knew that place. Beyond the cape a river has its entrance, and through the jungle of that land there is a narrow path. We made a fire and cooked rice. Then we lay down to sleep on the soft sand in the shade of our canoe, while she watched. No sooner had I closed my eyes than I heard her cry of alarm. We leaped up. The sun was halfway down the sky already, and coming in sight in the opening of the bay we saw a prau[13] manned by many paddlers. We knew it at once; it was one of our Rajah's praus. They were watching the shore, and saw us. They beat the gong, and turned the head of the prau into the bay. I felt my heart become weak within my breast. Diamelen sat on the sand and covered her face. There was no escape by sea. My brother laughed. He had the gun you had given him, Tuan, before you went away, but there was only a handful of

13. **prau** (prou) swift Malayan boat with a large sail.

Think Aloud

Literary Analysis: Plot Devices
To model the process of working out the answer to the Literary Analysis question on the student page, use the following "think aloud." Say to students:

The question asks how the descriptions of the setting in which Arsat tells his tale provide a kind of commentary on his tale. First, I will look to find descriptions of the lagoon. The first paragraph on this page makes the lagoon sound eerie and lonely. The setting and the knowledge that Diamelen is very sick foreshadow how Arsat's story will end.

powder. He spoke to me quickly: 'Run with her along the path. I shall keep them back, for they have no firearms, and landing in the face of a man with a gun is certain death for some. Run with her. On the other side of that wood there is a fisherman's house—and a canoe. When I have fired all the shots I will follow. I am a great runner, and before they can come up we shall be gone. I will hold out as long as I can, for she is but a woman—that can neither run nor fight, but she has your heart in her weak hands.' He dropped behind the canoe. The prau was coming. She and I ran, and as we rushed along the path I heard shots. My brother fired—once—twice—and the booming of the gong ceased. There was silence behind us. That neck of land is narrow. Before I heard my brother fire the third shot I saw the shelving shore, and I saw the water again: the mouth of a broad river. We crossed a grassy glade. We ran down to the water. I saw a low hut above the black mud, and a small canoe hauled up. I heard another shot behind me. I thought, 'That is his last charge.' We rushed down to the canoe; a man came running from the hut, but I leaped on him, and we rolled together in the mud. Then I got up, and he lay still at my feet. I don't know whether I had killed him or not. I and Diamelen pushed the canoe afloat. I heard yells behind me, and I saw my brother run across the glade. Many men were bounding after him. I took her in my arms and threw her into the boat, then leaped in myself.

18 ▼ **Critical Viewing**
What aspects of Conrad's story does this photograph capture? **[Connect]**

19 ☑ Reading Check
What instructions does Arsat's brother give him?

"WE RAN OUR CANOE

ON THE WHITE BEACH

OF A LITTLE BAY..."

The Lagoon **1231**

18 Critical Viewing

Possible response: The image suggests some of the isolation of Conrad's story, but it does not capture the sense of danger or fear that pervades the story.

19 Reading Check

Answer: He tells Arsat to run while he holds off the Rajah's men with a gun. He says he will follow Arsat once he has fired all the shots.

Differentiated
Instruction · for Universal Access

Support for English Learners
English learners may find it especially difficult to detect the plot devices used by Conrad in "The Lagoon," because they are subtly interspersed with the story within a story. Have students read passages in which these devices are especially noticeable, and encourage students to identify them on their own or with teacher guidance.

20 Critical Thinking

Make a Judgment

1. **Ask** students why Arsat pushed the canoe away from the shore after his brother fell.
   Answer: He was afraid he would be killed along with his brother.
2. **Ask:** What does Arsat hope for after he leaves his brother behind?
   Answer: He hopes to live happily with Diamelen in "a country where death is forgotten."
3. Have students **make a judgment** about Arsat's actions. Was he right to leave his brother? Why or why not?
   Possible response: He was right to leave his brother. His brother was certainly going to be killed, and Arsat still had a chance to live.

When I looked back I saw that my brother had fallen. He fell and was up again, but the men were closing round him. He shouted, 'I am coming!' The men were close to him. I looked. Many men. Then I looked at her. Tuan, I pushed the canoe! I pushed it into deep water. She was kneeling forward looking at me, and I said, 'Take your paddle,' while I struck the water with mine. Tuan, I heard him cry. I heard him cry
20 my name twice; and I heard voices shouting, 'Kill! Strike!' I never turned back. I heard him calling my name again with a great shriek, as when life is going out together with the voice—and I never turned my head. My own name! . . . My brother! Three times he called—but I was not afraid of life. Was she not there in that canoe? And could I not with her find a country where death is forgotten—where death is unknown!"

The white man sat up. Arsat rose and stood, an indistinct and silent figure above the dying embers of the fire. Over the lagoon a mist drifting and low had crept, erasing slowly the glittering images of the stars. And now a great expanse of white vapor covered the land; it flowed cold and gray in the darkness, eddied in noiseless whirls round the tree-trunks and about the platform of the house, which seemed to float upon a restless and impalpable illusion of a sea. Only far away the tops of the trees stood outlined on the twinkle of heaven, like a somber and forbidding shore—a coast deceptive, pitiless and black.

Arsat's voice vibrated loudly in the profound peace.

"I had her there! I had her! To get her I would have faced all mankind. But I had her—and—"

His words went out ringing into the empty distances. He paused, and seemed to listen to them dying away very far—beyond help and beyond recall. Then he said quietly—

"Tuan, I loved my brother."

A breath of wind made him shiver. High above his head, high above the silent sea of mist the drooping leaves of the palms rattled together with a mournful and expiring sound. The white man stretched his legs. His chin rested on his chest, and he murmured sadly without lifting his head—

"We all love our brothers."

Think Aloud

Vocabulary: Using Context
Draw students to the word *eddied* in the second paragraph on this page. Use the following "think aloud" to model the skill of using context to infer the meaning of the word. Say to students:

I may not know the meaning of the word *eddied*. When I read the sentence, I realize that the writer is using *eddied* to describe the way vapor moves around the tree trunks and the platform of the house. The sentence also contains the word *whirls*. I can infer that *eddied* is a verb that describes a way of moving that involves whirling.

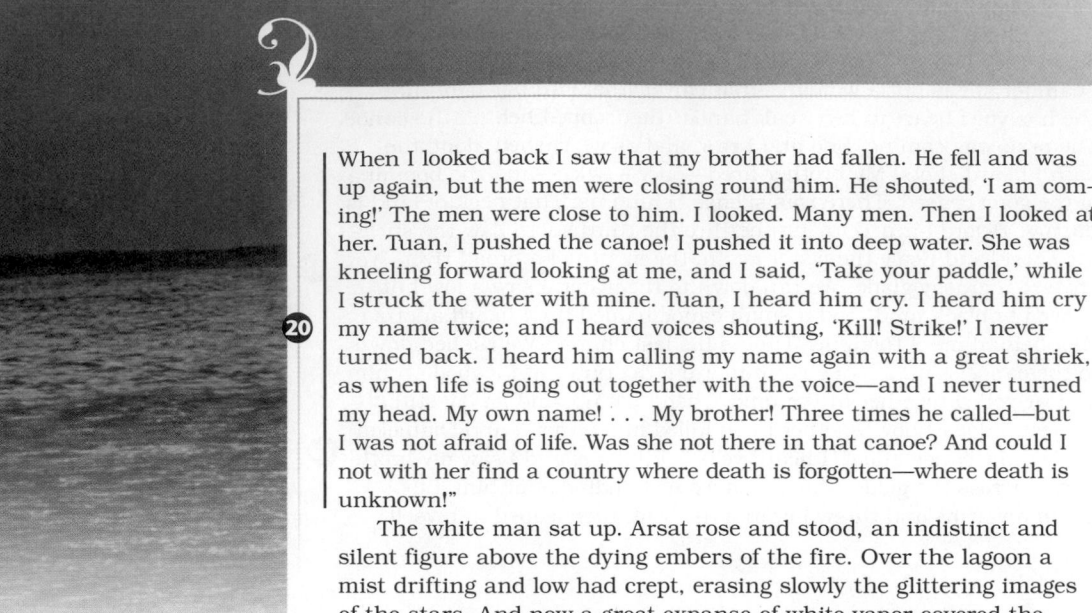

THEN HE SAID—
"SHE BURNS
NO MORE."

Arsat burst out with an intense whispering violence—

"What did I care who died? I wanted peace in my own heart."

He seemed to hear a stir in the house—listened—then stepped in noiselessly. The white man stood up. A breeze was coming in fitful puffs. The stars shone paler as if they had retreated into the frozen depths of immense space. After a chill gust of wind there were a few seconds of perfect calm and absolute silence. Then from behind the black and wavy line of the forests a column of golden light shot up into the heavens and spread over the semicircle of the eastern horizon. The sun had risen. The mist lifted, broke into drifting patches,
21 vanished into thin flying wreaths; and the unveiled lagoon lay, polished and black, in the heavy shadows at the foot of the wall of trees. A white eagle rose over it with a slanting and ponderous flight, reached the clear sunshine and appeared dazzlingly brilliant for a moment, then soaring higher, became a dark and motionless speck before it vanished into the blue as if it had left the earth forever. The white man, standing gazing upward before the doorway, heard in the hut a confused and broken murmur of distracted words ending with a loud groan. Suddenly Arsat stumbled out with outstretched hands, shivered, and stood still for some time with fixed eyes. Then he said—

"She burns no more."

Before his face the sun showed its edge above the treetops, rising steadily. The breeze freshened; a great brilliance burst upon the lagoon, sparkled on the rippling water. The forests came out of the clear shadows of the morning, became distinct, as if they had rushed nearer—to stop short in a great stir of leaves, of nodding boughs, of swaying branches. In the merciless sunshine the whisper of unconscious life grew louder, speaking in an incomprehensible voice round the dumb darkness of that human sorrow. Arsat's eyes wandered slowly, then stared at the rising sun.

"I can see nothing," he said half aloud to himself.

"There is nothing," said the white man, moving to the edge of the platform and waving his hand to his boat. A shout came faintly over the lagoon and the sampan began to glide toward the abode of the friend of ghosts.

"If you want to come with me, I will wait all the morning," said the white man, looking away upon the water.

Reading Strategy
Identifying Cause-and-Effect Relationships
What event causes Arsat to shiver? What else might have caused that reaction?

22 ☑ Reading Check
What happens to Arsat's brother?

Differentiated Instruction for Universal Access

Strategy for Less Proficient Readers
Encourage students to increase their understanding by rereading the page and listing each event that occurs. Have each student make a two-column chart, separating events into causes and effects.

Enrichment for Advanced Readers
Have students analyze the use of the eagle as a symbol in the third paragraph. Ask students to identify other symbolic objects in the text.

21 Reading Strategy
Identifying Cause-and-Effect Relationships

1. Remind students that there are often multiple causes for a particular effect.
2. Then, **ask** the Reading Strategy question: What event causes Arsat to shiver? What else might have caused that reaction?
   Answer: Arsat may be shivering because it has become cold or because Diamelen has died.

22 Reading Check
Answer: Arsat's brother is caught, and presumably killed, by the Rajah's men.

ASSESS

Answers

Before students respond, you may wish to have them write a brief objective summary of the selection. As they answer the questions below, remind them to support their answers with evidence from the text.

1. (a) He hopes the white man can cure Diamelen. (b) Arsat is disturbed and anxious.
2. (a) He shoots at the Rajah's henchmen and tries to escape, but he is captured and killed. (b) Arsat is desperate to escape with Diamelen. (c) He might have urged Diamelen to escape and gone back to help his brother; however, both brothers might have died.
3. (a) To Arsat, life means nothing now that Diamelen is dead. The white man means that there are no illusions to cling to. (b) Conrad is saying that all human life is illusion.
4. (a) **Possible responses:** Students may point to the descriptions of the gunshots, of the brother's screams across the water, and of the silence as the two men sit in front of the fire. These descriptions suggest that the act of storytelling involves representing both the silence and the noise of an episode, as well as the surroundings in which the episode is related. (b) Arsat is torn by guilt for acting out of passion and contributing to his brother's death. (c) If Arsat hoped to expunge his guilt for his brother's death, he has not succeeded.
5. (a) Conrad might say that a person must struggle to see through illusions to understand. (b) **Possible responses:** Students may agree or disagree but should provide reasons for their opinions.

Cite textual evidence to support your responses.

"No, Tuan," said Arsat softly. "I shall not eat or sleep in this house, but I must first see my road. Now I can see nothing—see nothing! There is no light and no peace in the world; but there is death—death for many. We were sons of the same mother—and I left him in the midst of enemies; but I am going back now."

He drew a long breath and went on in a dreamy tone:

"In a little while I shall see clear enough to strike—to strike. But she has died, and . . . now . . . darkness."

He flung his arms wide open, let them fall along his body, then stood still with unmoved face and stony eyes, staring at the sun. The white man got down into his canoe. The polers ran smartly along the sides of the boat, looking over their shoulders at the beginning of a weary journey. High in the stern, his head muffled up in white rags, the juragon sat moody, letting his paddle trail in the water. The white man, leaning with both arms over the grass roof of the little cabin, looked back at the shining ripple of the boat's wake. Before the sampan passed out of the lagoon into the creek he lifted his eyes. Arsat had not moved. He stood lonely in the searching sunshine; and he looked beyond the great light of a cloudless day into the darkness of a world of illusions.

Critical Reading

1. **Key Ideas and Details (a)** Why does Arsat ask the white man if he has medicine? **(b) Infer:** What is Arsat's state of mind?
2. **Key Ideas and Details (a)** What does Arsat's brother do while Arsat and Diamelen run to the canoe? **(b) Analyze Cause and Effect:** What motivates Arsat to leave his brother behind? **(c) Speculate:** How else could he have responded, and what might have been the results?
3. **Key Ideas and Details (a) Interpret:** Following Diamelen's death, Arsat says, "I can see nothing," and the white man replies, "There is nothing." What does each statement mean? **(b) Connect:** How might this dialogue relate to the story's final line?
4. **Craft and Structure (a) Analyze:** Find three examples of Conrad's descriptions of sounds, including descriptions of silence and speech. What do these images suggest about the act of storytelling? **(b) Draw Conclusions:** What is Arsat's purpose in telling his story? **(c) Evaluate:** Does he achieve it? Explain.
5. **Integration of Knowledge and Ideas (a) Draw Conclusions:** What do you think Conrad would recommend to people as a way to deal with past mistakes or regrets? **(b) Make a Judgment:** Would you agree? Explain.

23 # JAMES JOYCE

(1882–1941)

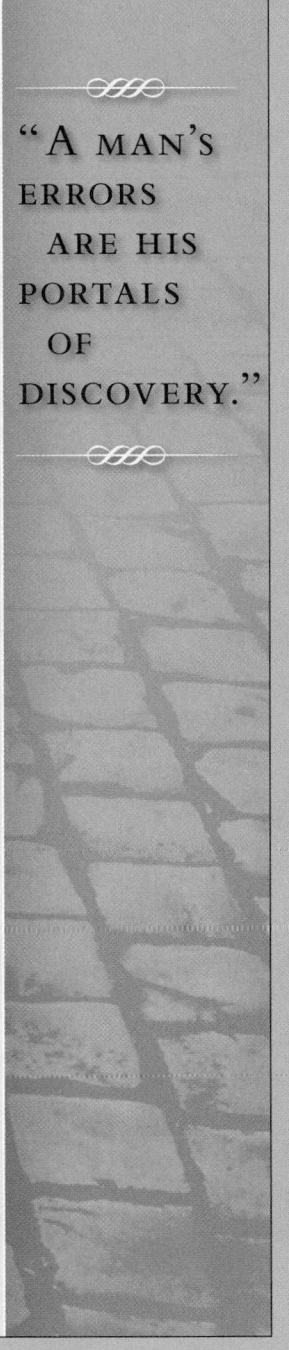

Author of "Araby"

The Dublin writer James Joyce's innovations in plot, character, and language make him one of the most challenging and distinguished writers of the twentieth century.

Experimentation Joyce's family and teachers wanted him to become a priest, but he pursued his own way as a writer. In 1904, he left Ireland for the continent. Ten years later, he published a landmark collection of short stories entitled *Dubliners.* These deceptively simple tales focus on the psychological conflicts of ordinary people. In the course of each story, the main character is forced to alter his or her perspective on life.

In 1916, Joyce published *A Portrait of the Artist as a Young Man,* a semiautobiographical work. Like Joyce, the novel's main character is in conflict with his Irish roots and chooses to become a writer.

Mature Fiction *A Portrait of the Artist* reveals a heightened awareness of language and an immersion in the minds of characters. Joyce carried these characteristics to a new level in *Ulysses* (1922). A stream-of-consciousness novel that roughly parallels Homer's *Odyssey,* the work presents a day in the life of three Dubliners. *Ulysses* represents a liberation of the novel from old ideas. Using a variety of styles and techniques, it places a new and thoroughly modern emphasis on the play of language.

In his final novel, *Finnegans Wake* (1939), Joyce took his fascination with words a step further. Written in what one scholar terms "a dream language of Joyce's own invention," it explores the author's view of human existence. With such radical innovations, Joyce guaranteed his place as one of the re-inventors of modern fiction.

"A MAN'S ERRORS ARE HIS PORTALS OF DISCOVERY."

23 Background

More About the Author

James Joyce came to fame relatively late in life. With the publication of *Ulysses* on his fortieth birthday, he was met with critical acclaim from Ezra Pound, T. S. Eliot, and Ernest Hemingway. His early influences included Ibsen (whom he greatly admired), Dante, and Yeats (who befriended Joyce). Many of Joyce's works were problematic—*Ulysses* was banned in the United States for a time because of its "pornographic" content; the proofs of *Dubliners* were destroyed in Dublin because the publisher feared a libel suit. Despite these and other setbacks, Joyce created some of the masterpieces of Modernism during his lifetime, many of which used the stream-of-consciousness narrative form in an innovative way.

Differentiated Instruction for Universal Access

Strategy for Advanced Readers
Have students read the description of the narrator's neighborhood in "Araby" independently. Then, tell them to write proposals for documentary film projects on Dublin's poor neighborhoods. Using James Joyce's descriptions, have students briefly describe the problems that Dublin's poor residents face and suggest topical angles for their documentaries.

Enrichment for Gifted/Talented Students
Encourage students to draw illustrations of the neighborhood described by the narrator of "Araby" in the first few paragraphs of the story. Tell them to focus on specific descriptions of the community and to reproduce them as accurately as possible. If the students are interested, have them draw the image of the narrator into the scenes they depict.

PHLit Online!

For more about the author, go online at **www.PHLitOnline.com.**

24 About the Selection

A boy has a deep crush on the older sister of a neighborhood friend. He watches her and dreams of their romantic future. Late one night, he goes on a mission to a bazaar called Araby to get her a gift, only to realize that Araby is not the exotic world he had imagined. In the darkness of the closing bazaar, he has a sudden vision of himself "as a creature driven and derided by vanity." This vision, provoking "anguish and anger," seems to take in his imaginary relationship with the girl and all his illusions.

24

Araby

JAMES JOYCE

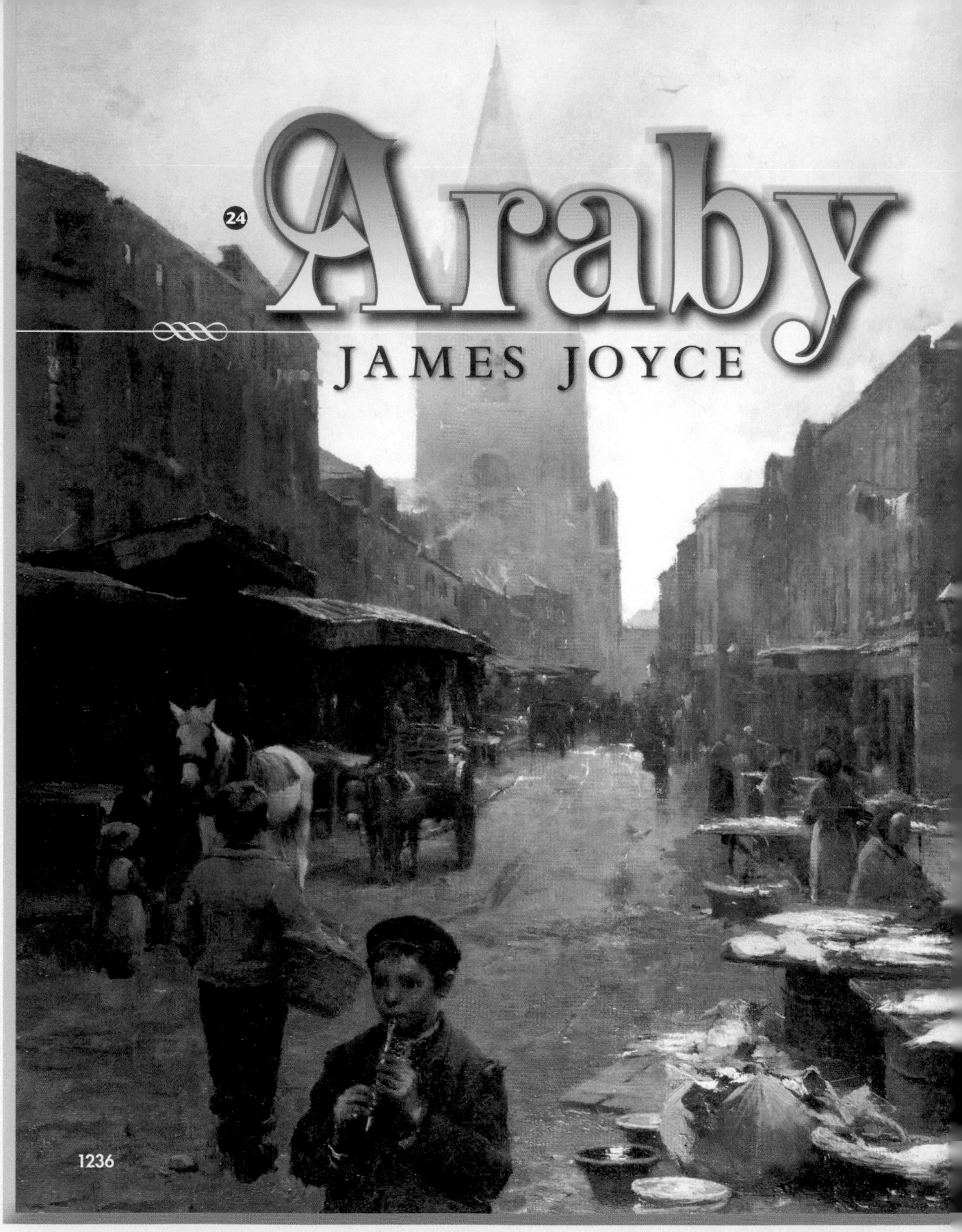

1236

Enrichment: Investigating Language

Epiphany

James Joyce uses epiphany moments frequently in his stories. An epiphany is a profound revelation experienced by a main character. The term was used in Greek mythology to describe an occasion when a god or goddess would suddenly reveal his or her true identity to a mortal. The word *epiphany* also has an ecclesiastical meaning. The Epiphany, or Twelfth Night, is a Christian holiday celebrated twelve days after Christmas. It commemorates the day that the Magi arrived to visit the Christ child and the beasts in the stable were able to talk.

Activity: Investigate Words from Greek Mythology Encourage interested students to investigate words that come from Greek mythology, such as *epiphany*, *arachnid*, *echo*, and *tantalize*. Suggest that they record what they learn on the **Enrichment: Investigating Language** worksheet, ***Professional Development Guidebook***, page 234.

North Richmond Street, being blind,[1] was a quiet street except at the hour when the Christian Brothers' School set the boys free. An uninhabited house of two stories stood at the blind end, detached from its neighbors in a square ground. The other houses of the street, conscious of decent lives within them, gazed at one another with brown imperturbable faces.

The former tenant of our house, a priest, had died in the back drawing room. Air, musty from having been long enclosed, hung in all the rooms, and the waste room behind the kitchen was littered with old useless papers. Among these I found a few paper-covered books, the pages of which were curled and damp: *The Abbot*, by Walter Scott, *The Devout Communicant* and *The Memoirs of Vidocq*.[2] I liked the last best because its leaves were yellow. The wild garden behind the house contained a central apple tree and a few straggling bushes under one of which I found the late tenant's rusty bicycle pump. He had been a very charitable priest: in his will he had left all his money to institutions and the furniture of his house to his sister.

When the short days of winter came dusk fell before we had well eaten our dinners. When we met in the street the houses had grown somber. The space of sky above us was the color of ever-changing violet and toward it the lamps of the street lifted their feeble lanterns. The cold air stung us and we played till our bodies glowed. Our shouts echoed in the silent street. The career of our play brought us through the dark muddy lanes behind the houses where we ran the gantlet of the rough tribes from the cottages, to the back doors of the dark dripping gardens where odors arose from the ashpits, to the dark odorous stables where a coachman smoothed and combed the horse or shook music from the buckled harness. When we returned to the street, light from the kitchen windows had filled the areas. If my uncle was seen turning the corner we hid in the shadow until we had seen him safely housed. Or if Mangan's sister came out on the doorstep to call her brother in to his tea we watched her from our shadow peer up and down the street. We waited to see whether she would remain or go in and, if she remained, we left our shadow and walked up to Mangan's steps resignedly. She was waiting for us, her figure defined by the light from the half-opened door. Her brother always teased her before he obeyed and I stood by the railings looking at her. Her dress swung as she moved her body and the soft rope of her hair tossed from side to side. (26)

Every morning I lay on the floor in the front parlor watching her door. The blind was pulled down to within an inch of the sash so that I could not be seen. When she came out on the doorstep my heart leaped. I ran to the hall, seized my books and followed her. I kept her brown figure always in my eye and, when we came near the point at

1. **blind** a dead end.
2. ***The Abbot . . . Vidocq*** a historical tale, a religious manual, and the remembrances of a French adventurer, respectively.

Vocabulary
imperturbable (im´ pər tur´ bə bəl) *adj.* calm; not easily ruffled

(25) **◀ Critical Viewing**
Why might the prospect of a fair or bazaar appeal to someone living on a street like this? **[Infer]**

Literary Analysis
Plot Devices What effect does the use of first-person point of view have on your impression of Mangan's sister?

(27) **Reading Check**
When and where does the story take place?

(25) Critical Viewing

Answer: Students may say that the allure of an exotic, romantic bazaar would be a welcome contrast to the bleak conditions of the neighborhood.

(26) Literary Analysis

Plot Devices

1. Review with students the different kinds of narrative points of view, focusing on the level of narrative information provided by each. If possible, have students identify examples of each type of point of view from selections they have previously read.
2. Then, **ask** students the Literary Analysis question: What effect does the use of first-person point of view have on your impression of Mangan's sister?
   Answer: Students should recognize that the first-person point of view makes us see Mangan's sister through the narrator's lovesick eyes.

(27) Reading Check

Answer: The story takes place on the dead-end North Richmond Street in the evening.

Differentiated Instruction for Universal Access

Support for Less Proficient Readers
Remind students to visualize the scenes Joyce describes. If it helps them picture the action, encourage them to sketch pictures in a notebook to help them remember what has occurred.

EL Support for English Learners
Students may have difficulty with some of the more complicated vocabulary Joyce's narrator uses to describe his situation. Encourage them to sound out any words that give them unusual difficulty and to try to put words into the context of sentences.

Enrichment for Gifted/Talented Students
Have students work with partners to role-play for the class the conversation from "Araby" between the boy and Mangan's sister. In addition to delivering their lines, tell students to concentrate on facial expressions, body language, and tone of voice.

28 Reading Strategy

Identifying Cause-and-Effect Relationships

1. As students read the passage, have them describe the behavior of the main character.
2. Then, **ask** students the Reading Strategy question: What is causing the narrator's distracted behavior? What do you think will happen to him?
   Possible response: He is distracted because of his feelings for his friend's sister. I think he will end up speaking to her.

29 Literary Analysis

Plot Devices and Epiphany

1. Review with students their understanding of the word *epiphany.*
2. Then, **ask** them the Literary Analysis question: In what way might the narrator's comments on his own past thoughts and feelings prepare for an epiphany?
   Answer: The narrator provides the background information that explains the buildup toward his epiphany.

26 which our ways diverged, I quickened my pace and passed her. This happened morning after morning. I had never spoken to her, except for a few casual words, and yet her name was like a summons to all my foolish blood.

Reading Strategy
Identifying Cause-and-Effect Relationships
What is causing the narrator's distracted behavior? What do you think will happen to him?

28 Her image accompanied me even in places the most hostile to romance. On Saturday evenings when my aunt went marketing I had to go to carry some of the parcels. We walked through the flaring streets, jostled by drunken men and bargaining women, amid the curses of laborers, the shrill litanies[3] of shop-boys who stood on guard by the barrels of pigs' cheeks, the nasal chanting of street singers, who sang a *come-all-you* about O'Donovan Rossa,[4] or a ballad about the troubles in our native land. These noises converged in a single sensation of life for me: I imagined that I bore my chalice safely through a throng of foes. Her name sprang to my lips at moments in strange prayers and praises which I myself did not understand. My eyes were often full of tears (I could not tell why) and at times a flood from my heart seemed to pour itself out into my bosom. I thought little of the future. I did not know whether I would ever speak to her or not or, if I spoke to her, how I could tell her of my confused adoration. But my body was like a harp and her words and gestures were like fingers running upon the wires.

Literary Analysis
Plot Devices and Epiphany
In what way might the narrator's comments on his own past thoughts and feelings prepare for an epiphany?

29 One evening I went into the back drawing room in which the priest had died. It was a dark rainy evening and there was no sound in the house. Through one of the broken panes I heard the rain impinge upon the earth, the fine incessant needles of water playing in the sodden beds. Some distant lamp or lighted window gleamed below me. I was thankful that I could see so little. All my senses seemed to desire to veil themselves and, feeling that I was about to slip from them, I pressed the palms of my hands together until they trembled, murmuring: *"O love! O love!"* many times.

At last she spoke to me. When she addressed the first words to me I was so confused that I did not know what to answer. She asked me was I going to *Araby.* I forget whether I answered yes or no. It would be a splendid bazaar, she said; she would love to go.

"And why can't you?" I asked.

While she spoke she turned a silver bracelet round and round her wrist. She could not go, she said, because there would be a retreat[5] that week in her convent.[6] Her brother and two other boys were fighting for their caps and I was alone at the railings. She held one of the spikes, bowing her head towards me. The light from the lamp opposite our door caught the white curve of her neck, lit up her hair that rested there and, falling, lit up the hand upon the railing. It fell over one side of her dress and caught the white border of a petticoat, just visible as she stood at ease.

---

3. **litanies** (lit′ ən ēz) *n* prayers in which a congregation repeats a fixed response; repetitive recitations.
4. ***come-all-you* . . . Rossa** opening of a ballad about an Irish hero.
5. **retreat** *n.* period of retirement or seclusion for prayer, religious study, and meditation.
6. **convent** *n.* school run by an order of nuns.

Enrichment: Investigating Popular Culture

Orientalism

People in the West have long been fascinated by the East. This phenomenon goes back at least to the 1200s, when Italian trader Marco Polo returned from China and central Asia and wrote a book about his fabulous adventures. In the 1800s, *The Arabian Nights*—a collection of two hundred folk tales from Arabia, Egypt, India, and Persia—was translated into English by the explorer and scholar Richard Francis Burton. The book, which became an instant classic in the West, reinforced people's impressions of the East as an exotic land of genies and flying carpets.

Activity: Learn More About Orientalism
Encourage interested students to learn more about Orientalism in European and American popular culture. Suggest that they record what they learn on the **Enrichment: Investigating Popular Culture** worksheet, ***Professional Development Guidebook,*** page 238.

"It's well for you," she said.

"If I go," I said, "I will bring you something."

What innumerable follies laid waste my waking and sleeping thoughts after that evening! I wished to annihilate the tedious intervening days. I chafed against the work of school. At night in my bedroom and by day in the classroom her image came between me and the page I strove to read. The syllables of the word *Araby* were called to me through the silence in which my soul luxuriated and cast an Eastern enchantment over me. I asked for leave to go to the bazaar on Saturday night. My aunt was surprised and hoped it was not some Freemason[7] affair. I answered few questions in class. I watched my master's face pass from amiability to sternness; he hoped I was not beginning to idle. I could not call my wandering thoughts together. I had hardly any patience with the serious work of life which, now that it stood between me and my desire, seemed to me child's play, ugly monotonous child's play.

On Saturday morning I reminded my uncle that I wished to go to the bazaar in the evening. He was fussing at the hallstand, looking for the hat brush, and answered me curtly:

"Yes, boy, I know."

As he was in the hall I could not go into the front parlor and lie at the window. I left the house in bad humor and walked slowly toward the school. The air was pitilessly raw and already my heart misgave me.

30 When I came home to dinner my uncle had not yet been home. Still it was early. I sat staring at the clock for some time and, when its ticking began to irritate me, I left the room. I mounted the staircase and gained the upper part of the house. The high cold empty gloomy rooms liberated me and I went from room to room singing. From the front window I saw my companions playing in the street. Their cries reached me weakened and indistinct and, leaning my forehead against the cool glass, I looked over at the dark house where she lived. I may have stood there for an hour, seeing nothing but the brown-clad figure cast by my imagination, touched discreetly by the lamplight at the curved neck, at the hand upon the railings and at the border below the dress.

When I came downstairs again I found Mrs. Mercer sitting at the fire. She was an old **garrulous** woman, a pawnbroker's widow, who collected used stamps for some pious purpose. I had to endure the gossip of the tea table. The meal was prolonged beyond an hour and still my uncle did not come. Mrs. Mercer stood up to go: she was sorry she couldn't wait any longer, but it was after eight o'clock and she did not like to be out late, as the night air was bad for her. When she had gone I began to walk up and down the room, clenching my fists. My aunt said:

"I'm afraid you may put off your bazaar for this night of Our Lord."

---

7. Freemason Free and Accepted Masons, an international secret society.

Spiral Review

Character Summarize the paragraph that begins "What innumerable follies. . . ." What can you conclude about the narrator's emotional state?

Reading Strategy

Identifying Cause-and-Effect Relationships Why does the narrator have to wait to go to the bazaar? What effect does his waiting have on his mood?

Vocabulary

garrulous (gar′ ə ləs) *adj.* talkative

31 Reading Check

What does the narrator promise Mangan's sister?

Spiral Review

Character

1. Remind students that they studied character in an earlier lesson.
2. **Ask** students the Spiral Review question.
   Possible response: The narrator is so obsessed that his view of the world and his priorities are completely changed.

30 Reading Strategy

Identifying Cause-and-Effect Relationships

1. Have students identify the sequence of events as the narrator waits to go to the bazaar.
2. Then, **ask** students the Reading Strategy question: Why does the narrator have to wait to go to the bazaar? What effect does his waiting have on his mood?
   Answer: He must wait for his uncle to come home. He becomes increasingly distressed and moody as he waits.

31 Reading Check

Answer: The narrator promises Mangan's sister something from the Araby bazaar.

Differentiated Instruction for Universal Access

Support for Less Proficient Readers

Have each student write a journal entry that the boy in "Araby" might have written upon returning home from the bazaar. Tell them to explain the hopes the boy had and his feelings about those hopes upon returning home.

EL Support for English Learners

Have students read the narrator's description of the bazaar with teacher guidance. Remind them that the narrator has been looking forward to the bazaar since his conversation with Mangan's sister.
As students read, encourage them to picture the action and situation.

Enrichment for Gifted/Talented Students

Tell students to create two drawings of the bazaar in "Araby." In one drawing, students should depict the bazaar as the boy imagines it before he arrives. In the other drawing, students should depict the contrasting reality of the bazaar.

㉜ The British Tradition

The Irish Tradition

Irish monasteries played a vital role as a cultural bridge between classical antiquity and the Middle Ages. This little-known story is brought to light in Thomas Cahill's slightly hyperbolic book *How the Irish Saved Civilization.*

Connect to the Literature

Ask students to make a list of clues from the story that reveal where the story takes place. Then, have them respond to the Connect to the Literature question.

Possible response: The narrator establishes numerous details throughout the story that are Irish in nature. An Irish hero is mentioned. The characters make time for tea. The names for units of currency are reflective of the British Isles. Students are likely to determine that the setting reflects Irish details more than the narrator.

㉜ *The* BRITISH TRADITION

The Irish Tradition

Joyce's stories are a modern addition to the rich cultural legacy of Ireland. Irish literature began with an oral tradition of epics and flourished through the medieval period. Bede's *History* is a culminating testament to the Irish preservation of learning on the islands—Irish books and Irish teaching flowing into Bede's England made the work possible.

Although the Irish cultural tradition is strong, centuries of rule by the English in Ireland and the Irish struggles against that rule have raised questions of cultural identity. When W. B. Yeats reinvigorated Irish poetry, he helped to launch the Irish Literary Revival. This literary assertion of Irish identity was also a political gesture reinforcing the movement to free Ireland. Since Yeats, writers such as Joyce, Louis MacNeice, and Seamus Heaney have made the Irish identity, as well as the splits it suffered under English rule, a theme for literary exploration.

Connect to the Literature

Which reflects more Irish details: the setting or the narrator? Explain.

At nine o'clock I heard my uncle's latchkey in the hall door. I heard him talking to himself and heard the hallstand rocking when it had received the weight of his overcoat. I could interpret these signs. When he was midway through his dinner I asked him to give me the money to go to the bazaar. He had forgotten.

"The people are in bed and after their first sleep now," he said.

I did not smile. My aunt said to him energetically:

"Can't you give him the money and let him go? You've kept him late enough as it is."

My uncle said he was very sorry he had forgotten. He said he believed in the old saying: *All work and no play makes Jack a dull boy.* He asked me where I was going and, when I had told him a second time he asked me did I know *The Arab's Farewell to His Steed.*[8] When I left the kitchen he was about to recite the opening lines of the piece to my aunt.

I held a florin[9] tightly in my hand as I strode down Buckingham Street toward the station. The sight of the streets thronged with buyers and glaring with gas recalled to me the purpose of my journey. I took my seat in a third-class carriage of a deserted train. After an intolerable delay the train moved out of the station slowly. It crept onward among ruinous houses and over the twinkling river. At Westland Row Station a crowd of people pressed to the carriage doors; but the porters moved them back, saying that it was a special train for the bazaar. I remained alone in the bare carriage. In a few minutes the train drew up beside an improvised wooden platform. I passed out onto the road and saw by the lighted dial of a clock that it was ten minutes to ten. In front of me was a large building which displayed the magical name.

I could not find any sixpenny entrance and, fearing that the bazaar would be closed, I passed in quickly through a turnstile, handing a shilling to a weary-looking man. I found myself in a big hall girdled at half its height by a gallery. Nearly all the stalls were closed and the greater part of the hall was in darkness. I recognized a silence like that which pervades a church after a service. I walked into the center of the bazaar timidly. A few people were gathered about the stalls which were still open. Before a curtain, over which the words *Café Chantant*[10] were written in colored lamps, two men were counting money on a salver.[11] I listened to the fall of the coins.

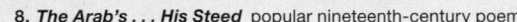

8. ***The Arab's . . . His Steed*** popular nineteenth-century poem.
9. **florin** two shilling coin of the time.
10. ***Café Chantant*** café with musical entertainment.
11. **salver** tray usually used for the presentation of letters or visiting cards.

Vocabulary Development

Vocabulary Knowledge Rating

When students have completed reading and discussing the selection, have them take out their **Vocabulary Knowledge Rating Charts** for the story. Read the words aloud and have students rate their knowledge of words again in the After Reading column. Clarify any words that are still problematic. Have students write their own definitions and example or sentence in the appropriate column. Then, have students complete the Vocabulary Practice at the end of the selection. Encourage students to use the words in further discussion and written work about the selection. Remind them that they will be accountable for these words on the **Selection Test, *Unit 6 Resources,*** pages 100–102 or 103–105.

Remembering with difficulty why I had come I went over to one of the stalls and examined porcelain vases and flowered tea sets. At the door of the stall a young lady was talking and laughing with two young gentlemen. I remarked their English accents and listened vaguely to their conversation.

"O, I never said such a thing!"

"O, but you did!"

"O, but I didn't!"

"Didn't she say that?"

"Yes. I heard her."

"O, there's a . . . fib!"

Observing me the young lady came over and asked me did I wish to buy anything. The tone of her voice was not encouraging; she seemed to have spoken to me out of a sense of duty. I looked humbly at the great jars that stood like Eastern guards at either side of the dark entrance to the stall and murmured:

"No, thank you."

The young lady changed the position of one of the vases and went back to the two young men. They began to talk of the same subject. Once or twice the young lady glanced at me over her shoulder.

I lingered before her stall, though I knew my stay was useless, to make my interest in her wares seem the more real. Then I turned away slowly and walked down the middle of the bazaar. I allowed the two pennies to fall against the sixpence in my pocket. I heard a voice call from one end of the gallery that the light was out. The upper part of the hall was now completely dark.

Gazing up into the darkness I saw myself as a creature driven and derided by vanity; and my eyes burned with anguish and anger.

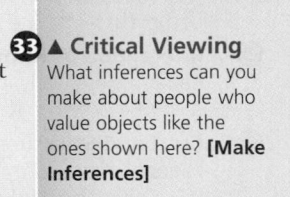

33 ▲ Critical Viewing
What inferences can you make about people who value objects like the ones shown here? **[Make Inferences]**

Vocabulary
derided (di rīd′ id) *v.* made fun of; ridiculed

Critical Reading

1. **Key Ideas and Details (a)** What does Mangan's sister do to make a trip to the bazaar so important to the narrator? **(b) Analyze:** Describe three scenes that establish the narrator's feelings for her.
2. **Key Ideas and Details** What features of the Araby bazaar conflict with the narrator's expectations?
3. **Key Ideas and Details (a) Draw Conclusions:** What has the narrator lost by the end of the story? **(b) Draw Conclusions:** What might he have gained?
4. **Integration of Knowledge and Ideas** Do the plot devices these writers use, story-within-a-story and epiphany, help convey the pain of wanting something very much and then failing to get it? Explain, using at least three of these Essential Question words: *imply, process, realization, epiphany, story-within-a-story.* *[Connecting to the Essential Question: What is the relationship of the writer to tradition?]*

Cite textual evidence to support your responses.

ASSESS

Answers

Before students respond, you may wish to have them write a brief objective summary of the selection. As they answer the questions below, remind them to support their answers with evidence from the text.

1. (a) Mangan's sister says that she would love to go and tells the narrator how fortunate he is to be able to go. (b) The narrator notices that she calls in her brother from play, he sees her leave for school, and he talks to her about the bazaar. Her lack of a name makes her seem more remote; it also shows how little the narrator knows about her.
2. He expects the Araby bazaar will be exotic, and the prospect of going "cast an Eastern enchantment" over him. Nothing he sees at the bazaar meets his expectations.
3. (a) The narrator has lost his illusions of Araby. (b) He might have gained the experience and maturity that come from encountering disappointment.
4. The *story-within-a-story* device allows readers to understand both the resulting feelings an incident has produced in a character as well as the *process* that brought the character to his or her present situation. *Epiphany* moments serve as moments of *realization* for the main characters, during which their failure to attain or retain what they want becomes clear.

33 Critical Viewing

Possible response: People who value such objects might believe a person's appearance or possessions mean more than attributes such as honesty or kindness.

Concept Connector

Reading Skill Graphic Organizer
Ask students to review the graphic organizers in which they have listed causes and effects in the story. Then, have students share their organizers and compare the causes and effects they identified.

Activating Prior Knowledge
Have students return to their responses to the Activating Prior Knowledge activity. Ask them to explain whether their thoughts have changed and, if so, how.

Writing About the Essential Question
Have students compare their responses to the prompt, completed before reading the story, with their thoughts afterward. Have them work individually or in groups, writing or discussing their thoughts, to formulate new responses. Then, lead a class discussion, probing for what students have learned that confirms or invalidates their initial thoughts. Encourage students to cite specific textual details to support their responses.

After You Read

The Lagoon • Araby

Literary Analysis

1. **Craft and Structure** Conrad uses the **plot device** of a **story-within-a-story** in "The Lagoon." What specific information would you lack if "The Lagoon" had been narrated entirely in the first person by Arsat?
2. **Craft and Structure** Why do you think Conrad chose to have Arsat narrate his own story?
3. **Key Ideas and Details** **(a)** Where in "Araby" does the **epiphany** occur? **(b)** What does the narrator in "Araby" suddenly realize?
4. **Integration of Knowledge and Ideas** Explain in what sense the narrator's epiphany in "Araby" is as much a loss of vision as it is a gain of insight.
5. **Craft and Structure** Contrast the mood of the parts of "The Lagoon" narrated by Arsat with the mood of the framing story, narrated in the third person.
6. **Comparing Literary Works** Use a chart like the one shown to compare how each story uses plot devices to establish distance between an experience of passion and the act of telling a story about passion.

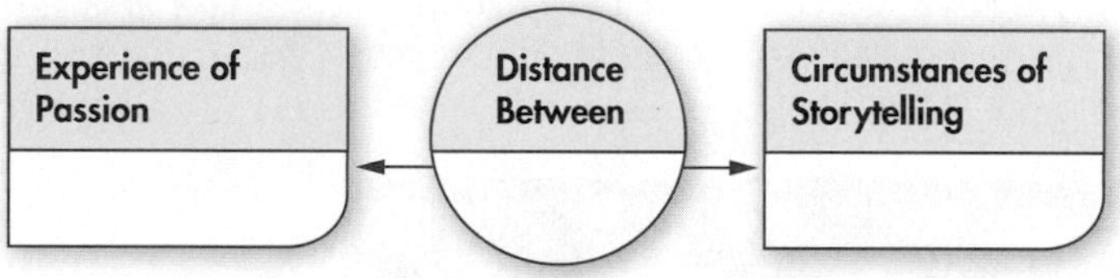

7. **Comparing Literary Works** **(a)** Compare the way that each story creates an "outsider's" perspective on a narrator's obsessive, passionate concerns. **(b)** Explain how plot devices add to the **theme** of each story.

Reading Strategy

8. **Identify cause and effect** in both stories. **(a)** What causes Arsat and the youngster in "Araby" to act? **(b)** In each case, what are the results of those actions?
9. What is the cause of the epiphany in "Araby"?
10. Explain how the story-within-a-story in "The Lagoon" is an effect of the story that frames it.
11. **(a)** Why do Arsat and the narrator in "Araby" tell the stories they tell? **(b)** What kind of reception do you think they expect to receive from their audience? Explain your answer.

Common Core State Standards

Reading Literature
9. Demonstrate knowledge of eighteenth-, nineteenth- and early-twentieth-century foundational works of American literature, including how two or more texts from the same period treat similar themes or topics. *(p. 1243)*

Writing
2. Write informative/explanatory texts to examine and convey complex ideas, concepts, and information clearly and accurately through the effective selection, organization, and analysis of content. *(p. 1243)*
2.b. Develop the topic thoroughly by selecting the most significant and relevant facts, extended definitions, concrete details, quotations, or other information and examples appropriate to the audience's knowledge of the topic. *(p. 1243)*
5. Develop and strengthen writing as needed by planning, revising, editing, rewriting, or trying a new approach, focusing on addressing what is most significant for a specific purpose and audience. *(p. 1243)*
9.a. Apply *grades 11–12 Reading standards* to literature. [RL.11-12.9] *(p. 1243)*

Language
5.b. Analyze nuances in the meaning of words with similar denotations. *(p. 1243)*

Answers

1. You would not know the antagonism the locals felt or the mystery that surrounds him.
2. Arsat can dramatize his story with his own emotions.
3. (a) The epiphany occurs at the bazaar. (b) The narrator realizes that his "romance" is imaginary.
4. The narrator loses an image of romance but gains an insight about reality.
5. The framing story has the objective mood of daylight. Arsat's story has an anguished mood of night.
6. "Lagoon"—Experience of Passion: Arsat's elopement/betrayal; Circumstances of Storytelling: Diamelen is dying; Distance Between: Passion is presented as a story told to a neutral character. "Araby"—Experience of Passion: narrator's crush on Mangan's sister; Circumstances of Storytelling: The events occurred in the past. Distance Between: The narrator tells of passion after losing his romantic illusions.
7. (a) "Lagoon": The white man listens to a story he is not involved in; "Araby": The narrator tells of a lost romantic illusion. (b) "Lagoon": The theme is the attempt to find meaning in loss; because the story-within-a-story gives us an outsider's view of Arsat's words, we can see their futility. "Araby": The theme is how passion thrives on possibility but dies in reality. Epiphany moves the speaker from the first to the second view.
8. (a) Arsat acts because he wants to escape with Diamelen. The narrator of "Araby" acts because he has a crush on a girl. (b) The result of Arsat's action is betrayal and regret. In "Araby," the result is that the narrator realizes his feelings are illusory.
9. The narrator feels the vacancy of the bazaar.
10. It contrasts an objective view of events with Arsat's personal view.
11. **Possible response:** (a) Arsat tells his story to unburden himself. Tuan is sympathetic. The narrator of "Araby" relates a life-changing event. He invites the audience to see the folly of his actions. (b) They expect others to be moved by their stories and understand their sense of loss.

Assessment Practice

Paired Passages (For more practice, see *All-in-One Workbook*.)

Many tests require students to compare and identify literary elements in two passages. The following sample item can teach students how to identify the tone of two passages. Have students reread the last paragraph on page 1232 ("The Lagoon") and the last three paragraphs on page 1241 ("Araby").

Which of the following statements best describes the tone of each passage?

A Both passages are playful and humorous.
B "The Lagoon" is morose, but "Araby" is cheerful.
C Both passages are mysterious and strange.
D "The Lagoon" is gloomy, while "Araby" is bitter.

Help students analyze the tone of each work. Choices *B* and C could describe "The Lagoon," but not "Araby." Choice *A* does not accurately describe either and can therefore be eliminated. Therefore, the correct answer is ***D***.

PERFORMANCE TASKS
Integrated Language Skills

Vocabulary Acquisition and Use

Word Analysis: Latin Root *-vinc-*

Early in "The Lagoon," you will find the word *invincible,* which means "unconquerable." *Invincible* is formed with the Latin root *-vinc-,* which comes from a Latin verb meaning "to conquer" and "to show conclusively." Some words use a variant spelling such as *-vict-,* which has the same meanings. Use the meaning of the root to define each of the following words. Then, write a sentence using each word appropriately.

1. convict
2. victory
3. vanquish
4. convince
5. evince
6. evict

Vocabulary: Synonyms

Synonyms are words with nearly the same meaning. Write the letter of the word that is a synonym of each word from the vocabulary list on page 1218. Then, explain the differences in meaning between the synonyms.

1. **derided: (a)** ejected, **(b)** exaggerated, **(c)** ridiculed
2. **imperturbable: (a)** calm, **(b)** indifferent, **(c)** ruthless
3. **invincible: (a)** facile, **(b)** warlike, **(c)** unconquerable
4. **garrulous: (a)** coy, **(b)** rich, **(c)** talkative
5. **conflagration: (a)** dispute, **(b)** fire, **(c)** battle
6. **propitiate: (a)** appease, **(b)** refuse, **(c)** resign

Writing

Informative Text James Joyce, an Irish author, and Ernest Hemingway, an American author, wrote several early twentieth-century masterpieces. Find a copy of Hemingway's short story "In Another Country," and read it carefully. Then, write an **essay** comparing and contrasting the first-person narrators in "Araby" and "In Another Country."

Prewriting Start by jotting down your impressions of the narrator in "Araby." Then jot down your impressions of the narrator in "In Another Country." Consider these questions: In what way is each narrator "wounded"? In each story, what events trigger an epiphany, or a moment of sudden insight?

Drafting As you draft your essay, use your prewriting notes as a guide, addressing the details you listed for each narrator. Link these details to broader considerations about how one narrator's characteristics are similar to or different from the other's. Support your ideas with quotations from each story.

Revising Review your draft, making sure that the sentences flow logically and that your ideas are well supported with details. Where evidence is lacking, review the stories to find relevant details to strengthen the support.

Model: Revising to Add Relevant Support

Nearly all the stalls are closed, and he remembers only "with difficulty why I had come. . . ."

In "Araby," the narrator rushes off to the bazaar, but he is disappointed.^

Citing specific textual details strengthens writing about literature.

Assessment Resources

Unit 6 Resources

L1 L2 EL **Selection Test A**, pp. 100–102. Administer Test A to less advanced readers.

L3 L4 EL **Selection Test B**, pp. 103–104. Administer Test B to on-level students and more advanced students.

L3 L4 **Open-Book Test**, pp. 97–99. As an alternative, give the Open-Book test.

All **Customizable Test Bank**

All **Self-tests**
Students may prepare for the **Selection Test** by taking the **Self-test** online.

PHLit Online! All assessment resources are available at **www.PHLitOnline.com**.

ASSESS/EXTEND

Answers

Vocabulary Acquisition and Use

Word Analysis

1. Convict: to show conclusively that someone is guilty of a crime; Sample answer: The jury decided to convict the defendant.
2. Victory: the defeat of an opponent; Sample answer: The basketball team scored a stunning victory.
3. Vanquish: to overwhelmingly defeat an enemy; Sample answer: The army hoped to vanquish the enemy.
4. Convince: to make someone believe that something is true; Sample answer: I hoped to convince my parents to let me go to the party.
5. Evince: to clearly show a feeling; Sample answer: Her smile was meant to evince her happiness.
6. Evict: to force someone to leave a place; Sample answer: The landlord chose to evict the tenant.

Vocabulary

Students should explain the differences in connotations between the two words.

1. c
2. b
3. c
4. c
5. b
6. a

Writing

1. To guide students in writing this informative text, give them the Support for Writing page (*Unit 6 Resources,* p. 95).
2. Remind students that a successful opening statement is very organized, with clearly defined arguments. It may help students to think of it as an outline that would guide a full court case.
3. Encourage students to focus on the tone of their address, which should be emphatic. Their introduction and conclusion sentences for each part of their argument should clearly and strongly state their ideas.
4. Use the **Speaking: Delivering a Persuasive Speech** rubric on page 301 in the *Professional Development Guidebook* to evaluate students' work.

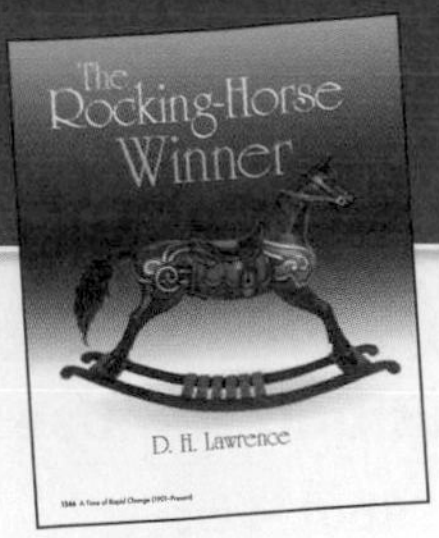

The Rocking-Horse Winner • A Shocking Accident

Lesson Pacing Guide

DAY 1 Preteach

- Administer the Reading and Vocabulary Warm-ups (*Unit 6 Resources*, pp. 106–109) as necessary.
- Introduce the Literary Analysis concept: Theme and Symbol.
- Introduce the Reading Strategy: Make Predictions.
- Build background with the author and Background features.
- Develop thematic thinking with Connecting to the Essential Questions.
- Teach the selection vocabulary.

DAYS 2–3 Preteach/Teach/Assess

- Distribute copies of the appropriate graphic organizer for the Reading Strategy (*Graphic Organizer Transparencies*, pp. 222–223).
- Distribute copies of the appropriate graphic organizer for Literary Analysis (*Graphic Organizer Transparencies*, pp. 224–225).
- Prepare students to read with the Activating Prior Knowledge activities (TE).
- Informally monitor comprehension while students read.
- Use the Reading Check questions to confirm comprehension.
- Develop students' understanding of theme and symbol using the Literary Analysis prompts.
- Develop students' ability to make predictions using the Reading Strategy prompts.
- Reinforce vocabulary with the Vocabulary notes.
- Assess students' comprehension and mastery of the skills by having them answer the Critical Reading, Literary Analysis, and Reading Strategy questions.
- Have students complete the Vocabulary Lesson.

DAY 4 Extend/Assess

- Have students complete the Writing Lesson and write a script for a scene. (You may assign as homework.)
- Administer Selection Test A or B (*Unit 6 Resources*, pp. 118–120 or 121–123).

Common Core State Standards

Reading Literature 3. Analyze the impact of the author's choices regarding how to develop and relate elements of a story.

Writing 3. Write narratives to develop real or imagined experiences or events using effective technique, well-chosen details, and well-structured event sequences.
5. Develop and strengthen writing as needed by planning, revising, editing, rewriting, or trying a new approach, focusing on addressing what is most significant for a specific purpose and audience.

Language 4.a. Use context as a clue to the meaning of a word or phrase.

Additional Standards Practice
Common Core Companion, pp. 28–35; 208–213; 226–227; 324–325

Daily Block Scheduling
Each day in this Lesson Pacing Guide represents a 40–50 minute period. Teachers using block scheduling may combine days to revise pacing. In addition, teachers may differentiate and support core instruction by integrating components for extended and intensive support as students require. See the Guide to Selected Leveled Resources (facing page).

Guide to Selected Leveled Resources

RTI **Tier 1** (students performing on level)			The Rocking-Horse Winner • A Shocking Accident
Warm Up	Whole class instruction; Group work	**Practice, model,** and **monitor** fluency, working **with the whole class** or **in groups**.	**Vocabulary and Reading Warm-ups B,** ***Unit 6 Resources,*** pp. 106–107, 109
Comprehension/Skills	Whole class instruction; Group work; Independent work	**Support** and **monitor** comprehension and skills development, having students complete the activities, graphic organizers, and interactive prompts **independently** or **as a class**.	• ***Reader's Notebook,*** adapted instruction and full selection EL ***Reader's Notebook: English Learner's Version,*** adapted instruction and adapted selection • **Reading Strategy Graphic Organizer B,** ***Graphic Organizer Transparencies,*** p. 233 • **Literary Analysis Graphic Organizer B,** ***Graphic Organizer Transparencies,*** p. 235
Monitor Progress	A	**Monitor** student progress with the differentiated curriculum-based assessment in the *Unit Resources.*	• **Selection Test B,** ***Unit 6 Resources,*** pp. 121–123 • **Open-Book Test,** ***Unit 6 Resources,*** pp. 115–117
Assess/ Screen	A	• **Assess** student progress using Benchmark Test. • **Preassess** instructional needs using the Vocabulary in Context section of the test.	• **Benchmark Test 10,** ***Unit 6 Resources,*** pp. 124–132, including Vocabulary in Context diagnostic items

RTI **Tier 2** (students requiring intervention)			The Rocking-Horse Winner • A Shocking Accident
Warm Up	Group work; One-on-one teaching	**Practice, model,** and **monitor** fluency **in groups** or **with individuals**.	• **Vocabulary and Reading Warm-ups A,** ***Unit 6 Resources,*** pp. 106–108 • ***Hear It!*** **Audio CD (adapted text)**
Comprehension/Skills	Group work; One-on-one teaching	• **Support** and **monitor** comprehension and skills development, working **in small groups** or **with individuals**. • As students complete the selection in the appropriate version of the *Reader's Notebook,* **monitor** comprehension frequently with group questions and individual instruction. • **Model** strategies while guiding students in completing the activities and prompts in the *Reader's Notebook,* as well as the graphic organizers. • **Practice** skills and **monitor** mastery with the *Reading Kit* worksheets.	• ***Reader's Notebook: Adapted Version,*** adapted instruction and adapted selection EL ***Reader's Notebook: English Learner's Version,*** adapted instruction and adapted selection • **Reading Strategy Graphic Organizer A,** ***Graphic Organizer Transparencies,*** p. 232 • **Literary Analysis Graphic Organizer A,** ***Graphic Organizer Transparencies,*** p. 234 • Practice worksheets
Monitor Progress	A	**Monitor** student progress with the differentiated curriculum-based assessment in the *Unit Resources* and in the *Reading Kit.*	• **Selection Test A,** ***Unit 6 Resources,*** pp. 118–120 • ***Reading Kit,*** Assess worksheets
Assess/ Screen	A	• **Assess** student progress using Benchmark Test. • **Preassess** instructional needs using the Vocabulary in Context section of the test.	**Benchmark Test 10,** ***Unit 6 Resources,*** pp. 124–132, including Vocabulary in Context diagnostic items

TIER 3 Tier 3 intervention may require consultation with the student's special-education or dyslexia specialist. For additional support, see the Tier 2 activities and resources listed above.

One-on-one teaching **Group work** **Whole class instruction** **Independent work** **A Assessment**

For a complete guide to selection support, including support for Advanced students, see the Overview of Resources in the frontmatter.

The Rocking-Horse Winner • A Shocking Accident

The Rocking-Horse Winner

D. H. Lawrence

1246 A Time of Rapid Change (1901–Present)

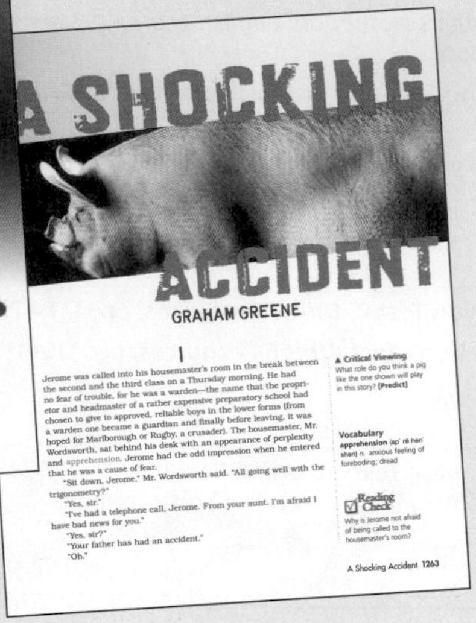
A SHOCKING ACCIDENT

GRAHAM GREENE

I

Jerome was called into his housemaster's room in the break between the second and the third class on a Thursday morning. He had no fear of trouble, for he was a warden—the name that the proprietor and headmaster of a rather expensive preparatory school had chosen to give to approved, reliable boys in the lower forms (from a warden one became a guardian and finally before leaving, it was hoped for Marlborough or Rugby, a crusader). The housemaster, Mr. Wordsworth, sat behind his desk with an appearance of perplexity and apprehension. Jerome had the odd impression when he entered that he was a cause of fear.

"Sit down, Jerome," Mr. Wordsworth said. "All going well with the trigonometry?"

"Yes, sir."

"I've had a telephone call, Jerome. From your aunt. I'm afraid I have bad news for you."

"Yes, sir?"

"Your father has had an accident."

"Oh."

▲ Critical Viewing What role do you think a pig like the one shown will play in this story? [Predict]

Vocabulary
apprehension (ap' rē hen' shən) n. anxious feeling of foreboding; dread

Reading Check
Why is Jerome not afraid of being called to the housemaster's room?

A Shocking Accident 1263

RESOURCES FOR:
- L1 Special-Needs Students
- L2 Below-Level Students (Tier 2)
- L3 On-Level Students (Tier 1)
- L4 Advanced Students (Tier 1)
- EL English Learners
- All All Students

Vocabulary/Fluency/Prior Knowledge

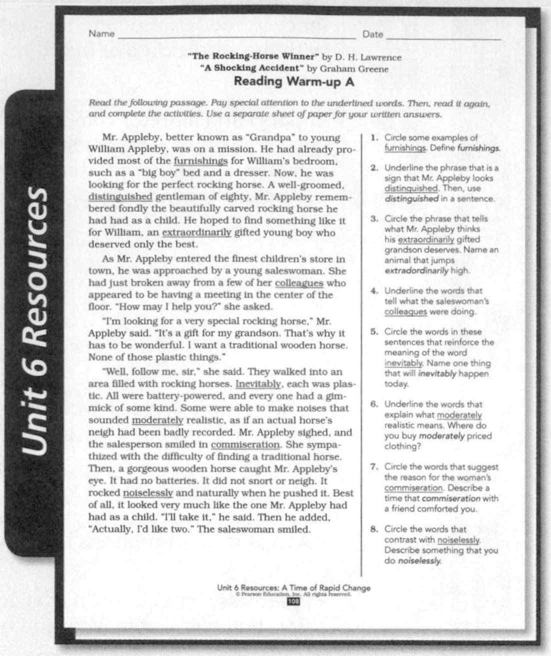
Unit 6 Resources

Name ______________________ Date ______________

"The Rocking-Horse Winner" by D. H. Lawrence
"A Shocking Accident" by Graham Greene
Reading Warm-up A

Read the following passage. Pay special attention to the underlined words. Then, read it again, and complete the activities. Use a separate sheet of paper for your written answers.

Mr. Appleby, better known as "Grandpa" to young William Appleby, was on a mission. He had already provided most of the furnishings for William's bedroom, such as a "big boy" bed and a dresser. Now, he was looking for the perfect rocking horse. A well-groomed, distinguished gentleman of eighty, Mr. Appleby remembered fondly the beautifully carved rocking horse he had had as a child. He hoped to find something like it for William, an extraordinarily gifted young boy who deserved only the best.

As Mr. Appleby entered the finest children's store in town, he was approached by a young saleswoman. She had just broken away from a few of her colleagues who appeared to be having a meeting in the center of the floor. "How may I help you?" she asked.

"I'm looking for a very special rocking horse," Mr. Appleby said. "It's a gift for my grandson. That's why it has to be wonderful. I want a traditional wooden horse. None of those plastic things."

"Well, follow me, sir," she said. They walked into an area filled with rocking horses. Inevitably, each was plastic. All were battery-powered, and every one had a gimmick of some kind. Some were able to make noises that sounded moderately realistic, as if an actual horse's neigh had been badly recorded. Mr. Appleby sighed, and the salesperson smiled in commiseration. She sympathized with the difficulty of finding a traditional horse. Then, a gorgeous wooden horse caught Mr. Appleby's eye. It had no batteries. It did not snort or neigh. It rocked noiselessly and naturally when he pushed it. Best of all, it looked very much like the one Mr. Appleby had had as a child. "I'll take it," he said. Then he added, "Actually, I'd like two." The saleswoman smiled.

1. Circle some examples of furnishings. Define *furnishings*.
2. Underline the phrase that is a sign that Mr. Appleby looks distinguished. Then, use *distinguished* in a sentence.
3. Circle the phrase that tells what Mr. Appleby thinks his extraordinarily gifted grandson deserves. Name an animal that jumps *extradordinarily* high.
4. Underline the words that tell what the saleswoman's colleagues were doing.
5. Circle the words in these sentences that reinforce the meaning of the word inevitably. Name one thing that will *inevitably* happen today.
6. Underline the words that explain what moderately realistic means. Where do you buy *moderately* priced clothing?
7. Circle the words that suggest the reason for the woman's commiseration. Describe a time that *commiseration* with a friend comforted you.
8. Circle the words that contrast with noiselessly. Describe something that you do *noiselessly*.

Unit 6 Resources: A Time of Rapid Change
© Pearson Education, Inc. All rights reserved.
108

EL L1 L2 **Reading Warm-ups A and B,** pp. 108–109

Also available for these selections:

EL L1 L2 **Vocabulary Warm-ups A and B,** pp. 106–107

All **Vocabulary Builder,** p. 112

Reader's Notebooks

Pre- and postreading pages for these selections appear in an interactive format in the *Reader's Notebooks*. Each *Notebook* is differentiated for a different group of learners. The selections in the Adapted and English Learner's versions are abridged.

L2 L3 ***Reader's Notebook***

L1 ***Reader's Notebook: Adapted Version***

EL ***Reader's Notebook: English Learner's Version***

EL ***Reader's Notebook: Spanish Version***

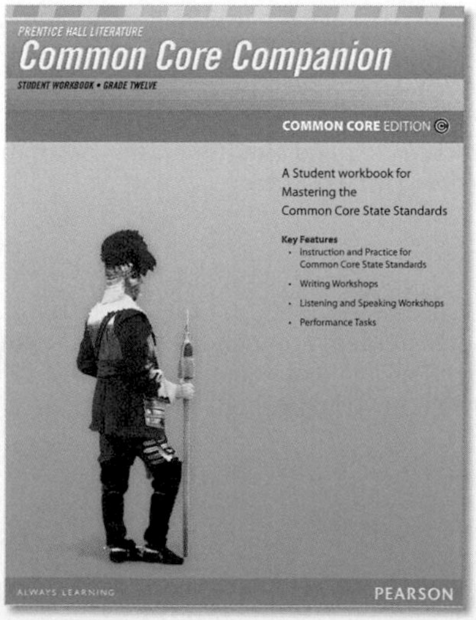

Common Core Companion

Additional instruction and practice for each Common Core State Standard

Selection Support

Graphic Organizer Transparencies

"The Rocking-Horse Winner" by D. H. Lawrence
"A Shocking Accident" by Graham Greene

Before You Read B: Make Predictions

Detail	Detail
Prediction	Prediction
Evaluation of Prediction	Evaluation of Prediction

Graphic Organizer Transparencies
© Pearson Education, Inc. All rights reserved.
223

EL L3 Reading: Graphic Organizer B, p. 223

Also available for these selections:

EL L1 L2 Reading: Graphic Organizer A, p. 222

EL L1 L2 Literary Analysis: Graphic Organizer A, (partially filled in), p. 224

EL L3 Literary Analysis: Graphic Organizer B, p. 225

Skills Development/Extension

Unit 6 Resources

Name ______________________ Date ______________

"The Rocking-Horse Winner" by D. H. Lawrence
"A Shocking Accident" by Graham Greene

Reading Strategy: Make and Confirm Predictions

While you are reading, incorporate your own background knowledge with the story's descriptions, events, and dialogue in order to **make predictions** about what might happen. Continue reading and collecting information that will either confirm your predictions or cause you to reformulate them. Once the actual situation is revealed, if the story has different events than you anticipated, your prediction needs to be revised. For example, predicting that Sally would laugh, like most other people did, when she found out about the cause of Jerome's father's death allowed tension to build. When it was revealed that she reacted differently, worried and somber, the prediction might then focus on the success of Jerome's relationship with Sally.

Directions: *Read the following passages from the stories. For each, make a prediction based on the information within the quote. Then discuss how those predictions would have worked out based on the actual events in the story.*

1. The boy saw she did not believe him; or rather, that she paid no attention to his assertion. This angered him somewhere, and made him want to compel her attention.
Prediction: ______________
Confirmation: ______________

2. "What, fifteen hundred pounds?"
"And twenty! And *forty*, that is, with the twenty he made on the course."
"It's amazing!" said the uncle.
"If Master Paul offers you to be partners, sir, I would, if I were you; if you'll excuse me," said Bassett.
Prediction: ______________
Confirmation: ______________

3. "I've had a telephone call, Jerome. From your aunt. I'm afraid I have bad news for you."
"Yes, sir?"
"Your father has had an accident."
"Oh."
"Mr. Wordsworth looked at him with some surprise. "A serious accident."
Prediction: ______________
Confirmation: ______________

4. He felt a longing to protect his memory, and uncertain whether this quite love of his would survive if Sally were so insensitive as to laugh when she heard the story of his father's death. Inevitably she would hear it when Jerome brought her to dinner with his aunt.

Unit 6 Resources: A Time of Rapid Change
© Pearson Education, Inc. All rights reserved.
111

All Reading: Make Predictions, p. 111

Also available for these selections:

All Literary Analysis: Theme and Symbol, p. 110

EL L3 L4 Support for Writing, p. 113

L4 Enrichment, p. 114

Assessment

Name ______________________ Date ______________

"The Rocking-Horse Winner" by D. H. Lawrence
"A Shocking Accident" by Graham Greene

Selection Test B

Critical Reading *Identify the letter of the choice that best completes the statement or answers the question.*

____ 1. In "The Rocking-Horse Winner," how is Paul's attitude toward luck different from his mother's?
A. He doesn't believe luck and money are related.
B. He believes people can create their own luck.
C. He blames other people for his bad luck.
D. He relies on luck to make up for recklessness.

____ 2. Based on the first paragraph of "The Rocking-Horse Winner," what would be the most logical prediction about the plot of the story?
A. The central problem is a woman's ceasing to love her husband.
B. The central problem is a woman's anxiety about her children.
C. The central problem is a woman's inability to love her family.
D. The central problem is a woman's selflessness.

____ 3. The rocking horse in "The Rocking-Horse Winner" adds to the story's fairy-tale style because it
A. is used as another character.
B. ultimately causes Paul's death.
C. brings Paul and his mother together.
D. seems to have supernatural powers.

____ 4. In "The Rocking-Horse Winner," the character of Paul is portrayed as
A. immoral beyond redemption.
B. victimized by his parents' greed.
C. spoiled and irresponsible.
D. passive in the face of opportunity.

____ 5. In "The Rocking-Horse Winner," Paul doesn't reveal the secret of his rocking horse because he
A. wants to preserve its special powers.
B. is a deceitful child.
C. fears ridicule.
D. has been sworn to secrecy by Bassett.

____ 6. One of Lawrence's themes in "The Rocking-Horse Winner" is the
A. ways that materialism can warp people psychologically.
B. power of supernatural forces over people's lives.
C. need children have for strict discipline.
D. high cost of taking unnecessary risks.

Unit 6 Resources: A Time of Rapid Change
© Pearson Education, Inc. All rights reserved.
121

EL L3 L4 Selection Test B, pp. 121–123

Also available for these selections:

L3 L4 Open-Book Test, pp. 115–117

EL L1 L2 Selection Test A, pp. 118–120

PHLit Online!
www.PHLitOnline.com

- complete narrated selection text
- a thematically related video with writing prompt
- an interactive graphic organizer
- highlighting feature
- access to all student print resources, adapted to individual student needs
- Spanish and English summaries
- adapted selection translations in Spanish

Online Resources: All print materials are also available online.

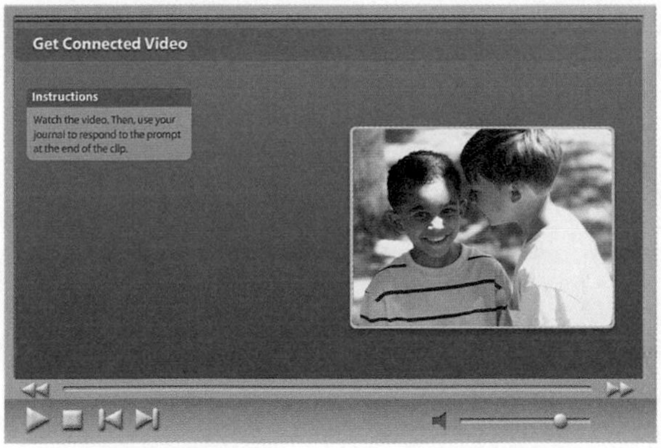

Get Connected! (thematic video with writing prompt)

Also available:

Background Video
All videos are available in Spanish.

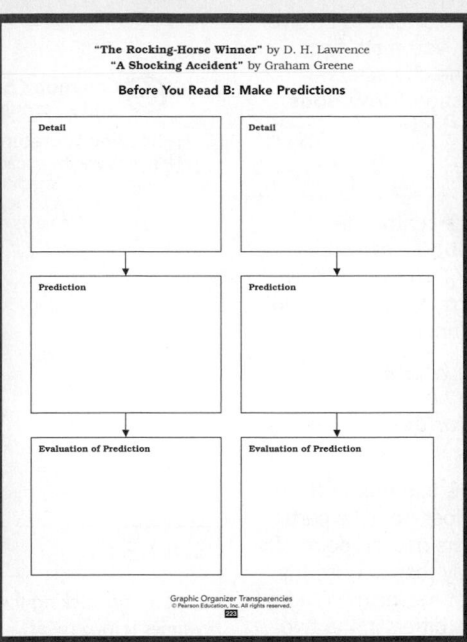

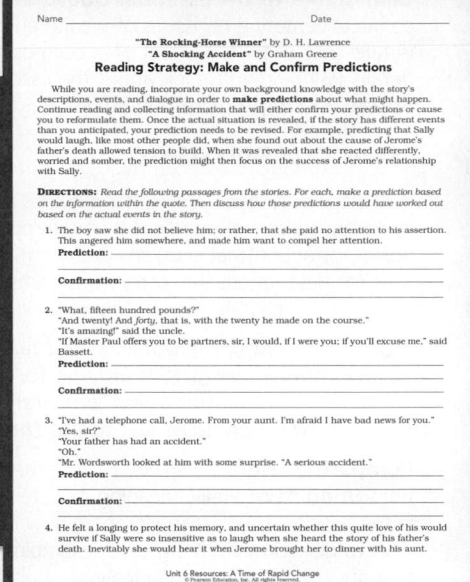

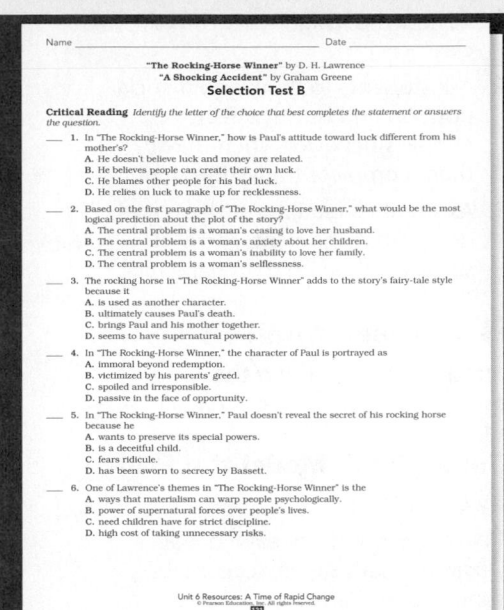

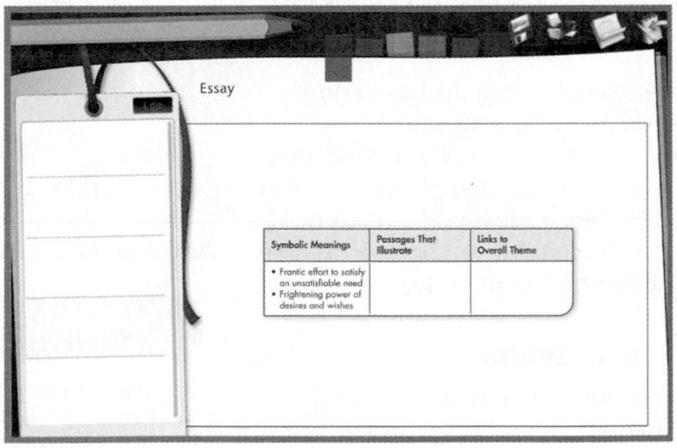

Writer's Journal (with graphics feature)

Also available:

Vocabulary Central (tools and activities for studying vocabulary)

❶ Connecting to the Essential Question

1. Review the assignment with the class.
2. Ask students to think about social position and how it affects people's behavior. Then, have them complete the assignment.
3. As students read, have them find details that show the effect of social position on the characters.

❷ Literary Analysis

Introduce the skill using the instruction on the student page.

Think Aloud: Model the Skill

Say to students:

We use symbols in real life. For example, let's say my classmate and I cannot agree on what to do for a school project. After talking it through, we decide to compromise. We shake hands to seal the deal. Our handshake is a symbol of the agreement that we have come to.

❸ Reading Strategy

1. Introduce the skill using the instruction on the student page.
2. Give students a copy of **Reading Strategy Graphic Organizer B,** page 223 in ***Graphic Organizer Transparencies,*** to fill out as they read.

Think Aloud: Model the Skill

Say to students:

We make predictions based on what people say and do. I may know that my friend is a good student and is capable of doing well in math. Since my friend studies hard, I can reasonably predict my friend's success on the math test.

❹ Vocabulary

1. Pronounce each word, giving its definition, and have students say it aloud.
2. For more guidance, see the ***Classroom Strategies and Teaching Routines*** card for introducing vocabulary.

Before You Read

The Rocking-Horse Winner • *A Shocking Accident*

❶ **Connecting to the Essential Question** Both of these stories involve conflicts centering on issues of wealth and class. As you read, find details that show the effect of social position on the characters. These details will help you think about the Essential Question: **How does literature shape or reflect society?**

Common Core State Standards

Reading Literature
3. Analyze the impact of the author's choices regarding how to develop and relate elements of a story.

❷ Literary Analysis

In most short stories, the writer explores a **theme,** a central idea or question. Writers often reveal theme through a **symbol,** a person, object, or action that suggests deeper meanings. To identify symbols, look for descriptions that carry special emphasis, such as the underlined words in this passage from "The Rocking-Horse Winner."

> *He knew the horse would take him to where there was luck, if only he forced it. So he would mount again, and start on his furious ride, hoping at last to get there.*

Comparing Literary Works Each of these stories is told from a **third-person point of view,** meaning that the narrator does not take part in the action. As you read, compare how both authors use this point of view to develop their themes, for example, in the way they disclose the thoughts of characters and create symbols to suggest meanings. In addition, ask yourself how the third-person point of view differs in the two stories. Consider, for instance, whether Greene's narrative has the same intensity as Lawrence's.

❸ Reading Strategy

Preparing to Read Complex Texts As you read, use the descriptions, events, and dialogue in the text—and your own background knowledge—to **make predictions** about what might happen. As you continue reading and learn more, you can confirm or revise those predictions. Use a graphic organizer like the one shown.

Detail
Paul misses picking the winner in two races.

↓

Prediction
He will be determined to pick the Derby winner.

↓

Evaluation of Prediction

❹ Vocabulary

discreet (di skrēt′) *adj.* wise; prudent (p. 1247)

obstinately (äb′ stə nət lē) *adv.* in a determined way; stubbornly (p. 1254)

uncanny (un kan′ ē) *adj.* mysterious; hard to explain (p. 1255)

apprehension (ap′ rē hen′ shən) *n.* anxious feeling of foreboding; dread (p. 1263)

embarked (em bärkt′) *v.* engaged in something, such as a conversation (p. 1265)

intrinsically (in trin′ sik lē) *adv.* at its core; innately (p. 1266)

PHLit Online! www.PHLitOnline.com

Vocabulary Development

Vocabulary Knowledge Rating

Create a **Vocabulary Knowledge Rating Chart** (***Professional Development Guidebook,*** p. 33) for the vocabulary words on the student page. Give each student a copy of the chart with the words on it. Read the words aloud, and have students mark their ratings in the Before Reading column. Urge students to attend to these words as they read and discuss the selections.

In order to gauge how much instruction you need to provide, tally how many students are confident in their knowledge of each word. As students read, point out the words and their context.

PHLit Online! **Vocabulary Central,** featuring tools and activities for studying vocabulary, is available online at **www.PHLitOnline.com.**

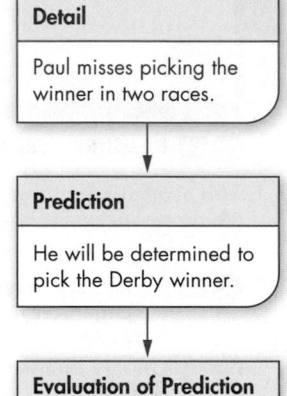

5 # D. H. Lawrence

(1885–1930)

Author of "The Rocking-Horse Winner"

During his lifetime, D. H. Lawrence's literary achievements were overshadowed by controversy. Like Percy Bysshe Shelley and Lord Byron in their day, Lawrence took unorthodox positions on politics and morality that shocked mainstream society.

Early Years Lawrence was born in Eastwood, Nottinghamshire, the son of an almost illiterate coal miner father and a more educated mother. Through her influence, he pursued a scholarship to the Nottingham High School, where he studied from 1898 to 1901. After leaving school for a job as a clerk, he contracted pneumonia and, on recovering, became a teacher.

Lawrence also began to write poems, stories, and novels, and his poetry attracted the attention of the well-known writer and editor Ford Madox Ford. In 1913, Lawrence published his first major novel, *Sons and Lovers,* a thinly disguised autobiography. Two years later, he published *The Rainbow,* which was banned in Britain.

Travels Abroad During World War I, Lawrence and his German wife, Frieda, lived in poverty in England and were unreasonably suspected of being German spies. At the end of the war, they left England and never returned. They traveled to Italy, Ceylon, Australia, Mexico, and the United States, and Lawrence used many of these locales in his fiction. In 1920, he published *Women in Love,* one of his greatest novels. A few years later, although suffering from tuberculosis, he completed *Lady Chatterley's Lover.* Shortly afterward, in the south of France, he died from that disease.

In the years since Lawrence's death, society's views of his writings have changed profoundly. Today, his fiction is widely admired for its vivid settings, fine craftsmanship, and psychological insight.

"THE HUMAN SOUL NEEDS ACTUAL BEAUTY MORE THAN bread."

Daily Bellringer

For each class during which you will teach this selection, have students complete one of the five activities for the appropriate week in the ***Daily Bellringer Activities*** booklet.

Multidraft Reading

To assist struggling readers and to enhance reading for all, assign the text in chunks, as warranted by length, and apply multidraft reading protocols. For each reading, have students set the purpose indicated:

- **First reading**—identifying key ideas and details and answering any Reading Checks.
- **Second reading**—analyzing craft and structure and responding to the side-column prompts.
- **Third reading**—integrating knowledge and ideas, connecting to other texts and the world, and answering the end-of-selection questions.

For more guidance, refer to the ***Classroom Strategies and Teaching Routines*** card on multidraft reading.

5 Background

More About the Author

D. H. Lawrence believed in the importance of instincts and intuitions, reflecting the ideas of philosopher Friedrich Nietzsche. Lawrence was tremendously influential in shaping twentieth-century fiction. His literary style is lush, sensuous, and incredibly descriptive. He was especially adept at creating a detailed sense of place and time.

PHLit Online!
www.PHLitOnline.com

Teaching From Technology

Preparing to Read
Go to **www.PHLitOnline.com** and display the ***Get Connected!*** slide show for these selections. Have the class brainstorm responses to the writing prompt, entering ideas in the interactive journal. Then, have students complete their written responses as homework.

To build background, display the Background and More About the Author features.

Using the Interactive Text
Go to **www.PHLitOnline.com** and display the **Enriched Online Student Edition.** As the class reads the selection or listens to the narration, record answers to side-column prompts using the graphic organizers accessible on the interactive page. Alternatively, have students use the online edition individually, answering the prompts as they read.

❶ About the Selection

In this parable about the ill effects of greed, a family is in constant need of money; at least that is what the mother tells her impressionable son. She says that having money is a matter of being lucky. Eager to please his mother and help her obtain the wealth she desires, the boy sets out to prove that he is lucky. His ability to choose winning racehorses and the price he pays for this ability will lead students to analyze their own ideas about luck and money.

❷ Activating Prior Knowledge

Before assigning the D. H. Lawrence story, write down a "secret" number between 1 and 10. Ask students to guess the number, record their guesses, and tally all responses on the chalkboard. Then, reveal the number you wrote. How many students guessed it correctly? If any did, have them tell how they made their choice: Luck? Intuition? Chance? Lead a discussion about the role of luck and chance in students' lives. Then, tell students that these elements play a very important role in these two stories.

Concept Connector →

Tell students they will return to their responses after reading the selection.

❶ ❷ The Rocking-Horse Winner

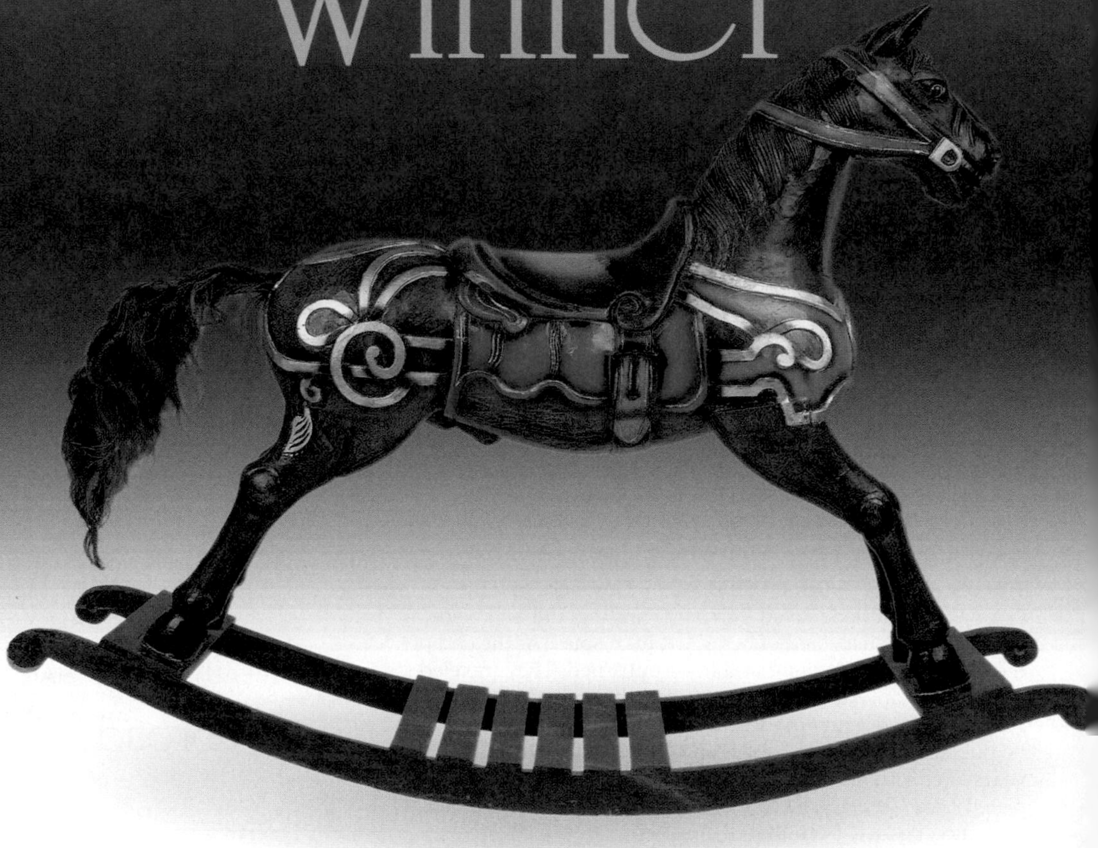

D. H. Lawrence

Text Complexity Rubric

	The Rocking-Horse Winner	A Shocking Accident
Qualitative Measures		
Context/ Knowledge Demands	Modernist story; cultural knowledge demands 1 2 ③ 4 5	Modernist story; cultural knowledge and life experience demands 1 2 3 ④ 5
Structure/Language Conventionality and Clarity	Extensive dialogue; accessible diction 1 ② 3 4 5	Long sentences; accessible diction 1 ② 3 4 5
Levels of Meaning/ Purpose/Concept Level	Moderate (greed, family ties, tragedy) 1 2 ③ 4 5	Moderate (humiliation; love and understanding) 1 2 ③ 4 5
Quantitative Measures		
Lexile/Text Length	650L / 5,436 words	980L / 2,026 words
Overall Complexity	**More accessible**	**More complex**

BACKGROUND DURING THE FIRST HALF OF THE TWENTIETH CENTURY, BRITAIN HAD A RIGID CLASS STRUCTURE. ITS UPPER CLASSES TRIED TO LIVE AT THE "RIGHT" ADDRESSES, ATTEND THE "RIGHT" SCHOOLS, AND HAVE THE "RIGHT" FRIENDS. IN "THE ROCKING-HORSE WINNER," PAUL'S MOTHER IS DESPERATE TO MAINTAIN UPPER-CLASS APPEARANCES DESPITE HER HUSBAND'S "SMALL INCOME." IN "A SHOCKING ACCIDENT," JEROME ATTENDS AN "EXPENSIVE PREPARATORY SCHOOL"—PRIVATE SCHOOLS IN BRITAIN ARE REFERRED TO AS PUBLIC SCHOOLS—AND MUST DEAL WITH CLASSMATES' REACTIONS TO A TRAGEDY THAT IS BIZARRELY IMPROPER.

There was a woman who was beautiful, who started with all the advantages, yet she had no luck. She married for love, and the love turned to dust. She had bonny children, yet she felt they had been thrust upon her, and she could not love them. They looked at her coldly, as if they were finding fault with her. And hurriedly she felt she must cover up some fault in herself. Yet what it was that she must cover up she never knew. Nevertheless,
41 when her children were present, she always felt the center of her heart go hard. This troubled her, and in her manner she was all the more gentle and anxious for her children, as if she loved them very much. Only she herself knew that at the center of her heart was a hard little place that could not feel love, no, not for anybody. Everybody else said of her: "She is such a good mother. She adores her children." Only she herself, and her children themselves, knew it was not so. They read it in each other's eyes.

There were a boy and two little girls. They lived in a pleasant house, with a garden and they had discreet servants, and felt themselves superior to anyone in the neighborhood.

Although they lived in style, they felt always an anxiety in the house. There was never enough money. The mother had a small income and the father had a small income, but not nearly enough for the social position which they had to keep up. The father went into town to some office. But though he had good prospects, these prospects never materialized. There was always the grinding sense of the shortage of money, though the style was always kept up.

At last the mother said, "I will see if *I* can't make something." But she did not know where to begin. She racked her brains, and tried this thing and the other, but could not find anything successful. The failure made deep lines come into her face. Her children were growing

3 ◀ Critical Viewing
What could someone riding a rocking horse like this one win? **[Speculate]**

Literary Analysis
Theme and Symbol
What ideas about the story's theme does this first paragraph suggest?

Vocabulary
discreet (di skrēt′) *adj.* wise; prudent

5 Reading Check
What does the mother feel toward her children?

3 Critical Viewing

Possible response: Students might suggest that the prize for riding the rocking horse pictured might be a toy or a piece of candy, because it looks like something a child would ride.

4 Literary Analysis

Theme and Symbol

1. Point out to students that this story begins much like a conventional fairy tale. **Ask** them what this choice of opening might symbolize.
   Possible response: Fairy tales generally have lessons to teach or morals to impart. Perhaps this story will do the same.
2. **Ask** students to describe what they have learned so far about the woman in the story.
   Answer: The woman is beautiful. She does not love her husband or her children and always feels at fault for something she cannot change.
3. **Ask** students the Literary Analysis question: What ideas about the story's theme does this first paragraph suggest?
   Possible response: The mother who does not love her children will experience some kind of setback, and she will not be the "winner" referred to in the title.

5 Reading Check

Answer: The mother does not love them; her heart goes "hard" in their presence.

Text Complexity: Reader and Task Suggestions

The Rocking-Horse Winner		A Shocking Accident	
Preparing to Read the Text	**Leveled Tasks**	**Preparing to Read the Text**	**Leveled Tasks**
• Using the Background on SE p. 1247, discuss the rigid class system in early twentieth-century Britain. • Discuss how financial worries can affect all members of a family. • Guide students to use Multidraft Reading strategies (TE p. 1245).	*Levels of Meaning* If students will have difficulty with the levels of meaning, have them first focus on the story's plot and the relationships of story characters. Then, as they reread, have students focus on the story's symbolism and moral message. *Analyzing* If students will not have difficulty with the levels of meaning, have them analyze the character of Paul, citing details to support their interpretation of his personality and motivation.	• Use the information on SE p. 1262 to discuss the psychological insights that good authors often bring to their characters. • Discuss with students the effects of embarrassment or humiliation on a person's relationships. • Guide students to use Multidraft Reading strategies (TE p. 1245).	*Levels of Meaning* If students will have difficulty with the levels of meaning, have them focus first on story events and Jerome's and Sally's reaction to them. Then, as they reread, have students consider what Jerome's experiences suggest about human relationships in general. *Evaluating* If students will not have difficulty with the meaning, have them evaluate the author's understanding of human behavior.

6 Literary Analysis

Theme and Symbol

1. **Ask** students if there is an actual whisper heard in the house. If not, what is it?
   Answer: No one is actually whispering, "There must be more money." The whisper is the message that the children discern from the behavior of the adults, particularly their mother.
2. **Ask** students the Literary Analysis question: How does this secret whispering help reveal a potential theme?
   Possible response: A potential theme is that what is communicated through feelings may be more important than what is spoken.

up, they would have to go to school. There must be more money, there must be more money. The father, who was always very handsome and expensive in his tastes, seemed as if he never *would* be able to do anything worth doing. And the mother, who had a great belief in herself, did not succeed any better, and her tastes were just as expensive.

Literary Analysis
Theme and Symbol
How does this secret whispering help reveal a potential theme?

And so the house came to be haunted by the unspoken phrase: *There must be more money! There must be more money!* The children could hear it all the time, though nobody said it aloud. They heard it at Christmas, when the expensive and splendid toys filled the nursery. Behind the shining modern rocking horse, behind the smart doll's house, a voice would start whispering: "There *must* be more money! There *must* be more money!" And the children would stop playing, to listen for a moment. They would look into each other's eyes to see if they had all heard. And each one saw in the eyes of the other two that they too had heard. "There *must* be more money! There *must* be more money!" 61

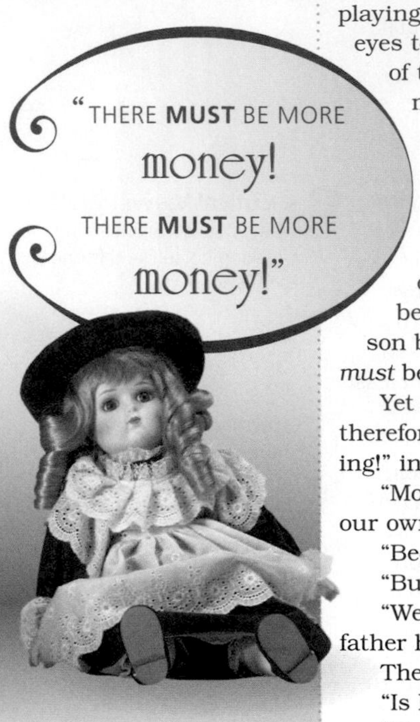
"THERE MUST BE MORE
money!
THERE MUST BE MORE
money!"

It came whispering from the springs of the still-swaying rocking horse, and even the horse, bending his wooden, champing head, heard it. The big doll, sitting so pink and smirking in her new pram,[1] could hear it quite plainly, and seemed to be smirking all the more self-consciously because of it. The foolish puppy, too, that took the place of the teddy bear, he was looking so extraordinarily foolish for no other reason but that he heard the secret whisper all over the house: "There *must* be more money."

Yet nobody ever said it aloud. The whisper was everywhere, and therefore no one spoke it. Just as no one ever says: "We are breathing!" in spite of the fact that breath is coming and going all the time.

"Mother!" said the boy Paul one day. "Why don't we keep a car of our own? Why do we always use uncle's, or else a taxi?"

"Because we're the poor members of the family," said the mother.

"But why *are* we, mother?"

"Well—I suppose," she said slowly and bitterly, "it's because your father has no luck."

The boy was silent for some time.

"Is luck money, mother?" he asked, rather timidly.

"No, Paul! Not quite. It's what causes you to have money."

"Oh!" said Paul vaguely. "I thought when Uncle Oscar said *filthy lucker,* it meant money."

"*Filthy lucre* does mean money," said the mother. "But it's lucre, not luck."

"Oh!" said the boy. "Then what *is* luck, mother?"

"It's what causes you to have money. If you're lucky you have money. That's why it's better to be born lucky than rich. If you're rich, you may lose your money. But if you're lucky, you will always get more money."

---

1. **pram** baby carriage.

Enrichment: Building Context

Greek Tragedy

In "The Rocking-Horse Winner," tragic consequences follow when a boy tries to "beat the odds." The struggle between fate and self-determination is a major theme in ancient Greek tragedies. Tell students as they read to look for how a basically noble hero is brought down by a tragic flaw such as hubris (excessive pride) and/or the will of the gods. In a twist on classical tragedy, some modern writers have used absurdity to emphasize humans' helplessness in an irrational world. Have students discuss how these stories and others they know illustrate the qualities of classical tragedy and the absurd.

Activity: Research Have students research elements of the Greek tragedy. Suggest that they record their findings in the **Enrichment: Building Context** worksheet, ***Professional Development Guidebook,*** page 222.

"Oh! Will you! And is father not lucky?"

"Very unlucky, I should say," she said bitterly.

The boy watched her with unsure eyes.

"Why?" he asked.

"I don't know. Nobody ever knows why one person is lucky and another unlucky."

"Don't they? Nobody at all? Does *nobody* know?"

"Perhaps God! But He never tells."

"He ought to, then. And aren't you lucky either, mother?"

"I can't be, if I married an unlucky husband."

"But by yourself, aren't you?"

"I used to think I was, before I married. Now I think I am very unlucky indeed."

"Why?"

"Well—never mind! Perhaps I'm not really," she said.

The child looked at her, to see if she meant it. But he saw, by the lines of her mouth, that she was only trying to hide something from him.

"Well, anyhow," he said stoutly, "I'm a lucky person."

"Why?" said his mother, with a sudden laugh.

He stared at her. He didn't even know why he had said it.

"God told me," he asserted, brazening[2] it out.

"I hope He did, dear!" she said, again with a laugh, but rather bitter.

7 "He did, mother!"

"Excellent!" said the mother, using one of her husband's exclamations.

The boy saw she did not believe him; or rather, that she paid no attention to his assertion. This angered him somewhere, and made him want to compel her attention.

He went off by himself, vaguely, in a childish way, seeking for the clue to "luck." Absorbed, taking no heed of other people, he went about with a sort of stealth, seeking inwardly for luck. He wanted luck, he wanted it, he wanted it. When the two girls were playing dolls, in the nursery, he would sit on his big rocking horse, charging madly into space, with a frenzy that made the little girls peer at him uneasily. Wildly the horse careered, the waving dark hair of the boy tossed, his eyes had a strange glare in them. The little girls dared not speak to him.

When he had ridden to the end of his mad little journey, he climbed down and stood in front of his rocking horse, staring fixedly into its lowered face. Its red mouth was slightly open, its big eye was wide and glassy bright.

"Now!" he would silently command the snorting steed. "Now take me to where there is luck! Now take me!"

And he would slash the horse on the neck with the little whip he had asked Uncle Oscar for. He *knew* the horse could take him to

2. **brazening** (brā′ zən iŋ) *v.* daring boldly or shamelessly.

Reading Strategy
Making and Confirming Predictions Based on what you have read, what do you think Paul will do? Why do you think so?

8 **Reading Check**
What does Paul do to find "the clue to 'luck'"?

7 Reading Strategy
Making and Confirming Predictions

1. Draw students' attention to the part of the text in which Paul tells his mother he is lucky. **Ask** students to describe his mother's reaction.
   Possible responses: Paul's mother laughs bitterly and clearly does not believe him.
2. **Ask** students to tell how Paul feels when he sees her reaction.
   Possible responses: Paul feels that his mother did not pay attention to his claim to being lucky; he is angered and wants to get her attention.
3. **Ask** students the Reading Strategy question: Based on what you have read, what do you think Paul will do?
   Possible responses: Paul will try to do something to get his mother's attention and prove to her that he is a lucky person.

8 Reading Check

Answer: Paul rides his rocking horse to find the clue to luck.

Differentiated Instruction for Universal Access

Vocabulary for Special-Needs Students
Prepare students by giving them the meanings of unfamiliar words or familiar words used in unfamiliar ways. Examples are *lucre* ("money gotten through questionable means"), *mad* ("crazy"), *go down* ("lose"), and *writs* ("legal documents ordering the payment of debts").

Strategy for Less Proficient Readers
Students may need assistance with unfamiliar cultural references. In addition, you may need to guide students to understand that the whispering is not really in the house but instead in the children's minds.

❾ Literary Analysis

Theme and Symbol

1. **Ask** students what they learn, during this exchange between Paul and Uncle Oscar, about why the rocking horse is so central to Paul's life.
   Possible response: Paul has become a horse-racing fan, and the rocking horse probably represents a racehorse.
2. Have students identify the source of Paul's information about horse racing.
   Answer: Paul learns about horse racing from Bassett, who is the gardener for Paul's family.
3. **Ask** students the Literary Analysis question: Bassett and the small boy "lived" in the racing events. What might this detail suggest about their lives?
   Answer: This detail suggests that both Bassett and Paul need an exciting and fulfilling escape from their daily lives.

where there was luck, if only he forced it. So he would mount again, and start on his furious ride, hoping at last to get there. He knew he could get there.

"You'll break your horse, Paul!" said the nurse.

"He's always riding like that! I wish he'd leave off!" said his elder sister Joan.

But he only glared down on them in silence. Nurse gave him up. She could make nothing of him. Anyhow he was growing beyond her.

One day his mother and his Uncle Oscar came in when he was on one of his furious rides. He did not speak to them.

"Hallo! you young jockey! Riding a winner?" said his uncle.

"Aren't you growing too big for a rocking horse? You're not a very little boy any longer, you know," said his mother.

But Paul only gave a blue glare from his big, rather close-set eyes. He would speak to nobody when he was in full tilt. His mother watched him with an anxious expression on her face.

At last he suddenly stopped forcing his horse into the mechanical gallop, and slid down.

"Well, I got there!" he announced fiercely, his blue eyes still flaring, and his sturdy long legs straddling apart.

> "AREN'T YOU GROWING TOO BIG FOR A rocking horse?"

"Where did you get to?" asked his mother.

"Where I wanted to go to," he flared back at her.

"That's right, son!" said Uncle Oscar. "Don't you stop till you get there. What's the horse's name?"

"He doesn't have a name," said the boy.

"Gets on without all right?" asked the uncle.

"Well, he has different names. He was called Sansovino last week."

"Sansovino, eh? Won the Ascot.[3] How did you know his name?"

"He always talks about horse races with Bassett," said Joan.

The uncle was delighted to find that his small nephew was posted with all the racing news. Bassett, the young gardener who had been wounded in the left foot in the war, and had got his present job through Oscar Cresswell, whose batman[4] he had been, was a perfect blade of the "turf."[5] He lived in the racing events, and the small boy lived with him. ❾

Literary Analysis
Theme and Symbol
Bassett and the small boy "lived" in the racing events. What might this detail suggest about their lives?

Oscar Cresswell got it all from Bassett.

"Master Paul comes and asks me, so I can't do more than tell him, sir," said Bassett, his face terribly serious, as if he were speaking of religious matters.

"And does he ever put anything on a horse he fancies?"

"Well—I don't want to give him away—he's a young sport, a fine sport, sir. Would you mind asking him yourself? He sort of takes a

3. Ascot major English horse race.
4. batman British military officer's orderly.
5. blade . . . "turf" horse-racing fan.

Enrichment: Investigating Career Connections

Financial Planning
Paul's mother and father cannot seem to manage their money. Today, professional financial planners help people to invest their money wisely. Career opportunities abound as companies grow and expand here and overseas, as computers process and provide information on a global scale, and as individuals become more savvy about saving or investing money.

Activity: Research Financial Planning Careers
Have students research opportunities in this field. Consider inviting a professional who is knowledgeable about the field to address the class and answer their questions about what opportunities are available. Suggest students record their findings in the **Enrichment: Investigating Career Connections** worksheet, *Professional Development Guidebook*, page 221.

pleasure in it, and perhaps he'd feel I was giving him away, sir, if you don't mind."

Bassett was serious as a church.

The uncle went back to his nephew, and took him off for a ride in the car.

"Say, Paul, old man, do you ever put anything on a horse?" the uncle asked.

The boy watched the handsome man closely.

"Why, do you think I oughtn't to?" he parried.

10 "Not a bit of it! I thought perhaps you might give me a tip for the Lincoln."[6]

The car sped on into the country, going down to Uncle Oscar's place in Hampshire.

"Honor bright?" said the nephew.

"Honor bright, son!" said the uncle.

"Well, then, Daffodil."

"Daffodil! I doubt it, sonny. What about Mirza?"

"I only know the winner," said the boy. "That's Daffodil!"

"Daffodil, eh?"

There was a pause. Daffodil was an obscure horse comparatively.

"Uncle!"

"Yes, son?"

"You won't let it go any further, will you? I promised Bassett."

"Bassett be hanged, old man! What's he got to do with it?"

"We're partners! We've been partners from the first! Uncle, he lent me my first five shillings, which I lost. I promised him, honor bright, it was only between me and him: only you gave me that ten-shilling note I started winning with, so I thought you were lucky. You won't let it go any further, will you?"

The boy gazed at his uncle from those big, hot, blue eyes, set rather close together. The uncle stirred and laughed uneasily.

"Right you are, son! I'll keep your tip private. Daffodil, eh! How much are you putting on him?"

"All except twenty pounds," said the boy. "I keep that in reserve."

The uncle thought it a good joke.

"You keep twenty pounds in reserve, do you, you young romancer? What are you betting, then?"

"I'm betting three hundred," said the boy gravely. "But it's between you and me, Uncle Oscar! Honor bright?"

The uncle burst into a roar of laughter.

"It's between you and me all right, you young Nat Gould,"[7] he said, laughing. "But where's your three hundred?"

---

6. **Lincoln** major English horse race.
7. **Nat Gould** famous English sportswriter and authority on horse racing.

Reading Strategy
Making and Confirming Predictions Which horse do you think will do better? Why?

11 **Reading Check**
What kind of a partnership does Paul have with Bassett?

10 Reading Strategy

Making and Confirming Predictions

1. **Ask** students who Paul and his uncle think will win the Lincoln.
   Answer: Paul thinks Daffodil will win the race, while Uncle Oscar thinks Mirza will win.
2. **Ask** students to recall the name that Paul gave his rocking horse last week, and what was special about it.
   Answer: Paul had given his rocking horse the name Sansovino. Sansovino was also the name of the horse that won the Ascot, an important race.
3. **Ask** students whether they think that the fact that Paul's rocking horse had the name Sansovino was a coincidence.
   Possible response: Students may say that they think Paul figures out which horse will win a given race by riding his rocking horse.
4. **Ask** students the Reading Strategy question: Which horse do you think will do better? Why?
   Possible responses: Students may reply that Daffodil will win the race. Students may determine that since Paul guessed the name of the Ascot winner, he will also correctly predict the winner of the Lincoln.

11 Reading Check

Answer: Paul and Bassett have a trusting partnership. Bassett keeps track of Paul's winnings for him.

Differentiated Instruction for Universal Access

EL Vocabulary for English Learners

Point out that the word *obscure* on page 1251 is formed by combining the prefix *ob-*, meaning "on" or "over," and the root *-scuro-*, meaning "to conceal or cover." By definition, something that is obscure lacks light, is dark, or is not easily perceived. Daffodil is what is known as a "dark horse," the unexpected winner of a race.

Enrichment for Gifted/Talented Students

Have students draw pictures of Paul based on one of the descriptions of him on pages 1250–1251. Encourage them to pay particular attention to his eyes as they are described in several places. They might draw Paul in conversation with his uncle or at the racetrack.

⓬ Literary Analysis

Theme, Symbol, and Third-Person Point of View

1. **Ask** students why Paul thinks his Uncle Oscar is lucky.
   Answer: Paul started winning on the races with a ten-shilling note his Uncle Oscar gave him.
2. Have students identify the information that shocks Uncle Oscar in this exchange.
   Answer: Uncle Oscar learns that Paul has won a significant amount of money betting on the races.
3. **Ask** students the Literary Analysis question: What does the narrator suggest about Paul's need by describing his eyes as "blue fire"?
   Possible response: Paul's need is great, because "blue fire" suggests something hot and intense.

⓭ Reading Strategy

Making and Confirming Predictions

1. **Ask** students to recall Paul's and Uncle Oscar's predictions of which horse would win the Ascot.
   Answer: Paul predicted that Daffodil would win the race, while Uncle Oscar predicted Mirza would win.
2. **Ask** students the results of the race.
   Answer: Daffodil came in first, Lancelot second, and Mirza third.
3. **Ask** students the Reading Strategy question: Based on what you have read, who do you think picks the winning horses? Why?
   Possible response: Students may say that since Paul predicted the winner correctly, that he has a talent or "luck" for picking winning horses.

"Bassett keeps it for me. We're partners."

"You are, are you! And what is Bassett putting on Daffodil?"

"He won't go quite as high as I do, I expect. Perhaps he'll go a hundred and fifty."

"What, pennies?" laughed the uncle.

"Pounds," said the child, with a surprised look at his uncle. "Bassett keeps a bigger reserve than I do."

Between wonder and amusement, Uncle Oscar was silent. He pursued the matter no further, but he determined to take his nephew with him to the Lincoln races.

"Now, son," he said, "I'm putting twenty on Mirza, and I'll put five for you on any horse you fancy. What's your pick?"

"Daffodil, uncle!"

"No, not the fiver on Daffodil!"

"I should if it was my own five," said the child.

"Good! Good! Right you are! A fiver for me and a fiver for you on Daffodil."

Literary Analysis
Theme, Symbol, and Third-Person Point of View What does the narrator suggest about Paul's need by describing his eyes as "blue fire"? ⓬

The child had never been to a race meeting before, and his eyes were blue fire. He pursed his mouth tight, and watched. A Frenchman just in front had put his money on Lancelot. Wild with excitement, he flayed his arms up and down, yelling *"Lancelot! Lancelot!"* in his French accent.

⓭ Daffodil came in first, Lancelot second, Mirza third. The child, flushed and with eyes blazing, was curiously serene. His uncle brought him five five-pound notes: four to one.

"What am I to do with these?" he cried, waving them before the boy's eyes.

"I suppose we'll talk to Bassett," said the boy. "I expect I have fifteen hundred now; and twenty in reserve; and this twenty."

His uncle studied him for some moments.

"Look here, son!" he said. "You're not serious about Bassett and that fifteen hundred, are you?"

Reading Strategy ⓯
Making and Confirming Predictions Based on what you have read, who do you think picks the winning horses? Why?

"Yes, I am. But it's between you and me, uncle! Honor bright!"

"Honor bright all right, son! But I must talk to Bassett."

"If you'd like to be a partner, uncle, with Bassett and me, we could all be partners. Only you'd have to promise, honor bright, uncle, not to let it go beyond us three. Bassett and I are lucky, and you must be lucky, because it was your ten shillings I started winning with. . . ."

⓮ ▶ **Critical Viewing**
Which details in this picture convey the feverish excitement that Paul and Bassett feel about horse racing? **[Analyze]**

Uncle Oscar took both Bassett and Paul into Richmond Park for an afternoon, and there they talked.

"It's like this, you see, sir," Bassett said. "Master Paul would get me talking about racing events, spinning yarns, you know, sir. And he was always keen on knowing if I'd made or if I'd lost. It's about a year since, now, that I put five shillings on Blush of Dawn for him—and we lost. Then the luck turned, with that ten shillings he had

Enrichment: Investigating a Literary Figure

Uncle Oscar/Oscar Wilde
Point out that Uncle Oscar is always joking, that he supplies Paul with the whip for his rocking horse, and that he gives Paul the incentive to keep wagering. Tell students that Uncle Oscar may be an allusion to Oscar Wilde. The character Uncle Oscar echoes Wilde's individualism and his ideas on morality. The "changeable" name of Paul's horse suggests a reference to Wilde's mother's pen name, Speranza. Just as Wilde firmly believed that art must stand apart from life, Uncle Oscar, like the story's omniscient narrator, stays emotionally aloof.

Activity: Research Have students research the life and work of Oscar Wilde. Suggest that they record their findings in the **Enrichment: Investigating a Literary Figure** worksheet, ***Professional Development Guidebook***, page 235.

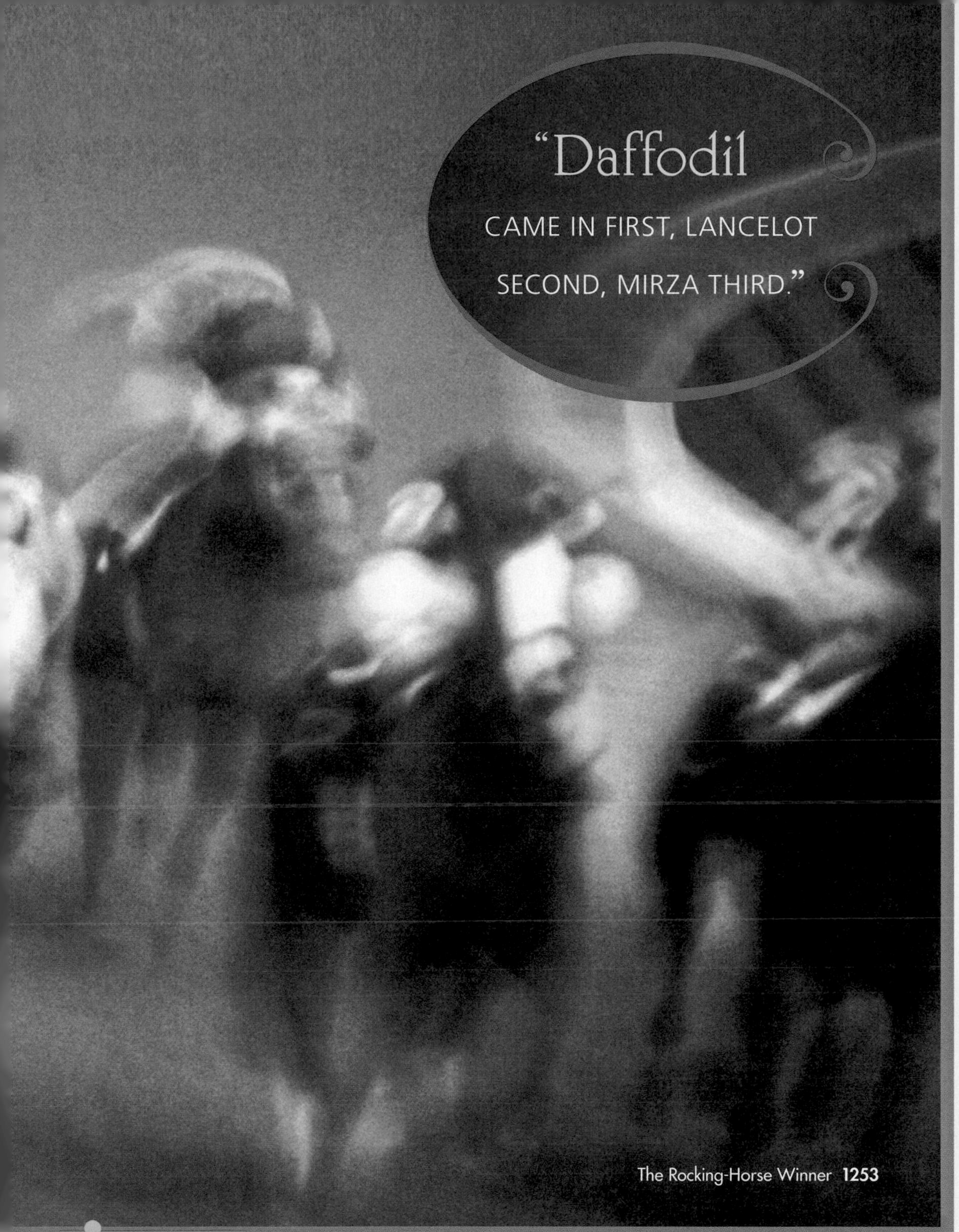
"Daffodil
CAME IN FIRST, LANCELOT
SECOND, MIRZA THIRD."

Differentiated Instruction for Universal Access

Support for Special-Needs Students
Have students work in groups of three to prepare the two scenes of dialogue on page 1252: the first among Uncle Oscar and Paul and the second between Bassett, Uncle Oscar, and Paul. Have them use their bodies and voices to communicate the excitement of the scenes.

Support for Less Proficient Readers
Have students decide whether there are other characters besides Paul in the story with whom they might identify. Have them make a character web for Uncle Oscar and Bassett, as well as for Paul's mother.

Strategy for English Learners
Have students use context to determine the meaning of the British usages in phrases such as "spinning yarns," "sure as eggs," and "I'll see the money."

⓮ Critical Viewing

Possible response: The speed at which the horses seem to be running and the intensity of the jockeys mirror the feverish excitement that Paul and Bassett feel about horse racing.

⓯ Critical Thinking

Define

1. Direct students' attention to the paragraph that begins "Yes, I am" near the bottom of page 1252.
2. **Ask** students to use context clues to determine the meaning of the phrase "honor bright" in the dialogue between Oscar and Paul.
   Answer: "Honor bright" means "honestly" or "truthfully." Students may offer "cross my heart" or "I promise" as well.

16 Critical Thinking

Deduce

1. Direct students' attention to the passage on the page beginning with "You see, it's all right, Uncle, when I'm *sure*!"
2. **Ask** students to deduce how Bassett and Paul became friends.
Answer: Paul asked Bassett about racing, and they found they had a common interest.
3. Have students **determine** whether Bassett and Paul have a trusting relationship. How do students know?
Answer: The two have a trusting relationship. They both contribute to telling stories about their escapades to Uncle Oscar. Bassett keeps silent about how much Paul has won until Paul tells Uncle Oscar. Paul also trusts Bassett to keep his winnings safe.

from you, that we put on Singhalese. And since that time, it's been pretty steady, all things considering. What do you say, Master Paul?"

"We're all right when we're *sure*," said Paul. "It's when we're not quite sure that we go down."

"Oh, but we're careful then," said Bassett.

"But when are you *sure*?" smiled Uncle Oscar.

"It's Master Paul, sir," said Bassett, in a secret, religious voice. "It's as if he had it from heaven. Like Daffodil now, for the Lincoln. That was as sure as eggs."

"Did you put anything on Daffodil?" asked Oscar Cresswell.

"Yes, sir. I made my bit."

"And my nephew?"

Bassett was obstinately silent, looking at Paul.

Vocabulary
obstinately (äb′ stə nət lē) *adv.* in a determined way; stubbornly

"I made twelve hundred, didn't I, Bassett? I told uncle I was putting three hundred on Daffodil."

"That's right," said Bassett, nodding.

"But where's the money?" asked the uncle.

"I keep it safe locked up, sir. Master Paul, he can have it any minute he likes to ask for it."

"What, fifteen hundred pounds?"

"And twenty! And *forty*, that is, with the twenty he made on the course."

"It's amazing!" said the uncle.

"If Master Paul offers you to be partners, sir, I would, if I were you; if you'll excuse me," said Bassett.

Oscar Cresswell thought about it.

"I'll see the money," he said.

They drove home again, and sure enough, Bassett came round to the garden house with fifteen hundred pounds in notes. The twenty pounds reserve was left with Joe Glee, in the Turf Commission deposit.

"You see, it's all right, uncle, when I'm *sure!* Then we go strong, for all we're worth. Don't we, Bassett?"

"We do that, Master Paul."

"And when are you sure?" said the uncle, laughing.

16 "Oh, well, sometimes I'm *absolutely* sure, like about Daffodil," said the boy, "and sometimes I have an idea; and sometimes I haven't even an idea, have I, Bassett? Then we're careful, because we mostly go down."

"You do, do you! And when you're sure, like about Daffodil, what makes you sure, sonny?"

"Oh, well, I don't know," said the boy uneasily. "I'm sure, you know, uncle; that's all."

"It's as if he had it from heaven, sir," Bassett reiterated.

"I should say so!" said the uncle.

But he became a partner. And when the Leger was coming on, Paul was "sure" about Lively Spark, which was a quite inconsiderable horse. The boy insisted on putting a thousand on the horse, Bassett went for five hundred, and Oscar Cresswell two hundred. Lively

Enrichment: Building Context

Probability

When Paul picks his winners, he pays no attention to which horses are favored and which are "dark horses." For him, the choice of a winner is based on a mysterious process of intuition, not on science or mathematics. The mathematical study of probability deals with the likelihood that events will occur. This field of study can be quite complex. A simple example of probability, however, involves the tossing of a die with six faces. The probability of one face appearing is equal to the ratio of that event (1) over the number of possible outcomes (6). Therefore, the probability of throwing a die and having a particular face come up is 1/6.

Activity: Research Have students research probability in horse racing. Suggest that they record their findings in the **Enrichment: Building Context** worksheet, ***Professional Development Guidebook,*** page 222.

Spark came in first, and the betting had been ten to one against him. Paul had made ten thousand.

17 "You see," he said. "I was absolutely sure of him."

Even Oscar Cresswell had cleared two thousand.

"Look here, son," he said, "this sort of thing makes me nervous."

"It needn't, uncle! Perhaps I shan't be sure again for a long time."

"But what are you going to do with your money?" asked the uncle.

"Of course," said the boy, "I started it for mother. She said she had no luck, because father is unlucky, so I thought if *I* was lucky, it might stop whispering."

"What might stop whispering?"

"Our house! I *hate* our house for whispering."

"What does it whisper?"

"Why—why"—the boy fidgeted—"why, I don't know! But it's always short of money, you know, uncle."

"I know it, son, I know it."

"You know people send mother writs, don't you, uncle?"

"I'm afraid I do," said the uncle.

"And then the house whispers like people laughing at you behind your back. It's awful, that is! I thought if I was lucky . . ."

"You might stop it," added the uncle.

The boy watched him with big blue eyes, that had an **uncanny** cold fire in them, and he said never a word.

"Well then!" said the uncle. "What are we doing?"

"I shouldn't like mother to know I was lucky," said the boy.

"Why not, son?"

"She'd stop me."

"I don't think she would."

"Oh!"—and the boy writhed in an odd way—"I *don't* want her to know, uncle."

"All right, son! We'll manage it without her knowing."

They managed it very easily. Paul, at the other's suggestion, handed over five thousand pounds to his uncle, who deposited it with the family lawyer, who was then to inform Paul's mother that a relative had put five thousand pounds into his hands, which sum was to be paid out a thousand pounds at a time, on the mother's birthday, for the next five years.

"So she'll have a birthday present of a thousand pounds for five successive years," said Uncle Oscar. "I hope it won't make it all the harder for her later."

Paul's mother had her birthday in November. The house had been "whispering" worse than ever lately, and even in spite of his luck, Paul could not bear up against it. He was very anxious to see the effect of the birthday letter, telling his mother about the thousand pounds.

When there were no visitors, Paul now took his meals with his parents, as he was beyond the nursery control. His mother went into

"OUR HOUSE! I **HATE** OUR HOUSE FOR whispering."

Vocabulary
uncanny (un kan' ē) *adj.* mysterious; hard to explain

18 **Reading Check**
Why does Paul want to win money?

17 Critical Thinking

Compare and Contrast

1. Direct students' attention to this line on the student page: "You see," he said, "I was absolutely sure of him."
2. **Ask** students to describe the hierarchy of sureness that Bassett and Paul use when betting on the horses.
   Answer: When Paul is absolutely sure, they bet a lot of money; when Paul has an idea, they bet less; and when Paul has no idea at all, they bet very little, because they usually lose.
3. **Ask** students to compare and contrast the beliefs of Bassett and Paul as to why Paul is able to predict the winning racers.
   Answer: Bassett thinks the answers come from God; Paul says he is just sure, but he does not know why.

18 Reading Check

Answer: Paul wants to win money so he can give it to his mother and so the house will stop whispering.

Differentiated Instruction for Universal Access

Strategy for Special-Needs Students
Guide students to understand that in households like this one, parents were relieved of the "burden" of messy meals with their small children. Paul is now at an age when he may dine with the grown-ups. Ask students to look for more evidence in the story that this family has a privileged place in society.

Enrichment for Gifted/Talented Students
Have each student design a sculpture, paint a picture, or choreograph a dance that captures the intensity of young Paul's trying to prevent his mother from sending him away before the Derby. Encourage students to consider abstract as well as representational possibilities.

19 Reading Strategy
Making and Confirming Predictions

1. Ask students if they ever received an expensive and unexpected gift. **Ask** them to describe how they reacted and how they felt.
   Answer: Students may say that they felt happy and excited; they may also say that they ended up wanting something different or something more.
2. **Ask** students to recall how Paul's mother felt about her job making sketches for advertisements.
   Answer: Students may say that Paul's mother was dissatisfied because she did not feel she was first, or successful.
3. **Ask** students the Reading Strategy question: How do you think Paul's mother will react to the letter about the money? Why?
   Possible response: Students may say that she will be dissatisfied because she will not think that it is enough.

20 Reading Strategy
Making and Confirming Predictions

1. Ask students to describe how Paul's mother answers when Paul asks her if she had received anything nice in the post for her birthday.
   Answer: Paul's mother answers him in a cold and absent voice, responding, "Quite moderately nice."
2. **Ask** students the Reading Strategy question: How accurate was your prediction about Paul's mother's reaction? How do you think Paul will respond to this result?
   Possible responses: Students may say that they thought Paul's mother would be delighted, but instead that she was dissatisfied. They may say that they think Paul will be very hurt and disappointed with her cold reaction.

Reading Strategy
Making and Confirming Predictions How do you think Paul's mother will react to the letter about the money? Why? 19

town nearly every day. She had discovered that she had an odd knack of sketching furs and dress materials, so she worked secretly in the studio of a friend who was the chief "artist" for the leading drapers. She drew the figures of ladies in furs and ladies in silk and sequins for the newspaper advertisements. This young woman artist earned several thousand pounds a year, but Paul's mother only made several hundreds, and she was again dissatisfied. She so wanted to be first in something, and she did not succeed, even in making sketches for drapery advertisements.

She was down to breakfast on the morning of her birthday. Paul watched her face as she read her letters. He knew the lawyer's letter. As his mother read it, her face hardened and became more expressionless. Then a cold, determined look came on her mouth. She hid the letter under the pile of others, and said not a word about it.

"Didn't you have anything nice in the post for your birthday, mother?" said Paul.

"Quite moderately nice," she said, her voice cold and absent.

She went away to town without saying more.

But in the afternoon Uncle Oscar appeared. He said Paul's mother had had a long interview with the lawyer, asking if the whole five thousand could not be advanced at once, as she was in debt.

"What do you think, uncle?" said the boy.

"I leave it to you, son."

"Oh, let her have it, then! We can get some more with the other," said the boy.

"A bird in the hand is worth two in the bush, laddie!" said Uncle Oscar.

"But I'm sure to *know* for the Grand National; or the Lincolnshire; or else the Derby.[8] I'm sure to know for *one* of them," said Paul.

So Uncle Oscar signed the agreement, and Paul's mother touched the whole five thousand. Then something very curious happened. The voices in the house suddenly went mad, like a chorus of frogs on a spring evening. There were certain new furnishings, and Paul had a tutor. He was *really* going to Eton,[9] his father's school, in the following autumn. There were flowers in the winter, and a blossoming of the luxury Paul's mother had been used to. And yet the voices in the house, behind the sprays of mimosa and almond blossom, and from under the piles of iridescent cushions, simply trilled and screamed in a sort of ecstasy: "There *must* be more money! Oh-h-h! There *must* be more money! Oh, now, now-w! now-w-w—there *must* be more money!—more than ever! More than ever!" 20

It frightened Paul terribly. He studied away at his Latin and Greek with his tutors. But his intense hours were spent with Bassett. The

"DIDN'T YOU HAVE ANYTHING NICE IN THE POST FOR YOUR BIRTHDAY, mother?"

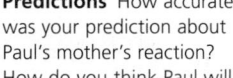

Reading Strategy
Making and Confirming Predictions How accurate was your prediction about Paul's mother's reaction? How do you think Paul will respond to this result?

8. **Grand National . . . Derby** major English horse races.
9. **Eton** prestigious private school in England.

Enrichment: Analyzing Historical Patterns, Trends, and Periods

British Empire
In an article entitled "A Rocking Horse: The Symbol, the Pattern, the Way to Live," critic W. D. Snodgrass examines the names of the horses on which Paul, Bassett, and Oscar gamble. He notes that the first winner, Singhalese, and his last, Malabar, have names of former British colonial regions in India. Snodgrass suggests that Lawrence deliberately selected these names and that he sees a parallel between Paul's fate and the fate of the British Empire.

Activity: Discuss Have students research the British Empire during the years of Lawrence's life. Have them analyze and discuss the parallel that Snodgrass draws. Suggest that they record their findings and ideas in the **Enrichment: Analyzing Historical Patterns, Trends, and Periods** worksheet, *Professional Development Guidebook,* page 231.

Grand National had gone by: he had not "known," and had lost a hundred pounds. Summer was at hand. He was in agony for the Lincoln. But even for the Lincoln he didn't "know," and he lost fifty pounds. He became wild-eyed and strange, as if something were going to explode in him.

"Let it alone, son! Don't you bother about it!" urged Uncle Oscar. But it was as if the boy couldn't really hear what his uncle was saying.

"I've got to know for the Derby! I've *got* to know for the Derby!" the child reiterated, his big blue eyes blazing with a sort of madness.

21 His mother noticed how overwrought he was.

"You'd better go to the seaside. Wouldn't you like to go now to the seaside, instead of waiting? I think you'd better," she said, looking down at him anxiously, her heart curiously heavy because of him.

But the child lifted his uncanny blue eyes.

22 "I couldn't possibly go before the Derby, mother!" he said. "I couldn't possibly!"

"Why not?" she said, her voice becoming heavy when she was opposed. "Why not? You can still go from the seaside to see the Derby with your Uncle Oscar, if that's what you wish. No need for you to wait here. Besides, I think you care too much about these races. It's a bad sign. My family has been a gambling family, and you won't know till you grow up how much damage it has done. But it has done damage. I shall have to send Bassett away, and ask Uncle Oscar not to talk racing to you, unless you promise to be reasonable about it; go away to the seaside and forget it. You're all nerves!"

"I'll do what you like, mother, so long as you don't send me away till after the Derby," the boy said.

"Send you away from where? Just from this house?"

"Yes," he said, gazing at her.

"Why, you curious child, what makes you care about this house so much, suddenly? I never knew you loved it!"

He gazed at her without speaking. He had a secret within a secret, something he had not divulged, even to Bassett or to his Uncle Oscar.

But his mother, after standing undecided and a little bit sullen for some moments, said:

"Very well, then! Don't go to the seaside till after the Derby, if you don't wish it. But promise me you won't let your nerves go to pieces! Promise you won't think so much about horse racing and *events,* as you call them!"

"Oh, no!" said the boy, casually. "I won't think much about them, mother. You needn't worry. I wouldn't worry, mother, if I were you."

"If you were me and I were you," said his mother, "I wonder what we should do!"

"But you know you needn't worry, mother, don't you?" the boy repeated.

"I should be awfully glad to know it," she said wearily.

Literary Analysis
Theme, Symbol, and Third-Person Point of View If the story were told from Paul's point of view, would you know about the mother's "curiously heavy" feelings concerning Paul? Why or why not?

23 ☑ Reading Check

What present does Paul give his mother?

Differentiated Instruction for Universal Access

Support for Less Proficient Readers
Guide students to understand that Paul's secret is that he finds his winners by riding furiously on the rocking horse.

EL Vocabulary for English Learners
Explain that Paul is obsessed with finding the Derby winner. Define *obsession* as "a persistent preoccupation with an idea or emotion." Point out that the word comes from the Latin *ob-* meaning "toward," "over," or "against," and *sedere,* meaning "to sit."

Support for Gifted/Talented Students
Ask students why they think the author left the father out of this story, except for introducing him at the beginning and having him go out to dinner with the mother toward the end. What plot reasons might Lawrence have had for making this decision? What thematic reasons might he have had?

21 Literary Analysis

Theme, Symbol, and Third-Person Point of View

1. **Ask** students what happens after Paul's mother gets the whole 5,000 pounds.
   Answer: She buys many new things, Paul gets a tutor, and the voices go mad.
2. Have students describe what happens to Paul's predictions of winners for the horse races.
   Answer: He does not "know" about winning horses for two major races and loses money on both of them.
3. **Ask** students what Paul's mother decides to do when she sees Paul getting so overwrought.
   Answer: She decides to send him to the seashore.
4. **Ask** students the Literary Analysis question: If the story were told from Paul's point of view, would you know about the mother's "curiously heavy" feelings concerning Paul? Why or why not?
   Answer: If the story were told from Paul's point of view, readers would know only the feelings of Paul.

22 Critical Thinking

Interpret

1. Direct students' attention to the passage on the student page that begins, "I couldn't possibly go before the Derby, mother!"
2. **Ask** why Paul does not want to go to the seashore before the Derby.
   Answer: Paul does not want to leave the house.
3. **Ask** students why they think Paul is desperate not to leave the house.
   Possible response: There is something about being in the house that allows Paul to be "sure" when he guesses the horse race winners.

23 Reading Check

Answer: Paul gives his mother 5,000 pounds of his winnings at the races.

㉔ Literary Analysis

Theme and Symbol

1. **Ask** what Paul's mother said when he asked to have his rocking horse moved to his bedroom.
   Answer: Paul's mother said, "Surely you're too big for a rocking horse!"
2. **Ask** students what is ironic about the mother's statement.
   Possible response: The statement is ironic because it indicates that the mother sees Paul as a child, when it is his acting like an adult that has brought her the recent 5,000 pounds.
3. **Ask** students the Literary Analysis question: In the paragraph beginning "Paul's secret . . . ," which words or phrases suggest that the rocking horse is a symbol?
   Answer: The phrase "that which had no name" suggests that the horse is a symbol for luck, for success—for that which will win him his mother's love.

㉕ Literary Analysis

Theme, Symbol, and Third-Person Point of View

1. **Ask** students to compare the house's "whispering" to Paul with his mother's seizures of anxiety about him.
   Answer: Paul's mother's sudden seizures of anxiety are symbolic of Paul's stress over the racing losses, just as the "whispering" is symbolic of his mother's fears about money.
2. **Ask** students the Literary Analysis question: Does the third-person narrator's insight into the mother's anxiety make you feel more sympathy for her? Explain.
   Possible response: Knowing that she can feel anxiety and worry about Paul makes her seem less cold and more concerned. This makes her more sympathetic to the readers.

"Oh, well, you *can*, you know. I mean you *ought* to know you needn't worry!" he insisted.

"Ought I? Then I'll see about it," she said.

Literary Analysis
Theme and Symbol ㉔ In the paragraph beginning, "Paul's secret . . . ," which words or phrases suggest that the rocking horse is a symbol?

Paul's secret of secrets was his wooden horse, that which had no name. Since he was emancipated from a nurse and a nursery governess, he had had his rocking horse removed to his own bedroom at the top of the house.

"Surely you're too big for a rocking horse!" his mother had remonstrated.

"Well, you see, mother, till I can have a *real* horse, I like to have *some* sort of animal about," had been his quaint answer.

"Do you feel he keeps you company?" she laughed.

"Oh, yes! He's very good, he always keeps me company, when I'm there," said Paul.

So the horse, rather shabby, stood in an arrested prance in the boy's bedroom.

The Derby was drawing near, and the boy grew more and more tense. He hardly heard what was spoken to him, he was very frail, and his eyes were really uncanny. His mother had sudden strange seizures of uneasiness about him. Sometimes, for half an hour, she would feel a sudden anxiety about him that was almost anguish. She wanted to rush to him at once, and know he was safe.

㉕ Two nights before the Derby, she was at a big party in town, when one of her rushes of anxiety about her boy, her firstborn, gripped her heart till she could hardly speak. She fought with the feeling, might and main, for she believed in common sense. But it was too strong. She had to leave the dance and go downstairs to telephone to the country. The children's nursery governess was terribly surprised and startled at being rung up in the night.

"Are the children all right, Miss Wilmot?"

"Oh yes, they are quite all right."

"Master Paul? Is he all right?"

"He went to bed as right as a trivet.[10] Shall I run up and look at him?"

"No!" said Paul's mother reluctantly. "No! Don't trouble. It's all right. Don't sit up. We shall be home fairly soon." She did not want her son's privacy intruded upon.

"Very good," said the governess.

Literary Analysis
Theme, Symbol, and Third-Person Point of View Does the third-person narrator's insight into the mother's anxiety make you feel more sympathy for her? Explain.

It was about one o'clock when Paul's mother and father drove up to their house. All was still. Paul's mother went to her room and slipped off her white fur cloak. She had told her maid not to wait up for her. She heard her husband downstairs, mixing a whisky-and-soda.

And then, because of the strange anxiety at her heart, she stole upstairs to her son's room. Noiselessly she went along the upper corridor. Was there a faint noise? What was it?

10. **right as a trivet** perfectly right.

Enrichment: Analyzing Film

***The Rocking-Horse Winner,* 1949, directed by Anthony Pelissier**

Show the film and invite students to compare and contrast it with Lawrence's story. Ask students to discuss whether the characters in the film are faithful to the story. Direct students to think about and discuss how the visual images in the film compare with the mental images they formed when reading the story. The movie version takes place much later, perhaps in the 1930s or 1940s, and the family's home is more opulent than readers of the story might have imagined.

Activity: Analyze the Film Have students analyze *The Rocking-Horse Winner.* Ask students to complete the **Enrichment: Analyzing Film** worksheet, ***Professional Development Guidebook,*** page 226.

26 She stood, with arrested muscles, outside his door, listening. There was a strange, heavy, and yet not loud noise. Her heart stood still. It was a soundless noise, yet rushing and powerful. Something huge, in violent, hushed motion. What was it? What in God's name was it? She ought to know. She felt that she *knew* the noise. She knew what it was.

Yet she could not place it. She couldn't say what it was. And on and on it went, like madness.

Softly, frozen with anxiety and fear, she turned the door handle.

The room was dark. Yet in the space near the window, she heard and saw something plunging to and fro. She gazed in fear and amazement.

27 Then suddenly she switched on the light, and saw her son, in his green pajamas, madly surging on his rocking horse. The blaze of light suddenly lit him up, as he urged the wooden horse, and lit her up, as she stood, blond, in her dress of pale green and crystal, in the doorway.

"Paul!" she cried. "Whatever are you doing?"

"It's Malabar!" he screamed, in a powerful, strange voice. "It's Malabar!"

His eyes blazed at her for one strange and senseless second, as he ceased urging his wooden horse. Then he fell with a crash to the ground, and she, all her tormented motherhood flooding upon her, rushed to gather him up.

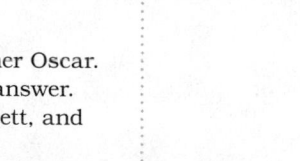

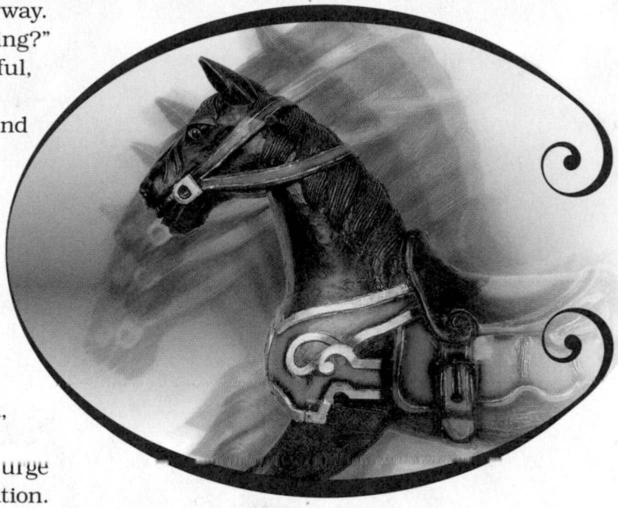

But he was unconscious, and unconscious he remained, with some brain fever. He talked and tossed, and his mother sat stonily by his side.

"Malabar! It's Malabar! Bassett, Bassett, I *know* it's Malabar!"

So the child cried, trying to get up and urge the rocking horse that gave him his inspiration.

"What does he mean by Malabar?" asked the heart-frozen mother.

"I don't know," said the father, stonily.

"What does he mean by Malabar?" she asked her brother Oscar.

"It's one of the horses running for the Derby," was the answer.

And, in spite of himself, Oscar Cresswell spoke to Bassett, and himself put a thousand on Malabar: at fourteen to one.

The third day of the illness was critical: they were watching for a change. The boy, with his rather long, curly hair, was tossing ceaselessly on the pillow. He neither slept nor regained consciousness, and his eyes were like blue stones. His mother sat, feeling her heart had gone, turned actually into a stone.

Literary Analysis
Theme and Symbol In what way is the rocking horse connected with the whispering of the house?

Reading Strategy
Making and Confirming Predictions What do you think will happen to Paul?

28 **Reading Check**
Why is Paul especially tense just before the Derby?

26 Literary Analysis
Theme and Symbol

1. Have students explain why the mother goes up to Paul's room when she returns from her evening out.
   Answer: She has been anxious about him all evening and she is still anxious even though she is now home.
2. **Ask** what the mother finds when she opens the door to Paul's bedroom.
   Answer: She finds Paul riding his rocking horse in a frenzy.
3. **Ask** students the Literary Analysis question: In what way is the rocking horse connected with the whispering of the house?
   Possible response: The noise of the rocking horse and the noise of the "whispering" are symbolic and reflect the anguished feelings of people in the house.

27 Reading Strategy
Making and Confirming Predictions

1. **Ask** students to describe Paul after he falls from the rocking horse.
   Possible responses: Paul talks and turns in an unconscious fever.
2. **Ask** what these details may indicate about Paul's condition.
   Possible responses: Students may say that the details show he is very ill or going crazy.
3. **Ask** students the Reading Strategy question: What do you think will happen to Paul?
   Possible response: Students may say they think Paul will die.

28 Reading Check

Answer: Paul has already lost money on two previous races because he had not "known" who the winner would be. He really wants to "know" which horse to choose for the Derby.

Differentiated Instruction for Universal Access

EL Pronunciation for English Learners

English learners may find it difficult to decipher the pronunciation of the word *unconscious.*

Write *un* and *conscious* on the board. Model the pronunciation of each for the students. Have students repeat the pronunciation. Explain that *un-* is a prefix that means the absence of a particular quality or state of being. Then define the word *conscious* as being aware of one's own surroundings or as being awake. Then write the word *unconscious* on the board. Model the pronunciation. Have the students repeat the word. Ensure that students place the stress on the correct syllable. Ask students to define *unconscious* based on the definitions of its separate word parts.

29 Critical Thinking

Deduce

1. **Direct** students' attention to the quote on page 1260.
2. **Ask** students who Malabar is and how they know.
   Answer: Since earlier hints suggest that the rocking horse has something to do with Paul's choices, and since Paul wants to stay in the house until the Derby, students can deduce that Malabar will be the Derby winner.

29
"It's Malabar!
BASSETT, BASSETT, I KNOW
IT'S MALABAR!"

30 In the evening, Oscar Cresswell did not come, but Bassett sent a message, saying could he come up for one moment, just one moment? Paul's mother was very angry at the intrusion, but on second thoughts she agreed. The boy was the same. Perhaps Bassett might bring him to consciousness.

The gardener, a shortish fellow with a little brown moustache and sharp little brown eyes, tiptoed into the room, touched his imaginary cap to Paul's mother, and stole to the bedside, staring with glittering, smallish eyes at the tossing, dying child.

"Master Paul!" he whispered. "Master Paul! Malabar came in first all right, a clean win. I did as you told me. You've made over seventy thousand pounds, you have; you've got over eighty thousand. Malabar came in all right, Master Paul."

"Malabar! Malabar! Did I say Malabar, mother? Did I say Malabar? Do you think I'm lucky, mother? I knew Malabar, didn't I? Over eighty thousand pounds! I call that lucky, don't you, mother? Over eighty thousand pounds! I knew, didn't I know I knew? Malabar came in all right. If I ride my horse till I'm sure, then I tell you, Bassett, you can go as high as you like. Did you go for all you were worth, Bassett?"

"I went a thousand on it, Master Paul."

"I never told you, mother, that if I can ride my horse, and *get there,* then I'm absolutely sure—oh, absolutely! Mother, did I ever tell you? I *am* lucky!"

"No, you never did," said the mother.

But the boy died in the night.

And even as he lay dead, his mother heard her brother's voice saying to her: "My God, Hester, you're eighty-odd thousand to the good, and a poor devil of a son to the bad. But, poor devil, poor devil, he's best gone out of a life where he rides his rocking horse to find a winner."

Spiral Review
Character What difficult problem does Paul face throughout the story?

Critical Reading

1. **Key Ideas and Details (a)** From the point of view of Paul's mother, what is the main problem of the family? **(b) Infer:** What does the mother's statement that the father is "unlucky" suggest about her values?
2. **Key Ideas and Details (a)** Over the course of the story, how does Paul react to the house's "whispers"? **(b) Analyze Cause and Effect:** Why is he affected as he is?
3. **Key Ideas and Details (a)** What does Uncle Oscar say at the end of the story? **(b) Interpret:** Do you think Uncle Oscar is speaking for the author? Why or why not?
4. **Integration of Knowledge and Ideas** What, if anything, is more important than the luck and money that Paul's mother wanted so desperately?

Cite textual evidence to support your responses.

30 Critical Thinking

Speculate

1. Direct students' attention to the first paragraph on the page.
2. **Ask** students why they think Bassett asks to see Paul.
   Answer: Bassett cares about Paul and also wants to tell him he chose the winning horse.
3. **Ask** students to speculate: In explaining the meaning of Paul's brief life, what would you add to his uncle's final words about him?
   Possible response: He died a victim of the family's greed.

Spiral Review

Character

Ask students the Spiral Review question.

Possible response: Throughout the story, the boy's problem is that he hopes to make his mother happy. He tries to use his "gift" to give his mother what she wants. However, she always envies what she does not have and so he is consumed by the effort to satisfy her.

ASSESS

Answers

Before students respond, you may wish to have them write a brief objective summary of the selection. As they answer the questions below, remind them to support their answers with evidence from the text.

1. (a) The family's main problem is that it is not lucky. (b) Her statement suggests that she believes one's life is ruled by fate, not by one's own actions.
2. (a) The continuing whispers fuel Paul's frenzied attempts to find luck. (b) He wants to help his mother so that she will love him.
3. (a) He says, "My God, Hester, you're eighty-odd thousand to the good, and a poor devil of a son to the bad. But, poor devil, poor devil, he's best gone out of a life where he rides his rocking horse to find a winner."
   (b) **Possible response:** Oscar seems to be speaking for the author because his statement forms a thematic summary of the story.
4. **Possible responses:** Love, satisfying work, and happiness are more important.

Differentiated Instruction for Universal Access

Enrichment for Gifted/Talented Students
Have students create a short sketch, loosely based on the events of "The Rocking-Horse Winner." Students might focus on one or more scenes from the story. They might choose a narrator, or simply rely on dialogue between the characters. Have students perform their sketch for the class.

Enrichment for Advanced Readers
Have students read other works by D. H. Lawrence. They might pick a short story or one of his novels. After they read their selections, have students summarize and report on what they read. Ask students to determine if any themes they visited in "The Rocking-Horse Winner" emerged in other of Lawrence's works.

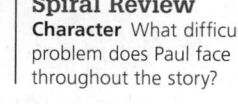

㉛ Background

More About the Author

Graham Greene was an inveterate traveler. Many of his stories, like "A Shocking Accident," use travel as an element of the plot. Greene's most popular works often feature an African or Latin American setting.

㉛ GRAHAM GREENE

(1904–1991)

Author of "A Shocking Accident"

The search for salvation, a theme addressed by poets like T. S. Eliot, is a central concern in the fiction of novelist Graham Greene. Like Eliot, Greene was a religious convert who wrote works exploring pain, fear, despair, and alienation.

Journalism and Travel The son of a school-master, Greene was born in Berkhamsted in Hertfordshire. He converted to Roman Catholicism after studying at Oxford University. Then, he began working as a copy editor in London and married. Eventually, he became a traveling freelance journalist.

Thrillers and More His journalism helped him develop the powers of observation, sensitivity to atmosphere, and simplicity of language that became hallmarks of his fiction. While traveling, he was able to scout out locations for his stories and novels.

Some of these novels, such as *Orient Express* (1932), he called "entertainments." These were an unusual type of thriller that went beyond the genre in its concern with moral issues.

Even more deeply involved with spiritual crisis, however, were such Greene classics as *Brighton Rock* (1938), *The Power and the Glory* (1940), and two novels set in Africa, *The Heart of the Matter* (1948) and *A Burnt-Out Case* (1961). In these works, Greene's concern with salvation burns with intensity.

Psychological Insight Greene's best fiction focuses on the psychology of human character rather than on plot. Many of his protagonists are people without roots or beliefs—people in pain. They may be odd, but they almost always excite the reader's curiosity and pity—and, almost always, Greene treats them with compassion as they strive to achieve salvation.

Enrichment: Investigating Psychology

Shame

This selection deals with the shame and embarrassment a young man experiences because of the way in which his father dies, accidentally. Shame can shape a person's psyche in powerful ways.

Activity: Research Have students research this topic and its effect on psychological development and psychological health and well-being. Have students record their findings in the Basic Concepts section of the **Enrichment: Investigating Psychology** worksheet, ***Professional Development Guidebook,*** page 239.

A SHOCKING ACCIDENT

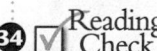

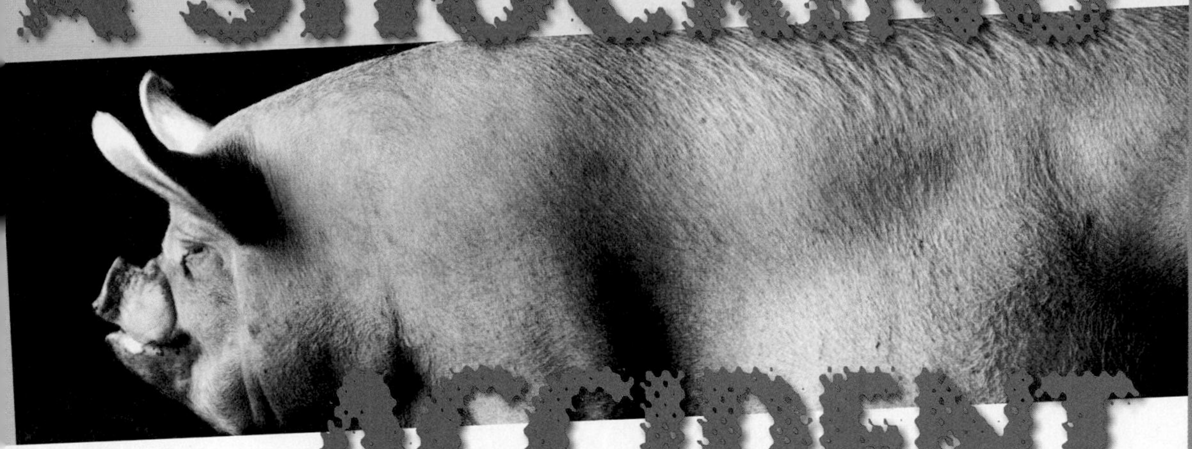

GRAHAM GREENE

I

Jerome was called into his housemaster's room in the break between the second and the third class on a Thursday morning. He had no fear of trouble, for he was a warden—the name that the proprietor and headmaster of a rather expensive preparatory school had chosen to give to approved, reliable boys in the lower forms (from a warden one became a guardian and finally before leaving, it was hoped for Marlborough or Rugby, a crusader). The housemaster, Mr. Wordsworth, sat behind his desk with an appearance of perplexity and apprehension. Jerome had the odd impression when he entered that he was a cause of fear.

"Sit down, Jerome," Mr. Wordsworth said. "All going well with the trigonometry?"

"Yes, sir."

"I've had a telephone call, Jerome. From your aunt. I'm afraid I have bad news for you."

"Yes, sir?"

"Your father has had an accident."

"Oh."

33 ▲ Critical Viewing
What role do you think a pig like the one shown will play in this story? **[Predict]**

Vocabulary
apprehension (ap´ rē hen´ shən) *n.* anxious feeling of foreboding; dread

34 ☑ Reading Check
Why is Jerome not afraid of being called to the housemaster's room?

A Shocking Accident **1263**

32 ⬤ About the Selection

In this story about the absurdities of life, a prep-school boy learns that his father, whom he hardly knows and whom he has romanticized, has died in an abrupt, embarrassing manner: A pig has fallen on him. The bizarre nature of this accident haunts the young man as he grows up, making him feel isolated and odd. In a surprising twist at the end of the story, his intended bride does not laugh when she hears the story for the first time. Her sympathetic response shows that even in the face of absurdity, people can find comfort and a measure of stability. Ironically, the young man's sense of humiliation ends when another person appreciates the ghastliness of his father's absurd death.

33 ⬤ Critical Viewing

Possible response: Students may predict that because an image of a pig is on the first page of the selection, that the story must be about an accident that happens to a pig.

34 ⬤ Reading Check

Possible response: Jerome is not afraid because he is a warden. Jerome even believes he is a cause of fear.

Differentiated
Instruction for Universal Access

Support for Special-Needs Students
Greene's long sentences may be hard for students to understand. Have them break down sentences, finding the meaning in the individual parts, and then put the sentences back together again. An example is the sentence beginning "He had no fear of trouble...," on page 1263.

Support for Less Proficient Readers
Guide students to understand the conflict here: The headmaster is trying to give Jerome the bad news, but the boy is still busy working on his fantasy.

35 Literary Analysis

Theme and Symbol

1. Direct students' attention to the second half of the student page, starting with "I'm afraid your father was very seriously hurt indeed."
2. **Ask** students how they think Jerome's father died.
   Possible response: Since Mr. Wordsworth says he died in a street accident, the father probably was hit by a car or a bus.
3. **Ask** students what their first response is on hearing that Jerome's father died because a pig fell on him.
   Possible response: Students will probably laugh and wonder how the accident happened. Some may worry about the pig.
4. **Ask** students the Literary Analysis question: Do you think that the way Jerome's father died could be symbolic? Why or why not?
   Possible response: The manner of death is symbolic of the absurdity and unexpectedness of life and death.

Mr. Wordsworth looked at him with some surprise. "A serious accident."

"Yes, sir?"

Jerome worshipped his father: the verb is exact. As man re-creates God, so Jerome re-created his father—from a restless widowed author into a mysterious adventurer who traveled in far places—Nice, Beirut, Majorca, even the Canaries. The time had arrived about his eighth birthday when Jerome believed that his father either "ran guns" or was a member of the British Secret Service. Now it occurred to him that his father might have been wounded in "a hail of machine-gun bullets."

Mr. Wordsworth played with the ruler on his desk. He seemed at a loss how to continue. He said, "You knew your father was in Naples?"

"Yes, sir."

"Your aunt heard from the hospital today."

"Oh."

Mr. Wordsworth said with desperation, "It was a street accident."

"Yes, sir?" It seemed quite likely to Jerome that they would call it a street accident. The police, of course, had fired first; his father would not take human life except as a last resort.

"I'm afraid your father was very seriously hurt indeed."

"Oh."

"In fact, Jerome, he died yesterday. Quite without pain."

"Did they shoot him through the heart?"

"I beg your pardon. What did you say, Jerome?"

"Did they shoot him through the heart?"

Literary Analysis
Theme and Symbol
Do you think that the way Jerome's father died could be symbolic? Why or why not? 35

"Nobody shot him, Jerome. A pig fell on him." An inexplicable convulsion took place in the nerves of Mr. Wordsworth's face; it really looked for a moment as though he were going to laugh. He closed his eyes, composed his features, and said rapidly, as though it were necessary to expel the story as rapidly as possible, "Your father was walking along a street in Naples when a pig fell on him. A shocking accident. Apparently in the poorer quarters of Naples they keep pigs on their balconies. This one was on the fifth floor. It had grown too fat. The balcony broke. The pig fell on your father."

Mr. Wordsworth left his desk rapidly and went to the window, turning his back on Jerome. He shook a little with emotion.

Jerome said, "What happened to the pig?"

"WHAT HAPPENED TO THE PIG?"

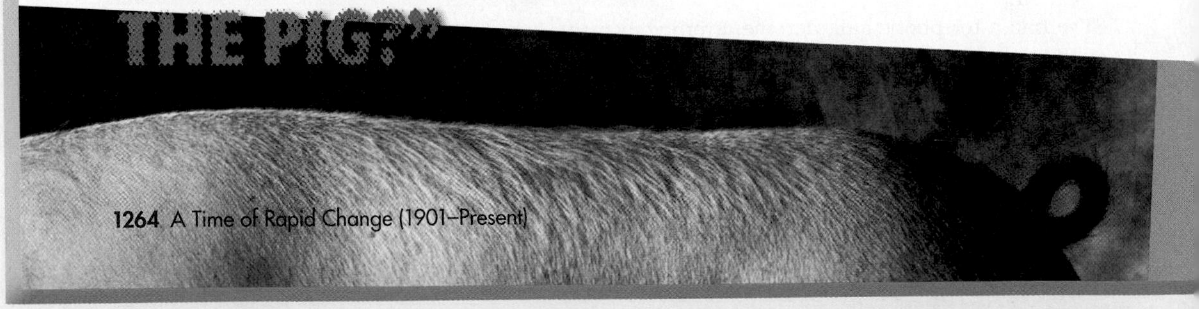

Enrichment: Investigating Career Connections

Travel Writing
Jerome's father was neither a Secret Service agent nor a mysterious adventurer. He did, in fact, have a job that many people would envy: He was a travel writer. Have students imagine a life that consists of exploring the world's exciting regions, acquainting oneself with the bounties of its cultures, tasting different foods, meeting all kinds of people, and staying in fine hotels and inns. Is travel writing a job students would want to have?

Activity: Investigating Travel Writing Have the class brainstorm a list of the pros and cons of such an occupation. Students can verify their suggestions by interviewing a travel writer or by reading travel writings. Have students record their pros and cons on the **Enrichment: Investigating Career Connections** worksheet, ***Professional Development Guidebook,*** page 221.

2

This was not callousness on the part of Jerome as it was interpreted by Mr. Wordsworth to his colleagues (he even discussed with them whether, perhaps, Jerome was not yet fitted to be a warden). Jerome was only attempting to visualize the strange scene and to get the details right. Nor was Jerome a boy who cried; he was a boy who brooded, and it never occurred to him at his preparatory school that the circumstances of his father's death were comic—they were still part of the mystery of life. It was later in his first term at his public school, when he told the story to his best friend, that he began to realize how it affected others. Naturally, after that disclosure he was known, rather unreasonably, as Pig.

Unfortunately his aunt had no sense of humor. There was an enlarged snapshot of his father on the piano: a large sad man in an unsuitable dark suit posed in Capri with an umbrella (to guard him against sunstroke), the Faraglioni rocks forming the background. By the age of sixteen Jerome was well aware that the portrait looked more like the author of *Sunshine and Shade* and *Rambles in the Balearics* than an agent of the Secret Service. All the same, he loved the memory of his father: he still possessed an album filled with picture-postcards (the stamps had been soaked off long ago for his other collection), and it pained him when his aunt **embarked** with strangers on the story of his father's death.

"A shocking accident," she would begin, and the stranger would compose his or her features into the correct shape for interest and commiseration. Both reactions, of course, were false, but it was terrible for Jerome to see how suddenly, midway in her rambling discourse, the interest would become genuine. "I can't think how such things can be allowed in a civilized country," his aunt would say. "I suppose one has to regard Italy as civilized. One is prepared for all kinds of things abroad, of course, and my brother was a great traveler. He always carried a water-filter with him. It was far less expensive, you know, than buying all those bottles of mineral water. My brother always said that his filter paid for his dinner wine. You can see from that what a careful man he was, but who could possibly have expected when he was walking along the Via Dottore Manuele Panucci on his way to the Hydrographic Museum that a pig would fall on him?" That was the moment when the interest became genuine.

36 Jerome's father had not been a distinguished writer, but the time always seems to come, after an author's death, when somebody thinks it worth his while to write a letter to *The Times Literary Supplement* announcing the preparation of a biography and asking to see any letters or documents or receive any anecdotes from friends of the dead man. Most of the biographies, of course, never appear—one

Spiral Review

Context What conclusions can you draw about the nuances in meaning of the word *disclosure* by analyzing the paragraph?

Vocabulary

embarked (em bärkt′) *v.* engaged in something, such as a conversation

37 Reading Check

What happened to Jerome's father?

Differentiated Instruction for Universal Access

EL Support for English Learners

Let students discuss the common practice of giving nicknames to friends. Some nicknames may be painful, while others might be a sign of affection. Do students think the nickname given to Jerome is meant in affection or as a joke?

Strategy for Gifted/Talented Students

Have students make a character web for Jerome. Have students note the specific description the author gives of Jerome; for example, he was not a "a boy who cried; he was a boy who brooded" and he did not think the manner of his father's death was comic.

Spiral Review

Context

1. Remind students that they studied context in an earlier lesson.
2. **Ask** students the Spiral Review question.

   Possible response: Because the boy has been sheltered from the world's reaction to the circumstances, and because the effect of the disclosure are extremely negative, in this context the *disclosure* is an unpleasant revelation.

36 Critical Thinking

Infer

1. Direct students' attention to the paragraph that begins "Jerome's father had not been a distinguished writer…"
2. Have students reread the paragraph.
3. **Ask:** Why might Jerome be concerned about someone doing research on his father?
   Answer: Jerome did not want any more people finding out how his father died.
4. **Ask:** What does the narrator mean by the line, "He did not realize how small the menace really was, nor that the danger period for someone of his father's obscurity had long passed"?
   Answer: Jerome had overestimated his father's importance. Eventually, the narrator implies, writers like his father disappear into obscurity.

37 Reading Check

Answer: Jerome's father was killed when a pig fell on him from a balcony above while he was walking on a street in Naples.

38 Critical Thinking

Analyze

1. Direct students' attention to the last six lines of the first paragraph on the page.
2. **Ask** students what Jerome fears will eventually happen in connection with his father.
   Answer: Since his father was an author, Jerome fears that someone will want to write a biography of him and will focus on the absurd manner of his death.
3. Have students **describe** how Jerome plans to counteract this possibility.
   Answer: Jerome rehearses how he will describe his father's death to any potential biographer.
4. **Ask** students: Why do you think Jerome is so desperate to reduce "the comic element" in the story of the accident?
   Answer: Jerome wants to control the way his father might be remembered in a book about his life. More deeply, the implied humiliation of his father's death causes him pain and diminishes his own self-esteem.

36 wonders whether the whole thing may not be an obscure form of blackmail and whether many a potential writer of a biography or thesis finds the means in this way to finish his education at Kansas or Nottingham. Jerome, however, as a chartered accountant, lived far from the literary world. He did not realize how small the menace really was, nor that the danger period for someone of his father's obscurity had long passed. 38 Sometimes he rehearsed the method of recounting his father's death so as to reduce the comic element to its smallest dimensions—it would be of no use to refuse information, for in that case the biographer would undoubtedly visit his aunt, who was living to a great old age with no sign of flagging.

It seemed to Jerome that there were two possible methods—the first led gently up to the accident, so well prepared that the death came really as an anticlimax. The chief danger of laughter in such a story was always surprise. When he rehearsed this method Jerome began boringly enough.

"You know Naples and those high tenement buildings? Somebody once told me that the Neapolitan always feels at home in New York just as the man from Turin feels at home in London because the river runs in much the same way in both cities. Where was I? Oh, yes, Naples, of course. You'd be surprised in the poorer quarters what things they keep on the balconies of those skyscraping tenements—not washing, you know, or bedding, but things like livestock, chickens or even pigs. Of course the pigs get no exercise whatever and fatten all the quicker." He could imagine how his hearer's eyes would have glazed by this time. "I've no idea, have you, how heavy a pig can be, but those old buildings are all badly in need of repair. A balcony on the fifth floor gave way under one of those pigs. It struck the third-floor balcony on its way down and sort of ricocheted into the street. My father was on the way to the Hydrographic Museum when the pig hit him. Coming from that height and that angle it broke his neck." This was really a masterly attempt to make an **intrinsically** interesting subject boring.

Vocabulary
intrinsically (in trin′ sik lē) *adv.* at its core; inherently; innately

The other method Jerome rehearsed had the virtue of brevity.

"My father was killed by a pig."

"Really? In India?"

"No, in Italy."

"How interesting. I never realized there was pig-sticking in Italy. Was your father keen on polo?"

In course of time, neither too early nor too late, rather as though, in his capacity as a chartered accountant, Jerome had studied the statistics and taken the average, he became engaged to be married: to a pleasant fresh-faced girl of twenty-five whose father was a doctor in Pinner. Her name was Sally, her favorite author was still Hugh

Vocabulary Development

Vocabulary Knowledge Rating

When students have completed reading and discussing the selection, have them take out their **Vocabulary Knowledge Rating Charts** for the story. Read the words aloud and have students rate their knowledge of words again in the After Reading column. Clarify any words that are still problematic. Have students write their own definitions and example or sentence in the appropriate column. Then, have students complete the Vocabulary Practice at the end of the selection. Encourage students to use the words in further discussion and written work about the selection. Remind them that they will be accountable for these words on the **Selection Test**, ***Unit 6 Resources,*** pages 118–120 or 121–123.

Walpole, and she had adored babies ever since she had been given a doll at the age of five which moved its eyes and made water. Their relationship was contented rather than exciting, as became the love affair of a chartered accountant; it would never have done if it had interfered with the figures.

39 One thought worried Jerome, however. Now that within a year he might himself become a father, his love for the dead man increased; he realized what affection had gone into the picture-postcards. He felt a longing to protect his memory, and uncertain whether this quiet love of his would survive if Sally were so insensitive as to laugh when she heard the story of his father's death. Inevitably she would hear it when Jerome brought her to dinner with his aunt. Several times he tried to tell her himself, as she was naturally anxious to know all she could that concerned him.

"You were very small when your father died?"

"Just nine."

"Poor little boy," she said.

"I was at school. They broke the news to me."

"Did you take it very hard?"

"I can't remember."

"You never told me how it happened."

"It was very sudden. A street accident."

"You'll never drive fast, will you, Jemmy?" (She had begun to call him "Jemmy.") It was too late then to try the second method—the one he thought of as the pig-sticking one.

They were going to marry quietly at a registry-office and have their honeymoon at Torquay. He avoided taking her to see his aunt until a week before the wedding, but then the night came, and he could not have told himself whether his apprehension was more for his father's memory or the security of his own love.

The moment came all too soon. "Is that Jemmy's father?" Sally asked, picking up the portrait of the man with the umbrella.

"Yes, dear. How did you guess?"

"He has Jemmy's eyes and brow, hasn't he?"

"Has Jerome lent you his books?"

"No."

"I will give you a set for your wedding. He wrote so tenderly about his travels. My own favorite is *Nooks and Crannies.* He would have had a great future. It made that shocking accident all the worse."

"Yes?"

Reading Strategy
Making and Confirming Predictions How do you think Sally will react to the story of Jerome's father's death? What impact will that have on Jerome?

40 **Reading Check**

What two methods of narrating his father's death does Jerome rehearse?

"IT WAS VERY SUDDEN. A STREET ACCIDENT."

39 Reading Strategy

Making and Confirming Predictions

1. Direct students' attention to the paragraph that begins "One thought worried Jerome, however."
2. Have students reread the paragraph.
3. **Ask** the Reading Strategy question: How do you think Sally will react to the story of Jerome's father's death? What impact will that have on Jerome?
Possible responses: Students might predict that, based on previous reactions, and based on the facts of the accident themselves, that Sally will laugh. If Sally laughs, Jerome would, once again, feel isolated. Other students might predict that Sally will not laugh. If she does not laugh, Jerome might find relief and understanding in her reaction.

40 Reading Check

Answer: Jerome rehearses a long and rambling account that blunts the shock of the ending, and a quick and to-the-point account.

Differentiated Instruction for Universal Access

Enrichment for Advanced Readers
Have students read another selection by Graham Greene. They might choose a short story, an excerpt from a novel, or a whole novel. What parallels might they draw in how Greene constructs his characters? Do they find other characters, like Jerome, in pain? How do those characters resolve or live with that pain? Have students share their findings with the class.

Enrichment for Gifted/Talented Students
Encourage students to rewrite the ending of this story. In what ways might they change either Sally's reaction, the aunt's retelling of the story, or Jerome's role in telling (or not telling) Sally about how his father died? Students can work in groups or individually. Have students share their alternative endings with one another and with the class.

41 Literary Analysis

Theme and Symbol

1. Have students **compare** Sally's and Jerome's responses to the story when they first hear it.
   Answer: Both ask what happened to the pig.
2. **Ask** students the Literary Analysis question: What does the contrast between Sally's reaction and those of other characters suggest about the theme?
   Possible responses: What is considered absurd and laughable to one person is a horror story to another. Life is full of surprises, some tragic, some joyful.

ASSESS

Answers

Before students respond, you may wish to have them write a brief objective summary of the selection. As they answer the questions below, remind them to support their answers with evidence from the text.

1. He develops a long, anticlimactic way and a short, quick way of telling the story of his father's death.
2. (a) Sally says the story is horrible and makes her think about how quickly life can change. (b) Sally's reaction tells Jerome she has a character he can trust. (c) Jerome's conflicts are resolved when his aunt tells Sally about the event, and Sally's reaction shows her understanding, concern, and sympathy.
3. Encourage students to support their opinions with details from their reading or experience.
4. **Possible response:** Because of the mores of *conventional* society, both main characters exhibited interesting *traits.* The *spontaneity* of Paul's racing choices and the squashed *emotions* of young Paul speak to the power of social mores, the pressure to conform, and the lengths to which a person will go to achieve his or her goals.

How Jerome longed to leave the room and not see that loved face crinkle with irresistible amusement.

"I had so many letters from his readers after the pig fell on him." She had never been so abrupt before.

And then the miracle happened. Sally did not laugh. Sally sat with open eyes of horror while his aunt told her the story, and at the end, "How horrible," Sally said. "It makes you think, doesn't it? Happening like that. Out of a clear sky."

Literary Analysis
Theme and Symbol 41
What does the contrast between Sally's reaction and those of other characters suggest about the theme?

Jerome's heart sang with joy. It was as though she had appeased his fear forever. In the taxi going home he kissed her with more passion than he had ever shown, and she returned it. There were babies in her pale blue pupils, babies that rolled their eyes and made water.

"A week today," Jerome said, and she squeezed his hand. "Penny for your thoughts, my darling."

"I was wondering," Sally said, "what happened to the poor pig?"

"They almost certainly had it for dinner," Jerome said happily and kissed the dear child again.

"WHAT HAPPENED TO THE POOR PIG?"

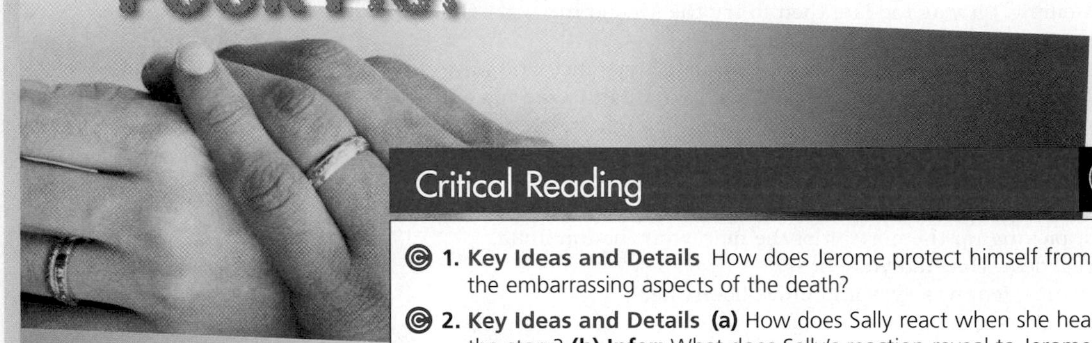

Critical Reading

1. **Key Ideas and Details** How does Jerome protect himself from the embarrassing aspects of the death?
2. **Key Ideas and Details (a)** How does Sally react when she hears the story? **(b) Infer:** What does Sally's reaction reveal to Jerome about her character? **(c) Draw Conclusions:** Are Jerome's conflicts about his father's death resolved at the end of the story? Why or why not?
3. **Integration of Knowledge and Ideas** One implication of the "shocking accident" might be that what happens in life is basically beyond our control. Do you agree with this idea? Why or why not?
4. **Integration of Knowledge and Ideas** Does the uniqueness of the main character in either or both of the stories suggest a message about society? Explain. In your response, use at least two of these Essential Question words: *emotion, spontaneity, conventional, trait.* ***[Connecting to the Essential Question: How does literature shape or reflect society?]***

Cite textual evidence to support your responses.

Concept Connector

Reading Strategy Graphic Organizer
Ask students to review the graphic organizers in which they have made and confirmed predictions. Then, have students share their organizers and compare the accuracy of their predictions.

Activating Prior Knowledge
Have students return to their responses to the Activating Prior Knowledge activity. Ask them to explain whether their thoughts have changed and, if so, how.

Writing About the Essential Question
Have students compare their responses to the prompt, completed before reading the selections, with their thoughts afterward. Have them work individually or in groups, writing or discussing their thoughts, to formulate new responses. Then, lead a class discussion, probing for what students have learned that confirms or invalidates their initial thoughts. Encourage students to cite specific textual details to support their responses.

After You Read

The Rocking-Horse Winner • A Shocking Accident

Literary Analysis

1. Key Ideas and Details Using the terms *love* and *money,* state a central question, issue, or concern that expresses one of the **themes** in "The Rocking-Horse Winner."

2. Integration of Knowledge and Ideas Complete a chart like this with **(a)** passages illustrating the **symbolic** meanings of the rocking horse and **(b)** explanations linking these meanings to the theme.

Symbolic Meanings	Passages That Illustrate	Links to Overall Theme
• Frantic effort to satisfy an unsatisfiable need • Frightening power of desires and wishes		

3. Key Ideas and Details For "A Shocking Accident," explain how the accident might symbolize either of these meanings: **(a)** that which makes no sense; **(b)** that which is unacceptable according to upper-class notions.

4. Key Ideas and Details Use the symbolic meanings of the accident to state the theme of "A Shocking Accident."

5. Craft and Structure For both "The Rocking-Horse Winner" and "A Shocking Accident," identify two passages that show the use of the **third-person point of view.**

6. Comparing Literary Works In which story does the third-person point of view work more effectively to reveal the theme? Explain, citing details from the stories.

7. Comparing Literary Works In which story is the third-person narrative more like a fairy tale and in which is it more like an anecdote? Explain.

Common Core State Standards

Writing

3. Write narratives to develop real or imagined experiences or events using effective technique, well-chosen details, and well-structured event sequences. *(p. 1270)*

5. Develop and strengthen writing as needed by planning, revising, editing, rewriting, or trying a new approach, focusing on addressing what is most significant for a specific purpose and audience. *(p. 1270)*

Language

4.a. Use context as a clue to the meaning of a word or phrase. *(p. 1270)*

Reading Strategy

8. (a) If "The Rocking-Horse Winner" continued, **predict** how Paul's mother might act in the future. **(b)** What information in the story and in your own *background knowledge* leads you to make that prediction?

9. What do you think Jerome would have done if Sally had responded with amusement to the story of his father's death? Explain.

10. Which story ending surprised you more? Why?

Assessment Practice

Revision Strategy (For more practice, see *All-in-One Workbook.*)

Many tests require students to apply revision strategies to a given passage. Use this sample item:

Your father was walking along a street in Naples when a pig fell on him.

The best place to add the words *on his way to the Hydrographic Museum* in this sentence is after ___.

A was
B walking
C Naples
D him

The first step in answering a question of this type is to use the phrase in each of the possible locations. If the phrase sounds awkward or the meaning of the sentence is changed, that choice is probably incorrect. The correct answer is **C**.

Answers

1. **Possible response:** The pursuit of money exhausts all energy for love.
2. **Sample answer:** (a) Symbolic Meanings: Frantic effort to satisfy an insatiable need; Passages that Illustrate: Any passage in which the mother talks about needing more money or Paul talks about needing to find luck; (b) Links to Overall Theme: Greed is destructive because all the frantic energy in the world is not enough to satisfy it.
3. (a) The accident symbolized "what makes no sense" because of its absurdity. (b) It symbolized "what is unacceptable to upper-class notions" that death be dignified.
4. Life is absurd, yet people deny the absurdity in their own lives and ideals.
5. Both stories reveal, through the third-person viewpoint, the thoughts and feelings of more than one character.
6. **Possible response:** The third-person narrative reveals the theme more effectively in "The Rocking-Horse Winner." The reader learns more about the characters, which helps relate the events to the theme of greed.
7. The third-person narrative is more like a fairy tale in "The Rocking-Horse Winner" because the characters are like stock figures—the bad mother, the kindly uncle, and so on. The narrative is more like an anecdote in "A Shocking Accident" because everything flows from a single event.
8. (a) Students' responses will vary. Some might offer that her son's death would be a revelation to her that her insatiable need for money cost her family dearly. Other students might offer that the mother might not experience any internal change. After all, she had a heart of "stone." (b) Students should relate information in the story to their own experiences.
9. Students' responses will vary. Students should support their responses with thoughtful reasons.
10. Students' responses will vary. Students should support their responses with thoughtful reasons.

EXTEND/ASSESS

Answers

Vocabulary Acquisition and Use

1. Introduce the skill.
2. Have students complete the Word Analysis activity and the Vocabulary practice.

Word Analysis

1. When his mother heard about his traffic ticket, she became unhinged.
2. Given the inclement weather, flight delays were unavoidable.
3. She hoped to sneak through the crowd unrecognized.
4. He needed to unclasp the hook in order to take off his jacket.
5. Thelma was unsure that she had made the best decision.
6. Population experts warn of the dangers of unchecked population growth in the years to come.

Vocabulary

1. Context: Though *the story itself was boring,* the storyteller made the story interesting.
2. Context: The investigator *raised no suspicions with his queries.*
3. Context: The camel *refused to budge.*
4. Context: The *sisters were reunited after ten years,* and then *recounted their lives* with each other.
5. Context: The *dark clouds* suggest the *worried farmer* may fear a storm will affect his crops.
6. Context: Her ability to predict the future *defied all logic.*

Writing

1. To guide students in writing this narrative text, give them the **Support for Writing** page (*Unit 6 Resources,* p. 113).
2. Remind students that their scripts should include descriptions of the scenery, dialogue, and directions regarding shots, camera movements, and scene changes.
3. If students have difficulty writing their scripts, have them work together to complete one.
4. Use the **Rubrics for Response to Literature,** ***Professional Development Guidebook,*** pages 250–251, to evaluate students' work.

PERFORMANCE TASKS

Integrated Language Skills

Vocabulary Acquisition and Use

Word Analysis: Anglo-Saxon prefix *un-*

Lawrence describes Paul's eyes as having an "uncanny" fire. The prefix *un-* means "not" or "the opposite or reversal of an action." It is used with adjectives, such as *unavailable* ("not available"), and verbs, such as *unlock* ("to reverse the action of locking"). The prefix comes from Anglo-Saxon, a Germanic language that is the basis for English. Write an original sentence that shows your understanding of the meaning of each of these words that begin with the prefix *un-*:

1. unhinge
2. unavoidable
3. unrecognized
4. unclasp
5. unsure
6. unchecked

Vocabulary: Context Clues

The context in which an unfamiliar word appears can give you clues to the word's meaning. For each sentence, explain how a context clue helps you identify the meaning of the italicized word from the vocabulary listed on page 1244.

1. The story was *intrinsically* boring, but the storyteller's style made it gripping.
2. The investigator's *discreet* queries raised no suspicions.
3. The camel *obstinately* refused to budge despite the owner's many efforts.
4. Reunited after ten years, the two sisters *embarked* on recounting their lives.
5. The dark clouds gave the worried farmer a feeling of *apprehension.*
6. Her *uncanny* ability to predict the future defied all logic.

Writing

Narrative Text Filmmakers use dialogue, images, and sounds to create symbols in films. Write a **script for a scene** from one of the stories. Include descriptions of the scenery, dialogue, and directions regarding shots, camera movement, and scene changes. Use some of the terms explained in the chart below.

Shots	Camera Movement	Scene Changes
• **Wide shot:** Camera captures a large area • **Medium shot:** Camera sees objects and surroundings • **Close-up:** Camera focuses on one object	• **Crane:** Camera moves in and out and up and down • **Pan:** Camera moves from side to side • **Zoom:** Camera moves in for a closer view	• **Dissolve:** Image grows faint as new image emerges • **Fade-out:** Image fades to black • **Montage:** Quick succession of unrelated images

Prewriting Choose the scene to script. Identify the symbols in that scene and their meaning. Decide how you want those symbols to appear.

Drafting Write a draft of your script. Be sure to describe what the camera sees, the movements of the characters, and the way the symbols will look. Include dialogue, indicating which character is speaking. Embellish your script with notes on how the scene should be shot and edited.

Revising Review your draft, making sure that the scene flows well, that directions are clear, and that you use the symbols effectively. Ensure that the descriptions and dialogue accurately and faithfully present the story.

Assessment Resources

Unit 6 Resources

L1 L2 EL **Selection Test A,** pp. 118–120. Administer Test A to less advanced readers.

L3 L4 EL **Selection Test B,** pp. 121–123. Administer Test B to on-level students and more advanced students.

L3 L4 **Open-Book Test,** pp. 115–117. As an alternative, give the Open-Book test.

All **Customizable Test Bank**

All **Self-tests**
Students may prepare for the **Selection Test** by taking the **Self-test** online.

PHLit Online! All assessment resources are available at **www.PHLitOnline.com.**

Conflicts at Home and Abroad

PART 3

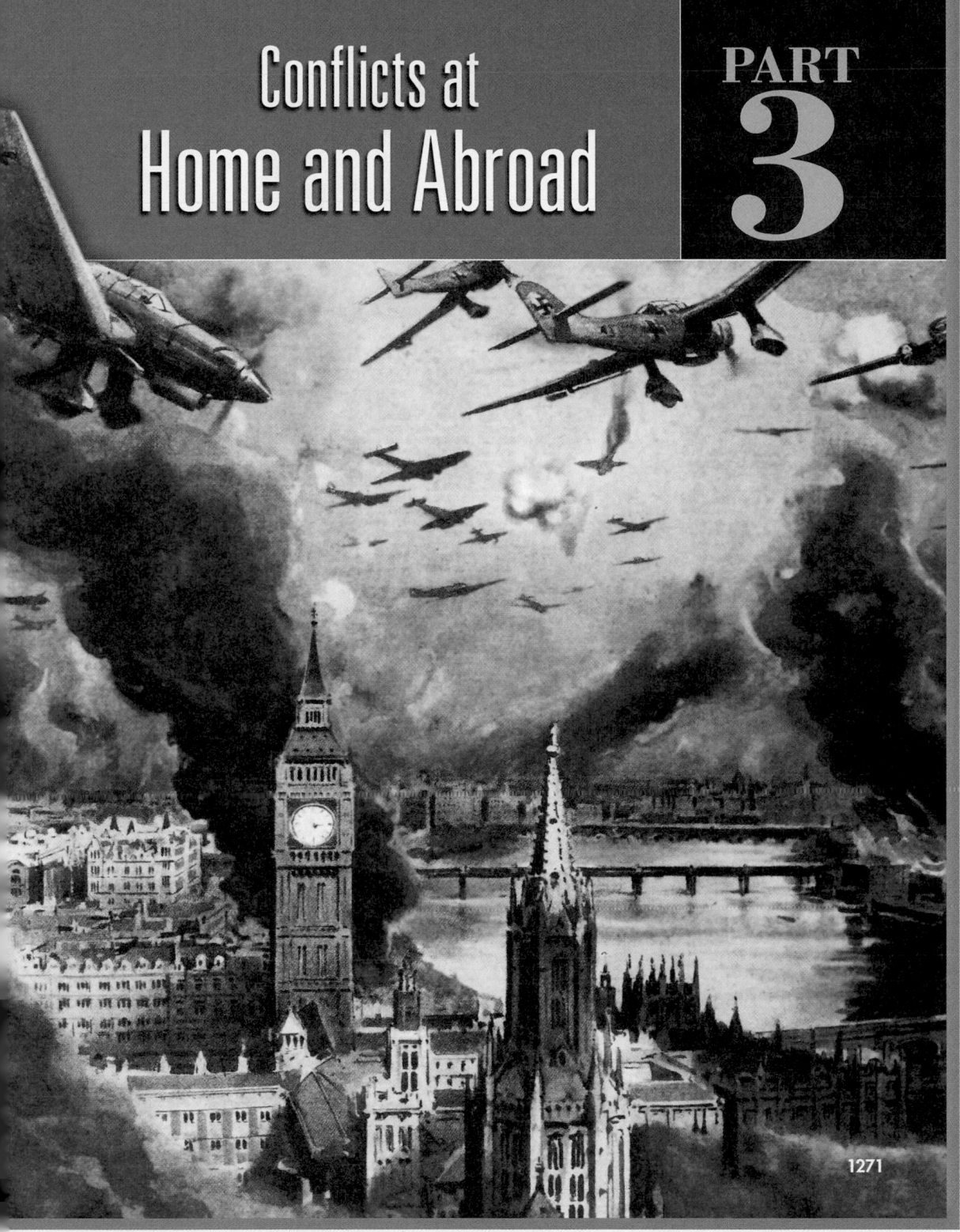

Selection Planning Guide

The violence of two world wars, as well as simmering conflicts at home and in British colonies abroad, left their mark on modern literature. Though courage in the face of conflict resounds in Churchill's speech, the work of the War Poets (Brooke, Sassoon, Owen, Douglas, Lewis, and Reed) provides readers with a sense of the horrors of war as seen from the battlefields. Bowen's ghost story, set during the very time illustrated by the opening art, suggests the vulnerability of those suffering from trauma. Conflicts within a community raise questions of Irish identity in the work of Heaney and Boland. For those affected by British colonialism, cultural conflict creates personal conflict, as demonstrated through the selections by Orwell, Lessing, Gordimer, Naipaul, and Walcott.

Humanities

German Airplanes Bombing the City of London, 1940, by Achille Beltrame (1871–1945), whose works often appeared on the cover of the Italian newspaper *The Sunday Courier,* captured this scene from the period referred to as the "Blitz." The Blitz was a period of 57 days during World War II in which Germans bombers attacked London nightly.

1. **Ask:** How might a citizen of London felt during the Blitz?
   Possible responses: Students may describe feelings of terror and fear. They may also suggest anger toward the attackers.
2. **Ask:** Why might someone affected by war be motivated to write about it?
   Possible responses: It is important to remember the events and details of a conflict, especially on a personal level. Additionally, the act of writing can be therapeutic. Finally, writing is a powerful way to address political and social issues.

Monitoring Progress

Before students read the selections in Part 3, refer to the results for the **Vocabulary in Context** items on **Benchmark Test 10** ***(Unit 6 Resources,*** p. 130). Use this diagnostic portion of the test to guide your choice of selections to teach as well as the depth of prereading preparation you will provide, based on students' readiness for the reading and vocabulary skills.

Text Complexity: At a Glance

This chart gives a general text complexity rating for the selections in this part of the unit to help guide instruction. For additional text complexity support, see the Test Complexity Rubric at point of use.

The Soldier	**More Accessible**	No Witchcraft for Sale	**More Accessible**
The Wirers	**More Accessible**	The Train From Rhodesia	**More Accessible**
Anthem for Doomed Youth	**More Complex**	B. Wordsworth	**More Complex**
The Demon Lover	**More Complex**	*from* Midsummer XXIII	**More Accessible**
Vergissmeinnicht	**More Complex**	*from* Omeros, Chapter XXVIII	**More Complex**
Postscript: For Gweno	**More Accessible**	Follower	**More Accessible**
Naming of Parts	**More Complex**	Two Lorries	**More Complex**
Shooting an Elephant	**More Complex**	Outside History	**More Complex**

COMMON CORE
Time and Resource Manager

The Soldier • Wirers • Anthem for Doomed Youth

Lesson Pacing Guide

DAY 1 Preteach

- Administer the Reading and Vocabulary Warm-ups (*Unit 6 Resources*, pp. 133–136) as necessary.
- Introduce the Literary Analysis concept: Tone.
- Introduce the Reading Strategy: Infer the Essential Message.
- Build background with the author and Background features.
- Develop thematic thinking with Connecting to the Essential Question.
- Teach the selection vocabulary.

DAYS 2–3 Preteach/Teach/Assess

- Distribute copies of the appropriate graphic organizer for the Reading Strategy (*Graphic Organizer Transparencies*, pp. 226–227).
- Distribute copies of the appropriate graphic organizer for Literary Analysis (*Graphic Organizer Transparencies*, pp. 228–229).
- Prepare students to read with the Activating Prior Knowledge activities (TE).
- Informally monitor comprehension while students read.
- Use the Reading Check questions to confirm comprehension.
- Develop students' understanding of tone using the Literary Analysis prompts.
- Develop students' ability to infer the essential message using the Reading Strategy prompts.
- Reinforce vocabulary with the Vocabulary notes.
- Assess students' comprehension and mastery of the skills by having them answer the Critical Reading, Literary Analysis, and Reading Strategy questions.
- Have students complete the Vocabulary Lesson.

DAY 4 Extend/Assess

- Have students complete the Writing Lesson and write a response to criticism. (You may assign as homework.)
- Administer Selection Test A or B (*Unit 6 Resources,* pp. 145–147 or 148–150).

Common Core State Standards

Reading Literature 4. Determine the meaning of words and phrases as they are used in the text, including figurative and connotative meanings; analyze the impact of specific word choices on meaning and tone, including words with multiple meanings or language that is particularly fresh, engaging, or beautiful.

Writing 1. Write arguments to support claims in an analysis of substantive topics or texts, using valid reasoning and relevant and sufficient evidence.

Language 5. Demonstrate understanding of figurative language, word relationships, and nuances in word meanings.

Additional Standards Practice
***Common Core Companion*, pp. 41–48; 185–195; 332–335**

Daily Block Scheduling
Each day in this Lesson Pacing Guide represents a 40–50 minute period. Teachers using block scheduling may combine days to revise pacing. In addition, teachers may differentiate and support core instruction by integrating components for extended and intensive support as students require. See the Guide to Selected Leveled Resources (facing page).

Guide to Selected Leveled Resources

RTI Tier 1 (students performing on level)

			The Soldier • Wirers • Anthem for Doomed Youth
Warm Up	Whole class instruction; Group work	**Practice, model,** and **monitor** fluency, working **with the whole class** or **in groups**.	**Vocabulary and Reading Warm-ups B,** ***Unit 6 Resources,*** pp. 133–134, 136
Comprehension/Skills	Whole class instruction; Group work; Independent work	**Support** and **monitor** comprehension and skills development, having students complete the activities, graphic organizers, and interactive prompts **independently** or **as a class**.	• ***Reader's Notebook,*** adapted instruction and full selection EL ***Reader's Notebook: English Learner's Version,*** adapted instruction and adapted selection • **Reading Strategy Graphic Organizer B,** ***Graphic Organizer Transparencies,*** p. 237 • **Literary Analysis Graphic Organizer B,** ***Graphic Organizer Transparencies,*** p. 239
Monitor Progress	A	**Monitor** student progress with the differentiated curriculum-based assessment in the *Unit Resources.*	• **Selection Test B,** ***Unit 6 Resources,*** pp. 148–150 • **Open-Book Test,** ***Unit 6 Resources,*** pp. 142–144

RTI Tier 2 (students requiring intervention)

			The Soldier • Wirers • Anthem for Doomed Youth
Warm Up	Group work; One-on-one teaching	**Practice, model,** and **monitor** fluency **in groups** or **with individuals**.	• **Vocabulary and Reading Warm-ups A,** ***Unit 6 Resources,*** pp. 133–135 • ***Hear It!*** **Audio CD (adapted text)**
Comprehension/Skills	Group work; One-on-one teaching	• **Support** and **monitor** comprehension and skills development, working **in small groups** or **with individuals**. • As students complete the selection in the appropriate version of the *Reader's Notebook,* **monitor** comprehension frequently with group questions and individual instruction. • **Model** strategies while guiding students in completing the activities and prompts in the *Reader's Notebook,* as well as the graphic organizers. • **Practice** skills and **monitor** mastery with the *Reading Kit* worksheets.	• ***Reader's Notebook: Adapted Version,*** adapted instruction and adapted selection EL ***Reader's Notebook: English Learner's Version,*** adapted instruction and adapted selection • **Reading Strategy Graphic Organizer A,** ***Graphic Organizer Transparencies,*** p. 236 • **Literary Analysis Graphic Organizer A,** ***Graphic Organizer Transparencies,*** p. 238 • ***Reading Kit,*** Practice worksheets
Monitor Progress	A	**Monitor** student progress with the differentiated curriculum-based assessment in the *Unit Resources* and in the *Reading Kit.*	• **Selection Test A,** ***Unit 6 Resources,*** pp. 145–147 • ***Reading Kit,*** Assess worksheets

TIER 3 Tier 3 intervention may require consultation with the student's special-education or dyslexia specialist. For additional support, see the Tier 2 activities and resources listed above.

One-on-one teaching **Group work** **Whole class instruction** **Independent work** **A Assessment**

For a complete guide to selection support, including support for Advanced students, see the Overview of Resources in the frontmatter.

The Soldier • Wirers • Anthem for Doomed Youth

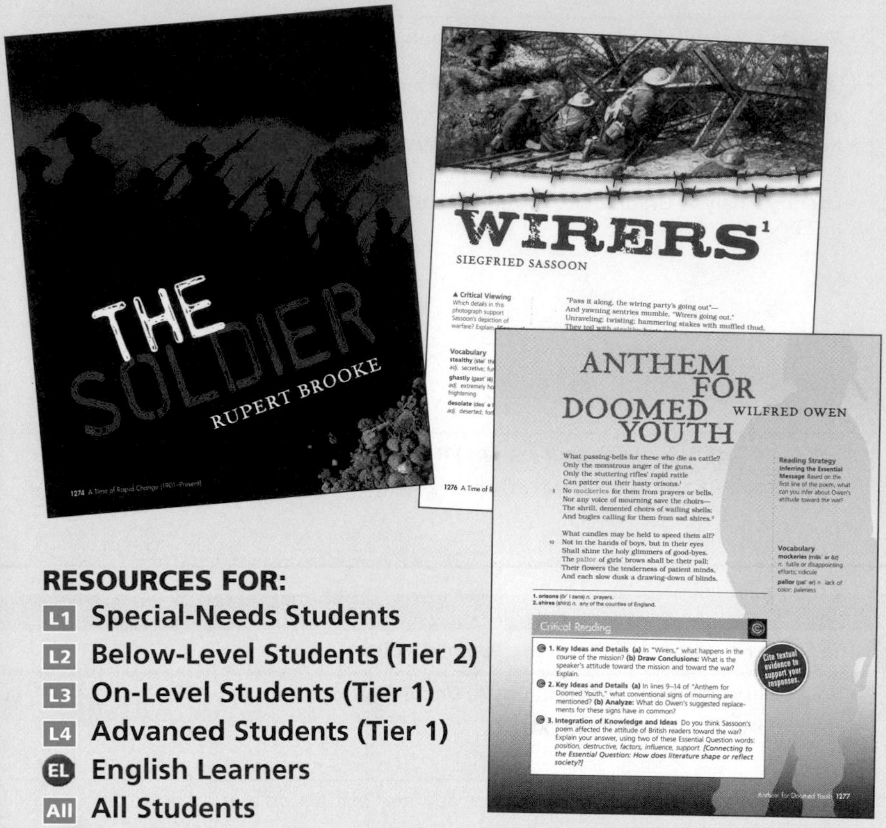

RESOURCES FOR:

- L1 Special-Needs Students
- L2 Below-Level Students (Tier 2)
- L3 On-Level Students (Tier 1)
- L4 Advanced Students (Tier 1)
- EL English Learners
- All All Students

Vocabulary/Fluency/Prior Knowledge

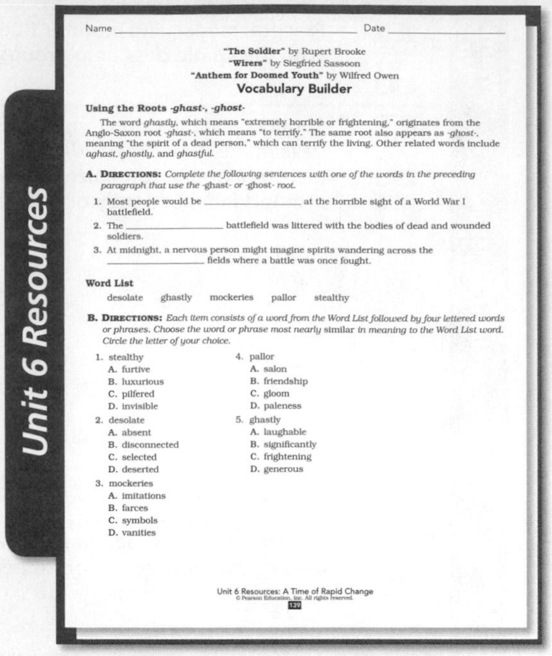

Name ______________________ Date ____________

"The Soldier" by Rupert Brooke
"Wirers" by Siegfried Sassoon
"Anthem for Doomed Youth" by Wilfred Owen
Vocabulary Builder

Using the Roots *-ghast-*, *-ghost-*

The word *ghastly*, which means "extremely horrible or frightening," originates from the Anglo-Saxon root *-ghast-*, which means "to terrify." The same root also appears as *-ghost-*, meaning "the spirit of a dead person," which can terrify the living. Other related words include *aghast*, *ghostly*, and *ghastful*.

A. Directions: *Complete the following sentences with one of the words in the preceding paragraph that use the -ghast- or -ghost- root.*

1. Most people would be ______________ at the horrible sight of a World War I battlefield.
2. The ______________ battlefield was littered with the bodies of dead and wounded soldiers.
3. At midnight, a nervous person might imagine spirits wandering across the ______________ fields where a battle was once fought.

Word List

desolate ghastly mockeries pallor stealthy

B. Directions: *Each item consists of a word from the Word List followed by four lettered words or phrases. Choose the word or phrase most nearly similar in meaning to the Word List word. Circle the letter of your choice.*

1. stealthy
 A. furtive
 B. luxurious
 C. pilfered
 D. invisible
2. desolate
 A. absent
 B. disconnected
 C. selected
 D. deserted
3. mockeries
 A. imitations
 B. farces
 C. symbols
 D. vanities
4. pallor
 A. salon
 B. friendship
 C. gloom
 D. paleness
5. ghastly
 A. laughable
 B. significantly
 C. frightening
 D. generous

Unit 6 Resources: A Time of Rapid Change
© Pearson Education, Inc. All rights reserved.
139

All **Vocabulary Builder,** p. 139

Also available for these selections:

EL L1 L2 **Vocabulary Warm-ups A and B,** pp. 133–134

EL L1 L2 **Reading Warm-ups A and B,** pp. 135–136

Reader's Notebooks

Pre- and postreading pages for these selections appear in an interactive format in the *Reader's Notebooks*. Each *Notebook* is differentiated for a different group of learners. The selections in the Adapted and English Learner's versions are abridged.

L2 L3 ***Reader's Notebook***

L1 ***Reader's Notebook: Adapted Version***

EL ***Reader's Notebook: English Learner's Version***

EL ***Reader's Notebook: Spanish Version***

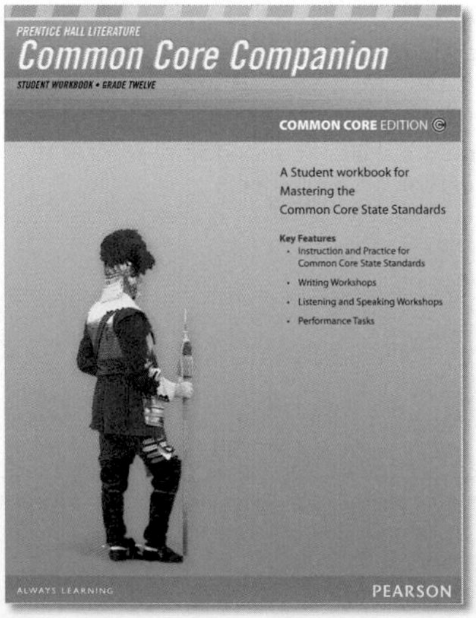

Common Core Companion

Additional instruction and practice for each Common Core State Standard

Selection Support

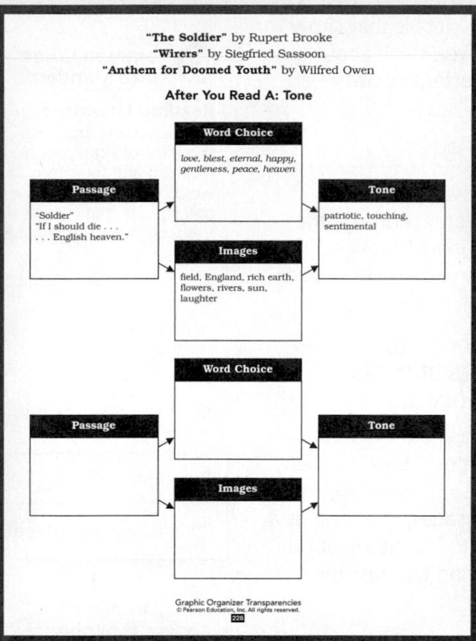
"**The Soldier**" by Rupert Brooke
"**Wirers**" by Siegfried Sassoon
"**Anthem for Doomed Youth**" by Wilfred Owen

After You Read A: Tone

Graphic Organizer Transparencies

228

EL L1 L2 **Literary Analysis: Graphic Organizer A,** (partially filled in), p. 228

Also available for these selections:

EL L1 L2 **Reading: Graphic Organizer A,** p. 226

EL L3 **Reading: Graphic Organizer B,** p. 227

EL L3 **Literary Analysis: Graphic Organizer B,** p. 229

Graphic Organizer Transparencies

Skills Development/Extension

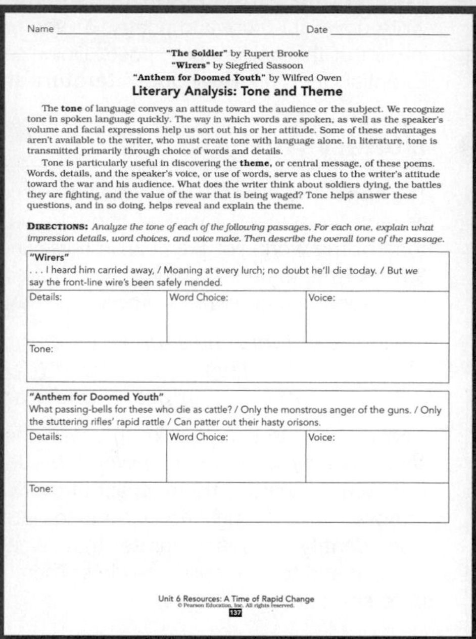
Name ______________________ Date ____________

"**The Soldier**" by Rupert Brooke
"**Wirers**" by Siegfried Sassoon
"**Anthem for Doomed Youth**" by Wilfred Owen

Literary Analysis: Tone and Theme

The **tone** of language conveys an attitude toward the audience or the subject. We recognize tone in spoken language quickly. The way in which words are spoken, as well as the speaker's volume and facial expressions help us sort out his or her attitude. Some of these advantages aren't available to the writer, who must create tone with language alone. In literature, tone is transmitted primarily through choice of words and details.

Tone is particularly useful in discovering the **theme,** or central message, of these poems. Words, details, and the speaker's voice, or use of words, serve as clues to the writer's attitude toward the war and his audience. What does the writer think about soldiers dying, the battles they are fighting, and the value of the war that is being waged? Tone helps answer these questions, and in so doing, helps reveal and explain the theme.

Directions: *Analyze the tone of each of the following passages. For each one, explain what impression details, word choices, and voice make. Then describe the overall tone of the passage.*

"Wirers" . . . I heard him carried away, / Moaning at every lurch; no doubt he'll die today. / But *we* say the front-line wire's been safely mended.		
Details:	Word Choice:	Voice:
Tone:		

"Anthem for Doomed Youth" What passing-bells for these who die as cattle? / Only the monstrous anger of the guns. / Only the stuttering rifles' rapid rattle / Can patter out their hasty orisons.		
Details:	Word Choice:	Voice:
Tone:		

Unit 6 Resources: A Time of Rapid Change

137

Unit 6 Resources

All **Literary Analysis: Tone,** p. 137

Also available for these selections:

All **Reading: Infer the Essential Message,** p. 138

EL L3 L4 **Support for Writing,** p. 140

L4 **Enrichment,** p. 141

Assessment

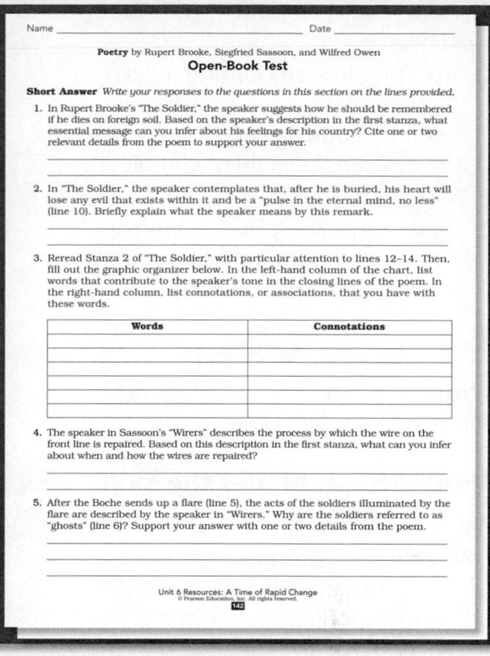
Name ______________________ Date ____________

Poetry by Rupert Brooke, Siegfried Sassoon, and Wilfred Owen

Open-Book Test

Short Answer *Write your responses to the questions in this section on the lines provided.*

1. In Rupert Brooke's "The Soldier," the speaker suggests how he should be remembered if he dies on foreign soil. Based on the speaker's description in the first stanza, what essential message can you infer about his feelings for his country? Cite one or two relevant details from the poem to support your answer.

2. In "The Soldier," the speaker contemplates that, after he is buried, his heart will lose any evil that exists within it and be a "pulse in the eternal mind, no less" (line 10). Briefly explain what the speaker means by this remark.

3. Reread Stanza 2 of "The Soldier," with particular attention to lines 12–14. Then, fill out the graphic organizer below. In the left-hand column of the chart, list words that contribute to the speaker's tone in the closing lines of the poem. In the right-hand column, list connotations, or associations, that you have with these words.

Words	Connotations

4. The speaker in Sassoon's "Wirers" describes the process by which the wire on the front line is repaired. Based on this description in the first stanza, what can you infer about when and how the wires are repaired?

5. After the Boche sends up a flare (line 5), the acts of the soldiers illuminated by the flare are described by the speaker in "Wirers." Why are the soldiers referred to as "ghosts" (line 6)? Support your answer with one or two details from the poem.

Unit 6 Resources: A Time of Rapid Change

142

L3 L4 **Open-Book Test,** pp. 142–144

Also available for these selections:

EL L1 L2 **Selection Test A,** pp. 145–147

EL L3 L4 **Selection Test B,** pp. 148–150

PHLit Online!
www.PHLitOnline.com

- complete narrated selection text
- a thematically related video with writing prompt
- an interactive graphic organizer
- highlighting feature
- access to all student print resources, adapted to individual student needs
- Spanish and English summaries
- adapted selection translations in Spanish

Online Resources: All print materials are also available online.

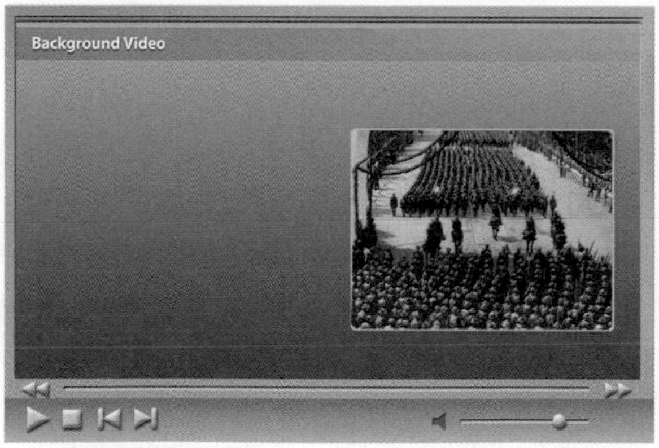

Background Video

Also available:

Get Connected! (thematic video with writing prompt)
All videos are available in Spanish.

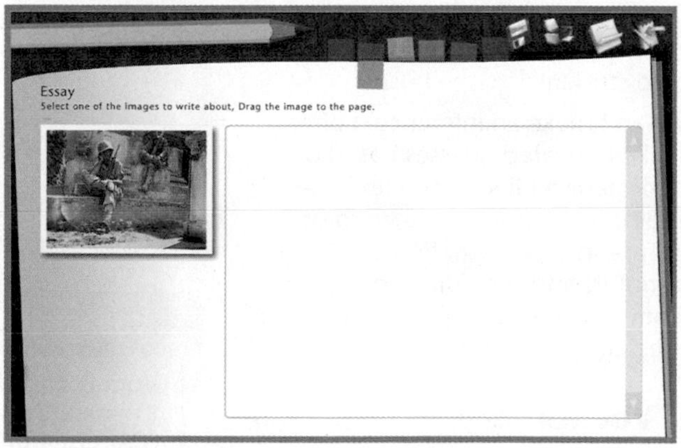

Writer's Journal (with graphics feature)

Also available:

Vocabulary Central (tools and activities for studying vocabulary)

PRETEACH

1 Connecting to the Essential Question

1. Review the assignment with the class.
2. Ask students why writing might be helpful for someone who has been through a powerful experience. Then, have them complete the assignment.
3. As students read, have them consider their feelings about war as written in the poems.

2 Literary Analysis

Introduce the skill using the instruction on the student page.

Think Aloud: Model the Skill

Say to students:

We analyze tone in real life all the time. For example, my Mother yells "Patricia Lucille Jones!" when she enters my room. I can infer that she is angry about something since she is yelling, calling me Patricia (rather than Patty) and using my middle name. From her use of words, I can tell how she feels.

3 Reading Strategy

1. Introduce the skill using the instruction on the student page.
2. Give students a copy of **Reading Strategy Graphic Organizer B,** page 227 in ***Graphic Organizer Transparencies,*** to fill out as they read.

Think Aloud: Model the Skill

Say to students:

When I make an inference, I often make educated guesses based on information I find in the text. For example, I will look at a word or phrase in a passage, find clues about it, and then draw inferences from the clues to figure out the message of the author.

4 Vocabulary

1. Pronounce each word, giving its definition, and have students say it aloud.
2. For more guidance, see the *Classroom Strategies and Teaching Routines* card for introducing vocabulary.

Before You Read

The Soldier • Wirers • Anthem for Doomed Youth

1 **Connecting to the Essential Question** War can lead soldiers to write powerful prose and poetry. As you read, notice details that show the impact of the war on these poets. Doing so will help you think about the Essential Question: **How does literature shape or reflect society?**

Common Core State Standards

Reading Literature
4. Analyze the impact of specific word choices on meaning and tone, including words with multiple meanings or language that is particularly fresh, engaging, or beautiful.

2 Literary Analysis

The **tone** of a literary work is the writer's attitude toward the readers and the subject. A writer's choice of words and details conveys the tone of the work. For example, in these lines from Rupert Brooke's "The Soldier," the underlined words and phrases communicate a tone of patriotic devotion and wistful memory:

Her sights and sounds; dreams happy as her day;
And laughter, learnt of friends; and gentleness,
In hearts at peace, under an English heaven.

Comparing Literary Works In a way, these selections are like letters sent home by soldiers during World War I. These "letters" each contain central messages, or **themes,** about the war for those back in England, removed from the fighting. In figuring out these messages, use tone as a clue. Identify words and phrases that reveal each writer's attitude about the war and toward civilian readers. Then, compare and contrast the different writers' messages.

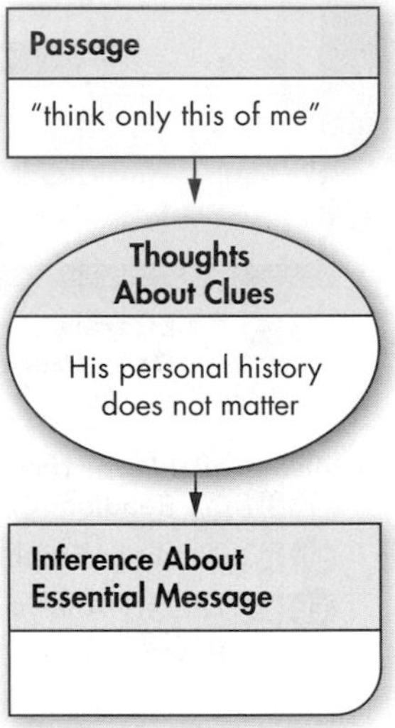

3 Reading Strategy

Preparing to Read Complex Texts Because writers often suggest rather than state elements like theme and speaker, readers must **infer the essential message,** or make educated guesses based on clues in the text. Use a chart like the one shown to make inferences about the essential message of these poems.

4 Vocabulary

stealthy (stel′ thē) *adj.* secretive; furtive (p. 1276)

ghastly (gast′ lē) *adj.* extremely horrible; frightening (p. 1276)

desolate (des′ ə lit) *adj.* deserted; forlorn (p. 1276)

mockeries (mäk′ ər ēz) *n.* futile or disappointing efforts; ridicule (p. 1277)

pallor (pal′ ər) *n.* lack of color; paleness (p. 1277)

PHLit Online! www.PHLitOnline.com

Vocabulary Development

Vocabulary Knowledge Rating

Create a **Vocabulary Knowledge Rating Chart** (***Professional Development Guidebook,*** p. 33) for the vocabulary words on the student page. Give each student a copy of the chart with the words on it. Read the words aloud, and have students mark their ratings in the Before Reading column. When students have completed reading and discussing the group of selections, have them take out their **Vocabulary Knowledge Rating** charts for the story. Read the words aloud and have students rate their knowledge again in the After Reading column. Clarify any words that are still problematic. Then, have students complete the Vocabulary practice at the end of the selections.

PHLit Online! **Vocabulary Central,** featuring tools and activities for studying vocabulary, is available online at **www.PHLitOnline.com.**

5 RUPERT BROOKE (1887–1915)

Author of "The Soldier"

Rupert Brooke had striking good looks, personal charm, and high intelligence. Before World War I began, Brooke had already established himself as a serious poet. He traveled a great deal, writing essays as well as poetry. When war broke out in 1914, he joined the Royal Navy. Tragically, he died from blood poisoning while on a mission to defeat the Turks.

Brooke's war sonnets, traditional and idealistic, were among the last from the soldier-poets of World War I to express wholehearted patriotism. The prolonged, inhuman slaughter of trench warfare extinguished the idealism of many of them.

5 SIEGFRIED SASSOON (1886–1967)

Author of "Wirers"

Born into a wealthy family in Kent, England, Siegfried Sassoon published poetry while still in his twenties. In 1914, he joined the army and showed such reckless courage in battle that he earned the nickname "Mad Jack," along with a medal for gallantry.

By 1916 or 1917, though, Sassoon's attitude toward war had changed. He began to write starkly realistic "trench poems" about war's agonies. He was wounded early in 1917 and, while recovering, wrote a statement condemning the war. Partly to defuse his criticism and partly to protect him from its consequences, he was placed in a hospital for victims of shell shock.

Sassoon survived the war and lived almost fifty years longer, but he wrote little to match his wartime verses.

5 WILFRED OWEN (1893–1918)

Author of "Anthem for Doomed Youth"

Always interested in literature, Wilfred Owen studied at London University and joined the army in 1915. He was wounded three times in 1917 and won a medal for outstanding bravery in 1918. Owen's work became grittier and angrier under the influence of Siegfried Sassoon, whom he had met at a military hospital in 1917. It was a terrible loss to English poetry when Owen was killed in battle just one week before the end of the war.

Owen was unknown as a poet until Sassoon published a collection of his work, *Poems*, in 1920. Today, Owen is regarded as one of the greatest war poets in the English language.

1273

Daily Bellringer

For each class during which you will teach these selections, have students complete one of the five activities for the appropriate week in the ***Daily Bellringer Activities*** booklet.

Multidraft Reading

To assist struggling readers and to enhance reading for all, assign the text in chunks, as warranted by length, and apply multidraft reading protocols. For each reading, have students set the purpose indicated:

- **First reading**—identifying key ideas and details and answering any Reading Checks.
- **Second reading**—analyzing craftand structure and responding to the side-column prompts.
- **Third reading**—integrating knowledge and ideas, connecting to other texts and the world, and answering the end-of-selection questions.

For more guidance, refer to the ***Classroom Strategies and Teaching Routines*** card on Multidraft Reading.

5 Background

More About the Authors

Rupert Brooke was a popular young man who counted among his friends E. M. Forster, Virginia Woolf, Maynard Keynes, and Edward Thomas.

Siegfried Sassoon was a British poet who fought during World War I, earning a Military Cross. He was so horrified by the brutalities and bloodshed of war, he threw his Military Cross into the river.

Wilfred Owen visited a hospital for the wounded in 1915, which spurred him to enlist. Years later he said that he wanted to help the soldiers by leading them well and by speaking on their behalf.

PHLit Online!
www.PHLitOnline.com

Teaching From Technology

Preparing to Read
Go to **www.PHLitOnline.com** and display the ***Get Connected!*** slide show for these selections. Have the class brainstorm responses to the writing prompt, entering ideas in the interactive journal. Then, have students complete their written responses as homework.

To build background, display the Background and More About the Author features.

Using the Interactive Text
Go to **www.PHLitOnline.com** and display the **Enriched Online Student Edition.** As the class reads the selection or listens to the narration, record answers to side-column prompts using the graphic organizers accessible on the interactive page. Alternatively, have students use the online edition individually, answering the prompts as they read.

❶ About the Selection

"The Soldier" records a soldier's love for his country and his wish to preserve all that he associates with that country. The speaker catalogs the features of his beloved England that he will never see again should he die in battle. His portrait of the Englishness he embodies—the sights, sounds, and very air that have shaped him—poignantly demonstrates the strong bond that can exist between the individual and society.

❷ Activating Prior Knowledge

Though students may see modern war in grisly detail on television, few will have heard firsthand accounts of war's battles, destruction, and horror. To prepare students for this selection's writings, discuss students' feelings about recent wars. Explain that the writers in this selection grouping—even while perhaps against the war or affected by its horrors—took their patriotic duty very seriously.

Concept Connector →

Tell students they will return to their responses after reading the selection.

① ②

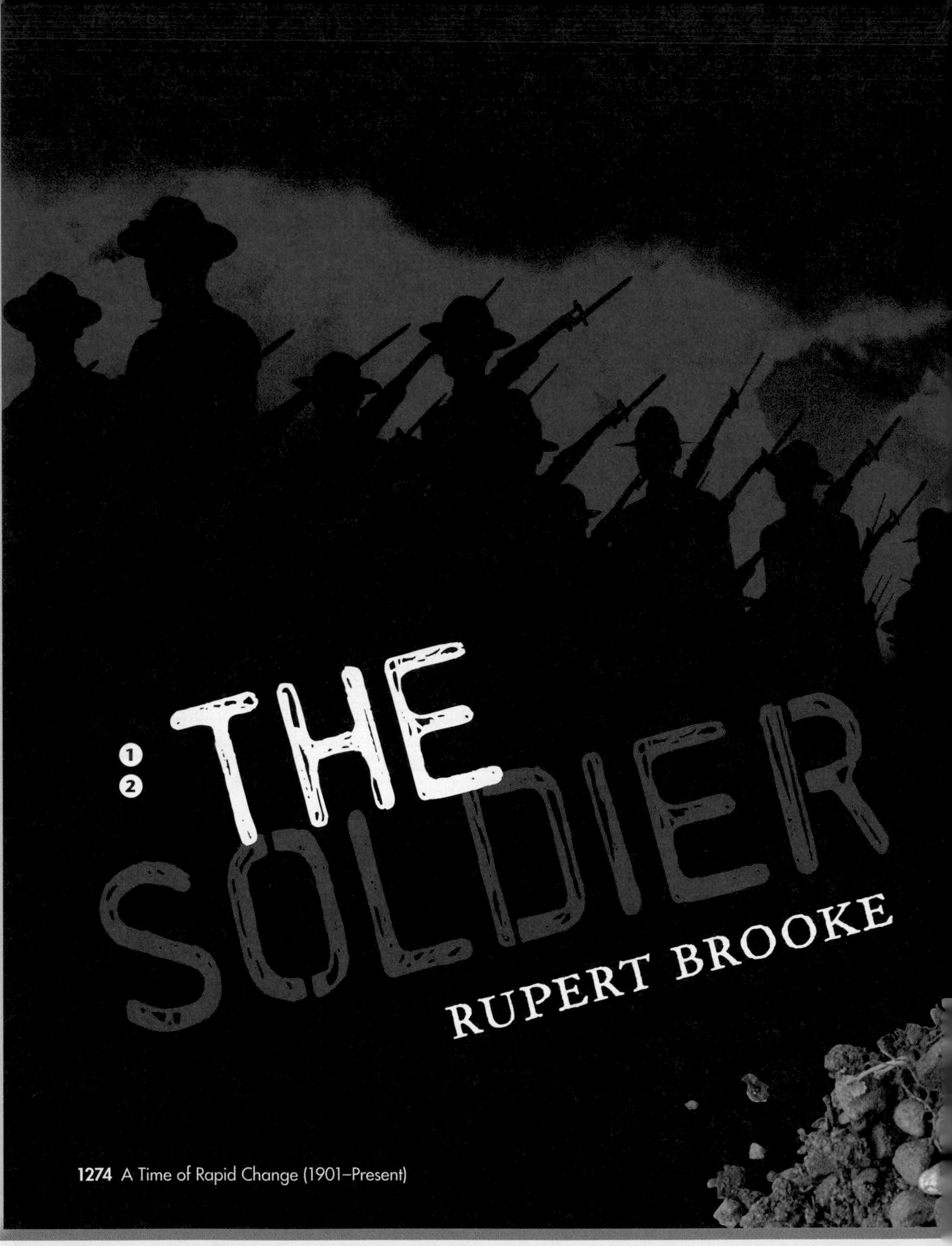

Text Complexity Rubric

	The Soldier	Wirers	Anthem for Doomed Youth
Qualitative Measures			
Context/Knowledge Demands	Modern war poem; historical knowledge demands 1 ② 3 4 5	Modern war poem; historical knowledge demands 1 ② 3 4 5	Modern war poem; historical and cultural knowledge demands 1 2 ③ 4 5
Structure/Language Conventionality and Clarity	Long sentences; accessible diction 1 ② 3 4 5	Dialogue; slang 1 ② 3 4 5	Rhetorical questions; accessible diction 1 2 3 ④ 5
Levels of Meaning/ Purpose/Concepts	Accessible (warfare; patriotism) 1 ② 3 4 5	Moderate (wartime cynicism; death) 1 ② 3 4 5	Moderate (death; wartime remorse) 1 2 ③ 4 5
Quantitative Measures			
Lexile/Text Length	NP / 112 words	NP / 108 words	NP / 109 words
Overall Complexity	**More accessible**	**More accessible**	**More complex**

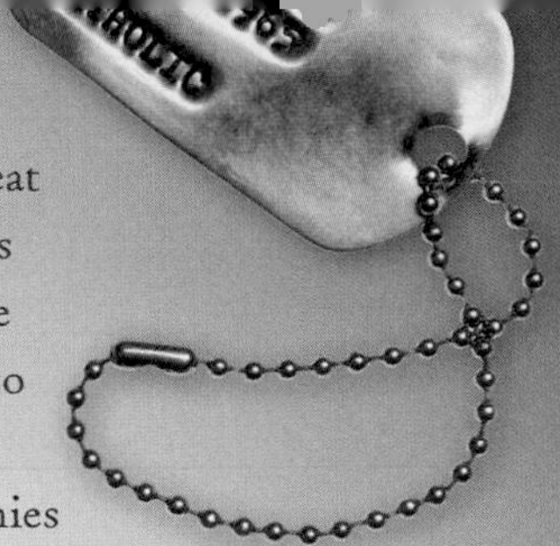

BACKGROUND World War I (1914–1918) pitted Great Britain, France, Russia, Japan, Italy, and, later, the United States (the Allies) against Germany, Austria-Hungary, and Turkey (the Central Powers). The war was fought not only in Europe but also in regions like the Middle East and Asia Minor. Typical of this conflict, especially in Western Europe, was trench warfare. Armies faced each other in defensive trenches protected by barbed wire. Periodically, one army would attack another in the face of machine-gun and artillery fire. Such warfare and the illnesses resulting from life in filthy trenches led to a total loss of about 8.5 million soldiers.

If I should die, think only this of me:
That there's some corner of a foreign field
That is forever England. There shall be
In that rich earth a richer dust concealed;
A dust whom England bore, shaped, made aware,
Gave, once, her flowers to love, her ways to roam,
A body of England's, breathing English air,
Washed by the rivers, blest by suns of home.

And think, this heart, all evil shed away,
A pulse in the eternal mind, no less
Gives somewhere back the thoughts by England given;
Her sights and sounds; dreams happy as her day;
And laughter, learnt of friends; and gentleness,
In hearts at peace, under an English heaven.

3 Literary Analysis
Tone What are three adjectives that describe the tone of this poem? Explain.

Critical Reading

1. **Key Ideas and Details** **(a)** How does the speaker ask his readers to remember him, should he die? **(b) Infer:** Why would the speaker go off to war, knowing he could be killed?
2. **Key Ideas and Details** **(a)** Name some of the things England has given the speaker. **(b) Interpret:** What is the "richer dust" to which the speaker refers?
3. **Key Ideas and Details** **(a)** In lines 9 and 10, what does the speaker say his "heart" will become? **(b) Interpret:** What does the speaker mean by this statement?
4. **Integration of Knowledge and Ideas** Brooke's attitude has been called a "ridiculous anachronism"—something outdated—in the face of modern warfare. Do you agree or disagree? Why?

Cite textual evidence to support your responses.

3 Literary Analysis

Tone

1. Read aloud the poem.
2. **Ask** students what ". . . the corner of a foreign field/That is forever England" is.
   Answer: It is the dead British soldier. If the narrator were to die while fighting abroad, his body would be a piece of England forever in the foreign soil.
3. Then, **ask** students the Literary Analysis question: What are three adjectives that describe the tone of the poem? Explain.
   Possible response: Three adjectives that describe this poem are *patriotic*—it deals with one's duty to country; *wistful*—it is written by a young man who may not return home to his beloved country; and *sentimental*—because it is filled with warm, positive feelings.

ASSESS

Answers

1. (a) The speaker asks the reader to think of him as being forever a part of England. (b) He believed that it was his duty and that England was worth defending.
2. (a) England gave the speaker flowers to appreciate, paths to roam, air, water, sun, and the laughter of friends. (b) The "richer dust" is human life.
3. (a) He says his heart will become "a pulse in the eternal mind." (b) The speaker's spirit will join other heavenly spirits.
4. **Possible responses:** Some students will agree, saying that today's governments do not deserve such loyalty. Others will disagree, saying that patriotism is never outdated.

Text Complexity: Reader and Task Suggestions

	The Soldier	Wirers	Anthem for Doomed Youth
Preparing to Read the Texts • Use the Background on SE p. 1275 to explain that the early glory many looked for in World War I soon turned to the horror of the trenches. • Discuss the different reactions soldiers may have to warfare, depending on their battlefield experiences. • Guide students to use Multidraft Reading strategies (TE p. 1273).	**Leveled Tasks** ***Structure/Language*** If students will have difficulty with the poem's long sentences, have them break the sentences into units of thought and focus on the key nouns and verbs. Then, have students explain how a portion of foreign soil became part of England. ***Analyzing*** If students will not have difficulty with the poem's sentences, have them analyze its controlling image of a foreign burial ground.	**Leveled Tasks** ***Knowledge Demands*** If students will have difficulty with the poem's context, first define war terminology. Then, have students read the poem, focusing on what is happening throughout. ***Evaluating*** If students will not have difficulty with the poem's context, have them evaluate the vividness with which the poem captures battlefield events.	**Leveled Tasks** ***Levels of Meaning*** If students will have difficulty with the meaning, explain first that passing-bells are funeral bells. Then, have students focus their reading on all the things the speaker says the "doomed youth" will and will not have. ***Analyzing*** If students will not have difficulty with the meaning, have them analyze the comparisons and contrasts that are central to the poem.

4 About the Selections

Both "Wirers" and "Anthem for Doomed Youth" focus on illustrating war's horrors. "Wirers" transports readers immediately into the experience of waiting out a battlefield night, watching with bated breath as the fence-menders risk almost-certain death. "Anthem for Doomed Youth" captures the sad despair of battlefield death that undergoes no loving rituals of peacetime mourning. Together, these poems convey the cynicism war often elicits.

5 Critical Viewing

Answer: Details in the photograph that support Sassoon's depiction of war include the wire fence, the wounded or dead soldiers lying in the grass, the soldiers moving toward the wire fence, perhaps to mend it, and the darkness-into-dawn feel of the colors.

6 Literary Analysis

Tone

1. Read aloud the bracketed passage.
2. **Ask** students what words characterize the actions of the wirers in the first stanza.
   Answer: Some words are "unraveling; twisting," "hammering" with "stealthy haste," and "anger in their blood."
3. Then, **ask** students how these words set the tone in the poem.
   Possible answer: The quick, tangled, and jarring action is analogous to the chaos, hatred, and broken bodies that are indicative of war.
   Monitor Progress: Ask students to describe the tone of the poem's final lines.
   Answer: Students should recognize that the tone is ironic. Sassoon creates the irony by trivializing the serious injury suffered by one of the wirers.
   Reteach: Have students reread the poem and decide whether the speaker thinks human life or a mended wire is more important.

4 # WIRERS[1]

SIEGFRIED SASSOON

5 **▲ Critical Viewing**
Which details in this photograph support Sassoon's depiction of warfare? Explain. **[Connect]**

Vocabulary

stealthy (stel′ thē) *adj.* secretive; furtive

ghastly (gast′ lē) *adj.* extremely horrible; frightening

desolate (des′ ə lit) *adj.* deserted; forlorn

6
"Pass it along, the wiring party's going out"—
And yawning sentries mumble, "Wirers going out."
Unraveling; twisting; hammering stakes with muffled thud,
They toil with stealthy haste and anger in their blood.

The Boche[2] sends up a flare. Black forms stand rigid there,
Stock-still like posts; then darkness, and the clumsy ghosts
Stride hither and thither, whispering, tripped by clutching
    snare
Of snags and tangles.
        Ghastly dawn with vaporous coasts
Gleams desolate along the sky, night's misery ended.

Young Hughes was badly hit; I heard him carried away,
Moaning at every lurch; no doubt he'll die today.
But *we* can say the front-line wire's been safely mended.

1. **Wirers** soldiers who were responsible for repairing the barbed-wire fences that protected the trenches in World War I.
2. **Boche** (bōsh) French slang for a German soldier.

Enrichment: Analyzing a Historical Event

War Memorials

War memorials throughout the world honor those who fought for their countries. The Vietnam Memorial in Washington, D.C. was designed by a college student named Maya Lin. She submitted her idea as part of a national design competition held in 1980–1981. Lin's memorial is a large V-shaped sculpture. Today, visitors gather in front of the memorial to search the inscribed names for a loved one or to honor those listed.

Activity: Research Have students visit war memorials in their own communities. What emotions do these visits stir? How do any words included in the memorials support their artistic intent? Suggest that they record information in the **Enrichment: Analyzing a Historical Event** worksheet, ***Professional Development Guidebook,*** page 230. Have students use the results of their research to write short poems about the memorials they have visited.

ANTHEM FOR DOOMED YOUTH

WILFRED OWEN

7 What passing-bells for these who die as cattle?
Only the monstrous anger of the guns.
Only the stuttering rifles' rapid rattle
Can patter out their hasty orisons.[1]
No **mockeries** for them from prayers or bells,
Nor any voice of mourning save the choirs—
The shrill, demented choirs of wailing shells;
And bugles calling for them from sad shires.[2]

What candles may be held to speed them all?
Not in the hands of boys, but in their eyes
Shall shine the holy glimmers of good-byes.
The **pallor** of girls' brows shall be their pall;
Their flowers the tenderness of patient minds,
And each slow dusk a drawing-down of blinds.

Reading Strategy
Inferring the Essential Message Based on the first line of the poem, what can you infer about Owen's attitude toward the war?

Vocabulary
mockeries (mäk′ ər ēz) *n.* futile or disappointing efforts; ridicule

pallor (pal′ ər) *n.* lack of color; paleness

1. **orisons** (ôr′ i zənz) *n.* prayers.
2. **shires** (shīrz) *n.* any of the counties of England.

Critical Reading

1. **Key Ideas and Details (a)** In "Wirers," what happens in the course of the mission? **(b) Draw Conclusions:** What is the speaker's attitude toward the mission and toward the war? Explain.
2. **Key Ideas and Details (a)** In lines 9–14 of "Anthem for Doomed Youth," what conventional signs of mourning are mentioned? **(b) Analyze:** What do Owen's suggested replacements for these signs have in common?
3. **Integration of Knowledge and Ideas** Do you think Sassoon's poem affected the attitude of British readers toward the war? Explain your answer, using two of these Essential Question words: *position, destructive, factors, influence, support. [Connecting to the Essential Question: How does literature shape or reflect society?]*

Cite textual evidence to support your responses.

7 Reading Strategy

Inferring the Essential Message

1. Direct students' attention to the first line of the poem.
2. **Ask** students: Based on the first line of the poem, what can you infer about Owen's attitude toward the war?
Answer: Owen refers to the dying as "cattle," which infers that they are blindly following orders and dying senseless deaths.

ASSESS

Answers

Before students respond, you may wish to have them write a brief objective summary of the selection. As they answer the questions below, remind them to support their answers with evidence from the text.

1. (a) The enemy sends up a flare to light the area, and the soldiers stand rigid to avoid being seen and shot. (b) The speaker is angry and hates the mission and war.
2. (a) Signs include passing-bells, candles, pall, flowers, and the drawing down of blinds. (b) The replacements are less ceremonial and more human.
3. **Possible response:** Sassoon's poem may have had a negative *influence* on the British attitude toward the war since his *position* was that the war was *destructive.*

Concept Connector

Reading Strategy Graphic Organizer

Ask students to review the graphic organizers in which they have found clues that point to the messages of these poems. Then, have students share their organizers and compare their thoughts and quotes.

Activating Prior Knowledge

Have students return to their responses to the Activating Prior Knowledge activity. Ask them to explain whether their thoughts have changed and, if so, how.

Writing About the Essential Question

Have students compare their responses to the prompt, completed before reading the poems, with their thoughts afterward. Have them work individually or in groups, writing or discussing their thoughts, to formulate new responses. Then, lead a class discussion, probing for what students have learned that confirms or invalidates their initial thoughts. Encourage students to cite specific textual details to support their responses.

After You Read

The Soldier • Wirers • Anthem for Doomed Youth

Literary Analysis

1. **Craft and Structure** Using a chart like the one shown, briefly describe the **tone** in two or three key passages from each poem.

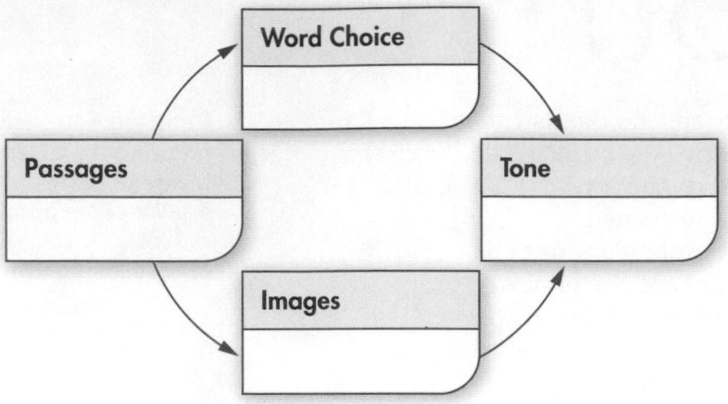

2. **Craft and Structure (a)** Of the three selections, which is the least angry in tone? Explain. **(b)** Which is the most sarcastic? Explain.
3. **Craft and Structure (a)** Which of the selections has the most surprising tone or mixture of tones? Why? **(b)** What is less surprising about the tone or tones of the other selections?
4. **Integration of Knowledge and Ideas** For English civilians of the time, which of these selections probably conveyed the most positive message about the war? Explain.
5. **Integration of Knowledge and Ideas (a)** Which poems are most concerned with war's destruction? Explain. **(b)** Which criticize how the war is being run? Explain.
6. **Comparing Literary Works** Compare the attitudes these writers have toward civilian readers.
7. **Key Ideas and Details** What do you think is Owen's purpose in altering funeral rituals in lines 9–14 of "Anthem for Doomed Youth"? Explain your reasoning.

Reading Strategy

8. **Infer the essential message** of "Wirers," explaining what details led you to your conclusion.
9. **(a)** Infer the essential message of "The Soldier" and "Anthem for Doomed Youth" and explain what details led you to that conclusion. **(b)** If Brooke had lived longer and experienced more of the war, do you think he would have produced poetry more like Owen's? Explain your answer.

Common Core State Standards

Writing
1. Write arguments to support claims in an analysis of substantive topics or texts, using valid reasoning and relevant and sufficient evidence. *(p. 1279)*

Language
5. Demonstrate understanding of figurative language, word relationships, and nuances in word meanings. *(p. 1279)*

Answers

1. **Sample response:** "The Soldier": Passage: lines 1–14; Word Choice: gentleness, peace, heaven; Images: field, England, rich earth, flowers, rivers, sun; Tone: patriotic, touching, sentimental
2. (a) **Possible response:** "The Soldier" is least angry in tone—it is very sentimental. (b) **Possible response:** Responses may vary.
3. (a) **Possible response:** Reponses may vary. (b) **Possible response:** The other selections are less surprising because their focus is on the effects of war on humans.
4. **Possible response:** "The Soldier" probably conveyed the most positive message because it is steeped in patriotism.
5. (a) "Wirers," and "Anthem for Doomed Youth" are both concerned with war's destruction—each describes the horror of war. (b) "Wirers" seems to criticize how the war is being run because it trivializes the fatally wounded soldier who tried to help mend the fence.
6. Brooke's attitude is one of conveying his patriotism and duty. The others seem to convey war's senselessness and destruction.
7. He alters funeral rituals to show the effect of the death of these soldiers and to underscore that no public acknowledgement equals the loss their deaths represent.
8. "Wirers" tells the reader that war is a deadly game with no winners. The final statement that follows Hughes's death, "*we* can say the front-line wire's been safely mended," is filled with sarcasm and negativity.
9. (a) The essential message of "The Soldier" is a soldier's reverence for England and his undying patriotism; in "Anthem for Doomed Youth," the speaker's message is that death is senseless, and the war is represented by the "monstrous anger of the guns." (b) Some students may say that in time, Brooke would have become embittered by the war; others may say that his patriotic nature would last.The selections describe bombs, machine guns, and fighter planes, which all made World War I so destructive.

Assessment Practice

Style (For more practice, see *All-in-One Workbook*.)

Many standardized tests require students to evaluate the appropriateness of a piece of writing for a particular audience. Use the following sample item to teach students how to recognize a text's intended audience.

Considering the enormous economic dislocation that the war operations have caused in the regions where the campaign is raging, there seems to be very little corresponding disturbance in the bird life of the same districts.

The language of this passage suggests it is written for an audience of—

A elementary school students
B a group of close friends
C bankers and brokers
D scientists who study the environment

Although the selection mentions economics briefly, it seems to introduce a discussion of birds, most appropriate for ***D***.

PERFORMANCE TASKS

Integrated Language Skills

Vocabulary Acquisition and Use

Word Analysis: Anglo-Saxon roots *-ghast-, -ghost-*

In "Wirers," Sassoon refers to the "ghastly" dawn. *Ghastly* comes from an Anglo-Saxon root, *-ghast-*, that means "to terrify." The same root also appears as *-ghost-*, which means "the spirit of a dead person," which can terrify the living. Use your understanding of these roots to determine the meaning of these words. Then use them in a sentence.

1. aghast
2. ghostly
3. ghosting
4. ghastful

Vocabulary: Synonyms

Synonyms are words that have similar meanings. Write the letter of the word that is the synonym of each word from the vocabulary list on page 1272. Then, explain the differences in meaning between the synonyms.

1. desolate: **(a)** crowded, **(b)** forlorn, **(c)** happy
2. ghastly: **(a)** frightening, **(b)** ghostly, **(c)** shocking
3. mockeries: **(a)** bravery, **(b)** praise, **(c)** ridicule
4. pallor: **(a)** care, **(b)** paleness, **(c)** friends
5. stealthy: **(a)** furtive, **(b)** honest, **(c)** smart

Writing

Argumentative Text When Irish poet William Butler Yeats selected poems for an anthology of modern English poetry, he left out Brooke, Sassoon, and Owen. Yeats explained his action this way: "I have a distaste for certain poems written in the midst of the great war. . . . The writers . . . were . . . officers of exceptional courage . . . but . . . passive suffering is not a theme for poetry." Write an **essay** that responds to Yeats based on your reading of these poets, particularly Sassoon and Owen. Cite evidence from the poems to support your point about the merits—or lack of merit—of these poets.

Prewriting Note uses of imagery, language, or ideas in the poems that reflect poetic skill or communicate important messages. Review your examples to see if they mainly support or refute Yeats's claim, and decide whether you agree or disagree with his view.

Drafting Begin your draft by summarizing Yeats's position and stating your response to it. Use detailed evidence and examples from the poems to support your points.

Revising Review your draft, highlighting generalizations and looking for supporting details for each. Where details are lacking, add them. Make sure that all quotations are accurate and properly referenced.

Clearly Stating Your Response
As I will demonstrate, Yeats misreads poems like "Wirers" when he dismisses them as representing "passive suffering."

Stating a position early and supporting it with evidence gives a clear picture of the argument.

ASSESS/EXTEND

Answers

Vocabulary Acquisition and Use

Word Analysis

Sample sentences:

1. The soldiers were aghast by the grisly horrors of wartime.
2. In the dark alley, the ghostly shadows looked menacing.
3. As I peered through the telescope, I was unable to differentiate between the real planets and the ghosting ones.
4. The earthquake caused ghastful destruction throughout the community.

Vocabulary

Students should explain the differences in connotations of the two words.

1. b
2. a
3. c
4. b
5. a

Writing

1. You may use this Writing Lesson as timed-writing practice, or you may allow students to develop the essay as a writing assignment over several days.
2. To give students guidance for writing this argumentative text, give them the Support for Writing Lesson page from *Unit 6 Resources,* page 140.
3. Prepare a model critical response ahead of time and have photocopies available to pass out to students.
4. Remind students to use details from the poems to support their positions.
5. Use the rubrics for **Response to Literature** in *Professional Development Guidebook,* pages 250–251, to evaluate student work.

Assessment Resources

Unit 6 Resources

L1 L2 EL **Selection Test A,** pp. 145–147. Administer Test A to less advanced readers.

L3 L4 EL **Selection Test B,** pp. 148–150. Administer Test B to on-level students and more advanced students.

L3 L4 **Open-Book Test,** pp. 142–144. As an alternative, give the Open-Book test.

All **Customizable Test Bank**

All **Self-tests**
Students may prepare for the **Selection Test** by taking the **Self-test** online.

PHLit Online! All assessment resources are available at **www.PHLitOnline.com**.

TEACH

Contemporary Connection

"Baghdad Burning" reproduces information first published in a blog on the Internet. Explain that the blog is written by a young Iraqi woman. She calls herself Riverbend to maintain her anonymity. Her journal documents the upheaval caused by the occupation of Baghdad. Depending on access, you may wish to use a computer in the classroom to present the latest information from this modern diarist and demonstrate the use of blogs. The Web site can be found at **http://riverbendblog.blogspot.com/**.

Connecting War Writings Past and Present

1. Because her blog has already been turned into two books and a stage production, some students may already be familiar with Riverbend's point of view. **Ask** students to share what they know. Students may explain that Riverbend is antiwar and sharply critical of the invasion. Others may comment that her writings allow us to see war from the Iraqis' point of view.
2. The text invites a comparison between "Baghdad Burning" and World War I British soldier Wilfred Owen's "War and the Pity of War" poetry. **Ask** students to compare and contrast the work of the two writers.
   Possible response: Students may note that both writers were youthful when they encountered the tragedy of war. Owen was an enlisted soldier on the front line defending his country, while Riverbend is a civilian forced by an invading army and the chaos in her homeland to become a refugee. Owen uses traditional poetry, while Riverbend uses the modern prose form of an online journal. Both writers document the events around them.

CONTEMPORARY CONNECTION

CONNECTING WAR WRITINGS PAST AND PRESENT

Wilfred Owen, British soldier and poet killed in battle one week before the end of World War I in 1918, wrote that "War and the Pity of War" were his chosen subject. The blogger Riverbend's subject is also the pity of war, a war that has forced her and her family, Iraqi Muslims, to realize that they must abandon their home in Baghdad, a city that in 2007 has all but disappeared into violence. Owen uses the traditional poetic form to describe the threat of "The shrill, demented choirs of wailing shells" in "Anthem for Doomed Youth." Riverbend's April 26, 2007 Web journal entry may be prose, yet it is just as fear-based: "It's difficult to decide which is more frightening—car bombs and militias, or having to leave everything you know and love. . . ."

Both writers are in their 20's when they confront the reality of war. Worlds of difference separate them—gender, religion, geography, technology, the patriotism of an enlisted soldier versus the witness a civilian woman must bear to the chaos surrounding her home—yet their concerns are remarkably similar: death, and the death of a way of life. Riverbend, 24 when she began to chronicle the details of daily life in her gripping blog, known in book form as *Baghdad Burning*, writes anonymously because, "I wouldn't feel free to write otherwise. . . ." Owen, at least, knows nothing of that kind of fear and publishes signed poetry describing the horror of what he witnesses. Both doomed soldier-poet and determined prose writer document events that overtake them, in the most effective and persuasive style they know.

RIVERBEND, AUTHOR OF

BAGHDAD BURNING

"I am female, Iraqi, and 24. I survived the war." With these words, the blogger who calls herself Riverbend begins her online journal one Sunday in August 2003. "That's all you need to know. That's all that matters these days," she writes. Her postings have been compiled into two books, *Baghdad Burning*, published in 2005, and *Baghdad Burning II*, which appeared the following year. Riverbend has become something of a blog celebrity, supplying her readers with a comprehensive local Iraqi view of the war. In fact, her blog has journeyed from cyberspace to the printed page to the stage, debuting in New York in 2005 in a blending of documentary drama and blog that became a play.

No journalist, Riverbend, who explains that she was forced from her job as a computer programmer, nonetheless exhibits a journalist's ability to describe everything around her, from the horror of looking for a missing neighbor to power failures that keep her from her computer. Her perspective is personal and her weapons are words, which survive beyond immediate events, just as the words of the war poets of World War I do.

"RIVERBEND" IS A STORYTELLER. HER "BAGHDAD BURNING" BLOG IS ONE PART ANNE FRANK, ANOTHER PART SCHEHERAZADE AND "A THOUSAND AND ONE ARABIAN NIGHTS."

—FROM CYBERSPACE
[PROMOTION BY HER PUBLISHER]

Riverbend

1. Review the information provided about Riverbend with students. You might point out that the author was educated for eight years in America. **Ask:** Why is it important that this woman share her story with the world?
   Possible response: Her blog journal provides intimate views of daily life from the Iraqi War not provided in the mainstream media, and from the firsthand perspective of someone who has experienced the events.
2. **Ask:** How is reading about these events in a blog different from reading a newspaper or a magazine article?
   Possible response: It is much more personal and immediate; she is able to share her thoughts and feelings with her readers as soon as events happen to her.

Baghdad Burning

1. Review with students their understanding about blogs. Many students may already know that *blog* comes from the term *Web log* and refers to a Web site in which entries are displayed in reverse chronological order, with the most recent shown first. Originally serving as online diaries or journals, they have evolved to serve as forums for news, discussion, and commentary on politics, hobbies, and other interests. Most blogs include a home page where the entries appear, links to other sites, and a commentary section for feedback.
2. Tell students that the text on these pages was posted on Riverbend's blog on April 26, 2007. Read the following quote aloud: "I'll meet you 'round the bend my friend, where hearts can heal and souls can mend . . ."
   Ask students: What do you think is the meaning of the reference for the quotation that opens Riverbend's online blog?
   Possible response: It represents her deeply felt desire to heal the wounds caused by the Iraqi War. It may possibly refer to the Tigris and Euphrates Rivers, which were the source of Iraq's early river valley civilization.

Baghdad Burning

1. As students read Riverbend's blog entry, have them pay attention to her tone and how she presents information about the Iraqi War. Explain that this entry describes her family's decision to leave their homeland. **Ask:** What events or conditions led to the family's decision to leave Baghdad? How does Riverbend feel about their decision?
   Possible responses: The war has brought turmoil and hostility between her former neighbors in Baghdad. She describes the choice between continuing to lead a nightmare existence, with raids in the middle of the night, and living a life that is more than mere survival. It also means leaving behind her childhood home for an uncertain future, so she is uneasy and troubled.
2. **Ask:** Why do you think that the author chose to remain anonymous and use *Riverbend* as a pseudonym?
   Answer: perhaps to protect her own safety in a world that has grown very hostile and dangerous

BAGHDAD BURNING

... I'LL MEET YOU 'ROUND THE BEND MY FRIEND, WHERE HEARTS CAN HEAL AND SOULS CAN MEND...

FROM THURSDAY, APRIL 26, 2007

I remember Baghdad before the war—one could live anywhere. We didn't know what our neighbors were—we didn't care. No one asked about religion or sect. No one bothered with what was considered a trivial topic: are you Sunni or Shia? You only asked something like that if you were uncouth and backward. Our lives revolve around it now. Our existence depends on hiding it or highlighting it—depending on the group of masked men who stop you or raid your home in the middle of the night.

On a personal note, we've finally decided to leave. I guess I've known we would be leaving for a while now. We discussed it as a family dozens of times. At first, someone would suggest it tentatively because, it was just a preposterous idea—leaving one's home and extended family—leaving one's country—and to what? To where?

Since last summer, we had been discussing it more and more. It was only a matter of time before what began as a suggestion—a last case scenario—soon took on solidity and developed into a plan. For the last couple of months, it has only been a matter of logistics. Plane or car? Jordan or Syria? Will we all leave together as a family? Or will it be only my brother and I at first?

After Jordan or Syria—where then? Obviously, either of those countries is going to be a transit to something else. They are both overflowing with Iraqi refugees, and every single Iraqi living in either country is complaining of the fact that work is difficult to come by, and getting a residency is even more difficult. There is also the little problem of being turned back at the border. Thousands of Iraqis aren't being let into Syria or Jordan—and there are no definite criteria for entry, the decision is based on the whim of the border patrol guard checking your passport.

An airplane isn't necessarily safer, as the trip to Baghdad International Airport is in itself risky and travelers are just as likely to be refused permission to enter the country (Syria and Jordan) if they arrive by airplane. And if you're wondering why Syria or Jordan, because they are the only two countries that will let Iraqis in without a visa. Following up visa issues with the few functioning embassies or consulates in Baghdad is next to impossible.

So we've been busy. Busy trying to decide what part of our lives to leave behind. Which memories are dispensable? We, like many Iraqis,

Enrichment: Investigating Culture

Iraqi Cultural Heritage
Iraq has a rich cultural heritage dating back to the Sumerians. After the period of Islamic rule, Baghdad became the capital of an empire ruled by caliphs. It was the center of a civilization rich in science, art, and literature. Later under Turkish rule, Britain occupied the region after the two world wars. Its monarchy was ended by a military coup in 1958. Saddam Hussein's regime that followed had a reputation for human rights abuses and terrorism. His dictatorship collapsed when U.S. and British military forces invaded in 2003.

Activity: Research Ask students to investigate Iraq's rich cultural history. Tell them to find more about family life, customs, music, art, religious rituals, and other practices. Suggest that they record their analyses in the **Investigating Culture** worksheet, *Professional Development Guidebook*, page 223.

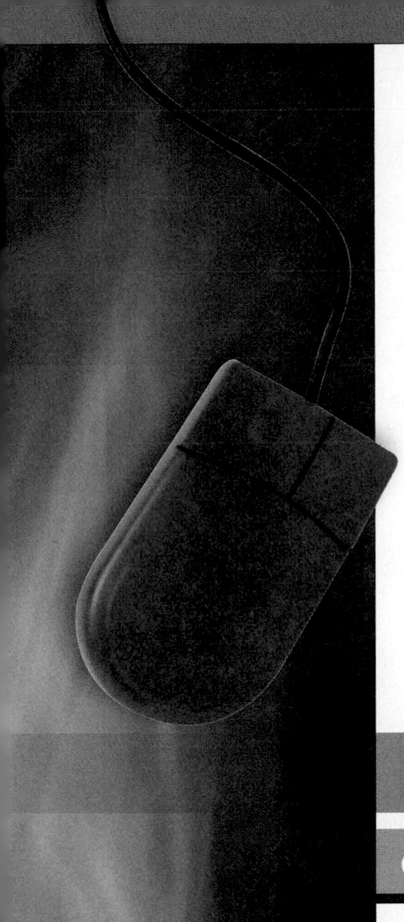

are not the classic refugees—the ones with only the clothes on their backs and no choice. We are choosing to leave because the other option is simply a continuation of what has been one long nightmare—stay and wait and try to survive.

On the one hand, I know that leaving the country and starting a new life somewhere else—as yet unknown—is such a huge thing that it should dwarf every trivial concern. The funny thing is that it's the trivial that seems to occupy our lives. We discuss whether to take photo albums or leave them behind. Can I bring along a stuffed animal I've had since the age of four? Is there room for E.'s guitar? What clothes do we take? Summer clothes? The winter clothes too? What about my books? What about the CDs, the baby pictures?

The problem is that we don't even know if we'll ever see this stuff again. We don't know if whatever we leave, including the house, will be available when and if we come back. There are moments when the injustice of having to leave your country, simply because someone got it into his head to invade it, is overwhelming. It is unfair that in order to survive and live normally, we have to leave our home and what remains of family and friends… And to what?

It's difficult to decide which is more frightening—car bombs and militias, or having to leave everything you know and love, to some unspecified place for a future where nothing is certain.

… WE'VE FINALLY DECIDED TO LEAVE

Critical Reading

1. **(a)** Why did Riverbend's family originally think leaving Iraq was a "preposterous" idea? **(b) Assess:** Was their idea to leave Iraq "preposterous"? Explain.
2. **(a)** What are the difficulties Riverbend anticipates her family will encounter as they try to leave Iraq?
   (b) Infer: How does Riverbend feel about these difficulties? Explain.
3. **(a)** What items might Riverbend's family take when they leave Iraq? **(b) Interpret:** Why does Riverbend's family want to bring these items?

Use these questions to focus a class discussion of "Baghdad Burning":

4. What can readers who are not involved in a war learn from the writings of Riverbend?
5. How is a blog posted on the Internet different from published essays, stories, or memoirs? How is it similar?

ASSESS

Answers

1. (a) Leaving felt unthinkable because they would leave behind loved ones and extended family. Also, trying to start a new life in an unknown place was scary. (b) **Possible response:** No, because conditions had became so intolerable that they decided becoming refugees was preferable to continuing to live where it was unsafe.
2. (a) They worry about logistics. Only certain countries (Syria and Jordan) are allowing Iraqi refugees in without a visa. Work and a temporary residence are difficult to find. (b) It is a huge decision to leave one's country, and she is surprised that the trivial questions about what to take and what to leave behind appear to dominate their lives.
3. (a) They bring photo albums, stuffed animals, musical instruments, clothing, and CDs. (b) They represent memories of their former lives, and they do not know if anything will remain if they return.
4. **Possible response:** They discover what daily life is like for those who must experience the chaos of the battlefield. They learn that war is dangerous, sometimes deadly, and not all heroism and daring.
5. **Possible response:** A blog entry is fresher and more immediate; it is similar to a diary or journal. It also avoids the delay of having to find a traditional publisher. Published essays, stories, and memoirs, however, allow the writer more time to reflect upon the events.

Differentiated Instruction for Universal Access

EL Support for English Learners

Build background knowledge by pointing out the location of Iraq on a map or globe and showing pictures of Iraq before, during, and after the war. You can download some images from the Internet to share with students. Have English learners read aloud from Riverbend's blog entry in pairs or in small groups. Help students with pronunciation. If students encounter unfamiliar words, stop and help them determine the meaning from context.

Enrichment for Gifted/Talented Students

Challenge students to develop a reader's theater presentation based on the events described in Riverbend's blog journal. Tell students to select a scene to dramatize. Have them work together to create any props they need and to write the script. Have them stage the dramatization for their classmates.

PRETEACH

Common Core State Standards

- **Reading Informational Text 2, 6**

❶ About the Text Forms

1. Introduce the speech and memorandum, using the instruction on the student page.
2. **Ask** students what the likely purpose would be of a wartime speech.
   Possible responses: The speech might be meant to encourage the soldiers or to update the public.
3. **Ask** students to predict the content of a memorandum titled "Government Evacuation Scheme."
   Possible response: This probably explains how people could leave a city.

❷ Reading Strategy

1. Introduce the strategy using the instruction on the student page.
2. Encourage students to use a chart like the one shown on p.1284 to take notes on the speech.

Think Aloud: Model the Skill

Model the strategy of determining the essential message. Say to students:

To determine the essential message of a document, I look for rhetorical devices as I read. These emphasize the point the writer is trying to make. Other clues can be found in any headings or lists.

❸ How does literature shape or reflect society?

1. Ask for a volunteer to read the Essential Question aloud.
2. Then, direct students to look for inspirational elements within Churchill's speech and consider how his words shaped society.

COMMON CORE ▪ RESEARCH PROJECT

Primary Sources

Speech
Wartime Speech
Memorandum
Evacuation Scheme

Common Core State Standards

Reading Informational Text
2. Determine two or more central ideas of a text and analyze their development over the course of the text, including how they interact and build on one another to provide a complex analysis; provide an objective summary of the text.
6. Determine an author's point of view or purpose in a text in which the rhetoric is particularly effective, analyzing how style and content contribute to the power, persuasiveness, or beauty of the text.

❶ About the Text Forms

A **speech** is an oral presentation on an important issue. Three elements of a speech are its *purpose,* the reason for its presentation; its *occasion,* the event that inspires it; and its *audience,* those who hear it at the time it is delivered or who hear or read it later. In the World War II era, before television, radio listeners were the largest audience for the speeches of national leaders and other important figures. Such speeches can be valuable primary sources in showing how both the authorities and the general public perceived and responded to events.

A **government memorandum** is a brief official message that summarizes reasons for a particular action and gives instructions on how it is to be performed. Since they affected large numbers of people, government memorandums from the past can be valuable primary sources about events and practices of those times.

❷ Reading Strategy

The central idea, or essential message, of a text is the main point the author expresses. It is closely tied to the author's purpose and his or her point of view on the issue. These texts, written during a period of crisis, reflect their authors' urgent purposes, including the need to ensure the public's willingness to endure hardship for the sake of survival and victory.

As you **determine the essential messages** of these documents, notice the *rhetorical devices and features* that the writers use to emphasize their *main points.*

For example, analyze Churchill's speech for **rhetorical devices** like *parallelism,* the use of similar grammatical structures to express ideas in a memorable way. Also analyze the speech for *emotional appeals,* such as the use of charged words like "victory." Analyze the memorandum for **text features** like headings and lists. Use a chart like the one shown to identify the essential message and the supporting devices and features.

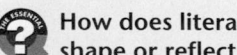

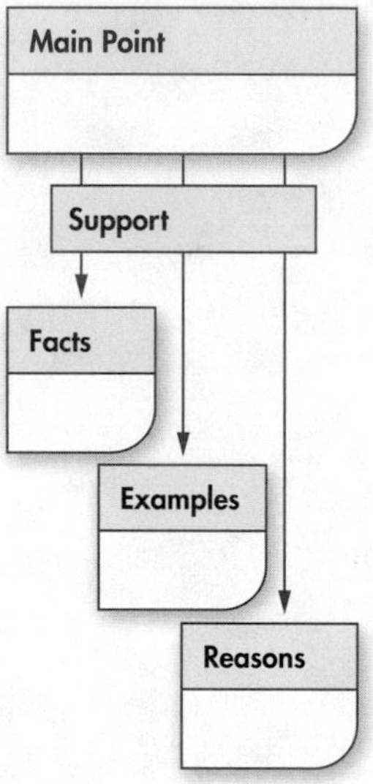

❸ How does literature shape or reflect society?

Winston Churchill was an inspirational leader at a time of great suffering for the British people. As you read, consider how his speech helped shape the public reaction to the hardships of World War II.

PHLit Online! www.PHLitOnline.com

Teaching Resources

The following resources can be used to enrich, extend, or differentiate the instruction.

All *Unit 6 Resources,* pp. 151–154

All **Enriched Online Student Edition**

PHLit Online! All resources are available at www.PHLITOnline.com.

❹ Note-Taking Guide

Primary-source documents are a rich source of information for researchers. As you read these documents, use a note-taking guide like the one shown here to organize relevant and accurate information.

1 Type of Document
☐ Newspaper Article ☐ Letter ☐ Diary ☐ Speech ☐ Map
☐ Government Document ☐ Advertisement ☐ Memorandum ☐ Other

2 Date of Document ______

3 Author ______
Author's Position ______

4 Original Audience ______

5 Purpose and Importance
a What was the original purpose? ______
Write down two details that support your answer. ______
b List two important ideas, statements, or observations from this document. ______
c What does this document show about the time and place in which it was composed? ______

Reading Strategy
Determine the Essential Message
Identifying the sources' main points and supporting features and devices will help you appreciate their purposes.

This guide was adapted from the **U.S. National Archives** document analysis worksheet.

❺ Vocabulary

intimidated (in tim′ ə dāt əd) *v.* made afraid; frightened (p. 1288)

endurance (en do͞or′ əns) *n.* ability to last or continue (p. 1288)

formidable (fôr′ mə də bəl) *adj.* causing fear or dread; hard to overcome (p. 1288)

invincible (in vin′ sə bəl) *adj.* unconquerable (p. 1288)

retaliate (ri tal′ ē āt′) *v.* fight in order to pay back an injury or wrong (p. 1289)

humanitarian (hyo͞o man′ ə ter′ ē ən) *adj.* acting to help humanity, especially by easing pain and suffering (p. 1291)

allocation (al′ ō kā′ shən) *n.* setting apart for a specific purpose; fixing the location of (p. 1291)

❹ Note-Taking Guide

1. Go over the sample note-taking guide on the student page.
2. Encourage students to use it to help them analyze the selections in this lesson.
3. Point out the Reading Strategy tip: Identifying the sources' main points and supporting features and devices will help you appreciate their purpose.

❺ Vocabulary

1. Have students preview the selection vocabulary, pronouncing the words and reading their definitions. Have students identify any words with which they are already familiar.
2. Use each word in a sentence with sufficient context to define the word. Then, repeat your definitional sentence with the vocabulary word missing, requiring the class to fill in the blank orally. Here is an example:
A formidable opponent is one who is difficult to overcome. When an opponent is tough to beat, he or she is [students say "formidable"].

Differentiated Instruction for Universal Access

Support for Special-Needs Students
Have students complete the **Before You Read** and the **Making Connections** pages for these selections in the ***Reader's Notebook: Adapted Version.*** These pages provide an abbreviated skills instruction, a selection summary, the **Before You Read** graphic organizer, and a **Note-Taking Guide.**

Support for Less Proficient Readers
Have students complete the **Before You Read** and the **Making Connections** pages for these selections in the ***Reader's Notebook.*** These pages provide an abbreviated skills instruction, a selection summary, the **Before You Read** graphic organizer, and a **Note-Taking Guide.**

EL Support for English Learners
Have students complete the **Before You Read** and the **Making Connections** pages for these selections in the ***Reader's Notebook: English Learner's Version.*** These pages provide additional vocabulary, vocabulary skills, and vocabulary practice, along with a **Getting Ready to Read** activity.

6 Background

The Story Behind the Documents

Sir Winston Churchill

Winston Churchill was a correspondent for *The Morning Post* in South Africa during the Boer War in 1899. During one battle, Churchill was captured and imprisoned by Louis Botha. He and other captured officers were kept in a school building in Pretoria. Churchill boldly escaped and made his way back to British lines—300 miles away! This action established Churchill as a war hero.

Churchill is one of the most-quoted speechwriters in history. His words inspired many in his lifetime and continue to inspire people today.

6 THE STORY BEHIND THE DOCUMENTS

Sir Winston Churchill

Sir Winston Churchill (1874–1965) first won fame as a soldier and journalist in colonial India and South Africa. His war-hero status earned him a seat in Parliament and several government posts, but he was out of power by the 1930s, when his repeated warnings about the dangers of Nazi Germany went unheeded. Only after World War II broke out did the British turn to the man who had been right about the Nazis all along. Churchill became prime minister in May of 1940 and went on to play a key role in the Allied victory five years later.

Churchill was a gifted orator who made dozens of memorable **speeches.** Many of these were delivered to Parliament or other live audiences and also broadcast on the radio; others were radio addresses made directly to the public. In the dark days of the war, when most of Europe had fallen and Britain faced the Nazis alone, it sometimes seemed that the fate of freedom itself depended on the gruff voice of the prime minister, infusing his fellow citizens with the strength and courage to endure.

In the autumn of 1940, a few months after the fall of France, the Germans concentrated their efforts on air attacks on Britain, hoping to bomb the nation into submission. In anticipation of the bombing attacks—and before the war actually began—the British government made plans for the evacuation of children, hospital patients, and some others in the urban areas likely to be targeted by German bombs. The British Ministry of Health outlined the evacuation plan in a 1939 **government memorandum.**

Evacuation was voluntary, but with the bombs flying, few families refused to participate. Because the likely targets for German bombs were factories, docks, and other industrial areas, the majority of the evacuated children were from poor working-class families who generally live in such areas. They were sent to the less populated countryside to live with farmers and villagers of the more prosperous middle class. The result was culture shock—but a culture shock that ultimately brought Britain closer together.

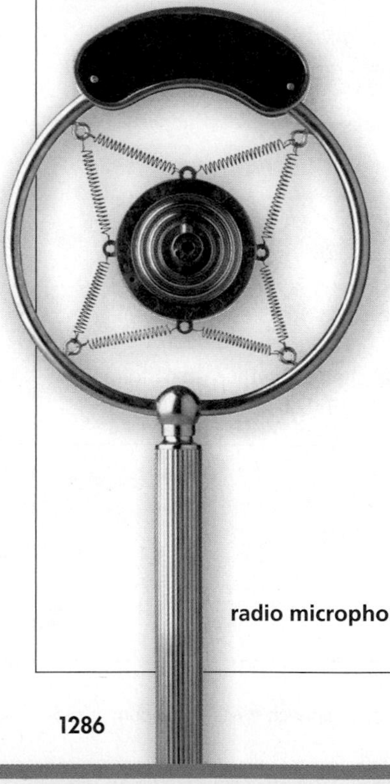

radio microphone

Enrichment: Building Context

World War II

World War II lasted from 1939–1945. Growing concerned with Germany's invasions of other European countries, England, and France declared war on Nazi Germany in September 1939. After a period of successive German victories, France sought an armistice, leaving England to fight on alone, in what Prime Minister Winston Churchill described as the country's "finest hour." With over forty million casualties, World War II was the bloodiest conflict in history. The endurance of the British forces was a source of pride for the British people.

The war changed the face of the world, leaving a divided Europe and the weakening of colonialism. The United States and Russia emerged as the predominant world powers, and colonialism effectively came to an end.

Activity: Research Have students do further research about England's involvement in World War II. Suggest that they record information on the **Enrichment: Building Context** worksheet, *Professional Development Guidebook*, page 222.

❶ WARTIME SPEECH

Sir Winston Churchill

BBC, London, 19 May 1940

I speak to you for the first time as Prime Minister in a solemn hour for the life of our country, of our Empire, of our Allies, and, above all, of the cause of Freedom. A tremendous battle is raging in France and Flanders.[1] The Germans, by a remarkable combination of air bombing and heavily armored tanks, have broken through the French defenses north of the Maginot Line,[2] and strong columns of their armored vehicles are ravaging the open country, which for the first day or two was without defenders. They have penetrated deeply and spread alarm and confusion in their track. Behind them there are now appearing infantry in lorries,[3] and behind them, again, the large masses are moving forward. The regroupment of the French armies to make head against, and also to strike at, this intruding wedge has

❷ **▼ Primary Source: Photographs**
Sir Winston Churchill is shown here making a radio broadcast. In what ways does the presentation of a radio speech differ from a speech given in person? **[Compare and Contrast]**

1. **Flanders** (flan′ dərz) region in northwest Europe, on the North Sea, that includes northern France and much of Belgium.
2. **Maginot** (mazh′ ə nō′) **Line** heavy fortifications built before World War II on the eastern frontier of France, in an unsuccessful effort to prevent a German invasion.
3. **infantry in lorries** (lôr′ ēz) foot soldiers in trucks.

❸ **Reading Check**
According to Churchill, what military victories have the Germans won?

Differentiated Instruction for Universal Access

Strategy for Special-Needs Students
Students may have difficulty understanding the speech because of the difficult language, historical context, and Briticisms. You may wish to group these students with more advanced students to discuss its meaning.

EL Strategy for English Learners
Show students a map of Allied and Axis battlefield movements during 1940. Have them use the map to clarify the references Churchill makes to specific locations in his speech.

TEACH

❶ Background
History

George VI appointed Winston Churchill as Prime Minister after the forced resignation of Neville Chamberlain. It weighed in Churchill's favor that he had expressed concerns about the rising forces in Nazi Germany prior to the war, whereas Chamberlain had underestimated the threat Germany posed.

Churchill delivered this speech in May 1940, when the Germans were advancing rapidly across France. Churchill sought to reassure and inspire the British armed services and the general population. He cites his confidence in the skill and courage of both French and British services and his expectation of loyalty and sacrifice by citizens at home. By linking his belief in the possibility of success with the difficulty of the challenges ahead, Churchill demonstrates his extraordinary power of confident leadership.

❷ Primary Source: Photographs

1. Have students look at the Primary Source Photograph on this page.
2. **Ask** students the Primary Source: Photograph question: In what ways does the presentation of a radio speech differ from a speech given in person?

Possible response: Students should note that a radio speech makes no allowance for gestures or body language, nor gives the speaker any emotional feedback from the audience.

❸ Reading Check

Answer: The Germans have penetrated the Maginot Line and have advanced deeply into French territory.

PHLit Online!

These selections are available in an interactive format in the **Enriched Online Student Edition,** at **www.PHLitOnline.com,** which includes a thematically related video with a writing prompt and an interactive graphic organizer

❹ Primary Source

Speech

1. Have students read the second page of the speech silently.
2. **Ask** the Primary Source question: What do Churchill's words in the third paragraph ("It would be foolish . . .") show about his opinion of the "concrete lines" of defense? **Possible response:** Churchill's words suggest that "concrete lines" are a thing of the past, and soldiers in modern wars must press on continually to defeat the enemy.

❺ Critical Thinking

Interpret

1. Read aloud the paragraph that begins with "In the air—."
2. Remind students that a topic sentence states the main point of the paragraph. **Ask** students to find the topic sentence.
   Answer: "My confidence in our ability to fight it out to the finish with the German Air Force has been strengthened by the fierce encounters which have taken place and are taking place."
3. Then, **ask:** What do you think is the purpose of this paragraph? **Possible response:** Students may say that the purpose of this paragraph is to boost morale—Churchill is telling of continued successes against the German Air Force and is, therefore, giving people reason to hope.

© COMMON CORE ▪ RESEARCH PROJECT

F
is for FRANCE
which we helped
to defend

been proceeding for several days, largely assisted by the magnificent efforts of the Royal Air Force.

We must not allow ourselves to be **intimidated** by the presence of these armored vehicles in unexpected places behind our lines. If they are behind our Front, the French are also at many points fighting actively behind theirs. Both sides are therefore in an extremely dangerous position. And if the French Army, and our own Army, are well handled, as I believe they will be; if the French retain that genius for recovery and counterattack for which they have so long been famous; and if the British Army shows the dogged **endurance** and solid fighting power of which there have been so many examples in the past—then a sudden transformation of the scene might spring into being.

❹ It would be foolish, however, to disguise the gravity of the hour. It would be still more foolish to lose heart and courage or to suppose that well-trained, well-equipped armies numbering three or four millions of men can be overcome in the space of a few weeks, or even months, by a scoop, or raid of mechanized vehicles, however **formidable**. We may look with confidence to the stabilization of the Front in France, and to the general engagement of the masses, which will enable the qualities of the French and British soldiers to be matched squarely against those of their adversaries. For myself, I have **invincible** confidence in the French Army and its leaders. Only a very small part of that splendid army has yet been heavily engaged; and only a very small part of France has yet been invaded. There is good evidence to show that practically the whole of the specialized and mechanized forces of the enemy have been already thrown into the battle; and we know that very heavy losses have been inflicted upon them. No officer or man, no brigade or division,[4] which grapples at close quarters with the enemy, wherever encountered, can fail to make a worthy contribution to the general result. The Armies must cast away the idea of resisting behind concrete lines or natural obstacles, and must realize that mastery can only be regained by furious and unrelenting assault. And this spirit must not only animate the High Command, but must inspire every fighting man.

❺ In the air—often at serious odds—often at odds hitherto[5] thought overwhelming—we have been clawing down three or four to one of our enemies; and the relative balance of the British and German Air Forces is now considerably more favorable to us than at the beginning of the battle. In cutting down the German bombers, we are fighting our own battle as well as that of France. My confidence in our ability to fight it out to the finish with the German Air Force has

Vocabulary

intimidated (in tim′ ə dāt əd) *v.* made afraid; frightened

endurance (en do͞or′ əns) *n.* ability to last or continue

formidable (fôr′ mə də bəl) *adj.* causing fear or dread; hard to overcome

invincible (in vin′ sə bəl) *adj.* unconquerable

Primary Source
Speech What do Churchill's words in the third paragraph show about his opinion of the "concrete lines" of defense?

4. **brigade or division** large units of soldiers.
5. **hitherto** (hith′ ər to͞o) *adv.* until this time.

Enrichment: Analyzing Historical Patterns, Trends, and Periods

Military Tactics
Encourage interested students to find out what was happening at the time of Churchill's speech. Have them find out where different countries' front lines were and then locate those places on a map.
Activity: Mapping the Military Have students do research in the library or on the Internet about new military tactics and weaponry that were being used during World War II. Suggest that they record information in the **Enrichment: Analyzing Historical Patterns, Trends, and Periods** worksheet, ***Professional Development Guidebook,*** page 231. Students can present to the class the information they have found, including maps showing the sites of engagement.

been strengthened by the fierce encounters which have taken place and are taking place. At the same time, our heavy bombers are striking nightly at the taproot of German mechanized power, and have already inflicted serious damage upon the oil refineries on which the Nazi effort to dominate the world directly depends. 5

We must expect that as soon as stability is reached on the Western Front, the bulk of that hideous apparatus of aggression which gashed Holland into ruin and slavery in a few days, will be turned upon us. I am sure I speak for all when I say we are ready to face it; to endure it; and to retaliate against it—to any extent that the unwritten laws of war permit. There will be many men, and many women, in this island who when the ordeal comes upon them, as come it will, will feel comfort, and even a pride—that they are sharing the perils of our lads at the Front—soldiers, sailors and airmen, God bless them—and are drawing away from them a part at least of the onslaught they have to bear. Is not this the appointed time for all to make the utmost exertions in their power? If the battle is to be won, we must provide our men with everincreasing quantities of the weapons and ammunition they need. We must have, and have quickly, more airplanes, more tanks, more shells, more guns. There is imperious need for these vital munitions.[6] They increase our strength against the powerfully armed enemy. They replace the wastage of the obstinate struggle; and the knowledge that wastage will speedily be replaced enables us to draw more readily upon our reserves and throw them in now that everything counts so much. 7

Our task is not only to win the battle—but to win the War. After this battle in France abates its force, there will come the battle for

6. **imperious** (im pir′ ē əs) **. . . munitions** (myo͞o nish′ ənz) urgent need for these vital weapons and ammunition.

6 ◄▲ **Primary Source: Art and Photographs** What mood about the war does the poster (left page) convey to British citizens? Does the photo above show Churchill conveying a similar mood? Explain. **[Compare and Contrast]**

Vocabulary
retaliate (ri tal′ ē āt′) *v.* fight in order to pay back an injury or wrong

8 ☑ Reading Check
What does Churchill say is the advantage of "the general engagement of the masses"?

Differentiated Instruction for Universal Access

Strategy for Special-Needs Students
Some students will have difficulty understanding the speech because of its formal style. Guide students through the difficult passages. Students may also benefit from listening to segments of the speech on the audio CD and then working together to paraphrase what they heard.

Support for Less Proficient Readers
Students may benefit from listening to this speech read aloud. Instruct students to read along as they listen to the speech on audio CD. Pause the recording periodically to check for understanding.

6 Primary Source: Art and Photographs

1. Have students look at the Primary Source Art and Photograph on this spread.
2. **Ask** students the Primary Source: Art question: What mood about the war is this poster trying to convey to British citizens?
   Possible response: The poster seeks to inspire a sense of honor and patriotism.
3. Then, **ask** students the Primary Source: Photographs question: Does the image above show Churchill conveying a similar mood?
   Possible response: The photograph of Churchill visiting a devastated area conveys a sense that all British people are in the war together and must support one another. The photograph's message is a more powerful version of the poster's message.

7 Critical Thinking

Evaluate

1. Ask a volunteer to read aloud the paragraph that begins with "We must expect . . . ."
2. Discuss with students Churchill's goal of inspiring popular support for the war and its necessary sacrifices.
3. **Ask** students how this passage serves that purpose.
   Possible response: Students should note that Churchill points out that many people will suffer hardship during the war, but that it is up to everyone to help in the war effort. He appeals to national pride and identifies for listeners specific ways that they can help, making them feel part of the team.

8 Reading Check

Answer: He says that the balance of British and German troops is considerably more favorable to the British forces now.

❾ Reading Strategy

Determining the Essential Message

1. Have students read the paragraph that begins with "Having received . . . ."
2. **Ask** students the Reading Strategy questions: What is the main point of this paragraph? What rhetorical devices does Churchill use to convey this point?
   Possible response: The main point is to affirm British unity and to inspire the British to heroic efforts by noting the international and historic significance of the war. To convey this point, Churchill uses loaded language, repetition, and parallelism.

❿ Primary Source: Photograph

1. Have students look at the Primary Source Photograph on this page.
2. **Ask** students the Primary Source: Photograph question: What does Churchill say have been the effects of having a strong air force with planes like the spitfire pictured here?

Answer: The effect of having a strong air force has been that the British bombers have inflicted serious damage on German power sources. The planes increase Britain's strength against a powerful enemy.

our island—for all that Britain is, and all that Britain means. That will be the struggle. In that supreme emergency we shall not hesitate to take every step, even the most drastic, to call forth from our people the last ounce and the last inch of effort of which they are capable. The interests of property, the hours of labor, are nothing compared with the struggle for life and honor, for right and freedom, to which we have vowed ourselves.

I have received from the Chiefs of the French Republic, and in particular from its indomitable Prime Minister, M. Reynaud,[7] the most sacred pledges that whatever happens they will fight to the end, be it bitter or be it glorious. Nay, if we fight to the end, it can only be glorious.

Reading Strategy
Determining the Essential Message What is the main point of this paragraph? What rhetorical devices does Churchill use to convey this point?

❾ Having received His Majesty's commission, I have found an administration of men and women of every party and of almost every point of view. We have differed and quarreled in the past; but now one bond unites us all—to wage war until victory is won, and never to surrender ourselves to servitude and shame, whatever the cost and the agony may be. This is one of the most awe-striking periods in the long history of France and Britain. It is also beyond doubt the most sublime. Side by side, unaided except by their kith and kin in the great Dominions and by the wide Empires which rest beneath their shield—side by side, the British and French peoples have advanced to rescue not only Europe but mankind from the foulest and most soul-destroying tyranny which has ever darkened and stained the pages of history. Behind them—behind us—behind the armies and fleets of Britain and France—gather a group of shattered States and bludgeoned[8] races: the Czechs, the Poles, the Norwegians, the Danes, the Dutch, the Belgians—upon all of whom the long night of barbarism will descend, unbroken even by a star of hope, unless we conquer, as conquer we must; as conquer we shall.

❿ **▼ Primary Source: Photograph** What does Churchill say have been the effects of having a strong air force with planes like the spitfire pictured here? **[Analyze Causes and Effects]**

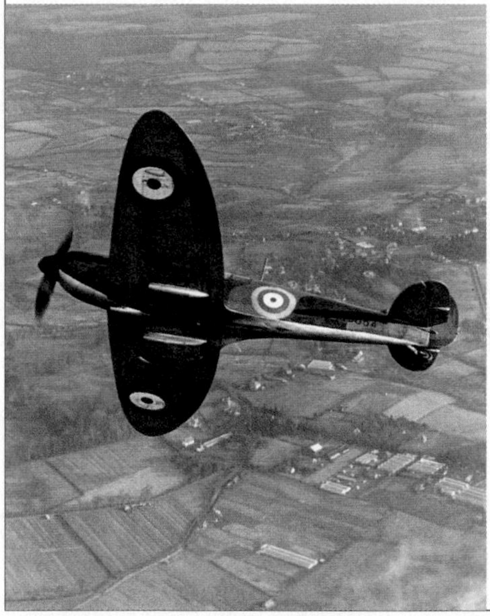

Today is Trinity Sunday.[9] Centuries ago words were written to be a call and a spur to the faithful servants of Truth and Justice; "Arm yourselves, and be ye men of valor, and be in readiness for the conflict; for it is better for us to perish in battle than to look upon the outrage of our nation and our altar. As the Will of God is in Heaven, even so let it be."[10]

7. **M. Reynaud** (rā nō´) Paul Reynaud (1878-1966), French politician who served as France's prime minister from March to June of 1940, when France fell to the Germans.
8. **bludgeoned** (bluj´ ənd) *adj.* beaten. Churchill goes on to name the people of nations that have been overrun by the Germans.
9. **Trinity Sunday** Christian holy day on the eighth Sunday after Easter.
10. **"Arm . . . be"** a quotation from the first book of Maccabees 3:58, a book that is part of Roman Catholic versions of the Bible but not Jewish and Protestant versions.

Enrichment: Investigating Daily Life

Wartime Communication

When Winston Churchill gave his wartime speech, listeners saw no accompanying graphic images of war and destruction. There was no fax, e-mail, or live television broadcast to speed news instantly around the globe. As a result, a speaker could craft a particular description of the situation designed to serve his or her purpose. In Churchill's case, public knowledge of just how bad the Allied situation was would not have helped him reassure the public or inspire its dedication to the war cause.

Activity: Debate Have interested students debate the issue of whether the media should report all facts during wartime or withhold information that may damage public morale. Ask students to analyze the opinions that are voiced in the debate, using the **Enrichment: Investigating Daily Life** worksheet, ***Professional Development Guidebook,*** page 224.

⓫ EVACUATION SCHEME

Memo. Ev. 4

GOVERNMENT EVACUATION SCHEME

MEMORANDUM.

4. The objective has been therefore to provide facilities for the removal from certain large crowded areas, in which the effects of air attack would be most serious, of certain groups of people whose removal is desirable on both national and humanitarian grounds, and to transfer them to districts where the primary purpose of dispersal can be achieved. This has involved an order of priority as regards both the classes of persons to be transferred and the towns to be evacuated, and the provisional allocation of other districts as receiving areas.

Priority classes.

5. The classes of person to whom priority is to be given under the Government Scheme are:—

(1) school children in organized units in charge of their teachers;
(2) children of pre-school age accompanied by their mothers or other persons responsible for looking after them;
(3) expectant mothers;
(4) the adult blind and cripple population so far as removal may be feasible.

The information to be given should include information as to the points of assembly and the amount and kind of hand luggage which can be conveyed. A full list should include the child's gas mask, a change of underclothing, night-clothes, house-shoes or plimsolls, spare stockings or socks, a toothbrush, comb, towel and handerkerchiefs, a warm coat or mackintosh, and a packet of food for the day. The children should be sent away wearing their thickest and warmest footwear.

⓬ **Reading Strategy**
Determining the Essential Message
What text features, such as fonts, heads, and design, are used to convey the essential message of this memorandum?

Vocabulary
humanitarian (hyo͞o man´ ə ter´ ē ən) *adj.* acting to help humanity, especially by easing pain and suffering

allocation (al´ ō kā´ shən) *n.* setting apart for a specific purpose; fixing the location of

Critical Reading

1. **Key Ideas and Details (a)** What major new development in the war does Churchill report in the beginning of his speech? **(b) Analyze:** What answer does Churchill provide to any concerns that this development might cause?
2. **Key Ideas and Details (a)** According to the memorandum, what is the "primary purpose" of the evacuation? **(b) Interpret:** What are the "national and humanitarian grounds" for the evacuation?

Cite textual evidence to support your responses.

Differentiated Instruction for Universal Access

Culturally Responsive Instruction
Culture Focus The evacuations of British citizens from urban areas meant that some family members were separated from one another during the war. Ask students to discuss what it would be like if women and children from all American cities were sent to the countryside, while the men were left behind to continue on as usual. What might be the local effects of such an evacuation?

⓫ Background

The memo included here is just one part of a larger document. To help the people who were having to evacuate, the Ministry of Health also provided lists of healthy meals for children to eat and other basic child care information.

⓬ Reading Strategy

Determining the Essential Message

Ask students the Reading Strategy question: What text features, such as fonts, heads, and design, are used to convey the essential message of this memorandum?
Possible response: The text features make the document look very formal and organized, as is expected for a government memorandum. This format conveys the sense that the information is important and the memo's directions should be followed.

ASSESS

Answers

Before students respond, you may wish to have them write a brief objective summary of the selection. As they answer the questions below, remind them to support their answers with evidence from the text.

1. (a) The Germans have broken through French defenses. (b) Churchill assures the public that British forces are strong and can match those of the German Army.
2. (a) The primary purpose of the evacuation is to protect people in crowded areas from air attacks. (b) On "national and humanitarian grounds"—for the future of the country and humanity as a whole—children, teachers, mothers of young children, pregnant women, and people with disabilities are to be taken out of harm's way.

⓭ Background

World War II photographers attempted to document every aspect of the conflict. Photographers were able to show the world the terrible effects of the bombings in London as well as the tremendous atrocities committed by the Nazis in concentration camps.

⓮ Primary Source: Art and Photographs

1. Have students look at the Primary Source Art and Photographs on this spread.
2. **Ask** students the Primary Source: Art and Photographs question: What story do the poster and the photographs tell you about the effects of the Blitz on England and its citizens?

Answer: The poster looks like it is meant to assure the British people of their future victory. The photographs show the devastation of the bombings and the tremendous hardships the British people were facing.

Ⓒ COMMON CORE ▪ RESEARCH PROJECT

⓭ PHOTOGRAPHS OF THE LONDON BLITZ

Churchill's promise of "conflict" in his Wartime Speech of May 19, 1940, was grimly fulfilled during the German bombing attack on London known as the Blitz (from the German *blitzkrieg*, meaning "lightning warfare"). The Blitz, which lasted from September 7, 1940, to May 11, 1941, caused many casualties and resulted in the damage or destruction of more than a million houses. Nevertheless, this bombardment strengthened rather than undermined Britain's resolve to fight. The photographs on this page show some of the physical effects of the Blitz.

V is for VICTORY
we never shall
be slaves

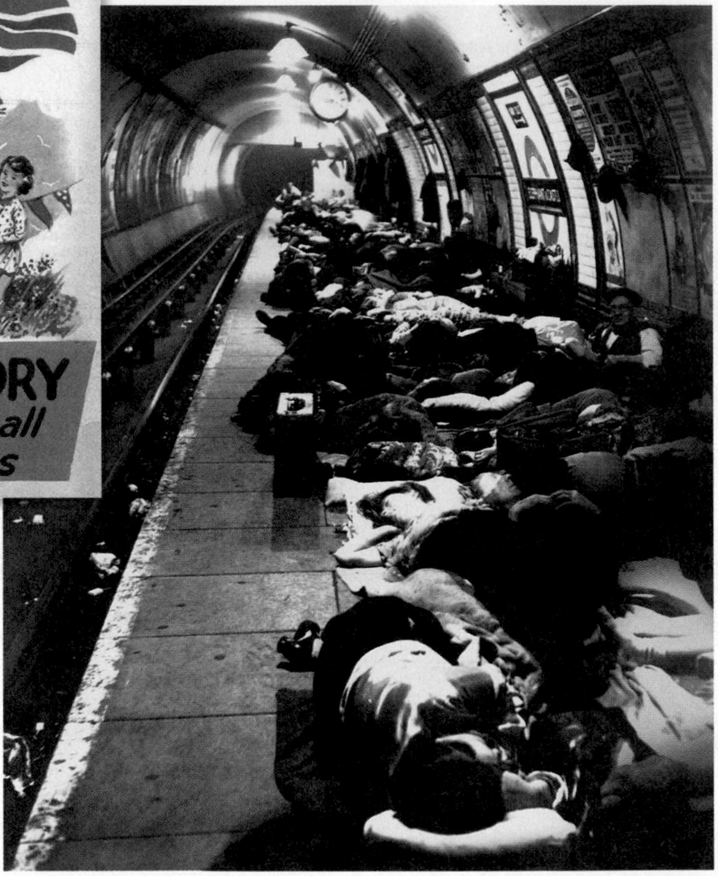

⓮ ▶ **Primary Source: Art and Photographs** What story do the poster (above) and the photographs (right) tell you about the effects of the Blitz on England and its citizens? **[Interpret]**

Enrichment: Analyzing a Historical Event

The Blitz

During the German bombings of 1940–1941, about 60 percent of the homes in London were destroyed, more than 60,000 civilians were killed, and more than 80,000 were injured. It was a time of immeasurable terror for the British people.

Activity: Examine Letters Have interested students locate letters and other primary source documents about the Blitz and its effects on London. Ask students to record what they learn, using the **Enrichment: Analyzing a Historical Event** worksheet, ***Professional Development Guidebook***, page 230.

15

Critical Thinking

15 Make a Judgment

1. Have students closely examine the photographs on this page.
2. Then **ask:** Which photograph do you find more emotionally powerful? Explain.
   Possible response: The photograph that shows people displaced from their homes is particularly moving. It puts a human face on the destruction.

COMMON CORE ▪ RESEARCH PROJECT

Speech • Memorandum

Comparing Primary Sources

Refer to your Note-Taking Guide to complete these questions:

1. **(a)** What is the specific occasion and purpose for Churchill's **speech** and the events to which the **government memorandum** responds? **(b)** What future occasion do both documents anticipate?
2. **(a)** Summarize one or more essential messages expressed in each document. **(b)** How is each document, in its own way, part of the British war effort?
3. **(a)** Who was the intended audience for each document? **(b)** What details and language used in each document reflect that audience? Use this chart to gather ideas and examples.

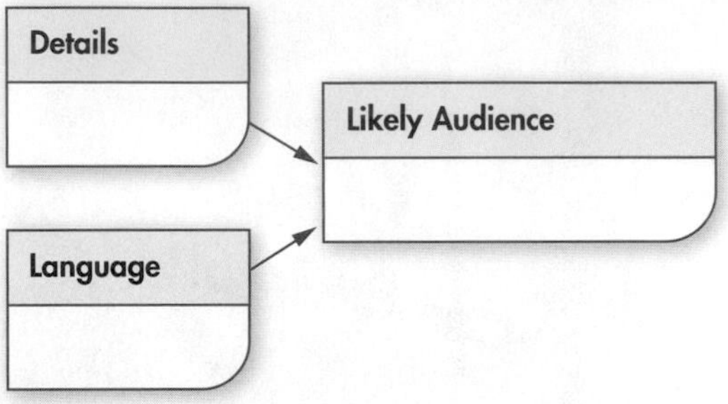

Common Core State Standards

Writing

7. Conduct short as well as more sustained research projects to answer a question or solve a problem; narrow or broaden the inquiry when appropriate; synthesize multiple sources on the subject, demonstrating understanding of the subject under investigation. *(p. 1295)*

8. Gather relevant information from multiple authoritative print and digital sources, using advanced searches effectively; assess the strengths and limitations of each source in terms of the task, purpose, and audience; integrate information into the text selectively to maintain the flow of ideas, avoiding plagiarism and overreliance on any one source and following a standard format for citation. *(p. 1295)*

Language

6. Acquire and use accurately general academic and domain-specific words and phrases, sufficient for reading, writing, speaking, and listening at the college and career readiness level.

Vocabulary Acquisition and Use

Antonyms For each word, choose the letter of its antonym, or opposite, and explain your choice.

1. intimidated: **(a)** astounded **(b)** soothed **(c)** yelled **(d)** arose
2. endurance: **(a)** disobedience **(b)** devotion **(c)** stability **(d)** brevity
3. formidable: **(a)** strong **(b)** weak **(c)** scary **(d)** lengthy
4. invincible: **(a)** conquerable **(b)** triumphant **(c)** wise **(d)** printable

Content-Area Vocabulary Indicate whether each statement is true or false and explain your answer.

5. Someone who wants revenge will not seek to *retaliate*.
6. A *humanitarian* effort does little to help others.
7. When you make an *allocation* of funds, you put the money aside for a specific purpose.

Etymology Study *Allocation* contains the Latin root *-loc-*, which means "place." When you make an *allocation*, you set something apart in a particular place or location. Explain the meaning of the following words, which also contain the Latin root *-loc-*. Then, use each word in a sentence.

dislocate	locality	locomotive
local	locomotion	relocate

Answers

Comparing Primary Sources

1. (a) Churchill's speech is in response to German troops crossing the Maginot Line; the memorandum is in response to the threat of bombings. (b) **Possible response:** Both are preparing British citizens for the war to continue.
2. (a) The main purpose of Churchill's speech is to prepare British citizens for the possibility that Germany will attack them; the purpose of the memo is to direct citizens on how to evacuate the cities that are likely to be bombed. (b) **Possible response:** Both documents are part of the war effort, because they prepare the citizenry for how to do its part.
3. (a) Churchill is speaking to both soldiers and civilians; the memo is for civilians. (b) Students' charts will vary, but should include appropriate details from each document.

Vocabulary Acquisition and Use

Antonyms

1. (b) soothed—Soothing someone is the opposite of intimidation.
2. (d) brevity—Shortness is the opposite of something that needs to be endured.
3. (b) weak—Someone weak would not be formidable.
4. (a) conquerable—Unconquerable would be equal to invincible.

Content-Area Vocabulary

5. False; retaliation is revenge.
6. False; humanitarians help others.
7. True: an allocation of funds is a particular savings account.

Etymology Study

- *dislocate*—move from its proper place. He dislocated his shoulder playing football.
- *local*—belonging to a place. She planned to join the local government.
- *locality*—a specific place. Before moving, they hoped to find a good school in the locality.
- *locomotion*—able to move from one place to another. She considered which form of locomotion to use on the trip.
- *locomotive*—a vehicle used for moving trains from one place to another. The huge freight train required a powerful locomotive.
- *relocate*—move from one place to another. Her father had to relocate to another city for his new job.

Research Task

Topic: Great Speeches

When Winston Churchill's speech beamed out on radio waves in 1940, it relied solely on the power of spoken words to connect with listeners. Twenty-five years later, Lyndon Johnson's "we shall overcome" speech to Congress, urging passage of civil rights legislation, was televised. Today, politicians' speeches can also be viewed on the Internet. How do various media affect the coverage—and the formality and tone—of major speeches like these?

On March 15, 1965, President Lyndon Johnson urged Congress to pass a major civil rights bill.

Assignment: Create a **multimedia presentation** in which you analyze media coverage of a major contemporary speech. Focus on how the presentation varies in different media—newspapers, magazines, radio, television, and the Internet. Consider such factors as bias and different audiences and purposes for the coverage.

Formulate a research plan. First, select the speech on which you will focus. Identify the different types of media used to cover the speech. Choose three types of media coverage you wish to research. Then, formulate questions such as these:

- Which medium is most complete and clear in its coverage?
- For each medium, how do different audiences and purposes affect the bias, formality, and tone of the coverage?
- Which medium seems the most unbiased? Explain.

RESEARCH TIP

In addition to the verbal commentary on the speech, pay attention to nonverbal elements such as music, sound effects, and displayed symbols.

Gather sources. Using print, broadcast, library, and online sources, research coverage of the speech. Keep accurate notations of the sources of all written, visual, and audio material to document your research.

Synthesize information. Based on your research plan, compare and contrast coverage of the speech. Pay special attention to changes in formality and tone across the various media.

Organize and present ideas. Use visuals, such as stills from a television report; sound, such as recording of a radio broadcast; and text to present your analysis. Tell the audience what to look for before showing each example. Then, present your analyses and conclusions.

Model: Presenting a Media Analysis

Step 1: Introduction	Listen for words: "thrilling occasion."
Step 2: Example	Show video clip.
Step 3: Analysis	Denotation and connotation of "thrilling occasion" show reporter may favor the speaker.
Step 4: Conclusion	This news outlet may be biased.

Use a checklist like the one shown to prepare a well-organized multimedia presentation.

Research Checklist

- ☐ Have I answered all the questions in my research plan?
- ☐ Have I properly identified every visual and audio excerpt in my presentation?
- ☐ Have I analyzed each medium's coverage objectively?
- ☐ Do my conclusions proceed logically from my analyses?

Great Speeches

Introduce the Assignment

1. Point out that the assignment calls for students to do two things—*analyze* media coverage, and then *compare and contrast* coverage in different media.
2. Ask students to list elements of media coverage. **Possible responses:** Commentary, choice of commentators, editing (verbal, visual, and sound), placement within a program or publication, length and time, stated and unstated bias.

Guide Student Research

1. Help students formulate research questions. Urge them to consider the intents and effects of elements such as commentary, tone, music, and visuals. Are they useful? Neutral? Do they distract? Enhance? Criticize?
2. Remind students not to confuse the formality and tone of the speech itself with the formality and tone of the media coverage. For example, a speech may be formal and serious, but its coverage may be informal, casual, ironic, or satiric.

Think Aloud: Model Analyzing Media Coverage of a Speech

Say to students: When I analyze coverage of a speech, I pay special attention to the purpose and audience of each media outlet. For example, in a newspaper for conservative readers, I expect coverage with a conservative bias. In magazines that target certain audiences—women, businesspeople, sports fans—I expect the coverage to be focused toward readers' views and interests.

Guide Student Writing

Remind students that media coverage usually identifies itself as "news" or "commentary." Students should also make this distinction and clearly identify each source.

Assessment Resources

Unit 6 Resources

- All **Selective Test**, pp. 153–154
- All **Customizable Test Bank**
- All **Self-tests**
  Students may prepare for the **Selection Test** by taking the **Self-test** online.

PHLit Online! Assessment resources are available at **www.PHLitOnline.com**.

• The Demon Lover
Lesson Pacing Guide

DAY 1 Preteach

- Administer the Reading and Vocabulary Warm-ups (*Unit 6 Resources*, pp. 155–158) as necessary.
- Introduce the Literary Analysis concept: The Ghost Story and Ambiguity.
- Introduce the Reading Strategy: Relate to Primary Source Documents.
- Build background with the author and Background features.
- Develop thematic thinking with Connecting to the Essential Question.
- Teach the selection vocabulary.

DAYS 2–3 Preteach/Teach/Assess

- Distribute copies of the appropriate graphic organizer for the Reading Strategy (*Graphic Organizer Transparencies*, pp. 232–233).
- Distribute copies of the appropriate graphic organizer for Literary Analysis (*Graphic Organizer Transparencies*, pp. 234–235).
- Prepare students to read with the Activating Prior Knowledge activities (TE).
- Informally monitor comprehension while students read.
- Use the Reading Check questions to confirm comprehension.
- Develop students' understanding of the ghost story and ambiguity using the Literary Analysis prompts.
- Develop students' ability to relate to primary source documents using the Reading Strategy prompts.
- Reinforce vocabulary with the Vocabulary notes.
- Assess students' comprehension and mastery of the skills by having them answer the Critical Reading, Literary Analysis, and Reading Strategy questions.
- Have students complete the Vocabulary Lesson.

DAY 4 Extend/Assess

- Have students complete the Writing Lesson and write a sequel. (You may assign as homework.)
- Administer Selection Test A or B (*Unit 6 Resources*, pp. 167–169 or 170–172).

Common Core State Standards

Reading Literature 3. Analyze the impact of the author's choices regarding how to develop and relate elements of a story or drama.

Writing 3.c. Use a variety of techniques to sequence events so that they build on one another to create a coherent whole and build toward a particular tone and outcome.
3.d. Use precise words and phrases, telling details, and sensory language to convey a vivid picture of the experiences, events, setting, and/or characters.

Language 4.a. Use context as a clue to the meaning of a word or phrase.

Additional Standards Practice
***Common Core Companion*, pp. 28–35; 208–218; 324–331**

Daily Block Scheduling
Each day in this Lesson Pacing Guide represents a 40–50 minute period. Teachers using block scheduling may combine days to revise pacing. In addition, teachers may differentiate and support core instruction by integrating components for extended and intensive support as students require. See the Guide to Selected Leveled Resources (facing page).

Guide to Selected Leveled Resources

RTI Tier 1 (students performing on level)

			The Demon Lover
Warm Up	Whole class instruction; Group work	**Practice, model,** and **monitor** fluency, working **with the whole class** or **in groups.**	**Vocabulary and Reading Warm-ups B,** ***Unit 6 Resources,*** pp. 173–174, 176
Comprehension/Skills	Whole class instruction; Group work; Independent work	**Support** and **monitor** comprehension and skills development, having students complete the activities, graphic organizers, and interactive prompts **independently** or **as a class.**	• ***Reader's Notebook,*** adapted instruction and full selection EL ***Reader's Notebook: English Learner's Version,*** adapted instruction and adapted selection • **Reading Strategy Graphic Organizer B,** ***Graphic Organizer Transparencies,*** p. 247 • **Literary Analysis Graphic Organizer B,** ***Graphic Organizer Transparencies,*** p. 249
Monitor Progress	A	**Monitor** student progress with the differentiated curriculum-based assessment in the *Unit Resources.*	• **Selection Test B,** ***Unit 6 Resources,*** pp. 188–190 • **Open-Book Test,** ***Unit 6 Resources,*** pp. 182–184

RTI Tier 2 (students requiring intervention)

			The Demon Lover
Warm Up	Group work; One-on-one teaching	**Practice, model,** and **monitor** fluency **in groups** or **with individuals.**	• **Vocabulary and Reading Warm-ups A,** ***Unit 6 Resources,*** pp. 173–175 • ***Hear It!*** **Audio CD (adapted text)**
Comprehension/Skills	Group work; One-on-one teaching	• **Support** and **monitor** comprehension and skills development, working **in small groups** or **with individuals.** • As students complete the selection in the appropriate version of the *Reader's Notebook,* **monitor** comprehension frequently with group questions and individual instruction. • **Model** strategies while guiding students in completing the activities and prompts in the *Reader's Notebook,* as well as the graphic organizers. • **Practice** skills and **monitor** mastery with the *Reading Kit* worksheets.	• ***Reader's Notebook: Adapted Version,*** adapted instruction and adapted selection EL ***Reader's Notebook: English Learner's Version,*** adapted instruction and adapted selection • **Reading Strategy Graphic Organizer A,** ***Graphic Organizer Transparencies,*** p. 246 • **Literary Analysis Graphic Organizer A,** ***Graphic Organizer Transparencies,*** p. 248 • ***Reading Kit,*** Practice worksheets
Monitor Progress	A	**Monitor** student progress with the differentiated curriculum-based assessment in the *Unit Resources* and in the *Reading Kit.*	• **Selection Test A,** ***Unit 6 Resources,*** pp. 185–187 • ***Reading Kit,*** Assess worksheets

TIER 3 Tier 3 intervention may require consultation with the student's special-education or dyslexia specialist. For additional support, see the Tier 2 activities and resources listed above.

One-on-one teaching **Group work** **Whole class instruction** **Independent work** **A Assessment**

For a complete guide to selection support, including support for Advanced students, see the Overview of Resources in the frontmatter.

• The Demon Lover

The
DEMON
LOVER
Elizabeth Bowen

BACKGROUND World War II was a fact of daily life in the
London of the 1940s. After decisive victories in Europe, Germany
determined to break Britain with a steady bombardment focused on
London. During the Blitz, from September 1940 to May 1941, German
planes dropped bombs on the city almost every night. Whole communities were evacuated periodically, leaving street after street of
deserted buildings. Elizabeth Bowen lived in London during this time,
and the eerie quality of "The Demon Lover" stems from her experience
of a time when war's horrors had become all too "ordinary."

Toward the end of her day in London Mrs. Drover went round to
her shut-up house to look for several things she wanted to take away.
Some belonged to herself, some to her family, who were by now used
to their country life. It was late August; it had been a steamy, showery day: at the moment the trees down the pavement glittered in an
escape of humid yellow afternoon sun. Against the next batch of
clouds, already piling up ink-dark, broken chimneys and parapets
stood out. In her once familiar street, as in any unused channel, an
unfamiliar queerness had silted up; a cat wove itself in and out of
railings, but no human eye watched Mrs. Drover's return. Shifting
some parcels under her arm, she slowly forced round her latchkey
in an unwilling lock, then gave the door, which had warped, a push
with her knee. Dead air came out to meet her as she went in.

1298 A Time of Rapid Change (1901–Present)

RESOURCES FOR:

- L1 Special-Needs Students
- L2 Below-Level Students (Tier 2)
- L3 On-Level Students (Tier 1)
- L4 Advanced Students (Tier 1)
- EL English Learners
- All All Students

Vocabulary/Fluency/Prior Knowledge

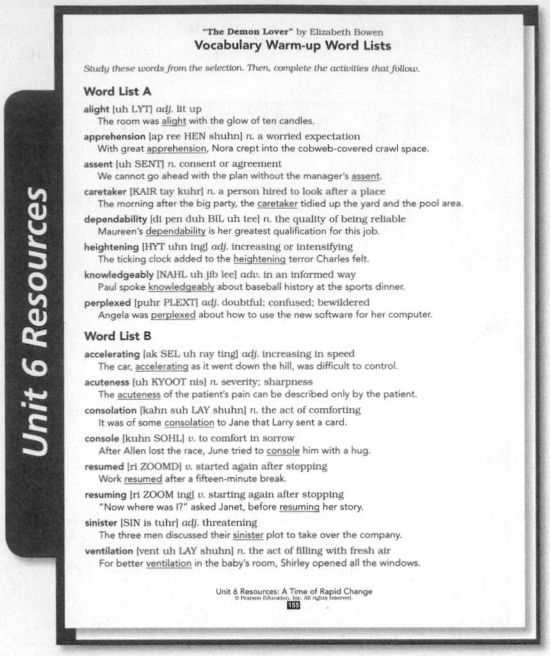

Unit 6 Resources

"The Demon Lover" by Elizabeth Bowen

Vocabulary Warm-up Word Lists

Study these words from the selection. Then, complete the activities that follow.

Word List A

alight [uh LYT] *adj.* lit up
The room was alight with the glow of ten candles.

apprehension [ap ree HEN shuhn] *n.* a worried expectation
With great apprehension, Nora crept into the cobweb-covered crawl space.

assent [uh SENT] *n.* consent or agreement
We cannot go ahead with the plan without the manager's assent.

caretaker [KAIR tay kuhr] *n.* a person hired to look after a place
The morning after the big party, the caretaker tidied up the yard and the pool area.

dependability [di pen duh BIL uh tee] *n.* the quality of being reliable
Maureen's dependability is her greatest qualification for this job.

heightening [HYT uhn ing] *adj.* increasing or intensifying
The ticking clock added to the heightening terror Charles felt.

knowledgeably [NAHL uh jib lee] *adv.* in an informed way
Paul spoke knowledgeably about baseball history at the sports dinner.

perplexed [puhr PLEXT] *adj.* doubtful; confused; bewildered
Angela was perplexed about how to use the new software for her computer.

Word List B

accelerating [ak SEL uh ray ting] *adj.* increasing in speed
The car, accelerating as it went down the hill, was difficult to control.

acuteness [uh KYOOT nis] *n.* severity; sharpness
The acuteness of the patient's pain can be described only by the patient.

consolation [kahn suh LAY shuhn] *n.* the act of comforting
It was of some consolation to Jane that Larry sent a card.

console [kuhn SOHL] *v.* to comfort in sorrow
After Allen lost the race, June tried to console him with a hug.

resumed [ri ZOOMD] *v.* started again after stopping
Work resumed after a fifteen-minute break.

resuming [ri ZOOM ing] *v.* starting again after stopping
"Now where was I?" asked Janet, before resuming her story.

sinister [SIN is tuhr] *adj.* threatening
The three men discussed their sinister plot to take over the company.

ventilation [vent uh LAY shuhn] *n.* the act of filling with fresh air
For better ventilation in the baby's room, Shirley opened all the windows.

Unit 6 Resources: A Time of Rapid Change
© Pearson Education, Inc. All rights reserved.
155

EL L1 L2 **Vocabulary Warm-ups A and B,** pp. 155–156

Also available for these selections:

EL L1 L2 **Reading Warm-ups A and B,** pp. 157–158

All **Vocabulary Builder,** pp. 161

Reader's Notebooks

Pre- and postreading pages for these selections appear in an interactive format in the *Reader's Notebooks*. Each *Notebook* is differentiated for a different group of learners. The selections in the Adapted and English Learner's versions are abridged.

- L2 L3 ***Reader's Notebook***
- L1 ***Reader's Notebook: Adapted Version***
- EL ***Reader's Notebook: English Learner's Version***
- EL ***Reader's Notebook: Spanish Version***

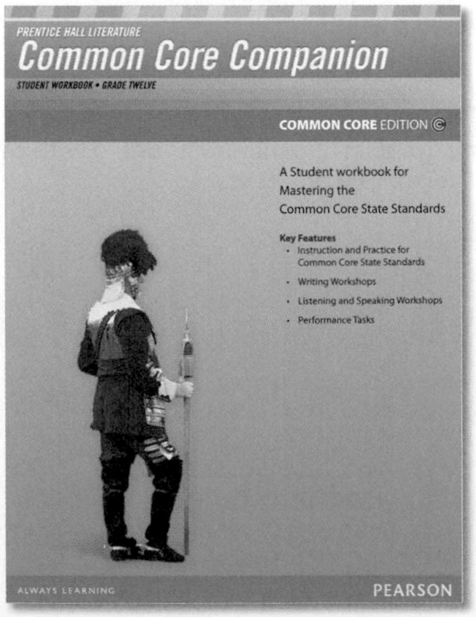

Common Core Companion

Additional instruction and practice for each Common Core State Standard

Selection Support

Graphic Organizer Transparencies

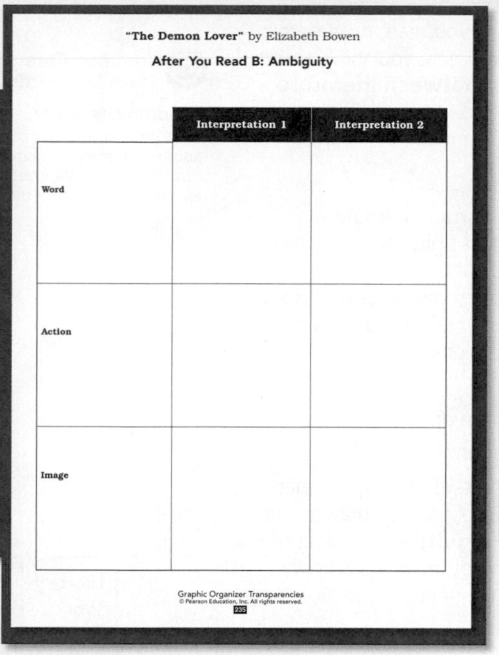
"The Demon Lover" by Elizabeth Bowen

After You Read B: Ambiguity

	Interpretation 1	Interpretation 2
Word		
Action		
Image		

Graphic Organizer Transparencies
© Pearson Education, Inc. All rights reserved.
235

EL L3 **Literary Analysis: Graphic Organizer B,** p. 235

Also available for these selections:

EL L1 L2 **Reading: Graphic Organizer A,** p. 232

EL L3 **Reading: Graphic Organizer B,** p. 233

EL L1 L2 **Literary Analysis: Graphic Organizer A,** (partially filled in), p. 234

Skills Development/Extension

Unit 6 Resources

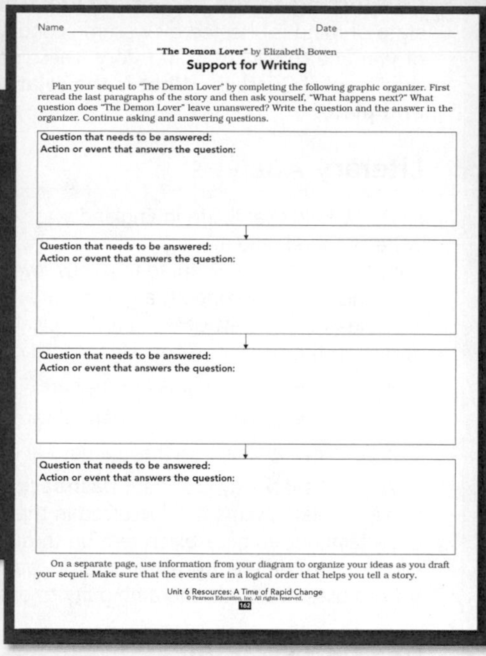
Name ______________ Date ______________

"The Demon Lover" by Elizabeth Bowen

Support for Writing

Plan your sequel to "The Demon Lover" by completing the following graphic organizer. First reread the last paragraphs of the story and then ask yourself, "What happens next?" What question does "The Demon Lover" leave unanswered? Write the question and the answer in the organizer. Continue asking and answering questions.

Question that needs to be answered:
Action or event that answers the question:

Question that needs to be answered:
Action or event that answers the question:

Question that needs to be answered:
Action or event that answers the question:

Question that needs to be answered:
Action or event that answers the question:

On a separate page, use information from your diagram to organize your ideas as you draft your sequel. Make sure that the events are in a logical order that helps you tell a story.

Unit 6 Resources: A Time of Rapid Change
© Pearson Education, Inc. All rights reserved.
162

EL L3 L4 **Support for Writing,** p. 162

Also available for these selections:

All **Literary Analysis: The Ghost Story and Ambiguity,** p. 159

All **Reading: Relate to Primary Source Documents,** p. 160

L4 **Enrichment,** p. 163

Assessment

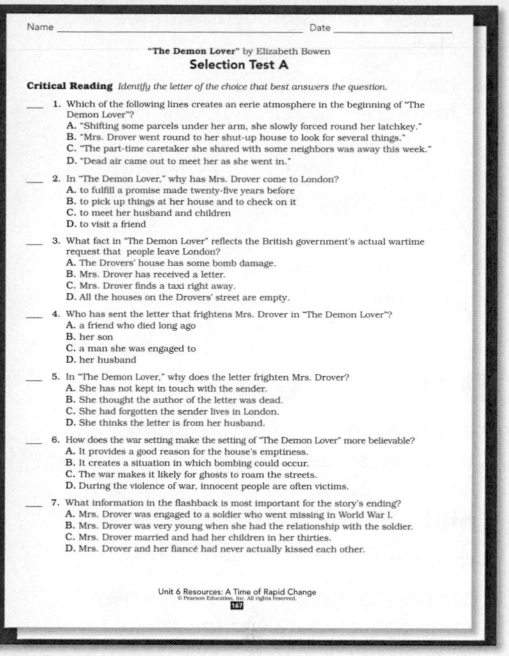
Name ______________ Date ______________

"The Demon Lover" by Elizabeth Bowen

Selection Test A

Critical Reading *Identify the letter of the choice that best answers the question.*

____ 1. Which of the following lines creates an eerie atmosphere in the beginning of "The Demon Lover"?
A. "Shifting some parcels under her arm, she slowly forced round her latchkey."
B. "Mrs. Drover went round to her shut-up house to look for several things."
C. "The part-time caretaker she shared with some neighbors was away this week."
D. "Dead air came out to meet her as she went in."

____ 2. In "The Demon Lover," why has Mrs. Drover come to London?
A. to fulfill a promise made twenty-five years before
B. to pick up things at her house and to check on it
C. to meet her husband and children
D. to visit a friend

____ 3. What fact in "The Demon Lover" reflects the British government's actual wartime request that people leave London?
A. The Drovers' house has some bomb damage.
B. Mrs. Drover has received a letter.
C. Mrs. Drover finds a taxi right away.
D. All the houses on the Drovers' street are empty.

____ 4. Who has sent the letter that frightens Mrs. Drover in "The Demon Lover"?
A. a friend who died long ago
B. her son
C. a man she was engaged to
D. her husband

____ 5. In "The Demon Lover," why does the letter frighten Mrs. Drover?
A. She has not kept in touch with the sender.
B. She thought the author of the letter was dead.
C. She had forgotten the sender lives in London.
D. She thinks the letter is from her husband.

____ 6. How does the war setting make the setting of "The Demon Lover" more believable?
A. It provides a good reason for the house's emptiness.
B. It creates a situation in which bombing could occur.
C. The war makes it likely for ghosts to roam the streets.
D. During the violence of war, innocent people are often victims.

____ 7. What information in the flashback is most important for the story's ending?
A. Mrs. Drover was engaged to a soldier who went missing in World War I.
B. Mrs. Drover was very young when she had the relationship with the soldier.
C. Mrs. Drover married and had her children in her thirties.
D. Mrs. Drover and her fiancé had never actually kissed each other.

Unit 6 Resources: A Time of Rapid Change
© Pearson Education, Inc. All rights reserved.
167

EL L1 L2 **Selection Test A,** pp. 167–169

Also available for these selections:

L3 L4 **Open-Book Test,** pp. 164–166

EL L3 L4 **Selection Test B,** pp. 170–172

PHLit Online!
www.PHLitOnline.com

- complete narrated selection text
- a thematically related video with writing prompt
- an interactive graphic organizer
- highlighting feature
- access to all student print resources, adapted to individual student needs
- Spanish and English summaries
- adapted selection translations in Spanish

Online Resources: All print materials are also available online.

Get Connected! (thematic video with writing prompt)

Also available:

Background video
All videos are available in Spanish.

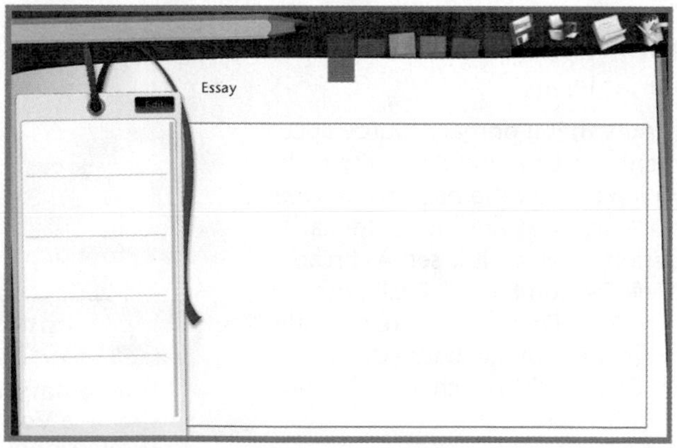

Writer's Journal (with graphics feature)

Also available:

Vocabulary Central (tools and activities for studying vocabulary)

PRETEACH

❶ Connecting to the Essential Question

1. Review the assignment with the class.
2. Have students discuss episodes from their own lives in which the setting or "sense of place" was significant to the experience. Then, have them complete the assignment.
3. As students read, have them look for details that create a wartime atmosphere.

❷ Literary Analysis

Introduce the skill using the instruction on the student page.

Think Aloud: Model the Skill

Say to students:

I know that ghost stories often play upon tension between the rational and the possibility of the supernatural. As I read the selection, I will look for places where Bowen suggests that there *could* be a logical explanation for the strange things happening to the main character.

❸ Reading Strategy

1. Introduce the skill using the instruction on the student page.
2. Give students a copy of **Reading Strategy Graphic Organizer B,** page 233 in ***Graphic Organizer Transparencies,*** to fill out as they read.

Think Aloud: Model the Skill

Say to students:

I know that a primary source document can be a useful lens through which to view the parallels between a literary work and the historical period in which it is set. As I read "The Demon Lover," I will note how Mrs. Drover's private struggle mirrors the public battle described by Churchill's speech.

❹ Vocabulary

1. Pronounce each word, giving its definition, and have students say it aloud.
2. For more guidance, see the *Classroom Strategies and Teaching Routines* card for introducing vocabulary.

Before You Read *The Demon Lover*

❶ **Connecting to the Essential Question** In this story, a woman's state of mind is affected by wartime conditions. As you read, note details of wartime conditions in the story. These details will help you think about the Essential Question: **What is the relationship between literature and place?**

Common Core State Standards

Reading Literature
3. Analyze the impact of the author's choices regarding how to develop and relate elements of a story or drama.

❷ Literary Analysis

During World War II, life in England was severely disrupted. Routines were changed, and anxiety replaced trust. The usual sights and sounds of daily life became doubtful, dangerous, even deadly.

In this historical context, a ghost story is right at home. A **ghost story** is a tale in which part of the past—typically, a dead person—seems to appear in the present. Ghost stories include these elements:

- An eerie or mysterious atmosphere
- The suggestion that supernatural forces are at work
- Eerie events that may have a natural explanation

A ghost story may include a **flashback,** a scene that interrupts a narrative to relate events that occurred in the past. Ghost stories may create uncertainty or an unresolved tension through **ambiguity**—the effect of two or more different possible interpretations. As you read, note how Bowen uses flashback and ambiguity to develop elements of the story.

❸ Reading Strategy

Preparing to Read Complex Texts "The Demon Lover" enables you to **relate a literary work to a primary-source document.** Bowen's fiction takes place in the real world described by Winston Churchill in his speech beginning on page 1287. As you read Bowen's story, use a graphic organizer like the one shown to relate Mrs. Drover's private battle to the public battle in Churchill's speech.

	Literary Work: Demon Lover	Primary Source: Wartime Speech
Source of Fear	Ghostly lover	German army
Atmosphere		
Weapons		
Tactics		
Main Goal		
End Result		

❹ Vocabulary

spectral (spek´ trəl) *adj.* ghostly (p. 1300)

dislocation (dis´ lō kā´ shən) *n.* condition of being out of place (p. 1303)

arboreal (är bor´ ē´ əl) *adj.* of, near, or among trees (p. 1303)

circumscribed (sʉr´ kəm skrībd´) *adj.* limited; having a definite boundary (p. 1303)

aperture (ap´ ər chər´) *n.* opening (p. 1305)

PHLit Online! www.PHLitOnline.com

Vocabulary Development

Vocabulary Knowledge Rating

Create a **Vocabulary Knowledge Rating Chart** (***Professional Development Guidebook,*** p. 33) for the vocabulary words on the student page. Give each student a copy of the chart with the words on it. Read the words aloud, and have students mark their ratings in the Before Reading column. Urge students to attend to these words as they read and discuss the selection.

In order to gauge how much instruction you need to provide, tally how many students are confident in their knowledge of each word. As students read, point out the words and their context.

PHLit Online! **Vocabulary Central,** featuring tools and activities for studying vocabulary, is available online at **www.PHLitOnline.com.**

5 Author of "The Demon Lover"

The fiction of Elizabeth Bowen is distinguished by her subtle observation of landscape, by her innovative and believable use of the supernatural, and by her haunting portrayal of England during one of the darkest eras of the country's history—World War II.

From Life Into Art Early in life, Bowen suffered serious losses. Her father had a breakdown when she was seven years old and was confined to an institution. When Bowen was thirteen, her mother died. As an adult, Bowen was to write about such experiences of the denial of emotion and the helplessness of the heart to understand itself or others in the absence of love. In her characters' insecure lives, in the damage that is done them when their feelings are not acknowledged, one can still trace the marks left by Bowen's own early abandonment.

A Writer's Life Bowen's one ambition was to write, and her family's money was enough to support her as she wrote her first short stories. Her first collection, published in 1923, received little attention. Through the 1930s, she perfected her craft, publishing regularly. In 1938, she completed *The Death of the Heart,* one of her best-known works. The novel is about the disillusionment of an innocent teenage girl, taken in by uncaring relatives after her mother's death.

The War and After During the war, Bowen observed England's hardships keenly and with compassion. She incorporated the brutal realities of the war—air raids, blackouts, betrayal—into some of her best stories. By using a wartime setting and playing on the heightened emotions and perceptions people have at such times, Bowen exposed the innermost workings of her characters' minds.

After the war, Bowen widened her literary activities to include literary criticism and book reviews. Her later novels exhibit a more symbolic, more poetic style than her earlier works. Bowen defined the novel as the "non-poetic statement of poetic truth." Guided by the hardships she had undergone, working in a deceptively simple style, she achieved this goal admirably.

Daily Bellringer

For each class during which you will teach this selection, have students complete one of the activities for the appropriate week in the *Daily Bellringer Activities* booklet.

Multidraft Reading

To assist struggling readers and to enhance reading for all, assign the text in chunks, as warranted by length, and apply multidraft reading protocols. For each reading, have students set the purpose indicated:

- **First reading**—identifying key ideas and details and answering any Reading Checks.
- **Second reading**—analyzing craft and structure and responding to the side-column prompts.
- **Third reading**—integrating knowledge and ideas, connecting to other texts and the world, and answering the end-of-selection questions.

For more guidance, refer to the ***Classroom Strategies and Teaching Routines*** card on Multidraft Reading.

5 Background
More About the Author

Elizabeth Dorothea Cole Bowen had a difficult childhood, but her inherited wealth allowed her to pursue her career as a writer. She was able to live independently in London and to winter in Italy before the war. She later inherited the family house at Kildorrery, County Cork. The history of the house is told in *Bowen's Court* (1942) and serves as the scene of her novel *The Last September* (1929).

PHLit Online!
www.PHLitOnline.com

Teaching From Technology

Preparing to Read
Go to **www.PHLitOnline.com** and display the ***Get Connected!*** slide show for this selection. Have the class brainstorm responses to the writing prompt, entering ideas in the interactive journal. Then, have students complete their written responses as homework.

To build background, display the Background and More About the Author features.

Using the Interactive Text
Go to **www.PHLitOnline.com** and display the **Enriched Online Student Edition.** As the class reads the selection or listens to the narration, record answers to side-column prompts using the graphic organizers accessible on the interactive page. Alternatively, have students use the online edition individually, answering the prompts as they read.

TEACH

❶ About the Selection

This chilling ghost story poses the question: Are there supernatural elements at work here, or is the inexplicable a product of the human imagination? When the story's main character, Mrs. Drover, returns to her deserted London home during a pause in World War II bombing, she discovers a letter that appears to be from a long-ago, and presumably dead, fiancé, calling for an assignation on that very day. Her responses to the letter demonstrate the vulnerability of the human psyche, especially during wartime. They also leave readers wondering: Is there really a ghost or is Mrs. Drover hallucinating? Even more profoundly, the story suggests a larger social meaning: A world that can go to war a second time is perhaps, like Mrs. Drover, in love with a demon.

❷ Activating Prior Knowledge

Have students imagine they are living in London during the Blitz (the place and time of this story). Have students describe daily life with nightly bombings under these conditions so they can better appreciate the eerie atmosphere of the story—especially its scanty references to the violence that was all around.

Concept Connector →

Tell students they will return to their responses after reading the selection.

1
2
The DEMON LOVER

Elizabeth Bowen

BACKGROUND World War II was a fact of daily life in the London of the 1940s. After decisive victories in Europe, Germany determined to break Britain with a steady bombardment focused on London. During the Blitz, from September 1940 to May 1941, German planes dropped bombs on the city almost every night. Whole communities were evacuated periodically, leaving street after street of deserted buildings. Elizabeth Bowen lived in London during this time, and the eerie quality of "The Demon Lover" stems from her experience of a time when war's horrors had become all too "ordinary."

Toward the end of her day in London Mrs. Drover went round to her shut-up house to look for several things she wanted to take away. Some belonged to herself, some to her family, who were by now used to their country life. It was late August; it had been a steamy, showery day: at the moment the trees down the pavement glittered in an escape of humid yellow afternoon sun. Against the next batch of clouds, already piling up ink-dark, broken chimneys and parapets stood out. In her once familiar street, as in any unused channel, an unfamiliar queerness had silted up; a cat wove itself in and out of railings, but no human eye watched Mrs. Drover's return. Shifting some parcels under her arm, she slowly forced round her latchkey in an unwilling lock, then gave the door, which had warped, a push with her knee. Dead air came out to meet her as she went in.

Text Complexity Rubric

The Demon Lover			
Qualitative Measures			
Context/Knowledge Demands	Modern horror story; historical knowledge demands 1 2 ③ 4 5		
Structure/Language Clarity	Accessible diction 1 2 ③ 4 5		
Levels of Meaning	Challenging (human vulnerability in wartime; possible supernatural explanations) 1 2 3 ④ 5		
Quantitative Measures			
Lexile	1010L	**Text Length**	2,763 words
Overall Complexity	**More complex**		

Reader and Task Suggestions

Preparing to Read the Text

- Use the information on SE p. 1297 to discuss Bowen's incorporation of World War II into her stories.
- Mention that in Bowen's horror story "The Demon Lover," readers are never sure whether the mysterious events are supernatural or not.
- Guide students to use Multidraft Reading strategies (TE p. 1297).

Leveled Tasks

Levels of Meaning If students will have difficulty with the story's levels of meaning, have them focus first on the ghostly elements. Then, have students reread the story and consider what it might be saying about war and its effects.

Evaluating If students will not have difficulty with levels of meaning, have them evaluate whether or not it is an effective ghost story.

The staircase window having been boarded up, no light came down into the hall. But one door, she could just see, stood ajar, so she went quickly through into the room and unshuttered the big window in there. Now the prosaic woman, looking about her, was more perplexed than she knew by everything that she saw, by traces of her long former habit of life—the yellow smoke stain up the white marble mantel-piece, the ring left by a vase on the top of the escritoire,[1] the bruise in the wallpaper where, on the door being thrown open widely, the china handle had always hit the wall. The piano, having gone away to be stored, had left what looked like claw marks on its part of the parquet.[2] Though not much dust had seeped in, each object wore a film of another kind; and, the only ventilation being the chimney, the whole drawing room smelled of the cold hearth. Mrs. Drover put down her parcels on the escritoire and left the room to proceed upstairs; the things she wanted were in a bedroom chest.

3 She had been anxious to see how the house was—the part-time caretaker she shared with some neighbors was away this week on his holiday, known to be not yet back. At the best of times he did not look in often, and she was never sure that she trusted him. There were some cracks in the structure, left by the last bombing, on which she was anxious to keep an eye. Not that one could do anything—

A shaft of refracted daylight now lay across the hall. She stopped dead and stared at the hall table—on this lay a letter addressed to her.

She thought first—then the caretaker *must* be back. All the same, who, seeing the house shuttered, would have dropped a letter in at the box? It was not a circular, it was not a bill. And the post office redirected, to the address in the country, everything for her that came through the post. The caretaker (even if he *were* back) did not know she was due in London today—her call here had been planned to be a surprise—so his 4 negligence in the manner of this letter, leaving it to wait in the dusk and the dust, annoyed her. Annoyed, she picked up the letter, which bore no stamp. But it cannot be important, or they would know . . . She took the letter rapidly upstairs with her, without a stop to look at the writing till she reached what had been her bedroom, where she let in light. The room looked over the garden and other gardens: the sun had gone in; as the clouds sharpened and lowered, the trees and rank lawns seemed already to smoke with dark. Her reluctance to look again at the letter came from the fact that she felt intruded upon—and by someone contemptuous of her ways. However, in the tenseness preceding the fall of rain she read it: it was a few lines.

DEAR KATHLEEN,

You will not have forgotten that today is our anniversary, and the day we said. The years have gone by at once slowly and fast. In view of the fact that nothing has changed, I shall rely upon you to

---

1. **escritoire** (es´ krə twär´) *n.* a writing desk or table.
2. **parquet** (pär kā´) *n.* flooring of inlaid woodwork in geometric forms.

Reading Strategy
Relate to Primary Source Documents Winston Churchill described "the gravity of the hour." How does the historical situation contribute to Mrs. Drover's anxiety?

Literary Analysis
The Ghost Story
How does Bowen prepare the reader for the suggestion that there is something supernatural about the letter?

5 **Reading Check**
What does Mrs. Drover unexpectedly discover in her vacant house?

❸ Reading Strategy
Relate to Primary Source Documents

1. Tell students to return to the second full paragraph on page 1288, in which Churchill describes "the gravity of the hour." **Ask:** To what is Churchill referring? **Answer:** He is referring to the serious wartime challenges England is facing from the German forces.
2. **Ask** students the Reading Strategy question: How did the historical situation contribute to Mrs. Drover's anxiety?
   Answer: London was under constant attack and Mrs. Drover's neighborhood was mostly abandoned.

❹ Literary Analysis
The Ghost Story

1. Have students read the first five paragraphs of the story, then pause to identify their reactions to the setting and opening exposition.
2. Review with students the three given traits of a ghost story, and have students identify which are evident in this passage. Have students identify specific passages, words, or phrases.
3. Then, **ask** students the Literary Analysis question: How does Bowen prepare the reader for the suggestion that there is something supernatural about the letter?
   Answer: The author hints at inexplicable aspects of the letter's arrival with clues such as the caretaker's absence and the lack of a stamp on the letter.

❺ Reading Check

Answer: Mrs. Drover unexpectedly discovers a letter addressed to her.

Differentiated Instruction for Universal Access

Support for Special-Needs Students
Have students complete the **Before You Read** and the **Making Connections** pages for this selection in the ***Reader's Notebook: Adapted Version.*** These pages provide an abbreviated skills instruction, a selection summary, the **Before You Read** graphic organizer, and a **Note-taking Guide.**

Support for Less Proficient Readers
Have students complete the **Before You Read** and the **Making Connections** pages for this selection in the ***Reader's Notebook.*** These pages provide an abbreviated skills instruction, a selection summary, the **Before You Read** graphic organizer, and a **Note-taking Guide.**

EL **Support for English Learners**
Have students complete the **Before You Read** and the **Making Connections** pages for this selection in the ***Reader's Notebook: English Learner's Version.*** These pages provide additional vocabulary, vocabulary skills, and vocabulary practice, along with a **Getting Ready to Read** activity.

PHLit Online!
This selection is available in interactive format in the **Enriched Online Student Edition,** at **www.PHLitOnline.com,** which includes a thematically related video with writing prompt and an interactive graphic organizer.

6 The British Tradition

War and Literature

"The Blitz" is derived from the German word *blitzkrieg*, meaning "lightning war." During the Blitz in World War II, the Germans conducted a number of surprise bombing attacks on heavily populated areas in England, especially London.

Connect to the Literature Have students read The British Tradition feature; next, present the additional background information above. Then, **ask** the Connect to the Literature question: Which details in the description of Mrs. Drover show the effects of war and a difficult life? **Possible response:** She has grown thinner and displays an aura of anxiety. Her appearance is unkempt at times and a muscular twitch beside her mouth is a reminder of a serious illness.

7 Literary Analysis

Flashback

1. Have students reread the last two paragraphs on this page. **Ask** them what Mrs. Drover's trailing thoughts at the end of the second-to-last paragraph signify.
   Answer: Her trailing thoughts indicate that she is trying to remember something from a long time ago.
2. Then, **ask** students the Literary Analysis question: What clues in the text signal the beginning of the flashback?
   Answer: Mrs. Drover's unfinished thought at the end of the second-to-last paragraph on the page, "'After twenty-five years. ...'" is one clue that there is going to be a flashback to twenty-five years ago. The young girl and the soldier in the garden mentioned at the beginning of the last paragraph on the page are also new characters, who are not with Mrs. Drover in the house, another clue that the story has moved to a different time and place.

6 *The* **BRITISH TRADITION**

War and Literature

In "The Demon Lover," Bowen hardly mentions World War II—the war appears only as the implied explanation for the Drovers' flight from their home. Bowen's story, though, captures the oppressive atmosphere of the Blitz, a time when familiar routines were routinely shattered by blackouts, airraid sirens, and explosions. The menace Mrs. Drover confronts is not a bombing raid, but like the Blitz itself, it is a menace that lurks behind the most ordinary scenes.

Literary works that reflect events of the day may satisfy a reader's need to find sense in the jumble of historical events. At the same time, these works may challenge events, refusing to assent to the values they represent. In her portrait of Mrs. Drover, who lives a life cracked by war, Bowen may be suggesting that our world is haunted by madness, a madness that spawned two world wars less than thirty years apart.

Connect to the Literature

Which details in the description of Mrs. Drover show the effects of war and a difficult life?

keep your promise. I was sorry to see you leave London, but was satisfied that you would be back in time. You may expect me, therefore, at the hour arranged. Until then . . . K.

Mrs. Drover looked for the date: it was today's. She dropped the letter onto the bedsprings, then picked it up to see the writing again—her lips, beneath the remains of lipstick, beginning to go white. She felt so much the change in her own face that she went to the mirror, polished a clear patch in it and looked at once urgently and stealthily in. She was confronted by a woman of forty-four, with eyes starting out under a hatbrim that had been rather carelessly pulled down. She had not put on any more powder since she left the shop where she ate her solitary tea. The pearls her husband had given her on their marriage hung loose round her now rather thinner throat, slipping into the V of the pink wool jumper her sister knitted last autumn as they sat round the fire. Mrs. Drover's most normal expression was one of controlled worry, but of assent. Since the birth of the third of her little boys, attended by a quite serious illness, she had had an intermittent muscular flicker to the left of her mouth, but in spite of this she could always sustain a manner that was at once energetic and calm.

Turning from her own face as precipitately as she had gone to meet it, she went to the chest where the things were, unlocked it, threw up the lid and knelt to search. But as rain began to come crashing down she could not keep from looking over her shoulder at the stripped bed on which the letter lay. Behind the blanket of rain the clock of the church that still stood struck six—with rapidly heightening apprehension she counted each of the slow strokes. "The hour arranged . . . My God," she said, "*What hour*? How should I . . .? After twenty-five years. . . ." 7

The young girl talking to the soldier in the garden had not ever completely seen his face. It was dark; they were saying goodbye under a tree. Now and then—for it felt, from not seeing him at this intense moment, as though she had never seen him at all—she verified his presence for these few moments longer by putting out a hand, which he each time pressed, without very much kindness, and painfully, on to one of the breast buttons of his uniform. That cut of the button on the palm of her hand was, principally, what she was to carry away. This was so near the end of a leave from France that she could only wish him already gone. It was August 1916. Being not kissed, being drawn away from and looked at intimidated Kathleen till she imagined **spectral** glitters in the place of his eyes. Turning away and looking back up the lawn she saw, through branches of trees, the drawing-room window alight; she caught a breath for the

Literary Analysis
Flashback What clues in the text signal the beginning of the flashback?

Vocabulary
spectral (spek′ trəl) *adj.* ghostly

Enrichment: Investigating Technology

World War I

Bowen's Mrs. Drover recalls parting with her fiancé, who served as a soldier in World War I. The war began in 1914. At first, Germany advanced quickly through Belgium and France. Soldiers from England and France dug themselves into trenches to fight off German attacks. Three horrible years followed, in which neither side gained much ground but both sides suffered great losses. This was warfare of a type Europeans had never seen before—poison gas, mud, and a shockingly high number of casualties. The lack of news from the front was difficult for those who, like Mrs. Drover, were waiting at home for loved ones.

Activity: Modern Warfare Have students conduct research on some of the new tools of warfare used during World War I (poison gas, bombs, airplanes). Suggest that they record information on the **Enrichment: Investigating Technology** worksheet, ***Professional Development Guidebook***, page 242. Have them use their research to discuss how technology has widened the ramifications of war for civilians.

8

9 ▲ **Critical Viewing** In what ways is the mood or atmosphere of the story reflected in this painting? **[Interpret]**

1301

8 Humanities

Portrait of N. Pietrunkevic, Nikolai Ge (1831–1894)
Nikolai Ge was a Russian realist painter. He studied at Petersburg Academy of Arts, and then worked and lived in Italy for twelve years. Ge painted religious scenes from the gospels. His rendition of the Last Supper spurred great public debate. After 1876, Ge retired to a farm in the Ukraine where he tried to simplify his life. Use this question for discussion:

1. **Ask** students to contemplate what the woman in the painting is reading. What types of literature would provide solace during times of war?
   Possible response: Students may suggest fiction, because it provides an escape from the chaos of war.

9 Critical Viewing

Possible response: Both are dark, quiet, and eerie.

Differentiated Instruction for Universal Access

Strategy for Less Proficient Readers

Clarify the jumps in time taking place in the story. Mrs. Drover's flashback begins, "The young girl . . ." (p. 1300). Explain that the leap from present to past occurs quickly, while the transition from past to present is gradual. Have students list the events in order.

EL Support for English Learners

Students might interpret the flashback as being about a different person. Explain the device of the flashback, and point out that early in the passage we learn that it is 1916. Help readers trace "Kathleen" until she becomes "Mrs. Drover."

Strategy for Advanced Readers

Have each student write a brief essay answering this question: How much more or less effective would it have been to have the story told in strict chronological order? Students with strong opinions might be invited to debate this point before the class.

⑩ Critical Viewing

Possible response: The furniture is very basic and the images are dark, like dust or soot. The occupant seems to have left quickly, and no attention has been paid to domestic details such as curtains or art.

⑪ Literary Analysis

Ambiguity

1. Have two volunteers act out the meeting between Kathleen and her fiancé. Remind these students to read the description of the meeting carefully so the interpretation is Bowen's, and not their own.
2. Discuss as a class how the scene could be interpreted. Keep a list of opinions on the board, as well as any supporting facts students mention.
3. Then, **ask** students the Literary Analysis question: In what two ways might Kathleen's fiancé's remarks be interpreted?
Answer: The fiancé's promises might mean just what they seem to—that the fiancé will not be that far away (France is close to Britain), and that he plans to return after the war ends. The remarks may also be interpreted to mean that he will return to haunt her.

⑩ **▲ Critical Viewing**
Which details in this painting suggest the dusty, abandoned quality of Mrs. Drover's room? **[Analyze]**

⑪ **Literary Analysis**
Ambiguity In what two ways might Kathleen's fiancé's remarks be interpreted?

moment when she could go running back there into the safe arms of her mother and sister, and cry: "What shall I do, what shall I do? He has gone."

Hearing her catch her breath, her fiancé said, without feeling: "Cold?"

"You're going away such a long way."

"Not so far as you think."

"I don't understand?"

"You don't have to," he said. "You will. You know what we said."

"But that was—suppose you—I mean, suppose."

"I shall be with you," he said, "sooner or later. You won't forget that. You need do nothing but wait."

Only a little more than a minute later she was free to run up the silent lawn. Looking in through the window at her mother and sister, who did not for the moment perceive her, she already felt that unnatural promise drive down between her and the rest of all humankind. No other way of having given herself could have made her feel so apart, lost and foresworn. She could not have plighted a more sinister troth.

Kathleen behaved well when, some months later, her fiancé was reported missing, presumed killed. Her family not only supported her

Enrichment: Investigating Psychology

More About Bowen
It has been said that Elizabeth Bowen had an extraordinary ability to get inside the minds of children. This was most likely a result of her own troubled childhood. She was intrigued by the psychological and emotional dynamics found in families. Bowen often returned to this theme, creating works in which children were orphaned, abandoned, misunderstood, and frequently sacrificed by an uncaring adult world.

Activity: Developmental Psychology In the past century, psychologists have progressed significantly in understanding how people's adult lives are affected by the formative experiences of childhood. Have students investigate some theories of developmental psychology and record them in the **Enrichment: Investigating Psychology** worksheet, ***Professional Development Guidebook,*** page 239. Have them relate these theories to Bowen's often topical writing style.

but were able to praise her courage without stint because they could not regret, as a husband for her, the man they knew almost nothing about. They hoped she would, in a year or two, console herself—and had it been only a question of consolation things might have gone much straighter ahead. But her trouble, behind just a little grief, was a complete **dislocation** from everything. She did not reject other lovers, for these failed to appear: for years she failed to attract men—and with the approach of her thirties she became natural enough to share her family's anxiousness on this score. She began to put herself out, to wonder; and at thirty-two she was very greatly relieved to find herself being courted by William Drover. She married him, and the two of them settled down in this quiet, **arboreal** part of Kensington; in this house the years piled up, her children were born and they all lived till they were driven out by the bombs of the next war. Her movements as Mrs. Drover were **circumscribed**, and she dismissed any idea that they were still watched.

As things were—dead or living the letter writer sent her only a threat. Unable, for some minutes, to go on kneeling with her back exposed to the empty room, Mrs. Drover rose from the chest to sit on an upright chair whose back was firmly against the wall. The desuetude[3] of her former bedroom, her married London home's whole air of being a cracked cup from which memory, with its reassuring power, had either evaporated or leaked away, made a crisis—and at just this crisis the letter writer had, knowledgeably, struck. The hollowness of the house this evening canceled years on years of voices, habits and steps. Through the shut windows she only heard rain fall on the roofs around. To rally herself, she said she was in a mood—and, for two or three seconds shutting her eyes, told herself that she imagined the letter. But she opened them—there it lay on the bed.

On the supernatural side of the letter's entrance she was not permitting her mind to dwell. Who, in London, knew she meant to call at the house today? Evidently, however, this had been known. The caretaker, *had* he come back, had had no cause to expect her: he would have taken the letter in his pocket, to forward it, at his own time, through the post. There was no other sign that the caretaker had been in—but, if not? Letters dropped in at doors of deserted houses do not fly or walk to tables in halls. They do not sit on the dust of empty tables with the air of certainty that they will be found. There is needed some human hand—but nobody but the caretaker had a key. Under circumstances she did not care to consider, a house can be entered without a key. It was possible that she was not alone now. She might be being waited for, downstairs. Waited for—until when? Until "the hour arranged." At least that was not six o'clock; six has struck.

She rose from the chair and went over and locked the door.

The thing was, to get out. To fly? No, not that: she had to catch

3. **desuetude** (des′ wi to͞od′) *adj.* condition of not being used any more.

12 **Vocabulary**

dislocation (dis′ lō kā′ shən) *n.* condition of being out of place

arboreal (är bôr′ ē′ əl) *adj.* of, near, or among trees

circumscribed (sʉr′ kəm skrībd′) *adj.* limited; having a definite boundary

13 **Reading Check**

What happens to Kathleen's fiancé after he returns to war?

12 Vocabulary Builder

Latin Root *-loc-*

1. Bowen writes that before her marriage, Kathleen experiences "a complete *dislocation* from everything." Have students read the meaning of the word in the margin.
2. Inform students that a second meaning of *dislocation* is "disruption of an established order."
3. Tell students that the word *dislocation* is built on the Latin root *-loc-*, meaning "place." Have them brainstorm for other words they know that might be built on the same root.
   Possible responses: Such words include *local, relocate, locus,* and *allocate.*
4. Have them check their suggestions in the dictionary to determine what the root contributes to the meaning of each word.

13 Reading Check

Answer: He was reported missing and presumed killed.

Differentiated Instruction for Universal Access

Enrichment for Less Proficient Readers
Have students each take a portion of the story to illustrate in a comic book manner—that is, with pictures and dialogue in speech balloons. Help them think of the story and how it could be scary, and urge them to illustrate the events in that manner.

Enrichment for Gifted/Talented Students
Have students work together to make a "silent movie" of the story. Students can add music that enhances the dramatics. Discuss what moments would be best emphasized by the music.

Enrichment for Advanced Readers
Encourage students to write their own short ghost stories. Review the reactions they experienced while reading "The Demon Lover" and how the author elicited those reactions. Remind them of the basic characteristics of a ghost story. Students can read their ghost stories to the class for review and comment.

⓮ Literary Analysis

The Ghost Story

1. Have students find details in the story that show Mrs. Drover's practical nature and those that support the feeling of the supernatural.
   Answer: She considers her alternatives in a practical manner, deciding to collect the objects she has come to fetch and to make her train; she plans to get a taxi and tries to calm herself. These details show her practicality. At the same time, the rush of her thoughts and the indications of her rapid breath and fumbling sustain the feelings of uncertainty and fear the letter has created. They suggest the possibility that something supernatural is about to happen.
2. Then, **ask** students the Literary Analysis question: In this paragraph, how do Mrs. Drover's fear of the supernatural and her attention to practical details blur the lines between the familiar world and the unknown?
   Answer: Her attention to practical details is motivated by her fear of the supernatural. In this way, ordinary reasoning is mixed up with fear of the unknown.

⓯ Critical Thinking

Connect

1. Encourage students to recognize the link between young Kathleen's inability to see her fiancé's face during the leave-taking and the mature Mrs. Drover's inability to recall that face.
2. Have students discuss whether the two represent related symptoms. **Ask:** Has Mrs. Drover built her practical personality around her refusal to look her demon "in the face"?
   Possible response: Her references to not being herself after her fiancé left and the unexplained emphasis on the idea that "under no conditions could she remember his face" show that she did not successfully deal with their traumatic parting. Her personality is a defense against the past trauma.

Literary Analysis
The Ghost Story
In this paragraph, how do Mrs. Drover's fear of the supernatural and her attention to practical details blur the lines between the familiar world and the unknown?

⓮ her train. As a woman whose utter dependability was the keystone of her family life she was not willing to return to the country, to her husband, her little boys and her sister, without the objects she had come up to fetch. Resuming work at the chest she set about making up a number of parcels in a rapid, fumbling-decisive way. These, with her shopping parcels, would be too much to carry; these meant a taxi—at the thought of the taxi her heart went up and her normal breathing resumed. I will ring up the taxi now; the taxi cannot come too soon; I shall hear the taxi out there running its engine, till I walk calmly down to it through the hall. I'll ring up—But no: the telephone is cut off . . . She tugged at a knot she had tied wrong.

The idea of flight . . . He was never kind to me, not really. I don't remember him kind at all. Mother said he never considered me. He was set on me, that was what it was—not love. Not love, not meaning a person well. What did he do, to make me promise like that? I can't remember—But she found that she could.

⓯ She remembered with such dreadful acuteness that the twenty-five years since then dissolved like smoke and she instinctively looked for the weal[4] left by the button on the palm of her hand. She remembered not only all that he said and did but the complete suspension of *her* existence during that August week. I was not myself—they all told me so at the time. She remembered—but with one white burning blank as where acid has dropped on a photograph: *under no conditions* could she remember his face.

So wherever he may be waiting, I shall not know him. You have no time to run from a face you do not expect.

The thing was to get to the taxi before any clock struck what could be the hour. She would slip down the street and round the side of the square to where the square gave on the main road. She would return in the taxi, safe, to her own door, and bring the driver into the house with her to pick up the parcels from room to room. The idea of the taxi driver made her decisive, bold; she unlocked her door, went to the top of the staircase and listened down.

She heard nothing—but while she was hearing nothing the passé[5] air of the staircase was disturbed by a draft that traveled up to her face. It emanated from the basement: down there a door or window was being opened by someone who chose this moment to leave the house.

⓰ The rain had stopped; the pavements steamily shone as Mrs. Drover let herself out by inches from her own front door into the empty street. The unoccupied houses opposite continued to meet her look with their damaged stare. Making toward the thoroughfare and the taxi, she tried not to keep looking behind. Indeed, the silence was so intense—one of those creeks of London silence exaggerated this summer by the damage of war—that no tread could have gained on hers unheard. Where her street debouched on the square where people went on living, she

4. **weal** *n.* raised mark, line, or ridge on the skin caused by an injury.
5. **passé** (pa sā´) *adj.* stale.

Vocabulary Development

Vocabulary Knowledge Rating
When students have completed reading and discussing the selection, have them take out their **Vocabulary Knowledge Rating Charts** for the story. Read the words aloud and have students rate their knowledge of words again in the After Reading column. Clarify any words that are still problematic. Have students write their own definitions and example or sentence in the appropriate column. Then, have students complete the Vocabulary Lesson at the end of the selection. Encourage students to use the words in further discussion and written work about the selection. Remind them that they will be accountable for these words on the **Selection Test,** ***Unit 6 Resources,*** pages 167–169 or 170–172.

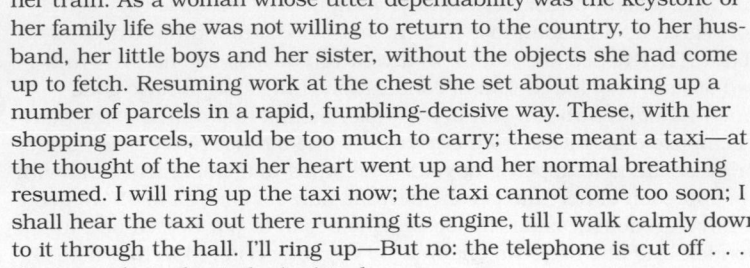

16 grew conscious of, and checked, her unnatural pace. Across the open end of the square two buses impassively passed each other; women, a perambulator,[6] cyclists, a man wheeling a barrow signalized, once again, the ordinary flow of life. At the square's most populous corner should be—and was—the short taxi rank. This evening, only one taxi —but this, although it presented its blank rump, appeared already to be alertly waiting for her. Indeed, without looking round the driver started his engine as she panted up from behind and put her hand on the door. As she did so, the clock struck seven. The taxi faced the main road. To make the trip back to her house it would have to turn—she had settled back on the seat and the taxi *had* turned before she, surprised by its knowing movement, recollected that she had not "said where." She leaned forward to scratch at the glass panel that divided the driver's head from her own.

The driver braked to what was almost a stop, turned round and slid the glass panel back. The jolt of this flung Mrs. Drover forward till her face was almost into the glass. Through the aperture driver and passenger, not six inches between them, remained for an eternity eye to eye. Mrs. Drover's mouth hung open for some seconds before she could issue her first scream. After that she continued to scream freely and to beat with her gloved hands on the glass all round as the taxi, accelerating without mercy, made off with her into the hinterland of deserted streets.

6. perambulator *n.* baby carriage.

Reading Strategy
Relate to a Primary Source
What effect does the war have on what Mrs. Drover sees and hears in the street?

Vocabulary
aperture (ap′ ər chər′) *n.* opening

Critical Reading

Cite textual evidence to support your responses.

1. **Key Ideas and Details (a)** Why is the appearance of the letter in Mrs. Drover's house unexpected? **(b) Infer:** Why is she so upset by it?
2. **Key Ideas and Details (a)** Before returning to the war, what had Mrs. Drover's fiancé promised her? **(b) Analyze:** Identify three points at which she feels she is being watched, and describe what each moment adds to the story.
3. **Key Ideas and Details (a) Analyze:** Identify three references in the story to "traces," marks left behind by objects or actions. **(b) Interpret:** In what sense are ghosts and memories also traces? **(c) Draw Conclusions:** How do the references to traces suggest and support the story's theme?
4. **Integration of Knowledge and Ideas** Beyond the physical effects of war on the home front, what emotional effects of the war does Bowen's story suggest? In your response, use at least two of these Essential Question words: *alter, vulnerable, unresolved. [Connecting to the Essential Question: What is the relationship between literature and place?]*

16 Reading Strategy
Relate to a Primary Source

Ask students the Reading Strategy question: What effect does the war have on what Mrs. Drover sees and hears in the street?
Answer: The street is silent and empty because many people have left London to avoid the bombings.

ASSESS
Answers

Before students respond, you may wish to have them write a brief objective summary of the selection. As they answer the questions below, remind them to support their answers with evidence from the text.

1. (a) The post office has been diverting their mail to the country house. (b) She is upset because it appears to be from her fiancé, whom she thought dead; the letter reminds her of a past promise.
2. (a) The fiancé had promised her that he would be with her, sooner or later. (b) She feels watched after the disappearance of her fiancé, when she is searching through the chest and when she feels the draft from the staircase. Each passage heightens the story's tension or links the present tension to an eerie past.
3. (a) Traces include a smoke stain, a bruise in the wallpaper, a ring left by a vase, claw marks from the piano, and the mark on Kathleen's palm from the button. (b) Ghosts and memories, like scars and stains, are a present indication of the past, of something or someone that is now absent. (c) The references to traces all suggest the ways in which an absence can make its presence felt.
4. War tends to unmoor people from the stabilizing touchstones of their lives. The alteration of the structure of daily life can leave people vulnerable to the uncertainty lying beneath even the most mundane activities.

Concept Connector

Reading Strategy Graphic Organizer
Ask students to review the graphic organizers in which they have related Mrs. Drover's private battle to the public battle in Churchill's primary source document. Then, have students share their organizers and compare the similarities they have identified.

Activating Prior Knowledge
Have students return to their responses to the Activating Prior Knowledge activity. Ask them to explain whether their thoughts have changed and, if so, how.

Writing About the Essential Question
Have students compare their responses to the prompt, completed before reading the story, with their thoughts afterward. Have them work individually or in groups, writing or discussing their thoughts, to formulate new responses. Then, lead a class discussion, probing for what students have learned that confirms or invalidates their initial thoughts. Encourage students to cite specific textual details to support their responses.

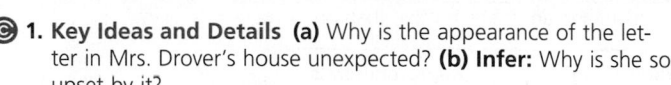

Answers

1. **Possible responses:** "In her once familiar street . . . an unfamiliar queerness had silted up . . . ," "each item wore a film of another kind . . . ," ". . . creeks of . . . silence exaggerated . . . by the damage of war . . ."
2. (a) Something inhuman might be watching her. (b) The dead air suggests the resurfacing of problems long ago laid to rest. (c) This line suggests that her promise to her dead lover was one that would come back to haunt her. (d) She is trying to rationalize the completely irrational and inexplicable appearance of the letter.
3. **Possible responses:** Mrs. Drover is hallucinating due to stress and isolation. Her lover may not have died in the war and has hunted her down.
4. (a) Mrs. Drover had a fiancé who died in the war. She spent her younger life single until marrying in her thirties. (b) She is haunted by the fact that her fiancé was presumed dead, but never found.
5. Students should pick appropriately ambiguous words, actions, and images. They should adequately justify two possible interpretations of each.
6. (a) The radio broadcasts allayed some of the population's fear by keeping them informed of what was happening. (b) The silence allows things Mrs. Drover might not have normally noticed to come to the forefront of her perception.
7. **Possible answer:** Students may note that the ghostly happenings intruding upon Mrs. Drover's life are, in a sense, like an "armored vehicle." That is, the events are resistant to the weapons of rationality that Mrs. Drover exerts against them. By nature of their imperviousness to rational thought, the events are an intimidating prospect.

After You Read *The Demon Lover*

Literary Analysis

1. **Key Ideas and Details** Bowen uses a historical period—the World War II home front—to create a haunting atmosphere of silence and emptiness. Identify three eerie details that show how ordinary life was affected during this period.
2. **Craft and Structure** A **ghost story** often suggests that supernatural forces are at work. Explain how Bowen creates that suggestion with each of the following sentences:
   - **a)** ". . . no human eye watched Mrs. Drover's return."
   - **b)** "Dead air came out to meet her as she went in."
   - **c)** "She could not have plighted a more sinister troth."
   - **d)** "On the supernatural side of the letter's entrance she was not permitting her mind to dwell."
3. **Integration of Knowledge and Ideas** A ghost story often keeps open the possibility that all the eerie events it recounts have a completely natural explanation. Explain all the events of "The Demon Lover" with completely natural causes.
4. **Craft and Structure** The **flashback** that returns Mrs. Drover and the reader to 1916 suggests an explanation for her state of mind in 1940. **(a)** What does the flashback tell you about Mrs. Drover? **(b)** In what sense is she "haunted" by an unresolved problem in her past?
5. **Craft and Structure** Bowen maintains **ambiguity**—the effect of two or more different interpretations—throughout the story. Use a chart like the one shown to interpret a word, an action, and an image in more than one way.

	Interpretation 1	Interpretation 2
Word		
Action		
Image		

Reading Strategy

6. **Relate a literary work to a primary-source document** by assessing Churchill and Bowen's sense of the power of the spoken word. **(a)** What do you think were some of the effects of a wartime radio broadcast? **(b)** What effect does Bowen create by emphasizing the intense silence of the city?
7. In his wartime speech, Winston Churchill says, "We must not allow ourselves to be intimidated by the presence of these armored vehicles in unexpected places behind our lines." Explain how Elizabeth Bowen, in her wartime story of terror, uses an "armored vehicle" and "unexpected" events to intimidate her main character.

Common Core State Standards

Writing
3.c. Use a variety of techniques to sequence events so that they build on one another to create a coherent whole and build toward a particular tone and outcome. *(p. 1307)*
3.d. Use precise words and phrases, telling details, and sensory language to convey a vivid picture of the experiences, events, setting, and/or characters. *(p. 1307)*

Language
4.a. Use context as a clue to the meaning of a word or phrase. *(p. 1307)*

Assessment Practice

Revision Strategy (For more practice, see *All-in-One Workbook*.)

Many tests require students to apply revision strategies to a given passage. Use the following sample test item to practice that skill.

Only a little more than a minute later she was free to run up the silent lawn. Looking in through the window at her mother and sister, who did not for the moment perceive her, she felt that unnatural promise drive between her and the rest of humankind.

Which of these sentences would best fit after the first sentence of the paragraph?

A Her palm was still bleeding.
B It was time for her favorite radio program.
C She ran quickly, eager to feel safe again.
D Her father had already gone to bed.

Lead students to recognize **C** is the best answer because it fits with the tone of the passage.

PERFORMANCE TASKS

Integrated Language Skills

Vocabulary Acquisition and Use

Word Analysis: Cognates

Cognates are words derived from the same original form. Cognates are often easy to spot because they have parts that look and sound alike.

Spectral, meaning "ghostly," is a cognate of *specter*, a word for "ghost." Both *specter* and *spectral* derive from the Latin word *spectrum*, meaning "appearance." When Isaac Newton experimented with light, he examined the spectrum, the colored bands that are visible when white light is refracted through a prism. Now a spectrum refers to any wide range, such as a spectrum of opinions.

Answer these questions:

1. Would you expect a *specter* to have a lively and vivid appearance? Why or why not?
2. If a store offers you a *spectrum* of choices, would you be a happier shopper? Explain.
3. If a landscape is described as *spectral*, what might it look like?

Vocabulary: Context Clues

Words take on meaning depending upon context—the meanings of the words around them. You can often use context clues to determine the meaning of an unfamiliar word.

Review the vocabulary list on page 1296. Then, in your notebook, explain whether the italicized word in each of the sentences below is used correctly, based on its context.

1. I was relieved when I touched not a *spectral* presence, but solid flesh.
2. Given the pollution in the world's waterways, I am surprised that more *arboreal* species are not endangered.
3. Take whatever you wish; my generosity is strictly *circumscribed.*
4. The letter fit through the *aperture.*
5. The doctor has caused a permanent *dislocation* of your shoulder; you should feel fine in a day or two.

Writing

Narrative Text Write a **sequel** to "The Demon Lover," answering the question *What happened next?* Continue the narrative logically. To ensure that your sequel also maintains the uneasy atmosphere that Bowen creates, use plenty of sensory details. Include an *interior monologue*—a speech that occurs only silently in a character's mind—to depict a character's feelings.

Prewriting Jot down questions that "The Demon Lover" leaves unanswered. Then, suggest answers to these questions. Select a few of these answers as a starting point.

Drafting Outline the events in your story in a logical way. As you draft, fill in background from the original story wherever you think it is necessary. In the interior monologue, include only what the character might know or feel.

Model: Revising to Add Sensory Details

As the taxi went down the ^fog-enshrouded^ street, the driver gave a ^blood-curdling^ laugh.

Sensory details make writing more vivid and interesting for the reader.

Revising Make sure that the events in your story are in the correct order. If you have used a *flashback*, make sure the reader knows where it begins and ends. Add sensory details to make the sights, sounds, and smells of a scene and the specific actions, movements, gestures, and feelings of the characters as vivid as possible.

Assessment Resources

Unit 6 Resources

L1 L2 EL **Selection Test A,** pp. 167–169. Administer Test A to less advanced readers.

L3 L4 EL **Selection Test B,** pp. 170–172. Administer Test B to on-level students and more advanced students.

L3 L4 **Open-Book Test,** pp. 164–166. As an alternative, give the Open-Book test.

All **Customizable Test Bank**

All **Self-tests**
Students may prepare for the **Selection Test** by taking the **Self-test** online.

PHLit Online! All assessment resources are available at **www.PHLitOnline.com**.

EXTEND/ASSESS

Answers

Vocabulary Acquisition and Use

Word Analysis

1. No, ghosts are often portrayed as unhappy entities that take a colorless and transparent form.
2. Yes, a wide range of choices would make it more likely that I would find something that I liked.
3. It would be poorly lit and misty, with solid objects appearing only as silhouettes.

Vocabulary

1. Yes, touching a spectral presence would be unpleasant, not relieving.
2. No, arboreal species live in trees and would not be as likely to be affected by water pollution as aquatic species.
3. No, a person who was circumscribed in their generosity would be unlikely to offer unlimited access to what they had.
4. Yes, a letter would fit through an opening, like a letter slot.
5. No, a doctor would not put a patient's shoulder out of place.

Writing

1. To give students guidance for writing this narrative text, give them the Support for Writing Lesson page from ***Unit 6 Resources,*** page 162.
2. During Prewriting, have students check with one another to be sure the "unanswered questions" have logical answers that grow out of the original story.
3. Students may want to first write the events of the original story in chronological order to determine where gaps in knowledge occur. They can then work toward filling in the gaps in their sequels.
4. For the students intending to narrate events out of order for dramatic effect, point out Bowen's use of line spaces to separate the narrative in the past from the narrative in the present in her story.
5. Use the **Rubrics for Narration: Short Story** in ***Professional Development Guidebook,*** pages 252–253, to evaluate students' work.

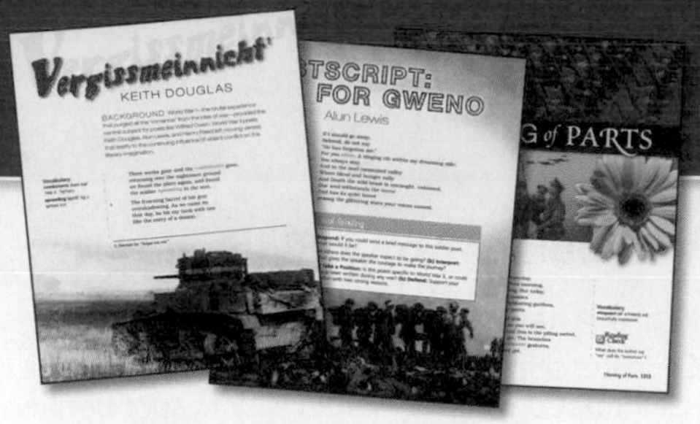

• World War II Poets

Lesson Pacing Guide

DAY 1 Preteach

- Administer the Reading and Vocabulary Warm-ups (*Unit 6 Resources*, pp. 173–176) as necessary.
- Introduce the Literary Analysis concept: Universal Theme.
- Introduce the Reading Strategy: Analyze Author's Purpose.
- Build background with the author and Background features.
- Develop thematic thinking with Connecting to the Essential Question.
- Teach the selection vocabulary.

DAY 2 Preteach/Teach/Extend

- Distribute copies of the appropriate graphic organizer for the Reading Strategy (*Graphic Organizer Transparencies*, pp. 236–237).
- Distribute copies of the appropriate graphic organizer for Literary Analysis (*Graphic Organizer Transparencies*, pp. 238–239).
- Prepare students to read with the Activating Prior Knowledge activities (TE).
- Informally monitor comprehension while students read.
- Use the Reading Check questions to confirm comprehension.
- Develop students' understanding of universal theme using the Literary Analysis prompts.
- Develop students' ability to analyze author's purpose using the Reading Strategy prompts.
- Reinforce vocabulary with the Vocabulary notes.
- Assess students' comprehension and mastery of the skills by having them answer the Critical Reading, Literary Analysis, and Reading Strategy questions.

DAY 3 Assess

- Have students complete the Vocabulary activity.
- Have students complete the Writing activity, writing a memorandum. (You may assign as homework.)
- Administer Selection Test A or B (*Unit 6 Resources*, pp. 185–187 or 188–190).

Common Core State Standards

Reading Literature 6. Analyze a case in which grasping point of view requires distinguishing what is directly stated in a text from what is really meant.

Writing 2. Write informative/explanatory texts to examine and convey complex ideas, concepts, and information clearly and accurately through effective selection, organization, and analysis of content.

Additional Standards Practice
***Common Core Companion**, pp. 61–62; 192–207*

Daily Block Scheduling
Each day in this Lesson Pacing Guide represents a 40–50 minute period. Teachers using block scheduling may combine days to revise pacing. In addition, teachers may differentiate and support core instruction by integrating components for extended and intensive support as students require. See the Guide to Selected Leveled Resources (facing page).

Guide to Selected Leveled Resources

RTI Tier 1 (students performing on level)

			World War II Poets
Warm Up	Whole class instruction; Group work	**Practice, model,** and **monitor** fluency, working **with the whole class** or **in groups.**	**Vocabulary and Reading Warm-ups B,** ***Unit 6 Resources,*** pp. 191–192, 194
Comprehension/Skills	Whole class instruction; Group work; Independent work	**Support** and **monitor** comprehension and skills development, having students complete the activities, graphic organizers, and interactive prompts **independently** or **as a class.**	• ***Reader's Notebook,*** adapted instruction and full selection EL ***Reader's Notebook: English Learner's Version,*** adapted instruction and adapted selection • **Reading Strategy Graphic Organizer B,** ***Graphic Organizer Transparencies,*** p. 251 • **Literary Analysis Graphic Organizer B,** ***Graphic Organizer Transparencies,*** p. 253
Monitor Progress	A	**Monitor** student progress with the differentiated curriculum-based assessment in the *Unit Resources.*	• **Selection Test B,** ***Unit 6 Resources,*** pp. 206–208 • **Open-Book Test,** ***Unit 6 Resources,*** pp. 200–202

RTI Tier 2 (students requiring intervention)

			World War II Poets
Warm Up	Group work; One-on-one teaching	**Practice, model,** and **monitor** fluency **in groups** or **with individuals.**	• **Vocabulary and Reading Warm-ups A,** ***Unit 6 Resources,*** pp. 191–193 • ***Hear It!*** **Audio CD (adapted text)**
Comprehension/Skills	Group work; One-on-one teaching	• **Support** and **monitor** comprehension and skills development, working **in small groups** or **with individuals.** • As students complete the selection in the appropriate version of the *Reader's Notebook,* **monitor** comprehension frequently with group questions and individual instruction. • **Model** strategies while guiding students in completing the activities and prompts in the *Reader's Notebook,* as well as the graphic organizers. • **Practice** skills and **monitor** mastery with the *Reading Kit* worksheets.	• ***Reader's Notebook: Adapted Version,*** adapted instruction and adapted selection EL ***Reader's Notebook: English Learner's Version,*** adapted instruction and adapted selection • **Reading Strategy Graphic Organizer A,** ***Graphic Organizer Transparencies,*** p. 250 • **Literary Analysis Graphic Organizer A,** ***Graphic Organizer Transparencies,*** p. 252 • ***Reading Kit,*** Practice worksheets
Monitor Progress	A	**Monitor** student progress with the differentiated curriculum-based assessment in the *Unit Resources* and in the *Reading Kit.*	• **Selection Test A,** ***Unit 6 Resources,*** pp. 203–205 • ***Reading Kit,*** Assess worksheets

TIER 3 Tier 3 intervention may require consultation with the student's special-education or dyslexia specialist. For additional support, see the Tier 2 activities and resources listed above.

One-on-one teaching | **Group work** | **Whole class instruction** | **Independent work** | **A Assessment**

For a complete guide to selection support, including support for Advanced students, see the Overview of Resources in the frontmatter.

• World War II Poets

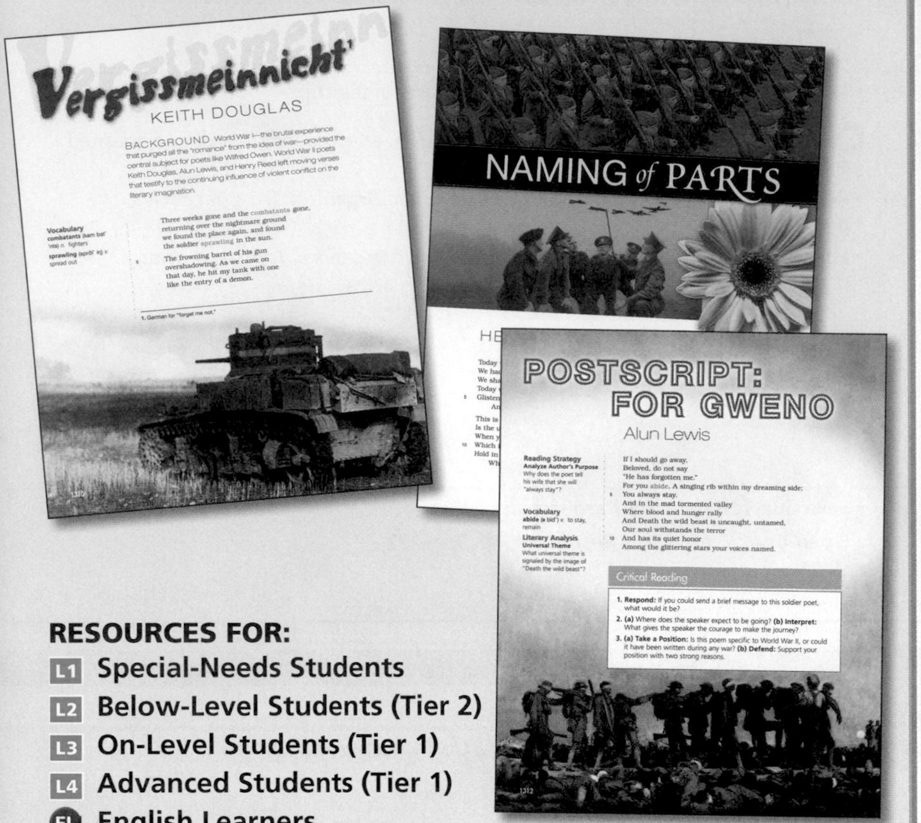

RESOURCES FOR:

- L1 Special-Needs Students
- L2 Below-Level Students (Tier 2)
- L3 On-Level Students (Tier 1)
- L4 Advanced Students (Tier 1)
- EL English Learners
- All All Students

Vocabulary/Fluency/Prior Knowledge

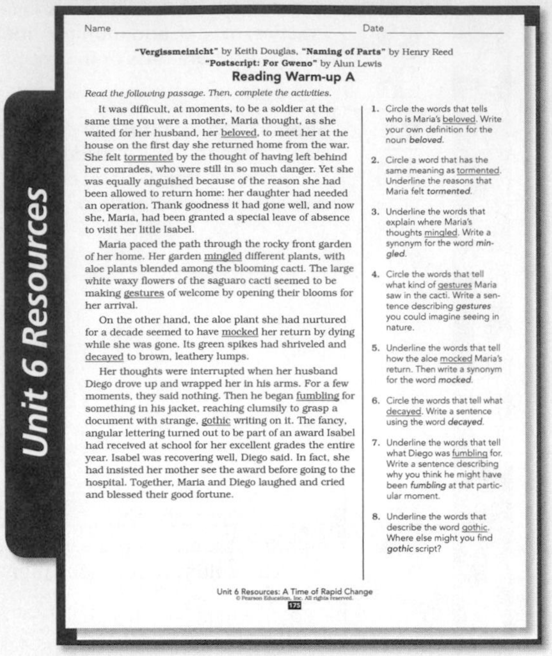

Unit 6 Resources

Name ______________________ Date ______________

"Vergissmeinicht" by Keith Douglas, **"Naming of Parts"** by Henry Reed
"Postscript: For Gweno" by Alun Lewis

Reading Warm-up A

Read the following passage. Then, complete the activities.

It was difficult, at moments, to be a soldier at the same time you were a mother, Maria thought, as she waited for her husband, her beloved, to meet her at the house on the first day she returned home from the war. She felt tormented by the thought of having left behind her comrades, who were still in so much danger. Yet she was equally anguished because of the reason she had been allowed to return home: her daughter had needed an operation. Thank goodness it had gone well, and now she, Maria, had been granted a special leave of absence to visit her little Isabel.

Maria paced the path through the rocky front garden of her home. Her garden mingled different plants, with aloe plants blended among the blooming cacti. The large white waxy flowers of the saguaro cacti seemed to be making gestures of welcome by opening their blooms for her arrival.

On the other hand, the aloe plant she had nurtured for a decade seemed to have mocked her return by dying while she was gone. Its green spikes had shriveled and decayed to brown, leathery lumps.

Her thoughts were interrupted when her husband Diego drove up and wrapped her in his arms. For a few moments, they said nothing. Then he began fumbling for something in his jacket, reaching clumsily to grasp a document with strange, gothic writing on it. The fancy, angular lettering turned out to be part of an award Isabel had received at school for her excellent grades the entire year. Isabel was recovering well, Diego said. In fact, she had insisted her mother see the award before going to the hospital. Together, Maria and Diego laughed and cried and blessed their good fortune.

1. Circle the words that tells who is Maria's beloved. Write your own definition for the noun *beloved*.
2. Circle a word that has the same meaning as tormented. Underline the reasons that Maria felt *tormented*.
3. Underline the words that explain where Maria's thoughts mingled. Write a synonym for the word *mingled*.
4. Circle the words that tell what kind of gestures Maria saw in the cacti. Write a sentence describing *gestures* you could imagine seeing in nature.
5. Underline the words that tell how the aloe mocked Maria's return. Then write a synonym for the word *mocked*.
6. Circle the words that tell what decayed. Write a sentence using the word *decayed*.
7. Underline the words that tell what Diego was fumbling for. Write a sentence describing why you think he might have been *fumbling* at that particular moment.
8. Underline the words that describe the word gothic. Where else might you find *gothic* script?

Unit 6 Resources: A Time of Rapid Change
© Pearson Education, Inc. All rights reserved.
175

EL L1 L2 **Reading Warm-ups A and B,** pp. 175–176

Also available for these selections:

EL L1 L2 **Vocabulary Warm-ups A and B,** pp. 173–174

All **Vocabulary Builder,** p. 179

L2 L3 ***Reader's Notebook***

L1 ***Reader's Notebook: Adapted Version***

EL ***Reader's Notebook: English Learner's Version***

EL ***Reader's Notebook: Spanish Version***

Reader's Notebooks

Pre- and postreading pages for these selections appear in an interactive format in the *Reader's Notebooks*. Each *Notebook* is differentiated for a different group of learners. The selections in the Adapted and English Learner's versions are abridged.

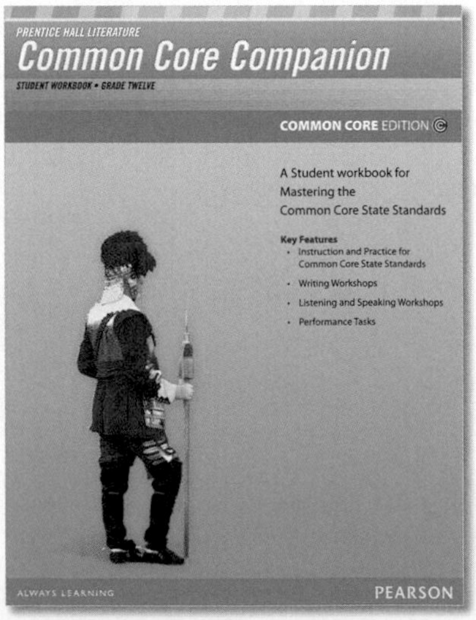

Common Core Companion

Additional instruction and practice for each Common Core State Standard

Selection Support

Graphic Organizer Transparencies

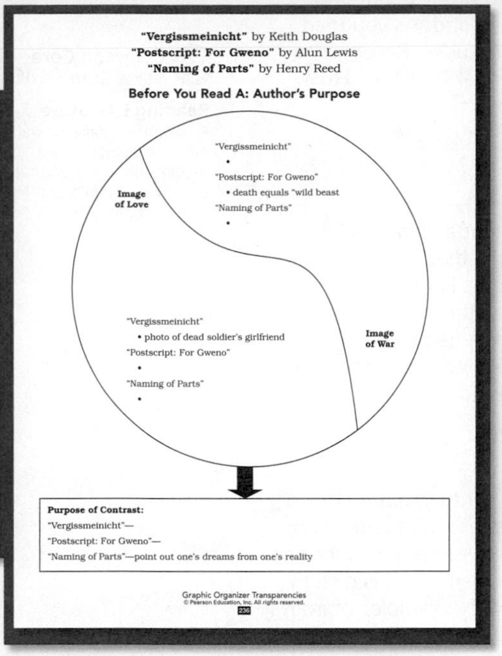
"Vergissmeinicht" by Keith Douglas
"Postscript: For Gweno" by Alun Lewis
"Naming of Parts" by Henry Reed

Before You Read A: Author's Purpose

Purpose of Contrast:
"Vergissmeinicht"—
"Postscript: For Gweno"—
"Naming of Parts"—point out one's dreams from one's reality

Graphic Organizer Transparencies
© Pearson Education, Inc. All rights reserved.
236

EL L1 L2 **Reading: Graphic Organizer A,** p. 236

Also available for these selections:

- EL L3 **Reading: Graphic Organizer B,** p. 237
- EL L1 L2 **Literary Analysis: Graphic Organizer A,** (partially filled in), p. 238
- EL L3 **Literary Analysis: Graphic Organizer B,** p. 239

Skills Development/Extension

Unit 6 Resources

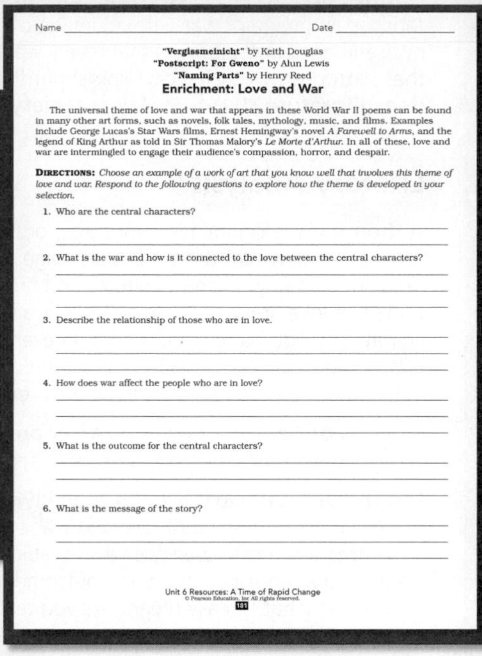
Name ______________________ Date ____________

"Vergissmeinicht" by Keith Douglas
"Postscript: For Gweno" by Alun Lewis
"Naming Parts" by Henry Reed

Enrichment: Love and War

The universal theme of love and war that appears in these World War II poems can be found in many other art forms, such as novels, folk tales, mythology, music, and films. Examples include George Lucas's Star Wars films, Ernest Hemingway's novel *A Farewell to Arms*, and the legend of King Arthur as told in Sir Thomas Malory's *Le Morte d'Arthur*. In all of these, love and war are intermingled to engage their audience's compassion, horror, and despair.

DIRECTIONS: *Choose an example of a work of art that you know well that involves this theme of love and war. Respond to the following questions to explore how the theme is developed in your selection.*

1. Who are the central characters?
2. What is the war and how is it connected to the love between the central characters?
3. Describe the relationship of those who are in love.
4. How does war affect the people who are in love?
5. What is the outcome for the central characters?
6. What is the message of the story?

Unit 6 Resources: A Time of Rapid Change
© Pearson Education, Inc All rights reserved.
181

L4 **Enrichment,** p. 181

Also available for these selections:

- All **Literary Analysis: Universal Theme,** p. 177
- All **Reading: Analyze Author's Purpose,** p. 178
- EL L3 L4 **Support for Writing,** p. 180

Assessment

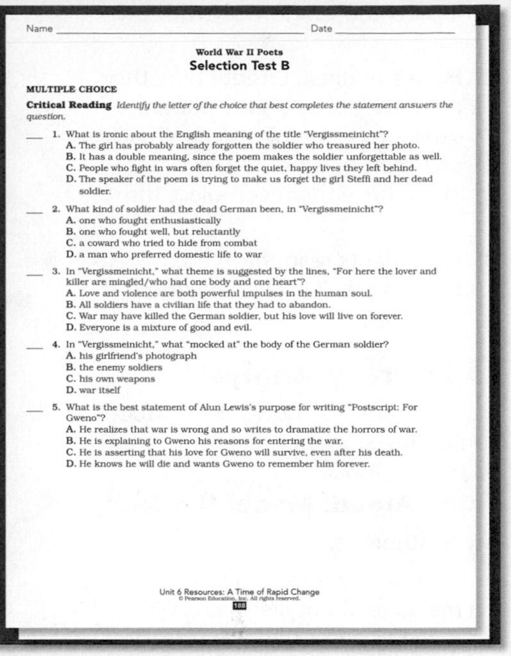
Name ______________________ Date ____________

World War II Poets
Selection Test B

MULTIPLE CHOICE

Critical Reading *Identify the letter of the choice that best completes the statement answers the question.*

___ 1. What is ironic about the English meaning of the title "Vergissmeinicht"?
A. The girl has probably already forgotten the soldier who treasured her photo.
B. It has a double meaning, since the poem makes the soldier unforgettable as well.
C. People who fight in wars often forget the quiet, happy lives they left behind.
D. The speaker of the poem is trying to make us forget the girl Steffi and her dead soldier.

___ 2. What kind of soldier had the dead German been, in "Vergissmeinicht"?
A. one who fought enthusiastically
B. one who fought well, but reluctantly
C. a coward who tried to hide from combat
D. a man who preferred domestic life to war

___ 3. In "Vergissmeinicht," what theme is suggested by the lines, "For here the lover and killer are mingled/who had one body and one heart"?
A. Love and violence are both powerful impulses in the human soul.
B. All soldiers have a civilian life that they had to abandon.
C. War may have killed the German soldier, but his love will live on forever.
D. Everyone is a mixture of good and evil.

___ 4. In "Vergissmeinicht," what "mocked at" the body of the German soldier?
A. his girlfriend's photograph
B. the enemy soldiers
C. his own weapons
D. war itself

___ 5. What is the best statement of Alun Lewis's purpose for writing "Postscript: For Gweno"?
A. He realizes that war is wrong and so writes to dramatize the horrors of war.
B. He is explaining to Gweno his reasons for entering the war.
C. He is asserting that his love for Gweno will survive, even after his death.
D. He knows he will die and wants Gweno to remember him forever.

Unit 6 Resources: A Time of Rapid Change
© Pearson Education, Inc. All rights reserved.
188

EL L3 L4 **Selection Test B,** pp. 188–190

Also available for these selections:

- L3 L4 **Open-Book Test,** pp. 182–184
- EL L1 L2 **Selection Test A,** pp. 185–187

PHLit Online!
www.PHLitOnline.com

- complete narrated selection text
- a thematically related video with writing prompt
- an interactive graphic organizer
- highlighting feature
- access to all student print resources, adapted to individual student needs
- Spanish and English summaries
- adapted selection translations in Spanish

Online Resources: All print materials are also available online.

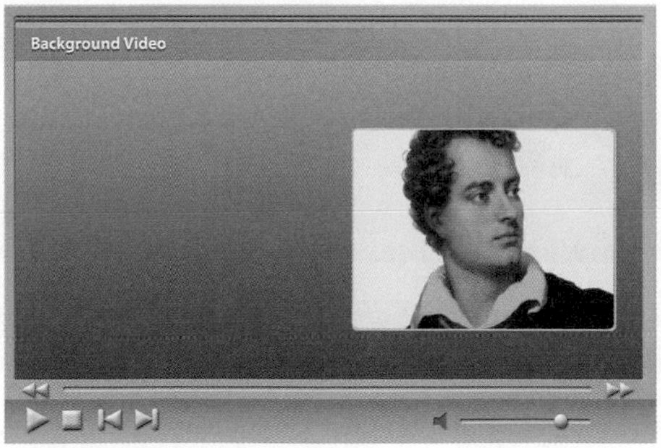

Background Video

Also available:

Get Connected! (thematic video with writing prompt)
All videos are available in Spanish.

Vocabulary Central (tools and activities for studying vocabulary)

Also available:

Writer's Journal (with graphics feature)

PRETEACH

1 Connecting to the Essential Question

1. Review the assignment with the class.
2. Have students consider how their own reactions toward war are similar to those of others. What common ground do they find? Then, have them complete the assignment.
3. As students read, have them identify images that reveal wartime attitudes.

2 Literary Analysis

Introduce the skill using the instruction on the student page.

Think Aloud: Model the Skill

Say to students:

I know that a universal theme is a message about life that can be applied to almost any culture, time, or place. One theme in the upcoming poems is that of the enduring quality of love amidst the losses of war.

I know that when something is ironic, it has an outcome that is different from expectations. I will look for uses of irony in the upcoming poems.

3 Reading Strategy

1. Introduce the skill using the instruction on the student page.
2. Give students a copy of **Reading Strategy Graphic Organizer B,** page 237 ***Graphic Organizer Transparencies,*** to fill out as they read.

Think Aloud: Model the Skill

Say to students:

When I consider the author's purpose, I think to myself, "What is the author trying to do?" What strategies are used to convey this purpose? I will keep an eye out in the following poems to see how the author conveys his purpose.

4 Vocabulary

1. Pronounce each word, giving its definition, and have students say it aloud.
2. For more guidance, see the ***Classroom Strategies and Teaching Routines*** card for introducing vocabulary.

Before You Read | *World War II Poets*

1 Connecting to the Essential Question Each of these poets juxtaposes an image of war with an image of another kind. As you read, notice images in the poems that reveal wartime attitudes. Recognizing these attitudes will help you think about the Essential Question: **How does literature shape or reflect society?**

Common Core State Standards

Reading Literature
6. Analyze a case in which grasping point of view requires distinguishing what is directly stated in a text from what is really meant.

2 Literary Analysis

A **theme** is the central idea, message, or insight that a literary work reveals. A **universal theme** is a message about life that is expressed regularly in many different cultures and time periods. For example, the power of love amid the horror of war is a universal theme because every culture and age has experienced it. In every war, the fierce fighter who kills and dies on a battlefield is also someone's beloved, someone's parent, someone's friend. As Keith Douglas expresses it,

> *For here the lover and killer are mingled*
> *who had one body and one heart.*

Comparing Literary Works In the twentieth century, authors who use the universal theme of love and war often express the theme with irony. **Irony** is a discrepancy or a contradiction between appearance and reality, between expectation and outcome, or between what is directly stated and what is really meant. As you read, identify examples of irony and consider what they suggest about the author's point of view.

3 Reading Strategy

Preparing to Read Complex Texts Each poet has a purpose in juxtaposing contrasting images of love and war. By **understanding the author's purpose,** you will gain an insight into love, war, or life in general. For example, the poet may want to celebrate the power of an undying love or lament the power of a death-dealing war. Use a graphic organizer like this one to help clarify each author's purpose.

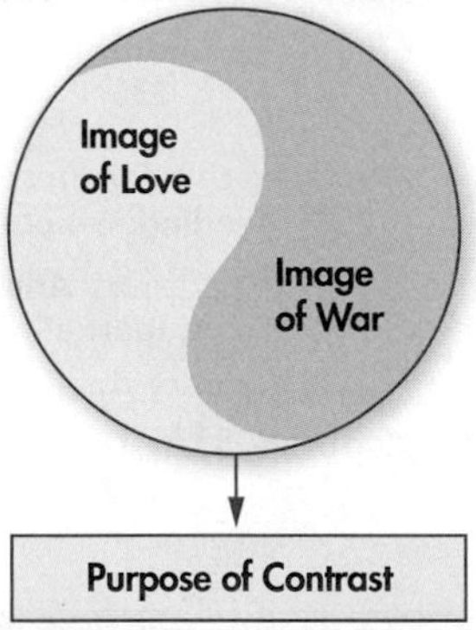

4 Vocabulary

combatants (kəm bat´ 'nts) *n.* fighters (p. 1310)

sprawling (sprôl´ iŋ) *v.* spread out (p. 1310)

abide (ə bīd´) *v.* stay, remain (p. 1312)

eloquent (el´ ə kwənt) *adj.* beautifully expressive (p. 1313)

www.PHLitOnline.com

Vocabulary Development

Vocabulary Knowledge Rating
Create a **Vocabulary Knowledge Rating Chart** (***Professional Development Guidebook,*** p. 33) for the vocabulary words on the student page. Give each student a copy of the chart with the words on it. Read the words aloud, and have students mark their ratings in the Before Reading column. Urge students to attend to these words as they read and discuss the selections.

In order to gauge how much instruction you need to provide, tally how many students are confident in their knowledge of each word. As students read, point out the words and their context.

Vocabulary Central, featuring tools and activities for studying vocabulary, is available online at **www.PHLitOnline.com.**

5 KEITH DOUGLAS (1920–1944)

Author of "Vergissmeinnicht"

Keith Douglas grew up wanting to be a soldier and needing to be a writer. As a boy at boarding school, he wrote poems and trained to become a military officer. When World War II erupted in 1939, Douglas immediately enlisted.

In 1942, when the tank battle of El Alamein began to rage in the desert, Douglas left his post, stole a truck, and drove out to join the fighting. The long battle left thousands of Allied and German troops killed and wounded. "Vergissmeinnicht" ("Forget me not") is Douglas's poetic response to his unforgettable discovery of one German corpse.

On D-Day, June 6, 1944, he commanded a tank troop in the main assault in Normandy. Near the little French village of St. Pierre, on June 9, a mortar shell killed him instantly.

ALUN LEWIS (1915–1944)

Author of "Postscript: For Gweno"

Born and raised in Wales, Alun Lewis began writing poems in college. He planned to become a teacher, but World War II intervened. Faced with the likelihood of being drafted, Lewis enlisted in 1940 but continued to write, and his collection *Raider's Dawn* appeared in 1942. He also wrote many emotional letters to his wife, Gweno, letters that helped him deal with frequent bouts of depression.

Posted to India in 1942, Lewis became deeply affected by Buddhist principles that coincided with his already strong impulses toward pacifism and social justice. Resistant to military life and reluctant to kill, he found in Buddhism "humility without submission . . . a service of perfect freedom." Lewis died in Burma in 1944.

HENRY REED (1914–1986)

Author of "Naming of Parts"

One poem—"Naming of Parts"—made Henry Reed famous. Readers immediately recognized its authentic voice and responded to its powerful opposition—life and love versus the mechanics of war and death. The poem became the best known verse inspired by the war, and for decades Reed struggled to become known for his other writing.

During the war, Reed served as a translator and as a cryptographer in Naval Intelligence. He survived World War II and forged a successful career writing radio plays and book reviews. In 1970, he published *Lessons of the War;* however, Reed never again wrote anything with the iron bite of "Naming of Parts."

Daily Bellringer

For each class during which you will teach these selections, have students complete one of the five activities for the appropriate week in the ***Daily Bellringer Activities*** booklet.

Multidraft Reading

To assist struggling readers and to enhance reading for all, assign the text in chunks, as warranted by length, and apply multidraft reading protocols. For each reading, have students set the purpose indicated:

- **First reading**—identifying key ideas and details and answering any Reading Checks.
- **Second reading**—analyzing craft and structure and responding to the side-column prompts.
- **Third reading**—integrating knowledge and ideas, connecting to other texts and the world, and answering the end-of-selection questions.

For more guidance, refer to the ***Classroom Strategies and Teaching Routines*** card on Multidraft Reading.

5 Background

More About the Authors

Keith Douglas

Keith Douglas's *Selected Poems* was published posthumously in 1951. Years later, a number of people, including Ted Hughes, edited other editions of Douglas's works.

Alun Lewis

Alun Lewis's first published collection, *Raider's Dawn and Other Poems,* established him as a great wartime poet.

Henry Reed

Henry Reed was a poet, radio dramatist, book reviewer, and translator. His poem "Naming of Parts" comes from "Lessons of War."

PHLit Online! Teaching From Technology

www.PHLitOnline.com

Preparing to Read

Go to **www.PHLitOnline.com** and display the ***Get Connected!*** slide show for these selections. Have the class brainstorm responses to the writing prompt, entering ideas in the interactive journal. Then, have students complete their written responses as homework.

To build background, display the Background and More About the Author features.

Using the Interactive Text

Go to **www.PHLitOnline.com** and display the **Enriched Online Student Edition.** As the class reads the selection or listens to the narration, record answers to side-column prompts using the graphic organizers accessible on the interactive page. Alternatively, have students use the online edition individually, answering the prompts as they read.

PHLit Online!

For more about the authors, for practice with the selection vocabulary, and for more background, go to **www.PHLitOnline.com**.

TEACH

❶ About the Selection

In this poem, Douglas recounts the moment he came upon a German corpse during the war.

❷ Activating Prior Knowledge

Show students a picture of a clean countryside next to a picture with heavy pollution. Ask students what reaction they have from seeing the two together. Tell students some of the poets they will be reading use this technique of juxtaposition.

Concept Connector →

Tell students they will return to their responses after reading the selection.

❸ Literary Analysis

Universal Theme

1. Have students reread lines 10–12.
2. **Ask:** What universal theme does the picture of the girl signal?
   Answer: The picture of the girl signals the theme that we all have loved ones who are dear to us.

❹ Reading Strategy

Analyze Author's Purpose

1. Have students reread lines 5–8.
2. **Ask:** What is the author's purpose in commenting on the soldier's equipment?
   Answer: If the German was not killed, he probably would have killed them.

❶ ❷ Vergissmeinnicht[1]

KEITH DOUGLAS

BACKGROUND World War I—the brutal experience that purged all the "romance" from the idea of war—provided the central subject for poets like Wilfred Owen. World War II poets Keith Douglas, Alun Lewis, and Henry Reed left moving verses that testify to the continuing influence of violent conflict on the literary imagination.

Vocabulary

combatants (kəm bat′ ′nts) *n.* fighters

sprawling (sprôl′ iŋ) *v.* spread out

Three weeks gone and the **combatants** gone,
returning over the nightmare ground
we found the place again, and found
the soldier **sprawling** in the sun.

❹ The frowning barrel of his gun
overshadowing. As we came on
that day, he hit my tank with one
like the entry of a demon.

1. German for "forget me not."

Text Complexity Rubric

	Vergissmeinnicht	Postscript: For Gweno	Naming of Parts
Qualitative Measures			
Context/Knowledge Demands	Modern war poem 1 2 (3) 4 5	Modern war poem 1 (2) 3 4 5	Modern war poem 1 (2) 3 4 5
Structure/Language Conventionality and Clarity	Accessible diction 1 (2) 3 4 5	Accessible diction 1 (2) 3 4 5	Jargon; poetic diction 1 2 (3) 4 5
Levels of Meaning/ Purpose/Concepts	Moderate (warfare, love, sympathy) 1 2 (3) 4 5	Accessible (love in wartime) 1 2 (3) 4 5	Moderate (war and nature) 1 2 (3) 4 5
Quantitative Measures			
Lexile/Text Length	NP / 154 words	NP / 62 words	NP / 276 words
Overall Complexity	**More complex**	**More accessible**	**More complex**

3 Look. Here in the gunpit spoil
the dishonored picture of his girl
who has put: *Steffi. Vergissmeinnicht*
in a copybook gothic script.

We see him almost with content
abased, and seeming to have paid
and mocked at by his own equipment
that's hard and good when he's decayed.

But she would weep to see today
how on his skin the swart flies move;
the dust upon the paper eye
and the burst stomach like a cave.

5 For here the lover and killer are mingled
who had one body and one heart.
And death who had the soldier singled
has done the lover mortal hurt.

Literary Analysis
Universal Theme
What universal theme does the picture of the girl signal?

Reading Strategy
Analyze Author's Purpose
What is the author's purpose in commenting on the soldier's equipment?

Literary Analysis
Universal Theme
Why is the theme expressed in the final two lines a *universal* theme?

Critical Reading

1. **Key Ideas and Details (a)** What personal object does the speaker find on the body of the German soldier? **(b) Analyze:** What insight does the object lead the speaker to realize?
2. **Integration of Knowledge and Ideas (a)** Despite his unemotional tone throughout the poem, what speculation does the speaker make about the girl's response? **(b) Infer:** What does his speculation reveal about human sympathy? **(c) Generalize:** What does his speculation say about the universal theme of love and war?

Cite textual evidence to support your responses.

5 Literary Analysis

Universal Theme

1. Have students reread lines 21–24.
2. **Ask:** Why is the theme expressed in the final two lines a *universal* theme?
   Answer: The theme is universal because when you kill someone during any war, you are killing the person who is also a lover, parent, or child of someone.

ASSESS

Answers

Before students respond, you may wish to have them write a brief objective summary of the selection. As they answer the questions below, remind them to support their answers with evidence from the text.

1. (a) a photograph; (b) The photo leads the speaker to realize that the German soldier was just as human as he is, and that he had loved ones who cared about him.
2. (a) He speculates that she would shed tears to know about her love's death. (b) It reveals that a person can feel sympathy toward someone who is different, even an enemy. (c) His speculation shows that regardless of what side of the war a person is fighting on, there is something that transcends allegiance, and that is a fragile human condition and our capacity to love and empathize.

Text Complexity: Reader and Task Suggestions

	Vergissmeinnicht	Postscript: For Gweno	Naming of Parts
Preparing to Read the Texts • Use the Background on SE p. 1310 to explain why World War II was particularly harrowing for the British. • Discuss the importance of loved ones back home to soldiers fighting a war. • Guide students to use Multidraft Reading strategies (TE p. 1309).	**Leveled Tasks** ***Context/Knowledge Demands*** If students will have difficulty with the poem's context, have them focus a British soldier encountering a dead enemy. Remind them that *Vergissmeinnicht* is German for "forget me not." ***Synthesizing*** If students will not have difficulty with the context, have them discuss what the juxtaposition of "lover" and "killer" images suggests about war.	**Leveled Tasks** ***Levels of Meaning*** If students will have difficulty with figurative language, have them first read to determine the speaker's feelings for Gweno. Then, have students discover the emotions behind specific figures of speech. ***Evaluating*** If students will not have difficulty with the figurative language, have them evaluate its power in conveying the speaker's emotions.	**Leveled Tasks** ***Language/Clarity*** If students will have difficulty with poem's language, have them use context clues to determine the speaker's situation in the first stanza. As they reread, have them focus on the contrasting tone in the descriptions of the classroom and the world outside. ***Synthesizing*** If students will not have difficulty with the language, have them contrast the events in the classroom with the world outside.

6 About the Selection

This love poem is addressed to Alun Lewis's wife, Gweno. In this poem, Lewis states that Gweno is always in his thoughts. He states, "You always stay." Although Death, the wild beast, is "uncaught, untamed," Lewis states that their love "withstands the terror."

7 Reading Strategy

Analyze Author's Purpose

1. Have students reread lines 4–5.
2. **Ask:** Why does the poet tell his wife that she will "always stay"?
   Answer: He says this because, although they are apart, he wants her to know she is always in his thoughts.

8 Literary Analysis

Universal Theme

1. Have students reread lines 6–8.
2. **Ask:** What universal theme is signaled by the image of "Death the wild beast"?
   Answer: The theme is that of Death as ravager and indiscriminate destroyer of physical life.

ASSESS

Answers

Before students respond, you may wish to have them write a brief objective summary of the selection. As they answer the questions below, remind them to support their answers with evidence from the text.

1. (a) He expects to be going to war. (b) The love of his wife, Gweno, gives him the courage to make the journey.
2. (a) It could have been written during any war. (b) There are no specific details that show that this is from World War II. The themes in this poem are universal and therefore can apply to almost any war.

6 POSTSCRIPT: FOR GWENO

Alun Lewis

Reading Strategy
Analyze Author's Purpose
Why does the poet tell his wife that she will "always stay"?

Vocabulary
abide (ə bīd′) *v.* stay, remain

Literary Analysis
Universal Theme
What universal theme is signaled by the image of "Death the wild beast"?

If I should go away,
Beloved, do not say
"He has forgotten me."
7 For you **abide**, A singing rib within my dreaming side;
You always stay.
8 And in the mad tormented valley
Where blood and hunger rally
And Death the wild beast is uncaught, untamed,
Our soul withstands the terror
And has its quiet honor
Among the glittering stars your voices named.

Critical Reading

Cite textual evidence to support your responses.

1. **Key Ideas and Details (a)** Where does the speaker expect to be going? **(b) Interpret:** What gives the speaker the courage to make the journey?
2. **Integration of Knowledge and Ideas (a) Take a Position:** Is this poem specific to World War II, or could it have been written during any war? **(b) Defend:** Support your position with two strong reasons.

9 NAMING *of* PARTS

HENRY REED

Today we have naming of parts. Yesterday,
We had daily cleaning. And tomorrow morning,
We shall have what to do after firing. But today,
Today we have naming of parts. Japonica
Glistens like coral in all of the neighboring gardens,
And today we have naming of parts.

This is the lower sling swivel. And this
Is the upper sling swivel, whose use you will see,
When you are given your slings. And this is the piling swivel,
Which in your case you have not got. The branches
Hold in the gardens their silent, eloquent gestures,
Which in our case we have not got.

Vocabulary
eloquent (el′ ə kwent) *adj.* beautifully expressive

10 **Reading Check**
What does the author say "we" will do "tomorrow"?

9 About the Selection

This poem describes a recruit in basic training who is learning to name the parts of a weapon. Reed juxtaposes the naming of parts of the weapon with images of nature.

10 Reading Check

Answer: Tomorrow morning they will have a training session called "what to do after firing."

11 Reading Strategy

Analyze Author's Purpose

1. Have students read the entire poem. Then, have them reread lines 25–30.
2. **Ask:** How does the author use contrast to emphasize his purpose?
   Answer: He contrasts the naming of parts with descriptions of nature to show how unnatural these preparations for war are.

12 Literary Analysis

Universal Theme and Irony

1. Direct students to the entire poem.
2. **Ask:** What is ironic about the juxtapositions of the images throughout the poem?
   Answer: The irony is that we do not expect, amidst the talk and training of war, descriptions of the beauty of nature.

ASSESS

Answers

Before students respond, you may wish to have them write a brief objective summary of the selection. As they answer the questions below, remind them to support their answers with evidence from the text.

1. (a) The preparation of soldiers for war and the daily habits of nature are shown side by side. (b) Although these events are happening simultaneously and are even described with some of the same language, they are very different and contradictory.
2. (a) He prefers the daily habits of nature. (b) I can tell by the diction he uses and his ironic juxtaposition of the two actions.
3. He is commenting that preparing people for war is unnatural.
4. **Possible response:** Our *relationships*, our vital social bonds, those of our family and of our own humanity, are violated by war. For example, in the last poem, there is a *disconnect* between the act of naming the parts of a gun with the natural world around the soldiers.

Reading Strategy
Analyze Author's Purpose How does the author use contrast to emphasize his purpose?

This is the safety-catch, which is always released
With an easy flick of the thumb. And please do not let me
See anyone using his finger. You can do it quite easy
If you have any strength in your thumb. The blossoms
Are fragile and motionless, never letting anyone see
    Any of them using their finger.

And this you can see is the bolt. The purpose of this
Is to open the breech, as you see. We can slide it
Rapidly backwards and forwards: we call this
Easing the spring. And rapidly backwards and forwards
The early bees are assaulting and fumbling the flowers:
    They call it easing the Spring.

12 **Literary Analysis**
Universal Theme and Irony What is ironic about the juxtaposition of the images throughout the poem?

11
They call it easing the Spring: it is perfectly easy
If you have any strength in your thumb: like the bolt,
And the breech, and the cocking-piece, and the point of balance,
Which in our case we have not got; and the almond-blossom
Silent in all of the gardens and the bees going backwards and
  forwards,
    For today we have naming of parts.

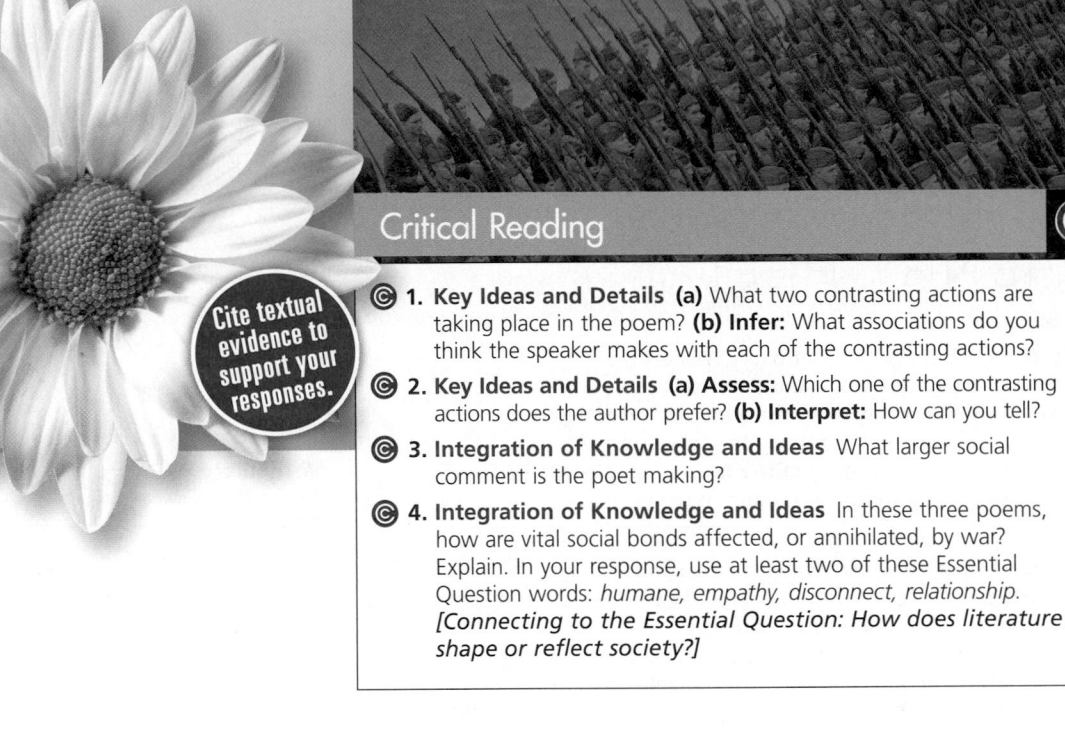

Cite textual evidence to support your responses.

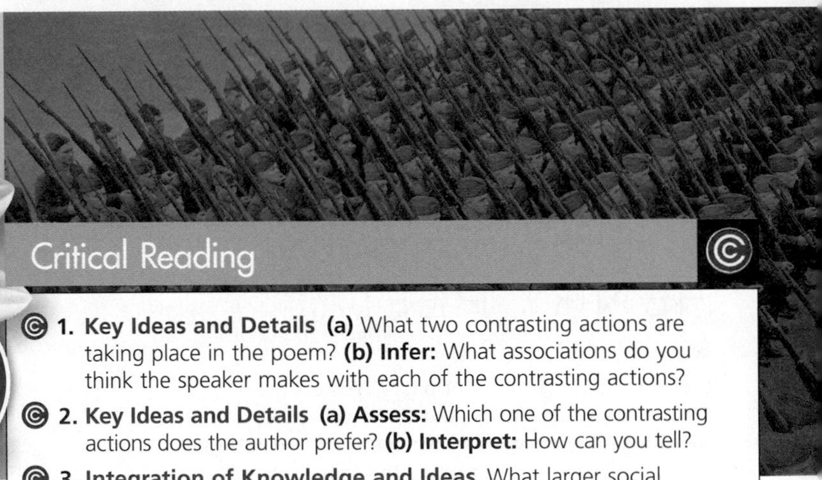

Critical Reading

1. **Key Ideas and Details (a)** What two contrasting actions are taking place in the poem? **(b) Infer:** What associations do you think the speaker makes with each of the contrasting actions?
2. **Key Ideas and Details (a) Assess:** Which one of the contrasting actions does the author prefer? **(b) Interpret:** How can you tell?
3. **Integration of Knowledge and Ideas** What larger social comment is the poet making?
4. **Integration of Knowledge and Ideas** In these three poems, how are vital social bonds affected, or annihilated, by war? Explain. In your response, use at least two of these Essential Question words: *humane, empathy, disconnect, relationship.* ***[Connecting to the Essential Question: How does literature shape or reflect society?]***

Assessment Practice

Assessment Practice (For more practice, see *All-in-One Workbook.*)

Diction and other aspects of a poem can set the tone of the work. Use the following to teach students to recognize the tone of a passage.

But she would weep to see today
how on his skin the swart flies move;
the dust upon the paper eye
and the burst stomach live a cave.
For here the lover and killer are mingled
who had one body and one heart.
And death who had the soldier singled
has done the lover mortal hurt.

Which of these *best* describes the tone of this excerpt from "Vergissmeinnicht"?

A humorous
B serious
C controversial
D satirical

Have students look for words that suggest tone. Guide students to words such as *weep, burst stomach,* and *death* that show that the tone is **B**, serious.

After You Read | *World War II Poets*

Literary Analysis

1. Craft and Structures Using a chart like the one shown, identify a word, phrase, or image from each poem that conveys its **universal theme.** Then state the universal theme it conveys.

Poem	Word, Phrase, or Image	Universal Theme
"Vergissmeinnicht"		
"Postscript: For Gweno"		
"Naming of Parts"		

2. Craft and Structure Compare and contrast the poets' use of **irony** in "Vergissmeinnicht" and "Naming of Parts."

Reading Strategy

3. In "Vergissmeinnicht," what is the **author's purpose** in calling the German girl's photograph "dishonored" (line 10)?

4. In "Naming of Parts," the author gives two different meanings of "easing the spring"—one military (line 22), one drawn from nature (line 24). What is his purpose in doing so?

Common Core State Standards

Writing
2. Write informative/explanatory texts to examine and convey complex ideas, concepts, and information clearly and accurately through the effective selection, organization, and analysis of content.

PERFORMANCE TASKS
Integrated Language Skills

Vocabulary Acquisition and Use

An analogy compares two relationships to show their basic similarity. For each item below, analyze the relationship between the first and second words. Then, select the word that best completes each analogy.

1. combatants : soldiers :: poets :
   a. writers **b.** boxers **c.** flyers **d.** drivers
2. sprawling : condensed :: gigantic :
   a. scary **b.** warlike **c.** normal **d.** tiny
3. abide : continue :: assist :
   a. destroy **b.** ignore **c.** help **d.** accompany
4. eloquent : awkward :: faithful :
   a. loyal **b.** charming **c.** foolish **d.** traitorous

Writing

Informative Text Imagine that you work for a foundation that gives a prize for Best War Poem. Write a **memo** stating the criteria for winning the prize. One of your criteria, for example, might be that the poem must convey a universal theme or that it must use irony effectively. Use a memo format.

Answers

1. For "Vergissmeinnicht": *Vergissmeinnicht;* this word means "forget-me-not" in German. Regardless of one's language or background, a person wants to be remembered by loved ones. For "Postscript: For Gweno": *you always stay;* this sentiment that loved ones are always with you in your thoughts is universal. For "Naming of Parts": *easing the Spring;* this phrase suggests that the natural order continues amidst all that is unnatural.
2. In "Naming of Parts," stanza 4 is ironic because it speaks of the spring of a gun and the season of spring, using the same terms.
3. The author's purpose in calling the photograph "dishonored" is to acknowledge the woman who had loved the killed soldier; this woman has feelings, too.
4. His purpose is to show that although the language is the same, they have opposing purposes: one brings life (bees and flowers), the other, death.

Vocabulary Acquisition and Use

1. a
2. d
3. c
4. d

Writing

Evaluate students' informative texts using the **Rubrics for Business Letter**, ***Professional Development Guidebook,*** pages 291–292.

Assessment Resources

Unit 6 Resources

L1 L2 EL **Selection Test A**, pp. 185–187. Administer Test A to less advanced readers.

L3 L4 EL **Selection Test B**, pp. 188–190. Administer Test B to on-level students and more advanced students.

L3 L4 **Open-Book Test**, pp. 182–184. As an alternative, give the Open-Book test.

All **Customizable Test Bank**

All **Self-tests**
Students may prepare for the **Selection Test** by taking the **Self-test** online.

PHLit Online! All assessment resources are available at **www.PHLitOnline.com**.

Shooting an Elephant • No Witchcraft for Sale

Lesson Pacing Guide

DAY 1 Preteach

- Administer the Reading and Vocabulary Warm-ups (*Unit 6 Resources*, pp. 191–194) as necessary.
- Introduce the Literary Analysis concept: Cultural Conflict and Irony.
- Introduce the Reading Strategy: Analyze and Evaluate Similar Themes.
- Build background with the author and Background features.
- Develop thematic thinking with Connecting to the Essential Question.
- Teach the selection vocabulary.

DAYS 2–3 Preteach/Teach/Assess

- Distribute copies of the appropriate graphic organizer for the Reading Skill (*Graphic Organizer Transparencies*, pp. 240–241).
- Distribute copies of the appropriate graphic organizer for Literary Analysis (*Graphic Organizer Transparencies*, pp. 242–243).
- Prepare students to read with the Activating Prior Knowledge activities (TE).
- Informally monitor comprehension while students read.
- Use the Reading Check questions to confirm comprehension.
- Develop students' understanding of cultural conflict and irony using the Literary Analysis prompts.
- Develop students' ability to analyze and evaluate similar themes using the Reading Strategy prompts.
- Reinforce vocabulary with the Vocabulary notes.
- Assess students' comprehension and mastery of the skills by having them answer the Critical Reading, Literary Analysis, and Reading Strategy questions.
- Have students complete the Vocabulary Lesson.

DAY 4 Extend/Assess

- Have students complete the Conventions and Style Lesson.
- Have students complete the Writing Lesson and write a problem-and-solution essay. (You may assign as homework.)
- Administer Selection Test A or B (*Unit 6 Resources,* pp. 204–206 or 207–209).

Common Core State Standards

Reading Informational Text
3. Analyze a complex set of ideas or sequence of events and explain how specific individuals, ideas, or events interact and develop over the course of a text.

Writing 2. Write informative/explanatory texts to examine and convey complex ideas, concepts, and information clearly and accurately through the effective selection, organization, and analysis of content.
2.d. Use precise language, domain-specific vocabulary, and techniques such as metaphor, simile, and analogy to manage the complexity of the topic.

Language 4.a. Use context as a clue to the meaning of a word or phrase.

Additional Standards Practice
***Common Core Companion**, pp. 15–22; 196–207; 324–331*

Daily Block Scheduling
Each day in this Lesson Pacing Guide represents a 40–50 minute period. Teachers using block scheduling may combine days to revise pacing. In addition, teachers may differentiate and support core instruction by integrating components for extended and intensive support as students require. See the Guide to Selected Leveled Resources (facing page).

Guide to Selected Leveled Resources

RTI Tier 1 (students performing on level)

			Shooting an Elephant • No Witchcraft for Sale
Warm Up	Whole class instruction; Group work	**Practice, model,** and **monitor** fluency, working **with the whole class** or **in groups.**	**Vocabulary and Reading Warm-ups B,** ***Unit 6 Resources,*** pp. 209–210, 212
Comprehension/Skills	Whole class instruction; Group work; Independent work	**Support** and **monitor** comprehension and skills development, having students complete the activities, graphic organizers, and interactive prompts **independently** or **as a class.**	• ***Reader's Notebook,*** adapted instruction and full selection EL ***Reader's Notebook: English Learner's Version,*** adapted instruction and adapted selection • **Reading Strategy Graphic Organizer B,** ***Graphic Organizer Transparencies,*** p. 255 • **Literary Analysis Graphic Organizer B,** ***Graphic Organizer Transparencies,*** p. 257
Monitor Progress	Assessment	**Monitor** student progress with the differentiated curriculum-based assessment in the *Unit Resources.*	• **Selection Test B,** ***Unit 6 Resources,*** pp. 225–227 • **Open-Book Test,** ***Unit 6 Resources,*** pp. 219–221

RTI Tier 2 (students requiring intervention)

			Shooting an Elephant • No Witchcraft for Sale
Warm Up	Group work; One-on-one teaching	**Practice, model,** and **monitor** fluency **in groups** or **with individuals.**	• **Vocabulary and Reading Warm-ups A,** ***Unit 6 Resources,*** pp. 209–211 • ***Hear It!*** **Audio CD (adapted text)**
Comprehension/Skills	Group work; One-on-one teaching	• **Support** and **monitor** comprehension and skills development, working **in small groups** or **with individuals.** • As students complete the selection in the appropriate version of the *Reader's Notebook,* **monitor** comprehension frequently with group questions and individual instruction. • **Model** strategies while guiding students in completing the activities and prompts in the *Reader's Notebook,* as well as the graphic organizers. • **Practice** skills and **monitor** mastery with the *Reading Kit* worksheets.	• ***Reader's Notebook: Adapted Version,*** adapted instruction and adapted selection EL ***Reader's Notebook: English Learner's Version,*** adapted instruction and adapted selection • **Reading Strategy Graphic Organizer A,** ***Graphic Organizer Transparencies,*** p. 254 • **Literary Analysis Graphic Organizer A,** ***Graphic Organizer Transparencies,*** p. 256 • ***Reading Kit,*** Practice worksheets
Monitor Progress	Assessment	**Monitor** student progress with the differentiated curriculum-based assessment in the *Unit Resources* and in the *Reading Kit.*	• **Selection Test A,** ***Unit 6 Resources,*** pp. 222–224 • ***Reading Kit,*** Assess worksheets

TIER 3 Tier 3 intervention may require consultation with the student's special-education or dyslexia specialist. For additional support, see the Tier 2 activities and resources listed above.

One-on-one teaching **Group work** **Whole class instruction** **Independent work** **A Assessment**

For a complete guide to selection support, including support for Advanced students, see the Overview of Resources in the frontmatter.

Shooting an Elephant • No Witchcraft for Sale

RESOURCES FOR:

- L1 Special-Needs Students
- L2 Below-Level Students (Tier 2)
- L3 On-Level Students (Tier 1)
- L4 Advanced Students (Tier 1)
- EL English Learners
- All All Students

Vocabulary/Fluency/Prior Knowledge

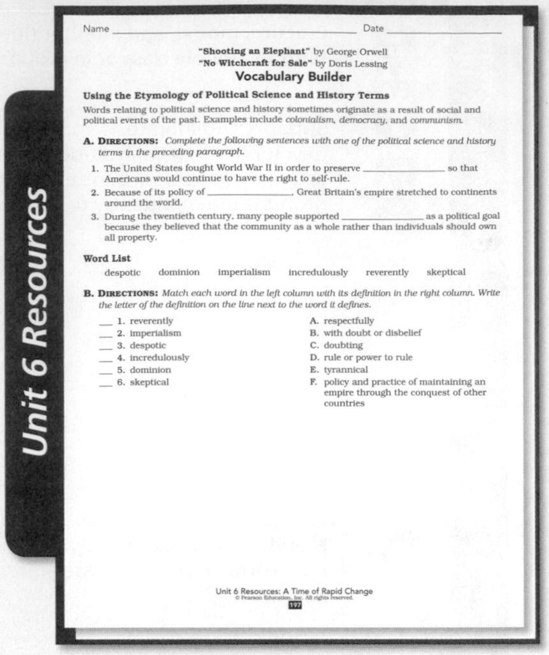
Unit 6 Resources

Name ______________________ Date ____________

"Shooting an Elephant" by George Orwell
"No Witchcraft for Sale" by Doris Lessing

Vocabulary Builder

Using the Etymology of Political Science and History Terms

Words relating to political science and history sometimes originate as a result of social and political events of the past. Examples include *colonialism, democracy,* and *communism.*

A. Directions: *Complete the following sentences with one of the political science and history terms in the preceding paragraph.*

1. The United States fought World War II in order to preserve ____________ so that Americans would continue to have the right to self-rule.
2. Because of its policy of ____________, Great Britain's empire stretched to continents around the world.
3. During the twentieth century, many people supported ____________ as a political goal because they believed that the community as a whole rather than individuals should own all property.

Word List

despotic dominion imperialism incredulously reverently skeptical

B. Directions: *Match each word in the left column with its definition in the right column. Write the letter of the definition on the line next to the word it defines.*

___ 1. reverently	A. respectfully
___ 2. imperialism	B. with doubt or disbelief
___ 3. despotic	C. doubting
___ 4. incredulously	D. rule or power to rule
___ 5. dominion	E. tyrannical
___ 6. skeptical	F. policy and practice of maintaining an empire through the conquest of other countries

Unit 6 Resources: A Time of Rapid Change
© Pearson Education, Inc. All rights reserved.
197

All **Vocabulary Builder,** p. 197

Also available for these selections:

EL L1 L2 **Vocabulary Warm-ups A and B,** pp. 191–192

EL L1 L2 **Reading Warm-ups A and B,** pp. 193–194

L2 L3 ***Reader's Notebook***

L1 ***Reader's Notebook: Adapted Version***

EL ***Reader's Notebook: English Learner's Version***

EL ***Reader's Notebook: Spanish Version***

Reader's Notebooks

Pre- and postreading pages for these selections, as well as "Shooting an Elephant" and "No Witchcraft for Sale," appear in an interactive format in the *Reader's Notebooks.* Each *Notebook* is differentiated for a different group of learners.
The selections in the Adapted and English Learner's versions are abridged.

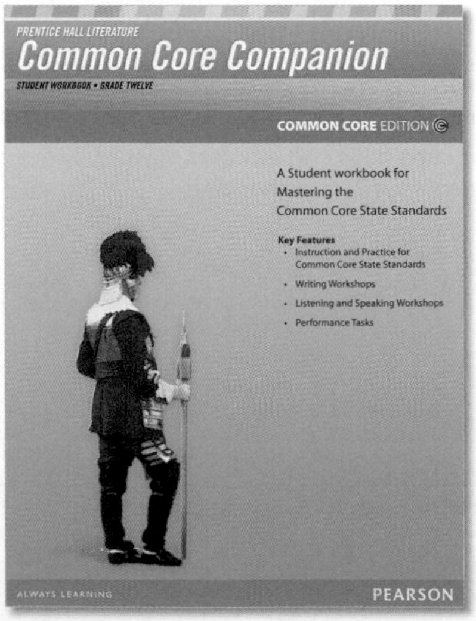

Common Core Companion

Additional instruction and practice for each Common Core State Standard

Selection Support

Graphic Organizer Transparencies

"Shooting an Elephant" by George Orwell
"No Witchcraft for Sale" by Doris Lessing

Before You Read B: Cultural Conflict

Aspect of Theme: Cultural Conflict	"Shooting an Elephant"	"No Witchcraft for Sale"
Source of Conflict		
Details of Conflict		
Result of Conflict		

Graphic Organizer Transparencies
© Pearson Education, Inc. All rights reserved.
241

EL L3 **Reading: Graphic Organizer B,** p. 241

Also available for these selections:

EL L1 L2 **Reading: Graphic Organizer A,** p. 240

EL L1 L2 **Literary Analysis: Graphic Organizer A,** (partially filled in), p. 242

EL L3 **Literary Analysis: Graphic Organizer B,** p. 243

Skills Development/Extension

Unit 6 Resources

Name ______________________ Date ____________

"Shooting an Elephant" by George Orwell
"No Witchcraft for Sale" by Doris Lessing

Reading Strategy: Analyze and Evaluate Similar Themes

A theme is the central idea or message of a piece of writing. Both the nonfiction work "Shooting an Elephant" and the short story "No Witchcraft for Sale" involve themes of cultural conflict. To understand these two pieces and how they relate, **analyze and evaluate the similar themes.**

Directions: *As you read "Shooting an Elephant" and "No Witchcraft for Sale," answer the following questions to analyze and evaluate the similar themes.*

1. What is the principal cultural conflict in "Shooting an Elephant"?
2. What is the principal cultural conflict in "No Witchcraft for Sale"?
3. How does the cultural conflict influence Orwell's actions in "Shooting an Elephant"?
4. How does the cultural conflict influence Gideon's actions in "No Witchcraft for Sale"?
5. How do the Farquars react to the cultural conflict with Gideon?
6. In your opinion, which character from the two selections responds most effectively to cultural conflict? Explain your answer.

Unit 6 Resources: A Time of Rapid Change
© Pearson Education, Inc. All rights reserved.
196

All **Reading: Analyze and Evaluate Similar Themes,** p. 196

Also available for these selections:

All **Literary Analysis: Cultural Conflict and Irony,** p. 195

EL L3 L4 **Grammar and Style,** p. 198

EL L3 L4 **Support for Writing,** p. 199

L4 **Enrichment,** p. 200

Assessment

Name ______________________ Date ____________

"Shooting an Elephant" by George Orwell; "No Witchcraft for Sale" by Doris Lessing

Open-Book Test

Short Answer *Write your responses to the questions in this section on the lines provided.*

1. Reread the opening section of Orwell's "Shooting an Elephant." How does Orwell seem to feel about his job as a police officer in Burma? Cite one or two details from the essay to support your response.
2. Explain the verbal irony in the following quotation from "Shooting an Elephant": "Feelings like these are the normal byproducts of imperialism: ask any Anglo-Indian official, if you can catch him off duty."
3. Before he sees the elephant in "Shooting an Elephant," Orwell prepares to shoot it only "to defend myself if necessary." However, Orwell shoots the elephant so that the Burmese people will not laugh at him. Explain why Orwell's decision to shoot the elephant in "Shooting an Elephant" is an example of irony of situation.
4. In "Shooting an Elephant," Orwell describes the behavior of the Burmese people throughout his account. Based on these descriptions, what seems to be Orwell's attitude toward the Burmese? Support your response with one or two examples from the text.
5. In "Shooting an Elephant," Orwell describes the behavior of the Burmese whom he polices. For example, after he shot the elephant, Orwell states that the Burmese raced to the animal's body and "had stripped his body almost to the bones by the afternoon." What can you conclude about the Burmese way of life under British rule, based on this description?

Unit 6 Resources: A Time of Rapid Change
© Pearson Education, Inc. All rights reserved.
201

L3 L4 **Open-Book Test,** pp. 201–203

Also available for these selections:

EL L1 L2 **Selection Test A,** pp. 204–206

EL L3 L4 **Selection Test B,** pp. 207–209

PHLit Online!
www.PHLitOnline.com

- complete narrated selection text
- a thematically related video with writing prompt
- an interactive graphic organizer
- highlighting feature
- access to all student print resources, adapted to individual student needs
- Spanish and English summaries
- adapted selection translations in Spanish

Online Resources: All print materials are also available online.

Get Connected! (thematic video with writing prompt)

Also available:

Background Video
All videos are available in Spanish.

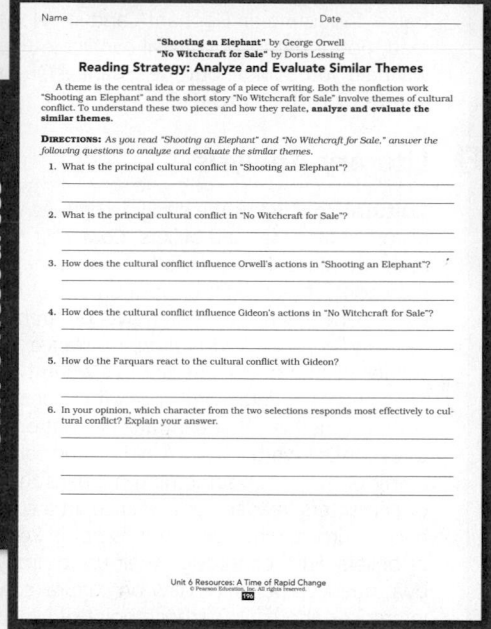

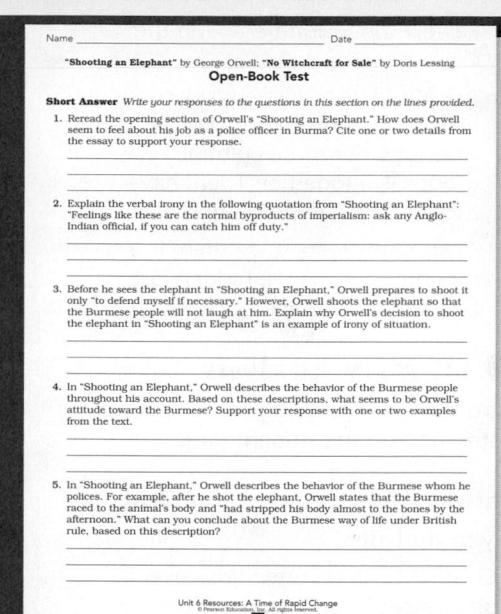

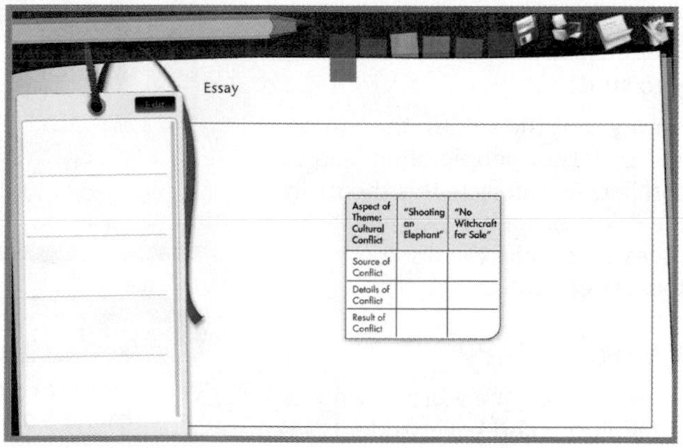

Writer's Journal (with graphics feature)

Also available:

Vocabulary Central (tools and activities for studying vocabulary)

PRETEACH

❶ Connecting to the Essential Question

1. Review the assignment with the class.
2. **Ask** students to name ways or reasons cultures might clash where two or more cultural groups live together. Then, have them complete the assignment.
3. As students read, have them look for emotions that lie hidden just beneath the surface.

❷ Literary Analysis

Introduce the skill using the instruction on the student page.

Think Aloud: Model the Skill

Say to students:

Cultural conflicts often arise over differences in beliefs and values, so as I read, I will look for differences in the attitudes of the colonizers and the people they rule. In looking for examples of irony, I will look for places where outward appearances differ sharply from what I would normally expect.

❸ Reading Strategy

1. Introduce the skill using the instruction on the student page.
2. Give students a copy of **Reading Strategy Graphic Organizer B,** page 241 in ***Graphic Organizer Transparencies,*** to fill out as they read.

Think Aloud: Model the Skill

Say to students:

I know that the values, thoughts, and beliefs of people often lead to conflict. As I analyze this theme in the selections, I can use self-stick notes to identify details about sources of conflict.

❹ Vocabulary

1. Pronounce each word, giving its definition, and have students say it aloud.
2. For more guidance, see the ***Classroom Strategies and Teaching Routines*** card for introducing vocabulary.

Before You Read

Shooting an Elephant • No Witchcraft for Sale

❶ **Connecting to the Essential Question** Cultural conflict is central in "Shooting an Elephant" and in "No Witchcraft for Sale." As you read, notice details of cultural conflict in these two selections. Doing so will help you think about the Essential Question: **How does literature shape or reflect society?**

Common Core State Standards

Reading Informational Text

3. Analyze a complex set of ideas or sequence of events and explain how specific individuals, ideas, or events interact and develop over the course of a text.

❷ Literary Analysis

Cultural conflict is the struggle between different social, economic, and historical attitudes and beliefs. *Conflict* is the word commonly applied to such situations. However, other words may be more useful and accurate than *conflict*—outright opposition and struggle—to describe what people experience in such a narrative: *difference, shock, ignorance, misunderstanding, misinterpretation, resistance.* As you read, be alert to subtle shades of thoughts and emotions when two cultural traditions meet.

Stories of cultural conflict often abound in **irony. Verbal irony** is saying something that contradicts what one means or believes. In a cultural conflict, verbal irony may be used for self-protection. **Situational irony** occurs when something happens that contradicts the expectations of characters, readers, or audience. In a cultural conflict, situations may become ironic when an action is not in keeping with a group's attitudes or beliefs. Further, through their use of irony, writers can convey their own nuanced points of view on cultural conflict. As you read, make inferences about the author's point of view by interpreting irony.

❸ Reading Strategy

Preparing to Read Complex Texts Both "Shooting an Elephant" and "No Witchcraft for Sale" involve themes of cultural conflict. As you read the selections, use a graphic organizer like the one shown to **analyze and evaluate the similar themes.**

"Shooting an Elephant"	"No Witchcraft for Sale"
Source of Conflict	Source of Conflict
Details of Conflict	Details of Conflict
Result of Conflict	Result of Conflict

❹ Vocabulary

imperialism (im pir´ ē əl iz em) *n.* creating and maintaining an empire; controlling other countries (p. 1320)

despotic (des pät´ ik) *adj.* with absolute power, like a tyrant (p. 1320)

dominion (də min´ yən) *n.* rule, authority (p. 1322)

reverently (re´ və rənt lē) *adv.* with great respect (p. 1329)

incredulously (in krej´ yoo ləs lē) *adv.* with doubt or disbelief (p. 1334)

skeptical (skep´ ti kəl) *adj.* doubting (p. 1334)

PHLit Online! www.PHLitOnline.com

Vocabulary Development

Vocabulary Knowledge Rating

Create a **Vocabulary Knowledge Rating Chart** (*Professional Development Guidebook,* p. 33) for the vocabulary words on the student page. Give each student a copy of the chart with the words on it. Read the words aloud, and have students mark their ratings in the Before Reading column. Urge students to attend to these words as they read and discuss the selections.

In order to gauge how much instruction you need to provide, tally how many students are confident in their knowledge of each word. As students read, point out the words and their context.

PHLit Online! **Vocabulary Central,** featuring tools and activities for studying vocabulary, is available online at **www.PHLitOnline.com.**

❺ # GEORGE ORWELL

1903-1950

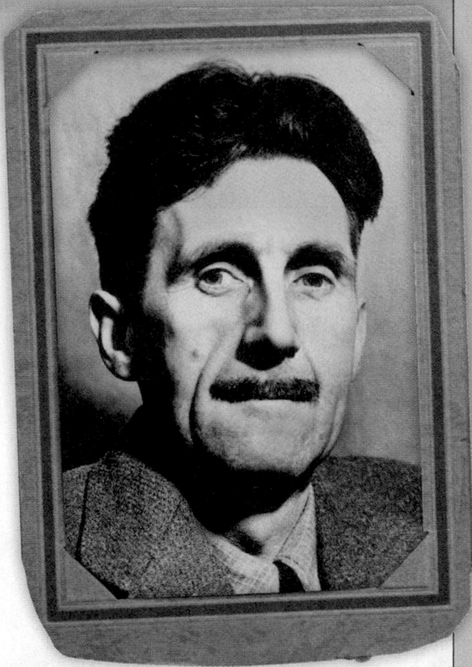

Author of **"Shooting an Elephant"**

Becoming an Officer Orwell was born Eric Blair in colonial India, was educated in England, and then joined the Imperial Police in Burma. Orwell was keenly aware of the inequities of imperialism. As an officer of the Burmese police, he headed a native-born police force of 13,000. Among the 90 officers, Englishmen held almost all the top ranks—a few white men governing 13 million Asians.

Disillusioned In 1928, after five years of service as an imperial police officer, the disillusioned Orwell resigned. His first novel, *Burmese Days* (1934), describes these bitter years. "Shooting an Elephant," one of his most famous essays, is based on a defining experience from this period.

Becoming George Orwell Orwell seemed to have a talent for immersing himself in difficult situations and then writing about them with extraordinary insight. Every book that emerged from an Orwell experience was a one-of-a-kind classic. In *Down and Out in Paris and London* (1933), for example, Orwell describes what it is like to be poor in two big cities. After his journeys on the seamier side of things, he published and lived under a new name: George Orwell.

Adventuring During the 1930s, Orwell gave himself to political causes. During the Spanish Civil War (1936–1939), he fought for democracy with anarchists and socialist Republicans. His book on that crisis, *Homage to Catalonia* (1938), is a gripping adventure story, one in which the narrator's cool presence of mind allows him to recall in precise detail his experience of being wounded.

A Political Prophet During World War II, Orwell wrote political and literary journalism. In 1945, he published *Animal Farm*, a satirical fable attacking both fascism and communism. In 1949, he shared a dark vision of the future in his novel *1984*, in which a dictator rules by controlling all thought and language. The year 1984 has passed, but George Orwell's lifelong commitment to political freedom and to the honest use of language is as relevant as ever.

Daily Bellringer

For each class during which you will teach these selections, have students complete one of the five activities for the appropriate week in the ***Daily Bellringer Activities*** booklet.

Multidraft Reading

To assist struggling readers and to enhance reading for all, assign the text in chunks, as warranted by length, and apply multidraft reading protocols. For each reading, have students set the purpose indicated:

- **First reading**—identifying key ideas and details and answering any Reading Checks.
- **Second reading**—analyzing craft and structure and responding to the side-column prompts.
- **Third reading**—integrating knowledge and ideas, connecting to other texts and the world, and answering the end-of-selection questions.

For more guidance, refer to the ***Classroom Strategies and Teaching Routines*** card on Multidraft Reading.

❺ Background

More About the Author

Orwell adopted his *nom de plume* from the beautiful River Orwell in East Anglia. In time, this name became so attached to him that few people other than close relatives ever knew him as Eric Arthur Blair.

Many phrases and words he used in his books have become catchphrases and buzzwords today. Orwell is responsible for such *bons mots* as "all animals are equal, but some animals are more equal than others," "Big Brother is watching you," "newspeak," and "doublethink."

PHLit Online!
www.PHLitOnline.com

Teaching From Technology

Preparing to Read
Go to **www.PHLitOnline.com** in class or in a lab and display the ***Get Connected!*** slide show for this grouping. Have the class brainstorm responses to the writing prompt, entering ideas in the interactive journal. Then, have students complete their written responses as homework.

To build background, display the Background and More About the Author feature.

Using the Interactive Text
Go to **www.PHLitOnline.com** and display the **Enriched Online Student Edition.** As the class reads the selection or listens to the narration, record answers to side-column prompts using the graphic organizers accessible on the interactive page. Alternatively, have students use the online edition individually, answering the prompts as they read.

❶ About the Selection

This essay reveals the ambivalence a person in a position of power may feel. On the one hand, young George Orwell (then Eric Blair) sympathizes with the Burmese people, who he feels are oppressed by the British colonists. On the other hand, Orwell, as a police officer, is committed to continuing and even defending that oppression. When an elephant goes wild in a Burmese marketplace, Orwell must act, making decisions more from his confused feelings than from common sense, and in the process revealing his intense human desire to avoid embarrassment.

❷ Activating Prior Knowledge

Have students imagine themselves in tense situations in which they must make quick decisions. They want to act one way, but they are expected to act in another. Now have them imagine that their decisions involve potentially dangerous situations. What would go through their minds? What kinds of feelings would they have? Tell students to write a paragraph describing the situation, their feelings, and what they would do about it.

Concept Connector →

Tell students they will return to their responses after reading the selection.

GEORGE ORWELL

❶ ❷ SHOOTING AN ELEPHANT

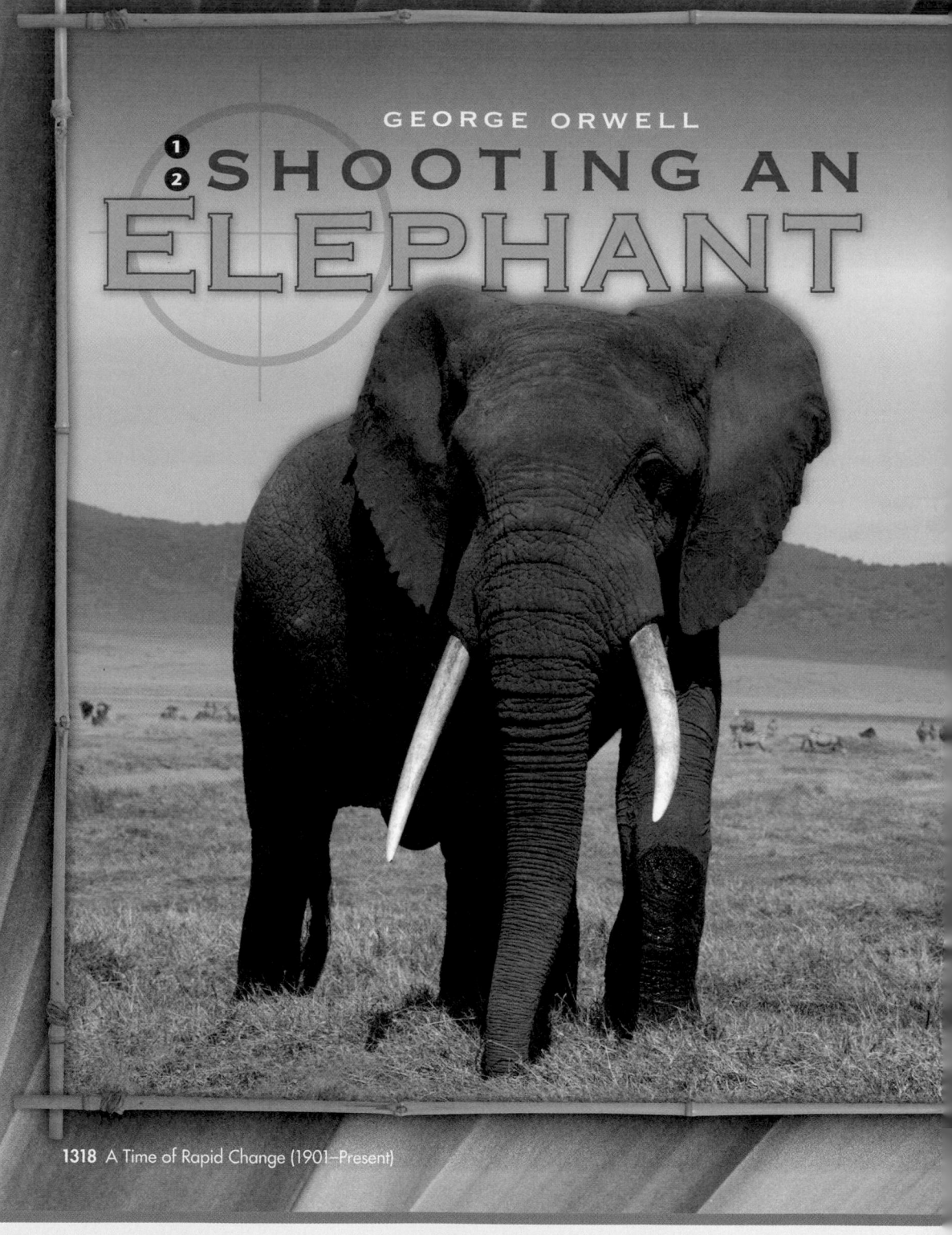

Text Complexity Rubric

	Shooting an Elephant	No Witchcraft for Sale
Qualitative Measures		
Context/ Knowledge Demands	Modern essay; historical and cultural knowledge demands 1 2 ③ 4 5	Modern story; historical and cultural knowledge demands 1 ② 3 4 5
Structure/Language Conventionality and Clarity	Regional terms 1 2 ③ 4 5	Regional terms and dialogue 1 ② 3 4 5
Levels of Meaning/ Purpose/Concept Level	Moderate (colonial experience; ambiguity of roles) 1 2 ③ 4 5	Moderate (cross-cultural experience) 1 2 ③ 4 5
Quantitative Measures		
Lexile/Text Length	1070L / 3,255 words	1000L / 3,143 words
Overall Complexity	**More complex**	**More accessible**

BACKGROUND *Hoping to secure a better trade route with China, Great Britain fought several wars against Burma (now also known as Myanmar) during the 1800s, finally conquering the country in 1885. Although the desired "golden path" to China did not prosper, Burma provided Britain with other economic opportunities, such as the export of Burmese rice. Many Burmese, however, were unwilling to accept British rule. Opponents of the British formed the Anti-Fascist People's Freedom League, led by Aung San. The group was instrumental in winning Burma's independence from Britain in 1948. In this essay, Orwell writes of the days of English rule in Burma.*

In Moulmein, in lower Burma, I was hated by large numbers of people—the only time in my life that I have been important enough for this to happen to me. I was subdivisional police officer of the town, and in an aimless, petty kind of way anti-European feeling was very bitter. No one had the guts to raise a riot, but if a European woman went through the bazaars alone somebody would probably spit betel juice over her dress. As a police officer I was an obvious target and was baited whenever it seemed safe to do so. When a nimble Burman tripped me up on the football field and the referee (another Burman) looked the other way, the crowd yelled with hideous laughter. This happened more than once. In the end the sneering yellow faces of young men that met me everywhere, the insults hooted after me when I was at a safe distance, got badly on my nerves. The young Buddhist priests were the worst of all. There were several thousands of them in the town and none of them seemed to have anything to do except stand on street corners and jeer at Europeans.

4 All this was perplexing and upsetting. For at that time I had already made up my mind that imperialism was an evil thing and the sooner I chucked up my job and got out of it the better. Theoretically—and secretly, of course—I was all for the Burmese and all against their oppressors, the British. As for the job I was doing, I hated it more bitterly than I can perhaps make clear. In a job like that you see the dirty work of Empire at close quarters. The wretched prisoners huddling in the stinking cages of the lockups, the gray, cowed faces of the long-term convicts, the scarred buttocks of the men who had been flogged with bamboos—all these oppressed me with an intolerable sense of guilt. But I could get nothing into
6 perspective. I was young and ill educated and I had had to think
7 out my problems in the utter silence that is imposed on every Englishman in the East. I did not even know that the British Empire

3 ◀ **Critical Viewing**
Does this photograph depict a useful beast or a dangerous menace? Explain. **[Make a Judgment]**

Literary Analysis
Cultural Conflict and Irony Explain the situational irony in the statement "I was all for the Burmese and all against their oppressors, the British."

5 **Reading Check**
According to Orwell, how do the Burmese view the English?

3 Critical Viewing

Answer: Students should recognize that the elephant has the potential to be either a useful or a dangerous beast, depending on the situation.

4 Literary Analysis

Cultural Conflict and Irony

1. **Ask** students to consider how Orwell felt about the Burmese, his job as a police officer, the treatment of Europeans in Burma, and British imperialism.
   Answer: Students should identify Orwell's sympathy for the Burmese, his dislike of imperialism, and his desire to leave his job. These attitudes conflict with his role as a police officer and British colonial representative.
2. Direct students to the bracketed passage. **Ask** students the Literary Analysis question: Explain the situational irony in the statement, "I was all for the Burmese and all against their oppressors, the British."
   Answer: Despite Orwell's sympathy for the Burmese people, he is British and his job as a police officer makes him an agent of the imperial system he dislikes, and one of those oppressors.

5 Reading Check

Answer: The Burmese hated the English and most Europeans.

PHLit Online!

These selections are available in interactive format in the **Enriched Online Student Edition** at **www.PHLitOnline.com**, which includes a thematically related video with writing prompt and an interactive graphic organizer.

Text Complexity: Reader and Task Suggestions

Shooting an Elephant		No Witchcraft for Sale	
Preparing to Read the Text	**Leveled Tasks**	**Preparing to Read the Text**	**Leveled Tasks**
• Use the information on SE p. 1317 to clarify that Burma, or Myanmar, is an independent nation of southeast Asia. • Discuss with students the distaste that Orwell had for his role as a police officer. • Guide students to use Multidraft Reading strategies (TE p. 1317).	***Levels of Meaning*** If students will have difficulty with the author's purpose, have them focus first on the events Orwell recounts and his feelings about them. Then, as they reread, have students concentrate on the author's comments about the political or social situation. ***Analyzing*** If students will not have difficulty with the author's purpose, have them analyze what the elephant symbolizes to the author.	• Use the information on SE p. 1327 to explain that Lessing often wrote about the injustice she saw in colonial Rhodesia. • Explain that British colonists in Africa often viewed tribal medical practices with contempt. • Guide students to use Multidraft Reading strategies (TE p. 1317).	***Levels of Meaning*** If students will have difficulty with the levels of meaning, have them focus first on story events and character relationships. Then, as they reread, have them focus on the characters' cultural differences. ***Evaluating*** If students will not have difficulty with the story's meaning, have them evaluate the effectiveness with which Lessing conveys her political and social message.

6 Critical Thinking

Connect

1. Direct students to the bracketed passage beginning with the words "But I could get nothing into perspective" on page 1319.
2. Remind students that Orwell was a young man of 19 when he went to serve in the imperial police in Burma. Ask students to consider how this fact may have affected his ambivalent feelings about the Burmese.
3. **Ask:** Would Orwell at this young age have had fixed, ready ways of responding to the world? Would he have felt differently about the British rule if he had been older?
Possible responses: Probably not; he was just starting to sort out his political beliefs. Perhaps; we know from the biographical note that this episode was a defining moment for Orwell, but people also tend to become more conservative as they age.
4. Have students brainstorm ideas about why Orwell did not speak up about the abuses he witnessed in Burma.

7 Reading Strategy

Analyze and Evaluate Similar Themes

1. Explain to students that the British Raj, or colonial government, on the subcontinent of India included the present-day countries of India, Pakistan, Bangladesh, and Burma. The Raj officially ended in 1947 with the partition of India and Pakistan.
2. **Ask** students: What result of long cultural conflict does Orwell say is now taking place?
Answer: The result is the death of the British Empire

Reading Strategy
Analyze and Evaluate Similar Themes
What result of long cultural conflict does Orwell say is now taking place? 6 7

Vocabulary
imperialism (im pir´ ē əl iz´əm) *n.* creating and maintaining an empire, especially by controlling other countries

despotic (de spät´ ik) *adj.* with absolute power, like a tyrant

is dying, still less did I know that it is a great deal better than the younger empires that are going to supplant it. All I knew was that I was stuck between my hatred of the empire I served and my rage against the evil-spirited little beasts who tried to make my job impossible. With one part of my mind I thought of the British Raj[1] as an unbreakable tyranny, as something clamped down, *in saecula saeculorum*,[2] upon the will of prostrate peoples; with another part I thought that the greatest joy in the world would be to drive a bayonet into a Buddhist priest's guts. Feelings like these are the normal byproducts of **imperialism**; ask any Anglo-Indian official, if you can catch him off duty.

One day something happened which in a roundabout way was enlightening. It was a tiny incident in itself, but it gave me a better glimpse than I had had before of the real nature of imperialism—the real motives for which **despotic** governments act. Early one morning the subinspector at a police station the other end of the town rang me up on the phone and said that an elephant was ravaging the bazaar. Would I please come and do something about it? I did not know what I could do, but I wanted to see what was happening and I got onto a pony and started out. I took my rifle, an old .44 Winchester and much too small to kill an elephant, but I thought the noise might be useful *in terrorem*.[3] Various Burmans stopped me on the way and told me about the elephant's doings. It was not, of course, a wild elephant, but a tame one which had gone "must."[4] It had been chained up, as tame elephants always are when their attack of "must" is due, but on the previous night it had broken its chain and escaped. Its mahout,[5] the only person who could manage it when it was in that state, had set out in pursuit, but had taken the wrong direction and was now twelve hours' journey away, and in the morning the elephant had suddenly reappeared in the town. The Burmese population had no weapons and were quite helpless against it. It had already destroyed somebody's bamboo hut, killed a cow and raided some fruit stalls and devoured the stock; also it had met the municipal rubbish van and, when the driver jumped out and took to his heels, had turned the van over and inflicted violences upon it.

The Burmese subinspector and some Indian constables were waiting for me in the quarter where the elephant had been seen. It was a very poor quarter, a labyrinth of squalid bamboo huts, thatched with palm leaf, winding all over a steep hillside. I remember that it was a cloudy, stuffy morning at the beginning of the rains. We began

1. **Raj** (räj) rule.
2. ***in saecula saeculorum*** (in sē´ ko͞o lə sē´ ko͞o lôr´ əm) Latin for "forever and ever."
3. ***in terrorem*** Latin for "for terror."
4. **must** into a dangerous, frenzied state.
5. **mahout** (mə ho͞ot´) elephant keeper and rider.

Enrichment: Analyzing Culture

British Imperialism in Burma
Orwell resented his position as an officer of the British Empire whose responsibility it was to enforce a system of imperialism he disliked. The Burmese had an even greater cause to resent the British for failing to recognize and respect differences in Burma's culture. For the sake of efficiency, the British treated Burma as a province of India. Not only was Burma different from India in language, race, religious traditions, and customs; India fought with the British in the wars that brought Burma into Britain's empire.

Activity: Analyze Burmese Culture Have students learn more about the customs and traditions of Burma. Tell students that the present name of this country is Myanmar. Suggest that they record their analyses in the **Enrichment: Investigating Culture** worksheet, ***Professional Development Guidebook,*** page 223.

questioning the people as to where the elephant had gone and, as usual, failed to get any definite information. That is invariably the case in the East; a story always sounds clear enough at a distance, but the nearer you get to the scene of events the vaguer it becomes. Some of the people said that the elephant had gone in one direction, some said that he had gone in another, some professed not even to have heard of any elephant. I had almost made up my mind that the whole story was a pack of lies, when we heard yells a little distance away. There was a loud scandalized cry of "Go away, child! Go away this instant!" and an old woman with a switch in her hand came round the corner of a hut, violently shooing away a crowd of naked children. Some more women followed, clicking their tongues and exclaiming; evidently there was something that the children ought not to have seen. I rounded the hut and saw a man's dead body sprawling in the mud. He was an Indian, a black Dravidian[6] coolie,[7] almost naked, and he could not have been dead many minutes. The people said that the elephant had come suddenly upon him round the corner of the hut, caught him with its trunk, put its foot on his back and ground him into the earth. This was the rainy season and the ground was soft, and his face had scored a trench a foot deep and a couple of yards long. He was lying on his belly with arms crucified and head sharply twisted to one side. His face was coated with mud, the eyes wide open, the teeth bared and grinning with an expression of unendurable agony. (Never tell me, by the way, that the dead look peaceful. Most of the corpses I have seen looked devilish.) The friction of the great beast's foot had stripped the skin from his back as neatly as one skins a rabbit. As soon as I saw the dead man I sent an orderly to a friend's house nearby to borrow an elephant rifle. I had already sent back the pony, not wanting it to go mad with fright and throw me if it smelled the elephant.

The orderly came back in a few minutes with a rifle and five cartridges, and meanwhile some Burmans had arrived and told us that the elephant was in the paddy fields[8] below, only a few hundred yards away. As I started forward practically the whole population of the quarter flocked out of the houses and followed me. They had seen the rifle and were all shouting excitedly that I was going to shoot the
10 elephant. They had not shown much interest in the elephant when he was merely ravaging their homes, but it was different now that he was going to be shot. It was a bit of fun to them, as it would be to

6. **Dravidian** (drə vid′ ē ən) belonging to the race of people inhabiting southern India.
7. **coolie** laborer.
8. **paddy fields** rice fields.

8 LITERATURE IN CONTEXT

Vocabulary of Empire

The key terms in Orwell's political vocabulary often have Latin origins:

- *Imperialism* comes from a Latin word for "command" or "empire."
- *Dominion* comes from a Latin word meaning "lord" or "master."

Supporters of British imperialism may have chosen Latinate words to describe the British Empire as a way of suggesting a comparison with the glory of the Roman Empire. However, critics like Orwell seized the word *imperialism*, and it gained strongly negative connotations.

Some meanings reflect history inaccurately. In an irony that Orwell would have appreciated, the word despot is derived from a Greek term for "ruler." Even though our ideas of democracy come from ancient Greece, where some rulers strove for democratic goals, the term has come to describe the opposite of a democratic leader—an oppressive tyrant.

Connect to the Literature

In what ways does the narrator fail to embody words like *imperialism* and *despotic*?

9 Reading Check

What has the elephant done that shows how dangerous it is?

8 Literature in Context

Vocabulary of Empire

Other important political words are derived from the Greek language. For example, the Greek word *kratos,* meaning "strength" or "power," forms the basis of many words describing different forms of government, including *democracy, monarchy, technocracy,* and *oligarchy*.

Connect to the Literature Have the class discuss the meanings of *imperialism* and *despotism* before students answer the question.

Ask students the Connect to the Literature question: In what ways does the narrator fail to embody words like *imperialism* and *despotic?*

Possible response: The style and tone of the author's commentary shows his frustration, compromise, and futility. He has inner conflicts stemming from the dilemma in which he finds himself. His thoughts and words also reflect an understanding of and empathy for the Burmese. These are not the notions of a typical despot. He is worried about justifying his actions in public as well as avoiding embarrassment and appeasing his guilt. He obviously responds to a conscience that questions blind duty.

9 Reading Check

Answer: The elephant destroyed a bamboo hut, killed a cow, raided some fruit stalls, overturned a van, and finally killed a man.

Differentiated Instruction for Universal Access

Strategy for Less Proficient Readers
Have students use flowcharts to track the decisions Orwell must make during this essay. Students can use different-colored pens or pencils to show the flow of events that actually occurred, through each decision he made.

Enrichment for Gifted/Talented Students
Have students research roles that elephants play in Asian countries. Suggest that they explore this topic from a variety of perspectives including cultural, religious, agricultural, and historical. Ask students to share their findings in oral reports. Encourage them to prepare multimedia presentations.

Background for Advanced Readers
Have advanced students research other British colonies that underwent similar difficulties under imperialism. Were these difficulties confined to British colonies, or did other nations have parallel troubles?

⑩ Literary Analysis

Irony

1. Direct students to the bracketed passage that starts: "As I started forward ..."
2. Review both verbal and situational irony with students, asking that they give an example of each.
3. Discuss with students any experiences they might have had facing a large crowd. Did the crowd make them feel safe or insecure? How did the crowd treat the student?
4. **Ask** students the Literary Analysis question: How does Orwell's description of the crowd's reaction create situational irony?
   Answer: Orwell claims that the crowd seemed indifferent about the threat of the elephant to their homes, reacting only to the prospect of seeing the animal shot. The contradiction in the situation is between the expected interests of homeowners (an interest in protecting their property) and the actual behavior of the crowd.

⑪ Literary Analysis

Irony

1. Have students skim the bracketed passage. Then, ask them to make a list of what Orwell thinks his relation to the crowd should be. Make another list of what his position really is.
2. Have students compare the two lists. **Ask:** Do the lists have anything in common?
   Possible response: Orwell thinks that as the lead actor he should dominate the situation, but instead he is controlled at every step by the natives' expectations.
3. **Ask** students the Literary Analysis question: What ironic observation does Orwell share here?
   Answer: Orwell has discovered that to rule the natives is actually to be ruled by them, since his conduct is guided at every moment by his need to impress them.

Literary Analysis
Irony How does Orwell's description of the crowd's reaction create situational irony? ⑩

an English crowd; besides they wanted the meat. It made me vaguely uneasy. I had no intention of shooting the elephant—I had merely sent for the rifle to defend myself if necessary— and it is always unnerving to have a crowd following you. I marched down the hill, looking and feeling a fool, with the rifle over my shoulder and an ever-growing army of people jostling at my heels. At the bottom, when you got away from the huts, there was a metaled road[9] and beyond that a miry waste of paddy fields a thousand yards across, not yet plowed but soggy from the first rains and dotted with coarse grass. The elephant was standing eight yards from the road, his left side toward us. He took not the slightest notice of the crowd's approach. He was tearing up bunches of grass, beating them against his knees to clean them, and stuffing them into his mouth.

I had halted on the road. As soon as I saw the elephant I knew with perfect certainty that I ought not to shoot him. It is a serious matter to shoot a working elephant—it is comparable to destroying a huge and costly piece of machinery—and obviously one ought not to do it if it can possibly be avoided. And at that distance, peacefully eating, the elephant looked no more dangerous than a cow. I thought then and I think now that his attack of "must" was already passing off; in which case he would merely wander harmlessly about until the mahout came back and caught him. Moreover, I did not in the least want to shoot him. I decided that I would watch him for a little while to make sure that he did not turn savage again, and then go home.

But at that moment I glanced round at the crowd that had followed me. It was an immense crowd, two thousand at the least and growing every minute. It blocked the road for a long distance on either side. I looked at the sea of yellow faces above the garish clothes—faces all happy and excited over this bit of fun, all certain that the elephant was going to be shot. They were watching me as they would watch a conjurer about to perform a trick. They did not like me, but with the magical rifle in my hands I was momentarily worth watching. And suddenly I realized that I should have to shoot the elephant after all. ⑪ The people expected it of me and I had got to do it; I could feel their two thousand wills pressing me forward, irresistibly. And it was at this moment, as I stood there with the rifle in my hands, that I first grasped the hollowness, the futility of the white man's **dominion** in the East. Here was I, the white man with his gun, standing in front of the unarmed native crowd—seemingly the leading actor of the piece; but in reality I was only an absurd puppet pushed to and fro by the will of those yellow faces behind. I perceived in this moment that when the white man turns tyrant it is his own freedom that he destroys. He becomes a sort of hollow, posing dummy, the conventionalized figure

Vocabulary
dominion (də min′ yən) *n.* rule, authority

Literary Analysis
Irony What ironic observation does Orwell share here?

9. **metaled road** road in which the pavement is reinforced with metal strips.

Think Aloud

Vocabulary: Using Context
Direct students' attention to the word *futility* on this page. Use the following "think aloud" to model the skill of using context to infer the meaning of the word. Say to students:

> I may not know the meaning of the word *futility*. When I read the sentence, however, I realize that Orwell is using *futility* to describe the frustration he feels regarding the white man's authority in his colonial empire. In the sentence, the word *futility* appears near the word *hollowness*. I know *hollow* means "empty." Later in the same paragraph Orwell says that the white man who tries to enforce colonial rule destroys his own freedom and becomes a "hollow dummy," so I think *futility* must refer to how *ineffective* Orwell feels trying to impress the natives with his power and authority.

"BUT I DID NOT WANT TO SHOOT THE ELEPHANT."

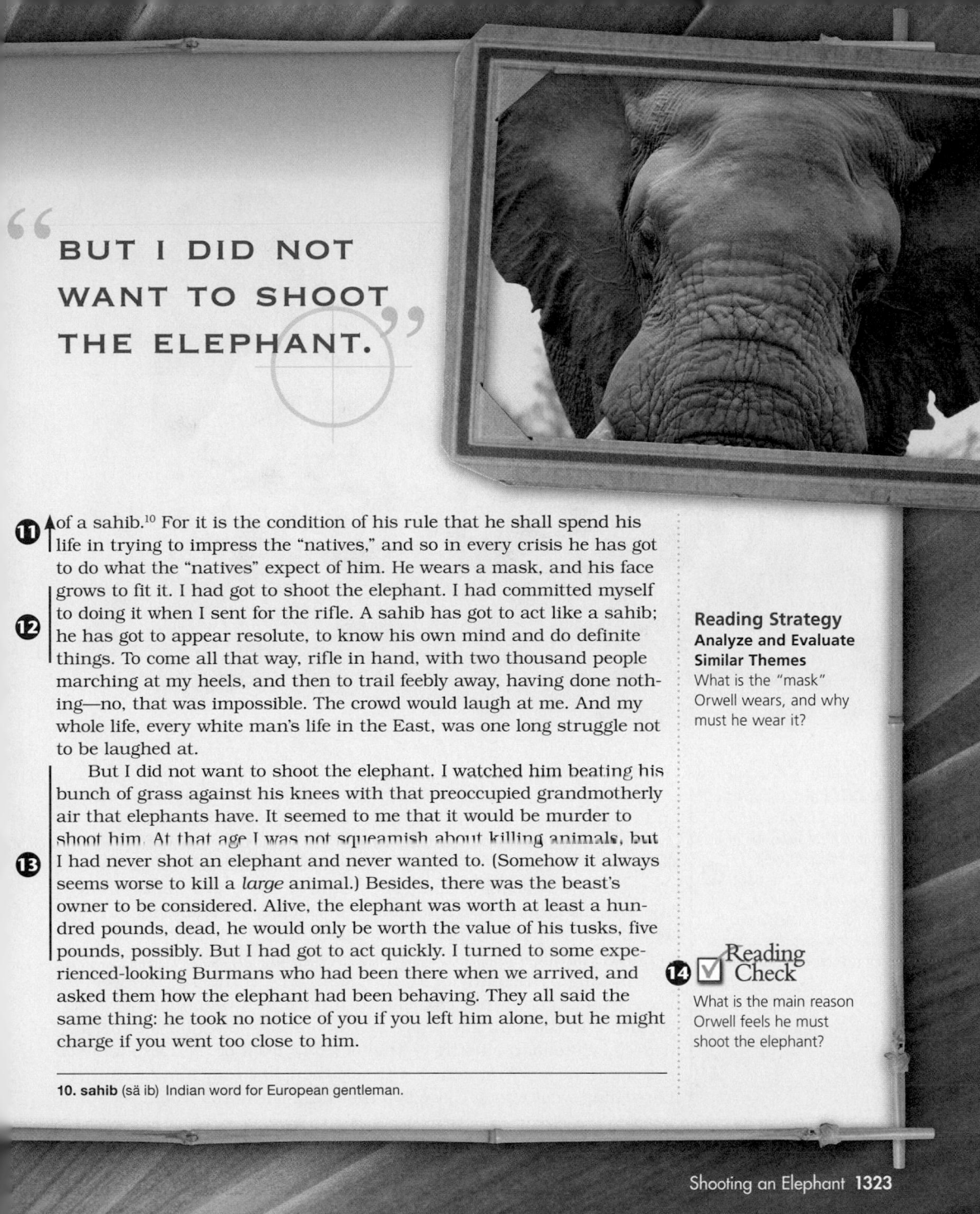

11 of a sahib.[10] For it is the condition of his rule that he shall spend his life in trying to impress the "natives," and so in every crisis he has got to do what the "natives" expect of him. He wears a mask, and his face grows to fit it. I had got to shoot the elephant. I had committed myself to doing it when I sent for the rifle. A sahib has got to act like a sahib; 12 he has got to appear resolute, to know his own mind and do definite things. To come all that way, rifle in hand, with two thousand people marching at my heels, and then to trail feebly away, having done nothing—no, that was impossible. The crowd would laugh at me. And my whole life, every white man's life in the East, was one long struggle not to be laughed at.

But I did not want to shoot the elephant. I watched him beating his bunch of grass against his knees with that preoccupied grandmotherly air that elephants have. It seemed to me that it would be murder to shoot him. At that age I was not squeamish about killing animals, but 13 I had never shot an elephant and never wanted to. (Somehow it always seems worse to kill a *large* animal.) Besides, there was the beast's owner to be considered. Alive, the elephant was worth at least a hundred pounds, dead, he would only be worth the value of his tusks, five pounds, possibly. But I had got to act quickly. I turned to some experienced-looking Burmans who had been there when we arrived, and asked them how the elephant had been behaving. They all said the same thing: he took no notice of you if you left him alone, but he might charge if you went too close to him.

10. **sahib** (sä ib) Indian word for European gentleman.

Reading Strategy
Analyze and Evaluate Similar Themes
What is the "mask" Orwell wears, and why must he wear it?

14 **Reading Check**
What is the main reason Orwell feels he must shoot the elephant?

12 Reading Strategy

Analyze and Evaluate Similar Themes

1. Direct students to the bracketed passage. **Ask** students how Orwell says he feels as he stands before the native crowd with his rifle.
   Answer: He feels like a puppet.
2. Then, **ask** students the Reading Strategy question: What is the "mask" that Orwell wears, and why must he wear it?
   Answer: Orwell wears the mask of a sahib, because he is the representative of the government.

13 Critical Thinking

Connect

1. Direct students to the bracketed passage.
2. **Ask** students to identify the reasons that Orwell gives for not shooting the elephant.
   Answer: It is a valuable working animal, and it is standing there peacefully eating.
3. **Ask:** What reason does he give for having to shoot the elephant?
   Answer: The natives expect him to, and he will look absurd if he does not use the rifle.

14 Reading Check

Answer: Orwell decides to shoot the elephant because the crowd expects him to do so and he would look foolish after sending for the rifle if he does not use it.

Differentiated Instruction for Universal Access

Support for Less Proficient Readers
Help readers understand the complexity of the situation in which Orwell found himself. Have students refer to the ***Reader's Notebook: Adapted Version.*** Discuss with them the forces that affected Orwell at this point.

EL Vocabulary for English Learners
Idiomatic expressions and informal speech may pose a challenge. Have students note phrases that do not translate literally, such as Orwell's comparison of his chances if the elephant charged to a "toad under a steamroller." Show them how to use an online dictionary to identify idioms.

Enrichment for Advanced Readers
Challenge advanced students to write about a time when they knew what they should do from a moral standpoint but accepted another course of action because of peer pressure. Have them relate their experiences to that of Orwell.

⓯ Critical Viewing

Possible response: The officers' formal dress, pith helmets, long coats, Sam Browne belts, and high boots would have been a stark contrast to the informal, loose clothing of the Burmese natives.

⓰ Literary Analysis

Irony

1. Have students read Orwell's description of his choices in dealing with the elephant independently. **Ask:** What does Orwell say he should do?
   Answer: He should test its behavior and only shoot if the elephant charges.
2. Direct students' attention to the memorable phrase "about as much chance as a toad under a steamroller."
3. **Ask:** What is ironic about Orwell's use of this phrase?
   Possible response: The phrase creates the mental image of the elephant squashing him flat if he misses. Yet even though Orwell knows he is a poor shot, what he keeps seeing is the eyes of the natives who are watching him.

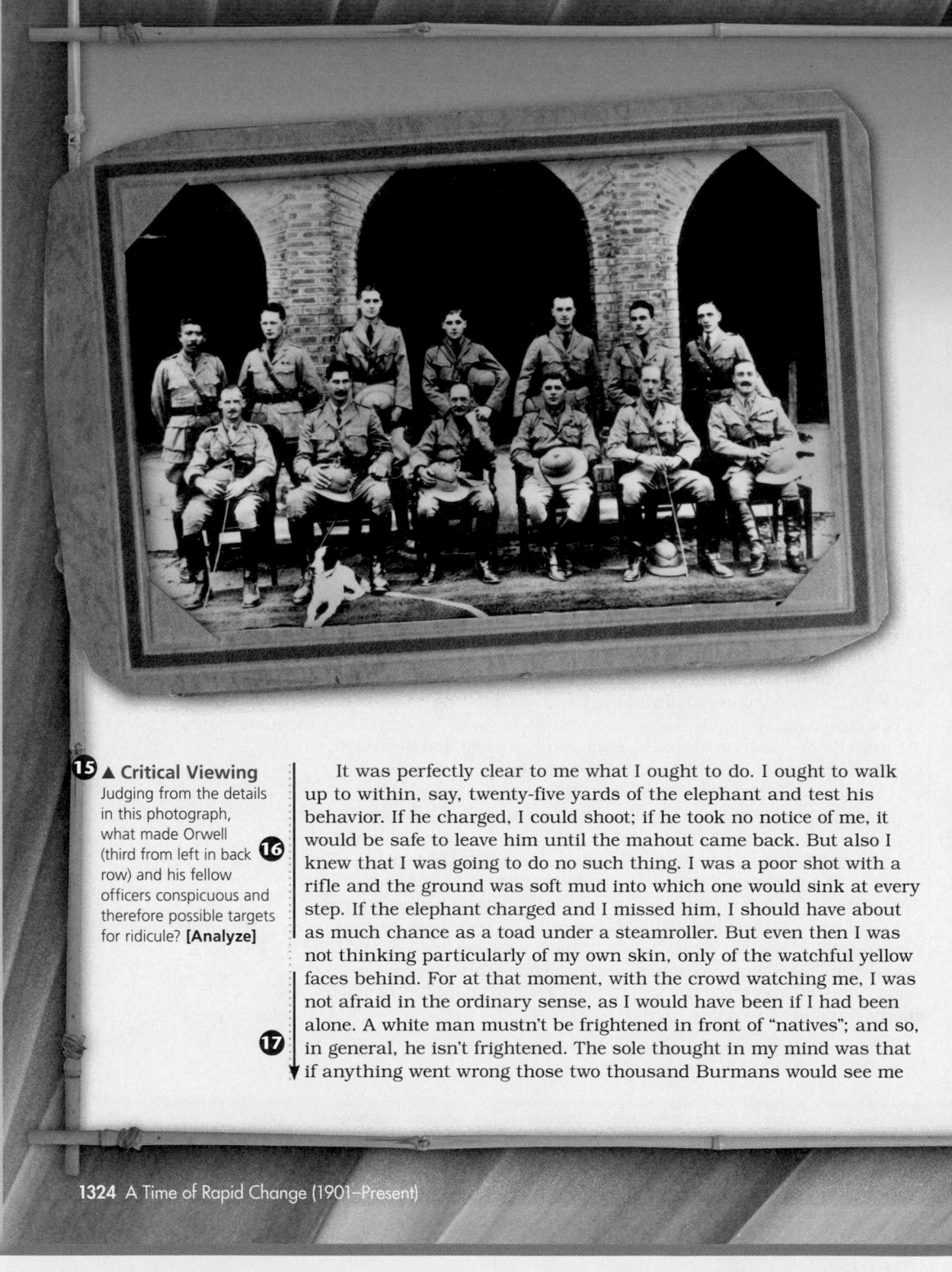

⓯ ▲ **Critical Viewing** Judging from the details in this photograph, what made Orwell (third from left in back row) and his fellow officers conspicuous and therefore possible targets for ridicule? **[Analyze]**

It was perfectly clear to me what I ought to do. I ought to walk up to within, say, twenty-five yards of the elephant and test his behavior. If he charged, I could shoot; if he took no notice of me, it would be safe to leave him until the mahout came back. But also I ⓰ knew that I was going to do no such thing. I was a poor shot with a rifle and the ground was soft mud into which one would sink at every step. If the elephant charged and I missed him, I should have about as much chance as a toad under a steamroller. But even then I was not thinking particularly of my own skin, only of the watchful yellow faces behind. For at that moment, with the crowd watching me, I was not afraid in the ordinary sense, as I would have been if I had been alone. A white man mustn't be frightened in front of "natives"; and so, ⓱ in general, he isn't frightened. The sole thought in my mind was that if anything went wrong those two thousand Burmans would see me

Enrichment: Investigating Career Connections

Police Officers

The speaker in this essay is a police officer attempting to defuse a tense situation. Police officers face duties ranging from monitoring political unrest to directing traffic around road construction. Depending on the area for which an officer is responsible, he or she may walk, ride a bicycle or horse, or drive a car.

Activity: Investigating Police Work and Training Have interested students inquire at a local police station about the types of police work done by that precinct and the related training officers receive in undertaking those duties. After reviewing those findings as a class, discuss the physical and emotional challenges police officers face in these various types of duties.

Suggest that students record their analyses in the **Enrichment: Investigating Career Connections** worksheet, ***Professional Development Guidebook,*** page 221.

17 pursued, caught, trampled on, and reduced to a grinning corpse like that Indian up the hill. And if that happened it was quite probable that some of them would laugh. That would never do. There was only one alternative. I shoved the cartridges into the magazine and lay down on the road to get a better aim.

The crowd grew very still, and a deep, low, happy sigh, as of people who see the theater curtain go up at last, breathed from innumerable throats. They were going to have their bit of fun, after all. The rifle was a beautiful German thing with cross-hair sights. I did not then know that in shooting an elephant one would shoot to cut an imaginary bar running from ear hole to ear hole. I ought, therefore, as the elephant was sideways on, to have aimed straight at his ear-hole; actually I aimed several inches in front of this, thinking the brain would be further forward.

18 When I pulled the trigger I did not hear the bang or feel the kick—one never does when a shot goes home—but I heard the devilish roar of glee that went up from the crowd. In that instant, in too short a time, one would have thought, even for the bullet to get there, a mysterious, terrible change had come over the elephant. He neither stirred nor fell, but every line of his body had altered. He looked suddenly stricken, shrunken, immensely old, as though the frightful impact of the bullet had paralyzed him without knocking him down. At last, after what seemed a long time—it might have been five seconds, I dare say—he sagged flabbily to his knees. His mouth slobbered. An enormous senility[11] seemed to have settled upon him. One could have imagined him thousands of years old. I fired again into the same spot. At the second shot he did not collapse but climbed with desperate slowness to his feet and stood weakly upright, with legs sagging and head drooping. I fired a third time. That was the shot that did for him. You could see the agony of it jolt his whole body and knock the last remnant of strength from his legs. But in falling he seemed for a moment to rise, for as his hind legs collapsed beneath him he seemed to tower upward like a huge rock toppling, his trunk reaching skyward like a tree. He trumpeted, for the first and only time. And then down he came, his belly toward me, with a crash that seemed to shake the ground even where I lay.

I got up. The Burmans were already racing past me across the mud. It was obvious that the elephant would never rise again, but he was not dead. He was breathing very rhythmically with long rattling gasps, his great mound of a side painfully rising and falling. His mouth was wide open—I could see far down into caverns of pale pink

Literary Analysis
Irony Why is Orwell's comment "That would never do" an example of verbal irony?

Reading Strategy
Analyze and Evaluate Similar Themes What does this long description of the elephant's death reveal about the cultural conflict Orwell faces?

19 **Reading Check**
What happens to the elephant after Orwell's first shot?

11. **senility** (si nil′ ə tē) *n.* mental deterioration due to old age.

17 Literary Analysis

Irony

1. Direct students' attention to the bracketed passage.
2. **Ask** the Literary Analysis question: Why is Orwell's statement "That will never do" an example of verbal irony?
   Answer: Orwell is talking about being trampled by an elephant, but all he is worried about is the natives laughing at his grinning corpse.

18 Reading Strategy

Analyze and Evaluate Similar Themes

1. Direct students to read the bracketed paragraph, in which Orwell describes the death of the elephant.
2. **Ask:** How does Orwell treat the scene? Does he make it attractive or repulsive?
   Answer: It sounds very ugly and brutal.
3. **Ask** the Reading Strategy question: What does this long description of the elephant's death reveal about the cultural conflict Orwell faces?
   Possible response: The crowd reacts like people attending a theater performance. His detailed description shows that Orwell was shocked by how long the death took and by the crowd's reaction, and that he was profoundly moved by the animal's agony.

19 Reading Check

Answer: The elephant seems to age and become immensely old, and its appearance alters as if the bullet paralyzed the animal without knocking him down.

Differentiated Instruction for Universal Access

Strategy for Less Proficient Readers
To help students better understand the concept of situational irony, work with students to complete a three-column chart with these heads: Subject, Expected Situation, and Actual Situation. Have students identify different ironic situations and then explain the clash or opposition that creates the irony in the situation.

Enrichment for Advanced Readers
George Orwell drew upon his life experiences and his political philosophy in many of his writings. Have students use online and library resources to research some of Orwell's other writings. Tell students to select one of his books, such as *Animal Farm* or *1984,* or another essay, such as "The Hanging," to read and then identify the personal experiences that influenced the work. Have them give presentations to the class summarizing what they learned.

⑳ Reading Strategy

Analyze and Evaluate Similar Themes

1. Direct students' attention to the bracketed passage. Have students read it independently.
2. **Ask:** How does Orwell's individual response mirror the end of the entire colonial enterprise?
   Possible response: Orwell is so disgusted that he just walks away. Britain tried to retain its colonies after World War II in small wars but gradually realized the empire was too expensive, and the nation too just walked away from many of its colonies.

ASSESS

Answers

Before students respond, you may wish to have them write a brief objective summary of the selection. As they answer the questions below, remind them to support their answers with evidence from the text.

1. (a) Orwell was hated because he was European and represented British-Indian rule. (b) He sympathized with the Burmese, but they bullied him constantly. (c) This conflict shows his ambivalence: He hates the imperialist system and sympathizes with the Burmese, but he despises his abusers and is honest enough to admit these feelings.
2. (a) The elephant is a costly working machine; it is probably unnecessary for public safety. (b) He shoots the elephant mostly to avoid looking foolish. (c) He was basically a moral person, but also he was weak enough to be influenced by others.

throat. I waited a long time for him to die, but his breathing did not weaken. Finally I fired my two remaining shots into the spot where I thought his heart must be. The thick blood welled out of him like red velvet, but still he did not die. His body did not even jerk when the shots hit him, the tortured breathing continued without a pause. He was dying, very slowly and in great agony, but in some world remote from me where not even a bullet could damage him further. I felt that I had got to put an end to that dreadful noise. It seemed dreadful to see the great beast lying there, powerless to move and yet powerless to die, and not even to be able to finish him. I sent back for my small rifle and poured shot after shot into his heart and down his throat. They seemed to make no impression. The tortured gasps continued as steadily as the ticking of a clock.

Reading Strategy
Analyze and Evaluate Similar Themes Read the first sentence of the paragraph beginning "In the end." How does Orwell's individual response mirror the end of the entire colonial enterprise? ⑳

In the end I could not stand it any longer and went away. I heard later that it took him half an hour to die. Burmans were bringing dahs[12] and baskets even before I left, and I was told they had stripped his body almost to the bones by the afternoon.

Afterward, of course, there were endless discussions about the shooting of the elephant. The owner was furious, but he was only an Indian and could do nothing. Besides, legally I had done the right thing, for a mad elephant has to be killed, like a mad dog, if its owner fails to control it. Among the Europeans opinion was divided. The older men said I was right, the younger men said it was a shame to shoot an elephant for killing a coolie, because an elephant was worth more than any Coringhee[13] coolie. And afterward I was very glad that the coolie had been killed; it put me legally in the right and it gave me a sufficient pretext for shooting the elephant. I often wondered whether any of the others grasped that I had done it solely to avoid looking a fool.

12. **dahs** (däz) knives.
13. **Coringhee** (cor in′ gē) Southern Indian.

Critical Reading

Cite textual evidence to support your responses.

1. **Key Ideas and Details (a)** Why did the Burmese hate George Orwell? **(b) Analyze:** Why does this hatred cause conflict in him? **(c) Interpret:** What does this internal conflict show about Orwell?
2. **Key Ideas and Details (a)** Why does Orwell think that the elephant need not be killed? **(b) Analyze:** What is the main factor in Orwell's decision to shoot the elephant? **(c) Interpret:** What does this decision, and his honesty about it, reveal about his character?

Enrichment: Investigating History

Britain's Asian Empire

The British Empire on the Indian subcontinent included present-day India, Pakistan, and various princely states. British families moved to many of these areas. In 1858, control reverted to the British Crown. Burma was added in 1886. When local independence movements began, Burma became a separate colony. After World War II, independence was granted to many former colonies.

Activity: Investigating the Legacy of the Colonial Period In order to keep colonies from uniting against British rule, the British often followed a policy of dividing subject peoples along ethnic and racial lines. This left an enduring legacy in its former colonies. Ask students to learn more about the impact of colonialism in India or Burma. Suggest that they record their analyses in the **Enrichment: Analyzing Historical Patterns, Trends, and Periods** worksheet, ***Professional Development Guidebook,*** page 231.

㉑ # Doris Lessing (b. 1919)

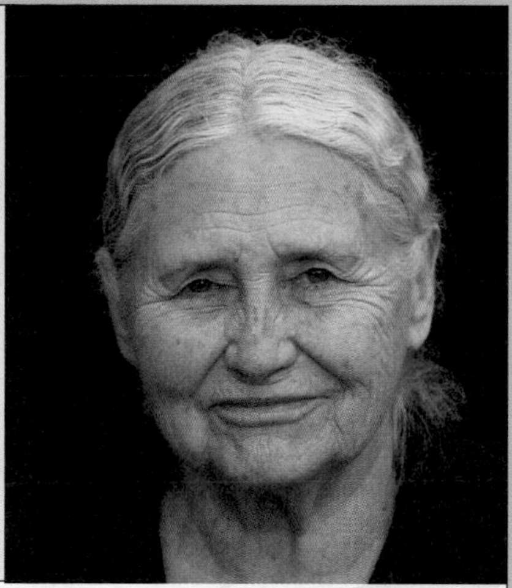

Author of "No Witchcraft for Sale"

Freely admitting her deep desire to influence others through her works of fiction, Doris Lessing has said that publishing a story or novel is "an attempt to impose one's personality and beliefs on other people. If a writer accepts this responsibility, he must see himself . . . as an architect of the soul."

Exposing Injustice One of the ways that Lessing fulfills this responsibility is by writing about social injustice, challenging ideas of race and women's roles. Her own experiences give her a unique perspective on the problems caused when cultures conflict. In much of her writing, Lessing explores the intricate connections between personal experience and political reality.

She was born in Persia (now Iran), the daughter of a British bank clerk. When she was five, her family moved to the British colony of Rhodesia (now the independent country of Zimbabwe) in southcentral Africa. Her memoir *Under My Skin* (1994) describes some ways that Europeans mistreated Africans, displacing them from their lands and suppressing their traditions.

Experience Shapes a Writer Lessing's talent for writing developed as a response to a variety of experiences, including a childhood she described as a mixture of some pleasure and much pain. Strictly disciplined by her mother at home and by teachers at school, the young Lessing sought refuge in reading and in explorations of nature.

Personal and Political Themes The turbulent influences that drove Lessing to write also taught her about the relationship between individuals and society. *The Golden Notebook* (1962), Lessing's best-known novel, explores social issues through one woman's persistent search for identity. The dominant theme in her works is the free woman who struggles for individuality and equality despite social assumptions and pressures. Lessing's fiction earned her the Nobel Prize for Literature in 2007.

㉑ Background

More About the Author

In her prolific career, Doris Lessing has not only shown her seemingly inexhaustible talent, but has also demonstrated her commitment to political issues by pursuing subjects of equality and civil rights in her fiction. In her 1950 book *The Grass Is Singing,* Lessing describes the complicated relationship between a white farmer's wife and her black servant. Lessing left school when she was 15 and worked variously as a nurse, a typist, and a telephone operator. After the end of her first marriage, she became involved in radical politics and moved to England with her son. There, she continued to support herself with her writing, turning to subjects as varied as mental breakdown, social disintegration, and technological disaster.

Differentiated Instruction for Universal Access

Culturally Responsive Instruction

Culture Connection Students may lack the background knowledge and context-building experiences necessary to comprehend the selection. Build background knowledge about the plant and animal life found in this region of Africa. Provide pictures of the grassland, the *bush* or *veld,* and of the tree snake that attacks Teddy. Discuss the context in which students might see them. Locate Rhodesia, or present-day Zimbabwe, on a map and show photographs of the people. Then, explain how a British family might come to live in Rhodesia in the days when Rhodesia was ruled by Great Britain.

㉒ About the Selection

The Farquars, a white family living on a homestead in Africa, employ Gideon, a local man, as their cook. He is kind and loving toward their young son, Teddy, but never forgets his place as a servant. When a medical emergency causes Gideon to use his traditional healing skills to restore Teddy's eyesight, the family is deeply grateful. But the incident leads to a cultural clash when the Farquars misunderstand Gideon's tribal position as a healer. The standoff between the Farquars and Gideon underscores a cultural gap that cannot be bridged.

㉓ Background

Medicine from Plants

Plants make their own chemical compounds to either attract or repel insects and animals or to defend against plant diseases. These chemicals are often used to fight human diseases. Medicine men like Gideon in this story have been acquiring knowledge about plants and their uses for thousands of years. Today, herbal remedies are receiving increasing attention in the scientific and medical world. Native plants, particularly from the major rain forests of Asia, Africa, and the Amazon, represent a resource with enormous potential for new medicines and food crops, as well as other useful products. Explain that folk medicine plays a key role in this story.

㉒ ㉓ No Witchcraft for Sale

Doris Lessing

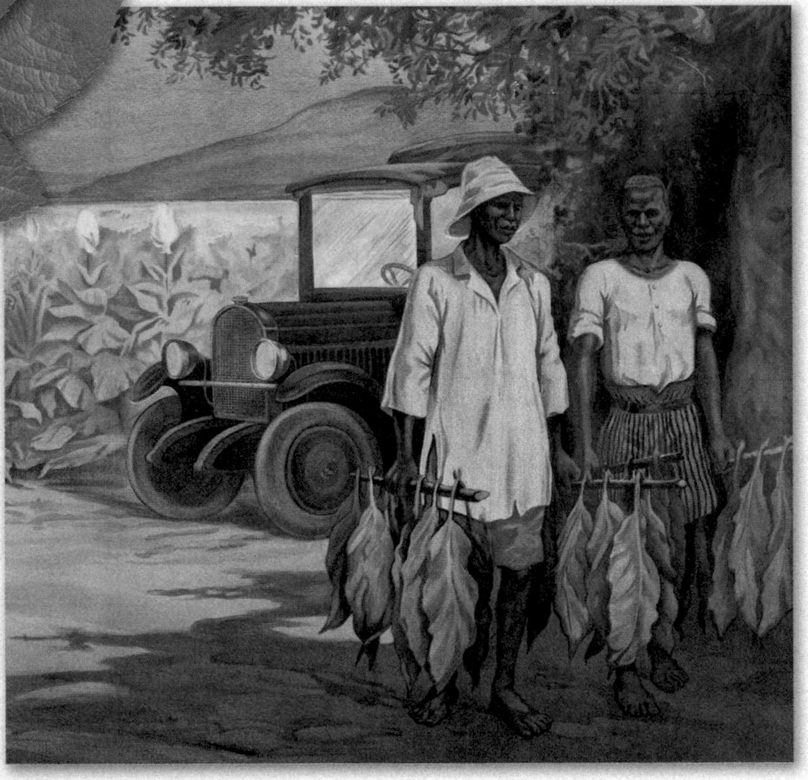

Enrichment: Investigating Daily Life

British Rhodesia

Present-day Zimbabwe, the former colony of Rhodesia, is a landlocked country in south-central Africa. Bantu tribes originally settled the region. Later the Ndelebele people established a powerful Zulu warrior kingdom. British explorers, colonists, and missionaries began arriving in the 1850s. The influx of these colonists and the discovery of gold led to the establishment of Rhodesia, named for British-born South African Cecil Rhodes.

Activity: Investigating Daily Life in Colonial Africa Have students learn more about what life was like for both colonists and natives in colonial Rhodesia. Tell them to compare and contrast life in colonial Rhodesia with life in modern Zimbabwe. Suggest that they record their analyses in the **Enrichment: Investigating Daily Life** worksheet, ***Professional Development Guidebook***, page 224.

㉔ Critical Viewing

Answer: Students may predict that the story will be about plants or animals used for ritual purposes.

㉕ Reading Check

Answer: Gideon's role in the Farquar household is that of cook.

BACKGROUND Doris Lessing's family moved to Southern Rhodesia (now Zimbabwe) in 1924. For two decades, British control had been forcing two vastly different cultures to live together. Every day, white European values and attitudes met face to face with black African values and attitudes. Traditions and beliefs inevitably clashed. However, although each culture exhibited distinctive characteristics, they also shared some fundamental cultural assumptions.

The Farquars had been childless for years when little Teddy was born; and they were touched by the pleasure of their servants, who brought presents of fowls and eggs and flowers to the homestead when they came to rejoice over the baby, exclaiming with delight over his downy golden head and his blue eyes. They congratulated Mrs. Farquar as if she had achieved a very great thing, and she felt that she had—her smile for the lingering, admiring natives was warm and grateful.

Later, when Teddy had his first haircut, Gideon the cook picked up the soft gold tufts from the ground, and held them **reverently** in his hand. Then he smiled at the little boy and said: "Little Yellow Head." That became the native name for the child. Gideon and Teddy were great friends from the first. When Gideon had finished his work, he would lift Teddy on his shoulders to the shade of a big tree, and play with him there, forming curious little toys from twigs and leaves and grass, or shaping animals from wetted soil. When Teddy learned to walk it was often Gideon who crouched before him, clucking encouragement, finally catching him when he fell, tossing him up in the air till they both became breathless with laughter. Mrs. Farquar was fond of the old cook because of his love for her child.

There was no second baby; and one day Gideon said: "Ah, missus, missus, the Lord above sent this one; Little Yellow Head is the most good thing we have in our house." Because of that "we" Mrs. Farquar
26 felt a warm impulse toward her cook; and at the end of the month she raised his wages. He had been with her now for several years; he was one of the few natives who had his wife and children in the compound and never wanted to go home to his kraal,[1] which was some hundreds of miles away. Sometimes a small piccanin who had been

㉔ ◀ Critical Viewing Using this picture and the title, predict what this story will be about. **[Predict]**

Vocabulary
reverently (rev′ ər ənt lē) *adv.* with great respect

㉕ Reading Check
What is Gideon's role in the Farquar household?

1. **kraal** (kräl) village of South African natives, usually fenced in with a stockade.

Differentiated Instruction for Universal Access

Vocabulary for Special-Needs Students
Encourage students to read aloud from the text with guidance. Tell them how to pronounce unfamiliar words. Remind them that the story is set in Africa and that many African terms may be unfamiliar. Encourage students to determine word meanings from context.

EL Vocabulary for English Learners
Students may find some African terms such as *baas, veld,* and *kaffir* in the story especially difficult. Encourage students to concentrate on the sounds of words with which they have trouble and to use the footnotes and margin definitions to enhance their understanding.

Strategy for Advanced Readers
Have students read independently. Remind them that as a child, Doris Lessing lived in Rhodesia, now called Zimbabwe. Ask students to research and create a timeline of the changes and turmoil it has undergone in the past century.

26 Reading Strategy

Analyze and Evaluate Similar Themes

1. Remind students that by paying attention to similarities and differences in cultural background, they may be able to identify cultural differences more readily.
2. Have students read the bracketed passage independently. Point out that it continues onto the next page. Then, **ask** students the Reading Strategy question: What cultural values do the Farquars and Gideon share?
   Answer: Both the Farquars and Gideon believe in God and destiny.

27 Literary Analysis

Cultural Conflict

1. Direct students to the bracketed passage.
2. Remind students that cultural conflict is often brought about by a difference in values or beliefs.
3. **Ask** them the Literary Analysis question: How do Gideon and Teddy manage the differences in their social status to protect their vulnerable emotions?
   Answer: Gideon and Teddy treat each other with formality and politeness; they do not touch each other.

born the same time as Teddy, could be seen peering from the edge of the bush, staring in awe at the little white boy with his miraculous fair hair and Northern blue eyes. The two little children would gaze at each other with a wide, interested gaze, and once Teddy put out his hand curiously to touch the black child's cheeks and hair.

26

Reading Strategy
Analyze and Evaluate Similar Themes What cultural values do the Farquars and Gideon share?

Gideon, who was watching, shook his head wonderingly, and said: "Ah, missus, these are both children, and one will grow up to be a baas, and one will be a servant"; and Mrs. Farquar smiled and said sadly, "Yes, Gideon, I was thinking the same." She sighed. "It is God's will," said Gideon, who was a mission boy. The Farquars were very religious people; and this shared feeling about God bound servant and masters even closer together.

Teddy was about six years old when he was given a scooter, and discovered the intoxications of speed. All day he would fly around the homestead, in and out of flowerbeds, scattering squawking chickens and irritated dogs, finishing with a wide dizzying arc into the kitchen door. There he would cry: "Gideon, look at me!" And Gideon would laugh and say: "very clever, Little Yellow Head." Gideon's youngest son, who was now a herdsboy, came especially up from the compound to see the scooter. He was afraid to come near it, but Teddy showed off in front of him. "Piccanin," shouted Teddy, "get out of my way!" And he raced in circles around the black child until he was frightened, and fled back to the bush.

"Why did you frighten him?" asked Gideon, gravely reproachful.[2]

Teddy said defiantly: "He's only a black boy," and laughed. Then, when Gideon turned away from him without speaking, his face fell. Very soon he slipped into the house and found an orange and brought it to Gideon, saying: "This is for you." He could not bring himself to say he was sorry; but he could not bear to lose Gideon's affection either. Gideon took the orange unwillingly and sighed. "Soon you will be going away to school, Little Yellow Head," he said wonderingly, "and then you will be grown up." He shook his head gently and said, "And that is how our lives go." He seemed to be putting a distance between himself and Teddy, not because of resentment, but in the way a person accepts something inevitable. The baby had lain in his arms and smiled up into his face: the tiny boy had swung from his shoulders and played with him by the hour. Now Gideon would not let his flesh touch the flesh of the white child. He was kind, but there was a grave formality in his voice that made Teddy pout and sulk away. Also, it made him into a man: with Gideon he was polite, and carried himself formally, and if he came into the kitchen to ask for something, it was in the way a white man uses toward a servant, expecting to be obeyed.

27

Literary Analysis
Cultural Conflict How do Gideon and Teddy manage the differences in their social status to protect their vulnerable emotions?

But on the day that Teddy came staggering into the kitchen with his fists to his eyes, shrieking with pain, Gideon dropped the pot full of hot soup that he was holding, rushed to the child, and forced aside

2. **reproachful** (ri prōch′ fəl) *adj.* expressing blame.

Enrichment: Investigating Health and Medicine

Folk Medicine

Long before people could obtain synthetic medicines from doctors, people all over the world relied on natural materials to battle illnesses or injuries. Aspirin contains salicylic acid, which relieves pain and reduces fever. Native Americans chewed willow bark for the same purpose. Some folk remedies use local plants or herbs for teas or poultices. Others combine minerals or animal products with plant matter to cure ailments.

Activity: Investigating Folk Remedies Have interested students use Internet and print resources to find information about natural medicines. They can learn about historic and promising new uses of plant materials for medical purposes. Suggest that they record their analyses in the **Enrichment: Investigating Health and Medicine** worksheet, ***Professional Development Guidebook,*** page 229.

his fingers. "A snake!" he exclaimed. Teddy had been on his scooter, and had come to a rest with his foot on the side of a big tub of plants. A treesnake, hanging by its tail from the roof, had spat full into his eyes. Mrs. Farquar came running when she heard the commotion. "He'll go blind," she sobbed, holding Teddy close against her. "Gideon,
28 he'll go blind!" Already the eyes, with perhaps half an hour's sight left in them, were swollen up to the size of fists: Teddy's small white face was distorted by great purple oozing protuberances.[3] Gideon said: "Wait a minute, missus, I'll get some medicine." He ran off into the bush.

Mrs. Farquar lifted the child into the house and bathed his eyes with permanganate.[4] She had scarcely heard Gideon's words; but when she saw that her remedies had no effect at all, and remembered how she had seen natives with no sight in their eyes, because of the spitting of a snake, she began to look for the return of her cook, remembering what she heard of the efficacy[5] of native herbs. She stood by the window, holding the terrified, sobbing little boy in her arms, and peered helplessly into the bush. It was not more than a few minutes before she saw Gideon come bounding back, and in his hand he held a plant.

"Do not be afraid, missus," said Gideon, "this will cure Little Yellow Head's eyes." He stripped the leaves from the plant, leaving a small white fleshy root. Without even washing it, he put the root in his mouth, chewed it vigorously, and then held the spittle there while he took the child forcibly from Mrs. Farquar. He gripped Teddy down
28 between his knees, and pressed the balls of his thumbs into the swollen eyes, so that the child screamed and Mrs. Farquar cried out in protest: "Gideon, Gideon!" But Gideon took no notice. He knelt over the writhing child, pushing back the puffy lids till chinks of eyeball showed, and then he spat hard, again and again, into first one eye, and then the other. He finally lifted Teddy gently into his mother's arms, and said: "His eyes will get better." But Mrs. Farquar was weeping with terror, and she could hardly thank him: it was impossible to believe that Teddy could keep his sight. In a couple of hours the swellings were gone: the eyes were inflamed and tender but Teddy could see. Mr. and Mrs. Farquar went to Gideon in the kitchen and thanked him over and over again. They felt helpless because of their gratitude: it seemed they could do nothing to express it. They gave Gideon presents for his wife and children, and a big increase in wages, but these things could not pay for Teddy's now completely cured eyes. Mrs. Farquar said: "Gideon, God chose you as an instrument for His goodness," and Gideon said: "Yes, missus, God is very good."

Now, when such a thing happens on a farm, it cannot be long before everyone hears of it. Mr. and Mrs. Farquar told their neighbors and the story was discussed from one end of the district to the other. The

---

3. **protuberances** (prō to͞o′ bər əns iz) *n.* bulges; swellings.
4. **permanganate** (pər maŋ′ gə nāt′) salt of permanganic acid.
5. **efficacy** (ef′ li kə sē) *n.* power to produce intended effects.

Reading Strategy
Analyze and Evaluate Similar Themes When Teddy is injured, what do the reactions of Mrs. Farquar and Gideon show about their cultural differences and similarities?

29 **Reading Check**
How is Teddy injured and who heals him?

28 Reading Strategy

Analyze and Evaluate Similar Themes

1. Direct students to read the bracketed passages.
2. Remind students that cultural differences and conflicts can be intensified by differences in customs and beliefs.
3. **Ask** students the Reading Strategy question: When Teddy is injured, what do the reactions of Mrs. Farquar and Gideon show about their cultural differences and similarities?
4. **Answer:** In this incident, Mrs. Farquar, the mistress of the house, is reduced to helplessness and tears, while Gideon, the servant, is the master of the situation. Both are afraid of the consequences of snake poison, but Gideon is confident that if he finds the plant remedy soon enough, he can save Teddy's sight.

29 Reading Check

Answer: A tree snake spat in his eyes. Gideon cures him with his knowledge of jungle medicine using native plants.

Differentiated Instruction for Universal Access

Strategy for Special-Needs Students
As students read the selection with guidance, have them identify some details that suggest differences between the Farquars and Gideon. Have students use a two-column chart to help them identify ways in which these differences result in cultural conflicts.

Strategy for Less Proficient Readers
Have students read the story with your guidance. Encourage students as they read to pay attention to the way in which the story is told in the third person. Ask them to consider Mrs. Farquar's perceptions of their family servant, Gideon. Tell them to write three diary entries for her, one from the day of the snakebite, one from the day of the scientist's visit, and one from years later, when Teddy is an adult.

30 Critical Viewing

Possible response: The cultivated farm area in the picture looks manicured and civilized, while the bush is open country filled with wild plants such as grasses, trees, vines, and shrubs.

30 ▶ **Critical Viewing**
How does the landscape in this picture contrast with the "bush" into which Gideon ventures for Teddy's medicine? **[Distinguish]**

bush is full of secrets. No one can live in Africa, or at least on the veld,[6] without learning very soon that there is an ancient wisdom of leaf and soil and season—and, too, perhaps most important of all, of the darker tracts of the human mind—which is the black man's heritage. Up and down the district people were telling anecdotes, reminding each other of things that had happened to them.

"But I saw it myself, I tell you. It was a puff-adder bite. The kaffir's[7] arm was swollen to the elbow, like a great shiny black bladder. He was groggy after half a minute. He was dying. Then suddenly a kaffir walked out of the bush with his hands full of green stuff. He smeared something on the place, and next day my boy was back at work, and all you could see was two small punctures in the skin."

This was the kind of tale they told. And, as always, with a certain amount of exasperation, because while all of them knew that in the

6. veld in South Africa, open grassy country, with few bushes and almost no trees.
7. kaffir's belonging to a black African; in South Africa, a contemptuous term.

Enrichment: Investigating Science

Ethnobotany
Most students know that botany is the scientific study of plants. The special area of botany that combines science with folk culture is ethnobotany. Specialists study the plant lore of a region or group of people and learn how they use plants for food, medicine, commerce, art, or other purposes. Unlike the scientist in the story, ethnobotanists are trained in botany and in anthropology, which enables them to respect the ancient lore and knowledge local people possess and to analyze their remedies scientifically.

Activity: Investigating Native Plant Lore Have students learn more about this exciting field. What do people in Africa, Central America, and South America have to teach us about herbal medicine and healing? Suggest that students record their analyses in the **Enrichment: Investigating Science** worksheet, ***Professional Development Guidebook,*** page 241.

bush of Africa are waiting valuable drugs locked in bark, in simple-looking leaves, in roots, it was impossible to ever get the truth about them from the natives themselves.

The story eventually reached town; and perhaps it was at a sundowner party, or some such function, that a doctor, who happened to be there, challenged it. "Nonsense," he said. "These things get exaggerated in the telling. We are always checking up on this kind of story, and we draw a blank every time."

Anyway, one morning there arrived a strange car at the homestead, and out stepped one of the workers from the laboratory in town, with cases full of test-tubes and chemicals.

Mr. and Mrs. Farquar were flustered and pleased and flattered. They asked the scientist to lunch, and they told the story all over again, for the hundredth time. Little Teddy was there too, his blue eyes sparkling with health, to prove the truth of it. The scientist explained how humanity might benefit if this new drug could be offered for sale; and the Farquars were even more pleased: they were kind, simple people, who liked to think of something good coming about because of them. But when the scientist began talking of the money that might result, their manner showed discomfort. Their feelings over the miracle (that was how they thought of it) were so strong and deep and religious, that it was distasteful to them to think of money. The scientist, seeing their faces, went back to his first point, which was the advancement of humanity. He was perhaps a trifle perfunctory:[8] it was not the first time he had come salting the tail of a fabulous bush secret.[9]

Eventually, when the meal was over, the Farquars called Gideon into their living room and explained to him that this baas, here, was a Big Doctor from the Big City, and he had come all that way to see Gideon. At this Gideon seemed afraid; he did not understand; and Mrs. Farquar explained quickly that it was because of the wonderful thing he had done with Teddy's eyes that the Big Baas had come.

Gideon looked from Mrs. Farquar to Mr. Farquar, and then at the little boy, who was showing great importance because of the occasion. At last he said grudgingly:[10] "The Big Baas want to know what medicine I used?" He spoke

8. **perfunctory** (pər fuŋk′ tə rē) *adj.* done without care or interest.
9. **salting . . . bush secret** allusion to the humororus and ironic advice given to children about how to catch a bird—by putting salt on its tail. In other words, the scientist does not really expect to capture a valuable bit of information.
10. **grudgingly** (gruj′ ing ly) adv. in a reluctant manner

31 LITERATURE IN CONTEXT

Colonial Rhodesia

Starting in the 1400s, Southern Rhodesia was ruled by a series of Shona empires. British exploitation of the area began in the late 1800s, when Cecil Rhodes brought the British South Africa Company to mine gold there, crushing outbursts of violent resistance by the local peoples. White Rhodesians voted to become a British colony in 1922.

In 1965, Rhodesia declared independence from Britain, and in 1969 a new constitution ensured that the black majority would never rule the country. It was only in the 1970s, after years of civil war, that blacks were granted equal rights. In 1980, Rhodesia became officially independent, changing its name to Zimbabwe ("house of stone"), the name of an ancient Shona city.

Connect to the Literature

In what ways might the relationship between the Farquars and Gideon differ had the story been set after 1980?

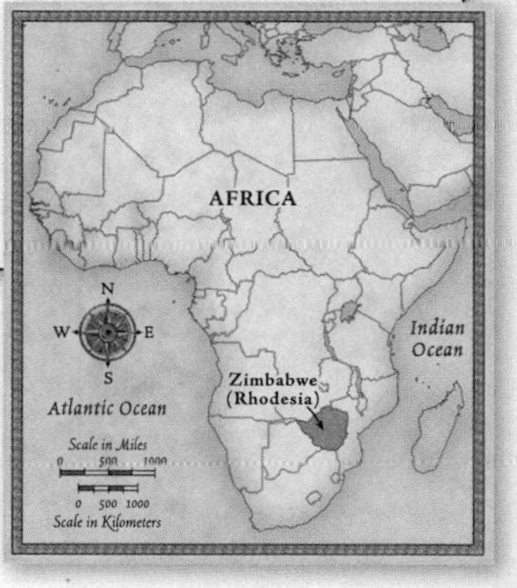

32 Reading Check

Why does the scientist visit the Farquars?

31 Literature in Context

Colonial Rhodesia

Cecil Rhodes (1853–1902) studied at Oxford University and built his fortune at the diamond mines in Kimberley, South Africa, before becoming a statesman of the British colony there. He was prime minister of Cape Colony from 1890 but resigned this post after being found guilty of a breach of duty for an unauthorized raid on Transvaal, the Dutch-controlled part of the region. Rhodes is famous today for the Rhodes scholarships he endowed at Oxford for students of the colonies, America, and Germany. Many Rhodes scholars have held important political posts, such as former President Bill Clinton and former New Jersey Governor Bill Bradley.

Connect to the Literature

1. **Ask** students to list reasons why governments are overthrown.
   Possible responses: tyranny, hunger, grinding poverty, interracial tensions, dissatisfaction with an existing government without a way to make needed changes peacefully
2. Then, **ask** the Connect to the Literature question: In what ways might the relationship between the Farquars and Gideon differ had the story been set after 1980?
   Possible responses: Some students may believe Gideon and the Farquars could become better friends and make a greater effort to understand each other's point of view since they would both be equal in the eyes of the law. Others may think that the native people will now be free to voice their anger over years of oppression.

32 Reading Check

Answer: The scientist visits the Farquars to inquire about selling the medicine from the root Gideon used to cure Teddy's eyes.

Differentiated Instruction for Universal Access

Support for Special-Needs Students
Have students read the story with your guidance. Remind them to pay attention to the characters and their conflicts as they read. Encourage them to read multiple times sections that give them difficulty.

EL Support for English Learners
English learners may find this story especially relevant, because they have no doubt encountered their own cultural conflicts as they have been learning a new language. Ask students to comment on the cultural conflicts in the story and suggest ways the conflicts could have been resolved.

Enrichment for Advanced Readers
Students may find the current interest in herbal remedies an interesting topic to pursue. Encourage them to prepare reports on herbal medicines—both traditional and experimental.

❸❸ Literary Analysis

Cultural Conflict

1. **Ask** students to compare Gideon's reaction with the Farquars' initial reaction to the scientist's proposal that Gideon tell him about the medicine he used to cure Teddy.
   Answer: The Farquars are pleased to think that the benefits of a new drug might come about because of them; Gideon feels personally betrayed.
2. Then, **ask** students: How is the way the Farquars react to the scientist's offer of money similar to Gideon's reaction to their request?
   Possible response: Both the Farquars and Gideon feel discomfort with the idea of sharing the healing secrets for profit. Gideon becomes hostile when the scientist offers him presents.

Spiral Review

Social Criticism

Ask students the Spiral Review question.

Possible response: Gideon's reaction shows that the conflict between cultures is costly to both: white Rhodesians denied effective drugs and treatments; African healing skills remain largely unused.

❸❹ Literary Analysis

Irony

1. Remind students that irony often involves the unexpected. **Ask:** What do the Farquars find unexpected about Gideon's behavior?
   Answer: Gideon, who is generally friendly, becomes angry and stubborn.
2. Then, **ask** the Literary Analysis question.
   Possible response: Gideon seems to agree to take them to find the root, but his behavior in walking them through the bush for more than two hours, when he had returned within minutes with the cure, shows that he does not intend to share his healing knowledge.

Vocabulary
incredulously (in krej′ oo ləs lē) *adv.* with doubt or disbelief

Vocabulary
skeptical (skep′ ti kəl) *adj.* doubting

Spiral Review
Social Criticism In this portrayal of Gideon's reaction, what point might the author be making about relations between those who ruled Rhodesia and those whom they excluded from power?

Literary Analysis
Irony Why is Gideon's statement, "I will show you the root," an example of verbal irony?

incredulously, as if he could not believe his old friends could so betray him. Mr. Farquar began explaining how a useful medicine could be made out of the root, and how it could be put on sale, and how thousands of people, black and white, up and down the continent of Africa, could be saved by the medicine when that spitting snake filled their eyes with poison. Gideon listened, his eyes bent on the ground, the skin of his forehead puckering in discomfort. When Mr. Farquar had finished he did not reply. The scientist, who all this time had been leaning back in a big chair, sipping his coffee and smiling with skeptical good humor, chipped in and explained all over again, in different words, about the making of drugs and the progress of science. Also, he offered Gideon a present.

There was silence after this further explanation, and then Gideon remarked indifferently that he could not remember the root. His face was sullen and hostile, even when he looked at the Farquars, whom he usually treated like old friends. They were beginning to feel annoyed; and this feeling annulled[11] the guilt that had been sprung into life by Gideon's accusing manner. They were beginning to feel that he was unreasonable. But it was at that moment that they all realized he would never give in. The magical drug would remain where it was, unknown and useless except for the tiny scattering of Africans who had the knowledge, natives who might be digging a ditch for the municipality in a ragged shirt and a pair of patched shorts, but who were still born to healing, hereditary healers, being the nephews or sons of the old witch doctors whose ugly masks and bits of bone and all the uncouth[12] properties of magic were the outward signs of real power and wisdom.

The Farquars might tread on that plant fifty times a day as they passed from house to garden, from cow kraal to mealie field, but they would never know it.

But they went on persuading and arguing, with all the force of their exasperation; and Gideon continued to say that he could not remember, or that there was no such root, or that it was the wrong season of the year, or that it wasn't the root itself, but the spit from his mouth that had cured Teddy's eyes. He said all these things one after another, and seemed not to care they were contradictory. He was rude and stubborn. The Farquars could hardly recognize their gentle, lovable old servant in this ignorant, perversely obstinate African, standing there in front of them with lowered eyes, his hands twitching his cook's apron, repeating over and over whichever one of the stupid refusals that first entered his head.

And suddenly he appeared to give in. He lifted his head, gave a long blank angry look at the circle of whites, who seemed to him like a circle of yelping dogs pressing around him, and said: "I will show you the root."

They walked single file away from the homestead down a kaffir path. It was a blazing December afternoon, with the sky full of hot

11. **annulled** (ə nuld′) *v.* did away with; neutralized.
12. **uncouth** (un ko͞oth′) *adj.* uncultured; crude; strange.

Vocabulary Development

Vocabulary Knowledge Rating

When students have completed reading and discussing the selection, have them take out their **Vocabulary Knowledge Rating Charts** for the story. Read the words aloud and have students rate their knowledge of words again in the After Reading column. Clarify any words that are still problematic. Have students write their own definitions and example or sentence in the appropriate column. Then, have students complete the Vocabulary Practice at the end of the selection. Encourage students to use the words in further discussion and written work about the selection. Remind them that they will be accountable for these words on the ***Selection Test, Unit 6 Resources,*** pages 204–206 or 207–209.

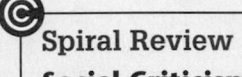

rain clouds. Everything was hot: the sun was like a bronze tray whirling overhead, there was a heat shimmer over the fields, the soil was scorching underfoot, the dusty wind blew gritty and thick and warm in their faces. It was a terrible day, fit only for reclining on a verandah with iced drinks, which is where they would normally have been at that hour.

34 From time to time, remembering that on the day of the snake it had taken ten minutes to find the root, someone asked: "Is it much further, Gideon?" And Gideon would answer over his shoulder, with angry politeness: "I'm looking for the root, baas." And indeed, he would frequently bend sideways and trail his hand among the grasses with a gesture that was insulting in its perfunctoriness. He walked them through the bush along unknown paths for two hours, in that melting destroying heat, so that the sweat trickled coldly down them and their heads ached. They were all quite silent: the Farquars because they were angry, the scientist because he was being proved right again; there was no such plant. His was a tactful silence.

At last, six miles from the house, Gideon suddenly decided they had had enough; or perhaps his anger evaporated at that moment. He picked up, without an attempt at looking anything but casual, a handful of blue flowers from the grass, flowers that had been growing plentifully all down the paths they had come.

He handed them to the scientist without looking at him, and marched off by himself on the way home, leaving them to follow him if they chose.

When they got back to the house, the scientist went to the kitchen to thank Gideon: he was being very polite, even though there was an amused look in his eyes. Gideon was not there. Throwing the flowers casually into the back of his car, the eminent visitor departed on his way back to his laboratory.

Gideon was back in his kitchen in time to prepare dinner, but he was sulking. He spoke to Mr. Farquar like an unwilling servant. It was days before they liked each other again.

The Farquars made inquiries about the root from their laborers. Sometimes they were answered with distrustful stares. Sometimes the natives said: "We do not know. We have never heard of the root." One, the cattle boy, who had been with them a long time, and had grown to trust them

35 ▼ Critical Viewing
Is this the way you pictured the landscape through which Gideon led the Farquars and the scientist? Explain. **[Relate]**

36 Reading Check
What does Gideon give the scientist?

35 Critical Viewing

Possible responses: Yes, I believed it would be fairly flat grassland with scrub grass under a baking hot sun; No, I thought it would look more like a jungle with heavy, thick plant growth.

36 Reading Check

Answer: Gideon gives the scientist a handful of blue flowers just like those that grew along the paths they had traveled for about two hours.

Differentiated Instruction for Universal Access

EL Pronunciation for English Learners

Direct students' attention to line 32 on page 1334. English learners may be uncertain about the correct way to pronounce the word *exasperation.* Tell students that the word means the same thing as "aggravation." Explain that the word has five syllables. Point out that the *ex-* at the beginning of this word has the same sound (ig) as the beginning sound in the words *example, exact,* or *exhaust.* Tell students that other words with the *ex-* spelling are pronounced with the letter (x) sound as in *exchange, extra,* or *export.* Still other *ex-* words are pronounced with the (iks) sound, as in *exposure* and *express.* Model the pronunciation of each word, with students repeating the words after you. Have fluent speakers help English learners discriminate among the sounds in the given words. Then return to the word from the selection, having them pronounce the word again.

ASSESS

Answers

Before students respond, you may wish to have them write a brief objective summary of the selection. As they answer the questions below, remind them to support their answers with evidence from the text.

1. (a) Gideon gives him his nickname when his hair is cut. (b) At first, "Little Yellow Head" is a term of affection. As Teddy grows, the term brings sadness at the loss of innocence and reinforces the fact that Gideon and Teddy have vastly different lives and positions in colonial society.
2. (a) Gideon uses a folk remedy to save his sight. (b) The incident reveals to the Farquars that Gideon has knowledge that is useful to their existence and well-being.
3. (a) When the scientist tries to get Gideon to reveal his secret, the Farquars do not understand Gideon's reluctance; that misunderstanding forces a wedge into their otherwise amicable relationship. (b) **Possible response:** He refuses to share his knowledge because it is part of his family's tradition, and not something to be shared with outsiders.
4. Gideon realizes that very soon Teddy will become a white master over the other black servants.
5. **Possible responses:** Yes, Gideon should hold his heritage with respect; no, he should pass on his knowledge to help other people.
6. **Possible responses:** This story suggests that some people *respond* to cultural differences by trying to bridge the differences with a sense of *humor,* while others use irony and sarcasm to protect the *integrity* of their culture. Ensure that students use at least three of the Essential Question words in their responses.

a little, said: "Ask your boy in the kitchen. Now, there's a doctor for you. He's the son of a famous medicine man who used to be in these parts, and there's nothing he cannot cure." Then he added politely: "Of course, he's not as good as the white man's doctor, we know that, but he's good for us."

After some time, when the soreness had gone from between the Farquars and Gideon, they began to joke: "When are you going to show us the snake-root, Gideon?" And he would laugh and shake his head, saying, a little uncomfortably: "But I did show you, missus, have you forgotten?"

Much later, Teddy, as a schoolboy, would come into the kitchen and say: "You old rascal, Gideon! Do you remember that time you tricked us all by making us walk miles all over the veld for nothing? It was so far my father had to carry me!"

And Gideon would double up with polite laughter. After much laughing, he would suddenly straighten himself up, wipe his old eyes, and look sadly at Teddy, who was grinning mischievously at him across the kitchen: "Ah, Little Yellow Head, how you have grown! Soon you will be grown up with a farm of your own . . ."

Cite textual evidence to support your responses.

Critical Reading

1. **Key Ideas and Details (a)** What is Teddy's nickname and how does he get it? **(b) Infer:** How does this nickname emphasize the differences between the Farquars and their servants?
2. **Key Ideas and Details (a)** How does Gideon save Teddy's sight? **(b) Interpret:** In what way does this incident reveal an aspect of Gideon previously unknown to the Farquars?
3. **Key Ideas and Details (a) Analyze:** What effect does the scientist's visit have on the Farquars' relationship with Gideon? **(b) Draw Conclusions:** Why does Gideon refuse to share his knowledge?
4. **Key Ideas and Details** What do Gideon's last words to Teddy mean?
5. **Integration of Knowledge and Ideas** Do you think Gideon's decision to withhold information about the plant is justified? Explain.
6. **Integration of Knowledge and Ideas** What insights do Orwell's essay and Lessing's story provide into how people deal with cultural differences? Use three of these Essential Question words in your answer: *differentiate, respond, acquiesce, integrity, understanding, humor.* ***[Connecting to the Essential Question: How does literature shape or reflect society?]***

Concept Connector

Reading Strategy Graphic Organizer

Ask students to review the graphic organizers in which they have listed the details that lead to cultural conflict. Then, have students share their organizers and compare the details and sources of conflict they have identified.

Activating Prior Knowledge

Have students return to their responses to the Activating Prior Knowledge activity. Ask them to explain whether their thoughts have changed and, if so, how.

Writing About the Essential Question

Have students compare their responses to the prompt, completed before reading the stories, with their thoughts afterward. Have them work individually or in groups, writing or discussing their thoughts, to formulate new responses. Then, lead a class discussion, probing for what students have learned that confirms or invalidates their initial thoughts. Encourage students to cite specific textual details to support their responses.

After You Read

Shooting an Elephant • *No Witchcraft for Sale*

Literary Analysis

1. **Key Ideas and Details** **Cultural conflict** often results when individuals or groups do not share a basic value or attitude with another individual or group. Use a chart like the one shown to identify the values in conflict in these selections.

What Orwell does not share with the Burmese	What the Burmese do not share with Orwell

What Gideon does not share with the Farquars	What the Farquars do not share with Gideon

2. **Key Ideas and Details** Refusal to betray values, traditions, or even history often causes cultural conflict. Gideon "could not believe his old friends could so betray him." Explain how Orwell, Gideon, and the Farquars all try to avoid some kind of betrayal.
3. **Key Ideas and Details** **Situational irony** results when expectations are not met. **(a)** Identify an example of situational irony in each of these selections. **(b)** What point of view about cultural conflict is revealed by each author's use of irony?
4. **Craft and Structure** Lessing builds **verbal irony** into the title of her story. Why is the title ironic?
5. **Integration of Knowledge and Ideas** Orwell conveys the theme of cultural conflict through nonfiction, Lessing through fiction. Which type of writing do you think suits the theme better? Why?

Common Core State Standards

Writing
2. Write informative/explanatory texts to examine and convey complex ideas, concepts, and information clearly and accurately through the effective selection, organization, and analysis of content. *(p. 1338)*
2.d. Use precise language, domain-specific vocabulary, and techniques such as metaphor, simile, and analogy to manage the complexity of the topic. *(p. 1338)*

Language
4.a. Use context as a clue to the meaning of a word or phrase. *(p. 1338)*

Reading Strategy

6. "Shooting an Elephant" and "No Witchcraft for Sale" offer an opportunity to **analyze and evaluate similar themes. (a)** How does Orwell's cultural background determine his actions against the elephant? **(b)** How does Gideon's cultural background determine his actions with the medicinal plant?
7. Cultural norms are sometimes contrary to what some people consider common sense. **(a)** In what way could common sense have solved Orwell's cultural conflict? **(b)** How could common sense have solved the conflict between Gideon and the Farquars?
8. Evaluate the degrees of success in resolving cultural conflict that is shown in these two selections. Who, in your opinion, does the best job—Orwell, Gideon, or the Farquars? Give reasons for your evaluation.

Assessment Practice

Analyze and Evaluate (For more practice, see *All-in-One Workbook*.)

Many tests require that students apply revision strategies to given passages. Use the following sample item to give students practice with this skill.

As soon as I saw the elephant, I knew with perfect certainty that I ought not to shoot him. It is a serious matter to shoot a working elephant–comparable to destroying a costly piece of machinery–and obviously one ought not do it if it can possibly be avoided.

To add more information, which of the following sentences would be suitable?

A This is clearly a working elephant. I had to figure out a way to avoid shooting it.
B I wished I had brought more ammunition.
C Elephants must reproduce.
D The elephant flapped its ears slowly.

Lead students to see that the correct answer is ***A***.

Answers

1. **Possible responses:** Orwell: his hatred for the imperial system; the Burmese: the best way to kill the elephant without causing him to suffer; Gideon: his native healing knowledge; Farquars: belief that white civilization is superior.
2. Orwell refuses to betray his duty as a police officer; the Farquars refuse to betray their position in colonial society; Gideon refuses to betray the trust given him by his teachers in native healing arts.
3. (a) Orwell is a minor colonial administrator, yet his actions are controlled by the Burmese; Gideon takes the Europeans on a two-hour trek through the bush looking for a root he found within minutes before. (b) The colonists represent the ruling class, so natives see them not as individuals but as members of their class/white society.
4. Lessing's title of "No Witchcraft for Sale" refers to Gideon's refusal to sell out his beliefs and values to someone who does not show proper respect for his healing tradition.
5. **Possible responses:** Nonfiction can use real examples of cultural conflict; fiction can use characters' thoughts and feelings to reveal conflicts in beliefs and values.
6. (a) Orwell's cultural background puts him in a position of authority, so in order not to appear foolish he shoots the elephant, even though he thinks it is too valuable to kill. (b) Gideon's cultural position as a tribal medicine man dictates that he not betray their secrets to outsiders.
7. (a) Instead of giving in to the crowd's frenzied excitement, Orwell could have sent for the elephant's mahout to control the animal. (b) Instead of demanding obedience, the Farquars could have treated Gideon as a friend and asked him to explain.
8. **Possible response:** Gideon does the best job because he is true to his personal beliefs and values and yet is able to accept a changed relationship with Teddy based on their differing roles in colonial society.

EXTEND/ASSESS

Answers

Vocabulary Acquisition and Use

1. Introduce the skill.
2. Have students complete the Word Analysis Activity and the Vocabulary Practice.

Word Analysis

1. colonialism—a government system based on sending a group of people to another place and gaining control of the land and resources, while authority remains in the hands of the home country; etymology from the Latin *colonus,* or "farmer"
2. democracy—a government based on a written constitution with written laws made by representatives elected by the people; etymology from the Greek *demokratia,* or "government of the people"
3. communism—a government system based on shared ownership of goods and the means of production; etymology from the Latin *commitat* for "community"

Vocabulary

1. skeptical; means doubtful
2. reverently; honor what you respect
3. despotic; a despot is cruel
4. dominion; control is to dominate
5. incredulously; refers to disbelief
6. imperialism; refers to empire

Writing

1. To give students guidance for writing this explanatory text, give them the **Support for Writing** page from ***Unit 6 Resources*** (p. 199).
2. Read with students the writing lesson on this page. Tell them to write a problem-solution essay offering a solution to either the conflict faced by Orwell or the one between Gideon and the Farquars.
3. Encourage students to formulate their ideas and solutions by outlining the conflicts precisely.
4. Use the **Rubrics for Problem-Solution Essay,** ***Professional Development Guidebook,*** pages 270–271, to evaluate students' work.

PERFORMANCE TASKS

Integrated Language Skills

Vocabulary Acquisition and Use

Word Analysis: Etymology of Political Science and History Terms

The etymology—the word origin—of a political science or history term is often tied to social and political events in the distant past. A powerful leader, an economic program, a war, a migration—all can give birth to words that enter the language and remain current.

For example, in the nineteenth century, when the British Empire was flourishing, the policy of *imperialism* was taken for granted. *Imperialism* derives from the Latin word for empire, *imperium.* Someone who supported such a policy of domination of weaker countries was an *imperialist.*

Write the definition of each of the following political science or history terms. Then, check each word in a dictionary to determine its etymology.

1. colonialism
2. democracy
3. communism

Vocabulary: Contexual Meaning

Select the word from the list on page 1316 that best completes each sentence. Use the meaning of the context to support your choice.

1. The scientist was _______ about the plant's medicinal value; he doubted it would work.
2. She handled the delicate sculpture _______ in honor of the brilliant artist who had made it.
3. His cruel and _______ behavior included imprisoning all his political opponents.
4. They controlled everything, and their _______ stretched from the river in the east to the mountains in the west.
5. He replied _______ because he could not believe the responses that he was hearing.
6. The effects of empire-building can still be seen in those countries that survived centuries of _______.

Writing

Explanatory Text In "Shooting an Elephant," Orwell must perform a violent act that he does not want to perform. In "No Witchcraft for Sale," the Farquars cannot understand Gideon's uncooperativeness, and he feels betrayed by them. In an **essay,** offer a solution to one of these problems.

Prewriting Reread both selections, jotting down details that both clarify the problems and suggest possible solutions.

Drafting In the introductory paragraph, state the problem accurately, identifying the causes of the problem and touching on your proposed solution. In the body of your essay, elaborate on your proposed solution, offering evidence that it will work and connecting it with the problem. Support your discussion of the problem and the solution with *accurate and detailed references* to the text.

Revising Be sure that you provide the possible effects of your proposed solution. Also, make sure that you have used precise language to clarify the causes of the problem.

Model: Identify the Causes of the Problem

Orwell's **problem is caused by** his position of authority conflicting with his personal beliefs. His position forces him to wear a "mask" and be something he is not. **As a result,** he faces the conflict of either sacrificing his authority or compromising his beliefs.

Precise language clarifies the sources of a problem.

Assessment Resources

Unit 6 Resources

L1 L2 EL **Selection Test A,** pp. 204–206. Administer Test A to less advanced readers.

L3 L4 EL **Selection Test B,** pp. 207–209. Administer Test B to on-level students and more advanced students.

L3 L4 **Open-Book Test,** pp. 201–203. As an alternative, give the Open-Book test.

All **Customizable Test Bank**

All **Self-tests**
Students may prepare for the **Selection Test** by taking the **Self-test** online.

PHLit Online! All assessment resources are available at **www.PHLitOnline.com.**

Conventions and Style: Variety in Sentence Beginnings

To avoid monotony in your sentences, use a variety of structures, lengths, and beginnings.

You can vary the beginnings of your sentences in a number of ways. The following chart illustrates a variety of sentence beginnings.

Subject	The elephant destroyed a hut, a cow, and a van in its rage.
Prepositional phrase	In its rage, the elephant destroyed a hut, a cow, and a van.
Participle	Enraged, the elephant destroyed a hut, a cow, and a van.
Adverb	Angrily, the elephant destroyed a hut, a cow, and a van.
Infinitive	To shoot the elephant was not what Orwell wanted to do.
Subordinate clause	As the elephant raged through the town, it destroyed a hut, a cow, and a van.

You may also invert normal sentence order so that the verb comes before the subject.

Normal Order (subject before verb): The elephant was eating grass in the field.

Inverted Order: There was the elephant eating grass in the field.

Practice Rewrite each sentence to begin with the item indicated in parentheses.

1. With gifts of chickens and flowers, the servants showed their delight in the baby. (subject)
2. Teddy, laughing, enjoyed being tossed in the air in play. (participle)
3. Respected and loved, Gideon was a valued servant. (subject)
4. Teddy sped around the homestead riding his scooter. (participle)
5. Shrieking with pain, Teddy staggered into the kitchen. (subject)
6. The plants held valuable secrets in their leaves, roots, and bark. (prepositional phrase)
7. A wind was blowing grit in their faces. (inverted order)
8. Gideon said he didn't remember to avoid answering the questions. (infinitive)
9. The crowd yelled loudly and laughed at Orwell. (adverb)
10. The crowd was behind as he pursued the elephant. (subordinate clause)

Writing and Speaking Conventions

A. Writing Write sentences beginning with the following words or phrases.

1. With insults **2.** Gideon **3.** Followed
4. As he had always done **5.** Carefully

Example: With insults
Sentence: With insults, the fans showed their dislike of the English.

B. Speaking Think of a conflict between two groups that you have read or heard about. Write and present to the class a headline and a brief news story to explain the conflict. Use at least three different kinds of sentence beginnings and one sentence with inverted order.

PH WRITING COACH
Further instruction and practice are available in *Prentice Hall Writing Coach.*

Extend the Lesson

Sentence Modeling

Display these sentences from the selections:

As for the job I was doing, I hated it more bitterly than I can make clear. (Orwell, "Shooting an Elephant")

Throwing the flowers casually into the back of his car, the eminent visitor departed on his way back to his laboratory. (Lessing, "No Witchcraft for Sale")

Finally, I fired my two remaining shots into the spot where I thought his heart must be. (Orwell, "Shooting an Elephant")

Ask students what they notice about the sentences. Elicit from them that they show ways to vary sentence structure. Then, ask what else they notice. (The first starts with a prepositional phrase, the second uses a participial phrase, and the third uses an adverb.)

Have students imitate the sentences in topics of their own choosing, matching each grammatical and stylistic feature discussed. Collect the sentences and share them with the class.

Conventions and Style

1. Introduce and discuss the skill, using the instruction on the student page.
2. Have students complete the Practice.

Practice

1. The servants showed their delight in the baby with gifts of chickens and flowers. (subject)
2. Laughing, Teddy enjoyed being tossed in the air in play. (participle)
3. Gideon was respected and loved as a valued servant. (subject)
4. Riding, Teddy sped around the homestead on his scooter. (participle)
5. Teddy, shrieking with pain, staggered into the kitchen. (subject)
6. In their leaves, roots, and bark, the plants held valuable secrets. (prepositional phrase)
7. There was a powerful wind blowing grit in their faces. (invert order)
8. To avoid answering the questions, Gideon said he did not remember. (infinitive)
9. Loudly, the crowd yelled and laughed at Orwell. (adverb)
10. As he pursued the elephant, the crowd followed behind. (subordinate clause)

Writing and Speaking Conventions

A. **Possible responses:**

1. With insults, they hooted at Orwell as he went past.
2. Gideon refused to share his knowledge of plants.
3. Followed by the crowd, Orwell checked the damage.
4. As he had always done, Teddy began to joke about the trek through the bush.
5. Carefully, he walked toward the huge beast.

B. Ensure that student responses use at least three kinds of sentence beginnings and one with inverted order.

PH WRITING COACH Grade 12

Further instruction on and practice with expository writing can be found in chapter 8.

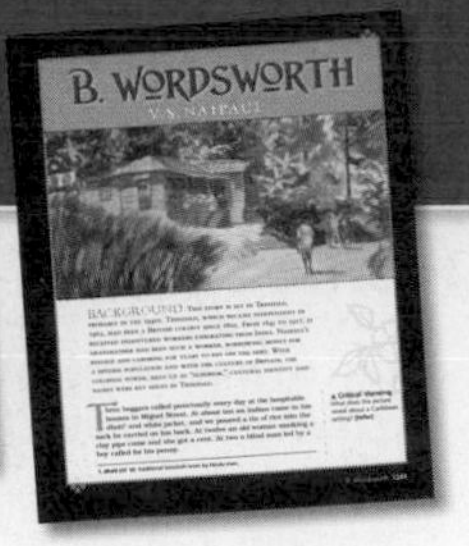

The Train from Rhodesia • B. Wordsworth
Lesson Pacing Guide

DAY 1 Preteach

- Administer the Reading and Vocabulary Warm-ups (*Unit 6 Resources*, pp. 228–231) as necessary.
- Introduce the Literary Analysis concept: Historical Period.
- Introduce the Reading Strategy: Apply Knowledge of Historical Background.
- Build background with the author and Background features.
- Develop thematic thinking with Connecting to the Essential Question.
- Teach the selection vocabulary.

DAYS 2–3 Preteach/Teach/Assess

- Distribute copies of the appropriate graphic organizer for the Reading Strategy (*Graphic Organizer Transparencies*, pp. 244–245).
- Distribute copies of the appropriate graphic organizer for Literary Analysis (*Graphic Organizer Transparencies*, pp. 246–247).
- Prepare students to read with the Activating Prior Knowledge activities (TE).
- Informally monitor comprehension while students read.
- Use the Reading Check questions to confirm comprehension.
- Develop students' understanding of historical period using the Literary Analysis prompts.
- Develop students' ability to apply knowledge of historical background using the Reading Strategy prompts.
- Reinforce vocabulary with the Vocabulary notes.
- Assess students' comprehension and mastery of the skills by having them answer the Critical Reading, Literary Analysis, and Reading Strategy questions.
- Have students complete the Vocabulary Lesson.

DAY 4 Extend/Assess

- Have students complete the Writing Lesson and write a biographical sketch. (You may assign as homework.)
- Administer Selection Test A or B (*Unit 6 Resources,* pp. 222–224 or 225–227).

Common Core State Standards

Reading Literature 1. Cite strong and thorough textual evidence to support analysis of what the text says explicitly as well as inferences drawn from the text, including determining where the text leaves matters uncertain.

Writing 3. Write narratives to develop real or imagined experiences or events using effective technique, well-chosen details, and well-structured event sequences.
3.d. Use precise words and phrases, telling details, and sensory language to convey a vivid picture of the experiences, events, setting, and/or characters.

Language 4.b. Identify and correctly use patterns of word changes that indicate different meanings or parts of speech.

Additional Standards Practice
Common Core Companion, pp. 208–218; 326–327

Daily Block Scheduling

Each day in this Lesson Pacing Guide represents a 40–50 minute period. Teachers using block scheduling may combine days to revise pacing. In addition, teachers may differentiate and support core instruction by integrating components for extended and intensive support as students require. See the Guide to Selected Leveled Resources (facing page).

Guide to Selected Leveled Resources

RTI Tier 1 (students performing on level)

			The Train from Rhodesia • B. Wordsworth
Warm Up	Whole class instruction; Group work	**Practice, model,** and **monitor** fluency, working **with the whole class** or **in groups.**	Vocabulary and Reading Warm-ups B, *Unit 6 Resources,* pp. 228–229, 231
Comprehension/Skills	Whole class instruction; Group work; Independent work	**Support** and **monitor** comprehension and skills development, having students complete the activities, graphic organizers, and interactive prompts **independently** or **as a class.**	• ***Reader's Notebook,*** adapted instruction and full selection EL ***Reader's Notebook: English Learner's Version,*** adapted instruction and adapted selection • **Reading Strategy Graphic Organizer B, *Graphic Organizer Transparencies,*** p. 259 • **Literary Analysis Graphic Organizer B, *Graphic Organizer Transparencies,*** p. 261
Monitor Progress	A	**Monitor** student progress with the differentiated curriculum-based assessment in the *Unit Resources.*	• **Selection Test B, *Unit 6 Resources,*** pp. 243–245 • **Open-Book Test, *Unit 6 Resources,*** pp. 237–239

RTI Tier 2 (students requiring intervention)

			The Train from Rhodesia • B. Wordsworth
Warm Up	Group work; One-on-one teaching	**Practice, model,** and **monitor** fluency **in groups** or **with individuals.**	• **Vocabulary and Reading Warm-ups A, *Unit 6 Resources,*** pp. 228–230 • ***Hear It!* Audio CD (adapted text)**
Comprehension/Skills	Group work; One-on-one teaching	• **Support** and **monitor** comprehension and skills development, working **in small groups** or **with individuals.** • As students complete the selection in the appropriate version of the *Reader's Notebook,* **monitor** comprehension frequently with group questions and individual instruction. • **Model** strategies while guiding students in completing the activities and prompts in the *Reader's Notebook,* as well as the graphic organizers. • **Practice** skills and **monitor** mastery with the *Reading Kit* worksheets.	• ***Reader's Notebook: Adapted Version,*** adapted instruction and adapted selection EL ***Reader's Notebook: English Learner's Version,*** adapted instruction and adapted selection • **Reading Strategy Graphic Organizer A, *Graphic Organizer Transparencies,*** p. 258 • **Literary Analysis Graphic Organizer A, *Graphic Organizer Transparencies,*** p. 260 • ***Reading Kit,*** Practice worksheets
Monitor Progress	A	**Monitor** student progress with the differentiated curriculum-based assessment in the *Unit Resources* and in the *Reading Kit.*	• **Selection Test A, *Unit 6 Resources,*** pp. 240–242 • ***Reading Kit,*** Assess worksheets

TIER 3 Tier 3 intervention may require consultation with the student's special-education or dyslexia specialist. For additional support, see the Tier 2 activities and resources listed above.

One-on-one teaching | Group work | Whole class instruction | Independent work | A Assessment

For a complete guide to selection support, including support for Advanced students, see the Overview of Resources in the frontmatter.

COMMON CORE
Visual Guide to Featured Selection Resources

The Train from Rhodesia • B. Wordsworth

RESOURCES FOR:

- L1 Special-Needs Students
- L2 Below-Level Students (Tier 2)
- L3 On-Level Students (Tier 1)
- L4 Advanced Students (Tier 1)
- EL English Learners
- All All Students

Vocabulary/Fluency/Prior Knowledge

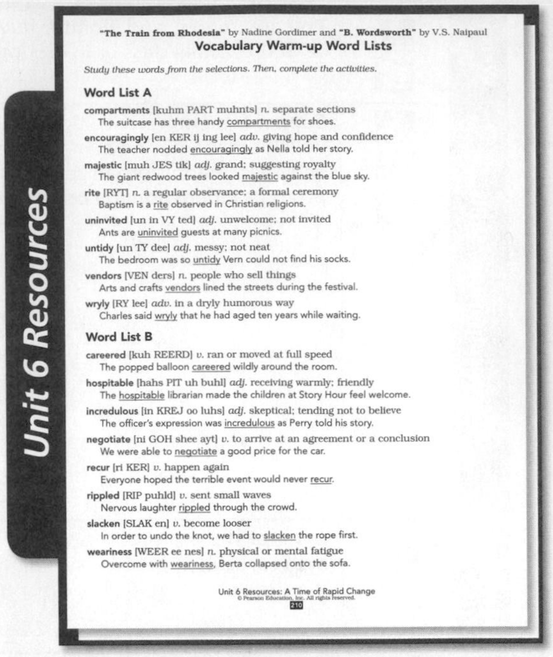

Unit 6 Resources

"The Train from Rhodesia" by Nadine Gordimer and "B. Wordsworth" by V.S. Naipaul

Vocabulary Warm-up Word Lists

Study these words from the selections. Then, complete the activities.

Word List A

compartments [kuhm PART muhnts] *n.* separate sections
The suitcase has three handy compartments for shoes.

encouragingly [en KER ij ing lee] *adv.* giving hope and confidence
The teacher nodded encouragingly as Nella told her story.

majestic [muh JES tik] *adj.* grand; suggesting royalty
The giant redwood trees looked majestic against the blue sky.

rite [RYT] *n.* a regular observance; a formal ceremony
Baptism is a rite observed in Christian religions.

uninvited [un in VY ted] *adj.* unwelcome; not invited
Ants are uninvited guests at many picnics.

untidy [un TY dee] *adj.* messy; not neat
The bedroom was so untidy Vern could not find his socks.

vendors [VEN ders] *n.* people who sell things
Arts and crafts vendors lined the streets during the festival.

wryly [RY lee] *adv.* in a dryly humorous way
Charles said wryly that he had aged ten years while waiting.

Word List B

careered [kuh REERD] *v.* ran or moved at full speed
The popped balloon careered wildly around the room.

hospitable [hahs PIT uh buhl] *adj.* receiving warmly; friendly
The hospitable librarian made the children at Story Hour feel welcome.

incredulous [in KREJ oo luhs] *adj.* skeptical; tending not to believe
The officer's expression was incredulous as Perry told his story.

negotiate [ni GOH shee ayt] *v.* to arrive at an agreement or a conclusion
We were able to negotiate a good price for the car.

recur [ri KER] *v.* happen again
Everyone hoped the terrible event would never recur.

rippled [RIP puhld] *v.* sent small waves
Nervous laughter rippled through the crowd.

slacken [SLAK en] *v.* become looser
In order to undo the knot, we had to slacken the rope first.

weariness [WEER ee nes] *n.* physical or mental fatigue
Overcome with weariness, Berta collapsed onto the sofa.

Unit 6 Resources: A Time of Rapid Change
© Pearson Education, Inc. All rights reserved.
210

EL L1 L2 **Vocabulary Warm-ups A and B,** pp. 210–211

Also available for these selections:

EL L1 L2 **Reading Warm-ups A and B,** pp. 212–213

All **Vocabulary Builder,** p. 216

Reader's Notebooks

Pre- and postreading pages for these selections appear in an interactive format in the *Reader's Notebooks*. Each *Notebook* is differentiated for a different group of learners. The selections in the Adapted and English Learner's versions are abridged.

L2 L3 ***Reader's Notebook***

L1 ***Reader's Notebook: Adapted Version***

EL ***Reader's Notebook: English Learner's Version***

EL ***Reader's Notebook: Spanish Version***

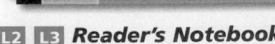

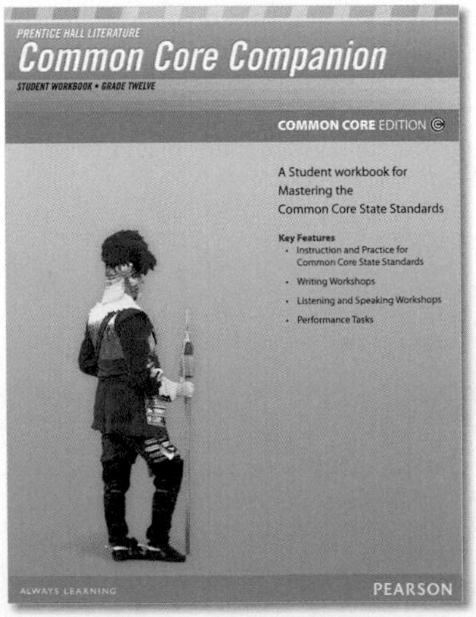

Common Core Companion

Additional instruction and practice for each Common Core State Standard

Selection Support

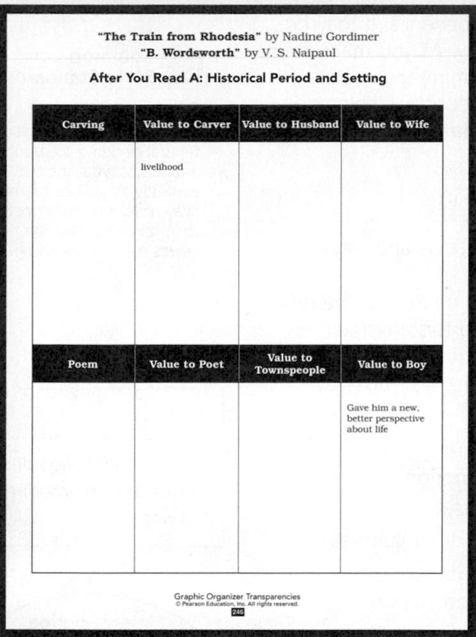
"The Train from Rhodesia" by Nadine Gordimer
"B. Wordsworth" by V. S. Naipaul
After You Read A: Historical Period and Setting

Carving	Value to Carver	Value to Husband	Value to Wife
	livelihood		
Poem	**Value to Poet**	**Value to Townspeople**	**Value to Boy**
			Gave him a new, better perspective about life

Graphic Organizer Transparencies
© Pearson Education, Inc. All rights reserved.
246

Graphic Organizer Transparencies

EL L1 L2 **Literary Analysis: Graphic Organizer A,** (partially filled in), p. 246

Also available for these selections:

EL L1 L2 **Reading: Graphic Organizer A,** p. 244

EL L3 **Reading: Graphic Organizer B,** p. 245

EL L3 **Literary Analysis: Graphic Organizer B,** p. 247

Skills Development/Extension

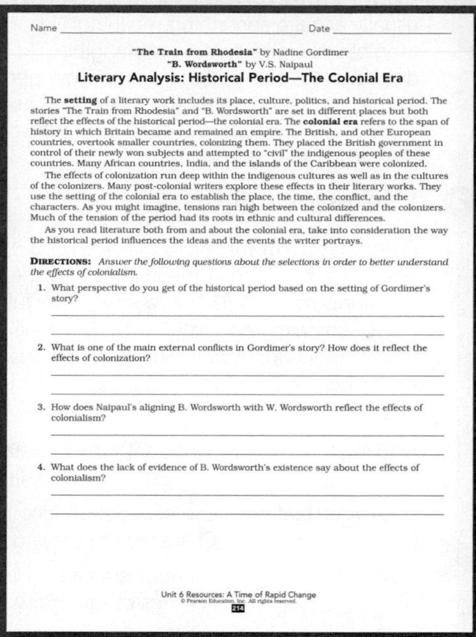
Name ______________________ Date ____________

"The Train from Rhodesia" by Nadine Gordimer
"B. Wordsworth" by V.S. Naipaul
Literary Analysis: Historical Period—The Colonial Era

The **setting** of a literary work includes its place, culture, politics, and historical period. The stories "The Train from Rhodesia" and "B. Wordsworth" are set in different places but both reflect the effects of the historical period—the colonial era. The **colonial era** refers to the span of history in which Britain became and remained an empire. The British, and other European countries, overtook smaller countries, colonizing them. They placed the British government in control of their newly won subjects and attempted to "civil" the indigenous peoples of these countries. Many African countries, India, and the islands of the Caribbean were colonized.

The effects of colonization run deep within the indigenous cultures as well as in the cultures of the colonizers. Many post-colonial writers explore these effects in their literary works. They use the setting of the colonial era to establish the place, the time, the conflict, and the characters. As you might imagine, tensions ran high between the colonized and the colonizers. Much of the tension of the period had its roots in ethnic and cultural differences.

As you read literature both from and about the colonial era, take into consideration the way the historical period influences the ideas and the events the writer portrays.

Directions: *Answer the following questions about the selections in order to better understand the effects of colonialism.*

1. What perspective do you get of the historical period based on the setting of Gordimer's story?
2. What is one of the main external conflicts in Gordimer's story? How does it reflect the effects of colonization?
3. How does Naipaul's aligning B. Wordsworth with W. Wordsworth reflect the effects of colonialism?
4. What does the lack of evidence of B. Wordsworth's existence say about the effects of colonialism?

Unit 6 Resources: A Time of Rapid Change
© Pearson Education, Inc. All rights reserved.
214

Unit 6 Resources

All **Literary Analysis: Historical Period,** p. 214

Also available for these selections:

All **Reading: Apply Knowledge of Historical Background,** p. 215

EL L3 L4 **Support for Writing,** p. 217

L4 **Enrichment,** p. 218

Assessment

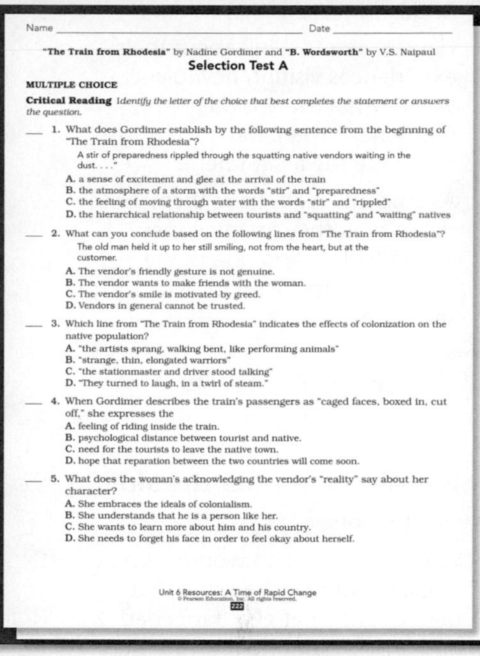
Name ______________________ Date ____________

"The Train from Rhodesia" by Nadine Gordimer and "B. Wordsworth" by V.S. Naipaul
Selection Test A

MULTIPLE CHOICE

Critical Reading *Identify the letter of the choice that best completes the statement or answers the question.*

___ 1. What does Gordimer establish by the following sentence from the beginning of "The Train from Rhodesia"?
A stir of preparedness rippled through the squatting native vendors waiting in the dust. . . ."
A. a sense of excitement and glee at the arrival of the train
B. the atmosphere of a storm with the words "stir" and "preparedness"
C. the feeling of moving through water with the words "stir" and "rippled"
D. the hierarchical relationship between tourists and "squatting" and "waiting" natives

___ 2. What can you conclude based on the following lines from "The Train from Rhodesia"?
The old man held it up to her still smiling, not from the heart, but at the customer.
A. The vendor's friendly gesture is not genuine.
B. The vendor wants to make friends with the woman.
C. The vendor's smile is motivated by greed.
D. Vendors in general cannot be trusted.

___ 3. Which line from "The Train from Rhodesia" indicates the effects of colonization on the native population?
A. "the artists sprang, walking bent, like performing animals"
B. "strange, thin, elongated warriors"
C. "the stationmaster and driver stood talking"
D. "They turned to laugh, in a twirl of steam."

___ 4. When Gordimer describes the train's passengers as "caged faces, boxed in, cut off," she expresses the
A. feeling of riding inside the train.
B. psychological distance between tourist and native.
C. need for the tourists to leave the native town.
D. hope that reparation between the two countries will come soon.

___ 5. What does the woman's acknowledging the vendor's "reality" say about her character?
A. She embraces the ideals of colonialism.
B. She understands that he is a person like her.
C. She wants to learn more about him and his country.
D. She needs to forget his face in order to feel okay about herself.

Unit 6 Resources: A Time of Rapid Change
© Pearson Education, Inc. All rights reserved.
222

EL L1 L2 **Selection Test A,** pp. 222–224

Also available for these selections:

L3 L4 **Open-Book Test,** pp. 219–221

EL L3 L4 **Selection Test B,** pp. 225–227

PHLit Online!
www.PHLitOnline.com

- complete narrated selection text
- a thematically related video with writing prompt
- an interactive graphic organizer
- highlighting feature
- access to all student print resources, adapted to individual student needs
- Spanish and English summaries
- adapted selection translations in Spanish

Online Resources: All print materials are also available online.

Background Video

Also available:

Get Connected! (thematic video with writing prompt)
All videos are available in Spanish.

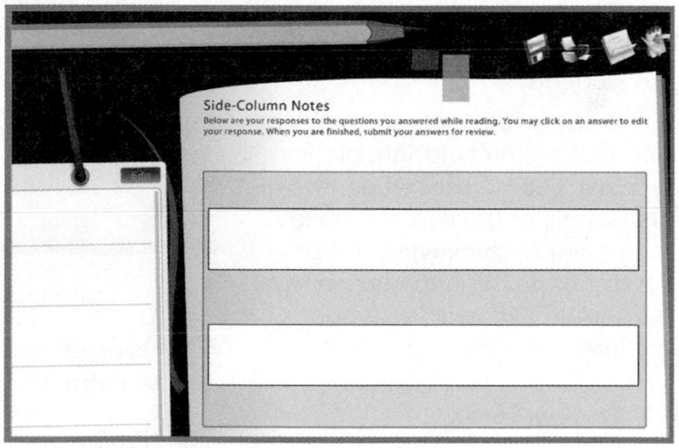

Writer's Journal (with graphics feature)

Also available:

Vocabulary Central (tools and activities for studying vocabulary)

PREETACH

1 Connecting to the Essential Question

1. Review the assignment.
2. Have students think about their experiences visiting new places. Do they have any vivid memories? Then, have them complete the assignment.
3. As students read, have them write down how they imagine they would feel visiting one of the characters described in the selections.

2 Literary Analysis

Introduce the skill.

Think Aloud: Model the Skill

Say to students:

When I read I often wonder who else lived during the same time period and what else happened. I find it interesting to look up more information about the time in the story and use that to expand my understanding of the story I am currently reading. This way I can picture the way things looked in that era.

3 Reading Strategy

1. Introduce the skill.
2. Give students a copy of **Reading Strategy Graphic Organizer B,** page 245 in ***Graphic Organizer Transparencies,*** to fill out as they read.

Think Aloud: Model the Skill

Say to students:

As I come across parts of the selection that seem confusing, particularly parts about the setting, the characters, or the conflict, I take a moment to think which historical fact or political situation in my background knowledge supports my interpretation of that text.

4 Vocabulary

1. Pronounce each word, giving its definition, and have students say it aloud.
2. For more guidance, see the ***Classroom Strategies and Teaching Routines*** card for introducing vocabulary.

Before You Read

The Train from Rhodesia* • *B. Wordsworth

1 Connecting to the Essential Question Travelers to distant places usually acquire something meaningful from their experience. It may be tangible, like a souvenir, or intangible, like a memory. As you read, notice details in the stories that suggest how people determine the values of things, places, or even other people. These observations will help you think about the Essential Question: **What is the relationship between literature and place?**

Common Core State Standards

Reading Literature
1. Cite strong and thorough textual evidence to support analysis of what the text says explicitly as well as inferences drawn from the text, including determining where the text leaves matters uncertain.

2 Literary Analysis

Every **historical period** is characterized by certain views and values, which are reflected in the literature of the period.

During the *colonial era,* a few powerful countries controlled the destiny of colonies that they "owned." Some supported this arrangement, while others opposed it. Following are ways in which this political conflict and other results of colonialism are reflected in stories like those by Gordimer and Naipaul:

Setting	Exotic settings in distant colonies Non-English vocabulary in descriptions
Characterization	Use of racial domination as a motive Characters becoming aware of other cultures
Conflict	Antagonism caused by cultural differences Feelings of inferiority in colonized culture

3 Reading Strategy

Preparing to Read Complex Texts As you read, **apply your background knowledge of a historical period** in order to analyze a setting, character, or conflict. Ask yourself, for example, "What historical fact or political situation or assumption explains this situation?" Make inferences and support them with evidence. Use a graphic organizer like the one shown.

Text
native vendors squatting in dust selling wooden carvings

Interpretation
Africans were so poor that they had to sell handmade artifacts to eke out a living.

Historical Background
Apartheid policies oppressed the black African majority.

4 Vocabulary

impressionistic (im presh ən is′ tik) *adj.* conveying a picture through quickly sketched suggestions of details (p. 1343)

segmented (seg′ ment id) *adj.* divided into joined parts (p. 1345)

atrophy (a′ trə fē) *v.* waste away (p. 1346)

patronize (pā′ trən īz) *v.* be a customer of a particular merchant or store (p. 1353)

distill (di stil′) *v.* obtain the essential part (p. 1353)

keenly (kēn′ lē) *adv.* sharply; intensely (p. 1354)

PHLit Online! www.PHLitOnline.com

Vocabulary Development

Vocabulary Knowledge Rating

Create a **Vocabulary Knowledge Rating Chart** (***Professional Development Guidebook,*** p. 33) for the vocabulary words on the student page. Give each student a copy of the chart with the words on it. Read the words aloud, and have students mark their ratings in the Before Reading column. Urge students to attend to these words as they read and discuss the selections.

In order to gauge how much instruction you need to provide, tally how many students are confident in their knowledge of each word. As students read, point out the words and their context.

PHLit Online! **Vocabulary Central,** featuring tools and activities for studying vocabulary, is available online at **www.PHLitOnline.com.**

5 # NADINE GORDIMER

(B. 1923)

Author of "The Train from Rhodesia"

The fiction of Nadine Gordimer has been shaped by her life in South Africa and by her firm opposition to the former government's policy of apartheid, an institutional form of racial separation and prejudice. In her longer works, as well as in her short stories, she has had a great deal to say about racial division and its harmful effects on both the oppressed and the oppressor. The South African government responded by banning some of her work. Nevertheless, Gordimer has built an international reputation as a writer.

Small Town Origins Gordimer was born in Springs, South Africa, a small town near Johannesburg. Her mother took her out of the local private school when she was eleven. From then until she was sixteen, she "read tremendously" and wrote much fiction. She published her first adult short story, "Come Again Tomorrow," when she was fifteen.

Literary Success *The Soft Voice of the Serpent* (1952) was the first collection of her stories to be published in the United States. Following the critical success of that book, Gordimer's stories appeared in leading American magazines such as *The New Yorker, The Atlantic Monthly,* and *Harper's Magazine.* These stories often describe the entrapment of whites who inherited political and economic power in the closed society of South Africa under apartheid. Frequently, as in "The Train from Rhodesia," she builds a tale around a fleeting but sharply focused moment of insight.

"Luminous Symbol" Until she was thirty, Gordimer had never been outside South Africa. Since then, however, she has traveled widely and lectured in a number of top United States universities, including Princeton, Columbia, and the University of Michigan. She has also won a great many literary awards, including the Nobel Prize for Literature in 1991. Called by one observer "a luminous symbol of at least one white person's understanding of the black man's burden," she is without doubt one of the leading novelists writing in English.

Daily Bellringer

For each class during which you will teach these selections, have students complete one of the five activities for the appropriate week in the ***Daily Bellringer Activities*** booklet.

Multidraft Reading

To assist struggling readers and to enhance reading for all, assign the text in chunks, as warranted by length, and apply multidraft reading protocols. For each reading, have students set the purpose indicated:

- **First reading**—identifying key ideas and details and answering any Reading Checks.
- **Second reading**—analyzing craft and structure and responding to the side-column prompts.
- **Third reading**—integrating knowledge and ideas, connecting to other texts and the world, and answering the end-of-selection questions.

For more guidance, refer to the ***Classroom Strategies and Teaching Routines*** card on Multidraft Reading.

5 Background

More About the Author

Nadine Gordimer was born into a white, middle-class family in South Africa. Her parents were Jewish immigrants—her father was from Lithuania (part of the Soviet Union when he left) and her mother from England. She was educated at a convent school and began writing at age nine. She was a voracious reader, and it was her reading that introduced her to the world outside of South Africa.

Gordimer's purpose has always been to show the effects of apartheid on both society and individuals. She understands that everyone suffers when injustice exists. She is the acknowledged "doyenne of South African letters" and has seen the end of the system against which she wrote.

PHLit Online!
www.PHLitOnline.com

Teaching From Technology

Preparing to Read
Go to **www.PHLitOnline.com** and display the ***Get Connected!*** slide show for these selections. Have the class brainstorm responses to the slide show writing prompt, entering ideas in the interactive journal. Then, have students complete their written responses individually, in a lab or as homework.

To build background, display the Background and More About the Author features.

Using the Interactive Text
Go to **www.PHLitOnline.com** and display the **Enriched Online Student Edition.** As the class reads the selection or listens to the narration, record answers to side-column prompts using the graphic organizers accessible on the interactive page. Alternatively, have students use the online edition individually, answering the prompts as they read.

1 About the Selection

The story "The Train from Rhodesia" illustrates how a moment in time can change and define a life. Though the incident described takes only an instant, it is an instant that not only shapes a marriage, but reflects the social and political situation of a whole country. On the surface, the incident is nothing more than a bargain sought and made over a carving, but below that surface, basic emotions stir, struggle, and finally emerge for a brief moment of both despair and clarity.

2 Activating Prior Knowledge

Ask students to think of a moment in their own lives when a person they had admired, trusted, or loved said or did something that shocked them or caused them to think differently about the person. Point out that the moment of revelation might have been a minor incident, but one that revealed a great character flaw. Read this passage from the story aloud: "'But how could you,' she said. He was shocked by the dismay of her face. 'Good Lord, he said, what's the matter?'" Have students use these lines to predict what might be wrong between the two characters. Then, have them read the story to find out if their predictions were correct.

Concept Connector →

Tell students they will return to their responses after reading the selection.

BACKGROUND

This story is set at a time when South Africa and Rhodesia (now Zimbabwe) enforced policies of racial separation, called apartheid in South Africa, ensuring the continued privileges of a white minority and its domination over the black majority.

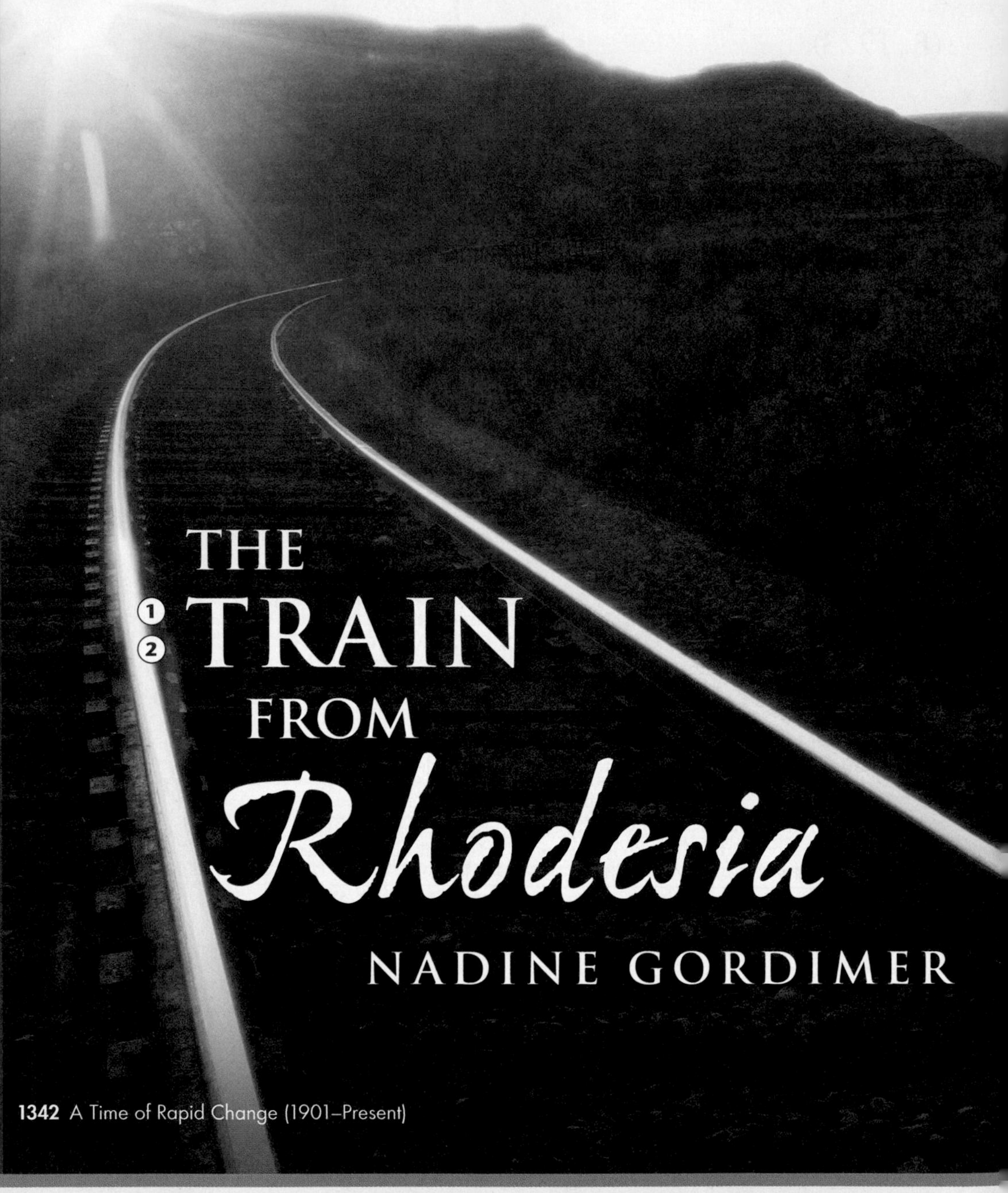

THE (1) (2) TRAIN FROM *Rhodesia*

NADINE GORDIMER

Text Complexity Rubric

	The Train from Rhodesia	B. Wordsworth
Qualitative Measures		
Context/ Knowledge Demands	Modern story; life experience demands 1 (2) 3 4 5	Modern story; historical and cultural knowledge demands 1 2 (3) 4 5
Structure/Language Conventionality and Clarity	Regional terms and dialogue 1 (2) 3 4 5	Regional terms and dialogue; dialect 1 2 (3) 4 5
Levels of Meaning/ Purpose/Concept Level	Moderate (apartheid and racism; marriage) 1 2 (3) 4 5	Challenging (colonialism and artistic expression; love of nature; coming of age) 1 2 3 (4) 5
Quantitative Measures		
Lexile/Text Length	870L / 2,004 words	600L / 2,306 words
Overall Complexity	**More accessible**	**More complex**

The train came out of the red horizon and bore down toward them over the single straight track. The stationmaster came out of his little brick station with its pointed chalet roof, feeling the creases in his serge uniform in his legs as well. A stir of preparedness rippled through the squatting native vendors waiting in the dust; the face of a carved wooden animal, eternally surprised, stuck out of a sack. The stationmaster's barefoot children wandered over. From the gray mud huts with the untidy heads that stood within a decorated mud wall, chickens, and dogs with their skin stretched like parchment over their bones, followed the piccanins[1] down to the track. The flushed and perspiring west cast a reflection, faint, without heat, upon the station, upon the tin shed marked "Goods," upon the walled kraal,[2] upon the gray tin house of the stationmaster and upon the sand, that lapped all around, from sky to sky, cast little rhythmical cups of shadow, so that the sand became the sea, and closed over the children's black feet softly and without imprint.

The stationmaster's wife sat behind the mesh of her veranda. Above her head the hunk of a sheep's carcass moved slightly, dangling in a current of air.

They waited.

The train called out, along the sky; but there was no answer; and the cry hung on: I'm coming . . . I'm coming . . .

The engine flared out now, big, whisking a dwindling body behind it; the track flared out to let it in.

Creaking, jerking, jostling, gasping, the train filled the station.

Here, let me see that one—the young woman curved her body farther out of the corridor window. Missus? smiled the old boy, looking at the creatures he held in his hand. From a piece of string on his gray finger hung a tiny woven basket; he lifted it, questioning. No, no, she urged, leaning down towards him, across the height of the train, towards the man in the piece of old rug; that one, that one, her hand commanded. It was a lion, carved out of soft dry wood that looked like spongecake; heraldic, black and, white, with **impressionistic** detail burnt in. The old man held it up to her still smiling, not from the heart, but at the customer. Between its Vandyke[3] teeth, in the mouth opened in an endless roar too terrible to be heard, it had a black tongue. Look, said the young husband, if you don't mind! And round the neck of the thing, a piece of fur (rat? rabbit? meerkat?); a real mane, majestic, telling you somehow that the artist had delight in the lion.

All up and down the length of the train in the dust the artists sprang, walking bent, like performing animals, the better to exhibit the fantasy held toward the faces on the train. Buck, startled and stiff, staring with round black and white eyes. More lions, standing erect, grappling with strange, thin, elongated warriors who clutched

1. **piccanins** *n.* native children.
2. **kraal** (kräl) *n.* fenced-in enclosure for cattle or sheep.
3. **Vandyke** (van dīk′) *adj.* tapering to a point, like a Vandyke beard.

3 ◄ **Critical Viewing** What does the landscape surrounding the tracks in the photo tell you about the area through which the train is traveling? **[Infer]**

4 **Literary Analysis** **Historical Period and Setting** Identify three details of the setting that indicate the economic condition of the native Africans.

Vocabulary
impressionistic (im presh ən is′ tik) *adj.* conveying a picture through quickly sketched suggestions of details

5 **Reading Check** What attracts the interest of the young woman on the train?

3 Critical Viewing

Answer: The landscape is harsh and isolated, and it would be a difficult place to make a living.

4 Literary Analysis

Historical Period and Setting

1. Remind students that the setting of a story often has direct consequences on the conflict and on the characters' actions. Ask students to name stories or movies in which setting plays a major role in shaping the events of the plot.
2. Next, ask students to think which of those stories, if any, portray economic conditions that are directly affected by the setting of the story. If so, ask students to describe the connection.
3. Finally, **ask** students to identify three details of the setting that indicate the economic condition of the native Africans.
   Possible responses: Natives "waiting in the dust," barefoot children, and "gray mud huts" are details that indicate the economic condition of the native Africans in this story.

5 Reading Check

Answer: A carving of a lion attracts the woman's attention.

PHLit Online!

These selections are available in interactive format in the **Enriched Online Student Edition** at **www.PHLitOnline.com**, which includes a thematically related video with writing prompt and an interactive graphic organizer.

Text Complexity: Reader and Task Suggestions

The Train from Rhodesia		B. Wordsworth	
Preparing to Read the Text	**Leveled Tasks**	**Preparing to Read the Text**	**Leveled Tasks**
• Use the Background on SE p. 1342 to explain the apartheid policies then in force in South Africa. • Discuss the idea that a single moment can reveal the essence of a person. • Guide students to use Multidraft Reading strategies (TE p. 1341).	***Levels of Meaning*** If students will have difficulty with the levels of meaning, have them focus first on the couple's changing relationship. Then, have students consider what that change suggests about South African society under apartheid. ***Analyzing*** If students will not have difficulty with the author's meaning, have them analyze the symbols of the train and station, explaining how they might relate to the story's central theme.	• Use the Background on SE p. 1349 to establish the importance of cultural identity in colonial Trinidad. • Discuss with students the effects of colonialism on both colonizers and colonized. • Guide students to use Multidraft Reading strategies (TE p. 1341).	***Levels of Meaning*** If students will have difficulty with the levels of meaning, have them focus first on B. Wordsworth's character and outlook and the way his life changes in the end. Then, have students consider the role that society plays in stifling B. Wordsworth's dreams. ***Evaluating*** If students will not have difficulty with the story's meaning, have them evaluate Naipaul's characterization of B. Wordsworth.

❻ Literature in Context

History Connection

Opposition to apartheid existed in South Africa since its establishment in 1948. In 1990 and 1991, after years of violent struggle involving government forces, pro-apartheid groups, and anti-apartheid forces, the government repealed most of the social legislation that had provided the basis for apartheid. In 1993, a new constitution was created. In 1994, all-race national elections were held and Nelson Mandela, a leader of the anti-apartheid African National Congress, was elected the country's first black president.

Connect to the Literature Have students define social class and then **ask:** Besides language, what other barriers exist between the young woman and the artists?
Possible responses: The woman and the artists are of different races and come from different social, economic, and cultural backgrounds.

❼ Reading Strategy

Apply Background Knowledge

1. Remind students to use their background knowledge to find explanations for things that happen in the text.
2. **Ask** students what effect it has when members of a basketball team attempt to tower over members of another basketball team.
   Possible response: The players are trying to convey superiority over the other players and to intimidate them.
3. **Ask:** How do the relative positions of the characters—the whites up on the train, the black natives on the ground—symbolize the policies of apartheid?
   Possible response: The policies of apartheid promoted the idea that the white population was morally, culturally, and economically elevated above the non-white population. This idea is represented symbolically when the white characters on the train are situated higher than the non-white characters on the ground.

❻ LITERATURE IN CONTEXT

History Connection

Apartheid

In Gordimer's story, the interactions between white passengers and black vendors reflect the social regime called apartheid ("apartness" in the language of Dutch South Africans). Under apartheid in South Africa, blacks were restricted to living in certain areas. To travel through a white area, they were required to carry passes—even if they worked every day in such areas. Public places—such as schools, restaurants, and hotels—were segregated by law. Whites lived as privileged rulers in the country. Blacks lived for the most part in poverty, stripped of political power. It was only in the closing decades of the twentieth century that blacks, after violent struggles, gained political rights in South Africa and Rhodesia.

Connect to the Literature

Besides language, what other barriers exist between the young woman and the artists?

spears and showed no fear in their slits of eyes. How much, they asked from the train, how much?

Give me penny, said the little ones with nothing to sell. The dogs went and sat, quite still, under the dining car, where the train breathed out the smell of meat cooking with onion.

A man passed beneath the arch of reaching arms meeting gray-black and white in the exchange of money for the staring wooden eyes, the stiff wooden legs sticking up in the air; went along under the voices and the bargaining, interrogating the wheels. Past the dogs; glancing up at the dining car where he could stare at the faces, behind glass, drinking beer, two by two, on either side of a uniform railway vase with its pale dead flower. Right to the end, to the guard's van, where the stationmaster's children had just collected their mother's two loaves of bread; to the engine itself, where the stationmaster and the driver stood talking against the steaming complaint of the resting beast.

The man called out to them, something loud and joking. They turned to laugh, in a twirl of steam. The two children careered over the sand, clutching the bread, and burst through the iron gate and up the path through the garden in which nothing grew.

Passengers drew themselves in at the corridor windows and turned into compartments to fetch money, to call someone to look. Those sitting inside looked up: suddenly different, caged faces, boxed in, cut off, after the contact of outside. There was an orange a piccanin would like. . . . What about that chocolate? It wasn't very nice. . . .

❼ **Reading Strategy**
Apply Background Knowledge How do the relative positions of the characters—the whites up on the train, the black natives on the ground—symbolize the policies of apartheid?

A young girl had collected a handful of the hard kind, that no one liked, out of the chocolate box, and was throwing them to the dogs, over at the dining car. But the hens darted in, and swallowed the chocolates, incredibly quick and accurate, before they had even dropped in the dust, and the dogs, a little bewildered, looked up with their brown eyes, not expecting anything.

—No, leave it, said the girl, don't take it. . . .

Too expensive, too much, she shook her head and raised her voice to the old boy, giving up the lion. He held it high where she had handed it to him. No, she said, shaking her head. Three-and-six?[4] insisted her husband, loudly. Yes baas! laughed the old man. Three-and-six?—The young man was incredulous. Oh leave it—she said. The young man stopped. Don't you want it? he said, keeping his face closed to the old man. No, never mind, she said, leave it. The old native kept his head on one side, looking at them sideways, holding the lion. Three-and-six, he murmured, as old people repeat things to themselves.

4. **three-and-six** three shillings and sixpence.

Enrichment: Investigating Geography

Local Trains

Point out that the social and economic activity of the town in the story seems centered on the train station. Explain that in many areas, trains are the main mode of transportation. Africa, especially, has a poor road system due to problems of topography and climate. In the south, where the story is set, railroad development has been vital to the economy. Ask students whether their community is served by a railroad, or if it was in the past. If so, have them explore how the coming of the railroad affected the community and, if it has stopped running, how its passing affected the area.

Activity: Investigating Geography and Railroads Encourage interested students to map the current railroad system in Zimbabwe. Suggest that they record their work in the **Enrichment: Investigating Geography** worksheet, ***Professional Development Guidebook***, page 228.

The young woman drew her head in. She went into the coupé[5] and sat down. Out of the window, on the other side, there was nothing; sand and bush; a thorn tree. Back through the open doorway, past the figure of her husband in the corridor, there was the station, the voices, wooden animals waving, running feet. Her eye followed the funny little valance of scrolled wood that outlined the chalet roof of the station; she thought of the lion and smiled. That bit of fur round the neck. But the wooden buck, the hippos, the elephants, the baskets that already bulked out of their brown paper under the seat and on the luggage rack! How will they look at home? Where will you put them? What will they mean away from the places you found them? Away from the unreality of the last few weeks? The young man outside. But he is not part of the unreality; he is for good now. Odd . . . somewhere there was an idea that he, that living with him, was part of the holiday, the strange places.

Outside, a bell rang. The stationmaster was leaning against the end of the train, green flag rolled in readiness. A few men who had got down to stretch their legs sprang onto the train, clinging to the observation platforms, or perhaps merely standing on the iron step, holding the rail; but on the train, safe from the one dusty platform, the one tin house, the empty sand.

There was a grunt. The train jerked. Through the glass the beer drinkers looked out, as if they could not see beyond it. Behind the flyscreen, the stationmaster's wife sat facing back at them beneath the darkening hunk of meat.

There was a shout. The flag drooped out. Joints not yet coordinated, the **segmented** body of the train heaved and bumped back against itself. It began to move; slowly the scrolled chalet moved past it, the yells of the natives, running alongside, jetted up into the air, fell back at different levels. Staring wooden faces waved drunkenly, there, then gone, questioning for the last time at the windows. Here, one-and-six baas!—As one automatically opens a hand to catch a thrown ball, a man fumbled wildly down his pocket, brought up the shilling and sixpence and threw them out; the old native, gasping, his skinny toes splaying the sand, flung the lion.

The piccanins were waving, the dogs stood, tails uncertain, watching the train go: past the mud huts, where a woman turned to look, up from the smoke of the fire, her hand pausing on her hip.

The stationmaster went slowly in under the chalet.

10 ↓ The old native stood, breath blowing out the skin between his

5. **coupé** (ko͞o pā′) *n.* half-compartment at the end of a train, with seats on only one side.

8 ▲ Critical Viewing
How do the figures in this photo compare with the lion figurine described in the story? **[Compare and Contrast]**

Vocabulary
segmented (seg′ ment id) *adj.* divided into joined parts

9 Reading Check
Why does the girl decide to leave the lion?

8 Critical Viewing

Answer: The figures in the photo are wooden carvings with carefully created and intricate details.

9 Reading Check

Answer: She thinks it is too expensive.

Differentiated Instruction for Universal Access

Enrichment for Special-Needs Students

Have students perform short skits reenacting the implications of the bygone glory of the native African cultures suggested by the statues as compared with the vendors' present circumstances. Have one student play a proud, traditional African and another play the role of one of the present-day vendors.

Strategy for Less Proficient Readers

Have students assume the role of a friend to the lady on the train. Then, have each write her a letter giving her advice about her new feelings of "shame" and "weariness."

Strategy for Advanced Readers

After students have finished reading the story, have each write an essay presenting his or her views as to whether the story is pessimistic or optimistic about the relations of blacks and whites in Southern Africa. Instruct them to use specific passages to support their arguments.

⑩ Literary Analysis

Historical Period and Characterization

1. Remind students that the values of a historical period are usually reflected in the literature of that period. Explain that the young man in the story behaves a certain way because it is encouraged by the culture of colonialism.
2. Ask students to think of other stories they have read in which a character acted in a certain way because it was expected by society.
3. **Ask** students the following: Explain how the young man's purchase of the lion reflects the social effects of colonialism.
   Possible response: The money the seller received was less than the lion was worth. This demonstrates how, native people are cheated by colonialism.

⑪ Reading Strategy

Apply Background Knowledge

1. Remind students to use their background knowledge to help them understand why characters behave or feel a certain way.
2. Next, ask students to use their background knowledge to consider the ways the people who rejected apartheid might have protested against it.
3. **Ask:** How does the woman's reaction convey a comment about the effects of apartheid on the entire society?
   Possible response: Through the woman's expression of disapproval for her husband's actions, the story makes clear that some members of the white population disagreed with the expectations established under apartheid.

Literary Analysis
Historical Period and Characterization Explain how the young man's purchase of the lion reflects the social effect of colonialism.

Reading Strategy
Apply Background Knowledge How does the woman's reaction convey a comment about the effects of apartheid on the entire society?

Vocabulary
atrophy (a´ trə fē) *v.* to waste away

⑩ ribs, feet tense, balanced in the sand, smiling and shaking his head. In his opened palm, held in the attitude of receiving, was the retrieved shilling and sixpence.

The blind end of the train was being pulled helplessly out of the station.

The young man swung in from the corridor, breathless. He was shaking his head with laughter and triumph. Here! he said. And waggled the lion at her. One-and-six!

What? she said.

He laughed. I was arguing with him for fun, bargaining—when the train had pulled out already, he came tearing after. . . . One-and-six baas! So there's your lion.

She was holding it away from her, the head with the open jaws, the pointed teeth, the black tongue, the wonderful ruff of fur facing her. She was looking at it with an expression of not seeing, of seeing something different. Her face was drawn up, wryly, like the face of a discomforted child. Her mouth lifted nervously at the corner. Very slowly, cautious, she lifted her finger and touched the mane, where it was joined to the wood.

But how could you, she said. He was shocked by the dismay of her face.

Good Lord, he said, what's the matter?

If you wanted the thing, she said, her voice rising and breaking with the shrill impotence of anger, why didn't you buy it in the first place? If you wanted it, why didn't you pay for it?

⑪ Why didn't you take it decently, when he offered it? Why did you have to wait for him to run after the train with it, and give him one-and-six? One-and-six!

She was pushing it at him, trying to force him to take it. He stood astonished, his hands hanging at his sides.

But you wanted it! You liked it so much?

—It's a beautiful piece of work, she said fiercely, as if to protect it from him.

You liked it so much! You said yourself it was too expensive—

Oh you—she said, hopeless and furious. You. . . . She threw the lion onto the seat.

He stood looking at her.

She sat down again in the corner and, her face slumped in her hand, stared out of the window. Everything was turning around inside her. One-and-six. One-and-six. One-and-six for the wood and the carving and the sinews of the legs and the switch of the tail. The mouth open like that and the teeth. The black tongue, rolling, like a wave. The mane round the neck. To give one-and-six for that. The heat of shame mounted through her legs and body and sounded in her ears like the sound of sand pouring. Pouring, pouring. She sat there, sick. A weariness, a tastelessness, the discovery of a void made her hands slacken their grip, atrophy emptily, as if the hour was not worth their grasp. She was feeling like this again. She had thought it was something to do with singleness, with being alone and belonging too much to oneself.

Enrichment: Analyzing an Image of South Africa

South Africa
Discuss with students the many levels of diversity found in South Africa. Not only is the population diverse, but the landscape is as well. In the reading, a passenger notices the bustle of the bartering townspeople on one side of the train and the desert landscape on the other side. South Africa is a place of opposite extremes—wealth and poverty, developing cities and extreme desert landscapes. Ask students to think about their community—who lives there, what businesses exist, and what the surrounding landscape is like. Have them describe any parallels to the diversity found in South Africa.

Activity: Analyzing an Image Ask students to search for an image that shows diversity of any kind in South Africa. Suggest that they record their work in the **Enrichment: Analyzing an Image** worksheet, ***Professional Development Guidebook,*** page 232.

THE TRAIN HAD CAST THE STATION *like a skin.*

She sat there not wanting to move or speak, or to look at anything, even; so that the mood should be associated with nothing, no object, word or sight that might recur and so recall the feeling again. . . . Smuts blew in grittily, settled on her hands. Her back remained at exactly the same angle, turned against the young man sitting with his hands drooping between his sprawled legs, and the lion, fallen on its side in the corner.

The train had cast the station like a skin. It called out to the sky, I'm coming, I'm coming; and again, there was no answer.

12 ▲ Critical Viewing
How does the facial expression of the woman in the photo reflect the feelings of the woman in the story? **[Connect]**

Critical Reading

Cite textual evidence to support your responses.

1. **Key Ideas and Details (a)** Who comes to meet the train from Rhodesia? **(b) Infer:** What does the interaction between these people and the passengers indicate about the story's theme?
2. **Key Ideas and Details (a) Analyze:** Why does the lion impress the young woman? **(b) Interpret:** Why is the young woman angry when her husband bargains for and obtains the lion at a low price?
3. **Key Ideas and Details (a) Draw Conclusions:** What have the husband and the wife discovered about each other by the end of the story? **(b) Speculate:** How might their marriage fare, given this episode? Explain.
4. **Integration of Knowledge and Ideas** What do you think the train and the station symbolize in this story?

12 Critical Viewing

Answer: The woman appears hopeless.

ASSESS

Answers

Before students respond, you may wish to have them write a brief objective summary of the selection. As they answer the questions below, remind them to support their answers with evidence from the text.

1. (a) The local African artists, vendors, children, and dogs come to meet the train. (b) The interactions reflect the insensitive attitude of the wealthy toward the poor.
2. (a) The lion impresses the woman because its details show that the artist had delight in the lion. (b) The woman is angry because her husband will enter the bargain only if he can best his social inferior, not simply to acquire something he wants or values.
3. (a) The woman has learned that her new husband is still really a stranger to her and has characteristics she cannot admire. The young man has learned little more than that he does not understand his new bride. (b) **Possible response:** The welfare of the marriage depends upon whether the young woman is able to communicate her convictions to her husband. If she cannot, she will remain isolated and lonely, and her husband will probably never understand why she becomes moody.
4. Students may respond that the train and station symbolize Africa. Others may feel it represents the point of connection between peoples.

Differentiated Instruction for Universal Access

Enrichment for Gifted/Talented Students
Have each student read another book about apartheid and write a report comparing and contrasting the two selections. What is the perspective of the second book? Do the characters in each book have any similar experiences?

Enrichment for Advanced Readers
Students may want to do some research into personal stories by South Africans who experienced apartheid firsthand and how it affected their lives. Ask them to present their findings to the class. How do the stories impact the student's feeling of apartheid? What were some especially moving or emotional parts of the story?

⓭ Background

More About the Author

Naipaul also writes nonfiction, including a report on a journey he took through the United States, apparently seeking connections between the American South and his own Trinidadian culture. Along with the issue of race, Naipaul considered features of southern Americana such as country-and-western music, conservative Christianity, and the ongoing obsession with Elvis Presley. V. S. Naipaul was awarded the 2001 Nobel Prize for Literature.

(B. 1932)

⓭ V. S. NAIPAUL

Author of "B. Wordsworth"

V. S. Naipaul, who grew up in Trinidad, has earned a reputation as a brilliant writer of fiction and nonfiction books about colonialism, exile, and issues of identity in the contemporary world. Although some writers have accused him of taking a snobbish attitude toward Third World cultures, he was awarded the Nobel Prize in Literature in 2001.

A "Many-Sided Background" Naipaul, whose family came from India, was born in Trinidad, then a part of the British West Indies. There, he grew up in the Hindu culture and attended British schools. These experiences, combined with living in England and traveling all over the world, make up what Naipaul calls his "many-sided background."

In his book of autobiographical writings, *Finding the Center: Two Narratives* (1984), Naipaul recounts how his grandfather came to Trinidad as an indentured laborer. The terms of indenture were not always strictly followed, and members of the Indian community faced many frustrations as a result. The next generation fared somewhat better; Naipaul's father became a popular journalist with the main Trinidadian newspaper.

Explorations in Writing Even as a student, Naipaul shared his father's talent for writing, and he won a scholarship to Oxford University. While in his final year there, he learned that his father had died. Naipaul's family wanted him to return to Trinidad, but he decided to remain in Britain. He soon found work in London writing about the West Indies for radio.

Far from home, he began to write stories that drew on his memories of Trinidad. Those early stories, including "B. Wordsworth," were eventually collected in *Miguel Street* (1959). In these tales, a young narrator describes the comic and absurd elements of growing up in the West Indies. To gain a full perspective of the community, he created a "narrator more in tune with the life of the street than I had been."

"Fiction Never Lies" *A House for Mr. Biswas* (1961) combines the comic perspective of his early tales with poignant and universal themes to tell the story of a man similar to his father. Naipaul returned to his own youth in the novelistic memoir *A Way in the World* (1994). In justifying his choice of fictional accounts over autobiography, Naipaul explains that "an autobiography can distort, facts can be realigned. But fiction never lies. It reveals the writer totally."

Enrichment: Analyzing Culture

Trinidad and Tobago

Today, the name of the country in which this story is set is Trinidad and Tobago. The country is made up of two islands in the Caribbean near the northeast coast of South America. The island of Trinidad makes up about 95 percent of the land area of Trinidad and Tobago, and 95 percent of the country's people live there. Trinidadians of African and Indian descent make up about 80 percent of the population. The rest of the people are of European, Chinese, or mixed European and African background.

English is the country's official language, though French, Spanish, and Hindi are also spoken. Trinidadian English is an island form of English influenced by both French and Spanish.

Activity: Analyzing Culture Ask students to research the culture of Trinidad and Tobago and provide the **Enrichment: Analyzing Culture** worksheet, ***Professional Development Guidebook***, page 223, for them to record their findings.

14 B. WORDSWORTH

V. S. NAIPAUL

BACKGROUND This story is set in Trinidad, probably in the 1940s. Trinidad, which became independent in 1962, had been a British colony since 1802. From 1845 to 1917, it received indentured workers emigrating from India. Naipaul's grandfather had been such a worker, borrowing money for passage and laboring for years to pay off the debt. With a diverse population and with the culture of Britain, the colonial power, held up as "superior," cultural identity and names were key issues in Trinidad.

Three beggars called punctually every day at the hospitable houses in Miguel Street. At about ten an Indian came in his dhoti[1] and white jacket, and we poured a tin of rice into the sack he carried on his back. At twelve an old woman smoking a clay pipe came and she got a cent. At two a blind man led by a boy called for his penny.

15 ▲ **Critical Viewing** What does this picture reveal about a Caribbean setting? **[Infer]**

1. **dhoti** (dō′ tē) traditional loincloth worn by Hindu men.

14 About the Selection

This story expresses the pain of life in colonial society by dramatizing the ways a Trinidadian poet is kept from success. An innocent narrator—a young boy—at first takes the poet at face value, noticing only his wondrous way of appreciating life's beauty. Gradually, however, the boy realizes the ways the poet's life has been limited so that his ability to produce written work has been stunted. By the story's end, the boy is brought to tears not only by the poet's approaching death but also by society's restrictions and life's tragedy: "I . . . ran home crying, like a poet, for everything I saw."

15 Critical Viewing

Answer: The setting is a beautiful place with lush vegetation.

Differentiated Instruction for Universal Access

Support for Special-Needs Students
Have students reread the Background on page 1349 and speculate on what effect British colonization might have had on Trinidadians. Also, have them guess why a poet of Trinidad might name himself "Black Wordsworth," the so-called brother of the British poet "White Wordsworth."

Strategy for Less Proficient Readers
Students may want to rephrase the dialect of the young narrator into standard English. For example, what would be the "translations" for "What you want?", "I ain't have the time," and "What you does do, mister?"

EL Strategy for English Learners
Help students find recorded examples of British and West Indian accents. Then, encourage them to prepare dramatic readings of parts of the story's dialogue, contrasting the narrator's and B. Wordsworth's ways of speaking.

16 Literary Analysis

Historical Period and Setting

1. Remind students that literature often reflects the social conditions of a particular time and place.
2. Ask students to think about the sorts of things that they can learn by paying attention to historical details.
3. **Ask** students the Literary Analysis question: What does the regular appearance of the beggars suggest about social conditions at this time?
   Possible response: It suggests that poverty was widespread, and people who were better off helped those who were poor.

Spiral Review

Characterization

Ask the Spiral Review question.

Possible response: Some students may say that B. Wordsworth's claims imply a strong sense of self-worth and confidence in his talents. Others may say that the claims reveal B. Wordsworth's need to appear greater than his circumstances. Still others may find B. Wordsworth to be delusional.

"I WANT TO WATCH YOUR BEES."

Sometimes we had a rogue.[2] One day a man called and said he was hungry. We gave him a meal. He asked for a cigarette and wouldn't go until we had lit it for him. That man never came again.

The strangest caller came one afternoon at about four o'clock. I had come back from school and was in my home-clothes. The man said to me, "Sonny, may I come inside your yard?"

He was a small man and he was tidily dressed. He wore a hat, a white shirt and black trousers.

I asked, "What you want?"

He said, "I want to watch your bees."

We had four small gru-gru palm trees[3] and they were full of uninvited bees.

I ran up the steps and shouted, "Ma, it have a man outside here. He say he want to watch the bees."

My mother came out, looked at the man and asked in an unfriendly way, "What you want?"

The man said, "I want to watch your bees."

His English was so good, it didn't sound natural, and I could see my mother was worried.

She said to me, "Stay here and watch him while he watch the bees."

The man said, "Thank you, Madam. You have done a good deed today."

He spoke very slowly and very correctly as though every word was costing him money.

We watched the bees, this man and I, for about an hour, squatting near the palm trees.

The man said, "I like watching bees. Sonny, do you like watching bees?"

I said, "I ain't have the time."

He shook his head sadly. He said, "That's what I do, I just watch. I can watch ants for days. Have you ever watched ants? And scorpions, and centipedes, and congorees[4]—have you watched those?"

I shook my head.

I said, "What you does do, mister?"

He got up and said, "I am a poet."

I said, "A good poet?"

He said, "The greatest in the world."

"What your name, mister?"

"B. Wordsworth."

"B for Bill?"

"Black. Black Wordsworth. White Wordsworth[5] was my brother.

16 Literary Analysis
Historical Period and Setting
What does the regular appearance of the beggars suggest about social conditions at this time?

Spiral Review
Characterization
What do B. Wordsworth's claims establish about his character?

2. **rogue** (rōg) *n.* wandering beggar or tramp; scoundrel.
3. **gru-gru** (gro͞o´ gro͞o´) **palm trees** West Indian palms that yield edible nuts.
4. **congorees** (käŋ´ gər ēz) Conger or Congo eels; large, scaleless eels found in the warm waters of the West Indies.
5. **White Wordsworth** English Romantic poet William Wordsworth (1770–1850).

Enrichment: Analyzing Calypso Music

Calypso

When asked what he does for a living, B. Wordsworth says that he sings calypsos. Calypso is a type of music that originated on the island of Trinidad and combines features of African and Spanish music with American jazz and blues. Calypso is often sung in French Creole dialect as well as in English. The songs are accompanied by such instruments as maracas—rattles traditionally made of dried gourds containing loose seeds; the cuatro—a stringed instrument; and guitar, flute, and saxophone. Calypso songs may also be accompanied by drums made from steel oil containers and played with sticks. The lyrics convey a variety of messages as each expresses the personal point of view of the singer-poet.

Activity: Analyzing Music Direct interested students to research calypso music and analyze a song. Have them record their work in the **Enrichment: Analyzing Music** worksheet, ***Professional Development Guidebook,*** page 236.

17 We share one heart. I can watch a small flower like the morning glory and cry."

I said, "Why you does cry?"

"Why, boy? Why? You will know when you grow up. You're a poet, too, you know. And when you're a poet you can cry for everything."

I couldn't laugh.

He said, "You like your mother?"

"When she not beating me."

He pulled out a printed sheet from his hip-pocket and said, "On this paper is the greatest poem about mothers and I'm going to sell it to you at a bargain price. For four cents."

I went inside and I said, "Ma, you want buy a poetry for four cents?"

My mother said, "Tell that blasted man I haul his tail away from my yard, you hear."

I said to B. Wordsworth, "My mother say she ain't have four cents."

B. Wordsworth said, "It is the poet's tragedy."

And he put the paper back in his pocket. He didn't seem to mind.

I said, "Is a funny way to go round selling poetry like

18 that. Only calypsonians[6] do that sort of thing. A lot of people does buy?"

He said, "No one has yet bought a single copy."

"But why you does keep on going round, then?"

He said, "In this way I watch many things, and I always hope to meet poets."

I said, "You really think I is a poet?"

"You're as good as me," he said.

And when B. Wordsworth left, I prayed I would see him again.

About a week later, coming back from school one afternoon, I met him at the corner of Miguel Street.

He said, "I have been waiting for you for a long time."

I said, "You sell any poetry yet?"

He shook his head.

He said, "In my yard I have the best mango tree in Port-of-Spain.[7] And now the mangoes are ripe and red and very sweet and juicy. I have waited here for you to tell you this and to invite you to come and eat some of my mangoes."

He lived in Alberto Street in a one-roomed hut placed right in the center of the lot. The yard seemed all green. There was the

6. **calypsonians** (kə lip sō′ nē ənz) those who sing calypso songs; the characteristic satirical street singers of Trinidad.

7. **Port-of-Spain** seaport capital of Trinidad and Tobago.

Reading Strategy
Apply Background Knowledge Based on what you know of Romantic poets, what quality of William Wordsworth does B. Wordsworth especially admire?

Literary Analysis
Historical Period and Setting How does background information about calypsonians clarify B. Wordsworth's profession?

19 **Reading Check**
How does the narrator meet B. Wordsworth?

17 Reading Strategy

Apply Background Knowledge

1. Remind students that background knowledge of other works of literature can be applied to what they are currently reading.
2. Next, **ask:** What do you know about the poet William Wordsworth?
   Possible response: Wordsworth was a Romantic writer who loved nature.
3. **Ask:** Based on what you know of Romantic poets, what quality of William Wordsworth does B. Wordsworth especially admire?
   Possible response: B. Wordsworth says that he can "watch a small flower like the morning glory and cry." This shows that he is moved by the beauty of nature, just as William Wordsworth was. This appreciation of nature is probably what he admires most in the Romantic poet's work.

18 Literary Analysis

Historical Period and Setting

1. Remind students that authors use historical details to convey ideas about characters.
2. Ask students to think about what it would be like to be a professional poet.
3. **Ask** students the Literary Analysis question: How does background information about calypsonians clarify B. Wordsworth's profession?
   Possible response: Knowing that calypsonians sing a special form of music with lyrics that express the poet's personal point of view makes clear the type of poetry B. Wordsworth writes.

19 Reading Check

Answer: He meets B. Wordsworth when the poet comes to his house and asks for permission to watch the bees.

Differentiated Instruction for Universal Access

Strategy for Less Proficient Readers
Ask students to list the characteristics of B. Wordsworth that they have learned about so far in the story that would make him a good poet. (He is observant and likes to watch things going on such as bees and the constellations; he is sensitive to the importance of words; he is a good storyteller; he is open to emotions; and so on.)

Enrichment for Advanced Readers
Students may want to do some research into constellations and present their findings to the class. Are the constellations students can see the same ones, or different ones, from those seen in the Caribbean? Which constellations are visible in the night sky at the time when students are reading this story?

⑳ Literary Analysis

Historical Period, Setting, and Characterization

1. Remind students to look for important details as they read.
2. Ask students to think about what the details of a person's living space can say about the person.
3. **Ask** students the Literary Analysis question: What does the wild array of trees suggest about B. Wordsworth's character?
   Possible response: The trees suggest B. Wordsworth's love for the wildness of nature. In addition, they suggest that he lives a somewhat secluded life in his own world, in a place that seemed "as though it wasn't in the city at all."

㉑ Reading Strategy

Apply Background Knowledge

1. Remind students that some themes appear over and over in literature.
2. Ask students to think of some examples of poetry or songs about stars.
3. **Ask** students the Reading Strategy question: Explain how B. Wordsworth's knowledge of the names of the stars links him with poets of the past.
   Possible response: Throughout the history of literature, poets have been fascinated by the stars, and many have used this theme in their work.

big mango tree. There was a coconut tree and there was a plum tree. The place looked wild, as though it wasn't in the city at all. You couldn't see all the big concrete houses in the street. 20

He was right. The mangoes were sweet and juicy. I ate about six, and the yellow mango juice ran down my arms to my elbows and down my mouth to my chin and my shirt was stained.

My mother said when I got home, "Where you was? You think you is a man now and could go all over the place? Go cut a whip for me."

She beat me rather badly, and I ran out of the house swearing that I would never come back. I went to B. Wordsworth's house. I was so angry, my nose was bleeding.

B. Wordsworth said, "Stop crying, and we will go for a walk."

I stopped crying, but I was breathing short. We went for a walk. We walked down St. Clair Avenue to the Savannah and we walked to the race-course.

B. Wordsworth said, "Now, let us lie on the grass and look up at the sky, and I want you to think how far those stars are from us."

Literary Analysis
Historical Period, Setting, and Characterization What does the wild array of trees suggest about B. Wordsworth's character?

I did as he told me, and I saw what he meant. I felt like nothing, and at the same time I had never felt so big and great in all my life. I forgot all my anger and all my tears and all the blows.

When I said I was better, he began telling me the names of the stars, and I particularly remembered the constellation of Orion
21 the Hunter,[8] though I don't really know why. I can spot Orion even today, but I have forgotten the rest.

Then a light was flashed into our faces, and we saw a policeman. We got up from the grass.

The policeman said, "What you doing here?"

B. Wordsworth said, "I have been asking myself the same question for forty years."

Reading Strategy
Apply Background Knowledge Explain how B. Wordsworth's knowledge of the names of the stars links him with poets of the past.

We became friends, B. Wordsworth and I. He told me, "You must never tell anybody about me and about the mango tree and the coconut tree and the plum tree. You must keep that a secret. If you tell anybody, I will know, because I am a poet."

I gave him my word and I kept it.

I liked his little room. It had no more furniture than George's front room,[9] but it looked cleaner and healthier. But it also looked lonely.

One day I asked him, "Mister Wordsworth, why you does keep

---

8. **constellation of Orion** (ō rī′ ən) **the Hunter** group of stars named after a mythological giant who was killed accidentally by the goddess of hunting, Diana.
9. **George's front room** George is a character in one of the companion stories in Naipaul's book, *Miguel Street*.

Enrichment: Investigating Language

Constellations

When B. Wordsworth and the narrator stargaze they see Orion the Hunter and other constellations. Orion is well-known because it is easily recognizable. Other constellations that are noticeable in the night sky are the Big Dipper and Little Dipper. Different constellations are visible at different times throughout the year, and some are seen all year round. Usually constellations have names that hold certain meanings. Typically, the name of a constellation is derived from an ancient language such as Latin, Greek, or Arabic because it was named when it was discovered in ancient times.

Activity: Investigating Language Suggest that each student research the name of a constellation. Which language did it come from? Who named it and what language did they speak? Suggest that they record their work in the **Enrichment: Investigating Language** worksheet, ***Professional Development Guidebook,*** page 234.

all this bush in your yard? Ain't it does make the place damp?"

He said, "Listen, and I will tell you a story. Once upon a time a boy and girl met each other and they fell in love. They loved each other so much they got married. They were both poets. He loved words. She loved grass and flowers and trees. They lived happily in a single room, and then one day, the girl poet said to the boy poet, 'We are going to have another poet in the family.' But this poet was never born, because the girl died, and the young poet died with her, inside her. And the girl's husband was very sad, and he said he would never touch a thing in the girl's garden. And so the garden remained, and grew high and wild." 22

I looked at B. Wordsworth, and as he told me this lovely story, he seemed to grow older. I understood his story.

We went for long walks together. We went to the Botanical Gardens and the Rock Gardens. We climbed Chancellor Hill in the late afternoon and watched the darkness fall on Port-of-Spain, and watched the lights go on in the city and on the ships in the harbor.

He did everything as though he were doing it for the first time in his life. He did everything as though he were doing some church rite.

He would say to me, "Now, how about having some ice cream?"

And when I said, yes, he would grow very serious and say, "Now, which café shall we **patronize**?" As though it were a very important thing. He would think for some time about it, and finally say, "I think I will go and negotiate the purchase with that shop."

The world became a most exciting place.

One day, when I was in his yard, he said to me, "I have a great secret which I am now going to tell you."

I said, "It really secret?"

"At the moment, yes."

I looked at him, and he looked at me. He said, " This is just between you and me, remember. I am writing a poem."

"Oh." I was disappointed.

He said, "But this is a different sort of poem. This is the greatest poem in the world."

I whistled.

He said, "I have been working on it for more than five years now. I will finish it in about twenty-two years from now, that is, if I keep on writing at the present rate."

"You does write a lot, then?"

He said, "Not any more. I just write one line a month. But I make sure it is a good line."

I asked, "What was last month's good line?"

He looked up at the sky, and said, *"The past is deep."*

I said, "It is a beautiful line."

B. Wordsworth said, "I hope to **distill** the experiences of a

Reading Strategy
Apply Background Knowledge Based on folk tales and fairy tales you know, how does B. Wordsworth deliberately make his story sound like an ancient tale?

Vocabulary
patronize (pā′ trən īz) *v.* to be a customer of a particular merchant or store

distill (di stil′) *v.* to obtain the essential part

23 **Reading Check**
What does B. Wordsworth do when the narrator, angry and crying, comes to see him?

22 Reading Strategy

Apply Background Knowledge

1. Remind students that when they read, they should ask themselves what other works the author may be alluding to.
2. Next, **ask:** What are some characteristics of folk tales and fairy tales?
   Possible response: Fairy tales often have "happy ever after" endings. They also include magical and strange events.
3. **Ask:** Based on folk tales and fairy tales you know, how does B. Wordsworth deliberately make his story sound like an ancient tale?
   Possible response:
   B. Wordsworth uses the phrases "once upon a time" and "they lived happily" (although the couple in the story does not live happily ever after). In addition, he moves swiftly through the events, glossing over the complexities of human experience the way some folk tales and fairy tales do.

23 Reading Check

Answer: He tells the narrator to lie on the grass looking up at the sky and think about how far away the stars are.

Differentiated Instruction for Universal Access

Support for Special-Needs Students
Have partners take turns presenting passages of the story that include dialogue between the narrator and B. Wordsworth. How would each student reading the narrator change his or her voice to show the difference between the narrator as a young boy and the narrator as the person telling the story?

Strategy for Less Proficient Readers
Ask students whether they have ever learned B. Wordsworth's real name. Then, ask them to see if they learn it before the end of the story. Have them discuss what the writer might be trying to express by not letting readers know the poet's true name.

EL Vocabulary for English Learners
Have students study the vocabulary words and use them in written sentences. Ask them to suggest words related to *patronize* and *distill.* (Students may cite *patron, patronizing, patronage, distilling, distilled, distillation.*)

24 World Literature Connection

Politics and Fiction

Thomas More's *Utopia* is one of the first examples of "political fiction," for his novel's story served as a harsh commentary on societal practices under King Henry VIII. Written against the backdrop of the coming Protestant Reformation, which officially began the year following *Utopia's* publication, the novel raised questions about the way in which religion was imposed and about division of wealth in society.

Connect to the Literature

Ask students the Connect to the Literature question: In what way does "B. Wordsworth" raise political or social questions?

Answer: In making references to the poor economic condition of both the narrator and B. Wordsworth, as well as comments about the narrator's mother hitting him, the story raises questions about the quality of life of the native population of Trinidad.

World 24 LITERATURE CONNECTION

Politics and Fiction

Because V. S. Naipaul's stories and novels examine how characters are affected by their societies, they are sometimes described as political fiction. The tradition of fiction that addresses political and social issues is a long one. British writer Thomas More published one of the first political novels, *Utopia,* in 1516. Eighteenth-century French writer Voltaire wrote *Candide,* one of the most famous political satires of all time. Russian author Leo Tolstoy took on Napoleon's invasion of Russia in *War and Peace,* and in the 1920s Franz Kafka addressed the issue of nightmarish government bureaucracies in *The Trial.*

More recently, novels by Latin American and Caribbean authors, including Juan Rulfo, Jacques Roumain, Carlos Fuentes, Isabel Allende, Julia Alvarez, and Edwidge Danticat, have dealt with political upheavals in their countries. Fiction by Chinua Achebe, Nadine Gordimer, and Ngugi wa Thiong'o has responded to the political turmoil of the African continent. Novels by Naguib Mahfouz, Ahdah Soueif, Anton Shammas, and Amos Oz speak about society in the Middle East.

Connect to the Literature

In what way does "B. Wordsworth" raise political or social questions?

Vocabulary
keenly (kēn′ lē)
adv. sharply; intensely

whole month into that single line of poetry. So, in twenty-two years, I shall have written a poem that will sing to all humanity."

I was filled with wonder.

Our walks continued. We walked along the sea-wall at Docksite one day, and I said, "Mr. Wordsworth, if I drop this pin in the water, you think it will float?"

He said, "This is a strange world. Drop your pin, and let us see what will happen."

The pin sank.

I said, "How is the poem this month?"

But he never told me any other line. He merely said, "Oh, it comes, you know. It comes."

Or we would sit on the sea-wall and watch the liners come into the harbor.

But of the greatest poem in the world I heard no more.

I felt he was growing older.

"How you does live, Mr. Wordsworth?" I asked him one day.

He said, "You mean how I get money?"

When I nodded, he laughed in a crooked way.

He said, "I sing calypsoes in the calypso season."

"And that last you the rest of the year?"

"It is enough."

"But you will be the richest man in the world when you write the greatest poem?"

He didn't reply.

One day when I went to see him in his little house, I found him lying on his little bed. He looked so old and so weak, that I found myself wanting to cry.

He said, "The poem is not going well."

He wasn't looking at me. He was looking through the window at the coconut tree, and he was speaking as though I wasn't there. He said, "When I was twenty I felt the power within myself." Then, almost in front of my eyes, I could see his face growing older and more tired. He said, "But that—that was a long time ago."

And then—I felt it so **keenly**, it was as though I had been slapped by my mother. I could see it clearly on his face. It was there for everyone to see. Death on the shrinking face.

He looked at me, and saw my tears and sat up.

He said, "Come." I went and sat on his knees.

He looked into my eyes, and he said, "Oh, you can see it, too. I always knew you had the poet's eye."

He didn't even look sad, and that made me burst out crying loudly.

Vocabulary Development

Vocabulary Knowledge Rating

When students have completed reading and discussing the selection, have them take out their **Vocabulary Knowledge Rating Charts** for the story. Read the words aloud and have students rate their knowledge of words again in the After Reading column. Clarify any words that are still problematic. Have students write their own definitions and example or sentence in the appropriate column. Then, have students complete the Vocabulary Practice at the end of the selection. Encourage students to use the words in further discussion and written work about the selection. Remind them that they will be accountable for these words on the **Selection Test, *Unit 6 Resources,*** pages 222–224 or 225–227.

He pulled me to his thin chest, and said, "Do you want me to tell you a funny story?" and he smiled encouragingly at me.

But I couldn't reply.

He said, "When I have finished this story, I want you to promise that you will go away and never come back to see me. Do you promise?"

I nodded.

He said, "Good. Well, listen. That story I told you about the boy poet and the girl poet, do you remember that? That wasn't true. It was something I just made up. All this talk about poetry and the greatest poem in the world, that wasn't true, either. Isn't that the funniest thing you have heard?"

But his voice broke.

I left the house, and ran home crying, like a poet, for everything I saw.

I walked along Alberto Street a year later, but I could find no sign of the poet's house. It hadn't vanished, just like that. It had been pulled down, and a big, two-storied building had taken its place. The mango tree and the plum tree and the coconut tree had all been cut down, and there was brick and concrete everywhere.

It was just as though B. Wordsworth had never existed.

"I WANT YOU TO PROMISE THAT YOU WILL GO AWAY AND NEVER COME BACK TO SEE ME."

Cite textual evidence to support your responses.

Critical Reading

1. **Key Ideas and Details (a)** What reason does B. Wordsworth give for wanting to come into the boy's yard? **(b) Compare and Contrast:** How is B. Wordsworth different from the other visitors who are described?
2. **Key Ideas and Details** What does B. Wordsworth mean when he calls the boy "a poet"?
3. **Key Ideas and Details** B. Wordsworth "did everything as though he were doing it for the first time." In what way does this help make B. Wordsworth "a poet"?
4. **Key Ideas and Details (a) Infer:** What do you think B. Wordsworth's motivation is for spending time with the boy? **(b) Draw Conclusions:** What does the boy gain from knowing B. Wordsworth?
5. **Integration of Knowledge and Ideas** Does B. Wordsworth's name reflect the harmful effects of colonialism on the identity of colonized peoples? Explain, using at least two of these Essential Question words: *authenticity, inherent, identity, influence.* ***[Connecting to the Essential Question: What is the relationship between literature and place?]***

ASSESS

Answers

Before students respond, you may wish to have them write a brief objective summary of the selection. As they answer the questions below, remind them to support their answers with evidence from the text.

1. (a) He wants to watch the bees that are in the narrator's palm trees. (b) The others are hoping to receive food or money, whereas B. Wordsworth just wants to watch the bees.
2. He means that the narrator is sensitive to the world around him.
3. He sees even the familiar world from a fresh perspective, which makes him creative.
4. (a) He may recognize the boy as a kindred spirit. He may also be lonely. (b) He discovers a new way of looking at the world.
5. **Possible response:** B. Wordsworth's choice of name reflects the harmful effects of colonialism in that he should not have to base his identity on that of a white poet. At the same time, it shows pride, because the poet takes the influence of William Wordsworth and turns it into something all his own.

Concept Connector

Reading Strategy Graphic Organizer

Ask students to review the graphic organizers in which they have applied background knowledge of a historical period. Then, have students share their organizers and compare what they have learned.

Activating Prior Knowledge

Have students return to their responses to the Activating Prior Knowledge activity. Ask them to explain whether their thoughts have changed and, if so, how.

Writing About the Essential Question

Have students compare their responses to the prompt, completed before reading the selections, with their thoughts afterward. Have them work individually or in groups, writing or discussing their thoughts, to formulate new responses. Then, lead a class discussion, probing for what students have learned that confirms or invalidates their initial thoughts. Encourage students to cite specific textual details to support their responses.

Answers

1. **Possible response:** Carving: lion; Value to Carver: livelihood, pride; Value to Husband: none, represented only his economic advantage/ability to exploit; Value to Wife: appreciated its fine craftsmanship; Poem: greatest in the world; Value to Poet: identity, beauty; Value to Townspeople: none; Value to Boy: provides new insight and awareness.
2. **Possible response:** Their fates suggest that colonialism was oppressive and dismissive of native people's talents.
3. **Possible response:** The student might answer that this shows the reluctance of some to support colonialism. The train is apartheid, trying to keep control and keep citizens in line.
4. **Possible response:** The student might offer that the woman's conflict represents the conflict of all anti-apartheid protesters.
5. **Possible response:** The student may say this helps him identify with different sides of the issue of colonialism. In addition, he has different influences from which to choose.
6. **Possible response:** His dark face and light hands emphasize his dual ethnicity. The unamused look on his face also emphasizes his demeanor.
7. **Possible response:** The student might answer that the wife's reaction showing her respect for the artist as an equal exhibits twentieth-century sensibility.
8. **Possible response:** The student may offer that Naipaul is using an example of someone held in high regard to highlight the devastating effects of colonialism, and that it can discourage even the greatest and most inspired minds.
9. **Possible responses:** (a) The student may respond that discrimination was the most harmful aspect of colonialism. (b) Exposure to the valuable talents and culture of native populations could be a positive aspect of colonialism, as could exposure of the native people to the talents and culture of the colonizing country.
10. **Possible response:** The student might say that the world has learned that subjugation of one culture by another is harmful.

After You Read *The Train from Rhodesia* • *B. Wordsworth*

Literary Analysis

1. **Key Ideas and Details** Gordimer and Naipaul use works of art (a carving, a poem) to show how **colonialism** affected people's values. Use a graphic organizer to compare the values placed on the carving in "The Train from Rhodesia" and the poem in "B. Wordsworth."

Carving	Value to Carver	Value to Husband	Value to Wife
Poem	Value to Poet	Value to Townspeople	Value to Boy

2. **Integration of Knowledge and Ideas** The carving is purchased cheaply and thrown into a corner. The poem of B. Wordsworth is stunted and never even comes into being. What do the fates of these objects say about colonialism?
3. **Craft and Structure** In "The Train from Rhodesia," the train itself is a major element of the *setting.* How might Gordimer be using "the segmented body of the train" to make a comment about colonialism?
4. **Integration of Knowledge and Ideas** Explain how the internal **conflict** experienced by the wife in "The Train from Rhodesia" reflects the external conflict created by colonialism and apartheid.
5. **Integration of Knowledge and Ideas** The *characterization* of B. Wordsworth presents him as a man who lives in two worlds, British and Trinidadian. Do you think this aspect of colonialism helped or hindered his development as a poet? Explain.
6. **Analyze Visual Information** What qualities of Naipaul does the caricature of him on this page emphasize?

Common Core State Standards

Writing

3. Write narratives to develop real or imagined experiences or events using effective technique, well-chosen details, and well-structured event sequences. *(p. 1357)*

3.d. Use precise words and phrases, telling details, and sensory language to convey a vivid picture of the experiences, events, setting, and/or characters. *(p. 1357)*

Language

4.b. Identify and correctly use patterns of word changes that indicate different meanings or parts of speech. *(p. 1357)*

Reading Strategy

7. In "The Train from Rhodesia," the husband manifests historical European assumptions about the colonial situation. Explain how the wife, by contrast, represents a twentieth-century sensibility.
8. William Wordsworth was a prolific writer who produced thousands of pages of lyric, narrative, and autobiographical poems. In Naipaul's story, B. Wordsworth is barely able to write one line per month. When you **apply this background knowledge,** what comment do you think Naipaul is making?
9. **(a)** Based on these two stories and your knowledge of history, which aspect of colonialism was most harmful to colonized people? **(b)** Was any aspect of colonialism positive? Explain.
10. Based on these two stories and your background knowledge, what important lessons do you think the nations of the world have learned about the relationships of colonized and colonizing peoples?

▼ David Levine caricature of V. S.Naipaul, Nov. 1, 2001. *http://www.nybooks.com/gallery/1851*

Assessment Practice

(For more practice, see *All-in-One Workbook.*)

Many tests ask students questions about a text's organization. Use the following sample item to teach students how to recognize patterns of organization within a paragraph. Have students read the second paragraph on page 1344.

Which of the following best expresses how the description in this paragraph is organized?

A spatially, from the sky to the ground
B from a general overview of the scene to specific details
C spatially, from one end of the train to the other
D from specific details to a general overview of the scene

Lead students to recognize that the description is arranged in spatial order. The description moves along with the man, who begins walking at the beginning of the passenger cars and ends at the engine. Students should determine that the correct answer is **C**.

PERFORMANCE TASKS

Integrated Language Skills

Vocabulary Acquisition and Use

Word Analysis: Patterns of Word Changes

Words often follow patterns as they change in function and in meaning. The word *patron*, for example, comes from a Latin root meaning "protector," "defender," or "father." Its various forms reflect these meanings.

- A *patron* (noun) of the arts is someone wealthy who supports artists.
- To *patronize* (verb) is to be kind but snobbish. *Patronize* also means to shop regularly in a particular store.
- *Patronage* (noun) is the power to grant political jobs or favors. *Patronage* also means business that customers give a store.

Complete each sentence using one of the following words: *patron, patronize, patronage.*

1. Some believe that _______ leads to corruption in politics.
2. A _______ of the arts, she gave generously to the orchestra.
3. I always _______ that vegetable market.

Vocabulary: Analogies

Analogies show the relationships between pairs of words. Complete each analogy using a word from the vocabulary list on page 1340. In each, your choice should create a word pair that matches the relationship between the first two words given. Then, explain your answers.

1. impressionistic : scientific :: subjective :
   a. objective **b.** perspective **c.** effective **d.** ineffective
2. segmented : separated :: fulfilled :
   a. abandoned **b.** emptied **c.** satisfied **d.** split
3. atrophy : develop :: grow :
   a. invest **b.** decay **c.** mature **d.** enlarge
4. patronize : patron :: advertise :
   a. store **b.** product **c.** customer **d.** advertiser
5. distill : dilute :: destroy :
   a. create **b.** smash **c.** distribute **d.** invent
6. keenly : intensely :: boldly :
   a. beautifully **b.** cowardly **c.** bravely **d.** awkwardly

Writing

Narrative Text The narrator of Naipaul's story will never forget the remarkable B. Wordsworth. Write a **biographical sketch** of a remarkable person you have known or met, using yourself as a first-person narrator.

Prewriting Jot down the traits that make your subject remarkable. Select a scene or an event that reveals this person's memorable personality.

Drafting As a first-person narrator, write an account of the scene. Like Naipaul, characterize your subject using your reactions and your subject's specific actions and words. Communicate the signficance of the scene or event to your audience.

Revising Review your account to replace vague adjectives with precise ones and add dialogue that conveys the flavor of the subject's personality.

Model: Revising to Add Precise Details as Support

Mrs. Walcott's ~~pleasant~~ resonant voice and lilting Jamaican accent made everything she said sound ~~true.~~ like a melody. On that occasion, she declared, "Hear the sounds behind the sounds."

The writer replaces vague language with precise adjectives and a simile and adds a vivid quotation.

EXTEND/ASSESS

Answers

Vocabulary Acquisition and Use

1. Introduce the skill using the instruction on the student page.
2. Have students complete the Word Analysis activity and the Vocabulary practice.

Word Analysis

1. patronage
2. patron
3. patronize

Vocabulary

1. a; objective
2. c; satisfied
3. b; decay
4. d; advertiser
5. a; create
6. c; bravely

Writing

1. To guide students in writing this narrative text, describe someone who has inspired you.
2. Remind students that each biography should describe the person's traits and personality as well as his or her motivation to do what it was that makes the person remarkable.
3. If students have difficulty thinking of someone to write about, suggest that they try to remember the person who comes to mind when they hear the words "admire," "respect," and "accomplishment."
4. Use the **Rubrics for Biography,** ***Professional Development Guidebook,*** pages 278–279, to evaluate students' work.

Assessment Resources

Unit 6 Resources

L1 L2 EL **Selection Test A,** pp. 222–224. Administer Test A to less advanced readers.

L3 L4 EL **Selection Test B,** pp. 225–227. Administer Test B to on-level students and more advanced students.

L3 L4 **Open-Book Test,** pp. 219–221. As an alternative, give the Open-Book test.

All **Customizable Test Bank**

All **Self-tests**
Students may prepare for the **Selection Test** by taking the **Self-test** online.

PHLit Online! All assessment resources are available at **www.PHLitOnline.com.**

from *Midsummer,* XXIII • from *Omeros,* from Chapter XXVIII

Lesson Pacing Guide

DAY 1 Preteach

- Administer the Reading and Vocabulary Warm-ups (*Unit 6 Resources,* pp. 228–231) as necessary.
- Introduce the Literary Analysis concept: Political Critique.
- Introduce the Reading Strategy: Repair Comprehension by Understanding Allusions.
- Build background with the author and Background features.
- Develop thematic thinking with Connecting to the Essential Question.
- Teach the selection vocabulary.

DAY 2 Preteach/Teach/Extend

- Distribute copies of the appropriate graphic organizer for the Reading Strategy (*Graphic Organizer Transparencies*, pp. 248–249).
- Distribute copies of the appropriate graphic organizer for Literary Analysis (*Graphic Organizer Transparencies*, pp. 250–251).
- Prepare students to read with the Activating Prior Knowledge activities (TE).
- Informally monitor comprehension while students read.
- Use the Reading Check questions to confirm comprehension.
- Develop students' understanding of political critiques using the Literary Analysis prompts.
- Develop students' ability to repair comprehension using the Reading Strategy prompts.
- Reinforce vocabulary with the Vocabulary notes.
- Assess students' comprehension and mastery of the skills by having them answer the Critical Reading, Literary Analysis, and Reading Strategy questions.

DAY 3 Assess

- Have students complete the Vocabulary Lesson.
- Have students complete the Writing activity, planning a multimedia presentation. (You may assign as homework.)
- Administer Selection Test A or B (*Unit 6 Resources,* pp. 240–242 or 243–245).

Common Core State Standards

Reading Literature 3. Analyze the impact of the author's choices regarding how to develop and relate elements of a story or drama.

Writing 7. Conduct short as well as more sustained research projects to answer a question or solve a problem.

Additional Standards Practice
Common Core Companion, *pp. 54–55; 196–207*

Daily Block Scheduling
Each day in this Lesson Pacing Guide represents a 40–50 minute period. Teachers using block scheduling may combine days to revise pacing. In addition, teachers may differentiate and support core instruction by integrating components for extended and intensive support as students require. See the Guide to Selected Leveled Resources (facing page).

Guide to Selected Leveled Resources

RTI Tier 1 (students performing on level)

		from Midsummer, XXIII • *from* Omeros, *from* Chapter XXVIII
Warm Up	**Practice, model,** and **monitor** fluency, working **with the whole class** or **in groups.**	**Vocabulary and Reading Warm-ups B,** ***Unit 6 Resources,*** pp. 248–249, 250
Comprehension/Skills	**Support** and **monitor** comprehension and skills development, having students complete the activities, graphic organizers, and interactive prompts **independently** or **as a class.**	• ***Reader's Notebook,*** adapted instruction and full selection EL ***Reader's Notebook: English Learner's Version,*** adapted instruction and adapted selection • **Reading Strategy Graphic Organizer B,** ***Graphic Organizer Transparencies,*** p. 263 • **Literary Analysis Graphic Organizer B,** ***Graphic Organizer Transparencies,*** p. 265
Monitor Progress	**Monitor** student progress with the differentiated curriculum-based assessment in the *Unit Resources.*	• **Selection Test B,** ***Unit 6 Resources,*** pp. 261–263 • **Open-Book Test,** ***Unit 6 Resources,*** pp. 255–257

RTI Tier 2 (students requiring intervention)

		from Midsummer, XXIII • *from* Omeros, *from* Chapter XXVIII
Warm Up	**Practice, model,** and **monitor** fluency **in groups** or **with individuals**	• **Vocabulary and Reading Warm-ups A,** ***Unit 6 Resources,*** pp. 247–249 • ***Hear It!*** **Audio CD (adapted text)**
Comprehension/Skills	• **Support** and **monitor** comprehension and skills development, working **in small groups** or **with individuals.** • As students complete the selection in the appropriate version of the *Reader's Notebook,* **monitor** comprehension frequently with group questions and individual instruction. • **Model** strategies while guiding students in completing the activities and prompts in the *Reader's Notebook,* as well as the graphic organizers. • **Practice** skills and **monitor** mastery with the *Reading Kit* worksheets.	• ***Reader's Notebook: Adapted Version,*** adapted instruction and adapted selection EL ***Reader's Notebook: English Learner's Version,*** adapted instruction and adapted selection • **Reading Strategy Graphic Organizer A,** ***Graphic Organizer Transparencies,*** p. 262 • **Literary Analysis Graphic Organizer A,** ***Graphic Organizer Transparencies,*** p. 264 • ***Reading Kit,*** Practice worksheets
Monitor Progress	**Monitor** student progress with the differentiated curriculum-based assessment in the *Unit Resources* and in the *Reading Kit.*	• **Selection Test A,** ***Unit 6 Resources,*** pp. 258–260 • ***Reading Kit,*** Assess worksheets

TIER 3 Tier 3 intervention may require consultation with the student's special-education or dyslexia specialist. For additional support, see the Tier 2 activities and resources listed above.

One-on-one teaching **Group work** **Whole class instruction** **Independent work** **Assessment**

For a complete guide to selection support, including support for Advanced students, see the Overview of Resources in the frontmatter.

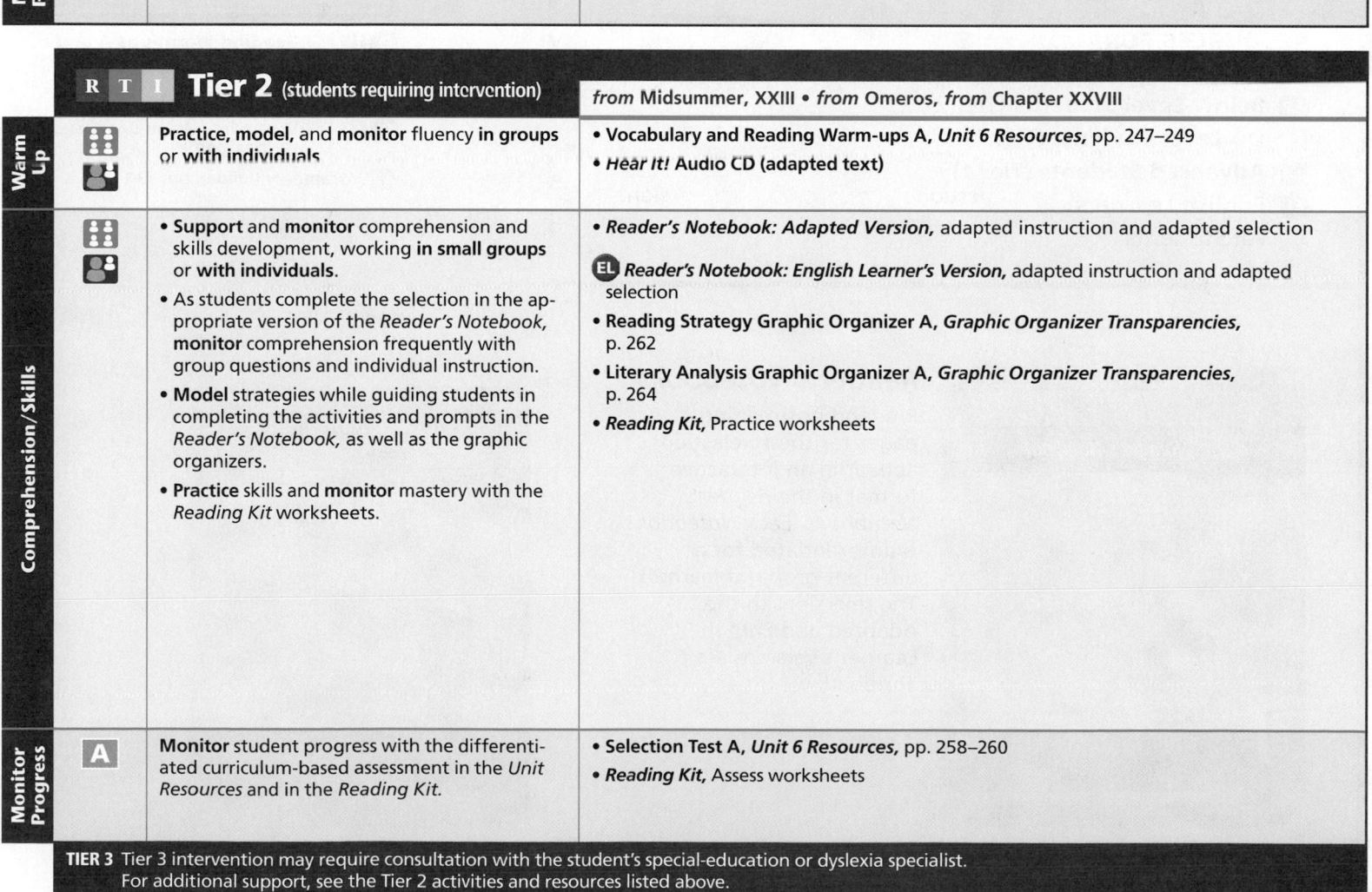

from *Midsummer,* XXIII • from *Omeros,* from Chapter XXVIII

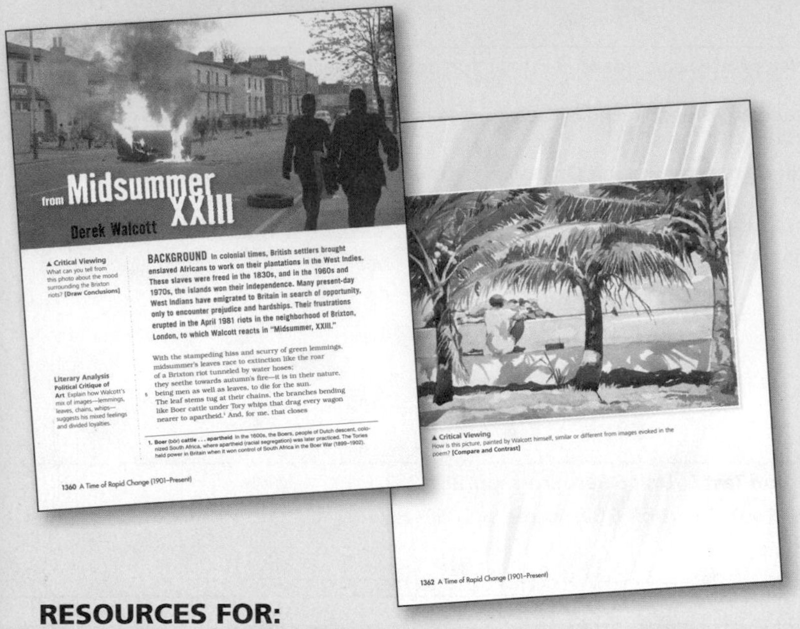

from Midsummer XXIII

Derek Walcott

▲ Critical Viewing What can you tell from this photo about the mood surrounding the Brixton riots? **[Draw Conclusions]**

BACKGROUND In colonial times, British settlers brought enslaved Africans to work on their plantations in the West Indies. These slaves were freed in the 1830s, and in the 1960s and 1970s, the islands won their independence. Many present-day West Indians have emigrated to Britain in search of opportunity, only to encounter prejudice and hardships. Their frustrations erupted in the April 1981 riots in the neighborhood of Brixton, London, to which Walcott reacts in "Midsummer, XXIII."

With the stampeding hiss and scurry of green lemmings,
midsummer's leaves race to extinction like the roar
of a Brixton riot tunneled by water hoses;
they seethe towards autumn's fire—it is in their nature,
being men as well as leaves, to die for the sun.
The leaf stems tug at their chains, the branches bending
like Boer cattle under Tory whips that drag every wagon
nearer to apartheid.[1] And, for me, that closes

Literary Analysis
Political Critique of Art Explain how Walcott's mix of images—lemmings, leaves, chains, whips—suggests his mixed feelings and divided loyalties.

1. **Boer** (bôr) **cattle . . . apartheid** In the 1600s, the Boers, people of Dutch descent, colonized South Africa, where apartheid (racial segregation) was later practiced. The Tories held power in Britain when it won control of South Africa in the Boer War (1899–1902).

1360 A Time of Rapid Change (1901–Present)

▲ Critical Viewing How is this picture, painted by Walcott himself, similar or different from images evoked in the poem? **[Compare and Contrast]**

1362 A Time of Rapid Change (1901–Present)

RESOURCES FOR:

- L1 Special-Needs Students
- L2 Below-Level Students (Tier 2)
- L3 On-Level Students (Tier 1)
- L4 Advanced Students (Tier 1)
- EL English Learners
- All All Students

Vocabulary/Fluency/Prior Knowledge

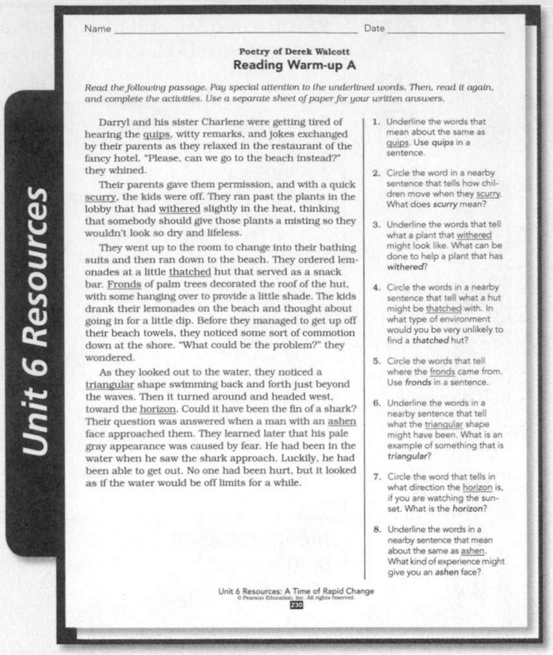

Unit 6 Resources

Name ______________________ Date ____________

Poetry of Derek Walcott
Reading Warm-up A

Read the following passage. Pay special attention to the underlined words. Then, read it again, and complete the activities. Use a separate sheet of paper for your written answers.

Darryl and his sister Charlene were getting tired of hearing the quips, witty remarks, and jokes exchanged by their parents as they relaxed in the restaurant of the fancy hotel. "Please, can we go to the beach instead?" they whined.

Their parents gave them permission, and with a quick scurry, the kids were off. They ran past the plants in the lobby that had withered slightly in the heat, thinking that somebody should give those plants a misting so they wouldn't look so dry and lifeless.

They went up to the room to change into their bathing suits and then ran down to the beach. They ordered lemonades at a little thatched hut that served as a snack bar. Fronds of palm trees decorated the roof of the hut, with some hanging over to provide a little shade. The kids drank their lemonades on the beach and thought about going in for a little dip. Before they managed to get up off their beach towels, they noticed some sort of commotion down at the shore. "What could be the problem?" they wondered.

As they looked out to the water, they noticed a triangular shape swimming back and forth just beyond the waves. Then it turned around and headed west, toward the horizon. Could it have been the fin of a shark? Their question was answered when a man with an ashen face approached them. They learned later that his pale gray appearance was caused by fear. He had been in the water when he saw the shark approach. Luckily, he had been able to get out. No one had been hurt, but it looked as if the water would be off limits for a while.

1. Underline the words that mean about the same as quips. Use *quips* in a sentence.
2. Circle the word in a nearby sentence that tells how children move when they scurry. What does *scurry* mean?
3. Underline the words that tell what a plant that withered might look like. What can be done to help a plant that has *withered*?
4. Circle the words in a nearby sentence that tell what a hut might be thatched with. In what type of environment would you be very unlikely to find a *thatched* hut?
5. Circle the words that tell where the fronds came from. Use *fronds* in a sentence.
6. Underline the words in a nearby sentence that tell what the triangular shape might have been. What is an example of something that is *triangular*?
7. Circle the word that tells in what direction the horizon is, if you are watching the sunset. What is the *horizon*?
8. Underline the words in a nearby sentence that mean about the same as ashen. What kind of experience might give you an *ashen* face?

Unit 6 Resources: A Time of Rapid Change
© Pearson Education, Inc. All rights reserved.
230

EL L1 L2 **Reading Warm-ups A and B,** pp. 230–231

Also available for these selections:

EL L1 L2 **Vocabulary Warm-ups A and B,** pp. 228–229

All **Vocabulary Builder,** pp. 234

Reader's Notebooks

Pre- and postreading pages for these selections appear in an interactive format in the *Reader's Notebooks.* Each *Notebook* is differentiated for a different group of learners. The selections in the Adapted and English Learner's versions are abridged.

L2 L3 ***Reader's Notebook***

L1 ***Reader's Notebook: Adapted Version***

EL ***Reader's Notebook: English Learner's Version***

EL ***Reader's Notebook: Spanish Version***

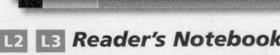

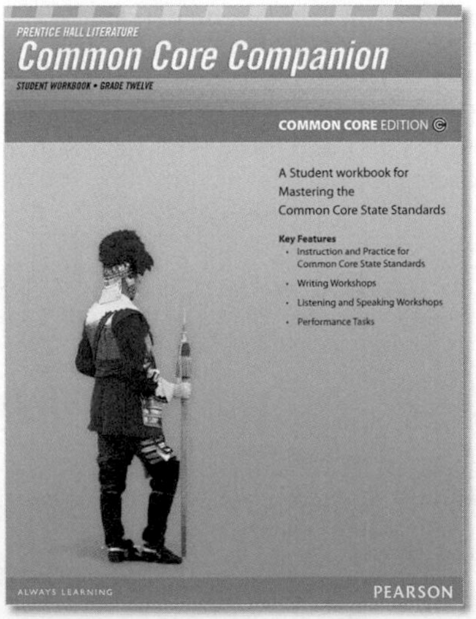

Common Core Companion

Additional instruction and practice for each Common Core State Standard

Selection Support

Graphic Organizer Transparencies

from *Midsummer, XXIII*
from *Omeros:* from *Chapter XXVIII* by Derek Walcott

After You Read B: Political Critique

Stance On . . .	Clarity	Consistency	Reasonableness
Slavery:			
Brixton Riot:			
Participating in Theater:			

Graphic Organizer Transparencies

251

EL L3 **Literary Analysis: Graphic Organizer B,** p. 251

Also available for these selections:

- EL L1 L2 **Reading: Graphic Organizer A,** p. 248
- EL L3 **Reading: Graphic Organizer B,** p. 249
- EL L1 L2 **Literary Analysis: Graphic Organizer A,** (partially filled in), p. 250

Skills Development/Extension

Unit 6 Resources

Name ______________________ Date ____________

from Midsummer, XXIII and from Omeros from Chapter XXVIII by Derek Walcott

Support for Writing

Use the graphic organizer below to collect and organize ideas for your multimedia presentation of either Walcott poem. First, write the poem you have chosen. List the theme and main images in the boxes on the left. Then, list ideas for photographs, artwork, music, video clips, and sound effects that may illustrate the poem.

Poem: ______________________ **Audiovisual Aids**

Theme:

Image:

Image:

Image:

Draw on details from your graphic organizer as you draft your script on a separate page. Show the line-by-line relationship between the text and the aids you will use.

Unit 6 Resources: A Time of Rapid Change

235

EL L3 L4 **Support for Writing,** p. 235

Also available for these selections:

- All **Literary Analysis: Political Critique,** p. 232
- All **Reading: Repair Comprehension by Understanding Allusions,** p. 233
- L4 **Enrichment,** p. 236

Assessment

Name ______________________ Date ____________

from* Midsummer, *XXIII and ***from* Omeros *Chapter XXVIII*** by Derek Walcott

Selection Test B

Critical Reading *Identify the letter of the choice that best completes the statement or answers the question.*

___ 1. What does Walcott describe in the first line of the poem *Midsummer,* XXIII?
"With the stampeding hiss and scurry of green lemmings"
A. the falling of leaves from the trees
B. the frantic nature of the rioters
C. the power of the sun
D. the history of apartheid

___ 2. What does Walcott's allusion to the history of apartheid contribute to the poem?
A. It provides the contemporary political context for the riots in Brixton.
B. It connects the experience of the rioters to the Tory party of today.
C. It provides a comment on the direction Walcott thinks society is headed.
D. It explains the difference between English and Dutch rule.

___ 3. What does Walcott imply when he writes, "the riot police and the skinheads exchanged quips"?
A. The riot police and the skinheads are "on the same side" during the riot.
B. The West Indians do not stand a chance against the riot police.
C. The riot police and the skinheads shared tactics for squelching the riot.
D. The riot police and the skinheads talked about the riot beforehand.

___ 4. How does Walcott's allusion to "the Moor's eclipse" reflect the contemporary event of the riots?
A. All West Indians share an original heritage with the Moors of North Africa.
B. The skinheads and the riot police are familiar with the story of *Othello.*
C. The smoke from the riot eclipsed, or blocked out, the light from the sun.
D. The black Othello is destroyed by the scheming and dishonest (white) Iago.

___ 5. In *Midsummer,* XXIII, Walcott refers to "Caedmon's raceless dew" and "Turner's ships" in order to
A. show how far the British Empire has fallen.
B. suggest past artistic glories are shamed by this age's brutality.
C. hint that these works of British art were never really of value.
D. imply that the demonstrators have totally missed the point.

___ 6. The excerpt from *Midsummer,* XXIII, primarily concerns
A. the passing of seasons in an English town.
B. a view of England from a nonwhite perspective.
C. race riots in England.
D. the failure of Shakespeare's drama in modern times.

___ 7. The selection from *Omeros,* Chapter XXVIII, takes as its topic the
A. destruction of African culture by modern life.
B. preservation of tradition orally by the griot.
C. speaker's struggle for his own identity.
D. dislocation and grief brought by the slave trade.

Unit 6 Resources: A Time of Rapid Change

243

EL L3 L4 **Selection Test B,** pp. 243–245

Also available for these selections:

- L3 L4 **Open-Book Test,** pp. 237–239
- EL L1 L2 **Selection Test A,** pp. 240–242

PHLit Online!
www.PHLitOnline.com

- complete narrated selection text
- a thematically related video with writing prompt
- an interactive graphic organizer
- highlighting feature
- access to all student print resources, adapted to individual student needs
- Spanish and English summaries
- adapted selection translations in Spanish

Online Resources: All print materials are also available online.

Get Connected! (thematic video with writing prompt)

Also available:

Background video
All videos are available in Spanish.

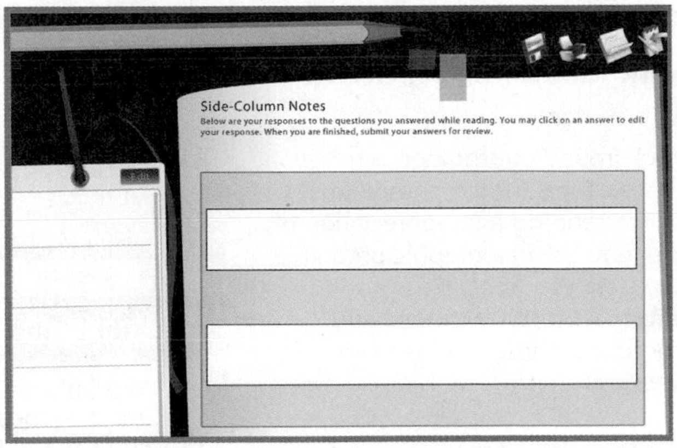

Writer's Journal (with graphics feature)

Also available:

Vocabulary Central (tools and activities for studying vocabulary)

PRETEACH

❶ Connecting to the Essential Question

1. Review the assignment.
2. Have students list major historical, political, or cultural events that have taken place during their lifetime, and **ask** them why these events were significant. Have them complete the assignment.
3. As students read, have them look for passages in which Walcott delves into his relationship with tradition.

❷ Literary Analysis

Introduce the skill.

Think Aloud: Model the Skill

Say to students:

In these readings you will focus on applying a political critique to Walcott's poems. A political critique looks at the way politics influence a work of art as well as the writer's attitudes toward the political climate. As you read, you should think about the poems and how politics and cultural experiences influenced the creation of the poems.

❸ Reading Strategy

1. Introduce the skill.
2. Give students a copy of **Reading Strategy Graphic Organizer B,** page 249 in ***Graphic Organizer Transparencies,*** to fill out as they read.

Think Aloud: Model the Skill

Say to students:

Background information is sometimes critical for the complete understanding and appreciation of a poem. Using a graphic organizer can help you apply background information to the theme and context of these poems as you interpret them.

❹ Vocabulary

1. Pronounce each word, giving its definition, and have students say it aloud.
2. For more guidance, see the ***Classroom Strategies and Teaching Routines*** card for introducing vocabulary.

Before You Read

from ***Midsummer, XXIII*** • from ***Omeros,*** from ***Chapter XXVIII***

❶ Connecting to the Essential Question Historical, political, and cultural events—important ones and trivial ones—can become part of tradition. As you read, notice historical events mentioned in the poems. These events will help you think about the Essential Question: **What is the relationship of the writer to tradition?**

Common Core State Standards

Reading Literature
3. Analyze the impact of the author's choices regarding how to develop and relate elements of a story or drama.

❷ Literary Analysis

It is important to analyze the clarity and consistency of political assumptions in a work of literature. You may, for example, apply a **political critique** to Derek Walcott's exploration of literary tradition. A political critique examines political influences and implications in a work of art, raising questions such as these:

- What political events have influenced a work of art?
- What political beliefs affect the writer's attitudes?
- Who "owns" a work of art?
- Who has the right to judge a work of art?
- What political or cultural experience must people have in order to appreciate a work of art?

Walcott's poems include **allusions**—references to persons, places, events, and artworks—that may help readers apply a political critique. Allusions use the past to gain perspective on the present. An allusion often implies that the writer and the reader "own" a common culture by jointly participating in it. Interpreting an allusion in a specific part of a poem helps you understand the meaning of the entire work.

❸ Reading Strategy

Preparing to Read Complex Texts Sometimes you can **repair comprehension by understanding allusions.** To understand Walcott's responses in *Midsummer,* you need to know that the Brixton riots erupted in London among Caribbean immigrants. You might find such information in footnotes, side glosses, background features, reference books, or the Internet. Use a chart like the one shown.

Passage
...a Brixton riot tunneled by water hoses;...

↓

Background Information
Residents of the South London district of Brixton rioted in April 1981.

↓

Interpretation
"Tunneled by water hoses": The police sprayed rioters with high-pressure water from firehoses to disperse them.

❹ Vocabulary

antic (an′ tik) *adj.* odd and funny; silly (p. 1361)

rancor (raŋ′ kər) *n.* continuing, bitter hate or ill will (p. 1361)

eclipse (i klips′) *n.* dimming or extinction of power or glory (p. 1361)

inducted (in duk′ tid) *v.* brought formally into an organization (p. 1361)

PHLit Online! www.PHLitOnline.com

Vocabulary Development

Vocabulary Knowledge Rating

Create a **Vocabulary Knowledge Rating Chart** (***Professional Development Guidebook,*** p. 33) for the vocabulary words on the student page. Give each student a copy of the chart with the words on it. Read the words aloud, and have students mark their rating of each in the Before Reading column. When students have completed reading and discussing the selections, have them take out their **Vocabulary Knowledge Rating Charts** for the selections. Read the words aloud and have students rate their knowledge again in the After Reading column. Clarify any words that are still problematic. Then, have students complete the Vocabulary practice at the end of the selections.

PHLit Online! **Vocabulary Central,** featuring tools and activities for studying vocabulary, is available online at **www.PHLitOnline.com.**

⑤ Derek Walcott
(b. 1930)

Author of *Midsummer*, XXIII • *Omeros*, Chapter XXVIII

Derek Walcott, one of the most renowned contemporary poets writing in English, has roots in two worlds. Both of his grandmothers were descendants of enslaved Africans, and both of his grandfathers were white colonials. He owes allegiance to his own rich native traditions, which can be traced back to African sources, yet he is also drawn to Western traditions that hearken back to ancient Greece. These foundations support the contexts of his poems, which carry a reader from Tropical Trinidad to ancient Greece to Shakespeare's England.

Early Poetry Walcott was born on the Caribbean Island of St. Lucia, where he spoke both the island dialect and English. He graduated from the University of the West Indies. Precocious and prolific, eighteen-year-old Walcott published the first of his many volumes of poetry, *Twenty-five Poems*, by using two hundred dollars that he borrowed, to print and distribute it on the street.

In 1959, Walcott, also an accomplished playwright, founded the Trinidad Theatre Workshop with his twin brother, Roderick. In his dramatic works, he explores his Caribbean roots more deeply than he does in his poetry. His play *Dream on Monkey Mountain*, a folk drama, won an Obie in 1971. More recently, Walcott collaborated with songwriter and composer Paul Simon on a Broadway musical, *The Capeman* (1997).

High Honors Walcott's 1990 book *Omeros*, which draws on the epics of the ancient Greek poet Homer, ensured him the Nobel Prize for Literature in 1992, making Walcott the first native Caribbean writer ever to win a Nobel Prize for literature. The Swedish Academy, when granting the award, concluded that "West Indian culture has found its great poet."

> **"I come from a place that likes grandeur."**

from Midsummer, XXIII • from Omeros, from Chapter XXVIII **1359**

Daily Bellringer

For each class during which you will teach these selections, have students complete one of the five activities for the appropriate week in the *Daily Bellringer Activities* booklet.

Multidraft Reading

To assist struggling readers and to enhance reading for all, assign the text in chunks, as warranted by length, and apply multidraft reading protocols. For each reading, have students set the purpose indicated:

- **First reading**—identifying key ideas and details and answering any Reading Checks.
- **Second reading**—analyzing craft and structure and responding to the side-column prompts.
- **Third reading**—integrating knowledge and ideas, connecting to other texts and the world, and answering the end-of-selection questions.

For more guidance, refer to the *Classroom Strategies and Teaching Routines* card, Multidraft Reading.

⑤ Background
More About the Author

The experience of growing up on the isolated volcanic island of St. Lucia, an ex-British colony, has had a strong influence on Walcott's life and work. Walcott has been an assiduous traveler to other countries but has always, not least in his efforts to create an indigenous drama, felt himself deeply rooted in Caribbean society, with its cultural fusion of African, Asian, and European elements.

www.PHLitOnline.com

Teaching From Technology

Preparing to Read
Go to **www.PHLitOnline.com** and display the *Get Connected!* slide show for these selections. Have the class brainstorm responses to the writing prompt, entering ideas in the interactive journal. Then, have students complete their written responses as homework.

To build background, display the Background and More About the Author features.

Using the Interactive Text
Go to **www.PHLitOnline.com** and display the **Enriched Online Student Edition.** As the class reads the selection or listens to the narration, record answers to side-column prompts using the graphic organizers accessible on the interactive page. Alternatively, have students use the online edition individually, answering the prompts as they read.

1 About the Selection

Derek Walcott wrestles with his conflicting loyalties as a black Caribbean poet accepted in British society.

2 Activating Prior Knowledge

To prepare students for these poems about West Indians adapting to European culture, have them share memories of times they visited places very different from their own homes. Have each student write a paragraph about his or her experiences.

Concept Connector →

Tell students they will return to their responses after reading the selection.

3 Critical Viewing

Answer: The mood is gloomy, dark, and frightening.

4 Literary Analysis

Political Critique of Art

1. Have students pay attention to the images in lines 1–7.
2. Then, **ask** the Literary Analysis question: Explain how Walcott's mix of images—lemmings, leaves, chains, whips—suggests his mixed feelings and divided loyalties.

Answer: The images compare man to both negative and positive images in nature: rodents and trees. They also reference the inhumanities done to man by man: "chains" and "whips."

1 from Midsummer XXIII

Derek Walcott

3 **▲ Critical Viewing** What can you tell from this photo about the mood surrounding the Brixton riots? **[Draw Conclusions]**

2 **BACKGROUND In colonial times, British settlers brought enslaved Africans to work on their plantations in the West Indies. These slaves were freed in the 1830s, and in the 1960s and 1970s, the islands won their independence. Many present-day West Indians have emigrated to Britain in search of opportunity, only to encounter prejudice and hardships. Their frustrations erupted in the April 1981 riots in the neighborhood of Brixton, London, to which Walcott reacts in "Midsummer, XXIII."**

Literary Analysis
Political Critique of Art Explain how Walcott's mix of images—lemmings, leaves, chains, whips—suggests his mixed feelings and divided loyalties.

With the stampeding hiss and scurry of green lemmings,
midsummer's leaves race to extinction like the roar
of a Brixton riot tunneled by water hoses;
4 they seethe towards autumn's fire—it is in their nature,
being men as well as leaves, to die for the sun.
The leaf stems tug at their chains, the branches bending
like Boer cattle under Tory whips that drag every wagon
nearer to apartheid.[1] And, for me, that closes

1. **Boer** (bör) **cattle . . . apartheid** In the 1600s, the Boers, people of Dutch descent, colonized South Africa, where apartheid (racial segregation) was later practiced. The Tories held power in Britain when it won control of South Africa in the Boer War (1899–1902).

Text Complexity Rubric

	from Midsummer XXIII	*from* Omeros, Chapter XXVIII
Qualitative Measures		
Context/ Knowledge Demands	Modern poetry; historical and literary knowledge demands 1 2 (3) 4 5	Modern epic; historical and cultural knowledge demands 1 2 (3) 4 5
Structure/Language Conventionality and Clarity	Poetic diction; slang 1 2 (3) 4 5	Poetic diction 1 2 (3) 4 5
Levels of Meaning/ Purpose/Concept Level	Challenging (racial tension; conflicting loyalties and traditions) 1 2 (3) 4 5	Challenging (Middle Passage and slavery; heritage) 1 2 3 (4) 5
Quantitative Measures		
Lexile/Text Length	NP / 191 words	NP / 298 words
Overall Complexity	**More accessible**	**More complex**

the child's fairy tale of an antic England—fairy rings,
thatched cottages fenced with dog roses,
a green gale lifting the hair of Warwickshire.
I was there to add some color to the British theater.
"But the blacks can't do Shakespeare, they have no experience."
This was true. Their thick skulls bled with rancor
when the riot police and the skinheads exchanged quips
you could trace to the Sonnets,[2] or the Moor's eclipse.[3]
Praise had bled my lines white of any more anger,
(5) and snow had inducted me into white fellowships,
while Calibans[4] howled down the barred streets of an empire
that began with Caedmon's raceless dew,[5] and is ending
in the alleys of Brixton, burning like Turner's ships.[6]

Vocabulary

antic (an′ tik) *adj.* odd and funny; silly

rancor (raŋ′ kər) *n.* continuing, bitter hate or ill will

eclipse (i klips′) *n.* dimming or extinction of power or glory

inducted (in dukt′ id) *v.* brought formally into an organization

2. **the Sonnets** William Shakespeare's sequence of 154 sonnets, noted for their passionate, often witty inquiries into love and rivalry.
3. **the Moor's eclipse** In Shakespeare's *Othello,* Othello the Moor (a black North African) is destroyed by the scheming of his white lieutenant, Iago.
4. **Calibans** Caliban is a deformed creature in Shakespeare's play *The Tempest.* Enslaved by the enchanter Prospero, Caliban has been interpreted as a native who rebels against his island's "colonizer," Prospero.
5. **Caedmon's** (kad′ mənz) **raceless dew** poetry written by the earliest known English poet, Caedmon (seventh century).
6. **Turner's ships** British artist J. M. W. Turner (1775–1851) rendered atmospheric oil paintings of, among other subjects, ships burning in battle.

Reading Strategy
Repair Comprehension by Understanding Allusions Some of Turner's paintings showed ships that carried slaves. How does this information help explain Walcott's final sentence?

Critical Reading

1. **Key Ideas and Details (a)** Toward what are midsummer's leaves racing? **(b) Interpret:** What mood does this race create for the poem?
2. **Key Ideas and Details (a)** What event "closes" for the speaker "the child's fairy tale of an antic England"? **(b) Infer:** Why is this event disillusioning? **(c) Connect:** Why does Walcott's reason for being in England at the time make the event especially significant for him?
3. **Key Ideas and Details (a) Draw Conclusions:** What does the speaker mean when he says that the "empire / . . . is ending / in the alleys of Brixton"? **(b) Connect:** What common idea or pattern connects the midsummer leaves, Walcott's disillusionment, and the crisis in England?
4. **Integration of Knowledge and Ideas** Judging by the poem, has Walcott come to terms with belonging to both black and white traditions? Explain.
5. **Integration of Knowledge and Ideas** Do you think black artists such as Walcott should withdraw from "white fellowships" to protest racial injustices? Explain.

Cite textual evidence to support your responses.

(5) Reading Strategy

Repair Comprehension by Understanding Allusions

1. Students should reread the final sentence of the poem, paying attention to the footnotes.
2. Pointing out that some of Turner's paintings showed ships carrying slaves, **ask:** How does this information help explain Walcott's final sentence?

   Answer: As in Brixton, Turner's ships represented racial destruction.

ASSESS

Answers

Remind students to support their answers with evidence from the text.

1. (a) The leaves are racing to extinction. (b) Students may respond that it suggests a frenzied, disturbed mood.
2. (a) The violence of the Brixton riots ends the speaker's romantic picture of England. The riots show that Britain is a troubled, divided, and violent society.
   (b) The event is disillusioning because its violence contrasts with the innocence of fairy tales.
   (c) Walcott was participating in a theatrical project, a sign of British acceptance of West Indians; the riots expose a more brutal truth about West Indians' place in Britain.
3. (a) West Indians were once ruled by the British, and West Indian immigration to Britain is an after-effect of the empire; the riots show that the empire failed to unite people and is torn apart by internal conflict. (b) The leaves are dead or dying. Walcott's innocence dies with them, and the crisis in England is an enactment of the empire's end.
4. Two societies battle within him—the educated style evokes the British tradition; the descriptions of British oppression suggest a West Indian perspective. The speaker seems torn between the two worlds.
5. Students may agree that black artists should reject white patronage. Other students may feel that artists can reduce injustice by maintaining ties with whites.

Text Complexity: Reader and Task Suggestions

	from Midsummer XXIII	*from* Omeros
Preparing to Read the Texts • Use the Background on SE p. 1360 to explain the origins of the Brixton riots in 1981. • Use the information on SE p. 1359 to explain that Omeros is Walcott's Homeric poem about his homeland. • Guide students to use Multidraft Reading strategies (TE p. 1359).	**Leveled Tasks** ***Knowledge Demands*** If students will have difficulty with the many footnoted allusions, have them first study the footnotes. Then, have them read to focus on the poem's key ideas. ***Analyzing*** If students will not have difficulty with the allusions, have them analyze the images of plants or greenery and explain how they help convey a central theme of the selection.	**Leveled Tasks** ***Levels of Meaning*** If students will have difficulty with the poem's meaning, have them first focus on the mood that the figurative language creates. Then, as they reread, have them infer the meaning of the figurative language. ***Evaluating*** If students will not have difficulty with the poem's meaning, have them evaluate its political criticism.

❻ About the Selection

This excerpt from Chapter XXVIII of Walcott's epic poem focuses on the painful legacies of the trade that brought enslaved Africans to America and the Caribbean. A West African griot, or storyteller, describes the Africans' experiences on the slave ships, and another speaker then comments on the legacy of those experiences.

❼ Critical Viewing

Answer: The setting in this picture is a calm and relaxing image of meditation and insight; it is a direct contrast from the disturbing images in the poem.

❼ **▲ Critical Viewing**
How is this picture, painted by Walcott himself, similar or different from images evoked in the poem? **[Compare and Contrast]**

Enrichment: Building Context

The Bight of Benin

A bight is a bay formed by a curve in a coastline. The Bight of Benin is on the west coast of Africa and forms the Gulf of Guinea. The land along the Bight of Benin was once home to the Kingdom of Benin. The residents were traders, and their king ruled from an affluent court. He often sent armies to raid rival villages to capture slaves to sell to European traders.

Benin today is a small country located between Nigeria and Togo. It is one of the poorest countries in West Africa, and most people there are subsistence farmers. Their crops include palm kernels, yams, and peanuts.

Activity: Investigating the Slave Coast
Encourage interested students to examine the physical or cultural geography of Benin, Togo, and western Nigeria. Suggest that students use the **Enrichment: Investigating Geography** worksheet, ***Professional Development Guidebook,*** page 228.

6 from *Omeros*

from CHAPTER XXVIII

Derek Walcott

8
Now he heard the griot[1] muttering his prophetic song
of sorrow that would be the past. It was a note, long-drawn
and endless in its winding like the brown river's tongue:

"We were the color of shadows when we came down
with tinkling leg-irons to join the chains of the sea,
for the silver coins multiplying on the sold horizon,

and these shadows are reprinted now on the white sand
of antipodal[2] coasts, your ashen ancestors
from the Bight of Benin, from the margin of Guinea.[3]

There were seeds in our stomachs, in the cracking pods
of our skulls on the scorching decks, the tubers[4]
withered in no time. We watched as the river-gods

changed from snakes into currents. When inspected,
our eyes showed dried fronds[5] in their brown irises,
and from our curved spines, the rib-cages radiated

like fronds from a palm-branch. Then, when the dead
palms were heaved overside, the ribbed corpses
floated, riding, to the white sand they remembered,

Literary Analysis
Political Critique of Art What political assumption is Walcott making by featuring the song of the griot?

9 **Reading Check**
To what does the griot compare the enslaved people?

1. **griot** (grē´ ō) *n.* in West African cultures, a poet/historian/performer who preserves and passes on the oral tradition.
2. **antipodal** (an tip´ ə dəl) *adj.* situated on opposite sides of the earth.
3. **the Bight** (bīt) **of Benin** (be nēn´) **. . . Guinea** (gin´ ē) area of west central Africa that came to be known as the Slave Coast.
4. **tubers** (to͞ob´ ərz) *n.* thick, fleshy parts of underground stems, such as potatoes.
5. **fronds** (frändz) *n.* leaves of a palm; also the leaflike parts of seaweed.

8 Literary Analysis

Political Critique of Art

1. Recall for students the characteristics of a political critique. Remind students to examine the political influences and implications of the poem as they read.
2. Have students read the first stanza. Then, **ask** them the Literary Analysis question: What political assumption is Walcott making by featuring the song of the griot?
   Answer: He invokes the oral traditions of the griot: a traveling poet, musician, or entertainer from North and West Africa, whose duties include the recitation of tribal and family histories. Because he uses the pronouns *we* and *our,* it can be assumed that the griot was a person of color or a slave.

9 Reading Check

Answer: The griot compares the enslaved people to shadows and palm trees.

Concept Connector

Literary Analysis Graphic Organizer

Ask students to review the graphic organizers in which they have recorded allusions to better understand the theme and context of the selections. Then, have students share their organizers and compare their interpretations.

Activating Prior Knowledge

Have students return to their responses to the Activating Prior Knowledge activity. Ask them to explain whether their thoughts have changed and, if so, how.

Writing About the Essential Question

Have students compare their responses to the prompt, completed before reading the selections, with their thoughts afterward. Have them work individually or in groups, writing or discussing their thoughts, to formulate their new responses. Then, lead a class discussion, probing for what students have learned that confirms or invalidates their initial thoughts. Encourage students to cite specific textual details to support their responses.

10 Reading Strategy

Repair Comprehension by Understanding Allusions

1. Have students read the third stanza, in which the Bight of Benin and New Guinea are mentioned. Tell them to reread the footnote.
2. Then, **ask** the Literary Analysis question: What contrast does Walcott set up by alluding to Benin and Guinea on one hand and the "stone-white hotel" on the other hand?

   Answer: He is setting up the racial contrast of the slaves and the whites; he then mentions the "black waiter bringing the bill" in line 24.

ASSESS/EXTEND

Answers

Remind students to support their answers with evidence from the text.

1. (a) The griot recalls the voyage of the Africans from the Slave Coast to the Caribbean. (b) Plant imagery is used to describe the bodies of enslaved Africans. The image of driftwood on the waves in the present is presented as an invitation to remember the enslaved Africans of the past.
2. (a) Different tribes, even families, were separated from one another. (b) Each man "was a nation in himself" because he was separated from his tribe, from his family, and from his friends.
3. Students may respond that Walcott has used the power of poetry to effectively portray the slaves's suffering through such imagery as "the cracking pods/ of our skulls on the scorching decks," "the ribbed corpses floated," and "the bolt rammed home its echo."
4. **Possible response:** Yes, Walcott includes his multiracial *origins* as he writes about each complex *situation* within the poems: the Brixton riot and the struggle of the slaves. His use of traditions focuses on his multiple references to storytelling.

Reading Strategy
Repair Comprehension by Understanding Allusions What contrast does Walcott set up by alluding to Benin and Guinea on the one hand and the "stone-white hotel" on the other hand?

to the Bight of Benin, to the margin of Guinea.
So, when you see burnt branches riding the swell,
trying to reclaim the surf through crooked fingers,

after a night of rough wind by some stone-white hotel,
10 past the bright triangular passage of the windsurfers,
remember us to the black waiter bringing the bill."

But they crossed, they survived. There is the epical splendor.
Multiply the rain's lances, multiply their ruin,
the grace born from subtraction as the hold's iron door

rolled over their eyes like pots left out in the rain,
and the bolt rammed home its echo, the way that thunder-
claps perpetuate their reverberation.

So there went the Ashanti one way, the Mandingo another,
the Ibo another, the Guinea.[6] Now each man was a nation
in himself, without mother, father, brother.

6. **the Ashanti** (ə shan′ tī) . . . **the Mandingo** (man diŋ′ gō) . . . **the Ibo** (ē′ bō′) . . . **the Guinea** (gin′ ē) names of West African peoples.

Critical Reading

Cite textual evidence to support your responses.

1. **Key Ideas and Details (a)** What event does the griot describe? **(b) Analyze:** How does the griot use plant imagery to link past and present?
2. **Key Ideas and Details (a)** What happens to members of the different West African peoples once they are brought across the sea? **(b) Interpret:** What does Walcott mean when he says, "Now each man was a nation / in himself"?
3. **Integration of Knowledge and Ideas** In this excerpt, does Walcott pass too quickly over the suffering inflicted by the slave trade? Explain.
4. **Integration of Knowledge and Ideas** Does Walcott effectively use traditions to address current controversies? Explain. In your response, use at least two of these Essential Question words: *origins, endurance, situation. [Connecting to the Essential Question: What is the relationship of the writer to tradition?]*

Assessment Practice

Style (For more practice, see *All-in-One Workbook*.)

Many tests require students to recognize stylistic devices and effective language. Use the following sample item to show students how to recognize the tone of a poem. Have students read page 1360 before answering this question.

> With the stampeding hiss and scurry of green lemmings,/midsummer's leaves race to extinction like the roar/of a Brixton riot tunneled by water hoses;/they seethe towards autumn's fire . . .

The tone in this passage can best be described as one of —

A hopelessness.
B urgency.
C acceptance.
D humor.

Point out the violent images in this passage: "stampeding hiss," "the roar of a Brixton riot." By considering the poem's diction, students should determine that the correct answer is ***B***.

After You Read

from *Midsummer, XXIII* • from *Omeros,* from *Chapter XXVIII*

Literary Analysis

1. **Integration of Knowledge and Ideas** Apply a **political critique** to Walcott's poems. First, identify their political stances, such as interpretations of history and individual actions. Then evaluate those stances for clarity, consistency, and reasonableness. Use a graphic organizer like the one shown.

Stance on...	Clarity	Consistency	Reasonableness
Slavery:			
Brixton Riot:			
Participating in Theater:			

2. **Integration of Knowledge and Ideas** In *Omeros*, Walcott makes the assumption that Homer, part of the European tradition, can be incorporated into the West Indian tradition. In what sense might a great artist of the past belong to everyone?

Common Core State Standards

Writing
7. Conduct short as well as more sustained research projects to answer a question or solve a problem.

Reading Strategy

3. In *Midsummer*, XXIII, how does **repairing your comprehension by understanding the allusion** to Caliban help you to appreciate Walcott's deeply mixed feelings about the Brixton riots?

PERFORMANCE TASKS
Integrated Language Skills

Vocabulary Acquisition and Use

Select the letter of the word that is a synonym for each of the words on the vocabulary list on page 1358.

1. **antic: (a)** oppositional **(b)** dangerous **(c)** disappointing **(d)** zany
2. **rancor: (a)** joyfulness **(b)** musicality **(c)** hatred **(d)** frustration
3. **eclipse: (a)** outburst **(b)** conflagration **(c)** extinction **(d)** omission
4. **inducted: (a)** anticipated **(b)** initiated **(c)** concluded **(d)** generalized

Writing

Informative Text Walcott's poems conjure up scenes. Plan a **multimedia presentation** of one of his poems. Identify print and nonprint media you would use to present the poem's images, speakers, rhythms, and language. Once you have organized your selected media, write responses to these questions:

- How would the media bring out qualities the poem possesses?
- What new qualities would the media add to the poem?
- How would the media help an audience to appreciate the poem?

Answers

1. In *Midsummer*, XXIII, Walcott observes that the racial divide continues despite the modern world. He also reveals his ambivalence because he is a multiracial man.
The experiences of slavery in *Omeros* have isolated and destroyed traditional culture, yet these oppressed people survive.
Possible answers to graphic organizer: *Midsummer*, XXIII: slavery: clarity, consistency
Brixton Riot: clarity, consistency
Participating in Theatre: clarity
Omeros: slavery: clarity, consistency
2. A great artist like Homer can relate to many historical situations and conflicts. Throughout history, societal struggles have maintained consistent themes.
3. The allusion to Caliban exemplifies Walcott's mixed feelings about the riots, since Caliban is used as a symbol for Walcott himself.

Vocabulary Acquisition and Use

1. d
2. c
3. c
4. b

Writing

Evaluate students' plans for an informative text using the **Rubrics for a Multimedia Report,** ***Professional Development Guidebook***, pp. 266–267.

Assessment Resources

Unit 6 Resources

L1 L2 EL **Selection Test A,** pp. 240–242. Administer Test A to less advanced readers.

L3 L4 EL **Selection Test B,** pp. 243–245. Administer Test B to on-level and more advanced students.

L3 L4 **Open-Book Test,** pp. 237–239. As an alternative, give the Open-Book Test.

All **Customizable Test Bank**

All **Self-tests**
Students may prepare for the **Selection Test** by taking the **Self-test** online.

PHLit Online! All assessment resources are available at **www.PHLitOnline.com.**

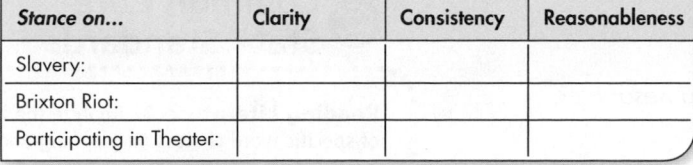

COMMON CORE
Time and Resource Manager

Follower • Two Lorries • Outside History

Lesson Pacing Guide

DAY 1 Preteach

- Administer the Reading and Vocabulary Warm-ups (*Unit 6 Resources*, pp. 246–249) as necessary.
- Introduce the Literary Analysis concept: Diction and Style.
- Introduce the Reading Strategy: Summarize.
- Build background with the author and Background features.
- Develop thematic thinking with Connecting to the Essential Question.
- Teach the selection vocabulary.

DAY 2 Preteach/Teach/Extend

- Distribute copies of the appropriate graphic organizer for the Reading Strategy (*Graphic Organizer Transparencies*, pp. 252–253).
- Distribute copies of the appropriate graphic organizer for Literary Analysis (*Graphic Organizer Transparencies*, pp. 254–255).
- Prepare students to read with the Activating Prior Knowledge activities (TE).
- Informally monitor comprehension while students read.
- Use the Reading Check questions to confirm comprehension.
- Develop students' understanding of diction and style using the Literary Analysis prompts.
- Develop students' ability to summarize using the Reading Strategy prompts.
- Reinforce vocabulary with the Vocabulary notes.
- Assess students' comprehension and mastery of the skills by having them answer the Critical Reading, Literary Analysis, and Reading Strategy questions.

DAY 3 Assess

- Have students complete the Vocabulary Lesson.
- Have students complete the Writing activity, writing directions. (You may assign as homework.)
- Administer Selection Test A or B (*Unit 6 Resources,* pp. 258–260 or 261–263).

Common Core State Standards

Reading Literature 4. Analyze the impact of specific word choices on meaning and tone.

Writing 2. Write informative/explanatory texts to examine and convey complex ideas, concepts, and information clearly and accurately through the effective selection, organization, and analysis of content.

Additional Standards Practice
Common Core Companion*, *pp. 41–48; 196–207

Daily Block Scheduling
Each day in this Lesson Pacing Guide represents a 40–50 minute period. Teachers using block scheduling may combine days to revise pacing. In addition, teachers may differentiate and support core instruction by integrating components for extended and intensive support as students require. See the Guide to Selected Leveled Resources (facing page).

Guide to Selected Leveled Resources

RTI Tier 1 (students performing on level)

			Follower • Two Lorries • Outside History
Warm Up	Whole class instruction; Group work	**Practice, model,** and **monitor** fluency, working **with the whole class** or **in groups.**	**Vocabulary and Reading Warm-ups B, *Unit 6 Resources,*** pp. 246–247, 249
Comprehension/Skills	Whole class instruction; Group work; Independent work	**Support** and **monitor** comprehension and skills development, having students complete the activities, graphic organizers, and interactive prompts **independently** or **as a class.**	• ***Reader's Notebook,*** adapted instruction and full selection EL ***Reader's Notebook: English Learner's Version,*** adapted instruction and adapted selection • **Reading Strategy Graphic Organizer B, *Graphic Organizer Transparencies,*** p. 267 • **Literary Analysis Graphic Organizer B, *Graphic Organizer Transparencies,*** p. 269
Monitor Progress	A	**Monitor** student progress with the differentiated curriculum-based assessment in the *Unit Resources.*	• **Selection Test B, *Unit 6 Resources,*** pp. 279–281 • **Open-Book Test, *Unit 6 Resources,*** pp. 273–275

RTI Tier 2 (students requiring intervention)

			Follower • Two Lorries • Outside History
Warm Up	Group work; One-on-one teaching	**Practice, model,** and **monitor** fluency **in groups** or **with individuals.**	• **Vocabulary and Reading Warm-ups A, *Unit 6 Resources,*** pp. 264–266 • ***Hear It!*** **Audio CD (adapted text)**
Comprehension/Skills	Group work; One-on-one teaching	• **Support** and **monitor** comprehension and skills development, working **in small groups** or **with individuals.** • As students complete the selection in the appropriate version of the *Reader's Notebook,* **monitor** comprehension frequently with group questions and individual instruction. • **Model** strategies while guiding students in completing the activities and prompts in the *Reader's Notebook,* as well as the graphic organizers. • **Practice** skills and **monitor** mastery with the *Reading Kit* worksheets.	• ***Reader's Notebook: Adapted Version,*** adapted instruction and adapted selection EL ***Reader's Notebook: English Learner's Version,*** adapted instruction and adapted selection • **Reading Strategy Graphic Organizer A, *Graphic Organizer Transparencies,*** p. 266 • **Literary Analysis Graphic Organizer A, *Graphic Organizer Transparencies,*** p. 268 • ***Reading Kit,*** Practice worksheets
Monitor Progress	A	**Monitor** student progress with the differentiated curriculum-based assessment in the *Unit Resources* and in the *Reading Kit.*	• **Selection Test A, *Unit 6 Resources,*** pp. 276–278 • ***Reading Kit,*** Assess worksheets

TIER 3 Tier 3 intervention may require consultation with the student's special-education or dyslexia specialist. For additional support, see the Tier 2 activities and resources listed above.

One-on-one teaching **Group work** **Whole class instruction** **Independent work** **A Assessment**

For a complete guide to selection support, including support for Advanced students, see the Overview of Resources in the frontmatter.

Follower • Two Lorries • Outside History

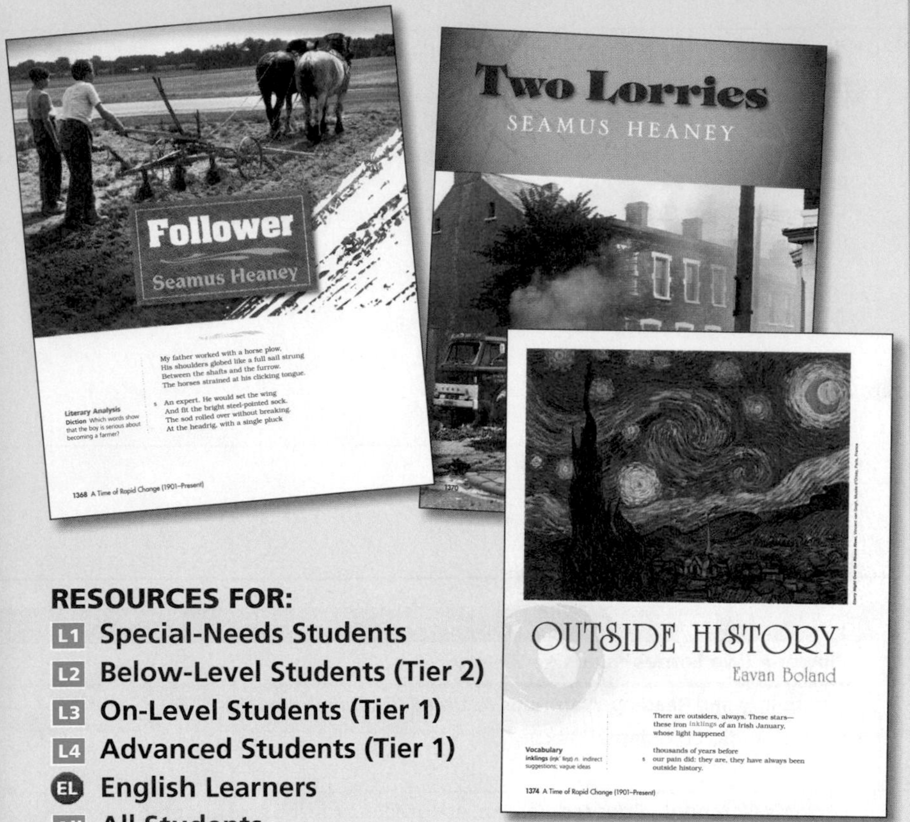

RESOURCES FOR:

- L1 Special-Needs Students
- L2 Below-Level Students (Tier 2)
- L3 On-Level Students (Tier 1)
- L4 Advanced Students (Tier 1)
- EL English Learners
- All All Students

Vocabulary/Fluency/Prior Knowledge

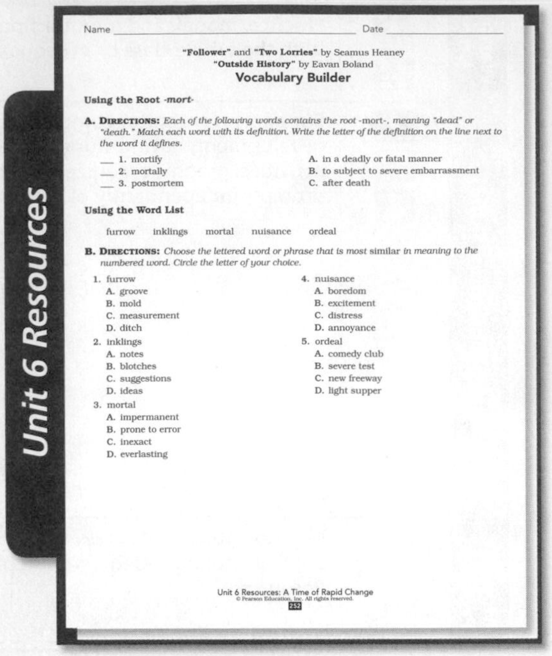
Unit 6 Resources

Name ______________________ Date ______________

"Follower" and "Two Lorries" by Seamus Heaney
"Outside History" by Eavan Boland
Vocabulary Builder

Using the Root *-mort-*

A. Directions: *Each of the following words contains the root -mort-, meaning "dead" or "death." Match each word with its definition. Write the letter of the definition on the line next to the word it defines.*

___ 1. mortify — A. in a deadly or fatal manner
___ 2. mortally — B. to subject to severe embarrassment
___ 3. postmortem — C. after death

Using the Word List

furrow inklings mortal nuisance ordeal

B. Directions: *Choose the lettered word or phrase that is most similar in meaning to the numbered word. Circle the letter of your choice.*

1. furrow
   A. groove
   B. mold
   C. measurement
   D. ditch
2. inklings
   A. notes
   B. blotches
   C. suggestions
   D. ideas
3. mortal
   A. impermanent
   B. prone to error
   C. inexact
   D. everlasting
4. nuisance
   A. boredom
   B. excitement
   C. distress
   D. annoyance
5. ordeal
   A. comedy club
   B. severe test
   C. new freeway
   D. light supper

Unit 6 Resources: A Time of Rapid Change
© Pearson Education, Inc. All rights reserved.
252

All **Vocabulary Builder,** p. 252

Also available for these selections:

EL L1 L2 **Vocabulary Warm-ups A and B,** pp. 246–247

EL L1 L2 **Reading Warm-ups A and B,** pp. 248–249

Reader's Notebooks

Pre- and postreading pages for these selections appear in an interactive format in the *Reader's Notebooks*. Each *Notebook* is differentiated for a different group of learners. The selections in the Adapted and English Learner's versions are abridged.

L2 L3 ***Reader's Notebook***

L1 ***Reader's Notebook: Adapted Version***

EL ***Reader's Notebook: English Learner's Version***

EL ***Reader's Notebook: Spanish Version***

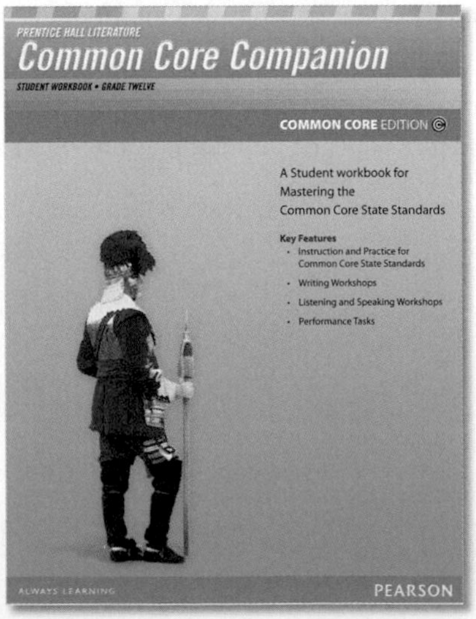

Common Core Companion

Additional instruction and practice for each Common Core State Standard

Selection Support

Graphic Organizer Transparencies

"**Follower**" and "**Two Lorries**" by Seamus Heaney
"**Outside History**" by Eavan Boland

Before You Read A: Summarizing

Passage

I have chosen:

Out of myth into history I move to be
part of that ordeal
whose darkness is

only now reaching me from those fields,
those rivers, those roads clotted as
firmaments with the dead.
("Outside History")

Main Points

- The speaker makes a conscious choice: earthly "ordeal" instead of stars' immortality.

Summary

Graphic Organizer Transparencies

252

EL L1 L2 **Reading: Graphic Organizer A,** p. 252

Also available for these selections:

EL L3 **Reading: Graphic Organizer B,** p. 253

EL L1 L2 **Literary Analysis: Graphic Organizer A,** (partially filled in), p. 254

EL L3 **Literary Analysis: Graphic Organizer B,** p. 255

Skills Development/Extension

Unit 6 Resources

Name ______________________ Date ____________

"**Follower**" and "**Two Lorries**" by Seamus Heaney
"**Outside History**" by Eavan Boland

Enrichment: Contemporary Farmer

In 1977, the U.S. Census Bureau revised the definition of "farm" to distinguish it from merely rural property. Under the new definition, a landowner who earns more than $1,000 annually from selling agricultural products is a farmer. In the United States, there are about two million farms so defined.

The nature of farming has changed much in recent history. Farm technology, farm markets (what products are needed and how much they sell for), and the business of running a farm have all become complex issues.

Consider the following statistics and what they mean in terms of being a farmer.

	1935	1992
Number of farms in U.S.	6.8 million	1.9 million
Acreage devoted to farming	982 million acres	126 million acres
Average farm size	155 acres	467 acres

The change in farm size reflects the changing nature of farming in general. The family-owned farm is becoming harder to find. Instead there are farmers or landowners who hire farm managers to make decisions about hundreds and hundreds of acres of land or perhaps thousands of head of livestock. Large farming corporations also operate farms.

Economic influences have brought about a radical change in farming. A single crop failure, or one year of low wheat prices, for example, can ruin a small farmer who has invested everything in that one crop. A large-scale farmer or corporation can afford to raise larger crops or more than one crop to ensure protection from crop failure or low prices.

Directions: *Refer to details in Seamus Heaney's poem "Follower," as well as to information on this page, to answer the following questions.*

1. The subject of Heaney's poem is probably a small farmer working his own farm in the 1940s. List the tools and equipment that are apparently in use by the farmer in "Follower."
2. What might the farmer in "Follower" need to know about "farm management?"
3. What do you think a contemporary farmer needs to know about farm management? List as many areas of knowledge as you can.

Unit 6 Resources: A Time of Rapid Change

254

L4 **Enrichment,** p. 254

Also available for these selections:

All **Literary Analysis: Diction and Style,** p. 250

All **Reading: Summarize,** p. 251

EL L3 L4 **Support for Writing,** p. 253

Assessment

Name ______________________ Date ____________

Poetry of Seamus Heaney and Eavan Boland

Open-Book Test

Short Answer *Write your responses to the questions in this section on the lines provided.*

1. In "Follower," Seamus Heaney presents a father-son relationship from the son's perspective. How does the son feel about his father? Cite one or two details from the poem to support your response.
2. The farmer's son, who is the speaker in "Follower," follows his father around the farm, watching him perform the daily chores. What is the main idea in stanza 2 of the poem?
3. Heaney chooses his words carefully in "Follower." Explain how the diction in Stanza 5 reflects the speaker's choice to be like his father.
4. In "Two Lorries," what does the speaker's account of the explosion of the second lorry (Stanzas 5 and 6) reveal about his attitude toward violence? Support your answer with one or two details from the poem.
5. In "Two Lorries," the sestina form causes certain key words in the poem to be repeated in important positions in the last three lines. What are three of these words, and what effect does this repetition have on the poem's overall mood?
6. In "Outside History" by Eavan Boland, the speaker refers to stars as "outside history" (line 6). Explain briefly how this choice of words provides a contrast to the speaker's own experience.

Unit 6 Resources: A Time of Rapid Change

255

L3 L4 **Open-Book Test,** pp. 255–257

Also available for these selections:

EL L1 L2 **Selection Test A,** pp. 258–260

EL L3 L4 **Selection Test B,** pp. 261–263

PHLit Online!
www.PHLitOnline.com

- complete narrated selection text
- a thematically related video with writing prompt
- an interactive graphic organizer
- highlighting feature
- access to all student print resources, adapted to individual student needs
- Spanish and English summaries
- adapted selection translations in Spanish

Online Resources: **All print materials are also available online.**

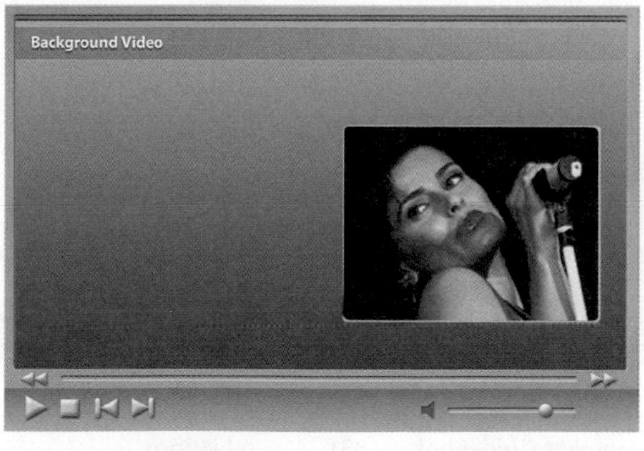

Background Video

Also available:

Get Connected! (thematic video with writing prompt)
All videos are available in Spanish.

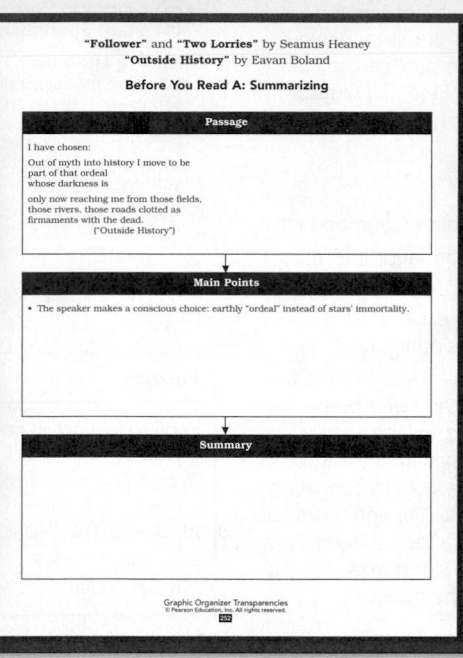

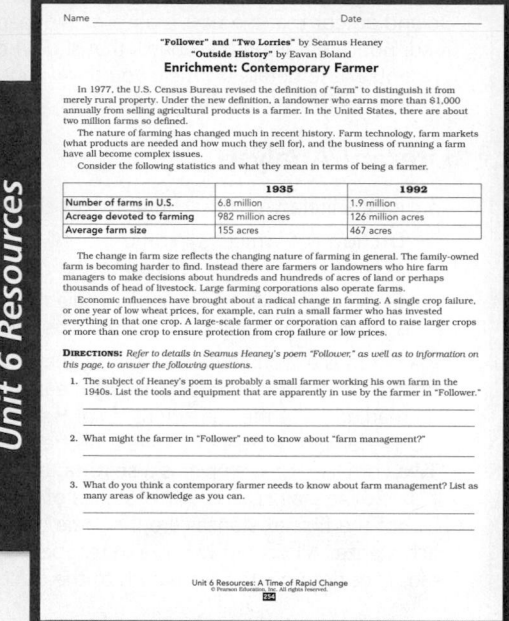

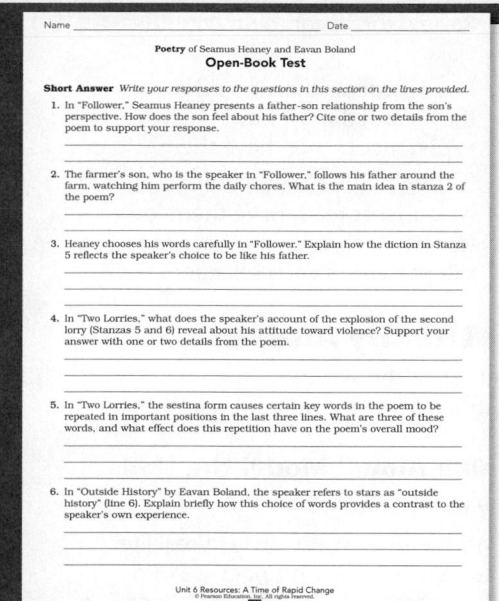

Vocabulary Central **(tools and activities for studying vocabulary)**

Also available:

Writer's Journal (with graphics feature)

PRETEACH

❶ Connecting to the Essential Question

1. Review the assignment with the class.
2. Have students talk about how they learned from past experiences. Then have them complete the assignment.
3. As students read, have them look for details about how the past is still present in each selection.

❷ Literary Analysis

Introduce the skill using the instruction on the student page.

Think Aloud: Model the Skill

Say to students:

We use diction and style in real life as well as in reading poetry aloud. For example, suppose I am talking on the telephone. If the other person asks me to repeat what I just said, I might change my pronunciation and choice of words. I want the other person to understand what I am saying.

❸ Reading Strategy

1. Introduce the skill using the instruction on the student page.
2. Give students a copy of **Reading Strategy Graphic Organizer B,** page 253 in ***Graphic Organizer Transparencies***, to fill out as they read.

Think Aloud: Model the Skill

Say to students:

We summarize events in real life as well as when discussing literature. Suppose I am late for an appointment and someone asks me, "What happened?" I would give a summary of the circumstances that led up to that moment. Whenever I tell what happened, I am summarizing.

❹ Vocabulary

1. Pronounce each word, giving its definition, and have students say it aloud.
2. For more guidance, see the ***Classroom Strategies and Teaching Routines*** card for introducing vocabulary.

Before You Read

Follower • Two Lorries • Outside History

Common Core State Standards

Reading Literature

4. Analyze the impact of specific word choices on meaning and tone, including words with multiple meanings or language that is particularly fresh, engaging, or beautiful.

❶ **Connecting to the Essential Question** Seamus Heaney and Eavan Boland accept that the past is always reappearing in our lives. As you read, notice details in the poems that show how the past can still be present. These details will help you think about the Essential Question: **How does literature shape or reflect society?**

❷ Literary Analysis

To create a literary work, a writer makes choices about diction and style.

- **Diction** is a writer's typical choice of words—formal or informal, abstract or concrete, scholarly or folksy.
- **Style** encompasses a writer's whole manner of expression. It includes word choice, forms, rhythms, themes, and imagery.

A poem is a work in words, and style and diction—both formed from patterns of words—are crucial to the meaning and tone of a poem. As you read, identify the characteristics of Heaney's and Boland's styles.

One element of Heaney's style is his frequent use of traditional forms. "Two Lorries," for example, is a **sestina,** an old French form consisting of six six-line stanzas and a final stanza of three lines. The end words of each of the first six stanzas are the same but are arranged differently in each stanza. All six end words also reappear in the final stanza. As you read, consider how this form adds to the effect of the poem.

❸ Reading Strategy

Preparing to Read Complex Texts To *determine the main idea* of a poem, it can be helpful to **summarize** it. Summarizing is restating key points in brief. Use a chart like the one shown to summarize the poems or individual stanzas in them.

Passage

I wanted to grow up and plow,
To close one eye, stiffen my arm.
All I ever did was follow
In his broad shadow round the farm.

↓

Main Points

Son following his father; looking up to him; wanting to be like him.

↓

Summary

I wanted to be a farmer, like my father.

❹ Vocabulary

furrow (fʉr´ ō) *n.* narrow groove made in the ground by a plow (p. 1369)

nuisance (no͞o´ səns) *n.* act, thing, or condition causing trouble (p. 1369)

inklings (iŋk´ liŋz) *n.* indirect suggestions; vague ideas (p. 1374)

mortal (môr´ təl) *adj.* of that which must eventually die (p. 1375)

ordeal (ôr dēl´) *n.* difficult or painful experience that tests one (p. 1375)

PHLit Online! www.PHLitOnline.com

Vocabulary Development

Vocabulary Knowledge Rating

Create a **Vocabulary Knowledge Rating Chart** (***Professional Development Guidebook***, p. 33) for the vocabulary words on the student page. Give each student a copy of the chart with the words on it. Read the words aloud, and have students mark their ratings in the Before Reading column. Urge students to attend to these words as they read and discuss the selections.

In order to gauge how much instruction you need to provide, tally how many students are confident in their knowledge of each word. As students read, point out the words and their context.

PHLit Online! **Vocabulary Central,** featuring tools and activities for studying vocabulary, is available online at **www.PHLitOnline.com.**

Author of "Follower" • "Two Lorries"

Born in County Derry, Northern Ireland, Seamus Heaney has devoted much of his poetry to the life and history of his homeland. He is a gifted traditionalist whom the American poet Robert Lowell called "the most important Irish poet since Yeats." Heaney has earned that high praise with visionary books of poetry, like *Seeing Things* (1991) and *The Spirit Level* (1996), and with his brilliant lectures on poetry, collected in *The Redress of Poetry* (1995).

A Happy Childhood The eldest of nine children, Heaney spent a happy childhood on a farm that had been in his family for generations. He has said that his deep regard for tradition grew from his early experiences in the countryside.

Leaving Home Heaney first published as an undergraduate at Queen's University in Belfast, Northern Ireland. In 1972, having struggled with the role of the artist in Northern Ireland's troubled political climate, he left and settled in the independent Irish Republic. His departure was called an artistic necessity by some and by others a betrayal. Heaney nevertheless remains the leading Irish poet—Republican or Northern.

Popular Success Heaney's accessible and deeply felt poetry has achieved a popularity that is rare among modern poets. Readers around the world have generated a strong demand for his poems, including his best-selling translation of *Beowulf* (2000). His readings are well attended by enthusiastic fans.

Since 1984, he has been Boylston Professor of Rhetoric and Poetry at Harvard. From 1989 to 1994 he also held the chair of Professor of Poetry at Oxford. In 1995, Heaney received the Nobel Prize for Literature.

5 Seamus Heaney

(b. 1939)

**"Between my finger
and my thumb
The squat pen rests.
I'll dig with it."**

Daily Bellringer

For each class during which you will teach these selections, have students complete one of the five activities for the appropriate week in the ***Daily Bellringer Activities*** booklet.

Multidraft Reading

To assist struggling readers and to enhance reading for all, assign the text in chunks, as warranted by length, and apply multidraft reading protocols. For each reading, have students set the purpose indicated:

- **First reading**—identifying key ideas and details and answering any Reading Checks.
- **Second reading**—analyzing craft and structure and responding to the side-column prompts.
- **Third reading**—integrating knowledge and ideas, connecting to other texts and the world, and answering the end-of-selection questions.

For more guidance, refer to the ***Classroom Strategies and Teaching Routines*** card on Multidraft Reading.

5 Background

More About the Author

Seamus Heaney belonged to a group of poets when he was in college at the University of Belfast in Northern Ireland. He has written of these friends: "[We] used to talk poetry day after day with an intensity and prejudice that cannot but have left a mark on us all." Heaney's modern translation of *Beowulf* was met with widespread acclaim.

PHLit Online!

Teaching From Technology

www.PHLitOnline.com

Preparing to Read

Go to **www.PHLitOnline.com** and display the ***Get Connected!*** slide show for these selections. Have the class brainstorm responses to the writing prompt, entering ideas in the interactive journal. Then, have students complete their written responses as homework.

To build background, display the Background and More About the Author features.

Using the Interactive Text

Go to **www.PHLitOnline.com** and display the **Enriched Online Student Edition.** As the class reads the selection or listens to the narration, record answers to side-column prompts using the graphic organizers accessible on the interactive page. Alternatively, have students use the online edition individually, answering the prompts as they read.

TEACH

1 About the Selection

In both of Seamus Heaney's poems, the speaker refers to his relationship with his parents and, by extension, with his Irish homeland. "Follower" focuses on the personal interaction between a small boy and his farmer father, poignantly conveying how the roles of parent and child shift as they age.

2 Activating Prior Knowledge

Ask the class to brainstorm for television shows, rock groups, cartoon shows, and fads that were popular when they were around eight years old. Ask students to write a paragraph about what they learned from those past entertainments. Then, tell students that the poems in this section all deal with how the poets' pasts shape their present.

Concept Connector →

Tell students they will return to their responses after reading the selection.

3 Literary Analysis

Diction

1. Have students read the two stanzas on the student page.
2. **Ask** the Literary Analysis question: Which words show that the boy is serious about becoming a farmer?
   Possible response: Words that show the boy is serious about becoming a farmer are *plow, furrow, sod,* and *horses.*

Follower

Seamus Heaney

My father worked with a horse plow,
His shoulders globed like a full sail strung
Between the shafts and the furrow.
The horses strained at his clicking tongue.

An expert. He would set the wing
And fit the bright steel-pointed sock.
The sod rolled over without breaking.
At the headrig, with a single pluck

3 **Literary Analysis**
Diction Which words show that the boy is serious about becoming a farmer?

Text Complexity Rubric

	Follower	Two Lorries	Outside History
Qualitative Measures			
Context/Knowledge Demands	Modern lyric; cultural knowledge and life experience demands 1 (2) 3 4 5	Modern lyric; historical and cultural knowledge demands 1 2 (3) 4 5	Modern poem; scientific knowledge demands 1 2 (3) 4 5
Structure/Language Conventionality and Clarity	Fairly simple diction 1 (2) 3 4 5	Fairly simple diction 1 2 (3) 4 5	Fairly simple diction 1 (2) 3 4 5
Levels of Meaning/ Purpose/Concepts	Accessible (family ties; aging or death) 1 2 (3) 4 5	Moderate (Northern Irish conflict) 1 2 (3) 4 5	Moderate (involvement and mortality) 1 2 3 (4) 5
Quantitative Measures			
Lexile/Text Length	NP / 155 words	NP / 625 words	NP / 123 words
Overall Complexity	**More accessible**	**More complex**	**More complex**

Of reins, the sweating team turned round
And back into the land. His eye
Narrowed and angled at the ground,
Mapping the furrow exactly.

I stumbled in his hobnailed wake,
Fell sometimes on the polished sod;
Sometimes he rode me on his back
Dipping and rising to his plod.

I wanted to grow up and plow,
To close one eye, stiffen my arm.
All I ever did was follow
In his broad shadow round the farm.

5 I was a nuisance, tripping, falling,
Yapping always. But today
It is my father who keeps stumbling
Behind me, and will not go away.

Vocabulary

furrow (fur´ ō) *n.* narrow groove made in the ground by a plow

nuisance (no͞o´ səns) *n.* act, thing, or condition causing trouble

◄ Critical Viewing
Which details in this picture convey the relationship described in the poem? **[Connect]**

Reading Strategy
Summarizing
Summarize the final stanza in one sentence.

Critical Reading

Cite textual evidence to support your responses.

1. **Key Ideas and Details (a)** In "Follower," what is the father doing? **(b) Interpret:** Why does the boy want to "close one eye" and "stiffen" his arm?
2. **Craft and Structure (a)** Give two examples of precise words Heaney uses to describe tools, actions, or other things associated with farming. **(b) Analyze:** How does the use of such words help convey the child's fascination with his father's life?
3. **Key Ideas and Details (a) Compare and Contrast:** How does the relationship between father and son shift at the end of "Follower"? **(b) Draw Conclusions:** What difference between his childhood view of his father and his own experience of adulthood does the speaker see?
4. **Integration of Knowledge and Ideas** Do people's relations with their parents always leave lasting marks or burdens? Explain.

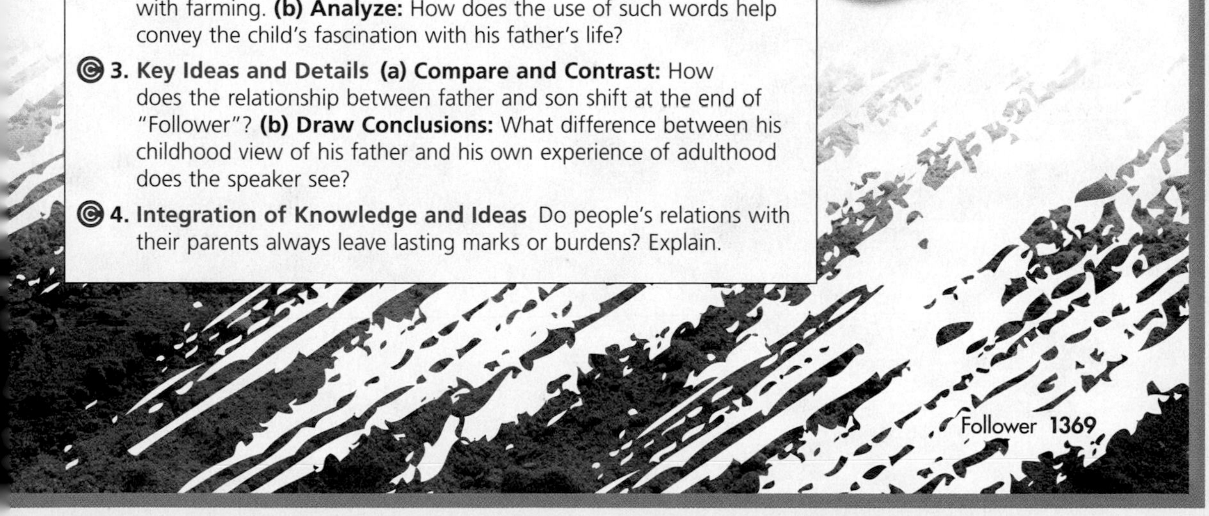

4 Critical Viewing

Answer: Two men are working with a horse plow, one watching, one working. Students might assume that both men are farmers.

5 Reading Strategy

Summarizing

1. Direct students' attention to the last stanza of the poem.
2. **Read** the Reading Strategy prompt: Summarize the final stanza in one sentence.
   Answer: As a child, the speaker was a bothersome child, but now it is his father who is a "nuisance."

ASSESS

Answers

1. (a) The father is plowing his farm fields. (b) The boy wants to imitate his father's expertise and mastery in every detail.
2. (a) Heaney uses such words as "shafts," "furrow," "wing," "steel-pointed sock," and "headrig." (b) The use of precise words echoes the boy's careful imitation of his father.
3. (a) The speaker has become an adult, and his father now seems dependent on him. (b) The speaker sees himself as a nuisance to his father when he was a boy, and his father as a kind of nuisance to him as an adult.
4. **Possible responses:** Parents can serve as their children's models into adulthood. Sometimes, living up to those ideals is a burden.

Text Complexity: Reader and Task Suggestions

	Follower	Two Lorries	Outside History
Preparing to Read the Text • Use the Background on SE p. 1371 to describe the violent past of Northern Ireland. • Discuss with students the role that family heritage may play in our life choices. • Guide students to use Multidraft Reading strategies (TE p. 1367).	**Leveled Tasks** *Levels of Meaning* If students will have difficulty with the poem's meaning, have them first focus on the speaker's father and his changing relationship with his son. Then, have students consider what the last three stanzas suggest about parent-child relationships. *Analyzing* If students will not have difficulty with the poem's meaning, have them analyze the significance of the poem's title.	**Leveled Tasks** *Levels of Meaning* If students will have difficulty with the poem's meaning, have them focus on the two lorry events. Then, have them reread to seek a connection between the events. *Synthesizing* If students will not have difficulty with the poem's meaning, have them discuss what the lorry events suggest about the human experience.	**Leveled Tasks** *Knowledge Demands* If students will have difficulty with the scientific context, clarify that light from the starts takes thousands of years to reach Earth. Then have students read the poem, focusing on the speaker's feelings about the human role in the universe. *Analyzing* If students will not have difficulty with the context, have them discuss what choice the speaker makes in the poem.

❻ About the Selection

In "Two Lorries," the poet laments the threat of Irish terrorism, contrasting a terrorist's truck bomb with a flirtatious delivery-truck driver—both might have taken his mother away from him, and both involve a "cheap," unreal passion. Both of Heaney's poems show the two faces of Ireland, one turned toward the past, the other turned toward the present; the strong emotions tying the Irish to their land; and the powerful ability of memories from daily life to focus those emotions.

❼ Critical Viewing

Answer: The scene is an ordinary city street,but clearly something destructive has happened.

❽ Critical Thinking

Connect

1. Have students read the first three stanzas of the poem.
2. **Ask** students: How does the speaker describe the woman in the poem?
   Answer: She is described as a "nineteen-forties" mother, who seems to be in a rush to leave her kitchen and go to the movies.

❻ # Two Lorries

SEAMUS HEANEY

1370

Enrichment: Investigating Geography

Ireland

The conflict in Ireland has socioeconomic causes. When English aristocrats seized land and instituted a feudal system, the Irish became dependent on foreign landowners.

Explain that Seamus Heaney made a significant choice about his Irish past when he settled in the Republic of Ireland in 1972. His own disquiet about living away from the continued conflict in Northern Ireland (his birthplace) might be compared to the father who follows him in "Follower." His regret at the terrorism in his homeland is evident in "Two Lorries."

Activity: Make a Political Map Encourage interested students to research the history of the conflict in Northern Ireland. Ask each to create a map that reflects how political borders changed. Suggest that they plan their map designs using the **Enrichment: Investigating Geography** worksheet, ***Professional Development Guidebook,*** page 228.

Background For large parts of its history, Ireland was under English control. In the 1920s, Ireland was partitioned into the Irish Republic in the South and Ulster, or Northern Ireland, which was allied with Great Britain. The Ulster Protestants generally supported British rule of Northern Ireland, while many Northern Irish Catholics wanted "the British out" and Ireland united. From the late 1960s on, this conflict has produced terrorism. It was only in 1998, with the signing of the Good Friday Agreement, that decisive steps were taken toward a peaceful sharing of power in Northern Ireland.

In their poems, both Heaney and Boland address the Irish past. Heaney views a childhood memory through the lens of a bombing incident sparked by the decades-long conflict. Boland reflects in more general terms on the responsibilities growing out of the Irish past.

It's raining on black coal and warm wet ashes.
There are tire-marks in the yard, Agnew's old lorry[1]
Has all its cribs down and Agnew the coalman
With his Belfast accent's sweet-talking my mother.
5 Would she ever go to a film in Magherafelt?
But it's raining and he still has half the load

To deliver farther on. This time the lode
Our coal came from was silk-black, so the ashes
Will be the silkiest white. The Magherafelt
10 (Via Toomebridge) bus goes by. The half-stripped lorry
With its emptied, folded coal-bags moves my mother:
The tasty ways of a leather-aproned coalman!

And films no less! The conceit of a coalman . . .
She goes back in and gets out the black lead
15 And emery paper, this nineteen-forties mother,
All business round her stove, half-wiping ashes
With a backhand from her cheek as the bolted lorry
Gets revved and turned and heads for Magherafelt

And the last delivery. Oh, Magherafelt!
20 Oh, dream of red plush and a city coalman
As time fastforwards and a different lorry
Groans into shot, up Broad Street, with a payload
That will blow the bus station to dust and ashes . . .
After that happened, I'd a vision of my mother,

1. **lorry** truck.

7 ◄ Critical Viewing
Identify ways in which this photograph, like Heaney's poem, conveys both the everyday and unusual.
[Interpret]

Literary Analysis
Diction and Style How does Heaney's repeated use of the word "Oh" help to convey the poem's meaning?

10 ☑ Reading Check
What does the coalman invite the speaker's mother to do?

Two Lorries 1371

9 Literary Analysis
Diction and Style

1. Encourage students to summarize what they have read by restating the key points to themselves.

2. Then, **ask** the Literary Analysis question: How does Heaney's repeated use of the word "Oh" help to convey the poem's meaning?
Answer: The use of "Oh" conveys meaning by exclaiming excitement at being done with deliveries and able to go to the movies.

10 Reading Check

Answer: The coalman asks the speaker's mother to go and see a film in Magherafelt.

Differentiated
Instruction for Universal Access

Strategy for Special-Needs Students	**Strategy for Less Proficient Readers**	**Strategy for Advanced Readers**
Students may find Heaney's comparison of two incidents in "Two Lorries" unusually daunting. Encourage them to break down each incident into its bare details—summarizing where necessary—to understand why he chooses to juxtapose these events.	Review with students what happens in "Two Lorries." Encourage them to give an account of the separate events in the poem by summarizing what occurs in each.	Remind students that Heaney's "Two Lorries" is a sestina—a sophisticated form that recycles the same six words at the end of each line in a stanza. Have students reread the poem to see the novel ways in which Heaney reuses each word.

11 Reading Strategy

Summarizing

1. Have students read the three stanzas on the student page.
2. **Read** the Reading Strategy prompt: The second half of the poem is Heaney's vision of his mother. Summarize his vision. **Possible response:** The speaker describes his mother as a ghost, with shopping bags full of ashes, in the middle of a deadly scene.

ASSESS

Answers

Before students respond, you may wish to have them write a brief objective summary of the selection. As they answer the questions below, remind them to support their answers with evidence from the text.

1. (a) In the first incident, the coal deliveryman asks Heaney's mother for a date to the movies. In the second incident, a bomb-carrying truck explodes, destroying a city bus station. (b) The movie and the bomb both are set in Magherafelt.
2. (a) The coalman who "sweet-talks" Heaney's mother is a threat because he is flirting with her and could upset domestic harmony. (b) The threat of Heaney's mother being taken away is similar to the threat of Heaney's motherland being destroyed by terrorism.
3. (a) The coalman's invitation might be a kind of empty tease—like the promises and results of terrorist politics. It might not lead to anything at all, or it might lead to something very bad. (b) The invitation to a movie is relatively benign flirtation, whereas the act of political violence is a profound threat.
4. (a) **Possible response:** He dislikes it for threatening to take away what he loves in Ireland, just as a sweet-talking coalman tried to steal away his mother. (b) **Possible response:** Students will probably say that Heaney's poem is a kind of political activism, because he takes a position on the evil of terrorism.

A revenant[2] on the bench where I would meet her
In that cold-floored waiting-room in Magherafelt,
Her shopping bags full up with shoveled ashes.
Death walked out past her like a dust-faced coalman
Refolding body-bags, plying his load
Empty upon empty, in a flurry

11 Of motes and engine-revs, but which lorry
Was it now? Young Agnew's or that other,
Heavier, deadlier one, set to explode
In a time beyond her time in Magherafelt . . .
So tally bags and sweet-talk darkness, coalman.
Listen to the rain spit in new ashes

As you heft a load of dust that was Magherafelt,
Then reappear from your lorry as my mother's
Dreamboat coalman filmed in silk-white ashes.

Reading Strategy
Summarizing The second half of the poem is Heaney's vision of his mother. Summarize his vision.

2. **revenant** (rev′ ə nənt) *n.* one who returns; ghost.

Critical Reading

Cite textual evidence to support your responses.

1. **Key Ideas and Details (a)** What are the two incidents described in "Two Lorries"? **(b) Analyze:** What details connect the two?
2. **Key Ideas and Details (a) Infer:** How is the coalman who "sweet-talk[s]" Heaney's mother a threat to the young Heaney? **(b) Connect:** What connection can you find between this threat and the threat of terrorism in Northern Ireland, Heaney's "motherland"?
3. **Integration of Knowledge and Ideas (a) Hypothesize:** In Heaney's view, what might the coalman's invitation to a movie, not meant or taken seriously, have in common with the promises and results of terrorist politics? **(b) Compare and Contrast:** What differences distinguish the two?
4. **Integration of Knowledge and Ideas (a) Draw Conclusions:** Judging from "Two Lorries," how would you describe Heaney's attitude toward the Irish conflicts? **(b) Evaluate:** Do you think that writing a poem like "Two Lorries" is a form of political activism? Explain.

Vocabulary Development

Vocabulary Knowledge Rating

When students have completed reading and discussing the selections, have them take out their **Vocabulary Knowledge Rating Charts** for the poems. Read the words aloud and have students rate their knowledge of words again in the After Reading column. Clarify any words that are still problematic. Have students write their own definitions and example or sentence in the appropriate column. Then, have students complete the Vocabulary practice at the end of the selections. Encourage students to use the words in further discussion and written work about the selections. Remind them that they will be accountable for these words on the Selection Test, ***Unit 6 Resources***, pages 258–260 or 261–262.

⓬ EAVAN BOLAND

(b. 1944)

Author of "Outside History"

Eavan Boland was born in Dublin, the capital of the Republic of Ireland. Her father was a diplomat who, she says, "recognized the importance of poetry to civilization." Her mother was a painter, who also "was totally in tune with what poetry tried to do."

Away From Ireland During much of Boland's early life, she was away from Ireland. When she was five, her father became ambassador to Great Britain and the family moved to London. Later, Boland was sent to school in New York City. There, she experienced anti-Irish hostility and felt "a great sense of isolation." Returning to Ireland when she was fifteen, Boland found "a great imaginative release."

A Personal Yet Public Poet Since 1967, she has published several acclaimed volumes of poetry, including *The War Horse* (1975), *In Her Own Image* (1980), *Night Feed* (1982), and *In a Time of Violence* (1994). Boland's poetry is notable for its intense focus on her personal experiences—she freely shares incidents from her life to uncover universal themes and insights. Her 1995 collection of essays, *Object Lessons: The Life of the Woman and Poet in Our Time,* combines her explorations of history, autobiography, and poetry. In addition to publishing poetry, she writes reviews and teaches at universities in both England and the United States.

Married to a novelist and the mother of two daughters, Boland often writes about domestic life, but she shuns the label "woman poet." She says poetry should create only statements that are "bound to be human." Unwilling to yoke poetry to a political program, she notes that "My poetry begins for me where certainty ends."

"What is a colony
if not the brutal truth
that when we speak
the graves open.
And the dead walk?"

⓬ Background

More About the Author

Eavan Boland's role in the poetic tradition in Ireland is an important one. She has secured a place for the feminine experience in the pantheon of Irish literature, traditionally a male domain. Boland's evocative poetry is often critical of the Irish political and cultural legacy.

Differentiated Instruction for Universal Access

Strategy for Less Proficient Readers
Students may have difficulty understanding the historical context of the Irish conflict. Review the Background note on page 1371, and ask for questions of clarification.

Enrichment for Gifted/Talented Students
Have students research current events in Ireland as they relate to the IRA and present-day conflicts between Protestants and Catholics. Students can present their findings to the class.

PHLit Online!
All video resources are available online at **www.PHLitOnline.com.**

⓭ About the Selection

This poem poses the choice between immortality—a place outside human history—and participation in the struggles of flawed life. The poet presents the stars as the symbol of immortality, a landscape impervious to history's pain. Against this image, she contrasts the many dead Irish whose memory clots the Earth's landscape. In choosing to join history, Boland engages in the fight to relieve pain and injustice, but she knows she will always be too late.

⓮ Humanities

Starry Night Over the Rhone River, 1888, by Vincent van Gogh

Vincent van Gogh, though virtually unknown and often impoverished in his lifetime, is today one of the best-known Postimpressionist painters. Born in the Netherlands, van Gogh turned to painting in his late twenties, around 1880, studying on his own as well as with other painters. Though he experienced periods of deep unhappiness and mental instability, van Gogh's short career was highly productive.

Use these questions for discussion:

1. What parts of the painting are most intense and alive?
   Possible response: The orange-yellow lights along the shore and their reflections in the water are the most intense and alive.
2. From these impressions, speculate about how van Gogh would respond to Boland's decision to move "inside" history.
   Possible response: He might respond that life within history is insubstantial unless a light burns through from outside.

⓯ Critical Viewing

Answer: Both the stars in the painting and those in Boland's poem suggest the eternal.

Starry Night Over the Rhone River, Vincent van Gogh, Musée d'Orsay, Paris, France

⓭ OUTSIDE HISTORY

Eavan Boland

Vocabulary
inklings (iŋk′ liŋz) *n.* indirect suggestions; vague ideas

There are outsiders, always. These stars—
these iron **inklings** of an Irish January,
whose light happened

thousands of years before
our pain did: they are, they have always been
outside history.

Concept Connector

Reading Skill Graphic Organizer

Ask students to review the graphic organizers in which they have summarized key point of the poems. Then, have students share their organizers and compare their analyses.

Activating Prior Knowledge

Have students return to their responses to the Activating Prior Knowledge activity. Ask them to explain whether their thoughts have changed and, if so, how.

Writing About the Essential Question

Have students compare their responses to the prompt, completed before reading the poems, with their thoughts afterward. Have them work individually or in groups, writing or discussing their thoughts, to formulate their new responses. Then, lead a class discussion, probing for what students have learned that confirms or invalidates their initial thoughts. Encourage students to cite specific textual details to support their responses.

They keep their distance. Under them remains
a place where you found
you were human, and

a landscape in which you know you are mortal.
And a time to choose between them.
I have chosen:

Out of myth into history I move to be
part of that ordeal
whose darkness is

16 only now reaching me from those fields,
those rivers, those roads clotted as
firmaments[1] with the dead.

How slowly they die
as we kneel beside them, whisper in their ear.
And we are too late. We are always too late.

1. **firmaments** *n.* the heavens.

15 ◄ **Critical Viewing**
Compare the stars in the painting with those in the poem. Do both suggest the eternal, or does one suggest the explosive? **[Compare and Contrast]**

Vocabulary
mortal (môr′ təl) *adj.* of that which must eventually die

ordeal (ôr dēl′) *n.* difficult or painful experience that tests one

Reading Strategy
Summarizing After the colon in line 12, Boland tells what she has "chosen." Summarize her choice.

Critical Reading

Cite textual evidence to support your responses.

1. **Key Ideas and Details (a)** What is the speaker viewing at the opening of the poem? **(b) Interpret:** Why does the speaker claim this sight is "outside history"?
2. **Key Ideas and Details (a) Interpret:** According to the speaker, what two things lie under the stars? **(b) Interpret:** Why must the speaker choose between them?
3. **Craft and Structure (a) Analyze:** What image does the speaker use to contrast the "ordeal" of history with the stars? **(b) Infer:** Who are "the dead" in line 18? **(c) Interpret:** Is acknowledging the dead a way of becoming part of the "ordeal"? Explain.
4. **Integration of Knowledge and Ideas** In writing this poem, does Boland become part of a larger "ordeal," or is that itself a myth? Explain.
5. **Integration of Knowledge and Ideas** How might an author justify remaining uninvolved in a conflict? Use three of these Essential Question words in your answer: *cite, doubt, position, rationalize, hindsight. [Connecting to the Essential Question: What is the relationship between literature and place?]*

16 Reading Strategy
Summarizing

1. Have students read the stanzas on the student page.
2. **Read** the Reading Strategy prompt: After the colon in line 12, Boland tells what she has "chosen." Summarize her choice.
   Possible responses: The speaker has chosen to be part of what is immortal.

ASSESS
Answers

Before students respond, you may wish to have them write a brief objective summary of the selection. As they answer the questions below, remind them to support their answers with evidence from the text.

1. (a) The speaker is viewing the stars. (b) She claims this sight is "outside history" because it takes thousands of years for a star's light to reach Earth.
2. (a) Beneath the stars lies a place where people discover they are human and a landscape in which they know they are mortal. (b) The speaker must choose between them because she wants to be part of history, inside history.
3. (a) She uses an image of darkness to contrast with the light of the stars. (b) The "dead" are those who have fallen, perhaps for a cause. (c) Yes, it requires involvement.
4. Boland becomes a part of the larger "ordeal" simply by the act of writing about it.
5. **Possible response:** An author might *rationalize* remaining uninvolved in a conflict, because he or she might *doubt* that any *position* taken would make a difference.

Assessment Practice

Style (For more practice, see *All-in-One Workbook.*)
Many tests require students to recognize stylistic devices and effective language. Use the following sample item to teach students how to describe a writer's diction.

An expert. He would set the wing
And fit the bright steel-pointed sock.
The sod rolled over without breaking.
At the headrig, with a single pluck

Heaney's diction in these lines is best characterized as—

A highly academic.
B frequently colloquial.
C alliterative.
D specific to a particular occupation.

Students should determine that the correct answer is ***D***, because this passage contains many terms related to farming.

Answers

1. Heaney's use of homespun diction, with precise terms for the work his father does; a rueful tone; and a reflective narrative style fit the subject.
2. **Possible responses:** Examples: Diction: "iron inklings," "mortal," "ordeal"; Imagery: "a landscape," "those fields," "roads clotted"; Rhythm/Rhyme: irregular; Form: 3-line stanza. Summary: Diction: philosophical/abstract diction; Imagery: simple, general imagery with abstract ideas; Rhythm/Rhyme: conversational; Form: simple
3. (a) The sestina requires Heaney to use the same six end words in each stanza. (b) The form allows variations on a theme.
4. (a) Heaney's diction in "Two Lorries" enables him to recreate the 1940s scene in which a coalman flirts with his mother. Heaney uses "old" words that bring us back to the scene. (b) Boland makes abstract ideas of history vivid in such lines as "those roads clotted as/firmaments with the dead."
5. In "Two Lorries," the speaker's mother chats with the coal deliveryman who invites her to see a film. She declines; the coalman drives off to the city. Then, a terrorist-driven truck explodes, destroying the bus station in which the speaker used to meet his mother. The main idea of the poem is that seemingly simple, individual choices can have ripple effects that last a long time.
6. People have a choice as to whether or not to engage in conflicts stemming from the past. In choosing to participate in Ireland's painful history, the speaker accepts that her efforts cannot undo past losses.

Vocabulary Acquisition and Use

1. nuisance
2. furrow
3. ordeal
4. inklings
5. mortal

Writing

Evaluate students' explanatory texts using the **Rubrics for a How-to Essay,** ***Professional Development Guidebook,*** pages 254–255.

After You Read

Follower • Two Lorries • Outside History

Literary Analysis

1. **Craft and Structure** Explain how Heaney's **diction** and **style** in "Follower" fit the subject of the poem.
2. **Craft and Structure** Complete this chart to analyze Boland's style in "Outside History." Then, summarize the distinctive elements of her style.

	Diction	Imagery	Rhythm/Rhyme	Form
Examples				
Summary of element				

3. **Craft and Structure (a)** What restrictions might the **sestina** form in "Two Lorries" place on Heaney? **(b)** What advantages might the form have?
4. **Craft and Structure (a)** How do Heaney's diction and style help him to re-create the past? Explain, using examples. **(b)** How does Boland make abstract ideas of history vivid?

Reading Strategy

5. **Summarize** "Two Lorries." Then, use your summary as a basis for stating the *main idea* of the poem.
6. Write a summary of "Outside History." Then, use your summary as a basis for stating the main idea of the poem.

Common Core State Standards

Writing

2. Write informative/explanatory texts to examine and convey complex ideas, concepts, and information clearly and accurately through the effective selection, organization, and analysis of content.

PERFORMANCE TASKS

Integrated Language Skills

Vocabulary Acquisition and Use

Identify the vocabulary word from page 1366 to fill in each blank. Use the contextual meaning of the paragraph to guide your choices.

When Heaney followed his father around the farm, he may have made a __1__ of himself. However, the boy's tripping over a __2__ was probably more a source of amusement than an __3__ for his father. One thing is certain, no __4__ that his father was __5__ had yet reached young Seamus.

Writing

Explanatory Text Use print or online resources to write **directions for traveling** by car from Belfast along the beautiful Antrim coast of Ireland. Identify and record streets, highways, and distances, and note beautiful sights along the route. Include a graphic with compass directions as well as ordered steps—what to do first, second, third, etc.

Assessment Resources

Unit 6 Resources

- L1 L2 EL **Selection Test A,** pp. 258–260. Administer Test A to less advanced readers.
- L3 L4 EL **Selection Test B,** pp. 261–263. Administer Test B to on-level and more advanced students.
- L3 L4 **Open-Book Test,** pp. 255–257. As an alternative, give the Open-Book Test.
- All **Customizable Test Bank**
- All **Self-tests** Students may prepare for the **Selection Test** by taking the **Self-test** online.

PHLit Online! All assessment resources are available at **www.PHLitOnline.com.**

The Postmodern and Beyond

PART 4

1377

Selection Planning Guide

The selections in this section are by modern writers nurtured in the British tradition. Poets Dylan Thomas, Ted Hughes, Philip Larkin, Peter Redgrove, and Stevie Smith are modern writers redefining that tradition. Writers Samuel Beckett, Harold Pinter, Penelope Shuttle, Carol Ann Duffy, Penelope Lively, and Anita Desai are leading voices of cultures once dominated by the British Empire, cultures with unique worldviews. Science-fiction writer Arthur C. Clarke addresses the daunting prospect of conquering space.

Humanities

The Postmodern and Beyond

This photograph depicts some office buildings in the Canary Wharf in London, England. The wharf is built on a site that was bombed and destroyed during World War II. The area's renovation was completed in 2002. It now includes major banks from across the globe and many important businesses and is an international hub of industry and finance.

Use these questions for discussion:

1. Canary Wharf has global influence in the financial world. Discuss how it can also affect the political concerns raised in the selections.
   Possible response: Students may say that because the banks influence the world of finance, they can have some control on the world as a whole.
2. What details in the photograph contribute to the impression of the power associated with the area?
   Possible response: Students may cite such details as the interesting architecture, bright lights, and high energy in the photograph.

Text Complexity: At a Glance

This chart gives a general text complexity rating for the selections in this part of the unit to help guide instruction. For additional text complexity support, see the Test Complexity Rubric at point of use.

Come and Go	**More Accessible**	Not Waving but Drowning	**More Accessible**
That's All	**More Complex**	Prayer	**More Accessible**
Do Not Go Gentle into That Good Night	**More Accessible**	In the Kitchen	**More Complex**
Fern Hill	**More Accessible**	A Devoted Son	**More Accessible**
The Horses	**More Complex**	Next Term, We'll Mash You	**More Accessible**
An Arundel Tomb	**More Complex**	*from* We'll Never Conquer Space	**More Complex**
The Explosion	**More Accessible**	I'm Like a Bird	**More Accessible**
On the Patio	**More Accessible**		

Monitoring Progress

Before students read the selections in Part 4, refer to the results for the **Vocabulary in Context** items on **Benchmark Test 10** (*Unit 6 Resources*, p. 130). Use this diagnostic portion of the test to guide your choice of selections to teach as well as the depth of prereading preparation you will provide, based on students' readiness for the reading and vocabulary skills.

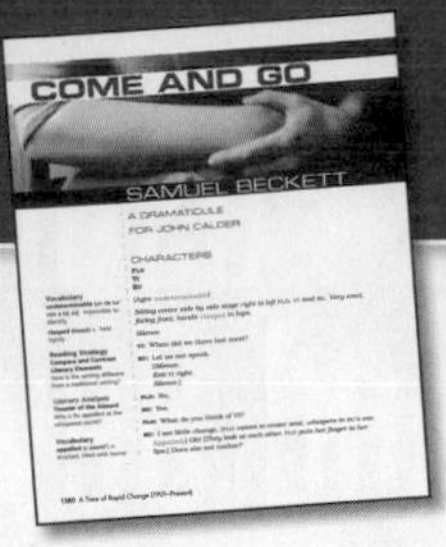

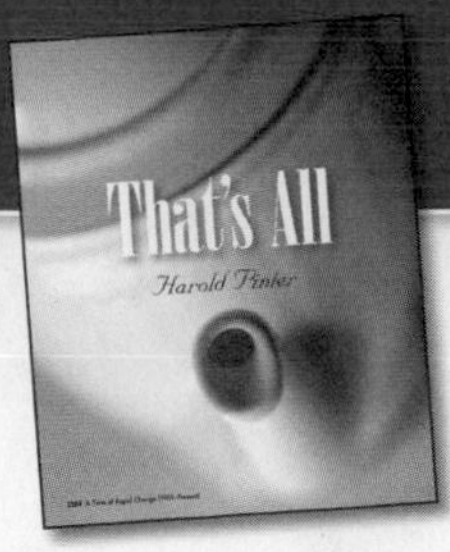

Come and Go • That's All
Lesson Pacing Guide

DAY 1 Preteach

- Administer the Reading and Vocabulary Warm-ups (*Unit 6 Resources*, pp. 264–267) as necessary.
- Introduce the Literary Analysis concept: Theatre of the Absurd.
- Introduce the Reading Strategy: Compare and Contrast Literary Elements.
- Build background with the author and Background features.
- Develop thematic thinking with Connecting to the Essential Question.
- Teach the selection vocabulary.

DAY 2 Preteach/Teach /Extend

- Distribute copies of the appropriate graphic organizer for the Reading Strategy (*Graphic Organizer Transparencies*, pp. 256–257).
- Distribute copies of the appropriate graphic organizer for Literary Analysis (*Graphic Organizer Transparencies*, pp. 258–259).
- Prepare students to read with the Activating Prior Knowledge activities (TE).
- Informally monitor comprehension while students read.
- Use the Reading Check questions to confirm comprehension.
- Develop students' understanding of Theater of the Absurd using the Literary Analysis prompts.
- Develop students' ability to compare and contrast literary elements using the Reading Strategy prompts.
- Reinforce vocabulary with the Vocabulary notes.
- Assess students' comprehension and mastery of the skills by having them answer the Critical Reading, Literary Analysis, and Reading Strategy questions.

DAY 3 Assess

- Have students complete the Vocabulary Lesson.
- Have students complete the Writing activity, writing a scene from an absurd drama. (You may assign as homework.)
- Administer Selection Test A or B (*Unit 6 Resources*, pp. 276–278 or 279–281).

Common Core State Standards

Reading Literature 3. Analyze the impact of the author's choices regarding how to develop and relate elements of a story or drama.

Writing 3. Write narratives to develop real or imagined experiences or events using effective technique, well-chosen details, and well-structured event sequences.

Additional Standards Practice
Common Core Companion, pp. 28–35; 208–218

Daily Block Scheduling
Each day in this Lesson Pacing Guide represents a 40–50 minute period. Teachers using block scheduling may combine days to revise pacing. In addition, teachers may differentiate and support core instruction by integrating components for extended and intensive support as students require. See the Guide to Selected Leveled Resources (facing page).

Guide to Selected Leveled Resources

RTI Tier 1 (students performing on level)		Come and Go • That's All
Warm Up	**Practice, model,** and **monitor** fluency, working **with the whole class** or **in groups.**	**Vocabulary and Reading Warm-ups B, *Unit 6 Resources,*** pp. 282–283, 285
Comprehension/Skills	**Support** and **monitor** comprehension and skills development, having students complete the activities, graphic organizers, and interactive prompts **independently** or **as a class.**	• ***Reader's Notebook,*** adapted instruction and full selection EL ***Reader's Notebook: English Learner's Version,*** adapted instruction and adapted selection • **Reading Strategy Graphic Organizer B, *Graphic Organizer Transparencies,*** p. 271 • **Literary Analysis Graphic Organizer B, *Graphic Organizer Transparencies,*** p. 273
Monitor Progress	**Monitor** student progress with the differentiated curriculum-based assessment in the *Unit Resources.*	• **Selection Test B, *Unit 6 Resources,*** pp. 297–299 • **Open-Book Test, *Unit 6 Resources,*** pp. 291–293
Assess/ Screen	**Assess** student progress using Benchmark Test 2.	• **Benchmark Test 11, *Unit 6 Resources,*** pp. 300–305

RTI Tier 2 (students requiring intervention)		Come and Go • That's All
Warm Up	**Practice, model,** and **monitor** fluency **in groups** or **with individuals.**	• **Vocabulary and Reading Warm-ups A, *Unit 6 Resources,*** pp. 282–284 • ***Hear It!* Audio CD (adapted text)**
Comprehension/Skills	• **Support** and **monitor** comprehension and skills development, working **in small groups** or **with individuals.** • As students complete the selection in the appropriate version of the *Reader's Notebook,* **monitor** comprehension frequently with group questions and individual instruction. • **Model** strategies while guiding students in completing the activities and prompts in the *Reader's Notebook,* as well as the graphic organizers. • **Practice** skills and **monitor** mastery with the *Reading Kit* worksheets.	• ***Reader's Notebook: Adapted Version,*** adapted instruction and adapted selection EL ***Reader's Notebook: English Learner's Version,*** adapted instruction and adapted selection • **Reading Strategy Graphic Organizer A, *Graphic Organizer Transparencies,*** p. 270 • **Literary Analysis Graphic Organizer A, *Graphic Organizer Transparencies,*** p. 272 • ***Reading Kit,*** Practice worksheets
Monitor Progress	**Monitor** student progress with the differentiated curriculum-based assessment in the *Unit Resources* and in the *Reading Kit.*	• **Selection Test A, *Unit 6 Resources,*** pp. 294–296 • ***Reading Kit,*** Assess worksheets
Assess/ Screen	**Assess** student progress using the Benchmark Test.	**Benchmark Test 11, *Unit 6 Resources,*** pp. 300–305

TIER 3 Tier 3 intervention may require consultation with the student's special-education or dyslexia specialist. For additional support, see the Tier 2 activities and resources listed above.

One-on-one teaching · Group work · Whole class instruction · Independent work · A Assessment

For a complete guide to selection support, including support for Advanced students, see the Overview of Resources in the frontmatter.

Come and Go • That's All

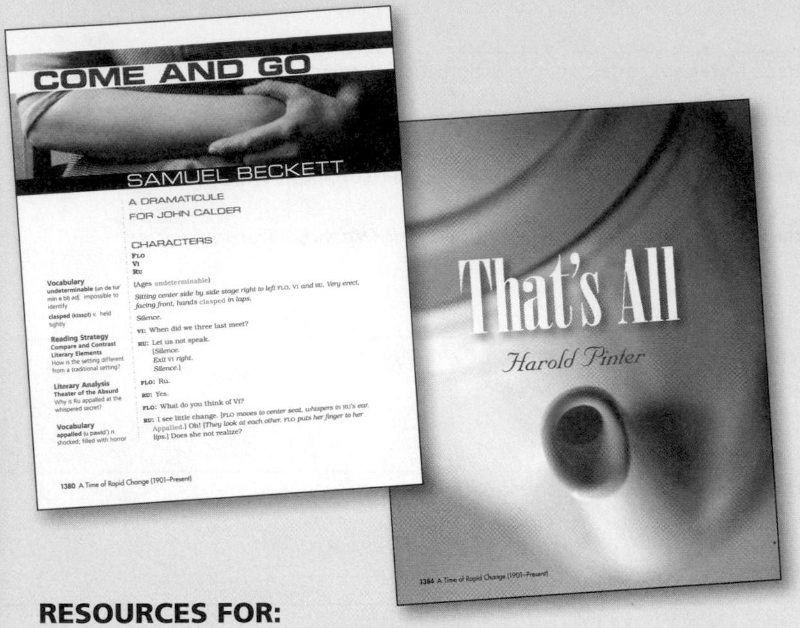

RESOURCES FOR:

- L1 Special-Needs Students
- L2 Below-Level Students (Tier 2)
- L3 On-Level Students (Tier 1)
- L4 Advanced Students (Tier 1)
- EL English Learners
- All All Students

Vocabulary/Fluency/Prior Knowledge

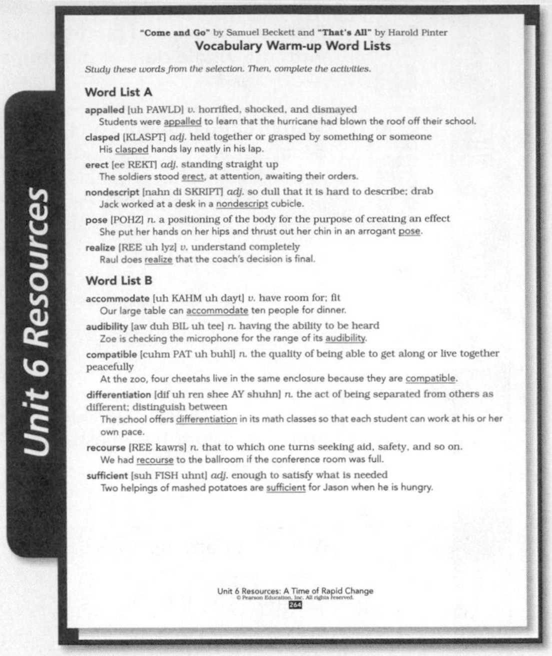
Unit 6 Resources

"Come and Go" by Samuel Beckett and "That's All" by Harold Pinter
Vocabulary Warm-up Word Lists

Study these words from the selection. Then, complete the activities.

Word List A

appalled [uh PAWLD] *v.* horrified, shocked, and dismayed
Students were appalled to learn that the hurricane had blown the roof off their school.
clasped [KLASPT] *adj.* held together or grasped by something or someone
His clasped hands lay neatly in his lap.
erect [ee REKT] *adj.* standing straight up
The soldiers stood erect, at attention, awaiting their orders.
nondescript [nahn di SKRIPT] *adj.* so dull that it is hard to describe; drab
Jack worked at a desk in a nondescript cubicle.
pose [POHZ] *n.* a positioning of the body for the purpose of creating an effect
She put her hands on her hips and thrust out her chin in an arrogant pose.
realize [REE uh lyz] *v.* understand completely
Raul does realize that the coach's decision is final.

Word List B

accommodate [uh KAHM uh dayt] *v.* have room for; fit
Our large table can accommodate ten people for dinner.
audibility [aw duh BIL uh tee] *n.* having the ability to be heard
Zoe is checking the microphone for the range of its audibility.
compatible [cuhm PAT uh buhl] *n.* the quality of being able to get along or live together peacefully
At the zoo, four cheetahs live in the same enclosure because they are compatible.
differentiation [dif uh ren shee AY shuhn] *n.* the act of being separated from others as different; distinguish between
The school offers differentiation in its math classes so that each student can work at his or her own pace.
recourse [REE kawrs] *n.* that to which one turns seeking aid, safety, and so on.
We had recourse to the ballroom if the conference room was full.
sufficient [suh FISH uhnt] *adj.* enough to satisfy what is needed
Two helpings of mashed potatoes are sufficient for Jason when he is hungry.

Unit 6 Resources: A Time of Rapid Change
© Pearson Education, Inc. All rights reserved.
264

EL L1 L2 **Vocabulary Warm-ups A and B,** pp. 264–265

Also available for these selections:

EL L1 L2 **Reading Warm-ups A and B,** pp. 266–267

All **Vocabulary Builder,** p. 270

Reader's Notebooks

Pre- and postreading pages for these selections appear in an interactive format in the *Reader's Notebooks*. Each *Notebook* is differentiated for a different group of learners. The selections in the Adapted and English Learner's versions are abridged.

L2 L3 ***Reader's Notebook***

L1 ***Reader's Notebook: Adapted Version***

EL ***Reader's Notebook: English Learner's Version***

EL ***Reader's Notebook: Spanish Version***

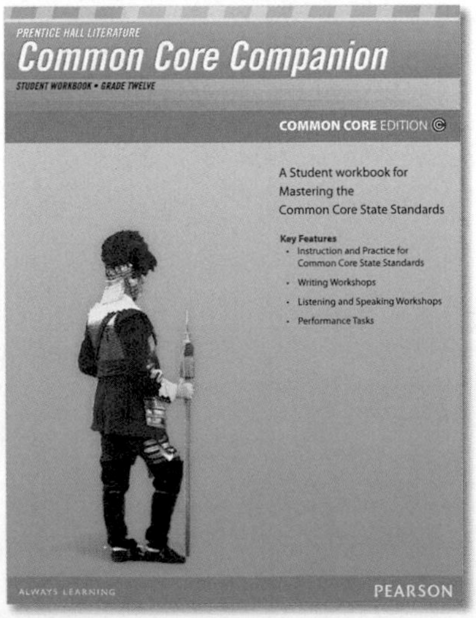

Common Core Companion

Additional instruction and practice for each Common Core State Standard

Selection Support

Graphic Organizer Transparencies

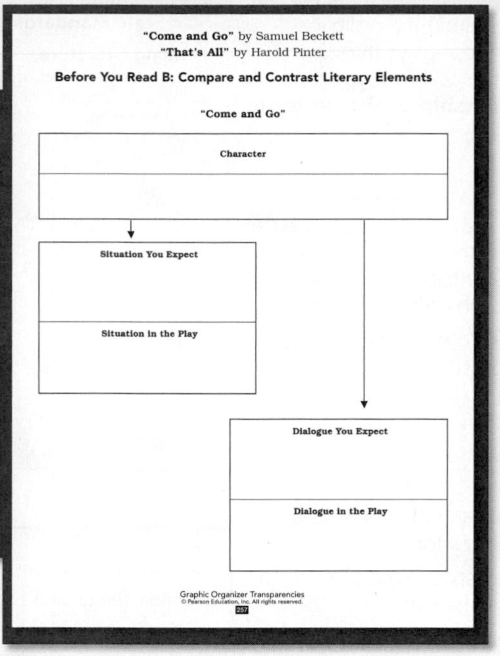
Name ____ Date ____

"Come and Go" by Samuel Beckett
"That's All" by Harold Pinter

Before You Read B: Compare and Contrast Literary Elements

"Come and Go"

Character

Situation You Expect

Situation in the Play

Dialogue You Expect

Dialogue in the Play

Graphic Organizer Transparencies
© Pearson Education, Inc. All rights reserved.
257

EL L3 **Reading: Graphic Organizer B,** p. 257

Also available for these selections:

EL L1 L2 **Reading: Graphic Organizer A,** p. 256

EL L1 L2 **Literary Analysis: Graphic Organizer A,** (partially filled in), p. 258

EL L3 **Literary Analysis: Graphic Organizer B,** p. 259

Skills Development/Extension

Unit 6 Resources

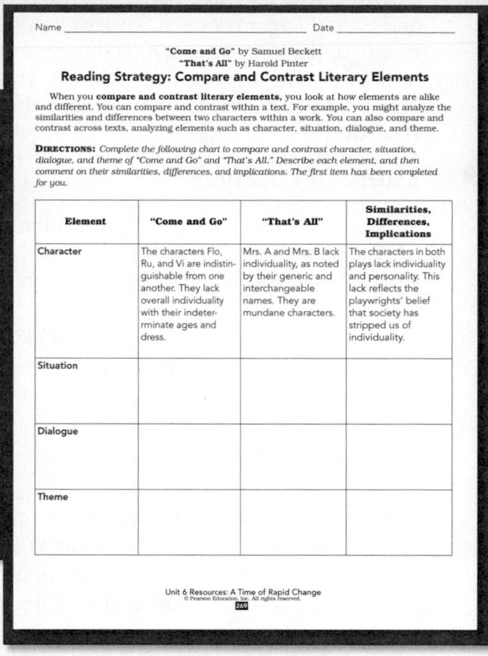
Name ____ Date ____

"Come and Go" by Samuel Beckett
"That's All" by Harold Pinter

Reading Strategy: Compare and Contrast Literary Elements

When you **compare and contrast literary elements,** you look at how elements are alike and different. You can compare and contrast within a text. For example, you might analyze the similarities and differences between two characters within a work. You can also compare and contrast across texts, analyzing elements such as character, situation, dialogue, and theme.

DIRECTIONS: *Complete the following chart to compare and contrast character, situation, dialogue, and theme of "Come and Go" and "That's All." Describe each element, and then comment on their similarities, differences, and implications. The first item has been completed for you.*

Element	"Come and Go"	"That's All"	Similarities, Differences, Implications
Character	The characters Flo, Ru, and Vi are indistinguishable from one another. They lack overall individuality with their indeterminate ages and dress.	Mrs. A and Mrs. B lack individuality, as noted by their generic and interchangeable names. They are mundane characters.	The characters in both plays lack individuality and personality. This lack reflects the playwrights' belief that society has stripped us of individuality.
Situation			
Dialogue			
Theme			

Unit 6 Resources: A Time of Rapid Change
© Pearson Education, Inc. All rights reserved.
269

All **Reading: Compare and Contrast Literary Elements,** p. 269

Also available for these selections:

All **Literary Analysis: Theater of the Absurd,** p. 268

EL L3 L4 **Support for Writing,** p. 271

L4 **Enrichment,** p. 272

Assessment

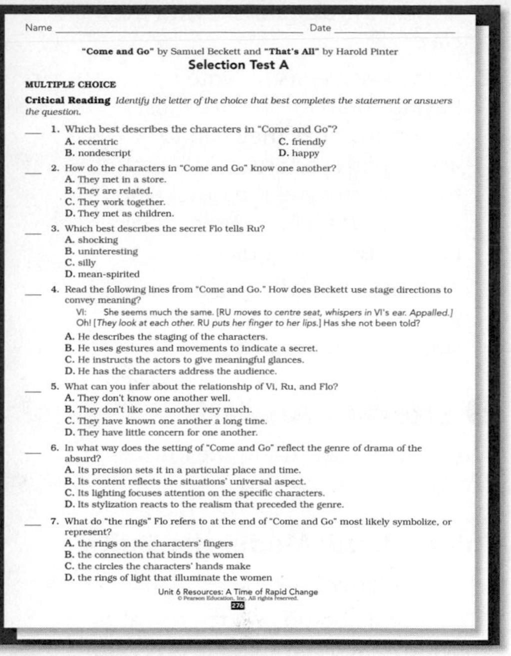
Name ____ Date ____

"Come and Go" by Samuel Beckett and "That's All" by Harold Pinter

Selection Test A

MULTIPLE CHOICE

Critical Reading *Identify the letter of the choice that best completes the statement or answers the question.*

___ 1. Which best describes the characters in "Come and Go"?
A. eccentric
B. nondescript
C. friendly
D. happy

___ 2. How do the characters in "Come and Go" know one another?
A. They met in a store.
B. They are related.
C. They work together.
D. They met as children.

___ 3. Which best describes the secret Flo tells Ru?
A. shocking
B. uninteresting
C. silly
D. mean-spirited

___ 4. Read the following lines from "Come and Go." How does Beckett use stage directions to convey meaning?
VI: She seems much the same. [RU *moves to centre seat, whispers in* VI's *ear. Appalled.*] Oh! [*They look at each other.* RU *puts her finger to her lips.*] Has she not been told?
A. He describes the staging of the characters.
B. He uses gestures and movements to indicate a secret.
C. He instructs the actors to give meaningful glances.
D. He has the characters address the audience.

___ 5. What can you infer about the relationship of Vi, Ru, and Flo?
A. They don't know one another well.
B. They don't like one another very much.
C. They have known one another a long time.
D. They have little concern for one another.

___ 6. In what way does the setting of "Come and Go" reflect the genre of drama of the absurd?
A. Its precision sets it in a particular place and time.
B. Its content reflects the situations' universal aspect.
C. Its lighting focuses attention on the specific characters.
D. Its stylization reacts to the realism that preceded the genre.

___ 7. What do "the rings" Flo refers to at the end of "Come and Go" most likely symbolize, or represent?
A. the rings on the characters' fingers
B. the connection that binds the women
C. the circles the characters' hands make
D. the rings of light that illuminate the women

Unit 6 Resources: A Time of Rapid Change
© Pearson Education, Inc. All rights reserved.
276

EL L1 L2 **Selection Test A,** pp. 276–278

Also available for these selections:

L3 L4 **Open-Book Test,** pp. 273–275

EL L3 L4 **Selection Test B,** pp. 279–281

PHLit Online!
www.PHLitOnline.com

- a thematically related video with writing prompt
- an interactive graphic organizer
- highlighting feature
- access to all student print resources, adapted to individual student needs
- Spanish and English summaries
- adapted selection translations in Spanish

Online Resources: All print materials are also available online.

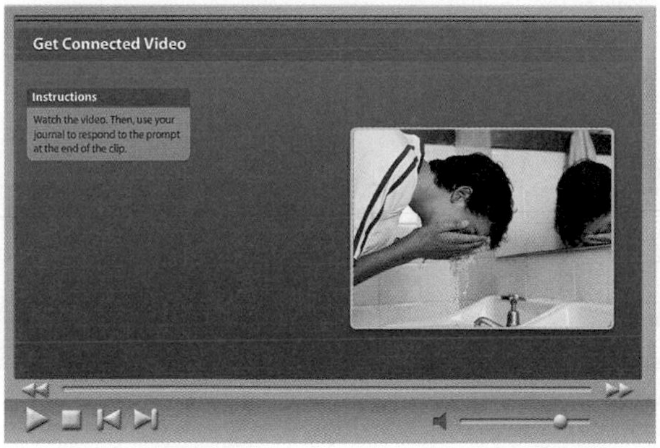

Get Connected! (thematic video with writing prompt)

All videos are available in Spanish.

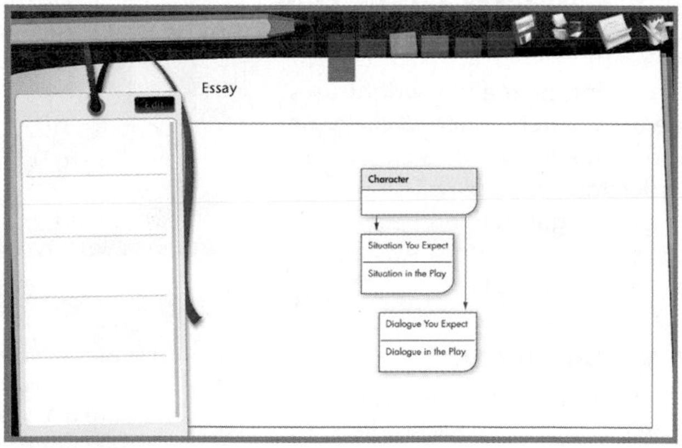

Writer's Journal (with graphics feature)

Also available:

Vocabulary Central (tools and activities for studying vocabulary)

PRETEACH

❶ Connecting to the Essential Question

1. Review the assignment with the class.
2. Prepare students to write by having them list the five most important tasks they had to accomplish yesterday. Then ask them to imagine the tasks' relative importance if an earthquake had occurred that day.
3. As students read, have them look for "pause" or "silence" in the stage directions.

❷ Literary Analysis

Introduce the skill using the instruction on the student page.

Think Aloud: Model the Skill

Say to students:

The atomic bomb and the threat of nuclear annihilation made everyday concerns seem absurd to many dramatists. Absurdist dramas tend to be essentially plotless. Sets are very simple, and movement is minimal.

❸ Reading Strategy

1. Introduce the skill using the instruction on the student page.
2. Give students a copy of **Reading Strategy Graphic Organizer B,** page 257 in ***Graphic Organizer Transparencies,*** to fill out as they read.

Think Aloud: Model the Skill

Say to students:

Examining how a playwright uses literary elements such as dialogue and characterization is critical for understanding a play. Using a graphic organizer can help you compare and contrast Absurdist and traditional plays.

❹ Vocabulary

1. Pronounce each word, giving its definition, and have students say it aloud.
2. For more guidance, see the *Classroom Strategies and Teaching Routines* card for introducing vocabulary.

Before You Read | *Come and Go • That's All*

❶ Connecting to the Essential Question The plays of Samuel Beckett and Harold Pinter convey a sense of bewilderment amid the ordinary events of daily life. As you read, notice details in these plays that show how they differ from plays of the past. These details will help you think about the Essential Question: **What is the relationship of the writer to tradition?**

Common Core State Standards

Reading Literature
3. Analyze the impact of the author's choices regarding how to develop and relate elements of a story or drama.

❷ Literary Analysis

Beckett and Pinter are major figures in the literary movement called **Theater of the Absurd.** The attitude of Absurdist writers is that human life has no inherent meaning and that human actions have essentially no purpose.

The techniques and characteristics of Theater of the Absurd grew directly out of these major themes and issues of the post–World War II era:

- After the horrors of World War II, the only possible way of living seemed to be a mixture of despair and humor.
- After decades of dealing with huge social issues—poverty, war, fascism, the Holocaust—writers turned inward to private, personal, familial, and everyday situations.
- After Modernism, many writers believed that the old structures of dramatic expression were no longer useful forms for a play.
- After centuries of manipulating language and style, writers began to mistrust language itself and its ability to communicate.

Look for moments in the plays that mix despair and humor or that seem to indicate that language has lost its power.

❸ Reading Strategy

Preparing to Read Complex Texts To recognize the absurdities in Theater of the Absurd, **compare and contrast literary elements.** Traditionally, characters, situations, and dialogue make logical sense, but in Theater of the Absurd, playwrights develop and relate these elements to defy logic and expectations. Use a chart like the one shown to compare and contrast characters, situations, and dialogue in an Absurdist play.

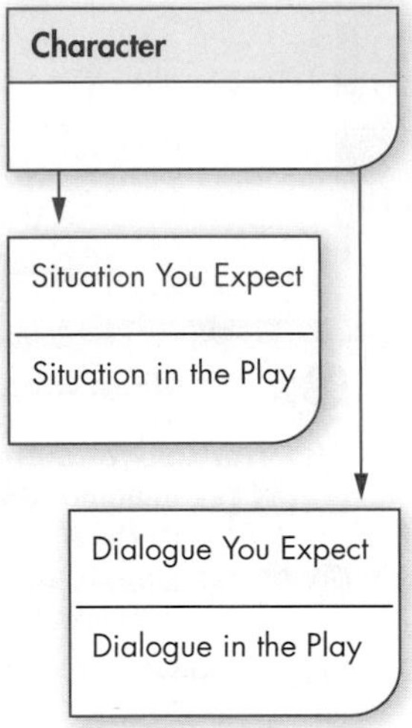

❹ Vocabulary

undeterminable (un di tur′ min ə bl) *adj.* impossible to identify (p. 1380)

clasped (klaspt) *v.* held tightly (p. 1380)

appalled (ə pôld′) *n.* shocked; filled with horror (p. 1380)

resume (ri zo͞om′) *v.* continue (p. 1381)

PHLit Online! www.PHLitOnline.com

Vocabulary Development

Vocabulary Knowledge Rating

Create a **Vocabulary Knowledge Rating Chart** (***Professional Development Guidebook,*** p. 33) for the vocabulary words on the student page. Give each student a copy of the chart with the words on it. Read the words aloud, and have students mark their ratings in the Before Reading column. Urge students to attend to these words as they read and discuss the selections.

In order to gauge how much instruction you need to provide, tally how many students are confident in their knowledge of each word. As students read, point out the words and their context.

PHLit Online! **Vocabulary Central,** featuring tools and activities for studying vocabulary, is available online at **www.PHLitOnline.com.**

5 SAMUEL BECKETT

1906–1989

Author of "Come and Go"

As a boy in Dublin, Ireland, young Samuel Beckett loved sports and languages, and, after studying at Trinity College in Dublin, he became as fluent in French as he was in English. In the late 1920s, Beckett settled in Paris, and throughout his life wrote novels and plays in both languages, often serving as his own translator. A major writer in the Modernist tradition, he was a friend of James Joyce and a brilliant critic of Marcel Proust.

Teacher and Resister For a while, Beckett taught French literature at Trinity College, and during World War II he worked as a courier for the French Resistance. He suffered terribly from depression, and during the war he wrote "to stay sane." Though he did travel in Europe and America, Beckett's life was primarily secluded and intensely private.

Waiting for Godot Beckett became suddenly famous in 1952 with what is still his best-known work, *Waiting for Godot*. In this revolutionary play, two tramps wait for someone named Godot. In the course of the play, their actions and inaction, their words spoken and left unspoken, their hesitant gestures and unmade decisions raise many disturbing questions about the meaning and value of human action—or its lack of meaning and value. Godot never arrives.

Prose Poetry Beckett's other major works include the trilogy of novels *Molloy, Malone Dies,* and *The Unnameable* (1951–1955) and the play *Endgame* (1957). Increasingly minimalistic, he developed a more and more compressed mode of expression as well as sparer and shorter forms—dramaticules (like "Come and Go") and micro-narratives. In effect, his distilled writing became a new kind of dramatic prose poetry. Beckett was awarded the Nobel Prize for literature in 1969.

"TRY AGAIN. FAIL AGAIN. FAIL BETTER."

PRETEACH

Daily Bellringer

For each class during which you will teach these selections, have students complete one of the five activities for the appropriate week in the ***Daily Bellringer Activities*** booklet.

Multidraft Reading

To assist struggling readers and to enhance reading for all, assign the text in chunks, as warranted by length, and apply multidraft reading protocols. For each reading, have students set the purpose indicated:

- **First reading**—identifying key ideas and details and answering any Reading Checks.
- **Second reading**—analyzing craft and structure and responding to the side-column prompts.
- **Third reading**—integrating knowledge and ideas, connecting to other texts and the world, and answering the end-of-selection questions.

For more guidance, refer to the ***Classroom Strategies and Teaching Routines*** card on Multidraft Reading.

5 Background

More About the Author

Like other Absurdist playwrights, Beckett was profoundly influenced by the events of World War II. He served as a courier for the French Resistance from 1940 to 1942, then fled to Roussillon in the south of France when his unit was betrayed to the Gestapo. He continued to assist the Resistance from his home in Roussillon and helped sabotage German operations in the nearby mountain areas. Following the war, Beckett wrote most of his plays in French, claiming that this enabled him to write simply, without concern for style or elaboration. The simple language and situations in Beckett's plays offer strong evidence of this.

PHLit Online!
www.PHLitOnline.com

Teaching From Technology

Preparing to Read
Go to **www.PHLitOnline.com** and display the ***Get Connected!*** slide show for these selections. Have the class brainstorm responses to the writing prompt, entering ideas in the interactive journal. Then, have students complete their written responses as homework.

To build background, display the Background and More About the Author features.

Using the Interactive Text
Go to **www.PHLitOnline.com** and display the **Enriched Online Student Edition.** As the class reads the selection or listens to the narration, record answers to side-column prompts using the graphic organizers accessible on the interactive page. Alternatively, have students use the online edition individually, answering the prompts as they read.

TEACH

❶ About the Selection

At the play's beginning, the three characters seem hesitant to talk. By the end of the play, all three drift into a sentimental longing.

❷ Activating Prior Knowledge

To prepare students for the plays they are about to read, have them share memories of a time when a major event suddenly made details of everyday life seem less important.

Concept Connector →

Tell students they will return to their responses after reading the selection.

Tell students they will return to their responses after reading the selection.

❸ Reading Strategy

Compare and Contrast Literary Elements

1. Remind students that Absurdist dramas tend to be minimalist.
2. **Ask** the Reading Strategy question: How is the setting different from a traditional setting?
   Answer: The playwright gives no information on where the scene takes place. The actual set is very simple.

❹ Literary Analysis

Theater of the Absurd

1. Explain that in the Theater of the Absurd, the audience hears private conversations.
2. **Ask** the Literary Analysis question: Why is Ru appalled at the whispered secret?
   Answer: Ru is hearing something unexpected and awful about Vi.

COME AND GO

SAMUEL BECKETT

A DRAMATICULE
FOR JOHN CALDER

CHARACTERS

FLO
VI
RU

(Ages **undeterminable**)

Sitting center side by side stage right to left FLO, VI *and* RU. *Very erect, facing front, hands* **clasped** *in laps.*

Silence.

VI: When did we three last meet?

RU: Let us not speak.
[*Silence.*
Exit VI *right.*
Silence.]

FLO: Ru.

RU: Yes.

FLO: What do you think of Vi?

RU: I see little change. [FLO *moves to center seat, whispers in* RU's *ear.* **Appalled.**] Oh! [*They look at each other.* FLO *puts her finger to her lips.*] Does she not realize?

Vocabulary
undeterminable (un de tur´ min e bl) *adj.* impossible to identify
clasped (klaspt) *v.* held tightly

Reading Strategy
Compare and Contrast Literary Elements
How is the setting different from a traditional setting?

Literary Analysis
Theater of the Absurd
Why is Ru appalled at the whispered secret?

Vocabulary
appalled (u pawld´) *n.* shocked; filled with horror

Text Complexity Rubric

	Come and Go	That's All
Qualitative Measures		
Context/ Knowledge Demands	Theater of the Absurd; life experience demands 1 2 ③ 4 5	Theater of the Absurd; life experience demands 1 2 ③ 4 5
Structure/Language Conventionality and Clarity	Simple diction 1 ② 3 4 5	Simple diction 1 ② 3 4 5
Levels of Meaning/ Purpose/Concept Level	Moderate (ambiguity; absurdist attitudes) 1 ② 3 4 5	Moderate (ambiguity; loneliness and meaninglessness) 1 2 3 ④ 5
Quantitative Measures		
Lexile/Text Length	NP / 542 words	NP / 423 words
Overall Complexity	**More accessible**	**More complex**

FLO: God grant not.

[*Enter* VI. FLO *and* RU *turn back front,* **resume** *pose.* VI *sits right. Silence.*]

Just sit together as we used to, in the playground at Miss Wade's.

RU: On the log.

[*Silence.*

Exit FLO *left.*

Silence.]

Vi.

VI: Yes.

RU: How do you find Flo?

VI: She seems much the same. [RU *moves to centre seat, whispers in* VI*'s ear. Appalled.*] Oh! [*They look at each other.* RU *puts her finger to her lips.*] Has she not been told?

RU: God forbid.

[*Enter* FLO, RU *and* VI *turn back front resume pose.* FLO *sits left.*]

Holding hands . . . that way.

FLO: Dreaming of . . . love.

[*Silence.*

Exit RU *right.*

Silence.]

VI: Flo.

FLO: Yes.

VI: How do you think Ru is looking?

FLO: One sees little in this light. [VI *moves to centre seat, whispers in* FLO*'s ear. Appalled.*] Oh! [*They look at each other.* VI *puts her finger to her lips.*] Does she not know?

VI: Please God not.

[*Enter* RU. VI *and* FLO *turn back front, resume pose.* RU *sits right. Silence.*]

May we not speak of the old days? [*Silence.*] Of what came after? [*Silence.*] Shall we hold hands in the old way?

[*After a moment they join hands as follows:* VI*'s right hand with* RU*'s right hand,* VI*'s left hand with* FLO*'s left hand,* FLO*'s right hand with* RU*'s left hand,* VI*'s arms being above* RU*'s left arm and* FLO*'s right arm. The three pairs of clasped hands rest on the three laps.*

Silence.]

FLO: I can feel the rings.

[*Silence.*]

CURTAIN

Vocabulary
resume (re zoom′) *v.* continue

5 Literary Analysis
Theater of the Absurd
Flo's exit and entrance mirror Vi's, and so will Ru's. What does this suggest about the women's lives?

ONE SEES LITTLE IN THIS LIGHT

6 Reading Check
How old are the characters?

5 Literary Analysis

Theater of the Absurd

1. Explain that movement in Absurdist plays is often circular. That is, characters may end up in the same place or position in which they began.
2. Suggest that students make maps of the characters' positions before and after each one exits.
3. **Ask** the Literary Analysis question: Flo's exit and entrance mirror Vi's, and so will Ru's. What does this suggest about the women's lives?
   Answer: Vi ends up back in the center, and Flo and Ru on either side of her, though their positions are reversed. The pattern of movement suggests that Vi has always been the leader, and Flo and Ru are the followers.

6 Reading Check

Answer: The characters are middle-aged or older, based on their reflections on their childhood and "the old days."

PHLit Online!

These selections are available in interactive format in the **Enriched Online Student Edition**, at **www.PHLitOnline.com,** which includes a thematically related video with writing prompt and an interactive graphic organizer.

Text Complexity: Reader and Task Suggestions

Come and Go		That's All	
Preparing to Read the Text	**Leveled Tasks**	**Preparing to Read the Text**	**Leveled Tasks**
• Using the Background on TE p. 1379, explain that Beckett wrote in French, then translated his plays into English. • Clarify that the absurdist idea that life has no purpose means that individuals must make their own. • Guide students to use Multidraft Reading strategies (TE p. 1379).	***Levels of Meaning*** If students will have difficulty with the play's ambiguity, tell them to use their knowledge of human nature as they read. Then, have students share their ideas. ***Analyzing*** If students will not have difficulty with the play's ambiguity, have them determine whether *Come and Go* is a dramatic fragment or a complete play.	• Using the Background on TE p. 1383, discuss the lasting effects that bombing raids might have had on the young Pinter. • Explain that minimalist dialogue can nevertheless reveal key details about the speakers. • Guide students to use Multidraft Reading strategies (TE p. 13791).	***Levels of Meaning*** If students will have difficulty with the play's ambiguity, have them use their knowledge of human nature to draw conclusions about Mrs. A and Mrs. B. Then, have them reread the play, trying to decide which character interpretations seem most likely. ***Evaluating*** If students will not have difficulty with the play's ambiguity, have them evaluate the realism of the repetitious dialogue.

❼ Literary Analysis

Theater of the Absurd

1. Have students reread the dialogue and stage directions on the previous page in which the women join hands.
2. **Ask** students the Literary Analysis question: Why do you think the women cross hands?
   Possible response: They are holding hands the way they did in the old days. By crossing hands, the women form a bond that seems more difficult to break than simply holding hands in a traditional way.

ASSESS/EXTEND

Answers

Before students respond, you may wish to have them write a brief objective summary of the selection. As they answer the questions below, remind them to support their answers with evidence from the text.

1. (a) The women sit side by side, not facing each other, and are very erect. (b) **Possible response:** They seem alienated from each other.
2. (a) When one woman exits, another slides over to her place and proceeds to whisper a secret about her to the third woman. (b) **Possible response:** Based on the characters' reactions, it is possible the secrets concern their health.
3. (a) Flo says, "Just sit together as we used to, in the playground at Miss Wade's." (b) **Possible response:** The women might talk about a shared experience or the liveliness they all had as young girls.
4. **Possible response:** Flo says she can feel "the rings," yet the notes say the women are not wearing rings. This helps readers to understand that she must be referring to the rings formed by how they have linked themselves together.

NOTES

Successive positions

1	FLO	VI	RU
2	FLO		RU
		FLO	RU
3	VI	FLO	RU
4	VI		RU
	VI	RU	
5	VI	RU	FLO
6	VI		FLO
		VI	FLO
7	RU	VI	FLO

Literary Analysis
Theater of the Absurd
Why do you think the women cross hands?

Hands

RU VI FLO

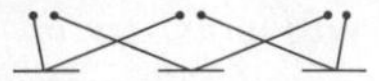

Lighting
Soft, from above only and concentrated on playing area. Rest of stage as dark as possible.

Costume
Full-length coats, buttoned high, dull violet (Ru), dull red (Vi), dull yellow (Flo). Drab nondescript hats with enough brim to shade faces. Apart from colour differentiation three figures as alike as possible. Light shoes with rubber soles. Hands made up to be as visible as possible. No rings apparent.

Seat
Narrow benchlike seat, without back, just long enough to accommodate three figures almost touching. As little visible as possible. It should not be clear what they are sitting on.

Exits
The figures are not seen to go off stage. They should disappear a few steps from lit area. If dark not sufficient to allow this, recourse should be had to screens or drapes as little visible as possible. Exits and entrances slow, without sound of feet.

Ohs
Three very different sounds.

Voices
As low as compatible with audibility. Colorless except for three 'ohs' and two lines following.

I CAN
FEEL
THE RINGS.

Critical Reading

1. **Key Ideas and Details (a)** How do the women sit on the stage? **(b) Interpret:** What do their posture and gestures suggest about their lives?
2. **Key Ideas and Details (a)** What happens each time one woman exits? **(b) Speculate:** What do you think each woman whispers?
3. **Key Ideas and Details (a)** Identify one line in which each woman shows she is thinking about the past. **(b) Speculate:** If the women were to "speak of the old days," what do you think they might say?
4. **Integration of Knowledge and Ideas** How do the notes add to your understanding of the play?

Cite textual evidence to support your responses.

Think Aloud

Literary Analysis: Theater of the Absurd
To model the process of working out the Literary Analysis question on the student page, use the following "think aloud." Say to students:

I might not be sure why the women have chosen to join hands at this point in the play. To fully understand their behavior, I can review the dialogue in the scene as well as any stage directions or notes from the playwright. This might help me locate details about the women's relationships that will help explain the gesture.

❽ # Harold Pinter *1930–2008*

Author of "That's All"

Although as a student his favorite authors were novelists—Franz Kafka and Ernest Hemingway—it was drama that most fascinated Harold Pinter. Born in East London, he acted in school plays, studied for two years at London's Royal Academy of Dramatic Art, and even worked as an actor on BBC radio. During the 1950s, Pinter acted and toured with several theater companies, learning the stagecraft and absorbing the dramatic forms and traditions that he would so radically alter.

Plays and Screenplays Pinter produced his first major play, *The Birthday Party*, in 1958, and a string of masterpieces followed: *The Dumb Waiter* (1959), *The Caretaker* (1960), and *The Homecoming* (1965). He has written the screenplays of numerous movies, including *The Servant* (1963), *Betrayal* (1983), and *Sleuth* (2007). Perhaps his greatest screenplay, an adaptation of Marcel Proust's *In Search of Lost Time*, was never filmed, though it was performed on stage in 2000.

Nobel Prize Pinter has also directed many plays and served as an associate director of the National Theatre. The award of the Nobel Prize for Literature in 2005 recognized his wide-ranging accomplishment, his technical innovation, and his profound contribution to the ability of drama to express some of the deepest anxieties of the twentieth and twenty-first centuries.

Menacing Silence Pinter usually presents his audiences with common speech and common situations that mask unnameable fears and forces. Menace always looms in a Pinter drama. Tense silence plays a major role. As in "That's All," Pinter's people may engage in small talk, but behind the banality lie loss, emptiness, deception, delusion, and despair.

"Apart from the known and the unknown, what else is there?"

❽ Background

More About the Author

As a child during World War II, Harold Pinter faced life-and-death scenarios almost daily: he was barely ten years old when Germany began bombing London in the infamous Blitz. The nightly air raids led Pinter's family to evacuate the city. The trauma of the raids and evacuation had a lasting effect on Pinter. The themes found in his work—loneliness, confusion, loss, separation, menace—can be attributed to wartime memories of London.

Differentiated Instruction for Universal Access

Strategy for Less Proficient Readers

Some students will be less comfortable reading a drama. Remind them to note who is speaking each line before reading the dialogue. Suggest that students form groups to act out the play and answer questions.

EL Vocabulary for English Learners

The two characters in Pinter's play are Mrs. A. and Mrs. B. Explain to students that *Mrs.* is an abbreviated title that indicates a woman is married. *A* and *B* could be the first initial of each woman's last name, or they might merely suggest "first woman" and "second woman."

PHLit Online!

All video resources are available online at **www.PHLitOnline.com.**

❾ About the Selection

In the dramatic sketch *That's All,* Pinter explores the difficulty people have in communicating. Two women sit without facing each other and carry on an extended conversation about a mutual acquaintance. Pinter's famous use of pauses underscores the tension surrounding the characters, who may or may not know that their seemingly meaningless conversation covers the emptiness of their lives.

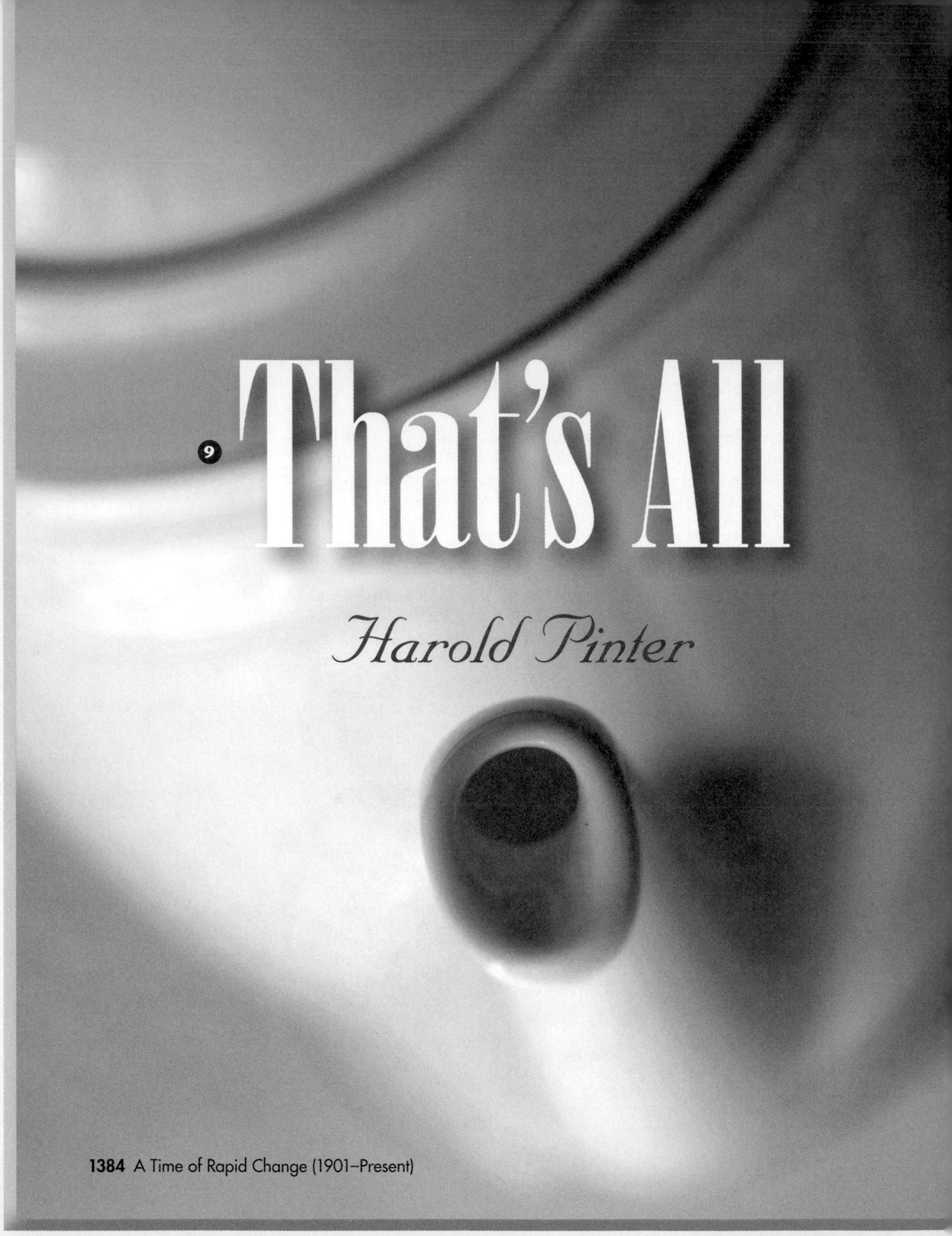

❾ That's All

Harold Pinter

Vocabulary Development

Vocabulary Knowledge Rating

When students have completed reading and discussing the selection, have them take out their **Vocabulary Knowledge Rating Charts** for the play. Read the words aloud and have students rate their knowledge of words again in the After Reading column. Clarify any words that are still problematic. Have students write their own definitions and example or sentence in the appropriate column. Then, have students complete the Vocabulary Practice at the end of the selection. Encourage students to use the words in further discussion and written work about the selection. Remind them that they will be accountable for these words on the **Selection Test,** ***Unit 6 Resources,*** pages 276–278 or 279–281.

MRS. A.: I always put the kettle on about that time.

MRS. B.: Yes. (*Pause.*)

MRS. A.: Then she comes round.

MRS. B.: Yes. (*Pause.*)

MRS. A.: Only on Thursdays.

MRS. B.: Yes. (*Pause.*)

MRS. A.: On Wednesdays I used to put it on. When she used to come round. Then she changed it to Thursdays.

MRS. B.: Oh yes.

MRS. A.: After she moved. When she used to live round the corner, then she always came in on Wednesdays, but then when she moved she used to come down to the butcher's on Thursdays. She couldn't find a butcher up there.

MRS. B.: No.

MRS. A.: Anyway, she decided she'd stick to her own butcher. Well, I thought, if she can't find a butcher, that's the best thing.

MRS. B.: Yes. (*Pause.*)

MRS. A.: So she started to come down on Thursdays. I didn't know she was coming down on Thursdays until one day I met her in the butcher.

MRS. B.: Oh yes.

MRS. A.: It wasn't my day for the butcher, I don't go to the butcher on Thursdays.

MRS. B.: No, I know. (*Pause.*)

MRS. A.: I go on Friday.

MRS. B.: Yes. (*Pause.*)

MRS. A.: That's where I see you.

MRS. B.: Yes. (*Pause.*)

MRS. A.: You're always in there on Fridays.

MRS. B.: Oh yes. (*Pause.*)

MRS. A.: But I happened to go in for a bit of meat, it turned out to be a Thursday. I wasn't going in for my usual weekly on Friday. I just slipped in, the day before.

MRS. B.: Yes.

MRS. A.: That was the first time I found out she couldn't find a butcher up there, so she decided to come back here, once a week, to her own butcher.

10 Reading Strategy
Compare and Contrast Literary Elements
How do the names of the characters contrast with the names of characters in traditional plays?

11 Literary Analysis
Theater of the Absurd
Summarize the event that Mrs. A. relates. What makes it "absurd"?

12 Reading Strategy
Compare and Contrast Literary Elements
What do Mrs. B.'s responses suggest about her character?

13 Reading Check
What day does Mrs. A. go to the butcher?

10 Reading Strategy

Compare and Contrast Literary Elements

1. Point out that in many Absurdist plays, character names are simple and may represent an idea the playwright wants to convey about the characters.
2. **Ask** students the first Reading Strategy question in the margin: How do the names of the characters contrast with the names of characters in traditional plays?
   Answer: Here, the names are simply letters of the alphabet, rather than the names of specific people, as in a traditional play.

11 Literary Analysis

Theater of the Absurd

1. Remind students that in Absurdist plays, characters experience great bewilderment over ordinary events.
2. **Ask** students the Literary Analysis question: Summarize the event that Mrs. A. relates. What makes it "absurd"?
   Answer: Mrs. A. describes how a former neighbor used to come over for tea on Wednesdays, but switched to visiting on Thursdays after she moved. The event is "absurd" because it is essentially meaningless, though Mrs. A. makes a complicated story about it, and also because the story ends up more or less in the same place where it started.

12 Reading Strategy

Compare and Contrast Literary Elements

1. Have students consider their responses to the Reading Strategy question above. Then, have them consider Mrs. B.'s responses in light of her character's name.
2. **Ask** students the second Reading Strategy question in the margin: What do Mrs. B.'s responses suggest about her character?
   Answer: Her brief and agreeable responses suggest that Mrs. B. is quiet and meek.

13 Reading Check

Answer: Mrs. A. usually goes to the butcher on Fridays.

Concept Connector

Reading Strategy Graphic Organizer
Ask students to review the graphic organizers in which they have compared and contrasted characters, situations, and dialogue. Have students share their organizers and compare the elements they examined.

Activating Prior Knowledge
Have students return to their responses to the Activating Prior Knowledge activity. Ask them to explain whether their thoughts have changed and, if so, how.

Writing About the Essential Question
Have students compare their responses to the prompt, completed before reading the plays, with their thoughts afterward. Have them work individually or in groups, writing or discussing their thoughts, to formulate new responses. Then, lead a class discussion, probing for what students have learned that confirms or invalidates their initial thoughts. Encourage students to cite specific textual details to support their responses.

⓮ Literary Analysis

Theater of the Absurd

1. Remind students that Pinter's characters often seem to feel trapped in a world that is small, empty, and full of despair.
2. **Ask** students the first Literary Analysis question in the margin: Why does Mrs. A. keep elaborating on her topic?
   Answer: Mrs. A. may have little else to talk about.

⓯ Literary Analysis

Theater of the Absurd

Ask students the second Literary Analysis question: What do Mrs. B.'s last two responses reveal about communication?
Possible response: Mrs. B. seems lonely and, as such, she is wanting to keep conversation going even if there is nothing to talk about.

ASSESS/EXTEND

Answers

Before students respond, you may wish to have them write a brief objective summary of the selection. As they answer the questions below, remind them to support their answers with evidence from the text.

1. (a) They are talking about Mrs. A.'s former neighbor.
   (b) **Possible responses:** Their lives are empty; they may be jealous of the neighbor who has moved away.
2. (a) pause; (b) **Possible response:** It provides a tense silence that underscores that the conversation is forced.
3. **Possible response:** The seemingly meaningless chatter allows Mrs. A. to be critical of the former neighbor without being openly hostile.
4. Pinter is commenting on the tendency of people to focus on mundane details that do not matter.
5. (The Essential Question) **Possible response:** The unadorned, minimalist approach allows Pinter to remove emotion and other very human essentials from the scene, which increases the possibilities for tension and anxiety in the audience.

Literary Analysis
Theatre of the Absurd
Why does Mrs. A. keep elaborating on her topic?

MRS. B.: Yes.

MRS. A.: She came on Thursday so she'd be able to get meat for the weekend. Lasted her till Monday, then from Monday to Thursday they'd have fish. She can always buy cold meat, if they want a change.

MRS. B.: Oh yes. (*Pause.*)

MRS. A.: So I told her to come in when she came down after she'd been to the butcher's and I'd put a kettle on. So she did. (*Pause.*)

MRS. B.: Yes (*Pause.*)

MRS. A.: It was funny because she always used to come in Wednesdays. (*Pause.*) Still, it made a break. (*Long pause.*)

MRS. B.: She doesn't come in no more, does she? (*Pause.*)

Literary Analysis
Theater of the Absurd
What do Mrs. B.'s last two responses reveal about communication?

MRS. A.: She comes in. She doesn't come in so much, but she comes in. (*Pause.*)

MRS. B.: I thought she didn't come in. (*Pause.*)

MRS. A.: She comes in. (*Pause.*) She just doesn't come in so much. That's all.

Critical Reading

Cite textual evidence to support your responses.

1. **Key Ideas and Details (a)** Who are Mrs. A. and Mrs. B. talking about? **(b) Interpret:** Why are they talking about her?
2. **Craft and Structure (a)** What stage direction follows most of Mrs. B.'s responses? **(b) Analyze:** What important quality does the stage direction add to the sketch?
3. **Key Ideas and Details** On the surface, the characters speak only ordinary chitchat or small talk. What do you think lies behind the surface of their chat?
4. **Integration of Knowledge and Ideas** What comment about the state of contemporary culture do you think Pinter is making? Explain.
5. **Integration of Knowledge and Ideas** In "That's All," Pinter reduces setting, plot, and characterization to the barest minimum. What effect do you think this has on the audience? Use three of these Essential Question words in your answer: *participate, essentials, imaginative, possibilities, unadorned. [Connecting to the Essential Question: What is the relationship of the writer to tradition?]*

Assessment Practice

Paired Passages (For more practice, see *All-in-One Workbook*.)

Many tests require students to compare literary elements in two passages. Have students reread the first page of *Come and Go*, page 1380, and the first page of *That's All*, page 1385.

Which statement best describes how the directions "Silence" and "Pause" help set the tone of each play?

A The directions increase the tension in both plays.
B In both plays, pauses give the actors time to move about the stage.
C The pauses are funny in *That's All* but gloomy in *Come and Go*.
D Pauses are used for humor in both plays.

Help students analyze the tone of each work. Choice ***B*** is incorrect because neither play contains any physical action. Choice **C** could describe *Come and Go* but not *That's All*. Neither play is humorous, which eliminates choice ***D***. The correct answer is ***A***.

After You Read | *Come and Go • That's All*

Literary Analysis

1. **Craft and Structure** Conflict lies at the heart of drama, but **Theater of the Absurd** deals with conflict in unusual ways. Use a graphic organizer like this one to analyze how Beckett's and Pinter's characters respond to conflict.

	Conflict	Characters' Actions	Resolution
Come and Go			
That's All			

2. **Craft and Structure** How do the titles of Beckett's and Pinter's short plays help to convey their themes?

Reading Strategy

3. Summarize the plot of "Come and Go." Then, **compare and contrast the literary element**—plot—with the plot of a traditional play.
4. Traditionally, dialogue can establish setting, reveal character, advance the plot, and convey the theme of a play. What does the dialogue accomplish in "That's All"?

Common Core State Standards

Writing
3. Write narratives to develop real or imagined experiences or events using effective technique, well-chosen details, and well-structured event sequences.

PERFORMANCE TASKS
Integrated Language Skills

Vocabulary Acquisition and Use

Select the word from the list on page 1378 that best completes each sentence. Then, use the context to explain your choices.

1. The workers stopped for lunch, but they planned to _______ at one o'clock.
2. Her locket meant a lot to him, so he _______ it tightly in his hand.
3. The audience was _______ by the shocking and outrageous show.
4. The sign was badly damaged, making the name of the town _______.

Writing

Narrative Text Write a **scene from an absurd drama** set in a school. Convey a Beckettian or Pinteresque sense of bewilderment or futility with these literary elements:

- Hopeless or confused characters
- Commonplace situations
- Banal dialogue and silence

Assessment Resources

Unit 6 Resources

L1 L2 EL **Selection Test A,** pp. 276–278. Administer Test A to less advanced readers.

L3 L4 EL **Selection Test B,** pp. 279–281. Administer Test B to on-level students and more advanced students.

L3 L4 **Open-Book Test,** pp. 273–275. As an alternative, give the Open-Book test.

All **Customizable Test Bank**

All **Self-tests**
Students may prepare for the **Selection Test** by taking the **Self-test** online.

PHLit Online! All assessment resources are available at **www.PHLitOnline.com**.

Answers

1. *Come and Go:* Conflict: A group of three former friends have grown apart. Characters' Actions: All the women are talking about each other behind one another's backs. Resolution: They join together. *That's All:* Conflict: Mrs. A.'s friend no longer comes to visit every week, so she is lonely. Characters' Actions: talking about it to someone else; Resolution: She is resigned to being lonely.
2. **Possible response:** Both titles are short and reveal little about what is really going on in the plays, just as the dialogue and lack of a clear plot reveal little of what is really going on in each play.
3. In *Come and Go,* three women sit side by side on a bench, talking. The woman in the center gets up and exits, after which one of the remaining women whispers a secret (which the audience never learns) to the other about the absent woman. The absent woman returns and sits in a different position. The scenario repeats with each of the remaining women. At the end, all three women link arms. Unlike a traditional play, there is no conflict to drive the action.
4. **Possible response:** The long pauses and meaningless chatter create a tense mood underscoring the feelings of loss, emptiness, and despair that plague the characters.

Vocabulary Acquisition and Use

1. resume; The workers want to resume work after stopping.
2. clasped; In order to avoid losing the locket, the man clasped, or tightly held onto, it.
3. appalled; To be appalled by something is to be shocked or horrified.
4. undeterminable; If a sign is badly damaged, any lettering on it will be hard to read, or undeterminable.

Writing

1. Remind students to cover all three of the bulleted elements.
2. Evaluate students' narrative texts using the **General (Holistic) Writing Rubric,** *Professional Development Guidebook,* pages 282–283.

Do Not Go Gentle into That Good Night • Fern Hill • The Horses

Lesson Pacing Guide

DAY 1 Preteach

- Administer the Reading and Vocabulary Warm-ups (*Unit 6 Resources,* pp. 288–291) as necessary.
- Introduce the Literary Analysis concept: Style.
- Introduce the Reading Strategy: Evaluate the Poet's Expression of the Theme.
- Build background with the author and Background features.
- Develop thematic thinking with Connecting to the Essential Question.
- Teach the selection vocabulary.

DAY 2 Preteach/Teach/Extend

- Distribute copies of the graphic organizer for the Reading Strategy (*Graphic Organizer Transparencies,* pp. 260–261).
- Distribute copies of the graphic organizer for Literary Analysis (*Graphic Organizer Transparencies,* pp. 262–263).
- Prepare students to read with the Activating Prior Knowledge activities (TE).
- Informally monitor comprehension while students read.
- Use the Reading Check questions to confirm comprehension.
- Develop students' understanding of style using the Literary Analysis prompts.
- Develop students' ability to evaluate expression of theme using the Reading Strategy prompts.
- Reinforce vocabulary with the Vocabulary notes.
- Assess students' comprehension and mastery of the skills by having them answer the Critical Reading, Literary Analysis, and Reading Strategy questions.

DAY 3 Assess

- Have students complete the Vocabulary Lesson.
- Have students complete the Writing activity, writing a parody. (You may assign as homework.)
- Administer Selection Test A or B (*Unit 6 Resources,* pp. 300–302 or 303–305).

Common Core State Standards

Reading Literature 2. Determine two or more themes or central ideas of a text and analyze their development over the course of the text, including how they interact and build on one another to produce a complex account.

Writing 4. Produce clear and coherent writing in which the development, organization, and style are appropriate to task, purpose, and audience.

Additional Standards Practice
Common Core Companion, *pp. 15–22; 219–220*

Daily Block Scheduling
Each day in this Lesson Pacing Guide represents a 40–50 minute period. Teachers using block scheduling may combine days to revise pacing. In addition, teachers may differentiate and support core instruction by integrating components for extended and intensive support as students require. See the Guide to Selected Leveled Resources (facing page).

Guide to Selected Leveled Resources

RTI **Tier 1** (students performing on level)		Do Not Go Gentle into That Good Night • Fern Hill • The Horses
Warm Up	**Practice, model,** and **monitor** fluency, working **with the whole class** or **in groups.**	**Vocabulary and Reading Warm-ups B,** ***Unit 6 Resources,*** pp. 306–307, 309
Comprehension/Skills	**Support** and **monitor** comprehension and skills development, having students complete the activities, graphic organizers, and interactive prompts **independently** or **as a class.**	• ***Reader's Notebook,*** adapted instruction and full selection EL ***Reader's Notebook: English Learner's Version,*** adapted instruction and adapted selection • **Reading Strategy Graphic Organizer B,** ***Graphic Organizer Transparencies,*** p. 275 • **Literary Analysis Graphic Organizer B,** ***Graphic Organizer Transparencies,*** p. 277
Monitor Progress	**Monitor** student progress with the differentiated curriculum-based assessment in the *Unit Resources.*	• **Selection Test B,** ***Unit 6 Resources,*** pp. 321–323 • **Open-Book Test,** ***Unit 6 Resources,*** pp. 315–317

RTI **Tier 2** (students requiring intervention)		Do Not Go Gentle into That Good Night • Fern Hill • The Horses
Warm Up	**Practice, model,** and **monitor** fluency **in groups** or **with individuals.**	• **Vocabulary and Reading Warm-ups A,** ***Unit 6 Resources,*** pp. 306–308 • ***Hear It!*** **Audio CD (adapted text)**
Comprehension/Skills	• **Support** and **monitor** comprehension and skills development, working **in small groups** or **with individuals.** • As students complete the selection in the appropriate version of the *Reader's Notebook,* **monitor** comprehension frequently with group questions and individual instruction. • **Model** strategies while guiding students in completing the activities and prompts in the *Reader's Notebook,* as well as the graphic organizers. • **Practice** skills and **monitor** mastery with the *Reading Kit* worksheets.	• ***Reader's Notebook: Adapted Version,*** adapted instruction and adapted selection EL ***Reader's Notebook: English Learner's Version,*** adapted instruction and adapted selection • **Reading Strategy Graphic Organizer A,** ***Graphic Organizer Transparencies,*** p. 277 • **Literary Analysis Graphic Organizer A,** ***Graphic Organizer Transparencies,*** p. 276 • ***Reading Kit,*** Practice worksheets
Monitor Progress	**Monitor** student progress with the differentiated curriculum-based assessment in the *Unit Resources* and in the *Reading Kit.*	• **Selection Test A,** ***Unit 6 Resources,*** pp. 318–320 • ***Reading Kit,*** Assess worksheets

TIER 3 Tier 3 intervention may require consultation with the student's special-education or dyslexia specialist. For additional support, see the Tier 2 activities and resources listed above.

One-on-one teaching **Group work** **Whole class instruction** **Independent work** **A Assessment**

For a complete guide to selection support, including support for Advanced students, see the Overview of Resources in the frontmatter.

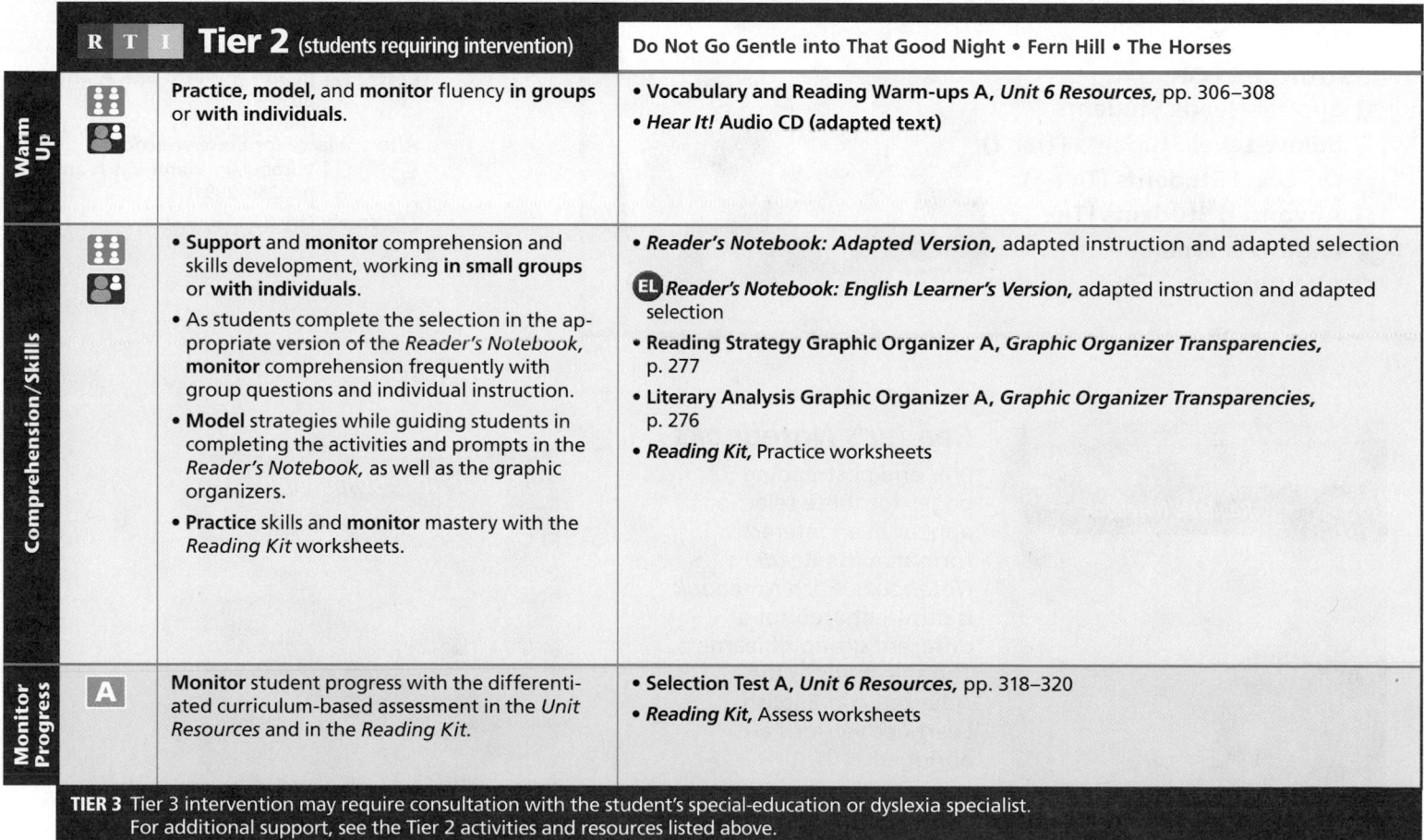

Do Not Go Gentle into That Good Night • Fern Hill • The Horses

RESOURCES FOR:

- L1 Special-Needs Students
- L2 Below-Level Students (Tier 2)
- L3 On-Level Students (Tier 1)
- L4 Advanced Students (Tier 1)
- EL English Learners
- All All Students

Vocabulary/Fluency/Prior Knowledge

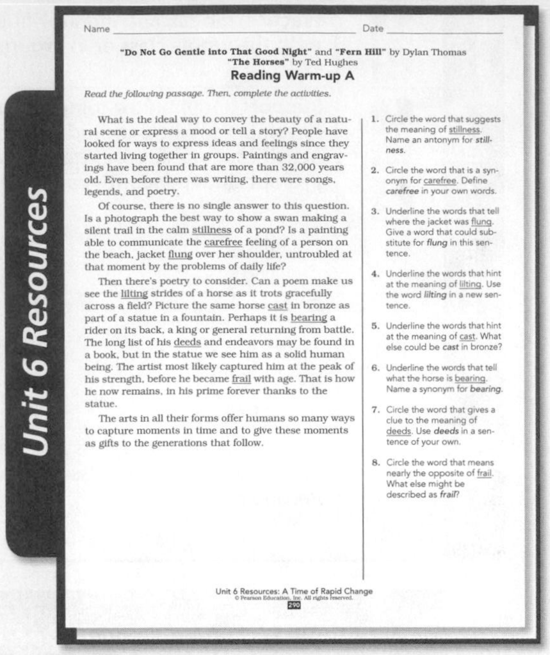

Unit 6 Resources

Name __________ Date __________

"Do Not Go Gentle into That Good Night" and **"Fern Hill"** by Dylan Thomas
"The Horses" by Ted Hughes

Reading Warm-up A

Read the following passage. Then, complete the activities.

What is the ideal way to convey the beauty of a natural scene or express a mood or tell a story? People have looked for ways to express ideas and feelings since they started living together in groups. Paintings and engravings have been found that are more than 32,000 years old. Even before there was writing, there were songs, legends, and poetry.

Of course, there is no single answer to this question. Is a photograph the best way to show a swan making a silent trail in the calm stillness of a pond? Is a painting able to communicate the carefree feeling of a person on the beach, jacket flung over her shoulder, untroubled at that moment by the problems of daily life?

Then there's poetry to consider. Can a poem make us see the lilting strides of a horse as it trots gracefully across a field? Picture the same horse cast in bronze as part of a statue in a fountain. Perhaps it is bearing a rider on its back, a king or general returning from battle. The long list of his deeds and endeavors may be found in a book, but in the statue we see him as a solid human being. The artist most likely captured him at the peak of his strength, before he became frail with age. That is how he now remains, in his prime forever thanks to the statue.

The arts in all their forms offer humans so many ways to capture moments in time and to give these moments as gifts to the generations that follow.

1. Circle the word that suggests the meaning of stillness. Name an antonym for *stillness*.
2. Circle the word that is a synonym for carefree. Define *carefree* in your own words.
3. Underline the words that tell where the jacket was flung. Give a word that could substitute for *flung* in this sentence.
4. Underline the words that hint at the meaning of lilting. Use the word *lilting* in a new sentence.
5. Underline the words that hint at the meaning of cast. What else could be *cast* in bronze?
6. Underline the words that tell what the horse is bearing. Name a synonym for *bearing*.
7. Circle the word that gives a clue to the meaning of deeds. Use *deeds* in a sentence of your own.
8. Circle the word that means nearly the opposite of frail. What else might be described as *frail*?

Unit 6 Resources: A Time of Rapid Change
© Pearson Education, Inc. All rights reserved.
290

EL L1 L2 **Reading Warm-ups A and B,** pp. 290–291

Also available for these selections:

EL L1 L2 **Vocabulary Warm-ups A and B,** pp. 288–289

All **Vocabulary Builder,** p. 294

Reader's Notebooks

Pre- and postreading pages for these selections appear in an interactive format in the *Reader's Notebooks*. Each *Notebook* is differentiated for a different group of learners. The selections in the Adapted and English Learner's versions are abridged.

L2 L3 ***Reader's Notebook***

L1 ***Reader's Notebook: Adapted Version***

EL ***Reader's Notebook: English Learner's Version***

EL ***Reader's Notebook: Spanish Version***

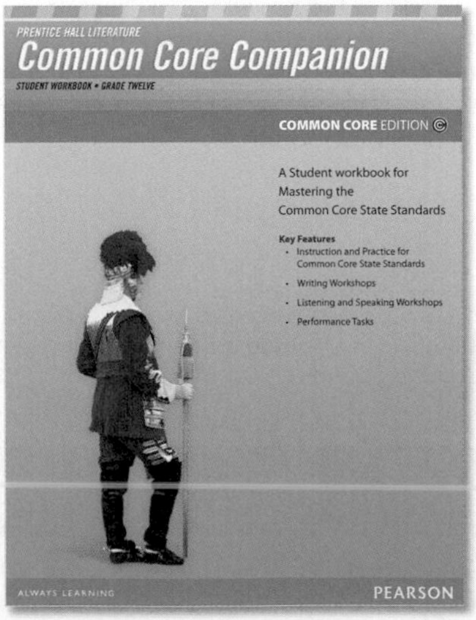

Common Core Companion

Additional instruction and practice for each Common Core State Standard

Selection Support

Graphic Organizer Transparencies

"Do Not Go Gentle into That Good Night" and **"Fern Hill"**
by Dylan Thomas
"The Horses" by Ted Hughes

After You Read A: Voice

Aspect of Style	Examples
Tumbles Out Words in a Rush	"Now as I was young and easy under the apple boughs / About the lilting house and happy as the grass was green."
Shows an Attitude of Wonder About Life	"Time to let me play and be / Golden in the mercy of his means."
Uses Complex Poetic Forms	
Chooses Evocative, Musical Words	
Uses Unusual, Almost Visionary Imagery	

Graphic Organizer Transparencies

262

EL L1 L2 **Literary Analysis: Graphic Organizer A** (partially filled in), p. 262

Also available for these selections:

EL L1 L2 **Reading: Graphic Organizer A,** p. 260

EL L3 **Reading: Graphic Organizer B,** p. 261

EL L3 **Literary Analysis: Graphic Organizer B,** p. 263

Skills Development/Extension

Unit 6 Resources

Name ______________________ Date ____________

"Do Not Go Gentle into That Good Night" and **"Fern Hill"** by Dylan Thomas
"The Horses" by Ted Hughes

Literary Analysis: Style and Theme, Villanelle

A writer's **style** encompasses his or her way of expressing ideas and emotions. To describe a writer's style, you must look at diction, syntax, form, as well as other literary techniques the writer uses, such as figurative language, sound devices, and imagery. Often writer's use style to support their expression of theme.

The **theme** of a selection is its central idea or message. When you analyze a work, look at its content, descriptions, and events, as well as style, to determine the central point the author is making.

Poets have the choice of a multitude of forms to express their themes. Some poets choose to write free verse, in which the rhythm, rhyme, and meter follow no specific pattern. Others choose to call upon traditional form in order to express their ideas. Thomas chooses the villanelle form for "Do Not Go Gentle into That Good Night." A **villanelle** is a nineteen-line poem that repeats lines 1 and 3 throughout. The rhyme scheme is set.

Directions: *Answer the following questions about Thomas's and Hughes's poems.*

1. How would you describe Thomas's style in "Do Not Go Gentle into That Good Night"? Give reasons for your evaluation.
2. How does Thomas's style in "Fern Hill" compare to that in his other poem?
3. How would you describe Hughes's style in relation to Thomas's two poems?
4. What common theme do these three poems address?

Unit 6 Resources: A Time of Rapid Change

292

All **Literary Analysis: Style,** p. 292

Also available for these selections:

All **Reading: Evaluate the Poet's Expression of the Theme,** p. 293

EL L3 L4 **Support for Writing,** p. 295

L4 **Enrichment,** p. 296

Assessment

Name ______________________ Date ____________

"Do Not Go Gentle into That Good Night" and **"Fern Hill"** by Dylan Thomas
"The Horses" by Ted Hughes

Selection Test B

Critical Reading *Identify the letter of the choice that best completes the statement or answers the question.*

___ 1. The speaker in "Do Not Go Gentle into That Good Night" tries to convince his father
A. to teach him about life.
B. to remember good men and wild men.
C. to go peacefully.
D. to resist death.

___ 2. In "Do Not Go Gentle into That Good Night," the wise men "[d]o not go gentle into that good night" because
A. they doubt their own wisdom.
B. they envy those who were less wise.
C. they are afraid of death.
D. their wisdom has not inspired others.

___ 3. The theme of "Do Not Go Gentle into That Good Night" is
A. people die in the same spirit in which they lived.
B. death comes too soon and should be resisted.
C. having regret at the end of one's life is pitiful.
D. people of all ranks and stations are equal in death.

___ 4. The use of the villanelle form allows Thomas to
A. enforce the theme through repetition of lines.
B. express ideas using a rhythm that mimics speech.
C. limit the extent of the poem's content.
D. experiment with different stanza and line lengths.

___ 5. How does Thomas use diction to creatively refer to death?
A. He experiments with different synonyms.
B. He uses a variety of figures of speech.
C. He personifies death repeatedly.
D. He avoids using the words *death* or *dying*.

___ 6. Which image in "Fern Hill" evokes the idea of natural simplicity and freshness?
A. ". . . happy as the grass was green . . ."
B. ". . . the pebbles of the holy streams."
C. ". . . fire green as grass."
D. ". . . a wanderer white / With the dew . . ."

___ 7. In "Fern Hill," Thomas's choice of descriptors, such as "lilting house" and "happy yard," helps express theme by
A. using figurative language.
B. giving the house a personality.
C. supporting new ideas about life.
D. reflecting his childhood emotions.

Unit 6 Resources: A Time of Rapid Change

303

EL L3 L4 **Selection Test B,** pp. 303–305

Also available for these selections:

L3 L4 **Open-Book Test,** pp. 297–299

EL L1 L2 **Selection Test A,** pp. 300–302

PHLit Online!
www.PHLitOnline.com

- complete narrated selection text
- a thematically related video with writing prompt
- an interactive graphic organizer
- highlighting feature
- access to all student print resources, adapted to individual student needs
- Spanish and English summaries
- adapted selection translations in Spanish

Online Resources: All print materials are also available online.

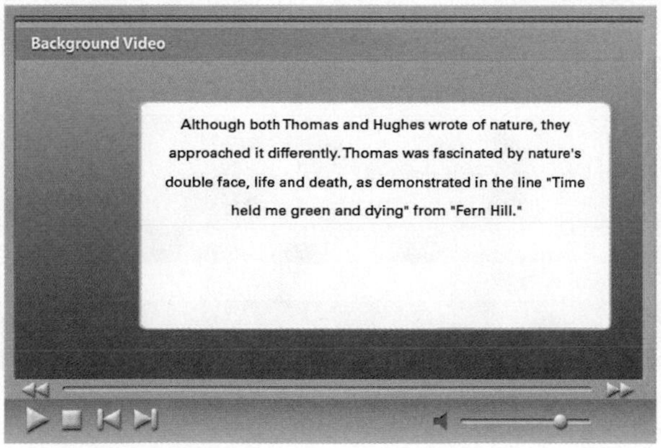

Background Video
Although both Thomas and Hughes wrote of nature, they approached it differently. Thomas was fascinated by nature's double face, life and death, as demonstrated in the line "Time held me green and dying" from "Fern Hill."

Background Video

Also available:

Get Connected! (thematic video with writing prompt)
All videos are available in Spanish.

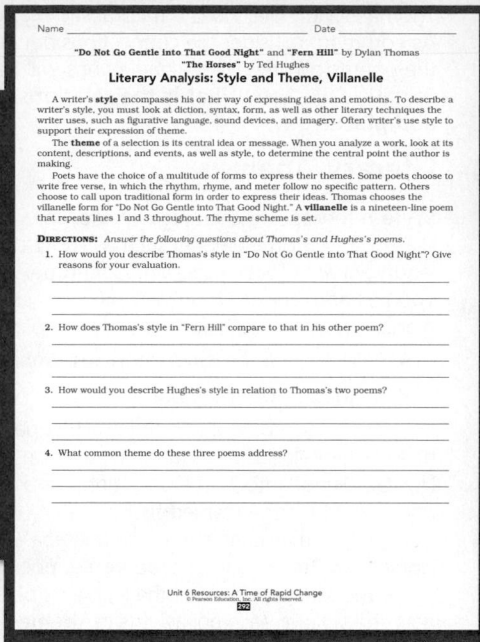

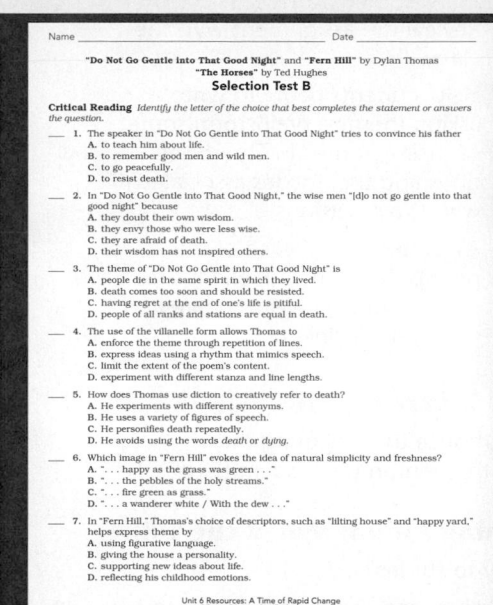

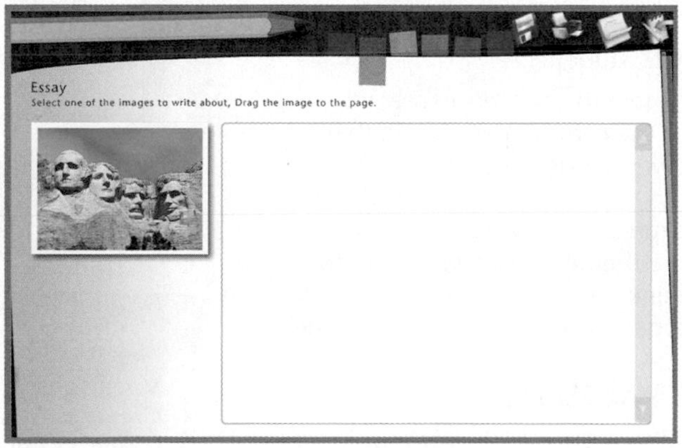

Select one of the images to write about, Drag the image to the page.

Writer's Journal (with graphics feature)

Also available:

Vocabulary Central (tools and activities for studying vocabulary)

PRETEACH

❶ Connecting to the Essential Question

1. Review the assignment with the class.
2. Help students begin to write by asking them to brainstorm some of their favorite childhood settings and the images associated with those settings.
3. As students read each of the poems, have them look for the connections between nature and the poets' insights.

❷ Literary Analysis

Introduce the skill using the instruction on the student page.

Think Aloud: Model the Skill

Say to students:

As we read the poetry, I want to be aware of each poet's style. I will be able to identify their styles by paying attention to elements such as rhyming patterns, the pace formed by the rhyming pattern, and the tone.

❸ Reading Strategy

1. Introduce the skill using the instruction on the student page.
2. Give students a copy of **Reading Strategy Graphic Organizer B**, page 261 in Graphic Organizer Transparencies, to fill out as they read.

Think Aloud: Model the Skill

Say to students:

I know that writers express theme, or the central message, in their own unique ways. To evaluate the effectiveness of the author's expression, I want to first identify the theme of each work and to think about the elements that work together to represent that theme.

❹ Vocabulary

1. Pronounce each word, giving its definition, and have students say it aloud.
2. For more guidance, see the card for introducing vocabulary.

Before You Read

Do Not Go Gentle into That Good Night • Fern Hill • The Horses

❶ **Connecting to the Essential Question** In "Fern Hill," poet Dylan Thomas vividly describes a natural setting he remembers from childhood. As you read, consider the connections between nature and the insights the poems convey. These connections will help you think about the Essential Question: **What is the relationship between literature and place?**

Common Core State Standards

Reading Literature
2. Determine two or more themes or central ideas of a text and analyze their development over the course of the text, including how they interact and build on one another to produce a complex account.

❷ Literary Analysis

Style refers to the characteristic way in which a writer writes. A poet's style is based on elements such as word choice, tone or attitude, line length, stanza form, pace, and sound devices or patterns of sound. Thomas and Hughes have very different styles, Thomas tumbling his words out in a rush, Hughes creating separate little pulses of images:

- Thomas: *"All the sun long it was running, it was lovely, . . ."*
- Hughes: *"Not a leaf, not a bird"*

Thomas's tumbled words fit into strict patterns, however. In "Fern Hill" he uses nine-line stanzas in which the line lengths form a pattern. "Do Not Go Gentle into That Good Night" is a **villanelle,** a nineteen-line poem in which the rhymed first and third lines repeat regularly to help form the rhyme scheme *aba aba aba aba aba abaa.* In contrast, "The Horses" by Ted Hughes is **free verse,** poetry with no fixed pattern.

As you read, consider all the elements of each poet's style. Also consider how the style of each poem suits its **themes**—its central ideas or concerns.

❸ Reading Strategy

Preparing to Read Complex Texts Different poems often express similar themes in different ways. To **evaluate the poet's expression of themes,** follow these three steps:

1. Identify two or more themes, or central ideas, of the poem.
2. Identify the details that work together to develop these themes, and consider how the themes interact to suggest a deeper meaning.
3. Evaluate how effectively those details communicate the themes. Use a chart like the one shown to help you organize your ideas.

Themes
Details That Convey Themes
Effectiveness

❹ Vocabulary

grieved (grēvd) *v.* felt deep sorrow for; mourned (p. 1390)

spellbound (spel′ bound) *adj.* held by a spell; enchanted; magical (p. 1393)

tortuous (tôr′cho͞o əs) *adj.* full of twists or curves (p. 1397)

dregs (dregz) *n.* particles of solid matter that settle in the bottom of a liquid; remnants; residue (p. 1397)

PHLit Online! www.PHLitOnline.com

Vocabulary Development

Vocabulary Knowledge Rating

Create a **Vocabulary Knowledge Rating Chart** (*Professional Development Guidebook*, p. 33) for the vocabulary words on the student page. Give each student a copy of the chart with the words on it. Read the words aloud, and have students mark their ratings in the Before Reading column. Urge students to attend to these words as they read and discuss the selections

In order to gauge how much instruction you need to provide, tally how many students are confident in their knowledge of each word. As students read, point out the words and their context.

PHLit Online! **Vocabulary Central,** featuring tools and activities for studying vocabulary, is available online at **www.PHLitOnline.com.**

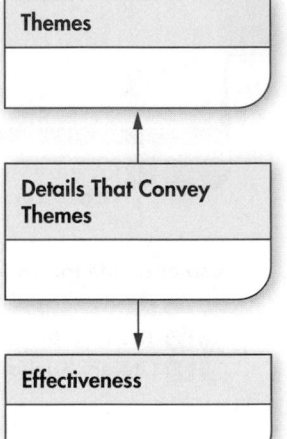

❺ # Dylan Thomas (1914–1953)

Author of "Do Not Go Gentle into That Good Night" • "Fern Hill"

Playful with language and exuberant about life, Thomas gained remarkable popularity in his lifetime. However, he also had a darker side, evident in his poems of death and the loss of childhood innocence.

A Young Poet Dylan Thomas was born in Swansea in southwestern Wales, an industrial city. However, he often visited his maternal grandfather's farm, which he describes in "Fern Hill." With the encouragement of his father, an English teacher, he became interested in poetry at an early age. Before turning twenty, he had already written—at least in early form—many of his best-known poems. As a teenager, he also produced source books of ideas that served as a basis for later works.

Journeys Abroad At the age of twenty-one, Thomas went to London, where he worked in journalism, broadcasting, and filmmaking for a number of years. In 1940, he published a collection of humorous stories about his childhood and youth, *Portrait of the Artist as a Young Dog.* In 1950, he made the first of four trips to the United States. Audiences here embraced him not only for his theatrical readings of his poems but also for the freshness and complexity of his poetic voice.

Though he continued to publish poetry, two of the later works for which he is best known are prose: *Under Milkwood,* a "play for voices," and "A Child's Christmas in Wales," a memoir.

An Artist's Problems Although acclaimed at an early age, Thomas struggled with poverty and alcoholism through most of his adult life. He died while on tour in the United States, where he had planned to collaborate on an opera with Igor Stravinsky.

1389

Daily Bellringer

For each class during which you will teach these selections, have students complete an activity for the appropriate week in the ***Daily Bellringer Activities*** booklet.

Multidraft Reading

To assist struggling readers and to enhance reading for all, apply multidraft reading protocols. For each reading, have students set the purpose indicated:

- **First reading**—identifying key ideas and details and answering any Reading Checks.
- **Second reading**—analyzing craft and structure and responding to the side-column prompts.
- **Third reading**—integrating knowledge and ideas, connecting to other texts and the world, and answering the end-of-selection questions.

For more guidance, refer to the ***Classroom Strategies and Teaching Routines*** card on Multidraft Reading.

❺ Background

More About the Author

Although Dylan Thomas's work appears to have flowed without stopping from his brain and through his pen, in fact the poet was a meticulous craftsman. He was almost obsessive in reworking his poems; he wrote many of them in the flush of his youth and refined them when he became an adult. One wonders what he would have produced had he lived beyond the age of 39.

PHLit Online!
www.PHLitOnline.com

Teaching From Technology

Preparing to Read
Go to **www.PHLitOnline.com** and display the ***Get Connected!*** slide show for this grouping. Have the class brainstorm responses to the writing prompt, entering ideas in the interactive journal. Then, have students complete their written responses individually, in a lab or as homework.

To build background, display the Background and More About the Authors features.

Using the Interactive Text
Go to **www.PHLitOnline.com** and display the **Enriched Online Student Edition**. As the class reads the selection or listens to the narration, record answers to side-column prompts using the graphic organizers accessible on the interactive page. Alternatively, have students use the online edition individually, answering the prompts as they read.

TEACH

❶ About the Selection

The speaker urges his father to resist death, to not "go gentle into that good night."

❷ Activating Prior Knowledge

Discuss with students the effectiveness of night and darkness as images of death.

❸ Literary Analysis

Style and Theme/Villanelle

1. **Ask** what is referred to in the phrase "that good night."
   Answer: It refers to death.
2. **Ask** students the Literary Analysis question.
   Answer: Each stanza ends with one of two imperatives: "Rage" (stanzas 1, 3, and 5) or "Do not go gentle" (stanzas 2 and 4).

ASSESS

Answers

Before students respond, you may wish to have them write a brief objective summary of the selection. As they answer the questions below, remind them to support their answers with evidence from the text.

1. (a) The speaker addresses his father. (b) The "good night" is death.
2. (a) It describes wise, good, wild, and grave men. (b) Each wishes he had taken advantage of some opportunity.
3. (a) Life is worth fighting for. (b) **Possible response:** *Good* is used ironically.

❶ ❷ Do Not Go Gentle into That Good Night

Dylan Thomas

Do not go gentle into that good night,
Old age should burn and rave at close of day;
Rage, rage against the dying of the light.

Though wise men at their end know dark is right,
Because their words had forked no lightning they
Do not go gentle into that good night.

Good men, the last wave by, crying how bright
Their frail deeds might have danced in a green bay,
Rage, rage against the dying of the light.

Wild men who caught and sang the sun in flight,
And learn, too late, they grieved it on its way,
Do not go gentle into that good night.

Grave men, near death, who see with blinding sight
Blind eyes could blaze like meteors and be gay,
Rage, rage against the dying of the light.

And you, my father, there on the sad height,
Curse, bless, me now with your fierce tears, I pray.
Do not go gentle into that good night.
Rage, rage against the dying of the light.

Vocabulary
grieved (grēvd) *v.* felt deep sorrow for; mourned

❸ **Literary Analysis**
Style and Theme/ Villanelle How does the last line of each stanza stop the movement of the poem and help stress the poem's theme?

Critical Reading

Cite textual evidence to support your responses.

1. **Key Ideas and Details (a)** Whom does the speaker address in the poem? **(b) Infer:** What is the "good night" to which the speaker refers?
2. **Key Ideas and Details (a)** What four types of men does the poem identify and describe? **(b) Interpret:** What regrets does each of these men have as he comes to the end of his life?
3. **Key Ideas and Details (a) Interpret:** What general advice about life and death is the speaker giving in lines 3, 9, 15, and 19? **(b) Analyze:** Considering the speaker's advice in these lines, why do you think he refers to the night as "good"?

Text Complexity Rubric

	Do Not Go Gentle into That Good Night	Fern Hill	The Horses
Qualitative Measures			
Context/Knowledge Demands	Modern villanelle; life experience demands 1 2 ③ 4 5	Modern lyric 1 2 ③ 4 5	Free verse 1 2 ③ 4 5
Structure/Language Conventionality and Clarity	Simple diction; unusual syntax 1 ② 3 4 5	Simple diction; unusual syntax 1 ② 3 4 5	Coined compounds 1 2 ③ 4 5
Levels of Meaning/ Purpose/Concepts	Accessible (family ties; death) 1 2 ③ 4 5	Moderate (childhood memories loss of) 1 2 ③ 4 5	Moderate (nature; primitive beauty; freedom) 1 2 ③ 4 5
Quantitative Measures			
Lexile/Text Length	NP / 169 words	NP / 468 words	NP / 274 words
Overall Complexity	**More accessible**	**More accessible**	**More complex**

LITERATURE IN CONTEXT

DYLAN THOMAS
❹ AND POETRY IN PERFORMANCE

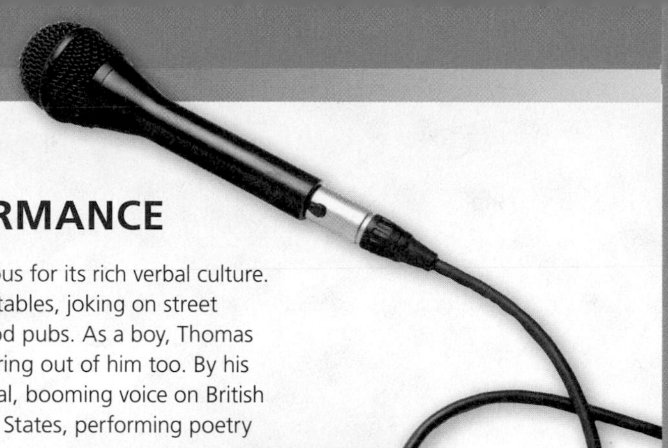

Dylan Thomas grew up in Wales, a country famous for its rich verbal culture. People spent hours conversing over their dinner tables, joking on street corners, and reciting poetry in their neighborhood pubs. As a boy, Thomas listened intently. Soon, rivers of words were pouring out of him too. By his early twenties, he was reading poetry in a musical, booming voice on British radio. A decade later, Thomas toured the United States, performing poetry to huge audiences.

Thomas was not the first lively poet to perform in America. In the 1920s, Langston Hughes and others had read their poems to jazz. Thomas, however, was the first to draw a large following, and he paved the way for performances by the Beat poets in the 1950s. Today, poets and rap artists like those shown here perform in theaters, clubs, and on the electronic media. They are participating in the revival of the spoken word that Dylan Thomas helped to start.

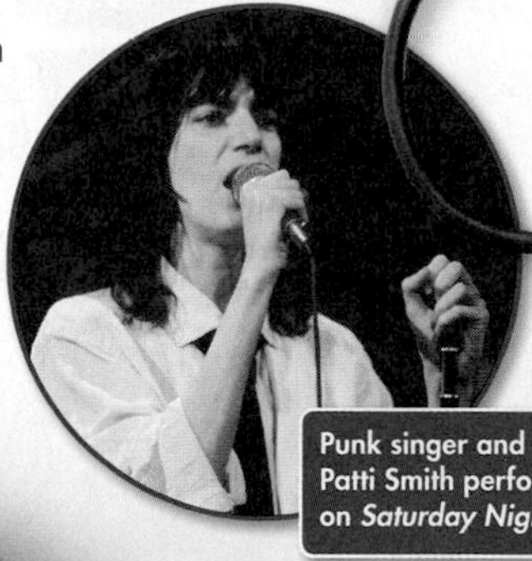

Punk singer and poet Patti Smith performing on *Saturday Night Live*

Poet Miguel Algarin, founder of The Nuyorican Poets Café, a home for poetry in performance on New York's Lower East Side for more than three decades

Rap star Saul Williams in performance

Dylan Thomas

CONNECT TO THE LITERATURE

How does reading Dylan Thomas's poetry aloud differ from reading it silently on the page?

❹ Literature in Context

Poetry in Performance

Many musical artists have explored and experimented with poetry. Popular artists such as John Lennon, Jim Morrison, and Tupac Shakur have written or performed poetry or had their poetry published. The popularity of hip-hop and rap music finds the connection between poetry and song stronger than ever, as the former employs many of the techniques—metaphor, simile, imagery, and allusion—found in the latter. A song, however, is not always derived from a poem. In fact, most songs need some form of instrumental accompaniment to convey their rhythm and musicality, while poetry—particularly lyrical poetry—contains sounds, words, and line breaks that convey a natural musical quality.

Connect to the Literature Allow students to read Thomas's poetry aloud and then **ask:** How does reading "Fern Hill" aloud differ from reading it silently on the page?

Possible responses: Students may prefer to read the poem aloud and may be more likely notice the repetition of words and sounds when doing so. Additionally, students will likely find the poem more expressive, enthusiastic, and lyrical when performed aloud.

PHLit Online!

This selection is available in interactive format in the **Enriched Online Student Edition**, at **www.PHLitOnline.com,** which includes a thematically related video with writing prompt and an interactive graphic organizer.

Text Complexity: Reader and Task Suggestions

	Do Not Go Gentle into That Good Night	Fern Hill	The Horses
Preparing to Read the Texts • Using the feature on TE p. 1391, stress that Dylan Thomas was famous for oral performance of his poems. • Discuss life experiences that would make good subjects for poetry. • Guide students to use Multidraft Reading strategies (TE p. 1389).	**Leveled Tasks** *Structure/Language* If students will have difficulty with the poem's structure, have them read it through for sense. As they reread, have them focus on repeated lines and their meaning for the father. *Evaluating* If students will not have difficulty with the poem's structure, have them evaluate the repetition and its effects on the poem's emotional impact and meaning.	**Leveled Tasks** *Levels of Meaning* If students will have difficulty with the poem's meaning, have them focus on the imagery. Then, have them reread the poem to focus on the speaker's life experiences. *Synthesizing* If students will not have difficulty with the poem's meaning, have them form a picture of the speaker as a youth and an adult.	**Leveled Tasks** *Levels of Meaning* If students will have difficulty with the levels of meaning, have them focus first on the feelings that the horses inspire in the speaker. As they reread, have them think what the horses might represent. *Synthesizing* If students will not have difficulty with the poem's meaning, have them compare it with other nature poems.

❺ About the Selection

From the perspective of adulthood, the speaker recalls the carefree and magical days he spent on a farm during his childhood—days when "Time let me play and be / Golden in the mercy of his means." At the end of the poem, the poet contrasts his former innocence with his present knowledge of the tyranny of time. He now knows that during childhood, "Time held me green and dying / Though I sang in my chains like the sea."

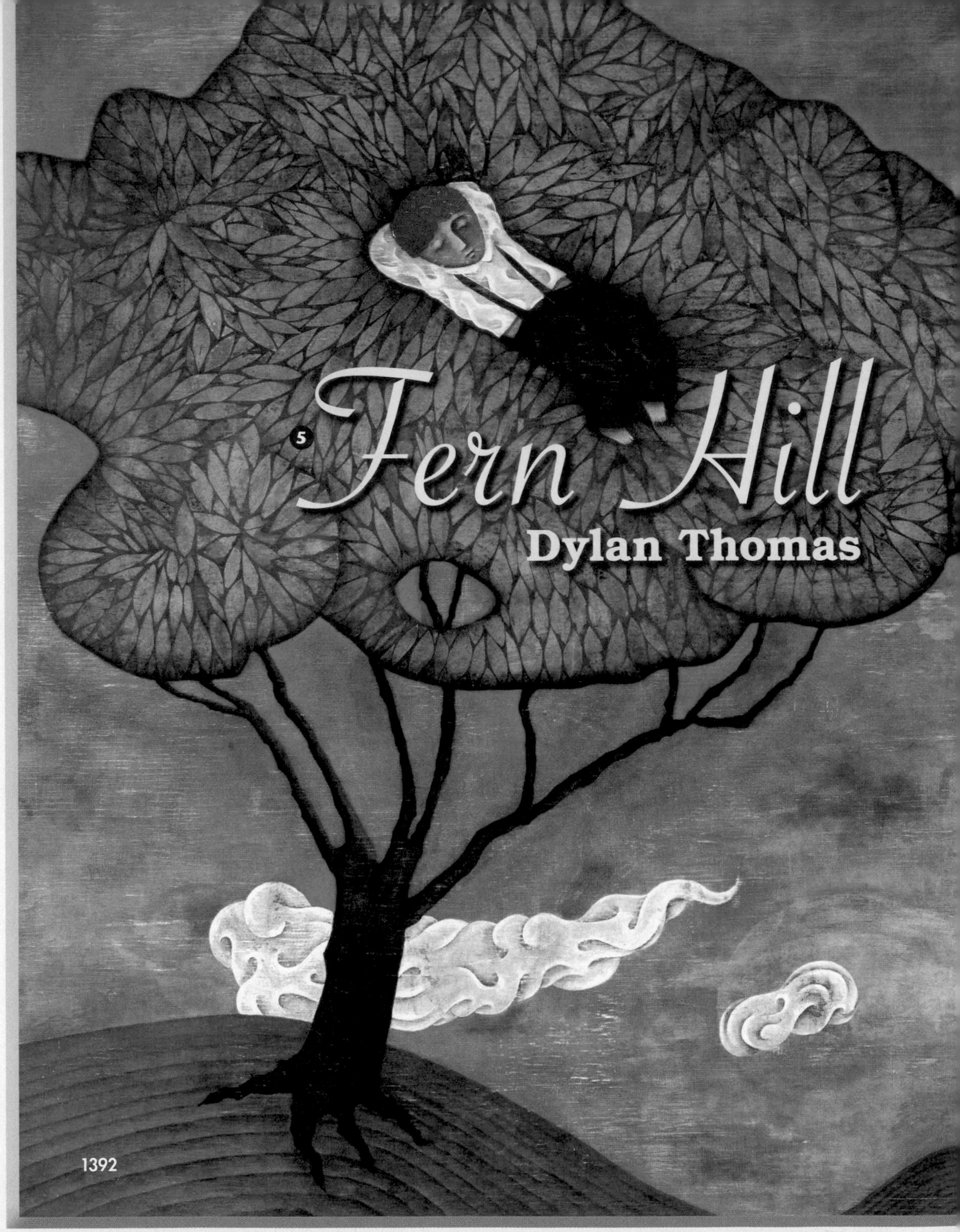

❺ Fern Hill

Dylan Thomas

1392

Enrichment: Analyzing a Literary Figure

Dylan Thomas

Read the following quotations to students or write them on the board:

> "[Dylan Thomas attempts] to express his highly intuitive, indeed mystical sense of reconciliation of opposites—life and death, beauty and horror, growth and decay . . . ."—William Vaughn Moody and Robert Morse Lovett
>
> "Thomas is a poet who takes care of the sound and lets the sense take care of itself."—Robert Graves

Activity: Analyzing Dylan Thomas Students will research Dylan Thomas and record their findings in the **Enrichment: Analyzing a Literary Figure** worksheet, ***Professional Development Guidebook***, page 235. Students may want to include analyses of the above quotes in the worksheet's section on style.

Now as I was young and easy under the apple boughs
About the lilting house and happy as the grass was green,
The night above the dingle starry,
Time let me hail and climb
Golden in the heydays of his eyes,
And honored among wagons I was prince of the apple towns
And once below a time I lordly had the trees and leaves
Trail with daisies and barley
Down the rivers of the windfall light.

And as I was green and carefree, famous among the barns
About the happy yard and singing as the farm was home,
In the sun that is young once only,
Time let me play and be
Golden in the mercy of his means,
And green and golden I was huntsman and herdsman, the calves
Sang to my horn, the foxes on the hills barked clear and cold,
And the sabbath rang slowly
In the pebbles of the holy streams.

All the sun long it was running, it was lovely, the hay
Fields high as the house, the tunes from the chimneys, it was air
And playing, lovely and watery
And fire green as grass.
And nightly under the simple stars
As I rode to sleep the owls were bearing the farm away,
All the moon long I heard, blessed among stables, the nightjars[1]
Flying with the ricks,[2] and the horses
Flashing into the dark.

And then to awake, and the farm, like a wanderer white
With the dew, come back, the cock on his shoulder; it was all
Shining, it was Adam and maiden,
The sky gathered again
And the sun grew round that very day.
So it must have been after the birth of the simple light
In the first, spinning place, the spellbound horses walking warm
Out of the whinnying green stable
On to the fields of praise.

---

1. **nightjars** *n.* common nocturnal birds, named for the whirring sound that the male makes.
2. **ricks** *n.* haystacks.

6 ◄ Critical Viewing What does the image suggest about the relationship of the poem to childhood? **[Infer]**

7 Literary Analysis
Style and Theme How does Thomas's tumbling rush of words contrast with the type of stanzas he uses?

Vocabulary
spellbound (spel′bound) *adj.* held by a spell; enchanted; magical

8 Reading Check
What jobs does the narrator have with the calves and foxes?

6 Critical Viewing

Possible response: The image, like the poem, conveys a nostalgia for childhood.

7 Literary Analysis

Style and Theme

1. **Ask** students what they think Thomas's view of nature is as they read the first three stanzas of the poem.
   Answer: Thomas views nature as surrounding him with beauty and lushness, particularly when he was a child.
2. **Ask** students the Literary Analysis question: How does Thomas's tumbling rush of words contrast with the type of stanzas he uses?
   Possible response: The structure of the poem does not "tumble." It is organized into six stanzas with the same number of lines and the same type of indentation. Thomas worked very hard to make it look as if the poem "just happened."

8 Reading Check

Answer: The narrator is both huntsman and herdsman.

Differentiated Instruction for Universal Access

Support for Special-Needs Students
Have students listen to a recording of the poem on the ***Hear It!* Audio CD**. Ask them to pay attention to the pacing, the pronunciation of words, and the ideas they get from listening. Then, ask volunteers to read individual stanzas aloud.

Strategy for Less Proficient Readers
Draw students' attention to Thomas's use of the words *green* and *golden* in lines 2, 5, 10, 14, 15, 22, 35, 44, and 53. Encourage them to comment on the meaning and significance of these two colors to the poet.

Strategy for Advanced Readers
Ask students what metaphor Thomas uses in stanza 4. That is, to what does he compare each new day to which he awakens? (The poet compares each new day to the first day of creation. "Adam and maiden" represent Adam and Eve.)

9 Reading Strategy
Evaluating Expression of Theme

1. **Ask** students to find examples of words and phrases that show time has a hold on the speaker.
   Possible responses: The author describes being in the "mercy of means," being held "green and dying," and being in "chains."
2. **Ask** students the Reading Strategy question.
   Possible response: The last stanza communicates the idea of a childhood that has fled by beginning with the phrase "lamb white days"—a reference to the innocence of childhood—but then quickly goes on to tell of "the moon that is always rising" and "riding to sleep"—night imagery associated with aging and with death.

ASSESS
Answers

Before students respond, you may wish to have them write a brief objective summary of the selection. As they answer the questions below, remind them to support their answers with evidence from the text.

1. (a) The speaker uses the colors *green* and *golden* to describe himself in his youth. (b) He feels that his childhood was a charmed, mythical time.
2. (a) I cared nothing about the passage of time when I was younger. One day I woke up and my childhood had fled. I realized that even as I felt young and immortal, I was already approaching death. (b) The mood changes from one of joy and celebration to one of sadness and loss. (c) These lines reflect the speaker's adult awareness of mortality.
3. Time has a hold on the narrator so that even as he experiences the joy of youth, he is growing old.
4. (a) The poem contrasts youth and adulthood. (b) The poem expresses an attitude of longing for youth and one of bitterness for adulthood.
5. Students' answers may include various stages of life: infancy, childhood, teenage, and early, middle, and late adulthood.

And honored among foxes and pheasants by the gay house
Under the new made clouds and happy as the heart was long,
In the sun born over and over,
I ran my heedless ways,
My wishes raced through the house-high hay
And nothing I cared, at my sky blue trades, that time allows
In all his tuneful turning so few and such morning songs
Before the children green and golden
Follow him out of grace,

Nothing I cared, in the lamb white days, that time would take me
Up to the swallow thronged loft by the shadow of my hand,
In the moon that is always rising,
Nor that riding to sleep
I should hear him fly with the high fields
And wake to the farm forever fled from the childless land.
Oh as I was young and easy in the mercy of his means,
Time held me green and dying
Though I sang in my chains like the sea.

Reading Strategy
Evaluating Expression of Theme How does the imagery in this stanza communicate the idea that childhood has fled? Cite details to support your evaluation.

Critical Reading

Cite textual evidence to support your responses.

1. **Key Ideas and Details (a)** Which two colors does the speaker use to describe himself in youth? **(b) Interpret:** What do the colors suggest that he feels about his childhood?
2. **Key Ideas and Details (a)** Paraphrase the last stanza. **(b) Analyze:** What change in mood occurs here? **(c) Infer:** What is the reason for the change?
3. **Key Ideas and Details** What is the meaning of lines 53–54?
4. **Key Ideas and Details (a)** What stages of life does the poem contrast? **(b) Draw Conclusions:** What attitude does the poem express toward the different stages of life?
5. **Integration of Knowledge and Ideas** Into what important stages would you divide human life? Explain.

Enrichment: Building Context

Fern Hill
As a youth, Dylan Thomas spent time visiting his grandfather's farm. In "Fern Hill," Thomas recalls many of these images. Students may want to develop concrete connections between Thomas's history and the scenes described in the poem. Alternatively, students may want to read some of Thomas's other writings or analyze how his work has affected others.

Activity: Building Context Students will research Fern Hill or elements of Thomas's other work and record their findings in the **Enrichment: Building Context** worksheet, ***Professional Development Guidebook***, page 222.

⑩ Ted Hughes

(1930–1998)

Author of "The Horses"

Born in rural West Yorkshire, Ted Hughes spent much of his youth hunting and fishing with his brother. These experiences contributed to his lifelong interest in the beauty and violence of nature, recurring themes in his work.

Hughes and His Father It would be a mistake, however, to ignore the violence of World War I as an influence on Hughes. He was born well after the war, but his father had had a traumatic experience in that conflict. He was among a handful of men to survive the destruction of his regiment. Hughes once said that as a child, he was strongly affected by his father's silence about this experience.

Hughes himself served in the Royal Air Force and then studied archaeology and anthropology at Pembroke College, Cambridge, where he met the American poet Sylvia Plath. He married Plath in 1956, but they later separated.

A Variety of Work Hughes is best known for his volumes of poetry *Hawk in the Rain, Crow,* and *Moortown*. In these and other works, he uses free verse and powerful, direct speech to express a yearning for a lost wholeness with the natural world. In exploring this theme, which appears in "The Horses," he was strongly influenced by the prose and poetry of D. H. Lawrence.

Hughes was a versatile writer who, in addition to poetry and fiction, wrote books for children. He even wrote a play in a language he invented. One of his final publications was *Tales from Ovid* (1997), a translation of many verse stories from the Latin poet Ovid's *Metamorphoses*. Hughes was poet laureate of England from 1984 until his death.

⑩ Background

More About the Author

The poet Ted Hughes also wrote books for children. One of them is *The Iron Man,* which was published as *The Iron Giant,* some say to avoid buyers confusing it with a book version of *Superman*. It is the story of a giant metal man whose competition with a monster from space brings peace to Earth. It was made into the animated film *The Iron Giant* in 1999.

Differentiated Instruction for Universal Access

Support for Special-Needs Students
Students may want to write their own horse poems and collect photos and illustrations from magazines and other sources. Point out that Hughes describes the horses as seen at dawn and just after sunrise. They might want to write a poem or draw an illustration of horses in bright sunlight or at night.

Strategy for Less Proficient Readers
Have students read the poem silently as they listen to a recitation of the piece. Then, have students rewrite the poem as prose and in their own words. Guide them to interpret as many of the symbolic words and phrases as possible.

Enrichment for Gifted/Talented Students
Students may want to draw or make sculptures of the group of horses as they envision the animals from the poet's description. Encourage students to use texture, color, and even abstract forms to convey their visions.

PHLit Online!

For more about the author, go online at **www.PHLitOnline.com.**

⓫ About the Selection

The speaker vividly describes an encounter with nature, as well as the sense of awe that accompanied it. He hopes that the image of these stalwart horses will remain with him through the years.

TED HUGHES

⓫ The Horses

BACKGROUND Although both Thomas and Hughes wrote of nature, they approached it differently. Thomas was fascinated by nature's double face, life and death, as demonstrated in the line "Time held me green and dying" from "Fern Hill." Hughes was often closely attuned to nature's remote, primitive, nonhuman beauty, as in "The Horses."

1396

Enrichment: Analyzing Symbols

Horses

Explain to students that symbols are images, characters, or events that represent a larger idea. While some symbols are universal, writers often add their own point of view. Ted Hughes's critics suggest that animals in his work symbolize the "instinctive power of nature that he finds lacking in human society." The symbols in this piece, obviously, are horses.

Activity: Analyzing Horses Ask students to record their analyses of horses as symbols and record their findings in the **Enrichment: Analyzing Themes and Symbols** worksheet, ***Professional Development Guidebook***, page 243.

I climbed through woods in the hour-before-dawn dark.
Evil air, a frost-making stillness,

Not a leaf, not a bird—
A world cast in frost. I came out above the wood

Where my breath left **tortuous** statues in the iron light.
But the valleys were draining the darkness

Till the moorline—blackening **dregs** of the brightening gray—
Halved the sky ahead. And I saw the horses:

Huge in the dense gray—ten together—
Megalith-still.[1] They breathed, making no move,

With draped manes and tilted hind-hooves,
Making no sound.

I passed: not one snorted or jerked its head.
Gray silent fragments

Of a gray silent world.

I listened in emptiness on the moor-ridge.
The curlew's[2] tear turned its edge on the silence.

---

1. **Megalith-still** still as the huge stones left by ancient peoples, such as those at Stonehenge.
2. **curlew's** (kur′ lo͞oz) *n.* of a large, brownish wading bird with long legs.

12 Literary Analysis
Style and Theme Identify three short bursts of images that help Hughes convey his theme.

Vocabulary
tortuous (tôr′cho͞o wəs) *adj.* full of twists or curves

dregs (dregz) *n.* particles of solid matter that settle in the bottom of a liquid; remnants; residue

13 ▼ Critical Viewing
Compare and contrast the horses in the poem with those in the picture. **[Compare and Contrast]**

14 Reading Check
What are the horses doing when Hughes sees them?

12 Literary Analysis
Style and Theme

1. **Ask** students to identify the personification in the first stanza. What is being personified, and how?
   Answer: The phrase "evil air" is personification, because it gives air a human quality. The poet calls the air evil because it is cold and still.
2. **Ask** students to paraphrase the second stanza as if they were writing a prose description.
   Possible response: I could not see a leaf on a tree and could not hear a single bird. My surroundings seemed to be a group of statues made of frost. I came out into the open above the wood.
3. **Ask** students the Literary Analysis question: Identify three short bursts of images that help Hughes convey his theme.
   Answer: Hughes conveys his theme in short bursts such as "Not a leaf," "not a bird," and "Megalith-still."

13 Critical Viewing
Answer: The horses in the photo are running, while the horses in the poem are still. Both convey power, but in different ways—the horses in the photo convey released energy, whereas those in the poem are filled with tension and potential energy.

14 Reading Check
Answer: The horses are standing as still as stone statues.

Concept Connector

Reading Skill Graphic Organizer
Ask students to review the graphic organizers in which they have made connections between the details and theme. Then, have students share their organizers and compare the connections they made.

Activating Prior Knowledge
Have students return to their responses to the Activating Prior Knowledge activity. Ask them to explain whether their thoughts have changed and, if so, how.

Connecting to the Essential Question
Have students compare their responses to the prompt, completed before reading the selections, with their thoughts afterward. Have them work individually or in groups, writing or discussing their thoughts, to formulate their new responses. Then, lead a class discussion, probing for connections between nature and the poets' insights.

⓯ Reading Strategy

Evaluating Expression of Theme

1. **Ask:** What is the theme, or central message, of "The Horses"? **Possible response:** Students may suggest that the central message entails the power, the beauty, and the wonder of nature.
2. **Ask** students to address the Reading Strategy directive: Contrast the images in lines 34–35 with earlier images. How effective is the contrast in helping to express the poem's theme? **Possible response:** Students may suggest that the contrast between the wooded setting, silent and wide-open, and the streets, noisy and crowded, is effective.

ASSESS

Answers

Before students respond, you may wish to have them write a brief objective summary of the selection. As they answer the questions below, remind them to support their answers with evidence from the text.

1. (a) The speaker walks up through a woodland area just before dawn, then as the sun rises he turns and walks back down the way he came. He sees the horses on each journey, both up and down. (b) **Possible response:** The poem suggests that nature is beautiful, powerful, mysterious, and timeless.
2. (a) The speaker wants to retain the memory of his encounter with the horses. (b) **Possible response:** He may find solace in the peacefulness of the scene when, later, he is surrounded by the "din of the crowded streets."
3. **Possible response:** Dramatic passages such as "emptiness on the moor-ridge," and "woods in the hour-before-dawn dark" are visual images that convey the quiet, lonely, and reflective theme of "The Horses." The setting of "Fern Hill" is emphasized through passages like "easy under the apple boughs" and "famous among the barns / about the happy yard."

Slowly detail leafed from the darkness. Then the sun
Orange, red, red erupted

Silently, and splitting to its core tore and flung cloud,
Shook the gulf open, showed blue,

And the big planets hanging—
I turned

Stumbling in the fever of a dream, down towards
The dark woods, from the kindling tops.

And came to the horses.
                    There, still they stood,
But now steaming and glistening under the flow of light,

Their draped stone manes, their tilted hind-hooves
Stirring under a thaw while all around them

The frost showed its fires. But still they made no sound.
Not one snorted or stamped,

Their hung heads patient as the horizons,
High over valleys, in the red leveling rays—

In din of the crowded streets, going among the years, the faces,
May I still meet my memory in so lonely a place

Between the streams and the red clouds, hearing curlews,
Hearing the horizons endure.

Reading Strategy
Evaluating Expression of Theme Contrast the images in lines 34–35 with earlier images. How effective is the contrast in helping to express the poem's theme?

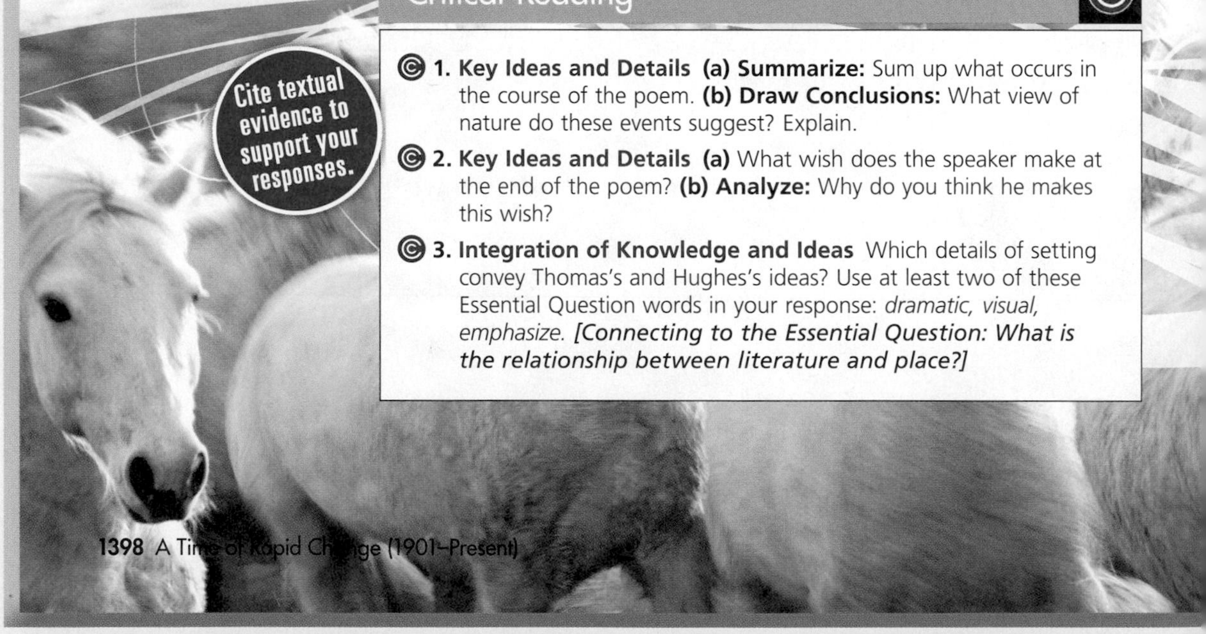
Cite textual evidence to support your responses.

Critical Reading

1. **Key Ideas and Details (a) Summarize:** Sum up what occurs in the course of the poem. **(b) Draw Conclusions:** What view of nature do these events suggest? Explain.
2. **Key Ideas and Details (a)** What wish does the speaker make at the end of the poem? **(b) Analyze:** Why do you think he makes this wish?
3. **Integration of Knowledge and Ideas** Which details of setting convey Thomas's and Hughes's ideas? Use at least two of these Essential Question words in your response: *dramatic, visual, emphasize. [Connecting to the Essential Question: What is the relationship between literature and place?]*

Assessment Practice

Sequential Order (For more practice, see *All-in-One Workbook.*)

Many tests require students to recognize stylistic devices and effective language. Use this sample item after students have read "Fern Hill."

The mood of this poem can best be described as

A optimistic.
B depressed.
C religious.
D dreamlike.

Review with students the definition of mood and lead them through the possible answers. Make sure students recognize that the question asks about the overall mood of the poem, not the mood in a particular stanza. Students should determine that the correct answer is *D*. The vivid, often surreal imagery contributes strongly to the poem's dreamlike quality.

After You Read

Do Not Go Gentle into That Good Night • Fern Hill • The Horses

Literary Analysis

1. **Craft and Structure** Fill in a chart like the one shown here to illustrate key aspects of Thomas's **style.** Then explain how these aspects convey the **theme** in "Fern Hill."

Aspect of Style	Examples
Tumbles out words in a rush	
Uses complex poetic forms	

2. **Craft and Structure** Fill out a chart for Hughes like the one above, and include his use of **free verse**. Then explain how aspects of Hughes's style help express the theme in "The Horses."

Common Core State Standards

Writing
4. Produce clear and coherent writing in which the development, organization, and style are appropriate to task, purpose, and audience.

Reading Strategy

3. How does the **villanelle's** repetition in "Do Not Go Gentle into That Good Night" help Thomas to **express his theme**?
4. Of "Fern Hill" and "The Horses," which do you think expresses its theme more effectively? Cite details to support your opinion.

PERFORMANCE TASKS
Integrated Language Skills

Vocabulary Acquisition and Use

Use a word from the vocabulary list on page 1388 to complete each sentence, and explain your choice. Use each word only once.

1. Instead of an easy path, we took a _______ route.
2. The _______ remained in the bottom of the cup.
3. When their beloved leader died, the whole nation _______.
4. She was _______ by the wizard's chant.

Writing

Poem Parody is writing that imitates and exaggerates an author's style and themes for humorous purposes. Write a **poem** that is a **parody** of the work of either Thomas or Hughes. Choose a subject or theme that exaggerates a subject from one of the poet's, and imitate and exaggerate that poet's imagery, word choice, tone, and sentence lengths or rhythms. For example, to exaggerate Thomas's style, you might make the tumble of words come even faster.

Assessment Resources

Unit 6 Resources

L1 L2 EL **Selection Test A,** pp. 300–302. Administer Test A to less advanced readers.

L3 L4 EL **Selection Test B,** pp. 303–305. Administer Test B to on-level and more advanced students.

L3 L4 **Open-Book Test,** pp. 297–299. As an alternative, give the Open-Book Test.

All **Customizable Test Bank**

All **Self-tests**
Students may prepare for the **Selection Test** by taking the **Self-test** online.

PHLit Online! All assessment resources are available at **www.PHLitOnline.com.**

Answers

1. **Possible responses:** Aspect of style: Tumbles out words in a rush; Example: "Now as I was young and easy under the apple boughs / About the lilting house and happy as the grass was green." Aspect of style: Uses complex poetic forms; Example: villanelle form of "Do Not Go Gentle into That Good Night." These aspects appear to be the exuberant description by an excited child, but are actually the thoughtful descriptions of a reflective adult who understands all that was lost.
2. Aspect of style: speaks in blips and pulses; Example: "Not a leaf, not a bird—"; Aspect of style: uses free verse; Example: "Slowly detail leafed from the darkness. Then the sun / Orange, red, red erupted." These aspects have the effect of coming across as the stream of consciousness of one who is remembering an event in photographic images and help convey the central message of wonder and awe of nature.
3. **Possible response:** The central message of the poem is to "rage" against death. Its repetition helps make the central message that much clearer.
4. Students' preferences will vary, but answers should be supported.

Vocabulary Acquisition and Use

1. tortuous
2. dregs
3. grieved
4. spellbound

Writing

1. Ask students to focus first on choosing a style or theme to exaggerate.
2. Encourage students to experiment with imagery, word choice, tone, sentence length, and rhythm in order to achieve the desired expression of theme.
3. Next, divide the class into small groups. Ask students to take turns reading their poems aloud to one another. Group members should listen and evaluate one another's expression of theme.
4. Allow students time to revise their poems based on their classmates' suggestions.

An Arundel Tomb • The Explosion • On the Patio • Not Waving but Drowning

Lesson Pacing Guide

DAY 1 Preteach

- Administer the Reading and Vocabulary Warm-ups (*Unit 6 Resources,* pp. 306–309) as necessary.
- Introduce the Literary Analysis concept: Meter and Free Verse.
- Introduce the Reading Strategy: Read Poetry in Sentences.
- Build background with the author and Background features.
- Develop thematic thinking with Connecting to the Essential Question.
- Teach the selection vocabulary.

DAY 2 Preteach/Teach/Extend

- Distribute copies of the appropriate graphic organizer for the Reading Strategy (*Graphic Organizer Transparencies,* pp. 264–265).
- Distribute copies of the appropriate graphic organizer for Literary Analysis (*Graphic Organizer Transparencies,* pp. 266–267).
- Prepare students to read with the Activating Prior Knowledge activities (TE).
- Informally monitor comprehension while students read.
- Use the Reading Check questions to confirm comprehension.
- Develop students' understanding of meter and free verse using the Literary Analysis prompts.
- Develop students' ability to read poetry in sentences using the Reading Strategy prompts.
- Reinforce vocabulary with the Vocabulary notes.
- Assess students' comprehension and mastery of the skills by having them answer the Critical Reading, Literary Analysis, and Reading Strategy questions.

DAY 3 Assess

- Have students complete the Vocabulary Lesson.
- Have students complete the Writing activity, writing a reflective essay. (You may assign as homework.)
- Administer Selection Test A or B (*Unit 6 Resources,* pp. 318–320 or 321–323).

Common Core State Standards

Reading Literature 5. Analyze how an author's choices concerning how to structure specific parts of a text contribute to its overall structure and meaning as well as its aesthetic impact.

Writing 3.e. Provide a conclusion that follows from and reflects on what is experienced, observed, or resolved over the course of the narrative.

Additional Standards Practice
***Common Core Companion,* pp. 54–55; 214–215**

Daily Block Scheduling
Each day in this Lesson Pacing Guide represents a 40–50 minute period. Teachers using block scheduling may combine days to revise pacing. In addition, teachers may differentiate and support core instruction by integrating components for extended and intensive support as students require. See the Guide to Selected Leveled Resources (facing page).

Guide to Selected Leveled Resources

RTI Tier 1 (students performing on level)		An Arundel Tomb • The Explosion • On the Patio • Not Waving but Drowning
Warm Up	**Practice, model,** and **monitor** fluency, working **with the whole class** or **in groups.**	Vocabulary and Reading Warm-ups B, *Unit 6 Resources,* pp. 324–325, 327
Comprehension/Skills	**Support** and **monitor** comprehension and skills development, having students complete the activities, graphic organizers, and interactive prompts **independently** or **as a class.**	• ***Reader's Notebook,*** adapted instruction and full selection EL ***Reader's Notebook: English Learner's Version,*** adapted instruction and adapted selection • **Reading Strategy Graphic Organizer B, *Graphic Organizer Transparencies,*** p. 279 • **Literary Analysis Graphic Organizer B, *Graphic Organizer Transparencies,*** p. 281
Monitor Progress	**Monitor** student progress with the differentiated curriculum-based assessment in the *Unit Resources.*	• **Selection Test B, *Unit 6 Resources,*** pp. 339–341 • **Open-Book Test, *Unit 6 Resources,*** pp. 333–335

RTI Tier 2 (students requiring intervention)		An Arundel Tomb • The Explosion • On the Patio • Not Waving but Drowning
Warm Up	**Practice, model,** and **monitor** fluency **in groups** or **with individuals.**	• **Vocabulary and Reading Warm-ups A, *Unit 6 Resources,*** pp. 324–326 • ***Hear It!* Audio CD (adapted text)**
Comprehension/Skills	• **Support** and **monitor** comprehension and skills development, working **in small groups** or **with individuals.** • As students complete the selection in the appropriate version of the *Reader's Notebook,* **monitor** comprehension frequently with group questions and individual instruction. • **Model** strategies while guiding students in completing the activities and prompts in the *Reader's Notebook,* as well as the graphic organizers. • **Practice** skills and **monitor** mastery with the *Reading Kit* worksheets.	• ***Reader's Notebook: Adapted Version,*** adapted instruction and adapted selection EL ***Reader's Notebook: English Learner's Version,*** adapted instruction and adapted selection • **Reading Strategy Graphic Organizer A, *Graphic Organizer Transparencies,*** p. 278 • **Literary Analysis Graphic Organizer A, *Graphic Organizer Transparencies,*** p. 280 • ***Reading Kit,*** Practice worksheets
Monitor Progress	**Monitor** student progress with the differentiated curriculum-based assessment in the *Unit Resources* and in the *Reading Kit.*	• **Selection Test A, *Unit 6 Resources,*** pp. 336–338 • ***Reading Kit,*** Assess worksheets

TIER 3 Tier 3 intervention may require consultation with the student's special-education or dyslexia specialist. For additional support, see the Tier 2 activities and resources listed above.

One-on-one teaching **Group work** **Whole class instruction** **Independent work** **A Assessment**

For a complete guide to selection support, including support for Advanced students, see the Overview of Resources in the frontmatter.

An Arundel Tomb • The Explosion • On the Patio • Not Waving but Drowning

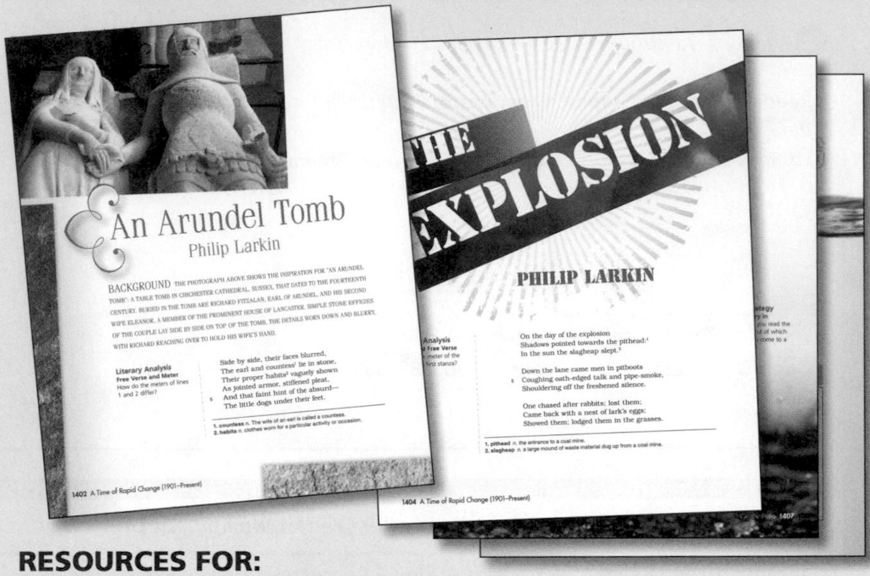

RESOURCES FOR:

- L1 Special-Needs Students
- L2 Below-Level Students (Tier 2)
- L3 On-Level Students (Tier 1)
- L4 Advanced Students (Tier 1)
- EL English Learners
- All All Students

Vocabulary/Fluency/Prior Knowledge

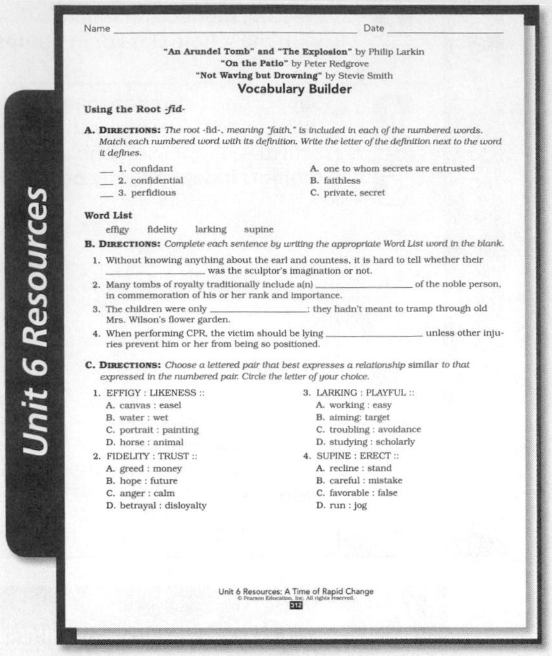

Unit 6 Resources

Name ______________________ Date ______________

"An Arundel Tomb" and **"The Explosion"** by Philip Larkin
"On the Patio" by Peter Redgrove
"Not Waving but Drowning" by Stevie Smith

Vocabulary Builder

Using the Root *-fid-*

A. DIRECTIONS: *The root -fid-, meaning "faith," is included in each of the numbered words. Match each numbered word with its definition. Write the letter of the definition next to the word it defines.*

___ 1. confidant — A. one to whom secrets are entrusted
___ 2. confidential — B. faithless
___ 3. perfidious — C. private, secret

Word List

effigy fidelity larking supine

B. DIRECTIONS: *Complete each sentence by writing the appropriate Word List word in the blank.*

1. Without knowing anything about the earl and countess, it is hard to tell whether their ______________ was the sculptor's imagination or not.
2. Many tombs of royalty traditionally include a(n) ______________ of the noble person, in commemoration of his or her rank and importance.
3. The children were only ______________; they hadn't meant to tramp through old Mrs. Wilson's flower garden.
4. When performing CPR, the victim should be lying ______________ unless other injuries prevent him or her from being so positioned.

C. DIRECTIONS: *Choose a lettered pair that best expresses a relationship similar to that expressed in the numbered pair. Circle the letter of your choice.*

1. EFFIGY : LIKENESS ::
   A. canvas : easel
   B. water : wet
   C. portrait : painting
   D. horse : animal
2. FIDELITY : TRUST ::
   A. greed : money
   B. hope : future
   C. anger : calm
   D. betrayal : disloyalty
3. LARKING : PLAYFUL ::
   A. working : easy
   B. aiming: target
   C. troubling : avoidance
   D. studying : scholarly
4. SUPINE : ERECT ::
   A. recline : stand
   B. careful : mistake
   C. favorable : false
   D. run : jog

Unit 6 Resources: A Time of Rapid Change
© Pearson Education, Inc. All rights reserved.
312

All **Vocabulary Builder,** p. 312

Also available for these selections:

EL L1 L2 **Vocabulary Warm-ups A and B,** pp. 306–307

EL L1 L2 **Reading Warm-ups A and B,** pp. 308–309

Reader's Notebooks

Pre- and postreading pages for these selections appear in an interactive format in the *Reader's Notebooks*. Each *Notebook* is differentiated for a different group of learners. The selections in the Adapted and English Learner's versions are abridged.

L2 L3 ***Reader's Notebook***

L1 ***Reader's Notebook: Adapted Version***

EL ***Reader's Notebook: English Learner's Version***

EL ***Reader's Notebook: Spanish Version***

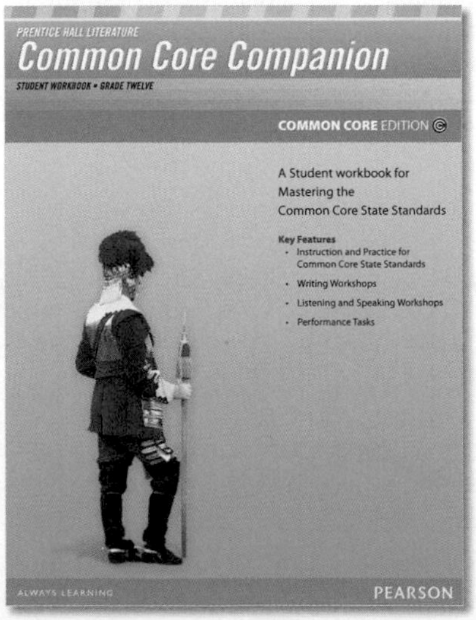

Common Core Companion

Additional instruction and practice for each Common Core State Standard

Selection Support

Graphic Organizer Transparencies

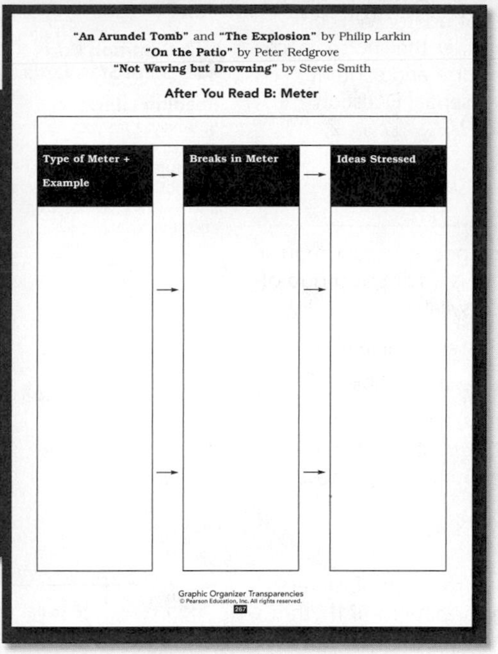
"An Arundel Tomb" and "The Explosion" by Philip Larkin
"On the Patio" by Peter Redgrove
"Not Waving but Drowning" by Stevie Smith

After You Read B: Meter

Type of Meter + Example	Breaks in Meter	Ideas Stressed

Graphic Organizer Transparencies
© Pearson Education, Inc. All rights reserved.
267

EL L3 Literary Analysis: Graphic Organizer B, p. 267

Also available for these selections:

- **EL L1 L2 Reading: Graphic Organizer A,** p. 264
- **EL L3 Reading: Graphic Organizer B,** p. 265
- **EL L1 L2 Literary Analysis: Graphic Organizer A** (partially filled in), p. 266

Skills Development/Extension

Unit 6 Resources

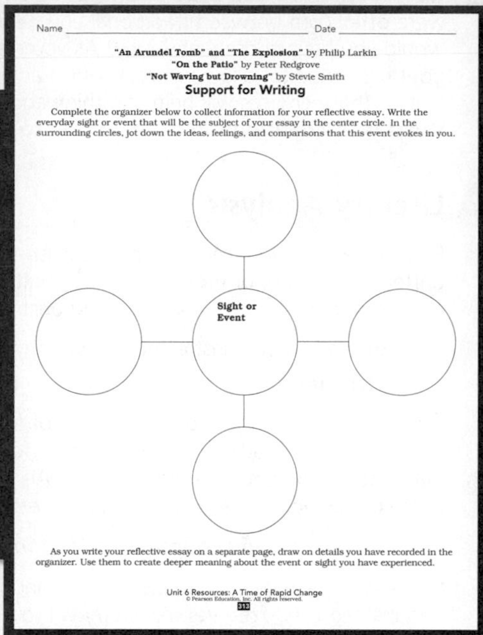
Name ____________ Date ____________

"An Arundel Tomb" and "The Explosion" by Philip Larkin
"On the Patio" by Peter Redgrove
"Not Waving but Drowning" by Stevie Smith

Support for Writing

Complete the organizer below to collect information for your reflective essay. Write the everyday sight or event that will be the subject of your essay in the center circle. In the surrounding circles, jot down the ideas, feelings, and comparisons that this event evokes in you.

As you write your reflective essay on a separate page, draw on details you have recorded in the organizer. Use them to create deeper meaning about the event or sight you have experienced.

Unit 6 Resources: A Time of Rapid Change
© Pearson Education, Inc. All rights reserved.
313

EL L3 L4 Support for Writing, p. 313

Also available for these selections:

- **All Literary Analysis: Meter and Free Verse,** p. 310
- **All Reading: Read Poetry in Sentences,** p. 311
- **L4 Enrichment,** p. 314

Assessment

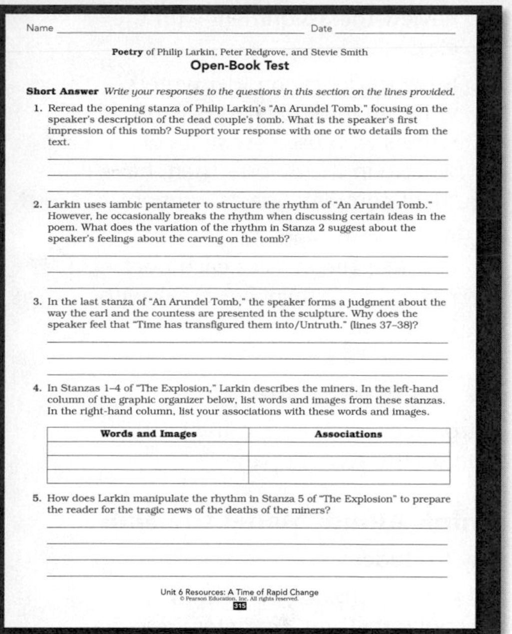
Name ____________ Date ____________

Poetry of Philip Larkin, Peter Redgrove, and Stevie Smith

Open-Book Test

Short Answer *Write your responses to the questions in this section on the lines provided.*

1. Reread the opening stanza of Philip Larkin's "An Arundel Tomb," focusing on the speaker's description of the dead couple's tomb. What is the speaker's first impression of this tomb? Support your response with one or two details from the text.

2. Larkin uses iambic pentameter to structure the rhythm of "An Arundel Tomb." However, he occasionally breaks the rhythm when discussing certain ideas in the poem. What does the variation of the rhythm in Stanza 2 suggest about the speaker's feelings about the carving on the tomb?

3. In the last stanza of "An Arundel Tomb," the speaker forms a judgment about the way the earl and the countess are presented in the sculpture. Why does the speaker feel that "Time has transfigured them into/Untruth." (lines 37–38)?

4. In Stanzas 1–4 of "The Explosion," Larkin describes the miners. In the left-hand column of the graphic organizer below, list words and images from these stanzas. In the right-hand column, list your associations with these words and images.

Words and Images	Associations

5. How does Larkin manipulate the rhythm in Stanza 5 of "The Explosion" to prepare the reader for the tragic news of the deaths of the miners?

Unit 6 Resources: A Time of Rapid Change
© Pearson Education, Inc. All rights reserved.
315

L3 L4 Open-Book Test, pp. 315–317

Also available for these selections:

- **EL L1 L2 Selection Test A,** pp. 318–320
- **EL L3 L4 Selection Test B,** pp. 321–323

PHLit Online!
www.PHLitOnline.com

- complete narrated selection text
- a thematically related video with writing prompt
- an interactive graphic organizer
- highlighting feature
- access to all student print resources, adapted to individual student needs
- Spanish and English summaries
- adapted selection translations in Spanish

Online Resources: All print materials are also available online.

Get Connected! (thematic video with writing prompt)

Also available:

Background Video
All videos are available in Spanish.

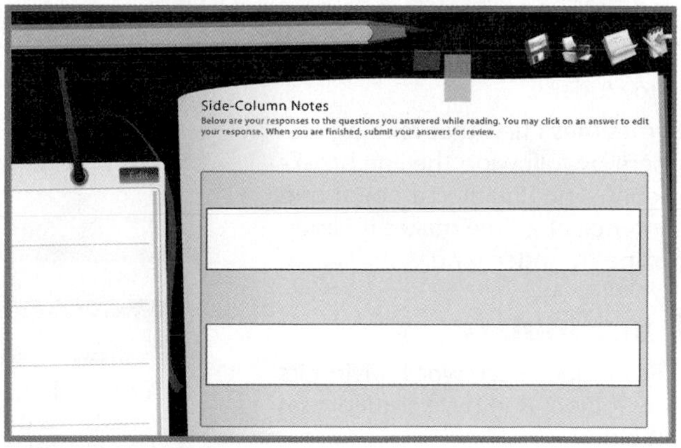

Writer's Journal (with graphics feature)

Also available:

Vocabulary Central (tools and activities for studying vocabulary)

PRETEACH

1 Connecting to the Essential Question

1. Review the assignment with the class.
2. Have students consider writers who use traditional forms and writers who use new styles of writing in their work. Then, have them complete the assignment.
3. As students read, have them consider the choices each poet has made to follow or break with tradition.

2 Literary Analysis

Introduce the skill using the instruction on the student page.

Think Aloud: Model the Skill

Say to students:

I know that poets can either use regular rhythms, or meter, in their work or can instead write in free verse, that is, poetry without a regular rhythm or rhyme. These choices lead to different effects, and I will watch for these effects in the upcoming poems.

3 Reading Strategy

1. Introduce the skill using the instruction on the student page.
2. Give students a copy of **Reading Strategy Graphic Organizer B,** page 265 in ***Graphic Organizer Transparencies,*** to fill out as they read.

Think Aloud: Model the Skill

Say to students:

Sometimes I find that reading a poem by following the line breaks is confusing. Reading a poem one sentence at a time makes it easier for me to understand.

4 Vocabulary

1. Pronounce each word, giving its definition, and have students say it aloud.
2. For more guidance, see the ***Classroom Strategies and Teaching Routines*** card for introducing vocabulary.

Before You Read

An Arundel Tomb • The Explosion • On the Patio • Not Waving but Drowning

1 Connecting to the Essential Question Twentieth-century poets were often torn between traditional and new styles of poetry. Which would you have chosen, and why? As you read, consider the choices each poet has made to follow or break with traditions in form and content. Noting these choices will help you think about the Essential Question: **What is the relationship of the writer to tradition?**

Common Core State Standards

Reading Literature
5. Analyze how an author's choices concerning how to structure specific parts of a text contribute to its overall structure and meaning as well as its aesthetic impact.

2 Literary Analysis

Before the twentieth century, most English-language poetry used a regular pattern of rhythm, or **meter.** The basic unit of meter is a **foot,** a group of one or more stressed, marked (´), and unstressed (˘) syllables.

- An **iamb** is one unstressed followed by one stressed syllable (˘ ´)
- A **trochee** is one stressed followed by one unstressed syllable (´ ˘)

Meter is described by its prevalent type of foot and number of feet per line. Three feet in a line is called *trimeter;* four feet, *tetrameter;* five feet, *pentameter;* six feet, *hexameter.* Thus, "An Arundel Tomb," with most lines containing four iambs, uses *iambic tetrameter*:

Thĕ éarl ănd cóuntĕss líe ĭn stóne, . . .

In the twentieth century, many poets abandoned the tradition of meter and instead used **free verse,** poetry without a regular pattern of rhythm or rhyme. Peter Redgrove uses free verse in "On the Patio."

Comparing Literary Works Compare and contrast the ways in which rhythm contributes to the **dramatic structure** of these poems—the use of contrasts to build toward a climax. Also, consider the ways in which the rhythm reinforces meaning and gives aesthetic pleasure.

3 Reading Strategy

Preparing to Read Complex Texts The best way to understand a poem is to **read it in sentences.** Focus on the units of thought, not on the rhythm or line breaks. As a reminder, use signs like these to mark the ends of lines in a copy of the poem.

Sign	Means
(arrow sign)	Continue without pause
(curved arrow sign)	Pause for comma, dash, or semicolon and continue
(stop sign)	Full stop for period

4 Vocabulary

effigy (ef′ i jē) *n.* portrait or statue of a person (p. 1403)

supine (so͞o′ pīn′) *adj.* lying on the back (p. 1403)

fidelity (fə del′ ə tē) *n.* faithfulness (p. 1403)

larking (lärk′ iŋ) *n.* free-spirited, whimsical fun (p. 1408)

PHLit Online! www.PHLitOnline.com

Vocabulary Development

Vocabulary Knowledge Rating

Create a **Vocabulary Knowledge Rating Chart** (***Professional Development Guidebook,*** p. 33) for the vocabulary words on the student page. Give each student a copy of the chart with the words on it. Read the words aloud, and have students mark their ratings in the Before Reading column. Urge students to attend to these words as they read and discuss the selections.

In order to gauge how much instruction you need to provide, tally how many students are confident in their knowledge of each word. As students read, point out the words and their context.

PHLit Online! **Vocabulary Central,** featuring tools and activities for studying vocabulary, is available online at **www.PHLitOnline.com.**

❺ # Philip Larkin

(1922–1985)

Author of **"An Arundel Tomb" • "The Explosion"**

Philip Larkin turned what could have been a discouragement into a reason for developing poetic skill and emotional restraint. As a child in Coventry, England, his home life was dominated by a father who held him accountable to rigid standards. Larkin escaped from these pressures by building a private childhood world rich in creativity and imagination.

Yeats Versus Hardy After graduating from St. John's College, Oxford, Larkin worked as a librarian for Hull University Library, a job he held for many years. His first book of poems, *The North Ship,* shows the strong influence of William Butler Yeats, but an encounter with Thomas Hardy's *Collected Poems* had a profound impact on Larkin. Larkin said, "When I came to Hardy it was with the sense of relief that I didn't have to try to jack myself up to a concept of poetry that lay outside my own life—this is perhaps what I felt Yeats was trying to make me do."

Deprivation Versus Daffodils Reflecting on his life, Larkin metaphorically explained how he drew inspiration from his difficult experiences when he told an interviewer, "Deprivation is for me what daffodils were for Wordsworth."

Although Larkin also developed a lifelong interest in jazz, which he came to love "even more than poetry," it was his clear-eyed, honest poetry, combining conversational language with well-crafted forms, that won him international fame. His poetry speaks of day-to-day realities, sometimes discouragingly, but is quietly haunted by realities beyond everyday life.

"Life has a practice of living you, if you don't live it."

Daily Bellringer

For each class during which you will teach these selections, have students complete one of the five activities for the appropriate week in the ***Daily Bellringer Activities*** booklet.

Multidraft Reading

To assist struggling readers and to enhance reading for all, assign the text in chunks, as warranted by length, and apply multidraft reading protocols. For each reading, have students set the purpose indicated:

- **First reading**—identifying key ideas and details and answering any Reading Checks.
- **Second reading**—analyzing craft and structure and responding to the side-column prompts.
- **Third reading**—integrating knowledge and ideas, connecting to other texts and the world, and answering the end-of-selection questions.

For more guidance, refer to the ***Classroom Strategies and Teaching Routines*** card on Multidraft Reading.

❺ Background

More About the Author

When Philip Larkin was offered the position of England's poet laureate in 1984, he turned it down, saying he had not published anything since 1974. The post went to Ted Hughes. Larkin's critical influence on British poetry helped to gain notice and eventual acceptance of Stevie Smith's poetry.

PHLit Online! www.PHLitOnline.com

Teaching From Technology

Preparing to Read

Go to **www.PHLitOnline.com** and display the ***Get Connected!*** slide show for this selection grouping. Have the class brainstorm responses to the slide show writing prompt, entering ideas in the interactive journal. Then, have students complete their written responses as homework.

To build background, display the More About the Authors feature.

Using the Interactive Text

Go to **www.PHLitOnline.com** and display the **Enriched Online Student Edition.** As the class reads the selection or listens to the narration, record answers to side-column prompts using the graphic organizers accessible on the interactive page. Alternatively, have students use the online edition individually, answering the prompts as they read.

TEACH

❶ About the Selections

In "An Arundel Tomb," Larkin points out an amusing misconception on the part of the tomb's visitors: Whereas those who view the effigy are comforted by the thought of love enduring through the centuries, the actual couple buried in the tomb had no intention of conveying such a message or serving as such an ideal.

In "The Explosion," Larkin vividly depicts the fatal suddenness of a coal mine's explosion and how it affects the town's women—the survivors.

❷ Activating Prior Knowledge

Invite volunteers to use body language to convey emotions, and encourage the rest of the class to guess the emotions. Discuss why body language is such a powerful tool in communication. Ask students to make a list of situations in which it is important to read body language. Tell students to watch for examples of "telling" body language in the following poems.

Concept Connector →

Tell students they will return to their responses after reading the selection.

❸ Literary Analysis

Free Verse and Meter

1. Have students read the first stanza aloud.
2. **Ask** students the Literary Analysis question: How do the meters of lines 1 and 2 differ? **Answer:** The first line is trochaic tetrameter, and the second line is iambic tetrameter.

An Arundel Tomb

Philip Larkin

❶ ❷

BACKGROUND THE PHOTOGRAPH ABOVE SHOWS THE INSPIRATION FOR "AN ARUNDEL TOMB": A TABLE TOMB IN CHICHESTER CATHEDRAL, SUSSEX, THAT DATES TO THE FOURTEENTH CENTURY. BURIED IN THE TOMB ARE RICHARD FITZALAN, EARL OF ARUNDEL, AND HIS SECOND WIFE ELEANOR, A MEMBER OF THE PROMINENT HOUSE OF LANCASTER. SIMPLE STONE EFFIGIES OF THE COUPLE LAY SIDE BY SIDE ON TOP OF THE TOMB, THE DETAILS WORN DOWN AND BLURRY, WITH RICHARD REACHING OVER TO HOLD HIS WIFE'S HAND.

Literary Analysis
Free Verse and Meter
How do the meters of lines 1 and 2 differ?

❸ Side by side, their faces blurred,
The earl and countess[1] lie in stone,
Their proper habits[2] vaguely shown
As jointed armor, stiffened pleat,
And that faint hint of the absurd—
The little dogs under their feet.

1. **countess** *n.* The wife of an earl is called a countess.
2. **habits** *n.* clothes worn for a particular activity or occasion.

Text Complexity Rubric

	An Arundel Tomb	The Explosion	On the Patio	Not Waving but Drowning
Qualitative Measures				
Context/Knowledge Demands	Modern lyric 1 2 (3) 4 5	Modern elegy 1 (2) 3 4 5	Free verse 1 (2) 3 4 5	Modern dramatic poem 1 (2) 3 4 5
Structure/Language Conventionality and Clarity	Unusual syntax 1 2 (3) 4 5	Unusual syntax 1 2 (3) 4 5	Unusual syntax; coined compounds 1 2 (3) 4 5	Simple diction 1 (2) 3 4 5
Levels of Meaning/ Purpose/Concepts	Challenging (love; irony) 1 2 3 (4) 5	Moderate (mining disaster) 1 2 (3) 4 5	Moderate (nature as benefactor) 1 2 (3) 4 5	Accessible (drowning; irony) 1 2 (3) 4 5
Quantitative Measures				
Lexile/Text Length	NP / 242 words	NP / 156 words	NP / 124 words	NP / 78 words
Overall Complexity	More complex	More accessible	More accessible	More accessible

Such plainness of the pre-baroque[3]
Hardly involves the eye, until
It meets his left-hand gauntlet,[4] still
Clasped empty in the other; and
One sees, with a sharp tender shock,
His hand withdrawn, holding her hand.

They would not think to lie so long.
Such faithfulness in **effigy**
Was just a detail friends would see:
A sculptor's sweet commissioned grace
Thrown off in helping to prolong
The Latin names around the base.

They would not guess how early in
Their **supine** stationary voyage
The air would change to soundless damage,
Turn the old tenantry[5] away;
How soon succeeding eyes begin
To look, not read. Rigidly they

❺
Persisted, linked, through lengths and breadths
Of time. Snow fell, undated. Light
Each summer thronged the glass. A bright
Litter of birdcalls strewed the same
Bone-riddled ground. And up the paths
The endless altered people came,

Washing at their identity.
Now, helpless in the hollow of
An unarmorial age, a trough
Of smoke in slow suspended skeins[6]
Above their scrap of history,
Only an attitude remains:

Time has transfigured them into
Untruth. The stone **fidelity**
They hardly meant has come to be
Their final blazon[7], and to prove
Our almost-instinct almost true:
What will survive of us is love.

---

3. **pre-baroque** (prē´ bə rōk´) *adj.* predating the Baroque Period (c. 1600–1750), when tombstone carvings along with other art and architecture grew far more ornate.
4. **gauntlet** (gônt´ or gänt´lĭt) *n.* armored glove.
5. **tenantry** *n.* peasants farming the nobles' land.
6. **skeins** (skānz) *n.* loosely coiled bunches of thread or yarn.
7. **blazon** (blā´ zən) *n.* coat of arms, emblem of a noble family.

❹ **◂ Critical Viewing**
Do engraved images such as the one on this tombstone always become an "untruth" in relation to life—as Larkin's poem seems to claim? **[Relate]**

Vocabulary
effigy (ef´ i jē) *n.* portrait, statue, or other likeness of a person

supine (so͞o´ pīn´) *adj.* lying on the back

Reading Strategy
Reading Poetry in Sentences Identify the full sentence in which line 25 appears.

Vocabulary
fidelity (fə del´ ə tē) *n.* faithfulness

❹ Critical Viewing

Answer: Students may say that an engraved image always becomes an "untruth" because later viewers can never see the original image as it was seen by people of the time. Other students may say that the passage of time offers new opportunities to see more truly.

❺ Reading Strategy

Reading Poetry in Sentences

1. Have students read the fourth stanza of the poem and determine how many sentences it contains.
   Answer: It contains one.
2. Now have students read the fifth stanza and identify the number of sentences it contains. **Ask** them if all the sentences both begin and end in the fifth stanza.
   Answer: There are three complete sentences, plus two partial sentences, one of which begins in the previous stanza, and one that ends in the next stanza.
3. **Ask** the Reading Strategy question: Identify the full sentence in which line 25 appears.
   Answer: "Rigidly they/Persisted, linked, through lengths and breadths/Of time."

PHLit Online!
This selection is available in interactive format in the **Enriched Online Student Edition** at **www.PHLitOnline.com,** which includes a thematically related video with writing prompt and an interactive graphic organizer.

Ⓒ Text Complexity: Reader and Task Suggestions

	An Arundel Tomb	The Explosion; On the Patio	Not Waving but Drowning
Preparing to Read the Texts • Point out that a poem can have dramatic structure even when its subject is not dramatic. • Discuss the idea that human beings often misunderstand the actions and motives of others. • Guide students to use Multidraft Reading strategies (TE p. 1401).	**Leveled Tasks** ***Levels of Meaning*** If students will have difficulty with the poem's meaning, have them focus on the carved effigies. As they reread, have students focus on why people misinterpret these figures. ***Synthesizing*** If students will not have difficulty with the poem's meaning, have them synthesize its details and explain how they lead to the final line.	**Leveled Tasks** ***Levels of Meaning*** If students will have difficulty with the levels of meaning, have them focus first on the events of each poem. Then, as they reread, have them consider the new understanding at each poem's end. ***Evaluating*** If students will not have difficulty with the meaning, have them judge which poem more effectively uses emotions and ideas.	**Leveled Tasks** ***Levels of Meaning*** If students have difficulty with the levels of meaning, have them first identify the different speakers in the first two stanzas and sum up what happened. Then, have them consider what the last stanza might mean. ***Analyzing*** If students will not have difficulty with the levels of meaning, have them analyze the poem's central metaphor.

❻ Literary Analysis

Meter and Free Verse

1. **Ask** students to read the first stanza for meaning. Ask if the description of the slagheap sleeping in the sun makes the reader see the scene as peaceful.
   Answer: Both the title and the first stanza use the word *explosion,* which suggests that despite the sleeping slagheap, something violent will happen in the poem.
2. Now **ask** students to read the first stanza again, this time being aware of the rhythm and meter. **Ask** them the Literary Analysis question: What is the meter of the lines in the first stanza? Explain.
   Answer: The first stanza is in trochaic tetrameter: There are four metrical feet, and each foot (except the very last) consists of a stressed syllable followed by an unstressed syllable.

❼ Literary Analysis

Meter and Free Verse

1. **Ask** students why Larkin uses a regular meter throughout much of his poem.
   Possible response: The regular meter creates a sense of ceremony appropriate for a tragedy.
2. **Ask** students the Literary Analysis question on the next page: What is the prevalent foot in this poem? How many feet does it typically have in each line?
   Answer: It is primarily trochaic. It generally has four feet to a line.

THE EXPLOSION

PHILIP LARKIN

Literary Analysis
Meter and Free Verse
What is the meter of the lines in the first stanza? Explain.

❻
On the day of the explosion
Shadows pointed towards the pithead:[1]
In the sun the slagheap slept.[2]

Down the lane came men in pitboots
Coughing oath-edged talk and pipe-smoke,
Shouldering off the freshened silence.

One chased after rabbits; lost them;
Came back with a nest of lark's eggs;
Showed them; lodged them in the grasses.

1. **pithead** *n.* the entrance to a coal mine.
2. **slagheap** *n.* a large mound of waste material dug up from a coal mine.

Enrichment: Analyzing Forms and Genres

Poetic Verse
Meter and Free Verse
The iamb is a metrical foot consisting of one unstressed syllable followed by a stressed syllable. The iamb is the most frequently used foot in English poetry; it is thought to mimic the natural rhythm of the language.

A trochee is a metrical foot consisting of a stressed syllable followed by an unstressed syllable. The word comes from the Greek *trokhaios,* meaning "running."

Free verse is rhymed or unrhymed poetry without any of the regular rhythms called meter. Free verse has lines of different lengths and an invented rhythm that suits its meaning.
Activity: Analyze Poetic Verse Instruct students to pick one form of poetic verse and research it. Suggest they record their research on the **Enrichment: Analyzing Forms and Genres** worksheet, ***Professional Development Guidebook,*** page 227.

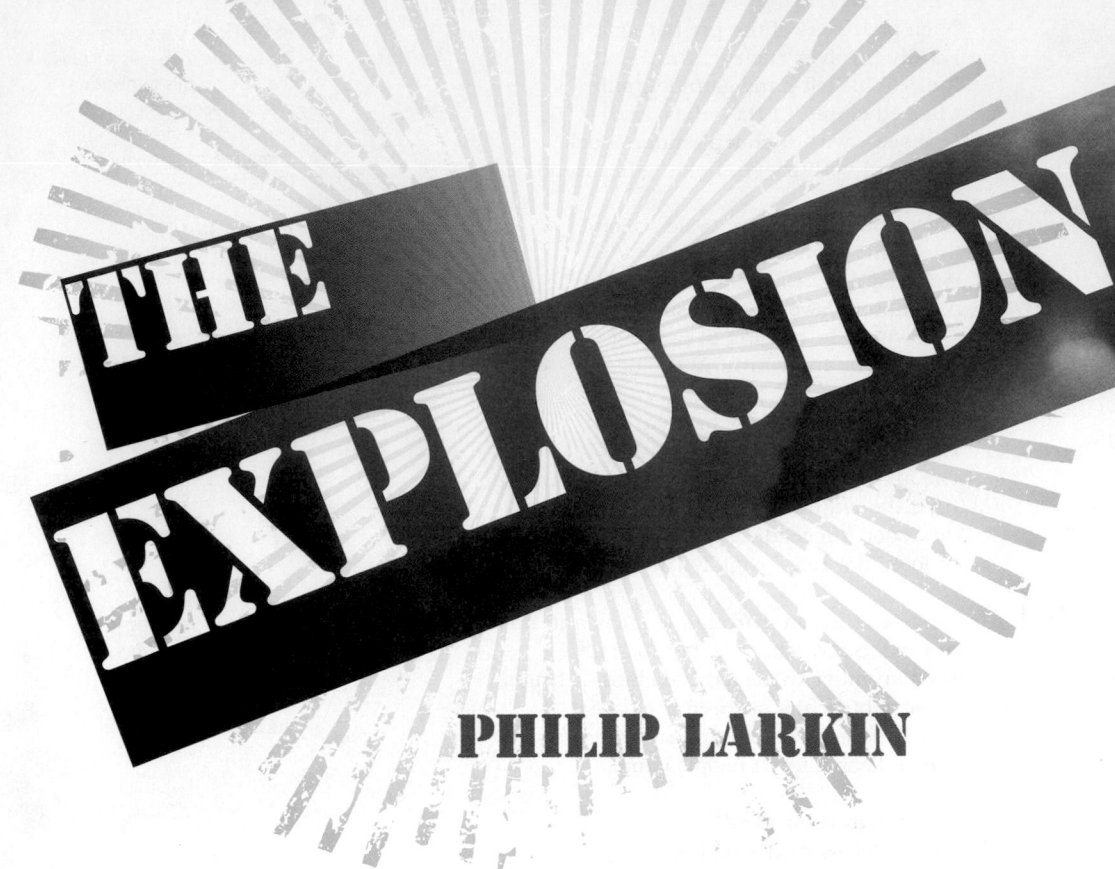

So they passed in beards and moleskins,[3]
Fathers, brothers, nicknames, laughter,
Through the tall gates standing open.

At noon, there came a tremor; cows
Stopped chewing for a second; sun,
Scarfed as in a heat-haze, dimmed.

The dead go on before us, they
Are sitting in God's house in comfort,
We shall see them face to face—

Plain as lettering in the chapels
It was said, and for a second
Wives saw men of the explosion

Larger than in life they managed—
Gold as on a coin, or walking
Somehow from the sun towards them,

One showing the eggs unbroken.

7 Literary Analysis
Meter and Free Verse
What is the prevalent foot in this poem? How many feet does it typically have in each line?

3. **moleskins** garments, especially trousers, of heavy cotton.

Critical Reading

Cite textual evidence to support your responses.

1. **Key Ideas and Details (a)** Describe the physical position of the sculptured couple in "An Arundel Tomb." **(b) Interpret:** What is the "supine stationary voyage" they have made?
2. **Key Ideas and Details (a)** What detail of the Arundel tomb catches the speaker's eye? **(b) Interpret:** What does he mean when he says that time has transfigured the couple into untruth?
3. **Key Ideas and Details (a)** Where are the men in "The Explosion" going? **(b) Infer:** What happens to them?
4. **Key Ideas and Details (a)** What events in "The Explosion" are said to last for a second? **(b) Connect:** What does the contrast between the things that take a second in the fifth and seventh stanzas suggest about life? **(c) Interpret:** What might the lark's egg symbolize about life?
5. **Integration of Knowledge and Ideas** What do both poems say about the traditional poetic subject of love? In your response, use at least two of these Essential Question words: *endure, transform, conventional. [Connecting to the Essential Question: What is the relationship of the writer to tradition?]*

ASSESS

Answers

Before students respond, you may wish to have them write a brief objective summary of the selection. As they answer the questions below, remind them to support their answers with evidence from the text.

1. (a) The couple lie side by side, his left hand free of his glove and holding one of hers. (b) Students may say that in death people may lie supine, without moving, yet be on a "voyage" to another physical state.
2. (a) The detail of the couple holding hands catches the eye. (b) The gesture was put in by the sculptor for artistic reasons; the couple might have considered it a detail for their friends to see. It is not true, however, that their loyalty to each other survives, since they are dead, nor did anyone intend the gesture as a message.
3. (a) They are going down into a mine. (b) They are killed in an explosion.
4. (a) Cows stopped chewing, and the wives saw their husbands walking toward them. (b) It suggests that both profound and meaningless things can happen in the blink of an eye. (c) The eggs symbolize the fragility of life, and also the randomness of what is saved versus what is destroyed.
5. "An Arundel Tomb" suggests that people in the present want to remember people in the past in comfortable and *conventional* terms. The love expressed by the gesture of the statues holding hands is an example of this convention, and therefore somewhat false. "The Explosion" suggests that the survivors will remember their husbands, fathers, and brothers with love that is able to *endure* death.

Differentiated Instruction for Universal Access

Strategy for Special-Needs Students
Have students outline the events in "The Explosion" and tell which stanzas describe each one. (Stanza one is the exposition, setting time and place. Stanzas two through eight are the rising action: The men walk to the mine as they do every day, laughing and talking. Time passes and the explosion occurs. More time passes and the villagers are sitting in the chapel during the funeral. The wives see the men as if they were still alive. The climax occurs when the wives see the unbroken eggs.)

Strategy for Less Proficient Readers
Have students note the change in meter between the fourth and fifth stanzas in "The Explosion." Ask them to identify the shift in meter and to speculate on why the poet made this choice. (The first four stanzas are written in trochaic tetrameter. The fifth stanza is written in iambic tetrameter.) The event that occurs in stanza five kills the miners and interrupts the lives of the survivors, and the poet emphasizes this by interrupting the regular rhythm.

❽ Background

More About the Authors

Peter Redgrove's vision was informed by his background in biology, chemistry, and other scientific fields. He blended his knowledge of the natural sciences with his own exhilarating vision of the world of nature.

Stevie Smith's radio broadcasts of her poems were popular in the 1960s, and her public readings were well attended. Public interest in her was extended by Hugh Whitemore's play *Stevie* (1978), which he later adapted as a film.

❾ About the Selections

Both poems use images of water, but in strikingly different ways. "On the Patio" uses the image of the poet draining a glass and allowing the thunderstorm to refill it as a symbol of a person willing to be open to nature and its bounty, someone who wants to get the most out of life, "draining" life's glass and coming back for a "refill." "Not Waving but Drowning" uses the water that drowned a man as a symbol of the coldness and isolation that plagued him his whole life—and finally led to his death.

Peter Redgrove ❽

(1932–2003)

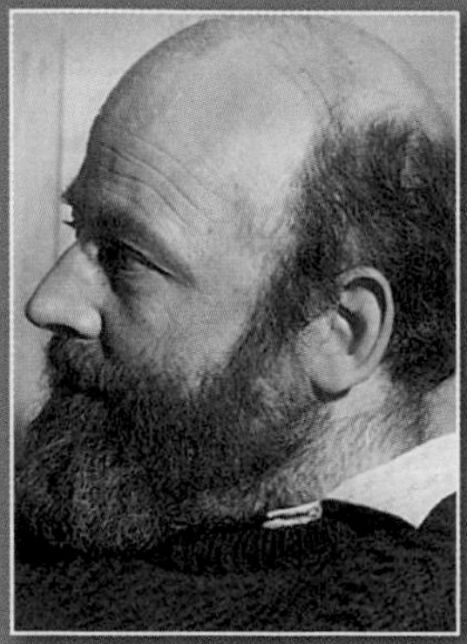

Author of "On the Patio"

Like William Blake, a visionary poet with whom he is sometimes compared, Peter Redgrove does not fit into the usual categories. He lived at a distance from the literary hub of London—in Falmouth, Cornwall, the southwestern tip of England. Redgrove lived at an imaginative distance from London as well, rejecting the drab, everyday qualities so prevalent in many post-World War II British poems.

Transformation Through Imagination In his poetry, novels, television scripts, and nonfiction works, Redgrove celebrates our power to reimagine and transform our lives. His rich visual imagery reflects a heightened awareness that borders on the mystical as he speaks for stones or sees the world through the eyes of a wandering dog.

Redgrove's poems have been widely acclaimed in England, and he was the recipient of the 1997 Queen's Medal for Poetry.

STEVIE SMITH ❽

(1902–1971)

Author of "Not Waving but Drowning"

Stevie Smith's poems cannot be easily classified. They are modeled, however, on familiar forms—hymns, popular songs, and nineteenth-century British and American poems. Using simple forms and language, she often evokes despair, perhaps relying on the poetic statement of bleak feelings to cleanse or banish them from life.

Auntie Lion The author of this unusual body of work was born Florence Margaret Smith in Hull, Yorkshire. Due to her mother's ill health, she was raised mostly by her beloved Auntie Lion, with whom she continued to live in a northern London suburb even as an adult. While working for a magazine, Smith wrote three novels and nine collections of poems.

Poems and Doodles Smith's poems can be humorous, macabre, surprising, and childlike, and she often illustrates them with sketches or doodles that echo her playful rhythms.

Some critics suggest that her work cunningly satirizes conventional forms of poetic expression, such as the hymn and the nursery rhyme, and adds dark new depths and keen irony to these traditional forms.

Vocabulary Development

Vocabulary Knowledge Rating

When students have completed reading and discussing the selection, have them take out their **Vocabulary Knowledge Rating Charts** for the story. Read the words aloud and have students rate their knowledge of the words again in the After Reading column. Clarify any words that are still problematic. Have students write their own definitions and example or sentence in the appropriate column. Then, have students complete the Vocabulary Practice at the end of the selection. Encourage students to use the words in further discussion and written work about the selection. Remind them that they will be accountable for these words on the **Selection Test,** ***Unit 6 Resources,*** pages 318–320 or 321–323.

PHLit Online!

For more about the authors, go online at **www.PHLitOnline.com.**

9 # On the Patio

Peter Redgrove

A wineglass overflowing with thunderwater
Stands out on the drumming steel table

Among the outcries of the downpour
Feathering chairs and rethundering on the awnings.

How the pellets of water shooting miles
Fly into the glass of swirl, and slop

Over the table's scales of rust
Shining like chained sores,

Because the rain eats everything except the glass
Of spinning water that is clear down here

But purple with rumbling depths above, and this cloud
Is transferring its might into a glass

In which thunder and lightning come to rest,
The cloud crushed into a glass.

Suddenly I dart out into the patio,
Snatch the bright glass up and drain it,

Bang it back down on the thundery steel table for a refill.

10 **Reading Strategy**
Reading Poetry in Sentences As you read the poem, at the end of which lines should you come to a complete stop?

Critical Reading

1. **Key Ideas and Details (a)** Describe the scene depicted in "On the Patio." **(b) Connect:** How do the images in the poem link what occurs above with what occurs below?
2. **Key Ideas and Details (a)** What does the speaker do at the end of the poem? **(b) Interpret:** What attitude toward life does the speaker's final gesture symbolize, or represent?

Cite textual evidence to support your responses.

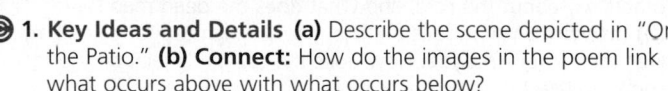

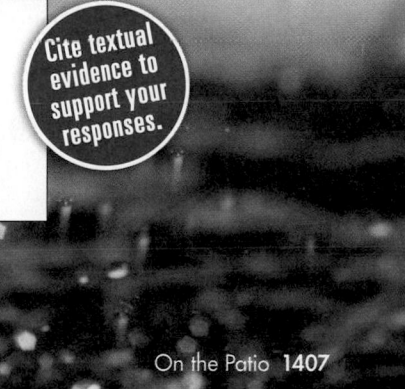

10 Reading Strategy

Reading Poetry in Sentences

1. Have students take turns reading the poem aloud.
2. **Ask** students why they might have to read lines 5–14 more than once to grasp the meaning.
   Answer: This part of the poem has few pauses, and the ideas continue for many lines.
3. **Ask** students the Reading Strategy question: As you read the poem, at the end of which lines would you come to a stop?
   Answer: Students should say they would stop at the end of lines 4, 14, and 17, because these lines are punctuated by periods.

ASSESS

Answers

Before students respond, you may wish to have them write a brief objective summary of the selection. As they answer the questions below, remind them to support their answers with evidence from the text.

1. (a) A wineglass has been left out on a table on a patio during a thunderstorm and is filling up with water. (b) The images concern both the violent descent of the rain from the clouds and its local effects on the patio.
2. (a) He drinks the glass of rainwater and puts it back to fill up again. (b) The gesture symbolizes the speaker's getting the most that life has to offer.

Concept Connector

Reading Strategy Graphic Organizer
Ask students to review their use of the signs to indicate how to read the poems in sentences. Then, have students share their marked copies and compare their placement of the symbols.

Activating Prior Knowledge
Have students return to their responses to the Activating Prior Knowledge activity. Ask them to explain whether their thoughts have changed and, if so, how.

Writing About the Essential Question
Have students compare their responses to the prompt, completed before reading the poems, with their thoughts afterward. Have them work individually or in groups, writing or discussing their thoughts, to formulate new responses. Then, lead a class discussion, probing for what students have learned that confirms or invalidates their initial thoughts. Encourage students to cite specific textual details to support their responses.

ASSESS

Answers

Before students respond, you may wish to have them write a brief objective summary of the selection. As they answer the questions below, remind them to support their answers with evidence from the text.

1. (a) He moans that he was farther out than people thought. (b) They think he is waving, when in fact he is drowning.
2. (a) They say the water must have been too cold for him. He says it was always too cold. (b) The dead man says that all his life he was unable to cope with the circumstances of his life. (c) People misinterpret his actions, and his cries for help go unnoticed.
3. Students may say that the subject matter is similar, in that topics such as nature and death are touched on. However, these subjects are seen from a different *perspective* than in earlier centuries. For example, "Not Waving but Drowning" takes an *ironic* perspective on the subject of death.

NOT WAVING BUT DROWNING

STEVIE SMITH

Nobody heard him, the dead man,
But still he lay moaning:
I was much further out than you thought
And not waving but drowning.

Poor chap, he always loved larking
And now he's dead
It must have been too cold for him his heart gave way,
They said.

Oh, no no no, it was too cold always
(Still the dead one lay moaning)
I was much too far out all my life
And not waving but drowning.

Vocabulary
larking (lärk´ iŋ) *n.* free-spirited, whimsical fun

Critical Reading

Cite textual evidence to support your responses.

1. **Key Ideas and Details (a)** What does the dead man moan in the first stanza? **(b) Infer:** How do others misinterpret his gestures?
2. **Key Ideas and Details (a) Compare and Contrast:** What do others say about the cold, and what does the dead man say? **(b) Interpret:** What does the line "I was much too far out all my life" mean? **(c) Analyze:** How does the speaker's relationship to society relate to drowning?
3. **Integration of Knowledge and Ideas** How is the subject matter of these poems like and unlike that of traditional poetry from earlier centuries? In answering, use at least two of these Essential Question words: *ironic, atypical,* and *perspective.* ***[Connecting to the Essential Question: What is the relationship of the writer to tradition?]***

Assessment Practice

Style (For more practice, see *All-in-One Workbook.*)

Many tests require students to recognize stylistic devices and effective language. Use this sample item:

One chased after rabbits; lost them;
Came back with a nest of lark's eggs;
Showed them; lodged them in the grasses.

Which of the following appears in these lines?

A parallel structure
B subject-verb disagreement
C personification
D dangling modifier

Review with students the definitions of each of the choices. Knowing that parallel structure is the repetition of a basic grammatical pattern should lead students to the correct answer, ***A***.

After You Read

An Arundel Tomb • The Explosion • On the Patio • Not Waving but Drowning

Literary Analysis

1. **Craft and Structure (a)** Identify the traditional **meter** in Larkin's poems. **(b)** Explain how breaks in the metrical pattern stress key ideas and build to a climax in the poem's **dramatic structure.** Use a chart like this to help you.

Type of Meter	Breaks in Meter	Ideas Stressed

2. **Craft and Structure** Explain how the use of **free verse** suits the content of "On the Patio."
3. **Craft and Structure** Traditional ballads often use four-line stanzas in which unrhymed lines of iambic tetrameter alternate with rhymed lines of iambic trimeter. How does Smith's poem modify this traditional ballad stanza?
4. **Comparing Literary Works** Compare and contrast the ways in which these poems use rhythm to enhance their dramatic structure.

Common Core State Standards

Writing

3.e. Provide a conclusion that follows from and reflects on what is experienced, observed, or resolved over the course of the narrative.

Reading Strategy

5. In **reading in sentences** lines 19–31 of "An Arundel Tomb," where should you make a full stop?
6. As you read lines 19–25 of "The Explosion," where should you pause or stop, and for how long?

PERFORMANCE TASKS

Integrated Language Skills

Vocabulary Acquisition and Use

For each word, choose the letter of its antonym, or opposite, and explain your choice.

1. effigy:	**(a)** scarecrow	**(b)** original	**(c)** likeness
2. supine:	**(a)** neat	**(b)** upright	**(c)** sloppy
3. fidelity:	**(a)** disloyalty	**(b)** cowardice	**(c)** faithfulness
4. larking:	**(a)** mischief	**(b)** laziness	**(c)** toil

Writing

Narrative Text Write a **reflective essay** in which you explain how an ordinary incident in your experience has taken on meaning as a general lesson about life. Begin by describing the incident. Then move from the specific to the general, providing a conclusion that explores the broader meaning of the incident.

Assessment Resources

Unit 6 Resources

L1 L2 EL **Selection Test A,** pp. 318–320. Administer Test A to less advanced readers.

L3 L4 EL **Selection Test B,** pp. 321–323. Administer Test B to on-level students and more advanced students.

L3 L4 **Open-Book Test,** pp. 315–317. As an alternative, give the Open-Book test.

All **Customizable Test Bank**

All **Self-tests**

Students may prepare for the **Selection Test** by taking the **Self-test** online.

PHLit Online! All assessment resources are available at **www.PHLitOnline.com**.

Answers

1. (a) Larkin uses trochaic tetrameter in "The Explosion" and iambic tetrameter in "An Arundel Tomb." (b) Students should note breaks in meter, such as the switch to iambs at the end of "The Explosion."
2. The free-verse lines of "On the Patio" convey the continuous drumming of the rain.
3. Smith alternates lines with more beats with lines with fewer. For example, line 8 has one beat and line 7 has six beats.
4. The use of free verse in "On the Patio" emphasizes the poem's description of the chaos of the downpour. The use of the modified ballad form in "Not Waving but Drowning" emphasizes the dead man's restraint and his inability to communicate effectively with people.
5. You should make a full stop after the periods in lines 24, 26, 27, 29, and 31.
6. You should pause briefly after the comma in line 20, pause longer after the dash in line 22, pause briefly after the commas in lines 23 and 24, and stop after the period at the end of line 25.

Vocabulary Acquisition and Use

1. b
2. b
3. a
4. c

Writing

1. You may use this Writing Lesson as timed-writing practice, or you may allow students to develop the essay as a writing assignment over several days.
2. To give students guidance for writing this narrative text, give them the Support for Writing Lesson page from *Unit 6 Resources,* page 313.
3. Tell students that ordinary events can inspire prose writing as well as poetry.
4. Encourage students to think of an ordinary event, sight, or feeling about which they feel strongly.
5. Use the rubrics for **Reflective Essay** in *Professional Development Guidebook,* pages 293–294, to evaluate students' work.

Prayer • In the Kitchen
Lesson Pacing Guide

DAY 1 Preteach

- Administer the Reading and Vocabulary Warm-ups (*Unit 6 Resources,* pp. 324–327) as necessary.
- Introduce the Literary Analysis concept: Form and Elegy.
- Introduce the Reading Strategy: Recognize Parallel Structure.
- Build background with the author and Background features.
- Develop thematic thinking with Connecting to the Essential Question.
- Teach the selection vocabulary.

DAY 2 Preteach/Teach/Extend

- Distribute copies of the appropriate graphic organizer for the Reading Strategy (*Graphic Organizer Transparencies,* pp. 268–269).
- Distribute copies of the appropriate graphic organizer for Literary Analysis (*Graphic Organizer Transparencies,* pp. 270–271).
- Prepare students to read with the Activating Prior Knowledge activities (TE).
- Informally monitor comprehension while students read.
- Use the Reading Check questions to confirm comprehension.
- Develop students' understanding of form and elegy using the Literary Analysis prompts.
- Develop students' ability to recognize parallel structure using the Reading Strategy prompts.
- Reinforce vocabulary with the Vocabulary notes.
- Assess students' comprehension and mastery of the skills by having them answer the Critical Reading, Literary Analysis, and Reading Strategy questions.

DAY 3 Assess

- Have students complete the Vocabulary Lesson.
- Have students complete the Writing activity, writing a radio introduction. (You may assign as homework.)
- Administer Selection Test A or B (*Unit 6 Resources,* pp. 336–338 or 339–341).

Common Core State Standards

Reading Literature 5. Analyze how an author's choices concerning how to structure specific parts of a text contribute to its overall structure and meaning as well as its aesthetic impact.

Writing 2.a. Introduce a topic; organize complex ideas, concepts, and information so that each new element builds on that which precedes it to create a unified whole.

Additional Standards Practice
***Common Core Companion,* pp. 54–55; 198–199**

Daily Block Scheduling
Each day in this Lesson Pacing Guide represents a 40–50 minute period. Teachers using block scheduling may combine days to revise pacing. In addition, teachers may differentiate and support core instruction by integrating components for extended and intensive support as students require. See the Guide to Selected Leveled Resources (facing page).

Guide to Selected Leveled Resources

RTI Tier 1 (students performing on level)			Prayer • In the Kitchen
Warm Up	Whole class instruction; Group work	**Practice, model,** and **monitor** fluency, working **with the whole class** or **in groups.**	**Vocabulary and Reading Warm-ups B,** ***Unit 6 Resources,*** pp. 342–343, 345
Comprehension/Skills	Whole class instruction; Group work; Independent work	**Support** and **monitor** comprehension and skills development, having students complete the activities, graphic organizers, and interactive prompts **independently** or **as a class.**	• ***Reader's Notebook,*** adapted instruction and full selection EL ***Reader's Notebook: English Learner's Version,*** adapted instruction and adapted selection • **Reading Strategy Graphic Organizer B,** ***Graphic Organizer Transparencies,*** p. 283 • **Literary Analysis Graphic Organizer B,** ***Graphic Organizer Transparencies,*** p. 285
Monitor Progress	A	**Monitor** student progress with the differentiated curriculum-based assessment in the *Unit Resources.*	• **Selection Test B,** ***Unit 6 Resources,*** pp. 357–359 • **Open-Book Test,** ***Unit 6 Resources,*** pp. 351–353

RTI Tier 2 (students requiring intervention)			Prayer • In the Kitchen
Warm Up	Group work; One-on-one teaching	**Practice, model,** and **monitor** fluency **in groups** or **with individuals.**	• **Vocabulary and Reading Warm-ups A,** ***Unit 6 Resources,*** pp. 342–344 • ***Hear It!*** **Audio CD (adapted text)**
Comprehension/Skills	Group work; One-on-one teaching	• **Support** and **monitor** comprehension and skills development, working **in small groups** or **with individuals.** • As students complete the selection in the appropriate version of the *Reader's Notebook,* **monitor** comprehension frequently with group questions and individual instruction. • **Model** strategies while guiding students in completing the activities and prompts in the *Reader's Notebook,* as well as the graphic organizers. • **Practice** skills and **monitor** mastery with the *Reading Kit* worksheets.	• ***Reader's Notebook: Adapted Version,*** adapted instruction and adapted selection EL ***Reader's Notebook: English Learner's Version,*** adapted instruction and adapted selection • **Reading Strategy Graphic Organizer A,** ***Graphic Organizer Transparencies,*** p. 282 • **Literary Analysis Graphic Organizer A,** ***Graphic Organizer Transparencies,*** p. 284 • ***Reading Kit,*** Practice worksheets
Monitor Progress	A	**Monitor** student progress with the differentiated curriculum-based assessment in the *Unit Resources* and in the *Reading Kit.*	• **Selection Test A,** ***Unit 6 Resources,*** pp. 354–356 • ***Reading Kit,*** Assess worksheets

TIER 3 Tier 3 intervention may require consultation with the student's special-education or dyslexia specialist. For additional support, see the Tier 2 activities and resources listed above.

One-on-one teaching **Group work** **Whole class instruction** **Independent work** **A Assessment**

For a complete guide to selection support, including support for Advanced students, see the Overview of Resources in the frontmatter.

Prayer • In the Kitchen

RESOURCES FOR:

- L1 Special-Needs Students
- L2 Below-Level Students (Tier 2)
- L3 On-Level Students (Tier 1)
- L4 Advanced Students (Tier 1)
- EL English Learners
- All All Students

Vocabulary/Fluency/Prior Knowledge

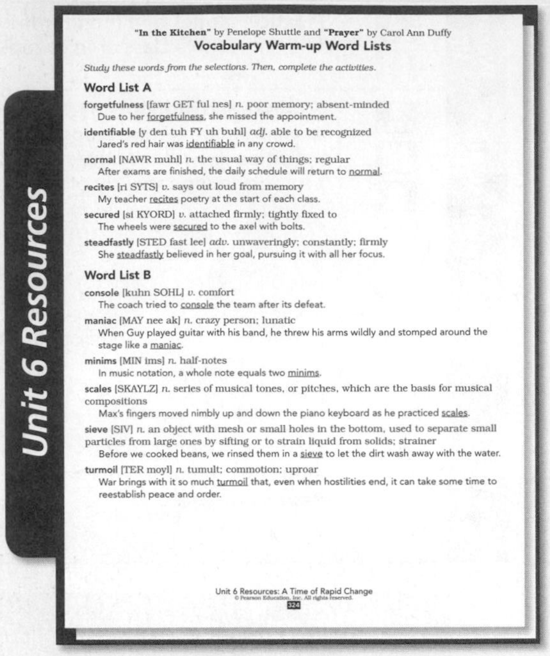

Unit 6 Resources

"In the Kitchen" by Penelope Shuttle and "Prayer" by Carol Ann Duffy
Vocabulary Warm-up Word Lists

Study these words from the selections. Then, complete the activities.

Word List A

forgetfulness [fawr GET ful nes] *n.* poor memory; absent-minded
Due to her forgetfulness, she missed the appointment.

identifiable [y den tuh FY uh buhl] *adj.* able to be recognized
Jared's red hair was identifiable in any crowd.

normal [NAWR muhl] *n.* the usual way of things; regular
After exams are finished, the daily schedule will return to normal.

recites [ri SYTS] *v.* says out loud from memory
My teacher recites poetry at the start of each class.

secured [si KYORD] *v.* attached firmly; tightly fixed to
The wheels were secured to the axel with bolts.

steadfastly [STED fast lee] *adv.* unwaveringly; constantly; firmly
She steadfastly believed in her goal, pursuing it with all her focus.

Word List B

console [kuhn SOHL] *v.* comfort
The coach tried to console the team after its defeat.

maniac [MAY nee ak] *n.* crazy person; lunatic
When Guy played guitar with his band, he threw his arms wildly and stomped around the stage like a maniac.

minims [MIN ims] *n.* half-notes
In music notation, a whole note equals two minims.

scales [SKAYLZ] *n.* series of musical tones, or pitches, which are the basis for musical compositions
Max's fingers moved nimbly up and down the piano keyboard as he practiced scales.

sieve [SIV] *n.* an object with mesh or small holes in the bottom, used to separate small particles from large ones by sifting or to strain liquid from solids; strainer
Before we cooked beans, we rinsed them in a sieve to let the dirt wash away with the water.

turmoil [TER moyl] *n.* tumult; commotion; uproar
War brings with it so much turmoil that, even when hostilities end, it can take some time to reestablish peace and order.

Unit 6 Resources: A Time of Rapid Change
324

EL L1 L2 **Vocabulary Warm-ups A and B,** p. 324–325

Also available for these selections:

EL L1 L2 **Reading Warm-ups A and B,** pp. 326–327

All **Vocabulary Builder,** pp. 330

Reader's Notebooks

Pre- and postreading pages for these selections appear in an interactive format in the *Reader's Notebooks*. Each *Notebook* is differentiated for a different group of learners. The selections in the Adapted and English Learner's versions are abridged.

L2 L3 ***Reader's Notebook***

L1 ***Reader's Notebook: Adapted Version***

EL ***Reader's Notebook: English Learner's Version***

EL ***Reader's Notebook: Spanish Version***

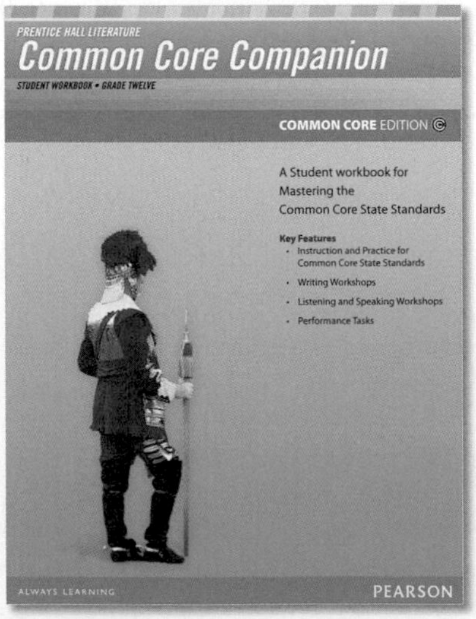

Common Core Companion

Additional instruction and practice for each Common Core State Standard

Graphic Organizer Transparencies

Selection Support

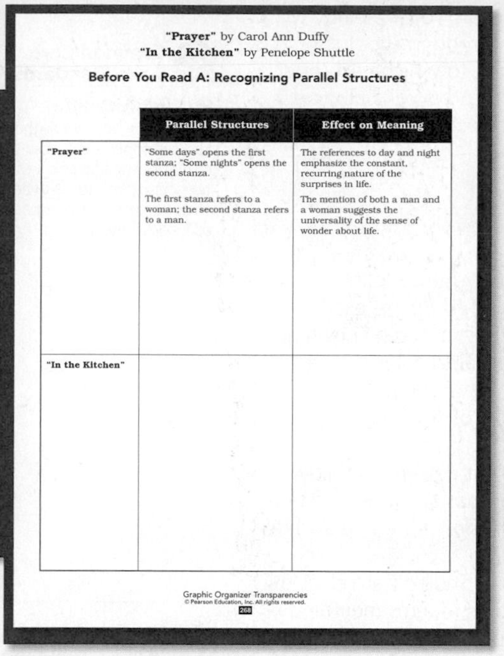

"Prayer" by Carol Ann Duffy
"In the Kitchen" by Penelope Shuttle

Before You Read A: Recognizing Parallel Structures

	Parallel Structures	Effect on Meaning
"Prayer"	"Some days" opens the first stanza; "Some nights" opens the second stanza. The first stanza refers to a woman; the second stanza refers to a man.	The references to day and night emphasize the constant, recurring nature of the surprises in life. The mention of both a man and a woman suggests the universality of the sense of wonder about life.
"In the Kitchen"		

Graphic Organizer Transparencies
© Pearson Education, Inc. All rights reserved.
268

EL L1 L2 **Reading: Graphic Organizer A,** p. 268

Also available for these selections:

- EL L3 **Reading: Graphic Organizer B,** p. 269
- EL L1 L2 **Literary Analysis: Graphic Organizer A** (partially filled in), p. 270
- EL L3 **Literary Analysis: Graphic Organizer B,** p. 271

Unit 6 Resources

Skills Development/Extension

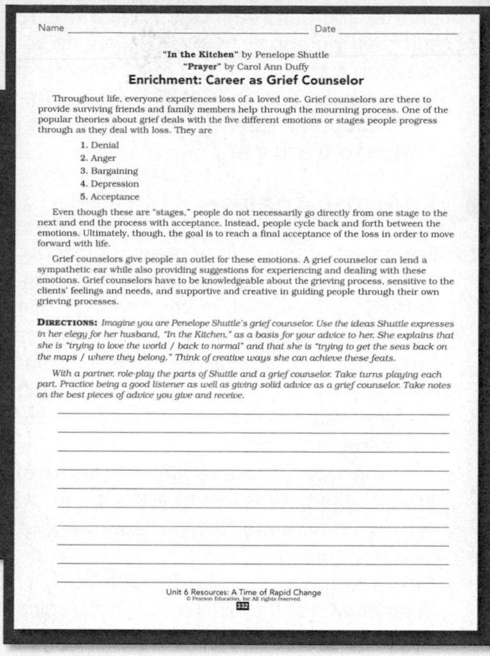

Name ______________________ Date ____________

"In the Kitchen" by Penelope Shuttle
"Prayer" by Carol Ann Duffy

Enrichment: Career as Grief Counselor

Throughout life, everyone experiences loss of a loved one. Grief counselors are there to provide surviving friends and family members help through the mourning process. One of the popular theories about grief deals with the five different emotions or stages people progress through as they deal with loss. They are

1. Denial
2. Anger
3. Bargaining
4. Depression
5. Acceptance

Even though these are "stages," people do not necessarily go directly from one stage to the next and end the process with acceptance. Instead, people cycle back and forth between the emotions. Ultimately, though, the goal is to reach a final acceptance of the loss in order to move forward with life.

Grief counselors give people an outlet for these emotions. A grief counselor can lend a sympathetic ear while also providing suggestions for experiencing and dealing with these emotions. Grief counselors have to be knowledgeable about the grieving process, sensitive to the clients' feelings and needs, and supportive and creative in guiding people through their own grieving processes.

Directions: *Imagine you are Penelope Shuttle's grief counselor. Use the ideas Shuttle expresses in her elegy for her husband, "In the Kitchen," as a basis for your advice to her. She explains that she is "trying to love the world / back to normal" and that she is "trying to get the seas back on the maps / where they belong." Think of creative ways she can achieve these feats.*

With a partner, role-play the parts of Shuttle and a grief counselor. Take turns playing each part. Practice being a good listener as well as giving solid advice as a grief counselor. Take notes on the best pieces of advice you give and receive.

Unit 6 Resources: A Time of Rapid Change
© Pearson Education, Inc All rights reserved.
332

L4 **Enrichment,** p. 332

Also available for these selections:

- All **Literary Analysis: Form and Elegy,** p. 328
- All **Reading: Recognize Parallel Structure,** p. 329
- EL L3 L4 **Support for Writing,** p. 331

Assessment

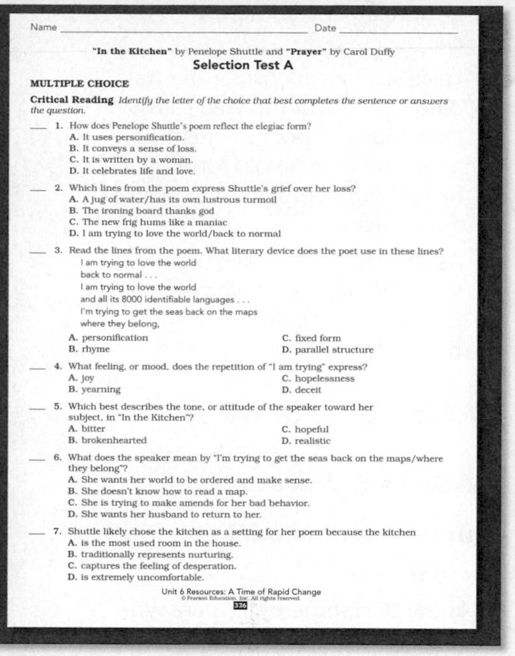

Name ______________________ Date ____________

"In the Kitchen" by Penelope Shuttle and **"Prayer"** by Carol Duffy

Selection Test A

MULTIPLE CHOICE

Critical Reading *Identify the letter of the choice that best completes the sentence or answers the question.*

____ 1. How does Penelope Shuttle's poem reflect the elegiac form?
A. It uses personification.
B. It conveys a sense of loss.
C. It is written by a woman.
D. It celebrates life and love.

____ 2. Which lines from the poem express Shuttle's grief over her loss?
A. A jug of water/has its own lustrous turmoil
B. The ironing board thanks god
C. The new frig hums like a maniac
D. I am trying to love the world/back to normal

____ 3. Read the lines from the poem. What literary device does the poet use in these lines?
I am trying to love the world
back to normal . . .
I am trying to love the world
and all its 8000 identifiable languages . . .
I'm trying to get the seas back on the maps
where they belong,
A. personification C. fixed form
B. rhyme D. parallel structure

____ 4. What feeling, or mood, does the repetition of "I am trying" express?
A. joy C. hopelessness
B. yearning D. deceit

____ 5. Which best describes the tone, or attitude of the speaker toward her subject, in "In the Kitchen"?
A. bitter C. hopeful
B. brokenhearted D. realistic

____ 6. What does the speaker mean by "I'm trying to get the seas back on the maps/where they belong"?
A. She wants her world to be ordered and make sense.
B. She doesn't know how to read a map.
C. She is trying to make amends for her bad behavior.
D. She wants her husband to return to her.

____ 7. Shuttle likely chose the kitchen as a setting for her poem because the kitchen
A. is the most used room in the house.
B. traditionally represents nurturing.
C. captures the feeling of desperation.
D. is extremely uncomfortable.

Unit 6 Resources: A Time of Rapid Change
© Pearson Education, Inc. All rights reserved.
336

EL L1 L2 **Selection Test A,** pp. 336–338

Also available for these selections:

- L3 L4 **Open-Book Test,** pp. 333–335
- EL L3 L4 **Selection Test B,** pp. 339–341

PHLit Online!
www.PHLitOnline.com

- complete narrated selection text
- a thematically related video with writing prompt
- an interactive graphic organizer
- highlighting feature
- access to all student print resources, adapted to individual student needs
- Spanish and English summaries
- adapted selection translations in Spanish

Online Resources: All print materials are also available online.

Background Video

Also available:

Get Connected! (thematic video with writing prompt)
All videos are available in Spanish.

Vocabulary Central (tools and activities for studying vocabulary)

Also available:

Writer's Journal (with graphics feature)

PRETEACH

1 Connecting to the Essential Question

1. Review the assignment with the class.
2. Have students consider the traditional form of the elegy. **Ask:** How would a poem benefit from a new take on an old form? Then, have them complete the assignment.
3. As students read, have them consider the degree to which each poet draws on poetic traditions of the past.

2 Literary Analysis

Introduce the skill using the instruction on the student page.

Think Aloud: Model the Skill

Say to students:

I know that some poems are written in a fixed form, which means that there is a set number of lines or stanzas with a set pattern of rhyme and meter. I can contrast this with free-form poems, which have no set pattern to follow. Another way a poem can be categorized is by content. One example, an elegy, is about loss. I will look for characteristics of elegies in the poems to come.

3 Reading Strategy

1. Introduce the skill using the instruction on the student page.
2. Give students a copy of **Reading Strategy Graphic Organizer B,** page 269 in ***Graphic Organizer Transparencies,*** to fill out as they read.

Think Aloud: Model the Skill

Say to students:

I know that looking for parallel structure in poems is a useful skill. It can help me to better understand the contents of what I read. I will look for these structures in the upcoming poems.

4 Vocabulary

1. Pronounce each word, giving its definition, and have students say it aloud.
2. For more guidance, see the ***Classroom Strategies and Teaching Routines*** card for introducing vocabulary.

Before You Read *Prayer • In the Kitchen*

1 Connecting to the Essential Question In their poems, Penelope Shuttle and Carol Ann Duffy adapt the traditional form of the elegy to suit their purposes. To what degree do you think a modern poet should draw on tradition? As you read, consider the degree to which each poet draws on poetic traditions of the past. These connections will help you think about the Essential Question: **What is the relationship of the writer to tradition?**

Common Core State Standards

Reading Literature
5. Analyze how an author's choices concerning how to structure specific parts of a text contribute to its overall structure and meaning as well as its aesthetic impact.

2 Literary Analysis

Form refers to the way a poem is organized. Some types of poems have a **fixed form**—a set number of lines or stanzas that usually follow a set pattern of rhyme and meter. *Sonnets, villanelles,* and *haiku* are examples. For instance, a *Shakespearean,* or *English, sonnet* has fourteen lines that break into three quatrains, or four-line stanzas, and a final couplet. The pattern of end rhymes is usually *abab cdcd efef gg,* and the meter is usually iambic pentameter. "Prayer" by Carol Ann Duffy is a Shakespearean sonnet.

Some types of poems have a **free form,** or no set pattern to follow. Instead, the poet is free to establish his or her own pattern or to use free verse with no pattern at all. Penelope Shuttle's "In the Kitchen" is such a free-form poem.

Comparing Literary Works Both Duffy's poem and Shuttle's are elegiac. In other words, they are written in the spirit of **elegies,** poems mourning the loss of someone or something. Compare and contrast these elegiac poems by considering who or what is being mourned and in how formal a manner.

3 Reading Strategy

Preparing to Read Complex Texts To appreciate the form of a poem and better understand how the structure of specific parts contributes to its overall structure and meaning, **recite the poem aloud.** Listen especially for *parallel structures* or other repeated structures. Use a chart like the one shown to identify the parallel structures.

Parallel Structures	Effect on Meaning
• ironing-board thanks . . . • fridge hums . . . • chair recites . . .	Personified kitchen items give support to speaker.

4 Vocabulary

utters (ut′ ərz) *v.* speaks (p. 1413)

scales (skālz) *n.* sequences of musical tones arranged to have a rising or falling pitch (p. 1413)

lustrous (lus′ trəs) *adj.* gleaming; shining (p. 1414)

steadfastly (sted′ fast′ lē) *adv.* in a firm manner; without wavering (p. 1414)

PHLit Online! www.PHLitOnline.com

Vocabulary Development

Vocabulary Knowledge Rating

Create a **Vocabulary Knowledge Rating Chart** (***Professional Development Guidebook,*** p. 33) for the vocabulary words on the student page. Give each student a copy of the chart with the words on it. Read the words aloud, and have students mark their ratings in the Before Reading column. When students have completed reading and discussing the group of selections, have them take out their **Vocabulary Knowledge Rating Charts** for the poems. Read the words aloud and have students rate their knowledge again in the After Reading column. Clarify any words that are still problematic. Then, have students complete the Vocabulary practice at the end of the selections.

PHLit Online! **Vocabulary Central,** featuring tools and activities for studying vocabulary, is available online at **www.PHLitOnline.com.**

❺ CAROL ANN DUFFY

(b. 1955)

Author of **"Prayer"**

One of contemporary Britain's most highly regarded poets, Carol Ann Duffy grew up in Staffordshire, England, to which her family moved from Scotland when she was just four years old. Her father was an unusual man—a machine fitter with the electric company, he also ran for Parliament and managed a local soccer team. Encouraged to follow her own path, Duffy studied philosophy at the University of Liverpool and then moved to London, where she worked as poetry editor for *Ambit* magazine. In 1996, she returned to northern England to teach poetry at Manchester Metropolitan University.

Dramatic Poetry A talented playwright as well as a poet, Duffy uses her dramatic skills in her verse, displaying a strong sense of dramatic timing and a deep understanding of human behavior. She also experiments with traditional poetic forms. "I write quite a lot of sonnets," she once noted. "I think of them almost as prayers: short and memorable, something you can recite."

PENELOPE SHUTTLE

(b. 1947)

Author of **"In the Kitchen"**

Penelope Shuttle won her first poetry award when she was in her twenties and has been writing ever since. One source of inspiration has been Cornwall, the remote, rocky coastal area of southwestern England to which she moved in 1970; another has been her husband, the noted poet Peter Redgrove, with whom she coauthored a book of poetry, two novels, and two works of nonfiction.

Poetry as Consolation Shuttle nursed her husband through years of debilitating illness until his death in 2003. During that harrowing time and in the aftermath of her great loss, poetry has provided an outlet for her emotions and a spur for entering the world again. "My years as a carer for Peter and the sadness of witnessing his decline," she observes, "were a time when I fought off depression and anger, not always successfully, but turned to poetry as a channel for and transformer of such emotions." Many of the poems Shuttle wrote in this period, including "In the Kitchen," appear in her collection *Redgrove's Wife* (2006).

Daily Bellringer

For each class during which you will teach these selections, have students complete one of the five activities for the appropriate week in the *Daily Bellringer Activities* booklet.

Multidraft Reading

To assist struggling readers and to enhance reading for all, assign the text in chunks, as warranted by length, and apply multidraft reading protocols. For each reading, have students set the purpose indicated:

- **First reading**—identifying key ideas and details and answering any Reading Checks.
- **Second reading**—analyzing craft and structure and responding to the side-column prompts.
- **Third reading**—integrating knowledge and ideas, connecting to other texts and the world, and answering the end-of-selection questions.

For more guidance, refer to the ***Classroom Strategies and Teaching Routines*** card on Multidraft Reading.

❺ Background

More About the Authors

Carol Ann Duffy

Carol Ann Duffy has the ability to deal with timeless, universal themes, yet write with a sensibility of contemporary life. Her distinct style has been mimicked by many.

Penelope Shuttle

In her poetry collection *Redgrove's Wife,* Penelope Shuttle remembers her late husband, Peter Redgrove, and also the death of her father. The collection of poetry was on the shortlist for the Forward Poetry Prize and the 2007 T. S. Eliot Prize.

PHLit Online!
www.PHLitOnline.com

Teaching From Technology

Preparing to Read
Go to **www.PHLitOnline.com** and display the ***Get Connected!*** slide show for these selections. Have the class brainstorm responses to the writing prompt, entering ideas in the interactive journal. Then, have students complete their written responses as homework.

To build background, display the Background and More About the Author features.

Using the Interactive Text
Go to **www.PHLitOnline.com** and display the **Enriched Online Student Edition.** As the class reads the selection or listens to the narration, record answers to side-column prompts using the graphic organizers accessible on the interactive page. Alternatively, have students use the online edition individually, answering the prompts as they read.

❶ About the Selection

This poem addresses the place of faith in certain people's lives. It states, "although we cannot pray, a prayer utters itself." It details small moments in which one can take comfort in "sudden gifts" of revelations.

❷ Activating Prior Knowledge

Lead a discussion about what qualities we take from our parents or guardians, and what qualities originate from ourselves. Have students write a paragraph about how they have modified something drawn from their parents or guardians and made it their own. Then, tell students that the writers they will read have drawn from tradition, but have made modifications to make their writing more modern.

Concept Connector →

Tell students they will return to their responses after reading the selection.

❶ ❷

PRAYER

CAROL ANN DUFFY

Text Complexity Rubric

	Prayer	In the Kitchen
Qualitative Measures		
Context/ Knowledge Demands	Contemporary lyric; cultural knowledge demands 1 2 (3) 4 5	Contemporary lyric; life experience demands 1 2 (3) 4 5
Structure/Language Conventionality and Clarity	Accessible diction 1 (2) 3 4 5	Simple diction 1 2 (3) 4 5
Levels of Meaning/ Purpose/Concept Level	Moderate (moments of faith in the modern world) 1 2 (3) 4 5	Moderate (everyday normality after a loss) 1 2 (3) 4 5
Quantitative Measures		
Lexile/Text Length	NP / 108 words	NP / 126 words
Overall Complexity	**More accessible**	**More complex**

Some days, although we cannot pray, a prayer
utters itself. So, a woman will lift
her head from the sieve of her hands and stare
at the minims[1] sung by a tree, a sudden gift.

Some nights, although we are faithless, the truth
enters our hearts, that small familiar pain;
then a man will stand stock-still,[2] hearing his youth
in the distant Latin chanting[3] of a train.

Pray for us now. Grade I piano scales
console the lodger looking out across
a Midlands[4] town. Then dusk, and someone calls
a child's name as though they named their loss.

Darkness outside. Inside, the radio's prayer—
Rockall. Malin. Dogger. Finisterre.[5]

Vocabulary
utters (ut′ ərz) *v.* speaks
scales (skālz) *n.* sequences of musical tones arranged to have a rising or falling pitch

3 ◄ Critical Viewing
Could this painting be said to represent the nights "we are faithless" described in the poem? Explain. **[Connect]**

4 Literary Analysis
Fixed and Free Forms Describe the pattern of rhyme and meter in this sonnet.

1. **minims** *n.* half notes in music.
2. **stock-still** *adj.* as still as a stock, or wooden block; perfectly motionless.
3. **Latin chanting** prayers in Latin.
4. **Midlands** *n.* the industrial middle of England.
5. **Rockall . . . Finisterre** (fin′ is târ′) Four places in the familiar listing of coastal areas traditionally named in shipping forecasts heard on British radio.

Critical Reading

1. **Key Ideas and Details (a)** What can the speaker and others not do on some days? **(b) Infer:** What is the woman trying to do in lines 2–3? Explain.
2. **Key Ideas and Details (a) Generalize:** Given what they cannot do on some days and nights, what do the speaker and others take comfort in instead? **(b) Support:** Cite images that support your generalization.
3. **Integration of Knowledge and Ideas (a) Compare and Contrast:** In what way are the words on the radio like a prayer? **(b) Analyze:** How do these words and all the other sounds that people hear in the poem relate to modern life? **(c) Interpret:** What does the poem imply about faith and modern life?

Cite textual evidence to support your responses.

3 Critical Viewing

Possible response: Students might say that, yes, it does represent the nights "we are faithless" because of the melancholic mood evoked by the colors used to paint the landscape.

4 Literary Analysis

Fixed and Free Forms

1. Have students reread the entire poem, noting the rhyme and meter used in this piece.
2. **Ask** the Literary Analysis question: Describe the pattern of rhyme and meter in this sonnet.
   Answer: The rhyme scheme is that of a traditional Shakespearean sonnet. The meter, however, is not quite iambic pentameter because there are numerous moments of variation and lines with extra syllables.

ASSESS

Answers

1. (a) pray; (b) She is lifting her head from her hands, possibly because she is tired or because she has been crying.
2. (a) They take comfort in everyday events that are like prayers uttering themselves. (b) the minims sung by a tree, "a sudden gift"; the distant chanting of a train; the radio's prayer.
3. (a) The words on the radio are like a prayer because they are familiar to the listener, and they have a rhythm to them. (b) Trains and the radio are part of modern life. (c) It implies that although we may not have time to pray, we can find truth and beauty and inspiration in the everyday.

Text Complexity: Reader and Task Suggestions

Prayer		In the Kitchen	
Preparing to Read the Text	**Leveled Tasks**	**Preparing to Read the Text**	**Leveled Tasks**
• Explain to students that the speaker in the poem finds spiritual content in the routines of daily life. • Have students consider when and where people experience moments of faith. • Guide students to use Multidraft Reading strategies (TE p. 1411).	***Levels of Meaning*** If students will have difficulty with the levels of meaning, have them focus on the various sounds of modern life and their effect on people. Then, have students consider what the poem suggests about modern life. ***Analyzing*** If students will not have difficulty with the poem's meaning, have them analyze what the various sounds of modern life, taken together, seem to symbolize in the poem.	• Use the information on SE p. 1411 to stress that many of Shuttle's poems are different approaches to the trauma of loss. • Discuss with students the comfort people sometimes take in everyday things following a traumatic event. • Guide students to use Multidraft Reading strategies (TE p. 1411).	***Levels of Meaning*** If students will have difficulty with the levels of meaning, have them focus first on what the speaker is trying to accomplish. Then, as they reread, have them consider what the poem implies about one's experience after a loss. ***Analyzing*** If students will not have difficulty with the poem's meaning, have them use the poem's details to help them analyze whether the speaker really means the final line.

❺ About the Selection

This poem establishes a domestic scene and personifies the objects in a kitchen. It creates an environment that is sympathetic to the speaker and her loss.

❻ Reading Strategy

Reciting Poetry Aloud

1. Have students reread the poem and come back to lines 7–8.
2. **Ask** the Reading Strategy question: Recite lines 7–8. Which other lines in the poem parallel these lines?
   Answers: Lines 13–14 and lines 16–17. They all start with the phrase "I am trying to . . ."

ASSESS

Answers

Before students respond, you may wish to have them write a brief objective summary of the selection. As they answer the questions below, remind them to support their answers with evidence from the text.

1. (a) She says that she is trying to "love the world back to normal." (b) **Possible response:** Students might say that the speaker is paying so much attention to the objects in her kitchen because she is feeling a great loss and needs immediate comfort from that which surrounds her.
2. **Possible response:** Duffy's sonnet and Shuttle's free-verse poem are extremely effective as elegies in their own ways. They both masterfully describe their loss in *contemporary* ways. Their words find comfort and *faith* in the everyday.

❺ In the Kitchen

PENELOPE SHUTTLE

A jug of water
has its own **lustrous** turmoil

The ironing-board thanks god
for its two good strong legs and sturdy back

The new fridge hums like a maniac
with helpfulness

❻ I am trying to love the world
back to normal

The chair recites its stand-alone prayer
again and again

The table leaves no stone unturned
The clock votes for the separate burial of hearts

I am trying to love the world
and all its 8000 identifiable languages

With the forgetfulness of a potter
I'm trying to get the seas back on the maps
where they belong,

secured to their rivers

The kettle alone knows the good he does,
here in the kitchen, loving the world,
steadfastly loving

See how easy it is, he whistles

Vocabulary
lustrous (lus′ trəs) *adj.* gleaming; shining

Reading Strategy
Reciting Poetry Aloud Recite lines 7-8. Which other lines in the poem parallel these lines?

Vocabulary
steadfastly (sted′ fast′ lē) *adv.* in a firm manner; without wavering

Critical Reading

Cite textual evidence to support your responses.

1. **Key Ideas and Details (a)** What does the speaker say she is trying to do? **(b) Infer:** Why is she paying so much attention to the objects in her kitchen?
2. **Integration of Knowledge and Ideas** Are Duffy's sonnet and Shuttle's free-verse poem equally effective as elegies? Explain. Use two of these Essential Question words in your response: *crafted, contemporary, faith. [Connecting to the Essential Question: What is the relationship of the writer to tradition?]*

Assessment Practice

Style (For more practice, see *All-in-One Workbook.*)

Many tests require students to recognize the use of the writer's diction. Use the following sample test item to teach students to describe the writer's use of diction.

In the poem "In the Kitchen," how would you describe the diction used?

A whimsical and informal
B domestic and simple
C ceremonial
D formal

Lead students to recognize the domestic and simple language used in the poem. Students should determine that the correct answer is ***B***, domestic and simple.

After You Read | *Prayer • In the Kitchen*

Literary Analysis

1. Craft and Structure Use a chart like this one to show how the two poems are like and unlike a traditional **elegy.**

Traditional Elegy	"Prayer"	"In the Kitchen"
Is about a great loss		
Mourns a death		
Uses a formal, sad, solemn tone		
Draws universal lessons		

2. Craft and Structure (a) In terms of both structure and content, how is "Prayer" like and unlike a traditional Shakespearean sonnet? **(b)** Given its content, why do you think Duffy chose to write this poem in sonnet form?

Common Core State Standards

Writing

2.a. Introduce a topic; organize complex ideas, concepts, and information so that each new element builds on that which precedes it to create a unified whole.

Reading Strategy

3. Recite aloud "In the Kitchen" to help you recognize the parallel structures in the poem. What are the two main parallel structures?

4. (a) Explain how the second stanza of "Prayer" parallels the first. **(b)** What parallel structures occur in the final couplet of "Prayer"? How would you read these lines aloud?

PERFORMANCE TASKS
Integrated Language Skills

Vocabulary Acquisition and Use

Indicate whether each statement is true or false, and explain your answer.

1. Some people use a special rinse to make their hair more *lustrous.*
2. A hesitant coward *steadfastly* defends others.
3. When there is total silence, no one *utters* a sound.
4. *Scales* on a piano are little weights that press down inside when someone plays the keyboard.

Writing

Informative Text Imagine that you must give a **brief introduction to a radio spot** in which both these poems will be read. Using a style that will hook your audience, write an introduction that meets your purpose of providing listeners with the information they will need to understand and appreciate these particular poems and their authors.

Answers

1. For "Prayer": no; no; yes; yes. For "In the Kitchen": yes, yes (it is suggested); no; yes.
2. (a) In most ways, the poem maintains the patterns of a Shakespearean sonnet. It has fourteen lines, and the correct rhyme scheme. It is unlike a Shakespearean sonnet because of its many moments of variation in meter. (b) **Possible response:** Duffy may have chosen to write in the form of a sonnet because using the sonnet with subject matter very different from our expectations of a traditional sonnet creates a fresh perspective on an old form. The structure of the traditional sonnet makes the poem almost seem like a modern prayer.
3. Structure 1: A [object][action verb] . . . ; Structure 2: I am trying to . . .
4. (a) They both start with *Some* and then *days* or *nights,* and then *although we* . . . . (b) It states what is happening outside and then inside. I would read the line with a brief pause at the two caesuras.

Vocabulary Acquisition and Use

1. True, people put products in their hair to make it shine.
2. False, a coward who is hesitant would waver in indecisiveness.
3. True, in total silence, no sound is spoken.
4. False, a scale is a sequence of musical tones, not little weights.

Writing

Evaluate students' informative texts using the **Rubric for Multimedia Presentation,** ***Professional Development Guidebook,*** pages 266–267.

Assessment Resources

Unit 6 Resources

L1 L2 EL **Selection Test A,** pp. 336–338. Administer Test A to less advanced readers.

L3 L4 EL **Selection Test B,** pp. 339–341. Administer Test B to on-level students and more advanced students.

L3 L4 **Open-Book Test,** pp. 333–335. As an alternative, give the Open-Book test.

All **Customizable Test Bank**

All **Self-tests**
Students may prepare for the **Selection Test** by taking the **Self-test** online.

PHLit Online! All assessment resources are available at **www.PHLitOnline.com**.

• A Devoted Son

Lesson Pacing Guide

DAY 1 Preteach

- Administer the Reading and Vocabulary Warm-ups (*Unit 6 Resources*, pp. 344–347) as necessary.
- Introduce the Literary Analysis concept: Conflict and Character.
- Introduce the Reading Strategy: Identify the Causes of the Characters' Actions.
- Build background with the author and Background features.
- Develop thematic thinking with Connecting to the Essential Question.
- Teach the selection vocabulary.

DAYS 2–3 Preteach/Teach/Assess

- Distribute copies of the appropriate graphic organizer for the Reading Strategy (*Graphic Organizer Transparencies*, pp. 272–273).
- Distribute copies of the appropriate graphic organizer for Literary Analysis (*Graphic Organizer Transparencies*, pp. 274–275).
- Prepare students to read with the Activating Prior Knowledge activities (TE).
- Informally monitor comprehension while students read.
- Use the Reading Check questions to confirm comprehension.
- Develop students' understanding of conflict and character using the Literary Analysis prompts.
- Develop students' ability to identify causes of characters' actions using the Reading Strategy prompts.
- Reinforce vocabulary with the Vocabulary notes.
- Assess students' comprehension and mastery of the skills by having them answer the Critical Reading, Literary Analysis, and Reading Strategy questions.
- Have students complete the Vocabulary Lesson.

DAY 4 Extend/Assess

- Have students complete the Writing activity, writing a response to literature. (You may assign as homework.)
- Administer Selection Test A or B (*Unit 6 Resources*, pp. 356–358 or 359–361).

Common Core State Standards

Reading Literature 3. Analyze the impact of the author's choices regarding how to develop and relate elements of a story or drama.

Writing 1.a. Introduce precise, knowledgeable claim(s), distinguish the claim(s) from alternate or opposing claims, and create an organization that logically sequences claim(s), counterclaims, reasons, and evidence.

1.b. Develop claim(s) and counterclaims fairly and thoroughly, supplying the most relevant evidence for each while pointing out the strengths and limitations of both in a manner that anticipates the audience's knowledge level, concerns, values, and possible biases.

Language 4.a. Use context as a clue to the meaning of a word or phrase.

Additional Standards Practice
Common Core Companion, pp. 28–35; 185–189

Daily Block Scheduling
Each day in this Lesson Pacing Guide represents a 40–50 minute period. Teachers using block scheduling may combine days to revise pacing. In addition, teachers may differentiate and support core instruction by integrating components for extended and intensive support as students require. See the Guide to Selected Leveled Resources (facing page).

Guide to Selected Leveled Resources

RTI **Tier 1** (students performing on level)			A Devoted Son
Warm Up	Whole class instruction; Group work	**Practice, model,** and **monitor** fluency, working **with the whole class** or **in groups.**	**Vocabulary** and **Reading Warm-ups B,** ***Unit 6 Resources,*** pp. 362–363, 365
Comprehension/Skills	Whole class instruction; Group work; Independent work	**Support** and **monitor** comprehension and skills development, having students complete the activities, graphic organizers, and interactive prompts **independently** or **as a class.**	• ***Reader's Notebook,*** adapted instruction and full selection EL ***Reader's Notebook: English Learner's Version,*** adapted instruction and adapted selection • **Reading Strategy Graphic Organizer B,** ***Graphic Organizer Transparencies,*** p. 287 • **Literary Analysis Graphic Organizer B,** ***Graphic Organizer Transparencies,*** p. 289
Monitor Progress	A	**Monitor** student progress with the differentiated curriculum-based assessment in the *Unit Resources.*	• **Selection Test B,** ***Unit 6 Resources,*** pp. 377–379 • **Open-Book Test,** ***Unit 6 Resources,*** pp. 371–373

RTI **Tier 2** (students requiring intervention)			A Devoted Son
Warm Up	Group work; One-on-one teaching	**Practice, model,** and **monitor** fluency **in groups** or **with individuals.**	• **Vocabulary and Reading Warm-ups A.** ***Unit 6 Resources,*** pp. 362–364 • ***Hear It!*** **Audio CD (adapted text)**
Comprehension/Skills	Group work; One-on-one teaching	• **Support** and **monitor** comprehension and skills development, working **in small groups** or **with individuals.** • As students complete the selection in the appropriate version of the *Reader's Notebook,* **monitor** comprehension frequently with group questions and individual instruction. • **Model** strategies while guiding students in completing the activities and prompts in the *Reader's Notebook,* as well as the graphic organizers. • **Practice** skills and **monitor** mastery with the *Reading Kit* worksheets.	• ***Reader's Notebook: Adapted Version,*** adapted instruction and adapted selection EL ***Reader's Notebook: English Learner's Version,*** adapted instruction and adapted selection • **Reading Strategy Graphic Organizer A,** ***Graphic Organizer Transparencies,*** p. 286 • **Literary Analysis Graphic Organizer A,** ***Graphic Organizer Transparencies,*** p. 288 • ***Reading Kit,*** Practice worksheets
Monitor Progress	A	**Monitor** student progress with the differentiated curriculum-based assessment in the *Unit Resources* and in the *Reading Kit.*	• **Selection Test A,** ***Unit 6 Resources,*** pp. 374–376 • ***Reading Kit,*** Assess worksheets

TIER 3 Tier 3 intervention may require consultation with the student's special-education or dyslexia specialist. For additional support, see the Tier 2 activities and resources listed above.

One-on-one teaching · Group work · Whole class instruction · Independent work · A Assessment

For a complete guide to selection support, including support for Advanced students, see the Overview of Resources in the frontmatter.

• A Devoted Son

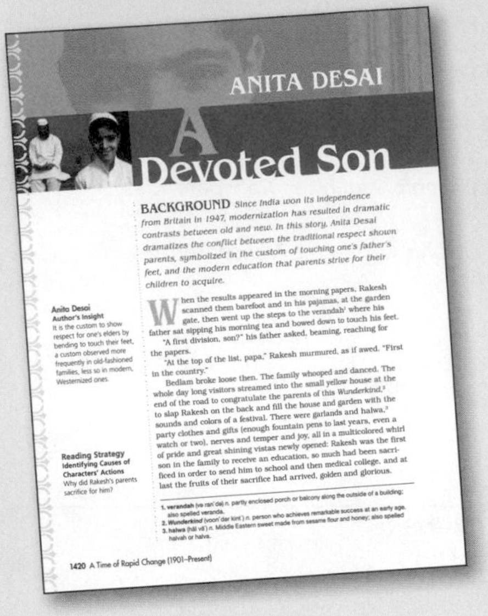
ANITA DESAI

A Devoted Son

BACKGROUND *Since India won its independence from Britain in 1947, modernization has resulted in dramatic contrasts between old and new. In this story, Anita Desai dramatizes the conflict between the traditional respect shown parents, symbolized in the custom of touching one's father's feet, and the modern education that parents strive for their children to acquire.*

When the results appeared in the morning papers, Rakesh scanned them barefoot and in his pajamas, at the garden gate, then went up the steps to the verandah[1] where his father sat sipping his morning tea and bowed down to touch his feet.

"A first division, son?" his father asked, beaming, reaching for the papers.

"At the top of the list, papa," Rakesh murmured, as if awed. "First in the country."

Bedlam broke loose then. The family whooped and danced. The whole day long visitors streamed into the small yellow house at the end of the road to congratulate the parents of this *Wunderkind*,[2] to slap Rakesh on the back and fill the house and garden with the sounds and colors of a festival. There were garlands and halwa,[3] party clothes and gifts (enough fountain pens to last years, even a watch or two), nerves and temper and joy, all in a multicolored whirl of pride and great shining vistas newly opened: Rakesh was the first son in the family to receive an education, so much had been sacrificed in order to send him to school and then medical college, and at last the fruits of their sacrifice had arrived, golden and glorious.

Anita Desai
Author's Insight
It is the custom to show respect for one's elders by bending to touch their feet, a custom observed more frequently in old-fashioned families, less so in modern, Westernized ones.

Reading Strategy
Identifying Causes of Characters' Actions
Why did Rakesh's parents sacrifice for him?

1. **verandah** (və ran′ də) *n.* partly enclosed porch or balcony along the outside of a building; also spelled veranda.
2. ***Wunderkind*** (voon′ dər kint′) *n.* person who achieves remarkable success at an early age.
3. **halwa** (häl vä′) *n.* Middle Eastern sweet made from sesame flour and honey; also spelled halvah or halva.

1420 A Time of Rapid Change (1901–Present)

RESOURCES FOR:

- L1 Special-Needs Students
- L2 Below-Level Students (Tier 2)
- L3 On-Level Students (Tier 1)
- L4 Advanced Students (Tier 1)
- EL English Learners
- All All Students

Vocabulary/Fluency/Prior Knowledge

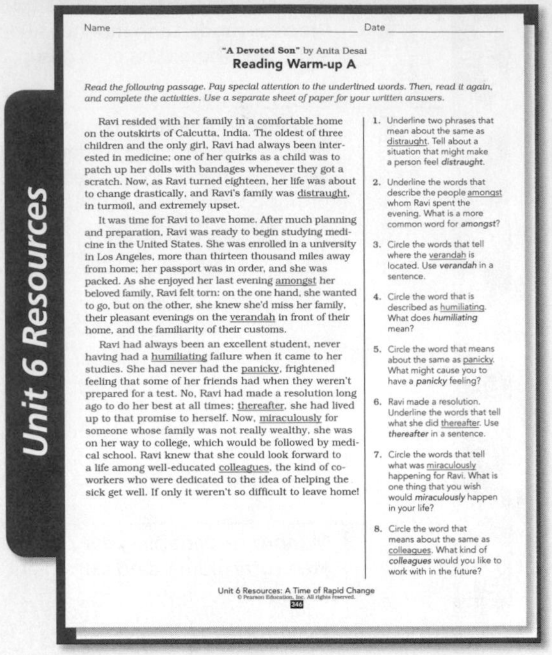
Unit 6 Resources

Name ____________ Date ____________

"A Devoted Son" by Anita Desai
Reading Warm-up A

Read the following passage. Pay special attention to the underlined words. Then, read it again, and complete the activities. Use a separate sheet of paper for your written answers.

Ravi resided with her family in a comfortable home on the outskirts of Calcutta, India. The oldest of three children and the only girl, Ravi had always been interested in medicine; one of her quirks as a child was to patch up her dolls with bandages whenever they got a scratch. Now, as Ravi turned eighteen, her life was about to change drastically, and Ravi's family was distraught, in turmoil, and extremely upset.

It was time for Ravi to leave home. After much planning and preparation, Ravi was ready to begin studying medicine in the United States. She was enrolled in a university in Los Angeles, more than thirteen thousand miles away from home; her passport was in order, and she was packed. As she enjoyed her last evening amongst her beloved family, Ravi felt torn: on the one hand, she wanted to go, but on the other, she knew she'd miss her family, their pleasant evenings on the verandah in front of their home, and the familiarity of their customs.

Ravi had always been an excellent student, never having had a humiliating failure when it came to her studies. She had never had the panicky, frightened feeling that some of her friends had when they weren't prepared for a test. No, Ravi had made a resolution long ago to do her best at all times; thereafter, she had lived up to that promise to herself. Now, miraculously for someone whose family was not really wealthy, she was on her way to college, which would be followed by medical school. Ravi knew that she could look forward to a life among well-educated colleagues, the kind of co-workers who were dedicated to the idea of helping the sick get well. If only it weren't so difficult to leave home!

1. Underline two phrases that mean about the same as distraught. Tell about a situation that might make a person feel *distraught*.
2. Underline the words that describe the people amongst whom Ravi spent the evening. What is a more common word for *amongst*?
3. Circle the words that tell where the verandah is located. Use *verandah* in a sentence.
4. Circle the word that is described as humiliating. What does *humiliating* mean?
5. Circle the word that means about the same as panicky. What might cause you to have a *panicky* feeling?
6. Ravi made a resolution. Underline the words that tell what she did thereafter. Use *thereafter* in a sentence.
7. Circle the words that tell what was miraculously happening for Ravi. What is one thing that you wish would *miraculously* happen in your life?
8. Circle the word that means about the same as colleagues. What kind of *colleagues* would you like to work with in the future?

Unit 6 Resources: A Time of Rapid Change
© Pearson Education, Inc. All rights reserved.
346

EL L1 L2 **Reading Warm-ups A and B,** pp. 346–347

Also available for these selections:

EL L1 L2 **Vocabulary Warm-ups A and B,** pp. 344–345

All **Vocabulary Builder,** p. 350

Reader's Notebooks

Pre- and postreading pages for this selection appear in an interactive format in the *Reader's Notebooks.* Each *Notebook* is differentiated for a different group of learners.
The selections in the Adapted and English Learner's versions are abridged.

L2 L3 ***Reader's Notebook***

L1 ***Reader's Notebook: Adapted Version***

EL ***Reader's Notebook: English Learner's Version***

EL ***Reader's Notebook: Spanish Version***

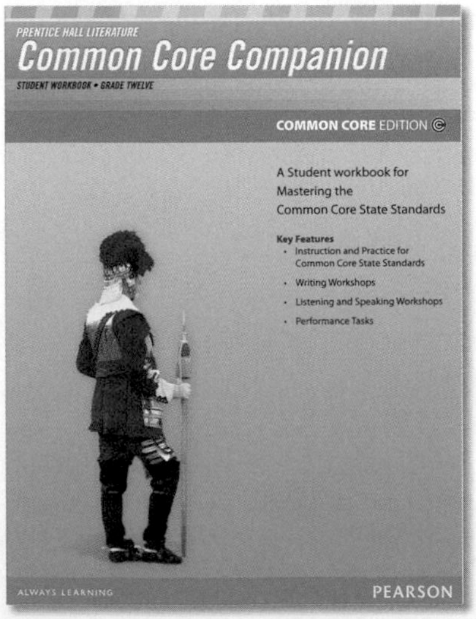

Common Core Companion

Additional instruction and practice for each Common Core State Standard

Selection Support

Graphic Organizer Transparencies

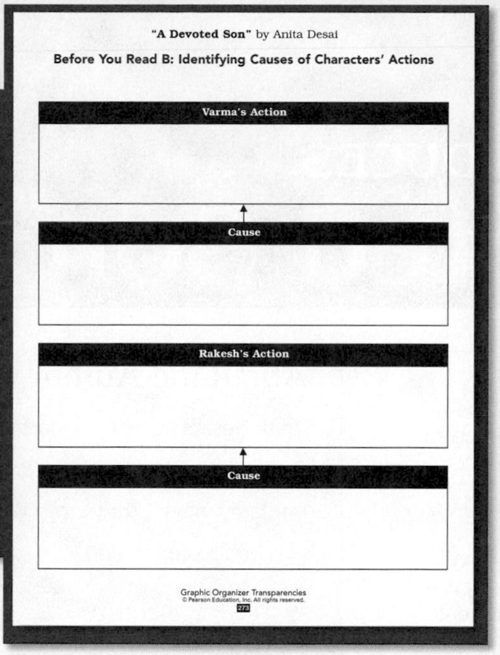
"A Devoted Son" by Anita Desai

Before You Read B: Identifying Causes of Characters' Actions

Varma's Action

Cause

Rakesh's Action

Cause

Graphic Organizer Transparencies

© Pearson Education, Inc. All rights reserved.

273

EL L3 **Reading: Graphic Organizer B,** p. 273

Also available for these selections:

EL L1 L2 **Reading: Graphic Organizer A,** p. 272

EL L1 L2 **Literary Analysis: Graphic Organizer A,** (partially filled in), p. 274

EL L3 **Literary Analysis: Graphic Organizer B,** p. 275

Skills Development/Extension

Unit 6 Resources

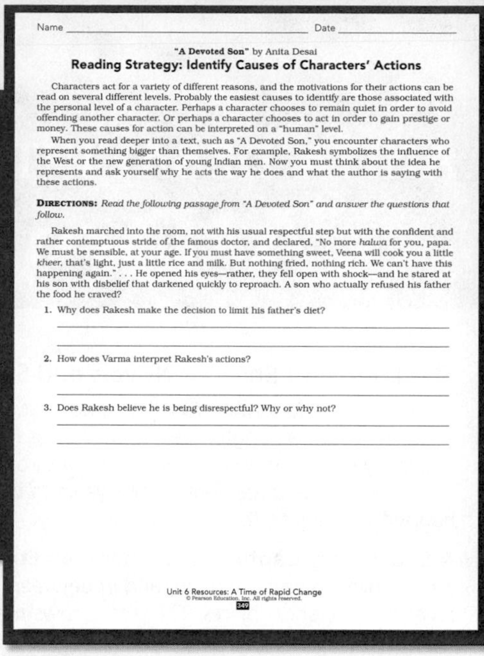
Name ______________________ Date ____________

"A Devoted Son" by Anita Desai

Reading Strategy: Identify Causes of Characters' Actions

Characters act for a variety of different reasons, and the motivations for their actions can be read on several different levels. Probably the easiest causes to identify are those associated with the personal level of a character. Perhaps a character chooses to remain quiet in order to avoid offending another character. Or perhaps a character chooses to act in order to gain prestige or money. These causes for action can be interpreted on a "human" level.

When you read deeper into a text, such as "A Devoted Son," you encounter characters who represent something bigger than themselves. For example, Rakesh symbolizes the influence of the West or the new generation of young Indian men. Now you must think about the idea he represents and ask yourself why he acts the way he does and what the author is saying with these actions.

Directions: *Read the following passage from "A Devoted Son" and answer the questions that follow.*

Rakesh marched into the room, not with his usual respectful step but with the confident and rather contemptuous stride of the famous doctor, and declared, "No more *halwa* for you, papa. We must be sensible, at your age. If you must have something sweet, Veena will cook you a little *kheer*, that's light, just a little rice and milk. But nothing fried, nothing rich. We can't have this happening again." . . . He opened his eyes—rather, they fell open with shock—and he stared at his son with disbelief that darkened quickly to reproach. A son who actually refused his father the food he craved?

1. Why does Rakesh make the decision to limit his father's diet?

2. How does Varma interpret Rakesh's actions?

3. Does Rakesh believe he is being disrespectful? Why or why not?

Unit 6 Resources: A Time of Rapid Change

© Pearson Education, Inc. All rights reserved.

349

All **Reading: Identify the Causes of the Character's Actions,** p. 349

Also available for these selections:

All **Literary Analysis: Conflict and Character,** p. 348

EL L3 L4 **Support for Writing,** p. 351

L4 **Enrichment,** p. 352

Assessment

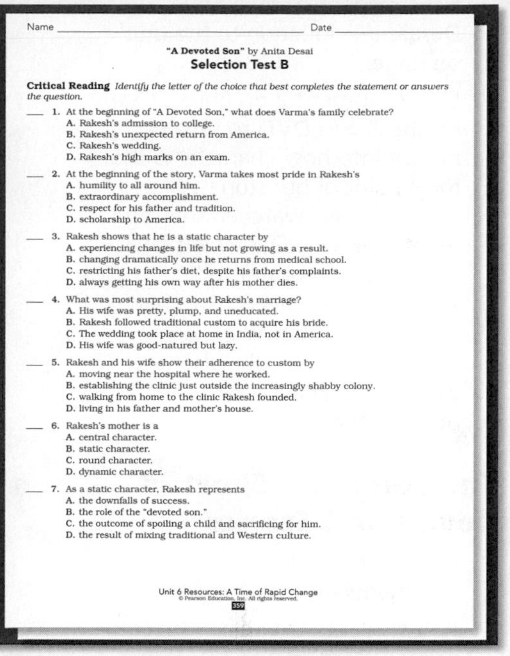
Name ______________________ Date ____________

"A Devoted Son" by Anita Desai

Selection Test B

Critical Reading *Identify the letter of the choice that best completes the statement or answers the question.*

___ 1. At the beginning of "A Devoted Son," what does Varma's family celebrate?
A. Rakesh's admission to college.
B. Rakesh's unexpected return from America.
C. Rakesh's wedding.
D. Rakesh's high marks on an exam.

___ 2. At the beginning of the story, Varma takes most pride in Rakesh's
A. humility to all around him.
B. extraordinary accomplishment.
C. respect for his father and tradition.
D. scholarship to America.

___ 3. Rakesh shows that he is a static character by
A. experiencing changes in life but not growing as a result.
B. changing dramatically once he returns from medical school.
C. restricting his father's diet, despite his father's complaints.
D. always getting his own way after his mother dies.

___ 4. What was most surprising about Rakesh's marriage?
A. His wife was pretty, plump, and uneducated.
B. Rakesh followed traditional custom to acquire his bride.
C. The wedding took place at home in India, not in America.
D. His wife was good-natured but lazy.

___ 5. Rakesh and his wife show their adherence to custom by
A. moving near the hospital where he worked.
B. establishing the clinic just outside the increasingly shabby colony.
C. walking from home to the clinic Rakesh founded.
D. living in his father and mother's house.

___ 6. Rakesh's mother is a
A. central character.
B. static character.
C. round character.
D. dynamic character.

___ 7. As a static character, Rakesh represents
A. the downfalls of success.
B. the role of the "devoted son."
C. the outcome of spoiling a child and sacrificing for him.
D. the result of mixing traditional and Western culture.

Unit 6 Resources: A Time of Rapid Change

© Pearson Education, Inc. All rights reserved.

359

EL L3 L4 **Selection Test B,** pp. 359–361

Also available for these selections:

L3 L4 **Open-Book Test,** pp. 353–355

EL L1 L2 **Selection Test A,** pp. 356–358

PHLit Online!

www.PHLitOnline.com

- complete narrated selection text
- a thematically related video with writing prompt
- an interactive graphic organizer
- highlighting feature
- access to all student print resources, adapted to individual student needs
- Spanish and English summaries
- adapted selection translations in Spanish

Online Resources: All print materials are also available online.

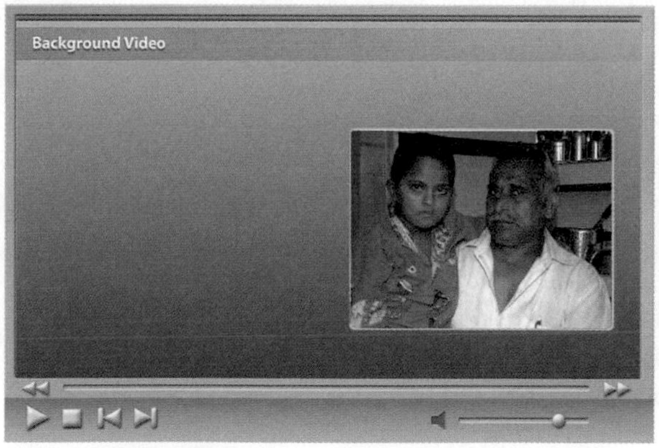

Background Video

Also available:

Get Connected! (thematic video with writing prompt)
All videos are available in Spanish.

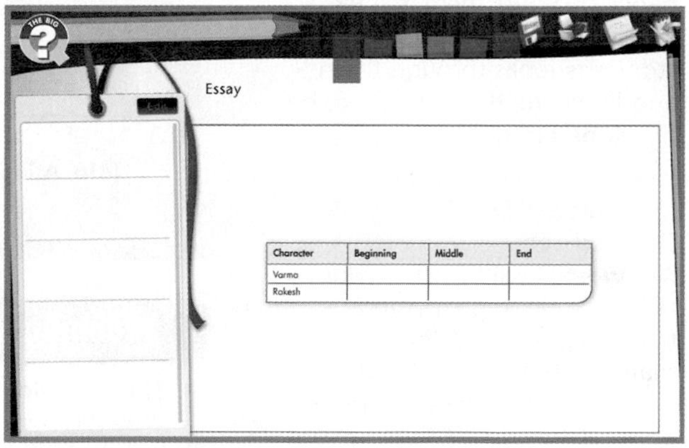

Writer's Journal (with graphics feature)

Also available:

Vocabulary Central (tools and activities for studying vocabulary)

TEACH

Themes Across Cultures

Anita Desai

1. Have students reread Anita Desai's introduction to the unit on pages 1135–1136.
2. Show Segment 2 on Anita Desai on the *See It!* **DVD** to provide insight into how character is the focal point of her stories. After students have watched the segment, **ask** why Desai feels character is so important to fiction. **Answer:** Desai feels that characters help determine where the plot is going. She also feels that characters are necessary to develop themes.

The Long and Short of Novels and Stories

1. Have students read Desai's comments on these pages.
2. **Ask** students to explain the comparison Desai makes between a story and a poem. **Answer:** Desai thinks that writing a story is like writing a poem because a story can focus on a single scene or event. Like a poem, a story is self-contained and complete when it is finished.

The Seeds of Stories

1. **Ask** a student to summarize Desai's process for writing a story. **Answer:** Desai jots down ideas, impressions, and bits of overheard conversation on pieces of paper and puts them in a file. When she needs an idea for a story, she looks through them and finds one that is ready to be developed into a story.
2. **Ask** a volunteer to explain the source of Desai's story "A Devoted Son." **Answer:** Desai heard an older neighbor singing a hymn at a family gathering. Although the man was not well and had had an unhappy life, Desai was moved by his story and his singing. The man made her think about the relationship between human life and art.

Ⓒ Themes Across Cultures: Author's Insights

ANITA DESAI INTRODUCES "A Devoted Son"

The Long and Short of Novels and Stories

I have always thought of myself as a novelist. What I like is to write slowly, at length, feeling my way as I go, getting to know my characters and following them through their lives. Such books take three, four, or five years to write, and I am happy to live inside them for that time.

A Short Story Captures a Moment, an Episode They are draining to write, though, and in between novels, it is a relief to write short pieces. This also throws me a different challenge: to put everything I want to say into a few pages, perhaps just one scene, and make my point sharply and concisely. Writing a short story is more like writing a poem than a novel. It captures a moment, an episode. It leads no further. It is complete in itself.

These moments come to me as one lives one's days—passing sensations or impressions. Often they don't seem important at the time. Often they are forgotten. But some stay in the mind, keep resurfacing in the memory, teasing and haunting one. Why? Mostly they are little things—words you heard someone say as you stood in line for coffee, an object you saw in your grandmother's house, a field or a bridge you passed in a train. Why do they linger in the mind? What do they mean? What is their significance?

Planting the Seeds of Stories In order to find out, I scribble down a few lines about them on a piece of paper. I put it away with other scraps of paper that live in a file. They may

About the Author

Anita Desai's novel *Baumgartner's Bombay* won the *Hadassah* Prize. Her latest novel, *The Zigzag Way*, was published in 2004.

Teaching Resources

The following resources can be used to enrich or extend the instruction for the Contemporary Commentary.

Unit 6 Resources
Contemporary Connection, Anita Desai, p. 342
Listening and Viewing, p. 343

See It! **DVD**
Anita Desai, Segment 2

PHLit Online! All resources are available at **www.PHLitOnline.com.**

stay there a long time, even years. Then one day I take them out and find that one is ready, ripe. It is as if they were seeds I planted that are now ready to come bursting out of the earth. In winding a story around them, I understand at last what they meant.

The Seed for "A Devoted Son" "A Devoted Son" occurred to me when I heard an old white-haired neighbor sing a hymn in ringing tones at a ceremony that was being held in his house for his newborn grandson. The old man often embarrassed his family by wandering about the streets and accosting people with wild language and gestures. It was said of him that he had lost his mind when he had to flee his country, leaving his home and lands behind. His son and daughter-in-law took care of him, but it must have been difficult. Yet he was capable of singing, in that incredibly moving way, a hymn of praise to God.

I wanted to capture that duality of human nature, of human life. Nothing is so simple as it seems; everything is complex, mysterious. Yet art—music, literature—can render it so that it becomes utterly pure, clear, and transparent.

▶ **Critical Viewing**
What messages about human nature and life does this picture capture? **[Interpret]**

"Nothing is so simple as it seems; everything is complex, mysterious."

Critical Reading

Cite textual evidence to support your responses.

1. **Key Ideas and Details (a)** What challenge does writing a short story pose for Desai? **(b) Infer:** How does she feel about such a challenge?
2. **Key Ideas and Details (a)** Where does Desai discover the ideas that eventually become stories? **(b) Interpret:** In your own words, explain why she does not develop these ideas immediately.

As You Read "A Devoted Son" . . .

3. **Integration of Knowledge and Ideas** As you read, consider ways in which "A Devoted Son" is similar to and different from the circumstances that first prompted Desai to write this story.
4. **Integration of Knowledge and Ideas** Explore ways in which "A Devoted Son" supports Desai's claim that literature can render the complexities in life so that they become "utterly pure, clear, and transparent."

Critical Viewing

Possible Response: Students may suggest that the picture illustrates the cycle of life—the power of new life to rejuvenate the old.

ASSESS

Answers

Before students respond, you may wish to have them write a brief objective summary of the selection. As they answer the questions below, remind them to support their answers with evidence from the text.

1. (a) For Desai, the challenge of writing a short story is to capture a moment or a scene in a few pages of writing. (b) She finds the challenge to be satisfying. It is a relief for her to write short stories after having written a novel.
2. (a) Desai discovers the ideas by being observant in her everyday life. She jots down the ideas and sets them aside to consider later. (b) **Possible response:** Desai waits for the ideas to develop, just as seeds in a garden germinate. She waits for the ideas to take on meaning.
3. The old man Desai saw in real life had lost his mind; the old man Varma in the story had not. He was similar to Varma because he was cared for by his son and daughter-in-law and took pride in the ceremony to celebrate a family member's accomplishment. Also, caring for both old men was difficult.
4. **Possible answer:** "A Devoted Son" shows the complexities of life in the duties, obligations, and desires of the son. At the end of the father's long life, any complexities he felt had been reduced to simple desires for familiar friends and tasty, familiar food. At the very end of the story, all the old man has left is a longing to be with God. Everything else in his life has been lost or stripped away from him.

PRETEACH

❶ Connecting to the Essential Question

1. Review the assignment with the class.
2. Ask students to discuss some reasons why children's attitudes about success change as they become adults. Display discussion notes on the board to aid students with their writing.
3. As students read, have them look for characters whose social attitudes change and the reasons for those changes.

❷ Literary Analysis

Introduce the skill using the instruction on the student page.

Think Aloud: Model the Skill

Say to students:

Identifying which characters undergo a change and which characters remain the same will help me understand the generational conflicts in this selection.

❸ Reading Strategy

1. Introduce the skill using the instruction on the student page.
2. Give students a copy of **Reading Strategy Graphic Organizer B,** page 273 in ***Graphic Organizer Transparencies,*** to fill out as they read.

Think Aloud: Model the Skill

Say to students:

In order to understand the behaviors of the characters in the story, I will try to identify the causes for those behaviors. To do this, I will pay attention to the author's descriptions of the characters' dominant traits and to the characters' dialogue. These story elements often reveal the reasons for particular behaviors and actions.

❹ Vocabulary

1. Pronounce each word, giving its definition, and have students say it aloud.
2. For more guidance, see the ***Classroom Strategies and Teaching Routines*** card for introducing vocabulary.

Before You Read *A Devoted Son*

❶ **Connecting to the Essential Question** In this story set in India, a father's attempt to help his son succeed backfires in unpredictable ways. As you read "A Devoted Son," notice details about changing social attitudes in India. Your ideas will help you respond to the Essential Question: **How does literature shape or reflect society?**

Common Core State Standards

Reading Literature

3. Analyze the impact of the author's choices regarding how to develop and relate elements of a story or drama.

❷ Literary Analysis

The plots of many stories center on **generational conflicts,** differences between older and younger generations. Sometimes these differences are based on personality, but often social factors play a role. For example, a parent's traditional values may conflict with a child's modern ones.

The way characters respond to these and other conflicts often depends on whether the characters can change and grow.

- **Static characters** are those who do not change in the course of a work. They often represent a social role or a particular trait or attitude.
- **Dynamic characters** are those who undergo a major change. They may change by choice or may have change thrust upon them.

As you read, consider why the author chose to present both static and dynamic characters in this story.

❸ Reading Strategy

Preparing to Read Complex Texts Whether a character is static or dynamic, you will understand his or her behavior better if you **identify the causes of the character's actions.** Use a chart like this to record behavior and its causes for the two main characters in "A Devoted Son."

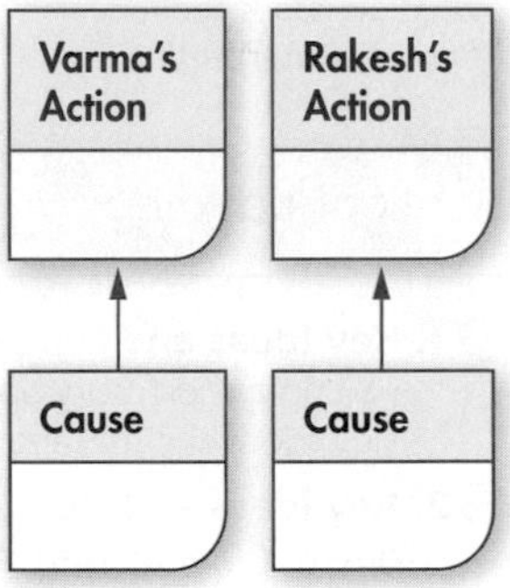

❹ Vocabulary

exemplary (eg zem′ plə rē) *adj.* worthy of serving as a model (p. 1421)

filial (fil′ ē əl) *adj.* of or due from a son or a daughter (p. 1421)

encomiums (en kō′ mē əmz) *n.* formal expressions of great praise (p. 1422)

complaisant (kəm plā′ zənt) *adj.* agreeable; willing to please (p. 1422)

fathom (fa*th*′ əm) *v.* understand thoroughly (p. 1423)

PHLit Online! www.PHLitOnline.com

Vocabulary Development

Vocabulary Knowledge Rating

Create a **Vocabulary Knowledge Rating Chart** (***Professional Development Guidebook***, p. 33) for the vocabulary words on the student page. Give each student a copy of the chart with the words on it. Read the words aloud, and have students mark their ratings in the Before Reading column. Urge students to attend to these words as they read and discuss the selection.

In order to gauge how much instruction you need to provide, tally how many students are confident in their knowledge of each word. As students read, point out the words and their context.

PHLit Online! **Vocabulary Central,** featuring tools and activities for studying vocabulary, is available online at **www.PHLitOnline.com.**

5 ANITA DESAI

(b. 1937)

Author of "A Devoted Son"

Anita Desai's father was Indian and her mother, German. This unusual heritage may have contributed to her understanding of people from many different cultures. She displays this understanding in finely crafted novels and short stories about conflicts among characters of different generations and backgrounds. These works of fiction have gained her a reputation as one of the most gifted Indian novelists writing in English.

A Diverse Heritage Desai was born in the northern Indian town of Mussoorie, located at the foot of the Himalaya Mountains. She grew up in the old section of Delhi, India's capital city. "There were a great many books in the house and we were all bookworms," Desai recalls.

Choosing a Language Because of its unique heritage, Desai's family spoke three languages: Hindi, English, and German. Desai first learned English at school. When asked why she chose to write in it, Desai explained, "It seemed to me the language of books. I just went on writing it because I always wanted to belong to this world of books." Desai became part of a new development in Indian literature—the Indian writing in English.

Recognition A precocious writer, Desai finished her first English story when she was seven and published for the first time when she was nine. After graduating from Delhi University, the newly married Desai joined the Writers Workshop in Calcutta. In 1963, she published her first novel, *Cry the Peacock,* a portrayal of the despair of a young married woman. This novel was followed by *Bye-Bye, Blackbird* (1968), *Fire on the Mountain* (1977), and *Clear Light of Day* (1980). This last novel, a study of complex family relationships, was nominated for England's prestigious Booker Prize. In many works, she with a quiet power explores the struggle of women in Indian culture to deal with the roles imposed on them by tradition.

"My style of writing is to allow the story to unfold on its own."

Daily Bellringer

For each class during which you will teach "A Devoted Son," have students complete one of the activities for the appropriate week in the *Daily Bellringer Activities* booklet.

Multidraft Reading

To assist struggling readers and to enhance reading for all, assign the text in chunks, as warranted by length, and apply multidraft reading protocols. For each reading, have students set the purpose indicated:

- **First reading**—identifying key ideas and details and answering any Reading Checks.
- **Second reading**—analyzing craft and structure and responding to the side-column prompts.
- **Third reading**—integrating knowledge and ideas, connecting to other texts and the world, and answering the end-of-selection questions.

For more guidance, refer to the *Classroom Strategies and Teaching Routines* card on Multidraft Reading.

5 Background

More About the Author

Desai's work is part of a new style of writing to come out of India, a style that is not nearly as conservative as Indian writing has been in the past. One concern evident in her work, especially the novel *Baumgartner's Bombay,* is cultural estrangement and dividedness. Desai grew up during World War II and could see the anxiety her German mother was experiencing about her family in Germany. After the war, when she realized the Germany she had known was devastated, her mother never returned there. Desai herself did not visit Germany until she was an adult.

PHLit Online!
www.PHLitOnline.com

Teaching From Technology

Preparing to Read
Go to **www.PHLitOnline.com** and display the ***Get Connected!*** slide show for this selection. Have the class brainstorm responses to the writing prompt, entering ideas in the interactive journal. Then, have students complete their written responses as homework.

To build background, display the Background and More About the Author features.

Using the Interactive Text
Go to **www.PHLitOnline.com** and display the **Enriched Online Student Edition.** As the class reads the selection or listens to the narration, record answers to side-column prompts using the graphic organizers accessible on the interactive page. Alternatively, have students use the online edition individually, answering the prompts as they read.

❶ About the Selection

In this ironically titled story, an Indian family sacrifices everything to send their son Rakesh to medical school. Rakesh's father is proud of his son's success and devotion—until the son begins to control his aging father's diet. The father's decline in body and spirit and his growing regret at the estrangement that a modern education has caused between his son and him make for a poignant story with a universal theme of generational conflict.

❷ Activating Prior Knowledge

Ask students what they know of care for the elderly in the United States today. Ask students to discuss to what extent children are responsible for their parents' care in their later years and the problems that arise from this intergenerational interaction.

Concept Connector →

Tell students they will return to their responses after reading the selection.

❸ Author's Insight

Direct students' attention to the Author's Insight note. **Ask** students to consider how time has changed attitudes and customs between older and younger generations.
Possible response: Students may suggest that respect for elders is not as common today as it was with previous generations.

❹ Reading Strategy

Identifying Causes of Characters' Actions

1. Read aloud the bracketed passage to students and then ask them to rephrase the material in their own words.
2. **Ask** students the Reading Strategy question: Why did Rakesh's parents sacrifice for him?
Answer: Rakesh was the first son in the family to receive an education, which they valued highly. His family knew he would succeed.

ANITA DESAI

❶ ❷ A Devoted Son

BACKGROUND *Since India won its independence from Britain in 1947, modernization has resulted in dramatic contrasts between old and new. In this story, Anita Desai dramatizes the conflict between the traditional respect shown parents, symbolized in the custom of touching one's father's feet, and the modern education that parents strive for their children to acquire.*

Anita Desai
Author's Insight ❸
It is the custom to show respect for one's elders by bending to touch their feet, a custom observed more frequently in old-fashioned families, less so in modern, Westernized ones.

When the results appeared in the morning papers, Rakesh scanned them barefoot and in his pajamas, at the garden gate, then went up the steps to the verandah[1] where his father sat sipping his morning tea and bowed down to touch his feet.

"A first division, son?" his father asked, beaming, reaching for the papers.

"At the top of the list, papa," Rakesh murmured, as if awed. "First in the country."

Bedlam broke loose then. The family whooped and danced. The whole day long visitors streamed into the small yellow house at the end of the road to congratulate the parents of this *Wunderkind*,[2] to slap Rakesh on the back and fill the house and garden with the sounds and colors of a festival. There were garlands and halwa,[3] party clothes and gifts (enough fountain pens to last years, even a watch or two), nerves and temper and joy, all in a multicolored whirl of pride and great shining vistas newly opened: Rakesh was the first son in the family to receive an education, so much had been sacrificed in order to send him to school and then medical college, and at last the fruits of their sacrifice had arrived, golden and glorious.

Reading Strategy
Identifying Causes of Characters' Actions ❹
Why did Rakesh's parents sacrifice for him?

1. **verandah** (və ran′ də) *n.* partly enclosed porch or balcony along the outside of a building; also spelled veranda.
2. ***Wunderkind*** (voon′ dər kint′) *n.* person who achieves remarkable success at an early age.
3. **halwa** (häl vä′) *n.* Middle Eastern sweet made from sesame flour and honey; also spelled halvah or halva.

Text Complexity Rubric

A Devoted Son	
Qualitative Measures	
Context/ Knowledge Demands	Contemporary Indian story; cultural knowledge and life experience demands 1 ② 3 4 5
Structure/Language Conventionality and Clarity	Accessible diction; dialogue 1 2 ③ 4 5
Levels of Meaning/ Purpose/Concept Level	Moderate (generational conflict; modern vs. traditional) 1 2 ③ 4 5
Quantitative Measures	
Lexile/Text Length	1440L / 3,989 words
Overall Complexity	**More accessible**

5 ◀ **Critical Viewing**
Identify two details in this photograph that illustrate the story's theme of the conflict between the modern and the traditional. **[Interpret]**

To everyone who came to him to say "*Mubarak*,[4] Varmaji, your son has brought you glory," the father said, "Yes, and do you know what is the first thing he did when he saw the results this morning? He came and touched my feet. He bowed down and touched my feet." This moved many of the women in the crowd so much that they were seen to raise the ends of their saris[5] and dab at their tears while the men reached out for the betel-leaves[6] and sweetmeats that were offered around on trays and shook their heads in wonder and approval of such **exemplary filial** behavior. "One does not often see such behavior
6 in sons any more," they all agreed, a little enviously perhaps. Leaving the house, some of the women said, sniffing, "At least on such an occasion they might have served pure *ghee*[7] sweets," and some of the men said, "Don't you think old Varma was giving himself airs? He needn't think we don't remember that he comes from the vegetable market himself, his father used to sell vegetables, and he has never seen the inside of a school." But there was more envy than rancor in their voices and it was, of course, inevitable—not every son in that shabby little colony at the edge of the city was destined to shine as Rakesh shone, and who knew that better than the parents themselves?

And that was only the beginning, the first step in a great, sweeping ascent to the radiant heights of fame and fortune. The thesis he wrote for his M.D. brought Rakesh still greater glory, if only in select medical circles. He won a scholarship. He went to the USA (that was what his father learnt to call it and taught the whole family to say—not America, which was what the ignorant neighbors called it, but, with a grand familiarity, "the USA") where he pursued his career

Literary Analysis
Generational Conflict Is there a generational conflict between Rakesh and his father at this point in the story? Explain.

Vocabulary
exemplary (eg zem′ plə rē) *adj.* worthy of serving as a model

filial (fil′ ē əl) *adj.* relating to a son or a daughter

7 **Reading Check**
Why is Rakesh's family celebrating?

4. **Mubarak** (mu bär′ək) greeting meaning "blessed one." The word, originally from Arabic, has become part of some languages spoken in India.
5. **saris** (sä′rēz) *n.* traditional garments worn by Indian women, consisting of lengths of cotton, silk, or other cloth wrapped around the waist and draped over one shoulder.
6. **betel-leaves** (bēt′l) *n.* leaves from an evergreen shrub, usually wrapped around seeds from that shrub and commonly chewed in Asia.
7. **ghee** (gē) *n.* clarified butter, often used in Indian cooking.

5 Critical Viewing

Possible responses: The theme of the story is conveyed through the differences shown on the busy street. The decorated elephant contrasts sharply with the other modern modes of transportation and the sign for the Internet-service provider.

6 Literary Analysis

Generational Conflict

1. Read aloud the bracketed passage to students and then ask them to rephrase the material in their own words.
2. **Ask** students the Literary Analysis question: Is there a generational conflict between Rakesh and his father at this point in the story? **Possible response:** At this point, there does not appear to be conflict. Rather, Rakesh is very respectful and his father is extremely proud.

7 Reading Check

Answer: Rakesh graduated at the top of his class, and he has managed to gain scholarships for study abroad in the United States to complete his medical training. His success has brought his family glory.

Text Complexity: Reader and Task Suggestions

A Devoted Son

Preparing to Read the Texts
- Using the Background feature on TE p. 1420, explain that India since World War II has seen many cultural changes that younger people usually embraced but older people did not.
- Discuss with students the theme of generational conflict. Point out that such conflicts are often stronger when the member of the older generation has ties to a culture or tradition that has far less influence on the member of the younger generation.
- Guide students to use Multidraft Reading strategies (TE p. 1419).

Leveled Tasks

Levels of Meaning If students will have difficulty with the story's irony, have them focus on what the father expected to happen when he educated his son Rakesh and what has happened instead. Then, as they reread, have them consider what the story says about change and generational conflict in general.

Analyzing If students will not have great difficulty with the story's irony, have them use story details to help them analyze why the title is ironic.

PHLit Online!

This selection is available in interactive format in the **Enriched Online Student Edition** at **www.PHLitOnline.com**, which includes a thematically related video with writing prompt and an interactive graphic organizer.

❽ Author's Insight

Point out Desai's comment about the shabby setting. **Ask** students how the choice of setting reveals insights about the character Rakesh. What does Rakesh's decision to come home reveal about him?

Possible response: Rakesh feels a loyalty to his family. His decision to come back to a small, shabby town shows the obligation he feels toward his family.

❾ Reading Strategy

Identify Causes of Characters' Actions

1. Remind students that identifying the causes of a character's actions will help them understand his or her behavior.
   Ask: How is Rakesh's behavior in this passage different from his behavior at the beginning of the story?
   Possible response: At the beginning of the story, Rakesh is very humble and is careful to first honor Varma before acknowledging his own success.
2. **Ask** students the Reading Strategy questions: Why does Rakesh take his parents to the clinic? What probably causes his fame to dim somewhat soon after that?
   Answer: Rakesh is proud and wants to show his parents his new clinic. Rakesh's fame begins to dim as people grow accustomed to his success and wealth.

❿ Author's Insight

Have a student read the Author's Insight note aloud to the class. **Ask** students if these possessions are signs of success in America.

Answer: Yes, expensive homes and new vehicles are symbols of success in America.

Vocabulary
encomiums (en kō′ mē əmz) *n.* formal expressions of great praise

Anita Desai ❽
Author's Insight I wanted to draw a quick sketch of a small town and its rather run-down outlying areas to show the humble beginnings of the famous man. Although he is exceptional in the eyes of his family and neighbors, he may not be so in the outer world. His light shines especially strong in this shabby setting.

Vocabulary
complaisant (kəm plā′ zənt) *adj.* agreeable; willing to please

Reading Strategy
Identifying Causes of Characters' Actions Why does Rakesh take his parents to the clinic? What probably causes his fame to dim somewhat soon after that? ❾

Anita Desai ❿
Author's Insight Acquiring a house and car are still signs of success in a country with much poverty.

in the most prestigious of all hospitals and won **encomiums** from his American colleagues which were relayed to his admiring and glowing family. What was more, he came *back,* he actually returned to that small yellow house in the once-new but increasingly shabby colony, right at the end of the road where the rubbish vans[8] tipped out their stinking contents for pigs to nose in and rag-pickers to build their shacks on, all steaming and smoking just outside the neat wire fences and welltended gardens. To this Rakesh returned and the first thing he did on entering the house was to slip out of the embraces of his sisters and brothers and bow down and touch his father's feet.

As for his mother, she gloated chiefly over the strange fact that he had not married in America, had not brought home a foreign wife as all her neighbors had warned her he would, for wasn't that what all Indian boys went abroad for? Instead he agreed, almost without argument, to marry a girl she had picked out for him in her own village, the daughter of a childhood friend, a plump and uneducated girl, it was true, but so old-fashioned, so placid, so **complaisant** that she slipped into the household and settled in like a charm, seemingly too lazy and too good-natured to even try and make Rakesh leave home and set up independently, as any other girl might have done. What was more, she was pretty—really pretty, in a plump, pudding way that only gave way to fat—soft, spreading fat, like warm wax—after the birth of their first baby, a son, and then what did it matter?

For some years Rakesh worked in the city hospital, quickly rising to the top of the administrative organization, and was made a director before he left to set up his own clinic. He took his parents in his car—a new, sky-blue Ambassador[9] with a rear window full of stickers and charms revolving on strings—to see the clinic when it was built, and the large sign-board over the door on which his name was printed in letters of red, with a row of degrees and qualifications to follow it like so many little black slaves of the regent.[10] Thereafter his fame seemed to grow just a little dimmer—or maybe it was only that everyone in town had grown accustomed to it at last—but it was also the beginning of his fortune for he now became known not only as the best but also the richest doctor in town.

However, all this was not accomplished in the wink of an eye. Naturally not. It was the achievement of a lifetime and it took up Rakesh's whole life. At the time he set up his clinic his father had grown into an old man and retired from his post at the kerosene dealer's depot at which he had worked for forty years, and his mother died soon after, giving up the ghost with a sigh that sounded positively happy, for it was her own son who ministered to her in her last illness and who sat pressing her feet at the last moment—such a son as few women had borne.

---

8. **rubbish vans** garbage trucks.
9. **Ambassador** popular model of car manufactured by Hindustan Motors of India.
10. **regent** (rē′ jənt) *n.* ruler; governor.

Enrichment: Investigating Careers

Physicians

The conflict in this story involves the sacrifices a family makes to send a son to medical school.

Activity: Investigating Physicians Ask students to research the duties, responsibilities, training, and skills required of physicians and to record their findings in the **Enrichment: Investigating Career Connections** worksheet, ***Professional Development Guidebook,*** page 221. Invite a medical student, intern, or resident physician to speak to the class about his or her training and the sacrifices and rewards of the chosen career. Students may want to compare their notes with the information provided by the guest speaker.

For it had to be admitted—and the most unsuccessful and most rancorous of neighbors eventually did so—that Rakesh was not only a devoted son and a miraculously good-natured man who contrived somehow to obey his parents and humor his wife and show concern equally for his children and his patients, but there was actually a brain inside this beautifully polished and formed body of good manners and kind nature and, in between ministering to his family and playing host to many friends and coaxing them all into feeling happy and grateful and content, he had actually trained his hands as well and emerged an excellent doctor, a really fine surgeon. How one man—and a man born to illiterate parents, his father having worked for a kerosene dealer and his mother having spent her life in a kitchen—had achieved, combined and conducted such a medley of virtues, no one could **fathom**, but all acknowledged his talent and skill.

It was a strange fact, however, that talent and skill, if displayed for too long, cease to dazzle. It came to pass that the most admiring of all eyes eventually faded and no longer blinked at his glory. Having retired from work and having lost his wife, the old father very quickly went to pieces, as they say. He developed so many complaints and fell ill so frequently and with such mysterious diseases that even his son could no longer make out when it was something of significance and when it was merely a peevish whim. He sat huddled on his string bed most of the day and developed an exasperating habit of stretching out suddenly and lying absolutely still, allowing the whole family to fly around him in a flap, wailing and weeping, and then suddenly sitting up, stiff and gaunt, and spitting out a big gob of betel-juice as if to mock their behavior.

11 He did this once too often: there had been a big party in the house, a birthday party for the youngest son, and the celebrations had to be suddenly hushed, covered up and hustled out of the way when the daughter-in-law discovered, or thought she discovered, that the old man, stretched out from end to end of his string bed, had lost his pulse; the party broke up, dissolved, even turned into a band of mourners, when the old man sat up and the distraught daughter-in-law received a gob of red spittle right on the hem of her organza[11] sari. After that no one much cared if he sat up crosslegged on his bed, hawking and spitting, or lay down flat and turned gray as a corpse. Except, of course, for that pearl amongst pearls, his son Rakesh.

It was Rakesh who brought him his morning tea, not in one of the china cups from which the rest of the family drank, but in the old man's favorite brass tumbler, and sat at the edge of his bed, comfortable and relaxed with the string of his pajamas dangling out from under his fine lawn night-shirt, and discussed or, rather, read out the morning news to his father. It made no difference to him that his father made no response apart from spitting. It was Rakesh, too, who,

11. **organza** (ôr gan′zə) *n.* stiff sheer fabric.

— such a son as few women had borne.

Vocabulary
fathom (fa*th*′ əm)
v. understand thoroughly

Anita Desai
Author's Insight He shows his bitterness and spite at the good health still enjoyed by the young.

12 Reading Check
Whom does Rakesh marry?

11 Author's Insight

Point out Desai's note on Rakesh's father. **Ask** students to discuss anyone they know who behaves like the father. Are they also showing bitterness at their loss of youth?
Possible response: Students may suggest a family member who behaves in such a way and may agree that people like Varma are bitter at their loss of youth.

12 Reading Check

Answer: Rakesh married a woman his mother had picked out for him.

Differentiated Instruction for Universal Access

Strategy for Less Proficient Readers
Have students write an essay addressing generational conflicts in American society. They might wish to draw upon their own experiences or address the challenges related to the assimilation of immigrants from one generation to the next.

Strategy for English Learners
The accessibility of its language and the ideas of this story serve as a good opportunity for English learners to focus on their speaking and presentation skills. As students read the story, have them collect information and citations for oral presentations.

Strategy for Advanced Readers
Have students read the story independently at their own pace. Desai has said that she is interested in discovering "the truth that is nine-tenths of the iceberg that lies submerged beneath the one-tenth visible portion we call Reality." Have each student write an essay discussing this statement.

⓭ Literary Analysis

Static and Dynamic Characters

1. Remind students that dynamic characters undergo major changes. Ask students to think of characters from other stories they have read who underwent changes. Encourage students to describe the factors that caused the characters' changes.
2. **Ask** students the Literary Analysis questions: Does Rakesh's stride show a change in his character? In what way is he still the ideal son?
   Possible response: Although Rakesh is acting more assertively and seems less concerned about pleasing his father, he is still an ideal, devoted son because he wants to do everything possible to keep his father alive and healthy.

⓮ Author's Insight

Direct students to the Author's Insight note. **Ask** if they think Desai effectively showed Rakesh taking over the role as senior family member.
Possible response: Some students may feel that Desai implemented Rakesh's new role effectively because it seems to occur naturally for good reasons.

⓯ Literary Analysis

Generational Conflict

1. Remind students that Varma and Rakesh no longer share the same values.
2. **Ask** students the Literary Analysis question: What role do traditional values play in the conflict that arises between Rakesh and his father?
   Answer: Varma clings to traditional values while Rakesh has given them up in favor of the values of his profession.

⓰ Author's Insight

Point out Desai's remark about defiance. **Ask** students to consider why the father would defy his son.
Possible response: Students may suggest that the father is trying to be independent.

Literary Analysis
Static and Dynamic Characters Does Rakesh's stride show a change in his character? In what way is he still the ideal son?

Anita Desai
Author's Insight By this act I want to show Rakesh taking over the role of the senior in the family and his father's shock at realizing he must relinquish it.

Literary Analysis
Generational Conflict What role do traditional values play in the conflict that arises between Rakesh and his father?

Anita Desai
Author's Insight In a traditional, well-ordered family, defiance is not permitted, so little acts of rebellion have to be devised.

on returning from the clinic in the evening, persuaded the old man to come out of his room, as bare and desolate as a cell, and take the evening air out in the garden, beautifully arranging the pillows and bolsters on the divan[12] in the corner of the open verandah. On summer nights he saw to it that the servants carried out the old man's bed onto the lawn and himself helped his father down the steps and onto the bed, soothing him and settling him down for a night under the stars.

All this was very gratifying for the old man. What was not so gratifying was that he even undertook to supervise his father's diet. One day when the father was really sick, having ordered his daughter-in-law to make him a dish of *soojie*[13] *halwa* and eaten it with a saucerful of cream, Rakesh marched into the room, not with his usual respectful step but with the confident and rather contemptuous stride of the famous doctor, and declared, "No more *halwa* for you, papa. We must be sensible, at your age. If you must have something sweet, Veena will cook you a little *kheer*,[14] that's light, just a little rice and milk. But nothing fried, nothing rich. We can't have this happening again."

The old man who had been lying stretched out on his bed, weak and feeble after a day's illness, gave a start at the very sound, the tone of these words. He opened his eyes—rather, they fell open with shock—and he stared at his son with disbelief that darkened quickly to reproach. A son who actually refused his father the food he craved? No, it was unheard of, it was incredible. But Rakesh had turned his back to him and was cleaning up the litter of bottles and packets on the medicine shelf and did not notice while Veena slipped silently out of the room with a little smirk that only the old man saw, and hated.

Halwa was only the first item to be crossed off the old man's diet. One delicacy after the other went—everything fried to begin with, then everything sweet, and eventually everything, everything that the old man enjoyed.

The meals that arrived for him on the shining stainless steel tray twice a day were frugal to say the least—dry bread, boiled lentils, boiled vegetables and, if there were a bit of chicken or fish, that was boiled too. If he called for another helping—in a cracked voice that quavered theatrically—Rakesh himself would come to the door, gaze at him sadly and shake his head, saying, "Now, papa, we must be careful, we can't risk another illness, you know," and although the daughter-in-law kept tactfully out of the way, the old man could just see her smirk sliding merrily through the air. He tried to bribe his grandchildren into buying him sweets (and how he missed his wife now, that generous, indulgent and illiterate cook), whispering, "Here's fifty paise,"[15] as he stuffed the coins into a tight, hot fist.

12. **divan** (də van´ or di van´) *n.* long backless sofa on which pillows or bolsters are usually arranged to support the back.
13. **soojie** n. Indian term for semolina, a coarse grain usually made from wheat; often spelled sooji or suji.
14. **kheer** (kir) *n.* rice pudding traditionally served as a dessert in southern India.
15. **paise** (pi´ se) *n.* plural of paisa, Indian money equal to 1/100 of a rupee.

Enrichment: Investigating Health

Cholesterol
In this story, a conflict arises over a son's attempts to control his father's diet, particularly the father's intake of fat and sugar. Explain to students that as societies become more affluent, people's diets tend to consist of fewer complex carbohydrates and more fats and animal proteins—many of which contain cholesterol.
Activity: Investigating Cholesterol Ask students to research information about cholesterol. Be sure to point out to students that there are two kinds of cholesterol: high-density lipoprotein (HDL), or "good cholesterol," and low-density lipoprotein (LDL), or "bad cholesterol." Students may record their findings in the **Enrichment: Investigating Health and Medicine** worksheet, ***Professional Development Guidebook***, page 229. Ask students to report their findings to the class.

17 "Run down to the shop at the crossroads and buy me thirty paise worth of *jalebis*,[16] and you can spend the remaining twenty paise on yourself. Eh? Understand? Will you do that?" He got away with it once or twice but then was found out, the conspirator was scolded by his father and smacked by his mother and Rakesh came storming into the room, almost tearing his hair as he shouted through compressed lips, "Now papa, are you trying to turn my little son into a liar? Quite apart from spoiling your own stomach, you are spoiling him as well—you are encouraging him to lie to his own parents. You should have heard the lies he told his mother when she saw him bringing back those *jalebis* wrapped up in filthy newspaper. I don't allow anyone in my house to buy sweets in the bazaar,[17] papa, surely you know that. There's cholera[18] in the city, typhoid, gastroenteritis—I see these cases daily in the hospital, how can I allow my own family to run such risks?" The old man sighed and lay down in the corpse position. But that worried no one any longer.

There was only one pleasure left in the old man now (his son's early morning visits and readings from the newspaper could no longer be called that) and those were visits from elderly neighbors. These were not frequent as his contemporaries were mostly as decrepit and helpless as he and few could walk the length of the road to visit him any more. 18 Old Bhatia, next door, however, who was still spry enough to refuse, adamantly, to bathe in the tiled bathroom indoors and to insist on carrying out his brass mug and towel, in all seasons and usually at impossible hours, into the yard and bathe noisily under the garden tap, would look over the hedge to see if Varma were out on his verandah and would call to him and talk while he wrapped his *dhoti*[19] about him and dried the sparse hair on his head, shivering with enjoyable exaggeration. Of course these conversations, bawled across the hedge by two rather deaf old men conscious of having their entire households overhearing them, were not very satisfactory but Bhatia occasionally came out of his yard, walked down the bit of road and came in at Varma's gate to collapse onto the stone plinth built under the temple tree.[20] If Rakesh was at home he would help his father down the steps into the garden and arrange him on his night bed under the tree and leave the two old men to chew betel-leaves and discuss the ills of their individual bodies with combined passion.

"At least you have a doctor in the house to look after you," sighed Bhatia, having vividly described his martyrdom to piles.[21]

16. ***jalebis*** (jä leb'ēz) *n.* Indian sweets made by frying a coil of batter and then soaking it in syrup.
17. **bazaar** (bə zär') *n.* open-air market.
18. **cholera** (käl'ər ə) . . . **typhoid** (tī'foid), **gastroenteritis** dangerous infectious diseases causing fever or intestinal problems.
19. ***dhoti*** (dō'tē) *n.* cloth worn by Hindu men in India, with the ends passing through the legs and tucked in at the waist.
20. **stone . . . tree** stone slab beneath the frangipani, an erect tree often grown in temple gardens in India.
21. **piles** *n.* hemorrhoids.

Reading Strategy
Identifying Causes of Characters Actions What does Rakesh's decision to forbid his father sweets cause his father to do?

Anita Desai
Author's Insight Bathing outdoors is what one might do when living on a farm or a village. Naturally, it cannot be done in a city. I wanted to show how my characters are people still making the transition from one to the other.

19 **Reading Check**
What does Varma complain about to his friend?

17 Reading Strategy
Identify Causes of Characters' Actions

1. **Ask** students if Rakesh's decision to ban sweets from the bazaar is based on logic or emotion.
   Answer: Though his desire to protect his family involves some emotion, Rakesh's decision is based mainly on logic: Eating sweets from the bazaar carries some risk of contracting diseases such as cholera, so there will be no sweets bought, no matter how happy they would make his father.
2. Then, **ask** students the Reading Strategy question: What does Rakesh's decision to forbid his father sweets cause his father to do?
   Answer: Varma bribes his grandchildren to go to the bazaar and buy sweets for him.

18 Author's Insight
Direct students' attention to Desai's note about bathing outside. **Ask** students to consider what the families of the two old men might be thinking when this occurs.
Possible response: The family members may be embarrassed at the behavior of the old men bathing outside. They may laugh at their inability to transition into city life.

19 Reading Check
Answer: Varma complains that his son does not give him enough to eat.

Differentiated Instruction for Universal Access

Culturally Responsive Instruction
Culture Focus
This story begins with an important act of filial devotion: a successful son's bowing down to touch his father's feet. Explain to students that one of the most important aspects of Indian culture is respect for one's elders. To bow down and touch someone's feet is a high sign of respect, for the feet are viewed as the most unclean part of the body. Parents and elders, in turn, place a hand on the head of the person bowing and give him or her a blessing. Have students share any gestures their own cultures use, and as they read encourage them to notice how characters use body language to express their feelings for one another.

⓴ Author's Insight

Point out Desai's note about disobedience. Tell students that this is another example of the changes in attitude and action between generations. It is also another instance when the reader sees Varma's relinquished role as head of the family.

㉑ Literary Analysis

Static and Dynamic Characters

1. Remind students of the difference between static and dynamic characters. Have them provide examples of each type of character from selections they have read in previous units.
2. Then, **ask** them the Literary Analysis question: In whose view has Rakesh's "sterling personality and character" undergone "a curious sea change"? Have students explain their answers.
Answer: Varma believes that Rakesh has transformed from a dutiful son into a cruel master.

Is it possible, even in this evil age, for a son to refuse his father food?

"Look after me?" cried Varma, his voice cracking like an ancient clay jar. "He—he does not even give me enough to eat."

"What?" said Bhatia, the white hairs in his ears twitching. "Doesn't give you enough to eat? Your own son?"

"My own son. If I ask him for one more piece of bread, he says no, papa, I weighed out the *ata*[22] myself and I can't allow you to have more than two hundred grams of cereal a day. He *weighs* the food he gives me, Bhatia—he has scales to weigh it on. That is what it has come to."

"Never," murmured Bhatia in disbelief. "Is it possible, even in this evil age, for a son to refuse his father food?"

"Let me tell you," Varma whispered eagerly. "Today the family was having fried fish—I could smell it. I called to my daughter-in-law to bring me a piece. She came to the door and said no. . . ." ⓴

"Said no?" It was Bhatia's voice that cracked. A *drongo*[23] shot out of the tree and sped away. *"No?"*

"No, she said no, Rakesh has ordered her to give me nothing fried. No butter, he says, no oil. . . ."

"No butter? No oil? How does he expect his father to live?"

Old Varma nodded with melancholy triumph. "That is how he treats me—after I have brought him up, given him an education, made him a great doctor. Great doctor! This is the way great doctors treat their fathers, Bhatia," for the son's sterling personality and character now underwent a curious sea change. Outwardly all might be the same but the interpretation had altered: his masterly efficiency was nothing but cold heartlessness, his authority was only tyranny in disguise. ㉑

There was cold comfort in complaining to neighbors and, on such a miserable diet, Varma found himself slipping, weakening and soon becoming a genuinely sick man. Powders and pills and mixtures were not only brought in when dealing with a crisis like an upset stomach

Anita Desai
Author's Insight
Her refusal is an incredible act of disobedience by a younger member of the family to an elder. I wanted to show the daughter-in-law as belonging to a traditional family but breaking out of it when she can.

Literary Analysis
Static and Dynamic Characters In whose view has Rakesh's "sterling personality and character" undergone "a curious sea change"? Explain.

22. **ata** (ä´tə) *n.* type of flour used in India.
23. **drongo** *n.* black bird with a long forked tail.

Enrichment: Investigating Religion

Hinduism
The story takes place in India, where more than 80 percent of the population practices the religion of Hinduism. Tell students that among the characteristics of Indian society traceable to Hinduism are the Indian caste system; the concepts of dharma, karma, and reincarnation; the practice of yoga; and the veneration of cows as sacred animals.

Activity: Investigating Hinduism Provide students with a copy of the **Enrichment: Investigating Religion and Myth** worksheet, ***Professional Development Guidebook,*** page 240, and ask them to research Hinduism and to record their findings on the worksheet. Provide time for students to report their findings to the class.

22 ◀ **Critical Viewing**
Why would Varma be tempted by an open-air market, like the one shown here? **[Analyze]**

but became a regular part of his diet—became his diet, complained Varma, supplanting the natural foods he craved. There were pills to regulate his bowel movements, pills to bring down his blood pressure, pills to deal with his arthritis and, eventually, pills to keep his heart beating. In between there were panicky rushes to the hospital, some humiliating experience with the stomach pump and enema, which left him frightened and helpless. He cried easily, shriveling up on his bed, but if he complained of a pain or even a vague, gray fear in the night, Rakesh would simply open another bottle of pills and force him to take one. "I have my duty to you papa," he said when his father begged to be let off.

"Let me be," Varma begged, turning his face away from the pills on the outstretched hand. "Let me die. It would be better. I do not want to live only to eat your medicines."

"Papa, be reasonable."

"I leave that to you," the father cried with sudden spirit. "Leave me alone, let me die now, I cannot live like this."

"Lying all day on his pillows, fed every few hours by his daughter-in-law's own hand, visited by every member of his family daily—and then he says he does not want to live 'like this,'" Rakesh was heard to say, laughing, to someone outside the door.

"Deprived of food," screamed the old man on the bed, "his wishes ignored, taunted by his daughter-in-law, laughed at by his grand-children—*that* is how I live." But he was very old and weak and all anyone heard was an incoherent croak, some expressive grunts and cries of genuine pain. Only once, when old Bhatia had come to see him and they sat together under the temple tree, they heard him cry, "God is calling me—and they won't let me go."

The quantities of vitamins and tonics he was made to take were not altogether useless. They kept him alive and even gave him a kind of strength that made him hang on long after he ceased to wish to hang on. It was as though he were straining at a rope, trying to break it, and it would not break, it was still strong. He only hurt himself, trying.

23 ☑ **Reading Check**
What becomes a regular part of Varma's diet?

22 Critical Viewing

Answer: In the open-air market, the scents and sights of Varma's favorite treats would likely be difficult to escape.

23 Reading Check

Answer: "Powders and pills and mixtures" become a "regular part of [Varma's] diet."

Differentiated Instruction for Universal Access

Strategy for Less Proficient Readers
Provide students with the character wheel graphic organizer on page 292 in ***Graphic Organizer Transparencies.*** Have them choose Rakesh or his father and fill in the character wheel, including information about the appearance, opinions, and habits of the character. Then, have each student write a brief summary of his or her character of choice at this point in the story.

Enrichment for Gifted/Talented Students
Have students work in small groups to choose a scene from the story. Then, have them write short scripts representative of their chosen scenes. Have them rehearse at a time convenient to all. Encourage them to use props and costumes, if appropriate. Then, have groups perform the scenes for an audience of classmates and possibly others.

24 Critical Thinking

Evaluate

1. Ask students to summarize Rakesh's "course of treatment" for his father. Encourage students to think of the changes in and supplements to Varma's diet, as well as the other ways he is cared for physically and socially.
2. **Ask** students to describe Varma's various reactions to Rakesh's caretaking methods.
   Possible response: Varma's reactions include complaining to his neighbors about Rakesh, bribing his grandchildren to buy him sweets, resisting letting Rakesh press his feet, and begging to be left alone so that he can die.
3. Then **ask**, What does Varma say while his son Rakesh is sitting at the edge of his bed?
   Possible response: Varma tells Rakesh that he is dying and that Rakesh should let him die.

. . . let me die now, I cannot live like this.

In the evening, that summer, the servants would come into his cell, grip his bed, one at each end, and carry it out to the verandah, there sitting it down with a thump that jarred every tooth in his head. In answer to his agonized complaints they said the doctor sahib[24] had told them he must take the evening air and the evening air they would make him take—thump. Then Veena, that smiling, hypocritical pudding in a rustling sari, would appear and pile up the pillows under his head till he was propped up stiffly into a sitting position that made his head swim and his back ache.

"Let me lie down," he begged. "I can't sit up any more."

"Try, papa, Rakesh said you can if you try," she said, and drifted away to the other end of the verandah where her transistor radio vibrated to the lovesick tunes from the cinema[25] that she listened to all day.

So there he sat, like some stiff corpse, terrified, gazing out on the lawn where his grandsons played cricket,[26] in danger of getting one of their hard-spun balls in his eye, and at the gate that opened onto the dusty and rubbish-heaped lane but still bore, proudly, a newly touched-up signboard that bore his son's name and qualifications, his own name having vanished from the gate long ago.

At last the sky-blue Ambassador arrived, the cricket game broke up in haste, the car drove in smartly and the doctor, the great doctor, all in white, stepped out. Someone ran up to take his bag from him, others to escort him up the steps. "Will you have tea?" his wife called, turning down the transistor set. "Or a Coca-Cola? Shall I fry you some *samosas?*"[27] But he did not reply or even glance in her direction. Ever a devoted son, he went first to the corner where his father sat gazing, stricken, at some undefined spot in the dusty yellow air that swam before him. He did not turn his head to look at his son. But he stopped gobbling air with his uncontrolled lips and set his jaw as hard as a sick and very old man could set it.

"Papa," his son said, tenderly, sitting down on the edge of the bed and reaching out to press his feet.

Old Varma tucked his feet under him, out of the way, and continued to gaze stubbornly into the yellow air of the summer evening.

"Papa, I'm home."

24 Varma's hand jerked suddenly, in a sharp, derisive movement, but he did not speak.

"How are you feeling, papa?"

Then Varma turned and looked at his son. His face was so out of control and all in pieces, that the multitude of expressions that crossed it could not make up a whole and convey to the famous man exactly what his father thought of him, his skill, his art.

"I'm dying," he croaked. "Let me die, I tell you."

---

24. **sahib** (sä´ib´, hib´, ēb´, or hĭb´) Indian term of respect.
25. **cinema** (sin´ə mə) *n.* movies.
26. **cricket** *n.* open-air game played between two teams using balls and bats.
27. **samosas** (sə mō´səz) *n.* fried triangular Indian pastries containing vegetables or meat.

Vocabulary Development

Vocabulary Knowledge Rating

When students have completed reading and discussing "A Devoted Son," have them take out their **Vocabulary Knowledge Rating Charts** for the story. Read the words aloud and have students rate their knowledge of words again in the After Reading column. Clarify any words that are still problematic. Have students write their own definitions and example or sentence in the appropriate column. Then, have students complete the Vocabulary Lesson at the end of the selection. Encourage students to use the words in further discussion and written work about the selection. Remind them that they will be accountable for these words on the **Selection Test, *Unit 6 Resources,*** pages 356–358 or 359–361.

"Papa, you're joking," his son smiled at him, lovingly. "I've brought you a new tonic to make you feel better. You must take it, it will make you feel stronger again. Here it is. Promise me you will take it regularly, papa."

Varma's mouth worked as hard as though he still had a gob of betel in it (his supply of betel had been cut off years ago). Then he spat out some words, as sharp and bitter as poison, into his son's face. "Keep your tonic—I want none—I want none—I won't take any more of—of your medicines. None. Never," and he swept the bottle out of his son's hand with a wave of his own, suddenly grand, suddenly effective. 25

26 His son jumped, for the bottle was smashed and thick brown syrup had splashed up, staining his white trousers. His wife let out a cry and came running. All around the old man was hubbub once again, noise, attention.

He gave one push to the pillows at his back and dislodged them so he could sink down on his back, quite flat again. He closed his eyes and pointed his chin at the ceiling, like some dire prophet, groaning, "God is calling me—now let me go."

Literary Analysis

Static and Dynamic Characters Compare the father's character at the end of the story with that of the betel-juice spitter of earlier scenes.

Anita Desai

Author's Insight

According to Hindu belief, a human life is divided into four stages—that of a student, a householder, a pilgrim, and, finally, a hermit. This belief is ingrained in the father, who sees the natural cycle thwarted by his son's modern ways, and chafes against it.

Critical Reading

Cite textual evidence to support your responses.

1. **Key Ideas and Details (a)** According to Varma, what is the first thing Rakesh does upon seeing his excellent exam results? **(b) Infer:** At this point in the story, what values does Rakesh's behavior reflect? **(c) Infer:** How does Varma feel about his son at this point in the story?
2. **Integration of Knowledge and Ideas (a) Evaluate:** After Rakesh becomes a doctor, would you say his behavior toward his father remains devoted? Explain. **(b) Generalize:** What does the story suggest about the relationship between devotion and compassion in caring for others?
3. **Integration of Knowledge and Ideas (a) Analyze:** Explain the irony of the title from Varma's perspective. **(b) Generalize:** In what ways is this conflict specifically Indian and in what ways is it universal?
4. **Integration of Knowledge and Ideas (a) Evaluate:** Do you think Rakesh's behavior is truly devoted? Explain. **(b) Generalize:** What lessons about hopes or expectations does the story teach to parents like Varma and to people in general?
5. **Integration of Knowledge and Ideas** What does the story show about traditional values and changing times in India? Explain, using at least three of these Essential Question words: *respectful, clash, modernization,* and *westernization. [Connecting to the Essential Question: How does literature shape or reflect society?]*

25 Literary Analysis

Static and Dynamic Characters

1. Have students review some of the factors, besides his poor diet, that may have contributed to Varma's deterioration.
   Answer: Varma was idle after having retired from work, his wife passed away, and many of his friends and neighbors were also in poor health.
2. Then, **ask** students the Literary Analysis question: Compare the father's character at the end of the story with that of the betel-juice spitter of earlier scenes.
   Possible responses: After his initial sulks and irritable posing, he has now given up and truly withdrawn, which gives him more dignity. Varma now seems victimized by the rest of the family, and the reader feels sorry for him.

26 Author's Insight

Draw students' attention to the Author's Insight note. Ask students to contemplate whether they think Rakesh will understand his father's decision to take no more medicine.

ASSESS

Answers

Before students respond, you may wish to have them write a brief objective summary of the selection. As they answer the questions below, remind them to support their answers with evidence from the text.

1. (a) Rakesh bowed down to touch his father's feet. (b) Rakesh's behavior reflects traditional values. (c) Varma is glowing with pride for his son.
2. (a) Some students may say Rakesh's behavior seems truly devoted. Others may say that his medical training blinds him to his father's misery. (b) Students may respond that true devotion calls for a deep awareness of a person's suffering, coupled with the wish to relieve it.
3. (a) Varma probably does not think his son is devoted, while Rakesh probably believes he is. (b) This conflict is Indian in some of the customs, such as bowing, and in the foods it describes. It is universal in that all children and their parents struggle with one another from time to time.
4. (a) Some students may say Rakesh's behavior seems truly devoted. Others may say that his medical training blinds him to his father's misery. (b) Parents would hope that the things that make their children successful are in keeping with the family's other social values.
5. **Possible response:** This story demonstrates how the modernization and westernization of India have resulted in conflict: the younger generation—once expected, at all times, to be respectful and deferential—clashes with the older, traditional generation.

Answers

1. (a) Rakesh and Varma disagree about Varma's diet, whether Varma should be taken outside when he prefers to stay indoors, and whether or not Varma can lie down during the daytime. (b) These disagreements reflect the central conflict, because in order to adhere to his professional ethos, Rakesh ignores the traditional idea that he should respect his father's autonomy.
2. (a) This conflict is specific to Indian customs, such as bowing, and to the Indian foods it describes. (b) It is universal in that all children and their parents struggle with one another from time to time.
3. In the beginning of the story, both Rakesh and Varma are traditional. In the middle of the story, both characters are traditional, though Rakesh has begun to observe some modern practices. By the end of the story, Varma remains traditional, while Rakesh is a combination of traditional and modern. Rakesh, therefore, is the dynamic character.
4. Varma believes that his son has transformed from a "devoted son" to a tyrant.
5. Throughout the story, both women observe traditional customs such as choosing a wife for her son, as in the case of Rakesh's mother, or following her husband's directives, as in the case of Veena.
6. Desai contrasts the ideas of the dynamic, modern generation—"No more *halwa* for you, papa"—with those of the static, traditional generation—"This is the way great doctors treat their fathers, Bhatia. . . ."
7. **Possible response:** It would be possible to show generational conflict using static characters only. However, in doing so, it would be difficult to develop or resolve the conflict and, therefore, not as interesting for the reader.
8. (a) The family values education and has great faith that Rakesh will succeed and bring them glory. (b) **Possible response:** Though Varma comes to view his decision as unwise, most students will probably say that it is important to provide a child with an education.

After You Read *A Devoted Son*

Literary Analysis

1. **Key Ideas and Details (a)** Name three things about which Rakesh and Varma come to disagree. **(b)** How do these disagreements reflect a **generational conflict** central to the story?
2. **Integration of Knowledge and Ideas (a)** In what ways is the story's generational conflict specific to the Indian setting? **(b)** In what ways is it more universal?
3. **Craft and Structure** Use a chart like this one to compare and contrast Varma and Rakesh in the beginning, middle, and end of the story. Which of the two do you think is a more **dynamic character**? Why?

Character	Beginning	Middle	End
Varma			
Rakesh			

4. **Key Ideas and Details** By the end of the story, what new perspective has Varma developed on his "devoted son"?
5. **Craft and Structure** Are Rakesh's mother and wife **static** or **dynamic characters**? Cite story details to explain your classifications.
6. **Craft and Structure** How does Desai use static and dynamic characters to explore ideas about traditional beliefs in the modern world? Use the characters' dialogue to support your answer.
7. **Integration of Knowledge and Ideas** Would it be possible to show a generational conflict using static characters only? Why or why not?

Reading Strategy

8. **(a) Identify the causes** that lead to the family's sacrifices for Rakesh's education. **(b)** Was this decision unwise? Explain.
9. Explain the causes of each of these actions on the part of Varma or Rakesh:
   (a) Varma hosts a party for the neighbors.
   (b) Rakesh touches his father's feet.
   (c) Varma "goes to pieces."
   (d) Rakesh puts his father on a strict diet.
   (e) Varma smashes the tonic his son brings him.
10. **(a)** In what sense does Varma cause his own problems in this story? **(b)** What role do his traditional values play in causing his problems?

Common Core State Standards

Writing
1.a. Introduce precise, knowledgeable claim(s), distinguish the claim(s) from alternate or opposing claims, and create an organization that logically sequences claim(s), counterclaims, reasons, and evidence. *(p. 1431)*
1.b. Develop claim(s) and counterclaims fairly and thoroughly, supplying the most relevant evidence for each while pointing out the strengths and limitations of both in a manner that anticipates the audience's knowledge level, concerns, values, and possible biases. *(p. 1431)*

Language
4.a. Use context as a clue to the meaning of a word or phrase. *(p. 1431)*

9. (a) Varma is proud of his son.
(b) Rakesh wants to honor his father, as is customary in India.
(c) Varma gets older, he retires, and his wife dies.
(d) Rakesh wants his father to be well.
(e) Varma is frustrated that he is treated like a patient.

10. (a) Varma very much wanted his son to be a good doctor and therefore is responsible for the way Rakesh treats him. Also, Varma refuses to acknowledge that his son's advice might be good. (b) Varma's traditional values expect that sons honor fathers at all times. This belief conflicts with the supervision under which Rakesh places his father.

Vocabulary Acquisition and Use

Vocabulary Lesson: Latin Root *-fil-*

The word *filial,* meaning "relating to a son or a daughter," contains the Latin root *-fil-,* which means "son or daughter." The same root occurs in the word *affiliate*, which goes back to a Latin word *affiliare*, meaning "to adopt as a son or daughter."

Forms of the word *affiliate* are often used in the fields of *history* and *political science.* Explain the meaning of each form of *affiliate* used in the following sentences, using a dictionary if necessary. Then, use the forms in sentences of your own.

1. With which political party is he *affiliated*?
2. She is an *affiliate* of the Whig party.
3. Is that nation in one of the international alliances, or is it *unaffiliated*?
4. What is your political *affiliation*?

Vocabulary: Context Clues

Context clues are words and phrases in a text that help you reason out the meaning of an unfamiliar word. Use context clues in the sentences below to choose the word from the vocabulary list on page 1418 that best completes the meaning. Then, explain how you arrived at your answers.

1. Rakesh was a(n) _______ student, earning the best grades in his division.
2. He was also a model of _______ devotion, showing much respect to his parents.
3. His father received many _______ for raising such a wonderful son.
4. Rakesh's wife was an easygoing, _______ local girl who tried hard to please her in-laws.
5. Varma could not _______ how Rakesh made him so unhappy when for years he had seemed such a devoted son.

Writing

Argumentative Text On page 1417, Anita Desai explains the original inspiration of this story. Write an **essay** comparing her original concept with the final product and arguing either that her original plan was fulfilled or that it fell short.

Prewriting Reread the story, jotting down details that do and do not conform to Desai's original concept. Evaluate whether or not the story as a whole effectively illustrates the original concept.

Drafting

- Begin by quoting Desai's original plan of capturing "that duality of human nature" and showing that "nothing is so simple as it seems."
- State whether Desai's story lives up to her plan.
- Defend your opinion by citing details from the story.

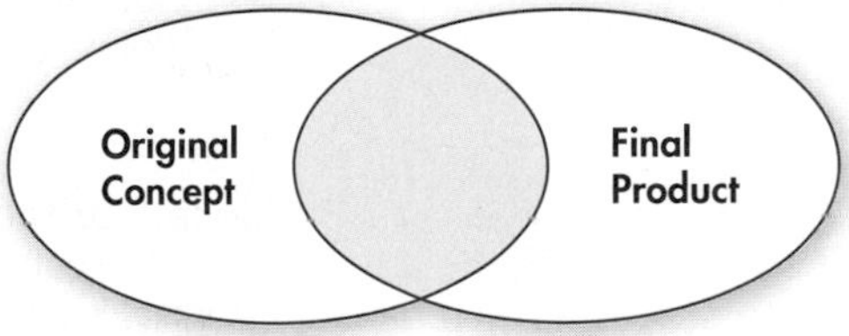

Revising If your answer to any of the following questions is "no," make suitable revisions:

- Did I accurately state Desai's original plan?
- Did I clearly state my opinion of whether or not she fulfilled her plan?
- Did I provide enough story details to support my opinion?

EXTEND/ASSESS

Answers

Vocabulary Acquisition and Use

Word Analysis

1. affiliated—connected to a group or family; sentences will vary
2. affiliate—member of a group or family; sentences will vary
3. unaffiliated—not associated with a group or family; sentences will vary
4. affiliation—membership in a group or family; sentences will vary

Vocabulary

Students should explain their answers.

1. exemplary
2. filial
3. encomiums
4. complaisant
5. fathom

Writing

1. Ask students to reread Desai's explanation for the origin of her story on page 1417.
2. To give students guidance in writing this argumentative text, provide them with the **Support for Writing Lesson** page from ***Unit 6 Resources,*** page 351.
3. Remind students to be clear about whether or not they believe Desai's story lives up to her original plan. Ask volunteers to share their thesis statements and supporting evidence. Make suggestions to help students improve the focus and organization of their responses.
4. Use the **Rubrics for Self-Assessment: Response to Literature resources** in ***Professional Development Guidebook,*** pages 250–251, to evaluate student work.
5. After students revise their argumentative texts, display their final papers around the room.

Assessment Resources

Unit 6 Resources

L1 L2 EL **Selection Test A,** pp. 356–358. Administer Test A to less advanced readers.

L3 L4 EL **Selection Test B,** pp. 359–361. Administer Test B to on-level and more advanced students.

L3 L4 **Open-Book Test,** pp. 353–355. As an alternative, give the Open Book Test.

All **Customizable Test Bank**

All **Self-tests**
Students may prepare for the Selection Test by taking the Self-test online.

PHLit Online! All assessment resources are available at **www.PHLitOnline.com.**

Contemporary British Fiction

1. Discuss with students how they have reacted to defining historical moments, social trends, and advances in technology in their own lifetimes. How have students' thoughts and attitudes been influenced because of these changes?
2. After students have discussed changes that have occurred in their own lifetimes, have them read about the influencing factors of contemporary British writers.

Background

Arundhati Roy

Born in Kerala, India, Roy is the first Indian citizen to win the prestigious Booker Prize for her first novel, *The God of Small Things*. The novel is the poetic story of Indian twins, Estha and Rahel, and what happens to the family when the laws of India's caste system are broken. Roy's Syrian mother Mary fought against India's Christian inheritance laws, so her daughter grew up in an atmosphere of social activism. Roy's novel indicts the legacy of British imperialism and Christianity in her nation as deepening the more oppressive effects of the Hindu caste system.

LITERARY HISTORY

"In this world without quiet corners, there can be no easy escapes from history, from hullabaloo, from terrible unquiet fuss."

– SALMAN RUSHDIE

Arundhati Roy

Contemporary British Fiction

A popular World War II song promised "love and laughter and peace ever after" when the world was free again. The truth was that years of air-raids, rationings, casualties, and bombed cities had worn out British citizens. The air breathed by modern writers now seemed stale and rarified. In the 1940s and 50s a new Britain began to emerge—one more critical of class privileges and more multicultural in make-up. This Britain looked different and sounded different. Contemporary British literature reflects this difference. Even more recently, British fiction has explored what it means to live in the consumerist, technological postmodern age, "wired" for fast connection—if not always for satisfying human relationships.

The Sun Never Sets on the British Empire At the height of its imperial power, Great Britain held great influence over its colonies and in world affairs. Throughout the twentieth century, British colonies demanded independence, and England's power waned. Numerous important British authors have written works that re-imagine major historical events in order to re-evaluate the effect they had on British society. Kazuo Ishiguro, a Japanese-born writer who settled in Britain at the age of five, wrote *The Remains of the Day*. Set on an English estate just before World War II and narrated by a butler who serves his master so well he cannot see the master's flaws, the novel chronicles the erosion of the British upper-class influence in domestic and world affairs. Pat Barker's trilogy of books about World War I (*Regeneration*, *The Eye in the Door*, *The Ghost Road*) shows the effects of the war on women and on members of the working class. Ian McEwan's *Atonement* sets its story in World War II and explores the British class system, showing how the life of a servant's son is forever changed by a careless lie.

"Glocal" Britain After World War II, any citizen from the British Commonwealth could immigrate to the United Kingdom, and numerous people from India, Bangladesh, South Africa, the Caribbean, Hong Kong, Nigeria, and Kenya resettled, particularly in London. England's capital city quickly became a teeming mixture of various ethnic identities, with a diversity of languages, customs, and religions. The epic novels of Salman Rushdie, an Indian-British novelist, are among the most critically acclaimed of the past 25 years. *Midnight's Children*, Rushdie's most popular work, tells the story of 1001 children born within an hour of India's independence and endowed with super powers. Rushdie's novels, which mix East and West, natural and supernatural, and the tragic and the comic, have influenced a generation of younger writers, including Zadie Smith. Smith, a woman of Jamaican and English heritage, also continues the great urban comic tradition of Charles Dickens. Her novels *White Teeth* and *On Beauty* celebrate the rich possibilities of hybrid ethnic identities and cross-cultural exchange in contemporary "glocal" (global and local) England.

Common Core State Standards

SL.11-12.1.a, SL.11-12.1.b, SL.11-12.1.c, SL.11-12.1.d
[For the full wording of the standards, see the standards chart in the front of your textbook.]

The Empire Writes Back On the other hand, writers from former colonies, such as South Africa's J. M. Coetzee and India's Arundhati Roy, depict the disfiguring legacies of colonialism in their novels. Both are considerably less optimistic about how deeply or quickly humans can recover from experiences of prejudice, conflict, or violence. Ireland, Great Britain's oldest colony and closest neighbor, continues to produced gifted writers, including Roddy Doyle, whose novels often are set in working class Dublin. Doyle has comically rewritten the pivotal event of Irish rebellion, the 1916 Easter Uprising in *A Star Called Henry*.

Hyperreality British literature also reflects the changes brought about by the computer age and by new scientific technologies. Kazuo Ishiguro's novel *Never Let Me Go* describes what seems like a fairly typical English boarding school—until the reader realizes that the students are clones. Ian McEwan's *Saturday* begins with the world's most famous 9/11 image, a plane off-course, and reflects on how life has changed in the United Kingdom since it supported the American occupation of Iraq. Nick Hornby's *About a Boy* examines the connection between loneliness and acquisitiveness, of living amid lots of great stuff—the best musical equipment, the fastest computers—but still not achieving the kind of human connections that make life meaningful.

Roddy Doyle

Zadie Smith

Speaking and Listening: Discussion

Comprehension and Collaboration With a small group, conduct a **panel discussion** on new British fiction, particularly any of the authors mentioned in this feature. As a group, choose an author and conduct research. Then, assign roles and responsibilities for each panelist. For example, decide who will introduce, moderate, and conclude the discussion.

During the discussion, work to clarify each others' ideas in a respectful manner, especially when there are disagreements. Invite questions and comments from the audience, and respond thoughtfully.

Background

Postcolonial Literature

Much of what is generally defined as postcolonial literature represents the novels, short stories, poetry, and essays written in countries formally colonized by Western nations, including Great Britain. However, some scholars consider the term misleading because some works given this label were actually written while the nations in question were still colonies. Other critics argue that the term implies that colonialism is over, when in fact many nations, though technically independent, are still culturally or economically subject to neocolonialism by wealthy industrial states. Irish writers, such as Roddy Doyle, are often included within this group as a postcolonial people because of their nationalist struggle.

Speaking and Listening: Discussion

1. Read the Panel Discussion instructions with the class. Have volunteers choose authors and play the role of those authors in the panel discussion. You may prefer to create a list of general questions or topics that the students on the panel should consider when researching their chosen authors. Here are some possible questions: What is the author's background? How does the author's identity influence his or her writing and response to the world? How has the author reacted to the trends of his or her times? Have students on the panel use these questions as a springboard to other questions that pertain to their selected authors.
2. Have students not on the panel research the authors under discussion by consulting print and online resources. Have them draw from these sources to generate questions that delve deeper into the authors' backgrounds.
3. Allow class time for the panel discussion and then lead a final discussion that ties the major themes together.

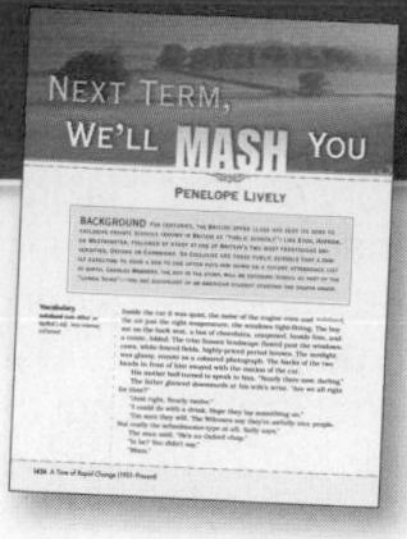

• Next Term, We'll Mash You

Lesson Pacing Guide

DAY 1 Preteach

- Administer the Reading and Vocabulary Warm-ups (*Unit 6 Resources,* pp. 362–365) as necessary.
- Introduce the Literary Analysis concept: Characterization.
- Introduce the Reading Strategy: Evaluate Social Influences of the Period.
- Build background with the author and Background features.
- Develop thematic thinking with Connecting to the Essential Question.
- Teach the selection vocabulary.

DAY 2 Preteach/Teach/Extend

- Distribute copies of the appropriate graphic organizer for the Reading Strategy (*Graphic Organizer Transparencies,* pp. 276–277).
- Distribute copies of the appropriate graphic organizer for Literary Analysis (*Graphic Organizer Transparencies,* pp. 278–279).
- Prepare students to read with the Activating Prior Knowledge activities (TE).
- Informally monitor comprehension while students read.
- Use the Reading Check questions to confirm comprehension.
- Develop students' understanding of characterization using the Literary Analysis prompts.
- Develop students' ability to evaluate social influences using the Reading Strategy prompts.
- Reinforce vocabulary with the Vocabulary notes.
- Assess students' comprehension and mastery of the skills by having them answer the Critical Reading, Literary Analysis, and Reading Strategy questions.

DAY 3 Assess

- Have students complete the Vocabulary Lesson.
- Have students complete the Writing activity, writing a magazine advertisement. (You may assign as homework.)
- Administer Selection Test A or B (*Unit 6 Resources,* pp. 374–376 or 377–379).

Common Core State Standards

Reading Literature 3. Analyze the impact of the author's choices regarding how to develop and relate elements of a story or drama.

Writing 4. Produce clear and coherent writing in which the development, organization, and style are appropriate to task, purpose, and audience.

Additional Standards Practice
***Common Core Companion,* pp. 28–35; 219–220**

Daily Block Scheduling
Each day in this Lesson Pacing Guide represents a 40–50 minute period. Teachers using block scheduling may combine days to revise pacing. In addition, teachers may differentiate and support core instruction by integrating components for extended and intensive support as students require. See the Guide to Selected Leveled Resources (facing page).

Guide to Selected Leveled Resources

RTI Tier 1 (students performing on level)

			Next Term, We'll Mash You
Warm Up	Whole class instruction; Group work	**Practice, model,** and **monitor** fluency, working **with the whole class** or **in groups.**	**Vocabulary** and **Reading Warm-ups B,** ***Unit 6 Resources,*** pp. 380–381, 383
Comprehension/Skills	Whole class instruction; Group work; Independent work	**Support** and **monitor** comprehension and skills development, having students complete the activities, graphic organizers, and interactive prompts **independently** or **as a class.**	• ***Reader's Notebook,*** adapted instruction and full selection EL ***Reader's Notebook: English Learner's Version,*** adapted instruction and adapted selection • **Reading Strategy Graphic Organizer B,** ***Graphic Organizer Transparencies,*** p. 291 • **Literary Analysis Graphic Organizer B,** ***Graphic Organizer Transparencies,*** p. 293
Monitor Progress	Assessment	**Monitor** student progress with the differentiated curriculum-based assessment in the *Unit Resources.*	• **Selection Test B,** ***Unit 6 Resources,*** pp. 395–397 • **Open-Book Test,** ***Unit 6 Resources,*** pp. 389–391

RTI Tier 2 (students requiring intervention)

			Next Term, We'll Mash You
Warm Up	Group work; One-on-one teaching	**Practice, model,** and **monitor** fluency **in groups** or **with individuals.**	• **Vocabulary and Reading Warm-ups A,** ***Unit 6 Resources,*** pp. 380–382 • ***Hear It!*** **Audio CD (adapted text)**
Comprehension/Skills	Group work; One-on-one teaching	• **Support** and **monitor** comprehension and skills development, working **in small groups** or **with individuals.** • As students complete the selection in the appropriate version of the *Reader's Notebook,* **monitor** comprehension frequently with group questions and individual instruction. • **Model** strategies while guiding students in completing the activities and prompts in the *Reader's Notebook,* as well as the graphic organizers. • **Practice** skills and **monitor** mastery with the *Reading Kit* worksheets.	• ***Reader's Notebook: Adapted Version,*** adapted instruction and adapted selection EL ***Reader's Notebook: English Learner's Version,*** adapted instruction and adapted selection • **Reading Strategy Graphic Organizer A,** ***Graphic Organizer Transparencies,*** p. 290 • **Literary Analysis Graphic Organizer A,** ***Graphic Organizer Transparencies,*** p. 292 • ***Reading Kit,*** Practice worksheets
Monitor Progress	Assessment	**Monitor** student progress with the differentiated curriculum-based assessment in the *Unit Resources* and in the *Reading Kit.*	• **Selection Test A,** ***Unit 6 Resources,*** pp. 392–394 • ***Reading Kit,*** Assess worksheets

TIER 3 Tier 3 intervention may require consultation with the student's special-education or dyslexia specialist. For additional support, see the Tier 2 activities and resources listed above.

One-on-one teaching **Group work** **Whole class instruction** **Independent work** **A Assessment**

For a complete guide to selection support, including support for Advanced students, see the Overview of Resources in the frontmatter.

• Next Term, We'll Mash You

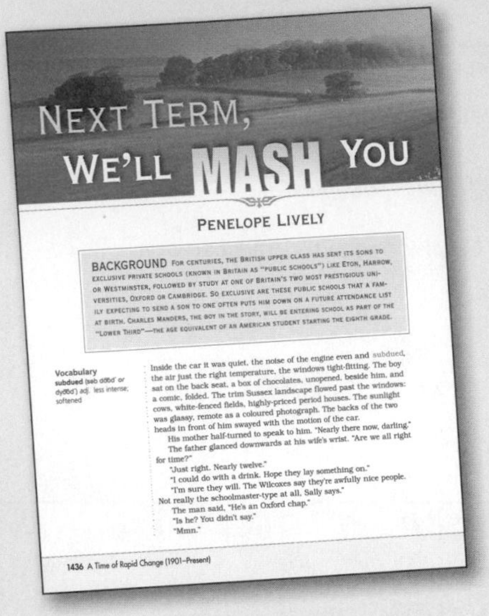

NEXT TERM, WE'LL MASH YOU

PENELOPE LIVELY

BACKGROUND For centuries, the British upper class has sent its sons to exclusive private schools (known in Britain as "public schools") like Eton, Harrow, or Westminster, followed by study at one of Britain's two most prestigious universities, Oxford or Cambridge. So exclusive are these public schools that a family expecting to send a son to one often puts him down on a future attendance list at birth. Charles Manders, the boy in the story, will be entering school as part of the "Lower Third"—the age equivalent of an American student starting the eighth grade.

Vocabulary
subdued (səb dōōd' or dyōōd') adj. less intense; softened

Inside the car it was quiet, the noise of the engine even and subdued, the air just the right temperature, the windows tight-fitting. The boy sat on the back seat, a box of chocolates, unopened, beside him, and a comic, folded. The trim Sussex landscape flowed past the windows: cows, white-fenced fields, highly-priced period houses. The sunlight was glassy, remote as a coloured photograph. The backs of the two heads in front of him swayed with the motion of the car.

His mother half-turned to speak to him. "Nearly there now, darling."

The father glanced downwards at his wife's wrist. "Are we all right for time?"

"Just right. Nearly twelve."

"I could do with a drink. Hope they lay something on."

"I'm sure they will. The Wilcoxes say they're awfully nice people. Not really the schoolmaster-type at all, Sally says."

The man said, "He's an Oxford chap."

"Is he? You didn't say."

"Mmn."

1436 A Time of Rapid Change (1901–Present)

RESOURCES FOR:

- L1 Special-Needs Students
- L2 Below-Level Students (Tier 2)
- L3 On-Level Students (Tier 1)
- L4 Advanced Students (Tier 1)
- EL English Learners
- All All Students

Vocabulary/Fluency/Prior Knowledge

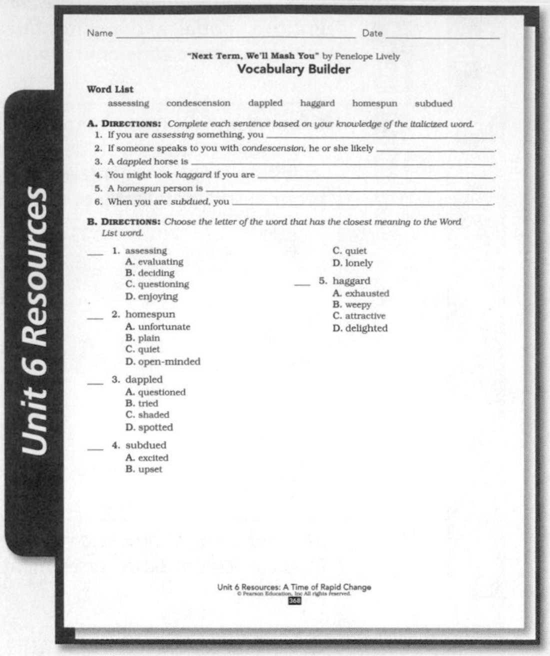

Unit 6 Resources

Name ______________________ Date ______________

"Next Term, We'll Mash You" by Penelope Lively
Vocabulary Builder

Word List

assessing condescension dappled haggard homespun subdued

A. DIRECTIONS: *Complete each sentence based on your knowledge of the italicized word.*

1. If you are *assessing* something, you ______________________.
2. If someone speaks to you with *condescension,* he or she likely ______________________.
3. A *dappled* horse is ______________________.
4. You might look *haggard* if you are ______________________.
5. A *homespun* person is ______________________.
6. When you are *subdued,* you ______________________.

B. DIRECTIONS: *Choose the letter of the word that has the closest meaning to the Word List word.*

___ 1. assessing
A. evaluating
B. deciding
C. questioning
D. enjoying

___ 2. homespun
A. unfortunate
B. plain
C. quiet
D. open-minded

___ 3. dappled
A. questioned
B. tried
C. shaded
D. spotted

___ 4. subdued
A. excited
B. upset
C. quiet
D. lonely

___ 5. haggard
A. exhausted
B. weepy
C. attractive
D. delighted

Unit 6 Resources: A Time of Rapid Change
© Pearson Education, Inc. All rights reserved.
368

All **Vocabulary Builder,** p. 368

Also available for these selections:

EL L1 L2 **Vocabulary Warm-ups A and B,** pp. 362–363

EL L1 L2 **Reading Warm-ups A and B,** pp. 362–365

Reader's Notebooks

Pre- and postreading pages for this selection appear in an interactive format in the *Reader's Notebooks.* Each *Notebook* is differentiated for a different group of learners.
The selections in the Adapted and English Learner's versions are abridged.

L2 L3 ***Reader's Notebook***

L1 ***Reader's Notebook: Adapted Version***

EL ***Reader's Notebook: English Learner's Version***

EL ***Reader's Notebook: Spanish Version***

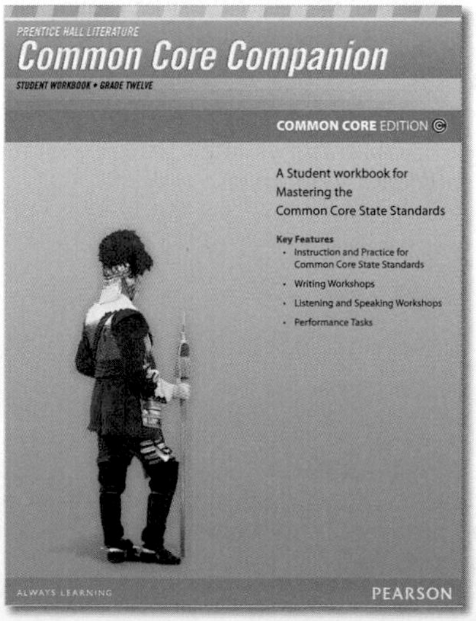

Common Core Companion

Additional instruction and practice for each Common Core State Standard

Selection Support

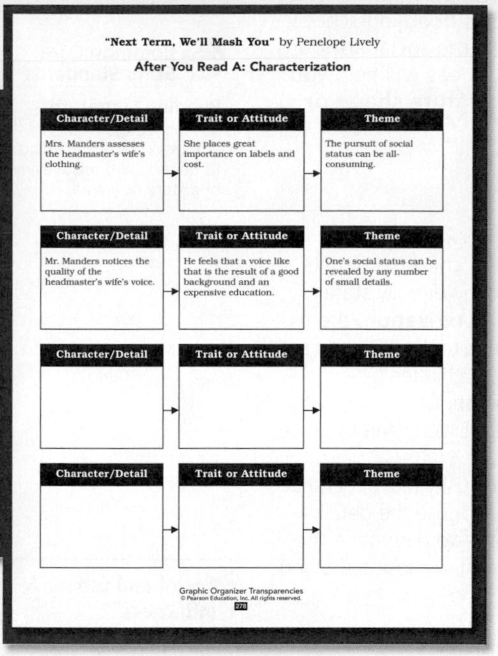

"Next Term, We'll Mash You" by Penelope Lively

After You Read A: Characterization

Character/Detail	Trait or Attitude	Theme
Mrs. Manders assesses the headmaster's wife's clothing.	She places great importance on labels and cost.	The pursuit of social status can be all-consuming.
Mr. Manders notices the quality of the headmaster's wife's voice.	He feels that a voice like that is the result of a good background and an expensive education.	One's social status can be revealed by any number of small details.

Graphic Organizer Transparencies
© Pearson Education, Inc. All rights reserved.
278

Graphic Organizer Transparencies

L1 L2 **Literary Analysis: Graphic Organizer A,** (partially filled in), p. 278

Also available for these selections:

L1 L2 **Reading: Graphic Organizer A,** p. 276

EL L3 **Reading: Graphic Organizer B,** p. 277

EL L3 **Literary Analysis: Graphic Organizer B,** p. 279

Skills Development/Extension

Unit 6 Resources

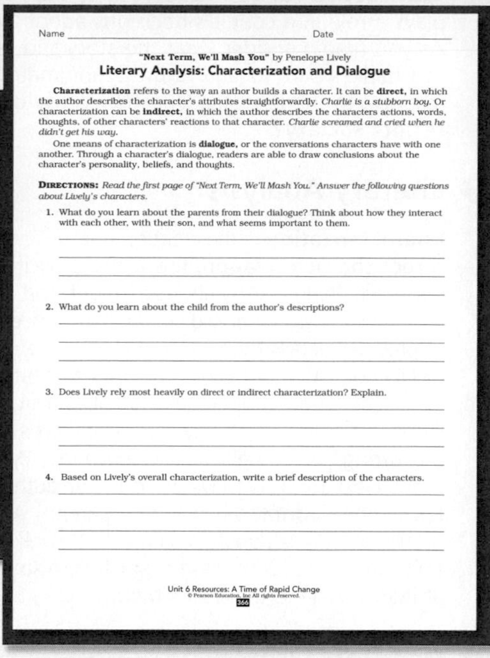

Name ______ Date ______

"Next Term, We'll Mash You" by Penelope Lively

Literary Analysis: Characterization and Dialogue

Characterization refers to the way an author builds a character. It can be **direct**, in which the author describes the character's attributes straightforwardly. *Charlie is a stubborn boy.* Or characterization can be **indirect**, in which the author describes the characters actions, words, thoughts, of other characters' reactions to that character. *Charlie screamed and cried when he didn't get his way.*

One means of characterization is **dialogue**, or the conversations characters have with one another. Through a character's dialogue, readers are able to draw conclusions about the character's personality, beliefs, and thoughts.

Directions: *Read the first page of "Next Term, We'll Mash You." Answer the following questions about Lively's characters.*

1. What do you learn about the parents from their dialogue? Think about how they interact with each other, with their son, and what seems important to them.
2. What do you learn about the child from the author's descriptions?
3. Does Lively rely most heavily on direct or indirect characterization? Explain.
4. Based on Lively's overall characterization, write a brief description of the characters.

Unit 6 Resources: A Time of Rapid Change
© Pearson Education, Inc. All rights reserved.
366

All **Literary Analysis: Characterization,** p. 366

Also available for these selections:

All **Reading: Evaluate Social Influences of the Period,** p. 367

EL L3 L4 **Support for Writing,** p. 369

L4 **Enrichment,** p. 370

Assessment

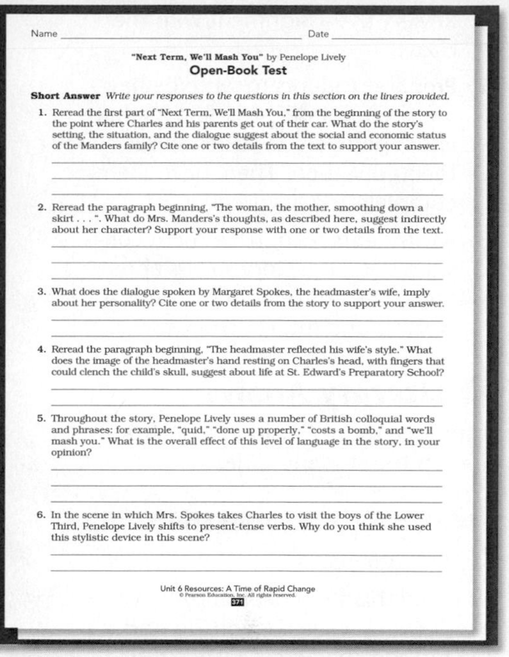

Name ______ Date ______

"Next Term, We'll Mash You" by Penelope Lively

Open-Book Test

Short Answer *Write your responses to the questions in this section on the lines provided.*

1. Reread the first part of "Next Term, We'll Mash You," from the beginning of the story to the point where Charles and his parents get out of their car. What do the story's setting, the situation, and the dialogue suggest about the social and economic status of the Manders family? Cite one or two details from the text to support your answer.
2. Reread the paragraph beginning, "The woman, the mother, smoothing down a skirt . . .". What do Mrs. Manders's thoughts, as described here, suggest indirectly about her character? Support your response with one or two details from the text.
3. What does the dialogue spoken by Margaret Spokes, the headmaster's wife, imply about her personality? Cite one or two details from the story to support your answer.
4. Reread the paragraph beginning, "The headmaster reflected his wife's style." What does the image of the headmaster's hand resting on Charles's head, with fingers that could clench the child's skull, suggest about life at St. Edward's Preparatory School?
5. Throughout the story, Penelope Lively uses a number of British colloquial words and phrases: for example, "quid," "done up properly," "costs a bomb," and "we'll mash you." What is the overall effect of this level of language in the story, in your opinion?
6. In the scene in which Mrs. Spokes takes Charles to visit the boys of the Lower Third, Penelope Lively shifts to present-tense verbs. Why do you think she used this stylistic device in this scene?

Unit 6 Resources: A Time of Rapid Change
© Pearson Education, Inc. All rights reserved.
371

L3 L4 **Open-Book Test,** pp. 371–373

Also available for these selections:

EL L1 L2 **Selection Test A,** pp. 374–376

EL L3 L4 **Selection Test B,** pp. 377–379

PHLit Online!
www.PHLitOnline.com

- complete narrated selection text
- a thematically related video with writing prompt
- an interactive graphic organizer
- highlighting feature
- access to all student print resources, adapted to individual student needs
- Spanish and English summaries
- adapted selection translations in Spanish

Online Resources: All print materials are also available online.

Get Connected! (thematic video with writing prompt)

Also available:

Background Video
All videos are available in Spanish.

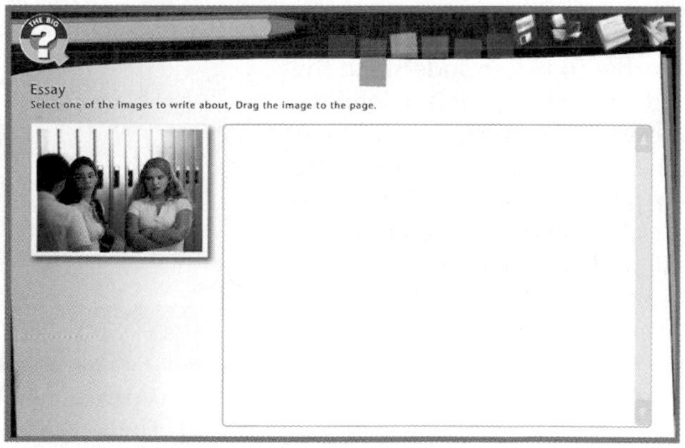

Writer's Journal (with graphics feature)

Also available:

Vocabulary Central (tools and activities for studying vocabulary)

PRETEACH

1 Connecting to the Essential Question

1. Review the assignment with the class.
2. Prepare students to write by having them list different factors that affect people's decisions about their education. Then, have them complete the assignment.
3. As students read, have them consider what the story shows about the social attitudes of Charles's parents and future schoolmates.

2 Literary Analysis

Introduce the skill using the instruction on the student page.

Think Aloud: Model the Skill

Say to students:

I know this story deals mostly with indirect characterization. To understand the characters in this story, I will have to pay special attention to what they say, how they act, and what they look like.

3 Reading Strategy

1. Introduce the skill using the instruction on the student page.
2. Give students a copy of **Reading Strategy Graphic Organizer B,** page 277 in ***Graphic Organizer Transparencies,*** to fill out as they read.

Think Aloud: Model the Skill

Say to students:

In order to better understand the author's message, it is helpful to know what was happening during the time period the author wrote the piece. Knowing about the social influences of the time period will probably help me understand the message Lively is trying to send by writing this story.

4 Vocabulary

1. Pronounce each word, giving its definition, and have students say it aloud.
2. For more guidance, see the ***Classroom Strategies and Teaching Routines*** card for introducing vocabulary.

Before You Read *Next Term, We'll Mash You*

1 Connecting to the Essential Question In this story, social status plays a role in a couple's decisions about their son's boarding school. As you read, consider what the story shows about the social attitudes of Charlie's parents and future schoolmates. Your ideas will help you respond to the Essential Question: **How does literature shape or reflect society?**

Common Core State Standards

Reading Literature
3. Analyze the impact of the author's choices regarding how to develop and relate elements of a story or drama.

2 Literary Analysis

Characterization is the creation and development of a character. In **direct characterization,** the writer explicitly states a character's traits. For example, in a story about a knight, the author may directly state "The knight was cruel and violent." In **indirect characterization,** the writer provides details from which you infer the character's traits: "'Do as I say or I'll chop off your heads,' the knight sneered to the children."

Characterization often helps point to a story's **theme.** For example, the story about the knight may express a theme such as "Cruelty and violence are wrong" or "Cruelty and violence may backfire."

In "Next Term, We'll Mash You," the author uses mostly indirect characterization to portray a boy and his parents. As you read, use the details—particularly the *dialogue,* or characters' spoken words—to determine the traits and attitudes of these characters. Also consider how those traits and attitudes relate to the story's theme.

3 Reading Strategy

Preparing to Read Complex Texts The society in which a work is produced or set usually influences that work. When you **evaluate social influences of the period,** you determine the value of social trends, ideas, or attitudes that a work's characters, plot, or setting reveals. Use a diagram like this to help you evaluate the contemporary British social influences in Lively's story.

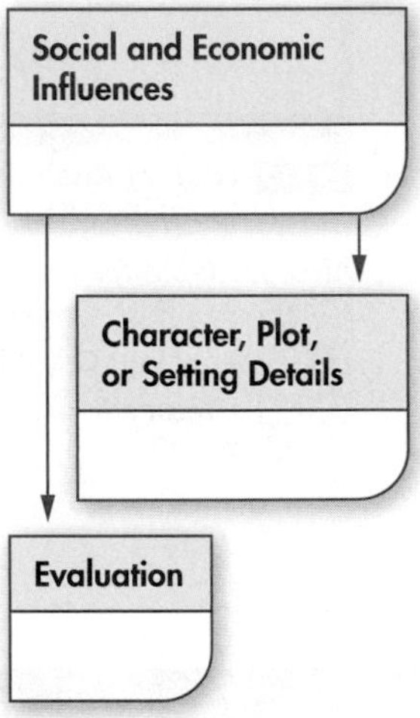

4 Vocabulary

subdued (səb do͞od′ *or* dyo͞od′) *adj.* less intense; softened (p. 1436)

dappled (dap′ əld) *adj.* covered with spots of shade or anything else of a different color (p. 1438)

assessing (ə ses′ iŋ) *v.* determining the value of (p. 1439)

homespun (hōm′ spun′) *adj.* plain; homely (p. 1439)

condescension (kän′ di sen′ shən) *n.* an attitude of lowering oneself to deal with others not considered one's equal; haughtiness (p. 1440)

haggard (hag′ ərd) *adj.* wild-eyed or tired looking; gaunt (p. 1442)

PHLit Online! www.PHLitOnline.com

Vocabulary Development

Vocabulary Knowledge Rating

Create a **Vocabulary Knowledge Rating Chart** (***Professional Development Guidebook,*** p. 33) for the vocabulary words on the student page. Give each student a copy of the chart with the words on it. Read the words aloud, and have students mark their ratings in the Before Reading column. Urge students to attend to these words as they read and discuss the selection.

In order to gauge how much instruction you need to provide, tally how many students are confident in their knowledge of each word. As students read, point out the words and their context.

PHLit Online! **Vocabulary Central,** featuring tools and activities for studying vocabulary, is available online at **www.PHLitOnline.com.**

❺ PENELOPE LIVELY
(B. 1933)

Author of "Next Term, We'll Mash You"

One of contemporary Britain's most acclaimed fiction writers, Penelope Lively was born in Cairo, Egypt, when it was still an outpost of the British Empire. In 1945, when she was twelve years old, her parents sent her to a boarding school in Sussex, an English county south of London. For someone who had grown up in the multicultural world of British Egypt, England seemed an alien place. "There were all sorts of codes that I couldn't follow," she recalls; "I was always getting things wrong." Only later did Lively come to realize that being forced to observe English society as an outsider probably helped hone her skills as a writer.

A Late Bloomer After studying history in college, Lively married and began to raise a family. She gave no thought to becoming a writer until, in her late thirties, she tried her hand at writing a book for children. Several more children's books followed until, in 1977, she published her first novel for adults, *The Road to Lichfield*. That book, like much of Lively's fiction, explores the relationship between memory and the past, a subject that had interested Lively since her college days as a student of history.

Crafting the Past Lively sets some of her fiction in the Egypt of her childhood and has also written a nonfiction memoir about growing up there. Her 1987 novel *Moon Tiger*, which earned her Britain's prestigious Booker Prize, is about a historian who grew up in Egypt and decides to write a novel about it. Popular with critics as well as everyday readers, Lively is often praised for her polished, evocative prose, in which not a word is wasted. "Next Term, We'll Mash You" is from her 1986 story collection *Pack of Cards*.

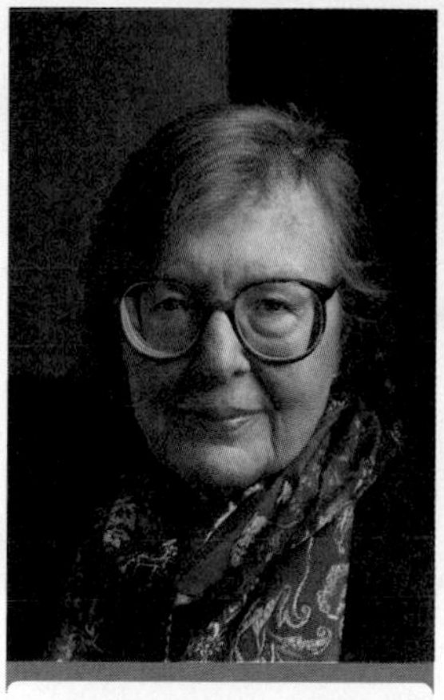

"IN WRITING FICTION I AM TRYING TO IMPOSE ORDER UPON CHAOS, TO GIVE STRUCTURE AND MEANING TO WHAT IS APPARENTLY RANDOM."

Daily Bellringer

For each class during which you will teach this selection, have students complete one of the five activities for the appropriate week in the *Daily Bellringer Activities* booklet.

Multidraft Reading

To assist struggling readers and to enhance reading for all, assign the text in chunks, as warranted by length, and apply multidraft reading protocols. For each reading, have students set the purpose indicated:

- **First reading**—identifying key ideas and details and answering any Reading Checks.
- **Second reading**—analyzing craft and structure and responding to the side-column prompts.
- **Third reading**—integrating knowledge and ideas, connecting to other texts and the world, and answering the end-of-selection questions.

For more guidance, refer to the ***Classroom Strategies and Teaching Routines*** card on Multidraft Reading.

❺ Background

The British Class System

British society is roughly divided into three classes. The upper class consists of old families, aristocrats, and those with inherited wealth. The upper class are defined by their education and title, as well as their pastimes. The majority of the population makes up the middle class, which includes businesspeople, shop owners, industrialists, and people with similar professions. The working class are laborers who work in the manufacturing, mining, and agricultural industries. It is usually evident to which class one belongs by the way he or she dresses, speaks, educates his or her children, or even by what foods are eaten.

PHLit Online!
www.PHLitOnline.com

Teaching From Technology

Preparing to Read
Go to **www.PHLitOnline.com** and display the ***Get Connected!*** slide show for this selection. Have the class brainstorm responses to the writing prompt, entering ideas in the interactive journal. Then, have students complete their written responses as homework.

To build background, display the Background and More About the Author features.

Using the Interactive Text
Go to **www.PHLitOnline.com** and display the **Enriched Online Student Edition.** As the class reads the selection or listens to the narration, record answers to side-column prompts using the graphic organizers accessible on the interactive page. Alternatively, have students use the online edition individually, answering the prompts as they read.

TEACH

1 About the Selection

"Next Term, We'll Mash You" is about a young boy named Charles whose parents are trying to find a good school for him to attend. This story focuses on their visit to St. Edward's Preparatory School, where the family meets the headmaster and his wife. Meanwhile, Charles meets the schoolboys and finds out what he is in for. The story makes a strong statement about the way class influenced the society of the period.

2 Activating Prior Knowledge

Ask students to write a paragraph about how they would feel if their parents decided which schools they attended, especially if they based their decisions solely on appearances. Such is the case for the main character in this story. Have students keep these thoughts in mind as they read the story.

Concept Connector →

Tell students they will return to their responses after reading the selection.

1 2 Next Term, We'll MASH You

Penelope Lively

> **BACKGROUND** For centuries, the British upper class has sent its sons to exclusive private schools (known in Britain as "public schools") like Eton, Harrow, or Westminster, followed by study at one of Britain's two most prestigious universities, Oxford or Cambridge. So exclusive are these public schools that a family expecting to send a son to one often puts him down on a future attendance list at birth. Charles Manders, the boy in the story, will be entering school as part of the "Lower Third"—the age equivalent of an American student starting the eighth grade.

Vocabulary
subdued (səb do͞od′ *or* dyo͞od′) *adj.* less intense; softened

Inside the car it was quiet, the noise of the engine even and **subdued**, the air just the right temperature, the windows tight-fitting. The boy sat on the back seat, a box of chocolates, unopened, beside him, and a comic, folded. The trim Sussex landscape flowed past the windows: cows, white-fenced fields, highly-priced period houses. The sunlight was glassy, remote as a coloured photograph. The backs of the two heads in front of him swayed with the motion of the car.

His mother half-turned to speak to him. "Nearly there now, darling."

The father glanced downwards at his wife's wrist. "Are we all right for time?"

"Just right. Nearly twelve."

"I could do with a drink. Hope they lay something on."

"I'm sure they will. The Wilcoxes say they're awfully nice people. Not really the schoolmaster-type at all, Sally says."

The man said, "He's an Oxford chap."

"Is he? You didn't say."

"Mmn."

Text Complexity Rubric

Next Term, We'll Mash You			
Qualitative Measures			
Context/Knowledge Demands	Contemporary story; cultural knowledge demands 1 2 ③ 4 5		
Structure/Language Clarity	Anglicisms and British slang; dialogue 1 ② 3 4 5		
Levels of Meaning	Accessible (social status; parent-child relationships) 1 2 ③ 4 5		
Quantitative Measures			
Lexile	780L	**Text Length**	1,844 words
Overall Complexity	**More accessible**		

Reader and Task Suggestions

Preparing to Read the Text

- Using the Background on TE p. 1435, explain that, despite far more social mobility today, Britain still has a class system. To be upper class, one must go to the "proper" school.
- Discuss the role of status in determining what some parents want for their children.
- Guide students to use Multidraft Reading strategies (TE p. 1435).

Leveled Tasks

Context/Knowledge Demands: If students will have difficulty with context, have them focus on the mother's and the son's impressions of the school. Then, have students decide what the contrast suggests about social status.

Analyzing: If students will not have difficulty with context, have them analyze how contrasting family views point to the story's theme.

"Of course, the fees are that much higher than the Seaford place." 3

"Fifty quid[1] or so. We'll have to see."

The car turned right, between white gates and high, dark, tight-clipped hedges. The whisper of the road under the tyres changed to the crunch of gravel. The child, staring sideways, read black lettering on a white board: "St Edward's Preparatory School. Please Drive Slowly'. He shifted on the seat, and the leather sucked at the bare skin under his knees, stinging.

The mother said, "It's a lovely place. Those must be the playing-fields. Look, darling, there are some of the boys.' She clicked open her handbag, and the sun caught her mirror and flashed in the child's eyes; the comb went through her hair and he saw the grooves it left, neat as distant ploughing.

"Come on, then, Charles, out you get."

The building was red brick, early nineteenth century, spreading out long arms in which windows glittered blackly. Flowers, trapped in neat beds, were alternate red and white. They went up the steps, the man, the woman, and the child two paces behind.

4 The woman, the mother, smoothing down a skirt that would be ridged from sitting, thought: I like the way they've got the maid all done up properly. The little white apron and all that. She's foreign, I suppose. Au pair.[2] Very nice. If he comes here there'll be Speech Days[3] and that kind of thing. Sally Wilcox says it's quite dressy—she got that cream linen coat for coming down here. You can see why it costs a bomb. Great big grounds and only an hour and a half from London.

1. **quid** *n.* slang for pounds, the chief monetary unit of Britain.
2. **Au pair** (ō per′) someone—often a student from a foreign country—who helps with the housework in exchange for room and board.
3. **Speech Days** special days for presenting awards in schools, usually marked by ceremony and speeches.

3 **▲ Critical Viewing**
Compare and contrast the author's description of the landscape in the first paragraph with the landscape shown in this image. **[Compare and Contrast]**

Literary Analysis
Characterization and Theme What do the mother's thoughts about the school reveal about the kind of person she is? To what story theme might this characterization point?

5 **Reading Check**

Where are Charles's parents taking him?

3 Critical Viewing

Possible response: The landscape is similar because of the lush, trim grassy fields; however, the picture does not feature the fences and houses mentioned in the story.

4 Literary Analysis

Characterization and Theme

1. Have students reread the last paragraph on page 1437.
2. Remind students that indirect characterization is a way of describing a character without providing a direct description. The reader must infer character traits using details from the text.
3. Then, **ask** students the Literary Analysis question: What do the mother's thoughts about the school reveal about the kind of person she is?
   Possible response: The mother's thoughts reveal how important appearances are for her. She is very superficial and feels that the more expensive and attractive the school, the better it is.
   Ask: To what story theme might this characterization point?
   Possible response: Her characterization might point to the theme of being improperly concerned about education and too concerned with prestige and appearances.

5 Reading Check

Answer: Charles's parents are taking him to visit St. Edward's Preparatory School.

Differentiated Instruction for Universal Access

Support for Special-Needs Students
Have students complete the **Before You Read** and the **Making Connections** pages for this selection in the ***Reader's Notebook: Adapted Version.*** These pages provide an abbreviated skills instruction, a selection summary, the **Before You Read** graphic organizer, and a **Note-taking Guide.**

Support for Less Proficient Readers
Have students complete the **Before You Read** and the **Making Connections** pages for this selection in the ***Reader's Notebook.*** These pages provide an abbreviated skills instruction, a selection summary, the **Before You Read** graphic organizer, and a **Note-taking Guide.**

EL **Support for English Learners**
Have students complete the **Before You Read** and the **Making Connections** pages for this selection in the ***Reader's Notebook: English Learner's Version.*** These pages provide additional vocabulary, vocabulary skills, and vocabulary practice, along with a **Getting Ready to Read** activity.

PHLit Online!
This selection is available in interactive format in the **Enriched Online Student Edition** at **www.PHLitOnline.com,** which includes a thematically related video with writing prompt and an interactive graphic organizer.

❻ Critical Viewing

Possible response: The furniture and decorations look expensive and regal. A person might get the impression that the owners of the place are wealthy and prestigious.

❼ Critical Thinking

Infer

1. Have a volunteer read aloud the first paragraph on page 1438. Remind them that this is a description of a room in the school.
2. Inform the students that *Country Life, The Field,* and *The Economist* are magazines. The first two are well-known British magazines geared toward upper-class rural pursuits. The third is a British-based international magazine that covers serious political and economic issues and is widely read by people of influence.
3. **Ask** students: What information about the school can you glean from the detailed description of the room and its view?
   Possible answer: The room seems somewhat noble and refined because of the books and leather chairs. The upper-class magazines indicate that the school is distinguished and reputable. The view tells me the school is in a high-class area.
4. **Ask:** Why do you think the author included these specific details?
   Possible response: The author included these details to further reinforce this society's emphasis on material and superficial ideals.

❻ ▲ **Critical Viewing**
What sort of effect would a room like the one shown ❼ have on a person's perception of a new place? **[Relate]**

Vocabulary
dappled (dap′ əld) *adj.* covered with spots of shade or anything else of a different color

They went into a room looking out into a terrace. Beyond, **dappled** lawns, gently shifting trees, black and white cows grazing behind iron railings. Books, leather chairs, a table with magazines—*Country Life, The Field, The Economist.* "Please, if you would wait here. The Headmaster won't be long."

Alone, they sat, inspected. "I like the atmosphere, don't you, John?"

"Very pleasant, yes. Four hundred a term, near enough. You can tell it's a cut above the Seaford place, though, or the one at St Albans. Bob Wilcox says quite a few City people send their boys here. One or two of the merchant bankers, those kind of people. It's the sort of contact that would do no harm at all. You meet someone, get talking at a cricket match[4] or what have you . . . Not at all a bad thing."

"All right, Charles? You didn't get sick in the car, did you?"

The child had black hair, slicked down smooth to his head. His ears, too large, jutted out, transparent in the light from the window, laced with tiny, delicate veins. His clothes had the shine and crease of newness. He looked at the books, the dark brown pictures, his parents, said nothing.

"Come here, let me tidy your hair."

The door opened. The child hesitated, stood up, sat, then rose again with his father.

"Mr and Mrs Manders? How very nice to meet you—I'm Margaret Spokes, and will you please forgive my husband who is tied up with some wretch who broke the cricket pavilion window and will be just a few more minutes. We try to be organised but a schoolmaster's day is

"I LIKE THE ATMOSPHERE, DON'T YOU, JOHN?"

4. **cricket match** game of cricket, a popular British outdoor sport played with balls and bats on an area called a pitch.

Think Aloud

Vocabulary: Using Context
Direct students' attention to the word *geniality* at the bottom of page 1439. Use the following "think aloud" to model the skill of using context to infer the meaning of the word. Say to students:

I may not know the meaning of the word *geniality.* When I read the sentence, however, I realize that the writer is using it to describe the headmaster's attitude. The sentence says his *geniality* is free of any *condescension.* We just learned that *condescension* is a demeaning attitude. *Geniality* must have something to do with his attitude. The next sentence expresses his deep regret at having kept the parents waiting. Expressing a genuine apology is a sign of a good person. This man must have a good attitude. I think *geniality* is a good and friendly attitude.

always just that bit unpredictable. Do please sit down and what will you have to revive you after that beastly drive? You live in Finchley, is that right?"

"Hampstead, really," said the mother. "Sherry would be lovely." She worked over the headmaster's wife from shoes to hairstyle, pricing and assessing. Shoes old but expensive—Russell and Bromley. Good skirt. Blouse could be Marks and Sparks[5]—not sure. Real pearls. Super Victorian ring. She's not gone to any particular trouble—that's just what she'd wear anyway. You can be confident, with a voice like that, of course. Sally Wilcox says she knows all sorts of people.

The headmaster's wife said, "I don't know how much you know about us. Prospectuses[6] don't tell you a thing, do they? We'll look round everything in a minute, when you've had a chat with my husband. I gather you're friends of the Wilcoxes, by the way. I'm awfully fond of Simon—he's down for Winchester, of course, but I expect you know that."

The mother smiled over her sherry. Oh, I know that all right. Sally Wilcox doesn't let you forget that.

"And this is Charles? My dear, we've been forgetting all about you! In a minute I'm going to borrow Charles and take him off to meet some of the boys because after all you're choosing a school for him,
8 aren't you, and not for you, so he ought to know what he might be letting himself in for and it shows we've got nothing to hide."

The parents laughed. The father, sherry warming his guts, thought that this was an amusing woman. Not attractive, of course, a bit homespun, but impressive all the same. Partly the voice, of course; it takes a bloody expensive education to produce a voice like that. And other things, of course. Background and all that stuff.

"I think I can hear the thud of the Fourth Form coming in from games, which means my husband is on the way, and then I shall leave you with him while I take Charles off to the common-room."[7]

For a moment the three adults centred on the child, looking, judging. The mother said, "He looks so hideously pale, compared to those boys we saw outside."

"My dear, that's London, isn't it? You just have to get them out, to get some colour into them. Ah, here's James. James—Mr and Mrs Manders. You remember, Bob Wilcox was mentioning at Sports Day . . ."

The headmaster reflected his wife's style, like paired cards in Happy Families.[8] His clothes were mature rather than old, his skin well-scrubbed, his shoes clean, his geniality untainted by the least

---

5. **Marks and Sparks** nickname for Marks & Spencer, well-known British department store chain that generally sells less expensive items than, for example, the shoe store Russell and Bromley.
6. **Prospectuses** (prō *or* prə spek′ təs əz) *n.* statements, often in booklet form, outlining the attractions of a business or an institution such as a school.
7. **common-room** room where students relax and socialize.
8. **Happy Families** British version of the card game Go Fish, played with a special deck of forty-four cards depicting the mother, father, son, and daughter in eleven families.

Vocabulary
assessing (ə ses′ iŋ) *v.* determining the value of

Vocabulary
homespun (hōm′ spun′) *adj.* plain; homely

9 **Reading Check**

Where are the Manders from?

8 Critical Thinking

Modify

1. After students read pages 1438–1439, ask them to recall the parents' thoughts about the appearances of the headmaster and his wife.
2. Have students imagine that instead of being well-spoken, confident, and dressed nicely, the headmaster and his wife wore less classy clothes, were a bit more reserved, and did not show signs of such an impressive background.
3. **Ask** students how they think the parents would have reacted toward the headmaster and his wife in those circumstances. **Possible response:** The parents most likely would have acted completely differently if the headmaster and his wife put off a different, slightly less classy first impression. If the parents were not impressed by their clothes and mien, they probably would not be impressed by the school as a whole.
4. **Ask** them how this helps support one of the story's themes. **Possible response:** This supports the theme of superficiality and the flaws of the educational system.

9 Reading Check

Answer: The Manders are from Hampstead.

⑩ Critical Viewing

Possible response: The uniforms and buildings make me think this is a more expensive school. Charles might have to deal with a strict curriculum and tense atmosphere, much like the one he would have to face if he were to attend the school in the story.

⑪ Literary Analysis

Characterization

1. Read aloud to the students the bracketed paragraphs starting with the one that begins "And the child is borne away…" to the one ending with "She is gone."
2. **Ask** students the Literary Analysis question: What do the details about the headmaster's wife and the students' behavior toward her show about the kind of person she is?
   Answer: There is a lot of attention given to her strong voice and how confident she is. When she enters the room, "silence fall[s]," and the students act very obediently and nicely while she is there, even opening and closing the door for her. She must be very strict to be able to elicit such a response from children who turn around and talk the way they do to Charles.

Vocabulary
condescension
(kän′ di sen′ shən) *n.* an attitude of lowering oneself to deal with others not considered one's equal; haughtiness

⑩ ▲ **Critical Viewing**
What do you think Charles's experience will be in a school like the one shown in these photographs? **[Speculate]**

Literary Analysis
Characterization
What do the details about the headmaster's wife and the students' behavior toward her show about the kind of person she is?

⑧ condescension. He was genuinely sorry to have kept them waiting, but in this business one lurches from one minor crisis to the next . . . And this is Charles? Hello, there, Charles. His large hand rested for a moment on the child's head, quite extinguishing the thin, dark hair. It was as though he had but to clench his fingers to crush the skull. But he took his hand away and moved the parents to the window, to observe the mutilated cricket pavilion, with indulgent laughter.

And the child is borne away by the headmaster's wife. She never touches him or tells him to come, but simply bears him away like some relentless tide, down corridors and through swinging glass doors, towing him like a frail craft, not bothering to look back to see if he is following, confident in the strength of magnetism, or obedience.

And delivers him to a room where boys are scattered among inky tables and rungless chairs and sprawled on a mangy carpet. There is a scampering, and a rising, and a silence falling, as she opens the door.

⑪ "Now this is the Lower Third, Charles, who you'd be with if you come to us in September. Boys, this is Charles Manders, and I want you to tell him all about things and answer any questions he wants to ask. You can believe about half of what they say, Charles, and they will tell you the most fearful lies about the food, which is excellent."

The boys laugh and groan; amiable, exaggerated groans. They must like the headmaster's wife: there is licensed repartee.[9] They look at her with bright eyes in open, eager faces. Someone leaps to hold the door for her, and close it behind her. She is gone.

The child stands in the center of the room, and it draws in around him. The circle of children contracts, faces are only a yard or so from him; strange faces, looking, assessing.

9. **licensed repartee** (rep′ ər tē′) witty replies permitted or encouraged by the students.

Vocabulary Development

Vocabulary Knowledge Rating

When students have completed reading and discussing the selection, have them take out their **Vocabulary Knowledge Rating Charts** for the story. Read the words aloud and have students rate their knowledge of words again in the After Reading column. Clarify any words that are still problematic. Have students write their own definitions and example or sentence in the appropriate column. Then, have students complete the vocabulary practice at the end of the selection. Encourage students to use the words in further discussion and written work about the selection. Remind them that they will be accountable for these words on the **Selection Test,** ***Unit 6 Resources,*** pages 374–376 or 377–379.

Asking questions. They help themselves to his name, his age, his school. Over their heads he sees beyond the window an inaccessible world of shivering trees and high racing clouds and his voice which has floated like a feather in the dusty schoolroom air dies altogether and he becomes mute, and he stands in the middle of them with shoulders humped, staring down at feet: grubby plimsolls[10] and kicked brown sandals. There is a noise in his ears like rushing water, a torrential din out of which voices boom, blotting each other out so that he cannot always hear the words. Do you? they say, and Have you? and What's your? and the faces, if he looks up, swing into one another in kaleidoscopic patterns and the floor under his feet is unsteady, lifting and falling.

And out of the noises comes one voice that is complete, that he can hear. "Next term, we'll mash you,' it says. "We always mash new boys."

And a bell goes, somewhere beyond doors and down corridors, and suddenly the children are all gone, clattering away and leaving him there with the heaving floor and the walls that shift and swing, and the headmaster's wife comes back and tows him away, and he is with his parents again, and they are getting into the car, and the high hedges skim past the car windows once more, in the other direction, and the gravel under the tyres changes to black tarmac.

"Well?"

"I liked it, didn't you?" The mother adjusted the car around her, closing windows, shrugging into her seat.

12 "Very pleasant, really. Nice chap."

"I liked him. Not quite so sure about her."

"It's pricey, of course."

"All the same . . ."

10. **plimsolls** (plim′ səlz) *n.* British term for sneakers.

"NEXT TERM, WE'LL MASH YOU. WE ALWAYS MASH NEW BOYS."

13 **Reading Check**

To whom does the headmaster's wife introduce Charles?

12 Critical Thinking

Make a Judgment

1. Choose two students to read aloud the dialogue between Charles's parents starting at the bottom of page 1441 and the top of page 1442.
2. **Ask** students what they think about the parents' decision to send Charles to that school and whether or not they think his parents did the right thing. Have them keep in mind the social influences of the time, and ask if it makes any difference.
   Possible response: I think Charles's parents were wrong to send Charles to that school. They were obviously only concerned with how the school looked and how much money they would have to spend to send him there. The more money they spent, the better it would make them look. The social influences of the time do not make it right. Even if a whole group of people is doing the same thing, that does not automatically make something right.

13 Reading Check

Answer: The headmaster's wife introduces Charles to the boys in the Lower Third class—students who would be his classmates.

Concept Connector

Reading Strategy Graphic Organizer

Ask students to review the graphic organizers in which they have evaluated the contemporary British social influences in Lively's story. Then, have students share their organizers and compare their evaluations.

Activating Prior Knowledge

Have students return to their responses to the Activating Prior Knowledge activity. Ask them to explain whether their thoughts have changed and, if so, how.

Writing About the Essential Question

Have students compare their responses to the prompt, completed before reading the story, with their thoughts afterward. Have them work individually or in groups, writing or discussing their thoughts, to formulate their new responses. Then, lead a class discussion, probing for what students have learned that confirms or invalidates their initial thoughts. Encourage students to cite specific textual details to support their responses.

14 Reading Strategy

Evaluate Social Influences of the Period

1. Briefly discuss with students their thoughts about the cost of a quality education.
2. **Ask** students the Reading Strategy question: What social influences prompt the father to think the high school fees are "money well spent"?
   Answer: Society seems to say that the more money spent on an education, the better it will be, the more high-class you will appear to others, and the higher you will sit on the status ladder. These things are important to the father.

ASSESS

Answers

Before students respond, you may wish to have them write a brief objective summary of the selection. As they answer the questions below, remind them to support their answers with evidence from the text.

1. (a) They are going to St. Edward's Preparatory School. (b) The headmaster and his wife wear quality clothing and are both very confident. Evidently, the school is prestigious.
2. (a) They like the superficial aspects of the school, such as the gym and the swimming pool. (b) **Possible response:** I don't think Charles's parents are properly concerned. They seem to care only about how it will look to others if Charles attends such a prestigious school, not about the way the school is run or what is taught.
3. (a) Students in the Lower Third "always mash new boys." (b) The warning suggests school will be tough for Charles.
4. **Possible response:** This story shows how important status was to British society. The more prestigious the school their child attended, the better the parents looked. Academics did not matter as much as access. The act of calling out the problem to the reader is an attempt to change society.

Reading Strategy
Evaluate Social Influences of the Period What social influences prompt the father to think the high school fees are "money well spent"?

Vocabulary
haggard (hag´ ərd) *adj.* wild-eyed or tired looking; gaunt

14 "Money well spent, though. One way and another."
"Shall we settle it, then?"
"I think so. I'll drop him a line."

The mother pitched her voice a notch higher to speak to the child in the back of the car. "Would you like to go there, Charles? Like Simon Wilcox. Did you see that lovely gym, and the swimming-pool? And did the other boys tell you all about it?"

The child does not answer. He looks straight ahead of him, at the road coiling beneath the bonnet of the car. His face is **haggard** with anticipation.

Cite textual evidence to support your responses.

> "MONEY WELL SPENT, THOUGH. ONE WAY AND ANOTHER."

Critical Reading

1. **Key Ideas and Details (a)** To what school is the Manders family going? **(b) Analyze:** What do the descriptions of the headmaster and his wife show about the kind of school it is?
2. **Key Ideas and Details (a) Summarize:** What do Charles's parents like about the school? **(b) Evaluate:** Do the parents seem properly concerned with Charles's education and happiness? Explain your opinion.
3. **Key Ideas and Details (a)** According to one boy, what do students in the Lower Third always do to newcomers? **(b) Infer:** What does the boy's warning suggest that school will be like for Charles?
4. **Integration of Knowledge and Ideas** What does this story show about class and its effects on British society? Explain, using at least two of these Essential Question words in your answer: *prestige, access, influential,* and *status. [Connecting to the Essential Question: How does literature shape or reflect society?]*

1442

Assessment Practice

Persuasion (For more practice, see *All-in-One Workbook.*)

Many tests require students to identify persuasive technique. The following sample item can teach students how to identify elements of persuasive writing. Have students recall the selection they have just read.

Which of the following best describes how the author persuades her audience?

A direct characterization
B satire
C indirect characterization
D irony

The tone of the piece is not quite satirical, so students can eliminate choice ***B.*** While she uses irony at the end of her story, it is not her chief means of conveyance, so choice ***D*** can be eliminated. She does use characterization, but she definitely uses more indirect characterization than direct characterization, so the correct answer is **C.**

After You Read | Next Term, We'll Mash You

Literary Analysis

1. **Craft and Structure** Choose one character, and show how the author uses **indirect characterization** to reveal what the character is like.
2. **Craft and Structure** Explain how **characterization** reflects the story's **themes.** First, identify details that point to a particular trait or attitude in character. Then, show how the portrayal of that trait or attitude reflects a theme. Use a chart like this:

Character/Detail	→	Trait or Attitude	→	Theme

Common Core State Standards

Writing
4. Produce clear and coherent writing in which the development, organization, and style are appropriate to task, purpose, and audience.

Reading Strategy

3. **(a)** What **social trends** does the story seem to be criticizing through the characters of the parents? **(b)** What social trends might it be criticizing through the characters of the students?
4. Based on this story, how does class seem to affect the British education system?

PERFORMANCE TASKS
Integrated Language Skills

Vocabulary Acquisition and Use

Complete the following analogies, using the words from the vocabulary list on page 1434. Use each word only once, and explain your choice.

1. *Counting* is to *enumeration* as _______ is to *evaluation.*
2. *Glamorous* is to *supermodel* as _______ is to *frump.*
3. *Courage* is to *hero* as _______ is to *snob.*
4. *Striped* is to *lines* as _______ is to *spots.*
5. *Loud* is to *scream* as _______ is to *whisper.*
6. *Skinny* is to *thin* as _______ is to *worn.*

Writing

Argumentative Text Write a **magazine advertisement** for St. Edward's Preparatory School that would attract a couple like the Manders. Think about the persuasive techniques you might employ. To what emotions should you appeal? What tone and language should you use? Would the Manders respond to a **bandwagon** approach ("everybody's doing it"), or to **testimonials,** in which people of stature praise the school? Write your final copy along with a description of visuals that would accompany the text.

Answers

1. **Possible response:** Lively reveals what Charles's mother is like by revealing her thought processes as the story goes on. When the parents meet the headmaster's wife, she focuses mainly on what the woman is wearing. This shows how superficial the woman is and reflects one of Lively's main themes: the superficiality of British society at the time.
2. **Possible response:** *Character/Detail:* Charles's father; *Trait or Attitude:* He believes the school is money well spent. *Theme:* Parents are improperly concerned about their children's education.
3. (a) The parents' attitudes seem to be a way of criticizing the superficial attitudes of the society. (b) The attitudes of the students might be a way of criticizing the way the society was bringing up its children. They appear to develop unhealthy inferiority complexes in such environments.
4. Class affects the education system because it seems that people who are so concerned with appearances and expense forget about the quality of education.

Vocabulary Acquisition and Use

1. assessing
2. homespun
3. condescension
4. dappled
5. subdued
6. haggard

Writing

Evaluate students' argumentative texts using the **General (Holistic) Writing Rubrics,** ***Professional Development Guidebook,*** pages 282–283.

Assessment Resources

Unit 6 Resources

L1 L2 EL **Selection Test A,** pp. 374–376. Administer Test A to less advanced readers.

L3 L4 EL **Selection Test B,** pp. 377–379. Administer Test B to on-level students and more advanced students.

L3 L4 **Open-Book Test,** pp. 371–373. As an alternative, give the Open-Book test.

All **Customizable Test Bank**

All **Self-tests**
Students may prepare for the **Selection Test** by taking the **Self-test** online.

PHLit Online! All assessment resources are available at **www.PHLitOnline.com.**

• *from* We'll Never Conquer Space

Lesson Pacing Guide

DAY 1 Preteach

- Administer the Reading and Vocabulary Warm-ups (*Unit 6 Resources*, pp. 380–383) as necessary.
- Introduce the Literary Analysis concept: Argumentative Essay.
- Introduce the Reading Strategy: Critique an Argument.
- Build background with the author and Background features.
- Develop thematic thinking with Connecting to the Essential Question.
- Teach the selection vocabulary.

DAY 2 Preteach/Teach/Extend

- Distribute copies of the graphic organizer for the Reading Strategy (*Graphic Organizer Transparencies*, pp. 280–281).
- Distribute copies of the graphic organizer for Literary Analysis (*Graphic Organizer Transparencies*, pp. 282–283).
- Prepare students to read with the Activating Prior Knowledge activities (TE).
- Informally monitor comprehension while students read.
- Use the Reading Check questions to confirm comprehension.
- Develop students' understanding of arugmentative essays using the Literary Analysis prompts.
- Develop students' ability to critique an argument using the Reading Strategy prompts.
- Reinforce vocabulary with the Vocabulary notes.
- Assess students' comprehension and mastery of the skills by having them answer the Critical Reading, Literary Analysis, and Reading Strategy questions.

DAY 3 Assess

- Have students complete the Vocabulary Lesson.
- Have students complete the Writing activity, writing an expository essay. (You may assign as homework.)
- Administer Selection Test A or B (*Unit 6 Resources,* pp. 392–394 or 395–397).

Common Core State Standards

Reading Informational Texts
2. Determine two or more central ideas of a text and analyze their development over the course of the text, including how they interact and build on one another to provide a complex analysis; provide an objective summary of the text.
4. Determine the meaning of words and phrases as they are used in a text, including figurative, connotative, and technical meanings; analyze how an author uses and refines the meaning of a key term or terms over the course of a text.
Writing 2. Write informative/explanatory texts to examine and convey complex ideas, concepts, and information clearly and accurately through the effective selection, organization, and analysis of content.

Additional Standards Practice
***Common Core Companion**, pp. 103–110; 123–130; 196–207*

Daily Block Scheduling
Each day in this Lesson Pacing Guide represents a 40–50 minute period. Teachers using block scheduling may combine days to revise pacing. In addition, teachers may differentiate and support core instruction by integrating components for extended and intensive support as students require. See the Guide to Selected Leveled Resources (facing page).

Guide to Selected Leveled Resources

RTI Tier 1 (students performing on level)

			from We'll Never Conquer Space
Warm Up	Whole class instruction; Group work	**Practice, model,** and **monitor** fluency, working **with the whole class** or **in groups.**	**Vocabulary** and **Reading Warm-ups B,** ***Unit 6 Resources,*** pp. 398–399, 401
Comprehension/Skills	Whole class instruction; Group work; Independent work	**Support** and **monitor** comprehension and skills development, having students complete the activities, graphic organizers, and interactive prompts **independently** or **as a class.**	• ***Reader's Notebook,*** adapted instruction and full selection EL ***Reader's Notebook: English Learner's Version,*** adapted instruction and adapted selection • **Reading Strategy Graphic Organizer B,** ***Graphic Organizer Transparencies,*** p. 295 • **Literary Analysis Graphic Organizer B,** ***Graphic Organizer Transparencies,*** p. 297
Monitor Progress	A	**Monitor** student progress with the differentiated curriculum-based assessment in the *Unit Resources.*	• **Selection Test B,** ***Unit 6 Resources,*** pp. 413–415 • **Open-Book Test,** ***Unit 6 Resources,*** pp. 407–409

RTI Tier 2 (students requiring intervention)

			from We'll Never Conquer Space
Warm Up	Group work; One-on-one teaching	**Practice, model,** and **monitor** fluency **in groups** or **with individuals**	• **Vocabulary and Reading Warm-ups A,** ***Unit 6 Resources,*** pp. 398–400 • ***Hear It!*** **Audio CD (adapted text)**
Comprehension/Skills	Group work; One-on-one teaching	• **Support** and **monitor** comprehension and skills development, working **in small groups** or **with individuals.** • As students complete the selection in the appropriate version of the *Reader's Notebook,* **monitor** comprehension frequently with group questions and individual instruction. • **Model** strategies while guiding students in completing the activities and prompts in the *Reader's Notebook,* as well as the graphic organizers. • **Practice** skills and **monitor** mastery with the *Reading Kit* worksheets.	• ***Reader's Notebook: Adapted Version,*** adapted instruction and adapted selection EL ***Reader's Notebook: English Learner's Version,*** adapted instruction and adapted selection • **Reading Strategy Graphic Organizer A,** ***Graphic Organizer Transparencies,*** p. 294 • **Literary Analysis Graphic Organizer A,** ***Graphic Organizer Transparencies,*** p. 296 • ***Reading Kit,*** Practice worksheets
Monitor Progress	A	**Monitor** student progress with the differentiated curriculum-based assessment in the *Unit Resources* and in the *Reading Kit.*	• **Selection Test A,** ***Unit 6 Resources,*** pp. 410–412 • ***Reading Kit,*** Assess worksheets

TIER 3 Tier 3 intervention may require consultation with the student's special-education or dyslexia specialist. For additional support, see the Tier 2 activities and resources listed above.

One-on-one teaching **Group work** **Whole class instruction** **Independent work** **A Assessment**

For a complete guide to selection support, including support for Advanced students, see the Overview of Resources in the frontmatter.

• *from* We'll Never Conquer Space

from We'll Never Conquer Space

Arthur C. Clarke

Background Clarke wrote this essay in 1960, at the brink of the era of space exploration. Three years earlier, in 1957, Sputnik had become the first satellite launched into space. The year after Clarke wrote the essay, in 1961, Alan Shepard became the first American to enter space. Over the next decades, human beings were to land on the moon (1969) and explore Mars via remote probes (1997). Yet Clarke's caution about the limits on the human conquest of space has yet to be tested.

Vocabulary
ludicrous (lōō di krəs) adj. absurd; ridiculous

Man will never conquer space. Such a statement may sound ludicrous, now that our rockets are already 100 million miles beyond the moon and the first human travelers are preparing to leave the atmosphere. Yet it expresses a truth which our forefathers knew, one we have forgotten—and our descendants must learn again, in heartbreak and loneliness.

Our age is in many ways unique, full of events and phenomena which never occurred before and can never happen again. They distort our thinking, making us believe that what is true now will be true forever, though perhaps on a larger scale. Because we have annihilated distance on this planet, we imagine that we can do it once

▲ Critical Viewing
Does this picture support or challenge Clarke's statement, "Man will never conquer space"? Explain. **[Connect]**

1446 A Time of Rapid Change (1901–Present)

RESOURCES FOR:

- L1 Special-Needs Students
- L2 Below-Level Students (Tier 2)
- L3 On-Level Students (Tier 1)
- L4 Advanced Students (Tier 1)
- EL English Learners
- All All Students

Vocabulary/Fluency/Prior Knowledge

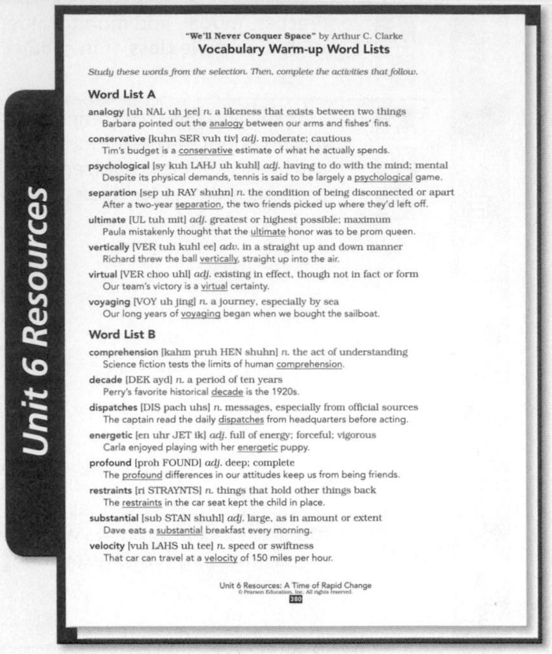

Unit 6 Resources

"We'll Never Conquer Space" by Arthur C. Clarke
Vocabulary Warm-up Word Lists

Study these words from the selection. Then, complete the activities that follow.

Word List A

analogy [uh NAL uh jee] *n.* a likeness that exists between two things
Barbara pointed out the analogy between our arms and fishes' fins.

conservative [kuhn SER vuh tiv] *adj.* moderate; cautious
Tim's budget is a conservative estimate of what he actually spends.

psychological [sy kuh LAHJ uh kuhl] *adj.* having to do with the mind; mental
Despite its physical demands, tennis is said to be largely a psychological game.

separation [sep uh RAY shuhn] *n.* the condition of being disconnected or apart
After a two-year separation, the two friends picked up where they'd left off.

ultimate [UL tuh mit] *adj.* greatest or highest possible; maximum
Paula mistakenly thought that the ultimate honor was to be prom queen.

vertically [VER tuh kuhl ee] *adv.* in a straight up and down manner
Richard threw the ball vertically, straight up into the air.

virtual [VER choo uhl] *adj.* existing in effect, though not in fact or form
Our team's victory is a virtual certainty.

voyaging [VOY uh jing] *n.* a journey, especially by sea
Our long years of voyaging began when we bought the sailboat.

Word List B

comprehension [kahm pruh HEN shuhn] *n.* the act of understanding
Science fiction tests the limits of human comprehension.

decade [DEK ayd] *n.* a period of ten years
Perry's favorite historical decade is the 1920s.

dispatches [DIS pach uhs] *n.* messages, especially from official sources
The captain read the daily dispatches from headquarters before acting.

energetic [en uhr JET ik] *adj.* full of energy; forceful; vigorous
Carla enjoyed playing with her energetic puppy.

profound [proh FOUND] *adj.* deep; complete
The profound differences in our attitudes keep us from being friends.

restraints [ri STRAYNTS] *n.* things that hold other things back
The restraints in the car seat kept the child in place.

substantial [sub STAN shuhl] *adj.* large, as in amount or extent
Dave eats a substantial breakfast every morning.

velocity [vuh LAHS uh tee] *n.* speed or swiftness
That car can travel at a velocity of 150 miles per hour.

Unit 6 Resources: A Time of Rapid Change
© Pearson Education, Inc. All rights reserved.
380

EL L1 L2 **Vocabulary Warm-ups A and B,** pp. 380–381

Also available for these selections:

EL L1 L2 **Reading Warm-ups A and B,** pp. 382–383

All **Vocabulary Builder,** p. 386

Reader's Notebooks

Pre- and postreading pages for this selection appear in an interactive format in the *Reader's Notebooks.* Each *Notebook* is differentiated for a different group of learners.
The selections in the Adapted and English Learner's versions are abridged.

L2 L3 ***Reader's Notebook***

L1 ***Reader's Notebook: Adapted Version***

EL ***Reader's Notebook: English Learner's Version***

EL ***Reader's Notebook: Spanish Version***

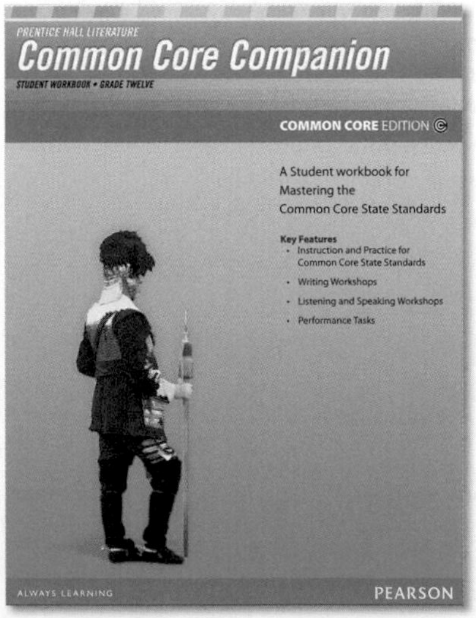

Common Core Companion

Additional instruction and practice for each Common Core State Standard

Selection Support

Graphic Organizer Transparencies

"We'll Never Conquer Space" by Arthur C. Clarke

After You Read B: Argumentative Essay

Argument:	
Facts	*Reasons*

Graphic Organizer Transparencies
© Pearson Education, Inc. All rights reserved.
283

EL L3 **Literary Analysis: Graphic Organizer B,** p. 283

Also available for these selections:

EL L1 L2 **Reading: Graphic Organizer A,** p. 280

EL L3 **Reading: Graphic Organizer B,** p. 281

EL L1 L2 **Literary Analysis: Graphic Organizer A, (partially filled in),** p. 282

Skills Development/Extension

Unit 6 Resources

Name ______________________ Date ____________

from **"We'll Never Conquer Space"** by Arthur C. Clarke

Support for Writing

Use the chart below to gather details for your analysis of an argument. Review the essay, and identify Clarke's assumptions. Write them in the left column. Then, analyze each assumption. In the right column, list evidence and reasons that support or contradict each assumption.

Clarke's Assumptions	Support or Evidence For or Against

Use information from the chart as you draft your analysis on a separate page. As you write, include an evaluation of whether Clarke's assumptions make sense.

Unit 6 Resources: A Time of Rapid Change
© Pearson Education, Inc. All rights reserved.
387

EL L3 L4 **Support for Writing,** p. 387

Also available for these selections:

All **Literary Analysis: Argumentative Essay,** p. 384

All **Reading: Critique and Argument,** p. 385

L4 **Enrichment,** p. 388

Assessment

Name ______________________ Date ____________

from **"We'll Never Conquer Space"** by Arthur C. Clarke

Selection Test A

Critical Reading *Identify the letter of the choice that best completes the statement or answers the question.*

____ 1. Which sentence from Clarke's essay states his main argument?
A. "Man will never conquer space."
B. "Psychologically as well as physically, there are no longer any remote places on earth."
C. "In a very few years, . . . we will be able to see friends on the far side of the earth."
D. "It [time barrier] will be a perpetual reminder of universal laws and limitations."

____ 2. What rhetorical strategy does Clarke use in the following sentence?
Yet it expresses a truth which our forefathers knew, one we have forgotten—and our descendants must learn again, in heartbreak and loneliness.
A. rhetorical question
B. analogy
C. anticipating objections
D. emotional appeal

____ 3. How might a reader challenge this statement from "We'll Never Conquer Space":
It will never be possible to converse with anyone on another planet.
A. A reader would know that Clarke can support his statement.
B. A reader would assume that Clarke is exaggerating.
C. A reader would agree, wishing this were not the case.
D. A reader would want to see proof of Clarke's statement.

____ 4. In which quotation is Clarke making an analogy, or a comparison, in "We'll Never Conquer Space"?
A. "Man will never conquer space."
B. "Every technical device is always developed to its limit."
C. "Saturn or Jupiter [will play] the same role . . . [as] Africa or Asia today."
D. "Space can be mapped and crossed and occupied."

____ 5. Which analogy does Clarke make in "We'll Never Conquer Space" to emphasize his prediction?
A. It will not be possible to talk with people on other planets.
B. Voyages that last many years will be taken.
C. It is hard to imagine the number of planets that exist.
D. What we think of as news would actually be history.

____ 6. Why does Clarke argue in "We'll Never Conquer Space" that colonies established around other stars would be independent of Earth?
A. They would be too distant in time and space for Earth to control them.
B. Aliens on other planets would quickly take over these colonies.
C. People who travel in space would be independent by nature and rebel.
D. Communications would not reach that far, so they would not receive orders.

Unit 6 Resources: A Time of Rapid Change
© Pearson Education, Inc. All rights reserved.
392

EL L1 L2 **Selection Test A,** pp. 392–394

Also available for these selections:

L3 L4 **Open-Book Test,** pp. 389–391

EL L3 L4 **Selection Test B,** pp. 395–397

PHLit Online!

www.PHLitOnline.com

- complete narrated selection text
- a thematically related video with writing prompt
- an interactive graphic organizer
- highlighting feature
- access to all student print resources, adapted to individual student needs
- Spanish and English summaries
- adapted selection translations in Spanish

Online Resources: All print materials are also available online.

Background Video

Also available:

Get Connected! (thematic video with writing prompt)
All videos are available in Spanish.

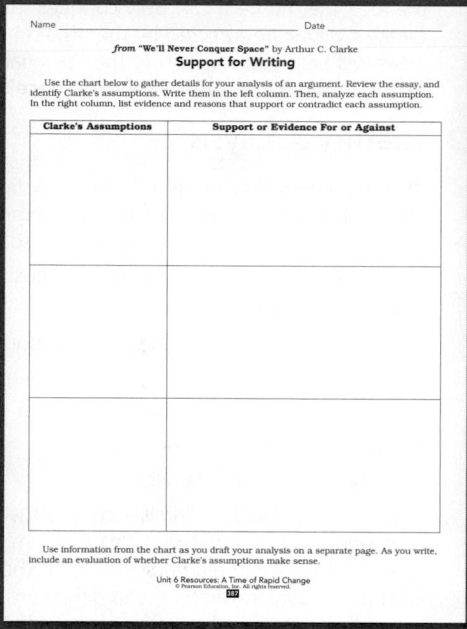

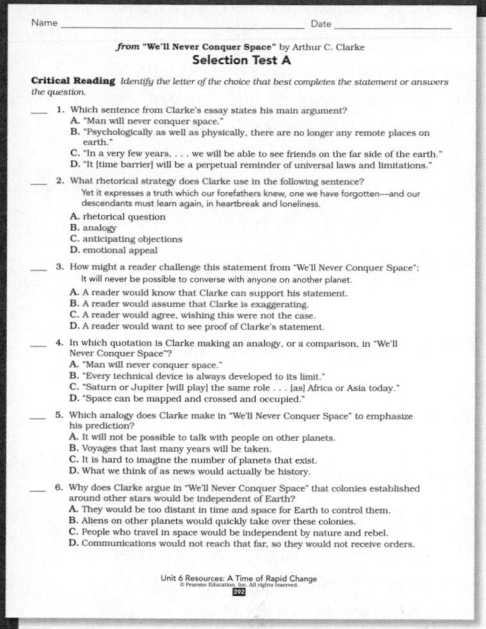

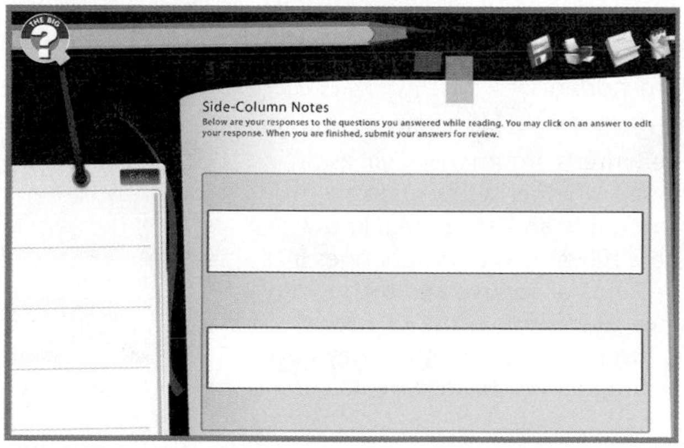

Writer's Journal (with graphics feature)

Also available:

Vocabulary Central (tools and activities for studying vocabulary)

PRETEACH

1 Connecting to the Essential Question

1. Review the assignment with the class.
2. Have small groups of students brainstorm lists of all that we have achieved in space exploration. Then have them complete the assignment.
3. As students read, have them look for how Clarke's ideas are affected by the nature of space.

2 Literary Analysis

Introduce the skill using the instruction on the student page.

Think Aloud: Model the Skill

Say to students:

As I read, I will look for a statement of Clarke's position, his tone, the facts he uses to support his arguments, any appeals to emotion that he makes, and any memorable phrases that he uses to convey his message. I will also examine the claims or counterclaims that Clarke uses to address readers' concerns.

3 Reading Strategy

1. Introduce the skill using the instruction on the student page.
2. Give students a copy of **Reading Strategy Graphic Organizer B,** page 281 in ***Graphic Organizer Transparencies,*** to fill out as they read.

Think Aloud: Model the Skill

Say to students:

As I read this essay, I will critique the writer's argument. I will ask myself whether his position seems reasonable and accurate. I know there have been many changes in the fields of science and technology since Clarke first wrote this essay, so I will consider whether they have any impact on his arguments.

4 Vocabulary

1. Pronounce each word, giving its definition, and have students say it aloud.
2. For more guidance, see the ***Classroom Strategies and Teaching Routines*** card for introducing vocabulary.

Before You Read from *We'll Never Conquer Space*

1 Connecting to the Essential Question Arthur C. Clarke challenges the idea that humans can truly conquer space. As you read, notice how Clarke's views are affected by the physical nature of outer space. Your ideas will help you respond to the Essential Question: **What is the relationship between literature and place?**

Common Core State Standards

Reading Informational Text
2. Determine two or more central ideas of a text and analyze their development over the course of the text, including how they interact and build on one another to provide a complex analysis; provide an objective summary of the text.
4. Determine the meaning of words and phrases as they are used in a text, including figurative, connotative, and technical meanings; analyze how an author uses and refines the meaning of a key term or terms over the course of a text.

2 Literary Analysis

An **argumentative essay** is a short nonfiction piece that argues a particular position. It may develop a number of central ideas that reinforce each other. It typically displays some or all of these features:

- A clear statement of the author's position
- A formal, informative tone
- Carefully researched facts that support general statements
- Ringing phrases to make the argument memorable
- Appeals to reason and/or emotion to convince readers
- Details that address reader concerns and counterclaims
- Clarification of unfamiliar concepts or a refinement of familiar ones

One way to clarify unfamiliar concepts is to use **analogies,** or extended comparisons of an unfamiliar idea to a familiar one. To refine the meaning of a familiar term, the author may apply the term repeatedly, using examples, counterexamples, and definitions to shape readers' understanding of the term. To advance his argument, Clarke refines the meaning of terms such as *space* and *distance.*

3 Reading Strategy

Preparing to Read Complex Texts Applying an expository critique means evaluating the power and truthfulness of an author's argument. As you read, use a checklist like the one shown to prepare an expository critique of Clarke's argument. Use textual evidence to support your inferences.

Criteria	Evaluation
Power of arguments	
Validity and truthfulness of arguments	
Appeal to friendly readers	
Appeal to hostile readers	
Anticipation of reader concerns	

4 Vocabulary

ludicrous (lo͞o′ di krəs) *adj.* absurd; ridiculous (p. 1446)

irrevocable (ir rev′ ə kə bəl) *adj.* unable to be undone or canceled (p. 1447)

instantaneous (in′ stən tā′ nē əs) *adj.* done or happening in an instant (p. 1449)

enigma (e nig′ mə) *n.* riddle; puzzling situation; mystery (p. 1450)

inevitable (in ev′ i tə bəl) *adj.* unavoidable; certain to happen (p. 1451)

PHLit Online! www.PHLitOnline.com

Vocabulary Development

Vocabulary Knowledge Rating

Create a **Vocabulary Knowledge Rating Chart** (***Professional Development Guidebook,*** p. 33) for the vocabulary words on the student page. Give each student a copy of the chart with the words on it. Read the words aloud, and have students mark their ratings in the Before Reading column. Urge students to attend to these words as they read and discuss the selection.

In order to gauge how much instruction you need to provide, tally how many students are confident in their knowledge of each word. As students read, point out the words and their context.

PHLit Online! **Vocabulary Central,** featuring tools and activities for studying vocabulary, is available online at **www.PHLitOnline.com.**

❺ Arthur C. Clarke (1917–2008)

Author of "We'll Never Conquer Space"

With more than one hundred million copies of his books in print worldwide, Arthur C. Clarke may have been the most successful science-fiction writer of all time. The extensive appeal of his books is probably due to their distinctive combination of technical expertise and touches of poetry.

A Scientific Start As a child, Clarke's natural curiosity led him to explore science and space with unflagging enthusiasm. He created his own map of the moon based on observations he made with a homemade telescope. At the age of twelve, when he started to read a magazine called *Amazing Stories,* Clarke discovered science fiction.

Imagining Satellites During World War II, Clarke's interest in scientific matters led to his service as a radar instructor in the Royal Air Force. At the end of the war, he drew on his wartime experience and his passion for space in an article for *Wireless World* magazine. The piece, entitled "Extra-Terrestrial Relays" (see page 1455) explained how television and telephone signals could be bounced off relay stations—satellites—sent into orbit by rocket. Clarke described, in essence, the methods used today for television and other broadcasting. Many consider Clarke "the godfather of global communication."

A Writer's Perspective From the early 1950s, Clarke worked full time as a writer, producing more than seventy works of fiction and non-fiction. One of his earliest stories, "The Sentinel" (1951), provided the germ of an idea for the epic film *2001: A Space Odyssey* (1968). Clarke summarized the film as an exploration of "man's place in the pecking order of cosmic intelligence."

Exploration of the Possible Clarke established credibility with his audience through an impressive command of science. However, while his speculations are grounded in hard facts, he turns them to lyrical, romantic ends in his science-fiction works. Challenging the notion that science fiction is escapism, Clarke asserted that the genre is "virtually the only kind of writing that's dealing with real problems and possibilities. . . ."

"The only way of finding the limits of the possible is by going beyond them into the impossible."

Daily Bellringer

For each class during which you will teach this selection, have students complete one of the five activities for the appropriate week in the ***Daily Bellringer Activities*** booklet.

Multidraft Reading

To assist struggling readers and to enhance reading for all, assign the text in chunks, as warranted by length, and apply multidraft reading protocols. For each reading, have students set the purpose indicated:

- **First reading**—literal comprehension: answering the Reading Check questions.
- **Second reading**—application of skills: answering the Literary Analysis and Reading Strategy questions.
- **Third reading**—interpretation: answering the end-of-selection questions.

For more guidance, refer to the ***Classroom Strategies and Teaching Routines*** card on Multidraft Reading.

❺ Background

More About the Author

The article Clarke published in 1945 on satellite relay stations laid down the principles of satellite communication, which was realized 25 years later. In 1956, Clarke moved to the island of Sri Lanka, which was then called Ceylon. Fascinated by the region's underwater realm, Clarke became an avid scuba diver and undersea explorer. His inventiveness brought him numerous honors, such as the 1982 Marconi International Fellowship and a gold medal from the Franklin Institute. Clarke's detailed descriptions of supercomputers, space shuttles, and future communication systems inspired millions of readers. This visionary passed away at the age of 90 in March 2008.

PHLit Online!
www.PHLitOnline.com

Teaching From Technology

Preparing to Read

Go to **www.PHLitOnline.com** in class or in a lab and display the ***Get Connected!*** slide show for this selection. Have the class brainstorm responses to the slide show writing prompt, entering ideas in the interactive journal. Then, have students complete their written responses individually, in a lab or as homework.

To build background, display the Background and More About the Author features.

Using the Interactive Text

Go to **www.PHLitOnline.com** and display the **Enriched Online Student Edition.** As the class reads the selection or listens to the narration, record answers to side-column prompts using the graphic organizers accessible on the interactive page. Alternatively, have students use the online edition individually, answering the prompts as they read.

❶ About the Selection

In this essay, Arthur C. Clarke challenges the idea that humans may ever truly "conquer" space. He stresses the improbability that humans will ever travel fast enough to make it possible to maintain a true connection with those left behind.

❷ Activating Prior Knowledge

Students may be familiar with science-fiction films such as *2001: A Space Odyssey* and the *Star Trek* television series, in which space travel is a basic premise. Have students discuss the extent to which they believe that people will make themselves at home in space in their lifetimes. Have each student write a paragraph considering what might be some of the practical and psychological benefits associated with space travel for the human race.

Concept Connector →

Tell students they will return to their responses after reading the selection.

❸ Critical Viewing

Possible responses: This picture of a satellite in orbit around Earth challenges Clarke's statement because it suggests that people have conquered space and left the planet Earth behind in the time since the article was written. Other students may say it neither supports nor challenges his statement since the satellite is still held by Earth's gravity.

① ② from We'll Never Conquer Space

Arthur C. Clarke

Background **Clarke wrote this essay in 1960, at the brink of the era of space exploration. Three years earlier, in 1957, Sputnik had become the first satellite launched into space. The year after Clarke wrote the essay, in 1961, Alan Shepard became the first American to enter space. Over the next decades, human beings were to land on the moon (1969) and explore Mars via remote probes (1997). Yet Clarke's caution about the limits on the human conquest of space has yet to be tested.**

Vocabulary
ludicrous (lo͞o di krəs) *adj.* absurd; ridiculous

④ Man will never conquer space. Such a statement may sound ludicrous, now that our rockets are already 100 million miles beyond the moon and the first human travelers are preparing to leave the atmosphere. Yet it expresses a truth which our forefathers knew, one we have forgotten—and our descendants must learn again, in heartbreak and loneliness.

Our age is in many ways unique, full of events and phenomena which never occurred before and can never happen again. They distort our thinking, making us believe that what is true now will be true forever, though perhaps on a larger scale. Because we have annihilated distance on this planet, we imagine that we can do it once

③ **▲ Critical Viewing**
Does this picture support or challenge Clarke's statement, "Man will never conquer space"? Explain. **[Connect]**

Text Complexity Rubric

from We'll Never Conquer Space			
Qualitative Measures			
Context/Knowledge Demands	Contemporary nonfiction; scientific knowledge demands 1 2 ③ 4 5		
Structure/Language Clarity	Accessible diction; technical terms 1 2 ③ 4 5		
Levels of Meaning	Challenging (space exploration, science controversy) 1 2 3 ④ 5		
Quantitative Measures			
Lexile	1310L	**Text Length**	1,870 words
Overall Complexity	**More complex**		

Reader and Task Suggestions

Preparing to Read the Text

- Using the Background on TE p. 1445, stress that Clarke was a respected scientist whose works often accurately envisioned the future.
- Discuss with students the phrase "conquer space" in Clarke's title. Ask them if unmanned exploration counts as "conquest."
- Guide students to use Multidraft Reading strategies (TE p. 1445).

Leveled Tasks

Levels of Meaning If students will have difficulty with the selection's meaning, have them focus on the author's idea. Then, as they reread, have them consider the evidence and logical arguments he provides.

Evaluating If students will not have difficulty with the meaning, have them evaluate the logic of Clarke's thesis.

again. The facts are far otherwise, and we will see them more clearly if we forget the present and turn our minds towards the past.

To our ancestors, the vastness of the earth was a dominant fact controlling their thoughts and lives. In all earlier ages than ours, the world was wide indeed, and no man could ever see more than a tiny fraction of its immensity. A few hundred miles—a thousand, at the most—was infinity. Only a lifetime ago, parents waved farewell to their emigrating children in the virtual certainty that they would never meet again.

And now, within one incredible generation, all this has changed. Over the seas where Odysseus wandered for a decade, the Rome-Beirut Comet whispers its way within the hour. And above that, the closer satellites span the distance between Troy and Ithaca[1] in less than a minute.

Psychologically as well as physically, there are no longer any remote places on earth. When a friend leaves for what was once a far country, even if he has no intention of returning, we cannot feel that same sense of irrevocable separation that saddened our forefathers. We know that he is only hours away by jet liner, and that we have merely to reach for the telephone to hear his voice.

In a very few years, when the satellite communication network is established, we will be able to see friends on the far side of the earth as easily as we talk to them on the other side of the town. Then the world will shrink no more, for it will have become a dimensionless point.

Forever Too Large

But the new stage that is opening up for the human drama will never shrink as the old one has done. We have abolished space here on the little earth; we can never abolish the space that yawns between the stars. Once again we are face to face with immensity and must accept its grandeur and terror, its inspiring possibilities and its dreadful restraints. From a world that has become too small, we are moving out into one that will be forever too large, whose frontiers will recede from us always more swiftly than we can reach out towards them.

Consider first the fairly modest solar, or planetary, distances which we are now preparing to assault. The very first Lunik[2] made a substantial impression upon them, traveling more than 200 million miles from the earth—six times the distance to Mars. When we have harnessed nuclear energy for spaceflight, the solar system will contract until it is little larger than the earth today. The remotest of the

1. **Odysseus . . . Troy and Ithaca** Odysseus was the King of Ithaca and hero of Homer's *Odyssey.* Troy and Ithaca are the ancient cities marking the beginning and end of his wanderings across the Mediterranean Sea in the *Odyssey.* The Comet was an airplane, one of the fastest at the time the essay was written.
2. **Lunik** name given by American journalists to Luna I, an unmanned Soviet space probe of 1959.

4 Reading Strategy
Applying an Expository Critique What is the effect of Clarke's suggesting—in the first paragraph—that his own argument may sound ludicrous?

Vocabulary
irrevocable (ir rəv´ ə kə bəl) *adj.* unable to be undone or canceled

5 Reading Check
What effect does Clarke say technology is having on distances on Earth?

4 Reading Strategy
Applying an Expository Critique

1. Have students read the bracketed passage. Remind them that they need to challenge the text.
2. **Ask** the Reading Strategy question: What is the effect of Clarke's suggesting—in the first paragraph—that his own argument may seem ludicrous?
   Possible response: It implies that modern readers might well consider space as conquerable in view of the fact that we have been to the moon and back, make daily use of orbital satellites, and have launched space probes to explore the solar system and beyond.

5 Reading Check
Answer: Clarke argues that advances in technology are decreasing distances on Earth.

Differentiated Instruction for Universal Access

Support for Special-Needs Students
Have students complete the **Before You Read** and the **Making Connections** pages for this selection in the *Reader's Notebook: Adapted Version.* These pages provide an abbreviated skills instruction, a selection summary, the **Before You Read** graphic organizer, and a **Note-taking Guide.**

Support for Less Proficient Readers
Have students complete the **Before You Read** and the **Making Connections** pages for this selection in the *Reader's Notebook.* These pages provide an abbreviated skills instruction, a selection summary, the **Before You Read** graphic organizer, and a **Note-taking Guide.**

EL Support for English Learners
Have students complete the **Before You Read** and the **Making Connections** pages for this selection in the *Reader's Notebook: English Learner's Version.* These pages provide additional vocabulary, vocabulary skills, and vocabulary practice, along with a **Getting Ready to Read** activity.

PHLit Online!
This selection is available in interactive format in the **Enriched Online Student Edition,** at **www.PHLitOnline.com,** which includes a thematically related video with writing prompt and an interactive graphic organizer.

❻ Reading Strategy

Applying an Expository Critique

1. Read aloud the bracketed passage. **Ask** students to summarize Clarke's comments on communication in space.
   Possible response: Today, telephone and television make possible instant communication on our planet, but beyond the orbit of the moon we meet the first barrier that we will not be able to penetrate.
2. **Ask** students what barrier Clarke is referring to in this paragraph.
   Answer: the speed of light
3. **Ask** students the Reading Strategy question: What counterclaim about conquering space does this paragraph anticipate?
   Answer: the idea that distances in the solar system will contract until it appears only a little larger than Earth does today
4. **Ask** students to consider e-mail, invented after Clarke wrote the essay. How important is instantaneous conversation today in conducting business across a distance?
   Possible response: People use e-mail regularly to conduct business today. Personal conversation may not be as important as Clarke appears to think. People could conduct business by sending messages and awaiting replies, as in the time of the American frontier.

❼ Critical Viewing

Answer: The speed of light and radio waves limits direct communication over the vast distances of space.

Reading Strategy
Applying an Expository Critique What counterclaim about conquering space does this paragraph anticipate?

planets will be perhaps no more than a week's travel from the earth, while Mars and Venus will be only a few hours away.

This achievement, which will be witnessed within a century, might appear to make even the solar system a comfortable, homely place, with such giant planets as Saturn and Jupiter playing much the same role in our thoughts as do Africa or Asia today. (Their qualitative differences of climate, atmosphere and gravity, fundamental though they are, do not concern us at the moment.) To some extent this may be true, yet as soon as we pass beyond the orbit of the moon, a mere quarter-million miles away, we will meet the first of the barriers that will separate the earth from her scattered children.

❻ The marvelous telephone and television network that will soon enmesh the whole world, making all men neighbors, cannot be extended into space. It will never be possible to converse with anyone on another planet.

Do not misunderstand this statement. Even with today's radio equipment, the problem of sending speech to the other planets is almost trivial. But the messages will take minutes—sometimes hours—on their journey, because radio and light waves travel at the same limited speed of 186,000 miles a second.

⑦ ▼ **Critical Viewing** What does Clarke say are the limitations of today's radio equipment like the dish shown below? **[Support]**

Twenty years from now you will be able to listen to a friend on Mars, but the words you hear will have left his mouth at least three minutes earlier, and your reply will take a corresponding time to reach him. In such circumstances, an exchange of verbal messages is possible—but not a conversation.

Even in the case of the nearby moon, the 2½ second time-lag will be annoying. At distances of more than a million miles, it will be intolerable.

It will never be possible to converse with anyone on another planet.

Enrichment: Investigating Technology

Artificial Satellites
Explain that there are six different types of satellites: (1) Earth-observation satellites take pictures of Earth. (2) Communications satellites receive radio signals and transmit them to other locations. (3) Research satellites gather information about space, the planets, and Earth's atmosphere. (4) Weather satellites relay information about weather patterns. (5) Navigation satellites determine locations on land, on sea, and in the air by sending signals to a transmitter. (6) Military satellites help to pinpoint locations of weapons and troops.

Activity: Investigating Satellite Networks Ask students to use Internet and print resources to learn more about satellite technology. Ask them to create a timeline of related inventions. Suggest that they record their analyses in the **Enrichment: Investigating Technology** worksheet, ***Professional Development Guidebook,*** page 242.

"Time Barrier"

To a culture which has come to take **instantaneous** communication for granted, as part of the very structure of civilized life, this "time barrier" may have a profound psychological impact. It will be a perpetual reminder of universal laws and limitations against which not all our technology can ever prevail. For it seems as certain as anything can be that no signal—still less any material object—can ever travel faster than light.

The velocity of light is the ultimate speed limit, being part of the very structure of space and time. Within the narrow confines of the solar system, it will not handicap us too severely, once we have accepted the delays in communication which it involves. At the worst, these will amount to 20 hours—the time it takes a radio signal to span the orbit of Pluto, the outermost planet.

Between the three inner worlds the earth, Mars, and Venus, it will never be more than 20 minutes—not enough to interfere seriously with commerce or administration, but more than sufficient to shatter those personal links of sound or vision that can give us a sense of direct contact with friends on earth, wherever they may be.

It is when we move out beyond the confines of the solar system that we come face to face with an altogether new order of cosmic reality. Even today, many otherwise educated men—like those savages who can count to three but lump together all numbers beyond four—cannot grasp the profound distinction between solar and stellar space. The first is the space enclosing our neighboring worlds, the planets; the second is that which embraces those distant suns, the stars, and it is literally millions of times greater.

8 There is no such abrupt change of scale in terrestrial affairs. To obtain a mental picture of the distance to the nearest star, as compared with the distance to the nearest planet, you must imagine a world in which the closest object to you is only five feet away—and then there is nothing else to see until you have traveled a thousand miles.

Many conservative scientists, appalled by these cosmic gulfs, have denied that they can ever be crossed. Some people never learn; those who 60 years ago scoffed at the possibility of flight, and ten (even five!) years ago laughed at the idea of travel to the planets, are now quite sure that the stars will always be beyond our reach. And again they are wrong, for they have failed to grasp the great lesson of our age—that if something is possible in theory, and no fundamental scientific laws oppose its realization, then sooner or later it will be achieved.

One day, it may be in this century, or it may be a thousand years from now, we shall discover a really efficient means of propelling our space vehicles. Every technical device is always developed to its limit (unless it is superseded by something better) and the ultimate speed for spaceships is the velocity of light. They will never reach that goal, 9 but they will get very close to it. And then the nearest star will be less than five years' voyaging from the earth.

Vocabulary
instantaneous (in′ stən tā′ nē əs) *adj.* done or happening in an instant

Literary Analysis
Analogy What is the purpose of the analogy in this paragraph?

Reading Check
What barrier will space travel force people to confront?

8 Literary Analysis

Analogy

1. Ask students to read the bracketed passage independently.
2. **Ask** the Literary Analysis question: What is the purpose of the analogy in this paragraph?
   Answer: to help the reader visualize the vast distances in space

9 Reading Check

Answer: Space travel will force people to confront the time barrier imposed by the speed of light.

Differentiated Instruction for Universal Access

Enrichment for Special-Needs Students
Have students view *2001: A Space Odyssey* and make oral presentations to the class explaining the different issues the film posed. Are the concerns the film raises with respect to computer technology unrealistic? In what ways was Clarke's vision prophetic?

Enrichment for Gifted/Talented Students
Have students construct a three-dimensional model, using whatever materials they find appropriate to illustrate different points of Clarke's essay. For example, they may design something that gives an accessible representation of the relationships of distance and scale in space.

⑩ The British Tradition

Finding a Place in the World

While Clarke's subject is largely informed by science, it is not entirely different from many of the other authors students have been studying throughout this text. Indeed, many of these authors share a common theme in assessing humanity's proper place in the scheme of things. Whether this theme takes the guise of England as a homeland or Earth as our mother planet, there is a common concern for the question of home and homelessness.

Connect to the Literature Have students discuss the pros and cons of the various assertions in the essay. Then, **ask** them to reply to the Connect to the Literature question: What effect does the complexity of the universe have on our own sense of size?

Possible responses: Answers may vary. Students may comment on how insignificant their size is in relation to the vastness of the universe. Others may observe that all matter in the universe is made up of atoms that are much smaller than a human being. Others still may remark that their size in relation to the universe is irrelevant because the size of the universe is so incomprehensible that it simply is an abstraction.

⑩ *The* BRITISH TRADITION

Finding a Place in the World

Clarke's essay poses the question, What is the place of humanity in the universe? With each shift in history, the literature of the British tradition has returned to this question—whether it is in the mingled yearnings for home and for the sea in the Anglo-Saxon poem "The Seafarer" (p. 20) or in Bede's definition of England as a homeland (p. 84) or in Milton's cosmic explorations in *Paradise Lost* (p. 524). Swift brought his satirical eye to the question in *Gulliver's Travels* (p. 606), finding that we are neither small enough (nor unreasonable enough) for Lilliput nor big enough (nor good enough) for Brobdingnag. Sydney Smith took on the issue in perhaps its smallest form: How physically comfortable can we be in the world? (see p. 1065).

Many of these writers, like Clarke, uncover a kind of universal human homelessness—a way in which the world leaves us with persistent, unsatisfied desires or unanswered questions. By affirming this condition, these writers remind us of our limits and challenge us to celebrate the life they define.

Connect to the Literature

What effect does the complexity of the universe have on our own sense of size? Explain.

Our exploring ships will spread outwards from their home over an ever-expanding sphere of space. It is a sphere which will grow at almost—but never quite—the speed of light. Five years to the triple system of Alpha Centauri, 10 to the strangely-matched doublet Sirius A and B, 11 to the tantalizing **enigma** of 61 Cygni,[3] the first star suspected to possess a planet. These journeys are long, but they are not impossible. Man has always accepted whatever price was necessary for his explorations and discoveries, *and the price of Space is Time.*

Even voyages which may last for centuries or millennia will one day be attempted. Suspended animation has already been achieved in the laboratory, and may be the key to interstellar travel. Self-contained cosmic arks which will be tiny traveling worlds in their own right may be another solution, for they would make possible journeys of unlimited extent, lasting generation after generation.

The famous Time Dilation effect predicted by the Theory of Relativity,[4] whereby time appears to pass more slowly for a traveler moving at almost the speed of light, may be yet a third. And there are others.

Looking far into the future, therefore, we must picture a slow (little more than half a billion miles an hour!) expansion of human activities outwards from the solar system, among the suns scattered across the region of the galaxy in which we now find ourselves. These suns are on the average five light-years apart; in other words, we can never get from one to the next in less than five years.

To bring home what this means, let us use a down-to-earth analogy. Imagine a vast ocean, sprinkled with islands—some desert, others perhaps inhabited. On one of these islands an energetic race has just discovered the art of building ships. It is preparing to explore the ocean, but must face the fact that the very nearest island is five years' voyaging away, and that no possible improvement in the technique of ship-building will ever reduce this time.

In these circumstances (which are those in which we will soon find ourselves) what could the islanders achieve?

Vocabulary
enigma (e nig′ mə) *n.* riddle; puzzling situation; mystery

3. **Alpha Centauri . . . 61 Cygni** Alpha Centauri is a system of three stars in the constellation of the Centaur; one of these, Proxima Centauri, is the star closest to Earth besides the sun. Sirius, known as the Dog Star, is the brightest star in Earth's sky; it is actually two stars orbiting each other, one of which (Sirius B), is only as big as the earth. 61 Cygni is a binary star in the constellation Cygnus, the Swan.
4. **Theory of Relativity** In physics, the theory that measurements of an object's physical properties will vary depending on the relative motion of the observer and the observed object: Only the speed of light is constant. One consequence of the theory is that time, as measured by an external observer, will slow down on an object moving close to the speed of light. In theory, a person traveling near the speed of light would age at a slower rate than a person traveling more slowly (the "Time Dilation effect" referred to by Clarke).

Vocabulary Development

Vocabulary Knowledge Rating

When students have completed reading and discussing the selection, have them take out their **Vocabulary Knowledge Rating Charts** for the story. Read the words aloud and have students rate their knowledge of words again in the After Reading column. Clarify any words that are still problematic. Have students write their own definitions and example or sentence in the appropriate column. Then, have students complete the Vocabulary Practice at the end of the selection. Encourage students to use the words in further discussion and written work about the selection. Remind them that they will be accountable for these words on the **Selection Test, *Unit 6 Resources,*** pages 392–394 or 395–397.

Man has always accepted whatever price was necessary for his explorations and discoveries, *and the price of Space is Time.*

After a few centuries, they might have established colonies on many of the nearby islands and have briefly explored many others. The daughter colonies might themselves have sent out further pioneers, and so a kind of chain reaction would spread the original culture over a steadily expanding area of the ocean.

But now consider the effects of the **inevitable**, unavoidable time-lag. There could be only the most tenuous contact between the home island and its offspring. Returning messengers could report what had happened on the nearest colony—five years ago. They could never bring information more up to date than that, and dispatches from the more distant parts of the ocean would be from still further in the past—perhaps centuries behind the times. There would never be news from the other islands, but only history.

Vocabulary
inevitable (in ev´ i tə bəl) *adj.* unavoidable; certain to happen

Critical Reading

Cite textual evidence to support your responses.

1. **Key Ideas and Details (a)** What reason does Clarke offer for claiming that a true conversation with someone on another planet is impossible? **(b) Classify:** What distinction does Clarke make between exchanging messages and having a conversation?
2. **Key Ideas and Details (a) Compare and Contrast:** According to Clarke, how is conquering space different from conquering regions of the Earth? **(b) Infer:** What implications does Clarke think that conquering space would have for human society?
3. **Integration of Knowledge and Ideas** What broader lesson about human limitations does Clarke's essay contain?
4. **Integration of Knowledge and Ideas** How does Clarke's view of space as a "place" inform the argument he makes? In your response, use at least two of these Essential Question words: *interplanetary, stellar, limitation.* ***[Connecting to the Essential Question: What is the relationship between literature and place?]***

ASSESS

Answers

Before students respond, you may wish to have them write a brief objective summary of the selection. As they answer the questions below, remind them to support their answers with evidence from the text.

1. (a) Clarke points out that even radio waves travel too slowly to allow for a true "conversation" across the vast distances of space. Communication would have to be in message form, which could take years, decades, or even centuries to arrive. (b) Clarke thinks of conversation as immediate and messages as entailing delay. That delay would mean that the messages would be more like "history" than communication.
2. (a) For Clarke, conquering space is different from conquering Earth as a result of the sheer size of space, especially when measured against the life span of the human being. The closest we would come, in his view, would be by bridging space with generation after generation of explorers, with no one to whom any given expedition could report results. (b) Attempting to conquer space would divide and scatter human society and culture over a wide area of space.
3. Some students may respond that Clarke would have a dampening effect on our pride and ambition. Others may feel his observations help rein in human arrogance.
4. **Possible response:** Clarke argues that *interplanetary* distances in space are so great that direct communication across the vast distances will not be possible. He asks us to imagine space like a vast ocean with other stars and planets scattered like islands within the galaxy. Because of the *limitations* imposed by the speed of light, Clarke says that any colonies that we created would be divided by this time barrier. Ensure that students' responses include at least two of the Essential Question Words.

Concept Connector

Literary Analysis Graphic Organizer
Ask students to review the graphic organizers in which they have listed analogies and comparisons used in the essay. Then, have students share their organizers and compare the analogies and comparisons they identified.

Activating Prior Knowledge
Have students return to their responses to the Activating Prior Knowledge activity. Ask them to explain whether their thoughts have changed and, if so, how.

Writing About the Essential Question
Have students compare their responses to the prompt, completed before reading the selection, with their thoughts afterward. Have them work individually or in groups, writing or discussing their thoughts, to formulate new responses. Then, lead a class discussion, probing for what students have learned that confirms or invalidates their initial thoughts. Encourage students to cite specific textual details to support their responses.

⓫ Literature in Context

In Bede's history of the English people, he described Britain as an island in the middle of the ocean. He depicts the island as the homeland of the original Britons, the Picts, the Scots, and the Irish, who are united by their Christian faith. Arthur C. Clarke in turn describes Earth itself as an island in the middle of the vastness of space.

Connect to the Literature Have students identify what each of the images represents: the architecture of modern London, a map of Great Britain, our planet seen from space, and the Milky Way galaxy. Then, **ask** them to reply to the Connect to the Literature question: As your eye moves upward on this page, consider how Clarke might answer the questions about a Londoner's home.

Possible response: Some students might respond that Clarke would answer yes to each of these questions except the last. Though he argues that eventually we will solve the technological problems of exploring space, Clarke does not seem to be completely at home in the Milky Way galaxy, because of the limitations imposed by the human life span and the difficulties of communicating across the distances.

11 LITERATURE IN CONTEXT

WHERE IS OUR ISLAND HOME?

In the Venerable Bede's *History of the English Church and People,* England makes its debut on the world stage as a remote but fertile island in the North Atlantic. To Arthur C. Clarke, writing well over a thousand years later, the Earth itself is an island home in an unimaginably vast ocean of space.

Is home the Milky Way Galaxy?

Is home the planet Earth?

Is home the British Isles?

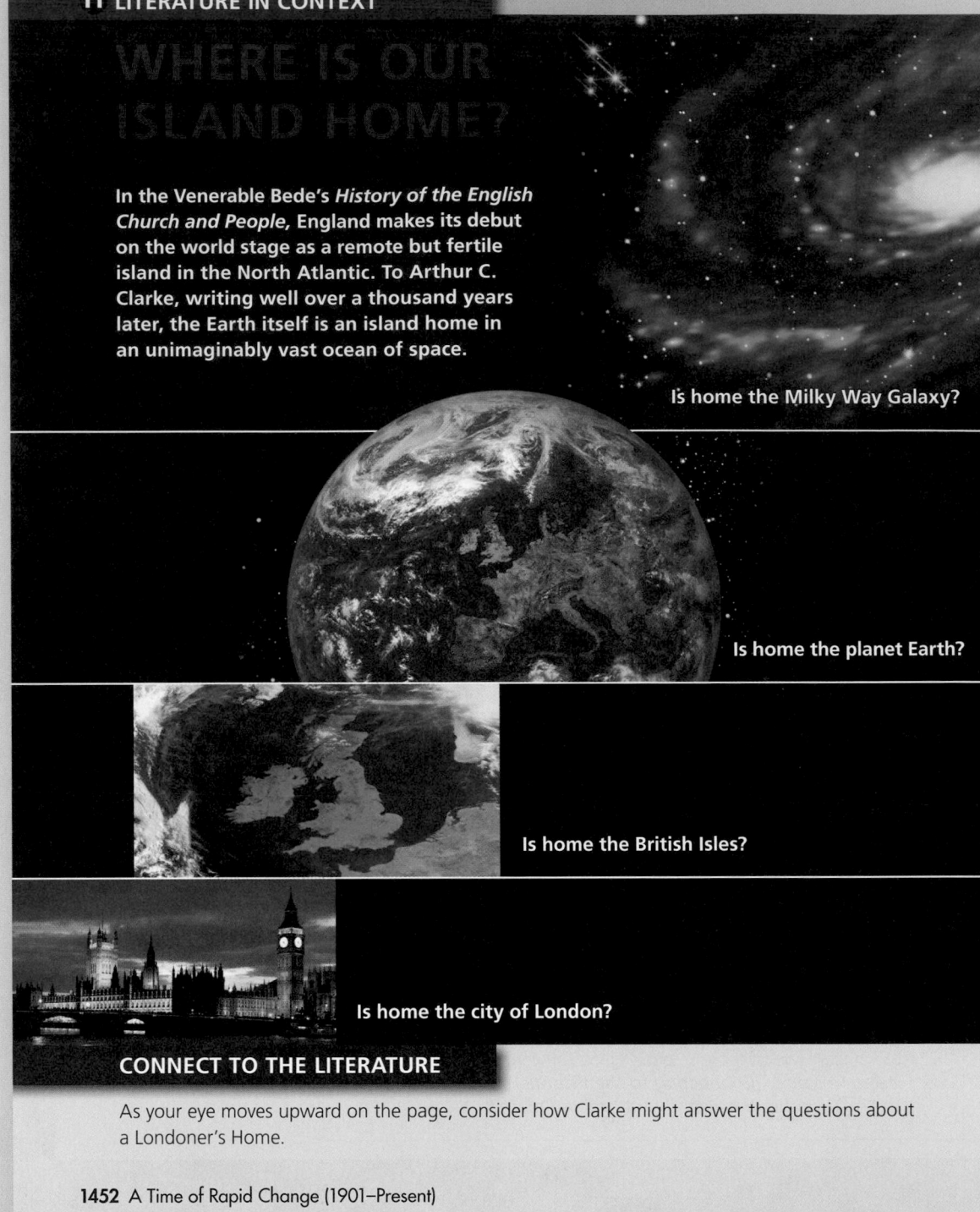

Is home the city of London?

CONNECT TO THE LITERATURE

As your eye moves upward on the page, consider how Clarke might answer the questions about a Londoner's Home.

Assessment Practice

Challenging (For more practice, see *All-in-One Workbook.*)

Tests often require students to apply revision strategies to passages in order to evaluate the appropriateness of a sentence. Use the following sample test item to give students practice:

> Self-contained cosmic arks . . . may be another solution, for they would make possible journeys of unlimited extent, lasting generation after generation.

To add information about these spaceships, which of the following would be most suitable?

A Spacesuits have sophisticated air conditioning systems.

B Space travelers would need special training.

C These vessels would require heavy shielding against the dangerous solar radiation.

D Movies and television shows have been made about space travel.

The correct answer is **C**. The other choices are not specifically about the spaceships.

After You Read from *We'll Never Conquer Space*

Literary Analysis

1. **Key Ideas and Details (a)** Summarize the argument that Clarke makes in this **argumentative essay.** Explain how the two central ideas of limits to communication and expanding exploration build on each other. **(b)** What facts and reasons does he provide to support his argument? Use a chart like this to gather your ideas.

Argument:	
Facts	Reasons

2. **Craft and Structure (a)** Explain Clarke's **analogy** involving islands in the ocean. **(b)** What general point does Clarke make with the analogy?
3. **Craft and Structure (a)** Explain how Clarke refines the term *space* in the essay, leading to the distinction between solar and stellar space. **(b)** In what way does his refinement of the term support his argument?
4. **Integration of Knowledge and Ideas** Has Clarke made a persuasive argument about the impossibility of conquering space? Explain.

Common Core State Standards

Writing
2. Write informative/explanatory texts to examine and convey complex ideas, concepts, and information clearly and accurately through the effective selection, organization, and analysis of content.

Reading Strategy

5. **(a)** In **applying an expository critique** to this essay, what logical and emotional appeals would you cite as especially effective? **(b)** What ringing phrases make the essay memorable?
6. Explain how well Clarke addresses counterclaims to his argument.

PERFORMANCE TASKS
Integrated Language Skills

Vocabulary Acquisition and Use

For each word, choose the letter of its antonym, and explain your choice.

1. ludicrous: **(a)** sensible **(b)** puzzling **(c)** unwise **(d)** tiresome
2. irrevocable: **(a)** tangible **(b)** changeable **(c)** laughable **(d)** doable
3. instantaneous: **(a)** momentous **(b)** large **(c)** wasteful **(d)** slow
4. enigma: **(a)** explanation **(b)** complexity **(c)** puzzle **(d)** stain
5. inevitable: **(a)** wishful **(b)** hopeless **(c)** avoidable **(d)** endurable

Writing

Informative Text Write a brief **essay** in which you *verify and clarify* the facts and explanations that Clarke provides. Using reliable print or online sources, confirm the distances, times, and other factual information in the essay. Remember to attribute your sources of information.

Answers

1. (a) Argument: Clarke predicts that man will not conquer space. (b) Facts: Radio and light waves travel at the speed of light—186,000 miles a second. Reasons: The speed of light is so slow that it would prevent direct contact with Earth.
2. (a) Clarke asks us to compare the distances between stars and habitable planets to islands in an ocean so vast that no improvement in shipbuilding can reduce the 5-year journey between them. (b) Islands represent isolation. Clarke is pointing out how isolated, by both space and time, future space explorers would be.
3. Some may feel Clarke's argument is persuasive because it considers the psychological impact of isolation on the human spirit. Others may say that an unanticipated breakthrough may enable us to conquer the technical problems.
4. Students' answers may vary but should be supported by evidence from the selection.
5. (a) Logical Appeals: scientific information about the effect of satellite communications, relativity, and the speed of light. Emotional Appeals: Ensure that students cite specific text details. (b) Clark's comparison of the spread of ant colonies to the spread of human colonies is memorable.
6. Clark addresses concerns in his opening statement and in arguing about the vastly different scale of the universe. It has the effect of further clarifying his position and of disarming rebuttal arguments.

Vocabulary Acquisition and Use

1. A; ludicrous, without sense
2. B; irrevocable, is not changeable
3. D; instantaneous, happens immediately, not slowly
4. A; an enigma is difficult to explain
5. C; inevitable, cannot be avoided

Writing

Evaluate students' informative texts using the rubrics for a *Persuasive Essay, Professional Development Guidebook,* pages 256–257.

Assessment Resources

Unit 6 Resources

L1 L2 EL **Selection Test A,** pp. 392–394. Administer Test A to less advanced readers.

L3 L4 EL **Selection Test B,** pp. 395–397. Administer Test B to on-level students and more advanced students.

L3 L4 **Open-Book Test,** pp. 389–391. As an alternative, give the Open-Book test.

All **Customizable Test Bank**

All **Self-tests**
Students may prepare for the **Selection Test** by taking the **Self-test** online.

PHLit Online! All assessment resources are available at **www.PHLitOnline.com.**

PRETEACH

Common Core State Standards

- Reading Informational Text 5
- Writing 2
- Language 4.d

About the Texts

1. Introduce the technical article and press release using the instruction on the student page.
2. Direct students to look for the bulleted features of each type of technical document as they read the selections.

Reading Strategy

1. Introduce the skill using the instruction and chart on the student page.
2. Tell students they will analyze cause-and-effect relationships as they read the two documents.

Think Aloud: Model the Skill

Model the strategy of analyzing cause-and-effect relationships. Say to students:

Even before I read this article, I look at the title and wonder about the cause-and-effect relationship between rocket stations and radio coverage. Since the article was written in 1945, I am also curious as to how technology was used at that time. I am interested to see what effect the combination of rocket stations and worldwide radios has had on society.

Content-Area Vocabulary

1. Have students say each word aloud.
2. Then, use each word in a sentence that makes its meaning clear. Repeat your sentence with the vocabulary word missing and have students fill in the blank.

For more guidance, consult the *Classroom Strategies and Teaching Routines* card on introducing vocabulary.

Reading for Information

Analyzing Functional and Expository Texts

Technical Article • Press Release

Common Core State Standards

Reading Informational Text
5. Analyze and evaluate the effectiveness of the structure an author uses in his or her exposition or argument, including whether the structure makes points clear, convincing, and engaging.

About the Texts

A **technical article** provides information on a scientific or technological subject. Many technical articles propose new ideas or announce breakthroughs in research. They often include statistical information and factual details explaining the idea; charts, graphs, illustrations, and other visual aids; and conclusions, references, appendices, and footnoted commentary.

A **press release** is a document that an organization sends to the news media to announce developments or events. Written to influence as well as inform media coverage, press releases contain these features:

- An extended headline or subhead summarizing the announcement
- Together with the date of the release, a brief description of key facts answering questions like *Who?, What?, When?, Where?, Why?,* and *How?*
- Supporting quotations from experts or those involved in the project

Reading Strategy

Informational writing uses *text structures* such as cause-and-effect relationships, which show how one thing brings about another. Consequently, **analyzing cause-and-effect relationships** can help you better understand an informational document. As you read, look for explanations of how a particular event or situation produced or might produce particular effects. Use a chart like the one shown to help you identify causes and effects.

Event	Causes	Effects

Content-Area Vocabulary

These words appear in the selections that follow. They may also appear in other content-area texts:

satellite (sat′ ’l īt) *n.* a man-made object that revolves around the Earth or another celestial body to relay data

atmosphere (at′ məs fir′) *n.* the mass of gas surrounding any star or planet

velocity (və läs′ ə tē) *n.* the speed and direction of a moving object

orbits (ôr′bits) *n.* paths of celestial bodies revolving around other bodies, like planets or stars

Teaching Resources

Reading Support

L2 L3 *Readers Notebook*

L1 *Readers Notebook: Adapted*

EL *Reader's Notebook: English Learner's Version*

In this article, Clarke proposed a new form of world-wide communication based on "stationary" artificial satellites that could hover in place above a single spot on the Earth. Today, such **satellite** communication is common, but it was a revolutionary idea when scientist and science-fiction writer Arthur C. Clarke first proposed it in the October, 1945, issue of the journal *Wireless World.* (October, 1945, pp. 305–308).

The author is suggesting that the answer to the question in the title is yes. He is also implying that the article will reveal the cause-and-effect chain leading to such "radio coverage."

Extra-Terrestrial Relays: Can Rocket Stations Give World-wide Radio Coverage?

By Arthur C. Clarke

The author makes a prediction that, if true, will make possible the kind of rocket stations he refers to in his title.

. . . A rocket which achieved a sufficiently great speed in flight outside the earth's **atmosphere** would never return. This "orbital" **velocity** is 8 km per sec (5 miles per sec), and a rocket which attained it would become an artificial satellite, circling the world for ever with no expenditure of power—a second moon, in fact. . . .

It will be possible in a few more years to build radio controlled rockets which can be steered into such **orbits** beyond the atmosphere and left to broadcast scientific information back to the earth. A little later, manned rockets will be able to make similar flights with sufficient excess power to break the orbit and return to earth.

There are an infinite number of possible stable orbits, circular and elliptical, in which a rocket would remain, if the initial conditions were correct. The velocity of 8 km/sec. applies only to the closest possible orbit, one just outside the atmosphere . . .

The fact the author points out in this paragraph is extremely important and lays the causal basis for his proposal.

It will be observed that one orbit, with a radius of 42,000 km, has a period of exactly 24 hours. A body in such an orbit, if its plane coincided with that of the earth's equator, would revolve with the earth and would thus be stationary above the same spot on the planet. It would remain fixed in the sky of a whole hemisphere and unlike all other heavenly bodies would neither rise nor set. A body in a smaller orbit would revolve more quickly than the earth and so would rise in the west, as indeed happens with the inner moon of Mars.

Using material ferried up by rockets, it would be possible to construct a "space station" in such an orbit. The station could be provided with living quarters, laboratories and everything needed for the comfort of its crew, who would be relieved and provisioned by a regular rocket service. This project might be undertaken for purely scientific reasons as it would contribute enormously to our knowledge of astronomy, physics, and meteorology. . . .

Differentiated Instruction for Universal Access

Strategy for Special-Needs Students

A technical article often contains technical terms that will need to be defined for special-needs students. Encourage students to read through the article with a partner, looking up words in a dictionary as needed for comprehension.

Strategy for Less Proficient Readers

Students may have difficulty separating the important details in the article from the minor details. Have them look for how the described events cause specific results. These are cause-and-effect relationships. Students should underline each instance in the article when one event leads to another.

TEACH

About Technical Articles

1. Tell students this is an article from a technical journal; students should also note the early publication date.
2. Have students read "Extra-Terrestrial Relays: Can Rocket Stations Give World-wide Radio Coverage?"
3. **Ask** students to explain why an article from 1945 is worth reading today.
   Answer: Although satellite communication is common today, it was a groundbreaking idea in 1945.

Analyzing Cause-and-Effect Relationships

1. Tell students that looking for cause-and-effect relationships within a technical article can enhance understanding.
2. **Ask** students how Clarke's idea to utilize "stationary" artificial satellites could have seemed outrageous in 1945.
   Possible response: At the time, no one had considered that technology could be used to benefit society in that way.
3. **Ask** students to read the second paragraph of the article and explain Clarke's theory on the effects of utilizing rockets in space.
   Answer: He intended to first build radio-controlled rockets. Then he planned to create manned rockets to orbit Earth. The effect would be that these rockets would broadcast scientific information back to Earth.
4. **Ask** students to reread the last paragraph on this page and discuss the intended benefits of manning the "space stations" with humans.
   Answer: The crew could contribute to different scientific studies: astronomy, physics, and meteorology.

Analyzing Cause-and-Effect Relationships

1. The author describes the space station as "fantastic."
   Ask students to explain his choice of words and how this relates to cause and effect.
   Possible response: At that time, it was outlandish to think that people could live and study in space. But his "fantasy" will lead to the space stations of today.
2. **Ask** students how the diagrams and captions help readers visualize the author's ideas.
   Possible response: They help readers imagine what the author describes by organizing the ideas in a different way.
3. **Ask** students to find the main idea of the article. Remind them to focus on the cause-and-effect relationship between the space stations and society.
   Possible response: Space stations should be built in order to increase worldwide communication and further scientific study.

Technical Article

Although such an undertaking may seem fantastic, it requires for its fulfillment rockets only twice as fast as those already in the design stage. Since the gravitational stresses involved in the structure are negligible, only the very lightest materials would be necessary and the station could be as large as required.

Let us now suppose that such a station were built in this orbit. It could be provided with receiving and transmitting equipment . . . and could act as a repeater to relay transmissions between any two points on the hemisphere beneath . . .

A single station could only provide coverage to half the globe, and for a world service three would be required, though more could be readily utilized. Figure 3 shows the simplest arrangement. The stations would be arranged approximately equidistantly around the earth . . .

Diagrams and captions help readers to imagine what the author describes.

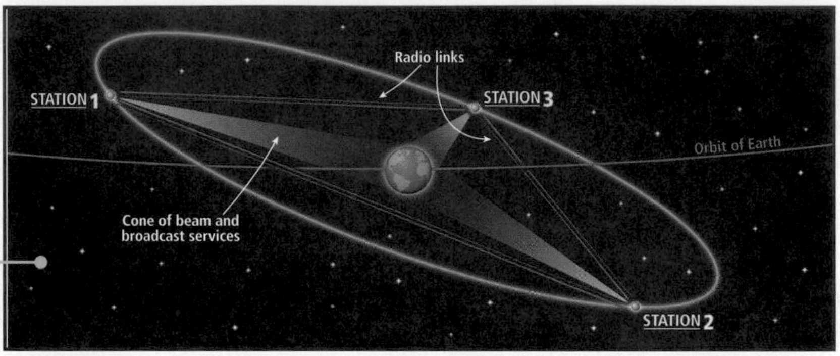

Figure 3. The stations in the chain would be linked by radio or optical beams and thus any conceivable beam or broadcast service could be provided. . . .

The author summarizes the advantages of "the space station," which can also be thought of as a series of results.

Conclusion

Briefly summarized, the advantages of the space station are as follows:

(1) It is the only way in which true world coverage can be achieved for all possible types of service.

(2) . . . an almost unlimited number of channels available would be.

(3) The power requirements are extremely small . . . Moreover, the cost of the power would be very low.

(4) However great the initial expense, it would only be a fraction of that required for the world networks replaced, and the running costs would be incomparably less.

Vocabulary Development

Content-Area Vocabulary: Science

Review the definitions of the cross-curricular vocabulary with students: *atmosphere, orbit, velocity,* and *satellite*. Then, examine each word in its context in the technical article.

When you have finished with the four listed words, ask students to identify other words in the document that fit the context of space technology, such as *meteorology, gravitational, hemisphere,* and *equidistantly*. Have students look up their definitions in a science reference book or dictionary and then use them in sentences about a space station.

Press Release

This catchy title helps to define the purpose of this press release.

Press releases often have a specific date and a specific place from which they are issued.

This paragraph, like others in the body of the release, details the benefits of the invention.

Contact:

Jen O'Leary (SSEC)

Russ Dengel (SSEC)

Weather in the palm of your hand

10 January 2006

Dengel created and maintains the PDA Animated Weather service known as PAW, which provides real time weather information in a format accesible to PDAs.

MADISON—Weather lovers have a new tool at hand to obtain weather information on demand through a PDA-friendly weather Web service created by Russ Dengel at the University of Wisconsin-Madison.

Dengel's PDA Animated Weather service, known as PAW, benefits a diverse community from long-haul truck drivers to firefighters in Puerto Rico to commuters trying to get to work safely on a snowy morning. The free service allows PDA users to access real-time radar and satellite weather images and forecasts whenever and wherever. "It's like a meteorologist's dream," says Dengel, a senior information technologist at UW-Madison's Space Science and Engineering Center, where he has access to numerous products.

Dengel frequently updates and expands the service's capabilities to meet the needs of his users. "I want to show people what's possible," Dengel says. PAW users can choose from a multitude of geographic regions and data options, including functions like animation, zoom and roam. Dengel creates these products using data from SSEC's Data Center.

Recently, he tailored the service to meet the needs of the fire department in Puerto Rico. Dengel set up a radar loop centered on San Juan and added satellite data showing clouds over the area. The PAW, he discovered, is "a fairly decent unit for first responders." He plans to continue to work with fire fighters in Puerto Rico to help them get the most out of the PAW service. Dengel also accommodated the fire department in Boise, ID by outfitting PAW with region-specific radar products.

Working with the Wisconsin Department of Transportation, Dengel now offers a PAW version of the DOT's winter road condition information. He created an option that permits users to superimpose road conditions

About Press Releases

1. Tell students this is a press release about the development of the PDA Animated Weather service known as PAW.
2. Have students read the first page of "Weather in the palm of your hand."
3. **Ask** students why a press release is an effective means of distributing this information.
   Answer: A press release provides an overall summary of the most important information on a newsworthy topic.

Analyzing Cause-and-Effect Relationships

1. Remind students that they are to look for cause-and-effect relationships throughout the press release in order to analyze the document.
2. **Ask** students to identify the cause-and-effect relationship within the second paragraph of this press release.
   Answer: PAW was developed as a means of disseminating meteorological information to many groups of people, including truck drivers, firefighters, and commuters.
3. **Ask** students to reread the third and fourth paragraphs on this page and identify how the PAW system meets a variety of needs.
   Answer: PAW's creator, Russ Dengel, updates and expands the service's capabilities, such as tailoring the service to the needs of firefighters in Puerto Rico and Boise, Idaho.

Differentiated Instruction for Universal Access

Culturally Responsive Instruction

Culture Connection This press release is about efforts to disseminate meteorological information to many groups of people. All over the world, people have a need to monitor weather conditions. Meteorological events such as snowstorms, hurricanes, tornadoes, and sudden changes in conditions can have disastrous effects. Ask students to think back to the most recent meteorological event in your community or your state. Provide newspaper articles about the event to refresh students' memory. Have students summarize what role the PAW system might have played in this event. Ask for volunteers to share their summaries with the class.

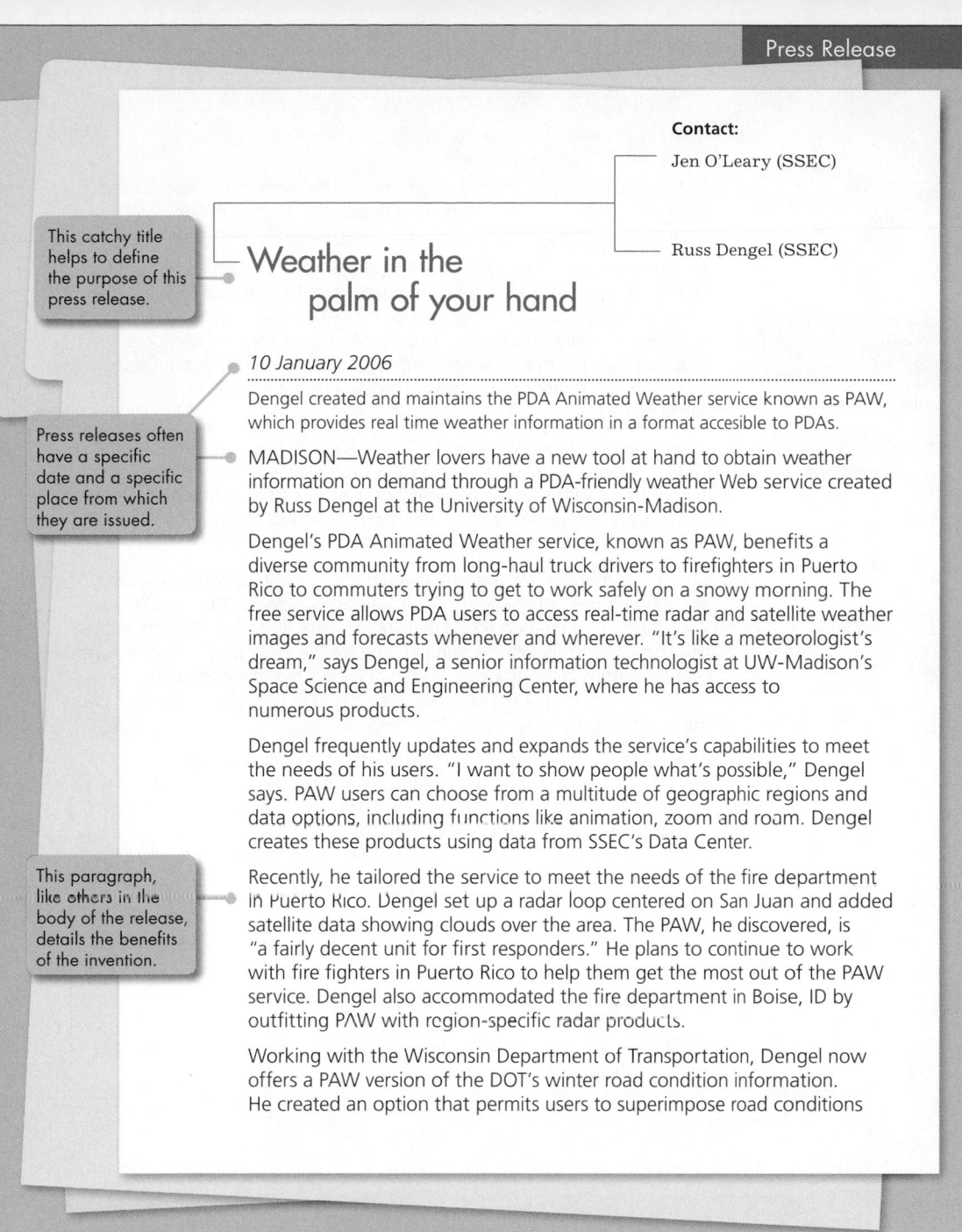

Analyze Cause-and-Effect Relationships

1. **Ask** students to locate a cause-and-effect relationship in the first full paragraph.
   Answer: Dengel developed his idea for the PAW system when he used a cell phone service to try to accurately predict snow while on a trip. The cell phone service indicated no snow would be present; he arrived to three inches of snow.
2. **Ask** students to summarize the second and third paragraphs in a sentence, demonstrating the cause-and-effect relationship.
   Answer: Dengel developed his own Web site to access images using a PDA; before long, hundreds of people around the country began to adopt his system.
3. **Ask** students to rewrite the last paragraph on this page as a cause-and-effect statement.
   Answer: As Dengel continues to respond to feedback, update the site, and add new features, more and more people are using PAW.

Press Release

on top of current satellite and radar images. By giving "motorists all the information they need to make good decisions," Dengel makes PAW invaluable to "the average Joe who's driving to work every morning."

These paragraphs explain what caused Russ Dengel to develop the PDA-friendly weather Web service.

Winter weather in Wisconsin inspired Dengel to develop PAW. Waiting for a flight out of the Milwaukee airport last winter, Dengel checked the weather in Madison using a service on his cell phone to get an idea of how long it would take to get from the Madison airport to his home in a suburb. While the mobile service indicated no snow in Madison, Dengel arrived to find three inches of snow on the ground and flakes falling rapidly.

When he made it into work at the Space Science and Engineering Center, Dengel decided to create a small Web site that allowed him to access radar images using a PDA. In the company of many weather enthusiasts, Dengel expanded the program to meet the needs of several co-workers. However, Dengel soon found out that "nothing can hide on the Web."

Only a few months after Dengel made himself a system with a few radar images, hundreds of people from all walks of life began to adopt PAW. With the help of co-workers Bill Bellon and Jerry Robaidek, Dengel created and continues to maintain a dynamic site for the PAW products. In August, over two thousand Web users landed at PAW's humble internet home. During December, the site received over 100,000 hits. The amount of Web traffic reflects the value of the PAW service.

New users keep picking up PAW products and spreading word of the site's usefulness. In response to feedback and suggestions from these users, Dengel constantly adds new products and features. He aims to increase functionality for private pilots and other speciality users. "I'm a meteorologist and I like looking at weather," says Dengel. "I found a lot of people like me."

After You Read

Technical Article • Press Release

Critical Reading

1. **(a)** What central question does the technical article ask and answer? **(b)** How does Clarke build support for his response to the question? **(c)** Is the structure he uses effective for communicating his response to the question clearly? Explain.
2. **(a)** What concepts explained verbally does the diagram illustrate? **(b)** According to Clarke, what advantages would ensue from this technology?
3. **(a)** Based on the press release, what prompted Dengel to create the PAW service? **(b)** What is the basic premise of this service? **(c)** What caused Dengel to add new features to this service?
4. **Content-Area Vocabulary (a)** The word *atmosphere* derives from the Greek root *-sphere-*, which means "globe, ball" Explain how the meaning of the Greek root informs the meaning of *atmosphere.* **(b)** Define the following words derived from the same Latin word: *spherical, hemisphere,* and *stratosphere.* **(c)** Use a dictionary to verify your definitions.

Common Core State Standards

Writing
2. Write informative/explanatory texts to examine and convey complex ideas, concepts, and information clearly and accurately through the effective selection, organization, and analysis of content.

Language
4.d. Verify the preliminary determination of the meaning of a word or phrase.

Timed Writing

Informative Text [40 minutes]

Format
In an **analytical essay,** you break a topic into smaller, meaningful segments and discuss them in a logical order. Support your ideas with sound reasons and evidence.

Write an **analytical essay** in which you explain the different uses and the benefits of satellite technology you read about in the technical article and the press release. You should use examples from the documents, but you may also draw on your knowledge of other areas in which the technology is used. Gather ideas by **synthesizing ideas and making logical connections** between the technical article and the press release.

Academic Vocabulary
When you **synthesize ideas and make logical connections,** you reach conclusions based on the relationship between the two texts.

5-Minute Planner

Complete these steps before you begin to write:

1. Read the prompt carefully and list key words.
2. Scan the text for details that relate to the prompt. **TIP** As you scan, take quick notes by jotting down key words and phrases rather than full sentences.
3. Before writing, sketch a rough outline to guide your work.
4. Reread the prompt, and begin drafting your essay.

Extend the Lesson

Connecting to the Students' World

To give students more practice with technical articles and to help them apply the material to their own world, divide the class into small groups. Have each group select a local communications company (telephone, Internet, or cable provider). Tell the groups they are to do an Internet search to find a technical article or press release by or about that company. Have students write a summary of their findings and present it to the class.

ASSESS

Answers

Critical Reading

1. (a) Can rocket stations give worldwide radio coverage? (b) He provides technical data to show that rocket stations could achieve fixed-position orbits and that three stations would be needed to provide worldwide coverage. (c) **Possible response:** Clarke's response is clear and effective because his data is arranged in logical sequence and he uses a diagram to illustrate his ideas.
2. (a) The diagram illustrates the simplest arrangement of three stations that could provide world service. (b) The costs of set-up and the running expenses would be lower than the alternatives.
3. (a) He was prompted by the winter weather in Wisconsin. (b) It provides real-time weather information in a format accessible to PDAs. (c) He updates and expands features to meet the needs of his users.
4. (a) *Atmosphere* is the air that surrounds the globe. (b) and (c) *Spherical* describes something in the shape of a globe. *Hemisphere* is half of a sphere. *Stratosphere* is a region of Earth's atmosphere. Students should verify their definitions.

Timed Writing

1. Before students begin the assignment, guide them in analyzing key words and phrases in the prompt, using the highlighted notes.
2. Work with students to draw up guidelines for their analytical essays based on the key words they identified.
3. Have students use the 5-Minute Planner to structure their time.
4. Allow students 40 minutes to complete the assignment. Evaluate their work using the guidelines they have developed.

Writing About the World Beyond Britain

1. Discuss with students their own experiences with nonfiction about faraway places. Have volunteers talk about books or articles that they have recently read.
2. After students have discussed the books and articles with which they are familiar, have them read the article about new British nonfiction.

LITERARY HISTORY

In the British journalistic tradition, writers are encouraged to inject their personality into their reporting and to express their *opinions*.

New British Nonfiction: Writing About the World Beyond Britain

Sofka Zinovieff

Simon Schama

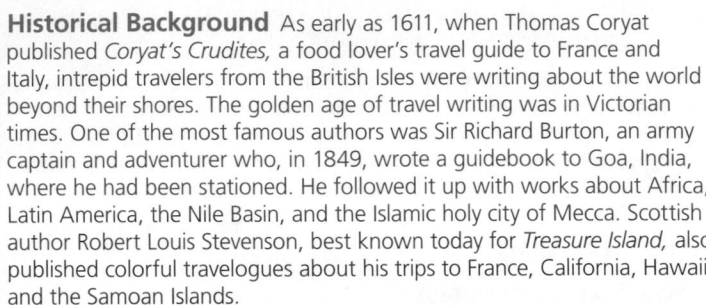

Historical Background As early as 1611, when Thomas Coryat published *Coryat's Crudites,* a food lover's travel guide to France and Italy, intrepid travelers from the British Isles were writing about the world beyond their shores. The golden age of travel writing was in Victorian times. One of the most famous authors was Sir Richard Burton, an army captain and adventurer who, in 1849, wrote a guidebook to Goa, India, where he had been stationed. He followed it up with works about Africa, Latin America, the Nile Basin, and the Islamic holy city of Mecca. Scottish author Robert Louis Stevenson, best known today for *Treasure Island,* also published colorful travelogues about his trips to France, California, Hawaii, and the Samoan Islands.

By this time, men were not the only ones traveling and writing about their voyages. Lady Anne Blunt went with her husband to the Middle East to buy horses and ended up writing *Bedouin Tribes of the Euphrates.* Mary Kingsley traveled alone to Africa and wrote the best-selling *Travels in West Africa.* Most astonishing of all was writer, political strategist, and spy Gertrude Bell. Bell published *Syria: The Desert and the Sown,* which brought images of Arabian deserts into many English parlors. Along with T. E. Lawrence, known as "Lawrence of Arabia," she helped engineer the Arab revolt against the Ottoman Empire during World War I, and then drew up the borders for modern Iraq.

Britain's role as the dominant colonial power of the nineteenth century enabled many of its writers to travel the world with relative ease, often by working for their government. Some, like Gertrude Bell, embraced the ideology of the British Empire; others energetically questioned it. All were motivated by a deep curiosity about the wider world.

Current Nonfiction In the twentieth and twenty-first centuries, British writers have continued to explore the world and to consider Britain's role in it. Working as newspaper reporters, travel writers, book authors, and essayists, they have tackled war and peace, culture and politics. Britain's flourishing publishing industry has encouraged many writers to produce carefully observed, insightful nonfiction and has provided a market for them. With one-fifth the population of the United States, Britain publishes more new book titles every year than any other country.

Today, many of the finest nonfiction writers in the English language are British. Their work can be found in newspapers, magazines, Web sites, and books. It runs the gamut from wryly nostalgic books like *Outposts: Journeys to the Surviving Relics of the British Empire* by author Simon Winchester to the sharply critical reportage of journalist Robert Fisk, author of *The Great War for Civilization: The Conquest of the Middle East.*

Newspapers and Magazines In the British journalistic tradition, writers are encouraged to inject their personality into their reporting and to express their opinions. Newspapers like *The Times, The Independent,* and *The Guardian* have nurtured writers with strong voices and helped fuel debate about many international issues.

Magazines have also contributed to the rich nonfiction tradition. One, *Granta,* has had an especially big impact by running long pieces by people who travel the world and report from their very personal perspectives. "Britain is particularly good at narrative writing, and *Granta* has played a major part in the rise of nonfiction amid what is perceived as literature," said Ian Jack, who edited the magazine for twelve years. The thoughtful personal pieces in *Granta* by writers such as James Fenton, Dilip Hiro, Jenny Diski, Simon Schama, and Sofka Zinovieff have shown that fine reporting can be a literary form.

British reportage and writing about the world is as exciting now as ever before. Those publishing today range across several generations, from writers like Jan Morris, who began her career covering the Middle East just after World War II to Robert MacFarlane, who published his first book, *Mountains of the Mind,* in 2003. American readers will discover that while we share a common language, these writers speak in a distinctly British voice.

Robert MacFarlane

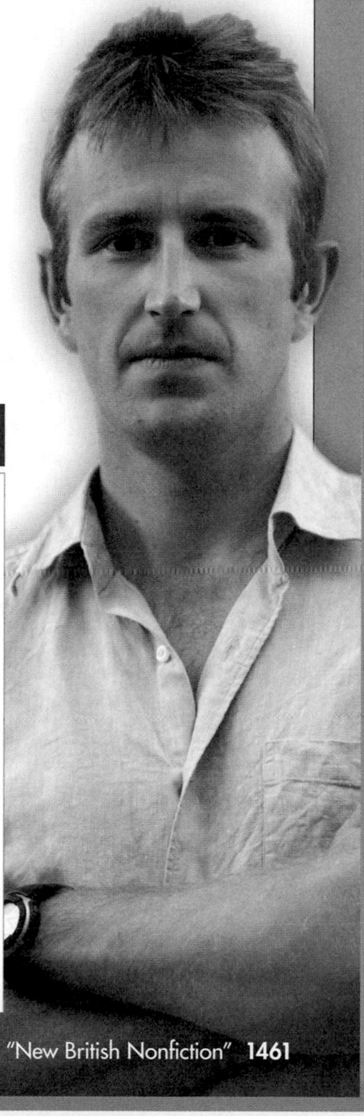

Speaking and Listening: Research

Comprehension and Collaboration Besides writing for newspapers, magazines, and Web sites, many British nonfiction writers have published books. Compile an **annotated bibliography** of five books by contemporary British writers who have explored beyond British shores and whose books you might like to read. Briefly explain your choices. Your annotated bibliography should include the book title, its author, and your comments.

To find books for your bibliography, use the Internet. You can browse the Web sites of British publications to find writers whose books have been reviewed recently. Following are the names of some prominent nonfiction writers you might want to research:

Julian Barnes	Pico Iyer	Jan Morris
Liam D'Arcy Brown	Ian Jack	Simon Schama
Jenny Diski	Robert MacFarlane	Tahir Shah
James Fenton	Catherine Merridale	Simon Winchester
Robert Fisk	Anne Mustoe	Gary Younge
Dilip Hiro	Tim Moore	Sofka Zinovieff

Background

Granta

Granta originated as a magazine created by students of Cambridge University in 1889. It originally featured political and literary writing. Some of Britain's best-known authors got their start at the magazine.

In 1979, interest in *Granta* was flagging. The publication was then taken up by postgraduates who reworked it into a collection of fiction, reporting, and photography. Today, *Granta* continues to promote the work of young writers.

Speaking and Listening: Research

1. Read the Annotated Bibliography instructions with the class. Remind students that an annotated bibliography lists citations and then gives a brief description and evaluation of the source. The purpose of the annotation is to inform the reader about the relevance and accuracy of the sources cited.
2. Encourage students to explore both library and Internet resources in order to find books for their bibliographies. Students may wish to focus on books about a single topic of interest or choose books that cover a range of topics.
3. Have each student share the contents of his or her bibliography with a partner. Students should discuss what they have learned about each book and why they think it looks interesting. Encourage students to find one or more of the books in their school or local library and read them.

• *from* Songbook: "I'm Like a Bird"

Lesson Pacing Guide

DAY 1 Preteach

- Administer the Reading and Vocabulary Warm-ups (*Unit 6 Resources*, pp. 398–401) as necessary.
- Introduce the Literary Analysis concept: Personal Essay.
- Introduce the Reading Strategy: Outlining Arguments and Strategies.
- Build background with the author and Background features.
- Develop thematic thinking with Connecting to the Essential Question.
- Teach the selection vocabulary.

DAY 2 Preteach/Teach/Extend

- Distribute copies of the appropriate graphic organizer for the Reading Strategy (*Graphic Organizer Transparencies*, pp. 284–285).
- Distribute copies of the appropriate graphic organizer for Literary Analysis (*Graphic Organizer Transparencies*, pp. 286–287).
- Prepare students to read with the Activating Prior Knowledge activities (TE).
- Informally monitor comprehension while students read.
- Use the Reading Check questions to confirm comprehension.
- Develop students' understanding of a personal essay using the Literary Analysis prompts.
- Develop students' ability to outline arguments and strategies using the Reading Strategy prompts.
- Reinforce vocabulary with the Vocabulary notes.
- Assess students' comprehension and mastery of the skills by having them answer the Critical Reading, Literary Analysis, and Reading Strategy questions.

DAY 3 Assess

- Have students complete the Vocabulary activities.
- Have students complete the Writing activity, writing explanatory notes. (You may assign as homework.)
- Administer Selection Test A or B (*Unit 6 Resources*, pp. 410–412 or 413–415).

Common Core State Standards

Reading Informational Text 5. Analyze and evaluate the effectiveness of the structure an author uses in his or her exposition or argument, including whether the structure makes points clear, convincing, and engaging.

Writing 2. Write informative/explanatory texts to examine and convey complex ideas, concepts, and information clearly and accurately through the effective selection, organization, and analysis of content.

Additional Standards Practice
***Common Core Companion*, pp. 136–137; 196–207**

Daily Block Scheduling
Each day in this Lesson Pacing Guide represents a 40–50 minute period. Teachers using block scheduling may combine days to revise pacing. In addition, teachers may differentiate and support core instruction by integrating components for extended and intensive support as students require. See the Guide to Selected Leveled Resources (facing page).

Guide to Selected Leveled Resources

RTI Tier 1 (students performing on level)

			from Songbook: "I'm Like a Bird"
Warm Up	Whole class instruction; Group work	**Practice, model,** and **monitor** fluency, working **with the whole class** or **in groups.**	**Vocabulary** and **Reading Warm-ups B,** ***Unit 6 Resources,*** pp. 416–417, 419
Comprehension/Skills	Whole class instruction; Group work; Independent work	**Support** and **monitor** comprehension and skills development, having students complete the activities, graphic organizers, and interactive prompts **independently** or **as a class.**	• ***Reader's Notebook,*** adapted instruction and full selection EL ***Reader's Notebook: English Learner's Version,*** adapted instruction and adapted selection • **Reading Strategy Graphic Organizer B,** ***Graphic Organizer Transparencies,*** p. 299 • **Literary Analysis Graphic Organizer B,** ***Graphic Organizer Transparencies,*** p. 301
Monitor Progress	A	**Monitor** student progress with the differentiated curriculum-based assessment in the *Unit Resources.*	• **Selection Test B,** ***Unit 6 Resources,*** pp. 431–433 • **Open-Book Test,** ***Unit 6 Resources,*** pp. 425–427
Assess/Screen	A	• **Assess** student progress using Benchmark Test 2. • **Preassess** instructional needs using the Vocabulary in Context section of the test.	• **Benchmark Test 12,** ***Unit 6 Resources,*** pp. 439–444

RTI Tier 2 (students requiring intervention)

			from Songbook: "I'm Like a Bird"
Warm Up	Group work; One-on-one teaching	**Practice, model,** and **monitor** fluency **in groups** or **with individuals.**	• **Vocabulary and Reading Warm-ups A,** ***Unit 6 Resources,*** pp. 416–418 • ***Hear It!*** **Audio CD (adapted text)**
Comprehension/Skills	Group work; One-on-one teaching	• **Support** and **monitor** comprehension and skills development, working **in small groups** or **with individuals.** • As students complete the selection in the appropriate version of the *Reader's Notebook,* **monitor** comprehension frequently with group questions and individual instruction. • **Model** strategies while guiding students in completing the activities and prompts in the *Reader's Notebook,* as well as the graphic organizers. • **Practice** skills and **monitor** mastery with the *Reading Kit* worksheets.	• ***Reader's Notebook: Adapted Version,*** adapted instruction and adapted selection EL ***Reader's Notebook: English Learner's Version,*** adapted instruction and adapted selection • **Reading Skill Graphic Organizer A,** ***Graphic Organizer Transparencies,*** p. 298 • **Literary Analysis Graphic Organizer A,** ***Graphic Organizer Transparencies,*** p. 300 • ***Reading Kit,*** Practice worksheets
Monitor Progress	A	**Monitor** student progress with the differentiated curriculum-based assessment in the *Unit Resources* and in the *Reading Kit.*	• **Selection Test A,** ***Unit 6 Resources,*** pp. 428–430 • ***Reading Kit,*** Assess worksheets
Assess/Screen	A	• **Assess** student progress using the Benchmark Test. • **Preassess** instructional needs using the Vocabulary in Context section of the test.	**Benchmark Test 12,** ***Unit 6 Resources,*** pp. 439–444

TIER 3 Tier 3 intervention may require consultation with the student's special-education or dyslexia specialist. For additional support, see the Tier 2 activities and resources listed above.

One-on-one teaching | Group work | Whole class instruction | Independent work | A Assessment

For a complete guide to selection support, including support for Advanced students, see the Overview of Resources in the frontmatter.

• *from* Songbook: "I'm Like a Bird"

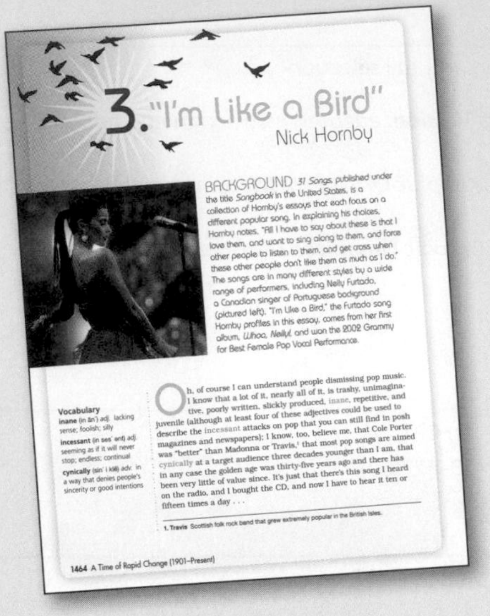

3. "I'm Like a Bird"
Nick Hornby

BACKGROUND *31 Songs*, published under the title *Songbook* in the United States, is a collection of Hornby's essays that each focus on a different popular song. In explaining his choices, Hornby notes, "All I have to say about these is that I love them, and want to sing along to them, and force other people to listen to them, and get cross when these other people don't like them as much as I do." The songs are in many different styles by a wide range of performers, including Nelly Furtado, a Canadian singer of Portuguese background (pictured left). "I'm Like a Bird," the Furtado song Hornby profiles in this essay, comes from her first album, *Whoa, Nelly!*, and won the 2002 Grammy for Best Female Pop Vocal Performance.

Vocabulary
inane (in ān') adj. lacking sense; foolish; silly
incessant (in ses' ənt) adj. seeming as if it will never stop; endless; continual
cynically (sin' i klē) adv. in a way that denies people's sincerity or good intentions

Oh, of course I can understand people dismissing pop music. I know that a lot of it, nearly all of it, is trashy, unimaginative, poorly written, slickly produced, inane, repetitive, and juvenile (although at least four of these adjectives could be used to describe the incessant attacks on pop that you can still find in posh magazines and newspapers); I know, too, believe me, that Cole Porter was "better" than Madonna or Travis,[1] that most pop songs are aimed cynically at a target audience three decades younger than I am, that in any case the golden age was thirty-five years ago and there has been very little of value since. It's just that there's this song I heard on the radio, and I bought the CD, and now I have to hear it ten or fifteen times a day . . .

1. Travis Scottish folk rock band that grew extremely popular in the British Isles.

1464 A Time of Rapid Change (1901–Present)

RESOURCES FOR:

- L1 Special-Needs Students
- L2 Below-Level Students (Tier 2)
- L3 On-Level Students (Tier 1)
- L4 Advanced Students (Tier 1)
- EL English Learners
- All All Students

Vocabulary/Fluency/Prior Knowledge

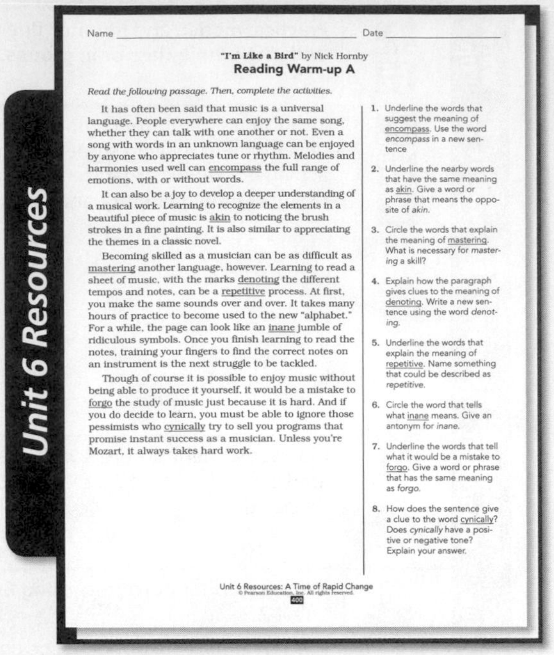

Name ______________ Date ______________

"I'm Like a Bird" by Nick Hornby
Reading Warm-up A

Read the following passage. Then, complete the activities.

It has often been said that music is a universal language. People everywhere can enjoy the same song, whether they can talk with one another or not. Even a song with words in an unknown language can be enjoyed by anyone who appreciates tune or rhythm. Melodies and harmonies used well can encompass the full range of emotions, with or without words.

It can also be a joy to develop a deeper understanding of a musical work. Learning to recognize the elements in a beautiful piece of music is akin to noticing the brush strokes in a fine painting. It is also similar to appreciating the themes in a classic novel.

Becoming skilled as a musician can be as difficult as mastering another language, however. Learning to read a sheet of music, with the marks denoting the different tempos and notes, can be a repetitive process. At first, you make the same sounds over and over. It takes many hours of practice to become used to the new "alphabet." For a while, the page can look like an inane jumble of ridiculous symbols. Once you finish learning to read the notes, training your fingers to find the correct notes on an instrument is the next struggle to be tackled.

Though of course it is possible to enjoy music without being able to produce it yourself, it would be a mistake to forgo the study of music just because it is hard. And if you do decide to learn, you must be able to ignore those pessimists who cynically try to sell you programs that promise instant success as a musician. Unless you're Mozart, it always takes hard work.

1. Underline the words that suggest the meaning of encompass. Use the word *encompass* in a new sentence
2. Underline the nearby words that have the same meaning as akin. Give a word or phrase that means the opposite of *akin*.
3. Circle the words that explain the meaning of mastering. What is necessary for *mastering* a skill?
4. Explain how the paragraph gives clues to the meaning of denoting. Write a new sentence using the word *denoting*.
5. Underline the words that explain the meaning of repetitive. Name something that could be described as *repetitive*.
6. Circle the word that tells what inane means. Give an antonym for *inane*.
7. Underline the words that tell what it would be a mistake to forgo. Give a word or phrase that has the same meaning as *forgo*.
8. How does the sentence give a clue to the word cynically? Does *cynically* have a positive or negative tone? Explain your answer.

Unit 6 Resources: A Time of Rapid Change
© Pearson Education, Inc. All rights reserved.
400

EL L1 L2 **Reading Warm-ups A and B,** pp. 400–401

Also available for these selections:

EL L1 L2 **Vocabulary Warm-ups A and B,** pp. 398–399

All **Vocabulary Builder,** pp. 404

Reader's Notebooks

Pre- and postreading pages for this selection appear in an interactive format in the *Reader's Notebooks*. Each *Notebook* is differentiated for a different group of learners.
The selections in the Adapted and English Learner's versions are abridged.

L2 L3 ***Reader's Notebook***

L1 ***Reader's Notebook: Adapted Version***

EL ***Reader's Notebook: English Learner's Version***

EL ***Reader's Notebook: Spanish Version***

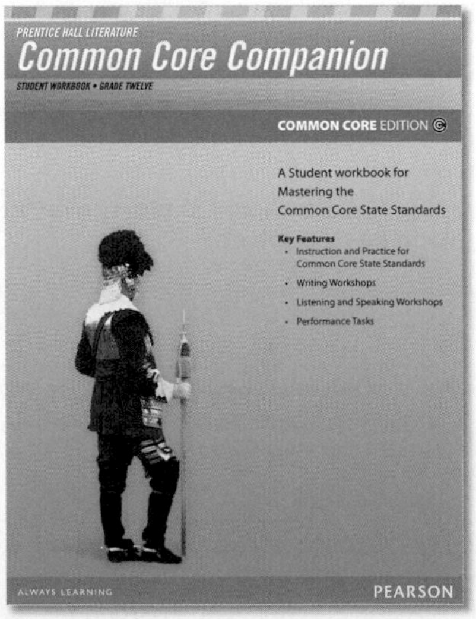

Common Core Companion

Additional instruction and practice for each Common Core State Standard

Selection Support

Graphic Organizer Transparencies

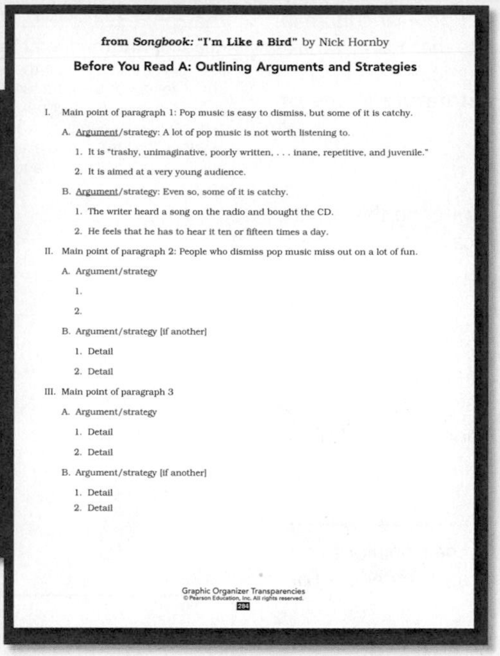
from *Songbook:* "I'm Like a Bird" by Nick Hornby

Before You Read A: Outlining Arguments and Strategies

I. Main point of paragraph 1: Pop music is easy to dismiss, but some of it is catchy.
A. Argument/strategy: A lot of pop music is not worth listening to.
1. It is "trashy, unimaginative, poorly written, . . . inane, repetitive, and juvenile."
2. It is aimed at a very young audience.
B. Argument/strategy: Even so, some of it is catchy.
1. The writer heard a song on the radio and bought the CD.
2. He feels that he has to hear it ten or fifteen times a day.
II. Main point of paragraph 2: People who dismiss pop music miss out on a lot of fun.
A. Argument/strategy
1.
2.
B. Argument/strategy [if another]
1. Detail
2. Detail
III. Main point of paragraph 3
A. Argument/strategy
1. Detail
2. Detail
B. Argument/strategy [if another]
1. Detail
2. Detail

Graphic Organizer Transparencies
© Pearson Education, Inc. All rights reserved.
284

EL L1 L2 **Reading: Graphic Organizer A,** p. 284

Also available for these selections:

EL L3 **Reading: Graphic Organizer B,** p. 285

EL L1 L2 **Literary Analysis: Graphic Organizer A,** (partially filled in), p. 286

EL L3 **Literary Analysis: Graphic Organizer B,** p. 287

Skills Development/Extension

Unit 6 Resources

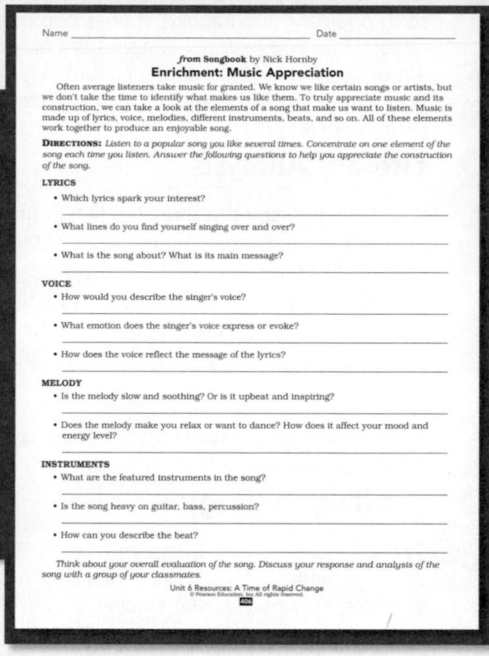
Name ______________ Date ______________

from **Songbook** by Nick Hornby

Enrichment: Music Appreciation

Often average listeners take music for granted. We know we like certain songs or artists, but we don't take the time to identify what makes us like them. To truly appreciate music and its construction, we can take a look at the elements of a song that make us want to listen. Music is made up of lyrics, voice, melodies, different instruments, beats, and so on. All of these elements work together to produce an enjoyable song.

Directions: *Listen to a popular song you like several times. Concentrate on one element of the song each time you listen. Answer the following questions to help you appreciate the construction of the song.*

LYRICS
- Which lyrics spark your interest?
- What lines do you find yourself singing over and over?
- What is the song about? What is its main message?

VOICE
- How would you describe the singer's voice?
- What emotion does the singer's voice express or evoke?
- How does the voice reflect the message of the lyrics?

MELODY
- Is the melody slow and soothing? Or is it upbeat and inspiring?
- Does the melody make you relax or want to dance? How does it affect your mood and energy level?

INSTRUMENTS
- What are the featured instruments in the song?
- Is the song heavy on guitar, bass, percussion?
- How can you describe the beat?

Think about your overall evaluation of the song. Discuss your response and analysis of the song with a group of your classmates.

Unit 6 Resources: A Time of Rapid Change
© Pearson Education, Inc. All rights reserved.
406

L4 **Enrichment,** p. 406

Also available for these selections:

All **Literary Analysis: Personal Essay,** p. 402,

All **Reading: Outlining Arguments and Strategies,** p. 403

EL L3 L4 **Support for Writing,** p. 405

Assessment

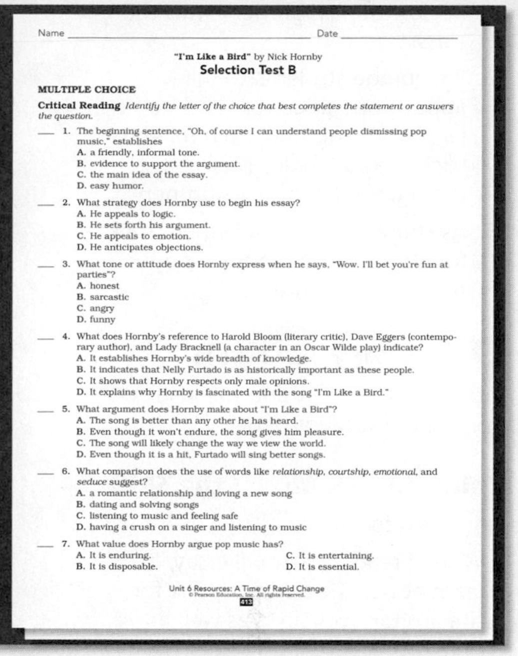
Name ______________ Date ______________

"I'm Like a Bird" by Nick Hornby

Selection Test B

MULTIPLE CHOICE

Critical Reading *Identify the letter of the choice that best completes the statement or answers the question.*

___ 1. The beginning sentence, "Oh, of course I can understand people dismissing pop music," establishes
A. a friendly, informal tone.
B. evidence to support the argument.
C. the main idea of the essay.
D. easy humor.

___ 2. What strategy does Hornby use to begin his essay?
A. He appeals to logic.
B. He sets forth his argument.
C. He appeals to emotion.
D. He anticipates objections.

___ 3. What tone or attitude does Hornby express when he says, "Wow. I'll bet you're fun at parties"?
A. honest
B. sarcastic
C. angry
D. funny

___ 4. What does Hornby's reference to Harold Bloom (literary critic), Dave Eggers (contemporary author), and Lady Bracknell (a character in an Oscar Wilde play) indicate?
A. It establishes Hornby's wide breadth of knowledge.
B. It indicates that Nelly Furtado is as historically important as these people.
C. It shows that Hornby respects only male opinions.
D. It explains why Hornby is fascinated with the song "I'm Like a Bird."

___ 5. What argument does Hornby make about "I'm Like a Bird"?
A. The song is better than any other he has heard.
B. Even though it won't endure, the song gives him pleasure.
C. The song will likely change the way we view the world.
D. Even though it is a hit, Furtado will sing better songs.

___ 6. What comparison does the use of words like *relationship, courtship, emotional,* and *seduce* suggest?
A. a romantic relationship and loving a new song
B. dating and solving songs
C. listening to music and feeling safe
D. having a crush on a singer and listening to music

___ 7. What value does Hornby argue pop music has?
A. It is enduring. C. It is entertaining.
B. It is disposable. D. It is essential.

Unit 6 Resources: A Time of Rapid Change
© Pearson Education, Inc. All rights reserved.
413

EL L3 L4 **Selection Test B,** pp. 413–415

Also available for these selections:

EL L1 L2 **Selection Test A, pp. 410–412**

L3 L4 **Open-Book Test, pp. 407–409**

PHLit Online!
www.PHLitOnline.com

Online Resources: All print materials are also available online.

- complete narrated selection text
- a thematically related video with writing prompt
- an interactive graphic organizer
- highlighting feature
- access to all student print resources, adapted to individual student needs
- Spanish and English summaries
- adapted selection translations in Spanish

Background Video

Also available:

Get Connected! (thematic video with writing prompt)
All videos are available in Spanish.

Vocabulary Central (tools and activities for studying vocabulary)

Also available:

Writer's Journal (with graphics feature)

PRETEACH

1 Connecting to the Essential Question

1. Review the assignment with the class.
2. Encourage students to think about popular culture and popular music, and how each reflects society as a whole. Then, have them complete the assignment.
3. As students read, have them look for Hornby's opinions on popular music and culture.

2 Literary Analysis

Introduce the skill using the instruction on the student page.

Think Aloud: Model the Skill

Say to students:

When I read a personal essay, I learn about the author. I look for the author's opinions as well as details that reveal his or her personality and life experiences. I also look for the author's tone. I know that in personal essays, the tone is usually less formal and more easygoing, and that frequently humor is employed by the essayist.

3 Reading Strategy

1. Introduce the skill using the instruction on the student page.
2. Give students a copy of **Reading Strategy Graphic Organizer B,** page 285 in *Graphic Organizer Transparencies,* to fill out as they read.

Think Aloud: Model the Skill

Say to students:

When I read a personal essay, I look for the arguments and strategies the essayist uses. Some authors might use emotion or humor. Other authors might use logic and persuasive techniques. How each author approaches his or her personal essay shapes the tone and overall effect of the piece.

4 Vocabulary

1. Pronounce each word, giving its definition, and have students say it aloud.
2. For more guidance, see the *Classroom Strategies and Teaching Routines* card for introducing vocabulary.

Before You Read

"I'm Like a Bird"
from ***Songbook***

1 Connecting to the Essential Question What makes a popular song popular? To what extent does pop music reflect popular culture in general? As you read, think about the broader points that Hornby makes about pop music and popular culture in general. Your ideas will help you respond to the Essential Question: **How does literature shape or reflect society?**

Common Core State Standards

Reading Informational Text
5. Analyze and evaluate the effectiveness of the structure an author uses in his or her exposition or argument, including whether the structure makes points clear, convincing, and engaging.

2 Literary Analysis

A **personal essay** is a short nonfiction prose piece offering the writer's personal observations on a particular subject. It typically contains some or all of these features:

- A friendly, informal tone, with easy humor
- Opinions about the subject
- Details that reveal the writer's life or personality
- Comments on life in general

Notice not only what Hornby's essay says about pop music but also what it reveals about Hornby himself and about life in general.

3 Reading Strategy

Preparing to Read Complex Texts To present their opinions convincingly, essayists often use a variety of arguments and strategies. For example, they may do the following:

- Appeal to emotions based on common experiences
- Anticipate and refute opinions different from their own
- Use logic to argue particular points
- Use humor to make their arguments appealing

Outlining the arguments and strategies will help you understand the essayist's points. Use an outline form like the one shown. Then, evaluate the effectiveness of the essay's organizational structure by considering how clearly and effectively Hornby communicates his ideas.

Outlining

I. Main point of paragraph 1
A. Argument/strategy
1. Detail
2. Detail
B. Argument/strategy [if another]
1. Detail
2. Detail
II. Main point of paragraph 2

4 Vocabulary

inane (in ān′) *adj.* lacking sense; foolish; silly (p. 1464)

incessant (in ses′ ənt) *adj.* seeming as if it will never stop; endless; continual (p. 1464)

cynically (sin′ i klē) *adv.* in a way that denies people's sincerity or good intentions (p. 1464)

languor (laŋ′ gər) *n.* lack of vitality; sluggishness (p. 1465)

anemic (ə nē′ mik) *adj.* lacking vigor; weak; lifeless (p. 1465)

disposable (di spō′ zə bəl) *adj.* able to be discarded; having only a short period of usefulness (p. 1465)

PHLit Online! www.PHLitOnline.com

Vocabulary Development

Vocabulary Knowledge Rating

Create a **Vocabulary Knowledge Rating Chart** (*Professional Development Guidebook,* p. 33) for the vocabulary words on the student page. Give each student a copy of the chart with the words on it. Read the words aloud, and have students mark their rating of each in the Before Reading column. When students have completed reading and discussing this selection, have them take out their **Vocabulary Knowledge Rating Charts** for the story. Read the words aloud and have students rate their knowledge again in the After Reading column. Clarify any words that are still problematic. Then, have students complete the Vocabulary practice at the end of the selection.

PHLit Online! **Vocabulary Central,** featuring tools and activities for studying vocabulary, is available online at **www.PHLitOnline.com.**

5 Nick Hornby

(b. 1957)

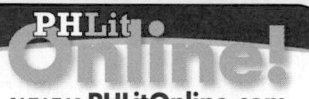

Author of "I'm Like a Bird"

Work, romance, parenthood, pop music, sports—these are some of the everyday subjects that Nick Hornby explores in his fiction and nonfiction. A noted commentator on popular culture, Hornby has won fame on both sides of the Atlantic for his ability to capture, with sympathy and humor, the ordinary concerns and anxieties of contemporary life.

A Disconcerting Childhood Hornby learned something about anxiety in his own childhood. The son of Sir Derek Hornby, a wealthy and influential businessman, Nick Hornby was raised by his schoolteacher mother after his parents divorced. Yet periodically he left his normal middle-class existence to visit the exotic world his father inhabited. "I never wanted to be in that world," Hornby once told an interviewer. "I was much happier with my mates at home."

From Books to Screen The dual nature of Hornby's life is evident in *Fever Pitch* (1992), the book that established his writing career. An autobiographical work focusing on his obsession with a London soccer team called Arsenal, *Fever Pitch* was hugely popular in Britain, where it was made into a 1997 film starring Colin Firth. Some years later, Jimmy Fallon starred in an American version in which the team was changed to baseball's Boston Red Sox.

Other Hornby books adapted for film include *High Fidelity* (1995), which draws on another of Hornby's passions, popular music; and *About a Boy* (1998), which explores the relationship between aimless Will Freeman and the twelve-year-old boy who claims him as a mentor.

Writing for Charity Hornby faced anguish in his relationship with his own son when Danny was diagnosed as autistic. Determined to do something about this development disorder, Hornby in 1997 helped found TreeHouse, a London school for autistic children. Among his fundraising ventures, he persuaded a number of talented writers to contribute to *Speaking with the Angel* (2000), a story collection he edited, which was then sold to benefit the TreeHouse project.

"It seemed obvious to me that popular culture is an important part of all our lives and it should have some kind of reflection in the books we are reading."

Daily Bellringer

For each class during which you will teach this selection, have students complete one of the activities for the appropriate week in the ***Daily Bellringer Activities*** booklet.

Multidraft Reading

To assist struggling readers and to enhance reading for all, assign the text in chunks, as warranted by length, and apply multidraft reading protocols. For each reading, have students set the purpose indicated:

- **First reading**—identifying key ideas and details and answering any Reading Checks.
- **Second reading**—analyzing craft and structure and responding to the side-column prompts.
- **Third reading**—integrating knowledge and ideas, connecting to other texts and the world, and answering the end-of-selection questions.

For more guidance, refer to the ***Classroom Strategies and Teaching Routines*** card on Multidraft Reading.

5 Background

More About the Author

After attending university, Nick Hornby began his career writing plays, and he later worked as a journalist. He has also written for *The New Yorker* as a pop music critic. Hornby's writing deals with ordinary, daily things, and is sometimes described as "domestic"—a moniker he actually welcomes.

PHLit Online! Teaching From Technology

www.PHLitOnline.com

Preparing to Read

Go to **www.PHLitOnline.com** and display the ***Get Connected!*** slide show for this selection. Have the class brainstorm responses to the writing prompt, entering ideas in the interactive journal. Then, have students complete their written responses as homework.

To build background, display the Background and More About the Author features.

Using the Interactive Text

Go to **www.PHLitOnline.com** and display the **Enriched Online Student Edition.** As the class reads the selection or listens to the narration, record answers to side-column prompts using the graphic organizers accessible on the interactive page. Alternatively, have students use the online edition individually, answering the prompts as they read.

TEACH

❶ About the Selection

This personal essay is a short reflection on popular music. Specifically, in this selection, Nick Hornby discusses the song "I'm Like a Bird," by Nelly Furtado. This song is the latest in his list of "favorite songs," and he takes time here to discuss the joys found in loving a song, listening to it over and over again, and watching others enjoy the same song as well.

❷ Activating Prior Knowledge

Popular culture and popular music infuse many parts of our lives. Have students think about a particular song, musical group, or musical genre that speaks to them. Have each student write a short paragraph about his or her choice.

Concept Connector →

Tell students they will return to their responses after reading the selection.

❶ ❷ 3. "I'm Like a Bird"

Nick Hornby

BACKGROUND *31 Songs,* published under the title *Songbook* in the United States, is a collection of Hornby's essays that each focus on a different popular song. In explaining his choices, Hornby notes, "All I have to say about these is that I love them, and want to sing along to them, and force other people to listen to them, and get cross when these other people don't like them as much as I do." The songs are in many different styles by a wide range of performers, including Nelly Furtado, a Canadian singer of Portuguese background (pictured left). "I'm Like a Bird," the Furtado song Hornby profiles in this essay, comes from her first album, *Whoa, Nelly!,* and won the 2002 Grammy for Best Female Pop Vocal Performance.

Vocabulary

inane (in ān′) *adj.* lacking sense; foolish; silly

incessant (in ses′ ənt) *adj.* seeming as if it will never stop; endless; continual

cynically (sin′ i klē) *adv.* in a way that denies people's sincerity or good intentions

Oh, of course I can understand people dismissing pop music. I know that a lot of it, nearly all of it, is trashy, unimaginative, poorly written, slickly produced, **inane**, repetitive, and juvenile (although at least four of these adjectives could be used to describe the **incessant** attacks on pop that you can still find in posh magazines and newspapers); I know, too, believe me, that Cole Porter was "better" than Madonna or Travis,[1] that most pop songs are aimed **cynically** at a target audience three decades younger than I am, that in any case the golden age was thirty-five years ago and there has been very little of value since. It's just that there's this song I heard on the radio, and I bought the CD, and now I have to hear it ten or fifteen times a day . . .

1. **Travis** Scottish folk rock band that grew extremely popular in the British Isles.

Ⓒ Text Complexity Rubric

"I'm Like a Bird"			
Qualitative Measures			
Context/Knowledge Demands	Contemporary nonfiction; cultural knowledge demands 1 2 ③ 4 5		
Structure/Language Clarity	Accessible diction 1 ② 3 4 5		
Levels of Meaning	Accessible (pop music; cultural commentary) 1 2 ③ 4 5		
Quantitative Measures			
Lexile	1460L	**Text Length**	748 words
Overall Complexity	**More accessible**		

Reader and Task Suggestions

Preparing to Read the Text

- Using the Background on TE p. 1463, note that Hornby, well known for his autobiographical writings, has also served as a pop music critic.
- Discuss with students the role of music in popular culture. Ask whether pop music has a unifying social effect.
- Guide students to use Multidraft Reading strategies (TE p. 1463).

Leveled Tasks

Levels of Meaning If students will have difficulty with the selection's meaning, have them read to determine the author's main ideas about Furtado's song. Then have them reread to focus on supporting details.

Evaluating If students will not have difficulty with the meaning, have them evaluate whether or not Hornby makes a persuasive case.

4 That's the thing that puzzles me about those who feel that contemporary pop (and I use the word to encompass soul, reggae, country, rock—anything and everything that might be regarded as trashy) is beneath them, or behind them, or beyond them—some preposition denoting distance, anyway: Does this mean that you never hear, or at least never enjoy, new songs, that everything you whistle or hum was written years, decades, centuries ago? Do you really deny yourselves the pleasure of mastering a tune (a pleasure, incidentally, that your generation is perhaps the first in the history of mankind to forgo) because you are afraid it might make you look as if you don't know who Harold Bloom[2] is? Wow. I'll bet you're fun at parties.

The song that has been driving me pleasurably potty recently is "I'm Like a Bird" by Nelly Furtado. Only history will judge whether Ms. Furtado turns out to be any kind of artist, and though I have my suspicions that she will not change the way we look at the world, I can't say that I'm very bothered: I will always be grateful to her for creating in me the narcotic need to hear her song again and again. It is, after all, a harmless need, easily satisfied, and there are few enough of those in the world. I don't even want to make a case for this song, as opposed to any other—although I happen to think that it's a very good pop song, with a dreamy **languor** and a bruised optimism that immediately distinguishes it from its **anemic** and stunted peers. The point is that a few months ago it didn't exist, at least as far as we are concerned, and now here it is, and that, in itself, is a small miracle.

Dave Eggers[3] has a theory that we play songs over and over, those of us who do, because we have to "solve" them, and it's true that in our early relationship with, and courtship of, a new song, there is a stage which is akin to a sort of emotional puzzlement. There's a little bit in "I'm Like a Bird," for example, about halfway through, where the voice is double-tracked on a phrase, and the effect—especially on someone who is not a musician, someone who loves and appreciates music but is baffled and seduced by even the simplest musical tricks—is rich and fresh and addictive.

Sure, it will seem thin and stale soon enough. Before very long I will have "solved" "I'm Like a Bird," and I won't want to hear it very much anymore—a three-minute pop song can only withhold its mysteries for so long, after all. So, yes, it's **disposable**, as if that makes any difference to anyone's perceptions of the value of pop music. But then, shouldn't we be sick of the *Moonlight* Sonata by now? Or *Christina's World?*[4] Or *The Importance of Being Earnest?* They're

2. **Harold Bloom** (b. 1930) Yale University professor who has written and edited numerous books on English literature.
3. **Dave Eggers** (b. 1970) American author whose publishing company published Hornby's *Songbook*.
4. ***Christina's World*** famous painting by American artist Andrew Wyeth (b. 1917).

3 Reading Strategy
Outlining Arguments and Strategies
What logical and emotional appeals does Hornby use to make his argument about pop music more convincing?

Vocabulary
languor (laŋ′ gər) *n.* lack of vitality; sluggishness
anemic (ə nē′ mik) *adj.* lacking vigor; weak; lifeless
disposable (di spō′ zə bəl) *adj.* able to be discarded; having only a short period of usefulness

5 Reading Check
What song is "driving" Hornby "potty"?

3 Reading Strategy

Outlining Arguments and Strategies

1. Direct students' attention to the second paragraph of the essay.
2. **Ask** the Reading Strategy question: What logical and emotional appeals does Hornby use to make his argument about pop music more convincing?
3. **Possible responses:** Students might offer that Hornby appeals to logic by discussing his simple enjoyment of "I'm Like a Bird." Hornby appeals to emotion by stating that those who denigrate contemporary pop puzzle him. He expresses concern, of a sort, that the current generation considers itself above or beyond contemporary pop. By implying that he does not believe that people dislike contemporary pop, his argument is more convincing.

4 Critical Thinking

Infer

1. Direct students' attention to the first paragraph on page 1465.
2. **Ask** students: Why might Hornby be referring to Harold Bloom?
3. Direct students' attention to footnote 2, which describes Harold Bloom.
4. **Possible responses:** Students might offer that Bloom is the author of *The Closing of the American Mind,* which presents a low opinion of popular culture and music. Hornby is inferring that people might deny that they listen to and enjoy popular music because they might want to seem more erudite than they are.

5 Reading Check

Answer: "I'm Like a Bird" by Nelly Furtado

Concept Connector

Reading Strategy Graphic Organizer

Ask students to review the graphic organizers in which they have outlined arguments and strategies. Then, have students share their organizers and compare their outlines.

Activating Prior Knowledge

Have students return to their responses to the Activating Prior Knowledge activity. Ask them to explain whether their thoughts have changed and, if so, how.

Writing About the Essential Question

Have students compare their responses to the prompt, completed before reading the essay, with their thoughts afterward. Have them work individually or in groups, writing or discussing their thoughts, to formulate new responses. Then, lead a class discussion, probing for what students have learned that confirms or invalidates their initial thoughts. Encourage students to cite specific textual details to support their responses.

PHLit Online!

This selection is available in interactive format in the **Enriched Online Student Edition**, at **www.PHLitOnline.com,** which includes a thematically related video with writing prompt and an interactive graphic organizer.

6 Literary Analysis

Personal Essay

1. Have students reread the last paragraph.
2. **Ask** students the Literary Analysis questions: What does the last paragraph reveal about Hornby? At what broader comment about life does the final sentence hint?
   Answers: The last paragraph reveals that Hornby loves to discover new songs and never really believes the next song will be as good as the one he currently loves. The last sentence tells us that Hornby has an insatiable appetite for new music and that it makes his "life worth living."

ASSESS

Answers

Remind students to support their answers with evidence from the text.

1. (a) Hornby's definition includes soul, reggae, rock, and anything that might be considered "trashy" music. (b) People who consider this music trashy are those who feel they are above it. (c) He does not share that opinion. He implies that everyone, at some point, has enjoyed pop music.
2. (a) He likes "I'm Like a Bird" because of its "dreamy languor" and "bruised optimism." (b) He uses Eggers's theory of loving songs as puzzles to be solved. Hornby writes that at some point he will "solve" "I'm Like a Bird."
3. (a) Hornby compares *Moonlight Sonata, Christina's World,* and *The Importance of Being Earnest* to contemporary pop music. (b) Hornby believes the cultural establishment holds them in high esteem.
4. (a) Hornby watched as the four girls in the waiting room sang the song, danced, and outwardly enjoyed "I'm Like a Bird." (b) This incident suggests that pop music cuts across racial, class, ethnic, and generational lines.
5. Hornby's essay criticizes the cultural establishment calling it *elitist* and *condescending.* His essay might cause some to rethink their narrow definitions of art, but that does not seem to be Hornby's intent.

empty! Nothing left! We sucked 'em dry! That's what gets me: The very people who are snotty about the disposability of pop will go over and over again to see Lady Bracknell say "A handbag?" in a funny voice.[5] They don't think that joke's exhausted itself? Maybe disposability is a sign of pop music's maturity, a recognition of its own limitations, rather than the converse. And anyway, I was sitting in a doctor's waiting room the other day, and four little Afro-Caribbean girls, patiently sitting out their mother's appointment, suddenly launched into Nelly Furtado's song. They were word perfect, and they had a couple of dance moves, and they sang with enormous appetite and glee, and I liked it that we had something in common, temporarily; I felt as though we all lived in the same world, and that doesn't happen so often.

Literary Analysis
Personal Essay What does the last paragraph reveal about Hornby? At what broader comment about life does the final sentence hint?

6 A couple of times a year I make myself a tape to play in the car, a tape full of all the new songs I've loved over the previous few months, and every time I finish one I can't believe that there'll be another. Yet there always is, and I can't wait for the next one; you need only a few hundred more things like that, and you've got a life worth living.

5. **Lady Bracknell . . . voice** In *The Importance of Being Earnest,* Lady Bracknell's line "A handbag?" has become very famous.

Critical Reading

Cite textual evidence to support your responses.

1. **Key Ideas and Details (a)** What is Hornby's definition of contemporary pop music? **(b) Infer:** Who does he suggest regards this music as "trashy"? **(c) Analyze:** Does he share this negative opinion? Explain.
2. **Key Ideas and Details (a) Summarize:** What does Hornby like about Nelly Furtado's "I'm Like a Bird"? **(b) Connect:** How does Dave Eggers's theory help explain Hornby's reaction to the song?
3. **Key Ideas and Details (a)** What three works of music, art, and literature does Hornby contrast with pop music? **(b) Interpret:** What is his view of the cultural establishment's reactions to these works?
4. **Key Ideas and Details (a) Summarize:** Sum up the incident with the four little girls in the doctor's waiting room. **(b) Generalize:** What does the incident suggest about the cultural value of pop music in general?
5. **Integration of Knowledge and Ideas** What comment does this essay make about the cultural establishment? Explain. In your response, use at least two of these Essential Question words: *intellectual, condescending, elitist, offend. [Connecting to the Essential Question: How does literature shape or reflect society?]*

Assessment Practice

Persuasive Forms (For more practice, see *All-in-One Workbook.*)

Many tests require students to recognize persuasive devices. Use this item to show that sometimes stating the opposition's viewpoint is a persuasive device in a personal essay.

In his essay, Nick Hornby believes that contemporary pop music is —

A the most artistic form of music yet developed.
B short-lived and disposable.
C silly and not worth consideration.
D worthy of serious attention.

Hornby agrees that contemporary pop songs are short-lived and disposable. He believes that is part of their charm. The correct answer is ***B***.

After You Read "I'm Like a Bird"

Literary Analysis

1. **Key Ideas and Details** What does this **personal essay** reveal about Hornby's background, personality, and outlook? Gather your ideas and details on a chart like the one below.

Autobiographical and Other Details	What They Reveal or Suggest

2. **Key Ideas and Details** Which details help Hornby achieve the informal tone and easy humor typical of personal essays? Cite at least five examples.
3. **Integration of Knowledge and Ideas** What does the essay suggest about life in general? Show how the essay's details lead to at least two broader comments on life.

Reading Strategy

4. **(a) Outline the arguments and strategies** of Hornby's opening paragraph. What criticisms of popular music does he anticipate? **(b)** How does the paragraph's last sentence refute those criticisms?
5. **(a)** What emotional appeals support Hornby's views on the value of pop music? **(b)** What logical explanation does he also offer?

Common Core State Standards

Writing
2. Write informative/explanatory texts to examine and convey complex ideas, concepts, and information clearly and accurately through the effective selection, organization, and analysis of content.

PERFORMANCE TASKS
Integrated Language Skills

Vocabulary Acquisition and Use

Use a word from the vocabulary list to complete each sentence and explain your choice. Use each word only once.

1. That remark is _______; why don't you say something sensible?
2. Unlike real china, paper plates are _______.
3. The voice of the ailing patient was quite _______.
4. "All people are dishonest," she said _______.
5. The _______ chirping of crickets gave me a headache.
6. I had no energy; the hot weather put me in a state of _______.

Writing

Informative Text Write the "liner notes" that might appear in the packaging of a recording of your favorite song. Your notes should give technical details about the composition, instrumentation, and performance of the song. They should also draw on ideas about music that Hornby expresses.

Answers

1. This essay reveals that Nick Hornby is well acquainted with the cultural establishment, and yet he does not accept it as the only authority on art and culture. Students should use the chart to demonstrate ideas.
2. Hornby's tone is easygoing: "Oh, of course I can understand people dismissing pop music." Hornby uses humor: "Wow. I'll bet you're fun at parties." He somewhat ironically refers to the song as a "small miracle." Hornby has definite opinions on the subject: "So, yes, it's disposable, as if that makes any difference to anyone's perceptions of the value of pop music." Hornby reveals his personality and shares friendly detail: "The song that has been driving me pleasurably potty recently is 'I'm Like a Bird' by Nelly Furtado."
3. This essay suggests that life in general is serious enough and hard enough, and that people need to find simple things to make them happy.
4. (a) Hornby anticipates criticisms of popular music as trashy, repetitive, juvenile, and poorly written. (b) The last sentence refutes these critiques, in a way, because this highly educated, celebrated writer admits to having bought a CD and listened to a particular song over and over again.
5. (a) Hornby uses emotional appeals by asking people to be honest about their music-listening habits. (b) He also offers a logical explanation saying that people listen to songs over and over again to "solve the puzzle" of those songs.

Vocabulary Acquisition and Use

1. inane
2. disposable
3. anemic
4. cynically
5. incessant
6. languor

Writing

Evaluate students' informative texts using the **Rubrics for Response to Literature,** *Professional Development Guidebook,* pages 250–251.

Assessment Resources

Unit 6 Resources

L1 L2 EL **Selection Test A,** pp. 410–412. Administer Test A to less advanced readers.

L3 L4 EL **Selection Test B,** pp. 413–415. Administer Test B to on-level students and more advanced students.

L3 L4 **Open-Book Test,** pp. 407–409. As an alternative, give the Open-Book test.

All **Customizable Test Bank**

All **Self-tests**
Students may prepare for the **Selection Test** by taking the **Self-test** online.

PHLit Online! All assessment resources are available at **www.PHLitOnline.com**.

PREteach

Common Core State Standards

- **Writing 3, 3.a, b, d; 5**
- **Language 2, 2.b**

Introducing the Assignment

Review the assignment and the criteria using the instructions on the student page.

What Do You Notice?

1. Read the excerpt from "Next Term, We'll Mash You." Discuss the passage with students.
2. Have a student read the highlighted sentence aloud. **Ask** students what makes the writing special. (**Possible responses:** its vivid verbs; its concrete details)
3. Direct students' attention to the participle *stinging* at the end of the sentence. **Ask** students what the word modifies. (**Answer:** *skin*)
4. Have students imagine pulling their own legs away from a leather seat. **Ask** when, specifically, they feel the sting, and how long it lasts. (**Answer:** just after the skin is pulled away; it lingers a few seconds) **Ask** why it is fitting that the modifier *stinging* falls at the end of the sentence. (**Possible response:** It parallels the slight delay and the lingering of the stinging itself.)
5. Encourage students to experiment with the placement of participles in their own stories.

Penelope Lively on Short Stories

Show students Segment 3 on Penelope Lively on the *See It!* DVD or via the link in the **Enriched Online Student Edition** at **www.PHLitOnline.com**. Discuss Lively's approach to writing short stories.

Writing Workshop

Write a Short Story

Short Story A short story can be set in any time and place, from historic Athens to a future settlement orbiting Jupiter. It can tell about any conflict, from a minor disagreement to a major battle. All short stories do not follow the same plan, but many focus on a single event that reveals an insight about a main character. When you follow the steps in this workshop, you will create an effective short story that brings to life a fictional world.

Assignment Write a short story that tells about a fictional character who faces a compelling conflict.

What to Include Your short story should have these elements:

- A setting that presents a time and place, using concrete sensory details
- A main character who experiences a conflict, or problem to be solved
- A plot that includes a clear sequence of events related to the conflict
- Dialogue that reveals personality and moves the plot forward
- Effective pacing and plot devices, like flashback and foreshadowing

To preview the criteria on which your short story may be assessed, see the rubric on page 1475.

Common Core State Standards

Writing

3. Write narratives to develop real or imagined experiences or events using effective techniques, well-chosen details, and well-structured event sequences.

3.a. Engage and orient the reader by setting out a problem, situation, or observation and its significance, establishing one or multiple point(s) of view, and introducing a narrator and/or characters; create a smooth progression of experiences or events.

3.b. Use narrative techniques, such as dialogue, pacing, description, reflection, and multiple plot lines, to develop experiences, events, and/or characters.

PHLit Online! www.PHLitOnline.com

To see how a short-story writer combines elements, read this excerpt from a story in this textbook (p. 1436). In a few lines, the writer establishes the setting and introduces two characters, using dialogue to reveal their relationship.

from: "Next Term, We'll Mash You"

The car turned right, between white gates and high, dark, tight-clipped hedges. The whisper of the road under the tires changed to the crunch of gravel. The child, staring sideways, read black lettering on a white board: "St Edwards's Preparatory School. Please Drive Slowly." He shifted on the seat, and the leather sucked at the bare skin under his knees, stinging.

The mother said, "It's a lovely place. Those must be the playing-fields. Look, darling, there are some of the boys." She clicked open her handbag, and the sun caught her mirror and flashed in the child's eyes; the comb went through her hair and he saw the grooves it left, neat as distant ploughing.

WRITE GUY
Jeff Anderson, M.Ed.

What Do You Notice?

Read the highlighted sentence several times. Then, with a partner, discuss the qualities that make it special. You might consider the following elements:

- Word choice
- Sentence length
- Use of punctuation
- Vivid details

Share your group's observations with the class.

Teaching Resources

The following resources can be used to enrich or extend the instruction.

All ***Unit 6 Resources***
Writing Workshop, pp. 416–417
Common Core Companion, pp. 16–31; 40–49

All ***Professional Development Guidebook***
Rubric for Self-Assessment: Short Stories, pp. 252–253

All ***Graphic Organizer Transparencies***
Rubric for Self-Assessment: Short Stories, p. 288

All ***See It!* DVD**
Penelope Lively, Segments 3 and 4

PHLit Online! All resources, including print and video, are available at **www.PHLitOnline.com**.

Prewriting and Planning

Choosing Your Topic

To choose a topic for your short story, use one of these strategies:

- **Draw a setting.** A unique setting can trigger story ideas. Sketch any setting: historic, realistic, or fantastic. Then, consider characters and a conflict that might go with the setting you have drawn.
- **Choose a real-life inspiration.** Your story might be loosely based on an event from real life, either one from your own experience or something you heard about in the news or read in a history book. Jot down elements that inspire you and list ways you might change or expand them in a fictional story.

Narrowing Your Topic

Create a story chart. A short story should follow a clear narrative. Using a story chart will help you focus your tale by planning the four stages of a story.

Use your chart to decide whether you will *foreshadow,* or give hints about what will happen. You might also choose to use *flashbacks,* which give readers information about events that happened before the beginning of the story.

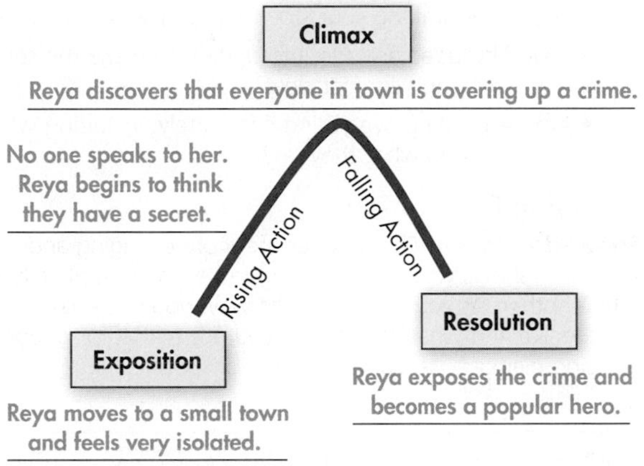

Climax
Reya discovers that everyone in town is covering up a crime.
No one speaks to her. Reya begins to think they have a secret.
Rising Action
Falling Action
Exposition
Reya moves to a small town and feels very isolated.
Resolution
Reya exposes the crime and becomes a popular hero.

Gathering Details

Improvise dialogue. Using a character's thoughts and words can help you move your story in an entertaining way. Role-playing alone or with a partner can help you generate ideas for dialogue.

- *Dialogue* between two or more characters can reveal character traits and move the plot forward.
- If you decide to use a first-person point of view, an *interior monologue,* or stream of thoughts and feelings going through the narrator's mind, can reveal his or her reactions to present or remembered events.

Role-play the parts of your characters to find their speech patterns and ways of talking. You can make audio recordings of your improvisations to capture specific words and phrases.

Applying Understanding by Design Principles

Clarifying Expected Outcomes: Using Rubrics

- Before students begin work on this assignment, have them preview the **Rubric for Self-Assessment,** page 1475, to learn what qualities their short stories must have. A copy of this rubric appears in the ***Professional Development Guidebook,*** page 252.
- Review the criteria in the Rubric with the class. Before students use the Rubric to assess their own writing, work with them to rate the Model (p. 1471) using the Rubric.
- If you wish to assess students' short stories with either a 4-point or 6-point scoring rubric, see the ***Professional Development Guidebook,*** pages 252–253.

TEACH

Prewriting and Planning

1. Introduce the prewriting strategies using the instruction on the student page.
2. Have students apply the strategies to choose a topic and draw a setting.

Teaching the Strategies

1. Have students share their sketches in small groups. Ask students what details made a strong impression on them and why.
2. Have students share their story ideas using the four stages of a story, and give them time to help one another brainstorm their plots.
3. Then, have students sketch Story Maps similar to the one in their books. Have them plot out the major points of the story on their Story Maps.

Think Aloud: Model Choosing a Real-Life Inspiration

Model the strategy of choosing a real-life inspiration, using the following "think aloud." Say to students:

Before I write a short story, I reflect on parts of my life that interest me. For example, if I moved to the United States as a child, I might wonder what the circumstances were in my home country that made my parents want to move. I would try to recall the items we brought and what we had to leave behind. If I recall concrete details to include in my story, I know that it will be vivid and entertaining.

Six Traits Focus

✔	Ideas		Word Choice
✔	Organization		Sentence Fluency
	Voice		Conventions

PH WRITING COACH Grade 12

Students will find additional information on short stories in Chapter 6.

Drafting

1. Introduce the drafting strategies using the instruction on the student page.
2. Have students apply the strategies as they draft their short stories.

Teaching the Strategies

1. Explain to students that establishing whether they tell the story in past or present tense and what narrative point of view to use are important first steps. Students do not want to be switching their tenses back and forth unintentionally because they did not consider what tense they wanted established.
2. Have students consider who their audience is. Do they know the setting in which the story takes place? What other details need to be further developed in order for the story to be clear?
3. Review the idea of "show, don't tell" with students. Remind students that a story is more believable with concrete images that "prove" the authenticity of the story.

Think Aloud: Model "Show, Don't Tell"

Model the strategy of showing and not telling the story, using the following "think aloud." Say to students:

> Why is it important to show, and not to just tell the story? How interesting would it be if the reader were just told about the action and how to feel and judge the action and characters? For example, "The day was tragic, and the man was angry." I think to myself, "how so?" Different people judge tragedy and anger in different ways. If you said instead that the man, walking to an interview, had a large cup of coffee spilled all over his newly pressed white shirt, and his face turned bright red, that would be more interesting and vivid. Ultimately, it would make a better story.

Six Traits Focus

✔	Ideas	✔	Word Choice
	Organization		Sentence Fluency
✔	Voice		Conventions

Drafting

Common Core State Standards

Writing
3.d. Use precise words and phrases, telling details, and sensory language to convey a vivid picture of the experiences, events, setting, and/or characters.

Shaping Your Writing

Establish a tense and point of view. Decide if you will tell your story using the past or present tense. Also, choose the narrative point of view from the options shown in this chart.

Narrator	Description	Example
First-person	The story is told by one of the characters involved. You might choose the main character, or a minor character who observes and comments on the action.	*I was sure I could be a great artist, despite what anyone thought.*
Third-person omniscient	The narrator is outside the story and knows everything that happened.	*Vic was a talented art student, but Mr. Watts doubted his dedication.*
Third-person limited	The narrator is outside the story but knows only what one character does and thinks.	*Vic knew he could be a great artist. But what did Mr. Watts think?*

Remember your audience. Think about what your audience needs to know as you are drafting your story. Ask yourself these questions:

- Have I included enough information to make the setting, characters, and conflict clear?
- Am I explaining everything completely, including why characters do what they do?

Providing Elaboration

Show; do not tell. Short stories are more engaging and involving when the writer shows what is happening rather than simply telling one event after another. As you draft, think of ways you can show what your characters are like and what they do. As you draft, look for opportunities to show by using dialogue, sensory language, or specific images.

Telling	*The crowd reacted angrily to the mayor's speech.*
Showing	*The mayor was only through half his speech when the shouting began. Soon, the mayor's soft voice was drowned out by the loud cries from the audience.*

Model: Showing, Not Telling
Her fingers were mottled with ink from the fierceness with which she dotted her *i's* and crossed her *t's* as page after page of final exams was blanketed with precise small lettering.

The writer shows us evidence of her character's strong concentration, rather than simply telling us that she was a hard worker.

Strategies for Using Vivid Language in Short Stories

Tell students to try to include details that appeal to each of the senses. Look for places in the story—particularly in descriptive passages—where a detail that appeals to sight, hearing, smell, taste, or touch can make their ideas more vivid for readers. Remind students that the more concrete the details that they provide, the more believable the story will be.

Writers on Writing

Anita Desai On Writing Vivid Descriptions

Anita Desai is the author of *A Devoted Son* (p. 1420).

My most vivid memory of childhood in India is of the heat and stillness of summer afternoons when we could do nothing but lie under a slowly revolving fan and read, or doze, waiting for the release brought by the cooler air of evening,

When I wrote a story about children's play—how intense it is and how seriously children take it—I started with an evocation of that heat and stillness. Then the children's games could erupt out of it noisily, almost violently, as a contrast.

"I started with an evocation of that heat and stillness."
—Anita Desai

from *Games at Twilight*

They faced the afternoon. It was too hot. Too bright. The white walls of the veranda glared stridently in the sun. The bougainvillea hung about it, purple and magenta, in livid balloons. The garden outside was like a tray made of beaten brass, flattened out on the red gravel and the stony soil in all shades of metal—aluminum, tin, copper and brass. No life stirred at this arid time of day—the birds still drooped, like dead fruit, in the papery tents of the trees; some squirrels lay limp on the wet earth under the garden tap. The outdoor dog lay stretched as if dead on the veranda mat, his paws and ears and tail all reaching out like dying travelers in search of water. He rolled his eyes at the children—two white marbles rolling in the purple sockets, begging for sympathy—and attempted to lift his tail in a wag but could not. It only twitched and lay still.

Then, perhaps roused by the shrieks of the children, a band of parrots suddenly fell out of the eucalyptus tree, tumbled frantically in the still, sizzling air, then sorted themselves out into battle formation and streaked away across the sky.

I needed bright, glaring colors to emphasize the heat of summer.

Metal can become white-hot in the sun, so I named different metals to convey that impression of heat.

I needed images of the inactivity and passivity that great heat imposes on one, so all the creatures I named are described as comatose.

Then, out of all that stillness, I wanted action to burst forth, startling the reader.

Anita Desai on Writing Vivid Descriptions

Review the passage on the student page with the class, using Anita Desai's comments to deepen students' understanding of the process of writing a short story.

Teaching From the Professional Model

1. Show students Segment 4 on Anita Desai on the ***From the Author's Desk* DVD** or from this page in the **Enriched Online Student Edition.** Discuss how even though Desai was living in the United States, she was still able to recreate vivid descriptions of a summer day in India from her memories.
2. Point out how even though Desai lives in the United States, she often returns to her native India in her writing. Living outside of her native culture enables her to see it in a new way. Students should understand that the process of finding her voice was a difficult one for Desai.
3. Review Desai's comments about how rewarding it is to be a writer. Ask students if their own writing has produced similar feelings of pride.
4. Talk with students about how Desai changed the mood in "Games at Twilight" by shifting abruptly from stillness to action. Ask students to think about the effects on the reader of such a sudden shift. Elicit from students that a sudden shift can help keep readers' interest. Challenge students to think about how they can achieve similar changes in tone or mood in their short stories or other forms of writing.

Differentiated Instruction for Universal Access

EL Support for English Learners

English learners may have difficulty expressing vivid descriptions through the adjectives in their short stories. Help students gain access to richer vocabulary words by having them look up choice adjectives in a thesaurus and dictionary. Have them make a list of possible adjectives. Then, help them decide which adjectives are most effective for the element they are describing.

Enrichment for Gifted/Talented Students

Artistic students may enjoy illustrating the vivid language in their short stories. Have them choose passages from their stories and illustrate them using any medium they wish. Have them include on the illustration, in some way, the words they have chosen to illustrate. Have students share their work with the class.

PHLit Online!

Enriched Online Student Edition
Show or assign the video online at **www.PHLitOnline.com.**

Revising

1. Introduce the revising strategies using the instruction on the student page.
2. Have students apply the strategies as they revise their short stories.

Teaching the Strategies

1. When asking students to think about the episodes of their scenes as photographs of moments in time, you may suggest that they return to their initial sketches to see if they inspire them in any way. What details are absolutely essential in conveying the desired mood and tone? What details just muddle the scene? You can have students use a dictionary to look up words and use them with precision. Encourage the use of figurative language to add depth to their writing.
2. Remind students that in the drafting phase, they chose a tense and perspective from which to write. Have them revisit their stories, with these choices in mind, and fix any unintentional shifts in tense or perspective.
3. Tell students to pay special attention to tenses of such verbs as *to be* (*is/are, was/were*) and *to have* (*has/have, had*).

Six Traits Focus

	Ideas	✔	Word Choice
✔	Organization		Sentence Fluency
	Voice		Conventions

Revising

Revising Your Overall Structure

Using snapshots to grab the reader's attention. Think of each episode in your story as a photograph of a moment in time. Review your scenes to identify places where the view could be made clearer. Add details like these to make the picture more vivid:

- Descriptive language that is precise and evocative
- Sensory language (appeal to senses of sight, touch, hearing, taste, or smell)
- Figurative language (similes, metaphors, personification) to explain what events, people, and setting are like

Common Core State Standards

Writing
5. Develop and strengthen writing as needed by revising, rewriting, or trying a new approach, focusing on addressing what is most significant for a specific purpose and audience.

Language
2. Demonstrate command of the conventions of standard English capitalization, punctuation, and spelling when writing.

Model: Revising to Create Snapshots

perched on a bleached-white oak log,
trapped by some long-ago flood on
On the longest day of the year, Rose sat ~~near~~ the riverbank, waiting for the boy. Minutes passed. He was late, and, as her mind listlessly created teasing rebukes, her ears caught
faint moan ,long and seductive and inhuman
a ~~sound~~ in the distance.

Where is Rose sitting? What sound does she hear?

Peer Review Exchange drafts with a partner. Identify two or three episodes in your partner's story that feel too short or somewhat vague. Consider how envisioning a snapshot of each episode will help the writer add effective details.

Revising Your Word Choice

Check for consistency. Your story could be confusing if you have unintentional shifts in tense or perspective.

Tense. Review your verb tenses. For example, if you are telling the story in the present tense, check that you have not slipped into the past by mistake.	***Narrative point of view.*** Be sure your narrative point of view is consistent. If you are using a first-person narrator, do not slip into the third-person.
Replace: I tried the door, but I'm locked inside. **With**: I tried the door, but I was locked inside.	**Replace**: We did not trust the newcomer, so they kept her under close surveillance. **With**: We did not trust the newcomer, so we kept her under close surveillance.

Strategies for Creating Stronger Sentences

Have students review the "Model: Revising to Create Snapshots." Point out that it demonstrates the use of stronger language to convey a clearer image. Tell students that a strong verb in a sentence can have a great impact on the reader's comprehension and visualization. Have students compare the verbs in these two sentences: *Sadie sat down on the couch. Sadie plopped down on the couch.* Explain to students that the second sentence contains a stronger, more vivid verb that gives the reader a clearer picture. While revising, have students substitute weak verbs with stronger, more effective verbs where appropriate. Have them use a thesaurus if necessary.

SIX TRAITS WRITER'S TOOLBOX SIX TRAITS

Sentence Fluency | Voice | Organization | Word Choice | Ideas | **Conventions**

Developing Your Style

Using Punctuation in Dialogue

Dialogue shows what people say—the punctuation in dialogue can help to show how they say it. The punctuation at the end of a sentence helps to indicate the tone of a sentence. Other forms of punctuation help readers hear the rhythms and pauses of natural speech. Follow these strategies to use punctuation effectively.

You might also use these punctuation strategies in your narration if your story has a first-person point of view.

Rule	Example
Use commas to indicate short pauses.	"Well, sure, we can do that."
Use ellipses to show a longer pause or hesitation. Ellipsis points can also suggest a voice trailing off.	"Yes. . . I suppose that's right." "Maybe we should. . ."
Use a dash to indicate a sudden stop, such as an interruption.	"Hey —" "Wait! Don't forget to —"
Use italics to emphasize a word.	"*What* are you doing here?" "What are you doing *here*?"
Use apostrophes to show dropped letters in dialect.	"That's nothin' special."

Find It in Your Reading

Review the dialogue in "Next Term, We'll Mash You" by Penelope Lively.

1. Look for examples of dialogue that are especially vivid or effective.
2. Explain how the punctuation contributes to the effect of each example.
3. **Discuss:** Choose a line of dialogue from the story and consider how adding a dash or ellipsis points would affect the impact of the line. Read both the original sentence and your revised version aloud to a partner. Without looking at your writing, can your partner tell what punctuation you added?

Apply It to Your Writing

To improve the dialogue in your story, follow these steps:

1. Read each line aloud. Listen for whether or not it sounds natural. Consider adding punctuation to indicate natural pauses in your character's voice.
2. Decide if there is more than one possible reading for the line. For important lines, consider using italics to show which word the character emphasizes.
3. Be careful not to overuse special punctuation, such as ellipsis points, dashes, and italics. Limit exclamation points, as well—they're more effective when used sparingly. Reread all of the dialogue in your story, paying attention to the balance of punctuation.

PH WRITING COACH
Further instruction and practice are available in *Prentice Hall Writing Coach*.

Developing Your Style

1. Introduce the punctuation strategies to students, using the instruction on the student page.
2. Have students complete the Find It in Your Reading and Apply It to Your Writing activities.

Teaching the Strategy

1. Remind students that the effective use of punctuation is important in setting the pace and the tone. Remind students that tone is the attitude they project in their writing. Punctuation can help to indicate how the speaker or narrator is feeling.
2. Students should understand that punctuation helps to emphasize the rhythms and pauses of a story. For example, commas in a series might slow down the pace and emphasize certain words, such as in the play *Macbeth,* in which Macbeth utters, "Tomorrow, and tomorrow, and tomorrow, / Creeps in this petty pace from day to day . . ." In this excerpt, the commas between the *tomorrows* make the whole line literally "creep" at a slow, drawn-out pace.
3. Have students read the dialogue in "Next Term, We'll Mash You." Have the class consider how adding certain punctuation, such as an ellipsis or dash, affects the impact of the line.
4. Have students keep in mind the steps in Apply It to Your Writing in order to improve their own dialogue. Remind students that reading their writing aloud is a key strategy they can use to hear whether the sentences sound natural or awkward. Adjusting the punctuation may help in achieving the desired effects.

Six Traits Focus

	Ideas		Word Choice
	Organization	✔	Sentence Fluency
	Voice		Conventions

Strategies for Punctuation in Dialogue

Give students these suggestions for developing their style by focusing on the proper use of punctuation.

1. Select a passage on which you would like to work. Think about the content and tone, and consider the best ways to convey them with your use of punctuation. Consider the example from Shakespeare's *Macbeth* as a classic example of effective use of punctuation to convey the tone and express the content.
2. Read your passage aloud. What sounds natural to you? What sounds awkward? Would the awkward sections be improved with a more effective use of punctuation?
3. Be careful not to overuse punctuation in your passage. Each punctuation mark has its own purpose, and being aware of the functions of these marks will help you use them more effectively. Make sure that the use of punctuation makes sense and has a clear purpose.

Student Model

Review the Student Model with the class, using the annotations to analyze the writer's incorporation of the elements of a short story.

Teaching the Strategies

1. Explain that the Student Model is a sample and that students' short stories may be longer.
2. Briefly review the five elements of a short story on page 1468. Point out that Elizabeth included all of these elements in "A Love Story."
3. **Ask** students to identify these five elements in "A Love Story." List their answers on the board. **Answer:** *Setting:* begins in a school, moves to the riverbank, through the woods, and ends on a train; *Main character/conflict:* Rose hears a noise and runs through the woods to find its source; *Plot:* Rose at school, Rose at the riverbank, Rose runs through the woods, Rose discovers the train, Rose on the train; *Dialogue:* details in first and second paragraph establish Rose's character and set up the rest of the story; *Plot devices:* Rose running through the woods is a chase scene; unexpected ending is a twist ending.

Connecting to Real-Life Writing

Short stories began through the ancient tradition of storytelling. They have existed over the centuries as short myths, legends, allegories, romances, and anecdotes. It was not until the early nineteenth century, however, that the short story became a recognized genre. American writers such as Nathaniel Hawthorne and Mark Twain contributed to the newly established genre. The respect for the short story grew as great writers continued to add new pieces and with the amount of critical attention the genre received. Many periodicals published short stories in every issue to satisfy eager readers. In the twentieth century, the short story became more complex and varied; however, the number of periodicals featuring short stories dwindled to a select few as the public turned to television and movies.

Student Model: Elizabeth Dumas, East Stroudsburg, PA

A Love Story

At eighteen, Rose had spent twelve years in the brick school that would catch the summer wind blowing in from the farmland, coating the last week of June in a haze of warm animals and clover. The wooden desks, scarred with jagged hearts and the initials of long-gone students, began to sweat furniture polish, and she could smell the cloying pine scent in her hands even over the heady outdoor mixture. Her fingers were mottled with ink from the fierceness with which she dotted her *i*'s and crossed her *t*'s as page after page of final exams was blanketed with precise small lettering.

> Elizabeth uses sensory language to establish the setting, and, at the end of the paragraph, reveals character through action.

She loved a boy, too, who had a solemn blue gaze and gentle words. They would meet barefoot at the great flat rock on the shore of the creek and wade until their clothes clung to their shaking frames, forcing them to lie in the sun, touching hands, hips, mouths. The fabric would wrinkle and tear, stiff strong fibers meeting stiffer, stronger stone, and the sun would fade the dye, aging their apparel to the nebulous clothing of romantic watercolors. Rose's affection for this boy was simple, an adoration of his smile, his voice, his rough strong hands. She loved his bouquets of wildflowers and the way his hair smelled after he had picked them. She loved how her cheek fit perfectly against his collarbone. She loved him.

> Notice how in this paragraph, Elizabeth conveys emotion through sensory details.

On the longest day of the year, Rose sat perched on a bleached-white oak log, trapped by some long-ago flood on the riverbank, waiting for the boy. Minutes passed. He was late, and, as her mind listlessly created teasing rebukes, her ears caught a faint moan in the distance, long and seductive and inhuman. Senses blazing, she slipped off her seat and plunged through the verdant forest, forcing away from the smell of water to the scent of mystery. Again, the sound came, louder and shriller, and she redoubled her struggle through the undergrowth, small branches whipping across her face. A rhythmic pounding could be felt through the soil, in her heart. It was ahead of her, the moaning and the pounding and a fierce sensation of speed and power.

Bursting through the last line of oaks, she almost fell gasping to her knees in bewilderment. A train, acres long, was ripping across the landscape, in a place where she could only remember ferns and dragonflies and dust in sunlight. And, miraculously, there was a tiny wooden depot and platform clinging next to the tracks; a sign hanging from the window proclaimed "TICKETS" in scarlet paint. Rose staggered over to the building, mind racing but filled with a steadily growing warmth. There was no attendant at the window, only a stack of handwritten slips that said, simply, "Admit One." Vaguely wondering when the next train arrived, she took one and leaned against the rough wall, twisting the slip idly through her fingers until it was soft and powdery.

> The details in this section are symbolic. They point to a resolution of the conflict, which involves the loss of the relationship.

Minutes or hours later, a vermillion engine roared into the station, and Rose clambered into a car and slipped into a seat without hesitation. The boy was across the aisle from her, looking out the opposite window. They smiled nervously at each other, eyes flicking back and forth over the other's features, but neither spoke or moved. Trying to recall his name as the train lurched forward, she found it gone.

> Elizabeth reveals the outcome of the relationship through showing, not telling.

Strategies for Using Plot Devices

Inform students that plot devices contribute to the plot by moving it along and further engaging the reader. Review with them a few of the most common devices, such as foreshadowing (subtle hints of events yet to come), flashback (an event from the past appearing within the present chronological order of the plot), a chase scene (a scene between plot points that does not develop the plot but creates tension), a cliffhanger (an abrupt ending that allows the story to continue in a separate work), a reversal (a complete change or reversal in the action), or a twist ending (an unexpected ending). Inform them that a skilled writer can incorporate plot devices smoothly, without any awkward pauses or transitions. Have students share with the class what plot devices they included in their short stories and how they did it.

Editing and Proofreading

Focus on punctuation in dialogue. Use quotation marks only for direct quotations. Check that you have used commas and capital letters correctly.

Direct Quotation: *"We're gonna win for sure," said Max.*
Indirect Quotation: *Max thought we would certainly win.*

Focus on spelling. To add *-ing*, *-ish*, or *-ist* to words that end in *y*, keep the *y* and add the suffix. For example, *worry* becomes *worrying*, *gray* becomes *grayish*, and *essay* becomes *essayist*.

Spiral Review: Conventions Earlier in this unit, you learned about avoiding sentence fragments and run-ons (p. 1151) and using transitional expressions to show the relationship between two ideas (p. 1169). Review your writing. Make sure you have used at least two transitional expressions to relate ideas.

Publishing, Presenting, and Reflecting

Consider one of the following ways to share your writing:

Record your story. Rehearse your story alone or with a group of classmates. Look for ways to communicate both the narration and dialogue using effective intonation, pauses, and pacing. Make an audio recording of your final reading, and make the recording available for others to borrow.

Create a layout. Use desktop-publishing software to create a final layout for your story, including appropriate illustrations, as well as margins that are not too wide and an effective type design for the title and text.

Reflect on your writing. Jot down your thoughts about the experience of writing a short story. Begin by answering this question: What did you learn about yourself as a writer while creating a short story?

Rubric for Self-Assessment

Evaluate your short story using the following criteria and rating scale, or, with your classmates, determine your own reasonable evaluation criteria.

Criteria	Rating Scale (not very — very)
Focus: How well do you tell a clear story from beginning to end?	1 2 3 4 5
Organization: How effectively do the events in your story build to a strong climax and satisfying resolution?	1 2 3 4 5
Support/Elaboration: How well do you use dialogue to reveal characters' actions and personalities?	1 2 3 4 5
Style: How effective are your sentences and their punctuation, both in dialogue and narration?	1 2 3 4 5
Conventions: How correct is your use of grammar, especially the punctuation of dialogue?	1 2 3 4 5

Common Core State Standards

Writing
5. Develop and strengthen writing as needed by editing, focusing on addressing what is most significant for a specific purpose and audience.

Language
2.b. Spell correctly.

PH WRITING COACH
Further instruction and practice are available in *Prentice Hall Writing Coach.*

Strategy for Test Taking

A reading passage on the SAT or ACT may require students to identify different elements of the plot. Review with students and have them commit to memory the Story Chart on page 1469, featuring the Exposition, Rising Action, Climax, Falling Action, and Resolution. Remind students to draw on their own experiences writing short stories when faced with these questions.

Editing and Proofreading

1. Introduce the editing and proofreading focuses using the instruction on the student page.
2. Have students read their short stories carefully, marking them for line edits. Make sure they check for errors of the type noted on the student page.

Teaching the Strategy

1. Have students go through their short stories, identifying any errors in grammar, spelling, or punctuation.
2. Remind students to analyze their use of punctuation. Remind students not to overuse punctuation without purpose, as their effects will be diminished from overuse.

Six Traits Focus

	Ideas		Word Choice
	Organization	✔	Sentence Fluency
	Voice		Conventions

ASSESS

Publishing, Presenting, and Reflecting

1. Remind students to use intonation, pauses, and pacing to communicate the narration and dialogue effectively, if they have chosen to record or present their stories.
2. If students have chosen to create layouts or visual aids, they should consider how different text and graphic features will aid in the telling of the story. The overall visual presentation should reflect the ideas of theme and mood.
3. Encourage students to discuss their processes and key strategies in writing their short stories.
4. Ask what plot changes might have made their stories more effective.

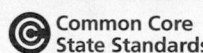

Common Core State Standards

- Speaking and Listening 2

Compare Media Coverage of the Same Event

1. Present some of the ways that students may consume news media, using the instruction on the student page. Discuss how the students' manner of processing news is shaped by the context in which information is presented.
2. Explain to students that, despite the purported objectivity with which news media outlets disseminate information, the public understanding of a given event is very much shaped by the manner in which it is covered.

Print Media Formats

1. Explain to students that there are two basic types of print media. Newspapers are usually daily, driving news coverage to be succinct and grounded in fact. Magazines (also called periodicals) tend to appear less frequently, allowing contributors further time to editorialize and analyze the events at hand.
2. As many papers relay news to a local audience, they may feature local stories more prominently. Magazines tend to serve a national audience and put national issues at the forefront of their coverage.

MEDIA LITERACY

Communications Workshop

Compare Media Coverage of Same Event

Common Core State Standards

Speaking and Listening
2. Integrate multiple sources of information presented in diverse formats and media in order to make informed decisions and solve problems, evaluating the credibility and accuracy of each source and noting any discrepancies among the data.

In today's fast-paced world, coverage of news events bombards us from print media like newspapers and magazines and nonprint media like television, radio, and the Internet. News media are the vehicles that bring us our daily dose of current events. Of course, in today's world, it is hard to limit ourselves to one dose per day. As you navigate the world of news media, it is important to understand that facts are not just facts; how stories are covered shapes public understanding of current events.

Print Media Formats

Print news media relies primarily on text to deliver information. There are two basic types of print news media:

- **Newspapers** are often published daily. The constant deadlines require stories to be concise and fact-driven. Newspapers often provide objective, unbiased reporting, but opinion pieces such as editorials take up a large portion of papers. Because many newspapers serve a local audience, they focus on local news and have a close relationship with their readers.
- **Magazines,** also known as periodicals or journals, appear less frequently than newspapers. This allows writers to deliver an in-depth analysis of an event and to inject commentary and opinions into a story. Visual elements, such as pictures and graphics, have a more prominent role. Most magazines serve a national audience and focus on national events.

News Coverage

Before you analyze the coverage of an event, you should assess the media source. Use a chart like the one below:

Factors of Print News Coverage	
Purpose	Most news articles are written to inform, but some media makers may also want to influence opinion or entertain. The purpose of a story will affect the information the reporter writes and the editors include.
Author's Perspective	News articles are meant to be objective. Sometimes, however, a writer may omit certain facts or emphasize others that implicitly express an opinion or shape a particular perception.
Audience	Some publications target specific populations and cater to the interests, needs, or even biases of those groups. Understanding the target audience can help you identify possible slants in the presentation of a news story.

News Coverage

1. Explain to students that, in order to obtain the most accurate possible impression of a given event, they should take into account the factors listed in the chart on the student page when analyzing the source of information.
2. Explain that, depending on the forum, a number of factors may influence the way in which information is conveyed. Facts may be omitted, overstated, or rearranged to appeal to a certain audience or to suit the editorial agenda of the author or media group.
3. Students may discuss how being cognizant of the efforts of the media to shape their perceptions of the world can make them more engaged and critical consumers of information.

Elements of News Presentations

As you read a print media source, notice how the following elements affect your understanding of a story:

- **Headline:** This provides basic information and sets the tone of the story. Look for *charged language*—words with strong positive or negative connotations.
- **Visual elements:** Images and photos affect how a reader understands a story.
- **Placement of story:** Editors will emphasize a story's importance by placing it on the front page of the newspaper.
- **Duration of coverage:** The length of time a story is covered—one day, a week, a month—also indicates its importance.

Activities: Compare Media Coverage

Comprehension and Collaboration For both activities, use an evaluation form like the one shown below.

A. Select a news event, and examine its coverage in three different newspapers or magazines. Look for similarities and differences in the ways each outlet approaches its coverage, and examine how the coverage emphasizes different elements.

Evaluation Form for Print Media Coverage

News Event: ____________

Three Sources in Which It Is Covered: ____________

Intended Audience of Each Publication: ____________

How are the headlines different? ____________

Are the stories placed differently? Explain. ____________

Do any of the stories seem to favor one side? Explain. ____________

What information is the same? What is different? ____________

How does each story provide a different understanding of the event? ____________

____

B. Find coverage of the same event in broadcast media (television or radio). Compare the broadcast coverage to the print media versions of the story. Determine if specific information was added or omitted. Write a paragraph explaining your findings.

Differentiated Instruction for Universal Access

EL Support for English Learners
Some English learners may encounter difficulty in understanding the semantic distinctions between words with similar meanings used in headlines. Have them explore these distinctions by parsing the language in several headlines about the same event. For example, how might a headline about a "heated debate" imply a different atmosphere than one announcing an "explosive debate"?

Support for Less Proficient Learners
Some students may find it difficult to discern some less obvious instances of bias in news coverage. In order to illustrate this issue, it may be instructive to have students examine the different ways in which explicitly partisan publications present the same news story.

Elements of News Presentations

1. Present the aspects of print media that may affect how a reader understands a report, using the instruction on the student page.
2. Explain that the presentation of information in current print media formats creates a necessarily hierarchical arrangement. By placing a story on the front page or cover, with a catchy headline and striking photograph, the media outlet in question is making an implicit value judgment that grants primacy to one story while subordinating others.
3. Point out that while such aspects of media presentation do not *necessarily* reflect on the objectivity of the publication, it is still important to consider the contextual elements of a story in attempting to form a thorough analysis.
4. It may be helpful for students to view these contextual elements as the bones of the "narrative" created from the facts available. By noting the situation of headlines, photos, and the story itself, students can conceptualize the narrative vehicle through which they are receiving information in the same way that they might interrogate the methods of a fictional narrator.

Activities: Compare Media Coverage

A. 1. Have each student choose a news event and compare its coverage in three separate media outlets.

2. Students should look for similarities and differences in coverage. They should examine which elements are emphasized or omitted in each example.

3. Students should record their observations on the Evaluation Form provided on the student page.

B. Students may also find coverage of the same event in broadcast media. They can compare the omission and inclusion of information between the two types of coverage and write a paragraph explaining their findings.

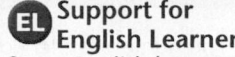

EXTEND

Common Core State Standards

- **Language 4.a, c**

Cognates and Borrowed Words

1. Teach the skill, using the instruction on the student page.
2. If possible, **ask** students to flip through a dictionary as they work in groups. Have them write down three cognates or borrowed words, as well as their origins.

Think Aloud: Model the Skill

Say to students:

I know that many English words correlate to words in other languages, both in origin and meaning. Additionally, some words have been co-opted wholesale into the English lexicon. When I come across words that do not contain roots or constructions with which I am familiar, I know that it is possible that they were taken from other languages. By defining these words and researching their origins, I will heighten my awareness of the fluidity of language.

Vocabulary Workshop

Cognates and Borrowed Words

Cognates are words that share origins and meanings with words in other languages. These words are often spelled similarly. For example, *candeur* in French and *candor* in English are cognates. Both are derived from the Latin word *candere,* meaning "honesty."

English also has many borrowed words that have been taken intact from other languages. Some of these words are so familiar that English speakers often do not realize their foreign origins. Study the borrowed words in the chart below.

Common Core State Standards

Language

4.a. Use context as a clue to the meaning of a word or phrase.

4.c. Consult general and specialized reference materials, both print and digital, to find the pronunciation of a word or determine or clarify its precise meaning, its part of speech, its etymology, or its standard usage.

French	German	Indian	Italian	Native American	West Indian
envoy	frankfurter	bungalow	alfresco	caribou	barbecue
potpourri	hamburger	cashmere	fiasco	chipmunk	canoe
rendezvous	rucksack	jungle	incognito	moccasin	maize

Practice

Directions: Identify the source of each borrowed word and use it in a sentence. If necessary, use a dictionary to aid you.

1. blitz
2. toboggan
3. kowtow
4. chocolate
5. banana
6. pundit
7. chili
8. boomerang
9. hammock
10. algebra

Directions: Find a newspaper or magazine article and identify five or more borrowed words in it. Then, trace the origin of three of these words.

Practice

Answers

1. German; The debate team really *blitzed* their opponents last night.
2. Native American; We laughed as the *toboggan* rocketed down the slick hill.
3. Chinese; The ambassador spent the whole party *kowtowing* to the president in an effort to get her to reconsider the treaty.
4. Spanish/Nahuatl; The confectioner mixed a massive amount of *chocolate* into the frosting.
5. Spanish/Portuguese; An aroma of ripe *bananas* lay heavy in the air.
6. Hindi; A firestorm of criticism arose over comments made during the debate between the two *pundits.*
7. Spanish/Nahuatl; He dusted the dish with *chili* powder.
8. Australian Aboriginal; The hunters launched their *boomerangs* at the flock of birds.
9. Spanish/Taino; A light breeze stirred her hair as she dozed in the swaying *hammock.*
10. Arabic; *Algebra* requires the memorization of many complex formulas.

Students should accurately identify three borrowed words in the article and trace their origins.

Vocabulary Acquisition and Use: Context Clues

Context clues are words or phrases that help readers clarify the meanings of unfamiliar words in a text. By using context clues, you can determine the word or words that complete a sentence. Sentence Completion questions appear in most standardized tests. These questions test your vocabulary skills as well as your understanding of sentence structure. In these types of questions, you are given sentences with one or more missing words. Your task is to use the context to choose the correct word or words to complete each sentence logically. Try this strategy: (1) Read the sentence. (2) Read *all* of the answer choices, and mark those that might work. (3) Of the ones you marked, choose the answer that works best.

Practice

This exercise is modeled after the Sentence Completion exercises that appear in the Critical Reading section of the SAT.

Directions: Each of the following sentences is missing one or two words. Choose the word or set of words that best completes each sentence.

Test-Taking Tip
Work on the sentence completion questions before the passage-based reading questions. They take less time.

1. The determined __?__ of the Roman Empire brought an army of 40,000 men to England in 42 A.D.
A. conflagration
B. aperture
C. languor
D. imperialism
E. condescension

2. The British tribesman were terrifying __?__ when they painted their bodies blue for battle.
A. combatants
B. upbraidings
C. enigmas
D. effigies
E. inklings

3. The conquered British natives were somewhat __?__ and did little to overthrow their invaders.
A. complaisant
B. exemplary
C. lustrous
D. despotic
E. circumscribed

4. The Romans' __?__ need to spread their form of civilization spurred them to build baths and ampitheaters in every land they conquered.
A. inane
B. incessant
C. impressionistic
D. invincible
E. desolate

5. The Roman roads remain a __?__ wonder, raised up out of the landscape with rock dug from __?__ on either side of the road bed.
A. supine . . . encomiums
B. filial . . . mockeries
C. undeterminable . . . tendrils
D. topographical . . . furrows
E. transient . . . intrigues

6. __?__ citizens from all walks of life __?__ the baths, less for cleanliness than to socialize.
A. Garrulous . . . patronized
B. Vivacious . . . endowed
C. Clamorous . . . distilled
D. Segmented . . . eclipsed
E. Irrevocable . . . recalled

ASSESS/EXTEND

Practice

1. Introduce the skill, using the instruction on the student page. Be sure students understand how context clues can reveal the meaning of an unknown word.
2. You may wish to go over the first item with students. Read the first item to the class, including all of the answer choices. As you read the list of choices the second time, ask students to raise their hands when they think a choice might work. Point out that *conflagration,* which means a large, destructive fire; *aperture,* which means an opening or gap; and *languor,* which means listlessness or weariness, clearly do not fit the context of the sentence. *Condescension,* which means behavior that implies feelings of superiority, seems like a possibility. However, *imperial-ism,* the policy of extending the rule or influence of one country over other states, is clearly the correct choice within the context of the sentence. So choice *D* is correct.
3. Assign the remaining items in the Practice Test. Point out that some questions require pairs of words, rather than a single word, for completion. Allow students 6 minutes to complete the questions.

Answers

1. D
2. A
3. A
4. B
5. D
6. A

Strategies for Test Taking

Tell students that they should read the passage carefully to find text that relates to each question. They should avoid the distraction of an answer choice that has information that does not relate directly to the question. Have students make sure that there are specific details in the passage that match what the question is asking and that support their chosen answers. Explain that these specific details are proof that their answers are correct.

MONITORING PROGRESS

Using the Test-Taking Practice

In this Test-Taking Practice (pp. 1480–1483), students apply the skills in Unit 6. The Practice is divided into three sections.

1. Before assigning each section, review the relevant Unit skills with students. Discuss the characteristics of each type of test and specific strategies for test questions, using the instruction that precedes each Practice.
2. Set a time limit for the multiple-choice items in each Practice, allowing a little more than 1 minute per question. Use the designated time allowance set for the Timed Writing section.
3. Administer each section. Have students write the starting time at the top of their papers. When half of the time for the multiple-choice items has elapsed, ask students to write the time next to the answer on which they are working. Have them make similar notes when the time is three-quarters through and again when time is up. Follow a similar procedure for the Timed Writing assignment.
4. Review with students the pacing reflected in their notes.

Reteaching

Have students complete each Practice. Then, use the Reteach charts to determine which skills require reteaching, based on the items students answer incorrectly. Reteach these skills prior to assigning the **Benchmark Test** (*Unit 6 Teaching Resources,* pp. 421–426)

Test-Taking Practice

Critical Reading: Short Reading Passages

The **short reading passages** of standardized tests ask you to read selections that may only be a paragraph or two in length or about 100 words. They may be poetry or fiction selections, or readings from natural science, social studies, and the humanities. They may include narrative, expository, and argumentative elements. The majority of the questions require extended reasoning in which you analyze and synthesize information. You will also be required to comment on the assumptions and the style of the author.

Common Core State Standards

RL.11-12.1, RL.11-12.2, RL.11-12.4; W.11-12.5; L.11-12.3, L.11-12.3.a

[For the full wording of the standards, see the standards chart in the front of your textbook.]

Practice

The following exercise is modeled after the SAT Short Passage Critical Reading section.

Directions: Read the following passage, taken from "An Arundel Tomb" by Philip Larkin. Then, choose the best answer to each question.

Side by side, their faces blurred,
The earl and countess lie in stone,
Their proper habits vaguely shown
As jointed armor, stiffened pleat,
And that faint hint of the absurd—
The little dogs under their feet.

Such plainness of the pre-baroque
Hardly involves the eye, until
It meets his left-hand gauntlet, still
Clasped empty in the other; and
One sees, with a sharp tender shock,
His hand withdrawn, holding her hand.

They would not think to lie so long.
Such faithfulness in effigy
Was just a detail friends would see:
A sculptor's sweet commissioned grace
Thrown off in helping to prolong
The Latin names around the base.

Strategy

- **Read carefully** to find text directly related to the question.
- **Avoid being misled** by an answer that looks correct but is not supported by information directly stated.
- When you match specific details in the text to what a question is asking, you have proof of your answer.

Strategies for Test Taking

Point out that a reading passage on the SAT or ACT may be accompanied by visuals and include questions that ask about the relationship between the visual and the text. The visual may be a photograph or illustration, or it may be a graph or chart. Remind students to draw upon their own experiences preparing multimedia reports when faced with these questions. Students should always take a moment to figure out how a visual supports the text in a test.

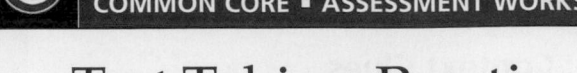

SAT® PREP ACT

1. What basic philosophy does the poet assume?
   A. belief in reincarnation
   B. rebirth after death
   C. eternal life
   D. sacredness in natural things
   E. the absence of God
2. Why does the author make an allusion to the "pre-baroque" in line 7?
   A. to emphasize the tomb's lack of ornamentation
   B. to contrast the time period in which the author writes to the time of the pre-baroque
   C. to suggest the beliefs and customs of the pre-baroque
   D. to compare the Roman period to the Baroque
   E. to allow readers to consider how the earl felt
3. In line 16, the word *commissioned* most nearly means
   A. friendly
   B. paid for
   C. uncompensated
   D. skilled
   E. offered up
4. It can be inferred that the earl and countess are
   A. knights
   B. still alive
   C. married
   D. unhappy
   E. Romans
5. In line 2, how does the figurative language of the poet "the earl and countess lie in stone" compare to the flashback in line 16?
   A. The sculptor's distortion has carried through to today.
   B. The poet gives life to them and brings the sculptor back to life.
   C. The poet suggests that the sculptor made them lie in peace.
   D. The sculptor has outlived both the earl and countess in stone.
   E. The earl and countess lie inside of stone while the sculptor is forgotten.
6. Answering which of these questions would increase your comprehension of the poem?
   A. What do the other tombs in Arundel look like?
   B. What does "jointed armor, stiffened pleat" mean?
   C. How would the sculptor know what they looked like?
   D. Why would someone feel "sharp tender shock"?
   E. Who is really buried in this tomb?
7. What clues does the poet give to place the subject matter in its historical period?
   A. armor, gauntlet
   B. hint of the absurd
   C. effigy, detail
   D. faithfulness in effigy
   E. pleat, dogs
8. The main idea of the poem would most likely be which of the following?
   A. The sculptor was trying to protect their Latin names.
   B. The earl and the countess never expected to live on so long.
   C. The affection of the long dead husband and wife is surprising.
   D. The plainness of the tomb and its inhabitants shocks.
   E. Little dogs do not belong on the tomb of a ruler.

GO ON

Differentiated Instruction for Universal Access

Support for Less Proficient Students

Read the passage with students and help them to summarize it. Then, go over the first test item as a class, guiding students to eliminate incorrect answer choices.

EL Support for English Learners

Read the entire passage with the class and help students to summarize each stanza. Review the questions, making sure that students understand *allusion* and *Baroque Period* in question 2 and *figurative* and *distortion* in question 5. Allow students to ask clarifying questions about any of the question choices, being careful not to reveal correct answers. Once students understand the questions, have them complete the test on their own. Allow 5 minutes for reading the passage and 12 minutes for the questions.

Critical Reading Test

Short Reading Passages

1. Introduce the passage using the instruction on page 1480.
2. Have students read the poem silently; then, as a class, analyze each choice in the first test item.

   A—The poem contains no suggestion that Larkin believes the earl and countess will be reincarnated. (Eliminate)

   B—As with Choice *A*, there is no suggestion of rebirth. (Eliminate)

   C—Correct answer. Line 13 suggests belief in eternal life after death.

   D—The passage contains no suggestions about nature. (Eliminate)

   E—Larkin does not mention an explicit belief or nonbelief in God. (Eliminate)
3. Assign the Practice exercise. Allow 15 minutes for this process, and announce to students when they have 5 minutes and 1 minute remaining.

Answers

1. C
2. A
3. B
4. C
5. C
6. D
7. A
8. C

Reteach

Question	Pages to Reteach
1	1138
2	1358
3	1400
4	1272
5	1154
6	1191
7	1340
8	1366

Grammar and Writing

Improving Paragraphs

1. Introduce the skill using the instruction on the student page. Be sure students understand the strategy set off in the boxed section.
2. Read the first paragraph of the Practice passage; then, go over the first test item with students, modeling the "focus only on the answers provided" strategy.
3. Point out that the original sentence consists of two clauses strung together in a run-on sentence. Though the clauses are separated by a comma, the sentence is awkward, so Choice *A* can be eliminated. Choice *B* also can be eliminated, since it offers the same run-on sentence without the comma. Choice *C* is the correct choice, because it divides the run-on sentence into two complete sentences. Choice *D* is still a run-on sentence and can be eliminated. Choice *E* can be eliminated. Though it divides the sentence into two complete sentences, it inverts the order and makes the progression of meaning illogical.
4. Have students complete questions 2–6 on their own. Allow students 6 minutes to complete the questions.

Grammar and Writing: Improving Paragraphs

Improving Paragraphs exercises often appear in the writing sections of standardized tests. They are made up of a reading passage with numbered sentences. The passages are usually drafts of student essays that contain errors in grammar, style, and usage. For each question, you must decide which of five possible answers will best correct the given sentence.

Practice

This exercise is modeled after the Improving Paragraphs portion of the SAT Writing Test.

Directions: Questions 1–6 refer to the following draft of a student essay.

[1] The Romans enjoyed a prosperous and peaceful existence in Britain, they did not extend their rule into Scotland and Wales. [2] They neglected to settle these areas, farm lands held greater interest, and it was too hard to settle these hostile landscapes. [3] Two-thirds of the troops in Rome guarded Wales alone to keep warlike tribes at bay.

[4] Stable society in Britain allowed the establishment of the villas of the wealthy who had grown fabulously rich in the grain trade. [5] Most villas began as simple farm compounds. [6] Yet before long, they featured <u>stone walls, water running through pipes, a way to heat the rooms, multiple rooms, bathing in bath houses</u>, and mosaics. [7] A golden age of villa building ensued with details only great fortunes could afford. [8] Highly elaborate and complex mosaic decorations were often found in the finest homes.

[9] A central forum with a town hall and merchant's trading area was a feature of most towns. [10] Other improvements included small theaters for plays, larger amphitheaters for gladiator combat, and baths for men and women. [11] Because nothing was too good for the Romans living in Britain.

1. Which revision is most needed in sentence 1?

A. (As it is now)
B. The Romans enjoyed a prosperous and peaceful existence in Britain they did not extend their rule into Scotland and Wales.
C. The Romans enjoyed a prosperous and peaceful existence in Britain. They did not extend their rule into Scotland and Wales.
D. The Romans enjoyed a prosperous and peaceful existence in Britain, in addition to which they did not extend their rule into Scotland and Wales.
E. They did not extend their rule into Scotland and Wales. The Romans enjoyed a prosperous and peaceful existence in Britain.

Strategy

Focus only on the answers provided. As you read, you will notice errors. Do not edit these errors the way you might improve them. Select the best of the answer choices.

Strategies for Test Taking

Point out to students that in Editing in Context Tests such as the one on this page, some test items simply list choices; students, following the general directions, are expected to choose the best alternative phrase or sentence. Items 1 and 2 are of this type.

Other test items require more careful interpretation. Often this involves adding or eliminating transitional words or expressions, or making revisions that might affect tone or structure. Items 3, 4, 5, and 6 are of this type.

Tell students to read these questions twice, making sure they understand exactly what change the writer is contemplating before testing out the item's choices.

Since these questions may take more time, students might work through the "simpler" test items first and then go back to the more detailed test items. Also, if students complete the test with time remaining, they should review their answers to the detailed test items.

SAT® PREP ACT

2. To add rhythm and emphasize key ideas, what would be the best version of sentence 2?
   A. (As it is now)
   B. They neglected to settle these areas. They thought farm lands held greater interest. It was too hard to conquer these hostile landscapes.
   C. They neglected to settle these areas, felt farm lands held greater interest, and believed it was too hard to conquer these hostile landscapes.
   D. They neglected to settle these areas, they felt farm lands held greater interest, and they believed it was too hard to settle these hostile landscapes.
   E. These areas they neglected to settle, farm lands held greater interest, it was too hard to conquer hostile landscapes.

3. Which is the best version of the underlined portion of sentence 6?
   A. (As it is now)
   B. stone walls, water, heating, multiple rooms, bathing
   C. walls made of stone, water running through pipes, heating in the rooms, multiple rooms, bathing in bath houses
   D. stone walls, piped water, a way to heat multiple rooms, bathing in bath houses
   E. stone walls, water pipes, a heating system, multiple rooms, bath houses

4. Which transition would show the relationship between sentences 7 and 8?
   A. moreover
   B. for example
   C. nevertheless
   D. all in all
   E. consequently

5. Which sentence would be the best transition between the second and third paragraphs?
   A. Life in the towns changed greatly under Roman rule.
   B. Villas were not the only signs of increased wealth in Britain.
   C. Only Romans living abroad could afford to live in the cities.
   D. The effects of Roman civilization greatly altered Britain.
   E. The first step to conquering Britain was to change its people.

6. Which part of sentence 10 should be revised to help the essay best express equal ideas?
   A. (As it is now)
   B. "smaller open-air theaters for religious festivals, pantomime, and plays,"
   C. "larger amphitheaters for gladiator combats and executions,"
   D. "and open baths for men and women"
   E. "as well as"

Timed Writing: Position Statement [25 minutes]

In the final stanza of Philip Larkin's poem "An Arundel Tomb," after examining the weathered stone remnants of a culture dating from nearly two centuries earlier, he concludes, "What will survive of us is love."

Write an essay in which you agree or disagree with Larkin's poetic prediction. Provide reasons why your opinions are correct based on your encounters with elements of today's culture, like art and science, as well as your personal philosophy. Feel free to speculate what, if anything, will survive of our culture. This assignment is similar to the Essay portion of the SAT Writing section.

Academic Vocabulary

Perspective is both a way of looking at things and a personal definition. In your essay, discuss the author's perspective before stating your opinion.

STOP

ASSESS/RETEACH

Answers

1. C
2. C
3. E
4. B
5. B
6. E

Timed Writing

Position Statement

1. Go over the two paragraphs of the timed writing assignment on the student page.
2. Tell students that they can quickly formulate thesis statements for their position statements.
3. Encourage students to budget adequate time for prewriting and revising/editing. Students should spend about 8 minutes in the prewriting stage, 12 minutes drafting, and 5 minutes revising and editing. Reinforce this by announcing elapsed time at the 8- and 20-minute marks as students respond to the assignment.
4. Use the **Rubric for Writing for Assessment**, *Professional Development Guidebook*, pages 258–259, to evaluate students' work.

Benchmark

Reteach skills as indicated by students' performance, following the Reteach charts on pages 1481 and 1483. Then, administer the end-of-unit **Benchmark Test** (*Unit 6 Resources*, pp. 421–426). The Benchmark Test concludes instruction in the Unit skills. Follow the **Interpretation Guide** for the test (*Unit 6 Resources*, p. 429) to assign reteaching pages as necessary in the *Reading Kit*. Use **Success Tracker** online to automatically assign these pages.

Reteach

Question	Pages to Reteach
1	1151
2	1207
3	1207
4	1169
5	1169
6	1169

PHLit Online!

The **Benchmark Tests** and **Success Tracker** are available online at **www.PHLitOnline.com.**

Performance Tasks

Assigning Tasks/Reteaching Skills

Use the chart below to choose appropriate Performance Tasks by identifying which tasks assess lessons in the textbook that you have taught. Use the same lessons for reteaching when students' performance indicates a failure to fully master a standard. For additional instruction and practice, assign the *Common Core Companion* pages indicated for each task.

Task	Where Taught/ Pages to Reteach	*Common Core Companion* Pages
1	1191, 1216, 1218, 1340, 1378, 1418, 1468	28–40, 196–207, 261–268
2	1218, 1244, 1272, 1308, 1316, 1434	15–27, 219–225, 261–268
3	1207, 1284, 1400, 1410, 1468	136–142, 185–195, 261–268
4	1136, 1284, 1444, 1454	103–115, 297–303, 306–312
5	1138, 1205, 1209, 1272, 1366, 1388	41–53, 306–312
6	1191, 1206, 1209, 1216, 1218, 1244, 1470	61–67, 306–312

Assessment Pacing

In assigning the Writing Tasks allow a class period for the completion of a task. As an alternative, assign tasks as homework. In assigning the Speaking and Listening Tasks consider having students do preparation as a homework assignment. Then, allow a class period for the presentations.

Evaluating Performance Tasks

Use the rubric at the bottom of this Teacher Edition page to evaluate students' mastery of the standards in their Performance Task responses. Review the rubric with students before they begin work so they know the criteria by which their work will be evaluated.

Performance Tasks

Follow the instructions to complete the tasks below as required by your teacher. As you work on each task, incorporate both general academic vocabulary and literary terms you learned in this unit.

Common Core State Standards

RL.11-12.2, RL.11-12.3, RL.11-12.4, RL.11-12.6; RI.11-12.2, RI.11-12.5; W.11-12.1, W.11-12.2, W.11-12.4, W.11-12.9.a, W.11-12.9.b; SL.11-12.4, SL.11-12.6

[For the full wording of the standards, see the standards chart in the front of your textbook.]

Writing

Task 1: Literature [RL.11-12.3; W.11-12.2, W.11-12.9.a]

Analyze a Key Narrative Element

*Write an **essay** in which you analyze the development of a key narrative element in a story from this unit.*

- Identify the story you will discuss and provide a brief summary.
- Explain which key narrative element—setting, characters, conflict, or plot sequence—you will analyze in depth.
- Analyze how the author introduces and develops the narrative element you have chosen as a focus. Discuss specific literary techniques, such as the use of descriptive language or dialogue, the author uses to establish this narrative component and engage the reader.
- Discuss the interactions between the narrative element that is your focus and other critical aspects of the story. For example, consider whether the setting is a source of conflict.
- Quote details from the story that support your analysis. Provide smooth transitions that clearly connect the details you cite.

Task 2: Literature [RL.11-12.2; W.11-12.4, W.11-12.9.a]

Analyze Themes in Literature

*Write an **essay** in which you analyze the development of two or more themes in a literary work from this unit.*

- Explain which literary work you will discuss. Introduce your analysis by summarizing the work and clearly identifying two distinct themes it conveys.
- Explain how the author develops the themes over the course of the work. For example, consider descriptions of the setting, characters' actions and reactions, and specific events. Also, consider symbols, imagery, or other literary elements that add to the development of two or more themes.
- Explain how the two themes interact and build on one another throughout the work.
- Express a clear thesis and supply relevant evidence from the story to support your interpretation. Clearly link textual evidence to your ideas.
- Develop and organize your ideas logically to produce coherent and clear support for your analysis.

Task 3: Informational Text [RI.11-12.5; W.11-12.1, W.11-12.9.b]

Analyze and Evaluate Structure

*Write an **essay** in which you analyze and evaluate the structure of a nonfiction work from this unit.*

- State which work you chose and briefly summarize the author's purpose and central ideas.
- Provide an outline or description of the structure of its exposition or argument. Consider whether the structure involves a formal pattern of organization, such as compare and contrast, cause and effect, or main idea and supporting details.
- Evaluate the clarity and logic of the structure, identifying whether it makes the author's ideas clear, convincing, and engaging.
- State a clear main idea, or thesis, and develop and organize your argument logically. Cite specific details from the text as support, and use appropriate transitions to link your ideas.
- End with a conclusion that follows from and supports your evaluation of the author's choices concerning structure.

Performance Task Rubric: Standards Mastery	Rating Scale (*not very* – *very*)
Critical Thinking: How clearly and consistently does the student pursue the specific mode of reasoning or discourse required by the standard, as specified in the prompt (e.g., comparing and contrasting, analyzing, explaining)?	1 2 3 4 5
Focus: How well does the student understand and apply the focus concepts of the standard, as specified in the prompt (e.g., development of theme or of complex characters, effects of structure, and so on)?	1 2 3 4 5
Support/Elaboration: How well does the student support points with textual or other evidence? How relevant, sufficient, and varied is the evidence provided?	1 2 3 4 5
Insight: How original, sophisticated, or compelling are the insights the student achieves by applying the standard to the text(s)?	1 2 3 4 5
Expression of Ideas: How well does the student organize and support ideas? How well does the student use language, including word choice and conventions, in the expression of ideas?	1 2 3 4 5

Speaking and Listening

Task 4: Informational Text [RI.11-12.2; SL.11-12.4, SL.11-12.6]
Analyze Development of Central Ideas

With a partner, deliver a ***presentation with visuals*** *in which you analyze the development of two central ideas in a nonfiction work from this unit.*

- To prepare, choose a work and analyze two or more central ideas it expresses. Determine whether the author has used a clear formal structure or a variety of structures. Note how ideas are introduced, developed, and refined and how specific supporting ideas relate to the main ideas. Explain how the central ideas combine to create a complex account or analysis.
- Capture your ideas in a combination of notes for your own use during the presentation and visuals to share with your audience. Consider such visuals as an idea web, a cause-and-effect chart, an outline, or a sequence-of-events chart. In addition, consider providing copies of annotated or highlighted text.
- Introduce your presentation by stating which work you chose and providing a brief summary. Then, present your analysis with accompanying visual elements.
- As you speak, use academic and content-area vocabulary accurately to clarify ideas and maintain a formal tone.

Task 5: Literature [RL.11-12.4; SL.11-12.6]
Analyze Word Choice, Meaning, and Tone

Deliver an ***oral presentation*** *in which you analyze the relationship between word choice, tone, and meaning in a literary work from this unit.*

- Identify which work you chose and explain why the author's use of language merits deeper analysis.
- Provide a general description of the types of language—complex, simple, figurative, technical, descriptive, etc.—the author uses in the work.
- Explain the author's overall tone, as well as any changes in tone that occur throughout the work.
- Cite specific examples of each broad type of language you noted. Interpret figures of speech and explain nuances and connotations in word meanings. Discuss how each example you cite adds to the overall meaning and tone of the work.
- As you present your work, take your audience's needs into account. Set a pace, neither too slow nor too fast, that allows you to communicate ideas clearly while maintaining listeners' interest.

Task 6: Literature [RL.11-12.6; SL.11-12.6]
Analyze Complex Point of View

Deliver an ***analysis and assessment*** *of the point of view in a literary work from this unit.*

- Identify a literary work from this unit in which the author's point of view is complicated by the use of satire, irony, understatement, or another literary construct in which stated meaning and actual meaning differ. Explain which story you chose and why you chose it.
- Briefly summarize the work. Identify the specific passages or sections you will analyze in depth.
- Discuss how irony, understatement, satire, or tone function in the work by exploring the differences between surface meanings and actual meanings. Explain how these double meanings help to express the author's point of view, or perspective.
- Cite specific details from the text that support your ideas.
- Use formal English as you present your analysis.

What is the relationship between literature and place?

Lives and Places Groups of writers often "belong" to a place because their work reflects its characters, settings, conflicts, or ideals.

Assignment Write a short **collective biography** of a group of British writers that is defined by a place. For example, consider writers associated with the English countryside or with a neighborhood in London; writers who lived in Ireland or Wales; or writers who fought on the battlefields of World War I. Research the lives of the writers in that place, and relate the place to the literary works created there.

Differentiated Instruction for Universal Access

Strategy for Less Proficient Readers
Assign a Performance Task, and then have students meet in groups to review the standard assessed in that task. Remind students of the selections or independent readings to which they have previously applied the standard. Have groups summarize what they learned in applying the standard and then present their summaries. Discuss, clarifying any points of confusion. After students have completed their tasks, have groups meet again to evaluate members' work. Encourage members to revise their work based on the feedback they receive.

EL Strategy for English Learners
For each Performance Task, review the instructions with students. Clarify the meaning of unfamiliar vocabulary, emphasizing classroom words such as *conflict* and *transition* and academic vocabulary such as *perspective.*

Next, have students note ideas for their responses. Pair students, and have them review each other's notes, asking questions to clarify meaning and suggesting improvements. Encourage students to ask for your assistance in supplying English words or expressions they may require.

Supporting Speaking and Listening

1. Consider having students work with partners or in groups to complete Performance Tasks involving listening and speaking. For tasks that you assign for individual work, you may still wish to have students rehearse with partners, who can provide constructive feedback.
2. As students rehearse, have them keep in mind these tips:
   - Present findings and evidence clearly and concisely.
   - Observe conventions of standard English grammar and usage.
   - Be relaxed and friendly but maintain a formal tone.
   - Make eye contact with the audience, pronounce words clearly, and vary your pace.
   - When working with a group, respond thoughtfully to others' positions, modifying your own in response to new evidence.

Linking Performance Tasks to Independent Reading

If you wish to cover the standards with students' independent reading, adapt Performance Tasks of your choice to the works they have selected. (Independent reading suggestions appear on the next page.)

What is the relationship between literature and place?

1. Remind students of the Essential Question, "What is the relationship between literature and place?"
2. Have students complete their responses to the prompt on the student page. Point out that in this unit, they have read a variety of literature of the modern and postmodern periods and that they should draw on these selections in their responses. Remind them that they can also draw on their own experiences and what they have learned in other subject areas in formulating their answers.

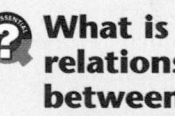

Independent Reading

Titles featured on the Independent Reading pages at the end of each unit represent a range of reading, including stories, dramas, and poetry, as well as literary nonfiction and other types of informational text. Throughout, labels indicate the works that are CCSS Exemplar Texts. Choosing from among these featured titles will help students read works at increasing levels of text complexity in the grades 11–12 text complexity band.

Using Literature Circles

A literature circle is a temporary group in which students independently discuss a book.

Use the guidance in the *Professional Development Guidebook*, pp. 47–49, as well as the teaching notes on the facing page, for additional suggestions for literature circles.

Meeting Unit 6 CCS Standards

Students can use books listed on this page to apply and reinforce their mastery of the CCS Standards covered in this unit.

Introducing Featured Titles

Have students choose a book or books for independent reading. Assist them by previewing the titles, noting their subject matter and level of difficulty. **Note:** Before recommending a work to students, preview it, taking into account the values of your community as well as the maturity of your students.

Featured Titles

In this unit, you have read a variety of literature of the modern and postmodern periods. Continue to read works related to this era on your own. Select books that you enjoy, but challenge yourself to explore new topics, new authors, and works offering varied perspectives or approaches. The titles suggested below will help you get started.

LITERATURE

Heart of Darkness and The Secret Sharer
Joseph Conrad

Fiction *Heart of Darkness* reveals the darkness within the human spirit during an ominous journey to the heart of the colonial African jungle. "The Secret Sharer" tells the tale of the promising journey of a young sea captain who finds help from an unexpected source.

[Conrad's short story "The Lagoon" appears on page 1220 of this book. Build knowledge by reading more fiction by this author.]

The Importance of Being Earnest
Oscar Wilde — EXEMPLAR TEXT

Drama Mistaken identities, clever plot twists, and witty dialogue will keep you entertained as you read this popular comedy of manners by Oscar Wilde. Look beneath the surface and you will find an incisive satire of late-Victorian British society.

Early Short Stories: 1883–1888
Anton Chekhov
Modern Library, 1999 — EXEMPLAR TEXT

Short Stories This collection of seventy early short stories by Russian writer Anton Chekhov, which includes the masterful story "Home," demonstrates the author's artistry at revealing the breadth of human emotions through seemingly ordinary experiences.

White Teeth
Zadie Smith

Novel After fighting together for the British army in World War II, Archibald Jones and Samad Iqbal settle in London. This extraordinary novel, which tells the story of Archibald's and Samad's lives, is an exploration of immigrant experiences, family, poverty, and friendship.

INFORMATIONAL TEXTS

Historical Texts

Testament of Youth
Vera Brittain
WN, 2009

Autobiography In 1915, Vera Brittain was about to return for her second year as a student at Oxford University. Instead, with the outbreak of World War I, she became a nurse and served through much of the war. In this much-admired memoir, she tells the story of a generation forever affected by the tragic conflict.

All Art Is Propaganda: Critical Essays
George Orwell
First Mariner Books, 2009 — EXEMPLAR TEXT

Criticism Orwell critiques literary figures such as T. S. Eliot and Graham Greene and presents his views on everything from greed and politics to poverty and homelessness. Included in the book is the essay "Politics and the English Language."

[Orwell's essay "Shooting an Elephant" appears on page 1318 of this book. Build knowledge by reading more nonfiction by this author.]

Once There Was a War
John Steinbeck

Journalism In 1943, journalist John Steinbeck was on assignment for *The New York Herald Tribune* in Italy, North Africa, and England during the London blitz. In his dispatches, he focuses on the human impacts of the war.

Contemporary Scholarship

Yeats
Harold Bloom
Oxford University Press, 1972

Literary Criticism Bloom presents his insightful interpretations of William Butler Yeats's poems and plays, and explains how Yeats was influenced by the writers of the Romantic movement. A must-read for anyone interested in learning more about the work of Yeats.

Text Complexity: Aligning Texts With Readers and Tasks

TEXTS	READERS AND TASKS
• *White Teeth* (Lexile: 960L) • *Once There Was a War*	**Below-Level Readers** Allow students to focus on reading for content, and challenge them to interpret multiple perspectives.
• *Heart of Darkness and The Secret Sharer* (Lexile: 1020L) • *The Importance of Being Earnest* • *Early Short Stories* • *Testament of Youth*	**Below-Level Readers** Challenge students as they read for content. **On-Level Readers** Allow students to focus on reading for content, and challenge them to interpret multiple perspectives. **Advanced Readers** Allow students to focus on interpreting multiple perspectives.
• *All Art is Propaganda* • *Yeats* (Lexile: 1500L)	**On-Level Readers** Challenge students as they read for content. **Advanced Readers** Allow students to focus on reading for content, and challenge them to interpret multiple perspectives.

Preparing to Read Complex Texts

Reading for College and Career In both college and the workplace, readers must analyze texts independently, draw connections among works that offer varied perspectives, and develop their own ideas and informed opinions. The questions shown below, and others that you generate on your own, will help you more effectively read and analyze complex college-level texts.

Common Core State Standards

Reading Literature/Informational Text
10. By the end of grade 12, read and comprehend literature, including stories, dramas, and poems and literary nonfiction, at the high end of the grades 11-CCR text complexity band independently and proficiently.

When reading analytically, ask yourself...

- What idea, experience, or story seems to have compelled the author to write? Has the author presented that idea, experience, or story in a way that I, too, find compelling?
- How might the author's era, social status, belief system, or personal experiences have affected the point of view he or she expresses in the text?
- How do my circumstances affect what I understand and feel about this text?
- What key idea does the author state explicitly? What key idea does he or she suggest or imply? Which details in the text help me to perceive implied ideas?
- Do I find multiple layers of meaning in the text? If so, what relationships do I see among these layers of meaning?
- How do details in the text connect or relate to one another? Do I find any details unconvincing, unrelated, or out of place?
- Do I find the text believable and convincing?

Key Ideas and Details

- What patterns of organization or sequences do I find in the text? Do these patterns help me understand the ideas better?
- What do I notice about the author's style, including his or her diction, uses of imagery and figurative language, and syntax?
- Do I like the author's style? Is the author's style memorable?
- What emotional attitude does the author express toward the topic, the story, or the characters? Does this attitude seem appropriate?
- What emotional attitude does the author express toward me, the reader? Does this attitude seem appropriate?
- What do I notice about the author's voice—his or her personality on the page? Do I like this voice? Does it make me want to read on?

Craft and Structure

- Is the work fresh and original?
- Do I agree with the author's ideas entirely, or are there elements I find unconvincing?
- Do I disagree with the author's ideas entirely, or are there elements I can accept as true?
- Based on my knowledge of British literature, history, and culture, does this work reflect the British tradition? Why or why not?

Integration of Ideas

Text Complexity: Reader and Task Support Suggestions

INDEPENDENT READING

Increased Support	Increased Challenge
Increased Support Suggest that students choose a book that they feel comfortable reading and one that is a bit more challenging. Pair a more proficient reader with a less proficient reader and have them work together on the more challenging text. Partners can prepare to read the book by reviewing questions on this student page. They can also read difficult passages together, sharing questions and insights. They can use the questions on the student page to guide after-reading discussion.	*Increased Challenge* Encourage students to integrate knowledge and ideas by combining the Essential Questions and the unit concepts in their approach to two or more featured titles. For example, students might consider the effects that World War I and World War II had on the people of Europe. Students can focus on the experiences of the characters in *White Teeth,* Brittain's descriptions in *Testament of Youth,* and Steinbeck's journalism in *Once There Was a War.*

Preparing to Read Complex Texts

1. Tell students they can be attentive readers by bringing their experience and imagination to the texts they read and by actively questioning those texts. Explain that the questions on the student page are examples of questions to ask about works of fiction and nonfiction.
2. Point out that, like writing, reading is a "multidraft" process, involving several readings of complete works or passages, revising and refining one's understanding each time.

Key Ideas and Details

3. **Ask:** What key ideas and details had particular relevance to you? How did these details affect your overall experience of the text?

   Possible response: Students may point out details that had a personal impact and describe how these details made the text resonate on a deeper level.

Craft and Structure

4. **Ask:** How does the organization help you grasp the author's ideas?

   Possible response: Chronological order in a narrative helps readers follow plot and character development. Cause-and-effect or problem-solution organization helps readers see the author's support for his or her argument.

Integration of Ideas

5. **Ask:** What characteristics or techniques might you find in a twentieth-century work that reflects the British tradition?

   Possible response: Some poets might use traditional forms, such as the sonnet or lyric poetry, to convey themes more relevant to today. Some current writers might expand on themes from past British literary movements.
6. Finally, explain to students that they should cite key ideas and details, examples of craft and structure, or instances of the integration of ideas as evidence to support their points during a discussion of fiction, nonfiction, or drama.

Resources

English Glossary

Essential Question vocabulary appears in **blue type**. High-utility Academic vocabulary is **underlined**.

A

abasement (uh BAYS muhnt) *n.* condition of being put down or humbled

abated (uh BAYT ihd) *v.* lessened

abide (uh BYD) *v.* to stay; remain

absolution (AB suh LOO shuhn) *n.* act of freeing someone of a sin or criminal charge

acceded (ak SEED uhd) *v.* yielded; agreed

accounts (uh KOWNTS) *n.* records of money received and paid out; financial records

adjure (uh JUR) *v.* request solemnly; appeal to earnestly

admonish (ad MON ihsh) *v.* caution

adroitly (uh DROYT lee) *adv.* with physical or mental skill

adulterations (uh duhl tuh RAY shuhnz) *n.* impurities; added ingredients that are improper or inferior

adversary (AD vuhr sehr ee) *n.* opponent; enemy

advocate (AD vuh kayt) *v.* speak or write in support of

affably (AF uh blee) *adv.* in a friendly manner

affinities (uh FIHN uh teez) *n.* family connections; sympathies

affluence (AF loo uhns) *n.* abundant wealth

ague (AY gyoo) *n.* a chill or fit of shivering

alderman (AWL duhr muhn) *n.* chief officers in a shire or county

alters (AWL tuhrz) *v.* changes

amiable (AY mee uh buhl) *adj.* friendly; agreeable

amorous (AM uhr uhs) *adj.* full of love or desire

anarchy (AN uhr kee) *n.* absence of government; disorder

anatomize (uh NAT uh myz) *v.* to dissect in order to examine structure

ancestral (an SEHS truhl) *adj.* inherited

anemic (uh NEE mihk) *adj.* lacking power, vigor, vitality, or colorfulness; listless; weak

annotate (AN uh tayt) *v.* note or mark with explanation

antic (AN tihk) *adj.* odd and funny; silly

antidote (AN tee doht) *n.* something that works against an unwanted condition; remedy

aperture (AP uhr chur) *n.* opening

apothecary (uh POTH uh kehr ee) *n.* pharmacist; druggist

appalled (uh PAWLD) *v.* filled with consternation or dismay

appendage (uh PEHN dihj) *n.* something added on

apprehension (ap rih HEHN shuhn) *n.* anxious feeling of foreboding; dread

apprehensions (ap rih HEHN shuhnz) *n.* fears; concerns

approbation (AP ruh BAY shuhn) *n.* official approval or sanction

arboreal (ahr BAWR ee uhl) *adj.* of, near, or among trees

articulate (ahr TIHK yuh layt) *v.* express clearly

artifice (AHR tuh fihs) *n.* skill; the product of skill, especially a skillful deception

artificiality (AHR tuh fihsh ee AL uh tee) *n.* unnatural; unreal

aspire (uh SPYR) *v.* have high ambitions; yearn or seek after

assault (uh SAWLT) *v.* violently attack

assessing (uh SEHS ihng) *v.* to estimate the value of (property) for taxation

assiduous (uh SIHJ oo uhs) *adj.* constant in application or attention

assignations (AS ihg NAY shuhn) *n.* appointments to meet

asunder (uh SUHN duhr) *adj.* into parts or pieces

atrophy (AT ruh fee) *v.* to waste away

augment (awg MEHNT) *v.* make greater; enlarge

authentic (aw THEHN tihk) *adj.* genuine; real

avarice (AV uhr ihs) *n.* greed

averred (uh VURD) *v.* stated to be true

awe (aw) *n.* mixed feeling of reverence, fear, and wonder

B

balm (bahm) *n.* ointment or other thing that heals or soothes

bar (bahr) *n.* one of the vertical lines dividing written music into equal sections called measures

beliefs (bih LEEFS) *n.* what is held to be true

bequeath (bih KWEETH) *v.* hand down as an inheritance

bilious (BIHL yuhs) *adj.* peevish; irritable; crank

blight (blyt) *n.* condition of withering

blithe (blyTH) *adj.* cheerful

boundary (BOWN duhr ee) *n.* limiting line; border

breach (breech) *n.* breaking or being broken; failure to observe the terms of an agreement

brink (brihngk) *n.* edge; margin

burden (BUR duhn) *n.* something that weighs one down; a heavy load or responsibility

C

cadence (KAY duhns) *n.* measured movement

caprices (kuh PREES ez) *n.* whims

capitalism (KAP uh tuh lihz uhm) *n.* economic system in which private individuals or groups of individuals own land, factories, and other means of production

categorize (KAT uh guh ryz) *v.* place in related groups

censure (SEHN shuhr) *v.* strongly disapprove; condemn

certify (SUR tuh fy) *v.* declare a thing true or accurate; verify; attest

characterize (KAR ihk tuh ryz) *v.* describe features, qualities, or traits

chronicle (KRON uh kuhl) *n.* historical record of events in chronological order

chrysalis (KRIHS uh lihs) *n.* the third stage in the development of a moth or butterfly

circumscribed (SUR kuhm skrybd) *v.* limited; having a definite boundary

cite (syt) *v.* quote from a text

city (SIHT ee) *n.* large and heavily populated town

clamorous (KLAM uhr uhs) *adj.* loud and confused; noisy

clarify (KLAR uh fy) *v.* make clear

clasped (klaspt) *v.* firmly grasped or gripped

classics (KLAS ihks) *n.* books or paintings of the highest quality

classify (KLAS uh fy) *v.* assign to a category

climacteric (kly MAK tuhr ihk) *n.* any critical period

colonize (KOL uh nyz) *v.* establish a settlement

combatants (KOM buh tuhnts) *n.* fighters

combustible (kuhm BUHS tuh buhl) *adj.* capable of being ignited and burned; flammable

commentary (KOM uhn TEHR ee) *n.* a series of comments

commission (kuh MIHSH uhn) *n.* authorization; act of giving authority to an individual

commodity (kuh MOD uh tee) *n.* product that is bought or sold

compassionate (kuhm PASH uh niht) *adj.* sympathizing

compile (kuhm PYL) *v.* put together

complaisant (kuhm PLAY zuhnt) *adj.* agreeable; willing to please

comprised (kuhm PRYZD) *v.* consisted of; included

concord (KON kawrd) *n.* friendly relations; harmony

condescension (kon dih SEHN shuhn) *n.* a patronizing act

conflagration (KON fluh GRAY shuhn) *n.* great fire

conflict (KON flihkt) *n.* a fight or struggle

conjecture (kuhn JEHK chuhr) *v.* guess

connote (kuh NOHT) *v.* suggest or convey

conquest (KON kwehst) *n.* act of conquering

consciousness (KON shuhs nihs) *n.* state of being aware

constituency (kuhn STIHCH oo uhn see) *n.* the people making up a body of voters

construct (kuhn STRUHKT) *v.* build by fitting parts together systematically

contemporary (kuhn TEHM puh rehr ee) *adj.* belonging to the same period of time

contemptuous (kuhn TEHMP choo uhs) *adj.* scornful

contend (kuhn TEHND) *v.* assert or argue

contention (kuhn TEHN shuhn) *n.* dispute; argument

contentious (kuhn TEHN shuhs) *adj.* quarrelsome

contextualize (kuhn TEHKS choo uh lyz) *v.* place information within a larger background

contrite (kuhn TRYT) *adj.* willing to repent or atone

controversy (KON truh vur see) *n.* act of arguing a question about which differences of opinion exist

contusions (kuhn TOO zhuhnz) *n.* an injury in which the skin is not broken; a bruise

conventional (kuhn VEHN shuh nuhl) *adj.* acting or behaving according to commonly accepted or approved ways

coordinate (koh AWR duh nayt) *v.* relate or link

country (KUHN tree) *n.* land; nation

covetousness (KUHV uh tuhs nuhs) *n.* greediness

conviction (kuhn VIHK shuhn) *n.* belief; faith

countenance (KOWN tuh nuhns) *n.* face

courtly (KAWRT lee) *adj.* elegantly dignified; polite

cower (KOW uhr) *v.* crouched, as from fear or cold

coyness (KOY nuhs) *n.* shyness; aloofness, often as part of a flirtation

credulity (kruh DOO luh tee) *n.* tendency to believe too readily

credulous (KREHJ uh luhs) *adj.* tending to believe too readily

critique (krih TEEK) *v.* examine critically; review

cultivated (KUHL tuh vay tihd) *v.* grown

cynically (SIHN uh kuhl ee) *adv.* like or characteristic of a cynic; distrusting or disparaging the motives of other

D

dappled (DAP uhld) *adj.* a spot or mottled marking, usually occurring in clusters

dauntless (DAWNT lihs) *adj.* fearless; cannot be intimidated

debate (dih BAYT) *v.* discuss opposing reasons

deduce (dih DOOS) *v.* infer from a general principle

deference (DEHF uhr uhns) *n.* courteous regard or respect

deficient (dih FIHSH uhnt) *adj.* lacking an essential quality

define (dih FYN) *v.* tell the qualities that make something what it is

deftly (DEHFT lee) *adv.* with ease and quickness

deism (DEE ihz uhm) *n.* belief in God on the evidence of reason and nature

deliberation (dih lihb uh RAY shuhn) *n.* careful consideration and discussion before reaching a decision

delirious (dih LIHR ee uhs) *adj.* having hallucinations; ranting

demonstrate (DEHM uhn strayt) *v.* show by reasoning or examples

denote (dih NOHT) *v.* refer to clearly

depict (dih PIHKT) *v.* portray an image using words

depredation (dep ruh DAY shuhn) *n.* a predatory attack; a raid

derided (dih RYD ihd) *v.* made fun of; ridiculed

design (dih ZYN) *v.* condescend; lower oneself

desolate (DEHS uh liht) *adj.* deserted; forlorn

despondent (dih SPON duhnt) *adj.* hopeless; dejected

despotic (dehs POT ihk) *adj.* tyrannical

destitute (DEHS tuh toot) *adj.* lacking

destruction (dih STRUHK shuhn) *n.* act of destroying

devise (dih VYZ) *v.* work out or create; plan

diffusive (dih FYOO sihv) *adj.* tending to spread out

disabused (dihs uh BYOOZ) *v.* freed from false ideas

discern (duh ZURN) *v.* recognize as separate or different

discreet (dihs KREET) *adj.* wise; prudent

discretion (dihs KREHSH uhn) *n.* care in what one does and says; good judgment; prudence

dislocation (dihs loh KAY shuhn) *n.* condition of being out of place

dispensation (dihs puhn SAY shuhn) *n.* religious system or beliefs

disposable (dihs POH zuh buhl) *adj.* free for use; available

dissatisfaction (dihs sat ihs FAK shuhn) *n.* state of being discontent

dissect (dih SEHKT) *v.* analyze and interpret minutely

distemper (dihs TEHM puhr) *n.* infectious disease such as the plague

distill (dihs TIHL) *v.* to obtain the essential part

divine (duh VYN) *adj.* heavenly; holy

dominion (duh MIHN yuhn) *n.* rule or power over a territory; authority or control

dominions (duh MIHN yuhnz) *n.* governed territories or lands

dowry (DOW ree) *n.* property brought by a woman's family to her husband upon their marriage

dregs (drehgz) *n.* a small amount; a residue

E

eclipse (ih KLIHPS) *v.* dimming or extinction of power or glory

economic (ee kuh NOM ihk) *adj.* having to do with the management of the income

edit (EHD iht) *v.* alter, adapt, or refine

effigy (EHF uh jee) *n.* portrait or statue of a person

electors (ih LEHK tuhrz) *n.* those who vote

eloquent (EHL uh kwuhnt) *adj.* beautifully expressive

eludes (ih LOODZ) *v.* avoids or escapes

embarked (ehm BAHRKT) *v.* engaged in something, such as a journey

embellishments (ehm BEHL ihsh muhnts) *n.* decorative touches; ornamentation

eminent (EHM uh nuhnt) *adj.* noteworthy; of high rank; distinguished

empire (EHM pyr) *n.* group of nations or states under one ruler or government

encomiums (ehn KOH mee uhmz) *n.* formal expressions of great praise

endeavored (ehn DEHV uhrd) *n.* made a serious attempt; tried

enhance (ehn HANS) *v.* improve or heighten

enigma (ih NIHG muh) *n.* riddle; perplexing statement, person, or situation

entreated (ehn TREET uhd) *v.* begged; pleaded with

enumerate (ih NOO muh rayt) *v.* specify a list

epic (EHP ihk) *n.* long poem that tells of the adventures of one or more great heroes

equate (ih KWAYT) *v.* consider one thing the same as another

equivocate (ih KWIHV uh kayt) *v.* to use terms that have two or more meanings to mislead purposely or deceive

escapade (EHS kuh payd) *n.* adventurous action, especially one that breaks ordinary rules of conduct

esteemed (ehs TEEMD) *adj.* highly respected; held in high regard

etymology (eht uh MOL uh jee) *n.* the study of word origins

evaluate (ih VAL yoo ayt) *v.* determine something's significance, worth, or condition

evanescence (ehv uh NEHS uhns) *n.* vanishing or tendency to vanish

evoke (ih VOHK) *v.* draw out a reaction

exemplary (ehg ZEHM pluhr ee) *adj.* of that which should serve as a model

exile (EHG zyl) *v.* force a person to leave home or country

exotic (ehg ZOT ihk) *adj.* from a foreign country

expedient (ehk SPEE dee uhnt) *n.* device used in an emergency

expiated (EHKS pee ayt uhd) *v.* atoned; made amends for, especially by suffering

extract (ehk STRAKT) *v.* draw out information

extravagant (ehk STRAV uh guhnt) *adj.* going beyond reasonable limits; excessive

F

fantastic (fan TAS tihk) *adj.* very fanciful; unbelievably good

fastidious (fas TIHD ee uhs) *adj.* particular; difficult to please

fate (fayt) *n.* destiny

fathom (FATH uhm) *v.* understand thoroughly

fervent (FUR vuhnt) *adj.* having great warmth of feeling

fidelity (fy DEHL uh tee) *n.* faithfulness

filial (FIHL ee uhl) *adj.* expected of a son or a daughter

form (FAWR myuh layt) *v.* give shape to

format (FAWR mat) *v.* arrange according to a plan

formulate (FAWR myuh layt) *v.* express fully and clearly; devise

fortitude (FAWR tuh tood) *n.* courage; strength to endure

fracture (FRAK chuhr) *n.* the act of breaking; state of being broken

frugally (FROO guhl ee) *adv.* in a way that is careful with money

furrow (FUR oh) *n.* narrow groove made in the ground by a plow

G

gall (gawl) *n.* bitter feeling; deep spite

galled (gawld) *adj.* injured or made sore by rubbing or chafing

galleons (GAL ee uhnz) *n.* large sailing ships used for war or trade

garnished (GAHR nihsht) *v.* decorated; trimmed

garrulous (GAR uh luhs) *adj.* talkative

gaunt (gawnt) *adj.* thin and bony, as from great hunger or age

geography (jee OG ruh fee) *n.* surface features of a place or region

ghastly (GAST lee) *adj.* terrible; very bad

gleaned (gleend) *v.* collected from bit by bit, as when gathering stray grain after a harvest

gout (gowt) *n.* a mass or splash, as of blood; spurt

grandeur (GRAN juhr) *n.* splendor; magnificence

gravity (GRAV uh tee) *n.* weight; seriousness

grievances (GREE vuhns ez) *n.* circumstances that cause people to complain

grieved (greevd) *v.* felt deep grief for; mourned

guile (gyl) *n.* artful trickery

H

haggard (HAG uhrd) *adj.* appearing worn and exhausted; gaunt

harbingers (HAHR bihn juhrz) *n.* forerunners

heedless (HEED lihs) *adj.* not taking notice; inattentive

highlight (HY lyt) *v.* emphasize

hoary (HAWR ee) *adj.* white or gray with age

homespun (hohm spuhn) *adj.* spun or made at home; plain

hypothesize (hy POTH uh syz) *v.* suggest a possible explanation

I

ideal (y DEE uhl) *n.* perfect type

idealism (y DEE uh lihz uhm) *n.* a belief in or pursuit of things as they should be

ignoble (ihg NOH buhl) *adj.* not noble; common

ignominy (IHG nuh mihn ee) *n.* humiliation; dishonor

illumine (ih LOO muhn) *v.* light up

illusion (ih LOO zhuhn) *n.* appearance or feeling that misleads because it is not real

immigrant (IHM uh gruhnt) *n.* person who comes into a foreign country to live

immortal (ih MAWR tuhl) *adj.* living or lasting forever; not dying

impediments (ihm PEHD uh muhnts) *n.* obstacles

imperceptibly (ihm puhr SEHP tuh buhl ee) *adv.* without being noticed

imperial (ihm PIHR ee uhl) *adj.* of an empire; having supreme authority

imperialism (ihm PIHR ee uh lihz uhm) *n.* policy of forming an empire by conquest and colonization

impertinence (ihm PUR tuh nuhns) *n.* rudeness; impudence

imperturbable (ihm puhr TUR buh buhl) *adj.* calm; not easily ruffled

implored (ihm PLAWRD) *v.* begged earnestly

importuning (ihm pawr TOON ihng) *v.* pleading with

impressionistic (ihm prehsh uh NIHS tihk) *adj.* conveying a picture through quickly sketched suggestions of details

impudence (IHM pyuh duhns) *n.* lack of shame; rudeness

impulse (IHM puhls) *n.* force driving forward

inane (ihn AYN) *adj.* lacking sense, significance, or ideas; silly

incessant (ihn SEHS uhnt) *adj.* continuing without interruption; ceaseless

incitement (ihn SYT muhnt) *n.* act of urging; encouragement

inconstancy (ihn KON stuhn see) *n.* fickleness; changeableness

inconstantly (ihn KON stuhnt lee) *adv.* changeably; in a fickle way

incredulously (ihn KR uh luhs lee) *adv.* in a manner expressing doubt or disbelief

independence (ihn dih PEHN duhns) *n.* freedom from the control of others

indignant (ihn DIHG nuhnt) *adj.* outraged; filled with righteous anger

indissoluble (ihn dih SOL yuh buhl) *adj.* not able to be dissolved or undone

inducted (ihn DUHKT ihd) *v.* brought formally into an organization

industry (IHN duh stree) *n.* any branch of business, trade, or manufacture

inevitable (ihn EHV uh tuh buhl) *adj.* unavoidable; certain to happen

infamy (IHN fuh mee) *n.* very bad reputation; disgrace; dishonor

infirmity (n FUR muh tee) *n.* physical or mental defect; illness

ingenuous (ihn JEHN yoo uhs) *adj.* naïve; simple

ingratiating (ihn GRAY shee ay tihng) *adj.* charming; agreeable; pleasing

inheritance (ihn HEHR uh tuhns) *n.* act of inheriting

inklings (IHNGK lihngz) *n.* indirect suggestions; vague ideas

innumerable (ih NOO muhr uh buhl) *adj.* too many to count

insatiableness (ihn SAY shuh buhl nuhs) *n.* the quality of being impossible to fill

instantaneous (IHN stuhn TAY nee uhs) *adj.* done or happening in an instant

integrate (IHN tuh grayt) *v.* bring together distinct parts

intemperance (ihn TEHM puhr uhns) *n.* lack of restraint

interpret (ihn TUR priht) *v.* explain the meaning

interpretation (ihn tur pruh TAY shuhn) *n.* act of explaining

interred (ihn TURD) *v.* buried in the earth

intrigues (ihn TREEGZ) *n.* plots or schemes

intrinsically (ihn TRIHN suh kuhl ee) *adv.* at its core; inherently; innately

invasion (ihn VAY zhuhn) *n.* entering by force

invincible (ihn VIHN suh buhl) *adj.* unconquerable

irrevocable (ih REHV uh kuh buhl) *adj.* unable to be undone or cancelled

isolation (y suh LAY shuhn) *n.* state of being completely separated from others

J

judicious (joo DIHSH uhs) *adj.* showing good judgment

K

keenly (KEEN lee) *adv.* sharply; intensely

ken (kehn) *n.* range of sight or knowledge

kindred (KIHN drihd) *n.* a person's relatives collectively

kingdoms (KIHNG duhm) *n.* countries that are governed by a king or queen

L

label (LAY buhl) *v.* describe or designate

laity (LAY uh tee) *n.* those not initiated into a priesthood

lament (luh MEHNT) *v.* to express grief over; to mourn

lamentable (LAM uhn tuh buhl) *adj.* causing grief; distressing

lamentations (lam uhn TAY shuhnz) *n.* expressions of grief or mourning

languish (LANG gwihsh) *v.* become weak; droop; suffer from longing

languished (LANG gwihsht) *v.* weakened; dulled

languor (LANG guhr) *n.* lack of energy or vitality; sluggishness

largesse (LAHR jihs) *n.* nobility of spirit

larking (LAHRK ihng) *v.* free-spirited, whimsical fun

legacy (LEHG uh see) *n.* money or other property left to a person by the will of someone who has died

lintel (LIHN tuhl) *n.* horizontal bar above a door

loathsome (LOHTH suhm) *adj.* disgusting

loyalties (LOY uhl teez) *n.* loyal feelings or behaviors; faithfulness

loyalty (LOY uhl tee) *n.* loyal feeling or behavior; faithfulness

ludicrous (LOO duh kruhs) *adj.* absurd; ridiculous

lustrous (LUHS truhs) *adj.* having luster; shining; luminous

M

macadam (muh KAD uhm) *n.* the broken stone used in making a road

madrigals (MAD ruh guhlz) *n.* short love poems set to music

magistrate (MAJ uh strayt) *n.* a local official who administers the law or serves as a judge

malevolence (muh LEHV uh luhns) *n.* ill will; spitefulness

malicious (muh LIHSH uhs) *adj.* deliberately harmful; destructive

massive (MAS ihv) *adj.* big and solid; bulky

measure (MEHZH uhr) *n.* a section of written music between two vertical lines called bars; a bill, resolution, or something else proposed or enacted to improve a situation

melodious (muh LOH dee uhs) *adj.* sweet-sounding; tuneful

melody (MEHL uh dee) *n.* a sequence of single tones that together create a tune or song

migrated (MY grayt uhd) *v.* moved from one region or country to another

mobility (moh BIHL uh tee) *n.* ability to move

mockeries (MOK uhr eez) *n.* futile or disappointing efforts; ridicule

modernization (mod uhr nuh ZAY shuhn) *n.* bringing up to the present ways or standards

monarch (MON uhrk) *n.* country ruled by one person

monotonous (muh NOT uh nuhs) *adj.* without variation

morose (muh ROHS) *adj.* gloomy; sullen

mortal (MAWR tuhl) *adj.* of that which must eventually die

multitudinous (muhl tuh TOO duh nuhs) *adj.* existing in great numbers

munificence (myoo NIHF uh suhns) *n.* lavish generosity

N

nature (NAY chuhr) *n.* all things except those made by man

nimble (NIHM buhl) *adj.* able to move quickly and lightly

nocturnal (nok TUR nuhl) *adj.* occurring at night

notorious (noh TAWR ee uhs) *adj.* widely but unfavorably known; having a bad reputation

nuisance (NOO suhns) *n.* act, thing, or condition causing trouble

O

obdurate (OB duhr iht) *adj.* stubborn

obedience (oh BEE dee uhns) *n.* the act of following orders or instructions

obliquely (uh BLEEK lee) *adv.* at a slant; indirectly

obscure (uhb SKYUR) *adj.* not easily seen; not generally known

obscure (uhb SKYUR) *v.* making difficult to see

obstinate (OB stuh niht) *adj.* stubborn; dogged

obstinately (OB stuh niht lee) *adv.* in a determined way; stubbornly

officious (uh FIHSH uhs) *adj.* meddlesome

ordeal (awr DEEL) *n.* difficult or painful experience that tests one

order (AWR duhr) *n.* way one thing follows another

orthodox (AWR thuh doks) *adj.* conforming to established beliefs

outcast (OWT KAST) *n.* person cast out from home and friends

outline (OWT LYN) *v.* develop a general plan

P

pallor (PAL uhr) *n.* unnatural lack of color; paleness

palpable (PAL puh buhl) *adj.* capable of being touched or felt

palpitation (pal puh TAY shuhn) *n.* an unusually or abnormally rapid or violent beating of the heart

paltry (PAWL tree) *adj.* practically worthless; insignificant

paradox (PAR uh doks) *n.* statement that may be true but seems to say two opposite things

paraphrase (PAR uh frayz) *v.* reword something spoken or written

pastoral (PAS tuhr uhl) *n.* simple or naturally beautiful like the country

pathos (PAY thos) *n.* quality that evokes sorrow or compassion

patronize (PAY truh nyz) *v.* to be a customer of a particular merchant or store

penury (PEHN yuhr ee) *n.* poverty

perceive (puhr SEEV) *v.* recognize through the senses

peril (PEHR uhl) *n.* exposure to harm or injury

pernicious (puhr NIHSH uhs) *adj.* causing great injury, destruction, or ruin; fatal; deadly

phantasm (FAN taz uhm) *n.* supernatural form or shape; ghost; figment of the imagination

philosophy (fuh LOS uh fee) *n.* system for guiding life

piety (PY uh tee) *n.* devotion to religion

platitude (PLAT uh tood) *n.* commonplace or overused statement

plebeian (plih BEE uhn) *adj.* common; not aristocratic

power (POW uhr) *n.* strength or force

predominance (prih DOM uh nuhns) *n.* superiority

predominant (prih DOM uh nuhnt) *adj.* foremost; powerful

prefiguring (pree FIHG yuhr ihng) *v.* resembling and so suggesting beforehand

prenatal (pree NAY tuhl) *adj.* existing or taking place before birth

presumed (prih ZOOMD) *v.* taken for granted; assumed

presumption (prih ZUHMP shuhn) *n.* audacity

prevail (prih VAYL) *v.* to succeed; become dominant; win out

prevarication (pree VAR uh KAY shuhn) *n.* evasion of truth

prime (prym) *n.* best stage of a thing or process

pristine (PRIHS teen) *adj.* original; unspoiled

probe (prohb) *v.* search into and explore thoroughly

prodding (PROD ihng) *v.* poking, jabbing, seeking

prodigal (PROD uh guhl) *adj.* recklessly wasteful

prodigious (pruh DIHJ uhs) *adj.* enormous; huge

profanation (PROF uh NAY shuhn) *n.* action showing disrespect for something sacred

proferring (PROF uhr ihng) n. offering

profuse (pruh FYOOS) *adj.* abundant; pouring out

progress (PROG rehs) *n.* growth; improvement

promontories (PROM uhn tawr eez) *n.* peaks of high land sticking out into a body of water

prophet (PROF iht) *n.* person who tells what will happen

propitiate (pruh PIHSH ee ayt) *v.* win the good-will of; appease

propose (pruh POHZ) *v.* set forth a plan or intention

propriety (pruh PRY uh tee) *n.* quality or condition of being proper

prosper (PROS puhr) *v.* to thrive

prowess (PROW ihs) *n.* heroism; distinction

prudence (PROO duhns) *n.* careful management of resources; economy

pulp (puhlp) *n.* the soft, juicy, edible part of a fruit

purge (purj) *v.* purify; cleanse

R

rancor (RANG kuhr) *n.* ill will; continuing and bitter hate

ransacked (RAN sakt) *v.* searched through to find goods to rob; Looted

rapture (RAP chuhr) *n.* joy; great pleasure

rapturous (RAP chuhr uhs) *adj.* filled with joy and love; ecstatic

rational (RASH uh nuhl) *adj.* sensible; reasonable

realms (rehlmz) *n.* regions under the rule of a king or queen

rebellious (rih BEHL yuhs) *adj.* defying authority

rebuild (ree BIHLD) *v.* build or create again

rebuke (rih BYOOK) *v.* criticize strongly

recall (rih KAWL) *v.* remember

reckoning (REHK uhn ihng) *n.* accounting

recoil (rih KOYL) *v.* to draw back in fear, surprise, or disgust

recommend (rehk uh MEHND) *v.* suggest favorably

recompense (REHK uhm pehns) *n.* payment in return for something

recount (rih KOWNT) *v.* tell in detail

reform (rih FAWRM) *v.* make better

reformation (REHF uhr MAY shuhn) *n.* change for the better; improvement

refractory (rih FRAK tuhr ee) *adj.* hard to manage; stubborn

refute (rih FYOOT) *v.* prove wrong

reiterate (ree IHT uh rayt) *v.* state or do over again

relates (rih LAYTS) *v.* tells

remnant (REHM nuhnt) *n.* what is left over; remainder

Renaissance (REHN uh sahns) *n.* great revival of art and learning in Europe during the 1300s, 1400s, and 1500s

reparation (rehp uh RAY shuhn) *n.* compensation for a wrong

reprove (rih PROOV) *v.* to disapprove of strongly; censure

requiem (REHK wee uhm) *n.* musical composition honoring the dead

resolution (rehz uh LOO shuhn) *n.* a resolve or determination

resume (rih ZOOM) *v.* to take up or go on with again after interruption

reticent (REHT uh suhnt) *adj.* silent; reserved

reverence (REHV uhr uhns) *n.* deep respect

reverently (REHV uhr uhnt lee) *adv.* with deep respect or awe

revolution (rehv uh LOO shuhn) *n.* complete overthrow of an established government or political system

righteousness (RY chuhs nihs) *n.* the characteristic of acting in a just, virtuous manner

risible (RIHZ uh buhl) *adj.* prompting laughter

rites (ryts) *n.* ceremonies; rituals

role (rohl) *n.* part or function assumed by any person or thing

roused (rowzd) *v.* stirred up

rue (roo) *n.* sorrow; regret

rummage (RUHM ihj) *v.* to search thoroughly or actively through

S

sanguine (SANG gwihn) *adj.* confident; cheerful

satiety (suh TY uh tee) *n.* state of being filled with enough or more than enough

sauntered (SAWN tuhrd) *v.* walked at an unhurried pace

scales (skaylz) *n.* thin, platelike pieces on an animal or plant

schism (SIHZ uhm) *n.* division of a group into factions

scope (skohp) *n.* range of perception or understanding

scurry (SKUR ee) *v.* to run hastily; to scamper

segmented (SEHG muhnt uhd) *v.* divided into joined parts

semblance (SEHM bluhns) *n.* appearance; image

sentinel (SEHN tuh nuhl) *n.* person or animal that guards

sepulcher (SEHP uhl kuhr) *n.* tomb

sequestered (sih KWEHS tuhrd) *v.* kept apart from others

shrill (shrihl) *adj.* high and sharp in tone; high-pitched

sinews (SIHN yooz) *n.* tendons

sinuous (SIHN yu uhs) *adj.* bending; winding

skeptical (SKEHP tuh kuhl) *adj.* doubting; not easily persuaded

smudge (smuhj) *n.* a smear or stain of dirt

sojourn (SOH jurn) *n.* short stay someplace; visit

solace (SOL ihs) *n.* comfort; relief

solicitous (suh LIHS uh tuhs) *adj.* showing care or concern

sordid (SAWR dihd) *adj.* dirty

sound (sownd) *adj.* healthy; undamaged

sovereign (SOV ruhn) *adj.* supreme in power, rank, or authority

specious (SPEE shuhs) *adj.* deceptively attractive or valid; false

spectral (SPEHK truhl) *adj.* ghostly

spellbound (SPEHL BOWND) *adj.* bound by or as if by a spell

spirit (SPIHR iht) *n.* immaterial part of man

sprawling (SPRAWL ihng) *adj.* spread out

stagnant (STAG nuhnt) *adj.* motionless; foul

stature (STACH uhr) *n.* height; level of achievement

stead (stehd) *n.* position being filled by a replacement

steadfastly (STEHD fast lee) *adv.* fixed in direction; steadily directed

stealthy (STEHL thee) *adj.* secretive; furtive; sly

stoic (STOH ihk) *n.* person indifferent to joy, grief, pleasure, or pain

struggle (STRUHG uhl) *v.* work hard against difficulties

subdued (suhb DOOD) *adj.* quiet; inhibited; repressed; controlled

substantial (suhb STAN shuhl) *adj.* having substance, large in size or strength

succor (SUHK uhr) *v.* help; aid; relief

suffused (suh FYOOZD) *v.* spread throughout; filled

sulk (suhlk) *v.* to show resentment by refusing to interact with others

sullen (SUHL uhn) *adj.* gloomy; dismal

sundry (SUHN dree) *adj.* various; miscellaneous

supine (soo PAHYN) *adj.* lying on the back

supplication (suhp luh KAY shuhn) *n.* act of praying or pleading

surmise (suhr MYZ) *n.* imaginings; speculation; guess

sustenance (SUHS tuh nuhns) *n.* food or money to support life

symbolize (SIHM buh lyz) *v.* represent a thing or concept

symmetry (SIHM uh tree) *n.* balanced form; the beauty resulting from such balance

syntax (SIHN taks) *n.* the study of sentence structure

T

tarry (TAR ee) *v.* to delay or linger

technology (tehk NOL uh jee) *n.* science of the mechanical and industrial arts

teeming (TEE mihng) *v.* filled to overflowing

temperate (TEHM puhr iht) *adj.* mild

tempestuous (tehm PEHS chu uhs) *adj.* turbulent; stormy

tenacity (tih NAS uh tee) *n.* persistence; stubbornness

terrestrial (tuh REHS tree uhl) *adj.* relating to the earth or to this world

topographical (top uh GRAF uh kuhl) *adj.* representing the surface features of a region

tortuous (TAWR chu uhs) *adj.* full of twists, turns, or bends; twisting, winding, or crooked

traditional (truh DIHSH uh nuhl) *adj.* customary

transformation (trans fuhr MAY shuhn) *n.* act or process of changing

transgress (tranz GREHS) *v.* violate a law or command

transgressed (tranz GREHST) *v.* overstepped or broke (a law or commandment)

tranquil (TRANG kwuhl) *adj.* calm; serene; peaceful

transcendent (tran SEHN duhnt) *adj.* exceeding beyond all limits

transient (TRAN shuhnt) *adj.* temporary; passing

treachery (TREHCH uhr ee) *n.* betrayal of trust, faith, or allegiance

treasons (TREE zuhnz) *n.* betrayals of one's country or oath of loyalty

trends (trehndz) *n.* general directions; fashions or styles

trepidation (TREHP uh DAY shuhn) *n.* trembling

tribe (tryb) *n.* group of people united by race and customs

trifles (TRY fuhlz) *n.* things of little value or importance

truculent (TRUHK yuh luhnt) *adj.* cruel; fierce

tumid (TOO mihd) *adj.* swollen

tumult (TOO muhlt) *n.* noisy commotion, often caused by a crowd

turbid (TUR bihd) *adj.* muddy or cloudy; stirred up and confused

turmoil (TUR moyl) *n.* a state of great commotion, confusion, or disturbance

tyrants (TY ruhnts) *n.* cruel, oppressive rulers

U

uncanny (uhn KAN ee) *adj.* mysterious; hard to explain

undeterminable (uhn dih TUR muh nuh buhl) *adj.* not able to be decided or settled

ungenial (uhn JEEN yuhl) *adj.* disagreeable; characterized by bad weather

upbraidings (uhp BRAY dihngz) *n.* stern words of disapproval; scoldings

urban (UR buhn) *adj.* that is or has the essential characteristics of a city

utters (UHT uhrz) *v.* sends forth with the voice

V

vales (vaylz) *n.* valleys; hollows; depressed stretches of ground

valor (VAL uhr) *n.* courageous behavior; bravery

values (VAL yooz) *n.* principles

venerable (VEHN uhr uh buhl) *adj.* commanding respect because of age, character, or social rank

verge (vurj) *n.* edge; rim

vindication (vihn duh KAY shuhn) *n.* act of providing justification or support for

vintage (VIHN tihj) *n.* wine of fine quality

vivacious (vy VAY shuhs) *adj.* lively, spirited

vulnerable (VUHL nuhr uh buhl) *adj.* exposed to attack or harm

W

wallowed (WOL ohd) *v.* rolled around in mud, water, etc.

wan (won) *adj.* sickly pale; faint or weak

waning (WAY nihng) *v.* gradually becoming dimmer or weaker

welfare (WEHL FAIR) *n.* condition of being well; health

winsome (WIHN suhm) *adj.* having a charming appearance or way

wither (WIHTH uhr) *v.* fade or waste away

wreath (reeth) *n.* circle of flowers

writhes (rythz) *v.* twists and turns the body, as in agony

writhing (RYTH ihng) *n.* twisting or turning motion

Spanish Glossary

El vocabulario de Pregunta Essential aparece en **azul**. El vocabulario academico de alta utilidad está **<u>subrayado</u>**.

A

abasement / humillación *s.* condición de ser degradado o rebajado

abated / disminuido *v.* reducido

abide / permanecer *v.* quedarse; mantenerse

absolution / absolución *s.* acto de librar a alguien de un pecado o acusación criminal

acceded / accedió *v.* cedió; acordó

accounts / cuentas *s.* registros de dinero recibido y pagado; registros financieros

adjure / implorar *v.* solicitar solemnemente; conjurar seriamente

admonish / amonestar *v.* advertir

adroitly / diestramente *adv.* con destreza física o mental

adulterations / adulteraciones *s.* impurezas; ingredientes agregados que son inadecuados o inferiores

adversary / adversario *s.* opositor; enemigo

<u>advocate</u> / <u>abogar</u> *v.* hablar o escribir en apoyo de

affably / afablemente *adv.* de manera amistosa

affinities / afinidades *s.* conexiones familiares; simpatías

affluence / opulencia *s.* riqueza abundante

ague / escalofrío *s.* enfriamiento o estremecimiento

alderman / concejal *s.* funcionario principal en un pueblo o condado

alters / altera *v.* cambia

amiable / amigable *adj.* amistoso; afable

amorous / amoroso *adj.* lleno de amor o deseo

anarchy / anarquía *s.* ausencia de gobierno; desorden

anatomize / anatomizar *v.* disecar a fin de examinar su estructura

ancestral / ancestral *adj.* heredado

anemic / anémico *adj.* que le falta fuerza, vigor, vitalidad o colorido; desganado; débil

<u>annotate</u> / <u>anotar</u> *v.* hacer anotaciones o señalar con una explicación

antic / bufonesco *adj.* raro y cómico; ridículo

antidote / antídoto *s.* algo que sirve para combatir una condición no deseada; remedio

aperture / abertura *s.* orificio

apothecary / boticario *s.* farmacéutico; titular de droguería

appalled / pasmó *v.* que se llenó de consternación o desaliento

appendage / apéndice *s.* algo que se agrega

apprehension / aprensión *s.* sentimiento ansioso de presentimiento; pavor

apprehensions / aprensiones *s.* temores; preocupaciones

approbation / aprobación *s.* aceptación o ratificación oficial

arboreal / arbóreo *adj.* de, cerca o entre los árboles

<u>articulate</u> / <u>articular</u> *v.* expresar claramente

artifice / artificio *s.* habilidad; el producto de una destreza, especialmente un engaño astuto

artificiality / artificialidad *s.* que no es natural; irreal

aspire / aspirar *v.* tener grandes ambiciones; desear o buscar

assault / asaltar *v.* atacar violentamente

assessing / avaluando *v.* estimando el valor (de una propiedad) para fines de impuestos

assiduous / asiduo *adj.* constante en cuanto a aplicación o atención

assignations / asignaciones *s.* citas que deben cumplirse

asunder / en partes *adj.* roto en partes o pedazos

atrophy / atrofiar *v.* deteriorar

augment / aumentar *v.* hacer más grande; expandir

authentic / auténtico *adj.* genuino; real

avarice / avaricia *s.* codicia

averred / afirmó *v.* verificó

awe / asombro *s.* sensación mixta de reverencia, temor y asombro

B

balm / bálsamo *s.* ungüento u otra cosa que sana o alivia

bar / barra *s.* una de las líneas verticales que divide la música escrita en secciones iguales llamadas compases

bequeath / heredar *v.* pasar como una herencia

beliefs / creencias *s.* lo que uno sostiene que es cierto

bilious / colérico *adj.* malgeniado; irritable; malhumorado

blight / plaga *s.* condición de estar marchito

blithe / alegre *adj.* Animado

boundary / límite *s.* línea divisoria; frontera

breach / ruptura *s.* rompimiento o estar roto; dejar de cumplir con los términos de un acuerdo

brink / borde *s.* orilla; margen

burden / carga *s.* algo que pone un peso sobre uno; una pesada obligación o responsabilidad

C

cadence / cadencia *s.* movimiento medido

capitalism / capitalismo *s.* sistema económico en el cual personas particulares o grupos de personas son propietarias de tierras, fábricas y otros medios de producción.

caprices / caprichos *s.* extravagancias

<u>categorize</u> / <u>categorizar</u> *v.* colocar en grupos relacionados

censure / censurar *v.* desaprobar con firmeza; condenar

certify / certificar *v.* declarar que una cosa es cierta o exacta; verificar; atestar

<u>characterize</u> / <u>caracterizar</u> *v.* describir aspectos, cualidades o rasgos

chronicle / crónica *s.* registro histórico de eventos en orden cronológico

chrysalis / crisálida *s.* la tercera fase en el desarrollo de una polilla o mariposa

circumscribed / circunscrito *v.* delimitado; que tiene un lindero definido

<u>cite</u> / <u>citar</u> *v.* referirse a un texto

city / ciudad *s.* pueblo grande densamente poblado

clamorous / clamoroso *adj.* bullicioso y confuso; ruidoso

<u>clarify</u> / <u>aclarar</u> *v.* poner en claro

clasped / agarrado *v.* sujetado o estrechado firmemente

classics / clásicos *s.* libros o pinturas de las más alta calidad

<u>classify</u> / <u>clasificar</u> *v.* asignar a una categoría climacteric / crisis *s.* cualquier período crítico

colonize / colonizar *v.* establecer un asentamiento

combatants / combatientes *s.* luchadores

combustible / combustible *adj.* capaz de ser encendido y quemado; inflamable

commentary / comentario *s.* serie de observaciones

commission / comisión *s.* autorización; acto de dar autoridad a un individuo

commodity / mercancía *s.* producto que es comprado o vendido

compassionate / compasivo *adj.* simpatizante con

compile / compilar *v.* reunir

complaisant / complaciente *adj.* afable; dispuesto a agradar

comprised / comprendió *v.* consistió de; incluyó

concord / concordia *s.* relaciones amistosas; armonía

condescension / condescendencia *s.* el acto o instancia de condescender

conflagration / conflagración *s.* gran incendio

conflict / conflicto *s.* lucha o contienda

conjecture / conjeturar *v.* adivinar

connote / connotar *v.* sugerir o comunicar

conquest / conquista *s.* acto de conquistar

consciousness / conciencia *s.* estar consciente de

constituency / distrito electoral *s.* la gente que compone un grupo de votantes

construct / construir *v.* colocar partes sistemáticamente para armar algo

contemporary / contemporáneo *adj.* que pertenece al mismo período de tiempo

contemptuous / desdeñoso *adj.* despreciativo

contend / contender *v.* aseverar o disputar

contention / contienda *s.* disputa, argumento

contentious / contencioso *adj.* disputador

contextualize / contextualizar *v.* colocar información dentro de un plano más amplio

contrite / contrito *adj.* dispuesto a arrepentirse o a expiar

controversy / controversia *s.* acto de disputar un tema sobre el cual existen varios puntos de vista

contusions / contusiones *s.* herida en la que la piel no se rompe; magulladura

conventional / convencional *adj.* que actúa o se comporta de manera usualmente aceptada o aprobada

conviction / convicción *s.* creencia; fe

coordinate / coordinar *v.* relacionar o vincular

countenance / semblante *s.* cara

country / país *s.* territorio; nación

courtly / cortésmente *adj.* elegantemente digno; decoroso

covetousness / codicia *s.* avaricia

cower / agachar *v.* encogerse, como de miedo o frío

coyness / modestia *s.* timidez; afectación, a menudo como parte de un coqueteo

credulity / credulidad *s.* tendencia a creer con demasiada facilidad

credulous / crédulo *adj.* que tiende a creer con demasiada facilidad

critique / criticar *v.* examinar críticamente, revisar

cultivated / cultivó *v.* sembró

cynically / cínicamente *adv.* semejante o característico de un cínico; desconfiado o que menosprecia los motivos de otro

D

dappled / manchado *adj.* pinto o moteado, usualmente en montones

dauntless / intrépido *adj.* valiente; que nada le intimida

debate / debatir *v.* discutir razonamientos opuestos

deduce / deducir *v.* inferir algo de un principio general

deference / deferencia *s.* consideración o respeto hacia otros

deficient / deficiente *adj.* que carece de una cualidad esencial

define / definir *v.* mencionar las cualidades que describen algo

deftly / diestramente *adv.* con facilidad y rapidez

deism / deísmo *s.* creencia en Dios basada en la evidencia de la razón y la naturaleza

deliberation / deliberación *s.* consideración y discusión cuidadosa antes de tomar una decisión

delirious / delirante *adj.* que tiene alucinaciones; desvariado

demonstrate / demostrar *v.* mostrar usando el razonamiento o ejemplos

denote / denotar *v.* referirse claramente a algo

depict / representar *v.* describir una imagen utilizando palabras

depredation / depredación *s.* un ataque predatorio; pillaje

derided / mofó *v.* burló; ridiculizó

deign / dignarse *v.* condescender; rebajarse a

desolate / desolado *adj.* desierto; solitario

despondent / desalentado *adj.* desanimado; abatido

despotic / despótico *adj.* tiránico

destitute / desprovisto *adj.* Carente

destruction / destrucción *s.* el acto de destruir

devise / idear *v.* inventar o crear; planear

diffusive / difusivo *adj.* tendiente a esparcirse

disabused / desengañó *v.* liberó de ideas falsas

discern / discernir *v.* reconocer como separado o diferente

discreet / discreto *adj.* sabio; prudente

discretion / discreción *s.* cuidado en lo que uno hace y dice; buen criterio; prudencia

dislocation / dislocación *s.* condición de estar fuera de lugar

dispensation / designio divino *s.* sistema religioso o creencias

disposable / disponible *adj.* libre para usar; a disposición

dissatisfaction / descontento *s.* estado de disgusto

dissect / disecar *v.* analizar e interpretar minuciosamente

distemper / distémper *s.* enfermedad infecciosa, como la plaga

distill / destilar *v.* obtener la parte esencial

divine / divino *adj.* celestial; sagrado

dominion / dominio *s.* soberanía o poder sobre un territorio; autoridad o control

dominions / dominios *s.* territorios o tierras gobernadas

dowry / dote *s.* propiedad que aporta la familia de la mujer a su marido cuando se casan

dregs / vestigios *s.* una pequeña cantidad; residuo

E

eclipse / eclipsar *v.* desvanecer o extinguir el poder o la gloria

economic / económico *adj.* relacionado al manejo de los ingresos

edit / editar *v.* alterar, adaptar o refinar

effigy / efigie *s.* retrato o estatua de una persona

electors / electores *s.* aquellos que votan

eloquent / elocuente *adj.* bellamente expresivo

eludes / elude *v.* evita o escapa

embarked / enfrascó *v.* que participó en algo, como en una conversación

embellishments / adornos *s.* toques decorativos; ornamentos

eminent / eminente *adj.* notable; de algo rango; distinguido

empire / imperio *s.* grupo de naciones o estados bajo un solo soberano o gobierno

encomiums / encomios *s.* expresiones formales de gran elogio

endeavored / esforzó *s.* hizo un intento serio; trató

enhance / realzar *v.* mejorar o elevar

enigma / enigma *s.* acertijo; declaración, persona o situación perpleja

entreated / suplicó *v.* imploró; rogó

enumerate / enumerar *v.* especificar en una lista

epic / epopeya *s.* poema largo sobre las aventuras de uno o más grandes héroes

equate / igualar *v.* considerar que una cosa es igual que otra

equivocate / emplear lenguaje ambiguo *v.* usar términos que tienen dos o más significados para despistar intencionalmente o engañar

escapade / escapada *s.* aventura, especialmente una que rompe con las reglas normales de conducta

esteemed / estimado *adj.* altamente respetado; tener en alta estima

etymology / etimología *s.* el estudio de los orígenes de las palabras

evaluate / evaluar *v.* establecer el significado, valor o condición de algo

evanescence / desvanecimiento *s.* desaparición o tendencia a desaparecer

evoke / evocar *v.* provocar una reacción

exemplary / ejemplar *adj.* dícese de algo que podría servir de modelo

exile / exiliar *v.* obligar a una persona a abandonar su hogar o país

exotic / exótico *adj.* de un país extranjero

expedient / recurso *s.* dispositivo usado en una emergencia

expiated / expió *v.* reparó; dio cumplida satisfacción, especialmente mediante el sufrimiento

extract / extraer *v.* sonsacar información

extravagant / extravagante *adj.* ir más allá de los límites razonables; excesivo

F

fantastic / fantástico *adj.* muy extravagante; increíblemente bueno

fastidious / quisquilloso *adj.* exigente; difícil de satisfacer

fate / sino *s.* destino

fathom / comprender *v.* entender cabalmente

fervent / ferviente *adj.* tener gran calidez de sentimientos

fidelity / fidelidad *s.* lealtad

filial / filial *adj.* lo que se espera de un hijo o hija

form / moldear *v.* dar forma a

format / formatear *v.* disponer de acuerdo a un plan

formulate / formular *v.* expresar completa y claramente; idear

fortitude / fortaleza *s.* valor; fuerza para resistir

fracture / fractura *s.* el acto de quebrar; condición de estar roto

frugally / frugalmente *adv.* forma de ser cuidadoso con el dinero

furrow / surco *s.* carril angosto hecho en la tierra con un arado

G

gall / amargura *s.* sentimiento amargo; rencor profundo

galled / irritado *adj.* lastimado o excoriado por rozadura

galleons / galeones *s.* grandes veleros usados para la guerra o el comercio

garnished / adornó *v.* decoró; guarneció

garrulous / gárrulo *adj.* parlanchín

gaunt / demacrado *adj.* flaco y huesudo, como por desnutrición o edad avanzada

geography / geografía *s.* aspectos de la superficie de un lugar o región

ghastly / horriblemente *adv.* terriblemente; muy malo

gleaned / espigó *v.* juntó poco a poco, como cuando se recolecta granos que quedan después de una cosecha

gout / gota *s.* una masa o salpicadura de un líquido como la sangre

grandeur / grandeza *s.* esplendor; magnificencia

gravity / gravedad *s.* peso; seriedad

grievances / agravios *s.* circunstancias que hacen que la gente se queje

grieved / afligió *v.* sintió mucho pesar; lamentó

guile / maña *s.* embuste habilidoso

H

haggard / demacrado *adj.* que aparenta estar consumido y agotado; ojeroso

harbingers / precursores *s.* heraldos

heedless / incauto *adj.* descuidado; desatento

highlight / realzar *v.* destacar

hoary / canoso *adj.* blanco o encanecido con la edad

homespun / doméstico *adj.* hilado o hecho en casa

hypothesize / formular una hipótesis *v.* sugerir una explicación posible

I

ideal / ideal *s.* modelo de perfección

idealism / idealismo *s.* acto de descuidar asuntos prácticos por seguir los ideales

ignoble / innoble *adj.* que no es noble; plebeyo

ignominy / ignominia *s.* humillación; deshonra

illumine / iluminar *v.* alumbrar

illusion / ilusión *s.* apariencia o sentimiento que engaña porque no es real

immigrant / inmigrante *s.* persona que llega a vivir a un país extranjero

immortal / inmortal *adj.* que vive o perdura para siempre; que no muere

impediments / impedimentos *s.* obstáculos

imperceptibly / imperceptiblemente *adv.* sin que se note

imperial / imperial *adj.* de un imperio; que tiene autoridad suprema

imperialism / imperialismo *s.* política de crear un imperio por medio de la conquista y la colonización

impertinence / impertinencia *s.* descortesía; insolencia

imperturbable / imperturbable *adj.* calmado; que no se enfada fácilmente

implored / imploró *v.* rogó seriamente

importuning / importunando *v.* insistiendo con

impressionistic / impresionista *adj.* que comunica un dibujo mediante sugerencias de detalles con un trazo rápido

impudence / impudencia *s.* falta de vergüenza; descortesía

impulse / impulso *s.* fuerza que empuja hacia adelante

inane / vacío *adj.* que le falta sentido, significado o ideas; necio

incessant / incesante *adj.* que continúa sin interrupción; perenne

incitement / incitación *s.* acto de apremiar; estímulo

inconstancy / inconstancia *s.* inestabilidad; veleidad

inconstantly / inconstantemente *adv.* inestablemente; veleidosamente

incredulously / incrédulamente *adv.* de forma que expresa duda o escepticismo

independence / independencia *s.* estar libre del control de los demás

indignant / indignado *adj.* enfurecido; lleno de cólera justa

indissoluble / indisoluble *adj.* que no puede ser disuelto o deshecho

inducted / admitió *v.* introdujo formalmente a una organización

industry / industria *s.* cualquier rama empresarial, comercial o manufacturera

inevitable / inevitable *adj.* ineludible; que sucederá con seguridad

infamy / infamia *s.* muy mala reputación; desgracia; deshonra

infirmity / enfermedad *s.* defecto físico o mental; dolencia

ingenuous / ingenuo *adj.* inocente; sencillo

ingratiating / congraciador *adj.* encantador; ameno; complaciente

inheritance / herencia *s.* acto de heredar

inklings / indicios *s.* sugerencias indirectas; ideas vagas

innumerable / innumerable *adj.* mucha cantidad para contar

insatiableness / insaciabilidad *s.* la cualidad de ser imposible de satisfacer

instantaneous / instantáneo *adj.* que se hace o sucede en un instante

integrate / integrar *v.* reunir partes distintas

intemperance / intemperancia *s.* falta de moderación

interpret / interpretar *v.* explicar el significado

interpretation / interpretación *s.* el acto de explicar

interred / sepultó *v.* enterró

intrigues / intrigas *s.* tramas o maquinaciones

intrinsically / intrínsecamente *adv.* en su meollo; inherentemente; de manera innata

invasion / invasión *s.* entrar a la fuerza

invincible / invencible *adj.* inconquistable

irrevocable / irrevocable *adj.* incapaz de ser deshecho o cancelado

isolation / aislamiento *s.* acto de estar completamente separado de los demás

J

judicious / juicioso *adj.* que muestra buen criterio

K

keenly / profundamente *adv.* agudamente; intensamente

ken / vista *s.* alcance de la vista o comprensión

kindred / parentela *s.* el grupo de parientes de una persona

kingdoms / reinos *s.* países bajo el mandato de un rey o una reina

L

label / calificar *v.* describir o designar

laity / laicos *s.* aquéllos que no pertenecen al sacerdocio

lament / lamentar *v.* expresar dolor; afligirse

lamentable / lamentable *adj.* que causa dolor; perturbador

lamentations / lamentaciones *s.* expresiones de dolor o aflicción

languish / languidecer *v.* debilitar; marchitar; suspirar por

languished / languideció *v.* se debilitó; se entorpeció

languor / languidez *s.* falta de energía o vitalidad; lentitud

largesse / generosidad *s.* nobleza de espíritu

larking / retozar *v.* divertirse despreocupada y caprichosamente

legacy / legado *s.* dinero u otras pertenencias heredadas a una persona por voluntad de alguien que haya muerto

lintel / dintel *s.* barra horizontal sobre una puerta

loathsome / repulsivo *adj.* repugnante

loyalties / lealtades *s.* sentimientos o comportamientos leales; fidelidad

loyalty / lealtad *s.* sentimiento o comportamiento leal; fidelidad

ludicrous / risible *adj.* absurdo; ridículo

lustrous / lustroso *adj.* que tiene lustre; brillante; luminoso

M

macadam / macadán *s.* piedra quebrada que se usa para hacer una calle con el mismo nombre

madrigals / madrigales *s.* poemas cortos de amor con música

magistrate / magistrado *s.* un funcionario local que hace cumplir la ley o funge como juez

malevolence / malevolencia *s.* mala voluntad; despecho

malicious / malicioso *adj.* deliberadamente dañino; destructivo

massive / masivo *adj.* grande y sólido; voluminoso

measure / medida *s.* una sección de música escrita entre dos líneas verticales llamadas barras; ley, resolución o algo parecido que se propone o ratifica para mejorar una situación

melodious / melodioso *adj.* de sonido placentero; armonioso

melody / melodía *s.* secuencia de tonos solos que juntos crean una tonada o canción

migrated / emigró *v.* que se mudó de una región o país a otro

mobility / movilidad *s.* habilidad de movimiento

mockeries / burlas *s.* esfuerzos fútiles o decepcionantes; ridículo

modernization / modernización *s.* llevar a la actualidad las costumbres o normas

monarch / monarca *s.* persona que gobierna un país

monotonous / monótono *adj.* sin variación

morose / malhumorado *adj.* triste; adusto

mortal / mortal *adj.* dícese de todo lo que eventualmente morirá

multitudinous / numeroso *adj.* que existe en grandes cantidades

munificence / munificencia *s.* esplendidez

N

nature / naturaleza *s.* todas las cosas, excepto aquellas creadas por el hombre

nimble / ágil *adj.* capaz de moverse rápidamente y con ligereza

nocturnal / nocturno *adj.* que ocurre de noche

notorious / notorio *adj.* ampliamente conocido pero desfavorablemente; que tiene una mala reputación

nuisance / fastidio *s.* acto, cosa o condición que causa molestia

O

obdurate / inexorable *adj.* obstinado

obedience / obediencia *s.* el acto de seguir órdenes o instrucciones

obliquely / oblicuamente *adv.* sesgadamente; indirectamente

obscure / oscuro *adj.* que no se ve fácilmente; que por lo general no se conoce

obscure / oscurecer *v.* que hace difícil ver

obstinate / obstinado *adj.* testarudo; terco

obstinately / obstinadamente *adv.* de forma determinante; testarudamente

officious / oficioso *adj.* entremetido

ordeal / prueba severa *s.* experiencia difícil o penosa que lo pone a uno a prueba

order / orden *s.* manera en que una cosa sigue después de otra

orthodox / ortodoxo *adj.* que se conforma a las creencias establecidas

outcast / desterrado *s.* persona exiliada de su hogar y amistades

outline / esbozar *v.* desarrollar un plan general

P

pallor / palor *s.* falta no natural de color; palor

palpable / palpable *adj.* capaz de ser tocado o sentido

palpitation / palpitación *s.* latido del corazón inusual o anormalmente rápido o violento

paltry / miserable *adj.* prácticamente inútil; insignificante

paradox / paradoja *s.* afirmación que puede ser verdadera pero pareciera expresar dos cosas opuestas

paraphrase / parafrasear *v.* poner en otras palabras algo dicho o escrito

pastoral / pastoral *s.* simple o naturalmente bello, como el campo

pathos / patetismo *s.* cualidad que evoca tristeza o compasión

patronize / frecuentar *v.* ser cliente asiduo de un determinado negocio o almacén

penury / penuria *s.* pobreza

perceive / percibir *v.* reconocer a través de los sentidos

peril / peligro *s.* exposición a situación peligrosa o arriesgada

pernicious / pernicioso *adj.* que causa un gran daño, destrucción o ruina; fatal; mortal

pernicious / pernicioso *adj.* que causa un gran daño, destrucción o ruina; mortal

phantasm / fantasma *s.* forma o figura sobrenatural; espectro; producto de la imaginación

philosophy / filosofía *s.* sistema que sirve de guía para la vida

piety / piedad *s.* devoción a una religión

platitude / perogrullada *s.* declaración que carece de autoridad

plebeian / plebeyo *adj.* común; no aristocrático

power / poder *s.* fuerza o vigor

predominance / predominio *s.* superioridad

predominant / predominante *adj.* en primer lugar; poderoso

prefiguring / prefigurando *v.* que se parece, por lo que se sugiere de antemano

prenatal / prenatal *adj.* que existe o tiene lugar antes del nacimiento

presumed / presumió *v.* que dio por sentado; supuso

presumption / presunción *s.* atrevimiento

prevail / prevalecer *v.* tener éxito; obtener el dominio; terminar ganando

prevarication / engaño *s.* evasión de la verdad

prime / plenitud *s.* la mejor etapa de una cosa o proceso

pristine / prístino *adj.* original; intacto

probe / indagar *v.* investigar y explorar minuciosamente

prodding / aguijoneando *v.* picando, punzando, buscando

prodigal / pródigo *adj.* despilfarrador

prodigious / prodigioso *adj.* enorme; inmenso

profanation / profanación *s.* acción que muestra irreverencia hacia algo sagrado

proferring / ofrecimiento *s.* ofrenda

profuse / profuso *adj.* abundante; que se derrama

progress / progreso *s.* crecimiento; mejora

promontories / promontorios *s.* colinas de tierras altas que se introducen en una masa de agua

prophet / profeta *s.* persona que dice lo que ocurrirá

propitiate / propiciar *v.* ganarse la buena voluntad de; aplacar

propose / proponer *v.* presentar un plan o intención

propriety / propiedad *s.* cualidad o condición de ser correcto

prosper / prosperar *v.* medrar

prowess / proeza *s.* heroísmo; distinción

prudence / prudencia *s.* cuidadoso manejo de recursos; economía

pulp / pulpa *s.* la parte suave, jugosa y comestible de una fruta

purge / purgar *v.* purificar; limpiar

R

rancor / rencor *s.* mala voluntad; odio amargo y persistente

ransacked / saqueó *v.* buscó por todo para hallar bienes para robar; pilló

rapture / éxtasis *s.* embeleso; gran placer

rapturous / extasiado *adj.* lleno de embeleso y amor; extático

rational / racional *adj.* sensato; razonable

realms / reinos *s.* regiones bajo el gobierno de un rey o reina

rebellious / rebelde *adj.* que desafía a la autoridad

rebuild / reconstruir *v.* construir o crear de nuevo

rebuke / increpar *v.* criticar fuertemente

recall / recordar *v.* rememorar

reckoning / cálculo *s.* contabilidad

recoil / recular *v.* retroceder por temor, sorpresa o disgusto

recommend / recomendar *v.* sugerir favorablemente

recompense / recompensar *v.* pagar en compensación por algo

recount / narrar *v.* contar con detalles

reform / reformar *v.* mejorar

reformation / reforma *s.* cambio positivo; mejora

refractory / recalcitrante *adj.* difícil de manejar; terco

refute / refutar *v.* demostrar lo contrario

reiterate / reiterar *v.* decir o hacer de nuevo

relates / relata *v.* cuenta

remnant / remanente *s.* lo que queda; residuo

renaissance / renacimiento *s.* gran renacer del arte y de los conocimientos en Europa durante los siglos XIV, XV y XVI

reparation / reparación *s.* compensación por un mal

reprove / criticar *v.* desaprobar con firmeza; censurar

requiem / réquiem *s.* composición musical para honrar a los muertos

resolution / resolución *s.* propósito o determinación

resume / reasumir *v.* asumir de nuevo o continuar con algo después de una interrupción

reticent / discreto *adj.* callado; reservado

reverence / reverencia *s.* respeto profundo

reverently / reverentemente *adv.* con profundo respeto o admiración

revolution / revolución *s.* derrocamiento total de un gobierno o sistema político establecido

righteousness / rectitud *s.* la característica de actuar de forma justa y virtuosa

risible / risible *adj.* que causa risa

rites / ritos *s.* ceremonias; rituales

role / papel *s.* rol o función desempeñada por una persona o cosa

roused / suscitó *v.* agitó

rue / desilusión *s.* tristeza; arrepentimiento

rummage / registrar *v.* buscar detenidamente o activamente

S

sanguine / optimista *adj.* confiado; esperanzado

satiety / saciedad *s.* condición de estar lleno con suficiente o más que suficiente

sauntered / deambuló *v.* caminó a un paso pausado

scales / escamas *s.* parte delgada, escariosa o membranosa de una planta, como la bráctea de un amento o candelilla

schism / cisma *s.* separación de un grupo en facciones

scope / alcance *s.* rango de percepción o entendimiento

scurry / escabullir *v.* correr rápidamente; escurrirse

segmented / segmentó *v.* dividió en partes unidas

semblance / apariencia *s.* aspecto exterior; imagen

sentinel / centinela *s.* persona o animal que vigila

sepulcher / sepulcro *s.* tumba

sequestered / secuestró *v.* mantuvo alejado de los demás

shrill / agudo *adj.* tono alto y agudo; estridente

sinews / tendones *s.* fibras

sinuous / sinuoso *adj.* ondulado; tortuoso

skeptical / escéptico *adj.* dudoso; que no se persuade fácilmente

smudge / mancha *s.* un tiznajo o mancha de tierra

sojourn / estada *s.* corta estadía en algún lugar; visita

solace / solaz *s.* confortación; desahogo

solicitous / solícito *adj.* que muestra interés o preocupación

sordid / sórdido *adj.* sucio

sound / íntegro *adj.* sano; ileso

sovereign / soberano *adj.* supremo en poder, rango o autoridad

specious / especioso *adj.* engañosamente atractivo o válido; falso

spectral / espectral *adj.* fantasmal

spellbound / encantado *adj.* atado como por un hechizo

spirit / espíritu *s.* parte inmaterial del ser humano

sprawling / extendido *adj.* irregular y grande

stagnant / estancado *adj.* estático; fétido

stature / estatura *s.* altura; nivel de realización

stead / lugar *s.* posición ocupada por un reemplazo

steadfastly / resueltamente *adv.* con dirección fija; dirigido con firmeza

stealthy / furtivo *adj.* secreto; clandestino; disimulado

stoic / estoico *s.* persona indiferente a la alegría, pena, placer o dolor

struggle / luchar *v.* esforzarse para vencer vicisitudes

subdued / reprimido *adj.* quieto; inhibido, dominado; controlado

substantial / sustancial *adj.* que tiene sustancia; grande en tamaño o fuerza

succor / socorrer *v.* ayudar; asistir; aliviar

suffused / bañó *v.* se dispersó por todo; llenó

sulk / enfurruñar *v.* mostrar resentimiento, rehusándose a interactuar con otros

sullen / malhumorado *adj.* triste; sombrío

sundry / diversos *adj.* varios; misceláneos

supine / supino *adj.* que yace sobre su espalda

supplication / súplica *s.* acto de rezar o rogar

surmise / conjetura *s.* imaginación; especulación; suposición

sustenance / sustento *s.* alimento o dinero para subsistir

symbolize / simbolizar *v.* representar una cosa o un concepto

symmetry / simetría *s.* forma balanceada; la belleza que resulta de un balance tal

syntax / sintaxis *s.* el estudio de la estructura de las oraciones

T

tarry / aguardar *v.* demorarse o quedarse atrás

technology / tecnología *s.* ciencia de las artes industriales y mecánicas

teeming / rebosar *v.* llenar hasta que se desborda

temperate / temperado *adj.* leve

tempestuous / tempestuoso *adj.* turbulento; tormentoso

tenacity / tenacidad *s.* persistencia; terquedad

terrestrial / terrestre *adj.* relativo a la tierra o a este mundo

topographical / topográfico *adj.* que representa las características superficiales de una región

tortuous / tortuoso *adj.* lleno de curvas, vueltas o giros; que es sinuoso, curveado o torcido

traditional / tradicional *adj.* habitual

transformation / transformación *s.* acto o proceso de cambio

transgress / transgredir *v.* violar una ley u orden

transgressed / transgredió *v.* propasó o violó (una ley o mandamiento)

tranquil / tranquilo *adj.* calmado; sereno; apacible

transcendent / trascendente *adj.* que excede todos los límites

transient / pasajero *adj.* temporal; transitorio

treachery / engaño *s.* el acto de traicionar la confianza, fe o lealtad

treasons / traiciones *s.* deslealtades hacia su propio país o hacia un juramento de lealtad

trends / tendencias *s.* direcciones generales; modas o estilos

trepidation / trepidación *s.* estremecimiento

trifles / bagatelas *s.* cosas de poco valor o importancia

truculent / truculento *adj.* cruel; feroz

tumid / túmido *adj.* hinchado

tumult / tumulto *s.* conmoción ruidosa, a menudo causada por una muchedumbre

turbid / turbio *adj.* lodoso o lechoso; revuelto y confuso

turmoil / disturbio *s.* estado de gran conmoción, confusión o alboroto

tyrants / tiranos *s.* gobernantes crueles y opresivos

U

uncanny / extraño *adj.* misterioso; difícil de explicar

undeterminable / indeterminable *adj.* no determinable; incierto

ungenial / desfavorable *adj.* desagradable; caracterizado por el mal tiempo

upbraidings / reproches *s.* palabras fuertes de desaprobación; regaños

urban / urbano *adj.* que es o posee las características principales de una ciudad

utters / pronuncia *v.* transmite con la voz

V

vales / valles *s.* hondonadas; hundimientos; depresiones en la superficie terrestre

valor / valor *s.* comportamiento valeroso; coraje

values / valores *s.* valor real; precio correcto

venerable / venerable *adj.* que exige respeto debido a edad, carácter o posición social

verge / borde *s.* filo; margen

vindication / reivindicación *s.* acto de dar justificación o apoyo por

vintage / vendimia *s.* vino de alta calidad

vivacious / vivaz *adj.* vivaracho, fogoso

vulnerable / vulnerable *adj.* expuesto a ataque o perjuicio

W

wallowed / revolcó *v.* rodó por el fango, agua, etc.

wan / pálido *adj.* con palidez enfermiza; desfallecido o débil

waning / menguando *v.* haciendo gradualmente más oscuro o débil

welfare / **bienestar** *s.* condición de estar bien; salud

winsome / atractivo *adj.* que tiene una apariencia o comportamiento encantador

wither / marchitar *v.* languidecer o deteriorarse

wreath / corona *s.* círculo de flores

writhes / retuerce *v.* que tuerce y contorsiona el cuerpo, como en agonía

writhing / retorciendo *v.* haciendo movimientos de retorcimiento y contorsión

Life of the English Language

The life of every language depends on the people who use it. Whenever you use English by asking a question, talking on the phone, going to a movie, reading a magazine, or writing an e-mail, you keep it healthy and valuable.

Using a Dictionary

Use a **dictionary** to find the meaning, the pronunciation, and the part of speech of a word. Consult a dictionary also to trace the word's *etymology,* or its origin. Etymology explains how words change, how they are borrowed from other languages, and how new words are invented, or "coined."

Here is an entry from a dictionary. Notice what it tells about the word *anthology.*

> **anthology** (an thäl′ ə jè) *n., pl.* –gies [Gr. anthologia, a garland, collection of short poems < *anthologos,* gathering flowers < *anthos,* flower + *legein,* to gather] a collection of poems, stories, songs, excerpts, etc., chosen by the compiler.

Dictionaries provide the *denotation* of each word, or its objective meaning. The symbol < means "comes from" or "is derived from." In this case, the Greek words for "flower" and "gather" combined to form a Greek word that meant a garland, and then that word became an English word that means a collection of literary flowers—a collection of literature like the one you are reading now.

Using a Thesaurus

Use a **thesaurus** to increase your vocabulary. In a thesaurus, you will find synonyms, or words that have similar meanings, for most words. Follow these guidelines to use a thesaurus:

- Do not choose a word just because it sounds interesting or educated. Choose the word that expresses exactly the meaning you intend.
- To avoid errors, look up the word in a dictionary to check its precise meaning and to make sure you are using it properly.

Here is an entry from a thesaurus. Notice what it tells about the word *book.*

> **book** *noun* A printed and bound work: tome, volume. See WORDS.
>
> **book** *verb* **1.** To register in or as if in a book: catalog, enroll, inscribe, list, set down, write down. *See* REMEMBER. **2.** To cause to be set aside, as for one's use, in advance: bespeak, engage, reserve. *See* GET.

If the word can be used as different parts of speech, as book can, the thesaurus entry provides synonyms for the word as each part of speech. Many words also have connotations, or emotional associations that the word calls to mind. A thesaurus entry also gives specific synonyms for each connotation of the word.

Activity Look up the words *knight* and *chivalry* in a dictionary. **(a)** What are their etymologies?
(b) Explain what their etymologies reveal about the development of English. Then, check the word *chivalry* in a thesaurus.
(c) What are two synonyms for this word?
(d) In what way do the connotations of the synonyms differ?

The Origin and Development of English

Old Engish English began about the year 500 when Germanic tribes settled in Britain. The language of these peoples—the Angles, Saxons, and Jutes—combined with Danish and Norse when Vikings attacked Britain and added some Latin elements when Christian missionaries arrived. The result was Old English, which looked like this:

> *Hwaet! We Gar-Dena in gear-dagum,*
> *peod-cyninga, prym gefrunon,*
> *hu da aepelingas ellen fremedon!*

These words are the opening lines of the Old English epic poem *Beowulf,* probably composed in the eighth century. In modern English, they mean: "Listen! We know the ancient glory of the Spear-Danes, and the heroic deeds of those noble kings!"

Middle English The biggest change in English took place after the Norman Conquest of Britain in 1066. The Normans spoke a dialect of Old French, and Old English changed dramatically when the Normans became the new aristocracy. From about 1100 to 1500, the people of Britain spoke what we now call Middle English.

> *A Knyght ther was, and that a worthy man,*
> *That fro the tyme that he first bigan*
> *To riden out, he loved chivalrie,*
> *Trouthe and honour, fredom and curtesie.*

These lines from the opening section of Chaucer's *Canterbury Tales* (c. 1400) are much easier for us to understand than the lines from *Beowulf.* They mean: "There was a knight, a worthy man who, from the time he began to ride, loved chivalry, truth, honor, freedom, and courtesy."

Modern English During the Renaissance, with its emphasis on reviving classical culture, Greek and Latin languages exerted a strong influence on the English language. In addition, Shakespeare added about two thousand words to the language. Grammar, spelling, and pronunciation continued to change. Modern English was born.

But soft! What light through yonder window breaks?
It is the East, and Juliet is the sun!

These lines from Shakespeare's *Romeo and Juliet* (c. 1600) need no translation, although it is helpful to know that "soft" means "speak softly." Since Shakespeare's day, conventions of usage and grammar have continued to change. For example, the *th* at the ends of many verbs has become s. In Shakespeare's time, it was correct to say "Romeo *hath* fallen in love." In our time, it is right to say "he *has* fallen in love." However, the changes of the past five hundred years are not nearly as drastic as the changes from Old English to Middle English, or from Middle English to Modern English. We still speak Modern English.

Old Words, New Words

Modern English has a larger vocabulary than any other language in the world. The *Oxford English Dictionary* contains about a half million words, and it is estimated that another half million scientific and technical terms do not appear in the dictionary. Here are the main ways that new words enter the language:

- **War**—Conquerors introduce new terms and ideas—and new vocabulary, such as *anger,* from Old Norse.
- **Immigration**—When large groups of people move from one country to another, they bring their languages with them, such as *boycott,* from Ireland.
- **Travel and Trade**—Those who travel to foreign lands and those who do business in faraway places bring new words back with them, such as *shampoo,* from Hindi.
- **Science and Technology**—In our time, the amazing growth of science and technology adds multitudes of new words to English, such as *Internet.*

English is also filled with **borrowings,** words taken directly from other languages. Sometimes borrowed words keep basically the same meanings they have in their original languages: *pajamas* (Hindi), *sauna* (Finnish), *camouflage* (French), *plaza* (Spanish). Sometimes borrowed words take on new meanings. *Sleuth,* for example, an Old Norse word for trail, has come to mean the person who follows a *trail*—a detective.

Mythology contributed to our language too. Some of the days of the week are named after Norse gods—Wednesday was Woden's Day, Thursday was Thor's Day. Greek and Roman myths have given us many words, such as *jovial* (from Jove), *martial* (from Mars), *mercurial* (from Mercury), and *herculean* (from Hercules).

Americanisms are words, phrases, usages, or idioms that originated in American English or that are unique to the way Americans speak. They are expressions of our national character in all its variety: *easy as pie, prairie dog, bamboozle, panhandle, halftime, fringe benefit, bookmobile, jackhammer, southpaw, lickety split.*

Activity Look up the following words in a dictionary. Describe the ways in which you think these words entered American English.

sabotage *burrito* *moccasin* *mecca* *megabyte*

The Influence of English

English continues to have an effect on world cultures and literature. There are about three hundred million native English speakers, and about the same number who speak English as a second language. Although more people speak Mandarin Chinese, English is the dominant language of trade, tourism, international diplomacy, science, and technology.

Language is a vehicle of both communication and culture, and the cultural influence of English in the twenty-first century is unprecedented in the history of the world's languages. Beyond business and science, English spreads through sports, pop music, Hollywood movies, television, and journalism. A book that is translated into English reaches many more people than it would in its native language alone. Perhaps most significantly, English dominates the Internet. The next time you log on, notice how many Web sites from around the world also have an English version. The global use of English is the closest the world has ever come to speaking an international language.

Activity Choose one area of culture—such as sports, fashion, the arts, or technology—and identify three new words that English has recently added to the *world's* vocabulary.
(a) How do you think non-English speakers feel about the spread of English? **(b)** Do you think English helps to bring people together? Why or why not?

Tips for Improving Fluency

When you were younger, you learned to read. Then, you read to expand your experiences or for pure enjoyment. Now, you are expected to read to learn. As you progress in school, you are given more and more material to read. The tips on these pages will help you improve your reading fluency, or your ability to read easily, smoothly, and expressively. Use these tips as you read daily.

Keeping Your Concentration

One common problem that readers face is the loss of concentration. When you are reading an assignment, you might find yourself rereading the same sentence several times without really understanding it. The first step in changing this behavior is to notice that you do it. Becoming an active, aware reader will help you get the most from your assignments. Practice using these strategies:

- Cover what you have already read with a note card as you go along. Then, you will not be able to reread without noticing that you are doing it.
- Set a purpose for reading beyond just completing the assignment. Then, read actively by pausing to ask yourself questions about the material as you read. Check the accuracy of your answers as you continue to read.
- Use the Reading Strategy instruction and notes that appear with each selection in this textbook.
- Look at any art or illustrations that accompany the reading and use picture clues to help your comprehension.
- Stop reading after a specified period of time (for example, 5 minutes) and summarize what you have read. To help you with this strategy, use the Reading Check questions that appear with each selection in this textbook. Reread to find any answers you do not know.

Reading Phrases

Fluent readers read phrases rather than individual words. Reading this way will speed up your reading and improve your comprehension. Here are some useful ideas:

- Experts recommend rereading as a strategy to increase fluency. Choose a passage of text that is neither too hard nor too easy. Read the same passage aloud several times until you can read it smoothly. When you can read the passage fluently, pick another passage and keep practicing.
- Read aloud into a tape recorder. Then, listen to the recording, noting your accuracy, pacing, and expression. You can also read aloud and share feedback with a partner.
- Use the *Pearson Prentice Hall Literature Audio Program Hear It!* to hear the selections read aloud. Read along silently in your textbook, noticing how the reader uses his or her voice and emphasizes certain words and phrases.
- Set a target reading rate. Time yourself as you read and work to increase your speed without sacrificing the level of your comprehension.

Understanding Key Vocabulary

If you do not understand some of the words in an assignment, you may miss out on important concepts. Therefore, it is helpful to keep a dictionary nearby when you are reading. Follow these steps:

- Before you begin reading, scan the text for unfamiliar words or terms. Find out what those words mean before you begin reading.
- Use context—the surrounding words, phrases, and sentences—to help you determine the meanings of unfamiliar words.
- If you are unable to understand the meaning through context, refer to the dictionary.

Paying Attention to Punctuation

When you read, pay attention to punctuation. Commas, periods, exclamation points, semicolons, and colons tell you when to pause or stop. They also indicate relationships between groups of words. When you recognize these relationships you will read with greater understanding and expression. Look at the chart below.

Punctuation Mark	Meaning
comma	brief pause
period	pause at the end of a thought
exclamation point	pause that indicates emphasis
semicolon	pause between related but distinct thoughts
colon	pause before giving explanation or examples

Using the Reading Fluency Checklist

Use the checklist below each time you read a selection in this textbook. In your Language Arts journal or notebook, note which skills you need to work on and chart your progress each week.

Reading Fluency Checklist
❑ Preview the text to check for difficult or unfamiliar words.
❑ Practice reading aloud.
❑ Read according to punctuation.
❑ Break down long sentences into the subject and its meaning.
❑ Read groups of words for meaning rather than reading single words.
❑ Read with expression (change your tone of voice to add meaning to the word).

Reading is a skill that can be improved with practice. The key to improving your fluency is to read. The more you read, the better your reading will become.

READING AND VOCABULARY HANDBOOK

Approaches to Criticism

By writing **criticism**—writing that analyzes literature—readers share their responses to a written work. Criticism is also a way for a reader to deepen his or her own understanding and appreciation of the work, and to help others to deepen theirs.

The information in this handbook will guide you through the process of writing criticism. In addition, it will help you to refine your critical perceptions to ensure that you are ready to produce work at the college level.

Understanding Criticism

There are a few different types of criticism. Each can enhance understanding and deepen appreciation of literature in a distinctive way. All types share similar functions.

The Types of Criticism

Analysis Students are frequently asked to analyze, or break into parts and examine, a passage or a work. When you write an analysis, you must support your ideas with references to the text.

Archetypal Criticism Archetypal criticism evaluates works of literature by identifying and analyzing the archetypes contained within them. An archetype, sometimes called a "universal symbol," is a plot, character, symbol, image, setting, or idea that recurs in the literature of many different cultures. Archetypes and patterns of archetypes can be seen as representing common patterns of human life and experience.

Biographical Criticism Biographical criticism uses information about a writer's life to shed light on his or her work.

Historical Criticism Historical criticism traces connections between an author's work and the events, circumstances, or ideas that shaped the writer's historical era.

Political Criticism Political criticism involves viewing an author's work with a focus on political assumptions and content—whether explicit or implicit—and, possibly, assessing the political impact of the work. Similar to historical criticism, political criticism draws connections between an author's work and the political issues and assumptions of the times.

Philosophical Criticism In philosophical criticism, the elements of a literary work such as plot, characters, conflict, and motivations are examined through the lens of the author's philosophical arguments and stances. The critic taking a philosophical approach will analyze philosophical arguments presented in a literary work and determine how those arguments have molded the work.

The Functions of Criticism

Critical writing serves a variety of important functions:

Making Connections All criticism makes connections between two or more things. For instance, an analysis of a poem may show similarities among different images.

Making Distinctions Criticism must make distinctions as well as connections. In an analysis of a poem, a critic may distinguish between two possible purposes for poetry: first, to create an enduring image and, second, to present a deeper meaning.

Achieving Insight By making connections and distinctions, criticism achieves insight. An analysis of a poem may reach the insight that the poem stands on its own as a work of beauty apart from any deeper meaning.

Making a Judgment Assessing the value of a work is an important function of criticism. A critic may assess a work by comparing it with other works and by using a standard such as enjoyment, insight, or beauty.

"Placing" the Work Critics guide readers not by telling them *what* to think but by giving them *terms in which to think.* Critical writing may help readers apply varied perspectives to illuminate different aspects of a work.

Writing Criticism

Like all solid writing, a work of criticism presents a thesis (a central idea) and supports it with arguments and evidence. Follow the strategies below to develop a critical thesis and gather support for it.

Formulate a Working Thesis

Once you have chosen a work or works on which to write, formulate a working thesis. First, ask yourself questions like these:

- What strikes you most about the work or the writer that your paper will address? What puzzles you most?
- In what ways is the work unlike others you have read?
- What makes the techniques used by the writer so well-suited to (or so poorly chosen for) conveying the theme of the work?

Jot down notes answering your questions. Then, reread passages that illustrate your answers, jotting down notes about what each passage contributes to the work. Review your notes, and write a sentence that draws a conclusion about the work.

If your thesis concerns . . .	look for support in the form of . . .
Character	• dialogue • character's actions • writer's descriptions of the character • other characters' reactions to the character
Theme	• fate of characters • patterns and contrasts of imagery, character, or events • mood • writer's attitude toward the action
Style	• memorable descriptions, observations • passages that "sound like" the writer • examples of rhetorical devices, such as exaggeration and irony
Historical Context	• references to historical events and personalities • evidence of social or political pressures on characters • socially significant contrasts between characters (for example, between the rich and the poor)
Literary Influences	• writer's chosen form or genre • passages that "sound like" another writer • events or situations that resemble those in other works • evidence of an outlook similar to that of another writer

Gather Support

Taking Notes From the Work

Once you have a working thesis, take notes on passages in the work that confirm it. To aid your search for support, consider the type of support suited to your thesis, as in the chart.

Conducting Additional Research If you are writing biographical or historical criticism, you will need to consult sources on the writer's life and era. Even if you are writing a close analysis of a poem, you should consider consulting the works of critics to benefit from their insights and understanding.

LITERARY HANDBOOK

Take Notes

Consider recording notes from the works you are analyzing, as well as from any critical works you consult, on a set of note cards. A good set of note cards enables you to recall details accurately, to organize your ideas effectively, and to see connections between ideas.

One Card, One Idea If you use note cards while researching, record each key passage, theme, critical opinion, or fact on a separate note card. A good note card includes a brief quotation or summary of an idea and a record of the source, including the page number, in which you found the information. When copying a sentence from a work, use quotation marks and check to make sure you have copied it correctly.

Coding Sources Keep a working bibliography, a list of all works you consult, as you conduct research. Assign a code, such as a letter, to each work on the list. For each note you take, include the code for the source.

Coding Cards Organize your note cards by labeling each with the subtopic it concerns.

Present Support Appropriately

As you draft, consider how much support you need for each point and the form that support should take. You can provide support in the following forms:

- **Summaries** are short accounts in your own words of important elements of the work, such as events, a character's traits, or the writer's ideas. They are appropriate for background information.
- **Paraphrases** are restatements of passages from a work in your own words. They are appropriate for background and for information incidental to your main point.
- **Quotations of key passages** are direct transcriptions of the writer's words, enclosed in quotation marks or, if longer than three lines, set as indented text. If a passage is crucial to your thesis, you should quote it directly and at whatever length is necessary.

Quotations of multiple examples are required to support claims about general features of a work, such as a claim about the writer's ironic style or use of cartoonlike characters.

DOs and DON'Ts of Academic Writing

Avoid gender and cultural bias. Certain terms and usages reflect the bias of past generations. To eliminate bias in any academic work you do, edit with the following rules in mind:

- **Pronoun usage** When referring to an unspecified individual in a case in which his or her gender is irrelevant, use forms of the pronoun phrase *he or she.* Example: "A lawyer is trained to use his or her mind."
- **"Culture-centric" terms** Replace terms that reflect a bias toward one culture with more generally accepted synonyms. For instance, replace terms such as primitive (used of hunting-gathering peoples), the Orient (used to refer to Asia), and Indians (used of Native Americans), all of which suggest a view of the world centered in Western European culture.

Avoid plagiarism. Presenting someone else's ideas, research, or exact words as your own is plagiarism, the equivalent of stealing or fraud. Laws protect the rights of writers and researchers in cases of commercial plagiarism. Academic standards protect their rights in cases of academic plagiarism.

To avoid plagiarism, follow these practices:

- Read from several sources.
- Synthesize what you learn.
- Let the ideas of experts help you draw your own conclusions.
- Always credit your sources properly when using someone else's ideas to support your view.

By following these guidelines, you will also push yourself to think independently.

Forming Your Critical Vocabulary

To enhance your critical perceptions—the connections you find and the distinctions you make—improve your critical vocabulary. The High-Utility Academic Words that appear in this textbook and are underlined in the Glossary (pp. R1–R13) are useful in critical writing.

Citing Sources and Preparing Manuscript

In research writing, cite your sources. In the body of your paper, provide a footnote, an endnote, or an internal citation, identifying the sources of facts, opinions, or quotations. At the end of your paper, provide a bibliography or a Works Cited list, a list of all the sources you cite. Follow an established format, such as Modern Language Association (MLA) Style or American Psychological Association (APA) Style.

Works Cited List (MLA Style)

A Works Cited list must contain accurate information sufficient to enable a reader to locate each source you cite. The basic components of an entry are as follows:

- Name of the author, editor, translator, or group responsible for the work
- Title
- Place and date of publication
- Publisher

For print materials, the information required for a citation generally appears on the copyright and title pages of a work. For the format of Works Cited list entries, consult the examples at right and in the chart on page R22.

Parenthetical Citations (MLA Style)

A parenthetical citation briefly identifies the source from which you have taken a specific quotation, factual claim, or opinion. It refers the reader to one of the entries on your Works Cited list. A parenthetical citation has the following features:

- It appears in parentheses.
- It identifies the source by the last name of the author, editor, or translator.
- It gives a page reference, identifying the page of the source on which the information cited can be found.

Punctuation A parenthetical citation generally falls outside a closing quotation mark but within the final punctuation of a clause or sentence. For a long quotation set off from the rest of your text, place the citation at the end of the excerpt without any punctuation following.

Special Cases

- If the author is an organization, use the organization's name, in a shortened version if necessary.
- If you cite more than one work by the same author, add the title or a shortened version of the title.

Sample Works-Cited Lists (MLA 7th Edition)

Carwardine, Mark, Erich Hoyt, R. Ewan Fordyce, and Peter Gill. *The Nature Company Guides: Whales, Dolphins, and Porpoises.* New York: Time-Life, 1998. Print.

"Discovering Whales." *Whales on the Net.* 1998. Whales in Danger Information Service. Web. 18 Oct. 1999.

Neruda, Pablo. "Ode to Spring." *Odes to Opposites.* Trans. Ken Krabbenhoft. Ed. and illus. Ferris Cook. Boston: Little, 1995. Print.

The Saga of the Volsungs. Trans. Jesse L. Byock. London: Penguin, 1990. Print.

List an anonymous work by title.

List both the title of the work and the collection in which it is found.

Sample Parenthetical Citations

It makes sense that baleen whales such as the blue whale, the bowhead whale, the humpback whale, and the sei whale (to name just a few) grow to immense sizes (Carwardine, Hoyt, and Fordyce 19–21). The blue whale has grooves running from under its chin to partway along the length of its underbelly. As in some other whales, these grooves expand and allow even more food and water to be taken in (Ellis 18–21).

Author's last name

Page numbers where information can be found

MLA Style for Listing Sources

Book with one author	Pyles, Thomas. *The Origins and Development of the English Language.* 2nd ed. New York: Harcourt, 1971. Print.
Book with two or three authors	McCrum, Robert, William Cran, and Robert MacNeil. *The Story of English.* New York: Penguin, 1987. Print.
Book with an editor	Truth, Sojourner. *Narrative of Sojourner Truth.* Ed. Margaret Washington. New York: Vintage, 1993. Print.
Book with more than three authors or editors	Donald, Robert B., et al. *Writing Clear Essays.* Upper Saddle River: Prentice, 1996. Print.
Single work in an anthology	Hawthorne, Nathaniel. "Young Goodman Brown." *Literature: An Introduction to Reading and Writing.* Ed. Edgar V. Roberts and H. E. Jacobs. Upper Saddle River: Prentice, 1998. 376–385. Print. [Indicate pages for the entire selection.]
Introduction to a work in a published edition	Washington, Margaret. Introduction. *Narrative of Sojourner Truth.* By Sojourner Truth. Ed. Washington. New York: Vintage, 1993. v–xi. Print.
Signed article from an encyclopedia	Askeland, Donald R. "Welding." *World Book Encyclopedia.* 1991 ed. Print.
Signed article in a weekly magazine	Wallace, Charles. "A Vodacious Deal." *Time* 14 Feb. 2000: 63. Print.
Signed article in a monthly magazine	Gustaitis, Joseph. "The Sticky History of Chewing Gum." *American History* Oct. 1998: 30–38. Print.
Newspaper	Thurow, Roger. "South Africans Who Fought for Sanctions Now Scrap for Investors." *Wall Street Journal* 11 Feb. 2000: A1+. Print. [For a multipage article that does not appear on consecutive pages, write only the first page number on which it appears, followed by the plus sign.]
Unsigned editorial or story	"Selective Silence." Editorial. *Wall Street Journal* 11 Feb. 2000: A14. Print. [If the editorial or story is signed, begin with the author's name.]
Signed pamphlet or brochure	[Treat the pamphlet as though it were a book.]
Work from a library subscription service	Ertman, Earl L. "Nefertiti's Eyes." *Archaeology* Mar.–Apr. 2008: 28–32. *Kids Search.* EBSCO. New York Public Library. Web. 18 June 2008 [Indicate the date you accessed the information.]
Filmstrips, slide programs, videocassettes, DVDs, and other audiovisual media	*The Diary of Anne Frank.* Dir. George Stevens. Perf. Millie Perkins, Shelley Winters, Joseph Schildkraut, Lou Jacobi, and Richard Beymer. 1959. Twentieth Century Fox, 2004. DVD.
CD-ROM (with multiple publishers)	Simms, James, ed. *Romeo and Juliet.* By William Shakespeare. Oxford: Attica Cybernetics; London: BBC Education; London: Harper, 1995. CD-ROM.
Radio or television program transcript	"Washington's Crossing of the Delaware." *Weekend Edition Sunday.* Natl. Public Radio. WNYC, New York. 23 Dec. 2003. Television transcript.
Internet Web page	"Fun Facts About Gum." NACGM site. 1999. National Association of Chewing Gum Manufacturers. Web. 19 Dec. 1999 [Indicate the date you accessed the information.]
Personal interview	Smith, Jane. Personal interview. 10 Feb. 2000.

All examples follow the style given in the *MLA Handbook for Writers of Research Papers,* seventh edition, by Joseph Gibaldi.

APA Style for Listing Sources

Book with one author	Pyles, T. (1971). *The origins and development of the English language* (2nd ed.). New York: Harcourt Brace Jovanovich.
Book with two or three authors	McCrum, R., Cran, W., & MacNeil, R. (1987). *The story of English.* New York: Penguin Books.
Book with an editor	Truth, S. (1993). *Narrative of Sojourner Truth* (M. Washington, Ed.). New York: Vintage Books.
Book with more than three authors or editors	Donald, R. B., Morrow, B. R., Wargetz, L. G., & Werner, K. (1996). *Writing clear essays.* Upper Saddle River, NJ: Prentice Hall. [With eight or more authors, abbreviate all authors after the sixth as "et al."]
Single work from an anthology	Hawthorne, N. (1998). Young Goodman Brown. In E. V. Roberts, & H. E. Jacobs (Eds.), *Literature: An introduction to reading and writing* (pp. 376–385). Upper Saddle River, NJ: Prentice Hall.
Introduction in a published edition	Washington, M. (1993). Introduction. In M. Washington (Ed.), S. Truth, *Narrative of Sojourner Truth* (pp. v–xi). New York: Vintage Books.
Signed article from an encyclopedia	Askeland, D. R. (1991). Welding. In *World Book Encyclopedia.* (Vol. 21, pp. 190–191). Chicago: World Book.
Signed article in a weekly magazine	Wallace, C. (2000, February 14). A vodacious deal. *Time, 155,* 63. [The volume number appears in italics before the page number.]
Signed article in a monthly magazine	Gustaitis, J. (1998, October). The sticky history of chewing gum. *American History, 33,* 30–38.
Newspaper	Thurow, R. (2000, February 11). South Africans who fought for sanctions now scrap for investors. *Wall Street Journal,* pp. A1, A4. [If an article appears on discontinuous pages, give all page numbers and separate the numbers with a comma.]
Unsigned editorial or story	Selective silence [Editorial]. (2000, February 11). *Wall Street Journal,* p. A14.
Signed pamphlet	Pearson Education. (2000). *LifeCare* (2nd ed.) [Pamphlet]. New York: Smith, John: Author.
Work from a library subscription service	Ertman, Earl L. (2008, March–April). "Nefertiti's Eyes." *Archaeology, 61,* 28–32. Retrieved June 18, 2008, from EBSCO Science Reference Center database.
Filmstrips, slide programs, videocassettes, DVDs, and other audiovisual media	Wallis, H. B. (Producer), & Curtiz, M. (Director). (1942). *Casablanca* [Motion picture]. United States: Warner.
Radio or television program transcript	Hackett Fisher, D. (Guest), Hansen, L. (Host). (2003, December 23). Washington's crossing of the Delaware. [Radio series installment]. *Weekend Edition Sunday.* New York: National Public Radio. Retrieved March 6, 2008 from http://www.npr.org/templates/story/story.php?storyId=1573202
Internet	National Association of Chewing Gum Manufacturers. (1999).Retrieved December 19, 1999, from http://www.nacgm.org/consumer/funfacts.html [References to Websites should begin with the author's last name, if available. Indicate the site name and the available path or URL address.]
CD	Shakespeare, W. (1995). *Romeo and Juliet.* (J. Simms, Ed.) [CD-ROM] Oxford: Attica Cybernetics.
Personal interview	[APA states that, since interviews (and other personal communications) do not provide "recoverable data," they should only be cited in text.]

Literary Terms

ALLEGORY An ***allegory*** is a literary work with two or more levels of meaning—a literal level and one or more symbolic levels. The events, settings, objects, or characters in an allegory—the literal level—stand for ideas or qualities, such as goodness, tyranny, salvation, and so on. Allegorical writing was common in the Middle Ages. Spenser revived the form in *The Faerie Queene,* and John Bunyan revived it yet again in *The Pilgrim's Progress.* Some modern novels, such as George Orwell's *Animal Farm,* can be read as allegories.

ALLITERATION ***Alliteration*** is the repetition of initial consonant sounds in accented syllables. Coleridge uses the alliteration of both *b* and *f* sounds in this line from "The Rime of the Ancient Mariner":

> The fair breeze blew, the white foam flew.

Especially in poetry, alliteration is used to emphasize and to link words, as well as to create musical sounds.

See also ***Anglo-Saxon Poetry.***

ALLUSION ***Allusion*** is a reference to a well-known person, place, event, literary work, or work of art.

AMBIGUITY ***Ambiguity*** is the effect created when words suggest and support two or more divergent interpretations. Ambiguity may be used in literature to express experiences or truths that are complex or even contradictory. For instance, the title of Elizabeth Bowen's short story "The Demon Lover," on page 1298, is ambiguous: It can refer either to the main character, who is a lover of a "demon" (a past love that she has not resolved), to the past that haunts her, or to her demonic lover, a ghost who haunts her. This ambiguous use of words reflects a larger ambiguity in the story.

See also ***Irony.***

ANALOGY An ***analogy*** is an extended comparison of relationships. It is based on the idea or insight that the relationship between one pair of things is like the relationship between another pair. Unlike a metaphor, another form of comparison, an analogy involves an explicit comparison, often using the word *like* or *as.*

See also ***Metaphor*** and ***Simile.***

ANAPEST See ***Meter.***

ANGLO-SAXON POETRY The rhythmic poetry composed in the Old English language before A.D. 1100 is known as ***Anglo-Saxon poetry***. It generally has four accented syllables and an indefinite number of unaccented syllables in each line. Each line is divided in half by a caesura, or pause, and the halves are linked by the alliteration of two or three of the accented syllables. The following translation from "Wulf and Eadwacer" shows the alliteration and caesuras used in Anglo-Saxon poetry:

> I waited for my Wulf // with far-Wandering yearnings,
> When it was rainy weather // and I sat weeping.

Anglo-Saxon poetry was sung or chanted to the accompaniment of a primitive harp; it was not written but was passed down orally.

See also ***Alliteration, Caesura,*** and ***Kenning.***

ARCHETYPAL LITERARY ELEMENTS ***Archetypal literary elements*** are patterns in literature found around the world. For instance, the occurrence of events in threes is an archetypal element of fairy tales. Certain character types, such as mysterious guides, are also archetypal elements of such traditional stories. According to some critics, these elements express in symbolic form truths about the human mind.

ARGUMENT See ***Persuasion.***

ASSONANCE ***Assonance*** is the repetition of vowel sounds in stressed syllables containing dissimilar consonant sounds. Robert Browning uses assonance in this line in "Andrea del Sarto":

> Ah, but man's reach should exceed his grasp. . . .

The long ***e*** sound is repeated in the words *reach* and *exceed.* The syllables containing these sounds are stressed and contain different consonants: ***r-ch*** and ***c-d.***

See also ***Consonance.***

BALLAD A ***ballad*** is a song that tells a story, often about adventure or romance, or a poem imitating such a song. Most ballads are divided into four- or six-line stanzas, are rhymed, use simple language, and depict dramatic action. Many ballads employ a repeated refrain. Some use incremental repetition, in which the refrain is varied slightly each time it appears.

BLANK VERSE ***Blank verse*** is unrhymed poetry usually written in iambic pentameter (see Meter). Occasional variations in rhythm are introduced in blank verse to create emphasis, variety, and naturalness of sound. Because blank verse sounds much like ordinary spoken English, it is often used in drama, as by Shakespeare, and in poetry.

See also ***Meter.***

CAESURA A ***caesura*** is a natural pause in the middle of a line of poetry. In Anglo-Saxon poetry, a caesura divides each four-stress line in half and thus is essential to the rhythm.

See also ***Anglo-Saxon Poetry.***

CARPE DIEM A Latin phrase, ***carpe diem*** means "seize the day" or "make the most of passing time." Many great literary works have been written with the *carpe diem* theme.

CHARACTER The personality that takes part in the action of a literary work is known as a character. Characters can be classified in different ways. A character who plays an important role is called a ***major character.*** A character who does not is called a ***minor character.*** A character who plays the central role in a story is called the ***protagonist.*** A character who opposes the protagonist is called the ***antagonist.*** A ***round character*** has many aspects to his or her personality. A ***flat character*** is defined by only a few qualities. A character who changes is called ***dynamic;*** a character who does not change is called ***static.***

See also ***Characterization.***

CHARACTERIZATION ***Characterization*** is the act of creating and developing a character. A writer uses ***direct characterization*** when he or she describes a character's traits explicitly. Writers also use ***indirect characterization.*** A character's traits can be revealed indirectly in what he or she says, thinks, or does; in a description of his or her appearance; or in the statements, thoughts, or actions of other characters.

See also ***Character.***

CLIMAX The ***climax*** is the high point of interest or suspense in a literary work. Often, the climax is also the crisis in the plot, the point at which the protagonist changes his or her understanding or situation. Sometimes, the climax coincides with the ***resolution***, the point at which the central conflict is ended.

See also ***Plot.***

COMEDY A ***comedy*** is a literary work, especially a play, that has a happy ending. A comedy often shows ordinary characters in conflict with their society. Types of comedy include ***romantic comedy,*** which involves problems among lovers, and the ***comedy of manners,*** which satirically challenges the social customs of a sophisticated society. Comedy is often contrasted with tragedy, in which the protagonist meets an unfortunate end.

See also ***Drama*** and ***Tragedy.***

CONCEIT A ***conceit*** is an unusual and surprising comparison between two very different things. This special kind of metaphor or complicated analogy is often the basis for a whole poem. During the Elizabethan Age, sonnets commonly included Petrarchan conceits. ***Petrarchan conceits*** make extravagant claims about the beloved's beauty or the speaker's suffering, with comparisons to divine beings, powerful natural forces, and objects that contain a given quality in the highest degree. Spenser uses a Petrarchan conceit when he claims in Sonnet 1, on page 254, that the "starry light" of his beloved's eyes will make his book happy when she reads it. Seventeenth-century ***metaphysical*** poets used elaborate, unusual, and highly intellectual conceits, as in the conceit of the compass in John Donne's "A Valediction: Forbidding Mourning," on page 484.

See also ***Metaphor.***

CONFLICT A ***conflict*** is a struggle between opposing forces. Sometimes, this struggle is internal, or within a character. At other times, the struggle is external, or between the character and some outside force. The outside force may be another character, nature, or some element of society such as a custom or a political institution. Often, the conflict in a work combines several of these possibilities.

See also ***Plot.***

CONNOTATION ***Connotation*** refers to the associations that a word calls to mind in addition to its dictionary meaning. For example, the words *home* and *domicile* have the same dictionary meaning. However, the first has positive connotations of warmth and security, whereas the second does not.

See also ***Denotation.***

CONSONANCE ***Consonance*** is the repetition of final consonant sounds in stressed syllables containing dissimilar vowel sounds. Samuel Taylor Coleridge uses consonance in these lines from "The Rime of the Ancient Mariner," on page 820:

> a frightful fie***nd*** / Doth close behi***nd*** him tread.

Fiend and the stressed syllable in *behind* have the same final consonat sounds but different vowel sounds.

See also ***Assonance.***

COUPLET A ***couplet*** is a pair of rhyming lines written in the same meter. A ***heroic couplet*** is a rhymed pair of iambic pentameter lines. In a ***closed couplet***, the meaning and syntax are completed within the two lines. These lines from Alexander Pope's "An Essay on Criticism" are a closed heroic couplet:

> True ease in writing comes from art, not chance,
> As those move easiest who have learned to dance.

Shakespearean sonnets usually end with heroic couplets.

See also ***Sonnet.***

DACTYL See ***Meter.***

DENOTATION ***Denotation*** is the objective meaning of a word—that to which the word refers, independent of other associations that the word calls to mind. Dictionaries list the denotative meanings of words.

See also ***Connotation.***

DIALECT ***Dialect*** is the form of a language spoken by people in a particular region or group. Dialects differ from one another in grammar, vocabulary, and pronunciation.

DIALOGUE ***Dialogue*** is a conversation between characters. Writers use dialogue to reveal character, to present events, to add variety to narratives, and to interest readers. Dialogue in a story is usually set off by quotation marks and paragraphing. Dialogue in a play script generally follows the name of the speaker.

DIARY A ***diary*** is a personal record of daily events, usually written in prose. Most diaries are not written for publication; sometimes, however, interesting diaries or diaries written by influential people are published. One example of a published diary is that of Samuel Pepys, a selection from which appears on page 571.

See also ***Journal.***

DICTION ***Diction*** is a writer's word choice. It can be a major determinant of the writer's style. Diction can be described as formal or informal, abstract or concrete, plain or ornate, ordinary or technical.

See also ***Style.***

DIMETER See ***Meter.***

DRAMA A ***drama*** is a story written to be performed by actors. It may consist of one or more large sections, called acts, which are made up of any number of smaller sections, called scenes.

Drama originated in the religious rituals and symbolic reenactments of primitive peoples. The ancient Greeks, who developed drama into a sophisticated art form, created such dramatic forms as tragedy and comedy.

The first dramas in England were the miracle plays and morality plays of the Middle Ages. Miracle plays told biblical stories. Morality plays, such as *Everyman,* were allegories dealing with personified virtues and vices. The English Renaissance saw a flowering of drama in England, culminating in the works of William Shakespeare, who wrote many of the world's greatest comedies, tragedies, histories, and romances. During the Neoclassical Age, English drama turned to satirical comedies of manners that probed the virtues of upper-class society. In the Romantic and Victorian ages, a few good verse plays were written, including Percy Bysshe Shelley's *The Cenci* and *Prometheus Unbound.* The end of the nineteenth and beginning of the twentieth centuries saw a resurgence of the drama in England and throughout the English-speaking world. Great plays of the Modern period include works by Bernard Shaw, Christopher Fry, T. S. Eliot, Harold Pinter, and Samuel Beckett.

DRAMATIC MONOLOGUE A ***dramatic monologue*** is a poem in which an imaginary character speaks to a silent listener. Robert Browning's "My Last Duchess," on page 978, is a dramatic monologue.

ELEGY An ***elegy*** is a solemn and formal lyric poem about death. It may mourn a particular person or reflect on a serious or tragic theme, such as the passing of youth or beauty. See Thomas Gray's "Elegy Written in a Country Churchyard," on page 666.

See also ***Lyric Poem.***

END-STOPPED LINE An ***end-stopped line*** is a line of poetry concluding with a break in the meter and in the meaning. This pause at the end of a line is often punctuated by a period, comma, dash, or semicolon. These lines from "Away, Melancholy," by Stevie Smith, are end-stopped:

Are not the trees green,
The earth as green?
Does not the wind blow,
Fire leap and the rivers flow?

See also ***Run-on Line.***

EPIC An ***epic*** is a long narrative poem about the adventures of gods or of a hero. *Beowulf,* on page 40, is a ***folk epic***, one that was composed orally and passed from storyteller to storyteller. The ancient Greek epics attributed to Homer—the *Iliad* and the *Odyssey*—are also folk epics. The *Aeneid,* by the Roman poet Virgil, and *The Divine Comedy,* by the Italian poet Dante Alighieri, are examples of literary epics from the Classical and Medieval periods, respectively. John Milton's *Paradise Lost,* a selection from which appears on page 524, is also a literary epic.

Epic conventions are traditional characteristics of epic poems, including an opening statement of the theme; an appeal for supernatural help in telling the story (an invocation); a beginning ***in medias res*** (Latin: "in the middle of things"); catalogs of people and things; accounts of past events; and descriptive phrases. See also ***Kenning.***

EPIGRAM An ***epigram*** is a brief statement in prose or in verse. The concluding couplet in an English sonnet may be epigrammatic. An essay may be written in an epigrammatic style.

EPIPHANY ***Epiphany*** is a term introduced by James Joyce to describe a moment of insight in which a character recognizes a truth. In Joyce's "Araby," on page 1236, the boy has an epiphany when he sees the falsity of his dream.

EPITAPH An ***epitaph*** is an inscription written on a tomb or burial place. In literature, epitaphs include serious or humorous lines written as if intended for such use, like the epitaph in Thomas Gray's "Elegy Written in a Country Churchyard," on page 666.

ESSAY An ***essay*** is a short nonfiction work about a particular subject. Essays are of many types but may be classified by tone or style as formal or informal. Addison's breezy style and tongue-in-cheek descriptions make "The Aims of *The Spectator,*" on page 682, an instance of an informal essay. An essay is often classed by its main purpose as descriptive, narrative, expository, argumentative, or persuasive.

EXTENDED METAPHOR See ***Metaphor.***

FICTION ***Fiction*** is prose writing about imaginary characters and events. Some writers of fiction base their stories on real events, whereas others rely solely on their imaginations.

See also ***Narration*** and ***Prose.***

FIGURATIVE LANGUAGE ***Figurative language*** is writing or speech not meant to be interpreted literally. Poets and other writers use figurative language to paint vivid word pictures, to make their writing emotionally intense and concentrated, and to state their ideas in new and unusual ways. Among the figures of speech making up figurative language are hyperbole, irony, metaphor, metonymy, oxymoron, paradox, personification, simile, and synecdoche.

See also the entries for individual figures of speech.

FOLKLORE The stories, legends, myths, ballads, riddles, sayings, and other traditional works produced orally by illiterate or semiliterate peoples are known as ***folklore***. Folklore influences written literature in many ways. The beheading contest in *Sir Gawain and the Green Knight,* on page 170, is an example of folklore.

FOOT See ***Meter.***

FREE VERSE ***Free verse*** is poetry not written in a regular, rhythmical pattern, or meter. Instead of having metrical feet and lines, free verse has a rhythm that suits its meaning and that uses the sounds of spoken language in lines of different lengths. Free verse has been widely used in twentieth-century poetry. An example is "The Galloping Cat," by Stevie Smith:

> All the same I
> Intend to go on being
> A cat that likes to
> Gallop about doing good
> So
> Now with my bald head I go,
> Chopping the untidy flowers down, to and fro.

GOTHIC ***Gothic*** is a term used to describe literary works that make extensive use of primitive, medieval, wild, mysterious, or natural elements. Gothic novels, such as Mary Wollstonecraft Shelley's *Frankenstein,* the Introduction to which appears on page 760, often depict horrifying events set in gloomy castles.

HEPTAMETER See ***Meter.***

HEXAMETER See ***Meter.***

HYPERBOLE ***Hyperbole*** is a deliberate exaggeration or overstatement. In "Song," on page 482, John Donne uses this figure of speech:

> When thou sigh'st, thou sigh'st not wind,
> but sigh'st my soul away

See also ***Figurative Language.***

IAMBIC PENTAMETER See ***Meter.***

IMAGE An ***image*** is a word or phrase that appeals to one or more of the senses—sight, hearing, touch, taste, or smell. In a famous essay on *Hamlet,* T. S. Eliot explained how a group of images can be used as an "objective correlative." By this phrase, Eliot meant that a complex emotional state can be suggested by images that are carefully chosen to evoke this state.

See also ***Imagery.***

IMAGERY ***Imagery*** is the descriptive language used in literature to re-create sensory experiences. Imagery enriches writing by making it more vivid, setting a tone, suggesting emotions, and guiding readers' reactions.

IRONY ***Irony*** is the general name given to literary techniques that involve surprising, interesting, or amusing contradictions. In ***verbal irony***, words are used to suggest the opposite of their usual meaning. In ***dramatic irony***, there is a contradiction between what a character thinks and what the reader or audience knows to be true. In ***irony of situation***, an event occurs that directly contradicts expectations.

JOURNAL A ***journal*** is a daily autobiographical account of events and personal reactions. Daniel Defoe adapted this form to fictional use in *A Journal of the Plague Year,* an excerpt from which appears on page 590.

See also ***Diary.***

KENNING A ***kenning*** is a metaphorical phrase used in Anglo-Saxon poetry to replace a concrete noun. In "The Seafarer," on page 20, the cuckoo is called "summer's sentinel" and the sea, "the whale's home."

See also ***Anglo-Saxon Poetry*** and ***Epic.***

LEGEND A ***legend*** is a widely told story about the past that may or may not be based in fact. A legend often reflects a people's identity or cultural values, generally with more historical truth than that in a myth. English legends include the stories of King Arthur (retold in *Morte d'Arthur,* a selection from which appears on page 185) and Robin Hood.

See also ***Myth.***

LETTER A ***letter*** addresses a specific person or group and is meant to be read within a specific time.

LYRIC POEM A ***lyric poem*** is a poem expressing the observations and feelings of a single speaker. Unlike a narrative poem, it presents an experience or a single effect, but it does not tell a full story. Types of lyric poems include the elegy, the ode, and the sonnet.

METAPHOR A ***metaphor*** is a figure of speech in which one thing is spoken of as though it were something else, as in "death, that long sleep." Through this identification of dissimilar things, a comparison is suggested or implied.

An ***extended metaphor*** is developed at length and involves several points of comparison. A mixed metaphor occurs when two metaphors are jumbled together, as in "The thorns of life rained down on him."

A ***dead metaphor*** is one that has been so overused that its original metaphorical impact has been lost. Examples of dead metaphors include "the foot of the bed" and "toe the line."

See also ***Figurative Language.***

METAPHYSICAL POETRY The term ***metaphysical poetry*** describes the works of such seventeenth-century English poets as Richard Crashaw, John Donne, George Herbert, and Andrew Marvell. Characteristic features of metaphysical poetry include intellectual playfulness, argument, paradoxes, irony, elaborate and unusual conceits, incongruity, and the rhythms of ordinary speech. Examples of metaphysical poems in this textbook include Donne's "Song," on page 482, and Marvell's "To His Coy Mistress," on page 506.

METER ***Meter*** is the rhythmical pattern of a poem. This pattern is determined by the number and types of stresses, or beats, in each line. To describe the meter of a poem, you must scan its lines. Scanning involves marking the stressed and unstressed syllables, as follows:

> I ween | that, when | the grave's | dark wall
> Did first | her form | retain,
> They thought | their hearts | could ne'er | recall
> The light | of joy | again.
>
> —Emily Brontë, "Song"

As you can see, each stressed syllable is marked with a slanted line (´) and each unstressed syllable with a horseshoe symbol (˘). The stresses are then divided by vertical lines into groups called feet. The following types of feet are common in English poetry:

1. ***Iamb:*** a foot with one unstressed syllable followed by one stressed syllable, as in the word ***afraid***
2. ***Trochee:*** a foot with one stressed syllable followed by one unstressed syllable, as in the word ***heather***
3. ***Anapest:*** a foot with two unstressed syllables followed by one stressed syllable, as in the word ***disembark***
4. ***Dactyl:*** a foot with one stressed syllable followed by two unstressed syllables, as in the word ***solitude***
5. ***Spondee:*** a foot with two stressed syllables, as in the word ***workday***
6. ***Pyrrhic:*** a foot with two unstressed syllables, as in the last foot of the word ***unspeak | ably***
7. ***Amphibrach:*** a foot with an unstressed syllable, one stressed syllable, and another unstressed syllable, as in the word ***another***
8. ***Amphimacer:*** a foot with a stressed syllable, one unstressed syllable, and another stressed syllable, as in ***up and down***

A line of poetry is described as ***iambic***, ***trochaic***, ***anapestic***, or ***dactylic*** according to the kind of foot that appears most often in the line. Lines are also described in terms of the number of feet that occur in them, as follows:

1. ***Monometer:*** verse written in one-foot lines:

   Sound the Flute!
   Now it's mute.
   Birds delight
   Day and Night.

   —William Blake, "Spring"

2. ***Dimeter:*** verse written in two-foot lines:

   O Rose | thou art sick.
   The invis | ible worm.
   That flies | in the night
   In the how | ling storm:
   Has found | out thy bed
   Of crim | son joy: . . .

   —William Blake, "The Sick Rose"

3. ***Trimeter:*** verse written in three-foot lines:

   I went | to the Gard | en of Love
   And saw | what I nev | er had seen:
   A Chap | el was built | in the midst,
   Where I used | to play | on the green.

   —William Blake, "The Garden of Love"

4. ***Tetrameter:*** verse written in four-foot lines:

   I wand | er thro' | each chart | er'd street
   Near where | the chart | er'd Thames |
   does flow
   And mark | in ev | ery face | I meet
   Marks of | weakness, | marks of | woe.

   —William Blake, "London"

A six-foot line is called a ***hexameter.*** A line with seven feet is a ***heptameter.***

A complete description of the meter of a line tells both how many feet there are in the line and what kind of foot is most common. Thus, the stanza from Emily Brontë's poem, quoted at the beginning of this entry, would be described as being made up of alternating iambic tetrameter and iambic trimeter lines. Poetry that does not have a regular meter is called ***free verse.***

See also ***Free Verse.***

METONYMY ***Metonymy*** is a figure of speech that substitutes something closely related for the thing actually meant. In the opening line of "The Lost Leader," Robert Browning says, "Just for a handful of silver he left us," using "silver" to refer to money paid for a betrayal.

See also ***Figurative Language.***

MIRACLE PLAY See ***Drama.***

MOCK EPIC A ***mock epic*** is a poem about a trivial matter written in the style of a serious epic. The incongruity of style and subject matter produces comic effects. Alexander Pope's "The Rape of the Lock," on page 632, is a mock epic.

See also ***Epic.***

MODERNISM ***Modernism*** describes an international movement in the arts during the early twentieth century. Modernists rejected old forms and experimented with the new. Literary Modernists—such as James Joyce, W. B. Yeats, and T. S. Eliot—used images as symbols. They presented human experiences in fragments, rather than as a coherent whole, which led to new experiments in the forms of poetry and fiction.

MONOLOGUE A ***monologue*** is a speech or performance given entirely by one person or by one character.

See also ***Dramatic Monologue*** and ***Soliloquy.***

MOOD ***Mood***, or ***atmosphere***, is the feeling created in the reader by a literary work or passage. Mood may be suggested by the writer's choice of words, by events in the work, or by the physical setting. Nadine Gordimer begins "The Train from Rhodesia," on page 1342, with a description of the hot, sandy train station that sets a mood mixing boredom and confinement with the eager expectation of the train.

See also ***Setting*** and ***Tone.***

MORALITY PLAY See ***Drama.***

MYTH A ***myth*** is a fictional tale, originally with religious significance, that explains the actions of gods or heroes, the causes of natural phenomena, or both. Allusions to characters and motifs from Greek, Roman, Norse, and Celtic myths are common in English literature. In addition, mythological stories are often retold or adapted.

See also ***Legend.***

NARRATION ***Narration*** is writing that tells a story. The act of telling a story is also called narration. The ***narrative,*** or story, is told by a character or speaker called the ***narrator.*** Biographies, autobiographies, journals, reports, novels, short stories, plays, narrative poems, anecdotes, fables, parables, myths, legends, folk tales, ballads, and epic poems are all narratives, or types of narration.

See also ***Point of View.***

NARRATIVE POEM A ***narrative poem*** is a poem that tells a story in verse. Three traditional types of narrative poems include ballads, epics, and metrical romances.

NATURALISM ***Naturalism*** was a literary movement among writers at the end of the nineteenth century and during the early decades of the twentieth century. The Naturalists depicted life in its grimmer details and viewed people as hopeless victims of natural laws.

See also ***Realism.***

NEOCLASSICISM ***Neoclassicism*** was a literary movement of the late seventeenth and the eighteenth centuries in which writers turned to classical Greek and Roman literary models and standards. Like the ancients, Neoclassicists, such as Alexander Pope, stressed order, harmony, restraint, and the ideal. Much Neoclassical literature dealt with themes related to proper human conduct. The most popular literary forms of the day—essays, letters, early novels, epigrams, parodies, and satires—reflected this emphasis.

See also ***Romanticism.***

NONFICTION ***Nonfiction*** is prose writing that presents and explains ideas or tells about real places, objects or events. To be classified as nonfiction, a work must be true.

NOVEL A ***novel*** is an extended work of fiction that often has a complicated plot, many major and minor characters, a unifying theme, and several settings. Novels can be grouped in many ways, based on the historical periods in which they are written (such as Victorian), on the subjects and themes that they treat (such as Gothic or regional), on the techniques used in them (such as stream of consciousness), or on their part in literary movements (such as Naturalism or Realism). Among the early novels were Samuel Richardson's *Pamela* and *Clarissa* and Henry Fielding's *Tom Jones.* Other classic English novels include Jane Austen's *Pride and Prejudice,* Sir Walter Scott's *Waverley,* Charles Dickens's *David Copperfield,* and George Eliot's *The Mill on the Floss.* Major twentieth-century novelists include James Joyce, Virginia Woolf, D. H. Lawrence, Henry James, Graham Greene, and Patrick White. A ***novella***—for example, Joseph Conrad's *Heart of Darkness*—is not as long as a novel but is longer than a short story.

OBJECTIVE CORRELATIVE See ***Image.***

OCTAVE See ***Stanza.***

ODE An ***ode*** is a long, formal lyric poem with a serious theme. It may have a traditional structure with stanzas grouped in threes, called the ***strophe,*** the ***antistrophe,*** and the ***epode.*** Odes often honor people, commemorate events, or respond to natural scenes.

See also ***Lyric Poem.***

ONOMATOPOEIA ***Onomatopoeia*** is the use of words that imitate sounds. Examples of such words are *buzz, hiss, murmur,* and *rustle.* Onomatopoeia is used to create musical effects and to reinforce meaning.

ORAL TRADITION ***Oral tradition*** is the body of songs, stories, and poems preserved by being passed from generation to generation by word of mouth. Among the many materials composed or preserved through oral tradition in Great Britain are *Beowulf,* on page 40, and the folk ballads on pages 205–211. In his *Morte d'Arthur,* a selection from which begins on page 185, Sir Thomas Malory drew on Arthurian legends from the oral tradition. Shakespeare drew on materials from the oral tradition to create the sprites and fairies of *A Midsummer Night's Dream* and the witches of *Macbeth,* on page 322. Folk epics, ballads, myths, legends, folk tales, folk songs, proverbs, and nursery rhymes are all products of the oral tradition.

See also ***Ballad, Folklore, Legend,*** and ***Myth.***

OXYMORON An ***oxymoron*** is a figure of speech that fuses two contradictory ideas, such as "freezing fire" or "happy grief," thus suggesting a paradox in just a few words.

See also ***Figurative Language*** and ***Paradox.***

PARABLE A ***parable*** is a short, simple story from which a moral or religious lesson can be drawn. The most famous parables are those in the New Testament, an example of which appears on page 302.

PARADOX A ***paradox*** is a statement that seems to be contradictory but that actually presents a truth. In "Love's Growth," John Donne presents the following paradox:

> Methinks I lied all winter, when I swore
> My love was infinite, if spring make it more.

Because a paradox is surprising or even shocking, it draws the reader's attention to what is being said.

See also ***Figurative Language*** and ***Oxymoron.***

PARODY A ***parody*** is a humorous imitation of another work or of a type of work.

PASTORAL ***Pastoral*** refers to literary works that deal with the pleasures of a simple rural life or with escape to a simpler place and time. The tradition of pastoral literature began in ancient Greece with the poetic idylls of Theocritus. The Roman poet Virgil also wrote a famous collection of pastoral poems, the *Eclogues.*

During the European Renaissance, pastoral writing became quite popular. Two famous examples are *The Countess of Pembroke's Arcadia,* by Sir Philip Sidney, and Christopher Marlowe's "The Passionate Shepherd to His Love," on page 266.

Today, the term ***pastoral*** is commonly applied to any work in which a speaker longs to escape to a simpler rural life. By this definition, both William Wordsworth's "The World Is Too Much With Us," on page 790, and William Butler Yeats's "The Lake Isle of Innisfree," on page 1141, are pastoral poems.

PENTAMETER See ***Meter.***

PERSONIFICATION ***Personification*** is a figure of speech in which a nonhuman subject is given human characteristics. Percy Bysshe Shelley uses personification in these lines:

> Swiftly walk o'er the western wave,
> Spirit of the Night!

Effective personification of things or ideas makes their qualities seem unified, like the characteristics of a person, and their relationship with the reader seem closer.

See also ***Figurative Language*** and ***Metaphor.***

PERSUASION ***Persuasion*** is writing or speech that attempts to convince a reader to think or act in a particular way. Persuasion is used in advertising, in editorials, in sermons, and in political speeches. An ***argument*** is a logical way of presenting a belief, conclusion, or stance. A good argument is supported with reasoning and evidence.

PLOT ***Plot*** is the sequence of events in a literary work. The two primary elements of any plot are characters and a conflict. Most plots can be analyzed into many or all of the following parts:

1. The ***exposition*** introduces the setting, the characters, and the basic situation.
2. The ***inciting incident*** introduces the central conflict and develops the rising action.
3. During the ***development,*** or rising action, the conflict runs its course and usually intensifies.
4. At the ***climax,*** the conflict reaches a high point of interest or suspense.
5. The ***denouement,*** or ***falling action,*** ties up loose ends that remain after the climax of the conflict.
6. At the ***resolution,*** the story is resolved and an insight is revealed.

There are many variations on the standard plot structure. Some stories begin ***in medias res*** ("in the middle of things"), after the inciting incident has already occurred. In some stories, the expository material appears toward the middle, in flashbacks. In many stories, there is no denouement. Occasionally, the conflict is left unresolved.

POETRY ***Poetry*** is one of the three major types, or genres, of literature, the others being prose and drama. Poetry defies simple definition because there is no single characteristic that is found in all poems and not found in all nonpoems.

Often, poems are divided into lines and stanzas. Poems such as sonnets, odes, villanelles, and sestinas are governed by rules regarding the number of lines, the number and placement of stressed syllables in each line, and the rhyme scheme. In the case of villanelles and sestinas, the repetition of words at the ends of lines or of entire lines is required. (An example of a sestina, Seamus Heaney's "Two Lorries," appears on page 1370. An example of a villanelle, Dylan Thomas's "Do Not Go Gentle into That Good Night," appears on page 1390.) However, some poems are written in free verse. Most poems make use of highly concise, musical, and emotionally charged language. Many also use imagery, figurative language, and devices of sound like rhyme.

Types of poetry include ***narrative poetry*** (ballads, epics, and metrical romances); ***dramatic poetry*** (dramatic monologues and dramatic dialogues); ***lyrics*** (sonnets, odes, elegies, and love poems); and ***concrete poetry*** (a poem presented on the page in a shape that suggests its subject).

POINT OF VIEW The perspective, or vantage point, from which a story is told is its ***point of view.*** If a character within the story narrates, then it is told from the ***first-person point of view.*** If a voice from outside the story tells it, then the story is told from the ***third-person point of view***. If the knowledge of the storyteller is limited to the internal states of one character, then the storyteller has a ***limited point of view.*** If the storyteller's knowledge extends to the internal states of all the characters, then the storyteller has an ***omniscient point of view.***

POLITICAL COMMENTARY ***Political commentary*** offers opinions on political issues, building arguments on evidence and assumptions. Using writing forms such as speeches, poems, and letters, commentators seek to persuade using persuasive devices such as rhetorical questions and balanced clauses.

PROSE ***Prose*** is the ordinary form of written language and one of the three major types of literature. Most writing that is not poetry, drama, or song is considered prose. Prose occurs in two major forms: fiction and nonfiction.

PSALM A ***psalm*** is a sacred song or lyric poem in praise of God.

PYRRHIC See ***Meter.***

QUATRAIN See ***Stanza.***

REALISM ***Realism*** is the presentation in art of details from actual life. During the last part of the nineteenth century and the first part of the twentieth, Realism enjoyed considerable popularity among writers in the English-speaking world. Novels often dealt with grim social realities and presented realistic portrayals of the psychological states of characters.

REFRAIN A ***refrain*** is a regularly repeated line or group of lines in a poem or song.

See also ***Ballad.***

REGIONALISM ***Regionalism*** is the tendency to confine one's writing to the presentation of the distinct culture of an area, including its speech, customs, and history. For example, the Brontës wrote about Yorkshire, Thomas Hardy wrote about Dorset and Wessex, and D. H. Lawrence wrote about Nottinghamshire.

RHYME ***Rhyme*** is the repetition of sounds at the ends of words. ***End rhyme*** occurs when rhyming words appear at the ends of lines. ***Internal rhyme*** occurs when rhyming words fall within a line. ***Exact rhyme*** is the use of identical rhyming sounds, as in *love* and *dove*. ***Approximate,*** or ***slant, rhyme*** is the use of sounds that are similar but not identical, as in *prove* and *glove*.

RHYME SCHEME ***Rhyme scheme*** is the regular pattern of rhyming words in a poem or stanza. To indicate a rhyme scheme, assign a different letter to each final sound in the poem or stanza. The following lines from Charlotte Brontë's "On the Death of Anne Brontë" have been marked:

There's little joy in life for me,	**a**
And little terror in the grave;	**b**
I've lived the parting hour to see	**a**
Of one I would have died to save.	**b**

RHYTHM See ***Meter.***

ROMANCE A ***romance*** is a story that presents remote or imaginative incidents rather than ordinary, realistic experience. The term ***romance*** was originally used to refer to medieval tales of the deeds and loves of noble knights and ladies. These early romances, or tales of chivalry and courtly love, are exemplified by *Sir Gawain and the Green Knight,* on page 170, and by the extract from Malory's *Morte d'Arthur,* on page 185. During the Renaissance in England, many writers, such as Edmund Spenser in ***The Faerie Queene,*** drew heavily on the romance tradition. From the eighteenth century on, the term ***romance*** has been used to describe sentimental novels about love.

ROMANTICISM ***Romanticism*** was a literary and artistic movement of the eighteenth and nineteenth centuries. In reaction to Neoclassicism, the Romantics emphasized imagination, fancy, freedom, emotion, wildness, the beauty of the untamed natural world, the rights of the individual, the nobility of the common man, and the attractiveness of pastoral life. Important figures in the Romantic Movement included William Wordsworth, Samuel Taylor Coleridge, Percy Bysshe Shelley, John Keats, and George Gordon, Lord Byron.

RUN-ON LINE A ***run-on line*** is a line that does not contain a pause or a stop at the end. It ends in the middle of a statement and a grammatical unit, and the reader must read the next line to find the end of the statement and the completion of the grammatical unit. The beginning of Molly Holden's "The Double Nature of White" illustrates the run-on line:

White orchards are the earliest, stunning
the spirit resigned to winter's black, white thorn
sprays first the bare wet branches of the hedge.

See also ***End-Stopped Line.***

SATIRE ***Satire*** is writing that ridicules or holds up to contempt the faults of individuals or groups. Satires include Jonathan Swift's prose work *Gulliver's Travels,* on page 606, and Alexander Pope's poem *The Rape of the Lock,* on page 632. Although a satire is often humorous, its purpose is not simply to make readers laugh but also to correct the flaws and shortcomings that it points out.

SCANSION ***Scansion*** is the process of analyzing the metrical pattern of a poem.

See also ***Meter.***

SERMON A ***sermon*** is a speech offering religious or moral instruction. For example, the Sermon on the Mount, on page 301, given by Jesus on a mountain in Galilee, contains the basic teachings of Christianity.

SESTET See ***Stanza.***

SETTING The ***setting*** is the time and place of the action of a literary work. A setting can provide a backdrop for the action. It can be the force that the protagonist struggles against and thus the source of the central conflict. It can also be used to create an atmosphere. In many works, the setting symbolizes a point that the author wishes to emphasize.

See also ***Mood*** and ***Symbol.***

SHORT STORY A ***short story*** is a brief work of fiction. The short story resembles the longer novel, but it generally has a simpler plot and setting. In addition, a short story tends to reveal character at a crucial moment, rather than to develop it through many incidents.

SIMILE A ***simile*** is a figure of speech that compares two apparently dissimilar things using ***like*** or ***as.*** Christina Rossetti uses simile in "Goblin Market" to describe two sisters:

Like two blossoms on one stem,
Like two flakes of new-fallen snow,
Like two wands of ivory
Tipped with gold for awful kings.

By comparing apparently dissimilar things, the writer of a simile surprises the reader into an appreciation of the hidden similarities of the things being compared.

See also ***Figurative Language.***

SOCIAL COMMENTARY ***Social commentary*** is writing that offers insight into society, its values, and its customs. For example, Mary Wollstonecraft's *A Vindication of the Rights of Woman* (p. 916) offers social commentary on the debate over women's rights and seeks to attribute this problem to social customs.

SOLILOQUY A ***soliloquy*** is a long speech in a play or in a prose work made by a character who is alone and thus reveals private thoughts and feelings to the audience or reader. William Shakespeare opens Act III of ***Macbeth,*** on page 361, with a soliloquy in which Banquo speculates on Macbeth's reaction to the witches' prophecy.

See also ***Monologue.***

SONNET A sonnet is a fourteen-line lyric poem with a single theme. Sonnets are usually written in iambic pentameter. The ***Petrarchan***, or ***Italian sonnet,*** is divided into two parts, an eight-line octave and a six-line sestet. The octave rhymes ***abba abba***, while the sestet generally rhymes ***cde cde*** or uses some combination of ***cd*** rhymes. The octave raises a question, states a problem, or presents a brief narrative, and the sestet answers the question, solves the problem, or comments on the narrative.

The ***Shakespearean***, or ***English***, ***sonnet*** has three four-line quatrains plus a concluding two-line couplet. The rhyme scheme of such a sonnet is usually ***abab cdcd efef gg***. Each of the three quatrains usually explores a different variation of the main theme. Then, the couplet presents a summarizing or concluding statement.

The ***Spenserian*** sonnet has three quatrains and a couplet, but the quatrains are joined by linking rhymes like those of an Italian sonnet. The rhyme scheme of this type of sonnet is ***abab bcbc cdcd ee***.

See also ***Lyric Poem*** and ***Sonnet Sequence.***

SONNET SEQUENCE A ***sonnet sequence*** is a series or group of sonnets, most often written to or about a beloved. Although each sonnet can stand alone as a separate poem, the sequence lets the poet trace the development of a relationship or examine different aspects of a single subject. Examples of sonnet sequences are Sir Philip Sidney's *Astrophel and Stella,* Edmund Spenser's *Amoretti,* and Elizabeth Barrett Browning's *Sonnets from the Portuguese.*

See also ***Sonnet.***

SPEAKER The ***speaker*** is the imaginary voice assumed by the writer of a poem; the character who "says" the poem. This character is often not identified by name but may be identified otherwise. For example, the title of William Blake's poem "The Chimney Sweeper," on page 751, identifies the speaker, a child who gives an account of his life.

Recognizing the speaker and thinking about his or her characteristics are often central to interpreting a lyric poem. In Blake's poem, for instance, the speaker's acceptance of his oppressive life is offered for the reader's evaluation.

See also ***Point of View.***

SPONDEE See ***Meter.***

SPRUNG RHYTHM The term ***sprung rhythm*** was used by Gerard Manley Hopkins to describe the idiosyncratic meters of his poems. The rhythm is quite varied and contains such violations of traditional metrical rules as several strong stresses in a row or feet containing more than two weak stresses.

STANZA A ***stanza*** is a group of lines in a poem, which is seen as a unit. Many poems are divided into stanzas that are separated by spaces. Stanzas often function like paragraphs in prose. Each stanza states and develops one main idea.

Stanzas are commonly named according to the number of lines found in them, as follows:

1. ***Couplet:*** a two-line stanza
2. ***Tercet:*** a three-line stanza
3. ***Quatrain:*** a four-line stanza
4. ***Cinquain:*** a five-line stanza
5. ***Sestet:*** a six-line stanza
6. ***Heptastich:*** a seven-line stanza
7. ***Octave:*** an eight-line stanza

See also ***Sonnet.***

STYLE ***Style*** is a writer's typical way of writing. Determinants of a writer's style include formality, use of figurative language, use of rhythm, typical grammatical patterns, typical sentence lengths, and typical methods of organization. John Milton is noted for a grand, heroic style that contrasts with John Keats's rich, sensory style and with T. S. Eliot's allusive, ironic style.

See also ***Diction.***

SUBLIME The ***sublime*** is an effect created in literature when a writer confronts a power or mystery in nature that exceeds human understanding. The effect is achieved by representing the infinite or endless in sensory terms, as when Byron characterizes the inexhaustible power of the ocean in the "Apostrophe to the Ocean" in *Childe Harold's Pilgrimage,* on page 856.

SYMBOL A ***symbol*** is a sign, word, phrase, image, or other object that stands for or represents something else. Thus, a flag can symbolize a country, a spoken word can symbolize an object, a fine car can symbolize wealth, and so on. In literary criticism, a distinction is often made between traditional or conventional symbols—those that are part of our general cultural inheritance—and ***personal symbols***—those that are created by particular authors for use in particular works. For example, the lamb in William Blake's poem "The Lamb," on page 748, is a conventional symbol for peace, gentleness, and innocence. However, the tiger in Blake's poem "The Tyger," on page 749, is not a conventional or inherited symbol. Blake created this symbol specifically for this poem.

Conventional symbolism is often based on elements of nature. For example, youth is often symbolized by greenery or springtime, middle age by summer, and old age by autumn or winter. Conventional symbols are also borrowed from religion and politics. For example, a cross may be a symbol of Christianity, or the color red may be a symbol of Marxist ideology.

SYNECDOCHE ***Synecdoche*** is a figure of speech in which a part of something is used to stand for the whole. In the preface to his long poem entitled *Milton,* William Blake includes these lines: "And did those feet in ancient time / Walk upon England's mountains green?" The "feet" stand for the whole body, and "England's mountains green" stand for England.

See also ***Figurative Language.***

SYNTAX ***Syntax*** is the way words are organized—for example, their order is a sentence or phrase.

TETRAMETER See ***Meter.***

THEME ***Theme*** is the central idea, concern, or purpose in a literary work. In an essay, the theme might be directly stated in what is known as a thesis statement. In a serious literary work, the theme is usually expressed indirectly rather than directly. A light work, one written strictly for entertainment, may not have a theme.

TONE ***Tone*** is the writer's attitude toward the readers and toward the subject. It may be formal or informal, friendly or distant, personal or pompous. For example, John Keats's tone in his poem "On First Looking into Chapman's Homer," on page 882, is earnest and respectful, while James Boswell's tone in *The Life of Samuel Johnson,* which begins on page 655, is familiar and engaging.

See also ***Mood.***

TRADITION In literary study and practice, a ***tradition*** is a past body of work, developed over the course of history. A literary tradition may be unified by form (the tradition of the sonnet), by language (literature in English), or by nationality (English literature). A tradition develops through the acknowledgment of works, forms, and styles as classic. It also develops through critical reappraisals, as when T. S. Eliot, in the early twentieth century, elevated seventeenth-century poet John Donne out of the shadows of critical obscurity and disfavor. Writers participate in a tradition if only by following conventions about the suitable forms and subjects for literature. They make conscious use of the tradition when they use references, stories, or forms from old literature to give authority to their work. For example, John Milton uses the classical form of the epic in *Paradise Lost,* page 524, to retell the biblical story of the Fall. Writers may also break from a tradition, as when Wordsworth rejects elevated poetic language in favor of conversational speech in poems such as "London, 1802," page 791. A tradition may also be used to question itself. For example, Derek Walcott in the extract from *Midsummer,* page 1360, uses references to Shakespeare's works to question the extent to which he, a black poet, can participate in a tradition largely maintained by white society for white society.

TRAGEDY ***Tragedy*** is a type of drama or literature that shows the downfall or destruction of a noble or outstanding person, traditionally one who possesses a character weakness called a ***tragic flaw.*** Macbeth, for example, is a brave and noble figure led astray by ambition. The ***tragic hero*** is caught up in a sequence of events that inevitably results in disaster. Because the protagonist is neither a wicked villain nor an innocent victim, the audience reacts with mixed emotions—both pity and fear, according to the Greek philosopher Aristotle, who defined tragedy in the *Poetics.* The outcome of a tragedy, in which the protagonist is isolated from society, contrasts with the happy resolution of a comedy, in which the protagonist makes peace with society.

See also ***Comedy*** and ***Drama.***

TRIMETER See ***Meter.***

TROCHEE See ***Meter.***

VOICE The ***voice*** of a writer is his or her "sound" on the page. It is based on elements such as word choice, sound devices, pace, and attitude.

College Application Essay

If you are applying for admission to a college, you will probably need to submit an essay as part of your application. This essay will help admissions committee members get a sense of you as a person and as a student. Review the chart at right for general strategies, and follow the guidelines below to produce an effective college application essay.

Strategies for Writing an Effective College Application Essay

- **Choose the right topic**. If you have a choice of essay topics, choose one that truly interests you.
- **Organize.** Use a strong organization that carries the reader from introduction to conclusion.
- **Begin Strongly.** Open with an introduction that has a good chance of sparking the reader's interest.
- **Elaborate.** Be sure to explain why the experiences you discuss are important to you or what you learned from them.
- **Show style.** Bring life to your essay through vivid descriptions, precise word choice, and sophisticated sentence structure, such as parallelism. Consider including dialogue where appropriate.
- **Close with a clincher.** Write a conclusion that effectively sums up your ideas.
- **Do a clean job**. Proofread your essay carefully. It should be error-free.

Selecting a Topic

Read the essay question on the application form with care. Mark key criteria and direction words such as *describe* and *explain*. After you have written a first draft, check to make sure you have met all of the requirements of the question. Your essay has a better chance of succeeding if it meets the requirements exactly.

General Questions About You

The essay question on a college application may be as general as "Describe a significant experience or event in your life and explain its consequences for you." To choose the right topic for such a question, think of an event or experience that truly is meaningful to you—a camping trip, a volunteer event, a family reunion. Test the subject by drafting a letter about it to a good friend or relative. If you find that your enthusiasm for the subject grows as you write, and if your discussion reveals something about your growth or your outlook on life, the topic may be the right one for your essay.

Directed Questions

The essay question on an application may be a directed question, rather than a general question. For instance, you may be asked to select three figures from history you would like to meet and to explain your choices.

In such cases, do not give an answer just because you think it will please reviewers. Rely on your own interests and instincts. Your most convincing writing will come from genuine interest in the subject.

Style

Remember that an essay is a formal document addressed to strangers. Use a formal to semiformal style. Avoid incomplete sentences and slang unless you are using them for clear stylistic effect. Use words with precision, selecting one or two accurate words to express your meaning. Do not use a word if you are unsure of its meaning.

Format

Most applications limit the length of essays. Do not exceed the allowed space or word count. Your college application essay should be neatly typed or printed, using adequate margins. Proofread your final draft carefully. If you submit a separate copy of the essay (rather than writing on the application form), number the pages and include your name and contact information on each page.

Reusing Your Essay

Most students apply to a number of different colleges. Once you have written a strong essay for one application, you may adapt it for others. However, do not submit a single essay to several schools blindly. Always read the application essay question carefully to ensure that the essay you submit fulfills all of its requirements.

Job Search Document: Cover Letter

A cover letter is a formal letter in which the writer asks to be considered for a job. It usually accompanies, or "covers," a completed job application, a résumé, or both. A good cover letter relates specifically to the job for which the writer is applying.

Write a Cover Letter

Consider a part-time job or a summer job you would like to have. Then, write a cover letter to accompany a job application. Include a header, an inside address, an introductory paragraph, one or two body paragraphs, a closing paragraph, and a signature. Mention your main qualifications, and explain how they make you a good fit for the job.

Cesar Moreno
000 Park Avenue
San Marcos, Texas 00000
512-000-0000
emailaddress@theinternet.com

January 15, 20—

> The heading should include the writer's name, address, phone number, e-mail address, and the date of the letter.

Barbara Jones, Director
River Place Day Camp
500 S. Camp Street
Austin, TX 00000

> The inside address includes the name, title, and address of the recipient.

Dear Ms. Jones:

I am writing to apply for the position of Activities Coordinator for your summer camp. The job description posted on the Texas Summer Camps job board perfectly parallels my own interests and experience.

As noted on the enclosed résumé, I have four years' experience as a camp counselor, including one as Lead Counselor and one as Assistant Activities Director. In these roles, I learned not only to work as a team leader, but also to help tailor a camp's programs to the needs of its campers. As an education student at Texas State University, I have completed basic education courses as well as electives in counseling, recreational learning, and youth leadership. These courses, along with my volunteer work as an after-school mentor, have sparked my interest in non-classroom education. In fact, I plan to base my entire career on the idea that learning can be fun—and can happen anywhere.

> The body paragraph describes how the writer's experiences relate specifically to the job responsibilities.

I hope to help make River Place Day Camp a fun, educational, and well-organized experience for both its campers and its staff. I look forward to meeting with you and discussing my qualifications in more detail.

Sincerely,

Cesar Moreno

Job Search Document: Résumé

A **résumé** is a written summary or outline of a person's job qualifications. It plays a key part in most career or job searches. An effective résumé has the following elements:

- candidate's name, current address, phone number, and e-mail address;
- educational background, work experience, and other relevant life experiences;
- logical organization;
- clearly labled sections.

Compile a Résumé

Write a résumé to use in a job search. Consider a specific job you would like to pursue. Then, brainstorm for relevant information in your schooling, work experience, including important details and maintaining a professional tone. As you develop your document, experiment with different fonts to create a professional, readable document.

CESAR MORENO
000 Park Avenue
San Marcos, Texas 00000
512-000-0000 • emailaddress@theinternet.com

> Place contact information at the top of the résumé.

EDUCATION
- **Texas State University**, San Marcos, TX
  Bachelor of Science in Education
  Expected: May, 20—
- **Austin High School**, Austin, TX
  Graduated with honors, May, 20—

WORK EXPERIENCE
- **Summer 2008–Summer 2010**
  Camp Lazy J, Fredericksburg, TX
  Camp Counselor: Supervised groups of campers aged 8–12. Served as Lead Counselor in 20– and as Assistant Activities Director in 20–.
- **2009–2010**
  YMCA, Austin, Texas
  Life Guard and Swim Instructor: Guarded weekend free-swim sessions and taught beginning and intermediate youth swim classes.

> The headings *Education, Work Experience*, and so on indicate that this résumé is organized by topic.

> The items under each topic are bulleted and arranged from most to least recent.

VOLUNTEER EXPERIENCE
- **2009–present**
  San Marcos Community Center, San Marcos, TX
  After-School Mentor: Help elementary and middle school students organize and complete schoolwork, develop skills and interests, and resolve personal issues.
- **2008–2009**
  Stepping Up Preschool, Austin, TX
  Teacher's Aide: Assisted in the 3- and 4-year-old classroom; helped plan and execute special summer programs.

ADDITIONAL SKILLS AND CERTIFICATIONS
- CPR certified, 2007 to the present
- Fluent in Spanish
- Proficient in water sports, including rowing, kayaking, and rafting
- Proficient in Microsoft Word, Excel, and PowerPoint
- Completed childcare training course, YMCA, 2007

REFERENCES
Furnished on request.

> A résumé should be no longer than a single page.

Job Search Document: Job Application

Many employers require job applicants to complete a **job application.** A job application is a standard form that asks for particular kinds of information, including the candidate's contact information, education, and work experience.

Complete a Job Application

Consider a part-time job you would like to have. Then, copy and complete the job application shown here using your own information.

Employment Application

PERSONAL INFORMATION

Full Name: Cesar Moreno
Address: 000 Park Ave., San Marcos, TX 00000
Phone Number: (512) 000-0000
E-mail Address: emailaddress@theinternet.com

POSITION AND AVAILABILITY

Position Applied For: Activities Coordinator

EDUCATION

School	Degree/Diploma	Graduation Date
Texas State University	B.S./Education	expected 5/20—
Austin High School	diploma	May, 20—

Additional Skills, Qualifications, Licenses, Training, Awards
CPR and childcare certified, 2007–present Fluent in Spanish

EMPLOYMENT HISTORY

Present/Last Position and Dates: Camp Counselor, Summer 2006–Summer 2009
Employer: Camp Lazy J
Responsibilities: supervised campers aged 8–12
Supervisor: Mr. Smith
May we contact Supervisor? If so, phone number: yes; (512) 000-0000

Previous Position: Lifeguard and Swim Instructor, 2007–2008
Employer: Austin YMCA
Responsibilities: Guarded free-swim sessions; taught youth swim classes
Supervisor: Mrs. Smith
May we contact Supervisor? If so, phone number: yes; (512) 000-0000

Please list additional employment information on a separate sheet of paper.

I certify that the information contained in this application is true and complete.
I authorize the verification of any or all information listed above.

Signature: *Cesar Moreno*
Date: January 15, 20—

Include only relevant information, and condense it to fit the space available.

Get your former supervisor's permission before responding "yes" to this item.

The applicant's signature gives the employer permission to check the information provided.

Business Communications: Business Letter

Business letters are formal letters in which the content is other than personal. Whatever the subject, an effective business letter has the following elements:

- a heading, inside address, salutation or greeting, body, closing, and signature
- one of several acceptable formats, including *block format,* in which each part of the letter begins at the left margin, and *modified block format,* in which the heading, closing, and signature are indented to the center of the page
- formal and courteous language

Write a Business Letter

Choose one of the following purposes and write a business letter to accomplish it. Include heading, inside address, salutation, body, closing, and signature. Use polite and formal language.

- complain about poor service in a restaurant
- accompany a short story you hope to have published
- praise the work of an artist or musician
- gain support for a beautification plan in your community

Bright Orange Lodge
000 Orange Dr.
Orchard, FL 00000

May 1, 20—

Tom Manager, Business Manager
Universal Bank, Inc.
00000 Adams Park Drive
Miami, FL 00000

The inside address includes the name, title, company, and address of the recipient.

Dear Mr. Manager:

I am writing to confirm the reservation you have made for your organization's annual corporate retreat.

Per our phone conversation of April 28, you requested that the Bright Orange Lodge facilities be reserved for Universal Bank, Inc. from Friday, June 10, at 6:00 p.m. to Sunday, June 12, at 3:00 p.m. Facilities are to include the large meeting room, the kitchen, and a block of between 20 and 30 double-occupancy rooms. As we discussed, I anticipate a firm room count from you by the end of this month.

This letter is organized in modified block format.

Per the same conversation, I understand that Universal Bank is planning to use its own caterers for all meals. Should this change, Bright Orange can provide food services in its main dining hall, but we will need advance notice.

A bill for the above-specified services will be sent to your attention under separate cover.

Thank you for choosing Bright Orange for your corporate retreat. If I can be of any further assistance, or if you have any questions, please contact me directly at (352) 000-0000.

Sincerely,
Pat Brown

Pat Brown
Event Coordinator

Business letters end with formal closings, such as *Sincerely* or *Respectfully yours,* followed by the writer's signature and typed name.

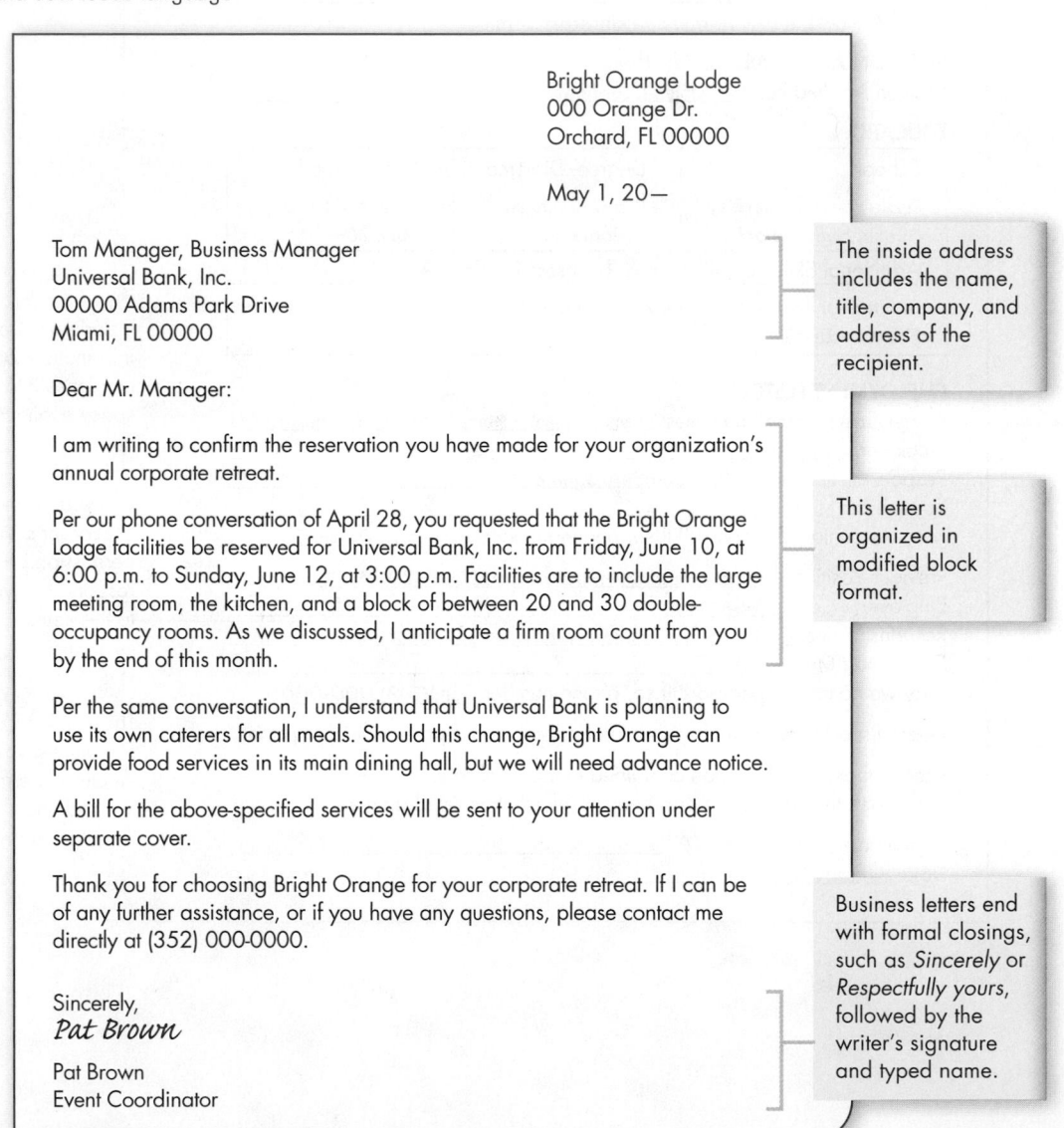

Business Communications: Memo

A **memo**—short for *memorandum*—is a brief printed message between co-workers. It usually focuses on information necessary for the completion of a particular task or project. An effective memo has the following elements:

- block organization, with each new element beginning at the left margin
- sender's name, intended audience, date, and topic
- clear and brief description, including statement of actions required

MEMO

TO: Members of the Corporate Retreat Staff
FROM: Ann Smith, Vice President
DATE: May 11, 20—
RE: PLANNING SESSION

Our annual corporate retreat is fast approaching. To ensure that all aspects of the retreat are coordinated, let's meet this Friday, May 14, at 9:00 a.m. in the second-floor conference room.

We will discuss the following topics, so please be prepared to report the status of your assigned area of responsibility.

- finalized dates, times, and location of the retreat (Tom)
- schedule of sessions and events (Bruno)
- presenters and topics (Yolanda)
- caterers and pricing (Barry)
- employee communications—invitations, RSVPs, etc. (DeShon)

I appreciate the many hours you have already invested in the planning process, and I hope that our meeting on Friday will be brief and productive.

AS

Most memos follow this format: To, From, Date, and Re (Regarding). The word *re:* is Latin for "about." It introduces the subject of the memo.

The body of a memo is brief and informative, and should clearly state a course of action.

Memos are often initialed (either at the conclusion or next to the "FROM" line) in order to indicate that the contents have been approved by the sender.

Business Communications: E-Mail

An **e-mail** is a message sent through an electronic communication system such as a computer network or the Internet. Like a memo, an e-mail may be sent to many recipients at once; however, an e-mail has the added benefit of traveling instantaneously. It can also be used to send an attachment—a file that travels with the e-mail but that must be opened using a separate application. While e-mail messages are often more casual than memos, a workplace e-mail (unlike a personal e-mail) should maintain an appropriately formal tone.

Write a Memo and an E-mail

Choose one of the topics below and write a memo that states the message quickly and efficiently. Then, recast the memo as an e-mail.

- announcement of an upcoming event to members of a club or organization
- reminder to fellow workers in a gift shop about store procedures
- information about a surprise party for a teacher
- details about transportation to a sports competition

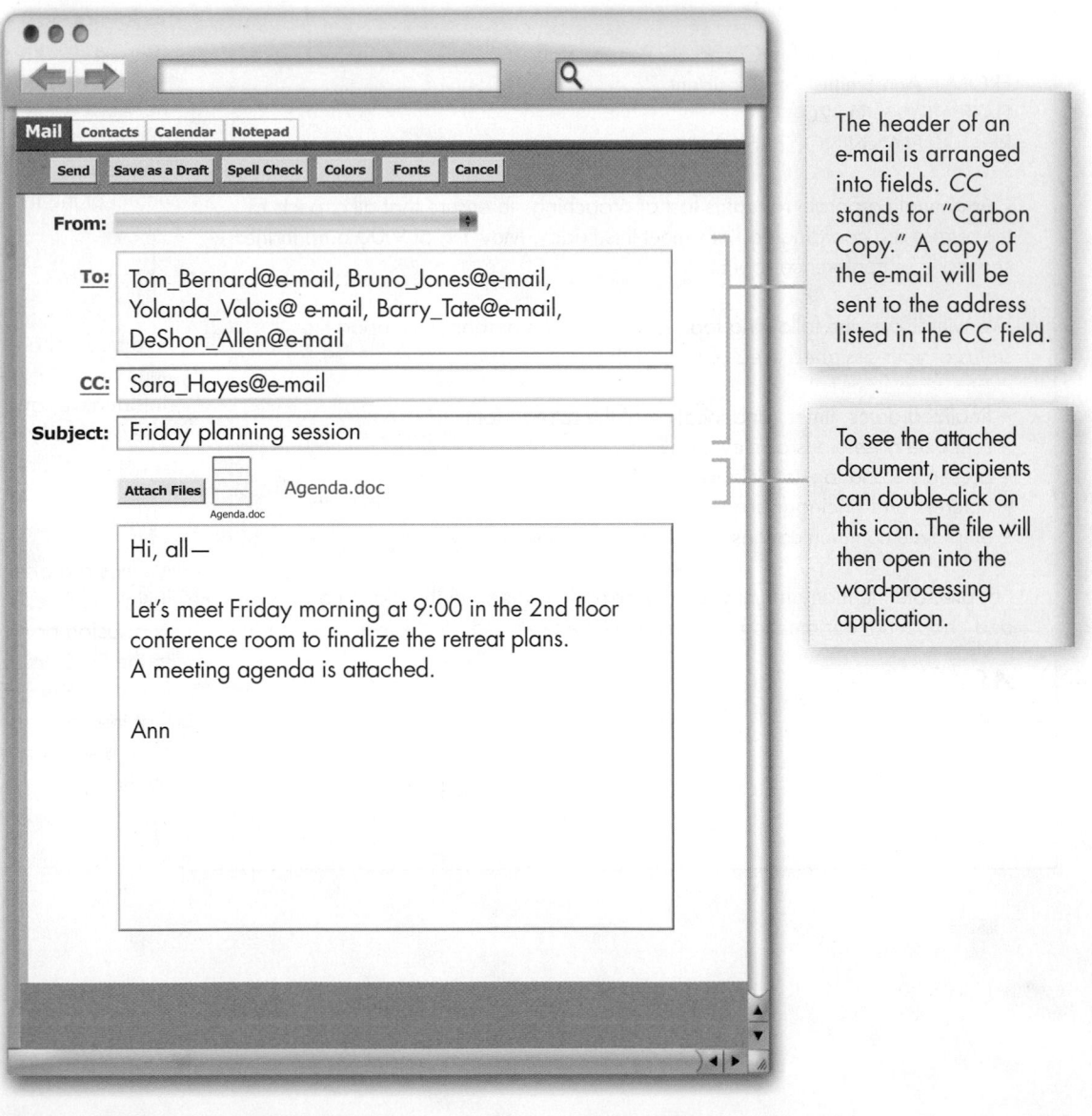

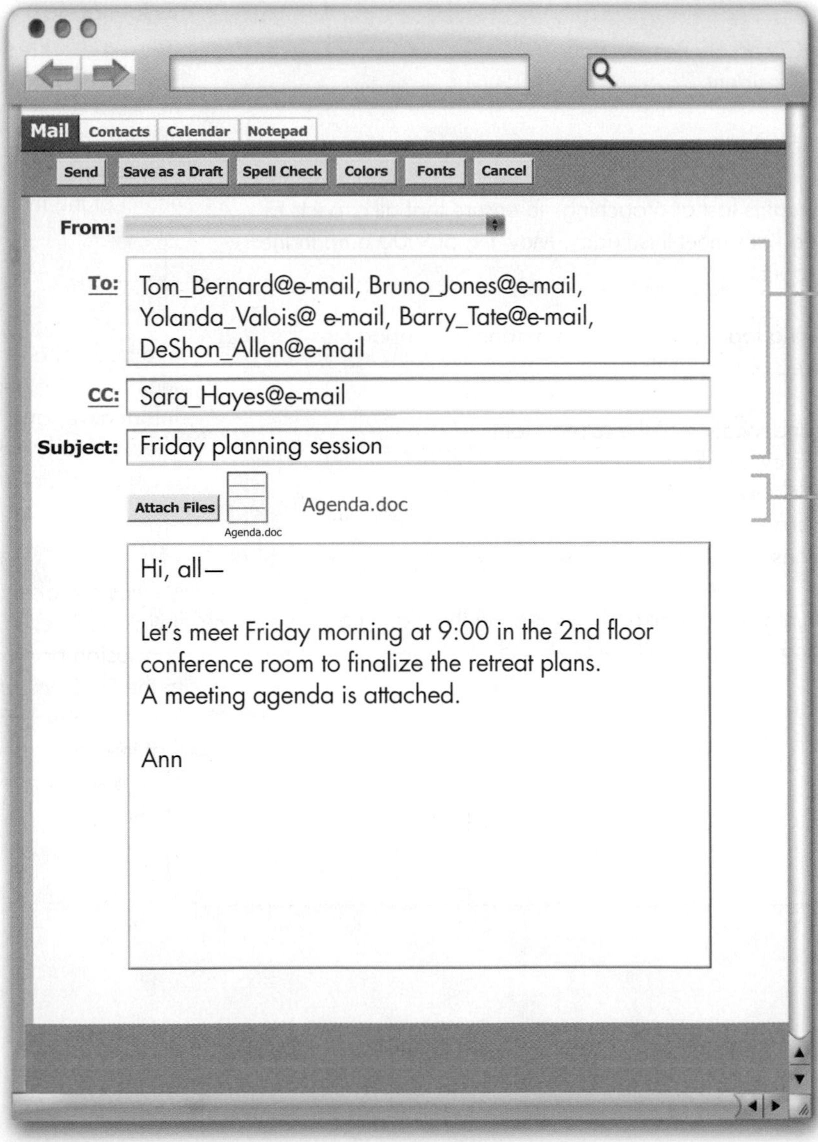

The header of an e-mail is arranged into fields. *CC* stands for "Carbon Copy." A copy of the e-mail will be sent to the address listed in the CC field.

To see the attached document, recipients can double-click on this icon. The file will then open into the word-processing application.

Business Communications: Meeting Minutes

Meeting minutes are notes that tell what transpired at a meeting: what was said, what was decided, and what was left unresolved. Often, the person taking the minutes will jot down abbreviated notes during the meeting, and then rewrite the minutes afterward to distribute to meeting participants.

Write Meeting Minutes

In a small group, conduct a business meeting. Take notes during the meeting. Afterward, write a set of minutes to distribute to your fellow group members.

Meeting to Finalize Corporate Retreat Plans
Friday, May 14, 20–
Main Office, 2nd Floor Conference Room, 9:00 a.m.

The header should include the name of the meeting and its date, location, and time.

Committee Members Present: Ann Smith, Tom Bernard, Yolanda Valois, DeShon Allen
Committee Members Absent: Bruno Jones
Others Present: Sara Hayes, assistant to Ann Smith

Proceedings:
Meeting called to order at 9:00 a.m. by Ann Smith.
Agenda was distributed by Sara Hayes.

First Agenda Item: Retreat dates, times, and location, presented by Tom Bernard.
Tom reported that he has received a letter from Bright Orange Lodge that confirms reservation of their retreat facilities for Universal Bank, Inc. from Friday, June 10, at 6:00 p.m. through Sunday, June 12, at 3:00 p.m. A copy of this letter is attached to the minutes.

These minutes are formatted to show that the meeting followed an agenda.

Second Agenda Item: Schedule of sessions and events, presented by Ann Smith for Bruno Jones.
Bruno is out of the office today, but e-mailed Ann the finalized retreat schedule. Ann distributed copies of the schedule to all members. MOTION to approve schedule; passed unanimously.

A *motion* is a proposal to vote on something. All motions and their results should be carefully noted in meeting minutes.

Assessment of the meeting: Members agreed that the retreat promises to be very successful. Jeff congratulated committee members on a job well done.

Meeting adjourned at 10:05 a.m.
Meeting minutes compiled by Sarah Hayes.

Business Communications: Technical Writing

Technical writing refers to any kind of writing that presents specialized information to help someone perform a task. Scientific reports, troubleshooting guides, assembly instructions, and school handbooks are all examples of technical writing. Although the format varies with the purpose, all technical writing must be clear and easy to use—in other words, "user friendly." It must also be absolutely precise.

Write a Section of a Technical Document

Think of something you know how to do well and write a set of procedures for completing the task. Remember to use specific language that accurately describes the details of the task.

Porterdale Community Library rev. 7/09
Policies and Procedures
Section IV: Collection Maintenance

A page header identifies the publication title, the section, and the revision date.

IV.D. PROCESSING NEW MATERIALS
When new items are delivered to the library, they must be processed, or prepared for use by patrons. The steps for processing a new shipment of items are as follows.

A brief introduction tells the reader what is included in this section.

1. Before unpacking the items:
- **a.** Remove the packing slip from the box.
- **b.** Find the matching order form in the main filing cabinet. Order forms are filed alphabetically by vendor.

2. Unpacking the items:
- **a.** Check each item against both the order form and the packing slip.
- **b.** Place a checkmark on each document next to the title of the item.
- **c.** If all items in the shipment correspond with those on the order form, send the order form and invoice to the business office for payment. The invoice is usually inside the shipment or affixed to the outside in an envelope.
- **d.** If an item is missing or damaged, make a note and/or set the item aside. (See section IV.B. for Ordering and Returning procedures.)

(To process books, see item 3, below. To process other media items, proceed to item 4 on the following page.)

Cross-references and navigational guides are included to help the reader find additional needed information with ease.

3. Processing books:
- **a.** Attach a bar code label to the upper left-hand corner of the front cover.
- **b.** Stamp books with the library name on the front inside cover and back inside cover.
- **c.** Prepare a spine label for books. (See section II.A. for call number designation.) Affix the label to the spine with a label protector.
- **d.** Enter information for the new item into the library catalog database. (See section III.B. for cataloging procedures.)

Guide to Rubrics

What is a rubric?

A rubric is a tool, often in the form of a chart or a grid, that helps you assess your work. Rubrics are particularly helpful for writing and speaking assignments.

To help you or others assess, or evaluate, your work, a rubric offers several specific criteria to be applied to your work. Then the rubric helps you or an evaluator indicate your range of success or failure according to those specific criteria. Rubrics are often used to evaluate writing for standardized tests.

Using a rubric will save you time, focus your learning, and improve the work you do. When you know what the rubric will be before you begin writing a persuasive essay, for example, you will be aware as you write of specific criteria that are important in that kind of an essay. As you evaluate the essay before giving it to your teacher, you will focus on the specific areas that your teacher wants you to master—or on areas that you know present challenges for you. Instead of searching through your work randomly for any way to improve it or correct its errors, you will have a clear and helpful focus on specific criteria.

How are rubrics constructed?

Rubrics can be constructed in several ways.

- Your teacher may assign a rubric for a specific assignment.
- Your teacher may direct you to a rubric in your textbook.
- Your teacher and your class may construct a rubric for a particular assignment together.
- You and your classmates may construct a rubric together.
- You may create your own rubric with criteria you want to evaluate in your work.

How will a rubric help me?

A rubric will help you assess your work on a scale. Scales vary from rubric to rubric but usually range from 6 to 1, 5 to 1, or 4 to 1, with 6, 5, or 4 being the highest score and 1 being the lowest. If someone else is using the rubric to assess your work, the rubric will give your evaluator a clear range within which to place your work. If you are using the rubric yourself, it will help you make improvements to your work.

What are the types of rubrics?

- A holistic rubric has general criteria that can apply to a variety of assignments. See p. R45 for an example of a holistic rubric.
- An analytic rubric is specific to a particular assignment. The criteria for evaluation address the specific issues important in that assignment. See p. R44 for examples of analytic rubrics.

Sample Analytic Rubrics

Rubric With a 4-point Scale

The following analytic rubric is an example of a rubric to assess a persuasive essay. It will help you evaluate focus, organization, support/elaboration, and style/convention.

	Focus	Organization	Support/Elaboration	Style/Convention
4	Demonstrates highly effective word choice; clearly focused on task.	Uses clear, consistent organizational strategy.	Provides convincing, well-elaborated reasons to support the position.	Incorporates transitions; includes very few mechanical errors.
3	Demonstrates good word choice; stays focused on persuasive task.	Uses clear organizational strategy with occasional inconsistencies.	Provides two or more moderately elaborated reasons to support the position.	Incorporates some transitions; includes few mechanical errors.
2	Shows some good word choices; minimally stays focused on persuasive task.	Uses inconsistent organizational strategy; presentation is not logical.	Provides several reasons, but few are elaborated; only one elaborated reason.	Incorporates few transitions; includes many mechanical errors.
1	Shows lack of attention to persuasive task.	Demonstrates lack of organizational strategy.	Provides no specific reasons or does not elaborate.	Does not connect ideas; includes many mechanical errors.

Rubric With a 6-point Scale

The following analytic rubric is an example of a rubric to assess a persuasive essay. It will help you evaluate presentation, position, evidence, and arguments.

	Presentation	Position	Evidence	Arguments
6	Essay clearly and effectively addresses an issue with more than one side.	Essay clearly states a supportable position on the issue.	All evidence is logically organized, well presented, and supports the position.	All reader concerns and counterarguments are effectively addressed.
5	Most of essay addresses an issue that has more than one side.	Essay clearly states a position on the issue.	Most evidence is logically organized, well presented, and supports the position.	Most reader concerns and counterarguments are effectively addressed.
4	Essay adequately addresses issue that has more than one side.	Essay adequately states a position on the issue.	Many parts of evidence support the position; some evidence is out of order.	Many reader concerns and counterarguments are adequately addressed.
3	Essay addresses issue with two sides but does not present second side clearly.	Essay states a position on the issue, but the position is difficult to support.	Some evidence supports the position, but some evidence is out of order.	Some reader concerns and counterarguments are addressed.
2	Essay addresses issue with two sides but does not present second side.	Essay states a position on the issue, but the position is not supportable.	Not much evidence supports the position, and what is included is out of order.	A few reader concerns and counterarguments are addressed.
1	Essay does not address issue with more than one side.	Essay does not state a position on the issue.	No evidence supports the position.	No reader concerns or counterarguments are addressed.

Sample Holistic Rubric

Holistic rubrics are sometimes used to assess writing assignments on standardized tests. Notice that the criteria for evaluation are focus, organization, support, and use of conventions.

Points	Criteria
6 Points	• The writing is strongly focused and shows fresh insight into the writing task. • The writing is organized with a logical progression of ideas. • A main idea is fully developed, and support is specific and substantial. • A mature command of the language is evident. • Sentence structure is varied, and writing is free of all but purposefully used fragments. • Virtually no errors in writing conventions appear.
5 Points	• The writing is clearly focused on the task. • The writing is well organized and generally shows a logical progression of ideas. • A main idea is well developed and supported with relevant detail. • Sentence structure is varied, and the writing is free of unintended fragments. • Writing conventions are followed correctly.
4 Points	• The writing is clearly focused on the task, but extraneous material may intrude at times. • Clear organizational pattern is present, though lapses may occur. • A main idea is adequately supported, but development may be uneven. • Sentence structure is generally fragment free but shows little variation. • Writing conventions are generally followed correctly.
3 Points	• Writing is generally focused on the task, but extraneous material may intrude at times. • An organizational pattern is evident, but writing may lack a logical progression of ideas. • Support for the main idea is generally present but is sometimes illogical. • Sentence structure is generally free of fragments, but there is almost no variation. • The work generally demonstrates a knowledge of writing conventions, with occasional misspellings.
2 Points	• The writing is related to the task but generally lacks focus. • There is little evidence of organizational pattern, and there is little sense of cohesion. • Support for the main idea is generally inadequate, illogical, or absent. • Sentence structure is unvaried, and serious errors may occur. • Errors in writing conventions and spellings are frequent.
1 Point	• The writing may have little connection to the task and is generally unfocused. • There has been little attempt at organization or development. • The paper seems fragmented, with no clear main idea. • Sentence structure is unvaried, and serious errors appear. • Poor word choice and poor command of the language obscure meaning. • Errors in writing conventions and spelling are frequent.
Unscorable	The paper is considered unscorable if: • The response is unrelated to the task or is simply a rewording of the prompt. • The response has been copied from a published work. • The student did not write a response. • The response is illegible. • The words in the response are arranged with no meaning. • There is an insufficient amount of writing to score.

Student Model

Persuasive Writing

This persuasive letter, which would receive a top score according to a persuasive rubric, is a response to the following writing prompt, or assignment:

Write a letter to a government official strongly supporting an environmental issue that is important to you and urging the official to take a specific action that supports your cause.

Dear Secretary of the Interior:

It's a normal carefree day in the forest. The birds are singing and all of the animals are relaxing under the refreshing glow of the sun. But suddenly the thunderous sound of a chainsaw echoes throughout the woodlands, and trees fall violently. The creatures of the forest run in terror. Many of these beautiful creatures will starve to death slowly and painfully as their homes are destroyed, and this precious ecosystem will not be able to regrow to its previous greatness for many years to come.

A descriptive and interesting introduction grabs the reader's attention and shows a persuasive focus.

This sad story is a true one in many places around the globe. We must slow deforestation and replant trees immediately to save our breathable air, fertile soil, and fragile ecosystems.

If entire forests continue to be obliterated, less oxygen will be produced and more CO_2 emitted. In fact, deforestation accounts for a quarter of the CO_2 released into the atmosphere each year: about 1–2 billion tons. Forests provide the majority of the oxygen on earth, and if these forests disappear our air will soon be unbreathable.

Second, deforestation results in a loss of topsoil. Many of the companies who are involved in deforestation claim that the land is needed for farms, but deforestation makes the land much less fertile because it accelerates the process of erosion. According to the UN Food and Agriculture Organization, deforestation has damaged almost 6 million square kilometers of soil.

Finally, if cutting doesn't slow, many species will die off and many ecosystems will be destroyed. The 2000 UN Global Environment Outlook says that forests and rain forests have the most diverse plant and animal life in the world. The GEO also notes that there are more than 1,000 threatened species living in the world's forests. Imagine someone destroying all the houses in your neighborhood and leaving all of the residents homeless. This is how it is for the organisms that live in the forests.

The writer supports the argument with facts and evidence, and also uses the persuasive appeal to the reader's emotions.

In conclusion, deforestation must slow down and trees must be replanted immediately, or we will lose clean air, topsoil, and many precious organisms. Furthermore, a loss in forests will result in a generation that knows very little about nature. So, to prevent the chaotic disturbance of peace in the forests, please do whatever you can to prevent deforestation. Vote YES on any UN bills that would help the condition of our world's forests.

The conclusion restates the argument and presents a call to action.

Sincerely Yours,
Jamil Khouri

21st Century Skills

Changing technology creates new ways to communicate. This handbook provides an overview of some ways you can use today's technology to create, share, and find information. You will find brief descriptions of the following topics in this section:

- ✔ Blogs
- ✔ Social Networking
- ✔ Widgets and Feeds
- ✔ Podcasts
- ✔ Wikis
- ✔ Internet Research Guide

BLOGS

A **blog** is a common form of online writing. The word *blog* is a contraction of *Web log.* Most blogs include a series of entries known as posts. The posts appear in a single column and are displayed in reverse chronological order. That means that the most recent post is at the top of the page. As you scroll down, you will find earlier posts.

Blogs have become increasingly popular. Researchers estimate that 75,000 new blogs are launched every day. Blog authors are often called bloggers. They can use their personal sites to share ideas, experiences, and impressions. Because blogs are designed so that they are easy to update, bloggers can post new messages as often as they like, often daily.

Another key component of blogs is interactivity with their audience. Many blogs allow readers to post their responses by using a comments feature found in each new post. Popular blog entries often inspire extended conversations and debates.

Kinds of Blogs

Not all blogs are the same. Many blogs have a single author, but others are group projects.

Blogs also serve a variety of purposes. Here are some common types of blog:

- Personal blogs often have a general focus. Bloggers post about any topic they find interesting in their daily lives.
- Topical blogs focus on a specific theme, such as movie reviews, political news, class assignments, or health care opportunities.
- Open Forum blogs are open to any Internet user.
- Closed Forum blogs are allowed only to members of a site. Bloggers can further limit readership by giving only invited users full access to their site.

Web Safety

Always be aware of the information you post on the Internet. Remember that whatever information you post can be read by everyone with access to that page. Once you post a picture or text, it can be saved on someone else's computer, even if you later remove it.

Using the Internet safely means keeping personal information personal. Do not post sensitive information. Never include your address (e-mail or real), last name, telephone numbers, or mention places you can be frequently found. Do not give out this information for other people. Never give out passwords you use to access other Web sites and do not respond to e-mails from strangers.

Anatomy of a Blog

Here are some of the features you can include in a blog.

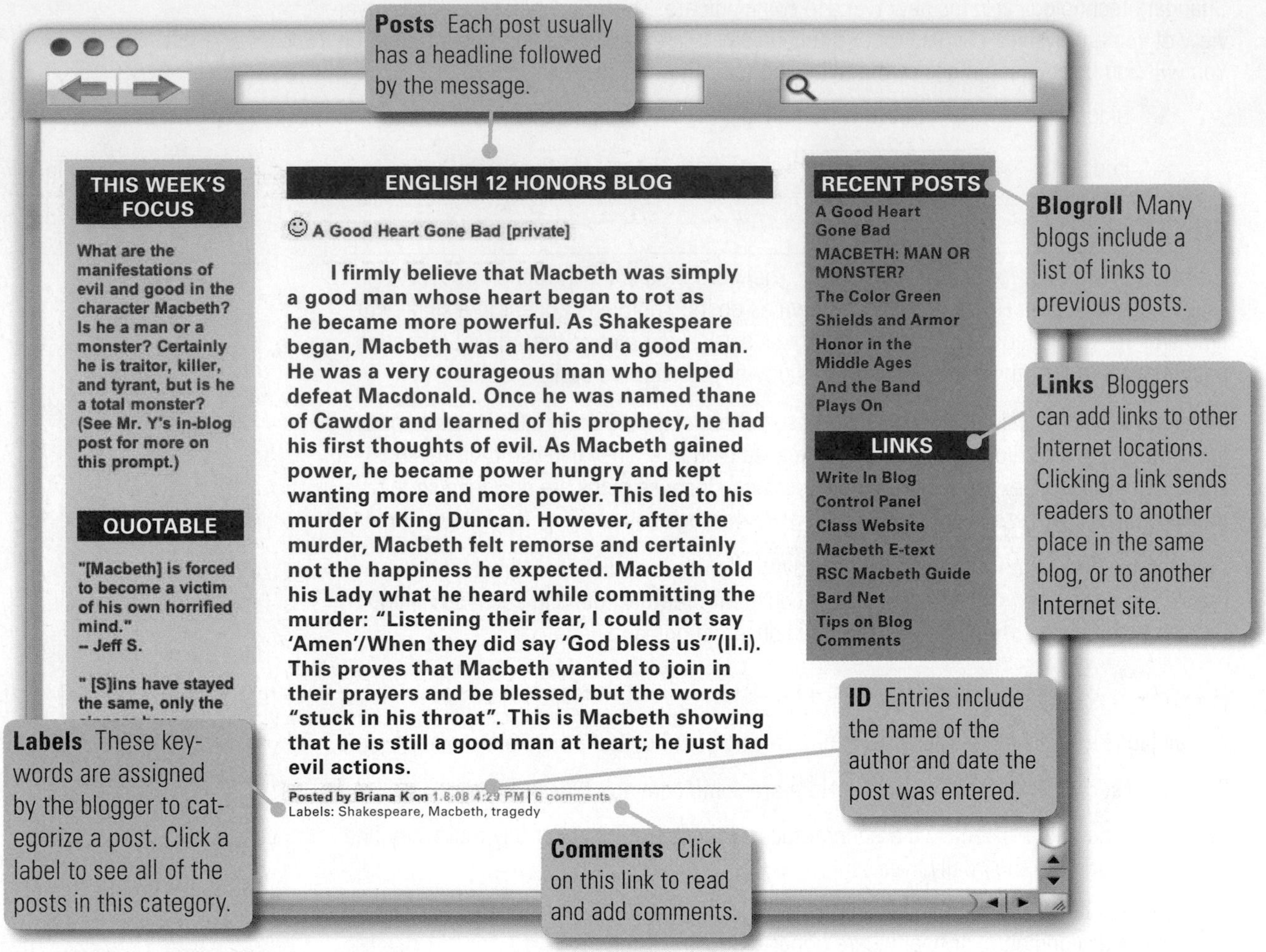

Posts Each post usually has a headline followed by the message.
THIS WEEK'S FOCUS
What are the manifestations of evil and good in the character Macbeth? Is he a man or a monster? Certainly he is traitor, killer, and tyrant, but is he a total monster? (See Mr. Y's in-blog post for more on this prompt.)
QUOTABLE
"[Macbeth] is forced to become a victim of his own horrified mind." – Jeff S.
" [S]ins have stayed the same, only the
ENGLISH 12 HONORS BLOG
A Good Heart Gone Bad [private]
I firmly believe that Macbeth was simply a good man whose heart began to rot as he became more powerful. As Shakespeare began, Macbeth was a hero and a good man. He was a very courageous man who helped defeat Macdonald. Once he was named thane of Cawdor and learned of his prophecy, he had his first thoughts of evil. As Macbeth gained power, he became power hungry and kept wanting more and more power. This led to his murder of King Duncan. However, after the murder, Macbeth felt remorse and certainly not the happiness he expected. Macbeth told his Lady what he heard while committing the murder: "Listening their fear, I could not say 'Amen'/When they did say 'God bless us'"(II.i). This proves that Macbeth wanted to join in their prayers and be blessed, but the words "stuck in his throat". This is Macbeth showing that he is still a good man at heart; he just had evil actions.
Posted by Briana K on 1.8.08 4:29 PM | 6 comments
Labels: Shakespeare, Macbeth, tragedy
RECENT POSTS
A Good Heart Gone Bad
MACBETH: MAN OR MONSTER?
The Color Green
Shields and Armor
Honor in the Middle Ages
And the Band Plays On
LINKS
Write In Blog
Control Panel
Class Website
Macbeth E-text
RSC Macbeth Guide
Bard Net
Tips on Blog Comments
Blogroll Many blogs include a list of links to previous posts.
Links Bloggers can add links to other Internet locations. Clicking a link sends readers to another place in the same blog, or to another Internet site.
ID Entries include the name of the author and date the post was entered.
Labels These key-words are assigned by the blogger to categorize a post. Click a label to see all of the posts in this category.
Comments Click on this link to read and add comments.

Creating a Blog

Like any form of writing, blogging is a form of communication. Keep these hints and strategies in mind to help you create an interesting and fair blog:

- Focus each blog entry on a single topic. If you have two ideas you want to write about, create two separate blog entries. This can help readers find topics that interest them.
- Vary the length of your posts. Sometimes, all you need is a line or two to share a quick thought. Other posts will be much longer.
- Make your main ideas pop out by using clear or clever headlines and boldfacing key terms.
- Use labels to categorize entries, allowing readers to find material that interests them.
- Give credit to other people's work and ideas. Mention the names of people whose ideas you are quoting. You can also add a link that will take readers directly to that person's blog or site.
- If you post comments, try to make them brief and polite. Even if you disagree, state the reasons for your disagreement clearly and without exaggeration.

SOCIAL NETWORKING

Social networking refers to any interaction between members of an online community. People can exchange many different kinds of information, from text and voice messages to video images.

Many social network communities, such as MySpace and Facebook, allow users to create permanent pages that describe themselves. Users create home pages to share ideas about their lives and post messages to other members in the network. Each user is responsible for adding and updating the content on his or her profile page. You can create a social network page for an individual or a group, such as a school or special interest club. Many hosting sites do not charge to register, so you can also have fun by creating a page for a pet or a fictional character.

Here are some features you are likely to find on a social network profile:

- A biographical description, including photographs and artwork.
- Lists of favorite things, such as books, movies, music, and fashions.
- Playable media elements, such as videos and sound recordings.
- Message boards, or "walls," in which members of the community can exchange messages.

Privacy in Social Networks

Social networks allow users to decide how open their profiles will be. Be sure to read introductory information carefully before you register at a new site. Once you have a personal profile page, monitor your privacy settings regularly. Remember that any information you post will be available to anyone in your network.

Users often post messages anonymously or using false names, or pseudonyms. People can also post using someone else's name. Judge all information on the net critically. Do not assume that you know who posted information simply because you recognize the name of the post author. The rapid speed of communication on the Internet can make it easy to jump to conclusions. Be careful to avoid this trap.

Think twice before posting anything on a social networking page or blog. Once you have posted a photo or text, it can be saved on someone else's computer. Even if you remove the material later, the Web user still has a copy. Once another user has your photo, he or she might post it to other sites, or alter it using photo editing software. This practice may not be legal, but many users are not familiar with privacy laws, or choose to ignore them.

In fact, the user might not even be a person. A Web crawler is a computer program that browses the Internet and collects and saves data posted on Web sites. Also known as Web spiders or Web robots, these automated programs might gather information for marketing research or targeted sales.

Tips for Sending Effective Messages

Technology makes it easy to share ideas quickly, but writing for the Internet also poses some special challenges. The writing style for blogs and social networks is usually conversational. In blog posts and comments, instant messages, and e-mails, writers express themselves very quickly, using relaxed language, short sentences, and abbreviations. However, in a conversation, we get a lot of information from a speaker's tone of voice and body language. On the Internet, those clues are missing. As a result, Internet writers sometimes use italics or bracketed labels to indicate emotions. An alternative is using emoticons—strings of characters that give visual clues to indicate emotion:

:-) smile (happy)	**:-(** frown (unhappy)	**;-)** wink (light sarcasm)

Direct Tone	That's just great! That's just great. :-) That's just *great.*
Sarcastic Tone	That's just great. ;-) <sarcasm> That's just great. <end sarcasm>

Here are some additional strategies you can use for communicating effectively when using technology:

- Reread your messages. Before you click **Send,** read your message through and make sure that your tone will be clear to the reader
- Don't jump to conclusions—ask for clarification first. Make sure you really understand what someone is saying before you respond.
- Remember that during chat sessions, messages often cross. As a result, messages may not always refer to the message immediately above. Read carefully to make sure you understand which topic a message refers to. If you're not sure, say so.
- Avoid using ALL CAPS. Many people feel this is like shouting for an entire conversation.

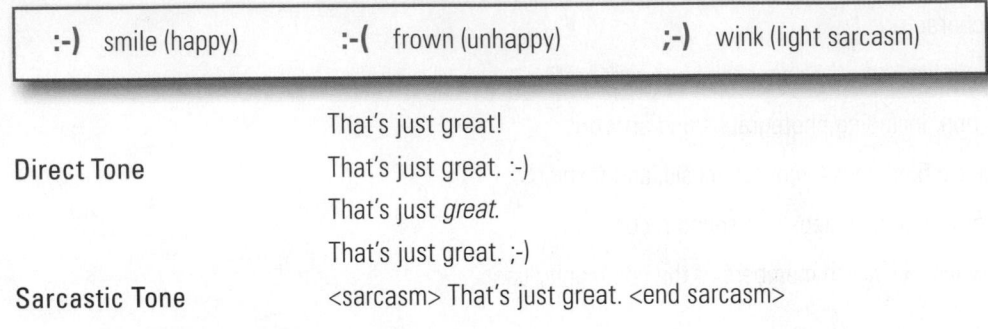

WIDGETS and FEEDS

A **widget** is a small application that can be found on many blogs, social network profiles, and other Web sites. Each widget performs a specific task. You might find widgets that give weather predictions, offer dictionary definitions or translations, or provide entertainment such as games. Other widgets present a new item each day, such as a joke, vocabulary word, sports photograph, brain teaser, or inspirational quotation.

A **feed** is a special kind of widget. It displays headlines taken from the latest content on a specific media source. Clicking on the headline will take you to the full article. Feeds can connect you to the latest news or sports. Feeds are convenient because they automatically send new data to your web page. You get news when it occurs.

Many social network communities and other Web sites allow you to personalize your home page by adding widgets and feeds. Browse through the options available to find the applications that are most useful to you. Be aware that loading widgets onto your page can affect the speed with which your page loads and updates. Test a new widget for one or two sessions—if you do not like the way it performs, simply delete it.

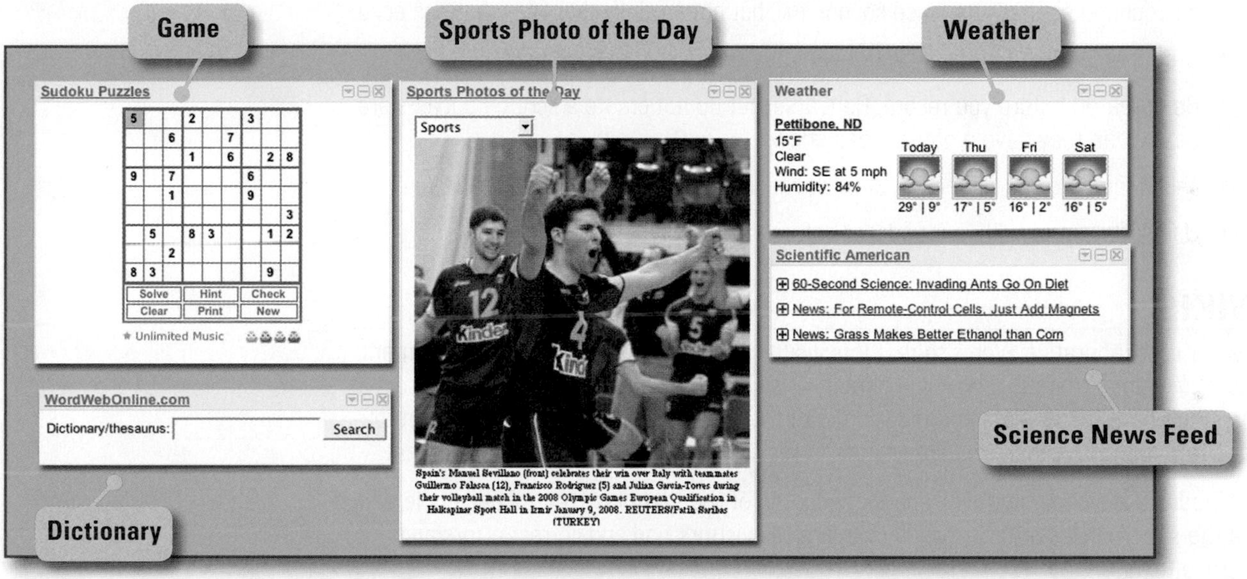

Widget and feeds on a home page.

PODCASTS

A **podcast** is a digital audio or video recording of a program that is made available on the Internet. Users can replay the podcast on a computer, or download and replay it on a personal audio player. You might think of podcasts as radio or television programs that you create yourself. They can be embedded on a Web site or fed to a Web page through a podcast widget.

Creating an Effective Podcast

To make a podcast, you will need a recording device, such as a microphone or digital video camera, as well as editing software. Open source editing software is widely available and free of charge. Most audio podcasts are converted into the MP3 format. Bulleted list of hints and strategies for creating a podcast that is clear and entertaining (such as rehearsing before recording, preparing a time outline, limiting length, and so on).

- Listen to several podcasts by different authors to get a feeling for the medium. Make a list of features and styles you like, as well as those you want to avoid.
- Test your microphone to find the best recording distance. You will stand close to the microphone so that your voice sounds full, but not so close that you create an echo.
- Create an outline that gives your estimated timing for each element.
- Be prepared before you record. Rehearse, but do not create a script. Podcasts are best when they have a natural, easy flow.
- Talk directly to your listeners. Slow down enough so they can understand you.
- Use software to edit your podcast before publishing it.

WIKIS

A **wiki** is collaborative Web site that lets visitors create, add, remove, and edit content. The term comes from the Hawaiian phrase *wiki wiki,* which means "quick." Web users at a wiki are both the readers and the writers of the site. Some wikis are open to contributions from anyone. Others require visitors to register before they can edit the content.

Wikipedia is a well-known wiki encyclopedia. All of the text was created by people who use the site. Articles are constantly changing, as visitors find and correct errors and improve texts.

Wikis have both advantages and disadvantages as sources of information. They are valuable open forums for the exchange of ideas. The unique collaborative writing process allows entries to change over time. However, entries can also be modified incorrectly. Careless or malicious users can delete good content and add inappropriate or inaccurate information.

You can change the information on a wiki, but be sure your information is correct and clear before you add it. Wikis keep track of all changes, so your work will be recorded and can be evaluated by other users.

Wiki users must agree to use the sites responsibly so they can offer accurate information. As with blogs and social networking pages, the informal nature of wikis can lead to trouble. Remember that all information you post to a wiki—including text or images you erase—can not only be seen but also tracked, since all versions of the wiki are saved for security purposes.

USING THE INTERNET FOR RESEARCH

Key Word Search

Before you begin a search, you should identify your specific topic. To make searching easier, narrow your subject to a key word or a group of key words. These are your search terms, and they should be as specific as possible. For example, if you are looking for the latest concert dates for your favorite musical group, you might use the band's name as a key word. However, if you were to enter the name of the group in the query box of the search engine, you might be presented with thousands of links to information about the group that is unrelated to what you want to know. You might locate such information as band member biographies, the group's history, fan reviews of concerts, and hundreds of sites with related names containing information that is irrelevant to your search. Because you used such a broad key word, you might need to navigate through all that information before you could find a link or subheading for concert dates. In contrast, if you were to type in "Duplex Arena and [band name]," you would have a better chance of locating pages that contain this information.

How to Narrow Your Search

If you have a large group of key words and still do not know which ones to use, write out a list of all the words you are considering. Once you have completed the list, scrutinize it. Then, delete the words that are least important to your search, and highlight those that are most important.

These **key search connectors** can help you fine-tune your search:

AND: Narrows a search by retrieving documents that include both terms. For example: ***baseball*** AND ***playoffs***

OR: Broadens a search by retrieving documents including any of the terms. For example: ***playoffs*** OR ***championships***

NOT: Narrows a search by excluding documents containing certain words. For example: ***baseball*** NOT ***history of***

Tips for an Effective Search

1. Remember that search engines can be case-sensitive. If your first attempt at searching fails, check your search terms for misspellings and try again.
2. If you are entering a group of key words, present them in order from the most important to the least important key word.
3. Avoid opening the link to every single page in your results list. Search engines present pages in descending order of relevancy. The most useful pages will be located at the top of the list. However, read the description of each link before you open the page.
4. Some search engines provide helpful tips for specializing your search. Take the opportunity to learn more about effective searching.

Other Ways to Search

Using Online Reference Sites How you search should be tailored to what you are hoping to find. If you are looking for data and facts, use reference sites before you jump onto a simple search engine. For example, you can find reference sites to provide definitions of words, statistics about almost any subject, biographies, maps, and concise information on many topics. Here are some useful online reference sites:

Online libraries
Online periodicals
Almanacs
Encyclopedias

You can find these sources using subject searches.

Conducting Subject Searches As you prepare to go online, consider your subject and the best way to find information to suit your needs. If you are looking for general information on a topic and you want your search results to be extensive, consider the subject search indexes on most search engines. These indexes, in the form of category and subject lists, often appear on the first page of a search engine. When you click on a specific highlighted word, you will be presented with a new screen containing subcategories of the topic you chose.

Evaluating the Reliability of Internet Resources

Just as you would evaluate the quality, bias, and validity of any other research material you locate, check the source of information you find online. Compare these two sites containing information about the poet and writer Langston Hughes:

Site A is a personal Web site constructed by a college student. It contains no bibliographic information or links to sites that he used. Included on the site are several poems by Langston Hughes and a student essay about the poet's use of symbolism. It has not been updated in more than six months.

Site B is a Web site constructed and maintained by the English Department of a major university. Information on Hughes is presented in a scholarly format, with a bibliography and credits for the writer. The site includes links to other sites and indicates new features that are added weekly.

For your own research, consider the information you find on Site B to be more reliable and accurate than that on Site A. Because it is maintained by experts in their field who are held accountable for their work, the university site will be a better research tool than the student-generated one.

Tips for Evaluating Internet Sources

1. Consider who constructed and who now maintains the Web page. Determine whether this author is a reputable source. Often, the URL endings indicate a source.
   - Sites ending in ***.edu*** are maintained by educational institutions.
   - Sites ending in ***.gov*** are maintained by government agencies (federal, state, or local).
   - Sites ending in ***.org*** are normally maintained by nonprofit organizations and agencies.
   - Sites ending in ***.com*** are commercially or personally maintained.
2. Skim the official and trademarked Web pages first. It is safe to assume that the information you draw from Web pages of reputable institutions, online encyclopedias, online versions of major daily newspapers, or government-owned sites produce information as reliable as the material you would find in print. In contrast, unbranded sites or those generated by individuals tend to borrow information from other sources without providing documentation. As information travels from one source to another, it could have been muddled, misinterpreted, edited, or revised.
3. You can still find valuable information in the less "official" sites. Check for the writer's credentials, and then consider these factors:
   - Do not be misled by official-looking graphics or presentations.
   - Make sure that the information is updated enough to suit your needs. Many Web pages will indicate how recently they have been updated.
   - If the information is borrowed, notice whether you can trace it back to its original source.

Respecting Copyrighted Material

Because the Internet is a relatively new and quickly growing medium, issues of copyright and ownership arise almost daily. As laws begin to govern the use and reuse of material posted online, they may change the way that people can access or reprint material.

Text, photographs, music, and fine art printed online may not be reproduced without acknowledged permission of the copyright owner.

Tips for Discussing Literature

As you read and study literature, discussions with other readers can help you understand, enjoy, and develop interpretations of what you read. Use the following tips to practice good speaking and listening skills in group discussions of literature.

- **Understand the purpose of your discussion.**
  Your purpose when you discuss literature is to broaden your understanding and appreciation of a work by testing your own ideas and hearing the ideas of others. Be sure to stay focused on the literature you are discussing and to keep your comments relevant to that literature. Starting with one focus question will help to keep your discussion on track.

- **Communicate effectively.**
  Effective communication requires thinking before speaking. Plan the points that you want to make and decide how you will express them. Organize these points in logical order and cite details from the work to support your ideas. Jot down informal notes to help keep your ideas focused.

  Remember to speak clearly, pronouncing words slowly and carefully so that your listeners will understand your ideas. Also, keep in mind that some literature touches readers deeply—be aware of the possibility of counterproductive emotional responses and work to control them.

- **Make relevant contributions.**
  Especially when responding to a short story or a novel, avoid simply summarizing the plot. Instead, consider *what* you think might happen next, *why* events take place as they do, or *how* a writer provokes a response in you. Let your ideas inspire deeper thought or discussion about the literature.

- **Consider other ideas and interpretations.**
  A work of literature can generate a wide variety of responses in different readers—and that can make your discussions really exciting. Be open to the idea that many interpretations can be valid. To support your own ideas, point to the events, descriptions, characters, or other literary elements in the work that led to your interpretation. To consider someone else's ideas, decide whether details in the work support the interpretation he or she presents. Be sure to convey your criticism of the ideas of others in a respectful and supportive manner.

- **Ask questions and extend the contributions of others.**
  Get in the habit of asking questions to help you clarify your understanding of another reader's ideas. You can also use questions to call attention to possible areas of confusion, to points that are open to debate, or to errors in the speaker's points.

  In addition, offer elaboration of the points that others make by providing examples and illustrations from the literature. To move a discussion forward, summarize and evaluate tentative conclusions reached by the group members.

Oral and Visual Communication

You use speaking and listening skills every day. When you talk with your friends, teachers, or parents, or when you interact with store clerks, you are communicating orally. In addition to everyday conversation, oral communication includes class discussions, speeches, interviews, presentations, debates, and performances. The following terms will give you a better understanding of the many elements that are part of communication and help you eliminate barriers to listening by managing any distractions:

Body language refers to the use of facial expressions, eye contact, gestures, posture, and movement to communicate a feeling or an idea.

Connotation is the set of associations a word calls to mind. The connotations of the words you choose influence the message you send. For example, most people respond more favorably to being described as "slim" rather than as "skinny." The connotation of *slim* is more appealing than that of *skinny.*

Eye contact is direct visual contact with another person's eyes.

Feedback is the set of verbal and nonverbal reactions that indicate to a speaker that a message has been received and understood.

Gestures are the movements made with arms, hands, face and fingers to communicate.

Listening is understanding and interpreting sound in a meaningful way. You listen differently for different purposes.

Listening for key information: For example, when a teacher gives an assignment, or when someone gives you directions to a place, you listen for key information.

Listening for main points: In a classroom exchange of ideas or information, or while watching a television documentary, you listen for main points.

Listening critically: When you evaluate a performance, song, or a persuasive or political speech, you listen critically, questioning and judging the speaker's message.

Medium is the material or technique used to present a visual image. Common media include paint, clay, and film.

Nonverbal communication is communication without the use of words. People communicate nonverbally through gestures, facial expressions, posture, and body movements. Sign language is an entire language based on nonverbal communication. Be aware of your nonverbal communication and make sure that your gestures and facial expressions do not conflict with your words.

Projection is speaking in such a way that the voice carries clearly to an audience. It's important to project your voice when speaking in a large space like a classroom or an auditorium.

Viewing is observing, understanding, analyzing, and evaluating information presented through visual means. You might use the following questions to help you interpret what you view:

- What subject is presented?
- What is communicated about the subject?
- Which parts are factual? Which are opinion?
- What mood, attitude, or opinion is conveyed?
- What is your emotional response?

Vocal delivery is the way in which you present a message. Your vocal delivery involves all of the following elements:

Volume: the loudness or quietness of your voice

Pitch: the high or low quality of your voice

Rate: the speed at which you speak; also called pace

Stress: the amount of emphasis placed on different syllables in a word or on different words in a sentence

All of these elements individually, and the way in which they are combined, contribute to the meaning of a spoken message.

Speaking, Listening, and Viewing Situations

Here are some of the many types of situations in which you apply speaking, listening, and viewing skills:

Audience Your audience in any situation refers to the person or people to whom you direct your message. An audience can be a group of people observing a performance or just one person. When preparing for any speaking situation, it's useful to analyze your audience, so that you can tailor your message to them.

Charts and graphs are visual representations of statistical information. For example, a pie chart might indicate how the average dollar is spent by government, and a bar graph might compare populations in cities over time.

Debate A debate is a formal public-speaking situation in which participants prepare and present arguments on opposing sides of a question, states as a **proposition.**

The two sides in a debate are the *affirmative* (pro) and the *negative* (con). The affirmative side argues in favor of the proposition, while the negative side argues against it. Each side has an opportunity for *rebuttal,* in which they may challenge or question the other side's argument.

Documentaries are nonfiction films that analyze news events or other focused subjects. You can watch a documentary for the information on its subject.

Graphic organizers summarize and present information in ways that can help you understand the information. Graphic organizers include charts, outlines, webs, maps, lists, and diagrams. For example, a graphic organizer for a history chapter might be an outline. A Venn diagram is intersecting circles that display information showing how concepts are alike and different.

Group discussion results when three or more people meet to solve a common problem, arrive at a decision, or answer a question of mutual interest. Group discussion is one of the most widely used forms or interpersonal communication in modern society.

Interview An interview is a form of interaction in which one person, the interviewer, asks questions of another person, the interviewee. Interviews may take place for many purposes: to obtain information, to discover a person's suitability for a job or a college, or to inform the public of a notable person's opinions.

Maps are visual representations of Earth's surface. Maps may show political boundaries and physical features and provide information on a variety of other topics. A map's titles and its key identify the content of the map.

Oral interpretation is the reading or speaking of a work of literature aloud for an audience. Oral interpretation involves giving expression to the ideas, meaning, or even the structure of a work of literature. The speaker interprets the work through his or her vocal delivery. **Storytelling,** in which a speaker reads or tells a story expressively, is a form of oral interpretation.

Panel discussion is a group discussion on a topic of interest common to all members of a panel and to a listening audience. A panel is usually composed of four to six experts on a particular topic who are brought together to share information and opinions.

Pantomime is a form of nonverbal communication in which an idea or a story is communicated completely through the use of gesture, body language, and facial expressions, without any words at all.

Political cartoons are drawings that comment on important political or social issues. Often, these cartoons use humor to convey a message about their subject. Viewers use their own knowledge of events to evaluate the cartoonist's opinion.

Readers theatre is a dramatic reading of a work of literature in which participants take parts from a story or play and read them aloud in expressive voices. Unlike a play, however, sets and costumes are not part of the performance, and the participants remain seated as they deliver their lines.

Role play To role-play is to take the role of a person or character and act out a given situation, speaking, acting, and responding in the manner of the character.

Speech A speech is a talk or address given to an audience. A speech may be **impromptu** or **extemporaneous**—delivered on the spur of the moment with no preparation—or formally prepared and delivered for a specific purpose or occasion.

- ***Purposes:*** the most common purposes of speeches are to persuade, to entertain, to explain, and to inform.
- ***Occasions:*** Different occasions call for different types of speeches. Speeches given on these occasions could be persuasive, entertaining, or informative, as appropriate.

Visual representation refers to informative texts, such as newspapers and advertisements, and entertaining texts, such as magazines. Visual representations use elements of design—such as texture and color, shapes, drawings, and photographs—to convey the meaning, message, or theme.

Grammar, Usage, and Mechanics Handbook

Parts of Speech

Every English word, depending on its meaning and its use in a sentence, can be identified as one of the eight parts of speech. These are nouns, pronouns, verbs, adjectives, adverbs, prepositions, conjunctions, and interjections. Understanding the parts of speech will help you learn the rules of English grammar and usage.

Part of Speech	Definition	Examples
Noun	**Names a person, place, or thing**	
Common	• Names any one of a class of persons, places, or things	writer, country, novel
Proper	• Names a specific person, place or thing	Charles Dickens, Great Britain, *Hard Times*
Pronoun	**Stands for a noun or for a word that takes the place of a noun**	
Personal	• Refers to the person speaking (first person); the person spoken to (second person); or the person, place, or thing spoken about (third person)	I, me, my, mine, we, us, our, ours, you, our, yours, he, him, his, she, her, hers, it, its, they, them, their, theirs, myself, ourselves, yourself, yourselves, himself, herself, itself, themselves
Reflexive	• Names the person or thing receiving an action when that person or thing is the same as the one performing the action	"They click upon *themselves*/ As the breeze rises,…" –Robert Frost
Intensive	• Adds emphasis to a noun or pronoun	"The United States *themselves* are essentially the greatest poem…" –Walt Whitman
Demonstrative	• Singles out specific person(s), place(s), or thing(s)	this, that, these, those
Relative	• Begins a subordinate clause and connects it to another idea in the sentence	that, which, who, whom, whose
Interrogative	• Begins a question	what, which, who, whom, whose
Indefinite	• Refers to a person, place, or thing that may or may not be specifically named	another, everyone, nobody, one, both, few, all, most, none

(Parts of Speech continued)

(continued)

Part of Speech	Definition	Examples
Verb	**Expresses time while showing an action, condition, or the fact that something exists**	
Action	• Tells what action someone or something is performing	gather, read, work, jump, imagine, analyze, conclude
Linking	• Connects the subject with another word that identifies or describes the subject	appear, be, become, feel, look,remain, sound, stay, taste
Helping	• Added to another verb to make a verb phrase	be, do, have, should, can, could, may
Adjective	**Used to describe a noun or pronoun or give it a more specific meaning**	*purple* hat, *happy* face, *this* bowl, *three* cars, *enough* food, *a loud* sound
Adverb	**Modifies a verb, an adjective, or another adverb by telling *where, when, how* or *to what extent***	will answer *soon, extremely* sad, calls *more* often
Preposition	**Relates a noun or pronoun that appears with it to another word in the sentence**	Dad made a meal *for* us. We talked *till* dusk. Bo missed school *because of* his illness.
Conjunction	**Connects words or groups of words**	
Coordinating	• Connects equal words or word groups	bread *and* cheese, brief *but* powerful
Correlative	• Used in pairs to connect equal words or word groups	*both* Luis *and* Rosa, neither you *nor I*
Subordinating	• Indicates the connection between two ideas by placing one below the other in rank or importance	We will miss her *if* she leaves. Hank shrieked *when* he slipped on the ice.
Interjection	**Expresses feeling or emotion**	ah, hey, ouch, well, yippee

Phrases and Clauses

Phrases A **phrase** is a group of words that does not have a subject and verb and that functions as one part of speech.

Prepositional Phrases A **prepositional phrase** is a group of words that includes a preposition and a noun or pronoun.

before dawn **as a result of** the rain

An **adjective phrase** is a prepositional phrase that modifies a noun or pronoun.

Eliza appreciates the beauty of a well-crafted poem.

An **adverb phrase** is a prepositional phrase that modifies a verb, an adjective, or an adverb.

She reads Spenser's sonnets **with great pleasure.**

Appositive Phrases An **appositive phrase** is a noun or pronoun with modifiers, placed next to a noun or pronoun to add information.

Mr. Roth, **my music teacher,** is sick.

Verbal Phrases A **participial phrase** is a participle that is modified by an adverb or an adverb phrase or that has a complement. The entire phase acts as an adjective.

Jenna's backpack, **loaded with equipment,** was heavy.

A **gerund** is a noun formed from the present participle of a verb (ending in *–ing*). A **gerund phrase** is a gerund with modifiers or a complement, all acting together as a noun.

Taking photographs of wildlife **is her main hobby.**

An **infinitive phrase** is an infinitive with modifiers, complements, or a subject, all acting together as a single part of speech.

She tries **to get out into the wilderness often.**

Clauses A **clause** is a group of words with its own subject and verb.

Independent Clauses An independent clause can stand by itself as a complete sentence.

George Orwell wrote with extraordinary insight.

Subordinate Clauses A subordinate clause cannot stand by itself as a complete sentence.

George Orwell, **who wrote with extraordinary insight,** produced many politically relevant works.

An **adjective clause** is a subordinate clause that modifies a noun or pronoun by telling *what kind* or *which one*.

"The Lamb" is the poem **that I memorized for class.**

An **adverb clause** is a subordinate clause that modifies a verb, an adjective, an adverb, or a verbal by telling *where, when, in what way, to what extent, under what condition,* or *why*.

When I recited the poem, Mr. Lopez was impressed.

A **noun clause** is a subordinate clause that acts as a noun.

William Blake survived on **whatever he made as an engraver.**

Sentence Structure

Subject and Predicate A **sentence** is a group of words with two main parts: a *subject* and a *predicate*. Together, these parts express a complete thought.

The **complete subject** tells *whom* or *what* the sentence is about. The **complete predicate** tells what the complete subject of the sentence does or is.

Complete Subject	**Complete Predicate**
Both of those girls	have already read *Macbeth.*

The **simple subject** is the essential noun, pronoun, or group of words acting as a noun that cannot be left out of the complete subject. The **simple predicate** is the essential verb or verb phrase that cannot be left out of the complete predicate.

Simple Subject	**Simple Predicate**
Both of those girls	I **have** already **read** *Macbeth.*

Complements A **complement** is a word or word group that completes the meaning of the predicate. There are five kinds of complements: *direct objects, indirect objects, objective complements, predicate nominatives,* and *predicate adjectives.*

A **direct object** is a noun, a pronoun, or a group of words acting as a noun that receives the action of a transitive verb.

Joseph Addison held important political **posts.**

An **indirect object** is a noun or pronoun that appears with a direct object and names the person or thing that something is given to or done for.

Oxford awarded **Samuel Johnson** an honorary degree. [The direct object is *degree.*]

An **objective complement** is an adjective or noun that appears with a direct object and describes or renames it.

Many consider Shakespeare the greatest **playwright.** [The direct object is *Shakespeare.*]

A **predicate nominative** is a noun or pronoun that appears with a linking verb and tells something about the subject.

"A Modest Proposal" is a **pamphlet.**

A **predicate adjective** is an adjective that appears with a linking verb and describes the subject of the sentence.

"A Modest Proposal" is **satirical.**

Classifying Sentences by Structure

Sentences are often classified according to the kind and number of clauses they contain. The four basic sentence structures are *simple, compound, complex,* and *compound-complex.*

A **simple sentence** consists of one independent clause.

Terrence enjoys modern British literature.

A **compound sentence** consists or two or more independent clauses.

Terrence enjoys modern British literature, but his brother prefers the classics.

A **complex sentence** consists of one independent clause and one or more subordinate clauses.

Terrence, who reads voraciously, enjoys modern British literature.

A **compound-complex sentence** consists of two or more independent clauses and one or more subordinate clauses.

Terrence, who reads voraciously, enjoys modern British literature, but his brother prefers the classics.

Paragraph Structure

An effective paragraph is organized around one **main idea,** which is often stated in a **topic sentence**. The other sentences support the main idea. To give the paragraph **unity**, make sure the connection between each sentence and the main idea is clear.

Usage

Lessons throughout your literature book will help you with many usage problems. See Unit 1 for help with **using coordinating conjunctions** (p. 67) and **using correlative conjunctions** (p. 154). See Unit 2 for help with **using subordinating conjunctions** (p.263) and **using adjective and adverb clauses** (p. 419). In Unit 3 you will find lessons on **comparative and superlative adjectives** and **adverbs** (p. 493), **using participles, gerunds,** and **infinitives** (p. 503), and **misplaced and dangling modifiers** (p. 539). Unit 4 has lessons on the following topics: **introductory phrases** and **clauses** (p. 755), **subject-verb agreement problems** (p. 767), and **pronoun-antecedent agreement problems** (p. 795). See Unit 5 for help with **avoiding shifts in verb tense** (p. 1009) and **using active, not passive, voice** (p. 1085). Go to Unit 6 for lessons on **sentence fragments** and **run-ons** (p. 1151), **transitional expressions** (p. 1169), **using parallel structure** (p. 1207), and **creating sentence variety** (p. 1339).

Unintended Shift in Person

Do not change needlessly from one person to another. Keep the person consistent in your sentences.

Max went to the bakery, but ***you*** can't buy mints there. [shift from third person to second person]

Max went to the bakery, but **he** can't buy mints there. [consistent]

Modifier Placement

To avoid confusion, a modifying word, phrase, or clause should be placed as close as possible to the word or words it is supposed to modify.

My cousin has a ferret **who works in a pet store.** [misplaced modifier]

My cousin, **who works in a pet store,** has a ferret. [correct placement]

Agreement

Subject and Verb Agreement

A singular subject must have a singular verb. A plural subject must have a plural verb.

Dr. Boone uses a telescope to view the night sky.

The **students use** a telescope to view the night sky.

A phrase or clause that comes between a subject and verb does not affect subject-verb agreement.

His **theory,** as well as his claims, **lacks** support.

Two subjects joined by *and* usually take a plural verb.

The **dog** and the **cats are** healthy.

Two singular subject joined by *or* or *nor* must have a singular verb.

The **dog** or the **cat is** hiding.

Two plural subjects joined by *or* or *nor* must have a plural verb.

The **dogs** and the **cats are** coming home with us.

Pronoun and Antecedent Agreement

Pronouns must agree with their antecedents in number and gender. Use singular pronouns with singular antecedents and plural pronouns with plural antecedents.

Doris Lessing uses **her** writing to challenge ideas about women's roles.

Writers often use **their** skills to effect social change.

Use a singular pronoun when the antecedent is a singular indefinite pronoun such as *anybody, each, either, everybody, neither, no one, one,* or *someone.*

Judge **each** of the articles on **its** merits.

Use a plural pronoun when the antecedent is a plural indefinite pronoun (*both, few, many,* or *several*).

Both of the articles have **their** flaws.

The indefinite pronouns *all, any, more, most, none,* and *some* can be singular or plural depending on the number of the word to which they refer.

Most of the books are in **their** proper places.

Most of the *book* has been torn from **its** binding.

Using Verbs

Principal Parts of Regular and Irregular Verbs

A verb has four principal parts:

Present	Present Participle	Past	Past Participle
learn	learning	learned	learned
discuss	discussing	discussed	discussed
stand	standing	stood	stood
begin	beginning	began	begun

Regular verbs such as *learn* and *discuss* form the past and past participle by adding *–ed* to the present form. **Irregular verbs** such as *stand* and *begin* form the past and past participle in other ways. If you are in doubt about the principal parts of an irregular verb, check a dictionary.

The Tenses of Verbs

The different tenses of verbs indicate the time an action or condition occurred.

The **present tense** is most often used to show one of the following:

Present action or condition:	Jamal **hikes** to the lake. The sky **is** clear.
Regularly occurring action or condition:	Tourists **flock** to the site yearly. **I am** usually tired by 9:00.
Constant action or condition:	The earth **orbits** the sun. Pets **are** good for our health.

The **past tense** is used to express a completed action or condition.

The squirrel **dropped** the nut and **ran** up the tree.

The **present perfect tense** is used to express (1) an action or condition that happened at an indefinite time in the past or (2) an action or condition from the past that is continuing into the present.

We **have seen** improvements in the neighborhood.

The puppy **has been** under the bed all day.

The **past perfect tense** shows an action or condition completed before another past action or condition.

Gerard **had revised** his essay before he turned it in.

The **future tense** is used to show a future action or condition.

The Glazers **will visit** us tomorrow.

The future perfect tense is used to show a future action or condition that is completed before another future action or condition.

Mimi **will have painted** the kitchen by the time we finish the shutters.

Using Modifiers

Degrees of Comparison

Adjectives and adverbs take different forms to show the three degrees of comparison: the *positive,* the *comparative,* and the *superlative.*

Positive	Comparative	Superlative
fast	faster	fastest
crafty	craftier	craftiest
abruptly	more abruptly	most abruptly
badly	worse	worst
much	more	most

Using Comparative and Superlative Adjectives and Adverbs

Use comparative adjectives and adverbs to compare two things. Use superlative adjectives and adverbs to compare three or more things.

Jake practices **more often** than Jamal.

Of everyone in the band, Jake practices **most often.**

Using Pronouns

Pronoun Case

The **case** of a pronoun is the form it takes to show its use in a sentence. There are three pronoun cases: *nominative, objective,* and *possessive.*

Nominative	Objective	Possessive
I, you, he, she, it, we, you, they	me, you, him, her, it, us, you, them	my, your, his, her, its, our, their, mine, yours, his, hers, its, ours, theirs

Use the **nominative case** for the *subject* or for a *predicate nominative.*

They are going to the movies. [subject]

The biggest movie fan is **she.** [predicate nominative]

Use the **objective case** for a *direct object,* an *indirect object,* or the *object of a preposition.*

The ending of the play surprised **me.** [direct object]

Mary gave **us** two tickets to the play. [indirect object]

The audience cheered for **him.** [object of preposition]

The **possessive case** is used to show ownership.

The red suitcase is **hers.**

Commonly Confused Words

Diction refers to word choice. The words you choose contribute to the overall effectiveness of your writing. One aspect of diction has to do with choosing between commonly confused words, such as the pairs listed below.

amount, number

Amount refers to quantity or a unit. *Number* refers to individual items that can be counted.

The **amount** of attention that great writers have paid to Faust is remarkable.

A **number** of important English writers have been fascinated by the legend of King Arthur.

bad, badly

Use bad after a linking verb such as *feel, look,* or *seem.* Use *badly* when an adverb is required.

In "My Last Duchess," the duke does not seem to feel **bad** about the death of his wife.

The announcement of Lady Macbeth's death **badly** unnerves Macbeth.

fewer, less

Use *fewer* for things that can be counted. Use *less* for amounts of quantities that cannot be counted.

Wordsworth uses **fewer** end-stopped lines than Pope does.

The prodigal son shows **less** respect for the father than the older son does.

lay, lie

Lay is a transitive verb meaning "to set or put something down." Its principal parts are *lay, laying, laid, laid. Lie* is an intransitive verb meaning "to recline." Its principal parts are *lie, lying, lay, lain.*

Coleridge implies that the mariner's reckless act of killing the albatross **lays** a curse on the crew.

By the end of D.H. Lawrence's story, Paul **lies** dead.

who, whom

Remember to use *who* only as a subject in clauses and sentences and *whom* only as an object.

V.S. Naipaul, **who** wrote "B. Wordsworth," has also written some well-received novels.

V.S. Naipaul, **whom** many critics have praised as one of the best contemporary writers in English, was born and raised in Trinidad.

Editing For English Language Conventions

Capitalization

First Words

Capitalize the first word of a sentence.

Stories about knights and their deeds interest me.

Capitalize the first word of a direct quotation.

Sharon asked, "**D**o you like stories about knights?"

Proper Nouns and Proper Adjectives

Capitalize all proper nouns.

Thames **R**iver　**J**ohn **K**eats　the **R**enaissance

Capitalize all proper adjectives.

Shakespearean play　**D**anish invaders
Elizabethan period　**B**ritish literature

Academic Course Names

Capitalize course names only if they are language courses, are followed by a number, or are preceded by a proper noun or adjective.

Spanish　**H**onors Chemistry　**H**istory 101
geology　**a**lgebra　**s**ocial **s**tudies

Titles

Capitalize titles showing family relationships when they refer to a specific person unless they are preceded by a possessive noun or pronoun.

Uncle Oscar　Mangan's **s**ister　his **a**unt Tessa

Capitalize the first word and all other key words in the titles of books, stories, songs, and other works of art.

Frankenstein　"**S**hooting an **E**lephant"

Punctuation

End Marks

Use a **period** to end a declarative sentence or an imperative sentence.

We are studying the structure of sonnets.

Read the biography of Mary Shelley.

Use periods with abbreviations.

D.H. Lawrence　Mrs. Browning

Use a **question mark** to end an interrogative sentence.

What is Macbeth's fatal flaw**?**

Use an **exclamation mark** after an exclamatory sentence or a forceful imperative sentence.

That's a beautiful painting**!**　Let me go now**!**

Commas

Use a **comma** before the conjunction to separate two independent clauses in a compound sentence.

The game was very close**,** but we were victorious.

Use commas to separate three or more words, phrases, or clauses in a series.

William Blake was a writer**,** artist**,** and printer.

Use a comma after an introductory word, phrase, or clause.

When Grendel was killed**,** his mother sought revenge.

Use commas to set off nonessential expressions.

Old English**,** of course**,** requires translation.

Use commas with places and dates.

Coventry**,** England　September 1**,** 1939

Semicolons

Use a **semicolon** to join closely related independent clauses that are not already joined by a conjunction.

Tanya likes to write poetry; Heather prefers prose.

Use semicolons to avoid confusion when items in a series contain commas.

They traveled to London, England; Madrid, Spain; and Rome, Italy.

Colons

Use a **colon** before a list of items following an independent clause.

Notable Victorian poets include the following: Tennyson, Arnold, Housman, and Hopkins.

Use a colon to introduce an independent clause that summarizes or explains the sentence before it.

Malcolm loves volunteering: He reads to sick children every Saturday afternoon.

Quotation Marks

Use **quotation marks** to enclose a direct quotation.

"Short stories," Ms. Hildebrand said, "should have rich, well-developed characters."

An **indirect quotation** does not require quotation marks.

Ms. Hildebrand said that short stories should have well-developed characters.

Use quotation marks around the titles of short written works, episodes in a series, songs, and titles of works mentioned as parts of collections.

"The Lagoon" "Boswell Meets Johnson"

Italics

Italicize the titles of long written works, movies, television and radio shows, lengthy works of music, paintings, and sculptures.

Howards End *60 Minutes* *Guernica*

For handwritten material, you can use underlining instead of italics.

The Princess Bride Mona Lisa

Dashes

Use **dashes** to indicate an abrupt change of thought, a dramatic interrupting idea, or a summary statement.

I read the entire first act of *Macbeth*—you won't believe this—in less than an hour.

Parentheses

Use **parentheses** to set off asides and explanations when the material is not essential or when it consists of one or more sentences.

He listened intently (it was too dark to see who was speaking) to try to identify the voices.

In the example above, the sentence in parentheses interrupts the larger sentence, so it does not have a capital letter and a period. When a sentence in parentheses falls between two other complete sentences, it should start with a capital letter and end with a period.

The quarterback threw three touchdown passes. (We knew he could do it.) Our team won the game by two points.

Apostrophes

Add an **apostrophe** and an *s* to show the possessive case of most singular nouns and of plural nouns that do not end in *–s* or *–es*.

Blake's poems the mice's whiskers

Names ending in *s* form their possessives in the same way, except for classical and biblical names, which add only an apostrophe to form the possessive.

Dickens's Hercules'

Add an apostrophe to show the possessive case of plural nouns ending in *–s* and *–es*.

the girls' songs the Ortizes' car

Use an apostrophe in a contraction to indicate the position of the missing letter or letters.

She's never read a Coleridge poem she didn't like.

Brackets

Use **brackets** to enclose a word or words you insert in a quotation when you are quoting someone else.

Use brackets to enclose a word or words you insert in a quotation when you are quoting someone else.
Arthur C. Clarke writes about changes in travel: "Over the seas where Odysseus wandered for a decade, the Rome-Beirut Comet [an airplane] whispers its way within the hour."

Ellipses

Use three **ellipses** to indicate where you have omitted words from quoted material.

Wollestonecraft wrote, "The education of women has of late been more attended to than formerly; yet they are still . . . ridiculed or pitied . . . ."

In the example above, the four dots at the end of the sentence are the three ellipses plus the period from the original sentence.

Spelling

Spelling Rules

Learning the rules of English spelling will help you make **generalizations** about how to spell words.

Rules for Spelling with Word Parts

The three word parts that can combine to form a word are roots, prefixes, and suffixes. Many of these word parts come from the Greek, Latin, and Anglo-Saxon languages.

The **root word** carries a word's basic meaning.

Root and Origin	Meaning	Examples
-leg- (-log-) [Gr.]	to say, speak	*leg*al, *log*ic
-pon- (-pos-) [L.]	to put, place	post*pone*, deposit

A **prefix** is one or more syllables at the beginning of a word. A prefix adds to the meaning of the root.

Prefix and Origin	Meaning	Examples
anti- [Gr.]	against	*anti*pathy
inter- [L.]	between	*inter*national
mis- [A.S.]	wrong	*mis*place

A **suffix** is added to the end of a root word and can change the word's meaning or part of speech.

Suffix and Origin	Meaning	Part of Speech
-ful [A.S.]	full of: scorn*ful*	adjective
-ity [L.]	state of being: advers*ity*	noun
-ize (-ise) [Gr.]	to make: idol*ize*	verb
-ly [A.S.]	in a manner: calm*ly*	adverb

Rules for Adding Suffixes to Root Words

When adding a suffix to a root word ending in *y* preceded by a consonant, change *y* to *i* unless the suffix begins with *i*.

ply + -able = pliable   happy + -ness = happiness
defy + -ing = defying   cry + -ing = crying

For a root word ending in *e*, drop the *e* when adding a suffix beginning with a vowel.

drive + -ing = driving   move + -able = movable
SOME EXCEPTIONS: traceable, seeing, dyeing

For root words ending with a consonant + vowel + consonant in a stressed syllable, double the final consonant when adding a suffix that begins with a vowel.

mud + -y = muddy   submit + -ed = submitted
SOME EXCEPTIONS: mixing, reference

Rules for Adding Prefixes to Root Words

When a prefix is added to a root word, the spelling of the root remains the same.

un- + certain = uncertain   mis- + spell = misspell

With some prefixes, the spelling of the prefix changes when joined to the root to make the pronunciation easier.

in- + mortal = immortal   ad- + vert = avert

Orthographic Patterns

Certain letter combinations in English make certain sounds. For instance, *ph* sounds like *f*, *eigh* usually makes a long *a* sound, and the *k* before an *n* is often silent.

pharmacy   n**eigh**bor   ac**k**nowledge

Understanding **orthographic patterns** such as these can help you improve your spelling.

Forming Plurals

The plural form of most nouns is formed by adding *–s* or *–es* to the singular.

computer**s**   gadget**s**   Washington**s**

For words ending in *s, ss, x, z, sh, ch,* add *–es.*

circus**es**   tax**es**   wish**es**   bench**es**

For words ending in *y* or *o* preceded by a vowel, add *–s.*

key**s**   patio**s**

For words ending in *y* preceded by a consonant, change the *y* to an *i* and add *–es.*

cit**ies**   enem**ies**   troph**ies**

For most words ending in *o* preceded by consonant, add *–es.*

echo**es**   tomato**es**

Some words form the plural in irregular ways.

oxen   children   teeth   deer

Foreign Words Used in English

Some words used in English are actually foreign words we have adopted. Learning to spell these words requires memorization. When in doubt, check a dictionary.

sushi   enchilada   au pair   fiancé
laissez faire   croissant

GRAMMAR, USAGE, AND MECHANICS HANDBOOK

Index of Authors and Titles

Note: Page numbers in *italics* refer to biographical information for authors, or commentary on titles or literary and historical issues. Nonfiction and informational text appears in red.

Index of Skills

Boldface numbers indicate pages where terms are defined.

Literary Analysis

Reading for Information

Reading Strategies

Vocabulary

Essential Question Vocabulary

Grammar, Usage and Mechanics

Word Analysis

Writing Applications

Writing Strategies

Prewriting

Drafting

Revising

More Skills . . .

Research and Technology

Speaking, Listening, and Viewing

Test-Taking Practice

Index of Features

Extended Study

Independent Reading,

Integrate and Evaluate Information

Literary Criticism

Literary History

Literature In Context

Reading for Information

Recent Scholarship

Story Behind the Documents

Test-Taking Practice

Themes Across Centuries/ Cultures

Unit Introduction

Vocabulary Workshop

Writing Workshop

Acknowledgments

Grateful acknowledgment is made to the following for copyrighted material:

Aitken Alexander Associates Ltd "B. Wordsworth" from *Miguel Street* by V. S. Naipaul. Copyright © 1959 by V. S. Naipaul. Used with permission of Aitken Alexander Associates Limited.

Anvil Press Poetry Ltd. "Prayer" from *Mean Time* by Carol Ann Duffy. Published by Anvil Press Poetry in 1993. Copyright © Carol Ann Duffy, 1985, 1987, 1990, 1993, 1994. Used by permission of Anvil Press Poetry.

Georges Borchardt, Inc. From "Disappearing Act" by John Lahr from *The New Yorker,* February 12, 2007. Used by permission of Georges Borchardt, Inc.

Professor Geoffrey Bownas "When I went to visit" by Ki Tsurayuki, "Was it that I went to sleep" by Ono Kamachi, "Once cannot ask loneliness" by Priest Jakuren. Copyright © 1964 by Penguin Books, revised edition 1998. Translation copyright © Geoffrey Bownas and Anthony Thwaite, 1964, 1998. Used by permission of Geoffrey Bownas.

Broadway Video "Where's Frankenstein" from a *Saturday Night Live* episode that originally aired on October 28, 2006, hosted by Hugh Laurie. Copyright © 2006 NBC Studios, Inc. Distributed by Broadway Video Enterprises. Courtesy of Broadway Video Enterprises and NBC Studios, Inc.

Curtis Brown London "Be Ye Men of Valor" (retitled "Wartime Speech"), BBC London, May 19, 1940, from *Blood, Toil, Tears and Sweat: The Speeches of Winston Churchill* edited and with an introduction by David Cannadine. Speeches Copyright © 1989 by Winston Churchill. Used courtesy of Curtis Brown Ltd. on behalf of The Estate of Winston Churchill.

California State Parks Jack London State Historic Park brochure, copyright © 2001 California State Parks. Used by permission of California State Parks.

Cambridge University Press, NY Excerpt from "Letter to Thomas Flower Ellis from Thomas Babington Macaulay on the Passing of the Reform Bill" written in 1831, from *The Selected Letters of Thomas Babington Macaulay,* ed. Thomas Pinney, 5 vols. Used with the permission of Cambridge University Press.

Citysearch.com "A Thoughtful, Poignant, and Chilling Macbeth" October 7, 1999 from *www.shakespearefest.org/macbeth_99.htm#Reviews.* Copyright © Citysearch.com. Citysearch is a registered trademark of Bluefoot Ventures, Inc. and is used under license. Used by permission of Citysearch.com.

Arthur C. Clarke "Extra-Terrestrial Relays" by Arthur C. Clarke from *Wireless World,* October 1945, pp 305-308 © 1945. Used by permission of the author and the author's agents, Scovil Chichak Galen Literary Agency, Inc.

Jonathan Clowes Ltd. "No Witchcraft for Sale," from *African Short Stories* by Doris Lessing. Copyright © 1981 Doris Lessing. Used by kind permission of Jonathan Clowes, Ltd., London, on behalf of Doris Lessing.

Copyright Clearance Center, Inc. for Hearst Communications, Inc. 'Kingdom of Desire' a sensual 'Macbeth' remake Peking opera style" by Robert Hurwitt from San Francisco Chronicle, May 23, 2005, *www.sfgate.com/cgi-bin/article.cgi?f=/c/a/2005/05/23/DDG9LCSI0H1.DTL&hw=kingdom+of+desire&sn=002&sc=981.* Copyright © 2005 by San Francisco Chronicle. Reproduced with permission of San Francisco Chronicle via Copyright Clearance Center.

Cumbria County Council Table of Traffic Flow at Waterhead, Ambleside. A591 from *Transport and Policies 1999/2000, and Local Transport Plan 2001/2–2005/6.* Copyright © Cumbria County Council. Used by permission of Cumbria County Council.

The Charles Dickens Museum Charles Dickens Museum in London Homepage & Online Tour retrieved from *http://www.dickensmuseum.com.* Copyright © 2005 Charles Dickens Museum. Reproduced courtesy of The Charles Dickens Museum, London.

Dorling Kindersley Ltd. "Lancashire and the Lakes" from *DK Eyewitness Travel Guides: Great Britain* by Michael Leapman. Copyright © 1995, 2001 Dorling Kindersley Limited, London. Reproduced by permission of Dorling Kindersley Ltd.

Dutton Signet From *Beowulf* by Burton Raffel, translator. Translation copyright © 1963, renewed © 1991 by Burton Raffel. Used by permission of Dutton Signet, a division of Penguin Group (USA) Inc.

Encyclopædia Britannica Search results: Anglo-Saxon Poetry from *http://search.eb.com/search?query=anglo+saxon+poetry&x=0&y=0.* "English Literature: The Old English Period: Poetry: The major manuscripts" from *http://search.eb.com/eb/article-12747.* Copyright © 2007 by Encyclopædia Britannica. Used with permission from Encyclopædia Britannica, Inc.

Faber and Faber Limited "Journey of the Magi" from *Collected Poems 1909–1962* by T. S. Eliot, copyright 1936, copyright © 1964, 1963 by T. S. Eliot. "The Horses" from *New Selected Poems* by Ted Hughes. Copyright © 1957, 1960 by Ted Hughes. Published in the UK in The Hawk in the Rain by Ted Hughes. "Follower" from *Poems 1965–1975* by Seamus Heaney. Copyright © 1980 by Seamus Heaney. "The Hollow Men" from *Collected Poems 1909–1962* by T. S. Eliot, copyright 1936 and renewed 1964, 1963 by T. S. Eliot. "Two Lorries" from *The Spirit Level* by Seamus Heaney. Copyright © 1996 by Seamus Heaney. "The Explosion" from *Collected Poems* by Philip Larkin. Copyright © 1988, 1989 by the Estate of Philip Larkin. "An Arundel Tomb" from *Collected Poems* by Philip Larkin. Copyright © 1988, 1989 by the Estate of Philip Larkin. "That's All" from *Complete Works: Three* by Harold Pinter. Copyright © 1966 by H. Pinter Ltd. "Not Palaces" by Stephen Spender. From *Collected Poems 1928–1985.* Copyright © 1986 by Stephen Spender. Copyright © 1934 by The Modern Library, Inc. and renewed 1962, 1964, 1986 by Stephen Spender. Used by permission of Faber and Faber.

Farrar, Straus & Giroux, LLC "Follower" from *Poems 1965–1975* by Seamus Heaney. Copyright © 1980 by Seamus Heaney. "The Horses" from *Collected Poems* by Ted Hughes. Copyright © 2003 by The Estate of Ted Hughes. "Two Lorries" from *The Spirit Level* by Seamus Heaney. Copyright © 1996 by Seamus Heaney. "The Explosion" from *Collected Poems* by Philip Larkin. Copyright © 1988, 1989 by the Estate of Philip Larkin. "An Arundel Tomb" from *Collected Poems* by Philip Larkin. Copyright © 1988, 1989 by the Estate of Philip Larkin. "Chapter XXVIII, Part I" from *Omeros* by Derek Walcott. Copyright © 1990 by Derek Walcott. "Midsummer XXIII" from *Collected Poems 1948–1984* by Derek Walcott. Copyright © 1986 by Derek Walcott. Used by permission of Farrar, Straus and Giroux, LLC.

Florida Department of Environmental Protection Marjorie Kinnan Rawlings Historic State Park Brochure from *http://www.floridastateparks.org/marjoriekinnanrawlings/docs/brochure.pdf.* Printed 02/07. Used by permission of Florida Department of Environmental Protection.

Fondo de Cultura Economica From *The Nine Guardians* by Rosario Castellanos, translated by Irene Nicholson. Balún Canán de Rosario Castellanos. D.R. © 1957 Fondo de Cultura Economica. Carretera Picacho-Ajusco 227, C.P. 14200, Mexico, D.F. Used by permission of Fondo de Cultura Económica.

Professor Norman Gash "The case for parliamentary reform: 1831: Lord John Russell: 1 March 1831" by Lord John Russell from *The Age of Peel* by Norman Gash (London, Edward Arnold, 1973) *www.dialspace.dial.pipex.com/town/terrace/adw03/peel/refact/refbill.htm.* Copyright © Norman Gash. "A conservative criticism of parliamentary reform: 1831" by Sir Robert Peel, 2nd Baronet from *The Age of Peel* by Norman Gash (London, Edward Arnold, 1973) *www.dialspace.dial.pipex.com/town/terrace/adw03/peel/refact/refpeel.htm.* Copyright © Norman Gash. Used by permission of Norman Gash.

Greater London Authority From *The Mayor's Annual Report 2004* from *http://www.london.gov.uk/mayor/annual_report/docs/ann_rpt_2004.pdf.* Copyright April 2004, Greater London Authority. Used by permission.

Grove/Atlantic, Inc. "That's All" from *Complete Works: Three* by Harold Pinter. Copyright © 1966 by H. Pinter Ltd. "Come and Go" from Collected Shorter Plays by Samuel Beckett. Copyright © 1968, 1984 by Samuel Beckett. "Next Term We'll Mash You" from *Pack of Cards* by Penelope Lively. Copyright © 1978, 1980 1981, 1982, 1984, 1985, 1986 by Penelope Lively. Used by permission of Grove/Atlantic, Inc.

Grove/Atlantic, Inc. From *Pedro Paramo* by Juan Rulfo, translated by Margaret Sayers Peden. Originally published in Mexico in 1955. English translation by Margaret Sayers Peden. Copyright © 1994 by Northwestern University Press.

J.C. Hall "Vergissmeinnicht" by Keith Douglas from *The Complete Poems of Keith Douglas,* Faber and Faber Ltd. Used by permission of Faber and Faber Ltd. and J.C. Hall.

Harcourt, Inc. Excerpt from *Mrs. Dalloway* by Virginia Woolf, copyright 1925 by Harcourt, Inc. and renewed 1953 by Leonard Woolf. Used by permission of the publisher. "The Hollow Men" from Collected Poems 1909–1962 by T. S. Eliot, copyright 1936 by Harcourt, Inc. and renewed 1964 by T. S. Eliot. "The Lady in the Looking Glass: A Reflection" from *A Haunted House and Other Short Stories* by Virginia Woolf, copyright 1944 and renewed 1972 by Harcourt, Inc. "Shooting an Elephant" from *Shooting an Elephant and Other Essays* by George Orwell, copyright 1950 by Sonia Brownell Orwell and renewed 1978 by Sonia Pitt-Rivers. "Journey of the Magi" from *Collected Poems 1909–1962* by T. S. Eliot, copyright 1936 by Harcourt Brace & Company, copyright © 1964, 1963 by T. S. Eliot. "Charles Baudelaire: L'Invitation au Voyage" from *Things of This World,* copyright © 1956 and renewed 1984 by Richard Wilbur. From A Room of One's Own by Virginia Woolf, copyright 1929 by Harcourt, Inc. and renewed 1957 by Leonard Woolf. Used by permission of the publisher. This material may not be reproduced in any form or by any means without the prior written permission of the publisher.

HarperCollins Publishers, Inc. "A Devoted Son" from *Games at Twilight and Other Stories* by Anita Desai. Copyright © 1978 by Anita Desai. Used by permission of HarperCollins Publishers, Inc.

HarperCollins Publishers, Ltd. UK "Post-Script: For Gweno" from *Raiders' Dawn and Other Poems* by Alun Lewis. First published in March, 1942. Second Impression June, 1942. Third Impression August, 1942. Fourth Impression October, 1943. Fifth Impression 1945. Reprinted 1946. Copyright © Alun Lewis. Used by permission of HarperCollins Publishers Ltd.

A.M. Heath & Company Limited "Shooting an Elephant" from *Shooting an Elephant and Other Essays* by George Orwell. Copyright © George Orwell, 1936. Used by permission of Bill Hamilton as the Literary Executor of the Estate of the Late Sonia Brownell Orwell and Secker & Warburg Ltd.

David Higham Associates Limited "On the Patio" from *Poems 1954–1987* by Peter Redgrove. Copyright © Peter Redgrove, 1959, 1961, 1963, 1966, 1972, 1973, 1975, 1977, 1979, 1981, 1985, 1986, 1987. "A Shocking Accident" from *Collected Stories of Graham Greene* by Graham Greene. Copyright © 1957 by Graham Greene. "In the Kitchen" from *Redgrove's Wife* by Penelope Shuttle. First published 2006 by Bloodaxe Books Ltd. Copyright © Penelope Shuttle 2006. "from Faust" from *Goethe's Faust: Parts I and II* by Louis Macneice. Originally published by Faber and Faber Limited. "Next Term We'll Mash You" from Pack of Cards by Penelope Lively. Copyright © 1978, 1980 1981, 1982, 1984, 1985, 1986 by Penelope Lively. Used by permission of David Higham Associates.

Hughes Network Systems, LLC "Satellite Network Keeps Florida Communicating During Emergencies" from *http://www.hughes.com/HUGHES/Doc/0/P6KO209FSOKK3E3H417TPTVSD6/florida_emergency.pdf.* Used by permission of Hughes Network Systems, LLC, www.hughes.com.

Johnson & Alcock Ltd. (formerly John Johnson Ltd.) "I have visited again" by Alexander Pushkin. Copyright © *The Bronze Horseman: Selected Poems of Alexander Pushkin,* translated by D.M. Thomas, Secker & Warburg UK 1981/Viking US 1982. Used by permission of Johnson & Alcock Ltd.

Alfred A. Knopf, Inc. "The Demon Lover" from *The Collected Stories of Elizabeth Bowen* by Elizabeth Bowen, copyright © 1981 by Curtis Brown Ltd., Literary Executors of the Estate of Elizabeth Bowen. Used by permission of Alfred A. Knopf, a division of Random House, Inc.

Lake District National Park Authority Education Service Tracking Management from *Education Service Traffic Management.* Copyright © Lake District National Park Authority. Used by permission of Lake District National Park Authority.

Barbara Levy Literary Agency "Wirers" from *Collected Poems Of Siegfried Sasson* by Siegfried Sassoon, copyright 1918, 1920 by E. P. Dutton. Used by kind permission of George Sassoon.

MARTA Metropolitan Atlanta Rapid Transit Authority Map and Schedule" from *www.itsmarta.com/getthere/schedules/index-rail.htm.* Copyright © 2004 MARTA. All rights reserved. Used by permission of MARTA.

Metropolitan Transportation Authority Go Metro Map and Metro Red Line East Schedule from *www.mta.net/riding_metro/riders_guide/planning_trip.htm.* Copyright © 2007 LACMTA. Used by permission of Metropolitan Transportation Authority.

Michelin Travel Publications "Tintern Abbey" by Staff from *The Green Guide.* Copyright © Michelin et Cie, proprietaires-editeurs. Used by permission of Michelin Travel Publications.

William Morrow & Company, Inc. From *Neverwhere* by Neil Gaiman. Copyright © 1996, 1997 by Neil Gaiman. Used by permission of HarperCollins Publishers.

NASA Johnson Space Center "Anticipating Earthquakes" by Patrick L. Barry from *www.nasa.gov/vision/earth/environment/earthquakes_prt.htm.* Copyright © National Aeronautics and Space Administration.

The National Archives of the UK "Government Evacuation Scheme (Source 1)" from *Learning Curve: The National Archives of the UK.* www.learningcurve.gov.uk/homefront/evacuation/britain/source1.htm. "The Interrogation of Don Lewes from Cordoba in Andalucia, Simplified Transcript (Source 4)" by from Learning Curve: The National Archives of the UK *www.learningcurve.gov.uk/snapshots/snapshot39/39_images_am/39_trans/SP63_1137Am4_pg1_simp.htm.*

New Beacon Books Ltd. "Time Removed" from *Fractured Circles* by James Berry, published by New Beacon Books Ltd. Copyright © 1979, James Berry. "Freedom" from *Fractured Circles* by James Berry, published by New Beacon Books Ltd. Copyright © 1979, James Berry. From "Lucy: Englan' Lady" from *Lucy's Letter and Loving* by James Berry. Copyright © 1982 by James Berry. First published by New Beacon Books Ltd. in 1982. Used by permission of New Beacon Books, Ltd

New Directions Publishing Corporation "Do Not Go Gentle Into That Good Night" by Dylan Thomas, from *The Poems of Dylan Thomas.* Copyright © 1952 by Dylan Thomas. "Anthem for Doomed Youth" by Wilfred Owen, from *The Collected Poems Of Wilfred Owen,* copyright © 1963 by Chatto & Windus, Ltd. "Jade Flower Palace" by Tu Fu, translated by Kenneth Rexroth from *One Hundred Poems from The Chinese.* Copyright © 1971 by Kenneth Rexroth. "Not Waving But Drowning" by Stevie Smith, from *Collected Poems of Stevie Smith,* copyright © 1972 by Stevie Smith. "Fern Hill" by Dylan Thomas, from *The Poems of Dylan Thomas,* copyright © 1945 by The Trustees for the Copyrights of Dylan Thomas. Used by permission of New Directions Publishing Corp.

The New York Times Agency c/o PARS International "The Scottish Play, Told With Sound and Fury and Puppets" by Lawrence Van Gelder from The New York Times Arts & Culture Section, 4/26/2007 Issue, Page E5, *http://theater2.nytimes.com/2007/04/26/theater/reviews/26macb.html?pagewanted=print. Copyright* © 2007 The New York Times. All rights reserved. Used by permission and protected by the Copyright Laws of the United States. The printing, copying, redistribution, or retransmission of the Material without express written permission is prohibited. www.nytimes.com.

W. W. Norton & Company, Inc. "Outside History" from *Outside History: Selected Poems, 1980–1990* by Eavan Boland. Copyright © 1990 by Eavan Boland. "The Inferno: Canto XXXIV", from *The Divine Comedy* by Dante Alighieri, translated by John Ciardi. Copyright 1954, 1957, 1959, 1960, 1961, 1965, 1967, 1970 by the Ciardi Family Publishing Trust. From *Sir Gawain And The Green Knight: A New Verse Translation* by Marie Borroff, translator. Copyright © 1967 by W.W. Norton & Company, Inc. Used by permission of W.W. Norton & Company, Inc.

The Flannery O'Connor-Andalusia Foundation Andalusia: Home of Flannery O'Connor brochure. Used courtesy of Flannery O'Connor-Andalusia Foundation.

Jen O'Leary "Weather in the Palm of Your Hand" by Jennifer O'Leary, University of Wisconsin-Madison Space Science and Engineering Center from *www.ssec.wisc.edu/media/features/jan10_06.htm.* Used by permission of the author.

Oxford University Press, Inc. "The Wanderer," from *An Anthology of Old English Poetry,* edited and translated by Charles W. Kennedy. Copyright © 1960 by Oxford University Press, Inc. Used by permission of Oxford University Press, Inc.

Oxford University Press, UK "The Naming of Parts," from *A Map of Verona* by Henry Reed, 1946, copyright © by Henry Reed. Used by permission of Oxford University Press, UK.

Oxford University Press, UK "To Lucasta, Going To the Wars" from *The Poems Of Richard Lovelace,* edited by C.H. Wilkinson, copyright © 1953. "To the Virgins, to Make Much of Time" from The Poems of Robert Herrick, edited by L.C. Martin.

Penguin Books Ltd., London "The Wife of Bath's Tale" from *The Canterbury Tales* by Geoffrey Chaucer, translated by Nevill Coghill (Penguin Classics 1951, Fourth revised edition 1977). Copyright 1951 by Nevill Coghill. Copyright © the Estate of Nevill Coghill, 1958, 1960, 1975, 1977. From *A History of The English Church and People* by Bede (pp 37-40), translated by Leo Sherley-Price, revised by R.E. Latham (Penguin Classics 1955, Revised edition 1968). Copyright © Leo Sherley-Price, 1955, 1968. "Prologue" from *The Canterbury Tales* by Geoffrey Chaucer, translated by Nevill Coghill (Penguin Classics 1951, Fourth revised edition 1977). Copyright 1951 by Nevill Coghill. Copyright © the Estate of Nevill Coghill, 1958, 1960, 1975, 1977. "Pardoner's Tale" from *The Canterbury Tales* by Geoffrey Chaucer, translated by Nevill Coghill (Penguin Classics 1951, Fourth revised edition 1977). Copyright 1951 by Nevill Coghill. Copyright © the Estate of Nevill Coghill, 1958, 1960, 1975, 1977. From *The Decameron* by Giovanni Boccaccio, translated with an introduction and notes by G. H. McWilliam (Penguin Classics 1972, Second Edition 1995). Copyright © G. H. McWilliam, 1972, 1995. "Next Term We'll Mash You" from Pack of Cards by Penelope Lively. Copyright © 1978, 1980 1981, 1982, 1984, 1985, 1986 by Penelope Lively. Used by permission of Penguin Group Ltd., UK.

Random House, Inc. "In Memory of W. B. Yeats", copyright 1940 & renewed 1968 by W.H. Auden from *Collected Poems* by W.H. Auden. "Musee des Beaux Arts", copyright 1940 & renewed 1968 by W.H. Auden from *Collected Poems* by W.H. Auden. Used by permission of Random House, Inc. "Home" by Anton Chekhov from *Modern Library,* copyright © 1999 by Random House, Inc.

Riverbend From "Baghdad Burning" by Riverbend (baghdad.burning@gmail.com)from *The Great Wall of Segregation…, http://riverbendblog.blogspot.com,* April 26, 2007.

Riverhead Books, an imprint of Penguin Group (USA) Inc. "I'm Like a Bird" from *Songbook* by Nick Hornby, copyright © 2002 by Nick Hornby. Used by permission of Riverhead Books, an imprint of Penguin Group (USA) Inc.

Rogers, Coleridge & White Ltd. "A Devoted Son" from *Games at Twilight and Other Stories* by Anita Desai. Copyright © 1978 Anita Desai. Reproduced by permission of the author c/o Rogers, Coleridge & White Ltd., 20 Powis Mews, London W11 1JN.

Russell & Volkening, Inc. "The Train from Rhodesia" from *Selected Stories* by Nadine Gordimer. Copyright © 1950 by Nadine Gordimer, renewed in 1978 by Nadine Gordimer. Used by the permission of Russell & Volkening as agents for the author.

Scovil Chichak Galen Literary Agency, Inc. "We'll Never Conquer Space" by Arthur C. Clarke, from *Science Digest,* June 1960. Copyright © 1960 by Popular Mechanics Company. Used by permission of the author and the author's agents, Scovil Chichak Galen Literary Agency, Inc.

Scribner, an imprint of Simon & Schuster "The Second Coming" from *The Collected Works of W.B. Yeats, Volume 1: The Poems* edited by Richard J. Finneran. Copyright © 1924 by The Macmillan Company; copyright renewed © 1952 by Bertha Georgie Yeats. Used with the permission of Scribner, an imprint of Simon & Schuster Adult Publishing Group, All rights reserved.

Smithsonian Institution "Recasting Shakespeare's Stage" by Eric Jaffe from *www.smithsonianmag.com/arts-culture/globe.html.* Copyright 2008 Smithsonian Institution. Used with permission from Smithsonian Business Ventures. All rights reserved. Reproduction in any medium is strictly prohibited without permission from Smithsonian Institution. Such permission may be requested from Smithsonian Business Ventures.

Stage Three Music (US) Inc. "Eli, the Barrow Boy" written by Colin Meloy from *Picaresque.* Copyright © 2005 music of Stage Three/Osterozhna! Music (BMI). Used by permission of Stage Three Music (US), Inc.

The Estate of Ann Stanford "The Wife's Lament" by Ann Stanford from *The Women Poets In English: An Anthology.* Copyright © 1972 by Ann Stanford. Used with permission of the Estate of Ann Stanford.

Taylor & Francis From "The Rape Of The Lock", reprinted from *The Poems of Alexander Pope,* edited by John Butt. Reproduced by permission of Taylor & Francis Books UK.

University of California Press & Carmen Balcells Agencia Literaria *Selected Odes of Pablo Neruda,* by Pablo Neruda, translated by Margaret Sayers Peden, copyright © 1990 by the Fundacion Pablo Neruda, published by the University of California Press. All rights reserved.

The University of Chicago Press Excerpt from "Oedipus The King" by Sophocles, D. Grene, trans., from *The Complete Greek Tragedies,* R. Lattimore and D. Grene, eds. Used with permission of The University of Chicago Press.

Ed Victor, Ltd. "Not Palaces" from *Collected Poems 1928–1985* by Stephen Spender, copyright © 2004 by Stephen Spender. Used by permission of Ed Victor Ltd.

Viking Penguin, Inc. "Araby", from *Dubliners* by James Joyce, copyright 1916 by B. W. Heubsch. Definitive text Copyright © 1967 by The Estate of James Joyce. "Wirers" from *Collected Poems Of Siegfried Sasson* by Siegfried Sassoon, copyright 1918, 1920 by E. P. Dutton. Copyright 1936, 1946, 1947, 1948 by Siegfried Sassoon. "The Rocking-Horse Winner" from *Complete Short Stories Of D.H. Lawrence* by D.H. Lawrence. Copyright © 1933 by the Estate of D. H. Lawrence, renewed © 1961 by Angelo Ravagli and C. M. Weekley, Executors of the Estate of Frieda Lawrence. "The Book of Sand", from *Collected Fictions,* by Jorge Luis Borges, translated by Andrew Hurley, copyright © 1998 by Maria Kodama; translation copyright © 1998 by Penguin Putnam, Inc. From "In Athens Once", from *Days Of Obligation* by Richard Rodriguez, copyright © 1992 by Richard Rodriguez. Used by permission of Viking Penguin, a division of Penguin Group (USA) Inc. All rights reserved.

Wake Forest University Press "Carrick Revisited" from *Selected Poems of Louis MacNeice,* edited by Michael Longley. Copyright © Wake Forest University Press, 1990. Used by permission of Wake Forest University Press.

The Arthur Waley Estate Excerpts from *The Analects of Confucius,* translated and annotated by Arthur Waley. Copyright © 1938 by George Allen and Unwin Ltd, London. From "The Book of Songs, Song 34 (Thick Grow the Rush Leaves)" translated by Arthur Waley from *The Book Of Songs.* Copyright © 1919, 1941 by Alfred A. Knopf, Inc. Used by permission of The Arthur Waley Estate.

Wikipedia.org "Zorro" retrieved from http://en.wikipedia.org accessed on 6/6/07. "Space Mirror Memorial" retrieved from http://en.wikipedia.org accessed on 6/15/07. "Davy Crockett" retrieved from http://en.wikipedia.org accessed on 6/18/07.

Yale University Press "The Seafarer" from *Poems from the Old English,* translated by Burton Raffel. Copyright © 1960, 1964; renewed 1988, 1922 by The University of Nebraska Press. Copyright © 1994 by Burton Raffel. Used by permission of Yale University Press.

Note: Every effort has been made to locate the copyright owner of material reproduced on this component. Omissions brought to our attention will be corrected in subsequent editions.

Credits

Photo Credits

xlvi: Amra Pasic/Shutterstock; **1:** Bridgeman Art Library, London/ SuperStock; **2:** r. **2:** m. © The Board of Trinity College, Dublin, Ireland/ The Bridgeman Art Library; **2:** l. Stapleton Collection/CORBIS; **3:** rt. Erich Lessing/Art Resource, NY; **3:** rm. British Museum/Art Resource, NY; **3:** rb. Andy Crawford/© Dorling Kindersley; **3:** bl. Historical Picture Archive/CORBIS; **3:** tl. Werner Forman/CORBIS; **4:** br. Archivo Iconografico, S.A./CORBIS; **4:** bl. The Art Archive / British Museum / Eileen Tweedy; **5:** br. **5:** bl. Abbie Enock; Travel Ink/CORBIS; **6:** bm. The Granger Collection, New York; **6:** br. The Art Archive / British Library; **7:** bl. Christophe Boisvieux/CORBIS; **7:** br. Frans Lanting/CORBIS; **8:** br. The Granger Collection, New York; **9:** br. The Granger Collection, New York; **9:** bl. Werner Forman/CORBIS; **10:** bl. The Gallery Collection/CORBIS; **10:** br. The Granger Collection, New York; **11:** bl. The Granger Collection, New York; **11:** br. Bettmann/CORBIS; **12:** bl. Archivo Iconografico, SA/ CORBIS; **12:** br. Danny Lehman/CORBIS; **13:** br. Stephano Bianchetti/ CORBIS; **13:** bl. HIP/Art Resource, NY; **15:** br. Prentice Hall; **17:** Bridgeman Art Library, London/SuperStock; **20–21:** Barry Lewis/CORBIS; **24:** t. St. Cuthbert's Holy Island, 1797 (w/c over pencil on textured paper) by Thomas Girtin (1775–1802); Yale Center for British Art, Paul Mellon Collection, USA/ / The Bridgeman Art Library; **26:** Matthias Kulka/ CORBIS; **31:** r. Clive Druett;Papilio/CORBIS; **33:** The Grandsons of Gostosmysl: Rurick, Truvori and Sineus, 1986 (oil on canvas), Glazunov, Ilya (b. 1930) / Private Collection, / The Bridgeman Art Library; **34:** The Granger Collection, New York; **37:** Boris Vallejo, Inc.; **42:** b. Kerstin Hamburg/CORBIS; **46:** l. istockphoto.com; **47:** b. ©The Trustees of the British Museum; **47:** TR ©The Trustees of the British Museum; **49:** r. HIP/Art Resource, NY; **55:** tr. British Museum/Art Resource, NY; **59:** BEOWULF: A TALE OF BLOOD, HEAT, AND ASHES. Text copyright ©27 by Nicky Raven. Illustrations copyright ©27 by John Howe. Reproduced by permission of the publisher Candlewick Press, Inc., Cambridge, MA; **61:** t. **62:** bl. The Granger Collection, New York; **63:** t. BEOWULF: A TALE OF BLOOD, HEAT, AND ASHES. Text copyright ©27 by Nicky Raven. Illustrations copyright ©27 by John Howe. Reproduced by permission of the publisher Candlewick Press, Inc., Cambridge, MA; **68:** t. ©Smith Richard Frank/CORBIS Sygma; **68:** m. Concept and design by Cynthia Krupt; b. The Art Archive/British Library; **69:** tr. Richard Cummings/CORBIS; **76:** b. **77: 78: 80:** t. **83:** tr. David Reed/CORBIS; **84: 87:** tr. M-Sat Ltd / Photo Researchers, Inc.; **90:** l. The Granger Collection, New York; **92–93:** The Granger Collection, New York; **93:** t. Stapleton Collection/CORBIS; **96–97:** Reproduced with the cooperation of Alexandra Szyk Bracie and Historicana www.szyk.com; **100:** l. The Yeoman, Arthur Szyk for The CANTERBURY TALES, Reproduced with permission of Alexadra Szyk Bracie and Irvin Ungar; **102:** l. The Monk, Arthur Szyk for The CANTERBURY TALES, Reproduced with permission of Alexadra Szyk Bracie and Irvin Ungar; **104:** l. The Student, Arthur Szyk for The CANTERBURY TALES, Reproduced with permission of Alexadra Szyk Bracie and Irvin Ungar; **109:** The Wife of Bath, Arthur Szyk for The CANTERBURY TALES, Reproduced with permission of Alexadra Szyk Bracie and Irvin Ungar; **111:** r. Matt Stroshane/Getty Images, Inc.; **111:** no credit necessry; **111:** The Miller, Arthur Szyk for The CANTERBURY TALES, Reproduced with permission of Alexadra Szyk Bracie and Irvin Ungar; **112:** Richard Ross/CORBIS; **113:** The Summoner Arthur Szyk for The CANTERBURY TALES, Reproduced with permission of Alexadra Szyk Bracie and Irvin Ungar; **114:** l. The Pardoner, Arthur Szyk for The Canterbury Tales, Reproduced with permission of Alexadra Szyk Bracie and Irvin Ungar; **118:** b. Three Monks, Arthur Szyk for The CANTERBURY TALES, Reproduced with permission of Alexadra Szyk Bracie and Irvin Ungar; **124: 131:** t. Lambeth Palace Library, London, UK/ Bridgeman Art Library, London/New York; **144:** Bridgeman Art Library; **151:** br. www.cartoonStock.com; **157:** r. Summerfield Press/CORBIS; **158:** The Decameron, 1916 (oil on canvas), Waterhouse, John William (1849–1917) / © Lady Lever Art Gallery, National Museums Liverpool, / The Bridgeman Art Library; **160:** b. Scala/Art Resource; **162:** l. The Granger Collection, New York; **167:** St. George and the Dragon, c.1606 (oil on canvas), Rubens, Peter Paul (1577–1640) / Prado, Madrid, Spain, Giraudon / The Bridgeman Art Library; **185:** Michel Setboun/CORBIS; **188–189:** Photo by Mansell/Time & Life Pictures/Getty Images; **190–191:** Fine Art Photographic Library, London/Art Resource, NY; **193** Giraudon/Art Resource, NY; **193:** Giraudon/Art Resource, NY; **196:** b. www.cartoonStock.com; **201:** Photographersdirect.com; **207:** tr. The Granger Collection, New York; **211:** t. The Gallery Collection/CORBIS; **211:** bl. Geoff Dann/© Dorling Kindersley, Courtesy of the Anthony Barton Collection; **211:** bmr. Geoff Dann/© Dorling Kindersley, Courtesy of the Anthony Barton Collection; **211:** bml. Geoff Dann/© Dorling Kindersley, Courtesy of the Anthony Barton Collection; **211:** br. Geoff Dann/© Dorling Kindersley, Courtesy of the Anthony Barton Collection; **214:** b. CORBIS; **234–235:** Scala/ Art Resource, NY; **236:** br. Private Collection/ The Stapleton Collection/ The Bridgeman Art Library; **236:** t. **237:** br. Scala/Art Resource, NY; **237:** bl. The Granger Collection, New York; **237:** bmr. The Granger Collection, New York; **237:** bml. Science Museum/Science & Society Picture Library; **238:** br. Gianni Dagli Orti/CORBIS; **238:** bl. Bettmann/CORBIS; **239:** King Richard I and his Barons, Anonymous / British Library, London, UK, © British Library Board. All Rights Reserved / The Bridgeman Art Library; **239:** bl. Jim Zuckerman/CORBIS; **239:** br. **240:** bl. Paule Seux/Hemis/CORBIS; **241:** bl. The Granger Collection, New York; **242:** b. The Granger Collection, New York; **243:** tr. National Trust/Art Resource, NY; **243:** br. Gregg Newton/ Gregg Newton/CORBIS; **243:** bl. Andy Willimams/Loop Images/CORBIS; **243:** rm. Victoria & Albert Museum, London / Art Resource, NY; **244:** bl. Blue Lantern Studio/CORBIS; **244:** Bettmann/CORBIS; **245:** br. Bettmann/CORBIS; **247:** br. Bettmann/CORBIS; **249:** b. Prentice Hall; **249:** t. ©Edinburgh University Library, Scotland/ The Bridgeman Art Library; **250:** t. ©Hatfield House, Hertfordshire, UK/ The Bridgeman Art Library; **251:** Burstein Collection/CORBIS; **251: 253:** r. **255:** Burstein Collection/CORBIS; **257:** r. **258:** Victoria & Albert Museum, London/Art Resource, NY; 265 rt. www.cartoonStock.com; **267–268:** Museum of Fine Arts, Houston, Texas, USA/ Agnes Cullen Arnold Endowment Fund/ The Bridgeman Art Library; **273:** r. **274:** Private Collection/ The Stapleton Collection/ The Bridgeman Art Library; **277:** tr. The Granger Collection, New York; **277:** ml. Private Collection/ © Philip Mould Ltd, London/ The Bridgeman Art Library; **277:** rm. **277:** rb. No. 3856 Henry Wriothesley, 3rd Earl of Southampton (1573–1624), c.1594 (gouache on vellum) by Nicholas Hilliard (1547–1619) Fitzwilliam Museum, University of Cambridge, UK/ The Bridgeman Art Library; **277:** bml. **277:** bl. North Wind Picture Archives; **277:** tl. The Art Archive/Victoria and Albert Museum London/Sally Chappell; **277:** tm. The Art Archive/Victoria and Albert Museum London/Sally Chappell; **277:** tr. Judith Miller/© Dorling Kindersley/Joseph H. Bonner; **277:** ml. istockphoto.com; **281:** Hans the Younger Holbein (1497/8–1543), Dutch, "Portrait of Henry VIII", 16th century. Oil on canvas. Belvoir Castle, Leicestershire. The Bridgeman Art Library Ltd.; **285:** tr. "Dangers Averted" medal, celebrating the defeat of the Spanish Armada, c. 1589, gold cast and chased by Nicholas Hilliard (1537–1619) Fitzwilliam Museum, University of Cambridge/Bridgeman Art Library , London/New York; **286:** Elizabeth I, Armada Portrait, c. 1588 (oil on panel) by George Gower (1540–1596) (attr. to). Woburn Abbey, Bedfordshire, UK/Bridgeman Art Library, London/New York; **288:** bl. Picture Desk, Inc./Kobal Collection; **290:** t. istockphoto.com; **292:** m. Getty Images; **292:** bl. Getty Images; **293:** t. **294:** l. Polygram/The Kobal Collection, Bailey, Alex; **295:** t. Studio Canal/Working Title/The Koball Collection/Sparham, Laurie; **297:** Private Collection/The Bridgeman Art Library; **298:** RÈunion des MusÈes Nationaux / Art Resource, NY; **303:** The Return of the Prodigal Son, Lionello Spada/Erich Lessing/Art Resource, NY; **307:** Ellen Terry (as Lady Macbeth), 1889, oil on canvas 87" x 45", Tate Gallery on loan to National Portrait Gallery London, Art Resource, NY; **313:** b. Photofest; **313:** tr. MIRISCH-7 ARTS/UNITED ARTISTS / THE KOBAL COLLECTION; **313:** tl. MGM / THE KOBAL COLLECTION; **316:** b. National Portrait Gallery, London/Superstock.; **318:** ml. Mary Evans Picture Library; **318–319:** b. **324:** t. Erich Lessing / Art Resource, NY; **328:** t. New Walk Museum, Leicester City Museum Service, UK/ The Bridgeman Art Library; **330:** b. Darren Robb/Getty Images; **332:** b. t. City of Westminster Archive Centre, London, UK/ The Bridgeman Art Library; **343:** t. Steve Gorton/© Dorling Kindersley; **347:** Photofest; **350:** b. The Pierpont Morgan Library, Art Resource, NY; **352:** t. The Granger Collection, New York; **366:** t. The Art Archive / Garrick Club; **371:** t. Scene from Macbeth, Cattermole, By Permission of the Folger Shakespeare Library, Washington, D.C.; **379:** t. Earl & Nazima Kowall/CORBIS; **380:** Victoria & Albert Museum, London / Art Resource, NY; **387:** b. The Granger Collection, New York; **393:** b. Corel Professional Photos CD-ROMÔ; **394: 399:** r. Yale Center for British Art, Paul Mellon Collection, USA/ The Bridgeman Art Library; **401:** r. Geoff Dann© Dorling Kindersley, Courtesy of David Edge; **402:** RÈunion des MusÈes Nationaux / Art Resource, NY; **410:** t. The Art

CREDITS

Archive / Garrick Club; **414:** CORBIS; **422:** tl. Museo Archeologico Nazionale, Naples, Italy, / The Bridgeman Art Library International; **423:** r. Boden/ Ledingham/Masterfile; **427:** b. Robbie Jack/CORBIS; **437:** OMD Corp.; **438:** Jason Hawkes/CORBIS; **439:** Peter Bennett/Ambient Images; **439:** t. Nathan Benn/CORBIS; **440:** Nigel Hicks/© Dorling Kindersley; **460:** br. National Portrait Gallery, London; **462–463:** **464:** r. The Granger Collection, New York; **464:** l. Bibliotheque Nationale, Paris, France, Archives Charmet / The Bridgeman Art Library International; **465:** m. British Museum, London, UK/ The Bridgeman Art Library; **465:** bl. The Granger Collection, New York; **465:** m. FoodCollection / SuperStock; **465:** b. Image Source Black / SuperStock; **466:** BL Anatomical drawing of hearts and blood vessels from Quaderni di Anatomia vol 2, folio 3v, 1499, Vinci, Leonardo da (1452–1519) / Private Collection, / The Bridgeman Art Library; **466:** br. Private Collection, © Look and Learn / The Bridgeman Art Library International; **466:** t. The Granger Collection, New York; **467:** b. © Leeds Museums and Galleries (City Art Gallery) U.K., / The Bridgeman Art Library International; **467:** t. © Museum of London, UK, / The Bridgeman Art Library International; **468:** t. Yale Center for British Art, Paul Mellon Collection, USA, / The Bridgeman Art Library International; **468:** b. Blue Lantern Studio/CORBIS; **469:** b. The Granger Collection, New York; **469:** t. Archivo Iconografico, S.A./CORBIS; **470:** l. Getty Images; **470:** m. Tibor Bogn-r/CORBIS; **470:** r. Matthias Kulka/ zefa/Corbis; **471:** l. Marylebone Cricket Club, London/Bridgeman Art Library, London/New York; **471:** r. istockphoto.com; **472:** l. DE AGOSTINI EDITORE PICTURE LIBRARY/Getty Images; **472:** r. Bettmann/CORBIS; **473:** b. Bettmann/CORBIS; **473:** tl. Time Life Pictures/Getty Images; **473:** tr. istockphoto.com; **474:** mt. Private Collection, / The Bridgeman Art Library International; **474:** b. Bettmann/CORBIS; **474:** MB istockphoto. com; **475:** The Gallery Collection/CORBIS; **477:** r. Prentice Hall; **477:** l. Patrick Ingrand/Getty Images; **478:** The Art Archive/BibliothÈque des Arts DÈcoratifs Paris/Dagli Orti; **478:** b. ©Guildhall Library, City of London/ The Bridgeman Art Library; **479:** The Trustees of the Goodwood Collection/ The Bridgeman Art Library; **481:** Michael Nicholson/CORBIS; **482:** Fair is My Love, 19 (oil on canvas) by Edwin A. Abbey (1852–1911), Harris Museum and Art Gallery, Preston, Lancashire, UK/Bridgeman Art Library; **486:** Sir Thomas Aston at the Deathbed of His Wife, John Souch ©Manchester City Art Galleries; **488–489:** Simon Plant/zefa/CORBIS; **496:** © Lenore Weber/omniphoto.com.; **496:** Lebrecht Music & Arts Photo Library; **499:** Portrait of Mrs. Richard Brinsley Sheriden, Thomas Gainsborough, Andrew W. Mellon Collection ©Board of Trustees, National Gallery of Art, Washington; **500:** The Granger Collection, New York; **505:** © Ferens Art Gallery, Hull City Museums and Art Galleries, / The Bridgeman Art Library International; **506:** Image copyright © The Metropolitan Museum of Art / Art Resource, NY; **509:** t. The Granger Collection, New York; **509:** b. **510:** Private Collection, © Odon Wagner Gallery, Toronto, Canada / The Bridgeman Art Library International; **511:** The Granger Collection, New York; **512:** Young Man Writing , Joos van Craesbeeck (follower of), Musee des Beaux-Arts, Nantes, France, Giraudon/The Bridgeman Art Library, London/New York; **513:** **515:** ©Print Collector / HIP / The Image Works; **516:** The Annunciation, 1425–1428. Expulsion from Paradise/Museo del Prado, Madrid, Spain/Photo Credit: Erich Lessing/Art Resource, NY; **518:** r. The Pierpont Morgan Library / Art Resource, NY; **518:** r. Image Select / Art Resource, NY; **519:** b. The Granger Collection, New York; **519:** t. The Granger Collection, New York; **520:** mr. Twentieth Century Fox Film Corp.; **520:** ml. Universal Pictures/ Photofest; **520:** b. LUCASFILM/20TH CENTURY FOX / THE KOBAL COLLECTION; **520:** t. istockphoto.com; **525:** The Granger Collection, New York; **533:** The Granger Collection, New York; **535:** **536:** ©The New Yorker Collection 1988 J.B. Handelsman from cartoonbank.com. All Rights Reserved.; **540:** MR Mary Evans Picture Library; **540:** tl. © Stapleton Collection/Corbis; **540:** bl. © Geoffrey Clements/CORBIS; **540:** tr. © Nik Wheeler/CORBIS; **540:** br. Blue Lantern Studios/CORBIS; **540:** ml. Mary Evans Picture Library; **542:** Museo Nazionale del Bargello, Florence, Italy, Alinari / The Bridgeman Art Library International; **543:** Gustave Dore, Judecca—Lucifer, Inferno XXXIV, 1862. New York Public Library Special Collections, L'Enfer de Dante Alighieri avec dessins de Gustave Dore, 1862. The New York Public Library / Art Resource, NY; **545:** The Granger Collection, New York; **546:** Bettmann/CORBIS; **548:** Gustave Dore, "Poets emerge from Hell, Inferno XXXIV, 139," 1862. New York Public Library Special Collections, L'Enfer de Dante Alighieri avec dessins de Gustave Dore, 1862. The New York Public Library / Art Resource, NY; **553:** Hulton-Deutsch Collection/CORBIS; **554:** CORBIS; **559:** Erich Lessing / Art Resource, NY; **559:** t. Private Collection/The Bridgeman Art Library; **560:** Private Collection/The Bridgeman Art Library; **562:** The Granger Collection, New York; **563:** Annette Fournet/ CORBIS; **564–565:** Brendan Regan/CORBIS; **567:** The Art Archive/Galleria Sabauda Turin/Dagli Orti; **570:** b. The Bridgeman Art Library; **570:** t. The Granger Collection, New York; **571:** The Granger Collection, New York; **573:** The Art Archive / London Museum / Eileen Tweedy; **574:** **576:** The Granger Collection, New York; **578:** ing Charles II (1630–1685) the Great Fire of London, 1666 (gouache on paper), Doughty, C.L. (1913–1985) / Private Collection, © Look and Learn / The Bridgeman Art Library International; **582:** Eric Fougere/VIP Images/CORBIS; **582–583:** Pete Turner/Getty Images; **583:** Avon Books. Jacket desgin by Amy Halperin.; **585:** Alan Sirulnikoff/Getty Images; **586:** Alan Sirulnikoff/Getty Images; **589:** Lebrecht Music & Arts Photo Library; **589:** Private Collection, / The Bridgeman Art Library InternationalPrivate Collection/ The Bridgeman Art Library; **590:** Courtesy of the Trustees of British Library; **594:** The Granger Collection, New York; **604:** Judith Miller / Dorling Kindersley / The Blue Pump; **605:** The Granger Collection, New York; **605:** t. National Portrait Gallery, London, UK, / The Bridgeman Art Library International; **605:** b. Garry Gay /Getty Images; **606:** The Granger Collection, New York; **607:** Tom Grill/Corbis; **608:** Siede Preis/Getty Images; **611:** The Granger Collection, New York; **617:** © Sotheby's / akg-images; **619:** The Granger Collection, New York; **623:** The Granger Collection, New York; **624:** ©The Trustees of The British Museum; **626:** ©The New Yorker Collection 1988 J.B. Handelsman from cartoonbank.com. All Rights Reserved.; **629:** The Granger Collection, New York; **630:** **633:** The Granger Collection, New York; **636:** The Granger Collection, New York; **638:** The Granger Collection, New York; **640:** Historical Picture Archive/CORBIS; **641:** The Granger Collection, New York; **647:** The Granger Collection, New York; **648:** Private Collection/ The Bridgeman Art Library; **649:** The Granger Collection, New York; **652:** Private Collection, / The Bridgeman Art Library; **654:** The Granger Collection, New York; **655:** The Granger Collection, New York; **657:** The Granger Collection, New York; **658:** ©British Museum; **662:** ©The New Yorker Collection 1995 Ed Fisher from cartoonbank.com. All Rights Reserved.; **672:** The Granger Collection, New York; **673:** Victoria & Albert Museum, London / Art Resource, NY; **677:** Girl Writing by Lamplight, c. 1850, by William Henry Hunt (1790–1864), The Maas Gallery London/ Bridgeman Art Library, London/New York; **681:** The Granger Collection, New York; **682:** The Granger Collection, New York; **686:** Prentice Hall; **687:** The Granger Collection, New York; **689:** Neil Emmerson/Getty Images; **690:** Dave G. Houser/CORBIS; **691:** Bill Ross/CORBIS; **692:** Mark Karrass/CORBIS; **697:** Prentice Hall; **714–715:** Two Men Observing the Moon, Caspar David Friedrich, oil on canvas, 35 x 44.5 cm, (1819–1820), Staatl, Kunstsammlungen, Neue Meister, Dresden, Germany, Erich Lessing/Art Resource, NY; **716:** ©Mary Evans Picture Library/The Image Works; **717:** bm. Derby Museum and Art Gallery, UK, / The Bridgeman Art Library International; **717:** bl. Private Collection, / The Bridgeman Art Library International; **717:** br. The Wanderer Over the Sea of Clouds, 1818, by Caspar-David Friedrich (1774–1840), Kunsthalle, Hamburg/Bridgeman Art Library, London/New York; **717:** tr. Warren Faidley/CORBIS; **717:** m. age fotostock / SuperStock; **717:** tm. Tate, London / Art Resource, NY; **717:** tl. Image copyright Photo credit : The Metropolitan Museum of Art / Art Resource, NY; **718:** bl. The Gallery Collection/CORBIS; **718:** br. istockphoto.com; **718:** t. **719:** r. Fine Art Photographic Library/CORBIS; **719:** l. Leonard de Selva/CORBIS; **720:** The Granger Collection, New York; **721:** l. rivate Collection/ Archives Charmet/ The Bridgeman Art Library; **721:** r. National Portrait Gallery, London, UK/ The Bridgeman Art Library; **722:** t. The Granger Collection, New York; **722:** b. Bettmann/CORBIS; **723:** BL istockphoto.com; **724:** t. The Granger Collection, New York; **724:** BL Bettmann/ CORBIS; **724:** br. The Art Archive / British Museum / Eileen Tweedy; **725:** b. Hulton-Deutsch Collection/CORBIS; **725:** t. Erich Lessing / Art Resource, NY; **726:** b. The Granger Collection, New York; **726:** t. Hulton-Deutsch Collection/CORBIS; **727:** r. The Granger Collection, New York; **727:** l. Bettmann/CORBIS; **729:** tr. Prentice Hall; **729:** tl. Bettmann/CORBIS; **729:** b. Bettmann/CORBIS; **730:** ORION / THE KOBAL COLLECTION; **731:** British Museum, London, UK/ The Bridgeman Art Library; **733:** **734:** istockphoto.com; **736:** l. istockphoto.com; **737:** The Bow, Talbot Hughes, Warrington Museum and Art Gallery, Cheshire, UK/Bridgeman Art Library; **740:** **741:** t. M. Angelo/CORBIS; **741:** b. **742:** The Village Wedding, detail, by Sir Luke Fildes (1844–1927), Christopher Wood Gallery, London/Bridgeman Art Library, London/New York; **747:** Blue Lantern Studio/CORBIS; **748:** The Granger Collection, New York; **750:** The Pierpont Morgan Library / Art Resource, NY; **751:** The Granger Collection, New York; **752:** **753:** ©The New Yorker Collection 1991 Mick Stevens from cartoonbank.com. All Rights Reserved.; **756:** b. Prentice Hall; **756:** t. Charles O'Rear/CORBIS; **757:** Bettmann/CORBIS; **759:** Bettmann/ CORBIS; **760:** Douglas Pearson/CORBIS; **762:** border Werner H.Mueller/

zefa/Corbis; **764:** border rubberball; **765:** ©The New Yorker Collection 1995 Ed Fisher from cartoonbank.com. All Rights Reserved.; **771:** Courtesy of Broadway Video Enterprises and NBC Studios, Inc.; **773:** The Wanderer Over the Sea of Clouds, 1818, by Caspar-David Friedrich (1774–1840), Kunsthalle, Hamburg/Bridgeman Art Library, London/New York; **776:** m. Michael Nicholson/CORBIS; **776–777:** Peter Adams/JAI/CORBIS; **777:** HIP / Art Resource, NY; **778:** Roy Rainford/Robert Harding World Imagery/CORBIS; **780: 785:** Private Collection/ © Agnew's, London, UK/ The Bridgeman Art Library; **786–787:** border Corbis / SuperStock; **787:** Stefano Bianchetti/CORBIS; **789: 790:** Jose Fuste Raga/CORBIS; **791:** Comstock / SuperStock; **793:** George Logan/zefa/CORBIS; **796:** l. Massimo Listri/CORBIS; **796:** m. Terje Kveen; **798:** t. State Russian Museum, St. Petersburg, Russia/The Bridgeman Art Library; **798:** b. Stapleton Collection/CORBIS; **799:** "Lake Scene in France", 19th century, oil on canvas. The Bowes Museum, Barnard Castle, County Durham, UK, The Bridgeman Art Library, New York.; **802:** "Lake Scene in France", 19th century, oil on canvas. The Bowes Museum, Barnard Castle, County Durham, UK, The Bridgeman Art Library, New York.; **804:** Art Resource/The New York Public Library Photographic Services; **805:** PoodlesRock/CORBIS; **806:** l. Demetrio Carrasco/JAI/ CORBIS; **806:** r. ©Steven Bourelle; **807:** Heibonsha/Pacific Press Service; **808:** Heibonsha/Pacific Press Service; **814:** Kim Sayer/© Dorling Kindersley; **815:** Charles Bowman/Robert Harding World Imagery; **816:** Kevin Jones/© Dorling Kindersley; **819:** Bettmann/CORBIS; **820:** The Granger Collection, New York; **822:** Engraving by Gust·ve DorÈ for The Rime of the Ancient Mariner by Samuel Taylor Coleridge ©1970 by Dover Publications, Inc.; **823:** Creativ Studio Heinemann; **825:** The Granger Collection, New York; **827:** The Granger Collection, New York; **833:** The Granger Collection, New York; **836:** The Granger Collection, New York; **838:** The Granger Collection, New York; **838:** imagewerks; **840:** The Granger Collection, New York; **843:** The Granger Collection, New York; **846:** Box and Cover, Ming Dynasty, first half of 16th century, lacquer, black; mother-of-pearl; wood; fabric. H. 4 in. The Seattle Art Museum, Gift of Mr. and Mrs. Louis Brechemin, Photo by Paul Macapia.; **848:** Werner Forman / Art Resource, NY; **853:** Chris Hellier/Corbis; **854:** Erich Lessing / Art Resource, NY; **857: 857:** Bkgrnd istockphoto.com; 859: Bkgrnd istockphoto.com; **860:** Michael Nicholson/CORBIS; **867:** Gustavo Tomsich/CORBIS; **868:** Kazuyoshi Nomachi/CORBIS; **871:** Alinari / Art Resource, NY; **895:** Science Museum, London, UK/ The Bridgeman Art Library; **898:** b. The Granger Collection, New York; **898:** m. The Granger Collection, New York; **898:** t. Sean Sexton Collection/CORBIS; **899:** Alamy; **900: 903:** b. Courtesy of the Trustees of Sir John Soane's Museum, London, / The Bridgeman Art Library International; **903:** t. The Granger Collection, New York; **905:** Courtesy of the Trustees of Sir John Soane's Museum, London, / The Bridgeman Art Library International; **906:** Grace Bergenicht Gallery, New York; **911:** t. Bettmann/CORBIS; **911:** b. The Granger Collection, New York; **912: 916:** Jean Georges Ferry; **938:** tr. ©Stock Montage/SuperStock; **938:** cr. ©Stock Montage/SuperStock; **938:** bl. ©Lebrecht Music and Arts Photo Library/Alamy Images; **940–941:** The Railway Station, 1862, by William Powell Frith (1819–1909), Royal Holloway and Bedford New College, Surrey, UK/Bridgeman Art Library, London/New York; **942:** BR Hulton-Deutsch Collection/CORBIS; **942:** BL Joseph Sohm/Visions of America/ CORBIS; **942:** t. The Granger Collection, New York; **942:** The Granger Collection, New York; **942:** m. The Art Archive / Alfredo Dagli Orti; **943:** t. Bettmann/CORBIS; **943:** BL Michael Nicholson/CORBIS; **943:** br. The Granger Collection, New York; **943:** tl. Historical Picture Archive/ CORBIS; **943:** tr. Hulton-Deutsch Collection/CORBIS; **943:** bl. Guildhall Library, City of London/ The Bridgeman Art Library; **943:** tl. Hulton-Deutsch Collection/CORBIS; **943:** m. Bettmann/CORBIS; **943:** br. ©Private Collection/ The Stapleton Collection/ The Bridgeman Art Library; **944:** tr. Medford Historical Society Collection/CORBIS; **944:** tl. Bettmann/ CORBIS; **944:** b. CORBIS; **945:** BL Stapleton Collection/CORBIS; **945:** br. Bettmann/CORBIS; **945:** t. Day Dream, 1880, Dante Gabriel Rosetti, Victoria & Albert Museum, London, UK/ The Bridgeman Art Library, London/New York; **946:** bm. Brooklyn Museum/CORBIS; **946:** bl. Bettmann/CORBIS; **946:** br. Bettmann/CORBIS; **946:** t. The Granger Collection, New York; **947:** bl. The Gallery Collection/CORBIS; **947:** br. istockphoto.com; **947:** t. istockphoto.com; **948:** m. Hulton-Deutsch Collection/CORBIS; **948:** b. Underwood & Underwood/CORBIS; **949:** l. Bettmann/CORBIS; **949:** m. Hulton-Deutsch Collection/CORBIS; **949:** r. istockphoto.com; **950:** t. Mary Evans Picture Library; **950:** CORBIS; **951:** br. Bettmann/CORBIS; **951:** BL Bettmann/CORBIS; **951:** bm. istock-photo.com; **953:** r. gezette.de Buro fur Fotografie; **953:** l. Mick Roessler / SuperStock; **954:** l. ©Alamy Images; **954:** r. age fotostock / SuperStock; **957:** ©Archivo Iconografico/CORBIS; **959:** Hulton-Deutsch Collection/ CORBIS; **960:** The Stages of Life, c.1835 (oil on canvas) by Caspar-David Friedrich (1774–1840), Museum der Bildenden Kunste, Leipzig/ Bridgeman Art Library, London/New York; **962:** ©Tate Gallery, London/ Art Resource, NY. Tate Gallery, London, Great Britain; **969:** Don Farrall/ Getty Images; **970:** Jean-Auguste-Dominique Ingres, Ulysses, 1827, Chester Dale Collection, Photograph ©Board of Trustees, National Gallery of Art, Washington; **977:** Hulton-Deutsch Collection/CORBIS; **978:** North Carolina Museum of Art/CORBIS; **981:** The Bridgeman Art Library International; **983:** Erich Lessing / Art Resource, NY; **985:** Michael Nicholson/CORBIS; **987: 989:** The Reader, Silvestro Lega, Alinari/Art Resource, NY; **992:** Illustration from The Oxford Illustrated Dickens; **994:** t. Hulton-Deutsch Collection/CORBIS; **994:** SuperStock, Inc. / SuperStock; **995:** Stapleton Collection/CORBIS; **996:** Robbie Jack/ CORBIS; **1005: 1012:** Lebrecht Music & Arts Photo Library; **1013:** The Bridgeman Art Library; **1016:** The Bridgeman Art Library; **1020:** The Bridgeman Art Library; **1023:** t. Stapleton Collection/CORBIS; **1023:** b. © Michael Nicholson/CORBIS; **1024:** b. © Michael Nicholson/ CORBIS; **1025:** b. © Raymond Gehman/CORBIS; **1025:** t. photo by JohnMoranPhoto.com; 1026: AP/Wide World Photos; **1029: 1030:** Private Collection, © The Maas Gallery, London, UK / The Bridgeman Art Library International; **1033:** Underwood & Underwood/CORBIS; **1039:** Private Collection/ The Bridgeman Art Library; **1041:** Michael Nicholson/CORBIS; **1042:** UK21 / Alamy; **1044:** The Granger Collection, New York; **1045:** Hulton Archive Photos/Getty Images Inc.; **1046:** Private Collection/Bridgeman Art Library, London/New York; **1047:** Judith Miller / Dorling Kindersley / Thos. Wm. Gaze & Son; **1048:** r. Private Collection/ The Bridgeman Art Library; **1048:** l. The Granger Collection, New York; **1050:** ©The New Yorker Collection 1988 J.B. Handelsman from cartoonbank.com. All Rights Reserved.; **1052:** t. gezette.de Buro fur Fotografie; **1052:** b. Glyn Thomas/Alamy; **1053:** ©David Noton/Masterfile; **1054:** t. Reuters Photographer / Reuters/Reuters/CORBIS; **1054:** m. ©Corbis / SuperStock; **1055:** Inset Bettmann/CORBIS; **1056:** Judith Miller / Dorling Kindersley / Thos. Wm. Gaze & Son; **1058:** b. age fotostock / SuperStock; **1058:** t. age fotostock / SuperStock; **1060–1061:** Mario Anzuoni/Reuters/CORBIS; **1064:** t. Hulton Archive Photos/Getty Images; **1064:** b. The Granger Collection, New York; **1064: 1067:** m. Two mousetrap cameras, c.1835 (wood), English School, (19th century) / NMPFT, Bradford, West Yorkshire, / The Bridgeman Art Library International; **1067:** tl. Ironbridge Gorge Museum, Telford, Shropshire, UK/The Bridgeman Art Library; **1067:** tr. ©The Art Archive / Musee de l'Affiche Paris / Dagli Orti; **1067:** br. The Science Museum/ Science & Society Picture Library; **1067:** tm. The Granger Collection, New York; **1067:** BL The Granger Collection, New York; **1068:** Image courtesy of The Advertising Archives; **1071:** Past and Present (no.2), Augustus Leopold Egg, Tate Gallery, London/Art Resource, NY; **1073: 1074:** The Soul of the Rose, 1908, John William Waterhouse, Private Collection/Julian Hartnoll, London, UK/Bridgeman Art Library; **1077:** Hulton-Deutsch Collection/CORBIS; **1079:** he Art Archive / MusÈe d'Orsay Paris / Gianni Dagli Orti; **1080:** RÈunion des MusÈes Nationaux / Art Resource, NY; **1083: 1086:** Alinari / Art Resource, NY; **1087:** ©Mary Evans/Jeffrey Morgan Collection/ The Image Works; **1091:** Hulton-Deutsch Collection/CORBIS; **1093:** age fotostock / SuperStock; **1109:** bl. The Granger Collection, New York; **1118:** bcr. ©Bettmann/Corbis; **1118–1119:** ©Musee National d'Art Moderne, Centre Pompidou, Paris, France/ Peter Willi/ The Bridgeman Art Library; **1124:** BL Hulton-Deutsch Collection/CORBIS: **1124:** bm. Bettmann/CORBIS; **1124:** t. The Granger Collection, New York; **1124:** br. istockphoto.com; **1125:** bl. Hulton-Deutsch Collection/CORBIS; **1125:** BR The Granger Collection, New York; **1125:** m. The Granger Collection, New York; **1125:** t. The Granger Collection, New York; **1126:** Swim Ink 2, LLC/CORBIS; **1126:** l. Bettmann/CORBIS; **1126:** tl. Bettmann/CORBIS; **1127:** br. David J. & Janice L. Frent Collection/ CORBIS; **1127:** bl. The Granger Collection, New York; **1127:** t. Private Collection/ The Bridgeman Art Library; **1128:** l. Bettmann/CORBIS; **1128:** r. The Granger Collection, New York; **1129:** t. Bettmann/CORBIS; **1129:** br. The Granger Collection, New York; **1129:** bl. istockphoto.com; **1129:** l. Stockbyte; **1130:** t. Photofest; bl. Hulton Archive/Getty Images; br. Corbis; **1131:** m. David Reed/CORBIS; **1131:** r. © Wojtek Buss; **1132:** tl. Owen Franken/CORBIS; **1132:** b. Igor Kostin/Sygma/CORBIS; **1132:** tr. Dario Mitidieri/Getty Images; **1133:** t. Anthony Correia/Getty Images; **1133:** b. Paula Bronstein/Getty Images; **1135:** tr. Colin McPherson/ CORBIS; **1135:** tl. Pete Turner/Getty Images; **1135:** b. The Granger Collection, New York; **1136:** Topham/The Image Works; **1136:** Art Resource, NY; **1139:** Hulton-Deutsch Collection/CORBIS; **1141:** Christie's Images/CORBIS; **1142:** John Conrad/CORBIS; **1143:** Photodisc/Getty

Images; **1144:** Underwood & Underwood/CORBIS; **1144:** age fotostock / SuperStock; **1145:** The Image Bank/Getty Images; **1147:** Gilles Mermet / Art Resource, NY; **1147:** Gilles Mermet / Art Resource, NY; **1148:** Gilles Mermet / Art Resource, NY; **1155:** Hulton-Deutsch Collection/CORBIS; **1156:** E.O. HoppÈ/CORBIS; **1158:** Jean Kugler/Getty Images; **1163:** PhotothÈque R. Magritte-ADAGP / Art Resource, NY, ©1998 C. Herscovici, Brussels/ Artists Rights Society (ARS), New York.; **1171:** Bettmann/CORBIS; **1172:** The Granger Collection, New York; **1172:** Bkgrnd Freyda Miller/CORBIS; **1174:** Michael Goldman/Getty Images; **1176:** Art Projects International; **1177: 1179:** Getty Images; **1180:** Michael St. Maur Sheil/CORBIS; **1182:** Sophie Bassouls/Sygma/CORBIS; **1182: 1183:** Paul Hardy/CORBIS; **1184:** Paul Hardy/CORBIS; **1187:** © Gilles Mermet / Art Resource; **1188:** Getty Images; **1189:** t. Private Collection, © The Bloomsbury Workshop, London / The Bridgeman Art Library International; **1189:** b. Private Collection, The Stapleton Collection/ The Bridgeman Art Library International; **1189: 1190:** t. Marilyn Monroe, Andy Warhol, © Andy Warhol Foundation/CORBIS. TM 2006 Marilyn Monroe, LLC by CMG Worldwide, Inc / www.MarilynMonroe.com © Andy Warhol Foundation for the Visual Arts / ARS, New York; **1190:** br. Getty Images; **1190:** bl. **1192:** RÈunion des MusÈes Nationaux / Art Resource, NY; **1193: 1195:** The Garden of Love, Walter Richard Sickert, Fitzwilliam Museum, Cambridge; **1196:** RÈunion des MusÈes Nationaux / Art Resource, NY; **1197:** age fotostock / SuperStock; **1198:** Private Collection, / The Bridgeman Art Library International; **1200:** Julian Barrow/Getty Images; **1200: 1201:** Andreas Altwein/dpa/CORBIS; **1210:** b. Library of Congress, Prints & Photographs Division, NYWT&S Collection; **1217:** Getty Images **1219:** Hulton-Deutsch Collection/CORBIS; **1220–1221:** Ron Dahlquist / Super; **1223:** Image1 / SuperStock; **1224–1225:** border Gala / SuperStock; **1226:** Michael Halminski / SuperStock; **1228–1229:** Steve Vidler / SuperStock; **1230–1231:** age fotostock / SuperStock; **1231:** Ben Mangor / SuperStock; **1232:** Digital Vision Ltd. / SuperStock; **1233:** The Granger Collection, New York; **1234:** St. Patrick's Close, Walter Osborne, National Gallery of Ireland; **1235:** Robbie Pleck / SuperStock; **1238:** © The Metropolitan Museum of Art / Art Resource, NY; **1239:** British Museum / Art Resource, NY; **1243:** Bettmann/CORBIS; **1244:** Stockbyte /Getty Images; **1245:** Stockbyte /Getty Images; **1247:** Izzy Schwartz/Getty Images; **1249:** Marvin E. Newman/Getty Images; **1250:** Jonathan Kitchen/ Getty Images; **1251:** C Squared Studios/Getty Images; **1255:** Stockbyte / Getty Images; **1256:** Marvin E. Newman/Getty Images; **1258:** Bettmann/ CORBIS; **1259:** Kevin Summers/Getty Images; **1260:** Kevin Summers/ Getty Images; **1262:** Kevin Summers/Getty Images; **1264:** Beth Dixson/ Getty Images; **1267:** Bildarchiv Preussischer Kulturbesitz / Art Resource, NY; **1269:** t. Michael Nicholson/CORBIS; **1269:** m. Hulton-Deutsch Collection/CORBIS; **1269:** b. The Granger Collection, New York; **1270:** Bettmann/CORBIS; **1271:** t. Nathan Benn/CORBIS; **1272:** Bettmann/ CORBIS; **1276:** Getty Images; **1278–1279:** AFP/Getty Images; **1282:** Bettmann/ CORBIS; **1283:** Snark/Art Resource, NY; **1293:** Hulton-Deutsch Collection/ CORBIS; **1296:** Portrait of N. Pietrunkevic, Nikolai Ge, Scala/Art Resource, NY; **1297:** Sleepless Night, Nikolai Romadin, Scala/Art Resource, NY; **1302–1303:** Hulton-Deutsch Collection/CORBIS; **1305:** b. courtesy of Royal Literary Fund and Special Collections, U of Birmingham; **1306:** Hulton-Deutsch Collection/CORBIS; **1308:** The Art Archive / Imperial War Museum; **1308:** The Art Archive / Imperial War Museum; **1313:** The Granger Collection, New York; **1314:** Paul Souders/ CORBIS; **1319:** Steve McDonough/CORBIS; **1320:** ©Orwell Archive; **1323:** Colin McPherson/CORBIS; **1324:** HIP / Art Resource, NY; **1327:** HIP / Art Resource, NY; **1330:** Private Collection/ The Stapleton Collection/ The Bridgeman Art Library; **1337:** Micheline Pelletier/CORBIS; **1338:** Ron Stroud/Masterfile; **1340:** Jean Miele/CORBIS; **1343:** Peter Turnley/ CORBIS; **1344:** David Bergman/CORBIS; **1355:** BASSOULS SOPHIE/ CORBIS SYGMA; **1356:** ©Bettmann/CORBIS; **1358:** "Boy on a Wall: Rat Island, 1989" from TIEPOLO'S HOUND by Derek Walcott. Copyright © 20 by Derek Walcott. Reprinted ty Permission of Farrar, Straus and Giroux, LLC. From the collection of Michael and Judy Chastanet.; **1358:** Ryan McVay/Getty Images; 1363: ©Smith Richard Frank/CORBIS Sygma; **1366:** Hulton-Deutsch Collection/CORBIS; **1369:** The Irish Times; **1370:** Starry Night, Vincent van Gogh, Digital Image © The Museum of Modern Art/Licensed by SCALA / Art Resource, NY; **1373:** JLImages / Alamy; **1375:** Thierry Orban/CORBIS SYGMA; **1376:** Ulrik Tofte/Getty Images; **1376:** Ulrik Tofte/Getty Images; **1379:** Getty Images; **1380:** Getty Images; **1385:** Getty Images; **1386:** Arthur S. AubryGetty Images; **1388:** Daniel Nevins / SuperStock; **1391:** AP/Wide World Photos; **1392:** Scott Stulberg/CORBIS; **1394:** Scott Stulberg/CORBIS; **1397:** Getty Images; **1398:** image reproduced with the kind permission of the Dean and Chapter of Chichester Cathedral; **1402:** t. Nicolas Elder/Globe Photos; **1402:** b. Hulton-Deutsch Collection/CORBIS; **1403:** GK Hart/Vicky Hart/Getty Images; **1404:** PIER/Getty Images; **1406:** Getty Images; **1407:** t. Colin McPherson/CORBIS; **1407:** b. Getty Images; **1408:** Artkey/ CORBIS; **1408:** Artkey/CORBIS; **1410:** Getty Images; **1410:** Getty Images; **1412:** l. Fridmar Damm/zefa/Corbis; **1412:** r. Colin McPherson/CORBIS; **1413:** istockphoto.com; **1415:** Colin McPherson/CORBIS; **1416:** Franck Guiziou/Hemis/CORBIS; **1417:** Martin Harvey/CORBIS; **1422:** Grace Davies/Omni-Photo Communications, Inc.; **1423:** Blaine Harrington III/ CORBIS; **1431:** Getty Images; **1432:** © David Noton Photography / Alamy; **1434:** © Orit Allush / Alamy; **1434:** © Orit Allush / Alamy; **1436:** Christopher Pillitz/Getty Images; **1438:** Tim Graham/Getty Images; **1441:** William Coupon/CORBIS; **1442:** Steve Nagy/Design Pics/CORBIS; **1443:** NASA/ JPL; **1444:** US Geological Service; **1444:** Hiroyuki Matsumoto /Getty Images; **1448:** AITCH/Getty Images; **1449:** t. CORBIS; **1449:** b. istockphoto. com; **1449:** mb. ESA/K. Horgan/Getty Images; **1449:** mt. DRA/Getty Images; **1459:** mc. PHERSON COLIN/CORBIS SYGMA; **1460:** Luke MacGregor/Reuters/CORBIS; **1462:** Tim Mosenfelder/CORBIS; **1462:** Tim Mosenfelder/CORBIS; **1486:** bcl. ©Bettmann/Corbis

Staff Credits

The people who made up the Pearson Prentice Hall Literature team—representing design, editorial, editorial services, education technology, manufacturing and inventory planning, market research, marketing services, planning and budgeting, product planning, production services, project office, publishing processes, and rights and permissions—are listed below. Boldface type denotes the core team members.

Tobey Antao, Margaret Antonini, Rosalyn Arcilla, Penny Baker, James Ryan Bannon, Stephan Barth, **Tricia Battipede,** Krista Baudo, Rachel Beckman, Julie Berger, Lawrence Berkowitz, Melissa Biezin, **Suzanne Biron,** Rick Blount, **Marcela Boos, Betsy Bostwick,** Kay Bosworth, Jeff Bradley, Andrea Brescia, Susan Brorein, Lois Brown, **Pam Carey,** Lisa Carrillo, **Geoffrey Cassar,** Patty Cavuoto, Doria Ceraso, Jennifer Ciccone, Jaime Cohen, Rebecca Cottingham, Joe Cucchiara, Jason Cuoco, **Alan Dalgleish, Karen Edmonds, Irene Ehrmann,** Stephen Eldridge, Amy Fleming, Dorothea Fox, Steve Frankel, Cindy Frederick, Philip Fried, Diane Fristachi, Phillip Gagler, **Pamela Gallo,** Husain Gatlin, **Elaine Goldman,** Elizabeth Good, John Guild, Phil Hadad, Patricia Hade, Monduane Harris, Brian Hawkes, Jennifer B. Heart, Martha Heller, John Hill, Beth Hyslip, Mary Jean Jones, Grace Kang, Nathan Kinney, Roxanne Knoll, **Kate Krimsky,** Monisha Kumar, Jill Kushner, Sue Langan, Melisa Leong, Susan Levine, Dave Liston, **Mary Luthi, George Lychock, Gregory Lynch, Joan Mazzeo, Sandra McGloster,** Salita Mehta, Eve Melnechuk, Kathleen Mercandetti, Artur Mkrtchyan, Karyn Mueller, Alison Muff, Christine Mulcahy, Kenneth Myett, Elizabeth Nemeth, Stefano Nese, Carrie O'Connor, April Okano, Kim Ortell, Sonia Pap, Raymond Parenteau, Dominique Pickens, Linda Punskovsky, **Sheila Ramsay,** Maureen Raymond, Mairead Reddin, **Erin Rehill-Seker, Renee Roberts, Laura Ross,** Bryan Salacki, Sharon Schultz, Jennifer Serra, **Melissa Shustyk,** Rose Sievers, Christy Singer, Yvonne Stecky, **Cynthia Summers,** Steve Thomas, Merle Uuesoo, Roberta Warshaw, Patricia Williams, Daniela Velez

Additional Credits

Lydie Bemba, Victoria Blades, Denise Data, Rachel Drice, Eleanor Kostyk, Jill Little, Loraine Machlin, Evan Marx, Marilyn McCarthy, Patrick O'Keefe, Shelia M. Smith, Lucia Tirondola, Laura Vivenzio, Linda Waldman, Angel Weyant